Official
BASEBA
REGIST

1989 EDITION

Editor/Baseball Register
BARRY SIEGEL

Contributing Editors/Baseball Register
CRAIG CARTER
JOHN DUXBURY
DOUG GREEN

President-Chief Executive Officer
RICHARD WATERS

Editor
TOM BARNIDGE

Director of Books and Periodicals
RON SMITH

Published by

The Sporting News

1212 North Lindbergh Boulevard
P.O. Box 56 — St. Louis, MO 63166

ISBN 0-89204-293-1 ISSN 0067-4281

Table of CONTENTS

Players included are those who played in at least one game in the major leagues in 1988, those who were part of a team's 40-man roster and selected invitees to spring training.

ON THE COVER: Minnesota lefthander Frank Viola enjoyed his finest major league season in 1988, carving out a 24-7 record en route to the American League Cy Young Award.

— Photo by Photo Editor Rich Pilling

EXPLANATION OF ABBREVIATIONS

G—Games played. Pos.—Position. AB—At Bats. R—Runs. H—Hits. 2B—Two-Base Hits. 3B—Three-Base Hits. HR—Home Runs. RBI—Runs Batted In. B.A.—Batting Average. PO—Putouts. A—Assists. E—Errors. F.A.—Fielding Average. IP—Innings Pitched. W—Won. L—Lost. Pct.—Winning percentage. ER—Earned Runs. SO—Strikeouts. BB—Bases on Balls. ERA—Earned-Run Average.

Players

Please note for statistical comparisons: In 1972, 10 days were missed, as well as 50 days in 1981, due to the cancellation of games because of players' strike.
★Denotes led league. ●Tied for lead. Mark before position (where more than one position is given) denotes where played as leader in department shown.

DONALD WILLIAM AASE

Name pronounced AH-see.

(Don)

Born September 8, 1954, at Orange, Calif.
Height, 6.03. Weight, 222.
Throws and bats righthanded.
Attended California State University, Fullerton, Calif.

Major League saves: 1979 (2), 1980 (2), 1981 (11), 1982 (4), 1984 (8), 1985 (14), 1986 (34), 1987 (2). Total—77.

Led International League pitchers in games started with 29 in 1975.

Led Carolina League pitchers in games started with 30, complete games with 18 and tied for lead in shutouts with 4 in 1974.

Named Carolina League Pitcher of the Year, 1974.

Year Club	League	G.	IP.	W.	L.	Pct.	H.	R.	ER.	SO.	BB.	ERA.
1972—Williamsport	NYP	12	62	0	★10	.000	60	48	40	40	34	5.81
1973—Winter Haven	Florida St.	29	170	12	●15	.444	153	82	68	127	73	3.60
1974—Winston-Salem	Carolina	32	★230	★17	8	.680	185	72	62	★176	84	★2.43
1975—Pawtucket	Int'national	29	186	8	13	.381	173	85	75	125	88	3.63
1976—Rhode Island†	Int'national	10	54	5	2	.714	42	23	20	40	34	3.33
1977—Pawtucket	Int'national	18	109	6	6	.500	118	67	61	64	60	5.04
1977—Boston‡	American	13	92	6	2	.750	85	36	32	49	19	3.13
1978—California	American	29	179	11	8	.579	185	88	80	93	80	4.02
1979—California	American	37	185	9	10	.474	200	104	99	96	77	4.82
1980—California	American	40	175	8	13	.381	193	83	79	74	66	4.06
1981—California	American	39	65	4	4	.500	56	17	17	38	24	2.35
1982—California§	American	24	52	3	3	.500	45	20	20	40	23	3.46
1983—California x	American	(Did not play)										
1984—Redwood y	California	4	12⅓	0	1	.000	9	9	7	10	7	5.11
1984—California z	American	23	39	4	1	.800	30	7	7	28	19	1.62
1985—Baltimore	American	54	88	10	6	.625	83	44	37	67	35	3.78
1986—Baltimore	American	66	81⅔	6	7	.462	71	29	27	67	28	2.98
1987—Baltimore a	American	7	8	1	0	1.000	8	2	2	3	4	2.25
1988—Rochester b	Int'national	7	7⅓	0	0	.000	5	1	1	6	3	1.23
1988—Baltimore c	American	35	46⅔	0	0	.000	40	22	21	28	37	4.05
Major League Totals—11 Years		367	1011⅓	62	54	.534	996	452	421	583	412	3.75

Selected by Boston Red Sox' organization in 6th round of free-agent draft, June 6, 1972.
†On disabled list, June 23, 1976 through remainder of season.
‡Traded with cash to California Angels for Second Baseman Jerry Remy, December 8, 1977.
§On disabled list, June 3 to June 27 and July 20 to September 7, 1982.
xOn disabled list, March 30, 1983 through remainder of season.
yOn California disabled list, March 27 to June 13, 1984; included rehabilitation disability assignment to Redwood, May 10 to May 30, 1984.
zGranted free agency, November 8, 1984; signed by Baltimore Orioles, December 13, 1984.
aOn disabled list, April 15 to May 13 and May 27, 1987 through remainder of season.
bOn Baltimore disabled list, March 30 to May 10, 1988; included rehabilitation disability assignment to Rochester, April 21 to May 10, 1988.
cReleased, October 3, 1988.

CHAMPIONSHIP SERIES RECORD

Year Club	League	G.	IP.	W.	L.	Pct.	H.	R.	ER.	SO.	BB.	ERA.
1979—California	American	2	5	1	0	1.000	4	1	1	6	2	1.80

ALL-STAR GAME RECORD

Year League	IP.	W.	L.	Pct.	H.	R.	ER.	SO.	BB.	ERA.
1986—American	⅔	0	0	.000	0	0	0	0	0	0.00

PAUL DAVID ABBOTT

Born September 15, 1967, at Van Nuys, Calif.
Height, 6.03. Weight, 185.
Throws and bats righthanded.

Pitched 3-0 no-hit victory against Palm Springs, June 26, 1988 (seven innings).

Tied for California League lead in games started by pitchers with 28 in 1988.

Year Club	League	G.	IP.	W.	L.	Pct.	H.	R.	ER.	SO.	BB.	ERA.
1985—Elizabethton	Ap'lachian	10	35	1	5	.167	33	32	27	34	32	6.94
1986—Kenosha	Midwest	25	98	6	10	.375	102	62	49	73	73	4.50
1987—Kenosha	Midwest	26	145⅓	13	6	.684	102	76	59	138	103	3.65
1988—Visalia	California	28	172⅓	11	9	.550	141	95	80	★205	★143	4.18

Selected by Minnesota Twins' organization in 3rd round of free-agent draft, June 3, 1985.

SHAWN WESLEY ABNER

Born June 17, 1966, at Hamilton, O.
Height, 6.01. Weight, 190.
Throws and bats righthanded.
Brother of Ben Abner, outfielder in Montreal Expos' and Pittsburgh Pirates' organizations, 1984 through 1987.

Major League stolen bases: 1987 (1).
Tied for Texas League lead in being hit by pitch with 7 in 1986.
Led Texas League outfielders in total chances with 352 in 1986.
Led Carolina League outfielders in total chances with 352 in 1985.
Named Carolina League Player of the Year, 1985.

Year Club	League	Pos.	G.	AB.	R.	H.	2B.	3B.	HR.	RBI.	B.A.	PO.	A.	E.	F.A.
1984—Kingsport	Appal.	OF	46	183	32	50	8	0	10	35	.273	87	1	1	.989
1984—Little Falls	NYP	OF	18	68	7	18	2	0	1	5	.265	40	2	1	.977
1985—Lynchburg	Carol.	OF	139	*542	71	*163	*30	*11	16	*89	.301	*332	8	12	.966
1986—Jackson†	Texas	OF	*134	511	80	136	29	•8	14	76	.266	*338	10	4	.989
1987—Las Vegas	P. C.	OF	105	406	60	122	14	11	11	85	.300	238	9	4	.984
1987—San Diego	Nat.	OF	16	47	5	13	3	1	2	7	.277	23	2	2	.926
1988—San Diego	Nat.	OF	37	83	6	15	3	0	2	5	.181	55	1	1	.982
1988—Las Vegas	P. C.	OF	63	252	35	64	16	2	4	34	.254	147	1	6	.961
Major League Totals—2 Years			53	130	11	28	6	1	4	12	.215	78	3	3	.964

Selected by New York Mets' organization in 1st round (first player selected) of free-agent draft, June 4, 1984.
†Traded with Outfielders Stanley Jefferson and Kevin Mitchell and Pitchers Kevin Armstrong and Kevin Brown to San Diego Padres for Outfielder Kevin McReynolds, Pitcher Gene Walter and Infielder Adam Ging, December 11, 1986.

JAMES JUSTIN ACKER
(Jim)

Born September 24, 1958, at Freer, Tex.
Height, 6.02. Weight, 212.
Throws and bats righthanded.
Attended University of Texas, Austin, Tex.
Brother of Bill Acker, nose tackle with St. Louis Cardinals, Kansas City Chiefs, Cincinnati Bengals and Buffalo Bills, 1980 through 1984.

Major League saves: 1983 (1), 1984 (1), 1985 (10), 1987 (14). Total—26.

Year Club	League	G.	IP.	W.	L.	Pct.	H.	R.	ER.	SO.	BB.	ERA.
1980—Bradenton Braves	Gulf Coast	1	5	1	0	1.000	1	0	0	5	0	0.00
1980—Savannah	Southern	13	95	5	5	.500	84	33	28	47	29	2.65
1981—Savannah	Southern	10	77	5	5	.500	57	34	23	37	34	2.69
1981—Richmond	Int'national	21	118	8	7	.533	112	63	55	72	74	4.19
1982—Savannah†‡	Southern	26	142	9	14	.391	120	96	70	96	86	4.44
1983—Toronto	American	38	97⅔	5	1	.833	103	52	47	44	38	4.33
1984—Toronto§	American	32	72	3	5	.375	79	39	35	33	25	4.38
1985—Toronto	American	61	86⅓	7	2	.778	86	35	31	42	43	3.23
1986—Toronto x	American	23	60	2	4	.333	63	34	29	32	22	4.35
1986—Atlanta	National	21	95	3	8	.273	100	47	40	37	26	3.79
1987—Atlanta	National	68	114⅔	4	9	.308	109	57	53	68	51	4.16
1988—Atlanta y	National	21	42	0	4	.000	45	26	22	25	14	4.71
1988—Greenville z	Southern	8	15⅔	0	0	.000	7	3	3	5	3	1.72
American League Totals—4 Years		154	316	17	12	.586	331	160	142	151	128	4.04
National League Totals—3 Years		110	251⅔	7	21	.250	254	130	115	130	91	4.11
Major League Totals—6 Years		264	567⅔	24	33	.421	585	290	257	281	219	4.07

Selected by Atlanta Braves' organization in 1st round (21st player selected) of free-agent draft, June 3, 1980.
†On disabled list, April 9 to April 20, 1982.
‡Drafted by Toronto Blue Jays, December 6, 1982.
§On disabled list, August 16 to September 1, 1984.
xTraded to Atlanta Braves for Pitcher Joe Johnson, July 6, 1986.
yOn disabled list, May 9 to August 19, 1988; included rehabilitation disability assignment to Greenville, July 30 to August 18, 1988.
zGranted free agency, November 4, 1988.

CHAMPIONSHIP SERIES RECORD

Year Club	League	G.	IP.	W.	L.	Pct.	H.	R.	ER.	SO.	BB.	ERA.
1985—Toronto	American	2	6	0	0	.000	2	0	0	5	0	0.00

JAMES DAVID ADDUCI

Name pronounced Uh-DOO-see.

(Jim)

Born August 9, 1959, at Chicago, Ill.
Height, 6.04. Weight, 200.
Throws and bats lefthanded.
Attended Southern Illinois University, Carbondale, Ill.

Led American Association batters in game-winning RBIs with 14 and tied for lead in strikeouts with 103 in 1983.
Led Texas League in game-winning RBIs with 14 in 1982.
Tied for Pacific Coast League lead in errors by first basemen with 15 in 1985.

Year	Club	League	Pos.	G.	AB.	R.	H.	2B.	3B.	HR.	RBI.	B.A.	PO.	A.	E.	F.A.
1980	—Johnson City	Appal.	OF	17	63	15	21	4	0	5	16	.333	27	2	1	.967
1980	—St. Petersburg	Fla. St.	OF	37	118	29	32	4	0	2	13	.271	62	3	2	.970
1981	—St. Petersburg	Fla. St.	OF	92	321	44	87	12	7	7	45	.271	185	4	7	.964
1981	—Arkansas	Texas	OF	40	131	16	36	8	3	5	14	.275	55	3	1	.983
1982	—Arkansas	Texas	OF	121	392	64	117	28	5	22	92	.298	178	6	3	.984
1983	—Louisville	A. A.	OF-1B	129	467	81	131	29	7	25	*101	.281	327	17	14	.961
1983	—St. Louis	Nat.	1B-OF	10	20	0	1	0	0	0	0	.050	47	4	0	1.000
1984	—Louisville†‡	A. A.	OF-1B	113	412	62	119	25	6	12	58	.289	252	13	5	.981
1985	—Vancouver	P. C.	1B-OF	112	393	63	109	28	2	20	77	.277	788	65	16	.982
1986	—Vancouver	P. C.	OF-1B	113	425	71	144	26	5	4	53	.339	418	31	7	.985
1986	—Milwaukee	Amer.	1B	3	11	2	1	1	0	0	0	.091	25	3	0	1.000
1987	—Denver§x	A. A.	OF-1B	16	59	9	17	3	0	2	15	.288	25	4	0	1.000
1987	—Taiyo y	Japan	OF	82	280	....	75	....	....	13	48	.268	Figures Unavailable			
1988	—Milwaukee	Amer.	OF-1B	44	94	8	25	6	1	1	15	.266	40	3	1	.977
1988	—Denver	A. A.	OF-1B	13	49	3	13	4	0	0	5	.265	43	4	1	.979
American League Totals—2 Years				47	105	10	26	7	1	1	15	.248	65	6	1	.986
National League Totals—1 Year				10	20	0	1	0	0	0	0	.050	47	4	0	1.000
Major League Totals—3 Years				57	125	10	27	7	1	1	15	.216	112	10	1	.992

Selected by Philadelphia Phillies' organization in 28th round of free-agent draft, June 7, 1977.

Selected by St. Louis Cardinals' organization in 7th round of free-agent draft, June 3, 1980.

†On disabled list, April 25 to May 22, 1984.

‡Traded with Outfielder Paul Householder to Milwaukee Brewers for Pitchers Rich Buonantony and Jim Koontz and Infielder Ron Koenigsfeld, October 3, 1984.

§Sold to San Francisco Giants' organization, April 19, 1987; returned, April 26, 1987.

xReleased, June 4, 1987; signed by Taiyo Whales of Japanese Baseball League.

yReleased by Taiyo Whales; re-signed by Milwaukee Brewers, January 18, 1988.

JUAN ROBERTO AGOSTO

Born February 23, 1958, at Rio Piedras, P.R.
Height, 6.02. Weight, 190.
Throws and bats lefthanded.

Major League saves: 1983 (7), 1984 (7), 1985 (1), 1986 (1), 1987 (2), 1988 (4). Total—22.

Led Carolina League in balks with 4 in 1977 and 5 in 1978.

Year	Club	League	G.	IP.	W.	L.	Pct.	H.	R.	ER.	SO.	BB.	ERA.
1975	—Winter Haven	Florida St.	6	28	0	4	.000	35	23	18	19	24	5.79
1975	—Elmira	NYP	9	23	1	4	.200	27	37	22	22	34	8.61
1976	—Winter Haven	Florida St.	28	107	5	11	.313	97	70	55	80	69	4.63
1977	—Winston-Salem	Carolina	30	119	4	9	.308	128	106	79	98	*111	5.97
1978	—Winter Haven	Florida St.	1	1	0	0	.000	5	2	2	0	0	27.00
1978	—Winston-Salem†	Carolina	23	120	5	11	.313	114	76	51	74	89	3.83
1979	—Puerto Rico‡	Int.-Amer.	10	31	3	2	.600	31	13	9	9	17	2.61
1980	—Glens Falls	Eastern	8	22	1	0	1.000	26	18	17	8	18	6.95
1980	—Appleton	Midwest	23	144	11	6	.647	118	60	43	93	52	2.69
1981	—Edmonton	P. Coast	48	120	7	10	.412	128	61	52	57	49	3.90
1981	—Chicago	American	2	6	0	0	.000	5	3	3	3	0	4.50
1982	—Edmonton	P. Coast	50	95⅓	3	4	.429	101	63	53	39	49	5.00
1982	—Chicago	American	1	2	0	0	.000	7	4	4	1	0	18.00
1983	—Denver	Am. Assoc.	19	26	4	1	.800	19	8	6	19	10	2.08
1983	—Chicago	American	39	41⅔	2	2	.500	41	20	19	29	11	4.10
1984	—Chicago	American	49	55⅓	2	1	.667	54	20	19	26	34	3.09
1985	—Chicago	American	54	60⅓	4	3	.571	45	27	24	39	23	3.58
1985	—Buffalo	Am. Assoc.	6	12⅔	0	0	.000	13	3	3	11	2	2.13
1986	—Chicago§-Minnesota	American	26	25	1	4	.200	49	30	24	12	18	8.64
1986	—Toledo x	Int'national	21	35	4	3	.571	33	11	9	29	14	2.31
1987	—Tucson	P. Coast	44	50	4	2	.667	48	16	11	31	19	1.98
1987	—Houston	National	27	27⅓	1	1	.500	26	12	8	6	10	2.63
1988	—Houston	National	75	91⅔	10	2	.833	74	27	23	33	30	2.26
American League Totals—6 Years			171	190⅓	9	10	.474	201	104	93	110	86	4.40
National League Totals—2 Years			102	119	11	3	.786	100	39	31	39	40	2.34
Major League Totals—8 Years			273	309⅓	20	13	.606	301	143	124	149	126	3.61

Signed as free agent by Boston Red Sox' organization, August 29, 1974.

†Released, September 21, 1978; signed by Puerto Rico of Inter-American League, March 10, 1979.

‡Declared free agent when Inter-American League folded, June 15, 1979; signed by Chicago White Sox' organization, January 18, 1980.

§Sold to Minnesota Twins in exchange for loaning Pitcher Pete Filson to Buffalo (Chicago White Sox' organization), April 30, 1986; Filson was returned to Minnesota and traded to Chicago White Sox for Pitcher Kurt Walker, September 3, 1986.

xReleased, December 20, 1986; signed by Tucson (Houston Astros' organization), February 13, 1987.

CHAMPIONSHIP SERIES RECORD

Year	Club	League	G.	IP.	W.	L.	Pct.	H.	R.	ER.	SO.	BB.	ERA.
1983	—Chicago	American	1	⅓	0	0	.000	0	0	0	0	0	0.00

—DID YOU KNOW—

That the Kansas City Royals won all 12 games they played against the Baltimore Orioles in 1988?

LUIS AGUAYO (MURIEL)

Name pronounced Uh-GWY-oh.

Born March 13, 1959, at Vega Baja, P.R.
Height, 5.09. Weight, 195.
Throws and bats righthanded

Major League stolen bases: 1980 (1), 1981 (1), 1982 (1), 1985 (1), 1986 (1), 1988 (2). Total—7.
Led Carolina League second basemen in assists with 365, errors with 30 and fielding percentage with .953 in 1977.

Year Club	League	Pos.	G.	AB.	R.	H.	2B.	3B.	HR.	RBI.	B.A.	PO.	A.	E.	F.A.
1976—Spartanburg	W. Car.	2B	3	11	0	1	0	0	0	0	.091	5	2	1	.875
1976—Auburn	NYP	2B-3B-SS	51	197	27	49	9	2	0	23	.249	79	99	10	.947
1977—Peninsula	Carol.	2B-SS	130	497	73	127	28	2	9	41	.256	271	409	34	.952
1978—Reading	East.	SS-2B	115	378	49	74	19	5	4	33	.196	198	341	25	.956
1979—Oklahoma City	A. A.	SS-2B	113	370	54	101	21	1	8	46	.273	191	320	27	.950
1980—Philadelphia†	Nat.	2B-SS	20	47	7	13	1	2	1	8	.277	44	44	3	.967
1980—Oklahoma City‡	A. A.	SS	84	291	37	71	19	2	9	40	.244	154	268	*28	.938
1981—Philadelphia	Nat.	2B-SS-3B	45	84	11	18	4	0	1	7	.214	39	63	5	.953
1982—Philadelphia	Nat.	2B-SS-3B	50	56	11	15	1	2	3	7	.268	27	49	4	.950
1983—Philadelphia§	Nat.	SS	2	4	1	1	0	0	0	0	.250	3	0	0	1.000
1983—Portland	P. C.	SS-2B	71	229	38	65	14	3	5	33	.284	121	216	10	.971
1984—Philadelphia	Nat.	3B-2B-SS	58	72	15	20	4	0	3	11	.278	18	55	3	.161
1984—Portland	P. C.	SS	3	13	3	7	1	0	1	2	.538	6	7	1	.929
1985—Philadelphia	Nat.	SS-2B-3B	91	165	27	46	7	3	6	21	.279	92	158	9	.965
1986—Philadelphia	Nat.	2B-SS-3B	62	133	17	28	6	1	4	13	.211	57	90	5	.967
1987—Philadelphia x	Nat.	SS-2B-3B	94	209	25	43	9	1	12	21	.206	86	172	7	.974
1988—Philadelphia y	Nat.	SS-3B-2B	49	97	9	24	3	0	3	5	.247	47	75	7	.946
1988—New York z	Amer.	3B-2B-SS	50	140	12	35	4	0	3	8	.250	36	81	6	.951
National League Totals—9 Years			471	867	123	208	35	9	33	93	.240	413	706	43	.963
American League Totals—1 Year			50	140	12	35	4	0	3	8	.250	36	81	6	.951
Major League Totals—9 Years			521	1007	135	243	39	9	36	101	.241	449	787	49	.962

Signed as free agent by Philadelphia Phillies' organization, December 27, 1975.
†On disabled list, May 7 to May 22, 1980.
‡On disabled list, May 22 to August 30, 1980.
§On disabled list, March 23 to June 13, 1983.
xOn disabled list, June 1 to June 16, 1987.
yTraded to New York Yankees for Pitcher Amalio Carreno, July 15, 1988.
zGranted free agency, November 4, 1988; signed by Cleveland Indians, December 2, 1988.

DIVISION SERIES RECORD

Year Club	League	Pos.	G.	AB.	R.	H.	2B.	3B.	HR.	RBI.	B.A.	PO.	A.	E.	F.A.
1981—Philadelphia	Nat.	PR	2	0	1	0	0	0	0	0	.000	0	0	0	.000

RICHARD WARREN AGUILERA

Name pronounced Ag-ah-lair-uh.

(Rick)

Born December 31, 1961, at San Gabriel, Calif.
Height, 6.05. Weight, 200.
Throws and bats righthanded.
Attended Brigham Young University, Provo, Utah.

Tied for Carolina League lead in shutouts with 3 in 1984.
Tied for New York-Pennsylvania League lead in shutouts with 2 in 1983.

Year Club	League	G.	IP.	W.	L.	Pct.	H.	R.	ER.	SO.	BB.	ERA.
1983—Little Falls	NYP	16	104	5	6	.455	*109	55	43	84	26	3.72
1984—Lynchburg	Carolina	13	88⅓	8	3	.727	72	29	23	101	28	2.34
1984—Jackson†	Texas	11	67	4	4	.500	68	37	34	71	19	4.57
1985—Tidewater	Int'national	11	79	6	4	.600	64	24	22	55	17	2.51
1985—New York	National	21	122⅓	10	7	.588	118	49	44	74	37	3.24
1986—New York	National	28	141⅔	10	7	.588	145	70	61	104	36	3.88
1987—New York‡	National	18	115	11	3	.786	124	53	46	77	33	3.60
1987—Tidewater	Int'national	3	13	1	1	.500	8	2	1	10	1	0.69
1988—New York§	National	11	24⅔	0	4	.000	29	20	19	16	10	6.93
1988—St. Lucie	Florida St.	2	7	0	0	.000	8	1	1	5	1	1.29
1988—Tidewater	Int'national	1	6	0	0	.000	6	1	1	4	1	1.50
Major League Totals—4 Years		78	403⅔	31	21	.596	416	192	170	271	116	3.79

Selected by St. Louis Cardinals' organization in 37th round of free-agent draft, June 3, 1980.
Selected by New York Mets' organization in 3rd round of free-agent draft, June 6, 1983.
†On disabled list, September 3 to September 15, 1985.
‡On disabled list, May 23 to August 24, 1987; included rehabilitation disability assignment to Tidewater, August 10 to August 24, 1987.
§On disabled list, April 19 to June 19 and July 12 to September 7, 1988; included rehabilitation disability assignment to St. Lucie, June 7 to June 14, 1988; and Tidewater, June 15 to June 19, 1988.

CHAMPIONSHIP SERIES RECORD

Year Club	League	G.	IP.	W.	L.	Pct.	H.	R.	ER.	SO.	BB.	ERA.
1986—New York	National	2	5	0	0	.000	2	1	0	2	2	0.00
1988—New York	National	3	7	0	0	.000	3	1	1	4	2	1.29
Championship Series Totals—2 Years		5	12	0	0	.000	5	2	1	6	4	0.75

WORLD SERIES RECORD

Year	Club	League	G.	IP.	W.	L.	Pct.	H.	R.	ER.	SO.	BB.	ERA.
1986	New York	National	2	3	1	0	1.000	8	4	4	4	1	12.00

DARREL WAYNE AKERFELDS

Born June 12, 1962, at Denver, Colo.
Height, 6.02. Weight, 210.
Throws and bats righthanded.
Attended Mesa College, Grand Junction, Colo., and
University of Arkansas, Fayetteville, Ark.

Tied for Midwest League lead in wild pitches with 19 in 1984.

Year	Club	League	G.	IP.	W.	L.	Pct.	H.	R.	ER.	SO.	BB.	ERA.
1983	Bellingham†	Northwest	12	68⅓	5	3	.625	62	36	34	85	36	4.48
1984	Madison	Midwest	24	151	11	6	.647	156	86	74	137	74	4.41
1985	Huntsville‡	Southern	17	96⅓	9	6	.600	75	42	37	56	64	3.46
1986	Tacoma	P. Coast	25	150	8	12	.400	158	91	79	91	62	4.74
1986	Oakland	American	2	5⅓	0	0	.000	7	5	4	5	3	6.75
1987	Tacoma§	P. Coast	19	129⅔	10	3	.769	117	52	51	84	57	3.54
1987	Cleveland	American	16	74⅔	2	6	.250	84	60	56	42	38	6.75
1988	Colorado Springs x	P. Coast	49	58	3	7	.300	70	43	28	50	26	4.34
Major League Totals—2 Years			18	80	2	6	.250	91	65	60	47	41	6.75

Selected by Atlanta Braves' organization in 9th round of free-agent draft, June 3, 1980.
Selected by Seattle Mariners' organization in 1st round (seventh player selected) of free-agent draft, June 6, 1983.
†Traded to Oakland A's, December 7, 1983, completing deal in which Seattle Mariners traded Pitcher Bill Caudill and a player to be named later to Oakland for Pitcher Dave Beard and Catcher Bob Kearney, November 21, 1983.
‡On disabled list, May 22 to June 13 and July 5 to August 20, 1985.
§Traded with Catcher Brian Dorsett to Cleveland Indians for Second Baseman Tony Bernazard, July 15, 1987.
xDrafted by Texas Rangers, December 5, 1988.

GIBSON ROBERTO ALBA (ROSADO)

Born January 18, 1960, at Santiago, D.R.
Height, 6.02. Weight, 160.
Throws and bats lefthanded.

Year	Club	League	G.	IP.	W.	L.	Pct.	H.	R.	ER.	SO.	BB.	ERA.
1977	Bradenton Pirates	Gulf Coast	6	27	1	1	.500	27	21	13	6	18	4.33
1978	Bradenton Pirates†	Gulf Coast	1	0	0	1	.000	4	4	4	0	1	....
1979-80			(Out of Organized Baseball)										
1981	Gastonia	S. Atlantic	5	12	0	0	.000	7	5	5	13	8	3.75
1981	St. Petersburg	Florida St.	6	10	0	0	.000	18	10	9	4	8	8.10
1981	Erie‡	NYP	16	44	1	2	.333	42	31	28	48	34	5.73
1982	Florence	S. Atlantic	32	114	6	9	.400	117	86	65	107	98	5.13
1983	Kingston§	Carolina	23	29⅔	2	3	.400	18	25	22	51	34	6.67
1984	Knoxville	Southern	45	110⅔	11	9	.550	89	69	57	100	81	4.64
1985	Syracuse	Int'national	17	55⅔	2	3	.400	48	41	35	33	51	5.66
1985	Knoxville	Southern	11	31⅔	0	3	.000	25	29	29	24	38	8.24
1986	Syracuse x	Int'national	28	37	2	1	.667	36	21	19	27	28	4.62
1986	Knoxville y	Southern	8	9⅔	0	0	.000	6	5	4	11	6	3.72
1987	Buffalo z-Denver a	Am. Assoc.	27	73	6	5	.545	95	75	69	46	47	8.51
1988	Louisville	Am. Assoc.	*58	81	4	0	1.000	66	37	35	80	40	3.89
1988	St. Louis	National	3	3⅓	0	0	.000	1	2	1	3	2	2.70
Major League Totals—1 Year			3	3⅓	0	0	.000	1	2	1	3	2	2.70

Signed as free agent by Pittsburgh Pirates' organization November 26, 1976.
†Released, July 1, 1978; signed by Johnson City (St. Louis Cardinals' organization), November 15, 1980.
‡Drafted by Knoxville (Toronto Blue Jays' organization), December 8, 1981.
§On disabled list, April 8 to June 15, 1983.
xOn disabled list, June 28 to July 8, 1986.
yDrafted by Buffalo (Cleveland Indians' organization), December, 1986.
zReleased, June 10, 1987; signed by Denver (Milwaukee Brewers' organization), June, 1987.
aDrafted by Louisville (St. Louis Cardinals' organization), December 8, 1987.

MICHAEL PETER ALDRETE

Name pronounced Owl-DRET-ee.

(Mike)

Born January 29, 1961, at Carmel, Calif.
Height, 5.11. Weight, 185.
Throws and bats lefthanded.
Received bachelor of arts degree in communication from
Stanford University, Stanford, Calif.
Brother of Rich Aldrete, first baseman in San Francisco Giants' organization.

Major League stolen bases: 1986 (1), 1987 (6), 1988 (6). Total—13.
Led California League in total bases with 225 in 1984.

Year	Club	League	Pos.	G.	AB.	R.	H.	2B.	3B.	HR.	RBI.	B.A.	PO.	A.	E.	F.A.
1983	Great Falls	Pion.	1B-OF	38	132	30	55	11	2	4	31	.417	257	17	4	.986
1983	Fresno	Calif.	1B	20	68	5	14	4	0	1	12	.206	189	9	2	.990
1984	Fresno	Calif.	1B	136	457	89	155	28	3	12	72	.339	1180	74	8	*.994
1985	Shreveport	Texas	1B-OF	127	441	80	147	32	1	15	77	.333	854	41	9	.990

Year	Club	League	Pos.	G.	AB.	R.	H.	2B.	3B.	HR.	RBI.	B.A.	PO.	A.	E.	F.A.
1985	Phoenix	P. C.	OF	3	8	0	1	1	0	0	1	.125	3	0	0	1.000
1986	Phoenix	P. C.	OF-1B	47	159	36	59	14	0	6	35	.371	131	8	1	.993
1986	San Francisco	Nat.	1B-OF	84	216	27	54	18	3	2	25	.250	317	36	1	.997
1987	San Francisco	Nat.	OF-1B	126	357	50	116	18	2	9	51	.325	328	18	3	.991
1988	San Francisco†	Nat.	OF-1B	139	389	44	104	15	0	3	50	.267	272	8	4	.986
Major League Totals—3 Years				349	962	121	274	51	5	14	126	.285	917	62	8	.992

Selected by San Francisco Giants' organization in 7th round of free-agent draft, June 6, 1983.
†Traded to Montreal Expos for Outfielder Tracy Jones, December 8, 1988.

CHAMPIONSHIP SERIES RECORD

Year	Club	League	Pos.	G.	AB.	R.	H.	2B.	3B.	HR.	RBI.	B.A.	PO.	A.	E.	F.A.
1987	San Francisco	Nat.	PH-OF	5	10	0	1	0	0	0	1	.100	5	0	0	1.000

DOYLE LAFAYETTE ALEXANDER

Born September 4, 1950, at Cordova, Ala.
Height, 6.03. Weight, 200.
Throws and bats righthanded.
Attended Jefferson State Junior College, Birmingham, Ala.

Tied National League record for most consecutive home runs allowed, inning (3), July 26, 1987, eighth inning.
Major League saves: 1972 (2), 1975 (1). Total—3.

Year	Club	League	G.	IP.	W.	L.	Pct.	H.	R.	ER.	SO.	BB.	ERA.
1968	Tri-City	Northwest	13	70	3	*9	.250	66	47	32	58	47	4.11
1969	Daytona Beach	Florida St.	30	185	13	9	.591	154	75	56	140	100	2.72
1969	Albuquerque	Texas	3	15	0	3	.000	19	10	10	3	12	6.00
1970	Albuquerque	Texas	10	80	4	3	.571	72	29	28	60	20	3.15
1970	Spokane	P. Coast	19	137	9	7	.563	137	66	55	78	26	3.61
1971	Spokane	P. Coast	15	110	6	3	.667	114	49	42	65	31	3.44
1971	Los Angeles†	National	17	92	6	6	.500	105	45	39	30	18	3.82
1972	Baltimore	American	35	106	6	8	.429	78	36	29	49	30	2.46
1973	Baltimore‡	American	29	175	12	8	.600	169	85	75	63	52	3.86
1974	Baltimore	American	30	114	6	9	.400	127	65	51	40	43	4.03
1975	Baltimore	American	32	133	8	8	.500	127	47	45	46	47	3.05
1976	Baltimore§-New York x	American	30	201	13	9	.591	172	81	75	58	63	3.36
1977	Texas	American	34	237	17	11	.607	221	103	96	82	82	3.65
1978	Texas	American	31	191	9	10	.474	198	84	82	81	71	3.86
1979	Texas y	American	23	113	5	7	.417	114	65	56	50	69	4.46
1980	Atlanta z	National	35	232	14	11	.560	227	120	108	114	74	4.19
1981	San Francisco a	National	24	152	11	7	.611	156	51	49	77	44	2.90
1982	Fort Lauderdale	Florida St.	2	11	0	1	.000	12	5	5	4	2	4.09
1982	New York bc	American	16	66⅔	1	7	.125	81	52	45	26	14	6.08
1982	Columbus	Int'national	1	3⅔	0	0	.000	5	4	4	1	2	9.82
1983	New York d-Toronto	American	25	145	7	8	.467	157	76	71	63	33	4.41
1983	Kinston	Carolina	1	6	0	0	.000	3	0	0	4	0	0.00
1984	Toronto	American	36	261⅔	17	6	*.739	238	99	91	139	59	3.13
1985	Toronto	American	36	260⅔	17	10	.630	268	105	100	142	67	3.45
1986	Toronto e	American	17	111	5	4	.556	120	56	55	65	20	4.46
1986	Atlanta f	National	17	117⅓	6	6	.500	135	58	50	74	17	3.84
1987	Atlanta g	National	16	117⅔	5	10	.333	115	57	54	64	27	4.13
1987	Detroit	American	11	88⅓	9	0	1.000	63	16	15	44	26	1.53
1988	Detroit h	American	34	229	14	11	.560	260	122	110	126	46	4.32
National League Totals—5 Years			109	711	42	40	.512	738	331	300	359	180	3.80
American League Totals—15 Years			419	2432⅓	146	116	.557	2393	1092	996	1074	722	3.69
Major League Totals—18 Years			528	3143⅓	188	156	.547	3131	1423	1296	1433	902	3.71

Selected by Los Angeles Dodgers' organization in 44th round of free-agent draft, June 7, 1968.

†Traded with Pitcher Bob O'Brien, Catcher Sergio Robles and First Baseman-Outfielder Royle Stillman to Baltimore Orioles for Pitcher Pete Richert and Outfielder Frank Robinson, December 2, 1971.

‡On disabled list, July 10 to August 6, 1973.

§Traded with Pitchers Ken Holtzman and Grant Jackson, Catcher Elrod Hendricks and Pitcher Jimmy Freeman to New York Yankees for Pitchers Rudy May, Tippy Martinez, Dave Pagan, Scott McGregor and Catcher Rick Dempsey, June 15, 1976.

xPlayed out option year and granted free agency, November 1, 1976; signed as free agent by Texas Rangers, November 23, 1976.

yTraded with Shortstop Larvell Blanks to Atlanta Braves for Pitcher Adrian Devine, Shortstop Pepe Frias and a player to be named later, December 7, 1979; Atlanta received $50,000 to complete deal when Outfielder Jeff Burroughs exercised no-trade clause.

zTraded to San Francisco Giants for Pitcher John Montefusco and Outfielder Craig Landis, December 12, 1980.

aTraded to New York Yankees for Pitcher Andy McGaffigan and Outfielder Ted Wilborn, March 30, 1982.

bOn disabled list, May 10 to July 8, 1982; included rehabilitation disability assignment to Columbus, June 22 to July 8, 1982.

cOn disabled list, August 11 to September 10, 1982.

dReleased, May 31, 1983; signed by Toronto Blue Jays' organization, June 21, 1983.

eTraded to Atlanta Braves for Pitcher Duane Ward, July 6, 1986.

fGranted free agency, November 12, 1986; re-signed by Braves, May 5, 1987.

gTraded to Detroit Tigers for Pitcher John Smoltz, August 12, 1987.

hGranted free agency, October 24, 1988.

CHAMPIONSHIP SERIES RECORD

Established Championship Series records for most runs and earned runs allowed, five-game Series (10), 1987.

Tied Championship Series record for most games lost, Series (2), 1987.

Established American League Championship Series record for most games lost, total Series (4).

Established American League Championship Series record for most runs and most earned runs allowed, seven-game Series (10), 1985.

Year	Club	League	G.	IP.	W.	L.	Pct.	H.	R.	ER.	SO.	BB.	ERA.
1973	—Baltimore	American	1	3⅔	0	1	.000	5	3	2	1	0	4.91
1985	—Toronto	American	2	10⅓	0	1	.000	14	10	10	9	3	8.71
1987	—Detroit	American	2	9	0	2	.000	14	10	10	5	1	10.00
Championship Series Total—3 Years			5	23	0	4	.000	33	23	22	15	4	8.61

WORLD SERIES RECORD

Year	Club	League	G.	IP.	W.	L.	Pct.	H.	R.	ER.	SO.	BB.	ERA.
1976	—New York	American	1	6	0	1	.000	9	5	5	1	2	7.50

ALL-STAR GAME RECORD

Member of American League All-Star Team in 1988; did not play.

LUIS RENE ALICEA

Born July 29, 1965, at Santurce, P. R.
Height, 5.09. Weight, 165.
Throws right and bats left and righthanded.
Attended Florida State University, Tallahassee, Fla.

Major League stolen bases: 1988 (1).

Named second baseman on THE SPORTING NEWS College Baseball All-America Team, 1986.

Year	Club	League	Pos.	G.	AB.	R.	H.	2B.	3B.	HR.	RBI.	B.A.	PO.	A.	E.	F.A.
1986	—Erie	NYP	2B	47	163	40	46	6	1	3	18	.282	94	163	12	.955
1986	—Arkansas	Texas	2B-SS	25	68	8	16	3	0	0	3	.235	39	63	4	.962
1987	—Arkansas	Texas	2B	101	337	57	91	14	3	4	47	.270	184	251	11	*.975
1987	—Louisville	A. A.	2B	29	105	18	32	10	2	2	20	.305	69	81	4	.974
1988	—Louisville	A. A.	2B-SS-OF	49	191	21	53	11	6	1	21	.277	116	165	0	1.000
1988	—St. Louis	Nat.	2B	93	297	20	63	10	4	1	24	.212	206	240	14	.970
Major League Totals—1 Year				93	297	20	63	10	4	1	24	.212	206	240	14	.970

Selected by St. Louis Cardinals' organization in 1st round (23rd player selected) of free-agent draft, June 2, 1986.

ANDREW NEAL ALLANSON
(Andy)

Born December 22, 1961, at Richmond, Va.
Height, 6.05. Weight, 225.
Throws and bats righthanded.
Attended University of Richmond, Richmond, Va.

Major League stolen bases: 1986 (10), 1987 (1), 1988 (5). Total—16.

Led American League catchers in total chances with 762 and double plays with 11 in 1988.

Year	Club	League	Pos.	G.	AB.	R.	H.	2B.	3B.	HR.	RBI.	B.A.	PO.	A.	E.	F.A.
1983	—Waterloo	Midw.	C	17	50	4	10	0	0	0	0	.200	99	8	3	.973
1983	—Batavla	NYP	C	51	145	27	38	3	0	0	6	.262	372	27	5	.988
1984	—Buffalo†	East.	C	39	111	12	28	4	0	0	11	.252	154	15	3	.983
1984	—Waterloo	Midw.	C	46	144	14	39	5	0	0	10	.271	68	9	1	.987
1985	—Waterbury	East.	C	120	420	69	131	17	1	0	47	*.312	578	64	10	.985
1986	—Cleveland	Amer.	C	101	293	30	66	7	3	1	29	.225	446	33	*20	.960
1987	—Buffalo	A.A.	C	76	276	21	75	8	0	4	39	.272	428	30	•12	.974
1987	—Cleveland	Amer.	C	50	154	17	41	6	0	3	16	.266	252	22	4	.986
1988	—Cleveland‡	Amer.	C	133	434	44	114	11	0	5	50	.263	*691	60	•11	.986
Major League Totals—3 Years				284	881	91	221	24	3	9	95	.251	1389	115	35	.977

Selected by Cleveland Indians' organization in 2nd round of free-agent draft, June 6, 1983.

†On disabled list, June 19 to June 29, 1984.

‡On disabled list, July 16 to August 5, 1988.

NEIL PATRICK ALLEN

Born January 24, 1958, at Kansas City, Kan.
Height, 6.02. Weight, 190.
Throws and bats righthanded.

Major League saves: 1979 (8), 1980 (22), 1981 (18), 1982 (19), 1983 (2), 1984 (3), 1985 (3). Total—75.

Tied for Carolina League lead in complete games with 11 in 1977.

Year	Club	League	G.	IP.	W.	L.	Pct.	H.	R.	ER.	SO.	BB.	ERA.
1976	—Marion	Ap'lachian	6	33	2	0	1.000	23	8	7	29	6	1.91
1976	—Wausau	Midwest	6	48	4	2	.667	51	27	20	34	20	3.75
1977	—Lynchburg†	Carolina	20	142	10	2	.833	136	55	44	*126	43	2.79
1978	—Jackson	Texas	16	120	5	9	.357	88	38	28	111	38	*2.10
1978	—Tidewater	Int'national	10	57	2	7	.222	65	35	28	30	12	4.42
1979	—New York‡	National	50	99	6	10	.375	100	46	39	65	47	3.55
1980	—New York	National	59	97	7	10	.412	87	43	40	79	40	3.71
1981	—New York	National	43	67	7	6	.538	64	26	22	50	26	2.96
1982	—New York	National	50	64⅔	3	7	.300	65	22	22	59	30	3.06
1983	—New York§-St. Louis	National	46	175⅔	12	13	.480	179	84	77	106	84	3.94
1984	—St. Louis	National	57	119	9	6	.600	105	54	47	66	49	3.55

Year Club	League	G.	IP.	W.	L.	Pct.	H.	R.	ER.	SO.	BB.	ERA.
1985—St. Louis x	National	23	29	1	4	.200	32	22	18	10	17	5.59
1985—New York y	American	17	29⅓	1	0	1.000	26	9	9	16	13	2.76
1986—Chicago z	American	22	113	7	2	.778	101	50	48	57	38	3.82
1987—Chicago ab-New York	American	23	74⅓	0	8	.000	97	52	49	42	36	5.93
1987—Daytona Beach	Florida St.	4	18	0	1	.000	17	6	4	17	7	2.00
1988—Fort Lauderdale c	Florida St.	3	9	0	0	.000	2	0	0	5	1	0.00
1988—Columbus	Int'national	2	15	0	1	.000	7	2	1	7	0	0.60
1988—New York d	American	41	117⅓	5	3	.625	121	51	50	61	37	3.84
National League Totals—7 Years		328	651⅓	45	56	.446	632	297	265	435	293	3.66
American League Totals—4 Years		103	334	13	13	.500	345	162	156	176	124	4.20
Major League Totals—10 Years		431	985⅓	58	69	.457	977	459	421	611	417	3.85

Selected by New York Mets' organization in 11th round of free-agent draft, June 8, 1976.
†On disabled list, July 26 to September 1, 1977.
‡On disabled list, June 1 to June 25, 1979.
§Traded with Pitcher Rick Ownbey to St. Louis Cardinals for First Baseman Keith Hernandez, June 15, 1983.
xTraded to New York Yankees for a player to be named later, July 17, 1985; deal settled with cash.
yTraded with Catcher Scott Bradley, Outfielder Glen Braxton and cash to Chicago White Sox for Catchers Ron Hassey and Chris Alvarez, Pitcher Eric Schmidt and Outfielder Matt Winters, February 13, 1986.
zOn disabled list, August 6 to September 10, 1986.
aOn disabled list, April 19 to May 26 and June 17 to July 20, 1987; included rehabilitation disability assignment to Daytona Beach, May 6 to May 26, 1987.
bReleased, August 29, 1987; signed by New York Yankees, September 4, 1987.
cOn New York disabled list, March 21 to May 10, 1988; included rehabilitation disability assignment to Fort Lauderdale, April 16 to May 6, 1988.
dGranted free agency, November 4, 1988.

RODERICK BERNET ALLEN
(Rod)

Born October 5, 1959, at Los Angeles, Calif.
Height, 6.02. Weight, 200.
Throws and bats righthanded.

Major League stolen bases: 1984 (1).
Led Pacific Coast League in total bases with 265 in 1988.

Year Club	League	Pos.	G.	AB.	R.	H.	2B.	3B.	HR.	RBI.	B.A.	PO.	A.	E.	F.A.
1977—Sarasota W. Sox	Gulf C.	OF	43	176	21	54	5	2	1	23	.307	60	2	2	.969
1978—Appleton	Midw.	OF	100	342	48	83	16	4	7	55	.243	134	7	8	.946
1979—Knoxville	South.	OF	86	281	32	75	12	2	6	45	.267	98	6	5	.954
1980—Glens Falls†	East.	OF	31	121	26	43	5	4	3	27	.355	29	1	0	1.000
1980—Iowa‡	A. A.	OF	38	131	23	34	4	0	6	24	.260	42	0	0	1.000
1981—Edmonton§	P. C.	OF	109	388	47	114	25	3	11	52	.294	144	12	4	.975
1982—Salt Lake City	P. C.	OF	117	436	82	141	25	2	15	75	.323	178	8	6	.969
1983—Seattle	Amer.	OF	11	12	1	2	0	0	0	0	.167	5	0	0	1.000
1983—Salt Lake City x	P. C.	OF	81	290	48	94	17	4	12	69	.324	55	1	1	.982
1984—Detroit	Amer.	OF	15	27	6	8	1	0	0	3	.296	2	0	0	1.000
1984—Evansville y	A. A.	OF	74	234	24	66	14	4	1	25	.282	106	5	1	.991
1985—Rochester za	Int.	OF	102	333	36	78	17	3	7	32	.234	145	3	6	.961
1986—Nuevo Laredo b	Mex.	OF	20	72	10	21	4	0	2	10	.292	20	0	1	.952
1986—Waterbury	East.	OF	31	103	18	30	10	1	0	9	.291	46	3	1	.980
1986—Maine	Int.	OF	73	252	33	67	7	1	10	52	.266	64	2	0	1.000
1987—Buffalo	A. A.	OF	126	474	85	143	28	7	17	92	.302	1	0	0	1.000
1988—Colorado Springs	P. C.	OF	124	469	84	152	36	4	23	*100	.324	32	1	2	.943
1988—Cleveland c	Amer.	PH-DH	5	11	1	1	1	0	0	0	.091	0	0	0	.000
Major League Totals—3 Years			31	50	8	11	2	0	0	3	.220	7	0	0	1.000

Selected by Chicago White Sox' organization in 6th round of free-agent draft, June 7, 1977.
†On disabled list, August 1 to August 31, 1980.
‡On disabled list, July 8 to July 30, 1980.
§Traded with Catcher Jim Essian and Shortstop Todd Cruz to Seattle Mariners for Outfielder Tom Paciorek, December 11, 1981.
xGranted free agency, October 20, 1983; signed by Evansville (Detroit Tigers' organization), February 14, 1984.
yTraded to Baltimore Orioles for Catcher Luis Rosado, April 9, 1985.
zGranted free agency, October 15, 1985; signed by Charlotte (Baltimore Orioles' organization), January 8, 1986.
aReleased, April 3, 1986; signed by Nuevo Laredo of Mexican League, 1986.
bReleased, 1986; signed by Waterbury (Cleveland Indians' organization), May 20, 1986.
cReleased, November 28, 1988.

WILLIAM FRANCIS ALMON
(Bill)

Born November 21, 1952, at Providence, R. I.
Height, 6.03. Weight, 170.
Throws and bats righthanded.
Received bachelor of arts degree from Brown University, Providence, R. I., in 1979.
Brother of John Almon, outfielder in San Diego Padres' organization, 1977 through 1979.

Major League stolen bases: 1974 (1), 1976 (3), 1977 (20), 1978 (17), 1979 (6), 1980 (2), 1981 (16), 1982 (10), 1983 (26), 1984 (5), 1985 (10), 1986 (11), 1987 (1). Total—128.
Led National League in sacrifice hits with 20 in 1977.
Led National League shortstops in total chances with 882 in 1977.

Led Pacific Coast League shortstops in total chances with 792 in 1975.
Tied for Pacific Coast League lead in stolen bases with 33 in 1975.
Named College Player of the Year by THE SPORTING NEWS, 1974.
Received reported $100,000 bonus to sign with San Diego Padres, 1974.
Named shortstop on THE SPORTING NEWS College Baseball All-America Team, 1974.

Year Club	League	Pos.	G.	AB.	R.	H.	2B.	3B.	HR.	RBI.	B.A.	PO.	A.	E.	F.A.
1974—Hawaii	P. C.	SS	14	36	6	8	0	0	0	3	.222	16	33	7	.875
1974—Alexandria	Texas	SS	25	97	9	18	2	2	0	5	.186	48	70	8	.937
1974—San Diego	Nat.	SS	16	38	4	12	1	0	0	3	.316	13	30	4	.915
1975—Hawaii	P. C.	SS	•144	496	76	113	22	0	1	47	.228	*288	456	*48	.939
1975—San Diego	Nat.	SS	6	10	0	4	0	0	0	0	.400	6	5	0	1.000
1976—Hawaii	P. C.	SS	129	454	67	132	16	2	3	44	.291	*248	395	*36	.947
1976—San Diego	Nat.	SS	14	57	6	14	3	0	1	6	.246	23	52	3	.962
1977—San Diego	Nat.	SS	155	613	75	160	18	11	2	43	.261	*303	538	*41	.954
1978—San Diego	Nat.	3B-SS-2B	138	405	39	102	19	2	0	21	.252	102	255	23	.939
1979—San Diego†	Nat.	2B-SS-OF	100	198	20	45	3	0	1	8	.227	142	193	7	.980
1980—Mtl.‡-N.Y.§	Nat.	SS-2B-3B	66	150	15	29	4	3	0	7	.193	79	134	12	.947
1981—Chicago	Amer.	SS	103	349	46	105	10	2	4	41	.301	190	340	17	.969
1982—Chicago x	Amer.	SS	111	308	40	79	10	4	4	26	.256	164	317	•26	.949
1983—Oakland	Amer.	S-3-1-O-2	143	451	45	120	29	1	4	63	.266	327	176	20	.962
1984—Oakland y	Amer.	O-1-3-S-C	106	211	24	47	11	0	7	16	.223	255	15	2	.993
1985—Pittsburgh	Nat.	S-O-1-3	88	244	33	66	17	0	6	29	.270	104	108	5	.977
1986—Pittsburgh	Nat.	O-3-S-1	102	196	29	43	7	2	7	27	.219	80	45	8	.940
1987—Pitt.z-N.Y. ab	Nat.	S-2-O-1-3	68	74	13	17	4	0	0	5	.230	26	42	3	.958
1988—Philadelphia c	Nat.	3B-SS-1B	20	26	1	3	2	0	0	1	.115	20	15	2	.946
National League Totals—11 Years			773	2011	235	495	78	18	17	150	.246	898	1417	108	.955
American League Totals—4 Years			463	1319	155	351	60	7	19	146	.266	936	848	65	.965
Major League Totals—15 Years			1236	3330	390	846	138	25	36	296	.254	1834	2265	173	.960

Selected by San Diego Padres' organization in 10th round of free-agent draft, June 8, 1971.
Selected by San Diego Padres' organization in 1st round (first player selected) of free-agent draft, June 5, 1974.
†Traded with First Baseman-Outfielder Dan Briggs to Montreal Expos for Second Baseman Dave Cash, November 27, 1979.
‡Became free agent after refusing option to Denver, July 7, 1980; signed by New York Mets, July 11, 1980.
§Released, December 19, 1980; signed by Chicago White Sox' organization, February 4, 1981.
xGranted free agency, November 10, 1982; signed by Oakland A's, January 18, 1983.
yGranted free agency, November 8, 1984; signed by Pittsburgh Pirates, April 8, 1985.
zTraded to New York Mets for Infielder Al Pedrique and Outfielder Scott Little, May 29, 1987.
aGranted free agency, November 9, 1987; re-signed by Mets, January 9, 1988.
bTraded to Philadelphia Phillies for Pitchers Shawn Barton and Vladimir Perez, March 21, 1988.
cReleased, June 16, 1988.

ROBERTO ALOMAR (VELAZQUEZ)

Born February 5, 1968, at Salinas, Puerto Rico.
Height, 6.00. Weight, 155.
Throws right and bats left and righthanded.
Son of Sandy Alomar Sr., infielder with Milwaukee-Atlanta Braves, New York Mets, Chicago White Sox, California Angels, New York Yankees and Texas Rangers, 1964 through 1978; minor league instructor, San Diego Padres' organization, 1985; and coach with San Diego Padres since 1986; and brother of Sandy Alomar, Jr., catcher in San Diego Padres' organization.

Major League stolen bases: 1988 (24).
Led Texas League shortstops in putouts with 167 and errors with 34 in 1987.
Led South Atlantic League second basemen in errors with 35 in 1985.

Year Club	League	Pos.	G.	AB.	R.	H.	2B.	3B.	HR.	RBI.	B.A.	PO.	A.	E.	F.A.
1985—Charleston	S. Atl.	2B-SS	*137	*546	89	160	14	3	0	54	.293	298	339	36	.947
1986—Reno	Calif.	2B	90	356	53	123	16	4	4	49	*.346	198	265	18	.963
1987—Wichita	Texas	SS-2B	130	536	88	171	41	4	12	68	.319	188	309	36	.932
1988—Las Vegas	P. C.	2B	9	37	5	10	1	0	2	14	.270	22	29	1	.981
1988—San Diego	Nat.	2B	143	545	84	145	24	6	9	41	.266	319	459	16	.980
Major League Totals—1 Year			143	545	84	145	24	6	9	41	.266	319	459	16	.980

Signed as free agent by San Diego Padres' organization, February 16, 1985.

SANTOS ALOMAR JR. (VELAZQUEZ)
(Sandy)

Born June 18, 1966, at Salinas, Puerto Rico.
Height, 6.05. Weight, 200.
Throws and bats righthanded.
Son of Sandy Alomar, Sr., infielder with Milwaukee-Atlanta Braves, New York Mets, Chicago White Sox, California Angels, New York Yankees and Texas Rangers, 1964 through 1978; minor league instructor, San Diego Padres' organization, 1985; and coach with San Diego Padres since 1986; and brother of Roberto Alomar, infielder with San Diego Padres.

Led Pacific Coast League catchers in putouts with 573 and total chances with 633 in 1988.
Led Northwest League catchers in putouts with 421 in 1984.
Named Minor League Co-Player of the Year by THE SPORTING NEWS, 1988.
Named Pacific Coast League Player of the Year, 1988.

Year Club	League	Pos.	G.	AB.	R.	H.	2B.	3B.	HR.	RBI.	B.A.	PO.	A.	E.	F.A.
1984—Spokane†	N'west	*C-1B	59	219	13	47	5	0	0	21	.215	465	51	8	*.985
1985—Charleston†	S. Atl.	C-OF	100	352	38	73	7	0	3	43	.207	779	75	18	.979

Year	Club	League	Pos.	G.	AB.	R.	H.	2B.	3B.	HR.	RBI.	B.A.	PO.	A.	E.	F.A.
1986	—Beaumont†	Texas	C	100	346	36	83	15	1	4	27	.240	505	60	★18	.969
1987	—Wichita	Texas	C	103	375	50	115	19	1	8	65	.307	★606	50	★15	.978
1988	—Las Vegas	P. C.	C-OF	93	337	59	100	9	5	16	71	.297	574	46	★14	.978
1988	—San Diego	Nat.	PH	1	1	0	0	0	0	0	0	.000	0	0	0	.000
Major League Totals—1 Year				1	1	0	0	0	0	0	0	.000	0	0	0	.000

Signed as free agent by San Diego Padres' organization, October 21, 1983.
†Batted left and righthanded.

JOSE LINO ALVAREZ

Born April 12, 1956, at Tampa, Fla.
Height, 5.11. Weight, 175.
Throws and bats righthanded.
Attended Hillsborough Junior College, Tampa, Fla., and
University of Southwestern Louisiana, Lafayette, La.

Major League saves: 1988 (3).
Tied for International League lead in shutouts with 2 in 1987.

Year	Club	League	G.	IP.	W.	L.	Pct.	H.	R.	ER.	SO.	BB.	ERA.
1978	—Kingsport	Ap'lachian	8	54	3	3	.500	38	15	8	45	22	1.33
1978	—Greenwood	W. Carolina	7	34	3	1	.750	25	15	13	28	22	3.44
1979	—Savannah	Southern	29	186	11	11	.500	165	87	62	120	73	3.00
1980	—Savannah†	Southern	12	31	2	2	.500	15	5	4	35	11	1.16
1980	—Bradenton	Gulf Coast	4	21	1	0	1.000	16	4	3	16	7	1.29
1980	—Durham	Carolina	2	18	2	0	1.000	14	6	4	12	5	2.00
1981	—Richmond	Int'national	39	71	7	5	.583	51	29	17	61	31	2.15
1981	—Atlanta	National	1	2	0	0	.000	0	0	0	2	0	0.00
1982	—Richmond	Int'national	36	111	5	5	.500	111	54	49	91	50	3.97
1982	—Atlanta	National	7	7⅔	0	0	.000	8	4	4	6	2	4.70
1983	—Richmond‡§	Int'national	33	81⅔	8	2	.800	67	50	48	61	53	5.29
1984	—Tucson x	P. Coast	33	87	4	3	.571	91	56	52	69	48	5.38
1985	—Memphis y-Jacksonville z	Southern	23	101	3	7	.300	90	59	51	78	63	4.54
1986	—Greenville	Southern	36	149⅔	11	6	.647	123	70	59	133	63	3.55
1986	—Richmond	Int'national	5	9⅓	0	0	.000	9	5	3	6	4	2.89
1987	—Greenville	Southern	9	21⅓	1	0	1.000	14	2	2	20	8	0.84
1987	—Richmond	Int'national	22	145	9	•13	.409	142	80	70	108	53	4.34
1988	—Richmond	Int'national	10	14⅓	2	1	.667	13	2	2	10	6	1.26
1988	—Atlanta	National	60	102⅓	5	6	.455	88	34	34	81	53	2.99
Major League Totals—3 Years			68	112	5	6	.455	96	38	38	89	55	3.05

Selected by Atlanta Braves' organization in 8th round of free-agent draft, June 6, 1978.
†On disabled list, April 11 to June 19, 1980.
‡On disabled list, July 10 to August 3, 1983.
§Traded to Houston Astros' organization for Pitcher Ron Meridith, February 16, 1984.
xGranted free agency, October 15, 1984; signed by Memphis (Kansas City Royals' organization), May 6, 1985.
yReleased, July 5, 1985; signed by Jacksonville (Montreal Expos' organization), July 19, 1985.
zReleased, March 31, 1986; signed by Greenville (Atlanta Braves' organization), April 4, 1986.

LARRY EUGENE ANDERSEN

Born May 6, 1953, at Portland, Ore.
Height, 6.03. Weight, 205.
Throws and bats righthanded.
Attended Bellevue Community College, Bellevue, Wash.

Pitched 6-0 no-hit victory against Victoria, June 1, 1974.
Major League saves: 1981 (5), 1982 (1), 1984 (4), 1985 (3), 1986 (1), 1987 (5), 1988 (5). Total—24.
Led Pacific Coast League in saves with 25 in 1978 and 22 in 1983.
Led American Association in balks with 4 in 1975.

Year	Club	League	G.	IP.	W.	L.	Pct.	H.	R.	ER.	SO.	BB.	ERA.
1971	—Reno	California	7	24	1	0	1.000	37	20	18	10	9	6.75
1971	—Sarasota Indians	Gulf Coast	4	15	0	3	.000	15	7	5	10	7	3.00
1972	—Reno	California	27	124	4	14	.222	166	102	90	79	57	6.53
1973	—Reno	California	29	164	10	8	.556	173	91	72	115	67	3.95
1974	—San Antonio	Texas	25	169	10	6	.625	176	84	72	64	51	3.83
1975	—Oklahoma City	Am. Assoc.	25	156	10	11	.476	179	87	73	64	52	4.21
1975	—Cleveland	American	3	6	0	0	.000	4	3	3	4	2	4.50
1976	—Toledo	Int'national	6	23	0	2	.000	47	33	33	8	6	12.91
1976	—Williamsport	Eastern	21	133	9	6	.600	117	47	40	74	34	2.71
1977	—Toledo†	Int'national	45	65	5	6	.455	52	20	14	40	37	1.94
1977	—Cleveland	American	11	14	0	1	.000	10	7	5	8	9	3.21
1978	—Portland	P. Coast	57	99	10	7	.588	92	42	38	65	45	3.45
1979	—Tacoma	P. Coast	27	112	10	6	.625	124	59	50	52	32	4.02
1979	—Cleveland‡	American	8	17	0	0	.000	25	14	14	7	4	7.41
1980	—Portland§	P. Coast	52	93	5	7	.417	78	24	18	65	16	1.74
1981	—Seattle	American	41	68	3	3	.500	57	27	20	40	18	2.65
1982	—Seattle x	American	40	79⅔	0	0	.000	100	56	53	32	23	5.99
1982	—Salt Lake City y	P. Coast	5	6⅔	1	0	1.000	2	0	0	8	3	0.00
1983	—Portland	P. Coast	52	70⅓	7	8	.467	63	35	16	64	30	2.05
1983	—Philadelphia	National	17	26⅓	1	0	1.000	19	7	7	14	9	2.39
1984	—Philadelphia	National	64	90⅔	3	7	.300	85	32	24	54	25	2.38
1985	—Philadelphia	National	57	73	3	3	.500	78	41	35	50	26	4.32
1986	—Philadelphia z-Houston a	National	48	77⅓	2	1	.667	83	30	26	42	26	3.03

Year	Club	League	G.	IP.	W.	L.	Pct.	H.	R.	ER.	SO.	BB.	ERA.
1987—	Houston b	National	67	101⅔	9	5	.643	95	46	39	94	41	3.45
1988—	Houston c	National	53	82⅔	2	4	.333	82	29	27	66	20	2.94
	American League Totals—5 Years		103	184⅔	3	4	.429	196	107	95	91	56	4.63
	National League Totals—6 Years		306	451⅔	20	20	.500	442	185	158	320	147	3.15
	Major League Totals—11 Years		409	636⅓	23	24	.489	638	292	253	411	203	3.58

Selected by Cleveland Indians' organization in 7th round of free-agent draft, June 8, 1971.
†Appeared as first baseman with no chances.
‡Traded to Pittsburgh Pirates for Outfielder Larry Littleton and Pitcher John Burden, December 21, 1979.
§Traded to Seattle Mariners, October 29, 1980, completing deal in which Seattle traded Pitcher Odell Jones to Pittsburgh Pirates for a player to be named later, April 1, 1980.
xOn disabled list, August 11 to September 1, 1982; included rehabilitation disability assignment to Salt Lake City, August 11 to August 31, 1982.
yLoaned to Portland (Philadelphia Phillies' organization), April 1, 1983; sold to Philadelphia Phillies, July 29, 1983.
zReleased, May 13, 1986; signed by Houston Astros, May 16, 1986.
aGranted free agency, November 12, 1986; re-signed by Astros, December 21, 1986.
bGranted free agency, November 9, 1987; re-signed by Astros, January 8, 1988.
cOn disabled list, April 26 to May 11, 1988.

CHAMPIONSHIP SERIES RECORD

Year	Club	League	G.	IP.	W.	L.	Pct.	H.	R.	ER.	SO.	BB.	ERA.
1986—	Houston	National	2	5	0	0	.000	1	0	0	3	2	0.00

WORLD SERIES RECORD

Year	Club	League	G.	IP.	W.	L.	Pct.	H.	R.	ER.	SO.	BB.	ERA.
1983—	Philadelphia	National	2	4	0	0	.000	4	1	1	1	0	2.25

ALLAN LEE ANDERSON

Born January 7, 1964, at Lancaster, O.
Height, 6.00. Weight, 194.
Throws and bats lefthanded.

Led California League in shutouts with 5 in 1984.

Year	Club	League	G.	IP.	W.	L.	Pct.	H.	R.	ER.	SO.	BB.	ERA.
1983—	Wisconsin Rapids	Midwest	7	30⅓	0	4	.000	36	28	23	46	17	6.82
1983—	Elizabethton	Ap'lachian	6	12⅔	1	3	.250	17	12	12	12	7	8.53
1984—	Visalia	California	26	188⅔	12	7	.632	152	80	60	151	105	2.86
1985—	Toledo	Int'national	27	176	7	11	.389	176	81	67	94	79	3.43
1986—	Toledo	Int'national	11	67	2	5	.286	78	39	34	37	31	4.57
1986—	Minnesota†	American	21	84⅓	3	6	.333	106	54	52	51	30	5.55
1987—	Portland	P. Coast	19	98	4	8	.333	127	77	61	45	49	5.60
1987—	Minnesota	American	4	12⅓	1	0	1.000	20	15	15	3	10	10.95
1988—	Portland	P. Coast	3	14⅓	1	1	.500	11	4	2	9	5	1.26
1988—	Minnesota	American	30	202⅓	16	9	.640	199	70	55	83	37	*2.45
	Major League Totals—3 Years		55	299	20	15	.571	325	139	122	137	77	3.67

Selected by Minnesota Twins' organization in 2nd round of free-agent draft, June 7, 1982.
†Appeared in one game as a pinch-runner.

BRADY KEVIN ANDERSON

Born January 18, 1964, at Silver Spring, Md.
Height, 6.01. Weight, 186.
Throws and bats lefthanded.
Attended University of California, Irvine, Calif.

Major League stolen bases: 1988 (10).
Led New York-Pennsylvania League in bases on balls received with 67 in 1985.
Led Florida State League in bases on balls received with 107 in 1986.

Year	Club	League	Pos.	G.	AB.	R.	H.	2B.	3B.	HR.	RBI.	B.A.	PO.	A.	E.	F.A.
1985—	Elmira	NYP	OF	71	215	36	55	7	•6	5	21	.256	119	5	3	.976
1986—	Winter Haven	Fla. St.	OF	126	417	86	133	19	11	12	87	.319	280	5	1	*.997
1987—	New Britain	East.	OF	52	170	30	50	4	3	6	35	.294	127	2	2	.985
1987—	Pawtucket	Int.	OF	23	79	18	30	4	0	2	8	.380	48	1	0	1.000
1988—	Bos.†-Balt.	Amer.	OF	94	325	31	69	13	4	1	21	.212	243	4	4	.984
1988—	Pawtucket	Int.	OF	49	167	27	48	6	1	4	19	.287	115	4	2	.983
	Major League Totals—1 Year			94	325	31	69	13	4	1	21	.212	243	4	4	.984

Selected by Boston Red Sox' organization in 10th round of free-agent draft, June 3, 1985.
†Traded with Pitcher Curt Schilling to Baltimore Orioles for Pitcher Mike Boddicker, July 29, 1988.

DAVID CARTER ANDERSON
(Dave)

Born August 1, 1960, at Louisville, Ky.
Height, 6.02. Weight, 191.
Throws and bats righthanded.
Attended Memphis State University, Memphis, Tenn.

Major League stolen bases: 1983 (6), 1984 (15), 1985 (5), 1986 (5), 1987 (9), 1988 (4). Total—44.
Led Pacific Coast League shortstops in double plays with 81 in 1982.

Year Club	League	Pos.	G.	AB.	R.	H.	2B.	3B.	HR.	RBI.	B.A.	PO.	A.	E.	F.A.
1981—Vero Beach	Fla. St.	SS	65	200	44	54	8	1	0	18	.270	109	218	23	.934
1982—Albuquerque	P. C.	SS	132	507	100	174	19	7	5	76	.343	223	397	*34	.948
1983—Albuquerque	P. C.	SS	9	27	10	11	1	1	0	3	.407	17	26	1	.977
1983—Los Angeles	Nat.	SS-3B	61	115	12	19	4	2	1	2	.165	56	100	5	.969
1984—Los Angeles	Nat.	SS-3B	121	374	51	94	16	2	3	34	.251	176	359	19	.966
1985—Los Angeles†	Nat.	3B-SS-2B	77	221	24	44	6	0	4	18	.199	61	187	9	.965
1985—Albuquerque	P. C.	SS-3B-2B	28	97	23	28	7	0	3	16	.289	29	62	11	.892
1986—Los Angeles‡	Nat.	3B-SS-2B	92	216	31	53	9	0	1	15	.245	77	159	11	.955
1987—Los Angeles§	Nat.	SS-3B-2B	108	265	32	62	12	3	1	13	.234	103	207	7	.978
1988—Los Angeles	Nat.	SS-3B-2B	116	285	31	71	10	2	2	20	.249	139	244	5	.987
Major League Totals—6 Years			575	1476	181	343	57	9	12	102	.232	612	1256	56	.971

Selected by Los Angeles Dodgers' organization in 1st round (22nd player selected) of free-agent draft, June 8, 1981.

†On disabled list, April 29 to June 2 and July 31 to September 1, 1985; included rehabilitation disability assignment to Albuquerque, May 17 to June 1 and August 17 to August 31, 1985.

‡On disabled list, June 22 to August 19, 1986.

§On disabled list, August 11 to September 2, 1987.

CHAMPIONSHIP SERIES RECORD

Year Club	League	Pos.	G.	AB.	R.	H.	2B.	3B.	HR.	RBI.	B.A.	PO.	A.	E.	F.A.
1985—Los Angeles	Nat.	PR-SS-3B	4	5	1	0	0	0	0	0	.000	3	4	0	1.000

WORLD SERIES RECORD

Year Club	League	Pos.	G.	AB.	R.	H.	2B.	3B.	HR.	RBI.	B.A.	PO.	A.	E.	F.A.
1988—Los Angeles	Nat.	PH-DH	1	1	0	0	0	0	0	0	.000	0	0	0	.000

RICHARD ARLEN ANDERSON
(Rick)

Born November 29, 1956, at Everett, Wash.
Height, 6.00. Weight, 175.
Throws and bats righthanded.
Attended Everett Community College, Everett, Wash., and University of Washington, Seattle, Wash.

Pitched 8-0 no-hit victory against Shreveport, May 12, 1979.

Major League saves: 1986 (1).

Year Club	League	G.	IP.	W.	L.	Pct.	H.	R.	ER.	SO.	BB.	ERA.
1978—Little Falls	NYP	14	40	2	3	.400	48	25	10	40	20	2.25
1979—Jackson	Texas	25	131	8	11	.421	124	72	56	71	43	3.85
1980—Jackson	Texas	25	64	3	2	.600	57	24	23	48	17	3.23
1980—Tidewater	Int'national	14	40	1	3	.250	36	18	17	25	15	3.83
1981—Tidewater	Int'national	37	89	3	5	.375	68	34	33	41	45	3.34
1982—Tidewater	Int'national	31	80	4	2	.667	84	35	29	49	23	3.26
1983—Jackson	Texas	13	77⅔	5	1	.833	77	40	31	48	29	3.59
1983—Tidewater	Int'national	15	40	2	1	.667	37	19	18	23	22	4.05
1984—Tidewater†	Int'national	26	130⅓	6	9	.400	118	59	49	93	48	3.38
1985—Tidewater	Int'national	48	95⅓	6	3	.667	79	28	21	54	33	1.98
1986—Tidewater	Int'national	22	84	7	2	.778	76	26	25	56	16	2.68
1986—New York‡	National	15	49⅔	2	1	.667	45	17	15	21	11	2.72
1987—Kansas City	American	6	13	0	2	.000	26	22	20	12	9	13.85
1987—Omaha	Am. Assoc.	15	79⅔	6	5	.545	94	44	40	47	22	4.52
1988—Omaha	Am. Assoc.	14	99⅔	7	4	.636	92	37	29	54	23	2.62
1988—Kansas City§x	American	7	34	2	1	.667	41	17	16	9	9	4.24
National League Totals—1 Year		15	49⅔	2	1	.667	45	17	15	21	11	2.72
American League Totals—2 Years		13	47	2	3	.400	67	39	36	21	18	6.89
Major League Totals—3 Years		28	96⅔	4	4	.500	112	56	51	42	29	4.75

Selected by New York Mets' organization in 24th round of free-agent draft, June 6, 1978.

†Granted free agency, October 15, 1984; re-signed by Mets' organization, February 2, 1985.

‡Traded with Catcher Ed Hearn and Pitcher Mauro Gozzo to Kansas City Royals for Pitcher David Cone and Catcher Chris Jelic, March 27, 1987.

§On disabled list, July 30 to August 15, 1988.

xGranted free agency, October 15, 1988.

JOAQUIN ANDUJAR

Name pronounced Wah-KEEN AHN-doo-hahr.

Born December 21, 1952, at San Pedro de Macoris, D. R.
Height, 6.00. Weight, 180.
Throws right and bats left and righthanded.

Major League saves: 1978 (1), 1979 (4), 1980 (2), 1983 (1), 1986 (1). Total—9.

Led National League in hit batsmen with 11 in 1985 and tied for lead with 7 in 1984.

Tied for National League lead in shutouts with 4 in 1984.

Tied for National League lead in balks with 5 in 1976.

Named National League Comeback Player of the Year by THE SPORTING NEWS, 1984.

Named pitcher on THE SPORTING NEWS National League All-Star fielding team, 1984.

Year Club	League	G.	IP.	W.	L.	Pct.	H.	R.	ER.	SO.	BB.	ERA.
1970—Bradenton Reds	Gulf Coast	12	82	3	5	.375	*86	*58	*38	88	56	4.17
1971—Sioux Falls	Northern	19	75	4	7	.364	61	67	53	82	63	6.36

Year	Club	League	G.	IP.	W.	L.	Pct.	H.	R.	ER.	SO.	BB.	ERA.
1972	Three Rivers	Eastern	22	112	7	6	.538	87	59	44	101	73	3.54
1973	Indianapolis	Am. Assoc.	11	40	2	5	.286	42	45	40	23	45	9.00
1973	Three Rivers†	Eastern	10	59	5	2	.714	38	29	13	39	38	1.98
1974	Indianapolis	Am. Assoc.	33	111	8	8	.500	85	62	44	92	93	3.57
1975	Three Rivers‡§	Eastern	18	62	4	8	.333	57	36	28	44	40	4.06
1976	Houston	National	28	172	9	10	.474	163	74	69	59	75	3.61
1977	Houston	National	26	159	11	8	.579	149	80	65	69	64	3.68
1978	Houston x	National	35	111	5	7	.417	88	45	42	55	58	3.41
1979	Houston	National	46	194	12	12	.500	168	86	74	77	88	3.43
1980	Houston	National	35	122	3	8	.273	132	59	53	75	43	3.91
1981	Houston y-St. Louis z	National	20	79	8	4	.667	85	41	36	37	23	4.10
1982	St. Louis	National	38	265⅔	15	10	.600	237	85	73	137	50	2.47
1983	St. Louis	National	39	225	6	16	.273	215	112	104	125	75	4.16
1984	St. Louis	National	36	*261⅓	*20	14	.588	218	104	97	147	70	3.34
1985	St. Louis a	National	38	269⅔	21	12	.636	265	113	102	112	82	3.40
1986	Oakland bc	American	28	155⅓	12	7	.632	139	70	66	72	56	3.82
1987	Oakland de	American	13	60⅔	3	5	.375	63	43	41	32	26	6.08
1988	Houston f	National	23	78⅔	2	5	.286	94	43	35	35	21	4.00
1988	Osceola g	Florida St.	2	10	1	0	1.000	8	5	3	4	3	2.70
National League Totals—11 Years			364	1937⅓	112	106	.514	1814	842	750	928	649	3.48
American League Totals—2 Years			41	216	15	12	.556	202	113	107	104	82	4.46
Major League Totals—13 Years			405	2153⅓	127	118	.518	2016	955	857	1032	731	3.58

Signed as free agent by Cincinnati Reds' organization, November 14, 1969.

†On disabled list, August 5 to August 15, 1973.

‡On disabled list, May 11 to July 4, 1975.

§Traded to Houston Astros for two minor league players to be named later, October 24, 1975; Cincinnati Reds' organization acquired Pitchers Carlos Alfonso and Luis Sanchez to complete deal, December 12, 1975.

xOn disabled list, July 8 to July 30, 1978.

yTraded to St. Louis Cardinals for Outfielder Tony Scott, June 7, 1981.

zGranted free agency, November 13, 1981; re-signed by Cardinals, December 29, 1981.

aTraded to Oakland A's for Catcher Mike Heath and Pitcher Tim Conroy, December 10, 1985.

bOn suspended list, April 7 to April 12, 1986.

cOn disabled list, June 7 to July 18, 1986.

dOn disabled list, March 25 to April 28, April 29 to May 25, June 11 to June 26 and August 4, 1987 through remainder of season.

eGranted free agency, November 9, 1987; signed by Houston Astros, January 8, 1988.

fOn disabled list, April 5 to May 11, 1988.

gGranted free agency, November 4, 1988.

CHAMPIONSHIP SERIES RECORD

Established National League Championship Series record for most runs allowed (10) and most earned runs allowed (8), six-game Series, 1985.

Year	Club	League	G.	IP.	W.	L.	Pct.	H.	R.	ER.	SO.	BB.	ERA.
1980	Houston	National	1	1	0	0	.000	0	0	0	0	1	0.00
1982	St. Louis	National	1	6⅔	1	0	1.000	6	2	2	4	2	2.70
1985	St. Louis	National	2	10⅓	0	1	.000	14	10	8	9	4	6.97
Championship Series Totals—3 Years			4	18	1	1	.500	20	12	10	13	7	5.00

WORLD SERIES RECORD

Year	Club	League	G.	IP.	W.	L.	Pct.	H.	R.	ER.	SO.	BB.	ERA.
1982	St. Louis	National	2	13⅓	2	0	1.000	10	3	2	4	1	1.35
1985	St. Louis	National	2	4	0	1	.000	10	4	4	3	4	9.00
World Series Totals—2 Years			4	17⅓	2	1	.667	20	7	6	7	5	3.12

ALL-STAR GAME RECORD

Year	League	IP.	W.	L.	Pct.	H.	R.	ER.	SO.	BB.	ERA.
1979	National	2	0	0	.000	2	2	1	0	1	4.50

Named to National League All-Star Team for 1985 game; declined and replaced by Ron Darling.

Named to National League All-Star Team for 1984 game; replaced due to injury by Fernando Valenzuela.

Member of National League All-Star Team in 1977; did not play.

LUIS ANTONIO AQUINO (COLON)

Name pronounced A-Keno.

Born May 19, 1965, at Rio Piedras, Puerto Rico.
Height, 6.01. Weight, 175.
Throws and bats righthanded.

Pitched 2-0 no-hit victory against Columbus, June 20, 1988.

Led Southern League in saves with 20 and tied for lead in games finished in relief with 42 in 1985.

Led Carolina League in games finished in relief with 42 in 1984.

Year	Club	League	G.	IP.	W.	L.	Pct.	H.	R.	ER.	SO.	BB.	ERA.
1982	Bradenton Blue Jays	Gulf Coast	13	73⅓	4	7	.364	60	33	27	52	17	3.31
1983	Florence	S. Atlantic	29	133⅔	7	9	.438	128	91	78	104	61	5.25
1984	Kinston	Carolina	*53	70	5	6	.455	50	21	21	78	37	2.70
1984	Knoxville	Southern	3	4	0	0	.000	3	4	4	7	3	9.00
1985	Knoxville	Southern	50	83	5	7	.417	58	29	24	82	32	2.60
1986	Syracuse	Int'national	43	84⅓	3	7	.300	70	30	27	60	34	2.88

Year	Club	League	G.	IP.	W.	L.	Pct.	H.	R.	ER.	SO.	BB.	ERA.
1986	—Toronto	American	7	11⅓	1	1	.500	14	8	8	5	3	6.35
1987	—Syracuse†	Int'national	26	84⅔	6	7	.462	75	46	45	68	51	4.78
1987	—Omaha	Am. Assoc.	14	50⅔	3	2	.600	42	15	13	29	16	2.31
1988	—Omaha	Am. Assoc.	25	129⅓	8	3	.727	106	43	41	93	50	2.85
1988	—Kansas City	American	7	29	1	0	1.000	33	15	9	11	17	2.79
	Major League Totals—2 Years		14	40⅓	2	1	.667	47	23	17	16	20	3.79

Signed as free agent by Toronto Blue Jays' organization, June 15, 1981.
†Traded to Kansas City Royals' organization for Outfielder Juan Beniquez, July 14, 1987.

ANTONIO RAFAEL ARMAS (MACHADO)
(Tony)

Born July 2, 1953, at Anzoatequi, Venezuela.
Height, 6.01. Weight, 224.
Throws and bats righthanded.
Brother of Marcos Armas, first baseman in Oakland Athletics' organization.

Established major league records for most putouts (11) and chances accepted by right fielder, game (12), June 12, 1982.

Tied major league records for most doubles, inning (2), July 8, 1988 (fourth inning); fewest double plays by outfielder, season, for leader in most double plays (4), 1977.

Major League stolen bases: 1977 (1), 1978 (1), 1979 (1), 1980 (5), 1981 (5), 1982 (2), 1984 (1), 1987 (1), 1988 (1). Total—18.

Led American League in total bases with 339 in 1984.
Led American League batters in strikeouts with 115 in 1981 and 156 in 1984.
Tied for American League lead in grounding into double plays with 31 in 1983.
Tied for American League lead in double plays by outfielders with 4 in 1977.
Named American League Player of the Year by THE SPORTING NEWS, 1981.
Named outfielder on THE SPORTING NEWS American League All-Star Team, 1981 and 1984.
Named outfielder on THE SPORTING NEWS American League Silver Slugger team, 1984.

Year	Club	League	Pos.	G.	AB.	R.	H.	2B.	3B.	HR.	RBI.	B.A.	PO.	A.	E.	F.A.
1971	—Monroe	W. Car.	OF	31	88	7	20	3	0	1	10	.227	37	3	6	.870
1971	—Bradenton Pir.	Gulf C.	OF	43	169	12	39	3	3	0	17	.231	*98	5	3	.972
1972	—Gastonia	W. Car.	OF	117	399	50	106	18	4	9	51	.266	165	7	8	.956
1973	—Sherbrooke†	East.	OF	84	302	46	91	15	5	11	45	.301	150	6	8	.951
1974	—Thetford Mines	East.	OF	*137	476	64	132	26	3	15	81	.277	*329	18	10	.972
1975	—Charleston	Int.	OF	128	450	65	135	28	4	12	72	.300	220	•14	3	.987
1976	—Charleston	Int.	OF-1B	114	409	62	96	24	1	21	67	.235	210	8	7	.969
1976	—Pittsburgh‡	Nat.	OF	4	6	0	2	0	0	0	1	.333	3	0	0	1.000
1977	—Oakland§	Amer.	OF-SS	118	363	26	87	8	2	13	53	.240	294	9	6	.981
1978	—Oakland x	Amer.	OF	91	239	17	51	6	1	2	13	.213	214	3	2	.991
1979	—Oakland y	Amer.	OF	80	278	29	69	9	3	11	34	.248	194	7	5	.976
1980	—Oakland	Amer.	OF	158	628	87	175	18	8	35	109	.279	374	17	10	.975
1981	—Oakland	Amer.	OF	•109	440	51	115	24	3	•22	76	.261	259	8	2	.993
1982	—Oakland za	Amer.	OF	138	536	58	125	19	2	28	89	.233	333	9	6	.983
1983	—Boston	Amer.	OF	145	574	77	125	23	2	36	107	.218	326	5	5	.985
1984	—Boston	Amer.	OF	157	639	107	171	29	5	*43	*123	.268	329	4	9	.974
1985	—Boston b	Amer.	OF	103	385	50	102	17	5	23	64	.265	173	3	3	.983
1986	—Boston cd	Amer.	OF	121	425	40	112	21	4	11	58	.264	247	4	8	.969
1987	—Edmonton	P. C.	OF	29	108	11	27	4	1	3	16	.250	60	1	0	1.000
1987	—California	Amer.	OF	28	81	8	16	3	1	3	9	.198	36	0	0	1.000
1988	—California	Amer.	OF	120	368	42	100	20	2	13	49	.272	212	5	3	.986
	National League Totals—1 Year			4	6	0	2	0	0	0	1	.333	3	0	0	1.000
	American League Totals—12 Years			1368	4956	592	1248	197	38	240	784	.252	2991	74	59	.981
	Major League Totals—13 Years			1372	4962	592	1250	197	38	240	785	.252	2994	74	59	.981

Signed as free agent by Pittsburgh Pirates' organization, January 18, 1971.
†On disabled list, May 27 to July 12, 1973.
‡Traded with Pitchers Dave Giusti, Doc Medich, Doug Bair and Rick Langford and Outfielder Mitchell Page to Oakland A's for Infielders Tommy Helms and Phil Garner and Pitcher Chris Batton, March 15, 1977.
§On disabled list, August 5 to September 1, 1977.
xOn disabled list, April 28 to June 2, 1978.
yOn disabled list, April 15 to June 5, 1979.
zOn disabled list, May 13 to May 28, 1982.
aTraded with Catcher Jeff Newman to Boston Red Sox for Third Baseman Carney Lansford, Outfielder Garry Hancock and a player to be named later, December 6, 1982; Oakland A's acquired Pitcher Jerry King to complete deal, December 20, 1982.
bOn disabled list, June 17 to July 26, 1985.
cOn disabled list, July 12 to July 27, 1986.
dGranted free agency, November 12, 1986; signed by California Angels' organization, July 1, 1987.

DIVISION SERIES RECORD

Year	Club	League	Pos.	G.	AB.	R.	H.	2B.	3B.	HR.	RBI.	B.A.	PO.	A.	E.	F.A.
1981	—Oakland	Amer.	OF	3	11	1	6	2	0	0	3	.545	6	0	1	.857

CHAMPIONSHIP SERIES RECORD

Year	Club	League	Pos.	G.	AB.	R.	H.	2B.	3B.	HR.	RBI.	B.A.	PO.	A.	E.	F.A.
1981	—Oakland	Amer.	OF	3	12	0	2	0	0	0	0	.167	5	2	0	1.000
1986	—Boston	Amer.	OF	5	16	1	2	1	0	0	0	.125	12	0	0	1.000
	Championship Series Totals—2 Years			8	28	1	4	1	0	0	0	.143	17	2	0	1.000

WORLD SERIES RECORD

Year	Club	League	Pos.	G.	AB.	R.	H.	2B.	3B.	HR.	RBI.	B.A.	PO.	A.	E.	F.A.
1986—Boston		Amer.	PH	1	1	0	0	0	0	0	0	.000	0	0	0	.000

ALL-STAR GAME RECORD

Year	League	Pos.	AB.	R.	H.	2B.	3B.	HR.	RBI.	B.A.	PO.	A.	E.	F.A.
1981—American		OF	1	0	0	0	0	0	0	.000	0	0	0	.000

Member of American League All-Star Team in 1984; did not play.

JACK WILLIAM ARMSTRONG

Born March 7, 1965, at Englewood, N.J.
Height, 6.05. Weight, 220.
Throws and bats righthanded.
Attended Rider College, Lawrenceville, N.J., and received degree in economics from University of Oklahoma, Norman, Okla., in 1987.

Pitched 4-0 no-hit victory against Indianapolis, August 7, 1988.

Year	Club	League	G.	IP.	W.	L.	Pct.	H.	R.	ER.	SO.	BB.	ERA.
1987—Billings		Pioneer	5	20⅓	2	1	.667	16	7	6	29	12	2.66
1987—Vermont		Eastern	5	35⅔	1	2	.333	24	12	12	39	23	3.03
1988—Nashville		Am. Assoc.	17	120	5	5	.500	84	44	40	116	38	3.00
1988—Cincinnati		National	14	65⅓	4	7	.364	63	44	42	45	38	5.79
Major League Totals—1 Year			14	65⅓	4	7	.364	63	44	42	45	38	5.79

Selected by San Francisco Giants' organization in 3rd round of free-agent draft, June 2, 1986.
Selected by Cincinnati Reds' organization in 1st round (18th player selected) of free-agent draft, June 2, 1987.

SCOTT GENTRY ARNOLD

Born August 18, 1962, at Lexington, Ky.
Height, 6.02. Weight, 210.
Throws and bats righthanded.
Attended Miami University, Oxford, O.

Led Texas League pitchers in games started with 29, wild pitches with 17 and tied for lead in shutouts with 2 in 1987.
Tied for Appalachian League lead in games started by pitchers with 13 in 1984.

Year	Club	League	G.	IP.	W.	L.	Pct.	H.	R.	ER.	SO.	BB.	ERA.
1984—Johnson City		Ap'lachian	14	91⅓	4	5	.444	80	38	31	90	38	3.05
1984—Springfield		Midwest	1	6	0	1	.000	6	6	6	9	0	9.00
1985—Savannah		S. Atlantic	24	169	8	9	.471	131	76	62	169	70	3.30
1986—St. Petersburg		Florida St.	22	136⅓	10	5	.667	121	57	41	85	39	2.71
1986—Arkansas		Texas	5	28⅓	4	1	.800	24	15	12	23	14	3.81
1987—Arkansas		Texas	29	169	12	9	.571	151	84	76	120	74	4.05
1988—St. Louis		National	6	6⅔	0	0	.000	9	4	4	8	4	5.40
1988—Louisville		Am. Assoc.	3	8⅓	0	3	.000	12	12	9	5	12	9.72
1988—Arkansas		Texas	21	130⅔	10	4	.714	108	42	37	103	52	2.55
Major League Totals—1 Year			6	6⅔	0	0	.000	9	4	4	8	4	5.40

Selected by New York Yankees' organization in 40th round of free-agent draft, June 6, 1983.
Selected by St. Louis Cardinals' organization in 5th round of free-agent draft, June 4, 1984.

BRADLEY JAMES ARNSBERG
(Brad)

Born August 20, 1963, at Seattle, Wash.
Height, 6.04. Weight, 205.
Throws and bats righthanded.
Attended Merced College, Merced, Calif.
Brother of Tim Arnsberg, pitcher in Houston Astros' organization, 1985 through 1987.

Pitched 5-0 no-hit victory against Savannah, May 24, 1984.
Led International League in complete games with 9 and tied for lead in shutouts with 2 in 1987.
Led International League pitchers in games started with 28 and balks with 5 in 1986.
Tied for South Atlantic League lead in complete games with 10 and shutouts with 4 in 1984.
Named International League Pitcher of the Year, 1987.
Named Eastern League Pitcher of the Year, 1985.

Year	Club	League	G.	IP.	W.	L.	Pct.	H.	R.	ER.	SO.	BB.	ERA.
1984—Greensboro		S. Atlantic	23	158⅔	12	5	.706	121	61	52	112	59	2.95
1985—Albany†		Eastern	20	141⅓	•14	2	*.875	105	34	25	82	35	*1.59
1986—Columbus		Int'national	28	*177⅓	8	•12	.400	168	*106	•83	96	53	4.21
1986—New York		American	2	8	0	0	.000	13	3	3	3	1	3.38
1987—Columbus		Int'national	19	144	12	5	.706	140	55	46	83	37	2.88
1987—New York‡§		American	6	19⅓	1	3	.250	22	12	12	14	13	5.59
1988—Texas x		American					(Did not play)						
Major League Totals—2 Years			8	27⅓	1	3	.250	35	15	15	17	14	4.94

Selected by Cleveland Indians' organization in 19th round of free-agent draft, June 8, 1981.
Selected by St. Louis Cardinals' organization in secondary phase of free-agent draft, January 12, 1982.
Selected by Baltimore Orioles' organization in secondary phase of free-agent draft, June 7, 1982.
Selected by California Angels' organization in secondary phase of free-agent draft, January 11, 1983.
Selected by New York Yankees' organization in secondary phase of free-agent draft, June 6, 1983.
†On disabled list, May 12 to May 24 and June 23 to July 22, 1985.

‡On disabled list, August 23 to September 14, 1987.

§Traded to Texas Rangers, November 10, 1987, completing deal in which Texas traded Catcher Don Slaught to New York Yankees for a player to be named later, November 2, 1987.

xOn disabled list, March 29 to September 1, 1988.

ALAN DEAN ASHBY

Born July 8, 1951, at Long Beach, Calif.
Height, 6.02. Weight, 195.
Throws right and bats left and righthanded.
Attended Los Angeles Harbor Junior College, Wilmington, Calif.

Tied National League record for most no-hit games caught, lifetime (3).
Major League stolen bases: 1975 (3), 1978 (1), 1982 (2), 1986 (1). Total—7.
Led National League in passed balls with 14 in 1980.
Led California League catchers in double plays with 12 in 1971.

Year Club	League	Pos.	G.	AB.	R.	H.	2B.	3B.	HR.	RBI.	B.A.	PO.	A.	E.	F.A.
1969—Sarasota Indians...	Gulf C.	C	48	117	10	28	3	1	0	14	.239	219	20	2	★.992
1970—Reno†	Calif.	C	40	121	15	23	5	1	3	18	.190	321	27	7	.980
1971—Jacksonville	South.	C	13	35	4	7	2	0	0	8	.200	76	6	1	.988
1971—Reno‡	Calif.	C-3B	77	239	52	70	14	1	18	60	.293	492	59	10	.982
1972—Portland	P. C.	C	95	291	33	65	9	2	9	28	.223	601	50	8	.988
1973—Ok.C.§-Evan.	A. A.	C-OF	41	124	20	28	8	0	3	16	.226	253	26	2	.993
1973—Cleveland	Amer.	C	11	29	4	5	1	0	1	3	.172	45	0	1	.978
1974—Oklahoma City	A. A	C	66	211	26	60	19	1	2	24	.284	405	33	8	.982
1974—Cleveland	Amer.	C	10	7	1	1	0	0	0	0	.143	12	0	0	1.000
1975—Cleveland	Amer.	C-1B-3B	90	254	32	57	10	1	5	32	.224	450	43	6	.988
1976—Cleveland xy	Amer.	C-1B-3B	89	247	26	59	5	1	4	32	.239	476	52	7	.987
1977—Toronto	Amer.	C	124	396	25	83	16	3	2	29	.210	619	71	11	.984
1978—Toronto z	Amer.	C	81	264	27	69	15	0	9	29	.261	399	38	6	.986
1979—Houston a	Nat.	C	108	336	25	68	15	2	2	35	.202	548	57	8	.987
1980—Houston	Nat.	C	116	352	30	90	19	2	3	48	.256	608	60	6	.991
1981—Houston	Nat.	C	83	255	20	69	13	0	4	33	.271	434	58	9	.982
1982—Houston b	Nat.	C	100	339	40	87	14	2	12	49	.257	530	55	14	.977
1983—Houston c	Nat.	C	87	275	31	63	18	1	8	34	.229	435	56	13	.974
1984—Houston d	Nat.	C	66	191	16	50	7	0	4	27	.262	303	42	5	.986
1985—Houston e	Nat.	C	65	189	20	53	8	0	8	25	.280	312	37	8	.978
1986—Houston f	Nat.	C	120	315	24	81	15	0	7	38	.257	632	43	10	.985
1987—Houston	Nat.	C	125	386	53	111	16	0	14	63	.288	778	46	6	★.993
1988—Houston g	Nat.	C	73	227	19	54	10	0	7	33	.238	414	23	4	.991
1988—Tucson	P. C.	C	2	4	1	0	0	0	0	0	.000	6	2	0	1.000
American League Totals—6 Years			405	1197	115	274	47	5	21	125	.229	2001	204	31	.986
National League Totals—10 Years			943	2865	278	726	135	7	69	385	.253	4994	477	83	.985
Major League Totals—16 Years			1348	4062	393	1000	182	12	90	510	.246	6995	681	114	.985

Selected by Cleveland Indians' organization in 3rd round of free-agent draft, June 5, 1969.

†On military list, January 1 to May 23, 1970.

‡On temporary inactive list, August 27 to September 13, 1971.

§Loaned to Evansville (Milwaukee Brewers' organization), May 22, 1973; returned, July 2, 1973.

xOn disabled list, August 9, 1976 through remainder of season.

yTraded with Outfielder-First Baseman Doug Howard to Toronto Blue Jays for Pitcher Al Fitzmorris, November 5, 1976.

zTraded to Houston Astros for Pitcher Mark Lemongello, Outfielder Joe Cannon and Shortstop Pedro Hernandez, November 27, 1978.

aOn disabled list, August 30 to September 17, 1979.

bGranted free agency, November 10, 1982; re-signed by Astros, December 21, 1982.

cOn disabled list, June 27 to July 24, 1983.

dOn disabled list, April 25 to May 31, 1984.

eOn disabled list, July 29 to September 7, 1985.

fGranted free agency, November 12, 1986; re-signed by Astros, December 19, 1986.

gOn disabled list, June 22 to August 30, 1988; included rehabilitation disability assignment to Tucson, August 28 and 29, 1988.

DIVISION SERIES RECORD

Year Club	League	Pos.	G.	AB.	R.	H.	2B.	3B.	HR.	RBI.	B.A.	PO.	A.	E.	F.A.
1981—Houston	Nat.	C	3	9	1	1	0	0	1	2	.111	24	2	0	1.000

CHAMPIONSHIP SERIES RECORD

Year Club	League	Pos.	G.	AB.	R.	H.	2B.	3B.	HR.	RBI.	B.A.	PO.	A.	E.	F.A.
1980—Houston	Nat.	C-PH	2	8	0	1	0	0	0	1	.125	11	2	0	1.000
1986—Houston	Nat.	C	6	23	2	3	1	0	1	2	.130	59	1	0	1.000
Championship Series Totals—2 Years			8	31	2	4	1	0	1	3	.129	70	3	0	1.000

PAUL ANDRE ASSENMACHER

Born December 10, 1960, at Detroit, Mich.
Height, 6.03. Weight, 200.
Throws and bats lefthanded.
Received degree in business administration from Aquinas College, Grand Rapids, Mich.

Major League saves: 1986 (7), 1987 (2), 1988 (5). Total—14.

Year	Club	League	G.	IP.	W.	L.	Pct.	H.	R.	ER.	SO.	BB.	ERA.
1983	—Bradenton Braves	Gulf Coast	10	36⅔	1	0	1.000	35	14	9	44	4	2.21
1984	—Durham	Carolina	26	147⅓	6	11	.353	153	78	70	147	52	4.28
1985	—Durham	Carolina	14	38⅓	3	2	.600	38	16	14	36	13	3.29
1985	—Greenville	Southern	29	52⅔	6	0	1.000	47	16	15	59	11	2.56
1986	—Atlanta	National	61	68⅓	7	3	.700	61	23	19	56	26	2.50
1987	—Atlanta†	National	52	54⅔	1	1	.500	58	41	31	39	24	5.10
1987	—Richmond	Int'national	4	24⅔	1	2	.333	30	11	10	21	8	3.65
1988	—Atlanta‡	National	64	79⅓	8	7	.533	72	28	27	71	32	3.06
Major League Totals—3 Years			177	202⅓	16	11	.593	191	92	77	166	82	3.43

Signed as free agent by Atlanta Braves' organization, July 10, 1983.
†On disabled list, April 29 to May 9, 1987.
‡On disabled list, August 10 to August 25, 1988.

KEITH ROWE ATHERTON

Born February 19, 1959, at Mathews, Va.
Height, 6.04. Weight, 200.
Throws and bats righthanded.

Major League saves: 1983 (4), 1984 (2), 1985 (3), 1986 (10), 1987 (2), 1988 (3). Total—24.
Led Eastern League in complete games with 13 in 1980.
Tied for Northwest League lead in shutouts with 2 in 1978.

Year	Club	League	G.	IP.	W.	L.	Pct.	H.	R.	ER.	SO.	BB.	ERA.
1978	—Bend	Northwest	12	92	7	3	.700	86	44	35	81	40	3.42
1979	—Waterbury	Eastern	4	21	0	3	.000	28	23	13	7	13	5.57
1979	—Modesto	California	21	146	9	8	.529	190	107	97	103	51	5.98
1980	—West Haven	Eastern	27	190	11	12	.478	185	101	87	117	58	4.12
1981	—West Haven	Eastern	27	175	11	13	.458	174	83	70	116	64	3.60
1982	—Tacoma	P. Coast	28	*200	12	9	.571	214	108	97	128	54	4.37
1983	—Tacoma	P. Coast	26	120⅓	3	8	.273	117	60	53	93	44	3.96
1983	—Oakland†	American	29	68⅓	2	5	.286	53	22	21	40	23	2.77
1984	—Oakland	American	57	104	7	6	.538	110	51	50	58	39	4.33
1985	—Oakland‡	American	56	104⅔	4	7	.364	89	51	50	77	42	4.30
1986	—Oakland§-Minnesota	American	60	97	6	10	.375	100	47	44	67	46	4.08
1987	—Minnesota	American	59	79⅓	7	5	.583	81	46	40	51	30	4.54
1988	—Minnesota	American	49	74	7	5	.583	65	29	28	43	22	3.41
Major League Totals—6 Years			310	527⅓	33	38	.465	498	246	233	336	202	3.98

Selected by Oakland A's organization in 2nd round of free-agent draft, June 6, 1978.
†Struck out in only at bat during season when designated hitter took the field.
‡On disabled list, July 24 to August 13, 1985.
§Traded to Minnesota Twins for a player to be named later and cash, May 20, 1986; Oakland A's organization acquired Pitcher Eric Broersma to complete deal, May 23, 1986.

CHAMPIONSHIP SERIES RECORD

Year	Club	League	G.	IP.	W.	L.	Pct.	H.	R.	ER.	SO.	BB.	ERA.
1987	—Minnesota	American	1	⅓	0	0	.000	1	0	0	0	0	0.00

WORLD SERIES RECORD

Year	Club	League	G.	IP.	W.	L.	Pct.	H.	R.	ER.	SO.	BB.	ERA.
1987	—Minnesota	American	2	1⅓	0	0	.000	0	1	1	0	1	6.75

DONALD GLENN AUGUST
(Don)

Born July 3, 1963, at Inglewood, Calif.
Height, 6.03. Weight, 190.
Throws and bats righthanded.
Attended Chapman College, Orange, Calif.

Tied for Pacific Coast League lead in games started by pitchers with 27 in 1986.
Member of 1984 U.S. Olympic baseball team.

Year	Club	League	G.	IP.	W.	L.	Pct.	H.	R.	ER.	SO.	BB.	ERA.
1985	—Columbus	Southern	27	176⅓	14	8	.636	183	77	58	78	49	2.96
1986	—Tucson†-Vancouver	P. Coast	27	179	10	10	.500	192	88	67	70	51	3.37
1987	—Denver	Am. Assoc.	28	179⅓	10	9	.526	*220	*124	*111	91	55	5.57
1988	—Denver	Am. Assoc.	10	71⅔	4	1	.800	79	37	28	58	14	3.52
1988	—Milwaukee	American	24	148⅓	13	7	.650	137	55	51	66	48	3.09
Major League Totals—1 Year			24	148⅓	13	7	.650	137	55	51	66	48	3.09

Selected by Houston Astros' organization in 1st round (17th player selected) of free-agent draft, June 4, 1984.
†Traded with a player to be named later to Milwaukee Brewers for Pitcher Danny Darwin, August 15, 1986; Milwaukee organization acquired Pitcher Mark Knudson to complete deal, August 21, 1986.

WALTER WAYNE BACKMAN
(Wally)

Born September 22, 1959, at Hillsboro, Ore.
Height, 5.09. Weight, 168.
Throws right and bats right and lefthanded.

Major League stolen bases: 1980 (2), 1981 (1), 1982 (8), 1984 (32), 1985 (30), 1986 (13), 1987 (11), 1988 (9). Total—106.

Tied for National League lead in sacrifice hits with 14 in 1985.
Led International League in bases on balls received with 87 in 1980.
Led Carolina League in caught stealing with 17 in 1978.

Year	Club	League	Pos.	G.	AB.	R.	H.	2B.	3B.	HR.	RBI.	B.A.	PO.	A.	E.	F.A.
1977	—Little Falls	NYP	SS-3B	69	255	44	83	10	2	6	30	.325	96	185	19	.937
1978	—Lynchburg	Carol.	SS	132	494	86	149	19	•9	3	38	.302	★202	★329	30	★.947
1979	—Jackson	Texas	SS-2B	110	404	63	114	11	5	2	19	.282	184	259	31	.935
1980	—Tidewater	Int.	2B-SS	125	400	53	117	15	5	1	51	.293	237	320	22	.962
1980	—New York	Nat.	2B-SS	27	93	12	30	1	1	0	9	.323	62	55	1	.992
1981	—New York	Nat.	2B-3B	26	36	5	10	2	0	0	0	.278	14	21	2	.946
1981	—Tidewater†‡	Int.	SS-3B-2B	21	59	6	9	3	1	0	6	.153	12	38	1	.980
1982	—New York§	Nat.	2B-3B-SS	96	261	37	71	13	2	3	22	.272	173	209	16	.960
1983	—New York	Nat.	2B-3B	26	42	6	7	0	1	0	3	.167	16	15	2	.939
1983	—Tidewater	Int.	2B-SS-3B	101	361	69	114	11	3	1	28	.316	175	278	13	.972
1984	—New York	Nat.	2B-SS	128	436	68	122	19	2	1	26	.280	223	306	10	.981
1985	—New York	Nat.	★2B-SS	145	520	77	142	24	5	1	38	.275	273	370	7	★.989
1986	—New York	Nat.	2B	124	387	67	124	18	2	1	27	.320	186	290	17	.966
1987	—New Yorkx	Nat.	2B	94	300	43	75	6	1	1	23	.250	131	210	6	.983
1988	—New York yz	Nat.	2B	99	294	44	89	12	0	0	17	.303	128	219	4	.989
Major League Totals—9 Years				765	2369	359	670	95	14	7	165	.283	1206	1695	65	.978

Selected by New York Mets' organization in 1st round (16th player selected) of free-agent draft, June 7, 1977.
†On suspended list, June 18 to June 20, 1981.
‡On disabled list, July 9 to September 1, 1981.
§On disabled list, August 15 to September 8, 1982.
xOn disabled list, June 9 to June 29, 1987.
yOn disabled list, August 27 to September 11, 1988.
zTraded with Pitcher Mike Santiago to Minnesota Twins for Pitchers Jeff Bumgarner, Steve Gasser and Toby Nivens, December 7, 1988.

CHAMPIONSHIP SERIES RECORD

Year	Club	League	Pos.	G.	AB.	R.	H.	2B.	3B.	HR.	RBI.	B.A.	PO.	A.	E.	F.A.
1986	—New York	Nat.	2B-PH	6	21	5	5	0	0	0	2	.238	9	17	0	1.000
1988	—New York	Nat.	2B	7	22	2	6	1	0	0	2	.273	7	19	2	.929
Championship Series Totals—2 Years				13	43	7	11	1	0	0	4	.256	16	36	2	.963

WORLD SERIES RECORD

Year	Club	League	Pos.	G.	AB.	R.	H.	2B.	3B.	HR.	RBI.	B.A.	PO.	A.	E.	F.A.
1986	—New York	Nat.	PR-2B	6	18	4	6	0	0	0	1	.333	9	13	0	1.000

SCOTT BAILES

Born December 18, 1962, at Chillicothe, O.
Height, 6.02. Weight, 175.
Throws and bats lefthanded.
Attended St. Louis Community College at Meramec, St. Louis, Mo.

Major League saves: 1986 (7), 1987 (6). Total—13.

Year	Club	League	G.	IP.	W.	L.	Pct.	H.	R.	ER.	SO.	BB.	ERA.
1982	—Greenwood†	S. Atlantic	3	13⅔	0	1	.000	17	12	11	8	6	7.24
1983	—Alexandria	Carolina	52	75	5	2	.714	67	38	28	101	45	3.36
1984	—Nashua	Eastern	54	87	6	8	.429	80	43	33	61	46	3.41
1985	—Nashua‡-Waterbury	Eastern	42	126⅓	9	6	.600	123	58	38	93	43	2.71
1986	—Cleveland	American	62	112⅔	10	10	.500	123	70	62	60	43	4.95
1987	—Cleveland	American	39	120⅓	7	8	.467	145	75	62	65	47	4.64
1988	—Cleveland	American	37	145	9	14	.391	149	89	79	53	46	4.90
Major League Totals—3 Years			138	378	26	32	.448	417	234	203	178	136	4.83

Selected by Texas Rangers' organization in 7th round of free-agent draft, January 12, 1982.
Selected by Pittsburgh Pirates' organization in secondary phase of free-agent draft, June 7, 1982.
†On disabled list, August 12, 1982 through remainder of season.
‡Traded to Cleveland Indians' organization, July 3, 1985, completing deal in which Cleveland traded Shortstop Johnnie LeMaster to Pittsburgh Pirates for a player to be named later, May 30, 1985.

JOHN MARK BAILEY

(Known by middle name.)

Born November 4, 1961, at Springfield, Mo.
Height, 6.05. Weight, 200.
Throws right and bats right and lefthanded.
Attended Southwest Missouri State University, Springfield, Mo.

Major League stolen bases: 1986 (1), 1987 (1). Total—2.
Switch-hit home runs in one game, September 16, 1984.
Led National League in passed balls with 17 in 1984 and 19 in 1985.
Led South Atlantic League catchers in fielding percentage with .989 in 1983.

Year	Club	League	Pos.	G.	AB.	R.	H.	2B.	3B.	HR.	RBI.	B.A.	PO.	A.	E.	F.A.
1982	—Auburn	NYP	1B-3B-OF	65	230	46	69	10	1	11	40	.300	195	29	5	.978
1983	—Asheville	S. Atl.	C-1B	122	410	68	108	23	1	19	62	.263	767	77	7	.992
1984	—Columbus	South.	C-1B-OF	17	53	5	15	3	2	0	9	.283	83	11	0	1.000
1984	—Houston	Nat.	C	108	344	38	73	16	1	9	34	.212	629	56	12	.983
1985	—Houston	Nat.	•C-1B	114	332	47	88	14	0	10	45	.265	566	52	•13	.979
1986	—Houston	Nat.	C-1B	57	153	9	27	5	0	4	15	.176	322	33	4	.989

Year	Club	League	Pos.	G.	AB.	R.	H.	2B.	3B.	HR.	RBI.	B.A.	PO.	A.	E.	F.A.
1986	—Tucson†	P. C.	C-1B	35	123	22	42	8	1	1	19	.341	120	10	3	.977
1987	—Houston	Nat.	C	35	64	5	13	1	0	0	3	.203	126	7	2	.985
1987	—Tucson	P. C.	C-1B	11	29	1	4	0	0	0	2	.138	32	6	1	.974
1988	—Houston‡	Nat.	C	8	23	1	3	0	0	0	0	.130	48	3	1	.981
1988	—Tucson§	P. C.	C-1B-OF	37	111	6	19	7	1	0	9	.171	113	9	1	.992
1988	—Indianapolis	A. A.	C	20	51	10	12	2	0	2	6	.235	99	7	3	.972
Major League Totals—5 Years				322	916	100	204	36	1	23	97	.223	1691	151	32	.983

Selected by Houston Astros' organization in 6th round of free-agent draft, June 7, 1982.
†On disabled list, August 6 to August 16, 1986.
‡On disabled list, May 9 to June 2, 1988.
§Traded to Montreal Expos for Infielder Casey Candaele, July 23, 1988.

HAROLD DOUGLAS BAINES

Born March 15, 1959, at Easton, Md.
Height, 6.02. Weight, 195.
Throws and bats lefthanded.

Tied major league record for most plate appearances, game (12), May 8, finished May 9, 1984 (25 innings).

Tied American League records for longest errorless game and most innings by outfielder, game (25), May 8, finished May 9, 1984.

Major League stolen bases: 1980 (2), 1981 (6), 1982 (10), 1983 (7), 1984 (1), 1985 (1), 1986 (2). Total—29.
Hit three home runs in a game, July 7, 1982 and September 17, 1984.
Led American League in slugging percentage with .541 in 1984.
Led American League in game-winning RBIs with 22 in 1983.
Tied for American Association lead in double plays by outfielders with 4 in 1979.
Named designated hitter on THE SPORTING NEWS American League All-Star Team, 1988.
Named outfielder on THE SPORTING NEWS American League All-Star Team, 1985.

Year	Club	League	Pos.	G.	AB.	R.	H.	2B.	3B.	HR.	RBI.	B.A.	PO.	A.	E.	F.A.
1977	—Appleton	Midw.	OF	69	222	37	58	11	2	5	29	.261	94	10	7	.937
1978	—Knoxville	South.	OF-1B	137	502	70	138	16	6	13	72	.275	291	22	13	.960
1979	—Iowa	A. A.	OF	125	466	87	139	25	8	22	87	.298	222	•16	11	.956
1980	—Chicago	Amer.	OF	141	491	55	125	23	6	13	49	.255	229	6	9	.963
1981	—Chicago	Amer.	OF	82	280	42	80	11	7	10	41	.286	120	10	2	.985
1982	—Chicago	Amer.	OF	161	608	89	165	29	8	25	105	.271	326	10	7	.980
1983	—Chicago	Amer.	OF	156	596	76	167	33	2	20	99	.280	312	10	9	.973
1984	—Chicago	Amer.	OF	147	569	72	173	28	10	29	94	.304	307	8	6	.981
1985	—Chicago	Amer.	OF	160	640	86	198	29	3	22	113	.309	318	8	2	.994
1986	—Chicago	Amer.	OF	145	570	72	169	29	2	21	88	.296	295	15	5	.984
1987	—Chicago†	Amer.	OF	132	505	59	148	26	4	20	93	.293	13	0	0	1.000
1988	—Chicago	Amer.	OF	158	599	55	166	39	1	13	81	.277	14	1	2	.882
Major League Totals—9 Years				1282	4858	606	1391	247	43	173	763	.286	1934	68	42	.979

Selected by Chicago White Sox' organization in 1st round (first player selected) of free-agent draft, June 7, 1977.
†On disabled list, April 7 to May 8, 1987.

CHAMPIONSHIP SERIES RECORD

Year	Club	League	Pos.	G.	AB.	R.	H.	2B.	3B.	HR.	RBI.	B.A.	PO.	A.	E.	F.A.
1983	—Chicago	Amer.	OF	4	16	0	2	0	0	0	0	.125	5	1	0	1.000

ALL-STAR GAME RECORD

Year	League	Pos.	AB.	R.	H.	2B.	3B.	HR.	RBI.	B.A.	PO.	A.	E.	F.A.
1985	—American	PH	1	0	1	0	0	0	0	1.000	0	0	0	.000
1986	—American	PH	1	0	0	0	0	0	0	.000	0	0	0	.000
1987	—American	PH	1	0	0	0	0	0	0	.000	0	0	0	.000
All-Star Game Totals—3 Years			3	0	1	0	0	0	0	.333	0	0	0	.000

CHARLES DOUGLAS BAIR
(Doug)

Born August 22, 1949, at Defiance, O.
Height, 6.00. Weight, 180.
Throws and bats righthanded.
Received bachelor of science degree in industrial education from
Bowling Green State University, Bowling Green, O.

Major League saves: 1977 (8), 1978 (28), 1979 (16), 1980 (6), 1981 (1), 1982 (8), 1983 (5), 1984 (4), 1986 (4). Total—80.
Led Carolina League in complete games with 15 in 1972.
Named Carolina League Pitcher of the Year, 1972.

Year	Club	League	G.	IP.	W.	L.	Pct.	H.	R.	ER.	SO.	BB.	ERA.
1971	—Salem†	Carolina	6	29	2	3	.400	35	22	19	18	26	5.90
1971	—Waterbury	Eastern	1	7	1	0	1.000	5	0	0	2	0	0.00
1972	—Salem	Carolina	24	180	15	7	.682	170	•86	57	186	*95	2.85
1972	—Charleston	Int'national	1	4	0	1	.000	5	3	3	5	0	6.75
1973	—Charleston	Int'national	26	158	7	11	.389	173	103	77	94	87	4.39
1974	—Charleston‡	Int'national	26	170	7	*16	.304	166	87	77	117	91	4.08
1975	—Charleston	Int'national	26	167	9	12	.429	157	72	56	113	58	3.02
1976	—Charleston	Int'national	45	122	7	10	.412	102	48	43	108	57	3.17
1976	—Pittsburgh§	National	4	6	0	0	.000	4	4	4	4	5	6.00
1977	—San Jose	P. Coast	20	33	5	2	.714	24	8	8	49	17	2.18
1977	—Oakland x	American	45	83	4	6	.400	78	39	32	68	57	3.47

Year Club	League	G.	IP.	W.	L.	Pct.	H.	R.	ER.	SO.	BB.	ERA.
1978—Cincinnati	National	70	100	7	6	.538	87	23	22	91	38	1.98
1979—Cincinnati	National	65	94	11	7	.611	93	47	45	86	51	4.31
1980—Cincinnati	National	61	85	3	6	.333	91	42	40	62	39	4.24
1981—Cincinnati y-St. Louis	National	35	55	4	2	.667	55	34	31	30	19	5.07
1982—St. Louis	National	63	91⅔	5	3	.625	69	27	26	68	36	2.55
1983—St. Louis z	National	26	29⅔	1	1	.500	24	11	10	21	13	3.03
1983—Detroit a	American	27	55⅔	7	3	.700	51	27	24	39	19	3.88
1984—Detroit	American	47	93⅔	5	3	.625	82	42	39	57	36	3.75
1985—Detroit b	American	21	49	2	0	1.000	54	38	34	30	25	6.24
1985—St. Louis c	National	2	2	0	0	.000	1	0	0	0	2	0.00
1986—Tacoma	P. Coast	8	12	3	1	.750	8	3	0	13	6	0.00
1986—Oakland d	American	31	45	2	3	.400	37	15	15	40	18	3.00
1987—Maine	Int'national	45	72⅓	6	3	.667	56	27	24	63	32	2.99
1987—Philadelphia e	National	11	13⅔	2	0	1.000	17	9	9	10	5	5.93
1988—Syracuse	Int'national	39	65⅓	3	4	.429	41	19	17	60	20	2.34
1988—Toronto f	American	10	13⅓	0	0	.000	14	6	6	8	3	4.05
National League Totals—9 Years		337	477	33	25	.569	441	197	187	372	208	3.53
American League Totals—6 Years		181	339⅔	20	15	.571	316	167	150	242	158	3.97
Major League Totals—13 Years		518	816⅔	53	40	.570	757	364	337	614	366	3.71

Selected by Pittsburgh Pirates' organization in 2nd round of free-agent draft, June 8, 1971.
†On temporary inactive list, June 23 to July 22, 1971.
‡Conditionally released to Detroit Tigers' organization, December 17, 1974; returned, March 28, 1975.
§Traded with Pitchers Doc Medich, Dave Giusti and Rick Langford, Outfielders Mitchell Page and Tony Armas to Oakland A's for Infielders Phil Garner and Tommy Helms, and Pitcher Chris Batton, March 15, 1977.
xTraded to Cincinnati Reds for First Baseman Dave Revering and cash, February 25, 1978.
yTraded to St. Louis Cardinals for Pitcher Joe Edelen and Second Baseman Neil Fiala, September 10, 1981.
zTraded to Detroit Tigers for a player to be named later, June 21, 1983; St. Louis Cardinals acquired Pitcher Dave Rucker to complete deal, July 5, 1983.
aGranted free agency, November 7, 1983; re-signed by Tigers, December 23, 1983.
bReleased, August 22, 1985; signed by St. Louis Cardinals, September 2, 1985.
cGranted free agency, November 12, 1985; signed by Oakland A's organization, May 19, 1986.
dGranted free agency, November 10, 1986; signed by Maine (Philadelphia Phillies' organization), July 23, 1987.
eReleased, March 26, 1988; signed by Syracuse (Toronto Blue Jays' organization), April 7, 1988.
fReleased, October 31, 1988.

CHAMPIONSHIP SERIES RECORD

Year Club	League	G.	IP.	W.	L.	Pct.	H.	R.	ER.	SO.	BB.	ERA.
1979—Cincinnati	National	1	1	0	1	.000	2	1	1	0	1	9.00
1982—St. Louis	National	1	1	0	0	.000	2	0	0	0	3	0.00
Championship Series Totals—2 Years		2	2	0	1	.000	4	1	1	0	4	4.50

WORLD SERIES RECORD

Year Club	League	G.	IP.	W.	L.	Pct.	H.	R.	ER.	SO.	BB.	ERA.
1982—St. Louis	National	3	2	0	1	.000	2	2	2	3	2	9.00
1984—Detroit	American	1	⅔	0	0	.000	0	0	0	1	0	0.00
World Series Totals—2 Years		4	2⅔	0	1	.000	2	2	2	4	2	6.75

DOUGLAS LEE BAKER
(Doug)

Born April 3, 1961, at Fullerton, Calif.
Height, 5.09. Weight, 165.
Throws right and bats left and righthanded.
Attended Arizona State University, Tempe, Ariz.
Brother of Dave Baker, third baseman with Toronto Blue Jays, 1982.

Major League stolen bases: 1984 (3).
Led Southern League in sacrifice hits with 18 and being hit by pitch with 13 in 1983.
Led Pacific Coast League shortstops in double plays with 80 in 1988.
Led Southern League shortstops in total chances with 747 in 1983.

Year Club	League	Pos.	G.	AB.	R.	H.	2B.	3B.	HR.	RBI.	B.A.	PO.	A.	E.	F.A.
1982—Birmingham	South.	SS	70	213	28	48	3	4	1	21	.225	115	190	14	.956
1983—Birmingham	South.	SS	*146	452	72	109	18	3	5	51	.241	238	*482	27	.964
1984—Evansville†	A. A.	SS	77	243	34	63	21	1	8	30	.259	152	270	16	.963
1984—Detroit	Amer.	SS-2B	43	108	15	20	4	1	0	12	.185	56	86	5	.966
1985—Detroit	Amer.	SS-2B	15	27	4	5	1	0	0	1	.185	12	12	1	.960
1985—Nashville	A. A.	SS	107	325	42	71	9	4	2	30	.218	179	318	22	.958
1986—Detroit	Amer.	SS-2B	13	24	1	3	1	0	0	0	.125	17	21	1	.974
1986—Nashville	A. A.	SS	112	369	46	101	14	6	2	40	.274	*208	291	15	*.971
1987—Toledo	Int.	SS	117	376	40	93	14	2	2	27	.247	190	342	*24	.957
1987—Detroit ‡	Amer.	SS-2B-3B	8	1	0	0	0	0	0	0	.000	2	8	0	1.000
1988—Portland	P. C.	*SS-3B	121	417	52	102	17	4	2	45	.245	194	340	21	*.962
1988—Minnesota	Amer.	SS-3B-2B	11	7	1	0	0	0	0	0	.000	5	7	0	1.000
Major League Totals—5 Years			90	167	21	28	6	1	0	13	.168	92	134	7	.970

Selected by Oakland A's organization in 9th round of free-agent draft, January 13, 1981.
Selected by Detroit Tigers' organization in 9th round of free-agent draft, June 7, 1982.
†On disabled list, June 10 to June 21, 1984.
‡Traded to Minnesota Twins for Shortstop Julius McDougal, February 24, 1988.

CHAMPIONSHIP SERIES RECORD

Year	Club	League	Pos.	G.	AB.	R.	H.	2B.	3B.	HR.	RBI.	B.A.	PO.	A.	E.	F.A.
1984	Detroit	Amer.	SS	1	0	0	0	0	0	0	0	.000	0	0	0	.000

STEPHEN CHARLES BALBONI
(Steve)

Born January 16, 1957, at Brockton, Mass.
Height, 6.03. Weight, 225.
Throws and bats righthanded.
Attended Eckerd College, St. Petersburg, Fla.

Major League stolen bases: 1985 (1).
Led American League batters in strikeouts with 166 in 1985.
Led American League first basemen in total chances with 1,686 in 1985.
Led International League batters in strikeouts with 146 in 1981.
Led Southern League in total bases with 288 and intentional bases on balls received with 17 in 1980.
Led Florida State League batters in strikeouts with 154 in 1979.
Led Florida State League first basemen in double plays with 106 in 1979 and Southern League first basemen with 125 in 1980.
Named Southern League Most Valuable Player, 1980.
Named Florida State League Most Valuable Player, 1979.
Named designated hitter on THE SPORTING NEWS College Baseball All-America Team, 1978.

Year	Club	League	Pos.	G.	AB.	R.	H.	2B.	3B.	HR.	RBI.	B.A.	PO.	A.	E.	F.A.
1978	West Haven	East.	DH	2	2	0	0	0	0	0	0	.000	0	0	0	.000
1978	Fort Lauderdale	Fla. St.	1B	60	176	19	36	5	0	1	19	.205	475	19	4	.992
1979	Fort Lauderdale	Fla. St.	1B	★140	★504	69	127	19	2	★26	★91	.252	★1297	★97	11	★.992
1980	Nashville	South.	1B	141	521	★101	157	25	2	★34	★122	.301	★1218	76	13	★.990
1981	Columbus	Int.	1B	125	434	68	107	21	2	★33	★98	.247	631	55	★14	.980
1981	New York	Amer.	1B	4	7	2	2	1	1	0	2	.286	14	1	0	1.000
1982	Columbus	Int.	1B	83	313	57	89	17	1	★32	86	.284	426	38	8	.983
1982	New York	Amer.	1B	33	107	8	20	2	1	2	4	.187	194	13	2	.990
1983	Columbus	Int.	1B	84	317	72	87	14	0	27	81	.274	479	47	11	.980
1983	New York†	Amer.	1B	32	86	8	20	2	0	5	17	.233	178	9	3	.984
1984	Kansas City	Amer.	1B	126	438	58	107	23	2	28	77	.244	1102	79	●15	.987
1985	Kansas City	Amer.	1B	160	600	74	146	28	2	36	88	.243	★1573	101	12	.993
1986	Kansas City‡	Amer.	1B	138	512	54	117	25	1	29	88	.229	1236	98	★18	.987
1987	Kansas City§	Amer.	1B	121	386	44	80	11	1	24	60	.207	521	41	6	.989
1988	K.C.x-Sea	Amer.	1B	118	413	46	97	17	1	23	66	.235	428	30	4	.991
Major League Totals—8 Years				732	2549	294	589	109	9	147	402	.231	5246	372	60	.989

Selected by New York Yankees' organization in 4th round of free-agent draft, June 6, 1978.
†Traded with Pitcher Roger Erickson to Kansas City Royals for Pitcher Mike Armstrong and Catcher Duane Dewey, December 8, 1983.
‡Released, December 18, 1986; re-signed by Royals, February 25, 1987.
§Released, December 21, 1987; re-signed by Royals, February 18, 1988.
xReleased, May 27, 1988; signed by Seattle Mariners, June 1, 1988.

CHAMPIONSHIP SERIES RECORD

Tied American League Championship Series record for most strikeouts, seven-game Series (8), 1985.

Year	Club	League	Pos.	G.	AB.	R.	H.	2B.	3B.	HR.	RBI.	B.A.	PO.	A.	E.	F.A.
1984	Kansas City	Amer.	1B	3	11	0	1	0	0	0	0	.091	20	3	1	.958
1985	Kansas City	Amer.	1B	7	25	1	3	0	0	0	1	.120	72	7	2	.975
Championship Series Totals—2 Years				10	36	1	4	0	0	0	1	.111	92	10	3	.971

WORLD SERIES RECORD

Tied World Series record for most at-bats, inning (2), October 27, 1985 (fifth inning).

Year	Club	League	Pos.	G.	AB.	R.	H.	2B.	3B.	HR.	RBI.	B.A.	PO.	A.	E.	F.A.
1985	Kansas City	Amer.	1B	7	25	2	8	0	0	0	3	.320	70	3	0	1.000

JEFFREY SCOTT BALLARD
(Jeff)

Born August 13, 1963, at Billings, Mont.
Height, 6.02. Weight, 198.
Throws and bats lefthanded.
Attended Stanford University, Stanford, Calif.

Tied for New York-Pennsylvania League lead in shutouts with 3 in 1985.

Year	Club	League	G.	IP.	W.	L.	Pct.	H.	R.	ER.	SO.	BB.	ERA.
1985	Newark	NYP	13	96	●10	2	.833	78	20	15	91	20	1.41
1986	Hagerstown	Carolina	17	112	9	5	.643	106	39	23	115	32	★1.85
1986	Charlotte	Southern	10	59⅔	5	2	.714	70	29	22	35	20	3.32
1986	Rochester	Int'national	2	6⅓	0	2	.000	11	6	5	7	3	7.11
1987	Rochester	Int'national	23	160⅓	13	4	.765	151	60	55	114	35	3.09
1987	Baltimore	American	14	69⅔	2	8	.200	100	60	51	27	35	6.59
1988	Rochester	Int'national	9	60⅔	4	3	.571	56	26	20	32	11	2.97
1988	Baltimore	American	25	153⅓	8	12	.400	167	83	75	41	42	4.40
Major League Totals—2 Years			39	223	10	20	.333	267	143	126	68	77	5.09

Selected by Milwaukee Brewers' organization in 16th round of free-agent draft, June 8, 1981.
Selected by Baltimore Orioles' organization in 27th round of free-agent draft, June 4, 1984.
Selected by Baltimore Orioles' organizaton in 7th round of free-agent draft, June 3, 1985.

CHRISTOPHER MICHAEL BANDO
(Chris)

Born February 4, 1956, at Cleveland, O.
Height, 6.00. Weight, 195.
Throws right and bats left and righthanded
Attended Arizona State University, Tempe, Ariz.
Brother of Sal Bando, infielder with Kansas City Athletics, Oakland A's and Milwaukee Brewers, 1966 through 1981; Milwaukee Brewers' Special Assistant to the General Manager since 1982; and coach with Milwaukee Brewers, 1983.

Major League stolen bases: 1984 (1).
Received reported $25,000 bonus to sign with Cleveland Indians, 1978.

Year Club	League	Pos.	G.	AB.	R.	H.	2B.	3B.	HR.	RBI.	B.A.	PO.	A.	E.	F.A.
1978—Chattanooga	South.	C	76	241	30	55	12	0	4	21	.228	285	51	10	.971
1979—Chattanooga†	South.	C-3B	21	62	5	15	4	1	0	7	.242	61	13	0	1.000
1980—Chattanooga‡	South.	C-3B	121	404	78	141	31	3	12	73	*.349	480	97	12	.980
1981—Charleston	Int.	C-3B	96	320	47	98	16	2	11	45	.306	414	51	10	.979
1981—Cleveland	Amer.	C	21	47	3	10	3	0	0	6	.213	53	5	2	.967
1982—Cleveland§	Amer.	C-3B	66	184	13	39	6	1	3	16	.212	268	23	3	.990
1983—Cleveland	Amer.	C	48	121	15	31	3	0	4	15	.256	170	19	1	.995
1984—Maine x	Int.	C-1B	29	92	18	24	2	0	3	13	.261	138	12	5	.968
1984—Cleveland	Amer.	C-1B-3B	75	220	38	64	11	0	12	41	.291	307	30	6	.983
1985—Cleveland	Amer.	C	73	173	11	24	4	1	0	13	.139	251	28	4	.986
1986—Cleveland	Amer.	C	92	254	28	68	9	0	2	26	.268	359	30	4	.990
1987—Cleveland y	Amer.	C	89	211	20	46	9	0	5	16	.218	351	34	4	.990
1988—Clev.z-Det.a	Amer.	C	33	72	6	9	1	0	1	8	.125	123	14	3	.979
Major League Totals—8 Years			497	1282	134	291	46	2	27	141	.227	1882	183	27	.987

Selected by Milwaukee Brewers' organization in 22nd round of free-agent draft, June 7, 1977.
Selected by Cleveland Indians' organization in 2nd round of free-agent draft, June 6, 1978.
†On disabled list, April 16 to August 9, 1979.
‡On disabled list, April 24 to May 6, 1980.
§On disabled list, May 2 to June 17, 1982.
xOn Cleveland disabled list, March 28 to April 20, 1984.
yGranted free agency, November 9, 1987; re-signed by Indians, December 7, 1987.
zReleased, August 14, 1988; signed by Detroit Tigers, September 2, 1988.
aReleased, October 7, 1988.

MICHAEL SCOTT BANKHEAD

(Known by middle name.)

Born July 31, 1963, at Raleigh, N.C.
Height, 5.10. Weight, 185.
Throws and bats righthanded.
Attended University of North Carolina, Chapel Hill, N.C.

Member of 1984 U.S. Olympic baseball team.

Year Club	League	G.	IP.	W.	L.	Pct.	H.	R.	ER.	SO.	BB.	ERA.
1985—Memphis	Southern	24	140⅓	8	6	.571	117	63	56	•128	56	3.59
1986—Omaha	Am. Assoc.	7	48⅓	2	2	.500	31	11	8	34	14	1.49
1986—Kansas City†	American	24	121	8	9	.471	121	66	62	94	37	4.61
1987—Seattle‡	American	27	149⅓	9	8	.529	168	96	90	95	37	5.42
1988—San Bernardino§	California	2	11	0	0	.000	6	3	2	6	4	1.64
1988—Calgary	P. Coast	2	11	1	1	.500	15	9	9	5	5	7.36
1988—Seattle	American	21	135	7	9	.438	115	53	46	102	38	3.07
Major League Totals—3 Years		72	405⅓	24	26	.480	404	215	198	291	112	4.40

Selected by Pittsburgh Pirates' organization in 17th round of free-agent draft, June 8, 1981.
Selected by Kansas City Royals' organization in 1st round (16th player selected) of free-agent draft, June 4, 1984.
†Traded with Pitcher Steve Shields and Outfielder Mike Kingery to Seattle Mariners for Outfielder Danny Tartabull and Pitcher Rick Luecken, December 10, 1986.
‡On disabled list, June 24 to July 13, 1987.
§On Seattle disabled list, March 20 to May 14, 1988; included rehabilitation disability assignment to San Bernardino, April 23 to May 2, 1988, and Calgary, May 3 to May 10, 1988.

FLOYD FRANKLIN BANNISTER

Born June 10, 1955, at Pierre, S. Dakota.
Height, 6.01. Weight, 190.
Throws and bats lefthanded.
Attended Arizona State University, Tempe, Ariz.
Brother-in-law of Greg Cochran, pitcher in Oakland A's and New York Yankees' organizations, 1975 through 1982.

Named College Player of the Year by The Sporting News, 1976.
Named lefthanded pitcher on The Sporting News College Baseball All-America Team, 1975 and 1976.

Year Club	League	G.	IP.	W.	L.	Pct.	H.	R.	ER.	SO.	BB.	ERA.
1976—Covington	Ap'lachian	3	13	0	0	.000	3	0	0	27	2	0.00
1976—Columbus	Southern	3	24	1	0	1.000	16	4	4	20	14	1.50
1976—Memphis	Int'national	1	6	1	0	1.000	7	1	1	6	3	1.50
1977—Houston†	National	24	143	8	9	.471	138	70	64	112	68	4.03
1978—Houston‡	National	28	110	3	9	.250	120	59	59	94	63	4.83
1979—Seattle	American	30	182	10	15	.400	185	92	82	115	68	4.05
1980—Seattle	American	32	218	9	13	.409	200	96	84	155	66	3.47

Year	Club	League	G.	IP.	W.	L.	Pct.	H.	R.	ER.	SO.	BB.	ERA.
1981	—Seattle§	American	21	121	9	9	.500	128	62	60	85	39	4.46
1982	—Seattle x	American	35	247	12	13	.480	225	112	94	★209	77	3.43
1983	—Chicago	American	34	217⅓	16	10	.615	191	88	81	193	71	3.35
1984	—Chicago y	American	34	218	14	11	.560	211	127	117	152	80	4.83
1985	—Chicago	American	34	210⅔	10	14	.417	211	121	114	198	100	4.87
1986	—Chicago z	American	28	165⅓	10	14	.417	162	81	65	92	48	3.54
1987	—Chicago a	American	34	228⅔	16	11	.593	216	100	91	124	49	3.58
1988	—Kansas City	American	31	189⅓	12	13	.480	182	102	91	113	68	4.33
National League Totals—2 Years			52	253	11	18	.379	258	129	123	206	131	4.38
American League Totals—10 Years			313	1997⅓	118	123	.490	1911	981	879	1436	666	3.96
Major League Totals—12 Years			365	2250⅓	129	141	.478	2169	1110	1002	1642	797	4.01

Selected by Oakland A's organization in 3rd round of free-agent draft, June 5, 1973.
Selected by Houston Astros' organization in 1st round (first player selected) of free-agent draft, June 8, 1976.
†On disabled list, July 26 to August 22, 1977.
‡Traded to Seattle Mariners for Shortstop Craig Reynolds, December 8, 1978.
§On disabled list, August 8 to August 29, 1981.
xGranted free agency, November 10, 1982; signed by Chicago White Sox, December 13, 1982.
yHad one at-bat with no hits.
zOn disabled list, May 19 to June 17, 1986.
aTraded with Infielder Dave Cochrane to Kansas City Royals for Pitchers John Davis, Melido Perez, Chuck Mount and Greg Hibbard, December 10, 1987.

CHAMPIONSHIP SERIES RECORD

Year	Club	League	G.	IP.	W.	L.	Pct.	H.	R.	ER.	SO.	BB.	ERA.
1983	—Chicago	American	1	6	0	1	.000	5	4	3	5	1	4.50

ALL-STAR GAME RECORD

Year	League	IP.	W.	L.	Pct.	H.	R.	ER.	SO.	BB.	ERA.
1982	—American	1	0	0	.000	1	0	0	0	0	0.00

JESSE LEE BARFIELD

Born October 29, 1959, at Joliet, Ill.
Height, 6.01. Weight, 200.
Throws and bats righthanded.

Major League stolen bases: 1981 (4), 1982 (1), 1983 (2), 1984 (8), 1985 (22), 1986 (8), 1987 (3), 1988 (7). Total—55.
Led American League outfielders in double plays with 8 in 1985 and 1986.
Led Florida State League batters in strikeouts with 125 in 1978.
Named outfielder on THE SPORTING NEWS American League All-Star fielding team, 1986 and 1987.
Named outfielder on THE SPORTING NEWS American League Silver Slugger team, 1986.

Year	Club	League	Pos.	G.	AB.	R.	H.	2B.	3B.	HR.	RBI.	B.A.	PO.	A.	E.	F.A.
1977	—Utica	NYP	OF	70	234	37	53	9	3	5	35	.226	122	6	●13	.908
1978	—Dunedin	Fla. St.	OF	133	441	40	91	12	3	2	34	.206	229	★22	★15	.944
1979	—Kinston	Carol.	OF	136	477	66	126	24	5	8	71	.264	284	19	17	.947
1980	—Knoxville†	South.	OF	124	433	63	104	12	8	14	65	.240	309	14	12	.964
1981	—Knoxville	South.	OF	141	524	83	137	24	13	16	70	.261	270	★23	6	.980
1981	—Toronto	Amer.	OF	25	95	7	22	3	2	2	9	.232	71	2	0	1.000
1982	—Toronto	Amer.	OF	139	394	54	97	13	2	18	58	.246	217	15	9	.963
1983	—Toronto	Amer.	OF	128	388	58	98	13	3	27	68	.253	213	16	8	.966
1984	—Toronto	Amer.	OF	110	320	51	91	14	1	14	49	.284	190	9	10	.952
1985	—Toronto	Amer.	OF	155	539	94	156	34	9	27	84	.289	349	★22	4	.989
1986	—Toronto	Amer.	OF	158	589	107	170	35	2	★40	108	.289	368	★20	3	.992
1987	—Toronto	Amer.	OF	159	590	89	155	25	3	28	84	.263	341	●17	3	.992
1988	—Toronto‡	Amer.	OF	137	468	62	114	21	5	18	56	.244	325	12	4	.988
Major League Totals—8 Years				1011	3383	522	903	158	27	174	516	.267	2074	113	41	.982

Selected by Toronto Blue Jays' organization in 9th round of free-agent draft, June 7, 1977.
†On disabled list, August 15 to August 29, 1980.
‡On disabled list, May 16 to May 31, 1988.

CHAMPIONSHIP SERIES RECORD

Year	Club	League	Pos.	G.	AB.	R.	H.	2B.	3B.	HR.	RBI.	B.A.	PO.	A.	E.	F.A.
1985	—Toronto	Amer.	OF	7	25	3	7	1	0	1	4	.280	21	0	1	.955

ALL-STAR GAME RECORD

Year	League	Pos.	AB.	R.	H.	2B.	3B.	HR.	RBI.	B.A.	PO.	A.	E.	F.A.
1986	—American	PH-OF	3	0	0	0	0	0	0	.000	2	0	0	1.000

SALOME BAROJAS (ROMERO)

Name pronounced Sahl-low-MAY BAR-oh-hass.

Born June 16, 1957, at Cordoba, Veracruz, Mex.
Height, 5.09. Weight, 188.
Throws and bats righthanded.

Major League saves: 1982 (21), 1983 (12), 1984 (2). Total—35.
Led Mexican League in saves with 15 in 1987 and 17 in 1988.

Year	Club	League	G.	IP.	W.	L.	Pct.	H.	R.	ER.	SO.	BB.	ERA.
1976	—Cordoba	Mexican	15	43	3	1	.750	32	12	9	17	14	1.88
1977	—Cordoba	Mexican	41	126	5	4	.556	109	46	28	85	45	2.00

Year Club	League	G.	IP.	W.	L.	Pct.	H.	R.	ER.	SO.	BB.	ERA.
1978—Cordoba	Mexican	40	66	8	3	.727	54	22	18	27	34	2.45
1979—Cordoba	Mexican	41	148	7	6	.538	143	49	43	64	76	2.61
1980—Reynosa	Mexican	29	126	9	5	.643	105	40	33	82	49	2.36
1981—Mexico City Reds†	Mexican	50	98	12	3	.800	81	40	33	42	41	3.04
1982—Chicago	American	61	106⅔	6	6	.500	96	43	42	56	46	3.54
1983—Chicago	American	52	87⅓	3	3	.500	70	24	24	38	32	2.47
1984—Chicago‡-Seattle	American	43	134⅔	9	7	.563	136	70	62	55	60	4.14
1984—Denver	Am. Assoc.	3	9	1	0	1.000	6	1	1	3	5	1.00
1985—Seattle§x	American	17	52⅔	0	5	.000	65	40	35	27	33	5.98
1986—Mexico City Reds	Mexican	28	181⅔	11	9	.550	205	113	98	88	*99	4.86
1987—Mexico City Reds	Mexican	*53	124⅔	13	4	.764	119	47	43	62	70	3.10
1988—Mexico City Reds y	Mexican	51	103⅓	14	4	.778	89	40	36	60	54	3.14
1988—Philadelphia	National	6	8⅔	0	0	.000	7	9	8	1	8	8.31
American League Totals—4 Years		173	381⅓	18	21	.462	367	177	163	176	171	3.85
National League Totals—1 Year		6	8⅔	0	0	.000	7	9	8	1	8	8.31
Major League Totals—5 Years		179	390	18	21	.462	374	186	171	177	179	3.95

†Sold to Chicago White Sox, December 9, 1981.
‡Traded to Seattle Mariners for Pitchers Gene Nelson and Jerry Don Gleaton, June 27, 1984.
§On disabled list, June 5 to June 29, 1985.
xReleased, December 20, 1985; signed by Mexico City Reds of Mexican League, 1986.
ySold to Philadelphia Phillies, July 28, 1988 (sale to take affect after Mexican League season concludes); returned, September 29, 1988.

CHAMPIONSHIP SERIES RECORD

Year Club	League	G.	IP.	W.	L.	Pct.	H.	R.	ER.	SO.	BB.	ERA.
1983—Chicago	American	2	1	0	0	.000	4	2	2	0	0	18.00

MARTIN GLENN BARRETT
(Marty)

Born June 23, 1958, at Arcadia, Calif.
Height, 5.10. Weight, 175.
Throws and bats righthanded.
Attended Mesa Community College, Mesa, Ariz. and Arizona State University, Tempe, Ariz.
Brother of Charlie Barrett, pitcher in Los Angeles Dodgers' organization, 1973 through 1978; and Tom Barrett, infielder in Philadelphia Phillies' organization.

Major League stolen bases: 1984 (5), 1985 (7), 1986 (15), 1987 (15), 1988 (7). Total—49.
Led American League in sacrifice hits with 18 in 1986, 22 in 1987 and 20 in 1988.
Led American League second basemen in double plays with 110 in 1985.
Led Eastern League in sacrifice hits with 15 in 1980.
Led Florida State League in sacrifice flies with 9 in 1979.
Led International League second basemen in double plays with 99 in 1982.

Year Club	League	Pos.	G.	AB.	R.	H.	2B.	3B.	HR.	RBI.	B.A.	PO.	A.	E.	F.A.
1979—Winter Haven	Fla. St.	2B	57	178	25	53	7	0	1	28	.298	124	144	6	.978
1980—Bristol	East.	*2B-SS	128	475	72	130	17	2	1	41	.274	279	372	10	*.985
1981—Pawtucket†	Int.	2B	88	343	36	91	12	2	1	28	.265	186	254	10	.978
1982—Pawtucket	Int.	2B	131	477	72	143	27	1	5	57	.300	303	*415	11	*.985
1982—Boston	Amer.	2B	8	18	0	1	0	0	0	0	.056	11	21	0	1.000
1983—Boston	Amer.	2B	33	44	7	10	1	1	0	2	.227	32	28	1	.984
1983—Pawtucket	Int.	2B	36	119	24	41	4	2	1	18	.345	70	115	1	.995
1984—Boston	Amer.	2B	139	475	56	144	23	3	3	45	.303	245	417	9	*.987
1985—Boston	Amer.	2B	156	534	59	142	26	0	5	56	.266	*355	479	11	.987
1986—Boston	Amer.	2B	158	625	94	179	39	4	4	60	.286	303	*450	14	.982
1987—Boston‡	Amer.	2B	137	559	72	164	23	0	3	43	.293	320	438	9	*.988
1988—Boston	Amer.	2B	150	612	83	173	28	1	1	65	.283	312	402	7	.990
Major League Totals—7 Years			781	2867	371	813	140	9	16	271	.284	1578	2235	51	.987

Selected by California Angels' organization in 11th round of free-agent draft, January 11, 1977.
Selected by New York Mets' organization in 3rd round of free-agent draft, January 10, 1978.
Selected by Boston Red Sox' organization in secondary phase of free-agent draft, June 5, 1979.
†On disabled list, June 25 to July 15 and July 17 to August 4, 1981.
‡On disabled list, April 11 to April 27, 1987.

CHAMPIONSHIP SERIES RECORD

Established American League Championship Series record for most hits, seven-game Series (11), 1986.
Tied American League Championship Series record for most singles, seven-game Series (9), 1986.

Year Club	League	Pos.	G.	AB.	R.	H.	2B.	3B.	HR.	RBI.	B.A.	PO.	A.	E.	F.A.
1986—Boston	Amer.	2B	7	30	4	11	2	0	0	5	.367	19	21	0	1.000
1988—Boston	Amer.	2B	4	15	2	1	0	0	0	0	.067	6	8	0	1.000
Championship Series Totals—2 Years			11	45	6	12	2	0	0	5	.267	25	29	0	1.000

WORLD SERIES RECORD

Tied World Series records for most assists by second baseman, inning (3), October 23, 1986 (first inning); most hits, Series (13), 1986.

Year Club	League	Pos.	G.	AB.	R.	H.	2B.	3B.	HR.	RBI.	B.A.	PO.	A.	E.	F.A.
1986—Boston	Amer.	2B	7	30	1	13	2	0	0	4	.433	13	25	0	1.000

THOMAS LOREN BARRETT
(Tom)

Born April 2, 1960, at San Fernando, Calif.
Height, 5.10. Weight, 170.
Throws right and bats left and righthanded.
Attended Mesa Community College, Mesa, Ariz., and University of Arizona, Tucson, Ariz.
Brother of Charlie Barrett, pitcher in Los Angeles Dodgers' organization, 1973 through 1978; and Marty Barrett, second baseman with Boston Red Sox.

Led Eastern League in bases on balls received with 95 in 1987.
Led Eastern League in caught stealing with 21 in 1986.
Tied for International League lead in sacrifice flies with 8 in 1988.
Led International League second basemen in putouts with 177 and total chances with 456 in 1988.
Led Eastern League second basemen in putouts with 248, assists with 423, fielding percentage with .991 and double plays with 93 in 1987.

Year Club	League	Pos.	G.	AB.	R.	H.	2B.	3B.	HR.	RBI.	B.A.	PO.	A.	E.	F.A.
1982—Paintsville	Appal.	2B	61	231	59	84	5	2	0	21	.364	134	138	4	⋆.986
1983—Fort Lauderdale†	Fla. St.	3B-2B	103	397	80	130	21	1	0	32	⋆.327	99	207	25	.924
1984—Nashville	South.	2B	135	510	82	157	22	6	0	44	.308	325	365	⋆30	.958
1984—Columbus	Int.	3B	5	21	3	8	1	0	0	0	.381	2	3	0	1.000
1985—Columbus‡	Int.	3-O-2-S	55	169	27	44	11	1	1	11	.260	47	66	5	.958
1985—Albany	East.	2B-3B-OF	57	233	40	61	8	3	1	18	.262	69	79	12	.925
1986—Albany	East.	2B-OF-3B	132	498	75	133	20	2	3	45	.267	162	158	15	.955
1986—Columbus§	Int.	2B-3B	2	9	0	3	0	0	0	1	.333	3	5	0	1.000
1987—Reading	East.	2B-SS-OF	⋆136	485	107	162	20	9	1	55	.334	265	444	9	.987
1988—Maine	Int.	2B-SS	114	390	•69	111	16	4	1	33	.285	204	305	11	.979
1988—Philadelphia	Nat.	2B	36	54	5	11	1	0	0	3	.204	16	31	2	.959
Major League Totals—1 Year			36	54	5	11	1	0	0	3	.204	16	31	2	.959

Selected by New York Yankees' organization in 26th round of free-agent draft, June 7, 1982.
†On disabled list, July 26 to August 26, 1983.
‡On temporary inactive list, August 29, 1985 through remainder of season.
§Traded with Outfielder Mike Easler to Philadelphia Phillies for Pitchers Charles Hudson and Jeff Knox, December 11, 1986.

TIMOTHY WAYNE BARRETT
(Tim)

Born January 24, 1961, at Huntingsburg, Ind.
Height, 6.01. Weight, 185.
Throws right and bats lefthanded.
Attended Indiana State University, Terre Haute, Ind.

Major League saves: 1988 (1).

Year Club	League	G.	IP.	W.	L.	Pct.	H.	R.	ER.	SO.	BB.	ERA.
1984—Gastonia	S. Atlantic	13	88⅓	7	2	.778	63	25	19	96	31	1.94
1984—West Palm Beach	Florida St.	11	78⅓	5	4	.556	68	25	20	64	23	2.30
1984—Jacksonville	Southern	2	12⅓	1	1	.500	11	3	3	12	7	2.19
1985—Jacksonville	Southern	37	145⅓	13	8	.619	145	70	65	111	63	4.03
1985—Indianapolis	Am. Assoc.	4	11⅓	0	0	.000	9	1	1	4	6	0.79
1986—Indianapolis	Am. Assoc.	21	45	0	1	.000	40	22	20	25	22	4.00
1986—Jacksonville	Southern	11	60	3	4	.429	51	30	30	31	28	4.50
1987—Indianapolis	Am. Assoc.	46	93⅓	10	1	⋆.909	90	38	37	61	38	3.57
1988—Indianapolis	Am. Assoc.	42	72⅓	8	1	.889	54	19	16	51	29	1.99
1988—Montreal	National	4	9⅓	0	0	.000	10	6	6	5	2	5.79
Major League Totals—1 Year		4	9⅓	0	0	.000	10	6	6	5	2	5.79

Signed as free agent by Montreal Expos' organization, October 31, 1983.

KEVIN CHARLES BASS

Born May 12, 1959, at Redwood City, Calif.
Height, 6.00. Weight, 180.
Throws right and bats right and lefthanded.
Brother of Richard Bass, minor league outfielder, 1976 and 1977; cousin of James Lofton, wide receiver with Los Angeles Raiders.

Tied major league record for most games, switch-hit home runs, season (2), 1987.
Major League stolen bases: 1983 (2), 1984 (5), 1985 (19), 1986 (22), 1987 (21), 1988 (31). Total—100.
Switch-hit home runs in a game, August 3, 1987 and September 2, 1987.
Led Midwest League in being hit by pitch with 10 in 1978.
Led Eastern League outfielders in double plays with 7 in 1980.

Year Club	League	Pos.	G.	AB.	R.	H.	2B.	3B.	HR.	RBI.	B.A.	PO.	A.	E.	F.A.
1977—Newark	NYP	OF	48	189	30	56	11	•7	1	33	.296	56	2	3	.951
1978—Burlington	Midw.	OF	129	499	81	132	27	5	18	69	.265	⋆281	14	11	.964
1979—Holyoke	East.	OF	135	490	69	129	15	4	8	54	.263	280	•16	⋆17	.946
1980—Holyoke	East.	OF	136	490	79	147	⋆31	7	4	51	.300	305	14	⋆18	.947
1981—Vancouver†	P. C.	OF	97	339	40	87	10	5	2	30	.257	175	14	7	.964
1982—Milwaukee	Amer.	OF	18	9	4	0	0	0	0	0	.000	7	0	0	1.000
1982—Vancouver‡	P. C.	OF	102	413	70	130	23	7	17	65	.315	199	15	10	.955
1982—Houston	Nat.	OF	12	24	2	1	0	0	0	1	.042	11	0	1	.917

Year	Club	League	Pos.	G.	AB.	R.	H.	2B.	3B.	HR.	RBI.	B.A.	PO.	A.	E.	F.A.
1983	Houston	Nat.	OF	88	195	25	46	7	3	2	18	.236	68	1	4	.945
1984	Houston§	Nat.	OF	121	331	33	86	17	5	2	29	.260	149	4	4	.975
1985	Houston	Nat.	OF	150	539	72	145	27	5	16	68	.269	328	10	1	★.997
1986	Houston	Nat.	OF	157	591	83	184	33	5	20	79	.311	303	12	5	.984
1987	Houston	Nat.	OF	157	592	83	168	31	5	19	85	.284	287	11	4	.987
1988	Houston	Nat.	OF	157	541	57	138	27	2	14	72	.255	267	7	6	.979
American League Totals—1 Year				18	9	4	0	0	0	0	0	.000	7	0	0	1.000
National League Totals—7 Years				842	2813	355	768	142	25	73	352	.273	1413	45	25	.983
Major League Totals—7 Years				860	2822	359	768	142	25	73	352	.272	1420	45	25	.983

Selected by Milwaukee Brewers' organization in 2nd round of free-agent draft, June 7, 1977.

†On disabled list, July 29 to September 1, 1981.

‡Traded with Pitchers Mike Madden and Frank DiPino to Houston Astros, September 3, 1982, completing deal in which Houston traded Pitcher Don Sutton to Milwaukee Brewers for three players to be named later, August 30, 1982.

§On disabled list, March 29 to April 13, 1984.

CHAMPIONSHIP SERIES RECORD

Year	Club	League	Pos.	G.	AB.	R.	H.	2B.	3B.	HR.	RBI.	B.A.	PO.	A.	E.	F.A.
1986	Houston	Nat.	OF	6	24	0	7	2	0	0	0	.292	16	0	1	.941

ALL-STAR GAME RECORD

Year	League	Pos.	AB.	R.	H.	2B.	3B.	HR.	RBI.	B.A.	PO.	A.	E.	F.A.
1986	National	PH	1	0	0	0	0	0	0	.000	0	0	0	.000

JOSE JOAQUIN BAUTISTA

Name pronounced Bough-TEES-tuh.
Born July 25, 1964, at Bani, Dominican Republic.
Height, 6.02. Weight, 203.
Throws and bats righthanded.

Pitched 6-0 no-hit victory against Prince William, May 26, 1985 (first game).

Year	Club	League	G.	IP.	W.	L.	Pct.	H.	R.	ER.	SO.	BB.	ERA.
1981	Kingsport	Ap'lachian	13	66	3	6	.333	84	54	34	34	17	4.64
1982	Kingsport	Ap'lachian	14	38⅓	0	4	.000	61	44	38	13	19	8.92
1983	Sarasota Mets	Gulf Coast	13	81⅔	4	3	.571	66	31	21	44	32	2.31
1984	Columbia	S. Atlantic	19	135	13	4	.765	121	52	47	96	35	3.13
1985	Lynchburg	Carolina	27	169	15	8	.652	145	49	44	109	33	2.34
1986	Jackson	Texas	7	21⅔	0	1	.000	36	22	20	13	8	8.31
1986	Lynchburg	Carolina	18	118⅔	8	8	.500	120	58	52	62	24	3.94
1987	Jackson†	Texas	28	169⅓	10	5	.667	174	76	61	95	43	3.24
1988	Baltimore	American	33	171⅔	6	15	.286	171	86	82	76	45	4.30
Major League Totals—1 Year			33	171⅔	6	15	.286	171	86	82	76	45	4.30

Signed as free agent by New York Mets' organization, April 25, 1981.

†Drafted by Baltimore Orioles, December 7, 1987.

DONALD EDWARD BAYLOR
(Don)

Born June 28, 1949, at Austin, Tex.
Height, 6.01. Weight, 210.
Throws and bats righthanded.
Attended Miami-Dade Junior College, Miami, Fla., and
Blinn Junior College, Brenham, Tex.
Cousin of Pat Ballage, safety with Indianapolis Colts, 1986 and 1987.

Established major league record for most times hit by pitch, lifetime (255).

Tied major league records for most long hits, opening game of season (4), April 6, 1973 (2 doubles, 1 triple, 1 home run); most consecutive home runs, two consecutive games (4), July 1 and 2, 1975 (bases on balls included); most times caught stealing, inning (2), June 15, 1974, 9th inning.

Tied modern major league record for most at bats, game (7), August 25, 1979.

Established American League record for most times hit by pitch, season (35), 1986.

Tied American League record for most hits, two consecutive games (9), August 13 and 14, 1973.

Major League stolen bases: 1970 (1), 1972 (24), 1973 (32), 1974 (29), 1975 (32), 1976 (52), 1977 (26), 1978 (22), 1979 (22), 1980 (6), 1981 (3), 1982 (10), 1983 (17), 1984 (1), 1986 (3), 1987 (5). Total—285.

Hit three home runs in a game, July 2, 1975.

Led American League in game-winning RBIs with 21 in 1982.

Led American League in sacrifice flies with 12 in 1978.

Led American League in being hit by pitch with 13 in 1973, 20 in 1976, 18 in 1978, 23 in 1984, 24 in 1985, 35 in 1986, 28 in 1987 and tied for lead with 13 in 1975.

Led International League in being hit by pitch with 19 in 1970 and 16 in 1971.

Led International League in total bases with 296 in 1970.

Led Texas League in being hit by pitch with 13 in 1969.

Led Appalachian League in stolen bases with 26, total bases with 135 and tied for lead in caught stealing with 6 in 1967.

Named American League Most Valuable Player by Baseball Writers' Association of America, 1979.

Named American League Player of the Year by The Sporting News, 1979.

Named designated hitter on The Sporting News American League All-Star Team, 1979, 1985 and 1986.

Named designated hitter on The Sporting News American League Silver Slugger team, 1983, 1985 and 1986.

Named Appalachian League Player of the Year, 1967.

Named Minor League Player of the Year by The Sporting News, 1970.

Year	Club	League	Pos.	G.	AB.	R.	H.	2B.	3B.	HR.	RBI.	B.A.	PO.	A.	E.	F.A.
1967	—Bluefield	Appal.	OF	•67	246	50	★85	10	★8	8	47	★.346	106	5	5	.957
1968	—Stockton	Calif.	OF	68	244	52	90	6	3	7	40	.369	135	3	7	.952
1968	—Elmira	East.	OF	6	24	4	8	1	1	1	3	.333	10	1	0	1.000
1968	—Rochester	Int.	OF	15	46	4	10	2	0	0	4	.217	29	1	4	.882
1969	—Miami	Fla. St.	OF	17	56	13	21	5	4	3	24	.375	30	2	3	.914
1969	—Dal.-Ft. Worth	Texas	OF	109	406	71	122	17	•10	11	57	.300	241	7	★13	.950
1970	—Rochester	Int.	OF	•140	508	★127	166	★34	★15	22	107	.327	286	5	7	.977
1970	—Baltimore	Amer.	OF	8	17	4	4	0	0	0	4	.235	15	0	0	1.000
1971	—Rochester	Int.	OF	136	492	104	154	•31	10	20	95	.313	210	4	9	.960
1971	—Baltimore	Amer.	OF	1	2	0	0	0	0	0	1	.000	4	0	0	1.000
1972	—Baltimore	Amer.	OF-1B	102	320	33	81	13	3	11	38	.253	206	4	5	.977
1973	—Baltimore	Amer.	OF-1B	118	405	64	116	20	4	11	51	.286	228	10	6	.975
1974	—Baltimore	Amer.	OF-1B	137	489	66	133	22	1	10	59	.272	260	2	5	.981
1975	—Baltimore†	Amer.	OF-1B	145	524	79	148	21	6	25	76	.282	286	8	5	.983
1976	—Oakland‡	Amer.	OF-1B	157	595	85	147	25	1	15	68	.247	781	45	12	.986
1977	—California	Amer.	OF-1B	154	561	87	141	27	0	25	75	.251	280	16	7	.977
1978	—California	Amer.	OF-1B	158	591	103	151	26	0	34	99	.255	194	9	6	.971
1979	—California	Amer.	OF-1B	•162	628	★120	186	33	3	36	★139	.296	203	3	5	.976
1980	—California§	Amer.	OF	90	340	39	85	12	2	5	51	.250	119	4	4	.969
1981	—California	Amer.	1B-OF	103	377	52	90	18	1	17	66	.239	38	3	0	1.000
1982	—California x	Amer.	DH	157	608	80	160	24	1	24	93	.263	0	0	0	.000
1983	—New York	Amer.	OF-1B	144	534	82	162	33	3	21	85	.303	23	2	1	.962
1984	—New York	Amer.	OF	134	493	84	129	29	1	27	89	.262	8	0	1	.889
1985	—New York y	Amer.	DH	142	477	70	110	24	1	23	91	.231	0	0	0	.000
1986	—Boston	Amer.	1B-OF	160	585	93	139	23	1	31	94	.238	71	4	1	.987
1987	—Bos.z-Minn.a	Amer.	DH	128	388	67	95	9	0	16	63	.245	0	0	0	.000
1988	—Oakland b	Amer.	DH	92	264	28	58	7	0	7	34	.220	0	0	0	.000
Major League Totals—19 Years				2292	8198	1236	2135	366	28	338	1276	.260	2716	110	58	.980

Selected by Baltimore Orioles' organization in 2nd round of free-agent draft, June 6, 1967.

†Traded with Pitchers Mike Torrez and Paul Mitchell to Oakland Athletics for Outfielder Reggie Jackson and Pitchers Ken Holtzman and Bill Van Bommel, April 2, 1976.

‡Played out option year and granted free agency, November 1, 1976; signed as free agent by California Angels, November 16, 1976.

§On disabled list, May 11 to June 26, 1980.

xGranted free agency, November 10, 1982; signed by New York Yankees, December 1, 1982.

yTraded to Boston Red Sox for Designated Hitter Mike Easler, March 28, 1986.

zTraded to Minnesota Twins for a player to be named later, August 31, 1987; Boston Red Sox acquired Pitcher Enrique Rios to complete deal, December 18, 1987.

aReleased, December 21, 1987; signed by Oakland Athletics, February 9, 1988.

bGranted free agency, November 4, 1988.

CHAMPIONSHIP SERIES RECORD

Established Championship Series records for most clubs, total Series (5); most runs batted in, five-game Series (10), 1982.

Tied Championship Series records for most times reached first base safely, game (5), October 8, 1986; most home runs with bases filled, game (1), October 9, 1982; most runs batted in, game (5), October 5, 1982; most runs batted in, inning (4), October 9, 1982 (eighth inning).

Established American League Championship Series record for most consecutive games, one or more hits (12).

Year	Club	League	Pos.	G.	AB.	R.	H.	2B.	3B.	HR.	RBI.	B.A.	PO.	A.	E.	F.A.
1973	—Baltimore	Amer.	OF-PH	4	11	3	3	0	0	0	1	.273	7	0	0	1.000
1974	—Baltimore	Amer.	OF	4	15	0	4	0	0	0	0	.267	9	0	0	1.000
1979	—California	Amer.	DH-OF	4	16	2	3	0	0	1	2	.188	4	0	0	1.000
1982	—California	Amer.	DH	5	17	2	5	1	1	1	10	.294	0	0	0	.000
1986	—Boston	Amer.	DH	7	26	6	9	3	0	1	2	.346	0	0	0	.000
1987	—Minnesota	Amer.	PH-DH	2	5	0	2	0	0	0	1	.400	0	0	0	.000
1988	—Oakland	Amer.	DH	2	6	0	0	0	0	0	1	.000	0	0	0	.000
Championship Series Totals—7 Years				28	96	13	26	4	1	3	17	.271	20	0	0	1.000

WORLD SERIES RECORD

Tied World Series records for most clubs, total Series (3); most at-bats, inning (2), October 17, 1987 (fourth inning).

Year	Club	League	Pos.	G.	AB.	R.	H.	2B.	3B.	HR.	RBI.	B.A.	PO.	A.	E.	F.A.
1986	—Boston	Amer.	DH-PH	4	11	1	2	1	0	0	1	.182	0	0	0	.000
1987	—Minnesota	Amer.	DH-PH	5	13	3	5	0	0	1	3	.385	0	0	0	.000
1988	—Oakland	Amer.	PH	1	1	0	0	0	0	0	0	.000	0	0	0	.000
World Series Totals—3 Years				10	25	4	7	1	0	1	4	.280	0	0	0	.000

ALL-STAR GAME RECORD

Year	League	Pos.	AB.	R.	H.	2B.	3B.	HR.	RBI.	B.A.	PO.	A.	E.	F.A.
1979	—American	OF	4	2	2	1	0	0	1	.500	1	0	0	1.000

WILLIAM DARO BEAN
(Billy)

Born May 11, 1964, at Santa Ana, Calif.
Height, 6.01. Weight, 185.
Throws and bats lefthanded.
Received bachelor of arts degree in business administration
from Loyola Marymount University, Los Angeles, Calif.

Tied modern major league record for most hits, first game in major leagues (nine innings) (4), April 25, 1987.
Major League stolen bases: 1987 (1).

Year Club	League	Pos.	G.	AB.	R.	H.	2B.	3B.	HR.	RBI.	B.A.	PO.	A.	E.	F.A.
1986—Glens Falls	East.	OF	80	279	43	77	10	3	8	49	.277	189	4	3	.985
1987—Toledo	Int.	OF	104	357	51	98	18	2	8	43	.275	228	1	7	.970
1987—Detroit	Amer.	OF	26	66	6	17	2	0	0	4	.258	54	1	0	1.000
1988—Toledo	Int.	OF-1B	•138	484	59	124	19	1	6	40	.256	664	43	12	.983
1988—Detroit	Amer.	OF-1B	10	11	2	2	0	1	0	0	.182	8	1	0	1.000
Major League Totals—2 Years			36	77	8	19	2	1	0	4	.247	62	2	0	1.000

Selected by New York Yankees' organization in 24th round of free-agent draft, June 3, 1985.
Selected by Detroit Tigers' organization in 4th round of free-agent draft, June 2, 1986.

WILLIAM LAMAR BEANE III

Name pronounced Been.

(Billy)

Born March 29, 1962, at Orlando, Fla.
Height, 6.04. Weight, 208.
Throws and bats righthanded.
Attended University of California at San Diego, La Jolla, Calif.

Major League stolen bases: 1986 (2).
Led Pacific Coast League outfielders in double plays with 5 in 1987.
Led International League batters in strikeouts with 130 in 1985.
Tied for Carolina League lead in sacrifice flies with 8 in 1981.
Led Texas League outfielders in fielding percentage with .994 in 1983.

Year Club	League	Pos.	G.	AB.	R.	H.	2B.	3B.	HR.	RBI.	B.A.	PO.	A.	E.	F.A.
1980—Little Falls	NYP	OF	43	138	10	29	3	2	1	14	.210	93	5	3	.970
1981—Lynchburg	Carol.	OF	114	403	47	108	13	•9	9	59	.268	233	8	11	.956
1982—Jackson	Texas	OF	126	418	39	88	13	4	5	36	.211	200	6	10	.954
1983—Jackson	Texas	OF-1B	121	423	53	104	14	1	11	75	.246	382	24	8	.981
1984—Jackson	Texas	OF	123	455	78	128	29	3	20	72	.281	180	5	7	.964
1984—New York	Nat.	OF	5	10	0	1	0	0	0	0	.100	2	0	0	1.000
1985—Tidewater	Int.	OF	135	504	63	143	*34	4	19	77	.284	255	10	6	.978
1985—New York†	Nat.	OF	8	8	0	2	1	0	0	1	.250	1	0	0	1.000
1986—Minnesota‡	Amer.	OF	80	183	20	39	6	0	3	15	.213	118	0	0	1.000
1986—Toledo	Int.	OF	32	126	17	37	5	0	5	17	.294	68	0	4	.944
1987—Portland	P. C.	OF-1B	123	463	63	132	28	8	8	71	.285	259	15	9	.968
1987—Minnesota§	Amer.	OF	12	15	1	4	2	0	0	1	.267	8	0	0	1.000
1988—Detroit	Amer.	OF	6	6	1	1	0	0	0	1	.167	5	0	0	1.000
1988—Toledo x	Int.	OF	110	361	33	85	15	2	9	39	.235	130	4	3	.978
National League Totals—2 Years			13	18	0	3	1	0	0	1	.167	3	0	0	1.000
American League Totals—3 Years			98	204	22	44	8	0	3	17	.216	131	0	0	1.000
Major League Totals—5 Years			111	222	22	47	9	0	3	18	.212	134	0	0	1.000

Selected by New York Mets' organization in 1st round (23rd player selected) of free-agent draft, June 3, 1980.
†Traded with Pitchers Bill Latham and Joe Klink to Minnesota Twins for Second Baseman Tim Teufel and Outfielder Pat Crosby, January 16, 1986.
‡On disabled list, April 1 to April 21, 1986.
§Traded to Detroit Tigers for Pitcher Balvino Galvez, March 24, 1988.
xGranted free agency, October 15, 1988.

GORDON BLAINE BEATTY

(Known by middle name.)

Born April 25, 1964, at Victoria, Tex.
Height, 6.02. Weight, 185.
Throws and bats lefthanded.
Attended San Jacinto College, Pasadena, Tex., and Baylor University, Waco, Tex.

Led Texas League pitchers in shutouts with 5, complete games with 12 and tied for lead in games started with 28 in 1988.
Led New York-Pennsylvania League pitchers in complete games with 8 in 1986.
Named Texas League Pitcher of the Year, 1988.
Named Carolina League Pitcher of the Year, 1987.

Year Club	League	G.	IP.	W.	L.	Pct.	H.	R.	ER.	SO.	BB.	ERA.
1986—Newark	NYP	15	*119⅓	*11	3	.786	98	37	28	93	30	2.11
1987—Hagerstown	Carolina	13	100	11	1	*.917	81	32	28	65	11	2.52
1987—Charlotte†	Southern	15	105⅔	6	5	.545	110	38	36	57	20	3.07
1988—Jackson	Texas	30	*208⅔	*16	8	.667	191	64	57	103	34	2.46

Selected by Baltimore Orioles' organization in 5th round of free-agent draft, January 17, 1984.
Selected by Baltimore Orioles' organization in secondary phase of free-agent draft, June 4, 1984.
Selected by St. Louis Cardinals' organization in secondary phase of free-agent draft, June 3, 1985.
Selected by Baltimore Orioles' organization in 9th round of free-agent draft, June 2, 1986.
†Traded with a player to be named later to New York Mets for Pitcher Doug Sisk, December 8, 1987; New York acquired Pitcher Greg Talamantez to complete deal, December 11, 1987.

STEPHEN WAYNE BEDROSIAN

Name pronounced Bed-ROHZ-ee-un.

(Steve)

Born December 6, 1957, at Methuen, Mass.
Height, 6.03. Weight, 205.
Throws and bats righthanded.
Attended North Essex Community College, Haverhill, Mass., and
University of New Haven, New Haven, Conn.

Established major league record for most games taken out as starting pitcher, season (37), 1985.
Major League saves: 1982 (11), 1983 (19), 1984 (11), 1986 (29), 1987 (40), 1988 (28). Total—138.
Led National League in saves with 40 in 1987.
Tied for Southern League lead in games started by pitchers with 29 in 1980.
Won National League Cy Young Memorial Award, 1987.
Named National League Fireman of the Year by THE SPORTING NEWS, 1987.
Named National League Rookie Pitcher of the Year by THE SPORTING NEWS, 1982.

Year Club	League	G.	IP.	W.	L.	Pct.	H.	R.	ER.	SO.	BB.	ERA.
1978—Kingsport	Ap'lachian	6	38	2	2	.500	38	18	13	29	25	3.08
1978—Greenwood	W. Carol.	8	55	5	1	.833	45	17	13	58	34	2.13
1979—Savannah†	Southern	13	89	5	5	.500	71	36	30	73	58	3.03
1980—Savannah	Southern	29	*203	14	10	.583	167	91	72	*161	96	3.19
1981—Richmond	Int'national	26	184	10	10	.500	143	76	55	144	99	2.69
1981—Atlanta	National	15	24	1	2	.333	15	14	12	9	15	4.50
1982—Atlanta	National	64	137⅔	8	6	.571	102	39	37	123	57	2.42
1983—Atlanta	National	70	120	9	10	.474	100	50	48	114	51	3.60
1984—Atlanta‡	National	40	83⅔	9	6	.600	65	23	22	81	33	2.37
1985—Atlanta§	National	37	206⅔	7	15	.318	198	101	88	134	111	3.83
1986—Philadelphia	National	68	90⅓	8	6	.571	79	39	34	82	34	3.39
1987—Philadelphia	National	65	89	5	3	.625	79	31	28	74	28	2.83
1988—Maine x	Int'national	5	6⅔	0	0	.000	6	0	0	5	2	0.00
1988—Philadelphia	National	57	74⅓	6	6	.500	75	34	31	61	27	3.75
Major League Totals—8 Years		416	825⅔	53	54	.495	713	331	300	678	356	3.27

Selected by Atlanta Braves' organization in 3rd round of free-agent draft, June 6, 1978.
†On disabled list, June 24 to September 18, 1979.
‡On disabled list, August 20 to September 4, 1984.
§Traded with Outfielder Milt Thompson to Philadelphia Phillies for Catcher Ozzie Virgil and Pitcher Pete Smith, December 10, 1985.
xOn Philadelphia disabled list, March 21 to May 20, 1988; included rehabilitation disability assignment to Maine, May 9 to May 19, 1988.

CHAMPIONSHIP SERIES RECORD

Year Club	League	G.	IP.	W.	L.	Pct.	H.	R.	ER.	SO.	BB.	ERA.
1982—Atlanta	National	2	1	0	0	.000	3	2	2	2	1	18.00

ALL-STAR GAME RECORD

Year League	IP.	W.	L.	Pct.	H.	R.	ER.	SO.	BB.	ERA.
1987—National	1	0	0	.000	0	0	0	0	2	0.00

TIMOTHY WAYNE BELCHER

(Tim)

Born October 19, 1961, at Mount Gilead, O.
Height, 6.03. Weight, 210.
Throws and bats righthanded.
Attended Mt. Vernon Nazarene College, Mt. Vernon, O.

Major League saves: 1988 (4).
Named National League Rookie Pitcher of the Year by THE SPORTING NEWS, 1988.
Named righhanded pitcher on THE SPORTING NEWS College Baseball All-America Team, 1983.

Year Club	League	G.	IP.	W.	L.	Pct.	H.	R.	ER.	SO.	BB.	ERA.
1984—Madison	Midwest	16	98⅓	9	4	.692	80	45	39	111	48	3.57
1984—Albany	Eastern	10	54	3	4	.429	37	30	20	40	41	3.33
1985—Huntsville	Southern	29	149⅔	11	10	.524	145	99	78	90	99	4.69
1986—Huntsville†	Southern	9	37	2	5	.286	50	28	27	25	22	6.57
1987—Tacoma‡	P. Coast	29	163	9	11	.450	143	89	80	136	*133	4.42
1987—Los Angeles	National	6	34	4	2	.667	30	11	9	23	7	2.38
1988—Los Angeles	National	36	179⅔	12	6	.667	143	65	58	152	51	2.91
Major League Totals—2 Years		42	213⅔	16	8	.667	173	76	67	175	58	2.82

Selected by Minnesota Twins' organization in 1st round (first player selected) of free-agent draft, June 6, 1983.
Selected by New York Yankees' organization in secondary phase of free-agent draft, January 17, 1984.
Selected by Oakland A's organization in player compensation pool draft, February 8, 1984. (Oakland received compensation for Baltimore Orioles' signing of free-agent Pitcher Tom Underwood, a Type A player, February 7, 1984.)
†On disabled list, April 10 to May 4 and May 5 to July 23, 1986.
‡Traded to Los Angeles Dodgers, September 3, 1987, completing deal in which Los Angeles traded Pitcher Rick Honeycutt to Oakland Athletics for a player to be named later, August 29, 1987.

CHAMPIONSHIP SERIES RECORD

Tied Championship Series record for most games won, seven-game Series (2), 1988.
Tied National League Championship Series record for most earned runs allowed, seven-game Series (7), 1988.

Year	Club	League	G.	IP.	W.	L.	Pct.	H.	R.	ER.	SO.	BB.	ERA.
1988	—Los Angeles	National	2	15⅓	2	0	1.000	12	7	7	16	4	4.11

WORLD SERIES RECORD

Year	Club	League	G.	IP.	W.	L.	Pct.	H.	R.	ER.	SO.	BB.	ERA.
1988	—Los Angeles	National	2	8⅔	1	0	1.000	10	7	6	10	6	6.23

STANLEY PETER BELINDA
(Stan)

Born August 6, 1966, at State College, Pa.
Height, 6.03. Weight, 185.
Throws and bats righthanded.
Attended Allegany Community College, Cumberland, Md.

Year	Club	League	G.	IP.	W.	L.	Pct.	H.	R.	ER.	SO.	BB.	ERA.
1986	—Watertown	NYP	5	8	0	0	.000	5	3	3	5	2	3.38
1986	—Bradenton Pirates†	Gulf Coast	17	20⅓	3	2	.600	23	12	6	17	2	2.66
1987	—Macon	S. Atlantic	50	82	6	4	.600	59	26	19	75	27	2.09
1988	—Salem	Carolina	53	71⅔	6	4	.600	54	33	22	63	32	2.76

Selected by Pittsburgh Pirates' organization in 10th round of free-agent draft, June 2, 1986.
†On disabled list, June 21 to June 30, 1986.

DAVID GUS BELL
(Buddy)

Born August 27, 1951, at Pittsburgh, Pa.
Height, 6.03. Weight, 200.
Throws and bats righthanded.
Attended Xavier University, Cincinnati, O., and Miami University, Oxford, O.
Son of Gus Bell, outfielder with Pittsburgh Pirates, Cincinnati Reds, New York Mets and Milwaukee Braves, 1950 through 1964; scout, Cleveland Indians, 1966, 1968 and 1969; and scout, Texas Rangers, 1985.

Tied major league record for most home runs, opening day of season (2), April 8, 1982.
Major League stolen bases: 1972 (5), 1973 (7), 1974 (1), 1975 (6), 1976 (3), 1977 (1), 1978 (1), 1979 (5), 1980 (3), 1981 (3), 1982 (5), 1983 (3), 1984 (2), 1985 (3), 1986 (2), 1987 (4), 1988 (1). Total—55.
Led American League in sacrifice flies with 10 in 1981.
Led American League third basemen in total chances with 495 in 1978, 361 in 1981, 540 in 1982 and 523 in 1983.
Led American League third basemen in assists with 364 in 1979 and 281 in 1981.
Led American League third basemen in putouts with 144 and double plays with 44 in 1973.
Tied for American League lead in game-winning RBIs with 16 in 1979.
Tied for American League lead in double plays by third basemen with 30 in 1978.
Led Gulf Coast League second basemen in double plays with 26 in 1969.
Named third baseman on THE SPORTING NEWS American League All-Star Team, 1981 and 1984.
Named third baseman on THE SPORTING NEWS American League All-Star fielding team, 1979 through 1984.
Named third baseman on THE SPORTING NEWS American League Silver Slugger team, 1984.

Year	Club	League	Pos.	G.	AB.	R.	H.	2B.	3B.	HR.	RBI.	B.A.	PO.	A.	E.	F.A.
1969	—Sarasota Ind.	Gulf C.	2B	51	170	18	39	4	•3	3	24	.229	119	108	7	*.970
1970	—Sumter	W. Car.	3B-2B-SS	121	442	81	117	19	3	12	75	.265	116	189	27	.919
1971	—Wichita	A. A.	*3-2-S-O	129	470	65	136	23	1	11	59	.289	*139	203	16	.955
1972	—Cleveland	Amer.	OF-3B	132	466	49	119	21	1	9	36	.255	284	23	3	.990
1973	—Cleveland	Amer.	3B-OF	156	631	86	169	23	7	14	59	.268	146	363	22	.959
1974	—Cleveland†	Amer.	3B	116	423	51	111	15	1	7	46	.262	112	274	15	.963
1975	—Cleveland	Amer.	3B	153	553	66	150	20	4	10	59	.271	*146	330	25	.950
1976	—Cleveland	Amer.	3B-1B	159	604	75	170	26	2	7	60	.281	109	331	20	.957
1977	—Cleveland	Amer.	3B-OF	129	479	64	140	23	4	11	64	.292	134	253	16	.960
1978	—Cleveland‡	Amer.	3B	142	556	71	157	27	8	6	62	.282	125	*355	15	.970
1979	—Texas	Amer.	3B-SS	•162	*670	89	200	42	3	18	101	.299	147	429	17	.971
1980	—Texas§	Amer.	*3B-SS	129	490	76	161	24	4	17	83	.329	125	282	8	*.981
1981	—Texas	Amer.	3B-SS	97	360	44	106	16	1	10	64	.294	67	284	14	.962
1982	—Texas	Amer.	*3B-SS	148	537	62	159	27	2	13	67	.296	*131	397	13	*.976
1983	—Texas	Amer.	3B	156	618	75	171	35	3	14	66	.277	123	*383	17	.967
1984	—Texas	Amer.	3B	148	553	88	174	36	5	11	83	.315	129	323	•20	.958
1985	—Texas x	Amer.	3B	84	313	33	74	13	3	4	32	.236	70	192	16	.942
1985	—Cincinnati	Nat.	3B	67	247	28	54	15	2	6	36	.219	54	105	9	.946
1986	—Cincinnati	Nat.	3B-2B	155	568	89	158	29	3	20	75	.278	105	291	10	.975
1987	—Cincinnati	Nat.	3B	143	522	74	148	19	2	17	70	.284	93	241	7	*.979
1988	—Cinc.yz-Hou.ab	Nat.	3B-1B	95	323	27	78	10	1	7	40	.241	88	140	15	.938
American League Totals—14 Years				1911	7253	929	2061	348	48	151	882	.284	1843	4218	221	.965
National League Totals—4 Years				460	1660	218	438	73	8	50	221	.264	340	777	41	.965
Major League Totals—17 Years				2371	8913	1147	2499	421	56	201	1103	.280	2183	4995	262	.965

Selected by Cleveland Indians' organization in 16th round of free-agent draft, June 5, 1969.
†On disabled list, May 27 to June 17 and August 8 to September 1, 1974.
‡Traded to Texas Rangers for Third Baseman Toby Harrah, December 8, 1978.
§On disabled list, June 9 to June 24, 1980.
xTraded to Cincinnati Reds for Outfielder Duane Walker and a player to be named later, July 19, 1985; Texas Rangers' organization acquired Pitcher Jeff Russell to complete deal, July 23, 1985.
yOn disabled list, March 26 to April 10 and April 14 to May 11, 1988.
zTraded to Houston Astros for a player to be named later, June 19, 1988; Cincinnati Reds' organization acquired Pitcher Carl Grovom to complete deal, October 20, 1988.
aOn disabled list, August 4 to August 19, 1988.
bReleased, December 21, 1988.

ALL-STAR GAME RECORD

Year League	Pos.	AB.	R.	H.	2B.	3B.	HR.	RBI.	B.A.	PO.	A.	E.	F.A.
1973—American	PH	1	0	1	0	1	0	0	1.000	0	0	0	.000
1980—American	3B	2	0	0	0	0	0	0	.000	0	2	0	1.000
1981—American	3B	1	0	0	0	0	0	1	.000	1	2	0	1.000
1982—American	PH-3B	3	0	0	0	0	0	0	.000	0	1	1	.500
1984—American	3B	1	0	0	0	0	0	0	.000	0	1	0	1.000
All-Star Game Totals—5 Years		8	0	1	0	1	0	1	.125	1	6	1	.875

GEORGE ANTONIO BELL (MATHEY)

Born October 21, 1959, at San Pedro de Macoris, D. R.
Height, 6.01. Weight, 202.
Throws and bats righthanded.
Brother of Juan Bell, shortstop in Baltimore Orioles' organization;
and Rolando Bell, infielder in Los Angeles Dodgers' organization, 1985 through 1987.

Major League stolen bases: 1981 (3), 1983 (1), 1984 (11), 1985 (21), 1986 (7), 1987 (5), 1988 (4). Total—52.
Hit three home runs in a game, April 4, 1988.
Led American League in total bases with 369 in 1987.
Tied for American League lead in game-winning RBIs with 15 in 1986.
Tied for International League lead in double plays by outfielders with 4 in 1983.
Led Western Carolinas League in total bases with 270 in 1979.
Named Major League Player of the Year by THE SPORTING NEWS, 1987.
Named American League Player of the Year by THE SPORTING NEWS, 1987.
Named American League Most Valuable Player by Baseball Writers' Association of America, 1987.
Named outfielder on THE SPORTING NEWS American League All-Star Team, 1986 and 1987.
Named outfielder on THE SPORTING NEWS American League Silver Slugger team, 1985 through 1987.

Year Club	League	Pos.	G.	AB.	R.	H.	2B.	3B.	HR.	RBI.	B.A.	PO.	A.	E.	F.A.
1978—Helena	Pion.	OF	33	106	20	33	6	1	0	14	.311	39	4	4	.915
1979—Spartanburg	W. Car.	OF	130	491	78	150	24	*15	22	*102	.305	206	14	8	.965
1980—Reading†‡	East.	OF	22	55	11	17	5	2	0	11	.309	24	0	1	.960
1981—Toronto	Amer.	OF	60	163	19	38	2	1	5	12	.233	92	3	3	.969
1982—Syracuse§	Int.	OF	37	125	11	25	5	4	3	19	.200	72	3	1	.987
1983—Syracuse	Int.	OF	85	317	37	86	11	4	15	59	.271	135	12	6	.961
1983—Toronto	Amer.	OF	39	112	5	30	5	4	2	17	.268	61	1	3	.954
1984—Toronto	Amer.	OF-3B	159	606	85	177	39	4	26	87	.292	289	13	9	.971
1985—Toronto	Amer.	•OF-1B	157	607	87	167	28	6	28	95	.275	320	14	•11	.968
1986—Toronto	Amer.	OF-3B	159	641	101	198	38	6	31	108	.309	270	17	10	.966
1987—Toronto	Amer.	OF-2B-3B	156	610	111	188	32	4	47	*134	.308	249	14	11	.960
1988—Toronto	Amer.	OF	156	614	78	165	27	5	24	97	.269	253	8	15	.946
Major League Totals—7 Years			886	3353	486	963	171	30	163	550	.287	1534	70	62	.963

Signed as free agent by Philadelphia Phillies' organization, June 23, 1978.
†On disabled list, June 22, 1980 through remainder of season.
‡Drafted by Toronto Blue Jays, December 8, 1980.
§On disabled list, April 20 to May 1, June 14 to June 30 and July 8, 1982 through remainder of season.

CHAMPIONSHIP SERIES RECORD

Year Club	League	Pos.	G.	AB.	R.	H.	2B.	3B.	HR.	RBI.	B.A.	PO.	A.	E.	F.A.
1985—Toronto	Amer.	OF	7	28	4	9	3	0	0	1	.321	13	0	0	1.000

ALL-STAR GAME RECORD

Year Club	League	Pos.	G.	AB.	R.	H.	2B.	3B.	HR.	RBI.	B.A.	PO.	A.	E.	F.A.
1987—Toronto	Amer.	OF	3	0	0	0	0	0	0	.000	1	0	0	0	1.000

JAY STUART BELL

Born December 11, 1965, at Pensacola, Fla.
Height, 6.01. Weight, 180.
Throws and bats righthanded.

Tied major league record by hitting home run in first major league at-bat, September 29, 1986.
Major League stolen bases: 1987 (2), 1988 (4). Total—6.
Led American Association shortstops in putouts with 198, assists with 322 and total chances with 550 in 1987.
Led Eastern League shortstops in total chances with 613 in 1986.
Led California League shortstops in double plays with 84 in 1985.
Led Appalachian League shortstops in double plays with 43 and total chances with 352 in 1984.

Year Club	League	Pos.	G.	AB.	R.	H.	2B.	3B.	HR.	RBI.	B.A.	PO.	A.	E.	F.A.
1984—Elizabethton	Appal.	SS	66	245	43	54	12	1	6	30	.220	*109	*218	25	.929
1985—Visalia†	Calif.	SS	106	376	56	106	16	6	9	59	.282	176	330	53	.905
1985—Waterbury	East.	SS	29	114	13	34	11	2	1	14	.298	41	79	6	.952
1986—Waterbury	East.	SS	138	494	86	137	28	4	7	74	.277	197	*371	*45	.927
1986—Cleveland	Amer.	2B	5	14	3	5	2	0	1	4	.357	1	6	2	.778
1987—Buffalo	A. A.	*SS-2B	110	362	71	94	15	4	17	60	.260	201	325	*30	.946
1987—Cleveland	Amer.	SS	38	125	14	27	9	1	2	13	.216	67	93	9	.947
1988—Cleveland	Amer.	SS	73	211	23	46	5	1	2	21	.218	103	170	10	.965
1988—Colorado Springs	P. C.	SS	49	181	35	50	12	2	7	24	.276	87	171	18	.935
Major League Totals—3 Years			116	350	40	78	16	2	5	38	.223	171	269	21	.954

Selected by Minnesota Twins' organization in 1st round (eighth player selected) of free-agent draft, June 4, 1984.
†Traded with Pitcher Curt Wardle, Outfielder Jim Weaver and a player to be named later to Cleveland Indians for Pitcher Bert Blyleven, August 1, 1985; Cleveland organization acquired Pitcher Rich Yett to complete deal, September 17, 1985.

JUAN BELL (MATHEY)

Born March 29, 1968 at San Pedro de Macoris, D. R.
Height, 5.11. Weight, 172.
Throws and bats righthanded.
Brother of George Bell, outfielder with Toronto Blue Jays; and Rolando Bell, infielder in Los Angeles Dodgers' organization, 1985 through 1987.

Led Gulf Coast League shortstops in total chances with 293 in 1986.
Led California League shortstops in total chances with 719 in 1987.

Year Club	League	Pos.	G.	AB.	R.	H.	2B.	3B.	HR.	RBI.	B.A.	PO.	A.	E.	F.A.
1985—Bradenton Dodg.†	Gulf C.	SS-2B	42	106	11	17	0	0	0	8	.160	56	73	20	.866
1986—Sarasota Dodg.	Gulf C.	SS	59	217	38	52	6	2	0	26	.240	78	★193	22	.925
1987—Bakersfield†	Calif.	SS	134	473	54	116	15	3	4	58	.245	235	★431	★53	.926
1988—San Antonio	Texas	SS	61	215	37	60	4	2	5	21	.279	106	182	20	.935
1988—Albuquerque†‡	P. C.	SS	73	257	42	77	9	3	8	45	.300	114	249	23	.940

Signed as free agent by Los Angeles Dodgers' organization, September 1, 1984.
†Batted left and righthanded.
‡Traded with Pitchers Brian Holton and Ken Howell to Baltimore Orioles for First Baseman Eddie Murray, December 4, 1988.

RAFAEL LEONIDAS BELLIARD (MATIAS)

Name pronounced BELL-ee-ard.

Born October 24, 1961, at Pueblo Nuevo, Mao, D. R.
Height, 5.06. Weight, 150.
Throws and bats righthanded.

Major League stolen bases: 1982 (1), 1984 (4), 1986 (12), 1987 (5), 1988 (7). Total—29.
Led National League shortstops in fielding percentage with .977 in 1988.
Led Carolina League in sacrifice hits with 12 and tied for lead in caught stealing with 15 in 1981.
Tied for Eastern League lead in double plays by shortstops with 69 in 1983.

Year Club	League	Pos.	G.	AB.	R.	H.	2B.	3B.	HR.	RBI.	B.A.	PO.	A.	E.	F.A.
1980—Bradenton Pir.	Gulf C.	SS-2B-3B	12	42	6	9	1	0	0	2	.214	24	39	1	.984
1980—Shelby	S. Atl.	SS	8	24	1	3	0	0	0	2	.125	10	27	5	.881
1981—Alexandria	Carol.	SS	127	472	58	102	6	5	0	33	.216	•205	330	29	.949
1982—Buffalo†	East.	SS	40	124	14	34	1	1	0	19	.274	56	87	5	.966
1982—Pittsburgh	Nat.	SS	9	2	3	1	0	0	0	0	.500	2	2	0	1.000
1983—Lynn	East.	SS-2B	127	431	63	113	13	2	2	37	.262	203	307	26	.951
1983—Pittsburgh	Nat.	SS	4	1	1	0	0	0	0	0	.000	1	3	0	1.000
1984—Pittsburgh‡	Nat.	SS-2B	20	22	3	5	0	0	0	0	.227	12	13	3	.893
1985—Pittsburgh	Nat.	SS	17	20	1	4	0	0	0	1	.200	13	23	2	.947
1985—Hawaii	P. C.	SS-2B	100	341	35	84	12	4	1	18	.246	172	289	5	.989
1986—Pittsburgh§	Nat.	SS-2B	117	309	33	72	5	2	0	31	.233	147	317	12	.975
1987—Pittsburgh x	Nat.	SS-2B	81	203	26	42	4	3	1	15	.207	113	191	6	.981
1987—Harrisburg	East.	SS	37	145	24	49	5	2	0	9	.338	59	115	7	.961
1988—Pittsburgh y	Nat.	SS-2B	122	286	28	61	0	4	0	11	.213	134	261	9	.978
Major League Totals—7 Years			370	843	95	185	9	9	1	58	.219	422	810	32	.975

Signed as free agent by Pittsburgh Pirates' organization, July 10, 1980.
†On disabled list, April 19 to July 24, 1982.
‡On disabled list, June 28 to August 28, 1984.
§On disabled list, July 28 to August 12, 1986.
xOn disabled list, August 27, 1987 through remainder of season.
yOn disabled list, May 19 to June 3, 1988.

BRUCE EDWIN BENEDICT

Born August 18, 1955, at Birmingham, Ala.
Height, 6.02. Weight, 195.
Throws and bats righthanded.
Attended University of Nebraska, Omaha, Neb.
Son of David Benedict, pitcher in New York Yankees', Washington Senators' and St. Louis Cardinals' organizations, 1950 through 1958.

Major League stolen bases: 1979 (1), 1980 (3), 1981 (1), 1982 (4), 1983 (1), 1984 (1), 1986 (1). Total—12.

Year Club	League	Pos.	G.	AB.	R.	H.	2B.	3B.	HR.	RBI.	B.A.	PO.	A.	E.	F.A.
1976—Kingsport	Appal.	C	17	63	10	18	1	0	0	4	.286	98	25	3	.976
1976—Greenwood	W. Car.	C	21	54	7	13	1	0	1	10	.241	93	12	5	.955
1976—Savannah	South.	C	24	73	10	21	1	0	0	7	.288	107	12	2	.983
1977—Savannah	South.	C	124	395	55	104	15	0	7	40	.263	★770	★112	13	.985
1978—Richmond	Int.	C	111	348	41	97	13	0	2	34	.279	592	56	4	★.994
1978—Atlanta	Nat.	C	22	52	3	13	2	0	0	1	.250	81	14	1	.990
1979—Atlanta	Nat.	C	76	204	14	46	11	0	0	15	.225	344	35	6	.984
1980—Richmond	Int.	C	3	10	0	3	0	0	0	0	.300	10	5	0	1.000
1980—Atlanta	Nat.	C	120	359	18	91	14	1	2	34	.253	502	76	7	.988
1981—Atlanta	Nat.	C	90	295	26	78	12	1	5	35	.264	404	★73	7	.986
1982—Atlanta	Nat.	C	118	386	34	95	11	1	3	44	.246	602	73	5	★.993
1983—Atlanta	Nat.	C	134	423	43	126	13	1	2	43	.298	738	91	7	.992
1984—Atlanta	Nat.	C	95	300	26	67	8	1	4	25	.223	504	37	5	.991
1985—Atlanta	Nat.	C	70	208	12	42	6	0	0	20	.202	314	35	4	.989
1986—Atlanta	Nat.	C	64	160	11	36	10	1	0	13	.225	252	28	2	.993
1987—Atlanta	Nat.	C	37	95	4	14	1	0	1	5	.147	165	21	2	.989

Year	Club	League	Pos.	G.	AB.	R.	H.	2B.	3B.	HR.	RBI.	B.A.	PO.	A.	E.	F.A.
1988	Atlanta	Nat.	C	90	236	11	57	7	0	0	19	.242	384	54	5	.989
Major League Totals—11 Years				916	2718	202	665	95	6	17	254	.245	4290	537	51	.990

Selected by Atlanta Braves' organization in 5th round of free-agent draft, June 8, 1976.

CHAMPIONSHIP SERIES RECORD

Year	Club	League	Pos.	G.	AB.	R.	H.	2B.	3B.	HR.	RBI.	B.A.	PO.	A.	E.	F.A.
1982	Atlanta	Nat.	C	3	8	1	2	1	0	0	0	.250	16	2	0	1.000

ALL-STAR GAME RECORD

Year	League	Pos.	AB.	R.	H.	2B.	3B.	HR.	RBI.	B.A.	PO.	A.	E.	F.A.
1981	National	C	1	0	0	0	0	0	0	.000	3	0	0	1.000
1983	National	C	1	0	1	0	0	0	0	1.000	5	0	0	1.000
All-Star Game Totals—2 Years			2	0	1	0	0	0	0	.500	8	0	0	1.000

JUAN JOSE BENIQUEZ (TORRES)

Name pronounced Be-NEE-kez.

Born May 13, 1950, at San Sebastian, P. R.
Height, 5.11. Weight, 175.
Throws and bats righthanded.

Established modern major league record for most errors, shortstop, two consective games (6), July 13 and 14, 1972.

Established American League record for most clubs played, lifetime (8).

Major League stolen bases: 1971 (3), 1972 (2), 1974 (19), 1975 (7), 1976 (17), 1977 (26), 1978 (10), 1979 (3), 1980 (2), 1981 (2), 1982 (3), 1983 (4), 1985 (4), 1986 (2). Total—104.

Hit three home runs in a game, June 12, 1986.

Led American League outfielders in putouts with 410 and total chances with 434 in 1976.

Led International League in sacrifice hits with 11 in 1971.

Led Florida State League shortstops in assists with 372 and double plays with 51 in 1969.

Named outfielder on THE SPORTING NEWS American League All-Star fielding team, 1977.

Year	Club	League	Pos.	G.	AB.	R.	H.	2B.	3B.	HR.	RBI.	B.A.	PO.	A.	E.	F.A.
1969	Winter Haven	Fla. St.	*SS-2B	120	426	59	111	15	*14	2	59	.261	175	373	*49	.918
1969	Winston-Salem	Carol.	SS	2	10	0	2	0	0	0	0	.200	2	6	0	1.000
1970	Winston-Salem	Carol.	SS	92	335	53	91	12	2	9	37	.272	144	275	35	.923
1970	Pawtucket	East.	SS	56	233	29	58	5	3	4	25	.249	105	167	29	.904
1971	Louisville	Int.	SS	132	534	82	149	12	*16	4	51	.279	205	364	*55	.912
1971	Boston	Amer.	SS	16	57	8	17	2	0	0	4	.298	24	27	6	.895
1972	Louisville	Int.	SS	66	277	40	82	10	7	5	32	.296	114	172	21	.932
1972	Boston	Amer.	SS	33	99	10	24	4	1	1	8	.242	38	88	14	.900
1973	Pawtucket	Int.	O-S-2-3	131	440	80	131	24	4	13	52	*.298	196	176	26	.934
1974	Boston†	Amer.	OF	106	389	60	104	14	3	5	33	.267	264	4	6	.978
1975	Boston‡§	Amer.	OF-3B	78	254	43	74	14	4	2	17	.291	110	17	1	.992
1976	Texas	Amer.	*OF-2B	145	478	49	122	14	4	0	33	.255	411	*18	7	.984
1977	Texas x	Amer.	OF	123	424	56	114	19	6	10	50	.269	311	10	4	.988
1978	Texas yz	Amer.	OF	127	473	61	123	17	3	11	50	.260	309	8	9	.972
1979	New York ab	Amer.	OF-3B	62	142	19	36	6	1	4	17	.254	100	15	2	.983
1980	Seattle cde	Amer.	OF	70	237	26	54	10	0	6	21	.228	176	3	8	.957
1981	California	Amer.	OF	58	166	18	30	5	0	3	13	.181	117	0	5	.959
1982	California	Amer.	OF	112	196	25	52	11	2	3	24	.265	113	4	2	.983
1983	California f	Amer.	OF	92	315	44	96	15	0	3	34	.305	174	8	6	.968
1984	California	Amer.	OF	110	354	60	119	17	0	8	39	.336	197	5	6	.971
1985	California g	Amer.	O-1-3-S	132	411	54	125	13	5	8	42	.304	439	26	4	.991
1986	Baltimore h	Amer.	OF-3B-1B	113	343	48	103	15	0	6	36	.300	211	56	13	.954
1987	K.C. i-Tor.	Amer.	OF-1B-3B	96	255	20	64	12	1	8	47	.251	97	5	2	.981
1987	Sarasota Royals j	G. Coast	OF-C	7	19	6	5	2	1	0	0	.263	6	0	0	1.000
1988	Toronto k	Amer.	OF	27	58	9	17	2	0	1	8	.293	0	0	0	.000
Major League Totals—17 Years				1500	4651	610	1274	190	30	79	476	.274	3091	294	96	.972

Signed as free agent by Boston Red Sox' organization, October 1, 1968.

†On disabled list, July 3 to July 28, 1974.

‡On disabled list, July 2 to July 18, 1975.

§Traded with Pitcher Steve Barr, a minor league player to be named later and an estimated $200,000 to Texas Rangers for Pitcher Ferguson Jenkins, November 17, 1975; Texas acquired Pitcher Craig Skok to complete deal, December 12, 1975.

xOn disabled list, July 31 to August 15, 1977.

yOn disabled list, June 13 to July 13, 1978.

zTraded with Pitchers Paul Mirabella, Mike Griffin and Dave Righetti and Outfielder Greg Jemison to New York Yankees for Pitchers Sparky Lyle, Larry McCall and Dave Rajsich, Catcher Mike Heath, Shortstop Domingo Ramos and cash, November 10, 1978.

aOn disabled list, July 9 to September 1, 1979.

bTraded with Catcher Jerry Narron and Pitchers Jim Beattie and Rick Anderson to Seattle Mariners for Outfielder Ruppert Jones and Pitcher Jim Lewis, November 1, 1979.

cOn disabled list, April 9 to June 2 and July 19 to August 8, 1980.

dOn suspended list, September 2 to September 7, 1980.

eGranted free agency, October 24, 1980; signed by California Angels, December 29, 1980.

fOn disabled list, June 20 to August 9, 1983.

gGranted free agency, November 12, 1985; signed by Baltimore Orioles, January 28, 1986.

hTraded to Kansas City Royals for Shortstop Joe Jarrell and Pitcher Jimmy Daniel, December 17, 1986.

iTraded to Toronto Blue Jays for Pitcher Luis Aquino, July 14, 1987.

jGranted free agency, January 22, 1988; re-signed by Blue Jays, January 25, 1988.

kReleased, May 31, 1988.

CHAMPIONSHIP SERIES RECORD

Tied American League Championship Series record for most stolen bases, three-game Series (2), 1975.

Year Club	League	Pos.	G.	AB.	R.	H.	2B.	3B.	HR.	RBI.	B.A.	PO.	A.	E.	F.A.
1975—Boston	Amer.	DH	3	12	2	3	0	0	0	1	.250	0	0	0	.000
1982—California	Amer.	OF	2	0	0	0	0	0	0	0	.000	1	0	0	1.000
Championship Series Totals—2 Years			5	12	2	3	0	0	0	1	.250	1	0	0	1.000

WORLD SERIES RECORD

Year Club	League	Pos.	G.	AB.	R.	H.	2B.	3B.	HR.	RBI.	B.A.	PO.	A.	E.	F.A.
1975—Boston	Amer.	OF-PH	3	8	0	1	0	0	0	1	.125	6	1	0	1.000

TODD ERIC BENZINGER

Born February 11, 1963, at Dayton, Ky.
Height, 6.01. Weight, 185.
Throws right and bats left and righthanded.
Nephew of Don Gross, pitcher with Cincinnati Reds and Pittsburgh Pirates, 1955 through 1960.

Major League stolen bases: 1987 (5), 1988 (2). Total—7.

Year Club	League	Pos.	G.	AB.	R.	H.	2B.	3B.	HR.	RBI.	B.A.	PO.	A.	E.	F.A.
1981—Elmira	NYP	OF-1B	41	141	21	34	10	1	2	8	.241	131	9	2	.986
1982—Winston-Salem	Carol.	OF-1B	121	443	54	97	19	1	5	46	.219	438	28	8	.983
1983—Winter Haven	Fla. St.	OF-1B-3B	125	480	56	134	34	5	7	68	.279	206	10	8	.964
1984—New Britain†	East.	OF-1B	110	391	49	101	25	5	10	60	.258	465	29	14	.972
1985—Pawtucket‡	Int.	OF	70	256	31	64	13	1	11	47	.250	106	3	3	.973
1986—Pawtucket§	Int.	OF-1B	90	314	41	79	13	2	11	32	.252	156	4	2	.988
1987—Pawtucket	Int.	OF-1B	65	257	47	83	17	3	13	49	.323	256	16	2	.993
1987—Boston	Amer.	OF-1B	73	223	36	62	11	1	8	43	.278	155	7	2	.988
1988—Boston xy	Amer.	1B-OF	120	405	47	103	28	1	13	70	.254	602	38	6	.991
Major League Totals—2 Years			193	628	83	165	39	2	21	113	.263	757	45	8	.990

Selected by Boston Red Sox' organization in 4th round of free-agent draft, June 8, 1981.
†On disabled list, August 10, 1984 through remainder of season.
‡On disabled list, April 10 to June 11, 1985.
§On disabled list, April 11 to April 21 and June 26 to July 17, 1986.
xOn disabled list, June 3 to June 22, 1988.
yTraded with Pitcher Jeff Sellers and a player to be named later to Cincinnati Reds for First Baseman Nick Esasky and Pitcher Rob Murphy, December 13, 1988.

CHAMPIONSHIP SERIES RECORD

Year Club	League	Pos.	G.	AB.	R.	H.	2B.	3B.	HR.	RBI.	B.A.	PO.	A.	E.	F.A.
1988—Boston	Amer.	1B-PH	4	11	0	1	0	0	0	0	.091	21	1	0	1.000

JUAN BAUTISTA BERENGUER

Name pronounced Bare-en-GARE.

Born November 30, 1954, at Aguadulce, Panama.
Height, 5.11. Weight, 223.
Throws and bats righthanded.

Major League saves: 1983 (1), 1986 (4), 1987 (4), 1988 (2). Total—11.
Led Carolina League pitchers in games started with 28 and hit batsmen with 13 in 1976.
Tied for American Association lead in complete games with 9 in 1982.
Tied for Texas League pitchers lead in games started with 26 in 1977.
Tied for Midwest League lead in hit batsmen with 8 in 1975.
Named International League Pitcher of the Year, 1978.

Year Club	League	G.	IP.	W.	L.	Pct.	H.	R.	ER.	SO.	BB.	ERA.
1975—Wausau	Midwest	18	95	5	4	.556	83	41	31	58	50	2.94
1976—Lynchburg	Carolina	28	187	10	13	.435	*175	89	*75	114	*118	3.61
1977—Jackson	Texas	26	181	9	8	.529	143	89	69	*160	*126	3.43
1978—Tidewater	Int'national	24	147	10	7	.588	117	60	60	130	91	3.67
1978—New York†	National	5	13	0	2	.000	17	12	12	8	11	8.31
1979—Tacoma	P. Coast	26	166	8	8	.500	128	101	90	*220	129	4.88
1979—New York	National	5	31	1	1	.500	28	13	10	25	12	2.90
1980—Tidewater	Int'national	27	157	9	●15	.375	122	78	67	*178	76	3.84
1980—New York‡	National	6	9	0	1	.000	9	9	6	7	10	6.00
1981—Kansas City§-Toronto x	American	20	91	2	*13	.133	84	62	53	49	51	5.24
1982—Evansville	Am. Assoc.	25	156⅓	11	10	.524	152	85	80	127	80	4.61
1982—Detroit	American	2	6⅔	0	0	.000	5	5	5	8	9	6.75
1983—Detroit	American	37	157⅔	9	5	.643	110	58	55	129	71	3.14
1984—Detroit	American	31	168⅓	11	10	.524	146	75	65	118	79	3.48
1985—Detroit y	American	31	95	5	6	.455	96	67	59	82	48	5.59
1986—San Francisco za	National	46	73⅓	2	3	.400	64	23	22	72	44	2.70
1987—Minnesota bc	American	47	112	8	1	.889	100	51	49	110	47	3.94
1988—Minnesota	American	57	100	8	4	.667	74	44	44	99	61	3.96
National League Totals—4 Years		62	126⅓	3	7	.300	118	57	50	112	77	3.56
American League Totals—7 Years		225	730⅔	43	39	.524	615	362	330	595	366	4.06
Major League Totals—11 Years		287	857	46	46	.500	733	419	380	707	443	3.99

Signed as free agent by New York Mets' organization, February 22, 1975.
†Loaned to Tacoma (Cleveland Indians' organization), March 24, 1979; returned August 29, 1979.
‡Traded to Kansas City for Outfielder Marvell Wynne and Pitcher John Skinner, March 31, 1981.

§Sold on waivers to Toronto Blue Jays, August 8, 1981.

xReleased, March 28, 1982; signed by Evansville (Detroit Tigers' organization), April 4, 1982.

yTraded with Catcher Bob Melvin and a player to be named later to San Francisco Giants for Pitchers Dave LaPoint and Eric King and Catcher Matt Nokes, October 7, 1985; San Francisco acquired Pitcher Scott Medvin to complete deal, December 11, 1985.

zOn disabled list, April 7 to April 28, 1986.

aReleased, December 9, 1986; signed by Minnesota Twins, January 9, 1987.

bOn disabled list, August 3 to August 22, 1987.

cGranted free agency, November 9, 1987; re-signed by Twins, December 22, 1987.

CHAMPIONSHIP SERIES RECORD

Tied American League Championship Series record for most games pitched, five-game Series (4), 1987.

Year Club	League	G.	IP.	W.	L.	Pct.	H.	R.	ER.	SO.	BB.	ERA.
1987—Minnesota	American	4	6	0	0	.000	1	1	1	6	3	1.50

WORLD SERIES RECORD

Year Club	League	G.	IP.	W.	L.	Pct.	H.	R.	ER.	SO.	BB.	ERA.
1987—Minnesota	American	3	$4\frac{1}{3}$	0	1	.000	10	5	5	1	0	10.38

DAVID BRUCE BERGMAN
(Dave)

Born June 6, 1953, at Evanston, Ill.
Height, 6.02. Weight, 190.
Throws and bats lefthanded.
Received bachelor of arts degree in business administration
from Illinois State University, Normal, Ill., in 1974.

Major League stolen bases: 1978 (2), 1980 (1), 1981 (2), 1982 (3), 1983 (2), 1984 (3). Total—13.
Led International League in bases on balls received with 95 in 1979.
Led International League first basemen in putouts with 1,199 in 1976.
Led Eastern League first basemen in assists with 58 in 1975.
Named Eastern League Most Valuable Player, 1975.
Named outfielder on THE SPORTING NEWS College Baseball All-America Team, 1974.

Year Club	League	Pos.	G.	AB.	R.	H.	2B.	3B.	HR.	RBI.	B.A.	PO.	A.	E.	F.A.
1974—Oneonta	NYP	1B	56	201	60	70	6	●7	10	48	*.348	494	*29	8	*.985
1975—West Haven	East.	1B-OF	124	399	76	124	15	6	11	60	*.311	610	61	5	.993
1975—New York	Amer.	OF	7	17	0	0	0	0	0	0	.000	10	1	1	.917
1976—Syracuse	Int.	*1B-OF	134	455	68	134	23	2	7	65	.295	1201	82	10	*.992
1977—Syracuse	Int.	OF-1B	132	468	88	146	29	4	16	59	.312	534	39	8	.986
1977—New York†	Amer.	OF-1B	5	4	1	1	0	0	0	1	.250	8	0	0	1.000
1978—Houston	Nat.	1B-OF	104	186	15	43	5	1	0	12	.231	328	16	4	.989
1979—Charleston	Int.	1B-OF	138	461	78	129	23	3	6	58	.280	910	61	11	.989
1979—Houston	Nat.	1B	13	15	4	6	0	0	1	2	.400	8	0	0	1.000
1980—Houston	Nat.	1B-OF	90	78	12	20	6	1	0	3	.256	187	16	1	.995
1981—Hou.‡-S.F.	Nat.	1B-OF	69	151	17	38	9	0	4	14	.252	255	25	3	.989
1982—San Francisco	Nat.	1B-OF	100	121	22	33	3	1	4	14	.273	321	20	4	.988
1983—San Francisco§	Nat.	1B-OF	90	140	16	40	4	1	6	24	.286	299	27	2	.994
1984—Detroit	Amer.	1B-OF	120	271	42	74	8	5	7	44	.273	658	75	8	.989
1985—Detroit x	Amer.	1B-OF	69	140	8	25	2	0	3	7	.179	306	25	3	.991
1985—Nashville	A. A.	1B	11	39	6	9	1	0	1	6	.231	87	8	1	.990
1986—Detroit	Amer.	1B-OF	65	130	14	30	6	1	1	9	.231	255	29	4	.986
1987—Detroit y	Amer.	1B-OF	91	172	25	47	7	3	6	22	.273	357	29	3	.992
1988—Detroit z	Amer.	1B-OF	116	289	37	85	14	0	5	35	.294	386	37	4	.991
National League Totals—6 Years			466	691	86	180	27	4	15	69	.260	1398	104	14	.991
American League Totals—7 Years			473	1023	127	262	37	9	22	118	.256	1980	196	23	.990
Major League Totals—13 Years			939	1714	213	442	64	13	37	187	.258	3378	300	37	.990

Selected by Chicago Cubs' organization in 12th round of free-agent draft, June 8, 1971.

Selected by New York Yankees' organization in 2nd round of free-agent draft, June 5, 1974.

†Traded to Houston Astros, November 23, 1977, completing deal in which Houston traded First Baseman-Catcher Cliff Johnson to New York Yankees for Infielder Mike Fischlin, Pitcher Randy Niemann and a player to be named later, June 15, 1977.

‡Traded with Outfielder Jeff Leonard to San Francisco Giants for First Baseman Mike Ivie, April 20, 1981.

§Traded to Philadelphia Phillies for Outfielder Alejandro Sanchez, March 24, 1984; Traded by Philadelphia with Pitcher Willie Hernandez to Detroit Tigers for Outfielder Glenn Wilson and Catcher-First Baseman John Wockenfuss, March 24, 1984.

xOn disabled list, April 22 to May 29, 1985; included rehabilitation disability assignment to Nashville, May 15 to May 29, 1985.

yOn disabled list, June 7 to June 22, 1987.

zGranted free agency, November 4, 1988; re-signed by Tigers, December 7, 1988.

CHAMPIONSHIP SERIES RECORD

Year Club	League	Pos.	G.	AB.	R.	H.	2B.	3B.	HR.	RBI.	B.A.	PO.	A.	E.	F.A.
1980—Houston	Nat.	PR-1B	4	3	0	1	0	1	0	2	.333	8	2	1	.909
1984—Detroit	Amer.	PR-1B	2	1	1	1	0	0	0	0	1.000	5	0	0	1.000
1987—Detroit	Amer.	PH-DH-1	4	4	0	1	0	0	0	2	.250	6	0	0	1.000
Championship Series Totals—3 Years			10	8	1	3	0	1	0	4	.375	19	2	1	.955

WORLD SERIES RECORD

Year Club	League	Pos.	G.	AB.	R.	H.	2B.	3B.	HR.	RBI.	B.A.	PO.	A.	E.	F.A.
1984—Detroit	Amer.	PR-1B	5	5	0	0	0	0	0	0	.000	22	4	0	1.000

GERONIMO EMILIANO BERROA

Born March 18, 1965, at Santo Domingo, D. R.
Height, 6.00. Weight, 165.
Throws and bats righthanded.

Led International League in being hit by pitch with 10 and tied for lead in sacrifice flies with 8 in 1988.
Led Southern League in total bases with 297 in 1987.

Year	Club	League	Pos.	G.	AB.	R.	H.	2B.	3B.	HR.	RBI.	B.A.	PO.	A.	E.	F.A.
1984	Bradenton Jays	Gulf C.	OF	62	235	31	59	16	1	3	34	.251	75	2	5	.939
1985	Kinston	Carol.	OF	19	43	4	8	0	0	1	4	.186	13	1	1	.933
1985	Medicine Hat	Pion.	OF	54	201	39	69	★22	2	6	45	.343	58	3	3	.953
1985	Florence	S. Atl.	OF	19	66	7	21	2	0	3	20	.318	24	0	2	.923
1986	Ventura	Calif.	OF	128	459	76	137	22	5	21	73	.298	194	9	14	.935
1986	Knoxville	South.	OF	1	4	0	0	0	0	0	0	.000	2	0	0	1.000
1987	Knoxville	South.	OF	134	523	87	150	33	3	36	108	.287	236	6	●15	.942
1988	Syracuse†	Int.	OF	131	470	55	122	●29	1	8	64	.260	243	12	5	.981

Signed as free agent by Toronto Blue Jays' organization, September 4, 1983.
†Drafted by Atlanta Braves, December 5, 1988.

DAMON SCOTT BERRYHILL

Born December 3, 1963, at South Laguna, Calif.
Height, 6.00. Weight, 205.
Throws right and bats right and lefthanded.
Attended Orange Coast College, Costa Mesa, Calif.

Major League stolen bases: 1988 (1).
Led American Association catchers in putouts with 603, assists with 66, double plays with 11, passed balls with 15 and total chances with 676 in 1987.
Led Carolina League in passed balls with 18 in 1985.

Year	Club	League	Pos.	G.	AB.	R.	H.	2B.	3B.	HR.	RBI.	B.A.	PO.	A.	E.	F.A.
1984	Quad Cities†	Midw.	C-1B	62	217	30	60	14	0	0	31	.276	314	31	8	.977
1985	Winston-Salem	Carol.	C-1B	117	386	31	90	25	1	9	50	.233	625	71	11	.984
1986	Pittsfield	East.	C-OF	112	345	33	71	13	1	6	35	.206	449	61	12	.977
1987	Iowa	A. A.	★C-1B	121	429	54	123	22	1	18	67	.287	607	67	7	★.990
1987	Chicago	Nat.	C	12	28	2	5	1	0	0	1	.179	37	3	4	.909
1988	Iowa	A. A.	C	21	73	11	16	5	1	2	11	.219	117	15	0	1.000
1988	Chicago‡	Nat.	C	95	309	19	80	19	1	7	38	.259	448	54	9	.982
Major League Totals—2 Years				107	337	21	85	20	1	7	39	.252	485	57	13	.977

Selected by Chicago White Sox' organization in 13th round of free-agent draft, January 11, 1983.
Selected by Chicago Cubs' organization in 1st round (fourth player selected) of free-agent draft, January 17, 1984.
†Batted righthanded.
‡On disabled list, June 30 to July 15, 1988.

KARL JON BEST

Born March 6, 1959, at Aberdeen, Wash.
Height, 6.04. Weight, 210.
Throws and bats righthanded.

Major League saves: 1985 (4), 1986 (1). Total—5.
Led Pacific Coast League in saves with 21 in 1988.

Year	Club	League	G.	IP.	W.	L.	Pct.	H.	R.	ER.	SO.	BB.	ERA.
1978	Stockton	California	12	40	1	5	.167	42	37	21	32	33	4.73
1978	Bellingham	Northwest	10	54	3	3	.500	58	32	30	47	32	5.00
1979	Alexandria	Carolina	24	167	8	11	.421	150	74	60	108	85	3.23
1980	Lynn	Eastern	26	154	9	14	.391	144	116	95	92	★106	5.55
1981	Lynn†	Eastern	13	71	4	4	.500	73	37	30	50	31	3.80
1982	Lynn	Eastern	21	138⅓	9	4	.692	104	63	53	125	90	3.45
1983	Salt Lake City	P. Coast	51	84	7	4	.636	86	51	45	108	64	4.82
1983	Seattle	American	4	5⅓	0	1	.000	14	9	8	3	5	13.50
1984	Salt Lake City	P. Coast	46	76	6	5	.545	69	52	44	77	55	5.21
1984	Seattle	American	5	6	1	1	.500	7	2	2	6	0	3.00
1985	Calgary	P. Coast	4	5⅓	0	0	.000	2	1	0	8	4	0.00
1985	Seattle‡	American	15	32⅓	2	1	.667	25	9	7	32	6	1.95
1986	Seattle§	American	26	35⅔	2	3	.400	35	19	16	23	21	4.04
1986	Calgary	P. Coast	16	17	0	1	.000	16	6	3	20	12	1.59
1987	Calgary x	P. Coast	27	37⅓	2	6	.250	34	23	18	35	27	4.34
1987	Toledo y	Int'national	28	40⅓	3	5	.375	34	12	12	43	19	2.68
1988	Portland z-Phoenix	P. Coast	39	41⅔	0	3	.000	36	22	20	34	17	4.32
1988	Minnesota	American	11	12	0	0	.000	15	9	8	9	7	6.00
Major League Totals—5 Years			61	91⅓	5	6	.455	96	48	41	73	39	4.04

Selected by Seattle Mariners' organization in 12th round of free-agent draft, June 7, 1977.
†On disabled list, May 9 to July 25, 1981.
‡On disabled list, June 24, 1985 through remainder of season.
§On disabled list, March 30 to April 18, 1986.
xTraded to Detroit Tigers' organization for Pitcher Bryan Kelly, June 22, 1987.
yTraded to Minnesota Twins for Pitcher Don Schulze, March 28, 1988.
zSold to San Francisco Giants, August 12, 1988.

ALPHONSE DANTE BICHETTE

(Known by middle name.)
Born November 18, 1963, at West Palm Beach, Fla.
Height, 6.03. Weight, 215.
Throws and bats righthanded.
Attended Palm Beach Junior College, Lake Worth, Fla.

Led Midwest League in game-winning RBIs with 13 in 1985.

Year	Club	League	Pos.	G.	AB.	R.	H.	2B.	3B.	HR.	RBI.	B.A.	PO.	A.	E.	F.A.
1984	—Salem	N'west	OF-1B-3B	64	250	27	58	9	2	4	30	.232	224	24	11	.958
1985	—Quad Cities	Midw.	1B-OF-C	137	547	58	145	28	4	11	78	.265	300	21	15	.955
1986	—Palm Springs	Calif.	OF-3B	68	290	39	79	15	0	10	73	.272	78	68	11	.930
1986	—Midland	Texas	OF-3B	62	243	43	69	16	2	12	36	.284	131	30	11	.936
1987	—Edmonton	P. C.	OF-3B	92	360	54	108	20	3	13	50	.300	169	21	9	.955
1988	—Edmonton	P. C.	OF	132	509	64	136	29	•10	14	81	.267	218	*22	*15	.941
1988	—California	Amer.	OF	21	46	1	12	2	0	0	8	.261	44	2	1	.979
Major League Totals—1 Year				21	46	1	12	2	0	0	8	.261	44	2	1	.979

Selected by California Angels' organization in 16th round of free-agent draft, June 4, 1984.

MICHAEL JOSEPH BIELECKI

Name pronounced Bill-LECK-ee.

(Mike)

Born July 31, 1959, at Baltimore, Md.
Height, 6.03. Weight, 195.
Throws and bats righthanded.
Attended Loyola College, Baltimore, Md. and Valencia Community College, Orlando, Fla.

Tied for Eastern League lead in home runs allowed with 24 in 1982.
Tied for South Atlantic League lead in games started with 28 in 1981.

Year	Club	League	G.	IP.	W.	L.	Pct.	H.	R.	ER.	SO.	BB.	ERA.
1979	—Bradenton Pirates	Gulf Coast	9	51	1	4	.200	48	21	13	35	21	2.29
1980	—Shelby	S. Atlantic	29	99	3	5	.375	106	60	50	78	58	4.55
1981	—Greenwood	S. Atlantic	28	192	12	11	.522	172	95	73	163	82	3.42
1982	—Buffalo	Eastern	25	157⅓	7	12	.368	165	96	•85	135	75	4.86
1983	—Lynn	Eastern	25	163⅔	•15	7	.682	126	73	58	*143	69	3.19
1984	—Hawaii	P. Coast	28	187⅔	*19	3	*.864	162	70	62	*162	88	2.97
1984	—Pittsburgh	National	4	4⅓	0	0	.000	4	0	0	1	0	0.00
1985	—Pittsburgh	National	12	45⅔	2	3	.400	45	26	23	22	31	4.53
1985	—Hawaii	P. Coast	20	129⅓	8	6	.571	117	58	55	111	56	3.83
1986	—Pittsburgh	National	31	148⅔	6	11	.353	149	87	77	83	83	4.66
1987	—Vancouver	P. Coast	26	181	12	10	.545	194	89	76	140	78	3.78
1987	—Pittsburgh†	National	8	45⅔	2	3	.400	43	25	24	25	12	4.73
1988	—Chicago	National	19	48⅓	2	2	.500	55	22	18	33	16	3.35
1988	—Iowa	Am. Assoc.	23	54⅔	3	2	.600	34	19	16	50	20	2.63
Major League Totals—5 Years			74	292⅔	12	19	.387	296	160	142	164	142	4.37

Selected by Kansas City Royals' organization in 6th round of free-agent draft, January 9, 1979.
Selected by Pittsburgh Pirates' organization in secondary phase of free-agent draft, June 5, 1979.
†Traded to Chicago Cubs for Pitcher Mike Curtis, March 31, 1988.

CRAIG ALAN BIGGIO

Born December 14, 1965, at Smithtown, N. Y.
Height, 5.11. Weight, 180.
Throws and bats righthanded.
Attended Seton Hall University, South Orange, N. J.

Major League stolen bases: 1988 (6).
Named catcher on THE SPORTING NEWS College Baseball All-America Team, 1987.

Year	Club	League	Pos.	G.	AB.	R.	H.	2B.	3B.	HR.	RBI.	B.A.	PO.	A.	E.	F.A.
1987	—Asheville	S. Atl.	C-OF	64	216	59	81	17	2	9	49	.375	378	46	2	.995
1988	—Tucson	P. C.	C-OF	77	281	60	90	21	4	3	41	.320	318	33	6	.983
1988	—Houston	Nat.	C	50	123	14	26	6	1	3	5	.211	292	28	3	.991
Major League Totals—1 Year				50	123	14	26	6	1	3	5	.211	292	28	3	.991

Selected by Houston Astros' organization in 1st round (22nd player selected) of free-agent draft, June 2, 1987.

MICHAEL LAURENCE BIRKBECK

(Mike)

Born March 10, 1961, at Orrville, O.
Height, 6.02. Weight, 185.
Throws and bats righthanded.
Attended University of Akron, Akron, O.

Year	Club	League	G.	IP.	W.	L.	Pct.	H.	R.	ER.	SO.	BB.	ERA.
1983	—Paintsville	Ap'lachian	7	28⅔	3	1	.750	17	12	6	38	17	1.88
1983	—Beloit	Midwest	7	42	2	4	.333	35	22	16	38	17	3.43
1984	—Beloit	Midwest	26	177⅔	14	3	.824	134	57	43	164	64	2.18
1985	—El Paso	Texas	24	155	9	9	.500	154	67	59	103	64	3.43
1986	—Vancouver	P. Coast	23	134⅓	12	6	.667	160	82	69	81	39	4.62

Year Club	League	G.	IP.	W.	L.	Pct.	H.	R.	ER.	SO.	BB.	ERA.
1986—Milwaukee	American	7	22	1	1	.500	24	12	11	13	12	4.50
1987—Milwaukee†	American	10	45	1	4	.200	63	33	31	25	19	6.20
1987—Beloit	Midwest	1	4⅓	0	0	.000	4	4	1	7	1	2.08
1987—Denver	Am. Assoc.	1	4⅔	0	1	.000	9	11	5	1	3	9.64
1988—Milwaukee	American	23	124	10	8	.556	141	69	65	64	37	4.72
1988—Denver	Am. Assoc.	5	44⅔	4	1	.800	30	10	10	30	10	2.01
Major League Totals—3 Years		40	191	12	13	.480	228	114	107	102	68	5.04

Selected by Chicago Cubs' organization in 11th round of free-agent draft, June 7, 1982.
Selected by Milwaukee Brewers' organization in 4th round of free-agent draft, June 8, 1983.
†On disabled list, June 2 to September 15, 1987; included rehabilitation disability assignment to Beloit, June 19 to June 23, 1987, and Denver, June 24 to July 1, 1987.

TIMOTHY DEAN BIRTSAS
(Tim)

Born September 5, 1960, at Clarkston, Mich.
Height, 6.07. Weight, 240.
Throws and bats lefthanded.
Received bachelor of science degree in recreation from Michigan State University, East Lansing, Mich.

Year Club	League	G.	IP.	W.	L.	Pct.	H.	R.	ER.	SO.	BB.	ERA.
1982—Oneonta	NYP	6	16⅓	1	1	.500	19	13	7	24	17	3.86
1983—Fort Lauderdale	Florida St.	23	167⅔	12	8	.600	120	57	44	*160	88	2.36
1984—Fort Lauderdale†	Florida St.	11	57⅔	5	1	.833	51	23	23	62	37	3.59
1985—Tacoma	P. Coast	4	26⅔	2	2	.500	21	10	9	25	14	3.04
1985—Oakland	American	29	141⅓	10	6	.625	124	72	63	94	91	4.01
1986—Oakland	American	2	2	0	0	.000	2	5	5	1	4	22.50
1986—Tacoma‡	P. Coast	19	92⅓	3	7	.300	94	59	52	75	71	5.07
1987—Huntsville	Southern	17	114⅔	5	10	.333	109	54	46	75	53	3.61
1987—Tacoma§	P. Coast	10	66⅓	7	2	.778	46	26	23	50	54	3.12
1988—Nashville	Am. Assoc.	8	49⅔	1	3	.250	33	20	17	48	21	3.08
1988—Cincinnati	National	36	64⅓	1	3	.250	61	34	30	38	24	4.20
American League Totals—2 Years		31	143⅓	10	6	.625	126	77	68	95	95	4.27
National League Totals—1 Year		36	64⅓	1	3	.250	61	34	30	38	24	4.20
Major League Totals—3 Years		67	207⅔	11	9	.550	187	111	98	133	119	4.25

Selected by New York Yankees' organization in 2nd round of free-agent draft, June 7, 1982.
†Traded with Outfielder Stan Javier and Pitchers Jay Howell, Eric Plunk and Jose Rijo to Oakland A's for Outfielder Rickey Henderson, Pitcher Bert Bradley and cash, December 5, 1984.
‡On disabled list, July 18 to August 26, 1986.
§Traded with Pitcher Jose Rijo to Cincinnati Reds for Outfielder Dave Parker, December 8, 1987.

JEFFREY SCOTT BITTIGER
(Jeff)

Born April 13, 1962, at Jersey City, N.J.
Height, 5.10. Weight, 175.
Throws and bats righthanded.
Attended Montclair State College, Upper Montclair, N.J., and Jersey City State College, Jersey City, N.J.
Tied for Pacific Coast League lead in complete games with 9 in 1987.
Tied for International League lead in games started by pitchers with 28 in 1983.
Named Texas League Pitcher of the Year, 1982.

Year Club	League	G.	IP.	W.	L.	Pct.	H.	R.	ER.	SO.	BB.	ERA.
1980—Little Falls	NYP	7	26	0	1	.000	10	6	3	33	20	1.04
1981—Lynchburg	Carolina	24	137	11	7	.611	121	72	60	*168	79	3.94
1981—Jackson	Texas	4	33	2	1	.667	24	4	4	27	8	1.09
1982—Jackson	Texas	25	164	12	5	.706	106	59	54	*190	94	2.96
1983—Tidewater	Int'national	28	163	12	10	.545	175	90	79	110	*111	4.36
1984—Tidewater†	Int'national	24	134⅔	8	8	.500	124	72	58	70	53	3.88
1985—Tidewater‡	Int'national	24	131⅔	11	7	.611	131	62	54	66	52	3.69
1986—Portland	P. Coast	27	171⅓	13	8	.619	181	83	79	101	58	4.15
1986—Philadelphia§x	National	3	14⅔	1	1	.500	16	10	9	8	7	5.52
1987—Portland	P. Coast	26	180	12	10	.545	171	84	68	94	57	3.40
1987—Minnesota y	American	3	8⅓	1	0	1.000	11	5	5	5	0	5.40
1988—Vancouver	P. Coast	7	52	4	1	.800	35	9	6	49	6	1.04
1988—Chicago z	American	25	61⅔	2	4	.333	59	31	29	33	29	4.23
National League Totals—1 Year		3	14⅔	1	1	.500	16	10	9	8	7	5.52
American League Totals—2 Years		28	70	3	4	.429	70	36	34	38	29	4.37
Major League Totals—3 Years		31	84⅔	4	5	.444	86	46	43	46	36	4.57

Selected by New York Mets' organization in 7th round of free-agent draft, June 3, 1980.
†On disabled list, June 13 to June 24, 1984.
‡Traded with Catcher Ronn Reynolds to Philadelphia Phillies for Pitcher Rodger Cole and First Baseman Ronnie Gideon, January 16, 1986.
§Released, December 8, 1986; signed by Richmond (Atlanta Braves' organization), December 20, 1986.
xReleased, April 4, 1987; signed by Portland (Minnesota Twins' organization), April 15, 1987.
yReleased, November 12, 1987; signed by Chicago White Sox, January 22, 1988.
zOn disabled list, July 20 to August 9, 1988.

RECORD AS THIRD BASEMAN

Year	Club	League	Pos.	G.	AB.	R.	H.	2B.	3B.	HR.	RBI.	B.A.	PO.	A.	E.	F.A.
1980	Little Falls	NYP	3B-P	22	37	4	7	0	1	0	3	.189	11	24	8	.814

HARRY RALSTON BLACK
(Bud)

Born June 30, 1957, at San Mateo, Calif.
Height, 6.02. Weight, 180.
Throws and bats lefthanded.
Attended Lower Columbia College, Longview, Wash. and received bachelor of arts degree in finance from San Diego State University, San Diego, Calif. in 1979.
Son of Harry Black, Sr., former minor league hockey player.

Major League saves: 1986 (9), 1987 (1), 1988 (1). Total—11.
Led American League in balks with 7 in 1982.

Year	Club	League	G.	IP.	W.	L.	Pct.	H.	R.	ER.	SO.	BB.	ERA.
1979	Bellingham	Northwest	2	5	0	0	.000	3	0	0	8	5	0.00
1979	San Jose	California	17	27	0	1	.000	17	11	9	24	16	3.00
1980	San Jose	California	32	86	5	3	.625	67	34	33	73	49	3.45
1981	Lynn	Eastern	22	87	2	6	.250	78	38	29	86	23	3.00
1981	Spokane	P. Coast	4	8	1	0	1.000	12	4	4	4	2	4.50
1981	Seattle†	American	2	1	0	0	.000	2	0	0	0	3	0.00
1982	Kansas City	American	22	88⅓	4	6	.400	92	48	45	40	34	4.58
1982	Omaha	Am. Assoc.	4	29	3	1	.750	23	9	8	20	10	2.48
1983	Omaha	Am. Assoc.	5	35	3	1	.750	31	13	13	32	13	3.34
1983	Kansas City	American	24	161⅓	10	7	.588	159	75	68	58	43	3.79
1984	Kansas City	American	35	257	17	12	.586	226	99	89	140	64	3.12
1985	Kansas City	American	33	205⅔	10	15	.400	216	111	99	122	59	4.33
1986	Kansas City	American	56	121	5	10	.333	100	49	43	68	43	3.20
1987	Kansas City‡	American	29	122⅓	8	6	.571	126	63	49	61	35	3.60
1988	Kansas City§-Cleveland x	American	33	81	4	4	.500	82	47	45	63	34	5.00
1988	Williamsport y	Eastern	1	5	1	0	1.000	0	0	0	5	0	0.00
	Major League Totals—8 Years		234	1037⅔	58	60	.492	1003	492	438	552	315	3.80

Selected by San Francisco Giants' organization in 3rd round of free-agent draft, January 11, 1977.
Selected by New York Mets' organization in secondary phase of free-agent draft, June 7, 1977.
Selected by Seattle Mariners' organization in 17th round of free-agent draft, June 5, 1979.
†Traded to Kansas City Royals, March 2, 1982, completing deal in which Kansas City traded Infielder Manny Castillo to Seattle Mariners for a player to be named later, October 23, 1981.
‡On disabled list, June 8 to July 4, 1987.
§Traded to Cleveland Indians for First Baseman Pat Tabler, June 3, 1988.
xOn disabled list, July 19 to August 21, 1988; included rehabilitation disability assignment to Williamsport, August 16 to August 21, 1988.
yGranted free agency, November 4, 1988; re-signed by Indians, December 5, 1988.

CHAMPIONSHIP SERIES RECORD

Year	Club	League	G.	IP.	W.	L.	Pct.	H.	R.	ER.	SO.	BB.	ERA.
1984	Kansas City	American	1	5	0	1	.000	7	4	4	3	1	7.20
1985	Kansas City	American	3	10⅔	0	0	.000	11	3	2	8	4	1.69
	Championship Series Totals—2 Years		4	15⅔	0	1	.000	18	7	6	11	5	3.45

WORLD SERIES RECORD

Year	Club	League	G.	IP.	W.	L.	Pct.	H.	R.	ER.	SO.	BB.	ERA.
1985	Kansas City	American	2	5⅓	0	1	.000	4	3	3	4	5	5.06

KEVIN DeWAYNE BLANKENSHIP

Born January 26, 1963, at Anaheim, Calif.
Height, 6.00. Weight, 185.
Throws and bats righthanded.
Attended University of Arizona, Tucson, Ariz.

Year	Club	League	G.	IP.	W.	L.	Pct.	H.	R.	ER.	SO.	BB.	ERA.
1984	Bradenton Braves	Gulf Coast	19	53⅔	3	1	.750	48	20	8	27	16	1.34
1985	Durham	Carolina	29	116⅔	8	8	.500	124	63	49	89	53	3.78
1986	Greenville	Southern	38	123	6	7	.462	132	78	67	83	84	4.90
1987	Greenville	Southern	40	102⅓	4	7	.364	96	51	47	78	53	4.13
1988	Greenville	Southern	28	177	13	9	.591	132	58	46	127	83	2.34
1988	Atlanta†-Chicago	National	3	15⅔	1	1	.500	14	8	8	9	8	4.60
	Major League Totals—1 Year		3	15⅔	1	1	.500	14	8	8	9	8	4.60

Signed as free agent by Atlanta Braves' organization, June 19, 1984.
†Traded with Pitcher Kevin Coffman to Chicago Cubs for Catcher Jody Davis, September 29, 1988.

LANCE ROBERT BLANKENSHIP

Born December 6, 1963, at Portland, Ore.
Height, 6.00. Weight, 185.
Throws and bats righthanded.
Attended University of California, Berkeley, Calif.

Led Pacific Coast League in bases on balls received with 96 in 1988.

Led Pacific Coast League second basemen in total chances with 682 in 1988.
Named third baseman on THE SPORTING NEWS College Baseball All-America Team, 1985.

Year	Club	League	Pos.	G.	AB.	R.	H.	2B.	3B.	HR.	RBI.	B.A.	PO.	A.	E.	F.A.
1986	Medford	N'west	OF	14	52	22	21	3	0	2	17	.404	22	1	1	.958
1986	Modesto	Calif.	OF-3B	55	171	47	50	5	3	6	25	.292	88	27	7	.943
1987	Modesto	Calif.	3-O-S-2	22	84	14	23	9	2	0	17	.274	26	30	8	.875
1987	Huntsville	South.	OF-2B-3B	107	390	64	99	21	3	4	39	.254	185	99	8	.973
1988	Tacoma	P. C.	2B-OF	131	437	84	116	21	8	9	52	.265	272	★390	21	.969
1988	Oakland	Amer.	2B	10	3	1	0	0	0	0	0	.000	1	1	0	1.000
Major League Totals—1 Year				10	3	1	0	0	0	0	0	.000	1	1	0	1.000

Selected by Oakland Athletics' organization in 10th round of free-agent draft, June 2, 1986.

JEFFREY MICHAEL BLAUSER
(Jeff)

Born November 8, 1965, at Los Gatos, Calif.
Height, 6.00. Weight, 170.
Throws and bats righthanded.
Attended Sacramento City College, Sacramento, Calif.

Major League stolen bases: 1987 (7).
Led Carolina League shortstops in total chances with 506 in 1986.

Year	Club	League	Pos.	G.	AB.	R.	H.	2B.	3B.	HR.	RBI.	B.A.	PO.	A.	E.	F.A.
1984	Pulaski	Appal.	SS	62	217	41	54	6	1	3	24	.249	61	162	24	.903
1985	Sumter	S. Atl.	SS	125	422	74	99	19	0	5	49	.235	150	306	35	.929
1986	Durham	Carol.	SS	123	447	94	128	27	3	13	52	.286	167	★314	25	★.951
1987	Richmond	Int.	SS-2B	33	113	11	20	1	0	1	12	.177	56	106	9	.947
1987	Atlanta	Nat.	SS	51	165	11	40	6	3	2	15	.242	65	166	9	.962
1987	Greenville	South.	SS	72	265	35	66	13	3	4	32	.249	101	225	8	.976
1988	Richmond	Int.	SS	69	271	40	77	19	1	5	23	.284	93	156	15	.943
1988	Atlanta	Nat.	2B-SS	18	67	7	16	3	1	2	7	.239	35	59	4	.959
Major League Totals—2 Years				69	232	18	56	9	4	4	22	.241	100	225	13	.962

Selected by St. Louis Cardinals' organization in 1st round (eighth player selected) of free-agent draft, January 17, 1984.

Selected by Atlanta Braves' organization in secondary phase of free-agent draft, June 4, 1984.

TERRY FENNELL BLOCKER

Born August 18, 1960, at Columbia, S.C.
Height, 6.02. Weight, 195.
Throws and bats lefthanded.
Received degree in health and recreation from Tennessee State University, Nashville, Tenn. in 1981.

Major League stolen bases: 1988 (1).
Tied for International League lead in double plays by outfielders with 6 in 1987 and 4 in 1988.

Year	Club	League	Pos.	G.	AB.	R.	H.	2B.	3B.	HR.	RBI.	B.A.	PO.	A.	E.	F.A.
1981	Little Falls	NYP	OF	36	135	28	46	8	1	7	16	.341	72	6	7	.918
1982	Jackson	Texas	OF	118	438	69	114	20	2	5	38	.260	248	7	3	★.988
1983	Jackson	Texas	OF	66	263	38	81	16	7	3	54	.308	92	5	5	.951
1983	Tidewater	Int.	OF	72	239	26	73	7	2	2	32	.305	133	4	6	.958
1984	Tidewater	Int.	OF	115	386	45	85	10	1	3	31	.220	215	2	6	.973
1985	New York†	Nat.	OF	18	15	1	1	0	0	0	0	.067	4	0	0	1.000
1985	Tidewater	Int.	OF	75	267	40	82	8	4	5	38	.307	183	5	5	.974
1986	Tidewater	Int.	OF	117	434	53	125	13	5	9	47	.288	249	11	7	.974
1987	Tidewater‡	Int.	OF	124	525	89	164	21	5	6	37	.312	286	8	7	.977
1988	Atlanta	Nat.	OF	66	198	13	42	4	2	2	10	.212	164	1	1	.994
1988	Richmond	Int.	OF	69	266	34	60	3	1	2	9	.226	175	6	0	1.000
Major League Totals—2 Years				84	213	14	43	4	2	2	10	.202	168	1	1	.994

Selected by New York Mets' organization in 1st round (fourth player selected) of free-agent draft, June 8, 1981.
†On disabled list, June 10 to June 25, 1985.
‡Traded to Atlanta Braves for a player to be named later, November 11, 1987; New York Mets acquired Pitcher Kevin Dewayne Brown, December 8, 1987.

RIK AALBERT BLYLEVEN
(Bert)

Born April 6, 1951, at Zeist, The Netherlands.
Height, 6.03. Weight, 205.
Throws and bats righthanded.

Established major league record for most home runs allowed, season (50), 1986.
Tied major league record for most putouts by pitcher, nine-inning game (6), June 24, 1984.
Established American League record for most years, 200 or more strikeouts (8).
Tied American League records for longest one-hit complete game (10 innings), June 21, 1976; most seasons, 200 or more strikeouts (7).
Pitched 6-0 no-hit victory against California Angels, September 22, 1977.
Led American League in home runs allowed with 50 in 1986 and 46 in 1987.
Led American League pitchers in complete games with 24 and tied for lead in games started with 37 in 1985.
Led American League in hit batsmen with 12 in 1976 and 16 in 1988.
Led American League in shutouts with 9 in 1973 and 5 in 1985.
Tied for American League lead in balks with 3 in 1970.
Named American League Rookie Pitcher of the Year by THE SPORTING NEWS, 1970.

Year	Club	League	G.	IP.	W.	L.	Pct.	H.	R.	ER.	SO.	BB.	ERA.
1969	Sarasota Twins	Gulf Coast	7	32	2	2	.500	31	13	10	39	11	2.81
1969	Orlando	Florida St.	6	37	5	0	1.000	36	6	6	41	14	1.46
1970	Evansville	Am. Assoc.	8	54	4	2	.667	48	18	15	63	12	2.50
1970	Minnesota	American	27	164	10	9	.526	143	66	58	135	47	3.18
1971	Minnesota	American	38	278	16	15	.516	267	95	87	224	59	2.82
1972	Minnesota	American	39	287	17	17	.500	247	93	87	228	69	2.73
1973	Minnesota	American	40	325	20	17	.541	296	109	91	258	67	2.52
1974	Minnesota	American	37	281	17	17	.500	244	99	83	249	77	2.66
1975	Minnesota	American	35	276	15	10	.600	219	104	92	233	84	3.00
1976	Minnesota†-Texas	American	36	298	13	16	.448	283	106	95	219	81	2.87
1977	Texas‡	American	30	235	14	12	.538	181	81	71	182	69	2.72
1978	Pittsburgh	National	34	244	14	10	.583	217	94	82	182	66	3.02
1979	Pittsburgh	National	37	237	12	5	.706	238	102	95	172	92	3.61
1980	Pittsburgh§	National	34	217	8	13	.381	219	102	92	168	59	3.82
1981	Cleveland	American	20	159	11	7	.611	145	52	51	107	40	2.89
1982	Cleveland x	American	4	20⅓	2	2	.500	16	14	11	19	11	4.87
1983	Cleveland	American	24	156⅓	7	10	.412	160	74	68	123	44	3.91
1984	Cleveland y	American	33	245	19	7	.731	204	86	78	170	74	2.87
1985	Cleveland z-Minnesota	American	37	★293⅔	17	16	.515	264	121	103	★206	75	3.16
1986	Minnesota	American	36	★271⅔	17	14	.548	262	134	121	215	58	4.01
1987	Minnesota	American	37	267	15	12	.556	249	132	119	196	101	4.01
1988	Minnesota ab	American	33	207⅓	10	★17	.370	240	128	★125	145	51	5.43
National League Totals—3 Years			105	698	34	28	.548	674	298	269	522	217	3.47
American League Totals—16 Years			506	3764⅓	220	198	.526	3420	1494	1340	2909	1007	3.20
Major League Totals—19 Years			611	4462⅓	254	226	.529	4094	1792	1609	3431	1224	3.25

Selected by Minnesota Twins' organization in 3rd round of free-agent draft, June 5, 1969.

†Traded with Shortstop Danny Thompson to Texas Rangers for Pitcher Bill Singer, Infielders Roy Smalley and Mike Cubbage, Pitcher Jim Gideon and a reported $250,000 cash, June 1, 1976.

‡Traded with First Baseman-Outfielder John Milner to Pittsburgh Pirates for Outfielder-First Baseman Al Oliver and Infielder Nelson Norman, December 8, 1977.

§Traded with Catcher Manny Sanguillen to Cleveland Indians for Pitchers Bob Owchinko, Rafael Vasquez and Victor Cruz and Catcher Gary Alexander, December 9, 1980.

xOn disabled list, May 2, 1982 through remainder of season.

yOn disabled list, May 23 to June 10, 1984.

zTraded to Minnesota Twins for Pitcher Curt Wardle, Outfielder Jim Weaver, Infielder Jay Bell and a player to be named later, August 1, 1985; Cleveland Indians' organization acquired Pitcher Rich Yett to complete deal, September 17, 1985.

aOn disabled list, July 30 to August 15, 1988.

bTraded with Pitcher Kevin Trudeau to California Angels for Pitchers Mike Cook and Rob Wassenaar and First Baseman Paul Sorrento, November 3, 1988.

CHAMPIONSHIP SERIES RECORD

Year	Club	League	G.	IP.	W.	L.	Pct.	H.	R.	ER.	SO.	BB.	ERA.
1970	Minnesota	American	1	2	0	0	.000	2	1	0	2	0	0.00
1979	Pittsburgh	National	1	9	1	0	1.000	8	1	1	9	0	1.00
1987	Minnesota	American	2	13⅓	2	0	1.000	12	6	6	9	3	4.05
Championship Series Totals—3 Years			4	24⅓	3	0	1.000	22	8	7	20	3	2.59

WORLD SERIES RECORD

Year	Club	League	G.	IP.	W.	L.	Pct.	H.	R.	ER.	SO.	BB.	ERA.
1979	Pittsburgh	National	2	10	1	0	1.000	8	2	2	4	3	1.80
1987	Minnesota	American	2	13	1	1	.500	13	5	4	12	2	2.77
World Series Totals—2 Years			4	23	2	1	.667	21	7	6	16	5	2.35

ALL-STAR GAME RECORD

Year	League	IP.	W.	L.	Pct.	H.	R.	ER.	SO.	BB.	ERA.
1973	American	1	0	1	.000	2	2	2	0	2	18.00
1985	American	2	0	0	.000	3	2	2	1	1	9.00
All-Star Game Totals—2 Years		3	0	1	.000	5	4	4	1	3	12.00

RANDY WALTER BOCKUS

Born October 5, 1960, at Canton, O.
Height, 6.03. Weight, 205.
Throws right and bats lefthanded.
Attended Kent State University, Kent, O.

Led Texas League pitchers in complete games with 15 and tied for lead in games started with 27 in 1985.
Led California League pitchers in games started with 30 in 1983.
Tied for Texas League in shutouts with 3 in 1984.

Year	Club	League	G.	IP.	W.	L.	Pct.	H.	R.	ER.	SO.	BB.	ERA.
1982	Great Falls	Pioneer	18	53	2	0	1.000	60	38	27	42	22	4.58
1983	Fresno	California	30	196	14	6	.700	185	89	78	★144	78	3.58
1984	Shreveport	Texas	18	128⅓	8	5	.615	106	44	40	93	54	2.81
1985	Shreveport	Texas	28	★201	★14	11	.560	196	85	61	126	44	★2.73
1986	Phoenix	P. Coast	42	122⅔	11	6	.647	139	69	58	55	54	4.26
1986	San Francisco†	National	5	7	0	0	.000	7	5	2	4	6	2.57
1987	Phoenix	P. Coast	36	108⅓	7	5	.583	133	60	54	64	41	4.49
1987	San Francisco	National	12	17⅓	1	0	1.000	17	8	7	9	4	3.63

Year	Club	League	G.	IP.	W.	L.	Pct.	H.	R.	ER.	SO.	BB.	ERA.
1988	—Phoenix†	P. Coast	23	51⅓	4	3	.571	63	36	34	27	22	5.96
1988	—San Francisco‡	National	20	32	1	1	.500	35	19	17	18	13	4.78
	Major League Totals—3 Years		37	56⅓	2	1	.667	59	32	26	31	23	4.15

Selected by San Francisco Giants' organization in 34th round of free-agent draft, June 7, 1982.
†Appeared in one game as an outfielder with no chances.
‡Granted free agency, October 15, 1988.

MICHAEL JAMES BODDICKER

Name pronounced BOD-dick-er

(Mike)

Born August 23, 1957, at Cedar Rapids, Iowa.
Height, 5.11. Weight, 186.
Throws and bats righthanded.
Attended University of Iowa, Iowa City, Iowa.

Tied modern major league record for most putouts by pitcher, season (49), 1984.
Led American League in shutouts with 5 in 1983.
Named American League Rookie Pitcher of the Year by THE SPORTING NEWS, 1983.
Named righthanded pitcher on THE SPORTING NEWS American League All-Star Team, 1984.

Year	Club	League	G.	IP.	W.	L.	Pct.	H.	R.	ER.	SO.	BB.	ERA.
1978	—Bluefield	Ap'lachian	8	19	2	1	.667	9	2	1	28	10	0.47
1978	—Charlotte	Southern	10	65	4	3	.571	42	15	14	48	17	1.94
1978	—Rochester	Int'national	1	5	1	0	1.000	4	1	1	3	2	1.80
1979	—Charlotte	Southern	14	102	9	3	.750	82	40	34	89	36	3.00
1979	—Rochester	Int'national	15	72	4	6	.400	88	48	48	48	27	6.00
1980	—Rochester	Int'national	25	190	12	9	.571	149	57	46	109	35	2.18
1980	—Baltimore	American	1	7	0	1	.000	6	6	5	4	5	6.43
1981	—Rochester	Int'national	30	182	10	10	.500	182	91	85	109	66	4.20
1981	—Baltimore	American	2	6	0	0	.000	6	4	3	2	2	4.50
1982	—Rochester	Int'national	20	133⅓	10	5	.667	121	59	53	82	36	3.58
1982	—Baltimore	American	7	25⅔	1	0	1.000	25	10	10	20	12	3.51
1983	—Rochester	Int'national	4	23⅔	3	1	.750	17	6	5	18	13	1.90
1983	—Baltimore	American	27	179	16	8	.667	141	65	55	120	52	2.77
1984	—Baltimore†	American	34	261⅓	*20	11	.645	218	95	81	128	81	*2.79
1985	—Baltimore‡	American	32	203⅓	12	17	.414	227	104	92	135	89	4.07
1986	—Baltimore§	American	33	218⅓	14	12	.538	214	125	114	175	74	4.70
1987	—Baltimore	American	33	226	10	12	.455	212	114	105	152	78	4.18
1988	—Baltimore x-Boston	American	36	236	13	15	.464	234	102	89	156	77	3.39
	Major League Totals—9 Years		205	1362⅔	86	76	.531	1283	625	554	892	470	3.66

Selected by Montreal Expos' organization in 8th round of free-agent draft, June 4, 1975.
Selected by Baltimore Orioles' organization in 6th round of free-agent draft, June 6, 1978.
†Appeared in one game as a pinch-runner.
‡Appeared in two games as a pinch-runner.
§On disabled list, April 20 to May 10, 1986.
xTraded to Boston Red Sox for Outfielder Brady Anderson and Pitcher Curt Schilling, July 29, 1988.

CHAMPIONSHIP SERIES RECORD

Established Championship Series record for most strikeouts, four-game Series (14), 1983.
Tied Championship Series record for most strikeouts, game (14), October 6, 1983.

Year	Club	League	G.	IP.	W.	L.	Pct.	H.	R.	ER.	SO.	BB.	ERA.
1983	—Baltimore	American	1	9	1	0	1.000	5	0	0	14	3	0.00
1988	—Boston	American	1	2⅔	0	1	.000	8	6	6	2	1	20.25
	Championship Series Totals—2 Years		2	11⅔	1	1	.500	13	6	6	16	4	4.63

WORLD SERIES RECORD

Year	Club	League	G.	IP.	W.	L.	Pct.	H.	R.	ER.	SO.	BB.	ERA.
1983	—Baltimore	American	1	9	1	0	1.000	3	1	0	6	0	0.00

ALL-STAR GAME RECORD

Member of American League All-Star Team in 1984; did not play.

JOSEPH MARTIN BOEVER

Name pronounced BAY-vur.

(Joe)

Born October 4, 1960, at St. Louis, Mo.
Height, 6.01. Weight, 200.
Throws and bats righthanded.
Attended Crowder College, Neosho, Mo., St. Louis Community College at Meramec, St. Louis, Mo., and University of Nevada, Las Vegas, Nev.

Major League saves: 1988 (1).
Led International League in saves with 22 in 1988.
Led American Association in saves with 21 in 1987.
Led Florida State League in games finished in relief with 38 and tied for lead in saves with 14 in 1984.

Led Florida State League in games finished in relief with 46, saves with 26 and intentional bases on balls issued with 12 in 1983.

Tied for New York-Pennsylvania League lead in intentional bases on balls issued with 5 in 1982.

Year Club	League	G.	IP.	W.	L.	Pct.	H.	R.	ER.	SO.	BB.	ERA.
1982—Erie	NYP	19	32⅔	2	3	.400	20	8	7	63	12	1.93
1982—Springfield	Midwest	3	4	0	0	.000	3	1	1	7	2	2.25
1983—St. Petersburg	Florida St.	53	80⅓	5	6	.455	61	29	27	57	37	3.02
1984—Arkansas	Texas	8	11	0	1	.000	10	11	10	12	12	8.18
1984—St. Petersburg	Florida St.	48	77⅔	6	4	.600	52	31	26	81	45	3.01
1985—Arkansas	Texas	27	37⅔	3	1	.750	21	5	5	45	23	1.19
1985—Louisville	Am. Assoc.	21	35⅓	3	2	.600	28	11	8	37	22	2.04
1985—St. Louis	National	13	16⅓	0	0	.000	17	8	8	20	4	4.41
1986—St. Louis	National	11	21⅔	0	1	.000	19	5	4	8	11	1.66
1986—Louisville	Am. Assoc.	51	88	4	5	.444	71	25	22	75	48	2.25
1987—Louisville†	Am. Assoc.	43	59	3	2	.600	52	22	22	79	27	3.36
1987—Atlanta	National	14	18⅓	1	0	1.000	29	15	15	18	12	7.36
1987—Richmond	Int'national	6	9	1	0	1.000	8	1	1	8	4	1.00
1988—Richmond	Int'national	48	71⅓	6	3	.667	47	17	17	71	22	2.14
1988—Atlanta	National	16	20⅓	0	2	.000	12	4	4	7	1	1.77
Major League Totals—4 Years		54	76⅔	1	3	.250	77	32	31	53	28	3.64

Signed as free agent by St. Louis Cardinals' organization, June 25, 1982.

†Traded to Atlanta Braves for Pitcher Randy O'Neal, July 25, 1987.

WADE ANTHONY BOGGS

Born June 15, 1958, at Omaha, Neb.
Height, 6.02. Weight, 197.
Throws right and bats lefthanded.
Attended Hillsborough Community College, Tampa, Fla.

Tied major league record for most games, one or more hits, season (135), 1985.

Established American League records for highest batting average, rookie season, 100 or more games (.349), 1982; most consecutive years with 200 or more hits (6); most singles, season (187), 1985.

Tied American League record for fewest double plays, third baseman, season, 150 or more games (17), 1988.

Major League stolen bases: 1982 (1), 1983 (3), 1984 (3), 1985 (2), 1987 (1), 1988 (2). Total—12.

Led American League in intentional bases on balls received with 19 in 1987 and tied for lead with 18 in 1988.

Led American League in bases on balls received with 105 in 1986 and 125 in 1988.

Led American League in grounding into double plays with 23 in 1988.

Led American league third basemen in total chances with 486 in 1985.

Led American League third basemen in double plays with 30 in 1984 and 37 in 1987.

Named third baseman on THE SPORTING NEWS American League All-Star Team, 1983 and 1985 through 1988.

Named third baseman on THE SPORTING NEWS American League Silver Slugger team, 1983 and 1986 through 1988.

Year Club	League	Pos.	G.	AB.	R.	H.	2B.	3B.	HR.	RBI.	B.A.	PO.	A.	E.	F.A.
1976—Elmira	NYP	3B	57	179	29	47	6	0	0	15	.263	36	75	16	.874
1977—Winston-Salem	Carol.	3B-2B-SS	117	422	67	140	13	1	2	55	.332	145	223	27	.932
1978—Bristol	East.	3-S-2-O	109	354	63	110	14	2	1	32	.311	62	107	7	.960
1979—Bristol†	East.	*3-S-2	113	406	56	132	17	2	0	41	.325	94	213	15	*.953
1980—Pawtucket	Int.	3B-1B	129	418	51	128	21	0	1	45	.306	108	156	12	.957
1981—Pawtucket	Int.	3B-1B	137	498	67	*167	*41	3	5	60	*.335	359	238	26	.958
1982—Boston	Amer.	1B-3B-OF	104	338	51	118	14	1	5	44	.349	489	168	8	.988
1983—Boston	Amer.	3B	153	582	100	210	44	7	5	74	*.361	118	368	*27	.947
1984—Boston	Amer.	3B	158	625	109	203	31	4	6	55	.325	141	330	●20	.959
1985—Boston	Amer.	3B	161	653	107	*240	42	3	8	78	*.368	134	335	17	.965
1986—Boston	Amer.	3B	149	580	107	207	47	2	8	71	*.357	*121	267	19	.953
1987—Boston	Amer.	3B-1B	147	551	108	200	40	6	24	89	*.363	112	277	14	.965
1988—Boston	Amer.	3B	155	584	*128	214	*45	6	5	58	*.366	*122	250	11	.971
Major League Totals—7 Years			1027	3913	710	1392	263	29	61	469	.356	1237	1995	116	.965

Selected by Boston Red Sox' organization in 7th round of free-agent draft, June 8, 1976.

†On disabled list, April 20 to May 2, 1979.

CHAMPIONSHIP SERIES RECORD

Year Club	League	Pos.	G.	AB.	R.	H.	2B.	3B.	HR.	RBI.	B.A.	PO.	A.	E.	F.A.
1986—Boston	Amer.	3B	7	30	3	7	1	1	0	2	.233	7	13	2	.909
1988—Boston	Amer.	3B	4	13	2	5	0	0	0	3	.385	6	6	0	1.000
Championship Series Totals—2 Years			11	43	5	12	1	1	0	5	.279	13	19	2	.941

WORLD SERIES RECORD

Tied World Series record for most assists by third baseman, inning (3), October 19, 1986 (third inning).

Year Club	League	Pos.	G.	AB.	R.	H.	2B.	3B.	HR.	RBI.	B.A.	PO.	A.	E.	F.A.
1986—Boston	Amer.	3B	7	31	3	9	3	0	0	3	.290	4	15	0	1.000

ALL-STAR GAME RECORD

Year League	Pos.	AB.	R.	H.	2B.	3B.	HR.	RBI.	B.A.	PO.	A.	E.	F.A.
1985—American	3B	0	0	0	0	0	0	0	.000	0	0	0	.000
1986—American	3B	3	0	1	0	0	0	0	.333	0	1	0	1.000
1987—American	3B	3	0	0	0	0	0	0	.000	0	3	0	1.000
1988—American	3B	3	0	1	0	0	0	0	.333	0	1	0	1.000
All-Star Game Totals—4 Years		9	0	2	0	0	0	0	.222	0	5	0	1.000

THOMAS EDWARD BOLTON

(Tom)

Born May 6, 1962, at Nashville, Tenn.
Height, 6.03. Weight, 175.
Throws and bats lefthanded.

Major League saves: 1988 (1).

Year Club	League	G.	IP.	W.	L.	Pct.	H.	R.	ER.	SO.	BB.	ERA.
1980—Elmira	NYP	23	56	6	2	.750	43	26	15	43	22	2.41
1981—Winter Haven	Florida St.	24	92	2	9	.182	125	62	46	47	41	4.50
1982—Winter Haven	Florida St.	28	162⅔	9	8	.529	161	67	54	77	63	2.99
1983—New Britain†	Eastern	16	99⅔	7	3	.700	93	36	32	62	41	2.89
1983—Pawtucket	Int'national	6	29	0	5	.000	33	26	21	20	25	6.52
1984—New Britain	Eastern	33	87	4	5	.444	87	54	40	66	34	4.14
1985—New Britain	Eastern	34	101	5	6	.455	106	53	48	74	40	4.28
1986—Pawtucket‡	Int'national	29	86	3	4	.429	80	30	26	58	25	2.72
1987—Pawtucket	Int'national	5	21⅔	2	1	.667	25	14	13	8	12	5.40
1987—Boston	American	29	61⅔	1	0	1.000	83	33	30	49	27	4.38
1988—Pawtucket	Int'national	18	19⅓	3	0	1.000	17	7	6	15	10	2.79
1988—Boston	American	28	30⅓	1	3	.250	35	17	16	21	14	4.75
Major League Totals—2 Years		57	92	2	3	.400	118	50	46	70	41	4.50

Selected by Boston Red Sox organization in 20th round of free-agent draft, June 3, 1980.
†On disabled list, June 27 to July 9, 1983.
‡On disabled list, April 11 to May 26, 1986.

BARRY LAMAR BONDS

Born July 24, 1964, at Riverside, Calif.
Height, 6.01. Weight, 185.
Throws and bats lefthanded.
Attended Arizona State University, Tempe, Ariz.
Son of Bobby Bonds, outfielder with San Francisco, New York Yankees, California, Chicago White Sox, Texas, Cleveland, St. Louis and Chicago Cubs, 1968 through 1981; and coach with Cleveland Indians, 1984 through 1987.

Major League stolen bases: 1986 (36), 1987 (32), 1988 (17). Total—85.
Named outfielder on THE SPORTING NEWS College Baseball All-America Team, 1985.

Year Club	League	Pos.	G.	AB.	R.	H.	2B.	3B.	HR.	RBI.	B.A.	PO.	A.	E.	F.A.
1985—Prince William	Carol.	OF	71	254	49	76	16	4	13	37	.299	202	4	5	.976
1986—Hawaii	P. C.	OF	44	148	30	46	7	2	7	37	.311	109	4	2	.983
1986—Pittsburgh	Nat.	OF	113	413	72	92	26	3	16	48	.223	280	9	5	.983
1987—Pittsburgh	Nat.	OF	150	551	99	144	34	9	25	59	.261	330	15	5	.986
1988—Pittsburgh	Nat.	OF	144	538	97	152	30	5	24	58	.283	292	5	6	.980
Major League Totals—3 Years			407	1502	268	388	90	17	65	165	.258	902	29	16	.983

Selected by San Francisco Giants' organization in 2nd round of free-agent draft, June 7, 1982.
Selected by Pittsburgh Pirates' organization in 1st round (sixth player selected) of free-agent draft, June 3, 1985.

ROBERTO MARTIN ANTONIO BONILLA

Name pronounced Boh-NEE-yah.

(Bobby)

Born February 23, 1963, at New York, N.Y.
Height, 6.03. Weight, 230.
Throws right and bats left and righthanded.
Attended New York Technical College, Westbury, N.Y.

Major League stolen bases: 1986 (8), 1987 (3), 1988 (3). Total—14.
Switch-hit home runs in one game, July 3, 1987 and April 6, 1988.
Led National League third basemen in total chances with 489 in 1988.
Named third baseman on THE SPORTING NEWS National League All-Star Team, 1988.
Named third baseman on THE SPORTING NEWS National League Silver Slugger team, 1988.

Year Club	League	Pos.	G.	AB.	R.	H.	2B.	3B.	HR.	RBI.	B.A.	PO.	A.	E.	F.A.
1981—Bradenton Pir.	Gulf C.	1B-C-3B	22	69	6	15	5	0	0	7	.217	124	23	5	.967
1982—Bradenton Pir.	Gulf C.	1B	47	167	20	38	3	0	5	26	.228	318	36	*14	.962
1983—Alexandria	Carol.	OF-1B	●136	504	88	129	19	7	11	59	.256	259	12	15	.948
1984—Nashua	East.	*OF-1B	136	484	74	128	19	5	11	71	.264	312	8	*15	.955
1985—Prince William†‡	Carol.	1B-3B	39	130	15	34	4	1	3	11	.262	180	9	2	.990
1986—Chicago§	Amer.	OF-1B	75	234	27	63	10	2	2	26	.269	361	22	2	.995
1986—Pittsburgh	Nat.	OF-1B-3B	63	192	28	46	6	2	1	17	.240	90	16	3	.972
1987—Pittsburgh	Nat.	3B-OF-1B	141	466	58	140	33	3	15	77	.300	142	139	16	.946
1988—Pittsburgh	Nat.	3B	159	584	87	160	32	7	24	100	.274	121	*336	*32	.935
American League Totals—1 Year			75	234	27	63	10	2	2	26	.269	361	22	2	.995
National League Totals—3 Years			363	1242	173	346	71	12	40	194	.279	353	491	51	.943
Major League Totals—3 Years			438	1476	200	409	81	14	42	220	.277	714	513	53	.959

Signed as free agent by Pittsburgh Pirates' organization, July 11, 1981.
†On Pittsburgh disabled list, March 25 to July 19, 1985.
‡Drafted by Chicago White Sox, December 10, 1985.
§Traded to Pittsburgh Pirates for Pitcher Jose DeLeon, July 23, 1986.

ALL-STAR GAME RECORD

Year	League	Pos.	AB.	R.	H.	2B.	3B.	HR.	RBI.	B.A.	PO.	A.	E.	F.A.
1988	National	3B	4	0	0	0	0	0	0	.000	0	2	0	1.000

GREGORY SCOTT BOOKER

(Greg)

Born June 22, 1960, at Lynchburg, Va.
Height, 6.06. Weight, 245.
Throws and bats righthanded.
Attended Elon College, Elon College, N.C.
Son-in-law of Jack McKeon, minor league catcher, 1949 through 1959; minor league manager, 1955 through 1964, 1968 through 1972, 1976 and 1980; scout, Minnesota Twins, 1965 through 1967; manager, Kansas City Royals, 1973 through 1975; manager, Oakland A's, 1977 and 1978; Vice-President/Baseball Operations with San Diego Padres, 1980 through 1988; and manager of San Diego Padres since May 28, 1988; related to Richard (Buddy) Booker, catcher with Cleveland Indians and Chicago White Sox, 1966 and 1968.

Major League saves: 1987 (1).
Led California League in wild pitches with 20 in 1982.

Year	Club	League	G.	IP.	W.	L.	Pct.	H.	R.	ER.	SO.	BB.	ERA.
1981	Walla Walla	Northwest	11	53	2	3	.400	55	41	31	25	35	5.26
1982	Reno	California	27	161⅔	8	*13	.381	160	*133	*114	81	*157	6.35
1983	Las Vegas	P. Coast	46	102⅓	5	6	.455	120	77	63	58	68	5.54
1983	San Diego	National	6	11⅔	0	1	.000	18	10	10	5	9	7.71
1984	Las Vegas	P. Coast	9	55⅔	4	3	.571	66	39	34	23	24	5.50
1984	San Diego	National	32	57⅓	1	1	.500	67	27	21	28	27	3.30
1985	San Diego	National	17	22⅓	0	1	.000	20	17	17	7	17	6.85
1985	Las Vegas†	P. Coast	10	45	1	1	.500	46	34	27	16	34	5.40
1986	Las Vegas	P. Coast	36	128⅔	8	9	.471	148	89	75	71	65	5.25
1986	San Diego	National	9	11	1	0	1.000	10	5	2	7	4	1.64
1987	San Diego‡	National	44	68⅓	1	1	.500	62	29	24	17	30	3.16
1988	San Diego	National	34	63⅔	2	2	.500	68	31	24	43	19	3.39
Major League Totals—6 Years			142	234⅓	5	6	.455	245	119	98	107	106	3.76

Selected by Oakland A's organization in 32nd round of free-agent draft, June 6, 1978.
Selected by San Diego Padres' organization in 10th round of free-agent draft, June 8, 1981.
†On disabled list, July 18 to August 21, 1985.
‡On disabled list, March 29 to April 15, 1987.

CHAMPIONSHIP SERIES RECORD

Year	Club	League	G.	IP.	W.	L.	Pct.	H.	R.	ER.	SO.	BB.	ERA.
1984	San Diego	National	1	2	0	0	.000	2	0	0	2	1	0.00

WORLD SERIES RECORD

Year	Club	League	G.	IP.	W.	L.	Pct.	H.	R.	ER.	SO.	BB.	ERA.
1984	San Diego	National	1	1	0	0	.000	0	1	1	0	4	9.00

RECORD AS INFIELDER

Year	Club	League	Pos.	G.	AB.	R.	H.	2B.	3B.	HR.	RBI.	B.A.	PO.	A.	E.	F.A.
1981	Walla Walla	N'west	*P-1B	31	64	8	12	0	0	4	15	.188	26	14	0	*1.000

RODERICK STEWART BOOKER

(Rod)

Born September 4, 1958, at Los Angeles, Calif.
Height, 6.00. Weight, 175.
Throws right and bats lefthanded.
Attended Pasadena City College, Pasadena, Calif., and University of California, Berkeley, Calif.

Major League stolen bases: 1987 (2), 1988 (2). Total—4.

Year	Club	League	Pos.	G.	AB.	R.	H.	2B.	3B.	HR.	RBI.	B.A.	PO.	A.	E.	F.A.
1980	Visalia	Calif.	SS	69	242	45	68	5	4	0	26	.281	91	198	18	.941
1981	Orlando	South.	SS-3B	111	331	56	85	8	3	0	33	.257	145	304	30	.937
1982	Toledo†	Int.	SS-2B-3B	104	292	38	73	8	1	0	19	.250	177	272	36	.926
1983	Arkansas	Texas	SS-3B-2B	127	469	75	128	15	3	3	60	.273	153	343	19	.963
1984	Louisville	A. A.	2B-SS-3B	63	185	19	47	3	1	0	14	.254	100	167	8	.971
1984	Arkansas	Texas	SS	52	209	10	43	4	3	0	22	.206	87	160	15	.943
1985	Arkansas	Texas	SS	129	466	59	123	18	3	1	47	.264	198	362	26	*.956
1986	Arkansas	Texas	SS	36	151	20	48	7	2	0	20	.318	66	121	10	.949
1986	Louisville	A. A.	2B-SS-3B	78	289	51	81	11	5	1	30	.280	151	205	10	.973
1987	Louisville	A. A.	2B-SS-3B	34	135	25	47	3	1	1	21	.348	50	95	5	.967
1987	St. Louis	Nat.	2B-3B-SS	44	47	9	13	1	1	0	8	.277	25	28	2	.964
1988	St. Louis	Nat.	3B-2B	18	35	6	12	3	0	0	3	.343	3	15	2	.900
1988	Louisville	A. A.	2B-SS-OF	111	370	50	96	12	1	4	31	.259	197	330	20	.963
Major League Totals—2 Years				62	82	15	25	4	1	0	11	.305	28	43	4	.947

Selected by Detroit Tigers' organization in 14th round of free-agent draft, June 8, 1976.
Selected by Baltimore Orioles' organization in 10th round of free-agent draft, June 5, 1979.
Selected by Minnesota Twins' organization in 4th round of free-agent draft, June 3, 1980.
†Sold to St. Louis Cardinals' organization, April 5, 1983.

ROBERT RAYMOND BOONE
(Bob)

Born November 19, 1947, at San Diego, Calif.
Height, 6.02. Weight, 207.
Throws and bats righthanded.
Received bachelor of arts degree in psychology from Stanford University, Palo Alto, Calif. in 1969.
Son of Ray Boone, infielder with Cleveland, Detroit, Chicago A.L., Kansas City, Milwaukee and Boston, 1948 through 1960; and scout with Boston Red Sox since 1961; brother of Rodney Alan Boone, catcher-outfielder in Kansas City Royals' and Houston Astros' organization, 1972 through 1975; and father of Bret Boone, second baseman at University of Southern California.

Established major league records for most games by catcher, lifetime (2,056); most years, 100 or more games, catcher (14).

Major League stolen bases: 1972 (1), 1973 (3), 1974 (3), 1975 (1), 1976 (2), 1977 (5), 1978 (2), 1979 (1), 1980 (3), 1981 (2), 1983 (4), 1984 (3), 1985 (1), 1986 (1), 1988 (2). Total—34.

Led American League catchers in double plays with 12 in 1983, 15 in 1985 and 16 in 1986.

Led American League catchers in total chances with 745 in 1982.

Led National League catchers in fielding percentage with .991 in 1978.

Led National League catchers in total chances with 924 in 1974.

Led Pacific Coast League catchers in passed balls with 18 and double plays with 13 in 1972.

Tied for Carolina League lead in double plays by third basemen with 18 in 1969.

Named catcher on THE SPORTING NEWS National League All-Star Team, 1976.

Named catcher on THE SPORTING NEWS American League All-Star fielding team, 1982 and 1986 through 1988.

Named catcher on THE SPORTING NEWS National League All-Star fielding team, 1978 and 1979.

Year	Club	League	Pos.	G.	AB.	R.	H.	2B.	3B.	HR.	RBI.	B.A.	PO.	A.	E.	F.A.
1969	Raleigh-Dur.	Carol.	3B	80	300	45	90	13	1	5	46	.300	71	160	20	.920
1970	Reading†	East.	3B	20	80	12	23	2	0	2	10	.288	28	38	7	.904
1971	Reading‡	East.	3B-C-SS	92	328	41	87	14	3	4	37	.265	206	138	17	.953
1972	Eugene	P. C.	C	138	513	77	158	32	4	17	67	.308	*699	*77	*24	.970
1972	Philadelphia	Nat.	C	16	51	4	14	1	0	1	4	.275	66	7	5	.936
1973	Philadelphia	Nat.	C	145	521	42	136	20	2	10	61	.261	868	*89	10	.990
1974	Philadelphia	Nat.	C	146	488	41	118	24	3	3	52	.242	*825	77	*22	.976
1975	Philadelphia	Nat.	C-3B	97	289	28	71	14	2	2	20	.246	459	48	5	.990
1976	Philadelphia	Nat.	C-1B	121	361	40	98	18	2	4	54	.271	587	39	6	.990
1977	Philadelphia	Nat.	C-3B	132	440	55	125	26	4	11	66	.284	654	83	8	.989
1978	Philadelphia	Nat.	C-1B-OF	132	435	48	123	18	4	12	62	.283	650	55	8	.989
1979	Philadelphia	Nat.	C-3B	119	398	38	114	21	3	9	58	.286	527	66	8	.987
1980	Philadelphia	Nat.	C	141	480	34	110	23	1	9	55	.229	741	88	*18	.979
1981	Philadelphia§	Nat.	C	76	227	19	48	7	0	4	24	.211	365	32	6	.985
1982	California	Amer.	C	143	472	42	121	17	0	7	58	.256	*650	*87	8	.989
1983	California	Amer.	C	142	468	46	120	18	0	9	52	.256	606	*83	*14	.980
1984	California	Amer.	C	139	450	33	91	16	1	3	32	.202	660	*71	12	.984
1985	California	Amer.	C	150	460	37	114	17	0	5	55	.248	670	71	10	.987
1986	California x	Amer.	C	144	442	48	98	12	2	7	49	.222	812	*84	11	.988
1987	Palm Springs	Calif.	C	3	9	0	1	1	0	0	0	.111	17	4	1	.955
1987	California	Amer.	C	128	389	42	94	18	0	3	33	.242	684	56	*13	.983
1988	California y	Amer.	C	122	352	38	104	17	0	5	39	.295	506	*66	8	.986
National League Totals—10 Years				1125	3690	349	957	172	21	65	456	.259	5742	584	96	.958
American League Totals—7 Years				968	3033	286	742	115	3	39	318	.245	4588	518	76	.985
Major League Totals—17 Years				2093	6723	635	1699	287	24	104	774	.253	10330	1102	172	.985

Selected by Philadelphia Phillies' organization in 20th round of free-agent draft, June 5, 1969.
†On military list, May 26, 1970 through remainder of season.
‡On disabled list, April 10 to June 4, 1971.
§Sold to California Angels, December 6, 1981.
xGranted free agency, November 12, 1986; re-signed by Angels, May 1, 1987.
yGranted free agency, October 24, 1988; signed by Kansas City Royals, November 30, 1988.

DIVISION SERIES RECORD

Year	Club	League	Pos.	G.	AB.	R.	H.	2B.	3B.	HR.	RBI.	B.A.	PO.	A.	E.	F.A.
1981	Philadelphia	Nat.	C	3	5	0	0	0	0	0	0	.000	10	2	0	1.000

CHAMPIONSHIP SERIES RECORD

Tied Championship Series record for most consecutive hits, one Series (5), 1986.

Established American League Championship Series record for highest batting average, seven-game Series (.455), 1986.

Tied American League Championship Series records for most consecutive hits, total Series (5); most singles, seven-game Series (9), 1986.

Year	Club	League	Pos.	G.	AB.	R.	H.	2B.	3B.	HR.	RBI.	B.A.	PO.	A.	E.	F.A.
1976	Philadelphia	Nat.	C	3	7	0	2	0	0	0	1	.286	8	2	0	1.000
1977	Philadelphia	Nat.	C	4	10	1	4	0	0	0	0	.400	18	2	0	1.000
1978	Philadelphia	Nat.	C	3	11	0	2	0	0	0	0	.182	16	2	1	.947
1980	Philadelphia	Nat.	C	5	18	1	4	0	0	0	2	.222	22	3	0	1.000
1982	California	Amer.	C	5	16	3	4	0	0	1	4	.250	30	3	0	1.000
1986	California	Amer.	C	7	22	4	10	0	0	1	2	.455	33	3	0	1.000
Championship Series Totals—6 Years				27	84	9	26	0	0	2	9	.310	127	15	1	.993

WORLD SERIES RECORD

Year	Club	League	Pos.	G.	AB.	R.	H.	2B.	3B.	HR.	RBI.	B.A.	PO.	A.	E.	F.A.
1980	Philadelphia	Nat.	C	6	17	3	7	2	0	0	4	.412	49	3	0	1.000

ALL-STAR GAME RECORD

Year	League	Pos.	AB.	R.	H.	2B.	3B.	HR.	RBI.	B.A.	PO.	A.	E.	F.A.
1976	—National	C	2	0	0	0	0	0	0	.000	5	0	0	1.000
1978	—National	C	1	1	1	0	0	0	2	1.000	3	1	0	1.000
1979	—National	C	2	1	1	0	0	0	0	.500	0	0	0	.000
1983	—American	C	0	0	0	0	0	0	0	.000	1	0	0	1.000
All-Star Game Totals—4 Years			5	2	2	0	0	0	2	.400	9	1	0	1.000

PATRICK LANCE BORDERS
(Pat)

Born May 14, 1963, at Columbus, O.
Height, 6.02. Weight, 205.
Throws and bats righthanded.

Tied for Southern League in passed balls with 16 in 1987.

Year	Club	League	Pos.	G.	AB.	R.	H.	2B.	3B.	HR.	RBI.	B.A.	PO.	A.	E.	F.A.
1982	—Medicine Hat	Pion.	3B	61	217	30	66	12	2	5	33	.304	23	96	★25	.826
1983	—Florence	S. Atl.	3B	131	457	62	125	31	4	5	54	.274	70	233	★41	.881
1984	—Florence	S. Atl.	1B-3B-OF	131	467	69	129	32	5	12	85	.276	650	77	25	.967
1985	—Kinston	Carol.	1B	127	460	43	120	16	1	10	60	.261	854	42	★20	.978
1986	—Florence	S. Atl.	C-OF	16	40	8	15	7	0	3	9	.375	22	1	0	1.000
1986	—Knoxville	South.	C-1B	12	34	3	12	1	0	2	5	.353	45	5	3	.943
1986	—Kinston	Carol.	C-1B-OF	49	174	24	57	10	0	6	26	.328	211	26	7	.971
1987	—Dunedin	Fla. St.	1B	3	11	0	4	0	0	0	1	.364	21	1	0	1.000
1987	—Knoxville	South.	C-3B	94	349	44	102	14	1	11	51	.292	432	49	12	.976
1988	—Toronto†	Amer.	C-2B-3B	56	154	15	42	6	3	5	21	.273	205	19	7	.970
1988	—Syracuse	Int.	C	35	120	11	29	8	0	3	14	.242	202	17	2	.991
Major League Totals—1 Year				56	154	15	42	6	3	5	21	.273	205	19	7	.970

Selected by Toronto Blue Jays' organization in sixth round of free-agent draft, June 7, 1982.

†On disabled list, July 5 to August 19, 1988; included rehabilitation disability assignment to Syracuse, July 30 to August 19, 1988.

RICHARD ALBERT BORDI

Name pronounced BORD-ee.

(Rich)

Born April 18, 1959, at South San Francisco, Calif.
Height, 6.07. Weight, 220.
Throws and bats righthanded.
Attended Fresno State University, Fresno, Calif.

Major League saves: 1983 (1), 1984 (4), 1985 (2), 1986 (3). Total—10.
Tied for Pacific Coast League lead in complete games with 15 in 1981.

Year	Club	League	G.	IP.	W.	L.	Pct.	H.	R.	ER.	SO.	BB.	ERA.
1980	—West Haven	Eastern	11	76	4	6	.400	75	42	35	49	30	4.14
1980	—Oakland	American	1	2	0	0	.000	4	1	1	0	0	4.50
1981	—Tacoma	P. Coast	27	191	9	11	.450	197	98	78	101	66	3.68
1981	—Oakland†	American	2	2	0	0	.000	1	0	0	0	1	0.00
1982	—Salt Lake City	P. Coast	25	168⅓	12	9	.571	212	105	84	118	31	4.49
1982	—Seattle‡	American	7	13	0	2	.000	18	12	12	10	1	8.31
1983	—Iowa§	Am. Assoc.	18	111⅓	7	2	.778	134	62	57	80	21	4.61
1983	—Chicago	National	11	25⅓	0	2	.000	34	15	14	20	12	4.97
1984	—Chicago xy	National	31	83⅓	5	2	.714	78	37	32	41	20	3.46
1985	—New York za	American	51	98	6	8	.429	95	41	35	64	29	3.21
1986	—Baltimore b	American	52	107	6	4	.600	105	56	53	83	41	4.46
1987	—Columbus	Int'national	25	46⅔	2	2	.500	36	15	9	33	14	1.74
1987	—New York c	American	16	33	3	1	.750	42	28	28	23	12	7.64
1988	—Tacoma	P. Coast	40	119	7	7	.500	122	61	46	81	35	3.48
1988	—Oakland	American	2	7⅔	0	1	.000	6	6	4	6	5	4.70
American League Totals—7 Years			131	262⅔	15	16	.484	271	144	133	186	89	4.56
National League Totals—2 Years			42	108⅔	5	4	.556	112	52	46	61	32	3.81
Major League Totals—9 Years			173	371⅓	20	20	.500	383	196	179	247	121	4.34

Selected by Minnesota Twins' organization in 5th round of free-agent draft, June 7, 1977.

Selected by Oakland A's organization in 3rd round of free-agent draft, June 3, 1980.

†Traded to Seattle Mariners for Third Baseman-Outfielder Dan Meyer, December 9, 1981.

‡Traded to Chicago Cubs for Outfielder Steve Henderson, December 9, 1982.

§On disabled list, April 25 to May 10, 1983.

xOn disabled list, August 8 to August 23, 1984.

yTraded with Catcher Ron Hassey, Outfielder Henry Cotto and Pitcher Porfi Altamirano to New York Yankees for Pitcher Ray Fontenot and Outfielder Brian Dayett, December 4, 1984.

zOn disabled list, April 30 to May 15, 1985.

aTraded with Infielder Rex Hudler to Baltimore Orioles for Outfielder Gary Roenicke and a player to be named later, December 12, 1985; New York Yankees acquired Outfielder Leo Hernandez to complete deal, December 16, 1985.

bReleased, March 30, 1987; signed by Columbus (New York Yankees' organization), April 10, 1987.

cReleased, December 18, 1987; signed by Tacoma (Oakland Athletics' organization), January 29, 1988.

CHRISTOPHER LOUIS BOSIO

Name pronounced Boz-e-o.

(Chris)

Born April 3, 1963, at Carmichael, Calif.
Height, 6.03. Weight, 210.
Throws and bats righthanded.
Attended Sacramento City College, Sacramento, Calif.

Major League saves: 1987 (2), 1988 (6). Total—8.

Tied for Pacific Coast League lead in saves with 16 in 1986.

Year Club	League	G.	IP.	W.	L.	Pct.	H.	R.	ER.	SO.	BB.	ERA.
1982—Pikeville	Ap'lachian	13	51⅓	3	2	.600	60	31	28	53	17	4.91
1983—Beloit	Midwest	17	107⅔	3	10	.231	125	82	67	71	41	5.60
1983—Paintsville	Ap'lachian	7	44⅓	2	2	.500	30	18	14	43	18	2.84
1984—Beloit	Midwest	26	181	*17	6	.739	159	83	55	156	56	2.73
1985—El Paso	Texas	28	181⅓	11	6	.647	186	108	77	*155	49	3.82
1986—Vancouver	P. Coast	44	67	7	3	.700	47	18	17	60	13	2.28
1986—Milwaukee	American	10	34⅔	0	4	.000	41	27	27	29	13	7.01
1987—Milwaukee	American	46	170	11	8	.579	187	102	99	150	50	5.24
1988—Milwaukee	American	38	182	7	15	.318	190	80	68	84	38	3.36
1988—Denver	Am. Assoc.	2	14	1	0	1.000	13	6	6	12	4	3.86
Major League Totals—3 Years		94	386⅔	18	27	.400	418	209	194	263	101	4.52

Selected by Pittsburgh Pirates' organization in 29th round of free-agent draft, June 8, 1981.
Selected by Milwaukee Brewers' organization in secondary phase of free-agent draft, January 12, 1982.

THADDIS BOSLEY JR.

Name pronounced BAHZ-lee.

(Thad)

Born September 17, 1956, at Oceanside, Calif.
Height, 6.03. Weight, 175.
Throws and bats lefthanded.
Attended Mira Costa Community College, Oceanside, Calif.

Major League stolen bases: 1977 (5), 1978 (12), 1979 (4), 1980 (3), 1981 (2), 1982 (3), 1983 (1), 1984 (5), 1985 (5), 1986 (3), 1988 (1). Total—44.

Led California League in stolen bases with 90 and caught stealing with 17 in 1976.

Led Pioneer League in bases on balls received with 71 in 1974.

Named California League Most Valuable Player, 1976.

Year Club	League	Pos.	G.	AB.	R.	H.	2B.	3B.	HR.	RBI.	B.A.	PO.	A.	E.	F.A.
1974—Idaho Falls	Pion.	OF	68	223	55	54	3	4	0	14	.242	101	4	*11	.905
1975—Quad Cities†	Midw.	OF	108	379	67	113	12	3	1	50	.298	206	2	4	*.981
1976—Salinas	Calif.	OF	134	527	105	171	26	4	2	72	*.324	285	13	7	*.977
1977—Salt Lake City	P. C.	OF	69	298	55	97	22	2	2	38	.326	169	6	5	.972
1977—California‡§	Amer.	OF	58	212	19	63	10	2	0	19	.297	130	1	5	.963
1978—Iowa	A. A.	OF	47	179	27	52	3	0	3	15	.291	77	5	2	.976
1978—Chicago x	Amer.	OF	66	219	25	59	5	1	2	13	.269	155	3	4	.975
1979—Iowa y	A. A.	OF	95	382	62	101	14	5	1	24	.264	140	6	5	.967
1979—Chicago	Amer.	OF	36	77	13	24	1	1	1	8	.312	57	2	2	.967
1980—Chicago za	Amer.	OF	70	147	12	33	2	0	2	14	.224	91	1	4	.958
1981—Vancouver	P. C.	OF	34	122	15	39	5	2	0	14	.320	75	0	5	.938
1981—Milwaukee b	Amer.	OF	42	105	11	24	2	0	0	3	.229	55	1	2	.966
1982—Seattle	Amer.	OF	22	46	3	8	1	0	0	2	.174	12	1	0	1.000
1982—Salt Lake C. cdef	P. C.	OF	22	84	15	25	2	2	3	9	.298	24	2	0	1.000
1983—Mexico City	Mex.	OF	31	107	24	35	7	3	4	18	.327	24	1	0	1.000
1983—Iowa	A. A.	OF	39	124	22	36	11	0	7	24	.290	3	0	1	.750
1983—Chicago	Nat.	OF	43	72	12	21	4	1	2	12	.292	27	1	0	1.000
1984—Iowa	A. A.	OF	51	162	23	58	16	1	6	43	.358	31	4	2	.946
1984—Chicago	Nat.	OF	55	98	17	29	2	2	2	14	.296	39	2	1	.976
1985—Chicago	Nat.	OF	108	180	25	59	6	3	7	27	.328	84	0	1	.988
1986—Chicago g	Nat.	OF	87	120	15	33	4	1	1	9	.275	31	0	1	.969
1987—Kansas City h	Amer.	OF	80	140	13	39	6	1	1	16	.279	28	0	1	.966
1988—K.C. ij-Calif.	Amer.	OF	50	96	10	25	5	0	0	9	.260	59	0	2	.967
1988—Edmonton k	P.C.	OF	18	52	13	16	5	1	0	9	.308	20	1	0	1.000
American League Totals—8 Years			424	1042	106	275	32	5	6	84	.264	587	9	20	.968
National League Totals—4 Years			293	470	69	142	16	7	12	62	.302	181	3	3	.984
Major League Totals—12 Years			717	1512	175	417	48	12	18	146	.276	768	12	23	.971

Selected by California Angels' organization in 4th round of free-agent draft, June 5, 1974.

†On disabled list, April 19 to May 6, 1975.

‡On disabled list, June 29 to July 10, 1977.

§Traded with Outfielder Bobby Bonds and Pitcher Richard Dotson to Chicago White Sox for Pitchers Chris Knapp and Dave Frost and Catcher Brian Downing, December 5, 1977.

xOn disabled list, June 29 to July 17, 1978.

yOn disabled list, July 15 to July 25, 1979.

zOn disabled list, August 12, 1980 through remainder of season.

aTraded to Milwaukee Brewers' organization for First Baseman-Outfielder John Poff, April 1, 1981.

bTraded to Seattle Mariners for Pitcher Mike Parrott, March 5, 1982.

cOn disabled list, June 6 to July 1 and August 3 to September 2, 1982.

dGranted free agency, September 5, 1982; signed by Tacoma (Oakland A's organization), February 14, 1983.

eSold to Iowa (Chicago Cubs' organization), March 30, 1983.
fLoaned to Mexico City Tigers, April 3, 1983; returned, May 28, 1983.
gTraded with Pitcher Dave Gumpert to Kansas City Royals for Catcher Jim Sundberg, March 30, 1987.
hGranted free agency, November 9, 1987; re-signed by Royals, January 5, 1988.
iOn disabled list, May 11 to May 27, 1988.
jReleased, May 27, 1988; signed by Edmonton (California Angels' organization), June 7, 1988.
kGranted free agency, November 4, 1988.

DIVISION SERIES RECORD

Year	Club	League	Pos.	G.	AB.	R.	H.	2B.	3B.	HR.	RBI.	B.A.	PO.	A.	E.	F.A.
1981	Milwaukee	Amer.	PR-DH	1	0	0	0	0	0	0	0	.000	0	0	0	.000

CHAMPIONSHIP SERIES RECORD

Year	Club	League	Pos.	G.	AB.	R.	H.	2B.	3B.	HR.	RBI.	B.A.	PO.	A.	E.	F.A.
1984	Chicago	Nat.	PH	2	2	0	0	0	0	0	0	.000	0	0	0	.000

DARYL LAMONT BOSTON

Born January 4, 1963, at Cincinnati, O.
Height, 6.03. Weight, 203.
Throws and bats lefthanded.

Major League stolen bases: 1984 (6), 1985 (8), 1986 (9), 1987 (12), 1988 (9). Total—44.
Led Eastern League batters in strikeouts with 133 in 1983.
Led Midwest League outfielders in total chances with 312 in 1982.
Tied for American Association lead in sacrifice flies with 11 in 1984.
Tied for American Association lead in double plays by outfielders with 4 in 1984.

Year	Club	League	Pos.	G.	AB.	R.	H.	2B.	3B.	HR.	RBI.	B.A.	PO.	A.	E.	F.A.
1981	Sarasota W. S.	Gulf C.	OF	56	189	30	55	6	3	1	30	.291	84	9	3	.969
1982	Appleton	Midw.	OF	★139	512	86	143	19	9	15	77	.279	★293	9	10	.968
1983	Glens Falls	East.	OF	113	435	65	104	15	1	18	50	.239	271	8	13	.955
1983	Denver	A. A.	OF	14	51	11	13	4	1	2	7	.255	26	1	5	.844
1984	Denver	A. A.	OF	127	471	94	147	21	★19	15	82	.312	311	11	●10	.970
1984	Chicago	Amer.	OF	35	83	8	14	3	1	0	3	.169	59	2	6	.910
1985	Chicago	Amer.	OF	95	232	20	53	13	1	3	15	.228	179	7	2	.989
1985	Buffalo	A. A.	OF	63	241	45	66	12	1	10	36	.274	151	3	3	.981
1986	Buffalo	A. A.	OF	96	360	57	109	16	3	5	41	.303	210	1	5	.977
1986	Chicago	Amer.	OF	56	199	29	53	11	3	5	22	.266	152	3	5	.969
1987	Chicago	Amer.	OF	103	337	51	87	21	2	10	29	.258	207	3	2	.991
1987	Hawaii	P. C.	OF	21	77	14	23	3	0	5	13	.299	43	3	0	1.000
1988	Chicago	Amer.	OF	105	281	37	61	12	2	15	31	.217	190	4	10	.951
Major League Totals—5 Years				394	1132	145	268	60	9	33	100	.237	787	19	25	.970

Selected by Chicago White Sox' organization in 1st round (seventh player selected) of free-agent draft, June 8, 1981.

DENNIS RAY BOYD
(Oil Can)

(Given nickname from beer drinking friends in Meridian, Miss. where beer is referred to as oil.)
Born October 6, 1959, at Meridian, Miss.
Height, 6.01. Weight, 160.
Throws and bats righthanded.
Attended Jackson State University, Jackson, Miss.
Brother of Don Boyd, outfielder in St. Louis Cardinals' organization, 1973.

Led Florida State League pitchers in games started with 28 and home runs allowed with 11 in 1981.
Tied for Eastern League lead in games started by pitchers with 27 and complete games with 13 in 1982.

Year	Club	League	G.	IP.	W.	L.	Pct.	H.	R.	ER.	SO.	BB.	ERA.
1980	Elmira	NYP	12	69	7	1	.875	54	20	19	79	30	2.48
1981	Winter Haven	Florida St.	28	186	14	8	.636	★195	90	75	154	54	3.63
1982	Bristol	Eastern	27	★205	14	8	.636	190	71	64	★191	49	2.81
1982	Boston	American	3	8⅓	0	1	.000	11	5	5	2	2	5.40
1983	Pawtucket	Int'national	20	122⅔	5	8	.385	119	69	55	129	41	4.04
1983	Boston	American	15	98⅔	4	8	.333	103	46	36	43	23	3.28
1984	Boston	American	29	197⅔	12	12	.500	207	109	96	134	53	4.37
1984	Pawtucket	Int'national	5	37⅓	3	1	.750	30	12	12	45	12	2.89
1985	Boston	American	35	272⅓	15	13	.536	★273	117	112	154	67	3.70
1986	Boston	American	30	214⅓	16	10	.615	222	99	90	129	45	3.78
1987	Pawtucket†	Int'national	3	12	1	1	.500	12	6	6	8	4	4.50
1987	Boston	American	7	36⅔	1	3	.250	47	31	24	12	9	5.89
1988	Boston‡	American	23	129⅔	9	7	.563	147	82	77	71	41	5.34
Major League Totals—7 Years			142	957⅔	57	54	.514	1010	489	440	545	240	4.14

Selected by Boston Red Sox' organization in 16th round of free-agent draft, June 3, 1980.
†On Boston disabled list, March 29 to June 22 and July 31, 1987 through remainder of season; included rehabilitation disability assignment to Pawtucket, June 8 to June 22, 1987.
‡On disabled list, July 27 to August 20 and August 31, 1988 through remainder of season.

CHAMPIONSHIP SERIES RECORD

Year	Club	League	G.	IP.	W.	L.	Pct.	H.	R.	ER.	SO.	BB.	ERA.
1986	Boston	American	2	13⅔	1	1	.500	17	7	7	8	3	4.61

WORLD SERIES RECORD

Year	Club	League	G.	IP.	W.	L.	Pct.	H.	R.	ER.	SO.	BB.	ERA.
1986	Boston	American	1	7	0	1	.000	9	6	6	3	1	7.71

PHILIP POOLE BRADLEY
(Phil)

Born March 11, 1959, at Bloomington, Ind.
Height, 6.00. Weight, 185.
Throws and bats righthanded.
Received bachelor of science degree in personnel management from
University of Missouri, Columbia, Mo., in 1982.

Major League stolen bases: 1983 (3), 1984 (21), 1985 (22), 1986 (21), 1987 (40), 1988 (11). Total—118.
Led National League in being hit by pitch with 16 in 1988.
Named outfielder on THE SPORTING NEWS American League All-Star Team, 1985.

Year	Club	League	Pos.	G.	AB.	R.	H.	2B.	3B.	HR.	RBI.	B.A.	PO.	A.	E.	F.A.
1981	Bellingham	N'west	OF	53	193	38	58	12	5	1	20	.301	94	3	1	*.990
1982	Bakersfield	Calif.	OF	109	405	98	134	17	10	0	37	.331	226	13	6	.976
1983	Salt Lake City	P. Coast	OF	130	458	100	148	14	4	2	41	.323	284	13	1	*.997
1983	Seattle	Amer.	OF	23	67	8	18	2	0	0	5	.269	36	1	1	.974
1984	Seattle	Amer.	OF	124	322	49	97	12	4	0	24	.301	235	3	2	.992
1985	Seattle	Amer.	OF	159	641	100	192	33	8	26	88	.300	336	10	5	.986
1986	Seattle†	Amer.	OF	143	526	88	163	27	4	12	50	.310	250	11	1	.996
1987	Seattle‡	Amer.	OF	158	603	101	179	38	10	14	67	.297	273	13	5	.983
1988	Philadelphia§	Nat.	OF	154	569	77	150	30	5	11	56	.264	298	14	3	.990
American League Totals—5 Years				607	2159	346	649	112	26	52	234	.301	1130	38	14	.988
National League Totals—1 Year				154	569	77	150	30	5	11	56	.264	298	14	3	.990
Major League Totals—6 Years				761	2728	423	799	142	31	63	290	.293	1428	52	17	.989

Selected by Seattle Mariners' organization in 3rd round of free-agent draft, June 8, 1981.
†On disabled list, May 26 to June 12, 1986.
‡Traded with Pitcher Tim Fortugno to Philadelphia Phillies for Outfielders Glenn Wilson and Dave Brundage and Pitcher Mike Jackson, December 9, 1987.
§Traded to Baltimore Orioles for Pitchers Ken Howell and Gordon Dillard, December 8, 1988.

ALL-STAR GAME RECORD

Year	League	Pos.	AB.	R.	H.	2B.	3B.	HR.	RBI.	B.A.	PO.	A.	E.	F.A.
1985	American	OF	1	0	0	0	0	0	0	.000	1	0	0	1.000

SCOTT WILLIAM BRADLEY

Born March 22, 1960, at Montclair, N.J.
Height, 5.11. Weight, 185.
Throws right and bats lefthanded.
Received bachelor of science degree in business administration
from University of North Carolina, Chapel Hill, N.C.

Major League stolen bases: 1986 (1), 1988 (1). Total—2.
Tied for International League lead in game-winning RBIs with 14 in 1984.
Tied for Florida State League lead in game-winning RBIs with 13 in 1982.
Named International League Player of the Year, 1984.

Year	Club	League	Pos.	G.	AB.	R.	H.	2B.	3B.	HR.	RBI.	B.A.	PO.	A.	E.	F.A.
1981	Oneonta	NYP	C-OF	71	276	48	85	17	4	4	54	.308	323	40	9	.976
1982	Nashville	South.	C	5	19	2	2	1	0	0	0	.105	44	2	2	.958
1982	Fort Lauderdale	Fla. St.	C-1B-3B	121	439	52	130	28	4	3	66	.296	407	57	10	.979
1983	Nashville	South.	C-3B	137	525	83	142	33	4	8	76	.270	475	88	13	.977
1984	Columbus	Int.	C-OF-3B	*138	*538	84	*180	31	2	6	●84	*.335	432	50	9	.982
1984	New York	Amer.	OF-C	9	21	3	6	1	0	0	2	.286	10	0	0	1.000
1985	New York†	Amer.	C	19	49	4	8	2	1	0	1	.163	12	0	1	.923
1985	Albany	East.	3B	6	24	2	3	1	0	0	2	.125	8	14	4	.846
1985	Columbus‡	Int.	C-3B	43	163	17	49	10	0	4	27	.301	118	53	4	.977
1986	Buffalo	A. A.	C-OF	33	126	14	42	3	3	5	20	.333	165	9	0	1.000
1986	Chi.§-Sea	Amer.	C-OF	77	220	20	66	8	3	5	28	.300	281	21	3	.990
1987	Seattle	Amer.	C-3B-OF	102	342	34	95	15	1	5	43	.278	438	39	8	.984
1988	Seattle	Amer.	C-O-3-1	103	335	45	86	17	1	4	33	.257	543	42	6	.990
Major League Totals—5 Years				310	967	106	261	43	6	14	107	.270	1284	102	18	.987

Selected by Minnesota Twins' organization in 12th round of free-agent draft, June 6, 1978.
Selected by New York Yankees' organization in 3rd round of free-agent draft, June 8, 1981.
†On disabled list, April 24 to June 17, 1985; included rehabilitation disability assignment to Sarasota, June 5 and June 6, 1985, and Albany, June 7 to June 17, 1985.
‡Traded with Pitcher Neil Allen, Outfielder Glen Braxton and cash to Chicago White Sox for Catchers Ron Hassey and Chris Alvarez, Pitcher Eric Schmidt and Outfielder Matt Winters, February 13, 1986.
§Traded to Seattle Mariners for a player to be named later, June 26, 1986; Chicago White Sox' organization acquired Outfielder Ivan Calderon to complete deal, July 1, 1986.

GLENN ERICK BRAGGS

Born October 17, 1962, at San Bernardino, Calif.
Height, 6.03. Weight, 210.
Throws and bats righthanded.
Attended University of Hawaii, Honolulu, Hawaii.

Major League stolen bases: 1986 (1), 1987 (12), 1988 (6). Total—19.
Led Texas League in being hit by pitch with 10 in 1985.
Led Appalachian League in total bases with 164, bases on balls received with 54 and intentional bases on balls received with 6 in 1983.
Named California League Most Valuable Player, 1984.
Named Appalachian League Player of the Year, 1983.
Received reported $50,000 bonus to sign with Milwaukee Brewers, 1983.

Year Club	League	Pos.	G.	AB.	R.	H.	2B.	3B.	HR.	RBI.	B.A.	PO.	A.	E.	F.A.
1983—Paintsville	Appal.	OF	•73	241	*65	*94	*20	1	•16	*74	*.390	115	8	6	.953
1984—Stockton	Calif.	OF	108	399	76	118	29	2	15	86	.296	158	4	6	.964
1985—El Paso	Texas	OF	117	448	105	139	26	4	20	103	.310	239	10	11	.958
1986—Vancouver	P. C.	OF	90	325	80	117	26	6	15	75	.360	218	8	2	.991
1986—Milwaukee	Amer.	OF	58	215	19	51	8	2	4	18	.237	116	5	12	.910
1987—Milwaukee	Amer.	OF	132	505	67	136	28	7	13	77	.269	301	6	9	.972
1988—Milwaukee†	Amer.	OF	72	272	30	71	14	0	10	42	.261	134	1	3	.978
Major League Totals—3 Years			262	992	116	258	50	9	27	137	.260	551	12	24	.959

Selected by New York Yankees' organization in 6th round of free-agent draft, June 3, 1980.
Selected by Milwaukee Brewers' organization in 2nd round of free-agent draft, June 6, 1983.
†On disabled list, July 2, 1988 through remainder of season.

CLIFFORD BRANTLEY
(Cliff)

Born April 12, 1968, at Staten Island, N.Y.
Height, 6.01. Weight, 195.
Throws and bats righthanded.

Led Florida State League in wild pitches with 20 in 1988.

Year Club	League	G.	IP.	W.	L.	Pct.	H.	R.	ER.	SO.	BB.	ERA.
1986—Utica	NYP	11	60⅔	3	5	.375	68	37	29	42	25	4.30
1987—Spartanburg	S. Atlantic	20	110⅓	3	10	.231	114	69	59	86	58	4.81
1988—Clearwater	Florida St.	24	166⅔	8	11	.421	126	55	48	124	74	2.59
1988—Reading	Eastern	1	6	1	0	1.000	5	4	4	5	2	6.00

Selected by Philadelphia Phillies' organization in 2nd round of free-agent draft, June 2, 1986.

MICHAEL CHARLES BRANTLEY
(Mickey)

Born June 17, 1961, at Catskill, N.Y.
Height, 5.10. Weight, 180.
Throws and bats righthanded.
Attended Columbia-Greene Community College, Hudson, N.Y., and Coastal Carolina Community College, Jacksonville, N.C.

Major League stolen bases: 1986 (1), 1987 (13), 1988 (18). Total—32.
Hit three home runs in a game, September 14, 1987.
Tied for Southern League lead in sacrifice flies with 10 in 1984.

Year Club	League	Pos.	G.	AB.	R.	H.	2B.	3B.	HR.	RBI.	B.A.	PO.	A.	E.	F.A.
1983—Bakersfield	Calif.	OF	53	185	33	55	9	3	6	29	.297	59	3	1	.984
1984—Chattanooga	South.	OF-3B	131	472	73	149	21	9	11	76	.316	211	14	8	.966
1984—Salt Lake City	P. C.	OF	4	17	2	4	0	0	0	1	.235	8	0	0	1.000
1985—Calgary†	P. C.	OF	74	279	52	68	13	6	11	45	.244	165	1	3	.982
1986—Calgary	P. C.	OF	106	396	*104	126	18	4	30	92	.318	201	9	4	.981
1986—Seattle	Amer.	OF	27	102	12	20	3	2	3	7	.196	54	3	1	.983
1987—Seattle‡	Amer.	OF	92	351	52	106	23	2	14	54	.302	163	3	3	.982
1987—Calgary	P. C.	OF	13	50	13	12	0	1	2	6	.240	6	1	1	.875
1988—Seattle	Amer.	OF	149	577	76	152	25	4	15	56	.263	327	5	6	.982
Major League Totals—3 Years			268	1030	140	278	51	8	32	117	.270	544	11	10	.982

Selected by Cincinnati Reds' organization in 8th round of free-agent draft, June 7, 1982.
Selected by Seattle Mariners' organization in 2nd round of free-agent draft, June 6, 1983.
†On disabled list, August 20 to September 9, 1985.
‡On disabled list, April 19 to June 4, 1987; included rehabilitation disability assignment to Calgary, May 9 to May 29, 1987.

SIDNEY EUGENE BREAM
(Sid)

Born August 3, 1960, at Carlisle, Pa.
Height, 6.04. Weight, 220.
Throws and bats lefthanded.
Attended Liberty Baptist College, Lynchburg, Va.

Established National League record for most assists by first baseman, season (166), 1986.
Major League stolen bases: 1984 (1), 1986 (13), 1987 (9), 1988 (9). Total—32.
Led National League first basemen in total chances with 1,503 in 1986.
Led Pacific Coast League first basemen in total chances with 1,411 in 1983 and 1,200 in 1984.
Led Pacific Coast League first basemen in double plays with 106 in 1984.

Year Club	League	Pos.	G.	AB.	R.	H.	2B.	3B.	HR.	RBI.	B.A.	PO.	A.	E.	F.A.
1981—Vero Beach	Fla. St.	1B	70	260	35	85	12	5	1	47	.327	613	45	10	.985
1982—Vero Beach	Fla. St.	1B	63	226	41	70	13	5	4	43	.310	523	40	5	.991
1982—San Antonio	Texas	1B	70	259	43	83	18	0	8	50	.320	621	40	12	.982

Year	Club	League	Pos.	G.	AB.	R.	H.	2B.	3B.	HR.	RBI.	B.A.	PO.	A.	E.	F.A.
1982	—Albuquerque	P. C.	1B	3	8	3	3	1	0	1	2	.375	11	0	0	1.000
1983	—Albuquerque	P. C.	1B	138	485	115	149	23	4	•32	*118	.307	1264	*123	24	.983
1983	—Los Angeles	Nat.	1B	15	11	0	2	0	0	0	2	.182	8	0	0	1.000
1984	—Albuquerque	P. C.	1B	114	429	82	147	25	4	20	90	.343	1071	*112	17	.986
1984	—Los Angeles	Nat.	1B	27	49	2	9	3	0	0	6	.184	95	11	0	1.000
1985	—L.A.†-Pitt.	Nat.	1B	50	148	18	34	7	0	6	21	.230	367	35	3	.993
1985	—Albuquerque	P. C.	1B-OF	85	297	51	110	25	3	17	57	.370	381	51	2	.995
1986	—Pittsburgh	Nat.	*1B-OF	154	522	73	140	37	5	16	77	.268	1320	*166	*17	.989
1987	—Pittsburgh	Nat.	1B	149	516	64	142	25	3	13	65	.275	1236	127	*17	.988
1988	—Pittsburgh	Nat.	1B	148	462	50	122	37	0	10	65	.264	1118	*140	6	.995
Major League Totals—6 Years				543	1708	207	449	109	8	45	236	.263	4144	479	43	.991

Selected by Los Angeles Dodgers' organization in 2nd round of free-agent draft, June 8, 1981.

†Traded with Outfielder Cecil Espy, September 9, 1985, completing deal in which Los Angeles Dodgers acquired Third Baseman Bill Madlock for three players to be named later, August 31, 1985. Pittsburgh Pirates acquired Outfielder R. J. Reynolds as partial completion of deal, September 3, 1985.

ROBERT EARL BRENLY
(Bob)

Born February 25, 1954, at Coshocton, O.
Height, 6.02. Weight, 205.
Throws and bats righthanded.
Received bachelor of science degree in health education from
Ohio University, Athens, O. in 1976.

Tied major league record for most errors by third baseman, inning (4), September 14, 1986 (fourth inning).
Major League stolen bases: 1982 (6), 1983 (10), 1984 (6), 1985 (1), 1986 (10), 1987 (10), 1988 (1). Total—44.
Led National League catchers in assists with 83 in 1987.
Led National League catchers in fielding percentage with .995 in 1986.
Led California League third basemen in double plays with 30 in 1978.
Led Midwest League third basemen in double plays with 21 in 1977.

Year	Club	League	Pos.	G.	AB.	R.	H.	2B.	3B.	HR.	RBI.	B.A.	PO.	A.	E.	F.A.
1976	—Great Falls	Pion.	3B	25	86	16	27	5	1	1	17	.314	10	16	2	.929
1976	—Fresno	Calif.	3B	17	60	16	22	3	1	1	9	.367	2	6	1	.889
1977	—Cedar Rapids	Midw.	*•3B-OF	136	499	85	135	16	1	22	73	.271	90	*263	•31	.919
1978	—Fresno	Calif.	3B	135	489	102	139	34	5	17	89	.284	*118	247	27	.931
1979	—Fresno	Calif.	3B	56	212	49	65	11	2	9	37	.307	39	133	17	.910
1979	—Shreveport	Texas	C-3-O-1	64	193	33	57	8	1	9	30	.295	199	55	7	.973
1980	—Shreveport	Texas	3B	2	10	2	3	0	0	1	3	.300	1	2	0	1.000
1980	—Phoenix	P. C.	3-C-S-O	84	287	34	74	9	6	7	45	.258	183	110	20	.936
1981	—Phoenix	P. C.	C-OF-3B	76	257	42	75	11	3	7	41	.292	177	41	9	.960
1981	—San Francisco	Nat.	C-3B-OF	19	45	5	15	2	1	1	4	.333	52	6	4	.935
1982	—San Francisco†	Nat.	C-3B	65	180	26	51	4	1	4	15	.283	265	32	12	.961
1983	—San Francisco	Nat.	C-1B-OF	104	281	36	63	12	2	7	34	.224	465	73	9	.984
1984	—San Francisco	Nat.	C-1B-OF	145	506	74	147	28	0	20	80	.291	807	76	13	.985
1985	—San Francisco	Nat.	C-3B-1B	133	440	41	97	16	1	19	56	.220	719	85	17	.979
1986	—San Francisco	Nat.	C-3B-1B	149	472	60	116	26	0	16	62	.246	688	118	16	.981
1987	—San Francisco	Nat.	C-1B-3B	123	375	55	100	19	1	18	51	.267	685	86	9	.988
1988	—San Francisco‡	Nat.	C	73	206	13	39	7	0	5	22	.189	334	27	6	.984
Major League Totals—8 Years				811	2505	310	628	114	6	90	324	.251	4015	503	86	.981

Signed as free agent by San Francisco Giants' organization, June 21, 1976.
†On disabled list, March 25 to May 13, 1982.
‡Released, December 21, 1988.

CHAMPIONSHIP SERIES RECORD

Year	Club	League	Pos.	G.	AB.	R.	H.	2B.	3B.	HR.	RBI.	B.A.	PO.	A.	E.	F.A.
1987	—San Francisco	Nat.	C-PH	6	17	3	4	1	0	1	2	.235	28	2	0	1.000

ALL-STAR GAME RECORD

Year	League	Pos.	AB.	R.	H.	2B.	3B.	HR.	RBI.	B.A.	PO.	A.	E.	F.A.
1984	—National	PH	1	0	0	0	0	0	0	.000	0	0	0	.000

WILLIAM RAYMOND BRENNAN

Born January 15, 1963, at Tampa, Fla.
Height, 6.03. Weight, 194.
Throws and bats righthanded.
Attended Mercer University, Macon, Ga.

Year	Club	League	G.	IP.	W.	L.	Pct.	H.	R.	ER.	SO.	BB.	ERA.
1985	—Vero Beach	Florida St.	22	142	10	9	.526	121	64	45	74	59	2.85
1986	—San Antonio†	Texas	26	146⅔	7	9	.438	149	75	63	83	61	3.87
1987	—Albuquerque	P. Coast	28	171⅓	10	9	.526	188	95	82	95	67	4.31
1988	—Albuquerque	P. Coast	29	167⅓	14	8	.636	177	85	71	83	51	3.82
1988	—Los Angeles	National	4	9⅓	0	1	.000	13	7	7	7	6	6.75
Major League Totals—1 Year			4	9⅓	0	1	.000	13	7	7	7	6	6.75

Signed as free agent by Los Angeles Dodgers' organization, September 1, 1984.
†On disabled list, August 14 to August 28, 1986.

GEORGE HOWARD BRETT

Born May 15, 1953, at Glen Dale, W. Va.
Height, 6.00. Weight, 200.
Throws right and bats lefthanded.
Attended Longview Community College, Lee's Summit, Mo. and
El Camino College, Torrance, Calif.
Brother of Ken Brett, pitcher with Boston, Milwaukee, Philadelphia, Pittsburgh, New York AL,
Chicago AL, California, Minnesota, Los Angeles and Kansas City, 1967 and 1969 through 1981;
and manager of Utica (Co-op) in New York-Pennsylvania League, 1985;
John Brett, third baseman in Boston Red Sox' organization, 1968;
and Bob Brett, outfielder in Kansas City Royals' organization, 1972.

Established major league record for most consecutive games, three or more hits, season (6), May 8 through 13, 1976.

Tied major league records for most consecutive seasons leading major league in triples (2), 1975 and 1976; most home runs, month of October (4), 1985.

Established American League record for fewest putouts by third baseman for leader in most putouts, season (140), 1976.

Became sixth major-league player to collect 20 or more doubles, triples and home runs in one season, 1979.

Hit three home runs in a game, July 22, 1979 and April 20, 1983.

Hit for the cycle, May 28, 1979.

Major League stolen bases: 1974 (8), 1975 (13), 1976 (21), 1977 (14), 1978 (23), 1979 (17), 1980 (15), 1981 (14), 1982 (6), 1985 (9), 1986 (1), 1987 (6), 1988 (14). Total—161.

Led American League in intentional bases on balls received with 31 in 1985 and 18 in 1986.

Led American League in slugging percentage with .664 in 1980, .563 in 1983 and .585 in 1985.

Led American League in total bases with 298 in 1976.

Led American League third basemen in double plays with 33 in 1985.

Led American League third basemen in assists with 373, errors with 30 and total chances with 532 in 1979.

Led American League third baseman in putouts with 140 in 1976.

Led California League in sacrifice hits with 8 in 1972.

Led California League third basemen in assists with 172 in 1972.

Named Man of the Year by THE SPORTING NEWS, 1980.

Named Major League Player of the Year by THE SPORTING NEWS, 1980.

Named American League Player of the Year by THE SPORTING NEWS, 1980.

Named American League Most Valuable Player by Baseball Writers' Association of America, 1980.

Named first baseman on THE SPORTING NEWS American League All-Star Team, 1988.

Named third baseman on THE SPORTING NEWS American League All-Star Team, 1976, 1979 and 1980.

Named third baseman on THE SPORTING NEWS American League All-Star fielding team, 1985.

Named first baseman on THE SPORTING NEWS American League Silver Slugger Team, 1988.

Named third baseman on THE SPORTING NEWS Silver Slugger team, 1980 and 1985.

Year Club	League	Pos.	G.	AB.	R.	H.	2B.	3B.	HR.	RBI.	B.A.	PO.	A.	E.	F.A.
1971—Billings	Pion.	SS-3B	68	258	44	75	8	5	5	44	.291	87	140	28	.890
1972—San Jose†	Calif.	★3-S-2	117	431	66	118	13	5	10	68	.274	101	213	★30	.913
1973—Omaha	A. A.	3B-OF	117	405	66	115	16	4	8	64	.284	92	219	26	.923
1973—Kansas City	Amer.	3B	13	40	2	5	2	0	0	0	.125	9	28	1	.974
1974—Omaha	A. A.	3B	16	64	9	17	2	0	2	14	.266	8	31	4	.907
1974—Kansas City	Amer.	3B-SS	133	457	49	129	21	5	2	47	.282	102	279	21	.948
1975—Kansas City	Amer.	●3B-SS	159	★634	84	★195	35	●13	11	89	.308	132	356	●26	.949
1976—Kansas City	Amer.	3B-SS	159	★645	94	★215	34	★14	7	67	★.333	146	350	26	.950
1977—Kansas City	Amer.	3B-SS	139	564	105	176	32	13	22	88	.312	115	325	21	.954
1978—Kansas City‡	Amer.	3B-SS	128	510	79	150	★45	8	9	62	.294	104	289	16	.961
1979—Kansas City	Amer.	3B-1B	154	645	119	★212	42	★20	23	107	.329	176	378	31	.947
1980—Kansas City§	Amer.	3B-1B	117	449	87	175	33	9	24	118	★.390	107	256	17	.955
1981—Kansas City	Amer.	3B	89	347	42	109	27	7	6	43	.314	74	170	14	.946
1982—Kansas City	Amer.	3B-OF	144	552	101	166	32	9	21	82	.301	130	295	17	.962
1983—Kansas City x	Amer.	3B-1B-OF	123	464	90	144	38	2	25	93	.310	210	192	25	.941
1984—Kansas City y	Amer.	3B	104	377	42	107	21	3	13	69	.284	59	201	14	.949
1985—Kansas City	Amer.	3B	155	550	108	184	38	5	30	112	.335	107	★339	15	.967
1986—Kansas City	Amer.	3B-SS	124	441	70	128	28	4	16	73	.290	97	218	16	.952
1987—Kansas City z	Amer.	1B-3B	115	427	71	124	18	2	22	78	.290	805	69	9	.990
1988—Kansas City	Amer.	1B-SS	157	589	90	180	42	3	24	103	.306	1126	70	10	.992
Major League Totals—16 Years			2013	7691	1233	2399	488	117	255	1231	.312	3499	3815	279	.963

Selected by Kansas City Royals' organization in 2nd round of free-agent draft, June 8, 1971.

†On disabled list, April 29 to May 11, 1972.

‡On disabled list, May 4 to May 19 and July 27 to August 14, 1978.

§On disabled list, June 11 to July 10, 1980.

xOn disabled list, June 8 to June 29, 1983.

yOn disabled list, April 1 to May 18, 1984.

zOn disabled list, April 20 to May 13 and May 16 to June 12, 1987.

DIVISION SERIES RECORD

Year Club	League	Pos.	G.	AB.	R.	H.	2B.	3B.	HR.	RBI.	B.A.	PO.	A.	E.	F.A.
1981—Kansas City	Amer.	3B	3	12	0	2	0	0	0	0	.167	1	6	1	.876

CHAMPIONSHIP SERIES RECORD

Established Championship Series records for most games with one club (27); highest slugging average, total Series, 50 or more at-bats (.728); most runs, total Series (22); most three-base hits, total Series (4); most runs, four-game Series (7), 1978; most home runs, total Series (9); most Series, two or more home runs (3); most total bases, total Series (75); most long hits, total Series (18).

Tied Championship Series records for most runs, game (4), October 11, 1985; most three-base hits, Series (2), 1977; most home runs, game (3), October 6, 1978; most times hitting home run as leadoff batter, start of game (1), October 6, 1978.

Established American League Championship Series records for highest slugging average, seven-game Series (.826), 1985; most runs, total Series (16); highest slugging average, four-game Series (1.056), 1978; most hits, four-game Series (7), 1978; most home runs, seven-game Series (3), 1985; most total bases, four-game Series (19), 1978; most long hits, four-game Series (5), 1978 and seven-game Series (5), 1985; most long hits, two consecutive games, one series (4), October 6 and 7, 1978; most total bases (19) and most bases on balls (7), seven-game Series, 1985; most total bases, game (12), October 6, 1978.

Tied American League Championship Series records for most at-bats, four-game Series (18), 1978; most home runs, four-game Series (3), 1978; most Series, one or more home runs (4); most long hits, game (3), October 6, 1978 and October 11, 1985; most consecutive games, one or more hits (9); most home runs, three-game Series (2), 1980.

Year Club	League	Pos.	G.	AB.	R.	H.	2B.	3B.	HR.	RBI.	B.A.	PO.	A.	E.	F.A.
1976—Kansas City	Amer.	3B	5	18	4	8	1	1	1	5	.444	3	7	3	.769
1977—Kansas City	Amer.	3B	5	20	2	6	0	2	0	2	.300	5	12	2	.895
1978—Kansas City	Amer.	3B	4	18	7	7	1	1	3	3	.389	3	8	1	.917
1980—Kansas City	Amer.	3B	3	11	3	3	1	0	2	4	.273	2	7	0	1.000
1984—Kansas City	Amer.	3B	3	13	0	3	0	0	0	0	.231	2	7	0	1.000
1985—Kansas City	Amer.	3B	7	23	6	8	2	0	3	5	.348	7	8	2	.882
Championship Series Totals—6 Years			27	103	22	35	5	4	9	19	.340	22	49	8	.899

WORLD SERIES RECORD

Tied World Series record for most times reached first base safely, game (batting 1.000) (5), October 22, 1985.

Year Club	League	Pos.	G.	AB.	R.	H.	2B.	3B.	HR.	RBI.	B.A.	PO.	A.	E.	F.A.
1980—Kansas City	Amer.	3B	6	24	3	9	2	1	1	3	.375	4	17	1	.955
1985—Kansas City	Amer.	3B	7	27	5	10	1	0	0	1	.370	10	19	1	.967
World Series Totals—2 Years			13	51	8	19	3	1	1	4	.373	14	36	2	.962

ALL-STAR GAME RECORD

Year League	Pos.	AB.	R.	H.	2B.	3B.	HR.	RBI.	B.A.	PO.	A.	E.	F.A.
1976—American	3B	2	0	0	0	0	0	0	.000	0	1	0	1.000
1977—American	3B	2	0	0	0	0	0	0	.000	2	1	0	1.000
1978—American	3B	3	1	2	1	0	0	2	.667	0	2	0	1.000
1979—American	3B	3	1	0	0	0	0	0	.000	1	2	0	1.000
1981—American	3B	3	0	0	0	0	0	0	.000	0	1	0	1.000
1982—American	3B	2	0	2	0	0	0	0	1.000	0	0	0	.000
1983—American	3B	4	2	2	1	1	0	1	.500	1	5	0	1.000
1984—American	3B	3	1	1	0	0	1	1	.333	3	0	0	1.000
1985—American	3B	1	0	0	0	0	0	1	.000	2	1	0	1.000
1988—American	PH	1	0	0	0	0	0	0	.000	0	0	0	.000
All-Star Game Totals—10 Years		24	5	7	2	1	1	5	.292	9	13	0	1.000

Named to American League All-Star Team in 1980 game; replaced due to injury.
Named to American League All-Star Team for 1986 game; replaced due to injury by Brook Jacoby.
Named to American League All-Star Team for 1987 game; replaced due to injury by Kevin Seitzer.

GREGORY BRILEY
(Greg)

Born May 24, 1965, at Bethel, N. C.
Height, 5.08. Weight, 165.
Throws right and bats lefthanded.
Attended Louisburg College, Louisburg, N. C., and
North Carolina State University, Raleigh, N. C.

Year Club	League	Pos.	G.	AB.	R.	H.	2B.	3B.	HR.	RBI.	B.A.	PO.	A.	E.	F.A.
1986—Bellingham	N'west	2B	63	218	52	65	12	●4	7	46	.298	132	146	24	.921
1987—Chattanooga	South.	2B	137	539	81	148	21	5	7	61	.275	221	346	★29	.951
1988—Calgary	P. C.	OF-2B	112	445	74	139	29	9	11	66	.312	237	132	15	.961
1988—Seattle	Amer.	OF	13	36	6	9	2	0	1	4	.250	13	0	1	.929
Major League Totals—1 Year			13	36	6	9	2	0	1	4	.250	13	0	1	.929

Selected by Los Angeles Dodgers' organization in 3rd round of free-agent draft, January 9, 1985.
Selected by Cleveland Indians' organization in secondary phase of free-agent draft, June 3, 1985.
Selected by Seattle Mariners' organization in secondary phase of free-agent draft, June 2, 1986.

GREGORY ALLEN BROCK
(Greg)

Born June 14, 1957, at McMinnville, Ore.
Height, 6.03. Weight, 205.
Throws right and bats lefthanded.
Attended University of Wyoming, Laramie, Wyo.
Brother of Eric Brock, shortstop in Los Angeles Dodgers' organization, 1983 and 1984.

Major League stolen bases: 1983 (5), 1984 (8), 1985 (4), 1986 (2), 1987 (5), 1988 (6). Total—30.

Led Pacific Coast League in bases on balls received with 105 and intentional bases on balls received with 15 in 1982.

Led Pioneer League in bases on balls received with 54 in 1979.

Led Pacific Coast League first basemen in double plays with 106 in 1982.

Year Club	League	Pos.	G.	AB.	R.	H.	2B.	3B.	HR.	RBI.	B.A.	PO.	A.	E.	F.A.
1979—Lethbridge	Pion.	1B	66	247	61	88	18	2	16	77	.356	543	★36	8	★.986
1980—Lodi	Calif.	1B	121	418	72	125	19	3	★29	95	.299	906	★79	5	★.995

Year	Club	League	Pos.	G.	AB.	R.	H.	2B.	3B.	HR.	RBI.	B.A.	PO.	A.	E.	F.A.
1981	—San Antonio	Texas	1B	128	499	86	147	25	3	*32	106	.295	1071	*90	9	.992
1982	—Albuquerque	P. C.	1B	135	480	118	149	21	8	44	138	.310	*1076	*106	*20	.983
1982	—Los Angeles	Nat.	1B	18	17	1	2	1	0	0	1	.118	9	0	0	1.000
1983	—Los Angeles	Nat.	1B	146	455	64	102	14	2	20	66	.224	1162	106	12	.991
1984	—Los Angeles†	Nat.	1B	88	271	33	61	6	0	14	34	.225	703	65	4	.995
1984	—Albuquerque	P. C.	1B-3B	24	93	19	29	7	0	6	15	.312	134	38	11	.940
1985	—Los Angeles	Nat.	1B	129	438	64	110	19	0	21	66	.251	1113	84	7	.994
1986	—Los Angeles‡§	Nat.	1B	115	325	33	76	13	0	16	52	.234	726	87	3	.996
1987	—Milwaukee x	Amer.	1B	141	532	81	159	29	3	13	85	.299	1065	109	8	.993
1988	—Milwaukee y	Amer.	1B	115	364	53	77	16	1	6	50	.212	915	102	7	.993
National League Totals—5 Years				496	1506	195	351	53	2	71	219	.233	3713	342	26	.994
American League Totals—2 Years				256	896	134	236	45	4	19	135	.263	1980	211	15	.993
Major League Totals—7 Years				752	2402	329	587	98	6	90	354	.244	5693	553	41	.993

Selected by Los Angeles Dodgers' organization in 13th round of free-agent draft, June 5, 1979.
†On disabled list, May 12 to June 7, 1984.
‡On disabled list, June 19 to July 10, 1986.
§Traded to Milwaukee Brewers for Pitchers Tim Leary and Tim Crews, December 10, 1986.
xOn disabled list, June 12 to June 27, 1987.
yOn disabled list, June 7 to July 23, 1988.

CHAMPIONSHIP SERIES RECORD

Year	Club	League	Pos.	G.	AB.	R.	H.	2B.	3B.	HR.	RBI.	B.A.	PO.	A.	E.	F.A.
1983	—Los Angeles	Nat.	1B	3	9	1	0	0	0	0	0	.000	13	0	0	1.000
1985	—Los Angeles	Nat.	1B-PH	5	12	2	1	0	0	1	2	.083	35	4	0	1.000
Championship Series Totals—2 Years				8	21	3	1	0	0	1	2	.048	48	4	0	1.000

THOMAS DALE BROOKENS
(Tom)

Born August 10, 1953, at Chambersburg, Pa.
Height, 5.10. Weight, 170.
Throws and bats righthanded.
Attended Mansfield State College, Mansfield, Pa.
Twin brother of Tim Brookens, infielder-outfielder in Detroit Tigers' organization, 1975 through 1978; cousin of Ike Brookens, pitcher with Detroit Tigers, 1975.

Tied American League record for most errors by third baseman, game (4), September 6, 1980.

Major League stolen bases: 1979 (10), 1980 (13), 1981 (5), 1982 (5), 1983 (10), 1984 (6), 1985 (14), 1986 (11), 1987 (7), 1988 (4). Total—85.

Tied for American League lead in errors by third basemen with 23 in 1985.

Year	Club	League	Pos.	G.	AB.	R.	H.	2B.	3B.	HR.	RBI.	B.A.	PO.	A.	E.	F.A.
1975	—Montgomery	South.	SS	100	329	37	73	11	2	7	36	.222	139	298	31	.934
1976	—Montgomery	South.	2B	137	492	76	127	22	5	11	56	.258	310	*389	*25	.965
1977	—Evansville	A. A.	3B-2B	118	440	70	127	22	5	8	52	.289	132	250	25	.939
1978	—Evansville†	A. A.	3B-2B-1B	65	206	27	58	11	1	6	25	.282	76	100	20	.898
1979	—Evansville	A. A.	3B-2B	77	265	51	81	23	2	14	46	.306	71	166	16	.937
1979	—Detroit	Amer.	3B-2B	60	190	23	50	5	2	4	21	.263	76	141	11	.952
1980	—Detroit	Amer.	*3-2-S	151	509	64	140	25	9	10	66	.275	127	307	*29	.937
1981	—Detroit‡	Amer.	3B	71	239	19	58	10	1	4	25	.243	58	139	10	.952
1982	—Detroit	Amer.	3-2-S-O	140	398	40	92	15	3	9	58	.231	119	276	20	.952
1983	—Detroit	Amer.	3B-SS-2B	138	332	50	71	13	3	6	32	.214	97	254	22	.941
1984	—Detroit§	Amer.	3B-SS-2B	113	224	32	55	11	4	5	26	.246	98	187	12	.960
1985	—Detroit x	Amer.	3-S-2-C	156	485	54	115	34	6	7	47	.237	135	277	24	.944
1986	—Detroit	Amer.	3-2-S-O	98	281	42	76	11	2	3	25	.270	106	144	7	.973
1987	—Detroit y	Amer.	3B-SS-2B	143	444	59	107	15	3	13	59	.241	119	256	19	.952
1988	—Detroit	Amer.	3B-SS-2B	136	441	62	107	23	5	5	38	.243	101	235	17	.952
Major League Totals—10 Years				1206	3543	445	871	162	38	66	397	.246	1036	2216	171	.950

Selected by Detroit Tigers' organization in 1st round (fourth player selected) of free-agent draft, January 9, 1975.
†On disabled list, April 14 to May 9 and June 4 to June 21, 1978.
‡On disabled list, March 30 to May 4, 1981.
§On disabled list, August 19 to September 4, 1984.
xGranted free agency, November 12, 1985; re-signed by Tigers, January 8, 1986.
yGranted free agency, January 22, 1988; re-signed by Tigers, February 9, 1988.

CHAMPIONSHIP SERIES RECORD

Year	Club	League	Pos.	G.	AB.	R.	H.	2B.	3B.	HR.	RBI.	B.A.	PO.	A.	E.	F.A.
1984	—Detroit	Amer.	2B-3B	2	2	0	0	0	0	0	0	.000	0	2	1	.667
1987	—Detroit	Amer.	3B	5	13	0	0	0	0	0	0	.000	3	15	0	1.000
Championship Series Totals—2 Years				7	15	0	0	0	0	0	0	.000	3	17	1	.952

WORLD SERIES RECORD

Year	Club	League	Pos.	G.	AB.	R.	H.	2B.	3B.	HR.	RBI.	B.A.	PO.	A.	E.	F.A.
1984	—Detroit	Amer.	PH-3B	3	3	0	0	0	0	0	0	.000	0	3	0	1.000

—DID YOU KNOW—

That the Toronto Blue Jays were shut out just three times in 1988 while the Atlanta Braves were blanked 17 times?

HUBERT BROOKS JR.
(Hubie)

Born September 24, 1956, at Los Angeles, Calif.
Height, 6.00. Weight, 200.
Throws and bats righthanded.
Attended Mesa Community College, Mesa, Ariz., and received bachelor of science degree in health science from Arizona State University, Tempe, Ariz.
Grandson of Leandrus Brooks, player with Philadelphia of Negro National League; and cousin of Donnie Moore, pitcher with Chicago Cubs, St. Louis Cardinals, Milwaukee Brewers, Atlanta Braves and California Angels, 1975 and 1977 through 1988.

Major League stolen bases: 1980 (1), 1981 (9), 1982 (6), 1983 (6), 1984 (6), 1985 (6), 1986 (4), 1987 (4), 1988 (7). Total—49.

Led International League in game-winning RBIs with 12 in 1980.

Named shortstop on THE SPORTING NEWS National League Silver Slugger team, 1985 and 1986.

Named shortstop on THE SPORTING NEWS College Baseball All-America Team, 1978.

Named outfielder on THE SPORTING NEWS College Baseball All-America Team, 1977.

Year Club	League	Pos.	G.	AB.	R.	H.	2B.	3B.	HR.	RBI.	B.A.	PO.	A.	E.	F.A.
1978—Jackson	Texas	SS-OF-3B	45	153	19	33	8	1	3	16	.216	49	84	14	.905
1979—Jackson	Texas	3B-SS	112	406	68	124	21	2	3	28	.305	92	218	29	.942
1979—Tidewater	Int.	SS-3B-OF	5	15	1	6	1	0	1	3	.400	4	8	1	.923
1980—Tidewater	Int.	OF-3B-SS	113	417	50	124	18	5	3	50	.297	152	90	18	.931
1980—New York	Nat.	3B	24	81	8	25	2	1	1	10	.309	16	40	2	.966
1981—New York	Nat.	*3-O-S	98	358	34	110	21	2	4	38	.307	67	193	*21	.925
1982—New York†	Nat.	3B	126	457	40	114	21	2	2	40	.249	89	237	24	.931
1983—New York	Nat.	3B-2B	150	586	53	147	18	4	5	58	.251	116	303	21	.952
1984—New York‡	Nat.	3B-SS	153	561	61	159	23	2	16	73	.283	112	284	29	.932
1985—Montreal	Nat.	SS	156	605	67	163	34	7	13	100	.269	203	441	28	.958
1986—Montreal §	Nat.	SS	80	306	50	104	18	5	14	58	.340	116	222	15	.958
1987—Montreal x	Nat.	SS	112	430	57	113	22	3	14	72	.263	131	271	20	.953
1988—Montreal	Nat.	OF	151	588	61	164	35	2	20	90	.279	261	8	9	.968
Major League Totals—9 Years			1050	3972	431	1099	194	28	89	539	.277	1111	1999	169	.948

Selected by Montreal Expos' organization in 19th round of free-agent draft, June 5, 1974.
Selected by Kansas City Royals' organization in secondary phase of free-agent draft, January 7, 1976.
Selected by Chicago White Sox' organization in secondary phase of free-agent draft, June 8, 1976.
Selected by Oakland A's organization in secondary phase of free-agent draft, January 11, 1977.
Selected by Chicago White Sox' organization in secondary phase of free-agent draft, June 7, 1977.
Selected by New York Mets' organization in 1st round (third player selected) of free-agent draft, June 6, 1978.
†On disabled list, June 28 to July 22, 1982.
‡Traded with Catcher Mike Fitzgerald, Outfielder Herm Winningham and Pitcher Floyd Youmans to Montreal Expos for Catcher Gary Carter, December 10, 1984.
§On disabled list, August 2, 1986 through remainder of season.
xOn disabled list, April 11 to May 25, 1987.

ALL-STAR GAME RECORD

Year League	Pos.	AB.	R.	H.	2B.	3B.	HR.	RBI.	B.A.	PO.	A.	E.	F.A.
1986—National	PH-SS	2	1	0	0	0	0	0	.000	1	0	0	1.000
1987—National	SS	3	1	1	0	0	0	0	.333	1	2	0	1.000
All-Star Game Totals—2 Years		5	2	1	0	0	0	0	.200	2	2	0	1.000

ROBERT RICHARD BROWER
(Bob)

Born January 10, 1960, at Queens, N.Y.
Height, 6.00. Weight, 190.
Throws and bats righthanded.
Attended Duke University, Durham, N.C.

Major League stolen bases: 1986 (1), 1987 (15), 1988 (10). Total—26.

Led American Association in bases on balls received with 94 in 1986.

Led American Association outfielders in total chances with 382 in 1986.

Year Club	League	Pos.	G.	AB.	R.	H.	2B.	3B.	HR.	RBI.	B.A.	PO.	A.	E.	F.A.
1982—Sarasota Rangers	Gulf C.	OF	36	122	25	35	7	2	0	7	.287	53	3	0	1.000
1983—Burlington	Midw.	OF	43	138	35	43	4	6	5	28	.312	60	4	4	.941
1983—Tulsa	Texas	OF	69	252	41	59	4	1	3	17	.234	138	4	4	.973
1984—Tulsa	Texas	OF	96	344	69	98	14	9	7	30	.285	209	10	3	.986
1984—Oklahoma City	A. A.	OF	35	107	18	24	2	2	1	8	.224	69	7	2	.974
1985—Oklahoma City	A. A.	OF	133	445	56	111	13	*18	5	50	.249	282	8	3	.990
1986—Oklahoma City	A. A.	OF	•140	*550	*130	•158	25	7	13	72	.287	*366	8	8	.979
1986—Texas	Amer.	OF	21	9	3	1	1	0	0	0	.111	9	0	0	1.000
1987—Texas	Amer.	OF	127	303	63	79	10	3	14	46	.261	183	2	7	.964
1988—Texas†‡	Amer.	OF	82	201	29	45	7	0	1	11	.224	104	2	3	.972
Major League Totals—3 Years			230	513	95	125	18	3	15	57	.244	296	4	10	.968

Signed as free agent by Texas Rangers' organization, July 1, 1982.
†On disabled list, April 4 to April 27, 1988.
‡Traded to New York Yankees for Shortstop Bobby Meacham, December 5, 1988.

JAMES KEVIN BROWN

(Known by middle name.)

Born March 14, 1965, at McIntyre, Ga.
Height, 6.04. Weight, 188.
Throws and bats righthanded.
Attended Georgia Tech, Atlanta, Ga.

Named as righthanded pitcher on THE SPORTING NEWS College Baseball All-America Team, 1986.

Year	Club	League	G.	IP.	W.	L.	Pct.	H.	R.	ER.	SO.	BB.	ERA.
1986	Sarasota Rangers	Gulf Coast	3	6	0	0	.000	7	4	4	1	2	6.00
1986	Tulsa	Texas	3	10	0	0	.000	9	7	5	10	5	4.50
1986	Texas	American	1	5	1	0	1.000	6	2	2	4	0	3.60
1987	Tulsa	Texas	8	42	1	4	.200	53	36	34	26	18	7.29
1987	Oklahoma City	Am. Assoc.	5	24⅓	0	5	.000	32	32	29	9	17	10.73
1987	Port Charlotte	Florida St.	6	36⅓	0	2	.000	33	14	11	21	17	2.72
1988	Tulsa	Texas	26	174⅓	12	10	.545	174	94	68	118	61	3.51
1988	Texas	American	4	23⅓	1	1	.500	33	15	11	12	8	4.24
Major League Totals—2 Years			5	28⅓	2	1	.667	39	17	13	16	8	4.13

Selected by Texas Rangers' organization in 1st round (fourth player selected) of free-agent draft, June 2, 1986.

JOHN CHRISTOPHER BROWN
(Chris)

Born August 15, 1961, at Jackson, Miss.
Height, 6.02. Weight, 210.
Throws and bats righthanded.

Major League stolen bases: 1984 (2), 1985 (2), 1986 (13), 1987 (4). Total—21.
Led National League in being hit by pitch with 11 in 1985.

Year	Club	League	Pos.	G.	AB.	R.	H.	2B.	3B.	HR.	RBI.	B.A.	PO.	A.	E.	F.A.
1979	Great Falls	Pion.	3B	47	171	24	46	5	3	5	30	.269	31	77	11	.908
1980	Clinton	Midw.	3B-1B	103	337	38	80	5	3	7	35	.237	352	132	19	.962
1981	Fresno	Calif.	3B-OF-1B	85	291	37	84	11	2	8	44	.289	89	156	23	.914
1982	Shreveport	Texas	3B-2B	58	185	26	49	14	0	1	21	.265	51	82	9	.937
1982	Fresno	Calif.	3B-1B-SS	41	133	22	39	9	1	4	31	.293	41	71	6	.949
1983	Shreveport	Texas	3B	102	322	44	88	21	0	10	58	.273	63	182	17	.935
1984	Phoenix†	P. C.	3B	84	283	41	80	13	5	9	64	.283	43	119	17	.905
1984	San Francisco	Nat.	3B	23	84	6	24	7	0	1	11	.286	23	40	7	.900
1985	San Francisco	Nat.	3B	131	432	50	117	20	3	16	61	.271	94	243	10	★.971
1986	San Francisco	Nat.	3B-SS	116	416	57	132	16	3	7	49	.317	73	181	18	.934
1987	S.F.‡§-S.D.	Nat.	3B-SS	82	287	34	68	9	0	12	40	.237	60	132	16	.923
1988	San Diego x	Nat.	3B	80	247	14	58	6	0	2	19	.235	54	131	10	.949
Major League Totals—5 Years				432	1466	161	399	58	6	38	180	.272	304	727	61	.944

Selected by San Francisco Giants' organization in 2nd round of free-agent draft, June 5, 1979.
†On disabled list, April 11 to April 21 and July 30 to August 11, 1984.
‡On disabled list, May 5 to June 18, 1987.
§Traded with Pitchers Keith Comstock, Mark Davis and Mark Grant to San Diego Padres for Pitchers Dave Dravecky and Craig Lefferts and Infielder Kevin Mitchell, July 4, 1987.
xTraded with Infielder Keith Moreland to Detroit Tigers for Pitcher Walt Terrell, October 28, 1988.

ALL-STAR GAME RECORD

Year	League	Pos.	AB.	R.	H.	2B.	3B.	HR.	RBI.	B.A.	PO.	A.	E.	F.A.
1986	National	3B	2	1	1	1	0	0	0	.500	1	0	0	1.000

KEITH EDWARD BROWN

Born February 14, 1964, at Flagstaff, Ariz.
Height, 6.04. Weight, 205.
Throws right and bats left and righthanded.
Attended College of the Siskiyous, Weed, Calif.,
and California State University, Sacramento, Calif.

Year	Club	League	G.	IP.	W.	L.	Pct.	H.	R.	ER.	SO.	BB.	ERA.
1986	Sarasota Reds	Gulf Coast	7	47⅓	4	1	.800	29	15	5	26	5	0.95
1986	Billings	Pioneer	4	21⅓	2	0	1.000	18	6	5	14	7	2.11
1986	Vermont	Eastern	4	14	1	1	.500	12	10	8	11	8	5.14
1987	Cedar Rapids	Midwest	17	124⅓	13	4	.765	91	28	22	86	27	★1.59
1988	Chattanooga	Southern	10	69⅔	9	1	★.900	47	11	11	34	20	1.42
1988	Nashville	Am. Assoc.	12	85⅓	6	3	.667	72	33	18	43	28	1.90
1988	Cincinnati	National	4	16⅓	2	1	.667	14	5	5	6	4	2.76
Major League Totals—1 Year			4	16⅓	2	1	.667	14	5	5	6	4	2.76

Selected by Cincinnati Reds' organization in 21st round of free-agent draft, June 2, 1986.

MARTY LEO BROWN

Born January 23, 1963, at Lawton, Okla.
Height, 6.01. Weight, 195.
Throws and bats righthanded.
Attended Crowder College, Neosho, Mo., and
University of Georgia, Athens, Ga.

Tied for Midwest League lead in caught stealing with 20 in 1986.

Led Eastern League third basemen in assists with 234 and fielding percentage with .957 in 1987.
Led Pioneer League first basemen in assists with 49 in 1985.

Year Club	League	Pos.	G.	AB.	R.	H.	2B.	3B.	HR.	RBI.	B.A.	PO.	A.	E.	F.A.
1985—Billings	Pion.	1B-OF	68	248	50	84	21	3	10	45	.339	592	50	10	.985
1986—Cedar Rapids	Midw.	3B-1B	•139	508	85	152	19	8	18	83	.299	86	249	40	.893
1987—Vermont	East.	3B-1B	134	470	69	124	17	5	15	74	.264	132	237	14	.963
1988—Nashville	A. A.	3B-OF-SS	135	484	50	128	15	4	7	55	.264	93	227	22	.936
1988—Cincinnati	Nat.	3B	10	16	0	3	1	0	0	2	.188	1	9	0	1.000
Major League Totals—1 Year			10	16	0	3	1	0	0	2	.188	1	9	0	1.000

Selected by Cincinnati Reds' organization in 12th round of free-agent draft, June 3, 1985.

MICHAEL CHARLES BROWN
(Mike)

Born December 29, 1959, at San Francisco, Calif.
Height, 6.02. Weight, 195.
Throws and bats righthanded.
Attended San Jose State University, San Jose, Calif.

Major League stolen bases: 1983 (1), 1985 (2), 1986 (2). Total—5.

Year Club	League	Pos.	G.	AB.	R.	H.	2B.	3B.	HR.	RBI.	B.A.	PO.	A.	E.	F.A.
1980—Salinas	Calif.	OF-C	47	152	24	40	7	0	5	35	.263	72	4	5	.938
1981—Holyoke	East.	OF	135	499	64	160	25	8	6	83	.321	182	9	9	.955
1982—Spokane	P. C.	OF	134	476	74	135	30	7	11	73	.284	261	20	14	.957
1983—Edmonton	P. C.	OF	115	442	91	157	39	6	22	106	.355	190	11	2	.990
1983—California	Amer.	OF	31	104	12	24	5	1	3	9	.231	52	4	3	.949
1984—Edmonton	P. C.	OF	26	102	22	35	9	4	4	24	.343	50	5	0	1.000
1984—California	Amer.	OF	62	148	19	42	8	3	7	22	.284	57	4	2	.968
1985—California†	Amer.	OF	60	153	23	41	9	1	4	20	.268	78	3	0	1.000
1985—Pittsburgh	Nat.	OF	57	205	29	68	18	2	5	33	.332	87	3	6	.938
1986—Pittsburgh	Nat.	OF	87	243	18	53	7	0	4	26	.218	107	3	3	.973
1986—Hawaii‡	P. C.	OF	24	87	14	33	8	0	1	12	.379	38	2	1	.976
1987—Richmond§	Int.	OF	25	83	6	18	2	0	0	7	.217	34	1	2	.946
1987—Hawaii x	P. C.	OF	67	230	46	67	13	2	7	32	.291	156	7	2	.988
1988—Toledo y	Int.	OF	79	244	22	68	17	2	3	21	.279	89	1	3	.968
1988—Edmonton	P. C.	OF	33	118	21	41	6	1	3	21	.347	55	0	0	1.000
1988—California	Amer.	OF	18	50	4	11	2	0	0	3	.220	33	2	2	.946
American League Totals—4 Years			171	455	58	118	24	5	14	54	.259	220	13	7	.971
National League Totals—2 Years			144	448	47	121	25	2	9	59	.270	194	6	9	.957
Major League Totals—5 Years			315	903	105	239	49	7	23	113	.265	414	19	16	.964

Selected by California Angels' organization in 7th round of free-agent draft, June 3, 1980.

†Traded with Pitcher Pat Clements and a player to be named later to Pittsburgh Pirates for Pitchers John Candelaria and Al Holland and Outfielder George Hendrick, August 2, 1985; Pittsburgh organization acquired Pitcher Bob Kipper to complete deal, August 16, 1985.

‡Released, March 31, 1987; signed by Atlanta Braves' organization, April 8, 1987.

§Released, May 15, 1987; signed by Chicago White Sox' organization, June 1, 1987.

xReleased, December 13, 1987; signed by Toledo (Detroit Tigers' organization), December 30, 1987.

ySold to Edmonton (California Angels' organization), July 14, 1988.

JEROME A. BROWNE
(Jerry)

Born February 13, 1966, at St. Croix, Virgin Islands.
Height, 5.10. Weight, 170.
Throws right and bats left and righthanded.

Major League stolen bases: 1987 (27), 1988 (7). Total—34.
Led Texas League second basemen in fielding percentage with .984 in 1986.
Led Carolina League second basemen in total chances with 675 in 1985.

Year Club	League	Pos.	G.	AB.	R.	H.	2B.	3B.	HR.	RBI.	B.A.	PO.	A.	E.	F.A.
1983—Sarasota Rangers	Gulf C.	2B	48	181	34	51	2	2	0	20	.282	92	123	14	.939
1984—Burlington	Midw.	SS-2B	127	420	70	99	10	1	0	18	.236	231	311	43	.926
1985—Salem	Carol.	2B	122	460	69	123	18	4	3	58	.267	*265	*390	20	.970
1986—Tulsa	Texas	2B-SS	128	491	82	149	15	7	2	57	.303	282	307	19	.969
1986—Texas	Amer.	2B	12	24	6	10	2	0	0	3	.417	9	15	2	.923
1987—Texas†	Amer.	2B	132	454	63	123	16	6	1	38	.271	258	338	12	.980
1988—Texas	Amer.	2B	73	214	26	49	9	2	1	17	.229	112	139	11	.958
1988—Oklahoma City‡	A. A.	2B	76	286	45	72	15	2	5	34	.252	190	231	10	.977
Major League Totals—3 Years			217	692	95	182	27	8	2	58	.263	379	492	25	.972

Signed as free agent by Texas Rangers' organization, March 3, 1983.

†On disabled list, August 24 to September 8, 1987.

‡Traded with First Baseman Pete O'Brien and Outfielder Oddibe McDowell to Cleveland Indians for Second Baseman Julio Franco, December 6, 1988.

—DID YOU KNOW—

That in 1988, California's Chili Davis became only the third player in big-league history to homer from both sides of the plate in both leagues? Reggie Smith and Ted Simmons also accomplished the feat.

THOMAS LEO BROWNING
(Tom)

Born April 28, 1960, at Casper, Wyo.
Height, 6.01. Weight, 190.
Throws and bats lefthanded.
Attended Tennessee Wesleyan College, Athens, Tenn., and
Le Moyne College, Syracuse, N.Y.

Pitched 1-0 perfect game against Los Angeles Dodgers, September 16, 1988.
Pitched seven-inning, 2-0 no-hit victory against Iowa, July 31, 1984.
Led National League in home runs allowed with 36 in 1988.
Tied for National League lead in games started by pitchers with 39 in 1986 and 36 in 1988.
Tied for American Association lead in home runs allowed with 24 in 1984.
Named National League Rookie Pitcher of the Year by THE SPORTING NEWS, 1985.

Year Club	League	G.	IP.	W.	L.	Pct.	H.	R.	ER.	SO.	BB.	ERA.
1982—Billings	Pioneer	14	88	4	•8	.333	96	53	38	*87	41	3.89
1983—Tampa	Florida St.	11	78⅔	8	1	.889	53	19	13	101	36	1.49
1983—Waterbury	Eastern	18	117⅓	4	10	.286	100	62	46	101	63	3.53
1984—Wichita	Am. Assoc.	30	189⅓	12	10	.545	169	88	83	*160	73	3.95
1984—Cincinnati	National	3	23⅓	1	0	1.000	27	4	4	14	5	1.54
1985—Cincinnati	National	38	261⅓	20	9	.690	242	111	103	155	73	3.55
1986—Cincinnati	National	39	243⅓	14	13	.519	225	123	103	147	70	3.81
1987—Cincinnati	National	32	183	10	13	.435	201	107	102	117	61	5.02
1987—Nashville	Am. Assoc.	5	29⅔	2	3	.400	37	22	20	28	12	6.07
1988—Cincinnati	National	36	250⅔	18	5	.783	205	98	95	124	64	3.41
Major League Totals—5 Years		148	961⅔	63	40	.612	900	443	407	557	273	3.81

Selected by Cincinnati Reds' organization in 9th round of free-agent draft, June 7, 1982.

ANTHONY MICHAEL BRUMLEY
(Mike)

Born April 9, 1963, at Oklahoma City, Okla.
Height, 5.10. Weight, 165.
Throws right and bats left and righthanded.
Attended University of Texas, Austin, Tex.
Son of Mike Brumley, catcher with Washington Senators, 1964 through 1966.

Major League stolen bases: 1987 (7).
Led American Association shortstops in total chances with 597 in 1986.

Year Club	League	Pos.	G.	AB.	R.	H.	2B.	3B.	HR.	RBI.	B.A.	PO.	A.	E.	F.A.
1983—Winter Haven	Fla. St.	SS-OF	44	153	25	48	6	4	1	18	.314	51	92	20	.877
1984—New Britain†	East.	OF-SS	34	121	14	28	6	2	0	9	.231	71	6	6	.928
1984—Midland	Texas	OF	73	255	37	55	11	3	6	21	.216	128	4	5	.964
1985—Pittsfield	East.	SS-OF	131	460	66	127	23	*14	3	58	.276	182	333	33	.940
1986—Iowa	A. A.	SS	139	458	74	103	21	5	10	44	.225	177	*400	20	.966
1987—Iowa	A. A.	SS-2B-OF	92	319	44	81	20	5	6	42	.254	147	240	24	.942
1987—Chicago‡	Nat.	SS-2B	39	104	8	21	2	2	1	9	.202	43	93	5	.965
1988—Las Vegas	P. C.	S-O-3-2	113	425	77	134	16	7	3	41	.315	139	322	28	.943
Major League Totals—1 Year			39	104	8	21	2	2	1	9	.202	43	93	5	.965

Selected by Philadelphia Phillies' organization in 16th round of free-agent draft, June 3, 1980.
Selected by Boston Red Sox' organization in 2nd round of free-agent draft, June 6, 1983.
†Traded with Pitcher Dennis Eckersley to Chicago Cubs for First Baseman-Outfielder Bill Buckner, May 25, 1984.
‡Traded with Infielder Keith Moreland to San Diego Padres for Pitchers Rich Gossage and Ray Hayward, February 12, 1988.

THOMAS ANDREW BRUNANSKY
(Tom)

Born August 20, 1960, at Covina, Calif.
Height, 6.04. Weight, 216.
Throws and bats righthanded.
Attended California State Poly University, Pomona, Calif.
Brother-in-law of Dave Engle, catcher with Minnesota Twins,
Detroit Tigers and Montreal Expos, 1981 through 1988.

Major League stolen bases: 1981 (1), 1982 (1), 1983 (2), 1984 (4), 1985 (5), 1986 (12), 1987 (11), 1988 (17). Total—53.
Led American League outfielders in double plays with 8 in 1983 and 6 in 1984.
Tied for Texas League lead in double plays by outfielders with 4 in 1980.
Received reported $100,000 bonus to sign with California Angels, 1978.

Year Club	League	Pos.	G.	AB.	R.	H.	2B.	3B.	HR.	RBI.	B.A.	PO.	A.	E.	F.A.
1978—Idaho Falls	Pioneer	OF	48	190	55	63	14	4	6	45	.332	85	1	8	.915
1979—Salinas	Calif.	OF	*140	485	85	131	23	1	23	76	.270	279	11	6	.980
1980—El Paso	Texas	OF	128	495	103	160	24	8	24	97	.323	306	17	*14	.958
1980—Salt Lake City	P. C.	OF	9	32	7	11	2	2	1	8	.344	28	1	0	1.000
1981—Salt Lake City†	P. C.	OF	96	343	61	114	17	10	22	81	.332	250	14	5	.981
1981—California	Amer.	OF	11	33	7	5	0	0	3	6	.152	27	3	2	.938
1982—Spokane‡	P. C.	OF	25	88	12	18	6	1	1	6	.205	44	7	1	.981
1982—Minnesota	Amer.	OF	127	463	77	126	30	1	20	46	.272	343	8	5	.986
1983—Minnesota	Amer.	OF	151	542	70	123	24	5	28	82	.227	375	16	6	.985
1984—Minnesota	Amer.	OF	155	567	75	144	21	0	32	85	.254	304	13	5	.984
1985—Minnesota	Amer.	OF	157	567	71	137	28	4	27	90	.242	300	14	5	.984

Year	Club	League	Pos.	G.	AB.	R.	H.	2B.	3B.	HR.	RBI.	B.A.	PO.	A.	E.	F.A.
1986—	Minnesota	Amer.	OF	157	593	69	152	28	1	23	75	.256	315	10	6	.982
1987—	Minnesota	Amer.	OF	155	532	83	138	22	2	32	85	.259	273	10	3	.990
1988—	Minnesota§	Amer.	OF	14	49	5	9	1	0	1	6	.184	19	0	3	.864
1988—	St. Louis	Nat.	OF	143	523	69	128	22	4	22	79	.245	267	10	1	*.996
American League Totals—8 Years				927	3346	457	834	154	13	166	475	.249	1956	74	35	.983
National League Totals—1 Year				143	523	69	128	22	4	22	79	.245	267	10	1	.996
Major League Totals—8 Years				1070	3869	526	962	176	17	188	554	.249	2223	84	36	.985

Selected by California Angels' organization in 1st round (14th player selected) of free-agent draft, June 6, 1978.

†On disabled list, August 8 to August 31, 1981.

‡Traded with Pitcher Mike Walters and cash to Minnesota Twins for Pitcher Doug Corbett and Second Baseman Rob Wilfong, May 12, 1982.

§Traded to St. Louis Cardinals for Second Baseman Tom Herr, April 22, 1988.

CHAMPIONSHIP SERIES RECORD

Tied Championship Series record for most long hits, Series (6), 1987.

Established American League Championship Series record for highest slugging average, five-game Series (1.000), 1987.

Tied American League Championship Series record for most doubles, five-game Series (4), 1987.

Year	Club	League	Pos.	G.	AB.	R.	H.	2B.	3B.	HR.	RBI.	B.A.	PO.	A.	E.	F.A.
1987—	Minnesota	Amer.	OF	5	17	5	7	4	0	2	9	.412	10	0	0	1.000

WORLD SERIES RECORD

Year	Club	League	Pos.	G.	AB.	R.	H.	2B.	3B.	HR.	RBI.	B.A.	PO.	A.	E.	F.A.
1987—	Minnesota	Amer.	OF	7	25	5	5	0	0	0	2	.200	14	0	0	1.000

ALL-STAR GAME RECORD

Year	League	Pos.	AB.	R.	H.	2B.	3B.	HR.	RBI.	B.A.	PO.	A.	E.	F.A.
1985—	American	OF	1	0	0	0	0	0	0	.000	0	0	0	.000

WILLIAM JOSEPH BUCKNER
(Bill)

Born December 14, 1949, at Vallejo, Calif.
Height, 6.01. Weight, 195.
Throws and bats lefthanded.
Attended University of Southern California, Los Angeles, Calif., and
Arizona State University, Tempe, Ariz.
Brother of Jim Buckner, minor league outfielder, 1972 through 1981;
and Bob Buckner, minor league infielder, 1966 through 1970;
and part-time scout with Chicago Cubs, 1977 through 1979.

Established major league record for most assists, first baseman, season (184), 1985.

Tied major league record for most games, first baseman, season (162), 1985.

Tied National League records for fewest double plays, first baseman, season, 150 or more games (89), 1982; fewest errors by first baseman for leader in errors, season (13), 1983.

Major League stolen bases: 1971 (4), 1972 (10), 1973 (12), 1974 (31), 1975 (8), 1976 (28), 1977 (7), 1978 (7), 1979 (9), 1980 (1), 1981 (5), 1982 (15), 1983 (12), 1984 (2), 1985 (18), 1986 (6), 1987 (2), 1988 (5). Total—182.

Led Pioneer League first basemen in double plays with 37 in 1968.

Year	Club	League	Pos.	G.	AB.	R.	H.	2B.	3B.	HR.	RBI.	B.A.	PO.	A.	E.	F.A.
1968—	Ogden	Pion.	1B	*64	*256	54	*88	10	*8	4	41	*.344	468	28	4	*.992
1969—	Albuquerque	Texas	OF-1B	70	257	44	79	7	3	7	50	.307	220	15	3	.987
1969—	Spokane	P. C.	OF-1B	36	143	21	45	1	1	2	27	.315	128	12	5	.966
1969—	Los Angeles	Nat.	PH	1	1	0	0	0	0	0	0	.000	0	0	0	.000
1970—	Spokane	P. C.	1B-OF	111	465	78	156	33	2	3	74	.335	582	22	7	.989
1970—	Los Angeles	Nat.	OF-1B	28	68	6	13	3	1	0	4	.191	37	1	0	1.000
1971—	Los Angeles	Nat.	OF-1B	108	358	37	99	15	1	5	41	.277	235	11	1	.996
1972—	Los Angeles	Nat.	OF-1B	105	383	47	122	14	3	5	37	.319	434	22	4	.991
1973—	Los Angeles	Nat.	1B-OF	140	575	68	158	20	0	8	46	.275	981	50	3	.997
1974—	Los Angeles	Nat.	OF-1B	145	580	83	182	30	3	7	58	.314	284	5	7	.976
1975—	Los Angeles†	Nat.	OF	92	288	30	70	11	2	6	31	.243	138	4	2	.986
1976—	Los Angeles‡	Nat.	OF-1B	154	642	76	193	28	4	7	60	.301	315	7	5	.985
1977—	Chicago§	Nat.	1B	122	426	40	121	27	0	11	60	.284	966	58	10	.990
1978—	Chicago x	Nat.	1B	117	446	47	144	26	1	5	74	.323	1075	83	6	.995
1979—	Chicago	Nat.	1B	149	591	72	168	34	7	14	66	.284	1258	124	7	.995
1980—	Chicago	Nat.	1B-OF	145	578	69	187	41	3	10	68	*.324	916	78	8	.992
1981—	Chicago	Nat.	1B	106	421	45	131	*35	3	10	75	.311	996	81	*17	.984
1982—	Chicago	Nat.	1B	161	*657	93	201	34	5	15	105	.306	1547	*159	12	.993
1983—	Chicago	Nat.	*●1B-OF	153	626	79	175	●38	6	16	66	.280	1391	*161	●13	.992
1984—	Chicago y	Nat.	1B-OF	21	43	3	9	0	0	0	2	.209	71	6	0	1.000
1984—	Boston	Amer.	1B	114	439	51	122	21	2	11	67	.278	974	96	●15	.986
1985—	Boston	Amer.	1B	162	673	89	201	46	3	16	110	.299	1384	*184	12	.992
1986—	Boston	Amer.	1B	153	629	73	168	39	2	18	102	.267	1067	*157	14	.989
1987—	Bos. za-Cal.	Amer.	1B	132	469	39	134	18	2	5	74	.286	640	60	6	.992
1988—	Cal.b-K.C.c	Amer.	1B	108	285	19	71	14	0	3	43	.249	161	13	1	.994
National League Totals—16 Years				1747	6683	795	1973	356	39	119	793	.295	10644	850	95	.992
American League Totals—5 Years				669	2495	271	696	138	9	53	396	.279	4226	510	48	.990
Major League Totals—20 Years				2416	9178	1066	2669	494	48	172	1189	.291	14870	1360	143	.991

Selected by Los Angeles Dodgers' organization in 2nd round of free-agent draft, June 7, 1968.

†On disabled list, April 21 to May 12, 1975.

‡Traded with Infielder Ivan DeJesus and Pitcher Jeff Albert to Chicago Cubs for Outfielder Rick Monday and Pitcher Mike Garman, January 11, 1977.

§On disabled list, March 28 to April 19, 1977.

xOn disabled list, June 22 to July 7, 1978.

yTraded to Boston Red Sox for Pitcher Dennis Eckersley and Outfielder Mike Brumley, May 25, 1984.

zOn disabled list, June 10 to June 26, 1987.

aReleased, July 23, 1987; signed by California Angels, July 28, 1987.

bReleased, May 9, 1988; signed by Kansas City Royals, May 13, 1988.

cGranted free agency, November 4, 1988; re-signed by Royals, December 6, 1988.

CHAMPIONSHIP SERIES RECORD

Year Club	League	Pos.	G.	AB.	R.	H.	2B.	3B.	HR.	RBI.	B.A.	PO.	A.	E.	F.A.
1974—Los Angeles	Nat.	OF	4	18	0	3	1	0	0	0	.167	6	0	0	1.000
1986—Boston.....................	Amer.	1B	7	28	3	6	1	0	0	3	.214	49	5	0	1.000
Championship Series Totals—2 Years.....			11	46	3	9	2	0	0	3	.196	55	5	0	1.000

WORLD SERIES RECORD

Year Club	League	Pos.	G.	AB.	R.	H.	2B.	3B.	HR.	RBI.	B.A.	PO.	A.	E.	F.A.
1974—Los Angeles	Nat.	OF	5	20	1	5	1	0	1	1	.250	11	0	0	1.000
1986—Boston.....................	Amer.	1B	7	32	2	6	0	0	0	1	.188	53	7	1	.984
World Series Totals—2 Years			12	52	3	11	1	0	1	2	.212	64	7	1	.986

ALL-STAR GAME RECORD

Year League	Pos.	AB.	R.	H.	2B.	3B.	HR.	RBI.	B.A.	PO.	A.	E.	F.A.
1981—National...	PH	1	0	0	0	0	0	0	.000	0	0	0	.000

STEVEN BERNARD BUECHELE

Name pronounced BOO-shell.

(Steve)

Born September 26, 1961, at Lancaster, Calif.
Height, 6.02. Weight, 190.
Throws and bats righthanded.
Attended Stanford University, Stanford, Calif.

Major League stolen bases: 1985 (3), 1986 (5), 1987 (2), 1988 (2). Total—12.

Named American Association Most Valuable Player, 1985.

Year Club	League	Pos.	G.	AB.	R.	H.	2B.	3B.	HR.	RBI.	B.A.	PO.	A.	E.	F.A.
1982—Tulsa.......................	Texas	2B-3B	62	213	21	63	12	2	5	33	.296	111	174	8	.973
1983—Tulsa.......................	Texas	2B-3B	117	437	62	121	12	4	14	62	.277	182	259	18	.961
1983—Oklahoma City.....	A. A.	2B-3B	9	34	6	9	5	0	1	4	.265	17	22	1	.975
1984—Oklahoma City.....	A. A.	2B-3B	131	447	48	118	25	3	7	59	.264	236	329	17	.971
1985—Oklahoma City.....	A. A.	3B-2B	89	350	56	104	20	7	9	64	.297	84	170	7	.973
1985—Texas.....................	Amer.	3B-2B	69	219	22	48	6	3	6	21	.219	52	138	6	.969
1986—Texas.....................	Amer.	3B-2B-OF	153	461	54	112	19	2	18	54	.243	174	292	12	.975
1987—Texas.....................	Amer.	3B-2B-OF	136	363	45	86	20	0	13	50	.237	89	211	9	.971
1988—Texas.....................	Amer.	3B-2B	155	503	68	126	21	4	16	58	.250	114	300	16	.963
Major League Totals—4 Years................			513	1546	189	372	66	9	53	183	.241	429	941	43	.970

Selected by Chicago White Sox' organization in 1st round (ninth player selected) of free-agent draft, June 5, 1979.

Selected by Texas Rangers' organization in 5th round of free-agent draft, June 7, 1982.

JAY CAMPBELL BUHNER

Born August 13, 1964, at Louisville, Ky.
Height, 6.03. Weight, 205.
Throws and bats righthanded.
Attended McLennan Community College, Waco, Tex.

Major League stolen bases: 1988 (1).

Led Florida State League in game-winning RBIs with 15 in 1985.

Tied for International League lead in double plays by outfielders with 6 in 1987.

Year Club	League	Pos.	G.	AB.	R.	H.	2B.	3B.	HR.	RBI.	B.A.	PO.	A.	E.	F.A.
1984—Watertown†	NYP	OF	65	229	43	74	16	3	9	•58	.323	106	8	1	.991
1985—Fort Lauderdale..	Fla. St.	OF	117	409	65	121	18	10	11	76	.296	235	12	7	.972
1986—Fort Lauderdale‡	Fla. St.	OF	36	139	24	42	9	1	7	31	.302	84	7	3	.968
1987—Columbus..............	Int.	OF	134	502	83	140	23	1	★31	85	.279	275	★20	6	.980
1987—New York.............	Amer.	OF	7	22	0	5	2	0	0	1	.227	11	1	0	1.000
1988—Columbus..............	Int.	OF	38	129	26	33	5	0	8	18	.256	83	3	1	.989
1988—N.Y.§-Sea.	Amer.	OF	85	261	36	56	13	1	13	38	.215	186	9	3	.985
Major League Totals—2 Years................			92	283	36	61	15	1	13	39	.216	197	10	3	.986

Selected by Atlanta Braves' organization in 9th round of free-agent draft, June 6, 1983.

Selected by Pittsburgh Pirates' organization in secondary phase of free-agent draft, January 17, 1984.

†Traded with Infielder Dale Berra and Pitcher Alfonso Pulido to New York Yankees for Outfielder Steve Kemp, Infielder Tim Foli and $800,000, December 20, 1984.

‡On disabled list, April 11 to July 28, 1986.

§Traded with Pitcher Rich Balabon and a player to be named later to Seattle Mariners for Designated Hitter Ken Phelps, July 21, 1988; Seattle acquired Pitcher Troy Evers to complete deal, October 12, 1988.

DeWAYNE ALLISON BUICE

Name pronounced Byce.

Born August 20, 1957, at Lynwood, Calif.
Height, 5.11. Weight, 170.
Throws and bats righthanded.
Attended California State University at Dominguez Hills, Carson, Calif.;
Los Angeles Harbor Junior College, Wilmington, Calif.,
and Cypress College, Cypress, Calif.

Major League saves: 1987 (17), 1988 (3). Total—20.

Year Club	League	G.	IP.	W.	L.	Pct.	H.	R.	ER.	SO.	BB.	ERA.
1977—Great Falls	Pioneer	15	37	1	4	.200	48	34	15	30	24	3.65
1978—Cedar Rapids	Midwest	36	74	3	5	.375	58	30	14	68	41	1.70
1979—Fresno	California	46	97	7	5	.583	83	51	40	86	44	3.71
1980—Fresno†	California	36	100	7	4	.636	101	42	37	88	38	3.33
1981—West Haven	Eastern	*58	82	8	3	.727	75	24	19	88	41	2.09
1981—Tacoma	P. Coast	2	3	1	0	1.000	0	0	0	2	3	0.00
1982—Tacoma‡	P. Coast	19	41	4	2	.667	51	22	19	36	19	4.17
1982—West Haven	Eastern	8	23⅔	1	1	.500	18	11	9	40	8	3.42
1983—Tacoma §xy	P. Coast	32	52⅓	5	3	.625	44	27	20	41	22	3.44
1984—Nuevo Laredo	Mexico	14	40	4	1	.800	26	12	10	35	17	2.25
1985—Nuevo Laredo	Mexico	24	33⅔	0	1	.000	33	13	12	37	15	3.21
1986—Midland	Texas	45	78⅓	8	6	.571	70	34	30	73	22	3.45
1986—Edmonton	P. Coast	8	12⅓	2	1	.667	6	2	1	11	3	0.73
1987—Edmonton	P. Coast	5	8⅓	1	1	.500	4	5	1	7	7	1.08
1987—California	American	57	114	6	7	.462	87	45	43	109	40	3.39
1988—California z	American	32	41⅓	2	4	.333	45	29	27	38	19	5.88
1988—Edmonton	P. Coast	9	11⅔	0	0	.000	9	4	3	17	2	2.31
Major League Totals—2 Years		89	155⅓	8	11	.421	132	74	70	147	59	4.06

Signed as free agent by San Francisco Giants' organization, May 19, 1977.
†Drafted by West Haven (Oakland A's organization), December 9, 1980.
‡On disabled list, July 3 to July 13 and August 12, 1982 through remainder of season.
§On disabled list, June 8 to June 28 and July 13, 1983 through remainder of season.
xGranted free agency, October 15, 1983; signed by Maine (Cleveland Indians' organization), January 14, 1984.
yReleased, April 7, 1984; signed by Edmonton (California Angels' organization), November 19, 1985.
zOn disabled list, June 16 to August 5, 1988; included rehabilitation disability assignment to Edmonton, July 17 to August 5, 1988.

ERIC JERALD BULLOCK

Born February 16, 1960, at Los Angeles, Calif.
Height, 5.11. Weight, 185.
Throws and bats lefthanded.
Attended Los Angeles Harbor Junior College, Woodland Hills, Calif.
and California State University, Fullerton, Calif.
Son of Eddie Bullock, minor league outfielder, 1955.

Major League stolen bases: 1986 (2), 1988 (1). Total—3.
Led Pacific Coast League in stolen bases with 51 in 1988.
Tied for Pacific Coast League lead in being hit by pitch with 7 in 1985.

Year Club	League	Pos.	G.	AB.	R.	H.	2B.	3B.	HR.	RBI.	B.A.	PO.	A.	E.	F.A.
1981—Sarasota Orange	Gulf C.	OF	56	184	38	54	8	3	1	15	.293	67	6	3	.961
1981—Daytona Beach	Fla. St.	DH	1	2	1	1	0	0	0	1	.500	0	0	0	.000
1982—Daytona Beach	Fla. St.	OF	117	442	90	150	24	11	5	•85	.339	180	11	5	.974
1982—Columbus	South.	OF	18	66	6	20	1	0	2	13	.303	21	1	0	1.000
1983—Columbus	South.	OF	130	475	65	131	15	6	9	59	.276	196	9	3	.986
1984—Columbus	South.	OF	71	265	47	77	15	2	3	41	.291	133	3	4	.971
1984—Tucson	P. C.	OF	60	185	22	51	6	2	1	16	.276	96	2	5	.951
1985—Tucson	P. C.	OF	124	467	81	149	26	8	4	57	.319	199	5	7	.967
1985—Houston	Nat.	OF	18	25	3	7	2	0	0	2	.280	6	0	2	.750
1986—Houston	Nat.	OF	6	21	0	1	0	0	0	1	.048	7	0	1	.875
1986—Tucson†	P. C.	OF	42	151	28	58	8	2	3	21	.384	73	2	1	.987
1987—Tuc.‡-Port.§	P. C.	OF	106	330	42	88	13	6	2	34	.267	145	5	2	.987
1988—Portland	P. C.	OF	117	434	69	134	20	8	2	46	.309	211	11	3	*.987
1988—Minnesota x	Amer.	OF	16	17	3	5	0	0	0	3	.294	7	0	1	.875
National League Totals—2 Years			24	46	3	8	2	0	0	3	.174	13	0	3	.813
American League Totals—1 Year			16	17	3	5	0	0	0	3	.294	7	0	1	.875
Major League Totals—3 Years			40	63	6	13	2	0	0	6	.206	20	0	4	.833

Selected by Los Angeles Dodgers' organization in 18th round of free-agent draft, June 6, 1978.
Selected by San Diego Padres' organization in 1st round (fifth player selected) of free-agent draft, January 13, 1981.
Selected by Houston Astros' organization in secondary phase of free-agent draft, June 8, 1981.
†On disabled list, May 6 to July 7, 1986.
‡Traded to Minnesota Twins' organization for Pitcher Clay Christiansen, June 2, 1987.
§Granted free agency, October 15, 1987; re-signed by Twins' organization, November 7, 1987.
xTraded with Second Baseman Tom Herr and Catcher Tom Nieto to Philadelphia Phillies for Pitcher Shane Rawley and cash, October 24, 1988.

—DID YOU KNOW—

That the St. Louis Cardinals, who weren't shut out until their 113th game in 1987, were shut out 16 times in 1988?

JEFFREY BENTON BUMGARNER
(Jeff)

Born June 12, 1967, at Spokane, Wash.
Height, 6.05. Weight, 205.
Throws and bats righthanded.

Tied for Southern League lead in shutouts with 3 in 1987.
Tied for Midwest League lead in wild pitches with 19 in 1986.
Received reported $175,000 bonus to sign with Minnesota Twins, 1985.

Year Club	League	G.	IP.	W.	L.	Pct.	H.	R.	ER.	SO.	BB.	ERA.
1985—Elizabethton	Ap'lachian	10	55⅓	5	5	.500	56	33	19	36	31	3.09
1986—Kenosha	Midwest	23	153⅓	7	14	.333	128	81	59	102	80	3.46
1987—Orlando	Southern	26	168⅓	13	10	.565	174	96	82	87	94	4.38
1988—Portland	P. Coast	7	25⅔	2	3	.400	34	26	22	17	32	7.71
1988—Orlando†	Southern	20	117⅓	3	11	.214	129	66	50	68	56	3.84

Selected by Minnesota Twins' organization in 1st round (13th player selected) of free-agent draft, June 3, 1985.
†Traded with Pitchers Steve Gasser and Toby Nivens to New York Mets for Second Baseman Wally Backman and Pitcher Mike Santiago, December 7, 1988.

TIMOTHY PHILIP BURKE
(Tim)

Born February 19, 1959, at Omaha, Neb.
Height, 6.03. Weight, 200.
Throws and bats righthanded.
Attended University of Nebraska, Lincoln, Neb.

Established National League record for most games pitched by rookie, season (78), 1985.
Major League saves: 1985 (8), 1986 (4), 1987 (18), 1988 (18). Total—48.

Year Club	League	G.	IP.	W.	L.	Pct.	H.	R.	ER.	SO.	BB.	ERA.
1980—Salem†	Carolina					(Did not play)						
1981—Alexandria	Carolina	23	149	8	10	.444	139	67	57	111	48	3.44
1982—Buffalo‡	Eastern	25	144	7	10	.412	162	93	83	93	57	5.19
1983—Columbus	Eastern	4	12	1	0	1.000	15	9	9	6	8	6.75
1983—Nashville§x	Southern	20	129	12	4	.750	124	63	46	64	37	3.21
1984—Indianapolis	Am. Assoc.	35	180⅔	11	8	.579	192	81	70	108	61	3.49
1985—Montreal	National	*78	120⅓	9	4	.692	86	32	32	87	44	2.39
1986—Montreal	National	68	101⅓	9	7	.563	103	37	33	82	46	2.93
1987—Montreal y	National	55	91	7	0	1.000	64	18	12	58	17	1.19
1988—Montreal	National	61	82	3	5	.375	84	36	31	42	25	3.40
Major League Totals—4 Years		262	394⅔	28	16	.636	337	123	108	269	132	2.46

Selected by Pittsburgh Pirates' organization in 2nd round of free-agent draft, June 3, 1980.
†On disabled list, July 12, 1980 through remainder of season.
‡Traded with Catcher John Holland, Infielder Jose Rivera and Outfielder Don Aubin to New York Yankees' organization for Outfielder Lee Mazzilli, December 22, 1982.
§On disabled list, May 4 to May 23, 1983.
xTraded to Montreal Expos' organization for Outfielder Pat Rooney, December 19, 1983.
yOn disabled list, March 28 to April 22, 1987.

JOHN DAVID BURKETT

Born November 28, 1964, at New Brighton, Pa.
Height, 6.02. Weight, 180.
Throws and bats righthanded.

Year Club	League	G.	IP.	W.	L.	Pct.	H.	R.	ER.	SO.	BB.	ERA.
1983—Great Falls	Pioneer	13	50⅓	2	6	.250	73	44	35	38	30	6.26
1984—Clinton	Midwest	20	126⅔	7	6	.538	128	81	61	83	38	4.33
1985—Fresno	California	20	109⅔	7	4	.636	98	43	35	72	46	2.87
1986—Fresno	California	4	24⅔	0	3	.000	34	19	15	14	8	5.47
1986—Shreveport	Texas	22	128⅔	10	6	.625	99	46	38	73	42	2.66
1987—Shreveport	Texas	27	*177⅔	•14	8	.636	181	75	66	126	53	3.34
1987—San Francisco	National	3	6	0	0	.000	7	4	3	5	3	4.50
1988—Phoenix	P. Coast	21	114	5	11	.313	141	79	66	74	49	5.21
1988—Shreveport	Texas	7	50⅔	5	1	.833	33	15	12	34	18	2.13
Major League Totals—1 Year		3	6	0	0	.000	7	4	3	5	3	4.50

Selected by San Francisco Giants' organization in 6th round of free-agent draft, June 6, 1983.

ELLIS RENA BURKS

Born September 11, 1964, at Vicksburg, Miss.
Height, 6.02. Weight, 188.
Throws and bats righthanded.
Attended Ranger Junior College, Ranger, Tex.

Major League stolen bases: 1987 (27), 1988 (25). Total—52.
Tied for Florida State League lead in double plays by outfielders with 6 in 1984.

Year Club	League	Pos.	G.	AB.	R.	H.	2B.	3B.	HR.	RBI.	B.A.	PO.	A.	E.	F.A.
1983—Elmira	NYP	OF	53	174	30	42	9	0	2	23	.241	89	5	2	.979
1984—Winter Haven	Fla. St.	OF	112	375	52	96	15	4	6	43	.256	196	12	5	.977
1985—New Britain	East.	OF	133	476	66	121	25	7	10	61	.254	306	9	8	.975
1986—New Britain	East.	OF	124	462	70	126	20	3	14	55	.273	318	5	5	.985

Year	Club	League	Pos.	G.	AB.	R.	H.	2B.	3B.	HR.	RBI.	B.A.	PO.	A.	E.	F.A.
1987	Pawtucket	Int.	OF	11	40	11	9	3	1	3	6	.225	25	0	0	1.000
1987	Boston	Amer.	OF	133	558	94	152	30	2	20	59	.272	320	15	4	.988
1988	Boston†	Amer.	OF	144	540	93	159	37	5	18	92	.294	370	9	9	.977
Major League Totals—2 Years				277	1098	187	311	67	7	38	151	.283	690	24	13	.982

Selected by Boston Red Sox' organization in 1st round (20th player selected) of free agent draft, January 11, 1983.
†On disabled list, March 26 to April 12, 1988.

CHAMPIONSHIP SERIES RECORD

Year	Club	League	Pos.	G.	AB.	R.	H.	2B.	3B.	HR.	RBI.	B.A.	PO.	A.	E.	F.A.
1988	Boston	Amer.	OF	4	17	2	4	1	0	0	1	.235	10	0	0	1.000

TODD EDWARD BURNS

Born July 6, 1963, at Maywood, Calif.
Height, 6.02. Weight, 186.
Throws and bats righthanded.
Attended Oral Roberts University, Tulsa, Okla.

Major League saves: 1988 (1).
Tied for Southern League lead in shutouts with 3 in 1986.

Year	Club	League	G.	IP.	W.	L.	Pct.	H.	R.	ER.	SO.	BB.	ERA.
1984	Medford	Northwest	22	36⅓	3	0	1.000	21	4	2	63	12	0.50
1984	Madison	Midwest	10	14	3	2	.600	11	4	4	20	3	2.57
1985	Madison	Midwest	20	123	8	8	.500	109	55	50	94	40	3.66
1985	Huntsville	Southern	4	22⅔	3	1	.750	16	6	3	8	13	1.19
1986	Huntsville	Southern	20	124⅔	7	7	.500	122	59	52	77	39	3.75
1986	Tacoma	P.Coast	11	16⅔	0	1	.000	11	4	4	14	12	2.16
1987	Huntsville	Southern	34	63⅔	3	4	.429	49	24	21	54	17	2.97
1987	Tacoma	P. Coast	21	27⅔	2	2	.500	27	16	15	30	16	4.88
1988	Tacoma	P. Coast	21	73⅓	4	3	.571	74	39	30	59	26	3.68
1988	Oakland	American	17	102⅔	8	2	.800	93	38	36	57	34	3.16
Major League Totals—1 Year			17	102⅔	8	2	.800	93	38	36	57	34	3.16

Selected by Oakland A's organization in 7th round of free-agent draft, June 4, 1984.

WORLD SERIES RECORD

Year	Club	League	G.	IP.	W.	L.	Pct.	H.	R.	ER.	SO.	BB.	ERA.
1988	Oakland	American	1	⅓	0	0	.000	0	0	0	0	0	0.00

ROBERT RANDALL BUSH
(Randy)

Born October 5, 1958, at Dover, Del.
Height, 6.01. Weight, 184.
Throws and bats lefthanded.
Attended Miami-Dade Community College (North), Miami, Fla.,
and University of New Orleans, New Orleans, La.

Tied American League record for most home runs by pinch-hitter, consecutive at-bats (2), June 20 and 23, 1986.
Major League stolen bases: 1984 (1), 1985 (3), 1986 (5), 1987 (10), 1988 (8). Total—27.
Led Southern League in being hit by pitch with 8 in 1979 and 12 in 1981.

Year	Club	League	Pos.	G.	AB.	R.	H.	2B.	3B.	HR.	RBI.	B.A.	PO.	A.	E.	F.A.
1979	Orlando	South.	1B	76	243	33	62	12	2	6	34	.255	653	38	13	.982
1980	Toledo†	Int.	OF-1B	40	108	11	21	1	0	1	7	.194	112	6	1	.992
1980	Orlando	South.	1B	51	175	32	41	2	1	7	26	.234	458	28	4	.992
1981	Orlando	South.	OF-1B	136	482	98	140	26	3	22	94	.290	174	7	5	.973
1982	Toledo	Int.	OF	49	160	21	52	14	0	8	27	.325	68	0	1	.986
1982	Minnesota	Amer.	OF	55	119	13	29	6	1	4	13	.244	7	0	0	1.000
1983	Minnesota	Amer.	1B	124	373	43	93	24	3	11	56	.249	21	3	0	1.000
1984	Minnesota	Amer.	1B	113	311	46	69	17	1	11	43	.222	5	0	0	1.000
1985	Minnesota	Amer.	OF-1B	97	234	26	56	13	3	10	35	.239	79	0	2	.975
1986	Minnesota	Amer.	OF-1B	130	357	50	96	19	7	7	45	.269	182	2	4	.979
1987	Minnesota	Amer.	OF-1B	122	293	46	74	10	2	11	46	.253	164	5	4	.977
1988	Minnesota‡	Amer.	OF-1B	136	394	51	103	20	3	14	51	.261	206	5	4	.981
Major League Totals—7 Years				777	2081	275	520	109	20	68	289	.250	664	15	14	.980

Selected by Minnesota Twins' organization in 2nd round of free-agent draft, June 5, 1979.
†On disabled list, May 25 to June 27, 1980.
‡Granted free agency, November 4, 1988; re-signed by Twins, December 12, 1988.

CHAMPIONSHIP SERIES RECORD

Tied American League Championship Series record for most stolen bases, five-game Series (3), 1987.

Year	Club	League	Pos.	G.	AB.	R.	H.	2B.	3B.	HR.	RBI.	B.A.	PO.	A.	E.	F.A.
1987	Minnesota	Amer.	DH	4	12	4	3	0	1	0	2	.250	0	0	0	.000

WORLD SERIES RECORD

Year	Club	League	Pos.	G.	AB.	R.	H.	2B.	3B.	HR.	RBI.	B.A.	PO.	A.	E.	F.A.
1987	Minnesota	Amer.	DH-PH	4	6	1	1	1	0	0	2	.167	0	0	0	.000

SALVATORE PHILIP BUTERA
(Sal)

Born September 25, 1952, at Richmond Hill, N.Y.
Height, 6.00. Weight, 189.
Throws and bats righthanded.
Attended Suffolk Community College, Selden, N.Y.

Led Carolina League in passed balls with 20 in 1974.
Tied for Carolina League lead in double plays by catchers with 9 in 1974.

Year Club	League	Pos.	G.	AB.	R.	H.	2B.	3B.	HR.	RBI.	B.A.	PO.	A.	E.	F.A.
1972—Sarasota W. Sox†	Gulf C.	C	36	114	18	28	7	0	0	16	.246	253	20	10	.965
1973—Fort Lauderdale	Fla. St.	C	99	319	21	76	12	1	1	32	.238	503	*86	10	.983
1974—Lynchburg	Carol.	C	124	417	35	90	16	2	3	55	.216	589	*102	7	*.990
1975—Orlando	South.	C	20	51	8	9	2	0	0	4	.176	61	14	0	1.000
1975—Tacoma	P. C.	C	73	215	21	52	9	0	2	26	.242	376	36	6	.986
1976—Orlando	South.	C	90	267	45	73	8	0	3	28	.273	326	41	6	.984
1977—Tacoma	P. C.	C	87	252	27	70	13	0	4	45	.278	257	49	9	.971
1978—Toledo	Int.	C	74	206	20	52	7	0	4	28	.252	334	32	5	.987
1979—Toledo	Int.	C	78	236	20	70	13	0	2	29	.297	392	33	11	.975
1980—Minnesota	Amer.	C	34	85	4	23	1	0	0	2	.271	106	9	6	.950
1981—Minnesota	Amer.	C-1B	62	167	13	40	7	1	0	18	.240	256	41	9	.971
1982—Minnesota‡	Amer.	C	54	126	9	32	2	0	0	8	.254	230	26	3	.988
1983—Detroit	Amer.	C	4	5	1	1	0	0	0	0	.200	12	1	1	.929
1983—Evansville§	A. A.	C	67	219	23	65	11	0	2	21	.297	300	26	11	.967
1984—Indianapolis	A. A.	C	111	283	36	76	11	0	7	41	.269	588	54	6	*.991
1984—Montreal	Nat.	C	3	3	0	0	0	0	0	0	.000	9	0	0	1.000
1985—Indianapolis	A. A.	C	5	18	2	4	0	0	1	4	.222	27	4	0	1.000
1985—Montreal x	Nat.	C-P	67	120	11	24	1	0	3	12	.200	227	20	4	.984
1986—Cincinnati	Nat.	C-P	56	113	14	27	6	1	2	16	.239	215	17	5	.979
1987—Cincinnati y	Nat.	C	5	11	1	2	0	0	1	2	.182	19	4	2	.920
1987—Portland	P. C.	C	10	26	4	4	1	0	1	3	.154	46	7	0	1.000
1987—Minnesota za	Amer.	C	51	111	7	19	5	0	1	12	.171	213	21	4	.983
1988—Syracuse	Int.	C	42	127	8	20	5	0	0	5	.157	245	23	2	.993
1988—Toronto	Amer.	C	23	60	3	14	2	1	1	6	.233	97	10	1	.991
American League Totals—6 Years			228	554	37	129	17	2	2	46	.233	914	108	24	.977
National League Totals—4 Years			131	247	26	53	7	1	6	30	.215	470	41	11	.979
Major League Totals—9 Years			359	801	63	182	24	3	8	76	.227	1384	149	35	.978

Signed as free agent by Minnesota Twins' organization, May 15, 1972.
†Loaned to Sarasota White Sox (Chicago White Sox' organization), June 26, 1972; returned, September 14, 1972.
‡Traded to Detroit Tigers for Catcher Stine Poole, March 25, 1983.
§Released, October 21, 1983; signed by Indianapolis (Montreal Expos' organization), December 23, 1983.
xTraded with Pitcher Bill Gullickson to Cincinnati Reds for Pitchers Jay Tibbs, Andy McGaffigan and John Stuper and Catcher Dann Bilardello, December 19, 1985.
yReleased, May 19, 1987; signed by Portland (Minnesota Twins' organization), May 22, 1987.
zReleased, December 21, 1987; re-signed by Twins, January 5, 1988.
aReleased, March 18, 1988; signed by Syracuse (Toronto Blue Jays' organization), March 24, 1988.

CHAMPIONSHIP SERIES RECORD

Year Club	League	Pos.	G.	AB.	R.	H.	2B.	3B.	HR.	RBI.	B.A.	PO.	A.	E.	F.A.
1987—Minnesota	Amer.	C	1	3	0	2	0	0	0	0	.667	6	0	0	1.000

WORLD SERIES RECORD

Year Club	League	Pos.	G.	AB.	R.	H.	2B.	3B.	HR.	RBI.	B.A.	PO.	A.	E.	F.A.
1987—Minnesota	Amer.	C	1	0	0	0	0	0	0	0	.000	0	0	0	.000

PITCHING RECORD

Year Club	League	G.	IP.	W.	L.	Pct.	H.	R.	ER.	SO.	BB.	ERA.
1985—Montreal	National	1	1	0	0	.000	0	0	0	0	0	0.00
1986—Cincinnati	National	1	1	0	0	.000	0	0	0	1	1	0.00
Major League Totals—2 Years		2	2	0	0	.000	0	0	0	1	1	0.00

BRETT MORGAN BUTLER

Born June 15, 1957, at Los Angeles, Calif.
Height, 5.10. Weight, 160.
Throws and bats lefthanded.
Attended Arizona State University, Tempe, Ariz., and received bachelor of science degree in education from Southeastern Oklahoma State University, Durant, Okla., in 1979.

Tied major league record for fewest double plays by outfielder, season, for leader in most double plays (4), 1983.
Tied National League record for fewest assists, outfielder, season, 150 or more games (3), 1988.
Major League stolen bases: 1981 (9), 1982 (21), 1983 (39), 1984 (52), 1985 (47), 1986 (32), 1987 (33), 1988 (43). Total—276.
Led American League in caught stealing with 22 in 1984 and 20 in 1985.
Tied for National League lead in double plays by outfielders with 4 in 1983.
Led International League in bases on balls received with 103 in 1981.
Named International League Most Valuable Player, 1981.

Year Club	League	Pos.	G.	AB.	R.	H.	2B.	3B.	HR.	RBI.	B.A.	PO.	A.	E.	F.A.
1979—Greenwood	W. Car.	OF	35	117	26	37	2	4	1	11	.316	45	2	0	1.000
1979—Bradenton	Gulf C.	OF	30	111	36	41	7	5	3	20	.369	66	5	0	1.000

Year	Club	League	Pos.	G.	AB.	R.	H.	2B.	3B.	HR.	RBI.	B.A.	PO.	A.	E.	F.A.
1980	—Anderson	S. Atl.	OF	70	255	73	76	12	6	1	26	.298	190	5	1	.995
1980	—Durham	Carol.	OF	66	224	47	82	15	6	2	39	.366	156	4	3	.982
1981	—Richmond	Int.	OF	125	466	★93	156	19	4	3	36	.335	286	15	3	.990
1981	—Atlanta	Nat.	OF	40	126	17	32	2	3	0	4	.254	76	2	1	.987
1982	—Atlanta	Nat.	OF	89	240	35	52	2	0	0	7	.217	129	2	0	1.000
1982	—Richmond	Int.	OF	41	157	22	57	8	3	1	22	.363	101	2	1	.990
1983	—Atlanta†	Nat.	OF	151	549	84	154	21	★13	5	37	.281	284	13	4	.987
1984	—Cleveland	Amer.	OF	159	602	108	162	25	9	3	49	.269	448	13	4	.991
1985	—Cleveland	Amer.	OF	152	591	106	184	28	14	5	50	.311	437	19	1	★.998
1986	—Cleveland	Amer.	OF	161	587	92	163	17	★14	4	51	.278	434	9	3	.993
1987	—Cleveland‡§	Amer.	OF	137	522	91	154	25	8	9	41	.295	393	4	4	.990
1988	—San Francisco	Nat.	OF	157	568	★109	163	27	9	6	43	.287	395	3	5	.988
National League Totals—4 Years				437	1483	245	401	52	25	11	91	.270	884	20	10	.989
American League Totals—4 Years				609	2302	397	663	95	45	21	191	.288	1712	45	12	.993
Major League Totals—8 Years				1046	3785	642	1064	147	70	32	282	.281	2596	65	22	.992

Selected by Atlanta Braves' organization in 23rd round of free-agent draft, June 5, 1979.

†Traded with Infielder Brook Jacoby to Cleveland Indians, October 21, 1983, completing deal in which Atlanta Braves acquired Pitcher Len Barker for three players to be named later, August 28, 1983. Cleveland acquired Pitcher Rick Behenna as partial completion of deal, September 2, 1983.

‡On disabled list, April 11 to April 30, 1987.

§Granted free agency, November 9, 1987; signed by San Francisco Giants, December 1, 1987.

CHAMPIONSHIP SERIES RECORD

Year	Club	League	Pos.	G.	AB.	R.	H.	2B.	3B.	HR.	RBI.	B.A.	PO.	A.	E.	F.A.
1982	—Atlanta	Nat.	OF-PH	2	1	0	0	0	0	0	0	.000	0	0	0	.000

RANDELL PARKER BYERS

Born October 2, 1964, at Bridgeton, N.J.
Height, 6.02. Weight, 180.
Throws and bats lefthanded.
Attended Community College of Baltimore, Baltimore, Md.

Major League stolen bases: 1987 (1).

Led South Atlantic League in game-winning RBIs with 22 in 1985.

Year	Club	League	Pos.	G.	AB.	R.	H.	2B.	3B.	HR.	RBI.	B.A.	PO.	A.	E.	F.A.
1984	—Spokane	N'west	OF	67	273	34	63	9	●4	4	43	.231	146	6	9	.944
1985	—Charleston	S. Atl.	★3B-OF	133	501	79	160	32	●9	7	94	.319	72	181	★44	.852
1986	—Beaumont	Texas	OF	121	463	60	123	23	4	11	50	.266	204	●14	10	.956
1987	—Las Vegas	P. C.	OF	121	463	58	127	22	9	12	76	.274	189	14	1	★.995
1987	—San Diego	Nat.	OF	10	16	1	5	1	0	0	1	.313	6	1	0	1.000
1988	—Las Vegas	P. C.	OF	100	360	52	96	24	4	6	55	.267	126	9	2	.985
1988	—San Diego	Nat.	OF	11	10	0	2	1	0	0	0	.200	0	0	0	.000
Major League Totals—2 Years				21	26	1	7	2	0	0	1	.269	6	1	0	1.000

Selected by Toronto Blue Jays' organization in 22nd round of free-agent draft, June 7, 1982.

Selected by Detroit Tigers' organization in secondary phase of free-agent draft, January 11, 1983.

Selected by Boston Red Sox' organization in secondary phase of free-agent draft, June 6, 1983.

Selected by San Diego Padres' organization in secondary phase of free-agent draft, January 17, 1984.

FRANCISCO CABRERA (PAULINO)

Born October 10, 1966, at Santo Domingo, D.R.
Height, 6.04. Weight, 195.
Throws and bats righthanded.

Tied for New York-Pennsylvania League lead in game-winning RBIs with 10 in 1986.

Led Southern League catchers in total chances with 874 and tied for lead in double plays with 6 in 1988.

Led South Atlantic League catchers in total chances with 959 in 1987.

Year	Club	League	Pos.	G.	AB.	R.	H.	2B.	3B.	HR.	RBI.	B.A.	PO.	A.	E.	F.A.
1986	—Ventura County	Calif.	C	6	12	2	2	1	0	0	3	.167	26	3	1	.967
1986	—St. Catherines	NYP	C	68	246	31	73	13	2	6	35	.297	449	50	6	.988
1987	—Myrtle Beach	S. Atl.	C	129	449	61	124	27	1	14	72	.276	★849	89	●21	.978
1988	—Dunedin	Fla. St.	C	9	35	2	14	4	0	1	9	.400	74	9	3	.965
1988	—Knoxville	South.	C	119	429	59	122	19	1	20	54	.284	★783	★68	★230	.974

Signed as free agent by Toronto Blue Jays' organization, February 28, 1986.

GREGORY JAMES CADARET
(Greg)

Born February 27, 1962, at Detroit, Mich.
Height, 6.03. Weight, 205.
Throws and bats lefthanded.
Attended Grand Valley State College, Allendale, Mich.

Major League saves: 1988 (3).

Year	Club	League	G.	IP.	W.	L.	Pct.	H.	R.	ER.	SO.	BB.	ERA.
1983	—Medford	Northwest	12	64	7	3	.700	73	36	31	51	36	4.36
1984	—Modesto	California	26	171⅓	13	8	.619	162	79	58	138	82	3.05
1985	—Huntsville	Southern	17	82⅓	3	7	.300	96	61	56	60	57	6.12
1985	—Modesto	California	12	61⅓	3	9	.250	59	50	40	43	54	5.87

Year Club	League	G.	IP.	W.	L.	Pct.	H.	R.	ER.	SO.	BB.	ERA.
1986—Huntsville	Southern	28	141⅓	12	5	.706	166	106	85	113	98	5.41
1987—Huntsville	Southern	24	40⅓	5	2	.714	31	16	13	48	20	2.90
1987—Tacoma	P. Coast	7	13	1	2	.333	5	6	5	12	13	3.46
1987—Oakland	American	29	39⅔	6	2	.750	37	22	20	30	24	4.54
1988—Oakland	American	58	71⅔	5	2	.714	60	26	23	64	36	2.89
Major League Totals—2 Years		87	111⅓	11	4	.733	97	48	43	94	60	3.48

Selected by Oakland A's organization in 11th round of free-agent draft, June 6, 1983.

CHAMPIONSHIP SERIES RECORD

Year Club	League	G.	IP.	W.	L.	Pct.	H.	R.	ER.	SO.	BB.	ERA.
1988—Oakland	American	1	⅓	0	0	.000	1	1	1	0	0	27.00

WORLD SERIES RECORD

Year Club	League	G.	IP.	W.	L.	Pct.	H.	R.	ER.	SO.	BB.	ERA.
1988—Oakland	American	3	2	0	0	.000	2	0	0	3	0	0.00

IVAN CALDERON (PEREZ)

Name pronounced Call-durh-OWN.

Born March 19, 1962, at Fajardo, Puerto Rico.
Height, 6.01. Weight, 221.
Throws and bats righthanded.

Major League stolen bases: 1984 (1), 1985 (4), 1986 (3), 1987 (10), 1988 (4). Total—22.
Tied for Southern League lead in total bases with 267 in 1983.

Year Club	League	Pos.	G.	AB.	R.	H.	2B.	3B.	HR.	RBI.	B.A.	PO.	A.	E.	F.A.
1980—Bellingham	N'west	OF	57	195	44	62	7	★9	4	32	.318	56	4	7	.896
1981—Wausau	Midw.	OF-SS	117	402	79	123	19	1	20	62	.306	130	17	6	.961
1982—Wausau	Midw.	S-O-3-1	126	461	91	132	22	5	24	89	.286	215	202	45	.903
1983—Chattanooga	South.	OF	139	546	92	●170	34	★15	11	80	★.311	251	10	13	.953
1984—Salt Lake City†	P. C.	OF	66	255	61	93	7	9	4	45	.365	132	9	8	.946
1984—Seattle‡	Amer.	OF	11	24	2	5	1	0	1	1	.208	22	0	0	1.000
1985—Seattle	Amer.	OF-1B	67	210	37	60	16	4	8	28	.286	108	5	2	.983
1986—Sea.§-Chi.	Amer.	OF	50	164	16	41	7	1	2	15	.250	64	4	5	.932
1986—Calgary	P. C.	OF	24	81	17	27	3	0	3	18	.333	34	2	1	.973
1986—Buffalo	A. A.	OF	27	105	11	23	9	0	5	22	.219	30	1	5	.861
1987—Chicago x	Amer.	OF	144	542	93	159	38	2	28	83	.293	295	8	5	.984
1988—Chicago y	Amer.	OF	73	264	40	56	14	0	14	35	.212	141	5	7	.954
Major League Totals—5 Years			345	1204	188	321	76	7	53	162	.267	630	22	19	.972

Signed as free agent by Seattle Mariners' organization, July 30, 1979.
†On disabled list, May 25 to July 2, 1984.
‡On disabled list, August 26 to September 12, 1984.
§Traded to Chicago White Sox' organization, July 1, 1986, completing deal in which Chicago traded Catcher Scott Bradley to Seattle Mariners for a player to be named later, June 26, 1986.
xOn disabled list, May 16 to May 31, 1987.
yOn disabled list, June 27 to July 12 and July 31, 1988 through remainder of season.

JEFFREY WILTON CALHOUN
(Jeff)

Born April 11, 1958, at LaGrange, Ga.
Height, 6.02. Weight, 190.
Throws and bats lefthanded.
Received degree from University of Mississippi, University, Miss. in 1980.

Major League saves: 1985 (4), 1987 (1). Total—5.
Led Florida State League in wild pitches with 17 in 1982.

Year Club	League	G.	IP.	W.	L.	Pct.	H.	R.	ER.	SO.	BB.	ERA.
1980—Sarasota Astros	Gulf Coast	8	50	2	2	.500	38	18	10	41	21	1.80
1981—Daytona Beach†	Florida St.	21	111	6	6	.500	106	55	46	94	71	3.73
1982—Columbus	Southern	7	34⅔	1	3	.250	44	35	22	32	28	5.71
1982—Daytona Beach	Florida St.	21	116⅓	9	6	.600	126	71	60	62	55	4.64
1983—Columbus	Southern	27	151⅓	6	11	.353	157	103	78	93	83	4.64
1984—Columbus	Southern	37	63⅔	4	2	.667	52	21	20	51	26	2.83
1984—Tucson	P. Coast	14	21⅔	1	1	.500	16	4	4	20	12	1.66
1984—Houston	National	9	15⅓	0	1	.000	5	3	2	11	2	1.17
1985—Houston‡	National	44	63⅔	2	5	.286	56	21	18	47	24	2.54
1986—Houston	National	20	26⅔	1	0	1.000	28	16	11	14	12	3.71
1986—Tucson §x	P. Coast	22	39	1	3	.250	29	20	19	28	19	4.38
1987—Maine	Int'national	28	36⅓	1	1	.500	24	5	4	37	11	0.99
1987—Philadelphia y	National	42	42⅔	3	1	.750	25	13	7	31	26	1.48
1988—Philadelphia z	National	3	2⅓	0	0	.000	6	4	4	1	1	15.43
1988—Reading	Eastern	7	12	0	1	.000	6	2	1	8	4	0.75
1988—Maine a	Int'national	38	36⅔	1	1	.500	32	20	19	25	24	4.66
Major League Totals—5 Years		118	150⅔	6	7	.462	120	57	42	104	65	2.51

Selected by California Angels' organization in 28th round of free-agent draft, June 8, 1976.
Selected by Houston Astros' organization in 3rd round of free-agent draft, June 3, 1980.
†On disabled list, May 4 to May 16, 1981.
‡On disabled list, June 7 to June 22, 1985.

§On disabled list, July 21 to August 1, 1986.
xTraded to Philadelphia Phillies' organization for Catcher Ronn Reynolds, April 2, 1987.
yOn disabled list, June 27 to July 23, 1987.
zOn disabled list, April 15 to June 16, 1988; included rehabilitation disability assignment to Reading, May 13 to May 25, 1988, and to Maine, May 26 and June 12 to June 16, 1988.
aGranted free agency, October 15, 1988.

CHAMPIONSHIP SERIES RECORD

Year Club	League	G.	IP.	W.	L.	Pct.	H.	R.	ER.	SO.	BB.	ERA.
1986—Houston	National	1	1	0	0	.000	1	1	1	0	1	9.00

ERNIE CARLOS CAMACHO

Born February 1, 1956, at Salinas, Calif.
Height, 6.01. Weight, 180.
Throws and bats righthanded.
Attended Hartnell Junior College, Salinas, Calif.

Major League saves: 1984 (23), 1986 (20), 1987 (1), 1988 (1). Total—45.

Year Club	League	G.	IP.	W.	L.	Pct.	H.	R.	ER.	SO.	BB.	ERA.
1976—Modesto	California	10	56	3	4	.429	69	47	35	29	39	5.63
1977—Modesto†	California	5	32	2	1	.667	30	19	14	21	23	3.94
1977—Chattanooga	Southern	11	60	3	8	.273	74	50	43	20	28	6.45
1978—Modesto‡	California	1	2	0	0	.000	0	0	0	2	2	0.00
1979—Ogden	P. Coast	21	97	7	9	.438	102	86	71	60	70	6.59
1980—Ogden	P. Coast	33	64	5	3	.625	60	29	28	58	26	3.94
1980—Oakland§	American	5	12	0	0	.000	20	9	9	9	5	6.75
1981—Portland x	P. Coast	18	38	2	3	.400	45	24	20	31	22	4.74
1981—Pittsburgh y	National	7	22	0	1	.000	23	13	12	11	15	4.91
1982—Edmonton zab	P. Coast	7	19⅔	0	0	.000	10	8	7	18	16	3.20
1982—Mexico City Reds	Mexican	15	20⅓	3	1	.750	21	12	12	15	6	5.31
1982—Rochester c	Int'national	8	17⅔	0	1	.000	16	7	4	11	10	2.04
1983—Vancouver d	P. Coast	11	23⅔	0	2	.000	31	21	18	16	12	6.85
1983—Charleston	Int'national	24	33⅓	4	0	1.000	19	5	5	27	17	1.35
1983—Cleveland	American	4	5⅓	0	1	.000	5	3	3	2	2	5.06
1984—Cleveland	American	69	100	5	9	.357	83	31	27	48	37	2.43
1985—Cleveland e	American	2	3⅓	0	1	.000	4	3	3	2	1	8.10
1986—Cleveland f	American	51	57⅓	2	4	.333	60	26	26	36	31	4.08
1987—Cleveland	American	15	13⅔	0	1	.000	21	14	14	9	5	9.22
1987—Buffalo g	Am. Assoc.	23	29⅓	1	3	.250	33	14	6	18	16	1.84
1988—Tucson	P. Coast	36	42⅓	1	5	.167	47	24	20	26	27	4.25
1988—Houston h	National	13	17⅔	0	3	.000	25	15	15	13	12	7.64
American League Totals—6 Years		146	191⅔	7	16	.304	193	86	82	106	81	3.85
National League Totals—2 Years		20	39⅔	0	4	.000	48	28	27	24	27	6.13
Major League Totals—8 Years		166	231⅓	7	20	.259	241	114	109	130	108	4.24

Selected by Pittsburgh Pirates' organization in 12th round of free-agent draft, June 4, 1975.
Selected by California Angels' organization in secondary phase of free-agent draft, January 7, 1976.
Selected by Oakland A's organization in secondary phase of free-agent draft, June 8, 1976.
†On disabled list, April 23 to June 14, 1977.
‡On Jersey City temporary inactive list, April 14 to July 18, 1978; on Modesto temporary inactive list, July 18 to August 30, 1978.
§Traded to Pittsburgh Pirates, April 10, 1981, completing deal in which Pittsburgh traded Pitcher Bob Owchinko to Oakland A's for cash and player to be named later, April 6, 1981.
xOn disabled list, June 23 to July 15, 1981.
yTraded with Infielder Vance Law to Chicago White Sox for Pitchers Ross Baumgarten and Butch Edge, March 21, 1982.
zOn suspended list, April 5 to April 25, 1982.
aLoaned to Mexico City Reds, May 16, 1982; returned, August 2, 1982.
bLoaned to Rochester (Baltimore Orioles' organization), August 5, 1982; returned, September 17, 1982.
cGranted free agency, October 22, 1982; signed by Vancouver (Milwaukee Brewers' organization), December 19, 1982.
dTraded with Outfielder Gorman Thomas and Pitcher Jamie Easterly to Cleveland Indians for Outfielder Rick Manning and Pitcher Rick Waits, June 6, 1983.
eOn disabled list, April 13, 1985 through remainder of season.
fOn disabled list, May 14 to May 29, 1986.
gGranted free agency, October 15, 1987; signed by Houston Astros, March 10, 1988.
hGranted free agency, October 15, 1988.

KENNETH GENE CAMINITI
(Ken)

Born April 21, 1963, at Hanford, Calif.
Height, 6.00. Weight, 200.
Throws right and bats left and righthanded.
Attended San Jose State University, San Jose, Calif.

Led Pacific Coast League third basemen in double plays with 25 and total chances with 382 in 1988.
Led Southern League third basemen in double plays with 34 in 1986.
Named third baseman on THE SPORTING NEWS College Baseball All-America Team, 1984.

Year Club	League	Pos.	G.	AB.	R.	H.	2B.	3B.	HR.	RBI.	B.A.	PO.	A.	E.	F.A.
1985—Osceola	Fla. St.	3B	126	468	83	133	26	9	4	73	.284	53	193	20	.925

Year	Club	League	Pos.	G.	AB.	R.	H.	2B.	3B.	HR.	RBI.	B.A.	PO.	A.	E.	F.A.
1986—	Columbus	South.	3B	137	513	82	154	29	3	12	81	.300	105	*299	33	.924
1987—	Columbus	South.	3B	95	375	66	122	25	2	15	69	.325	55	205	21	.925
1987—	Houston	Nat.	3B	63	203	10	50	7	1	3	23	.246	50	98	8	.949
1988—	Tucson	P. C.	3B	109	416	54	113	24	7	5	66	.272	*105	*250	27	.929
1988—	Houston	Nat.	3B	30	83	5	15	2	0	1	7	.181	12	43	3	.948
Major League Totals—2 Years				93	286	15	65	9	1	4	30	.227	62	141	11	.949

Selected by Houston Astros' organization in 3rd round of free-agent draft, June 4, 1984.

MICHAEL THOMAS CAMPBELL
(Mike)

Born February 17, 1964, at Seattle, Wash.
Height, 6.03. Weight, 210.
Throws and bats righthanded.
Attended University of Hawaii, Honolulu, Haw.

Named Pacific Coast League Player of the Year, 1987.

Year	Club	League	G.	IP.	W.	L.	Pct.	H.	R.	ER.	SO.	BB.	ERA.
1985—	Salinas	California	10	50	4	4	.500	41	22	18	50	22	3.24
1986—	Chattanooga	Southern	12	75	9	1	*.900	69	32	29	80	22	3.48
1986—	Calgary†	P. Coast	1	3	0	1	.000	1	3	3	3	2	9.00
1987—	Calgary	P. Coast	24	162⅔	*15	2	*.882	136	65	48	130	72	2.66
1987—	Seattle	American	9	49⅓	1	4	.200	41	29	26	35	25	4.74
1988—	Seattle	American	20	114⅔	6	10	.375	128	81	75	63	43	5.89
1988—	Calgary	P. Coast	10	70⅓	4	4	.500	80	35	35	38	26	4.48
Major League Totals—2 Years			29	164	7	14	.333	169	110	101	98	68	5.54

Selected by Atlanta Braves' organization in 5th round of free-agent draft, June 7, 1982.
Selected by Seattle Mariners' organization in 1st round (seventh player selected) of free-agent draft, June 3, 1985.
†On disabled list, June 26, 1986 through remainder of season.

SILVESTRE CAMPUSANO
(Sil)

Born December 31, 1966, at Mano Guayabo, D. R.
Height, 6.00. Weight, 175.
Throws and bats righthanded.

Tied for Gulf Coast League lead in stolen bases with 21 in 1984.
Tied for International League lead in caught stealing with 15 in 1987.
Led Southern League outfielders in total chances with 437 and tied for lead in double plays with 6 in 1986.
Led South Atlantic League outfielders in double plays with 5 in 1985.
Named South Atlantic League Most Valuable Player, 1985.

Year	Club	League	Pos.	G.	AB.	R.	H.	2B.	3B.	HR.	RBI.	B.A.	PO.	A.	E.	F.A.
1984—	Bradenton Jays	Appal.	OF	●63	236	42	63	17	2	0	22	.267	128	7	*8	.944
1985—	Florence	S. Atl.	OF	88	348	80	109	31	1	15	56	.313	188	12	4	.980
1985—	Knoxville	South.	OF	45	178	30	54	9	0	6	29	.303	135	3	4	.972
1986—	Knoxville	South.	OF	132	493	89	126	32	6	14	59	.256	*401	21	15	.966
1987—	Syracuse	Int.	OF	129	481	70	127	28	●10	14	63	.264	324	8	*11	.968
1988—	Toronto†	Amer.	OF	73	142	14	31	10	2	2	12	.218	111	2	8	.934
1988—	Syracuse	Int.	OF	17	62	8	13	3	0	0	3	.210	44	0	1	.978
Major League Totals—1 Year				73	142	14	31	10	2	2	12	.218	111	2	8	.934

Signed as free agent by Toronto Blue Jays' organization, November 14, 1983.
†On disabled list, August 4 to September 2, 1988; included rehabilitation disability assignment to Syracuse, August 19 to September 2, 1988.

GEORGE ANTHONY CANALE IV

Born August 11, 1965, at Memphis, Tenn.
Height, 6.01. Weight, 190.
Throws right and bats lefthanded.
Attended Virginia Tech, Blacksburg, Va.

Led Texas League batters in strikeouts with 152 in 1988.
Led Pioneer League in bases on balls received with 54 in 1986.
Led Texas League first basemen in double plays with 106 in 1988.
Led Pioneer League first basemen in double plays with 47 in 1986.
Named first baseman on THE SPORTING NEWS College Baseball All-America Team, 1986.

Year	Club	League	Pos.	G.	AB.	R.	H.	2B.	3B.	HR.	RBI.	B.A.	PO.	A.	E.	F.A.
1986—	Helena	Pion.	1B	65	221	48	72	19	0	9	49	.326	*554	29	6	*.990
1987—	El Paso	Texas	1B	65	253	38	65	10	2	7	36	.257	639	35	3	.996
1987—	Stockton	Calif.	1B	66	246	42	69	18	1	7	48	.280	615	33	4	.994
1988—	El Paso	Texas	1B-3B-OF	132	496	77	120	23	2	23	93	.242	1231	71	12	.991

Selected by Milwaukee Brewers' organization in 6th round of free-agent draft, June 2, 1986.

—DID YOU KNOW—

That Roger Clemens' league-leading eight shutouts in 1988 equaled or exceeded the team totals of the Brewers (8), Tigers (8), Orioles (7) and Yankees (5)?

CASEY TODD CANDAELE

Named pronounced Kan-DELL.
Born January 12, 1961, at Lompoc, Calif.
Height, 5.09. Weight, 165.
Throws right and bats right and lefthanded.
Attended University of Arizona, Tucson, Ariz.
Son of Helen St. Aubin, former professional women's baseball player.

Major League stolen bases: 1986 (3), 1987 (7), 1988 (1). Total—11.
Led American Association in sacrifice hits with 11 in 1986.
Led Florida State League second basemen in assists with 391, double plays with 87 and errors with 30 in 1983.
Tied for American Association lead in double plays by second basemen with 68 in 1986.

Year Club	League	Pos.	G.	AB.	R.	H.	2B.	3B.	HR.	RBI.	B.A.	PO.	A.	E.	F.A.
1983—W. Palm Beach	Fla. St.	2-O-3-S	127	*511	77	156	26	9	0	45	.305	271	403	32	.955
1983—Memphis	South.	3B	5	19	4	4	1	0	0	1	.211	2	11	0	1.000
1984—Jacksonville	South.	S-O-2-3	132	532	68	145	23	2	2	53	.273	224	352	18	.970
1985—Indianapolis	A. A.	O-2-S-3	127	390	55	101	13	5	0	35	.259	266	160	6	.986
1986—Indianapolis	A. A.	2B-OF	119	480	77	145	32	6	2	42	.302	240	319	13	.977
1986—Montreal	Nat.	2B-3B	30	104	9	24	4	1	0	6	.231	45	74	2	.983
1987—Montreal	Nat.	2-O-S-1	138	449	62	122	23	4	1	23	.272	237	176	8	.981
1988—Mon.†-Hou.	Nat.	2B-OF-3B	57	147	11	25	8	1	0	5	.170	79	126	2	.990
1988—Indianapolis	A. A.	SS-2B-OF	60	239	23	63	11	6	2	36	.264	105	161	3	.989
1988—Tucson	P. C.	O-2-S-3	17	66	8	17	3	0	0	5	.258	35	29	3	.955
Major League Totals—3 Years			225	700	82	171	35	6	1	34	.244	361	376	12	.984

Signed as free agent by Montreal Expos' organization, August 15, 1982.
†Traded to Houston Astros for Catcher Mark Bailey, July 23, 1988.

JOHN ROBERT CANDELARIA

Born November 6, 1953, at Brooklyn, N.Y.
Height, 6.06. Weight, 225.
Throws left and bats righthanded.

Pitched 2-0 no-hit victory against Los Angeles Dodgers, August 9, 1976.
Major League saves: 1976 (1), 1978 (1), 1980 (1), 1982 (1), 1984 (2), 1985 (9), 1988 (1). Total—16.
Tied for National League lead in home runs allowed with 29 in 1977.
Led Carolina League in home runs allowed with 17 in 1974.
Named American League Comeback Player of the Year by THE SPORTING NEWS, 1986.
Received reported $40,000 bonus to sign with Pittsburgh Pirates, 1973.

Year Club	League	G.	IP.	W.	L.	Pct.	H.	R.	ER.	SO.	BB.	ERA.
1973—Charleston	W. Carol.	18	95	10	2	*.833	84	45	40	60	38	3.79
1974—Salem	Carolina	25	154	11	8	.579	146	80	63	147	63	3.68
1974—Charleston	Int'national	1	11	0	0	.000	7	2	2	10	1	1.64
1975—Charleston	Int'national	10	61	7	1	.875	53	15	12	48	17	1.77
1975—Pittsburgh	National	18	121	8	6	.571	95	47	37	95	36	2.75
1976—Pittsburgh	National	32	220	16	7	.696	173	87	77	138	60	3.15
1977—Pittsburgh	National	33	231	20	5	*.800	197	64	60	133	52	*2.34
1978—Pittsburgh	National	30	189	12	11	.522	191	73	68	94	49	3.24
1979—Pittsburgh	National	33	207	14	9	.609	201	83	74	101	41	3.22
1980—Pittsburgh	National	35	233	11	14	.440	246	114	104	97	50	4.02
1981—Pittsburgh†	National	6	41	2	2	.500	42	17	16	14	11	3.51
1982—Pittsburgh	National	31	174⅔	12	7	.632	166	62	57	133	37	2.94
1983—Pittsburgh	National	33	197⅔	15	8	.652	191	73	71	157	45	3.23
1984—Pittsburgh	National	33	185⅓	12	11	.522	179	69	56	133	34	2.72
1985—Pittsburgh‡	National	37	54⅓	2	4	.333	57	23	22	47	14	3.64
1985—California	American	13	71	7	3	.700	70	33	30	53	24	3.80
1986—California§	American	16	91⅔	10	2	.833	68	30	26	81	26	2.55
1986—Palm Springs	California	2	7	0	0	.000	4	2	2	8	2	2.57
1987—California xy	American	20	116⅔	8	6	.571	127	70	61	74	20	4.71
1987—New York z	National	3	12⅓	2	0	1.000	17	8	8	10	3	5.84
1988—New York	American	25	157	13	7	.650	150	69	59	121	23	3.38
National League Totals—12 Years		324	1866⅓	126	84	.600	1755	720	650	1152	430	3.13
American League Totals—4 Years		74	436⅓	38	18	.679	415	202	176	329	93	3.63
Major League Totals—14 Years		398	2302⅔	164	102	.617	2170	922	826	1481	523	3.23

Selected by Pittsburgh Pirates' organization in 2nd round of free-agent draft, June 6, 1972.
†On disabled list, May 11, 1981 through remainder of season.
‡Traded with Pitcher Al Holland and Outfielder George Hendrick to California Angels for Pitcher Pat Clements, Outfielder Mike Brown and a player to be named later, August 2, 1985; Pittsburgh Pirates' organization acquired Pitcher Bob Kipper to complete deal, August 16, 1985.
§On disabled list, April 15 to July 8, 1986; included rehabilitation disability assignment to Palm Springs, June 26 to July 2, 1986.
xOn disabled list, May 14 to May 29 and June 19 to August 5, 1987.
yTraded to New York Mets for Pitchers Shane Young and Jeff Richardson, September 15, 1987.
zGranted free agency, November 9, 1987; signed by New York Yankees, January 15, 1988.

CHAMPIONSHIP SERIES RECORD

Established Championship Series record for most strikeouts, three-game Series (14), 1975.
Tied Championship Series records for most strikeouts, game (14), October 7, 1975; most consecutive strikeouts, start of game (4), October 7, 1975.

Year	Club	League	G.	IP.	W.	L.	Pct.	H.	R.	ER.	SO.	BB.	ERA.
1975	—Pittsburgh	National	1	7⅔	0	0	.000	3	3	3	14	2	3.52
1979	—Pittsburgh	National	1	7	0	0	.000	5	2	2	4	1	2.57
1986	—California	American	2	10⅔	1	1	.500	11	8	1	7	6	0.84
Championship Series Totals—3 Years			4	25⅓	1	1	.500	19	13	6	25	9	2.13

WORLD SERIES RECORD

Year	Club	League	G.	IP.	W.	L.	Pct.	H.	R.	ER.	SO.	BB.	ERA.
1979	—Pittsburgh	National	2	9	1	1	.500	14	6	5	4	2	5.00

ALL-STAR GAME RECORD

Member of National League All-Star Team in 1977; did not play.

THOMAS CAESAR CANDIOTTI
(Tom)

Born August 31, 1957, at Walnut Creek, Calif.
Height, 6.02. Weight, 200.
Throws and bats righthanded.
Received bachelor of science degree in business administration from St. Mary's College, Moraga, Calif., in 1979.
Brother-in-law of Brad Wellman, infielder with Kansas City Royals.

Led American League in complete games with 17 in 1986.

Year	Club	League	G.	IP.	W.	L.	Pct.	H.	R.	ER.	SO.	BB.	ERA.
1979	—Victoria†	Northwest	12	70	5	1	.833	63	23	19	66	16	2.44
1980	—Fort Myers	Florida St.	7	44	3	2	.600	32	16	11	31	9	2.25
1980	—Jacksonville‡§	Southern	17	117	7	8	.467	98	45	36	93	40	2.77
1981	—El Paso x	Texas	21	119	7	6	.538	137	51	37	68	27	2.80
1982	—Vancouver y	P. Coast	(Did not play)										
1983	—El Paso	Texas	7	24⅔	1	0	1.000	23	10	8	18	7	2.92
1983	—Vancouver	P. Coast	15	99⅓	6	4	.600	87	35	31	61	16	2.81
1983	—Milwaukee	American	10	55⅔	4	4	.500	62	21	20	21	16	3.23
1984	—Vancouver z	P. Coast	15	96⅔	8	4	.667	96	36	31	53	22	2.89
1984	—Milwaukee a	American	8	32⅓	2	2	.500	38	21	19	23	10	5.29
1984	—Beloit	Midwest	2	10	0	1	.000	12	5	3	12	5	2.70
1985	—El Paso	Texas	4	29⅓	1	0	1.000	29	11	9	16	7	2.76
1985	—Vancouver b	P. Coast	24	150⅔	9	13	.409	178	83	66	97	36	3.94
1986	—Cleveland	American	36	252⅓	16	12	.571	234	112	100	167	106	3.57
1987	—Cleveland	American	32	201⅔	7	18	.280	193	132	107	111	93	4.78
1988	—Cleveland c	American	31	216⅔	14	8	.636	225	86	79	137	53	3.28
Major League Totals—5 Years			117	758⅔	43	44	.494	752	372	325	459	278	3.86

Signed as free-agent by Victoria (Independent), July 17, 1979.
†Released, January 4, 1980; signed by Ft. Myers (Kansas City Royals' organization), January 5, 1980.
‡On disabled list, June 7 to June 26, 1980.
§Drafted by Vancouver (Milwaukee Brewers' organization), December 9, 1980.
xOn disabled list, April 10 to May 12, 1981.
yOn disabled list, April 13, 1982 through remainder of season.
zOn disabled list, May 30 to June 15, 1984.
aOn disabled list, August 2 to September 1, 1984; included rehabilitation disability assignment to Beloit, August 24 to August 31, 1984.
bGranted free agency, October 15, 1985; signed by Cleveland Indians, December 12, 1985.
cOn disabled list, August 4 to August 19, 1988.

JOHN ANTHONY CANGELOSI

Born March 10, 1963, at Brooklyn, N.Y.
Height, 5.08. Weight, 150.
Throws left and bats right and lefthanded.
Attended Miami-Dade Community College (North), Miami, Fla.

Established American League record for most stolen bases by rookie (50), 1986.
Major League stolen bases: 1986 (50), 1987 (21), 1988 (9). Total—80.
Led Eastern League in bases on balls received with 101 in 1984.
Led Midwest League in stolen bases with 87 and caught stealing with 35 in 1983.
Tied for New York-Pennsylvania League lead in bases on balls received with 56 in 1982.

Year	Club	League	Pos.	G.	AB.	R.	H.	2B.	3B.	HR.	RBI.	B.A.	PO.	A.	E.	F.A.
1982	—Niagara Falls	NYP	OF	•76	277	60	80	15	4	5	38	.289	118	5	4	.969
1983	—Appleton	Midw.	OF	128	439	87	124	12	4	1	48	.282	262	10	6	.978
1984	—Glens Falls†	East.	OF	138	464	91	133	17	1	1	38	.287	310	11	11	.967
1985	—Mex. City Reds	Mex.	OF	61	201	46	71	9	4	1	30	.353	127	7	6	.957
1985	—Chicago	Amer.	OF	5	2	2	0	0	0	0	0	.000	1	0	0	1.000
1985	—Buffalo	A. A.	OF	78	244	34	58	8	5	1	21	.238	148	9	2	.987
1986	—Chicago‡	Amer.	OF	137	438	65	103	16	3	2	32	.235	276	7	9	.969
1987	—Pittsburgh	Nat.	OF	104	182	44	50	8	3	4	18	.275	74	3	3	.962
1988	—Pittsburgh§	Nat.	OF-P	75	118	18	30	4	1	0	8	.254	52	0	2	.963
1988	—Buffalo	A. A.	OF	37	145	23	48	6	0	0	10	.331	89	3	0	1.000
American League Totals—2 Years				142	440	67	103	16	3	2	32	.234	277	7	9	.969
National League Totals—2 Years				179	300	62	80	12	4	4	26	.267	126	3	5	.963
Major League Totals—4 Years				321	740	129	183	28	7	6	58	.247	403	10	14	.967

Selected by Chicago White Sox' organization in 4th round of free-agent draft, January 12, 1982.

†Loaned with Infielder Manny Salinas to Mexico City Reds, March 4, 1985, as part of deal in which Infielder Nelson Barrera was purchased by Chicago White Sox; returned, June 1, 1985.

‡Traded to Pittsburgh Pirates, March 30, 1987, completing deal in which Pittsburgh traded Pitcher Jim Winn to Chicago White Sox for a player to be named later, March 27, 1987.

§On disabled list, June 6 to June 27, 1988; included rehabilitation disability assignment to Buffalo, June 20 to June 27, 1988.

PITCHING RECORD

Year Club	League	G.	IP.	W.	L.	Pct.	H.	R.	ER.	SO.	BB.	ERA.
1988—Pittsburgh	National	1	2	0	0	.000	1	0	0	0	0	0.00

JOSE CANSECO JR.

Name pronounced CON-seko.

Born July 2, 1964, at Havana, Cuba.
Height, 6.03. Weight, 230.
Throws and bats righthanded.
Identical twin of Ozzie Canseco, outfielder in Oakland Athletics' organization.

Major League stolen bases: 1985 (1), 1986 (15), 1987 (15), 1988 (40). Total—71.
Hit three home runs in a game, July 3, 1988.
Led American League in slugging percentage with .569 in 1988.
Led Northwest League batters in strikeouts with 78 in 1983.
Led California League outfielders in double plays with 8 in 1984.
Named American League Player of the Year by THE SPORTING NEWS, 1988.
Named American League Most Valuable Player by Baseball Writers' Association of America, 1988.
Named outfielder on THE SPORTING NEWS American League All-Star Team, 1988.
Named outfielder on THE SPORTING NEWS American League Silver Slugger team, 1988.
Named American League Rookie Player of the Year by THE SPORTING NEWS, 1986.
Named American League Rookie of the Year by Baseball Writers' Association of America, 1986.
Named Minor League Player of the Year by THE SPORTING NEWS, 1985.
Named Southern League Most Valuable Player, 1985.

Year Club	League	Pos.	G.	AB.	R.	H.	2B.	3B.	HR.	RBI.	B.A.	PO.	A.	E.	F.A.
1982—Miami	Fla. St.	3B	6	9	0	1	0	0	0	0	.111	3	1	1	.800
1982—Idaho Falls	Pion.	3B-OF	28	57	13	15	3	0	2	7	.263	6	17	3	.885
1983—Madison	Midw.	OF	34	88	8	14	4	0	3	10	.159	23	2	1	.962
1983—Medford	N'west	OF	59	197	34	53	15	2	11	40	.269	46	5	5	.911
1984—Modesto	Calif.	OF	116	410	61	113	21	2	15	73	.276	216	17	9	.963
1985—Huntsville†	South.	OF	58	211	47	67	10	2	25	80	.318	117	9	7	.947
1985—Tacoma	P.C.	OF	60	233	41	81	16	1	11	47	.348	81	7	2	.978
1985—Oakland	Amer.	OF	29	96	16	29	3	0	5	13	.302	56	2	3	.951
1986—Oakland	Amer.	OF	157	600	85	144	29	1	33	117	.240	319	4	•14	.958
1987—Oakland	Amer.	OF	159	630	81	162	35	3	31	113	.257	263	12	7	.975
1988—Oakland	Amer.	OF	158	610	120	187	34	0	*42	*124	.307	304	11	7	.978
Major League Totals—4 Years			503	1936	302	522	101	4	111	367	.270	942	29	31	.969

Selected by Oakland A's organization in 15th round of free-agent draft, June 7, 1982.
†On disabled list, May 14 to June 3, 1985.

CHAMPIONSHIP SERIES RECORD

Tied American League Championship Series record for most home runs, four-game Series (3), 1988.

Year Club	League	Pos.	G.	AB.	R.	H.	2B.	3B.	HR.	RBI.	B.A.	PO.	A.	E.	F.A.
1988—Oakland	Amer.	OF	4	16	4	5	1	0	3	4	.313	6	0	0	1.000

WORLD SERIES RECORD

Tied World Series records for hitting home run in first Series at-bat, October 15 (second inning); most grand slams, game (1), October 15, 1988; most runs batted in, inning (4), October 15, 1988 (second inning); batting in all club's runs, game, most (4), October 15, 1988.

Year Club	League	Pos.	G.	AB.	R.	H.	2B.	3B.	HR.	RBI.	B.A.	PO.	A.	E.	F.A.
1988—Oakland	Amer.	OF	5	19	1	1	0	0	1	5	.053	8	0	0	1.000

ALL-STAR GAME RECORD

Year League	Pos.	AB.	R.	H.	2B.	3B.	HR.	RBI.	B.A.	PO.	A.	E.	F.A.
1988—American	OF	4	0	0	0	0	0	0	.000	3	0	0	1.000

Member of American League All-Star Team in 1986; did not play.

MICHAEL LEE CAPEL
(Mike)

Born October 13, 1961, at Marshall, Tex.
Height, 6.02. Weight, 175.
Throws and bats righthanded.
Attended University of Texas, Austin, Tex.

Led American Association in intentional bases on balls issued with 11 in 1987.

Year Club	League	G.	IP.	W.	L.	Pct.	H.	R.	ER.	SO.	BB.	ERA.
1983—Midland	Texas	3	14⅓	1	1	.500	22	12	11	8	8	6.91
1983—Quad Cities	Midwest	8	44⅔	3	2	.600	32	15	12	35	14	2.42
1984—Midland	Texas	16	61⅓	1	10	.091	69	53	43	20	37	6.31
1984—Lodi	California	20	69	0	7	.000	54	38	28	46	35	3.65

Year	Club	League	G.	IP.	W.	L.	Pct.	H.	R.	ER.	SO.	BB.	ERA.
1985—	Pittsfield	Eastern	33	73⅓	3	6	.333	74	44	40	53	47	4.91
1986—	Pittsfield†	Eastern	38	62⅔	4	4	.500	51	20	13	50	22	1.87
1987—	Iowa	Am. Assoc.	53	108⅓	7	10	.412	117	72	69	75	43	5.73
1988—	Iowa	Am. Assoc.	32	57⅔	3	2	.600	60	24	22	49	23	3.43
1988—	Chicago	National	22	29⅓	2	1	.667	34	19	16	19	13	4.91
	Major League Totals—1 Year		22	29⅓	2	1	.667	34	19	16	19	13	4.91

Selected by Philadelphia Phillies' organization in 24th round of free-agent draft, June 3, 1980.
Selected by Chicago Cubs' organization in 13th round of free-agent draft, June 6, 1983.
†On disabled list, May 26 to June 16, 1986.

NICK LEE CAPRA

Born March 8, 1958, at Denver, Colo.
Height, 5.08. Weight, 165.
Throws and bats righthanded.
Attended Blinn College, Brenham, Tex., Lamar Community College, Lamar, Colo. and University of Oklahoma, Norman, Okla.

Major League stolen bases: 1982 (2), 1988 (1). Total—3.
Led Texas League in stolen bases with 55 and tied for lead in game-winning RBIs with 13 in 1980.
Led American Association outfielders in total chances with 330 in 1983.
Named second baseman on THE SPORTING NEWS College Baseball All-America Team 1979.

Year	Club	League	Pos.	G.	AB.	R.	H.	2B.	3B.	HR.	RBI.	B.A.	PO.	A.	E.	F.A.
1979—	Tulsa†	Texas	3B-2B-SS	66	212	29	59	7	0	3	26	.278	60	173	22	.914
1980—	Tulsa	Texas	2B-OF-SS	117	440	90	127	25	9	6	53	.289	288	303	19	.969
1981—	Wichita	A. A.	OF	123	398	74	104	16	4	4	38	.261	226	6	7	.971
1982—	Denver	A. A.	OF	121	416	82	117	15	10	9	40	.281	275	11	3	.990
1982—	Texas	Amer.	OF	13	15	2	4	0	0	1	1	.267	14	2	0	1.000
1983—	Oklahoma City	A. A.	OF	124	441	84	113	17	4	13	41	.256	*307	12	11	.967
1983—	Texas	Amer.	OF	8	2	2	0	0	0	0	0	.000	0	0	0	.000
1984—	Oklahoma City‡	A. A.	OF-2B	123	442	68	113	18	1	2	21	.256	329	13	4	.988
1985—	Oklahoma City	A. A.	OF-2B	97	353	53	96	17	1	0	27	.272	201	70	2	.993
1985—	Texas§	Amer.	OF	8	8	1	1	0	0	0	0	.125	11	0	0	1.000
1986—	Buf.x-Ok. City y	A. A.	OF-2B	108	406	68	105	18	2	7	31	.259	231	58	6	.980
1987—	Oklahoma City z	A. A.	OF	97	353	69	107	18	3	1	39	.303	250	11	2	.992
1988—	Omaha	A. A.	OF	93	346	53	100	11	6	1	43	.289	169	10	4	.978
1988—	Kansas City a	Amer.	OF	14	29	3	4	1	0	0	0	.138	15	0	0	1.000
	Major League Totals—4 Years			43	54	8	9	1	0	1	1	.167	40	2	0	1.000

Selected by Montreal Expos' organization in 12th round of free-agent draft, June 8, 1976.
Selected by Texas Rangers' organization in 3rd round of free-agent draft, June 5, 1979.
†On disabled list, July 4 to July 19, 1979.
‡On disabled list, May 14 to June 1, 1984.
§Granted free agency, October 15, 1985; signed by Chicago White Sox' organization, January 18, 1986.
xLoaned to Oklahoma City (Texas Rangers' organization), June 17, 1986; returned, September 2, 1986.
yGranted free agency, October 15, 1986; signed by Oklahoma City (Texas Rangers' organization), January 10, 1987.
zGranted free agency, October 15, 1987; signed by Omaha (Kansas City Royals' organization), December 18, 1987.
aGranted free agency, October 15, 1988.

STEVEN NORMAN CARLTON
(Steve)

Born December 22, 1944, at Miami, Fla.
Height, 6.05. Weight, 210.
Throws and bats lefthanded.
Attended Miami-Dade Community College, Miami, Fla.

Established major league records for most consecutive starting assignments, lifetime (544); most strikeouts, game by lefthanded pitcher and losing pitcher (19), September 15, 1969; most balks, season (11), 1979.

Established National League records for most years and most consecutive years pitched (22); most games started, lifetime (677); most consecutive starting assignments, lifetime (534); most years, 100 or more strikeouts (18); most consecutive years, 100 or more strikeouts (18); most strikeouts, lifetime (4,000); most bases on balls issued, lifetime (1,717).

Tied National League record for most strikeouts, game (19), September 15, 1969.

Tied modern National League record for most games won, season, by lefthander (27), 1972.

Major League saves: 1987 (1).

Led National League pitchers in games started with 41 in 1972, 38 in 1982 and tied for lead with 40 in 1973 and 38 in 1980.

Led National League in shutouts with 6 in 1982.

Led National League in complete games with 30 in 1972, 19 in 1982 and tied for lead with 18 in 1973.

Led National League in balks with 7 in 1977, 11 in 1979, 7 in 1980 and 9 in 1982 and 1983 and tied for lead with 7 in 1975, 1978 and 1984.

Led National League in wild pitches with 17 in 1980.

Led National League in home runs allowed with 30 in 1978.

Won National League Cy Young Memorial Award, 1972, 1977, 1980 and 1982.

Named National League Pitcher of the Year by THE SPORTING NEWS, 1972, 1977, 1980 and 1982.

Named lefthanded pitcher on THE SPORTING NEWS National League All-Star Team, 1969, 1971, 1972, 1977, 1979, 1980 and 1982.

Named pitcher on THE SPORTING NEWS National League All-Star fielding team, 1981.

Year	Club	League	G.	IP.	W.	L.	Pct.	H.	R.	ER.	SO.	BB.	ERA.
1964—	Rock Hill	W. Carol.	11	79	10	1	.909	39	17	9	91	36	1.03
1964—	Winnipeg	Northern	12	75	4	4	.500	63	40	28	79	48	3.36

Year Club	League	G.	IP.	W.	L.	Pct.	H.	R.	ER.	SO.	BB.	ERA.
1964—Tulsa	Texas	4	24	1	1	.500	16	13	7	21	18	2.63
1965—St. Louis	National	15	25	0	0	.000	27	7	7	21	8	2.52
1966—Tulsa	P. Coast	19	128	9	5	.643	110	65	51	108	54	3.59
1966—St. Louis	National	9	52	3	3	.500	56	22	18	25	18	3.12
1967—St. Louis	National	30	193	14	9	.609	173	71	64	168	62	2.98
1968—St. Louis	National	34	232	13	11	.542	214	87	77	162	61	2.99
1969—St. Louis	National	31	236	17	11	.607	185	66	57	210	93	2.17
1970—St. Louis	National	34	254	10	*19	.345	239	123	105	193	109	3.72
1971—St. Louis†	National	37	273	20	9	.690	275	120	108	172	98	3.56
1972—Philadelphia	National	41	*346	*27	10	.730	*257	84	76	*310	87	*1.98
1973—Philadelphia	National	40	•293	13	*20	.394	*293	*146	*127	223	113	3.90
1974—Philadelphia	National	39	291	16	13	.552	249	118	104	*240	*136	3.22
1975—Philadelphia	National	37	255	15	14	.517	217	116	101	192	104	3.56
1976—Philadelphia	National	35	253	20	7	*.741	224	94	88	195	72	3.13
1977—Philadelphia	National	36	283	*23	10	.697	229	99	83	198	89	2.64
1978—Philadelphia	National	34	247	16	13	.552	228	91	78	161	63	2.84
1979—Philadelphia	National	35	251	18	11	.621	202	112	101	213	89	3.62
1980—Philadelphia	National	38	*304	*24	9	.727	243	87	79	*286	90	2.34
1981—Philadelphia	National	24	190	13	4	.765	152	59	51	179	62	2.42
1982—Philadelphia	National	38	*295⅔	*23	11	.676	*253	114	102	*286	86	3.10
1983—Philadelphia	National	37	*283⅔	15	16	.484	*277	117	98	*275	84	3.11
1984—Philadelphia	National	33	229	13	7	.650	214	104	91	163	79	3.58
1985—Philadelphia‡	National	16	92	1	8	.111	84	43	34	48	53	3.33
1986—Philadelphia§-San Francisco x	National	22	113	5	11	.313	138	90	74	80	61	5.89
1986—Chicago y	American	10	63⅓	4	3	.571	58	30	26	40	25	3.69
1987—Cleveland z-Minnesota a	American	32	152	6	14	.300	165	111	97	91	86	5.74
1988—Minnesota b	American	4	9⅔	0	1	.000	20	19	18	5	5	16.76
National League Totals—22 Years		695	4991⅓	319	226	.585	4429	1970	1723	4000	1717	3.11
American League Totals—3 Years		46	225	10	18	.357	243	160	141	136	116	5.64
Major League Totals—24 Years		741	5216⅓	329	244	.574	4672	2130	1864	4136	1833	3.22

Signed as free agent by St. Louis Cardinals' organization, October 8, 1963.
†Traded to Philadelphia Phillies for Pitcher Rick Wise, February 25, 1972.
‡On disabled list, June 21 to September 2, 1985.
§Released, June 24, 1986; signed by San Francisco Giants, July 4, 1986.
xReleased, August 7, 1986; signed by Chicago White Sox, August 12, 1986.
yGranted free agency, November 12, 1986; signed by Cleveland Indians, April 4, 1987.
zTraded to Minnesota Twins for a player to be named later, July 31, 1987; Cleveland Indians' organization acquired Pitcher Jeff Perry to complete deal, August 18, 1987.
aReleased, December 21, 1987; re-signed by Twins, January 29, 1988.
bReleased, April 28, 1988.

DIVISION SERIES RECORD

Year Club	League	G.	IP.	W.	L.	Pct.	H.	R.	ER.	SO.	BB.	ERA.
1981—Philadelphia	National	2	14	0	2	.000	14	6	6	13	8	3.86

CHAMPIONSHIP SERIES RECORD

Established Championship Series record for most bases on balls, total Series (28).

Tied Championship Series records for most games won, total Series (4); most games won, Series (2); most home runs hit by pitcher, total Series (1); most bases on balls, four-game Series (8), 1977; most bases on balls, five-game series (8), 1980.

Established National League Championship Series records for most strikeouts, total Series (39); most games started, total Series (8); most innings pitched, total Series (53⅔); most hits allowed, total Series (53); most earned runs allowed, total Series (21).

Tied National League Championship Series records for most strikeouts, four-game Series (13), 1983; most bases on balls, three-game Series (5), 1976.

Year Club	League	G.	IP.	W.	L.	Pct.	H.	R.	ER.	SO.	BB.	ERA.
1976—Philadelphia	National	1	7	0	1	.000	8	5	4	6	5	5.14
1977—Philadelphia	National	2	11⅔	0	1	.000	13	9	9	6	8	6.94
1978—Philadelphia	National	1	9	1	0	1.000	8	4	4	8	2	4.00
1980—Philadelphia	National	2	12⅓	1	0	1.000	11	3	3	6	8	2.19
1983—Philadelphia	National	2	13⅔	2	0	1.000	13	1	1	13	5	0.66
Championship Series Totals—5 Years		8	53⅔	4	2	.667	53	22	21	39	28	3.52

WORLD SERIES RECORD

Tied World Series record for most games won, losing none, six-game Series (2), 1980.

Year Club	League	G.	IP.	W.	L.	Pct.	H.	R.	ER.	SO.	BB.	ERA.
1967—St. Louis	National	1	6	0	1	.000	3	1	0	5	2	0.00
1968—St. Louis	National	2	4	0	0	.000	7	3	3	3	1	6.75
1980—Philadelphia	National	2	15	2	0	1.000	14	5	4	17	9	2.40
1983—Philadelphia	National	1	6⅔	0	1	.000	5	3	2	7	3	2.70
World Series Totals—4 Years		6	31⅔	2	2	.500	29	12	9	32	15	2.56

ALL-STAR GAME RECORD

Year League	IP.	W.	L.	Pct.	H.	R.	ER.	SO.	BB.	ERA.
1968—National	1	0	0	.000	0	0	0	1	0	0.00
1969—National	3	1	0	1.000	2	2	2	2	1	6.00
1972—National	1	0	0	.000	0	0	0	0	1	0.00
1979—National	1	0	0	.000	2	3	3	0	1	27.00
1982—National	2	0	0	.000	1	0	0	4	2	0.00
All-Star Game Totals—5 Years	8	1	0	1.000	5	5	5	7	5	5.63

Member of National League All-Star Team in 1971, 1974, 1977, 1980 and 1981; did not play.

DONALD WAYNE CARMAN
(Don)

Born August 14, 1959, at Oklahoma City, Okla.
Height, 6.03. Weight, 195.
Throws and bats lefthanded.
Attended Seminole Junior College, Seminole, Okla.,
and University of Oklahoma, Norman, Okla.

Major League saves: 1983 (1), 1985 (7), 1986 (1). Total—9.

Year Club	League	G.	IP.	W.	L.	Pct.	H.	R.	ER.	SO.	BB.	ERA.
1979—Spartanburg	W. Carol.	37	78	6	3	.667	72	36	34	70	28	3.92
1980—Peninsula	Carolina	27	150	14	5	.737	149	73	57	*141	53	3.42
1981—Reading	Eastern	28	176	12	13	.480	167	93	79	105	75	4.04
1982—Oklahoma City	Am. Assoc.	10	33	0	1	.000	37	29	25	29	23	6.82
1982—Reading	Eastern	20	97⅓	6	7	.462	99	58	45	81	62	4.16
1983—Reading	Eastern	*56	124⅓	8	5	.615	85	51	41	93	71	2.97
1983—Philadelphia	National	1	1	0	0	.000	0	0	0	0	0	0.00
1984—Portland	P. Coast	39	55⅔	3	3	.500	66	36	33	53	22	5.34
1984—Philadelphia	National	11	13⅓	0	1	.000	14	9	8	16	6	5.40
1985—Philadelphia	National	71	86⅓	9	4	.692	52	25	20	87	38	2.08
1986—Philadelphia	National	50	134⅓	10	5	.667	113	50	48	98	52	3.22
1987—Philadelphia	National	35	211	13	11	.542	194	110	99	125	69	4.22
1988—Philadelphia	National	36	201⅓	10	14	.417	211	101	96	116	70	4.29
Major League Totals—6 Years		204	647⅓	42	35	.545	584	295	271	442	235	3.77

Signed as free agent by Philadelphia Phillies' organization, August 25, 1978.

CRIS HOWELL CARPENTER

Born April 5, 1965, at St. Augustine, Fla.
Height, 6.01. Weight, 185.
Throws and bats righthanded.
Attended University of Georgia, Athens, Ga.

Received reported $160,000 bonus to sign with St. Louis Cardinals, 1987.

Year Club	League	G.	IP.	W.	L.	Pct.	H.	R.	ER.	SO.	BB.	ERA.
1988—Louisville	Am. Assoc.	13	87⅔	6	2	.750	81	28	28	45	26	2.87
1988—St. Louis	National	8	47⅔	2	3	.600	56	27	25	24	9	4.72
Major League Totals—1 Year		8	47⅔	2	3	.600	56	27	25	24	9	4.72

Selected by Toronto Blue Jays' organization in 7th round of free-agent draft, June 2, 1986.
Selected by St. Louis Cardinals' organization in 1st round (14th player selected) of free-agent draft, June 2, 1987.

MARK STEVEN CARREON

Born July 19, 1963, at Chicago, Ill.
Height, 6.00. Weight, 194.
Throws left and bats righthanded.
Son of Camilo Carreon, catcher with Chicago White Sox,
Cleveland Indians and Baltimore Orioles, 1959 through 1966.

Led International League in game-winning RBIs with 19 in 1987 and tied for lead with 11 in 1988.
Led Carolina League in sacrifice flies with 11 in 1983.
Tied for South Atlantic League lead in game-winning RBIs with 12 in 1982.

Year Club	League	Pos.	G.	AB.	R.	H.	2B.	3B.	HR.	RBI.	B.A.	PO.	A.	E.	F.A.
1981—Kingsport	Appal.	OF-C	64	232	30	67	8	0	1	36	.289	101	7	4	.964
1982—Shelby	S. Atl.	OF	133	486	*120	160	29	6	2	79	.329	183	8	5	.974
1983—Lynchburg	Carol.	OF	128	491	94	164	13	8	1	67	.334	173	8	14	.928
1984—Jackson	Texas	OF	119	435	64	122	14	3	1	43	.280	146	1	4	.974
1985—Tidewater	Int.	OF	7	15	1	2	1	0	1	2	.133	2	0	0	1.000
1985—Jackson	Texas	OF	123	447	96	140	23	5	6	51	.313	201	8	1	.995
1986—Tidewater	Int.	OF	115	426	62	123	23	2	10	64	.289	192	6	6	.971
1987—Tidewater	Int.	OF	133	525	83	164	*41	5	10	89	.312	237	8	5	.980
1987—New York	Nat.	OF	9	12	0	3	0	0	0	1	.250	4	0	1	.800
1988—Tidewater	Int.	OF	102	365	48	96	13	3	14	55	.263	111	6	2	.983
1988—New York	Nat.	OF	7	9	5	5	2	0	1	1	.556	1	0	0	1.000
Major League Totals—2 Years			16	21	5	8	2	0	1	2	.381	5	0	1	.833

Selected by New York Mets' organization in 8th round of free-agent draft, June 8, 1981.

MATIAS CARRILLO (GARCIA)

Born February 2, 1964, at Los Mochis Sinaloa, Mexico.
Height, 5.11. Weight, 185.
Throws and bats lefthanded.

Led Mexican League in stolen bases with 30 and tied for lead in intentional bases on balls received with 16 in 1984.
Tied for Mexican League lead in double plays by outfielders with 4 in 1985.

Year Club	League	Pos.	G.	AB.	R.	H.	2B.	3B.	HR.	RBI.	B.A.	PO.	A.	E.	F.A.
1982—Poza Rica	Mex.	OF-1B	99	301	59	93	9	5	0	29	.309	150	13	6	.964
1983—Poza Rica	Mex.	OF	91	360	54	112	13	11	6	39	.311	128	12	1	.993
1984—Mex. City Tigers	Mex.	OF	113	442	100	154	32	6	14	76	.348	281	13	12	.961
1985—Mex. City Tigers†	Mex.	OF	126	465	114	164	21	8	20	102	.353	320	13	10	.971
1986—Nashua‡	East.	OF	15	52	3	8	1	0	0	0	.154	28	0	0	1.000
1986—Mex. City Tigers	Mex.	OF	60	216	39	70	15	5	11	64	.324	123	6	1	.992

Year	Club	League	Pos.	G.	AB.	R.	H.	2B.	3B.	HR.	RBI.	B.A.	PO.	A.	E.	F.A.
1987	—Salem§x	Carol.	OF	90	284	42	77	11	3	8	37	.271	55	3	3	.951
1988	—El Paso	Texas	OF	106	396	76	118	17	2	12	55	.298	232	★18	2	★.992

†Sold to Hawaii (Pittsburgh Pirates' organization), December 15, 1985.
‡Loaned to Mexico City Tigers of Mexican League, May 8, 1986; returned, September, 1986.
§On suspended list, May 15 to May 29, 1988.
xDrafted by Milwaukee Brewers' organization, December 8, 1987.

GARY EDMUND CARTER

Born April 8, 1954, at Culver City, Calif.
Height, 6.02. Weight, 210.
Throws and bats righthanded.
Brother of Gordon Carter, outfielder in San Francisco Giants' organization, 1972 and 1973.

Established major league records for most putouts, catcher, lifetime (10,360); most chances accepted, catcher, lifetime (11,404); fewest passed balls, season, 150 or more games (1), 1978.

Tied major league records for most home runs, two consecutive games (5), September 3 and 4, 1985; most years leading league in chances accepted, catcher (8).

Established National League records for most seasons leading league in games by catcher (6); most years leading league in putouts by catcher (8); most years leading league in chances accepted by catcher (7); most putouts (9,563) and chances accepted (10,553) by catcher, lifetime.

Major League stolen bases: 1974 (2), 1975 (5), 1977 (5), 1978 (10), 1979 (3), 1980 (3), 1981 (1), 1982 (2), 1983 (1), 1984 (2), 1985 (1), 1986 (1). Total—36.

Hit three home runs in a game, April 20, 1977 and September 3, 1985.

Led National League in sacrifice flies with 15 and tied for lead in game-winning RBIs with 16 and grounding into double plays with 21 in 1986.

Led National League catchers in assists with 107 in 1983.

Led National League catchers in total chances with 921 in 1977, 874 in 1978, 848 in 1979, 937 in 1980, 571 in 1981, 1,068 in 1982 and 860 in 1988.

Led National League in passed balls with 12 in 1979.

Led National League catchers in putouts with 811 in 1977, 781 in 1978, 509 in 1981, 956 in 1985 and 797 in 1988.

Led National League catchers in double plays with 14 in 1977, 9 in 1978, 12 in 1979, 14 in 1983 and 13 in 1987.

Led International League catchers in putouts with 794, assists with 65, double plays with 15 and fielding percentage with .990 in 1974.

Named National League Rookie Player of the Year by THE SPORTING NEWS, 1975.

Named catcher on THE SPORTING NEWS National League All-Star Team, 1980 through 1982 and 1984 through 1986.

Named catcher on THE SPORTING NEWS National League All-Star fielding team, 1980 through 1982.

Named catcher on THE SPORTING NEWS National League Silver Slugger team, 1981, 1982 and 1984 through 1986.

Year	Club	League	Pos.	G.	AB.	R.	H.	2B.	3B.	HR.	RBI.	B.A.	PO.	A.	E.	F.A.
1972	—Cocoa Expos	Fla.E.C.	C-1B-3B	18	71	6	17	3	0	2	9	.239	111	12	10	.925
1972	—W. Palm Beach	Fla. St.	C	20	50	9	16	2	2	0	5	.320	84	12	2	.980
1973	—Quebec City	East.	C-1B-OF	130	439	65	111	16	1	15	68	.253	823	75	20	.978
1973	—Peninsula	Int.	C	8	25	2	7	2	0	0	1	.280	5	1	0	1.000
1974	—Memphis	Int.	C-1B-3B	135	441	62	118	14	7	23	83	.268	908	76	12	.988
1974	—Montreal	Nat.	C-OF	9	27	5	11	0	1	1	6	.407	28	4	0	1.000
1975	—Montreal	Nat.	OF-C-3B	144	503	58	136	20	1	17	68	.270	430	38	9	.981
1976	—Montreal†	Nat.	C-OF	91	311	31	68	8	1	6	38	.219	364	42	2	.995
1977	—Montreal	Nat.	★C-OF	154	522	86	148	29	2	31	84	.284	813	★101	9	.990
1978	—Montreal	Nat.	C-1B	157	533	76	136	27	1	20	72	.255	787	83	10	.989
1979	—Montreal	Nat.	C	141	505	74	143	26	5	22	75	.283	★751	★88	9	.989
1980	—Montreal	Nat.	C	154	549	76	145	25	5	29	101	.264	★822	★108	7	★.993
1981	—Montreal	Nat.	C-1B	100	374	48	94	20	2	16	68	.251	515	58	4	.993
1982	—Montreal	Nat.	C	154	557	91	163	32	1	29	97	.293	★954	★104	10	.991
1983	—Montreal	Nat.	★C-1B	145	541	63	146	37	3	17	79	.270	855	108	5	★.995
1984	—Montreal‡	Nat.	C-1B	159	596	75	175	32	1	27	●106	.294	990	78	7	.993
1985	—New York	Nat.	C-1B-OF	149	555	83	156	17	1	32	100	.281	987	70	8	.992
1986	—New York§	Nat.	C-1-O-3	132	490	81	125	14	2	24	105	.255	943	70	9	.991
1987	—New York	Nat.	C-1B-OF	139	523	55	123	18	2	20	83	.235	886	70	9	.991
1988	—New York	Nat.	C-1B-3B	130	455	39	110	16	2	11	46	.242	842	58	10	.989
Major League Totals—15 Years				1958	7041	941	1879	321	30	302	1128	.267	10967	1080	108	.991

Selected by Montreal Expos' organization in 3rd round of free-agent draft, June 6, 1972.
†On disabled list, June 6 to July 22, 1976.
‡Traded to New York Mets for Infielder Hubie Brooks, Catcher Mike Fitzgerald, Outfielder Herm Winningham and Pitcher Floyd Youmans, December 10, 1984.
§On disabled list, August 17 to September 1, 1986.

DIVISION SERIES RECORD

Year	Club	League	Pos.	G.	AB.	R.	H.	2B.	3B.	HR.	RBI.	B.A.	PO.	A.	E.	F.A.
1981	—Montreal	Nat.	C	5	19	3	8	3	0	2	6	.421	21	5	0	1.000

CHAMPIONSHIP SERIES RECORD

Tied National League Championship Series record for most at-bats, six-game Series (27), 1986.

Year	Club	League	Pos.	G.	AB.	R.	H.	2B.	3B.	HR.	RBI.	B.A.	PO.	A.	E.	F.A.
1981	—Montreal	Nat.	C	5	16	3	7	1	0	0	0	.438	27	3	0	1.000
1986	—New York	Nat.	C	6	27	1	4	1	0	0	2	.148	42	5	0	1.000
1988	—New York	Nat.	C	7	27	0	6	1	1	0	4	.222	58	1	0	1.000
Championship Series Totals—3 Years				18	70	4	17	3	1	0	6	.243	127	9	0	1.000

WORLD SERIES RECORD

Year	Club	League	Pos.	G.	AB.	R.	H.	2B.	3B.	HR.	RBI.	B.A.	PO.	A.	E.	F.A.
1986	New York	Nat.	C	7	29	4	8	2	0	2	9	.276	57	1	0	1.000

ALL-STAR GAME RECORD

Tied All-Star Game record for most home runs, game (2), August 9, 1981.

Year	League	Pos.	AB.	R.	H.	2B.	3B.	HR.	RBI.	B.A.	PO.	A.	E.	F.A.
1975	National	OF	0	0	0	0	0	0	0	.000	1	0	0	1.000
1979	National	C	2	0	1	0	0	0	1	.500	6	1	0	1.000
1980	National	C	1	0	0	0	0	0	0	.000	1	0	0	1.000
1981	National	C	3	2	2	0	0	2	2	.667	5	1	0	1.000
1982	National	C	3	0	1	0	0	0	1	.333	7	0	0	1.000
1983	National	C	2	0	0	0	0	0	0	.000	3	0	0	1.000
1984	National	C	2	1	1	0	0	1	1	.500	9	0	0	1.000
1986	National	C	3	0	0	0	0	0	0	.000	9	0	0	1.000
1987	National	C	1	0	0	0	0	0	0	.000	1	0	0	1.000
1988	National	C	3	0	1	0	0	0	0	.333	3	0	0	1.000
All-Star Game Totals—10 Years			20	3	6	0	0	3	5	.300	45	2	0	1.000

Named to National League All-Star Team for 1985 game; replaced due to injury by Terry Kennedy.

JOSEPH CHRIS CARTER
(Joe)

Born March 7, 1960, at Oklahoma City, Okla.
Height, 6.03. Weight, 215.
Throws and bats righthanded.
Attended Wichita State University, Wichita, Kan.
Brother of Fred Carter, outfielder in New York Yankees' and Cleveland Indians' organizations, 1985 through 1988.

Major League stolen bases: 1983 (1), 1984 (2), 1985 (24), 1986 (29), 1987 (31), 1988 (27). Total—114.
Hit three home runs in a game, August 29, 1986 and May 28, 1987.
Led American League first basemen in errors with 12 in 1987.
Led American Association in total bases with 265 and tied for lead in strikeouts by batters with 103 in 1983.
Named College Player of the Year by THE SPORTING NEWS, 1981.
Named outfielder on THE SPORTING NEWS College Baseball All-America Team, 1980 and 1981.
Received reported $150,000 bonus to sign with Chicago Cubs, 1981.

Year	Club	League	Pos.	G.	AB.	R.	H.	2B.	3B.	HR.	RBI.	B.A.	PO.	A.	E.	F.A.
1981	Midland	Texas	OF	67	249	42	67	15	3	5	35	.269	100	10	4	.965
1982	Midland†	Texas	OF	110	427	84	136	22	8	25	98	.319	182	6	5	.974
1983	Iowa	A. A.	OF	124	*522	82	160	27	6	22	83	.307	204	9	12	.947
1983	Chicago	Nat.	OF	23	51	6	9	1	1	0	1	.176	26	0	0	1.000
1984	Iowa‡	A. A.	OF	61	248	45	77	12	7	14	67	.310	142	6	2	.987
1984	Cleveland§	Amer.	OF-1B	66	244	32	67	6	1	13	41	.275	169	11	6	.968
1985	Cleveland	Amer.	O-1-2-3	143	489	64	128	27	0	15	59	.262	311	17	6	.982
1986	Cleveland	Amer.	OF-1B	162	663	108	200	36	9	29	*121	.302	800	55	10	.988
1987	Cleveland	Amer.	1B-OF	149	588	83	155	27	2	32	106	.264	782	46	17	.980
1988	Cleveland	Amer.	OF	157	621	85	168	36	6	27	98	.271	444	8	7	.985
National League Totals—1 Year				23	51	6	9	1	1	0	1	.176	26	0	0	1.000
American League Totals—5 Years				677	2605	372	718	132	18	116	425	.276	2506	137	46	.983
Major League Totals—6 Years				700	2656	378	727	133	19	116	426	.274	2532	137	46	.983

Selected by Chicago Cubs' organization in 1st round (second player selected) of free-agent draft, June 8, 1981.
†On disabled list, April 9 to April 19, 1982.
‡Traded with Outfielder Mel Hall and Pitchers Don Schulze and Darryl Banks to Cleveland Indians for Catcher Ron Hassey and Pitchers Rick Sutcliffe and George Frazier, June 13, 1984.
§On disabled list, July 2 to July 17, 1984.

CHARLES DOUGLAS CARY
(Chuck)

Born March 3, 1960, at Whittier, Calif.
Height, 6.04. Weight, 210.
Throws and bats lefthanded.
Attended University of California, Berkeley, Calif.

Major League saves: 1985 (2), 1987 (1). Total—3.
Tied for Southern League lead in balks with 3 in 1982.

Year	Club	League	G.	IP.	W.	L.	Pct.	H.	R.	ER.	SO.	BB.	ERA.
1981	Macon	S. Atlantic	13	87	5	5	.500	77	32	25	55	19	2.59
1982	Birmingham	Southern	28	166	8	14	.364	162	93	77	125	64	4.17
1983	Birmingham†	Southern	17	104⅔	6	8	.429	103	50	42	69	42	3.61
1983	Evansville	Am. Assoc.	15	16⅓	1	1	.500	21	10	8	8	8	4.41
1984	Birmingham‡	Southern	22	108⅓	6	4	.600	118	61	58	62	46	4.82
1985	Nashville	Am. Assoc.	48	66	2	1	.667	55	27	22	54	27	3.00
1985	Detroit	American	16	23⅔	0	1	.000	16	9	9	22	8	3.42
1986	Detroit	American	22	31⅔	1	2	.333	33	18	12	21	15	3.41
1986	Nashville§	Am. Assoc.	22	26⅓	1	4	.200	29	21	16	19	15	5.47
1987	Richmond	Int'national	40	105⅔	4	6	.400	104	64	55	128	43	4.68
1987	Atlanta	National	13	16⅔	1	1	.500	17	7	7	15	4	3.78
1988	Atlanta x	National	7	8⅓	0	0	.000	8	6	6	7	4	6.48

Year Club	League	G.	IP.	W.	L.	Pct.	H.	R.	ER.	SO.	BB.	ERA.
1988—Bradenton Braves	Gulf Coast	4	12	0	2	.000	11	10	5	18	2	3.75
1988—Richmond y	Int'national	5	6⅓	0	0	.000	4	1	1	3	2	1.42
American League Totals—2 Years		38	55⅓	1	3	.250	49	27	21	43	23	3.42
National League Totals—2 Years		20	25	1	1	.500	25	13	13	22	8	4.68
Major League Totals—4 Years		58	80⅓	2	4	.333	74	40	34	65	31	3.81

Selected by Detroit Tigers' organization in 7th round of free-agent draft, June 8, 1981.
†On disabled list, April 18 to May 12, 1983.
‡On disabled list, June 24 to July 11 and August 4 to August 17, 1984.
§Traded with Pitcher Randy O'Neal to Atlanta Braves for Outfielders Terry Harper and Freddy Tiburcio, January 27, 1987.
xOn disabled list, April 10 to August 17, 1988; included rehabilitation disability assignment to Bradenton, July 29 to August 10, 1988, and to Richmond, August 11 to August 17, 1988.
yReleased, December 4, 1988.

ANTONIO CASTILLO
(Tony)

Born March 1, 1963, at Lara, Venezuela.
Height, 5.10. Weight, 177.
Throws and bats lefthanded.

Year Club	League	G.	IP.	W.	L.	Pct.	H.	R.	ER.	SO.	BB.	ERA.
1983—Bradenton Jays	Gulf Coast	1	3	0	0	.000	3	1	1	4	0	3.00
1984—Florence	S. Atlantic	25	137⅓	11	8	.579	123	71	52	96	50	3.41
1985—Kinston	Carolina	36	127⅔	11	7	.611	111	44	27	136	48	1.90
1986—Knoxville†	Southern	(Did not play)										
1987—Dunedin	Florida St.	39	69⅔	6	2	.750	62	30	26	62	19	3.36
1988—Dunedin	Florida St.	30	42⅔	4	3	.571	31	9	7	46	10	1.48
1988—Knoxville	Southern	5	8	1	0	1.000	2	0	0	11	1	0.00
1988—Toronto	American	14	15	1	0	1.000	10	5	5	14	2	3.00
Major League Totals—1 Year		14	15	1	0	1.000	10	5	5	14	2	3.00

Signed as free agent by Toronto Blue Jays' organization, February 16, 1983.
†On disabled list, April 10, 1986 through entire season.

JUAN CASTILLO

Name pronounced Cas-TEE-yo.

Born January 25, 1962, at San Pedro de Macoris, D. R.
Height, 5.11. Weight, 155.
Throws right and bats left and righthanded.

Major league stolen bases: 1986 (1), 1987 (15), 1988 (2). Total—18.
Led Texas League in caught stealing with 17 in 1983.
Led Texas League second basemen in assists with 359 in 1984.
Led Texas League second basemen in putouts with 247, assists with 360, errors with 27, double plays with 79 and total chances with 634 in 1983.
Led California League second basemen in double plays with 88 in 1982.

Year Club	League	Pos.	G.	AB.	R.	H.	2B.	3B.	HR.	RBI.	B.A.	PO.	A.	E.	F.A.
1980—Burlington	Midw.	2B	30	103	12	22	0	0	0	6	.214	60	72	3	.978
1980—Butte	Pion.	2B	59	183	28	53	9	3	0	20	.290	87	99	18	.912
1981—Burlington	Midw.	2B	110	365	36	90	8	4	4	34	.247	244	284	18	*.967
1982—Stockton	Calif.	2B	134	483	60	130	9	8	0	42	.269	273	*428	23	.968
1983—El Paso	Texas	2B-SS-OF	123	461	79	125	24	2	8	62	.271	250	363	28	.956
1984—El Paso	Texas	2B-OF-SS	119	448	78	129	21	7	4	59	.288	273	360	17	.974
1984—Vancouver	P. C.	2B	8	30	6	10	0	0	0	2	.333	16	18	1	.971
1985—Vancouver	P. C.	SS-2B	118	440	71	119	17	3	1	32	.270	222	367	26	.958
1986—Milwaukee	Amer.	2-S-3-O	26	54	6	9	0	1	0	5	.167	41	46	4	.956
1986—Vancouver	P. C.	2B	26	73	10	14	3	0	0	4	.192	34	95	5	.963
1987—Milwaukee†	Amer.	2B-SS-3B	116	321	44	72	11	4	3	28	.224	190	251	12	.974
1987—Denver	A. A.	SS	1	2	2	1	0	0	0	1	.500	2	3	0	1.000
1988—Milwaukee‡	Amer.	2-3-S-O	54	90	10	20	0	0	0	2	.222	24	82	7	.938
Major League Totals—3 Years			196	465	60	101	11	5	3	35	.217	255	379	23	.965

Signed as free agent by Milwaukee Brewers' organization, October 11, 1979.
†On disabled list, July 16 to July 31, 1987; included rehabiliation disability assignment to Denver, July 27 to July 31, 1987.
‡On disabled list, April 2 to May 12, 1988.

MONTE CARMELO CASTILLO

Name pronounced Cas-TEE-yo.

(Carmen)

Born June 8, 1958, at San Francisco de Macoris, D. R.
Height, 6.01. Weight, 190.
Throws and bats righthanded.

Major League stolen bases: 1983 (1), 1984 (1), 1985 (3), 1986 (2), 1987 (1), 1988 (6). Total—14.

Year Club	League	Pos.	G.	AB.	R.	H.	2B.	3B.	HR.	RBI.	B.A.	PO.	A.	E.	F.A.
1978—Auburn†	NYP	OF	53	174	37	41	10	2	4	21	.236	109	6	11	.913
1978—Helena	Pion.	OF	5	15	1	6	2	0	0	2	.400	2	0	1	.667

Year Club	League	Pos.	G.	AB.	R.	H.	2B.	3B.	HR.	RBI.	B.A.	PO.	A.	E.	F.A.
1979—Waterloo	Midw.	OF	49	138	25	28	5	1	3	12	.203	54	1	7	.887
1979—Batavia	NYP	OF	36	128	29	43	8	1	8	28	.336	56	4	5	.923
1980—Waterloo	Midw.	OF	117	390	69	103	14	1	11	64	.264	173	10	14	.929
1981—Chattanooga	South.	OF	119	441	63	124	17	6	11	58	.281	236	13	15	.943
1982—Charleston	Int.	OF	71	281	46	78	12	1	9	39	.278	159	10	11	.939
1982—Cleveland	Amer.	OF	47	120	11	25	4	0	2	11	.208	91	0	2	.978
1983—Charleston‡	Int.	OF	36	148	29	40	5	2	4	22	.270	85	6	6	.938
1983—Cleveland	Amer.	OF	23	36	9	10	2	1	1	3	.278	23	3	2	.929
1984—Cleveland	Amer.	OF	87	211	36	55	9	2	10	36	.261	123	2	9	.933
1985—Cleveland	Amer.	OF	67	184	27	45	5	1	11	25	.245	101	0	5	.953
1985—Maine	Int.	OF	26	96	12	23	2	2	2	18	.240	9	0	0	1.000
1986—Cleveland	Amer.	OF	85	205	34	57	9	0	8	32	.278	58	4	4	.939
1987—Cleveland	Amer.	OF	89	220	27	55	17	0	11	31	.250	29	3	0	1.000
1988—Cleveland	Amer.	OF	66	176	12	48	8	0	4	14	.273	69	1	5	.933
Major League Totals—7 Years			464	1152	156	295	54	4	47	152	.256	494	13	27	.949

Signed as free agent by Philadelphia Phillies' organization, June 30, 1978.
†Drafted by Chattanooga (Cleveland Indians' organization), December 5, 1978.
‡On disabled list, May 5 to July 4, 1983.

JOSE ISABEL CECENA

Born August 20, 1963, at Ciudad Obregon, Sonora, Mex.
Height, 5.09. Weight, 180.
Throws and bats righthanded.

Major League saves: 1988 (1).

Year Club	League	G.	IP.	W.	L.	Pct.	H.	R.	ER.	SO.	BB.	ERA.
1983—Saltillo	Mexican	16	34⅓	1	2	.333	33	23	22	19	31	5.77
1984—Saltillo	Mexican	24	78⅓	1	4	.200	92	61	52	61	58	5.97
1985—Saltillo	Mexican	39	108⅔	7	13	.350	125	73	62	100	53	5.13
1986—Reading	Eastern	10	21⅓	1	2	.333	26	19	17	18	16	7.17
1986—Clearwater†	Florida St.	22	110⅓	8	4	.667	97	49	41	66	44	3.34
1987—Tulsa	Texas	43	61	3	3	.500	54	37	29	61	37	4.28
1988—Texas‡	American	22	26⅓	0	0	.000	20	16	14	27	23	4.78
1988—Oklahoma City	Am. Assoc.	5	3	0	0	.000	6	2	2	3	0	6.00
Major League Totals—1 Year		22	26⅓	0	0	.000	20	16	14	27	23	4.78

Signed as a free agent by Philadelphia Phillies' organization, December 10, 1985.
†Drafted by Oklahoma City (Texas Rangers' organization), December 9, 1986.
‡On disabled list, June 19 to September 1, 1988; included rehabilitation disability assignment to Oklahoma City, July 19 to August 5, 1988.

RICHARD ALDO CERONE

Name pronounced Ce-RONE.

(Rick)

Born May 19, 1954, at Newark, N. J.
Height, 5.11. Weight, 195.
Throws and bats righthanded.
Received bachelor of science degree in physical education from
Seton Hall University, South Orange, N. J. in 1975.

Major League stolen bases: 1979 (1), 1980 (1), 1984 (1), 1985 (1). Total—4.
Named catcher on The Sporting News American League All-Star Team, 1980.
Received reported $60,000 bonus to sign with Cleveland Indians, 1975.

Year Club	League	Pos.	G.	AB.	R.	H.	2B.	3B.	HR.	RBI.	B.A.	PO.	A.	E.	F.A.
1975—Oklahoma City	A. A.	C-OF	46	140	22	35	6	1	2	13	.250	178	30	3	.986
1975—Cleveland	Amer.	C	7	12	1	3	1	0	0	0	.250	18	1	0	1.000
1976—Toledo†	Int.	C	96	339	38	86	19	0	11	49	.254	351	50	*18	.957
1976—Cleveland‡	Amer.	C	7	16	1	2	0	0	0	1	.125	25	1	1	.963
1977—Charleston	Int.	C-OF	70	231	30	54	10	1	6	40	.234	254	32	5	.983
1977—Toronto	Amer.	C	31	100	7	20	4	0	1	10	.200	146	15	1	.944
1978—Toronto	Amer.	C	88	282	25	63	8	2	3	20	.223	426	44	4	.992
1979—Toronto§	Amer.	C	136	469	47	112	27	4	7	61	.239	560	68	13	.980
1980—New York	Amer.	C	147	519	70	144	30	4	14	85	.277	800	73	9	.990
1981—New York x	Amer.	C	71	234	23	57	13	2	2	21	.244	353	26	3	.992
1982—New York y	Amer.	C	89	300	29	68	10	0	5	28	.227	509	25	6	.989
1983—New York	Amer.	C-3B	80	246	18	54	7	0	2	22	.220	412	18	4	.991
1984—New York z	Amer.	C	38	120	8	25	3	0	2	13	.208	230	9	1	.996
1984—Columbus a	Int.	C	8	25	2	5	2	0	0	1	.200	42	5	1	.979
1985—Atlanta bc	Nat.	C	96	282	15	61	9	0	3	25	.216	384	48	6	.986
1986—Milwaukee d	Amer.	C	68	216	22	56	14	0	4	18	.259	391	44	4	.991
1987—New York e	Amer.	*C-1B-P	113	284	28	69	12	1	4	23	.243	542	38	1	*.998
1988—Boston	Amer.	C	84	264	31	71	13	1	3	27	.269	471	28	0	*1.000
American League Totals—13 Years			959	3062	310	744	142	14	47	329	.243	4883	390	47	.991
National League Totals—1 Year			96	282	15	61	9	0	3	25	.216	384	48	6	.986
Major League Totals—14 Years			1055	3344	325	805	151	14	50	354	.241	5267	438	53	.991

Selected by Cleveland Indians' organization in 1st round (seventh player selected) of free-agent draft, June 4, 1975.
†On disabled list, May 13 to May 24, 1976.
‡Traded with Infielder-Outfielder John Lowenstein to Toronto Blue Jays for Outfielder Rico Carty, December 6, 1976.

§Traded with Pitcher Tom Underwood and Outfielder Ted Wilborn to New York Yankees for First Baseman Chris Chambliss, Infielder Damaso Garcia and Pitcher Paul Mirabella, November 1, 1979.
xOn disabled list, April 19 to May 24, 1981.
yOn disabled list, May 12 to July 15, 1982.
zOn disabled list, May 7 to July 5, 1984; included rehabilitation disability assignment to Columbus, June 25 to July 5, 1984.
aTraded to Atlanta Braves for Pitcher Brian Fisher, December 5, 1984.
bOn disabled list, June 17 to July 2, 1985.
cTraded with Pitcher David Clay and Shortstop Flavio Alfaro to Milwaukee Brewers for Catcher Ted Simmons, March 5, 1986.
dGranted free agency, November 12, 1986; signed by New York Yankees, February 13, 1987.
eReleased, April 4, 1988; signed by Boston Red Sox, April 15, 1988.

DIVISION SERIES RECORD

Year Club	League	Pos.	G.	AB.	R.	H.	2B.	3B.	HR.	RBI.	B.A.	PO.	A.	E.	F.A.
1981—New York	Amer.	C	5	18	1	6	2	0	1	5	.333	42	1	1	.977

CHAMPIONSHIP SERIES RECORD

Tied Championsip Series record for hitting home run in first Series at-bat, October 8, 1980.

Year Club	League	Pos.	G.	AB.	R.	H.	2B.	3B.	HR.	RBI.	B.A.	PO.	A.	E.	F.A.
1980—New York	Amer.	C	3	12	1	4	0	0	1	2	.333	14	4	0	1.000
1981—New York	Amer.	C	3	10	1	1	0	0	0	0	.100	23	2	0	1.000
Championship Series Totals—2 Years			6	22	2	5	0	0	1	2	.227	37	6	0	1.000

WORLD SERIES RECORD

Year Club	League	Pos.	G.	AB.	R.	H.	2B.	3B.	HR.	RBI.	B.A.	PO.	A.	E.	F.A.
1981—New York	Amer.	C	6	21	2	4	1	0	1	3	.190	42	4	0	1.000

PITCHING RECORD

Year Club	League	G.	IP.	W.	L.	Pct.	H.	R.	ER.	SO.	BB.	ERA.
1987—New York	American	2	2	0	0	.000	0	0	0	1	1	0.00

JOHN JOSEPH CERUTTI

Born April 28, 1960, at Albany, N. Y.
Height, 6.02. Weight, 200.
Throws and bats lefthanded.
Received bachelor of arts degree in economics from Amherst College, Amherst, Mass.

Major League saves: 1986 (1), 1988 (1). Total—2.
Tied for Southern League lead in shutouts with 3 in 1983.
Tied for Pioneer League lead in home runs allowed with 8 and games started by pitchers with 14 in 1981.

Year Club	League	G.	IP.	W.	L.	Pct.	H.	R.	ER.	SO.	BB.	ERA.
1981—Medicine Hat	Pioneer	14	*107	8	4	.667	87	45	36	120	43	3.03
1982—Kinston	Carolina	16	113	10	5	.667	88	47	40	136	49	3.19
1982—Knoxville	Southern	4	32⅓	4	0	1.000	18	4	4	17	10	1.11
1982—Syracuse	Int'national	6	30	0	3	.000	42	25	22	20	16	6.60
1983—Knoxville	Southern	29	188⅔	9	13	.409	182	89	72	131	65	3.43
1984—Syracuse	Int'national	29	148	7	•13	.350	152	89	73	114	52	4.44
1985—Syracuse	Int'national	28	182	11	9	.550	165	84	60	110	60	2.97
1985—Toronto	American	4	6⅔	0	2	.000	10	7	4	5	4	5.40
1986—Syracuse	Int'national	7	43⅔	1	3	.250	44	27	20	22	16	4.12
1986—Toronto	American	34	145⅓	9	4	.692	150	73	67	89	47	4.15
1987—Toronto	American	44	151⅓	11	4	*.733	144	75	74	92	59	4.40
1988—Toronto	American	46	123⅔	6	7	.462	120	56	43	65	42	3.13
Major League Totals—4 Years		128	427	26	17	.605	424	211	188	251	152	3.96

Selected by Toronto Blue Jays' organization in 1st round (21st player selected) of free-agent draft, June 8, 1981.

CARROLL CHRISTOPHER CHAMBLISS
(Chris)

Born December 26, 1948, at Dayton, O.
Height, 6.01. Weight, 220.
Throws right and bats lefthanded.
Attended Mira Costa Junior College, Oceanside, Calif., and University of California, Los Angeles, Calif.; and received degree in physical education and recreation from Montclair State College, Upper Montclair, N.J.
Cousin of Jo Jo White, guard with Boston Celtics, Golden State Warriors and Kansas City Kings, 1969-70 through 1980-81.

Tied major league record for fewest caught stealing, season, 150 or more games (0), 1976 and 1977.
Major League stolen bases: 1971 (2), 1972 (3), 1973 (4), 1976 (1), 1977 (4), 1978 (2), 1979 (3), 1980 (7), 1981 (4), 1982 (7), 1983 (2), 1984 (1). Total—40.
Led National League first basemen in double plays with 144 in 1982.
Led National League first basemen in total chances with 1,739 in 1980 and 1,144 in 1981.
Led American League first basemen in total chances with 1,565 in 1973.
Named American League Rookie Player of the Year by The Sporting News, 1971.
Named American League Rookie of the Year by Baseball Writers' Association of America, 1971.
Named first baseman on The Sporting News American League All-Star Team, 1976.
Named first baseman on The Sporting News American League All-Star fielding team, 1978.

Year	Club	League	Pos.	G.	AB.	R.	H.	2B.	3B.	HR.	RBI.	B.A.	PO.	A.	E.	F.A.
1970	—Wichita†	A. A.	OF-1B	105	383	60	131	17	8	7	52	*.342	413	21	13	.971
1971	—Wichita	A. A.	OF-1B	13	42	8	12	3	0	2	6	.286	42	3	0	1.000
1971	—Cleveland	Amer.	1B	111	415	49	114	20	4	9	48	.275	943	55	8	.992
1972	—Cleveland‡	Amer.	1B	121	466	51	136	27	2	6	44	.292	1109	56	8	.993
1973	—Cleveland	Amer.	1B	155	572	70	156	30	2	11	53	.273	1437	114	*14	.991
1974	—Cleve.§-N.Y.	Amer.	1B	127	467	46	119	20	3	6	50	.255	1035	84	11	.990
1975	—New York	Amer.	1B	150	562	66	171	38	4	9	72	.304	1222	106	12	.991
1976	—New York	Amer.	1B	156	641	79	188	32	6	17	96	.293	1440	109	9	.994
1977	—New York	Amer.	1B	157	600	90	172	32	6	17	90	.287	1368	98	16	.989
1978	—New York	Amer.	1B	162	625	81	171	26	3	12	90	.274	1366	111	4	*.997
1979	—New York xy	Amer.	1B	149	554	61	155	27	3	18	63	.280	1299	95	7	.995
1980	—Atlanta	Nat.	1B	158	602	83	170	37	2	18	72	.282	*1626	101	12	.993
1981	—Atlanta	Nat.	1B	107	404	44	110	25	2	8	51	.272	1046	*94	4	.997
1982	—Atlanta	Nat.	1B	157	534	57	144	25	2	20	86	.270	1352	138	10	.993
1983	—Atlanta z	Nat.	1B	131	447	59	125	24	3	20	78	.280	1092	89	5	.996
1984	—Atlanta	Nat.	1B	135	389	47	100	14	0	9	44	.257	996	70	8	.993
1985	—Atlanta	Nat.	1B	101	170	16	40	7	0	3	21	.235	299	25	1	.997
1986	—Atlanta a	Nat.	1B	97	122	13	38	8	0	2	14	.311	141	6	1	.993
1988	—New York bc	Amer.	PH	1	1	0	0	0	0	0	0	.000	0	0	0	.000
American League Totals—10 Years				1289	4903	593	1382	252	33	105	606	.282	11219	828	89	.993
National League Totals—7 Years				886	2668	319	727	140	9	80	366	.272	6552	523	41	.994
Major League Totals—17 Years				2175	7571	912	2109	392	42	185	972	.279	17771	1351	130	.993

Selected by Cincinnati Reds' organization in 31st round of free-agent draft, June 6, 1967.

Selected by Cincinnati Reds' organization in secondary phase of free-agent draft, January 27, 1968.

Selected by Cleveland Indians' organization in 1st round (first player selected) of free-agent draft, January 17, 1970.

†On disabled list, May 25 to June 16, 1970.

‡On military list, June 23 to June 30, 1972.

§Traded with Pitchers Dick Tidrow and Cecil Upshaw to New York Yankees for Fritz Peterson, Steve Kline, Fred Beene and Tom Buskey, April 26, 1974.

xTraded with Infielder Damaso Garcia and Pitcher Paul Mirabella to Toronto Blue Jays for Catcher Rick Cerone, Pitcher Tom Underwood and Outfielder Ted Wilborn, November 1, 1979.

yTraded with Shortstop Luis Gomez to Atlanta Braves for Outfielder Barry Bonnell and Pitcher Joey McLaughlin, December 5, 1979.

zOn disabled list, August 8 to August 23, 1983.

aGranted free agency, November 12, 1986; named coach with New York Yankees, November 6, 1987.

bActivated by New York Yankees as a player, May 7, 1988.

cReleased as a player, May 10, 1988; named manager of London Tigers of Eastern League, November 3, 1988.

CHAMPIONSHIP SERIES RECORD

Established Championship Series records for highest slugging average, five-game Series (.952), 1976; most total bases, five-game Series (20), 1976.

Tied Championship Series records for most hits, five-game Series (11), 1976; most hits, two consecutive games, one Series (6), October 3 and 4, 1978; most consecutive hits, one Series (5), 1978.

Tied American League Championship Series records for most consecutive hits, total Series (5); most one-base hits, four-game Series (6), 1978; most home runs, five-game Series (2), 1976.

Year	Club	League	Pos.	G.	AB.	R.	H.	2B.	3B.	HR.	RBI.	B.A.	PO.	A.	E.	F.A.
1976	—New York	Amer.	1B	5	21	5	11	1	1	2	8	.524	50	3	1	.981
1977	—New York	Amer.	1B	5	17	0	1	0	0	0	0	.059	35	7	0	1.000
1978	—New York	Amer.	1B	4	15	1	6	0	0	0	2	.400	28	1	0	1.000
1982	—Atlanta	Nat.	1B	3	10	0	0	0	0	0	0	.000	30	5	0	1.000
Championship Series Totals—4 Years				17	63	6	18	1	1	2	10	.286	143	16	1	.994

WORLD SERIES RECORD

Tied World Series records for most errors by first baseman, four-game Series (1), 1976; one or more hits, each game, four-game Series, 1976.

Year	Club	League	Pos.	G.	AB.	R.	H.	2B.	3B.	HR.	RBI.	B.A.	PO.	A.	E.	F.A.
1976	—New York	Amer.	1B	4	16	1	5	1	0	0	1	.313	26	3	1	.967
1977	—New York	Amer.	1B	6	24	4	7	2	0	1	4	.292	55	5	0	1.000
1978	—New York	Amer.	1B	3	11	1	2	0	0	0	0	.182	17	1	0	1.000
World Series Totals—3 Years				13	51	6	14	3	0	1	5	.275	98	9	1	.991

ALL-STAR GAME RECORD

Year	League	Pos.	AB.	R.	H.	2B.	3B.	HR.	RBI.	B.A.	PO.	A.	E.	F.A.
1976	—American	PH	1	0	0	0	0	0	0	.000	0	0	0	.000

DARRIN JOHN CHAPIN

Born February 1, 1966, at Warren, O.
Height, 6.00. Weight, 170.
Throws and bats righthanded.
Attended Cuyahoga Community College, Cleveland, O.,
and Cleveland State University, Cleveland, O.

Tied for New York-Pennsylvania League lead in intentional bases on balls issued with 5 in 1987.

Year	Club	League	G.	IP.	W.	L.	Pct.	H.	R.	ER.	SO.	BB.	ERA.
1986	—Sarasota Yankees	Gulf Coast	13	83⅓	4	3	.571	71	●42	30	67	27	3.24
1987	—Oneonta	NYP	25	40	1	1	.500	31	8	3	26	17	0.68

Year	Club	League	G.	IP.	W.	L.	Pct.	H.	R.	ER.	SO.	BB.	ERA.
1988	—Fort Lauderdale	Florida St.	38	63	6	4	.600	39	8	6	57	19	0.86
1988	—Albany	Eastern	3	4	0	0	.000	11	7	5	4	2	11.25

Selected by New York Yankees' organization in 6th round of free-agent draft, January 14, 1986.

COLIN MARC CHARLAND

Born November 13, 1965, at New York, N.Y.
Height, 6.03. Weight, 205.
Throws and bats lefthanded.
Attended Dallas Baptist University, Dallas, Tex.

Led California League in complete games with 12 in 1988.
Named California League co-Pitcher of the Year, 1988.

Year	Club	League	G.	IP.	W.	L.	Pct.	H.	R.	ER.	SO.	BB.	ERA.
1986	—Salem	Northwest	5	31	4	0	1.000	16	7	5	49	15	1.45
1986	—Quad Cities	Midwest	10	59⅓	3	4	.429	55	29	23	61	29	3.49
1987	—Palm Springs	California	27	147⅓	6	12	.333	159	100	88	150	87	5.38
1988	—Palm Springs	California	27	204	•17	5	.773	187	76	57	183	71	2.51

Selected by California Angels' organization in 6th round of free-agent draft, June 2, 1986.

NORMAN WOOD CHARLTON
(Norm)

Born January 6, 1963, at Fort Polk, La.
Height, 6.03. Weight, 195.
Throws left and bats left and righthanded.
Received degree in political science, religion, and physical education
from Rice University, Houston, Tex.

Led American Association in wild pitches with 13 in 1988.

Year	Club	League	G.	IP.	W.	L.	Pct.	H.	R.	ER.	SO.	BB.	ERA.
1984	—West Palm Beach	Florida St.	8	39⅓	1	4	.200	51	27	20	27	22	4.58
1985	—West Palm Beach†	Florida St.	24	128	7	10	.412	135	79	65	71	79	4.57
1986	—Vermont	Eastern	22	136⅔	10	6	.625	109	55	43	96	74	2.83
1987	—Nashville‡	Am. Assoc.	18	98⅓	2	8	.200	97	57	47	74	44	4.30
1988	—Nashville	Am. Assoc.	27	182	11	10	.524	149	69	61	*161	56	3.02
1988	—Cincinnati	National	10	61⅓	4	5	.444	60	27	27	39	20	3.96
Major League Totals—1 Year			10	61⅓	4	5	.444	60	27	27	39	20	3.96

Selected by Montreal Expos' organization in 1st round (27th player selected) of free-agent draft, June 4, 1984.
†Traded with a player to be named later to Cincinnati Reds for Infielder Wayne Krenchicki, March 31, 1986; Cincinnati acquired Second Baseman Tim Barker to complete deal, April 2, 1986.
‡On Cincinnati disabled list, April 6 to June 26, 1987; included rehabilitation disability assignment to Nashville, June 9 to June 26, 1987.

RODNEY OSBORNE CHILDRESS
(Rocky)

Born February 18, 1962, at Santa Rosa, Calif.
Height, 6.02. Weight, 195.
Throws and bats righthanded.
Attended Santa Rosa Junior College, Santa Rosa, Calif.

Led Eastern League in intentional bases on balls issued with 13 in 1984.
Led Carolina League in saves with 16 and tied for lead in games finished in relief with 50 in 1983.

Year	Club	League	G.	IP.	W.	L.	Pct.	H.	R.	ER.	SO.	BB.	ERA.
1980	—Helena	Pioneer	15	68	3	4	.429	79	32	19	43	20	2.51
1981	—Bend	Northwest	25	46	4	5	.444	56	36	23	38	21	4.50
1982	—Spartanburg	S. Atlantic	46	92	4	4	.500	101	53	41	54	44	4.01
1983	—Peninsula	Carolina	*58	74⅓	4	7	.364	87	47	36	43	31	4.36
1984	—Reading	Eastern	•62	103⅓	7	6	.538	107	38	34	50	40	2.96
1985	—Portland	P. Coast	34	56⅔	5	2	.714	48	12	8	30	23	1.27
1985	—Philadelphia	National	16	33⅓	0	1	.000	45	23	23	14	9	6.21
1986	—Portland†-Tucson	P. Coast	61	83⅓	5	10	.333	99	69	63	40	46	6.80
1986	—Philadelphia‡	National	2	2⅔	0	0	.000	4	3	2	1	1	6.75
1987	—Tucson	P. Coast	33	42⅔	3	3	.500	49	23	18	23	19	3.80
1987	—Houston	National	32	48⅓	1	2	.333	46	17	16	26	18	2.98
1988	—Tucson	P. Coast	43	97⅓	6	4	.600	102	48	36	58	41	3.33
1988	—Houston	National	11	23⅓	1	0	1.000	26	17	16	24	9	6.17
Major League Totals—4 Years			61	107⅔	2	3	.400	121	60	57	65	37	4.76

Selected by Philadelphia Phillies' organization in 21st round of free-agent draft, June 3, 1980.
†Traded to Houston Astros' organization for Pitcher Mike Madden, June 20, 1986; deal voided, June 27, 1986.
‡Traded to Houston Astros for a player to be named later, November 17, 1986; deal settled with cash.

JOHN LAWRENCE CHRISTENSEN

Born September 5, 1960, at Downey, Calif.
Height, 6.00. Weight, 180.
Throws and bats righthanded.
Attended California State University, Fullerton, Calif.
Brother of Jim Christensen, second baseman with Minnesota Twins' and
Oakland A's organizations, 1977 through 1983.

Major League stolen bases: 1985 (1), 1987 (2). Total—3.

Led International League outfielders in fielding percentage with .994 in 1984.

Year Club	League	Pos.	G.	AB.	R.	H.	2B.	3B.	HR.	RBI.	B.A.	PO.	A.	E.	F.A.
1982—Shelby	S. Atl.	OF	125	440	100	147	24	2	22	*97	.334	156	9	2	.988
1982—Lynchburg	Carol.	OF	8	31	7	10	1	1	0	4	.323	11	1	1	.923
1983—Jackson	Texas	OF-1B-3B	109	405	76	135	26	2	12	72	.333	417	49	11	.977
1983—Tidewater	Int.	OF	20	80	12	21	0	0	2	15	.263	28	1	2	.935
1984—Tidewater	Int.	OF-1B	129	421	57	133	12	0	15	71	.316	177	7	1	.995
1984—New York	Nat.	OF	5	11	2	3	2	0	0	3	.273	1	0	1	.500
1985—New York	Nat.	OF	51	113	10	21	4	1	3	13	.186	41	2	2	.956
1985—Tidewater†	Int.	OF	43	156	14	33	4	1	1	13	.212	65	7	4	.947
1986—Pawtucket‡	Int.	OF	62	175	27	41	0	0	5	22	.234	83	2	0	1.000
1987—Calgary	P. C.	OF	13	46	11	15	4	0	1	12	.326	24	0	2	.923
1987—Seattle§	Amer.	OF	53	132	19	32	6	1	2	12	.242	60	3	0	1.000
1987—Chattanooga	South.	OF	12	39	8	15	5	0	0	6	.385	10	1	0	1.000
1988—Cal. x-Port.	P. C.	OF	106	385	57	117	23	3	9	49	.304	126	10	4	.971
1988—Minnesota y	Amer.	OF	23	38	5	10	4	0	0	5	.263	20	0	0	1.000
National League Totals—2 Years			56	124	12	24	6	1	3	16	.194	42	2	3	.936
American League Totals—2 Years			76	170	24	42	10	1	2	17	.247	80	3	0	1.000
Major League Totals—4 Years			132	294	36	66	16	2	5	33	.224	122	5	3	.977

Selected by California Angels' organization in 16th round of free-agent draft, June 6, 1978.

Selected by New York Mets' organization in 2nd round of free-agent draft, June 8, 1981.

†Traded with Pitchers Calvin Schiraldi and Wes Gardner and Outfielder LaSchelle Tarver to Boston Red Sox for Pitchers Bob Ojeda, Tom McCarthy, John Mitchell and Chris Bayer, November 13, 1985.

‡Traded to Seattle Mariners, September 25, 1986, completing deal in which Seattle traded Shortstop Spike Owen and Outfielder Dave Henderson to Boston Red Sox for Infielder Rey Quinones, a player to be named later and cash, August 19, 1986. As part of deal, Seattle claimed Pitchers Mike Brown and Mike Trujillo on waivers from Boston, August 22, 1986.

§On disabled list, July 23 to September 2, 1987; included rehabilitation disability assignment to Chattanooga, August 21 to September 2, 1987.

xReleased, May 23, 1988; signed by Portland (Minnesota Twins' organization), May 28, 1988.

yReleased, December 21, 1988.

JAMES CLANCY
(Jim)

Born December 18, 1955, at Chicago, Ill.
Height, 6.04. Weight, 220.
Throws and bats righthanded.

Major League saves: 1988 (1).

Led American League pitchers in games started with 40 in 1982 and tied for lead with 36 in 1984.

Tied for Gulf Coast League lead in shutouts with 2 in 1974.

Year Club	League	G.	IP.	W.	L.	Pct.	H.	R.	ER.	SO.	BB.	ERA.
1974—Sarasota Rangers	Gulf Coast	9	53	3	3	.500	40	21	16	58	28	2.72
1975—Anderson	W. Carol.	23	148	6	13	.316	139	85	63	109	91	3.83
1976—San Antonio†‡	Texas	23	125	6	8	.429	133	94	*89	77	98	6.41
1977—Jersey City	Eastern	20	118	5	13	.278	116	87	64	99	75	4.88
1977—Toronto	American	13	77	4	9	.308	80	47	43	44	47	5.03
1978—Toronto	American	31	194	10	12	.455	199	96	88	106	91	4.08
1979—Toronto§	American	12	64	2	7	.222	65	44	39	33	31	5.48
1980—Toronto	American	34	251	13	16	.448	217	108	92	152	*128	3.30
1981—Toronto	American	22	125	6	12	.333	126	77	68	56	64	4.90
1982—Toronto	American	40	266⅔	16	14	.533	251	122	110	139	77	3.71
1983—Toronto	American	34	223	15	11	.577	238	115	97	99	61	3.91
1984—Toronto	American	36	219⅔	13	15	.464	249	*132	*125	118	88	5.12
1985—Toronto x	American	23	128⅔	9	6	.600	117	54	54	66	37	3.78
1985—Knoxville	Southern	2	8	1	0	1.000	7	3	3	2	2	3.38
1986—Toronto y	American	34	219⅓	14	14	.500	202	100	96	126	63	3.94
1987—Toronto	American	37	241⅓	15	11	.577	234	103	95	180	80	3.54
1988—Toronto z	American	36	196⅓	11	13	.458	207	106	98	118	47	4.49
Major League Totals—12 Years		352	2206	128	140	.478	2185	1104	1005	1237	814	4.10

Selected by Texas Rangers' organization in 4th round of free-agent draft, June 5, 1974.

†On disabled list, June 15 to June 26, 1976.

‡Selected by Toronto Blue Jays from Texas Rangers in American League expansion draft, November 5, 1976.

§On disabled list, May 12 to July 4 and August 5, 1979 through remainder of season.

xOn disabled list, March 25 to April 30 and July 27 to September 2, 1985; included rehabilitation disability assignment to Knoxville, April 21 to April 30, 1985.

yGranted free agency, November 12, 1986; re-signed by Blue Jays, January 6, 1987.

zGranted free agency, October 24, 1988; signed by Houston Astros, December 16, 1988.

CHAMPIONSHIP SERIES RECORD

Year Club	League	G.	IP.	W.	L.	Pct.	H.	R.	ER.	SO.	BB.	ERA.
1985—Toronto	American	1	1	0	1	.000	2	1	1	0	1	9.00

ALL-STAR GAME RECORD

Year League	IP.	W.	L.	Pct.	H.	R.	ER.	SO.	BB.	ERA.
1982—American	1	0	0	.000	0	0	0	0	0	0.00

DAVID EARL CLARK
(Dave)

Born September 3, 1962, at Tupelo, Miss.
Height, 6.02. Weight, 200.
Throws right and bats lefthanded.
Attended Jackson State University, Jackson, Miss.
Brother of Lewis Clark, wide receiver with Seattle Seahawks.

Major League stolen bases: 1986 (1), 1987 (1). Total—2.

Named outfielder on THE SPORTING NEWS College Baseball All-America Team, 1983.

Year	Club	League	Pos.	G.	AB.	R.	H.	2B.	3B.	HR.	RBI.	B.A.	PO.	A.	E.	F.A.
1983	Waterloo	Midw.	OF	58	159	20	44	8	1	4	20	.277	37	4	1	.976
1984	Waterloo	Midw.	OF	110	363	74	112	16	3	15	63	.309	128	10	4	.972
1984	Buffalo	East.	OF	17	56	12	10	1	0	3	10	.179	23	2	1	.962
1985	Waterbury	East.	OF	132	463	75	140	24	7	12	64	.302	204	11	11	.951
1986	Maine	Int.	OF	106	355	56	99	17	2	19	58	.279	150	4	6	.963
1986	Cleveland	Amer.	OF	18	58	10	16	1	0	3	9	.276	26	0	0	1.000
1987	Buffalo	A. A.	OF	108	420	83	143	22	3	30	80	.340	181	*22	6	.971
1987	Cleveland	Amer.	OF	29	87	11	18	5	0	3	12	.207	24	1	0	1.000
1988	Cleveland	Amer.	OF	63	156	11	41	4	1	3	18	.263	36	0	2	.947
1988	Colorado Springs	P. C.	OF	47	165	27	49	10	2	4	31	.297	85	6	3	.968
Major League Totals—3 Years				110	301	32	75	10	1	9	39	.249	86	1	2	.978

Selected by Cleveland Indians' organization in 1st round (11th player selected) of free-agent draft, June 6, 1983.

JACK ANTHONY CLARK

Born November 10, 1955, at New Brighton, Pa.
Height, 6.03. Weight, 205.
Throws and bats righthanded.

Tied major league record for most errors by first baseman, inning (3), May 25, 1987, second inning.

Established National League record for most consecutive games, one or more bases on balls (16), July 18 through August 10, 1987.

Tied National League record for most bases on balls, doubleheader (6), July 8, 1987 (19 innings).

Major League stolen bases: 1975 (1), 1976 (6), 1977 (12), 1978 (15), 1979 (11), 1980 (2), 1981 (1), 1982 (6), 1983 (5), 1984 (1), 1985 (1), 1986 (1), 1987 (1), 1988 (3). Total—66.

Led National League in bases on balls received with 136 and slugging percentage with .597 in 1987.

Led National League in game-winning RBIs with 18 in 1980 and tied for lead with 21 in 1982.

Tied for National League lead in double plays by outfielders with 5 in 1978, 7 in 1979 and 4 in 1981.

Led Texas League in total bases with 239 in 1975.

Led California League in total bases with 254 in 1974.

Led Texas League third basemen in putouts with 102, assists with 278, double plays with 29 and fielding percentage with .872 in 1975.

Named first baseman on THE SPORTING NEWS National League All-Star Team, 1987.

Named outfielder on THE SPORTING NEWS National League All-Star Team, 1978.

Named first baseman on THE SPORTING NEWS National League Silver Slugger team, 1985 and 1987.

Year	Club	League	Pos.	G.	AB.	R.	H.	2B.	3B.	HR.	RBI.	B.A.	PO.	A.	E.	F.A.
1973	Great Falls	Pion.	OF-P-3B	65	234	46	75	20	1	9	54	.321	73	9	1	.988
1974	Fresno	Calif.	3B	131	495	88	156	23	9	19	*117	.315	100	204	*53	.852
1975	Lafayette	Texas	*3B-OF	126	466	94	141	25	2	•23	77	.303	107	279	*56	.873
1975	San Francisco	Nat.	OF-3B	8	17	3	4	0	0	0	2	.235	8	1	0	1.000
1976	Phoenix	P. C.	OF-3B	131	470	111	152	29	*16	17	86	.323	188	23	9	.959
1976	San Francisco	Nat.	OF	26	102	14	23	6	2	2	10	.225	71	3	1	.987
1977	San Francisco	Nat.	OF	136	413	64	104	17	4	13	51	.252	226	11	6	.975
1978	San Francisco	Nat.	OF	156	592	90	181	46	8	25	98	.306	320	16	6	.982
1979	San Francisco	Nat.	OF-3B	143	527	84	144	25	2	26	86	.273	262	13	5	.971
1980	San Francisco†	Nat.	OF	127	437	77	124	20	8	22	82	.284	229	7	8	.967
1981	San Francisco	Nat.	OF	99	385	60	103	19	2	17	53	.268	193	•14	4	.981
1982	San Francisco	Nat.	OF	157	563	90	154	30	3	27	103	.274	281	10	6	.980
1983	San Francisco	Nat.	OF-1B	135	492	82	132	25	0	20	66	.268	262	20	9	.969
1984	San Francisco‡§	Nat.	OF-1B	57	203	33	65	9	1	11	44	.320	120	9	2	.985
1985	St. Louis x	Nat.	*1B-OF	126	442	71	124	26	3	22	87	.281	1128	66	*14	.988
1986	St. Louis y	Nat.	1B	65	232	34	55	12	2	9	23	.237	623	35	3	.995
1987	St. Louis z	Nat.	1B-OF	131	419	93	120	23	1	35	106	.286	1152	77	14	.989
1988	New York ab	Amer.	OF-1B	150	496	81	120	14	0	27	93	.242	129	8	5	.965
National League Totals—13 Years				1366	4824	795	1333	258	36	229	811	.276	4875	282	78	.985
American League Totals—1 Year				150	496	81	120	14	0	27	93	.242	129	8	5	.965
Major League Totals—14 Years				1516	5320	876	1453	272	36	256	904	.273	5004	290	83	.985

Selected by San Francisco Giants' organization in 13th round of free-agent draft, June 5, 1973.

†On disabled list, August 23 to September 8, 1980.

‡On disabled list, June 25 to September 5, 1984.

§Traded to St. Louis Cardinals for First Basemen David Green and Gary Rajsich, Pitcher Dave LaPoint and Shortstop Jose Gonzalez (Jose Uribe), February 1, 1985.

xOn disabled list, August 24 to September 8, 1985.

yOn disabled list, June 25, 1986 through remainder of season.

zGranted free agency, November 9, 1987; signed by New York Yankees, January 6, 1988.

aOn disabled list, March 21 to April 15, 1988.

bTraded with Pitcher Pat Clements to San Diego Padres for Pitchers Jimmy Jones and Lance McCullers and Outfielder Stan Jefferson, October 24, 1988.

CHAMPIONSHIP SERIES RECORD

Tied Championship Series record for most hits, inning (2), October 13, 1985 (second inning).
Tied National League Championship Series records for most singles (7) and most bases on balls (5), six-game Series, 1985.

Year	Club	League	Pos.	G.	AB.	R.	H.	2B.	3B.	HR.	RBI.	B.A.	PO.	A.	E.	F.A.
1985	St. Louis	Nat.	1B	6	21	4	8	0	0	1	4	.381	55	0	0	1.000
1987	St. Louis	Nat.	PH	1	1	0	0	0	0	0	0	.000	0	0	0	.000
Championship Series Totals—2 Years				7	22	4	8	0	0	1	4	.364	55	0	0	1.000

WORLD SERIES RECORD

Year	Club	League	Pos.	G.	AB.	R.	H.	2B.	3B.	HR.	RBI.	B.A.	PO.	A.	E.	F.A.
1985	St. Louis	Nat.	1B	7	25	1	6	2	0	0	4	.240	49	4	0	1.000

ALL-STAR GAME RECORD

Year	League	Pos.	AB.	R.	H.	2B.	3B.	HR.	RBI.	B.A.	PO.	A.	E.	F.A.
1978	National	OF	1	0	0	0	0	0	0	.000	0	0	0	.000
1979	National	PH	1	0	0	0	0	0	0	.000	0	0	0	.000
1985	National	1B	1	0	0	0	0	0	0	.000	4	0	0	1.000
1987	National	1B	3	0	0	0	0	0	0	.000	7	1	0	1.000
All-Star Game Totals—4 Years			6	0	0	0	0	0	0	.000	11	1	0	1.000

PITCHING RECORD

Year	Club	League	G.	IP.	W.	L.	Pct.	H.	R.	ER.	SO.	BB.	ERA.
1973	Great Falls	Pioneer	5	15	0	2	.000	24	24	10	17	19	6.00

JERALD DWAYNE CLARK

Born August 10, 1963, at Crockett, Tex.
Height, 6.04. Weight, 189.
Throws and bats righthanded.
Attended Lamar University, Beaumont, Tex.
Brother of Phil Clark, catcher-outfielder in Detroit Tigers' organization;
and Isaiah Clark, shortstop in Oakland Athletics' organization.

Named Northwest League Most Valuable Player, 1985.

Year	Club	League	Pos.	G.	AB.	R.	H.	2B.	3B.	HR.	RBI.	B.A.	PO.	A.	E.	F.A.
1985	Spokane	N'west	OF	73	283	45	92	•24	3	2	50	.325	145	7	6	.962
1986	Reno	Calif.	OF	95	389	76	118	34	3	7	58	.303	135	6	5	.966
1986	Beaumont	Texas	OF	16	56	9	18	4	1	0	6	.321	39	1	2	.952
1987	Wichita	Texas	OF	132	531	86	165	36	8	18	95	.311	262	10	3	.989
1988	Las Vegas	P. C.	OF-3B-1B	107	408	65	123	27	7	9	67	.301	194	11	7	.967
1988	San Diego	Nat.	OF	6	15	0	3	1	0	0	3	.200	10	1	0	1.000
Major League Totals—1 Year				6	15	0	3	1	0	0	3	.200	10	1	0	1.000

Selected by Los Angeles Dodgers' organization in 23rd round of free-agent draft, June 4, 1984.
Selected by San Diego Padres' organization in 12th round of free-agent draft, June 3, 1985.

PHILLIP BENJAMIN CLARK
(Phil)

Born May 6, 1968, at Crockett, Tex.
Height, 6.00. Weight, 175.
Throws and bats righthanded.
Brother of Jerald Clark, outfielder in San Diego Padres' organization;
and Isaiah Clark, infielder in Oakland Athletics' organization.

Led South Atlantic League catchers in passed balls with 23 and tied for lead in errors with 21 in 1987.
Led Appalachian League catchers in errors with 11 in 1986.

Year	Club	League	Pos.	G.	AB.	R.	H.	2B.	3B.	HR.	RBI.	B.A.	PO.	A.	E.	F.A.
1986	Bristol	Appal.	C-OF	66	247	40	★82	4	2	4	36	★.332	354	25	11	.972
1987	Fayetteville	S. Atl.	C-OF-3B	135	★542	83	160	26	•9	8	79	.295	480	82	28	.953
1988	Lakeland	Fla. St.	C-OF	109	403	60	120	17	4	9	66	.298	413	35	8	.982

Selected by Detroit Tigers' organization in 1st round (18th player selected) of free-agent draft, June 2, 1986.

TERRY LEE CLARK

Born October 10, 1960, at Los Angeles, Calif.
Height, 6.02. Weight, 196.
Throws and bats righthanded.
Attended Mount San Antonio College, Walnut, Calif.

Led Florida State League in games finished in relief with 51 in 1982.
Led South Atlantic League in games finished in relief with 51 in 1981.
Led Appalachian League in saves with 8 in 1979.

Year	Club	League	G.	IP.	W.	L.	Pct.	H.	R.	ER.	SO.	BB.	ERA.
1979	Johnson City	Ap'lachian	•23	32	4	2	.667	31	10	7	22	11	1.97
1980	Gastonia	S. Atlantic	49	88	4	7	.364	82	34	31	50	22	3.17
1981	Gastonia	S. Atlantic	★53	75	4	5	.444	56	23	18	66	25	2.16
1982	St. Petersburg	Florida St.	★58	88⅓	10	7	.588	81	32	25	61	34	2.55
1983	Arkansas	Texas	52	81⅓	6	6	.500	68	31	29	63	19	3.21
1984	Louisville†	Am. Assoc.	18	34⅓	1	3	.250	41	19	18	24	12	4.72
1985	Arkansas‡	Texas	42	96⅔	6	5	.545	102	64	53	67	38	4.93

Year	Club	League	G.	IP.	W.	L.	Pct.	H.	R.	ER.	SO.	BB.	ERA.
1986	Midland	Texas	57	90⅓	9	4	.692	98	49	33	66	28	3.29
1987	Edmonton	P. Coast	33	154⅔	8	9	.471	140	79	66	88	56	3.84
1988	Edmonton	P. Coast	16	113⅔	7	6	.538	128	62	57	59	33	4.51
1988	California	American	15	94	6	6	.500	120	54	53	39	31	5.07
Major League Totals—1 Year			15	94	6	6	.500	120	54	53	39	31	5.07

Selected by St. Louis Cardinals' organization in 22nd round of free-agent draft, June 5, 1979.
†On disabled list, May 27 to August 22, 1984.
‡Granted free agency, October 15, 1985; signed by Midland (California Angels' organization), February 25, 1986.

WILLIAM NUSCHLER CLARK JR.
(Will)

Born March 13, 1964, at New Orleans, La.
Height, 6.01. Weight, 190.
Throws and bats lefthanded.
Attended Mississippi State University, Starkville, Miss.

Tied major league record by hitting home run in first major league at-bat, April 8, 1986.
Major League stolen bases: 1986 (4), 1987 (5), 1988 (9). Total—18.
Led National League in bases on balls received with 100 and intentional bases on balls received with 27 in 1988.
Led National League first basemen in total chances with 1,608 in 1988.
Led National League first baseman in double plays with 130 in 1987 and 126 in 1988.
Named first baseman on THE SPORTING NEWS National League All-Star Team, 1988.
Named first baseman on THE SPORTING NEWS College Baseball All-America Team, 1985.
Member of 1984 U.S. Olympic baseball team.
Named designated hitter on THE SPORTING NEWS College Baseball All-America Team, 1984.

Year	Club	League	Pos.	G.	AB.	R.	H.	2B.	3B.	HR.	RBI.	B.A.	PO.	A.	E.	F.A.
1985	Fresno	Calif.	1B-OF	65	217	41	67	14	0	10	48	.309	523	51	6	.990
1986	San Francisco†	Nat.	1B	111	408	66	117	27	2	11	41	.287	942	72	11	.989
1986	Phoenix	P. C.	DH	6	20	3	5	0	0	0	1	.250	0	0	0	.000
1987	San Francisco	Nat.	1B	150	529	89	163	29	5	35	91	.308	1253	103	13	.991
1988	San Francisco	Nat.	1B	*162	575	102	162	31	6	29	*109	.282	*1492	104	12	.993
Major League Totals—3 Years				423	1512	257	442	87	13	75	241	.292	3687	279	36	.991

Selected by Kansas City Royals' organization in 4th round of free-agent draft, June 7, 1982.
Selected by San Francisco Giants' organization in 1st round (second player selected) of free-agent draft, June 3, 1985.
†On disabled list, June 4 to July 24, 1986; included rehabilitation disability assignment to Phoenix, July 7 to July 24, 1986.

CHAMPIONSHIP SERIES RECORD

Year	Club	League	Pos.	G.	AB.	R.	H.	2B.	3B.	HR.	RBI.	B.A.	PO.	A.	E.	F.A.
1987	San Francisco	Nat.	1B	7	25	3	9	2	0	1	3	.360	63	7	1	.986

ALL-STAR GAME RECORD

Year	League	Pos.	AB.	R.	H.	2B.	3B.	HR.	RBI.	B.A.	PO.	A.	E.	F.A.
1988	National	1B	2	0	0	0	0	0	0	.000	4	1	0	1.000

DANNY BRUCE CLAY

Born October 24, 1961, at Sun Valley, Calif.
Height, 6.01. Weight, 190.
Throws and bats righthanded.
Attended Los Angeles Pierce Junior College, Woodland Hills, Calif., and Loyola Marymount University, Los Angeles, Calif.

Tied for Appalachian League lead in shutouts with 2 in 1983.

Year	Club	League	G.	IP.	W.	L.	Pct.	H.	R.	ER.	SO.	BB.	ERA.
1983	Wisconsin Rapids	Midwest	4	21	0	4	.000	18	17	14	15	12	6.00
1983	Elizabethton	Ap'lachian	15	*97⅔	6	7	.462	82	47	34	80	42	3.13
1984	Kenosha	Midwest	26	171⅔	9	8	.529	146	73	52	96	64	2.73
1985	Orlando	Southern	31	190⅔	13	9	.591	*195	112	95	79	89	4.48
1986	Toledo	Int'national	29	151⅔	8	11	.421	147	92	●83	105	*93	4.93
1987	Portland†	P. Coast	16	55⅔	1	5	.167	67	46	43	30	45	6.95
1987	Maine	Int'national	15	88⅔	4	6	.400	88	54	43	53	34	4.36
1988	Maine	Int'national	25	45⅓	5	1	.833	24	7	5	41	19	0.99
1988	Philadelphia	National	17	24	0	1	.000	27	17	16	12	21	6.00
Major League Totals—1 Year			17	24	0	1	.000	27	17	16	12	21	6.00

Selected by San Francisco Giants' organization in 30th round of free-agent draft, June 3, 1980.
Signed as free agent by Minnesota Twins' organization, November 27, 1982.
†Traded with Third Baseman Tom Schwarz to Philadelphia Phillies' organization for Pitcher Dan Schatzeder and cash, June 24, 1987.

MARK ALAN CLEAR

Born May 27, 1956, at Los Angeles, Calif.
Height, 6.04. Weight, 215.
Throws and bats righthanded.
Attended Mount San Antonio College, Walnut, Calif.
Nephew of Bob Clear, minor league pitcher, 1945 through 1955; minor league player-manager, 1956 through 1961; minor league manager, 1962 through 1973; scout with California Angels, 1974 and 1975; and coach with California Angels, 1976 through 1987.

Major League saves: 1979 (14), 1980 (9), 1981 (9), 1982 (14), 1983 (4), 1984 (8), 1985 (3), 1986 (16), 1987 (6). Total—83.
Led Appalachian League in hit batsmen with 11 in 1974.
Named American League Rookie Pitcher of the Year by THE SPORTING NEWS, 1979.

Year Club	League	G.	IP.	W.	L.	Pct.	H.	R.	ER.	SO.	BB.	ERA.
1974—Pulaski†	Ap'lachian	14	51	0	7	.000	73	★69	49	38	43	8.65
1975—Idaho Falls	Pioneer	13	28	1	2	.333	24	14	6	29	30	1.93
1976—Quad Cities	Midwest	30	144	8	10	.444	135	84	63	109	111	3.94
1977—Quad Cities	Midwest	13	74	6	3	.667	64	47	40	48	50	4.86
1977—Salinas	California	13	44	1	4	.200	49	36	32	26	45	6.55
1978—Salinas	California	10	53	3	5	.375	51	38	32	55	40	5.43
1978—El Paso	Texas	31	52	4	2	.667	28	14	14	80	32	2.42
1979—California	American	52	109	11	5	.688	87	48	44	98	68	3.63
1980—California‡	American	58	106	11	11	.500	82	51	39	105	65	3.31
1981—Boston	American	34	77	8	3	.727	69	36	35	82	51	4.09
1982—Boston	American	55	105	14	9	.609	92	39	35	109	61	3.00
1983—Boston	American	48	96	4	5	.444	101	71	67	81	68	6.28
1984—Boston	American	47	67	8	3	.727	47	38	30	76	70	4.03
1985—Boston§	American	41	55⅔	1	3	.250	45	26	23	55	50	3.72
1986—Milwaukee	American	59	73⅔	5	5	.500	53	23	18	85	36	2.20
1987—Milwaukee x	American	58	78⅓	8	5	.615	70	46	39	81	55	4.48
1988—Milwaukee yz	American	25	29	1	0	1.000	23	12	9	26	21	2.79
Major League Totals—10 Years		477	796⅔	71	49	.592	669	390	339	798	545	3.83

Selected by Philadelphia Phillies' organization in 8th round of free-agent draft, June 5, 1974.
†Released, April 2, 1975; signed by California Angels' organization, June 16, 1975.
‡Traded with Third Baseman Carney Lansford and Outfielder Rick Miller to Boston Red Sox for Shortstop Rick Burleson and Third Baseman Butch Hobson, December 10, 1980.
§Traded to Milwaukee Brewers for Infielder Ed Romero, December 11, 1985.
xGranted free agency, November 9, 1987; re-signed by Brewers, December 14, 1987.
yOn disabled list, July 21 to August 11 and August 22, 1988 through remainder of season.
zReleased, October 13, 1988.

CHAMPIONSHIP SERIES RECORD

Year Club	League	G.	IP.	W.	L.	Pct.	H.	R.	ER.	SO.	BB.	ERA.
1979—California	American	1	5⅔	0	0	.000	4	3	3	3	2	4.76

ALL-STAR GAME RECORD

Year League	IP.	W.	L.	Pct.	H.	R.	ER.	SO.	BB.	ERA.
1979—American	2	0	0	.000	2	1	1	0	1	4.50

Member of American League All-Star Team in 1982; did not play.

WILLIAM ROGER CLEMENS

(Known by middle name.)
Born August 4, 1962, at Dayton, O.
Height, 6.04. Weight, 220.
Throws and bats righthanded.
Attended San Jacinto College (North), Houston, Tex., and University of Texas, Austin, Tex.

Established major league record for most strikeouts, nine-inning game (20), April 29, 1986.
Tied American League record for most consecutive strikeouts, game (8), April 29, 1986.
Led American League in shutouts with 7 in 1987 and 8 in 1988.
Led American League in complete games with 18 in 1987 and tied for lead with 14 in 1988.
Named Major League Player of the Year by THE SPORTING NEWS, 1986.
Named American League Pitcher of the Year by THE SPORTING NEWS, 1986.
Won American League Cy Young Memorial Award, 1986 and 1987.
Named American League Most Valuable Player by Baseball Writers' Association of America, 1986.
Named righthanded pitcher on THE SPORTING NEWS American League All-Star Team, 1986 and 1987.

Year Club	League	G.	IP.	W.	L.	Pct.	H.	R.	ER.	SO.	BB.	ERA.
1983—Winter Haven	Florida St.	4	29	3	1	.750	22	4	4	36	0	1.24
1983—New Britain	Eastern	7	52	4	1	.800	31	8	8	59	12	1.38
1984—Pawtucket	Int'national	7	46⅔	2	3	.400	39	12	10	50	14	1.93
1984—Boston	American	21	133⅓	9	4	.692	146	67	64	126	29	4.32
1985—Boston†	American	15	98⅓	7	5	.583	83	38	36	74	37	3.29
1986—Boston	American	33	254	★24	4	★.857	179	77	70	238	67	★2.48
1987—Boston	American	36	281⅔	•20	9	.690	248	100	93	256	83	2.97
1988—Boston	American	35	264	18	12	.600	217	93	86	★291	62	2.93
Major League Totals—5 Years		140	1031⅓	78	34	.696	873	375	349	985	278	3.05

Selected by New York Mets' organization in 12th round of free-agent draft, June 8, 1981.
Selected by Boston Red Sox' organization in 1st round (19th player selected) of free-agent draft, June 6, 1983.
†On disabled list, July 8 to August 3 and August 21, 1985 through remainder of season.

CHAMPIONSHIP SERIES RECORD

Tied Championship Series record for most games started, Series (3), 1986.

Established American League Championship Series records for most innings pitched (22⅔) and most earned runs allowed (11), seven-game Series, 1986; most hits allowed, Series (22), 1986.

Tied American League Championship Series records for most runs (8) and earned runs (7) allowed, game, October 7, 1986.

Year Club	League	G.	IP.	W.	L.	Pct.	H.	R.	ER.	SO.	BB.	ERA.
1986—Boston	American	3	22⅔	1	1	.500	22	12	11	17	7	4.37
1988—Boston	American	1	7	0	0	.000	6	3	3	8	0	3.86
Championship Series Totals—2 Years		4	29⅔	1	1	.500	28	15	14	25	7	4.25

WORLD SERIES RECORD

Year Club	League	G.	IP.	W.	L.	Pct.	H.	R.	ER.	SO.	BB.	ERA.
1986—Boston	American	2	11⅓	0	0	.000	9	5	4	11	6	3.18

ALL-STAR GAME RECORD

Year League	IP.	W.	L.	Pct.	H.	R.	ER.	SO.	BB.	ERA.
1986—American	3	1	0	1.000	0	0	0	2	0	0.00
1988—American	1	0	0	.000	0	0	0	1	0	0.00
All-Star Game Totals—2 Years	4	1	0	1.000	0	0	0	3	0	0.00

PATRICK BRIAN CLEMENTS
(Pat)

Born February 2, 1962, at McCloud, Calif.
Height, 6.00. Weight, 180.
Throws left and bats righthanded.
Attended University of California, Los Angeles, Calif.

Major League saves: 1985 (3), 1986 (2), 1987 (7). Total—12.

Year Club	League	G.	IP.	W.	L.	Pct.	H.	R.	ER.	SO.	BB.	ERA.
1983—Peoria	Midwest	15	92⅓	4	7	.364	113	56	46	67	24	4.48
1984—Waterbury	Eastern	43	67	4	2	.667	59	28	20	44	29	2.69
1985—California†	American	41	62	5	0	1.000	47	23	23	19	25	3.34
1985—Pittsburgh	National	27	34⅓	0	2	.000	39	14	14	17	15	3.67
1986—Pittsburgh‡	National	65	61	0	4	.000	53	20	19	31	32	2.80
1987—New York	American	55	80	3	3	.500	91	45	44	36	30	4.95
1987—Columbus	Int'national	4	19	1	0	1.000	19	8	8	7	2	3.79
1988—Columbus	Int'national	32	144	6	7	.462	136	55	44	69	34	2.75
1988—New York§	American	6	8⅓	0	0	.000	12	8	6	3	4	6.48
American League Totals—2 Years		102	150⅓	8	3	.727	150	76	73	58	59	4.37
National League Totals—2 Years		92	95⅓	0	6	.000	92	34	33	48	47	3.12
Major League Totals—4 Years		194	245⅔	8	9	.471	242	110	106	106	106	3.88

Selected by New York Yankees' organization in 32nd round of free-agent draft, June 3, 1980.
Selected by California Angels' organization in 4th round of free-agent draft, June 6, 1983.

†Traded with Outfielder Mike Brown and a player to be named later to Pittsburgh Pirates for Pitchers John Candelaria and Al Holland and Outfielder George Hendrick, August 2, 1985; Pittsburgh organization acquired Pitcher Bob Kipper to complete deal, August 16, 1985.

‡Traded with Pitchers Rick Rhoden and Cecilio Guante to New York Yankees for Pitchers Doug Drabek, Brian Fisher and Logan Easley, November 26, 1986.

§Traded with First Baseman-Outfielder Jack Clark to San Diego Padres for Pitchers Jimmy Jones and Lance McCullers and Outfielder Stan Jefferson, October 24, 1988.

STEWART WALKER CLIBURN
(Stu)

Born December 19, 1956, at Jackson, Miss.
Height, 6.00. Weight, 187.
Throws and bats righthanded.
Attended Delta State University, Cleveland, Miss.
Identical twin of Stan Cliburn, catcher with California Angels, 1980.

Major League saves: 1985 (6).

Year Club	League	G.	IP.	W.	L.	Pct.	H.	R.	ER.	SO.	BB.	ERA.
1977—Salem	Carolina	15	97	8	5	.615	108	50	35	48	33	3.25
1978—Shreveport†	Texas	9	42	1	0	1.000	37	13	9	30	17	1.93
1979—Buffalo	Eastern	15	103	6	6	.500	110	50	37	62	43	3.23
1979—Portland‡	P. Coast	7	33	3	2	.600	43	19	18	17	17	4.91
1980—Buffalo§	Eastern	1	6	1	0	1.000	5	0	0	2	3	0.00
1980—Portland	P. Coast	17	82	2	9	.182	97	56	50	44	39	5.49
1981—Buffalo x	Eastern	28	85	5	8	.385	77	45	41	53	35	4.34
1981—Portland y	P. Coast	6	17	0	1	.000	32	18	18	7	6	9.53
1982—Holyoke	Eastern	22	103⅔	5	3	.625	91	48	41	78	42	3.56
1982—Spokane	P. Coast	8	38⅔	1	6	.143	51	37	33	28	17	7.68
1983—Nashua	Eastern	39	98⅔	6	7	.462	94	45	41	40	31	3.74
1984—Edmonton	P. Coast	45	75	7	7	.500	71	30	24	48	28	2.88
1984—California	American	1	2	0	0	.000	3	3	3	1	1	13.50
1985—Edmonton	P. Coast	2	3⅔	0	0	.000	3	0	0	2	0	0.00
1985—California	American	44	99	9	3	.750	87	25	23	48	26	2.09
1986—Edmonton z	P. Coast	20	23⅓	1	2	.333	36	18	18	17	7	6.94
1987—Edmonton a	P. Coast	16	15⅔	1	0	1.000	10	4	4	10	6	2.30
1988—California b	American	40	84	4	2	.667	83	45	38	42	32	4.07
Major League Totals—3 Years		85	185	13	5	.722	173	73	64	91	59	3.11

Selected by San Francisco Giants' organization in 16th round of free-agent draft, June 5, 1974.
Selected by Pittsburgh Pirates' organization in 4th round of free-agent draft, June 7, 1977.
†On disabled list, May 9 to May 24, May 26 to June 15 and July 2 to August 22, 1978.

‡On disabled list, July 22 to August 8, 1979.
§On disabled list, April 14 to April 26, 1980.
xOn disabled list, May 11 to May 27, 1981.
yReleased, April 8, 1982; signed by Holyoke (California Angels' organization), April 29, 1982.
zOn disabled list, April 22 to July 16, 1986.
aReleased, December 21, 1987; re-signed by Angels' organization, January 22, 1988.
bAppeared in one game as a pinch-runner.

BRYAN RICHARD CLUTTERBUCK

Born December 17, 1959, at Detroit, Mich.
Height, 6.04. Weight, 223.
Throws and bats righthanded.
Attended Eastern Michigan University, Ypsilanti, Mich.

Tied for Texas League lead in games started by pitchers with 27 in 1983 and 1984.
Tied for Midwest League lead in shutouts with 4 in 1982.

Year Club	League	G.	IP.	W.	L.	Pct.	H.	R.	ER.	SO.	BB.	ERA.
1981—Butte	Pioneer	6	16	1	1	.500	22	13	13	4	7	7.31
1982—Beloit	Midwest	26	173⅔	13	6	.684	165	84	70	138	56	3.63
1983—El Paso	Texas	27	166⅓	11	7	.611	204	118	96	86	78	5.19
1984—El Paso	Texas	27	179	10	9	.526	*198	*103	*79	112	52	3.97
1985—Vancouver	P. Coast	29	147⅔	11	7	.611	156	68	58	101	41	3.53
1986—Vancouver	P. Coast	17	115⅓	8	5	.615	121	60	59	63	30	4.60
1986—Milwaukee	American	20	56⅔	0	1	.000	68	32	27	38	16	4.29
1987—Denver†	Am. Assoc.	7	33⅓	3	2	.600	49	24	21	14	4	5.67
1988—Denver	Am. Assoc.	20	130⅔	9	3	*.750	133	54	50	88	32	3.44
Major League Totals—1 Year		20	56⅔	0	1	.000	68	32	27	38	16	4.29

Selected by Milwaukee Brewers' organization in 7th round of free-agent draft, June 8, 1981.
†Granted free agency, October 15, 1987; re-signed by Brewers, November 11, 1987.

CHRISTOPHER ALLEN CODIROLI

Name pronounced Coda-RO-lee.

(Chris)

Born March 26, 1958, at Oxnard, Calif.
Height, 6.01. Weight, 160.
Throws and bats righthanded.
Attended San Jose City College, San Jose, Calif., and San Jose State University, San Jose, Calif.

Major League saves: 1983 (1), 1984 (1), 1988 (1). Total—3.
Tied for American League lead in games started by pitchers with 37 in 1985.

Year Club	League	G.	IP.	W.	L.	Pct.	H.	R.	ER.	SO.	BB.	ERA.
1978—Lakeland	Florida St.	16	102	4	6	.400	93	44	37	72	40	3.26
1978—Montgomery	Southern	10	78	5	2	.714	60	20	17	57	24	1.96
1979—Montgomery†	Southern	8	49	2	3	.400	41	24	18	34	27	3.31
1980—Lakeland‡	Florida St.	9	50	1	1	.500	33	13	10	26	19	1.80
1980—Montgomery§	Southern	2	4	0	1	.000	6	7	6	1	4	13.50
1981—San Jose	California	14	35	3	2	.600	23	8	6	26	24	1.54
1981—West Haven	Eastern	21	50	3	2	.600	35	25	15	47	25	2.70
1982—West Haven x	Eastern	12	45	6	1	.857	37	14	12	45	19	2.40
1982—Tacoma	P. Coast	16	123⅓	10	3	*.769	100	36	26	85	21	*1.90
1982—Oakland	American	3	16⅔	1	2	.333	16	8	8	5	4	4.32
1983—Oakland	American	37	205⅔	12	12	.500	208	115	102	85	72	4.46
1984—Oakland	American	28	89⅓	6	4	.600	111	67	58	44	34	5.84
1984—Tacoma	P. Coast	9	57	2	1	.667	49	35	24	52	30	3.79
1985—Oakland	American	37	226	14	14	.500	228	125	112	111	78	4.46
1986—Oakland y	American	16	91⅔	5	8	.385	91	54	41	43	38	4.03
1987—Oakland	American	3	11⅓	0	2	.000	12	11	11	4	8	8.74
1987—Tacoma z	P. Coast	19	67⅔	2	7	.222	77	56	46	34	52	6.12
1988—Cleveland	American	14	19⅓	0	4	.000	32	22	20	12	10	9.31
1988—Colorado Springs a	P. Coast	17	96⅓	5	4	.556	104	64	52	51	42	4.86
Major League Totals—7 Years		138	660	38	46	.452	698	402	352	304	244	4.80

Selected by Detroit Tigers' organization in 1st round (11th player selected) of free-agent draft, January 10, 1978.
†On disabled list, May 25, 1979 through remainder of season.
‡On disabled list, April 11 to June 10, 1980.
§Released, April 3, 1981; signed by Oakland A's organization, April 14, 1981.
xOn disabled list, April 19 to April 29, 1982.
yOn disabled list, June 28, 1986 through remainder of season.
zGranted free agency, October 15, 1987; signed by Colorado Springs (Cleveland Indians' organization), February 22, 1988.
aReleased, September 6, 1988.

KEVIN REESE COFFMAN

Born January 19, 1965, at Austin, Tex.
Height, 6.03. Weight, 206.
Throws and bats righthanded.

Led Southern League in wild pitches with 21 in 1987.

Year	Club	League	G.	IP.	W.	L.	Pct.	H.	R.	ER.	SO.	BB.	ERA.
1983	—Bradenton Braves	Gulf Coast	6	28⅔	2	4	.333	27	29	21	25	39	6.59
1984	—Anderson	S. Atlantic	7	32⅔	1	4	.200	37	23	17	23	26	4.68
1984	—Pulaski	Ap'lachian	11	48	1	4	.200	41	26	22	41	33	4.13
1985	—Durham†	Carolina	3	4⅓	0	1	.000	4	5	5	1	11	10.38
1985	—Sumter‡	S. Atlantic	24	62⅔	1	3	.250	42	25	22	43	26	3.16
1986	—Durham	Carolina	3	13⅓	1	2	.333	11	12	11	7	17	7.43
1986	—Sumter	S. Atlantic	18	114⅓	10	3	.769	99	56	39	120	64	3.07
1986	—Greenville	Southern	8	48⅔	3	4	.429	43	24	24	43	30	4.44
1987	—Greenville	Southern	30	181⅔	11	11	.500	162	102	89	153	*130	4.41
1987	—Atlanta	National	5	25⅓	2	3	.400	31	14	13	14	22	4.62
1988	—Atlanta	National	18	67	2	6	.250	62	52	43	24	54	5.78
1988	—Durham	Carolina	8	10	1	1	.500	12	6	5	10	3	4.50
1988	—Richmond§	Int'national	9	19⅓	1	1	.500	15	10	9	18	20	4.19
Major League Totals—2 Years			23	92⅓	4	9	.308	93	66	56	38	76	5.46

Selected by Atlanta Braves' organization in 11th round of free-agent draft, June 6, 1983.
†On disabled list, April 24 to May 4, 1985.
‡On disabled list, May 4 to May 28, 1985.
§Traded with Pitcher Kevin Blankenship to Chicago Cubs for Catcher Jody Davis, September 29, 1988.

ALEXANDER COLE JR.
(Alex)

Born August 17, 1965, at Fayetteville, N. C.
Height, 6.02. Weight, 170.
Throws and bats lefthanded.
Attended Manatee Junior College, Bradenton, Fla.

Led Texas League in stolen bases with 68 and caught stealing with 29 in 1987.
Led Florida State League in caught stealing with 22 in 1986.
Led Appalachian League in stolen bases with 46 and caught stealing with 8 in 1985.
Tied for Texas League lead in double plays by outfielders with 5 in 1987.
Led Appalachian League outfielders in total chances with 142 in 1985.

Year	Club	League	Pos.	G.	AB.	R.	H.	2B.	3B.	HR.	RBI.	B.A.	PO.	A.	E.	F.A.
1985	—Johnson City	Appal.	OF	66	232	*60	61	5	1	1	13	.263	*127	*12	3	.979
1986	—St. Petersburg	Fla. St.	OF	74	286	76	98	9	1	0	26	.343	201	4	8	.962
1986	—Louisville	A. A.	OF	63	200	25	50	2	4	1	16	.250	135	6	9	.940
1987	—Arkansas	Texas	OF	125	477	68	122	12	4	2	27	.256	289	14	10	.968
1988	—Louisville	A. A.	OF	120	392	44	91	7	8	0	24	.232	276	13	1	.997

Selected by Pittsburgh Pirates' organization in 11th round of free-agent draft, January 17, 1984.
Selected by St. Louis Cardinals' organization in 2nd round of free-agent draft, January 9, 1985.

VINCENT MAURICE COLEMAN
(Vince)

Born September 22, 1961, at Jacksonville, Fla.
Height, 6.00. Weight, 170.
Throws right and bats left and righthanded.
Received degree in physical education from Florida A&M University, Tallahassee, Fla.
Cousin of Greg Coleman, punter with Washington Redskins.

Established major league records for most stolen bases (110) and most caught stealing (25), rookie season, 1985.
Tied major league records for most sacrifice flies, game (3), May 1, 1986; fewest errors by outfielder, season, for leader in errors (9), 1986.
Major League stolen bases: 1985 (110), 1986 (107), 1987 (109), 1988 (81). Total—407.
Led National League in stolen bases with 110 in 1985, 107 in 1986, 109 in 1987 and 81 in 1988.
Led National League in caught stealing with 25 in 1985, 22 in 1987 and tied for lead with 27 in 1988.
Led American Association in stolen bases with 101 and caught stealing with 36 in 1984.
Led South Atlantic League in stolen bases with 145 and caught stealing with 31 in 1983.
Tied for Appalachian League lead in stolen bases with 43 in 1982.
Led American Association outfielders in total chances with 381 in 1984.
Named National League Rookie Player of the Year by The Sporting News, 1985.
Named National League Rookie of the Year by Baseball Writers' Association of America, 1985.
Named South Atlantic League Most Valuable Player, 1983.

Year	Club	League	Pos.	G.	AB.	R.	H.	2B.	3B.	HR.	RBI.	B.A.	PO.	A.	E.	F.A.
1982	—Johnson City	Appal.	OF	58	212	40	53	2	1	0	16	.250	123	7	8	.942
1983	—Macon	S. Atl.	OF	113	446	99	156	8	7	0	53	*.350	225	18	8	.968
1984	—Louisville	A. A.	OF	152	*608	*97	156	21	7	4	48	.257	357	14	•10	.974
1985	—Louisville	A. A.	OF	5	21	1	3	0	0	0	0	.143	8	0	0	1.000
1985	—St. Louis	Nat.	OF	151	636	107	170	20	10	1	40	.267	305	16	7	.979
1986	—St. Louis	Nat.	OF	154	600	94	139	13	8	0	29	.232	300	12	•9	.972
1987	—St. Louis	Nat.	OF	151	623	121	180	14	10	3	43	.289	274	16	9	.970
1988	—St. Louis	Nat.	OF	153	616	77	160	20	10	3	38	.260	290	14	9	.971
Major League Totals—4 Years				609	2475	399	649	67	38	7	150	.262	1169	58	34	.973

Selected by Philadelphia Phillies' organization in 20th round of free-agent draft, June 8, 1981.
Selected by St. Louis Cardinals' organization in 10th round of free-agent draft, June 7, 1982.

CHAMPIONSHIP SERIES RECORD

Year	Club	League	Pos.	G.	AB.	R.	H.	2B.	3B.	HR.	RBI.	B.A.	PO.	A.	E.	F.A.
1985	—St. Louis	Nat.	OF	3	14	2	4	0	0	0	1	.286	8	0	0	1.000
1987	—St. Louis	Nat.	OF	7	26	3	7	1	0	0	4	.269	9	1	0	1.000
Championship Series Totals—2 Years				10	40	5	11	1	0	0	5	.275	17	1	0	1.000

WORLD SERIES RECORD

Year	Club	League	Pos.	G.	AB.	R.	H.	2B.	3B.	HR.	RBI.	B.A.	PO.	A.	E.	F.A.
1987	St. Louis	Nat.	OF	7	28	5	4	2	0	0	2	.143	10	2	0	1.000

ALL-STAR GAME RECORD

Year	League	Pos.	AB.	R.	H.	2B.	3B.	HR.	RBI.	B.A.	PO.	A.	E.	F.A.
1988	National	OF	2	1	1	0	0	0	0	.500	3	0	0	1.000

DARNELL COLES

First name pronounced Darr-NELL.

Born June 2, 1962, at San Bernardino, Calif.
Height, 6.01. Weight, 185.
Throws and bats righthanded.
Attended Orange Coast College, Costa Mesa, Calif.

Major League stolen bases: 1984 (2), 1986 (6), 1987 (1), 1988 (4). Total—13.
Hit three home runs in a game, September 20, 1987.
Led Midwest League shortstops in double plays with 66 in 1981.

Year	Club	League	Pos.	G.	AB.	R.	H.	2B.	3B.	HR.	RBI.	B.A.	PO.	A.	E.	F.A.
1980	Bellingham	N'west	SS	35	117	23	25	3	1	2	12	.214	37	80	★28	.807
1981	Wausau	Midw.	SS	111	354	53	97	20	3	9	48	.274	154	335	52	.904
1982	Bakersfield	Calif.	SS	136	482	91	146	24	4	11	55	.303	200	419	★73	.895
1983	Chattanooga	South.	SS	72	261	49	75	10	4	5	24	.287	131	232	30	.924
1983	Salt Lake City	P. C.	SS	61	234	43	74	12	5	10	41	.316	100	178	25	.917
1983	Seattle	Amer.	3B	27	92	9	26	7	0	1	6	.283	17	47	4	.941
1984	Salt Lake City†	P. C.	3B	69	242	57	77	22	3	14	68	.318	45	164	16	.929
1984	Seattle	Amer.	3B-OF	48	143	15	23	3	1	0	6	.161	31	63	8	.922
1985	Calgary‡	P. C.	3B-SS-OF	31	97	16	31	8	0	4	24	.320	16	49	5	.929
1985	Seattle§	Amer.	SS-3B-OF	27	59	8	14	4	0	1	5	.237	25	44	6	.920
1986	Detroit x	Amer.	3B-OF-SS	142	521	67	142	30	2	20	86	.273	111	242	23	.939
1987	Detroit y	Amer.	3-1-O-S	53	149	14	27	5	1	4	15	.181	84	67	17	.899
1987	Toledo z	Int.	3B-OF-SS	10	37	7	12	5	0	1	8	.324	7	8	1	.938
1987	Pittsburgh	Nat.	OF-3B-1B	40	119	20	27	8	0	6	24	.227	39	20	3	.952
1988	Pittsburgh a	Nat.	OF-1B-3B	68	211	20	49	13	1	5	36	.232	100	0	2	.980
1988	Seattle	Amer.	OF-1B	55	195	32	57	10	1	10	34	.292	66	3	1	.986
American League Totals—6 Years				352	1159	145	289	59	5	36	152	.249	334	466	59	.931
National League Totals—2 Years				108	330	40	76	21	1	11	60	.230	139	20	5	.970
Major League Totals—6 Years				460	1489	185	365	80	6	47	212	.245	473	486	64	.937

Selected by Seattle Mariners' organization in 1st round (sixth player selected) of free-agent draft, June 3, 1980.

†On Seattle disabled list, March 29 to April 24, 1984; included rehabilitation disability assignment to Salt Lake City, April 12 to April 24, 1984.

‡On disabled list, August 8 to September 9, 1985.

§Traded to Detroit Tigers for Pitcher Rich Monteleone, December 12, 1985.

xOn disabled list, June 16 to July 1, 1986.

yOn disabled list, May 25 to June 27, 1987; included rehabilitation disability assignment to Toledo, June 16 to June 27, 1987.

zTraded with a player to be named later to Pittsburgh Pirates for Third Baseman Jim Morrison, August 7, 1987; Pittsburgh organization acquired Pitcher Morris Madden to complete deal, August 12, 1987.

aTraded to Seattle Mariners for Outfielder Glenn Wilson, July 22, 1988.

DAVID S. COLLINS
(Dave)

Born October 20, 1952, at Rapid City, S. D.
Height, 5.10. Weight, 175.
Throws left and bats left and righthanded.
Attended Mesa Community College, Mesa, Ariz.

Major League stolen bases: 1975 (24), 1976 (32), 1977 (25), 1978 (7), 1979 (16), 1980 (79), 1981 (26), 1982 (13), 1983 (31), 1984 (60), 1985 (29), 1986 (27), 1987 (9), 1988 (7). Total—385.
Led Pioneer League outfielders in double plays with 3 in 1972.
Named Pioneer League Most Valuable Player, 1972.

Year	Club	League	Pos.	G.	AB.	R.	H.	2B.	3B.	HR.	RBI.	B.A.	PO.	A.	E.	F.A.
1972	Idaho Falls	Pion.	★OF-1B	68	252	40	69	8	★8	1	27	.274	101	★11	3	.974
1973	Quad Cities†	Midw.	OF	110	387	61	100	15	7	4	49	.258	229	10	11	.956
1974	Salinas	Calif.	OF-1B	39	143	30	49	3	5	1	21	.343	109	0	5	.956
1974	El Paso	Texas	1B-OF	82	324	64	114	15	4	4	49	★.352	381	14	12	.971
1975	Salt Lake City	P. C.	OF	51	193	41	60	7	6	0	24	.311	58	2	1	.984
1975	California	Amer.	OF	93	319	41	85	13	4	3	29	.266	159	3	2	.988
1976	Salt Lake City	P. C.	OF	35	136	28	49	13	4	0	12	.360	50	3	2	.964
1976	California‡	Amer.	OF	99	365	45	96	12	1	4	28	263	160	3	1	.994
1977	Seattle§	Amer.	OF	120	402	46	96	9	3	5	28	.239	124	6	2	.985
1978	Cincinnati	Nat.	OF	102	102	13	22	1	0	0	7	.216	30	1	1	.969
1979	Cincinnati	Nat.	OF-1B	122	396	59	126	16	4	3	35	.318	223	3	4	.983
1980	Cincinnati	Nat.	OF	144	551	94	167	20	4	3	35	.303	337	5	5	.986
1981	Cincinnati x	Nat.	OF	95	360	63	98	18	6	3	23	.272	167	4	4	.977
1982	New York y	Amer.	OF-1B	111	348	41	88	12	3	3	25	.253	498	28	7	.987
1983	Toronto z	Amer.	OF-1B	118	402	55	109	12	4	1	34	.271	270	9	3	.989
1984	Toronto a	Amer.	OF-1B	128	441	59	136	24	●15	2	44	.308	237	11	2	.992
1985	Oakland b	Amer.	OF	112	379	52	95	16	4	4	29	.251	221	1	5	.978

Year	Club	League	Pos.	G.	AB.	R.	H.	2B.	3B.	HR.	RBI.	B.A.	PO.	A.	E.	F.A.
1986—Detroit cd		Amer.	OF	124	419	44	113	18	2	1	27	.270	211	2	1	.995
1987—Nashville		A. A.	DH-PH	13	40	8	8	6	0	0	9	.200	0	0	0	.000
1987—Cincinnati e		Nat.	OF	57	85	19	25	5	0	0	5	.294	36	0	0	1.000
1988—Cincinnati f		Nat.	OF-1B	99	174	12	41	6	2	0	14	.236	66	2	4	.944
National League Totals—6 Years				619	1668	260	479	66	16	9	119	.287	859	15	18	.980
American League Totals—8 Years				905	3075	383	818	116	36	23	244	.266	1880	63	23	.988
Major League Totals—14 Years				1524	4743	643	1297	182	52	32	363	.273	2739	78	41	.986

Selected by Cincinnati Reds' organization in 23rd round of free-agent draft, June 8, 1971.
Selected by Kansas City Royals' organization in secondary phase of free-agent draft, January 12, 1972.
Selected by California Angels' organization in secondary phase of free-agent draft, June 6, 1972.
†On disabled list, May 21 to May 31, 1973.
‡Selected by Seattle Mariners in special American League expansion draft, November 5, 1976.
§Traded to Cincinnati Reds for Pitcher Shane Rawley, December 9, 1977.
xGranted free agency, November 13, 1981; signed by New York Yankees, December 23, 1981.
yTraded with Pitcher Mike Morgan, First Baseman Fred McGriff and a reported $400,000 to Toronto Blue Jays for Pitcher Dale Murray and Outfielder-Catcher Tom Dodd, December 9, 1982.
zOn disabled list, June 4 to June 22, 1983.
aTraded with Shortstop Alfredo Griffin and cash to Oakland A's for Pitcher Bill Caudill, December 8, 1984.
bTraded to Detroit Tigers for Infielder Barbaro Garbey, November 13, 1985.
cReleased, October 16, 1986; signed by Montreal Expos, November 13, 1986.
dReleased, March 31, 1987; signed by Nashville (Cincinnati Reds' organization), June 19, 1987.
eGranted free agency, November 9, 1987; re-signed by Reds, December 8, 1987.
fGranted free agency, November 4, 1988; re-signed by Reds, December 7, 1988.

CHAMPIONSHIP SERIES RECORD

Year	Club	League	Pos.	G.	AB.	R.	H.	2B.	3B.	HR.	RBI.	B.A.	PO.	A.	E.	F.A.
1979—Cincinnati		Nat.	OF	3	14	0	5	1	0	0	1	.357	5	0	0	1.000

KEITH MARTIN COMSTOCK

Born December 23, 1955, at San Francisco, Calif.
Height, 6.00. Weight, 174.
Throws and bats lefthanded.
Attended Canada College, Redwood City, Calif.
Brother of Brad Comstock, pitcher in San Francisco Giants' organization.

Major League saves: 1987 (1).
Tied for Southern League lead in shutouts with 3 in 1983.

Year	Club	League	G.	IP.	W.	L.	Pct.	H.	R.	ER.	SO.	BB.	ERA.
1976—Idaho Falls†		Pioneer	15	37	1	4	.200	33	18	16	45	32	3.89
1977—Quad Cities		Midwest	18	32	1	0	1.000	22	18	18	39	18	5.06
1977—Salinas		California	23	33	1	1	.500	35	26	17	41	18	4.64
1978—Salinas		California	27	82	6	4	.600	70	31	26	71	46	2.85
1979—El Paso‡		Texas	16	63	2	5	.286	95	64	50	18	35	7.14
1980—West Haven		Eastern	29	73	2	4	.333	64	40	34	52	37	4.19
1981—West Haven		Eastern	35	145	8	7	.533	123	76	66	133	80	4.10
1982—West Haven		Eastern	24	125	9	5	.643	99	48	42	132	69	3.02
1982—Tacoma§		P. Coast	5	27⅔	1	2	.333	34	24	22	22	12	7.16
1983—Birmingham x		Southern	37	145⅔	12	3	•.800	130	58	52	136	63	3.21
1984—Minnesota		American	4	6⅓	0	0	.000	6	6	6	2	4	8.53
1984—Toledo y		Int'national	23	164⅓	12	6	.667	132	58	51	154	56	2.79
1985—Yomiuri		Central	21	124	8	8	.500	....	....	58	87	76	4.19
1986—Yomiuri z		Central	3	10	0	2	.000	....	....	9	7	7	7.83
1987—Phoenix		P. Coast	17	39	4	2	.667	24	12	12	35	23	2.77
1987—San Francisco ab-San Diego		National	41	56⅔	2	1	.667	52	30	29	59	31	4.61
1988—Las Vegas		P. Coast	50	71⅔	5	4	.556	67	32	25	78	31	3.14
1988—San Diego c		National	7	8	0	0	.000	8	6	6	9	3	6.75
American League Totals—1 Year			4	6⅓	0	0	.000	6	6	6	2	4	8.53
National League Totals—2 Years			48	64⅔	2	1	.667	60	36	35	68	34	4.87
Major League Totals—3 Years			52	71	2	1	.667	66	42	41	70	38	5.20

Selected by California Angels' organization in 5th round of free-agent draft, January 7, 1976.
†On disabled list, July 29, 1976 through remainder of season.
‡Released, July 6, 1979; signed by West Haven (Oakland A's organization), February 29, 1980.
§Sold to Detroit Tigers' organization, March 28, 1983.
xGranted free agency, October 23, 1983; signed by Minnesota Twins' organization, October 23, 1983.
yReleased, November 6, 1984; signed by Yomiuri Giants of Japanese Baseball League.
zReleased by Yomiuri Giants; signed by San Francisco Giants, November 24, 1986.
aAppeared in one game as an outfielder with no chances.
bTraded with Third Baseman Chris Brown and Pitchers Mark Davis and Mark Grant to San Diego Padres for Pitchers Dave Dravecky and Craig Lefferts and Infielder Kevin Mitchell, July 4, 1987.
cGranted free agency, October 15, 1988.

—DID YOU KNOW—

That San Diego's Tony Gwynn hit .313 in 1988 to record the lowest average ever for a National League batting champion? Gwynn broke the record of .320 set by Larry Doyle of the New York Giants in 1915.

DAVID ISMAEL CONCEPCION (BENITEZ)

Name pronounced Con-sep-see-OHN.

(Dave)

Born June 17, 1948, at Ocumare de la Costa, Aragua, Venezuela.
Height, 6.01. Weight, 200.
Throws and bats righthanded.
Attended College Augustin Codazzi, Aragua, Venezuela.

Tied major league records for most stolen bases by pinch-runner, inning, (2), July 7, 1974 (1st game, 7th inning); most double plays by shortstop, game, (5), June 25, 1975.

Established National League record for fewest chances accepted by shortstop, season, 150 or more games (616), 1985.

Tied National League record for fewest double plays by shortstop, season, 150 or more games (64), 1985.

Major League stolen bases: 1970 (10), 1971 (9), 1972 (13), 1973 (22), 1974 (41), 1975 (33), 1976 (21), 1977 (29), 1978 (23), 1979 (19), 1980 (12), 1981 (4), 1982 (13), 1983 (14), 1984 (22), 1985 (16), 1986 (13), 1987 (4), 1988 (3). Total—321.

Led National League in game-winning RBIs with 14 in 1981.

Tied for National League lead in grounding into double plays with 21 in 1983.

Led National League shortstops in total chances with 805 in 1974 and 837 in 1976.

Tied for National League lead in double plays by shortstops with 102 in 1979.

Led Southern League shortstops in double plays with 64 in 1969.

Led Florida State League shortstops in fielding percentage with .953 in 1968.

Named shortstop on THE SPORTING NEWS National League All-Star Team, 1974, 1976, 1977 and 1981.

Named shortstop on THE SPORTING NEWS National League All-Star fielding team, 1974 through 1977 and 1979.

Named shortstop on THE SPORTING NEWS National League Silver Slugger team, 1981 and 1982.

Year Club	League	Pos.	G.	AB.	R.	H.	2B.	3B.	HR.	RBI.	B.A.	PO.	A.	E.	F.A.
1968—Tampa	Fla. St.	SS-2B	120	329	47	77	11	1	0	22	.234	151	239	20	.951
1969—Asheville	South.	SS	96	340	47	100	11	5	1	37	.294	★157	★292	★29	★.939
1969—Indianapolis	A. A.	S-2-3-O	42	167	29	57	7	1	0	17	.341	76	128	9	.958
1970—Cincinnati	Nat.	SS-2B	101	265	38	69	6	3	1	19	.260	144	247	22	.947
1971—Cincinnati†	Nat.	S-2-3-O	130	327	24	67	4	4	1	20	.205	182	310	13	.974
1972—Cincinnati	Nat.	SS-3B-2B	119	378	40	79	13	2	2	29	.209	197	372	19	.968
1973—Cincinnati‡	Nat.	SS-OF	89	328	39	94	18	3	8	46	.287	167	292	12	.975
1974—Cincinnati	Nat.	★SS-OF	160	594	70	167	25	1	14	82	.281	239	★536	30	.963
1975—Cincinnati	Nat.	SS-3B	140	507	62	139	23	1	5	49	.274	241	446	16	.977
1976—Cincinnati	Nat.	SS	152	576	74	162	28	7	9	69	.281	★304	★506	27	.968
1977—Cincinnati	Nat.	SS	156	572	59	155	26	3	8	64	.271	280	490	11	★.986
1978—Cincinnati	Nat.	SS	153	565	75	170	33	4	6	67	.301	255	459	23	.969
1979—Cincinnati	Nat.	SS	149	590	91	166	25	3	16	84	.281	284	495	27	.967
1980—Cincinnati	Nat.	SS-2B	156	622	72	162	31	8	5	77	.260	265	451	16	.978
1981—Cincinnati	Nat.	SS	106	421	57	129	28	0	5	67	.306	208	322	22	.960
1982—Cincinnati	Nat.	SS-1B-3B	147	572	48	164	25	4	5	53	.287	271	459	17	.977
1983—Cincinnati	Nat.	SS-3B-1B	143	528	54	123	22	0	1	47	.233	227	387	13	.979
1984—Cincinnati	Nat.	SS-3B-1B	154	531	46	130	26	1	4	58	.245	213	324	17	.969
1985—Cincinnati	Nat.	SS-3B	155	560	59	141	19	2	7	48	.252	214	405	24	.963
1986—Cincinnati§ x	Nat.	S-1-2-3	90	311	42	81	13	2	3	30	.260	153	223	10	.974
1987—Cincinnati	Nat.	2-1-3-S	104	279	32	89	15	0	1	33	.319	250	169	5	.988
1988—Cincinnati yz	Nat.	2-1-S-3-P	84	197	11	39	9	0	0	8	.198	151	131	2	.993
Major League Totals—19 Years			2488	8723	993	2326	389	48	101	950	.267	4245	7024	326	.972

Signed as free agent by Cincinnati Reds' organization, September 12, 1967.

†On disabled list March 21 to April 20, 1971.

‡On disabled list July 22, 1973 through remainder of season.

§On disabled list, July 11 to September 1, 1986.

xGranted free agency, November 12, 1986; re-signed by Reds, December 9, 1986.

yOn disabled list, July 16 to July 31, 1988.

zReleased, October 7, 1988.

CHAMPIONSHIP SERIES RECORD

Year Club	League	Pos.	G.	AB.	R.	H.	2B.	3B.	HR.	RBI.	B.A.	PO.	A.	E.	F.A.
1970—Cincinnati	Nat.	PR-SS	3	0	0	0	0	0	0	0	.000	1	1	0	1.000
1972—Cincinnati	Nat.	PH-S-PR	3	2	0	0	0	0	0	0	.000	0	0	0	.000
1975—Cincinnati	Nat.	SS	3	11	2	5	0	0	1	1	.455	6	8	1	.933
1976—Cincinnati	Nat.	SS	3	10	4	2	1	0	0	0	.200	2	12	0	1.000
1979—Cincinnati	Nat.	SS	3	14	1	6	1	0	0	0	.429	3	14	0	1.000
Championship Series Totals—5 Years			15	37	7	13	2	0	1	1	.351	12	35	1	.979

WORLD SERIES RECORD

Tied World Series records for most sacrifice flies, total Series (3); fewest chances accepted by shortstop, game (0), October 16, 1975; one or more hits, each game, four-game Series, 1976.

Year Club	League	Pos.	G.	AB.	R.	H.	2B.	3B.	HR.	RBI.	B.A.	PO.	A.	E.	F.A.
1970—Cincinnati	Nat.	SS	3	9	0	3	0	1	0	3	.333	2	2	0	1.000
1972—Cincinnati	Nat.	S-PR-PH	6	13	2	4	0	1	0	2	.308	4	11	1	.938
1975—Cincinnati	Nat.	SS	7	28	3	5	1	0	1	4	.179	12	22	1	.971
1976—Cincinnati	Nat.	SS	4	14	1	5	1	1	0	3	.357	6	11	1	.944
World Series Totals—4 Years			20	64	6	17	2	3	1	12	.266	24	46	3	.959

ALL STAR GAME RECORD

Year League	Pos.	AB.	R.	H.	2B.	3B.	HR.	RBI.	B.A.	PO.	A.	E.	F.A.
1975—National	SS	2	0	1	0	0	0	0	.500	1	1	1	.667
1976—National	SS	2	0	1	0	0	0	0	.500	2	3	0	1.000
1977—National	SS	1	0	0	0	0	0	0	.000	1	1	0	1.000

Year League	Pos.	AB.	R.	H.	2B.	3B.	HR.	RBI.	B.A.	PO.	A.	E.	F.A.
1978—National	SS	0	1	0	0	0	0	0	.000	2	0	0	1.000
1980—National	SS	1	1	0	0	0	0	0	.000	0	2	0	1.000
1981—National	SS	3	0	0	0	0	0	0	.000	0	0	0	.000
1982—National	SS	3	1	1	0	0	1	2	.333	1	1	0	1.000
All-Star Game Totals—7 Years		12	3	3	0	0	1	2	.250	7	8	1	.938

Named to National League All-Star Team for 1973 game; replaced due to injury.
Named to National League All-Star Team for 1979 game; replaced due to injury by Larry Parrish.

PITCHING RECORD

Year Club	League	G.	IP.	W.	L.	Pct.	H.	R.	ER.	SO.	BB.	ERA.
1988—Cincinnati	National	1	1⅓	0	0	.000	2	0	0	1	0	0.00

DAVID BRIAN CONE

Born January 2, 1963, at Kansas City, Mo.
Height, 6.01. Weight, 185.
Throws right and bats lefthanded.

Major League saves: 1987 (1).
Tied for National League lead in balks with 10 in 1988.
Led Southern League in wild pitches with 27 in 1984.

Year Club	League	G.	IP.	W.	L.	Pct.	H.	R.	ER.	SO.	BB.	ERA.
1981—Sarasota Royals-Blue	Gulf Coast	14	67	6	4	.600	52	24	19	45	33	2.55
1982—Charleston	S. Atlantic	16	104⅔	9	2	.818	84	38	24	87	47	2.06
1982—Fort Myers	Florida St.	10	72⅓	7	1	.875	56	21	17	57	25	2.12
1983—Jacksonville†	Southern					(Did not play)						
1984—Memphis	Southern	29	178⅔	8	12	.400	162	103	85	110	114	4.28
1985—Omaha	Am. Assoc.	28	158⅔	9	15	.375	157	90	82	115	*93	4.65
1986—Omaha	Am. Assoc.	39	71	8	4	.667	60	23	22	63	25	2.79
1986—Kansas City‡	American	11	22⅔	0	0	.000	29	14	14	21	13	5.56
1987—New York§	National	21	99⅓	5	6	.455	87	46	41	68	44	3.71
1987—Tidewater	Int'national	3	11	0	1	.000	10	8	7	7	6	5.73
1988—New York	National	35	231⅓	20	3	*.870	178	67	57	213	80	2.22
American League Totals—1 Year		11	22⅔	0	0	.000	29	14	14	21	13	5.56
National League Totals—2 Years		56	330⅔	25	9	.735	265	113	98	281	124	2.67
Major League Totals—3 Years		67	353⅓	25	9	.735	294	127	112	302	137	2.85

Selected by Kansas City Royals' organization in 3rd round of free-agent draft, June 8, 1981.
†On disabled list, April 8, 1983 through entire season.
‡Traded with Catcher Chris Jelic to New York Mets for Catcher Ed Hearn and Pitchers Rick Anderson and Mauro Gozzo, March 27, 1987.
§On disabled list, May 28 to August 14, 1987; included rehabilitation disability assignment to Tidewater, July 30 to August 14, 1987.

CHAMPIONSHIP SERIES RECORD

Year Club	League	G.	IP.	W.	L.	Pct.	H.	R.	ER.	SO.	BB.	ERA.
1988—New York	National	3	12	1	1	.500	10	6	6	9	5	4.50

ALL-STAR GAME RECORD

Year League	IP.	W.	L.	Pct.	H.	R.	ER.	SO.	BB.	ERA.
1988—National	1	0	0	.000	0	0	0	1	0	0.00

DENNIS BRYAN COOK

Born October 4, 1962, at Lamarque, Texas.
Height, 6.03. Weight, 185.
Throws and bats lefthanded.
Attended Angelina College, Lufkin, Tex., and University of Texas, Austin, Tex.

Named Texas League Pitcher of the Year, 1987.

Year Club	League	G.	IP.	W.	L.	Pct.	H.	R.	ER.	SO.	BB.	ERA.
1985—Clinton	Midwest	13	83	5	4	.556	73	35	31	40	27	3.36
1986—Fresno	California	27	170	12	7	.632	141	92	75	*173	100	3.97
1987—Shreveport	Texas	16	105⅔	9	2	.818	94	32	25	98	20	2.13
1987—Phoenix	P. Coast	12	62	2	5	.286	72	45	36	24	26	5.23
1988—Phoenix	P. Coast	26	141⅓	11	9	.550	138	73	61	110	51	3.88
1988—San Francisco	National	4	22	2	1	.667	9	8	7	13	11	2.86
Major League Totals—1 Year		4	22	2	1	.667	9	8	7	13	11	2.86

Selected by San Diego Padres' organization in 6th round of free-agent draft, January 11, 1983.
Selected by San Francisco Giants' organization in 18th round of free-agent draft, June 3, 1985.

JEFFREY DION COOK
(Jeff)

Born December 17, 1965, at Kansas City, Mo.
Height, 6.00. Weight, 185.
Throws right and bats left and righthanded.
Attended Johnson County Community College, Overland Park, Kan., and Phillips University, Enid, Okla.

Led Eastern League in sacrifice hits with 11 in 1988.

Led Eastern League outfielders in double plays with 4 in 1988.

Year	Club	League	Pos.	G.	AB.	R.	H.	2B.	3B.	HR.	RBI.	B.A.	PO.	A.	E.	F.A.
1985	Braden. Pirates†	Gulf C.	OF	46	167	32	44	1	1	1	13	.263	100	5	1	.991
1986	Prince William†	Carol.	OF	128	511	86	154	16	5	2	29	.301	259	17	7	.975
1987	Harrisburg	East.	OF	53	193	26	44	6	0	0	4	.228	103	2	0	1.000
1987	Salem†	Carol.	OF	69	298	48	101	9	4	1	26	.339	149	6	4	.975
1988	Harrisburg	East.	OF	127	490	55	126	9	2	1	29	.257	260	13	7	.975

Selected by Chicago Cubs' organization in 6th round of free-agent draft, January 17, 1984.
Selected by Pittsburgh Pirates' organization in 10th round of free-agent draft June 3, 1985.
†Batted righthanded only.

MICHAEL HORACE COOK
(Mike)

Born August 14, 1963, at Charleston, S. C.
Height, 6.03. Weight, 215.
Throws and bats righthanded.
Attended University of South Carolina, Columbia, S. C.

Year	Club	League	G.	IP.	W.	L.	Pct.	H.	R.	ER.	SO.	BB.	ERA.
1985	Quad Cities†	Midwest	2	10	0	0	.000	6	3	2	10	7	1.80
1986	Midland	Texas	15	105⅓	4	6	.400	101	54	41	82	52	3.50
1986	California	American	5	9	0	2	.000	13	12	9	6	7	9.00
1986	Edmonton	P. Coast	9	55⅓	4	1	.800	49	42	33	35	24	5.37
1987	California	American	16	34⅓	1	2	.333	34	21	21	27	18	5.50
1987	Edmonton	P. Coast	15	83⅓	4	7	.364	81	64	60	54	54	6.48
1988	Edmonton	P. Coast	51	91	5	9	.357	93	56	49	84	41	4.85
1988	California‡	American	3	3⅔	0	1	.000	4	2	2	2	1	4.91
Major League Totals—3 Years			24	47	1	5	.167	51	35	32	35	26	6.13

Selected by Philadelphia Phillies' organization in 6th round of free-agent draft, June 7, 1982.
Selected by California Angels' organization in 1st round (19th player selected) of free-agent draft, June 3, 1985.
†On temporary inactive list, July 9, 1985 through remainder of season.
‡Traded with Pitcher Rob Wassenaar and First Baseman Paul Sorrento to Minnesota Twins for Pitchers Bert Blyleven and Kevin Trudeau, November 3, 1988.

SCOTT KENDRICK COOPER

Born October 13, 1967, at St. Louis, Mo.
Height, 6.03. Weight, 200.
Throws right and bats lefthanded.

Led Carolina League in total bases with 234 in 1988.

Year	Club	League	Pos.	G.	AB.	R.	H.	2B.	3B.	HR.	RBI.	B.A.	PO.	A.	E.	F.A.
1986	Elmira	NYP	3B	51	191	23	55	9	0	9	43	.288	22	62	9	.903
1987	Greensboro	S. Atl.	3B-1B	119	370	52	93	21	2	15	63	.251	150	153	21	.935
1988	Lynchburg	Carol.	3B-1B-OF	130	497	90	•148	★45	7	9	73	.298	116	198	27	.921

Selected by Boston Red Sox' organization in 3rd round of free-agent draft, June 2, 1986.

JOSE MANUEL CORA
(Joey)

Born May 14, 1965, at Cuguas, Puerto Rico.
Height, 5.08. Weight, 150.
Throws right and bats left and righthanded.
Attended Vanderbilt University, Nashville, Tenn.

Major League stolen bases: 1987 (15).
Led Pacific Coast League second basemen in errors with 24 in 1988.

Year	Club	League	Pos.	G.	AB.	R.	H.	2B.	3B.	HR.	RBI.	B.A.	PO.	A.	E.	F.A.
1985	Spokane	N'west	2B	43	170	48	55	11	2	3	26	.324	92	123	9	.960
1986	Beaumont†	Texas	2B-SS	81	315	54	96	5	5	3	41	.305	217	267	19	.962
1987	San Diego	Nat.	2B-SS	77	241	23	57	7	2	0	13	.237	123	200	10	.970
1987	Las Vegas	P. C.	2B-SS	81	293	50	81	9	1	1	24	.276	186	249	9	.980
1988	Las Vegas	P. C.	2B-3B-OF	127	460	73	136	15	3	3	55	.296	285	346	26	.960
Major League Totals—1 Year				77	241	23	57	7	2	0	13	.237	123	200	10	.970

Selected by San Diego Padres' organization in 1st round (23rd player selected) of free-agent draft, June 3, 1985.
†On disabled list, June 22 to August 15, 1986.

SHERMAN STANLEY CORBETT

Born November 3, 1962, at New Braunfels, Tex.
Height, 6.04. Weight, 203.
Throws and bats lefthanded.
Attended Texas A&M University, College Station, Tex.

Major League saves: 1988 (1).
Tied for California League lead in shutouts with 3 and games started by pitchers with 28 in 1985.
Tied for Northwest League lead in shutouts with 2 in 1984.

Year	Club	League	G.	IP.	W.	L.	Pct.	H.	R.	ER.	SO.	BB.	ERA.
1984	Salem	Northwest	15	100⅓	7	6	.538	75	42	35	97	43	3.14
1985	Redwood	California	28	174	11	12	.478	165	108	78	122	101	4.03

Year	Club	League	G.	IP.	W.	L.	Pct.	H.	R.	ER.	SO.	BB.	ERA.
1986	—Midland	Texas	26	147⅔	7	10	.412	168	94	80	82	56	4.88
1987	—Edmonton	P. Coast	41	55⅔	6	6	.500	61	37	34	29	49	5.50
1988	—Midland	Texas	18	47⅔	3	2	.600	48	21	18	40	11	3.40
1988	—California	American	34	45⅔	2	1	.667	47	23	21	28	23	4.14
Major League Totals—1 Year			34	45⅔	2	1	.667	47	23	21	28	23	4.14

Selected by California Angels' organization in 3rd round of free-agent draft, June 4, 1984.

EDWIN JOSUE CORREA
(Ed)

Born April 29, 1966, at Hato Rey, Puerto Rico.
Height, 6.02. Weight, 215.
Throws and bats righthanded.
Brother of Ramser Correa, pitcher in Milwaukee Brewers' organization.

Year	Club	League	G.	IP.	W.	L.	Pct.	H.	R.	ER.	SO.	BB.	ERA.
1982	—Sarasota White Sox	Gulf Coast	10	59	5	2	.714	40	23	18	53	27	2.75
1983	—Appleton†	Midwest	19	95	3	9	.250	81	59	47	87	61	4.45
1984	—Appleton	Midwest	26	149⅓	10	6	.625	127	71	57	135	87	3.44
1985	—Glens Falls	Eastern	8	40	1	5	.167	37	41	30	34	35	6.75
1985	—Appleton	Midwest	18	139	13	3	•.813	93	45	39	128	56	2.53
1985	—Chicago‡	American	5	10⅓	1	0	1.000	11	9	8	10	11	6.97
1986	—Texas	American	32	202⅓	12	14	.462	167	102	95	189	126	4.23
1987	—Texas§	American	15	70	3	5	.375	83	63	59	61	52	7.59
1988	—Texas x	American					(Did not play)						
Major League Totals—3 Years			52	282⅔	16	19	.457	261	174	162	260	189	5.16

Signed as free agent by Chicago White Sox' organization, July 11, 1982.
†On disabled list, May 22 to June 12, 1983.
‡Traded with Infielder Scott Fletcher and a player to be named later to Texas Rangers for Infielder Wayne Tolleson and Pitcher Dave Schmidt, November 25, 1985; Texas acquired Infielder Jose Mota to complete deal, December 12, 1985.
§On disabled list, July 9 to September 10, 1987.
xOn disabled list, March 24 to September 1, 1988.

JAMES BERNARD CORSI
(Jim)

Born September 9, 1961, at Newton, Mass.
Height, 6.01. Weight, 210.
Throws and bats righthanded.
Received bachelor of arts degree in management from St. Leo College, St. Leo, Fla.

Led Pacific Coast League in games finished in relief with 45 in 1988.

Year	Club	League	G.	IP.	W.	L.	Pct.	H.	R.	ER.	SO.	BB.	ERA.
1982	—Oneonta	NYP	1	3⅓	0	0	.000	5	4	4	6	2	10.80
1982	—Paintsville	Ap'lachian	8	31	0	2	.000	32	11	10	20	13	2.90
1983	—Greensboro†	S. Atlantic	12	50⅔	2	2	.500	59	37	23	37	33	4.09
1983	—Oneonta‡	NYP	11	59⅓	3	6	.333	76	38	28	47	21	4.25
1984	—						(Out of Organized Baseball)						
1985	—Greensboro§	S. Atlantic	41	78⅔	5	8	.385	94	49	37	84	23	4.23
1986	—New Britain x	Eastern	29	51⅓	2	3	.400	52	13	13	38	20	2.28
1987	—Modesto	California	19	30	3	1	.750	23	16	12	45	10	3.60
1987	—Huntsville	Southern	28	48	8	1	.889	30	17	15	33	15	2.81
1988	—Tacoma	P. Coast	50	59	2	5	.286	60	25	18	48	23	2.75
1988	—Oakland	American	11	21⅓	0	1	.000	20	10	9	10	6	3.80
Major League Totals—1 Year			11	21⅓	0	1	.000	20	10	9	10	6	3.80

Selected by New York Yankees' organization in 25th round of free-agent draft, June 7, 1982.
†On Fort Lauderdale disabled list, April 8 to May 11, 1983.
‡Released, April 3, 1984; signed by Greensboro (Boston Red Sox' organization), April 1, 1985.
§Released, January 31, 1986; re-signed by Red Sox' organization, April 5, 1986.
xReleased, April 2, 1987; signed by Modesto (Oakland Athletics' organization), April 12, 1987.

FRED MICHAEL COSTELLO

Born December 1, 1966, at Clearlake, Calif.
Height, 6.04. Weight, 190.
Throws and bats righthanded.

Year	Club	League	G.	IP.	W.	L.	Pct.	H.	R.	ER.	SO.	BB.	ERA.
1986	—Sarasota Astros	Gulf Coast	14	66⅓	4	5	.444	74	•42	*35	51	26	4.75
1987	—Sarasota Astros	Gulf Coast	13	72⅔	5	7	.417	74	40	26	45	28	3.22
1988	—Asheville	S. Atlantic	51	76	6	7	.462	76	34	30	65	31	3.55

Selected by Houston Astros' organization in 4th round of free-agent draft, June 2, 1986.

JOHN REILLY COSTELLO

Born December 24, 1960, at New York, N. Y.
Height, 6.01. Weight, 180.
Throws and bats righthanded.
Received degree in police science from Mercyhurst College, Erie, Pa.

Major League saves: 1988 (1).

Year	Club	League	G.	IP.	W.	L.	Pct.	H.	R.	ER.	SO.	BB.	ERA.
1983	—Erie	NYP	15	63⅔	2	5	.286	79	51	47	41	21	6.64
1984	—Savannah	S. Atlantic	26	166	13	9	.591	142	80	62	114	86	3.36
1985	—Springfield	Midwest	28	188	8	13	.381	188	105	*87	127	60	4.16
1986	—St. Petersburg	Florida St.	15	71⅔	8	2	.800	65	21	19	32	24	2.39
1986	—Arkansas	Texas	10	15	0	0	.000	17	11	9	10	6	5.40
1987	—Arkansas	Texas	44	74	5	2	.714	64	27	19	67	22	2.31
1987	—Louisville	Am. Assoc.	6	10⅓	2	0	1.000	14	6	5	8	7	4.35
1988	—Louisville	Am. Assoc.	20	29⅓	1	1	.500	17	7	6	34	7	1.84
1988	—St. Louis	National	36	49⅔	5	2	.714	44	15	10	38	25	1.81
Major League Totals—1 Year			36	49⅔	5	2	.714	44	15	10	38	25	1.81

Selected by St. Louis Cardinals' organization in 24th round of free-agent draft, June 6, 1983.

HENRY COTTO (SUAREZ)

Name pronounced KOTT-oh.

Born January 5, 1961, at New York, N. Y.
Height, 6.02. Weight, 180.
Throws and bats righthanded.

Major League stolen bases: 1984 (9), 1985 (1), 1986 (3), 1987 (4), 1988 (27). Total—44.
Led Texas League in stolen bases with 52 in 1982.
Tied for American Association lead in caught stealing with 17 in 1983.
Led Texas League outfielders in total chances with 333 in 1982.
Tied for International League lead in double plays by outfielders with 3 in 1986.

Year	Club	League	Pos.	G.	AB.	R.	H.	2B.	3B.	HR.	RBI.	B.A.	PO.	A.	E.	F.A.
1980	—Sarasota Cubs	Gulf C.	OF	43	166	24	47	7	5	0	30	.283	93	6	3	.971
1980	—Quad Cities	Midw.	OF	19	78	9	22	1	1	0	5	.282	27	2	4	.879
1981	—Quad Cities	Midw.	OF	128	493	80	144	15	6	1	46	.292	249	*23	13	.954
1982	—Midland	Texas	OF	130	524	103	161	12	5	1	36	.307	*310	16	7	.979
1983	—Iowa†	A. A.	OF	104	426	52	111	7	10	0	35	.261	253	8	7	.974
1984	—Chicago	Nat.	OF	105	146	24	40	5	0	0	8	.274	117	3	2	.984
1984	—Iowa‡	A. A.	OF	8	30	3	6	2	0	0	0	.200	12	3	0	1.000
1985	—New York§	Amer.	OF	34	56	4	17	1	0	1	6	.304	41	2	1	.977
1985	—Columbus	Int.	OF	75	272	38	70	16	2	7	36	.257	158	5	2	.988
1986	—New York	Amer.	OF	35	80	11	17	3	0	1	6	.213	59	1	0	1.000
1986	—Columbus	Int.	OF	97	359	45	89	17	6	7	48	.248	215	5	8	.965
1987	—Columbus	Int.	OF	34	129	26	39	13	2	3	20	.302	73	3	2	.974
1987	—New York x	Amer.	OF	68	149	21	35	10	0	5	20	.235	89	2	1	.989
1988	—Seattle	Amer.	OF	133	386	50	100	18	1	8	33	.259	253	6	2	.992
National League Totals—1 Year				105	146	24	40	5	0	0	8	.274	117	3	2	.984
American League Totals—4 Years				270	671	86	169	32	1	15	65	.252	442	11	4	.991
Major League Totals—5 Years				375	817	110	209	37	1	15	73	.256	559	14	6	.990

Signed as free agent by Chicago Cubs' organization, June 7, 1980.
†On disabled list, May 10 to May 30, 1983.
‡Traded with Catcher Ron Hassey and Pitchers Rich Bordi and Porfi Altamirano to New York Yankees for Pitcher Ray Fontenot and Outfielder Brian Dayett, December 4, 1984.
§On disabled list, May 25 to July 5, 1985; included rehabilitation disability assignment to Columbus, June 19 to July 5, 1985.
xTraded with Pitcher Steve Trout to Seattle Mariners for Pitchers Lee Guetterman, Clay Parker and Wade Taylor, December 22, 1987.

CHAMPIONSHIP SERIES RECORD

Year	Club	League	Pos.	G.	AB.	R.	H.	2B.	3B.	HR.	RBI.	B.A.	PO.	A.	E.	F.A.
1984	—Chicago	Nat.	OF-PR	3	1	1	1	0	0	0	0	1.000	2	0	0	1.000

DANNY BRADFORD COX

Born September 21, 1959, at Northhampton, England.
Height, 6.04. Weight, 225.
Throws and bats righthanded.
Attended Chattahoochee Valley Community College, Phenix City, Ala.,
and Troy State University, Troy, Ala.

Pitched 11-0 no-hit victory against Bristol, August 9, 1981.
Tied for National League lead in hit batsmen with 7 in 1984.
Led Appalachian League in complete games with 10 and shutouts with 4 in 1981.
Named Appalachian League Player of the Year, 1981.

Year	Club	League	G.	IP.	W.	L.	Pct.	H.	R.	ER.	SO.	BB.	ERA.
1981	—Johnson City	Ap'lachian	13	*109	9	4	.692	80	27	25	*87	36	*2.06
1982	—Springfield	Midwest	15	84⅓	5	3	.625	82	46	24	68	29	2.56
1983	—St. Petersburg†	Florida St.	5	32	2	2	.500	26	10	9	22	14	2.53
1983	—Arkansas	Texas	11	86⅓	8	3	.727	60	31	22	73	24	2.29
1983	—Louisville	Am. Assoc.	2	11	0	0	.000	10	3	3	8	0	2.45
1983	—St. Louis	National	12	83	3	6	.333	92	38	30	36	23	3.25
1984	—St. Louis	National	29	156⅓	9	11	.450	171	81	70	70	54	4.03
1984	—Louisville	Am. Assoc.	6	42⅓	4	1	.800	34	16	10	34	7	2.13
1985	—St. Louis	National	35	241	18	9	.667	226	91	77	131	64	2.88
1986	—St. Louis‡	National	32	220	12	13	.480	189	85	71	108	60	2.90
1987	—St. Louis§	National	31	199⅓	11	9	.550	224	99	86	101	71	3.88

Year	Club	League	G.	IP.	W.	L.	Pct.	H.	R.	ER.	SO.	BB.	ERA.
1988	St. Louis x	National	13	86	3	8	.273	89	40	38	47	25	3.98
1988	Louisville	Am. Assoc.	3	11⅔	0	0	.000	11	7	4	7	6	3.09
	Major League Totals—6 Years		152	985⅔	56	56	.500	991	434	372	493	297	3.40

Selected by St. Louis Cardinals' organization in 13th round of free-agent draft, June 8, 1981.

†On Arkansas disabled list, April 8 to April 21, 1983.

‡On disabled list, March 30 to April 24, 1986; included rehabilitation disability assignment to Louisville, April 17 to April 24, 1986.

§On disabled list, July 10 to August 8, 1987.

xOn disabled list, April 30 to June 27 and August 7, 1988 through remainder of season; included rehabilitation disability assignment to Louisville, June 16 to June 27, 1988.

CHAMPIONSHIP SERIES RECORD

Tied Championship Series record for most complete games pitched, Series (2), 1987.

Tied National League Championship Series record for most complete games pitched, total Series (2).

Year	Club	League	G.	IP.	W.	L.	Pct.	H.	R.	ER.	SO.	BB.	ERA.
1985	St. Louis	National	1	6	1	0	1.000	4	1	1	4	5	1.50
1987	St. Louis	National	2	17	1	1	.500	17	4	4	11	3	2.12
	Championship Series Totals—2 Years		3	23	2	1	.667	21	5	5	15	8	1.96

WORLD SERIES RECORD

Tied World Series records for most games lost, seven-game Series (2), 1987; most earned runs allowed, nine-inning game (7), October 18, 1987; most earned runs allowed, inning (6), October 18, 1987 (fourth inning).

Year	Club	League	G.	IP.	W.	L.	Pct.	H.	R.	ER.	SO.	BB.	ERA.
1985	St. Louis	National	2	14	0	0	.000	14	2	2	13	4	1.29
1987	St. Louis	National	3	11⅔	1	2	.333	13	10	10	9	8	7.71
	World Series Totals—2 Years		5	25⅔	1	2	.333	27	12	12	22	12	4.21

STANLEY TIMOTHY CREWS
(Tim)

Born April 3, 1961, at Tampa, Fla.
Height, 6.00. Weight, 190.
Throws and bats righthanded.
Attended Valencia Community College, Orlando, Fla.

Major League saves: 1987 (3).

Led Texas League in home runs allowed with 25 and tied for lead in balks with 4 in 1983.

Tied for Midwest League lead in home runs allowed with 16 in 1981.

Year	Club	League	G.	IP.	W.	L.	Pct.	H.	R.	ER.	SO.	BB.	ERA.
1981	Burlington	Midwest	21	144	10	4	.714	148	82	67	98	27	4.19
1982	Stockton	California	19	139	10	4	.714	151	66	52	83	28	3.37
1983	El Paso	Texas	27	163⅓	9	8	.529	*207	*129	*119	99	53	6.56
1984	El Paso†	Texas	8	36	2	3	.400	56	32	27	22	10	6.75
1985	Stockton‡	California	16	90	8	1	.889	101	46	33	56	17	3.30
1986	El Paso	Texas	15	90⅔	5	5	.500	114	53	48	50	18	4.76
1986	Vancouver§	P. Coast	10	33⅓	2	1	.667	39	15	15	28	14	4.05
1987	Albuquerque	P. Coast	42	72	7	2	.778	73	34	29	60	25	3.63
1987	Los Angeles	National	20	29	1	1	.500	30	9	8	20	8	2.48
1988	Albuquerque	P. Coast	10	13⅓	1	1	.500	13	5	4	7	2	2.70
1988	Los Angeles	National	42	71⅔	4	0	1.000	77	29	25	45	16	3.14
	Major League Totals—2 Years		62	100⅔	5	1	.833	107	38	33	65	24	2.95

Selected by Kansas City Royals' organization in 2nd round of free-agent draft, January 8, 1980.

Selected by Milwaukee Brewers' organization in 2nd round of free-agent draft, January 13, 1981.

†On disabled list, June 9, 1984 through remainder of season.

‡On disabled list, May 17 to July 12, 1985.

§Traded with Pitcher Tim Leary to Los Angeles Dodgers for First Baseman Greg Brock, December 10, 1986.

CHARLES ROBERT CRIM
(Chuck)

Born July 23, 1961, at Van Nuys, Calif.
Height, 6.00. Weight, 185.
Throws and bats righthanded.
Attended University of Hawaii, Honolulu, Haw.

Major League saves: 1987 (12), 1988 (9). Total—21.

Led Appalachian League in complete games with 8 in 1982.

Tied for Midwest League lead in complete games with 11 in 1983.

Year	Club	League	G.	IP.	W.	L.	Pct.	H.	R.	ER.	SO.	BB.	ERA.
1982	Pikeville	Ap'lachian	11	77⅓	4	6	.400	62	32	22	76	18	2.56
1983	Beloit	Midwest	25	163⅓	11	10	.524	150	83	63	154	50	3.47
1984	El Paso	Texas	55	90	7	4	.636	77	20	15	69	25	1.50
1985	Vancouver	P. Coast	48	106⅔	3	6	.333	110	58	54	68	38	4.56
1986	Vancouver	P. Coast	26	45⅓	0	3	.000	64	32	25	26	15	4.96
1986	El Paso	Texas	16	39	2	4	.333	35	16	12	32	2	2.77
1987	Milwaukee	American	53	130	6	8	.429	133	60	53	56	39	3.67
1988	Milwaukee	American	*70	105	7	6	.538	95	38	34	58	28	2.91
	Major League Totals—2 Years		123	235	13	14	.481	228	98	87	114	67	3.33

Selected by Chicago Cubs' organization in 3rd round of free-agent draft, June 5, 1979.
Selected by Milwaukee Brewers' organization in 17th round of free-agent draft, June 7, 1982.

MATTHEW JAMES CROUCH
(Matt)

Born September 14, 1964, at Sacramento, Calif.
Height, 6.01. Weight, 170.
Throws and bats righthanded.
Attended Sacramento City College, Sacramento, Calif.

Year Club	League	G.	IP.	W.	L.	Pct.	H.	R.	ER.	SO.	BB.	ERA.
1984—Eugene	Northwest	16	57⅔	3	6	.333	45	28	18	42	34	2.81
1985—Eugene	Northwest	8	26	1	4	.200	35	25	22	21	17	7.62
1986—Burlington	Northwest	20	117⅓	6	6	.500	115	62	54	81	54	4.14
1987—Memphis	Southern	16	90	7	3	.700	103	49	40	47	26	4.00
1987—Fort Myers	Florida St.	10	73	5	1	.833	65	23	15	47	14	1.85
1988—Memphis	Southern	20	114	8	5	.615	107	48	37	110	36	2.92

Selected by Chicago Cubs' organization in 5th round of free-agent draft, January 17, 1984.
Selected by Kansas City Royals' organization in secondary phase of free-agent draft, June 4, 1984.

ZACHARY QUINN CROUCH
(Zach)

Born October 26, 1965, at Folsom, Calif.
Height, 6.03. Weight, 190.
Throws and bats lefthanded.

Pitched 4-0 no-hit victory against Miami, August 2, 1986 (five innings).

Year Club	League	G.	IP.	W.	L.	Pct.	H.	R.	ER.	SO.	BB.	ERA.
1985—Greensboro	S. Atlantic	26	131	8	5	.615	141	63	55	103	65	3.78
1986—Winter Haven†	Florida St.	30	139	9	6	.600	103	56	42	93	64	2.72
1987—New Britain	Eastern	24	131⅔	6	9	.400	129	63	57	90	61	3.90
1988—Pawtucket	Int'national	14	84⅔	2	8	.200	104	52	44	44	23	4.68
1988—Boston	American	3	1⅓	0	0	.000	4	1	1	0	2	6.75
1988—New Britain	Eastern	8	47⅓	2	3	.400	43	19	17	40	7	3.23
Major League Totals—1 Year		3	1⅓	0	0	.000	4	1	1	0	2	6.75

Selected by Boston Red Sox' organization in 13th round of free-agent draft, June 4, 1984.
†On Greensboro disabled list, April 9 to April 24, 1986.

JOSE CRUZ (DILAN)

Born August 8, 1947, at Arroyo, Puerto Rico.
Height, 6.00. Weight, 185.
Throws and bats lefthanded.
Brother of Hector Cruz, third baseman-outfielder with St. Louis, Chicago N.L., San Francisco and Cincinnati, 1973 and 1975 through 1982, and Yomiuri Giants of Japanese baseball, 1983; and Cirilo (Tommy) Cruz, outfielder with St. Louis Cardinals and Chicago White Sox, 1973 and 1977, and with Nippon Ham Fighters in Japanese Baseball League.

Tied major league record for fewest double plays by outfielder, season, 150 or more games (0), 1978.
Major League stolen bases: 1971 (6), 1972 (9), 1973 (10), 1974 (4), 1975 (6), 1976 (28), 1977 (44), 1978 (37), 1979 (36), 1980 (36), 1981 (5), 1982 (21), 1983 (30), 1984 (22), 1985 (16), 1986 (3), 1987 (4). Total—317.
Led National League outfielders in double plays with 5 in 1972.
Tied for National League lead in sacrifice flies with 10 in 1977 and 1984.
Named outfielder on THE SPORTING NEWS National League All-Star Team, 1984.
Named outfielder on THE SPORTING NEWS National League Silver Slugger team, 1983 and 1984.
Led Texas League in total bases with 254 in 1970.

Year Club	League	Pos.	G.	AB.	R.	H.	2B.	3B.	HR.	RBI.	B.A.	PO.	A.	E.	F.A.
1967—St. Petersburg	Fla. St.	OF-1B	78	205	33	57	8	9	1	20	.278	113	5	7	.944
1968—Modesto	Calif.	OF-SS	133	504	101	144	24	10	13	53	.286	219	10	11	.954
1969—Arkansas†	Texas	OF	102	400	56	109	18	9	6	49	.273	235	16	9	.965
1970—Arkansas	Texas	OF	133	493	89	148	*29	7	21	90	.300	*276	10	12	.960
1970—St. Louis	Nat.	OF	6	17	2	6	1	0	0	1	.353	16	0	0	1.000
1971—Tulsa	A. A.	OF	67	254	56	83	15	7	15	49	.327	146	1	7	.955
1971—St. Louis	Nat.	OF	83	292	46	80	13	2	9	27	.274	197	2	5	.975
1972—St. Louis	Nat.	OF	117	332	33	78	14	4	2	23	.235	220	9	5	.979
1973—St. Louis	Nat.	OF	132	406	51	92	22	5	10	57	.227	276	2	6	.979
1974—St. Louis‡	Nat.	OF-1B	107	161	24	42	4	3	5	20	.261	81	2	2	.976
1975—Houston	Nat.	OF	120	315	44	81	15	2	9	49	.257	187	6	4	.980
1976—Houston	Nat.	OF	133	439	49	133	21	5	4	61	.303	265	10	8	.972
1977—Houston	Nat.	OF	157	579	87	173	31	10	17	87	.299	311	11	9	.973
1978—Houston	Nat.	OF-1B	153	565	79	178	34	9	10	83	.315	328	5	8	.977
1979—Houston	Nat.	OF	157	558	73	161	33	7	9	72	.289	320	7	14	.959
1980—Houston	Nat.	OF	160	612	79	185	29	7	11	91	.302	323	16	●11	.969
1981—Houston	Nat.	OF	107	409	53	109	16	5	13	55	.267	237	5	4	.984
1982—Houston	Nat.	OF	155	570	62	157	27	2	9	68	.275	340	9	*13	.964
1983—Houston	Nat.	OF	160	594	85	●189	28	8	14	92	.318	322	9	7	.979
1984—Houston	Nat.	OF	160	600	96	187	28	13	12	95	.312	310	11	8	.976
1985—Houston	Nat.	OF	141	544	69	163	34	4	9	79	.300	257	12	8	.971
1986—Houston§	Nat.	OF	141	479	48	133	22	4	10	72	.278	237	5	4	.984

Year	Club	League	Pos.	G.	AB.	R.	H.	2B.	3B.	HR.	RBI.	B.A.	PO.	A.	E.	F.A.
1987	—Houston x	Nat.	OF	126	365	47	88	17	4	11	38	.241	178	5	3	.984
1988	—New York y	Amer.	OF	38	80	9	16	2	0	1	7	.200	8	0	1	.889
1988	—Columbus z	Int.	OF	5	17	3	4	2	0	1	5	.235	8	0	1	.889
National League Totals—18 Years				2315	7837	1027	2235	389	94	164	1070	.285	4405	126	119	.974
American League Totals—1 Year				38	80	9	16	2	0	1	7	.200	8	0	1	.889
Major League Totals—19 Years				2353	7917	1036	2251	391	94	165	1077	.284	4413	126	120	.974

Signed as free agent by St. Louis Cardinals' organization, October 27, 1966.
†On disabled list, April 8 to May 12, 1969.
‡Sold to Houston Astros, October 24, 1974.
§On disabled list, March 30 to April 19, 1986.
xGranted free agency, November 9, 1987; signed by New York Yankees, February 25, 1988.
yOn disabled list, May 7 to May 28, 1988; included rehabilitation disability assignment to Columbus, May 23 to May 28, 1988.
zReleased, July 22, 1988.

DIVISION SERIES RECORD

Year	Club	League	Pos.	G.	AB.	R.	H.	2B.	3B.	HR.	RBI.	B.A.	PO.	A.	E.	F.A.
1981	—Houston	Nat.	OF	5	20	0	6	1	0	0	0	.300	15	0	1	.938

CHAMPIONSHIP SERIES RECORD

Established Championship Series record for most walks, five-game series (8), 1980.

Year	Club	League	Pos.	G.	AB.	R.	H.	2B.	3B.	HR.	RBI.	B.A.	PO.	A.	E.	F.A.
1980	—Houston	Nat.	OF	5	15	3	6	1	1	0	4	.400	19	0	0	1.000
1986	—Houston	Nat.	OF	6	26	0	5	0	0	0	2	.192	11	0	0	1.000
Championship Series Totals—2 Years				11	41	3	11	1	1	0	6	.268	30	0	0	1.000

ALL-STAR GAME RECORD

Year	League	Pos.	AB.	R.	H.	2B.	3B.	HR.	RBI.	B.A.	PO.	A.	E.	F.A.
1985	—National	OF	1	0	0	0	0	0	0	.000	2	0	0	1.000

Member of National League All-Star Team in 1980; did not play.

STEVEN BRENT CUMMINGS
(Steve)

Born July 15, 1964, at Houston, Tex.
Height, 6.02. Weight, 200.
Throws right and bats left and righthanded.
Attended Blinn College, Brenham, Tex.,
and University of Houston, Houston, Tex.

Led Southern League in games started by pitchers with 33 in 1988.
Led Florida State League pitchers in games started with 29 in 1987.
Tied for New York-Pennsylvania League lead in games started by pitchers with 18 in 1986.

Year	Club	League	G.	IP.	W.	L.	Pct.	H.	R.	ER.	SO.	BB.	ERA.
1986	—St. Catharines	NYP	18	110⅓	9	5	.643	80	36	25	86	34	2.04
1987	—Dunedin	Florida St.	32	186⅔	*18	8	.692	189	80	61	111	60	2.94
1988	—Knoxville	Southern	35	*212⅔	14	11	.560	*206	88	65	131	64	2.75

Selected by Texas Rangers' organization in 5th round of free-agent draft, January 17, 1984.
Selected by Atlanta Braves' organization in secondary phase of free-agent draft, June 4, 1984.
Selected by Toronto Blue Jays' organization in 2nd round of free-agent draft, June 2, 1986.

STEPHEN T. CURRY
(Steve)

Born September 13, 1965, at Winter Park, Fla.
Height, 6.06. Weight, 217.
Throws and bats righthanded.
Attended Manatee Junior College, Bradenton, Fla.

Pitched 11-0 no-hit victory against Richmond, July 6, 1987.
Led Eastern League in complete games with 12 and tied for lead in balks with 5 in 1986.
Led Florida State League in balks with 11 in 1985.
Tied for International League lead in balks with 5 in 1987.

Year	Club	League	G.	IP.	W.	L.	Pct.	H.	R.	ER.	SO.	BB.	ERA.
1984	—Elmira	NYP	14	83⅓	6	4	.600	83	51	37	82	35	4.00
1985	—Winter Haven	Florida St.	27	161	9	10	.474	157	75	66	81	63	3.69
1986	—New Britain	Eastern	24	*177⅓	11	9	.550	163	66	55	94	76	2.79
1987	—Pawtucket	Int'national	28	184⅓	11	12	.478	175	85	78	112	74	3.81
1988	—Pawtucket	Int'national	23	146⅓	11	9	.550	125	56	50	110	69	3.08
1988	—Boston	American	3	11	0	1	.000	15	10	10	4	14	8.18
Major League Totals—1 Year			3	11	0	1	.000	15	10	10	4	14	8.18

Selected by Boston Red Sox' organization in 7th round of free-agent draft, June 4, 1984.

—DID YOU KNOW—

That the Cincinnati Reds scored 10 runs in the first inning of a July 19 game against the New York Mets? The Reds won, 11-2.

MILTON CUYLER JR.
(Milt)

Born October 7, 1968, at Macon, Ga.
Height, 5.10. Weight, 175.
Throws right and bats left and righthanded.

Led Florida State League in caught stealing with 25 in 1988.
Led South Atlantic League in sacrifice hits with 17 in 1987.

Year Club	League	Pos.	G.	AB.	R.	H.	2B.	3B.	HR.	RBI.	B.A.	PO.	A.	E.	F.A.
1986—Bristol	Appal.	OF	45	174	24	40	3	5	1	11	.230	97	0	4	.960
1987—Fayetteville	S. Atl.	OF	94	366	65	107	8	4	2	34	.292	237	13	7	.973
1988—Lakeland	Fla. St.	OF	132	483	*100	143	11	3	2	32	.296	257	8	4	.985

Selected by Detroit Tigers' organization in 2nd round of free-agent draft, June 2, 1986.

KALVOSKI DANIELS
(Kal)

Born August 20, 1963, at Vienna, Ga.
Height, 5.11. Weight, 195.
Throws right and bats lefthanded.
Attended Middle Georgia College, Cochran, Ga.

Major League stolen bases: 1986 (15), 1987 (26), 1988 (27). Total—68.
Led Eastern League in slugging percentage with .525 in 1984.
Tied for Pioneer League lead in game-winning RBIs with 9 and stolen bases with 27 in 1982.

Year Club	League	Pos.	G.	AB.	R.	H.	2B.	3B.	HR.	RBI.	B.A.	PO.	A.	E.	F.A.
1982—Billings	Pion.	OF	67	240	43	88	19	4	3	38	.367	104	4	5	.956
1983—Cedar Rapids	Midw.	OF	101	342	51	86	14	5	5	28	.251	130	5	2	.985
1984—Vermont	East.	OF	122	415	81	130	29	4	17	62	.313	143	2	5	.967
1985—Denver†	A. A.	OF	76	285	59	86	12	9	15	43	.302	83	5	4	.957
1986—Cincinnati	Nat.	OF	74	181	34	58	10	4	6	23	.320	88	0	3	.967
1986—Denver	A. A.	OF	42	132	33	49	12	2	8	32	.371	78	4	3	.965
1987—Cincinnati‡	Nat.	OF	108	368	73	123	24	1	26	64	.334	178	5	6	.968
1988—Cincinnati	Nat.	OF	140	495	95	144	29	1	18	64	.291	256	10	5	.982
Major League Totals—3 Years			322	1044	202	325	63	6	50	151	.311	522	15	14	.975

Selected by New York Mets' organization in 3rd round of free-agent draft, January 12, 1982.
Selected by Cincinnati Reds' organization in secondary phase of free-agent draft, June 7, 1982.
†On disabled list, July 7, 1985 through remainder of season.
‡On disabled list, July 6 to August 6, 1987.

RONALD MAURICE DARLING JR.
(Ron)

Born August 19, 1960, at Honolulu, Hawaii.
Height, 6.03. Weight, 195.
Throws and bats righthanded.
Attended Yale University, New Haven, Conn.
Brother of Eddie Darling, first baseman in New York Yankees' organization, 1981 and 1982.

Tied National League record for fewest assists by pitcher, season, for leader in assists (47), 1985 and 1986.

Year Club	League	G.	IP.	W.	L.	Pct.	H.	R.	ER.	SO.	BB.	ERA.
1981—Tulsa†	Texas	13	71	4	2	.667	72	43	35	53	33	4.44
1982—Tidewater	Int'national	26	152	7	9	.438	143	76	63	114	95	3.73
1983—Tidewater	Int'national	27	159	10	9	.526	137	83	71	107	102	4.02
1983—New York	National	5	35⅓	1	3	.250	31	11	11	23	17	2.80
1984—New York	National	33	205⅔	12	9	.571	179	97	87	136	104	3.81
1985—New York	National	36	248	16	6	.727	214	93	80	167	*114	2.90
1986—New York	National	34	237	15	6	.714	203	84	74	184	81	2.81
1987—New York‡	National	32	207⅔	12	8	.600	183	111	99	167	96	4.29
1988—New York	National	34	240⅔	17	9	.654	218	97	87	161	60	3.25
Major League Totals—6 Years		174	1174⅓	73	41	.640	1028	493	438	838	472	3.36

Selected by Texas Rangers' organization in 1st round (ninth player selected) of free-agent draft, June 8, 1981.
†Traded with Pitcher Walt Terrell to New York Mets' organization for Outfielder Lee Mazzilli, April 1, 1982.
‡On disabled list, September 12, 1987 through remainder of season.

CHAMPIONSHIP SERIES RECORD

Established National League Championship Series record for most runs allowed, seven-game Series (9), 1988.

Year Club	League	G.	IP.	W.	L.	Pct.	H.	R.	ER.	SO.	BB.	ERA.
1986—New York	National	1	5	0	0	.000	6	4	4	5	2	7.20
1988—New York	National	2	7	0	1	.000	11	9	6	7	4	7.71
Championship Series Totals—2 Years		3	12	0	1	.000	17	13	10	12	6	7.50

Appeared as pinch-runner for New York Mets in one game of 1988 Championship Series.

WORLD SERIES RECORD

Tied World Series records for most consecutive home runs allowed, inning (2), October 27, 1986 (second inning); most wild pitches, game (2), October 18, 1986.

Year Club	League	G.	IP.	W.	L.	Pct.	H.	R.	ER.	SO.	BB.	ERA.
1986—New York	National	3	17⅔	1	1	.500	13	4	3	12	10	1.53

ALL-STAR GAME RECORD

Member of National League All-Star Team in 1985; did not play.

DANIEL WAYNE DARWIN
(Danny)

Born October 25, 1955, at Bonham, Tex.
Height, 6.03. Weight, 190.
Throws and bats righthanded.
Attended Grayson County College, Denison, Tex.

Major League saves: 1980 (8), 1982 (7), 1985 (2), 1988 (3). Total—20.
Tied for American League lead in home runs allowed with 34 in 1985.
Tied for Texas League lead in shutouts with 4 and hit batsmen with 8 in 1977.
Tied for Western Carolinas League lead in balks with 5 in 1976.

Year Club	League	G.	IP.	W.	L.	Pct.	H.	R.	ER.	SO.	BB.	ERA.
1976—Asheville	W. Carol.	16	102	6	3	.667	96	54	41	76	48	3.62
1977—Tulsa†	Texas	23	154	13	4	.765	130	53	43	129	72	2.51
1978—Tucson	P. Coast	23	125	8	9	.471	147	100	87	126	83	6.26
1978—Texas	American	3	9	1	0	1.000	11	4	4	8	1	4.00
1979—Tucson	P. Coast	13	95	6	6	.500	89	43	38	65	42	3.60
1979—Texas	American	20	78	4	4	.500	50	36	35	58	30	4.04
1980—Texas‡	American	53	110	13	4	.765	98	37	32	104	50	2.62
1981—Texas	American	22	146	9	9	.500	115	67	59	98	57	3.64
1982—Texas	American	56	89	10	8	.556	95	38	34	61	37	3.44
1983—Texas§	American	28	183	8	13	.381	175	86	71	92	62	3.49
1984—Texas x	American	35	223⅔	8	12	.400	249	110	98	123	54	3.94
1985—Milwaukee y	American	39	217⅔	8	18	.308	212	112	92	125	65	3.80
1986—Milwaukee z	American	27	130⅓	6	8	.429	120	62	51	80	35	3.52
1986—Houston	National	12	54⅓	5	2	.714	50	19	14	40	9	2.32
1987—Houston a	National	33	195⅔	9	10	.474	184	87	78	134	69	3.59
1988—Houston	National	44	192	8	13	.381	189	86	82	129	48	3.84
American League Totals—9 Years		283	1186⅔	67	76	.469	1125	552	476	749	391	3.61
National League Totals—3 Years		89	442	22	25	.468	423	192	174	303	126	3.54
Major League Totals—11 Years		372	1628⅔	89	101	.468	1548	744	650	1052	517	3.59

Signed as free agent by Texas Rangers' organization, May 10, 1976.
†On disabled list, April 25 to May 4 and May 22 to June 11, 1977.
‡On disabled list, June 5 to June 26, 1980.
§On disabled list, March 25 to April 10 and August 9 to September 1, 1983.
xTraded with a player to be named later to Milwaukee Brewers as part of a six-player, four-team deal in which Kansas City Royals acquired Catcher Jim Sundberg from Milwaukee, Texas Rangers acquired Catcher Don Slaught from Kansas City, New York Mets' organization acquired Pitcher Frank Wills from Kansas City and Milwaukee organization acquired Pitcher Tim Leary from New York, January 18, 1985; Milwaukee organization acquired Catcher Bill Hance from Texas to complete deal, January 30, 1985.
yGranted free agency, November 12, 1985; re-signed by Brewers, December 22, 1985.
zTraded to Houston Astros for Pitcher Don August and a player to be named later, August 15, 1986; Milwaukee Brewers' organization acquired Pitcher Mark Knudson to complete deal, August 21, 1986.
aGranted free agency, November 9, 1987; re-signed by Astros, January 8, 1988.

DOUGLAS CRAIG DASCENZO
(Doug)

Born June 30, 1964, at Cleveland, O.
Height, 5.08. Weight, 160.
Throws left and bats left and righthanded.
Attended Florida College, Temple Terrace, Fla., and
Oklahoma State University, Stillwater, Okla.

Major League stolen bases: 1988 (6).
Led Carolina League in sacrifice hits with 12 in 1986.
Led Eastern League outfielders in total chances with 308 in 1987.

Year Club	League	Pos.	G.	AB.	R.	H.	2B.	3B.	HR.	RBI.	B.A.	PO.	A.	E.	F.A.
1985—Geneva	NYP	OF-1B	70	252	*59	84	15	1	3	23	.333	133	7	4	.972
1986—Winston-Salem	Carol.	OF	138	545	107	*178	29	11	6	83	.327	299	15	8	.975
1987—Pittsfield	East.	OF	134	496	84	152	32	6	3	56	.306	*299	5	4	*.987
1988—Iowa	A. A.	OF	132	505	73	149	22	5	6	49	.295	261	6	4	.985
1988—Chicago	Nat.	OF	26	75	9	16	3	0	0	4	.213	55	1	0	1.000
Major League Totals—1 Year			26	75	9	16	3	0	0	4	.213	55	1	0	1.000

Selected by Chicago Cubs' organization in 12th round of free-agent draft, June 3, 1985.

DARREN ARTHUR DAULTON

Born January 3, 1962, at Arkansas City, Kan.
Height, 6.02. Weight, 190.
Throws right and bats lefthanded.
Attended Cowley County Community College, Arkansas City, Kan.

Major League stolen bases: 1985 (3), 1986 (2), 1988 (2). Total—7.
Tied for Eastern League lead in sacrifice flies with 10 in 1983.

Year	Club	League	Pos.	G.	AB.	R.	H.	2B.	3B.	HR.	RBI.	B.A.	PO.	A.	E.	F.A.
1980	Helena	Pion.	C	37	100	13	20	2	1	1	10	.200	224	17	4	.984
1981	Spartanburg	S. Atl.	C-OF-3B	98	270	44	62	11	1	3	29	.230	378	34	4	.990
1982	Peninsula	Carol.	C-1B	110	324	65	78	21	2	11	44	.241	654	63	9	.990
1983	Reading	East.	C-1B-OF	113	362	77	95	16	4	19	83	.262	557	57	14	.978
1983	Philadelphia	Nat.	C	2	3	1	1	0	0	0	0	.333	8	0	0	1.000
1984	Portland†	P. C.	C	80	252	45	75	19	4	7	38	.298	322	26	6	.983
1985	Portland	P. C.	C	23	64	13	19	5	3	2	10	.297	110	9	0	1.000
1985	Philadelphia‡	Nat.	C	36	103	14	21	3	1	4	11	.204	160	15	1	.994
1986	Philadelphia§	Nat.	C	49	138	18	31	4	0	8	21	.225	244	21	4	.985
1987	Clearwater x	Fla. St.	C-1B	9	22	1	5	3	0	1	5	.227	27	5	3	.914
1987	Maine	Int.	C-1B	20	70	9	15	1	1	3	10	.214	138	12	0	1.000
1987	Philadelphia	Nat.	C-1B	53	129	10	25	6	0	3	13	.194	210	13	2	.991
1988	Philadelphia y	Nat.	C-1B	58	144	13	30	6	0	1	12	.208	205	15	6	.973
Major League Totals—5 Years				198	517	56	108	19	1	16	57	.209	827	64	13	.986

Selected by Philadelphia Phillies' organization in 25th round of free-agent draft, June 3, 1980.
†On disabled list, July 20 to August 28, 1984.
‡On disabled list, May 17 to August 9, 1985; included rehabilitation disability assignment to Portland, July 20 to August 7, 1985.
§On Philadelphia disabled list, June 22, 1986 through remainder of season.
xOn Philadelphia disabled list, April 1 to April 16, 1987.
yOn disabled list, August 28, 1988 through remainder of season.

JOHN MARK DAVIDSON

(Known by middle name.)

Born February 15, 1961, at Knoxville, Tenn.
Height, 6.02. Weight, 190.
Throws and bats righthanded.
Attended University of North Carolina, Charlotte, N.C.,
and Clemson University, Clemson, S.C.
Son of Max Davidson, minor league outfielder, 1947 through 1954.

Major League stolen bases: 1986 (2), 1987 (9), 1988 (3). Total—14.
Led Southern League in game-winning RBIs with 16 in 1985.

Year	Club	League	Pos.	G.	AB.	R.	H.	2B.	3B.	HR.	RBI.	B.A.	PO.	A.	E.	F.A.
1982	Wis. Rapids	Midw.	OF	79	247	54	74	11	0	10	41	.300	166	13	5	.973
1983	Wis. Rapids†	Midw.	OF	111	363	63	80	15	1	13	48	.220	181	6	6	.969
1984	Orlando‡	South.	OF-1B-3B	114	348	55	99	11	6	4	37	.284	243	13	3	.988
1985	Orlando	South.	OF-3B	134	453	93	137	17	2	25	106	.302	305	14	6	.982
1986	Toledo	Int.	OF	108	383	55	95	16	1	10	38	.248	290	8	8	.974
1986	Minnesota	Amer.	OF	36	68	5	8	3	0	0	2	.118	48	0	1	.980
1987	Minnesota	Amer.	OF	102	150	32	40	4	1	1	14	.267	102	3	0	1.000
1988	Minnesota	Amer.	OF-3B	100	106	22	23	7	0	1	10	.217	103	3	5	.955
1988	Portland	P. C.	OF-P	15	56	6	18	4	2	0	5	.321	35	2	0	1.000
Major League Totals—3 Years				238	324	59	71	14	1	2	26	.219	253	6	6	.977

Selected by Minnesota Twins' organization in 11th round of free-agent draft, June 7, 1982.
†On disabled list, April 15 to May 4, 1983.
‡On disabled list, July 16 to July 26, 1984.

CHAMPIONSHIP SERIES RECORD

Year	Club	League	Pos.	G.	AB.	R.	H.	2B.	3B.	HR.	RBI.	B.A.	PO.	A.	E.	F.A.
1987	Minnesota	Amer.	PR	1	0	0	0	0	0	0	0	.000	0	0	0	.000

WORLD SERIES RECORD

Year	Club	League	Pos.	G.	AB.	R.	H.	2B.	3B.	HR.	RBI.	B.A.	PO.	A.	E.	F.A.
1987	Minnesota	Amer.	OF-PH	2	1	0	0	0	0	0	0	.000	0	0	0	.000

PITCHING RECORD

Year	Club	League	G.	IP.	W.	L.	Pct.	H.	R.	ER.	SO.	BB.	ERA.
1988	Portland	P. Coast	1	1⅓	0	1	.000	2	1	1	0	2	6.75

JAMES P. DAVINS

(Jim)

Born May 23, 1964, at New Haven, Conn.
Height, 6.03. Weight, 215.
Throws and bats righthanded.
Attended University of Maine, Orono, Maine.

Year	Club	League	G.	IP.	W.	L.	Pct.	H.	R.	ER.	SO.	BB.	ERA.
1985	Watertown	NYP	16	29⅔	2	0	1.000	15	14	12	39	22	3.64
1986	Macon†	S. Atlantic	44	59	3	5	.375	49	27	25	58	42	3.81
1987	Kenosha	Midwest	48	85	6	4	.600	75	36	28	80	52	2.96
1988	Portland	P. Coast	41	61	0	5	.000	69	39	38	55	30	5.61

Selected by Pittsburgh Pirates' organization in 25th round of free-agent draft, January 17, 1984.
†Released, April 2, 1987; signed by Kenosha (Minnesota Twins' organization), April 5, 1987.

RECORD AS OUTFIELDER

Year	Club	League	Pos.	G.	AB.	R.	H.	2B.	3B.	HR.	RBI.	B.A.	PO.	A.	E.	F.A.
1984	Bradenton Pir.†	Gulf C.	OF	1	4	0	0	0	0	0	0	.000	2	0	0	1.000

†On disabled list, June 27, 1984 through remainder of season.

ALVIN GLENN DAVIS
(Al)

Born September 9, 1960, at Riverside, Calif.
Height, 6.01. Weight, 190.
Throws right and bats lefthanded.
Received bachelor of science degree in finance from Arizona State University, Tempe, Ariz.

Tied major league record for most putouts, first baseman, nine-inning game (22), May 28, 1988.
Tied American League record for most home runs, first two major league games (2), April 11 and 13, 1984.
Major League stolen bases: 1984 (5), 1985 (1), 1988 (1). Total—7.
Led Southern League in bases on balls received with 120 and sacrifice flies with 12 in 1983.
Led Southern League first basemen in total chances with 1,348 and double plays with 118 in 1983.
Named American League Rookie Player of the Year by THE SPORTING NEWS, 1984.
Named American League Rookie of the Year by Baseball Writers' Association of America, 1984.

Year	Club	League	Pos.	G.	AB.	R.	H.	2B.	3B.	HR.	RBI.	B.A.	PO.	A.	E.	F.A.
1982	Lynn	East	1B	74	225	37	64	10	1	12	56	.284	579	51	6	.991
1983	Chattanooga†	South.	*•1B-OF	131	422	87	125	24	3	18	83	.296	*1233	*99	•16	.988
1984	Salt Lake City	P. C.	1B	1	3	2	2	0	0	0	1	.667	2	0	0	1.000
1984	Seattle	Amer.	1B	152	567	80	161	34	3	27	116	.284	1271	94	11	.992
1985	Seattle	Amer.	1B	155	578	78	166	33	1	18	78	.287	1438	103	13	.992
1986	Seattle‡	Amer.	1B	135	479	66	130	18	1	18	72	.271	880	82	14	.986
1987	Seattle	Amer.	1B	157	580	86	171	37	2	29	100	.295	1386	96	9	.994
1988	Seattle§	Amer.	1B	140	478	67	141	24	1	18	69	.295	980	65	6	.994
Major League Totals—5 Years				739	2682	377	769	146	8	110	435	.287	5955	440	53	.992

Selected by San Francisco Giants' organization in 8th round of free-agent draft, June 6, 1978.
Selected by Oakland A's organization in 6th round of free-agent draft, June 8, 1981.
Selected by Seattle Mariners' organization in 6th round of free-agent draft, June 7, 1982.
†On disabled list, July 21 to July 31, 1983.
‡On disabled list, June 25 to July 17, 1986.
§On disabled list, June 26 to July 15, 1988.

ALL-STAR GAME RECORD

Year	League	Pos.	AB.	R.	H.	2B.	3B.	HR.	RBI.	B.A.	PO.	A.	E.	F.A.
1984	American	PH	1	0	0	0	0	0	0	.000	0	0	0	.000

CHARLES THEODORE DAVIS
(Chili)

(Original nickname was Chili Bowl, which was prompted by a friend who saw Davis after he received a haircut back in the sixth grade. The nickname was later shortened to Chili.)

Born January 17, 1960, at Kingston, Jamaica.
Height, 6.03. Weight, 210.
Throws right and bats left and righthanded.

Tied major league record for fewest errors by outfielder, season, for leader in errors (9), 1986.
Established National League record for most games, switch-hit home runs, lifetime (3).
Tied National League record for most games, switch-hit home runs, season (2), 1987.
Major League stolen bases: 1981 (2), 1982 (24), 1983 (10), 1984 (12), 1985 (15), 1986 (16), 1987 (16), 1988 (9). Total—104.
Switch-hit home runs in one game, June 5, 1983, June 27, 1987, September 15, 1987 and July 30, 1988.
Tied for American League lead in sacrifice flies with 10 in 1988.

Year	Club	League	Pos.	G.	AB.	R.	H.	2B.	3B.	HR.	RBI.	B.A.	PO.	A.	E.	F.A.
1978	Cedar Rapids	Midw.	C-OF	124	424	63	119	18	5	16	73	.281	365	45	25	.943
1979	Fresno	Calif.	OF-C	134	490	91	132	24	5	21	95	.269	339	43	20	.950
1980	Shreveport	Texas	OF-C	129	442	50	130	30	4	12	67	.294	184	20	12	.944
1981	San Francisco	Nat.	OF	8	15	1	2	0	0	0	0	.133	7	0	0	1.000
1981	Phoenix†	P. C.	OF	88	334	76	117	16	6	19	75	.350	175	7	6	.968
1982	San Francisco	Nat.	OF	154	641	86	167	27	6	19	76	.261	404	•16	12	.972
1983	San Francisco	Nat.	OF	137	486	54	113	21	2	11	59	.233	357	7	9	.976
1983	Phoenix	P. C.	OF	10	44	12	13	2	0	2	9	.295	15	0	2	.882
1984	San Francisco	Nat.	OF	137	499	87	157	21	6	21	81	.315	292	9	9	.971
1985	San Francisco	Nat.	OF	136	481	53	130	25	2	13	56	.270	279	10	6	.980
1986	San Francisco	Nat.	OF	153	526	71	146	28	3	13	70	.278	303	9	•9	.972
1987	San Francisco‡	Nat.	OF	149	500	80	125	22	1	24	76	.250	265	6	7	.975
1988	California	Amer.	OF	158	600	81	161	29	3	21	93	.268	299	10	*19	.942
National League Totals—7 Years				874	3148	432	840	144	20	101	418	.267	1907	57	52	.974
American League Totals—1 Year				158	600	81	161	29	3	21	93	.268	299	10	19	.942
Major League Totals—8 Years				1032	3748	513	1001	173	23	122	511	.267	2206	67	71	.970

Selected by San Francisco Giants' organization in 11th round of free-agent draft, June 7, 1977.
†On disabled list, August 19 to August 28, 1982.
‡Granted free agency, November 9, 1987; signed by California Angels, December 1, 1987.

CHAMPIONSHIP SERIES RECORD

Year	Club	League	Pos.	G.	AB.	R.	H.	2B.	3B.	HR.	RBI.	B.A.	PO.	A.	E.	F.A.
1987	San Francisco	Nat.	OF	6	20	2	3	1	0	0	0	.150	11	1	1	.923

ALL-STAR GAME RECORD

Year	League	Pos.	AB.	R.	H.	2B.	3B.	HR.	RBI.	B.A.	PO.	A.	E.	F.A.
1984	National	PH	1	0	0	0	0	0	0	.000	0	0	0	.000

Year League	Pos.	AB.	R.	H.	2B.	3B.	HR.	RBI.	B.A.	PO.	A.	E.	F.A.
1986—National	OF	1	0	0	0	0	0	0	.000	0	0	0	.000
All-Star Game Totals—2 Years		2	0	0	0	0	0	0	.000	0	0	0	.000

DOUGLAS RAYMOND DAVIS
(Doug)

Born September 24, 1962, at Bloomsburg, Pa.
Height, 6.00. Weight, 180.
Throws and bats righthanded.
Attended North Carolina State University, Raleigh, N. C.

Year Club	League	Pos.	G.	AB.	R.	H.	2B.	3B.	HR.	RBI.	B.A.	PO.	A.	E.	F.A.
1984—Peoria	Midw.	C	43	127	15	28	2	0	2	14	.220	273	25	9	.971
1985—Midland	Texas	C-OF-3B	79	252	26	65	11	0	6	29	.258	293	59	10	.972
1986—Midland	Texas	C-3-O-1	48	138	24	31	5	0	4	16	.225	225	35	6	.977
1986—Palm Springs	Calif.	C	31	100	20	29	3	0	3	20	.290	176	20	2	.990
1987—Midland	Texas	C-O-1-3	63	187	28	43	5	1	7	26	.230	335	50	5	.987
1988—Edmonton	P. C.	C	79	245	28	63	10	0	1	29	.257	377	48	6	.986
1988—California	Amer.	C-3B	6	12	1	0	0	0	0	0	.000	6	1	1	.875
Major League Totals—1 Year			6	12	1	0	0	0	0	0	.000	6	1	1	.875

Selected by California Angels' organization in 9th round of free-agent draft, June 4, 1984.

ERIC KEITH DAVIS

Born May 29, 1962, at Los Angeles, Calif.
Height, 6.03. Weight, 185.
Throws and bats righthanded.

Established major league record for most strikeouts, two consecutive games (9), April 24 and 25, 1987 (21 innings).
Tied major league record for most grand slams, one month (3), May, 1987.
Major League stolen bases: 1984 (10), 1985 (16), 1986 (80), 1987 (50), 1988 (35). Total—191.
Hit three home runs in a game, September 10, 1986 and May 3, 1987.
Led National League in game-winning RBIs with 21 in 1988.
Led National League outfielders in total chances with 394 in 1987.
Led Northwest League in stolen bases with 40 in 1981.
Named outfielder on THE SPORTING NEWS National League All-Star Team, 1987.
Named outfielder on THE SPORTING NEWS National League All-Star fielding team, 1987 and 1988.
Named outfielder on THE SPORTING NEWS National League Silver Slugger team, 1987.

Year Club	League	Pos.	G.	AB.	R.	H.	2B.	3B.	HR.	RBI.	B.A.	PO.	A.	E.	F.A.
1980—Eugene	N'west	SS-2B	33	73	12	16	1	0	1	11	.219	24	35	11	.843
1981—Eugene	N'west	OF	62	214	★67	69	10	4	11	39	.322	94	11	4	.963
1982—Cedar Rapids	Midw.	OF	111	434	80	120	20	5	15	56	.276	239	9	9	.965
1983—Waterbury	East.	OF	89	293	56	85	13	1	15	43	.290	214	8	2	.991
1983—Indianapolis	A. A.	OF	19	77	18	23	4	0	7	19	.299	61	1	1	.984
1984—Wichita	A. A.	OF	52	194	42	61	9	5	14	34	.314	110	5	5	.958
1984—Cincinnati†	Nat.	OF	57	174	33	39	10	1	10	30	.224	125	4	1	.992
1985—Cincinnati	Nat.	OF	56	122	26	30	3	3	8	18	.246	75	3	1	.987
1985—Denver	A. A.	OF	64	206	48	57	10	2	15	38	.277	94	5	3	.971
1986—Cincinnati	Nat.	OF	132	415	97	115	15	3	27	71	.277	274	2	7	.975
1987—Cincinnati	Nat.	OF	129	474	120	139	23	4	37	100	.293	★380	10	4	.990
1988—Cincinnati	Nat.	OF	135	472	81	129	18	3	26	93	.273	300	2	6	.981
Major League Totals—5 Years			509	1657	357	452	69	14	108	312	.273	1154	21	19	.984

Selected by Cincinnati Reds' organization in 8th round of free-agent draft, June 3, 1980.
†On disabled list, August 16 to September 1, 1984.

ALL-STAR GAME RECORD

Year League	Pos.	AB.	R.	H.	2B.	3B.	HR.	RBI.	B.A.	PO.	A.	E.	F.A.
1987—National	OF	3	0	0	0	0	0	0	.000	1	0	0	1.000

GEORGE EARL DAVIS JR.
(Storm)

(Nicknamed by mother after "Dr. Storm", a character in "Dates on Trial",
a book she was reading while pregnant with Storm.)

Born December 26, 1961, at Dallas, Tex.
Height, 6.04. Weight, 200.
Throws and bats righthanded.

Major League saves: 1984 (1).
Tied for American League lead in wild pitches with 16 in 1988.
Named American League Comeback Player of the Year by THE SPORTING NEWS, 1988.

Year Club	League	G.	IP.	W.	L.	Pct.	H.	R.	ER.	SO.	BB.	ERA.
1979—Bluefield	Ap'lachian.	10	58	4	4	.500	44	34	25	54	30	3.88
1980—Miami	Florida St.	25	151	9	12	.429	157	85	59	90	55	3.52
1981—Charlotte	Southern	28	187	14	10	.583	★215	86	72	119	65	3.47
1982—Rochester	Int'national	4	26⅔	2	1	.667	25	13	11	27	7	3.71
1982—Baltimore	American	29	100⅔	8	4	.667	96	40	39	67	28	3.49
1983—Baltimore	American	34	200⅓	13	7	.650	180	90	80	125	64	3.59
1984—Baltimore	American	35	225	14	9	.609	205	86	78	105	71	3.12
1985—Baltimore	American	31	175	10	8	.556	172	92	88	93	70	4.53

Year Club	League	G.	IP.	W.	L.	Pct.	H.	R.	ER.	SO.	BB.	ERA.
1986—Baltimore†	American	25	154	9	12	.429	166	70	62	96	49	3.62
1986—Hagerstown‡	Carolina	1	4	0	0	.000	3	0	0	6	3	0.00
1987—San Diego§	National	21	62⅔	2	7	.222	70	48	43	37	36	6.18
1987—Wichita	Texas	1	4	0	1	.000	4	3	0	2	0	0.00
1987—Reno x	California	1	5	0	0	.000	2	2	2	5	6	3.60
1987—Oakland	American	5	30⅓	1	1	.500	28	13	11	28	11	3.26
1988—Oakland	American	33	201⅔	16	7	.696	211	86	83	127	91	3.70
American League Totals—7 Years		192	1087	71	48	.597	1058	477	441	641	384	3.65
National League Totals—1 Year		21	62⅔	2	7	.222	70	48	43	37	36	6.18
Major League Totals—7 Years		213	1149⅔	73	55	.570	1128	525	484	678	420	3.79

Selected by Baltimore Orioles' organization in 7th round of free-agent draft, June 5, 1979.

†On disabled list, July 4 to July 22, 1986; included rehabilitation disability assignment to Hagerstown, July 18 to July 22, 1986.

‡Traded to San Diego Padres for Catcher Terry Kennedy and Pitcher Mark Williamson, October 30, 1986.

§On disabled list, June 30 to August 17, 1987; included rehabilitation disability assignment to Wichita, August 7 to August 11, and Reno, August 12 to August 17, 1987.

xTraded to Oakland Athletics for two players to be named later, August 30, 1987; San Diego Padres acquired Pitcher Dave Leiper, August 31, 1987, and First Baseman Rob Nelson, September 8, 1987, to complete deal.

CHAMPIONSHIP SERIES RECORD

Year Club	League	G.	IP.	W.	L.	Pct.	H.	R.	ER.	SO.	BB.	ERA.
1983—Baltimore	American	1	6	0	0	.000	5	0	0	2	2	0.00
1988—Oakland	American	1	6⅓	0	0	.000	2	2	0	4	5	0.00
Championship Series Totals—2 Years		2	12⅓	0	0	.000	7	2	0	6	7	0.00

WORLD SERIES RECORD

Tied World Series record for most games lost, five-game Series (2), 1988.

Year Club	League	G.	IP.	W.	L.	Pct.	H.	R.	ER.	SO.	BB.	ERA.
1983—Baltimore	American	1	5	1	0	1.000	6	3	3	3	1	5.40
1988—Oakland	American	2	8	0	2	.000	14	10	10	7	1	11.25
World Series Totals—2 Years		3	13	1	2	.333	20	13	13	10	2	9.00

GLENN EARL DAVIS

Born March 28, 1961, at Jacksonville, Fla.
Height, 6.03. Weight, 210.
Throws and bats righthanded.
Attended Manatee Junior College, Bradenton, Fla.,
and University of Georgia, Athens, Ga.

Tied National League record for fewest double plays by first baseman, season, 150 or more games (89), 1987.
Major League stolen bases: 1986 (3), 1987 (4), 1988 (4). Total—11.
Hit three home runs in a game, September 10, 1987.
Tied for National League lead in game-winning RBIs with 16 in 1986.
Led Gulf Coast League first basemen in total chances with 520 and tied for lead in double plays with 35 in 1981.
Named first baseman on THE SPORTING NEWS National League Silver Slugger team, 1986.

Year Club	League	Pos.	G.	AB.	R.	H.	2B.	3B.	HR.	RBI.	B.A.	PO.	A.	E.	F.A.
1981—Sara. Astros-Or.	Gulf C.	*1B-OF	54	188	27	49	7	1	6	35	.261	*469	*37	*14	.973
1982—Daytona Beach	Fla. St.	1B-3B	103	378	70	119	28	3	•19	79	.315	759	70	16	.981
1982—Columbus	South.	1B	26	97	14	24	6	1	4	8	.247	257	11	2	.993
1983—Columbus	South.	OF	118	445	68	133	19	3	•25	85	.299	186	17	9	.958
1983—Tucson	P. C.	OF-1B-3B	15	57	5	12	3	0	1	8	.211	52	4	2	.966
1984—Tucson	P. C.	1B-OF	131	471	66	140	28	7	16	94	.297	922	94	22	.979
1984—Houston	Nat.	1B	18	61	6	13	5	0	2	8	.213	151	15	2	.988
1985—Tucson	P. C.	1B-OF	60	220	22	67	24	2	5	35	.305	420	29	5	.989
1985—Houston	Nat.	1B-OF	100	350	51	95	11	0	20	64	.271	766	57	12	.986
1986—Houston	Nat.	1B	158	574	91	152	32	3	31	101	.265	1253	111	11	.992
1987—Houston	Nat.	1B	151	578	70	145	35	2	27	93	.251	1283	112	12	.991
1988—Houston	Nat.	1B	152	561	78	152	26	0	30	99	.271	1355	103	6	*.996
Major League Totals—5 Years			579	2124	296	557	109	5	110	365	.262	4808	398	43	.992

Selected by Baltimore Orioles' organization in 32nd round of free-agent draft, June 5, 1979.
Selected by Houston Astros' organization in secondary phase of free-agent draft, January 13, 1981.

CHAMPIONSHIP SERIES RECORD

Tied Championship Series records for most at-bats, game (7), October 15, 1986 (16 innings); hitting home run in first Series at-bat, October 8, 1986.

Year Club	League	Pos.	G.	AB.	R.	H.	2B.	3B.	HR.	RBI.	B.A.	PO.	A.	E.	F.A.
1986—Houston	Nat.	1B	6	26	3	7	1	0	1	3	.269	62	3	1	.985

ALL-STAR GAME RECORD

Year League	Pos.	AB.	R.	H.	2B.	3B.	HR.	RBI.	B.A.	PO.	A.	E.	F.A.
1986—National	PH	1	0	0	0	0	0	0	.000	0	0	0	.000

—DID YOU KNOW—

That four grand slams have been hit on the same day 11 times in major league history, the last time September 13, 1988?

JODY RICHARD DAVIS

Born November 12, 1956, at Gainesville, Ga.
Height, 6.03. Weight, 210.
Throws and bats righthanded.
Attended Middle Georgia College, Cochran, Ga.

Major League stolen bases: 1984 (5), 1985 (1), 1987 (1). Total—7.
Led National League catchers in total chances with 998 and double plays with 14 in 1986.
Led National League in passed balls with 21 in 1983.
Tied for National League lead in double plays by catchers with 11 in 1982.
Led Carolina League in sacrifice flies with 13 in 1978.
Led Carolina League catchers in double plays with 8 in 1978.
Named catcher on THE SPORTING NEWS National League All-Star fielding team, 1986.

Year Club	League	Pos.	G.	AB.	R.	H.	2B.	3B.	HR.	RBI.	B.A.	PO.	A.	E.	F.A.
1976—Marion	Appal.	C	50	164	20	38	5	1	5	19	.232	290	30	*13	.961
1977—Little Falls	NYP	C-1B	64	214	37	62	11	2	11	46	.290	369	50	12	.972
1978—Lynchburg	Carol.	C-1B-3B	120	408	57	107	24	2	16	94	.262	595	79	15	.978
1979—Jackson†	Texas	C-1B	132	433	57	128	23	4	21	91	.296	661	81	15	.980
1980—St. Petersburg	Fla. St.	C-1B	45	155	27	43	4	0	6	27	.277	171	20	5	.974
1980—Springfield‡§	A. A.	C-1B	13	36	3	6	1	0	0	2	.167	59	7	1	.985
1981—Chicago	Nat.	C	56	180	14	46	5	1	4	21	.256	274	44	9	.972
1982—Chicago	Nat.	C	130	418	41	109	20	2	12	52	.261	598	89	11	.984
1983—Chicago	Nat.	C	151	510	56	138	31	2	24	84	.271	730	75	13	.984
1984—Chicago	Nat.	C	150	523	55	134	25	2	19	94	.256	811	89	*15	.984
1985—Chicago	Nat.	C	142	482	47	112	30	0	17	58	.232	694	84	8	.990
1986—Chicago	Nat.	*C-1B	148	528	61	132	27	2	21	74	.250	*885	*105	8	.992
1987—Chicago	Nat.	C	125	428	57	106	12	2	19	51	.248	749	79	9	.989
1988—Chi.xy-Atl.	Nat.	C	90	257	21	59	9	0	7	36	.230	396	34	2	.995
Major League Totals—8 Years			992	3326	352	836	159	11	123	470	.251	5137	599	75	.987

Selected by New York Mets' organization in 3rd round of free-agent draft, January 7, 1976.
†Traded to St. Louis Cardinals' organization for Pitcher Ray Searage, December 10, 1979.
‡On disabled list, April 14 to June 20, 1980.
§Drafted by Chicago Cubs, December 8, 1980.
xOn disabled list, May 3 to May 19, 1988.
yTraded to Atlanta Braves for Pitchers Kevin Coffman and Kevin Blankenship, September 29, 1988.

CHAMPIONSHIP SERIES RECORD

Established National League Championship Series record for highest slugging average, five-game Series (.833), 1984.
Tied National League Championship Series record for most total bases, five-game Series (15), 1984.

Year Club	League	Pos.	G.	AB.	R.	H.	2B.	3B.	HR.	RBI.	B.A.	PO.	A.	E.	F.A.
1984—Chicago	Nat.	C	5	18	3	7	2	0	2	6	.389	23	2	0	1.000

ALL-STAR GAME RECORD

Year League	Pos.	AB.	R.	H.	2B.	3B.	HR.	RBI.	B.A.	PO.	A.	E.	F.A.
1984—National	C	1	0	0	0	0	0	0	.000	1	0	0	1.000
1986—National	C	1	0	1	0	0	0	0	1.000	3	0	0	1.000
All-Star Game Totals—2 Years		2	0	1	0	0	0	0	.500	4	0	0	1.000

JOEL CLARK DAVIS

Born January 30, 1965, at Jacksonville, Fla.
Height, 6.05. Weight, 205.
Throws right and bats lefthanded.

Year Club	League	G.	IP.	W.	L.	Pct.	H.	R.	ER.	SO.	BB.	ERA.
1983—Sarasota White Sox	Gulf Coast	12	75⅓	6	2	.750	51	23	16	95	26	1.91
1984—Appleton	Midwest	11	40⅓	1	2	.333	40	27	27	38	38	6.02
1984—Niagara Falls	NYP	11	69	3	4	.429	57	35	18	72	37	2.35
1984—Glens Falls	Eastern	4	11⅔	1	2	.333	12	13	10	9	14	7.71
1985—Glens Falls†	Eastern	4	25⅓	1	1	.500	21	8	8	20	16	2.84
1985—Buffalo	Am. Assoc.	10	56⅓	2	5	.286	61	39	29	31	35	4.63
1985—Chicago	American	12	71⅓	3	3	.500	71	34	33	37	26	4.16
1986—Chicago	American	19	105⅓	4	5	.444	115	64	55	54	51	4.70
1986—Buffalo	Am. Assoc.	6	39⅓	1	4	.200	41	24	20	30	11	4.58
1987—Chicago	American	13	55	1	5	.167	56	35	35	25	29	5.73
1987—Hawaii	P. Coast	17	111⅔	6	7	.462	90	54	46	52	45	3.71
1988—Vancouver	P. Coast	27	95⅔	7	1	.875	100	45	40	75	27	3.76
1988—Chicago	American	5	16	0	1	.000	21	12	12	10	5	6.75
Major League Totals—4 Years		49	247⅔	8	14	.364	263	145	135	126	111	4.91

Selected by Chicago White Sox' organization in 1st round (13th player selected) of free-agent draft, June 6, 1983.
†On disabled list, April 12 to May 28, 1985.

JOHN KIRK DAVIS

Born January 5, 1963, at Chicago, Ill.
Height, 6.07. Weight 215.
Throws and bats righthanded.

Major League saves: 1987 (2), 1988 (1). Total—3.
Tied for American League lead in intentional bases on balls issued with 10 in 1988.

Led Pioneer League in wild pitches with 12 in 1982.

Year Club	League	G.	IP.	W.	L.	Pct.	H.	R.	ER.	SO.	BB.	ERA.
1981—Sarasota Royals-Blue	Gulf Coast	10	30	2	2	.500	28	21	17	13	23	5.10
1982—Butte	Pioneer	14	80⅔	7	1	.875	100	62	*55	38	37	6.14
1983—Charleston	S. Atlantic	20	78	5	6	.455	104	64	57	48	40	6.58
1984—Fort Myers	Florida St.	25	153	7	11	.389	170	91	77	84	70	4.53
1985—Memphis	Southern	27	160⅓	6	15	.286	186	113	96	103	75	5.39
1986—Memphis	Southern	41	111⅓	6	6	.500	99	63	58	70	69	4.69
1986—Omaha	Am. Assoc.	2	2	0	0	.000	2	1	1	1	1	4.50
1987—Omaha	Am. Assoc.	43	50⅔	4	3	.571	34	16	15	44	27	2.66
1987—Kansas City†	American	27	43⅔	5	2	.714	29	13	11	24	26	2.27
1988—Chicago	American	34	63⅔	2	5	.286	77	58	47	37	50	6.64
1988—Vancouver	P. Coast	15	17⅓	1	0	1.000	15	7	6	9	7	3.06
Major League Totals—1 Year		61	107⅓	7	7	.500	106	71	58	61	76	4.86

Selected by Kansas City Royals' organization in 7th round of free-agent draft, June 8, 1981.

†Traded with Pitchers Melido Perez, Chuck Mount and Greg Hibbard to Chicago White Sox for Pitcher Floyd Bannister and Infielder Dave Cochrane, December 10, 1987.

MARK ANTHONY DAVIS

Born November 25, 1964, at Lemon Grove, Calif.
Height, 6.00. Weight, 170.
Throws and bats righthanded.
Attended Stanford University, Stanford, Calif.
Brother of Mike Davis, outfielder with Los Angeles Dodgers;
cousin of Dave Grayson, Sr., defensive back with Dallas Texans, Kansas City Chiefs
and Oakland Raiders, 1961 through 1970; and related to Dave Grayson, Jr., linebacker with Cleveland Browns.

Year Club	League	Pos.	G.	AB.	R.	H.	2B.	3B.	HR.	RBI.	B.A.	PO.	A.	E.	F.A.
1986—Appleton	Midw.	OF	77	272	37	62	10	4	3	22	.228	105	5	3	.973
1987—Peninsula	Carol.	OF	134	507	91	149	24	6	16	72	.294	214	9	7	.970
1988—Birmingham	South.	OF	66	248	52	72	18	3	6	27	.290	142	5	6	.961
1988—Vancouver	P. C.	OF	68	241	24	51	9	2	4	29	.212	114	6	5	.960

Selected by St. Louis Cardinals' organization in 5th round of free-agent draft, June 7, 1982.
Selected by San Diego Padres' organization in 9th round of free-agent draft, June 3, 1985.
Selected by Chicago White Sox' organization in 12th round of free-agent draft, June 2, 1986.

MARK WILLIAM DAVIS

Born October 19, 1960, at Livermore, Calif.
Height, 6.04. Weight, 200.
Throws and bats lefthanded.
Attended Chabot College, Hayward, Calif.

Major League saves: 1985 (7), 1986 (4), 1987 (2), 1988 (28). Total—41.

Led Western Carolinas League in shutouts with 5, home runs allowed with 18 and tied for lead in balks with 5 in 1979.

Tied for Eastern League lead in shutouts with 4 and in games started by pitchers with 28 in 1980.
Named Eastern League Most Valuable Player, 1980.

Year Club	League	G.	IP.	W.	L.	Pct.	H.	R.	ER.	SO.	BB.	ERA.
1979—Spartanburg	W. Carol.	26	166	11	9	.550	147	76	59	135	49	3.20
1980—Reading	Eastern	28	*193	*19	6	*.760	140	63	53	*185	75	*2.47
1980—Philadelphia	National	2	7	0	0	.000	4	2	2	5	5	2.57
1981—Oklahoma City†	Am. Assoc.	13	65	5	2	.714	66	34	28	56	47	3.88
1981—Philadelphia	National	9	43	1	4	.200	49	37	37	29	24	7.74
1982—Oklahoma City‡§	Am. Assoc.	21	96⅔	5	12	.294	111	75	67	95	50	6.24
1983—Phoenix	P. Coast	13	72⅔	6	3	.667	89	57	51	64	33	6.32
1983—San Francisco	National	20	111	6	4	.600	93	51	43	83	50	3.49
1984—San Francisco	National	46	174⅔	5	17	.227	201	113	*104	124	54	5.36
1985—San Francisco	National	77	114⅓	5	12	.294	89	49	45	131	41	3.54
1986—San Francisco	National	67	84⅓	5	7	.417	63	33	28	90	34	2.99
1987—San Francisco x - San Diego	National	63	133	9	8	.529	123	64	59	98	59	3.99
1988—San Diego	National	62	98⅓	5	10	.333	70	24	22	102	42	2.01
Major League Totals—8 Years		346	765⅔	36	62	.367	692	373	340	662	309	4.00

Selected by New York Mets' organization in 21st round of free-agent draft, June 6, 1978.
Selected by Philadelphia Phillies' organization in secondary phase of free-agent draft, January 9, 1979.
†On disabled list, April 14 to June 11, 1981.
‡On disabled list, August 3 to August 30, 1982.

§Traded with Pitcher Mike Krukow and Outfielder Charles Penigar to San Francisco Giants for Second Baseman Joe Morgan and Pitcher Al Holland, December 14, 1982.

xTraded with third Baseman Chris Brown and Pitchers Keith Comstock and Mark Grant to San Diego Padres for Pitchers Dave Dravecky and Craig Lefferts and Infielder Kevin Mitchell, July 4, 1987.

ALL-STAR GAME RECORD

Year League	IP.	W.	L.	Pct.	H.	R.	ER.	SO.	BB.	ERA.
1988—National	⅔	0	0	.000	1	0	0	0	0	0.00

—DID YOU KNOW—

That the Los Angeles Dodgers went from the worst team in the National League on artificial surfaces in 1987 (11-31, .262) to the best in 1988 (27-15, .643)?

MICHAEL DWAYNE DAVIS
(Mike)

Born June 11, 1959, at San Diego, Calif.
Height, 6.03. Weight, 185.
Throws and bats lefthanded.
Attended San Diego Mesa College, San Diego, Calif.
Brother of Mark A. Davis, outfielder in Chicago White Sox' organization; and cousin of Dave Grayson, Sr., defensive back with Dallas Texans, Kansas City Chiefs and Oakland Raiders, 1961 through 1970; and related to Dave Grayson, Jr., linebacker with Cleveland Browns.

Major League stolen bases: 1980 (2), 1982 (3), 1983 (32), 1984 (14), 1985 (24), 1986 (27), 1987 (19), 1988 (7). Total—128.

Year	Club	League	Pos.	G.	AB.	R.	H.	2B.	3B.	HR.	RBI.	B.A.	PO.	A.	E.	F.A.
1977	Medicine Hat	Pion.	★OF-1-2	59	213	53	67	5	3	2	18	.315	82	6	★15	.854
1978	Modesto	Calif.	OF-1B	106	406	74	136	12	4	2	35	.335	201	10	13	.942
1979	Modesto	Calif.	OF	41	161	48	63	10	4	0	19	.391	76	3	7	.919
1979	Waterbury	East.	OF	97	351	51	77	9	5	6	39	.219	208	7	15	.935
1980	Ogden	P. C.	OF	19	69	14	21	7	2	1	14	.304	34	2	1	.973
1980	Oakland	Amer.	OF-1B	51	95	11	20	2	1	1	8	.211	76	7	1	.988
1981	Tacoma	P. C.	OF-1B	133	515	84	148	28	6	6	71	.287	286	7	7	.977
1981	Oakland	Amer.	OF-1B	17	20	0	1	1	0	0	0	.050	3	0	0	1.000
1982	Tacoma†	P. C.	OF-1B	100	374	71	118	23	3	12	68	.316	197	13	9	.959
1982	Oakland	Amer.	OF-1B	23	75	12	30	4	0	1	10	.400	65	4	5	.932
1983	Oakland‡	Amer.	OF	128	443	61	122	24	4	8	62	.275	278	16	8	.974
1984	Oakland	Amer.	OF	134	382	47	88	18	3	9	46	.230	287	6	●12	.961
1985	Oakland	Amer.	OF	154	547	92	157	34	1	24	82	.287	370	6	8	.979
1986	Oakland	Amer.	OF	142	489	77	131	28	3	19	55	.268	310	9	9	.973
1987	Oakland§	Amer.	OF	139	494	69	131	32	1	22	72	.265	210	3	●13	.942
1988	Los Angeles	Nat.	OF	108	281	29	55	11	2	2	17	.196	121	3	5	.961
American League Totals—8 Years				788	2545	369	680	143	13	84	335	.267	1599	51	56	.967
National League Totals—1 Year				108	281	29	55	11	2	2	17	.196	121	3	5	.961
Major League Totals—9 Years				896	2826	398	735	154	15	86	352	.260	1720	54	61	.967

Selected by Minnesota Twins' organization in 31st round of free agent draft, June 8, 1976.
Selected by Oakland A's organization in 3rd round of free agent draft, June 7, 1977.
†On disabled list, April 13 to May 24, 1982.
‡On disabled list, July 13 to July 31, 1983.
§Granted free agency, November 9, 1987; signed by Los Angeles Dodgers, December 15, 1987.

CHAMPIONSHIP SERIES RECORD

Year	Club	League	Pos.	G.	AB.	R.	H.	2B.	3B.	HR.	RBI.	B.A.	PO.	A.	E.	F.A.
1981	Oakland	Amer.	PH	1	1	0	1	0	0	0	0	1.000	0	0	0	.000
1988	Los Angeles	Nat.	PH	4	2	0	0	0	0	0	0	.000	0	0	0	.000
Championship Series Totals—2 Years				5	3	0	1	0	0	0	0	.333	0	0	0	.000

WORLD SERIES RECORD

Year	Club	League	Pos.	G.	AB.	R.	H.	2B.	3B.	HR.	RBI.	B.A.	PO.	A.	E.	F.A.
1988	Los Angeles	Nat.	PH-DH-O	4	7	3	1	0	0	1	2	.143	0	0	0	.000

RONALD GENE DAVIS
(Ron)

Born August 6, 1955, at Houston Tex.
Height, 6.04. Weight, 198.
Throws and bats righthanded.
Attended Blinn Junior College, Brenham, Tex.

Established major league record for most consecutive strikeouts by relief pitcher, game (8), May 4, 1981.
Established American League record for most wins by rookie relief pitcher, season (14), 1979.
Tied American League record for most consecutive strikeouts, game (8), May 4, 1981.
Major League saves: 1979 (9), 1980 (7), 1981 (6), 1982 (22), 1983 (30), 1984 (29), 1985 (25), 1986 (2). Total—130.
Led American League in intentional bases on balls issued with 12 in 1982.

Year	Club	League	G.	IP.	W.	L.	Pct.	H.	R.	ER.	SO.	BB.	ERA.
1976	Pompano Beach	Florida St.	18	115	8	8	.500	110	62	48	78	51	3.76
1977	Midland†	Texas					(Did not play)						
1977	Pompano Beach	Florida St.	21	111	8	7	.533	119	63	51	58	59	4.14
1978	Midland‡	Texas	12	68	3	3	.500	80	51	48	45	38	6.35
1978	West Haven	Eastern	21	60	9	2	.818	41	14	10	39	27	1.50
1978	New York	American	4	2	0	0	.000	3	4	3	0	3	13.50
1979	Columbus	Int'national	11	19	0	1	.000	13	9	9	10	15	4.26
1979	New York	American	44	85	14	2	★.875	84	29	27	43	28	2.86
1980	New York	American	53	131	9	3	.750	121	50	43	65	32	2.95
1981	New York§	American	43	73	4	5	.444	47	22	22	83	25	2.71
1982	Minnesota	American	63	106	3	9	.250	106	53	52	89	47	4.42
1983	Minnesota	American	66	89	5	8	.385	89	34	33	84	33	3.34
1984	Minnesota	American	64	83	7	11	.389	79	44	42	74	41	4.55
1985	Minnesota	American	57	64⅔	2	6	.250	55	28	25	72	35	3.48
1986	Minnesota x	American	36	38⅔	2	6	.250	55	42	39	30	29	9.08
1986	Chicago	National	17	20	0	2	.000	31	18	17	10	3	7.65
1987	Chicago y-Los Angeles	National	25	36⅓	0	0	.000	50	27	24	32	18	5.94
1987	Iowa z	Am. Assoc.	1	2	0	0	.000	2	1	1	0	3	4.50

Year	Club	League	G.	IP.	W.	L.	Pct.	H.	R.	ER.	SO.	BB.	ERA.
1987	Albuquerque a	P. Coast	7	9⅓	0	1	.000	6	6	5	8	7	4.82
1988	Phoenix	P. Coast	42	43	7	3	.700	35	19	13	38	26	2.72
1988	San Francisco b	National	9	17⅓	1	1	.500	15	10	9	15	6	4.67
American League Totals—9 Years			430	672⅓	46	50	.479	639	306	286	540	273	3.83
National League Totals—3 Years			51	73⅔	1	3	.250	96	55	50	57	27	6.11
Major League Totals—11 Years			481	746	47	53	.470	735	361	336	597	300	4.05

Selected by Chicago Cubs' organization in 3rd round of free-agent draft, January 7, 1976.

†On disabled list, April 9 to May 6, 1977.

‡Traded to New York Yankees' organization, June 12, 1978; completing deal in which New York traded Pitcher Ken Holtzman to Chicago Cubs for a player to be named later, June 10, 1978.

§Traded with Pitcher Paul Boris and Shortstop Greg Gagne and a reported $400,000 to Minnesota Twins for Shortstop Roy Smalley, April 10, 1982.

xTraded with Pitcher Dewayne Coleman to Chicago Cubs for Pitchers George Frazier and Ray Fontenot and Shortstop Julius McDougal, August 13, 1986.

yOn disabled list, May 24 to June 14, 1987; included rehabilitation disability assignment to Iowa, June 10 to June 12, 1987.

zReleased, August 4, 1987; signed by Los Angeles Dodgers' organization, August 13, 1987.

aReleased, March 19, 1988; signed by Phoenix (San Francisco Giants' organization), May 11, 1988.

bGranted free agency, November 4, 1988.

DIVISION SERIES RECORD

Year	Club	League	G.	IP.	W.	L.	Pct.	H.	R.	ER.	SO.	BB.	ERA.
1981	New York	American	3	6	1	0	1.000	1	0	0	6	2	0.00

CHAMPIONSHIP SERIES RECORD

Year	Club	League	G.	IP.	W.	L.	Pct.	H.	R.	ER.	SO.	BB.	ERA.
1980	New York	American	1	4	0	0	.000	3	1	1	3	1	2.25
1981	New York	American	2	3⅓	0	0	.000	0	0	0	4	2	0.00
Championship Series Totals—2 Years			3	7⅓	0	0	.000	3	1	1	7	3	1.23

WORLD SERIES RECORD

Year	Club	League	G.	IP.	W.	L.	Pct.	H.	R.	ER.	SO.	BB.	ERA.
1981	New York	American	4	2⅓	0	0	.000	4	8	6	4	5	23.14

ALL-STAR GAME RECORD

Year	League	IP.	W.	L.	Pct.	H.	R.	ER.	SO.	BB.	ERA.
1981	American	1	0	0	.000	1	1	1	1	0	9.00

WALLACE McARTHUR DAVIS
(Butch)

Born June 19, 1958, at Williamston, N.C.
Height, 6.00. Weight, 185.
Throws and bats righthanded.
Attended St. Augustine's College, Raleigh, N.C., and received bachelor of science degree from East Carolina University, Greenville, N.C. in 1980.

Major League stolen bases: 1983 (4), 1984 (4), 1988 (1). Total—9.

Led Gulf Coast League in total bases with 105 and stolen bases with 31 in 1980.

Year	Club	League	Pos.	G.	AB.	R.	H.	2B.	3B.	HR.	RBI.	B.A.	PO.	A.	E.	F.A.
1980	Sarasota Royals	Gulf C.	OF	61	235	46	*74	*17	4	2	35	.315	117	5	3	.976
1981	Fort Myers	Fla. St.	OF	126	464	*89	139	17	10	13	70	.300	239	5	12	.953
1982	Jacksonville	South.	OF	122	450	64	115	18	4	10	57	.256	231	7	2	.992
1983	Jacksonville	South.	OF-1B	90	331	51	105	15	7	14	63	.317	117	4	4	.968
1983	Omaha	A. A.	OF	46	171	27	54	10	3	5	21	.316	10	0	1	.909
1983	Kansas City	Amer.	OF	33	122	13	42	2	6	2	18	.344	83	1	2	.977
1984	Kansas City	Amer.	OF	41	116	11	17	3	0	2	12	.147	69	2	3	.959
1984	Omaha	A. A.	OF-1B	83	314	45	102	15	5	7	43	.325	153	13	6	.965
1985	Omaha	A. A.	OF-1B	109	403	58	106	26	10	6	34	.263	209	3	9	.959
1986	Omaha†‡	A. A.					(Did not play)									
1987	Vancouver	P. C.	OF	111	424	58	115	17	7	7	57	.271	232	8	4	.984
1987	Pittsburgh§	Nat.	OF	7	7	3	1	1	0	0	0	.143	3	0	0	1.000
1988	Charlotte	South.	OF	101	412	62	124	23	7	13	82	*.301	116	3	3	.975
1988	Rochester	Int.	OF	8	28	4	4	0	2	0	0	.143	10	0	0	1.000
1988	Baltimore x	Amer.	OF	13	25	2	6	1	0	0	0	.240	16	1	0	1.000
American League Totals—3 Years				87	263	26	65	6	6	4	30	.247	168	4	5	.972
National League Totals—1 Year				7	7	3	1	1	0	0	0	.143	3	0	0	1.000
Major League Totals—4 Years				94	270	29	66	7	6	4	30	.244	171	4	5	.972

Selected by Kansas City Royals' organization in 12th round of free-agent draft, June 3, 1980.

†On disabled list, April 11, 1986 through entire season.

‡Granted free agency, October 15, 1986; signed by Pittsburgh Pirates, December 4, 1986.

§Granted free agency, October 15, 1987; signed by Charlotte (Baltimore Orioles' organization), May 3, 1988.

xGranted free agency, October 15, 1988; re-signed by Orioles' organization, November 21, 1988.

WILLIAM CHESTER DAWLEY
(Bill)

Born February 6, 1958, at Norwich, Conn.
Height, 6.04. Weight, 240.
Throws and bats righthanded.

Major League saves: 1983 (14), 1984 (5), 1985 (2), 1986 (2), 1987 (2). Total—25.

Led American Association pitchers in games started with 28 in 1982.

Year Club	League	G.	IP.	W.	L.	Pct.	H.	R.	ER.	SO.	BB.	ERA.
1976—Billings	Pioneer	13	78	6	4	.600	62	42	24	80	37	2.77
1977—Tampa	Florida St.	24	181	10	8	.556	151	69	57	110	69	2.83
1978—Nashville	Southern	27	141	7	13	.350	135	78	63	86	55	4.02
1979—Nashville†	Southern	25	140	9	9	.500	144	72	62	84	41	3.99
1980—Indianapolis	Am. Assoc.	25	77	4	6	.400	90	46	39	28	31	4.56
1980—Waterbury	Eastern	7	49	2	2	.500	43	18	16	33	25	2.94
1981—Indianapolis	Am. Assoc.	26	133	6	8	.429	141	77	73	109	69	4.94
1982—Indianapolis‡§	Am. Assoc.	29	★179	11	7	.611	196	86	76	106	48	3.82
1983—Houston	National	48	79⅔	6	6	.500	51	26	25	60	22	2.82
1984—Houston	National	60	98	11	4	.733	82	24	21	47	35	1.93
1985—Houston xy	National	49	81	5	3	.625	76	35	32	48	37	3.56
1986—Chicago z	American	46	97⅔	0	7	.000	91	38	36	66	28	3.32
1987—St. Louis a	National	60	96⅔	5	8	.385	93	51	48	65	38	4.47
1988—Maine	Int'national	22	38⅔	1	2	.333	30	13	12	29	11	2.79
1988—Philadelphia bc	National	8	8⅔	0	2	.000	16	13	13	3	4	13.50
National League Totals—5 Years		225	364	27	23	.540	318	149	139	223	136	3.44
American League Totals—1 Year		46	97⅔	0	7	.000	91	38	36	66	28	3.32
Major League Totals—6 Years		271	461⅔	27	30	.474	409	187	175	289	164	3.41

Selected by Cincinnati Reds' organization in 7th round of free-agent draft, June 8, 1976.

†On temporary inactive list, May 21 to May 31, 1979.

‡Appeared in one game as an outfielder with no chances.

§Traded with Outfielder Anthony Walker to Houston Astros' organization for Catcher Alan Knicely, March 31, 1983.

xOn disabled list, July 6 to July 24, 1985.

yReleased, April 1, 1986; signed by Chicago White Sox, April 15, 1986.

zTraded to St. Louis Cardinals for Infielder Fred Manrique, December 22, 1986.

aReleased, December 21, 1987; signed by Philadelphia Phillies' organization, February 10, 1988.

bOn disabled list, May 11 to August 19, 1988; included rehabilitation disability assignment to Maine, July 27 to August 16, 1988.

cReleased, October 7, 1988.

ALL-STAR GAME RECORD

Year League	IP.	W.	L.	Pct.	H.	R.	ER.	SO.	BB.	ERA.
1983—National	1⅓	0	0	.000	1	0	0	1	0	0.00

ANDRE FERNANDO DAWSON

Born July 10, 1954, at Miami, Fla.
Height, 6.03. Weight, 195.
Throws and bats righthanded.
Attended Florida A&M University, Tallahassee, Fla.
Nephew of Theodore Taylor, third baseman-outfielder in Pittsburgh Pirates' organization, 1967 through 1969.

Tied major league records for most total bases, inning (8); most home runs, inning (2), July 30, 1978 (third inning) and September 24, 1985 (fifth inning); most runs batted in, inning (6), September 24, 1985 (fifth inning); fewest double plays by outfielder, season, 150 or more games (0), 1987.

Major League stolen bases: 1976 (1), 1977 (21), 1978 (28), 1979 (35), 1980 (34), 1981 (26), 1982 (39), 1983 (25), 1984 (13), 1985 (13), 1986 (18), 1987 (11), 1988 (12). Total—276.

Hit for the cycle, April 29, 1987.

Hit three home runs in a game, September 24, 1985 and August 1, 1987.

Led National League in total bases with 341 in 1983 and 353 in 1987.

Led National League in sacrifice flies with 18 in 1983.

Led National League in being hit by pitch with 12 in 1978, 7 in 1981 and tied for lead with 6 in 1980 and 9 in 1983.

Tied for National League lead in game-winning RBIs with 16 in 1987.

Led National League outfielders in total chances with 344 in 1981, 435 in 1982 and 450 in 1983.

Led Pioneer League in total bases with 166, in being hit by pitch with 6 and tied for lead in sacrifice flies with 5 in 1975.

Named National League Player of the Year by THE SPORTING NEWS, 1981 and 1987.

Named National League Most Valuable Player by Baseball Writers' Association of America, 1987.

Named National League Rookie Player of the Year by THE SPORTING NEWS, 1977.

Named National League Rookie of the Year by Baseball Writers' Association of America, 1977.

Named outfielder on THE SPORTING NEWS National League All-Star Team, 1981, 1983 and 1987.

Named outfielder on THE SPORTING NEWS National League All-Star fielding team, 1980 through 1985, 1987 and 1988.

Named outfielder on THE SPORTING NEWS National League Silver Slugger team, 1980, 1981, 1983 and 1987.

Year Club	League	Pos.	G.	AB.	R.	H.	2B.	3B.	HR.	RBI.	B.A.	PO.	A.	E.	F.A.
1975—Lethbridge	Pion.	OF	●72	★300	52	★99	14	7	★13	50	.330	★142	7	★10	.937
1976—Quebec City	East.	OF	40	143	27	51	6	0	8	27	.357	89	3	6	.939
1976—Denver	A. A.	OF	74	240	51	84	19	4	20	46	.350	97	2	2	.980
1976—Montreal	Nat.	OF	24	85	9	20	4	1	0	7	.235	61	1	2	.969
1977—Montreal	Nat.	OF	139	525	64	148	26	9	19	65	.282	352	9	4	.989
1978—Montreal	Nat.	OF	157	609	84	154	24	8	25	72	.253	411	17	5	.988
1979—Montreal	Nat.	OF	155	639	90	176	24	12	25	92	.275	394	7	5	.988
1980—Montreal	Nat.	OF	151	577	96	178	41	7	17	87	.308	410	14	6	.986
1981—Montreal	Nat.	OF	103	394	71	119	21	3	24	64	.302	★327	10	7	.980
1982—Montreal	Nat.	OF	148	608	107	183	37	7	23	83	.301	★419	8	8	.982
1983—Montreal	Nat.	OF	159	633	104	●189	36	10	32	113	.299	★435	6	9	.980
1984—Montreal	Nat.	OF	138	533	73	132	23	6	17	86	.248	297	11	8	.975

Year	Club	League	Pos.	G.	AB.	R.	H.	2B.	3B.	HR.	RBI.	B.A.	PO.	A.	E.	F.A.
1985	—Montreal	Nat.	OF	139	529	65	135	27	2	23	91	.255	248	9	7	.973
1986	—Montreal†‡	Nat.	OF	130	496	65	141	32	2	20	78	.284	200	11	3	.986
1987	—Chicago	Nat.	OF	153	621	90	178	24	2	★49	★137	.287	271	12	4	.986
1988	—Chicago	Nat.	OF	157	591	78	179	31	8	24	79	.303	267	7	3	.989
Major League Totals—13 Years				1753	6840	996	1932	350	77	298	1054	.282	4092	122	71	.983

Selected by Montreal Expos' organization in 11th round of free-agent draft, June 4, 1975.
†On disabled list, June 5 to June 30, 1986.
‡Granted free agency, November 12, 1986; signed by Chicago Cubs, March 9, 1987.

DIVISION SERIES RECORD

Year	Club	League	Pos.	G.	AB.	R.	H.	2B.	3B.	HR.	RBI.	B.A.	PO.	A.	E.	F.A.
1981	—Montreal	Nat.	OF	5	20	1	6	0	1	0	0	.300	12	1	1	.929

CHAMPIONSHIP SERIES RECORD

Year	Club	League	Pos.	G.	AB.	R.	H.	2B.	3B.	HR.	RBI.	B.A.	PO.	A.	E.	F.A.
1981	—Montreal	Nat.	OF	5	20	2	3	0	0	0	0	.150	12	0	0	1.000

ALL-STAR GAME RECORD

Year	League	Pos.	AB.	R.	H.	2B.	3B.	HR.	RBI.	B.A.	PO.	A.	E.	F.A.
1981	—National	OF	4	0	1	0	0	0	0	.250	4	0	0	1.000
1982	—National	OF	4	0	1	0	0	0	0	.250	4	0	0	1.000
1983	—National	OF	3	0	0	0	0	0	0	.000	3	0	0	1.000
1987	—National	OF	3	0	1	1	0	0	0	.333	3	0	0	1.000
1988	—National	OF	2	0	1	0	0	0	0	.500	0	0	0	.000
All-Star Game Totals—5 Years			16	0	4	1	0	0	0	.250	14	0	0	1.000

KENNETH GRANT DAYLEY II
(Ken)

Born February 25, 1959, at Jerome, Ida.
Height, 6.00. Weight, 180.
Throws and bats lefthanded.
Attended University of Portland, Portland, Ore.

Major League saves: 1985 (11), 1986 (5), 1987 (4), 1988 (5). Total—25.
Led International League pitchers in games started with 31 in 1981.
Received reported $100,000 bonus to sign with Atlanta Braves, 1980.
Named lefthanded pitcher on THE SPORTING NEWS College Baseball All-America Team, 1980.

Year	Club	League	G.	IP.	W.	L.	Pct.	H.	R.	ER.	SO.	BB.	ERA.
1980	—Savannah	Southern	16	105	8	3	.727	86	38	30	104	54	2.57
1981	—Richmond	Int'national	31	★200	●13	8	.619	180	82	74	★162	★117	3.33
1982	—Richmond	Int'national	13	98⅓	8	3	.727	89	43	34	79	47	3.11
1982	—Atlanta	National	20	71⅓	5	6	.455	79	39	36	34	25	4.54
1983	—Richmond	Int'national	14	90⅔	9	3	.750	79	39	33	74	49	3.28
1983	—Atlanta	National	24	104⅔	5	8	.385	100	59	50	70	39	4.30
1984	—Atlanta†-St. Louis	National	7	23⅔	0	5	.000	44	28	21	10	11	7.99
1984	—Richmond	Int'national	9	62⅓	5	1	.833	66	31	28	45	24	4.04
1984	—Louisville	Am. Assoc.	13	96⅓	4	6	.400	86	42	35	79	22	3.27
1985	—St. Louis	National	57	65⅓	4	4	.500	65	24	20	62	18	2.76
1986	—St. Louis‡§	National	31	38⅔	0	3	.000	42	19	14	33	11	3.26
1987	—Louisville	Am. Assoc.	1	2	0	0	.000	1	1	1	1	1	4.50
1987	—Springfield	Midwest	2	3⅔	0	0	.000	1	0	0	3	1	0.00
1987	—St. Louis x	National	53	61	9	5	.643	52	21	18	63	33	2.66
1988	—St. Louis y	National	54	55⅓	2	7	.222	48	20	17	38	19	2.77
Major League Totals—7 Years			246	420	25	38	.397	430	210	176	310	156	3.77

Selected by Atlanta Braves' organization in 1st round (third player selected) of free-agent draft, June 3, 1980.
†Traded with First Baseman Mike Jorgensen to St. Louis Cardinals for Third Baseman Ken Oberkfell, June 15, 1984.
‡On disabled list, July 13, 1986 through remainder of season.
§Released, December 20, 1986; re-signed by Cardinals, January 19, 1987.
xOn St. Louis disabled list, April 5 to May 21, 1987; included rehabilitation disability assignment to Louisville, May 12 to May 21, 1987.
yOn disabled list, April 5 to May 9, 1988.

CHAMPIONSHIP SERIES RECORD

Established Championship Series record for most saves, seven-game Series (2), 1987.
Established National League Championship Series records for most games pitched (5) and most saves (2), six-game Series, 1985.

Year	Club	League	G.	IP.	W.	L.	Pct.	H.	R.	ER.	SO.	BB.	ERA.
1985	—St. Louis	National	5	6	0	0	.000	2	0	0	3	1	0.00
1987	—St. Louis	National	3	4	0	0	.000	1	0	0	4	2	0.00
Championship Series Totals—2 Years			8	10	0	0	.000	3	0	0	7	3	0.00

WORLD SERIES RECORD

Year	Club	League	G.	IP.	W.	L.	Pct.	H.	R.	ER.	SO.	BB.	ERA.
1985	—St. Louis	National	4	6	1	0	1.000	1	0	0	5	3	0.00
1987	—St. Louis	National	4	4⅔	0	0	.000	2	1	1	3	0	1.93
World Series Totals—2 Years			8	10⅔	1	0	1.000	3	1	1	8	3	0.84

BRIAN LOUIS DEAK

Born October 25, 1967, at Harrisburg, Pa.
Height, 6.00. Weight, 183.
Throws and bats righthanded.
Attended Yavapai College, Prescott, Ariz.

Led Midwest League in slugging percentage with .481 in 1988.
Led Appalachian League catchers in total chances with 419 in 1986.
Named Appalachian League Player of the Year, 1986.

Year Club	League	Pos.	G.	AB.	R.	H.	2B.	3B.	HR.	RBI.	B.A.	PO.	A.	E.	F.A.
1986—Pulaski	Appal.	C	62	197	45	64	15	2	12	43	.325	*391	24	4	.990
1987—Sumter	S. Atl.	C	92	252	50	51	6	0	15	49	.202	576	55	11	.983
1988—Burlington	Midw.	C	119	345	58	85	19	1	20	59	.246	604	87	12	.983

Selected by Atlanta Braves' organization in 3rd round of free-agent draft, January 14, 1986.

JEFFREY LINDEN DEDMON
(Jeff)

Born March 4, 1960, at Torrance, Calif.
Height, 6.02. Weight, 200.
Throws right and bats lefthanded.
Attended West Los Angeles College, Culver City, Calif.

Major League saves: 1984 (4), 1986 (3), 1987 (4), 1988 (1). Total—12.

Year Club	League	G.	IP.	W.	L.	Pct.	H.	R.	ER.	SO.	BB.	ERA.
1980—Bradenton Braves	Gulf Coast	10	64	3	4	.429	55	26	21	28	11	2.95
1980—Anderson	S. Atlantic	2	11	1	0	1.000	10	3	1	8	3	0.82
1981—Durham	Carolina	28	165	7	8	.467	178	97	79	115	50	4.31
1982—Durham	Carolina	31	121⅓	5	6	.455	113	57	37	102	54	2.74
1983—Savannah	Southern	21	50	4	1	.800	46	18	16	26	16	2.88
1983—Richmond	Int'national	21	36	2	2	.500	28	9	7	33	14	1.75
1983—Atlanta	National	5	4	0	0	.000	10	6	6	3	0	13.50
1984—Atlanta	National	54	81	4	3	.571	86	39	34	51	35	3.78
1984—Richmond	Int'national	6	10	1	2	.333	11	10	9	10	13	8.10
1985—Richmond	Int'national	10	12	1	1	.500	12	2	2	7	3	1.50
1985—Atlanta	National	60	86	6	3	.667	84	52	39	41	49	4.08
1986—Atlanta†	National	57	99⅔	6	6	.500	90	43	33	58	39	2.98
1987—Atlanta‡	National	53	89⅔	3	4	.429	82	46	39	40	42	3.91
1988—Cleveland	American	21	33⅔	1	0	1.000	35	20	17	17	21	4.54
1988—Colorado Springs	P. Coast	17	41⅓	2	3	.400	56	30	20	24	11	4.35
National League Totals—5 Years		229	360⅓	19	16	.543	352	186	151	193	165	3.77
American League Totals—1 Year		21	33⅔	1	0	1.000	35	20	17	17	21	4.54
Major League Totals—6 Years		250	394	20	16	.556	387	206	168	210	186	3.84

Selected by Houston Astros' organization in 1st round (seventh player selected), of free-agent draft, January 9, 1979.
Selected by Oakland A's organization in secondary phase of free-agent draft, June 5, 1979.
Selected by San Francisco Giants' organization in secondary phase of free-agent draft, January 8, 1980.
Selected by Atlanta Braves' organization in secondary phase of free-agent draft, June 3, 1980.
†Appeared in one game as an outfielder with no chances.
‡Traded to Cleveland Indians for a player to be named later, March 28, 1988; Atlanta Braves acquired Pitcher Tommy Kurczewski to complete deal, June 22, 1988.

ROBERT GEORGE DEER
(Rob)

Born September 29, 1960, at Orange, Calif.
Height, 6.03. Weight, 210.
Throws and bats righthanded.
Attended Fresno City College, Fresno, Calif.

Tied major league records for most grand slams, two consecutive games (2), August 19 and 20, 1987; most strikeouts, nine-inning game (5), August 8, first game, 1987.
Established American League record for most strikeouts, season (186), 1987.
Major League stolen bases: 1984 (1), 1986 (5), 1987 (12), 1988 (9). Total—27.
Led American League batters in strikeouts with 186 in 1987 and tied for lead with 153 in 1988.
Led Pacific Coast League batters in strikeouts with 175 in 1984.
Led Texas League batters in strikeouts with 177 in 1982 and 185 in 1983.
Tied for Texas League lead in game-winning RBIs with 13 in 1983.
Led California League batters in strikeouts with 146 in 1981.

Year Club	League	Pos.	G.	AB.	R.	H.	2B.	3B.	HR.	RBI.	B.A.	PO.	A.	E.	F.A.
1978—Great Falls	Pion.	OF	48	137	20	34	6	5	0	18	.248	83	3	4	.956
1979—Cedar Rapids	Midw.	OF	29	86	7	18	0	1	1	16	.209	35	1	4	.900
1979—Great Falls	Pion.	OF	63	218	49	69	18	7	7	44	.317	95	10	5	.955
1980—Clinton	Midw.	OF	127	434	60	114	31	5	13	58	.263	184	•17	11	.948
1981—Fresno	Calif.	OF	135	479	86	137	24	4	*33	107	.286	211	14	6	.974
1982—Shreveport	Texas	OF-1B	128	410	58	85	26	0	27	73	.207	184	10	11	.946
1983—Shreveport	Texas	OF	132	448	89	97	15	1	*35	99	.217	252	13	7	.974
1984—Phoenix	P. C.	OF	133	449	88	102	21	1	*31	69	.227	251	*19	9	.968
1984—San Francisco	Nat.	OF	13	24	5	4	0	0	3	3	.167	19	0	2	.905
1985—San Francisco†	Nat.	OF-1B	78	162	22	30	5	1	8	20	.185	127	2	2	.985
1986—Milwaukee	Amer.	OF-1B	134	466	75	108	17	3	33	86	.232	312	8	8	.976

Year	Club	League	Pos.	G.	AB.	R.	H.	2B.	3B.	HR.	RBI.	B.A.	PO.	A.	E.	F.A.
1987	—Milwaukee	Amer.	OF-1B	134	474	71	113	15	2	28	80	.238	304	16	8	.976
1988	—Milwaukee‡	Amer.	OF	135	492	71	124	24	0	23	85	.252	284	10	3	.990
National League Totals—2 Years				91	186	27	34	5	1	11	23	.183	146	2	4	.974
American League Totals—3 Years				403	1432	217	345	56	5	84	251	.241	900	34	19	.980
Major League Totals—5 Years				494	1618	244	379	61	6	95	274	.234	1046	36	23	.979

Selected by San Francisco Giants' organization in 4th round of free-agent draft, June 6, 1978.
†Traded to Milwaukee Brewers for Pitchers Dean Freeland and Eric Pilkington, December 18, 1985.
‡On disabled list, July 4 to July 27, 1988.

IVAN DeJESUS (ALVAREZ)

Name pronounced Day-HAY-soos.

Born January 9, 1953, at Santurce, Puerto Rico.
Height, 5.11. Weight, 185.
Throws and bats righthanded.
Attended University of Puerto Rico, Rio Piedras, Puerto Rico.

Tied Major League record for fewest double plays by shortstop, season, 150 or more games (64), 1983.

Major League stolen bases: 1975 (1), 1977 (24), 1978 (41), 1979 (24), 1980 (44), 1981 (21), 1982 (14), 1983 (11), 1984 (12), 1985 (2). Total—194.

Hit for the cycle, April 22, 1980.

Led National League shortstops in double plays with 81 in 1981.

Led Pacific Coast League shortstops in double plays with 114 in 1974.

Led California League shortstops in double plays with 87 in 1973.

Led California League shortstops in assists with 311, errors with 48 and double plays with 53 in 1971.

Led Florida State League shortstops in double plays with 56 in 1970.

Year	Club	League	Pos.	G.	AB.	R.	H.	2B.	3B.	HR.	RBI.	B.A.	PO.	A.	E.	F.A.
1970	—Daytona Beach	Fla. St.	SS	123	396	51	92	12	7	2	38	.232	164	361	38	.933
1971	—Bakersfield	Calif.	SS-2B	126	462	77	108	16	2	6	30	.234	159	323	49	.908
1972	—Daytona Beach	Fla. St.	SS	131	442	56	108	15	4	7	39	.244	187	*452	37	.945
1973	—Bakersfield	Calif.	SS	132	519	77	125	17	1	7	57	.241	221	*403	*47	.930
1974	—Albuquerque	P. C.	SS	140	510	81	152	17	5	7	55	.298	*268	*479	38	.952
1974	—Los Angeles	Nat.	SS	3	3	1	1	0	0	0	0	.333	1	0	0	1.000
1975	—Albuquerque	P. C.	SS	62	221	24	60	10	2	1	21	.271	97	265	24	.938
1975	—Los Angeles	Nat.	SS	63	87	10	16	2	1	0	2	.184	45	107	4	.974
1976	—Albuquerque	P. C.	SS-3B	108	405	69	123	27	7	7	64	.304	161	341	35	.935
1976	—Los Angeles†	Nat.	SS-3B	22	41	4	7	2	1	0	2	.171	20	47	3	.957
1977	—Chicago	Nat.	SS	155	624	91	166	31	7	3	40	.266	234	*595	33	.962
1978	—Chicago	Nat.	SS	160	619	*104	172	24	7	3	35	.278	232	*558	27	.967
1979	—Chicago	Nat.	SS	160	636	92	180	26	10	5	52	.283	235	507	32	.959
1980	—Chicago	Nat.	SS	157	618	78	160	26	3	3	33	.259	229	529	24	.969
1981	—Chicago‡	Nat.	SS	106	403	49	78	8	4	0	13	.194	*221	343	24	.959
1982	—Philadelphia	Nat.	SS-3B	161	536	53	128	21	5	3	59	.239	222	488	21	.971
1983	—Philadelphia	Nat.	SS	158	497	60	126	15	7	4	45	.254	214	438	23	.966
1984	—Philadelphia§	Nat.	SS	144	435	40	112	15	3	0	35	.257	166	400	29	.951
1985	—St. Louis x	Nat.	3B-SS	59	72	11	16	5	0	0	7	.222	15	40	2	.965
1986	—Columbus	Int.	SS-2B	25	84	10	22	3	1	0	15	.262	36	72	6	.947
1986	—New York y	Amer.	SS	7	4	1	0	0	0	0	0	.000	5	4	1	.900
1986	—Vermont z	East.	SS-3B	10	36	4	10	1	0	1	5	.278	9	23	0	1.000
1987	—Louisville a	A. A.	SS-3B	40	145	26	40	11	0	1	14	.276	57	111	6	.966
1987	—San Francisco	Nat.	SS	9	10	0	2	0	0	0	1	.200	7	14	4	.840
1987	—Phoenix b	P. C.	SS-2B-3B	17	54	8	14	4	1	0	2	.259	24	43	2	.971
1988	—Toledo	Int.	SS-3B	60	200	16	47	5	1	0	16	.235	74	150	9	.961
1988	—Detroit	Amer.	SS	7	17	1	3	0	0	0	0	.176	8	17	3	.893
National League Totals—13 Years				1357	4581	593	1164	175	48	21	324	.254	1841	4066	226	.963
American League Totals—2 Years				14	21	2	3	0	0	0	0	.143	13	21	4	.895
Major League Totals—15 Years				1371	4602	595	1167	175	48	21	324	.254	1854	4087	230	.963

Signed as free agent by Los Angeles Dodgers' organization, May 23, 1969.

†Traded with First Baseman Bill Buckner and Pitcher Jeff Albert to Chicago Cubs for Outfielder Rick Monday and Pitcher Mike Garman, January 11, 1977.

‡Traded to Philadelphia Phillies for Shortstop Larry Bowa and Infielder Ryne Sandberg, January 27, 1982.

§Traded with Pitcher Bill Campbell to St. Louis Cardinals for Pitcher Dave Rucker, April 6, 1985.

xGranted free agency, November 12, 1985; signed by Columbus (New York Yankees' organization), May 1, 1986.

yReleased, June 24, 1986; signed by Vermont (Cincinnati Reds' organization), July 16, 1986.

zReleased, July 28, 1986; signed by Louisville (St. Louis Cardinals' organization), February 20, 1987.

aSold to San Francisco Giants, June 5, 1987.

bReleased, July 17, 1987; signed by Toledo (Detroit Tigers' organization), June 22, 1988.

CHAMPIONSHIP SERIES RECORD

Year	Club	League	Pos.	G.	AB.	R.	H.	2B.	3B.	HR.	RBI.	B.A.	PO.	A.	E.	F.A.
1983	—Philadelphia	Nat.	SS	4	12	0	3	0	0	0	1	.250	4	11	2	.882

WORLD SERIES RECORD

Year	Club	League	Pos.	G.	AB.	R.	H.	2B.	3B.	HR.	RBI.	B.A.	PO.	A.	E.	F.A.
1983	—Philadelphia	Nat.	SS	5	16	0	2	0	0	0	0	.125	5	14	1	.950
1985	—St. Louis	Nat.	PH	1	1	0	0	0	0	0	0	.000	0	0	0	.000
World Series Totals—2 Years				6	17	0	2	0	0	0	0	.118	5	14	1	.950

JOSE LUIS DeJESUS (VELAZQUEZ)

Born January 6, 1965, at Brooklyn, N.Y.
Height, 6.05. Weight, 175.
Throws and bats righthanded.

Year Club	League	G.	IP.	W.	L.	Pct.	H.	R.	ER.	SO.	BB.	ERA.
1983—Sarasota Royals	Gulf Coast	10	24	1	2	.333	17	18	11	10	17	4.13
1984—Charleston	S. Atlantic	27	163	11	12	.478	152	98	80	85	69	4.42
1985—Fort Myers†	Florida St.	27	129⅔	8	10	.444	119	70	62	94	59	4.30
1986—Fort Myers	Florida St.	22	110	4	9	.308	87	64	42	97	82	3.44
1987—Memphis	Southern	25	130⅓	4	11	.267	106	78	65	79	99	4.49
1988—Memphis	Southern	20	116	9	9	.500	88	56	50	149	70	3.88
1988—Omaha	Am. Assoc.	7	49⅔	2	3	.400	44	22	19	57	14	3.44
1988—Kansas City	American	2	2⅔	0	1	.000	6	10	8	2	5	27.00
Major League Totals—1 Year		2	2⅔	0	1	.000	6	10	8	2	5	27.00

Signed as free agent by Kansas City Royals' organization, May 9, 1983.
†Drafted by Toronto Blue Jays, December 10, 1985; returned, April 3, 1986.

JOSE DeLEON (CHESTARO)

Born December 20, 1960, at Rancho Viejo, LaVega, D.R.
Height, 6.03. Weight, 211.
Throws and bats righthanded.

Major League saves: 1985 (3), 1986 (1). Total—4.
Led Gulf Coast League in home runs allowed with 7 in 1979.
Tied for South Atlantic League lead in home runs allowed with 19 in 1980.
Tied for Gulf Coast League lead in wild pitches with 9 in 1979.

Year Club	League	G.	IP.	W.	L.	Pct.	H.	R.	ER.	SO.	BB.	ERA.
1979—Bradenton Pirates	Gulf Coast	11	59	2	4	.333	76	47	42	33	38	6.41
1980—Shelby	S. Atlantic	26	168	10	15	.400	160	108	*90	118	69	4.82
1981—Buffalo	Eastern	25	159	12	6	.667	136	72	55	158	94	3.11
1982—Portland†	P. Coast	24	119	10	7	.588	138	81	79	94	65	5.97
1983—Hawaii	P. Coast	20	127⅓	11	6	.647	90	50	43	128	68	*3.04
1983—Pittsburgh	National	15	108	7	3	.700	75	36	34	118	47	2.83
1984—Pittsburgh	National	30	192⅓	7	13	.350	147	86	80	153	92	3.74
1985—Pittsburgh	National	31	162⅔	2	*19	.095	138	93	85	149	89	4.70
1985—Hawaii	P. Coast	5	41	4	0	1.000	15	4	4	45	10	0.88
1986—Hawaii	P. Coast	15	106	5	8	.385	87	32	29	83	44	2.46
1986—Pittsburgh‡	National	9	16⅓	1	3	.250	17	16	15	11	17	8.27
1986—Chicago	American	13	79	4	5	.444	49	30	26	68	42	2.96
1987—Chicago§	American	33	206	11	12	.478	177	106	92	153	97	4.02
1988—St. Louis x	National	34	225⅓	13	10	.565	198	95	92	208	86	3.67
National League Totals—5 Years		119	704⅔	30	48	.385	575	326	306	639	331	3.91
American League Totals—2 Years		46	285	15	17	.469	226	136	118	221	139	3.73
Major League Totals—6 Years		165	989⅔	45	65	.409	801	462	424	860	470	3.86

Selected by Pittsburgh Pirates' organization in 3rd round of free-agent draft June 5, 1979.
†On disabled list, July 5 to July 29, 1982.
‡Traded to Chicago White Sox for Outfielder Bobby Bonilla, July 23, 1986.
§Traded to St. Louis Cardinals for Pitcher Rick Horton, Outfielder Lance Johnson and cash, February 9, 1988.
xAppeared in one game as an outfielder with one putout.

RAFAEL ALONZO DeLIMA

Born December 21, 1967, at Valencia, Venezuela.
Height, 5.11. Weight, 175.
Throws and bats lefthanded.

Led Appalachian League in sacrifice flies with 6 in 1986.
Tied for Appalachian League lead in double plays by outfielders with 2 in 1986.

Year Club	League	Pos.	G.	AB.	R.	H.	2B.	3B.	HR.	RBI.	B.A.	PO.	A.	E.	F.A.
1986—Kenosha	Midw.	OF	20	35	2	1	0	0	0	0	.029	23	0	0	1.000
1986—Elizabethton	Appal.	OF	49	136	20	31	7	0	2	21	.228	82	5	2	.978
1987—Kenosha	Midw.	OF	131	494	75	135	24	9	9	67	.273	*272	6	10	.965
1988—Orlando	South.	OF	137	500	66	143	25	3	3	46	.286	330	8	5	*.985

Signed as free agent by Minnesota Twins' organization, October 10, 1985.

LUIS MANUEL DELOS SANTOS

Born December 29, 1966, at San Cristobal, D.R.
Height, 6.05. Weight, 190.
Throws and bats righthanded.

Led American Association in grounding into double plays with 20 in 1987 and 17 in 1988.
Led American Association first basemen in total chances with 1,050 in 1988.
Named American Association Most Valuable Player, 1988.

Year Club	League	Pos.	G.	AB.	R.	H.	2B.	3B.	HR.	RBI.	B.A.	PO.	A.	E.	F.A.
1984—Eugene	N'west	3B	67	257	27	69	10	2	2	30	.268	67	93	22	.879
1985—Fort Myers	Fla. St.	3B	123	454	44	120	18	2	0	48	.264	87	141	32	.877
1986—Memphis	South.	3B	135	525	72	159	21	5	3	84	.303	*136	244	*50	.884
1987—Omaha	A.A.	3B-1B	135	518	53	152	29	6	2	67	.293	401	116	27	.950
1988—Omaha	A.A.	1B	136	*535	62	*164	25	4	6	●87	.307	*971	68	*11	.990

Year	Club	League	Pos.	G.	AB.	R.	H.	2B.	3B.	HR.	RBI.	B.A.	PO.	A.	E.	F.A.
1988	Kansas City	Amer.	1B	11	22	1	2	1	1	0	1	.091	31	1	0	1.000
	Major League Totals—1 Year			11	22	1	2	1	1	0	1	.091	31	1	0	1.000

Selected by Kansas City Royals' organization in 2nd round of free-agent draft, June 4, 1984.

JOHN RIKARD DEMPSEY
(Rick)

Born September 13, 1949, at Fayetteville, Tenn.
Height, 6.00. Weight, 184.
Throws and bats righthanded.
Attended Pierce Junior College, Woodland Hills, Calif.
Brother of Pat Dempsey, catcher in Oakland A's, Baltimore Orioles', New York Yankees', Cleveland Indians' and Minnesota Twins' organizations, 1977 through 1987.

Tied major league record for most double plays by catcher, game (3), June 1, 1977.

Major League stolen bases: 1974 (1), 1976 (1), 1977 (2), 1978 (7), 1980 (3), 1983 (1), 1984 (1), 1986 (1), 1988 (1). Total—18.

Tied for American League lead in double plays by catchers with 14 in 1978.

Led International League in passed balls with 14 in 1973.

Led New York-Pennsylvania League catchers in putouts with 468, assists with 35, fielding percentage with .990 and tied for lead in double plays with 4 in 1968.

Year	Club	League	Pos.	G.	AB.	R.	H.	2B.	3B.	HR.	RBI.	B.A.	PO.	A.	E.	F.A.
1967	Sarasota Twins	Gulf C.	C-OF-1B	40	102	9	21	4	3	0	9	.206	133	16	2	.987
1968	Wisconsin Rapids	Midw.	C	11	35	12	8	2	0	1	6	.229	68	2	1	.986
1968	Auburn	NYP	C-1B-OF	73	270	48	79	10	7	7	61	.293	505	38	7	.987
1969	Wisconsin Rapids	Midw.	C	50	151	35	55	11	2	6	31	.364	341	30	•13	.966
1969	Minnesota	Amer.	C	5	6	1	3	1	0	0	0	.500	5	0	1	.833
1970	Charlotte	South	C-OF-2B	105	351	28	86	20	6	4	42	.245	506	76	18	.970
1970	Minnesota	Amer.	C	5	7	1	0	0	0	0	0	.000	12	0	1	.923
1971	Charlotte	South	C-OF	105	338	39	82	16	2	8	47	.243	599	65	8	.988
1971	Minnesota	Amer.	C	6	13	2	4	1	0	0	0	.308	30	4	2	.944
1972	Minnesota†	Amer.	C	25	40	0	8	1	0	0	0	.200	67	5	1	.986
1972	Tacoma	P. C.	C-OF	48	161	13	38	6	2	3	18	.236	284	33	5	.984
1973	Syracuse	Int.	C-OF-3B	122	387	53	96	14	4	6	47	.248	585	69	9	.986
1973	New York	Amer.	C	6	11	0	2	0	0	0	0	.182	9	0	2	.818
1974	New York	Amer.	C-OF	43	109	12	26	3	0	2	12	.239	152	22	4	.978
1975	New York	Amer.	C-OF-3B	71	145	18	38	8	0	1	11	.262	92	9	3	.971
1976	N.Y.‡-Balt.	Amer.	C-OF	80	216	12	42	2	0	0	12	.194	302	39	4	.988
1977	Baltimore§	Amer.	C	91	270	27	61	7	4	3	34	.226	416	52	11	.977
1978	Baltimore	Amer.	C	136	441	41	114	25	0	6	32	.259	636	79	11	.985
1979	Baltimore	Amer.	C	124	368	48	88	23	0	6	41	.239	615	*81	7	.990
1980	Baltimore	Amer.	C-OF-1B	119	362	51	95	26	3	9	40	.262	544	55	8	.987
1981	Baltimore	Amer.	C	92	251	24	54	10	1	6	15	.215	384	35	1	*.998
1982	Baltimore	Amer.	C	125	344	35	88	15	1	5	36	.256	491	46	5	.991
1983	Baltimore	Amer.	C	128	347	33	80	16	2	4	32	.231	591	65	2	*.997
1984	Baltimore	Amer.	C	109	330	37	76	11	0	11	34	.230	453	43	4	.992
1985	Baltimore	Amer.	C	132	362	54	92	19	0	12	52	.254	575	49	8	.987
1986	Baltimore x	Amer.	C	122	327	42	68	15	1	13	29	.208	659	53	7	.990
1987	Cleveland yz	Amer.	C	60	141	16	25	10	0	1	9	.177	293	18	5	.984
1988	Los Angeles	Nat.	C	77	167	25	42	13	0	7	30	.251	333	29	4	.989
	American League Totals—19 Years			1479	4090	454	964	193	12	79	389	.236	6326	655	87	.988
	National League Totals—1 Year			77	167	25	42	13	0	7	30	.251	333	29	4	.989
	Major League Totals—20 Years			1556	4257	479	1006	206	12	86	419	.236	6659	684	91	.988

Selected by Minnesota Twins' organization in 12th round of free-agent draft, June 6, 1967.

†Traded to New York Yankees' organization for Outfielder Danny Walton, October 27, 1972.

‡Traded with Pitchers Rudy May, Tippy Martinez, Dave Pagan and Scott McGregor to Baltimore Orioles for Pitchers Ken Holtzman, Doyle Alexander and Grant Jackson, Catcher Ellie Hendricks and Pitcher Jimmy Freeman, June 15, 1976.

§On disabled list, July 9 to August 21, 1977.

xGranted free agency, November 12, 1986; signed by Cleveland Indians, February 6, 1987.

yOn disabled list, July 22 to September 11, 1987.

zReleased, October 29, 1987; signed by Los Angeles Dodgers, March 30, 1988.

CHAMPIONSHIP SERIES RECORD

Year	Club	League	Pos.	G.	AB.	R.	H.	2B.	3B.	HR.	RBI.	B.A.	PO.	A.	E.	F.A.
1979	Baltimore	Amer.	C	3	10	3	4	2	0	0	2	.400	10	1	0	1.000
1983	Baltimore	Amer.	C	4	12	1	2	0	0	0	0	.167	29	5	1	.971
1988	Los Angeles	Nat.	PH-C	4	5	1	2	2	0	0	2	.400	7	0	0	1.000
	Championship Series Totals—3 Years			11	27	5	8	4	0	0	4	.296	46	6	1	.981

WORLD SERIES RECORD

Established World Series record for most long hits, five-game Series (5), 1983.

Tied World Series record for most two-base hits, five-game Series (4), 1983.

Year	Club	League	Pos.	G.	AB.	R.	H.	2B.	3B.	HR.	RBI.	B.A.	PO.	A.	E.	F.A.
1979	Baltimore	Amer.	C-PR	7	21	3	6	2	0	0	0	.286	38	2	0	1.000
1983	Baltimore	Amer.	C	5	13	3	5	4	0	1	2	.385	27	4	0	1.000
1988	Los Angeles	Nat.	C	2	5	0	1	1	0	0	1	.200	13	1	0	1.000
	World Series Totals—3 Years			14	39	6	12	7	0	1	3	.308	78	7	0	1.000

ANDREW DENSON JR.

Born November 16, 1965, at Cincinnati, O.
Height, 6.05. Weight, 210.
Throws right and bats left and righthanded.

Led Southern League first basemen in double plays with 111 in 1988.
Led Gulf Coast League in total bases with 133 and slugging percentage with .556 in 1984.

Year	Club	League	Pos.	G.	AB.	R.	H.	2B.	3B.	HR.	RBI.	B.A.	PO.	A.	E.	F.A.
1984	—Bradenton Brav.†	Gulf C.	OF	62	239	43	*77	*20	3	•10	*45	*.322	65	6	2	.973
1985	—Sumter†‡	S. Atl.	OF	111	383	59	115	18	4	14	74	.300	119	5	3	.976
1986	—Durham†§	Carol.	OF	72	231	31	54	6	3	4	23	.234	86	3	11	.890
1987	—Greenville†	South.	1B	128	447	54	98	23	1	14	55	.219	998	50	10	.991
1988	—Greenville	South.	1B-OF	140	507	85	136	26	4	13	78	.268	1148	73	18	.985

Selected by Atlanta Braves' organization in 1st round (19th player selected) of free-agent draft, June 4, 1984.
†Batted righthanded only.
‡On disabled list, April 24 to May 4, 1985.
§On disabled list, May 3 to May 24 and July 8 to August 8, 1986.

ROBERT EUGENE DERNIER

Name pronounced Dur-NEER.

(Bob)

Born January 5, 1957, at Kansas City, Mo.
Height, 6.00. Weight, 165.
Throws and bats righthanded.
Attended Longview Community College, Lee's Summit, Mo.

Major League stolen bases: 1980 (3), 1981 (2), 1982 (42), 1983 (35), 1984 (45), 1985 (31), 1986 (27), 1987 (16), 1988 (13). Total—214.

Led Carolina League in stolen bases with 77 in 1979, Eastern League with 71 in 1980 and American Association with 72 in 1981.

Led Carolina League outfielders in putouts with 315 in 1979.
Tied for Carolina League lead in sacrifice hits with 12 in 1979.
Tied for Pioneer League lead in double plays by third basemen with 9 in 1978.
Named outfielder on THE SPORTING NEWS National League All-Star fielding team, 1984.
Named Carolina League Most Valuable Player, 1979.

Year	Club	League	Pos.	G.	AB.	R.	H.	2B.	3B.	HR.	RBI.	B.A.	PO.	A.	E.	F.A.
1978	—Spartanburg	W. Car.	SS	22	57	9	8	1	0	0	5	.140	23	61	16	.840
1978	—Helena	Pion.	3B	53	186	49	56	6	2	4	27	.301	38	104	22	.866
1979	—Peninsula	Carol.	OF-3B	135	491	102	143	19	2	4	42	.291	331	23	10	.973
1980	—Reading	East.	OF	136	*536	*111	160	29	4	10	57	.299	*325	9	9	.974
1980	—Philadelphia	Nat.	OF	10	7	5	4	0	0	0	1	.571	9	0	0	1.000
1981	—Oklahoma City	A. A.	OF	127	497	*105	150	26	7	5	35	.302	*317	7	5	.985
1981	—Philadelphia	Nat.	OF	10	4	0	3	0	0	0	0	.750	2	0	0	1.000
1982	—Philadelphia	Nat.	OF	122	370	56	92	10	2	4	21	.249	255	5	5	.981
1983	—Philadelphia	Nat.	OF	122	221	41	51	10	0	1	15	.231	164	3	2	.988
1983	—Reading†	East.	OF	14	56	8	13	1	1	1	4	.232	36	0	0	1.000
1984	—Chicago	Nat.	OF	143	536	94	149	26	5	3	32	.278	355	5	5	.986
1985	—Chicago‡	Nat.	OF	121	469	63	119	20	3	1	21	.254	310	4	9	.972
1986	—Chicago§	Nat.	OF	108	324	32	73	14	1	4	18	.225	222	3	3	.987
1987	—Chicago x	Nat.	OF	93	199	38	63	4	4	8	21	.317	86	2	1	.989
1988	—Philadelphia y	Nat.	OF	68	166	19	48	3	1	1	10	.289	98	2	2	.980
Major League Totals—9 Years				797	2296	348	602	87	16	22	139	.262	1501	24	27	.983

Selected by Cincinnati Reds' organization in 12th round of free-agent draft, January 11, 1977.
Signed as free agent by Philadelphia Phillies' organization, August 5, 1977.
†Traded with Outfielder Gary Matthews and Pitcher Porfi Altamirano to Chicago Cubs for Pitcher Bill Campbell and Catcher Mike Diaz, March 27, 1984.
‡On disabled list, June 15 to July 7, 1985.
§On disabled list, June 15 to July 23, 1986.
xGranted free agency, November 9, 1987; signed by Philadelphia Phillies, December 8, 1987.
yOn disabled list, May 29 to June 16 and July 8 to July 29, 1988.

CHAMPIONSHIP SERIES RECORD

Tied Championship Series records for hitting home run in first Series at-bat, October 2, 1984; most times hitting home run as leadoff batter, start of game (1), October 2, 1984.

Year	Club	League	Pos.	G.	AB.	R.	H.	2B.	3B.	HR.	RBI.	B.A.	PO.	A.	E.	F.A.
1983	—Philadelphia	Nat.	OF	1	0	0	0	0	0	0	0	.000	0	0	0	.000
1984	—Chicago	Nat.	OF	5	17	5	4	2	0	1	1	.235	12	1	0	1.000
Championship Series Totals—2 Years				6	17	5	4	2	0	1	1	.235	12	1	0	1.000

WORLD SERIES RECORD

Year	Club	League	Pos.	G.	AB.	R.	H.	2B.	3B.	HR.	RBI.	B.A.	PO.	A.	E.	F.A.
1983	—Philadelphia	Nat.	PR	1	0	1	0	0	0	0	0	.000	0	0	0	.000

—DID YOU KNOW—

That 6-foot-10 Montreal righthander Randy Johnson, who debuted with the Expos on September 15, is the tallest man ever to play in the major leagues?

JAMES JOSEPH DESHAIES

Name pronounced Duh-SHAYS.

(Jim)

Born June 23, 1960, at Massena, N.Y.
Height, 6.04. Weight, 222.
Throws and bats lefthanded.
Received bachelor of arts degree from Le Moyne College, Syracuse, N.Y., in 1982.

Established modern major league record for most consecutive strikeouts at start of game (8), September 23, 1986.
Pitched seven-inning, 5-1 no-hit victory for Nashville against Columbus, May 4, 1984.
Led National League in balks with 7 in 1986.
Led International League in balks with 4 in 1985.
Tied for International League lead in shutouts with 4 in 1984.

Year Club	League	G.	IP.	W.	L.	Pct.	H.	R.	ER.	SO.	BB.	ERA.
1982—Oneonta	NYP	15	108⅓	6	5	.545	93	50	40	★137	40	3.32
1983—Fort Lauderdale	Florida St.	20	117⅔	11	3	.786	105	44	33	128	58	2.52
1984—Nashville	Southern	7	45	3	2	.600	33	20	14	42	29	2.80
1984—Columbus	Int'national	18	135⅔	10	5	.667	99	45	36	117	62	★2.39
1984—New York	American	2	7	0	1	.000	14	9	9	5	7	11.57
1985—Columbus†‡	Int'national	21	131⅔	8	6	.571	124	67	63	106	59	4.31
1985—Houston	National	2	3	0	0	.000	1	0	0	2	0	0.00
1986—Houston§	National	26	144	12	5	.706	124	58	52	128	59	3.25
1987—Houston x	National	26	152	11	6	.647	149	81	78	104	57	4.62
1988—Houston	National	31	207	11	14	.440	164	77	69	127	72	3.00
American League Totals—1 Year		2	7	0	1	.000	14	9	9	5	7	11.57
National League Totals—4 Years		85	506	34	25	.576	438	216	199	361	188	3.54
Major League Totals—5 Years		87	513	34	26	.567	452	225	208	366	195	3.65

Selected by Montreal Expos' organization in 13th round of free-agent draft, June 6, 1978.
Selected by New York Yankees' organization in 21st round of free-agent draft, June 7, 1982.
†On disabled list, April 10 to April 26 and August 4 to August 14, 1985.
‡Traded with a player to be named later to Houston Astros for Pitcher Joe Niekro, September 15, 1985; Houston organization acquired Infielder Neder Horta, September 24, 1985, and Pitcher Dody Rather, January 11, 1986, to complete deal.
§On disabled list, April 21 to May 7, 1986.
xOn disabled list, July 26 to August 16, 1987.

ORESTES DESTRADE

Name pronounced Des-TRAD-a.

Born May 8, 1962, at Santiago, Cuba.
Height, 6.04. Weight, 220.
Throws right and bats right and lefthanded.
Attended Florida College, Temple Terrace, Fla.

Led Eastern League batters in strikeouts with 129 in 1985.
Tied for Florida State League lead in bases on balls received with 82 and game-winning RBIs with 15 in 1983.
Led Eastern League first basemen in total chances with 1,194 and double plays with 99 in 1985.
Tied for Appalachian League lead in double plays by first basemen with 42 in 1981.

Year Club	League	Pos.	G.	AB.	R.	H.	2B.	3B.	HR.	RBI.	B.A.	PO.	A.	E.	F.A.
1981—Paintsville	Appal.	1B	63	208	51	57	12	1	★14	46	.274	461	22	11	.978
1982—Greensboro	S. Atl.	1B	43	122	9	22	4	1	1	14	.180	359	15	4	.989
1982—Oneonta	NYP	1B	64	194	44	45	12	1	4	30	.232	298	33	10	.971
1983—Fort Lauderdale	Fla. St.	OF-1B	127	425	61	124	24	5	18	74	.292	425	24	9	.980
1984—Nashville	South.	OF-1B	35	121	15	29	6	0	6	12	.240	56	2	3	.951
1984—Fort Lauderdale	Fla. St.	1B	95	308	40	68	14	2	12	57	.221	764	41	●16	.981
1985—Albany	East.	1B	136	471	82	119	24	5	23	72	.253	★1103	73	18	.985
1986—Columbus†	Int.	1B	98	359	59	99	21	4	19	56	.276	697	63	11	.986
1987—Columbus	Int.	1B	135	465	76	119	26	3	25	81	.256	509	47	6	.989
1987—New York‡	Amer.	1B	9	19	5	5	0	0	0	1	.263	20	1	0	1.000
1988—Buffalo	A. A.	1B	77	273	37	74	16	1	12	42	.271	732	43	9	.989
1988—Pittsburgh	Nat.	1B	36	47	2	7	1	0	1	3	.149	61	2	0	1.000
American League Totals—1 Year			9	19	5	5	0	0	0	1	.263	20	1	0	1.000
National League Totals—1 Year			36	47	2	7	1	0	1	3	.149	61	2	0	1.000
Major League Totals—2 Years			45	66	7	12	1	0	1	4	.182	81	3	0	1.000

Selected by California Angels' organization in 23rd round of free-agent draft, June 3, 1980.
Signed as free agent by New York Yankees' organization, May 17, 1981.
†On disabled list, July 24, 1986 through remainder of season.
‡Traded to Pittsburgh Pirates for Pitcher Hipolito Pena, March 30, 1988.

MICHAEL DEVEREAUX

(Mike)

Born April 10, 1963, at Casper, Wyo.
Height, 6.00. Weight, 195.
Throws and bats righthanded.
Attended Mesa Community College, Mesa, Ariz., and received bachelor of arts degree in finance from Arizona State University, Tempe, Ariz.

Major League stolen bases: 1987 (3).
Led Texas League in sacrifice flies with 11 in 1987.

Led Pioneer League in total bases with 152 and stolen bases with 40 in 1985.
Led Texas League outfielders in total chances with 349 in 1987.

Year	Club	League	Pos.	G.	AB.	R.	H.	2B.	3B.	HR.	RBI.	B.A.	PO.	A.	E.	F.A.
1985	Great Falls	Pion.	OF	•70	★289	★73	★103	17	10	4	★67	.356	100	4	5	.954
1986	San Antonio	Texas	OF	115	431	69	130	22	2	10	53	.302	292	13	4	.987
1987	San Antonio	Texas	OF	★135	★562	90	169	28	9	26	91	.301	★339	7	3	★.991
1987	Albuquerque	P. C.	OF	3	11	2	3	1	0	1	1	.273	4	1	0	1.000
1987	Los Angeles	Nat.	OF	19	54	7	12	3	0	0	4	.222	21	1	0	1.000
1988	Albuquerque	P. C.	OF	109	423	88	144	26	4	13	76	.340	211	5	7	.969
1988	Los Angeles	Nat.	OF	30	43	4	5	1	0	0	2	.116	29	0	0	1.000
Major League Totals—2 Years				49	97	11	17	4	0	0	6	.175	50	1	0	1.000

Selected by Cleveland Indians' organization in 26th round of free-agent draft, June 4, 1984.
Selected by Los Angeles Dodgers' organization in 5th round of free-agent draft, June 3, 1985.

BAUDILIO JOSE DIAZ (SEIJAS)

Name pronounced DEE-az.

(Bo)

Born March 23, 1953, at Cua, Miranda, Venezuela.
Height, 5.11. Weight, 205.
Throws and bats righthanded.

Major League stolen bases: 1980 (1), 1981 (2), 1982 (3), 1983 (1), 1986 (1), 1987 (1). Total—9.
Tied for International League lead in double plays by catchers with 7 in 1977.

Year	Club	League	Pos.	G.	AB.	R.	H.	2B.	3B.	HR.	RBI.	B.A.	PO.	A.	E.	F.A.
1971	Winter Haven	Fla. St.	C	4	10	1	0	0	0	0	0	.000	25	1	0	1.000
1971	Williamsport	NYP	PH	1	1	0	0	0	0	0	0	.000	0	0	0	.000
1971	Pawtucket	East.	C	1	2	0	0	0	0	0	0	.000	4	0	0	1.000
1971	Greenville	W. Car.	C	10	25	2	5	1	0	0	0	.200	35	2	2	.949
1972	Winter Haven	Fla. St.	C	14	44	3	7	1	0	0	0	.159	72	7	0	1.000
1973	Elmira	NYP	C	25	69	3	17	3	0	0	9	.246	107	16	1	.992
1974	Winter Haven	Fla. St.	C-3B	97	327	31	79	20	1	1	38	.242	476	75	14	.975
1975	Winston-Salem	Carol.	C	59	179	22	47	8	1	6	29	.263	271	45	9	.972
1976	Rhode Island	Int.	C-OF	62	117	10	29	1	0	4	18	.248	222	28	3	.988
1977	Pawtucket	Int.	★C-3B	105	308	37	81	14	1	7	54	.263	459	67	6	★.989
1977	Boston†	Amer.	C	2	1	0	0	0	0	0	0	.000	5	0	0	1.000
1978	Cleveland‡	Amer.	C	44	127	12	30	4	0	2	11	.236	183	18	6	.971
1979	Tacoma	P. C.	C	34	115	5	28	7	0	2	11	.243	223	24	5	.980
1979	Cleveland§	Amer.	C	15	32	0	5	2	0	0	1	.156	63	6	3	.958
1980	Cleveland	Amer.	C	76	207	15	47	11	2	3	32	.227	317	35	4	.989
1981	Cleveland x	Amer.	C	63	182	25	57	19	0	7	38	.313	247	27	7	.975
1982	Philadelphia	Nat.	C	144	525	69	151	29	1	18	85	.288	850	80	10	.989
1983	Philadelphia	Nat.	C	136	471	49	111	17	0	15	64	.236	903	97	★14	.986
1984	Philadelphia y	Nat.	C	27	75	5	16	4	0	1	9	.213	114	9	1	.992
1984	Reading	East.	C	3	7	2	3	0	0	1	3	.429	11	4	1	.938
1985	Phil. za-Cinc.	Nat.	C	77	237	21	58	13	1	5	31	.245	428	42	8	.983
1986	Cincinnati	Nat.	C	134	474	50	129	21	0	10	56	.272	732	83	13	.984
1987	Cincinnati	Nat.	C	140	496	49	134	28	1	15	82	.270	747	70	7	.992
1988	Cincinnati b	Nat.	C	92	315	26	69	9	0	10	35	.219	468	44	5	.990
American League Totals—5 Years				200	549	52	139	36	2	12	82	.253	815	86	20	.978
National League Totals—7 Years				750	2593	269	668	121	3	74	362	.258	4242	425	58	.988
Major League Totals—12 Years				950	3142	321	807	157	5	86	444	.257	5057	511	78	.986

Signed as free agent by Boston Red Sox' organization, November 25, 1970.

†Traded with Pitchers Rick Wise and Mike Paxton and Third Baseman Ted Cox to Cleveland Indians for Pitcher Dennis Eckersley and Catcher Fred Kendall, March 30, 1978.

‡On disabled list, April 16 to June 16, 1978.

§On disabled list, March 31 to April 17 and June 8 to July 20, 1979.

xTraded to Philadelphia Phillies for Outfielder Lonnie Smith and a player to be named later, November 20, 1981; Cleveland organization acquired Pitcher Scott Munninghoff to complete deal, December 9, 1981.

yOn disabled list, May 1 to May 31, June 21 to July 16 and August 20, 1984 through remainder of season; included rehabilitation disability assignment to Reading, July 11 to July 16, 1984.

zOn disabled list, April 19 to June 1, 1985.

aTraded with Pitcher Greg Simpson to Cincinnati Reds for Shortstop Tom Foley, Catcher Alan Knicely, a player to be named later and cash, August 8, 1985; Philadelphia Phillies acquired Pitcher Freddie Toliver to complete deal, August 27, 1985.

bOn disabled list, June 17 to July 2, 1988.

CHAMPIONSHIP SERIES RECORD

Year	Club	League	Pos.	G.	AB.	R.	H.	2B.	3B.	HR.	RBI.	B.A.	PO.	A.	E.	F.A.
1983	Philadelphia	Nat.	C	4	13	0	2	1	0	0	0	.154	32	2	0	1.000

WORLD SERIES RECORD

Year	Club	League	Pos.	G.	AB.	R.	H.	2B.	3B.	HR.	RBI.	B.A.	PO.	A.	E.	F.A.
1983	Philadelphia	Nat.	C	5	15	1	5	1	0	0	0	.333	37	1	1	.974

ALL-STAR GAME RECORD

Year	League	Pos.	AB.	R.	H.	2B.	3B.	HR.	RBI.	B.A.	PO.	A.	E.	F.A.
1981	American	C	1	0	0	0	0	0	0	.000	2	0	0	1.000
1987	National	C	1	0	0	0	0	0	0	.000	1	0	0	1.000
All-Star Game Totals—2 Years			2	0	0	0	0	0	0	.000	3	0	0	1.000

EDGAR SERRANO DIAZ

Name pronounced DEE-az.

Born February 8, 1964, at Santurce, Puerto Rico.
Height, 6.00. Weight, 160.
Throws and bats righthanded.

Led Texas League shortstops in total chances with 743 and double plays with 101 in 1985.

Year Club	League	Pos.	G.	AB.	R.	H.	2B.	3B.	HR.	RBI.	B.A.	PO.	A.	E.	F.A.
1982—Pikeville	Appal.	SS	15	24	4	2	0	0	0	0	.083	12	30	3	.933
1983—Beloit	Midw.	SS	107	307	29	64	2	0	0	15	.208	173	258	42	.911
1984—Stockton	Calif.	SS	123	419	58	108	1	7	0	35	.258	189	381	40	.934
1985—El Paso	Texas	SS	132	501	90	134	14	4	0	55	.267	*217	*489	37	.950
1986—Vancouver†	P. C.	*SS-2B	108	346	44	109	2	4	0	43	.315	173	311	*31	.940
1986—Milwaukee	Amer.	SS	5	13	0	3	0	0	0	0	.231	6	8	2	.875
1987—Denver‡	A. A.	SS	48	162	24	44	10	2	0	15	.272	95	144	10	.960
1988—Denver§	A. A.	SS	79	278	44	65	7	0	0	21	.234	161	221	18	.955
Major League Totals—1 Year			5	13	0	3	0	0	0	0	.231	6	8	2	.875

Signed as free agent by Milwaukee Brewers' organization, March 3, 1982.

†On disabled list, July 3 to July 17, 1986.

‡On Milwaukee disabled list, March 29 to June 3, 1987; included rehabilitation disability assignment to Denver, May 15 to June 3, 1987.

§On restricted list, July 28, 1988 through remainder of season.

MARIO RAFAEL DIAZ (TORRES)

Born January 10, 1962, at Humacao, P. R.
Height, 5.10. Weight, 160.
Throws and bats righthanded.

Led Southern League in sacrifice hits with 14 in 1985.

Year Club	League	Pos.	G.	AB.	R.	H.	2B.	3B.	HR.	RBI.	B.A.	PO.	A.	E.	F.A.
1979—Bellingham	N'west	SS-3B-2B	32	96	12	19	2	0	1	5	.198	28	69	8	.924
1980—Wausau	Midw.	SS-2B	110	349	28	63	5	0	3	21	.181	172	328	41	.924
1981—Lynn	East.	SS	106	314	16	63	8	1	1	22	.201	163	318	18	*.964
1982—Lynn	East.	SS-1B	53	162	19	35	7	1	1	13	.216	384	172	18	.969
1982—Salt Lake City	P. C.	SS	5	19	2	7	1	0	0	2	.368	4	15	1	.950
1982—Wausau	Midw.	SS	56	187	15	49	8	1	1	23	.262	78	148	16	.934
1983—Bakersfield	Calif.	SS-2B	51	171	23	41	5	1	0	10	.240	92	146	22	.915
1983—Chattanooga	South.	SS	33	111	18	30	6	5	2	13	.270	48	80	10	.928
1984—Chattanooga	South.	SS-2B	108	322	23	67	7	1	1	19	.208	179	313	26	.950
1985—Chattanooga	South.	SS	115	400	38	101	6	7	0	38	.253	186	314	31	.942
1986—Calgary	P. C.	SS	109	379	40	107	17	6	1	41	.282	194	302	16	.969
1987—Calgary	P. C.	SS	108	376	52	106	17	3	4	52	.282	195	280	21	.958
1987—Seattle	Amer.	SS	11	23	4	7	0	1	0	3	.304	10	25	1	.972
1988—Calgary	P. C.	SS	46	164	16	54	18	0	1	30	.329	65	138	12	.944
1988—Seattle†	Amer.	S-2-1-3	28	72	6	22	5	0	0	9	.306	31	47	1	.987
Major League Totals—2 Years			39	95	10	29	5	1	0	12	.305	41	72	2	.983

Signed as free agent by Seattle Mariners' organization, December 21, 1978.

†On disabled list, May 6 to May 23, 1988; included rehabilitation disability assignment to Calgary, May 16 to May 23, 1988.

MICHAEL ANTHONY DIAZ

Name pronounced DEE-az.

(Mike)

Born April 15, 1960, at San Francisco, Calif.
Height, 6.02. Weight, 220.
Throws and bats righthanded.

Major League stolen bases: 1987 (1).
Tied for Pacific Coast League lead in being hit by pitch with 7 in 1985.
Led Texas League catchers in total chances with 684 in 1981.

Year Club	League	Pos.	G.	AB.	R.	H.	2B.	3B.	HR.	RBI.	B.A.	PO.	A.	E.	F.A.
1978—Bradenton Cubs	Gulf C.	C-OF	26	68	10	19	3	0	1	7	.279	54	8	3	.954
1979—Geneva	NYP	C	63	237	45	74	*19	1	7	36	.312	*423	35	7	.985
1980—Davenport	Midw.	C	105	386	51	113	17	1	8	47	.293	*627	63	*16	.977
1981—Midland	Texas	C	110	390	56	103	19	2	10	60	.264	*593	*75	16	.977
1982—Midland	Texas	C	121	443	54	128	23	4	22	75	.289	417	42	15	.968
1983—Iowa	A. A.	C-1B-OF	74	238	43	77	13	3	15	47	.324	223	14	12	.952
1983—Chicago†	Nat.	C	6	7	2	2	1	0	0	1	.286	5	0	0	1.000
1984—Portland	P. C.	C-OF-1B	105	341	52	92	15	1	14	46	.270	373	16	14	.965
1985—Port.‡-Haw.	P. C.	C-O-1-3	128	445	65	139	29	4	22	85	.312	698	37	7	.991
1986—Pittsburgh	Nat.	O-1-3-C	97	209	22	56	9	0	12	36	.268	202	8	3	.986
1987—Pittsburgh	Nat.	OF-1B-C	103	241	28	58	8	2	16	48	.241	303	23	6	.982
1988—Pittsburgh§x	Nat.	OF-1B-C	47	74	6	17	3	0	0	5	.230	63	4	0	1.000
1988—Chicago y	Amer.	1B	40	152	12	36	6	0	3	12	.237	352	25	5	.987
National League Totals—4 Years			253	531	58	133	21	2	28	90	.250	573	35	9	.985
American League Totals—1 Year			40	152	12	36	6	0	3	12	.237	352	25	5	.987
Major League Totals—4 Years			293	683	70	169	27	2	31	102	.247	925	60	14	.986

Selected by Chicago Cubs' organization in 30th round of free-agent draft, June 6, 1978.

†Traded with Pitcher Bill Campbell to Philadelphia Phillies for Outfielders Bob Dernier and Gary Matthews and Pitcher Porfi Altamirano, March 27, 1984.
‡Traded to Pittsburgh Pirates' organization for Catcher Steve Herz, April 27, 1985.
§On disabled list, March 25 to May 7, 1988.
xTraded to Chicago White Sox for Outfielder Gary Redus, August 19, 1988.
yReleased, December 12, 1988.

ROBERT KEITH DIBBLE
(Rob)

Born January 24, 1964, at Bridgeport, Conn.
Height, 6.04. Weight, 235.
Throws right and bats lefthanded.
Attended Florida Southern College, Lakeland, Fla.

Year Club	League	G.	IP.	W.	L.	Pct.	H.	R.	ER.	SO.	BB.	ERA.
1983—Billings	Pioneer	5	12⅔	0	1	.000	18	13	11	7	11	7.82
1983—Eugene	Northwest	7	37⅔	3	2	.600	38	28	24	17	18	5.73
1984—Tampa	Florida St.	15	64⅔	5	2	.714	59	31	21	39	29	2.92
1985—Cedar Rapids	Midwest	45	65⅔	5	5	.500	67	37	28	73	28	3.84
1986—Vermont	Eastern	31	55⅓	3	2	.600	53	29	19	37	28	3.09
1986—Denver	Am. Assoc.	5	6⅔	1	0	1.000	9	4	4	3	2	5.40
1987—Nashville	Am. Assoc.	44	61	2	4	.333	72	34	32	51	27	4.72
1988—Nashville	Am. Assoc.	31	35	2	1	.667	21	9	9	41	14	2.31
1988—Cincinnati	National	37	59⅓	1	1	.500	43	12	12	59	21	1.82
Major League Totals—1 Year		37	59⅓	1	1	.500	43	12	12	59	21	1.82

Selected by St. Louis Cardinals' organization in 11th round of free-agent draft, June 7, 1982.
Selected by Cincinnati Reds' organization in secondary phase of free-agent draft, June 6, 1983.

GORDON LEE DILLARD

Born May 20, 1964, at Salinas, Calif.
Height, 6.01. Weight, 180.
Throws and bats lefthanded.
Attended Hartnell Community College, Salinas, Calif., Connors State College, Warner, Okla. and Oklahoma State University, Stillwater, Okla.

Year Club	League	G.	IP.	W.	L.	Pct.	H.	R.	ER.	SO.	BB.	ERA.
1986—Newark	NYP	27	63⅓	5	6	.455	55	37	30	77	34	4.26
1987—Hagerstown	Carolina	14	22	2	1	.667	12	5	5	26	11	2.05
1987—Charlotte	Southern	36	49	5	2	.714	44	18	18	53	19	3.31
1988—Charlotte	Southern	38	131⅔	7	5	.583	97	42	32	100	67	2.19
1988—Rochester	Int'national	5	11	0	2	.000	9	5	3	6	9	2.45
1988—Baltimore†	American	2	3	0	0	.000	3	2	2	2	4	6.00
Major League Totals—1 Year		2	3	0	0	.000	3	2	2	2	4	6.00

Selected by Texas Rangers' organization in 2nd round of free-agent draft, January 17, 1984.
Selected by Pittsburgh Pirates' organization in secondary phase of free-agent draft, June 4, 1984.
Selected by New York Mets' organization in secondary phase of free-agent draft, June 5, 1985.
Selected by Baltimore Orioles' organization in 14th round of free-agent draft, June 2, 1986.
†Traded with Pitcher Ken Howell to Philadelphia Phillies for Outfielder Phil Bradley, December 8, 1988.

DANIEL MARK DIMASCIO
(Dan)

Born October 8, 1964, at Chicago Heights, Ill.
Height, 6.01. Weight, 195.
Throws and bats righthanded.
Received bachelor of science degree in management science from University of California at San Diego, LaJolla, Calif.

Year Club	League	Pos.	G.	AB.	R.	H.	2B.	3B.	HR.	RBI.	B.A.	PO.	A.	E.	F.A.
1986—Lakeland	Fla. St.	C-OF	51	143	20	38	5	1	4	17	.266	118	20	8	.945
1987—Glens Falls	East.	C-OF	78	220	28	49	13	0	5	38	.233	297	49	10	.961
1988—Glens Falls	East.	C-OF-1B	79	211	30	59	8	1	6	31	.280	302	40	9	.974

Selected by Detroit Tigers' organization in 18th round of free-agent draft, June 2, 1986.

FRANK LAWRENCE DiMICHELE

Name pronounced Di-MY-kul.

Born February 16, 1965, at Philadelphia, Pa.
Height, 6.03. Weight, 205.
Throws left and bats righthanded.
Attended Philadelphia Community College, Philadelphia, Pa.

Tied for Midwest League lead in shutouts with 4 in 1986.

Year Club	League	G.	IP.	W.	L.	Pct.	H.	R.	ER.	SO.	BB.	ERA.
1985—Salem	Northwest	9	41⅔	1	5	.167	50	33	27	40	19	5.83
1986—Quad Cities†	Midwest	26	122⅔	7	10	.412	112	72	50	64	68	3.67
1987—Palm Springs	California	38	97⅔	6	9	.400	105	74	52	73	65	4.79
1988—California	American	4	4⅔	0	0	.000	5	5	5	1	2	9.64
1988—Edmonton	P. Coast	12	13⅓	0	0	.000	16	7	6	8	6	4.05

Year Club	League	G.	IP.	W.	L.	Pct.	H.	R.	ER.	SO.	BB.	ERA.
1988—Midland	Texas	37	37	1	4	.200	48	31	27	28	29	6.57
Major League Totals—1 Year		4	4⅔	0	0	.000	5	5	5	1	2	9.64

Selected by California Angels' organization in 15th round of free-agent draft, June 3, 1985.
†On disabled list, August 6 to August 20, 1986.

FRANK MICHAEL DiPINO

Born October 22, 1956, at Syracuse, N.Y.
Height, 6.00. Weight, 180.
Throws and bats lefthanded.
Attended St. Leo College, St. Leo, Fla.

Pitched seven-inning, 6-0 no-hit victory against Reading, June 8, 1980 (second game).
Major League saves: 1983 (20), 1984 (14), 1985 (6), 1986 (3), 1987 (4), 1988 (6). Total—53.

Year Club	League	G.	IP.	W.	L.	Pct.	H.	R.	ER.	SO.	BB.	ERA.
1977—Newark	NYP	14	29	1	3	.250	14	12	8	41	22	2.48
1978—Burlington	Midwest	15	88	5	4	.556	98	58	46	68	36	4.70
1979—Stockton†	California	16	99	5	3	.625	92	45	38	67	46	3.45
1980—Holyoke	Eastern	16	76	7	0	1.000	46	13	11	58	27	1.30
1980—Vancouver	P. Coast	24	28	3	1	.750	24	10	7	32	14	2.25
1981—Vancouver‡	P. Coast	27	81	3	5	.375	83	45	39	81	39	4.33
1981—Milwaukee	American	2	2	0	0	.000	0	0	0	3	3	0.00
1982—Vancouver§	P. Coast	26	189⅔	13	9	.591	187	102	85	115	86	4.03
1982—Houston	National	6	28⅓	2	2	.500	32	20	19	25	11	6.04
1983—Houston	National	53	71⅓	3	4	.429	52	21	21	67	20	2.65
1984—Houston	National	57	75⅓	4	9	.308	74	32	28	65	36	3.35
1985—Houston	National	54	76	3	7	.300	69	44	34	49	43	4.03
1986—Houston x-Chicago	National	61	80⅓	3	7	.300	74	45	39	70	30	4.37
1987—Chicago	National	69	80	3	3	.500	75	31	28	61	34	3.15
1988—Chicago y	National	63	90⅓	2	3	.400	102	54	50	69	32	4.98
American League Totals—1 Year		2	2	0	0	.000	0	0	0	3	3	0.00
National League Totals—7 Years		363	501⅔	20	35	.364	478	247	219	406	206	3.93
Major League Totals—8 Years		365	503⅔	20	35	.364	478	247	219	409	209	3.91

Signed as free agent by Milwaukee Brewers' organization, July 11, 1977.
†On disabled list, May 19 to June 11, 1979.
‡On disabled list, May 9 to June 10, 1981.
§Traded with Outfielder Kevin Bass and Pitcher Mike Madden to Houston Astros, September 3, 1982, completing deal in which Houston traded Pitcher Don Sutton to Milwaukee Brewers for three players to be named later, August 30, 1982.
xTraded to Chicago Cubs for Outfielder Davey Lopes, July 21, 1986.
yGranted free agency, November 4, 1988; signed by St. Louis Cardinals, December 21, 1988.

BENITO JAMES DISTEFANO JR.

Name pronounced Dis-tuh-FAHN-oh.

(Benny)

Born January 23, 1962, at Brooklyn, N.Y.
Height, 6.01. Weight, 200.
Throws and bats lefthanded.
Attended Alvin Community College, Alvin, Tex.

Led American Association in being hit by pitch with 12 in 1988.
Led Pacific Coast League in being hit by pitch with 15 in 1987.

Year Club	League	Pos.	G.	AB.	R.	H.	2B.	3B.	HR.	RBI.	B.A.	PO.	A.	E.	F.A.
1982—Greenwood	S. Atl.	1B	136	477	74	138	23	•8	15	89	.289	*1184	*104	19	.985
1983—Lynn	East.	OF-1B	*137	480	71	130	19	7	25	92	.271	271	13	13	.956
1984—Hawaii	P. C.	1B-OF	66	240	40	73	13	8	6	33	.304	334	30	0	1.000
1984—Pittsburgh	Nat.	OF-1B	45	78	10	13	1	2	3	9	.167	88	9	3	.970
1985—Hawaii	P. C.	OF-1B	136	480	74	114	27	8	14	67	.238	375	18	8	.980
1986—Hawaii	P. C.	OF-1B	111	402	58	104	25	9	13	57	.259	564	37	9	.985
1986—Pittsburgh	Nat.	OF-1B	31	39	3	7	1	0	1	5	.179	13	0	0	1.000
1987—Vancouver	P. C.	*1B-OF	130	431	67	120	20	4	15	77	.278	1042	67	6	*.995
1988—Buffalo	A. A.	OF-1B	135	482	69	127	26	1	19	63	.263	234	15	3	.988
1988—Pittsburgh	Nat.	1B-OF	16	29	6	10	3	1	1	6	.345	41	3	0	1.000
Major League Totals—3 Years			92	146	19	30	5	3	5	20	.205	142	12	3	.981

Selected by Los Angeles Dodgers' organization in 16th round of free-agent draft, January 13, 1981.
Selected by Toronto Blue Jays' organization in secondary phase of free-agent draft, June 8, 1981.
Selected by Pittsburgh Pirates' organization in secondary phase of free-agent draft, January 12, 1982.

REGINALD TERRENCE DOBIE

(Reggie)

Born August 17, 1964, at Rosedale, Miss.
Height, 6.01. Weight, 175.
Throws and bats righthanded.
Attended Triton College, River Grove, Ill., and
Chicago State University, Chicago, Ill.

Tied for Texas League lead in games started by pitchers with 27 and wild pitches with 15 in 1986.

Tied for Carolina League lead in games started by pitchers with 26 in 1985.
Tied for Gulf Coast League lead in balks with 3 in 1983.

Year Club	League	G.	IP.	W.	L.	Pct.	H.	R.	ER.	SO.	BB.	ERA.
1983—Sarasota Mets	Gulf Coast	12	44	0	4	.000	47	21	16	44	31	3.27
1984—Columbia	S. Atlantic	25	172⅓	10	9	.526	123	75	58	*128	*119	3.03
1985—Lynchburg	Carolina	26	167⅔	12	5	.706	118	61	49	144	77	2.63
1986—Jackson	Texas	28	155	13	7	.650	113	70	63	123	94	3.66
1987—Tidewater	Int'national	26	169⅓	12	10	.545	147	89	82	85	63	4.36
1988—Tidewater†	Int'national	20	112	8	5	.615	102	51	48	78	57	3.86

Selected by New York Mets' organization in 8th round of free-agent draft, January 11, 1983.
†Traded to Seattle Mariners for Outfielder Chuck Carr, November 20, 1988.

PATRICK NEAL DODSON
(Pat)

Born October 11, 1959, at Santa Monica, Calif.
Height, 6.04. Weight, 220.
Throws and bats lefthanded.
Attended University of California, Los Angeles, Calif.

Led International League in slugging percentage with .524 in 1986.
Led Florida State League in bases on balls received with 95 in 1981.
Tied for International League lead in intentional bases on balls received with 10 in 1987.
Led Florida State League first basemen in double plays with 100 and total chances with 1,223 in 1981.
Named International League Player of the Year, 1986.

Year Club	League	Pos.	G.	AB.	R.	H.	2B.	3B.	HR.	RBI.	B.A.	PO.	A.	E.	F.A.
1980—Winter Haven	Fla. St.	1B-OF	61	190	26	52	18	0	1	36	.274	437	28	3	.994
1981—Winter Haven	Fla. St.	1B	127	413	54	104	17	3	4	42	.252	*1134	76	13	*.989
1982—Winter Haven†	Fla. St.	1B-OF	104	345	50	87	16	0	15	69	.252	786	54	6	.993
1983—New Britain	East.	1B	118	383	55	100	25	1	12	70	.261	815	54	11	.988
1984—Pawtucket	Int.	1B-OF	114	292	51	75	17	0	16	51	.257	681	48	9	.988
1985—Pawtucket	Int.	*1B-OF-P	123	400	51	89	14	0	18	47	.223	942	83	8	*.992
1986—Pawtucket	Int.	1B	120	416	60	112	23	1	27	*102	.269	983	77	*14	.987
1986—Boston	Amer.	1B	9	12	3	5	2	0	1	3	.417	25	1	0	1.000
1987—Boston	Amer.	1B	26	42	4	7	3	0	2	6	.167	99	4	0	1.000
1987—Pawtucket	Int.	1B	111	367	59	101	15	1	18	72	.275	926	84	•14	.986
1988—Pawtucket	Int.	1B	64	197	25	45	7	0	7	28	.228	521	39	3	.995
1988—Boston‡	Amer.	1B	17	45	5	8	3	1	1	1	.178	87	12	0	1.000
Major League Totals—3 Years			52	99	12	20	8	1	4	10	.202	211	17	0	1.000

Selected by Boston Red Sox' organization in 6th round of free-agent draft, June 3, 1980.
†On disabled list, August 17, 1982 through remainder of season.
‡Granted free agency, October 15, 1988.

PITCHNG RECORD

Year Club	League	G.	IP.	W.	L.	Pct.	H.	R.	ER.	SO.	BB.	ERA.
1985—Pawtucket	Int'national	3	3⅔	0	0	.000	2	0	0	1	4	0.00

JOHN ROBERT DOPSON JR.

Born July 14, 1963, at Baltimore, Md.
Height, 6.04. Weight, 205.
Throws right and bats lefthanded.

Year Club	League	G.	IP.	W.	L.	Pct.	H.	R.	ER.	SO.	BB.	ERA.
1982—Jamestown	NYP	15	106⅔	6	•8	.429	117	58	47	62	34	3.97
1983—West Palm Beach	Florida St.	23	146⅔	13	6	.684	141	82	56	69	38	3.44
1984—Jacksonville†	Southern	26	170⅔	10	8	.556	198	83	70	76	41	3.69
1985—Jacksonville	Southern	5	32⅓	3	0	1.000	27	5	4	20	10	1.11
1985—Indianapolis‡	Am. Assoc.	18	95⅓	4	7	.364	88	44	40	48	44	3.78
1985—Montreal	National	4	13	0	2	.000	25	17	16	4	4	11.08
1986—West Palm Beach§	Florida St.	2	10⅔	2	0	1.000	8	0	0	8	4	0.00
1986—Indianapolis	Am. Assoc.	4	16	0	3	.000	18	12	8	6	11	4.50
1987—Jacksonville	Southern	21	118⅓	7	5	.583	123	58	50	75	30	3.80
1988—Indianapolis	Am. Assoc.	3	18	0	0	.000	19	7	7	15	5	3.50
1988—Montreal x	National	26	168⅔	3	11	.214	150	69	57	101	58	3.04
Major League Totals—2 Years		30	181⅔	3	13	.188	175	86	73	105	62	3.62

Selected by Montreal Expos' organization in 2nd round of free-agent draft, June 7, 1982.
†On suspended list, May 24 to May 31, 1984.
‡On disabled list, June 24 to July 15, 1985.
§On Indianapolis disabled list, April 10 to May 12, May 29 to June 23 and July 7, 1986 through remainder of season.
xTraded with Shortstop Luis Rivera to Boston Red Sox for Shortstop Spike Owen and Pitcher Dan Gakeler, December 8, 1988.

WILLIAM DONALD DORAN

Name pronounced DOOR-un.

(Bill)

Born May 28, 1958, at Cincinnati, O.
Height, 6.00. Weight, 175.
Throws right and bats right and lefthanded.
Attended Miami University, Oxford, O.

Major League stolen bases: 1982 (5), 1983 (12), 1984 (21), 1985 (23), 1986 (42), 1987 (31), 1988 (17). Total—151.
Led National League in caught stealing with 19 in 1986.
Led National League second basemen in fielding percentage with .992 in 1987.
Led Pacific Coast League second basemen in double plays with 123 in 1982.
Led Gulf Coast League second basemen in double plays with 33 in 1979.

Year Club	League	Pos.	G.	AB.	R.	H.	2B.	3B.	HR.	RBI.	B.A.	PO.	A.	E.	F.A.
1979—Sarasota Astros	Gulf C.	2B	44	164	21	42	6	0	1	16	.256	107	★144	11	.958
1980—Daytona Beach	Fla. St.	2B-SS	102	369	62	90	11	3	2	45	.244	232	259	21	.959
1981—Columbus	South.	2B-SS	124	427	83	120	17	7	5	56	.281	263	355	17	.973
1982—Tucson	P. C.	2B	★142	559	100	169	32	7	1	65	.302	★361	★424	★23	.972
1982—Houston	Nat.	2B	26	97	11	27	3	0	0	6	.278	41	78	3	.975
1983—Houston	Nat.	2B	154	535	70	145	12	7	8	39	.271	★347	461	17	.979
1984—Houston	Nat.	2B-SS	147	548	92	143	18	11	4	41	.261	274	440	12	.983
1985—Houston	Nat.	2B	148	578	84	166	31	6	14	59	.287	345	440	16	.980
1986—Houston	Nat.	2B	145	550	92	152	29	3	6	37	.276	262	329	16	.974
1987—Houston	Nat.	2B-SS	★162	625	82	177	23	3	16	79	.283	300	432	7	.991
1988—Houston	Nat.	2B	132	480	66	119	18	1	7	53	.248	260	371	8	★.987
Major League Totals—7 Years			914	3413	497	929	134	31	55	314	.272	1829	2551	79	.982

Selected by Houston Astros' organization in 6th round of free-agent draft, June 5, 1979.

CHAMPIONSHIP SERIES RECORD

Tied Championship Series record for most at-bats, game (7), October 15, 1986 (16 innings).
Tied National League Championship Series record for most at-bats, six-game Series (27), 1986.

Year Club	League	Pos.	G.	AB.	R.	H.	2B.	3B.	HR.	RBI.	B.A.	PO.	A.	E.	F.A.
1986—Houston	Nat.	2B	6	27	3	6	0	0	1	3	.222	9	17	0	1.000

BRIAN RICHARD DORSETT

Born April 9, 1961, at Terre Haute, Ind.
Height, 6.03. Weight, 215.
Throws and bats righthanded.
Attended Indiana State University, Terre Haute, Ind.

Year Club	League	Pos.	G.	AB.	R.	H.	2B.	3B.	HR.	RBI.	B.A.	PO.	A.	E.	F.A.
1983—Medford	N'west	C	14	48	11	13	2	1	1	10	.271	85	8	2	.979
1983—Madison	Midw.	C	58	204	16	52	7	0	3	27	.255	337	51	6	.985
1984—Modesto†	Calif.	C-1B	99	375	39	99	19	0	8	52	.264	511	76	13	.978
1985—Madison	Midw.	C	40	161	15	43	11	0	2	30	.267	194	40	5	.979
1985—Huntsville	South.	C	88	313	38	84	18	3	11	43	.268	437	51	10	.980
1986—Tacoma	P. C.	C	117	426	49	111	33	1	10	51	.261	420	54	18	.963
1987—Tacoma‡	P. C.	C	78	282	31	66	14	1	6	39	.234	341	51	4	.990
1987—Buffalo	A. A.	C	26	86	9	22	5	1	4	14	.256	119	9	1	.992
1987—Cleveland	Amer.	C	5	11	2	3	0	0	1	3	.273	12	0	0	1.000
1988—C. S. §x -Edm.	P. C.	C-1B	53	163	21	43	7	0	11	32	.264	283	37	5	.985
1988—California y	Amer.	C	7	11	0	1	0	0	0	2	.091	19	3	0	1.000
Major League Totals—2 Years			12	22	2	4	0	0	1	5	.182	31	3	0	1.000

Selected by Oakland A's organization in 10th round of free-agent draft, June 6, 1983.
†On disabled list, June 18 to July 24, 1984.
‡Traded with Pitcher Darrel Akerfelds to Cleveland Indians for Second Baseman Tony Bernazard, July 15, 1987.
§On Cleveland disabled list, March 26 to June 7, 1988.
xTraded to California Angels for a player to be named later, June 7, 1988.
yTraded to New York Yankees for Pitcher Eric Schmidt, November 17, 1988.

RICHARD ELLIOTT DOTSON

Born January 10, 1959, at Cincinnati, O.
Height, 6.00. Weight, 203.
Throws and bats righthanded.

Tied for American League lead in shutouts with 4 in 1981.

Year Club	League	G.	IP.	W.	L.	Pct.	H.	R.	ER.	SO.	BB.	ERA.
1977—Idaho Falls†	Pioneer	13	66	4	5	.444	65	61	42	83	63	5.73
1978—Knoxville	Southern	26	145	11	10	.524	128	85	69	152	★105	4.28
1979—Knoxville	Southern	25	163	9	9	.500	133	81	67	133	88	3.70
1979—Chicago	American	5	24	2	0	1.000	28	13	10	13	6	3.75
1980—Chicago	American	33	198	12	10	.545	185	105	94	109	87	4.27
1981—Chicago	American	24	141	9	8	.529	145	67	59	73	49	3.77
1982—Chicago	American	34	196⅔	11	15	.423	219	97	84	109	73	3.84
1983—Chicago	American	35	240	22	7	★.759	209	92	86	137	★106	3.23
1984—Chicago‡	American	32	245⅔	14	15	.483	216	110	98	120	103	3.59
1985—Chicago§	American	9	52⅓	3	4	.429	53	30	26	33	17	4.47
1986—Chicago	American	34	197	10	•17	.370	226	125	120	110	69	5.48
1987—Chicago x	American	31	211⅓	11	12	.478	201	109	98	114	86	4.17
1988—New York y	American	32	171	12	9	.571	178	103	95	77	72	5.00
Major League Totals—10 Years		269	1677	106	97	.522	1660	851	770	895	668	4.13

Selected by California Angels' organization in 1st round (seventh player selected) of free-agent draft, June 7, 1977.
†Traded with Outfielders Bobby Bonds and Thad Bosley to Chicago White Sox for Catcher Brian Downing and Pitchers Chris Knapp and Dave Frost, December 5, 1977.
‡Appeared in one game as a pinch-runner.
§On disabled list, April 7 to April 22 and June 11, 1985 through remainder of season.

xTraded with Pitcher Scott Nielsen to New York Yankees for Outfielder Dan Pasqua, Catcher Mark Salas and Pitcher Steve Rosenberg, November 12, 1987.
yOn disabled list, July 1 to July 18, 1988.

CHAMPIONSHIP SERIES RECORD

Year	Club	League	G.	IP.	W.	L.	Pct.	H.	R.	ER.	SO.	BB.	ERA.
1983	Chicago	American	1	5	0	1	.000	6	6	6	3	3	10.80

ALL-STAR GAME RECORD

Year	League	IP.	W.	L.	Pct.	H.	R.	ER.	SO.	BB.	ERA.
1984	American	2	0	0	.000	2	0	0	2	1	0.00

BRIAN JAY DOWNING

Born October 9, 1950, at Los Angeles, Calif.
Height, 5.10. Weight, 194.
Throws and bats righthanded.
Attended Cypress Junior College, Cypress, Calif.

Tied major league records for highest fielding percentage by outfielder, season, 150 or more games (1.000), 1982; fewest errors by outfielder, season, 150 or more games (0), 1982; fewest double plays by outfielder, season, 150 or more games (0), 1982.

Established American League record for most consecutive errorless games by an outfielder (244), May 25, 1981 through July 21, second game, 1983.

Major League stolen bases: 1975 (13), 1976 (7), 1977 (1), 1978 (3), 1979 (3), 1981 (1), 1982 (2), 1983 (1), 1985 (5), 1986 (4), 1987 (5), 1988 (3). Total—48.

Tied for American League lead in bases on balls received with 106 in 1987.

Year	Club	League	Pos.	G.	AB.	R.	H.	2B.	3B.	HR.	RBI.	B.A.	PO.	A.	E.	F.A.
1970	Sarasota W. S.	Gulf C.	C-OF	34	96	16	21	1	1	0	14	.219	167	11	1	.994
1971	Appleton	Midw.	3B-C-OF	99	333	51	82	6	3	3	22	.246	353	98	13	.972
1972	Knoxville	South.	OF-3B-C	135	442	75	123	24	7	15	67	.278	250	123	21	.947
1973	Iowa	A. A.	3B-OF-C	68	228	34	56	6	1	7	27	.246	84	90	8	.956
1973	Chicago†	Amer.	OF-C-3B	34	73	5	13	1	0	2	4	.178	72	17	5	.947
1974	Chicago	Amer.	C-OF	108	293	41	66	12	1	10	39	.225	337	30	2	.995
1975	Chicago	Amer.	C	138	420	58	101	12	1	7	41	.240	730	84	8	.990
1976	Chicago‡	Amer.	C	104	317	38	81	14	0	3	30	.256	450	38	6	.988
1977	Chicago§	Amer.	C-OF	69	169	28	48	4	2	4	25	.284	325	28	6	.983
1978	California	Amer.	C	133	412	42	105	15	0	7	46	.255	681	82	5	.993
1979	California	Amer.	C	148	509	87	166	27	3	12	75	.326	669	35	11	.985
1980	California x	Amer.	C	30	93	5	27	6	0	2	25	.290	69	6	0	1.000
1981	California	Amer.	OF-C	93	317	47	79	14	0	9	41	.249	237	18	2	.992
1982	California	Amer.	OF	158	623	109	175	37	2	28	84	.281	321	9	0	•1.000
1983	California y	Amer.	OF	113	403	68	99	15	1	19	53	.246	160	9	1	.994
1984	California	Amer.	OF	156	539	65	148	28	2	23	91	.275	272	5	0	*1.000
1985	California	Amer.	OF	150	520	80	137	23	1	20	85	.263	244	5	2	.992
1986	California z	Amer.	OF	152	513	90	137	27	4	20	95	.267	267	5	3	.989
1987	California	Amer.	OF	155	567	110	154	29	3	29	77	.272	47	2	0	1.000
1988	California a	Amer.	DH	135	484	80	117	18	2	25	64	.242	0	0	0	.000
Major League Totals—16 Years				1876	6252	953	1653	282	22	220	875	.264	4881	391	51	.990

Signed as free agent by Chicago White Sox' organization, August 19, 1969.
†On disabled list, June 1 to July 9, 1973.
‡On disabled list, July 30 to August 15, 1976.
§Traded with Pitchers Chris Knapp and Dave Frost to California Angels for Outfielders Bobby Bonds and Thad Bosley and Pitcher Richard Dotson, December 5, 1977.
xOn disabled list, April 20 to September 1, 1980.
yOn disabled list, May 10 to June 20, 1983.
zGranted free agency, November 12, 1986; re-signed by Angels, January 8, 1987.
aOn disabled list, April 20 to May 6, 1988.

CHAMPIONSHIP SERIES RECORD

Established American League Championship Series record for most runs batted in, seven-game Series (7), 1986.

Year	Club	League	Pos.	G.	AB.	R.	H.	2B.	3B.	HR.	RBI.	B.A.	PO.	A.	E.	F.A.
1979	California	Amer.	C	4	15	1	3	0	0	0	1	.200	27	0	0	1.000
1982	California	Amer.	C	5	19	3	3	1	0	0	0	.158	5	0	0	1.000
1986	California	Amer.	OF	7	27	2	6	0	0	1	7	.222	18	0	0	1.000
Championship Series Totals—3 Years				16	61	6	12	1	0	1	8	.197	50	0	0	1.000

ALL-STAR GAME RECORD

Year	League	Pos.	AB.	R.	H.	2B.	3B.	HR.	RBI.	B.A.	PO.	A.	E.	F.A.
1979	American	C	1	0	1	0	0	0	0	1.000	3	0	0	1.000

KELLY ROBERT DOWNS

Born October 25, 1960, at Ogden, Utah.
Height, 6.04. Weight, 200.
Throws and bats righthanded.
Brother of Dave Downs, pitcher with Philadelphia Phillies, 1972.

Major League saves: 1987 (1).
Tied for Pacific Coast League lead in games started by pitchers with 29 in 1983.

Year	Club	League	G.	IP.	W.	L.	Pct.	H.	R.	ER.	SO.	BB.	ERA.
1980	Spartanburg	W. Carol.	14	90	5	7	.417	85	41	26	40	17	2.60
1981	Peninsula	Carolina	25	175	13	7	.650	176	79	58	124	35	2.98
1982	Oklahoma City	Am. Assoc.	32	156⅔	2	★15	.118	182	★116	93	70	72	5.34
1983	Portland	P. Coast	29	159⅓	9	•13	.409	186	98	79	71	61	4.46
1984	Portland†	P. Coast	30	163	7	12	.368	166	106	96	104	65	5.30
1985	Phoenix	P. Coast	37	137	9	10	.474	138	69	61	109	56	4.01
1986	Phoenix	P. Coast	18	108	8	5	.615	116	54	41	68	28	3.42
1986	San Francisco	National	14	88⅓	4	4	.500	78	29	27	64	30	2.75
1987	San Francisco	National	41	186	12	9	.571	185	83	75	137	67	3.63
1988	San Francisco ‡	National	27	168	13	9	.591	140	67	62	118	47	3.32
	Major League Totals—3 Years		82	442⅓	29	22	.569	403	179	164	319	144	3.34

Selected by Philadelphia Phillies' organization in 26th round of free-agent draft, June 5, 1979.

†Traded with Pitcher George Riley to San Francisco Giants for First Baseman Al Oliver and a player to be named later, August 20, 1984; Philadelphia Phillies acquired Pitcher Renie Martin to complete deal, August 30, 1984.

‡On disabled list, August 31, 1988 through remainder of season.

CHAMPIONSHIP SERIES RECORD

Year	Club	League	G.	IP.	W.	L.	Pct.	H.	R.	ER.	SO.	BB.	ERA.
1987	San Francisco	National	1	1⅓	0	0	.000	1	0	0	0	0	0.00

DOUGLAS DEAN DRABEK
(Doug)

Born July 25, 1962, at Victoria, Tex.
Height, 6.01. Weight, 185.
Throws and bats righthanded.
Attended University of Houston, Houston, Tex.

Year	Club	League	G.	IP.	W.	L.	Pct.	H.	R.	ER.	SO.	BB.	ERA.
1983	Niagara Falls	NYP	16	103⅔	6	7	.462	99	52	42	103	48	3.65
1984	Appleton	Midwest	1	5	1	0	1.000	3	1	1	6	3	1.80
1984	Glens Falls†	Eastern	19	124⅔	12	5	.706	90	34	31	75	44	2.24
1984	Nashville	Southern	4	31	1	2	.333	30	11	8	22	10	2.32
1985	Albany	Eastern	26	★192⅔	13	7	.650	153	71	64	★153	55	2.99
1986	Columbus	Int'national	8	42	1	4	.200	50	36	34	23	25	7.29
1986	New York‡	American	27	131⅔	7	8	.467	126	64	60	76	50	4.10
1987	Pittsburgh§	National	29	176⅓	11	12	.478	165	86	76	120	46	3.88
1988	Pittsburgh	National	33	219⅓	15	7	.682	194	83	75	127	50	3.08
	American League Totals—1 Year		27	131⅔	7	8	.467	126	64	60	76	50	4.10
	National League Totals—2 Years		62	395⅔	26	19	.578	359	169	151	247	96	3.43
	Major League Totals—3 Years		89	527⅓	33	27	.550	485	233	211	323	146	3.60

Selected by Cleveland Indians' organization in 4th round of free-agent draft, June 3, 1980.

Selected by Chicago White Sox' organization in 11th round of free-agent draft, June 6, 1983.

†Traded with Pitcher Kevin Hickey to New York Yankees' organization, August 13, 1984, completing deal in which New York traded Infielder Roy Smalley to Chicago White Sox for two players to be named later, July 18, 1984.

‡Traded with Pitchers Brian Fisher and Logan Easley to Pittsburgh Pirates for Pitchers Rick Rhoden, Cecilio Guante and Pat Clements, November 26, 1986.

§On disabled list, April 26 to May 18, 1987.

DAVID FRANCIS DRAVECKY
(Dave)

Born February 14, 1956, at Youngstown, O.
Height, 6.01. Weight, 200.
Throws left and bats righthanded.
Attended Youngstown State University, Youngstown, Ohio.

Major League saves: 1982 (2), 1983 (8). Total—10.

Led Texas League in shutouts with 4 in 1981.

Year	Club	League	G.	IP.	W.	L.	Pct.	H.	R.	ER.	SO.	BB.	ERA.
1978	Charleston	W. Carol.	20	52	4	2	.667	54	30	24	31	32	4.15
1979	Buffalo	Eastern	35	114	6	7	.462	125	71	54	81	59	4.26
1980	Buffalo†	Eastern	27	161	13	7	.650	165	76	60	64	60	3.35
1981	Amarillo	Texas	30	172	•15	5	.750	157	69	51	141	45	2.67
1982	Hawaii	P. Coast	16	36⅓	4	1	.800	28	15	10	26	14	2.48
1982	San Diego	National	31	105	5	3	.625	86	37	30	59	33	2.57
1983	San Diego	National	28	183⅔	14	10	.583	181	78	73	74	44	3.58
1984	San Diego	National	50	156⅔	9	8	.529	125	53	51	71	51	2.93
1985	San Diego	National	34	214⅔	13	11	.542	200	79	70	105	57	2.93
1986	San Diego	National	26	161⅓	9	11	.450	149	68	55	87	54	3.07
1987	San Diego‡-San Francisco	National	48	191⅓	10	12	.455	186	82	73	138	64	3.43
1988	San Francisco§	National	7	37	2	2	.500	33	19	13	19	8	3.16
1988	Phoenix	P. Coast	1	2⅔	0	1	.000	11	5	5	1	0	16.88
	Major League Totals—7 Years		224	1049⅔	62	57	.521	960	416	365	553	311	3.13

Selected by Pittsburgh Pirates' organization in 21st round of free-agent draft, June 6, 1978.

†Traded to San Diego Padres' organization for Outfielder Robert D. (Bobby) Mitchell, April 5, 1981.

‡Traded with Pitcher Craig Lefferts and Infielder Kevin Mitchell to San Francisco Giants for Third Baseman Chris Brown and Pitchers Keith Comstock, Mark Davis and Mark Grant, July 4, 1987.

§On disabled list, May 3 to May 28 and May 31, 1988 through remainder of season; included rehabilitation disability assignment to Phoenix, August 10 to August 16, 1988.

CHAMPIONSHIP SERIES RECORD

Tied Championship Series record for fewest hits allowed, game (2), October 7, 1987.
Tied National League Championship Series record for most consecutive scoreless innings, total Series (16).

Year Club	League	G.	IP.	W.	L.	Pct.	H.	R.	ER.	SO.	BB.	ERA.
1984—San Diego	National	3	6	0	0	.000	2	0	0	5	0	0.00
1987—San Francisco	National	2	15	1	1	.500	7	1	1	14	4	0.60
Championship Series Totals—2 Years		5	21	1	1	.500	9	1	1	19	4	0.43

WORLD SERIES RECORD

Year Club	League	G.	IP.	W.	L.	Pct.	H.	R.	ER.	SO.	BB.	ERA.
1984—San Diego	National	2	4⅔	0	0	.000	3	0	0	5	1	0.00

ALL-STAR GAME RECORD

Year League	IP.	W.	L.	Pct.	H.	R.	ER.	SO.	BB.	ERA.
1983—National	2	0	0	.000	1	0	0	2	0	0.00

THOMAS KENT DREES
(Tom)

Born June 17, 1963, at Des Moines, Ia.
Height, 6.06. Weight, 210.
Throws left and bats left and righthanded.
Received degree from Creighton University, Omaha, Neb., in 1985.

Year Club	League	G.	IP.	W.	L.	Pct.	H.	R.	ER.	SO.	BB.	ERA.
1985—Sarasota White Sox	Gulf Coast	12	74⅓	6	3	.667	75	29	23	75	17	2.78
1986—Peninsula	Carolina	37	94⅔	5	7	.417	108	64	50	54	61	4.75
1987—Daytona Beach	Florida St.	27	168⅔	10	•14	.417	195	87	70	76	58	3.74
1988—Birmingham	Southern	22	158	9	7	.563	149	63	49	94	52	2.79

Selected by Chicago White Sox' organization in 17th round of free-agent draft, June 3, 1985.

CAMERON STEWARD DREW

Born February 12, 1964, at Boston, Mass.
Height, 6.05. Weight, 215.
Throws right and bats lefthanded.
Attended University of New Haven, New Haven, Conn.

Led South Atlantic League in total bases with 255 in 1986.
Tied for South Atlantic League lead in game-winning RBIs with 13 in 1986.
Named South Atlantic League Most Valuable Player, 1986.

Year Club	League	Pos.	G.	AB.	R.	H.	2B.	3B.	HR.	RBI.	B.A.	PO.	A.	E.	F.A.
1985—Auburn	NYP	OF	72	278	48	81	10	4	5	45	.291	152	1	4	.975
1986—Asheville	S. Atl.	OF	124	439	77	143	26	4	*26	*117	.326	172	6	2	.989
1987—Columbus	South.	OF	133	490	66	137	26	1	17	70	.280	298	8	5	.984
1988—Tucson	P. C.	OF	97	354	50	126	22	7	4	70	.356	137	4	6	.959
1988—Houston	Nat.	OF	7	16	1	3	0	1	0	1	.188	10	0	0	1.000
Major League Totals—1 Year			7	16	1	3	0	1	0	1	.188	10	0	0	1.000

Selected by Houston Astros' organization in 1st round (12th player selected) of free-agent draft, June 3, 1985.

TIMOTHY DARNELL DRUMMOND
(Tim)

Born December 24, 1964, at La Plata, Md.
Height, 6.03. Weight, 170.
Throws and bats righthanded.
Attended Charles County Community College, La Plata, Md.

Year Club	League	G.	IP.	W.	L.	Pct.	H.	R.	ER.	SO.	BB.	ERA.
1983—Bradenton Pirates	Gulf Coast	14	88	7	2	.778	73	20	14	40	21	1.43
1984—Macon	S. Atlantic	27	154⅔	7	*15	.318	139	93	67	76	81	3.90
1985—Macon	S. Atlantic	27	168⅓	8	11	.421	171	100	77	91	73	4.12
1986—Prince William	Carolina	47	73⅔	6	4	.600	71	39	31	55	34	3.79
1987—Vancouver	P. Coast	46	63⅔	2	6	.250	62	35	21	49	43	2.97
1987—Pittsburgh†	National	6	6	0	0	.000	5	3	3	5	3	4.50
1988—Tidewater	Int'national	38	82⅓	6	3	.667	71	33	30	62	28	3.28
Major League Totals—1 Year		6	6	0	0	.000	5	3	3	5	3	4.50

Selected by Pittsburgh Pirates' organization in 12th round of free-agent draft, January 11, 1983.
†Traded with Catcher Mackey Sasser to New York Mets for First Baseman Randy Milligan and Pitcher Scott Henion, March 26, 1988.

ROBERT THOMAS DUCEY
(Rob)

Born May 24, 1965, at Toronto, Canada.
Height, 6.02. Weight, 175.
Throws right and bats lefthanded.
Attended Seminole Community College, Sanford, Fla.

Major League stolen bases: 1987 (2), 1988 (1). Total—3.

Tied for Southern League lead in double plays by outfielders with 6 in 1986.

Year	Club	League	Pos.	G.	AB.	R.	H.	2B.	3B.	HR.	RBI.	B.A.	PO.	A.	E.	F.A.
1984—	Medicine Hat	Pion.	OF-1B	63	235	49	71	10	3	12	49	.302	185	11	6	.970
1985—	Florence	S. Atl.	OF-1B	134	529	78	133	22	2	13	86	.251	228	8	9	.963
1986—	Ventura	Calif.	OF-1B	47	178	36	60	11	3	12	38	.337	97	3	2	.980
1986—	Knoxville	South.	OF	88	344	49	106	22	3	11	58	.308	186	10	6	.970
1987—	Syracuse	Int.	OF	100	359	62	102	14	•10	10	60	.284	171	13	6	.968
1987—	Toronto	Amer.	OF	34	48	12	9	1	0	1	6	.188	31	0	0	1.000
1988—	Syracuse	Int.	OF	90	317	40	81	14	4	7	42	.256	233	6	4	.984
1988—	Toronto	Amer.	OF	27	54	15	17	4	1	0	6	.315	35	1	0	1.000
Major League Totals—2 Years				61	102	27	26	5	1	1	12	.255	66	1	0	1.000

Signed as free agent by Toronto Blue Jays' organization, May 16, 1984.

MARIANO DUNCAN

Born March 13, 1963, at San Pedro de Macoris, D. R.
Height, 6.00. Weight, 190.
Throws right and bats left and righthanded.

Major League stolen bases: 1985 (38), 1986 (48), 1987 (11). Total—97.
Led Florida State League in stolen bases with 56 in 1983.
Led Texas League second basemen in double plays with 84 in 1984.

Year	Club	League	Pos.	G.	AB.	R.	H.	2B.	3B.	HR.	RBI.	B.A.	PO.	A.	E.	F.A.
1982—	Lethbridge	Pion.	SS-2B	30	55	9	13	3	1	1	8	.236	23	35	15	.795
1983—	Vero Beach	Fla. St.	OF-SS-2B	109	384	73	102	10	★15	0	42	.266	169	157	37	.898
1984—	San Antonio	Texas	2B-OF-SS	125	502	80	127	14	•11	2	44	.253	283	335	22	.966
1985—	Los Angeles	Nat.	SS-2B	142	562	74	137	24	6	6	39	.244	224	430	30	.956
1986—	Los Angeles†	Nat.	SS	109	407	47	93	7	0	8	30	.229	172	317	25	.951
1987—	Los Angeles‡	Nat.	★S-2-O	76	261	31	56	8	1	6	18	.215	101	213	★21	.937
1987—	Albuquerque	P. C.	SS	6	22	6	6	0	0	0	0	.273	8	15	2	.920
1988—	Albuquerque	P. C.	SS-2B	56	227	48	65	4	8	0	25	.286	104	153	18	.935
Major League Totals—3 Years				327	1230	152	286	39	7	20	87	.233	497	960	76	.950

Signed as free agent by Los Angeles Dodgers' organization, January 17, 1982.
†On disabled list, August 19 to September 17, 1986.
‡On disabled list, June 19 to July 4 and August 16, 1987 through remainder of season.

CHAMPIONSHIP SERIES RECORD

Year	Club	League	Pos.	G.	AB.	R.	H.	2B.	3B.	HR.	RBI.	B.A.	PO.	A.	E.	F.A.
1985—	Los Angeles	Nat.	SS	5	18	2	4	2	1	0	1	.222	7	16	1	.958

MICHAEL DENNIS DUNNE
(Mike)

Born October 27, 1962, at South Bend, Ind.
Height, 6.04. Weight, 200.
Throws right and bats lefthanded.
Attended Bradley University, Peoria, Ill.

Led American Association pitchers in balks with 9 and tied for lead in games started with 28 in 1986.
Named National League Rookie Pitcher of the Year by THE SPORTING NEWS, 1987.
Member of 1984 U.S. Olympic baseball team.
Named righthanded pitcher on THE SPORTING NEWS College Baseball All-America Team, 1984.

Year	Club	League	G.	IP.	W.	L.	Pct.	H.	R.	ER.	SO.	BB.	ERA.
1985—	Arkansas†	Texas	23	146	4	9	.308	133	72	50	91	57	3.08
1986—	Louisville‡	Am. Assoc.	28	★185⅔	9	•12	.429	182	102	★94	94	82	4.56
1987—	Vancouver	P. Coast	9	61⅓	3	5	.375	61	21	12	41	23	1.76
1987—	Pittsburgh	National	23	163⅓	13	6	.684	143	66	55	72	68	3.03
1988—	Pittsburgh§	National	30	170	7	11	.389	163	88	74	70	88	3.92
Major League Totals—2 Years			53	333⅓	20	17	.541	306	154	129	142	156	3.48

Selected by St. Louis Cardinals' organization in 1st round (seventh player selected) of free-agent draft, June 4, 1984.
†On disabled list, May 31 to June 10, 1985.
‡Traded with Outfielder Andy Van Slyke and Catcher Mike LaValliere to Pittsburgh Pirates for Catcher Tony Pena, April 1, 1987.
§On disabled list, April 6 to April 28, 1988.

SHAWON DONNELL DUNSTON

Born March 21, 1963, at Brooklyn, N.Y.
Height, 6.01. Weight, 175.
Throws and bats righthanded.

Major League stolen bases: 1985 (11), 1986 (13), 1987 (12), 1988 (30). Total—66.
Led National League shortstops in total chances with 817 and tied for lead in double plays with 96 in 1986.
Received reported $150,000 bonus to sign with Chicago Cubs, 1982.

Year	Club	League	Pos.	G.	AB.	R.	H.	2B.	3B.	HR.	RBI.	B.A.	PO.	A.	E.	F.A.
1982—	Sarasota Cubs	Gulf C.	SS-3B	53	190	27	61	11	0	2	28	.321	61	129	24	.888
1983—	Quad Cities†	Midw.	SS	117	455	65	141	17	8	4	62	.310	172	326	47	.914
1984—	Midland	Texas	SS	73	298	44	98	13	3	3	34	.329	164	203	32	.920
1984—	Iowa	A. A.	SS	61	210	25	49	11	1	7	27	.233	90	165	26	.907
1985—	Chicago	Nat.	SS	74	250	40	65	12	4	4	18	.260	144	248	17	.958

Year	Club	League	Pos.	G.	AB.	R.	H.	2B.	3B.	HR.	RBI.	B.A.	PO.	A.	E.	F.A.
1985	Iowa	A. A.	SS	73	272	24	73	9	6	2	28	.268	138	176	12	.963
1986	Chicago	Nat.	SS	150	581	66	145	36	3	17	68	.250	*320	*465	*32	.961
1987	Chicago‡	Nat.	SS	95	346	40	85	18	3	5	22	.246	160	271	14	.969
1987	Iowa	A. A.	SS	5	19	1	8	1	0	0	2	.421	6	12	1	.947
1988	Chicago	Nat.	SS	155	575	69	143	23	6	9	56	.249	*257	455	20	.973
Major League Totals—4 Years				474	1752	215	438	89	16	35	164	.250	881	1439	83	.965

Selected by Chicago Cubs' organization in 1st round (first player selected) of free-agent draft, June 7, 1982.

†On disabled list, May 31 to June 10, 1983.

†On disabled list, June 16 to August 21, 1987; included rehabilitation disability assignment to Iowa, August 14 to August 21, 1987.

ALL-STAR GAME RECORD

Member of National League All-Star Team in 1988; did not play.

LEON DURHAM

Born July 31, 1957, at Cincinnati, O.
Height, 6.02. Weight, 210.
Throws and bats lefthanded.

Major League stolen bases: 1980 (8), 1981 (25), 1982 (28), 1983 (12), 1984 (16), 1985 (7), 1986 (8), 1987 (2). Total—106.

Tied major league record for most assists, first baseman, inning (3), July 22, 1986 (first inning).

Tied for National League lead in intentional bases on balls received with 24 in 1985.

Led Texas League first basemen in double plays with 96 in 1978.

Led Gulf Coast League first basemen in errors with 10 in 1976.

Named outfielder on THE SPORTING NEWS National League Silver Slugger team, 1982.

Year	Club	League	Pos.	G.	AB.	R.	H.	2B.	3B.	HR.	RBI.	B.A.	PO.	A.	E.	F.A.
1976	Sarasota Cards	Gulf C.	1B-OF	44	156	25	35	3	5	2	18	.224	296	5	12	.962
1977	Gastonia	W. Car.	1B	63	239	45	88	18	3	4	44	.368	492	28	8	.985
1977	St. Petersburg	Fla. St.	1B	63	209	26	60	3	6	0	25	.287	533	27	9	.984
1978	Arkansas†	Texas	1B	102	367	72	116	21	5	12	70	.316	931	42	8	*.992
1979	Springfield	A. A.	OF-1B	127	449	84	139	33	4	23	88	.310	304	19	6	.982
1980	Springfield	A. A.	OF-1B	32	128	20	33	5	5	5	23	.258	96	8	4	.963
1980	St. Louis‡	Nat.	OF-1B	96	303	42	82	15	4	8	42	.271	180	22	3	.985
1981	Chicago§	Nat.	OF-1B	87	328	42	95	14	6	10	35	.290	175	4	5	.973
1982	Chicago	Nat.	OF-1B	148	539	84	168	33	7	22	90	.312	311	12	12	.964
1983	Chicago x	Nat.	OF-1B	100	337	58	87	18	8	12	55	.258	203	4	6	.972
1984	Chicago y	Nat.	1B	137	473	86	132	30	4	23	96	.279	1162	96	7	.994
1985	Chicago	Nat.	1B	153	542	58	153	32	2	21	75	.282	1421	107	7	.995
1986	Chicago	Nat.	1B	141	484	66	127	18	7	20	65	.262	1231	80	7	.995
1987	Chicago	Nat.	1B	131	439	70	120	22	1	27	63	.273	1049	57	11	.990
1988	Chi.z-Cin.ab	Nat.	1B	45	124	14	27	9	1	4	8	.218	296	21	2	.994
Major League Totals—9 Years				1038	3569	520	991	191	40	147	529	.278	6028	403	60	.991

Selected by St. Louis Cardinals' organization in 1st round (15th player selected) of free-agent draft, June 8, 1976.

†On disabled list, April 23 to May 25, 1978.

‡Traded with Third Baseman Ken Reitz and a player to be named later to Chicago Cubs for Pitcher Bruce Sutter, December 9, 1980; Chicago acquired Third Baseman Tye Waller to complete deal, December 22, 1980.

§On disabled list, June 2 to August 9, 1981.

xOn disabled list, June 9 to June 24, 1983.

yOn disabled list, June 24 to July 12, 1984.

zTraded to Cincinnati Reds for Pitcher Pat Perry and cash, May 19, 1988.

aOn disabled list, May 24 to June 14 and July 11 to September 16, 1988.

bReleased, November 8, 1988.

CHAMPIONSHIP SERIES RECORD

Year	Club	League	Pos.	G.	AB.	R.	H.	2B.	3B.	HR.	RBI.	B.A.	PO.	A.	E.	F.A.
1984	Chicago	Nat.	1B	5	20	2	3	0	0	2	4	.150	47	3	1	.980

ALL-STAR GAME RECORD

Year	League	Pos.	AB.	R.	H.	2B.	3B.	HR.	RBI.	B.A.	PO.	A.	E.	F.A.
1983	National	OF	2	0	0	0	0	0	0	.000	0	0	0	.000

Member of National League All-Star Team in 1982; did not play.

JAMES EDWARD DWYER
(Jimmy)

Born January 3, 1950, at Evergreen Park, Ill.
Height, 5.10. Weight, 186.
Throws and bats lefthanded.
Received bachelor of arts degree in accounting from Southern Illinois University, Carbondale, Ill., in 1973.
Nephew of Don Dwyer, second baseman in New York Giants' organization, 1947.

Major League stolen bases: 1975 (4), 1978 (7), 1979 (3), 1980 (3), 1982 (2), 1983 (1), 1987 (4). Total—24.

Tied for American Association lead in caught stealing with 13 in 1977.

Year	Club	League	Pos.	G.	AB.	R.	H.	2B.	3B.	HR.	RBI.	B.A.	PO.	A.	E.	F.A.
1971	Cedar Rapids	Midw.	OF	58	201	30	63	6	6	2	15	.313	73	3	3	.962
1972	Modesto	Calif.	OF	92	354	87	115	15	*13	9	45	.325	149	8	4	.975
1972	Arkansas	Texas	OF	44	162	16	41	1	0	2	14	.253	101	6	2	.982

Year Club	League	Pos.	G.	AB.	R.	H.	2B.	3B.	HR.	RBI.	B.A.	PO.	A.	E.	F.A.
1973—Tulsa	A. A.	OF	87	349	63	135	22	8	1	40	*.387	127	8	5	.964
1973—St. Louis	Nat.	OF	28	57	7	11	1	1	0	0	.193	32	0	0	1.000
1974—Tulsa	A. A.	OF-1B	36	119	20	40	7	2	1	15	.336	120	13	3	.978
1974—St. Louis	Nat.	OF-1B	74	86	13	24	1	0	2	11	.279	31	3	0	1.000
1975—Tulsa	A. A.	OF	33	109	17	44	8	2	1	17	.404	49	2	2	.962
1975—St.L.†-Mont.	Nat.	OF	81	206	26	56	8	1	3	21	.272	104	8	4	.966
1976—Mont.‡-N.Y.§	Nat.	OF-PH	61	105	9	19	3	1	0	5	.181	35	0	1	.972
1976—Tidewater	Int.	OF	8	26	0	5	1	0	0	1	.192	14	0	1	.933
1977—Wichita x	A. A.	OF	130	464	*113	*154	*38	12	18	70	*.332	245	6	8	.969
1977—St. Louis	Nat.	OF	13	31	3	7	1	0	0	2	.226	16	0	0	1.000
1978—St.L. y-S.F. z	Nat.	OF-1B	107	238	30	53	12	2	6	26	.223	216	15	3	.987
1979—Boston	Amer.	1B-OF	76	113	19	30	7	0	2	14	.265	167	16	4	.979
1980—Boston a	Amer.	OF-1B	93	260	41	74	11	1	9	38	.285	143	15	4	.975
1981—Baltimore	Amer.	OF-1B	68	134	16	30	0	1	3	10	.224	97	2	2	.980
1982—Baltimore	Amer.	OF-1B	71	148	28	45	4	3	6	15	.304	87	0	2	.978
1983—Baltimore	Amer.	OF-1B	100	196	37	56	17	1	8	38	.286	123	2	4	.969
1984—Baltimore b	Amer.	OF	76	161	22	41	9	1	2	21	.255	83	3	3	.966
1985—Baltimore c	Amer.	OF	101	233	35	58	8	3	7	36	.249	131	4	1	.993
1986—Baltimore d	Amer.	OF-1B	94	160	18	39	13	1	8	31	.244	33	4	0	1.000
1987—Baltimore	Amer.	OF	92	241	54	66	7	1	15	33	.274	57	1	0	1.000
1988—Balt.ef-Minn.	Amer.	OF	55	94	9	24	1	0	2	18	.255	3	0	0	1.000
1988—Rochester g	Int.	DH	8	27	7	8	3	1	0	4	.296	0	0	0	.000
National League Totals—6 Years			364	723	88	170	26	5	11	65	.235	434	26	8	.983
American League Totals—10 Years			826	1740	279	463	77	12	62	254	.266	924	47	20	.980
Major League Totals—16 Years			1190	2463	367	633	103	17	73	319	.257	1358	73	28	.981

Selected by St. Louis Cardinals' organization in 11th round of free-agent draft, June 8, 1971.

†Traded to Montreal Expos for Infielder Larry Lintz, July 25, 1975.

‡Traded with Outfielder Jose (Pepe) Mangual to New York Mets for Outfielder Del Unser and Infielder Wayne Garrett, July 21, 1976.

§In three-club deal, Chicago Cubs traded Outfielder-First Baseman Pete LaCock to Kansas City Royals, the New York Mets traded Outfielder Jim Dwyer to Chicago Cubs' organization, and New York received a player to be named later, December 8, 1976; New York acquired Outfielder Sheldon Mallory from Kansas City to complete deal, December 13, 1976.

xReleased, September 7, 1977, signed by St. Louis Cardinals, September 13, 1977.

yTraded to San Francisco Giants, June 15, 1978, completing deal in which San Francisco traded Pitcher Frank Riccelli to St. Louis Cardinals for a player to be named later, October 25, 1977.

zSold to Boston Red Sox, March 15, 1979.

aGranted free agency, October 22, 1980; signed by Baltimore Orioles, December 23, 1980.

bOn disabled list, July 19 to August 29, 1984.

cGranted free agency, November 12, 1985; re-signed by Orioles, February 5, 1986.

dGranted free agency, November 12, 1986; re-signed by Orioles, November 20, 1986.

eOn disabled list, April 15 to May 14 and July 11 to August 1, 1988; included rehabilitation disability assignment to Rochester, May 6 to May 14, 1988.

fTraded to Minnesota Twins for a player to be named later, August 29, 1988; Baltimore Orioles acquired Pitcher Doug Kline to complete deal, August 31, 1988.

gGranted free agency, November 4, 1988; re-signed by Twins, December 6, 1988.

CHAMPIONSHIP SERIES RECORD

Year Club	League	Pos.	G.	AB.	R.	H.	2B.	3B.	HR.	RBI.	B.A.	PO.	A.	E.	F.A.
1983—Baltimore	Amer.	PH-OF	2	4	1	1	1	0	0	0	.250	4	0	0	1.000

WORLD SERIES RECORD

Tied World Series record for hitting home run in first Series at-bat, October 11, 1983 (first inning).

Year Club	League	Pos.	G.	AB.	R.	H.	2B.	3B.	HR.	RBI.	B.A.	PO.	A.	E.	F.A.
1983—Baltimore	Amer.	OF	2	8	3	3	1	0	1	1	.375	2	0	0	1.000

MICHAEL LAWRENCE DYER
(Mike)

Born September 8, 1966, at Upland, Calif.
Height, 6.03. Weight, 195.
Throws and bats righthanded.
Attended Citrus College, Glendora, Calif.

Tied for Appalachian League lead in games started by pitchers with 14 in 1986.

Year Club	League	G.	IP.	W.	L.	Pct.	H.	R.	ER.	SO.	BB.	ERA.
1986—Elizabethton	Ap'lachian	14	72⅓	5	7	.417	70	50	28	62	42	3.48
1987—Kenosha	Midwest	27	167	16	5	.762	124	72	57	163	84	3.07
1988—Orlando	Southern	27	162⅓	11	13	.458	155	84	72	125	86	3.99

Selected by Minnesota Twins' organization in 4th round of free-agent draft, January 14, 1986.

—DID YOU KNOW—

That Baltimore righthander Bob Milacki was 2-0 as a rookie last season and both his victories were 2-0 decisions? Milacki shut out Detroit on September 18 in his major league debut and then shut out the New York Yankees on September 28.

LEONARD KYLE DYKSTRA

Name pronounced DYK-struh.

(Lenny)

Born February 10, 1963, at Santa Ana, Calif.
Height, 5.10. Weight, 170.
Throws and bats lefthanded.
Grandson of Pete Leswick, forward with New York Americans and Boston Bruins of NHL, 1936-37 and 1944-45; nephew of Tony Leswick, forward with New York Rangers, Detroit Red Wings and Chicago Black Hawks of NHL, 1945-46 through 1955-56 and 1957-58; and brother of Kevin Dykstra, umpire in Northwest League, 1988.

Major League stolen bases: 1985 (15), 1986 (31), 1987 (27), 1988 (30). Total—103.
Led Carolina League in bases on balls received with 107, stolen bases with 105 and caught stealing with 23 in 1983.
Named Carolina League Player of the Year, 1983.

Year Club	League	Pos.	G.	AB.	R.	H.	2B.	3B.	HR.	RBI.	B.A.	PO.	A.	E.	F.A.
1981—Shelby	S. Atl.	OF-SS	48	157	34	41	7	2	0	18	.261	86	3	4	.957
1982—Shelby	S. Atl.	OF	120	413	95	120	13	7	3	38	.291	239	11	14	.947
1983—Lynchburg	Carol.	OF	•136	★525	★132	★188	24	★14	8	81	★.358	268	9	7	.975
1984—Jackson	Texas	OF	131	501	★100	138	25	7	6	52	.275	256	5	2	★.992
1985—Tidewater	Int.	OF	58	229	44	71	8	6	1	25	.310	184	4	5	.974
1985—New York	Nat.	OF	83	236	40	60	9	3	1	19	.254	165	6	1	.994
1986—New York	Nat.	OF	147	431	77	127	27	7	8	45	.295	283	8	3	.990
1987—New York	Nat.	OF	132	431	86	123	37	3	10	43	.285	239	4	3	.988
1988—New York	Nat.	OF	126	429	57	116	19	3	8	33	.270	270	3	1	.996
Major League Totals—4 Years			488	1527	260	426	92	16	27	140	.279	957	21	8	.992

Selected by New York Mets' organization in 12th round of free-agent draft, June 8, 1981.

CHAMPIONSHIP SERIES RECORD

Established National League Championship Series records for highest batting average, seven-game Series (.429), 1988; most doubles, seven-game Series (3), 1988.

Year Club	League	Pos.	G.	AB.	R.	H.	2B.	3B.	HR.	RBI.	B.A.	PO.	A.	E.	F.A.
1986—New York	Nat.	OF-PH	6	23	3	7	1	1	1	3	.304	10	0	0	1.000
1988—New York	Nat.	PH-OF	7	14	6	6	3	0	1	3	.429	9	0	0	1.000
Championship Series Totals—2 Years			13	37	9	13	4	1	2	6	.351	19	0	0	1.000

WORLD SERIES RECORD

Tied World Series record for most times home run as leadoff batter, start of game (1), October 21, 1986.

Year Club	League	Pos.	G.	AB.	R.	H.	2B.	3B.	HR.	RBI.	B.A.	PO.	A.	E.	F.A.
1986—New York	Nat.	OF-PH	7	27	4	8	0	0	2	3	.296	14	0	0	1.000

GARY LOUIS EAVE

Born July 22, 1963, at Monroe, La.
Height, 6.04. Weight, 190.
Throws and bats righthanded.
Attended Grambling State University, Grambling, La.

Year Club	League	G.	IP.	W.	L.	Pct.	H.	R.	ER.	SO.	BB.	ERA.
1985—Bradenton Braves	Gulf Coast	6	30⅔	2	1	.667	28	7	6	21	8	1.76
1986—Sumter	S. Atlantic	25	47	4	1	.800	34	18	15	61	21	2.87
1987—Durham	Carolina	16	87⅓	5	4	.556	90	51	47	82	35	4.84
1987—Greenville	Southern	25	54⅓	2	5	.286	39	19	17	52	23	2.82
1988—Richmond	Int'national	34	101	5	9	.357	100	49	40	81	31	3.56
1988—Atlanta	National	5	5	0	0	.000	7	5	5	0	3	9.00
Major League Totals—1 Year		5	5	0	0	.000	7	5	5	0	3	9.00

Selected by Atlanta Braves' organization in 12th round of free-agent draft, June 3, 1985.

DENNIS LEE ECKERSLEY

Born October 3, 1954, at Oakland, Calif.
Height, 6.02. Weight, 195.
Throws and bats righthanded.
Son-in-law of Al Jacinto, second baseman in Chicago White Sox' organization, 1947 through 1954.

Pitched 1-0 no-hit victory against California Angels, May 30, 1977.
Major League saves: 1975 (2), 1976 (1), 1987 (16), 1988 (45). Total—64.
Led American League in saves with 45 in 1988.
Led American League in home runs allowed with 30 in 1978.
Tied for American League lead in intentional bases on balls issued with 11 in 1977.
Led Texas League in hit batsmen with 10 in 1974.
Led California League pitchers in games started with 31 and tied for lead in shutouts with 5 in 1973.
Named American League Fireman of the Year by THE SPORTING NEWS, 1988.
Named American League Rookie Pitcher of the Year by THE SPORTING NEWS, 1975.
Received reported $32,000 bonus to sign with Cleveland Indians, 1972.

Year Club	League	G.	IP.	W.	L.	Pct.	H.	R.	ER.	SO.	BB.	ERA.
1972—Reno	California	12	75	5	5	.500	87	46	40	56	33	4.80
1973—Reno	California	31	202	12	8	.600	182	97	82	218	91	3.65
1974—San Antonio	Texas	23	167	•14	3	★.824	141	66	63	★163	60	3.40
1975—Cleveland	American	34	187	13	7	.650	147	61	54	152	90	2.60
1976—Cleveland	American	36	199	13	12	.520	155	82	76	200	78	3.44

Year Club	League	G.	IP.	W.	L.	Pct.	H.	R.	ER.	SO.	BB.	ERA.
1977—Cleveland†	American	33	247	14	13	.519	214	100	97	191	54	3.53
1978—Boston	American	35	268	20	8	.714	258	99	89	162	71	2.99
1979—Boston	American	33	247	17	10	.630	234	89	82	150	59	2.99
1980—Boston	American	30	198	12	14	.462	188	101	94	121	44	4.27
1981—Boston	American	23	154	9	8	.529	160	82	73	79	35	4.27
1982—Boston	American	33	224⅓	13	13	.500	228	101	93	127	43	3.73
1983—Boston	American	28	176⅓	9	13	.409	223	119	110	77	39	5.61
1984—Boston‡	American	9	64⅔	4	4	.500	71	38	36	33	13	5.01
1984—Chicago§	National	24	160⅓	10	8	.556	152	59	54	81	36	3.03
1985—Chicago x	National	25	169⅓	11	7	.611	145	61	58	117	19	3.08
1986—Chicago y	National	33	201	6	11	.353	226	109	102	137	43	4.57
1987—Oakland	American	54	115⅔	6	8	.429	99	41	39	113	17	3.03
1988—Oakland	American	60	72⅔	4	2	.667	52	20	19	70	11	2.35
American League Totals—12 Years		408	2153⅔	134	112	.545	2029	933	862	1475	554	3.60
National League Totals—3 Years		82	530⅔	27	26	.509	523	229	214	335	98	3.63
Major League Totals—14 Years		490	2684⅓	161	138	.538	2552	1162	1076	1810	652	3.61

Selected by Cleveland Indians' organization in 3rd round of free-agent draft, June 6, 1972.

†Traded with Catcher Fred Kendall to Boston Red Sox for Pitchers Rick Wise and Mike Paxton, Third Baseman Ted Cox and Catcher Bo Diaz, March 30, 1978.

‡Traded with Outfielder Mike Brumley to Chicago Cubs for First Baseman-Outfielder Bill Buckner, May 25, 1984.

§Granted free agency, November 8, 1984; re-signed by Cubs, November 28, 1984.

xOn disabled list, August 11 to September 7, 1985.

yTraded with Infielder Dan Rohn to Oakland Athletics for Outfielder Dave Wilder, Infielder Brian Guinn and Pitcher Mark Leonette, April 3, 1987.

CHAMPIONSHIP SERIES RECORD

Established Championship Series record for most saves, Series (4), 1988.
Tied Championship Series record for most games pitched, four-game Series (4), 1988.
Established American League Championship Series record for most saves, total Series (4).

Year Club	League	G.	IP.	W.	L.	Pct.	H.	R.	ER.	SO.	BB.	ERA.
1984—Chicago	National	1	5⅓	0	1	.000	9	5	5	0	0	8.44
1988—Oakland	American	4	6	0	0	.000	1	0	0	5	2	0.00
Championship Series Totals—2 Years		5	11⅓	0	1	.000	10	5	5	5	2	3.97

WORLD SERIES RECORD

Year Club	League	G.	IP.	W.	L.	Pct.	H.	R.	ER.	SO.	BB.	ERA.
1988—Oakland	American	2	1⅔	0	1	.000	2	2	2	2	1	10.80

ALL-STAR GAME RECORD

Year League	IP.	W.	L.	Pct.	H.	R.	ER.	SO.	BB.	ERA.
1977—American	2	0	0	.000	0	0	0	1	0	0.00
1982—American	3	0	1	.000	2	3	3	1	2	9.00
1988—American	1	0	0	.000	0	0	0	1	0	0.00
All-Star Game Totals—3 Years	6	0	1	.000	2	3	3	3	2	4.50

WAYNE MAURICE EDWARDS

Born March 7, 1964, at Burbank, Calif.
Height, 6.05. Weight, 185.
Throws and bats lefthanded.
Attended Azusa Pacific University, Azusa, Calif.

Led Southern League in wild pitches with 16 in 1988.
Led Florida State League in complete games with 15 and tied for lead in wild pitches with 17 in 1987.

Year Club	League	G.	IP.	W.	L.	Pct.	H.	R.	ER.	SO.	BB.	ERA.
1985—Sarasota White Sox	Gulf Coast	11	68⅔	•7	3	.700	52	26	19	61	18	2.49
1986—Peninsula	Carolina	24	128⅓	8	8	.500	149	80	60	86	68	4.21
1987—Daytona Beach	Florida St.	29	★199⅔	16	8	.667	★211	91	80	121	68	3.61
1988—Birmingham	Southern	27	167	9	12	.429	176	108	91	136	92	4.90
1988—Vancouver	P. Coast	2	3	0	0	.000	0	0	0	2	0	0.00

Selected by Chicago White Sox' organization in 10th round of free agent draft, June 3, 1985.

JUAN TYRONE EICHELBERGER

Name pronounced EYE-kul-burg-ur.

Born October 21, 1953, at St. Louis, Mo.
Height, 6.02. Weight, 195.
Throws and bats righthanded.
Attended University of California, Berkeley, Calif.

Tied major league record for most consecutive strikeouts as batter, season (14), 1980.
Tied for National League lead in balks with 5 in 1981.

Year Club	League	G.	IP.	W.	L.	Pct.	H.	R.	ER.	SO.	BB.	ERA.
1975—Reno	California	16	117	10	4	.714	105	52	36	92	54	2.77
1975—Alexandria	Texas	8	50	3	4	.429	52	31	24	31	21	4.32
1976—Amarillo	Texas	11	66	2	6	.250	77	50	41	41	45	5.59
1976—Reno	California	13	89	6	1	.857	71	48	35	77	63	3.54
1977—Amarillo†	Texas	25	162	12	7	.632	177	90	74	92	77	4.11

Year Club	League	G.	IP.	W.	L.	Pct.	H.	R.	ER.	SO.	BB.	ERA.
1978—Hawaii	P. Coast	26	156	8	13	.381	143	95	78	106	*113	4.50
1978—San Diego	National	3	3	0	0	.000	4	4	4	2	2	12.00
1979—Hawaii	P. Coast	28	195	13	9	.591	151	79	73	159	*137	3.37
1979—San Diego	National	3	21	1	1	.500	15	10	8	12	11	3.43
1980—Hawaii	P. Coast	11	77	7	3	.700	56	35	30	62	49	3.51
1980—San Diego‡	National	15	89	4	2	.667	73	41	36	43	55	3.64
1981—San Diego	National	25	141	8	8	.500	136	60	55	81	74	3.51
1982—San Diego§x	National	31	177⅔	7	14	.333	171	98	83	74	72	4.20
1983—Cleveland y	American	28	134	4	11	.267	132	80	73	56	59	4.90
1984—Vancouver za	P. Coast	25	139⅔	8	11	.421	136	84	77	91	75	4.96
1985—Miami b	Florida St.	7	42	2	3	.400	50	31	19	40	23	4.07
1985—Richmond c	Int'national	17	21	4	1	.800	20	7	7	15	7	3.00
1986—Richmond	Int'national	32	44	7	4	.636	40	22	20	44	25	4.09
1986—Greenville	Southern	18	23⅓	3	3	.500	18	8	7	25	8	2.70
1987—Richmond d	Int'national	40	127⅔	7	5	.583	105	53	48	86	38	3.38
1988—Richmond	Int'national	25	63	2	4	.333	58	24	22	44	13	3.14
1988—Atlanta e	National	20	37⅓	2	0	1.000	44	19	16	13	10	3.86
National League Totals—6 Years		97	469	22	25	.468	443	232	202	225	224	3.88
American League Totals—1 Year		28	134	4	11	.267	132	80	73	56	59	4.90
Major League Totals—7 Years		125	603	26	36	.419	575	312	275	281	283	4.10

Selected by San Francisco Giants' organization in 36th round of free-agent draft, June 8, 1971.
Selected by San Diego Padres' organization in secondary phase of free-agent draft, January 9, 1975.
†Appeared as outfielder in two games with 3 putouts.
‡On disabled list, July 18 to August 8, 1980.
§On disabled list, July 16 to August 6, 1982.
xTraded with First Baseman-Outfielder Broderick Perkins to Cleveland Indians for Pitcher Ed Whitson, November 18, 1982.
yReleased, April 1, 1984; signed by Vancouver (Milwaukee Brewers' organization), April 25, 1984.
zReleased, August 31, 1984; signed by Hawaii (Pittsburgh Pirates' organization), January 15, 1985.
aReleased, April 7, 1985; signed by Miami (Independent), April 12, 1985.
bReleased, May 15, 1985; signed by Richmond (Atlanta Braves' organization), June 3, 1985.
cOn disabled list, August 1, 1985 through remainder of season.
dGranted free agency, October 15, 1987; re-signed by Braves' organization, January 27, 1988.
eGranted free agency, October 15, 1988.

MARK ANTHONY EICHHORN

Name pronounced IKE-horn
Born November 21, 1960, at San Jose, Calif.
Height, 6.03. Weight, 200.
Throws and bats righthanded.
Attended Cabrillo Junior College, Aptos, Calif.

Tied American League record for most games, relief pitcher, season (89), 1987.
Major League saves: 1986 (10), 1987 (4), 1988 (1). Total—15.
Led American League in intentional bases on balls issued with 14 in 1986.
Tied for Southern League lead in games started by pitchers with 29 in 1981.
Named American League Rookie Pitcher of the Year by THE SPORTING NEWS, 1986.

Year Club	League	G.	IP.	W.	L.	Pct.	H.	R.	ER.	SO.	BB.	ERA.
1979—Medicine Hat	Pioneer	16	93	7	6	.538	101	62	35	66	26	3.39
1980—Kinston	Carolina	26	183	14	10	.583	158	72	59	119	56	2.90
1981—Knoxville	Southern	30	192	10	14	.417	202	112	85	99	57	3.98
1982—Syracuse	Int'national	27	156⅔	10	11	.476	158	92	79	71	83	4.54
1982—Toronto	American	7	38	0	3	.000	40	28	23	16	14	5.45
1983—Syracuse	Int'national	7	30⅔	0	5	.000	36	32	27	12	21	7.92
1983—Knoxville	Southern	21	120⅔	6	12	.333	124	65	58	54	47	4.33
1984—Syracuse	Int'national	36	117⅔	5	9	.357	147	92	78	54	51	5.97
1985—Knoxville	Southern	26	116⅓	5	1	.833	101	49	39	76	34	3.02
1985—Syracuse	Int'national	8	37⅓	2	5	.286	38	24	20	27	7	4.82
1986—Toronto†	American	69	157	14	6	.700	105	32	30	166	45	1.72
1987—Toronto	American	*89	127⅔	10	6	.625	110	47	45	96	52	3.17
1988—Toronto	American	37	66⅔	0	3	.000	79	32	31	28	27	4.19
1988—Syracuse	Int'national	18	38⅓	4	4	.500	35	9	5	34	15	1.17
Major League Totals—4 Years		202	389⅓	24	18	.571	334	139	129	306	138	2.98

Selected by Toronto Blue Jays' organization in 2nd round of free-agent draft, January 9, 1979.
†On disabled list, June 16 to July 1, 1986.

DAVID WILLIAM EILAND
(Dave)

Born July 5, 1966, at Dade City, Fla.
Height, 6.03. Weight, 210.
Throws and bats righthanded.
Attended University of Florida, Gainesville, Fla., and
University of South Florida, Tampa, Fla.

Tied for Eastern League lead in complete games with 7 in 1988.

Year Club	League	G.	IP.	W.	L.	Pct.	H.	R.	ER.	SO.	BB.	ERA.
1987—Oneonta	NYP	5	29⅓	4	0	1.000	20	6	6	16	3	1.84
1987—Fort Lauderdale	Florida St.	8	62⅓	5	3	.625	57	17	13	28	8	1.88

Year Club	League	G.	IP.	W.	L.	Pct.	H.	R.	ER.	SO.	BB.	ERA.
1988—Albany	Eastern	18	119⅓	9	5	.643	95	39	34	66	22	2.56
1988—Columbus	Int'national	4	24⅓	1	1	.500	25	8	7	13	6	2.59
1988—New York	American	3	12⅔	0	0	.000	15	9	9	7	4	6.39
Major League Totals—1 Year		3	12⅔	0	0	.000	15	9	9	7	4	6.39

Selected by New York Yankees' organization in 7th round of free-agent draft, June 2, 1987.

JAMES MICHAEL EISENREICH

Name pronounced EYES-en-rike.

(Jim)

Born April 18, 1959, at St. Cloud, Minn.
Height, 5.11. Weight, 195.
Throws and bats lefthanded.
Attended St. Cloud State University, St. Cloud, Minn.

Major League stolen bases: 1984 (2), 1987 (1), 1988 (9). Total—12.
Named Appalachian League Co-Player of the Year, 1980.

Year Club	League	Pos.	G.	AB.	R.	H.	2B.	3B.	HR.	RBI.	B.A.	PO.	A.	E.	F.A.
1980—Elizabethton	Appal.	OF	67	258	47	77	12	●4	3	41	.298	151	7	3	.981
1980—Wis. Rapids	Midw.	DH	5	16	4	7	0	0	0	5	.438	0	0	0	.000
1981—Wis. Rapids	Midw.	OF	★134	489	101	●152	★27	0	23	99	.311	★295	17	9	.972
1982—Minnesota†	Amer.	OF	34	99	10	30	6	0	2	9	.303	72	0	2	.973
1983—Minnesota‡	Amer.	OF	2	7	1	2	1	0	0	0	.286	6	1	0	1.000
1984—Minnesota§x	Amer.	OF	12	32	1	7	1	0	0	3	.219	5	0	0	1.000
1985-86—y					(Out of Organized Baseball)										
1987—Memphis	South.	DH	70	275	60	105	36	●10	11	57	.382	0	0	0	.000
1987—Kansas City z	Amer.	DH	44	105	10	25	8	2	4	21	.238	0	0	0	.000
1988—Kansas City	Amer.	OF	82	202	26	44	8	1	1	19	.218	109	0	4	.965
1988—Omaha	A. A.	OF	36	142	28	41	8	3	4	14	.289	73	1	1	.987
Major League Totals—5 Years			174	445	48	108	24	3	7	52	.243	192	1	6	.970

Selected by Minnesota Twins' organization in 16th round of free-agent draft, June 3, 1980.
†On disabled list, May 6 to May 28 and June 18 to September 1, 1982.
‡On disabled list, April 7, 1983; then transferred to voluntarily retired list, May 27, 1983 through remainder of season.
§On disabled list, April 26 to May 18, 1984.
xOn voluntarily retired list, June 4, 1984 through September 29, 1986.
yClaimed on waivers by Kansas City Royals, October 2, 1986.
zOn disabled list, August 25 to September 9, 1987.

STEVEN CLARK ELLSWORTH

(Steve)

Born July 30, 1960, at Chicago, Ill.
Height, 6.08. Weight, 220.
Throws and bats righthanded.
Attended Fresno City College, Fresno, Calif., and
California State University, Northridge, Calif.
Son of Dick Ellsworth, pitcher with Chicago Cubs, Philadelphia Phillies, Boston Red Sox,
Cleveland Indians and Milwaukee Brewers, 1958 and 1960 through 1971.

Tied for Carolina League lead in complete games with 7 in 1984.

Year Club	League	G.	IP.	W.	L.	Pct.	H.	R.	ER.	SO.	BB.	ERA.
1981—Elmira	NYP	1	1	0	1	.000	0	2	2	0	2	18.00
1982—Elmira†	NYP						(Did not play)					
1983—Winter Haven	Florida State	20	83⅓	1	11	.083	119	81	70	47	34	7.56
1984—Wintson-Salem	Carolina	26	164⅓	13	8	.619	158	79	60	104	68	3.29
1984—New Britain	Eastern	3	21⅓	1	1	.500	18	8	7	12	5	2.95
1985—New Britain	Eastern	20	120⅓	7	8	.467	136	66	57	63	31	4.26
1986—New Britain	Eastern	9	73	5	3	.625	57	19	16	41	18	1.97
1986—Pawtucket	Int'national	15	83	6	2	.750	82	33	31	43	19	3.36
1987—Pawtucket	Int'national	27	165⅔	11	8	.579	182	85	79	89	46	4.29
1988—Boston	American	8	36	1	6	.143	47	29	27	16	16	6.75
1988—Pawtucket	Int'national	18	108⅓	7	7	.500	105	49	45	58	23	3.74
Major League Totals—1 Year		8	36	1	6	.143	47	29	27	16	16	6.75

Selected by Minnesota Twins' organization in 7th round of free-agent draft, January 8, 1980.
Selected by Cleveland Indians' organization in secondary phase of free-agent draft, June 8, 1980.
Selected by Boston Red Sox' organization in secondary phase of free-agent draft, June 8, 1981.
†On disabled list, June 10, 1982 through entire season.

KEVIN DANIEL ELSTER

Born August 3, 1964, at San Pedro, Calif.
Height, 6.02. Weight, 195.
Throws and bats righthanded.
Attended Golden West College, Huntington Beach, Calif.

Major League stolen bases: 1988 (2).
Led Texas League shortstops in total chances with 589 and double plays with 83 in 1986.
Led New York-Pennsylvania League shortstops in double plays with 45 and total chances with 358 in 1984.

Year	Club	League	Pos.	G.	AB.	R.	H.	2B.	3B.	HR.	RBI.	B.A.	PO.	A.	E.	F.A.
1984	—Little Falls	NYP	SS	71	257	35	66	7	3	3	35	.257	★128	214	16	★.955
1985	—Lynchburg	Carol.	SS	59	224	41	66	9	0	7	26	.295	82	195	16	.945
1985	—Jackson†	Texas	SS	59	214	30	55	13	0	2	22	.257	107	220	10	.970
1986	—Jackson	Texas	SS	127	435	69	117	19	3	2	52	.269	★196	★365	28	★.952
1986	—New York	Nat.	SS	19	30	3	5	1	0	0	0	.167	16	35	2	.962
1987	—Tidewater	Int.	SS	134	★549	83	★170	33	7	8	74	.310	219	419	21	.968
1987	—New York	Nat.	SS	5	10	1	4	2	0	0	1	.400	4	6	1	.909
1988	—New York	Nat.	SS	149	406	41	87	11	1	9	37	.214	196	345	13	.977
Major League Totals—3 Years				173	446	45	96	14	1	9	38	.215	216	386	16	.974

Selected by New York Mets' organization in 2nd round of free-agent draft, January 17, 1984.
†On disabled list, August 11, 1985 through remainder of season.

CHAMPIONSHIP SERIES RECORD

Year	Club	League	Pos.	G.	AB.	R.	H.	2B.	3B.	HR.	RBI.	B.A.	PO.	A.	E.	F.A.
1986	—New York	Nat.	PR-SS	4	3	0	0	0	0	0	0	.000	2	3	0	1.000
1988	—New York	Nat.	SS-PR	5	8	1	2	1	0	0	1	.250	7	7	2	.875
Championship Series Totals—2 Years				9	11	1	2	1	0	0	1	.182	9	10	2	.905

WORLD SERIES RECORD

Year	Club	League	Pos.	G.	AB.	R.	H.	2B.	3B.	HR.	RBI.	B.A.	PO.	A.	E.	F.A.
1986	—New York	Nat.	SS	1	1	0	0	0	0	0	0	.000	3	3	1	.857

NARCISO ELVIRA

Born October 29, 1967, at Vera Cruz, Mexico.
Height, 5.10. Weight, 160.
Throws and bats lefthanded.

Year	Club	League	G.	IP.	W.	L.	Pct.	H.	R.	ER.	SO.	BB.	ERA.
1986	—Leon†	Mexican	31	127⅓	8	5	.615	128	81	68	86	84	4.81
1987	—Beloit‡	Midwest	4	27	3	0	1.000	15	5	4	29	12	1.33
1987	—Leon	Mexican	33	109⅓	6	8	.429	104	75	64	80	62	5.27
1988	—Stockton	California	25	135⅓	7	6	.538	87	49	44	161	79	2.93

†Sold to Milwaukee Brewers' organization, December, 1986.
‡Loaned to Leon of Mexican League.

RALPH DAVID ENGLE
(Dave)

Born November 30, 1956, at San Diego, Calif.
Height, 6.03. Weight, 216.
Throws and bats righthanded.
Attended University of Southern California, Los Angeles, Calif.
Brother-in-law of Tom Brunansky, outfielder with St. Louis Cardinals.

Major League stolen bases: 1983 (2), 1985 (2), 1987 (1). Total—5.

Year	Club	League	Pos.	G.	AB.	R.	H.	2B.	3B.	HR.	RBI.	B.A.	PO.	A.	E.	F.A.
1978	—Salinas†	Calif.	3B	53	203	34	62	11	0	6	40	.305	20	65	10	.895
1979	—Toledo	Int.	3B	106	363	46	104	17	1	7	51	.287	72	197	23	.921
1980	—Toledo	Int.	OF	133	489	74	150	27	3	7	73	★.307	225	16	5	.980
1981	—Minnesota	Amer.	OF-3B	82	248	29	64	14	4	5	32	.258	144	4	3	.980
1982	—Minnesota	Amer.	OF	58	186	20	42	7	2	4	16	.226	63	3	1	.985
1982	—Toledo	Int.	OF	9	34	14	15	1	1	5	12	.441	15	4	0	1.000
1983	—Minnesota	Amer.	C-OF	120	374	46	114	22	4	8	43	.305	306	26	9	.974
1984	—Minnesota	Amer.	C	109	391	56	104	20	1	4	38	.266	376	34	8	.981
1985	—Minnesota‡	Amer.	C-OF	70	172	28	44	8	2	7	25	.256	66	4	1	.986
1986	—Detroit§	Amer.	1B-OF-C	35	86	6	22	7	0	0	4	.256	185	14	0	1.000
1986	—Nashville x	A. A.	OF-C	8	24	5	4	0	0	2	7	.167	17	2	0	1.000
1987	—Montreal y	Nat.	O-C-1-3	59	84	7	19	4	0	1	14	.226	33	3	0	1.000
1988	—Montreal z	Nat.	C-OF-3B	34	37	4	8	3	0	0	1	.216	25	1	0	1.000
American League Totals—6 Years				474	1457	185	390	78	13	28	158	.268	1140	85	22	.982
National League Totals—2 Years				93	121	11	27	7	0	1	15	.223	58	4	0	1.000
Major League Totals—8 Years				567	1578	196	417	85	13	29	173	.264	1198	89	22	.983

Selected by California Angels' organization in 2nd round of free-agent draft, June 6, 1978.
†Traded with Outfielder Ken Landreaux and Pitchers Paul Hartzell and Brad Havens to Minnesota Twins for First Baseman Rod Carew, February 3, 1979.
‡Traded to Detroit Tigers for Infielder Chris Pittaro and Outfielder Alex Sanchez, January 16, 1986.
§On disabled list, April 29 to August 10, 1986; included rehabilitation disability assignment to Nashville, May 28 to June 6, 1986.
xReleased, August 10, 1986; signed by Montreal Expos' organization, January 19, 1987.
yGranted free agency, November 9, 1987; signed by Indianapolis (Montreal Expos' organization), December 7, 1987.
zReleased, July 14, 1988.

ALL-STAR GAME RECORD

Member of American League All-Star Team in 1984; did not play.

JAMES GERHARD EPPARD

(Jim)

Born April 27, 1960, at South Bend, Ind.
Height, 6.02. Weight, 180.
Throws and bats lefthanded.
Attended Citrus College, Azusa, Calif., and University of California, Berkeley, Calif.

Tied for California League lead in grounding into double plays with 19 in 1985.
Led California League first basemen in total chances with 1,341 in 1985.

Year Club	League	Pos.	G.	AB.	R.	H.	2B.	3B.	HR.	RBI.	B.A.	PO.	A.	E.	F.A.
1982—Medford	N'west	*1B-OF	64	242	58	*91	13	2	1	41	*.376	459	*38	10	.980
1983—Modesto	Calif.	1B	134	488	68	138	18	4	4	45	.283	1086	74	10	*.991
1984—Albany	East.	OF-1B	118	417	58	130	14	6	0	51	.312	551	41	4	.993
1985—Modesto	Calif.	1B	141	531	97	*183	23	4	3	88	*.345	1204	*125	12	.991
1986—Tacoma†‡	P. C.	OF-1B	95	321	39	88	15	1	0	34	.274	204	11	2	.991
1987—Edmonton	P. C.	1B-OF	132	446	68	152	*33	3	3	94	*.341	947	85	11	.989
1987—California	Amer.	OF	8	9	2	3	0	0	0	0	.333	1	0	0	1.000
1988—Edmonton	P. C.	1B	41	141	18	37	6	1	0	16	.262	322	31	4	.989
1988—California	Amer.	OF-1B	56	113	7	32	3	1	0	14	.283	63	4	2	.971
Major League Totals—2 Years			64	122	9	35	3	1	0	14	.287	64	4	2	.971

Selected by Chicago Cubs' organization in 11th round of free-agent draft, January 8, 1980.
Selected by Oakland A's organization in 13th round of free-agent draft, June 7, 1982.
†On disabled list, April 11 to April 21, 1986.
‡Sold to California Angels' organization, January 12, 1987.

NICHOLAS ANDREW ESASKY

Name pronounced Ee-SASS-kee.

(Nick)

Born February 24, 1960, at Hialeah, Fla.
Height, 6.03. Weight, 215.
Throws and bats righthanded.

Major League stolen bases: 1983 (6), 1984 (1), 1985 (3), 1988 (7). Total—17.
Led Eastern League batters in strikeouts with 131 and game-winning RBIs with 14 in 1980.

Year Club	League	Pos.	G.	AB.	R.	H.	2B.	3B.	HR.	RBI.	B.A.	PO.	A.	E.	F.A.
1978—Billings	Pion.	3B	64	213	38	65	10	5	4	48	.305	*62	88	22	.872
1979—Tampa	Fla. St.	3B	124	439	52	118	16	3	10	66	.269	91	234	27	.923
1980—Waterbury	East.	3B	135	425	79	115	18	4	*30	79	.271	98	241	23	.936
1981—Indianapolis	A. A.	3B	121	423	55	112	22	4	17	62	.265	99	220	*37	.896
1982—Indianapolis	A. A.	3B	105	341	59	90	15	3	27	62	.264	77	150	21	*.915
1983—Indianapolis	A. A.	3B	49	158	33	44	5	0	14	37	.278	27	71	14	.875
1983—Cincinnati	Nat.	3B	85	302	41	80	10	5	12	46	.265	53	133	13	.935
1984—Cincinnati	Nat.	3B-1B	113	322	30	62	10	5	10	45	.193	220	137	18	.952
1985—Cincinnati	Nat.	3B-OF-1B	125	413	61	108	21	0	21	66	.262	169	106	8	.972
1986—Cincinnati†	Nat.	1B-OF-3B	102	330	35	76	17	2	12	41	.230	585	33	5	.992
1987—Nashville‡	A. A.	1B	13	52	13	23	6	0	5	18	.442	102	7	0	1.000
1987—Cincinnati	Nat.	1B-3B-OF	100	346	48	94	19	2	22	59	.272	773	41	6	.993
1988—Cincinnati§x	Nat.	1B	122	391	40	95	17	2	15	62	.243	982	52	6	.994
Major League Totals—6 Years			647	2104	255	515	94	16	92	319	.245	2782	502	56	.983

Selected by Cincinnati Reds' organization in 1st round (17th player selected) of free-agent draft, June 6, 1978.
†On disabled list, June 15 to July 17, 1986.
‡On Cincinnati disabled list, March 23 to May 19, 1987; included rehabilitation disability assignment to Nashville, May 5 to May 19, 1987.
§On disabled list, May 11 to June 3, 1988.
xTraded with Pitcher Rob Murphy to Boston Red Sox for First Baseman Todd Benzinger, Pitcher Jeff Sellers and a player to be named later, December 13, 1988.

ANGEL RUBEN ESCOBAR (RIVAS)

Born May 12, 1965, at La Sabana, Vargas, Venezuela.
Height, 6.00. Weight, 160.
Throws right and bats left and righthanded.

Led Texas League in sacrifice hits with 11 in 1986.
Led Pacific Coast League shortstops in total chances with 617 in 1987.
Led Midwest League shortstops in double plays with 71 in 1984.

Year Club	League	Pos.	G.	AB.	R.	H.	2B.	3B.	HR.	RBI.	B.A.	PO.	A.	E.	F.A.
1983—Great Falls	Pion.	SS-2B	44	109	15	23	3	1	0	6	.211	50	64	17	.870
1984—Clinton	Midw.	SS	99	311	47	70	16	2	2	25	.225	175	295	*48	.907
1985—Fresno	Calif.	SS-2B	109	386	62	97	13	2	1	34	.251	174	290	36	.928
1986—Shreveport	Texas	*SS-2B	131	439	58	121	14	4	2	46	.276	185	349	*33	.942
1987—Phoenix	P. C.	SS	130	434	68	115	13	8	2	50	.265	*200	*378	*39	.937
1988—Phoenix	P. C.	SS	77	270	32	54	6	6	1	29	.200	93	189	21	.931
1988—San Francisco	Nat.	3B-SS	3	3	1	1	0	0	0	0	.333	2	1	0	1.000
1988—Shreveport†	Texas	SS	22	73	10	14	2	1	0	6	.192	55	67	7	.946
Major League Totals—1 Year			3	3	1	1	0	0	0	0	.333	2	1	0	1.000

Signed as free agent by San Francisco Giants' organization, June 10, 1982.
†Traded to Montreal Expos for Catcher Wil Tejada, November 20, 1988.

ALVARO ALBERTO ESPINOZA (RAMIREZ)

Name pronounced Ess-pin-OH-zuh.

Born February 19, 1962, at Valencia, Carabobo, Venezuela.
Height, 6.00. Weight, 170.
Throws and bats righthanded.

Tied for International League lead in sacrifice hits with 16 in 1984.
Led International League shortstops in putouts with 159 in 1986.
Led California League shortstops in total chances with 660 in 1983.
Led Gulf Coast League shortstops in assists with 217, double plays with 33 and total chances with 356 in 1980.

Year	Club	League	Pos.	G.	AB.	R.	H.	2B.	3B.	HR.	RBI.	B.A.	PO.	A.	E.	F.A.
1979	Sarasota Astros	Gulf C.	SS-2B-3B	11	32	3	7	0	0	0	5	.219	18	27	1	.978
1980	Sara. Astros-O.†	Gulf C.	★SS-3B	59	200	24	43	5	0	0	14	.215	★114	219	★25	.930
1981						(Out of Organized Baseball)										
1982	Wis. Rapids	Midw.	SS-3B-1B	112	379	41	101	9	0	5	29	.266	237	241	33	.935
1983	Visalia	Calif.	SS	130	486	57	155	20	1	4	57	.319	★256	364	40	.939
1984	Toledo‡	Int.	SS	104	344	22	80	12	5	0	30	.233	157	293	19	.959
1984	Minnesota	Amer.	SS	1	0	0	0	0	0	0	0	.000	0	0	0	.000
1985	Toledo§	Int.	SS	82	266	24	61	11	0	1	33	.229	132	245	16	.959
1985	Minnesota	Amer.	SS	32	57	5	15	2	0	0	9	.263	25	69	5	.949
1986	Toledo	Int.	SS-2B	73	253	18	71	8	1	2	27	.281	170	205	12	.969
1986	Minnesota	Amer.	2B-SS	37	42	4	9	1	0	0	1	.214	23	52	4	.949
1987	Portland x	P. C.	SS-3B-1B	91	291	28	80	3	2	4	28	.275	158	236	20	.952
1988	Columbus	Int.	SS-2B-3B	119	435	42	107	10	5	2	30	.246	221	404	19	.970
1988	New York	Amer.	2B-SS	3	3	0	0	0	0	0	0	.000	5	2	0	1.000
Major League Totals—3 Years				72	102	9	24	3	0	0	10	.235	53	123	9	.951

Signed as free agent by Houston Astros' organization, October 30, 1978.
†Released, September 30, 1980; signed by Wisconsin Rapids (Minnesota Twins' organization), March 18, 1982.
‡On disabled list, June 7 to June 25, 1984.
§On disabled list, June 6 to July 2, 1985.
xGranted free agency, October 15, 1987; signed by Columbus (New York Yankees' organization), November 17, 1987.

CECIL EDWARD ESPY

Born January 20, 1963, at San Diego, Calif.
Height, 6.03. Weight, 195.
Throws right and bats left and righthanded.
Son of Cecil Espy, scout with St. Louis Cardinals since 1979.

Major League stolen bases: 1987 (2), 1988 (33). Total—35.
Led Florida State League in stolen bases with 74 in 1982.
Tied for Texas League lead in caught stealing with 17 in 1985.
Led Texas League shortstops in errors with 50 in 1985.
Led Texas League outfielders in total chances with 365 in 1984.

Year	Club	League	Pos.	G.	AB.	R.	H.	2B.	3B.	HR.	RBI.	B.A.	PO.	A.	E.	F.A.
1980	Sarasota W. Sox	Gulf C.	OF	58	212	33	58	7	3	0	26	.274	138	4	7	.953
1981	Appleton	Midw.	OF	72	273	37	55	2	2	1	19	.201	143	5	5	.967
1981	Sarasota W. Sox†	Gulf C.	OF	43	142	24	40	3	1	0	16	.282	54	1	4	.932
1982	Vero Beach	Fla. St.	OF	131	★523	★100	★166	14	7	1	34	.317	275	9	10	.966
1983	San Antonio	Texas	OF	133	★564	88	151	16	11	4	38	.268	258	12	10	.964
1983	Los Angeles	Nat.	OF	20	11	4	3	1	0	0	1	.273	11	0	0	1.000
1984	San Antonio	Texas	★O-2-S	★133	★535	99	146	19	8	8	60	.273	★348	16	5	.986
1985	San Antonio‡	Texas	SS-OF	124	461	64	129	24	3	5	49	.280	183	346	51	.912
1986	Hawaii§	P. C.	OF-2B-SS	106	384	49	101	19	3	4	38	.263	172	8	5	.973
1987	Oklahoma City	A. A.	OF-SS	118	443	76	134	18	6	1	37	.302	195	161	16	.957
1987	Texas	Amer.	OF	14	8	1	0	0	0	0	0	.000	8	1	0	1.000
1988	Texas x	Amer.	O-S-C-1-2	123	347	46	86	17	6	2	39	.248	200	11	7	.968
National League Totals—1 Year				20	11	4	3	1	0	0	1	.273	11	0	0	1.000
American League Totals—2 Years				137	355	47	86	17	6	2	39	.242	208	12	7	.969
Major League Totals—3 Years				157	366	51	89	18	6	2	40	.243	219	12	7	.971

Selected by Chicago White Sox' organization in 1st round (eighth player selected) of free-agent draft, June 3, 1980.
†Traded with Pitcher Burt Geiger to Los Angeles Dodgers' organization for Outfielder Rudy Law, March 30, 1982.
‡Traded with First Baseman Sid Bream to Pittsburgh Pirates, September 9, 1985, completing deal in which Los Angeles Dodgers acquired Third Baseman Bill Madlock for three players to be named later, R. J. Reynolds as partial completion of deal, September 3, 1985.
§Drafted by Texas Rangers, December 8, 1986.
xOn disabled list, May 3 to May 18, 1988.

DARRELL WAYNE EVANS

Born May 26, 1947, at Pasadena, Calif.
Height, 6.02. Weight, 205.
Throws right and bats lefthanded.
Attended Pasadena City College, Pasadena, Calif. and
California State University, Los Angeles, Calif.
Grandson of David Salazar, former minor league player.

Established National League records for most double plays, third baseman, (45), 1974; most games, consecutive, one or more bases on balls (15), April 9 through 27, 1976.
Tied modern National League record for most errors in inning by third baseman (3), April 11, 1980 (7th inning).

Major League stolen bases: 1971 (2), 1972 (4), 1973 (6), 1974 (4), 1975 (12), 1976 (9), 1977 (9), 1978 (4), 1979 (6), 1980 (17), 1981 (2), 1982 (5), 1983 (6), 1984 (2), 1986 (3), 1987 (6), 1988 (1). Total—98.

Hit three home runs in a game, June 15, 1983.

Led National League in bases on balls received with 124 in 1973 and 126 in 1974.

Led National League third basemen in putouts with 161 and assists with 381 in 1975.

Led National League third basemen in double plays with 45 in 1974 and 41 in 1975.

Led National League third basemen in total chances with 471 in 1973, 578 in 1974, 578 in 1975, 520 in 1978 and 528 in 1979.

Led International League third basemen in fielding percentage with .951 in 1970.

Named third baseman on THE SPORTING NEWS National League All-Star Team, 1973.

Named Player of the Year in Gulf Coast League, 1967.

Year Club	League	Pos.	G.	AB.	R.	H.	2B.	3B.	HR.	RBI.	B.A.	PO.	A.	E.	F.A.
1967—Peninsula	Carol.	3B	8	28	4	11	1	1	0	6	.393	6	13	2	.905
1967—Bradenton A's	Gulf C.	3B-SS	14	45	13	22	3	3	2	11	.489	25	30	2	.965
1967—Leesburg	Fla. St.	3B-SS	39	142	18	37	4	2	0	12	.261	49	81	11	.922
1968—Birmingham†	South.	3B-1B-2B	56	187	18	45	6	3	3	25	.241	103	101	10	.953
1969—Richmond	Int.	3B	59	211	43	76	12	4	7	45	.360	51	103	19	.890
1969—Shreveport	Texas	3B-SS-OF	24	79	14	22	5	4	2	14	.278	25	40	3	.956
1969—Atlanta	Nat.	3B	12	26	3	6	0	0	0	1	.231	4	7	1	.917
1970—Richmond	Int.	3B-1B-OF	120	447	92	134	20	7	20	83	.300	99	220	16	.952
1970—Atlanta	Nat.	3B	12	44	4	14	1	1	0	9	.318	6	26	2	.941
1971—Richmond	Int.	OF-3B	31	101	20	31	2	2	6	30	.307	59	11	1	.986
1971—Atlanta	Nat.	3B-OF	89	260	42	63	11	1	12	38	.242	77	138	14	.939
1972—Atlanta‡	Nat.	3B	125	418	67	106	12	0	19	71	.254	126	273	25	.941
1973—Atlanta	Nat.	3B-1B	161	595	114	167	25	8	41	104	.281	266	335	24	.962
1974—Atlanta	Nat.	3B	160	571	99	137	21	3	25	79	.240	★185	367	26	.955
1975—Atlanta	Nat.	★3B-1B	156	567	82	138	22	2	22	73	.243	164	382	★36	.938
1976—Atl.§-S.F.	Nat.	1B-3B	136	396	53	81	9	1	11	46	.205	978	110	10	.991
1977—San Francisco	Nat.	OF-1B-3B	144	461	64	117	18	3	17	72	.254	324	83	13	.969
1978—San Francisco x	Nat.	3B	159	547	82	133	24	2	20	78	243	★147	★348	★25	.952
1979—San Francisco	Nat.	3B	160	562	68	142	23	2	17	70	.253	★129	★369	★30	.943
1980—San Francisco	Nat.	3B-1B	154	556	69	147	23	0	20	78	.264	232	340	27	.955
1981—San Francisco	Nat.	3B-1B	102	357	51	92	13	4	12	48	.258	188	202	14	.965
1982—San Francisco	Nat.	3B-1B-SS	141	465	64	119	20	4	16	61	.256	471	233	21	.971
1983—San Francisco y	Nat.	1B-3B-SS	142	523	94	145	29	3	30	82	.277	1001	164	19	.984
1984—Detroit	Amer.	1B-3B	131	401	60	93	11	1	16	63	.232	331	62	2	.995
1985—Detroit	Amer.	1B-3B	151	505	81	125	17	0	★40	94	.248	831	125	20	.980
1986—Detroit z	Amer.	1B-3B	151	507	78	122	15	0	29	85	.241	809	109	2	.998
1987—Detroit	Amer.	1B-3B	150	499	90	128	20	0	34	99	.257	815	108	4	.996
1988—Detroit a	Amer.	1B	144	437	48	91	9	0	22	64	.208	509	58	4	.993
National League Totals—15 Years			1853	6348	956	1607	251	34	262	910	.253	4298	3377	287	.964
American League Totals—5 Years			727	2349	357	559	72	1	141	405	.238	3295	462	32	.992
Major League Totals—20 Years			2580	8697	1313	2166	323	35	403	1315	.249	7593	3839	319	.973

Selected by Chicago Cubs' organization in 8th round of free-agent draft, June 22, 1965.

Selected by New York Yankees' organization in secondary phase of free-agent draft, January 29, 1966.

Selected by Detroit Tigers' organization in 5th round of free-agent draft, June 6, 1966.

Selected by Philadelphia Phillies' organization in 3rd round of free-agent draft, January 28, 1967.

Selected by Kansas City A's organization in secondary phase of free-agent draft, June 7, 1967.

†Drafted by Atlanta Braves, December 2, 1968.

‡On military list, June 17 to July 3, 1972.

§Traded with Shortstop Marty Perez to San Francisco Giants for First Baseman-Outfielder Willie Montanez, Shortstop Craig Robinson, Infielder Mike Eden and Outfielder Jake Brown, June 13, 1976.

xGranted free agency, November 2, 1978; re-signed by Giants, December 5, 1978.

yGranted free agency, November 7, 1983; signed by Detroit Tigers, December 17, 1983.

zReleased, December 20, 1986; re-signed by Tigers, February 24, 1987.

aGranted free agency, November 4, 1988; signed by Richmond (Atlanta Braves' organization), December 23, 1988.

CHAMPIONSHIP SERIES RECORD

Year Club	League	Pos.	G.	AB.	R.	H.	2B.	3B.	HR.	RBI.	B.A.	PO.	A.	E.	F.A.
1984—Detroit	Amer.	1B-3B	3	10	1	3	1	0	0	1	.300	22	4	0	1.000
1987—Detroit	Amer.	1B-3B	5	17	0	5	0	0	0	0	.294	43	4	3	.940
Championship Series Totals—2 Years			8	27	1	8	1	0	0	1	.296	65	8	3	.961

WORLD SERIES RECORD

Year Club	League	Pos.	G.	AB.	R.	H.	2B.	3B.	HR.	RBI.	B.A.	PO.	A.	E.	F.A.
1984—Detroit	Amer.	1B-3B	5	15	1	1	0	0	0	1	.067	18	5	0	1.000

ALL-STAR GAME RECORD

Year League	Pos.	AB.	R.	H.	2B.	3B.	HR.	RBI.	B.A.	PO.	A.	E.	F.A.
1973—National	PH	0	0	0	0	0	0	0	.000	0	0	0	.000
1983—National	1B	1	0	0	0	0	0	0	.000	2	1	0	1.000
All-Star Game Totals—2 Years		1	0	0	0	0	0	0	.000	2	1	0	1.000

DWIGHT MICHAEL EVANS

Born November 3, 1951, at Santa Monica, Calif.
Height, 6.03. Weight, 208.
Throws and bats righthanded.

Major League stolen bases: 1973 (5), 1974 (4), 1975 (3), 1976 (6), 1977 (4), 1978 (8), 1979 (6), 1980 (3), 1981 (3), 1982 (3), 1983 (3), 1984 (3), 1985 (7), 1986 (3), 1987 (4), 1988 (5). Total—70.

Hit for the cycle, June 28, 1984.

Led American League in bases on balls received with 85 in 1981, 114 in 1985 and tied for lead with 106 in 1987.

Led American League in total bases with 215 in 1981.

Led American League outfielders in double plays with 8 in 1975 and 7 in 1980.

Tied for American League lead in errors by first basemen with 12 in 1987.

Led Western Carolinas League in sacrifice flies with 8 in 1970.

Tied for Carolina League lead in double plays by outfielders with 3 in 1971.

Named outfielder on THE SPORTING NEWS American League All-Star Team, 1982, 1984 and 1987.

Named outfielder on THE SPORTING NEWS American League All-Star fielding team, 1976, 1978, 1979 and 1981 through 1985.

Named outfielder on THE SPORTING NEWS American League Silver Slugger team, 1981 and 1987.

Named International League Most Valuable Player, 1972.

Year Club	League	Pos.	G.	AB.	R.	H.	2B.	3B.	HR.	RBI.	B.A.	PO.	A.	E.	F.A.
1969—Jamestown	NYP	OF-3B	34	100	13	28	3	2	1	12	.280	44	10	3	.947
1970—Greenville	W. Car.	OF-3B	108	355	69	98	14	★11	7	68	.276	130	11	7	.953
1971—Winston-Salem	Carol.	OF-1B	118	402	63	115	20	4	12	63	.286	219	17	10	.959
1972—Louisville	Int.	OF	●144	496	90	149	23	8	17	★95	.300	270	12	6	.979
1972—Boston	Amer.	OF	18	57	2	15	3	1	1	6	.263	25	3	0	1.000
1973—Boston	Amer.	OF	119	282	46	63	13	1	10	32	.223	178	4	1	.995
1974—Boston	Amer.	OF	133	463	60	130	19	8	10	70	.281	294	8	3	.990
1975—Boston	Amer.	OF	128	412	61	113	24	6	13	56	.274	281	15	4	.987
1976—Boston	Amer.	OF	146	501	61	121	34	5	17	62	.242	324	15	2	★.994
1977—Boston†	Amer.	OF	73	230	39	66	9	2	14	36	.287	126	2	1	.992
1978—Boston	Amer.	OF	147	497	75	123	24	2	24	63	.247	305	14	6	.982
1979—Boston	Amer.	OF	152	489	69	134	24	1	21	58	.274	307	15	4	.988
1980—Boston	Amer.	OF	148	463	72	123	37	5	18	60	.266	268	11	5	.982
1981—Boston	Amer.	OF	108	412	84	122	19	4	●22	71	.296	259	9	2	.993
1982—Boston	Amer.	OF	●162	609	122	178	37	7	32	98	.292	346	9	10	.973
1983—Boston‡	Amer.	OF	126	470	74	112	19	4	22	58	.238	222	6	3	.987
1984—Boston	Amer.	OF	●162	630	★121	186	37	8	32	104	.295	311	7	2	.994
1985—Boston	Amer.	OF	159	617	110	162	29	1	29	78	.263	291	9	3	.990
1986—Boston	Amer.	OF	152	529	86	137	33	2	26	97	.259	280	10	5	.983
1987—Boston	Amer.	1B-OF	154	541	109	165	37	2	34	123	.305	753	46	13	.984
1988—Boston	Amer.	OF-1B	149	559	96	164	31	7	21	111	.293	611	34	9	.986
Major League Totals—17 Years			2236	7761	1287	2114	429	66	346	1183	.272	5181	217	73	.987

Selected by Boston Red Sox' organization in 5th round of free-agent draft, June 5, 1969.

†On disabled list, June 21 to July 8 and August 25 to September 21, 1977.

‡On disabled list, August 13 to September 1, 1983.

CHAMPIONSHIP SERIES RECORD

Year Club	League	Pos.	G.	AB.	R.	H.	2B.	3B.	HR.	RBI.	B.A.	PO.	A.	E.	F.A.
1975—Boston	Amer.	OF	3	10	1	1	1	0	0	0	.100	7	0	0	1.000
1986—Boston	Amer.	OF	7	28	2	6	1	0	1	4	.214	11	0	0	1.000
1988—Boston	Amer.	OF	4	12	1	2	1	0	0	1	.167	11	0	0	1.000
Championship Series Totals—3 Years			14	50	4	9	3	0	1	5	.180	29	0	0	1.000

WORLD SERIES RECORD

Tied World Series record for highest fielding average by outfielder, seven-game Series (1.000 with 24 chances), 1975.

Year Club	League	Pos.	G.	AB.	R.	H.	2B.	3B.	HR.	RBI.	B.A.	PO.	A.	E.	F.A.
1975—Boston	Amer.	OF	7	24	3	7	1	1	1	5	.292	23	1	0	1.000
1986—Boston	Amer.	OF	7	26	4	8	2	0	2	9	.308	16	1	1	.944
World Series Totals—2 Years			14	50	7	15	3	1	3	14	.300	39	2	1	.976

ALL-STAR GAME RECORD

Year League	Pos.	AB.	R.	H.	2B.	3B.	HR.	RBI.	B.A.	PO.	A.	E.	F.A.
1978—American	OF	1	0	0	0	0	0	0	.000	3	0	0	1.000
1981—American	PH-OF	2	1	1	0	0	0	0	.500	2	0	0	1.000
1987—American	OF	2	0	2	0	0	0	0	1.000	2	0	0	1.000
All-Star Game Totals—3 Years		5	1	3	0	0	0	0	.600	7	0	0	1.000

TROY MARK EVERS

Born February 4, 1964, at Kaukauna, Wis.
Height, 6.04. Weight, 205.
Throws and bats righthanded.
Attended Iowa State University, Ames, Ia.

Year Club	League	G.	IP.	W.	L.	Pct.	H.	R.	ER.	SO.	BB.	ERA.
1985—Oneonta	NYP	14	99⅓	●10	1	.909	69	21	13	85	25	★1.18
1986—Fort Lauderdale†‡	Florida St.	1	2⅔	1	0	1.000	2	0	0	1	0	0.00
1987—Fort Lauderdale	Florida St.	24	147⅔	13	5	.722	126	61	51	60	52	3.11

Selected by New York Mets' organization in 10th round of free-agent draft, June 7, 1982.

Selected by New York Yankees' organization in 2nd round of free-agent draft, June 3, 1985.

†On Albany disabled list, April 11 to July 3, 1986.

‡On disabled list, July 9, 1986, through remainder of season.

STEVEN MICHAEL FARR
(Steve)

Born December 12, 1956, at Cheverly, Md.
Height, 5.11. Weight, 200.
Throws and bats righthanded.
Attended American University, Washington, D. C.,
and Charles County Community College, La Plata, Md.

Major League saves: 1984 (1), 1985 (1), 1986 (8), 1987 (1), 1988 (20). Total—31.

Year Club	League	G.	IP.	W.	L.	Pct.	H.	R.	ER.	SO.	BB.	ERA.
1977—Niagara Falls	NYP	10	52	1	5	.167	53	30	23	43	30	3.98
1978—Charleston	W. Carol.	21	77	5	3	.625	72	45	36	54	63	4.21
1978—Salem	Ap'lachian	2	16	2	0	1.000	13	2	1	12	1	0.56
1979—Salem†	Carolina	26	119	3	10	.231	138	81	66	105	47	4.99
1980—Buffalo	Eastern	23	161	11	6	.647	158	84	71	71	64	3.97
1980—Portland	P. Coast	2	7	0	1	.000	11	9	8	0	2	10.29
1981—Buffalo	Eastern	29	106	8	3	.727	102	50	44	82	48	3.74
1981—Portland	P. Coast	4	23	0	3	.000	39	28	20	19	12	7.83
1982—Buffalo‡§	Eastern	25	76⅓	5	8	.385	72	40	34	84	38	4.01
1983—Buffalo	Eastern	18	112	13	1	*.929	88	28	20	108	50	*1.61
1984—Maine	Int'national	6	45	4	0	1.000	37	14	13	40	8	2.60
1984—Cleveland xy	American	31	116	3	11	.214	106	61	59	83	46	4.58
1985—Omaha	Am. Assoc.	17	133⅔	10	4	.714	105	36	30	98	41	*2.02
1985—Kansas City	American	16	37⅔	2	1	.667	34	15	13	36	20	3.11
1986—Kansas City	American	56	109⅓	8	4	.667	90	39	38	83	39	3.13
1987—Kansas City	American	47	91	4	3	.571	97	47	42	88	44	4.15
1987—Omaha	Am. Assoc.	8	12⅔	0	0	.000	6	3	2	15	6	1.42
1988—Kansas City	American	62	82⅔	5	4	.556	74	25	23	72	30	2.50
Major League Totals—5 Years		212	436⅔	22	23	.489	401	187	175	362	179	3.61

Signed as a free agent by Pittsburgh Pirates' organization, December 13, 1976.
†On disabled list, June 6 to June 22, 1979.
‡On Lynn suspended list, April 16, 1983; then transferred to restricted list, April 27 to June 8, 1983.
§Traded to Buffalo (Cleveland Indians' organization) for Catcher John Malkin, June 8, 1983.
xOn disabled list, June 20 to July 5, 1984.
yReleased, March 31, 1985; signed by Kansas City Royals' organization, May 9, 1985.

CHAMPIONSHIP SERIES RECORD

Year Club	League	G.	IP.	W.	L.	Pct.	H.	R.	ER.	SO.	BB.	ERA.
1985—Kansas City	American	2	6⅓	1	0	1.000	4	1	1	3	1	1.42

JOHN EDWARD FARRELL

Born August 4, 1962, at Monmouth Park, N. J.
Height, 6.04. Weight, 210.
Throws and bats righthanded.
Attended Oklahoma State University, Stillwater, Okla.

Led American Association in home runs allowed with 26 in 1987.
Tied for Eastern League lead in shutouts with 3 and hit batsmen with 10 in 1986.

Year Club	League	G.	IP.	W.	L.	Pct.	H.	R.	ER.	SO.	BB.	ERA.
1984—Waterloo	Midwest	9	43⅓	0	5	.000	59	34	31	29	33	6.44
1984—Maine	Int'national	5	26⅓	2	1	.667	20	11	11	12	20	3.76
1985—Waterbury	Eastern	25	149	7	13	.350	161	*106	86	75	76	5.19
1986—Waterbury	Eastern	26	173⅓	9	10	.474	158	82	59	104	54	3.06
1987—Buffalo	Am. Assoc.	25	156	6	12	.333	155	109	101	91	64	5.83
1987—Cleveland	American	10	69	5	1	.833	68	29	26	28	22	3.39
1988—Cleveland†	American	31	210⅓	14	10	.583	216	106	99	92	67	4.24
Major League Totals—2 Years		41	279⅓	19	11	.633	284	135	125	120	89	4.03

Selected by Oakland A's organization in 9th round of free-agent draft, June 3, 1980.
Selected by Cleveland Indians' organization in 16th round of free-agent draft, June 6, 1983.
Selected by Cleveland Indians' organization in 2nd round of free-agent draft, June 4, 1984.
†On disabled list, August 28 to September 20, 1988.

JEFFREY JOSEPH FASSERO
(Jeff)

Born January 5, 1963, at Springfield, Ill.
Height, 6.01. Weight, 180.
Throws and bats lefthanded.
Attended Lincoln Land Community College, Springfield, Ill.,
and University of Mississippi, Oxford, Miss.

Led Texas League in intentional bases on balls issued with 13 in 1988.
Tied for Florida State League lead in games started by pitchers with 26 in 1986.

Year Club	League	G.	IP.	W.	L.	Pct.	H.	R.	ER.	SO.	BB.	ERA.
1984—Johnson City	Ap'lachian	13	66⅔	4	7	.364	65	42	34	59	39	4.59
1985—Springfield	Midwest	29	119	4	8	.333	125	78	53	65	45	4.01
1986—St. Petersburg	Florida St.	26	*176	13	7	.650	156	63	48	112	56	2.45
1987—Arkansas	Texas	28	151⅓	10	7	.588	168	90	69	118	67	4.10
1988—Arkansas	Texas	*70	78	5	5	.500	97	48	31	72	41	3.58

Selected by St. Louis Cardinals' organization in 22nd round of free-agent draft, June 4, 1984.

MICHAEL OTIS FELDER
(Mike)

Born November 18, 1962, at Richmond, Calif.
Height, 5.08. Weight, 160.
Throws right and bats left and righthanded.
Attended Contra Costa College, San Pablo, Calif.

Major League stolen bases: 1985 (4), 1986 (16), 1987 (34), 1988 (8). Total—62.
Led Pacific Coast League in stolen bases with 61 in 1985.
Led Texas League in sacrifice flies with 9 in 1984.
Led Texas League in stolen bases with 71 in 1983 and 58 in 1984.
Led California League in stolen bases with 92 in 1982.
Led Texas League outfielders in putouts with 332, total chances with 363 and tied for lead in assists with 18 in 1983.

Year Club	League	Pos.	G.	AB.	R.	H.	2B.	3B.	HR.	RBI.	B.A.	PO.	A.	E.	F.A.
1981—Stockton	Calif.	2B-OF	91	338	66	91	8	1	3	30	.269	172	162	13	.963
1982—Stockton	Calif.	OF	137	524	102	138	18	11	7	47	.263	314	9	10	.970
1983—El Paso	Texas	•OF-2B	133	554	108	156	23	10	9	78	.282	334	24	•13	.965
1984—El Paso†	Texas	OF	122	496	98	144	19	2	9	72	.290	321	13	6	.982
1985—Vancouver	P. C.	OF-2B	137	563	91	177	16	11	2	43	.314	294	15	4	.987
1985—Milwaukee	Amer.	OF	15	56	8	11	1	0	0	0	.196	32	1	0	1.000
1986—Milwaukee‡	Amer.	OF	44	155	24	37	2	4	1	13	.239	98	0	0	1.000
1986—El Paso	Texas	OF	8	31	10	14	3	0	0	2	.452	14	0	0	1.000
1986—Vancouver	P. C.	OF	39	153	21	40	3	4	1	15	.261	83	4	4	.956
1987—Milwaukee	Amer.	OF-2B	108	289	48	77	5	7	2	31	.266	190	10	5	.976
1987—Denver	A. A.	OF-2B	27	113	26	41	6	2	2	20	.363	75	3	1	.987
1988—Milwaukee§	Amer.	OF-2B	50	81	14	14	1	0	0	5	.173	40	1	1	.976
1988—Denver	A. A.	OF	20	78	10	21	4	1	0	5	.269	55	1	1	.982
Major League Totals—4 Years			217	581	94	139	9	11	3	49	.239	360	12	6	.984

Selected by Milwaukee Brewers' organization in 3rd round of free-agent draft, January 13, 1981.
†On disabled list, April 15 to April 26, 1984.
‡On disabled list, May 3 to June 5, 1986; included rehabilitation disability assignment to El Paso, May 23 to June 5, 1986.
§On disabled list, May 31 to August 2, 1988; included rehabilitation disability assignment to Denver, June 24 to July 1 and July 15 to July 28, 1988.

FELIX JOSE FERMIN

Born October 9, 1963, at Mao, Valverde, D. R.
Height, 5.11 Weight, 170.
Throws and bats righthanded.

Major League stolen bases: 1988 (3).
Led Eastern League shortstops in fielding percentage with .968 in 1987.
Led Eastern League shortstops in total chances with 661 in 1985.
Tied for New York-Pennsylvania League lead in double plays by shortstops with 38 in 1983.

Year Club	League	Pos.	G.	AB.	R.	H.	2B.	3B.	HR.	RBI.	B.A.	PO.	A.	E.	F.A.
1983—Watertown	NYP	SS	67	234	27	46	6	1	0	14	.197	94	223	30	.914
1983—Brandenton Pir.	Gulf C.	SS	1	4	1	1	0	0	0	1	.250	1	4	0	1.000
1984—Prince William	Carol.	SS	119	382	34	94	13	1	0	41	.246	181	376	23	★.960
1985—Nashua	East.	★SS-2B	137	443	32	100	10	2	0	27	.226	★251	387	24	★.964
1986—Hawaii	P.C.	SS-2B	39	125	13	32	5	0	0	9	.256	60	99	7	.958
1986—Prince William	Carol.	SS	84	322	58	90	10	1	0	26	.280	158	205	19	.950
1987—Harrisburg	East.	SS-2B	100	399	62	107	9	5	0	35	.268	177	288	15	.969
1987—Pittsburgh†	Nat.	SS	23	68	6	17	0	0	0	4	.250	36	62	2	.980
1988—Buffalo	A. A.	SS	87	352	38	92	11	1	0	31	.261	131	268	10	.976
1988—Pittsburgh	Nat.	SS	43	87	9	24	0	2	0	2	.276	51	76	6	.955
Major League Totals—2 Years			66	155	15	41	0	2	0	6	.265	87	138	8	.966

Signed as free agent by Pittsburgh Pirates' organization, June 11, 1983.
†On disabled list, July 19 to August 24, 1987; included rehabilitation disability assignment to Harrisburg, August 12 to August 24, 1987.

CHARLES SIDNEY FERNANDEZ
(Sid)

Born October 12, 1962, at Honolulu, Haw.
Height, 6.01. Weight, 230.
Throws and bats lefthanded.

Pitched 1-0 no-hit victory against Fort Lauderdale, June 8, 1982.
Pitched 5-0 no-hit victory against Winter Haven, April 24, 1982.
Major League saves: 1986 (1).
Named Texas League Pitcher of the Year, 1983.

Year Club	League	G.	IP.	W.	L.	Pct.	H.	R.	ER.	SO.	BB.	ERA.
1981—Lethbridge	Pioneer	11	76	5	1	.833	43	21	13	★128	31	★1.54
1982—Vero Beach	Florida St.	12	84⅔	8	1	.889	38	19	18	★137	38	1.91
1982—Albuquerque	P. Coast	13	88	6	5	.545	76	54	53	86	52	5.42
1983—San Antonio	Texas	24	153	•13	4	.765	111	61	48	★209	96	★2.82
1983—Los Angeles†	National	2	6	0	1	.000	7	4	4	9	7	6.00
1984—Tidewater	Int'national	17	105⅔	6	5	.545	69	39	30	123	63	2.56

Year	Club	League	G.	IP.	W.	L.	Pct.	H.	R.	ER.	SO.	BB.	ERA.
1984	New York	National	15	90	6	6	.500	74	40	35	62	34	3.50
1985	Tidewater	Int'national	5	35⅓	4	1	.800	17	8	8	42	21	2.04
1985	New York	National	26	170⅓	9	9	.500	108	56	53	180	80	2.80
1986	New York	National	32	204⅓	16	6	.727	161	82	80	200	91	3.52
1987	New York‡	National	28	156	12	8	.600	130	75	66	134	67	3.81
1988	New York	National	31	187	12	10	.545	127	69	63	189	70	3.03
Major League Totals—6 Years			134	813⅔	55	40	.579	607	326	301	774	349	3.33

Selected by Los Angeles Dodgers' organization in 3rd round of free-agent draft, June 8, 1981.
†Traded with Infielder Ross Jones to New York Mets for Pitcher Carlos Diaz and a player to be named later, December 8, 1983; Los Angeles Dodgers acquired Infielder Bob Bailor to complete deal, December 12, 1983.
‡On disabled list, August 4 to August 22, 1987.

CHAMPIONSHIP SERIES RECORD

Year	Club	League	G.	IP.	W.	L.	Pct.	H.	R.	ER.	SO.	BB.	ERA.
1986	New York	National	1	6	0	1	.000	3	3	3	5	1	4.50
1988	New York	National	1	4	0	1	.000	7	6	6	5	1	13.50
Championship Series Totals—2 Years			2	10	0	2	.000	10	9	9	10	2	8.10

WORLD SERIES RECORD

Year	Club	League	G.	IP.	W.	L.	Pct.	H.	R.	ER.	SO.	BB.	ERA.
1986	New York	National	3	6⅔	0	0	.000	6	1	1	10	1	1.35

ALL-STAR GAME RECORD

Year	League	IP.	W.	L.	Pct.	H.	R.	ER.	SO.	BB.	ERA.
1986	National	1	0	0	.000	0	0	0	3	2	0.00
1987	National	1	0	0	.000	0	0	0	1	1	0.00
All-Star Game Totals—2 Years		2	0	0	.000	0	0	0	4	3	0.00

OCTAVIO ANTONIO FERNANDEZ (CASTRO)
(Tony)

Born June 30, 1962, at San Pedro de Macoris, D. R.
Height, 6.02. Weight, 175.
Throws right and bats right and lefthanded.

Established American League record for most games by shortstop, season (163), 1986.
Tied American League record for most games by switch-hitter, season (163), 1986.
Major League stolen bases: 1984 (5), 1985 (13), 1986 (25), 1987 (32), 1988 (15). Total—90.
Led American League shortstops in total chances with 791 in 1985.
Led International League shortstops in double plays with 87 in 1983.
Named shortstop on THE SPORTING NEWS American League All-Star Team, 1986.
Named shortstop on THE SPORTING NEWS American League All-Star fielding team, 1986 through 1988.

Year	Club	League	Pos.	G.	AB.	R.	H.	2B.	3B.	HR.	RBI.	B.A.	PO.	A.	E.	F.A.
1980	Kinston	Carol.	SS	62	187	28	52	6	2	0	12	.278	93	205	28	.914
1981	Kinston	Carol.	SS	75	280	57	89	10	6	1	13	.318	121	227	19	.948
1981	Syracuse†	Int.	SS	31	115	13	32	6	2	1	9	.278	69	80	3	.980
1982	Syracuse	Int.	SS	134	523	78	158	21	6	4	56	.302	*246	364	23	*.964
1983	Syracuse	Int.	SS	117	437	65	131	18	6	5	38	.300	*211	361	26	.957
1983	Toronto	Amer.	SS	15	34	5	9	1	1	0	2	.265	16	17	0	1.000
1984	Syracuse	Int.	SS	26	94	12	24	1	0	0	6	.255	46	72	5	.959
1984	Toronto	Amer.	SS-3B	88	233	29	63	5	3	3	19	.269	119	195	9	.972
1985	Toronto	Amer.	SS	161	564	71	163	31	10	2	51	.289	283	*478	30	.962
1986	Toronto	Amer.	SS	*163	*687	91	213	33	9	10	65	.310	*294	445	13	*.983
1987	Toronto	Amer.	SS	146	578	90	186	29	8	5	67	.322	*270	396	14	.979
1988	Toronto	Amer.	SS	154	648	76	186	41	4	5	70	.287	247	470	14	.981
Major League Totals—6 Years				727	2744	362	820	140	35	25	274	.299	1229	2001	80	.976

Signed as free agent by Toronto Blue Jays' organization, April 24, 1979.
†On disabled list, August 10 to August 27, 1981.

CHAMPIONSHIP SERIES RECORD

Year	Club	League	Pos.	G.	AB.	R.	H.	2B.	3B.	HR.	RBI.	B.A.	PO.	A.	E.	F.A.
1985	Toronto	Amer.	SS	7	24	2	8	2	0	0	2	.333	11	15	2	.929

ALL-STAR GAME RECORD

Year	League	Pos.	AB.	R.	H.	2B.	3B.	HR.	RBI.	B.A.	PO.	A.	E.	F.A.
1986	American	SS	0	0	0	0	0	0	0	.000	0	0	0	.000
1987	American	SS	2	0	0	0	0	0	0	.000	1	3	0	1.000
All-Star Game Totals—2 Years			2	0	0	0	0	0	0	.000	1	3	0	1.000

—DID YOU KNOW—

That the Chicago White Sox stopped both the Milwaukee Brewers' 13-game season-opening winning streak in 1987 and the Baltimore Orioles' 21-game season-opening losing streak in 1988?

MICHAEL LEE FETTERS
(Mike)

Born December 19, 1964, at Van Nuys, Calif.
Height, 6.04. Weight, 200.
Throws and bats righthanded.
Attended Pepperdine University, Malibu, Calif.

Year Club	League	G.	IP.	W.	L.	Pct.	H.	R.	ER.	SO.	BB.	ERA.
1986—Salem	Northwest	12	72	4	2	.667	60	39	27	72	51	3.38
1987—Palm Springs	California	19	116	9	7	.563	106	62	46	105	73	3.57
1988—Midland	Texas	20	114	8	8	.500	116	78	75	101	67	5.92
1988—Edmonton	P. Coast	2	14	2	0	1.000	8	3	3	11	10	1.93

Selected by Los Angeles Dodgers' organization in 22nd round of free-agent draft, June 6, 1983.
Selected by California Angels' organization in 1st round (compensation selection) of free-agent draft, June 2, 1986.

CECIL GRANT FIELDER

Born September 21, 1963, at Los Angeles, Calif.
Height, 6.03. Weight, 220.
Throws and bats righthanded.
Attended University of Nevada, Las Vegas, Nev.

Led Pioneer League in total bases with 176 and being hit by pitch with 8 in 1982.

Year Club	League	Pos.	G.	AB.	R.	H.	2B.	3B.	HR.	RBI.	B.A.	PO.	A.	E.	F.A.
1982—Butte†	Pion.	1B	69	273	73	88	*28	0	*20	68	.322	247	18	4	.985
1983—Florence	S. Atl.	1B	140	500	81	156	28	2	16	94	.312	957	64	16	.985
1984—Kinston	Carol.	1B	61	222	42	63	12	1	19	49	.284	533	24	9	.984
1984—Knoxville	South.	1B	64	236	33	60	12	2	9	44	.254	173	10	4	.979
1985—Knoxville	South.	1B	96	361	52	106	26	2	18	81	.294	444	26	6	.987
1985—Toronto	Amer.	1B	30	74	6	23	4	0	4	16	.311	171	17	4	.979
1986—Toronto	Amer.	1B-3B-OF	34	83	7	13	2	0	4	13	.157	37	4	1	.976
1986—Syracuse	Int.	OF-1B	88	325	47	91	13	3	18	68	.280	117	5	1	.992
1987—Toronto	Amer.	1B-3B	82	175	30	47	7	1	14	32	.269	98	6	0	1.000
1988—Toronto‡	Amer.	1B-3B-2B	74	174	24	40	6	1	9	23	.230	101	12	1	.991
Major League Totals—4 Years			220	506	67	123	19	2	31	84	.243	407	39	6	.987

Selected by Baltimore Orioles' organization in 31st round of free-agent draft, June 8, 1981.
Selected by Kansas City Royals' organization in secondary phase of free-agent draft, June 7, 1982.
†Traded to Toronto Blue Jays' organization for Outfielder Leon Roberts, February 4, 1983.
‡Sold to Hanshin Tigers of Japanese Baseball League, December 22, 1988.

CHAMPIONSHIP SERIES RECORD

Year Club	League	Pos.	G.	AB.	R.	H.	2B.	3B.	HR.	RBI.	B.A.	PO.	A.	E.	F.A.
1985—Toronto	Amer.	PH	3	3	0	1	1	0	0	0	.333	0	0	0	.000

BRUCE ALAN FIELDS

Born October 6, 1960, at Cleveland, O.
Height, 6.00. Weight, 185.
Throws right and bats lefthanded.
Attended Lansing Community College, Lansing, Mich.

Major League stolen bases: 1986 (1).

Year Club	League	Pos.	G.	AB.	R.	H.	2B.	3B.	HR.	RBI.	B.A.	PO.	A.	E.	F.A.
1978—Bristol	Appal.	OF-3B	46	159	15	32	6	2	0	11	.201	77	4	3	.964
1979—Lakeland	Fla. St.	OF	70	220	30	52	4	2	0	17	.236	120	2	3	.976
1979—Bristol	Appal.	OF-2B	41	138	23	32	4	1	1	7	.232	81	5	2	.977
1980—Lakeland	Fla. St.	OF	53	162	22	37	5	2	1	15	.228	113	1	4	.966
1980—Macon	S. Atl.	OF	67	240	40	71	7	1	2	27	.296	118	2	2	.984
1981—Lakeland	Fla. St.	OF	103	377	54	112	14	3	1	37	.297	225	11	4	*.983
1982—Birmingham	South.	OF	43	162	26	37	3	2	0	14	.228	102	0	6	.944
1982—Macon†	S. Atl.	OF	80	312	61	105	13	3	6	38	.337	162	4	3	.982
1983—San Jose	Calif.	OF	123	450	80	123	21	6	2	45	.273	234	6	7	.972
1984—Birmingham	South.	OF	93	307	49	92	11	3	4	38	.300	169	8	4	.978
1985—Birmingham‡	South.	OF	114	421	59	136	24	4	2	41	*.323	228	10	5	.979
1986—Nashville	A. A.	OF	116	383	57	141	31	5	1	53	*.368	177	10	4	.979
1986—Detroit	Amer.	OF	16	43	4	12	1	1	0	6	.279	25	0	1	.962
1987—Toledo§	Int.	OF	123	446	75	136	32	4	3	51	.305	194	8	5	.976
1988—Seattle	Amer.	OF	39	67	8	18	5	0	1	5	.269	23	0	0	1.000
1988—Calgary	P. C.	OF	42	168	31	54	6	1	4	19	.321	73	2	1	.987
Major League Totals—2 Years			55	110	12	30	6	1	1	11	.273	48	0	1	.980

Selected by Detroit Tigers' organization in 7th round of free-agent draft, June 6, 1978.
†Loaned to San Jose (Baltimore Orioles' organization), April 7, 1983; returned, September 8, 1983.
‡On disabled list, April 12 to April 22, 1985.
§Traded to Seattle Mariners for Pitcher Stan Clarke, October 5, 1987.

—DID YOU KNOW—

That Royals catcher Bob Boone, at age 40, compiled the highest batting average of his 17-year major league career in 1988 when he hit .295?

THOMAS CARSON FILER III
(Tom)

Born December 1, 1956, at Philadelphia, Pa.
Height, 6.01. Weight, 198.
Throws and bats righthanded.
Received bachelor of science degree in marketing from
La Salle College, Philadelphia, Pa., in 1978.

Tied for American Association lead in wild pitches with 11 in 1981.

Year Club	League	G.	IP.	W.	L.	Pct.	H.	R.	ER.	SO.	BB.	ERA.
1978—Oneonta	NYP	9	43	2	3	.400	30	14	8	34	14	1.67
1979—West Haven	Eastern	24	154	12	8	.600	132	73	62	80	53	3.62
1980—Nashville†	Southern	27	187	13	9	.591	168	94	61	112	86	2.94
1981—Columbus‡	Int'national	1	3	0	1	.000	6	5	5	3	4	15.00
1981—Iowa	Am. Assoc.	21	109	4	9	.308	123	64	58	61	57	4.79
1982—Iowa	Am. Assoc.	17	92⅓	6	7	.462	109	74	69	51	31	6.73
1982—Chicago	National	8	40⅔	1	2	.333	50	25	25	15	18	5.53
1983—Iowa	Am. Assoc.	27	108	5	6	.455	128	56	50	56	44	4.17
1984—Iowa §x	Am. Assoc.	26	123⅓	9	7	.563	149	86	67	80	48	4.89
1985—Syracuse y	Int'national	12	78⅓	7	2	.778	67	24	22	31	22	2.53
1985—Toronto z	American	11	48⅔	7	0	1.000	38	21	21	24	18	3.88
1986—Toronto a	American					(Did not play)						
1987—Syracuse	Int'national	8	24⅔	1	0	1.000	23	6	4	9	6	1.46
1987—Knoxville	Southern	6	20⅔	2	0	1.000	13	2	2	14	4	0.87
1987—Dunedin b	Florida St.	6	23	0	0	.000	20	5	2	13	0	0.78
1988—Denver	Am. Assoc.	8	55⅔	4	2	.667	40	14	13	34	9	2.10
1988—Milwaukee	American	19	101⅔	5	8	.385	108	54	50	39	33	4.43
National League Totals—1 Year		8	40⅔	1	2	.333	50	25	25	15	18	5.53
American League Totals—2 Years		30	150⅓	12	8	.600	146	75	71	63	51	4.25
Major League Totals—3 Years		38	191	13	10	.565	196	100	96	78	69	4.52

Signed as free agent by New York Yankees' organization, June 28, 1978.
†Drafted by Oakland A's, December 8, 1980; returned, April 9, 1981.
‡Traded with cash to Chicago Cubs' organization for Catcher Barry Foote, April 27, 1981.
§On disabled list, April 20 to May 12 and August 11 to August 22, 1984.
xGranted free agency, October 15, 1984; signed by Syracuse (Toronto Blue Jays' organization), November 21, 1984.
yOn disabled list, April 24 to May 4 and May 16 to May 26, 1985.
zOn disabled list, August 28 to September 12, 1985.
aOn disabled list, March 27, 1986 through entire season.
bSold to Denver (Milwaukee Brewers' organization), October 6, 1987.

CHARLES EDWARD FINLEY
(Chuck)

Born November 26, 1962 at Monroe, La.
Height, 6.06. Weight, 215.
Throws and bats lefthanded.
Attended Northeast Louisiana State University, Monroe, La.

Year Club	League	G.	IP.	W.	L.	Pct.	H.	R.	ER.	SO.	BB.	ERA.
1985—Salem	Northwest	18	29	3	1	.750	34	21	15	32	10	4.66
1986—Quad Cities	Midwest	10	12	1	0	1.000	4	0	0	16	3	0.00
1986—California	American	25	46⅓	3	1	.750	40	17	17	37	23	3.30
1987—California	American	35	90⅔	2	7	.222	102	54	47	63	43	4.67
1988—California	American	31	194⅓	9	15	.375	191	95	90	111	82	4.17
Major League Totals—3 Years		91	331⅓	14	23	.378	333	166	154	211	148	4.18

Selected by California Angels' organization in 15th round of free-agent draft, June 4, 1984.
Selected by California Angels' organization in secondary phase of free-agent draft, January 9, 1985.

CHAMPIONSHIP SERIES RECORD

Year Club	League	G.	IP.	W.	L.	Pct.	H.	R.	ER.	SO.	BB.	ERA.
1986—California	American	3	2	0	0	.000	1	0	0	1	0	0.00

DANIEL MICHAEL FIROVA
(Dan)

Born October 15, 1956, at Refugio, Tex.
Height, 6.00. Weight, 185.
Throws and bats righthanded.
Attended Bee County College, Beeville, Tex., and Pan American University, Edinburg, Tex.

Led Eastern League in passed balls with 20 in 1988.

Year Club	League	Pos.	G.	AB.	R.	H.	2B.	3B.	HR.	RBI.	B.A.	PO.	A.	E.	F.A.
1980—San Jose	Calif.	C	4	14	2	2	0	0	0	2	.143	29	1	1	.968
1980—Spokane	P. C.	C	11	28	1	2	1	0	0	0	.071	39	9	1	.980
1980—Jacksonville	South	C	3	9	0	5	2	0	0	1	.556	22	2	0	1.000
1980—Bellingham†	N'west	C-OF	63	218	33	44	6	3	1	31	.202	354	*77	11	.975
1981—Nuevo Laredo	Mex.	C	97	291	25	69	3	2	3	38	.237	417	67	8	.984
1981—Seattle‡	Amer.	C	13	2	0	0	0	0	0	0	.000	8	0	0	1.000
1982—Nuevo Laredo	Mex.	C	72	215	18	55	5	0	1	15	.256	257	51	8	.975
1982—Seattle§	Amer.	C	3	5	0	0	0	0	0	0	.000	8	1	1	.900

Year Club	League	Pos.	G.	AB.	R.	H.	2B.	3B.	HR.	RBI.	B.A.	PO.	A.	E.	F.A.
1982—Bakersfield x	Calif.	C	11	39	3	9	2	0	0	5	.231	48	8	3	.949
1983—Nuevo Laredo	Mex.	C	72	218	17	52	3	1	2	14	.239	318	34	10	.972
1984—Saltillo y	Mex.	C-1B	91	330	54	104	20	6	4	50	.315	389	61	10	.978
1985—Chattanooga	South.	C	110	346	28	83	14	2	3	22	.240	483	★89	14	.976
1986—Calgary	P. C.	C	67	209	19	52	9	0	3	22	.249	316	46	8	.978
1987—Salinas	Calif.	C	23	75	5	25	3	0	1	10	.333	170	21	0	1.000
1987—Chattanooga	South.	C	52	165	19	33	7	0	1	21	.200	303	33	2	.994
1987—Calgary z	P. C.	C	8	19	2	3	0	0	0	0	.158	37	4	1	.976
1988—Saltillo	Mex.	C	8	26	5	7	0	0	0	5	.269	47	4	1	.981
1988—Williamsport	East.	C	42	127	8	29	3	0	0	11	.228	194	41	6	.975
1988—Colorado Springs.	P. C.	C	17	55	7	17	2	0	0	4	.309	104	7	5	.957
1988—Cleveland a	Amer.	C	1	0	0	0	0	0	0	0	.000	0	0	0	.000
Major League Totals—3 Years			17	7	0	0	0	0	0	0	.000	16	1	1	.944

Selected by Montreal Expos' organization in 7th round of free-agent draft, January 11, 1977.
Selected by Milwaukee Brewers' organization in 28th round of free-agent draft, June 5, 1979.
Selected by Seattle Mariners' organization in secondary phase of free-agent draft, January 8, 1980.
†Loaned to Nuevo Laredo, March 20, 1981; returned, August 28, 1981.
‡Loaned to Nuevo Laredo, April 4, 1982; returned, May 13, 1982.
§Loaned to Nuevo Laredo, May 22, 1982; returned, August 15, 1982.
xLoaned to Nuevo Laredo, March 20, 1983; returned, August 7, 1983.
yOn Salt Lake City suspended list, April 7, 1984 through entire season.
zGranted free agency, October 15, 1987; signed by Williamsport (Cleveland Indians' organization), May 11, 1988.
aGranted free agency, October 15, 1988.

JEFFREY THOMAS FISCHER
(Jeff)

Born August 17, 1963, at West Palm Beach, Fla.
Height, 6.03. Weight, 180.
Throws and bats righthanded.
Attended University of Florida, Gainesville, Fla.

Year Club	League	G.	IP.	W.	L.	Pct.	H.	R.	ER.	SO.	BB.	ERA.
1985—West Palm Beach	Florida St.	13	84⅔	6	5	.545	92	40	33	40	18	3.51
1986—West Palm Beach	Florida St.	14	93⅔	10	2	●.833	74	24	15	64	20	1.44
1986—Jacksonville	Southern	11	70⅔	5	2	.714	70	35	29	39	16	3.69
1987—Indianapolis	Am. Assoc.	24	145⅔	7	9	.438	179	93	88	76	55	5.44
1987—Montreal	National	4	13⅔	0	1	.000	21	14	13	6	5	8.56
1988—Indianapolis†	Am. Assoc.	28	177⅓	13	8	.619	162	63	53	110	32	2.69
Major League Totals—1 Year		4	13⅔	0	1	.000	21	14	13	6	5	8.56

Selected by Montreal Expos' organization in 7th round of free-agent draft, June 3, 1985.
†Drafted by Los Angeles Dodgers, December 5, 1988.

JOHN ALAN FISHEL

Born November 8, 1962, at Fullerton, Calif.
Height, 5.11. Weight, 185.
Throws and bats righthanded.
Attended California State University, Fullerton, Calif.

Tied for Florida State League lead in sacrifice flies with 10 in 1986.
Led Florida State League third basemen in total chances with 418 and tied for lead in double plays with 20 in 1986.

Year Club	League	Pos.	G.	AB.	R.	H.	2B.	3B.	HR.	RBI.	B.A.	PO.	A.	E.	F.A.
1985—Auburn	NYP	OF-3B	●77	268	53	70	15	2	9	42	.261	108	44	9	.944
1986—Osceola	Fla. St.	3B	★137	490	82	132	★36	4	12	83	.269	99	★278	★41	.902
1987—Columbus	South.	OF-3B-C	130	457	78	126	29	2	24	88	.276	192	33	6	.974
1988—Tucson	P. C.	OF-3B	102	360	61	94	19	6	18	68	.261	128	12	2	.986
1988—Houston	Nat.	OF	19	26	1	6	0	0	1	2	.231	2	0	0	1.000
Major League Totals—1 Year			19	26	1	6	0	0	1	2	.231	2	0	0	1.000

Selected by New York Yankees' organization in 8th round of free-agent draft, June 8, 1981.
Selected by Oakland A's organization in 19th round of free-agent draft, June 4, 1984.
Selected by Houston Astros' organization in 9th round of free-agent draft, June 3, 1985.

BRIAN KEVIN FISHER

Born March 18, 1962, at Honolulu, Haw.
Height, 6.04. Weight, 210.
Throws and bats righthanded.
Attended Columbia College, Aurora, Colo.

Major League saves: 1985 (14), 1986 (6), 1988 (1). Total—21.
Led International League pitchers in games started with 29 in 1984.
Tied for South Atlantic League lead in balks with 4 in 1981.

Year Club	League	G.	IP.	W.	L.	Pct.	H.	R.	ER.	SO.	BB.	ERA.
1980—Bradenton Braves	Gulf Coast	12	61	5	3	.625	55	34	26	48	★53	3.84
1981—Anderson	S. Atlantic	25	152	6	8	.429	139	96	72	152	94	4.26
1982—Durham†	Carolina	18	104	6	6	.500	72	43	32	129	43	2.77
1983—Savannah	Southern	27	150	8	11	.421	172	101	87	103	56	5.22
1984—Richmond‡	Int'national	29	183	9	11	.450	188	●101	★87	122	●100	4.28
1985—Columbus	Int'national	7	11⅓	0	0	.000	8	4	3	12	7	2.38
1985—New York	American	55	98⅓	4	4	.500	77	32	26	85	29	2.38

Year	Club	League	G.	IP.	W.	L.	Pct.	H.	R.	ER.	SO.	BB.	ERA.
1986	New York	American	62	96⅔	9	5	.643	105	61	53	67	37	4.93
1986	Columbus§	Int'national	6	8⅔	0	0	.000	8	4	4	4	3	4.15
1987	Pittsburgh	National	37	185⅓	11	9	.550	185	99	93	117	72	4.52
1988	Pittsburgh x	National	33	146⅓	8	10	.444	157	78	75	66	57	4.61
American League Totals—2 Years			117	195	13	9	.591	182	93	79	152	66	3.65
National League Totals—2 Years			70	331⅔	19	19	.500	342	177	168	183	129	4.56
Major League Totals—4 Years			187	526⅔	32	28	.533	524	270	247	335	195	4.22

Selected by Atlanta Braves' organization in 2nd round of free-agent draft, June 3, 1980.
†On disabled list, May 18 to July 1, 1982.
‡Traded to New York Yankees for Catcher Rick Cerone, December 5, 1984.
§Traded with Pitchers Doug Drabek and Logan Easley to Pittsburgh Pirates for Pitchers Rick Rhoden, Cecilio Guante and Pat Clements, November 26, 1986.
xOn disabled list, April 30 to May 15, 1988.

CARLTON ERNEST FISK

Born December 26, 1947, at Bellows Falls, Vt.
Height, 6.02. Weight, 225.
Throws and bats righthanded.
Attended University of New Hampshire, Durham, N. H.
Brother of Calvin Fisk, former catcher in Baltimore Orioles' organization;
brother-in-law of Rick Miller, outfielder with Boston Red Sox and California Angels, 1971 through 1985;
and cousin of Dave Jennings, punter with New York Giants and New York Jets, 1974 through 1987.

Established major league records for longest game with no passed balls (25 innings), and most innings played by catcher, game (25), May 8, finished May 9, 1984.

Tied major league records for most at-bats (11) and plate appearances (12), game, May 8, finished May 9, 1984 (25 innings); most home runs, opening game of season (2), April 6, 1973.

Tied modern major league record for most long hits, inning (2), May 15, 1975 (eighth inning) and June 30, 1977 (eighth inning).

Established American League records for most games, catcher, lifetime (1,838); most home runs by catcher, season (33), 1985.

Tied American League record for fewest passed balls, season, 150 or more games (4), 1977.

Major League stolen bases: 1972 (5), 1973 (7), 1974 (5), 1975 (4), 1976 (12), 1977 (7), 1978 (7), 1979 (3), 1980 (11), 1981 (3), 1982 (17), 1983 (9), 1984 (6), 1985 (17), 1986 (2), 1987 (1). Total—116.

Hit for the cycle, May 16, 1984.
Led American League in being hit by pitch with 13 in 1980.
Led American League in passed balls with 11 in 1983.
Led American League catchers in double plays with 10 in 1981 and 15 in 1987.
Led American League catches in putouts with 470 in 1981.
Led American League catchers in errors with 10 in 1980.
Led American League catchers in total chances with 933 in 1972, 803 in 1973, 519 in 1981 and 871 in 1985.
Led International League catchers in double plays with 12 in 1971.
Named THE SPORTING NEWS American League Rookie Player of the Year, 1972.
Named American League Rookie of the Year by Baseball Writers' Association of America, 1972.
Named catcher on THE SPORTING NEWS American League All-Star Team, 1972, 1977, 1983 and 1985.
Named catcher on THE SPORTING NEWS American League All-Star fielding team, 1972.
Named catcher on THE SPORTING NEWS American League Silver Slugger team, 1981, 1985 and 1988.

Year	Club	League	Pos.	G.	AB.	R.	H.	2B.	3B.	HR.	RBI.	B.A.	PO.	A.	E.	F.A.
1967	Greenville†	W. Car.					(In Military Service)									
1968	Waterloo‡	Midw.	C	62	195	31	66	11	2	12	34	.338	385	42	8	.982
1969	Pittsfield	East.	C	97	309	38	75	18	3	10	41	.243	551	65	★22	.966
1969	Boston	Amer.	C	2	5	0	0	0	0	0	0	.000	2	0	0	1.000
1970	Pawtucket	East.	C-OF-1B	93	284	43	65	18	1	12	44	.229	482	50	7	.987
1971	Louisville	Int.	C-OF-3B	94	308	45	81	10	4	10	43	.263	588	51	13	.980
1971	Boston	Amer.	C	14	48	7	15	2	1	2	6	.313	72	6	2	.975
1972	Boston	Amer.	C	131	457	74	134	28	●9	22	61	.293	★846	★72	●15	.984
1973	Boston	Amer.	C	135	508	65	125	21	0	26	71	.246	★739	50	★14	.983
1974	Boston§	Amer.	C	52	187	36	56	12	1	11	26	.299	267	26	6	.980
1975	Boston x	Amer.	C	79	263	47	87	14	4	10	52	.331	347	30	8	.979
1976	Boston	Amer.	C	134	487	76	124	17	5	17	58	.255	649	73	12	.984
1977	Boston	Amer.	C	152	536	106	169	26	3	26	102	.315	779	69	11	.987
1978	Boston	Amer.	★C-OF	157	571	94	162	39	5	20	88	.284	734	90	★17	.980
1979	Boston y	Amer.	C-OF	91	320	49	87	23	2	10	42	.272	155	8	3	.982
1980	Boston z	Amer.	C-1-O-3	131	478	73	138	25	3	18	62	.289	543	56	11	.982
1981	Chicago	Amer.	C-1-3-O	96	338	44	89	12	0	7	45	.263	479	46	6	.989
1982	Chicago	Amer.	C-1B	135	476	66	127	17	3	14	65	.267	648	63	5	.993
1983	Chicago	Amer.	C	138	488	85	141	26	4	26	86	.289	★709	46	7	.991
1984	Chicago a	Amer.	C	102	359	54	83	20	1	21	43	.231	421	38	6	.987
1985	Chicago b	Amer.	C	153	543	85	129	23	1	37	107	.238	★801	60	10	.989
1986	Chicago	Amer.	C-OF	125	457	42	101	11	0	14	63	.221	455	44	8	.984
1987	Chicago c	Amer.	C-1B-OF	135	454	68	116	22	1	23	71	.256	597	66	7	.990
1988	Chicago d	Amer.	C	76	253	37	70	8	1	19	50	.277	338	36	2	.995
Major League Totals—19 Years				2038	7228	1108	1953	346	44	323	1098	.270	9581	879	150	.986

Selected by Baltimore Orioles' organization in 36th round of free-agent draft, June, 1965.
Selected by Boston Red Sox' organization in 1st round (fourth player selected) of free-agent draft, January, 1967.
†On temporary inactive list, April 17, 1967; transferred to military list, May 18, 1967 through April 9, 1968.
‡On temporary inactive list, August 5 to August 20, 1968.
§On disabled list, March 21 to April 26 and June 28, 1974 through remainder of season.
xOn disabled list, March 24 to June 23, 1975.

yOn disabled list, April 14 to May 21, 1979.
zGranted free agency by arbitrator's ruling, February 12, 1981; signed by Chicago White Sox, March 18, 1981.
aOn disabled list, June 13 to July 5, 1984.
bGranted free agency, November 12, 1985; re-signed by White Sox, January 8, 1986.
cGranted free agency, January 22, 1988; re-signed by White Sox, February 9, 1988.
dOn disabled list, May 11 to July 28, 1988.

CHAMPIONSHIP SERIES RECORD

Year	Club	League	Pos.	G.	AB.	R.	H.	2B.	3B.	HR.	RBI.	B.A.	PO.	A.	E.	F.A.
1975	Boston	Amer.	C	3	12	4	5	1	0	0	2	.417	15	0	0	1.000
1983	Chicago	Amer.	C	4	17	0	3	1	0	0	0	.176	27	3	0	1.000
Championship Series Totals—2 Years				7	29	4	8	2	0	0	2	.276	42	3	0	1.000

WORLD SERIES RECORD

Tied World Series records for most at bats inning and most times faced pitcher inning (2), October 15, 1975 (fourth inning); most errors by catcher, game (2), October 14, 1975.

Year	Club	League	Pos.	G.	AB.	R.	H.	2B.	3B.	HR.	RBI.	B.A.	PO.	A.	E.	F.A.
1975	Boston	Amer.	C	7	25	5	6	0	0	2	4	.240	37	3	2	.952

ALL-STAR GAME RECORD

Year	League	Pos.	AB.	R.	H.	2B.	3B.	HR.	RBI.	B.A.	PO.	A.	E.	F.A.
1972	American	C	2	1	1	0	0	0	0	.500	2	0	0	1.000
1973	American	C	2	0	0	0	0	0	0	.000	3	0	0	1.000
1976	American	C	1	0	0	0	0	0	0	.000	1	0	0	1.000
1977	American	C	2	0	0	0	0	0	0	.000	6	1	0	1.000
1978	American	C	2	0	0	0	0	0	1	.000	4	0	0	1.000
1980	American	C	2	0	0	0	0	0	0	.000	5	0	0	1.000
1981	American	C	3	1	1	0	0	0	0	.333	4	0	0	1.000
1982	American	C	2	0	0	0	0	0	0	.000	2	0	0	1.000
1985	American	C	2	0	0	0	0	0	0	.000	2	0	0	1.000
All-Star Game Totals—9 Years			18	2	2	0	0	0	1	.111	29	1	0	1.000

Named to American League All-Star Team for 1974 game; replaced due to injury.

MICHAEL PATRICK FITZGERALD
(Mike)

Born March 28, 1964, at Savannah, Ga.
Height, 6.01. Weight, 200.
Throws and bats righthanded.
Attended Middle Georgia College, Cochran, Ga.

Led Texas League in game-winning RBIs with 15 in 1987.
Led Midwest League in game-winning RBIs with 17 and sacrifice flies with 10 in 1986.
Led Midwest League in passed balls with 23 in 1985.
Led Appalachian League catchers in double plays with 4 and tied for lead in errors with 11 in 1984.

Year	Club	League	Pos.	G.	AB.	R.	H.	2B.	3B.	HR.	RBI.	B.A.	PO.	A.	E.	F.A.
1984	Johnson City	Appal.	C-OF	51	171	31	59	11	0	7	31	*.345	245	35	13	.956
1985	Springfield	Midw.	C	113	413	58	105	21	0	16	62	.254	673	56	17	.977
1986	Springfield	Midw.	1B-C	126	498	74	148	30	4	19	93	.297	819	63	22	.976
1987	Arkansas	Texas	1B	126	447	72	128	36	4	27	•108	.286	839	*76	*25	.973
1988	Louisville	A. A.	1B	106	382	33	92	14	1	10	50	.241	867	71	5	*.995
1988	St. Louis	Nat.	1B	13	46	4	9	1	0	0	1	.196	96	4	1	.990
Major League Totals—1 Year				13	46	4	9	1	0	0	1	.196	96	4	1	.990

Selected by San Francisco Giants' organization in 1st round (15th player selected) of free-agent draft, January 11, 1983.
Selected by Cleveland Indians' organization in 10th round of free-agent draft, January 17, 1984.
Selected by St. Louis Cardinals' organization in secondary phase of free-agent draft, June 4, 1984.

MICHAEL ROY FITZGERALD
(Mike)

Born July 13, 1960, at Long Beach, Calif.
Height, 5.11. Weight, 190.
Throws and bats righthanded.
Nephew of Dan Gausepohl, outfielder in San Diego
Padres' organization, 1979 through 1982.

Tied major league record by hitting home run in first major league at-bat, September 13, 1983.
Major League stolen bases: 1984 (1), 1985 (5), 1986 (3), 1987 (3), 1988 (2). Total—14.
Led Carolina League in sacrifice flies with 11 in 1979.

Year	Club	League	Pos.	G.	AB.	R.	H.	2B.	3B.	HR.	RBI.	B.A.	PO.	A.	E.	F.A.
1978	Little Falls	NYP	C	48	140	25	36	10	0	5	21	.257	230	37	1	.996
1979	Lynchburg	Carol.	C	117	368	55	93	16	4	13	*75	.253	424	60	10	.980
1980	Alex.†-Lynch.	Carol.	C-1B-OF	105	338	36	71	10	2	10	44	.210	438	45	7	.986
1981	Jackson	Texas	C-1-O-3	66	218	28	68	14	2	4	29	.312	344	52	3	.992
1981	Tidewater	Int.	C-OF	24	58	9	9	2	0	1	3	.155	124	9	2	.985
1982	Tidewater	Int.	C-1-O-3	94	302	33	74	9	2	4	36	.245	451	34	7	986
1983	Tidewater	Int.	C-1-3-O	111	370	64	105	17	1	14	65	.284	588	62	8	.988
1983	New York	Nat.	C	8	20	1	2	0	0	1	2	.100	37	8	2	.957
1984	New York‡	Nat.	C	112	360	20	87	15	1	2	33	.242	715	47	4	*.995

Year	Club	League	Pos.	G.	AB.	R.	H.	2B.	3B.	HR.	RBI.	B.A.	PO.	A.	E.	F.A.
1985	Montreal	Nat.	C	108	295	25	61	7	1	5	34	.207	542	46	8	.987
1986	Indianapolis	A. A.	C	10	32	4	11	3	0	0	4	.344	58	5	1	.984
1986	Montreal§	Nat.	C	73	209	20	59	13	1	6	37	.282	415	35	3	.993
1987	Montreal x	Nat.	C-1B-2B	107	287	32	69	11	0	3	36	.240	603	27	12	.981
1988	Montreal	Nat.	C-OF	63	155	17	42	6	1	5	23	.271	262	21	6	.979
1988	Indianapolis	A. A.	C	32	96	12	24	6	1	1	13	.250	234	11	2	.992
Major League Totals—6 Years				471	1326	115	320	52	4	22	165	.241	2574	184	35	.987

Selected by New York Mets' organization in 6th round of free-agent draft, June 6, 1978.
†Loaned to Alexandria (Co-op), April 8, 1980; returned, May 31, 1980.
‡Traded with Infielder Hubie Brooks, Outfielder Herm Winningham and Pitcher Floyd Youmans to Montreal Expos for Catcher Gary Carter, December 10, 1984.
§On disabled list, August 2, 1986 through remainder of season.
xOn disabled list, March 28 to April 20, 1987.

MICHAEL KENDALL FLANAGAN
(Mike)

Born December 16, 1951, at Manchester, N. H.
Height, 6.00. Weight, 195.
Throws and bats lefthanded.
Attended University of Massachusetts, Amherst, Mass.
Son of Ed Flanagan, Jr., minor league pitcher, 1947 through 1952.

Major League saves: 1977 (1).
Tied for American League lead in shutouts with 5 in 1979.
Tied for American League lead in games started by pitchers with 40 in 1978.
Tied for International League lead in shutouts with 4 in 1975.
Tied for Southern League lead in shutouts with 3 in 1974.
Named American League Pitcher of the Year by THE SPORTING NEWS, 1979.
Won American League Cy Young Memorial Award, 1979.
Named lefthanded pitcher on THE SPORTING NEWS American League All-Star Team, 1979.

Year	Club	League	G.	IP.	W.	L.	Pct.	H.	R.	ER.	SO.	BB.	ERA.
1973	Miami	Florida St.	11	61	4	1	.800	39	21	15	61	25	2.21
1974	Miami	Florida St.	14	103	6	6	.500	67	32	24	119	48	2.10
1974	Asheville	Southern	11	84	6	4	.600	61	19	17	62	18	1.82
1975	Rochester	Int'national	27	173	13	4	*.765	155	58	48	135	56	2.50
1975	Baltimore	American	2	10	0	1	.000	9	4	3	7	6	2.70
1976	Baltimore	American	20	85	3	5	.375	83	41	39	56	33	4.13
1976	Rochester	Int'national	7	51	6	1	.857	40	16	12	24	14	2.12
1977	Baltimore	American	36	235	15	10	.600	235	100	95	149	70	3.64
1978	Baltimore	American	40	281	19	15	.559	271	128	*126	167	87	4.04
1979	Baltimore	American	39	266	*23	9	.719	245	107	91	190	70	3.08
1980	Baltimore	American	37	251	16	13	.552	*278	121	115	128	71	4.12
1981	Baltimore	American	20	116	9	6	.600	108	55	54	72	37	4.19
1982	Baltimore	American	36	236	15	11	.577	233	110	104	103	76	3.97
1983	Baltimore†	American	20	125⅓	12	4	.750	135	53	46	50	31	3.30
1984	Baltimore	American	34	226⅔	13	13	.500	213	103	89	115	81	3.53
1985	Hagerstown‡	Carolina	1	6	0	0	.000	1	0	0	5	4	0.00
1985	Baltimore	American	15	86	4	5	.444	101	49	49	42	28	5.13
1986	Baltimore§	American	29	172	7	11	.389	179	95	81	96	66	4.24
1987	Baltimore xy-Toronto	American	23	144	6	8	.429	148	72	65	93	51	4.06
1987	Rochester	Int'national	3	12	0	0	.000	12	5	4	10	3	3.00
1988	Toronto z	American	34	211	13	13	.500	220	106	98	99	80	4.18
Major League Totals—14 Years			385	2445	155	124	.556	2458	1144	1055	1367	787	3.88

Selected by Houston Astros' organization in 15th round of free-agent draft, June 8, 1971.
Selected by Baltimore Orioles' organization in 7th round of free-agent draft, June 5, 1973.
†On disabled list, May 18 to August 7, 1983.
‡On Baltimore disabled list, March 26 to July 20, 1985; included rehabilitation disability assignment to Hagerstown, July 10 to July 20, 1985.
§On disabled list, May 31 to June 19, 1986.
xOn disabled list, May 18 to July 17, 1987; included rehabilitation disability assignment to Rochester, July 3 to July 17, 1987.
yTraded to Toronto Blue Jays for Pitcher Oswald Peraza and a player to be named later, August 31, 1987; Baltimore Orioles acquired Pitcher Jose Mesa to complete deal, September 4, 1987.
zGranted free agency, November 4, 1988; re-signed by Blue Jays, December 24, 1988.

CHAMPIONSHIP SERIES RECORD

Year	Club	League	G.	IP.	W.	L.	Pct.	H.	R.	ER.	SO.	BB.	ERA.
1979	Baltimore	American	1	7	1	0	1.000	6	6	4	2	1	5.14
1983	Baltimore	American	1	5	1	0	1.000	5	1	1	1	0	1.80
Championship Series Totals—2 Years			2	12	2	0	1.000	11	7	5	3	1	3.75

WORLD SERIES RECORD

Year	Club	League	G.	IP.	W.	L.	Pct.	H.	R.	ER.	SO.	BB.	ERA.
1979	Baltimore	American	3	15	1	1	.500	18	7	5	13	2	3.00
1983	Baltimore	American	1	4	0	0	.000	6	2	2	1	1	4.50
World Series Totals—2 Years			4	19	1	1	.500	24	9	7	14	3	3.32

ALL-STAR GAME RECORD

Named to American League All-Star Team for 1978 game; did not play.

TIMOTHY EARL FLANNERY
(Tim)

Born September 29, 1957, at Tulsa, Okla.
Height, 5.11. Weight, 181.
Throws right and bats lefthanded.
Attended Chapman College, Orange, Calif.
Nephew of Hal Smith, catcher with St. Louis Cardinals and Pittsburgh Pirates, 1956 through 1961 and 1965; minor league manager, 1966; coach, Pittsburgh Pirates, 1967; coach, Cincinnati Reds, 1968 and 1969; and scout with St. Louis Cardinals, 1970 through 1975 and since 1978.

Major League stolen bases: 1980 (2), 1981 (1), 1982 (1), 1983 (2), 1984 (4), 1985 (2), 1986 (3), 1987 (2), 1988 (3). Total—20.

Year Club	League	Pos.	G.	AB.	R.	H.	2B.	3B.	HR.	RBI.	B.A.	PO.	A.	E.	F.A.
1978—Reno	Calif.	2B-P	84	340	65	119	11	5	2	49	.350	213	269	19	.962
1979—Amarillo	Texas	2B-SS	125	524	88	•181	23	6	6	71	.345	287	374	28	.959
1979—San Diego	Nat.	2B	22	65	2	10	0	1	0	4	.154	45	60	1	.991
1980—Hawaii	P. C.	2B	47	182	27	63	10	3	1	16	.346	102	146	5	.980
1980—San Diego	Nat.	2B-3B	95	292	15	70	12	0	0	25	.240	140	204	8	.977
1981—Hawaii	P. C.	2B	21	78	16	22	3	1	0	10	.282	47	62	2	.982
1981—San Diego	Nat.	3B-2B	37	67	4	17	4	1	0	6	.254	16	32	2	.960
1982—San Diego	Nat.	2B-3B-SS	122	379	40	100	11	7	0	30	.264	226	278	14	.973
1983—San Diego	Nat.	3B-2B-SS	92	214	24	50	7	3	3	19	.234	63	156	4	.982
1984—San Diego	Nat.	2B-SS-3B	86	128	24	35	3	3	2	10	.273	36	69	5	.955
1985—San Diego	Nat.	2B-3B	126	384	50	108	14	3	1	40	.281	261	287	13	.977
1986—San Diego	Nat.	2B-3B-SS	134	368	48	103	11	2	3	28	.280	226	275	5	.990
1987—San Diego†	Nat.	2B-3B-SS	106	276	23	63	5	1	0	20	.228	142	226	7	.981
1988—San Diego‡	Nat.	3B-2B-SS	79	170	16	45	5	4	0	19	.265	28	76	3	.972
1988—Riverside	Calif.	DH	4	11	2	3	1	0	0	1	.273	0	0	0	.000
Major League Totals—10 Years			899	2343	246	601	72	25	9	201	.257	1183	1663	62	.979

Selected by San Diego Padres' organization in 6th round of free-agent draft, June 6, 1978.
†On disabled list, May 6 to May 31, 1987.
‡On disabled list, April 29 to May 23, 1988; included rehabilitation disability assignment to Riverside, May 18 to May 23, 1988.

CHAMPIONSHIP SERIES RECORD

Year Club	League	Pos.	G.	AB.	R.	H.	2B.	3B.	HR.	RBI.	B.A.	PO.	A.	E.	F.A.
1984—San Diego	Nat.	PH	3	2	2	1	0	0	0	0	.500	0	0	0	.000

WORLD SERIES RECORD

Year Club	League	Pos.	G.	AB.	R.	H.	2B.	3B.	HR.	RBI.	B.A.	PO.	A.	E.	F.A.
1984—San Diego	Nat.	PH-2B	1	1	0	1	0	0	0	0	1.000	1	0	0	1.000

PITCHING RECORD

Year Club	League	G.	IP.	W.	L.	Pct.	H.	R.	ER.	SO.	BB.	ERA.
1978—Reno	California	1	⅓	0	1	.000	3	6	5	0	1	135.00

SCOTT BRIAN FLETCHER

Born July 30, 1958, at Fort Walton Beach, Fla.
Height, 5.11. Weight, 173.
Throws and bats righthanded.
Attended University of Toledo, Toledo, O.; Valencia Community College, Orlando, Fla., and Georgia Southern College, Statesboro, Ga.
Son of Richard W. Fletcher, minor league pitcher, 1952 through 1959.

Major League stolen bases: 1982 (1), 1983 (5), 1984 (10), 1985 (5), 1986 (12), 1987 (13), 1988 (8). Total—54.
Led American Association in being hit by pitch with 9 and grounding into double plays with 20 in 1981.
Led American Association shortstops in total chances with 607 in 1982.
Led Texas League second basemen in double plays with 112 in 1980.

Year Club	League	Pos.	G.	AB.	R.	H.	2B.	3B.	HR.	RBI.	B.A.	PO.	A.	E.	F.A.
1979—Geneva	NYP	SS	67	261	59	81	12	3	4	43	.310	99	195	18	★.942
1980—Midland	Texas	★2B-SS	130	501	★111	164	16	★11	6	65	.327	★354	★390	★29	.962
1981—Iowa	A. A.	SS	119	458	66	117	26	4	4	33	.255	★222	337	28	.952
1981—Chicago	Nat.	2B-SS-3B	19	46	6	10	4	0	0	1	.217	34	44	3	.963
1982—Iowa	A. A.	SS	129	502	90	157	26	3	4	60	.313	224	•357	26	.957
1982—Chicago†	Nat.	SS	11	24	4	4	0	0	0	1	.167	11	23	0	1.000
1983—Chicago	Amer.	SS-2B-3B	114	262	42	62	16	5	3	31	.237	126	308	16	.964
1984—Chicago	Amer.	SS-2B-3B	149	456	46	114	13	3	3	35	.250	234	439	19	.973
1985—Chicago‡	Amer.	3B-SS-2B	119	301	38	77	8	1	2	31	.256	123	208	8	.976
1986—Texas	Amer.	SS-3B-2B	147	530	82	159	34	5	3	50	.300	216	388	16	.974
1987—Texas	Amer.	SS	156	588	82	169	28	4	5	63	.287	249	413	23	.966
1988—Texas§	Amer.	SS	140	515	59	142	19	4	0	47	.276	215	414	11	.983
National League Totals—2 Years			30	70	10	14	4	0	0	2	.200	45	67	3	.974
American League Totals—6 Years			825	2652	349	723	118	22	16	257	.273	1163	2170	93	.973
Major League Totals—8 Years			855	2722	359	737	122	22	16	259	.271	1208	2237	96	.973

Selected by Los Angeles Dodgers' organization in 33rd round of free-agent draft, June 8, 1976.
Selected by Oakland A's organization in secondary phase of free-agent draft, January 10, 1978.
Selected by Houston Astros' organization in secondary phase of free-agent draft, June 6, 1978.
Selected by Chicago Cubs' organization in secondary phase of free-agent draft, June 5, 1979.

†Traded with Pitchers Dick Tidrow and Randy Martz and Infielder Pat Tabler to Chicago White Sox for Pitchers Steve Trout and Warren Brusstar, January 25, 1983.

‡Traded with Pitcher Ed Correa and a player to be named later to Texas Rangers for Infielder Wayne Tolleson and Pitcher Dave Schmidt, November 25, 1985; Texas acquired Infielder Jose Mota to complete deal, December 12, 1985.

§Granted free agency, November 4, 1988; re-signed by Rangers, November 30, 1988.

CHAMPIONSHIP SERIES RECORD

Year	Club	League	Pos.	G.	AB.	R.	H.	2B.	3B.	HR.	RBI.	B.A.	PO.	A.	E.	F.A.
1983	Chicago	Amer.	SS	3	7	0	0	0	0	0	0	.000	3	8	0	1.000

THOMAS MICHAEL FOLEY
(Tom)

Born September 9, 1959, at Columbus, Ga.
Height, 6.01. Weight, 180.
Throws right and bats lefthanded.
Attended Miami-Dade Community College (South), Miami, Fla.

Major League stolen bases: 1983 (1), 1984 (3), 1985 (2), 1986 (10), 1987 (6), 1988 (2). Total—24.
Led Pioneer League in caught stealing with 10 in 1977.
Led Florida State League shortstops in double plays with 71 in 1979.
Led Western Carolinas League shortstops in double plays with 98 in 1978.

Year	Club	League	Pos.	G.	AB.	R.	H.	2B.	3B.	HR.	RBI.	B.A.	PO.	A.	E.	F.A.
1977	Billings	Pion.	3B-SS	59	209	37	53	7	1	2	21	.254	53	109	24	.871
1978	Shelby	W. Car.	SS	124	424	55	98	19	1	2	41	.231	★217	●352	30	★.950
1979	Tampa	Fla. St.	SS	125	414	38	95	12	6	0	37	.229	223	★394	35	.946
1980	Waterbury	East.	2B	131	477	49	119	16	4	4	41	.249	★222	329	31	.947
1981	Indianapolis	A. A.	SS	103	347	47	81	12	2	6	27	.233	175	267	27	.942
1982	Indianapolis	A. A.	SS	129	427	65	115	20	9	8	63	.269	★227	343	27	.955
1983	Cincinnati	Nat.	SS-2B	68	98	7	20	4	1	0	9	.204	54	76	2	.985
1984	Cincinnati	Nat.	SS-2B-3B	106	277	26	70	8	3	5	27	.253	119	228	11	.969
1985	Cinc.† - Phil.	Nat.	SS-2B-3B	89	250	24	60	13	1	3	23	.240	127	202	7	.979
1986	Reading‡	East.	SS-2B	3	11	2	2	2	0	0	0	.182	2	11	0	1.000
1986	Phil.§ - Mon.	Nat.	SS-2B-3B	103	263	26	70	15	3	1	23	.266	117	190	6	.981
1987	Montreal x	Nat.	SS-2B-3B	106	280	35	82	18	3	5	28	.293	134	190	9	.973
1988	Montreal	Nat.	2B-SS-3B	127	377	33	100	21	3	5	43	.265	204	324	15	.972
Major League Totals—6 Years				599	1545	151	402	79	14	19	153	.260	755	1210	50	.975

Selected by Cincinnati Reds' organization in 7th round of free-agent draft, June 7, 1977.

†Traded with Catcher Alan Knicely, a player to be named later and cash to Philadelphia Phillies for Catcher Bo Diaz and Pitcher Greg Simpson, August 8, 1985; Philadelphia acquired Pitcher Freddie Toliver to complete deal, August 27, 1985.

‡On Philadelphia disabled list, March 23 to April 29, 1986; included rehabilitation disability assignment to Reading, April 25 to April 29, 1986.

§Traded with Pitcher Lary Sorensen to Montreal Expos for Pitcher Dan Schatzeder and Infielder Skeeter Barnes, July 24, 1986.

xOn disabled list, May 17 to June 2, 1987.

CURTIS GLENN FORD
(Curt)

Born October 11, 1960, at Jackson, Miss.
Height, 5.10. Weight, 150.
Throws right and bats lefthanded.
Attended Jackson State University, Jackson, Miss.

Major League stolen bases: 1985 (1), 1986 (13), 1987 (11), 1988 (6). Total—31.
Led American Association in stolen bases with 45 and tied for lead in caught stealing with 17 in 1985.
Led Midwest League in total bases with 236 in 1983.
Named Midwest League Most Valuable Player, 1983.

Year	Club	League	Pos.	G.	AB.	R.	H.	2B.	3B.	HR.	RBI.	B.A.	PO.	A.	E.	F.A.
1981	Johnson City	Appal.	★2B-1B	63	218	36	65	11	2	5	38	.298	115	149	★18	.936
1982	St. Petersburg	Fla. St.	2B-OF	133	447	59	123	18	8	1	49	.275	292	294	22	.964
1983	Springfield	Midw.	OF-2B	126	465	80	135	27	7	20	★91	.290	181	7	8	.960
1984	Arkansas	Texas	OF-2B-3B	118	442	62	143	23	1	10	78	.324	224	102	8	.976
1984	Louisville	A. A.	OF-2B	13	38	5	10	2	0	0	1	.263	13	2	0	1.000
1985	Louisville	A. A.	OF-3B	127	475	73	121	20	6	7	45	.255	243	25	8	.971
1985	St. Louis	Nat.	OF	11	12	2	6	2	0	0	3	.500	3	0	1	.750
1986	Louisville	A. A.	OF	53	200	47	59	9	2	4	31	.295	120	2	1	.992
1986	St. Louis	Nat.	OF	85	214	30	53	15	2	2	29	.248	109	7	3	.975
1987	St. Louis†	Nat.	OF	89	228	32	65	9	5	3	26	.285	157	2	3	.981
1988	St. Louis‡	Nat.	OF-1B	91	128	11	25	6	0	1	18	.195	95	6	2	.981
Major League Totals—4 Years				276	582	75	149	32	7	6	76	.256	364	15	9	.977

Selected by St. Louis Cardinals' organization in 4th round of free-agent draft, June 8, 1981.

†On disabled list, August 10 to September 18, 1987.

‡Traded with Catcher Steve Lake to Philadelphia for Outfielder Milt Thompson, December 16, 1988.

CHAMPIONSHIP SERIES RECORD

Year	Club	League	Pos.	G.	AB.	R.	H.	2B.	3B.	HR.	RBI.	B.A.	PO.	A.	E.	F.A.
1987	St. Louis	Nat.	OF-PH	4	9	2	3	0	0	0	0	.333	6	0	0	1.000

WORLD SERIES RECORD

Year	Club	League	Pos.	G.	AB.	R.	H.	2B.	3B.	HR.	RBI.	B.A.	PO.	A.	E.	F.A.
1987—St. Louis		Nat.	OF-PH	5	13	1	4	0	0	0	2	.308	5	0	0	1.000

ROBERT HERBERT FORSCH
(Bob)

Born January 13, 1950, at Sacramento, Calif.
Height, 6.03. Weight, 215.
Throws and bats righthanded.
Attended Sacramento City College, Sacramento, Calif.
Brother of Ken Forsch, pitcher with Houston Astros and California Angels, 1970 through 1984 and 1986.

Pitched 3-0 no-hit victory against Montreal Expos, September 26, 1983.
Pitched 5-0 no-hit victory against Philadelphia Phillies, April 16, 1978.
Pitched 5-0 no-hit victory against Denver, May 25, 1973.
Pitched seven-inning, 4-0 no-hit victory against Memphis, May 13, 1972.
Major League saves: 1982 (1), 1985 (2). Total—3.
Led Midwest League in hit batsmen with 11 in 1971.
Tied for Texas League lead in hit batsmen with 10 in 1972.
Named pitcher on THE SPORTING NEWS National League Silver Slugger team, 1980 and 1987.
Received reported $25,000 bonus to sign with St. Louis Cardinals, 1968.

Year	Club	League	G.	IP.	W.	L.	Pct.	H.	R.	ER.	SO.	BB.	ERA.
1970—Cedar Rapids		Midwest	1	3	0	0	.000	6	4	4	1	2	12.00
1970—Lewiston		Northwest	7	28	2	3	.400	32	22	13	15	17	4.18
1971—Cedar Rapids		Midwest	23	158	11	7	.611	140	74	55	134	41	3.13
1972—Arkansas		Texas	24	153	8	10	.444	158	85	*74	109	47	4.35
1973—Tulsa		Am. Assoc.	27	166	12	12	.500	169	91	81	124	66	4.36
1974—Tulsa		Am. Assoc.	15	103	8	5	.615	95	49	42	71	33	3.67
1974—St. Louis		National	19	100	7	4	.636	84	38	33	39	34	2.97
1975—St. Louis		National	34	230	15	10	.600	213	89	73	108	70	2.86
1976—St. Louis		National	33	194	8	10	.444	209	112	85	76	71	3.94
1977—St. Louis		National	35	217	20	7	.741	210	97	84	95	69	3.48
1978—St. Louis		National	34	234	11	17	.393	205	110	96	114	97	3.69
1979—St. Louis		National	33	219	11	11	.500	215	102	93	92	52	3.82
1980—St. Louis		National	31	215	11	10	.524	225	102	90	87	33	3.77
1981—St. Louis		National	20	124	10	5	.667	106	47	44	41	29	3.19
1982—St. Louis		National	36	233	15	9	.625	238	95	90	69	54	3.48
1983—St. Louis		National	34	187	10	12	.455	190	104	89	56	54	4.28
1984—St. Louis†		National	16	52⅓	2	5	.286	64	38	35	21	19	6.02
1985—St. Louis		National	34	136	9	6	.600	132	63	59	48	47	3.90
1986—St. Louis‡		National	33	230	14	10	.583	211	91	83	104	68	3.25
1987—St. Louis§		National	33	179	11	7	.611	189	90	86	89	45	4.32
1988—St. Louis x-Houston y		National	36	136⅓	10	8	.556	153	73	65	54	44	4.29
Major League Totals—15 Years			461	2686⅔	164	131	.556	2644	1251	1105	1093	786	3.70

Selected by St. Louis Cardinals' organization in 38th round of free-agent draft, June 7, 1968.
†On disabled list, June 1 to September 3, 1984.
‡Granted free agency, November 12, 1986; re-signed by Cardinals, December 19, 1986.
§Released, December 21, 1987; re-signed by Cardinals, January 27, 1988.
xTraded to Houston Astros for Denny Walling, August 31, 1988.
yGranted free agency, November 4, 1988; re-signed by Astros, December 21, 1988.

CHAMPIONSHIP SERIES RECORD

Year	Club	League	G.	IP.	W.	L.	Pct.	H.	R.	ER.	SO.	BB.	ERA.
1982—St. Louis		National	1	9	1	0	1.000	3	0	0	6	0	0.00
1985—St. Louis		National	1	3⅓	0	0	.000	3	2	2	0	2	5.40
1987—St. Louis		National	3	3	1	1	.500	4	4	4	3	1	12.00
Championship Series Totals—3 Years			5	15⅓	2	1	.667	10	6	6	9	3	3.52

WORLD SERIES RECORD

Tied World Series record for most games lost, seven-game Series (2), 1982.

Year	Club	League	G.	IP.	W.	L.	Pct.	H.	R.	ER.	SO.	BB.	ERA.
1982—St. Louis		National	2	12⅔	0	2	.000	18	10	7	4	3	4.97
1985—St. Louis		National	2	3	0	1	.000	6	4	4	3	1	12.00
1987—St. Louis		National	3	6⅓	1	0	1.000	8	7	7	3	5	9.95
World Series Totals—3 Years			7	22	1	3	.250	32	21	18	10	9	7.36

RECORD AS INFIELDER

Year	Club	League	Pos.	G.	AB.	R.	H.	2B.	3B.	HR.	RBI.	B.A.	PO.	A.	E.	F.A.
1968—Sarasota Cards		Gulf C.	3B	44	143	17	32	5	0	0	16	.224	29	80	12	*.901
1969—Lewiston		N'west	3B-OF-2B	26	74	11	15	3	0	3	10	.203	12	45	13	.814
1969—Modesto		Calif.	3B-OF	33	119	8	28	2	0	1	7	.235	33	58	6	.938
1970—Modesto		Calif.	3B-OF	20	47	4	7	3	0	1	1	.149	19	20	3	.929
1970—Cedar Rapids		Midw.	3B-1B-P	19	34	2	3	2	0	0	1	.088	9	19	3	.903
1970—Lewiston		N'west	P-S-2-3	18	30	5	4	0	1	0	3	.133	9	13	6	.786

—DID YOU KNOW—

That there have been 505 World Series games played since the first Series in 1903? The American League has won 272 games, the N.L. 230, and there have been three ties.

EMILO ANTHONY FOSSAS
(Tony)

Born September 23, 1958, at Havana, Cuba.
Height, 6.00. Weight 180.
Throws and bats lefthanded.
Attended University of South Florida, Tampa, Fla.

Tied for South Atlantic League in games started by pitchers with 27 in 1980.

Year Club	League	G.	IP.	W.	L.	Pct.	H.	R.	ER.	SO.	BB.	ERA.
1979—Sarasota Rangers	Gulf Coast	10	60	6	3	.667	54	28	20	49	26	3.00
1979—Tulsa	Texas	2	11	1	1	.500	14	10	8	3	4	6.55
1980—Asheville	S. Atlantic	30	*197	8	2	.600	*187	84	69	140	69	3.15
1981—Tulsa†‡§	Texas	38	106	5	6	.455	113	65	49	57	44	4.16
1982—Burlington	Midwest	25	146⅓	8	9	.471	121	63	50	115	33	3.08
1983—Tulsa	Texas	24	133	8	7	.533	123	77	62	103	46	4.20
1983—Oklahoma City	Am. Assoc.	10	35⅓	1	2	.333	55	33	31	23	12	7.90
1984—Tulsa	Texas	4	10	0	1	.000	12	5	5	7	3	4.50
1984—Oklahoma City	Am. Assoc.	29	121	5	9	.357	143	65	58	74	34	4.31
1985—Oklahoma City x	Am. Assoc.	30	110	7	6	.538	121	65	58	49	36	4.75
1986—Edmonton y	P. Coast	7	43⅓	3	3	.500	53	23	22	15	12	4.57
1987—Edmonton z	P. Coast	40	117⅓	6	8	.429	152	76	65	54	29	4.99
1988—Oklahoma City	Am. Assoc.	52	66⅔	3	0	1.000	64	21	21	42	16	2.84
1988—Texas a	American	5	5⅔	0	0	.000	11	3	3	0	2	4.76
Major League Totals—1 Year		5	5⅔	0	0	.000	11	3	3	0	2	4.76

Selected by Minnesota Twins' organization in 9th round of free-agent draft, June 6, 1978.
Selected by Texas Rangers' organization in 12th round of free-agent draft, June 5, 1979.
†Released, February 18, 1982; signed by Midland (Chicago Cubs' organization), March 11, 1982.
‡Loaned to Tabasco of Mexican League, March 15, 1982; returned, April 7, 1982.
§Released, April 7, 1982; signed by Burlington (Texas Rangers' organization), May 3, 1982.
xGranted free agency, October 15, 1985; signed by Edmonton (California Angels' organization), December 13, 1985.
yOn disabled list, June 2, 1986 through remainder of season.
zGranted free agency, October 15, 1987; signed by Oklahoma City (Texas Rangers' organization), December 1, 1987.
aGranted free agency, October 15, 1988.

JOHN ANTHONY FRANCO

Born September 17, 1960, at Brooklyn, N.Y.
Height, 5.10. Weight, 185.
Throws and bats lefthanded.
Attended St. John's University, Jamaica, N.Y.

Major League saves: 1984 (4), 1985 (12), 1986 (29), 1987 (32), 1988 (39). Total—116.
Led National League in saves with 39 in 1988.
Led National League in games finished in relief with 60 in 1987 and 61 in 1988.
Named National League Fireman of the Year by The Sporting News, 1988.

Year Club	League	G.	IP.	W.	L.	Pct.	H.	R.	ER.	SO.	BB.	ERA.
1981—Vero Beach	Florida St.	13	79	7	4	.636	78	41	31	60	41	3.53
1982—Albuquerque	P. Coast	5	27⅓	1	2	.333	41	22	22	24	15	7.24
1982—San Antonio	Texas	17	105⅓	10	5	.667	137	70	58	76	46	4.96
1983—Albuquerque†	P. Coast	11	15	0	0	.000	10	11	9	8	11	5.40
1983—Indianapolis	Am. Assoc.	23	115	6	10	.375	148	69	62	54	42	4.85
1984—Wichita	Am. Assoc.	6	9⅓	1	0	1.000	8	6	6	11	4	5.79
1984—Cincinnati	National	54	79⅓	6	2	.750	74	28	23	55	36	2.61
1985—Cincinnati	National	67	99	12	3	.800	83	27	24	61	40	2.18
1986—Cincinnati	National	74	101	6	6	.500	90	40	33	84	44	2.94
1987—Cincinnati	National	68	82	8	5	.615	76	26	23	61	27	2.52
1988—Cincinnati	National	70	86	6	6	.500	60	18	15	46	27	1.57
Major League Totals—5 Years		333	447⅓	38	22	.633	383	139	118	307	174	2.37

Selected by Los Angeles Dodgers' organization in 5th round of free-agent draft, June 8, 1981.
†Traded with Pitcher Brett Wise to Cincinnati Reds' organization for Infielder Rafael Landestoy, May 9, 1983.

ALL-STAR GAME RECORD

Year League	IP.	W.	L.	Pct.	H.	R.	ER.	SO.	BB.	ERA.
1987—National	⅔	0	0	.000	0	0	0	0	0	0.00

Member of National League All-Star Team in 1986; did not play.

JULIO CESAR FRANCO

Name pronounced FRANHK-oh.

Born August 23, 1961, at San Pedro de Macoris, D. R.
Height, 6.00. Weight, 165.
Throws and bats righthanded.

Major League stolen bases: 1983 (32), 1984 (19), 1985 (13), 1986 (10), 1987 (32), 1988 (25). Total—131.
Led American League in grounding into double plays with 28 in 1986.
Led American League shortstops in errors with 35 in 1985.
Led Northwest League in total bases with 153 in 1979.
Led Carolina League shortstops in double plays with 73 in 1980.
Led Northwest League shortstops in double plays with 45 in 1979.
Named second baseman on The Sporting News American League Silver Slugger team, 1988.
Named Carolina League Most Valuable Player, 1980.

Year	Club	League	Pos.	G.	AB.	R.	H.	2B.	3B.	HR.	RBI.	B.A.	PO.	A.	E.	F.A.
1978	—Butte	Pion.	SS	47	141	34	43	5	2	3	28	.305	37	52	25	.781
1979	—Central Ore.	N'west	SS	•71	299	57	★98	15	5	•10	45	.328	103	★256	31	.921
1980	—Peninsula	Carol.	SS	•140	★555	105	178	25	6	11	★99	.321	179	★412	42	.934
1981	—Reading	East.	SS	★139	★532	70	160	17	3	8	74	.301	246	437	30	.958
1982	—Oklahoma City	A. A.	★SS-3B	120	463	80	139	19	5	21	66	.300	211	350	★42	.930
1982	—Philadelphia†	Nat.	SS-3B	16	29	3	8	1	0	0	3	.276	8	25	0	1.000
1983	—Cleveland	Amer.	SS	149	560	68	153	24	8	8	80	.273	247	438	28	.961
1984	—Cleveland	Amer.	SS	160	★658	82	188	22	5	3	79	.286	280	481	★36	.955
1985	—Cleveland	Amer.	SS-2B	160	636	97	183	33	4	6	90	.288	252	437	36	.950
1986	—Cleveland	Amer	SS-2B	149	599	80	183	30	5	10	74	.306	248	413	19	.972
1987	—Cleveland‡	Amer.	SS-2B	128	495	86	158	24	3	8	52	.319	175	313	18	.964
1988	—Cleveland§	Amer.	2B	152	613	88	186	23	6	10	54	.303	310	434	14	.982
National League Totals—1 Year				16	29	3	8	1	0	0	3	.276	8	25	0	1.000
American League Totals—6 Years				898	3561	501	1051	156	31	45	429	.295	1512	2516	151	.964
Major League Totals—7 Years				914	3590	504	1059	157	31	45	432	.295	1520	2541	151	.964

Signed as free agent by Philadelphia Phillies' organization, June 23, 1978.

†Traded with Second Baseman Manny Trillo, Outfielder George Vukovich, Pitcher Jay Baller and Catcher Jerry Willard to Cleveland Indians for Outfielder Von Hayes, December 9, 1982.

‡On disabled list, July 13 to August 8, 1987.

§Traded to Texas Rangers for First Baseman Pete O'Brien, Outfielder Oddibe McDowell and Second Baseman Jerry Browne, December 6, 1988.

TERRY JON FRANCONA

Born April 22, 1959, at New Brighton, Pa.
Height, 6.01. Weight, 175.
Throws and bats lefthanded.
Attended University of Arizona, Tucson, Ariz.
Son of John (Tito) Francona, outfielder-first baseman with Baltimore, Chicago A.L., Detroit, Cleveland, St. Louis, Philadelphia, Atlanta, Oakland and Milwaukee, 1956 through 1970.

Major League stolen bases: 1981 (1), 1982 (2), 1985 (5), 1987 (2). Total—10.
Named College Player of the Year by THE SPORTING NEWS, 1980.
Named outfielder on THE SPORTING NEWS College Baseball All-America Team, 1980.

Year	Club	League	Pos.	G.	AB.	R.	H.	2B.	3B.	HR.	RBI.	B.A.	PO.	A.	E.	F.A.
1980	—Memphis	South.	OF	60	210	20	63	13	2	1	23	.300	59	4	4	.940
1981	—Memphis	South.	OF-1B	41	161	20	56	8	1	0	18	.348	102	7	5	.956
1981	—Denver	A. A.	OF	93	355	53	125	17	★9	1	58	.352	158	7	3	.982
1981	—Montreal	Nat.	OF-1B	34	95	11	26	0	1	1	8	.274	41	5	0	1.000
1982	—Montreal†	Nat.	OF-1B	46	131	14	42	3	0	0	9	.321	65	0	3	.956
1983	—Montreal	Nat.	OF-1B	120	230	21	59	11	1	3	22	.257	172	10	3	.984
1984	—Montreal‡	Nat.	1B-OF	58	214	18	74	19	2	1	18	.346	431	50	3	.994
1985	—Montreal§	Nat.	1B-OF-3B	107	281	19	75	15	1	2	31	.267	431	40	6	.987
1986	—Chicago	Nat.	OF-1B	86	124	13	31	3	0	2	8	.250	123	7	0	1.000
1986	—Iowa x	A. A.	1B-OF	17	60	7	15	3	2	0	8	.250	82	3	1	.988
1987	—Cincinnati y	Nat.	1B-OF	102	207	16	47	5	0	3	12	.227	377	45	2	.995
1988	—Colorado Springs	P. C.	OF-1B	68	235	29	76	15	5	0	32	.329	115	11	3	.977
1988	—Cleveland z	Amer.	1B-OF	62	212	24	66	8	0	1	12	.311	47	5	1	.981
National League Totals—7 Years				553	1282	112	354	56	5	12	108	.276	1640	157	17	.991
American League Totals—1 Year				62	212	24	66	8	0	1	12	.311	47	5	1	.981
Major League Totals—8 Years				615	1494	136	420	64	5	13	120	.281	1687	162	18	.990

Selected by Chicago Cubs' organization in 2nd round of free-agent draft, June 7, 1977.
Selected by Montreal Expos' organization in 1st round (22nd player selected) of free-agent draft, June 3, 1980.
†On disabled list, June 17 to September 27, 1982.
‡On disabled list, June 15 to September 5, 1984.
§Released, April 1, 1986; signed by Chicago Cubs' organization, May 2, 1986.
xGranted free agency, October 18, 1986; signed by Cincinnati Reds, March 23, 1987.
yGranted free agency, November 12, 1987; signed by Colorado Springs (Cleveland Indians' organization), February 28, 1988.
zGranted free agency, November 4, 1988.

DIVISION SERIES RECORD

Year	Club	League	Pos.	G.	AB.	R.	H.	2B.	3B.	HR.	RBI.	B.A.	PO.	A.	E.	F.A.
1981	—Montreal	Nat.	OF	5	12	0	4	0	0	0	0	.333	8	0	0	1.000

CHAMPIONSHIP SERIES RECORD

Year	Club	League	Pos.	G.	AB.	R.	H.	2B.	3B.	HR.	RBI.	B.A.	PO.	A.	E.	F.A.
1981	—Montreal	Nat.	PH-OF	2	1	0	0	0	0	0	0	.000	0	0	0	.000

WILLIAM PATRICK FRASER
(Willie)

Born May 26, 1964, at New York, N.Y.
Height, 6.01. Weight, 208.
Throws and bats righthanded.
Attended Concordia College, Bronxville, N.Y.

Major League saves: 1987 (1).
Led American League in home runs allowed with 33 in 1988.

Year	Club	League	G.	IP.	W.	L.	Pct.	H.	R.	ER.	SO.	BB.	ERA.
1985—	Quad Cities	Midwest	13	81⅔	2	6	.250	95	53	49	72	32	5.40
1986—	Palm Springs	California	19	124⅓	9	2	.818	115	60	49	99	29	3.55
1986—	Edmonton	P. Coast	6	40	4	1	.800	25	15	14	24	8	3.15
1986—	California	American	1	4⅓	0	0	.000	6	4	4	2	1	8.31
1987—	California	American	36	176⅔	10	10	.500	160	85	77	106	63	3.92
1988—	California	American	34	194⅔	12	13	.480	203	129	117	86	80	5.41
	Major League Totals—3 Years		71	375⅔	22	23	.489	369	218	198	194	144	4.74

Selected by California Angels' organization in 1st round (15th player selected) of free-agent draft, June 3, 1985.

LaVEL MAURICE FREEMAN

Born February 18, 1963, at Oakland, Calif.
Height, 5.09. Weight, 170.
Throws and bats lefthanded.
Attended Sacramento City College, Sacramento, Calif.

Led Texas League in total bases with 330 and slugging percentage with .627 in 1987.
Led Appalachian League in game-winning RBIs with 9 in 1983.

Year	Club	League	Pos.	G.	AB.	R.	H.	2B.	3B.	HR.	RBI.	B.A.	PO.	A.	E.	F.A.
1983—	Paintsville	Appal.	OF	71	264	64	81	17	0	7	50	.307	96	5	6	.944
1984—	Stockton	Calif.	OF	80	290	41	68	10	4	0	22	.234	136	5	8	.946
1984—	Beloit	Midw.	OF	49	170	29	50	14	1	2	33	.294	65	2	3	.957
1985—	Stockton	Calif.	OF-P	137	544	89	171	25	2	7	92	.314	189	11	9	.957
1986—	El Paso	Texas	OF	128	*515	101	166	31	5	14	91	.322	165	9	4	.978
1987—	El Paso	Texas	OF	129	526	*117	*208	42	4	24	96	*.395	212	9	8	.965
1988—	Denver	A. A.	OF	111	384	54	122	26	7	5	59	*.318	176	7	5	.973

Selected by Chicago White Sox' organization in 30th round of free-agent draft, June 8, 1981.
Selected by Milwaukee Brewers' organization in 1st round (26th player selected) of free-agent draft, January 11, 1983.

PITCHING RECORD

Year	Club	League	G.	IP.	W.	L.	Pct.	H.	R.	ER.	SO.	BB.	ERA.
1985—	Stockton	California	1	2	0	0	.000	4	2	2	2	0	9.00

MARVIN FREEMAN

Born April 10, 1963, at Chicago, Ill.
Height, 6.06. Weight, 200.
Throws and bats righthanded.
Attended Jackson State University, Jackson, Miss.

Pitched 6-0 no-hit victory against Richmond, July 28, 1988 (second game).
Tied for Eastern League lead in games started by pitchers with 27 in 1986.
Tied for Northwest League lead in games started by pitchers with 15 in 1984.

Year	Club	League	G.	IP.	W.	L.	Pct.	H.	R.	ER.	SO.	BB.	ERA.
1984—	Bend	Northwest	15	89⅔	8	5	.615	64	41	26	79	52	2.61
1985—	Clearwater	Florida St.	14	88⅓	6	5	.545	72	32	30	55	36	3.06
1985—	Reading	Eastern	11	65⅓	1	7	.125	51	41	39	35	52	5.37
1986—	Reading	Eastern	27	163	13	6	.684	130	89	73	113	*111	4.03
1986—	Philadelphia	National	3	16	2	0	1.000	6	4	4	8	10	2.25
1987—	Maine	Int'national	10	46	0	7	.000	56	38	32	29	30	6.26
1987—	Reading	Eastern	9	49⅔	3	3	.500	45	30	28	40	32	5.07
1988—	Maine	Int'national	18	74	5	5	.500	62	43	38	37	46	4.62
1988—	Philadelphia	National	11	51⅔	2	3	.400	55	36	35	37	43	6.10
	Major League Totals—2 Years		14	67⅔	4	3	.571	61	40	39	45	53	5.19

Selected by Montreal Expos' organization in 9th round of free-agent draft, June 8, 1981.
Selected by Philadelphia Phillies' organization in 2nd round of free-agent draft, June 4, 1984.

TODD GERALD FROHWIRTH

Born September 28, 1962, at Milwaukee, Wis.
Height, 6.04. Weight, 195.
Throws and bats righthanded.
Attended Northwest Missouri State University, Maryville, Mo.

Led Eastern League in saves with 19 in 1987.
Led Carolina League in games finished in relief with 48 and saves with 18 in 1985.
Led Northwest League in games finished in relief with 25 and tied for lead in saves with 11 in 1984.
Tied for International League lead in intentional bases on balls issued with 7 in 1987.

Year	Club	League	G.	IP.	W.	L.	Pct.	H.	R.	ER.	SO.	BB.	ERA.
1984—	Bend	Northwest	29	49⅔	4	4	.500	26	17	9	60	31	1.63
1985—	Peninsula	Carolina	*54	82	7	5	.583	70	33	20	74	48	2.20
1986—	Clearwater	Florida St.	32	52	3	3	.500	54	29	23	39	18	3.98
1986—	Reading	Eastern	29	42	0	4	.000	39	20	15	23	10	3.21
1987—	Reading	Eastern	36	58	2	4	.333	36	14	12	44	13	1.86
1987—	Maine	Int'national	27	32⅓	1	4	.200	30	12	9	21	15	2.51
1987—	Philadelphia	National	10	11	1	0	1.000	12	0	0	9	2	0.00
1988—	Philadelphia	National	12	12	1	2	.333	16	11	11	11	11	8.25
1988—	Maine	Int'national	49	62⅔	7	3	.700	52	21	17	39	19	2.44
	Major League Totals—2 Years		22	23	2	2	.500	28	11	11	20	13	4.30

Selected by Philadelphia Phillies' organization in 13th round of free-agent draft, June 4, 1984.

GARY JOSEPH GAETTI

Name pronounced Guy-ETT-ee.

Born August 19, 1958, at Centralia, Ill.
Height, 6.00. Weight, 200.
Throws and bats righthanded.
Attended Lake Land College, Mattoon, Ill., and Northwest
Missouri State University, Maryville, Mo.

Tied major league records by hitting home run in first major league at-bat, September 20, 1981; most home runs, opening day of season (2), April 6, 1982; most sacrifice flies, rookie season (13), 1982.
Major League stolen bases: 1983 (7), 1984 (11), 1985 (13), 1986 (14), 1987 (10), 1988 (7). Total—62.
Led American League in grounding into double plays with 25 in 1987.
Led American League in sacrifice flies with 13 in 1982.
Led American League third basemen in putouts with 142 in 1984 and 146 in 1985.
Led American League third basemen in total chances with 496 in 1984 and 473 in 1986.
Led American League third basemen in assists with 334 in 1984 and 1986.
Led American League third basemen in double plays with 46 in 1983 and 36 in 1986.
Tied for American League lead in errors by third basemen with 20 in 1984.
Led Southern League third basemen in putouts with 122 and assists with 281 in 1981.
Led Midwest League third basemen in double plays with 35 in 1980.
Tied for Appalachian League lead in errors by third basemen with 18 in 1979.
Named third baseman on THE SPORTING NEWS American League All-Star fielding team, 1986 through 1988.

Year Club	League	Pos.	G.	AB.	R.	H.	2B.	3B.	HR.	RBI.	B.A.	PO.	A.	E.	F.A.
1979—Elizabethton	Appal.	3B-SS	66	230	50	59	15	2	14	42	.257	70	134	21	.907
1980—Wis. Rapids	Midw.	3B	138	503	77	134	27	3	*22	82	.266	*94	*363	●35	.929
1981—Orlando	South.	*3B-1B	137	495	92	137	19	2	30	93	.277	143	283	*32	.930
1981—Minnesota	Amer.	3B	9	26	4	5	0	0	2	3	.192	5	17	0	1.000
1982—Minnesota	Amer.	3B-SS	145	508	59	117	25	4	25	84	.230	106	291	17	.959
1983—Minnesota	Amer.	3B-SS	157	584	81	143	30	3	21	78	.245	*131	361	17	.967
1984—Minnesota	Amer.	3B-OF-SS	●162	588	55	154	29	4	5	65	.262	163	335	21	.960
1985—Minnesota	Amer.	3B-OF-1B	160	560	71	138	31	0	20	63	.246	162	316	18	.964
1986—Minnesota	Amer.	3-S-O-2	157	596	91	171	34	1	34	108	.287	120	335	21	.956
1987—Minnesota†	Amer.	3B	154	584	95	150	36	2	31	109	.257	●134	261	11	.973
1988—Minnesota‡	Amer.	3B-SS	133	468	66	141	29	2	28	88	.301	105	191	7	.977
Major League Totals—8 Years			1077	3914	522	1019	214	16	166	598	.260	926	2107	112	.964

Selected by St. Louis Cardinals' organization in 4th round of free-agent draft, January 10, 1978.
Selected by Chicago White Sox' organization in secondary phase of free-agent draft, June 6, 1978.
Selected by Minnesota Twins' organization in secondary phase of free-agent draft, June 5, 1979.
†Granted free agency, November 9, 1987; re-signed by Twins, January 7, 1988.
‡On disabled list, August 21 to September 5, 1988.

CHAMPIONSHIP SERIES RECORD

Established Championship Series record for hitting home run in first two Series at-bats, October 7, 1987.
Tied Championship Series record for hitting home run in first Series at-bat, October 7, 1987.

Year Club	League	Pos.	G.	AB.	R.	H.	2B.	3B.	HR.	RBI.	B.A.	PO.	A.	E.	F.A.
1987—Minnesota	Amer.	3B	5	20	5	6	1	0	2	5	.300	8	7	0	1.000

WORLD SERIES RECORD

Tied World Series records for most at-bats (2) and most hits (2), inning, October 17, 1987 (fourth inning).

Year Club	League	Pos.	G.	AB.	R.	H.	2B.	3B.	HR.	RBI.	B.A.	PO.	A.	E.	F.A.
1987—Minnesota	Amer.	3B	7	27	4	7	2	1	1	4	.259	6	15	0	1.000

ALL-STAR GAME RECORD

Year League	Pos.	AB.	R.	H.	2B.	3B.	HR.	RBI.	B.A.	PO.	A.	E.	F.A.
1988—American	PH	1	0	0	0	0	0	0	.000	0	0	0	.000

GREGORY CARPENTER GAGNE

Name pronounced GAG-nee.

(Greg)

Born November 12, 1961, at Fall River, Mass.
Height, 5.11. Weight, 177.
Throws and bats righthanded.

Tied Major League record for most inside-the-park home runs, game (2), October 4, 1986.
Major League stolen bases: 1985 (10), 1986 (12), 1987 (6), 1988 (15). Total—43.
Led International League shortstops in total chances with 599 in 1983.

Year Club	League	Pos.	G.	AB.	R.	H.	2B.	3B.	HR.	RBI.	B.A.	PO.	A.	E.	F.A.
1979—Paintsville	Appal.	SS	41	106	10	19	2	3	0	7	.179	28	62	14	.865
1980—Greensboro†	S. Atl.	SS-3B-2B	98	337	39	91	20	5	3	32	.270	133	233	35	.913
1981—Greensboro	S. Atl.	2B-SS-3B	104	364	71	108	21	3	9	48	.297	172	280	25	.948
1982—Fort Lauderdale‡	Fla. St.	SS	1	3	0	1	0	0	0	0	.333	3	5	0	1.000
1982—Orlando	South.	SS-2B	136	504	73	117	23	5	11	57	.232	185	403	39	.938
1983—Toledo	Int.	SS	119	392	61	100	22	4	17	66	.255	201	*364	*34	.943
1983—Minnesota	Amer.	SS	10	27	2	3	1	0	0	3	.111	10	14	2	.923
1984—Toledo§	Int.	3B-SS-2B	70	236	31	66	7	2	9	27	.280	58	168	20	.926
1984—Minnesota	Amer.	PR-PH	2	1	0	0	0	0	0	0	.000	0	0	0	.000
1985—Minnesota x	Amer.	SS	114	293	37	66	15	3	2	23	.225	149	269	14	.968
1986—Minnesota	Amer.	*SS-2B	156	472	63	118	22	6	12	54	.250	228	381	*26	.959

Year	Club	League	Pos.	G.	AB.	R.	H.	2B.	3B.	HR.	RBI.	B.A.	PO.	A.	E.	F.A.
1987—	Minnesota	Amer.	SS-OF-2B	137	437	68	116	28	7	10	40	.265	196	391	18	.970
1988—	Minnesota	Amer.	S-O-2-3	149	461	70	109	20	6	14	48	.236	202	373	18	.970
	Major League Totals—6 Years			568	1691	240	412	86	22	38	168	.244	785	1428	78	.966

Selected by New York Yankees' organization in 5th round of free-agent draft, June 5, 1979.

†On disabled list, September 4 to September 22, 1980.

‡Traded with Pitchers Ron Davis and Paul Boris and a reported $400,000 to Minnesota Twins for Shortstop Roy Smalley, April 10, 1982.

§On disabled list, June 13 to July 18, 1984.

xOn disabled list, August 10 to September 1, 1985.

CHAMPIONSHIP SERIES RECORD

Year	Club	League	Pos.	G.	AB.	R.	H.	2B.	3B.	HR.	RBI.	B.A.	PO.	A.	E.	F.A.
1987—	Minnesota	Amer.	SS	5	18	5	5	3	0	2	3	.278	9	13	2	.917

WORLD SERIES RECORD

Tied World Series record for most at-bats, inning (2), October 18, 1987 (fourth inning).

Year	Club	League	Pos.	G.	AB.	R.	H.	2B.	3B.	HR.	RBI.	B.A.	PO.	A.	E.	F.A.
1987—	Minnesota	Amer.	SS	7	30	5	6	1	0	1	3	.200	6	20	2	.929

ANDRES JOSE GALARRAGA

Name pronounced Gahl-ah-RAH-guh.

Born June 18, 1961, at Caracas, Venezuela.
Height, 6.03. Weight, 235.
Throws and bats righthanded.

Major League stolen bases: 1985 (1), 1986 (6), 1987 (7), 1988 (13). Total—27.

Led National League batters in total bases with 329 and strikeouts with 153 in 1988.

Led National League in being hit by pitch with 10 in 1987.

Led Southern League in total bases with 271, slugging percentage with .508, intentional bases on balls received with 10 and tied for lead in being hit by pitch with 9 in 1984.

Tied for American Association lead in game-winning RBIs with 13 in 1985.

Led Southern League first basemen in total chances with 1,428 and double plays with 130 in 1984.

Named first baseman on THE SPORTING NEWS National League Silver Slugger team, 1988.

Named Southern League Most Valuable Player, 1984.

Year	Club	League	Pos.	G.	AB.	R.	H.	2B.	3B.	HR.	RBI.	B.A.	PO.	A.	E.	F.A.
1979—	W. Palm Beach	Fla. St.	1B	7	23	3	3	0	0	0	1	.130	2	1	0	1.000
1979—	Calgary	Pion.	1B-3B-C	42	112	14	24	3	1	4	16	.214	187	21	5	.976
1980—	Calgary	Pion.	1-3-C-O	59	190	27	50	11	4	4	22	.263	287	52	21	.942
1981—	Jamestown	NYP	C-1-O-3	47	154	24	40	5	4	6	26	.260	154	15	0	1.000
1982—	W. Palm Beach	Fla. St.	1B-OF	105	338	39	95	20	2	14	51	.281	462	36	9	.982
1983—	W. Palm Beach	Fla. St.	1B-OF-3B	104	401	55	116	18	3	10	66	.289	861	77	13	.986
1984—	Jacksonville	South.	1B	143	533	81	154	28	4	27	87	.289	*1302	*110	16	.989
1985—	Indianapolis	A. A.	1B-OF	121	439	*75	118	15	8	25	87	.269	930	63	14	.986
1985—	Montreal	Nat.	1B	24	75	9	14	1	0	2	4	.187	173	22	1	.995
1986—	Montreal†	Nat.	1B	105	321	39	87	13	0	10	42	.271	805	40	4	.995
1987—	Montreal	Nat.	1B	147	551	72	168	40	3	13	90	.305	*1300	103	10	.993
1988—	Montreal	Nat.	1B	157	609	99	*184	*42	8	29	92	.302	1464	103	15	.991
	Major League Totals—4 Years			433	1556	219	453	96	11	54	228	.291	3742	268	30	.993

Signed as free agent by Montreal Expos' organization, January 19, 1979.

†On disabled list, July 10 to August 19 and August 20 to September 4, 1986.

ALL-STAR GAME RECORD

Year	League	Pos.	AB.	R.	H.	2B.	3B.	HR.	RBI.	B.A.	PO.	A.	E.	F.A.
1988—	National	1B	2	0	0	0	0	0	0	.000	6	0	0	1.000

DAVID THOMAS GALLAGHER
(Dave)

Born September 20, 1960, at Trenton, N.J.
Height, 6.00. Weight, 180.
Throws and bats righthanded.
Attended Mercer County Community College, Trenton, N.J.

Major League stolen bases: 1987 (2), 1988 (5). Total—7.

Led International League in sacrifice hits with 12 in 1986.

Led Midwest League in sacrifice hits with 21 in 1982.

Led International League outfielders in total chances with 369 in 1985.

Tied for Eastern League lead in double plays by outfielders with 4 in 1983.

Year	Club	League	Pos.	G.	AB.	R.	H.	2B.	3B.	HR.	RBI.	B.A.	PO.	A.	E.	F.A.
1980—	Batavia	NYP	OF	69	241	33	66	6	3	5	36	.274	114	4	2	.983
1981—	Waterloo	Midw.	OF-3B	127	435	55	102	22	1	3	34	.234	224	22	7	.972
1982—	Chattanooga	South.	OF	15	54	10	12	2	1	0	4	.222	32	1	0	1.000
1982—	Waterloo	Midw.	OF	110	409	61	118	25	7	6	47	.289	232	15	4	*.984
1983—	Buffalo†	East.	OF-3B	107	376	64	127	21	3	2	47	*.338	223	13	5	.979
1984—	Maine	Int.	OF	116	380	49	94	19	5	6	49	.247	208	7	3	.986
1985—	Maine	Int.	OF	132	488	71	118	22	3	9	55	.242	*357	9	3	*.992
1986—	Maine	Int.	OF	132	497	59	145	23	5	8	44	.292	341	*14	1	*.997
1987—	Cleveland	Amer.	OF	15	36	2	4	1	1	0	1	.111	34	1	1	.972

Year	Club	League	Pos.	G.	AB.	R.	H.	2B.	3B.	HR.	RBI.	B.A.	PO.	A.	E.	F.A.
1987	—Buffalo‡	A. A.	OF	12	46	10	12	4	0	0	6	.261	34	1	0	1.000
1987	—Calgary§	P. C.	OF	75	268	45	82	27	2	3	46	.306	143	5	4	.974
1988	—Vancouver	P. C.	OF	34	131	23	44	8	1	4	27	.336	79	2	0	1.000
1988	—Chicago	Amer.	OF	101	347	59	105	15	3	5	31	.303	228	5	0	1.000
Major League Totals—2 Years				116	383	61	109	16	4	5	32	.285	262	6	1	.996

Selected by Oakland A's organization in 1st round (third player selected) of free-agent draft, January 8, 1980.
Selected by Cleveland Indians' organization in secondary phase of free-agent draft, June 3, 1980.
†On disabled list, May 2 to June 6, 1983.
‡Traded to Seattle Mariners' organization for Pitcher Mark Huismann, May 12, 1987.
§Released, September 30, 1987; signed by Vancouver (Chicago White Sox' organization), December 7, 1987.

MICHAEL ANTHONY GALLEGO
(Mike)

Born October 31, 1960, at Whittier, Calif.
Height, 5.08. Weight, 160.
Throws and bats righthanded.
Attended University of California, Los Angeles, Calif.

Major League stolen bases: 1985 (1), 1988 (2). Total—3.
Led Pacific Coast League in being hit by pitch with 8 in 1986.

Year	Club	League	Pos.	G.	AB.	R.	H.	2B.	3B.	HR.	RBI.	B.A.	PO.	A.	E.	F.A.
1981	—Modesto	Calif.	2B	60	202	38	55	9	3	0	23	.272	127	161	13	.957
1982	—West Haven	East.	2B-SS	54	139	17	25	1	0	0	5	.180	85	111	4	.980
1982	—Tacoma	P. C.	2B-3B-SS	44	136	12	30	3	1	0	11	.221	73	111	8	.958
1983	—Tacoma†	P. C.	2B	2	2	0	0	0	0	0	0	.000	0	1	0	1.000
1983	—Albany	East.	2B-SS-3B	90	274	31	61	6	0	0	18	.223	184	260	4	.991
1984	—Tacoma	P. C.	2B-SS-3B	101	288	29	70	8	1	0	18	.243	167	231	13	.968
1985	—Oakland	Amer.	2B-SS-3B	76	77	13	16	5	1	1	9	.208	57	94	1	.993
1985	—Modesto	Calif.	2B-SS-3B	6	25	1	5	1	0	0	2	.200	12	11	1	.958
1986	—Tacoma	P. C.	SS-3B-2B	132	443	58	122	16	5	4	46	.275	197	417	23	.964
1986	—Oakland	Amer.	2B-3B-SS	20	37	2	10	2	0	0	4	.270	24	51	1	.987
1987	—Tacoma	P. C.	2B	10	41	6	11	0	2	0	6	.268	15	25	1	.976
1987	—Oakland‡	Amer.	2B-3B-SS	72	124	18	31	6	0	2	14	.250	75	122	8	.961
1988	—Oakland	Amer.	2B-SS-3B	129	277	38	58	8	0	2	20	.209	155	254	8	.981
Major League Totals—4 Years				297	515	71	115	21	1	5	47	.223	311	521	18	.979

Selected by Oakland A's organization in 2nd round of free-agent draft., June 8, 1981.
†On temporary inactive list, April 10 to May 20, 1983.
‡On disabled list, June 13 to July 29, 1987.

CHAMPIONSHIP SERIES RECORD

Year	Club	League	Pos.	G.	AB.	R.	H.	2B.	3B.	HR.	RBI.	B.A.	PO.	A.	E.	F.A.
1988	—Oakland	Amer.	2B	4	12	1	1	0	0	0	0	.083	7	6	0	1.000

WORLD SERIES RECORD

Year	Club	League	Pos.	G.	AB.	R.	H.	2B.	3B.	HR.	RBI.	B.A.	PO.	A.	E.	F.A.
1988	—Oakland	Amer.	PR-2B	1	0	0	0	0	0	0	0	.000	0	0	0	.000

BALVINO GALVEZ

Name pronounced Gal-VEZ.

Born March 31, 1964, at San Pedro de Macoris, D. R.
Height, 6.01. Weight, 180.
Throws and bats righthanded.

Year	Club	League	G.	IP.	W.	L.	Pct.	H.	R.	ER.	SO.	BB.	ERA.
1982	—Lethbridge	Pioneer	10	20⅓	0	0	.000	33	21	13	11	17	5.75
1983	—Bradenton Dodgers	Gulf Coast	13	66⅓	4	3	.571	62	33	22	51	19	2.98
1984	—Vero Beach	Florida St.	26	156⅔	12	11	.522	152	68	63	76	62	3.62
1985	—San Antonio	Texas	26	170⅔	10	9	.526	181	99	86	111	79	4.54
1986	—Albuquerque†	P. Coast	18	81	3	6	.333	82	50	44	32	43	4.89
1986	—Los Angeles	National	10	20⅔	0	1	.000	19	10	9	11	12	3.92
1987	—Vero Beach	Florida St.	6	39	2	3	.400	39	20	14	21	13	3.23
1987	—Glens Falls‡§	Eastern	22	116⅔	5	9	.357	148	69	60	53	54	4.63
1988	—Orlando	Southern	4	23⅔	2	0	1.000	23	11	8	19	8	3.04
1988	—Portland	P. Coast	23	143⅓	11	7	.611	149	69	60	60	63	3.77
Major League Totals—1 Year			10	20⅔	0	1	.000	19	10	9	11	12	3.92

Signed as free agent by Los Angeles Dodgers' organization, September 10, 1981.
†On disabled list, May 29 to July 13, 1986.
‡Traded to Detroit Tigers' organization for Catcher Orlando Mercado, May 5, 1987.
§Traded to Minnesota Twins for Outfielder Billy Beane, March 24, 1988.

RONALD EDWIN GANT
(Ronnie)

Born March 2, 1965, at Victoria, Tex.
Height, 6.00. Weight, 172.
Throws and bats righthanded.

Major League stolen bases: 1987 (4), 1988 (19). Total—23.

Led National League second baseman in errors with 26 in 1988.
Led Carolina League in total bases with 271 in 1986.
Led Southern League second basemen in double plays with 108 and total chances with 783 in 1987.
Led South Atlantic League second basemen in double plays with 75 in 1984.

Year Club	League	Pos.	G.	AB.	R.	H.	2B.	3B.	HR.	RBI.	B.A.	PO.	A.	E.	F.A.
1983—Bradenton Brav...	Gulf C.	SS	56	193	32	45	2	2	1	14	.233	68	134	22	.902
1984—Anderson	S. Atl.	2B	105	359	44	85	14	6	3	38	.237	248	263	31	.943
1985—Sumter	S. Atl.	2B-SS	102	305	46	78	14	4	7	37	.256	160	200	10	.973
1986—Durham	Carol.	2B	137	512	108	142	31	10	*26	102	.277	240	384	26	.960
1987—Greenville	South.	2B	140	527	78	130	27	3	14	82	.247	*328	*434	21	*.973
1987—Atlanta	Nat.	2B	21	83	9	22	4	0	2	9	.265	45	59	3	.972
1988—Richmond	Int.	2B	12	45	3	14	2	2	0	4	.311	22	23	5	.900
1988—Atlanta	Nat.	2B-3B	146	563	85	146	28	8	19	60	.259	316	417	31	.959
Major League Totals—2 Years			167	646	94	168	32	8	21	69	.260	361	476	34	.961

Selected by Atlanta Braves' organization in 4th round of free-agent draft, June 6, 1983.

JAMES ELMER GANTNER
(Jim)

Born January 5, 1954, at Eden, Wis.
Height, 5.11. Weight, 175.
Throws right and bats lefthanded.
Attended University of Wisconsin, Oshkosh, Wis.

Tied major league record for longest errorless game by second baseman (25 innings), May 8, finished May 9, 1984; fielded 24⅓ innings.

Tied American League record for most innings played by second baseman, game (25), May 8, finished May 9, 1984; fielded 24⅓ innings.

Major League stolen bases: 1976 (1), 1977 (2), 1978 (2), 1979 (3), 1980 (11), 1981 (3), 1982 (6), 1983 (5), 1984 (6), 1985 (11), 1986 (13), 1987 (6), 1988 (20). Total—89.

Led American League second basemen in total chances with 613 in 1981, 900 in 1983 and 844 in 1984.
Led American League second basemen in double plays with 95 in 1981 and 128 in 1983.
Led Pacific Coast League third basemen in putouts with 136 and in fielding percentage with .936 in 1977.
Led Eastern League third basemen in fielding percentage with .953 in 1976.
Led Eastern League third basemen in putouts with 118 and assists with 310 in 1975.

Year Club	League	Pos.	G.	AB.	R.	H.	2B.	3B.	HR.	RBI.	B.A.	PO.	A.	E.	F.A.
1974—Newark	NYP	SS-3B	62	177	35	54	6	2	5	21	.305	64	134	14	.934
1975—Thetford Mines	East.	3B-SS	•138	456	61	117	17	0	12	48	.257	129	317	33	.931
1976—Berkshire	East.	3B-SS	126	403	56	118	21	1	6	53	.293	120	294	20	.954
1976—Milwaukee	Amer.	3B	26	69	6	17	1	0	0	7	.246	17	37	1	.982
1977—Spokane	P. C.	*3B-OF	•143	541	98	152	35	5	15	80	.281	137	*321	31	.937
1977—Milwaukee	Amer.	3B	14	47	4	14	1	0	1	2	.298	8	29	4	.902
1978—Milwaukee	Amer.	2-3-S-1	43	97	14	21	1	0	1	8	.216	46	82	5	.962
1979—Milwaukee	Amer.	3-2-S-P	70	208	29	59	10	3	2	22	.284	80	161	7	.972
1980—Milwaukee	Amer.	3B-2B-SS	132	415	47	117	21	3	4	40	.282	159	335	15	.971
1981—Milwaukee	Amer.	2B	107	352	35	94	14	1	2	33	.267	251	352	10	.984
1982—Milwaukee	Amer.	2B	132	447	48	132	17	2	4	43	.295	307	398	13	.982
1983—Milwaukee	Amer.	2B	161	603	85	170	23	8	11	74	.282	374	*512	14	.984
1984—Milwaukee	Amer.	2B	153	613	61	173	27	1	3	56	.282	*362	469	13	.985
1985—Milwaukee	Amer.	2B-3B-SS	143	523	63	133	15	4	5	44	.254	278	436	11	.985
1986—Milwaukee	Amer.	2B-3B-SS	139	497	58	136	25	1	7	38	.274	309	353	10	.985
1987—Milwaukee†	Amer.	2B-3B	81	265	37	72	14	0	4	30	.272	119	193	6	.981
1988—Milwaukee‡	Amer.	*2B-3B	155	539	67	149	28	2	0	47	.276	*325	430	11	.986
Major League Totals—13 Years			1356	4675	554	1287	197	25	44	444	.275	2635	3787	120	.982

Selected by Milwaukee Brewers' organization in 12th round of free-agent draft, June 5, 1974.
†On disabled list, July 31 to September 3, 1987.
‡Granted free agency, November 4, 1988; re-signed by Brewers, December 20, 1988.

DIVISION SERIES RECORD

Year Club	League	Pos.	G.	AB.	R.	H.	2B.	3B.	HR.	RBI.	B.A.	PO.	A.	E.	F.A.
1981—Milwaukee	Amer.	2B	4	14	1	2	1	0	0	0	.143	3	15	2	.900

CHAMPIONSHIP SERIES RECORD

Year Club	League	Pos.	G.	AB.	R.	H.	2B.	3B.	HR.	RBI.	B.A.	PO.	A.	E.	F.A.
1982—Milwaukee	Amer.	2B	5	16	1	3	0	0	0	2	.188	12	8	0	1.000

WORLD SERIES RECORD

Established World Series records for most assists by second baseman, seven-game Series (33), 1982; most errors by second baseman, seven-game Series (5), 1982.

Year Club	League	Pos.	G.	AB.	R.	H.	2B.	3B.	HR.	RBI.	B.A.	PO.	A.	E.	F.A.
1982—Milwaukee	Amer.	2B	7	24	5	8	4	1	0	4	.333	9	33	5	.894

PITCHING RECORD

Year Club	League	G.	IP.	W.	L.	Pct.	H.	R.	ER.	SO.	BB.	ERA.
1979—Milwaukee	American	1	1	0	0	.000	2	0	0	0	0	0.00

HENRY EUGENE GARBER
(Gene)

Born November 13, 1947, at Lancaster, Pa.
Height, 5.10. Weight, 172.
Throws and bats righthanded.
Received bachelor of arts degree in history and political science from
Elizabethtown College, Elizabethtown, Pa. in 1969.

Established major league record for most games lost by relief pitcher, season (16), 1979.

Tied major league record for most consecutive games won by relief pitcher, three consecutive games (3), May 15 through 17, 1975.

Major League saves: 1973 (11), 1974 (5), 1975 (14), 1976 (11), 1977 (19), 1978 (25), 1979 (25), 1980 (7), 1981 (2), 1982 (30), 1983 (9), 1984 (11), 1985 (1), 1986 (24), 1987 (18), 1988 (6). Total—218.

Led National League in games finished in relief with 47 in 1975.

Tied for International League lead in complete games with 13 in 1972.

Named International League Pitcher of the Year, 1972.

Year Club	League	G.	IP.	W.	L.	Pct.	H.	R.	ER.	SO.	BB.	ERA.
1965—Salem	Ap'lachian	1	⅔	0	0	.000	0	0	0	2	2	0.00
1965—Batavia	NYP	11	72	4	3	.571	71	42	28	40	31	3.50
1966—Raleigh	Carolina	16	94	4	4	.500	106	53	48	76	28	4.60
1967—Raleigh	Carolina	18	138	8	6	.571	103	41	29	68	47	1.89
1968—York	Eastern	16	118	7	2	.778	79	33	21	86	30	1.60
1968—Columbus	Int'national	23	59	5	1	.833	62	21	16	32	17	2.44
1969—York	Eastern	11	73	5	3	.625	61	40	25	57	40	3.08
1969—Pittsburgh	National	2	5	0	0	.000	6	3	3	3	1	5.40
1969—Columbus†	Int'national	17	123	7	6	.538	116	51	42	74	37	3.07
1970—Columbus	Int'national	30	95	5	2	.714	96	57	50	75	38	4.74
1970—Pittsburgh	National	14	22	0	3	.000	22	13	13	7	10	5.32
1971—Charleston‡	Int'national	24	170	14	6	.700	*184	85	79	105	54	4.18
1972—Charleston	Int'national	20	163	14	3	*.824	131	49	41	103	45	*2.26
1972—Pittsburgh§	National	4	6	0	0	.000	7	5	5	3	3	7.50
1973—Kansas City	American	48	153	9	9	.500	164	78	72	60	49	4.24
1974—Kansas City x	American	17	28	1	2	.333	35	21	15	14	13	4.82
1974—Toledo	Int'national	3	22	2	1	.667	19	7	1	17	3	0.41
1974—Philadelphia	National	34	48	4	0	1.000	39	15	11	27	31	2.06
1975—Philadelphia	National	*71	110	10	12	.455	104	48	44	69	27	3.60
1976—Philadelphia	National	59	93	9	3	.750	78	33	29	92	30	2.81
1977—Philadelphia	National	64	103	8	6	.571	82	30	27	78	23	2.36
1978—Philadelphia y-Atlanta	National	65	117	6	5	.545	84	32	28	85	24	2.15
1979—Atlanta	National	68	106	6	16	.273	121	66	51	56	24	4.33
1980—Atlanta	National	68	82	5	5	.500	95	42	35	51	24	3.84
1981—Atlanta z	National	35	59	4	6	.400	49	23	17	34	20	2.59
1982—Atlanta	National	69	119⅓	8	10	.444	100	40	31	68	32	2.34
1983—Atlanta a	National	43	60⅔	4	5	.444	72	37	31	45	23	4.60
1984—Atlanta	National	62	106	3	6	.333	103	45	36	55	24	3.06
1985—Atlanta	National	59	97⅓	6	6	.500	98	41	39	66	25	3.61
1986—Atlanta	National	61	78	5	5	.500	76	23	22	56	20	2.54
1987—Atlanta b	National	49	69⅓	8	10	.444	87	39	34	48	28	4.41
1987—Kansas City c	American	13	14⅓	0	0	.000	13	5	4	3	1	2.51
1988—Kansas City d	American	26	32⅔	0	4	.000	29	15	13	20	13	3.58
American League Totals—4 Years		104	228	10	15	.400	241	119	104	97	76	4.11
National League Totals—17 Years		827	1281⅔	86	98	.467	1223	535	456	843	369	3.20
Major League Totals—19 Years		931	1509⅔	96	113	.459	1464	654	560	940	445	3.34

Selected by Pittsburgh Pirates' organization in 13th round of free-agent draft, June 14, 1965.

†On military list, September 2, 1969, through February 18, 1970.

‡On temporary inactive list, June 24 to July 12, 1971.

§Traded to Kansas City Royals for Pitcher Jim Rooker, October 25, 1972.

xSold to Philadelphia Phillies, July 12, 1974.

yTraded to Atlanta Braves for Pitcher Dick Ruthven, June 15, 1978.

zOn disabled list, May 4 to August 9, 1981.

aOn disabled list, June 25 to July 27, 1983.

bTraded to Kansas City Royals for a player to be named later, August 31, 1987; Atlanta Braves acquired Catcher Terry Bell to complete deal, September 3, 1987.

cGranted free agency, November 9, 1987; re-signed by Royals, December 7, 1987.

dReleased, July 4, 1988.

CHAMPIONSHIP SERIES RECORD

Year Club	League	G.	IP.	W.	L.	Pct.	H.	R.	ER.	SO.	BB.	ERA.
1976—Philadelphia	National	2	⅔	0	1	.000	2	2	1	0	1	13.50
1977—Philadelphia	National	3	5⅓	1	1	.500	4	3	2	3	0	3.38
1982—Atlanta	National	2	3⅓	0	1	.000	4	3	3	3	1	8.10
Championship Series Totals—3 Years		7	9⅓	1	3	.250	10	8	6	6	2	5.79

BARBARO GARBEY GARBEY

Name pronounced BAR-bar-o Gar-BAY.

Born December 4, 1957, at Santiago, Cuba.
Height, 5.10. Weight, 170.
Throws and bats righthanded.

Major League stolen bases: 1984 (6), 1985 (3). Total—9.

Tied for Southern League lead in double plays by outfielders with 5 in 1982.

Year Club	League	Pos.	G.	AB.	R.	H.	2B.	3B.	HR.	RBI.	B.A.	PO.	A.	E.	F.A.
1980—Lakeland	Fla. St.	OF	26	88	15	32	4	0	1	16	.364	60	4	3	.955
1981—Birmingham†	South.	OF	107	391	56	112	17	4	6	55	.286	106	3	5	.956
1981—Evansville	A. A.	OF	4	12	4	1	0	0	0	0	.083	7	0	0	1.000
1982—Birmingham‡	South.	OF-1B	120	480	69	143	32	4	17	99	.298	206	22	11	.956
1983—Evansville§	A. A.	OF-3B-1B	101	377	60	121	21	6	14	59	.321	147	55	12	.944
1984—Detroit	Amer.	1-3-0-2	110	327	45	94	17	1	5	52	.287	411	58	12	.975
1985—Detroit xy	Amer.	1B-OF-3B	86	237	27	61	9	1	6	29	.257	228	20	3	.988
1986—Nuevo Laredo	Mex.	OF	22	66	3	19	1	1	0	5	.288	22	2	1	.960
1987—Campeche z	Mex.	1B-2B-3B	24	82	15	16	5	0	2	11	.195	76	36	2	.982
1988—Oklahoma City	A. A.	OF-1B-3B	67	263	30	81	16	0	5	41	.308	81	6	1	.989
1988—Texas a	Amer.	OF-1B-3B	30	62	4	12	2	0	0	5	.194	45	8	1	.981
Major League Totals—3 Years			226	626	76	167	28	2	11	86	.267	684	86	16	.980

Signed as free agent by Detroit Tigers' organization, June 6, 1980.
†On disabled list, April 16 to May 4, 1981.
‡On disabled list, August 22, 1982 through remainder of season.
§On suspended list, July 1 to July 31, 1983.
xTraded to Oakland A's for Outfielder Dave Collins, November 13, 1985.
yReleased, March 21, 1986; signed by Nuevo Laredo of Mexican League.
zReleased by Campeche of Mexican League; signed by Oklahoma City (Texas Rangers' organization), December 13, 1987.
aOn disabled list, July 16 to August 19, 1988.

CHAMPIONSHIP SERIES RECORD

Year Club	League	Pos.	G.	AB.	R.	H.	2B.	3B.	HR.	RBI.	B.A.	PO.	A.	E.	F.A.
1984—Detroit	Amer.	DH-PH	3	9	1	3	0	0	0	0	.333	0	0	0	.000

WORLD SERIES RECORD

Tied World Series record for most at-bats, inning (2), October 12, 1984 (second inning).

Year Club	League	Pos.	G.	AB.	R.	H.	2B.	3B.	HR.	RBI.	B.A.	PO.	A.	E.	F.A.
1984—Detroit	Amer.	DH-PH	4	12	0	0	0	0	0	0	.000	0	0	0	.000

DAMASO DOMINGO GARCIA

First name pronounced Da-MAH-so.

Born February 7, 1957, at Moca, Dominican Republic.
Height, 6.00. Weight, 185.
Throws and bats righthanded.
Attended Madre y Maestra University, Santiago, Dominican Republic.

Major League stolen bases: 1978 (1), 1979 (2), 1980 (13), 1981 (13), 1982 (54), 1983 (31), 1984 (46), 1985 (28), 1986 (9), 1988 (1). Total—198.
Tied major league record for most doubles, game (4), June 27, 1986.
Led Florida State League second baseman in double plays with 83 in 1976.
Tied for New York-Pennsylvania League lead in double plays by second basemen with 33 in 1975.
Named second baseman on THE SPORTING NEWS American League All-Star Team, 1982 and 1985.
Named second baseman on THE SPORTING NEWS American League Silver Slugger team, 1982.

Year Club	League	Pos.	G.	AB.	R.	H.	2B.	3B.	HR.	RBI.	B.A.	PO.	A.	E.	F.A.
1975—Oneonta	NYP	2B	50	157	28	42	4	2	0	17	.268	103	118	★17	.929
1976—Fort Lauderdale†	Fla.St.	2B	124	412	55	109	•22	4	1	41	.265	★273	353	21	★.968
1977—West Haven	East.	2B	129	445	62	118	13	9	0	53	.265	263	382	19	.971
1978—Tacoma	P. C.	2B-SS	102	385	51	103	18	6	1	53	.268	217	345	25	.957
1978—New York	Amer.	2B-SS	18	41	5	8	0	0	0	1	.195	36	35	4	.947
1979—Columbus ‡	Int.	SS-1B	39	118	18	32	1	0	1	3	.271	53	85	6	.958
1979—New York §	Amer.	SS-3B	11	38	3	10	1	0	0	4	.263	9	28	4	.902
1980—Toronto	Amer.	2B	140	543	50	151	30	7	4	46	.278	316	471	16	.980
1981—Toronto x	Amer.	2B	64	250	24	63	8	1	1	13	.252	132	181	9	.972
1982—Toronto	Amer.	2B	147	597	89	185	32	3	5	42	.310	273	461	15	.980
1983—Toronto	Amer.	2B	131	525	84	161	23	6	3	38	.307	266	360	12	.981
1984—Toronto	Amer.	2B	152	633	79	180	32	5	5	46	.284	267	427	14	.980
1985—Toronto	Amer.	2B	146	600	70	169	25	4	8	65	.282	302	371	13	.981
1986—Toronto y	Amer.	2B-1B	122	424	57	119	22	0	6	46	.281	225	286	8	.985
1987—Richmond z	Int.	2B	1	1	0	0	0	0	0	0	.000	0	0	0	.000
1988—Atlanta a	Nat.	2B	21	60	3	7	1	0	1	4	.117	26	35	1	.984
1988—Albuquerque	P. C.	2B	3	5	1	2	1	0	0	1	.400	1	1	1	.667
National League Totals—1 Year			21	60	3	7	1	0	1	4	.117	26	35	1	.984
American League Totals—9 Years			931	3651	461	1046	173	26	32	301	.286	1826	2620	95	.979
Major League Totals—10 Years			952	3711	464	1053	174	26	33	305	.284	1852	2655	96	.979

Signed as free agent by New York Yankees' organization, March 10, 1975.
†On suspended list, June 4 to June 7, 1976.
‡On disabled list, May 14 to July 24 and July 31 to August 13, 1979.
§Traded with First Baseman Chris Chambliss and Pitcher Paul Mirabella to Toronto Blue Jays for Catcher Rick Cerone, Pitcher Tom Underwood and Outfielder Ted Wilborn, November 1, 1979.
xOn disabled list, August 22, 1981 through remainder of season.
yTraded with Pitcher Luis Leal to Atlanta Braves for Pitcher Craig McMurtry, February 2, 1987.
zOn Atlanta disabled list, March 29 to September 1, 1987; included rehabilitation disability assignment to Richmond, June 29 and June 30, 1987.
aReleased, May 17, 1988; signed by Albuquerque (Los Angeles Dodgers' organization), June 29, 1988.

CHAMPIONSHIP SERIES RECORD

Established American League Championship Series record for most doubles, seven-game Series (4), 1985.

Year	Club	League	Pos.	G.	AB.	R.	H.	2B.	3B.	HR.	RBI.	B.A.	PO.	A.	E.	F.A.
1985	Toronto	Amer.	2B	7	30	4	7	4	0	0	1	.233	10	12	0	1.000

ALL-STAR GAME RECORD

Year	League	Pos.	AB.	R.	H.	2B.	3B.	HR.	RBI.	B.A.	PO.	A.	E.	F.A.
1984	American	2B	1	0	0	0	0	0	0	.000	1	0	0	1.000
1985	American	2B	2	0	1	0	0	0	0	.500	0	3	0	1.000
All-Star Game Totals—2 Years			3	0	1	0	0	0	0	.333	1	3	0	1.000

LEONARDO ANTONIO GARCIA
(Leo)

Born November 6, 1962, at Santiago, D. R.
Height, 5.08. Weight, 165.
Throws and bats lefthanded.

Major League stolen bases: 1987 (3).

Year	Club	League	Pos.	G.	AB.	R.	H.	2B.	3B.	HR.	RBI.	B.A.	PO.	A.	E.	F.A.
1980	Sarasota W.S.	Gulf C.	OF	32	108	8	26	0	0	0	7	.241	60	3	2	.969
1981	Appleton†	Midw.	OF	107	395	55	103	14	6	1	38	.261	192	13	11	.949
1982	Appleton‡	Midw.	OF	117	435	56	115	17	6	2	37	.264	207	15	10	.957
1983	Waterbury	East.	OF	131	498	65	128	25	*11	5	47	.257	233	13	5	.980
1984	Wichita	A. A.	OF	117	336	47	95	12	6	3	39	.283	147	13	3	.982
1985	Denver	A. A.	OF	118	385	53	112	19	3	4	25	.291	198	14	*11	.951
1986	Denver	A. A.	OF	139	528	81	147	32	6	4	57	.278	317	10	6	.982
1987	Nashville	A. A.	OF	116	437	64	124	12	8	3	40	.284	262	13	5	.982
1987	Cincinnati	Nat.	OF	31	30	8	6	0	0	1	2	.200	19	0	0	1.000
1988	Nashville	A. A.	OF	48	178	21	46	5	5	1	17	.258	107	0	2	.982
1988	Cincinnati §	Nat.	OF	23	28	2	4	1	0	0	0	.143	12	0	0	1.000
Major League Totals—2 Years				54	58	10	10	1	0	1	2	.172	31	0	0	1.000

Signed as free agent by Chicago White Sox' organization after Inter-American League folded, January 26, 1980.

†On disabled list, July 6 to July 21, 1981.

‡Traded with Third Baseman Wade Rowdon to Cincinnati Reds' organization, September 7, 1982, completing deal in which Cincinnati traded Pitcher Jim Kern to Chicago White Sox for two players to be named later, August 23, 1982.

§Granted free agency, October 15, 1988.

MIGUEL ANGEL GARCIA

Born April 3, 1967, at Caracas, Venezuela.
Height, 6.01. Weight, 170.
Throws and bats lefthanded.

Year	Club	League	G.	IP.	W.	L.	Pct.	H.	R.	ER.	SO.	BB.	ERA.
1985	Quad City	Midwest	29	65⅓	3	2	.600	60	25	21	50	21	2.89
1986	Palm Springs	California	43	72⅔	8	3	.727	59	18	13	75	26	1.61
1987	Midland	Texas	50	87	10	6	.625	86	35	25	67	34	2.59
1987	California†	American	1	1⅔	0	0	.000	3	4	3	0	3	16.20
1987	Pittsburgh	National	1	⅔	0	0	.000	0	0	0	0	0	0.00
1988	Buffalo	Am. Assoc.	25	66⅓	6	2	.750	71	26	19	34	21	2.58
1988	Pittsburgh	National	1	2	0	0	.000	3	2	1	2	2	4.50
American League Totals—1 Year			1	1⅔	0	0	.000	3	4	3	0	3	16.20
National League Totals—2 Years			2	2⅔	0	0	.000	3	2	1	2	2	3.38
Major League Totals—2 Years			3	4⅓	0	0	.000	6	6	4	2	5	8.31

Signed as free agent by California Angels' organization, January 22, 1985.

†Traded to Pittsburgh Pirates, September 3, 1987, completing deal in which Pittsburgh traded Second Baseman Johnny Ray to California Angels for Third Baseman Billie Merrifield and a player to be named later, August 29, 1987.

MARK ALLAN GARDNER

Born March 1, 1962, at Clovis, Calif.
Height, 6.01. Weight, 190.
Throws and bats righthanded.
Attended Fresno City College, Fresno, Calif.,
and Fresno State University, Fresno, Calif.

Year	Club	League	G.	IP.	W.	L.	Pct.	H.	R.	ER.	SO.	BB.	ERA.
1985	Jamestown	NYP	3	13	0	0	.000	9	4	4	16	4	2.77
1985	West Palm Beach	Florida St.	10	60⅔	5	4	.556	54	24	16	44	18	2.37
1986	Jacksonville	Southern	29	168⅔	10	11	.476	144	88	72	140	90	3.84
1987	Indianapolis	Am. Assoc.	9	46	3	3	.500	48	32	29	41	28	5.67
1987	Jacksonville	Southern	17	101	4	6	.400	101	50	47	78	42	4.19
1988	Jacksonville	Southern	15	112⅓	6	3	.667	72	24	20	130	36	1.60
1988	Indianapolis	Am. Assoc.	13	84⅓	4	2	.667	65	30	26	71	32	2.77

Selected by California Angels' organization in 6th round of free-agent draft, January 11, 1983.
Selected by Cleveland Indians' organization in 17th round of free-agent draft, June 4, 1984.
Selected by Montreal Expos' organization in 8th round of free-agent draft, June 3, 1985.

WESLEY BRIAN GARDNER
(Wes)

Born April 29, 1961, at Benton, Ark.
Height, 6.04. Weight, 203.
Throws and bats righthanded.
Attended University of Central Arkansas, Conway, Ark.

Major League saves: 1984 (1), 1987 (10), 1988 (2). Total—13.
Led International League in saves with 20 in 1984 and tied for lead with 18 in 1985.
Led International League in games finished in relief with 37 in 1984.

Year Club	League	G.	IP.	W.	L.	Pct.	H.	R.	ER.	SO.	BB.	ERA.
1982—Little Falls	NYP	23	77⅔	3	6	.333	73	48	32	77	29	3.71
1983—Lynchburg	Carolina	49	62⅔	6	3	.667	55	16	13	67	32	1.87
1984—Tidewater	Int'national	40	56	1	2	.333	40	11	10	36	19	1.61
1984—New York	National	21	25⅓	1	1	.500	34	19	18	19	8	6.39
1985—Tidewater	Int'national	53	76⅔	7	6	.538	57	31	24	75	34	2.82
1985—New York†	National	9	12	0	2	.000	18	14	7	11	8	5.25
1986—Boston‡	American	1	1	0	0	.000	1	1	1	1	0	9.00
1987—Boston	American	49	89⅔	3	6	.333	98	55	54	70	42	5.42
1987—Pawtucket	Int'national	5	8⅔	1	0	1.000	8	3	3	9	3	3.12
1988—Boston §	American	36	149	8	6	.571	119	61	58	106	64	3.50
National League Totals—2 Years		30	37⅓	1	3	.250	52	33	25	30	16	6.03
American League Totals—3 Years		86	239⅔	11	12	.478	218	117	113	177	106	4.24
Major League Totals—5 Years		116	277	12	15	.444	270	150	138	207	122	4.48

Selected by New York Mets' organization in 22nd round of free-agent draft, June 7, 1982.
†Traded with Pitcher Calvin Schiraldi and Outfielders John Christensen and LaSchelle Tarver to Boston Red Sox for Pitchers Bob Ojeda, Tom McCarthy, John Mitchell and Chris Bayer, November 13, 1985.
‡On disabled list, April 14, 1986 through remainder of season; included rehabilitation disability assignment to Pawtucket, June 24 to July 1, 1986.
§On disabled list, May 29 to June 13, 1988.

CHAMPIONSHIP SERIES RECORD

Established Championship Series record for most strikeouts by relief pitcher, game (8), October 8, 1988.

Year Club	League	G.	IP.	W.	L.	Pct.	H.	R.	ER.	SO.	BB.	ERA.
1988—Boston	American	1	4⅔	0	0	.000	6	3	3	8	2	5.79

PHILIP MASON GARNER
(Phil)

Born April 30, 1949, at Jefferson City, Tenn.
Height, 5.10. Weight, 177.
Throws and bats righthanded.
Received bachelor of science degree in general business from
University of Tennessee, Knoxville, Tenn., in 1973.

Tied major league record for most home runs, bases filled, two consecutive games (2), September 14 and 15, 1978.
Tied National League record for most home runs, bases filled, month (2), September, 1978.
Major League stolen bases: 1974 (1), 1975 (4), 1976 (35), 1977 (32), 1978 (27), 1979 (17), 1980 (32), 1981 (10), 1982 (24), 1983 (18), 1984 (3), 1985 (4), 1986 (12), 1987 (6). Total—225.
Led American League second basemen in total chances with 865 in 1976.
Led National League second basemen in assists with 499, total chances with 869 and double plays with 116 in 1980.
Led Pacific Coast League third basemen in putouts with 104, assists with 261 and double plays with 23 in 1973.

Year Club	League	Pos.	G.	AB.	R.	H.	2B.	3B.	HR.	RBI.	B.A.	PO.	A.	E.	F.A.
1971—Burlington	Midw.	3B	116	439	73	122	22	4	11	70	.278	*122	203	29	.918
1972—Birmingham	South.	3B	71	264	45	74	10	6	12	40	.280	74	116	13	.936
1972—Iowa	A. A.	3B	70	247	33	60	18	4	9	22	.243	50	140	10	.950
1973—Tucson	P. C.	*3B-2B	138	516	87	149	23	12	14	73	.289	107	270	*35	.915
1973—Oakland	Amer.	3B	9	5	0	0	0	0	0	0	.000	2	3	0	1.000
1974—Tucson	P. C.	3B-SS	96	388	78	128	29	10	11	51	.330	92	182	15	.948
1974—Oakland	Amer.	3B-SS-2B	30	28	4	5	1	0	0	1	.179	11	24	1	.972
1975—Oakland	Amer.	*2B-SS	●160	488	46	120	21	5	6	54	.246	355	427	*26	.968
1976—Oakland†	Amer.	2B	159	555	54	145	29	12	8	74	.261	378	*465	22	.975
1977—Pittsburgh	Nat.	3B-2B-SS	153	585	99	152	35	10	17	77	.260	223	351	17	.971
1978—Pittsburgh	Nat.	3B-2B-SS	154	528	66	138	25	9	10	66	.261	258	389	28	.959
1979—Pittsburgh	Nat.	3B-2B-SS	150	549	76	161	32	8	11	59	.293	234	396	22	.966
1980—Pittsburgh	Nat.	*2B-SS	151	548	62	142	27	6	5	58	.259	349	500	*21	.976
1981—Pitt‡§-Hou.	Nat.	2B	87	294	35	73	9	3	1	26	.248	183	250	12	.973
1982—Houston	Nat.	2B-3B	155	588	65	161	33	8	13	83	.274	285	464	17	.978
1983—Houston	Nat.	3B	154	567	76	135	24	2	14	79	.238	100	311	24	.945
1984—Houston	Nat.	3B-2B	128	374	60	104	17	6	4	45	.278	136	251	12	.970
1985—Houston	Nat.	3B-2B	135	463	65	124	23	10	6	51	.268	101	229	21	.940
1986—Houston x	Nat.	3B-2B	107	313	43	83	14	3	9	41	.265	66	152	23	.905
1987—Hou.y-L.A.z	Nat.	3B-2B-SS	113	238	29	49	9	0	5	23	.206	65	144	13	.941
1988—San Francisco a	Nat.	3B	15	13	0	2	0	0	0	1	.154	0	0	0	.000
1988—Phoenix b	P. C.	2B-3B	17	45	5	12	2	1	1	5	.267	12	22	0	1.000
American League Totals—4 Years			358	1076	104	270	51	17	14	129	.251	746	919	49	.971
National League Totals—12 Years			1502	5060	676	1324	248	65	95	609	.262	2000	3437	210	.963
Major League Totals—16 Years			1860	6136	780	1594	299	82	109	738	.260	2746	4356	259	.965

Selected by Montreal Expos' organization in 8th round of free-agent draft, June 4, 1970.
Selected by Oakland A's organization in secondary phase of free-agent draft, January 13, 1971.

†Traded with Infielder Tommy Helms and Pitcher Chris Batton to Pittsburgh Pirates for Pitchers Doc Medich, Dave Giusti, Rick Langford and Doug Bair and Outfielders Mitchell Page and Tony Armas, March 15, 1977.

‡On disabled list, April 2 to April 23, 1981.

§Traded to Houston Astros for Second Baseman Johnny Ray and two players to be named later, August 31, 1981; Pittsburgh Pirates' organization acquired Outfielder Kevin Houston and Pitcher Randy Niemann to complete deal, September 9, 1981.

xGranted free agency, November 12, 1986; re-signed by Astros, January 6, 1987.

yTraded to Los Angeles Dodgers for a player to be named later, June 19, 1987; Houston Astros' organization acquired Pitcher Jeff Edwards to complete deal, June 26, 1987.

zGranted free agency, November 9, 1987; signed by San Francisco Giants, January 28, 1988.

aOn disabled list, April 13 to September 2, 1988; included rehabilitation disability assignment to Phoenix, August 5 to August 24, 1988.

bGranted free agency, November 4, 1988; named coach of Houston Astros.

DIVISION SERIES RECORD

Year	Club	League	Pos.	G.	AB.	R.	H.	2B.	3B.	HR.	RBI.	B.A.	PO.	A.	E.	F.A.
1981	—Houston	Nat.	2B	5	18	1	2	0	0	0	0	.111	6	8	1	.933

CHAMPIONSHIP SERIES RECORD

Year	Club	League	Pos.	G.	AB.	R.	H.	2B.	3B.	HR.	RBI.	B.A.	PO.	A.	E.	F.A.
1975	—Oakland	Amer.	2B	3	5	0	0	0	0	0	0	.000	7	4	1	.917
1979	—Pittsburgh	Nat.	2B-SS	3	12	4	5	0	1	1	1	.417	8	9	0	1.000
1986	—Houston	Nat.	3B	3	9	1	2	1	0	0	2	.222	1	9	0	1.000
Championship Series Totals—3 Years				9	26	5	7	1	1	1	3	.269	16	22	1	.974

WORLD SERIES RECORD

Established World Series record for most double plays by second baseman, seven-game Series (9), 1979.

Tied World Series records for highest batting average, seven-game Series (.500), 1979; one or more hits, each game, seven-game Series, 1979; most assists by second baseman, inning (3), October 13, 1979 (ninth inning).

Year	Club	League	Pos.	G.	AB.	R.	H.	2B.	3B.	HR.	RBI.	B.A.	PO.	A.	E.	F.A.
1979	—Pittsburgh	Nat.	2B	7	24	4	12	4	0	0	5	.500	21	23	2	.957

ALL-STAR GAME RECORD

Year	League	Pos.	AB.	R.	H.	2B.	3B.	HR.	RBI.	B.A.	PO.	A.	E.	F.A.
1976	—American	2B	1	0	0	0	0	0	0	.000	1	1	0	1.000
1980	—National	2B	2	1	1	0	0	0	0	.500	1	3	0	1.000
1981	—National	2B	0	0	0	0	0	0	0	.000	0	0	0	.000
All-Star Game Totals—3 Years			3	1	1	0	0	0	0	.333	2	4	0	1.000

SCOTT WILLIAM GARRELTS

Name pronounced Guh-RELTZ.

Born October 30, 1961, at Urbana, Ill.
Height, 6.04. Weight, 205.
Throws and bats righthanded.

Pitched seven-inning, 1-0 no-hit victory against Tacoma, August 20, 1983.
Major League saves: 1985 (13), 1986 (10), 1987 (12), 1988 (13). Total—48.
Tied for Midwest League lead in games started by pitchers with 27 in 1980.

Year	Club	League	G.	IP.	W.	L.	Pct.	H.	R.	ER.	SO.	BB.	ERA.
1979	—Great Falls	Pioneer	8	43	1	4	.200	45	37	28	26	40	5.86
1980	—Clinton	Midwest	27	176	11	11	.500	155	98	76	*159	*149	3.89
1981	—Shreveport†	Texas	14	71	3	8	.273	56	43	35	73	43	4.44
1982	—Shreveport	Texas	27	151⅓	9	10	.474	131	76	64	159	90	3.81
1982	—San Francisco	National	1	2	0	0	.000	3	3	3	4	2	13.50
1983	—Phoenix‡	P. Coast	21	97⅔	5	5	.500	86	64	50	89	81	4.61
1983	—San Francisco	National	5	35⅔	2	2	.500	33	11	10	16	19	2.52
1984	—Phoenix	P. Coast	21	97⅔	5	7	.417	97	75	64	69	82	5.90
1984	—San Francisco	National	21	43	2	3	.400	45	33	27	32	34	5.65
1985	—San Francisco	National	74	105⅔	9	6	.600	76	37	27	106	58	2.30
1986	—San Francisco	National	53	173⅔	13	9	.591	144	65	60	125	74	3.11
1987	—San Francisco	National	64	106⅓	11	7	.611	70	41	38	127	55	3.22
1988	—San Francisco	National	65	98	5	9	.357	80	42	39	86	46	3.58
Major League Totals—7 Years			283	564⅓	42	36	.538	451	232	204	496	288	3.25

Selected by San Francisco Giants' organization in 1st round (15th player selected) of free-agent draft, June 5, 1979.

†On disabled list, July 15 to August 16, 1981.

‡On disabled list, May 12 to June 6 and July 8 to July 24, 1983.

CHAMPIONSHIP SERIES RECORD

Year	Club	League	G.	IP.	W.	L.	Pct.	H.	R.	ER.	SO.	BB.	ERA.
1987	—San Francisco	National	2	2⅔	0	0	.000	2	2	2	4	4	6.75

ALL-STAR GAME RECORD

Member of National League All-Star Team in 1985; did not play.

—DID YOU KNOW—

That Kansas City's Kevin Seitzer compiled the fourth-best batting average in his league in each of his first four seasons of professional baseball?

RICHARD LEO GEDMAN JR.
(Rich)

Born September 26, 1959, at Worcester, Mass.
Height, 6.00. Weight, 215.
Throws right and bats lefthanded.

Established major league records for most putouts (36) and chances accepted (37) by catcher, two consecutive nine-inning games, April 29, 30, 1986.
Tied major league record for most putouts by catcher, nine-inning game (20), April 29, 1986.
Tied American League record for most chances accepted by catcher, nine-inning game (20), April 29, 1986.
Major League stolen bases: 1985 (2), 1986 (1). Total—3.
Hit for the cycle, September 18, 1985.
Led American League catchers in total chances with 937 and passed balls with 14 in 1986.
Led International League catchers in double plays with 13 in 1980.
Named catcher on THE SPORTING NEWS American League All-Star Team, 1986.
Named American League Rookie Player of the Year by THE SPORTING NEWS, 1981.

Year Club	League	Pos.	G.	AB.	R.	H.	2B.	3B.	HR.	RBI.	B.A.	PO.	A.	E.	F.A.
1978—Winter Haven	Fla. St.	C	98	297	35	89	17	3	3	32	.300	377	39	2	*.995
1979—Bristol	East.	C	130	470	48	129	25	1	12	63	.274	497	58	11	*.981
1980—Pawtucket	Int.	C	111	347	43	82	18	2	11	29	.236	367	*65	7	.984
1980—Boston	Amer.	C	9	24	2	5	0	0	0	1	.208	13	0	2	.867
1981—Pawtucket	Int.	C	25	81	8	24	3	0	2	11	.296	176	20	6	.969
1981—Boston	Amer.	C	62	205	22	59	15	0	5	26	.288	275	30	3	.990
1982—Boston	Amer.	C	92	289	30	72	17	2	4	26	.249	397	29	10	.977
1983—Boston	Amer.	C	81	204	21	60	16	1	2	18	.294	274	26	6	.980
1984—Boston	Amer.	C	133	449	54	121	26	4	24	72	.269	693	58	*18	.977
1985—Boston	Amer.	C	144	498	66	147	30	5	18	80	.295	768	*78	*15	.983
1986—Boston†	Amer.	C	135	462	49	119	29	0	16	65	.258	*866	65	6	.994
1987—Boston‡	Amer.	C	52	151	11	31	8	0	1	13	.205	306	14	8	.976
1988—Boston§	Amer.	C	95	299	33	69	14	0	9	39	.231	570	40	5	.992
1988—Pawtucket	Int.	C	4	15	2	7	1	0	1	1	.467	13	1	1	.933
Major League Totals—9 Years			803	2581	288	683	155	12	79	340	.265	4162	340	73	.984

Signed as free agent by Boston Red Sox' organization, August 5, 1977.
†Granted free agency, November 12, 1986; re-signed by Red Sox, May 2, 1987.
‡On disabled list, July 7 to July 22 and July 30, 1987 through remainder of season.
§On disabled list, April 26 to May 20, 1988; included rehabilitation disability assignment to Pawtucket, May 14 to May 20, 1988.

CHAMPIONSHIP SERIES RECORD

Tied Championship Series records for most hits, two consecutive games, one Series (6), October 12 (11 innings) and 14, 1986; most times reached first base safely, game (5), October 12, 1986 (11 innings).
Tied American League Championship Series record for most hits, two consecutive Series (15), 1986 and 1988.

Year Club	League	Pos.	G.	AB.	R.	H.	2B.	3B.	HR.	RBI.	B.A.	PO.	A.	E.	F.A.
1986—Boston	Amer.	C	7	28	4	10	1	0	1	6	.357	45	4	0	1.000
1988—Boston	Amer.	C	4	14	1	5	0	0	1	1	.357	34	5	0	1.000
Championship Series Totals—2 Years			11	42	5	15	1	0	2	7	.357	79	9	0	1.000

WORLD SERIES RECORD

Tied World Series record for most double plays by catcher, game (2), October 22, 1986.

Year Club	League	Pos.	G.	AB.	R.	H.	2B.	3B.	HR.	RBI.	B.A.	PO.	A.	E.	F.A.
1986—Boston	Amer.	C	7	30	1	6	1	0	1	1	.200	46	3	2	.961

ALL-STAR GAME RECORD

Year League	Pos.	AB.	R.	H.	2B.	3B.	HR.	RBI.	B.A.	PO.	A.	E.	F.A.
1985—American	C	1	0	0	0	0	0	0	.000	4	0	0	1.000
1986—American	C	0	0	0	0	0	0	0	.000	1	1	0	1.000
All-Star Game Totals—2 Years		1	0	0	0	0	0	0	.000	5	1	0	1.000

ROBERT PETER GEREN III
(Bob)

Born September 22, 1961, at San Diego, Calif.
Height, 6.03. Weight, 205.
Throws and bats righthanded.

Led Eastern League catchers in fielding percentage with .994 in 1987.
Led Texas League catchers in fielding percentage with .996 in 1985.
Led Midwest League catchers in putouts with 826, assists with 102 and total chances with 939 in 1983.

Year Club	League	Pos.	G.	AB.	R.	H.	2B.	3B.	HR.	RBI.	B.A.	PO.	A.	E.	F.A.
1979—Walla Walla	N'west	C	54	151	19	26	5	0	0	16	.172	183	23	9	.958
1980—Reno	Calif.	C	48	157	24	45	7	1	4	23	.287	89	17	4	.964
1980—Walla Walla†	N'west	C	51	177	19	45	8	1	2	28	.254	306	40	10	.972
1981—St. Petersburg	Fla. St.	C	64	167	15	37	9	1	0	13	.222	204	24	3	.987
1982—St. Petersburg	Fla. St.	*C-OF-1B	110	352	38	86	24	1	1	45	.244	500	*72	10	.983
1983—Springfield	Midw.	C-1B	124	434	67	115	21	3	24	73	.265	829	104	11	.988
1984—Arkansas	Texas	C-1B-3B	86	292	39	72	12	0	15	40	.247	545	56	8	.987
1984—Louisville	A. A.	C	15	40	3	7	1	0	0	3	.175	80	6	1	.989

Year Club	League	Pos.	G.	AB.	R.	H.	2B.	3B.	HR.	RBI.	B.A.	PO.	A.	E.	F.A.
1985—Arkansas	Texas	C-1B-OF	103	315	38	71	18	1	5	40	.225	562	60	4	.994
1985—Louisville‡	A. A.	C	5	14	2	5	2	0	1	3	.357	27	1	0	1.000
1986—Albany	East.	C-1B	11	27	3	4	1	0	0	0	.148	51	7	0	1.000
1986—Columbus	Int.	C-1B	68	205	24	52	15	3	7	25	.254	270	36	5	.984
1987—Albany	East.	C-1B-3B	78	213	33	47	7	2	11	31	.221	319	45	3	.992
1987—Columbus	Int.	C	5	20	1	3	0	0	1	3	.150	20	3	1	.958
1988—Columbus	Int.	C	95	321	37	87	13	2	8	35	.271	478	72	8	.986
1988—New York	Amer.	C	10	10	0	1	0	0	0	0	.100	18	3	0	1.000
Major League Totals—1 Year			10	10	0	1	0	0	0	0	.100	18	3	0	1.000

Selected by San Diego Padres' organization in 1st round (24th player selected) of free-agent draft, June 5, 1979.

†Traded to St. Louis Cardinals' organization, December 10, 1980, completing deal in which San Diego Padres traded Pitchers Rollie Fingers and Bob Shirley, Catcher-First Baseman Gene Tenace and a player to be named later to St. Louis Cardinals for Catchers Terry Kennedy and Steve Swisher, Pitchers John Littlefield, Al Olmsted, Kim Seaman and John Urrea and Infielder Mike Phillips, December 8, 1980.

‡Granted free agency, October 15, 1985; signed by Columbus (New York Yankees' organization), November 7, 1985.

HAROLD KENNETH GERHART
(Ken)

Born May 19, 1961, at Charleston, S. C.
Height, 6.01. Weight, 195.
Throws and bats righthanded.
Attended Middle Tennessee State University, Murfreesboro, Tenn.

Major League stolen bases: 1987 (9), 1988 (7). Total—16.
Led International League in total bases with 232 in 1986.
Led Carolina League in total bases with 275 in 1983.
Led Appalachian League in sacrifice flies with 8 in 1982.

Year Club	League	Pos.	G.	AB.	R.	H.	2B.	3B.	HR.	RBI.	B.A.	PO.	A.	E.	F.A.
1982—Bluefield	Appal.	OF	66	228	57	59	13	0	12	43	.259	105	3	2	.982
1983—Hagerstown	Carol.	OF	130	501	131	137	29	8	*31	86	.273	274	11	13	.956
1984—Charlotte	South.	OF	85	264	40	53	8	3	13	40	.201	183	5	4	.979
1984—Hagerstown	Carol.	OF	47	168	39	54	18	3	6	21	.321	108	1	5	.956
1985—Charlotte†	South.	OF	68	222	55	61	16	1	17	52	.275	177	4	1	.995
1986—Rochester	Int.	OF	124	453	73	124	18	3	*28	72	.274	216	11	7	.970
1986—Baltimore	Amer.	OF	20	69	4	16	2	0	1	7	.232	34	0	1	.971
1987—Baltimore‡	Amer.	OF	92	284	41	69	10	2	14	34	.243	174	3	5	.973
1988—Charlotte§	South.	OF	3	13	2	2	0	0	1	1	.154	5	0	0	1.000
1988—Baltimore	Amer.	OF	103	262	27	51	10	1	9	23	.195	192	3	5	.975
Major League Totals—3 Years			215	615	72	136	22	3	24	64	.221	400	6	11	.974

Selected by Baltimore Orioles' organization in 5th round of free-agent draft, June 7, 1982.

†On disabled list, July 8 to September 3, 1985.

‡On disabled list, August 13, 1987 through remainder of season.

§On Baltimore disabled list, March 26 to April 16, 1988; included rehabilitation disability assignment to Charlotte, April 10 to April 16, 1988.

KIRK HAROLD GIBSON

Born May 28, 1957, at Pontiac, Mich.
Height, 6.03. Weight, 215.
Throws and bats lefthanded.
Attended Michigan State University, East Lansing, Mich.

Tied major league record for most home runs, opening day of season (2), April 7, 1986.

Major League stolen bases: 1979 (3), 1980 (4), 1981 (17), 1982 (9), 1983 (14), 1984 (29), 1985 (30), 1986 (34), 1987 (26), 1988 (31). Total—197.

Named National League Most Valuable Player by Baseball Writers' Association of America, 1988.
Named outfielder on THE SPORTING NEWS National League Silver Slugger team, 1988.
Named as wide receiver on THE SPORTING NEWS College Football All-America Team, 1978.
Selected by St. Louis Cardinals in 7th round (173rd player selected) of 1979 NFL draft.
Received reported $200,000 bonus to sign with Detroit Tigers, 1978.
Named outfielder on THE SPORTING NEWS College Baseball All-America Team, 1978.

Year Club	League	Pos.	G.	AB.	R.	H.	2B.	3B.	HR.	RBI.	B.A.	PO.	A.	E.	F.A.
1978—Lakeland†	Fla. St.	OF	54	175	27	42	5	4	8	40	.240	115	2	6	.951
1979—Evansville‡	A. A.	OF	89	327	50	80	13	5	9	42	.245	100	5	9	.921
1979—Detroit	Amer.	OF	12	38	3	9	3	0	1	4	.237	15	0	0	1.000
1980—Detroit§	Amer.	OF	51	175	23	46	2	1	9	16	.263	122	1	1	.992
1981—Detroit	Amer.	OF	83	290	41	95	11	3	9	40	.328	142	1	4	.973
1982—Detroit x	Amer.	OF	69	266	34	74	16	2	8	35	.278	167	4	1	.994
1983—Detroit	Amer.	OF	128	401	60	91	12	9	15	51	.227	116	2	3	.975
1984—Detroit	Amer.	OF	149	531	92	150	23	10	27	91	.282	245	4	●12	.954
1985—Detroit y	Amer.	OF	154	581	96	167	37	5	29	97	.287	286	1	●11	.963
1986—Detroit z	Amer.	OF	119	441	84	118	11	2	28	86	.268	190	2	2	.990
1987—Toledo	Int.	DH	6	17	2	4	0	0	0	3	.235	0	0	0	.000
1987—Detroit ab	Amer.	OF	128	487	95	135	25	3	24	79	.277	253	6	7	.974
1988—Los Angeles	Nat.	OF	150	542	106	157	28	1	25	76	.290	311	6	*12	.964
American League Totals—9 Years			893	3210	528	885	140	35	150	499	.276	1536	21	41	.974
National League Totals—1 Year			150	542	106	157	28	1	25	76	.290	311	6	12	.964
Major League Totals—10 Years			1043	3752	634	1042	168	36	175	575	.278	1847	27	53	.972

Selected by Detroit Tigers' organization in 1st round (12th player selected) of free-agent draft, June 6, 1978.
†On restricted list, August 15, 1978, to March 1, 1979.
‡On disabled list, April 13 to May 21, 1979.
§On disabled list, June 18 to October 6, 1980.
xOn disabled list, July 11, 1982 through remainder of season.
yGranted free agency, November 12, 1985; re-signed by Tigers, January 8, 1986.
zOn disabled list, April 23 to June 2, 1986.
aOn Detroit disabled list, March 30 to May 5, 1987; included rehabilitation disability assignment to Toledo, April 28 to May 5, 1987.
bGranted free agency, January 22, 1988; signed by Los Angeles Dodgers, January 29, 1988.

CHAMPIONSHIP SERIES RECORD

Established American League Championship Series record for most strikeouts, five-game Series (8), 1987.
Tied American League Championship Series record for most stolen bases, five-game Series (3), 1987.

Year Club	League	Pos.	G.	AB.	R.	H.	2B.	3B.	HR.	RBI.	B.A.	PO.	A.	E.	F.A.
1984—Detroit	Amer.	OF	3	12	2	5	1	0	1	2	.417	7	0	0	1.000
1987—Detroit	Amer.	OF	5	21	4	6	1	0	1	4	.286	10	1	0	1.000
1988—Los Angeles	Nat.	OF	7	26	2	4	0	0	2	6	.154	17	1	1	.947
Championship Series Totals—3 Years			15	59	8	15	2	0	4	12	.254	34	2	1	.973

WORLD SERIES RECORD

Year Club	League	Pos.	G.	AB.	R.	H.	2B.	3B.	HR.	RBI.	B.A.	PO.	A.	E.	F.A.
1984—Detroit	Amer.	OF	5	18	4	6	0	0	2	7	.333	5	1	2	.750
1988—Los Angeles	Nat.	PH	1	1	1	1	0	0	1	2	1.000	0	0	0	.000
World Series Totals—2 Years			6	19	5	7	0	0	3	9	.368	5	1	2	.750

PAUL MARSHALL GIBSON

Born January 4, 1960, at Southampton, N.Y.
Height, 6.00. Weight, 165.
Throws left and bats righthanded.
Attended Suffolk County Community College, Selden, N.Y.

Tied for International League lead in shutouts with 2 in 1987.

Year Club	League	G.	IP.	W.	L.	Pct.	H.	R.	ER.	SO.	BB.	ERA.
1978—Shelby	W. Carol.	24	140	9	6	.600	106	57	47	71	71	3.02
1979—Tampa	Florida St.	24	129	3	8	.273	121	56	44	58	46	3.07
1980—Cedar Rapids†	Midwest	28	146	6	•15	.286	171	97	80	74	53	4.93
1981—Lakeland	Florida St.	20	64	4	3	.571	64	25	21	38	21	2.95
1982—Birmingham‡	Southern	44	77⅓	3	3	.500	60	25	23	71	39	2.68
1983—Orlando§	Southern	40	76⅔	1	7	.125	91	59	52	45	56	6.10
1984—Orlando x	Southern	27	121	7	7	.500	125	71	52	64	54	3.87
1985—Birmingham	Southern	36	144⅓	8	8	.500	135	73	66	79	63	4.12
1986—Glens Falls	Eastern	9	19⅔	3	1	.750	16	3	3	21	7	1.37
1986—Nashville	Am. Assoc.	30	113⅓	5	6	.455	121	58	50	91	40	3.97
1987—Toledo	Int'national	27	179	*14	7	.667	173	83	69	118	57	3.47
1988—Detroit	American	40	92	4	2	.667	83	33	30	50	34	2.93
Major League Totals—1 Year		40	92	4	2	.667	83	33	30	50	34	2.93

Selected by Cincinnati Reds' organization in 3rd round of free-agent draft, January 10, 1978.
†Released, April 8, 1981; signed by Lakeland (Detroit Tigers' organization), May 23, 1981.
‡Drafted by Minnesota Twins, December 6, 1982.
§On disabled list, August 4 to August 14, 1983.
xGranted free agency, October 15, 1984; signed by Birmingham (Detroit Tigers' organization), November 9, 1984.

BYRON BRETT GIDEON

(Known by middle name.)
Born August 8, 1963, at Ozona, Tex.
Height, 6.02. Weight, 195.
Throws and bats righthanded.
Attended Bee County College, Beeville, Tex., and University of Mary Hardin-Baylor, Belton, Tex.

Major League saves: 1987 (3).

Year Club	League	G.	IP.	W.	L.	Pct.	H.	R.	ER.	SO.	BB.	ERA.
1985—Macon	S. Atlantic	15	82⅓	4	7	.364	71	38	30	62	46	3.28
1986—Prince William	Carolina	26	55⅔	1	6	.143	60	43	34	41	37	5.50
1986—Macon	S. Atlantic	6	48	5	1	.833	33	16	14	38	35	2.63
1986—Nashua	Eastern	4	11⅔	0	1	.000	13	6	4	6	5	3.09
1987—Harrisburg	Eastern	26	36⅓	4	3	.571	27	10	8	39	10	1.98
1987—Pittsburgh	National	29	36⅔	1	5	.167	34	22	19	31	10	4.66
1988—Harrisburg	Eastern	25	39⅔	3	2	.600	27	8	6	30	21	1.36
1988—Buffalo	Am. Assoc.	24	42	1	6	.143	33	17	17	41	19	3.64
Major League Totals—1 Year		29	36⅔	1	5	.167	34	22	19	31	10	4.66

Selected by Houston Astros' organization in 8th round of free-agent draft, January 11, 1983.
Selected by Pittsburgh Pirates' organization in 6th round of free-agent draft, June 3, 1985.

JOSEPH ELLIOTT GIRARDI

(Joe)

Born October 14, 1964, at Peoria, Ill.
Height, 5.11. Weight, 195.
Throws and bats righthanded.
Received degree in industrial engineering from Northwestern University, Evanston, Ill., in 1986.

Led Eastern League catchers in putouts with 448, fielding percentage with .992, total chances with 528 and tied for lead in double plays with 5 in 1988.

Led Carolina League catchers in total chances with 661 and tied for lead in passed balls with 17 in 1987.

Year Club	League	Pos.	G.	AB.	R.	H.	2B.	3B.	HR.	RBI.	B.A.	PO.	A.	E.	F.A.
1986—Peoria†	Midw.	C	68	230	36	71	13	1	3	28	.309	405	34	5	.989
1987—Winston-Salem	Carol.	C	99	364	51	102	9	8	8	46	.280	*569	*74	18	.973
1988—Pittsfield‡	East.	*C-OF	104	357	44	97	14	1	7	41	.272	460	*76	6	.989

Selected by Chicago Cubs' organization in 5th round of free-agent draft, June 2, 1986.

†On disabled list, August 27, 1986 through remainder of season.

‡On disabled list, August 7, 1988 through remainder of season.

BRIAN ALLEN GIVENS

Born November 6, 1965, at Lompoc, Calif.
Height, 6.05. Weight, 220.
Throws left and bats righthanded.
Attended Trinidad State Junior College, Trinidad, Colo.

Led Carolina League in wild pitches with 19 in 1987.

Led Appalachian League in wild pitches with 20 in 1984.

Year Club	League	G.	IP.	W.	L.	Pct.	H.	R.	ER.	SO.	BB.	ERA.
1984—Kingsport	Ap'lachian	14	44⅓	4	1	.800	41	36	32	51	52	6.50
1985—Little Falls	NYP	11	73⅔	3	4	.429	54	28	24	81	43	2.93
1985—Columbia	S. Atlantic	3	21⅓	1	2	.333	15	7	7	25	13	2.95
1986—Columbia	S. Atlantic	27	172	8	7	.533	147	89	72	*189	100	3.77
1987—Lynchburg	Carolina	21	112⅓	6	8	.429	112	79	58	96	69	4.65
1987—Tidewater	Int'national	1	3⅔	0	1	.000	9	10	10	3	6	24.55
1988—Jackson	Texas	26	164⅓	6	*14	.300	140	78	69	*156	68	3.78

Selected by New York Mets' organization in 10th round of free-agent draft, January 17, 1984.

CLINTON DANIEL GLADDEN III

(Dan)

Born July 7, 1957, at San Jose, Calif.
Height, 5.11. Weight, 175.
Throws and bats righthanded.
Attended DeAnza College, Cupertino, Calif., and
Fresno State University, Fresno, Calif.
Brother of Jeff Gladden, pitcher in Kansas City Royals' and
San Francisco Giants' organization, 1980 through 1984.

Major League stolen bases: 1983 (4), 1984 (31), 1985 (32), 1986 (27), 1987 (25), 1988 (28). Total—147.

Tied for American League lead in double plays by outfielders with 5 in 1988.

Led Texas League in stolen bases with 52 and caught stealing with 26 in 1981.

Year Club	League	Pos.	G.	AB.	R.	H.	2B.	3B.	HR.	RBI.	B.A.	PO.	A.	E.	F.A.
1979—Fresno	Calif.	OF-2B-SS	60	228	41	70	9	1	3	31	.307	56	16	3	.960
1980—Fresno	Calif.	OF	62	237	46	72	10	2	9	41	.304	68	3	1	.986
1980—Shreveport	Texas	OF-SS	74	292	51	86	11	2	9	35	.295	169	14	5	.973
1981—Shreveport	Texas	OF-SS-2B	124	472	81	148	23	9	8	44	.314	211	12	3	.987
1982—Phoenix	P. C.	OF	130	503	93	155	40	5	10	74	.308	264	16	7	.976
1983—Phoenix	P. C.	OF	127	505	113	153	30	9	12	80	.303	319	6	7	.979
1983—San Francisco	Nat.	OF	18	63	6	14	2	0	1	9	.222	53	0	0	1.000
1984—Phoenix†	P. C.	OF	59	234	70	93	11	7	3	27	.397	130	4	2	.985
1984—San Francisco	Nat.	OF	86	342	71	120	17	2	4	31	.351	232	8	3	.988
1985—San Francisco	Nat.	OF	142	502	64	122	15	8	7	41	.243	273	3	7	.975
1986—San Francisco‡	Nat.	OF	102	351	55	97	16	1	4	29	.276	226	7	3	.987
1986—Phoenix§ x	P. C.	OF	7	27	5	9	4	0	0	0	.333	11	0	0	1.000
1987—Minnesota	Amer.	OF	121	438	69	109	21	2	8	38	.249	223	9	3	.987
1988—Minnesota	Amer.	O-2-3-P	141	576	91	155	32	6	11	62	.269	319	12	3	.991
National League Totals—4 Years			348	1258	196	353	50	11	16	110	.281	784	18	13	.984
American League Totals—2 Years			262	1014	160	264	53	8	19	100	.260	542	21	6	.989
Major League Totals—6 Years			610	2272	356	617	103	19	35	210	.272	1326	39	19	.986

Signed as free agent by San Francisco Giants' organization, June 17, 1979.

†On disabled list, April 19 to May 1, 1984.

‡On disabled list, June 4 to July 23, 1986; included rehabilitation disability assignment to Phoenix, July 14 to July 23, 1986.

§Batted left and righthanded.

xTraded with Pitcher David Blakley to Minnesota Twins for Pitchers Jose Dominguez and Ray Velasquez and a player to be named later, March 31 1987; San Francisco Giants' organization acquired Pitcher Bryan Hickerson to complete deal, June 15, 1987.

CHAMPIONSHIP SERIES RECORD

Year Club	League	Pos.	G.	AB.	R.	H.	2B.	3B.	HR.	RBI.	B.A.	PO.	A.	E.	F.A.
1987—Minnesota	Amer.	OF	5	20	5	7	2	0	0	5	.350	12	0	0	1.000

WORLD SERIES RECORD

Tied World Series records for most grand slams, game (1), October 17, 1987; most runs batted in, inning (4), October 17, 1987 (fourth inning).

Year	Club	League	Pos.	G.	AB.	R.	H.	2B.	3B.	HR.	RBI.	B.A.	PO.	A.	E.	F.A.
1987	Minnesota	Amer.	OF	7	31	3	9	2	1	1	7	.290	12	0	0	1.000

PITCHING RECORD

Year	Club	League	G.	IP.	W.	L.	Pct.	H.	R.	ER.	SO.	BB.	ERA.
1988	Minnesota	American	1	1	0	0	.000	0	0	0	0	0	0.00

THOMAS MICHAEL GLAVINE

Name pronounced GLA-vin.

(Tom)

Born March 25, 1966, at Concord, Mass.
Height, 6.00. Weight, 175.
Throws and bats lefthanded.

Led Gulf Coast League in wild pitches with 12 in 1984.

Drafted by Los Angeles Kings in 1984 NHL entry draft. Fourth Kings pick, 69th player overall, fourth round.

Year	Club	League	G.	IP.	W.	L.	Pct.	H.	R.	ER.	SO.	BB.	ERA.
1984	Bradenton Braves	Gulf Coast	8	32⅓	2	3	.400	29	17	12	34	13	3.34
1985	Sumter	S. Atlantic	26	168⅔	9	6	.600	114	58	44	174	73	*2.35
1986	Greenville	Southern	22	145⅓	11	6	.647	129	62	55	114	70	3.41
1986	Richmond	Int'national	7	40	1	5	.167	40	29	25	12	27	5.63
1987	Richmond	Int'national	22	150⅓	6	12	.333	142	70	56	91	56	3.35
1987	Atlanta	National	9	50⅓	2	4	.333	55	34	31	20	33	5.54
1988	Atlanta	National	34	195⅓	7	*17	.292	201	111	99	84	63	4.56
Major League Totals—2 Years			43	245⅔	9	21	.300	256	145	130	104	96	4.76

Selected by Atlanta Braves' organization in 2nd round of free-agent draft, June 4, 1984.

JERRY DON GLEATON

(Jerry Don)

Born September 14, 1957, at Brownwood, Tex.
Height, 6.03. Weight, 210.
Throws and bats lefthanded.
Attended University of Texas, Austin, Tex.

Major League saves: 1984 (2), 1985 (1), 1987 (5), 1988 (3). Total—11.

Tied for Eastern League lead in complete games with 13 in 1982.

Tied for Texas League lead in home runs allowed with 17 in 1980.

Year	Club	League	G.	IP.	W.	L.	Pct.	H.	R.	ER.	SO.	BB.	ERA.
1979	Tulsa	Texas	5	35	3	2	.600	37	19	19	21	15	4.89
1979	Texas	American	5	10	0	1	.000	15	7	7	2	2	6.30
1980	Tulsa	Texas	25	178	13	7	.650	179	83	72	138	68	3.64
1980	Texas†	American	5	7	0	0	.000	5	2	2	2	4	2.57
1981	Seattle	American	20	85	4	7	.364	88	50	45	31	38	4.76
1981	Spokane	P. Coast	13	91	5	7	.417	104	53	42	57	39	4.15
1982	Lynn	Eastern	24	182	15	7	.682	175	71	55	132	54	2.72
1982	Seattle	American	3	4⅔	0	0	.000	7	7	7	1	2	13.50
1983	Salt Lake City	P. Coast	24	137⅓	9	9	.500	189	112	102	73	81	6.68
1984	Salt Lake City‡	P. Coast	29	49⅔	4	1	.800	62	39	32	39	17	5.80
1984	Denver	Am. Assoc.	12	20	1	1	.500	20	5	4	10	4	1.80
1984	Chicago	American	11	18⅓	1	2	.333	20	12	7	4	6	3.44
1985	Buffalo	Am. Assoc.	38	55⅓	8	2	*.800	62	17	15	37	21	2.44
1985	Chicago	American	31	29⅔	1	0	1.000	37	19	19	22	13	5.76
1986	Buffalo§	Am. Assoc.	46	78⅓	4	3	.571	79	34	28	77	35	3.22
1987	Omaha	Am. Assoc.	6	15	2	0	1.000	14	6	5	9	6	3.00
1987	Kansas City	American	48	50⅔	4	4	.500	38	28	24	44	28	4.26
1988	Omaha	Am. Assoc.	15	37⅓	4	2	.667	30	7	6	40	14	1.45
1988	Kansas City	American	42	38	0	4	.000	33	17	15	29	17	3.55
Major League Totals—8 Years			165	243⅓	10	18	.357	243	142	126	135	110	4.66

Selected by Baltimore Orioles' organization in 2nd round of free-agent draft, June 8, 1976.

Selected by Texas Rangers' organization in 1st round (17th player selected) of free-agent draft, June 5, 1979.

†Traded with Pitchers Brian Allard, Ken Clay and Steve Finch, Shortstop Rick Auerbach and Outfielder Richie Zisk to Seattle Mariners for Catcher Larry Cox, Pitcher Rick Honeycutt, Outfielders Willie Horton and Leon Roberts and Shortstop Mario Mendoza, December 12, 1980.

‡Traded with Pitcher Gene Nelson to Chicago White Sox for Pitcher Salome Barojas, June 27, 1984.

§Granted free agency, October 15, 1986; signed by Kansas City Royals, November 15, 1986.

JERRY LEROY GOFF

Born April 12, 1964, at San Rafael, Calif.
Height. 6.03. Weight, 205.
Throws right and bats lefthanded.
Attended Marin Community College, Kentfield, Calif.,
and University of California, Berkeley, Calif.

Led Northwest League catchers in double plays with 7 in 1986.
Led Midwest League in passed balls with 32 in 1987.

Year Club	League	Pos.	G.	AB.	R.	H.	2B.	3B.	HR.	RBI.	B.A.	PO.	A.	E.	F.A.
1986—Bellingham	N'west	C	54	168	26	32	7	2	7	25	.190	286	35	12	.964
1987—Wausau	Midw.	C-1B	109	336	51	78	17	2	13	47	.232	583	73	15	.978
1988—San Bernardino	Calif.	C	65	215	38	62	11	0	13	43	.288	383	64	6	.987
1988—Vermont	East.	*C-OF	63	195	27	41	7	1	7	23	.210	283	40	*17	.950

Selected by Oakland A's organization in 7th round of free-agent draft, January 11, 1983.
Selected by New York Yankees' organization in 12th round of free-agent draft, January 17, 1984.
Selected by Seattle Mariners' organization in 3rd round of free-agent draft, June 2, 1986.

LEONARDO GOMEZ
(Leo)

Born March 2, 1967, in Puerto Rico.
Height, 6.00. Weight, 180.
Throws and bats righthanded.

Year Club	League	Pos.	G.	AB.	R.	H.	2B.	3B.	HR.	RBI.	B.A.	PO.	A.	E.	F.A.
1986—Bluefield†	Appal.	3B-2B-SS	27	88	23	31	7	1	7	28	.352	15	38	7	.883
1987—Hagerstown	Carol.	3B-SS	131	466	94	152	*38	2	19	110	*.326	75	233	33	.903
1988—Charlotte‡	South.	3B-1B	24	89	6	26	5	0	1	10	.292	19	50	8	.896

Signed as free agent by Baltimore Orioles' organization, December 13, 1985.
†On disabled list, July 3 to July 31, 1986.
‡On disabled list, May 3, 1988 through remainder of season.

RENE ADRIAN GONZALES

Born September 3, 1961, at Austin, Tex.
Height, 6.02. Weight, 191.
Throws and bats righthanded.
Attended Glendale College, Glendale, Calif.; and California State University, Los Angeles, Calif.

Major League stolen bases: 1987 (1), 1988 (2). Total—3.
Led American Association shortstops in double plays with 79 in 1985.
Led Southern League shortstops in double plays with 102 in 1983.

Year Club	League	Pos.	G.	AB.	R.	H.	2B.	3B.	HR.	RBI.	B.A.	PO.	A.	E.	F.A.
1982—Memphis	South.	SS	56	183	10	39	3	1	1	11	.213	77	183	14	.949
1983—Memphis	South.	SS	144	476	67	128	12	2	2	44	.269	*258	449	20	*.972
1984—Indianapolis	A. A.	SS-3B-2B	114	359	41	84	12	2	2	32	.234	161	349	13	.975
1984—Montreal	Nat.	SS	29	30	5	7	1	0	0	2	.233	17	28	2	.957
1985—Indianapolis	A. A.	SS	130	340	21	77	11	1	0	25	.226	203	*345	23	.960
1986—Indianapolis	A. A.	3B-SS-2B	116	395	57	108	14	2	3	43	.273	208	297	23	.956
1986—Montreal†	Nat.	SS-3B	11	26	1	3	0	0	0	0	.115	7	19	0	1.000
1987—Baltimore	Amer.	3B-2B-SS	37	60	14	16	2	1	1	7	.267	22	43	2	.970
1987—Rochester	Int.	3-S-2-1-O	42	170	20	51	9	3	0	24	.300	72	108	3	.984
1988—Baltimore	Amer.	3-2-S-1-O	92	237	13	51	6	0	2	15	.215	66	185	8	.969
National League Totals—2 Years			40	56	6	10	1	0	0	2	.179	24	47	2	.973
American League Totals—2 Years			129	297	27	67	8	1	3	22	.226	88	228	10	.969
Major League Totals—4 Years			169	353	33	77	9	1	3	24	.218	112	275	12	.970

Selected by Montreal Expos' organization in 5th round of free-agent draft, June 7, 1982.
†Traded to Baltimore Orioles, December 16, 1986, completing deals in which Baltimore traded Pitcher Dennis Martinez to Montreal Expos on June 16, 1986 and Catcher John Stefero to Montreal on December 8, 1986, both for a player to be named later.

DENIO MARIANO GONZALEZ (MANZUETA)
(Denny)

Born July 22, 1963, at Sabana Grande Boya, D.R.
Height, 5.11. Weight, 185.
Throws and bats righthanded.

Major League stolen bases: 1984 (1), 1985 (2). Total—3.

Year Club	League	Pos.	G.	AB.	R.	H.	2B.	3B.	HR.	RBI.	B.A.	PO.	A.	E.	F.A.
1981—Bradenton Pir.	Gulf C.	2B-3B	50	179	32	62	5	3	2	24	.346	102	113	14	.939
1982—Portland	P. C.	2B-3B	51	164	23	37	4	6	0	9	.226	106	133	20	.923
1982—Buffalo	East.	2B	68	252	28	70	5	4	3	21	.278	137	176	11	.966
1983—Hawaii	P. C.	SS-2B	125	449	76	121	18	8	9	48	.269	193	319	34	.938
1984—Hawaii	P. C.	OF-3B-2B	113	380	61	114	22	7	15	67	.300	121	84	5	.976
1984—Pittsburgh	Nat.	3B-SS-OF	26	82	9	15	3	1	0	4	.183	26	53	3	.963
1985—Hawaii	P. C.	3-O-2-S	106	365	68	105	21	6	12	57	.288	97	183	15	.949
1985—Pittsburgh	Nat.	3B-OF-2B	35	124	11	28	4	0	4	12	.226	44	42	8	.915
1986—Hawaii	P. C.	3B-SS	109	379	48	84	10	2	10	45	.222	64	157	18	.925
1987—Pittsburgh	Nat.	SS	5	7	1	0	0	0	0	0	.000	2	1	0	1.000
1987—Vancouver	P. C.	3B	113	413	62	108	20	0	13	57	.262	76	232	•25	.925
1988—Buffalo	A. A.	3B-2B	75	267	37	79	14	2	8	39	.296	64	166	17	.931
1988—Pittsburgh†	Nat.	SS-2B-3B	24	32	5	6	1	0	0	1	.188	20	22	2	.955
Major League Totals—4 Years			90	245	26	49	8	1	4	17	.200	92	118	13	.942

Signed as free agent by Pittsburgh Pirates' organization, June 25, 1981.
†Traded to Cleveland Indians for a player to be named later, November 28, 1988.

GERMAN JOSE GONZALEZ

Born October 3, 1965, at Rio Caribe, Venez.
Height, 6.00. Weight, 170.
Throws and bats righthanded.

Major League saves: 1988 (1).
Led Southern League in saves with 31 in 1988.
Named Southern League Pitcher of the Year, 1988.

Year Club	League	G.	IP.	W.	L.	Pct.	H.	R.	ER.	SO.	BB.	ERA.
1987—Kenosha	Midwest	47	82⅓	8	5	.615	70	26	23	92	22	2.51
1988—Orlando	Southern	50	61⅔	2	1	.667	41	9	7	69	19	1.02
1988—Minnesota	American	16	21⅓	0	0	.000	20	8	8	19	8	3.38
Major League Totals—1 Year		16	21⅓	0	0	.000	20	8	8	19	8	3.38

Signed as free agent by Minnesota Twins' organization, December 29, 1986.

JOSE RAFAEL GONZALEZ

Born November 23, 1964, at Puerto Plata, Dominican Republic.
Height, 6.02. Weight, 196.
Throws and bats righthanded.

Major League stolen bases: 1985 (1), 1986 (4), 1987 (5), 1988 (3). Total—13.
Tied for Texas League lead in caught stealing with 17 in 1985.
Led Texas League outfielders in total chances with 320 in 1985.

Year Club	League	Pos.	G.	AB.	R.	H.	2B.	3B.	HR.	RBI.	B.A.	PO.	A.	E.	F.A.
1981—Lethbridge	Pion.	OF	34	103	11	14	1	1	0	7	.136	65	6	5	.934
1982—Lethbridge	Pion.	OF	55	209	35	63	14	1	4	47	.301	112	7	1	.992
1983—Lodi†	Calif.	OF	76	310	48	91	17	4	6	36	.294	182	7	4	.979
1984—Bakersfield	Calif.	OF	129	484	86	107	26	1	11	59	.221	264	13	9	.969
1985—San Antonio	Texas	OF	128	448	82	137	22	6	13	62	.306	*294	15	11	.966
1985—Los Angeles	Nat.	OF	23	11	6	3	2	0	0	0	.273	10	0	0	1.000
1986—Albuquerque	P. C.	OF	89	303	39	84	20	3	6	37	.277	171	10	6	.968
1986—Los Angeles	Nat.	OF	57	93	15	20	5	1	2	6	.215	73	0	6	.924
1987—Albuquerque	P. C.	OF	116	339	67	95	22	3	13	61	.280	225	10	9	.963
1987—Los Angeles	Nat.	OF	18	16	2	3	2	0	0	1	.188	19	1	0	1.000
1988—Albuquerque	P. C.	OF	84	288	57	88	15	2	5	22	.306	177	7	6	.968
1988—Los Angeles	Nat.	OF	37	24	7	2	1	0	0	0	.083	15	0	1	.938
Major League Totals—4 Years			135	144	30	28	10	1	2	7	.194	117	1	7	.944

Signed as free agent by Los Angeles Dodgers' organization, August 12, 1980.
†On disabled list, July 7, 1983 through remainder of season.

CHAMPIONSHIP SERIES RECORD

Year Club	League	Pos.	G.	AB.	R.	H.	2B.	3B.	HR.	RBI.	B.A.	PO.	A.	E.	F.A.
1988—Los Angeles	Nat.	OF-PR	5	0	2	0	0	0	0	0	.000	3	0	0	1.000

WORLD SERIES RECORD

Year Club	League	Pos.	G.	AB.	R.	H.	2B.	3B.	HR.	RBI.	B.A.	PO.	A.	E.	F.A.
1988—Los Angeles	Nat.	PH-OF	4	2	0	0	0	0	0	0	.000	2	0	0	1.000

DWIGHT EUGENE GOODEN

Born November 16, 1964, at Tampa, Fla.
Height, 6.03. Weight, 203.
Throws and bats righthanded.
Uncle of Gary Sheffield, infielder with Milwaukee Brewers.

Established major league record for most strikeouts by rookie, season (276), 1984.
Tied modern major league record for most strikeouts, two consecutive games (32), September 12, 17, 1984.
Established National League record for most strikeouts, three consecutive games (43), September 7, 12, 17, 1984.
Led National League in complete games with 16 in 1985.
Tied for National League lead in balks with 7 in 1984.
Led Carolina League in shutouts with 6 in 1983.
Named National League Pitcher of the Year by The Sporting News, 1985.
Won National League Cy Young Memorial Award, 1985.
Named righthanded pitcher on The Sporting News National League All-Star Team, 1985.
Named National League Rookie Pitcher of the Year by The Sporting News, 1984.
Named National League Rookie of the Year by Baseball Writers' Association of America, 1984.
Named Carolina League Pitcher of the Year, 1983.
Received reported $125,000 bonus to sign with New York Mets, 1982.

Year Club	League	G.	IP.	W.	L.	Pct.	H.	R.	ER.	SO.	BB.	ERA.
1982—Kingsport	Ap'lachian	9	65⅔	5	4	.556	53	34	18	66	25	2.47
1982—Little Falls	NYP	2	13	0	1	.000	11	6	6	18	3	4.15
1983—Lynchburg	Carolina	27	191	*19	4	.826	121	58	53	*300	*112	*2.50
1984—New York	National	31	218	17	9	.654	161	72	63	*276	73	2.60
1985—New York	National	35	*276⅔	*24	4	.857	198	51	47	*268	69	*1.53
1986—New York	National	33	250	17	6	.739	197	92	79	200	80	2.84
1987—Tidewater†	Int'national	4	22	3	0	1.000	20	7	5	24	9	2.05
1987—Lynchburg	Carolina	1	4	0	0	.000	2	0	0	3	2	0.00
1987—New York	National	25	179⅔	15	7	.682	162	68	64	148	53	3.21
1988—New York	National	34	248⅓	18	9	.667	242	98	88	175	57	3.19
Major League Totals—5 Years		158	1172⅔	91	35	.722	960	381	341	1067	332	2.62

Selected by New York Mets' organization in 1st round (fifth player selected) of free-agent draft, June 7, 1982.
†On New York disabled list, April 1 to June 5, 1987; included rehabilitation disability assignment to Tidewater, May 12 to May 17 and May 21 to June 1, 1987.

CHAMPIONSHIP SERIES RECORD

Established National League Championship Series records for most bases on balls, seven-game Series (8), 1988; most strikeouts, seven-game Series (20), 1988.
Tied National League Championship Series record for most innings pitched, game (10), October 14, 1986.

Year Club	League	G.	IP.	W.	L.	Pct.	H.	R.	ER.	SO.	BB.	ERA.
1986—New York	National	2	17	0	1	.000	16	2	2	9	5	1.06
1988—New York	National	3	18⅓	0	0	.000	10	6	6	20	8	2.95
Championship Series Totals—2 Years		5	35⅓	0	1	.000	26	8	8	29	13	2.04

WORLD SERIES RECORD

Tied World Series record for most games lost, seven-game Series (2), 1986.

Year Club	League	G.	IP.	W.	L.	Pct.	H.	R.	ER.	SO.	BB.	ERA.
1986—New York	National	2	9	0	2	.000	17	10	8	9	4	8.00

ALL-STAR GAME RECORD

Tied All-Star Game record for most games lost, lifetime (2).

Year League	IP.	W.	L.	Pct.	H.	R.	ER.	SO.	BB.	ERA.
1984—National	2	0	0	.000	1	0	0	3	0	0.00
1986—National	3	0	1	.000	3	2	2	2	0	6.00
1988—National	3	0	1	.000	3	1	1	1	1	3.00
All-Star Game Totals—3 Years	8	0	2	.000	7	3	3	6	1	3.38

Member of National League All-Star Team in 1985; did not play.

DONALD THOMAS GORDON
(Don)

Born October 10, 1959, at New York, N.Y.
Height, 6.01. Weight, 185.
Throws and bats righthanded.
Attended The Citadel, Charleston, S.C., and University of South Carolina, Columbia, S.C.

Major League saves: 1986 (1), 1987 (1), 1988 (1). Total—3.

Year Club	League	G.	IP.	W.	L.	Pct.	H.	R.	ER.	SO.	BB.	ERA.
1982—Bristol	Ap'lachian	22	65⅔	4	4	.500	48	17	16	42	14	2.19
1983—Birmingham	Southern	43	102⅔	9	5	.643	104	50	39	50	23	3.42
1984—Birmingham†-Knoxville	Southern	54	109⅔	6	4	.600	103	47	41	51	21	3.36
1985—Syracuse	Int'national	51	113	8	5	.615	93	39	26	43	21	*2.07
1986—Toronto	American	14	21⅔	0	1	.000	28	20	17	13	8	7.06
1986—Syracuse	Int'national	25	109	8	5	.615	105	42	35	62	21	2.89
1987—Syracuse	Int'national	41	82⅓	4	6	.400	83	28	16	67	10	1.75
1987—Toronto‡-Cleveland	American	26	50⅔	0	3	.000	57	36	23	23	15	4.09
1988—Colorado Springs	P. Coast	21	57⅓	3	3	.500	62	34	27	19	13	4.24
1988—Cleveland	American	38	59⅓	3	4	.429	65	33	29	20	19	4.40
Major League Totals—3 Years		78	131⅔	3	8	.273	150	89	69	56	42	4.72

Selected by Detroit Tigers' organization in 31st round of free-agent draft, June 7, 1982.
†Released, June 23, 1984; signed by Knoxville (Toronto Blue Jays' organization), June 25, 1984.
‡Traded to Cleveland Indians, August 10, 1987, completing deal in which Cleveland traded Pitcher Phil Niekro to Toronto Blue Jays for Outfielder Darryl Landrum and a player to be named later, August 9, 1987.

THOMAS GORDON
(Tom)

Born November 18, 1967, at Sebring, Fla.
Height, 5.09. Weight, 160.
Throws and bats righthanded.

Tied for Northwest League lead in balks with 4 in 1987.

Year Club	League	G.	IP.	W.	L.	Pct.	H.	R.	ER.	SO.	BB.	ERA.
1986—Sarasota Royals	Gulf Coast	9	44	3	1	.750	31	12	5	47	23	1.02
1986—Omaha	Am. Assoc.	1	1⅓	0	0	.000	6	7	7	3	2	47.25
1987—Eugene	Northwest	15	72⅓	•9	0	•1.000	48	33	23	91	47	2.86
1987—Fort Myers	Florida St.	3	13⅔	1	0	1.000	5	4	4	11	17	2.63
1988—Appleton	Midwest	17	118	7	5	.583	69	30	27	*172	43	2.06
1988—Memphis	Southern	6	47⅓	6	0	1.000	16	3	2	62	17	0.38
1988—Omaha	Am. Assoc.	3	20⅓	3	0	1.000	11	3	3	29	15	1.33
1988—Kansas City	American	5	15⅔	0	2	.000	16	9	9	18	7	5.17
Major League Totals—1 Year		5	15⅔	0	2	.000	16	9	9	18	7	5.17

Selected by Kansas City Royals' organization in 6th round of free-agent draft, June 2, 1986.

RICHARD MICHAEL GOSSAGE
(Rich or Goose)

Born July 5, 1951, at Colorado Springs, Colo.
Height, 6.03. Weight, 226.
Throws and bats righthanded.
Attended Southern Colorado State College, Pueblo, Colo.

Established National League record for most strikeouts by relief pitcher, season (151), 1977.

Major League saves: 1972 (2), 1974 (1), 1975 (26), 1976 (1), 1977 (26), 1978 (27), 1979 (18), 1980 (33), 1981 (20), 1982 (30), 1983 (22), 1984 (25), 1985 (26), 1986 (21), 1987 (11), 1988 (13). Total—302.

Led American League in saves with 26 in 1975 and 27 in 1978.
Led American League in games finished in relief with 55 in 1978.
Tied for American League lead in saves with 33 in 1980.
Tied for American League lead in intentional bases on balls issued with 15 in 1975.
Led Midwest League in complete games with 15 and shutouts with 7 in 1971.
Named American League Fireman of the Year by THE SPORTING NEWS, 1975 and 1978.
Named Midwest League Player of the Year, 1971.

Year Club	League	G.	IP.	W.	L.	Pct.	H.	R.	ER.	SO.	BB.	ERA.
1970—Sarasota White Sox	Gulf Coast	3	16	0	0	.000	11	6	5	21	4	2.81
1970—Appleton	Midwest	10	35	0	3	.000	41	27	23	21	19	5.91
1971—Appleton	Midwest	25	187	*18	2	*.900	141	48	38	149	50	*1.83
1972—Chicago	American	36	80	7	1	.875	72	44	38	57	44	4.28
1973—Iowa	Am. Assoc.	12	71	5	4	.556	59	32	29	66	28	3.68
1973—Chicago	American	20	50	0	4	.000	57	44	41	33	37	7.38
1974—Appleton	Midwest	2	8	0	2	.000	8	6	3	5	4	3.38
1974—Chicago	American	39	89	4	6	.400	92	45	41	64	47	4.15
1975—Chicago	American	61	142	9	8	.529	99	32	29	130	70	1.84
1976—Chicago†	American	31	224	9	17	.346	214	104	98	135	90	3.94
1977—Pittsburgh‡	National	72	133	11	9	.550	78	27	24	151	49	1.62
1978—New York	American	63	134	10	11	.476	87	41	30	122	59	2.01
1979—New York§	American	36	58	5	3	.625	48	18	17	41	19	2.64
1980—New York	American	64	99	6	2	.750	74	29	25	103	37	2.27
1981—New York	American	32	47	3	2	.600	22	6	4	48	14	0.77
1982—New York	American	56	93	4	5	.444	63	23	23	102	28	2.23
1983—New York x	American	57	87⅓	13	5	.722	82	27	22	90	25	2.27
1984—San Diego	National	62	102⅓	10	6	.625	75	34	33	84	36	2.90
1985—San Diego y	National	50	79	5	3	.625	64	21	16	52	17	1.82
1986—San Diego z	National	45	64⅔	5	7	.417	69	36	32	63	20	4.45
1987—San Diego ab	National	40	52	5	4	.556	47	18	18	44	19	3.12
1988—Chicago c	National	46	43⅔	4	4	.500	50	23	21	30	15	4.33
National League Totals—6 Years		315	474⅔	40	33	.548	383	159	144	424	156	2.73
American League Totals—11 Years		496	1103⅓	70	64	.522	910	413	368	925	470	3.00
Major League Totals—17 Years		811	1578	110	97	.531	1293	572	512	1349	626	2.92

Selected by Chicago White Sox' organization in 9th round of free-agent draft, June 4, 1970.

†Traded with Pitcher Terry Forster to Pittsburgh Pirates for Outfielder Richie Zisk and Pitcher Silvio Martinez, December 10, 1976.

‡Granted free agency, October 28, 1977; signed by New York Yankees, November 23, 1977.
§On disabled list, April 21 to July 9, 1979.
xGranted free agency, November 7, 1983; signed by San Diego Padres, January 6, 1984.
yOn disabled list, August 8 to September 1, 1985.
zOn suspended list, August 29 to September 18, 1986.
aOn disabled list, April 15 to May 4, 1987.
bTraded with Pitcher Ray Hayward to Chicago Cubs for Infielders Keith Moreland and Mike Brumley, February 12, 1988.
cOn disabled list, June 16 to July 1, 1988.

DIVISION SERIES RECORD

Year Club	League	G.	IP.	W.	L.	Pct.	H.	R.	ER.	SO.	BB.	ERA.
1981—New York	American	3	6⅔	0	0	.000	3	0	0	8	2	0.00

CHAMPIONSHIP SERIES RECORD

Tied American League Championship Series record for most saves, total Series (2).

Year Club	League	G.	IP.	W.	L.	Pct.	H.	R.	ER.	SO.	BB.	ERA.
1978—New York	American	2	4	1	0	1.000	3	2	2	3	0	4.50
1980—New York	American	1	⅓	0	1	.000	3	2	2	0	0	54.00
1981—New York	American	2	2⅔	0	0	.000	1	0	0	2	0	0.00
1984—San Diego	National	3	4	0	0	.000	5	2	2	5	1	4.50
Championship Series Totals—4 Years		8	11	1	1	.500	12	6	6	10	1	4.91

WORLD SERIES RECORD

Tied World Series record for most saves, six-game Series (2), 1981.

Year Club	League	G.	IP.	W.	L.	Pct.	H.	R.	ER.	SO.	BB.	ERA.
1978—New York	American	3	6	1	0	1.000	1	0	0	4	1	0.00
1981—New York	American	3	5	0	0	.000	2	0	0	5	2	0.00
1984—San Diego	National	2	2⅔	0	0	.000	3	4	4	2	1	13.50
World Series Totals—3 Years		8	13⅔	1	0	1.000	6	4	4	11	4	2.63

ALL-STAR GAME RECORD

Established All-Star game record for most games finished (5).

Year League	IP.	W.	L.	Pct.	H.	R.	ER.	SO.	BB.	ERA.
1975—American	1	0	0	.000	1	1	1	0	0	9.00
1977—National	1	0	0	.000	1	2	2	2	1	18.00
1978—American	1	0	1	.000	4	4	4	1	1	36.00
1980—American	1	0	0	.000	1	0	0	0	0	0.00
1984—National	1	0	0	.000	1	0	0	2	0	0.00
1985—National	1	0	0	.000	0	0	0	2	1	0.00
All-Star Game Totals—6 Years	6	0	1	.000	8	7	7	7	3	10.50

Named to American League All-Star Team for 1981 game; replaced due to injury.
Member of American League All-Star Team in 1976 and 1982; did not play.

JAMES WILLIAM GOTT
(Jim)

Born August 3, 1959, at Hollywood, Calif.
Height, 6.04. Weight, 220.
Throws and bats righthanded.
Attended Brigham Young University, Provo, Utah.

Major League saves: 1984 (2), 1986 (1), 1987 (13), 1988 (34). Total—50.
Led Western Carolinas League in wild pitches with 21 in 1979.
Tied for Pioneer League lead in games started by pitchers with 14 in 1977.

Year Club	League	G.	IP.	W.	L.	Pct.	H.	R.	ER.	SO.	BB.	ERA.
1977—Calgary	Pioneer	14	65	3	4	.429	71	*82	*69	60	*83	9.55
1978—Gastonia	W. Carol.	22	145	9	6	.600	100	67	64	130	•113	3.97
1978—St. Petersburg	Flordia St.	5	28	1	3	.250	23	9	4	15	12	1.29
1979—St. Petersburg	Florida St.	4	18	0	3	.000	18	13	13	9	13	6.50
1979—Gastonia	W. Carol.	19	77	5	5	.500	63	57	48	102	88	5.61
1979—Arkansas†	Texas	2	5	0	1	.000	3	6	3	7	13	5.40
1980—St. Petersburg	Florida St.	25	137	5	11	.313	138	96	70	103	113	4.60
1981—Arkansas‡	Texas	28	131	5	9	.357	133	68	50	93	65	3.44
1982—Toronto	American	30	136	5	10	.333	134	76	67	82	66	4.43
1983—Toronto	American	34	176⅔	9	14	.391	195	103	93	121	68	4.74
1984—Toronto§	American	35	109⅔	7	6	.538	93	54	49	73	49	4.02
1985—San Francisco	National	26	148⅓	7	10	.412	144	73	64	78	51	3.88
1986—San Francisco x	National	9	13	0	0	.000	16	12	11	9	13	7.62
1986—Phoenix y	P. Coast	2	2⅔	0	0	.000	2	2	2	2	3	6.75
1987—San Francisco z-Pittsburgh	National	55	87	1	2	.333	81	43	33	90	40	3.41
1988—Pittsburgh	National	67	77⅓	6	6	.500	68	30	30	76	22	3.49
American League Totals—3 Years		99	422⅓	21	30	.412	422	233	209	276	183	4.45
National League Totals—4 Years		157	325⅔	14	18	.438	309	158	138	253	126	3.81
Major League Totals—7 Years		256	748	35	48	.422	731	391	347	529	309	4.18

Selected by St. Louis Cardinals' organization in 4th round of free-agent draft, June 7, 1977.
†On disabled list, August 16 to September 1, 1979.
‡Drafted by Toronto Blue Jays, December 7, 1981.
§Traded with Pitcher Jack McKnight and Infielder Augie Schmidt to San Francisco Giants for Pitcher Gary Lavelle, January 26, 1985.
xOn disabled list, May 9, 1986 through remainder of season; included rehabilitation disability assignment to Phoenix, June 9 to June 24, 1986.
yReleased, December 19, 1986; re-signed by Giants, April 7, 1987.
zClaimed on waivers by Pittsburgh Pirates, August 3, 1987.

MARK EUGENE GRACE

Born June 28, 1964, at Winston-Salem, N. C.
Height, 6.02. Weight, 190.
Throws and bats lefthanded.
Attended Saddleback College, Mission Viejo, Calif., and
San Diego State University, San Diego, Calif.

Major League stolen bases: 1988 (3).
Led Eastern League in slugging percentage with .545 in 1987.
Led Midwest League first basemen in double plays with 103 in 1986.
Named National League Rookie Player of the Year by The Sporting News, 1988.
Named Eastern League Most Valuable Player, 1987.

Year Club	League	Pos.	G.	AB.	R.	H.	2B.	3B.	HR.	RBI.	B.A.	PO.	A.	E.	F.A.
1986—Peoria	Midw.	1B-OF	126	465	81	159	30	4	15	95	*.342	1050	69	13	.989
1987—Pittsfield	East.	1B	123	453	81	151	29	8	17	*101	.333	1054	*96	6	*.995
1988—Iowa	A.A.	1B	21	67	11	17	4	0	0	14	.254	189	20	1	.995
1988—Chicago	Nat.	1B	134	486	65	144	23	4	7	57	.296	1182	87	•17	.987
Major League Totals—1 Year			134	486	65	144	23	4	7	57	.296	1182	87	17	.987

Selected by Minnesota Twins' organization in 15th round of free-agent draft, January 17, 1984.
Selected by Chicago Cubs' organization in 24th round of free-agent draft, June 3, 1985.

MARK ANDREW GRANT

Born October 24, 1963, at Aurora, Ill.
Height, 6.02. Weight, 205.
Throws and bats righthanded.
Cousin of Rick Ramos, pitcher in Montreal Expos' organization, 1978 through 1983; and nephew of Richard Ramos, pitcher in Chicago White Sox' organization, 1953 through 1958.

Pitched 9-0 no-hit victory against Danville, August 12, 1982.
Major League saves: 1984 (1), 1987 (1). Total—2.
Led Pacific Coast League pitchers in complete games with 10 and tied for lead in games started with 27 in 1986.
Led Pacific Coast League pitchers in wild pitches with 18 and tied for league lead in games started with 29 in 1985.
Tied for Pacific Coast League lead in shutouts with 3 in 1985 and 1986.
Tied for Midwest League lead in shutouts with 4 in 1982.

Year Club	League	G.	IP.	W.	L.	Pct.	H.	R.	ER.	SO.	BB.	ERA.
1981—Great Falls	Pioneer	10	64	2	6	.250	63	36	31	50	35	4.36
1982—Clinton	Midwest	27	*198⅔	*16	5	*.762	139	63	52	*243	60	2.36
1983—Shreveport	Texas	26	*186⅔	10	8	.556	182	83	76	159	71	3.66
1984—Phoenix	P. Coast	17	111⅓	5	7	.417	102	64	49	78	61	3.96
1984—San Francisco†	National	11	53⅔	1	4	.200	56	40	38	32	19	6.37
1985—Phoenix	P. Coast	29	183	8	•15	.348	182	101	92	133	90	4.52
1986—Phoenix	P. Coast	28	181⅔	*14	7	.667	204	105	99	93	46	4.90
1986—San Francisco	National	4	10	0	1	.000	6	4	4	5	5	3.60
1987—San Francisco‡-San Diego	National	33	163⅓	7	9	.438	170	88	77	90	73	4.24
1987—Phoenix	P. Coast	3	23	2	1	.667	20	8	8	12	5	3.13
1988—San Diego	National	33	97⅔	2	8	.200	97	41	40	61	36	3.69
Major League Totals—4 Years		81	324⅔	10	22	.313	329	173	159	188	133	4.41

Selected by San Francisco Giants' organization in 1st round (10th player selected) of free-agent draft, June 8, 1981.
†On disabled list, May 4 to May 23, 1984.
‡Traded with Third Baseman Chris Brown and Pitchers Keith Comstock and Mark Davis to San Diego Padres for Pitchers Dave Dravecky and Craig Lefferts and Infielder Kevin Mitchell, July 4, 1987.

JEFFREY EDWARD GRAY
(Jeff)

Born April 10, 1963, at Richmond, Va.
Height, 6.01. Weight, 175.
Throws and bats righthanded.
Attended Florida State University, Tallahassee, Fla.

Led Florida State League in games finished in relief with 47 in 1985.
Tied for Gulf Coast League lead in intentional bases on balls issued with 5 in 1984.

Year Club	League	G.	IP.	W.	L.	Pct.	H.	R.	ER.	SO.	BB.	ERA.
1984—Sarasota Phillies	Gulf Coast	26	41⅓	6	4	.600	35	9	6	26	10	1.31
1985—Clearwater†	Florida St.	55	87⅔	5	9	.357	80	38	31	80	33	3.18
1986—Vermont	Eastern	*55	84⅓	*14	2	*.875	71	24	22	65	26	2.35
1987—Nashville	Am. Assoc.	53	83⅓	4	10	.286	97	52	45	70	26	4.86
1988—Nashville	Am. Assoc.	42	73	8	5	.615	59	17	16	73	18	1.97
1988—Cincinnati	National	5	9⅓	0	0	.000	12	4	4	5	4	3.86
Major League Totals—1 Year		5	9⅓	0	0	.000	12	4	4	5	4	3.86

Signed as free agent by Philadelphia Phillies' organization, June 14, 1984.
†Traded with Pitcher John Denny to Cincinnati Reds for Outfielder Gary Redus and Pitcher Tom Hume, December 11, 1985.

IRA THOMAS GREENE
(Tommy)

Born April 6, 1967, at Lumberton, N. C.
Height, 6.05. Weight, 225.
Throws and bats righthanded.

Led South Atlantic League pitchers in games started with 28 and tied for lead in shutouts with 3 in 1986.
Tied for International League lead in shutouts with 3 in 1988.

Year Club	League	G.	IP.	W.	L.	Pct.	H.	R.	ER.	SO.	BB.	ERA.
1985—Pulaski	Ap'lachian	12	50⅔	2	5	.286	49	45	43	32	27	7.64
1986—Sumter	S. Atlantic	28	174⅔	11	7	.611	162	95	91	169	82	4.69
1987—Greenville	Southern	23	142⅓	11	8	.579	103	60	52	101	66	3.29
1988—Richmond	Int'national	29	177⅓	7	17	.292	169	98	94	130	70	4.77

Selected by Atlanta Braves' organization in 1st round (14th player selected) of free-agent draft, June 3, 1985.

MICHAEL LEWIS GREENWELL
(Mike)

Born July 18, 1963, at Louisville, Ky.
Height, 6.00. Weight, 195.
Throws right and bats lefthanded.

Established American League record for most game-winning runs batted in, season (23), 1988.
Hit for the cycle, September 14, 1988.
Major League stolen bases: 1985 (1), 1987 (5), 1988 (16). Total—22.
Led American League in game-winning RBIs with 23 and tied for lead in intentional bases on balls received with 18 in 1988.
Led Carolina League in being hit by pitch with 15 in 1984.
Named outfielder on THE SPORTING NEWS American League All-Star Team, 1988.
Named outfielder on THE SPORTING NEWS American League Silver Slugger team, 1988.

Year Club	League	Pos.	G.	AB.	R.	H.	2B.	3B.	HR.	RBI.	B.A.	PO.	A.	E.	F.A.
1982—Elmira	NYP	3B-2B	72	268	57	72	10	1	6	36	.269	96	151	31	.888
1983—Winston-Salem†	Carol.	OF	48	158	23	44	8	0	3	21	.278	28	1	1	.967

Year	Club	League	Pos.	G.	AB.	R.	H.	2B.	3B.	HR.	RBI.	B.A.	PO.	A.	E.	F.A.
1984	Winston-Salem	Carol.	3B-OF	130	454	70	139	23	6	16	84	.306	126	132	30	.896
1985	Pawtucket	Int.	OF	117	418	47	107	21	1	13	52	.256	178	8	7	.964
1985	Boston	Amer.	OF	17	31	7	10	1	0	4	8	.323	14	0	0	1.000
1986	Pawtucket	Int.	OF-3B	89	320	62	96	21	1	18	59	.300	130	20	8	.949
1986	Boston	Amer.	OF	31	35	4	11	2	0	0	4	.314	18	1	0	1.000
1987	Boston	Amer.	OF-C	125	412	71	135	31	6	19	89	.328	165	8	6	.966
1988	Boston	Amer.	OF	158	590	86	192	39	8	22	119	.325	302	6	6	.981
Major League Totals—4 Years				331	1068	168	348	73	14	45	220	.326	499	15	12	.977

Selected by Boston Red Sox' organization in 3rd round of free-agent draft, June 7, 1982.
†On disabled list, April 21 to May 2 and May 13 to July 25, 1983.

CHAMPIONSHIP SERIES RECORD

Year	Club	League	Pos.	G.	AB.	R.	H.	2B.	3B.	HR.	RBI.	B.A.	PO.	A.	E.	F.A.
1986	Boston	Amer.	PH	2	2	0	1	0	0	0	0	.500	0	0	0	.000
1988	Boston	Amer.	OF	4	14	2	3	1	0	1	3	.214	4	0	0	1.000
Championship Series Totals—2 Years				6	16	2	4	1	0	1	3	.250	4	0	0	1.000

WORLD SERIES RECORD

Year	Club	League	Pos.	G.	AB.	R.	H.	2B.	3B.	HR.	RBI.	B.A.	PO.	A.	E.	F.A.
1986	Boston	Amer.	PH	4	3	0	0	0	0	0	0	.000	0	0	0	.000

ALL-STAR GAME RECORD

Year	League	Pos.	AB.	R.	H.	2B.	3B.	HR.	RBI.	B.A.	PO.	A.	E.	F.A.
1988	American	OF	1	0	0	0	0	0	0	.000	1	0	0	1.000

WILLIAM THOMAS GREGG JR.
(Tommy)

Born July 29, 1963, at Boone, N. C.
Height, 6.01. Weight, 190.
Throws and bats lefthanded.
Attended Wake Forest University, Winston-Salem, N. C.

Led Eastern League in intentional bases on balls received with 14 in 1987.

Year	Club	League	Pos.	G.	AB.	R.	H.	2B.	3B.	HR.	RBI.	B.A.	PO.	A.	E.	F.A.
1985	Macon	S. Atl.	OF	72	259	43	81	14	2	1	18	.313	117	4	1	.992
1986	Nashua	East.	OF-1B	126	421	55	113	13	4	1	29	.268	216	7	4	.982
1987	Harrisburg	East.	OF	133	461	99	171	22	9	10	82	*.371	242	12	7	.973
1987	Pittsburgh	Nat.	OF	10	8	3	2	1	0	0	0	.250	1	0	0	1.000
1988	Buffalo	A. A.	OF	72	252	34	74	12	0	6	27	.294	134	3	2	.986
1988	Pitt.†-Atl.	Nat.	OF	25	44	5	13	4	0	1	7	.295	26	1	0	1.000
Major League Totals—2 Years				35	52	8	15	5	0	1	7	.288	27	1	0	1.000

Selected by Cleveland Indians' organization in 9th round of free-agent draft, June 8, 1981.
Selected by Cleveland Indians' organization in 32nd round of free-agent draft, June 4, 1984.
Selected by Pittsburgh Pirates' organization in 7th round of free-agent draft, June 3, 1985.
†Traded to Atlanta Braves, September 1, 1988, completing deal in which Atlanta traded Infielder Ken Oberkfell and cash to Pittsburgh Pirates for a player to be named later, August 28, 1988.

GEORGE KENNETH GRIFFEY
(Ken)

Born April 10, 1950, at Donora, Pa.
Height, 6.00. Weight, 210.
Throws and bats lefthanded.
Father of Ken Griffey Jr., outfielder in Seattle Mariners' organization.

Tied major league record for most at bats, game, since 1900 (7), June 13, 1975.
Major League stolen bases: 1973 (4), 1974 (9), 1975 (16), 1976 (34), 1977 (17), 1978 (23), 1979 (12), 1980 (23), 1981 (12), 1982 (10), 1983 (5), 1984 (2), 1985 (7), 1986 (14), 1987 (4), 1988 (1). Total—193.
Hit three home runs in a game, July 22, 1986.
Led American Association in stolen bases with 43 in 1973.
Tied for Eastern League lead in double plays by outfielders with 6 in 1972.
Named as outfielder on THE SPORTING NEWS National League All-Star Team, 1976.

Year	Club	League	Pos.	G.	AB.	R.	H.	2B.	3B.	HR.	RBI.	B.A.	PO.	A.	E.	F.A.
1969	Bradenton Reds	Gulf C.	*OF-1B	49	153	22	43	*11	1	1	12	.281	57	4	*10	.859
1970	Sioux Falls	North.	OF	51	164	20	40	2	1	2	24	.244	76	2	7	.918
1971	Tampa	Fla. St.	OF	88	281	60	96	7	11	3	33	.342	137	13	8	.949
1971	Three Rivers	East.	OF	9	32	1	13	1	2	0	4	.406	17	0	1	.944
1972	Three Rivers	East.	●OF-SS	128	472	*96	150	21	3	14	52	.318	212	10	●15	.937
1973	Indianapolis	A. A.	OF	107	397	88	130	18	5	10	58	.327	171	11	6	.968
1973	Cincinnati	Nat.	OF	25	86	19	33	5	1	3	14	.384	25	1	0	1.000
1974	Indianapolis	A. A.	OF	43	162	34	54	6	4	5	18	.333	70	4	1	.987
1974	Cincinnati	Nat.	OF	88	227	24	57	9	5	2	19	.251	115	5	0	1.000
1975	Cincinnati	Nat.	OF	132	463	95	141	15	9	4	46	.305	202	6	7	.967
1976	Cincinnati	Nat.	OF	148	562	111	189	28	9	6	74	.336	270	10	6	.976
1977	Cincinnati	Nat.	OF	154	585	117	186	35	8	12	57	.318	298	10	3	.990
1978	Cincinnati	Nat.	OF	158	614	90	177	33	8	10	63	.288	296	13	10	.969
1979	Cincinnati†	Nat.	OF	95	380	62	120	27	4	8	32	.316	175	8	3	.984
1980	Cincinnati	Nat.	OF	146	544	89	160	28	10	13	85	.294	266	5	6	.978
1981	Cincinnati‡	Nat.	OF	101	396	65	123	21	6	2	34	.311	268	8	3	.989

Year	Club	League	Pos.	G.	AB.	R.	H.	2B.	3B.	HR.	RBI.	B.A.	PO.	A.	E.	F.A.
1982	—New York	Amer.	OF	127	484	70	134	23	2	12	54	.277	282	8	5	.983
1983	—New York§	Amer.	1B-OF	118	458	60	140	21	3	11	46	.306	870	57	8	.991
1984	—New York	Amer.	OF-1B	120	399	44	109	20	1	7	56	.273	422	22	16	.965
1985	—New York x	Amer.	OF-1B	127	438	68	120	28	4	10	69	.274	227	8	7	.971
1986	—New York y	Amer.	OF	59	198	33	60	7	0	9	26	.303	96	5	3	.971
1986	—Atlanta	Nat.	OF-1B	80	292	36	90	15	3	12	32	.308	136	2	2	.986
1987	—Atlanta za	Nat.	OF-1B	122	399	65	114	24	1	14	64	.286	205	8	2	.991
1988	—Atl. b - Cinc. c	Nat.	OF-1B	94	243	26	62	6	0	4	23	.255	193	16	4	.981
National League Totals—12 Years				1343	4791	799	1452	246	64	90	543	.303	2449	92	46	.982
American League Totals—5 Years				551	1977	275	563	99	10	49	251	.285	1897	100	39	.981
Major League Totals—16 Years				1894	6768	1074	2015	345	74	139	794	.298	4346	192	85	.982

Selected by Cincinnati Reds' organization in 29th round of free-agent draft, June 5, 1969.

†On disabled list, August 14 to September 7, 1979.

‡Traded to New York Yankees for Pitcher Brian Ryder and a player to be named later, November 4, 1981; Cincinnati Reds' organization acquired Pitcher Freddie Toliver to complete deal, December 10, 1981.

§On disabled list, July 2 to August 2, 1983.

xOn disabled list, May 28 to June 12, 1985.

yTraded to Atlanta Braves for Outfielder Claudell Washington and Shortstop Paul Zuvella, June 30, 1986.

zOn disabled list, May 5 to May 10, 1987.

aGranted free agency, November 9, 1987; re-signed by Braves, November 13, 1987.

bReleased, July 28, 1988; signed by Cincinnati Reds, August 2, 1988.

cReleased, December 21, 1988.

CHAMPIONSHIP SERIES RECORD

Tied Championship Series record for most stolen bases, game (3), October 5, 1975.

Year	Club	League	Pos.	G.	AB.	R.	H.	2B.	3B.	HR.	RBI.	B.A.	PO.	A.	E.	F.A.
1973	—Cincinnati	Nat.	OF-PH	3	7	0	1	1	0	0	0	.143	2	0	0	1.000
1975	—Cincinnati	Nat.	OF	3	12	3	4	1	0	0	4	.333	4	1	0	1.000
1976	—Cincinnati	Nat.	OF	3	13	2	5	0	1	0	2	.385	11	0	0	1.000
Championship Series Totals—3 Years				9	32	5	10	2	1	0	6	.313	17	1	0	1.000

WORLD SERIES RECORD

Tied World Series record for fewest chances accepted by outfielder, extra-inning game (0), October 21, 1975 (12 innings); most at-bats, game, no hits (5), October 21, 1976.

Year	Club	League	Pos.	G.	AB.	R.	H.	2B.	3B.	HR.	RBI.	B.A.	PO.	A.	E.	F.A.
1975	—Cincinnati	Nat.	OF	7	26	4	7	3	1	0	4	.269	10	1	0	1.000
1976	—Cincinnati	Nat.	OF	4	17	2	1	0	0	0	1	.059	5	0	0	1.000
World Series Totals—2 Years				11	43	6	8	3	1	0	5	.186	15	1	0	1.000

ALL-STAR GAME RECORD

Year	League	Pos.	AB.	R.	H.	2B.	3B.	HR.	RBI.	B.A.	PO.	A.	E.	F.A.
1976	—National	OF	1	1	1	0	0	0	1	1.000	1	0	0	1.000
1980	—National	OF	3	1	2	0	0	1	1	.667	0	0	0	.000
All-Star Game Totals—2 Years			4	2	3	0	0	1	2	.750	1	0	0	1.000

Member of National League All-Star Team in 1977; did not play.

ALFREDO CLAUDINO GRIFFIN

Born March 6, 1957, at Santo Domingo, D. R.
Height, 5.11. Weight, 165.
Throws right and bats left and righthanded.

Major League stolen bases: 1977 (2), 1979 (21), 1980 (18), 1981 (8), 1982 (10), 1983 (8), 1984 (11), 1985 (24), 1986 (33), 1987 (26), 1988 (7). Total—168.

Led American League shortstops in putouts with 280 in 1983.

Led American League shortstops in total chances with 824 in 1982.

Named shortstop on The Sporting News American League All-Star fielding team, 1985.

Named American League Co-Rookie of the Year by the Baseball Writers' Association of America, 1979.

Year	Club	League	Pos.	G.	AB.	R.	H.	2B.	3B.	HR.	RBI.	B.A.	PO.	A.	E.	F.A.
1974	—Reno	Calif.	SS	11	35	4	9	0	0	0	1	.257	10	22	9	.780
1974	—Sarasota Ind.	Gulf C.	SS	49	158	17	41	1	0	0	11	.259	67	133	★25	.889
1975	—San Jose	Calif.	SS	124	358	42	82	4	3	0	25	.229	189	281	47	.909
1976	—San Jose	Calif.	SS	64	224	40	58	3	1	0	17	.259	91	145	24	.908
1976	—Williamsport	East.	SS	58	200	22	55	3	0	0	17	.275	86	172	17	.938
1976	—Toledo	Int.	SS	22	88	5	19	7	1	0	6	.216	44	71	7	.943
1976	—Cleveland	Amer.	SS	12	4	0	1	0	0	0	0	.250	1	2	1	.750
1977	—Toledo	Int.	SS	125	457	60	114	14	5	1	32	.249	★223	398	★49	.927
1977	—Cleveland	Amer.	SS	14	41	5	6	1	0	0	3	.146	17	30	3	.940
1978	—Portland	P. C.	★SS-OF	133	474	82	138	22	10	5	48	.291	201	395	★40	.937
1978	—Cleveland†	Amer.	SS	5	4	1	2	1	0	0	0	.500	4	7	1	.917
1979	—Toronto	Amer.	SS	153	624	81	179	22	10	2	31	.287	272	501	★36	.956
1980	—Toronto	Amer.	SS	155	653	63	166	26	●15	2	41	.254	295	489	★37	.955
1981	—Toronto	Amer.	★SS-3B-2B	101	388	30	81	19	6	0	21	.209	191	279	★31	.938
1982	—Toronto	Amer.	SS	●162	539	57	130	20	8	1	48	.241	★319	479	●26	.968
1983	—Toronto	Amer.	SS-2B	●162	528	62	132	22	9	4	47	.250	287	422	25	.966
1984	—Toronto‡	Amer.	SS-2B	140	419	53	101	8	2	4	30	.241	230	320	21	.963
1985	—Oakland	Amer.	SS	162	614	75	166	18	7	2	64	.270	278	440	30	.960
1986	—Oakland	Amer.	SS	162	594	74	169	23	6	4	51	.285	282	421	25	.966

Year	Club	League	Pos.	G.	AB.	R.	H.	2B.	3B.	HR.	RBI.	B.A.	PO.	A.	E.	F.A.
1987	Oakland§	Amer.	SS-2B	144	494	69	130	23	5	3	60	.263	250	389	24	.964
1988	Los Angeles xy	Nat.	SS	95	316	39	63	8	3	1	27	.199	145	264	15	.965
American League Totals—12 Years				1372	4902	570	1263	183	68	22	396	.258	2426	3779	260	.960
National League Totals—1 Year				95	316	39	63	8	3	1	27	.199	145	264	15	.965
Major League Totals—13 Years				1467	5218	609	1326	191	71	23	423	.254	2571	4043	275	.960

Signed as free agent by Cleveland Indians' organization, August 22, 1973.

†Traded with Third Baseman Phil Lansford to Toronto Blue Jays for Pitcher Victor Cruz, December 6, 1978.

‡Traded with Outfielder Dave Collins and cash to Oakland A's for Pitcher Bill Caudill, December 8, 1984.

§As part of an eight-player, three-team deal, New York Mets traded Pitcher Jesse Orosco to Oakland Athletics, December 11, 1987. Oakland then traded Orosco along with Shortstop Alfredo Griffin and Pitcher Jay Howell to Los Angeles Dodgers for Pitchers Bob Welch, Matt Young and Jack Savage. Oakland then traded Savage along with Pitchers Wally Whitehurst and Kevin Tapani to New York.

xOn disabled list, May 22 to July 25, 1988.

yGranted free agency, November 4, 1988; re-signed by Dodgers, November 7, 1988.

CHAMPIONSHIP SERIES RECORD

Year	Club	League	Pos.	G.	AB.	R.	H.	2B.	3B.	HR.	RBI.	B.A.	PO.	A.	E.	F.A.
1988	Los Angeles	Nat.	SS	7	25	1	4	1	0	0	3	.160	17	13	0	1.000

WORLD SERIES RECORD

Year	Club	League	Pos.	G.	AB.	R.	H.	2B.	3B.	HR.	RBI.	B.A.	PO.	A.	E.	F.A.
1988	Los Angeles	Nat.	SS	5	16	2	3	0	0	0	0	.188	7	13	1	.952

ALL-STAR GAME RECORD

Year	League	Pos.	AB.	R.	H.	2B.	3B.	HR.	RBI.	B.A.	PO.	A.	E.	F.A.
1984	American	SS	0	0	0	0	0	0	0	.000	0	1	0	1.000

JASON ALAN GRIMSLEY

Born August 7, 1967, at Cleveland, Tex.
Height, 6.03. Weight, 180.
Throws and bats righthanded.

Led New York-Pennsylvania League in hit batsmen with 11 and wild pitches with 18 in 1986.

Year	Club	League	G.	IP.	W.	L.	Pct.	H.	R.	ER.	SO.	BB.	ERA.
1985	Bend	Northwest	6	11⅓	0	1	.000	12	21	17	10	25	13.50
1986	Utica	NYP	14	64⅔	1	•10	.091	63	61	46	46	*77	6.40
1987	Spartanburg	S. Atlantic	23	88⅓	7	4	.636	59	48	31	98	54	3.16
1988	Clearwater	Florida St.	16	101⅓	4	7	.364	80	48	42	90	37	3.73
1988	Reading	Eastern	5	21⅓	1	3	.250	20	19	17	14	13	7.17

Selected by Philadelphia Phillies' organization in 10th round of free-agent draft, June 3, 1985.

GREGORY EUGENE GROSS
(Greg)

Born August 1, 1952, at York, Pa.
Height, 5.11. Weight, 180.
Throws and bats lefthanded.

Major League stolen bases: 1973 (2), 1974 (12), 1975 (2), 1976 (2), 1978 (3), 1979 (5), 1980 (1), 1981 (2), 1982 (4), 1983 (3), 1984 (1), 1985 (1), 1986 (1). Total—39.

Tied for Appalachian League lead in double plays by outfielders with 3 in 1970.

Named National League Rookie Player of the Year by THE SPORTING NEWS, 1974.

Named Appalachian League Player of the Year, 1970.

Year	Club	League	Pos.	G.	AB.	R.	H.	2B.	3B.	HR.	RBI.	B.A.	PO.	A.	E.	F.A.
1970	Covington	Appal.	OF	54	211	40	*74	8	3	2	27	.351	93	*10	3	.972
1971	Columbus	South.	OF-1B	132	494	57	144	14	4	2	33	.291	244	13	9	.966
1972	Columbus	South.	OF	101	367	55	111	14	2	0	25	.302	172	9	3	.984
1972	Okla. City	A. A.	OF	28	109	15	27	4	0	0	8	.248	64	4	1	.986
1973	Denver	A. A.	OF	131	528	98	*174	25	6	0	55	.330	226	11	10	.960
1973	Houston	Nat.	OF	14	39	5	9	2	1	0	1	.231	13	2	0	1.000
1974	Houston	Nat.	OF	156	589	78	185	21	8	0	36	.314	296	15	2	.994
1975	Houston†	Nat.	OF	132	483	67	142	14	10	0	41	.294	216	14	10	.958
1976	Houston‡	Nat.	OF	128	426	52	122	12	3	0	27	.286	208	13	5	.978
1977	Chicago	Nat.	OF	115	239	43	77	10	4	5	32	.322	109	3	1	.991
1978	Chicago§	Nat.	OF	124	347	34	92	12	7	1	39	.265	182	6	4	.979
1979	Philadelphia x	Nat.	OF	111	174	21	58	6	3	0	15	.333	82	5	2	.978
1980	Philadelphia	Nat.	OF-1B	127	154	19	37	7	2	0	12	.240	69	5	2	.974
1981	Philadelphia	Nat.	OF	83	102	14	23	6	1	0	7	.225	48	7	1	.982
1982	Philadelphia	Nat.	OF	119	134	14	40	4	0	0	10	.299	55	3	1	.983
1983	Philadelphia	Nat.	OF-1B	136	245	25	74	12	3	0	29	.302	105	1	1	.991
1984	Philadelphia	Nat.	OF-1B	112	202	19	65	9	1	0	16	.322	195	13	2	.990
1985	Philadelphia y	Nat.	OF-1B	93	169	21	44	5	2	0	14	.260	66	8	0	1.000
1986	Philadelphia	Nat.	OF-1B-P	87	101	11	25	5	0	0	8	.248	40	3	0	1.000
1987	Philadelphia	Nat.	OF-1B	114	133	14	38	4	1	1	12	.286	53	2	0	1.000
1988	Philadelphia z	Nat.	OF-1B	98	133	10	27	1	0	0	5	.203	108	7	1	.991
Major League Totals—16 Years				1749	3670	447	1058	130	46	7	304	.288	1845	107	32	.984

Selected by Houston Astros' organization in 4th round of free-agent draft, June 4, 1970.

†On disabled list, April 2 to April 24, 1975.
‡Traded to Chicago Cubs for Infielder Julio Gonzalez, December 8, 1976.
§Traded with Second Baseman Manny Trillo and Catcher Dave Rader to Philadelphia Phillies for Outfielder Jerry Martin, Catcher Barry Foote, Second Baseman Ted Sizemore and Pitchers Derek Botelho and Henry Mack, February 23, 1979.
xGranted free agency, November 1, 1979; re-signed by Phillies, December 13, 1979.
yOn disabled list, September 6, 1985 through remainder of season.
zGranted free agency, November 4, 1988.

DIVISION SERIES RECORD

Year Club	League	Pos.	G.	AB.	R.	H.	2B.	3B.	HR.	RBI.	B.A.	PO.	A.	E.	F.A.
1981—Philadelphia	Nat.	PH-OF	4	4	0	0	0	0	0	0	.000	0	0	0	.000

CHAMPIONSHIP SERIES RECORD

Year Club	League	Pos.	G.	AB.	R.	H.	2B.	3B.	HR.	RBI.	B.A.	PO.	A.	E.	F.A.
1980—Philadelphia	Nat.	PH-OF	4	4	2	3	0	0	0	1	.750	1	0	0	1.000
1983—Philadelphia	Nat.	OF-PH	4	5	1	0	0	0	0	0	.000	4	0	0	1.000
Championship Series Totals—2 Years			8	9	3	3	0	0	0	1	.333	5	0	0	1.000

WORLD SERIES RECORD

Year Club	League	Pos.	G.	AB.	R.	H.	2B.	3B.	HR.	RBI.	B.A.	PO.	A.	E.	F.A.
1980—Philadelphia	Nat.	PH-OF	4	2	0	0	0	0	0	0	.000	1	0	0	1.000
1983—Philadelphia	Nat.	OF	2	6	0	0	0	0	0	0	.000	8	0	0	1.000
World Series Totals—2 Years			6	8	0	0	0	0	0	0	.000	9	0	0	1.000

PITCHING RECORD

Year Club	League	G.	IP.	W.	L.	Pct.	H.	R.	ER.	SO.	BB.	ERA.
1986—Philadelphia	National	1	⅔	0	0	.000	1	0	0	2	1	0.00

KEVIN FRANK GROSS

Born June 8, 1961, at Downey, Calif.
Height, 6.05. Weight, 215.
Throws and bats righthanded.
Attended Oxnard College, Oxnard, Calif., and
California Lutheran College, Thousand Oaks, Calif.

Major League saves: 1984 (1).
Led National League in home runs allowed with 28 in 1986.
Led National League in hit batsmen with 11 in 1988 and tied for lead with 8 in 1986 and 10 in 1987.
Tied for South Atlantic League lead in games started by pitchers with 28 in 1981.

Year Club	League	G.	IP.	W.	L.	Pct.	H.	R.	ER.	SO.	BB.	ERA.
1981—Spartanburg	S. Atlantic	28	192	13	12	.520	173	94	76	123	62	3.56
1982—Reading	Eastern	26	151	10	15	.400	138	81	71	136	89	4.23
1983—Portland	P. Coast	15	80	3	5	.375	82	60	60	61	45	6.75
1983—Philadelphia	National	17	96	4	6	.400	100	46	38	66	35	3.56
1984—Philadelphia	National	44	129	8	5	.615	140	66	59	84	44	4.12
1985—Philadelphia	National	38	205⅔	15	13	.536	194	86	78	151	81	3.41
1986—Philadelphia	National	37	241⅔	12	12	.500	240	115	108	154	94	4.02
1987—Philadelphia	National	34	200⅔	9	16	.360	205	107	97	110	87	4.35
1988—Philadelphia†	National	33	231⅔	12	14	.462	209	101	95	162	*89	3.69
Major League Totals—6 Years		203	1104⅔	60	66	.476	1088	521	475	727	430	3.87

Selected by Baltimore Orioles' organization in 32nd round of free-agent draft, June 5, 1979.
Selected by Philadelphia Phillies' organization in secondary phase of free-agent draft, January 13, 1981.
†Traded to Montreal Expos for Pitchers Floyd Youmans and Jeff Parrett, December 6, 1988.

ALL-STAR GAME RECORD

Year League	IP.	W.	L.	Pct.	H.	R.	ER.	SO.	BB.	ERA.
1988—National	1	0	0	.000	0	0	0	1	0	0.00

KELLY WAYNE GRUBER

Born February 26, 1962, at Bellaire, Tex.
Height, 6.00. Weight, 185.
Throws and bats righthanded.
Attended University of Texas, Austin, Tex.

Major League stolen bases: 1986 (2), 1987 (12), 1988 (23). Total—37.
Led American League third basemen in assists with 349 and total chances with 477 in 1988.
Led International League in slugging percentage with .500 in 1984.
Led International League third basemen in total chances with 309 in 1985.
Led Southern League shortstops in errors with 43 in 1982.

Year Club	League	Pos.	G.	AB.	R.	H.	2B.	3B.	HR.	RBI.	B.A.	PO.	A.	E.	F.A.
1980—Batavia	NYP	SS	61	212	27	46	3	2	2	19	.217	87	155	21	.920
1981—Waterloo	Midw.	SS	127	458	64	133	25	4	14	59	.290	*180	*389	*56	.910
1982—Chattanooga	South.	SS-3B	128	441	53	107	18	4	13	54	.243	161	333	44	.918
1983—Buffalo†	East.	3B-SS-OF	111	403	60	106	20	4	15	54	.263	98	170	27	.908
1984—Toronto	Amer.	3B-OF-SS	15	16	1	1	0	0	1	2	.063	6	12	2	.900
1984—Syracuse	Int.	3B-OF	97	342	53	92	12	2	21	55	.269	76	156	18	.928
1985—Syracuse	Int.	3B	121	473	71	118	16	5	21	69	.249	78	*217	14	.955

Year	Club	League	Pos.	G.	AB.	R.	H.	2B.	3B.	HR.	RBI.	B.A.	PO.	A.	E.	F.A.
1985—	Toronto	Amer.	3B-2B	5	13	0	3	0	0	0	1	.231	2	6	0	1.000
1986—	Toronto	Amer.	3-2-O-S	87	143	20	28	4	1	5	15	.196	43	77	7	.945
1987—	Toronto	Amer.	3-S-2-O	138	341	50	80	14	3	12	36	.235	76	200	13	.955
1988—	Toronto	Amer.	3-2-O-S	158	569	75	158	33	5	16	81	.278	121	365	16	.968
Major League Totals—5 Years				403	1082	146	270	51	9	34	135	.250	248	660	38	.960

Selected by Cleveland Indians' organization in 1st round (10th player selected) of free-agent draft, June 3, 1980.
†Drafted by Toronto Blue Jays, December 5, 1983.

CECILIO GUANTE (MAGALLANES)

Name pronounced Goo-AHN-tay.

Born February 2, 1960, at Jacagua, D. R.
Height, 6.03. Weight, 205.
Throws and bats righthanded.

Major League saves: 1983 (9), 1984 (2), 1985 (5), 1986 (4), 1987 (1), 1988 (12). Total—33.
Led South Atlantic League in saves with 19 in 1980.

Year	Club	League	G.	IP.	W.	L.	Pct.	H.	R.	ER.	SO.	BB.	ERA.
1980—	Shelby	S. Atlantic	39	90	6	6	.500	58	32	29	114	25	2.90
1980—	Salem	Carolina	6	14	0	0	.000	7	2	2	18	8	1.29
1981—	Buffalo	Eastern	10	14	1	1	.500	8	3	1	17	9	0.64
1981—	Portland†	P. Coast	19	104	6	6	.500	110	64	62	70	58	5.37
1982—	Portland	P. Coast	21	35	3	2	.600	34	17	15	29	26	3.86
1982—	Pittsburgh	National	10	27	0	0	.000	28	16	10	26	5	3.33
1983—	Hawaii	P. Coast	15	25⅔	2	1	.667	22	12	10	24	12	3.51
1983—	Pittsburgh	National	49	100⅓	2	6	.250	90	45	37	82	46	3.32
1984—	Pittsburgh‡	National	27	41⅓	2	3	.400	32	12	12	30	16	2.61
1984—	Nashua	Eastern	1	3	0	0	.000	5	1	1	2	0	3.00
1985—	Pittsburgh	National	63	109	4	6	.400	84	34	33	92	40	2.72
1986—	Pittsburgh§x	National	52	78	5	2	.714	65	32	29	63	29	3.35
1987—	New York y	American	23	44	3	2	.600	42	30	28	46	20	5.73
1988—	New York z-Texas a	American	63	79⅔	5	6	.455	67	26	25	65	26	2.82
National League Totals—5 Years			201	355⅔	13	17	.433	299	139	121	293	136	3.06
American League Totals—2 Years			86	123⅔	8	8	.500	109	56	53	111	46	3.86
Major League Totals—7 Years			287	479⅓	21	25	.457	408	195	174	404	182	3.27

Signed as free agent by Pittsburgh Pirates' organization, November 24, 1979.
†On disabled list, July 25 to August 5, 1981.
‡On disabled list, July 13 to July 30, 1984.
§On disabled list, August 25 to September 24, 1986.
xTraded with Pitchers Rick Rhoden and Pat Clements to New York Yankees for Pitchers Doug Drabek, Brian Fisher and Logan Easley, November 26, 1986.
yOn disabled list, May 25 to June 9 and July 7 to September 14, 1987.
zTraded to Texas Rangers for Pitcher Dale Mohorcic, August 30, 1988.
aGranted free agency, November 4, 1988.

MARK STEVEN GUBICZA

Name pronounced GOO-ba-zah.

Born August 14, 1962, at Philadelphia, Pa.
Height, 6.05. Weight, 210.
Throws and bats righthanded.
Son of Anthony F. Gubicza, minor league pitcher, 1950 and 1951.

Year	Club	League	G.	IP.	W.	L.	Pct.	H.	R.	ER.	SO.	BB.	ERA.
1981—	Sarasota Royals-Gold	Gulf Coast	11	56	•8	1	*.889	39	18	14	40	23	2.25
1982—	Fort Myers†	Florida St.	11	48	2	5	.286	49	33	22	36	25	4.13
1983—	Jacksonville	Southern	28	196	14	12	.538	146	81	67	*146	93	3.08
1984—	Kansas City	American	29	189	10	14	.417	172	90	85	111	75	4.05
1985—	Kansas City	American	29	177⅓	14	10	.583	160	88	80	99	77	4.06
1986—	Kansas City‡	American	35	180⅔	12	6	.667	155	77	73	118	84	3.64
1987—	Kansas City	American	35	241⅔	13	18	.419	231	114	107	166	120	3.98
1988—	Kansas City	American	35	269⅔	20	8	.714	237	94	81	183	83	2.70
Major League Totals—5 Years			163	1058⅓	69	56	.552	955	463	426	677	439	3.62

Selected by Kansas City Royals' organization in 2nd round of free-agent draft, June 8, 1981.
†On disabled list, June 29, 1982 through remainder of season.
‡On disabled list, June 6 to June 21, 1986.

CHAMPIONSHIP SERIES RECORD

Year	Club	League	G.	IP.	W.	L.	Pct.	H.	R.	ER.	SO.	BB.	ERA.
1985—	Kansas City	American	2	8⅓	1	0	1.000	4	3	3	4	4	3.24

ALL-STAR GAME RECORD

Year	League	IP.	W.	L.	Pct.	H.	R.	ER.	SO.	BB.	ERA.
1988—	American	2	0	0	.000	3	1	1	2	0	4.50

—DID YOU KNOW—

That there were 421 more balks called in the American League (558-137) in 1988 than the year before?

PEDRO GUERRERO

Name pronounced Guh-RAIR-oh.

Born June 29, 1956, at San Pedro de Macoris, D. R.
Height, 6.00. Weight, 195.
Throws and bats righthanded.
Half-brother of Domingo Michel, outfielder in Los Angeles Dodgers' organization.

Established National League records for most home runs, month of June (15), 1985; most consecutive times reached base safely, season (14), July 23 through 26, 1985.

Major League stolen bases: 1979 (2), 1980 (2), 1981 (5), 1982 (22), 1983 (23), 1984 (9), 1985 (12), 1987 (9), 1988 (4). Total—88.

Led National League in slugging percentage with .577 in 1985.
Led National League third basemen in errors with 30 and tied for lead in total chances with 458 in 1983.
Led Pacific Coast League in sacrifice flies with 15 in 1978.
Tied for Northwest League lead in double plays by third basemen with 13 in 1974.
Named outfielder on THE SPORTING NEWS National League All-Star Team, 1981 and 1982.
Named outfielder on THE SPORTING NEWS National League Silver Slugger team, 1982.

Year Club	League	Pos.	G.	AB.	R.	H.	2B.	3B.	HR.	RBI.	B.A.	PO.	A.	E.	F.A.
1973—Sarasota Ind.†	Gulf C.	3B-SS	44	153	13	39	2	3	2	22	.255	32	82	11	.912
1974—Orangeburg	W. Car.	3B	19	55	3	8	1	0	0	1	.145	11	22	5	.868
1974—Bellingham	N'west	3B	82	297	49	94	•23	2	3	55	.316	*69	124	23	.894
1975—Danville	Midw.	3B-OF	104	351	81	121	25	5	10	76	*.345	111	168	31	.900
1976—Waterbury	East.	1B	132	495	73	151	*30	10	5	66	.305	1129	*96	*19	.985
1977—Albuquerque‡	P. C.	1B	32	129	30	52	11	4	4	39	.403	329	17	10	.972
1978—Albuquerque	P. C.	1B-3B	134	492	92	166	28	4	14	*116	.337	982	80	10	.991
1978—Los Angeles	Nat.	1B	5	8	3	5	0	1	0	1	.625	25	1	0	1.000
1979—Albuquerque	P. C.	OF-3B-1B	113	453	94	151	33	9	22	*103	.333	188	9	5	.975
1979—Los Angeles	Nat.	OF-1B-3B	25	62	7	15	2	0	2	9	.242	53	4	1	.983
1980—Los Angeles§	Nat.	O-2-3-1	75	183	27	59	9	1	7	31	.322	103	110	3	.986
1981—Los Angeles	Nat.	OF-3B-1B	98	347	46	104	17	2	12	48	.300	165	55	11	.952
1982—Los Angeles	Nat.	OF-3B	150	575	87	175	27	5	32	100	.304	282	53	12	.965
1983—Los Angeles	Nat.	3B-1B	160	584	87	174	28	6	32	103	.298	130	308	31	.934
1984—Los Angeles x	Nat.	3B-OF-1B	144	535	85	162	29	4	16	72	.303	271	151	22	.950
1985—Los Angeles	Nat.	OF-3B-1B	137	487	99	156	22	2	33	87	.320	251	123	13	.966
1986—Los Angeles y	Nat.	OF-1B	31	61	7	15	3	0	5	10	.246	39	1	0	1.000
1987—Los Angeles	Nat.	OF-1B	152	545	89	184	25	2	27	89	.338	482	44	12	.978
1988—L.A.zab-St.L.	Nat.	1B-3B-OF	103	364	40	104	14	2	10	65	.286	466	99	12	.979
1988—Albuquerque	P. C.	1B	5	12	3	5	0	0	1	4	.417	30	2	0	1.000
Major League Totals—11 Years			1080	3751	577	1153	176	25	176	615	.307	2267	949	117	.965

Signed as free agent by Cleveland Indians' organization, January 15, 1973.
†Traded to Los Angeles Dodgers for Pitcher Bruce Ellingsen, April 4, 1974.
‡On disabled list, May 19 to August 30, 1977.
§On disabled list, August 23 to September 15, 1980.
xOn disabled list, July 22 to August 6, 1984.
yOn disabled list, April 4 to July 30 and August 11 to September 3, 1986.
zOn suspended list, May 24 to May 28, 1988.
aOn disabled list, June 5 to July 29, 1988; included rehabilitation disability assignment to Bakersfield, July 23 to July 29, 1988.
bTraded to St. Louis Cardinals for Pitcher John Tudor, August 16, 1988.

DIVISION SERIES RECORD

Year Club	League	Pos.	G.	AB.	R.	H.	2B.	3B.	HR.	RBI.	B.A.	PO.	A.	E.	F.A.
1981—Los Angeles	Nat.	3B	5	17	1	3	1	0	1	1	.176	3	15	0	1.000

CHAMPIONSHIP SERIES RECORD

Tied National League Championship Series record for most bases on balls, six-game Series (5), 1985.

Year Club	League	Pos.	G.	AB.	R.	H.	2B.	3B.	HR.	RBI.	B.A.	PO.	A.	E.	F.A.
1981—Los Angeles	Nat.	OF	5	19	1	2	0	0	1	2	.105	9	2	0	1.000
1983—Los Angeles	Nat.	3B	4	12	1	3	1	1	0	2	.250	0	9	0	1.000
1985—Los Angeles	Nat.	OF	6	20	2	5	1	0	0	4	.250	11	0	0	1.000
Championship Series Totals—3 Years			15	51	4	10	2	1	1	8	.196	20	11	0	1.000

WORLD SERIES RECORD

Year Club	League	Pos.	G.	AB.	R.	H.	2B.	3B.	HR.	RBI.	B.A.	PO.	A.	E.	F.A.
1981—Los Angeles	Nat.	OF	6	21	2	7	1	1	2	7	.333	17	1	0	1.000

ALL-STAR GAME RECORD

Year League	Pos.	AB.	R.	H.	2B.	3B.	HR.	RBI.	B.A.	PO.	A.	E.	F.A.
1981—National	PH	1	0	0	0	0	0	0	.000	0	0	0	.000
1983—National	3B-OF	1	0	0	0	0	0	0	.000	0	0	1	.000
1987—National	PH	1	0	0	0	0	0	0	.000	0	0	0	.000
All-Star Game Totals—3 Years		3	0	0	0	0	0	0	.000	0	0	1	.000

Named to National League All-Star Team for 1985 game; replaced due to injury by Glenn Wilson.

—DID YOU KNOW—

That Oakland's Terry Steinbach is the only player in history to hit a homer in both his first major league at-bat and first All-Star Game at-bat?

ARTHUR LEE GUETTERMAN

(Known by middle name.)

Born November 22, 1958, at Chattanooga, Tenn.
Height, 6.08. Weight, 225.
Throws and bats lefthanded.
Received bachelor of science degree in physical education from
Liberty Baptist College, Lynchburg, Va. in 1981.

Year Club	League	G.	IP.	W.	L.	Pct.	H.	R.	ER.	SO.	BB.	ERA.
1981—Bellingham	Northwest	13	84	6	4	.600	85	36	25	55	42	2.68
1982—Bakersfield	California	26	154	7	11	.389	172	100	76	82	69	4.44
1983—Bakersfield	California	25	156⅓	12	6	.667	164	72	56	93	45	3.22
1984—Chattanooga†	Southern	24	157	11	7	.611	174	68	59	47	38	3.38
1984—Seattle	American	3	4⅓	0	0	.000	9	2	2	2	2	4.15
1985—Calgary‡	P. Coast	20	110⅓	5	8	.385	138	86	71	48	44	5.79
1986—Seattle	American	41	76	0	4	.000	108	67	62	38	30	7.34
1986—Calgary	P. Coast	4	19⅓	1	0	1.000	24	12	12	8	7	5.59
1987—Calgary	P. Coast	16	44	5	1	.833	41	14	14	29	17	2.86
1987—Seattle§	American	25	113⅓	11	4	*.733	117	60	48	42	35	3.81
1988—New York	American	20	40⅔	1	2	.333	49	21	21	15	14	4.65
1988—Columbus	Int'national	18	120⅔	9	6	.600	109	46	37	49	26	2.76
Major League Totals—4 Years		89	234⅓	12	10	.545	283	150	133	97	81	5.11

Selected by Seattle Mariners' organization in 4th round of free-agent draft, June 8, 1981.
†On disabled list, August 1 to August 15, 1984.
‡On disabled list, April 11 to May 31, 1985.
§Traded with Pitchers Clay Parker and Wade Taylor to New York Yankees for Pitcher Steve Trout and Outfielder Henry Cotto, December 22, 1987.

RONALD AMES GUIDRY

Name pronounced GID-ree.

(Ron)

Born August 28, 1950, at Lafayette, La.
Height, 5.11. Weight, 160.
Throws and bats lefthanded.
Attended University of Southwestern Louisiana, Lafayette, La.

Established major league record for highest winning percentage, season, 20 or more wins (.893), 1978.
Tied major league record for striking out side on nine pitches, August 7, 1984, second game (ninth inning).
Established American League record for most strikeouts by lefthanded pitcher, game (18), June 17, 1978.
Tied American League record for most shutouts by lefthanded pitcher, season (9), 1978.
Major League saves: 1977 (1), 1979 (2), 1980 (1). Total—4.
Led American League in complete games with 21 in 1983.
Led American League in shutouts with 9 in 1978.
Named Man of the Year by THE SPORTING NEWS, 1978.
Named Major League Player of the Year by THE SPORTING NEWS, 1978.
Named American League Pitcher of the Year by THE SPORTING NEWS, 1978.
Won American League Cy Young Memorial Award, 1978.
Named lefthanded pitcher on THE SPORTING NEWS American League All-Star Team, 1978, 1981, 1983 and 1985.
Named pitcher on THE SPORTING NEWS American League All-Star fielding team, 1982 through 1986.

Year Club	League	G.	IP.	W.	L.	Pct.	H.	R.	ER.	SO.	BB.	ERA.
1971—Johnson City	Ap'lachian	7	47	2	2	.500	34	13	11	61	27	2.11
1972—Fort Lauderdale†	Florida St.	15	66	2	4	.333	53	35	28	61	50	3.82
1973—Kinston‡	Carolina	20	101	7	6	.538	85	53	36	97	70	3.21
1974—West Haven§	Eastern	37	77	2	4	.333	80	48	45	79	53	5.26
1975—Syracuse	Int'national	42	62	6	5	.545	46	24	20	76	37	2.90
1975—New York	American	10	16	0	1	.000	15	6	6	15	9	3.38
1976—New York	American	7	16	0	0	.000	20	12	10	12	4	5.63
1976—Syracuse	Int'national	22	40	5	1	.833	16	5	3	50	13	0.68
1977—New York	American	31	211	16	7	.696	174	72	66	176	65	2.82
1978—New York	American	35	274	*25	3	*.893	187	61	53	248	72	*1.74
1979—New York x	American	33	236	18	8	.692	203	83	73	201	71	*2.78
1980—New York	American	37	220	17	10	.630	215	97	87	166	80	3.56
1981—New York y	American	23	127	11	5	.688	100	41	39	104	26	2.76
1982—New York	American	34	222	14	8	.636	216	104	94	162	69	3.81
1983—New York x	American	31	250⅓	21	9	.700	232	99	95	156	60	3.42
1984—New York za	American	29	195⅔	10	11	.476	223	102	98	127	44	4.51
1985—New York	American	34	259	*22	6	*.786	243	104	94	143	42	3.27
1986—New York b	American	30	192⅓	9	12	.429	202	94	85	140	38	3.98
1986—Albany c	Eastern	1	3	0	0	.000	1	1	1	3	2	3.00
1987—Fort Lauderdale	Florida St.	2	6	0	0	.000	4	0	0	7	1	0.00
1987—Columbus	Int'national	1	5	1	0	1.000	3	2	0	3	2	0.00
1987—New York	American	22	117⅔	5	8	.385	111	50	48	96	38	3.67
1988—Fort Lauderdale d	Florida St.	4	14⅔	0	0	.000	7	2	2	17	2	1.23
1988—New York ae	American	12	56	2	3	.400	57	28	26	32	15	4.18
Major League Totals—14 Years		368	2393	170	91	.651	2198	953	874	1778	633	3.29

Selected by New York Yankees' organization in 3rd round of free-agent draft, June 8, 1971.
†Appeared as outfielder in one game with one putout.
‡On temporary inactive list, July 13 to August 3, 1973.
§Appeared as outfielder with no chances.
xAppeared as outfielder in one game with no chances.

yGranted free agency, November 13, 1981; re-signed by Yankees, December 15, 1981.
zOn disabled list, August 16 to September 3, 1984.
aAppeared in one game as a pinch-runner.
bOn disabled list, July 3 to July 27, 1986; included rehabilitation disability assignment to Albany, July 23 to July 27, 1986.
cGranted free agency, November 12, 1986; re-signed by Yankees, May 1, 1987.
dOn New York disabled list, April 4 to May 22 and May 31 to July 1, 1988; included rehabilitation disability assignment to Fort Lauderdale, April 28 to May 18, 1988.
eGranted free agency, December 20, 1988.

DIVISION SERIES RECORD

Year Club	League	G.	IP.	W.	L.	Pct.	H.	R.	ER.	SO.	BB.	ERA.
1981—New York	American	2	8⅓	0	0	.000	11	5	5	8	3	5.40

CHAMPIONSHIP SERIES RECORD

Year Club	League	G.	IP.	W.	L.	Pct.	H.	R.	ER.	SO.	BB.	ERA.
1977—New York	American	2	11⅓	1	0	1.000	9	5	5	8	3	3.97
1978—New York	American	1	8	1	0	1.000	7	1	1	7	1	1.13
1980—New York	American	1	3	0	1	.000	5	4	4	2	4	12.00
Championship Series Totals—3 Years		4	22⅓	2	1	.667	21	10	10	17	8	4.03

Appeared as pinch-runner for New York Yankees in one game of 1976 Championship Series.

WORLD SERIES RECORD

Tied World Series record for most consecutive home runs allowed, inning (2), October 25, 1981 (seventh inning).

Year Club	League	G.	IP.	W.	L.	Pct.	H.	R.	ER.	SO.	BB.	ERA.
1977—New York	American	1	9	1	0	1.000	4	2	2	7	3	2.00
1978—New York	American	1	9	1	0	1.000	8	1	1	4	7	1.00
1981—New York	American	2	14	1	1	.500	8	3	3	15	4	1.93
World Series Totals—3 Years		4	32	3	1	.750	20	6	6	26	14	1.69

ALL-STAR GAME RECORD

Year League	IP.	W.	L.	Pct.	H.	R.	ER.	SO.	BB.	ERA.
1978—American	⅓	0	0	.000	0	0	0	0	0	0.00
1979—American	⅓	0	0	.000	0	0	0	0	1	0.00
All-Star Game Totals—2 Years	⅔	0	0	.000	0	0	0	0	1	0.00

Member of American League All-Star Team in 1982; did not play.
Named to American League All-Star Team for 1983 game; replaced due to injury by Tippy Martinez.

OSWALDO JOSE GUILLEN (BARRIOS)

Name pronounced GEY-un.

(Ozzie)

Born January 20, 1964, at Ocumare del Tuy, Miranda, Venezuela.
Height, 5.11. Weight, 153.
Throws right and bats lefthanded.

Tied major league record for fewest bases on balls received, 150 or more games, season (12), 1985, 1986.
Established American League record for fewest putouts, shortstop, season, 150 or more games (220), 1985.
Major League stolen bases: 1985 (7), 1986 (8), 1987 (25), 1988 (25). Total—65.
Led American League shortstops in total chances with 760 in 1987 and 863 in 1988.
Led American League shortstops in double plays with 105 in 1987.
Led Pacific Coast League shortstops in assists with 362 and total chances with 549 in 1984.
Tied for California League lead in sacrifice hits with 14 in 1982.
Named American League Rookie Player of the Year by THE SPORTING NEWS, 1985.
Named American League Rookie of the Year by Baseball Writers' Association of America, 1985.

Year Club	League	Pos.	G.	AB.	R.	H.	2B.	3B.	HR.	RBI.	B.A.	PO.	A.	E.	F.A.
1981—Bradenton Padr.†	Gulf C.	SS-2B	55	189	26	49	4	1	0	16	.259	105	135	15	.941
1982—Reno†	Calif.	SS	130	528	★103	★183	33	1	2	54	.347	★240	399	41	.940
1983—Beaumont†	Texas	SS	114	427	62	126	20	4	2	48	.295	185	327	★38	.931
1984—Las Vegas†‡	P. C.	SS-2B	122	463	81	137	26	6	5	53	.296	172	364	17	.969
1985—Chicago	Amer.	SS	150	491	71	134	21	9	1	33	.273	220	382	12	★.980
1986—Chicago	Amer.	SS	159	547	58	137	19	4	2	47	.250	261	459	22	.970
1987—Chicago	Amer.	SS	149	560	64	156	22	7	2	51	.279	266	475	19	.975
1988—Chicago	Amer.	SS	156	566	58	148	16	7	0	39	.261	273	★570	20	.977
Major League Totals—4 Years			614	2164	251	575	78	27	5	170	.266	1020	1886	73	.975

Signed as free agent by San Diego Padres' organization, December 17, 1980.
†Batted left and righthanded.
‡Traded with Pitchers Tim Lollar and Bill Long and Third Baseman Luis Salazar to Chicago White Sox for Pitchers LaMarr Hoyt, Kevin Kristan and Todd Simmons, December 6, 1984.

ALL-STAR GAME RECORD

Named to American League All-Star Team for 1988 game; replaced due to injury by Kurt Stillwell.

—DID YOU KNOW—

That righthander Nolan Ryan has won at least 100 games for one club in each league? Ryan won 138 games for the California Angels from 1972 through 1979 and 106 as a member of the Houston Astros from 1980 through 1988.

WILLIAM LEE GULLICKSON
(Bill)

Born February 20, 1959, at Marshall, Minn.
Height, 6.03. Weight, 220.
Throws and bats righthanded.

Tied modern major league record for most wild pitches, game (6), April 10, 1982.
Led National League in home runs allowed with 27 in 1984.
Named National League Rookie Pitcher of the Year by THE SPORTING NEWS, 1980.

Year Club	League	G.	IP.	W.	L.	Pct.	H.	R.	ER.	SO.	BB.	ERA.
1977—West Palm Beach	Florida St.	10	56	3	3	.500	67	30	25	35	17	4.02
1978—West Palm Beach	Florida St.	20	148	9	9	.500	121	45	30	127	52	1.82
1978—Memphis	Southern	8	50	1	4	.200	44	19	17	43	19	3.06
1979—Denver	Am. Assoc.	11	54	3	3	.500	65	44	40	31	26	6.67
1979—Memphis	Southern	16	116	10	3	.769	110	52	47	115	42	3.65
1979—Montreal	National	1	1	0	0	.000	2	0	0	0	0	0.00
1980—Denver	Am. Assoc.	9	66	6	2	.750	47	14	14	64	29	1.91
1980—Montreal	National	24	141	10	5	.667	127	53	47	120	50	3.00
1981—Montreal	National	22	157	7	9	.438	142	54	49	115	34	2.81
1982—Montreal	National	34	236⅔	12	14	.462	231	101	94	155	61	3.57
1983—Montreal	National	34	242⅓	17	12	.586	230	108	101	120	59	3.75
1984—Montreal†	National	32	226⅔	12	9	.571	230	100	91	100	37	3.61
1985—Montreal‡§	National	29	181⅓	14	12	.538	187	78	71	68	47	3.52
1986—Cincinnati	National	37	244⅔	15	12	.556	245	103	92	121	60	3.38
1987—Cincinnati x	National	27	165	10	11	.476	172	99	89	89	39	4.85
1987—New York y	American	8	48	4	2	.667	46	29	26	28	11	4.88
1988—Yomiuri Giants	Central	26	203⅓	14	9	.609	....	....	70	134	51	3.10
National League Totals—9 Years		240	1595⅔	97	84	.536	1566	696	634	888	387	3.58
American League Totals—1 Year		8	48	4	2	.667	46	29	26	28	11	4.88
Major League Totals—9 Years		248	1643⅔	101	86	.540	1612	725	660	916	398	3.61

Selected by Montreal Expos' organization in 1st round (second player selected) of free-agent draft, June 7, 1977.
†On disabled list, April 20 to May 8, 1984.
‡On disabled list, June 17 to July 8, 1985.
§Traded with Catcher Sal Butera to Cincinnati Reds for Pitchers Jay Tibbs, Andy McGaffigan and John Stuper and Catcher Dann Bilardello, December 19, 1985.
xTraded to New York Yankees for Pitcher Dennis Rasmussen, August 26, 1987.
yGranted free agency, November 9, 1987; signed by Yomiuri Giants of Japanese Baseball League, January 13, 1988.

DIVISION SERIES RECORD

Year Club	League	G.	IP.	W.	L.	Pct.	H.	R.	ER.	SO.	BB.	ERA.
1981—Montreal	National	1	7⅔	1	0	1.000	6	1	1	3	1	1.17

CHAMPIONSHIP SERIES RECORD

Tied Championship Series record for most games lost, Series (2), 1981.

Year Club	League	G.	IP.	W.	L.	Pct.	H.	R.	ER.	SO.	BB.	ERA.
1981—Montreal	National	2	14⅓	0	2	.000	12	5	4	12	6	2.51

JOAQUIN FERNANDO GUTIERREZ

Name pronounced Wah-KEEN Goo-TEE-erz.

(Jackie)

Born June 27, 1960, at Cartagena, Colombia.
Height, 6.01. Weight, 180.
Throws and bats righthanded.
Brother-in-law of Orlando Ramirez, shortstop with California Angels, 1974 through 1977 and 1979;
son of Campo Gutierrez, who competed in javelin event for Columbia in 1936 Olympics;
and brother of Freddie Gutierrez, who competed in 100 meter race in 1964 Olympics.

Established major league records for fewest assists (347), and chances accepted (575) by shortstop, season, 150 or more games, 1984.
Major League stolen bases: 1984 (12), 1985 (10), 1986 (3). Total—25.
Led Carolina League shortstops in assists with 423 and tied for lead in putouts with 205 and errors with 53 in 1981.

Year Club	League	Pos.	G.	AB.	R.	H.	2B.	3B.	HR.	RBI.	B.A.	PO.	A.	E.	F.A.
1978—Elmira	NYP	SS	63	216	23	42	8	0	0	18	.194	*131	197	20	*.943
1979—Elmira	NYP	SS-2B	63	183	29	46	4	2	0	14	.251	97	157	12	.955
1980—Winter Haven	Fla. St.	3B-SS-2B	111	368	46	94	4	1	1	40	.255	103	179	19	.937
1981—Winston-Salem	Carol.	SS-3B	137	507	56	126	14	5	1	45	.249	207	428	55	.920
1982—Bristol	East.	SS	138	468	64	130	20	2	1	44	.278	*199	368	37	*.939
1983—New Britain	East.	SS	67	248	36	69	7	2	4	25	.278	116	194	13	.960
1983—Pawtucket	Int.	SS	66	233	30	62	11	1	1	17	.266	109	211	20	.941
1983—Boston	Amer.	SS	5	10	2	3	0	0	0	0	.300	9	6	1	.938
1984—Boston	Amer.	SS	151	449	55	118	12	3	2	29	.263	228	347	31	.949
1985—Boston†	Amer.	SS	103	275	33	60	5	2	2	21	.218	143	238	23	.943
1986—Baltimore‡	Amer.	2B-3B	61	145	8	27	3	0	0	4	.186	96	108	4	.981
1986—Rochester	Int.	SS	54	198	29	60	7	2	1	22	.303	93	146	13	.948
1987—Baltimore	Amer.	2B-3B	3	1	0	0	0	0	0	0	.000	0	0	0	.000
1987—Rochester§	Int.	SS-2B-3B	92	333	32	85	9	3	2	25	.255	141	275	13	.970
1988—Maine	Int.	SS-3B	40	144	7	34	4	0	0	11	.236	50	72	4	.968

Year	Club	League	Pos.	G.	AB.	R.	H.	2B.	3B.	HR.	RBI.	B.A.	PO.	A.	E.	F.A.
1988—	Philadelphia x	Nat.	SS-3B	33	77	8	19	4	0	0	9	.247	28	59	8	.916
American League Totals—5 Years				323	880	98	208	20	5	4	54	.236	476	699	59	.952
National League Totals—1 Year				33	77	8	19	4	0	0	9	.247	28	59	8	.916
Major League Totals—6 Years				356	957	106	227	24	5	4	63	.237	504	758	67	.950

Signed as free agent by Boston Red Sox' organization, January 14, 1978.
†Traded to Baltimore Orioles for Pitcher Sammy Stewart, December 17, 1985.
‡On disabled list, May 12 to June 20, 1986; included rehabilitation disability assignment to Rochester, June 1 to June 20, 1986.
§Released, March 23, 1988; signed by Philadelphia Phillies, July 15, 1988.
xReleased, October 7, 1988.

JOSE ALBERTO GUZMAN (MIRABEL)

Born April 9, 1963, at Santa Isabel, Puerto Rico.
Height, 6.03. Weight, 185.
Throws and bats righthanded.

Year	Club	League	G.	IP.	W.	L.	Pct.	H.	R.	ER.	SO.	BB.	ERA.
1981—	Sarasota Rangers	Gulf Coast	14	39	3	3	.500	44	30	23	13	14	5.31
1982—	Sarasota Rangers	Gulf Coast	12	66	5	4	.556	51	21	16	42	13	2.18
1983—	Burlington	Midwest	25	154⅔	12	8	.600	135	68	51	146	52	2.97
1984—	Tulsa	Texas	25	140⅓	7	9	.438	137	75	65	82	55	4.17
1985—	Oklahoma City	Am. Assoc.	25	149⅔	10	5	.667	131	60	52	76	40	3.13
1985—	Texas	American	5	32⅔	3	2	.600	27	13	10	24	14	2.76
1986—	Texas	American	29	172⅓	9	15	.375	199	101	87	87	60	4.54
1987—	Texas	American	37	208⅓	14	14	.500	196	115	108	143	82	4.67
1988—	Texas	American	30	206⅔	11	13	.458	180	99	85	157	82	3.70
Major League Totals—4 Years			101	620	37	44	.457	602	328	290	411	238	4.21

Signed as free agent by Texas Rangers' organization, February 10, 1981.

JUAN ANDRES GUZMAN (CORREA)

Born October 28, 1966, at Santo Domingo, D. R.
Height, 6.00. Weight, 190.
Throws and bats righthanded.

Led Florida State League in wild pitches with 16 in 1986.
Led Gulf Coast League in wild pitches with 15 in 1985.

Year	Club	League	G.	IP.	W.	L.	Pct.	H.	R.	ER.	SO.	BB.	ERA.
1985—	Bradenton Dodgers	Gulf Coast	21	42	5	1	.833	39	26	18	43	25	3.86
1986—	Vero Beach	Florida St.	26	131⅓	10	9	.526	114	69	51	96	90	3.49
1987—	Bakersfield†	California	22	110	5	6	.455	106	71	58	113	84	4.75
1988—	Knoxville	Southern	46	84	4	5	.444	52	29	22	90	61	2.36

Signed as free agent by Los Angeles Dodgers' organization, March 16, 1985.
†Traded to Toronto Blue Jays for Infielder Mike Sharperson, September 22, 1987.

ANTHONY KEITH GWYNN

Name pronounced Gwin.

(Tony)

Born May 9, 1960, at Los Angeles, Calif.
Height, 5.11. Weight, 199.
Throws and bats lefthanded.
Attended San Diego State University, San Diego, Calif.
Brother of Chris Gwynn, outfielder in Los Angeles Dodgers' organization.

Established National League record for lowest average by batting leader, season (.313), 1988.
Tied modern National League record for most stolen bases, game (5), September 20, 1986.
Major League stolen bases: 1982 (8), 1983 (7), 1984 (33), 1985 (14), 1986 (37), 1987 (56), 1988 (26). Total—181.
Led National League outfielders in total chances with 360 in 1986.
Named outfielder on THE SPORTING NEWS National League All-Star Team, 1984, 1986 and 1987.
Named outfielder on THE SPORTING NEWS National League All-Star fielding team, 1986 and 1987.
Named outfielder on THE SPORTING NEWS National League Silver Slugger team, 1984, 1986 and 1987.
Named Northwest League Most Valuable Player, 1981.
Drafted by San Diego Clippers in 10th round (210th player selected) of NBA draft, June 9, 1981.

Year	Club	League	Pos.	G.	AB.	R.	H.	2B.	3B.	HR.	RBI.	B.A.	PO.	A.	E.	F.A.
1981—	Walla Walla	N'west	OF	42	178	46	59	12	1	12	37	⋆.331	76	2	3	.963
1981—	Amarillo	Texas	OF	23	91	22	42	8	2	4	19	.462	41	1	0	1.000
1982—	Hawaii	P. C.	OF	93	366	65	120	23	2	5	46	.328	208	11	4	.982
1982—	San Diego†	Nat.	OF	54	190	33	55	12	2	1	17	.289	110	1	1	.991
1983—	Las Vegas‡	P. C.	OF	17	73	15	25	6	0	0	7	.342	23	2	3	.893
1983—	San Diego	Nat.	OF	86	304	34	94	12	2	1	37	.309	163	9	1	.994
1984—	San Diego	Nat.	OF	158	606	88	⋆213	21	10	5	71	⋆.351	345	11	4	.989
1985—	San Diego	Nat.	OF	154	622	90	197	29	5	6	46	.317	337	14	4	.989
1986—	San Diego	Nat.	OF	160	⋆642	●107	⋆211	33	7	14	59	.329	⋆337	19	4	.989
1987—	San Diego	Nat.	OF	157	589	119	⋆218	36	13	7	54	⋆.370	298	13	6	.981
1988—	San Diego§	Nat.	OF	133	521	64	163	22	5	7	70	⋆.313	264	8	5	.982
Major League Totals—7 Years				902	3474	535	1151	165	44	41	354	.331	1854	75	25	.987

Selected by San Diego Padres' organization in 3rd round of free-agent draft, June 8, 1981.
†On disabled list, August 26 to September 10, 1982.

‡On San Diego disabled list, March 26 to June 21, 1983; included rehabilitation assignment to Las Vegas, May 31 to June 20, 1983.

§On disabled list, May 8 to May 29, 1988.

CHAMPIONSHIP SERIES RECORD

Tied Championship Series record for most runs, five-game Series (6), 1984.

Year Club	League	Pos.	G.	AB.	R.	H.	2B.	3B.	HR.	RBI.	B.A.	PO.	A.	E.	F.A.
1984—San Diego	Nat.	OF	5	19	6	7	3	0	0	3	.368	9	0	0	1.000

WORLD SERIES RECORD

Year Club	League	Pos.	G.	AB.	R.	H.	2B.	3B.	HR.	RBI.	B.A.	PO.	A.	E.	F.A.
1984—San Diego	Nat.	OF	5	19	1	5	0	0	0	0	.263	12	1	1	.929

ALL-STAR GAME RECORD

Year League	Pos.	AB.	R.	H.	2B.	3B.	HR.	RBI.	B.A.	PO.	A.	E.	F.A.
1984—National	OF	3	0	1	0	0	0	0	.333	0	0	0	.000
1985—National	OF	1	0	0	0	0	0	0	.000	1	0	0	1.000
1986—National	OF	3	0	0	0	0	0	0	.000	1	0	0	1.000
1987—National	PH	1	0	0	0	0	0	0	.000	0	0	0	.000
All-Star Game Totals—4 Years		8	0	1	0	0	0	0	.125	2	0	0	1.000

CHRISTOPHER KARLTON GWYNN

Name pronounced Gwin.

(Chris)

Born October 13, 1964, at Los Angeles, Calif.
Height, 6.00. Weight, 200.
Throws and bats lefthanded.
Attended San Diego State University, San Diego, Calif.
Brother of Tony Gwynn, outfielder with San Diego Padres.

Named outfielder on The Sporting News College Baseball All-America Team, 1985.
Member of 1984 U.S. Olympic baseball team.

Year Club	League	Pos.	G.	AB.	R.	H.	2B.	3B.	HR.	RBI.	B.A.	PO.	A.	E.	F.A.
1985—Vero Beach	Fla. St.	OF	52	179	19	46	8	6	0	17	.257	43	2	0	1.000
1986—San Antonio	Texas	OF	111	401	46	115	22	1	6	67	.287	186	11	2	.990
1987—Albuquerque	P. C.	OF	110	362	54	101	12	3	5	41	.279	141	5	1	.993
1987—Los Angeles	Nat.	OF	17	32	2	7	1	0	0	2	.219	12	0	0	1.000
1988—Albuquerque	P. C.	OF	112	411	57	123	22	•10	5	61	.299	134	3	4	.972
1988—Los Angeles	Nat.	OF	12	11	1	2	0	0	0	0	.182	0	0	0	.000
Major League Totals—2 Years			29	43	3	9	1	0	0	2	.209	12	0	0	1.000

Selected by California Angels' organization in 5th round of free-agent draft, June 7, 1982.
Selected by Los Angeles Dodgers' organization in 1st round (10th player selected) of free-agent draft, June 3, 1985.

JOHN GABRIEL HABYAN

Name pronounced HAY-bee-un.
Born January 29, 1964, at Bayshore, N. Y.
Height, 6.02. Weight, 198.
Throws and bats righthanded.

Pitched 6-0 no-hit victory against Columbus, May 13, 1985.
Major League saves: 1987 (1).

Year Club	League	G.	IP.	W.	L.	Pct.	H.	R.	ER.	SO.	BB.	ERA.
1982—Bluefield	Ap'lachian	12	81⅓	•9	2	.818	68	35	32	55	24	3.54
1982—Hagerstown	Carolina	1	⅔	0	0	.000	5	5	5	1	2	67.50
1983—Hagerstown	Carolina	11	48	2	3	.400	54	41	31	42	29	5.81
1983—Newark	NYP	11	71⅔	5	3	.625	68	34	27	64	29	3.39
1984—Hagerstown	Carolina	13	81⅓	9	4	.692	64	41	32	81	33	3.54
1984—Charlotte	Southern	13	77	4	7	.364	84	46	38	55	34	4.44
1985—Charlotte	Southern	28	189⅔	13	5	.722	157	73	69	123	90	3.27
1985—Baltimore	American	2	2⅔	1	0	1.000	3	1	0	2	0	0.00
1986—Rochester	Int'national	26	157⅓	12	7	.632	168	82	75	93	69	4.29
1986—Baltimore	American	6	26⅓	1	3	.250	24	17	13	14	18	4.44
1987—Rochester	Int'national	7	49	3	2	.600	47	23	21	39	20	3.86
1987—Baltimore	American	27	116⅓	6	7	.462	110	67	62	64	40	4.80
1988—Rochester	Int'national	23	147⅓	9	9	.500	161	78	73	91	46	4.46
1988—Baltimore	American	7	14⅔	1	0	1.000	22	10	7	4	4	4.30
Major League Totals—4 Years		42	160	9	10	.474	159	95	82	84	62	4.61

Selected by Baltimore Orioles' organization in 3rd round of free-agent draft, June 7, 1982.

JERRY WAYNE HAIRSTON

Born February 16, 1952, at Birmingham, Ala.
Height, 5.10. Weight, 196.
Throws right and bats left and righthanded.
Attended Lawson State Junior College, Birmingham, Ala.
Son of Sam Hairston, Sr., catcher with Chicago White Sox, 1951; scout and minor league instructor with Chicago White Sox, 1961 through 1982 and 1985; and minor league coach in Chicago White Sox' organization since 1986; brother of John Hairston, catcher-outfielder with Chicago Cubs, 1969; and Sam Hairston, Jr., second baseman in Chicago White Sox' organization, 1966.

Major League stolen bases: 1975 (1), 1976 (1), 1984 (2). Total—4.
Led Mexican League in bases on balls received with 122 in 1978, 77 in 1980 and 122 in 1981.
Led Midwest League second baseman in double plays with 77 in 1971.
Tied for Mexican League lead in double plays by outfielders with 4 in 1981.

Year Club	League	Pos.	G.	AB.	R.	H.	2B.	3B.	HR.	RBI.	B.A.	PO.	A.	E.	F.A.
1970—Sarasota W. Sox	Gulf C.	2B	56	183	37	61	8	2	1	36	.333	129	130	★19	.932
1971—Appleton	Midw.	2B	121	448	86	120	15	4	0	39	.268	★260	★333	★31	.950
1972—Knoxville	South.	2-1-O-3	132	459	82	134	19	●9	10	64	.292	591	225	27	.968
1973—Iowa	A. A.	O-2-3-1	84	274	51	95	18	6	9	65	.347	70	36	7	.938
1973—Chicago	Amer.	OF-1B	60	210	25	57	11	1	0	23	.271	194	13	5	.976
1974—Iowa	A. A.	OF	42	140	31	53	10	2	5	42	.379	48	1	2	.961
1974—Chicago†	Amer.	OF	45	109	8	25	7	0	0	8	.229	24	1	2	.926
1975—Denver	A. A.	DH	40	139	28	51	9	0	3	31	.367	0	0	0	.000
1975—Chicago	Amer.	OF	69	219	26	62	8	0	0	23	.283	111	6	6	.951
1976—Iowa	A. A.	OF-INF	94	325	53	94	24	3	5	64	.289	199	13	5	.977
1976—Chicago	Amer.	OF	44	119	20	27	2	2	0	10	.227	71	1	2	.973
1977—Chicago‡	Amer.	OF	13	26	3	8	2	0	0	4	.308	15	1	0	1.000
1977—Pittsburgh§	Nat.	OF-2B	51	52	5	10	2	0	2	6	.192	13	0	1	.929
1978—Durango	Mex.	OF	144	488	97	177	21	7	9	77	.363	297	19	11	.966
1979—Durango	Mex.	OF	128	427	87	151	22	5	12	56	.354	295	8	6	.981
1980—Campeche	Mex.	OF-1B	77	235	50	74	15	2	7	28	.315	189	11	3	.985
1981—Mex. C. Reds x	Mex.	OF	123	536	74	118	14	8	7	73	.296	★334	11	6	.983
1981—Chicago	Amer.	OF	9	25	5	7	1	0	1	6	.280	14	0	1	.933
1982—Chicago	Amer.	OF	85	90	11	21	5	0	5	18	.233	34	2	0	1.000
1983—Chicago	Amer.	OF	101	126	17	37	9	1	5	22	.294	29	1	1	.968
1984—Chicago	Amer.	OF	115	227	41	59	13	2	5	19	.260	57	2	2	.967
1985—Chicago	Amer.	OF	95	140	9	34	8	0	2	20	.243	5	0	0	1.000
1986—Chicago	Amer.	1B-OF	101	225	32	61	15	0	5	26	.271	132	9	0	1.000
1987—Chicago y	Amer.	OF-1B	66	126	14	29	8	0	5	20	.230	82	5	1	.989
1988—Chicago z	Amer.	PH	2	2	0	0	0	0	0	0	.000	0	0	0	.000
American League Totals—13 Years			805	1644	211	427	89	6	28	199	.260	768	41	20	.976
National League Totals—1 Year			51	52	5	10	2	0	2	6	.192	13	0	1	.929
Major League Totals—13 Years			856	1696	216	437	91	6	30	205	.258	781	41	21	.975

Selected by Chicago White Sox' organization in 3rd round of free-agent draft, June 4, 1970.
†On disabled list, June 27 to July 12, 1974.
‡Sold to Pittsburgh Pirates, June 13, 1977.
§Sold to Durango of Mexican League, March 2, 1978.
xSold to Chicago White Sox, September 10, 1981.
yReleased, March 25, 1988; signed by Chicago White Sox, August 31, 1988.
zReleased, October 19, 1988.

CHAMPIONSHIP SERIES RECORD

Year Club	League	Pos.	G.	AB.	R.	H.	2B.	3B.	HR.	RBI.	B.A.	PO.	A.	E.	F.A.
1983—Chicago	Amer.	PH-OF	2	3	0	0	0	0	0	0	.000	0	0	1	.000

ALBERT HALL

Born March 7, 1959, at Birmingham, Ala.
Height, 5.11. Weight, 158.
Throws right and bats left and righthanded.

Major League stolen bases: 1983 (1), 1984 (6), 1985 (1), 1986 (8), 1987 (33), 1988 (15). Total—64.
Hit for the cycle, September 23, 1987.
Led International League in stolen bases with 62 in 1982 and 72 in 1986.
Led International League in caught stealing with 16 in 1986.
Led Carolina League in being hit by pitch with 9, stolen bases with 100 and caught stealing with 27 in 1980.
Led Western Carolinas League in stolen bases with 66 in 1979.
Led Gulf Coast League shortstops in double plays with 23 in 1978.
Tied for Southern League lead in caught stealing with 17 in 1981.

Year Club	League	Pos.	G.	AB.	R.	H.	2B.	3B.	HR.	RBI.	B.A.	PO.	A.	E.	F.A.
1977—Kingsport	Appal.	SS	35	68	11	11	0	0	0	3	.162	10	28	10	.792
1978—Bradenton Brav.	Gulf C.	SS	34	123	15	36	4	2	0	14	.293	55	100	●15	.912
1979—Greenwood	W. Car.	SS	105	368	84	106	10	3	0	38	.288	120	288	★72	.850
1980—Durham	Carol.	OF-SS	125	491	95	139	16	7	4	41	.283	166	32	16	.925
1981—Savannah	South.	OF	133	487	83	150	28	10	5	27	.308	263	16	10	.965
1981—Atlanta	Nat.	OF	6	2	1	0	0	0	0	0	.000	0	0	0	.000
1982—Richmond	Int.	OF	129	528	97	139	18	★15	3	42	.263	297	6	7	.977
1982—Atlanta	Nat.	PR	5	0	1	0	0	0	0	0	.000	0	0	0	.000
1983—Richmond	Int.	★OF-SS	130	521	120	153	28	★11	1	42	.294	280	10	★12	.960
1983—Atlanta	Nat.	OF	10	8	2	0	0	0	0	0	.000	3	0	1	.750
1984—Atlanta	Nat.	OF	87	142	25	37	6	1	1	9	.261	64	4	5	.932
1985—Atlanta	Nat.	OF	54	47	5	7	0	1	0	3	.149	7	2	1	.900
1985—Richmond†	Int.	OF	38	98	12	22	0	3	0	5	.224	77	2	3	.963
1986—Richmond	Int.	OF	125	441	73	119	18	3	3	41	.270	264	8	7	.975
1986—Atlanta	Nat.	OF	16	50	6	12	2	0	0	1	.240	26	1	3	.900
1987—Atlanta‡	Nat.	OF	92	292	54	83	20	4	3	24	.284	148	5	3	.981
1988—Atlanta§	Nat.	OF	85	231	27	57	7	1	1	15	.247	137	7	4	.973
1988—Bradenton Brav.	Gulf C.	OF	2	8	1	2	0	0	0	1	.250	7	0	0	1.000
Major League Totals—8 Years			355	772	121	196	35	7	5	52	.254	385	19	17	.960

Selected by Atlanta Braves' organization in 6th round of free-agent draft, June 7, 1977.
†On disabled list, July 12 to July 26, 1985.

‡On disabled list, June 19 to July 5, 1987.

§On disabled list, July 2 to July 26 and July 28 to September 1, 1988; included rehabilitation disability assignment to Bradenton, July 17 to July 26, 1988.

ANDREW CLARK HALL
(Drew)

Born March 27, 1963, at Louisville, Ky.
Height, 6.04. Weight, 220.
Throws and bats lefthanded.
Attended Morehead State University, Morehead, Ky.

Major League saves: 1986 (1), 1988 (1). Total—2.
Tied for Eastern League lead in shutouts with 3 in 1986.
Named lefthanded pitcher on THE SPORTING NEWS College Baseball All-America Team, 1984.

Year Club	League	G.	IP.	W.	L.	Pct.	H.	R.	ER.	SO.	BB.	ERA.
1984—Lodi	California	8	48	3	3	.500	43	31	26	43	44	4.88
1985—Winston-Salem	Carolina	24	140⅔	10	7	.588	131	92	73	135	83	4.67
1986—Pittsfield	Eastern	24	158⅓	8	11	.421	130	77	63	115	84	3.58
1986—Chicago	National	5	23⅔	1	2	.333	24	12	12	21	10	4.56
1987—Iowa	Am. Assoc.	35	66⅓	6	3	.667	74	42	33	66	45	4.48
1987—Chicago	National	21	32⅔	1	1	.500	40	31	25	20	14	6.89
1988—Chicago	National	19	22⅓	1	1	.500	26	20	19	22	9	7.66
1988—Iowa†	Am. Assoc.	49	65⅓	4	3	.571	41	20	17	75	26	2.34
Major League Totals—3 Years		45	78⅔	3	4	.429	90	63	56	63	33	6.41

Selected by Chicago Cubs' organization in 1st round (third player selected) of free-agent draft, June 4, 1984.

†Traded with Outfielder Rafael Palmeiro and Pitcher Jamie Moyer to Texas Rangers for Pitchers Mitch Williams, Paul Kilgus and Steve Wilson, Infielder Curtis Wilkerson and Luis Benitez and Outfielder Pablo Delgado, December 5, 1988.

MELVIN HALL JR.
(Mel)

Born September 16, 1960, at Lyons, N. Y.
Height, 6.01. Weight, 205.
Throws and bats lefthanded.
Son of Melvin Hall Sr., minor league player in Cincinnati Reds' organization, 1949.

Major League stolen bases: 1983 (6), 1984 (3), 1986 (6), 1987 (5), 1988 (7). Total—27.
Led American Association in game-winning RBIs with 17 in 1982.
Led Texas League in total bases with 286 in 1981.
Led American Association outfielders in total chances with 339 in 1982.
Led Texas League outfielders in total chances with 324 and double plays with 5 in 1981.

Year Club	League	Pos.	G.	AB.	R.	H.	2B.	3B.	HR.	RBI.	B.A.	PO.	A.	E.	F.A.
1978—Bradenton Cubs	Gulf C.	OF	43	145	30	42	7	3	2	17	.290	*97	5	4	.962
1979—Geneva	NYP	OF	66	251	49	79	18	5	3	53	.315	113	5	7	.944
1980—Midland	Texas	OF	37	128	17	34	7	3	1	14	.266	58	3	3	.953
1980—Quad Cities	Midw.	OF	97	347	54	102	14	4	6	42	.294	171	9	5	.973
1981—Midland	Texas	OF	131	533	•98	*170	34	5	24	95	.319	*302	14	8	.975
1981—Chicago	Nat.	OF	10	11	1	1	0	0	1	2	.091	0	0	0	.000
1982—Iowa	A. A.	OF	133	502	*116	165	*34	6	32	125	.329	*317	13	•9	.973
1982—Chicago	Nat.	OF	24	80	6	21	3	2	0	4	.263	42	4	3	.939
1983—Chicago†	Nat.	OF	112	410	60	116	23	5	17	56	.283	239	8	3	.988
1983—Midland	Texas	OF	6	19	9	9	2	1	3	7	.474	8	0	0	1.000
1984—Chicago‡	Nat.	OF	48	150	25	42	11	3	4	22	.280	69	5	3	.961
1984—Cleveland	Amer.	OF	83	257	43	66	13	1	7	30	.257	143	3	1	.993
1985—Cleveland§	Amer.	OF	23	66	7	21	6	0	0	12	.318	18	0	0	1.000
1986—Cleveland	Amer.	OF	140	442	68	131	29	2	18	77	.296	233	7	7	.972
1987—Cleveland	Amer.	OF	142	485	57	136	21	1	18	76	.280	264	3	3	.989
1988—Cleveland	Amer.	OF	150	515	69	144	32	4	6	71	.280	288	3	10	.967
National League Totals—4 Years			194	651	92	180	37	10	22	84	.276	350	17	9	.976
American League Totals—5 Years			538	1765	244	498	101	8	49	266	.282	946	16	21	.979
Major League Totals—8 Years			732	2416	336	678	138	18	71	350	.281	1296	33	30	.978

Selected by Chicago Cubs' organization in 2nd round of free-agent draft, June 6, 1978.

†On disabled list, April 15 to May 31, 1983; included rehabilitation disability assignment to Midland, May 25 to May 31, 1983.

‡Traded with Outfielder Joe Carter and Pitchers Don Schulze and Darryl Banks to Cleveland Indians for Catcher Ron Hassey and Pitchers Rick Sutcliffe and George Frazier, June 13, 1984.

§On disabled list, May 10, 1985 through remainder of season.

MICHAEL DARREN HALL

(Known by middle name.)

Born July 14, 1964, at Marysville, O.
Height, 6.03. Weight, 205.
Throws and bats righthanded.
Attended Dallas Baptist University, Dallas, Tex.

Tied for Pioneer League lead in wild pitches with 12 and games started by pitchers with 16 in 1986.

Year Club	League	G.	IP.	W.	L.	Pct.	H.	R.	ER.	SO.	BB.	ERA.
1986—Medicine Hat	Pioneer	17	89⅓	5	7	.417	91	64	38	60	47	3.83

Year	Club	League	G.	IP.	W.	L.	Pct.	H.	R.	ER.	SO.	BB.	ERA.
1987	Myrtle Beach	S. Atlantic	41	66⅔	5	5	.500	57	31	26	68	28	3.51
1988	Dunedin	Florida St.	4	9⅓	1	1	.500	6	2	2	15	5	1.93
1988	Knoxville	Southern	37	40⅓	3	2	.600	28	11	10	33	17	2.23

Selected by Toronto Blue Jays' organization in 28th round of free-agent draft, June 2, 1986.

DARRYL QUINN HAMILTON

Born December 3, 1964, at Baton Rouge, La.
Height, 6.01. Weight, 180.
Throws right and bats lefthanded.
Attended Nicholls State University, Thibodaux, La.

Major League stolen bases: 1988 (7).
Led California League in intentional bases on balls received with 9 in 1987.

Year	Club	League	Pos.	G.	AB.	R.	H.	2B.	3B.	HR.	RBI.	B.A.	PO.	A.	E.	F.A.
1986	Helena	Pion.	OF	65	248	*72	●97	12	●6	0	35	*.391	132	9	0	*1.000
1987	Stockton	Calif.	OF	125	494	102	162	17	6	8	61	.328	221	8	1	*.996
1988	Denver	A. A.	OF	72	277	55	90	11	4	0	32	.325	160	2	2	.988
1988	Milwaukee	Amer.	OF	44	103	14	19	4	0	1	11	.184	75	1	0	1.000
Major League Totals—1 Year				44	103	14	19	4	0	1	11	.184	75	1	0	1.000

Selected by Milwaukee Brewers' organization in 11th round of free-agent draft, June 2, 1986.

JEFFREY ROBERT HAMILTON
(Jeff)

Born March 19, 1964, at Flint, Mich.
Height, 6.03. Weight, 214.
Throws and bats righthanded.

Led Florida State League third basemen in total chances with 395 and double plays with 25 in 1984.
Led Pioneer League third basemen in double plays with 16 in 1983.

Year	Club	League	Pos.	G.	AB.	R.	H.	2B.	3B.	HR.	RBI.	B.A.	PO.	A.	E.	F.A.
1983	Lodi	Calif.	3B-OF	44	141	15	28	4	0	0	10	.199	26	62	17	.838
1983	Lethbridge	Pion.	3B	68	*281	48	●94	*23	2	3	61	.335	38	118	17	.902
1984	Vero Beach	Fla. St.	3B	127	466	51	121	31	4	4	59	.260	*109	*259	*27	*.932
1985	San Antonio	Texas	3B-OF	101	377	48	125	14	3	13	59	.332	69	186	16	.941
1986	Albuquerque	P. C.	3B	71	288	40	90	21	3	10	42	.313	39	151	19	.909
1986	Los Angeles	Nat.	3B-SS	71	147	22	33	5	0	5	19	.224	40	87	4	.969
1987	Albuquerque	P. C.	3B	65	236	52	85	17	1	12	48	.360	43	102	11	.929
1987	Los Angeles†	Nat.	3B-SS	35	83	5	18	3	0	0	1	.217	27	60	6	.935
1988	Los Angeles‡	Nat.	3B-SS-1B	111	309	34	73	14	2	6	33	.236	67	160	14	.942
Major League Totals—3 Years				217	539	61	124	22	2	11	53	.230	134	307	24	.948

Selected by Los Angeles Dodgers' organization in 29th round of free-agent draft, June 7, 1982.
†On disabled list, August 14, 1987 through remainder of season.
‡On disabled list, July 27 to September 1, 1988.

CHAMPIONSHIP SERIES RECORD

Year	Club	League	Pos.	G.	AB.	R.	H.	2B.	3B.	HR.	RBI.	B.A.	PO.	A.	E.	F.A.
1988	Los Angeles	Nat.	3B	7	23	2	5	0	0	0	1	.217	9	10	2	.905

WORLD SERIES RECORD

Year	Club	League	Pos.	G.	AB.	R.	H.	2B.	3B.	HR.	RBI.	B.A.	PO.	A.	E.	F.A.
1988	Los Angeles	Nat.	3B	5	19	1	2	0	0	0	0	.105	2	5	1	.875

CHARLTON ATLEE HAMMAKER

(Known by middle name.)

Bor, January 24, 1958, at Carmel, Calif.
Height, 6.02. Weight, 200.
Throws left and bats right and lefthanded.
Attended East Tennessee State University, Johnson City, Tenn.

Major League saves: 1988 (5).

Year	Club	League	G.	IP.	W.	L.	Pct.	H.	R.	ER.	SO.	BB.	ERA.
1979	Sarasota Royals-Gold	Gulf Coast	1	5	1	0	1.000	3	1	1	6	1	1.80
1979	Fort Myers†	Florida St.	1	5	0	1	.000	9	5	1	5	0	1.80
1980	Jacksonville‡	Southern	20	137	8	9	.471	131	64	51	88	37	3.35
1981	Omaha	Am. Assoc.	21	146	11	5	.688	147	70	59	63	40	3.64
1981	Kansas City§	American	10	39	1	3	.250	44	24	24	11	12	5.54
1982	Phoenix	P. Coast	1	5⅔	0	1	.000	13	5	4	6	2	6.35
1982	San Francisco	National	29	175	12	8	.600	189	86	80	102	28	4.11
1983	San Francisco x	National	23	172⅓	10	9	.526	147	57	43	127	32	*2.25
1984	Phoenix y	P. Coast	2	8	0	1	.000	14	7	4	5	2	4.50
1984	San Francisco	National	6	33	2	0	1.000	32	10	8	24	9	2.18
1985	San Francisco	National	29	170⅔	5	12	.294	161	81	71	100	47	3.74
1986	San Francisco za	National	(Did not play)										
1987	Phoenix b	P. Coast	3	17⅓	1	2	.333	19	9	8	8	6	4.15
1987	Shreveport	Texas	1	7	0	1	.000	6	2	1	3	0	1.29
1987	San Francisco c	National	31	168⅓	10	10	.500	159	73	67	107	57	3.58

Year	Club	League	G.	IP.	W.	L.	Pct.	H.	R.	ER.	SO.	BB.	ERA.
1988	—San Francisco	National	43	144⅔	9	9	.500	136	68	60	65	41	3.73
American League Totals—1 Year			10	39	1	3	.250	44	24	24	11	12	5.54
National League Totals—6 Years			161	864	48	48	.500	824	375	329	525	214	3.43
Major League Totals—7 Years			171	903	49	51	.490	868	399	353	536	226	3.52

Selected by Kansas City Royals' organization in 1st round (21st player selected) of free-agent draft, June 5, 1979.

†On disabled list, July 6 to October 26, 1979.

‡On disabled list, August 3 to August 22, 1980.

§Traded with Pitchers Craig Chamberlain and Renie Martin and a player to be named later to San Francisco Giants for Pitchers Vida Blue and Bob Tufts, March 30, 1982; San Francisco organization acquired Second Baseman Brad Wellman to complete deal, April 19, 1982.

xOn disabled list, July 26 to August 21, 1983.

yOn San Francisco disabled list, April 2 to June 26 and August 4 to September 1, 1984; included rehabilitation disability assignment to Phoenix, June 16 to June 25, 1984.

zOn disabled list, April 7, 1986 through entire season.

aReleased, December 9, 1986; re-signed by Giants, February 4, 1987.

bOn San Francisco disabled list, April 2 to April 30, 1987; included rehabilitation disability assignment to Phoenix, April 10 to April 30, 1987.

cGranted free agency, November 9, 1987; re-signed by Giants, January 8, 1988.

CHAMPIONSHIP SERIES RECORD

Tied National League Championship Series record for most earned runs allowed, seven-game Series (7), 1987.

Year	Club	League	G.	IP.	W.	L.	Pct.	H.	R.	ER.	SO.	BB.	ERA.
1987	—San Francisco	National	2	8	0	1	.000	12	7	7	7	0	7.88

ALL-STAR GAME RECORD

Established All-Star Game and inning records for most runs and earned runs allowed (7), July 6, 1983 (third inning).

Tied All-Star Game record for most home runs allowed, inning (2), July 6, 1983 (third inning).

Year	League	IP.	W.	L.	Pct.	H.	R.	ER.	SO.	BB.	ERA.
1983	—National	⅔	0	0	.000	6	7	7	0	1	94.50

CHRISTOPHER ANDREW HAMMOND
(Chris)

Born January 21, 1966, at Atlanta, Ga.
Height, 6.01. Weight, 190.
Throws and bats lefthanded.
Attended Gulf Coast Community College, Panama City, Fla., and University of Alabama, Birmingham, Ala.

Year	Club	League	G.	IP.	W.	L.	Pct.	H.	R.	ER.	SO.	BB.	ERA.
1986	—Sarasota Reds	Gulf Coast	7	41⅔	3	2	.600	27	21	13	53	17	2.81
1986	—Tampa	Florida St.	5	21⅔	0	2	.000	25	8	8	5	13	3.32
1987	—Tampa	Florida St.	25	170	11	11	.500	174	81	67	126	60	3.55
1988	—Chattanooga	Southern	26	182⅔	★16	5	.762	127	48	35	127	77	★1.72

Selected by Cincinnati Reds' organization in 6th round of free-agent draft, January 14, 1986.

DAVID ANDREW HANSEN
(Dave)

Born November 24, 1968, at Long Beach, Calif.
Height, 6.00. Weight, 180.
Throws right and bats lefthanded.

Led Florida State League in total bases with 210, game-winning RBIs with 19 and tied for lead in sacrifice flies with 9 in 1988.

Led Florida State League third basemen in total chances with 383 and double plays with 24 in 1988.

Year	Club	League	Pos.	G.	AB.	R.	H.	2B.	3B.	HR.	RBI.	B.A.	PO.	A.	E.	F.A.
1986	—Great Falls	Pion.	OF-3B-C	61	204	39	61	7	3	1	36	.299	54	10	7	.901
1987	—Bakersfield	Calif.	★3B-OF	132	432	68	113	22	1	3	38	.262	79	198	★45	.860
1988	—Vero Beach	Fla. St.	3B	135	512	68	★149	•28	6	7	★81	.291	★102	★263	18	★.953

Selected by Los Angeles Dodgers' organization in 2nd round of free-agent draft, June 2, 1986.

ERIK B. HANSON

Born May 18, 1965, at Kinnelon, N. J.
Height, 6.06. Weight, 205.
Throws and bats righthanded.
Attended Wake Forest University, Winston-Salem, N. C.

Pitched 5-0 no-hit victory against Las Vegas, August 21, 1988 (second game).

Year	Club	League	G.	IP.	W.	L.	Pct.	H.	R.	ER.	SO.	BB.	ERA.
1986	—Chattanooga†	Southern	3	9⅓	0	0	.000	10	4	4	11	4	3.86
1987	—Chattanooga	Southern	21	131⅓	8	10	.444	102	56	38	131	43	2.60
1987	—Calgary	P. Coast	8	47⅓	1	3	.250	38	23	19	43	21	3.61
1988	—Calgary	P. Coast	27	161⅔	12	7	.632	167	92	76	★154	57	4.23
1988	—Seattle	American	6	41⅔	2	3	.400	35	17	15	36	12	3.24
Major League Totals—1 Year			6	41⅔	2	3	.400	35	17	15	36	12	3.24

Selected by Montreal Expos' organization in 7th round of free-agent draft, June 6, 1983.
Selected by Seattle Mariners' organization in 2nd round of free-agent draft, June 2, 1986.
†On inactive list, June 12 to August 18, 1986.

MICHAEL ANTHONY HARKEY
(Mike)

Born October 25, 1966, at San Diego, Calif.
Height, 6.05. Weight, 220.
Throws and bats righthanded.
Attended California State University, Fullerton, Calif.

Year Club	League	G.	IP.	W.	L.	Pct.	H.	R.	ER.	SO.	BB.	ERA.
1987—Peoria	Midwest	12	76	2	3	.400	81	45	30	48	28	3.55
1987—Pittsfield	Eastern	1	2	0	0	.000	1	0	0	2	0	0.00
1988—Pittsfield	Eastern	13	85⅔	9	2	*.818	66	29	13	73	35	1.37
1988—Iowa	Am. Assoc.	12	78⅔	7	2	.778	55	36	31	62	33	3.55
1988—Chicago	National	5	34⅔	0	3	.000	33	14	10	18	15	2.60
Major League Totals—1 Year		5	34⅔	0	3	.000	33	14	10	18	15	2.60

Selected by San Diego Padres' organization in 18th round of free-agent draft, June 4, 1984.
Selected by Chicago Cubs' organization in 1st round (fourth player selected) of free-agent draft, June 2, 1987.

PETER THOMAS HARNISCH
(Pete)

Born September 23, 1966, at Commack, N. Y.
Height, 6.00. Weight, 195.
Throws and bats righthanded.
Attended Fordham University, Bronx, N. Y.

Year Club	League	G.	IP.	W.	L.	Pct.	H.	R.	ER.	SO.	BB.	ERA.
1987—Bluefield	Ap'lachian	9	52⅔	3	1	.750	38	19	15	64	26	2.56
1987—Hagerstown	Carolina	4	20	1	2	.333	17	7	5	18	14	2.25
1988—Charlotte	Southern	20	132⅓	7	6	.538	113	55	38	141	52	2.58
1988—Rochester	Int'national	7	58⅓	4	1	.800	44	16	14	43	14	2.16
1988—Baltimore	American	2	13	0	2	.000	13	8	8	10	9	5.54
Major League Totals—1 Year		2	13	0	2	.000	13	8	8	10	9	5.54

Selected by Baltimore Orioles' organization in 1st round (27th player selected) of free-agent draft, June 2, 1987.

BRIAN DAVID HARPER

Born October 16, 1959, at Los Angeles, Calif.
Height, 6.02. Weight, 195.
Throws and bats righthanded.

Major League stolen bases: 1981 (1).
Led Pacific Coast League in total bases with 339 in 1981.
Led Pacific Coast League in sacrifice flies with 12 in 1987.
Led Pacific Coast League catchers in errors with 19 in 1981.
Led Texas League in passed balls with 19 in 1979.
Tied for American Association lead in errors by catchers with 13 in 1986.

Year Club	League	Pos.	G.	AB.	R.	H.	2B.	3B.	HR.	RBI.	B.A.	PO.	A.	E.	F.A.
1977—Idaho Falls	Pion.	C	52	186	28	60	9	3	1	33	.323	352	36	13	.968
1978—Quad Cities	Midw.	C	129	508	80	149	31	2	24	*101	.293	430	46	16	.967
1979—El Paso	Texas	C	132	531	85	167	*37	3	14	90	.315	443	66	*29	.946
1979—California	Amer.	DH	1	2	0	0	0	0	0	0	.000	0	0	0	.000
1980—El Paso†	Texas	C	105	400	61	114	23	3	12	66	.285	214	30	7	.972
1981—Salt Lake City	P. C.	C-OF-1B	134	549	99	*192	45	9	28	122	.350	421	30	24	.949
1981—California‡	Amer.	OF	4	11	1	3	0	0	0	1	.273	5	0	1	.833
1982—Pittsburgh	Nat.	OF	20	29	4	8	1	0	2	4	.276	10	0	0	1.000
1982—Portland	P. C.	OF-3B-C	101	395	71	112	29	8	17	73	.284	164	36	8	.962
1983—Pittsburgh	Nat.	OF-1B	61	131	16	29	4	1	7	20	.221	40	0	0	1.000
1984—Pittsburgh§ x	Nat.	OF-C	46	112	4	29	4	0	2	11	.259	57	3	1	.984
1985—St. Louis y	Nat.	O-3-C-1	43	52	5	13	4	0	0	8	.250	15	5	0	1.000
1986—Nashville	A. A.	C-OF-1B	95	317	41	83	11	1	11	45	.262	377	55	15	.966
1986—Detroit z	Amer.	OF-1B-C	19	36	2	5	1	0	0	3	.139	25	2	1	.964
1987—San Jose a	Calif.	3B-OF-C	8	29	5	9	0	0	3	8	.310	21	12	5	.868
1987—Tacoma	P. C.	OF-C-P	94	323	41	100	17	0	9	62	.310	163	10	5	.972
1987—Oakland b	Amer.	OF	11	17	1	4	1	0	0	3	.235	0	0	0	.000
1988—Portland	P. C.	C-3-O-P	46	170	34	60	10	1	13	42	.353	181	25	5	.976
1988—Minnesota	Amer.	C-3B	60	166	15	49	11	1	3	20	.295	208	15	2	.991
American League Totals—5 Years			95	232	19	61	13	1	3	27	.263	238	17	4	.985
National League Totals—4 Years			170	324	29	79	13	1	11	43	.244	122	8	1	.992
Major League Totals—9 Years			265	556	48	140	26	2	14	70	.252	360	25	5	.987

Selected by California Angels' organization in 4th round of free-agent draft, June 7, 1977.
†On disabled list, July 1 to July 17, 1980.
‡Traded to Pittsburgh Pirates for Shortstop Tim Foli, December 11, 1981.
§On disabled list, April 12 to May 10 and May 16 to June 4, 1984.
xTraded with Pitcher John Tudor to St. Louis Cardinals for Outfielder-First Baseman George Hendrick and Catcher Steve Barnard, December 12, 1984.

yReleased, April 1, 1986; signed by Detroit Tigers, April 25, 1986.
zReleased, March 23, 1987; signed by San Jose (Independent), May 3, 1987.
aSold to Oakland Athletics' organization, May 12, 1987.
bReleased, October 12, 1987; signed by Portland (Minnesota Twins' organization), January 4, 1988.

CHAMPIONSHIP SERIES RECORD

Year	Club	League	Pos.	G.	AB.	R.	H.	2B.	3B.	HR.	RBI.	B.A.	PO.	A.	E.	F.A.
1985	St. Louis	Nat.	PH	1	1	0	0	0	0	0	0	.000	0	0	0	.000

WORLD SERIES RECORD

Year	Club	League	Pos.	G.	AB.	R.	H.	2B.	3B.	HR.	RBI.	B.A.	PO.	A.	E.	F.A.
1985	St. Louis	Nat.	PH	4	4	0	1	0	0	0	1	.250	0	0	0	.000

PITCHING RECORD

Year	Club	League	G.	IP.	W.	L.	Pct.	H.	R.	ER.	SO.	BB.	ERA.
1987	Tacoma	P. Coast	1	3	0	0	.000	3	1	1	1	0	3.00
1988	Portland	P. Coast	1	1	0	0	.000	2	1	1	0	2	9.00

GREG ALLEN HARRIS

Born November 2, 1955, at Lynwood, Calif.
Height, 6.00. Weight, 165.
Throws right and bats left and righthanded.
Attended Long Beach City College, Long Beach, Calif.

Major League saves: 1981 (1), 1982 (1), 1984 (3), 1985 (11), 1986 (20), 1988 (1). Total—37.

Year	Club	League	G.	IP.	W.	L.	Pct.	H.	R.	ER.	SO.	BB.	ERA.
1977	Jackson	Texas	30	83	3	6	.333	96	63	50	56	36	5.42
1978	Lynchburg	Carolina	21	154	8	9	.471	114	52	37	102	74	2.16
1978	Jackson	Texas	6	33	2	3	.400	24	13	11	18	10	3.00
1979	Jackson	Texas	25	163	9	11	.450	125	58	41	89	81	*2.26
1980	Tidewater	Int'national	39	110	2	9	.182	99	45	33	92	40	2.70
1981	Tidewater	Int'national	7	48	4	0	1.000	37	14	11	26	16	2.06
1981	New York†	National	16	69	3	5	.375	65	36	34	54	28	4.43
1982	Indianapolis	Am. Assoc.	8	48	4	1	.800	27	18	16	44	24	3.00
1982	Cincinnati	National	34	91⅓	2	6	.250	96	56	49	67	37	4.83
1983	Indianapolis	Am. Assoc.	28	152⅓	9	12	.429	155	83	70	*146	66	4.14
1983	Cincinnati‡	National	1	1	0	0	.000	2	3	3	1	3	27.00
1984	Montreal§-San Diego	National	34	54⅓	2	2	.500	38	18	15	45	25	2.48
1984	Indianapolis x	Am. Assoc.	14	44⅔	4	4	.500	44	27	22	45	29	4.43
1985	Texas	American	58	113	5	4	.556	74	35	31	111	43	2.47
1986	Texas	American	73	111⅓	10	8	.556	103	40	35	95	42	2.83
1987	Texas yz	American	42	140⅔	5	10	.333	157	92	76	106	56	4.86
1988	Maine	Int'national	3	4⅔	0	1	.000	5	3	1	5	1	1.93
1988	Philadelphia a	National	66	107	4	6	.400	80	34	28	71	52	2.36
National League Totals—5 Years			151	322⅔	11	19	.367	281	147	129	238	145	3.60
American League Totals—3 Years			173	365	20	22	.476	334	167	142	312	141	3.50
Major League Totals—8 Years			324	687⅔	31	41	.431	615	314	271	550	286	3.55

Selected by California Angels' organization in 10th round of free-agent draft, June 5, 1974.
Selected by New York Mets' organization in secondary phase of free-agent draft, January 9, 1975.
Selected by New York Mets' organization in 7th round of free-agent draft, January 7, 1976.
Signed as free agent by New York Mets' organization, September 17, 1976.
†Traded with Catcher Alex Trevino and Pitcher Jim Kern to Cincinnati Reds for Outfielder George Foster, February 10, 1982.
‡Claimed on waivers by Montreal Expos, September 27, 1983.
§Traded to San Diego Padres for Infielder Al Newman, July 20, 1984.
xSold to Texas Rangers, February 13, 1985.
yReleased, December 21, 1987; signed by Cleveland Indians, January 19, 1988.
zReleased, March 24, 1988; signed by Maine (Philadelphia Phillies' organization), April 1, 1988.
aGranted free agency, November 4, 1988; re-signed by Phillies, December 7, 1988.

CHAMPIONSHIP SERIES RECORD

Tied Championship Series records for most runs, most earned runs and most hits allowed, inning (6), October 2, 1984 (fifth inning); most earned runs allowed, game (7), October 2, 1984.

Tied National League Championship Series record for most runs allowed, five-game Series (8), 1984.

Year	Club	League	G.	IP.	W.	L.	Pct.	H.	R.	ER.	SO.	BB.	ERA.
1984	San Diego	National	1	2	0	0	.000	9	8	7	2	3	31.50

WORLD SERIES RECORD

Year	Club	League	G.	IP.	W.	L.	Pct.	H.	R.	ER.	SO.	BB.	ERA.
1984	San Diego	National	1	5⅓	0	0	.000	3	0	0	5	3	0.00

GREGORY WADE HARRIS
(Greg)

Born December 1, 1963, at Greensboro, N. C.
Height, 6.02. Weight, 190.
Throws and bats righthanded.
Attended Elon College, Elon College, N. C.

Pitched 7-0 no-hit victory against Midland, August 26, 1987.

Led Texas League in complete games with 7, home runs allowed with 32, balks with 6 and tied for lead in shutouts with 2 in 1987.

Year	Club	League	G.	IP.	W.	L.	Pct.	H.	R.	ER.	SO.	BB.	ERA.
1985	Spokane	Northwest	13	87⅓	5	4	.556	80	36	33	90	36	3.40
1986	Charleston	S. Atlantic	27	*191⅓	13	7	.650	176	69	56	176	54	2.63
1987	Wichita	Texas	27	174⅓	12	11	.522	205	103	83	170	49	4.28
1988	Las Vegas	P. Coast	26	159⅔	9	5	.643	160	84	73	147	65	4.11
1988	San Diego	National	3	18	2	0	1.000	13	3	3	15	3	1.50
	Major League Totals—1 Year		3	18	2	0	1.000	13	3	3	15	3	1.50

Selected by San Diego Padres' organization in 10th round of free-agent draft, June 3, 1985.

LEONARD ANTHONY HARRIS
(Lenny)

Born October 28, 1964, at Miami, Fla.
Height, 5.10. Weight, 195.
Throws right and bats lefthanded.
Attended Miami-Dade Community College (North), Miami, Fla.

Major League stolen bases: 1988 (4).
Led American Association in stolen bases with 45 and caught stealing with 22 in 1988.
Led Eastern League in game-winning RBIs with 13 in 1986.
Led American Association second basemen in errors with 23 in 1988.
Led Eastern League third basemen in putouts with 116 and total chances with 360 in 1986.
Led Florida State League third basemen in double plays with 34 in 1985.

Year	Club	League	Pos.	G.	AB.	R.	H.	2B.	3B.	HR.	RBI.	B.A.	PO.	A.	E.	F.A.
1983	Billings	Pion.	3B	56	224	37	63	8	1	1	26	.281	34	95	22	.854
1984	Cedar Rapids	Midw.	3B	132	468	52	115	15	3	6	53	.246	111	204	*34	.903
1985	Tampa	Fla. St.	3B	132	499	66	129	11	8	3	51	.259	89	*277	*35	.913
1986	Vermont	East.	*3B-SS	119	450	68	114	17	2	10	52	.253	119	220	*28	.924
1987	Nashville	A. A.	SS-3B	120	403	45	100	12	3	2	31	.248	124	210	34	.908
1988	Nashville†	A. A.	2B-SS-3B	107	422	46	117	20	2	0	35	.277	203	247	25	.947
1988	Glens Falls	East.	2B	17	65	9	22	5	1	1	7	.338	40	49	5	.947
1988	Cincinnati	Nat.	3B-2B	16	43	7	16	1	0	0	8	.372	14	33	1	.979
	Major League Totals—1 Year			16	43	7	16	1	0	0	8	.372	14	33	1	.979

Selected by Cincinnati Reds' organization in 5th round of free-agent draft, June 6, 1983.
†Loaned to Glens Falls (Detroit Tigers' organization), May 6, 1988; returned, June 26, 1988.

TYRONE EUGENE HARRIS
(Gene)

Born December 5, 1964, at Sebring, Fla.
Height, 5.11. Weight, 190.
Throws and bats righthanded.
Attended Tulane University, New Orleans, La.

Led Southern League in complete games with 7 in 1988.

Year	Club	League	G.	IP.	W.	L.	Pct.	H.	R.	ER.	SO.	BB.	ERA.
1986	Jamestown	NYP	4	20⅓	0	2	.000	15	8	5	16	11	2.21
1986	Burlington	Midwest	7	53⅓	4	2	.667	37	12	8	32	15	1.35
1986	West Palm Beach	Florida St.	2	11	0	0	.000	14	7	5	5	7	4.09
1987	West Palm Beach	Florida St.	26	179	9	7	.563	178	101	87	121	77	4.37
1988	Jacksonville	Southern	18	126⅔	9	5	.643	95	43	37	103	45	2.63

Selected by Montreal Expos' organization in 5th round of free-agent draft, June 2, 1986.

MICHAEL EDWARD HARTLEY
(Mike)

Born August 31, 1961, at Hawthorne, Calif.
Height, 6.01. Weight, 192.
Throws and bats righthanded.
Attended Grossmont College, El Cajon, Calif.

Year	Club	League	G.	IP.	W.	L.	Pct.	H.	R.	ER.	SO.	BB.	ERA.
1982	Johnson City	Ap'lachian	8	29	3	1	.750	32	12	9	13	8	2.79
1983	St. Petersburg	Florida St.	9	29⅔	1	3	.250	25	14	11	18	24	3.34
1983	Macon	S. Atlantic	7	29	2	3	.400	36	36	33	12	30	10.24
1983	Erie	NYP	7	32	1	3	.250	36	27	24	25	31	6.75
1984	St. Petersburg	Florida St.	31	139⅓	8	14	.364	142	81	65	88	84	4.20
1985	Springfield	Midwest	33	114⅓	2	7	.222	119	77	65	100	62	5.12
1986	Springfield	Midwest	8	15	0	0	.000	22	17	16	10	14	9.60
1986	Savannah†	S. Atlantic	39	56	5	7	.417	38	31	18	55	37	2.89
1987	Bakersfield	California	33	56	5	4	.556	44	19	16	72	24	2.57
1987	San Antonio	Texas	25	41	3	4	.429	21	8	6	37	18	1.32
1987	Albuquerque	P. Coast	2	2⅔	0	1	.000	5	3	2	3	3	6.75
1988	San Antonio	Texas	30	45	5	1	.833	25	5	4	57	18	0.80
1988	Albuquerque	P. Coast	18	20⅔	2	2	.500	22	11	10	16	12	4.35

Signed as free agent by St. Louis Cardinals' organization, November 27, 1981.
†Drafted by San Antonio (Los Angeles Dodgers' organization), December 9, 1986.

BRYAN STANLEY HARVEY

Born June 2, 1963, at Chattanooga, Tenn.
Height, 6.02. Weight, 212.
Throws and bats righthanded.
Attended University of North Carolina, Charlotte, N. C.

Major League saves: 1988 (17).
Named American League Rookie Pitcher of the Year by THE SPORTING NEWS, 1988.

Year Club	League	G.	IP.	W.	L.	Pct.	H.	R.	ER.	SO.	BB.	ERA.
1985—Quad City†	Midwest	30	81⅔	5	6	.455	66	37	32	111	37	3.53
1986—Palm Springs	California	43	57	3	4	.429	38	24	17	68	38	2.68
1987—Midland	Texas	43	53	2	2	.500	40	14	12	78	28	2.04
1987—California	American	3	5	0	0	.000	6	0	0	3	2	0.00
1988—Edmonton	P. Coast	5	5⅔	0	0	.000	7	2	2	10	4	3.18
1988—California	American	50	76	7	5	.583	59	22	18	67	20	2.13
Major League Totals—2 Years		53	81	7	5	.583	65	22	18	70	22	2.00

Signed as free agent by California Angels' organization, August 20, 1984.
†On disabled list, April 12 to April 22, 1985.

RONALD WILLIAM HASSEY
(Ron)

Born February 27, 1953, at Tucson, Ariz.
Height, 6.02. Weight, 195.
Throws right and bats lefthanded.
Received degree in public administration from University of Arizona, Tucson, Ariz.
Son of Bill Hassey, minor league outfielder, 1949 through 1952.

Major League stolen bases: 1978 (2), 1979 (1), 1982 (3), 1983 (2), 1984 (1), 1986 (1), 1988 (2). Total—12.
Led American League in passed balls with 15 in 1985.

Year Club	League	Pos.	G.	AB.	R.	H.	2B.	3B.	HR.	RBI.	B.A.	PO.	A.	E.	F.A.
1976—San Jose	Calif.	C-3B	22	62	7	19	4	0	1	7	.306	55	2	2	.966
1976—Williamsport	East.	C	21	68	6	19	3	0	0	8	.279	63	10	4	.948
1977—Toledo	Int.	C-3-1-O	129	446	50	132	21	1	10	57	.296	484	82	21	.964
1978—Portland	P. C.	C-3B	72	235	42	76	12	1	12	52	.323	312	32	7	.980
1978—Cleveland	Amer.	C	25	74	5	15	0	0	2	9	.203	130	15	1	.993
1979—Tacoma	P. C.	C-3B	44	157	25	53	10	0	3	27	.338	282	44	2	.994
1979—Cleveland	Amer.	C-1B	75	223	20	64	14	0	4	32	.287	368	29	3	.993
1980—Cleveland	Amer.	C-1B	130	390	43	124	18	4	8	65	.318	564	52	4	.994
1981—Cleveland	Amer.	C-1B	61	190	8	44	4	0	1	25	.232	327	44	3	.992
1982—Cleveland	Amer.	C-1B	113	323	33	81	18	0	5	34	.251	566	38	4	.993
1983—Cleveland	Amer.	C	117	341	48	92	21	0	6	42	.270	514	43	3	.995
1984—Cleveland†	Amer.	C-1B	48	149	11	38	5	1	0	19	.255	210	16	1	.996
1984—Chicago‡§	Nat.	C-1B	19	33	5	11	0	0	2	5	.333	53	2	1	.982
1985—New York xy	Amer.	C-1B	92	267	31	79	16	1	13	42	.296	420	20	7	.984
1986—N.Y.z-Chi.	Amer.	C	113	341	45	110	25	1	9	49	.323	318	14	4	.988
1987—Chicago a	Amer.	C	49	145	15	31	9	0	3	12	.214	114	12	0	1.000
1987—Hawaii b	P. C.	DH	6	21	3	3	2	0	0	4	.143	0	0	0	.000
1988—Oakland	Amer.	C	107	323	32	83	15	0	7	45	.257	465	31	3	.994
American League Totals—11 Years			930	2766	291	761	145	7	58	374	.275	3996	314	33	.992
National League Totals—1 Year			19	33	5	11	0	0	2	5	.333	53	2	1	.982
Major League Totals—12 Years			949	2799	296	772	145	7	60	379	.276	4049	316	34	.992

Selected by Cincinnati Reds' organization in 23rd round of free-agent draft, June 6, 1972.
Selected by Kansas City Royals' organization in 22nd round of free-agent draft, June 4, 1975.
Selected by Cleveland Indians' organization in 18th round of free-agent draft, June 8, 1976.
†Traded with Pitchers Rick Sutcliffe and George Frazier to Chicago Cubs for Outfielders Mel Hall and Joe Carter and Pitchers Don Schulze and Darryl Banks, June 13, 1984.
‡On disabled list, July 5 to September 1, 1984.
§Traded with Outfielder Henry Cotto and Pitchers Rich Bordi and Porfi Altamirano to New York Yankees for Pitcher Ray Fontenot and Outfielder Brian Dayett, December 4, 1984.
xTraded with Pitcher Joe Cowley to Chicago White Sox for Pitcher Britt Burns, Shortstop Mike Soper and Outfielder Glen Braxton, December 12, 1985.
yTraded with Catcher Chris Alvarez, Pitcher Eric Schmidt and Outfielder Matt Winters to New York Yankees for Pitcher Neil Allen, Catcher Scott Bradley, Outfielder Glen Braxton and cash, February 13, 1986.
zTraded with Shortstop Carlos Martinez and a player to be named later to Chicago White Sox for Outfielder Ron Kittle, Infielder Wayne Tolleson and Catcher Joel Skinner, July 30, 1986; New York Yankees traded Catcher Bill Lindsey to Chicago organization to complete deal, December 24, 1986.
aOn disabled list, June 1 to August 7, 1987; included rehabilitation disability assignment to Hawaii, June 28 to August 2, 1987.
bGranted free agency, November 30, 1987; signed by Oakland Athletics, December 9, 1987.

CHAMPIONSHIP SERIES RECORD

Established Championship Series record for highest batting average, four-game Series (.500), 1988.

Year Club	League	Pos.	G.	AB.	R.	H.	2B.	3B.	HR.	RBI.	B.A.	PO.	A.	E.	F.A.
1988—Oakland	Amer.	C	4	8	2	4	1	0	1	3	.500	13	0	0	1.000

WORLD SERIES RECORD

Year Club	League	Pos.	G.	AB.	R.	H.	2B.	3B.	HR.	RBI.	B.A.	PO.	A.	E.	F.A.
1988—Oakland	Amer.	C-PH	5	8	0	2	0	0	0	1	.250	28	1	0	1.000

MICHAEL VAUGHN HATCHER JR.
(Mickey)

Born March 15, 1955, at Cleveland, O.
Height, 6.02. Weight, 202.
Throws and bats righthanded.
Attended Mesa Community College, Mesa, Ariz., and
University of Oklahoma, Norman, Okla.
Brother of Hal Hatcher, catcher in Kansas City Royals' organization, 1980 through 1985.

Major League stolen bases: 1979 (1), 1981 (3), 1983 (2), 1986 (2), 1987 (2). Total—10.

Year Club	League	Pos.	G.	AB.	R.	H.	2B.	3B.	HR.	RBI.	B.A.	PO.	A.	E.	F.A.
1977—Clinton	Midw.	OF	78	288	47	89	12	4	11	53	.309	126	9	4	.971
1978—San Antonio†	Texas	3B	83	334	60	111	12	6	8	62	.332	55	124	22	.891
1978—Albuquerque	P. C.	3B-OF	41	155	25	51	11	5	7	39	.329	24	63	8	.916
1979—Albuquerque	P. C.	3B-OF	103	420	88	156	29	12	10	93	*.371	127	156	12	.959
1979—Los Angeles	Nat.	OF-3B	33	93	9	25	4	1	1	5	.269	47	24	5	.934
1980—Albuquerque	P. C.	OF-3B	43	181	28	65	7	2	7	40	.359	52	32	9	.903
1980—Los Angeles‡	Nat.	3B-OF	57	84	4	19	2	0	1	5	.226	31	23	3	.947
1981—Minnesota	Amer.	OF-1B-3B	99	377	36	96	23	2	3	37	.255	296	11	3	.990
1982—Minnesota	Amer.	OF-3B	84	277	23	69	13	2	3	26	.249	81	17	1	.990
1983—Minnesota§	Amer.	OF-1B-3B	106	375	50	119	15	3	9	47	.317	199	11	3	.986
1984—Minnesota	Amer.	OF-1B-3B	152	576	61	174	35	5	5	69	.302	364	20	9	.977
1985—Minnesota x	Amer.	OF-1B	116	444	46	125	28	0	3	49	.282	246	7	3	.988
1986—Minnesota y	Amer.	OF-1B-3B	115	317	40	88	13	3	3	32	.278	220	16	4	.983
1987—Los Angeles	Nat.	3B-1B-OF	101	287	27	81	19	1	7	42	.282	277	105	11	.972
1988—Los Angeles z	Nat.	OF-1B-3B	88	191	22	56	8	0	1	25	.293	189	19	3	.986
National League Totals—4 Years			279	655	62	181	33	2	10	77	.276	544	171	22	.970
American League Totals—6 Years			672	2366	256	671	127	15	26	260	.284	1406	82	23	.985
Major League Totals—10 Years			951	3021	318	852	160	17	36	337	.282	1950	253	45	.980

Selected by Houston Astros' organization in 14th round of free-agent draft, June 5, 1974.
Selected by New York Mets' organization in 2nd round of free-agent draft, January 7, 1976.
Selected by Los Angeles Dodgers' organization in 5th round of free-agent draft, June 7, 1977.
†On disabled list, July 13 to July 23, 1978.
‡Traded with First Baseman Kelly Snider and Pitcher Matt Reeves to Minnesota Twins for Outfielder Ken Landreaux, March 30, 1981.
§On disabled list, June 21 to July 8 and August 1 to August 23, 1983.
xOn disabled list, July 10 to July 25, 1985.
yReleased, March 31, 1987; signed by Los Angeles Dodgers, April 10, 1987.
zOn disabled list, July 7 to July 22, 1988.

CHAMPIONSHIP SERIES RECORD

Year Club	League	Pos.	G.	AB.	R.	H.	2B.	3B.	HR.	RBI.	B.A.	PO.	A.	E.	F.A.
1988—Los Angeles	Nat.	1B-OF	6	21	4	5	2	0	0	3	.238	34	1	2	.946

WORLD SERIES RECORD

Tied World Series record for hitting home run in first Series at-bat, October 15, 1988 (first inning).

Year Club	League	Pos.	G.	AB.	R.	H.	2B.	3B.	HR.	RBI.	B.A.	PO.	A.	E.	F.A.
1988—Los Angeles	Nat.	OF	5	19	5	7	1	0	2	5	.368	8	0	0	1.000

WILLIAM AUGUSTUS HATCHER
(Billy)

Born October 4, 1960, at Williams, Ariz.
Height, 5.09. Weight, 175.
Throws and bats righthanded.
Attended Yavapai Community College, Prescott, Ariz.

Major League stolen bases: 1984 (2), 1985 (2), 1986 (38), 1987 (53), 1988 (32). Total—127.
Tied for National League lead in double plays by outfielders with 6 in 1987.
Led American Association in being hit by pitch with 9 in 1984.
Led New York-Pennsylvania League in being hit by pitch with 8 in 1981.

Year Club	League	Pos.	G.	AB.	R.	H.	2B.	3B.	HR.	RBI.	B.A.	PO.	A.	E.	F.A.
1981—Geneva	NYP	OF	•75	289	57	81	15	3	4	40	.280	138	7	11	.930
1982—Salinas	Calif.	OF	138	549	92	171	18	8	8	59	.311	235	10	12	.953
1983—Midland	Texas	OF	135	545	*132	163	33	11	10	80	.299	286	17	•13	.959
1984—Iowa	A. A.	OF	150	595	96	164	27	18	9	59	.276	303	15	7	.978
1984—Chicago	Nat.	OF	8	9	1	1	0	0	0	0	.111	2	1	0	1.000
1985—Iowa	A. A.	OF	67	279	39	78	14	5	5	19	.280	157	4	4	.976
1985—Chicago†‡	Nat.	OF	53	163	24	40	12	1	2	10	.245	77	2	1	.988
1986—Houston§	Nat.	OF	127	419	55	108	15	4	6	36	.258	226	7	4	.983
1987—Houston x	Nat.	OF	141	564	96	167	28	3	11	63	.296	276	16	4	.986
1988—Houston	Nat.	OF	145	530	79	142	25	4	7	52	.268	280	7	5	.983
Major League Totals—5 Years			474	1685	255	458	80	12	26	161	.272	861	33	14	.985

Selected by Chicago Cubs' organization in 6th round of free-agent draft, January 13, 1981.
†On disabled list, August 19 to September 3, 1985.
‡Traded with a player to be named later to Houston Astros for Outfielder Jerry Mumphrey, December 16, 1985; Houston organization acquired Pitcher Steve Engel to complete deal, July 24, 1986.
§On disabled list, June 28 to July 13, 1986.
xOn disabled list, July 7 to July 2, 1987.

CHAMPIONSHIP SERIES RECORD

Tied Championship Series record for most at-bats, game (7), October 15, 1986 (16 innings).
Established National League Championship Series record for most stolen bases, six-game Series (3), 1986.

Year	Club	League	Pos.	G.	AB.	R.	H.	2B.	3B.	HR.	RBI.	B.A.	PO.	A.	E.	F.A.
1986	Houston	Nat.	OF	6	25	4	7	0	0	1	2	.280	11	0	1	.917

BRADLEY DAVID HAVENS
(Brad)

Born November 17, 1959, at Highland Park, Mich.
Height, 6.01. Weight, 197.
Throws and bats lefthanded.

Major League saves: 1986 (1), 1987 (1), 1988 (1). Total—3.
Led International League in complete games with 12 in 1984.
Led California League in complete games with 12 in 1980.
Led Midwest League in complete games with 17 in 1978.
Tied for California League lead in games started by pitchers with 28 in 1980.
Named International League Pitcher of the Year, 1984.

Year	Club	League	G.	IP.	W.	L.	Pct.	H.	R.	ER.	SO.	BB.	ERA.
1978	Quad Cities†	Midwest	26	*200	13	10	.565	171	80	59	*197	74	2.66
1979	Orlando	Southern	19	94	4	10	.286	128	85	76	63	50	7.28
1979	Wisconsin Rapids	Midwest	10	73	6	1	.857	62	35	34	80	18	4.19
1980	Visalia	California	28	195	14	9	.609	186	90	72	*179	82	3.32
1981	Orlando	Southern	11	74	6	2	.750	81	38	29	58	20	3.53
1981	Minnesota	American	14	78	3	6	.333	76	33	31	43	24	3.58
1982	Minnesota	American	33	208⅔	10	14	.417	201	112	100	129	80	4.31
1983	Minnesota	American	16	80⅓	5	8	.385	110	75	73	40	38	8.18
1983	Toledo	Int'national	11	69⅔	6	3	.667	60	34	30	64	37	3.88
1984	Toledo‡	Int'national	25	169	11	10	.524	142	56	49	*169	70	2.61
1985	Rochester	Int'national	34	133⅔	8	10	.444	135	79	72	*129	52	4.85
1985	Baltimore	American	8	14⅓	0	1	.000	20	14	14	19	10	8.79
1986	Baltimore	American	46	71	3	3	.500	64	37	36	57	29	4.56
1987	Rochester§	Int'national	9	31⅓	2	3	.400	36	22	21	16	17	6.03
1987	Los Angeles x	National	31	35⅓	0	0	.000	30	18	17	23	23	4.33
1987	Albuquerque	P. Coast	3	7	0	1	.000	5	5	4	3	7	5.14
1988	Los Angeles y	National	9	9⅔	0	0	.000	15	5	5	8	4	4.66
1988	Colorado Springs	P. Coast	9	15	0	0	.000	12	4	4	7	4	2.40
1988	Cleveland	American	28	57⅓	2	3	.400	62	22	20	30	17	3.14
	American League Totals—6 Years		145	509⅔	23	35	.397	533	293	274	318	198	4.84
	National League Totals—2 Years		40	45	0	0	.000	45	23	22	31	27	4.40
	Major League Totals—7 Years		185	554⅔	23	35	.397	578	316	296	349	225	4.80

Selected by California Angels' organization in 8th round of free-agent draft, June 7, 1977.
†Traded with Outfielder Ken Landreaux, Pitcher Paul Hartzell and Third Baseman Dave Engle to Minnesota Twins for First Baseman Rod Carew, February 3, 1979.
‡Traded to Baltimore Orioles' organization for Pitcher Mark Brown, March 27, 1985.
§Traded with Outfielder John Shelby to Los Angeles Dodgers for Pitcher Tom Niedenfuer, May 22, 1987.
xOn disabled list, August 3 to August 29, 1987; included rehabilitation disability assignment to Albuquerque, August 20 to August 29, 1987.
yReleased, May 13, 1988; signed by Colorado Springs (Cleveland Indians' organization), May 24, 1988.

MELTON ANDREW HAWKINS
(Andy)

Born January 21, 1960, at Waco, Tex.
Height, 6.03. Weight, 217.
Throws and bats righthanded.

Led Pacific Coast League in shutouts with 6 in 1982.
Led Texas League in complete games with 14 and tied for lead in games started by pitchers with 27 in 1981.
Led Northwest League in balks with 4 in 1978.

Year	Club	League	G.	IP.	W.	L.	Pct.	H.	R.	ER.	SO.	BB.	ERA.
1978	Walla Walla	Northwest	14	102	8	3	.727	95	52	24	73	45	2.12
1979	Reno	California	27	188	8	13	.381	*232	143	*117	130	97	5.60
1980	Reno	California	26	171	13	10	.565	183	108	81	124	79	4.26
1981	Amarillo	Texas	27	200	11	10	.524	*209	100	*93	144	48	4.19
1982	Hawaii	P. Coast	18	132⅔	9	7	.563	108	49	32	91	47	2.17
1982	San Diego	National	15	63⅔	2	5	.286	66	33	29	25	27	4.10
1983	Las Vegas	P. Coast	14	85⅓	6	4	.600	110	67	61	50	27	6.43
1983	San Diego	National	21	119⅔	5	7	.417	106	50	39	59	48	2.93
1984	San Diego	National	36	146	8	9	.471	143	90	76	77	72	4.68
1985	San Diego	National	33	228⅔	18	8	.692	229	88	80	69	65	3.15
1986	San Diego	National	37	209⅓	10	8	.556	218	111	100	117	75	4.30
1987	San Diego†	National	24	117⅔	3	10	.231	131	71	66	51	49	5.05
1988	San Diego‡	National	33	217⅔	14	11	.560	196	88	81	91	76	3.35
	Major League Totals—7 Years		199	1102⅔	60	58	.508	1089	531	471	489	412	3.84

Selected by San Diego Padres' organization in 1st round (fifth player selected) of free-agent draft, June 6, 1978.
†On disabled list, July 29 to September 1, 1987.
‡Granted free agency, November 4, 1988; signed by New York Yankees, December 8, 1988.

CHAMPIONSHIP SERIES RECORD

Year	Club	League	G.	IP.	W.	L.	Pct.	H.	R.	ER.	SO.	BB.	ERA.
1984	San Diego	National	3	3⅔	0	0	.000	0	0	0	1	2	0.00

WORLD SERIES RECORD

Year	Club	League	G.	IP.	W.	L.	Pct.	H.	R.	ER.	SO.	BB.	ERA.
1984	San Diego	National	3	12	1	1	.500	4	1	1	4	6	0.75

CHARLES DEWAYNE HAYES
(Charlie)

Born May 29, 1965, at Hattiesburg, Miss.
Height, 6.00. Weight, 190.
Throws and bats righthanded.

Led Pacific Coast League in grounding into double plays with 19 in 1988.
Led Texas League third basemen in total chances with 334 in 1987.
Led Texas League third basemen in double plays with 27 in 1986.

Year	Club	League	Pos.	G.	AB.	R.	H.	2B.	3B.	HR.	RBI.	B.A.	PO.	A.	E.	F.A.
1983	Great Falls†	Pion.	3B-OF	34	111	9	29	4	2	0	9	.261	13	32	9	.833
1984	Clinton	Midw.	3B	116	392	41	96	17	2	2	51	.245	68	216	28	.910
1985	Fresno	Calif.	3B	131	467	73	132	17	2	4	68	.283	★100	233	18	★.949
1986	Shreveport	Texas	3B	121	434	52	107	23	2	5	45	.247	89	★259	25	.933
1987	Shreveport	Texas	3B	128	487	66	148	33	3	14	75	.304	★100	★212	22	★.934
1988	Phoenix	P. C.	OF-3B	131	492	71	151	26	4	7	71	.307	206	100	23	.930
1988	San Francisco	Nat.	OF-3B	7	11	0	1	0	0	0	0	.091	5	0	0	1.000
Major League Totals—1 Year				7	11	0	1	0	0	0	0	.091	5	0	0	1.000

Selected by San Francisco Giants' organization in 4th round of free-agent draft, June 6, 1983.
†On disabled list, July 20, 1983 through remainder of season.

VON FRANCIS HAYES

Born August 31, 1958, at Stockton, Calif.
Height, 6.05. Weight, 180.
Throws right and bats lefthanded.
Attended St. Mary's College, Moraga, Calif.

Tied major league record for most home runs (2) and most total bases (8), inning, June 11, 1985 (first inning).
Major League stolen bases: 1981 (8), 1982 (32), 1983 (20), 1984 (48), 1985 (21), 1986 (24), 1987 (16), 1988 (20). Total—189.
Led Midwest League third basemen in fielding percentage with .930 in 1980.
Named Midwest League Most Valuable Player, 1980.

Year	Club	League	Pos.	G.	AB.	R.	H.	2B.	3B.	HR.	RBI.	B.A.	PO.	A.	E.	F.A.
1980	Waterloo	Midw.	3B-SS	134	492	105	★162	★33	3	15	90	★.329	94	291	30	.928
1981	Cleveland	Amer.	OF-3B	43	109	21	28	8	2	1	17	.257	30	4	3	.919
1981	Charleston	Int.	3B-1B	105	382	58	120	19	6	10	73	.314	96	222	19	.944
1982	Cleveland†	Amer.	OF-3B-1B	150	527	65	132	25	3	14	82	.250	323	17	6	.983
1983	Philadelphia‡	Nat.	OF	124	351	45	93	9	5	6	32	.265	165	7	5	.972
1984	Philadelphia	Nat.	OF	152	561	85	164	27	6	16	67	.292	341	2	4	.988
1985	Philadelphia	Nat.	OF	152	570	76	150	30	4	13	70	.263	368	9	6	.984
1986	Philadelphia	Nat.	1B-OF	158	610	•107	186	★46	2	19	98	.305	1247	100	13	.990
1987	Philadelphia	Nat.	1B-OF	158	556	84	154	36	5	21	84	.277	1216	80	13	.990
1988	Philadelphia§	Nat.	1B-OF-3B	104	367	43	100	28	2	6	45	.272	756	58	9	.989
American League Totals—2 Years				193	636	86	160	33	5	15	99	.252	353	21	9	.977
National League Totals—6 Years				848	3015	440	847	176	24	81	396	.281	4093	256	50	.989
Major League Totals—8 Years				1041	3651	526	1007	209	29	96	495	.276	4446	277	59	.988

Selected by Cleveland Indians' organization in 7th round of free-agent draft, June 5, 1979.
†Traded to Philadelphia Phillies for Second Baseman Manny Trillo, Outfielder George Vukovich, Infielder Julio Franco, Pitcher Jay Baller and Catcher Jerry Willard, December 9, 1982.
‡On disabled list, March 27 to April 12, 1983.
§On disabled list, July 15 to September 2, 1988.

CHAMPIONSHIP SERIES RECORD

Year	Club	League	Pos.	G.	AB.	R.	H.	2B.	3B.	HR.	RBI.	B.A.	PO.	A.	E.	F.A.
1983	Philadelphia	Nat.	PH-OF	2	2	0	0	0	0	0	0	.000	0	0	0	.000

WORLD SERIES RECORD

Year	Club	League	Pos.	G.	AB.	R.	H.	2B.	3B.	HR.	RBI.	B.A.	PO.	A.	E.	F.A.
1983	Philadelphia	Nat.	PH-OF	4	3	0	0	0	0	0	0	.000	1	0	0	1.000

RAYMOND ALTON HAYWARD JR.
(Ray)

Born April 27, 1961, at Enid, Okla.
Height, 6.01. Weight, 194.
Throws and bats lefthanded.
Received degree in finance from University of Oklahoma, Norman, Okla., in 1983.

Tied for Pacific Coast League lead in hit batsmen with 6 in 1985.
Tied for Pacific Coast League lead in wild pitches with 16 in 1984.
Named lefthanded pitcher on The Sporting News College Baseball All-America Team, 1983.

Year	Club	League	G.	IP.	W.	L.	Pct.	H.	R.	ER.	SO.	BB.	ERA.
1983—Beaumont		Texas	10	66⅓	5	1	.833	45	16	13	71	30	1.76
1984—Las Vegas		P. Coast	26	129⅓	9	6	.600	129	78	70	91	79	4.87
1985—Las Vegas		P. Coast	28	*191⅓	11	10	.524	198	104	85	150	79	4.00
1986—Las Vegas		P. Coast	26	136	9	11	.450	156	87	70	100	65	4.63
1986—San Diego		National	3	10	0	2	.000	16	12	10	6	4	9.00
1987—Las Vegas		P. Coast	23	142⅓	8	5	.615	139	56	49	115	79	3.10
1987—San Diego†‡		National	4	6	0	0	.000	12	11	11	2	3	16.50
1988—Oklahoma City		Am. Assoc.	8	42	3	2	.600	36	21	18	31	18	3.86
1988—Texas§		American	12	62⅔	4	6	.400	63	44	38	37	35	5.46
National League Totals—2 Years			7	16	0	2	.000	28	23	21	8	7	11.81
American League Totals—1 Year			12	62⅔	4	6	.400	63	44	38	37	35	5.46
Major League Totals—3 Years			19	78⅔	4	8	.333	91	67	59	45	42	6.75

Selected by Pittsburgh Pirates' organization in 12th round of free-agent draft, June 7, 1982.

Selected by San Diego Padres' organization in 1st round (10th player selected) of free-agent draft, June 6, 1983.

†Traded with Pitcher Rich Gossage to Chicago Cubs for Infielders Keith Moreland and Mike Brumley, February 12, 1988.

‡Traded to Texas Rangers for Outfielder Dave Meier and Infielder Greg Tabor, March 17, 1988.

§On disabled list, July 6 to September 1, 1988; included rehabilitation disability assignment to Oklahoma City, July 20 to August 8, 1988.

EDWARD JOHN HEARN
(Ed)

Born August 23, 1960, at Stuart, Fla.
Height, 6.03. Weight, 210.
Throws and bats righthanded.

Year	Club	League	Pos.	G.	AB.	R.	H.	2B.	3B.	HR.	RBI.	B.A.	PO.	A.	E.	F.A.
1978—Helena		Pion.	C	47	173	34	49	3	1	13	45	.283	274	35	9	.972
1979—Helena†		Pion.					(Did not play)									
1980—Spartanburg		S. Atl.	1B	66	217	25	65	12	2	3	32	.300	68	7	1	.987
1981—Peninsula		Carol.	1B	101	317	61	96	29	2	10	44	.303	538	25	12	.979
1982—Peninsula		Carol.	C-1B	21	76	15	25	2	0	6	14	.329	69	2	2	.973
1982—Reading‡§		East.	1B-C	43	135	16	37	6	2	3	27	.274	204	16	7	.969
1983—Jackson		Texas	1B-C	5	20	4	6	1	0	0	2	.300	40	1	1	.976
1983—Lynchburg		Carol.	C-1-3-O	91	290	37	79	16	1	5	47	.272	333	37	9	.976
1984—Jackson x		Texas	C-1B	86	311	46	97	19	2	11	51	.312	613	54	6	.991
1985—Tidewater		Int.	C-1B	112	418	35	110	29	1	5	57	.263	543	45	5	.992
1986—Tidewater		Int.	1B-C	22	83	7	22	4	0	1	12	.265	170	15	1	.995
1986—New York y		Nat.	C	49	136	16	36	5	0	4	10	.265	223	11	3	.987
1987—Kansas City z		Amer.	C	6	17	2	5	2	0	0	3	.294	25	0	0	1.000
1988—Baseball City a		Fla. St.	C	17	56	3	17	4	0	0	5	.304	54	3	1	.983
1988—Kansas City		Amer.	C	7	18	1	4	2	0	0	1	.222	12	1	0	1.000
National League Totals—1 Year				49	136	16	36	5	0	4	10	.265	223	11	3	.987
American League Totals—2 Years				13	35	3	9	4	0	0	4	.257	37	1	0	1.000
Major League Totals—3 Years				62	171	19	45	9	0	4	14	.263	260	12	3	.989

Selected by Philadelphia Phillies' organization in 4th round of free-agent draft, June 6, 1978.

†On temporary inactive list, June 22, 1979 through remainder of season.

‡On disabled list, June 15 to July 6, 1982.

§Released, January 7, 1983; signed by Lynchburg (New York Mets' organization), February 3, 1983.

xGranted free agency, October 15, 1984; re-signed by Mets' organization, December 13, 1984.

yTraded with Pitchers Rick Anderson and Mauro Gozzo to Kansas City Royals for Pitcher David Cone and Catcher Chris Jelic, March 27, 1987.

zOn disabled list, April 19, 1987 through remainder of season.

aOn Kansas City disabled list, March 30 to September 1, 1988; included rehabilitation disability assignment to Baseball City, August 14 to September 1, 1988.

KELLY MARK HEATH

Born September 4, 1957, at Plattsburg, N.Y.
Height, 5.08. Weight, 165.
Throws and bats righthanded.
Attended Louisburg College, Louisburg, N.C.

Tied for International League lead in double plays by outfielders with 3 in 1986.

Year	Club	League	Pos.	G.	AB.	R.	H.	2B.	3B.	HR.	RBI.	B.A.	PO.	A.	E.	F.A.
1977—Daytona Beach		Fla. St.	SS	59	181	13	42	4	4	2	30	.232	108	147	19	.931
1978—Jacksonville†		South.	SS	70	231	29	62	6	0	3	24	.268	115	217	31	.915
1979—Jacksonville		South.	SS-2B	129	422	67	115	26	3	7	61	.273	167	348	31	.943
1980—Omaha		A. A.	SS	56	182	22	46	10	1	3	22	.253	75	128	11	.949
1980—Jacksonville		South.	SS	55	205	26	63	10	2	5	27	.307	75	186	12	.956
1981—Omaha		A. A.	2B-SS	111	387	52	93	21	5	3	37	.240	212	282	11	.978
1982—Omaha		A. A.	2B-SS	106	361	48	86	14	2	11	41	.238	232	285	17	.968
1982—Kansas City		Amer.	2B	1	1	0	0	0	0	0	0	.000	1	2	0	1.000
1983—Omaha‡		A. A.	2B-SS	129	460	71	110	16	6	13	61	.239	263	371	13	.980
1984—Columbus		Int.	2-3-S-O	108	350	72	87	17	5	8	38	.249	138	151	23	.926
1985—Columbus§		Int.	OF-2B	121	377	83	97	21	4	18	53	.257	151	55	7	.967
1986—Richmond		Int.	O-3-S-2	102	300	46	80	17	2	11	47	.267	148	124	16	.944
1987—Richmond x		Int.	2-3-O-S	114	352	49	86	21	1	8	30	.244	151	198	15	.959
1988—Syracuse		Int.	3B-2B-OF	90	287	48	89	22	0	5	41	.310	40	64	7	.937
Major League Totals—1 Year				1	1	0	0	0	0	0	0	.000	1	2	0	1.000

Selected by Kansas City Royals' organization in 7th round of free-agent draft, June 7, 1977.
†On disabled list, May 8 to June 30, 1978.
‡Granted free agency, October 20, 1983; signed by New York Yankees' organization, December 2, 1983.
§Granted free agency, October 15, 1985; signed by Atlanta Braves, December 26, 1985.
xGranted free agency, October 15, 1987; signed by Syracuse (Toronto Blue Jays' organization), January, 1988.

MICHAEL THOMAS HEATH
(Mike)

Born February 5, 1955, at Tampa, Fla.
Height, 5.11. Weight, 180.
Throws and bats righthanded.

Major League stolen bases: 1979 (1), 1980 (3), 1981 (3), 1982 (8), 1983 (3), 1984 (7), 1985 (7), 1986 (6), 1987 (1), 1988 (1). Total—40.

Led New York-Pennsylvania League shortstops in double plays with 42 in 1974.
Tied for Appalachian League lead in sacrifice hits with 7 in 1973.

Year Club	League	Pos.	G.	AB.	R.	H.	2B.	3B.	HR.	RBI.	B.A.	PO.	A.	E.	F.A.
1973—Johnson City	Appal.	SS-2B-3B	48	166	17	29	5	2	0	10	.175	83	137	24	.902
1974—Oneonta	NYP	SS	65	234	51	66	6	3	3	34	.282	114	170	★27	.913
1975—Fort Lauderdale†	Fla. St.	SS	98	376	43	87	7	3	1	23	.231	184	256	31	.934
1976—Fort Lauderdale‡	Fla. St.	SS-3B-C-P	80	267	28	71	16	3	2	30	.266	143	121	16	.943
1977—West Haven	East.	C-3B	98	352	58	94	13	5	8	42	.267	492	72	16	.972
1978—West Haven	East.	C-SS	66	217	43	64	16	1	8	27	.295	335	53	10	.975
1978—New York§	Amer.	C	33	92	6	21	3	1	0	8	.228	151	11	5	.970
1979—Tucson x	P. C.	C	54	196	21	53	8	2	1	28	.270	183	24	7	.967
1979—Oakland	Amer.	OF-C-3B	74	258	19	66	8	0	3	27	.256	167	32	5	.975
1980—Oakland	Amer.	C-OF	92	305	27	74	10	2	1	33	.243	292	20	4	.987
1981—Oakland	Amer.	★C-OF	84	301	26	71	7	1	8	30	.236	399	45	★10	.978
1982—Oakland y	Amer.	C-OF-3B	101	318	43	77	18	4	3	39	.242	368	54	12	.972
1983—Oakland z	Amer.	C-OF-3B	96	345	45	97	17	0	6	33	.281	362	47	11	.974
1984—Oakland	Amer.	C-O-3-S	140	475	49	118	21	5	13	64	.248	495	56	8	.986
1985—Oakland a	Amer.	C-OF-3B	138	436	71	109	18	6	13	55	.250	539	67	12	.981
1986—St. Louis b	Nat.	C-OF	65	190	19	39	8	1	4	25	.205	260	30	10	.967
1986—Detroit	Amer.	C-3B	30	98	11	26	3	0	4	11	.265	145	9	3	.981
1987—Detroit c	Amer.	C-O-I	93	270	34	76	16	0	8	33	.281	384	43	5	.988
1988—Detroit	Amer.	C-OF	86	219	24	54	7	2	5	18	.247	361	24	6	.985
American League Totals—11 Years			967	3117	355	789	128	21	64	351	.253	3663	408	81	.980
National League Totals—1 Year			65	190	19	39	8	1	4	25	.205	260	30	10	.967
Major League Totals—11 Years			1032	3307	374	828	136	22	68	376	.250	3923	438	91	.980

Selected by New York Yankees' organization in 2nd round of free-agent draft, June 5, 1973.
†On Syracuse disabled list, August 2 to September 16, 1975.
‡On disabled list, June 29 to July 13, 1976.
§Traded with Pitchers Sparky Lyle, Larry McCall and Dave Rajsich, Shortstop Domingo Ramos and cash to Texas Rangers for Outfielders Juan Beniquez and Greg Jemison and Pitchers Mike Griffin, Paul Mirabella and Dave Righetti, November 10, 1978.
xTraded with Third Baseman Dave Chalk and cash to Oakland A's for Pitcher John Henry Johnson, June 15, 1979.
yOn disabled list, March 28 to April 20, 1982.
zOn disabled list, April 25 to May 25, 1983.
aTraded with Pitcher Tim Conroy to St. Louis Cardinals for Pitcher Joaquin Andujar, December 10, 1985.
bTraded to Detroit Tigers for Pitcher Ken Hill and a player to be named later, August 10, 1986; St. Louis Cardinals acquired First Baseman Mike Laga to complete deal, September 2, 1986.
cGranted free agency, November 9, 1987; re-signed by Tigers, December 1, 1987.

DIVISION SERIES RECORD

Year Club	League	Pos.	G.	AB.	R.	H.	2B.	3B.	HR.	RBI.	B.A.	PO.	A.	E.	F.A.
1981—Oakland	Amer.	C	2	8	0	0	0	0	0	0	.000	9	1	0	1.000

CHAMPIONSHIP SERIES RECORD

Year Club	League	Pos.	G.	AB.	R.	H.	2B.	3B.	HR.	RBI.	B.A.	PO.	A.	E.	F.A.
1981—Oakland	Amer.	C-OF	3	6	1	2	0	0	0	0	.333	3	1	0	1.000
1987—Detroit	Amer.	C	3	7	1	2	0	0	1	2	.286	14	0	0	1.000
Championship Series Totals—2 Years			6	13	2	4	0	0	1	2	.308	17	1	0	1.000

WORLD SERIES RECORD

Year Club	League	Pos.	G.	AB.	R.	H.	2B.	3B.	HR.	RBI.	B.A.	PO.	A.	E.	F.A.
1978—New York	Amer.	C	1	0	0	0	0	0	0	0	.000	0	0	0	.000

PITCHING RECORD

Year Club	League	G.	IP.	W.	L.	Pct.	H.	R.	ER.	SO.	BB.	ERA.
1976—Fort Lauderdale	Florida St.	1	1	0	0	.000	1	0	0	1	0	0.00

—DID YOU KNOW—

That lefthander John Tudor beat the Philadelphia Phillies twice within a week in 1988 for two different teams? Tudor beat the Phils, 1-0, August 10 in his last game for the St. Louis Cardinals and 7-2 August 17 in his first start for the Los Angeles Dodgers.

RONALD JEFFREY HEATHCOCK
(Jeff)

Born November 18, 1959, at West Covina, Calif.
Height, 6.04. Weight, 195.
Throws and bats righthanded.
Attended Golden West College, Huntington Beach, Calif., and Oral Roberts University, Tulsa, Okla.

Major League saves: 1983 (1), 1985 (1), 1987 (1). Total—3.
Led Southern League in home runs allowed with 26 in 1982.
Tied for Pacific Coast League lead in games started by pitchers with 27 in 1986.
Tied for Southern League lead in shutouts with 3 in 1983.

Year Club	League	G.	IP.	W.	L.	Pct.	H.	R.	ER.	SO.	BB.	ERA.
1981—Daytona Beach	Florida St.	11	85	9	0	1.000	67	20	12	77	21	1.27
1981—Columbus	Southern	16	101	4	7	.364	104	57	52	59	35	4.63
1982—Columbus	Southern	29	191	13	13	.500	216	*119	*101	108	56	4.76
1983—Columbus	Southern	14	91⅓	4	4	.500	82	32	23	69	22	2.27
1983—Tucson	P. Coast	15	110⅓	10	3	.769	104	45	34	65	26	2.77
1983—Houston	National	6	28	2	1	.667	19	14	10	12	4	3.21
1984—Tucson†	P. Coast	4	16⅔	1	1	.500	12	8	8	8	6	4.32
1985—Tucson	P. Coast	23	141⅔	7	10	.412	180	91	80	59	27	5.08
1985—Houston	National	14	56⅓	3	1	.750	50	25	21	25	13	3.36
1986—Tucson	P. Coast	27	164⅔	10	8	.556	*211	100	93	69	42	5.08
1987—Tucson	P. Coast	22	142⅔	11	6	.647	145	67	55	71	28	3.47
1987—Houston	National	19	42⅔	4	2	.667	44	15	15	15	9	3.16
1988—Houston	National	17	31	0	5	.000	33	25	20	12	16	5.81
1988—Tucson	P. Coast	16	79⅔	3	5	.375	88	45	45	49	19	5.08
Major League Totals—4 Years		56	158	9	9	.500	146	79	66	64	42	3.76

Selected by Milwaukee Brewers' organization in 2nd round of free-agent draft, January 9, 1979.
Selected by San Diego Padres' organization in secondary phase of free-agent draft, June 5, 1979.
Selected by Houston Astros' organization in secondary phase of free-agent draft, June 3, 1980.
†On disabled list, April 25, 1984 through remainder of season.

NEAL HEATON

Born March 3, 1960, at Jamaica, N. Y.
Height, 6.01. Weight, 195.
Throws and bats lefthanded.
Attended University of Miami, Coral Gables, Fla.

Major League saves: 1983 (7), 1986 (1), 1988 (2). Total—10.
Named lefthanded pitcher on THE SPORTING NEWS College Baseball All-America Team, 1981.

Year Club	League	G.	IP.	W.	L.	Pct.	H.	R.	ER.	SO.	BB.	ERA.
1981—Chattanooga	Southern	11	77	4	4	.500	61	42	34	50	27	3.97
1982—Charleston	Int'national	29	172⅔	10	5	.667	194	97	77	105	66	4.01
1982—Cleveland	American	8	31	0	2	.000	32	21	18	14	16	5.23
1983—Cleveland	American	39	149⅓	11	7	.611	157	79	69	75	44	4.16
1984—Cleveland	American	38	198⅔	12	15	.444	231	128	115	75	75	5.21
1985—Cleveland	American	36	207⅔	9	17	.346	244	119	113	82	80	4.90
1986—Cleveland†-Minnesota‡	American	33	198⅔	7	15	.318	201	102	90	90	81	4.08
1987—Montreal	National	32	193⅓	13	10	.565	207	103	97	105	37	4.52
1988—Montreal§	National	32	97⅓	3	10	.231	98	54	54	43	43	4.99
American League Totals—5 Years		154	785⅓	39	56	.411	865	449	405	336	296	4.64
National League Totals—2 Years		64	290⅔	16	20	.444	305	157	151	148	80	4.68
Major League Totals—7 Years		218	1076	55	76	.420	1170	606	556	484	376	4.65

Selected by New York Mets' organization in 1st round (first player selected) of free-agent draft, January 9, 1979.
Selected by Cleveland Indians' organization in 2nd round of free-agent draft, June 8, 1981.
†Traded to Minnesota Twins for Pitcher John Butcher, June 20, 1986.
‡Traded with Pitchers Al Cardwood and Yorkis Perez and Catcher Jeff Reed to Montreal Expos for Pitcher Jeff Reardon and Catcher Tom Nieto, February 3, 1987.
§On disabled list, April 8 to April 29, 1988.

DANIEL WILLIAM HEEP
(Danny)

Born July 3, 1957, at San Antonio, Tex.
Height, 5.11. Weight, 177.
Throws and bats lefthanded.
Received degree in teaching and political science from St. Mary's University, San Antonio, Tex.

Major League stolen bases: 1983 (3), 1984 (3), 1985 (2), 1986 (1), 1987 (1), 1988 (2). Total—12.
Led Southern League in total bases with 274 in 1979.
Named Southern League co-Most Valuable Player, 1979.

Year Club	League	Pos.	G.	AB.	R.	H.	2B.	3B.	HR.	RBI.	B.A.	PO.	A.	E.	F.A.
1978—Daytona Beach	Fla. St.	OF	66	212	29	72	18	2	2	24	.340	89	9	2	.980
1979—Columbus	South.	OF	138	523	103	*171	30	5	21	84	.327	211	12	6	.974
1979—Houston	Nat.	OF	14	14	0	2	0	0	0	2	.143	7	0	0	1.000
1980—Tucson	P. C.	1B-OF	96	376	63	129	28	5	17	69	*.343	810	53	8	.991
1980—Houston	Nat.	1B	33	87	6	24	8	0	0	6	.276	188	8	2	.990
1981—Houston†	Nat.	1B-OF	33	96	6	24	3	0	0	11	.250	198	9	2	.990

Year	Club	League	Pos.	G.	AB.	R.	H.	2B.	3B.	HR.	RBI.	B.A.	PO.	A.	E.	F.A.
1981	—Tuscon	P. C.	1B-OF	78	285	55	96	23	5	11	60	.337	635	44	12	.983
1982	—Houston‡	Nat.	OF-1B	85	198	16	47	14	1	4	22	.237	192	6	1	.995
1983	—New York	Nat.	OF-1B	115	253	30	64	12	0	8	21	.253	159	11	0	1.000
1984	—New York	Nat.	OF-1B	99	199	36	46	9	2	1	12	.231	137	7	4	.973
1985	—New York	Nat.	OF-1B	95	271	26	76	17	0	7	42	.280	154	5	4	.975
1986	—New York§	Nat.	OF	86	195	24	55	8	2	5	33	.282	83	2	1	.988
1987	—San Antonio	Texas	OF	11	47	6	16	1	0	2	9	.340	9	1	0	1.000
1987	—Los Angeles	Nat.	OF-1B	60	98	7	16	4	0	0	9	.163	52	6	1	.983
1988	—Los Angeles x	Nat.	OF-1B-P	95	149	14	36	2	0	0	11	.242	129	10	3	.979
Major League Totals—10 Years				715	1560	165	390	77	5	25	169	.250	1299	64	18	.987

Selected by Houston Astros' organization in 2nd round of free-agent draft, June 6, 1978.
†On disabled list, April 19 to May 4, 1981.
‡Traded to New York Mets for Pitcher Mike Scott, December 10, 1982.
§Granted free agency, November 12, 1986; signed by Los Angeles Dodgers' organization, June 12, 1987.
x Released, December 21, 1988.

CHAMPIONSHIP SERIES RECORD

Year	Club	League	Pos.	G.	AB.	R.	H.	2B.	3B.	HR.	RBI.	B.A.	PO.	A.	E.	F.A.
1980	—Houston	Nat.	PH	1	1	0	0	0	0	0	0	.000	0	0	0	.000
1986	—New York	Nat.	PH-OF	5	4	0	1	0	0	0	1	.250	0	0	0	.000
1988	—Los Angeles	Nat.	PH	3	1	0	0	0	0	0	0	.000	0	0	0	.000
Championship Series Totals—3 Years				9	6	0	1	0	0	0	1	.167	0	0	0	.000

WORLD SERIES TOTALS

Year	Club	League	Pos.	G.	AB.	R.	H.	2B.	3B.	HR.	RBI.	B.A.	PO.	A.	E.	F.A.
1986	—New York	Nat.	PH-O-DH	5	11	0	1	0	0	0	2	.091	1	0	0	1.000
1988	—Los Angeles	Nat.	PH-O-DH	3	8	0	2	1	0	0	0	.250	0	0	0	.000
World Series Totals—2 Years				8	19	0	3	1	0	0	2	.158	1	0	0	1.000

PITCHING RECORD

Year	Club	League	G.	IP.	W.	L.	Pct.	H.	R.	ER.	SO.	BB.	ERA.
1988	—Los Angeles	National	1	2	0	0	.000	2	2	2	0	0	9.00

DONALD ELLIOTT HEINKEL
(Don)

Born October 20, 1959, at Racine, Wis.
Height, 6.00. Weight, 185.
Throws right and bats lefthanded.
Received bachelor of science degree in biology from
Wichita State University, Wichita, Kan., in 1982.

Major League saves: 1988 (1).

Led Southern League pitchers in games started with 30, complete games with 13 and home runs allowed with 26 in 1983.

Tied for International League lead in home runs allowed with 24, shutouts with 2 and balks with 5 in 1987.
Tied for American Association lead in shutouts with 3 in 1984.
Named Southern League Pitcher of the Year, 1983.

Year	Club	League	G.	IP.	W.	L.	Pct.	H.	R.	ER.	SO.	BB.	ERA.
1982	—Bristol	Ap'lachian	1	9	1	0	1.000	2	1	0	11	0	0.00
1982	—Lakeland	Florida St.	4	31⅔	3	0	1.000	27	7	6	14	12	1.71
1982	—Birmingham	Southern	9	64	4	5	.444	59	25	20	44	15	2.81
1983	—Birmingham	Southern	30	★207⅓	★19	6	.760	★212	87	78	113	57	3.39
1984	—Evansville	Am. Assoc.	30	178⅓	11	13	.458	205	101	79	75	58	3.99
1985	—Nashville	Am. Assoc.	8	41⅔	1	3	.250	49	36	33	18	14	7.13
1985	—Birmingham†	Southern	10	57	2	5	.286	77	31	31	33	18	4.89
1986	—Glens Falls	Eastern	10	67	3	5	.375	61	30	21	49	22	2.82
1986	—Nashville	Am. Assoc.	9	59⅓	5	2	.714	48	18	18	32	14	2.73
1987	—Toledo	Int'national	29	★187⅓	8	10	.444	★208	●103	83	132	49	3.99
1988	—Detroit‡	American	21	36⅓	0	0	.000	30	17	16	30	12	3.96
1988	—Toledo§	Int'national	8	28⅓	1	0	1.000	25	7	6	30	8	1.91
Major League Totals—1 Year			21	36⅓	0	0	.000	30	17	16	30	12	3.96

Selected by Kansas City Royals' organization in 15th round of free-agent draft, June 6, 1978.
Selected by Detroit Tigers' organization in 30th round of free-agent draft, June 7, 1982.
†On disabled list, July 16, 1985 though remainder of season.
‡On disabled list, June 7 to July 26, 1988; included rehabilitation disability assignment to Toledo, July 6 to July 25, 1988.

§Released, October 14, 1988.

SCOTT MATHEW HEMOND

Born November 18, 1965, at Taunton, Mass.
Height, 6.00. Weight, 205.
Throws and bats righthanded.
Attended University of South Florida, Tampa, Fla.

Led Southern League third basemen in assists with 299 and total chances with 427 in 1988.
Named catcher on THE SPORTING NEWS College Baseball All-America Team, 1986.

Year	Club	League	Pos.	G.	AB.	R.	H.	2B.	3B.	HR.	RBI.	B.A.	PO.	A.	E.	F.A.
1986	—Madison	Midw.	C	22	85	9	26	2	0	2	13	.306	121	11	2	.985
1987	—Madison	Midw.	C-OF	90	343	60	99	21	4	8	52	.289	408	53	16	.966
1987	—Huntsville	South.	C-3B	33	110	10	20	3	1	1	8	.182	161	32	6	.970
1988	—Huntsville	South.	3B-C	133	482	51	106	22	4	9	53	.220	93	302	38	.912

Selected by Kansas City Royals' organization in 5th round of free-agent draft, June 6, 1983.
Selected by Oakland Athletics' organization in 1st round (12th player selected) of free-agent draft, June 2, 1986.

DAVID LEE HENDERSON
(Dave)

Born July 21, 1958, at Dos Palos, Calif.
Height, 6.02. Weight, 210.
Throws and bats righthanded.
Nephew of Joe Henderson, pitcher with Chicago
White Sox and Cincinnati Reds, 1974, 1976 and 1977.

Major League stolen bases: 1981 (2), 1982 (2), 1983 (9), 1984 (5), 1985 (6), 1986 (2), 1987 (3), 1988 (2). Total—31.

Year	Club	League	Pos.	G.	AB.	R.	H.	2B.	3B.	HR.	RBI.	B.A.	PO.	A.	E.	F.A.
1977	—Bellingham	N'west	OF	65	251	47	79	14	2	•16	63	.315	136	5	*11	.928
1978	—Stockton	Calif.	OF	117	409	48	95	16	4	7	63	.232	204	12	14	.939
1979	—San Jose	Calif.	OF	136	507	103	152	23	3	27	99	.300	264	18	4	.986
1980	—Spokane†	P. C.	OF	109	341	48	95	26	1	7	50	.279	258	9	7	.974
1981	—Seattle	Amer.	OF	59	126	17	21	3	0	6	13	.167	105	4	0	1.000
1981	—Spokane	P. C.	OF	80	272	47	76	23	1	12	50	.279	146	7	3	.981
1982	—Seattle‡	Amer.	OF	104	324	47	82	17	1	14	48	.253	249	11	4	.985
1983	—Seattle	Amer.	OF	137	484	50	130	24	5	17	55	.269	304	17	6	.982
1984	—Seattle§	Amer.	OF	112	350	42	98	23	0	14	43	.280	242	11	3	.988
1985	—Seattle	Amer.	OF	139	502	70	121	28	2	14	68	.241	335	8	5	.986
1986	—Sea. x-Bos.	Amer.	OF	139	388	59	103	22	4	15	47	.265	231	11	5	.980
1987	—Boston y	Amer.	OF	75	184	30	43	10	0	8	25	.234	114	0	5	.958
1987	—San Francisco z	Nat.	OF	15	21	2	5	2	0	0	1	.238	10	1	0	1.000
1988	—Oakland a	Amer.	OF	146	507	100	154	38	1	24	94	.304	382	5	7	.982
American League Totals—8 Years				911	2865	415	752	165	13	112	393	.262	1962	67	35	.983
National League Totals—1 Year				15	21	2	5	2	0	0	1	.238	10	1	0	1.000
Major League Totals—8 Years				926	2886	417	757	167	13	112	394	.262	1972	68	35	.983

Selected by Seattle Mariners' organization in 1st round (26th player selected) of free-agent draft, June 7, 1977.
†On disabled list, June 26 to July 22, 1980.
‡On disabled list, May 3 to May 18, 1982.
§On disabled list, August 10 to August 29, 1984.
xTraded with Infielder Spike Owen to Boston Red Sox for Infielder Rey Quinones, a player to be named later and cash, August 19, 1986; as part of deal, Seattle Mariners claimed Pitchers Mike Brown and Mike Trujillo on waivers from Boston, August 22, 1986. Seattle acquired Outfielder John Christensen to complete deal, September 25, 1986.
yTraded to San Francisco Giants for a player to be named later, September 1, 1987; Boston Red Sox acquired Outfielder Randy Kutcher to complete deal, December 9, 1987.
zGranted free agency, November 9, 1987; signed by Oakland A's, December 21, 1987.
aGranted free agency, November 4, 1988; re-signed by Athletics, December 1, 1988.

CHAMPIONSHIP SERIES RECORD

Established Championship Series record for most strikeouts, four-game Series (7), 1988.

Year	Club	League	Pos.	G.	AB.	R.	H.	2B.	3B.	HR.	RBI.	B.A.	PO.	A.	E.	F.A.
1986	—Boston	Amer.	OF	5	9	3	1	0	0	1	4	.111	11	0	0	1.000
1988	—Oakland	Amer.	OF	4	16	2	6	1	0	1	4	.375	11	0	2	.846
Championship Series Totals—2 Years				9	25	5	7	1	0	2	8	.280	22	0	2	.917

WORLD SERIES RECORD

Year	Club	League	Pos.	G.	AB.	R.	H.	2B.	3B.	HR.	RBI.	B.A.	PO.	A.	E.	F.A.
1986	—Boston	Amer.	OF	7	25	6	10	1	1	2	5	.400	22	0	0	1.000
1988	—Oakland	Amer.	OF	5	20	1	6	2	0	0	1	.300	12	0	0	1.000
World Series Totals—2 Years				12	45	7	16	3	1	2	6	.356	34	0	0	1.000

RICKEY HENLEY HENDERSON

Born December 25, 1958, at Chicago, Ill.
Height, 5.10. Weight, 195.
Throws left and bats righthanded.

Established modern major league record for most stolen bases, season (130), 1982.
Established major league record for most times caught stealing, season (42), 1982.
Tied major league record for most home runs as leadoff batter, lifetime (35).
Established American League records for most home runs as leadoff batter, season (9), 1986; most consecutive years, 50 or more stolen bases (7).
Tied American League records for most years with 50 or more stolen bases (8); most stolen bases, two consecutive games (7), July 3, 4, 1983.
Major League stolen bases: 1979 (33), 1980 (100), 1981 (56), 1982 (130), 1983 (108), 1984 (66), 1985 (80), 1986 (87), 1987 (41), 1988 (93). Total—794.
Led American League in bases on balls received with 116 in 1982 and 103 in 1983.
Led American League in stolen bases with 100 in 1980, 56 in 1981, 130 in 1982, 108 in 1983, 66 in 1984, 80 in 1985, 87 in 1986 and 93 in 1988.

Led American League in caught stealing with 26 in 1980, 22 in 1981, 42 in 1982, 19 in 1983 and tied for lead with 18 in 1986.

Led American League outfielders in total chances with 341 in 1981.

Tied for American League lead in double plays by outfielders with 5 in 1988.

Led Eastern League in stolen bases with 81 and caught stealing with 28 in 1978.

Led California League in stolen bases with 95 and caught stealing with 22 in 1977.

Led Eastern League outfielders in double plays with 4 in 1978.

Won THE SPORTING NEWS Golden Shoe Award, 1983.

Won THE SPORTING NEWS Silver Shoe Award, 1982.

Named outfielder on THE SPORTING NEWS American League All-Star Team, 1981 and 1985.

Named outfielder on THE SPORTING NEWS American League All-Star fielding team, 1981.

Named outfielder on THE SPORTING NEWS American League Silver Slugger team, 1981 and 1985.

Year Club	League	Pos.	G.	AB.	R.	H.	2B.	3B.	HR.	RBI.	B.A.	PO.	A.	E.	F.A.
1976—Boise	N'west.	OF	46	140	34	47	13	2	3	23	.336	99	3	*12	.895
1977—Modesto	Calif.	OF	134	481	120	166	18	4	11	69	.345	278	15	*20	.936
1978—Jersey City	East.	OF	133	455	81	141	14	4	0	34	.310	305	●15	7	.979
1979—Ogden	P. C.	OF	71	259	66	80	11	8	3	26	.309	149	6	6	.963
1979—Oakland	Amer.	OF	89	351	49	96	13	3	1	26	.274	215	5	6	.973
1980—Oakland	Amer.	OF	158	591	111	179	22	4	9	53	.303	407	15	7	.984
1981—Oakland	Amer.	OF	108	423	*89	*135	18	7	6	35	.319	*327	7	7	.979
1982—Oakland	Amer.	OF	149	536	119	143	24	4	10	51	.267	379	2	9	.977
1983—Oakland	Amer.	OF	145	513	105	150	25	7	9	48	.292	349	9	3	.992
1984—Oakland†	Amer.	OF	142	502	113	147	27	4	16	58	.293	341	7	11	.969
1985—Fort Lauderdale‡	Fla. St.	OF	3	6	5	1	0	1	0	3	.167	6	0	0	1.000
1985—New York	Amer.	OF	143	547	*146	172	28	5	24	72	.314	439	7	9	.980
1986—New York	Amer.	OF	153	608	*130	160	31	5	28	74	.263	426	4	6	.986
1987—New York§	Amer.	OF	95	358	78	104	17	3	17	37	.291	189	3	4	.980
1988—New York	Amer.	OF	140	554	118	169	30	2	6	50	.305	320	7	12	.965
Major League Totals—10 Years			1322	4983	1058	1455	235	44	126	504	.292	3392	66	74	.979

Selected by Oakland A's organization in 4th round of free-agent draft, June 8, 1976.

†Traded with Pitcher Bert Bradley and cash to New York Yankees for Outfielder Stan Javier and Pitchers Jay Howell, Jose Rijo, Eric Plunk and Tim Birtsas, December 5, 1984.

‡On New York disabled list, March 30 to April 22, 1985; included rehabilitation disability assignment to Fort Lauderdale, April 19 to April 22, 1985.

§On disabled list, June 5 to June 29 and July 26 to September 1, 1987.

DIVISION SERIES RECORD

Year Club	League	Pos.	G.	AB.	R.	H.	2B.	3B.	HR.	RBI.	B.A.	PO.	A.	E.	F.A.
1981—Oakland	Amer.	OF	3	11	3	2	0	0	0	0	.182	8	0	0	1.000

CHAMPIONSHIP SERIES RECORD

Tied American League Championship Series record for most stolen bases, three-game Series (2), 1981.

Year Club	League	Pos.	G.	AB.	R.	H.	2B.	3B.	HR.	RBI.	B.A.	PO.	A.	E.	F.A.
1981—Oakland	Amer.	OF	3	11	0	4	2	1	0	1	.364	6	0	1	.857

ALL-STAR GAME RECORD

Tied All-Star Game record for most one-base hits, game (3), July 13, 1982.

Year League	Pos.	AB.	R.	H.	2B.	3B.	HR.	RBI.	B.A.	PO.	A.	E.	F.A.
1980—American	OF	1	0	0	0	0	0	0	.000	0	0	0	.000
1982—American	OF	4	1	3	0	0	0	0	.750	3	0	1	.750
1983—American	OF	1	0	0	0	0	0	1	.000	0	0	0	.000
1984—American	OF	2	0	0	0	0	0	0	.000	0	0	0	.000
1985—American	OF	3	1	1	0	0	0	0	.333	1	0	0	1.000
1986—American	OF	3	0	0	0	0	0	0	.000	2	0	0	1.000
1987—American	OF	3	0	1	0	0	0	0	.333	0	0	0	.000
1988—American	OF	2	0	1	0	0	0	0	.500	1	0	0	1.000
All-Star Game Totals—8 Years		19	2	6	0	0	0	1	.316	7	0	1	.875

STEPHEN CURTIS HENDERSON
(Steve)

Born November 18, 1952, at Houston, Tex.
Height, 6.01. Weight, 185.
Throws and bats righthanded.
Attended Prairie View A & M University, Prairie View, Tex.

Major League stolen bases: 1977 (6), 1978 (13), 1979 (13), 1980 (23), 1981 (5), 1982 (6), 1983 (10), 1984 (2), 1988 (1). Total—79.

Led National League in grounding into double plays with 24 in 1978.

Led Eastern League in total bases with 255 and caught stealing with 17 in 1976.

Year Club	League	Pos.	G.	AB.	R.	H.	2B.	3B.	HR.	RBI.	B.A.	PO.	A.	E.	F.A.
1974—Billings	Pion.	OF	72	249	*60	72	19	5	●8	●44	.289	114	6	6	*.952
1975—Tampa	Fla. St.	OF-SS	123	413	59	115	9	*16	0	54	.278	263	7	8	.971
1976—Three Rivers	East.	OF	134	506	90	●158	24	*11	17	61	.312	260	12	8	.971
1977—Indianapolis†	A. A.	OF	60	233	35	76	12	6	7	25	.326	107	3	3	.973
1977—New York	Nat.	OF	99	350	67	104	16	6	12	65	.297	189	4	4	.980
1978—New York	Nat.	OF	157	587	83	156	30	9	10	65	.266	315	18	11	.968
1979—New York‡	Nat.	OF	98	350	42	107	16	8	5	39	.306	201	6	2	.990
1980—New York§	Nat.	OF	143	513	75	149	17	8	8	58	.290	299	7	6	.981
1981—Chicago x	Nat.	OF	82	287	32	84	9	5	5	35	.293	152	4	*8	.951

Year Club	League	Pos.	G.	AB.	R.	H.	2B.	3B.	HR.	RBI.	B.A.	PO.	A.	E.	F.A.
1982—Chicago y	Nat.	OF	92	257	23	60	12	4	2	29	.233	126	5	6	.956
1983—Seattle z	Amer.	OF	121	436	50	128	32	3	10	54	.294	182	15	6	.970
1984—Seattle ab	Amer.	OF	109	325	42	85	12	3	10	35	.262	84	4	6	.936
1985—Oakland	Amer.	OF	85	193	25	58	8	3	3	31	.301	79	3	4	.953
1986—Oakland c	Amer.	OF	11	26	2	2	1	0	0	3	.077	8	0	2	.800
1986—Buffalo de	A. A.	OF	72	240	37	69	8	1	5	39	.288	60	1	2	.968
1987—Tacoma	P. C.	OF	74	255	45	77	12	4	2	33	.302	122	4	2	.984
1987—Oakland f	Amer.	OF	46	114	14	33	7	0	3	9	.289	33	0	2	.943
1988—Houston	Nat.	OF-1B	42	46	4	10	2	0	0	5	.217	14	1	0	1.000
1988—Tucson g	P.C.	OF	42	133	17	37	8	0	4	18	.278	61	1	3	.954
National League Totals—7 Years			713	2390	326	670	102	40	42	296	.280	1296	45	37	.973
American League Totals—5 Years			372	1094	133	306	60	9	26	132	.280	386	22	20	.953
Major League Totals—12 Years			1085	3484	459	976	162	49	68	428	.280	1682	67	57	.968

Selected by Cincinnati Reds' organization in 5th round of free-agent draft, June 5, 1974.

†Traded with Infielder Doug Flynn, Outfielder Dan Norman and Pitcher Pat Zachry to New York Mets for Pitcher Tom Seaver, June 15, 1977.

‡On disabled list, July 31 to September 17, 1979.

§Traded with cash to Chicago Cubs for Outfielder Dave Kingman, February 28, 1981.

xOn disabled list, May 29 to August 11, 1981.

yTraded to Seattle Mariners for Pitcher Rich Bordi, December 9, 1982.

zGranted free agency, November 7, 1983; re-signed by Mariners, January 26, 1984.

aOn disabled list, June 10 to June 25, 1984.

bGranted free agency, November 8, 1984; signed by Oakland A's, March 31, 1985.

cReleased, May 29, 1986; signed by Buffalo (Chicago White Sox' organization), June 20, 1986.

dReleased, September 2, 1986; signed by Seattle Mariners' organization, February 4, 1987.

eReleased, March 31, 1987; signed by Oakland Athletics' organization, April 17, 1987.

fGranted free agency, November 9, 1987; signed by Houston Astros, March 10, 1988.

gReleased, October 3, 1988.

GEORGE ANDREW HENDRICK JR.

Born October 18, 1949, at Los Angeles, Calif.
Height, 6.03. Weight, 195.
Throws and bats righthanded.
Attended East Los Angeles Junior College, Los Angeles, Calif.
Father of Brian Hendrick, forward at University of California.

Major League stolen bases: 1972 (3), 1973 (7), 1974 (6), 1975 (6), 1976 (4), 1977 (11), 1978 (2), 1979 (2), 1980 (6), 1981 (4), 1982 (3), 1983 (3), 1985 (1), 1986 (1). Total—59.

Hit three home runs in a game, June 19, 1973.

Led National League in sacrifice flies with 14 in 1982.

Led American League outfielders in double plays with 6 in 1976.

Tied for National League lead in double plays by outfielders with 7 in 1979.

Named first baseman on THE SPORTING NEWS National League All-Star Team, 1983.

Named outfielder on THE SPORTING NEWS National League All-Star Team, 1980.

Named first baseman on THE SPORTING NEWS National League Silver Slugger team, 1983.

Named outfielder on THE SPORTING NEWS National League Silver Slugger team, 1980.

Year Club	League	Pos.	G.	AB.	R.	H.	2B.	3B.	HR.	RBI.	B.A.	PO.	A.	E.	F.A.
1968—Burlington	Midw.	OF	103	364	58	119	•25	4	5	60	★.327	134	8	8	.947
1969—Lodi	Calif.	OF	86	316	47	97	13	2	4	28	.307	121	5	4	.969
1970—Burlington	Midw.	OF	54	198	37	61	9	3	12	43	.308	80	1	5	.942
1970—Birmingham	South.	OF	54	199	30	57	12	0	6	20	.286	115	4	5	.960
1971—Iowa	A. A.	OF	63	249	57	83	9	2	21	63	.333	113	5	3	.975
1971—Oakland	Amer.	OF	42	114	8	27	4	1	0	8	.237	52	1	1	.981
1972—Iowa	A. A.	OF	8	33	0	9	0	0	0	4	.273	14	2	0	1.000
1972—Oakland†	Amer.	OF	58	121	10	22	1	1	4	15	.182	68	0	0	1.000
1973—Cleveland‡	Amer.	OF	113	440	64	118	18	0	21	61	.268	242	7	3	.988
1974—Cleveland	Amer.	OF	139	495	65	138	23	1	19	67	.279	355	9	4	.989
1975—Cleveland	Amer.	OF	145	561	82	145	21	2	24	86	.258	338	4	6	.983
1976—Cleveland§	Amer.	OF	149	551	72	146	20	3	25	81	.265	288	13	4	.987
1977—San Diego	Nat.	OF	152	541	75	168	25	2	23	81	.311	386	11	7	.983
1978—S.D. x-St.L.	Nat.	OF	138	493	64	137	31	1	20	75	.278	313	6	2	.994
1979—St. Louis	Nat.	OF	140	493	67	148	27	1	16	75	.300	254	★20	2	.993
1980—St. Louis	Nat.	OF	150	572	73	173	33	2	25	109	.302	322	10	2	.994
1981—St. Louis	Nat.	OF	101	394	67	112	19	3	18	61	.284	227	6	4	.983
1982—St. Louis	Nat.	OF	136	515	65	145	20	5	19	104	.282	238	6	5	.980
1983—St. Louis	Nat.	1B-OF	144	529	73	168	33	3	18	97	.318	904	79	8	.992
1984—St. Louis y	Nat.	OF-1B	120	441	57	122	28	1	9	69	.277	189	9	2	.990
1985—Pittsburgh z	Nat.	OF	69	256	23	59	15	0	2	25	.230	133	2	4	.971
1985—California	Amer.	OF	16	41	5	5	1	0	2	6	.122	18	1	0	1.000
1986—California	Amer.	OF-1B	102	283	45	77	13	1	14	47	.272	188	9	5	.975
1987—California a	Amer.	OF-1B	65	162	14	39	10	0	5	25	.241	114	5	3	.975
1988—California b	Amer.	OF-1B	69	127	12	31	1	0	3	19	.244	129	9	3	.979
American League Totals—10 Years			898	2895	377	748	112	9	117	415	.258	1792	58	29	.985
National League Totals—9 Years			1150	4234	564	1232	231	18	150	696	.291	2966	149	36	.989
Major League Totals—18 Years			2048	7129	941	1980	343	27	267	1111	.278	4758	207	65	.987

Selected by Oakland A's organization in 1st round (first player selected) of free-agent draft, January 27, 1968.

†Traded with Catcher Dave Duncan to Cleveland Indians for Catcher Ray Fosse and Infielder Jack Heidemann, March 24, 1973.

‡On disabled list, August 14 to September 29, 1973.
§Traded to San Diego Padres for Outfielder John Grubb, Catcher Fred Kendall and Shortstop Hector Torres, December 8, 1976.
xTraded to St. Louis Cardinals for Pitcher Eric Rasmussen, May 26, 1978.
yTraded with Catcher Steve Barnard to Pittsburgh Pirates for Pitcher John Tudor and Outfielder Brian Harper, December 12, 1984.
zTraded with Pitchers John Candelaria and Al Holland to California Angels for Pitcher Pat Clements, Outfielder Mike Brown and a player to be named later, August 2, 1985; Pittsburgh Pirates' organization acquired Pitcher Bob Kipper to complete deal, August 16, 1985.
aOn disabled list, April 22 to June 9, 1987.
bGranted free agency, November 4, 1988.

CHAMPIONSHIP SERIES RECORD

Tied American League Championship Series record for most positions played, total Series (3).

Year Club	League	Pos.	G.	AB.	R.	H.	2B.	3B.	HR.	RBI.	B.A.	PO.	A.	E.	F.A.
1972—Oakland	Amer.	PH-OF	5	7	2	1	0	0	0	0	.143	1	0	0	1.000
1982—St. Louis	Nat.	OF	3	13	2	4	0	0	0	2	.308	5	0	0	1.000
1986—California	Amer.	OF-1B	3	12	0	1	0	0	0	0	.083	16	2	0	1.000
Championship Series Totals—3 Years			11	32	4	6	0	0	0	2	.188	22	2	0	1.000

WORLD SERIES RECORD

Tied World Series record for most times awarded first base on catcher's interference, game (1), October 15, 1982.

Year Club	League	Pos.	G.	AB.	R.	H.	2B.	3B.	HR.	RBI.	B.A.	PO.	A.	E.	F.A.
1972—Oakland	Amer.	OF	5	15	3	2	0	0	0	0	.133	12	0	0	1.000
1982—St. Louis	Nat.	OF	7	28	5	9	0	0	0	5	.321	10	1	0	1.000
World Series Totals—2 Years			12	43	8	11	0	0	0	5	.256	22	1	0	1.000

ALL-STAR GAME RECORD

Year League	Pos.	AB.	R.	H.	2B.	3B.	HR.	RBI.	B.A.	PO.	A.	E.	F.A.
1974—American	OF	2	0	1	0	0	0	0	.500	3	0	0	1.000
1975—American	PR-OF	1	1	1	0	0	0	0	1.000	0	0	0	.000
1980—National	OF	2	0	1	0	0	0	1	.500	0	0	0	.000
All-Star Game Totals—3 Years		5	1	3	0	0	0	1	.600	3	0	0	1.000

Member of National League All-Star Team in 1983; did not play.

DAVID LEE HENGEL

(Dave)

Born December 18, 1961, at Oakland, Calif.
Height, 6.00. Weight, 195.
Throws and bats righthanded.
Attended University of California, Berkeley, Calif.

Led Midwest League in slugging percentage with .565 in 1984.
Led Pacific Coast League outfielders in double plays with 5 in 1986.

Year Club	League	Pos.	G.	AB.	R.	H.	2B.	3B.	HR.	RBI.	B.A.	PO.	A.	E.	F.A.
1983—Bellingham	N'west	OF	9	27	4	9	4	0	0	6	.333	10	0	0	1.000
1984—Wausau	Midw.	OF	120	441	68	136	31	2	26	98	.308	109	9	9	.929
1985—Chattanooga	South.	OF	122	460	71	132	30	5	17	89	.287	277	14	6	.980
1985—Calgary	P. C.	OF	6	23	1	2	1	0	0	3	.087	13	0	0	1.000
1986—Calgary†	P. C.	OF	113	407	73	116	22	1	27	94	.285	217	•16	8	.967
1986—Seattle	Amer.	OF	21	63	3	12	1	0	1	6	.190	9	1	0	1.000
1987—Calgary	P. C.	OF	117	448	80	132	25	2	★23	★103	.295	180	10	•11	.945
1987—Seattle	Amer.	OF	10	19	2	6	0	0	1	4	.316	7	0	1	.875
1988—Calgary	P. C.	OF	62	222	29	51	17	1	6	37	.230	67	4	3	.959
1988—Seattle	Amer.	OF	26	60	3	10	1	0	2	7	.167	20	0	1	.952
Major League Totals—3 Years			57	142	8	28	2	0	4	17	.197	36	1	2	.949

Selected by San Francisco Giants' organization in 6th round of free-agent draft, June 3, 1980.
Selected by Seattle Mariners' organization in 3rd round of free-agent draft, June 6, 1983.
†On disabled list, August 5 to August 23, 1986.

THOMAS ANTHONY HENKE

Name pronounced HEN-key.

(Tom)

Born December 21, 1957, at Kansas City, Mo.
Height, 6.05. Weight, 225.
Throws and bats righthanded.
Attended East Central College, Union, Mo.

Major League saves: 1983 (1), 1984 (2), 1985 (13), 1986 (27), 1987 (34), 1988 (25). Total—102.
Led American League in games finished in relief with 62 and saves with 34 in 1987.
Tied for International League lead in saves with 18 in 1985.
Named International League Pitcher of the Year, 1985.

Year Club	League	G.	IP.	W.	L.	Pct.	H.	R.	ER.	SO.	BB.	ERA.
1980—Sarasota Rangers	Gulf Coast	8	38	3	3	.500	33	11	4	34	12	0.95
1980—Asheville	S. Atlantic	5	23	0	2	.000	25	21	20	19	20	7.83
1981—Asheville	S. Atlantic	28	92	8	6	.571	77	36	30	67	35	2.93
1981—Tulsa	Texas	15	32	4	3	.571	31	16	14	37	14	3.94

Year	Club	League	G.	IP.	W.	L.	Pct.	H.	R.	ER.	SO.	BB.	ERA.
1982	—Tulsa	Texas	*52	87⅔	3	6	.333	69	35	26	100	40	2.67
1982	—Texas	American	8	15⅔	1	0	1.000	14	2	2	9	8	1.15
1983	—Oklahoma City	Am. Assoc.	47	77⅔	9	6	.600	71	33	26	90	33	3.01
1983	—Texas	American	8	16	1	0	1.000	16	6	6	17	4	3.38
1984	—Texas	American	25	28⅓	1	1	.500	36	21	20	25	20	6.35
1984	—Oklahoma City†	Am. Assoc.	39	64⅔	6	2	.750	59	21	19	65	25	2.64
1985	—Syracuse	Int'national	39	51⅓	2	1	.667	13	5	5	60	18	0.88
1985	—Toronto	American	28	40	3	3	.500	29	12	9	42	8	2.03
1986	—Toronto	American	63	91⅓	9	5	.643	63	39	34	118	32	3.35
1987	—Toronto	American	72	94	0	6	.000	62	27	26	128	25	2.49
1988	—Toronto	American	52	68	4	4	.500	60	23	22	66	24	2.91
	Major League Totals—7 Years		256	353⅓	19	19	.500	280	130	119	405	121	3.03

Selected by Seattle Mariners' organization in 20th round of free-agent draft, June 5, 1979.

Selected by Chicago Cubs' organization in secondary phase of free-agent draft, January 8, 1980.

Selected by Texas Rangers' organization in secondary phase of free-agent draft, June 3, 1980.

†Selected by Toronto Blue Jays' organization in player compensation pool draft, January 24, 1985. (Toronto received compensation for Texas Rangers' signing of free agent Designated Hitter Cliff Johnson, a Type A player, December 5, 1984.

CHAMPIONSHIP SERIES RECORD

Tied Championship Series record for most games won, seven-game Series (2), 1985.

Year	Club	League	G.	IP.	W.	L.	Pct.	H.	R.	ER.	SO.	BB.	ERA.
1985	—Toronto	American	3	6⅓	2	0	1.000	5	3	3	4	4	4.26

ALL-STAR GAME RECORD

Year	League	IP.	W.	L.	Pct.	H.	R.	ER.	SO.	BB.	ERA.
1987	—American	2⅔	0	0	.000	2	0	0	1	0	0.00

MICHAEL ALAN HENNEMAN
(Mike)

Born December 11, 1961, at St. Charles, Mo.
Height, 6.04. Weight, 195.
Throws and bats righthanded.
Attended Oklahoma State University, Stillwater, Okla.

Major League saves: 1987 (7), 1988 (22). Total—29.

Tied for American League lead in intentional bases on balls issued with 10 in 1988.

Named American League Rookie Pitcher of the Year by THE SPORTING NEWS, 1987.

Year	Club	League	G.	IP.	W.	L.	Pct.	H.	R.	ER.	SO.	BB.	ERA.
1984	—Birmingham	Southern	29	59⅓	4	2	.667	48	22	16	39	33	2.43
1985	—Birmingham	Southern	46	70⅓	3	5	.375	88	50	45	40	28	5.76
1986	—Nashville	Am. Assoc.	31	58	2	5	.286	57	27	19	39	23	2.95
1987	—Toledo	Int'national	11	18⅓	1	1	.500	5	3	3	19	3	1.47
1987	—Detroit†	American	55	96⅔	11	3	.786	86	36	32	75	30	2.98
1988	—Detroit‡	American	65	91⅓	9	6	.600	72	23	19	58	24	1.87
	Major League Totals—2 Years		120	188	20	9	.690	158	59	51	133	54	2.44

Selected by Toronto Blue Jays' organization in 27th round of free-agent draft, June 7, 1982.

Selected by Philadelphia Phillies' organization in secondary phase of free-agent draft, June 6, 1983.

Selected by Detroit Tigers' organization in 4th round of free-agent draft, June 4, 1984.

†Struck out in only at-bat.

‡On disabled list, May 22 to June 6, 1988.

CHAMPIONSHIP SERIES RECORD

Year	Club	League	G.	IP.	W.	L.	Pct.	H.	R.	ER.	SO.	BB.	ERA.
1987	—Detroit	American	3	5	1	0	1.000	6	6	6	3	6	10.80

DWAYNE ALLEN HENRY

Born February 16, 1962, at Elkton, Md.
Height, 6.03. Weight, 205.
Throws and bats righthanded.

Major League saves: 1985 (3), 1988 (1). Total—4.

Year	Club	League	G.	IP.	W.	L.	Pct.	H.	R.	ER.	SO.	BB.	ERA.
1980	—Sarasota Rangers	Gulf Coast	11	54	5	1	.833	36	23	16	47	28	2.67
1981	—Asheville	S. Atlantic	25	134	8	7	.533	120	81	66	86	58	4.43
1982	—Burlington†	Midwest	4	18⅔	2	0	1.000	6	0	0	25	6	0.00
1983	—Tulsa‡	Texas	9	14	0	0	.000	16	14	9	14	19	5.79
1983	—Sarasota Rangers	Gulf Coast	3	9	0	0	.000	10	6	4	11	1	4.00
1984	—Tulsa	Texas	33	85	5	8	.385	65	42	32	79	60	3.39
1984	—Texas	American	3	4⅓	0	1	.000	5	4	4	2	7	8.31
1985	—Tulsa	Texas	34	81⅓	7	6	.538	51	32	24	97	44	2.66
1985	—Texas	American	16	21	2	2	.500	16	7	6	20	7	2.57
1986	—Texas§	American	19	19⅓	1	0	1.000	14	11	10	17	22	4.66
1986	—Oklahoma City	Am. Assoc.	28	44⅓	2	1	.667	51	30	29	41	27	5.89
1987	—Oklahoma City	Am. Assoc.	30	69	4	4	.500	66	39	38	55	50	4.96
1987	—Texas	American	5	10	0	0	.000	12	10	10	7	9	9.00
1988	—Oklahoma City	Am. Assoc.	46	75⅔	5	5	.500	57	51	47	98	54	5.59

Year	Club	League	G.	IP.	W.	L.	Pct.	H.	R.	ER.	SO.	BB.	ERA.
1988	—Texas	American	11	10⅓	0	1	.000	15	10	10	10	9	8.71
	Major League Totals—5 Years		54	65	3	4	.429	62	42	40	56	54	5.54

Selected by Texas Rangers' organization in 2nd round of free-agent draft, June 3, 1980.
†On disabled list, May 4, 1982 through remainder of season.
‡On disabled list, April 8 to July 9, 1983.
§On disabled list, May 31 to July 8, 1986; included rehabilitation disability assignment to Oklahoma City, June 18 to July 8, 1986.

RICHARD DOUGLAS HENRY
(Doug)

Born December 10, 1963, at Sacramento, Calif.
Height, 6.04. Weight, 185.
Throws and bats righthanded.
Attended Arizona State University, Tempe, Ariz.

Year	Club	League	G.	IP.	W.	L.	Pct.	H.	R.	ER.	SO.	BB.	ERA.
1986	—Beloit	Midwest	27	143⅓	7	8	.467	153	95	74	115	56	4.65
1987	—Beloit	Midwest	31	132⅔	8	9	.471	145	83	72	106	51	4.88
1988	—Stockton	California	23	70⅔	7	1	.875	46	19	14	71	31	1.78
1988	—El Paso	Texas	14	45⅔	4	0	1.000	33	16	16	50	19	3.15

Selected by New York Mets' organization in 16th round of free-agent draft, June 7, 1982.
Selected by Milwaukee Brewers' organization in 8th round of free-agent draft, June 3, 1985.

CARLOS ALBERTO HERNANDEZ

Born May 24, 1967, at Bolivar, Venezuela.
Height, 5.11. Weight, 185.
Throws and bats righthanded.

Tied for Gulf Coast League lead in double plays by catcher with 3 in 1986.

Year	Club	League	Pos.	G.	AB.	R.	H.	2B.	3B.	HR.	RBI.	B.A.	PO.	A.	E.	F.A.
1985	—Braden. Dodgers	Gulf C.	3B-1B	22	49	3	12	1	0	0	0	.245	48	16	2	.970
1986	—Sarasota Dodgers	Gulf C.	C-3B	57	205	19	64	7	0	1	31	.312	217	36	10	.962
1987	—Bakersfield	Calif.	C	48	162	22	37	6	1	3	22	.228	181	26	8	.963
1988	—Bakersfield	Calif.	C	92	333	37	103	15	2	5	52	.309	480	88	14	.976
1988	—Albuquerque	P. C.	C	3	8	0	1	0	0	0	1	.125	11	0	1	.917

Signed as free agent by Los Angeles Dodgers' organization, October 10, 1984.

CESAR DARIO HERNANDEZ (PEREZ)

Born September 28, 1966, at Yamasa, Dominican Republic.
Height, 6.00. Weight, 160.
Throws and bats righthanded.
Attended University of Autonona, Santo Domingo, Dominican Republic.

Year	Club	League	Pos.	G.	AB.	R.	H.	2B.	3B.	HR.	RBI.	B.A.	PO.	A.	E.	F.A.
1985	—		(Played in Dominican Republic League)													
1986	—Burlington†‡	Midw.	OF	38	104	12	26	11	0	1	12	.250	62	1	3	.955
1987	—W. Palm Beach	Fla. St.	OF	32	106	14	25	3	1	2	6	.236	60	4	3	.955
1988	—Rockford	Midw.	OF	117	411	71	101	20	4	19	60	.246	188	9	16	.925

Signed as free agent by Montreal Expos' organization, March 2, 1985.
†Switch-hitter.
‡On disabled list, June 3, 1986 through remainder of season.

FRANCIS XAVIER HERNANDEZ

(Known by middle name.)

Born August 16, 1965, at Port Arthur, Tex.
Height, 6.02. Weight, 185.
Throws right and bats lefthanded.
Attended University of Southwestern Louisiana, Lafayette, La.

Year	Club	League	G.	IP.	W.	L.	Pct.	H.	R.	ER.	SO.	BB.	ERA.
1986	—St. Catharines	NYP	13	70⅔	5	5	.500	55	27	21	69	16	2.67
1987	—St. Catharines	NYP	13	55	3	3	.500	57	39	31	49	16	5.07
1988	—Myrtle Beach	S. Atlantic	23	148	13	6	.684	116	52	42	111	28	2.55
1988	—Knoxville	Southern	11	68⅓	2	4	.333	73	32	22	33	15	2.90

Selected by Toronto Blue Jays' organization in 4th round of free-agent draft, June 2, 1986.

GUILLERMO HERNANDEZ (VILLANUEVA)

Born November 14, 1954, at Aguada, Puerto Rico.
Height, 6.02. Weight, 185.
Throws and bats lefthanded.

Tied National League record for most consecutive strikeouts by relief pitcher, game (6), July 3, 1983.
Major League saves: 1977 (4), 1978 (3), 1981 (2), 1982 (10), 1983 (8), 1984 (32), 1985 (31), 1986 (24), 1987 (8), 1988 (10). Total—132.
Led American League in games finished in relief with 68 in 1984.
Led Western Carolinas League pitchers in games started with 26 and complete games with 13 in 1977.

Named American League Most Valuable Player by Baseball Writers' Association of America, 1984.
Named American League Pitcher of the Year by THE SPORTING NEWS, 1984.
Won American League Cy Young Memorial Award, 1984.
Named lefthanded pitcher on THE SPORTING NEWS American League All-Star Team, 1984.
Received reported $25,000 bonus to sign with Philadelphia Phillies, 1974.

Year Club	League	G.	IP.	W.	L.	Pct.	H.	R.	ER.	SO.	BB.	ERA.
1974—Spartanburg	W. Carol.	26	*190	11	11	.500	169	82	58	*179	49	2.75
1975—Reading	Eastern	13	91	8	2	.800	79	32	30	46	25	2.97
1975—Toledo	Int'national	13	80	6	4	.600	86	43	29	46	26	3.26
1976—Oklahoma City†	Am. Assoc.	25	135	8	9	.471	154	82	68	88	30	4.53
1977—Chicago	National	67	110	8	7	.533	94	42	37	78	28	3.03
1978—Chicago	National	54	60	8	2	.800	57	26	25	38	35	3.75
1979—Chicago	National	51	79	4	4	.500	85	50	44	53	39	5.01
1980—Chicago	National	53	108	1	9	.100	115	58	53	75	45	4.42
1981—Iowa	Am. Assoc.	18	74	4	5	.444	84	39	32	41	27	3.89
1981—Chicago	National	12	14	0	0	.000	14	7	6	13	8	3.86
1982—Chicago	National	75	75	4	6	.400	74	26	25	54	24	3.00
1983—Chicago‡-Philadelphia§	National	74	115⅓	9	4	.692	109	47	42	93	32	3.28
1984—Detroit	American	*80	140⅓	9	3	.750	96	30	30	112	36	1.92
1985—Detroit x	American	74	106⅔	8	10	.444	82	38	32	76	14	2.70
1986—Detroit	American	64	88⅔	8	7	.533	87	35	35	77	21	3.55
1987—Detroit y	American	45	49	3	4	.429	53	27	20	30	20	3.67
1987—Toledo	Int'national	2	3	0	0	.000	4	1	1	2	1	3.00
1988—Detroit	American	63	67⅔	6	5	.545	50	24	23	59	31	3.06
National League Totals—7 Years		386	561⅓	34	32	.515	548	256	232	404	211	3.72
American League Totals—5 Years		326	452⅓	34	29	.540	368	154	140	354	122	2.79
Major League Totals—12 Years		712	1013⅔	68	61	.527	916	410	372	758	333	3.30

Signed as free agent by Philadelphia Phillies' organization, September 11, 1973.
†Drafted by Chicago Cubs, December 6, 1976.
‡Traded to Philadelphia Phillies for Pitchers Dick Ruthven and Bill Johnson, May 22, 1983.
§Traded with First Baseman Dave Bergman to Detroit Tigers for Outfielder Glenn Wilson and Catcher-First Baseman John Wockenfuss, March 24, 1984.
xGrounded out in only at-bat.
yOn disabled list, April 9 to May 5 and May 6 to May 30, 1987; included rehabilitation disability assignment to Toledo, May 1 to May 5, 1987.

CHAMPIONSHIP SERIES RECORD

Tied Championship Series record for most games pitched, three-game Series (3), 1984.

Year Club	League	G.	IP.	W.	L.	Pct.	H.	R.	ER.	SO.	BB.	ERA.
1984—Detroit	American	3	4	0	0	.000	3	1	1	3	1	2.25
1987—Detroit	American	1	⅓	0	0	.000	2	0	0	0	0	0.00
Championship Series Totals—2 Years		4	4⅓	0	0	.000	5	1	1	3	1	2.08

WORLD SERIES RECORD

Tied World Series record for most saves, five-game Series (2), 1984.

Year Club	League	G.	IP.	W.	L.	Pct.	H.	R.	ER.	SO.	BB.	ERA.
1983—Philadelphia	National	3	4	0	0	.000	0	0	0	4	1	0.00
1984—Detroit	American	3	5⅓	0	0	.000	4	1	1	0	0	1.69
World Series Totals—2 Years		6	9⅓	0	0	.000	4	1	1	4	1	0.96

ALL-STAR GAME RECORD

Year League	IP.	W.	L.	Pct.	H.	R.	ER.	SO.	BB.	ERA.
1984—American	1	0	0	.000	1	1	1	1	0	9.00
1985—American	⅔	0	0	.000	1	0	0	2	1	0.00
All-Star Game Totals—2 Years	1⅔	0	0	.000	2	1	1	3	1	5.40

Member of American League All-Star Team in 1986; did not play.

KEITH HERNANDEZ

Born October 20, 1953, at San Francisco, Calif.
Height, 6.00. Weight, 205.
Throws and bats lefthanded.
Attended College of San Mateo, San Mateo, Calif.
Son of John Hernandez, minor league infielder, 1941 through 1950; and brother of Gary Hernandez, first baseman-outfielder in St. Louis Cardinals' organization, 1972 through 1975.

Established major league records for most game-winning RBIs, season (24), 1985; most game-winning RBIs, lifetime (129); most years leading league in double plays by first baseman (6); most assists by first baseman, lifetime (1,631).

Tied National League records for most home runs with bases filled, month (2), September, 1977; fewest errors by first baseman for leader in errors, season (13), 1983.

Major League stolen bases: 1976 (4), 1977 (7), 1978 (13), 1979 (11), 1980 (14), 1981 (12), 1982 (19), 1983 (9), 1984 (2), 1985 (3), 1986 (2), 1988 (2). Total—98.

Hit for the cycle, July 4, 1985.

Led National League in bases on balls received with 94 in 1986.

Led National League in intentional bases on balls received with 19 in 1982.

Led National League first basemen in putouts with 1,054 in 1981 and 1,586 in 1982.

Led National League first basemen in double plays with 146 in 1977, 145 in 1979, 146 in 1980, 99 in 1981, 147 in 1983 and 127 in 1984.

Led National League first basemen in total chances with 1,643 in 1979, 1,732 in 1982, 1,578 in 1983 and 1,457 in 1987.

Led National League in game-winning RBIs with 24 in 1985 and tied for lead with 21 in 1982.
Led Texas League first basemen in double plays with 101 in 1973.
Named National League Player of the Year by THE SPORTING NEWS, 1979.
Named National League co-Most Valuable Player by Baseball Writers' Association of America, 1979.
Named first baseman on THE SPORTING NEWS National League All-Star Team, 1979, 1980 and 1984 through 1986.
Named first baseman on THE SPORTING NEWS National League All-Star fielding team, 1978 through 1988.
Named first baseman on THE SPORTING NEWS National League Silver Slugger team, 1980 and 1984.

Year Club	League	Pos.	G.	AB.	R.	H.	2B.	3B.	HR.	RBI.	B.A.	PO.	A.	E.	F.A.
1972—St. Petersburg†	Fla. St.	1B	84	309	38	79	16	5	5	41	.256	682	52	7	.991
1972—Tulsa	A. A.	1B	11	29	5	7	1	0	0	1	.241	54	2	0	1.000
1973—Arkansas	Texas	1B	105	388	62	101	20	2	3	52	.260	960	61	9	★.991
1973—Tulsa	A. A.	1B	31	120	20	40	6	1	5	25	.333	289	15	1	.997
1974—Tulsa‡	A. A.	1B-OF	102	353	67	124	18	6	14	63	★.351	690	50	12	.984
1974—St. Louis	Nat.	1B	14	34	3	10	1	2	0	2	.294	70	1	2	.973
1975—Tulsa	A. A.	●1B-OF	85	324	70	107	29	3	10	48	.330	597	53	●13	.980
1975—St. Louis	Nat.	1B	64	188	20	47	8	2	3	20	.250	469	36	2	.996
1976—St. Louis	Nat.	1B	129	374	54	108	21	5	7	46	.289	862	●107	10	.990
1977—St. Louis	Nat.	1B	161	560	90	163	41	4	15	91	.291	1453	106	12	.992
1978—St. Louis	Nat.	1B	159	542	90	138	32	4	11	64	.255	1436	96	10	.994
1979—St. Louis	Nat.	1B	161	610	★116	210	★48	11	11	105	★.344	★1489	★146	8	.995
1980—St. Louis	Nat.	1B	159	595	★111	191	39	8	16	99	.321	1572	115	9	.995
1981—St. Louis	Nat.	1B-OF	103	376	65	115	27	4	8	48	.306	1056	86	3	.997
1982—St. Louis	Nat.	1B-OF	160	579	79	173	33	6	7	94	.299	1591	135	11	.994
1983—St.L.§-N.Y.	Nat.	1B	150	538	77	160	23	7	12	63	.297	★1418	147	●13	.992
1984—New York	Nat.	1B	154	550	83	171	31	0	15	94	.311	1214	★142	8	.994
1985—New York	Nat.	1B	158	593	87	183	34	4	10	91	.309	1310	★139	4	★.997
1986—New York	Nat.	1B	149	551	94	171	34	1	13	83	.310	1199	149	5	★.996
1987—New York	Nat.	1B	154	587	87	170	28	2	18	89	.290	1298	★149	10	.993
1988—New York x	Nat.	1B	95	348	43	96	16	0	11	55	.276	734	77	2	.998
Major League Totals—15 Years			1970	7025	1099	2106	416	60	157	1044	.300	17171	1631	109	.994

Selected by St. Louis Cardinals' organization in 42nd round of free-agent draft, June 8, 1971.
†On disabled list, April 10 to May 30, 1972.
‡On disabled list, April 16 to May 20, 1974.
§Traded to New York Mets for Pitchers Neil Allen and Rick Ownbey, June 15, 1983.
xOn disabled list, June 7 to June 22 and June 24 to August 5, 1988.

CHAMPIONSHIP SERIES RECORD

Tied Championship Series record for most at-bats, game (7), October 15, 1986 (16 innings).
Established National League Championship Series record for most bases on balls, seven-game Series (6), 1988.

Year Club	League	Pos.	G.	AB.	R.	H.	2B.	3B.	HR.	RBI.	B.A.	PO.	A.	E.	F.A.
1982—St. Louis	Nat.	1B	3	12	3	4	0	0	0	1	.333	35	1	0	1.000
1986—New York	Nat.	1B	6	26	3	7	1	1	0	3	.269	67	12	0	1.000
1988—New York	Nat.	1B	7	26	2	7	0	0	1	5	.269	57	4	1	.984
Championship Series Totals—3 Years			16	64	8	18	1	1	1	9	.281	159	17	1	.994

WORLD SERIES RECORD

Year Club	League	Pos.	G.	AB.	R.	H.	2B.	3B.	HR.	RBI.	B.A.	PO.	A.	E.	F.A.
1982—St. Louis	Nat.	1B	7	27	4	7	2	0	1	8	.259	62	7	2	.972
1986—New York	Nat.	1B	7	26	1	6	0	0	0	4	.231	48	4	1	.981
World Series Totals—2 Years			14	53	5	13	2	0	1	12	.245	110	11	3	.976

ALL-STAR GAME RECORD

Year League	Pos.	AB.	R.	H.	2B.	3B.	HR.	RBI.	B.A.	PO.	A.	E.	F.A.
1979—National	PH	1	0	0	0	0	0	0	.000	0	0	0	.000
1980—National	PH-1B	2	0	2	0	0	0	0	1.000	5	0	0	1.000
1984—National	1B	1	0	0	0	0	0	0	.000	1	0	0	1.000
1986—National	1B	4	0	0	0	0	0	0	.000	5	0	0	1.000
1987—National	1B	2	0	1	0	0	0	0	.500	4	2	0	1.000
All-Star Game Totals—5 Years		10	0	3	0	0	0	0	.300	15	2	0	1.000

LARRY LEE HERNDON

Born November 3, 1953, at Sunflower, Miss.
Height, 6.03. Weight, 200.
Throws and bats righthanded.
Attended Tennessee State University, Nashville, Tenn.; and Skyline College, San Bruno, Calif.

Tied major league record for most consecutive home runs, two consecutive games (4), May 16 and 18, 1982.
Major League stolen bases: 1976 (12), 1977 (4), 1978 (13), 1979 (8), 1980 (8), 1981 (15), 1982 (12), 1983 (9), 1984 (6), 1985 (2), 1986 (2), 1987 (1). Total—92.
Hit three home runs in a game, May 18, 1982.
Led Texas League in stolen bases with 50 and caught stealing with 16 in 1974.
Tied for Texas League lead in double plays by outfielders with 4 in 1974.
Named National League Rookie Player of the Year by THE SPORTING NEWS, 1976.

Year Club	League	Pos.	G.	AB.	R.	H.	2B.	3B.	HR.	RBI.	B.A.	PO.	A.	E.	F.A.
1971—Sarasota Cards	Gulf C.	OF	40	138	13	33	2	0	0	8	.239	68	4	3	.960
1972—St. Petersburg	Fla. St.	OF	7	28	2	4	0	0	0	0	.143	12	1	2	.867
1972—Sarasota R. B.	Gulf C.	OF	31	113	16	29	5	3	0	9	.257	50	5	3	.948
1972—Cedar Rapids†	Midw.	OF	7	21	1	6	0	0	0	1	.286	10	0	0	1.000
1973—St. Petersburg	Fla. St.	OF	141	485	83	139	9	5	3	41	.287	233	10	8	.968

Year Club	League	Pos.	G.	AB.	R.	H.	2B.	3B.	HR.	RBI.	B.A.	PO.	A.	E.	F.A.
1974—Arkansas	Texas	OF	132	498	74	142	16	•10	2	41	.285	325	★24	16	.956
1974—St. Louis	Nat.	OF	12	1	3	1	0	0	0	0	1.000	1	0	0	1.000
1975—Tulsa‡	A. A.	OF	22	96	13	23	5	0	1	5	.240	35	2	3	.925
1975—Phoenix	P. C.	OF	115	427	49	115	6	4	2	44	.269	287	10	10	.967
1976—Phoenix	P. C.	OF	14	57	8	14	2	1	1	5	.246	38	3	0	1.000
1976—San Francisco	Nat.	OF	115	337	42	97	11	3	2	23	.288	226	8	8	.967
1977—San Francisco§x	Nat.	OF	49	109	13	26	4	3	1	5	.239	87	2	4	.957
1978—San Francisco	Nat.	OF	151	471	52	122	15	9	1	32	.259	369	3	10	.974
1979—San Francisco	Nat.	OF	132	354	35	91	14	5	7	36	.257	196	10	8	.963
1980—San Francisco	Nat.	OF	139	493	54	127	17	11	8	49	.258	247	8	•11	.959
1981—San Francisco y	Nat.	OF	96	364	48	105	15	8	5	41	.288	207	8	5	.977
1982—Detroit	Amer.	OF	157	614	92	179	21	13	23	88	.292	328	11	6	.983
1983—Detroit	Amer.	OF	153	603	88	182	28	9	20	92	.302	283	6	★15	.951
1984—Detroit	Amer.	OF	125	407	52	114	18	5	7	43	.280	199	7	3	.986
1985—Detroit	Amer.	OF	137	442	45	108	12	7	12	37	.244	273	7	7	.976
1986—Detroit z	Amer.	OF	106	283	33	70	13	1	8	37	.247	156	2	2	.988
1987—Detroit a	Amer.	OF	89	225	32	73	13	2	9	47	.324	82	4	1	.989
1988—Detroit b	Amer.	OF	76	174	16	39	5	0	4	20	.224	21	0	0	1.000
National League Totals—7 Years			694	2129	247	569	76	39	24	186	.267	1333	39	46	.968
American League Totals—7 Years			843	2748	358	765	110	37	83	364	.278	1342	37	34	.976
Major League Totals—14 Years			1537	4877	605	1334	186	76	107	550	.274	2675	76	80	.972

Selected by St. Louis Cardinals' organization in 3rd round of free-agent draft, June 8, 1971.
†On disabled list, August 11, 1972 through remainder of season.
‡Traded with Pitcher Tony Gonzalez to San Francisco Giants for Pitcher Ron Bryant, May 9, 1975.
§On disabled list, June 19 to August 26, 1977.
xOn disqualified list, August 26, 1977 through remainder of season.
yTraded to Detroit Tigers for Pitchers Dan Schatzeder and Mike Chris, December 9, 1981.
zGranted free agency, November 12, 1986; re-signed by Tigers, December 5, 1986.
aGranted free agency, November 9, 1987; re-signed by Tigers, December 14, 1987.
bGranted free agency, November 4, 1988.

CHAMPIONSHIP SERIES RECORD

Year Club	League	Pos.	G.	AB.	R.	H.	2B.	3B.	HR.	RBI.	B.A.	PO.	A.	E.	F.A.
1984—Detroit	Amer.	OF	2	5	1	1	0	0	1	1	.200	6	0	0	1.000
1987—Detroit	Amer.	O-PH-DH	3	9	1	3	1	0	0	2	.333	2	0	1	.667
Championship Series Totals—2 Years			5	14	2	4	1	0	1	3	.286	8	0	1	.889

WORLD SERIES RECORD

Year Club	League	Pos.	G.	AB.	R.	H.	2B.	3B.	HR.	RBI.	B.A.	PO.	A.	E.	F.A.
1984—Detroit	Amer.	OF-PH	5	15	1	5	0	0	1	3	.333	6	0	0	1.000

THOMAS MITCHELL HERR
(Tom)

Born April 4, 1956, at Lancaster, Pa.
Height, 6.00. Weight, 185.
Throws right and bats left and righthanded.
Attended University of Delaware, Newark, Del.

Tied National League record for most sacrifice flies by switch-hitter, season (13), 1985.

Major League stolen bases: 1979 (1), 1980 (9), 1981 (23), 1982 (25), 1983 (6), 1984 (13), 1985 (31), 1986 (22), 1987 (19), 1988 (13). Total—162.

Led National League in sacrifice flies with 13 in 1985 and 12 in 1987.

Led National League second basemen in double plays with 74 in 1981, 106 in 1984 and 121 in 1986.

Led National League second basemen in total chances with 590 in 1981.

Led Florida State League in stolen bases with 50 in 1977.

Led Florida State League second basemen in double plays with 91 in 1977.

Named second baseman on THE SPORTING NEWS National League All-Star Team, 1985.

Year Club	League	Pos.	G.	AB.	R.	H.	2B.	3B.	HR.	RBI.	B.A.	PO.	A.	E.	F.A.
1975—Johnson City	Appal.	2B-SS	42	133	29	41	8	1	0	15	.308	74	125	5	.975
1976—St. Petersburg	Fla. St.	SS-2B	82	275	47	74	6	1	0	21	.269	133	211	18	.950
1977—St. Petersburg	Fla. St.	2B	136	★515	★80	★156	13	7	1	53	.303	★348	★430	21	★.974
1978—Arkansas	Texas	2B	89	335	70	98	23	4	3	45	.293	207	280	13	.974
1978—Springfield	A. A.	2B	33	86	16	24	6	1	0	8	.279	45	63	7	.939
1979—Springfield	A. A.	2B	109	423	74	124	20	6	6	48	.293	225	324	10	★.982
1979—St. Louis	Nat.	2B	14	10	4	2	0	0	0	1	.200	12	11	0	1.000
1980—Springfield	A. A.	2B-3B	37	141	29	44	6	2	1	16	.312	29	52	1	.988
1980—St. Louis	Nat.	2B-SS	76	222	29	55	12	5	0	15	.248	124	184	7	.978
1981—St. Louis	Nat.	2B	103	411	50	110	14	9	0	46	.268	211	★374	5	★.992
1982—St. Louis	Nat.	2B	135	493	83	131	19	4	0	36	.266	263	427	9	.987
1983—St. Louis†	Nat.	2B	89	313	43	101	14	4	2	31	.323	178	245	6	.986
1983—Arkansas	Texas	2B	3	9	0	4	3	0	0	1	.444	4	9	0	1.000
1984—St. Louis	Nat.	2B	145	558	67	154	23	2	4	49	.276	328	452	6	.992
1985—St. Louis	Nat.	2B	159	596	97	180	38	3	8	110	.302	337	448	12	.985
1986—St. Louis	Nat.	2B	152	559	48	141	30	4	2	61	.252	352	414	9	.988
1987—St. Louis‡	Nat.	2B	141	510	73	134	29	0	2	83	.263	306	350	7	.989
1988—St. Louis§	Nat.	2B	15	50	4	13	0	0	1	3	.260	28	35	1	.984

Year	Club	League	Pos.	G.	AB.	R.	H.	2B.	3B.	HR.	RBI.	B.A.	PO.	A.	E.	F.A.
1988—	Minnesota xyz	Amer.	2B-SS	86	304	42	80	16	0	1	21	.263	140	195	4	.988
National League Totals—10 Years				1029	3722	498	1021	179	31	19	435	.274	2139	2940	62	.988
American League Totals—1 Year				86	304	42	80	16	0	1	21	.263	140	195	4	.988
Major League Totals—10 Years				1115	4026	540	1101	195	31	20	456	.273	2279	3135	66	.988

Signed as free agent by St. Louis Cardinals' organization, August 22, 1974.

†On disabled list, March 25 to April 29 and August 9, 1983 through remainder of season; included rehabilitation disability assignment to Arkansas, April 18 to April 29, 1983.

‡On disabled list, April 24 to May 12, 1987.

§Traded to Minnesota Twins for Outfielder Tom Brunansky, April 22, 1988.

xOn disabled list, June 21 to July 22 and July 25 to August 18, 1988.

yTraded with Catcher Tom Nieto and Outfielder Eric Bullock to Philadelphia Phillies for Pitcher Shane Rawley and cash, October 24, 1988.

zGranted free agency, November 4, 1988; re-signed by Phillies, November 17, 1988.

CHAMPIONSHIP SERIES RECORD

Tied Championship Series record for most consecutive games, one or more runs batted in (4), 1985.

Established National League Championship Series records for most doubles (4) and most long hits (5), six-game Series, 1985.

Tied National League Championship Series record for most bases on balls, six-game Series (5), 1985.

Year	Club	League	Pos.	G.	AB.	R.	H.	2B.	3B.	HR.	RBI.	B.A.	PO.	A.	E.	F.A.
1982—	St. Louis	Nat.	2B	3	13	1	3	1	0	0	0	.231	6	10	0	1.000
1985—	St. Louis	Nat.	2B	6	21	2	7	4	0	1	6	.333	13	12	0	1.000
1987—	St. Louis	Nat.	2B	7	27	0	6	0	0	0	3	.222	12	11	1	.958
Championship Series Totals—3 Years				16	61	3	16	5	0	1	9	.262	31	33	1	.985

WORLD SERIES RECORD

Established World Series record for most double plays started, second baseman, seven-game Series (5), 1985.

Established World Series record for most runs batted in on sacrifice fly (2), October 16, 1982 (second inning).

Year	Club	League	Pos.	G.	AB.	R.	H.	2B.	3B.	HR.	RBI.	B.A.	PO.	A.	E.	F.A.
1982—	St. Louis	Nat.	2B	7	25	2	4	2	0	0	5	.160	11	19	1	.968
1985—	St. Louis	Nat.	2B	7	26	2	4	2	0	0	0	.154	11	13	0	1.000
1987—	St. Louis	Nat.	2B	7	28	2	7	0	0	1	1	.250	23	17	0	1.000
World Series Totals—3 Years				21	79	6	15	4	0	1	6	.190	45	49	1	.989

ALL-STAR GAME RECORD

Year	League	Pos.	AB.	R.	H.	2B.	3B.	HR.	RBI.	B.A.	PO.	A.	E.	F.A.
1985—	National	2B	3	1	1	1	0	0	0	.333	0	1	0	1.000

OREL LEONARD HERSHISER IV

Name pronounced Hersh-HYZ-ur.

Born September 16, 1958, at Buffalo, N. Y.

Height, 6.03. Weight, 190.

Throws and bats righthanded.

Attended Bowling Green State University, Bowling Green, O.

Brother of Gordie Hershiser, pitcher in Los Angeles Dodgers' organization.

Established major league record for most consecutive scoreless innings, season (59), August 30, sixth inning, through September 28, tenth inning, 1988.

Tied National League record for most shutouts, month (5), September, 1988.

Major League saves: 1983 (1), 1984 (2), 1987 (1), 1988 (1). Total—5.

Led National League in shutouts with 8 in 1988 and tied for lead with 4 in 1984.

Tied for National League lead in complete games with 15 in 1988.

Tied for National League lead in sacrifice hits by batters with 19 in 1988.

Led Pacific Coast League in intentional bases on balls issued with 8 in 1983.

Named Major League Player of the Year by The Sporting News, 1988.

Named National League Pitcher of the Year by The Sporting News, 1988.

Won National League Cy Young Memorial Award, 1988.

Named righthanded pitcher on The Sporting News National League All-Star Team, 1988.

Named pitcher on The Sporting News National League All-Star fielding team, 1988.

Year	Club	League	G.	IP.	W.	L.	Pct.	H.	R.	ER.	SO.	BB.	ERA.
1979—	Clinton	Midwest	15	43	4	0	1.000	33	15	10	33	17	2.09
1980—	San Antonio	Texas	49	109	5	9	.357	120	59	43	75	59	3.55
1981—	San Antonio	Texas	42	102	7	6	.538	94	54	53	95	50	4.68
1982—	Albuquerque	P. Coast	47	123⅔	9	6	.600	121	73	51	93	63	3.71
1983—	Albuquerque	P. Coast	49	134⅓	10	8	.556	132	73	61	95	57	4.09
1983—	Los Angeles	National	8	8	0	0	.000	7	6	3	5	6	3.38
1984—	Los Angeles	National	45	189⅔	11	8	.579	160	65	56	150	50	2.66
1985—	Los Angeles	National	36	239⅔	19	3	*.864	179	72	54	157	68	2.03
1986—	Los Angeles	National	35	231⅓	14	14	.500	213	112	99	153	86	3.85
1987—	Los Angeles	National	37	*264⅔	16	16	.500	247	105	90	190	74	3.06
1988—	Los Angeles	National	35	*267	•23	8	.742	208	73	67	178	73	2.26
Major League Totals—6 Years			196	1200⅓	83	49	.629	1014	433	369	833	357	2.77

Selected by Los Angeles Dodgers' organization in 17th round of free-agent draft, June 5, 1979.

CHAMPIONSHIP SERIES RECORD

Established Championship Series record for most innings pitched, Series (24⅔), 1988.

Tied Championship Series records for most games pitched, seven-game Series (4); most games started, Series (3), 1988.

Established National League Championship Series records for most hits allowed, six-game Series, (17), 1985; most hits allowed, seven-game Series (18), 1988.

Tied National League Championship Series record for most complete games pitched, total Series (2).

Year Club	League	G.	IP.	W.	L.	Pct.	H.	R.	ER.	SO.	BB.	ERA.
1985—Los Angeles	National	2	15⅓	1	0	1.000	17	6	6	5	6	3.52
1988—Los Angeles	National	4	24⅔	1	0	1.000	18	5	3	15	7	1.09
Championship Series Totals—2 Years		6	40	2	0	1.000	35	11	9	20	13	2.03

WORLD SERIES RECORD

Year Club	League	G.	IP.	W.	L.	Pct.	H.	R.	ER.	SO.	BB.	ERA.
1988—Los Angeles	National	2	18	2	0	1.000	7	2	2	17	6	1.00

ALL-STAR GAME RECORD

Year League	IP.	W.	L.	Pct.	H.	R.	ER.	SO.	BB.	ERA.
1987—National	2	0	0	.000	1	0	0	0	1	0.00
1988—National	1	0	0	.000	0	0	0	0	0	0.00
All-Star Game Totals—2 Years	3	0	0	.000	1	0	0	0	1	0.00

JOSEPH THOMAS HESKETH
(Joe)

Born February 15, 1959, at Lackawanna, N. Y.
Height, 6.02. Weight, 170.
Throws and bats lefthanded.
Attended State University of New York, Buffalo, N. Y.

Major League saves: 1984 (1), 1987 (1), 1988 (9). Total—11.
Tied for American Association lead in shutouts with 2 in 1983.
Named American Association Pitcher of the Year, 1984.

Year Club	League	G.	IP.	W.	L.	Pct.	H.	R.	ER.	SO.	BB.	ERA.
1980—West Palm Beach	Florida St.	11	75	8	2	.800	71	30	16	43	32	1.92
1980—Memphis	Southern	3	20	1	0	1.000	20	13	9	20	7	4.05
1981—Memphis†	Southern					(Did Not Play)						
1982—Memphis‡	Southern					(Did Not Play)						
1982—West Palm Beach	Florida St.	8	45⅔	3	2	.600	41	16	14	24	16	2.76
1983—Memphis	Southern	11	74	6	4	.600	82	38	25	22	25	3.04
1983—Wichita	Am. Assoc.	15	88⅓	5	5	.500	98	53	50	41	46	5.09
1984—Indianapolis	Am. Assoc.	22	147⅔	12	3	.800	120	60	50	135	54	3.05
1984—Montreal	National	11	45	2	2	.500	38	12	9	32	15	1.80
1985—Montreal§	National	25	155⅓	10	5	.667	125	52	43	113	45	2.49
1986—Montreal x	National	15	82⅔	6	5	.545	92	46	46	67	31	5.01
1987—Bradenton Expos	Gulf Coast	2	4⅓	0	0	.000	7	4	4	8	0	8.31
1987—Jacksonville	Southern	6	19⅔	1	0	1.000	18	6	5	22	4	2.29
1987—Montreal	National	18	28⅔	0	0	.000	23	12	10	31	15	3.14
1988—Indianapolis	Am. Assoc.	8	11	0	0	.000	10	5	4	16	5	3.27
1988—Montreal	National	60	72⅔	4	3	.571	63	30	23	64	35	2.85
Major League Totals—5 Years		129	384⅓	22	15	.595	341	152	131	307	141	3.07

Selected by Montreal Expos' organization in 2nd round of free-agent draft, June 3, 1980.
†On disabled list, April 9, 1981, through remainder of season.
‡On disabled list, April 8 to July 8, 1982.
§On disabled list, August 24, 1985 through remainder of season.
xOn disabled list, July 4, 1986 through remainder of season.

ERIC PAUL HETZEL

Born September 25, 1963, at Crowley, La.
Height, 6.03. Weight, 175.
Throws and bats righthanded.
Attended Eastern Oklahoma State College, Wilburton, Okla., and Louisiana State University, Baton Rouge, La.

Year Club	League	G.	IP.	W.	L.	Pct.	H.	R.	ER.	SO.	BB.	ERA.
1985—Greensboro	S. Atlantic	15	76	7	5	.853	87	54	47	82	48	5.57
1986—Greensboro†	S. Atlantic					(Did not play)						
1987—Winter Haven	Florida St.	26	192⅔	10	12	.455	186	94	76	136	87	3.55
1988—Pawtucket	Int'national	22	127⅓	6	10	3.75	129	67	56	122	51	3.96

Selected by Boston Red Sox' organization in 5th round of free-agent draft, January 11, 1983.
Selected by Kansas City Royals' organization in 2nd round of free-agent draft, January 17, 1984.
Selected by Pittsburgh Pirates' organization in secondary phase of free-agent draft, June 4, 1984.
Selected by Boston Red Sox' organization in secondary phase of free-agent draft, June 3, 1985.
†On disabled list, April 9, 1986 through entire season.

—DID YOU KNOW—

That the Oakland Athletics were shut out in both games of a doubleheader at home last year? The Minnesota Twins delivered the double-whammy, beating the Athletics 11-0 and 5-0 June 26.

JAMES GREGORY HIBBARD
(Greg)

Born September 13, 1964, at New Orleans, La.
Height, 6.00. Weight, 180.
Throws and bats lefthanded.
Attended Mississippi Gulf Coast Junior College, Perkinston, Miss., and University of Alabama, Tuscaloosa, Ala.

Year Club	League	G.	IP.	W.	L.	Pct.	H.	R.	ER.	SO.	BB.	ERA.
1986—Eugene	Northwest	26	39	5	2	.714	30	23	15	44	19	3.46
1987—Appleton	Midwest	9	64⅔	7	2	.778	53	17	8	61	18	1.11
1987—Fort Myers	Florida St.	3	24	2	1	.667	20	5	5	20	3	1.88
1987—Memphis†	Southern	16	106	7	6	.538	102	48	38	56	21	3.23
1988—Vancouver	P. Coast	25	144⅓	11	11	.500	155	74	66	65	44	4.12

Selected by Houston Astros' organization in 8th round of free-agent draft, January 17, 1984.
Selected by Kansas City Royals' organization in 16th round of free-agent draft, June 2, 1986.
†Traded with Pitchers Melido Perez, John Davis and Chuck Mount to Chicago White Sox for Pitcher Floyd Bannister and Third Baseman Dave Cochrane, December 10, 1987.

TEODORO HIGUERA (VALENZUELA)

Name pronounced Tea-O-door-RO Hugh-gare-a Val-en-ZWAY-luh.

(Ted)

Born November 9, 1958, at Las Mochis, Mexico.
Height, 5.10. Weight, 180.
Throws left and bats left and righthanded.

Tied for Mexican League lead in games started by pitchers with 27 and complete games with 18 in 1983.
Named lefthanded pitcher on The Sporting News American League All-Star Team, 1986.
Named American League Rookie Pitcher of the Year by The Sporting News, 1985.

Year Club	League	G.	IP.	W.	L.	Pct.	H.	R.	ER.	SO.	BB.	ERA.
1979—Ciudad Juarez	Mexican	2	1	0	1	.000	4	5	5	1	4	45.00
1980—Ciudad Juarez†	Mexican	19	117	8	3	.727	111	30	24	76	59	1.85
1980—Ciudad Juarez‡	Mexican	8	49	2	5	.286	44	22	20	29	17	3.67
1981—Ciudad Juarez	Mexican	28	203	16	9	.640	207	81	70	157	69	3.10
1982—Ciudad Juarez	Mexican	24	142⅓	9	12	.429	163	77	64	74	53	4.05
1983—Ciudad Juarez§	Mexican	27	*222	•17	8	.680	177	61	50	*165	68	2.03
1984—El Paso	Texas	19	121	8	7	.533	116	57	35	99	43	*2.60
1984—Vancouver	P. Coast	8	40	1	4	.200	49	26	21	29	14	4.73
1985—Milwaukee	American	32	212⅓	15	8	.652	186	105	92	127	63	3.90
1986—Milwaukee	American	34	248⅓	20	11	.645	226	84	77	207	74	2.79
1987—Milwaukee	American	35	261⅔	18	10	.643	236	120	112	240	87	3.85
1988—Milwaukee	American	31	227⅓	16	9	.640	168	66	62	192	59	2.45
Major League Totals—4 Years		132	949⅔	69	38	.645	816	375	343	766	283	3.25

†20-team season.
‡6-team season.
§Sold to Vancouver (Milwaukee Brewers' organization), September 13, 1983.

ALL-STAR GAME RECORD

Year League	IP.	W.	L.	Pct.	H.	R.	ER.	SO.	BB.	ERA.
1986—American	3	0	0	.000	1	0	0	2	1	0.00

DONALD EARL HILL
(Donnie)

Born November 12, 1960, at Pomona, Calif.
Height, 5.10. Weight, 160.
Throws right and bats left and righthanded.
Attended Orange Coast College, Costa Mesa, Calif.; and Arizona State University, Tempe, Ariz.

Major League stolen bases: 1983 (1), 1984 (1), 1985 (9), 1986 (5), 1987 (1), 1988 (3). Total—20.
Tied for Eastern League lead in sacrifice flies with 8 in 1982.

Year Club	League	Pos.	G.	AB.	R.	H.	2B.	3B.	HR.	RBI.	B.A.	PO.	A.	E.	F.A.
1981—Modesto	Calif.	SS-2B	46	149	21	29	3	0	6	22	.195	44	84	22	.853
1982—West Haven†	East.	SS-3B	132	405	66	103	21	3	10	59	.254	141	301	29	.938
1983—Tacoma‡	P. C.	SS	93	322	45	101	19	2	14	63	.314	148	256	18	.957
1983—Oakland	Amer.	SS	53	158	20	42	7	0	2	15	.266	87	136	9	.961
1984—Oakland§	Amer.	SS-2B-3B	73	174	21	40	6	0	2	16	.230	102	128	12	.950
1984—Tacoma	P. C.	SS-2B	42	141	28	46	12	3	2	24	.326	71	92	4	.976
1985—Oakland	Amer.	2B	123	393	45	112	13	2	3	48	.285	228	320	15	.973
1986—Oakland x	Amer.	2B-3B-SS	108	339	37	96	16	2	4	29	.283	104	213	9	.972
1987—Chicago y	Amer.	2B-3B	111	410	57	98	14	6	9	46	.239	167	278	14	.969
1987—Hawaii	P. C.	2B	7	23	10	9	2	0	2	6	.391	11	11	0	1.000
1988—Chicago	Amer.	2B-3B	83	221	17	48	6	1	2	20	.217	118	152	8	.971
1988—Vancouver	P. C.	2B	7	26	5	9	4	0	0	7	.346	4	10	1	.933
Major League Totals—6 Years			551	1695	197	436	62	11	22	174	.257	806	1227	67	.968

Selected by Houston Astros' organization in 5th round of free-agent draft, January 8, 1980.
Selected by San Francisco Giants' organization in secondary phase of free-agent draft, June 3, 1980.
Selected by Oakland A's organization in secondary phase of free-agent draft, June 8, 1981.
†On temporary inactive list, April 13 to April 23, 1982.

‡On disabled list, April 30 to May 10, 1983.
§On disabled list, May 3 to May 18, 1984.
xTraded to Chicago White Sox for Pitcher Gene Nelson and a player to be named later, December 11, 1986; Oakland A's acquired Pitcher Bruce Tanner to complete deal, December 18, 1986.
yOn disabled list, May 30 to June 14 and July 29 to August 13, 1987; included rehabilitation disability assignment to Hawaii, June 6 to June 14, 1987.

KENNETH WADE HILL
(Ken)

Born December 14, 1965, at Lynn, Mass.
Height, 6.02. Weight, 175.
Throws and bats righthanded.

Year Club	League	G.	IP.	W.	L.	Pct.	H.	R.	ER.	SO.	BB.	ERA.
1985—Gastonia	S. Atlantic	15	69	3	6	.333	60	51	38	48	57	4.96
1986—Gastonia	S. Atlantic	22	122⅔	9	5	.643	95	51	38	86	80	2.79
1986—Glens Falls†	Eastern	1	7	0	1	.000	4	4	4	4	6	5.14
1986—Arkansas	Texas	3	18	1	2	.333	18	10	9	9	7	4.50
1987—Arkansas	Texas	18	53⅔	3	5	.375	60	33	31	48	30	5.20
1988—St. Louis‡	National	4	14	0	1	.000	16	9	8	6	6	5.14
1988—Arkansas	Texas	22	115⅓	9	9	.500	129	76	63	107	50	4.92
Major League Totals—1 Year		4	14	0	1	.000	16	9	8	6	6	5.14

Signed as free agent by Detroit Tigers' organization, February 14, 1985.
†Traded with a player to be named later to St. Louis Cardinals for Catcher Mike Heath, August 10, 1986; St. Louis acquired First Baseman Mike Laga to complete deal, September 2, 1986.
‡On disabled list, March 26 to May 9, 1988.

SHAWN PATRICK HILLEGAS

Name pronounced HILL-uh-gus.

Born August 21, 1964, at Dos Palos, Calif.
Height, 6.02. Weight, 208.
Throws and bats righthanded.
Attended Middle Georgia College, Cochran, Ga.

Year Club	League	G.	IP.	W.	L.	Pct.	H.	R.	ER.	SO.	BB.	ERA.
1984—Vero Beach	Florida St.	13	93⅓	5	3	.625	71	25	19	64	33	1.83
1985—San Antonio	Texas	23	139⅓	4	10	.286	134	72	49	56	67	3.17
1986—San Antonio	Texas	17	132⅓	9	5	.643	107	60	45	97	58	3.06
1986—Albuquerque	P. Coast	9	46⅔	1	5	.167	48	35	32	43	31	6.17
1987—Albuquerque	P. Coast	24	165⅔	13	5	.722	172	79	62	105	64	3.37
1987—Los Angeles	National	12	58	4	3	.571	52	27	23	51	31	3.57
1988—Albuquerque	P. Coast	16	100⅔	6	4	.600	93	44	39	66	22	3.49
1988—Los Angeles†	National	11	56⅔	3	4	.429	54	26	26	30	17	4.13
1988—Chicago	American	6	40	3	2	.600	30	16	14	26	18	3.15
National League Totals—2 Years		23	114⅔	7	7	.500	106	53	49	81	48	3.85
American League Totals—1 Year		6	40	3	2	.600	30	16	14	26	18	3.15
Major League Totals—2 Years		29	154⅔	10	9	.526	136	69	63	107	66	3.67

Selected by California Angels' organization in 26th round of free-agent draft, June 6, 1983.
Selected by Los Angeles Dodgers' organization in secondary phase of free-agent draft, January 17, 1984.
†Traded to Chicago White Sox, September 2, 1988, completing deal in which Chicago traded Pitcher Rick Horton to Los Angeles Dodgers for a player to be named later, August 30, 1988.

THOMAS LEE HINZO
(Tommy)

Born June 18, 1964, at San Diego, Calif.
Height, 5.10. Weight, 175.
Throws right and bats left and righthanded.
Attended Southwestern College, Chula Vista, Calif., and
University of Arizona, Tucson, Ariz.

Major League stolen bases: 1987 (9).
Led Pacific Coast League second basemen in double plays with 94 in 1988.

Year Club	League	Pos.	G.	AB.	R.	H.	2B.	3B.	HR.	RBI.	B.A.	PO.	A.	E.	F.A.
1986—Batavia	NYP	2B	55	219	35	73	7	3	1	15	*.333	112	135	12	.954
1987—Kinston	Carol.	2B	65	266	64	74	11	1	0	25	.278	129	186	13	.960
1987—Williamsport	East.	2B	26	99	16	24	2	1	0	9	.242	58	78	3	.978
1987—Cleveland	Amer.	2B	67	257	31	68	9	3	3	21	.265	115	204	9	.973
1988—Colorado Springs	P. C.	2B-SS	119	449	67	104	16	4	1	29	.232	236	391	19	.971
Major League Totals—1 Year			67	257	31	68	9	3	3	21	.265	115	204	9	.973

Selected by Cleveland Indians' organization in 1st round (third player selected) of free-agent draft, January 17, 1984.
Selected by New York Mets' organization in secondary phase of free-agent draft, June 4, 1984.
Selected by Pittsburgh Pirates' organization in secondary phase of free-agent draft, June 3, 1985.
Selected by Cleveland Indians' organization in 7th round of free-agent draft, June 2, 1986.

GUY ALAN HOFFMAN

Born July 9, 1956, at Ottawa, Ill.
Height, 5.09. Weight, 175.
Throws and bats lefthanded.
Attended Bradley University, Peoria, Ill.

Major League saves: 1979 (2), 1980 (1). Total—3.

Year Club	League	G.	IP.	W.	L.	Pct.	H.	R.	ER.	SO.	BB.	ERA.
1978—Appleton	Midwest	7	34	2	0	1.000	22	10	9	31	15	2.38
1979—Appleton	Midwest	2	5	0	0	.000	2	0	0	4	1	0.00
1979—Iowa	Am. Assoc.	13	70	6	0	1.000	62	30	26	34	40	3.34
1979—Chicago	American	24	30	0	5	.000	30	18	18	18	23	5.40
1980—Iowa	Am. Assoc.	15	75	6	3	.667	59	31	30	56	34	3.60
1980—Chicago	American	23	38	1	0	1.000	38	12	11	24	17	2.61
1981—Edmonton	P. Coast	20	111	4	6	.400	117	70	53	71	60	4.30
1982—Edmonton	P. Coast	28	138⅓	8	•14	.364	186	129	106	72	67	6.90
1983—Denver	Am. Assoc.	32	52⅔	5	3	.625	49	23	22	50	23	3.76
1983—Chicago	American	11	6	1	0	1.000	14	5	5	2	2	7.50
1984—Denver†	Am. Assoc.	35	112	4	8	.333	124	71	59	76	40	4.74
1985—Iowa‡	Am. Assoc.	9	36	4	0	1.000	23	9	6	37	17	1.50
1986—Iowa	Am. Assoc.	9	59⅓	4	0	1.000	50	14	14	48	20	2.12
1986—Chicago§	National	32	84	6	2	.750	92	37	36	47	29	3.86
1987—Cincinnati x	National	36	158⅔	9	10	.474	160	83	77	87	49	4.37
1988—Texas	American	11	22⅓	0	0	.000	22	14	13	9	8	5.24
1988—Oklahoma City yz	Am. Assoc.	7	41	3	2	.600	40	14	14	26	11	3.07
American League Totals—4 Years		69	96⅓	2	5	.286	104	49	47	53	50	4.39
National League Totals—2 Years		68	242⅔	15	12	.556	252	120	113	134	78	4.19
Major League Totals—6 Years		137	339	17	17	.500	356	169	160	187	128	4.25

Signed as free agent by Chicago White Sox' organization, July 17, 1978.

†Released, October 19, 1984; signed by Chicago Cubs' organization, January 3, 1985.

‡On disabled list, April 12 to May 31 and June 1 to July 12, 1985.

§Traded to Cincinnati Reds for a player to be named later, February 17, 1987; Chicago Cubs' organization acquired Infielder Wade Rowdon to complete deal, February 23, 1987.

xReleased, March 29, 1988; signed by Texas Rangers, April 4, 1988.

yOn disabled list, May 5 to June 1, 1988.

zReleased, October 11, 1988.

CHRISTOPHER ALLEN HOILES
(Chris)

Born March 20, 1965, at Bowling Green, O.
Height, 6.00. Weight, 195.
Throws and bats righthanded.
Attended Eastern Michigan University, Ypsilanti, Mich.

Led Eastern League in slugging percentage with .500 in 1988.

Led Appalachian League in game-winning RBIs with 10 and total bases with 143 in 1986.

Led Appalachian League first basemen in putouts with 515, total chances with 551 and fielding percentage with .996 in 1986.

Tied for Eastern League lead in double plays by catchers with 5 in 1988.

Year Club	League	Pos.	G.	AB.	R.	H.	2B.	3B.	HR.	RBI.	B.A.	PO.	A.	E.	F.A.
1986—Bristol	Appal.	1B-C	•68	253	42	81	*19	2	13	*57	.320	563	38	4	.993
1987—Glens Falls	East.	C-1B-3B	108	380	47	105	12	0	13	53	.276	406	88	11	.978
1988—Glens Falls†	East.	C-1B	103	360	67	102	21	3	•17	73	.283	438	57	7	.986
1988—Toledo	Int.	C	22	69	4	11	1	0	2	6	.159	71	2	1	.986

Selected by Detroit Tigers' organization in 19th round of free-agent draft, June 2, 1986.

†Traded with Pitchers Cesar Mejia and Robinson Garces to Baltimore Orioles, September 9, 1988, to complete deal in which Baltimore traded Outfielder Fred Lynn to Detroit Tigers for three players to be named later, August 31, 1988.

BRIAN SCOTT HOLMAN

Born January 25, 1965, at Denver, Colo.
Height, 6.04. Weight, 185.
Throws and bats righthanded.

Led Southern League in complete games with 6 in 1987.

Named Southern League Pitcher of the Year, 1987.

Year Club	League	G.	IP.	W.	L.	Pct.	H.	R.	ER.	SO.	BB.	ERA.
1983—Jamestown†	NYP	2	5⅓	0	0	.000	7	7	7	5	4	11.81
1984—West Palm Beach	Florida St.	4	8	0	3	.000	14	19	16	14	21	18.00
1984—Gastonia	S. Atlantic	20	90⅔	5	8	.385	76	58	48	94	98	4.76
1985—West Palm Beach	Florida St.	25	143⅓	9	9	.500	124	79	63	103	90	3.96
1986—Jacksonville	Southern	27	157⅔	11	9	.550	146	111	90	118	*122	5.14
1987—Jacksonville	Southern	22	151⅓	14	5	.737	114	52	42	115	56	*2.50
1987—Indianapolis	Am. Assoc.	6	34⅔	0	4	.000	41	28	24	27	33	6.23
1988—Indianapolis	Am. Assoc.	14	91⅓	8	1	.889	78	26	24	70	30	2.36
1988—Montreal	National	18	100⅓	4	8	.333	101	39	36	58	34	3.23
Major League Totals—1 Year		18	100⅓	4	8	.333	101	39	36	58	34	3.23

Selected by Montreal Expos' organization in 1st round (16th player selected) of free-agent draft, June 6, 1983.

†On disabled list, August 3, 1983 through remainder of season.

SHAWN LeROY HOLMAN

Born November 10, 1964, at Sewickley, Pa.
Height, 6.02. Weight, 185.
Throws and bats righthanded.

Year Club	League	G.	IP.	W.	L.	Pct.	H.	R.	ER.	SO.	BB.	ERA.
1982—Bradenton Pirates	Gulf Coast	7	47	5	1	.833	35	20	14	33	11	2.68
1983—Greenwood	S. Atlantic	22	102⅔	5	9	.357	126	80	66	60	49	5.79
1984—Macon	S. Atlantic	9	46⅔	3	2	.600	48	19	10	32	25	1.93
1984—Prince William	Carolina	15	77⅔	7	4	.636	74	46	35	47	49	4.06
1985—Prince William	Carolina	24	141⅓	10	11	.476	123	69	56	65	53	3.54
1985—Nashua	Eastern	2	8	0	1	.000	10	6	4	2	7	4.50
1986—Nashua	Eastern	25	109⅓	4	•13	.235	108	61	58	39	67	4.77
1987—Harrisburg†-Glens Falls	Eastern	45	104⅓	5	6	.455	116	65	54	49	60	4.66
1988—Glens Falls	Eastern	52	91⅔	8	3	.727	82	36	19	44	26	1.87

Selected by Pittsburgh Pirates' organization in 14th round of free-agent draft, June 7, 1982.
†Traded with First Baseman Pete Rice to Detroit Tigers for Outfielder Terry Harper, June 26, 1987.

BRIAN JOHN HOLTON

Born November 29, 1959, at McKeesport, Pa.
Height, 6.00. Weight, 195.
Throws and bats righthanded.
Attended Louisburg College, Louisburg, N. C.

Major League saves: 1987 (2), 1988 (1). Total—3.
Tied for Pacific Coast League lead in games started by pitchers with 27 in 1986.
Tied for Texas League lead in complete games with 16 in 1980.
Tied for California League lead in shutouts with 3 in 1979.

Year Club	League	G.	IP.	W.	L.	Pct.	H.	R.	ER.	SO.	BB.	ERA.
1978—Clinton†	Midwest	14	79	6	4	.600	94	51	38	54	23	4.33
1979—Lodi	California	10	72	7	0	1.000	47	26	21	72	32	2.63
1979—San Antonio	Texas	13	51	3	5	.375	50	24	21	40	25	3.71
1980—San Antonio	Texas	27	207	•15	10	.600	204	93	79	139	65	3.43
1981—Albuquerque	P. Coast	26	191	16	6	.727	215	94	73	73	51	3.44
1982—Albuquerque	P. Coast	32	161⅓	12	8	.600	191	102	92	76	60	5.13
1983—Albuquerque‡	P. Coast	20	97⅔	7	5	.583	113	76	69	70	50	6.36
1984—Albuquerque §x	P. Coast	12	32	0	0	.000	39	23	20	15	9	5.63
1985—Albuquerque	P. Coast	27	179⅔	9	10	.474	183	83	72	86	40	3.61
1985—Los Angeles	National	3	4	1	1	.500	9	7	4	1	1	9.00
1986—Albuquerque	P. Coast	27	★182⅔	10	10	.500	200	90	74	105	20	3.78
1986—Los Angeles	National	12	24⅓	2	3	.400	28	13	12	24	6	4.44
1987—Los Angeles	National	53	83⅓	3	2	.600	87	39	36	58	32	3.89
1988—Los Angeles y	National	45	84⅔	7	3	.700	69	19	16	49	26	1.70
Major League Totals—4 Years		113	196⅓	13	9	.591	193	78	68	132	65	3.12

Selected by Los Angeles Dodgers' organization in 1st round (22nd player selected) of free-agent draft, January 10, 1978.
†On temporary inactive list, June 12 to July 7, 1978.
‡On disabled list, June 28 to July 15, 1983.
§On disabled list, April 7 to July 11, 1984.
xGranted free agency, October 15, 1984; re-signed by Dodgers' organization, October 22, 1984.
yTraded with Pitcher Ken Howell and Shortstop Juan Bell to Baltimore Orioles for First Baseman Eddie Murray, December 4, 1988.

CHAMPIONSHIP SERIES RECORD

Year Club	League	G.	IP.	W.	L.	Pct.	H.	R.	ER.	SO.	BB.	ERA.
1988—Los Angeles	National	3	4	0	0	.000	2	1	1	2	1	2.25

WORLD SERIES RECORD

Year Club	League	G.	IP.	W.	L.	Pct.	H.	R.	ER.	SO.	BB.	ERA.
1988—Los Angeles	National	1	2	0	0	.000	0	0	0	0	1	0.00

FREDERICK WAYNE HONEYCUTT
(Rick)

Born June 29, 1954, at Chattanooga, Tenn.
Height, 6.01. Weight, 190.
Throws and bats lefthanded.
Received bachelor of science degree in health education from
University of Tennessee, Knoxville, Tenn.

Major League saves: 1985 (1), 1988 (7). Total—8.
Tied for New York-Pennsylvania League lead in complete games with 7 in 1976.

Year Club	League	G.	IP.	W.	L.	Pct.	H.	R.	ER.	SO.	BB.	ERA.
1976—Niagara Falls†	NYP	13	★97	5	3	.625	91	36	28	★98	20	2.60
1977—Shreveport‡§	Texas	21	135	10	6	.625	144	53	37	82	42	★2.47
1977—Seattle	American	10	29	0	1	.000	26	16	14	17	11	4.34
1978—Seattle x	American	26	134	5	11	.313	150	81	73	50	49	4.90
1979—Seattle	American	33	194	11	12	.478	201	103	87	83	67	4.04
1980—Seattle y	American	30	203	10	17	.370	221	99	89	79	60	3.95
1981—Texas	American	20	128	11	6	.647	120	49	47	40	17	3.30
1982—Texas	American	30	164	5	17	.227	201	103	96	64	54	5.27

Year	Club	League	G.	IP.	W.	L.	Pct.	H.	R.	ER.	SO.	BB.	ERA.
1983	—Texas z	American	25	174⅔	14	8	.636	168	59	47	56	37	*2.42
1983	—Los Angeles	National	9	39	2	3	.400	46	26	25	18	13	5.77
1984	—Los Angeles	National	29	183⅔	10	9	.526	180	72	58	75	51	2.84
1985	—Los Angeles	National	31	142	8	12	.400	141	71	54	67	49	3.42
1986	—Los Angeles	National	32	171	11	9	.550	164	71	63	100	45	3.32
1987	—Los Angeles a	National	27	115⅔	2	12	.143	133	74	59	92	45	4.59
1987	—Oakland	American	7	23⅔	1	4	.200	25	17	14	10	9	5.32
1988	—Oakland b	American	55	79⅔	3	2	.600	74	36	31	47	25	3.50
American League Totals—9 Years			236	1130	60	78	.435	1186	563	498	446	329	3.97
National League Totals—5 Years			128	651⅓	33	45	.423	664	314	259	352	203	3.58
Major League Totals—12 Years			364	1781⅓	93	123	.431	1850	877	757	798	532	3.82

Selected by Baltimore Orioles' organization in 14th round of free-agent draft, June 6, 1972.

Selected by Pittsburgh Pirates' organization in 17th round of free-agent draft, June 8, 1976.

†Played two games as first baseman and one game as shortstop.

‡Traded to Seattle Mariners, August 22, 1977, completing deal in which Seattle traded Pitcher Dave Pagan to Pittsburgh Pirates for a player to be named later, July 27, 1977.

§Appeared as shortstop with no chances.

xOn disabled list, May 20 to June 26, 1978.

yTraded with Catcher Larry Cox, Outfielders Willie Horton and Leon Roberts and Shortstop Mario Mendoza to Texas Rangers for Pitchers Brian Allard, Ken Clay, Steve Finch and Jerry Don Gleaton, Shortstop Rick Auerbach and Outfielder Richie Zisk, December 12, 1980.

zTraded to Los Angeles Dodgers for Pitcher Dave Stewart and a player to be named later, August 19, 1983; Texas Rangers acquired Pitcher Ricky Wright to complete deal, September 16, 1983.

aTraded to Oakland Athletics for a player to be named later, August 29, 1987; Los Angeles Dodgers acquired Pitcher Tim Belcher to complete deal, September 3, 1987.

bGranted free agency, November 4, 1988; re-signed by Athletics, December 21, 1988.

CHAMPIONSHIP SERIES RECORD

Year	Club	League	G.	IP.	W.	L.	Pct.	H.	R.	ER.	SO.	BB.	ERA.
1983	—Los Angeles	National	2	1⅔	0	0	.000	4	4	4	2	0	21.60
1985	—Los Angeles	National	2	1⅓	0	0	.000	4	2	2	1	2	13.50
1988	—Oakland	American	3	2	1	0	1.000	0	0	0	0	2	0.00
Championship Series Totals—3 Years			7	5	1	0	1.000	8	6	6	3	4	10.80

WORLD SERIES RECORD

Year	Club	League	G.	IP.	W.	L.	Pct.	H.	R.	ER.	SO.	BB.	ERA.
1988	—Oakland	American	3	3⅓	1	0	1.000	0	0	0	5	0	0.00

ALL-STAR GAME RECORD

Year	League	IP.	W.	L.	Pct.	H.	R.	ER.	SO.	BB.	ERA.
1983	—American	2	0	0	.000	5	2	2	0	0	9.00

Member of American League All-Star Team in 1980; did not play.

DENNIS RAY HOOD

Born July 3, 1966, at Glendale, Calif.
Height, 6.02. Weight, 170.
Throws and bats righthanded.

Led Southern League batters in strikeouts with 139 in 1988.

Led South Atlantic League outfielders in total chances with 328 in 1986.

Year	Club	League	Pos.	G.	AB.	R.	H.	2B.	3B.	HR.	RBI.	B.A.	PO.	A.	E.	F.A.
1984	—Bradenton Brav.	Gulf C.	OF	49	155	16	31	7	0	1	18	.200	96	3	3	.971
1985	—Bradenton Brav.	Gulf C.	OF	59	204	19	49	14	0	1	17	.240	103	8	●6	.949
1986	—Sumter	S. Atl.	OF	*135	*562	104	142	25	3	7	42	.253	*305	11	12	.963
1987	—Durham	Carol.	OF	120	438	73	118	19	4	13	62	.269	275	15	9	.970
1988	—Greenville	South.	OF	141	525	85	135	15	●8	14	47	.257	271	21	6	.980

Selected by Atlanta Braves' organization in 12th round of free-agent draft, June 4, 1984.

SAMUEL LEE HORN
(Sam)

Born November 2, 1963, at Dallas, Tex.
Height, 6.05. Weight, 240.
Throws and bats lefthanded.

Tied American League record for most home runs, first two major league games (2), July 25 and 26, 1987.

Led International League in slugging percentage with .649 in 1987.

Led Carolina League in slugging percentage with .538 in 1984.

Tied for International League lead in intentional bases on balls received with 10 in 1988.

Year	Club	League	Pos.	G.	AB.	R.	H.	2B.	3B.	HR.	RBI.	B.A.	PO.	A.	E.	F.A.
1982	—Elmira	NYP	1B	61	213	47	64	13	1	11	48	.300	368	29	11	.973
1983	—Winston-Salem†	Carol.	1B	68	217	33	52	9	0	9	29	.240	363	24	10	.975
1984	—Winston-Salem	Carol.	1B	127	403	67	126	22	3	21	89	.313	978	*70	*29	.973
1985	—New Britain	East.	1B	134	457	64	129	*32	0	11	82	.282	751	63	*23	.973
1986	—New Britain	East.	1B	100	345	41	85	13	0	8	46	.246	356	28	9	.977
1986	—Pawtucket	Int.	1B	20	77	8	15	2	0	3	14	.195	61	4	0	1.000
1987	—Pawtucket	Int.	1B	94	333	57	107	19	0	30	84	.321	28	2	2	.938
1987	—Boston	Amer.	DH	46	158	31	44	7	0	14	34	.278	0	0	0	.000

Year	Club	League	Pos.	G.	AB.	R.	H.	2B.	3B.	HR.	RBI.	B.A.	PO.	A.	E.	F.A.
1988—	Boston	Amer.	DH	24	61	4	9	0	0	2	8	.148	0	0	0	.000
1988—	Pawtucket	Int.	1B	83	279	33	65	10	0	10	31	.233	6	1	1	.875
Major League Totals—2 Years				70	219	35	53	7	0	16	42	.242	0	0	0	.000

Selected by Boston Red Sox' organization in 1st round (16th player selected) of free-agent draft, June 7, 1982.
†On disabled list, April 28 to June 23, 1983.

JAMES ROBERT HORNER
(Bob)

Born August 6, 1957, at Junction City, Kan.
Height, 6.01. Weight, 215.
Throws and bats righthanded.
Attended Arizona State University, Tempe, Ariz.

Tied major league record for most home runs, game (4), July 6, 1986.
Major League stolen bases: 1980 (3), 1981 (2), 1982 (3), 1983 (4), 1985 (1), 1986 (1). Total—14.
Hit four home runs in a game, July 6, 1986.
Led National League first basemen in double plays with 138 in 1986.
Named National League Rookie Player of the Year by THE SPORTING NEWS, 1978.
Named National League Rookie of the Year by Baseball Writers' Association of America, 1978.
Named College Player of the Year by THE SPORTING NEWS, 1978.
Received reported $175,000 bonus to sign with Atlanta Braves, 1978.
Named second baseman on THE SPORTING NEWS College Baseball All-America Team, 1977 and 1978.

Year	Club	League	Pos.	G.	AB.	R.	H.	2B.	3B.	HR.	RBI.	B.A.	PO.	A.	E.	F.A.
1978—	Atlanta	Nat.	3B	89	323	50	86	17	1	23	63	.266	81	199	13	.956
1979—	Atlanta†	Nat.	3B-1B	121	487	66	153	15	1	33	98	.314	470	167	22	.967
1980—	Atlanta‡	Nat.	3B-1B	124	463	81	124	14	1	35	89	.268	80	253	23	.935
1981—	Atlanta	Nat.	3B	79	300	42	83	10	0	15	42	.277	51	129	12	.938
1982—	Atlanta	Nat.	3B	140	499	85	130	24	0	32	97	.261	102	217	10	.970
1983—	Atlanta§	Nat.	3B-1B	104	386	75	117	25	1	20	68	.303	78	153	10	.959
1984—	Atlanta x	Nat.	3B	32	113	15	31	8	0	3	19	.274	21	61	3	.965
1985—	Atlanta	Nat.	1B-3B	130	483	61	129	25	3	27	89	.267	917	119	11	.989
1986—	Atlanta y	Nat.	1B	141	517	70	141	22	0	27	87	.273	*1378	102	8	.995
1987—	Yakult z	Cent	1B-3B	93	303	60	99	....	....	31	73	.327	figures unavailable			
1988—	St. Louis ab	Nat.	1B	60	206	15	53	9	1	3	33	.257	463	40	5	.990
Major League Totals—10 Years				1020	3777	560	1047	169	8	218	685	.277	3641	1440	117	.977

Selected by Oakland A's organization in 15th round of free-agent draft, June 4, 1975.
Selected by Atlanta Braves' organization in 1st round (first player selected) of free-agent draft, June 6, 1978.
†On disabled list, April 11 to April 26, 1979.
‡On disqualified list when refused option to Richmond (International), April 28, 1980; reinstated, May 10, 1980.
§On disabled list, August 16, 1983 through remainder of season.
xOn disabled list, April 28 to May 17 and June 4, 1984 through remainder of season.
yGranted free agency, November 12, 1986; signed by Yakult Swallows of Japanese Baseball League, April 14, 1987.
zReleased by Yakult Swallows; signed by St. Louis Cardinals, January 14, 1988.
aOn disabled list, June 20, 1988 through remainder of season.
bReleased, December 21, 1988.

CHAMPIONSHIP SERIES RECORD

Year	Club	League	Pos.	G.	AB.	R.	H.	2B.	3B.	HR.	RBI.	B.A.	PO.	A.	E.	F.A.
1982—	Atlanta	Nat.	3B	3	11	0	1	0	0	0	0	.091	2	5	0	1.000

ALL-STAR GAME RECORD

Year	League	Pos.	AB.	R.	H.	2B.	3B.	HR.	RBI.	B.A.	PO.	A.	E.	F.A.
1982—	National	PH	1	0	0	0	0	0	0	.000	0	0	0	.000

RICKY NEAL HORTON
(Rick)

Born July 30, 1959, at Poughkeepsie, N.Y.
Height, 6.02. Weight, 197.
Throws and bats lefthanded.
Received bachelor of science degree in engineering from
University of Virginia, Charlottesville, Va. in 1982.
Brother of David Horton, infielder in St. Louis Cardinals' organization, 1986 and 1987.

Major League saves: 1984 (1), 1985 (1), 1986 (3), 1987 (7), 1988 (2). Total—14.
Led American Association in balks with 7 in 1983.

Year	Club	League	G.	IP.	W.	L.	Pct.	H.	R.	ER.	SO.	BB.	ERA.
1980—	St. Petersburg	Florida St.	6	25	0	2	.000	29	18	17	13	17	6.12
1980—	Gastonia	S. Atlantic	14	42	2	4	.333	30	21	17	30	25	3.64
1981—	St. Petersburg	Florida St.	28	100	7	3	.700	101	52	49	66	49	4.41
1982—	Arkansas	Texas	16	108⅔	9	6	.600	83	45	38	90	52	3.15
1982—	Louisville	Am. Assoc.	8	36⅓	2	3	.400	47	31	27	37	11	6.69
1983—	Louisville	Am. Assoc.	30	157	10	6	.625	177	99	84	92	58	4.82
1984—	St. Louis	National	37	125⅔	9	4	.692	140	53	48	76	39	3.44
1985—	St. Louis	National	49	89⅔	3	2	.600	84	30	29	59	34	2.91
1986—	St. Louis†	National	42	100⅓	4	3	.571	77	25	25	49	26	2.24
1986—	Springfield	Midwest	1	2	0	0	.000	2	0	0	2	0	0.00
1987—	St. Louis‡§	National	67	125	8	3	.727	127	58	53	55	42	3.82

Year Club	League	G.	IP.	W.	L.	Pct.	H.	R.	ER.	SO.	BB.	ERA.
1988—Chicago x	American	52	109⅓	6	10	.375	120	64	59	28	36	4.86
1988—Los Angeles	National	12	9	1	1	.500	11	7	5	8	2	5.00
National League Totals—5 Years		207	449⅔	25	13	.658	439	173	160	247	143	3.20
American League Totals—1 Year		52	109⅓	6	10	.375	120	64	59	28	36	4.86
Major League Totals—5 Years		259	559	31	23	.574	559	237	219	275	179	3.53

Selected by San Francisco Giants' organization in 20th round of free-agent draft, June 7, 1977.

Selected by St. Louis Cardinals' organization in 4th round of free-agent draft, June 3, 1980.

†On disabled list, May 25 to June 24, 1986; included rehabilitation disability assignment to Springfield, June 20 to June 24, 1986.

‡Appeared as an outfielder with no chances.

§Traded with Outfielder Lance Johnson and cash to Chicago White Sox for Pitcher Jose DeLeon, February 9, 1988.

xTraded to Los Angeles Dodgers for a player to be named later, August 30, 1988; Chicago White Sox acquired Pitcher Shawn Hillegas to complete deal, September 2, 1988.

CHAMPIONSHIP SERIES RECORD

Tied Championship Series record for most games pitched, seven-game Series (4), 1988.

Year Club	League	G.	IP.	W.	L.	Pct.	H.	R.	ER.	SO.	BB.	ERA.
1985—St. Louis	National	3	3	0	0	.000	4	4	4	1	2	12.00
1987—St. Louis	National	1	3	0	0	.000	2	0	0	2	0	0.00
1988—Los Angeles	National	4	4⅓	0	0	.000	4	0	0	3	2	0.00
Championship Series Totals—3 Years		8	10⅓	0	0	.000	10	4	4	6	4	3.48

WORLD SERIES RECORD

Year Club	League	G.	IP.	W.	L.	Pct.	H.	R.	ER.	SO.	BB.	ERA.
1985—St. Louis	National	3	4	0	0	.000	4	3	3	5	5	6.75
1987—St. Louis	National	2	3	0	0	.000	5	2	2	1	0	6.00
World Series Totals—2 Years		5	7	0	0	.000	9	5	5	6	5	6.43

DAVID ALAN HOSTETLER
(Dave)

Born March 27, 1956, at Pasadena, Calif.
Height, 6.03. Weight, 220.
Throws and bats righthanded.
Attended Citrus College, Azusa, Calif., and University of Southern California, Los Angeles, Calif.

Major League stolen bases: 1982 (2).

Led Southern League in intentional bases on balls received with 13 in 1979.

Named first baseman on THE SPORTING NEWS College Baseball All-America Team, 1977.

Year Club	League	Pos.	G.	AB.	R.	H.	2B.	3B.	HR.	RBI.	B.A.	PO.	A.	E.	F.A.
1978—W. Palm Beach	Fla. St.	1B	75	249	27	67	12	0	5	29	.269	541	36	11	.981
1979—Memphis	South.	1B	•145	548	77	148	28	4	20	*114	.270	959	55	9	.991
1980—Denver	A. A.	1B	126	453	62	122	17	1	9	58	.269	1039	63	*16	.986
1981—Denver	A. A.	1B	125	440	91	140	14	7	27	103	.318	1104	66	*13	.989
1981—Montreal†	Nat.	1B	5	6	1	3	0	0	1	1	.500	4	0	0	1.000
1982—Denver	A. A.	1B	36	128	24	34	8	0	12	36	.266	123	8	3	.978
1982—Texas	Amer.	1B	113	418	53	97	12	3	22	67	.232	1099	48	12	.990
1983—Texas	Amer.	1B	94	304	31	67	9	2	11	46	.220	11	0	0	1.000
1984—Texas	Amer.	1B	37	82	7	18	2	1	3	10	.220	90	8	0	1.000
1984—Oklahoma City‡	A. A.	1B	64	227	28	69	9	2	11	43	.304	305	35	6	.983
1985—Indy§-Iowa x	A. A.	1B	132	465	69	119	18	2	*29	*89	.256	983	79	11	.990
1986—Nankai	Japan	1B	130	487	....	139	....	....	25	74	.285	figures unavailable			
1987—Nankai y	Japan	1B	124	391	....	98	....	....	17	68	.251	figures unavailable			
1988—Pittsburgh	Nat.	1B-C	6	8	0	2	0	0	0	0	.250	15	2	1	.944
1988—Buffalo z	A. A.	1B	84	225	21	42	8	4	4	29	.187	141	6	2	.987
National League Totals—2 Years			11	14	1	5	0	0	1	1	.357	19	2	1	.955
American League Totals—3 Years			244	804	91	182	23	6	36	123	.226	1200	56	12	.991
Major League Totals—5 Years			255	818	92	187	23	6	37	124	.229	1219	58	13	.990

Selected by San Francisco Giants' organization in 4th round of free-agent draft, January 9, 1975.

Selected by San Francisco Giants' organization in 4th round of free-agent draft, January 7, 1976.

Selected by Cleveland Indians' organization in secondary phase of free-agent draft, June 8, 1976.

Selected by San Francisco Giants' organization in secondary phase of free-agent draft, June 7, 1977.

Selected by Montreal Expos' organization in 3rd round of free-agent draft, June 6, 1978.

†Traded with Third Baseman Larry Parrish to Texas Rangers for First Baseman-Outfielder Al Oliver, March 31, 1982.

‡Traded to Montreal Expos' organization for Pitcher Chris Welsh, November 7, 1984.

§Sold to Iowa (Chicago Cubs' organization), May 12, 1985.

xGranted free agency, October 22, 1985; signed by Nankai Hawks of Japanese Baseball League.

yReleased by Nankai Hawks; signed by Vancouver (Pittsburgh Pirates' organization), January 20, 1988.

zReleased, August 28, 1988.

—DID YOU KNOW—

That Toronto's George Bell hit three homers in the Blue Jays' first game of the 1988 season but didn't hit more than one homer in any other game the rest of the year?

CHARLES OLIVER HOUGH

Name pronounced Huff.

(Charlie)

Born January 5, 1948, at Honolulu, Haw.
Height, 6.02. Weight, 190.
Throws and bats righthanded.
Son of Dick Hough, minor league third baseman, 1933.

Tied major league record for most strikeouts, inning (4), July 4, 1988 (first inning).
Established American League record for most balks, season (9), 1987.
Major League saves: 1970 (2), 1973 (5), 1974 (1), 1975 (4), 1976 (18), 1977 (22), 1978 (7), 1980 (1), 1981 (1). Total—61.
Led American League in hit batsmen with 19 and balks with 9 in 1987.
Led American League in games started with 40 in 1987 and tied for lead with 36 in 1984.
Led American League pitchers in complete games with 17 in 1984.
Led Pacific Coast League in intentional bases on balls issued with 13 in 1972.
Led Pacific Coast League in saves with 18 in 1970.
Led Texas League in home runs allowed with 17 in 1969.
Named Pacific Coast League Pitcher of the Year, 1972.

Year Club	League	G.	IP.	W.	L.	Pct.	H.	R.	ER.	SO.	BB.	ERA.
1966—Ogden	Pioneer	21	68	5	•7	.417	82	56	36	68	29	4.76
1967—Santa Barbara	California	20	165	14	4	*.778	129	50	41	138	43	2.24
1967—Albuquerque	Texas	7	36	2	1	.667	57	31	28	25	10	7.00
1968—Albuquerque†	Texas	27	121	6	10	.375	145	72	53	74	26	3.94
1969—Albuquerque	Texas	27	163	10	9	.526	190	87	74	113	42	4.09
1970—Spokane	P. Coast	49	134	12	8	.600	98	43	29	90	44	1.95
1970—Los Angeles	National	8	17	0	0	.000	18	11	10	8	11	5.29
1971—Spokane‡	P. Coast	47	117	10	8	.556	95	56	51	104	52	3.92
1971—Los Angeles	National	4	4	0	0	.000	3	3	2	4	3	4.50
1972—Albuquerque§	P. Coast	58	125	14	5	.737	109	47	33	95	60	2.38
1972—Los Angeles	National	2	3	0	0	.000	2	1	1	4	2	3.00
1973—Los Angeles	National	37	72	4	2	.667	52	24	22	70	45	2.75
1974—Los Angeles	National	49	96	9	4	.692	65	45	40	63	40	3.75
1975—Los Angeles	National	38	61	3	7	.300	43	25	20	34	34	2.95
1976—Los Angeles	National	77	143	12	8	.600	102	43	35	81	77	2.20
1977—Los Angeles	National	70	127	6	12	.333	98	53	47	105	70	3.33
1978—Los Angeles	National	55	93	5	5	.500	69	38	34	66	48	3.29
1979—Los Angeles	National	42	151	7	5	.583	152	88	80	76	66	4.77
1980—Los Angeles x	National	19	32	1	3	.250	37	21	20	25	21	5.63
1980—Texas	American	16	61	2	2	.500	54	30	27	47	37	3.98
1981—Texas	American	21	82	4	1	.800	61	30	27	69	31	2.96
1982—Texas	American	34	228	16	13	.552	217	111	100	128	72	3.95
1983—Texas	American	34	252	15	13	.536	219	96	89	152	95	3.18
1984—Texas	American	36	266	16	14	.533	*260	127	111	164	94	3.76
1985—Texas	American	34	250⅓	14	16	.467	198	102	92	141	83	3.31
1986—Oklahoma City y	Am. Assoc.	1	5	0	1	.000	7	5	5	3	1	9.00
1986—Texas	American	33	230⅓	17	10	.630	188	115	97	146	89	3.79
1987—Texas	American	40	*285⅓	18	13	.581	238	*159	120	223	124	3.79
1988—Texas	American	34	252	15	16	.484	202	111	93	174	*126	3.32
National League Totals—11 Years		401	799	47	46	.505	641	352	311	536	417	3.50
American League Totals—9 Years		282	1907	117	98	.544	1637	881	756	1244	751	3.57
Major League Totals—19 Years		683	2706	164	144	.532	2278	1233	1067	1780	1168	3.55

Selected by Los Angeles Dodgers' organization in 8th round of free-agent draft, June 9, 1966.
†On temporary inactive list, June 19 to July 1, 1968.
‡On temporary inactive list, July 10 to July 24, 1971.
§On temporary inactive list June 12 to June 15, July 22 to July 24 and August 7 to August 12, 1972.
xSold to Texas Rangers, July 11, 1980.
yOn Texas disabled list, March 25 to May 6, 1986; included rehabilitation disability assignment to Oklahoma City, May 2 to May 6, 1986.

CHAMPIONSHIP SERIES RECORD

Year Club	League	G.	IP.	W.	L.	Pct.	H.	R.	ER.	SO.	BB.	ERA.
1974—Los Angeles	National	1	2⅓	0	0	.000	4	2	2	2	0	7.71
1977—Los Angeles	National	1	2	0	0	.000	2	1	1	3	0	4.50
1978—Los Angeles	National	1	2	0	0	.000	1	1	1	1	0	4.50
Championship Series Totals—3 Years		3	6⅓	0	0	.000	7	4	4	6	0	5.68

WORLD SERIES RECORD

Tied World Series record for most wild pitches, inning and game (2), October 15, 1978 (seventh inning).

Year Club	League	G.	IP.	W.	L.	Pct.	H.	R.	ER.	SO.	BB.	ERA.
1974—Los Angeles	National	1	2	0	0	.000	0	0	0	4	1	0.00
1977—Los Angeles	National	2	5	0	0	.000	3	1	1	5	0	1.80
1978—Los Angeles	National	2	5⅓	0	0	.000	10	5	5	5	2	8.44
World Series Totals—3 Years		5	12⅓	0	0	.000	13	6	6	14	3	4.38

ALL-STAR GAME RECORD

Year League	IP.	W.	L.	Pct.	H.	R.	ER.	SO.	BB.	ERA.
1986—American	1⅔	0	0	.000	2	2	1	3	0	5.40

BATTING RECORD

Year	Club	League	Pos.	G.	AB.	R.	H.	2B.	3B.	HR.	RBI.	B.A.	PO.	A.	E.	F.A.
1967	—Santa Barbara	Calif.	P-1B	28	72	8	14	2	0	0	4	.194	15	25	2	.953
1968	—Albuquerque	Texas	P-1B-3B	56	83	10	21	4	0	0	6	.253	43	25	4	.944
1969	—Albuquerque	Texas	P-3B	31	57	10	12	0	0	1	9	.211	10	19	2	.935
1970	—Spokane	P. C.	P-OF-1B	49	33	1	6	0	0	1	3	.182	7	28	3	.921
1971	—Spokane	P. C.	P-OF	48	36	2	10	0	0	0	3	.278	6	20	1	.963
1972	—Albuquerque	P. C.	P-OF	58	34	4	9	1	0	0	5	.265	3	27	0	1.000

STEVEN BERNARD HOWARD
(Steve)

Born December 7, 1963, at Oakland, Calif.
Height, 6.02. Weight, 205.
Throws and bats righthanded.
Attended Laney College, Oakland, Calif.

Led Southern League in being hit by pitch with 12 in 1987.
Led Northwest League batters in strikeouts with 89 in 1984.

Year	Club	League	Pos.	G.	AB.	R.	H.	2B.	3B.	HR.	RBI.	B.A.	PO.	A.	E.	F.A.
1983	—Idaho Falls	Pion.	OF	61	203	40	45	4	4	6	33	.222	77	2	6	.929
1984	—Madison	Midw.	OF	44	123	13	21	4	0	2	14	.171	36	0	4	.900
1984	—Medford	N'west	OF	53	185	26	39	4	1	4	24	.211	55	2	5	.919
1985	—Modesto	Calif.	OF	110	349	59	77	15	3	14	64	.221	101	1	11	.903
1986	—Modesto†	Calif.	OF	98	302	64	70	11	4	9	53	.232	156	2	12	.929
1987	—Huntsville	South.	OF	133	439	79	112	17	4	13	66	.255	197	1	•15	.930
1988	—Huntsville	South.	OF	128	461	70	114	19	6	17	78	.247	211	5	11	.952

Selected by Oakland Athletics' organization in 8th round of free-agent draft, January 11, 1983.
†On disabled list, June 30 to July 22, 1986.

THOMAS SYLVESTER HOWARD
(Tom)

Born December 11, 1964, at Middletown, O.
Height, 6.00. Weight, 200.
Throws right and bats left and righthanded.
Attended Ball State University, Muncie, Ind.

Named outfielder on THE SPORTING NEWS College Baseball All-America Team, 1986.

Year	Club	League	Pos.	G.	AB.	R.	H.	2B.	3B.	HR.	RBI.	B.A.	PO.	A.	E.	F.A.
1986	—Spokane	N'west	OF	13	55	16	23	3	3	2	17	.418	24	3	0	1.000
1986	—Reno	Calif.	OF	61	223	35	57	7	3	10	39	.256	104	5	6	.948
1987	—Wichita	Texas	OF	113	401	72	133	27	4	14	60	.332	226	6	6	.975
1988	—Wichita	Texas	OF	29	103	15	31	9	2	0	16	.301	51	2	2	.964
1988	—Las Vegas	P. C.	OF	44	167	29	42	9	1	0	15	.251	74	3	2	.975

Selected by San Diego Padres' organization in 1st round (11th player selected) of free-agent draft, June 2, 1986.

JACK ROBERT HOWELL

Born August 18, 1961, at Tucson, Ariz.
Height, 6.00. Weight, 201.
Throws right and bats lefthanded.
Attended Pima Community College, Tucson, Ariz., and University of Arizona, Tucson, Ariz.

Major League stolen bases: 1985 (1), 1986 (2), 1987 (4), 1988 (2). Total—9.
Led California League third basemen in fielding percentage with .943, assists with 259, double plays with 23 and total chances with 368 in 1984.

Year	Club	League	Pos.	G.	AB.	R.	H.	2B.	3B.	HR.	RBI.	B.A.	PO.	A.	E.	F.A.
1983	—Salem	N'west	3B-2B	21	76	23	30	2	5	3	12	.395	19	32	11	.823
1984	—Redwood	Calif.	3B-1B	135	451	62	111	21	5	5	64	.246	96	260	21	.944
1985	—Edmonton†	P. C.	3B-SS	79	284	55	106	22	3	13	48	.373	67	130	12	.943
1985	—California	Amer.	3B	43	137	19	27	4	0	5	18	.197	33	75	8	.931
1986	—Edmonton	P. C.	3B	44	156	39	56	17	3	3	28	.359	28	84	8	.933
1986	—California	Amer.	3B-OF	63	151	26	41	14	2	4	21	.272	38	57	2	.979
1987	—California	Amer.	OF-3B-2B	138	449	64	110	18	5	23	64	.245	185	95	7	.976
1988	—California	Amer.	3B-OF	154	500	59	127	32	2	16	63	.254	97	249	17	.953
Major League Totals—4 Years				398	1237	168	305	68	9	48	166	.247	353	476	34	.961

Signed as free agent by California Angels' organization, August 6, 1983.
†On disabled list, June 21 to July 7, 1985.

CHAMPIONSHIP SERIES RECORD

Year	Club	League	Pos.	G.	AB.	R.	H.	2B.	3B.	HR.	RBI.	B.A.	PO.	A.	E.	F.A.
1986	—California	Amer.	PH	2	1	0	0	0	0	0	0	.000	0	0	0	.000

JAY CANFIELD HOWELL

Born November 26, 1955, at Miami, Fla.
Height, 6.03. Weight, 205.
Throws and bats righthanded.
Attended University of Colorado, Boulder, Colo.

Major League saves: 1984 (7), 1985 (29), 1986 (16), 1987 (16), 1988 (21). Total—89.
Tied for American Association lead in shutouts with 2 in 1982.
Tied for American Association lead in balks with 6 in 1981.
Named American Association Pitcher of the Year, 1982.

Year Club	League	G.	IP.	W.	L.	Pct.	H.	R.	ER.	SO.	BB.	ERA.
1976—Eugene	Northwest	13	73	5	4	.556	65	30	24	79	34	2.96
1977—Tampa	Florida St.	23	158	7	13	.350	141	60	52	99	52	2.96
1978—Nashville	Southern	28	166	9	14	.391	134	70	57	*173	55	3.09
1979—Indianapolis	Am. Assoc.	24	128	10	10	.500	121	82	73	79	84	5.13
1980—Indianapolis	Am. Assoc.	25	98	5	11	.313	95	70	55	73	71	5.05
1980—Cincinnati†	National	5	3	0	0	.000	8	5	5	1	0	15.00
1981—Iowa	Am. Assoc.	23	144	5	10	.333	141	74	60	90	62	3.75
1981—Chicago	National	10	22	2	0	1.000	23	13	12	10	10	4.91
1982—Iowa‡	Am. Assoc.	20	141⅓	13	4	*.765	102	45	37	139	48	*2.36
1982—Columbus	Int'national	5	37⅓	2	1	.667	18	13	10	33	19	2.41
1982—New York	American	6	28	2	3	.400	42	25	24	21	13	7.71
1983—New York§	American	19	82	1	5	.167	89	53	49	61	35	5.38
1984—New York x	American	61	103⅔	9	4	.692	86	33	31	109	34	2.69
1985—Oakland	American	63	98	9	8	.529	98	32	31	68	31	2.85
1986—Oakland y	American	38	53⅓	3	6	.333	53	23	20	42	23	3.38
1986—Modesto	California	2	2	0	0	.000	5	3	3	1	1	13.50
1987—Oakland za	American	36	44⅓	3	4	.429	48	30	29	35	21	5.89
1988—Los Angeles b	National	50	65	5	3	.625	44	16	15	70	21	2.08
National League Totals—3 Years		65	90	7	3	.700	75	34	32	81	31	3.20
American League Totals—6 Years		223	409⅓	27	30	.474	416	196	184	336	157	4.05
Major League Totals—9 Years		288	499⅓	34	33	.507	491	230	216	417	188	3.89

Selected by Cincinnati Reds' organization in 12th round of free-agent draft, June 5, 1973.
Selected by Cincinnati Reds' organization in 31st round of free-agent draft, June 8, 1976.
†Traded to Chicago Cubs for Catcher Mike O'Berry, October 17, 1980.
‡Traded to New York Yankees' organization, August 2, 1982, completing deal in which Chicago Cubs acquired Second Baseman Pat Tabler from New York on waivers for two players to be named later, August 19, 1981; New York acquired Pitcher Bill Caudill as partial completion of deal, April 1, 1982.
§On disabled list, August 3, 1983 through remainder of season.
xTraded with Outfielder Stan Javier and Pitchers Jose Rijo, Eric Plunk and Tim Birtsas to Oakland A's for Outfielder Rickey Henderson, Pitcher Bert Bradley and cash, December 5, 1984.
yOn disabled list, April 30 to May 18 and May 27 to July 20, 1986; included rehabilitation disability assignment to Modesto, July 11 to July 16, 1986.
zOn disabled list, August 25, 1987 through remainder of season.
aAs part of an eight-player, three-team deal, New York Mets traded Pitcher Jesse Orosco to Oakland Athletics, December 11, 1987. Oakland then traded Orosco along with Shortstop Alfredo Griffin and Pitcher Jay Howell to Los Angeles Dodgers for Pitchers Bob Welch, Matt Young and Jack Savage. Oakland then traded Savage along with Pitchers Wally Whitehurst and Kevin Tapani to New York.
bOn disabled list, June 21 to July 7, 1988.

CHAMPIONSHIP SERIES RECORD

Year Club	League	G.	IP.	W.	L.	Pct.	H.	R.	ER.	SO.	BB.	ERA.
1988—Los Angeles	National	2	⅔	0	1	.000	1	2	2	1	2	27.00

WORLD SERIES RECORD

Year Club	League	G.	IP.	W.	L.	Pct.	H.	R.	ER.	SO.	BB.	ERA.
1988—Los Angeles	National	2	2⅔	0	1	.000	3	1	1	2	1	3.38

ALL-STAR GAME RECORD

Year League	IP.	W.	L.	Pct.	H.	R.	ER.	SO.	BB.	ERA.
1987—American	2	0	1	.000	3	2	2	3	0	9.00

Member of American League All-Star Team in 1985; did not play.

KENNETH HOWELL JR.
(Ken)

Born November 28, 1960, at Detroit, Mich.
Height, 6.03. Weight, 228.
Throws and bats righthanded.
Attended Tuskegee Institute, Tuskegee Institute, Ala.

Major League saves: 1984 (6), 1985 (12), 1986 (12), 1987 (1). Total—31.
Tied for Texas League lead in games started by pitchers with 27 in 1983.

Year Club	League	G.	IP.	W.	L.	Pct.	H.	R.	ER.	SO.	BB.	ERA.
1982—Vero Beach	Florida St.	11	59⅔	5	4	.556	58	40	28	37	36	4.22
1983—San Antonio	Texas	27	169⅓	8	11	.421	171	98	83	116	101	4.41
1983—Albuquerque	P. Coast	1	3	0	0	.000	4	3	3	1	1	9.00
1984—Albuquerque†	P. Coast	18	72⅓	8	2	.800	79	48	37	58	37	4.60
1984—Los Angeles	National	32	51⅓	5	5	.500	51	21	19	54	9	3.33
1985—Los Angeles	National	56	86	4	7	.364	66	41	36	85	35	3.77
1986—Los Angeles	National	62	97⅔	6	12	.333	86	48	42	104	63	3.87
1987—Los Angeles	National	40	55	3	4	.429	54	32	30	60	29	4.91
1987—Albuquerque	P. Coast	2	13	1	0	1.000	6	1	0	13	7	0.00
1988—Bakersfield‡	California	3	13⅔	0	1	.000	8	5	2	13	9	1.32
1988—Albuquerque	P. Coast	18	107⅓	10	1	*.909	92	43	39	95	42	3.27
1988—Los Angeles§x	National	4	12⅔	0	1	.000	16	10	9	12	4	6.39
Major League Totals—5 Years		194	302⅔	18	29	.383	273	152	136	315	140	4.04

Selected by Los Angeles Dodgers' organization in 3rd round of free-agent draft, June 7, 1982.

†On disabled list, April 7 to April 17, 1984.

‡On Los Angeles disabled list, March 20 to May 25 and June 17 to July 8, 1988; included rehabilitation disability assignment to Bakersfield, May 7 to May 11 and May 17 to May 25, 1988; and to Albuquerque, May 12 to May 16 and June 24 to July 8, 1988.

§Traded with Pitcher Brian Holton and Shortstop Juan Bell to Baltimore Orioles for First Baseman Eddie Murray, December 4, 1988.

xTraded with Pitcher Gordon Dillard by Baltimore Orioles to Philadelphia Phillies for Outfielder Phil Bradley, December 8, 1988.

CHAMPIONSHIP SERIES RECORD

Year Club	League	G.	IP.	W.	L.	Pct.	H.	R.	ER.	SO.	BB.	ERA.
1985—Los Angeles	National	1	2	0	0	.000	0	0	0	2	0	0.00

KENT ALAN HRBEK

Name pronounced HER-beck.

Born May 21, 1960, at Minneapolis, Minn.
Height, 6.04. Weight, 250.
Throws right and bats lefthanded.

Major League stolen bases: 1982 (3), 1983 (4), 1984 (1), 1985 (1), 1986 (2), 1987 (5). Total—16.

Led California League in slugging percentage with .630 and tied for lead in sacrifice flies with 9 in 1981.

Named California League Most Valuable Player, 1981.

Year Club	League	Pos.	G.	AB.	R.	H.	2B.	3B.	HR.	RBI.	B.A.	PO.	A.	E.	F.A.
1979—Elizabethton†‡	Appal.	1B	17	59	5	12	2	0	1	11	.203	126	11	2	.986
1980—Wisc. Rapids§	Midw.	1B	115	419	74	112	16	0	19	76	.267	1005	81	★20	.982
1981—Visalia	Calif.	1B	121	462	119	175	25	5	27	111	★.379	1034	53	11	★.989
1981—Minnesota	Amer.	1B	24	67	5	16	5	0	1	7	.239	124	4	0	1.000
1982—Minnesota	Amer.	1B	140	532	82	160	21	4	23	92	.301	1174	88	9	.993
1983—Minnesota	Amer.	1B	141	515	75	153	41	5	16	84	.297	1151	89	13	.990
1984—Minnesota	Amer.	1B	149	559	80	174	31	3	27	107	.311	1320	99	14	.990
1985—Minnesota	Amer.	1B	158	593	78	165	31	2	21	93	.278	1339	114	8	.995
1986—Minnesota	Amer.	1B	149	550	85	147	27	1	29	91	.267	1218	104	10	.992
1987—Minnesota	Amer.	1B	143	477	85	136	20	1	34	90	.285	1179	68	5	.996
1988—Minnesota	Amer.	1B	143	510	75	159	31	0	25	76	.312	842	57	3	.997
Major League Totals—8 Years			1047	3803	565	1110	207	16	176	640	.292	8347	623	62	.993

Selected by Minnesota Twins' organization in 17th round of free-agent draft, June 6, 1978.

†On Wisconsin Rapids disabled list, April 13 to June 21, 1979.

‡On Elizabethton disabled list, July 22 to September 6, 1979.

§On disabled list, May 27 to June 6, 1980.

CHAMPIONSHIP SERIES RECORD

Year Club	League	Pos.	G.	AB.	R.	H.	2B.	3B.	HR.	RBI.	B.A.	PO.	A.	E.	F.A.
1987—Minnesota	Amer.	1B	5	20	4	3	0	0	1	1	.150	40	3	0	1.000

WORLD SERIES RECORD

Tied World Series records for most grand slams, game (1), October 24, 1987; most runs batted in, inning (4), October 24, 1987 (sixth inning).

Year Club	League	Pos.	G.	AB.	R.	H.	2B.	3B.	HR.	RBI.	B.A.	PO.	A.	E.	F.A.
1987—Minnesota	Amer.	1B	7	24	4	5	0	0	1	6	.208	68	2	0	1.000

ALL-STAR GAME RECORD

Year League	Pos.	AB.	R.	H.	2B.	3B.	HR.	RBI.	B.A.	PO.	A.	E.	F.A.
1982—American	PH	1	0	0	0	0	0	0	.000	0	0	0	.000

GLENN DEE HUBBARD

Born September 25, 1957, at Hahn Air Force Base, Germany.
Height, 5.07. Weight, 169.
Throws and bats righthanded.

Tied major league record for most assists by second baseman, nine-inning game (12), April 14, 1985.

Major League stolen bases: 1978 (2), 1980 (7), 1981 (4), 1982 (4), 1983 (3), 1984 (4), 1985 (4), 1986 (3), 1987 (1), 1988 (1). Total—33.

Led National League in sacrifice hits with 20 in 1982.

Led National League second basemen in total chances with 888 in 1985.

Led National League second basemen in double plays with 111 in 1982, 127 in 1985 and 114 in 1987.

Led Appalachian League third basemen in fielding percentage with .932 in 1975.

Named second baseman on THE SPORTING NEWS National League All-Star Team, 1983.

Year Club	League	Pos.	G.	AB.	R.	H.	2B.	3B.	HR.	RBI.	B.A.	PO.	A.	E.	F.A.
1975—Kingsport	Appal.	3B-SS-2B	53	136	31	39	6	4	2	21	.287	44	88	9	.936
1976—Kingsport	Appal.	2B	37	136	29	40	8	0	2	15	.294	96	122	1	.995
1976—Greenwood†	W. Car.	2B	33	126	26	40	8	1	4	21	.317	62	83	6	.960
1977—Greenwood	W. Car.	2B	45	182	39	70	10	1	5	44	.385	114	133	4	.984
1977—Savannah	South.	2B	87	298	49	67	15	2	6	32	.225	209	239	10	.978
1978—Richmond	Int.	2B	80	301	58	101	12	3	14	36	.336	208	243	11	.976
1978—Atlanta‡	Nat.	2B	44	163	15	42	4	0	2	13	.258	102	130	5	.979
1979—Richmond	Int.	3B-2B	34	125	21	42	5	1	2	17	.336	83	109	7	.965
1979—Atlanta	Nat.	2B	97	325	34	75	12	0	3	29	.231	193	268	●15	.968
1980—Richmond	Int.	2B	38	143	23	45	11	2	2	25	.315	89	127	4	.982

Year	Club	League	Pos.	G.	AB.	R.	H.	2B.	3B.	HR.	RBI.	B.A.	PO.	A.	E.	F.A.
1980	—Atlanta	Nat.	2B	117	431	55	107	21	3	9	43	.248	268	405	15	.978
1981	—Atlanta	Nat.	2B	99	361	39	85	13	5	6	33	.235	188	344	5	.991
1982	—Atlanta	Nat.	2B	145	532	75	132	25	1	9	59	.248	312	505	14	.983
1983	—Atlanta	Nat.	2B	148	517	65	136	24	6	12	70	.263	313	484	12	.985
1984	—Atlanta	Nat.	2B	120	397	53	93	27	2	9	43	.234	237	405	8	.988
1985	—Atlanta	Nat.	2B	142	439	51	102	21	0	5	39	.232	339	*539	10	.989
1986	—Atlanta	Nat.	2B	143	408	42	94	16	1	4	36	.230	282	487	19	.976
1987	—Atlanta§	Nat.	2B	141	443	69	117	33	2	5	38	.264	284	*478	11	.986
1988	—Oakland x	Amer.	2B	105	294	35	75	12	2	3	33	.255	195	267	6	.987
National League Totals—10 Years				1196	4016	498	983	196	20	64	403	.245	2518	4045	114	.983
American League Totals—1 Year				105	294	35	75	12	2	3	33	.255	195	267	6	.987
Major League Totals—11 Years				1301	4310	533	1058	208	22	67	436	.245	2713	4312	120	.983

Selected by Atlanta Braves' organization in 20th round of free-agent draft, June 4, 1975.
†On temporary inactive list, May 17 to June 22, 1976.
‡On disabled list, July 22 to August 23, 1978.
§Granted free agency, November 9, 1987; signed by Oakland Athletics, January 11, 1988.
xOn disabled list, March 26 to April 15, 1988.

CHAMPIONSHIP SERIES RECORD

Year	Club	League	Pos.	G.	AB.	R.	H.	2B.	3B.	HR.	RBI.	B.A.	PO.	A.	E.	F.A.
1982	—Atlanta	Nat.	2B	3	9	1	2	0	0	0	1	.222	4	11	0	1.000

WORLD SERIES RECORD

Year	Club	League	Pos.	G.	AB.	R.	H.	2B.	3B.	HR.	RBI.	B.A.	PO.	A.	E.	F.A.
1988	—Oakland	Amer.	2B	4	12	2	3	0	0	0	0	.250	5	7	1	.923

ALL-STAR GAME RECORD

Year	League	Pos.	AB.	R.	H.	2B.	3B.	HR.	RBI.	B.A.	PO.	A.	E.	F.A.
1983	—National	2B	1	0	1	0	0	0	0	1.000	0	0	0	.000

REX ALLEN HUDLER

Born September 2, 1960, at Tempe, Ariz.
Height, 6.02. Weight, 180.
Throws and bats righthanded.

Major League stolen bases: 1986 (1), 1988 (29). Total—30.
Led International League second basemen in double plays with 95 in 1984.

Year	Club	League	Pos.	G.	AB.	R.	H.	2B.	3B.	HR.	RBI.	B.A.	PO.	A.	E.	F.A.
1978	—Oneonta	NYP	SS	58	221	33	62	5	5	0	24	.281	123	21	22	.906
1979	—Fort Lauderdale†	Fla. St.	S-3-2-O	116	414	37	104	14	1	1	25	.251	164	314	45	.914
1980	—Fort Lauderdale‡	Fla. St.	3-2-O-1	37	125	14	26	4	0	0	6	.208	55	71	5	.962
1980	—Greensboro	S. Atl.	2B	20	75	7	17	3	1	2	9	.227	51	52	5	.954
1981	—Fort Lauderdale§	Fla. St.	2-S-3-O	79	259	35	77	11	1	2	26	.297	104	238	19	.947
1982	—Nashville	South.	2B-SS-OF	89	299	27	71	14	1	0	24	.237	136	219	20	.947
1982	—Fort Lauderdale	Fla. St.	2B	9	32	2	8	1	0	1	6	.250	23	25	2	.960
1983	—Fort Lauderdale	Fla. St.	2B-SS	91	345	55	93	15	2	2	50	.270	195	245	15	.967
1983	—Columbus	Int.	2B-3B-SS	40	118	17	36	5	0	1	11	.305	55	95	4	.974
1984	—Columbus	Int.	2B	114	394	49	115	26	1	1	35	.292	266	348	16	.975
1984	—New York	Amer.	2B	9	7	2	1	1	0	0	0	.143	4	7	0	1.000
1985	—Columbus	Int.	2-S-O-3-1	106	380	62	95	13	4	3	18	.250	192	234	17	.962
1985	—New York x	Amer.	2B-1B-SS	20	51	4	8	0	1	0	1	.157	42	51	2	.979
1986	—Rochester	Int.	2-3-O-S	77	219	29	57	12	3	2	13	.260	135	191	15	.956
1986	—Baltimore	Amer.	2B-3B	14	1	1	0	0	0	0	0	.000	2	3	1	.833
1987	—Rochester yz	Int.	OF-2B-SS	31	106	22	27	5	1	5	10	.255	51	15	2	.971
1988	—Indianapolis	A. A.	O-2-S-3	67	234	36	71	11	3	7	25	.303	102	96	4	.980
1988	—Montreal	Nat.	2B-SS-OF	77	216	38	59	14	2	4	14	.273	116	168	10	.966
American League Totals—3 Years				43	59	7	9	1	1	0	1	.153	48	61	3	.973
National League Totals—1 Year				77	216	38	59	14	2	4	14	.273	116	168	10	.966
Major League Totals—4 Years				120	275	45	68	15	3	4	15	.247	164	229	13	.968

Selected by New York Yankees' organization in 1st round (18th player selected) of free-agent draft, June 6, 1978.
†On disabled list, May 18 to May 31, 1979
‡On disabled list, May 10 to June 15, 1980.
§On disabled list, May 11 to June 11, 1981.
xTraded with Pitcher Rich Bordi to Baltimore Orioles for Oufielder Gary Roenicke and a player to be named later, December 12, 1985; New York Yankees acquired Outfielder Leo Hernandez to complete deal, December 16, 1985.
yOn Baltimore disabled list, March 23 to June 16, 1987; included rehabilitation disability assignment to Rochester, May 28 to June 16, 1987.
zGranted free agency, October 15, 1987; signed by Indianapolis (Montreal Expos' organization) December 18, 1987.

CHARLES LYNN HUDSON

Born March 16, 1959, at Ennis, Tex.
Height, 6.03. Weight, 185.
Throws right and bats left and righthanded.
Received bachelor of business administration degree in management from
Prairie View A&M University, Prairie View, Tex., in 1981.

Major League saves: 1988 (2).
Tied for Carolina League lead in shutouts with 3 in 1982.

Tied for Carolina League lead in games started by pitchers with 14 in 1981.
Named Carolina League Pitcher of the Year, 1982.

Year Club	League	G.	IP.	W.	L.	Pct.	H.	R.	ER.	SO.	BB.	ERA.
1981—Helena	Pioneer	14	87	5	5	.500	92	53	37	67	27	3.83
1982—Peninsula	Carolina	27	185	•15	5	.750	143	56	38	147	64	*1.85
1983—Portland	P. Coast	10	64	6	3	.667	48	19	19	51	16	2.67
1983—Philadelphia	National	26	169⅓	8	8	.500	158	73	63	101	53	3.35
1984—Philadelphia†	National	30	173⅔	9	11	.450	181	101	78	94	52	4.04
1985—Philadelphia	National	38	193	8	13	.381	188	92	81	122	74	3.78
1986—Philadelphia‡	National	33	144	7	10	.412	165	87	79	82	58	4.94
1987—New York	American	35	154⅔	11	7	.611	137	63	62	100	57	3.61
1987—Columbus	Int'national	5	13⅔	0	2	.000	22	11	9	13	5	5.93
1988—New York§	American	28	106⅓	6	6	.500	93	53	53	58	36	4.49
National League Totals—4 Years		127	680	32	42	.432	692	353	301	399	237	3.98
American League Totals—2 Years		63	261	17	13	.567	230	116	115	158	93	3.97
Major League Totals—6 Years		190	941	49	55	.471	922	469	416	557	330	3.98

Selected by Philadelphia Phillies' organization in 12th round of free-agent draft, June 8, 1981.
†On disabled list, August 10 to September 1, 1984.
‡Traded with Pitcher Jeff Knox to New York Yankees for Outfielder Mike Easler and Infielder Tom Barrett, December 11, 1986.
§On disabled list, July 19 to August 22, 1988.

CHAMPIONSHIP SERIES RECORD

Year Club	League	G.	IP.	W.	L.	Pct.	H.	R.	ER.	SO.	BB.	ERA.
1983—Philadelphia	National	1	9	1	0	1.000	4	2	2	9	2	2.00

WORLD SERIES RECORD

Tied World Series records for most games lost, five-game Series (2), 1983; most home runs allowed, five-game Series (4), 1983.

Year Club	League	G.	IP.	W.	L.	Pct.	H.	R.	ER.	SO.	BB.	ERA.
1983—Philadelphia	National	2	8⅓	0	2	.000	9	8	8	6	1	8.64

KEITH WILLS HUGHES

Born September 12, 1963, at Bryn Mawr, Pa.
Height, 6.03. Weight, 210.
Throws and bats lefthanded.

Major League stolen bases: 1988 (1).
Tied for South Atlantic League lead in intentional bases on balls received with 5 in 1983.

Year Club	League	Pos.	G.	AB.	R.	H.	2B.	3B.	HR.	RBI.	B.A.	PO.	A.	E.	F.A.
1982—Bend	N'west	OF	55	179	29	46	10	2	3	26	.257	90	6	5	.950
1983—Spartanburg	S. Atl.	OF-1B	131	484	80	159	31	4	15	90	.329	171	5	7	.962
1984—Reading†	East.	OF-1B	70	230	35	60	7	5	2	20	.261	117	7	9	.932
1984—Nashville	South.	OF	21	50	6	9	0	0	0	5	.180	19	0	0	1.000
1985—Albany	East.	OF-2B	104	361	53	97	22	5	10	54	.269	218	18	3	.988
1985—Columbus	Int.	OF	18	54	7	16	4	0	3	8	.296	25	0	2	.926
1986—Albany‡	East.	OF-1B	94	323	44	99	21	3	7	37	.307	247	17	7	.974
1986—Columbus	Int.	OF	2	8	0	1	0	0	0	0	.125	6	0	1	.857
1987—Col.-Maine	Int.	OF-1B	90	316	48	93	15	4	17	57	.294	149	2	7	.956
1987—New York§	Amer.	PH	4	4	0	0	0	0	0	0	.000	0	0	0	.000
1987—Philadelphia x	Nat.	OF	37	76	8	20	2	0	0	10	.263	26	0	1	.963
1988—Rochester	Int.	OF	77	274	44	74	13	2	7	49	.270	159	2	3	.982
1988—Baltimore	Amer.	OF	41	108	10	21	4	2	2	14	.194	59	4	2	.969
American League Totals—2 Years			45	112	10	21	4	2	2	14	.188	59	4	2	.969
National League Totals—1 Year			37	76	8	20	2	0	0	10	.263	26	0	1	.963
Major League Totals—2 Years			82	188	18	41	6	2	2	24	.218	85	4	3	.967

Signed as free agent by Philadelphia Phillies' organization, August 24, 1981.
†Traded with Pitcher Marty Bystrom to New York Yankees for Pitcher Shane Rawley, June 30, 1984.
‡On disabled list, July 22 to August 26, 1986.
§Traded with Infielder Shane Turner to Philadelphia Phillies' organization for Outfielder Mike Easler, June 10, 1987.
xTraded with Infielder Rick Schu and Outfielder Jeff Stone to Baltimore Orioles for Outfielder Mike Young and a player to be named later, March 21, 1988; Philadelphia Phillies acquired Outfielder Frank Bellino to complete deal, June 14, 1988.

MARK LAWRENCE HUISMANN

Born May 11, 1958, at Lincoln, Neb.
Height, 6.03. Weight, 195.
Throws and bats righthanded.
Received bachelor of science degree in business and finance from
Colorado State University, Fort Collins, Colo., in 1980.

Major League saves: 1984 (3), 1986 (5), 1987 (2). Total—10.
Led International League in games finished in relief with 45 in 1988.
Led American Association in saves with 33 and games finished in relief with 56 in 1985.
Named American Association Pitcher of the Year, 1985.

Year Club	League	G.	IP.	W.	L.	Pct.	H.	R.	ER.	SO.	BB.	ERA.
1980—Sarasota Royals-Blue	Gulf Coast	28	59	1	2	.333	50	20	16	46	14	2.44
1981—Charleston	S. Atlantic	28	44	3	2	.600	36	16	8	42	17	1.64

Year Club	League	G.	IP.	W.	L.	Pct.	H.	R.	ER.	SO.	BB.	ERA.
1981—Fort Myers	Florida St.	14	21	3	1	.750	15	9	8	19	16	3.43
1982—Fort Myers	Florida St.	14	23	3	1	.750	16	1	1	21	4	0.39
1982—Jacksonville	Southern	36	54⅔	4	4	.500	52	18	13	60	15	2.14
1983—Jacksonville	Southern	37	61⅓	6	3	.667	60	25	22	46	25	3.23
1983—Omaha	Am. Assoc.	17	24⅓	0	2	.000	16	7	5	25	9	1.85
1983—Kansas City	American	13	30⅔	2	1	.667	29	20	19	20	17	5.58
1984—Kansas City	American	38	75	3	3	.500	84	38	35	54	21	4.20
1984—Omaha	Am. Assoc.	15	19	2	0	1.000	11	0	0	18	5	0.00
1985—Omaha	Am. Assoc.	*59	89⅓	5	5	.500	70	20	20	70	14	2.01
1985—Kansas City	American	9	18⅔	1	0	1.000	14	4	4	9	3	1.93
1986—Kansas City†-Seattle	American	46	97⅓	3	4	.429	98	47	41	72	25	3.79
1987—Seattle‡-Cleveland	American	26	50	2	3	.400	48	32	28	38	12	5.04
1987—Buffalo§	Am. Assoc.	13	33⅓	1	1	.500	43	32	28	31	8	7.56
1988—Toledo	Int'national	48	57⅔	4	6	.400	50	20	12	61	15	1.87
1988—Detroit	American	5	5⅓	1	0	1.000	6	3	3	6	2	5.06
Major League Totals—6 Years		137	277	12	11	.522	279	144	130	199	80	4.22

Selected by Chicago Cubs' organization in 23rd round of free-agent draft, June 5, 1979.
Signed as free agent by Kansas City Royals' organization, June 16, 1980.
†Traded to Seattle Mariners for Catcher Terry Bell, May 21, 1986.
‡Traded to Cleveland Indians for Outfielder Dave Gallagher, May 12, 1987.
§Released, March 17, 1988; signed by Toledo (Detroit Tigers' organization), March 23, 1988.

CHAMPIONSHIP SERIES RECORD

Year Club	League	G.	IP.	W.	L.	Pct.	H.	R.	ER.	SO.	BB.	ERA.
1984—Kansas City	American	1	2⅔	0	0	.000	6	3	2	2	1	6.75

DARREN SCOTT HURSEY

Born August 1, 1968, at Urbana, Ill.
Height, 6.06. Weight, 180.
Throws and bats lefthanded.

Year Club	League	G.	IP.	W.	L.	Pct.	H.	R.	ER.	SO.	BB.	ERA.
1986—Bristol	Ap'lachian	13	66⅔	5	3	.625	58	29	20	44	21	2.70
1987—Fayetteville	S. Atlantic	25	139	11	8	.579	132	65	48	77	57	3.11
1988—Lakeland	Florida St.	26	166	15	8	.652	148	56	44	82	68	2.39

Selected by Detroit Tigers' organization in 17th round of free-agent draft, June 2, 1986.

BRUCE VEE HURST

Born March 24, 1958, at St. George, Utah.
Height, 6.03. Weight, 215.
Throws and bats lefthanded.
Attended Dixie College, St. George, Utah.

Led American League in balks with 4 in 1985.

Year Club	League	G.	IP.	W.	L.	Pct.	H.	R.	ER.	SO.	BB.	ERA.
1976—Elmira	NYP	9	42	3	2	.600	25	18	14	40	38	3.00
1977—Winter Haven†	Florida St.	13	91	5	4	.556	77	28	21	69	25	2.08
1978—Bristol‡	Eastern	6	33	1	3	.250	32	15	10	35	17	2.73
1979—Winter Haven	Florida St.	12	84	8	2	.800	57	22	18	64	20	1.93
1979—Bristol	Eastern	16	113	9	4	.692	108	56	45	91	49	3.58
1980—Pawtucket	Int'national	17	105	8	6	.571	101	52	46	54	50	3.94
1980—Boston	American	12	31	2	2	.500	39	33	31	16	16	9.00
1981—Pawtucket	Int'national	32	157	12	7	.632	143	68	50	99	71	2.87
1981—Boston	American	5	23	2	0	1.000	23	11	11	11	12	4.30
1982—Boston	American	28	117	3	7	.300	161	87	75	53	40	5.77
1983—Boston	American	33	211⅓	12	12	.500	241	102	96	115	62	4.09
1984—Boston	American	33	218	12	12	.500	232	106	95	136	88	3.92
1985—Boston	American	35	229⅓	11	13	.458	243	123	115	189	70	4.51
1986—Boston§	American	25	174⅓	13	8	.619	169	63	58	167	50	2.99
1987—Boston	American	33	238⅔	15	13	.536	239	124	117	190	76	4.41
1988—Boston xy	American	33	216⅔	18	6	.750	222	98	88	166	65	3.66
Major League Totals—9 Years		237	1459⅓	88	73	.547	1569	747	686	1043	479	4.23

Selected by Boston Red Sox' organization in 1st round (22nd player selected) of free-agent draft, June 8, 1976.
†On disabled list, August 8 to September 14, 1977.
‡On disabled list, May 23 to September 21, 1978.
§On disabled list, June 3 to July 18, 1986.
xOn disabled list, July 8 to July 24, 1988.
yGranted free agency, November 4, 1988; signed by San Diego Padres, December 8, 1988.

CHAMPIONSHIP SERIES RECORD

Tied Championship Series record for most games lost, Series (2), 1988.

Year Club	League	G.	IP.	W.	L.	Pct.	H.	R.	ER.	SO.	BB.	ERA.
1986—Boston	American	2	15	1	0	1.000	18	5	4	8	1	2.40
1988—Boston	American	2	13	0	2	.000	10	4	4	12	5	2.77
Championship Series Totals—2 Years		4	28	1	2	.333	28	9	8	20	6	2.57

WORLD SERIES RECORD

Year Club	League	G.	IP.	W.	L.	Pct.	H.	R.	ER.	SO.	BB.	ERA.
1986—Boston	American	3	23	2	0	1.000	18	5	5	17	6	1.96

ALL-STAR GAME RECORD

Member of American League All-Star Team in 1987; did not play.

JEFFREY KENT HUSON
(Jeff)

Born August 15, 1964, at Scottsdale, Ariz.
Height, 6.03. Weight, 170.
Throws right and bats lefthanded.
Attended Glendale Community College, Glendale, Ariz., and University of Wyoming, Laramie, Wyo.

Major League stolen bases: 1988 (2).
Led Southern League in stolen bases with 56 in 1988.

Year Club	League	Pos.	G.	AB.	R.	H.	2B.	3B.	HR.	RBI.	B.A.	PO.	A.	E.	F.A.
1986—Burlington	Midw.	SS-3B-2B	133	457	85	132	19	1	16	72	.289	183	324	37	.932
1986—Jacksonville	South.	3B	1	4	0	0	0	0	0	0	.000	0	1	0	1.000
1987—W. Palm Beach	Fla. St.	SS-OF-2B	131	455	54	130	15	4	1	53	.286	234	347	34	.945
1988—Jacksonville	South.	S-2-O-3	128	471	72	117	18	1	0	34	.248	217	285	26	.951
1988—Montreal	Nat.	S-2-3-O	20	42	7	13	2	0	0	3	.310	18	41	4	.937
Major League Totals—1 Year			20	42	7	13	2	0	0	3	.310	18	41	4	.937

Signed as free agent by Montreal Expos' organization, August 18, 1985.

PETER JOSEPH INCAVIGLIA
(Pete)

Born April 2, 1964, at Pebble Beach, Calif.
Height, 6.01. Weight, 220.
Throws and bats righthanded.
Attended Oklahoma State University, Stillwater, Okla.
Son of Tom Incaviglia, minor league infielder, 1948 through 1950 and 1955; and brother of Tony Incaviglia, minor league third baseman, 1979 through 1983.

Tied major league record for most doubles, inning (2), May 11, 1986, second game (fourth inning).
Major League stolen bases: 1986 (3), 1987 (9), 1988 (6). Total—18.
Led American League batters in strikeouts with 185 in 1986 and tied for lead with 153 in 1988.
Received reported $175,000 bonus to sign with Texas Rangers, 1985.
Named designated hitter on THE SPORTING NEWS College Baseball All-America Team, 1985.

Year Club	League	Pos.	G.	AB.	R.	H.	2B.	3B.	HR.	RBI.	B.A.	PO.	A.	E.	F.A.
1986—Texas†	Amer.	OF	153	540	82	135	21	2	30	88	.250	157	6	●14	.921
1987—Texas	Amer.	OF	139	509	85	138	26	4	27	80	.271	216	8	●13	.945
1988—Texas	Amer.	OF	116	418	59	104	19	3	22	54	.249	172	12	2	.989
Major League Totals—3 Years			408	1467	226	377	66	9	79	222	.257	545	26	29	.952

Selected by San Francisco Giants' organization in 10th round of free-agent draft, June 7, 1982.
Selected by Montreal Expos' organization in 1st round (eighth player selected) of free-agent draft, June 3, 1985.
†Traded to Texas Rangers' organization for Pitcher Bob Sebra and Infielder Jim Anderson, November 2, 1985.

FERMIN ALEXIS INFANTE

Name pronounced En-fawn-tay.
(Known by middle name.)
Born December 4, 1961, at Barquisimeto, Venezuela.
Height, 5.11. Weight, 182.
Throws and bats righthanded.

Led International League shortstops in errors with 23 in 1988.
Led International League shortstops in total chances with 699 and double plays with 84 in 1985.
Led South Atlantic League shortstops in total chances with 646 in 1983.

Year Club	League	Pos.	G.	AB.	R.	H.	2B.	3B.	HR.	RBI.	B.A.	PO.	A.	E.	F.A.
1982—Bradenton Jays	Gulf C.	SS	37	137	17	40	7	2	0	15	.292	47	117	5	.970
1983—Florence	S. Atl.	SS	128	480	88	134	25	3	4	56	.279	★197	393	★56	.913
1984—Knoxville	South.	SS	67	253	28	67	13	1	2	29	.265	92	204	18	.943
1984—Syracuse	Int.	SS	72	225	27	50	6	1	0	7	.222	88	229	21	.938
1985—Syracuse	Int.	SS	136	453	63	109	10	5	2	39	.241	★225	★432	★42	.940
1986—Syracuse†	Int.	SS	57	193	27	53	6	2	0	15	.275	73	172	14	.946
1987—Syracuse	Int.	S-3-O-2	107	319	40	72	7	4	2	30	.226	111	260	20	.949
1987—Toronto	Amer.	PR	1	0	0	0	0	0	0	0	.000	0	0	0	.000
1988—Syracuse	Int.	SS-3B-2B	97	340	48	102	15	4	2	28	.300	143	240	25	.939
1988—Toronto	Amer.	3B-SS	19	15	7	3	0	0	0	0	.200	4	6	1	.909
Major League Totals—2 Years			20	15	7	3	0	0	0	0	.200	4	6	1	.909

Signed as free agent by Toronto Blue Jays' organization, December 8, 1981.
†On disabled list, June 18, 1986 through remainder of season.

—DID YOU KNOW—

That Mike Maddux of the Phillies beat younger brother Greg of the Cubs in Philadelphia's 6-3 victory over Chicago on July 31?

JEFFREY DAVID INNIS
(Jeff)

Born July 5, 1962, at Decatur, Ill.
Height, 6.00. Weight, 170.
Throws and bats righthanded.
Attended University of Illinois, Champaign, Ill.

Led Texas League in saves with 25 in 1986.

Year Club	League	G.	IP.	W.	L.	Pct.	H.	R.	ER.	SO.	BB.	ERA.
1983—Little Falls	NYP	28	46	8	0	1.000	29	8	7	68	28	1.37
1984—Jackson	Texas	42	59⅓	6	5	.545	65	34	28	63	40	4.25
1985—Lynchburg	Carolina	53	77	6	3	.667	46	26	20	91	40	2.34
1986—Jackson	Texas	56	92	4	5	.444	69	30	25	75	24	2.45
1987—Tidewater	Int'national	29	44⅓	6	1	.857	26	10	10	28	16	2.03
1987—New York	National	17	25⅔	0	1	.000	29	9	9	28	4	3.16
1988—Tidewater	Int'national	34	48⅓	0	5	.000	43	22	19	43	25	3.54
1988—New York	National	12	19	1	1	.500	19	6	4	14	2	1.89
Major League Totals—2 Years		29	44⅔	1	2	.333	48	15	13	42	6	2.62

Selected by New York Mets' organization in 13th round of free-agent draft, June 6, 1983.

CHARLES LEO JACKSON
(Chuck)

Born March 19, 1963, at Seattle, Wash.
Height, 6.00. Weight, 185.
Throws and bats righthanded.
Attended University of Hawaii, Honolulu, Haw.

Major League stolen bases: 1987 (1), 1988 (1). Total—2.
Led Southern League third basemen in errors with 30 in 1985.

Year Club	League	Pos.	G.	AB.	R.	H.	2B.	3B.	HR.	RBI.	B.A.	PO.	A.	E.	F.A.
1984—Auburn	NYP	OF	10	38	4	14	0	2	1	4	.368	9	3	0	1.000
1984—Asheville	S. Atl.	OF	59	199	42	52	12	0	5	32	.261	98	6	4	.963
1985—Tucson	P. C.	OF	19	61	7	11	2	1	1	4	.180	43	3	1	.979
1985—Columbus	South.	3B-OF	108	361	62	112	10	8	8	46	.310	98	232	32	.912
1986—Tucson	P. C.	*3B-OF	127	448	83	137	27	5	11	62	.306	91	202	*29	.910
1987—Tucson	P. C.	3B-SS-OF	80	291	51	84	10	4	3	43	.289	79	124	20	.910
1987—Houston	Nat.	3B-OF-SS	35	71	3	15	3	0	1	6	.211	12	39	2	.962
1988—Houston	Nat.	3B-SS-OF	46	83	7	19	5	1	1	8	.229	12	51	7	.900
1988—Tucson	P. C.	SS-OF-3B	48	151	21	45	8	0	2	11	.298	55	95	9	.943
Major League Totals—2 Years			81	154	10	34	8	1	2	14	.221	24	90	9	.927

Selected by Cleveland Indians' organization in 21st round of free-agent draft, June 8, 1981.
Selected by Houston Astros' organization in 7th round of free-agent draft, June 4, 1984.

DANNY LYNN JACKSON

Born January 5, 1962, at San Antonio, Tex.
Height, 6.00. Weight, 205.
Throws left and bats righthanded.
Attended University of Oklahoma, Norman, Okla., and
Trinidad State Junior College, Trinidad, Colo.
Brother of Mike Jackson, fourth-round selection of Kansas City Kings in 1983 NBA draft.

Major League saves: 1986 (1).
Tied for National League lead in complete games with 15 in 1988.
Tied for American Association lead in complete games with 10 in 1984.
Tied for American Association lead in shutouts with 2 in 1983 and 3 in 1984.
Named lefthanded pitcher on The Sporting News National League All-Star Team, 1988.

Year Club	League	G.	IP.	W.	L.	Pct.	H.	R.	ER.	SO.	BB.	ERA.
1982—Charleston	S. Atlantic	13	96⅓	10	1	.909	80	37	28	62	39	2.62
1982—Jacksonville†	Southern	14	98	7	2	.778	78	30	26	74	42	2.39
1983—Omaha	Am. Assoc.	23	136	7	8	.467	126	74	60	93	73	3.97
1983—Kansas City	American	4	19	1	1	.500	26	12	11	9	6	5.21
1984—Kansas City	American	15	76	2	6	.250	84	41	36	40	35	4.26
1984—Omaha	Am. Assoc.	16	110⅓	5	8	.385	91	50	45	82	45	3.67
1985—Kansas City	American	32	208	14	12	.538	209	94	79	114	76	3.42
1986—Kansas City ‡	American	32	185⅔	11	12	.478	177	83	66	115	79	3.20
1987—Kansas City§	American	36	224	9	18	.333	219	115	100	152	109	4.02
1988—Cincinnati	National	35	260⅔	•23	8	.742	206	86	79	161	71	2.73
American League Totals—5 Years		119	712⅔	37	49	.430	715	345	292	430	305	3.69
National League Totals—1 Year		35	260⅔	23	8	.742	206	86	79	161	71	2.73
Major League Totals—6 Years		154	973⅓	60	57	.513	921	431	371	591	376	3.43

Selected by Oakland A's organization in 24th round of free-agent draft, June 3, 1980.
Selected by Kansas City Royals' organization in secondary phase of free-agent draft, January 17, 1982.
†On disabled list, September 8, 1982 through remainder of season.
‡On disabled list, April 4 to April 21, 1986.
§Traded with Shortstop Angel Salazar to Cincinnati Reds for Pitcher Ted Power and Shortstop Kurt Stillwell, November 6, 1987.

CHAMPIONSHIP SERIES RECORD

Year	Club	League	G.	IP.	W.	L.	Pct.	H.	R.	ER.	SO.	BB.	ERA.
1985	Kansas City	American	2	10	1	0	1.000	10	0	0	7	1	0.00

WORLD SERIES RECORD

Tied World Series record for most consecutive times striking out, Series (5), 1985.

Year	Club	League	G.	IP.	W.	L.	Pct.	H.	R.	ER.	SO.	BB.	ERA.
1985	Kansas City	American	2	16	1	1	.500	9	3	3	12	5	1.69

ALL-STAR GAME RECORD

Member of National League All-Star Team in 1988; did not play.

DARRIN JAY JACKSON

Born August 22, 1963, at Los Angeles, Calif.
Height, 6.00. Weight, 185.
Throws and bats righthanded.

Major League stolen bases: 1988 (4).
Led Gulf Coast League outfielders in total chances with 127 in 1981.
Tied for American Association lead in double plays by outfielders with 6 in 1987.
Tied for Texas League lead in double plays with 6 in 1984.

Year	Club	League	Pos.	G.	AB.	R.	H.	2B.	3B.	HR.	RBI.	B.A.	PO.	A.	E.	F.A.
1981	Sarasota Cubs	Gulf C.	OF	62	210	29	39	5	0	1	15	.186	*121	5	1	.992
1982	Quad Cities	Midw.	OF	132	529	86	146	23	5	5	48	.276	266	9	8	.972
1983	Salinas	Calif.	OF	129	509	70	126	18	5	6	54	.248	237	15	13	.951
1984	Midland	Texas	OF	132	496	63	134	18	2	15	54	.270	286	*19	8	.974
1985	Iowa	A. A.	OF	10	40	0	7	2	1	0	1	.175	19	0	0	1.000
1985	Pittsfield	East.	OF	91	325	38	82	10	1	3	30	.252	221	5	0	1.000
1985	Chicago	Nat.	OF	5	11	0	1	0	0	0	0	.091	7	0	0	1.000
1986	Pittsfield	East.	OF	137	•520	82	139	28	2	15	64	.267	320	*16	7	.980
1987	Iowa	A. A.	OF	132	474	81	130	32	5	23	81	.274	290	15	6	.981
1987	Chicago	Nat.	OF	7	5	2	4	1	0	0	0	.800	1	0	0	1.000
1988	Chicago	Nat.	OF	100	188	29	50	11	3	6	20	.266	116	1	2	.983
Major League Totals—3 Years				112	204	31	55	12	3	6	20	.270	124	1	2	.984

Selected by Chicago Cubs' organization in 2nd round of free-agent draft, June 8, 1981.

MICHAEL RAY JACKSON
(Mike)

Born December 22, 1964, at Houston, Tex.
Height, 6.00. Weight, 185.
Throws and bats righthanded.
Attended Hill Junior College, Hillsboro, Tex.

Major League saves: 1987 (1), 1988 (4). Total—5.
Tied for American League lead in intentional bases on balls issued with 10 in 1988.
Tied for National League lead in balks with 8 in 1987.
Led Carolina League in balks with 7 in 1985.

Year	Club	League	G.	IP.	W.	L.	Pct.	H.	R.	ER.	SO.	BB.	ERA.
1984	Spartanburg	S. Atlantic	14	$80\frac{2}{3}$	7	2	.778	53	35	24	77	50	2.68
1985	Peninsula	Carolina	31	$125\frac{1}{3}$	7	9	.438	127	71	64	96	53	4.60
1986	Reading	Eastern	30	$43\frac{1}{3}$	2	3	.400	25	9	8	42	22	1.66
1986	Portland	P. Coast	17	$22\frac{2}{3}$	3	1	.750	18	8	8	23	13	3.18
1986	Philadelphia	National	9	$13\frac{1}{3}$	0	0	.000	12	5	5	3	4	3.38
1987	Philadelphia†	National	55	$109\frac{1}{3}$	3	10	.231	88	55	51	93	56	4.20
1987	Maine‡	Int'national	2	11	1	0	1.000	9	2	1	13	5	0.82
1988	Seattle	American	62	$99\frac{1}{3}$	6	5	.545	74	37	29	76	43	2.63
National League Totals—2 Years			64	$122\frac{2}{3}$	3	10	.231	100	60	56	96	60	4.11
American League Totals—1 Year			62	$99\frac{1}{3}$	6	5	.545	74	37	29	76	43	2.63
Major League Totals—3 Years			126	222	9	15	.375	174	97	85	172	103	3.45

Selected by Philadelphia Phillies' organization in 29th round of free-agent draft, June 6, 1983.
Selected by Philadelphia Phillies' organization in secondary phase of free-agent draft, January 17, 1984.
†On disabled list, August 6 to August 21, 1987.
‡Traded with Outfielders Glenn Wilson and Dave Brundage to Seattle Mariners for Outfielder Phil Bradley and Pitcher Tim Fortugno, December 9, 1987.

VINCENT EDWARD JACKSON
(Bo)

Born November 30, 1962, at Bessemer, Ala.
Height, 6.01. Weight, 222.
Throws and bats righthanded.
Attended Auburn University, Auburn, Ala.

Tied major league records for most strikeouts, nine-inning game (5), April 18, 1987; most strikeouts, inning (2), April 8, 1987, fourth inning.
Major League stolen bases: 1986 (3), 1987 (10), 1988 (27). Total—40.

Year	Club	League	Pos.	G.	AB.	R.	H.	2B.	3B.	HR.	RBI.	B.A.	PO.	A.	E.	F.A.
1986	—Memphis†	South.	OF	53	184	30	51	9	3	7	25	.277	116	8	7	.947
1986	—Kansas City	Amer.	OF	25	82	9	17	2	1	2	9	.207	29	2	4	.886
1987	—Kansas City	Amer.	OF	116	396	46	93	17	2	22	53	.235	180	9	9	.955
1988	—Kansas City‡	Amer.	OF	124	439	63	108	16	4	25	68	.246	246	11	7	.973
Major League Totals—3 Years				265	917	118	218	35	7	49	130	.238	455	22	20	.960

Selected by New York Yankees' organization in 2nd round of free-agent draft, June 7, 1982.
Selected by California Angels' organization in 20th round of free-agent draft, June 3, 1985.
Selected by Kansas City Royals' organization in 4th round of free-agent draft, June 2, 1986.
†On temporary inactive list, June 20 to June 30, 1986.
‡On disabled list, June 1 to July 2, 1988.

RECORD AS FOOTBALL PLAYER

Heisman Trophy winner, 1985.
Named college football Player of the Year by THE SPORTING NEWS, 1985.
Named as running back on THE SPORTING NEWS College All-America Team, 1985.
Selected by Tampa Bay in 1st round (1st player selected) of 1986 NFL draft.
Selected by Birmingham in 1986 USFL territorial draft.
On reserve/did not sign entire 1986 football season through April 27, 1987.
Selected by Los Angeles Raiders in 7th round (183rd player selected) of 1987 NFL draft.
Signed by Los Angeles Raiders, July 17, 1987.

			RUSHING				PASS RECEIVING				TOTAL		
Year	Club	G.	Att.	Yds.	Avg.	TD.	P.C.	Yds.	Avg.	TD.	TD.	Pts.	F.
1987	—Los Angeles Raiders NFL	7	81	554	6.8	4	16	136	8.5	2	6	36	2
1988	—Los Angeles Raiders NFL	10	136	580	4.3	3	9	79	8.8	0	3	18	5
Pro Totals—2 Years		17	217	1134	5.2	7	25	215	8.6	2	9	54	7

Additional pro statistics: Recovered one fumble, 1987.

BROOK WALLACE JACOBY JR.

Born November 23, 1959, at Philadelphia, Pa.
Height, 5.11. Weight, 195.
Throws and bats righthanded.
Attended Ventura College, Ventura, Calif.
Son of Brook Jacoby Sr., minor league pitcher, 1956 through 1958.

Major League stolen bases: 1984 (3), 1985 (2), 1986 (2), 1987 (2), 1988 (2). Total—11.
Hit three home runs in a game, July 3, 1987.
Tied for American League lead in putouts by third basemen with 134 in 1987.
Led International League third basemen in total chances with 331 and double plays with 22 in 1982.

Year	Club	League	Pos.	G.	AB.	R.	H.	2B.	3B.	HR.	RBI.	B.A.	PO.	A.	E.	F.A.
1979	—Kingsport	Appal.	OF	8	28	3	7	2	0	0	1	.250	9	0	0	1.000
1979	—Bradenton	Gulf C.	OF	42	160	24	43	11	1	3	35	.269	65	7	4	.947
1980	—Anderson	S. Atl.	OF-3B	132	496	82	147	★40	4	19	★108	.296	219	30	10	.961
1980	—Savannah	South.	3B	3	8	0	1	0	0	0	0	.125	0	2	0	1.000
1981	—Savannah	South.	3B-OF	140	507	59	148	28	3	24	82	.292	103	232	31	.915
1981	—Atlanta	Nat.	3B	11	10	0	2	0	0	0	1	.200	3	4	0	1.000
1982	—Richmond	Int.	3B	134	501	74	150	21	3	18	58	.299	83	★229	★19	★.943
1983	—Richmond	Int.	3B	133	489	88	154	32	2	25	100	.315	62	247	18	.945
1983	—Atlanta†	Nat.	3B	4	8	0	0	0	0	0	0	.000	0	2	0	1.000
1984	—Cleveland‡	Amer.	3B-SS	126	439	64	116	19	3	7	40	.264	86	188	14	.951
1985	—Cleveland	Amer.	3B-2B	161	606	72	166	26	3	20	87	.274	114	319	19	.958
1986	—Cleveland	Amer.	3B	158	583	83	168	30	4	17	80	.288	109	292	25	.941
1987	—Cleveland	Amer.	•3B-1B	155	540	73	162	26	4	32	69	.300	192	261	•22	.954
1988	—Cleveland	Amer.	3B	152	552	59	133	25	0	9	49	.241	99	298	10	.975
National League Totals—2 Years				15	18	0	2	0	0	0	1	.111	3	6	0	1.000
American League Totals—5 Years				752	2720	351	745	126	14	85	325	.274	600	1358	90	.956
Major League Totals—7 Years				767	2738	351	747	126	14	85	326	.273	603	1364	90	.956

Selected by Atlanta Braves' organization in 7th round of free-agent draft, January 9, 1979.

†Traded with Outfielder Brett Butler to Cleveland Indians, October 21, 1983, completing deal in which Atlanta Braves acquired Pitcher Len Barker for three players to be named later, August 28, 1983. Cleveland acquired Pitcher Rick Behenna as partial completion of deal, September 2, 1983.

‡On disabled list, August 20, 1984 through remainder of season.

ALL-STAR GAME RECORD

Year	League	Pos.	AB.	R.	H.	2B.	3B.	HR.	RBI.	B.A.	PO.	A.	E.	F.A.
1986	—American	PH-3B	1	0	0	0	0	0	0	.000	1	1	0	1.000

DION JAMES

Born November 9, 1962, at Philadelphia, Pa.
Height, 6.01. Weight, 170.
Throws and bats lefthanded.

Major League stolen bases: 1983 (1), 1984 (10), 1987 (10), 1988 (9). Total—30.
Led California League outfielders in fielding percentage with .988 in 1981.

Year	Club	League	Pos.	G.	AB.	R.	H.	2B.	3B.	HR.	RBI.	B.A.	PO.	A.	E.	F.A.
1980	—Butte	Pion.	OF-1B	59	224	57	71	14	1	0	27	.317	80	4	7	.923
1980	—Burlington	Midw.	OF	3	10	0	1	0	0	0	1	.100	8	1	0	1.000
1981	—Stockton	Calif.	OF-1B	124	451	70	137	17	3	2	49	.304	250	10	3	.989

Year	Club	League	Pos.	G.	AB.	R.	H.	2B.	3B.	HR.	RBI.	B.A.	PO.	A.	E.	F.A.
1982	—El Paso†	Texas	OF	106	422	103	136	25	3	9	72	.322	237	9	7	.972
1983	—Vancouver	P. C.	OF	129	467	84	157	29	5	8	68	.336	289	6	2	.993
1983	—Milwaukee	Amer.	OF	11	20	1	2	0	0	0	1	.100	12	1	0	1.000
1984	—Milwaukee	Amer.	OF	128	387	52	114	19	5	1	30	.295	252	7	3	.989
1985	—Vancouver‡	P. C.	OF	10	37	2	4	2	0	0	5	.108	17	0	0	1.000
1985	—Milwaukee	Amer.	OF	18	49	5	11	1	0	0	3	.224	20	0	0	1.000
1986	—Vancouver§	P. C.	OF-1B	130	485	85	137	25	6	6	55	.282	348	7	5	.986
1987	—Atlanta	Nat.	OF	134	494	80	154	37	6	10	61	.312	262	4	1	*.996
1988	—Atlanta	Nat.	OF	132	386	46	99	17	5	3	30	.256	222	5	3	.987
American League Totals—3 Years				157	456	58	127	20	5	1	34	.279	284	8	3	.990
National League Totals—2 Years				266	880	126	253	54	11	13	91	.288	484	9	4	.992
Major League Totals—5 Years				423	1336	184	380	74	16	14	125	.284	768	17	7	.991

Selected by Milwaukee Brewers' organization in 1st round (25th player selected) of free-agent draft, June 3, 1980.

†On disabled list, July 1 to August 1, 1982.

‡On Milwaukee disabled list, March 31 to April 28 and May 20 to September 1, 1985; included rehabilitation disability assignment to Vancouver, April 12 to April 28, 1985.

§Traded to Atlanta Braves for Outfielder Brad Komminsk, January 20, 1987.

DONALD CHRISTOPHER JAMES
(Chris)

Born October 4, 1962, at Rusk, Tex.
Height, 6.01. Weight, 190.
Throws and bats righthanded.
Attended Blinn College, Brenham, Tex.
Brother of Craig James, running back with New England Patriots.

Major League stolen bases: 1987 (3), 1988 (7). Total—10.
Tied for Pacific Coast League lead in being hit by pitch with 7 in 1985.
Led South Atlantic League in total bases with 257 and tied for lead in being hit by pitch with 12 in 1983.
Led Pacific Coast League outfielders in total chances with 351 in 1985.

Year	Club	League	Pos.	G.	AB.	R.	H.	2B.	3B.	HR.	RBI.	B.A.	PO.	A.	E.	F.A.
1982	—Bend	N'west	3B-OF	63	227	47	72	*19	3	12	50	.317	93	54	10	.936
1983	—Spartanburg	S. Atl.	OF-3B	129	499	94	148	23	4	26	*121	.297	150	88	16	.937
1984	—Reading	East.	*3B-OF	128	457	66	117	19	*12	8	57	.256	104	209	*39	.889
1985	—Portland	P. C.	OF	135	507	78	160	35	8	11	73	.316	*328	16	7	.980
1986	—Portland	P. C.	OF-3B	69	266	30	64	6	2	12	41	.241	83	44	8	.941
1986	—Philadelphia†	Nat.	OF	16	46	5	13	3	0	1	5	.283	19	0	0	1.000
1987	—Philadelphia	Nat.	OF	115	358	48	105	20	6	17	54	.293	198	5	2	.990
1987	—Maine	Int.	OF-3B	13	40	5	9	2	1	0	3	.225	22	4	0	1.000
1988	—Philadelphia	Nat.	OF-3B	150	566	57	137	24	1	19	66	.242	282	51	9	.974
Major League Totals—3 Years				281	970	110	255	47	7	37	125	.263	499	56	11	.981

Signed as free agent by Philadelphia Phillies' organization, October 30, 1981.

†On disabled list, May 6 to July 21, 1986; included rehabilitation disability assignment to Portland, July 3 to July 21, 1986.

STANLEY JULIAN JAVIER

Name pronounced HAAV-e-AIR.

(Stan)

Born January 9, 1965, at San Francisco Macoris, D. R.
Height, 6.00. Weight, 185.
Throws right and bats left and righthanded.
Son of Julian Javier, infielder with St. Louis Cardinals and Cincinnati Reds, 1960 through 1972.

Major League stolen bases: 1986 (8), 1987 (3), 1988 (20). Total—31.
Led Southern League in bases on balls received with 112 in 1985.

Year	Club	League	Pos.	G.	AB.	R.	H.	2B.	3B.	HR.	RBI.	B.A.	PO.	A.	E.	F.A.
1981	—Johnson City	Appal.	OF	53	144	30	36	5	4	3	19	.250	53	2	3	.948
1982	—Johnson City†	Appal.	OF	57	185	45	51	3	●4	8	36	.276	94	8	4	.962
1983	—Greensboro	S. Atl.	OF	129	489	109	152	*34	6	12	77	.311	250	10	15	.945
1984	—New York	Amer.	OF	7	7	1	1	0	0	0	0	.143	3	0	0	1.000
1984	—Nashville‡	South.	OF	76	262	40	76	17	4	7	38	.290	202	4	7	.967
1984	—Columbus	Int.	OF	32	99	12	22	3	1	0	7	.222	77	4	2	.976
1985	—Huntsville	South.	OF	140	486	105	138	22	8	9	64	.284	363	8	7	.981
1986	—Tacoma	P. C.	OF-1B	69	248	50	81	16	2	4	51	.327	172	9	6	.968
1986	—Oakland	Amer.	OF	59	114	13	23	8	0	0	8	.202	118	1	0	1.000
1987	—Oakland§	Amer.	OF-1B	81	151	22	28	3	1	2	9	.185	149	5	3	.981
1987	—Tacoma	P. C.	OF-1B	15	51	6	11	2	0	0	2	.216	26	0	2	.929
1988	—Oakland x	Amer.	OF-1B	125	397	49	102	13	3	2	35	.257	274	7	5	.983
Major League Totals—4 Years				272	669	85	154	24	4	4	52	.230	544	13	8	.986

Signed as free agent by St. Louis Cardinals' organization, March 26, 1981.

†Traded with shortstop Bob Meacham to New York Yankees' organization for Outfielder Bob Helsom and Pitchers Marty Mason and Steve Fincher, December 14, 1982.

‡Traded with Pitchers Jay Howell, Jose Rijo, Eric Plunk and Tim Birtsas to Oakland A's for Outfielder Rickey Henderson, Pitcher Bert Bradley and cash, December 5, 1984.

§On disabled list, August 3 to September 1, 1987; included rehabilitation disability assignment to Tacoma, August 20 to September 1, 1987.

xOn disabled list, August 18 to September 2, 1988.

CHAMPIONSHIP SERIES RECORD

Year	Club	League	Pos.	G.	AB.	R.	H.	2B.	3B.	HR.	RBI.	B.A.	PO.	A.	E.	F.A.
1988	—Oakland	Amer.	OF-PR	2	4	0	2	0	0	0	1	.500	5	0	0	1.000

WORLD SERIES RECORD

Year	Club	League	Pos.	G.	AB.	R.	H.	2B.	3B.	HR.	RBI.	B.A.	PO.	A.	E.	F.A.
1988	—Oakland	Amer.	PR-OF	3	4	0	2	0	0	0	2	.500	1	0	0	1.000

JAMES MICHAEL JEFFCOAT
(Mike)

Born August 3, 1959, at Pine Bluff, Ark.
Height, 6.02. Weight, 189.
Throws and bats lefthanded.
Attended Louisiana Tech University, Ruston, La.

Major League saves: 1984 (1).

Year	Club	League	G.	IP.	W.	L.	Pct.	H.	R.	ER.	SO.	BB.	ERA.
1980	—Waterloo	Midwest	4	6	0	0	.000	12	12	4	7	3	6.00
1980	—Batavia	NYP	12	68	4	3	.571	65	40	30	71	45	3.97
1981	—Waterloo	Midwest	25	147	10	8	.556	151	71	63	109	78	3.86
1982	—Waterloo	Midwest	9	62	5	4	.556	58	29	28	68	15	4.06
1982	—Chattanooga	Southern	18	128⅓	8	8	.500	122	49	41	107	51	2.88
1983	—Charleston	Int'natonal	26	167	12	8	.600	187	95	84	96	46	4.53
1983	—Cleveland	American	11	32⅔	1	3	.250	32	13	12	9	13	3.31
1984	—Cleveland	American	63	75⅓	5	2	.714	82	28	25	41	24	2.99
1985	—Cleveland†	American	9	9⅔	0	0	.000	8	5	3	4	6	2.79
1985	—Phoenix	P. Coast	10	59⅔	4	5	.444	64	26	24	28	9	3.62
1985	—San Francisco	National	19	22	0	2	.000	27	13	13	10	6	5.32
1986	—Phoenix‡	P. Coast	54	75	7	2	.778	81	40	35	57	31	4.20
1987	—Oklahoma City	Am. Assoc.	26	159⅔	11	8	.579	193	99	85	101	41	4.79
1987	—Texas	American	2	7	0	1	.000	11	10	10	1	4	12.86
1988	—Texas	American	5	10	0	2	.000	19	13	13	5	5	11.70
1988	—Oklahoma City	Am. Assoc.	22	157⅓	9	5	.643	137	53	49	95	41	2.80
American League Totals—5 Years			90	134⅔	6	8	.429	152	69	63	60	52	4.21
National League Totals—1 Year			19	22	0	2	.000	27	13	13	10	6	5.32
Major League Totals—5 Years			109	156⅔	6	10	.375	179	82	76	70	58	4.37

Selected by St. Louis Cardinals' organization in 30th round of free-agent draft, June 7, 1977.
Selected by Cleveland Indians' organization in 13th round of free-agent draft, June 3, 1980.
†Traded with Infielder Luis Quinones to San Francisco Giants' organization for Shortstop Johnnie LeMaster, May 7, 1985.
‡Released, October 21, 1986; signed by Texas Rangers' organization, December 18, 1986.

GREGORY SCOTT JEFFERIES
(Gregg)

Born August 1, 1967, at Burlingame, Calif.
Height, 5.10. Weight, 175.
Throws right and bats left and righthanded.

Major League stolen bases: 1988 (5).
Tied for International League lead in intentional bases on balls received with 10 in 1988.
Led Texas League in intentional bases on balls received with 18 in 1987.
Led Carolina League in slugging percentage with .549 in 1986.
Led International League third basemen in assists with 240 in 1988.
Named Texas League Most Valuable Player, 1987.
Named Carolina League Most Valuable Player, 1986.
Named Appalachian League Player of the Year, 1985.

Year	Club	League	Pos.	G.	AB.	R.	H.	2B.	3B.	HR.	RBI.	B.A.	PO.	A.	E.	F.A.
1985	—Kingsport	Appal.	SS-2B	47	166	27	57	18	2	3	29	.343	78	130	21	.908
1985	—Columbia	S. Atl.	2B-SS	20	64	7	18	2	2	1	12	.281	28	26	2	.964
1986	—Columbia	S. Atl.	SS	25	112	29	38	6	1	5	24	.339	36	83	7	.944
1986	—Lynchburg	Carol.	SS	95	390	66	138	25	9	11	80	*.354	138	273	20	.954
1986	—Jackson	Texas	SS-3B	5	19	1	8	1	1	0	7	.421	7	9	1	.941
1987	—Jackson	Texas	SS-3B	134	510	81	187	*48	5	20	101	.367	167	388	35	.941
1987	—New York	Nat.	PH	6	6	0	3	1	0	0	2	.500	0	0	0	.000
1988	—Tidewater	Int.	3-S-2-O	132	504	62	142	28	4	7	61	.282	110	330	27	.942
1988	—New York	Nat.	3B-2B	29	109	19	35	8	2	6	17	.321	33	46	2	.975
Major League Totals—2 Years				35	115	19	38	9	2	6	19	.330	33	46	2	.975

Selected by New York Mets' organization in 1st round (20th player selected) of free-agent draft, June 3, 1985.

CHAMPIONSHIP SERIES RECORD

Year	Club	League	Pos.	G.	AB.	R.	H.	2B.	3B.	HR.	RBI.	B.A.	PO.	A.	E.	F.A.
1988	—New York	Nat.	3B	7	27	2	9	2	0	0	1	.333	5	8	1	.929

—DID YOU KNOW—

That Pittsburgh's Bobby Bonilla, who twice has homered from both sides of the plate in the same game, is the only Pittsburgh player ever to accomplish the feat?

REGINALD JIROD JEFFERSON
(Reggie)

Born September 25, 1968, at Tallahassee, Fla.
Height, 6.04. Weight, 210.
Throws left and bats right and lefthanded.

Led Gulf Coast League first basemen in total chances with 624 in 1986.

Year Club	League	Pos.	G.	AB.	R.	H.	2B.	3B.	HR.	RBI.	B.A.	PO.	A.	E.	F.A.
1986—Sarasota Reds	Gulf C.	1B	59	208	28	54	4	●5	3	33	.260	★581	★36	7	.989
1987—Billings	Pion.	1B	8	22	10	8	1	0	1	9	.364	21	1	0	1.000
1987—Cedar Rapids†	Midw.	1B	15	54	9	12	5	0	3	11	.222	120	11	1	.992
1988—Cedar Rapids†	Midw.	1B	135	517	76	149	26	2	18	★90	.288	1084	91	13	.989

Selected by Cincinnati Reds' organization in 3rd round of free-agent draft, June 2, 1986.
†Batted lefthanded only.

STANLEY JEFFERSON
(Stan)

Born December 4, 1962, at New York, N.Y.
Height, 5.11. Weight, 175.
Throws right and bats left and righthanded.
Attended Bethune-Cookman College, Daytona Beach, Fla.

Major League stolen bases: 1987 (34), 1988 (5). Total—39.
Led Texas League in stolen bases with 39 in 1985.
Led New York-Pennsylvania League in stolen bases with 35 in 1983.
Named outfielder on THE SPORTING NEWS College Baseball All-America Team, 1983.

Year Club	League	Pos.	G.	AB.	R.	H.	2B.	3B.	HR.	RBI.	B.A.	PO.	A.	E.	F.A.
1983—Little Falls †	NYP	OF	71	281	57	90	5	1	9	36	.320	★153	7	4	.976
1984—Lynchburg †	Carol.	OF	128	493	★113	142	20	●9	5	47	.288	265	11	8	.972
1985—Jackson	Texas	OF	133	524	97	145	21	6	8	30	.277	276	9	7	.976
1986—Tidewater‡	Int.	OF	95	369	60	107	19	4	2	37	.290	219	5	2	.991
1986—New York§	Nat.	OF	14	24	6	5	1	0	1	3	.208	13	0	0	1.000
1987—San Diego x	Nat.	OF	116	422	59	97	8	7	8	29	.230	232	3	3	.987
1988—San Diego	Nat.	OF	49	111	16	16	1	2	1	4	.144	62	0	0	1.000
1988—Las Vegas y	P. C.	OF	74	278	60	88	14	6	4	33	.317	163	4	7	.960
Major League Totals—3 Years			179	557	81	118	10	9	10	36	.212	307	3	3	.990

Selected by New York Mets' organization in 1st round (20th player selected) of free-agent draft, June 6, 1983.
†Batted righthanded only.
‡On disabled list, July 25 to August 14, 1986.
§Traded with Outfielders Shawn Abner and Kevin Mitchell and Pitchers Kevin Armstrong and Kevin Brown to San Diego Padres for Outfielder Kevin McReynolds, Pitcher Gene Walter and Infielder Adam Ging, December 11, 1986.
xOn disabled list, April 13 to May 7 and May 30 to June 14, 1987.
yTraded with Pitchers Jimmy Jones and Lance McCullers to New York Yankees for First Baseman-Outfielder Jack Clark and Pitcher Pat Clements, October 24, 1988.

LARRY STEVEN JELTZ
(Steve)

Born May 28, 1959, at Paris, France.
Height, 5.11. Weight, 180.
Throws right and bats left and righthanded.
Attended University of Kansas, Lawrence, Kan.

Major League stolen bases: 1984 (2), 1985 (1), 1986 (6), 1987 (1), 1988 (3). Total—13.
Led Carolina League second basemen in double plays with 84 in 1981.
Tied for Carolina League lead in caught stealing with 15 in 1981.

Year Club	League	Pos.	G.	AB.	R.	H.	2B.	3B.	HR.	RBI.	B.A.	PO.	A.	E.	F.A.
1980—Spartanburg†	S. Atl.	2B	31	107	19	31	2	1	0	8	.290	51	61	4	.966
1981—Peninsula	Carol.	2B	133	482	81	112	18	0	2	32	.232	★293	★369	25	.964
1982—Reading	East.	2B-SS-3B	126	380	61	92	10	3	7	28	.242	251	297	22	.961
1983—Portland	P. C.	3-2-S-O	71	181	34	48	6	1	0	16	.265	106	113	11	.952
1983—Philadelphia	Nat.	2B-SS-3B	13	8	0	1	0	1	0	1	.125	4	5	0	1.000
1984—Portland	P. C.	S-2-O-3	134	436	68	96	10	9	2	46	.220	270	349	28	.957
1984—Philadelphia	Nat.	SS-3B	28	68	7	14	0	1	1	7	.206	37	93	1	.992
1985—Philadelphia	Nat.	SS	89	196	17	37	4	1	0	12	.189	106	215	14	.958
1985—Portland	P. C.	SS	21	71	6	21	4	1	1	9	.296	28	66	4	.959
1986—Philadelphia	Nat.	SS	145	439	44	96	11	4	0	36	.219	229	406	22	.967
1987—Philadelphia	Nat.	SS-OF	114	293	37	68	9	6	0	12	.232	192	271	14	.971
1987—Maine	Int.	SS	24	72	6	24	7	0	0	3	.333	45	79	6	.954
1988—Philadelphia	Nat.	SS	148	379	39	71	11	4	0	27	.187	195	368	14	.976
Major League Totals—6 Years			537	1383	144	287	35	17	1	95	.208	763	1358	65	.970

Selected by Philadelphia Phillies' organization in 9th round of free-agent draft, June 3, 1980.
†On disabled list, July 27, 1980 through remainder of season.

—DID YOU KNOW—

That the New York Mets set an Opening Day record when they hit six home runs against Montreal on April 4?

JAMES DOUGLAS JENNINGS
(Doug)

Born September 30, 1964, at Atlanta, Ga.
Height, 5.10. Weight, 165.
Throws and bats lefthanded.
Attended Brevard Community College, Cocoa, Fla.

Led Texas League in bases on balls received with 94 and being hit by pitch with 13 in 1987.
Led California League in bases on balls received with 117 in 1986.

Year Club	League	Pos.	G.	AB.	R.	H.	2B.	3B.	HR.	RBI.	B.A.	PO.	A.	E.	F.A.
1984—Salem	N'west	OF	52	173	29	45	7	1	1	17	.260	82	5	9	.906
1985—Quad Cities	Midw.	OF	95	319	50	81	17	7	5	54	.254	187	12	11	.948
1986—Palm Springs	Calif.	OF	129	429	95	136	31	9	17	89	.317	205	10	6	.973
1987—Midland†	Texas	OF	126	464	106	157	33	1	•30	104	.338	145	6	6	.962
1988—Oakland‡	Amer.	OF-1B	71	101	9	21	6	0	1	15	.208	85	5	1	.989
1988—Tacoma	P. C.	OF-1B	16	49	12	16	1	0	0	9	.327	26	1	1	.964
Major League Totals—1 Year			71	101	9	21	6	0	1	15	.208	85	5	1	.989

Selected by California Angels' organization in 2nd round of free-agent draft, January 17, 1984.
†Drafted by Oakland Athletics, December 7, 1987.
‡On disabled list, June 27 to July 31, 1988; included rehabilitation disability assignment to Tacoma, July 15 to July 31, 1988.

ALFONSO JIMENEZ (GONZALEZ)

Name pronounced Him-MEN-ez.

(Houston)

(Nicknamed when he was five years old after a television Western character.)
Born October 30, 1957, at Mexico City, Mex.
Height, 5.07. Weight, 150.
Throws and bats righthanded.

Led Mexican League in sacrifice hits with 25 in 1978 and tied for lead with 19 in 1979.
Led Florida State League in bases on balls received with 105 in 1975.
Led Mexican League shortstops in double plays with 105 in 1979.
Led Mexican League shortstops in double plays with 108 and total chances with 856 in 1978.
Led Florida State League shortstops in putouts with 232, assists with 444, fielding percentage with .951, total chances with 711 and tied for lead in double plays with 73 in 1975.

Year Club	League	Pos.	G.	AB.	R.	H.	2B.	3B.	HR.	RBI.	B.A.	PO.	A.	E.	F.A.
1974—Puelba	Mex.	SS	20	33	4	7	1	0	1	3	.212	15	34	8	.860
1975—Key West	Fla. St.	SS-2B-OF	132	446	63	96	17	5	2	34	.215	242	452	35	.952
1976—Puelba	Mex.	SS	131	427	51	98	12	2	6	42	.230	250	476	28	.963
1977—Puebla	Mex.	SS	145	482	66	146	22	7	0	56	.303	*293	*527	32	.962
1978—Puebla	Mex.	SS-2B	142	538	74	144	14	10	1	35	.268	*286	*544	26	.970
1978—Iowa	A. A.	SS	13	41	7	9	2	0	0	6	.220	18	40	2	.967
1979—Puebla	Mex.	SS	132	442	62	135	23	5	1	42	.305	243	513	27	.966
1980—Puebla†‡	Mex.	SS	75	254	29	62	8	1	1	24	.244	139	263	20	.953
1981—Reynosa	Mex.					(Did not play)									
1982—Reynosa§	Mex.					(Did not play)									
1982—Toledo	Int.	SS	37	115	7	26	3	0	0	12	.226	54	122	5	.972
1983—Toledo	Int.	SS	22	64	13	16	3	0	3	6	.250	31	56	3	.967
1983—Minnesota	Amer.	SS	36	86	5	15	5	1	0	9	.174	43	83	4	.969
1984—Minnesota	Amer.	SS	108	298	28	60	11	1	0	19	.201	145	273	18	.959
1985—Toledo x	Int.	SS-2B	113	390	47	87	14	1	3	25	.223	201	340	19	.966
1986						(Out of Organized Baseball)									
1987—Vancouver	P. C.	2B-SS-3B	49	131	16	31	3	2	0	6	.237	31	64	5	.950
1987—Pittsburgh y	Nat.	SS-2B	5	6	0	0	0	0	0	0	.000	3	8	0	1.000
1988—Colorado Springs	P. C.	3-S-2-1	22	58	11	17	5	1	0	6	.293	18	47	4	.942
1988—Cleveland	Amer.	2B-SS	9	21	1	1	0	0	0	1	.048	13	28	1	.976
American League Totals—3 Years			153	405	34	76	16	2	0	29	.188	201	384	23	.962
National League Totals—1 Year			5	6	0	0	0	0	0	0	.000	3	8	0	1.000
Major League Totals—4 Years			158	411	34	76	16	2	0	29	.185	204	392	23	.963

Signed as free agent by Puebla of Mexican League, September 13, 1973.
†Released, July 2, 1980; signed as free agent by Minnesota Twins' organization, October 28, 1980.
‡Sold by Minnesota Twins' organization to Reynosa of Mexican League, April 1, 1981.
§Sold to Toledo (Minnesota Twins' organization), July 21, 1982.
xReleased, April 8, 1986; signed by Vancouver (Pittsburgh Pirates' organization), December 10, 1986.
yGranted free agency, October 15, 1987; signed by Colorado Springs (Cleveland Indians' organization), June 2, 1988.

GERMAN JIMENEZ

Born December 5, 1962, at Santiago Ixcuintala, Nayarit, D.R.
Height, 5.11. Weight, 185.
Throws and bats lefthanded.

Year Club	League	G.	IP.	W.	L.	Pct.	H.	R.	ER.	SO.	BB.	ERA.
1981—Campeche	Mexican	35	117	7	6	.538	115	47	37	68	37	2.85
1982—Campeche	Mexican	29	164⅓	11	10	.524	157	47	41	74	61	2.25
1983—Campeche	Mexican	25	184	13	9	.591	183	64	49	114	75	2.40
1984—Toluca	Mexican	25	167⅓	11	6	.647	227	90	85	98	75	4.57
1985—Puebla	Mexican	27	195⅓	18	9	.667	186	75	68	130	54	3.13

Year Club	League	G.	IP.	W.	L.	Pct.	H.	R.	ER.	SO.	BB.	ERA.
1986—Puebla	Mexican	24	170⅔	★17	6	.739	183	76	64	115	37	3.37
1987—Puebla	Mexican	23	168⅓	12	9	.571	178	72	62	108	42	3.31
1988—Jalisco†	Mexican	18	148⅔	14	2	.875	173	55	45	95	32	2.72
1988—Atlanta	National	15	55⅔	1	6	.143	65	39	31	26	12	5.01
Major League Totals—1 Year		15	55⅔	1	6	.143	65	39	31	26	12	5.01

†Sold to Atlanta Braves, June 26, 1988.

THOMAS EDWARD JOHN
(Tommy)

Born May 22, 1943, at Terre Haute, Ind.
Height, 6.03. Weight, 203.
Throws left and bats righthanded.
Attended Indiana State College, Terre Haute, Ind.

Tied major league records for most years pitched (25); most errors, pitcher, inning (3), July 27, 1988 (fourth inning).

Tied American League record for most hit batsmen, game, nine-innings (4), June 15, 1968.
Major League saves: 1978 (1).
Led American League in shutouts with 6 in 1980.
Tied for American League lead in shutouts with 5 in 1966 and 6 in 1967.
Tied for American League lead in wild pitches with 17 and in intentional bases on balls issued with 16 in 1970.
Named National League Comeback Player of the Year by THE SPORTING NEWS, 1976.
Named lefthanded pitcher on THE SPORTING NEWS American League All-Star Team, 1980.
Received reported $40,000 bonus to sign with Cleveland Indians, 1961.

Year Club	League	G.	IP.	W.	L.	Pct.	H.	R.	ER.	SO.	BB.	ERA.
1961—Dubuque	Midwest	14	88	10	4	.714	74	47	31	99	59	3.17
1962—Charleston	Eastern	21	128	6	8	.429	129	67	55	114	71	3.87
1962—Jacksonville	Int'national	8	34	2	2	.500	29	20	18	27	16	4.76
1963—Charleston	Eastern	12	95	9	2	.818	85	25	17	45	12	1.61
1963—Jacksonville	Int'national	18	102	6	8	.429	115	53	40	63	39	3.53
1963—Cleveland	American	6	20	0	2	.000	23	10	5	9	6	2.25
1964—Cleveland	American	25	94	2	9	.182	97	53	41	65	35	3.93
1964—Portland†	P. Coast	13	74	6	6	.500	75	38	35	72	24	4.26
1965—Chicago	American	39	184	14	7	.667	162	67	63	126	58	3.08
1966—Chicago	American	34	223	14	11	.560	195	76	65	138	57	2.62
1967—Chicago	American	31	178	10	13	.435	143	62	49	110	47	2.48
1968—Chicago‡	American	25	177	10	5	.667	135	45	39	117	49	1.98
1969—Chicago	American	33	232	9	11	.450	230	91	84	128	90	3.26
1970—Chicago	American	37	269	12	17	.414	253	117	98	138	101	3.28
1971—Chicago§	American	38	229	13	16	.448	244	115	92	131	58	3.62
1972—Los Angeles	National	29	187	11	5	.688	172	68	60	117	40	2.89
1973—Los Angeles	National	36	218	16	7	★.696	202	88	75	116	50	3.10
1974—Los Angeles x	National	22	153	13	3	.813	133	51	44	78	42	2.59
1975—Los Angeles y	National					(Did not play)						
1976—Los Angeles	National	31	207	10	10	.500	207	76	71	91	61	3.09
1977—Los Angeles	National	31	220	20	7	.741	225	82	68	123	50	2.78
1978—Los Angeles z	National	33	213	17	10	.630	230	95	78	124	53	3.30
1979—New York	American	37	276	21	9	.700	268	109	91	111	65	2.97
1980—New York	American	36	265	22	9	.710	270	115	101	78	56	3.43
1981—New York a	American	20	140	9	8	.529	135	50	41	50	39	2.64
1982—New York b-California	American	37	221⅓	14	12	.538	239	102	91	68	39	3.69
1983—California	American	34	234⅔	11	13	.458	★287	126	113	65	49	4.33
1984—California	American	32	181⅓	7	13	.350	223	97	91	47	56	4.52
1985—California c-Oakland	American	23	86⅓	4	10	.286	117	59	53	25	28	5.53
1985—Modesto	California	2	4	0	0	.000	12	8	7	11	6	5.73
1985—Madison d	Midwest	1	6	0	0	.000	4	2	2	3	4	3.00
1986—New York e	American	13	70⅔	5	3	.625	73	27	23	28	15	2.93
1986—Fort Lauderdale f	Florida St.	3	13⅔	2	0	1.000	7	2	0	7	1	0.00
1987—New York g	American	33	187⅔	13	6	.684	212	95	84	63	47	4.03
1988—New York h	American	35	176⅓	9	8	.529	221	96	88	81	46	4.49
American League Totals—19 Years		568	3445⅔	199	182	.522	3527	1512	1312	1578	941	3.43
National League Totals—6 Years		182	1198	87	42	.674	1169	460	396	649	296	2.97
Major League Totals—25 Years		750	4643⅔	286	224	.561	4696	1972	1708	2227	1237	3.31

Signed as free agent by Cleveland Indians' organization, June 12, 1961.

†Traded to Chicago White Sox with Catcher John Romano and Outfielder Tommie Agee for Catcher Camilo Carreon and Outfielder Rocky Colavito, January 20, 1965, as part of three-way deal which saw Chicago obtain Colavito from Kansas City Athletics earlier same day for Outfielders Jim Landis and Mike Hershberger and a pitcher to be named later; Kansas City acquired Pitcher Fred Talbot to complete deal, February 10, 1965.

‡On disabled list, August 22, 1968 through remainder of season.

§Traded with Infielder Steve Huntz to Los Angeles Dodgers for Infielder-Outfielder Richie Allen, December 2, 1971.

xOn disabled list, July 17, 1974 through remainder of season.

yOn disabled list, April 6, 1975 through remainder of season.

zGranted free agency, November 2, 1978; signed by New York Yankees, November 21, 1978.

aOn disabled list, June 1 to August 5, 1981.

bTraded to California Angels for a player to be named later, August 31, 1982; New York Yankees acquired Pitcher Dennis Rasmussen to complete deal, November 24 1982.

cReleased, June 19, 1985; signed by Modesto (Oakland A's organization), July 12, 1985.

dGranted free agency, November 12, 1985; signed by New York Yankees, May 2, 1986.

eOn disabled list, June 9 to August 8, 1986; included rehabilitation disability assignment to Fort Lauderdale, July 27 to August 8, 1986.

fGranted free agency, November 12, 1986; re-signed by Yankees, January 8, 1987.

gGranted free agency, November 9, 1987; re-signed by Yankees, December 18, 1987.

hReleased, November 10, 1988.

DIVISION SERIES RECORD

Year Club	League	G.	IP.	W.	L.	Pct.	H.	R.	ER.	SO.	BB.	ERA.
1981—New York	American	1	7	0	1	.000	8	5	5	0	2	6.43

CHAMPIONSHIP SERIES RECORD

Tied Championship Series record for most games won, total Series (4).

Tied National League Championship Series record for most complete games, total Series (2).

Year Club	League	G.	IP.	W.	L.	Pct.	H.	R.	ER.	SO.	BB.	ERA.
1977—Los Angeles	National	2	13⅔	1	0	1.000	11	5	1	11	5	0.66
1978—Los Angeles	National	1	9	1	0	1.000	4	0	0	4	2	0.00
1980—New York	American	1	6⅔	0	0	.000	8	2	2	3	1	2.70
1981—New York	American	1	6	1	0	1.000	6	1	1	3	1	1.50
1982—California	American	2	12⅓	1	1	.500	11	9	7	6	6	5.11
Championship Series Totals—5 Years		7	47⅔	4	1	.800	40	17	11	27	15	2.08

WORLD SERIES RECORD

Year Club	League	G.	IP.	W.	L.	Pct.	H.	R.	ER.	SO.	BB.	ERA.
1977—Los Angeles	National	1	6	0	1	.000	9	5	4	7	3	6.00
1978—Los Angeles	National	2	14⅔	1	0	1.000	14	8	5	6	4	3.07
1981—New York	American	3	13	1	0	1.000	11	1	1	8	0	0.69
World Series Totals—3 Years		6	33⅔	2	1	.667	34	14	10	21	7	2.67

ALL-STAR GAME RECORD

Year League	IP.	W.	L.	Pct.	H.	R.	ER.	SO.	BB.	ERA.
1968—American	⅔	0	0	.000	1	0	0	0	0	0.00
1980—American	2⅓	0	1	.000	4	3	3	1	0	11.57
All-Star Game Totals—2 Years	3	0	1	.000	5	3	3	1	0	9.00

Member of National League All-Star Team for 1978 game; did not play.

Member of American League All-Star Team for 1979 game; did not play.

HOWARD MICHAEL JOHNSON

Born November 29, 1960, at Clearwater, Fla.
Height, 5.10. Weight, 195.
Throws right and bats right and lefthanded.
Attended St. Petersburg Junior College, St. Petersburg, Fla.

Established National League record for most home runs, switch-hitter, season (36), 1987.

Major League stolen bases: 1982 (7), 1984 (10), 1985 (6), 1986 (8), 1987 (32), 1988 (23). Total—86.

Tied for National League lead in game-winning RBIs with 16 in 1987.

Led Florida State League in sacrifice hits with 16 in 1980.

Led American Association third basemen in double plays with 19 in 1982.

Led Florida State League third basemen in double plays with 21 in 1980.

Year Club	League	Pos.	G.	AB.	R.	H.	2B.	3B.	HR.	RBI.	B.A.	PO.	A.	E.	F.A.
1979—Lakeland	Fla. St.	3B-SS-OF	132	456	49	107	9	6	3	49	.235	130	240	36	.911
1980—Lakeland	Fla. St.	3B	130	474	83	135	*28	1	10	69	.285	*110	*264	13	*.966
1981—Birmingham	South.	3B	138	488	84	130	28	7	22	83	.266	103	218	26	.925
1982—Evansville	A. A.	3B-OF	98	366	70	116	16	4	23	67	.317	69	139	23	.900
1982—Detroit	Amer.	3B-OF	54	155	23	49	5	0	4	14	.316	36	40	7	.916
1983—Detroit	Amer.	3B	27	66	11	14	0	0	3	5	.212	10	30	7	.851
1983—Evansville†	A. A.	3B	3	9	1	2	1	0	0	0	.222	1	11	2	.857
1984—Detroit‡	Amer.	3-S-1-O	116	355	43	88	14	1	12	50	.248	63	150	14	.938
1985—New York	Nat.	3B-SS-OF	126	389	38	94	18	4	11	46	.242	78	190	18	.937
1986—New York§	Nat.	3B-SS-OF	88	220	30	54	14	0	10	39	.245	52	136	20	.904
1987—New York	Nat.	3B-SS-OF	157	554	93	147	22	1	36	99	.265	118	305	26	.942
1988—New York	Nat.	3B-SS	148	495	85	114	21	1	24	68	.230	110	274	18	.955
American League Totals—3 Years			197	576	77	151	19	1	19	69	.262	109	220	28	.922
National League Totals—4 Years			519	1658	246	409	75	6	81	252	.247	358	905	82	.939
Major League Totals—7 Years			716	2234	323	560	94	7	100	321	.251	467	1125	110	.935

Selected by New York Yankees' organization in 23rd round of free-agent draft, June 6, 1978.

Selected by Detroit Tigers' organization in secondary phase of free-agent draft, January 9, 1979.

†On disabled list, June 2 to August 8, 1983.

‡Traded to New York Mets for Pitcher Walt Terrell, December 7, 1984.

§On disabled list, June 2 to June 23, 1986.

CHAMPIONSHIP SERIES RECORD

Year Club	League	Pos.	G.	AB.	R.	H.	2B.	3B.	HR.	RBI.	B.A.	PO.	A.	E.	F.A.
1986—New York	Nat.	PH	2	2	0	0	0	0	0	0	.000	0	0	0	.000
1988—New York	Nat.	SS-3-PH	6	18	3	1	0	0	0	0	.056	6	9	1	.938
Championship Series Totals—2 Years			8	20	3	1	0	0	0	0	.050	6	9	1	.938

WORLD SERIES RECORD

Year	Club	League	Pos.	G.	AB.	R.	H.	2B.	3B.	HR.	RBI.	B.A.	PO.	A.	E.	F.A.
1984	Detroit	Amer.	PH	1	1	0	0	0	0	0	0	.000	0	0	0	.000
1986	New York	Nat.	3B-PH-SS	2	5	0	0	0	0	0	0	.000	1	0	0	1.000
World Series Totals—2 Years				3	6	0	0	0	0	0	0	.000	1	0	0	1.000

KENNETH LANCE JOHNSON

(Known by middle name.)
Born July 7, 1963, at Lincoln Heights, O.
Height, 5.11. Weight, 155.
Throws and bats lefthanded.
Attended Triton College, River Grove, Ill.,
and University of South Alabama, Mobile, Ala.

Major League stolen bases: 1987 (6), 1988 (6). Total—12.
Led Texas League in stolen bases with 49 and caught stealing with 15 in 1986.
Led Pacific Coast League outfielders in double plays with 5 in 1988.
Led American Association outfielders in total chances with 333 in 1987.
Led New York-Pennsylvania League outfielders in total chances with 201 in 1984.
Named American Association Most Valuable Player, 1987.

Year	Club	League	Pos.	G.	AB.	R.	H.	2B.	3B.	HR.	RBI.	B.A.	PO.	A.	E.	F.A.
1984	Erie	NYP	OF	71	283	*63	*96	7	5	1	28	.339	*188	5	8	.960
1985	St. Petersburg	Fla. St.	OF	129	497	68	134	17	10	2	55	.270	338	16	5	.986
1986	Arkansas	Texas	OF	127	445	82	128	24	6	2	33	.288	262	11	7	.975
1987	Louisville	A. A.	OF	116	477	89	159	21	11	5	50	.333	*319	6	●8	.976
1987	St. Louis†	Nat.	OF	33	59	4	13	2	1	0	7	.220	27	0	2	.931
1988	Chicago	Amer.	OF	33	124	11	23	4	1	0	6	.185	63	1	2	.970
1988	Vancouver	P. C.	OF	100	411	71	126	12	6	2	36	.307	262	9	5	.982
National League Totals—1 Year				33	59	4	13	2	1	0	7	.220	27	0	2	.931
American League Totals—1 Year				33	124	11	23	4	1	0	6	.185	63	1	2	.970
Major League Totals—2 Years				66	183	15	36	6	2	0	13	.197	90	1	4	.958

Selected by Pittsburgh Pirates' organization in 30th round of free-agent draft, June 8, 1981.
Selected by Seattle Mariners' organization in 31st round of free-agent draft, June 7, 1982.
Selected by St. Louis Cardinals' organization in 6th round of free-agent draft, June 4, 1984.
†Traded with Pitcher Rick Horton and cash to Chicago White Sox for Pitcher Jose DeLeon, February 9, 1988.

CHAMPIONSHIP SERIES RECORD

Year	Club	League	Pos.	G.	AB.	R.	H.	2B.	3B.	HR.	RBI.	B.A.	PO.	A.	E.	F.A.
1987	St. Louis	Nat.	PR	1	0	1	0	0	0	0	0	.000	0	0	0	.000

WORLD SERIES RECORD

Year	Club	League	Pos.	G.	AB.	R.	H.	2B.	3B.	HR.	RBI.	B.A.	PO.	A.	E.	F.A.
1987	St. Louis	Nat.	PR	1	0	0	0	0	0	0	0	.000	0	0	0	.000

RANDALL DAVID JOHNSON
(Randy)

Born September 10, 1963, at Walnut Creek, Calif.
Height, 6.10. Weight, 225.
Throws left and bats righthanded.
Attended University of Southern California, Los Angeles, Calif.

Led American Association in balks with 20 in 1988.
Tied for Florida State League lead in games started by pitchers with 26 in 1986.

Year	Club	League	G.	IP.	W.	L.	Pct.	H.	R.	ER.	SO.	BB.	ERA.
1985	Jamestown	NYP	8	27⅓	0	3	.000	29	22	18	21	24	5.93
1986	West Palm Beach	Florida St.	26	119⅔	8	7	.533	89	49	42	133	*94	3.16
1987	Jacksonville	Southern	25	140	11	8	.579	100	63	58	*163	128	3.73
1988	Indianapolis	Am. Assoc.	20	113⅓	8	7	.533	85	52	41	111	72	3.26
1988	Montreal	National	4	26	3	0	1.000	23	8	7	25	7	2.42
Major League Totals—1 Year			4	26	3	0	1.000	23	8	7	25	7	2.42

Selected by Atlanta Braves' organization in 3rd round of free-agent draft, June 7, 1982.
Selected by Montreal Expos' organization in 2nd round of free-agent draft, June 3, 1985.

RONDIN ALLEN JOHNSON
(Ron)

Born December 16, 1958, at Bremerton, Wash.
Height, 5.10, Weight, 160.
Throws right and bats left and righthanded.
Attended University of Washington, Seattle, Wash.

Tied for Gulf Coast League lead in caught stealing with 10 in 1980.
Led American Association second basemen in double plays with 76 in 1988.
Led American Association second basemen in total chances with 581 in 1986.
Led Florida State League second basemen in fielding percentage with .979 in 1981.
Led Southern League second basemen in double plays with 89 in 1983.
Tied for American Association lead in assists by second basemen with 393 in 1987.

Year Club	League	Pos.	G.	AB.	R.	H.	2B.	3B.	HR.	RBI.	B.A.	PO.	A.	E.	F.A.
1980—Sarasota Royals	Gulf C.	2B	*63	*266	43	70	5	2	0	21	.263	154	*183	12	*.966
1981—Fort Myers†	Fla. St.	2B-SS	107	424	49	92	16	3	0	29	.217	183	339	14	.974
1982—Jacksonville	South.	2B	128	494	59	109	8	3	1	28	.221	268	315	9	*.985
1983—Jacksonville	South.	2B	140	555	74	147	12	5	0	30	.265	274	•416	18	*.975
1984—Omaha	A. A.	2B	131	488	60	123	18	4	1	49	.252	219	342	17	.971
1985—Omaha‡	A. A.	2B	99	366	44	86	8	1	0	22	.235	181	257	10	.978
1986—Omaha§	A. A.	2B	127	484	57	140	15	*14	1	60	.289	*239	*333	9	*.985
1986—Kansas City	Amer.	2B	11	31	1	8	0	1	0	2	.258	14	32	0	1.000
1987—Omaha	A. A.	2B-SS	134	503	58	128	14	7	2	53	.254	281	423	20	.972
1988—Omaha x	A. A.	2B	121	465	48	122	13	3	1	41	.262	225	360	13	.978
Major League Total—1 Year			11	31	1	8	0	1	0	2	.258	14	32	0	1.000

Selected by Kansas City Royals' organization in 6th round of free-agent draft, June 3, 1980.
†Batted righthanded only.
‡On disabled list, April 29 to May 10 and July 9 to July 26, 1985.
§On disabled list, April 11 to April 21, 1986.
xGranted free agency, October 15, 1988.

WALLACE DARNELL JOHNSON
(Wally)

Born December 25, 1956, at Gary, Ind.
Height, 5.11. Weight, 185.
Throws right and bats right and lefthanded.
Received degree in accounting from Indiana State University, Terre Haute, Ind., in 1979.

Major League stolen bases: 1981 (1), 1982 (4), 1983 (1), 1986 (6), 1987 (5). Total—17.
Led Florida State League in stolen bases with 58 and caught stealing with 22 in 1980.
Named Florida State League Southern Division Most Valuable Player, 1980.

Year Club	League	Pos.	G.	AB.	R.	H.	2B.	3B.	HR.	RBI.	B.A.	PO.	A.	E.	F.A.
1979—Jamestown	NYP	2B	70	*284	60	96	11	6	6	42	.338	157	155	17	.948
1980—W. Palm Beach	Fla. St.	2B-OF	126	488	86	*163	17	5	3	49	*.334	294	350	31	.954
1980—Memphis	South.	2B	4	13	1	1	1	0	0	0	.077	5	12	0	1.000
1981—Memphis†	South.	2B-OF	28	102	15	37	9	0	1	18	.363	44	52	10	.906
1981—Denver	A. A.	2B-OF	59	215	39	64	13	4	0	16	.298	72	116	7	.964
1981—Montreal	Nat.	PH	11	9	1	2	0	1	0	3	.222	1	2	0	1.000
1982—Montreal	Nat.	2B	36	57	5	11	0	2	0	2	.193	22	18	2	.952
1982—Wichita	A. A.	2B-OF	76	298	62	105	12	4	6	36	.352	128	79	12	.945
1983—Wichita	A. A.	OF	16	53	7	14	3	1	0	6	.264	26	0	2	.929
1983—Mont.‡-S. F.	Nat.	2B	10	10	1	2	0	0	0	1	.200	3	2	0	1.000
1983—Phoenix§	P. C.	2B	63	229	42	66	8	2	2	26	.288	105	150	15	.944
1984—Jacksonville	South.	DH	31	117	18	35	5	0	1	12	.299	0	0	0	.000
1984—Indianapolis	A. A.	OF-1B-2B	97	357	50	101	12	2	3	38	.283	350	39	5	.987
1984—Montreal	Nat.	1B	17	24	3	5	0	0	0	4	.208	27	3	1	.968
1985—Indianapolis x	A. A.	OF-1B-2B	127	431	68	133	13	3	3	36	.309	240	14	5	.981
1986—Indianapolis	A. A.	1B-OF	61	225	27	58	15	4	0	26	.258	188	14	3	.985
1986—Montreal	Nat.	1B	61	127	13	36	3	1	1	10	.283	204	17	2	.991
1987—Montreal	Nat.	1B	75	85	7	21	5	0	1	14	.247	68	2	2	.972
1988—Montreal	Nat.	1B-2B	86	94	7	29	5	1	0	3	.309	80	9	1	.989
Major League Totals—7 Years			296	406	37	106	13	5	2	37	.261	405	53	8	.983

Selected by Montreal Expos' organization in 6th round of free-agent draft, June 5, 1979.
†On disabled list, April 29 to May 15, 1981.
‡Traded to San Francisco Giants for Outfielder Mike Vail, May 25, 1983.
§Released, March 27, 1984; signed by Jacksonville (Montreal Expos' organization), April 1, 1984.
xGranted free agency, October 15, 1985; re-signed by Expos, January 22, 1986.

DIVISION SERIES RECORD

Year Club	League	Pos.	G.	AB.	R.	H.	2B.	3B.	HR.	RBI.	B.A.	PO.	A.	E.	F.A.
1981—Montreal	Nat.	PH	2	2	0	1	0	0	0	1	.500	0	0	0	.000

BARRY LOUIS JONES

Born February 15, 1963, at Centerville, Ind.
Height, 6.04. Weight, 225.
Throws and bats righthanded.
Attended Indiana University, Bloomington, Ind.

Major League saves: 1986 (3), 1987 (1), 1988 (3). Total—7.

Year Club	League	G.	IP.	W.	L.	Pct.	H.	R.	ER.	SO.	BB.	ERA.
1984—Watertown	NYP	14	86⅔	6	3	.667	75	41	33	61	49	3.43
1985—Prince William	Carolina	28	37⅓	3	2	.600	26	7	5	42	19	1.21
1985—Nashua	Eastern	23	29	3	2	.600	19	6	5	24	10	1.55
1985—Hawaii	P. Coast	1	3	0	0	.000	5	5	3	2	1	9.00
1986—Hawaii	P. Coast	35	48	3	6	.333	41	20	19	28	20	3.56
1986—Pittsburgh	National	26	37⅓	3	4	.429	29	16	12	29	21	2.89
1987—Pittsburgh	National	32	43⅓	2	4	.333	55	34	27	28	23	5.61
1987—Vancouver	P. Coast	20	25⅓	1	2	.333	21	9	9	27	14	3.20
1988—Pittsburgh†	National	42	56⅓	1	1	.500	57	21	19	31	21	3.04

Year Club	League	G.	IP.	W.	L.	Pct.	H.	R.	ER.	SO.	BB.	ERA.
1988—Chicago	American	17	26	2	2	.500	15	7	7	17	17	2.42
National League Totals—3 Years		100	137	6	9	.400	141	71	58	88	65	3.81
American League Totals—1 Year		17	26	2	2	.500	15	7	7	17	17	2.42
Major League Totals—3 Years		117	163	8	11	.421	156	77	65	105	82	3.59

Selected by Texas Rangers' organization in 6th round of free-agent draft, June 8, 1981.
Selected by Pittsburgh Pirates' organization in 3rd round of free-agent draft, June 4, 1984.
†Traded to Chicago White Sox for Pitcher Dave LaPoint, August 13, 1988.

CHRISTOPHER NEIL JONES
(Chris)

Born December 17, 1963, at Glen Dale, W. Va.
Height, 6.01. Weight, 195.
Throws and bats righthanded.
Attended Ohio State University, Columbus, O.

Tied for New York-Pennsylvania League lead in games started by pitchers with 18 in 1986.

Year Club	League	G.	IP.	W.	L.	Pct.	H.	R.	ER.	SO.	BB.	ERA.
1985—Medicine Hat†	Pioneer	11	34	0	6	.000	31	23	21	23	18	5.56
1986—Florence	S. Atlantic	14	54	1	7	.125	54	42	29	53	54	4.28
1986—St. Catharines	NYP	18	101⅓	7	4	.636	81	36	29	103	46	2.58
1987—Dunedin	Florida St.	27	157⅓	11	6	.647	119	48	46	95	57	2.63
1988—Knoxville‡	Southern	35	134⅔	6	9	.400	133	74	64	119	61	4.28

Selected by Toronto Blue Jays' organization in 4th round of free-agent draft, June 3, 1985.
†On disabled list, June 20 to July 20, 1985.
‡Drafted by Los Angeles Dodgers, December 5, 1988.

DENNIS RAY JONES

Born July 26, 1966, at Gadsden, Ala.
Height, 6.06. Weight, 195.
Throws and bats lefthanded.
Attended Gadsden State Junior College, Gadsden, Ala.

Year Club	League	G.	IP.	W.	L.	Pct.	H.	R.	ER.	SO.	BB.	ERA.
1985—Bradenton Blue Jays	Gulf Coast	15	58	2	6	.250	45	35	22	77	41	3.41
1986—Florence†	S. Atlantic	17	55⅓	0	5	.000	45	44	36	62	49	5.86
1987—Myrtle Beach	S. Atlantic	21	68⅔	6	5	.545	51	37	21	78	50	2.75
1988—Knoxville‡	Southern	19	89⅓	8	5	.615	57	32	26	106	64	2.62

Selected by Toronto Blue Jays' organization in 8th round of free-agent draft, January 9, 1985.
†On disabled list, May 19 to June 23, 1986.
‡On disabled list, July 1 to July 22 and July 30, 1988 through remainder of season.

DOUGLAS REID JONES
(Doug)

Born June 24, 1957, at Covina, Calif.
Height, 6.02. Weight, 195.
Throws and bats righthanded.
Attended Central Arizona College, Coolidge, Ariz., and Butler University, Indianapolis, Ind.

Major League saves: 1986 (1), 1987 (8), 1988 (37). Total—46.
Led Midwest League in complete games with 16 and tied for lead in shutouts with 3 in 1979.
Tied for Eastern League lead in intentional bases on balls issued with 8 in 1985.

Year Club	League	G.	IP.	W.	L.	Pct.	H.	R.	ER.	SO.	BB.	ERA.
1978—Newark†	NYP	15	38	2	4	.333	49	30	22	27	15	5.21
1979—Burlington	Midwest	28	★190	10	10	.500	144	63	37	115	73	★1.75
1980—Stockton	California	11	76	6	2	.750	63	32	24	54	31	2.84
1980—Vancouver	P. Coast	8	53	3	2	.600	52	19	19	28	15	3.23
1980—Holyoke	Eastern	8	62	5	3	.625	57	23	20	39	26	2.90
1981—El Paso	Texas	15	90	5	7	.417	121	67	58	62	28	5.80
1981—Vancouver	P. Coast	11	80	5	3	.625	79	29	27	38	22	3.04
1982—Milwaukee	American	4	2⅔	0	0	.000	5	3	3	1	1	10.13
1982—Vancouver	P. Coast	23	106	5	8	.385	109	48	35	60	31	2.97
1983—Vancouver‡	P. Coast	3	7	0	1	.000	10	8	8	4	5	10.29
1984—Vancouver§	P. Coast	3	8	1	0	1.000	9	9	9	2	3	10.13
1984—El Paso x	Texas	16	109⅓	6	8	.429	120	61	52	62	35	4.28
1985—Waterbury	Eastern	39	116	9	4	.692	123	59	47	113	36	3.65
1986—Maine	Int'national	43	116⅓	5	6	.455	105	35	27	98	27	★2.09
1986—Cleveland	American	11	18	1	0	1.000	18	5	5	12	6	2.50
1987—Cleveland	American	49	91⅓	6	5	.545	101	45	32	87	24	3.15
1987—Buffalo	Am. Assoc.	23	61⅔	5	2	.714	49	18	14	61	12	2.04
1988—Cleveland	American	51	83⅓	3	4	.429	69	26	21	72	16	2.27
Major League Totals—4 Years		115	195⅓	10	9	.526	193	79	61	172	47	2.81

Selected by Milwaukee Brewers' organization in 3rd round of free-agent draft, January 10, 1978.
†On disabled list, June 20 to July 12, 1978.
‡On disabled list, April 11 to September 1, 1983.
§On disabled list, April 25 to May 30, 1984.
xGranted free agency, October 15, 1984; signed by Waterbury (Cleveland Indians' organization), April 3, 1985.

ALL-STAR GAME RECORD

Year League	IP.	W.	L.	Pct.	H.	R.	ER.	SO.	BB.	ERA.
1988—American	⅔	0	0	.000	0	0	0	1	0	0.00

JAMES CONDIA JONES
(Jimmy)

Born April 20, 1964, at Dallas, Tex.
Height, 6.02. Weight, 190.
Throws and bats righthanded.

Tied modern major league record for fewest hits allowed, first major league game, nine innings (1), September 21, 1986.

Tied for Pacific Coast League lead in games started by pitchers with 27 in 1986.

Year Club	League	G.	IP.	W.	L.	Pct.	H.	R.	ER.	SO.	BB.	ERA.
1982—Walla Walla	Northwest	14	78⅓	4	6	.400	64	49	28	78	71	3.22
1983—Reno	California	17	116⅔	7	5	.583	96	50	35	79	49	2.70
1984—Beaumont†	Texas	13	85⅔	7	2	.778	63	28	20	49	39	2.10
1985—Beaumont‡	Texas	16	85	7	5	.583	84	51	44	57	66	4.66
1986—Las Vegas	P. Coast	28	157⅔	9	10	.474	168	84	77	114	72	4.40
1986—San Diego	National	3	18	2	0	1.000	10	6	5	15	3	2.50
1987—Las Vegas	P. Coast	4	24⅓	2	0	1.000	24	16	16	11	8	5.92
1987—San Diego	National	30	145⅔	9	7	.563	154	85	67	51	54	4.14
1988—San Diego§	National	29	179	9	14	.391	192	98	82	82	44	4.12
Major League Totals—3 Years		62	342⅔	20	21	.488	356	189	154	148	101	4.04

Selected by San Diego Padres' organization in 1st round (third player selected) of free-agent draft, June 7, 1982.

†On disabled list, July 13, 1984 through remainder of season.

‡On disabled list, June 29 to July 11 and July 28, 1985 through remainder of season.

§Traded with Pitcher Lance McCullers and Outfielder Stan Jefferson to New York Yankees for First Baseman-Outfielder Jack Clark and Pitcher Pat Clements, October 24, 1988.

LaBARRY JONES
(Barry)

Born February 14, 1965, at Jackson, Ala.
Height, 6.02. Weight, 195.
Throws right and bats lefthanded.

Led Southern League in slugging percentage with .497 in 1988.

Tied for South Atlantic League lead in intentional bases on balls received with 4 in 1986.

Year Club	League	Pos.	G.	AB.	R.	H.	2B.	3B.	HR.	RBI.	B.A.	PO.	A.	E.	F.A.
1984—Braden. Braves	Gulf C.	OF	21	55	9	16	0	1	2	9	.291	27	2	3	.906
1985—Sumter	S. Atl.	OF	52	138	21	29	0	3	0	8	.210	67	1	3	.958
1986—Sumter	S. Atl.	OF	98	288	60	78	11	0	6	51	.271	127	4	6	.956
1986—Durham	Carol.	OF	10	27	2	4	1	0	0	3	.148	11	2	1	.929
1987—Durham	Carol.	OF	117	424	72	120	23	4	15	52	.283	210	*16	5	.978
1988—Greenville	South.	OF	101	384	56	109	18	•8	16	55	.284	166	3	9	.949
1988—Richmond	Int.	OF	35	126	12	35	7	0	3	10	.278	75	6	1	.988

Signed as free agent by Atlanta Braves' organization, July 3, 1984.

ODELL JONES JR.

Born January 13, 1953, at Tulare, Calif.
Height, 6.03. Weight, 175.
Throws and bats righthanded.
Attended Compton College, Compton, Calif.
Cousin of Charles Jackson, linebacker with Kansas City Chiefs and New York Jets, 1978 through 1986.

Pitched 7-0 no-hit victory against Pittsfield, April 29, 1974.

Major League saves: 1983 (10), 1984 (2), 1988 (1). Total—13.

Led Eastern League in balks with 3 in 1974.

Tied for International League lead in home runs allowed with 24 in 1987.

Year Club	League	G.	IP.	W.	L.	Pct.	H.	R.	ER.	SO.	BB.	ERA.
1972—Niagara Falls	NYP	11	79	7	3	.700	78	34	27	53	20	3.08
1973—Charleston	W. Carol.	10	62	2	3	.400	42	22	10	62	29	1.45
1973—Salem	Carolina	11	67	5	4	.556	64	40	36	55	38	4.84
1974—Thetford Mines	Eastern	24	161	11	8	.579	103	63	58	153	*120	3.24
1975—Charleston	Int'national	26	*188	•14	9	.609	133	67	56	*157	88	2.68
1975—Pittsburgh	National	2	3	0	0	.000	1	0	0	2	0	0.00
1976—Charleston†	Int'national	16	84	2	7	.222	81	49	46	47	43	4.93
1977—Pittsburgh	National	34	108	3	7	.300	118	63	61	66	31	5.08
1978—Columbus	Int'national	28	181	12	9	.571	174	100	*92	*169	69	4.57
1978—Pittsburgh‡	National	3	9	2	0	1.000	7	3	2	10	4	2.00
1979—Seattle§	American	25	119	3	11	.214	151	90	80	72	58	6.05
1980—Portland x	P. Coast	19	98	6	7	.462	96	49	45	89	46	4.13
1981—Portland	P. Coast	23	153	12	6	.667	138	73	60	*135	68	3.53
1981—Pittsburgh	National	13	54	4	5	.444	51	23	20	30	23	3.33
1982—Portland y	P. Coast	28	190⅓	*16	9	.640	162	103	90	*172	94	4.26
1983—Texas z	American	42	67	3	6	.333	56	28	23	50	22	3.09
1984—Texas a	American	33	59⅓	2	4	.333	62	28	24	28	23	3.64
1985—Rochester	Int'national	41	105	4	6	.400	97	52	49	104	45	4.20
1986—Rochester	Int'national	17	83⅔	7	3	*.700	73	38	34	69	42	3.66

Year	Club	League	G.	IP.	W.	L.	Pct.	H.	R.	ER.	SO.	BB.	ERA.
1986	—Baltimore b	American	21	49⅓	2	2	.500	58	22	21	32	23	3.83
1987	—Syracuse c	Int'national	31	167⅔	12	7	.632	142	80	75	★147	81	4.03
1988	—Milwaukee d	American	28	80⅔	5	0	1.000	75	47	39	48	29	4.35
National League Totals—4 Years			52	174	9	12	.429	177	89	83	108	58	4.29
American League Totals—5 Years			149	375⅓	15	23	.395	402	215	187	230	155	4.48
Major League Totals—9 Years			201	549⅓	24	35	.407	579	304	270	338	213	4.42

Signed as free agent by Pittsburgh Pirates' organization, November 25, 1971.

†On disabled list, July 13 to August 24, 1976.

‡Traded with Shortstop Mario Mendoza and Pitcher Rafael Vasquez to Seattle Mariners for Pitchers Enrique Romo and Rick Jones and Shortstop Tom McMillan, December 5, 1978.

§Traded to Pittsburgh Pirates' organization for a player to be named later, April 1, 1980; Seattle Mariners acquired Pitcher Larry Andersen to complete deal, October 29, 1980.

xOn disabled list, June 16 to July 6 and July 13 to August 3, 1980.

yDrafted by Texas Rangers, December 6, 1982.

zOn disabled list, August 19 to September 9, 1983.

aGranted free agency, December 20, 1984; signed by Baltimore Orioles, February 1, 1985.

bReleased, March 27, 1987; signed by Syracuse (Toronto Blue Jays' organization), April 4, 1987.

cGranted free agency, October 15, 1987; signed by Milwaukee Brewers' organization, November 10, 1987.

dGranted free agency, November 4, 1988; re-signed by Brewers' organization, December 7, 1988.

RONALD GLEN JONES
(Ron)

Born June 11, 1964, at Seguin, Tex.
Height, 5.10. Weight, 200.
Throws right and bats lefthanded.
Attended Wharton County Junior College, Wharton, Tex.
Nephew of Alvin Jones, outfielder in Atlanta Braves' organization, 1973 through 1976.

Led Florida State League in total bases with 216 and slugging percentage with .524 in 1986.
Led Northwest League in game-winning RBIs with 10 in 1985.
Tied for International League lead in game-winning RBIs with 11 and sacrifice flies with 8 in 1988.
Tied for International League lead in double plays by outfielders with 4 in 1988.
Named Florida State League Most Valuable Player, 1986.

Year	Club	League	Pos.	G.	AB.	R.	H.	2B.	3B.	HR.	RBI.	B.A.	PO.	A.	E.	F.A.
1985	—Bend	N'west	OF	73	286	54	90	13	1	10	60	.315	88	4	★11	.893
1986	—Clearwater	Fla. St.	OF	108	412	76	●153	18	★12	7	73	★.371	196	9	2	.990
1986	—Portland†	P. C.	OF	11	34	4	4	1	0	0	2	.118	11	2	0	1.000
1987	—Maine	Int.	OF	90	316	33	78	13	4	7	32	.247	178	4	3	.984
1988	—Maine	Int.	OF	125	445	64	119	15	3	16	★75	.267	191	14	7	.967
1988	—Philadelphia	Nat.	OF	33	124	15	36	6	1	8	26	.290	70	1	0	1.000
Major League Totals—1 Year				33	124	15	36	6	1	8	26	.290	70	1	0	1.000

Selected by Toronto Blue Jays' organization in 14th round of free-agent draft, June 7, 1982.

Selected by Montreal Expos' organization in secondary phase of free-agent draft, January 11, 1983.

Signed as free agent by Philadelphia Phillies' organization, October 20, 1984.

†On disabled list, August 8, 1986 through remainder of season.

TRACY DONALD JONES

Born March 31, 1961, at Inglewood, Calif.
Height, 6.03. Weight, 220.
Throws and bats righthanded.
Attended Loyola Marymount University, Los Angeles, Calif.
Brother of Terry Jones, infielder in Kansas City Royals organization.

Major League stolen bases: 1986 (7), 1987 (31), 1988 (18). Total—56.

Year	Club	League	Pos.	G.	AB.	R.	H.	2B.	3B.	HR.	RBI.	B.A.	PO.	A.	E.	F.A.
1983	—Tampa	Fla. St.	O-3-1-S	53	118	27	32	5	3	1	15	.271	54	12	11	.857
1983	—Eugene	N'west	2B-3B-OF	55	203	42	54	12	0	1	26	.266	81	68	12	.925
1984	—Tampa†	Fla. St.	OF	86	307	50	95	14	3	4	41	.309	150	6	0	1.000
1985	—Vermont	East.	OF	75	284	40	90	12	3	4	31	.317	117	4	1	.992
1985	—Denver	A. A.	OF	51	205	43	69	12	0	10	31	.337	93	2	0	1.000
1986	—Cincinnati‡	Nat.	OF-1B	46	86	16	30	3	0	2	10	.349	46	1	0	1.000
1987	—Cincinnati	Nat.	OF	117	359	53	104	17	3	10	44	.290	189	2	2	.990
1988	—Cinc.§x-Mon.	Nat.	OF	90	224	29	66	6	1	3	24	.295	96	2	2	.980
1988	—Nashville y	A. A.	OF	2	6	2	3	1	0	0	1	.500	2	1	0	1.000
Major League Totals—3 Years				253	669	98	200	26	4	15	78	.299	331	5	4	.988

Selected by New York Mets' organization in 4th round of free-agent draft, June 7, 1982.

Selected by Cincinnati Reds' organization in secondary phase of free-agent draft, January 11, 1983.

†On disabled list, July 18 to September 18, 1984.

‡On disabled list, May 23 to June 15 and July 10 to September 1, 1986.

§On disabled list, May 5 to May 22 and May 26 to June 20, 1988; included rehabilitation disability assignment to Nashville, June 18 and June 19, 1988.

xTraded with Pitcher Pat Pacillo to Montreal Expos for Catcher Jeff Reed, Outfielder Herm Winningham and Pitcher Randy St. Claire, July 13, 1988.

yTraded to San Francisco Giants for Outfielder Mike Aldrete, December 8, 1988.

WILLIAM TIMOTHY JONES
(Tim)

Born December 1, 1962, at Sumter, S. C.
Height, 5.10. Weight, 172.
Throws right and bats lefthanded.
Received degree in health service from The Citadel, Charleston, S.C., in 1985.

Major League stolen bases: 1988 (4).
Tied for Appalachian League lead in sacrifice flies with 5 in 1985.
Led Appalachian League shortstops in putouts with 105 and double plays with 30 in 1985.

Year Club	League	Pos.	G.	AB.	R.	H.	2B.	3B.	HR.	RBI.	B.A.	PO.	A.	E.	F.A.
1985—Johnson City	Appal.	SS-3B	68	*235	33	75	10	1	3	48	.319	109	148	23	.918
1986—St. Petersburg	Fla. St.	SS	39	142	19	43	3	2	0	27	.254	67	125	8	.960
1986—Arkansas	Texas	SS	96	284	36	76	15	1	2	27	.268	142	277	24	.946
1987—Arkansas	Texas	SS-2B	61	176	23	58	12	0	3	26	.330	80	151	9	.963
1987—Louisville	A. A.	SS	73	276	48	78	14	3	4	43	.283	112	221	13	.962
1988—Louisville	A. A.	SS	103	370	63	95	21	2	6	38	.257	145	302	15	*.968
1988—St. Louis	Nat.	SS-2B-3B	31	52	2	14	0	0	0	3	.269	26	40	1	.985
Major League Totals—1 Year			31	52	2	14	0	0	0	3	.269	26	40	1	.985

Selected by St. Louis Cardinals' organization in 2nd round of free-agent draft, June 3, 1985.

PAUL SCOTT JORDAN
(Ricky)

Born May 26, 1965, at Richmond, Calif.
Height, 6.03. Weight, 210.
Throws and bats righthanded.

Major League stolen bases: 1988 (1).
Tied for Eastern League lead in sacrifice flies with 9 in 1987.
Led Eastern League first basemen in total chances with 1,255 and double plays with 110 in 1987.
Led Eastern League first basemen in double plays with 100 in 1986.

Year Club	League	Pos.	G.	AB.	R.	H.	2B.	3B.	HR.	RBI.	B.A.	PO.	A.	E.	F.A.
1983—Helena	Pion.	1B	60	247	32	73	7	1	5	33	.296	486	35	7	.986
1984—Spartanburg	S. Atl.	1B	128	490	72	143	23	4	10	76	.292	1129	69	14	.988
1985—Clearwater	Fla. St.	1B	*139	528	60	146	22	8	7	62	.277	1252	86	*20	.985
1986—Reading	East.	*1B-OF	133	478	44	131	19	3	2	60	.274	1052	87	*17	.985
1987—Reading	East.	1B	132	475	78	151	28	3	16	95	.318	*1193	54	8	.994
1988—Maine	Int.	1B	87	338	42	104	23	1	7	36	.308	809	41	4	.995
1988—Philadelphia	Nat.	1B	69	273	41	84	15	1	11	43	.308	579	35	5	.992
Major League Totals—1 Year			69	273	41	84	15	1	11	43	.308	579	35	5	.992

Selected by Philadelphia Phillies' organization in 1st round (22nd player selected) of free-agent draft, June 6, 1983.

SCOTT ALLAN JORDAN

Born May 23, 1963, at Waco, Tex.
Height, 6.00. Weight, 180.
Throws and bats righthanded.
Attended Georgia Tech, Atlanta, Ga.

Led Eastern League outfielders in total chances with 325 in 1988.

Year Club	League	Pos.	G.	AB.	R.	H.	2B.	3B.	HR.	RBI.	B.A.	PO.	A.	E.	F.A.
1985—Waterbury†	East.	OF	8	27	2	2	1	0	0	2	.074	20	1	0	1.000
1985—Batavia	NYP	OF	20	68	8	14	3	0	3	9	.206	35	1	0	1.000
1986—Waterloo	Midw.	OF	117	434	88	108	17	4	13	55	.249	212	12	8	.966
1987—Kinston	Carol.	OF	123	447	97	126	21	8	11	73	.282	260	6	12	.957
1988—Williamsport	East.	OF	129	481	68	122	17	3	4	33	.254	*312	3	10	.969
1988—Cleveland	Amer.	OF	7	9	0	1	0	0	0	1	.111	10	0	0	1.000
Major League Totals—1 Year			7	9	0	1	0	0	0	1	.111	10	0	0	1.000

Selected by Boston Red Sox' organization in 16th round of free-agent draft, June 4, 1984.
Selected by Cleveland Indians' organization in 4th round of free-agent draft, June 3, 1985.
†On temporarily inactive list, June 23 to July 25, 1985.

DOMINGO FELIX JOSE

(Known by middle name.)

Born May 8, 1965, at Santo Domingo, D. R.
Height, 6.01. Weight, 190.
Throws right and bats left and righthanded.

Major League stolen bases: 1988 (1).

Year Club	League	Pos.	G.	AB.	R.	H.	2B.	3B.	HR.	RBI.	B.A.	PO.	A.	E.	F.A.
1984—Idaho Falls	Pion.	OF	45	152	16	33	6	0	1	18	.217	48	6	1	.982
1985—Madison	Midw.	OF	117	409	46	89	13	3	3	33	.218	187	9	12	.942
1986—Modesto	Calif.	OF	127	516	77	147	22	8	14	77	.285	215	12	14	.942
1987—Huntsville	South.	OF	91	296	29	67	11	1	5	42	.226	131	7	8	.945
1988—Tacoma	P. C.	OF	134	508	72	161	29	5	12	83	.317	253	11	8	.971
1988—Oakland	Amer.	OF	8	6	2	2	1	0	0	1	.333	8	0	0	1.000
Major League Totals—1 Year			8	6	2	2	1	0	0	1	.333	8	0	0	1.000

Signed as free agent by Oakland A's organization, January 3, 1984.

WALLACE KEITH JOYNER
(Wally)

Born June 16, 1962, at Atlanta, Ga.
Height, 6.02. Weight, 198.
Throws and bats lefthanded.
Attended Brigham Young University, Provo, Utah.

Tied major league record for most home runs, month of October (4), 1987.
Major League stolen bases: 1986 (5), 1987 (8), 1988 (8). Total—21.
Hit three home runs in a game, October 3, 1987.
Led American League in sacrifice flies with 12 in 1986.
Led American League first basemen in total chances with 1,520 and double plays with 148 in 1988.
Tied for Eastern League lead in intentional bases on balls received with 8 in 1984.
Led Pacific Coast League first basemen in total chances with 1,229 and double plays with 121 in 1985.

Year Club	League	Pos.	G.	AB.	R.	H.	2B.	3B.	HR.	RBI.	B.A.	PO.	A.	E.	F.A.
1983—Peoria	Midw.	1B	54	192	25	63	16	2	3	33	.328	480	45	6	.989
1984—Waterbury	East.	1B-OF	134	467	81	148	24	7	12	72	.317	906	86	9	.991
1985—Edmonton	P. C.	1B	126	477	68	135	29	5	12	73	.283	⋆1107	⋆107	•15	.988
1986—California	Amer.	1B	154	593	82	172	27	3	22	100	.290	1222	139	15	.989
1987—California	Amer.	1B	149	564	100	161	33	1	34	117	.285	1276	92	10	.993
1988—California	Amer.	1B	158	597	81	176	31	2	13	85	.295	⋆1369	⋆143	8	.995
Major League Totals—3 Years			461	1754	263	509	91	6	69	302	.290	3867	374	33	.992

Selected by California Angels' organization in 3rd round of free-agent draft, June 6, 1983.

CHAMPIONSHIP SERIES RECORD

Year Club	League	Pos.	G.	AB.	R.	H.	2B.	3B.	HR.	RBI.	B.A.	PO.	A.	E.	F.A.
1986—California	Amer.	1B	3	11	3	5	2	0	1	2	.455	24	1	0	1.000

ALL-STAR GAME RECORD

Year League	Pos.	AB.	R.	H.	2B.	3B.	HR.	RBI.	B.A.	PO.	A.	E.	F.A.
1986—American	1B	1	0	0	0	0	0	0	.000	3	1	0	1.000

EDWARD JAMES JURAK

Name pronounced YOU-rack.

(Ed)

Born October 24, 1957, at Los Angeles, Calif.
Height, 6.02. Weight, 187.
Throws and bats righthanded.

Major League stolen bases: 1983 (1).
Led Pacific Coast League in sacrifice flies with 10 in 1988.
Led Eastern League shortstops in double plays with 76 in 1979.

Year Club	League	Pos.	G.	AB.	R.	H.	2B.	3B.	HR.	RBI.	B.A.	PO.	A.	E.	F.A.
1975—Elmira	NYP	SS	68	250	41	63	9	3	0	25	.252	104	192	⋆43	.873
1976—Winston-Salem	Carol.	SS	113	401	49	88	6	2	4	35	.219	168	346	⋆55	.903
1977—Bristol	East.	SS	123	441	74	116	12	8	1	36	.263	173	345	26	.952
1978—Pawtucket	Int.	SS-3B	23	46	9	12	1	1	0	6	.261	11	34	8	.849
1978—Winter Haven†	Fla. St.	SS-3B-1B	38	139	14	37	0	1	0	11	.266	49	99	16	.902
1979—Bristol	East.	SS	135	435	50	96	17	2	0	41	.221	⋆208	⋆374	⋆40	.936
1980—Pawtucket‡	Int.	SS-3B	83	221	16	58	8	1	3	31	.262	72	130	19	.914
1981—Bristol§	East.	SS-3B-2B	87	297	63	101	19	3	1	25	⋆.340	114	194	29	.914
1981—Pawtucket	Int.	SS	23	90	13	27	3	2	1	9	.300	39	81	10	.923
1982—Pawtucket	Int.	3B-SS	81	284	39	84	14	1	9	43	.296	53	177	17	.931
1982—Boston	Amer.	3B-OF	12	21	3	7	0	0	0	7	.333	7	17	2	.923
1983—Boston	Amer.	S-1-3-2	75	159	19	44	8	4	0	18	.277	197	117	11	.966
1984—Boston	Amer.	1-2-3-S	47	66	6	16	3	1	1	7	.242	92	40	3	.978
1985—Pawtucket	Int.	3B-OF-1B	72	263	33	68	11	2	6	38	.259	183	75	8	.970
1985—Boston x	Amer.	3-S-1-O	26	13	4	3	0	0	0	0	.231	5	10	2	.882
1986—San Jose y	Calif.	SS-3B	28	71	14	23	0	0	3	10	.324	55	66	9	.931
1987—Tulsa	Texas	SS-3B	98	338	67	117	19	3	10	47	.346	153	247	19	.955
1987—Oklahoma City z	A. A.	3B-SS	31	94	9	29	0	1	3	8	.309	29	62	4	.958
1988—Tacoma	P. C.	SS-3B-1B	126	448	63	132	22	2	7	67	.295	188	280	23	.953
1988—Oakland a	Amer.	3B	31	1	1	0	0	0	0	0	.000	0	0	0	.000
Major League Totals—5 Years			163	260	33	70	11	5	1	32	.269	301	184	18	.964

Selected by Boston Red Sox' organization in 3rd round of free-agent draft, June 4, 1975.
†On disabled list, May 4 to June 16, 1978.
‡On disabled list, April 16 to April 28 and May 28 to June 7, 1980.
§On disabled list, June 10 to July 4, 1981.
xReleased, March 19, 1986; signed by San Jose (Independent), August 2, 1986.
yReleased, December 31, 1986; signed by Tulsa (Texas Rangers' organization), February 17, 1987.
zGranted free agency, October 15, 1987; signed by Oakland Athletics' organization, November 10, 1987.
aGranted free agency, October 15, 1988.

—DID YOU KNOW—

That Dave Dravecky won on opening day last season as a member of the Giants after losing to San Francisco in San Diego's 1987 season opener while pitching for the Padres?

DAVID CHRISTOPHER JUSTICE
(Dave)

Born April 14, 1966, at Cincinnati, O.
Height, 6.03. Weight, 195.
Throws and bats lefthanded.
Attended Thomas More College, Crestview Hills, Ky.

Tied for Appalachian League lead in sacrifice flies with 5 in 1985.

Year Club	League	Pos.	G.	AB.	R.	H.	2B.	3B.	HR.	RBI.	B.A.	PO.	A.	E.	F.A.
1985—Pulaski	Appal.	OF	66	204	39	50	8	0	•10	46	.245	86	2	4	.957
1986—Sumter	S. Atl.	OF	61	220	48	66	16	0	10	61	.300	124	7	4	.970
1986—Durham	Carol.	OF-1B	67	229	47	64	9	1	12	44	.279	163	5	1	.994
1987—Greenville	South.	OF	93	348	38	79	12	4	6	40	.227	199	4	8	.962
1988—Richmond	Int.	OF	70	227	27	46	9	1	8	28	.203	136	5	4	.972
1988—Greenville	South.	OF	58	198	34	55	13	1	9	37	.278	100	3	5	.954

Selected by Atlanta Braves' organization in 4th round of free-agent draft, June 3, 1985.

JEFFREY PATRICK KAISER
(Jeff)

Born July 24, 1960, at Wyandotte, Mich.
Height, 6.03. Weight, 195.
Throws left and bats righthanded.
Received bachelor of arts degree in business administration from
Western Michigan University, Kalamazoo, Mich.

Year Club	League	G.	IP.	W.	L.	Pct.	H.	R.	ER.	SO.	BB.	ERA.
1982—Medford	Northwest	15	78	8	1	*.889	91	56	46	69	57	5.31
1983—Modesto	California	25	164⅔	12	9	.571	160	84	70	102	80	3.83
1984—Albany	Eastern	7	47⅔	5	1	.833	36	11	10	20	15	1.89
1984—Tacoma†	P. Coast	14	74⅔	4	7	.364	81	52	38	38	28	4.58
1985—Oakland	American	15	16⅔	0	0	.000	25	32	27	10	20	14.58
1985—Tacoma‡	P. Coast	27	46⅓	4	2	.667	33	10	9	36	18	1.75
1986—Tacoma§x	P. Coast	34	110⅔	4	4	.500	123	70	53	63	52	4.31
1987—Buffalo	Am. Assoc.	22	71⅓	5	3	.625	87	52	41	53	32	5.17
1987—Cleveland y	American	2	3⅓	0	0	.000	4	6	6	2	3	16.20
1988—Colorado Springs	P. Coast	36	53	3	2	.600	56	23	22	47	19	3.74
1988—Cleveland	American	3	2⅔	0	0	.000	2	0	0	0	1	0.00
Major League Totals—3 Years		20	22⅔	0	0	.000	31	38	33	12	24	13.10

Selected by Toronto Blue Jays' organization in 7th round of free-agent draft, June 8, 1981.
Selected by Oakland A's organization in 10th round of free-agent draft, June 7, 1982.
†On disabled list, July 20 to August 3, 1984.
‡On disabled list, June 21 to July 7, 1985.
§On disabled list, May 4 to May 14, 1986.
xTraded to Cleveland Indians for Pitcher Curt Wardle, February 23, 1987.
yOn disabled list, August 9 to August 31, 1987.

KEITH WADE KAISER

Born May 24, 1967, at San Antonio, Tex.
Height, 6.04. Weight, 200.
Throws right and bats left and righthanded.
Attended New Mexico State University, Las Cruces, N.M.

Led South Atlantic League in wild pitches with 17 in 1988.

Year Club	League	G.	IP.	W.	L.	Pct.	H.	R.	ER.	SO.	BB.	ERA.
1986—Sarasota Reds	Gulf Coast	11	28⅓	0	4	.000	28	22	10	14	25	3.18
1987—Billings	Pioneer	13	76	6	5	.545	67	37	26	71	39	3.08
1988—Greensboro	S. Atlantic	28	186	11	9	.550	135	67	52	159	*101	2.52

Selected by Cincinnati Reds' organization in 21st round of free-agent draft, June 3, 1985.
Signed as free agent by Cincinnati Reds' organization, July 7, 1986.

RONALD JOSEPH KARKOVICE

Name pronounced CAR-koh-vice.

(Ron)

Born August 8, 1963, at Union, N. J.
Height, 6.01. Weight, 215.
Throws and bats righthanded.

Major League stolen bases: 1986 (1), 1987 (3), 1988 (4). Total—8.
Led Gulf Coast League batters in strikeouts with 73 in 1982.
Led Eastern League catchers in double plays with 13 in 1985.
Led Midwest League catchers in fielding percentage with .996 in 1983.
Led Gulf Coast League catchers in total chances with 394 and tied for lead in double plays with 5 in 1982.

Year Club	League	Pos.	G.	AB.	R.	H.	2B.	3B.	HR.	RBI.	B.A.	PO.	A.	E.	F.A.
1982—Sarasota W.S.	Gulf C.	C	60	214	34	56	6	0	7	32	.262	*331	*51	12	.970
1983—Appleton	Midw.	C-OF	97	326	54	78	17	3	13	48	.239	682	91	4	.995
1984—Glens Falls	East.	C	88	260	37	56	9	1	13	39	.215	442	*68	11	.979
1984—Denver	A. A.	C	31	86	7	19	1	0	2	10	.221	149	28	3	.983
1985—Glens Falls	East.	C	99	324	37	70	9	3	11	37	.216	573	*103	*14	.980

Year	Club	League	Pos.	G.	AB.	R.	H.	2B.	3B.	HR.	RBI.	B.A.	PO.	A.	E.	F.A.
1986	—Birmingham	South.	C	97	319	63	90	13	1	20	53	.282	463	72	10	.982
1986	—Chicago	Amer.	C	37	97	13	24	7	0	4	13	.247	227	19	1	.996
1987	—Chicago	Amer.	C	39	85	7	6	0	0	2	7	.071	147	20	3	.982
1987	—Hawaii	P. C.	C-OF	34	104	15	19	3	0	4	11	.183	108	13	3	.976
1988	—Vancouver	P. C.	C	39	116	12	29	10	0	2	13	.250	202	16	3	.986
1988	—Chicago	Amer.	C	46	115	10	20	4	0	3	9	.174	190	24	1	.995
Major League Totals—3 Years				122	297	30	50	11	0	9	29	.168	564	63	5	.992

Selected by Chicago White Sox' organization in 1st round (14th player selected) of free-agent draft, June 7, 1982.

ROBERTO CONRADO KELLY

Born October 1, 1964, at Panama City, Panama.
Height, 6.04. Weight, 185.
Throws and bats righthanded.
Attended Jose Dolores Moscote College, Panama.

Major League stolen bases: 1987 (9), 1988 (5). Total—14.
Led International League in stolen bases with 51 in 1987.
Led International League outfielders in total chances with 345 in 1987.

Year	Club	League	Pos.	G.	AB.	R.	H.	2B.	3B.	HR.	RBI.	B.A.	PO.	A.	E.	F.A.
1982	—Bradenton Yanks	Gulf C.	SS-OF	31	86	13	17	1	1	1	18	.198	47	79	19	.869
1983	—Oneonta	NYP	OF-3B	48	167	17	36	1	2	2	17	.216	70	3	5	.936
1983	—Greensboro	S. Atl.	OF	20	49	6	13	0	0	0	3	.265	30	2	0	1.000
1984	—Greensboro	S. Atl.	Of-1B	111	361	68	86	13	2	1	26	.238	228	5	4	.983
1985	—Fort Lauderdale†	Fla. St.	OF	114	417	86	103	4	*13	3	38	.247	187	1	1	.995
1986	—Albany‡	East.	OF	86	299	42	87	11	4	2	43	.291	206	8	7	.968
1987	—Columbus	Int.	OF	118	471	77	131	19	8	13	62	.278	*331	4	10	.971
1987	—New York	Amer.	OF	23	52	12	14	3	0	1	7	.269	42	0	2	.955
1988	—New York§	Amer.	OF	38	77	9	19	4	1	1	7	.247	70	1	1	.986
1988	—Columbus	Int.	OF	30	120	25	40	8	1	3	16	.333	51	1	0	1.000
Major League Totals—2 Years				61	129	21	33	7	1	2	14	.256	112	1	3	.974

Signed as free agent by New York Yankees' organization, February 21, 1982.
†Batted left and righthanded.
‡On disabled list, July 10 to August 23, 1986.
§On disabled list, June 29 to September 1, 1988.

STEVEN F. KEMP
(Steve)

Born August 7, 1954, at San Angelo, Tex.
Height, 6.00. Weight, 190.
Throws and bats lefthanded.
Attended University of Southern California, Los Angeles, Calif.

Major League stolen bases: 1977 (3), 1978 (2), 1979 (5), 1980 (5), 1981 (9), 1982 (7), 1983 (1), 1984 (4), 1985 (1), 1986 (1), 1988 (1). Total—39.
Received reported $50,000 bonus to sign with Detroit Tigers, 1976.
Named outfielder on THE SPORTING NEWS College Baseball All-America Team, 1975.

Year	Club	League	Pos.	G.	AB.	R.	H.	2B.	3B.	HR.	RBI.	B.A.	PO.	A.	E.	F.A.
1976	—Montgomery	South.	OF-1B	73	256	41	74	17	2	8	43	.289	91	4	2	.979
1976	—Evansville	A. A.	OF	52	171	37	66	14	3	11	38	.386	91	2	5	.945
1977	—Detroit	Amer.	OF	151	552	75	142	29	4	18	88	.257	252	10	5	.981
1978	—Detroit	Amer.	OF	159	582	75	161	18	4	15	79	.277	325	11	8	.977
1979	—Detroit	Amer.	OF	134	490	88	156	26	3	26	105	.318	229	12	6	.976
1980	—Detroit	Amer.	OF	135	508	88	149	23	3	21	101	.293	197	4	1	.995
1981	—Detroit†	Amer.	OF	105	372	52	103	18	4	9	49	.277	207	4	3	.986
1982	—Chicago‡	Amer.	OF	160	580	91	166	23	1	19	98	.286	280	6	7	.976
1983	—New York§	Amer.	OF	109	373	53	90	17	3	12	49	.241	215	5	3	.987
1984	—New York xy	Amer.	OF	94	313	37	91	12	1	7	41	.291	138	2	4	.972
1985	—Pittsburgh z	Nat.	OF	92	236	19	59	13	2	2	21	.250	105	1	0	1.000
1986	—Pittsburgh a	Nat.	OF	13	16	1	3	0	0	1	1	.188	9	0	0	1.000
1986	—Las Vegas b	P. C.	OF	48	160	27	43	10	2	5	27	.269	32	0	0	1.000
1987	—Oklahoma City c	A. A.	OF	121	421	73	112	28	6	20	84	.266	49	6	1	.982
1988	—Texas de	Amer.	OF-1B	16	36	2	8	0	0	0	2	.222	6	0	0	1.000
1988	—Oklahoma City	A. A.	OF-1B	37	121	12	33	6	0	2	19	.273	97	4	3	.971
American League Totals—9 Years				1063	3806	561	1066	166	23	127	612	.280	1849	54	37	.981
National League Totals—2 Years				105	252	20	62	13	2	3	22	.246	114	1	0	1.000
Major League Totals—11 Years				1168	4058	581	1128	179	25	130	634	.278	1963	55	37	.982

Selected by Detroit Tigers' organization in 1st round (first player selected) of free-agent draft, January 7, 1976.
†Traded to Chicago White Sox for Outfielder Chet Lemon, November 27, 1981.
‡Granted free agency, November 10, 1982; signed by New York Yankees as Type A player, December 8, 1982. (Pitcher Steve Mura was selected from player compensation pool by Chicago White Sox, January 26, 1983.)
§On disabled list, September 15, 1983 through remainder of season.
xOn disabled list, April 4 to April 20, 1984.
yTraded with Infielder Tim Foli and $800,000 to Pittsburgh Pirates for Infielder Dale Berra, Pitcher Alfonso Pulido and Outfielder Jay Buhner, December 20, 1984.
zOn disabled list, April 6 to April 21, 1985.
aReleased, May 8, 1986; signed by Las Vegas (San Diego Padres' organization), June 22, 1986.
bReleased, September 18, 1986; signed by Oklahoma City (Texas Rangers' organization), March 4, 1987.

cReleased, October 15, 1987; re-signed by Texas Rangers, January 19, 1988.
dReleased, May 25, 1988; re-signed by Oklahoma City (Texas Rangers' organization), June 9, 1988.
eOn voluntarily retired list, July 20, 1988.

ALL-STAR GAME RECORD

Year League	Pos.	AB.	R.	H.	2B.	3B.	HR.	RBI.	B.A.	PO.	A.	E.	F.A.
1979—American	PH	1	0	0	0	0	0	0	.000	0	0	0	.000

TERRENCE EDWARD KENNEDY
(Terry)

Born June 4, 1956, at Euclid, O.
Height, 6.04. Weight, 224.
Throws right and bats lefthanded.
Attended Florida State University, Tallahassee, Fla.
Son of Bob Kennedy, third baseman-outfielder with Chicago AL, Cleveland, Baltimore, Detroit and Brooklyn, 1939 through 1957; scout, Cleveland, 1958 through 1961; minor league manager, Chicago Cubs' organization, 1962; coach, Chicago Cubs, 1963 and 1964; Chicago Cubs executive, 1965; minor league manager, Los Angeles Dodgers' organization, 1966; coach, Atlanta Braves, 1967; manager, Oakland A's, 1968; Director of Player Development, St. Louis Cardinals, 1969 through 1976; Executive Vice President, Chicago Cubs, 1977 through 1981; Houston Astros Vice-President-Baseball Operations, 1982 through 1985; and San Francisco Giants Vice-President-Baseball Operations since 1986; brother of Bob Kennedy Jr., pitcher in St. Louis Cardinals' organization, 1971 through 1975; scout, Seattle Mariners, 1976; scout, Chicago Cubs, 1977 through 1981; scout with Houston Astros, 1982 through 1985.

Tied National League record for most two-base hits by catcher, season (40), 1982.
Major League stolen bases: 1982 (1), 1983 (1), 1984 (1), 1987 (1). Total—4.
Led National League catchers in double plays with 12 in 1981 and tied for lead with 11 in 1982 and 12 in 1985.
Named catcher on The Sporting News National League Silver Slugger team, 1983.
Named College Player of the Year by The Sporting News, 1977.
Received reported $100,000 bonus to sign with St. Louis Cardinals, 1977.
Named catcher on The Sporting News College Baseball All-America Team, 1976 and 1977.

Year Club	League	Pos.	G.	AB.	R.	H.	2B.	3B.	HR.	RBI.	B.A.	PO.	A.	E.	F.A.
1977—Johnson City	Appal.	C-1B	12	39	14	23	7	2	3	15	.590	66	3	1	.986
1977—St. Petersburg	Fla. St.	C	45	166	22	41	8	0	4	22	.247	168	22	6	.969
1978—Arkansas	Texas	C-OF	69	239	55	69	14	0	10	54	.289	365	30	7	.983
1978—Springfield	A. A.	C-1B	64	230	35	76	13	0	10	46	.330	331	26	7	.981
1978—St. Louis	Nat.	C	10	29	0	5	0	0	0	2	.172	46	4	1	.980
1979—Springfield	A. A.	C	84	294	35	86	18	1	13	64	.293	434	38	13	.973
1979—St. Louis	Nat.	C	33	109	11	31	7	0	2	17	.284	135	7	1	.993
1980—St. Louis†	Nat.	C-OF	84	248	28	63	12	3	4	34	.254	231	22	7	.973
1981—San Diego	Nat.	C	101	382	32	115	24	1	2	41	.301	465	63	*20	.964
1982—San Diego	Nat.	C-1B	153	562	75	166	42	1	21	97	.295	777	66	9	.989
1983—San Diego	Nat.	C-1B	149	549	47	156	27	2	17	98	.284	807	82	12	.987
1984—San Diego	Nat.	C	148	530	54	127	16	1	14	57	.240	708	54	14	.982
1985—San Diego	Nat.	C-1B	143	532	54	139	27	1	10	74	.261	662	68	10	.986
1986—San Diego‡	Nat.	C	141	432	46	114	22	1	12	57	.264	692	70	8	.990
1987—Baltimore	Amer.	C	143	512	51	128	13	1	18	62	.250	750	*58	6	.993
1988—Baltimore	Amer.	C	85	265	20	60	10	0	3	16	.226	332	23	2	.994
National League Totals—9 Years			962	3373	347	916	177	10	82	477	.272	4523	436	82	.984
American League Totals—2 Years			228	777	71	188	23	1	21	78	.242	1082	81	8	.993
Major League Totals—11 Years			1190	4150	418	1104	200	11	103	555	.266	5605	517	90	.986

Selected by St. Louis Cardinals' organization in 1st round (sixth player selected) of free-agent draft, June 7, 1977.

†Traded with Catcher Steve Swisher, Pitchers John Littlefield, Al Olmsted, Kim Seaman and John Urrea and Infielder Mike Phillips to San Diego Padres for Pitchers Rollie Fingers and Bob Shirley, Catcher-First Baseman Gene Tenace and a player to be named later, December 8, 1980; St. Louis Cardinals' organization acquired catcher Bob Geren to complete deal, December 10, 1980.

‡Traded with Pitcher Mark Williamson to Baltimore Orioles for Pitcher Storm Davis, October 30, 1986.

CHAMPIONSHIP SERIES RECORD

Year Club	League	Pos.	G.	AB.	R.	H.	2B.	3B.	HR.	RBI.	B.A.	PO.	A.	E.	F.A.
1984—San Diego	Nat.	C	5	18	2	4	0	0	0	1	.222	28	4	0	1.000

WORLD SERIES RECORD

Year Club	League	Pos.	G.	AB.	R.	H.	2B.	3B.	HR.	RBI.	B.A.	PO.	A.	E.	F.A.
1984—San Diego	Nat.	C	5	19	2	4	1	0	1	3	.211	30	2	0	1.000

ALL-STAR GAME RECORD

Year League	Pos.	AB.	R.	H.	2B.	3B.	HR.	RBI.	B.A.	PO.	A.	E.	F.A.
1981—National	PH	1	0	0	0	0	0	0	.000	0	0	0	.000
1985—National	C	2	0	1	0	0	0	1	.500	0	0	1	.000
1987—American	C	2	0	0	0	0	0	0	.000	3	1	0	1.000
All-Star Game Totals—3 Years		5	0	1	0	0	0	1	.200	3	1	1	.800

Member of National League All-Star Team in 1983; did not play.

—DID YOU KNOW—

That Jerry Reuss and Milt Pappas are the only 200-game winners in major league history never to have recorded a 20-victory season?

CHARLES PATRICK KERFELD
(Charley)

Born September 28, 1963, at Knob Noster, Mo.
Height, 6.07. Weight, 250.
Throws and bats righthanded.
Attended Yavapai College, Prescott, Ariz.

Major League saves: 1986 (7)
Led South Atlantic League pitchers in complete games with 12 and tied for lead in games started with 28 in 1983.
Named South Atlantic League Pitcher of the Year, 1983.

Year Club	League	G.	IP.	W.	L.	Pct.	H.	R.	ER.	SO.	BB.	ERA.
1983—Asheville	S. Atlantic	28	*192	*16	10	.615	171	84	62	189	85	2.91
1984—Columbus†	Southern	24	162⅔	14	9	.609	140	80	54	118	79	2.99
1984—Tucson	P. Coast	1	3⅔	0	1	.000	6	4	4	3	1	9.82
1985—Tucson	P. Coast	26	163⅓	10	11	.476	176	95	80	123	74	4.41
1985—Houston	National	11	44⅓	4	2	.667	44	22	20	30	25	4.06
1986—Houston‡	National	61	93⅔	11	2	.846	71	32	27	77	42	2.59
1987—Houston§	National	21	29⅔	0	2	.000	34	22	22	17	21	6.67
1987—Tucson	P. Coast	32	62⅔	4	4	.500	61	36	33	59	27	4.74
1988—Columbus x	Southern	13	64	2	7	.222	63	36	32	63	21	4.50
Major League Totals—3 Years		93	167⅔	15	6	.714	149	76	69	124	88	3.70

Selected by Philadelphia Phillies' organization in 24th round of free-agent draft, June 8, 1981.
Selected by Seattle Mariners' organization in secondary phase of free-agent draft, January 12, 1982.
Selected by Houston Astros' organization in secondary phase of free-agent draft, June 7, 1982.
†On disabled list, June 4 to June 28, 1984.
‡On disabled list, June 14 to July 2, 1986.
§On disabled list, July 31 to September 21, 1987.
xOn Houston disabled list, March 27 to April 21, 1988.

CHAMPIONSHIP SERIES RECORD

Year Club	League	G.	IP.	W.	L.	Pct.	H.	R.	ER.	SO.	BB.	ERA.
1986—Houston	National	3	4	0	1	.000	2	1	1	4	1	2.25

JAMES EDWARD KEY
(Jimmy)

Born April 22, 1961, at Huntsville, Ala.
Height, 6.01. Weight, 190.
Throws left and bats righthanded.
Attended Clemson University, Clemson, S. C.

Major League saves: 1984 (10).
Named American League Pitcher of the Year by THE SPORTING NEWS, 1987.
Named lefthanded pitcher on THE SPORTING NEWS American League All-Star Team, 1987.

Year Club	League	G.	IP.	W.	L.	Pct.	H.	R.	ER.	SO.	BB.	ERA.
1982—Medicine Hat	Pioneer	5	31⅓	2	1	.667	27	12	8	25	10	2.30
1982—Florence	S. Atlantic	9	58	5	2	.714	59	33	24	49	18	3.72
1983—Knoxville	Southern	14	101	6	5	.545	86	35	32	57	40	2.85
1983—Syracuse	Int'national	16	89⅓	4	8	.333	87	58	41	71	33	4.13
1984—Toronto	American	63	62	4	5	.444	70	37	32	44	32	4.65
1985—Toronto†	American	35	212⅔	14	6	.700	188	77	71	85	50	3.00
1986—Toronto	American	36	232	14	11	.560	222	98	92	141	74	3.57
1987—Toronto	American	36	261	17	8	.680	210	93	80	161	66	*2.76
1988—Toronto‡	American	21	131⅓	12	5	.706	127	55	48	65	30	3.29
1988—Dunedin	Florida St.	4	21⅓	2	0	1.000	15	2	0	11	1	0.00
Major League Totals—5 Years		191	899	61	35	.635	817	360	323	496	252	3.23

Selected by Chicago White Sox' organization in 10th round of free-agent draft, June 5, 1979.
Selected by Toronto Blue Jays' organization in 3rd round of free-agent draft, June 7, 1982.
†Appeared in one game as a pinch-runner.
‡On disabled list, April 15 to June 29, 1988; included rehabilitation disability assignment to Dunedin, June 10 to June 27, 1988.

CHAMPIONSHIP SERIES RECORD

Year Club	League	G.	IP.	W.	L.	Pct.	H.	R.	ER.	SO.	BB.	ERA.
1985—Toronto	American	2	8⅔	0	1	.000	15	5	5	5	2	5.19

ALL-STAR GAME RECORD

Year League	IP.	W.	L.	Pct.	H.	R.	ER.	SO.	BB.	ERA.
1985—American	⅓	0	0	.000	0	0	0	0	0	0.00

SAM KHALIFA

Name pronounced Kuh-LEE-fuh.

(Sammy)

Born December 5, 1963, at Fontana, Calif.
Height, 5.11. Weight, 177.
Throws and bats righthanded.

Major League stolen bases: 1985 (5).

Year	Club	League	Pos.	G.	AB.	R.	H.	2B.	3B.	HR.	RBI.	B.A.	PO.	A.	E.	F.A.
1982—	Bradenton Pir.	Gulf. C.	SS	6	25	1	2	0	0	0	0	.080	12	26	4	.905
1982—	Greenwood	S. Atl.	SS	48	177	29	54	6	1	0	19	.305	69	136	19	.915
1983—	Alexandria†	Carol.	*SS-2B	103	356	42	96	19	6	1	49	.270	156	279	*33	.929
1983—	Lynn	East.	SS	5	15	1	3	0	0	0	1	.200	8	9	0	1.000
1984—	Nashua‡	East.	SS	91	344	39	82	12	4	1	36	.238	151	266	24	.946
1985—	Hawaii	P. C.	SS-2B	67	217	36	61	14	5	1	22	.281	89	193	11	.962
1985—	Pittsburgh	Nat.	SS	95	.320	30	76	14	3	2	31	.238	156	316	16	.967
1986—	Pittsburgh	Nat.	SS-2B	64	151	8	28	6	0	0	4	.185	94	168	10	.963
1986—	Hawaii	P. C.	SS-2B	50	200	30	63	9	4	1	26	.315	82	165	7	.972
1987—	Vancouver	P. C.	SS-OF	111	367	39	83	12	5	0	31	.226	193	325	35	.937
1987—	Pittsburgh	Nat.	SS	5	17	1	3	0	0	0	2	.176	5	6	1	.917
1988—	Buffalo	A. A.	3B-SS	66	215	30	49	9	3	5	21	.228	45	154	7	.966
1988—	Harrisburg	East.	SS	41	142	21	47	4	4	2	15	.331	57	113	13	.929
Major League Totals—3 Years				164	488	39	107	20	3	2	37	.219	255	490	27	.965

Selected by Pittsburgh Pirates' organization in 1st round (seventh player selected) of free-agent draft, June 7, 1982.
†On disabled list, May 6 to May 21, 1983.
‡On disabled list, April 13 to May 9 and August 11, 1984 through remainder of season.

STEVEN GEORGE KIEFER

Name pronounced Key-fer.

(Steve)

Born October 18, 1960, at Chicago, Ill.
Height, 6.01. Weight, 180.
Throws and bats righthanded.
Attended Cerritos College, Norwalk, Calif. and Fullerton College, Fullerton, Calif.

Led American Association in slugging percentage with .668 in 1987.
Led Pacific Coast League shortstops in errors with 35 in 1984.
Tied for Eastern League lead in sacrifice hits with 12 in 1983.

Year	Club	League	Pos.	G.	AB.	R.	H.	2B.	3B.	HR.	RBI.	B.A.	PO.	A.	E.	F.A.
1981—	Medford	N'west	SS-3B	55	192	38	47	7	5	4	22	.245	68	175	17	.935
1982—	Madison	Midw.	SS	124	415	72	97	24	1	15	58	.234	173	395	44	.928
1983—	Albany	East.	SS-3B-OF	123	415	68	102	18	1	19	81	.246	186	306	38	.928
1984—	Tacoma	P. C.	SS-3B	125	455	63	122	18	3	16	54	.268	189	328	38	.932
1984—	Oakland	Amer.	SS-3B	23	40	7	7	1	2	0	2	.175	15	35	5	.909
1985—	Tacoma†	P. C.	3B-SS	85	331	41	87	25	2	12	53	.263	80	171	13	.951
1985—	Oakland‡	Amer.	3B	40	66	8	13	1	1	1	10	.197	15	37	7	.881
1986—	Vancouver	P. C.	3B-2B-SS	126	426	67	114	22	6	15	69	.268	123	266	24	.942
1986—	Milwaukee	Amer.	SS	2	6	0	0	0	0	0	0	.000	7	8	0	1.000
1987—	Denver	A. A.	3B	90	361	90	119	21	4	31	95	.330	60	161	15	.936
1987—	Milwaukee	Amer.	3B-2B	28	99	17	20	4	0	5	17	.202	16	50	2	.971
1988—	Milwaukee	Amer.	2B-3B	7	10	2	3	1	0	1	1	.300	4	8	1	.923
1988—	Denver§	A. A.	3B-2B-1B	79	294	47	63	11	8	10	45	.214	93	137	15	.929
Major League Totals—5 Years				100	221	34	43	7	3	7	30	.195	57	138	15	.929

Selected by Oakland A's organization in 1st round (16th player selected) of free-agent draft, January 13, 1981.
†On disabled list, May 6 to May 20, 1985.
‡Traded with Pitchers Mike Fulmer and Pete Kendrick and Catcher Charlie O'Brien to Milwaukee Brewers for Pitcher Moose Haas, March 30, 1986.
§Granted free agency, October 15, 1988.

PAUL NELSON KILGUS

Born February 2, 1962, at Bowling Green, Ky.
Height, 6.01. Weight, 175.
Throws and bats lefthanded.
Received bachelor of science degree in biology from University of Kentucky, Lexington, Ky., in 1984.

Year	Club	League	G.	IP.	W.	L.	Pct.	H.	R.	ER.	SO.	BB.	ERA.
1984—	Tri-Cities	Northwest	14	78⅓	7	5	.583	87	38	25	60	31	2.87
1985—	Salem	Carolina	38	84⅓	3	1	.750	69	28	19	67	26	2.03
1986—	Tulsa	Texas	41	103⅔	3	7	.300	102	56	43	59	36	3.73
1987—	Oklahoma City	Am. Assoc.	21	24⅔	2	0	1.000	23	12	11	14	10	4.01
1987—	Texas	American	25	89⅓	2	7	.222	95	45	41	42	31	4.13
1988—	Texas†	American	32	203⅓	12	15	.444	190	105	94	88	71	4.16
Major League Totals—2 Years			57	292⅔	14	22	.389	285	150	135	130	102	4.15

Selected by Texas Rangers' organization in 43rd round of free-agent draft, June 4, 1984.
†Traded with Pitchers Mitch Williams and Steve Wilson, Infielders Curtis Wilkerson and Luis Benitez and Outfielder Pablo Delgado to Chicago Cubs for Outfielder Rafael Palmeiro and Pitchers Jamie Moyer and Drew Hall, December 5, 1988.

ERIC STEVEN KING

Born April 10, 1964, at Oxnard, Calif.
Height, 6.02. Weight, 180.
Throws and bats righthanded.

Tied major league record for most putouts by pitcher, nine-inning game (6), July 8, 1986.
Major League saves: 1986 (3), 1987 (9), 1988 (3). Total—15.

Year	Club	League	G.	IP.	W.	L.	Pct.	H.	R.	ER.	SO.	BB.	ERA.
1983	Great Falls	Pioneer	20	56⅓	3	4	.429	58	31	27	61	14	4.31
1984	Clinton	Midwest	35	147⅓	5	10	.333	142	74	55	124	76	3.36
1985	Shreveport†‡	Texas	15	104⅔	5	3	.625	74	34	27	80	30	2.32
1986	Nashville	Am. Assoc.	6	38⅓	3	2	.600	29	16	15	38	16	3.52
1986	Detroit	American	33	138⅓	11	4	.733	108	54	54	79	63	3.51
1987	Detroit	American	55	116	6	9	.400	111	67	63	89	60	4.89
1988	Toledo	Int'national	10	69	3	4	.429	54	26	25	51	23	3.26
1988	Detroit	American	23	68⅔	4	1	.800	60	28	26	45	34	3.41
Major League Totals—3 Years			111	323	21	14	.600	279	149	143	213	157	3.98

Signed as free agent by San Francisco Giants' organization, June 11, 1983.

†On suspended list, July 3 to July 13, 1985, then transferred to disabled list, July 13 to July 27, 1985.

‡Traded with Pitcher Dave LaPoint and Catcher Matt Nokes to Detroit Tigers for Pitcher Juan Berenguer, Catcher Bob Melvin and a player to be named later, October 7, 1985; San Francisco Giants acquired Pitcher Scott Medvin to complete deal, December 11, 1985.

CHAMPIONSHIP SERIES RECORD

Year	Club	League	G.	IP.	W.	L.	Pct.	H.	R.	ER.	SO.	BB.	ERA.
1987	Detroit	American	2	5⅓	0	0	.000	3	1	1	4	2	1.69

JEFFREY WAYNE KING
(Jeff)

Born December 26, 1964, at Marion, Ind.
Height, 6.01. Weight, 175.
Throws and bats righthanded.
Attended University of Arkansas, Fayetteville, Ark.
Son of Jack King, minor league catcher, 1954 and 1955; and brother of James King, shortstop drafted by Philadelphia Phillies' organization in 1982 and Seattle Mariners' organization in 1984.

Led Carolina League in slugging percentage with .565 in 1987.
Received reported $180,000 bonus to sign with Pittsburgh Pirates, 1986.
Named College Player of the Year by THE SPORTING NEWS, 1986.
Named third baseman on THE SPORTING NEWS College Baseball All-America Team, 1986.

Year	Club	League	Pos.	G.	AB.	R.	H.	2B.	3B.	HR.	RBI.	B.A.	PO.	A.	E.	F.A.
1986	Prince William	Carol.	3B	37	132	18	31	4	1	6	20	.235	25	50	8	.904
1987	Salem	Carol.	1B-3B	90	310	68	86	9	1	26	71	.277	572	106	13	.981
1987	Harrisburg	East.	1B	26	100	12	24	7	0	2	25	.240	107	10	1	.992
1988	Harrisburg	East.	3B	117	411	49	105	21	1	14	66	.255	97	208	24	.927

Selected by Chicago Cubs' organization in 23rd round of free-agent draft, June 6, 1983.
Selected by Pittsburgh Pirates' organization in 1st round (first player selected) of free-agent draft, June 2, 1986.

MICHAEL SCOTT KINGERY
(Mike)

Born March 29, 1961, at St. James, Minn.
Height, 6.00. Weight, 180.
Throws and bats lefthanded.
Attended Willmar Community College, Willmar, Minn.; and St. Cloud State University, St. Cloud, Minn.

Major League stolen bases: 1986 (7), 1987 (7), 1988 (3). Total—17.
Led Florida State League in intentional bases on balls received with 11 in 1983.
Tied for South Atlantic League lead in double plays by outfielders with 5 in 1982.

Year	Club	League	Pos.	G.	AB.	R.	H.	2B.	3B.	HR.	RBI.	B.A.	PO.	A.	E.	F.A.
1980	K.C. Royals-Gold	Gulf C.	OF	44	143	12	32	3	3	0	13	.224	78	5	2	.976
1981	Charleston†	S. Atl.	OF	69	213	33	57	3	4	3	25	.268	80	7	4	.956
1982	Charleston	S. Atl.	OF	140	513	65	163	19	4	8	75	.318	250	21	7	.975
1983	Fort Myers	Fla. St.	OF	123	436	68	116	9	7	2	51	.266	200	16	5	.977
1984	Memphis	South.	OF	139	455	65	135	19	3	4	58	.297	291	18	6	.981
1985	Omaha	A. A.	OF	132	444	51	113	25	6	2	49	.255	247	17	5	.981
1986	Omaha	A. A.	OF	79	298	47	99	14	8	3	47	.332	171	10	1	.995
1986	Kansas City‡	Amer.	OF	62	209	25	54	8	5	3	14	.258	102	6	3	.973
1987	Seattle	Amer.	OF	120	354	38	99	25	4	9	52	.280	226	15	2	.992
1988	Seattle	Amer.	OF-1B	57	123	21	25	6	0	1	9	.203	102	6	2	.982
1988	Calgary	P. C.	OF-1B	47	170	29	54	12	2	1	14	.318	144	4	3	.980
Major League Totals—3 Years				239	686	84	178	39	9	13	75	.259	430	27	7	.985

Signed as free agent by Kansas City Royals' organization, August 27, 1979.

†On disabled list, July 29 to August 15, 1981.

‡Traded with Pitchers Scott Bankhead and Steve Shields to Seattle Mariners for Outfielder Danny Tartabull and Pitcher Rick Luecken, December 10, 1986.

MATTHEW ROY KINZER
(Matt)

Born June 17, 1963, at Indianapolis, Ind.
Height, 6.02. Weight, 210.
Throws and bats righthanded.
Attended Purdue University, West Lafayette, Ind.

Year Club	League	G.	IP.	W.	L.	Pct.	H.	R.	ER.	SO.	BB.	ERA.
1984—Arkansas	Texas	14	82⅔	5	6	.455	97	48	41	41	27	4.46
1985—Springfield†	Midwest	11	58⅓	5	4	.556	56	26	24	36	21	3.70
1986—St. Petersburg	Florida St.	22	134	10	7	.588	129	49	43	80	42	2.89
1987—Arkansas	Texas	17	91⅓	5	6	.455	82	57	48	74	34	4.73
1988—Arkansas	Texas	16	29	3	0	1.000	26	11	10	34	3	3.10
1988—Louisville	Am. Assoc.	46	80	6	2	.750	73	34	33	53	24	3.71

Selected by Cleveland Indians' organization in 2nd round of free-agent draft, June 8, 1981.
Selected by St. Louis Cardinals' organization in 6th round of free-agent draft, June 4, 1984.
†On disabled list, August 2, 1985 through remainder of season.

ROBERT WAYNE KIPPER
(Bob)

Born July 8, 1964, at Aurora, Ill.
Height, 6.02. Weight, 175.
Throws left and bats righthanded.

Pitched seven-inning, 9-0 no-hit victory against San Jose, June 10, 1984 (second game).
Named California League Pitcher of the Year, 1984.

Year Club	League	G.	IP.	W.	L.	Pct.	H.	R.	ER.	SO.	BB.	ERA.
1982—Salem	Northwest	13	76⅔	6	5	.545	62	46	38	65	52	4.46
1983—Peoria†	Midwest	22	127⅔	5	8	.385	112	77	66	105	52	4.65
1984—Redwood	California	26	185	*18	8	.692	147	61	42	98	65	*2.04
1985—California	American	2	3⅓	0	1	.000	7	8	8	0	3	21.60
1985—Midland‡	Texas	9	49⅔	3	3	.500	52	22	17	31	10	3.08
1985—Edmonton§x-Hawaii	P. Coast	7	49⅔	3	0	1.000	36	15	11	42	12	1.99
1985—Pittsburgh	National	5	24⅔	1	2	.333	21	16	14	13	7	5.11
1986—Pittsburgh y	National	20	114	6	8	.429	123	60	51	81	34	4.03
1986—Nashua	Eastern	4	18⅓	0	1	.000	14	7	7	19	3	3.44
1987—Pittsburgh	National	24	110⅔	5	9	.357	117	74	73	83	52	5.94
1987—Vancouver	P. Coast	6	25⅓	0	2	.000	23	7	5	22	4	1.78
1988—Pittsburgh	National	50	65	2	6	.250	54	33	27	39	26	3.74
American League Totals—1 Year		2	3⅓	0	1	.000	7	8	8	0	3	21.60
National League Totals—4 Years		99	314⅓	14	25	.359	315	183	165	216	119	4.72
Major League Totals—4 Years		101	317⅔	14	26	.350	322	191	173	216	122	4.90

Selected by California Angels' organization in 1st round (eighth player selected) of free-agent draft, June 7, 1982.
†On disabled list, July 20 to August 8, 1983.
‡On disabled list, May 31 to June 10, 1985.
§Loaned to Hawaii (Pittsburgh Pirates' organization), August 2, 1985; returned, August 16, 1985.
xTraded to Pittsburgh Pirates' organization, August 16, 1985, completing deal in which Pittsburgh traded Pitchers John Candelaria and Al Holland and Outfielder George Hendrick to California Angels for Pitcher Pat Clements, Outfielder Mike Brown and a player to be named later, August 2, 1985.
yOn disabled list, June 29 to September 1, 1986; included rehabilitation disability assignment to Nashua, August 14 to September 1, 1986.

RONALD DALE KITTLE
(Ron)

Born January 5, 1958, at Gary, Ind.
Height, 6.04. Weight, 220.
Throws and bats righthanded.

Tied major league record for most home runs, month of October (4), 1985.
Major League stolen bases: 1983 (8), 1984 (3), 1985 (1), 1986 (4). Total—16.
Led American League batters in strikeouts with 150 in 1983.
Led Pacific Coast League in total bases with 355, slugging percentage with .752 and tied for lead in being hit by pitch with 10 in 1982.
Led Eastern League in total bases with 270 and slugging percentage with .694 in 1981.
Named American League Rookie Player of the Year by The Sporting News, 1983.
Named American League Rookie of the Year by Baseball Writers' Association of America, 1983.
Named Minor League Player of the Year by The Sporting News, 1982.
Named Pacific Coast League Most Valuable Player, 1982.
Named Eastern League Most Valuable Player, 1981.

Year Club	League	Pos.	G.	AB.	R.	H.	2B.	3B.	HR.	RBI.	B.A.	PO.	A.	E.	F.A.
1977—Clinton†	Midw.	OF	22	53	9	10	4	0	0	3	.189	16	0	0	1.000
1977—Lethbridge	Pion.	OF	34	100	22	25	3	0	7	21	.250	29	2	6	.838
1978—Clinton‡	Midw.	OF	13	35	2	5	2	1	0	4	.143	4	1	1	.833
1979—Knoxville	South.	OF-C	53	157	28	43	9	1	6	26	.274	44	1	6	.980
1979—Appleton	Midw.	OF-C	35	120	18	31	3	1	2	12	.258	33	1	2	.972
1980—Appleton	Midw.	C-OF	61	209	31	66	15	3	12	56	.316	56	9	1	.985
1980—Glens Falls§	East.	OF	17	65	11	20	3	1	4	9	.308	24	4	3	.903
1981—Glens Falls x	East.	OF	109	389	97	127	17	3	*40	*103	.326	28	0	3	.903
1982—Edmonton	P. C.	OF-C	127	472	*121	163	22	10	*50	*144	.345	149	15	8	.953
1982—Chicago	Amer.	OF	20	29	3	7	2	0	1	7	.241	3	0	0	1.000
1983—Chicago	Amer.	OF	145	520	75	132	19	3	35	100	.254	234	7	9	.964
1984—Chicago	Amer.	OF	139	466	67	100	15	0	32	74	.215	226	14	7	.972
1985—Chicago y	Amer.	OF	116	379	51	87	12	0	26	58	.230	88	2	1	.989
1985—Buffalo	A. A.	OF	6	21	3	7	2	0	2	5	.333	2	0	0	1.000
1986—Chi. z-N.Y.	Amer.	OF	116	376	42	82	13	0	21	60	.218	39	3	0	1.000

Year	Club	League	Pos.	G.	AB.	R.	H.	2B.	3B.	HR.	RBI.	B.A.	PO.	A.	E.	F.A.
1987	—New York a	Amer.	OF	59	159	21	44	5	0	12	28	.277	4	1	0	1.000
1987	—Columbus b	Int.	DH	4	18	3	4	0	0	0	1	.222	0	0	0	.000
1988	—Cleveland c	Amer.	DH	75	225	31	58	8	0	18	43	.258	0	0	0	.000
Major League Totals—7 Years				670	2154	290	510	74	3	145	370	.237	594	27	17	.973

Signed as free agent by Los Angeles Dodgers' organization, July 5, 1977.
†On disabled list, April 30 to May 14, 1977.
‡Released, July 7, 1978; signed by Knoxville (Chicago White Sox' organization), September 4, 1978.
§On disabled list, July 27 to August 31, 1980.
xOn disabled list, April 21 to May 10, 1981.
yOn disabled list, July 4 to July 25, 1985; included rehabilitation disability assignment to Buffalo, July 19 to July 25, 1985.
zTraded with Infielder Wayne Tolleson and Catcher Joel Skinner to New York Yankees for Catcher Ron Hassey, Shortstop Carlos Martinez and a player to be named later, July 30, 1986; New York traded Catcher Bill Lindsey to Chicago White Sox' organization to complete deal, December 24, 1986.
aOn disabled list, July 7 to August 16, 1987; included rehabilitation disability assignment to Columbus, August 14 to August 16, 1987.
bReleased, December 21, 1987; signed by Cleveland Indians, February 9, 1988.
cGranted free agency, November 4, 1988; signed by Chicago White Sox, November 26, 1988.

CHAMPIONSHIP SERIES RECORD

Year	Club	League	Pos.	G.	AB.	R.	H.	2B.	3B.	HR.	RBI.	B.A.	PO.	A.	E.	F.A.
1983	—Chicago	Amer.	OF	3	7	1	2	1	0	0	0	.286	3	0	0	1.000

ALL-STAR GAME RECORD

Year	League	Pos.	AB.	R.	H.	2B.	3B.	HR.	RBI.	B.A.	PO.	A.	E.	F.A.
1983	—American	OF	2	1	1	0	0	0	0	.500	1	0	0	1.000

ROBERT WESLEY KNEPPER

Name pronounced NEPP-ur.

(Bob)

Born May 25, 1954, at Akron, O.
Height, 6.02. Weight, 210.
Throws and bats lefthanded.

Tied National League record for fewest assists by pitcher, season, for leader in assists (47), 1986.
Major League saves: 1982 (1).
Led National League in shutouts with 6 in 1978 and tied for lead with 5 in 1986.
Tied for National League lead in hit batsmen with 8 in 1980.
Led California League pitchers in games started with 30 and tied for lead in complete games with 16 in 1974.
Tied for Pacific Coast League lead in shutouts with 3 in 1976.
Named National League Comeback Player of the Year by THE SPORTING NEWS, 1981.

Year	Club	League	G.	IP.	W.	L.	Pct.	H.	R.	ER.	SO.	BB.	ERA.
1972	—Great Falls	Pioneer	12	68	7	1	.875	53	20	11	75	19	1.46
1973	—Decatur	Midwest	11	79	7	2	.778	65	28	17	68	23	1.94
1973	—Fresno	California	13	71	2	8	.200	78	54	32	66	35	4.06
1974	—Fresno	California	30	*238	*20	5	●.800	*239	103	84	*247	80	3.18
1975	—Phoenix	P. Coast	26	155	11	11	.500	169	101	79	94	78	4.59
1976	—Phoenix	P. Coast	29	205	14	10	.583	209	105	98	130	64	4.30
1976	—San Francisco	National	4	25	1	2	.333	26	9	9	11	7	3.24
1977	—Phoenix	P. Coast	10	51	3	6	.333	68	51	42	24	25	7.41
1977	—San Francisco	National	27	166	11	9	.550	151	73	62	100	72	3.36
1978	—San Francisco	National	36	260	17	11	.607	218	85	76	147	85	2.63
1979	—San Francisco	National	34	207	9	12	.429	241	117	107	123	77	4.65
1980	—San Francisco†	National	35	215	9	16	.360	242	114	98	103	61	4.10
1981	—Houston	National	22	157	9	5	.643	128	41	38	75	38	2.18
1982	—Houston	National	33	180	5	15	.250	193	100	89	108	60	4.45
1983	—Houston	National	35	203	6	13	.316	202	93	72	125	71	3.19
1984	—Houston	National	35	233⅔	15	10	.600	223	93	83	140	55	3.20
1985	—Houston	National	37	241	15	13	.536	253	●119	95	131	54	3.55
1986	—Houston	National	40	258	17	12	.586	232	100	90	143	62	3.14
1987	—Houston	National	33	177⅔	8	*17	.320	226	118	104	76	54	5.27
1988	—Houston	National	27	175	14	5	.737	156	70	61	103	67	3.14
Major League Totals—13 Years			398	2498⅓	136	140	.493	2491	1132	984	1385	763	3.54

Selected by San Francisco Giants' organization in 2nd round of free-agent draft, June 6, 1972.
†Traded with Outfielder Chris Bourjos to Houston Astros for Third Baseman Enos Cabell, December 8, 1980.

DIVISION SERIES RECORD

Year	Club	League	G.	IP.	W.	L.	Pct.	H.	R.	ER.	SO.	BB.	ERA.
1981	—Houston	National	1	5	0	1	.000	6	3	3	4	2	5.40

CHAMPIONSHIP SERIES RECORD

Year	Club	League	G.	IP.	W.	L.	Pct.	H.	R.	ER.	SO.	BB.	ERA.
1986	—Houston	National	2	15⅓	0	0	.000	13	7	6	9	1	3.52

ALL-STAR GAME RECORD

Year	League	IP.	W.	L.	Pct.	H.	R.	ER.	SO.	BB.	ERA.
1981	—National	2	0	0	.000	1	0	0	3	2	0.00
1988	—National	1	0	0	.000	2	1	1	0	1	9.00
All-Star Game Totals—2 Years		3	0	0	.000	3	1	1	3	3	3.00

CHARLES RAY KNIGHT

(Known by middle name.)

Born December 28, 1952, at Albany, Ga.
Height, 6.02. Weight, 190.
Throws and bats righthanded.
Attended Albany Junior College, Albany, Ga.
Husband of Nancy Lopez Knight, professional golfer.

Tied major league records for most home runs, inning (2) and most total bases, inning (8), May 13, 1980 (fifth inning).

Major League stolen bases: 1977 (1), 1979 (4), 1980 (1), 1981 (2), 1982 (2), 1985 (1), 1986 (2), 1988 (1). Total—14.

Led National League in grounding into double plays with 18 in 1981 and tied for lead with 24 in 1980.

Led American Association third basemen in putouts with 102 in 1976.

Tied for American Association lead in double plays by third basemen with 24 in 1974.

Named National League Comeback Player of the Year by THE SPORTING NEWS, 1986.

Year	Club	League	Pos.	G.	AB.	R.	H.	2B.	3B.	HR.	RBI.	B.A.	PO.	A.	E.	F.A.
1971	Sioux Falls	North.	O-INF-P	64	239	34	68	5	2	6	31	.285	69	79	17	.897
1972	Three Rivers	East.	O-INF-P	97	302	25	64	8	1	2	35	.212	102	142	20	.924
1973	Three Rivers	East.	O-3-1-2	57	193	41	54	14	2	2	22	.280	76	57	7	.950
1973	Indianapolis	A. A.	3-O-1-P	78	253	20	55	10	4	1	16	.217	72	126	11	.947
1974	Indianapolis	A. A.	*3B-OF	107	352	36	80	13	4	5	37	.227	94	177	11	*.961
1974	Cincinnati	Nat.	3B	14	11	1	2	1	0	0	2	.182	2	8	0	1.000
1975	Indianapolis	A. A.	*3B-1B	123	434	58	118	16	5	4	48	.272	*116	227	17	.953
1976	Indianapolis†	A. A.	3B-1B	110	396	47	106	24	3	10	41	.268	136	181	13	.961
1977	Cincinnati	Nat.	3-2-O-S	80	92	8	24	5	1	1	13	.261	45	45	4	.957
1978	Cincinnati‡	Nat.	3-2-O-S-1	83	65	7	13	3	0	1	4	.200	13	41	7	.885
1979	Cincinnati	Nat.	3B	150	551	64	175	37	4	10	79	.318	120	262	15	.962
1980	Cincinnati	Nat.	3B	162	618	71	163	39	7	14	78	.264	120	291	13	.969
1981	Cincinnati§	Nat.	3B	106	386	43	100	23	1	6	34	.259	69	176	11	.957
1982	Houston	Nat.	1B-3B	158	609	72	179	36	6	6	70	.294	1002	186	17	.986
1983	Houston	Nat.	1B	145	507	43	154	36	4	9	70	.304	1285	73	9	.993
1984	Hou. x-N.Y.	Nat.	3B-1B	115	371	28	88	14	0	3	35	.237	256	132	9	.977
1985	New York y	Nat.	3B-2B-1B	90	271	22	59	12	0	6	36	.218	56	113	7	.960
1986	New York z	Nat.	3B-1B	137	486	51	145	24	2	11	76	.298	94	204	16	.949
1987	Baltimore a	Amer.	3B-1B	150	563	46	144	24	0	14	65	.256	169	284	19	.960
1988	Detroit b	Amer.	1B-3B-OF	105	299	34	65	12	2	3	33	.217	438	42	4	.992
National League Totals—11 Years				1240	3967	410	1102	230	25	67	497	.278	3062	1531	108	.977
American League Totals—2 Years				255	862	80	209	36	2	17	98	.242	607	326	23	.976
Major League Totals—13 Years				1495	4829	490	1311	266	27	84	595	.271	3669	1857	131	.977

Selected by Cincinnati Reds' organization in 10th round of free-agent draft, June 4, 1970.

†On disabled list, June 21 to July 2, 1976.

‡On disabled list, April 17 to May 8, 1978.

§Traded to Houston Astros for First Baseman-Outfielder Cesar Cedeno, December 18, 1981.

xTraded to New York Mets for three players to be named later, August 28, 1984; Houston Astros acquired Outfielder Gerald Young and Infielder Manny Lee, August 31, 1984, and Pitcher Mitch Cook, September 10, 1984, to complete deal.

yOn disabled list, March 30 to April 20, 1985.

zGranted free agency, November 12, 1986; signed by Baltimore Orioles, February 12, 1987.

aTraded to Detroit Tigers for Pitcher Mark Thurmond, February 27, 1988.

bReleased, November 16, 1988.

CHAMPIONSHIP SERIES RECORD

Year	Club	League	Pos.	G.	AB.	R.	H.	2B.	3B.	HR.	RBI.	B.A.	PO.	A.	E.	F.A.
1979	Cincinnati	Nat.	3B	3	14	0	4	1	0	0	0	.286	0	5	0	1.000
1986	New York	Nat.	3B	6	24	1	4	0	0	0	2	.167	5	19	1	.960
Championship Series Totals—2 Years				9	38	1	8	1	0	0	2	.211	5	24	1	.967

WORLD SERIES RECORD

Year	Club	League	Pos.	G.	AB.	R.	H.	2B.	3B.	HR.	RBI.	B.A.	PO.	A.	E.	F.A.
1986	New York	Nat.	3B	6	23	4	9	1	0	1	5	.391	5	6	1	.917

ALL-STAR GAME RECORD

Year	League	Pos.	AB.	R.	H.	2B.	3B.	HR.	RBI.	B.A.	PO.	A.	E.	F.A.
1980	National	3B	1	1	1	0	0	0	0	1.000	0	1	0	1.000
1982	National	3B	3	0	0	0	0	0	0	.000	1	4	0	1.000
All-Star Game Totals—2 Years			4	1	1	0	0	0	0	.250	1	5	0	1.000

PITCHING RECORD

Year	Club	League	G.	IP.	W.	L.	Pct.	H.	R.	ER.	SO.	BB.	ERA.
1971	Sioux Falls	Northern	3	4	1	1	.500	5	6	5	4	5	11.25
1972	Three Rivers	Eastern	2	4	0	0	.000	3	1	1	2	4	2.25
1973	Indianapolis	Am. Assoc.	1	2	0	0	.000	2	1	1	0	4	4.50

—DID YOU KNOW—

That no American League West Division team has a winning record in League Championship Series play? The Oakland Athletics (13-14, .481) have the best record and the Kansas City Royals (12-15, .444) are second.

MARK RICHARD KNUDSON

Name pronounced NOOD-sun.

Born October 28, 1960, at Denver, Colo.
Height, 6.05. Weight, 215.
Throws and bats righthanded.
Attended Colorado State University, Fort Collins, Colo.

Year Club	League	G.	IP.	W.	L.	Pct.	H.	R.	ER.	SO.	BB.	ERA.
1982—Daytona Beach	Florida St.	12	60⅓	2	6	.250	75	35	32	15	23	4.77
1983—Daytona Beach	Florida St.	12	78⅔	5	3	.625	80	29	21	47	22	2.40
1983—Columbus	Southern	13	69⅔	4	5	.444	82	40	33	28	21	4.26
1984—Columbus	Southern	14	101	4	5	.444	100	32	25	54	27	2.23
1984—Tucson	P. Coast	13	84	4	6	.400	93	41	34	42	20	3.64
1985—Tucson	P. Coast	24	146	8	5	.615	171	69	65	68	37	4.01
1985—Houston†	National	2	11	0	2	.000	21	11	11	4	3	9.00
1986—Tucson‡-Vancouver	P. Coast	17	106⅔	6	6	.500	124	54	49	63	26	4.13
1986—Houston	National	9	42⅔	1	5	.167	48	23	20	20	15	4.22
1986—Milwaukee	American	4	17⅔	0	1	.000	22	15	15	9	5	7.64
1987—Denver	Am. Assoc.	14	78⅓	7	2	.778	89	53	51	37	30	5.86
1987—Milwaukee	American	15	62	4	4	.500	88	46	37	26	14	5.37
1988—Denver	Am. Assoc.	24	164⅓	11	8	.579	180	67	62	66	33	3.40
1988—Milwaukee	American	5	16	0	0	.000	17	3	2	7	2	1.13
National League Totals—2 Years		11	53⅔	1	7	.167	69	34	31	24	18	5.20
American League Totals—3 Years		24	95⅔	4	5	.444	127	64	54	42	21	5.08
Major League Totals—4 Years		35	149⅓	5	12	.294	196	98	85	66	39	5.12

Selected by Houston Astros' organization in 3rd round of free-agent draft, June 7, 1982.

†On disabled list, July 15 to August 5, 1985.

‡Traded to Milwaukee Brewers' organization, August 21, 1986, completing deal in which Milwaukee traded Pitcher Danny Darwin to Houston Astros for Pitcher Don August and a player to be named later, August 15, 1986.

RANDALL JOHN KRAMER
(Randy)

Born September 20, 1960, at Palo Alto, Calif.
Height, 6.02. Weight, 180.
Throws right and bats left and righthanded.
Attended San Jose City College, San Jose, Calif.

Tied for Northwest League lead in games started by pitchers with 15 and wild pitches with 13 in 1984.

Year Club	League	G.	IP.	W.	L.	Pct.	H.	R.	ER.	SO.	BB.	ERA.
1982—Sarasota Rangers	Gulf Coast	2	2⅔	0	0	.000	2	0	0	0	0	0.00
1983—Burlington	Midwest	26	132⅔	6	8	.429	131	97	76	113	92	5.16
1984—Salem	Carolina	12	53	2	8	.200	63	66	58	35	34	9.85
1984—Tri-Cities	Northwest	15	84	5	6	.455	83	62	47	74	*58	5.04
1985—Salem	Carolina	25	115⅓	7	11	.389	143	*99	*86	86	77	6.71
1986—Kinston†-Salem	Carolina	25	43⅓	3	3	.500	43	26	23	38	28	4.78
1986—Tulsa‡	Texas	26	39	0	3	.000	40	22	19	32	19	4.38
1987—Harrisburg	Eastern	26	49⅔	4	5	.444	62	43	35	43	29	6.34
1987—Vancouver	P. Coast	11	17⅔	0	0	.000	16	14	12	16	19	6.11
1988—Buffalo	Am. Assoc.	28	*198⅓	10	8	.556	161	85	69	120	50	3.13
1988—Pittsburgh	National	5	10	1	2	.333	12	6	6	7	1	5.40
Major League Totals—1 Year		5	10	1	2	.333	12	6	6	7	1	5.40

Selected by San Diego Padres' organization in 26th round of free-agent draft, June 6, 1978.

Selected by Houston Astros' organization in 2nd round of free-agent draft, January 12, 1982.

Selected by Texas Rangers' organization in secondary phase of free-agent draft, June 7, 1982.

†Loaned to Kinston (Independent), April 2, 1986; returned, May 20, 1986.

‡Traded to Pittsburgh Pirates for Pitcher Jeff Zaske, September 30, 1986.

RAYMOND ALLEN KRAWCZYK

Name pronounced KRAH-sick.

(Ray)

Born October 9, 1959, at Pittsburgh, Pa.
Height, 6.01. Weight, 184.
Throws and bats righthanded.
Attended Golden West College, Huntington Beach, Calif., and Oral Roberts University, Tulsa, Okla.

Major League saves: 1988 (1).

Led Pacific Coast League in saves with 20 in 1985.

Year Club	League	G.	IP.	W.	L.	Pct.	H.	R.	ER.	SO.	BB.	ERA.
1981—Bradenton Pirates	Gulf Coast	4	18	0	1	.000	11	5	3	14	7	1.50
1981—Alexandria	Carolina	8	46	2	4	.333	48	32	25	41	14	4.89
1982—Alexandria	Carolina	6	18⅔	1	0	1.000	10	1	1	25	13	0.48
1982—Buffalo	Eastern	38	101⅓	3	5	.375	93	59	53	102	59	4.71
1983—Hawaii	P. Coast	41	88⅔	5	7	.417	80	46	37	88	33	3.76
1984—Hawaii	P. Coast	43	72	4	5	.444	57	21	17	77	36	2.13
1984—Pittsburgh	National	4	5⅓	0	0	.000	7	2	2	3	4	3.38
1985—Hawaii†‡	P. Coast	38	55⅔	5	3	.625	35	15	14	54	22	2.26
1985—Pittsburgh	National	8	8⅓	0	2	.000	20	13	13	9	6	14.04
1986—Hawaii	P. Coast	32	47⅓	3	6	.333	51	29	26	40	21	4.94

Year Club	League	G.	IP.	W.	L.	Pct.	H.	R.	ER.	SO.	BB.	ERA.
1986—Pittsburgh§x	National	12	12⅓	0	1	.000	17	13	10	7	10	7.30
1987—Hawaii y	P. Coast	35	120	11	6	.647	124	59	55	78	38	4.13
1988—California	American	14	24⅓	0	1	.000	29	13	13	17	8	4.81
1988—Edmonton z	P. Coast	20	94⅔	4	9	.308	101	58	48	70	25	4.56
National League Totals—3 Years		24	26	0	3	.000	44	28	25	19	20	8.65
American League Totals—1 Year		14	24⅓	0	1	.000	29	13	13	17	8	4.81
Major League Totals—4 Years		38	50⅓	0	4	.000	73	41	38	36	28	6.79

Selected by Boston Red Sox' organization in 1st round (23rd player selected) of free-agent draft, January 8, 1980.
Selected by St. Louis Cardinals' organization in secondary phase of free-agent draft, June 3, 1980.
Selected by Pittsburgh Pirates' organization in secondary phase of free-agent draft, June 8, 1981.
†Appeared in one game as a first baseman with no chances.
‡On disabled list, June 10 to June 20, 1985.
§On disabled list, April 23 to June 18, 1986; included rehabilitation disability assignment to Prince William, June 1 to June 18, 1986.
xReleased, November 12, 1986; signed by Hawaii (Chicago White Sox' organization), April 17, 1987.
yReleased, November 22, 1987; signed by California Angels, December 22, 1987.
zGranted free agency, October 15, 1988.

CHAD MICHAEL KREUTER

Born August 26, 1964, in Marin County, Calif.
Height, 6.02. Weight, 190.
Throws right and bats left and righthanded.
Attended Pepperdine University, Malibu, Calif.

Tied major league record for most hits, inning, first major league game (2), September 14, 1988 (fifth inning).
Tied for Texas League lead in double plays by catchers with 9 in 1988.
Led Carolina League catchers in double plays with 17 and tied for lead in assists with 113 in 1986.

Year Club	League	Pos.	G.	AB.	R.	H.	2B.	3B.	HR.	RBI.	B.A.	PO.	A.	E.	F.A.
1985—Burlington†	Midw.	C	69	199	25	53	9	0	4	26	.266	349	34	8	.980
1986—Salem†	Carol.	C-OF-3B	125	387	55	85	21	2	6	49	.220	613	115	*21	.972
1987—Charlotte†	Fla. St.	C-OF-3B	85	281	36	61	18	1	9	40	.217	380	54	8	.982
1988—Tulsa	Texas	C	108	358	46	95	24	6	3	51	.265	603	71	●13	.981
1988—Texas	Amer.	C	16	51	3	14	2	1	1	5	.275	93	8	1	.990
Major League Totals—1 Year			16	51	3	14	2	1	1	5	.275	93	8	1	.990

Selected by Texas Rangers' organization in 5th round of free-agent draft, June 3, 1985.
†Batted righthanded only.

WILLIAM CULP KRUEGER

Name pronounced KREW-ger.

(Bill)

Born April 24, 1958, at Waukegan, Ill.
Height, 6.05. Weight, 210.
Throws and bats lefthanded.
Received bachelor of arts degree in business administration from University of Portland, Portland, Ore. in 1979.

Pitched seven-inning 2-0 no-hit victory against Phoenix, August 14, 1987 (second game).
Major League saves: 1986 (1).
Led Pacific Coast League in shutouts with 4 in 1988.
Tied for Eastern League lead in games started by pitchers with 27 and shutouts with 3 in 1982.

Year Club	League	G.	IP.	W.	L.	Pct.	H.	R.	ER.	SO.	BB.	ERA.
1980—Medford	Northwest	9	44	0	4	.000	54	38	25	48	29	5.11
1981—Modesto	California	16	98	3	5	.375	87	49	40	76	52	3.67
1981—West Haven	Eastern	11	68	3	6	.333	74	36	27	36	31	3.57
1982—West Haven	Eastern	28	181	15	9	.625	160	69	57	163	81	2.83
1983—Oakland†	American	17	109⅔	7	6	.538	104	54	44	58	53	3.61
1984—Tacoma	P. Coast	5	31⅔	2	2	.500	29	17	13	20	21	3.69
1984—Oakland	American	26	142	10	10	.500	156	95	75	61	85	4.75
1985—Oakland	American	32	151⅓	9	10	.474	165	95	76	56	69	4.52
1985—Tacoma	P. Coast	2	9⅔	0	1	.000	12	10	10	10	6	9.31
1986—Oakland‡	American	11	34⅓	1	2	.333	40	25	23	10	13	6.03
1986—Madison	Midwest	1	2	0	0	.000	1	0	0	1	1	0.00
1986—Tacoma	P. Coast	8	52⅓	3	3	.500	53	32	27	41	27	4.64
1987—Oakland	American	9	5⅔	0	3	.000	9	7	6	2	8	9.53
1987—Tacoma§-Albuquerque	P. Coast	24	146⅓	9	7	.563	158	74	66	97	66	4.06
1987—Los Angeles x	National	2	2⅓	0	0	.000	3	2	0	2	1	0.00
1988—Albuquerque	P. Coast	27	173⅓	*15	5	.750	167	74	58	114	69	*3.01
1988—Los Angeles y	National	1	2⅓	0	0	.000	4	3	3	1	2	11.57
American League Totals—5 Years		95	443	27	31	.466	474	276	224	187	228	4.55
National League Totals—2 Years		3	4⅔	0	0	.000	7	5	3	3	3	5.79
Major League Totals—6 Years		98	447⅔	27	31	.466	481	281	227	190	231	4.56

Signed as free agent by Oakland A's organization, July 12, 1980.
†On disabled list, August 5, 1983 through remainder of season.
‡On disabled list, May 6 to August 8, 1986; included rehabilitation disability assignment to Madison, July 4 to July 8, and Tacoma, July 10 to July 18 and July 21 to July 27, 1986.
§Traded to Los Angeles Dodgers' organization for Pitcher Tim Meeks, June 23, 1987.

xReleased, November 12, 1987; re-signed by Dodgers' organization, January 1, 1988.
yTraded to Pittsburgh Pirates for Pitcher Jim Neidlinger, October 3, 1988.

JOHN MARTIN KRUK

Born February 9, 1961, at Charleston, W. Va.
Height, 5.10. Weight, 195.
Throws and bats lefthanded.
Attended Allegany Community College, Cumberland, Md.

Major League stolen bases: 1986 (2), 1987 (18), 1988 (5). Total—25.
Led Texas League in sacrifice flies with 13 in 1983.
Led Pacific Coast League outfielders in double plays with 4 in 1984.

Year Club	League	Pos.	G.	AB.	R.	H.	2B.	3B.	HR.	RBI.	B.A.	PO.	A.	E.	F.A.
1981—Walla Walla	N'west	OF-1B	63	157	31	38	10	0	1	13	.242	108	5	2	.983
1982—Reno	Calif.	OF-1B	125	441	82	137	30	8	11	92	.311	253	11	7	.974
1983—Beaumont	Texas	OF-1B-P	133	498	94	170	41	9	10	88	.341	304	22	8	.976
1984—Las Vegas	P. C.	OF	115	340	56	111	25	6	11	57	.326	183	7	2	.990
1985—Las Vegas	P. C.	OF-1B	123	422	61	148	29	4	7	59	★.351	356	18	7	.982
1986—San Diego	Nat.	OF-1B	122	278	33	86	16	2	4	38	.309	139	6	3	.980
1986—Las Vegas	P. C.	OF-1B	6	28	6	13	3	1	0	9	.464	22	1	0	1.000
1987—San Diego	Nat.	1B-OF	138	447	72	140	14	2	20	91	.313	911	78	5	.995
1988—San Diego	Nat.	1B-OF	120	378	54	91	17	1	9	44	.241	634	37	3	.996
Major League Totals—3 Years			380	1103	159	317	47	5	33	173	.287	1684	121	11	.994

Selected by Pittsburgh Pirates' organization in 3rd round of free-agent draft, January 13, 1981.
Selected by San Diego Padres' organization in secondary phase of free-agent draft, June 8, 1981.

PITCHING RECORD

Year Club	League	G.	IP.	W.	L.	Pct.	H.	R.	ER.	SO.	BB.	ERA.
1983—Beaumont	Texas	3	5	0	0	.000	5	0	0	3	2	0.00

MICHAEL EDWARD KRUKOW

Name pronounced KROO-koh.

(Mike)

Born January 21, 1952, at Long Beach, Calif.
Height, 6.04. Weight, 205.
Throws and bats righthanded.
Attended California Poly State University, San Luis Obispo, Calif.

Major League saves: 1984 (1).
Tied for National League lead in games started by pitchers with 25 in 1981.
Tied for National League lead in hit batsmen with 8 in 1980.
Led Gulf Coast League in intentional bases on balls issued with 4 and tied for lead in complete games with 4 in 1973.

Year Club	League	G.	IP.	W.	L.	Pct.	H.	R.	ER.	SO.	BB.	ERA.
1973—Bradenton Cubs	Gulf Coast	13	77	4	3	.571	76	32	27	★80	28	3.16
1974—Midland	Texas	6	30	1	1	.500	42	24	17	21	19	5.10
1974—Key West	Florida St.	20	130	5	10	.333	121	66	46	94	47	3.18
1975—Midland†	Texas	24	153	13	6	.684	143	65	58	100	66	3.41
1976—Wichita	Am. Assoc.	26	144	7	9	.438	142	61	53	108	47	3.31
1976—Chicago	National	2	4	0	0	.000	6	4	4	1	2	9.00
1977—Chicago	National	34	172	8	14	.364	195	96	84	106	61	4.40
1978—Wichita	Am. Assoc.	7	53	2	3	.400	51	27	23	29	21	3.91
1978—Chicago	National	27	138	9	3	.750	125	62	60	81	53	3.91
1979—Chicago	National	28	165	9	9	.500	172	84	77	119	81	4.20
1980—Chicago	National	34	205	10	15	.400	200	117	100	130	80	4.39
1981—Chicago‡	National	25	144	9	9	.500	146	68	59	101	55	3.69
1982—Philadelphia§	National	33	208	13	11	.542	211	87	72	138	82	3.12
1983—San Francisco x	National	31	184⅓	11	11	.500	189	95	81	136	76	3.95
1984—San Francisco	National	35	199⅓	11	12	.478	★234	★117	101	141	78	4.56
1985—San Francisco	National	28	194⅔	8	11	.421	176	80	73	150	49	3.38
1986—San Francisco y	National	34	245	20	9	.690	204	90	83	178	55	3.05
1987—San Francisco z	National	30	163	5	6	.455	182	98	87	104	46	4.80
1988—San Francisco a	National	20	124⅔	7	4	.636	111	51	49	75	31	3.54
1988—Phoenix	P. Coast	1	5	1	0	1.000	0	0	0	5	0	0.00
Major League Totals—13 Years		361	2147	120	114	.513	2151	1049	930	1460	749	3.90

Selected by California Angels' organization in 32nd round of free-agent draft, June 4, 1970.
Selected by Chicago Cubs' organization in 8th round of free-agent draft, June 5, 1973.
†On disabled list, May 19 to June 7, 1975.
‡Traded with cash to Philadelphia Phillies for Catcher Keith Moreland and Pitchers Dan Larson and Dickie Noles, December 8, 1981.
§Traded with Pitcher Mark Davis and Outfielder Charles Penigar to San Francisco Giants for Second Baseman Joe Morgan and Pitcher Al Holland, December 14, 1982.
xOn disabled list, April 11 to May 8, 1983.
yOn disabled list, July 23 to August 7, 1986.
zOn disabled list, June 6 to June 25, 1987.
aOn disabled list, June 26 to August 13, 1988; included rehabilitation disability assignment to Phoenix, August 9 to August 13, 1988.

CHAMPIONSHIP SERIES RECORD

Year	Club	League	G.	IP.	W.	L.	Pct.	H.	R.	ER.	SO.	BB.	ERA.
1987—	San Francisco	National	1	9	1	0	1.000	9	2	2	3	1	2.00

ALL—STAR GAME RECORD

Year	League	IP.	W.	L.	Pct.	H.	R.	ER.	SO.	BB.	ERA.
1986—	National	1	0	0	.000	0	0	0	0	0	0.00

JEFFREY WILLIAM KUNKEL
(Jeff)

Born March 25, 1962, at West Palm Beach, Fla.
Height, 6.02. Weight, 190.
Throws and bats righthanded.
Attended Rider College, Lawrenceville, N.J.
Son of Bill Kunkel, pitcher with Kansas City A's and New York Yankees, 1961 through 1963; umpire, Florida State League, 1966; Southern League, 1967 and 1968; and American League umpire, 1968 through 1984.

Major League stolen bases: 1984 (4).
Named shortstop on THE SPORTING NEWS College Baseball All-America Team, 1983.

Year	Club	League	Pos.	G.	AB.	R.	H.	2B.	3B.	HR.	RBI.	B.A.	PO.	A.	E.	F.A.
1983—	Burlington	Midw.	SS	31	122	22	35	7	1	6	18	.287	38	88	13	.906
1983—	Tulsa	Texas	SS-2B	37	130	21	37	14	0	5	25	.285	68	106	9	.951
1984—	Tulsa†	Texas	SS	47	177	30	56	16	1	4	22	.316	64	103	16	.913
1984—	Texas	Amer.	SS	50	142	13	29	2	3	3	7	.204	81	120	17	.922
1985—	Oklahoma City	A. A.	SS-OF	99	370	40	72	8	6	5	43	.195	152	308	26	.947
1985—	Texas	Amer.	SS	2	4	1	1	0	0	0	0	.250	2	5	0	1.000
1986—	Oklahoma City	A. A.	55	111	409	50	100	16	4	11	51	.244	135	272	19	.955
1986—	Texas	Amer.	SS	8	13	3	3	0	0	1	2	.231	4	6	3	.769
1987—	Oklahoma City‡	A. A.	S-O-2-3	58	193	31	49	9	3	9	34	.254	65	100	5	.971
1987—	Texas	Amer.	2-3-O-1-S	15	32	1	7	0	0	1	2	.219	19	27	3	.939
1988—	Oklahoma City	A. A.	SS-OF	56	203	28	44	11	4	5	21	.217	68	151	7	.969
1988—	Texas	Amer.	2-S-3-O-P	55	154	14	35	8	3	2	15	.227	78	119	8	.961
Major League Totals—5 Years				130	345	32	75	10	6	7	26	.217	184	277	31	.937

Selected by Texas Rangers' organization in 1st round (third player selected) of free-agent draft, June 6, 1983.
†On disabled list, April 10 to May 12 and May 17 to June 4, 1984.
‡On Texas disabled list, March 25 to May 6, 1987; included rehabilitation disability assignment to Oklahoma City, April 17 to May 6, 1987.

PITCHING RECORD

Year	Club	League	G.	IP.	W.	L.	Pct.	H.	R.	ER.	SO.	BB.	ERA.
1988—	Texas	American	1	1	0	0	.000	0	0	0	1	0	0.00

RANDY SCOTT KUTCHER

Born April 20, 1960, at Anchorage, Alaska.
Height, 5.11. Weight, 175.
Throws and bats righthanded.

Major League stolen bases: 1986 (6), 1987 (1). Total—7.
Led International League third basemen in errors with 21 in 1988.

Year	Club	League	Pos.	G.	AB.	R.	H.	2B.	3B.	HR.	RBI.	B.A.	PO.	A.	E.	F.A.
1979—	Great Falls	Pion.	SS	65	245	55	62	8	2	2	25	.253	79	109	29	.866
1980—	Clinton	Midw.	SS-3B	138	525	72	133	17	•8	3	46	.253	204	365	39	.936
1981—	Fresno	Calif.	S-O-2-3	41	161	28	44	10	2	3	26	.273	66	80	18	.890
1981—	Shreveport	Texas	SS	77	249	36	71	13	4	4	20	.285	112	212	18	.947
1982—	Shreveport	Texas	SS-OF	116	397	56	98	18	2	3	31	.247	183	142	18	.948
1983—	Phoenix	P. C.	S-O-2-3-C	104	275	45	75	11	4	3	45	.273	152	138	15	.951
1984—	Phoenix	P. C.	O-S-3-2-C	103	336	37	93	17	3	2	31	.277	177	80	11	.959
1985—	Phoenix†	P. C.	OF-2B	97	228	36	54	15	2	1	20	.237	143	9	4	.974
1986—	Phoenix	P. C.	S-O-2-3-C	55	208	47	72	14	4	11	39	.346	93	89	16	.919
1986—	San Francisco	Nat.	O-S-3-2	71	186	28	44	9	1	7	16	.237	111	11	1	.992
1987—	Phoenix	P. C.	O-3-2-S-1	92	349	68	89	15	5	6	53	.255	153	116	15	.947
1987—	San Francisco‡	Nat.	O-2-3-S	14	16	7	3	1	1	0	1	.188	14	5	0	1.000
1988—	Pawtucket	Int.	3B-OF-2B	86	331	40	77	12	2	4	27	.233	73	138	22	.906
1988—	Boston	Amer.	OF-3B	19	12	2	2	1	0	0	0	.167	6	5	1	.917
National League Totals—2 Years				85	202	35	47	10	2	7	17	.233	125	16	1	.993
American League Totals—1 Year				19	12	2	2	1	0	0	0	.167	6	5	1	.917
Major League Totals—3 Years				104	214	37	49	11	2	7	17	.229	131	21	2	.987

Selected by San Francisco Giants' organization in 4th round of free-agent draft, June 5, 1979.
†Granted free agency, October 15, 1985; re-signed by Giants, February 3, 1986.
‡Traded to Boston Red Sox, December 9, 1987, completing deal in which Boston traded Outfielder Dave Henderson to San Francisco Giants for a player to be named later, September 1, 1987.

MICHAEL JAMES LaCOSS
(Mike)

Born May 30, 1956, at Glendale, Calif.
Height, 6.04. Weight, 200.
Throws and bats righthanded.

Major League saves: 1981 (1), 1983 (1), 1984 (3), 1985 (1). Total—6.
Tied for American Association lead in shutouts with 3 in 1978.

Year	Club	League	G.	IP.	W.	L.	Pct.	H.	R.	ER.	SO.	BB.	ERA.
1974	—Billings	Pioneer	13	87	6	5	.545	81	40	27	58	38	2.79
1975	—Tampa	Florida St.	23	151	4	7	.412	131	61	48	72	41	2.86
1976	—Three Rivers	Eastern	25	162	12	10	.545	148	66	53	80	53	2.94
1977	—Indianapolis	Am. Assoc.	27	186	11	*13	.458	181	93	80	104	65	3.87
1978	—Indianapolis	Am. Assoc.	19	130	11	5	.688	129	62	50	67	49	3.46
1978	—Cincinnati	National	16	96	4	8	.333	104	56	48	31	46	4.50
1979	—Cincinnati	National	35	206	14	8	.636	202	92	80	73	79	3.50
1980	—Cincinnati	National	34	169	10	12	.455	207	101	87	59	68	4.63
1981	—Cincinnati†	National	20	78	4	7	.364	102	55	53	22	30	6.12
1982	—Houston	National	41	115	6	6	.500	107	41	37	51	54	2.90
1983	—Houston‡	National	38	138	5	7	.417	142	81	68	53	56	4.43
1984	—Houston§	National	39	132	7	5	.583	132	64	59	86	55	4.02
1985	—Kansas City	American	21	40⅔	1	1	.500	49	25	23	26	29	5.09
1985	—Omaha x	Am. Assoc.	4	22⅓	1	2	.333	23	12	8	11	15	3.22
1986	—San Francisco y	National	37	204⅓	10	13	.435	179	99	81	86	70	3.57
1987	—San Francisco z	National	39	171	13	10	.565	184	78	70	79	63	3.68
1988	—San Francisco a	National	19	114⅓	7	7	.500	99	55	46	70	47	3.62
National League Totals—10 Years			318	1423⅔	80	83	.491	1458	722	629	610	568	3.98
American League Totals—1 Year			21	40⅔	1	1	.500	49	25	23	26	29	5.09
Major League Totals—11 Years			339	1464⅓	81	84	.491	1507	747	652	636	597	4.01

Selected by Cincinnati Reds' organization in 3rd round of free-agent draft, June 5, 1974.
†Sold on waivers to Houston Astros, April 4, 1982.
‡On disabled list, June 17 to July 8, 1983.
§Granted free agency, November 8, 1984; signed by Kansas City Royals' organization, February 19, 1985.
xReleased, November 6, 1985; signed by San Francisco Giants' organization, February 3, 1986.
yGranted free agency, November 12, 1986; re-signed by Giants, December 12, 1986.
zGranted free agency, November 9, 1987; re-signed by Giants, November 24, 1987.
aOn disabled list, July 17 to September 8, 1988.

CHAMPIONSHIP SERIES RECORD

Year	Club	League	G.	IP.	W.	L.	Pct.	H.	R.	ER.	SO.	BB.	ERA.
1979	—Cincinnati	National	1	1⅔	0	1	.000	1	2	2	0	4	10.80
1987	—San Francisco	National	2	3⅓	0	0	.000	1	0	0	2	3	0.00
Championship Series Totals—2 Years			3	5	0	1	.000	2	2	2	2	7	3.60

ALL-STAR GAME RECORD

Year	League	IP.	W.	L.	Pct.	H.	R.	ER.	SO.	BB.	ERA.
1979	—National	1⅓	0	0	.000	1	0	0	0	0	0.00

MICHAEL RUSSELL LAGA
(Mike)

Born June 14, 1960, at Ridgewood, N. J.
Height, 6.02. Weight, 210.
Throws and bats lefthanded.
Attended Bergen Community College, Paramus, N. J.,
and Fairleigh Dickinson University, Teaneck, N. J.

Major League stolen bases: 1982 (1).
Led American Association in intentional bases on balls received with 12 in 1987.
Led American Association in sacrifice flies with 7 in 1985.
Led American Association in being hit by pitch with 13 in 1982.
Led American Association first basemen in double plays with 101 in 1985.
Led American Association first basemen in total chances with 1,221 in 1982 and 1,146 in 1985.

Year	Club	League	Pos.	G.	AB.	R.	H.	2B.	3B.	HR.	RBI.	B.A.	PO.	A.	E.	F.A.
1980	—Lakeland	Fla. St.	1B	122	407	60	111	14	6	12	74	.273	1025	84	*18	.984
1981	—Birmingham	South.	1B	142	547	89	158	28	7	31	86	.289	1193	*105	*23	.983
1982	—Evansville	A. A.	1B	126	444	77	111	15	3	34	90	.250	*1135	68	18	.985
1982	—Detroit	Amer.	1B	27	88	6	23	9	0	3	11	.261	163	4	1	.994
1983	—Evansville	A. A.	1B	105	355	46	82	24	1	16	58	.231	835	62	*11	.988
1983	—Detroit	Amer.	1B	12	21	2	4	0	0	0	2	.190	9	1	0	1.000
1984	—Evansville	A. A.	1B	•153	569	86	151	30	9	30	94	.265	1008	92	14	.987
1984	—Detroit	Amer.	1B	9	11	1	6	0	0	0	1	.545	12	1	0	1.000
1985	—Nashville	A. A.	1B	117	430	58	113	30	2	20	79	.263	*1024	*111	11	.990
1985	—Detroit	Amer.	1B	9	36	3	6	1	0	2	6	.167	33	5	1	.974
1986	—Detroit†	Amer.	1B	15	45	6	9	1	0	3	8	.200	98	7	0	1.000
1986	—Nashville	A. A.	1B	12	41	4	9	3	0	2	7	.220	109	16	2	.984
1986	—St. Louis‡	Nat.	1B	18	46	7	10	4	0	3	8	.217	109	14	0	1.000
1987	—St. Louis	Nat.	1B	17	29	4	4	1	0	1	4	.138	66	7	2	.973
1987	—Louisville	A. A.	1B	116	418	80	127	35	2	29	91	.304	922	67	11	.989
1988	—Louisville§	A. A.	1B	13	49	4	10	2	0	1	5	.204	74	3	1	.987
1988	—St. Louis x	Nat.	1B	41	100	5	13	0	0	1	4	.130	293	17	0	1.000
American League Totals—5 Years				72	201	18	48	11	0	8	28	.239	315	18	2	.994
National League Totals—3 Years				76	175	16	27	5	0	5	16	.154	468	38	2	.996
Major League Totals—7 Years				148	376	34	75	16	0	13	44	.199	783	56	4	.995

Selected by Detroit Tigers' organization in 1st round (17th player selected) of free-agent draft, January 8, 1980.

†On disabled list, May 15 to September 1, 1986; included rehabilitation disability assignment to Nashville, August 8 to August 27, 1986.

‡Traded to St. Louis Cardinals, September 2, 1986, completing deal in which St. Louis traded Catcher Mike Heath to Detroit Tigers for Pitcher Ken Hill and a player to be named later, August 10, 1986.

§On St. Louis disabled list, March 26 to July 14, 1988; included rehabilitation disability assignment to Louisville, June 28 to July 14, 1988.

xReleased, November 8, 1988.

STEVEN MICHAEL LAKE
(Steve)

Born March 14, 1957, at Inglewood, Calif.
Height, 6.01. Weight, 190.
Throws and bats righthanded.
Cousin of Mike Lake, minor league pitcher, 1941 through 1946.

Major League stolen bases: 1985 (1).

Led Appalachian League in passed balls with 15 in 1975.

Year Club	League	Pos.	G.	AB.	R.	H.	2B.	3B.	HR.	RBI.	B.A.	PO.	A.	E.	F.A.
1975—Bluefield	Appal.	C	49	162	17	45	12	0	3	24	.278	254	*39	9	.970
1976—Miami	Fla. St.	PH	1	1	0	1	0	0	0	1	1.000	0	0	0	.000
1977—Miami	Fla. St.	C	79	232	25	55	10	1	2	24	.237	357	47	6	.985
1978—Miami†‡	Fla. St.	C	69	223	19	57	10	0	2	26	.256	300	49	6	.983
1979—Stockton§	Calif.	C	94	329	36	93	12	3	6	40	.283	504	73	8	.986
1980—Holyoke	East.	C-OF	102	325	26	84	9	2	2	44	.258	445	107	10	.982
1981—Vancouver x	P. C.	C	109	348	27	80	14	1	2	38	.230	502	102	7	.989
1982—Tucson y	P. C.	C	112	378	42	100	15	4	3	45	.265	504	91	12	.980
1983—Chicago	Nat.	C	38	85	9	22	4	1	1	7	.259	115	22	0	1.000
1984—Chicago z	Nat.	C	25	54	4	12	4	0	2	7	.222	72	13	4	.955
1984—Midland	Texas	C	9	25	2	4	0	0	0	1	.160	46	7	0	1.000
1985—Chicago	Nat.	C	58	119	5	18	2	0	1	11	.151	182	25	1	.995
1986—Chi. a-St.L.	Nat.	C	36	68	8	20	2	0	2	14	.294	105	9	2	.983
1986—Iowa-Louisville	A. A.	C	33	98	5	24	6	0	0	13	.245	140	21	2	.988
1987—St. Louis	Nat.	C	74	179	19	45	7	2	2	19	.251	253	21	1	.996
1988—St. Louis b	Nat.	C	36	54	5	15	3	0	1	4	.278	51	8	1	.983
Major League Totals—6 Years			267	559	50	132	22	3	9	62	.236	778	98	9	.990

Selected by Baltimore Orioles' organization in 3rd round of free-agent draft, June 4, 1975.

†On disabled list, April 17 to May 16, 1978.

‡Sold to Milwaukee Brewers' organization, December 21, 1978.

§On disabled list, June 20 to July 6, 1979.

xLoaned to Tucson (Houston Astros' organization), April 5, 1982; returned, September 7, 1982.

yTraded to Chicago Cubs for a player to be named later, April 1, 1983; Milwaukee Brewers' organization acquired Pitcher Rich Buonantony to complete deal, October 24, 1983.

zOn disabled list, May 14 to August 3, 1984; included rehabilitation disability assignment to Midland, July 23 to August 3, 1984.

aReleased, July 15, 1986; signed by Louisville (St. Louis Cardinals' organization), July 24, 1986.

bTraded with Outfielder Curt Ford to Philadelphia Phillies for Outfielder Milt Thompson, December 16, 1988.

CHAMPIONSHIP SERIES RECORD

Year Club	League	Pos.	G.	AB.	R.	H.	2B.	3B.	HR.	RBI.	B.A.	PO.	A.	E.	F.A.
1984—Chicago	Nat.	C	1	1	0	1	1	0	0	0	1.000	0	0	0	.000

WORLD SERIES RECORD

Year Club	League	Pos.	G.	AB.	R.	H.	2B.	3B.	HR.	RBI.	B.A.	PO.	A.	E.	F.A.
1987—St. Louis	Nat.	C	3	3	0	1	0	0	0	1	.333	8	1	0	1.000

DENNIS PATRICK LAMP

Born September 23, 1952, at Los Angeles, Calif.
Height, 6.03. Weight, 215.
Throws and bats righthanded.

Major League saves: 1982 (5), 1983 (15), 1984 (9), 1985 (2), 1986 (2). Total—33.

Year Club	League	G.	IP.	W.	L.	Pct.	H.	R.	ER.	SO.	BB.	ERA.
1971—Caldwell	Pioneer	14	46	1	2	.333	51	39	33	43	32	6.46
1972—Bradenton Cubs	Gulf Coast	14	70	7	2	.778	56	20	15	56	21	1.93
1973—Quincy	Midwest	13	89	6	4	.600	67	32	26	71	29	2.63
1973—Midland	Texas	9	48	2	4	.333	54	29	25	23	11	4.69
1974—Key West	Florida St.	8	49	1	5	.167	39	15	8	20	14	1.47
1974—Midland	Texas	24	60	1	1	.500	70	38	31	42	22	4.65
1975—Midland	Texas	37	127	7	5	.583	112	52	47	71	54	3.33
1976—Wichita	Am. Assoc.	30	153	8	*14	.364	182	94	69	98	52	4.06
1977—Wichita	Am. Assoc.	20	129	11	4	*.733	116	54	42	52	23	2.93
1977—Chicago	National	11	30	0	2	.000	43	21	21	12	8	6.30
1978—Chicago	National	37	224	7	15	.318	221	96	82	73	56	3.29
1979—Chicago	National	38	200	11	10	.524	223	96	78	86	46	3.51
1980—Chicago†	National	41	203	10	14	.417	259	*123	*117	83	82	5.19
1981—Chicago	American	27	127	7	6	.538	103	41	34	71	43	2.41
1982—Chicago	American	44	189⅔	11	8	.579	206	96	84	78	59	3.99
1983—Chicago‡	American	49	116⅓	7	7	.500	123	52	48	44	29	3.71
1984—Toronto	American	56	85	8	8	.500	97	53	43	45	38	4.55
1985—Toronto	American	53	105⅔	11	0	1.000	96	42	39	68	27	3.32

Year	Club	League	G.	IP.	W.	L.	Pct.	H.	R.	ER.	SO.	BB.	ERA.
1986—	Toronto§ x	American	40	73	2	6	.250	93	50	41	30	23	5.05
1987—	Tacoma	P. Coast	6	12⅓	1	0	1.000	9	4	4	10	8	2.92
1987—	Oakland y	American	36	56⅔	1	3	.250	76	38	32	36	22	5.08
1988—	Boston za	American	46	82⅔	7	6	.538	92	39	32	49	19	3.48
National League Totals—4 Years			127	657	28	41	.406	746	336	298	254	192	4.08
American League Totals—8 Years			351	836	54	44	.551	886	411	353	421	260	3.80
Major League Totals—12 Years			478	1493	82	85	.491	1632	747	651	675	452	3.92

Selected by Chicago Cubs' organization in 3rd round of free-agent draft, June 8, 1971.
†Traded to Chicago White Sox for Pitcher Ken Kravec, March 28, 1981.
‡Granted free agency, November 7, 1983; signed by Toronto Blue Jays as Type A player, January 10, 1984. (Pitcher Tom Seaver selected from player compensation pool by Chicago White Sox, January 20, 1984.)
§Released, October 20, 1986; signed by Cleveland Indians, February 5, 1987.
xReleased, March 23, 1987; signed by Oakland Athletics' organization, April 27, 1987.
yGranted free agency, October 19, 1987; signed by Pawtucket (Boston Red Sox' organization), January 5, 1988.
zOn disabled list, August 9 to August 27, 1988.
aGranted free agency, November 4, 1988; re-signed by Red Sox, November 20, 1988.

CHAMPIONSHIP SERIES RECORD

Tied American League Championship Series record for most strikeouts by a relief pitcher, game (5), October 15, 1985.

Year	Club	League	G.	IP.	W.	L.	Pct.	H.	R.	ER.	SO.	BB.	ERA.
1983—	Chicago	American	3	2	0	0	.000	0	1	0	1	2	0.00
1985—	Toronto	American	3	9⅓	0	0	.000	2	0	0	10	1	0.00
Championship Series Totals—2 Years			6	11⅓	0	0	.000	2	1	0	11	3	0.00

THOMAS MICHAEL LAMPKIN
(Tom)

Born March 4, 1964, at Cincinnati, O.
Height, 5.11. Weight, 185.
Throws right and bats lefthanded.
Attended University of Portland, Portland, Ore.

Year	Club	League	Pos.	G.	AB.	R.	H.	2B.	3B.	HR.	RBI.	B.A.	PO.	A.	E.	F.A.
1986—	Batavia	NYP	C	63	190	24	49	5	1	1	20	.258	323	36	8	.978
1987—	Waterloo	Midw.	C	118	398	49	106	19	2	7	55	.266	689	*100	15	.981
1988—	Williamsport	East.	C	80	263	38	71	10	0	3	23	.270	431	60	9	.982
1988—	Colorado Springs	P. C.	C	34	107	14	30	5	0	0	7	.280	171	28	5	.975
1988—	Cleveland	Amer.	C	4	4	0	0	0	0	0	0	.000	3	0	0	1.000
Major League Totals—1 Year				4	4	0	0	0	0	0	0	.000	3	0	0	1.000

Selected by Cleveland Indians' organization in 11th round of free-agent draft, June 2, 1986.

LESTER WAYNE LANCASTER
(Les)

Born April 21, 1962, at Dallas, Tex.
Height, 6.02. Weight, 200.
Throws and bats righthanded.
Attended Dallas Baptist College, Dallas, Tex., and University of Arkansas, Fayetteville, Ark.

Major League saves: 1988 (5).
Tied for National League lead in balks with 8 in 1987.
Led Appalachian League in complete games with 7 and intentional bases on balls issued with 5 in 1985.

Year	Club	League	G.	IP.	W.	L.	Pct.	H.	R.	ER.	SO.	BB.	ERA.
1985—	Wytheville	Ap'lachian	20	*102	7	4	.636	*98	49	41	*81	24	3.62
1986—	Winston-Salem	Carolina	13	97	8	3	.727	88	37	30	52	30	2.78
1986—	Pittsfield	Eastern	14	88	5	6	.455	105	46	41	49	34	4.19
1987—	Chicago	National	27	132⅓	8	3	.727	138	76	72	78	51	4.90
1987—	Iowa	Am. Assoc.	15	67	5	3	.625	59	24	24	62	17	3.22
1988—	Chicago†	National	44	85⅔	4	6	.400	89	42	36	36	34	3.78
Major League Totals—2 Years			71	218	12	9	.571	227	118	108	114	85	4.46

Selected by New York Yankees' organization in 24th round of free-agent draft, June 8, 1981.
Selected by Texas Rangers' organization in 39th round of free-agent draft, June 6, 1983.
Signed as free agent by Chicago Cubs' organization, June 13, 1985.
†On disabled list, July 24 to August 14 and August 20 to September 4, 1988.

TERRY LEE LANDRUM
(Tito)

Born October 25, 1954, at Joplin, Mo.
Height, 5.11. Weight, 175.
Throws and bats righthanded.
Attended Eastern Oklahoma State, Wilburton, Okla.

Major League stolen bases: 1980 (3), 1981 (4), 1983 (1), 1984 (3), 1985 (1), 1986 (3), 1987 (2). Total—17.
Led Florida State League in stolen bases with 68 in 1978.

Year	Club	League	Pos.	G.	AB.	R.	H.	2B.	3B.	HR.	RBI.	B.A.	PO.	A.	E.	F.A.
1973—	Orangeburg	W. Car.	OF	70	262	30	73	7	3	1	27	.279	168	7	1	.994
1974—	St. Petersburg†	Fla. St.	OF	87	309	38	73	5	9	3	39	.236	214	7	8	.965

Year	Club	League	Pos.	G.	AB.	R.	H.	2B.	3B.	HR.	RBI.	B.A.	PO.	A.	E.	F.A.
1975	—St. Petersburg	Fla. St.	OF	132	435	76	96	21	4	11	45	.221	*313	5	7	.978
1976	—Arkansas‡	Texas	OF	99	359	49	99	13	3	7	45	.276	201	12	7	.968
1976	—Tulsa	A. A.	OF	9	24	1	6	1	0	0	1	.250	17	0	0	1.000
1977	—Arkansas	Texas	OF	26	84	11	18	3	1	2	13	.214	50	5	1	.982
1977	—St. Petersburg	Fla. St.	OF	67	249	40	61	15	3	4	40	.245	157	7	1	.994
1978	—St. Petersburg	Fla. St.	OF	117	434	66	129	*25	1	4	45	.297	*305	8	3	.991
1979	—Arkansas	Texas	OF	71	265	44	71	20	5	3	33	.268	134	7	4	.972
1979	—Springfield	A. A.	OF	61	193	28	50	8	2	6	34	.259	126	5	2	.985
1980	—Springfield	A. A.	OF	93	350	55	106	23	6	12	46	.303	193	6	4	.980
1980	—St. Louis	Nat.	OF	35	77	6	19	2	2	0	7	.247	40	1	1	.976
1981	—St. Louis	Nat.	OF	81	119	13	31	5	4	0	10	.261	72	6	0	1.000
1982	—St. Louis	Nat.	OF	79	72	12	20	3	0	2	14	.278	50	2	0	1.000
1982	—Louisville	A. A.	OF	25	94	10	19	2	1	0	6	.202	46	0	2	.958
1983	—St. Louis	Nat.	OF	6	5	0	1	0	1	0	0	.200	1	0	0	1.000
1983	—Louisville§	A. A.	OF	111	431	79	126	23	*12	18	77	.292	286	8	8	.974
1983	—Baltimore x	Amer.	OF	26	42	8	13	2	0	1	4	.310	39	0	0	1.000
1984	—St. Louis	Nat.	OF	105	173	21	47	9	1	3	26	.272	93	1	2	.979
1985	—St. Louis y	Nat.	OF	85	161	21	45	8	2	4	21	.280	91	2	0	1.000
1986	—St. Louis	Nat.	OF	96	205	24	43	7	1	2	17	.210	131	6	1	.993
1987	—St. L. za-L. A.	Nat.	OF-1B	81	117	13	26	4	0	1	10	.222	77	2	1	.988
1987	—Louisville b	A. A.	OF	5	16	2	3	1	0	0	1	.188	7	1	0	1.000
1988	—Baltimore	Amer.	OF	13	24	2	3	0	1	0	2	.125	15	0	0	1.000
1988	—Rochester c	Int.	OF	5	17	2	4	2	0	1	4	.235	9	1	0	1.000
1988	—Oklahoma City d	A. A.	OF	69	229	29	58	6	6	3	25	.253	110	4	2	.983
National League Totals—8 Years				568	929	110	232	38	11	12	105	.250	555	20	5	.991
American League Totals—2 Years				39	66	10	16	2	1	1	6	.242	54	0	0	1.000
Major League Totals—10 Years				607	995	120	248	40	12	13	111	.249	609	20	5	.992

Signed as free agent by St. Louis Cardinals' organization, October 10, 1972.

†On disabled list, July 19 to September 20, 1974.

‡On disabled list, April 24 to May 10, 1976.

§Sold to Baltimore Orioles, August 31, 1983, completing deal in which Baltimore traded Infielder-Catcher Floyd Rayford to St. Louis Cardinals for a player to be named later, June 13, 1983.

xTraded to St. Louis Cardinals for Pitcher Jose Brito and cash, March 25, 1984.

yOn disabled list, April 17 to May 8, 1985.

zOn disabled list, May 2 to June 5, 1987; included rehabilitation disability assignment to Louisville, May 30 to June 5, 1987.

aReleased, July 4, 1987; signed by Los Angeles Dodgers, July 10, 1987.

bReleased, April 4, 1988; signed by Baltimore Orioles, April 12, 1988.

cReleased, May 10, 1988; signed by Oklahoma City (Texas Rangers' organization), May 17, 1988.

dGranted free agency, October 15, 1988.

CHAMPIONSHIP SERIES RECORD

Tied Championship Series record for most hits, inning (2), October 13, 1985 (second inning).

Tied National League Championship Series record for most hits, game (4), October 13, 1985.

Year	Club	League	Pos.	G.	AB.	R.	H.	2B.	3B.	HR.	RBI.	B.A.	PO.	A.	E.	F.A.
1983	—Baltimore	Amer.	PR-O-PH	4	10	2	2	0	0	1	1	.200	5	0	0	1.000
1985	—St. Louis	Nat.	PH-OF	5	14	2	6	0	0	0	4	.429	6	0	0	1.000
Championship Series Totals—2 Years				9	24	4	8	0	0	1	5	.333	11	0	0	1.000

WORLD SERIES RECORD

Year	Club	League	Pos.	G.	AB.	R.	H.	2B.	3B.	HR.	RBI.	B.A.	PO.	A.	E.	F.A.
1983	—Baltimore	Amer.	PR-OF	3	0	0	0	0	0	0	0	.000	1	0	0	1.000
1985	—St. Louis	Nat.	OF	7	25	3	9	2	0	1	1	.360	12	1	0	1.000
World Series Totals—2 Years				10	25	3	9	2	0	1	1	.360	13	1	0	1.000

THOMAS WILLIAM LANDRUM
(Bill)

Born August 17, 1958, at Columbia, S.C.
Height, 6.02. Weight, 185.
Throws and bats righthanded.
Attended Spartanburg Methodist College, Spartanburg, S.C., and received bachelor of science degree from University of South Carolina, Columbia, S.C. in 1980.
Son of Joe Landrum, pitcher with Brooklyn Dodgers, 1950 and 1952.

Major League saves: 1987 (2).

Year	Club	League	G.	IP.	W.	L.	Pct.	H.	R.	ER.	SO.	BB.	ERA.
1980	—Sarasota Cubs†	Gulf Coast	11	37	2	0	1.000	37	21	17	27	11	4.14
1981	—Tampa	Florida St.	17	83	6	8	.42	87	44	35	52	22	3.80
1982	—Waterbury	Eastern	*58	112⅓	10	6	.625	109	63	51	104	65	4.09
1983	—Waterbury	Eastern	17	29⅔	1	1	.500	17	5	5	33	14	1.52
1983	—Indianapolis‡	Am. Assoc.	15	17⅔	1	3	.250	20	6	6	21	6	3.06
1984	—Wichita§	Am. Assoc.	47	130⅓	7	4	.636	12	58	50	120	52	3.45
1985	—Denver	Am. Assoc.	29	138	6	6	.500	148	72	61	88	49	3.98
1986	—Denver x	Am. Assoc.	24	36⅓	1	3	.250	36	20	14	36	25	3.47
1986	—Cincinnati	National	10	13⅓	0	0	.000	23	11	10	14	4	6.75
1987	—Cincinnati	National	44	65	3	2	.600	68	35	34	42	34	4.71
1987	—Nashville y	Am. Assoc.	19	38⅔	4	0	1.000	30	9	9	47	19	2.09

Year	Club	League	G.	IP.	W.	L.	Pct.	H.	R.	ER.	SO.	BB.	ERA.
1988	Iowa	Am. Assoc.	9	21⅓	1	0	1.000	13	7	7	22	6	2.95
1988	Chicago z	National	7	12⅓	1	0	1.000	19	8	8	6	3	5.84
Major League Totals—3 Years			61	90⅔	4	2	.667	110	54	52	62	41	5.16

Signed as free agent by Chicago Cubs' organization, June 22, 1980.
†Released, October 20, 1980; signed by Billings (Cincinnati Reds' organization), February 7, 1981.
‡On disabled list, July 19 to August 4, 1983.
§Drafted by Chicago White Sox, December 3, 1984; returned, March 30, 1985.
xOn disabled list, April 29 to June 21, 1986.
yTraded to Chicago Cubs for Infielder Luis Quinones, April 1, 1988.
zGranted free agency, October 15, 1988.

MARK EDWARD LANGSTON

Born August 20, 1960, at San Diego, Calif.
Height, 6.02. Weight, 183.
Throws left and bats righthanded.
Attended San Jose State University, San Jose, Calif.

Named pitcher on THE SPORTING NEWS American League All-Star fielding team, 1987 and 1988.
Named American League Rookie Pitcher of the Year by THE SPORTING NEWS, 1984.

Year	Club	League	G.	IP.	W.	L.	Pct.	H.	R.	ER.	SO.	BB.	ERA.
1981	Bellingham	Northwest	13	85	7	3	.700	81	37	32	97	46	3.39
1982	Bakersfield	California	26	177⅓	12	7	.632	143	71	50	161	102	2.54
1983	Chattanooga	Southern	28	198	14	9	.609	187	104	79	142	102	3.59
1984	Seattle	American	35	225	17	10	.630	188	99	85	*204	*118	3.40
1985	Seattle†	American	24	126⅔	7	14	.333	122	85	77	72	91	5.47
1986	Seattle	American	37	239⅓	12	14	.462	234	*142	*129	*245	123	4.85
1987	Seattle	American	35	272	19	13	.594	242	132	116	*262	114	3.84
1988	Seattle	American	35	261⅓	15	11	.577	222	108	97	235	110	3.34
Major League Totals—5 Years			166	1124⅓	70	62	.530	1008	566	504	1018	556	4.03

Selected by Chicago Cubs' organization in 15th round of free-agent draft, June 6, 1978.
Selected by Seattle Mariners' organization in 3rd round of free-agent draft, June 8, 1981.
†On disabled list, June 7 to July 22, 1985.

ALL-STAR GAME RECORD

Year	League	IP.	W.	L.	Pct.	H.	R.	ER.	SO.	BB.	ERA.
1987	American	2	0	0	.000	0	0	0	3	0	0.00

CARNEY RAY LANSFORD

Born February 7, 1957, at San Jose, Calif.
Height, 6.02. Weight, 195.
Throws and bats righthanded.
Brother of Phil Lansford, infielder in Cleveland Indians' and Toronto Blue Jays' organizations, 1978 through 1981; and Joe Lansford, first baseman with San Diego Padres, 1982 and 1983.

Major League stolen bases: 1978 (20), 1979 (20), 1980 (14), 1981 (15), 1982 (9), 1983 (3), 1984 (9), 1985 (2), 1986 (16), 1987 (28), 1988 (29). Total—164.
Hit three home runs in a game, September 1, 1979.
Led American League in sacrifice flies with 11 in 1980.
Led American League third basemen in fielding percentage with .980 in 1987 and .979 in 1988.
Led Texas League third basemen in double plays with 16 in 1977.
Named third baseman on THE SPORTING NEWS American League Silver Slugger team, 1981.

Year	Club	League	Pos.	G.	AB.	R.	H.	2B.	3B.	HR.	RBI.	B.A.	PO.	A.	E.	F.A.
1975	Idaho Falls†	Pion.	3B-SS	8	27	5	6	2	0	1	1	.222	8	14	9	.710
1976	Quad Cities	Midw.	3B-OF-SS	121	418	87	120	19	5	14	86	.287	130	215	36	.906
1977	El Paso	Texas	3B	120	443	98	147	17	3	18	94	.332	*110	*210	15	*.955
1978	California‡	Amer.	3B-SS	121	453	63	133	23	2	8	52	.294	94	186	18	.940
1979	California	Amer.	3B	157	654	114	188	30	5	19	79	.287	*135	263	7	*.983
1980	California§	Amer.	3B	151	602	87	157	27	3	15	80	.261	*151	250	19	.955
1981	Boston	Amer.	3B	102	399	61	134	23	3	4	52	*.336	70	180	13	.951
1982	Boston xy	Amer.	3B	128	482	65	145	28	4	11	63	.301	83	216	10	.968
1983	Oakland z	Amer.	3B-SS	80	299	43	92	16	2	10	45	.308	60	163	10	.957
1984	Oakland	Amer.	3B	151	597	70	179	31	5	14	74	.300	137	268	18	.957
1985	Oakland a	Amer.	3B	98	401	51	111	18	2	13	46	.277	85	119	5	.976
1986	Oakland	Amer.	3B-1B-2B	151	591	80	168	16	4	19	72	.284	480	170	6	.991
1987	Oakland	Amer.	3B-1B	151	554	89	160	27	4	19	76	.289	156	258	7	.983
1988	Oakland	Amer.	3B-1B-2B	150	556	80	155	20	2	7	57	.279	125	221	7	.980
Major League Totals—11 Years				1440	5588	803	1622	259	36	139	696	.290	1576	2294	120	.970

Selected by California Angels' organization in 3rd round of free-agent draft, June 4, 1975.
†On disabled list, July 21 to September 30, 1975.
‡On disabled list, June 11 to July 7, 1978.
§Traded with Pitcher Mark Clear and Outfielder Rick Miller to Boston Red Sox for Shortstop Rick Burleson and Third Baseman Butch Hobson, December 10, 1980.
xOn disabled list, June 24 to July 21, 1982.
yTraded with Outfielder Garry Hancock and a player to be named later to Oakland A's for Outfielder Tony Armas and Catcher Jeff Newman, December 6, 1982; Oakland acquired Pitcher Jerry King to complete deal, December 20, 1982.
zOn disabled list, May 19 to June 7, 1983.
aOn disabled list, July 26 to August 28, 1985.

CHAMPIONSHIP SERIES RECORD

Year	Club	League	Pos.	G.	AB.	R.	H.	2B.	3B.	HR.	RBI.	B.A.	PO.	A.	E.	F.A.
1979—	California	Amer.	3B	4	17	2	5	0	0	0	3	.294	4	8	0	1.000
1988—	Oakland	Amer.	3B	4	17	4	5	1	0	1	2	.294	7	8	0	1.000
Championship Series Totals—2 Years				8	34	6	10	1	0	1	5	.294	11	16	0	1.000

WORLD SERIES RECORD

Year	Club	League	Pos.	G.	AB.	R.	H.	2B.	3B.	HR.	RBI.	B.A.	PO.	A.	E.	F.A.
1988—	Oakland	Amer.	3B	5	18	2	3	0	0	0	1	.167	8	7	0	1.000

ALL-STAR GAME RECORD

Year	League	Pos.	AB.	R.	H.	2B.	3B.	HR.	RBI.	B.A.	PO.	A.	E.	F.A.
1988—	American	3B	1	0	0	0	0	0	0	.000	0	1	0	1.000

DAVID JEFFREY LaPOINT
(Dave)

Born July 29, 1959, at Glens Falls, N. Y.
Height, 6.03. Weight, 215.
Throws and bats lefthanded.

Pitched 4-0 no-hit victory against Reno, July 25, 1979.
Major League saves: 1980 (1).
Led National League in wild pitches with 15 in 1984.
Tied for American Association lead in complete games with 9 in 1981.
Tied for California League lead in shutouts with 3 and complete games with 11 in 1979.
Tied for Midwest League lead in home runs allowed with 20 in 1978.

Year	Club	League	G.	IP.	W.	L.	Pct.	H.	R.	ER.	SO.	BB.	ERA.
1977—	Newark	NYP	13	69	5	2	.714	73	40	36	60	22	4.70
1978—	Burlington	Midwest	25	161	12	12	.500	177	98	72	134	41	4.02
1979—	Stockton	California	27	180	12	10	.545	144	74	63	*208	85	3.15
1980—	Vancouver†	P. Coast	17	93	7	4	.636	71	48	29	64	45	2.81
1980—	Milwaukee‡	American	5	15	1	0	1.000	17	14	10	5	13	6.00
1981—	Springfield	Am. Assoc.	25	172	13	9	.591	160	83	61	*129	66	3.19
1981—	St. Louis	National	3	11	1	0	1.000	12	5	5	4	2	4.09
1982—	St. Louis	National	42	152⅔	9	3	.750	170	63	58	81	52	3.42
1983—	St. Louis	National	37	191⅓	12	9	.571	191	92	84	113	84	3.95
1984—	St. Louis§x	National	33	193	12	10	.545	205	94	85	130	77	3.96
1985—	San Francisco y	National	31	206⅔	7	17	.292	215	99	82	122	74	3.57
1986—	Detroit z	American	16	67⅔	3	6	.333	85	49	43	36	32	5.72
1986—	San Diego a	National	24	61⅓	1	4	.200	67	37	29	41	24	4.26
1987—	St. Louis	National	6	16	1	1	.500	26	12	12	8	5	6.75
1987—	Louisville b	Am. Assoc.	14	91⅔	5	5	.500	93	45	41	70	27	4.03
1987—	Chicago c	American	14	82⅔	6	3	.667	69	29	27	43	31	2.94
1988—	Chicago d	American	25	161⅓	10	11	.476	151	69	61	79	47	3.40
1988—	Pittsburgh e	National	8	52	4	2	.667	54	18	16	19	10	2.77
American League Totals—4 Years			60	326⅔	20	20	.500	322	161	141	163	123	3.88
National League Totals—8 Years			184	884	47	46	.505	940	420	371	518	328	3.78
Major League Totals—9 Years			244	1210⅔	67	66	.504	1262	581	512	681	451	3.81

Selected by Milwaukee Brewers' organization in 10th round of free-agent draft, June 7, 1977.

†On disabled list, May 6 to May 17 and June 6 to July 15, 1980.

‡Traded with Pitcher Lary Sorensen and Outfielders Sixto Lezcano and David Green to St. Louis Cardinals for Pitchers Pete Vuckovich and Rollie Fingers and Catcher Ted Simmons, December 12, 1980.

§On disabled list, June 15 to June 30, 1984.

xTraded with First Basemen David Green and Gary Rajsich and Shortstop Jose Gonzalez (Jose Uribe) to San Francisco Giants for Outfielder-First Baseman Jack Clark, February 1, 1985.

yTraded with Catcher Matt Nokes and Pitcher Eric King to Detroit Tigers for Pitcher Juan Berenguer, Catcher Bob Melvin and a player to be named later, October 7, 1985; San Francisco Giants acquired Pitcher Scott Medvin to complete deal, December 11, 1985.

zTraded to San Diego Padres for Pitcher Mark Thurmond, July 9, 1986.

aReleased, December 20, 1986; signed by St. Louis Cardinals, January 19, 1987.

bTraded to Chicago White Sox for Pitcher Bryce Hulstrom, July 30, 1987.

cGranted free agency, November 9, 1987; re-signed by White Sox, February 9, 1988.

dTraded to Pittsburgh Pirates for Pitcher Barry Jones, August 13, 1988.

eGranted free agency, November 4, 1988; signed by New York Yankees, December 3, 1988.

WORLD SERIES RECORD

Year	Club	League	G.	IP.	W.	L.	Pct.	H.	R.	ER.	SO.	BB.	ERA.
1982—	St. Louis	National	2	8⅓	0	0	.000	10	6	3	3	2	3.24

BARRY LOUIS LARKIN

Born April 28, 1964, at Cincinnati, O.
Height, 6.00. Weight, 185.
Throws and bats righthanded.
Attended University of Michigan, Ann Arbor, Mich.

Major League stolen bases: 1986 (8), 1987 (21), 1988 (40). Total—69.
Led American Association in slugging percentage with .525 in 1986.
Named shortstop on THE SPORTING NEWS National League All-Star Team, 1988.

Named shortstop on THE SPORTING NEWS National League Silver Slugger team, 1988.
Named American Association Most Valuable Player, 1986.
Named shortstop on THE SPORTING NEWS College Baseball All-America Team, 1985.
Member of 1984 U.S. Olympic baseball team.

Year Club	League	Pos.	G.	AB.	R.	H.	2B.	3B.	HR.	RBI.	B.A.	PO.	A.	E.	F.A.
1985—Vermont	East.	SS	72	255	42	68	13	2	1	31	.267	110	166	17	.942
1986—Denver	A. A.	SS-2B	103	413	67	136	31	10	10	51	.329	172	287	18	.962
1986—Cincinnati	Nat.	SS-2B	41	159	27	45	4	3	3	19	.283	51	125	4	.978
1987—Cincinnati†	Nat.	SS	125	439	64	107	16	2	12	43	.244	168	358	19	.965
1988—Cincinnati	Nat.	SS	151	588	91	174	32	5	12	56	.296	231	470	•29	.960
Major League Totals—3 Years			317	1186	182	326	52	10	27	118	.275	450	953	52	.964

Selected by Cincinnati Reds' organization in 2nd round of free-agent draft, June 7, 1982.
Selected by Cincinnati Reds' organization in 1st round (fourth player selected) of free-agent draft, June 3, 1985.
†On disabled list, April 13 to May 2, 1987.

ALL-STAR GAME RECORD

Year League	Pos.	AB.	R.	H.	2B.	3B.	HR.	RBI.	B.A.	PO.	A.	E.	F.A.
1988—National	SS	2	0	0	0	0	0	0	.000	0	1	0	1.000

EUGENE THOMAS LARKIN
(Gene)

Born October 24, 1962, at Flushing, N. Y.
Height, 6.03. Weight, 212.
Throws right and bats left and righthanded.
Received degree from Columbia University, New York, N. Y.

Major League stolen bases: 1987 (1), 1988 (3). Total—4.
Led American League in being hit by pitch with 15 in 1988.
Led California League in sacrifice flies with 14 in 1985.
Tied for Southern League lead in sacrifice flies with 13 in 1986.
Led California League first basemen in double plays with 140 in 1985.
Led Appalachian League first basemen in double plays with 54 in 1984.

Year Club	League	Pos.	G.	AB.	R.	H.	2B.	3B.	HR.	RBI.	B.A.	PO.	A.	E.	F.A.
1984—Elizabethton	Appal.	1B	57	193	29	63	13	1	6	37	.326	478	19	6	★.988
1985—Visalia	Calif.	1B	•142	528	90	161	25	3	13	•106	.305	★1227	62	12	.991
1986—Orlando	South.	1B-3B	142	529	85	•170	29	6	15	104	.321	923	53	13	.987
1987—Portland	P. C.	1B-OF	35	129	17	39	9	0	1	14	.302	191	22	4	.982
1987—Minnesota	Amer.	1B	85	233	23	62	11	2	4	28	.266	165	10	2	.989
1988—Minnesota	Amer.	1B	149	505	56	135	30	2	8	70	.267	466	28	3	.994
Major League Totals—2 Years			234	738	79	197	41	4	12	98	.267	631	38	5	.993

Selected by Minnesota Twins' organization in 20th round of free-agent draft, June 4, 1984.

CHAMPIONSHIP SERIES RECORD

Year Club	League	Pos.	G.	AB.	R.	H.	2B.	3B.	HR.	RBI.	B.A.	PO.	A.	E.	F.A.
1987—Minnesota	Amer.	PH	1	1	0	1	1	0	0	1	1.000	0	0	0	.000

WORLD SERIES RECORD

Year Club	League	Pos.	G.	AB.	R.	H.	2B.	3B.	HR.	RBI.	B.A.	PO.	A.	E.	F.A.
1987—Minnesota	Amer.	1B-PH	5	3	1	0	0	0	0	0	.000	1	0	0	1.000

WILLIAM ALAN LASKEY
(Bill)

Born December 20, 1957, at Toledo, O.
Height, 6.05. Weight, 190.
Throws and bats righthanded.
Attended Monroe County Community College, Monroe, Mich., and
Kent State University, Kent, O.

Major League saves: 1986 (1), 1988 (1). Total—2.

Year Club	League	G.	IP.	W.	L.	Pct.	H.	R.	ER.	SO.	BB.	ERA.
1978—Sarasota Royals	Gulf Coast	4	23	1	2	.333	13	7	5	9	11	1.96
1978—Jacksonville	Southern	7	27	3	2	.600	23	14	13	13	15	4.33
1979—Fort Myers	Florida St.	13	93	7	4	.636	71	24	23	72	35	2.23
1979—Jacksonville	Southern	15	97	4	3	.571	78	44	38	53	46	3.53
1980—Omaha	Am. Assoc.	27	145	5	8	.385	155	81	67	77	72	4.16
1981—Omaha†	Am. Assoc.	23	138	10	8	.556	136	67	60	87	52	3.91
1982—Phoenix	P. Coast	2	14	1	0	1.000	12	5	2	10	2	1.29
1982—San Francisco	National	32	189⅓	13	12	.520	186	74	66	88	43	3.14
1983—San Francisco	National	25	148⅓	13	10	.565	151	75	69	81	45	4.19
1984—San Francisco	National	35	207⅔	9	14	.391	222	112	100	71	50	4.33
1985—San Francisco‡-Montreal§	National	30	148⅓	5	16	.238	165	91	81	60	53	4.91
1986—San Francisco	National	20	27⅓	1	1	.500	28	14	13	8	13	4.28
1986—Phoenix x	P. Coast	14	86⅔	5	5	.500	101	40	33	47	22	3.43
1987—Toledo y	Int'national	56	100⅓	12	6	.667	90	51	43	73	31	3.86
1988—Cleveland	American	17	24⅓	1	0	1.000	32	16	14	17	6	5.18
1988—Colorado Springs z	P. Coast	12	25⅔	1	1	.500	38	22	16	15	6	5.61
National League Totals—5 Years		142	721	41	53	.436	752	366	329	308	204	4.11
American League Totals—1 Year		17	24⅓	1	0	1.000	32	16	14	17	6	5.18
Major League Totals—6 Years		159	745⅓	42	53	.442	784	382	343	325	210	4.14

Selected by Detroit Tigers' organization in 8th round of free-agent draft, January 11, 1977.
Selected by Detroit Tigers' organization in secondary phase of free-agent draft, June 7, 1977.
Selected by Kansas City Royals' organization in secondary phase of free-agent draft, June 6, 1978.
†Traded with Pitcher Rich Gale to San Francisco Giants for Outfielder Jerry Martin, December 10, 1981.
‡Traded with First Baseman Scot Thompson and a player to be named later to Montreal Expos for First Baseman Dan Driessen, August 1, 1985.
§Traded to San Francisco Giants for Pitcher George Riley and Outfielder Alonzo Powell, October 24, 1985 (this deal settled earlier deal of Laskey going from San Francisco to Montreal on August 1, 1985).
xReleased, November 10, 1986; signed by Toledo (Detroit Tigers' organization), February 4, 1987.
yGranted free agency, October 15, 1987; signed by Colorado Springs (Cleveland Indians' organization), January 1, 1988.
zReleased, August 21, 1988.

TIMOTHY JON LAUDNER

Name pronounced LAWD-ner.

(Tim)

Born June 7, 1958, at Mason City, Ia.
Height, 6.03. Weight, 208.
Throws and bats righthanded.
Attended University of Missouri, Columbia, Mo.

Tied American League record for most home runs, first two major league games (2), August 28 and 29, 1981.
Major League stolen bases: 1986 (1), 1987 (1). Total—2.
Led Southern League in slugging percentage with .628 and game-winning RBIs with 14 in 1981.
Named Southern League Most Valuable Player, 1981.

Year Club	League	Pos.	G.	AB.	R.	H.	2B.	3B.	HR.	RBI.	B.A.	PO.	A.	E.	F.A.
1979—Orlando	South.	C	45	141	17	34	7	0	3	20	.241	224	29	6	.977
1980—Orlando†	South.	C	17	61	7	14	5	0	2	5	.230	81	10	1	.989
1980—Visalia	Calif.	C	56	186	23	42	13	0	10	29	.226	251	36	5	.983
1981—Orlando	South.	C-1B	130	433	87	123	21	1	*42	104	.284	631	66	15	.979
1981—Minnesota	Amer.	C	14	43	4	7	2	0	2	5	.163	49	5	0	1.000
1982—Toledo	Int.	C	20	71	4	12	2	0	2	12	.169	121	9	0	1.000
1982—Minnesota	Amer.	C	93	306	37	78	19	1	7	33	.255	454	41	*12	.976
1983—Minnesota	Amer.	C	62	168	20	31	9	0	6	18	.185	259	22	4	.986
1984—Minnesota	Amer.	C	87	262	31	54	16	1	10	35	.206	362	38	9	.978
1985—Minnesota	Amer.	C-1B	72	164	16	39	5	0	7	19	.238	236	19	8	.970
1986—Minnesota	Amer.	C	76	193	21	47	10	0	10	29	.244	299	13	5	.984
1987—Minnesota‡	Amer.	C-1B	113	288	30	55	7	1	16	43	.191	547	29	7	.988
1988—Minnesota§	Amer.	C-1B	117	375	38	94	18	1	13	54	.251	624	35	5	.992
Major League Totals—8 Years			634	1799	197	405	86	4	71	236	.225	2830	202	50	.984

Selected by Cincinnati Reds' organization in 33rd round of free-agent draft, June 8, 1976.
Selected by Minnesota Twins' organization in 3rd round of free-agent draft, June 5, 1979.
†On disabled list, April 11 to April 21, 1980.
‡Granted free agency, November 9, 1987; re-signed by Twins, February 3, 1988.
§Granted free agency, November 4, 1988; re-signed by Twins, December 19, 1988.

CHAMPIONSHIP SERIES RECORD

Year Club	League	Pos.	G.	AB.	R.	H.	2B.	3B.	HR.	RBI.	B.A.	PO.	A.	E.	F.A.
1987—Minnesota	Amer.	C	5	14	1	1	1	0	0	2	.071	31	2	0	1.000

WORLD SERIES RECORD

Year Club	League	Pos.	G.	AB.	R.	H.	2B.	3B.	HR.	RBI.	B.A.	PO.	A.	E.	F.A.
1987—Minnesota	Amer.	C	7	22	4	7	1	0	1	4	.318	46	2	0	1.000

ALL-STAR GAME RECORD

Year League	Pos.	AB.	R.	H.	2B.	3B.	HR.	RBI.	B.A.	PO.	A.	E.	F.A.
1988—American	C	1	0	1	1	0	0	0	1.000	3	0	0	1.000

MICHAEL EUGENE LaVALLIERE

Name pronounced Luh-VAHL-yur.

(Mike)

Born August 18, 1960, at Charlotte, N. C.
Height, 5.09. Weight, 190.
Throws right and bats lefthanded.
Attended University of Lowell, Lowell, Mass.
Son of Guy LaValliere, minor league catcher, 1952 and 1955 through 1961.

Major League stolen bases: 1988 (3).
Named catcher on THE SPORTING NEWS National League All-Star Team, 1988.
Named catcher on THE SPORTING NEWS National League All-Star fielding team, 1987.

Year Club	League	Pos.	G.	AB.	R.	H.	2B.	3B.	HR.	RBI.	B.A.	PO.	A.	E.	F.A.
1981—Spartanburg	S. Atl.	3B-OF	39	123	15	33	9	0	2	23	.268	16	32	5	.906
1982—Peninsula	Carol.	C-3B	66	178	20	49	4	2	2	23	.275	306	35	6	.983
1983—Reading	East.	C-3B-P	81	218	24	64	16	2	4	43	.294	243	59	4	.987
1984—Reading	East.	C-3-2-P	55	147	19	37	6	0	6	22	.252	113	45	2	.988
1984—Portland	P. C.	C	37	122	20	38	6	3	5	21	.311	186	16	1	.995
1984—Philadelphia†‡	Nat.	C	6	7	0	0	0	0	0	0	.000	20	2	0	1.000

Year	Club	League	Pos.	G.	AB.	R.	H.	2B.	3B.	HR.	RBI.	B.A.	PO.	A.	E.	F.A.
1985	—St. Louis	Nat.	C	12	34	2	5	1	0	0	6	.147	48	5	0	1.000
1985	—Louisville§	A. A.	C	83	231	19	47	12	1	4	26	.203	420	53	5	.990
1986	—St. Louis x	Nat.	C	110	303	18	71	10	2	3	30	.234	468	47	6	.988
1987	—Pittsburgh	Nat.	C	121	340	33	102	19	0	1	36	.300	584	70	5	.992
1988	—Pittsburgh	Nat.	C	120	352	24	92	18	0	2	47	.261	565	55	8	.987
Major League Totals—5 Years				369	1036	77	270	48	2	6	119	.261	1685	179	19	.990

Signed as free agent by Philadelphia Phillies' organization, July 12, 1981.

†Traded to St. Louis Cardinals for a player to be named later, December 3, 1984; returned due to injured status, December 13, 1984.

‡Granted free agency, December 23, 1984; signed by Louisville (St. Louis Cardinals' organization), January 23, 1985.

§On disabled list, July 18 to July 29, 1985.

xTraded with Outfielder Andy Van Slyke and Pitcher Mike Dunne to Pittsburgh Pirates for Catcher Tony Pena, April 1, 1987.

PITCHING RECORD

Year	Club	League	G.	IP.	W.	L.	Pct.	H.	R.	ER.	SO.	BB.	ERA.
1983	—Reading	Eastern	4	3⅓	0	0	.000	3	3	2	2	2	5.40
1984	—Reading	Eastern	1	1	0	0	.000	3	2	2	1	1	18.00

JOSEPH MICHAEL LAW
(Joe)

Born February 4, 1962, at Pittsburgh, Pa.
Height, 6.02. Weight, 200.
Throws and bats righthanded.
Attended Pensacola Junior College, Pensacola, Fla.

Pitched 1-0 no-hit victory against Stockton, August 14, 1987.

Year	Club	League	G.	IP.	W.	L.	Pct.	H.	R.	ER.	SO.	BB.	ERA.
1983	—Idaho Falls	Pioneer	14	15⅔	0	3	.000	17	12	6	20	7	3.45
1983	—Albany	Eastern	2	3	0	0	.000	1	1	1	2	3	3.00
1984	—Modesto	California	29	143	11	2	*.846	114	47	41	105	71	2.58
1985	—Huntsville	Southern	37	106	8	8	.500	115	86	72	53	78	6.11
1986	—Huntsville	Southern	8	39⅓	1	4	.200	55	37	36	12	28	8.24
1986	—Madison	Midwest	19	123	6	9	.400	117	58	48	80	61	3.51
1987	—Modesto	California	18	118⅔	10	1	*.909	87	45	38	123	40	2.88
1987	—Tacoma	P. Coast	2	7	0	1	.000	4	5	2	7	4	2.57
1988	—Tacoma	P. Coast	12	66⅓	5	3	.625	62	31	29	46	19	3.93
1988	—Huntsville	Southern	17	116	9	3	.750	100	42	33	67	33	2.56

Signed as free agent by Oakland A's organization, July 4, 1983.

VANCE AARON LAW

Born October 1, 1956, at Boise, Ida.
Height, 6.01. Weight, 190.
Throws and bats righthanded.
Attended Brigham Young University, Provo, Utah.
Son of Vern Law, pitcher with Pittsburgh Pirates, 1950, 1951 and 1954 through 1967.

Established American League record for longest errorless game by third baseman (25 innings), May 8, finished May 9, 1984.

Tied American League record for most innings played by third baseman, game (25), May 8, finished May 9, 1984.

Major League stolen bases: 1980 (2), 1981 (1), 1982 (4), 1983 (3), 1984 (4), 1985 (6), 1986 (3), 1987 (8), 1988 (1). Total—32.

Led Pacific Coast League in sacrifice hits with 14 in 1979.

Year	Club	League	Pos.	G.	AB.	R.	H.	2B.	3B.	HR.	RBI.	B.A.	PO.	A.	E.	F.A.
1978	—Bradenton Pir.	Gulf C.	SS	1	3	0	1	0	0	0	0	.333	2	5	0	1.000
1978	—Salem	Carol.	SS	60	213	48	68	13	7	2	30	.319	96	180	22	.926
1979	—Portland	P. C.	SS-3B-2B	131	448	62	139	16	8	2	52	.310	201	308	22	.959
1980	—Portland	P. C.	SS	96	339	59	100	23	5	5	54	.295	169	295	14	.971
1980	—Pittsburgh	Nat.	2B-SS-3B	25	74	11	17	2	2	0	3	.230	31	54	3	.966
1981	—Pittsburgh	Nat.	2B-SS-3B	30	67	1	9	0	1	0	3	.134	50	58	0	1.000
1981	—Portland†‡	P. C.	2B-SS-3B	88	310	55	86	14	9	5	43	.277	168	218	9	.977
1982	—Chicago	Amer.	S-3-2-O	114	359	40	101	20	1	5	54	.281	156	313	26	.947
1983	—Chicago	Amer.	3-2-S-O	145	408	55	99	21	5	4	42	.243	94	311	14	.967
1984	—Chicago§	Amer.	3-2-O-S	151	481	60	121	18	2	17	59	.252	119	246	16	.958
1985	—Montreal	Nat.	2-1-3-O	147	519	75	138	30	6	10	52	.266	420	402	12	.986
1986	—Montreal	Nat.	2-1-3-P-O	112	360	37	81	17	2	5	44	.225	273	299	4	.993
1987	—Montreal x	Nat.	2-1-3-P	133	436	52	119	27	1	12	56	.273	258	308	11	.981
1988	—Chicago	Nat.	3B-OF	151	556	73	163	29	2	11	78	.293	112	272	19	.953
National League Totals—6 Years				598	2012	249	527	105	14	38	236	.262	1144	1393	49	.981
American League Totals—3 Years				410	1248	155	321	59	8	26	155	.257	369	870	56	.957
Major League Totals—9 Years				1008	3260	404	848	164	22	64	391	.260	1513	2263	105	.973

Selected by Pittsburgh Pirates' organization in 38th round of free-agent draft, June 6, 1978.

†On disabled list, July 5 to July 15, 1981.

‡Traded with Pitcher Ernie Camacho to Chicago White Sox for Pitchers Ross Baumgarten and Butch Edge, March 21, 1982.

§Traded to Montreal Expos for Pitcher Bob James, December 7, 1984.

xGranted free agency, November 9, 1987; signed by Chicago Cubs, December 14, 1987.

CHAMPIONSHIP SERIES RECORD

Year	Club	League	Pos.	G.	AB.	R.	H.	2B.	3B.	HR.	RBI.	B.A.	PO.	A.	E.	F.A.
1983	—Chicago	Amer.	3B	4	11	0	2	0	0	0	1	.182	1	9	1	.909

ALL-STAR GAME RECORD

Year	League	Pos.	AB.	R.	H.	2B.	3B.	HR.	RBI.	B.A.	PO.	A.	E.	F.A.
1988	—National	2B	0	0	0	0	0	0	0	.000	0	0	0	.000

PITCHING RECORD

Year	Club	League	G.	IP.	W.	L.	Pct.	H.	R.	ER.	SO.	BB.	ERA.
1986	—Montreal	National	3	4	0	0	.000	3	2	1	0	2	2.25
1987	—Montreal	National	3	3⅓	0	0	.000	5	2	2	2	0	5.40
Major League Totals—2 Years			6	7⅓	0	0	.000	8	4	3	2	2	3.68

THOMAS JAMES LAWLESS
(Tom)

Born December 19, 1956, at Erie, Pa.
Height, 5.11. Weight, 165.
Throws and bats righthanded.
Received bachelor of arts degree in political science from
Pennsylvania State University-Behrend, Erie, Pa.

Major League stolen bases: 1982 (16), 1984 (7), 1985 (2), 1986 (8), 1987 (2), 1988 (6). Total—41.
Led American Association in stolen bases with 46 in 1983.
Led Florida State League in sacrifice hits with 13 and stolen bases with 60 in 1979.
Led Pioneer League shortstops in putouts with 116 in 1978.

Year	Club	League	Pos.	G.	AB.	R.	H.	2B.	3B.	HR.	RBI.	B.A.	PO.	A.	E.	F.A.
1978	—Billings	Pioneer	SS-2B	63	254	64	70	5	•7	5	35	.276	117	186	24	.927
1979	—Tampa	Fla. St.	2B	131	469	66	126	9	5	1	39	.269	★296	376	17	★.975
1980	—Waterbury	East.	2B	130	498	83	137	20	7	2	29	.275	★316	333	14	.979
1981	—Waterbury	East.	2B	136	522	77	152	20	10	8	50	.291	323	379	15	.979
1982	—Indianapolis	A. A.	2B-SS	86	351	76	108	18	6	2	28	.308	185	251	13	.971
1982	—Cincinnati	Nat.	2B	49	165	19	35	6	0	0	4	.212	87	136	5	.978
1983	—Indianapolis	A. A.	2B	115	423	93	118	23	3	13	35	.279	255	303	17	.970
1984	—Cinc.†-Mont.	Nat.	2B-3B	54	97	11	23	3	0	1	2	.237	50	52	1	.990
1984	—Wich.-Ind.‡	A. A.	3B-2B-SS	50	173	36	47	5	5	4	23	.272	53	103	4	.975
1985	—Louisville	A. A.	3B-OF	31	124	16	36	9	1	1	12	.290	20	58	3	.963
1985	—St. Louis	Nat.	3B-2B	47	58	8	12	3	1	0	8	.207	19	44	1	.984
1986	—St. Louis	Nat.	3B-2B-OF	46	39	5	11	1	0	0	3	.282	11	15	2	.929
1987	—St. Louis§	Nat.	2B-3B-OF	19	25	5	2	1	0	0	0	.080	5	15	0	1.000
1988	—St. Louis x	Nat.	3-O-2-1	54	65	9	10	2	1	1	3	.154	23	29	0	1.000
Major League Totals—6 Years				269	449	57	93	16	2	2	20	.207	195	291	9	.982

Selected by Cincinnati Reds' organization in 17th round of free-agent draft, June 6, 1978.
†Traded to Montreal Expos' organization for First Baseman-Outfielder Pete Rose, August 16, 1984.
‡Sold to Louisville (St. Louis Cardinals' organization), March 25, 1985, completing deal in which St. Louis traded Pitcher Mickey Mahler to Montreal Expos for a player to be named later, February 6, 1985.
§On disabled list, August 21 to September 5, 1987.
xReleased, December 21, 1988.

CHAMPIONSHIP SERIES RECORD

Year	Club	League	Pos.	G.	AB.	R.	H.	2B.	3B.	HR.	RBI.	B.A.	PO.	A.	E.	F.A.
1987	—St. Louis	Nat.	3B-PH-O	3	6	0	2	0	0	0	0	.333	1	4	0	1.000

WORLD SERIES RECORD

Year	Club	League	Pos.	G.	AB.	R.	H.	2B.	3B.	HR.	RBI.	B.A.	PO.	A.	E.	F.A.
1985	—St. Louis	Nat.	PR	1	0	0	0	0	0	0	0	.000	0	0	0	.000
1987	—St. Louis	Nat.	3B	3	10	1	1	0	0	1	3	.100	3	6	1	.900
World Series Totals—2 Years				4	10	1	1	0	0	1	3	.100	3	6	1	.900

MARCUS DWAYNE LAWTON

Born August 18, 1965, at Gulfport, Miss.
Height, 6.01. Weight, 160.
Throws right and bats left and righthanded.

Led Carolina League in bases on balls received with 102 in 1986.
Led South Atlantic League in stolen bases with 111 in 1985.
Led Carolina League outfielders in total chances with 359 in 1986.
Tied for Texas League lead in errors by outfielders with 13 in 1987.

Year	Club	League	Pos.	G.	AB.	R.	H.	2B.	3B.	HR.	RBI.	B.A.	PO.	A.	E.	F.A.
1983	—Sarasota Mets†	Gulf C.	SS-3B	51	187	25	48	3	1	0	16	.257	75	128	24	.894
1984	—Kingsport†	Appal.	SS	54	191	43	57	10	1	1	15	.298	86	126	20	.914
1984	—Lynchburg†	Carol.	2B	3	9	3	2	0	0	0	1	.222	3	8	1	.917
1985	—Columbia	S. Atl.	OF-SS-2B	128	470	113	126	11	5	1	53	.268	223	129	39	.900
1986	—Lynchburg	Carol.	OF	★141	★567	★118	158	22	★16	4	66	.279	★336	17	6	★.983
1987	—Jackson	Texas	OF-2B	133	530	99	159	20	★10	5	36	.300	265	18	14	.953
1988	—Jackson	Texas	OF	54	205	42	61	12	0	2	20	.298	129	7	6	.958
1988	—Tidewater‡	Int.	OF	94	335	46	78	16	4	0	17	.233	202	5	3	.986

Selected by New York Mets' organization in 6th round of free-agent draft, June 6, 1983.

†Batted righthanded only.
‡Drafted by California Angels, December 5, 1988.

JACK THOMAS LAZORKO

Name pronounced La-ZOR-ko.

Born March 30, 1956, at Hoboken, N.J.
Height, 5.11. Weight, 218.
Throws and bats righthanded.
Attended Miami-Dade Community College (South), Miami, Fla.; and received bachelor of science degree in business administration and management from Mississippi State University, Mississippi State, Miss. in 1978.

Major League saves: 1984 (1), 1985 (1). Total—2.
Led Pacific Coast League in complete games with 10 in 1988.
Led Texas League in intentional bases on balls issued with 12 in 1980.
Led Texas League in games finished in relief with 37 in 1981.
Tied for American Association lead in shutouts with 2 in 1986.
Tied for Pacific Coast League lead in hit batsmen with 6 in 1985.

Year Club	League	G.	IP.	W.	L.	Pct.	H.	R.	ER.	SO.	BB.	ERA.
1978—Sarasota Astros	Gulf Coast	3	4	0	1	.000	7	2	1	5	2	2.25
1978—Daytona Beach	Florida St.	13	27	3	0	1.000	21	8	8	8	10	2.67
1979—Daytona Beach†	Florida St.	17	29	2	1	.667	38	15	15	17	12	4.66
1979—Asheville	W. Carolinas	23	37	4	3	.571	33	19	13	22	12	3.16
1980—Tulsa	Texas	55	82	6	5	.545	78	50	34	47	53	3.73
1981—Tulsa	Texas	47	67	4	8	.333	54	31	25	36	23	3.36
1981—Wichita	Am. Assoc.	8	13	1	0	1.000	14	4	4	9	8	2.77
1982—Denver	Am. Assoc.	23	43⅓	1	2	.333	63	38	33	32	23	6.85
1982—Tulsa‡	Texas	15	39⅔	2	2	.500	27	9	9	40	7	2.04
1983—El Paso§	Texas	46	80⅓	7	1	.875	102	62	53	55	34	5.94
1984—Vancouver	P. Coast	28	52⅔	2	3	.400	43	24	22	35	15	3.76
1984—Milwaukee x	American	15	39⅔	0	1	.000	37	19	19	24	22	4.31
1985—Phoenix y-Calgary z	P. Coast	44	74⅓	5	5	.500	56	20	17	52	21	2.06
1985—Seattle a	American	15	20⅓	0	0	.000	23	10	8	7	8	3.54
1986—Nashville	Am. Assoc.	29	154⅔	8	6	.571	146	63	55	*119	72	3.20
1986—Detroit b	American	3	6⅔	0	0	.000	8	3	3	3	4	4.05
1987—Edmonton	P. Coast	10	69⅓	8	1	.889	63	32	27	35	32	3.50
1987—California	American	26	117⅔	5	6	.455	108	68	60	55	44	4.59
1988—Edmonton	P. Coast	21	149	11	8	.579	156	72	64	59	33	3.87
1988—California	American	10	37⅔	0	1	.000	37	15	14	19	16	3.35
Major League Totals—5 Years		69	222	5	8	.385	213	115	104	108	94	4.22

Selected by Philadelphia Phillies' organization in 8th round of free-agnt draft, January 9, 1975.
Selected by Philadelphia Phillies' organization in 1st round (18th player selected) of free-agent draft, January 7, 1976.
Selected by Philadelphia Phillies' organization in secondary phase of free-agent draft, June 8, 1976.
Selected by New York Yankees' organization in secondary phase of free-agent draft, June 7, 1977.
Selected by Houston Astros' organization in 11th round of free-agent draft, June 6, 1978.
†Sold to Texas Rangers' organization, June 27, 1979.
‡Released, April 5, 1983; signed by El Paso (Milwaukee Brewers' organization), April 10, 1984.
§On disabled list, April 27 to May 7, 1984.
xGranted free agency, October 15, 1984; signed by Phoenix (San Francisco Giants' organization), April 10, 1985.
ySold to Calgary (Seattle Mariners' organization), June 13, 1985.
zAppeared in one game as a third baseman and outfielder with no chances.
aReleased, November 1, 1985; signed by Nashville (Detroit Tigers' organization), February 7, 1986.
bGranted free agency, October 15, 1986; signed by Edmonton (California Angels' organization), January 6, 1987.

CHARLES WILLIAM LEA

Name pronounced Lee.

(Charlie)

Born December 25, 1956, at Orleans, France.
Height, 6.04. Weight, 200.
Throws and bats righthanded.
Attended University of Mississippi, University, Miss., Shelby State Community College, Memphis, Tenn., and Memphis State University, Memphis, Tenn.

Pitched 4-0 no-hit victory against San Francisco Giants, May 10, 1981 (second game).

Year Club	League	G.	IP.	W.	L.	Pct.	H.	R.	ER.	SO.	BB.	ERA.
1978—Memphis	Southern	12	68	3	3	.500	57	34	27	37	32	3.57
1979—Memphis	Southern	24	162	8	8	.500	161	88	79	81	71	4.39
1980—Memphis	Southern	9	75	9	0	1.000	34	10	7	54	21	0.84
1980—Denver	Am. Assoc.	2	12	0	0	.000	8	2	2	9	5	1.50
1980—Montreal	National	21	104	7	5	.583	103	51	43	56	55	3.72
1981—Montreal	National	16	64	5	4	.556	63	34	33	31	26	4.64
1982—Montreal	National	27	177⅔	12	10	.545	145	70	64	115	56	3.24
1983—Montreal	National	33	222	16	11	.593	195	87	77	137	84	3.12
1984—Montreal	National	30	224⅓	15	10	.600	198	82	72	123	68	2.89
1985—Montreal†	National					(Did not play)						
1986—Montreal‡§	National					(Did not play)						
1987—West Palm Beach	Florida St.	19	71	2	6	.250	70	33	29	54	27	3.68
1987—Indianapolis	Am. Assoc.	5	24⅓	1	2	.333	23	13	12	19	15	4.44

Year	Club	League	G.	IP.	W.	L.	Pct.	H.	R.	ER.	SO.	BB.	ERA.
1987—Montreal x		National	1	1	0	1	.000	4	4	4	1	2	36.00
1988—Minnesota yz		American	24	130	7	7	.500	156	79	70	72	50	4.85
National League Totals—6 Years			128	793	55	41	.573	708	328	293	463	291	3.33
American League Totals—1 Year			24	130	7	7	.500	156	79	70	72	50	4.85
Major League Totals—7 Years			152	923	62	48	.564	864	407	363	535	341	3.54

Selected by New York Mets' organization in 15th round of free-agent draft, June 4, 1975.
Selected by St. Louis Cardinals' organization in secondary phase of free-agent draft, June 8, 1976.
Selected by Chicago White Sox' organization in secondary phase of free-agent draft, January 11, 1977.
Selected by Montreal Expos' organization in 9th round of free-agent draft, June 6, 1978.
†On disabled list, March 24, 1985 through entire season.
‡On disabled list, March 24, 1986 through entire season.
§Granted free agency, November 12, 1986; re-signed by Expos' organization, February 16, 1987.
xGranted free agency, November 9, 1987; signed by Portland (Minnesota Twins' organization), February 4, 1988.
yOn disabled list, August 24 to September 14, 1988.
zGranted free agency, November 4, 1988.

ALL-STAR GAME RECORD

Year	League	IP.	W.	L.	Pct.	H.	R.	ER.	SO.	BB.	ERA.
1984—	National	2	1	0	1.000	3	1	1	2	0	4.50

RICHARD MAX LEACH JR.
(Rick)

Born May 4, 1957, at Ann Arbor, Mich.
Height, 6.00. Weight, 195.
Throws and bats lefthanded.
Attended University of Michigan, Ann Arbor, Mich.

Major League stolen bases: 1982 (4), 1983 (2). Total—6.
Led International League in sacrifice flies with 12 in 1985.
Tied for International League lead in assists by outfielders with 13 in 1985.
Selected by Denver Broncos in 5th round of 1979 NFL draft.
Received reported $200,000 bonus to sign with Detroit Tigers, 1979.
Named outfielder on THE SPORTING NEWS College Baseball All-America Team, 1979.

Year	Club	League	Pos.	G.	AB.	R.	H.	2B.	3B.	HR.	RBI.	B.A.	PO.	A.	E.	F.A.
1979—	Lakeland†	Fla. St.	OF	48	168	21	51	10	1	2	23	.304	104	8	3	.974
1980—	Evansville	A. A.	1B-OF	126	430	69	117	14	1	5	58	.272	767	62	9	.989
1981—	Evansville	A. A.	1B	13	44	8	18	5	0	2	16	.409	129	16	2	.986
1981—	Detroit	Amer.	1B-OF	54	83	9	16	3	1	1	11	.193	149	14	0	1.000
1982—	Detroit‡	Amer.	1B-OF	82	218	23	52	7	2	3	12	.239	430	29	2	.996
1982—	Evansville	A. A.	DH	11	38	6	11	2	0	0	2	.289	0	0	0	.000
1983—	Detroit§	Amer.	1B-OF	99	242	22	60	17	0	3	26	.248	465	45	4	.992
1984—	Syracuse	Int.	OF-1B	23	79	16	24	6	2	3	8	.304	70	4	2	.974
1984—	Toronto	Amer.	OF-1B-P	65	88	11	23	6	2	0	7	.261	92	14	0	1.000
1985—	Syracuse	Int.	OF-1B	136	533	77	151	24	2	15	79	.283	675	66	10	.987
1985—	Toronto	Amer.	1B-OF	16	35	2	7	0	1	0	1	.200	78	6	1	.988
1986—	Toronto	Amer.	OF-1B	110	246	35	76	14	1	5	39	.309	107	5	3	.974
1987—	Toronto	Amer.	OF-1B	98	195	26	55	13	1	3	25	.282	57	1	1	.993
1988—	Toronto x	Amer.	OF-1B	87	199	21	55	13	1	0	23	.276	93	5	0	1.000
Major League Totals—8 Years				611	1306	149	344	73	9	15	144	.263	1471	119	11	.993

Selected by Philadelphia Phillies' organization in 11th round of free-agent draft, June 4, 1975.
Selected by Philadelphia Phillies' organization in 24th round of free-agent draft, June 6, 1978.
Selected by Detroit Tigers' organization in 1st round (13th player selected) of free-agent draft, June 5, 1979.
†On disabled list, June 18 to June 29, 1979.
‡On disabled list, April 12 to May 17, 1982; included rehabilitation disability assignment to Evansville, May 6 to May 17, 1982.
§Released, March 24, 1984; signed by Toronto Blue Jays' organization, April 3, 1984.
xGranted free agency, November 4, 1988.

PITCHING RECORD

Year	Club	League	G.	IP.	W.	L.	Pct.	H.	R.	ER.	SO.	BB.	ERA.
1984—	Toronto	American	1	1	0	0	.000	2	3	3	0	2	27.00

TERRY HESTER LEACH

Born March 13, 1954, at Selma, Ala.
Height, 6.00. Weight, 191.
Throws and bats righthanded.
Received business administration degree in personnel management-industrial relations from Auburn University, Auburn University, Ala.

Major League saves: 1982 (3), 1985 (1), 1988 (3). Total—7.
Led Gulf States League in home runs allowed with 12 in 1976.

Year	Club	League	G.	IP.	W.	L.	Pct.	H.	R.	ER.	SO.	BB.	ERA.
1976—	Baton Rouge†‡	Gulf States	5	19	2	0	1.000	43	21	13	15	14	6.16
1977—	Greenwood	W. Carol.	20	67	3	2	.600	47	25	19	67	24	2.55
1978—	Savannah§	Southern	9	25	1	0	1.000	24	17	14	21	13	5.04
1978—	Kinston	Carolina	34	66	5	4	.556	57	29	24	46	25	3.27
1979—	Savannah	Southern	40	92	2	9	.182	77	33	20	68	26	1.96
1979—	Richmond	Int'national	7	14	3	1	.750	14	3	3	12	4	1.93

Year Club	League	G.	IP.	W.	L.	Pct.	H.	R.	ER.	SO.	BB.	ERA.
1980—Savannah xy	Southern	22	87	5	1	.833	83	36	31	58	17	3.21
1980—Jackson	Texas	8	54	5	1	.833	50	16	9	30	15	1.50
1981—Tidewater	Int'national	15	76	5	2	.714	63	27	23	42	19	2.72
1981—Jackson	Texas	8	58	5	1	.833	47	14	11	43	12	1.71
1981—New York	National	21	35	1	1	.500	26	11	10	16	12	2.57
1982—Tidewater	Int'national	30	48⅔	4	1	.800	48	20	16	34	19	2.96
1982—New York	National	21	45⅓	2	1	.667	46	22	21	30	18	4.17
1983—Tidewater za	Int'national	37	113	5	7	.417	120	66	56	66	42	4.46
1984—Richmond b-Tidewater	Int'national	43	95	11	4	.733	98	42	32	59	30	3.03
1985—Tidewater	Int'national	24	45⅓	1	0	1.000	33	12	8	25	8	1.59
1985—New York	National	22	55⅔	3	4	.429	48	19	18	30	14	2.91
1986—Tidewater	Int'national	34	79⅔	4	4	.500	69	30	22	55	21	2.49
1986—New York	National	6	6⅔	0	0	.000	6	3	2	4	3	2.70
1987—New York c	National	44	131⅓	11	1	.917	132	54	47	61	29	3.22
1988—New York	National	52	92	7	2	.778	95	32	26	51	24	2.54
Major League Totals—6 Years		166	366	24	9	.727	353	141	124	192	100	3.05

Selected by Boston Red Sox' organization in 7th round of free-agent draft, January 7, 1976.
†Signed as free agent by Baton Rouge (Independent), June 29, 1976; released when Baton Rouge withdrew from league, August 13, 1976.
‡Signed by Greenwood (Atlanta Braves' organization) as free agent, May 28, 1977.
§Loaned to Kinston (Independent), June 3, 1978; returned, October 25, 1978.
xOn disabled list, June 12 to July 23, 1980.
yReleased, July 23, 1980; signed by Jackson (New York Mets' organization), July 27, 1980.
zTraded to Chicago Cubs' organization for Pitchers Jim Adamczak and Mitch Cook, September 26, 1983.
aTraded by Chicago Cubs' organization to Atlanta Braves' organization for Pitcher Ron Meridith, April 4, 1984.
bReleased, May 25, 1984; signed by New York Mets' organization, May 26, 1984.
cOn disabled list, July 12 to July 27, 1987.

CHAMPIONSHIP SERIES RECORD

Year Club	League	G.	IP.	W.	L.	Pct.	H.	R.	ER.	SO.	BB.	ERA.
1988—New York	National	3	5	0	0	.000	4	0	0	4	1	0.00

TIMOTHY JAMES LEARY
(Tim)

Born December 23, 1958, at Santa Monica, Calif.
Height, 6.03. Weight, 208.
Throws and bats righthanded.
Attended University of California, Los Angeles, Calif.

Major League saves: 1987 (1).
Led Texas League in shutouts with 6 in 1980.
Named National League Comeback Player of the Year by THE SPORTING NEWS, 1988.
Named pitcher on National League Silver Slugger team, 1988.
Named Texas League Most Valuable Player, 1980.
Named righthanded pitcher on THE SPORTING NEWS College Baseball All-America Team, 1979.

Year Club	League	G.	IP.	W.	L.	Pct.	H.	R.	ER.	SO.	BB.	ERA.
1979—Jackson†	Texas					(Did not play)						
1980—Jackson	Texas	26	173	•15	8	.652	150	67	53	138	62	2.76
1981—New York‡	National	1	2	0	0	.000	0	0	0	3	1	0.00
1981—Tidewater	Int'national	6	34	1	3	.250	27	16	14	15	27	3.71
1982—Tidewater§	Int'national					(Did not play)						
1983—Tidewater	Int'national	27	160⅓	8	*16	.333	170	100	78	106	73	4.38
1983—New York	National	2	10⅔	1	1	.500	15	10	4	9	4	3.38
1984—New York	National	20	53⅔	3	3	.500	61	28	24	29	18	4.02
1984—Tidewater x	Int'national	10	53⅓	4	4	.500	47	26	24	27	42	4.05
1985—Vancouver	P. Coast	27	177⅔	10	7	.588	174	85	79	136	57	4.00
1985—Milwaukee	American	5	33⅓	1	4	.200	40	18	15	29	8	4.05
1986—Milwaukee y	American	33	188⅓	12	12	.500	216	97	88	110	53	4.21
1987—Los Angeles	National	39	107⅔	3	11	.214	121	62	57	61	36	4.76
1988—Los Angeles	National	35	228⅔	17	11	.607	201	87	74	180	56	2.91
National League Totals—5 Years		97	402⅔	24	26	.480	398	187	159	282	115	3.55
American League Totals—2 Years		38	221⅔	13	16	.448	256	115	103	139	61	4.18
Major League Totals—7 Years		135	624⅓	37	42	.468	654	302	262	421	176	3.78

Selected by New York Mets' organization in 1st round (second player selected) of free-agent draft, June 5, 1979.
†On disabled list, July 19 to October 1, 1979.
‡On disabled list, April 16 to August 1, 1981.
§On disabled list, April 13, 1982 through remainder of season.
xTraded to Milwaukee Brewers' organization as part of a six-player, four-team deal in which Kansas City Royals acquired Catcher Jim Sundberg from Milwaukee, Texas Rangers acquired Catcher Don Slaught from Kansas City, New York Mets' organization acquired Pitcher Frank Wills from Kansas City and Milwaukee acquired Pitcher Danny Darwin and a player to be named later from Texas, January 18, 1985; Milwaukee organization acquired Catcher Bill Hance from Texas to complete deal, January 30, 1985.
yTraded with Pitcher Tim Crews to Los Angeles Dodgers for First Baseman Greg Brock, December 10, 1986.

CHAMPIONSHIP SERIES RECORD

Year Club	League	G.	IP.	W.	L.	Pct.	H.	R.	ER.	SO.	BB.	ERA.
1988—Los Angeles	National	2	4⅓	0	1	.000	8	4	3	3	3	6.23

WORLD SERIES RECORD

Year	Club	League	G.	IP.	W.	L.	Pct.	H.	R.	ER.	SO.	BB.	ERA.
1988	Los Angeles	National	2	6⅔	0	0	.000	6	1	1	4	2	1.35

MANUEL LORA LEE
(Manny)

Born June 17, 1965, at San Pedro de Macoris, D. R.
Height, 5.09. Weight, 161.
Throws right and bats left and righthanded.

Major League stolen bases: 1985 (1), 1987 (2), 1988 (3). Total—6.

Year	Club	League	Pos.	G.	AB.	R.	H.	2B.	3B.	HR.	RBI.	B.A.	PO.	A.	E.	F.A.
1982	Kingsport	Appal.	2B-SS	16	54	2	12	1	0	0	3	.222	34	34	6	.919
1983	Sarasota Mets	Gulf C.	2B-SS	32	97	8	24	2	1	0	12	.247	44	79	8	.939
1983	Little Falls	NYP	2B	17	45	10	13	0	0	0	5	.289	34	40	3	.961
1984	Columbia†‡§	S. Atl.	SS-2B	102	346	84	114	12	5	2	33	*.329	126	277	34	.922
1985	Toronto	Amer.	2B-SS-3B	64	40	9	8	0	0	0	0	.200	34	56	3	.968
1986	Syracuse	Int.	SS-2B	76	236	34	58	6	1	1	19	.246	132	237	18	.953
1986	Knoxville	South.	SS-2B	41	158	21	43	1	2	0	11	.272	70	117	8	.959
1986	Toronto	Amer.	2B-SS-3B	35	78	8	16	0	1	1	7	.205	36	76	2	.982
1987	Toronto	Amer.	2B-SS	56	121	14	31	2	3	1	11	.256	77	110	5	.974
1987	Syracuse	Int.	SS	74	251	25	71	9	5	3	26	.283	120	177	23	.928
1988	Toronto x	Amer.	2B-SS-3B	116	381	38	111	16	3	2	38	.291	250	308	12	.979
Major League Totals—4 Years				271	620	69	166	18	7	4	56	.268	397	550	22	.977

Signed as free agent by New York Mets' organization, May 10, 1982.
†On disabled list, April 9 to April 22, 1984.
‡Traded with Outfielder Gerald Young to Houston Astros, August 31, 1984, as partial completion of deal in which New York Mets acquired Infielder Ray Knight for three players to be named later, August 28, 1984; Houston acquired Pitcher Mitch Cook to complete deal, September 10, 1984.
§Drafted by Toronto Blue Jays, December 3, 1984.
xOn disabled list, March 28 to April 12 and May 12 to June 1, 1988.

CHAMPIONSHIP SERIES RECORD

Year	Club	League	Pos.	G.	AB.	R.	H.	2B.	3B.	HR.	RBI.	B.A.	PO.	A.	E.	F.A.
1985	Toronto	Amer.	PR-2B	1	0	0	0	0	0	0	0	.000	0	0	0	.000

MARK OWEN LEE

Born July 20, 1964, at Williston, N. D.
Height, 6.03. Weight, 198.
Throws and bats lefthanded.
Attended Trinidad State Junior College, Trinidad, Colo., and Florida International University, Miami, Fla.

Year	Club	League	G.	IP.	W.	L.	Pct.	H.	R.	ER.	SO.	BB.	ERA.
1985	Bristol	Ap'lachian	15	33	3	0	1.000	18	5	4	40	12	1.09
1986	Lakeland	Florida St.	41	62⅔	2	5	.286	73	44	36	39	21	5.17
1987	Glens Falls	Eastern	7	8⅓	0	0	.000	13	9	8	3	1	8.64
1987	Lakeland	Florida St.	30	53	3	2	.600	48	17	15	42	18	2.55
1988	Lakeland	Florida St.	10	19	1	0	1.000	16	7	3	15	4	1.42
1988	Glens Falls	Eastern	14	26	3	0	1.000	27	10	7	25	4	2.42
1988	Toledo†	Int'national	22	19⅓	0	1	.000	18	7	6	13	7	2.79
1988	Kansas City	American	4	5	0	0	.000	6	2	2	0	1	3.60
Major League Totals—1 Year			4	5	0	0	.000	6	2	2	0	1	3.60

Selected by Detroit Tigers' organization in 15th round of free-agent draft, June 3, 1985.
†Traded with Catcher Rey Palacios to Kansas City Royals for Pitcher Ted Power, August 31, 1988.

CRAIG LINDSAY LEFFERTS

Born September 29, 1957, in Munich, West Germany.
Height, 6.01. Weight, 210.
Throws and bats lefthanded.
Attended University of Arizona, Tucson, Ariz.

Major League saves: 1983 (1), 1984 (10), 1985 (2), 1986 (4), 1987 (6), 1988 (11). Total—34.

Year	Club	League	G.	IP.	W.	L.	Pct.	H.	R.	ER.	SO.	BB.	ERA.
1980	Geneva	NYP	12	94	9	1	*.900	74	35	29	*99	24	2.78
1981	Midland	Texas	26	185	12	•12	.500	203	95	85	135	36	4.14
1982	Iowa†	Am.Assoc.	18	97⅓	8	5	.615	97	50	33	71	25	3.05
1983	Chicago‡	National	56	89	3	4	.429	80	35	31	60	29	3.13
1984	San Diego	National	62	105⅔	3	4	.429	88	29	25	56	24	2.13
1985	San Diego	National	60	83⅓	7	6	.538	75	34	31	48	30	3.35
1986	San Diego	National	*83	107⅔	9	8	.529	98	41	37	72	44	3.09
1987	San Diego§-San Francisco	National	77	98⅔	5	5	.500	92	47	42	57	33	3.83
1988	San Francisco	National	64	92⅓	3	8	.273	74	33	30	58	23	2.92
Major League Totals—6 Years			402	576⅔	30	35	.462	507	219	196	351	183	3.06

Selected by Kansas City Royals' organization in 6th round of free-agent draft, June 5, 1979.
Selected by Chicago Cubs' organization in 9th round of free-agent draft, June 3, 1980.
†On disabled list, April 24 to June 4, 1982.

‡Traded with First Baseman Carmelo Martinez and Third Baseman Fritz Connally to San Diego Padres for Pitcher Scott Sanderson, December 7, 1983.

§Traded with Pitcher Dave Dravecky and Infielder Kevin Mitchell to San Francisco Giants for Third Baseman Chris Brown and Pitchers Keith Comstock, Mark Davis and Mark Grant, July 4, 1987.

CHAMPIONSHIP SERIES RECORD

Tied Championship Series record for most games won, Series (2), 1984.

Year Club	League	G.	IP.	W.	L.	Pct.	H.	R.	ER.	SO.	BB.	ERA.
1984—San Diego	National	3	4	2	0	1.000	1	0	0	1	1	0.00
1987—San Francisco	National	3	2	0	0	.000	3	0	0	0	1	0.00
Championship Series Totals—2 Years		6	6	2	0	1.000	4	0	0	1	2	0.00

WORLD SERIES RECORD

Year Club	League	G.	IP.	W.	L.	Pct.	H.	R.	ER.	SO.	BB.	ERA.
1984—San Diego	National	3	6	0	0	.000	2	0	0	7	1	0.00

CHARLES LOUIS LEIBRANDT JR.
(Charlie)

Born October 4, 1956, at Chicago, Ill.
Height, 6.03. Weight, 200.
Throws left and bats righthanded.
Received bachelor of science degree in business management from
Miami University, Oxford, O.

Established major league record for fewest assists by pitcher, for leader in assists (43), 1986.
Major League saves: 1982 (2).
Tied for American Association lead in shutouts with 3 in 1984.
Tied for American Association lead in games started by pitchers with 26 in 1979.

Year Club	League	G.	IP.	W.	L.	Pct.	H.	R.	ER.	SO.	BB.	ERA.
1978—Eugene	Northwest	3	20	2	0	1.000	24	13	9	18	5	4.05
1978—Tampa	Florida St.	6	47	4	1	.800	26	4	4	40	17	0.77
1978—Indianapolis	Am. Assoc	4	29	2	1	.667	20	9	9	12	12	2.79
1979—Indianapolis	Am. Assoc.	27	162	8	*14	.364	146	67	53	100	65	2.94
1979—Cincinnati	National	3	4	0	0	.000	2	2	0	1	2	0.00
1980—Cincinnati	National	36	174	10	9	.526	200	84	82	62	54	4.24
1981—Indianapolis	Am. Assoc.	25	169	9	7	.563	149	76	55	101	75	2.93
1981—Cincinnati	National	7	30	1	1	.500	28	12	12	9	15	3.60
1982—Cincinnati	National	36	107⅔	5	7	.417	130	68	61	34	48	5.10
1983—Indianapolis†-Omaha	Am. Assoc.	27	185⅓	9	10	.474	181	113	88	128	77	4.27
1984—Omaha	Am. Assoc.	9	72⅔	7	1	.875	51	14	10	38	16	1.24
1984—Kansas City	American	23	143⅔	11	7	.611	158	65	58	53	38	3.63
1985—Kansas City	American	33	237⅔	17	9	.654	223	86	71	108	68	2.69
1986—Kansas City	American	35	231⅓	14	11	.560	238	112	105	108	63	4.09
1987—Kansas City‡	American	35	240⅓	16	11	.593	235	104	91	151	74	3.41
1988—Kansas City	American	35	243	13	12	.520	244	98	86	125	62	3.19
National League Totals—4 Years		82	315⅔	16	17	.485	360	166	155	106	119	4.42
American League Totals—5 Years		161	1096	71	50	.587	1098	465	411	545	305	3.38
Major League Totals—9 Years		243	1411⅔	87	67	.565	1458	631	566	651	424	3.61

Selected by Cincinnati Reds' organization in 9th round of free-agent draft, June 6, 1978.
†Traded to Kansas City Royals for Pitcher Bob Tufts, June 7, 1983.
‡Granted free agency, November 9, 1987; re-signed by Royals, January 7, 1988.

CHAMPIONSHIP SERIES RECORD

Established American League Championship Series record for most hits allowed, seven-game Series (17), 1985.
Tied Championship Series record for most games lost, Series (2), 1985.
Tied American League Championship Series record for most strikeouts by a relief pitcher, game (5), October 16, 1985.

Year Club	League	G.	IP.	W.	L.	Pct.	H.	R.	ER.	SO.	BB.	ERA.
1979—Cincinnati	National	1	⅓	0	0	.000	0	0	0	0	0	0.00
1984—Kansas City	American	1	8	0	1	.000	3	1	1	6	4	1.13
1985—Kansas City	American	3	15⅓	1	2	.333	17	9	9	6	4	5.28
Championship Series Totals—3 Years		5	23⅔	1	3	.250	20	10	10	12	8	3.80

WORLD SERIES RECORD

Year Club	League	G.	IP.	W.	L.	Pct.	H.	R.	ER.	SO.	BB.	ERA.
1985—Kansas City	American	2	16⅓	0	1	.000	10	5	5	10	4	2.76

DAVID PAUL LEIPER
(Dave)

Born June 18, 1962, at Whittier, Calif.
Height, 6.01. Weight, 160.
Throws and bats lefthanded.
Attended Fullerton College, Fullerton, Calif.

Major League saves: 1986 (1), 1987 (2), 1988 (1). Total—4.

Year	Club	League	G.	IP.	W.	L.	Pct.	H.	R.	ER.	SO.	BB.	ERA.
1982	—Idaho Falls	Pioneer	14	85⅓	9	3	.750	94	49	39	77	27	4.11
1983	—Madison	Midwest	16	79⅓	5	4	.556	89	43	33	60	37	3.74
1984	—Modesto	California	19	35⅓	5	0	1.000	12	2	1	30	14	0.25
1984	—Tacoma	P. Coast	28	32⅔	2	3	.400	33	11	11	13	14	3.03
1984	—Oakland	American	8	7	1	0	1.000	12	7	7	3	5	9.00
1985	—Tacoma†	P. Coast	15	23⅓	0	1	.000	29	16	14	7	12	5.40
1985	—Modesto	California	21	30	1	0	1.000	53	31	26	24	19	7.80
1986	—Tacoma	P. Coast	20	26	2	1	.667	30	17	14	13	9	4.85
1986	—Oakland	American	33	31⅔	2	2	.500	28	17	17	15	18	4.83
1987	—Tacoma	P. Coast	5	9	0	0	.000	3	0	0	6	1	0.00
1987	—Oakland‡	American	45	52⅓	2	1	.667	49	28	22	33	18	3.78
1987	—San Diego	National	12	16	1	0	1.000	16	8	8	10	5	4.50
1988	—San Diego§	National	35	54	3	0	1.000	45	19	13	33	14	2.17
American League Totals—3 Years			86	91	5	3	.625	89	52	46	51	41	4.55
National League Totals—2 Years			47	70	4	0	1.000	61	27	21	43	19	2.70
Major League Totals—4 Years			133	161	9	3	.750	150	79	67	94	60	3.75

Selected by Texas Rangers' organization in 2nd round of free-agent draft, January 13, 1981.
Selected by San Francisco Giants' organization in secondary phase of free-agent draft, June 8, 1981.
Selected by Oakland A's organization in secondary phase of free-agent draft, January 12, 1982.
†On disabled list, April 11 to May 13, 1985.
‡Traded to San Diego Padres, August 31, 1987, as partial completion of deal in which San Diego traded Pitcher Storm Davis to Oakland Athletics for two players to be named later, August 30, 1987. San Diego acquired First Baseman Rob Nelson to complete deal, September 8, 1987.
§On disabled list, March 27 to April 18 and May 3 to May 23, 1988.

ALOIS TERRY LEITER

Name pronounced Li-ter.

(Al)

Born October 23, 1965, at Toms River, N. J.
Height, 6.03. Weight, 210.
Throws and bats lefthanded.
Brother of Kurt Leiter, pitcher in Baltimore Orioles' organization, 1982 through 1984; and Miami (Independent), 1986; and brother of Mark Leiter, pitcher in Baltimore Orioles' organization, 1983 through 1985.

Year	Club	League	G.	IP.	W.	L.	Pct.	H.	R.	ER.	SO.	BB.	ERA.
1984	—Oneonta	NYP	10	57	3	2	.600	52	32	23	48	26	3.63
1985	—Oneonta	NYP	6	38	3	2	.600	27	14	10	34	25	2.37
1985	—Fort Lauderdale	Florida St.	17	82	1	6	.143	87	70	59	44	57	6.48
1986	—Fort Lauderdale	Florida St.	22	117⅔	4	8	.333	96	64	53	101	90	4.05
1987	—Columbus	Int'national	5	23⅓	1	4	.200	21	18	16	23	15	6.17
1987	—Albany	Eastern	15	78	3	3	.500	64	34	29	71	37	3.35
1987	—New York	American	4	22⅔	2	2	.500	24	16	16	28	15	6.35
1988	—New York†	American	14	57⅓	4	4	.500	49	27	25	60	33	3.92
1988	—Columbus	Int'national	4	13	0	2	.000	5	7	5	12	14	3.46
Major League Totals—2 Years			18	80	6	6	.500	73	43	41	88	48	4.61

Selected by New York Yankees' organization in 2nd round of free-agent draft, June 4, 1984.
†On disabled list, June 22 to July 26, 1988; included rehabilitation disability assignment to Columbus, July 17 to July 25, 1988.

SCOTT THOMAS LEIUS

Born September 24, 1965, at Yonkers, N.Y.
Height, 6.03. Weight, 185.
Throws and bats righthanded.
Attended Concordia College, Bronxville, N.Y.

Led Midwest League shortstops in double plays with 74 in 1987.
Led Appalachian League shortstops in assists with 174 and double plays with 33 in 1986.

Year	Club	League	Pos.	G.	AB.	R.	H.	2B.	3B.	HR.	RBI.	B.A.	PO.	A.	E.	F.A.
1986	—Elizabethton	Appal.	SS-3B	61	237	37	66	14	1	4	23	.278	67	176	18	.931
1987	—Kenosha	Midw.	SS	126	414	65	99	16	4	8	51	.239	183	331	31	.943
1988	—Visalia	Calif.	SS	93	308	44	73	14	4	3	46	.237	154	234	15	.963

Selected by Minnesota Twins' organization in 13th round of free-agent draft, June 2, 1986.

MARK ALAN LEMKE

Born August 13, 1965, at Utica, N.Y.
Height, 5.09. Weight, 165.
Throws right and bats left and righthanded.

Led Southern League in total bases with 239 in 1988.
Led Southern League second basemen in total chances with 739 and double plays with 105 in 1988.
Led Carolina League second basemen in double plays with 83 in 1987.
Led Gulf Coast League second basemen in assists with 207, total chances with 391 and double plays with 39 in 1984.

Year	Club	League	Pos.	G.	AB.	R.	H.	2B.	3B.	HR.	RBI.	B.A.	PO.	A.	E.	F.A.
1983	—Bradenton Brav.	Gulf C.	2B	53	209	37	55	6	0	0	19	.263	81	101	11	.943
1984	—Anderson	S. Atl.	2B-3B	42	121	18	18	2	0	0	5	.149	67	83	4	.974
1984	—Bradenton Brav.	Gulf C.	*2B-SS	●63	*243	41	67	11	0	3	32	.276	*175	209	9	*.977
1985	—Sumter	S. Atl.	2B	90	231	25	50	6	0	0	20	.216	119	174	11	.964

Year	Club	League	Pos.	G.	AB.	R.	H.	2B.	3B.	HR.	RBI.	B.A.	PO.	A.	E.	F.A.
1986	Sumter	S. Atl.	3B-2B	126	448	99	122	24	2	18	66	.272	134	274	16	.962
1987	Durham	Carol.	★2B-3B	127	489	75	143	28	3	20	68	.292	248	★355	11	★.982
1987	Greenville	South.	3B	6	26	0	6	0	0	0	4	.231	4	12	1	.941
1988	Greenville	South.	2B	●143	★567	81	★153	30	4	16	80	.270	★281	★440	18	.976
1988	Atlanta	Nat.	2B	16	58	8	13	4	0	0	2	.224	47	51	3	.970
Major League Totals—1 Year				16	58	8	13	4	0	0	2	.224	47	51	3	.970

Selected by Atlanta Braves' organization in 27th round of free-agent draft, June 6, 1983.

CHESTER EARL LEMON
(Chet)

Born February 12, 1955, at Jackson, Miss.
Height, 6.00. Weight, 190.
Throws and bats righthanded.
Attended Pepperdine University, Malibu, Calif., and Cerritos College, Norwalk, Calif.
Cousin of Eric Yarber, wide receiver-kick returner with Washington Redskins.

Established American League records for most chances accepted by outfielder, season (524), 1977; most putouts by outfielder, season (512), 1977; most years by outfielder, 400 or more putouts (5).

Tied American League record for most years by outfielder, 500 or more putouts (1), 1977.

Major League stolen bases: 1975 (1), 1976 (13), 1977 (8), 1978 (5), 1979 (7), 1980 (6), 1981 (5), 1982 (1), 1984 (5), 1986 (2), 1988 (1). Total—54.

Led American League in being hit by pitch with 13 in 1979, 13 in 1981, 15 in 1982 and 20 in 1983.

Led American League outfielders in total chances with 536 in 1977.

Year	Club	League	Pos.	G.	AB.	R.	H.	2B.	3B.	HR.	RBI.	B.A.	PO.	A.	E.	F.A.
1972	Coos Bay-N. B.	N'west	SS-3B	38	140	33	40	8	1	2	16	.286	56	94	16	.904
1972	Burlington	Midw.	3B-SS	33	129	18	33	5	0	1	8	.256	24	62	13	.869
1973	Burlington	Midw.	3B-SS	113	392	73	121	21	1	19	★88	.309	102	215	36	.898
1974	Birmingham†	South.	3B-SS	79	272	52	79	22	2	10	61	.290	84	135	23	.905
1975	Tucson‡	P. C.	3B-OF	65	243	43	68	7	2	5	33	.280	60	70	19	.872
1975	Denver	A. A.	3B-OF	70	254	40	78	15	6	8	49	.307	39	76	19	.858
1975	Chicago	Amer.	3B-OF	9	35	2	9	2	0	0	1	.257	5	7	1	.923
1976	Chicago	Amer.	OF	132	451	46	111	15	5	4	38	.246	353	12	3	.992
1977	Chicago	Amer.	OF	150	553	99	151	38	4	19	67	.273	★512	12	12	.978
1978	Chicago§	Amer.	OF	105	357	51	107	24	6	13	55	.300	284	8	5	.983
1979	Chicago	Amer.	OF	148	556	79	177	●44	2	17	86	.318	411	10	10	.977
1980	Chicago	Amer.	OF-2B	147	514	76	150	32	6	11	51	.292	347	11	7	.981
1981	Chicago x	Amer.	OF	94	328	50	99	23	6	9	50	.302	240	2	4	.948
1982	Detroit	Amer.	OF	125	436	75	116	20	1	19	52	.266	242	11	4	.984
1983	Detroit	Amer.	OF	145	491	78	125	21	5	24	69	.255	406	6	5	.988
1984	Detroit	Amer.	OF	141	509	77	146	34	6	20	76	.287	427	6	2	.995
1985	Detroit	Amer.	OF	145	517	69	137	28	4	18	68	.265	411	6	4	.990
1986	Detroit	Amer.	OF	126	403	45	101	21	3	12	53	.251	316	6	5	.985
1987	Detroit	Amer.	OF	146	470	75	130	30	3	20	75	.277	350	4	3	.992
1988	Detroit	Amer.	OF	144	512	67	135	29	4	17	64	.264	296	8	8	.974
Major League Totals—14 Years				1757	6132	889	1694	361	55	203	805	.276	4600	109	73	.985

Selected by Oakland A's organization in 1st round (20th player selected) of free-agent draft, June 6, 1972.

†On disabled list, July 16 to September 16, 1974.

‡Traded with Pitcher Dave Hamilton to Chicago White Sox for Pitchers Stan Bahnsen and Lee (Skip) Pitlock, June 15, 1975.

§On disabled list, August 12 to August 27, 1978.

xTraded to Detroit Tigers for Outfielder Steve Kemp, November 27, 1981.

CHAMPIONSHIP SERIES RECORD

Year	Club	League	Pos.	G.	AB.	R.	H.	2B.	3B.	HR.	RBI.	B.A.	PO.	A.	E.	F.A.
1984	Detroit	Amer.	OF	3	13	1	0	0	0	0	0	.000	9	0	0	1.000
1987	Detroit	Amer.	OF	5	18	4	5	0	0	2	4	.278	13	0	0	1.000
Championship Series Totals—2 Years				8	31	5	5	0	0	2	4	.161	22	0	0	1.000

WORLD SERIES RECORD

Year	Club	League	Pos.	G.	AB.	R.	H.	2B.	3B.	HR.	RBI.	B.A.	PO.	A.	E.	F.A.
1984	Detroit	Amer.	OF	5	17	1	5	0	0	0	1	.294	15	0	0	1.000

ALL-STAR GAME RECORD

Year	League	Pos.	AB.	R.	H.	2B.	3B.	HR.	RBI.	B.A.	PO.	A.	E.	F.A.
1978	American	OF	0	0	0	0	0	0	0	.000	0	0	1	.000
1979	American	OF	2	1	0	0	0	0	0	.000	2	0	0	1.000
1984	American	OF	2	0	1	0	0	0	0	.500	0	0	0	.000
All-Star Game Totals—3 Years			4	1	1	0	0	0	0	.250	2	0	1	.667

PATRICK ORLANDO LENNON

Born April 27, 1968, at Whiteville, N.C.
Height, 6.02. Weight, 200.
Throws and bats righthanded.

Led Midwest League third basemen in errors with 39 in 1987.

Year	Club	League	Pos.	G.	AB.	R.	H.	2B.	3B.	HR.	RBI.	B.A.	PO.	A.	E.	F.A.
1986	Bellingham	N'west	SS-3B	51	169	35	41	5	2	3	27	.243	57	90	27	.845
1987	Wausau	Midw.	3B-SS	98	319	54	80	21	3	7	34	.251	73	190	40	.868
1988	Vermont	East.	3B	95	321	44	83	9	3	9	40	.259	81	143	*28	.889

Selected by Seattle Mariners' organization in 1st round (eighth player selected) of free-agent draft, June 2, 1986.

DANILO ENRIQUE LEON

Born April 3, 1967, at LaConcepcion, Venezuela.
Height, 6.01. Weight, 150.
Throws and bats righthanded.

Tied for New York-Pennsylvania League lead in shutouts with 4 in 1988.

Year	Club	League	G.	IP.	W.	L.	Pct.	H.	R.	ER.	SO.	BB.	ERA.
1986	Bradenton Expos	Gulf Coast	15	29⅓	1	2	.333	32	18	14	21	13	4.30
1987	Jamestown	NYP	3	1⅔	0	0	.000	4	3	3	3	1	16.20
1988	Jamestown	NYP	15	116	10	3	.769	75	29	15	100	48	1.16
1988	West Palm Beach	Florida St.	6	14	0	0	.000	12	6	5	15	5	3.21

Signed as free agent by Montreal Expos' organization, July 11, 1986.

JEFFREY N. LEONARD

Born September 22, 1955, at Philadelphia, Pa.
Height, 6.04. Weight, 200.
Throws and bats righthanded.

Major League stolen bases: 1979 (23), 1980 (4), 1981 (5), 1982 (18), 1983 (26), 1984 (17), 1985 (11), 1986 (16), 1987 (16), 1988 (17). Total—153.

Hit for the cycle, June 27, 1985.

Named National League Rookie Player of the Year by THE SPORTING NEWS, 1979.

Year	Club	League	Pos.	G.	AB.	R.	H.	2B.	3B.	HR.	RBI.	B.A.	PO.	A.	E.	F.A.
1973	Bellingham	N'west	OF	55	187	30	52	4	3	2	20	.278	46	2	5	.906
1974	Orangeburg	W. Car.	OF	8	15	0	1	0	0	0	1	.067	5	1	1	.857
1974	Bellingham	N'west	OF	78	278	47	90	12	4	3	43	.324	115	7	6	.953
1975	Bakersfield	Calif.	OF	106	320	44	89	11	3	4	37	.278	137	5	7	.953
1976	Lodi	Calif.	OF	133	509	93	168	29	9	8	85	.330	214	13	*15	.938
1976	Albuquerque	P. C.	OF	7	27	2	8	2	1	1	6	.296	14	0	0	1.000
1977	San Antonio	Texas	OF	122	468	75	147	17	10	12	70	.314	241	12	8	.969
1977	Los Angeles	Nat.	OF	11	10	1	3	0	1	0	2	.300	7	0	0	1.000
1978	Albuquerque†	P. C.	OF	133	502	111	*183	23	14	11	93	*.365	216	8	6	.974
1978	Houston	Nat.	OF	8	26	2	10	2	0	0	4	.385	16	1	0	1.000
1979	Houston	Nat.	OF	134	411	47	119	15	5	0	47	.290	227	6	10	.959
1980	Houston	Nat.	OF	88	216	29	46	7	5	3	20	.213	161	9	3	.983
1981	Hou.‡-S.F.	Nat.	OF-1B	44	145	21	42	12	4	4	29	.290	152	5	1	.994
1981	Phoenix	P. C.	OF	47	187	38	75	17	3	7	45	.401	90	2	2	.979
1982	San Francisco§	Nat.	OF-1B	80	278	32	72	16	1	9	49	.259	137	2	9	.939
1982	Phoenix	P. C.	OF	17	59	14	21	5	0	4	12	.356	5	0	0	1.000
1983	San Francisco	Nat.	OF	139	516	74	144	17	7	21	87	.279	253	17	7	.975
1984	San Francisco	Nat.	OF	136	514	76	155	27	2	21	86	.302	247	14	8	.970
1985	San Francisco	Nat.	OF	133	507	49	122	20	3	17	62	.241	203	10	5	.977
1986	San Francisco x	Nat.	OF	89	341	48	95	11	3	6	42	.279	158	4	5	.970
1987	San Francisco	Nat.	OF	131	503	70	141	29	4	19	63	.280	193	7	7	.966
1988	San Francisco yz	Nat.	OF	44	160	12	41	8	1	2	20	.256	74	0	1	.987
1988	Milwaukee a	Amer.	OF	94	374	45	88	19	0	8	44	.235	191	4	3	.985
	National League Totals—12 Years			1037	3627	461	990	164	36	102	511	.273	1828	75	56	.971
	American League Totals—1 Year			94	374	45	88	19	0	8	44	.235	191	4	3	.985
	Major League Totals—12 Years			1131	4001	506	1078	183	36	110	555	.269	2019	79	59	.973

Signed as free agent by Los Angeles Dodgers' organization, June 7, 1973.

†Traded to Houston Astros, September 11, 1978, completing deal in which Los Angeles Dodgers acquired Catcher Joe Ferguson for two players to be named later, July 1, 1978; Houston acquired Shortstop Rafael Landestoy as partial completion of deal, July 7, 1978.

‡Traded with First Baseman-Outfielder Dave Bergman to San Francisco Giants for First Baseman Mike Ivie, April 20, 1981.

§On disabled list, May 23 to July 19, 1982; included rehabilitation disability assignment to Phoenix, July 1 to July 19, 1982.

xOn disabled list, July 31, 1986 through remainder of season.

yOn disabled list, March 29 to April 13, 1988.

zTraded to Milwaukee Brewers for Shortstop Ernest Riles, June 8, 1988.

aGranted free agency, November 4, 1988; signed by Seattle Mariners, December 7, 1988.

CHAMPIONSHIP SERIES RECORD

Tied Championship Series records for most home runs, seven-game Series (4), 1987; most total bases, Series (22), 1987; most consecutive games, one or more runs batted in (4), 1987.

Established National League Championship Series records for highest slugging average (.917), most hits (10), most runs batted in (5), seven-game Series, 1987.

Year	Club	League	Pos.	G.	AB.	R.	H.	2B.	3B.	HR.	RBI.	B.A.	PO.	A.	E.	F.A.
1980	Houston	Nat.	PH-OF	3	3	0	0	0	0	0	0	.000	2	1	0	1.000
1987	San Francisco	Nat.	OF	7	24	5	10	0	0	4	5	.417	14	1	0	1.000
	Championship Series Totals—2 Years			10	27	5	10	0	0	4	5	.370	16	2	0	1.000

ALL-STAR GAME RECORD

Year League	Pos.	AB.	R.	H.	2B.	3B.	HR.	RBI.	B.A.	PO.	A.	E.	F.A.
1987—National	OF	2	0	0	0	0	0	0	.000	0	0	0	.000

DEREK JANSEN LILLIQUIST

Born February 20, 1966, at Winter Park, Fla.
Height, 6.00. Weight, 200.
Throws and bats lefthanded.
Attended University of Georgia, Athens, Ga.

Named lefthanded pitcher on THE SPORTING NEWS College Baseball All-America Team, 1987.

Year Club	League	G.	IP.	W.	L.	Pct.	H.	R.	ER.	SO.	BB.	ERA.
1987—Bradenton Braves	Gulf Coast	2	13	0	0	.000	3	0	0	16	2	0.00
1987—Durham	Carolina	3	25	2	1	.667	13	9	8	29	6	2.88
1988—Richmond	Int'national	28	170⅔	10	12	.455	179	70	64	80	36	3.38

Selected by Boston Red Sox' organization in 15th round of free-agent draft, June 4, 1984.
Selected by Atlanta Braves in 1st round (sixth player selected) of free-agent draft, June 2, 1987.

JOSE LIND (SALGADO)

Name pronounced Leend.

Born May 1, 1964, at Toabaja, P. R.
Height, 5.11. Weight, 170.
Throws and bats righthanded.
Brother of Orlando Lind, pitcher in Pittsburgh Pirates' organization; and cousin of Onix Concepcion, infielder with Kansas City Royals and Pittsburgh Pirates, 1980 through 1985 and 1987.

Major League stolen bases: 1987 (2), 1988 (15). Total—17.
Led Pacific Coast League second basemen in double plays with 84 and total chances with 764 in 1987.
Led Eastern League second basemen in total chances with 705 and double plays with 84 in 1986.

Year Club	League	Pos.	G.	AB.	R.	H.	2B.	3B.	HR.	RBI.	B.A.	PO.	A.	E.	F.A.
1983—Bradenton Pir.	Gulf C.	2B-SS	45	163	26	49	3	4	0	18	.301	102	125	9	.962
1984—Macon	S. Atl.	2B-SS	121	396	39	82	5	2	0	30	.207	271	306	32	.947
1985—Prince William	Carol.	2-S-3-O	105	377	42	104	9	4	0	28	.276	164	221	14	.965
1986—Nashua	East.	2B	134	•520	58	137	18	5	1	33	.263	★314	★378	13	★.982
1987—Vancouver	P. C.	2B	128	★533	75	143	16	3	3	30	.268	★311	★432	21	.973
1987—Pittsburgh	Nat.	2B	35	143	21	46	8	4	0	11	.322	53	139	1	.995
1988—Pittsburgh	Nat.	2B	154	611	82	160	24	4	2	49	.262	333	473	11	.987
Major League Totals—2 Years			189	754	103	206	32	8	2	60	.273	386	612	12	.988

Signed as free agent by Pittsburgh Pirates' organization, December 3, 1982.

JAMES WILLIAM LINDEMAN
(Jim)

Born January 10, 1962, at Evanston, Ill.
Height, 6.01. Weight, 200.
Throws and bats righthanded.
Attended Bradley University, Peoria, Ill.

Major League stolen bases: 1986 (1), 1987 (3). Total—4.

Year Club	League	Pos.	G.	AB.	R.	H.	2B.	3B.	HR.	RBI.	B.A.	PO.	A.	E.	F.A.
1983—St. Petersburg	Fla. St.	3B	70	232	45	64	13	1	8	37	.276	36	98	26	.838
1984—Springfield	Midw.	3B-SS	94	354	69	169	15	2	18	66	.271	78	175	30	.894
1984—Arkansas	Texas	3B	40	137	14	26	4	3	0	13	.190	26	67	6	.939
1985—Arkansas	Texas	3B	128	450	54	127	30	6	10	63	.282	74	238	24	.929
1986—Louisville	A. A.	1B-3B-OF	139	509	82	128	38	5	20	★96	.251	718	110	19	.978
1986—St. Louis	Nat.	1B-3B-OF	19	55	7	14	1	0	1	6	.255	118	10	1	.992
1987—St. Louis†	Nat.	OF-1B	75	207	20	43	13	0	8	28	.208	196	14	3	.986
1987—Louisville	A. A.	OF	20	78	11	24	3	1	4	10	.308	14	1	1	.938
1988—St. Louis‡	Nat.	OF-1B	17	43	3	9	1	0	2	7	.209	36	2	1	.974
1988—Louisville	A. A.	OF-1B	73	261	32	66	18	4	2	30	.253	308	23	4	.988
Major League Totals—3 Years			111	305	30	66	15	0	11	41	.216	350	26	5	.987

Selected by St. Louis Cardinals' organization in 1st round (24th player selected) of free-agent draft, June 6, 1983.
†On disabled list, May 12 to May 29 and June 4 to July 4, 1987; included rehabilitation disability assignment to Louisville, May 26 to May 29 and June 17 to July 4, 1987.
‡On disabled list, April 22 to July 5, 1988; included rehabilitation disability assignment to Louisville, June 16 to July 5, 1988.

CHAMPIONSHIP SERIES RECORD

Year Club	League	Pos.	G.	AB.	R.	H.	2B.	3B.	HR.	RBI.	B.A.	PO.	A.	E.	F.A.
1987—St. Louis	Nat.	1B-PH	5	13	1	4	0	0	1	3	.308	33	2	0	1.000

WORLD SERIES RECORD

Year Club	League	Pos.	G.	AB.	R.	H.	2B.	3B.	HR.	RBI.	B.A.	PO.	A.	E.	F.A.
1987—St. Louis	Nat.	1B-PH-O	6	15	3	5	1	0	0	2	.333	28	2	3	.909

NELSON ARTURO LIRIANO

Name pronounced Leer-EEE-anno.

Born June 3, 1964, at Puerto Plata, D. R.
Height, 5.10. Weight, 165.
Throws right and bats left and righthanded.

Major League stolen bases: 1987 (13), 1988 (12). Total—25.
Led International League second basemen in double plays with 96 and total chances with 611 in 1987.
Led Carolina League second basemen in double plays with 79 in 1985.

Year Club	League	Pos.	G.	AB.	R.	H.	2B.	3B.	HR.	RBI.	B.A.	PO.	A.	E.	F.A.
1983—Florence	S. Atl.	2B	129	478	87	124	24	5	6	57	.259	214	323	34	.940
1984—Kinston	Carol.	2B	132	*512	68	126	22	4	5	50	.246	260	*357	*21	.967
1985—Kinston	Carol.	2B	134	451	68	130	23	1	6	36	.288	*261	328	●25	.959
1986—Knoxville	South.	2B-3B-SS	135	557	88	159	25	*15	7	59	.285	239	324	22	.962
1987—Syracuse	Int.	2B	130	531	72	133	19	●10	10	55	.250	*246	*346	*19	.969
1987—Toronto	Amer.	2B	37	158	29	38	6	2	2	10	.241	83	107	1	.995
1988—Toronto	Amer.	2B-3B	99	276	36	73	6	2	3	23	.264	121	177	12	.961
1988—Syracuse	Int.	2B	8	31	2	6	1	1	0	1	.194	14	23	0	1.000
Major League Totals—2 Years			136	434	65	111	12	4	5	33	.256	204	284	13	.974

Signed as free agent by Toronto Blue Jays' organization, November 1, 1982.

PHILLIP ARDEN LOMBARDI
(Phil)

Born February 20, 1963, at Abilene, Tex.
Height, 6.02. Weight, 205.
Throws and bats righthanded.

Led Florida State League catchers in fielding percentage with .985 in 1984.

Year Club	League	Pos.	G.	AB.	R.	H.	2B.	3B.	HR.	RBI.	B.A.	PO.	A.	E.	F.A.
1981—Bradenton Yanks	Gulf C.	C	20	53	9	13	3	0	0	6	.245	94	17	4	.965
1982—Paintsville	Appal.	C	50	180	26	45	8	0	0	14	.250	323	*50	8	.979
1983—Greensboro	S. Atl.	C-OF	94	330	63	99	15	0	7	43	.300	564	52	14	.978
1983—Fort Lauderdale	Fla. St.	C	17	49	1	11	2	0	0	3	.224	77	6	5	.943
1984—Fort Lauderdale	Fla. St.	C-O-1-3	127	393	58	115	20	2	8	70	.293	669	61	14	.990
1985—Albany†	East.	C-O-3-S	76	250	44	64	13	2	5	32	.256	390	48	11	.976
1986—Columbus‡	Int.	C-OF	75	277	43	81	12	4	8	28	.292	222	16	7	.971
1986—New York	Amer.	OF-C	20	36	6	10	3	0	2	6	.278	22	3	3	.893
1987—Columbus	Int.	3B-OF-C	67	209	32	56	13	1	6	33	.268	101	55	15	.912
1987—Albany	East.	C	20	60	9	15	3	0	3	8	.250	29	7	1	.973
1987—New York§	Amer.	C	5	8	0	1	0	0	0	0	.125	7	1	0	1.000
1988—Tidewater x	Int.	OF-1B-C	85	292	49	90	14	0	9	44	.308	383	29	5	.988
Major League Totals—2 Years			25	44	6	11	3	0	2	6	.250	7	1	0	1.000

Selected by New York Yankees' organization in 3rd round of free-agent draft, June 8, 1981.
†On disabled list, July 20 to September 16, 1985.
‡On disabled list, June 19 to July 16, 1986.
§Traded with Outfielder Darren Reed and Pitcher Steve Frey to New York Mets for Shortstop Rafael Santana and Pitcher Victor Garcia, December 11, 1987.
xOn disabled list, July 18, 1988 through remainder of season.

STEPHEN PAUL LOMBARDOZZI
(Steve)

Born April 26, 1960, at Malden, Mass.
Height, 6.00. Weight, 183.
Throws and bats righthanded.
Attended Gulf Coast Community College, Panama City, Fla.,
and University of Florida, Gainesville, Fla.
Brother of Chris Lombardozzi, shortstop in New York Yankees' organization, 1985 through 1988.

Major League stolen bases: 1985 (3), 1986 (3), 1987 (5), 1988 (2). Total—13.
Led California League shortstops in fielding percentage with .947 in 1982.

Year Club	League	Pos.	G.	AB.	R.	H.	2B.	3B.	HR.	RBI.	B.A.	PO.	A.	E.	F.A.
1981—Elizabethton	Appal.	SS	65	246	48	79	13	2	6	38	.321	89	192	14	*.953
1982—Visalia	Calif.	SS-OF-P	122	441	81	131	24	1	6	67	.297	185	393	33	.946
1983—Orlando	South.	SS-2B	137	492	76	143	23	6	3	52	.291	203	364	33	.945
1984—Toledo	Int.	2B-SS	119	385	57	96	15	1	9	31	.249	237	310	14	.975
1985—Toledo	Int.	2B-3B-SS	118	451	55	119	21	3	14	48	.264	272	324	17	.972
1985—Minnesota	Amer.	2B	28	54	10	20	4	1	0	6	.370	31	80	2	.982
1986—Minnesota	Amer.	2B	156	453	53	103	20	5	8	33	.227	289	407	6	*.991
1987—Minnesota	Amer.	2B	136	432	51	103	19	3	8	38	.238	245	356	14	.977
1988—Minnesota	Amer.	2B-SS-3B	103	287	34	60	15	2	3	27	.209	152	237	5	.987
Major League Totals—4 Years			423	1226	148	286	58	11	19	104	.233	717	1080	27	.985

Selected by Minnesota Twins' organization in 9th round of free-agent draft, June 8, 1981.

CHAMPIONSHIP SERIES RECORD

Year Club	League	Pos.	G.	AB.	R.	H.	2B.	3B.	HR.	RBI.	B.A.	PO.	A.	E.	F.A.
1987—Minnesota	Amer.	2B-PR	5	15	2	4	7	0	0	1	.267	8	9	1	.944

WORLD SERIES RECORD

Year	Club	League	Pos.	G.	AB.	R.	H.	2B.	3B.	HR.	RBI.	B.A.	PO.	A.	E.	F.A.
1987	—Minnesota	Amer.	2B	6	17	3	7	1	0	1	4	.412	9	24	0	1.000

PITCHING RECORD

Year	Club	League	G.	IP.	W.	L.	Pct.	H.	R.	ER.	SO.	BB.	ERA.
1982	—Visalia	California	1	1	0	1	.000	5	4	4	2	0	36.00

WILLIAM DOUGLAS LONG
(Bill)

Born February 29, 1960, at Cincinnati, O.
Height, 6.00. Weight, 185.
Throws and bats righthanded.
Attended Miami University, Oxford, O.

Major League saves: 1987 (1), 1988 (2). Total—3.

Year	Club	League	G.	IP.	W.	L.	Pct.	H.	R.	ER.	SO.	BB.	ERA.
1981	—Salem	Carolina	14	87	9	2	.818	81	31	27	80	28	2.79
1982	—Amarillo	Texas	27	*198⅓	12	10	.545	*222	116	97	117	53	4.40
1983	—Las Vegas	P. Coast	18	62⅓	5	5	.500	99	66	53	41	28	7.65
1983	—Beaumont	Texas	10	65⅓	2	5	.286	80	47	41	33	28	5.65
1984	—Beaumont†	Texas	25	159⅔	•14	5	.737	149	56	52	114	67	2.93
1985	—Buffalo	Am. Assoc.	25	151⅓	*13	6	.684	146	69	59	71	43	3.51
1985	—Chicago	American	4	14	0	1	.000	25	17	16	13	5	10.29
1986	—Buffalo‡	Am. Assoc.	22	146	9	9	.500	159	73	63	86	44	3.88
1987	—Hawaii	P. Coast	2	13	2	0	1.000	15	7	6	6	4	4.15
1987	—Chicago	American	29	169	8	8	.500	179	85	82	72	28	4.37
1988	—Chicago	American	47	174	8	11	.421	187	89	78	77	43	4.03
Major League Totals—3 Years			80	357	16	20	.444	391	191	176	162	76	4.44

Selected by San Diego Padres' organization in 2nd round of free-agent draft, June 8, 1981.
†Traded with Pitcher Tim Lollar, Third Baseman Luis Salazar and Shortstop Ozzie Guillen to Chicago White Sox for Pitchers LaMarr Hoyt, Kevin Kristan and Todd Simmons, December 6, 1984.
‡On disabled list, May 12 to June 16, 1986.

VANCE ODELL LOVELACE

Born August 9, 1963, at Tampa, Fla.
Height, 6.05. Weight, 235.
Throws and bats lefthanded.

Led Florida State League in hit batsmen with 25, wild pitches with 25 and tied for lead in balks with 6 in 1983.

Year	Club	League	G.	IP.	W.	L.	Pct.	H.	R.	ER.	SO.	BB.	ERA.
1981	—Sarasota Cubs	Gulf Coast	7	30	0	5	.000	27	22	11	31	26	3.30
1982	—Quad Cities†‡	Midwest	21	94	4	6	.400	62	67	52	107	94	4.98
1983	—Vero Beach	Florida St.	24	115	8	10	.444	104	80	61	95	93	4.77
1984	—San Antonio§	Texas	16	65	3	7	.300	48	39	28	52	73	3.88
1985	—San Antonio	Texas	7	23⅔	0	4	.000	22	27	20	12	30	7.61
1985	—Vero Beach x	Florida St.	11	29⅓	1	2	.333	31	22	20	26	23	6.14
1986	—Midland	Texas	23	42⅓	2	4	.333	45	46	42	27	58	8.93
1986	—Palm Springs	California	6	17⅔	0	1	.000	21	23	18	16	30	9.17
1987	—Midland	Texas	53	83⅔	3	3	.500	73	40	30	91	60	3.23
1988	—Edmonton	P. Coast	46	69⅓	1	3	.250	79	48	47	56	57	6.10
1988	—California	American	3	1⅓	0	0	.000	2	2	2	0	3	13.50
Major League Totals—1 Year			3	1⅓	0	0	.000	2	2	2	0	3	13.50

Selected by Chicago Cubs' organization in 1st round (16th player selected) of free-agent draft, June 8, 1981.
†On disabled list, April 20 to May 6, 1982.
‡Traded with Outfielder Dan Cataline to Los Angeles Dodgers' organization for Third Baseman Ron Cey, January 19, 1983.
§On disabled list, April 28 to May 24, 1984.
xDrafted by California Angels' organization, December 11, 1985.

SALVATORE ANTHONY LOVULLO
(Torey)

Born July 25, 1965, at Santa Monica, Calif.
Height, 6.00. Weight, 180.
Throws right and bats left and righthanded.
Attended University of California, Los Angeles, Calif.

Named second baseman on THE SPORTING NEWS College Baseball All-America Team, 1987.

Year	Club	League	Pos.	G.	AB.	R.	H.	2B.	3B.	HR.	RBI.	B.A.	PO.	A.	E.	F.A.
1987	—Fayetteville	S. Atl.	3B-2B	55	191	34	49	13	0	8	32	.257	41	133	22	.888
1987	—Lakeland	Fla. St.	3B	18	60	11	16	3	0	1	16	.267	11	30	2	.953
1988	—Glens Falls	East.	3B-2B	78	270	37	74	17	1	9	50	.274	63	173	21	.918
1988	—Toledo	Int.	2B-3B-SS	57	177	18	41	8	1	5	20	.232	120	149	5	.982
1988	—Detroit	Amer.	2B-3B	12	21	2	8	1	1	1	2	.381	12	19	0	1.000
Major League Totals—1 Year				12	21	2	8	1	1	1	2	.381	12	19	0	1.000

Selected by Kansas City Royals' organization in 27th round of free-agent draft, June 2, 1986.
Selected by Detroit Tigers' organization in 5th round of free-agent draft, June 2, 1987.

DWIGHT LOWRY

Born October 23, 1957, in Robeson County, N. C.
Height, 6.03. Weight, 210.
Throws right and bats lefthanded.
Received degree in industrial relations from University of North Carolina, Chapel Hill, N. C.

Led Florida State League catchers in double plays with 8 in 1982.

Year Club	League	Pos.	G.	AB.	R.	H.	2B.	3B.	HR.	RBI.	B.A.	PO.	A.	E.	F.A.
1980—Lakeland	Fla. St.	C	45	142	18	28	5	0	0	16	.197	171	25	4	.980
1981—Birmingham	South.	C	19	52	3	8	2	0	0	4	.154	108	11	3	.975
1981—Macon	S. Atl.	C	67	231	30	58	6	0	2	32	.251	225	22	5	.980
1982—Lakeland	Fla. St.	C	93	278	33	77	11	2	7	28	.277	350	53	3	★.993
1983—Birmingham	South.	C-OF	90	288	42	77	9	2	9	44	.267	424	51	6	.988
1984—Detroit	Amer.	C	32	45	8	11	2	0	2	7	.244	87	8	0	1.000
1984—Evansville	A. A.	C	61	177	23	39	5	1	5	28	.220	240	45	6	.979
1985—Nashville	A. A.	C	74	203	20	37	7	1	2	13	.182	318	45	12	.968
1986—Nashville	A. A.	C-1B	18	57	5	14	1	0	1	6	.246	91	6	1	.990
1986—Detroit	Amer.	C-1B-OF	56	150	21	46	4	0	3	18	.307	250	17	2	.993
1987—Detroit	Amer.	C-1B	13	25	0	5	2	0	0	1	.200	40	2	0	1.000
1987—Toledo†	Int.	C-1B	42	93	8	18	3	0	0	3	.194	107	13	3	.976
1988—Minnesota	Amer.	C	7	7	0	0	0	0	0	0	.000	12	1	0	1.000
1988—Portland‡	P. C.	C-1B	79	244	33	63	13	3	5	32	.258	246	25	8	.971
Major League Totals—4 Years			108	227	29	62	8	0	5	26	.273	389	28	2	.995

Selected by Detroit Tigers' organization in 11th round of free-agent draft, June 3, 1980.
†Released, October 16, 1987; signed by Minnesota Twins, October 23, 1987.
‡Granted free agency, October 15, 1988.

RICHARD FRED LUECKEN
(Rick)

Born November 15, 1960, at McAllen, Tex.
Height, 6.06. Weight, 210.
Throws and bats righthanded.
Attended Texas A&M University, College Station, Tex.

Year Club	League	G.	IP.	W.	L.	Pct.	H.	R.	ER.	SO.	BB.	ERA.
1983—Bellingham	Northwest	14	78⅓	5	4	.556	70	39	31	83	37	3.56
1984—Chattanooga	Southern	26	163⅔	11	★13	.458	166	85	69	90	88	3.79
1985—Calgary†	P. Coast	18	111	4	8	.333	111	70	66	44	39	6.93
1986—Chattanooga‡§	Southern	17	88⅔	6	7	.462	106	57	52	55	42	5.28
1987—Memphis	Southern	28	146	9	9	.500	163	86	77	88	53	4.75
1988—Memphis	Southern	21	24⅔	4	1	.800	17	8	6	30	7	2.19
1988—Omaha	Am. Assoc.	26	40	5	0	1.000	45	10	9	27	15	2.03

Selected by San Francisco Giants' organization in 1st round (18th player selected) of free-agent draft, June 5, 1979.
Selected by Cincinnati Reds' organization in 12th round of free-agent draft, June 7, 1982.
Selected by Seattle Mariners' organization in 27th round of free-agent draft, June 6, 1983.
†On disabled list, April 11 to April 25, June 9 to July 2 and August 20, 1985 through remainder of season.
‡On disabled list, June 18 to August 14, 1986.
§Traded with Outfielder Danny Tartabull to Kansas City Royals for Pitchers Scott Bankhead and Steve Shields and Outfielder Mike Kingery, December 10, 1986.

URBANO RAFAEL LUGO

Born August 12, 1962, at Falcon, Venezuela.
Height, 5.11. Weight, 197.
Throws and bats righthanded.
Son of Urbano Lugo, pitcher in Mexican League, 1967 through 1970 and 1973.

Year Club	League	G.	IP.	W.	L.	Pct.	H.	R.	ER.	SO.	BB.	ERA.
1982—Danville	Midwest	10	24	0	2	.000	35	30	27	13	16	10.13
1982—Salem	Northwest	14	90⅔	7	3	.700	74	45	29	62	61	2.88
1983—Peoria	Midwest	15	107	8	5	.615	82	39	30	96	28	2.52
1983—Redwood	California	11	64⅔	5	5	.500	59	36	28	58	31	3.90
1984—Waterbury	Eastern	24	164⅓	13	8	.619	135	63	51	117	68	2.79
1985—Edmonton	P. Coast	4	25⅔	2	0	1.000	20	14	13	19	14	4.56
1985—California†	American	20	83	3	4	.429	86	36	34	42	29	3.69
1986—Midland‡	Texas	2	11	1	1	.500	9	2	2	4	4	1.64
1986—Edmonton	P. Coast	16	100⅓	8	6	.571	110	58	52	53	41	4.66
1986—California	American	6	21⅓	1	1	.500	21	9	9	9	6	3.80
1987—California	American	7	28	0	2	.000	42	34	29	24	18	9.32
1987—Edmonton	P. Coast	15	90⅔	4	3	.571	89	46	37	47	46	3.67
1988—Edmonton	P. Coast	38	116⅓	9	6	.600	148	74	68	69	47	5.26
1988—California	American	1	2	0	0	.000	2	2	2	1	1	9.00
Major League Totals—4 Years		34	134⅓	4	7	.364	151	81	74	76	54	4.96

Signed as free agent by California Angels' organization, January 31, 1982.
†On disabled list, August 22 to September 6, 1985.
‡On California disabled list, March 31 to June 5, 1986; included rehabilitation disability assignment to Midland, May 15 to June 4, 1986.

SCOTT EDWARD LUSADER

Named pronounced Loo-SAY-der.

Born September 30, 1964, at Chicago, Ill.
Height, 5.10. Weight, 165.
Throws and bats lefthanded.
Received bachelor of science degree in marketing
from University of Florida, Gainesville, Fla.

Major League stolen bases: 1987 (1).

Year	Club	League	Pos.	G.	AB.	R.	H.	2B.	3B.	HR.	RBI.	B.A.	PO.	A.	E.	F.A.
1985	Lakeland	Fla. St.	OF	27	97	16	28	5	1	2	22	.289	47	3	3	.943
1985	Birmingham	South.	OF	21	77	13	26	3	4	2	14	.338	49	1	0	1.000
1986	Glens Falls	East.	OF	136	479	74	134	23	3	11	59	.280	275	13	•11	.963
1987	Toledo	Int.	OF	136	505	78	136	29	8	17	80	.269	274	11	6	.979
1987	Detroit	Amer.	OF	23	47	8	15	3	1	1	8	.319	29	0	1	.967
1988	Toledo	Int.	OF-1B	89	329	38	86	11	5	4	46	.261	193	0	3	.985
1988	Detroit	Amer.	OF	16	16	3	1	0	0	1	3	.063	7	0	0	1.000
Major League Totals—2 Years				39	63	11	16	3	1	2	11	.254	36	0	1	.973

Selected by Detroit Tigers' organization in 6th round of free-agent draft, June 3, 1985.

FREDRIC MICHAEL LYNN
(Fred)

Born February 3, 1952, at Chicago, Ill.
Height, 6.01. Weight, 190.
Throws and bats lefthanded.
Attended University of Southern California, Los Angeles, Calif.

Established American League record for most doubles, rookie season (47), 1975.
Tied American League record for most total bases, game (16), June 18, 1975.
Major League stolen bases: 1975 (10), 1976 (14), 1977 (2), 1978 (3), 1979 (2), 1980 (12), 1981 (1), 1982 (7), 1983 (2), 1984 (2), 1985 (7), 1986 (2), 1987 (3), 1988 (2). Total—69.
Hit three home runs in a game, June 18, 1975.
Hit for the cycle, May 13, 1980.
Led American League in slugging percentage with .566 in 1975 and .637 in 1979.
Named American League Player of the Year by THE SPORTING NEWS, 1975.
Named American League Most Valuable Player by Baseball Writers' Association of America, 1975.
Named American League Rookie of the Year by Baseball Writers' Association of America, 1975.
Named American League Rookie Player of the Year by THE SPORTING NEWS, 1975.
Named outfielder on THE SPORTING NEWS American League All-Star Team, 1975, 1978 and 1979.
Named outfielder on THE SPORTING NEWS American League All-Star fielding team, 1975 and 1978 through 1980.
Received reported $40,000 bonus to sign with Boston Red Sox, 1973.
Named outfielder on THE SPORTING NEWS College Baseball All-America Team, 1972 and 1973.

Year	Club	League	Pos.	G.	AB.	R.	H.	2B.	3B.	HR.	RBI.	B.A.	PO.	A.	E.	F.A.
1973	Bristol	East.	OF	53	162	26	42	9	4	6	36	.259	79	3	5	.943
1974	Pawtucket	Int.	OF	124	415	65	117	19	2	21	68	.282	247	12	7	.974
1974	Boston	Amer.	OF	15	43	5	18	2	2	2	10	.419	18	2	0	1.000
1975	Boston	Amer.	OF	145	528	*103	175	*47	7	21	105	.331	404	11	7	.983
1976	Boston	Amer.	OF	132	507	76	159	32	8	10	65	.314	367	13	6	.984
1977	Boston†	Amer.	OF	129	497	81	129	29	5	18	76	.260	333	7	2	.994
1978	Boston	Amer.	OF	150	541	75	161	33	3	22	82	.298	408	11	7	.984
1979	Boston	Amer.	OF	147	531	116	177	42	1	39	122	*.333	381	10	5	.987
1980	Boston‡	Amer.	OF	110	415	67	125	32	3	12	61	.301	302	11	2	.994
1981	California	Amer.	OF	76	256	28	56	8	1	5	31	.219	176	4	4	.978
1982	California	Amer.	OF	138	472	89	141	38	1	21	86	.299	317	6	3	.991
1983	California	Amer.	OF	117	437	56	119	20	3	22	74	.272	274	8	2	.993
1984	California§	Amer.	OF	142	517	84	140	28	4	23	79	.271	321	12	6	.982
1985	Baltimore	Amer.	OF	124	448	59	118	12	1	23	68	.263	314	6	2	.994
1986	Baltimore x	Amer.	OF	112	397	67	114	13	1	23	67	.287	244	2	4	.984
1987	Baltimore y	Amer.	OF	111	396	49	100	24	0	23	60	.253	229	2	2	.991
1988	Balt. za-Det	Amer.	OF	114	391	46	96	14	1	25	56	.246	257	3	2	.992
Major League Totals—15 Years				1762	6376	1001	1828	374	41	289	1042	.287	4345	108	54	.988

Selected by New York Yankees' organization in 3rd round of free-agent draft, June 4, 1970.
Selected by Boston Red Sox' organization in 2nd round of free-agent draft, June 5, 1973.
†On disabled list, March 24 to May 6, 1977.
‡Traded with Pitcher Steve Renko to California Angels for Pitchers Frank Tanana and Jim Dorsey and Outfielder Joe Rudi, January 23, 1981.
§Granted free agency, November 8, 1984; signed by Baltimore Orioles, December 11, 1984. (Pitcher Donnie Moore selected from player compensation pool by California Angels, January 24, 1985.)
xOn disabled list, June 11 to June 27, 1986.
yOn disabled list, July 21 to August 5, 1987.
zOn disabled list, July 15 to August 12, 1988.
aTraded to Detroit Tigers for three players to be named later, August 31, 1988; Baltimore Orioles acquired Catcher Chris Hoiles and Pitchers Cesar Mejia and Robinson Garces to complete deal, September 9, 1988.

CHAMPIONSHIP SERIES RECORD

Established Championship Series record for highest batting average, five-game Series (.611), 1982.
Tied Championship Series records for most hits, five-game Series (11), 1982; most one-base hits, five-game Series (8), 1982.
Tied American League Championship Series record for most hits, two consecutive Series (15), 1975 and 1982.

Year	Club	League	Pos.	G.	AB.	R.	H.	2B.	3B.	HR.	RBI.	B.A.	PO.	A.	E.	F.A.
1975—Boston		Amer.	OF	3	11	1	4	1	0	0	3	.364	12	1	1	.929
1982—California		Amer.	OF	5	18	5	11	2	0	1	5	.611	16	0	1	.941
Championship Series Totals—2 Years				8	29	6	15	3	0	1	8	.517	28	1	2	.935

WORLD SERIES RECORD

Tied World Series record for highest fielding average by outfielder, seven-game Series (1.000 with 24 chances), 1975.

Year	Club	League	Pos.	G.	AB.	R.	H.	2B.	3B.	HR.	RBI.	B.A.	PO.	A.	E.	F.A.
1975—Boston		Amer.	OF	7	25	3	7	1	0	1	5	.280	23	1	0	1.000

ALL-STAR GAME RECORD

Hit only All-Star Game home run with bases loaded, July 6, 1983.
Established All-Star Game record for most runs batted in, inning (4), July 6, 1983.

Year	League	Pos.	AB.	R.	H.	2B.	3B.	HR.	RBI.	B.A.	PO.	A.	E.	F.A.
1975—American		PH-OF	2	0	0	0	0	0	0	.000	1	0	0	1.000
1976—American		OF	3	1	1	0	0	1	1	.333	0	0	0	1.000
1977—American		OF	1	1	0	0	0	0	0	.000	2	0	0	1.000
1978—American		OF	4	0	1	0	0	0	0	.250	3	0	0	1.000
1979—American		OF	1	1	1	0	0	1	2	1.000	0	0	0	.000
1980—American		OF	3	1	1	0	0	1	2	.333	2	0	0	1.000
1981—American		PH	1	0	1	0	0	0	1	1.000	0	0	0	.000
1982—American		OF	2	0	0	0	0	0	0	.000	0	0	0	.000
1983—American		OF	3	1	1	0	0	1	4	.333	1	0	0	1.000
All-Star Game Totals—9 Years			20	5	6	0	0	4	10	.300	9	0	0	1.000

BARRY STEPHEN LYONS

Born June 3, 1960, at Biloxi, Miss.
Height, 6.01. Weight, 205.
Throws and bats righthanded.
Attended Delta State University, Cleveland, Miss.

Led Texas League in grounding into double plays with 19 and tied for lead in game-winning RBIs with 16 in 1985.
Led Texas League catchers in errors with 19 in 1985.
Led Carolina League catchers in assists with 72 and fielding percentage with .989 in 1984.
Named Carolina League Player of the Year, 1984.

Year	Club	League	Pos.	G.	AB.	R.	H.	2B.	3B.	HR.	RBI.	B.A.	PO.	A.	E.	F.A.
1982—Shelby		S. Atl.	C-1B	45	164	23	46	12	0	4	46	.280	226	21	8	.969
1983—Lynchburg		Carol.	C	2	7	0	1	0	0	0	2	.143	21	4	0	1.000
1983—Columbia		S. Atl.	C-1B-OF	92	316	55	94	9	2	5	45	.297	387	33	17	.961
1984—Lynchburg		Carol.	C-1B-OF	115	412	59	130	17	3	12	87	.316	894	86	13	.987
1985—Jackson		Texas	C-1B	126	486	69	149	34	6	11	108	.307	834	65	23	.975
1986—New York		Nat.	C	6	9	1	0	0	0	0	2	.000	16	0	1	.941
1986—Tidewater†		Int.	1B-C	61	234	28	69	16	0	4	46	.295	423	25	6	.987
1987—New York		Nat.	C	53	130	15	33	4	1	4	24	.254	223	17	4	.984
1988—New York		Nat.	C-1B	50	91	5	21	7	1	0	11	.231	130	9	3	.979
Major League Totals—3 Years				109	230	21	54	11	2	4	37	.235	369	26	8	.980

Selected by Detroit Tigers' organization in 25th round of free-agent draft, June 8, 1981.
Selected by New York Mets' organization in 15th round of free-agent draft, June 7, 1982.
†On disabled list, August 4, 1986 through remainder of season.

STEPHEN JOHN LYONS
(Steve)

Born June 3, 1960, at Tacoma, Wash.
Height, 6.03. Weight, 195.
Throws right and bats lefthanded.
Attended Oregon State University, Corvallis, Ore.

Major League stolen bases: 1985 (12), 1986 (4), 1987 (3), 1988 (1). Total—20.
Led American League third basemen in double plays with 36 in 1988.
Led International League third basemen in putouts with 98, errors with 25 and total chances with 332 in 1984.

Year	Club	League	Pos.	G.	AB.	R.	H.	2B.	3B.	HR.	RBI.	B.A.	PO.	A.	E.	F.A.
1981—Winston-Salem		Carol.	OF-SS	64	252	43	61	9	3	6	40	.242	137	23	8	.952
1982—Bristol		East.	OF-SS	135	460	86	112	23	3	13	58	.243	275	11	9	.969
1983—New Britain		East.	3-O-S-P	132	456	83	112	24	7	7	62	.246	145	207	17	.954
1984—Pawtucket		Int.	3B-OF-SS	131	444	80	119	21	2	17	62	.268	141	211	26	.931
1985—Boston		Amer.	OF-3B-SS	133	371	52	98	14	3	5	30	.264	253	6	7	.974
1986—Bos.†-Chi.		Amer.	OF-3B-1B	101	247	30	56	9	3	1	20	.227	175	11	4	.979
1986—Buffalo		A. A.	3-S-O-1	20	74	18	22	5	1	3	8	.297	36	41	4	.951
1987—Chicago		Amer.	3B-OF-2B	76	193	26	54	11	1	1	19	.280	69	101	4	.977
1987—Hawaii		P. C.	O-2-3-S	47	167	26	48	11	0	2	16	.285	73	71	3	.980
1988—Chicago		Amer.	3-O-2-C-1	146	472	59	127	28	3	5	45	.269	128	243	29	.928
Major League Totals—4 Years				456	1283	167	335	62	10	12	114	.261	625	361	44	.957

Selected by Boston Red Sox' organization in 1st round (19th player selected) of free-agent draft, June 8, 1981.
†Traded to Chicago White Sox for Pitcher Tom Seaver, June 29, 1986.

PITCHING RECORD

Year	Club	League	G.	IP.	W.	L.	Pct.	H.	R.	ER.	SO.	BB.	ERA.
1983—New Britain		Eastern	3	3⅔	1	0	1.000	3	1	1	2	1	2.45

KEVIN CHRISTIAN MAAS

Born January 20, 1965, at Castro Valley, Calif.
Height, 6.03. Weight, 195.
Throws and bats lefthanded.
Attended University of California, Berkeley, Calif.
Brother of Jason Maas, outfielder-third baseman
in New York Yankees' organization.

Year Club	League	Pos.	G.	AB.	R.	H.	2B.	3B.	HR.	RBI.	B.A.	PO.	A.	E.	F.A.
1986—Oneonta	NYP	1B	28	101	14	36	10	0	0	18	.356	222	19	1	.996
1987—Fort Lauderdale	Fla. St.	1B	116	439	77	122	28	4	11	73	.278	667	51	10	.986
1988—Prince William	Carol.	1B	29	108	24	32	7	0	12	35	.296	288	25	5	.984
1988—Albany	East.	1B	109	372	66	98	14	3	16	55	.263	902	73	12	.988

Selected by New York Yankees' organization in 22nd round of free-agent draft, June 2, 1986.

MICHAEL ANDREW MACFARLANE
(Mike)

Born April 12, 1964, at Stockton, Calif.
Height, 6.01. Weight, 200.
Throws and bats righthanded.
Attended University of Santa Clara, Santa Clara, Calif.

Year Club	League	Pos.	G.	AB.	R.	H.	2B.	3B.	HR.	RBI.	B.A.	PO.	A.	E.	F.A.
1985—Memphis	South.	C	65	223	29	60	15	4	8	39	.269	295	24	9	.973
1986—Memphis†	South.	DH	40	141	26	34	7	2	12	29	.241	0	0	0	.000
1987—Omaha	A. A.	C	87	302	53	79	25	1	13	50	.262	408	37	6	.987
1987—Kansas City	Amer.	C	8	19	0	4	1	0	0	3	.211	29	2	0	1.000
1988—Kansas City	Amer.	C	70	211	25	56	15	0	4	26	.265	309	18	2	.994
1988—Omaha	A. A.	C	21	76	8	18	7	2	2	8	.237	85	5	1	.989
Major League Totals—2 Years			78	230	25	60	16	0	4	29	.261	338	20	2	.994

Selected by Kansas City Royals' organization in 4th round of free-agent draft, June 3, 1985.
†On disabled list, April 9 to July 9, 1986.

SHANE LEE MACK

Born December 7, 1963, at Los Angeles, Calif.
Height, 6.00. Weight, 185.
Throws and bats righthanded.
Attended University of California, Los Angeles, Calif.

Major League stolen bases: 1987 (4), 1988 (5). Total—9.
Tied for Texas League lead in being hit by pitch with 7 in 1986.
Led Texas League outfielders in double plays with 4 in 1986.
Member of 1984 U.S. Olympic baseball team.
Named outfielder on THE SPORTING NEWS College Baseball All-America Team, 1984.

Year Club	League	Pos.	G.	AB.	R.	H.	2B.	3B.	HR.	RBI.	B.A.	PO.	A.	E.	F.A.
1985—Beaumont	Texas	OF-3B	125	430	59	112	23	3	6	55	.260	252	12	7	.974
1986—Beaumont	Texas	OF	115	452	61	127	26	3	15	68	.281	255	•14	8	.971
1986—Las Vegas	P. C.	OF	19	69	13	25	1	6	0	6	.362	43	0	2	.956
1987—Las Vegas	P. C.	OF	39	152	38	51	11	1	5	26	.336	97	3	1	.990
1987—San Diego	Nat.	OF	105	238	28	57	11	3	4	25	.239	159	1	3	.982
1988—Las Vegas	P. C.	OF	55	196	43	68	7	1	10	40	.347	116	7	3	.976
1988—San Diego	Nat.	OF	56	119	13	29	3	0	0	12	.244	110	4	2	.983
Major League Totals—2 Years			161	357	41	86	14	3	4	37	.241	269	5	5	.982

Selected by Kansas City Royals' organization in 4th round of free-agent draft, June 8, 1981.
Selected by San Diego Padres' organization in 1st round (11th player selected) of free-agent draft, June 4, 1984.

MORRIS DeWAYNE MADDEN

Born August 31, 1960, at Laurens, S. C.
Height, 6.00. Weight, 165.
Throws and bats lefthanded.
Attended Spartanburg Methodist College, Spartanburg, S. C.

Year Club	League	G.	IP.	W.	L.	Pct.	H.	R.	ER.	SO.	BB.	ERA.
1979—Lethbridge	Pioneer	13	83	6	1	.857	62	44	27	106	45	2.93
1980—Vero Beach	Florida St.	27	171	11	9	.550	129	79	64	141	★127	3.37
1981—San Antonio	Texas	4	11	0	3	.000	22	17	17	6	14	13.91
1981—Vero Beach	Florida St.	21	146	6	12	.333	148	76	60	108	79	3.70
1982—San Antonio	Texas	4	19	1	1	.500	26	19	18	18	15	8.53
1982—Lodi†	California	12	72⅔	3	7	.300	67	32	21	47	36	2.60
1983—Vero Beach	Florida St.	16	46	2	4	.333	50	33	22	44	25	4.30
1983—San Antonio‡	Texas	27	72⅓	6	5	.545	77	49	44	60	59	5.47
1984—Tampa	Florida St.	29	132	6	9	.400	123	71	64	103	98	4.36
1985—Tampa	Florida St.	23	82⅓	6	8	.429	76	48	31	78	64	3.39
1985—Vermont§	Eastern	6	32⅓	1	3	.250	25	11	11	31	19	3.06
1986—Glens Falls	Eastern	35	91⅓	7	5	.583	87	52	41	64	55	4.04
1987—Toledo	Int'national	24	58⅓	4	2	.667	58	37	29	41	36	4.47
1987—Detroit x	American	2	1⅔	0	0	.000	4	3	3	0	3	16.20
1987—Vancouver	P. Coast	6	7⅓	0	0	.000	8	8	7	4	10	8.59
1988—Buffalo	Am. Assoc.	21	108⅔	5	6	.455	84	55	42	56	65	3.48

Year	Club	League	G.	IP.	W.	L.	Pct.	H.	R.	ER.	SO.	BB.	ERA.
1988	Pittsburgh	National	5	5⅔	0	0	.000	5	0	0	3	7	0.00
	Major League Totals—2 Years		7	7⅓	0	0	.000	9	3	3	3	10	3.68

Selected by Los Angeles Dodgers' organization in 24th round of free-agent draft, June 5, 1979.

†On disabled list, May 22 to July 4, 1982.

‡Drafted by Indianapolis (Cincinnati Reds' organization), December 6, 1983.

§Granted free agency, October 15, 1985; signed by Nashville (Detroit Tigers' organization), November 23, 1985.

xTraded to Pittsburgh Pirates' organization, August 12, 1987, completing deal in which Pittsburgh traded Third Baseman Jim Morrison to Detroit Tigers for Third Baseman Darnell Coles and a player to be named later, August 7, 1987.

GREGORY ALAN MADDUX
(Greg)

Born April 14, 1966, at San Angelo, Tex.
Height, 6.00. Weight, 170.
Throws and bats righthanded.
Brother of Mike Maddux, pitcher with Philadelphia Phillies.

Led National League in intentional bases on balls issued with 16 in 1988.
Led American Association in hit batsmen with 12 in 1986.
Led Appalachian League in hit batsmen with 8 and tied for lead in shutouts with 2 in 1984.
Tied for American Association lead in shutouts with 2 in both 1986 and 1987.

Year	Club	League	G.	IP.	W.	L.	Pct.	H.	R.	ER.	SO.	BB.	ERA.
1984	Pikeville	Ap'lachian	14	85⅔	6	2	.750	63	35	25	62	41	2.63
1985	Peoria	Midland	27	186	13	9	.591	176	86	66	125	52	3.19
1986	Pittsfield	Eastern	8	62⅔	4	3	.571	49	22	19	35	15	2.69
1986	Iowa	Am. Assoc.	18	128⅓	10	1	*.909	127	49	43	65	30	3.02
1986	Chicago	National	6	31	2	4	.333	44	20	19	20	11	5.52
1987	Chicago	National	30	155⅔	6	14	.300	181	111	97	101	74	5.61
1987	Iowa	Am. Assoc.	4	27⅔	3	0	1.000	17	3	3	22	12	0.98
1988	Chicago	National	34	249	18	8	.692	230	97	88	140	81	3.18
	Major League Totals—3 Years		70	435⅔	26	26	.500	455	228	204	261	166	4.21

Selected by Chicago Cubs' organization in 2nd round of free-agent draft, June 4, 1984.

ALL-STAR GAME RECORD

Member of National League All-Star team in 1988; did not play.

MICHAEL AUSLEY MADDUX
(Mike)

Born August 27, 1961, at Dayton, O.
Height, 6.02. Weight, 180.
Throws and bats righthanded.
Attended University of Texas, El Paso, Tex.
Brother of Greg Maddux, pitcher with Chicago Cubs.

Year	Club	League	G.	IP.	W.	L.	Pct.	H.	R.	ER.	SO.	BB.	ERA.
1982	Bend	Northwest	11	65⅓	3	6	.333	68	35	29	59	26	3.99
1983	Spartanburg	S. Atlantic	13	84⅓	4	6	.400	98	62	51	85	47	5.44
1983	Peninsula	Carolina	14	99⅓	8	4	.667	92	46	40	78	35	3.62
1983	Reading	Eastern	1	3	0	0	.000	4	2	2	2	1	6.00
1984	Reading	Eastern	20	116	3	•12	.200	143	82	65	77	49	5.04
1984	Portland	P. Coast	8	44⅔	2	4	.333	58	32	29	22	17	5.84
1985	Portland	P. Coast	27	166	9	12	.429	195	106	98	96	51	5.31
1986	Portland	P. Coast	12	84	5	2	.714	70	26	22	65	22	2.36
1986	Philadelphia	National	16	78	3	7	.300	88	56	47	44	34	5.42
1987	Maine	Int'national	18	103⅓	6	6	.500	116	58	50	71	26	4.35
1987	Philadelphia	National	7	17	2	0	1.000	17	5	5	15	5	2.65
1988	Philadelphia†	National	25	88⅔	4	3	.571	91	41	37	59	34	3.76
1988	Maine	Int'national	5	23⅔	0	2	.000	25	18	11	18	10	4.18
	Major League Totals—3 Years		48	183⅔	9	10	.474	196	102	89	118	73	4.36

Selected by Cincinnati Reds' organization in 36th round of free-agent draft, June 5, 1979.

Selected by Philadelphia Phillies' organization in 5th round of free-agent draft, June 7, 1982.

†On disabled list, April 21 to June 1, 1988; included rehabilitation disability assignment to Maine, May 13 to May 22, 1988.

CHARLES SCOTT MADISON
(Scotti)

Born September 12, 1959, at Pensacola, Fla.
Height, 5.11. Weight, 185.
Throws right and bats left and righthanded.

Received bachelor of science degree in business administration from Vanderbilt University, Nashville, Tenn.

Major League stolen bases: 1988 (1).
Led American Association in slugging percentage with .590 in 1985.
Named catcher on THE SPORTING NEWS College Baseball All-America Team, 1980.

Year	Club	League	Pos.	G.	AB.	R.	H.	2B.	3B.	HR.	RBI.	B.A.	PO.	A.	E.	F.A.
1980	Orlando	South.	C-1B-OF	81	282	31	65	9	4	6	32	.230	185	24	4	.981
1981	Visalia†	Calif.	*C-1B	133	459	109	157	*32	3	26	110	.342	542	66	11	*.982

Year Club	League	Pos.	G.	AB.	R.	H.	2B.	3B.	HR.	RBI.	B.A.	PO.	A.	E.	F.A.
1982—San Antonio‡	Texas	3-C-2-O	88	294	39	69	11	2	7	35	.235	167	75	16	.938
1982—Albuquerque	P. C.	C	11	36	5	8	1	0	0	2	.222	6	0	0	1.000
1983—San Antonio	Texas	C-3B	80	259	54	79	11	4	11	57	.305	423	55	11	.978
1983—Albuquerque§	P. C.	C-3B	23	65	10	19	2	0	2	12	.292	103	18	7	.945
1984—Birmingham	South.	C-1-3-2	133	473	82	129	23	4	15	83	.273	773	109	18	.980
1985—Birmingham	South	C-1B-3B	37	121	28	39	8	1	5	25	.322	205	27	2	.991
1985—Nashville	A. A.	C-3-1-O	86	317	59	108	23	4	16	54	*.341	352	74	11	.975
1985—Detroit	Amer.	C	6	11	0	0	0	0	0	1	.000	1	0	0	1.000
1986—Detroit x	Amer.	3B	2	7	0	0	0	0	0	1	.000	1	1	1	.667
1986—Nashville yz	A. A.	1-3-C-O	106	354	52	91	15	4	10	41	.257	425	95	10	.981
1987—Omaha	A. A.	3-1-C-O-2	125	454	68	123	31	2	22	83	.271	375	149	14	.974
1987—Kansas City	Amer.	1B-C	7	15	4	4	3	0	0	0	.267	28	3	3	.912
1988—Kansas City	Amer.	C-OF-1B	16	35	4	6	2	0	0	2	.171	23	1	0	1.000
1988—Omaha a	A. A.	O-1-C-3	36	104	14	25	4	3	2	12	.240	107	15	1	.992
Major League Totals—4 Years			31	68	8	10	5	0	0	4	.147	53	5	4	.935

Selected by Cincinnati Reds' organization in 35th round of free-agent draft, June 8, 1976.
Selected by San Francisco Giants' organization in 10th round of free-agent draft, June 5, 1979.
Selected by Minnesota Twins' organization in 3rd round of free-agent draft, June 3, 1980.
†Traded with Pitcher Paul Voigt to Los Angeles Dodgers' organization for Pitcher Bobby Castillo and Outfielder Bobby Mitchell, January 7, 1982.
‡On disabled list, June 25 to July 16, 1982.
§Sold to Birmingham (Detroit Tigers' organization), March 19, 1984.
xOn disabled list, March 26 to April 29, 1986.
yOn suspended list, May 15 to May 17, 1986.
zGranted free agency, October 15, 1986; signed by Kansas City Royals' organization, November 14, 1986.
aGranted free agency, October 15, 1988.

ALEXANDER MADRID JR.
(Alex)

Born April 18, 1963, at Springerville, Ariz.
Height, 6.02. Weight, 200.
Throws and bats righthanded.
Attended Yavapai College, Prescott, Ariz.

Tied for Texas League lead in games started by pitchers with 27 and balks with 6 in 1986.

Year Club	League	G.	IP.	W.	L.	Pct.	H.	R.	ER.	SO.	BB.	ERA.
1984—Beloit†	Midwest	22	118	6	7	.462	113	59	55	92	49	4.19
1985—Beloit	Midwest	19	135$\frac{2}{3}$	8	5	.615	144	55	43	99	26	2.85
1985—Stockton	California	8	59$\frac{1}{3}$	7	0	1.000	53	16	13	52	15	1.97
1986—El Paso	Texas	27	158$\frac{1}{3}$	12	9	.571	*213	*119	*106	99	51	6.03
1987—Denver	Am. Assoc.	27	99$\frac{1}{3}$	5	7	.417	114	64	59	50	31	5.35
1987—Milwaukee	American	3	5$\frac{1}{3}$	0	0	.000	11	9	9	1	1	15.19
1988—Denver‡	Am. Assoc.	31	88$\frac{2}{3}$	5	2	.714	95	47	40	52	20	4.06
1988—Maine	Int'national	2	11$\frac{2}{3}$	0	0	.000	10	3	3	9	0	2.31
1988—Philadelphia	National	5	16$\frac{1}{3}$	1	1	.500	15	5	5	2	6	2.76
American League Totals—1 Year		3	5$\frac{1}{3}$	0	0	.000	11	9	9	1	1	15.19
National League Totals—1 Year		5	16$\frac{1}{3}$	1	1	.500	15	5	5	2	6	2.76
Major League Totals—2 Years		8	21$\frac{2}{3}$	1	1	.500	26	14	14	3	7	5.82

Selected by Chicago Cubs' organization in 2nd round of free-agent draft, January 12, 1982.
Selected by Cincinnati Reds' organization in secondary phase of free-agent draft, June 7, 1982.
Selected by Texas Rangers' organization in secondary phase of free-agent draft, January 11, 1983.
Selected by Milwaukee Brewers' organization in secondary phase of free-agent draft, June 6, 1983.
†On disabled list, June 15 to June 29, 1984.
‡Traded to Philadelphia Phillies for Outfielder Mike Young, August 24, 1988.

DAVID JOSEPH MAGADAN
(Dave)

Born September 30, 1962, at Tampa, Fla.
Height, 6.03. Weight, 195.
Throws right and bats lefthanded.
Attended University of Alabama, University, Ala.
Cousin of Lou Piniella, outfielder with Baltimore Orioles, Cleveland Indians, Kansas City Royals and New York Yankees, 1964 and 1968 through 1984; coach, New York Yankees, June 25, 1984 through 1985; manager, New York Yankees, 1986, 1987 and June 23, 1988 through remainder of season; and General Manager of New York Yankees, beginning of 1988 through June 22, 1988.

Led Texas League in bases on balls received with 106 in 1985.
Led Carolina League in intentional bases on balls received with 10 in 1984.
Led International League third basemen in fielding percentage with .934, assists with 283 and double plays with 31 in 1986.
Led Texas League third basemen in putouts with 87, assists with 275 and total chances with 393 in 1985.
Named designated hitter on THE SPORTING NEWS College Baseball All-America Team, 1983.

Year Club	League	Pos.	G.	AB.	R.	H.	2B.	3B.	HR.	RBI.	B.A.	PO.	A.	E.	F.A.
1983—Columbia	S. Atl.	1B	64	220	41	74	13	1	3	32	.336	520	37	7	.988
1984—Lynchburg†	Carol.	1B	112	371	78	130	22	4	0	62	*.350	896	64	16	.984
1985—Jackson	Texas	*3B-1B	134	466	84	144	22	0	0	76	.309	106	276	*31	.925
1986—Tidewater	Int.	3B-1B	133	473	68	147	33	6	1	64	.311	78	284	25	.935

Year	Club	League	Pos.	G.	AB.	R.	H.	2B.	3B.	HR.	RBI.	B.A.	PO.	A.	E.	F.A.
1986	—New York	Nat.	1B	10	18	3	8	0	0	0	3	.444	48	5	0	1.000
1987	—New York‡	Nat.	3B-1B	85	192	21	61	13	1	3	24	.318	88	92	4	.978
1988	—New York§	Nat.	1B-3B	112	314	39	87	15	0	1	35	.277	459	99	10	.982
Major League Totals—3 Years				207	524	63	156	28	1	4	62	.298	595	196	14	.983

Selected by Boston Red Sox' organization in 12th round of free-agent draft, June 3, 1980.
Selected by New York Mets' organization in 2nd round of free-agent draft, June 6, 1983.
†On disabled list, August 7 to September 10, 1984.
‡On disabled list, March 29 to April 17, 1987.
§On disabled list, May 5 to May 20, 1988.

CHAMPIONSHIP SERIES RECORD

Year	Club	League	Pos.	G.	AB.	R.	H.	2B.	3B.	HR.	RBI.	B.A.	PO.	A.	E.	F.A.
1988	—New York	Nat.	PH	3	3	0	0	0	0	0	0	.000	0	0	0	.000

WARREN JEROME MAGEE

Born May 26, 1966, at Seaford, Del.
Height, 6.00. Weight, 195.
Throws right and bats left and righthanded.
Attended Ferrum College, Ferrum, Va.

Year	Club	League	G.	IP.	W.	L.	Pct.	H.	R.	ER.	SO.	BB.	ERA.
1986	—Utica	NYP	24	54⅔	4	3	.571	44	30	25	60	29	4.12
1987	—Clearwater	Florida St.	28	66⅔	6	5	.545	39	32	25	60	38	3.38
1987	—Reading	Eastern	13	55	4	4	.500	50	36	30	43	36	4.91
1988	—Reading	Eastern	42	108⅔	6	6	.500	88	50	45	90	52	3.73

Signed as free agent by Philadelphia Phillies' organization, June 7, 1986.

JOSEPH DAVID MAGRANE
(Joe)

Born July 2, 1964, at Des Moines, Ia.
Height, 6.06. Weight, 230.
Throws left and bats righthanded.
Attended University of Arizona, Tucson, Ariz.

Tied for National League lead in hit batsmen with 10 in 1987.
Tied for American Association lead in shutouts with 2 and complete games with 8 in 1986.

Year	Club	League	G.	IP.	W.	L.	Pct.	H.	R.	ER.	SO.	BB.	ERA.
1985	—Johnson City	Ap'lachian	6	30	2	1	.667	15	4	2	31	11	0.60
1985	—St. Petersburg	Florida St.	5	34⅔	3	1	.750	21	8	4	17	14	1.04
1986	—Arkansas	Texas	13	89⅓	8	4	.667	66	29	24	66	31	2.42
1986	—Louisville	Am. Assoc.	15	113⅓	9	6	.600	93	34	26	72	33	2.06
1987	—Louisville	Am. Assoc.	3	23⅓	1	0	1.000	16	7	5	17	3	1.93
1987	—St. Louis†	National	27	170⅓	9	7	.563	157	75	67	101	60	3.54
1988	—St. Louis‡	National	24	165⅓	5	9	.357	133	57	40	100	51	*2.18
1988	—Louisville	Am. Assoc.	4	20	2	1	.667	19	7	7	18	7	3.15
Major League Totals—2 Years			51	335⅔	14	16	.467	290	132	107	201	111	2.87

Selected by Pittsburgh Pirates' organization in 3rd round of free-agent draft, June 7, 1982.
Selected by St. Louis Cardinals' organization in 1st round (18th player selected) of free-agent draft, June 3, 1985.
†On disabled list, May 30 to June 18, 1987.
‡On disabled list, April 17 to June 11, 1988; included rehabilitation disability assignment to Louisville, May 23 to June 11, 1988.

CHAMPIONSHIP SERIES RECORD

Year	Club	League	G.	IP.	W.	L.	Pct.	H.	R.	ER.	SO.	BB.	ERA.
1987	—St. Louis	National	1	4	0	0	.000	4	4	4	3	2	9.00

WORLD SERIES RECORD

Year	Club	League	G.	IP.	W.	L.	Pct.	H.	R.	ER.	SO.	BB.	ERA.
1987	—St. Louis	National	2	7⅓	0	1	.000	9	7	7	5	5	8.59

RICHARD KEITH MAHLER

Name pronounced MAY-ler.

(Rick)

Born August 5, 1953, at Austin, Tex.
Height, 6.01. Weight, 202.
Throws and bats righthanded.
Attended Trinity University, San Antonio, Tex.
Brother of Mickey Mahler, pitcher with Atlanta Braves,
Pittsburgh Pirates, California Angels, Montreal Expos, Detroit Tigers,
Texas Rangers and Toronto Blue Jays, 1977 through 1982, 1985 and 1986.

Established major league record for most game-winning runs batted in by pitcher, season (3), 1985.
Tied National League record for most shutouts in season openers, lifetime (3).
Major League saves: 1981 (2).
Led National League pitchers in games started with 39 in 1985 and tied for lead with 39 in 1986.

Year	Club	League	G.	IP.	W.	L.	Pct.	H.	R.	ER.	SO.	BB.	ERA.
1975—	Kingsport	Ap'lachian	26	64	2	2	.500	52	23	21	58	26	2.95
1976—	Greenwood	W. Carol.	31	105	6	6	.500	96	49	34	68	49	2.91
1977—	Savannah	Southern	17	86	6	2	.750	71	31	22	53	38	2.30
1977—	Richmond	Int'national	14	40	0	2	.000	45	29	27	25	23	6.08
1978—	Richmond	Int'national	32	126	9	5	.643	130	65	55	66	53	3.93
1979—	Richmond	Int'national	24	54	4	6	.400	46	26	20	40	18	3.33
1979—	Atlanta	National	15	22	0	0	.000	28	16	15	12	11	6.14
1980—	Richmond	Int'national	29	188	12	6	.667	172	68	54	101	80	2.59
1980—	Atlanta	National	2	4	0	0	.000	2	1	1	1	0	2.25
1981—	Atlanta	National	34	112	8	6	.571	109	41	35	54	43	2.81
1982—	Atlanta	National	39	205⅓	9	10	.474	213	105	96	105	62	4.21
1983—	Atlanta	National	10	14⅓	0	0	.000	16	8	8	7	9	5.02
1983—	Richmond	In'national	24	162⅔	12	7	.632	165	102	89	103	85	4.92
1984—	Atlanta	National	38	222	13	10	.565	209	86	77	106	62	3.12
1985—	Atlanta	National	39	266⅔	17	15	.531	*272	116	103	107	79	3.48
1986—	Atlanta	National	39	237⅔	14	*18	.438	*283	*139	*129	137	95	4.88
1987—	Atlanta	National	39	197	8	13	.381	212	118	109	95	85	4.98
1988—	Atlanta†	National	39	249	9	16	.360	*279	*125	*102	131	42	3.69
Major League Totals—10 Years			294	1530	78	88	.470	1623	755	675	755	488	3.97

Signed as free agent by Atlanta Braves' organization, June 16, 1975.
†Granted free agency, November 4, 1988; signed by Cincinnati Reds, December 2, 1988.

CHAMPIONSHIP SERIES RECORD

Year	Club	League	G.	IP.	W.	L.	Pct.	H.	R.	ER.	SO.	BB.	ERA.
1982—	Atlanta	National	1	1⅔	0	0	.000	3	0	0	0	2	0.00

CANDIDO MALDONADO (GUADARRAMA)
(Candy)

Born September 5, 1960, at Humacao, Puerto Rico.
Height, 6.00. Weight, 195.
Throws and bats righthanded.

Tied major league record for most sacrifice flies, game (3), August 29, 1987.
Major League stolen bases: 1985 (1), 1986 (4), 1987 (8), 1988 (6). Total—19.
Hit for the cycle, May 4, 1987.
Led California League in total bases with 247 in 1980.
Tied for Pioneer League lead in sacrifice flies with 6 in 1978.
Named California League co-Most Valuable Player, 1980.

Year	Club	League	Pos.	G.	AB.	R.	H.	2B.	3B.	HR.	RBI.	B.A.	PO.	A.	E.	F.A.
1978—	Lethbridge	Pion.	OF	57	210	45	61	15	5	12	48	.290	112	6	8	.937
1979—	Clinton	Midw.	OF	50	158	25	37	13	1	2	26	.234	81	5	2	.977
1979—	Lethbridge	Pion.	OF	59	234	42	70	*20	3	5	33	.299	81	5	4	.956
1980—	Lodi†	Calif.	OF	121	456	75	139	27	3	25	*102	.305	211	13	11	.953
1981—	Albuquerque	P. C.	OF	126	460	96	154	40	9	21	104	.335	221	21	8	.968
1981—	Los Angeles	Nat.	OF	11	12	0	1	0	0	0	0	.083	8	0	0	1.000
1982—	Albuquerque	P. C.	OF	138	541	91	163	28	6	24	96	.301	303	15	10	.970
1982—	Los Angeles	Nat.	OF	6	4	0	0	0	0	0	0	.000	5	0	0	1.000
1983—	Los Angeles	Nat.	OF	42	62	5	12	1	1	1	6	.194	26	0	0	1.000
1983—	Albuquerque	P. C.	OF-3B	38	144	23	46	6	1	4	20	.319	66	11	4	.951
1984—	Los Angeles	Nat.	OF-3B	116	254	25	68	14	0	5	28	.268	124	5	8	.942
1985—	Los Angeles‡	Nat.	OF	121	213	20	48	7	1	5	19	.225	121	6	2	.984
1986—	San Francisco	Nat.	OF-3B	133	405	49	102	31	3	18	85	.252	161	11	3	.983
1987—	San Francisco§	Nat.	OF	118	442	69	129	28	4	20	85	.292	176	7	5	.973
1988—	San Francisco	Nat.	OF	142	499	53	127	23	1	12	68	.255	251	5	10	.962
Major League Totals—8 Years				689	1891	221	487	104	10	61	291	.258	872	34	28	.970

Signed as free agent by Los Angeles Dodgers' organization, June 6, 1978.
†On disabled list, August 16 to September 16, 1980.
‡Traded to San Francisco Giants for Catcher Alex Trevino, December 11, 1985.
§On disabled list, June 28 to August 7, 1987.

CHAMPIONSHIP SERIES RECORD

Year	Club	League	Pos.	G.	AB.	R.	H.	2B.	3B.	HR.	RBI.	B.A.	PO.	A.	E.	F.A.
1983—	Los Angeles	Nat.	PH	2	2	0	0	0	0	0	0	.000	0	0	0	.000
1985—	Los Angeles	Nat.	OF-PH	4	7	0	1	0	0	0	1	.143	4	0	1	.800
1987—	San Francisco	Nat.	OF	5	19	2	4	1	0	0	2	.211	7	0	0	1.000
Championship Series Totals—3 Years				11	28	2	5	1	0	0	3	.179	11	0	1	.917

CHARLES RAY MALONE JR.
(Chuck)

Born July 8, 1965, at Harrisburg, Ark.
Height, 6.07. Weight, 250.
Throws and bats righthanded.
Attended Arkansas State University, State University, Ark.,
and Three Rivers Community College, Poplar Bluff, Mo.

Year	Club	League	G.	IP.	W.	L.	Pct.	H.	R.	ER.	SO.	BB.	ERA.
1986	—Bend	Northwest	21	54⅔	2	6	.250	47	38	31	60	50	5.10
1987	—Clearwater	Florida St.	34	120	6	8	.429	105	55	52	100	63	3.90
1988	—Reading	Eastern	22	126⅔	12	7	.632	107	63	53	117	*88	3.77
1988	—Maine	Int'national	6	27⅔	1	4	.200	28	27	21	38	24	6.83

Selected by Philadelphia Phillies' organization in 5th round of free-agent draft, January 14, 1986.

KELLY JOHN MANN

Born August 17, 1967, at Santa Monica, Calif.
Height, 6.03. Weight, 215.
Throws and bats righthanded.

Tied for New York-Pennsylvania League lead in double plays by catchers with 7 in 1986.

Year	Club	League	Pos.	G.	AB.	R.	H.	2B.	3B.	HR.	RBI.	B.A.	PO.	A.	E.	F.A.
1985	—Wytheville	Appal.	C	26	75	6	15	3	0	1	10	.200	118	11	5	.963
1986	—Geneva	NYP	C	60	191	17	37	1	0	2	15	.194	419	49	8	.983
1986	—Peoria	Midw.	C	3	13	4	6	2	0	0	4	.462	26	1	1	.964
1987	—Peoria	Midw.	C	95	287	24	73	16	1	4	45	.254	582	63	9	.986
1988	—Winston-Salem	Carol.	C	94	307	32	84	11	0	8	40	.274	668	52	13	.982
1988	—Pittsfield	East.	C	22	51	7	10	3	0	0	3	.196	95	20	4	.966

Selected by Chicago Cubs' organization in 20th round of free-agent draft, June 3, 1985.

REYES FRED ELOY MANRIQUE
(Fred)

Name pronounced Man-ree-KEE.

Born November 5, 1961, at Bolivar, Venezuela.
Height, 6.01. Weight, 175.
Throws and bats righthanded.

Major League stolen bases: 1986 (1), 1987 (5), 1988 (6). Total—12.
Led American Association in grounding into double plays with 19 in 1986.
Led American Association shortstops in errors with 25 and double plays with 86 in 1986.
Led International League second basemen in errors with 22 in 1983 and 24 in 1984.

Year	Club	League	Pos.	G.	AB.	R.	H.	2B.	3B.	HR.	RBI.	B.A.	PO.	A.	E.	F.A.
1979	—Dunedin	Fla. St.	SS	5	15	0	2	0	0	0	0	.133	4	7	3	.786
1979	—Medicine Hat	Pion.	SS	66	270	47	81	8	•10	2	30	.300	103	208	*37	.894
1980	—Kinston	Carol.	SS-OF	111	390	49	108	9	5	7	50	.277	120	192	37	.894
1981	—Knoxville†	South.	SS	115	469	62	131	15	6	5	42	.279	161	330	45	.916
1981	—Toronto	Amer.	SS-3B	14	28	1	4	0	0	0	1	.143	10	27	3	.925
1982	—Syracuse‡	Int.	2B-3B-SS	103	362	41	91	9	2	4	37	.251	186	255	24	.948
1983	—Syracuse	Int.	2-S-3-O	128	485	55	130	22	8	10	50	.268	211	351	36	.940
1984	—Syracuse	Int.	2B-SS-3B	129	517	63	146	15	5	6	45	.282	233	389	28	.957
1984	—Toronto§	Amer.	2B	10	9	0	3	0	0	0	1	.333	5	10	1	.938
1985	—Indianapolis	A. A.	3B-SS-2B	123	409	46	98	21	5	8	37	.240	126	249	19	.952
1985	—Montreal x	Nat.	2B-SS-3B	9	13	5	4	1	1	1	1	.308	5	10	0	1.000
1986	—Louisville	A. A.	SS-2B	133	520	79	148	19	6	9	51	.285	208	421	26	.960
1986	—St. Louis y	Nat.	3B-2B	13	17	2	3	0	0	1	1	.176	1	3	0	1.000
1987	—Chicago	Amer.	2B-SS	115	298	30	77	13	3	4	29	.258	176	286	7	.985
1988	—Chicago	Amer.	2B-SS	140	345	43	81	10	6	5	37	.235	241	343	13	.978
American League Totals—4 Years				279	680	74	165	23	9	9	68	.243	432	666	24	.979
National League Totals—2 Years				22	30	7	7	1	1	2	2	.233	6	13	0	1.000
Major League Totals—6 Years				301	710	81	172	24	10	11	70	.242	438	679	24	.979

Signed as free agent by Toronto Blue Jays' organization, November 24, 1978.
†On disabled list, April 9 to April 19, 1981.
‡On disabled list, June 27 to July 12, 1982.
§Sold to Montreal Expos, April 7, 1985.
xTraded to St. Louis Cardinals for Catcher Tom Nieto, March 31, 1986.
yTraded to Chicago White Sox for Pitcher Bill Dawley, December 22, 1986.

JEFFREY PAUL MANTO
(Jeff)

Born August 23, 1964, at Bristol, Pa.
Height, 6.03. Weight, 210.
Throws and bats righthanded.
Attended Temple University, Philadelphia, Pa.

Led Texas League in grounding into double plays with 17 in 1988.
Led California League third basemen in assists with 245 and total chances with 365 in 1987.

Year	Club	League	Pos.	G.	AB.	R.	H.	2B.	3B.	HR.	RBI.	B.A.	PO.	A.	E.	F.A.
1985	—Quad Cities	Midw.	OF-3B	74	233	34	46	5	2	11	34	.197	87	8	3	.969
1986	—Quad Cities†	Midw.	3B	73	239	31	59	13	0	8	49	.247	48	114	28	.853
1987	—Palm Springs	Calif.	3B-1B	112	375	61	96	21	4	7	63	.256	93	246	37	.902
1988	—Midland	Texas	•3B-2B-1B	120	408	88	123	23	3	24	101	.301	82	208	•32	.901

Selected by New York Yankees' organization in 35th round of free-agent draft, June 7, 1982.
Selected by California Angels' organization in 14th round of free-agent draft, June 3, 1985.
†On disabled list, July 16, 1986 through remainder of season.

KIRT DEAN MANWARING

Born July 15, 1965, at Elmira, N. Y.
Height, 5.11. Weight, 185.
Throws and bats righthanded.
Attended Coastal Carolina College, Conway, S. C.

Led Texas League catchers in double plays with 8 and total chances with 688 in 1987.

Year Club	League	Pos.	G.	AB.	R.	H.	2B.	3B.	HR.	RBI.	B.A.	PO.	A.	E.	F.A.
1986—Clinton	Midw.	C	49	147	18	36	7	1	2	16	.245	243	31	5	.982
1987—Shreveport	Texas	C	98	307	27	82	13	2	2	22	.267	603	★81	4	.994
1987—San Francisco	Nat.	C	6	7	0	1	0	0	0	0	.143	9	1	1	.909
1988—Phoenix	P. C.	C	81	273	29	77	12	2	2	35	.282	411	51	6	.987
1988—San Francisco	Nat.	C	40	116	12	29	7	0	1	15	.250	162	24	4	.979
Major League Totals—2 Years			46	123	12	30	7	0	1	15	.244	171	25	5	.975

Selected by Boston Red Sox' organization in 12th round of free-agent draft, June 6, 1983.
Selected by San Francisco Giants' organization in 2nd round of free-agent draft, June 2, 1986.

RAVELO MANZANILLO

Name pronounced Mahn-zuh-NEE-yoh.

Born October 17, 1963, at San Pedro de Macoris, D. R.
Height, 5.10. Weight, 190.
Throws and bats lefthanded.

Year Club	League	G.	IP.	W.	L.	Pct.	H.	R.	ER.	SO.	BB.	ERA.
1981—Bradenton Pirates	Gulf Coast	9	48	3	1	.750	35	11	6	34	10	1.13
1982—Greenwood	S. Atlantic	27	157⅔	9	9	.500	156	•108	87	93	109	4.97
1983—Alexandria	Carolina	22	105⅓	7	7	.500	107	68	52	66	79	4.44
1984—Nashua†	Eastern	14	74⅓	4	4	.500	56	40	35	50	62	4.24
1985—Nashua	Eastern	33	123⅓	6	10	.375	99	70	64	62	96	4.67
1986—Vera Cruz‡	Mexican	5	21	1	3	.250	19	16	13	16	20	5.57
1987—						(Out of Organized Baseball)						
1988—Tampa	Florida St.	24	130⅓	10	6	.625	93	53	44	140	49	3.04
1988—Chicago	American	2	9⅓	0	1	.000	7	6	6	10	12	5.79
Major League Totals—1 Year		2	9⅓	0	1	.000	7	6	6	10	12	5.79

Signed as free agent by Pittsburgh Pirates' organization, August 21, 1980.
†On disabled list, July 30, 1984 through remainder of season.
‡Released, May 1, 1986; signed by Tampa (Chicago White Sox' organization), March, 1988.

MICHAEL ALLEN MARSHALL
(Mike)

Born January 12, 1960, at Libertyville, Ill.
Height, 6.05. Weight, 220.
Throws and bats righthanded.

Major League stolen bases: 1982 (2), 1983 (7), 1984 (4), 1985 (3), 1986 (4), 1988 (4). Total—24.
Led California League in total bases with 301 in 1979.
Led Pacific Coast League first basemen in double plays with 136 in 1981.
Led Texas League first basemen in double plays with 120 in 1980.
Named Minor League Player of the Year by THE SPORTING NEWS, 1981.
Named Pacific Coast League Most Valuable Player, 1981.
Named California League co-Most Valuable Player, 1979.

Year Club	League	Pos.	G.	AB.	R.	H.	2B.	3B.	HR.	RBI.	B.A.	PO.	A.	E.	F.A.
1978—Lethbridge	Pion.	1B-OF	65	256	48	83	15	2	12	70	.324	308	16	7	.979
1979—Lodi	Calif.	1B	137	525	101	★186	★37	3	24	116	★.354	1173	71	20	.984
1980—San Antonio	Texas	1B	134	470	95	151	21	6	16	82	.321	★1157	64	•16	.987
1981—Albuquerque	P. C.	1B	128	467	★114	174	25	7	★34	★137	★.373	1127	54	9	.992
1981—Los Angeles	Nat.	1B-3B-OF	14	25	2	5	3	0	0	1	.200	14	2	0	1.000
1982—Albuquerque	P. C.	OF-1B-3B	66	255	74	99	20	1	14	58	.388	113	3	4	.966
1982—Los Angeles	Nat.	OF-1B	49	95	10	23	3	0	5	9	.242	122	5	2	.984
1983—Los Angeles	Nat.	OF-1B	140	465	47	132	17	1	17	65	.284	395	21	6	.986
1984—Los Angeles†	Nat.	OF-1B	134	495	68	127	27	0	21	65	.257	331	17	5	.986
1985—Los Angeles‡	Nat.	OF-1B	135	518	72	152	27	2	28	95	.293	265	12	4	.986
1986—Los Angeles§	Nat.	OF	103	330	47	77	11	0	19	53	.233	149	8	6	.963
1987—Los Angeles x	Nat.	OF	104	402	45	118	19	0	16	72	.294	147	4	2	.987
1988—Los Angeles y	Nat.	OF-1B	144	542	63	150	27	2	20	82	.277	605	49	7	.989
Major League Totals—8 Years			823	2872	354	784	134	5	126	442	.273	2028	118	32	.985

Selected by Los Angeles Dodgers' organization in 6th round of free-agent draft, June 6, 1978.
†On disabled list, May 13 to June 3, 1984.
‡On disabled list, June 20 to July 18, 1985.
§On disabled list, July 20 to August 4, 1986.
xOn disabled list, May 6 to May 29 and August 21 to September 5, 1987.
yGranted free agency, November 4, 1988; re-signed by Dodgers, November 13, 1988.

DIVISION SERIES RECORD

Year Club	League	Pos.	G.	AB.	R.	H.	2B.	3B.	HR.	RBI.	B.A.	PO.	A.	E.	F.A.
1981—Los Angeles	Nat.	PH	1	1	0	0	0	0	0	0	.000	0	0	0	.000

CHAMPIONSHIP SERIES RECORD

Tied National League Championship Series records for most at-bats, seven-game Series (30), 1988; most strikeouts, four-game Series (6), 1983.

Year	Club	League	Pos.	G.	AB.	R.	H.	2B.	3B.	HR.	RBI.	B.A.	PO.	A.	E.	F.A.
1983	Los Angeles	Nat.	1B-OF	4	15	1	2	1	0	1	2	.133	22	2	0	1.000
1985	Los Angeles	Nat.	OF	6	23	1	5	2	0	1	3	.217	8	0	0	1.000
1988	Los Angeles	Nat.	OF	7	30	3	7	1	1	0	5	.233	14	0	0	1.000
Championship Series Totals—3 Years				17	68	5	14	4	1	2	10	.206	44	2	0	1.000

WORLD SERIES RECORD

Year	Club	League	Pos.	G.	AB.	R.	H.	2B.	3B.	HR.	RBI.	B.A.	PO.	A.	E.	F.A.
1988	Los Angeles	Nat.	OF	5	13	2	3	0	1	1	3	.231	6	0	0	1.000

ALL-STAR GAME RECORD

Member of National League All-Star Team in 1984; did not play.

CARLOS ALBERTO MARTINEZ

Born August 11, 1965, at La Guaira, Venezuela.
Height, 6.05. Weight, 175.
Throws and bats righthanded.

Major League stolen bases: 1988 (1).

Year	Club	League	Pos.	G.	AB.	R.	H.	2B.	3B.	HR.	RBI.	B.A.	PO.	A.	E.	F.A.
1984	Sara. Yankees	Gulf C.	SS	31	91	9	14	1	1	0	4	.154	53	103	14	.918
1985	Fort Lauderdale	Fla. St.	SS	93	311	39	77	15	7	6	44	.248	123	254	25	.938
1986	Fort Lauderdale†	Fla. St.	SS	5	16	1	1	0	0	0	0	.063	7	18	0	1.000
1986	Albany‡	East.	SS-3B	69	253	34	70	18	2	8	39	.277	120	161	32	.898
1986	Buffalo	A. A.	SS-3B	17	54	6	16	1	0	2	6	.296	24	20	5	.898
1987	Birmingham	South.	3B	9	30	2	7	1	0	0	0	.233	5	17	2	.917
1987	Hawaii	P. C.	OF-3B-SS	83	304	32	75	15	1	3	36	.247	109	91	18	.917
1988	Birmingham	South.	OF-3B-SS	133	498	67	138	22	3	14	73	.277	196	139	20	.944
1988	Chicago	Amer.	3B	17	55	5	9	1	0	0	0	.164	7	33	4	.909
Major League Totals—1 Year				17	55	5	9	1	0	0	0	.164	7	33	4	.909

Signed as free agent by New York Yankees' organization, November 17, 1983.
†On disabled list, April 11 to May 1, 1986.
‡Traded with Catcher Ron Hassey and a player to be named later to Chicago White Sox for Catcher Joel Skinner, Infielder Wayne Tolleson and Outfielder-Designated Hitter Ron Kittle, July 30, 1986; New York Yankees traded Catcher Bill Lindsey to Chicago organization to complete deal, December 24, 1986.

CARMELO MARTINEZ (SALGADO)

Born July 28, 1960, at Dorado, Puerto Rico.
Height, 6.02. Weight, 220.
Throws and bats righthanded.
Attended Central College of Bayamon, Bayamon, Puerto Rico.
Cousin of Edgar Martinez, third baseman in Seattle Mariners' organization.

Tied major league record by hitting home run in first major league at-bat, August 22, 1983.
Major League stolen bases: 1984 (1), 1986 (1), 1987 (5), 1988 (1). Total—8.
Tied for National League lead in sacrifice flies with 10 in 1984.
Led American Association first basemen in total chances with 1,283 and tied for lead in double plays with 99 in 1983.
Led Texas League first basemen in putouts with 1,087, total chances with 1,180 and double plays with 102 in 1982.

Year	Club	League	Pos.	G.	AB.	R.	H.	2B.	3B.	HR.	RBI.	B.A.	PO.	A.	E.	F.A.
1979	Sarasota Cubs	Gulf C.	OF-1B	40	143	18	29	4	0	1	23	.203	139	9	6	.961
1980	Quad Cities	Midw.	O-1-3-2-S	128	460	65	118	23	0	12	64	.257	433	99	13	.976
1981	Midland	Texas	3-O-2-1	116	392	65	116	22	1	21	84	.296	61	80	24	.855
1982	Midland	Texas	1B-OF	131	467	100	156	35	4	27	93	.334	1098	78	17	.986
1983	Iowa	A. A.	★1B-2B	123	458	76	115	25	1	★31	94	.251	★1191	★83	9	.993
1983	Chicago†	Nat.	1B-3B-OF	29	89	8	23	3	0	6	16	.258	233	17	2	.992
1984	San Diego	Nat.	OF-1B	149	488	64	122	28	2	13	66	.250	317	15	8	.976
1985	San Diego‡	Nat.	OF-1B	150	514	64	130	28	1	21	72	.253	302	14	7	.978
1986	San Diego	Nat.	OF-1B-3B	113	244	28	58	10	0	9	25	.238	142	14	2	.987
1987	San Diego	Nat.	OF-1B	139	447	59	122	21	2	15	70	.273	591	42	9	.986
1988	San Diego	Nat.	OF-1B	121	365	48	86	12	0	18	65	.236	430	32	4	.991
Major League Totals—6 Years				701	2147	271	541	102	5	82	314	.252	2015	134	32	.985

Signed as free agent by Chicago Cubs' organization, December 9, 1978.
†Traded with Pitcher Craig Lefferts and Third Baseman Fritz Connally to San Diego Padres for Pitcher Scott Sanderson, December 7, 1983.
‡On disabled list, March 31 to April 15, 1985.

CHAMPIONSHIP SERIES RECORD

Year	Club	League	Pos.	G.	AB.	R.	H.	2B.	3B.	HR.	RBI.	B.A.	PO.	A.	E.	F.A.
1984	San Diego	Nat.	OF	5	17	1	3	0	0	0	0	.176	6	0	0	1.000

WORLD SERIES RECORD

Established World Series record for most strikeouts, five-game Series (9), 1984.

Year	Club	League	Pos.	G.	AB.	R.	H.	2B.	3B.	HR.	RBI.	B.A.	PO.	A.	E.	F.A.
1984	San Diego	Nat.	OF	5	17	0	3	0	0	0	0	.176	7	0	1	.875

DAVID MARTINEZ
(Dave)

Born September 26, 1964, at New York, N.Y.
Height, 5.10, Weight, 150.
Throws and bats lefthanded.
Attended Valencia Community College, Orlando, Fla.

Major League stolen bases: 1986 (4), 1987 (16), 1988 (23). Total—43.

Year	Club	League	Pos.	G.	AB.	R.	H.	2B.	3B.	HR.	RBI.	B.A.	PO.	A.	E.	F.A.
1983	Quad Cities	Midw.	OF	44	119	17	29	6	2	0	10	.244	47	8	1	.982
1983	Geneva	NYP	OF	64	241	35	63	15	2	5	33	.261	132	6	8	.945
1984	Quad Cities†	Midw.	OF	12	41	6	9	2	2	0	5	.220	13	2	1	.938
1985	Winston-Salem	Carol.	OF	115	386	52	132	14	4	5	54	*.342	206	11	7	.969
1986	Iowa	A. A.	OF	83	318	52	92	11	5	5	32	.289	214	7	2	.991
1986	Chicago	Nat.	OF	53	108	13	15	1	1	1	7	.139	77	2	1	.988
1987	Chicago	Nat.	OF	142	459	70	134	18	8	8	36	.292	283	10	6	.980
1988	Chi.‡-Mon.	Nat.	OF	138	447	51	114	13	6	6	46	.255	281	4	6	.979
Major League Totals—3 Years				333	1014	134	263	32	15	15	89	.259	641	16	13	.981

Selected by Texas Rangers' organization in 40th round of free-agent draft, June 7, 1982.
Selected by Chicago Cubs' organization in secondary phase of free-agent draft, January 11, 1983.
†On disabled list, April 27, 1984 through remainder of season.
‡Traded to Montreal Expos for Outfielder Mitch Webster, July 14, 1988.

EDGAR MARTINEZ

Born January 2, 1963, at New York, N. Y.
Height, 5.11. Weight, 175.
Throws and bats righthanded.
Attended American College, Puerto Rico.
Cousin of Carmelo Martinez, outfielder-first baseman with San Diego Padres.

Led Southern League in sacrifice flies with 12 in 1985.
Led Pacific Coast League third basemen in double plays with 31 and total chances with 389 in 1987.
Led Southern League third basemen in double plays with 34 and total chances with 360 in 1985.

Year	Club	League	Pos.	G.	AB.	R.	H.	2B.	3B.	HR.	RBI.	B.A.	PO.	A.	E.	F.A.
1983	Bellingham	N'west	3B	32	104	14	18	1	1	0	5	.173	22	58	6	.930
1984	Wausau	Midw.	3B	126	433	72	131	32	2	15	66	.303	85	246	25	.930
1985	Chattanooga	South.	3B	111	357	43	92	15	5	3	47	.258	*94	*247	19	*.947
1985	Calgary	P. C.	3B-2B	20	68	8	24	7	1	0	14	.353	15	44	4	.937
1986	Chattanooga	South.	*3B-2B	132	451	71	119	29	5	6	74	.264	94	263	15	*.960
1987	Calgary	P. C.	3B	129	438	75	144	31	1	10	66	.329	*91	*278	20	.949
1987	Seattle	Amer.	3B	13	43	6	16	5	2	0	5	.372	13	19	0	1.000
1988	Calgary	P. C.	3B-2B	95	331	63	120	19	4	8	64	*.363	48	185	20	.921
1988	Seattle	Amer.	3B	14	32	0	9	4	0	0	5	.281	5	8	1	.929
Major League Totals—2 Years				27	75	6	25	9	2	0	10	.333	18	27	1	.978

Signed as free agent by Seattle Mariners' organization, December 19, 1982.

FELIX ANTHONY MARTINEZ
(Tippy)

Born May 31, 1950, at La Junta, Colo.
Height, 5.10. Weight, 175.
Throws and bats lefthanded.
Attended Colorado State University, Fort Collins, Colo.

Major League saves: 1975 (8), 1976 (10), 1977 (9), 1978 (5), 1979 (3), 1980 (10), 1981 (11), 1982 (16), 1983 (21), 1984 (17), 1985 (4), 1986 (1). Total—115.

Led American League in intentional bases on balls issued with 13 in 1984.
Tied for Carolina League lead in saves with 15 and wild pitches with 17 in 1973.

Year	Club	League	G.	IP.	W.	L.	Pct.	H.	R.	ER.	SO.	BB.	ERA.
1972	Oneonta	NYP	2	9	1	0	1.000	3	2	2	9	10	2.00
1972	Kinston	Carolina	5	20	0	0	.000	22	10	10	18	13	4.50
1973	Kinston	Carolina	54	105	13	8	.619	74	38	31	160	61	2.66
1974	Syracuse	Int'national	36	64	7	5	.583	49	29	27	70	32	3.80
1974	New York	American	10	13	0	0	.000	14	7	6	10	9	4.15
1975	Syracuse	Int'national	14	110	8	2	.800	91	39	25	105	35	2.05
1975	New York	American	23	37	1	2	.333	27	15	11	20	32	2.68
1976	New York†-Baltimore	American	39	70	5	1	.833	50	19	18	45	42	2.31
1977	Baltimore	American	41	50	5	1	.833	47	17	15	29	27	2.70
1978	Baltimore	American	42	69	3	3	.500	77	41	37	57	40	4.83
1979	Baltimore	American	39	78	10	3	.769	59	29	25	61	31	2.88
1980	Baltimore	American	53	81	4	4	.500	69	30	27	68	34	3.00
1981	Baltimore	American	37	59	3	3	.500	48	21	19	50	32	2.90
1982	Baltimore	American	76	95	8	8	.500	81	39	36	78	37	3.41
1983	Baltimore‡	American	65	103⅓	9	3	.750	76	30	27	81	37	2.35

Year	Club	League	G.	IP.	W.	L.	Pct.	H.	R.	ER.	SO.	BB.	ERA.
1984	—Baltimore	American	55	89⅔	4	9	.308	88	42	39	72	51	3.91
1985	—Baltimore	American	49	70	3	3	.500	70	48	42	47	37	5.40
1986	—Baltimore§	American	14	16	0	2	.000	18	10	10	11	12	5.63
1986	—Rochester	Int'national	3	6	0	1	.000	7	4	4	4	3	6.00
1987	—Hagerstown xy	Carolina	6	7	1	0	1.000	6	4	3	8	5	3.86
1988	—Minnesota z	American	3	4	0	0	.000	8	9	8	3	4	18.00
Major League Totals—14 Years			546	835	55	42	567	732	357	320	632	425	3.45

Selected by Washington Senators' organization in 35th round of free-agent draft, June 5, 1969.
Signed as free agent by New York Yankees' organization, July 22, 1972.
†Traded with Pitchers Rudy May, Dave Pagan and Scott McGregor and Catcher Rick Dempsey to Baltimore Orioles for Pitchers Ken Holtzman, Doyle Alexander and Grant Jackson, Catcher Ellie Hendricks and Pitcher Jimmy Freeman, June 15, 1976.
‡On disabled list, July 9 to July 31, 1983.
§On disabled list, April 20 to May 29, June 19 to July 4 and July 14, 1986 through remainder of season; included rehabilitation disability assignment to Rochester, May 19 to May 29, 1986.
xOn Baltimore disabled list, March 30 to June 4, 1987; included rehabilitation disability assignment to Hagerstown, May 15 to June 4, 1987.
yReleased, June 4, 1987; signed by Minnesota Twins, April 4,1988.
zReleased, April 21, 1988.

CHAMPIONSHIP SERIES RECORD

Year	Club	League	G.	IP.	W.	L.	Pct.	H.	R.	ER.	SO.	BB.	ERA.
1983	—Baltimore	American	2	6	1	0	1.000	5	0	0	5	3	0.00

WORLD SERIES RECORD

Tied World Series record for most saves, five-game Series (2), 1983.

Year	Club	League	G.	IP.	W.	L.	Pct.	H.	R.	ER.	SO.	BB.	ERA.
1979	—Baltimore	American	3	1⅓	0	0	.000	3	1	1	1	0	6.75
1983	—Baltimore	American	3	3	0	0	.000	3	1	1	0	0	3.00
World Series Totals—2 Years			6	4⅓	0	0	.000	6	2	2	1	0	4.15

ALL-STAR GAME RECORD

Member of American League All-Star Team in 1983; did not play.

JOSE DENNIS MARTINEZ

(Known by middle name.)

Born May 14, 1955, at Granada, Nicaragua.
Height, 6.01. Weight, 183.
Throws and bats righthanded.

Major League saves: 1977 (4), 1980 (1). Total—5.
Led American League pitchers in games started with 39 and complete games with 18 in 1979.
Tied for National League lead in balks with 10 in 1988.
Led International League in complete games with 16 in 1976.
Named International League Pitcher of the Year, 1976.

Year	Club	League	G.	IP.	W.	L.	Pct.	H.	R.	ER.	SO.	BB.	ERA.
1974	—Miami	Florida St.	25	179	15	6	.714	124	48	41	162	53	2.06
1975	—Miami	Florida St.	20	145	12	4	.750	125	54	42	114	35	2.61
1975	—Asheville	Southern	6	45	4	1	.800	45	16	13	18	12	2.60
1975	—Rochester	Int'national	2	5	0	0	.000	7	4	3	4	2	5.40
1976	—Rochester	Int'national	25	180	*14	8	.636	148	64	50	*140	50	*2.50
1976	—Baltimore	American	4	28	1	2	.333	23	8	8	18	8	2.57
1977	—Baltimore	American	42	167	14	7	.667	157	86	76	107	64	4.10
1978	—Baltimore	American	40	276	16	11	.593	257	121	108	142	93	3.25
1979	—Baltimore	American	40	*292	15	16	.484	279	129	119	132	78	3.67
1980	—Baltimore†	American	25	100	6	4	.600	103	44	44	42	44	3.96
1980	—Miami	Florida St.	2	12	0	0	.000	3	1	0	7	5	0.00
1981	—Baltimore	American	25	179	•14	5	.737	173	84	66	88	62	3.32
1982	—Baltimore	American	40	252	16	12	.571	262	123	118	111	87	4.21
1983	—Baltimore	American	32	153	7	16	.304	209	108	94	71	45	5.53
1984	—Baltimore	American	34	141⅔	6	9	.400	145	81	79	77	37	5.02
1985	—Baltimore	American	33	180	13	11	.542	203	110	103	68	63	5.15
1986	—Baltimore‡	American	4	6⅔	0	0	.000	11	5	5	2	2	6.75
1986	—Rochester§	Int'national	4	19⅓	2	1	.667	18	14	13	14	9	6.05
1986	—Montreal x	National	19	98	3	6	.333	103	52	50	63	28	4.59
1987	—Miami y	Florida St.	3	19	1	1	.500	21	14	13	11	3	6.16
1987	—Indianapolis	Am. Assoc.	7	38⅓	3	2	.600	32	20	19	30	13	4.46
1987	—Montreal z	National	22	144⅔	11	4	*.733	133	59	53	84	40	3.30
1988	—Montreal	National	34	235⅓	15	13	.536	215	94	71	120	55	2.72
American League Totals—11 Years			319	1775⅓	108	93	.537	1822	899	820	858	583	4.16
National League Totals—3 Years			75	478	29	23	.558	451	205	174	267	123	3.28
Major League Totals—13 Years			394	2253⅓	137	116	.542	2273	1104	994	1125	706	3.97

Signed as free agent by Baltimore Orioles' organization, December 10, 1973.
†On disabled list, March 28 to April 20 and June 3 to July 10, 1980; included rehabilitation disability assignment to Miami, July 1 to July 10, 1980.
‡On disabled list, April 28 to June 16, 1986; included rehabilitation disability assignment to Rochester, May 21 to June 10, 1986.

§Traded to Montreal Expos for a player to be named later, June 16, 1986; Baltimore Orioles acquired Infielder Rene Gonzales to complete deal, December 16, 1986.

xGranted free agency, November 12, 1986; signed by Miami (Independent), April 14, 1987.

yReleased, May 6, 1987; signed by Montreal Expos' organization, May 6, 1987.

zGranted free agency, November 9, 1987; re-signed by Expos, December 18, 1987.

CHAMPIONSHIP SERIES RECORD

Year Club	League	G.	IP.	W.	L.	Pct.	H.	R.	ER.	SO.	BB.	ERA.
1979—Baltimore	American	1	8⅓	0	0	.000	8	3	3	4	0	3.24

WORLD SERIES RECORD

Year Club	League	G.	IP.	W.	L.	Pct.	H.	R.	ER.	SO.	BB.	ERA.
1979—Baltimore	American	2	2	0	0	.000	6	4	4	0	0	18.00

RAMON JAIME MARTINEZ

Born March 22, 1968, at Santo Domingo, D. R.
Height, 6.04. Weight, 172.
Throws and bats righthanded.

Member of 1984 Dominican Republic Olympic baseball team.

Year Club	League	G.	IP.	W.	L.	Pct.	H.	R.	ER.	SO.	BB.	ERA.
1985—Bradenton Dodgers	Gulf Coast	23	59	4	1	.800	57	30	17	42	23	2.59
1986—Bakersfield	California	20	106	4	8	.333	119	73	56	78	63	4.75
1987—Vero Beach	Florida St.	25	170⅓	16	5	.762	128	45	41	148	78	2.17
1988—San Antonio	Texas	14	95	8	4	.667	79	29	26	89	34	2.46
1988—Albuquerque	P. Coast	10	58⅔	5	2	.714	43	24	18	49	32	2.76
1988—Los Angeles	National	9	35⅔	1	3	.250	27	17	15	23	22	3.79
Major League Totals—1 Year		9	35⅔	1	3	.250	27	17	15	23	22	3.79

Signed as free agent by Los Angeles Dodgers' organization, September 1, 1984.

JOHN ROBERT MARZANO

Born February 14, 1963, at Philadelphia, Pa.
Height, 5.11. Weight, 197.
Throws and bats righthanded.
Attended Temple University, Philadelphia, Pa.

Led Eastern League in being hit by pitch with 12 in 1986.
Member of 1984 U.S. Olympic baseball team.
Named catcher on The Sporting News College Baseball All-America Team, 1984.

Year Club	League	Pos.	G.	AB.	R.	H.	2B.	3B.	HR.	RBI.	B.A.	PO.	A.	E.	F.A.
1985—New Britain	East.	C	103	350	36	86	14	6	4	51	.246	530	70	12	.980
1986—New Britain†	East.	C-3B	118	445	55	126	28	2	10	62	.283	509	76	14	.977
1987—Pawtucket	Int.	C	70	255	46	72	22	0	10	35	.282	326	36	8	.978
1987—Boston	Amer.	C	52	168	20	41	11	0	5	24	.244	337	24	5	.986
1988—Boston	Amer.	C	10	29	3	4	1	0	0	1	.138	77	4	0	1.000
1988—Pawtucket	Int.	C	33	111	7	22	2	1	0	5	.198	151	24	8	.956
1988—New Britain	East.	C	35	112	11	23	6	1	0	5	.205	117	11	3	.977
Major League Totals—2 Years			62	197	23	45	12	0	5	25	.228	414	28	5	.989

Selected by Minnesota Twins' organization in 3rd round of free-agent draft, June 8, 1981.
Selected by Boston Red Sox' organization in 1st round (14th player selected) of free-agent draft, June 4, 1984.
†On disabled list, June 13 to June 28, 1986.

MICHAEL PAUL MASON
(Mike)

Born November 21, 1958, at Faribault, Minn.
Height, 6.02. Weight, 205.
Throws and bats lefthanded.
Attended Normandale Community College, Bloomington, Minn., and
Oral Roberts University, Tulsa, Okla.

Tied for Texas League lead in balks with 4 in 1982.

Year Club	League	G.	IP.	W.	L.	Pct.	H.	R.	ER.	SO.	BB.	ERA.
1980—Sarasota Rangers	Gulf Coast	12	61	6	1	.857	40	17	14	*55	46	2.07
1981—Asheville†	S. Atlantic	12	85	8	3	.727	58	28	20	39	35	2.12
1982—Tulsa	Texas	26	155	10	9	.526	153	84	67	111	46	3.89
1982—Texas	American	4	23	1	2	.333	21	13	13	8	9	5.09
1983—Texas	American	5	10⅔	0	2	.000	10	7	7	9	6	5.91
1983—Oklahoma City‡	Am. Assoc.	16	88⅔	5	5	.500	100	50	41	50	26	4.16
1984—Texas	American	36	184⅓	9	13	.409	159	78	74	113	51	3.61
1985—Texas	American	38	179	8	15	.348	212	113	96	92	73	4.83
1986—Texas§	American	27	135	7	3	.700	135	71	65	85	56	4.33
1986—Oklahoma City	Am. Assoc.	1	3	0	1	.000	2	5	1	1	3	3.00
1987—Texas x	American	8	29	0	2	.000	37	20	18	21	22	5.59
1987—Chicago y	National	17	38	4	1	.800	43	25	24	28	23	5.68
1987—Iowa z	Am. Assoc.	9	54	4	2	.667	53	28	21	41	27	3.50
1988—Portland	P. Coast	23	52⅔	2	2	.500	62	35	34	25	33	5.81

Year	Club	League	G.	IP.	W.	L.	Pct.	H.	R.	ER.	SO.	BB.	ERA.
1988—Minnesota		American	5	6⅔	0	1	.000	8	8	8	7	9	10.80
American League Totals—7 Years			123	567⅔	25	38	.397	582	310	281	335	226	4.46
National League Totals—1 Year			17	38	4	1	.800	43	25	24	28	23	5.68
Major League Totals—7 Years			140	605⅔	29	39	.426	625	335	305	363	249	4.53

Selected by Detroit Tigers' organization in 14th round of free-agent draft, June 6, 1978.
Selected by Minnesota Twins' organization in secondary phase of free-agent draft, January 9, 1979.
Selected by St. Louis Cardinals' organization in secondary phase of free-agent draft, June 5, 1979.
Selected by Texas Rangers' organization in secondary phase of free-agent draft, June 3, 1980.
†On disabled list, July 26, 1981 through remainder of season.
‡On disabled list, June 17 to July 15, 1983.
§On disabled list, June 7 to June 26 and July 21 to August 6, 1986; included rehabilitation disability assignment to Oklahoma City, June 24 to June 26, 1986.
xTraded to Chicago Cubs for a player to be named later, May 15, 1987; Texas Rangers' organization acquired Pitcher Dave Pavlas to complete deal, June 6, 1987.
yOn disabled list, August 15 to September 1, 1987.
zReleased, March 21, 1988; signed by Portland (Minnesota Twins' organization), May 10, 1988.

GREGORY INMAN MATHEWS
(Greg)

Born May 17, 1962, at Harbor City, Calif.
Height, 6.02. Weight, 180.
Throws left and bats righthanded.
Attended Santa Ana College, Santa Ana, Calif.; and
California State University, Fullerton, Calif.

Tied for American Association lead in shutouts with 2 in 1986 and 1987.

Year	Club	League	G.	IP.	W.	L.	Pct.	H.	R.	ER.	SO.	BB.	ERA.
1984—Erie		NYP	3	15	0	1	.000	16	15	15	9	8	9.00
1984—Johnson City		Ap'lachian	5	31⅓	2	3	.400	27	12	9	21	13	2.59
1984—Savannah		S. Atlantic	6	27⅓	1	0	1.000	24	10	9	21	15	2.96
1985—St. Petersburg		Florida St.	16	122	13	1	*.929	76	17	15	96	47	*1.11
1985—Louisville		Am. Assoc.	12	74	6	4	.600	61	33	24	47	26	2.92
1986—Louisville†		Am. Assoc.	7	45⅓	3	3	.500	44	19	13	20	14	2.58
1986—St. Louis		National	23	145⅓	11	8	.579	139	61	59	67	44	3.65
1987—St. Louis		National	32	197⅔	11	11	.500	184	87	82	108	71	3.73
1987—Louisville		Am. Assoc.	3	22	3	0	1.000	18	5	5	20	3	2.05
1988—St. Louis‡		National	13	68	4	6	.400	61	34	32	31	33	4.24
1988—Louisville		Am. Assoc.	5	16	0	1	.000	15	14	13	8	9	7.31
Major League Totals—3 Years			68	411	26	25	.510	384	182	173	206	148	3.79

Selected by Minnesota Twins' organization in 9th round of free-agent draft, January 12, 1982.
Selected by St. Louis Cardinals' organization in 10th round of free-agent draft, June 4, 1984.
†On disabled list, April 25 to May 12, 1986.
‡On disabled list, May 14 to August 16, 1988; included rehabilitation disability assignment to Arkansas, June 7 to June 13, 1988; and Louisville, July 26 to August 12, 1988.

CHAMPIONSHIP SERIES RECORD

Year	Club	League	G.	IP.	W.	L.	Pct.	H.	R.	ER.	SO.	BB.	ERA.
1987—St. Louis		National	2	10⅓	1	0	1.000	6	5	4	10	3	3.48

WORLD SERIES RECORD

Year	Club	League	G.	IP.	W.	L.	Pct.	H.	R.	ER.	SO.	BB.	ERA.
1987—St. Louis		National	1	3⅔	0	0	.000	2	1	1	3	2	2.45

DONALD ARTHUR MATTINGLY
(Don)

Born April 20, 1961, at Evansville, Ind.
Height, 6.00. Weight, 175.
Throws and bats lefthanded.

Established major league records for most home runs, seven consecutive games (9), July 8 through 17, 1987, and eight consecutive games (10), July 8 through 18, 1987; most grand slams, season (6), 1987.
Tied major league records for most doubles, inning (2), April 11, 1987, seventh inning; most consecutive games, one or more home runs (8), July 8 through 18, 1987; most sacrifice flies, game (3), May 3, 1986; most putouts and chances accepted by first baseman, nine-inning game (22), July 20, 1987.
Established American League record for most at-bats by lefthander, season (677), 1986; most consecutive games, one or more long hits, season (10), July 7 through 19, 1987.
Major League stolen bases: 1984 (1), 1985 (2), 1987 (1), 1988 (1). Total—5.
Led American League in total bases with 370 in 1985 and 388 in 1986.
Led American League in slugging percentage with .573 in 1986.
Led American League in game-winning RBIs with 21 in 1985 and tied for lead with 15 in 1986.
Led American League in sacrifice flies with 15 in 1985.
Led American League first basemen in fielding percentage with .996 in 1984 and 1986.
Led American League first basemen in putouts with 1,377 and total chances with 1,483 in 1986.
Tied for American League lead in double plays by first basemen with 154 in 1985.
Led South Atlantic League in sacrifice flies with 12 in 1980.
Named Major League Player of the Year by THE SPORTING NEWS, 1985.
Named American League Player of the Year by THE SPORTING NEWS, 1984 through 1986.
Named American League Most Valuable Player by Baseball Writers' Association of America, 1985.

Named first baseman on THE SPORTING NEWS American League All-Star Team, 1984 through 1987.
Named first baseman on THE SPORTING NEWS American League All-Star fielding team, 1985 through 1988.
Named first baseman on THE SPORTING NEWS American League Silver Slugger team, 1985 through 1987.
Named South Atlantic League Most Valuable Player, 1980.
Received reported $22,000 bonus to sign with New York Yankees, 1979.

Year Club	League	Pos.	G.	AB.	R.	H.	2B.	3B.	HR.	RBI.	B.A.	PO.	A.	E.	F.A.
1979—Oneonta	NYP	OF-1B	53	166	20	58	10	2	3	31	.349	29	2	2	.939
1980—Greensboro	S. Atl.	OF-1B	133	494	92	*177	32	5	9	105	*.358	205	16	8	.976
1981—Nashville	South.	OF-1B	141	547	74	173	*35	4	7	98	.316	846	69	12	.987
1982—Columbus	Int.	OF-1B	130	476	67	150	24	2	10	75	.315	271	17	5	.983
1982—New York	Amer.	OF-1B	7	12	0	2	0	0	0	1	.167	15	1	0	1.000
1983—New York	Amer.	OF-1B-2B	91	279	34	79	15	4	4	32	.283	350	15	3	.992
1983—Columbus	Int.	1B-OF	43	159	35	54	11	3	8	37	.340	325	29	1	.997
1984—New York	Amer.	1B-OF	153	603	91	*207	*44	2	23	110	*.343	1143	126	6	.995
1985—New York	Amer.	1B	159	652	107	211	*48	3	35	*145	.324	1318	87	7	*.995
1986—New York	Amer.	1B-3B	162	677	117	*238	*53	2	31	113	.352	1378	111	7	.995
1987—New York†	Amer.	1B	141	569	93	186	38	2	30	115	.327	1239	91	5	*.996
1988—New York‡	Amer.	1B-OF	144	599	94	186	37	0	18	88	.311	1250	99	9	.993
Major League Totals—7 Years			857	3391	536	1109	235	13	141	604	.327	6693	530	37	.995

Selected by New York Yankees' organization in 19th round of free-agent draft, June 5, 1979.
†On disabled list, June 9 to June 24, 1987.
‡On disabled list, May 27 to June 14, 1988.

ALL-STAR GAME RECORD

Year League	Pos.	AB.	R.	H.	2B.	3B.	HR.	RBI.	B.A.	PO.	A.	E.	F.A.
1984—American	PH	1	0	0	0	0	0	0	.000	0	0	0	.000
1985—American	1B	1	0	0	0	0	0	0	.000	4	0	0	1.000
1986—American	PH-1B	3	0	0	0	0	0	0	.000	7	0	0	1.000
1987—American	1B	1	0	0	0	0	0	0	.000	10	0	0	1.000
1988—American	1B	2	0	0	0	0	0	0	.000	2	1	1	.750
All-Star Game Totals—5 Years		8	0	0	0	0	0	0	.000	23	1	1	.960

DERRICK BRANT MAY

Born July 14, 1968, at Rochester, N.Y.
Height, 6.04. Weight, 210.
Throws right and bats lefthanded.
Son of Dave May, outfielder with Baltimore Orioles, Milwaukee Brewers, Atlanta Braves, Texas Rangers and Pittsburgh Pirates, 1967 through 1978.

Tied for Carolina League lead in double plays by outfielders with 4 in 1988.

Year Club	League	Pos.	G.	AB.	R.	H.	2B.	3B.	HR.	RBI.	B.A.	PO.	A.	E.	F.A.
1986—Wytheville	Appal.	OF	54	178	25	57	6	1	0	23	.320	47	3	5	.909
1987—Peoria	Midw.	OF	128	439	60	131	19	8	9	52	.298	181	13	8	.960
1988—Winston-Salem	Carol.	OF	130	485	76	•148	29	*9	8	65	.305	209	13	10	.957

Selected by Chicago Cubs' organization in 1st round (ninth player selected) of free-agent draft, June 2, 1986.

SCOTT FRANCIS MAY

Born November 11, 1961, at West Bend, Wis.
Height, 6.00. Weight, 185.
Throws and bats righthanded.
Attended University of Wisconsin, Stevens Point, Wis.

Year Club	League	G.	IP.	W.	L.	Pct.	H.	R.	ER.	SO.	BB.	ERA.
1983—Lethbridge	Pioneer	13	46⅔	2	1	.667	46	29	26	36	30	5.01
1984—Bakersfield	California	25	152⅔	8	10	.444	128	78	65	107	81	3.83
1985—San Antonio	Texas	26	191⅔	10	6	.625	181	85	74	125	*99	3.47
1986—Albuquerque	P. Coast	27	65	0	7	.000	97	59	50	57	39	6.92
1986—San Antonio	Texas	4	24	2	0	1.000	31	15	14	12	7	5.25
1987—San Antonio†	Texas	30	111⅓	8	8	.500	136	83	74	108	52	5.98
1988—Oklahoma City	Am. Assoc.	36	151⅔	8	7	.533	132	56	50	103	57	2.97
1988—Texas	American	3	7⅓	0	0	.000	8	7	7	4	4	8.59
Major League Totals—1 Year		3	7⅓	0	0	.000	8	7	7	4	4	8.59

Selected by Los Angeles Dodgers' organization in 6th round of free-agent draft, June 6, 1983.
†Traded to Texas Rangers' organization for Outfielder Javier Ortiz, December 23, 1987.

MATTHEW SAMUEL MAYSEY
(Matt)

Born January 8, 1967, at Hamilton, Ontario, Can.
Height, 6.04. Weight, 210.
Throws and bats righthanded.

Tied for Texas League lead in games started by pitchers with 28 in 1988.

Year Club	League	G.	IP.	W.	L.	Pct.	H.	R.	ER.	SO.	BB.	ERA.
1985—Spokane	Northwest	7	29	0	3	.000	27	18	15	18	16	4.66
1986—Charleston†	S. Atlantic	18	43	3	2	.600	43	28	24	39	24	5.02
1987—Charleston	S. Atlantic	41	150⅓	14	11	.560	112	71	53	143	59	3.17
1988—Wichita	Texas	28	187	9	9	.500	180	88	77	120	68	3.71

Selected by San Diego Padres' organization in 7th round of free-agent draft, June 3, 1985.
†On disabled list, May 4 to July 9, 1986.

LEE LOUIS MAZZILLI

Born March 25, 1955, at Brooklyn, N. Y.
Height, 6.01. Weight, 195.
Throws right and bats left and righthanded.
Son of Libero Mazzilli, former professional welterweight boxer.

Major League stolen bases: 1976 (5), 1977 (22), 1978 (20), 1979 (34), 1980 (41), 1981 (17), 1982 (13), 1983 (15), 1984 (8), 1985 (4), 1986 (4), 1987 (5), 1988 (4). Total—192.

Led Texas League in bases on balls received with 111, caught stealing with 15 and tied for lead in being hit by pitch with 7 in 1976.

Led California League in caught stealing with 16 in 1975.

Received reported $50,000 bonus to sign with New York Mets, 1973.

Year Club	League	Pos.	G.	AB.	R.	H.	2B.	3B.	HR.	RBI.	B.A.	PO.	A.	E.	F.A.
1974—Anderson	W. Car.	OF	132	472	82	127	24	3	11	48	.269	227	9	9	.963
1975—Visalia	Calif.	OF-1B	125	430	103	121	10	4	13	52	.281	185	9	9	.956
1976—Jackson	Texas	OF	131	439	91	128	21	6	13	43	.292	262	8	8	.971
1976—New York	Nat.	OF	24	77	9	15	2	0	2	7	.195	55	2	1	.983
1977—New York	Nat.	OF	159	537	66	134	24	3	6	46	.250	386	9	3	.992
1978—New York	Nat.	OF	148	542	78	148	28	5	16	61	.273	386	8	5	.987
1979—New York	Nat.	OF-1B	158	597	78	181	34	4	15	79	.303	480	24	5	.990
1980—New York	Nat.	1B-OF	152	578	82	162	31	4	16	76	.280	874	53	14	.985
1981—New York†	Nat.	OF	95	324	36	74	14	5	6	34	.228	192	5	6	.970
1982—Tex.‡§-N.Y. x	Amer.	OF-1B	95	323	43	81	10	0	10	34	.251	234	8	4	.984
1983—Pittsburgh	Nat.	OF-1B	109	246	37	59	9	0	5	24	.240	173	3	4	.978
1984—Pittsburgh y	Nat.	OF-1B	111	266	37	63	11	1	4	21	.237	103	2	1	.991
1985—Pittsburgh	Nat.	1B-OF	92	117	20	33	8	0	1	9	.282	152	6	3	.981
1986—Pit. z-N.Y.	Nat.	OF-1B	100	151	28	37	5	1	3	15	.245	128	2	0	1.000
1986—Tidewater	Int.	1B-OF	6	20	3	6	1	0	1	1	.300	28	1	0	1.000
1987—New York a	Nat.	1B-OF	88	124	26	38	8	1	3	24	.306	82	3	0	1.000
1988—New York	Nat.	OF-1B	68	116	9	17	2	0	0	12	.147	114	4	3	.975
National League Totals—12 Years			1304	3675	506	961	176	24	77	408	.261	3125	121	45	.986
American League Totals—1 Year			95	323	43	81	10	0	10	34	.251	234	8	4	.984
Major League Totals—13 Years			1399	3998	549	1042	186	24	87	442	.261	3359	129	49	.986

Selected by New York Mets' organization in 1st round (14th player selected) of free-agent draft, June 5, 1973.
†Traded to Texas Rangers for Pitchers Ron Darling and Walt Terrell, April 1, 1982.
‡On disabled list, May 20 to June 29, 1982.
§Traded to New York Yankees for Shortstop Bucky Dent, August 8, 1982.
xTraded to Pittsburgh Pirates for Outfielder Don Aubin, Pitcher Tim Burke, Catcher John Holland and Infielder Jose Rivera, December 22, 1982.
yOn disabled list, August 28 to September 11, 1984.
zReleased, July 23, 1986; signed by New York Mets' organization, August 3, 1986.
aGranted free agency, November 9, 1987; re-signed by Mets, December 17, 1987.

CHAMPIONSHIP SERIES RECORD

Year Club	League	Pos.	G.	AB.	R.	H.	2B.	3B.	HR.	RBI.	B.A.	PO.	A.	E.	F.A.
1986—New York	Nat.	PH	5	5	0	1	0	0	0	0	.200	0	0	0	.000
1988—New York	Nat.	PH	3	2	0	1	0	0	0	0	.500	0	0	0	.000
Championship Series Totals—2 Years			8	7	0	2	0	0	0	0	.286	0	0	0	.000

WORLD SERIES RECORD

Year Club	League	Pos.	G.	AB.	R.	H.	2B.	3B.	HR.	RBI.	B.A.	PO.	A.	E.	F.A.
1986—New York	Nat.	PH-OF	4	5	2	2	0	0	0	0	.400	1	0	0	1.000

ALL-STAR GAME RECORD

Tied All-Star Game record for most home runs by pinch-hitter, game (1), July 17, 1979.

Year League	Pos.	AB.	R.	H.	2B.	3B.	HR.	RBI.	B.A.	PO.	A.	E.	F.A.
1979—National	PH-OF	1	1	1	0	0	1	2	1.000	0	0	0	.000

THOMAS MICHAEL McCARTHY
(Tom)

Born June 18, 1961, at Lundstahl, W. Germany.
Height 6.00. Weight, 180.
Throws and bats righthanded.

Major League saves: 1988 (1).

Year Club	League	G.	IP.	W.	L.	Pct.	H.	R.	ER.	SO.	BB.	ERA.
1979—Elmira	NYP	18	46	2	6	.250	67	50	36	26	37	7.04
1980—Elmira	NYP	3	20	2	1	.667	10	7	7	14	13	3.15
1980—Winston-Salem	Carolina	11	61	4	4	.500	55	32	27	28	46	3.98
1981—Winston-Salem	Carolina	28	105	3	7	.300	123	99	85	75	99	7.29
1982—Winston-Salem	Carolina	30	103⅓	3	11	.214	128	95	75	75	65	6.53
1983—Winston-Salem	Carolina	35	98	8	6	.571	91	56	45	100	54	4.13
1984—New Britain	Eastern	38	79⅓	8	5	.615	71	35	27	65	56	3.06
1985—Pawtucket	Int'national	26	85⅓	5	6	.455	72	48	34	65	62	3.59
1985—Boston†	American	3	5	0	0	.000	7	6	6	2	4	10.80
1986—Tidewater‡	Int'national	22	84⅔	3	2	.600	89	43	38	30	37	4.04
1987—Tidewater	Int'national	10	19	0	2	.000	22	17	9	7	16	4.26
1987—Jackson	Texas	37	54⅓	1	4	.200	57	18	16	30	21	2.65
1988—Tidewater§	Int'national	34	57⅓	8	3	.727	49	19	17	28	29	2.67

Year Club	League	G.	IP.	W.	L.	Pct.	H.	R.	ER.	SO.	BB.	ERA.
1988—Vancouver	P. Coast	9	18⅔	1	0	1.000	11	0	0	11	4	0.00
1988—Chicago	American	6	13	2	0	1.000	9	2	2	5	2	1.38
Major League Totals—2 Years		9	18	2	0	1.000	16	8	8	7	6	4.00

Selected by Boston Red Sox' organization in 7th round of free-agent draft, June 5, 1979.

†Traded with Pitchers Bob Ojeda, John Mitchell and Chris Bayer to New York Mets for Pitchers Calvin Schiraldi and West Gardner and Outfielders John Christensen and LaSchelle Tarver, November 13, 1985.

‡On disabled list, July 21, 1986 through remainder of season.

§Traded with Infielder Steve Springer to Chicago White Sox for Outfielder Vince Harris and First Baseman Mike Maksodian, August 4, 1988.

KIRK EDWARD McCASKILL

Born April 9, 1961, at Kapuskasing, Ont., Canada.
Height, 6.01. Weight, 195.
Throws and bats righthanded.
Attended University of Vermont, Burlington, Vt.
Son of Ted McCaskill, center with Minnesota North Stars (NHL)
and Los Angeles Sharks (WHA), 1967-68, 1972-73 and 1973-74.

Year Club	League	G.	IP.	W.	L.	Pct.	H.	R.	ER.	SO.	BB.	ERA.
1982—Salem	Northwest	11	71⅓	5	5	.500	63	43	34	87	51	4.29
1983—Redwood	California	16	108⅓	6	5	.545	78	39	28	100	60	2.33
1983—Nashua†	Eastern	13	87	4	8	.333	90	47	43	63	43	4.45
1984—Edmonton	P. Coast	24	143	7	11	.389	162	104	91	75	74	5.73
1985—Edmonton	P. Coast	3	17⅔	1	1	.500	17	7	4	18	6	2.04
1985—California	American	30	189⅔	12	12	.500	189	105	99	102	64	4.70
1986—California	American	34	246⅓	17	10	.630	207	98	92	202	92	3.36
1987—California‡	American	14	74⅔	4	6	.400	84	52	47	56	34	5.67
1987—Palm Springs	California	2	10	2	0	1.000	4	1	0	7	3	0.00
1987—Edmonton	P. Coast	1	6	1	0	1.000	3	2	2	4	4	3.00
1988—California§	American	23	146⅓	8	6	.571	155	78	70	98	61	4.31
Major League Totals—4 Years		101	657	41	34	.547	635	333	308	458	251	4.22

Selected by California Angels' organization in 4th round of free-agent draft, June 7, 1982.

†On suspended list, August 30, 1983; then transferred to disqualified list, September 26, 1983 through April 25, 1984.

‡On disabled list, April 24 to July 11, 1987; included rehabilitation disability assignment to Palm Springs, June 24 tc July 2, and Edmonton, July 3 to July 8, 1987.

§On disabled list, August 9, 1988 through remainder of season.

CHAMPIONSHIP SERIES RECORD

Tied Championship Series records for most games lost, Series (2), 1986; most hits allowed, inning (6), October 14, 1986 (third inning).

Established American League Championship Series record for most runs allowed, seven-game Series (13), 1986.

Year Club	League	G.	IP.	W.	L.	Pct.	H.	R.	ER.	SO.	BB.	ERA.
1986—California	American	2	9⅓	0	2	.000	16	13	8	7	5	7.71

RECORD AS HOCKEY PLAYER

Year Team	League	Games	G.	A.	Pts.	Pen.
1983-84—Sherbrooke Jets (a)	AHL	78	10	12	22	21

(a)—June, 1981—Drafted by Winnipeg Jets in 1981 NHL entry draft. Fourth Jets pick, 64th overall, fourth round.

PAUL WILLIAM McCLELLAN

Born February 8, 1966, at San Mateo, Calif.
Height, 6.02. Weight, 180.
Throws and bats righthanded.
Attended College of San Mateo, San Mateo, Calif.

Led Texas League in balks with 22 in 1988.

Year Club	League	G.	IP.	W.	L.	Pct.	H.	R.	ER.	SO.	BB.	ERA.
1986—Everett	Northwest	13	86⅓	5	4	.556	71	39	32	74	46	3.34
1987—Clinton	Midwest	28	177⅓	12	10	.545	141	86	64	*209	100	3.25
1988—Shreveport	Texas	27	167	10	12	.455	146	89	75	128	62	4.04

Selected by Atlanta Braves' organization in 25th round of free-agent draft, June 3, 1985.

Selected by San Francisco Giants' organization in secondary phase of free-agent draft, January 14, 1986.

LLOYD GLENN McCLENDON

Born January 11, 1959, at Gary, Ind.
Height, 5.11. Weight, 195.
Throws and bats righthanded.
Attended Valparaiso University, Valparaiso, Ind.

Major League stolen bases: 1987 (1), 1988 (4). Total—5.

Year Club	League	Pos.	G.	AB.	R.	H.	2B.	3B.	HR.	RBI.	B.A.	PO.	A.	E.	F.A.
1980—Kingsport	Appal.	C	14	46	7	15	2	0	1	9	.326	19	5	3	.889
1980—Little Falls	NYP	C	40	117	25	32	9	1	3	20	.274	203	20	7	.970
1981—Lynchburg	Carol.	C-3B	103	363	55	91	12	6	7	57	.251	437	74	17	.968
1982—Lynchburg†‡	Carol.	C-3B	108	384	61	105	25	1	18	78	.273	492	87	15	.975
1983—Waterbury	East.	C-3B-1B	123	434	58	114	19	2	15	57	.263	466	99	8	.986
1984—Vermont	East.	C-1-3-O	60	202	36	56	16	0	7	27	.277	174	24	3	.985

Year	Club	League	Pos.	G.	AB.	R.	H.	2B.	3B.	HR.	RBI.	B.A.	PO.	A.	E.	F.A.
1984	—Wichita	A.A.	3B-1B-C	48	152	28	45	13	1	6	28	.296	143	45	4	.979
1985	—Denver	A.A.	1-3-C-O	114	379	57	105	18	5	16	79	.277	470	104	17	.971
1986	—Denver	A.A.	1-O-C-3	132	433	75	112	30	1	*24	88	.259	656	45	11	.985
1987	—Cincinnati	Nat.	C-1-3-O	45	72	8	15	5	0	2	13	.208	80	5	2	.977
1987	—Nashville	A. A.	1B-C	26	84	11	24	6	0	3	14	.286	72	3	1	.987
1988	—Cincinnati	Nat.	C-O-1-3	72	137	9	30	4	0	3	14	.219	197	13	4	.981
1988	—Nashville§	A. A.	OF-C	2	7	0	1	0	0	0	0	.143	12	2	0	1.000
Major League Totals—2 Years				117	209	17	45	9	0	5	27	.215	277	18	6	.980

Selected by New York Mets' organization in 8th round of free-agent draft, June 3, 1980.

†On disabled list, April 4 to April 27, 1982.

‡Traded with Pitcher Charlie Puleo and Outfielder Jason Felice to Cincinnati Reds for Pitcher Tom Seaver, December 16, 1982.

§Traded to Chicago Cubs for Outfielder Rolando Roomes, December 9, 1988.

ROBERT CRAIG McCLURE
(Bob)

Born April 29, 1953, at Oakland, Calif.
Height, 5.11. Weight, 170.
Throws left and bats left and righthanded.
Attended College of San Mateo, San Mateo, Calif.

Major League saves: 1975 (1), 1977 (6), 1978 (9), 1979 (5), 1980 (10), 1984 (1), 1985 (3), 1986 (6), 1987 (5), 1988 (3). Total—49.

Led American League in balks with 6 in 1983.

Tied for Pioneer League lead in shutouts with 3 in 1973.

Year	Club	League	G.	IP.	W.	L.	Pct.	H.	R.	ER.	SO.	BB.	ERA.
1973	—Billings	Pioneer	14	94	*10	2	.833	64	41	22	110	67	2.11
1974	—Omaha	Am. Assoc.	21	136	5	8	.385	140	71	58	88	65	3.84
1975	—Jacksonville†	Southern	9	42	3	2	.600	31	18	11	39	23	2.36
1975	—Kansas City	American	12	15	1	0	1.000	4	0	0	15	14	0.00
1976	—Omaha	Am. Assoc.	21	133	9	8	.529	133	61	44	91	41	2.98
1976	—Kansas City‡	American	8	4	0	0	.000	3	4	4	3	8	9.00
1977	—Milwaukee	American	68	71	2	1	.667	64	25	20	57	34	2.54
1978	—Milwaukee	American	44	65	2	6	.250	53	30	27	47	30	3.74
1979	—Milwaukee	American	36	51	5	2	.714	53	29	22	37	24	3.88
1980	—Milwaukee	American	52	91	5	8	.385	83	34	31	47	37	3.07
1981	—Burlington	Midwest	4	14	0	2	.000	19	15	15	11	11	9.64
1981	—Milwaukee§	American	4	8	0	0	.000	7	3	3	6	4	3.38
1982	—Milwaukee x	American	34	172⅔	12	7	.632	160	90	81	99	74	4.22
1983	—Milwaukee y	American	24	142	9	9	.500	152	75	71	68	68	4.50
1984	—Milwaukee	American	39	139⅔	4	8	.333	154	76	68	68	52	4.38
1985	—Milwaukee	American	38	85⅔	4	1	.800	91	43	41	57	30	4.31
1986	—Milwaukee z	American	13	16⅓	2	1	.667	18	7	7	11	10	3.86
1986	—Montreal	National	52	62⅔	2	5	.286	53	22	21	42	23	3.02
1987	—Montreal a	National	52	52⅓	6	1	.857	47	30	20	33	20	3.44
1988	—Montreal b-New York c	National	33	30	2	3	.400	35	18	18	19	8	5.40
American League Totals—12 Years			372	861⅓	46	43	.517	842	416	375	515	385	3.92
National League Totals—3 Years			137	145	10	9	.526	135	70	59	94	51	3.66
Major League Totals—14 Years			509	1006⅓	56	52	.519	977	486	434	609	436	3.88

Selected by Los Angeles Dodgers' organization in 3rd round of free-agent draft, January 10, 1973.

Selected by Kansas City Royals' organization in secondary phase of free-agent draft, June 5, 1973.

†On disabled list, April 15 to May 13 and June 5 to July 25, 1975.

‡Traded to Milwaukee Brewers, March 15, 1977; completing deal in which Kansas City Royals traded Infielder Jamie Quirk, Outfielder Jim Wohlford and a player to be named later to Milwaukee for Pitcher Jim Colborn and Catcher Darrell Porter, December 6, 1976.

§On disabled list, March 28 to September 1, 1981; included rehabilitation disability assignment to Burlington, August 7 to August 24, 1981.

xGranted free agency, November 10, 1982; re-signed by Brewers, December 6, 1982.

yOn disabled list, August 22 to September 12, 1983.

zSold to Montreal Expos, June 8, 1986.

aGranted free agency, November 9, 1987; re-signed by Expos, December 7, 1987.

bReleased, July 2, 1988; signed by New York Mets, July 13, 1988.

cReleased, October 27, 1988.

DIVISION SERIES RECORD

Year	Club	League	G.	IP.	W.	L.	Pct.	H.	R.	ER.	SO.	BB.	ERA.
1981	—Milwaukee	American	3	3⅓	0	0	.000	4	0	0	2	0	0.00

CHAMPIONSHIP SERIES RECORD

Year	Club	League	G.	IP.	W.	L.	Pct.	H.	R.	ER.	SO.	BB.	ERA.
1982	—Milwaukee	American	1	1⅔	1	0	1.000	2	0	0	0	0	0.00

WORLD SERIES RECORD

Tied World Series record for most games lost, seven-game Series (2), 1982.

Year	Club	League	G.	IP.	W.	L.	Pct.	H.	R.	ER.	SO.	BB.	ERA.
1982	—Milwaukee	American	5	4⅓	0	2	.000	5	2	2	5	3	4.15

JAMES ANTHONY McCOLLOM
(Jim)

Born April 23, 1963, at New York, N.Y.
Height, 6.01. Weight, 195.
Throws and bats righthanded.
Attended Clemson University, Clemson, S.C.

Led Texas League in slugging percentage with .560 in 1988.
Led Northwest League in being hit by pitch with 10 in 1985.

Year	Club	League	Pos.	G.	AB.	R.	H.	2B.	3B.	HR.	RBI.	B.A.	PO.	A.	E.	F.A.
1985—	Salem	N'west	1B	73	267	48	85	18	0	11	47	.318	571	*50	8	*.987
1986—	Quad Cities†	Midw.					(Did not play)									
1987—	Quad Cities	Midw.	1B-OF	88	322	35	88	21	0	8	36	.273	559	29	11	.982
1988—	Midland	Texas	1B-OF	118	452	95	155	32	3	20	75	.343	778	62	16	.981

Selected by California Angels' organization in 9th round of free-agent draft, June 3, 1985.
†On disabled list, April 5, 1986 through entire season.

LANCE GRAYE McCULLERS

Born March 8, 1964, at Tampa, Fla.
Height, 6.01. Weight, 218.
Throws right and bats right and lefthanded.

Major League saves: 1985 (5), 1986 (5), 1987 (16), 1988 (10). Total—36.
Tied for Pacific Coast League lead in hit batsmen with 6 in 1985.

Year	Club	League	G.	IP.	W.	L.	Pct.	H.	R.	ER.	SO.	BB.	ERA.
1982—	Helena	Pioneer	13	87	6	4	.600	89	44	36	62	33	3.72
1983—	Spartanburg†	S. Atlantic	22	136⅓	9	6	.600	139	79	61	87	57	4.03
1984—	Miami	Florida St.	22	106⅓	6	4	.600	92	37	30	94	45	2.54
1984—	Beaumont‡	Texas	8	55⅓	4	1	.800	38	13	13	48	35	2.11
1985—	Las Vegas	P. Coast	24	149⅓	11	8	.579	135	75	66	148	83	3.98
1985—	San Diego	National	21	35	0	2	.000	23	15	9	27	16	2.31
1986—	San Diego	National	70	136	10	10	.500	103	46	42	92	58	2.78
1987—	San Diego	National	78	123⅓	8	10	.444	115	60	51	126	59	3.72
1988—	San Diego§	National	60	97⅔	3	6	.333	70	29	27	81	55	2.49
Major League Totals—4 Years			229	392	21	28	.429	311	150	129	326	188	2.96

Selected by Philadelphia Phillies' organization in 2nd round of free-agent draft, June 7, 1982.
†Traded with Pitchers Marty Decker, Darren Burroughs and Ed Wojna to San Diego Padres, September 20, 1983, as partial completion of deal in which San Diego traded Outfielder Sixto Lezcano and a player to be named later to Philadelphia Phillies for four players to be named later, August 31, 1983; Philadelphia organization acquired Pitcher Steve Fireovid to complete deal, October 11, 1983.
‡On disabled list, September 7, 1984 through remainder of season.
§Traded with Pitcher Jimmy Jones and Outfielder Stan Jefferson to New York Yankees for First Baseman-Outfielder Jack Clark and Pitcher Pat Clements, October 24, 1988.

JACK BURNS McDOWELL

Born January 16, 1966, at Van Nuys, Calif.
Height, 6.05. Weight, 179.
Throws and bats righthanded.
Attended Stanford University, Stanford, Calif.

Received reported $175,000 bonus to sign with Chicago White Sox, 1987.

Year	Club	League	G.	IP.	W.	L.	Pct.	H.	R.	ER.	SO.	BB.	ERA.
1987—	Sarasota White Sox	Gulf Coast	2	7	0	1	.000	4	3	2	12	1	2.57
1987—	Birmingham	Southern	4	20⅔	1	2	.333	19	20	18	17	8	7.84
1987—	Chicago	American	4	28	3	0	1.000	16	6	6	15	6	1.93
1988—	Chicago	American	26	158⅔	5	10	.333	147	85	70	84	68	3.97
Major League Totals—2 Years			30	186⅔	8	10	.444	163	91	76	99	74	3.66

Selected by Boston Red Sox' organization in 20th round of free-agent draft, June 4, 1984.
Selected by Chicago White Sox' organization in 1st round (fifth player selected) of free-agent draft, June 2, 1987.

ODDIBE McDOWELL JR.

First name pronounced OH-da-bee.

Born August 25, 1962, at Hollywood, Fla.
Height, 5.09. Weight, 160.
Throws and bats lefthanded.
Attended Miami-Dade Community College (North), Miami, Fla., and
Arizona State University, Tempe, Ariz.

Tied major league record for most putouts by outfielder, game (12), July 20, 1985, 15 innings.
Tied American League record for most chances accepted by outfielder, game (12), July 20, 1985, 15 innings.
Major League stolen bases: 1985 (25), 1986 (33), 1987 (24), 1988 (33). Total—115.
Hit for the cycle, July 23, 1985.
Member of 1984 U.S. Olympic baseball team.
Named outfielder on THE SPORTING NEWS College Baseball All-America Team, 1983 and 1984.

Year	Club	League	Pos.	G.	AB.	R.	H.	2B.	3B.	HR.	RBI.	B.A.	PO.	A.	E.	F.A.
1985—	Oklahoma City	A. A.	OF	31	125	32	50	7	8	2	18	.400	72	4	1	.987
1985—	Texas	Amer.	OF	111	406	63	97	14	5	18	42	.239	282	9	2	.993
1986—	Texas	Amer.	OF	154	572	105	152	24	7	18	49	.266	325	13	3	.991

Year	Club	League	Pos.	G.	AB.	R.	H.	2B.	3B.	HR.	RBI.	B.A.	PO.	A.	E.	F.A.
1987	—Texas	Amer.	OF	128	407	65	98	26	4	14	52	.241	263	5	3	.989
1988	—Texas	Amer.	OF	120	437	55	108	19	5	6	37	.247	267	2	3	.989
1988	—Oklahoma City†	A. A.	OF	18	70	9	20	3	1	1	6	.286	50	1	0	1.000
Major League Totals—4 Years				513	1822	288	455	83	21	56	180	.250	1137	29	11	.991

Selected by St. Louis Cardinals' organization in 4th round of free-agent draft, January 13, 1981.
Selected by Texas Rangers' organization in secondary phase of free-agent draft, June 8, 1981.
Selected by New York Yankees' organization in secondary phase of free-agent draft, January 12, 1982.
Selected by Toronto Blue Jays' organization in secondary phase of free-agent draft, June 7, 1982.
Selected by Minnesota Twins' organization in secondary phase of free-agent draft, June 6, 1983.
Selected by Texas Rangers' organization in 1st round (12th player selected) of free-agent draft, June 4, 1984.
†Traded with First Baseman Pete O'Brien and Second Baseman Jerry Browne to Cleveland Indians for Second Baseman Julio Franco, December 6, 1988.

ROGER ALAN McDOWELL

Born December 21, 1960, at Cincinnati, O.
Height, 6.01. Weight, 185.
Throws and bats righthanded.
Attended Bowling Green State University, Bowling Green, O.

Major League saves: 1985 (17), 1986 (22), 1987 (25), 1988 (16). Total—80.

Year	Club	League	G.	IP.	W.	L.	Pct.	H.	R.	ER.	SO.	BB.	ERA.
1982	—Shelby	S. Atlantic	12	71⅓	6	4	.600	61	34	26	40	30	3.28
1982	—Lynchburg	Carolina	4	29⅓	2	0	1.000	26	12	7	23	11	2.15
1983	—Jackson	Texas	27	172⅓	11	12	.478	203	111	93	115	71	4.86
1984	—Jackson†	Texas	3	7⅓	0	0	.000	9	3	3	8	1	3.68
1985	—New York	National	62	127⅓	6	5	.545	108	43	40	70	37	2.83
1986	—New York‡	National	75	128	14	9	.609	107	48	43	65	42	3.02
1987	—New York§	National	56	88⅔	7	5	.583	95	41	41	32	28	4.16
1988	—New York	National	62	89	5	5	.500	80	31	26	46	31	2.63
Major League Totals—4 Years			255	433	32	24	.571	390	163	150	213	138	3.12

Selected by New York Mets' organization in 3rd round of free-agent draft, June 7, 1982.
†On disabled list, April 10 to August 14, 1984.
‡Appeared in one game as an outfielder with no chances.
§On disabled list, March 29 to May 14, 1987.

CHAMPIONSHIP SERIES RECORD

Tied Championship Series record for most games pitched, seven-game Series (4), 1988.

Year	Club	League	G.	IP.	W.	L.	Pct.	H.	R.	ER.	SO.	BB.	ERA.
1986	—New York	National	2	7	0	0	.000	1	0	0	3	0	0.00
1988	—New York	National	4	6	0	1	.000	6	3	3	5	2	4.50
Championship Series Totals—2 Years			6	13	0	1	.000	7	3	3	8	2	2.08

WORLD SERIES RECORD

Year	Club	League	G.	IP.	W.	L.	Pct.	H.	R.	ER.	SO.	BB.	ERA.
1986	—New York	National	5	7⅓	1	0	1.000	10	5	4	2	6	4.91

CHARLES DWAYNE McELROY
(Chuck)

Born October 1, 1967, at Galveston, Tex.
Height, 6.00. Weight, 160.
Throws and bats lefthanded.

Year	Club	League	G.	IP.	W.	L.	Pct.	H.	R.	ER.	SO.	BB.	ERA.
1986	—Utica	NYP	14	94⅔	4	6	.400	85	40	31	91	28	2.95
1987	—Spartanburg	S. Atlantic	24	130⅓	14	4	.778	117	51	45	115	48	3.11
1987	—Clearwater	Florida St.	2	7⅓	1	0	1.000	1	1	0	7	4	0.00
1988	—Reading	Eastern	28	160	9	12	.429	•173	89	*80	92	70	4.50

Selected by Philadelphia Phillies' organization in 8th round of free-agent draft, June 2, 1986.

ANDREW JOSEPH McGAFFIGAN
(Andy)

Born October 25, 1956, at West Palm Beach, Fla.
Height, 6.03. Weight, 190.
Throws and bats righthanded.
Attended Palm Beach Junior College, Lake Worth, Fla., and received degree from Florida Southern College, Lakeland, Fla., in 1978.

Major League saves: 1983 (2), 1984 (1), 1986 (2), 1987 (12), 1988 (4). Total—21.
Named Southern League Pitcher of the Year, 1980.

Year	Club	League	G.	IP.	W.	L.	Pct.	H.	R.	ER.	SO.	BB.	ERA.
1978	—Oneonta	NYP	2	12	0	1	.000	14	8	6	13	9	4.50
1978	—Fort Lauderdale	Florida St.	11	66	4	5	.444	45	28	21	36	20	2.86
1979	—West Haven	Eastern	23	144	10	6	.625	136	75	61	113	54	3.81
1980	—Nashville†	Southern	31	170	15	5	.750	139	62	45	125	62	*2.38
1981	—Columbus‡	Int'national	17	103	8	6	.571	85	45	37	57	37	3.23
1981	—New York§	American	2	7	0	0	.000	5	3	2	2	3	2.57
1982	—Phoenix x	P. Coast	18	96	1	6	.143	115	72	64	64	51	6.00

Year	Club	League	G.	IP.	W.	L.	Pct.	H.	R.	ER.	SO.	BB.	ERA.
1982	—San Francisco	National	4	8	1	0	1.000	5	1	0	4	1	0.00
1983	—San Francisco y	National	43	134⅓	3	9	.250	131	67	64	93	39	4.29
1984	—Montreal z-Cincinnati	National	30	69	3	6	.333	60	28	27	57	23	3.52
1985	—Denver	Am. Assoc.	26	106⅔	11	5	.688	105	43	35	91	37	2.95
1985	—Cincinnati a	National	15	94⅓	3	3	.500	88	40	39	83	30	3.72
1986	—Montreal	National	48	142⅔	10	5	.667	114	49	42	104	55	2.65
1987	—Montreal	National	69	120⅓	5	2	.714	105	38	32	100	42	2.39
1988	—Montreal b	National	63	91⅓	6	0	1.000	81	31	28	71	37	2.76
American League Totals—1 Year			2	7	0	0	.000	5	3	2	2	3	2.57
National League Totals—7 Years			272	660	31	25	.554	584	254	232	512	227	3.19
Major League Totals—8 Years			274	667	31	25	.554	589	257	234	514	230	3.16

Selected by Cincinnati Reds' organization in 36th round of free-agent draft, June 5, 1974.
Selected by Chicago White Sox' organization in 5th round of free-agent draft, January 7, 1976.
Selected by New York Yankees' organization in 6th round of free-agent draft, June 6, 1978.
†On disabled list, September 1 to September 22, 1980.
‡On disabled list, April 10 to June 14, 1981.
§Traded with Outfielder Ted Wilborn to San Francisco Giants' organization for Pitcher Doyle Alexander, March 30, 1982.
xOn disabled list, June 20 to August 13, 1982.
yTraded to Montreal Expos, March 31, 1984, as compensation for the injury that Pitcher Fred Breining arrived with in trade of February 27, 1984, which sent Breining and Outfielder Max Venable to Montreal for First Baseman Al Oliver. (Breining remained with Montreal.)
zTraded with Pitcher Jim Jefferson to Cincinnati Reds for First Baseman Dan Driessen, July 26, 1984.
aTraded with Pitchers Jay Tibbs and John Stuper and Catcher Dann Bilardello to Montreal Expos for Pitcher Bill Gullickson and Catcher Sal Butera, December 19, 1985.
bOn disabled list, June 15 to July 2, 1988.

WILLIE DEAN McGEE

Born November 2, 1958, at San Francisco, Calif.
Height, 6.01. Weight, 176.
Throws right and bats right and lefthanded.
Attended Diablo Valley College, Pleasant Hill, Calif.

Established modern National League record for highest batting average, switch-hitter, season, 100 or more games (.353), 1985.
Major League stolen bases: 1982 (24), 1983 (39), 1984 (43), 1985 (56), 1986 (19), 1987 (16), 1988 (41). Total—238.
Hit for the cycle, June 23, 1984.
Led National League in grounding into double plays with 24 in 1987.
Named National League Player of the Year by THE SPORTING NEWS, 1985.
Named National League Most Valuable Player by Baseball Writers' Association of America, 1985.
Named outfielder on THE SPORTING NEWS National League All-Star Team, 1985.
Named outfielder on THE SPORTING NEWS National League All-Star fielding team, 1983, 1985 and 1986.
Named outfielder on THE SPORTING NEWS National League Silver Slugger team, 1985.

Year	Club	League	Pos.	G.	AB.	R.	H.	2B.	3B.	HR.	RBI.	B.A.	PO.	A.	E.	F.A.
1977	—Oneonta	NYP	OF	65	225	31	53	4	3	2	22	.236	103	5	10	.915
1978	—Fort Lauderdale	Fla. St.	OF	124	423	62	106	6	6	0	37	.251	243	12	9	.966
1979	—West Haven	East.	OF	49	115	21	28	3	1	1	8	.243	88	3	3	.968
1979	—Fort Lauderdale	Fla. St.	OF	46	176	25	56	8	3	1	18	.318	103	3	2	.981
1980	—Nashville†	South.	OF	78	223	35	63	4	5	1	22	.283	127	6	6	.957
1981	—Nashville‡§	South.	OF	100	388	77	125	20	5	7	63	.322	203	10	6	.973
1982	—Louisville x	A. A.	OF	13	55	11	16	2	2	1	3	.291	40	0	1	.976
1982	—St. Louis	Nat.	OF	123	422	43	125	12	8	4	56	.296	245	3	11	.958
1983	—St. Louis y	Nat.	OF	147	601	75	172	22	8	5	75	.286	385	7	5	.987
1983	—Arkansas	Texas	OF	7	29	5	8	1	1	0	2	.276	7	0	0	1.000
1984	—St. Louis z	Nat.	OF	145	571	82	166	19	11	6	50	.291	374	10	6	.985
1985	—St. Louis	Nat.	OF	152	612	114	*216	26	*18	10	82	*.353	382	11	9	.978
1986	—St. Louis a	Nat.	OF	124	497	65	127	22	7	7	48	.256	325	9	3	*.991
1987	—St. Louis	Nat.	OF-SS	153	620	76	177	37	11	11	105	.285	354	10	7	.981
1988	—St. Louis	Nat.	OF	137	562	73	164	24	6	3	50	.292	348	9	9	.975
Major League Totals—7 Years				981	3885	528	1147	162	69	46	466	.295	2413	59	50	.980

Selected by Chicago White Sox' organization in 7th round of free-agent draft, June 8, 1976.
Selected by New York Yankees' organization in secondary phase of free-agent draft, January 11, 1977.
†On disabled list, May 22 to June 7 and July 14 to August 7, 1980.
‡On disabled list, April 24 to June 4, 1981.
§Traded to St. Louis Cardinals' organization for Pitcher Bob Sykes, October 21, 1981.
xOn disabled list, April 13 to April 23, 1982.
yOn disabled list, March 30 to April 29, 1983; included rehabilitation disability assignment to Arkansas, April 18 to April 29, 1983.
zOn disabled list, July 12 to July 27, 1984.
aOn disabled list, August 3 to August 27, 1986.

CHAMPIONSHIP SERIES RECORD

Tied Championship Series record for most three-base hits, Series (2), 1982.
Established National League Championship Series records for most runs, six-game Series (6), 1985; most triples, total Series (3).

Year	Club	League	Pos.	G.	AB.	R.	H.	2B.	3B.	HR.	RBI.	B.A.	PO.	A.	E.	F.A.
1982	—St. Louis	Nat.	OF	3	13	4	4	0	2	1	5	.308	12	0	1	.923
1985	—St. Louis	Nat.	OF	6	26	6	7	1	0	0	3	.269	18	0	0	1.000

Year	Club	League	Pos.	G.	AB.	R.	H.	2B.	3B.	HR.	RBI.	B.A.	PO.	A.	E.	F.A.
1987	—St. Louis	Nat.	OF	7	26	2	8	1	1	0	2	.308	16	0	0	1.000
Championship Series Totals—3 Years				16	65	12	19	2	3	1	10	.292	46	0	1	.979

WORLD SERIES RECORD

Tied World Series record for most putouts, inning, center fielder (3), October 22, 1987 (eighth inning).

Tied World Series records for most home runs, game, by rookie (2), October 15, 1982; highest fielding average by outfielder, seven-game Series (1.000 with 24 chances), 1982; most putouts by outfielder, seven-game Series (24), 1982.

Year	Club	League	Pos.	G.	AB.	R.	H.	2B.	3B.	HR.	RBI.	B.A.	PO.	A.	E.	F.A.
1982	—St. Louis	Nat.	OF	6	25	6	6	0	0	2	5	.240	24	0	0	1.000
1985	—St. Louis	Nat.	OF	7	27	2	7	2	0	1	2	.259	15	0	0	1.000
1987	—St. Louis	Nat.	OF	7	27	2	10	2	0	0	4	.370	21	1	1	.957
World Series Totals—3 Years				20	79	10	23	4	0	3	11	.291	60	1	1	.984

ALL-STAR GAME RECORD

Year	League	Pos.	AB.	R.	H.	2B.	3B.	HR.	RBI.	B.A.	PO.	A.	E.	F.A.
1983	—National	OF	2	0	1	0	0	0	0	.500	2	0	0	1.000
1985	—National	OF	2	0	1	1	0	0	2	.500	1	0	0	1.000
1987	—National	OF	4	0	0	0	0	0	0	.000	2	0	0	1.000
1988	—National	PR-OF	2	0	0	0	0	0	0	.000	1	0	0	1.000
All-Star Game Totals—4 Years			10	0	2	1	0	0	2	.200	6	0	0	1.000

RUSSELL BRENT McGINNIS
(Russ)

Born June 18, 1963, at Coffeyville, Kan.
Height, 6.03. Weight, 215.
Throws and bats righthanded.
Attended University of Oklahoma, Norman, Okla.

Year	Club	League	Pos.	G.	AB.	R.	H.	2B.	3B.	HR.	RBI.	B.A.	PO.	A.	E.	F.A.
1985	—Helena	N'west	1B-3B-C	48	150	33	46	7	0	5	38	.307	200	51	10	.962
1986	—Beloit	Midw.	1B-C-3B	124	413	62	102	24	2	16	59	.247	929	66	17	.983
1987	—Beloit†	Midw.	1B-C-3B	51	189	34	58	10	0	13	35	.307	384	33	7	.983
1987	—Modesto	Calif.	C-3B-1B	47	165	24	42	9	0	8	31	.255	137	21	4	.975
1988	—Huntsville	South.	C-1B	23	77	9	20	9	0	2	15	.260	82	11	2	.979
1988	—Tacoma	P. C.	C-1B	63	186	25	47	13	1	2	22	.253	309	30	9	.974

Selected by Milwaukee Brewers' organization in 14th round of free-agent draft, June 3, 1985.

†Traded to Oakland Athletics' organization for Pitcher Bill Mooneyham, June 29, 1987.

SCOTT HOUSTON McGREGOR

Born January 18, 1954, at Inglewood, Calif.
Height, 6.01. Weight, 190.
Throws left and bats right and lefthanded.
Attended El Camino Junior College, Torrance, Calif. and Loyola Marymount University, Los Angeles, Calif.

Major League saves: 1977 (4), 1978 (1). Total—5.
Tied for American League lead in home runs allowed with 34 in 1985.
Led International League in complete games with 12 and tied for lead in balks with 3 in 1974.
Led Eastern League pitchers in complete games with 14 and tied for lead in games started with 27 in 1973.
Led International League in shutouts with 6 in 1976.
Named International League Pitcher of the Year, 1974.
Received reported $80,000 bonus to sign with New York Yankees, 1972.

Year	Club	League	G.	IP.	W.	L.	Pct.	H.	R.	ER.	SO.	BB.	ERA.
1972	—Fort Lauderdale	Florida St.	11	79	7	3	.700	66	30	24	54	25	2.73
1973	—West Haven	Eastern	27	*197	•12	•13	.480	*197	95	72	126	63	3.29
1974	—Syracuse	Int'national	27	*199	13	10	.565	204	88	76	124	75	3.44
1975	—Syracuse†	Int'national	21	124	6	9	.400	134	73	55	72	60	3.99
1976	—Syracuse‡-Rochester	Int'national	24	162	12	6	.667	159	59	55	83	40	3.06
1976	—Baltimore	American	3	15	0	1	.000	17	7	6	6	5	3.60
1977	—Baltimore	American	29	114	3	5	.375	119	57	56	55	30	4.42
1978	—Baltimore	American	35	233	15	13	.536	217	98	86	94	47	3.32
1979	—Baltimore	American	27	175	13	6	.684	165	70	65	81	23	3.34
1980	—Baltimore	American	36	252	20	8	.714	254	101	93	119	58	3.32
1981	—Baltimore	American	24	160	13	5	.722	167	63	58	82	40	3.26
1982	—Baltimore	American	37	226⅓	14	12	.538	238	126	116	84	52	4.61
1983	—Baltimore	American	36	260	18	7	.720	271	101	92	86	45	3.18
1984	—Baltimore§	American	30	196⅓	15	12	.556	216	93	86	67	54	3.94
1985	—Baltimore	American	35	204	14	14	.500	226	118	109	86	65	4.81
1986	—Baltimore	American	34	203	11	15	.423	216	110	102	95	57	4.52
1987	—Baltimore x	American	26	85⅓	2	7	.222	112	69	63	39	35	6.64
1987	—Rochester	Int'national	3	17⅔	0	2	.000	17	6	6	15	5	3.06
1988	—Baltimore y	American	4	17⅓	0	3	.000	27	18	17	10	7	8.83
Major League Totals—13 Years			356	2141⅓	138	108	.561	2245	1031	949	904	518	3.99

Selected by New York Yankees' organization in 1st round (14th player selected) of free-agent draft, June 6, 1972.

†On disabled list, August 1 to August 29, 1975.

‡Traded with Pitchers Rudy May, Tippy Martinez and Dave Pagan, and Catcher Rick Dempsey to Baltimore Orioles for Pitchers Ken Holtzman, Doyle Alexander and Grant Jackson, Catcher Ellie Hendricks and Pitcher Jimmy Freeman, June 15, 1976.

§On disabled list, August 29, 1984 through remainder of season.
xOn disabled list, August 8 to September 5, 1987.
yReleased, May 2, 1988.

CHAMPIONSHIP SERIES RECORD

Year Club	League	G.	IP.	W.	L.	Pct.	H.	R.	ER.	SO.	BB.	ERA.
1979—Baltimore	American	1	9	1	0	1.000	6	0	0	4	1	0.00
1983—Baltimore	American	1	6⅔	0	1	.000	6	2	1	2	3	1.35
Championship Series Totals—2 Years		2	15⅔	1	1	.500	12	2	1	6	4	0.57

WORLD SERIES RECORD

Year Club	League	G.	IP.	W.	L.	Pct.	H.	R.	ER.	SO.	BB.	ERA.
1979—Baltimore	American	2	17	1	1	.500	16	6	6	8	2	3.18
1983—Baltimore	American	2	17	1	1	.500	9	2	2	12	2	1.06
World Series Totals—2 Years		4	34	2	2	.500	25	8	8	20	4	2.12

ALL-STAR GAME RECORD

Member of American League All-Star Team in 1981; did not play.

FREDERICK STANLEY McGRIFF
(Fred)

Born October 31, 1963, at Tampa, Fla.
Height, 6.03. Weight, 208.
Throws and bats lefthanded.

Major League stolen bases: 1987 (3), 1988 (6). Total—9.

Tied for International League lead in intentional bases on balls received with 8 and grounding into double plays with 16 in 1986.

Led Gulf Coast League in bases on balls received with 48 and tied for lead in game-winning RBIs with 6 in 1982.

Led International League first basemen in total chances with 1,314 and double plays with 108 in 1986.

Year Club	League	Pos.	G.	AB.	R.	H.	2B.	3B.	HR.	RBI.	B.A.	PO.	A.	E.	F.A.
1981—Bradenton Yanks	Gulf C.	1B	29	81	6	12	2	0	0	9	.148	176	8	7	.963
1982—Braden. Yanks†	Gulf C.	1B	62	217	38	59	11	1	★9	●41	.272	514	★56	8	.986
1983—Florence	S. Atl.	1B	33	119	26	37	3	1	7	26	.311	250	14	6	.978
1983—Kinston	Carol.	1B	94	350	53	85	14	1	21	57	.243	784	57	10	.988
1984—Knoxville	South.	1B	56	189	29	47	13	2	9	25	.249	481	45	10	.981
1984—Syracuse	Int.	1B	70	238	28	56	10	1	13	28	.235	644	45	3	.996
1985—Syracuse‡	Int.	1B	51	176	19	40	8	2	5	20	.227	433	37	5	.989
1986—Syracuse	Int.	★1B-OF	133	468	69	121	23	4	19	74	.259	★1219	★85	10	★.992
1986—Toronto	Amer.	1B	3	5	1	1	0	0	0	0	.200	3	0	0	1.000
1987—Toronto	Amer.	1B	107	295	58	73	16	0	20	43	.247	108	7	2	.983
1988—Toronto	Amer.	1B	154	536	100	151	35	4	34	82	.282	1344	93	5	★.997
Major League Totals—3 Years			264	836	159	225	51	4	54	125	.269	1455	100	7	.996

Selected by New York Yankees' organization in 9th round of free-agent draft, June 8, 1981.

†Traded with Outfielder Dave Collins, Pitcher Mike Morgan and a reported $400,000 to Toronto Blue Jays for Outfielder-Catcher Tom Dodd and Pitcher Dale Murray, December 9, 1982.

‡On disabled list, June 5 to August 14, 1985.

TERENCE ROY McGRIFF
(Terry)

Born September 23, 1963, at Fort Pierce, Fla.
Height, 6.02. Weight, 195.
Throws and bats righthanded.

Major League stolen bases: 1988 (1).

Led American Association catchers in double plays with 8 and passed balls with 10 in 1986.

Led Eastern League catchers in total chances with 731 in 1985.

Year Club	League	Pos.	G.	AB.	R.	H.	2B.	3B.	HR.	RBI.	B.A.	PO.	A.	E.	F.A.
1981—Billings	Pion.	C-1B	42	96	15	26	3	0	1	15	.271	166	14	7	.963
1982—Eugene	N'west	C	53	190	23	46	10	2	4	31	.242	320	★43	8	.978
1983—Tampa	Fla. St.	C	87	260	21	66	11	3	5	45	.254	403	67	7	.985
1984—Tampa	Fla. St.	C	110	345	48	96	19	0	7	41	.278	576	88	16	.976
1985—Vermont	East.	C	110	363	52	92	10	4	13	60	.253	★636	89	6	★.992
1986—Denver	A. A.	C	108	340	54	99	22	1	9	54	.291	411	★59	11	.977
1987—Nashville	A. A.	C	67	228	36	62	11	3	10	33	.272	343	36	3	.992
1987—Cincinnati	Nat.	C	34	89	6	20	3	0	2	11	.225	160	14	3	.983
1988—Cincinnati	Nat.	C	35	96	9	19	3	0	1	4	.198	177	14	2	.990
1988—Nashville	A. A.	C	35	97	8	21	3	1	1	12	.216	175	10	4	.979
Major League Totals—2 Years			69	185	15	39	6	0	3	15	.211	337	28	5	.986

Selected by Cincinnati Reds' organization in 8th round of free-agent draft, June 8, 1981.

WILLIAM PATRICK McGUIRE JR.
(Bill)

Born February 14, 1964, at Omaha, Neb.
Height, 6.03. Weight, 215.
Throws and bats righthanded.
Attended University of Nebraska, Lincoln, Neb.

Led California League catchers in double plays with 16 in 1986.

Year	Club	League	Pos.	G.	AB.	R.	H.	2B.	3B.	HR.	RBI.	B.A.	PO.	A.	E.	F.A.
1985—	Wausau	Midw.	C	56	191	24	47	9	0	3	15	.246	304	26	9	.973
1986—	Salinas	Calif.	C	116	368	49	110	22	1	6	62	.299	713	83	★20	.975
1987—	Chattanooga	South.	C	79	259	21	59	10	0	3	29	.228	477	43	6	.989
1988—	Vermont	East.	C	49	136	16	28	3	0	5	24	.206	280	43	7	.979
1988—	Calgary	P. C.	C	37	117	17	27	7	0	2	15	.231	215	19	1	.996
1988—	Seattle	Amer.	C	9	16	1	3	0	0	0	2	.188	29	3	0	1.000
Major League Totals—1 Year				9	16	1	3	0	0	0	2	.188	29	3	0	1.000

Selected by Cleveland Indians' organization in 25th round of free-agent draft, June 7, 1982.
Selected by Seattle Mariners' organization in 1st round (27th player selected) of free-agent draft, June 3, 1985.

MARK DAVID McGWIRE

Born October 1, 1963, at Pomona, Calif.
Height, 6.05. Weight, 225.
Throws and bats righthanded.
Attended University of Southern California, Los Angeles, Calif.
Brother of Dan McGwire, quarterback at San Diego State University.

Established major league records for most home runs (49) and extra bases on long hits (183) by rookie, season, 1987.
Tied major league record for most home runs, two consecutive games (5), June 27 and 28, 1987.
Tied modern major league record for most runs, two consecutive games (9), June 27 and 28, 1987.
Established American League record for highest slugging average by rookie, season (.618), 1987.
Hit three home runs in a game, June 27, 1987.
Major League stolen bases: 1987 (1).
Led American League in slugging percentage with .618 in 1987.
Led California League third basemen in assists with 239 and total chances with 354 in 1985.
Named American League Rookie Player of the Year by The Sporting News, 1987.
Named American League Rookie of the Year by Baseball Writers' Association of America, 1987.
Member of 1984 U.S. Olympic baseball team.
Named College Player of the Year by The Sporting News, 1984.
Named first baseman on The Sporting News College Baseball All-America Team, 1984.

Year	Club	League	Pos.	G.	AB.	R.	H.	2B.	3B.	HR.	RBI.	B.A.	PO.	A.	E.	F.A.
1984—	Modesto	Calif.	1B	16	55	7	11	3	0	1	1	.200	107	6	1	.991
1985—	Modesto	Calif.	3B-1B	138	489	95	134	23	3	•24	•106	.274	105	240	33	.913
1986—	Huntsville	South	3B	55	195	40	59	15	0	10	53	.303	34	124	16	.908
1986—	Tacoma	P. C.	3B	78	280	42	89	21	5	13	59	.318	53	126	25	.877
1986—	Oakland	Amer.	3B	18	53	10	10	1	0	3	9	.189	10	20	6	.833
1987—	Oakland	Amer.	1B-3B-OF	151	557	97	161	28	4	★49	118	.289	1176	101	13	.990
1988—	Oakland	Amer.	1B-OF	155	550	87	143	22	1	32	99	.260	1228	88	9	.993
Major League Totals—3 Years				324	1160	194	314	51	5	84	226	.271	2414	209	28	.989

Selected by Montreal Expos' organization in 8th round of free-agent draft, June 8, 1981.
Selected by Oakland A's organization in 1st round (10th player selected) of free-agent draft, June 4, 1984.

CHAMPIONSHIP SERIES RECORD

Year	Club	League	Pos.	G.	AB.	R.	H.	2B.	3B.	HR.	RBI.	B.A.	PO.	A.	E.	F.A.
1988—	Oakland	Amer.	1B	4	15	4	5	0	0	1	3	.333	24	2	0	1.000

WORLD SERIES RECORD

Year	Club	League	Pos.	G.	AB.	R.	H.	2B.	3B.	HR.	RBI.	B.A.	PO.	A.	E.	F.A.
1988—	Oakland	Amer.	1B	5	17	1	1	0	0	1	1	.059	40	3	0	1.000

ALL-STAR GAME RECORD

Year	League	Pos.	AB.	R.	H.	2B.	3B.	HR.	RBI.	B.A.	PO.	A.	E.	F.A.
1987—	American	1B	3	0	0	0	0	0	0	.000	7	0	1	.875
1988—	American	1B	2	0	1	0	0	0	0	.500	8	0	0	1.000
All-Star Game Totals—2 Years			5	0	1	0	0	0	0	.200	15	0	1	.938

TIMOTHY ALLEN McINTOSH
(Tim)

Born March 21, 1965, at Crystal, Minn.
Height, 5.11. Weight, 195.
Throws and bats righthanded.
Attended University of Minnesota, Minneapolis, Minn.

Led Midwest League in game-winning RBIs with 14 in 1987.
Led California League catchers in assists with 99 and double plays with 14 in 1988.

Year	Club	League	Pos.	G.	AB.	R.	H.	2B.	3B.	HR.	RBI.	B.A.	PO.	A.	E.	F.A.
1986—	Beloit	Midw.	OF	49	173	26	45	3	2	4	21	.260	98	4	4	.962
1987—	Beloit	Midw.	C	130	461	83	139	30	3	20	85	.302	624	71	6	★.991
1988—	Stockton	Calif.	C-OF	138	519	81	147	32	6	15	92	.283	779	101	17	.981

Selected by Milwaukee Brewers' organization in 3rd round of free-agent draft, June 2, 1986.

COLIN MICHAEL McLAUGHLIN

Born June 9, 1959, at Winchester, Mass.
Height, 6.06. Weight, 205.
Throws right and bats left and righthanded.
Attended Amherst College, Amherst, Mass., and University of Connecticut, Storrs, Conn.

Year Club	League	G.	IP.	W.	L.	Pct.	H.	R.	ER.	SO.	BB.	ERA.
1980—Kinston	Carolina	18	102	6	8	.429	97	58	46	90	70	4.06
1981—Knoxville	Southern	16	86	5	8	.385	77	54	47	81	73	4.92
1981—Syracuse	Int'national	14	61	3	5	.375	62	54	48	49	57	7.08
1982—Knoxville†	Southern	20	123⅔	8	7	.533	104	60	47	103	89	3.42
1983—Syracuse	Int'national	25	84⅓	4	6	.400	78	64	57	62	92	6.08
1984—Knoxville	Southern	27	63⅔	1	5	.167	63	48	44	52	59	6.22
1984—Syracuse	Int'national	5	24⅔	2	1	.667	16	11	10	21	17	3.65
1985—Syracuse‡	Int'national	34	101⅓	4	3	.571	91	56	49	73	66	4.35
1986—Knoxville§	Southern	31	59	2	1	.667	49	26	21	51	21	3.20
1986—Syracuse	Int'national	6	11⅓	0	0	.000	8	1	1	13	1	0.79
1987—Syracuse	Int'national	46	74	4	5	.444	53	41	34	91	39	4.14
1988—Syracuse x	Int'national	47	68⅔	9	4	.692	47	24	22	62	37	2.88

Selected by Toronto Blue Jays' organization in 1st round (first player selected) of free-agent draft, January 8, 1980.
†On disabled list, July 14 to August 12, 1982.
‡On disabled list, June 19 to July 15, 1985.
§On disabled list, June 16, 1986.
xDrafted by Seattle Mariners, December 5, 1988.

MARK TREMELL McLEMORE

Born October 4, 1964, at San Diego, Calif.
Height, 5.11. Weight, 195.
Throws right and bats left and righthanded.

Major League stolen bases: 1987 (25), 1988 (13). Total—38.
Led California League second basemen in assists with 400 and double plays with 84 in 1984.

Year Club	League	Pos.	G.	AB.	R.	H.	2B.	3B.	HR.	RBI.	B.A.	PO.	A.	E.	F.A.
1982—Salem	N'west	2B-SS	55	165	42	49	6	2	0	25	.297	81	125	11	.947
1983—Peoria	Midw.	2B-SS	95	329	42	79	7	3	0	18	.240	170	250	24	.946
1984—Redwood	Calif.	2B-SS	134	482	102	142	8	3	0	45	.295	274	429	25	.966
1985—Midland†	Texas	2B-SS	117	458	80	124	17	6	2	46	.271	301	339	19	.971
1986—Midland	Texas	2B	63	237	54	75	9	1	1	29	.316	155	194	13	.964
1986—Edmonton	P. C.	2B	73	286	41	79	13	1	0	23	.276	173	215	7	.982
1986—California	Amer.	2B	5	4	0	0	0	0	0	0	.000	3	10	0	1.000
1987—California	Amer.	2B-SS	138	433	61	102	13	3	3	41	.236	293	363	17	.975
1988—California‡	Amer.	2B-3B	77	233	38	56	11	2	2	16	.240	108	178	6	.979
1988—Palm Springs	Calif.	2B	11	44	9	15	3	1	0	6	.341	18	24	1	.977
1988—Edmonton	P. C.	2B	12	45	7	12	3	0	0	6	.267	35	33	1	.986
Major League Totals—3 Years			220	670	99	158	24	5	5	57	.236	404	551	23	.976

Selected by California Angels' organization in 9th round of free-agent draft, June 7, 1982.
†On disabled list, May 15 to May 27, 1985.
‡On disabled list, May 24 to August 2, 1988; included rehabilitation disability assignment to Palm Springs, July 7 to July 21, 1988; and Edmonton, July 22 to July 27, 1988.

JOE CRAIG McMURTRY

(Known by middle name.)
Born November 5, 1959, at Temple, Tex.
Height, 6.05. Weight, 195.
Throws and bats righthanded.
Attended McLennan Community College, Waco, Tex.

Major League saves: 1985 (1), 1988 (3). Total—4.
Tied for International League lead in games started by pitchers with 32 in 1982.
Named National League Rookie Pitcher of the Year by The Sporting News, 1983.
Named International League Pitcher of the Year, 1982.

Year Club	League	G.	IP.	W.	L.	Pct.	H.	R.	ER.	SO.	BB.	ERA.
1980—Savannah	Southern	14	86	7	4	.636	82	40	34	37	35	3.56
1981—Savannah	Southern	28	202	*15	11	.577	168	87	62	111	95	2.76
1982—Richmond	Int'national	32	*210	*17	9	.654	198	98	89	96	107	3.81
1983—Atlanta	National	36	224⅔	15	9	.625	204	86	77	105	88	3.08
1984—Atlanta	National	37	183⅓	9	17	.346	184	100	88	99	102	4.32
1985—Atlanta	National	17	45	0	3	.000	56	36	33	28	27	6.60
1985—Richmond	Int'national	16	107⅓	7	5	.583	88	43	39	74	51	3.27
1986—Atlanta†	National	37	79⅔	1	6	.143	82	46	42	50	43	4.74
1986—Greenville‡	Southern	3	15	1	1	.500	13	10	10	12	9	6.00
1987—Knoxville§	Southern	12	78	4	2	.667	64	28	24	56	20	2.77
1987—Syracuse x	Int'national	9	53⅔	5	3	.625	46	23	21	31	15	3.52
1988—Oklahoma City	Am. Assoc.	9	49⅔	2	5	.286	55	27	24	35	21	4.35
1988—Texas	American	32	60	3	3	.500	37	16	15	35	24	2.25
National League Totals—4 Years		127	532⅔	25	35	.417	526	268	240	282	260	4.06
American League Totals—1 Year		32	60	3	3	.500	37	16	15	35	24	2.25
Major League Totals—5 Years		159	592⅔	28	38	.424	563	284	255	317	284	3.87

Selected by Atlanta Braves' organization in 1st round (fourth player selected) of free-agent draft, January 8, 1980.

†On disabled list, July 27 to September 1, 1986; included rehabilitation disability assignment to Greenville, August 14 to September 1, 1986.

‡Traded to Toronto Blue Jays for Second Baseman Damaso Garcia and Pitcher Luis Leal, February 2, 1987.

§On Toronto disabled list, March 30 to June 18, 1987; included rehabilitation disability assignment to Knoxville, May 29 to June 17, 1987.

xGranted free agency, November 22, 1987; signed by Texas Rangers, December 8, 1987.

WALTER KEVIN McREYNOLDS

(Known by middle name.)
Born October 16, 1959, at Little Rock, Ark.
Height, 6.01. Weight, 215.
Throws and bats righthanded.
Attended University of Arkansas, Fayetteville, Ark.

Established major league record for most stolen bases with no caught stealing, season (21), 1988.
Tied major league record for fewest double plays by outfielder, season, 150 or more games (0), 1987.
Major League stolen bases: 1983 (2), 1984 (3), 1985 (4), 1986 (8), 1987 (14), 1988 (21). Total—52.
Led National League outfielders in double plays with 5 in 1988.
Led National League outfielders in total chances with 436 in 1984 and 445 in 1985.
Led Pacific Coast League in total bases with 328 in 1983.
Named outfielder on THE SPORTING NEWS National League All-Star Team, 1988.
Named Minor League Player of the Year by THE SPORTING NEWS, 1983.
Named Pacific Coast League Player of the Year, 1983.
Named California League Most Valuable Player, 1982.
Received reported $125,000 bonus to sign with San Diego Padres, 1982.
Named outfielder on THE SPORTING NEWS College Baseball All-America Team, 1981.

Year Club	League	Pos.	G.	AB.	R.	H.	2B.	3B.	HR.	RBI.	B.A.	PO.	A.	E.	F.A.
1982—Reno	Calif.	OF	90	338	83	127	17	5	*28	98	*.376	52	7	3	.952
1982—Amarillo	Texas	OF	40	162	30	57	8	3	5	39	.352	76	3	2	.975
1983—Las Vegas	P. C.	OF	113	446	98	168	*46	9	•32	116	.377	257	3	9	.967
1983—San Diego	Nat.	OF	39	140	15	31	3	1	4	14	.221	87	4	1	.989
1984—San Diego	Nat.	OF	147	525	68	146	26	6	20	75	.278	*422	10	4	.991
1985—San Diego	Nat.	OF	152	564	61	132	24	4	15	75	.234	*430	12	3	.993
1986—San Diego†	Nat.	OF	158	560	89	161	31	6	26	96	.288	332	9	8	.977
1987—New York	Nat.	OF	151	590	86	163	32	5	29	95	.276	286	8	4	.987
1988—New York	Nat.	OF	147	552	82	159	30	2	27	99	.288	252	*18	4	.985
Major League Totals—6 Years			794	2931	401	792	146	24	121	454	.270	1809	61	24	.987

Selected by Milwaukee Brewers' organization in 18th round of free-agent draft, June 6, 1978.
Selected by San Diego Padres' organization in 1st round (sixth player selected) of free-agent draft, June 8, 1981.
†Traded with Pitcher Gene Walter and Infielder Adam Ging to New York Mets for Outfielders Shawn Abner, Stanley Jefferson and Kevin Mitchell and Pitchers Kevin Armstrong and Kevin Brown, December 11, 1986.

CHAMPIONSHIP SERIES RECORD

Tied National League Championship Series record for most hits, game (4), October 11, 1988.

Year Club	League	Pos.	G.	AB.	R.	H.	2B.	3B.	HR.	RBI.	B.A.	PO.	A.	E.	F.A.
1984—San Diego	Nat.	OF	4	10	2	3	0	0	1	4	.300	10	0	0	1.000
1988—New York	Nat.	OF	7	28	4	7	2	0	2	4	.250	19	0	0	1.000
Championship Series Totals—2 Years			11	38	6	10	2	0	3	8	.263	29	0	0	1.000

LARRY DEAN McWILLIAMS

Born February 10, 1954, at Wichita, Kan.
Height, 6.05. Weight, 181.
Throws and bats lefthanded.
Attended Paris Junior College, Paris, Tex.

Tied major league record for most strikeouts by batter, inning (2), April 22, 1979 (fourth inning).
Major League saves: 1982 (1), 1984 (1), 1988 (1). Total—3.
Named lefthanded pitcher on THE SPORTING NEWS National League All-Star Team, 1983.

Year Club	League	G.	IP.	W.	L.	Pct.	H.	R.	ER.	SO.	BB.	ERA.
1974—Greenwood†	W. Carol.	11	64	4	3	.571	64	26	20	61	23	2.81
1975—Greenwood‡	W. Carol.	17	93	8	4	.667	83	36	29	71	18	2.81
1976—Greenwood	W. Carol.	8	48	2	2	.500	40	19	14	44	13	2.63
1976—Savannah	Southern	16	74	3	8	.273	82	41	38	37	33	4.62
1977—Savannah	Southern	26	158	8	9	.471	153	70	59	139	64	3.36
1978—Richmond	Int'national	15	108	6	5	.545	87	36	34	78	41	2.83
1978—Atlanta	National	15	99	9	3	.750	84	38	31	42	35	2.82
1979—Atlanta§	National	13	66	3	2	.600	69	41	41	32	22	5.59
1980—Atlanta	National	30	164	9	14	.391	188	97	90	77	39	4.94
1981—Richmond	Int'national	29	178	•13	10	.565	174	98	•86	157	79	4.35
1981—Atlanta	National	6	38	2	1	.667	31	13	13	23	8	3.08
1982—Atlanta x-Pittsburgh	National	46	159⅓	8	8	.500	158	79	68	118	44	3.84
1983—Pittsburgh	National	35	238	15	8	.652	205	99	86	199	87	3.25
1984—Pittsburgh	National	34	227⅓	12	11	.522	226	86	74	149	78	2.93
1985—Pittsburgh y	National	30	126⅓	7	9	.438	139	70	66	52	62	4.70
1986—Pittsburgh z	National	49	122⅓	3	11	.214	129	75	70	80	49	5.15
1987—Greenville	Southern	7	33	1	2	.333	33	24	20	27	26	5.45
1987—Atlanta a	National	9	20⅓	0	1	.000	25	15	13	13	7	5.75
1987—Oklahoma City b	Am. Assoc.	7	22⅓	1	4	.200	44	29	28	13	20	11.28
1988—St. Louis c	National	42	136	6	9	.400	130	64	59	70	45	3.90
Major League Totals—11 Years		309	1396⅔	74	77	.490	1384	677	611	855	476	3.94

Selected by Atlanta Braves' organization in 1st round (sixth player selected) of free-agent draft, January 9, 1974.
†On disabled list, July 22 to September 25, 1974.
‡On disabled list, April 11 to June 3, 1975.
§On disabled list, May 18 to June 15 and July 7 to September 1, 1979.
xTraded to Pittsburgh Pirates for Pitcher Pascual Perez and a player to be named later, June 30, 1982; Atlanta Braves' organization acquired Shortstop Carlos Rios to complete deal, September 8, 1982.
yOn disabled list, May 17 to June 8 and August 18 to September 3, 1985.
zReleased, April 6, 1987; signed by Greenville (Atlanta Braves' organization), May 18, 1987.
aReleased, July 25, 1987; signed by Oklahoma City (Texas Rangers' organization), August 6, 1987.
bReleased, February 2, 1988; signed by St. Louis Cardinals, February 12, 1988.
cGranted free agency, November 4, 1988.

ROBERT ANDREW MEACHAM
(Bobby)

Born August 25, 1960, at Los Angeles, Calif.
Height, 6.01. Weight, 180.
Throws and bats righthanded.
Attended San Diego State University, San Diego, Calif.

Major League stolen bases: 1983 (8), 1984 (9), 1985 (25), 1986 (3), 1987 (6), 1988 (7). Total—58.
Led American League in sacrifice hits with 14 in 1984 and 23 in 1985.
Named shortstop on THE SPORTING NEWS College Baseball All-America Team, 1981.

Year Club	League	Pos.	G.	AB.	R.	H.	2B.	3B.	HR.	RBI.	B.A.	PO.	A.	E.	F.A.
1981—Gastonia	S. Atl.	SS	74	274	24	50	8	2	1	18	.182	107	235	25	.932
1982—St. Petersburg†	Fla. St.	SS	120	421	57	109	15	4	0	37	.259	201	306	★47	.915
1983—Columbus‡	Int.	SS	120	423	58	111	18	3	9	60	.262	206	348	30	.949
1983—New York‡	Amer.	SS-3B	22	51	5	12	2	0	0	4	.235	16	64	6	.930
1984—Nashville‡	South.	SS	8	31	3	9	0	0	0	3	.290	16	25	1	.976
1984—Columbus‡	Int.	SS	46	187	35	53	13	•6	2	13	.283	67	133	14	.935
1984—New York‡	Amer.	SS-2B	99	360	62	91	13	4	2	25	.253	140	272	19	.956
1985—New York‡	Amer.	SS	156	481	70	105	16	2	1	47	.218	236	390	24	.963
1986—New York‡	Amer.	SS	56	161	19	36	7	1	0	10	.224	70	149	12	.948
1986—Columbus‡	Int.	SS-2B	46	150	14	21	0	5	0	11	.140	81	133	12	.947
1987—Columbus	Int.	2B-SS	40	154	28	42	5	3	3	23	.273	82	124	4	.981
1987—New York§	Amer.	SS-2B	77	203	28	55	11	1	5	21	.271	110	184	10	.967
1988—New York xy	Amer.	SS-2B-3B	47	115	18	25	9	0	0	7	.217	56	85	7	.953
Major League Totals—6 Years			457	1371	202	324	58	8	8	114	.236	628	1144	78	.958

Selected by Chicago White Sox' organization in 14th round of free agent draft, June 6, 1978.
Selected by St. Louis Cardinals' organization in 1st round (eighth player selected) of free-agent draft, June 8, 1981.
†Traded with Outfielder Stan Javier to New York Yankees' organization for Pitchers Marty Mason and Steve Fincher and Outfielder Bob Helsom, December 14, 1982.
‡Batted left and righthanded.
§On disabled list, July 2 to July 17, 1987.
xOn disabled list, July 14, 1988 through remainder of season.
yTraded to Texas Rangers for Outfielder Bob Brower, December 5, 1988.

MICHAEL RAY MEADOWS
(Louie)

Born April 29, 1961, in Onslow County, N. C.
Height, 5.11. Weight, 190.
Throws and bats lefthanded.
Attended North Carolina State University, Raleigh, N. C.

Major League stolen bases: 1986 (1), 1988 (4). Total—5.

Year Club	League	Pos.	G.	AB.	R.	H.	2B.	3B.	HR.	RBI.	B.A.	PO.	A.	E.	F.A.
1982—Asheville	S. Atl.	OF	66	228	43	72	9	1	10	41	.316	87	4	13	.875
1983—Daytona Beach	Fla. St.	OF	112	382	68	112	25	14	9	71	.293	169	5	4	.978
1984—Daytona Beach	Fla. St.	OF-1B	70	252	49	76	14	10	6	44	.302	323	17	5	.986
1984—Columbus	South.	OF-1B	65	225	33	63	17	4	8	36	.280	150	6	3	.981
1985—Columbus	South.	OF-1B	140	476	76	111	16	8	14	67	.233	514	32	12	.978
1986—Tucson†	P. C.	OF-1B	82	290	42	87	14	8	10	52	.300	203	15	9	.960
1986—Houston	Nat.	OF	6	6	1	2	0	0	0	0	.333	0	0	0	.000
1987—Tucson	P. C.	OF-1B	129	426	70	110	21	★14	10	76	.258	252	8	7	.974
1988—Tucson	P. C.	OF-1B	85	280	42	71	16	9	5	43	.254	415	28	5	.989
1988—Houston	Nat.	OF	35	42	5	8	0	1	2	3	.190	18	1	0	1.000
Major League Totals—2 Years			41	48	6	10	0	1	2	3	.208	18	1	0	1.000

Selected by Houston Astros' organization in 2nd round of free-agent draft, June 7, 1982.
†On disabled list, July 21, 1986 through remainder of season.

DAVID DONALD MEADS III
(Dave)

Born January 7, 1964, at Montclair, N. J.
Height, 6.00. Weight, 175.
Throws and bats lefthanded.
Attended Middlesex County College, Edison, N. J.

Year Club	League	G.	IP.	W.	L.	Pct.	H.	R.	ER.	SO.	BB.	ERA.
1984—Sarasota Astros	Gulf Coast	7	29⅓	2	2	.500	22	11	4	28	2	1.23
1984—Auburn†	NYP	10	28	5	1	.833	31	17	16	29	12	5.14

Year	Club	League	G.	IP.	W.	L.	Pct.	H.	R.	ER.	SO.	BB.	ERA.
1985—Gastonia		S. Atlantic	33	146⅓	3	10	.231	160	91	71	118	50	4.37
1986—Asheville		S. Atlantic	19	54⅓	4	3	.571	51	25	12	50	14	1.99
1986—Osceola		Florida St.	11	15⅓	2	4	.333	24	14	13	10	7	7.63
1986—Columbus		Southern	16	22⅓	1	1	.500	22	11	11	26	13	4.43
1987—Houston		National	45	48⅔	5	3	.625	60	31	30	32	16	5.55
1987—Tucson		P. Coast	10	9⅔	1	0	1.000	7	4	3	6	6	2.79
1988—Tucson		P. Coast	32	46	3	4	.429	45	12	10	46	10	1.96
1988—Houston		National	22	39⅔	3	1	.750	37	20	14	27	14	3.18
Major League Totals—2 Years			67	88⅓	8	4	.667	97	51	44	59	30	4.48

Selected by Houston Astros' organization in 6th round of free-agent draft, January 17, 1984.
†Loaned to Gastonia (Independent), April 4, 1985; returned, October 15, 1985.

LUIS MAIN MEDINA

Born March 26, 1963, at Santa Monica, Calif.
Height, 6.03. Weight, 195.
Throws left and bats righthanded.
Attended Cerritos College, Norwalk, Calif., and Arizona State University, Tempe, Ariz.

Led Pacific Coast League in slugging percentage with .616 in 1988.
Led Midwest League in total bases with 300 in 1986.
Named Midwest League Most Valuable Player, 1986.

Year	Club	League	Pos.	G.	AB.	R.	H.	2B.	3B.	HR.	RBI.	B.A.	PO.	A.	E.	F.A.
1985—Batavia		NYP	OF-1B	76	290	43	77	16	0	12	43	.266	101	3	1	.990
1986—Waterloo		Midw.	OF	136	505	*107	*160	25	5	*35	*110	.317	208	8	5	.977
1987—Williamsport		East.	OF-1B	96	341	61	109	15	6	16	68	.320	260	10	4	.985
1988—Colorado Springs		P. C.	OF-1B	111	406	81	126	28	6	*28	81	.310	374	26	10	.976
1988—Cleveland		Amer.	1B	16	51	10	13	0	0	6	8	.255	137	9	0	1.000
Major League Totals—1 Year				16	51	10	13	0	0	6	8	.255	137	9	0	1.000

Selected by New York Mets' organization in 33rd round of free-agent draft, June 8, 1981.
Selected by New York Mets' organization in secondary phase of free-agent draft, January 12, 1982.
Selected by New York Yankees' organization in secondary phase of free-agent draft, June 7, 1982.
Selected by Cincinnati Reds' organization in secondary phase of free-agent draft, January 11, 1983.
Selected by Oakland Athletics' organization in secondary phase of free-agent draft, June 6, 1983.
Selected by Houston Astros' organization in secondary phase of free-agent draft, June 4, 1984.
Selected by Cleveland Indians' organization in 9th round of free-agent draft, June 3, 1985.

SCOTT HOWARD MEDVIN

Born September 16, 1961, at North Olmsted, O.
Height, 6.00. Weight, 190.
Throws and bats righthanded.
Received bachelor of arts degree in management from Baldwin-Wallace College, Berea, O.

Year	Club	League	G.	IP.	W.	L.	Pct.	H.	R.	ER.	SO.	BB.	ERA.
1984—Wausau†		Midwest	40	65⅔	4	2	.667	62	36	26	53	35	3.56
1985—Lakeland‡		Florida St.	31	51⅓	5	4	.556	48	20	16	47	20	2.79
1985—Birmingham		Southern	13	23	3	3	.500	14	10	8	17	12	3.13
1986—Shreveport		Texas	49	93⅔	8	6	.571	71	32	25	68	42	2.40
1987—Shreveport		Texas	37	78⅔	7	1	.875	59	19	15	71	41	1.72
1987—Phoenix§-Vancouver x		P. Coast	13	22⅓	0	1	.000	22	17	13	16	18	5.24
1988—Buffalo		Am. Assoc.	39	56	5	4	.556	38	18	15	49	25	2.41
1988—Pittsburgh		National	17	27⅔	3	0	1.000	23	16	15	16	9	4.88
Major League Totals—1 Year			17	27⅔	3	0	1.000	23	16	15	16	9	4.88

Signed as free agent by Detroit Tigers' organization, September 27, 1983.
†Loaned to Wausau (Seattle Mariners' organization), April 4, 1984; returned, September 5, 1984.
‡Traded to San Francisco Giants, December 11, 1985, completing deal in which San Francisco traded Pitchers Dave LaPoint and Eric King and Catcher Matt Nokes to Detroit Tigers for Pitcher Juan Berenguer, Catcher Bob Melvin and a player to be named later, October 7, 1985.
§Traded with Pitcher Jeff Robinson to Pittsburgh Pirates for Pitcher Rick Reuschel, August 21, 1987.
xDrafted by Houston Astros, December 7, 1987; returned, April 4, 1988.

DAVID KEITH MEIER

Name pronounced MY-er.

(Dave)

Born August 8, 1959, at Helena, Mont.
Height, 6.00. Weight, 185.
Throws and bats righthanded.
Attended Fresno City College, Fresno, Calif., and received bachelor of arts degree in economics from Stanford University, Stanford, Calif. in 1981.

Led American Association in game-winning RBIs with 16 in 1988.
Tied for Southern League lead in double plays by outfielders with 5 in 1982.

Year	Club	League	Pos.	G.	AB.	R.	H.	2B.	3B.	HR.	RBI.	B.A.	PO.	A.	E.	F.A.
1981—Visalia		Calif.	SS-OF-3B	71	273	53	92	12	0	9	50	.337	65	85	13	.920
1982—Orlando		South.	O-3-2-S	134	474	71	136	19	7	8	63	.287	254	27	6	.979
1983—Toledo		Int.	OF-P	126	426	63	143	21	6	8	68	.336	224	6	7	.970
1984—Minnesota		Amer.	OF-3B	59	147	18	35	8	1	0	13	.238	87	2	2	.978

Year	Club	League	Pos.	G.	AB.	R.	H.	2B.	3B.	HR.	RBI.	B.A.	PO.	A.	E.	F.A.
1985	Minnesota†	Amer.	OF	71	104	15	27	6	0	1	8	.260	77	1	1	.987
1986	—					(Out of Organized Baseball)										
1987	Oklahoma City	A. A.	OF-3B	129	447	72	143	36	4	18	86	.320	171	31	6	.971
1987	Texas‡	Amer.	OF	13	21	4	6	1	0	0	0	.286	11	0	1	.917
1988	Iowa	A. A.	3-O-1-P	125	456	69	139	19	7	20	83	.305	207	72	12	.959
1988	Chicago	Nat.	3B	2	5	0	2	0	0	0	1	.400	1	0	0	1.000
American League Totals—3 Years				143	272	37	68	15	1	1	21	.250	175	3	4	.978
National League Totals—1 Year				2	5	0	2	0	0	0	1	.400	1	0	0	1.000
Major League Totals—4 Years				145	277	37	70	15	1	1	22	.253	176	3	4	.978

Selected by California Angels' organization in 31st round of free-agent draft, June 7, 1977.
Selected by St. Louis Cardinals' organization in secondary phase of free-agent draft, January 10, 1978.
Selected by Minnesota Twins' organization in 5th round of free-agent draft, June 8, 1981.
†Released, December 20, 1985; signed by Texas Rangers' organization, December 9, 1986.
‡Traded with Infielder Greg Tabor to Chicago Cubs for Pitcher Ray Hayward, March 17, 1988.

PITCHING RECORD

Year	Club	League	G.	IP.	W.	L.	Pct.	H.	R.	ER.	SO.	BB.	ERA.
1983	Toledo	Int'national	1	1	0	0	.000	2	1	1	0	0	9.00
1988	Iowa	Am. Assoc.	1	1	0	0	.000	0	0	0	0	0	0.00

CESAR EMILIO MEJIA (PEREZ)

Born October 10, 1966, at Azua, Dominican Republic.
Height, 6.02. Weight, 160.
Throws and bats righthanded.

Pitched 3-0 no-hit victory against Albany, April 17, 1988.
Led Eastern League in shutouts with 4 and tied for lead in complete games with 7 in 1988.
Named Eastern League Pitcher of the Year, 1988.

Year	Club	League	G.	IP.	W.	L.	Pct.	H.	R.	ER.	SO.	BB.	ERA.
1985	Bradenton Blue Jays	Gulf Coast	10	38	3	1	.750	31	12	10	26	7	2.37
1985	Florence	S. Atlantic	7	18⅔	0	0	.000	20	14	10	19	12	4.82
1986	Florence	S. Atlantic	37	131	9	7	.563	122	61	51	122	62	3.50
1987	Myrtle Beach†	S. Atlantic	33	125⅓	7	4	.636	108	42	38	90	27	2.73
1988	Glens Falls‡	Eastern	25	162⅔	14	5	.737	132	53	44	99	50	2.43

Signed as free agent by Toronto Blue Jays' organization, August 23, 1984.
†Drafted by Detroit Tigers' organization, December 8, 1987.
‡Traded with Pitcher Robinson Garces and Catcher Chris Hoiles to Baltimore Orioles, September 9, 1988, to complete deal in which Baltimore traded Outfielder Fred Lynn to Detroit Tigers for three players to be named later, August 31, 1988.

FRANCISCO JAVIER MELENDEZ (VILLEGAS)

Born January 25, 1964, at Rio Piedras, Puerto Rico.
Height, 6.00. Weight, 185.
Throws and bats lefthanded.

Led Pacific Coast League in intentional bases on balls received with 11 in 1987.
Led Pacific Coast League first basemen in putouts with 1,085 in 1984.
Led Eastern League first basemen in putouts with 1,081, total chances with 1,166 and double plays with 99 in 1983.
Tied for Pacific Coast League lead in errors by first basemen with 13 in 1987.

Year	Club	League	Pos.	G.	AB.	R.	H.	2B.	3B.	HR.	RBI.	B.A.	PO.	A.	E.	F.A.
1981	Peninsula	Carol.	1B-OF	32	74	6	10	3	0	0	6	.135	154	13	6	.965
1981	Spartanburg	S. Atl.	1B-OF	85	306	44	82	13	1	3	36	.268	760	57	17	.980
1982	Peninsula	Carol.	1B	118	424	54	124	*33	3	4	69	.292	739	75	11	.987
1983	Reading	East.	1B-OF	126	450	81	134	17	4	5	75	.298	1082	73	12	.990
1984	Portland	P. C.	*1B-OF	128	506	63	158	36	8	3	65	.312	1090	85	11	*.991
1984	Philadelphia	Nat.	1B	21	23	0	3	0	0	0	2	.130	37	4	0	1.000
1985	Portland	P. C.	•1B-OF	130	397	41	111	25	2	2	54	.280	974	69	•15	.986
1986	Portland	P. C.	1B-OF	96	356	47	113	21	2	4	57	.318	778	68	12	.986
1986	Philadelphia†	Nat.	1B	9	8	0	2	0	0	0	0	.250	1	0	0	1.000
1987	Phoenix	P. C.	1B-OF	138	514	78	*168	20	9	3	85	.327	1036	87	14	.988
1987	San Francisco	Nat.	OF	12	16	2	5	0	0	1	1	.313	19	0	0	1.000
1988	Phoenix‡	P. C.	1B-OF	96	368	61	133	26	2	4	58	.361	752	45	12	.985
1988	San Francisco	Nat.	1B-OF	23	26	1	5	0	0	0	3	.192	27	0	0	1.000
Major League Totals—4 Years				65	73	3	15	0	0	1	6	.205	84	4	0	1.000

Signed as free agent by Philadelphia Phillies' organization, October 4, 1980.
†Sold to Phoenix (San Francisco Giants' organization), March 22, 1987.
‡On San Francisco disabled list, March 26 to May 13, 1988; included rehabilitation disability assignment to Phoenix, May 6 to May 13, 1988.

ROBERT PAUL MELVIN
(Bob)

Born October 28, 1961, at Palo Alto, Calif.
Height, 6.04. Weight, 205.
Throws and bats righthanded.
Attended University of California, Berkeley, Calif.,
and Canada College, Redwood City, Calif.

Major League stolen bases: 1986 (3).

Year	Club	League	Pos.	G.	AB.	R.	H.	2B.	3B.	HR.	RBI.	B.A.	PO.	A.	E.	F.A.
1981	—Macon	S. Atl.	C	114	412	56	112	19	1	14	64	.272	456	67	2	★.996
1982	—Birmingham†	South.	★C-1B-3B	98	364	33	86	12	1	13	52	.236	638	54	9	★.987
1983	—Birmingham	South.	C-1B-2B	78	285	43	82	14	2	10	56	.288	404	30	2	.995
1983	—Evansville	A. A.	C-1B	45	142	10	27	6	0	2	11	.190	213	16	1	.996
1984	—Evansville	A. A.	C-1B	44	141	12	35	13	0	0	11	.248	214	21	1	.996
1984	—Birmingham	South.	C-1B-3B	69	271	34	73	14	1	2	33	.269	341	38	4	.990
1985	—Nashville	A. A.	C-1B-OF	53	177	27	48	7	1	9	24	.271	276	28	2	.993
1985	—Detroit‡	Amer.	C	41	82	10	18	4	1	0	4	.220	175	13	2	.989
1986	—San Francisco	Nat.	C-3B	89	268	24	60	14	2	5	25	.224	443	60	6	.988
1987	—San Francisco§	Nat.	C-1B	84	246	31	49	8	0	11	31	.199	414	44	1	.998
1988	—San Francisco	Nat.	C-1B	92	273	23	64	13	1	8	27	.234	406	31	7	.984
1988	—Phoenix	P. C.	C	21	75	11	23	5	0	2	9	.307	123	6	1	.992
American League Totals—1 Year				41	82	10	18	4	1	0	4	.220	175	13	2	.989
National League Totals—3 Years				265	787	78	173	35	3	24	83	.220	1263	135	14	.990
Major League Totals—4 Years				306	869	88	191	39	4	24	87	.220	1438	148	16	.990

Selected by Baltimore Orioles' organization in 3rd round of free-agent draft, June 5, 1979.

Selected by Detroit Tigers' organization in secondary phase of free-agent draft, January 13, 1981.

†On disabled list, May 1 to May 25, 1982.

‡Traded with Pitcher Juan Berenguer and a player to be named later to San Francisco Giants for Pitchers Dave LaPoint and Eric King and Catcher Matt Nokes, October 7, 1985; San Francisco acquired Pitcher Scott Medvin to complete deal, December 11, 1985.

§On disabled list, July 11 to July 26, 1987.

CHAMPIONSHIP SERIES RECORD

Year	Club	League	Pos.	G.	AB.	R.	H.	2B.	3B.	HR.	RBI.	B.A.	PO.	A.	E.	F.A.
1987	—San Francisco	Nat.	PH-C	3	7	0	3	0	0	0	0	.429	14	1	0	1.000

ORLANDO MERCADO (RODRIGUEZ)

Born November 7, 1961, at Arecibo, Puerto Rico.
Height, 6.00. Weight, 195.
Throws and bats righthanded.

Major League stolen bases: 1983 (2), 1984 (1). Total—3.

Led Eastern League in passed balls with 23 in 1980.

Led California League in passed balls with 24 in 1979.

Year	Club	League	Pos.	G.	AB.	R.	H.	2B.	3B.	HR.	RBI.	B.A.	PO.	A.	E.	F.A.
1978	—Bellingham	N'west	C	38	49	7	6	2	0	0	5	.122	184	20	4	.981
1979	—San Jose	Calif.	C-1B	110	335	53	86	18	2	10	54	.257	629	71	17	.976
1980	—Lynn	East.	C-1B	117	396	55	101	25	6	11	71	.255	607	78	11	.984
1981	—Spokane	P. C.	C-OF	95	312	32	67	21	2	4	31	.215	446	60	13	.975
1982	—Salt Lake City	P. C.	C-O-1-3	90	321	43	90	19	2	16	66	.280	497	43	13	.976
1982	—Seattle	Amer.	C	9	17	1	2	0	0	1	6	.118	31	1	0	1.000
1983	—Seattle	Amer.	C	66	178	10	35	11	2	1	16	.197	342	27	2	.995
1983	—Salt Lake City	P. C.	C-3B	26	88	12	20	2	1	2	12	.227	131	13	2	.986
1984	—Seattle	Amer.	C	30	78	5	17	3	1	0	5	.218	118	10	1	.992
1984	—Salt Lake City†	P. C.	C-1B-OF	29	109	18	39	9	2	6	22	.358	169	18	2	.989
1985	—Oklahoma City‡	A. A.	C	59	206	20	52	7	1	8	29	.252	268	26	4	.987
1986	—Oklahoma City	A. A.	C	48	172	20	47	11	1	3	25	.273	234	29	8	.970
1986	—Texas§	Amer.	C	46	102	7	24	1	1	1	7	.235	240	25	1	.996
1987	—Detroit x	Amer.	C	10	22	2	3	0	0	0	1	.136	40	8	1	.980
1987	—Albuquerque	P. C.	C	69	205	22	57	18	0	2	27	.278	327	47	6	.984
1987	—Los Angeles y	Nat.	C	7	5	1	3	1	0	0	1	.600	13	0	0	1.000
1988	—Oakland	Amer.	C	16	24	3	3	0	0	1	1	.125	45	2	2	.959
1988	—Tacoma z	P. C.	C-1B-OF	53	148	16	33	6	0	2	19	.223	228	22	2	.992
American League Totals—6 Years				177	421	28	84	15	4	4	36	.200	816	73	7	.992
National League Totals—1 Year				7	5	1	3	1	0	0	1	.600	13	0	0	1.000
Major League Totals—6 Years				184	426	29	87	16	4	4	37	.204	829	73	7	.992

Signed as free agent by Seattle Mariners' organization, January 6, 1978.

†Traded to Texas Rangers' organization for Catcher Donnie Scott, April 4, 1985.

‡On disabled list, July 10 to September 19, 1985.

§Traded to Detroit Tigers for a player to be named later, March 24, 1987; Texas Rangers' organization acquired Outfielder Ruben Guzman to complete deal, May 8, 1987.

xTraded to Los Angeles Dodgers' organization for Pitcher Balvino Galvez, May 5, 1987.

yReleased, November 12, 1987; signed by Tacoma (Oakland Athletics' organization), January 14, 1988.

zGranted free agency, October 15, 1988.

KENT FRANKLIN MERCKER

Born February 1, 1968, at Dublin, O.
Height, 6.01. Weight, 175.
Throws and bats lefthanded.

Named Carolina League co-Pitcher of the Year, 1988.

Year	Club	League	G.	IP.	W.	L.	Pct.	H.	R.	ER.	SO.	BB.	ERA.
1986	—Bradenton Braves	Gulf Coast	9	47⅓	4	3	.571	37	21	13	42	16	2.47
1987	—Durham	Carolina	3	11⅔	0	1	.000	11	8	7	14	6	5.40
1988	—Durham	Carolina	19	127⅔	11	4	.733	102	44	39	159	47	★2.75
1988	—Greenville	Southern	9	48⅓	3	1	.750	36	20	18	60	26	3.35

Selected by Atlanta Braves' organization in 1st round (fifth player selected) of free-agent draft, June 2, 1986.

JOSE RAMON MESA

Born May 22, 1966, at Azua, Dominican Republic.
Height, 6.03. Weight, 210.
Throws and bats righthanded.

Led Southern League pitchers in games started with 35 in 1987.
Led Gulf Coast League in shutouts with 3 in 1982.
Tied for Carolina League lead in hit batsmen with 9 in 1985.

Year Club	League	G.	IP.	W.	L.	Pct.	H.	R.	ER.	SO.	BB.	ERA.
1982—Bradenton Blue Jays	Gulf Coast	13	83⅓	6	4	.600	58	34	25	40	20	2.70
1983—Florence	S. Atlantic	28	141⅓	6	12	.333	153	*116	86	91	93	5.48
1984—Florence	S. Atlantic	7	38⅓	4	3	.571	38	24	16	35	25	3.76
1984—Kinston†	Carolina	10	50⅔	5	2	.714	51	23	22	24	28	3.91
1985—Kinston	Carolina	30	106⅔	5	10	.333	110	89	73	71	79	6.16
1986—Ventura County	California	24	142⅓	10	6	.625	141	71	61	113	58	3.86
1986—Knoxville	Southern	9	41⅓	2	2	.500	40	32	20	30	23	4.35
1987—Knoxville‡	Southern	35	*193⅓	10	•13	.435	*206	*131	*112	115	104	5.21
1987—Baltimore	American	6	31⅓	1	3	.250	38	23	21	17	15	6.03
1988—Rochester§	Int'national	11	15⅔	0	3	.000	21	20	15	15	14	8.62
Major League Totals—1 Year		6	31⅓	1	3	.250	38	23	21	17	15	6.03

Signed as free agent by Toronto Blue Jays' organization, October 31, 1981.
†On disabled list, August 27, 1984 through remainder of season.
‡Traded to Baltimore Orioles, September 4, 1987, completing deal in which Baltimore traded Pitcher Mike Flanagan to Toronto Blue Jays for Pitcher Oswald Peraza and a player to be named later, August 31, 1987.
§On disabled list, April 18 to May 16 and June 30, 1988 through remainder of season.

HENSLEY FILEMON MEULENS

Born June 23, 1967, at Curacao, Netherlands Antilles.
Height, 6.03. Weight, 190.
Throws and bats righthanded.

Led Gulf Coast League batters in strikeouts with 66 in 1986.
Led Gulf Coast League third basemen in total chances with 178 in 1986.
Tied for Eastern League lead in double plays by third basemen with 18 in 1988.

Year Club	League	Pos.	G.	AB.	R.	H.	2B.	3B.	HR.	RBI.	B.A.	PO.	A.	E.	F.A.
1986—Sarasota Yankees	Gulf C.	3B	59	219	36	51	10	4	4	31	.233	*40	*118	20	.888
1987—Prince William	Carol.	3B	116	430	76	129	23	2	28	103	.300	96	224	*37	.896
1987—Fort Lauderdale	Fla. St.	3B	17	58	2	10	3	0	0	2	.172	18	37	7	.887
1988—Albany	East.	3B	79	278	50	68	9	1	13	40	.245	57	162	23	.905
1988—Columbus	Int.	3B	55	209	27	48	9	1	6	22	.230	39	111	14	.915

Signed as free agent by New York Yankees' organization, October 31, 1985.

BRIAN S. MEYER

Born January 29, 1963, at Camden, N. J.
Height, 6.01. Weight, 190.
Throws and bats rigthanded.
Attended Rollins College, Winter Park, Fla.

Led Southern League in games finished in relief with 59 in 1988.
Led Florida State League in saves with 25 in 1987.
Led New York-Pennsylvania League in games finished in relief with 28 in 1986.

Year Club	League	G.	IP.	W.	L.	Pct.	H.	R.	ER.	SO.	BB.	ERA.
1986—Auburn	NYP	*32	56⅔	5	2	.714	44	14	9	66	10	1.43
1987—Osceola	Florida St.	52	77	8	9	.471	58	26	17	58	23	1.99
1988—Columbus	Southern	62	83⅓	4	3	.571	61	23	21	68	36	2.27
1988—Houston	National	8	12⅓	0	0	.000	9	2	2	10	4	1.46
Major League Totals—1 Year		8	12⅓	0	0	.000	9	2	2	10	4	1.46

Selected by Houston Astros' organization in 16th round of free-agent draft, June 2, 1986.

TANNER JOE MEYER JR.
(Joey)

Born May 10, 1962, at Honolulu, Haw.
Height, 6.03. Weight, 260.
Throws and bats righthanded.
Attended University of Hawaii, Honolulu, Haw.

Tied major league record for most strikeouts, nine-inning game (5), September 20, 1988.
Led Midwest League in total bases with 264 in 1984.
Named Midwest League Most Valuable Player, 1984.

Year Club	League	Pos.	G.	AB.	R.	H.	2B.	3B.	HR.	RBI.	B.A.	PO.	A.	E.	F.A.
1984—Beloit	Midw.	1B	128	475	73	152	22	0	*30	*102	*.320	560	34	11	.982
1985—El Paso	Texas	1B	131	506	79	154	17	2	*37	123	.304	252	15	6	.978
1986—Vancouver	P. C.	1B	126	451	65	115	16	0	24	98	.255	784	41	15	.982
1987—Denver†	A. A.	1B	79	296	58	92	23	0	29	92	.311	392	23	8	.981
1988—Milwaukee	Amer.	1B	103	327	22	86	18	0	11	45	.263	190	18	3	.986
Major League Totals—1 Year			103	327	22	86	18	0	11	45	.263	190	18	3	.986

Selected by California Angels' organization in 8th round of free-agent draft, June 8, 1981.
Selected by Milwaukee Brewers' organization in 5th round of free-agent draft, June 6, 1983.
†On disabled list, July 8, 1987 through remainder of season.

ROBERT MILACKI
(Bob)

Born July 28, 1964, at Trenton, N. J.
Height, 6.04. Weight, 220.
Throws and bats righthanded.
Attended Yavapai College, Prescott, Ariz.

Lost no-hitter in 12th inning against Chattanooga, May 28, 1987.
Led International League in complete games with 11 and tied for lead in shutouts with 3 in 1988.

Year	Club	League	G.	IP.	W.	L.	Pct.	H.	R.	ER.	SO.	BB.	ERA.
1984	Hagerstown†	Carolina	15	$77\frac{2}{3}$	4	5	.444	69	35	29	62	48	3.36
1985	Daytona Beach‡	Florida St.	8	$38\frac{1}{3}$	1	4	.200	32	23	17	24	26	3.99
1985	Hagerstown§	Carolina	7	$40\frac{2}{3}$	3	2	.600	32	16	12	37	22	2.66
1986	Hagerstown	Carolina	13	$60\frac{2}{3}$	4	5	.444	69	59	32	46	37	4.75
1986	Miami	Florida St.	12	$67\frac{1}{3}$	4	4	.500	70	36	28	41	27	3.74
1986	Charlotte	Southern	1	$5\frac{1}{3}$	0	1	.000	7	4	4	6	4	6.75
1987	Charlotte	Southern	29	148	11	9	.550	168	86	75	101	66	4.56
1988	Charlotte	Southern	5	$37\frac{2}{3}$	3	1	.750	26	11	10	29	12	2.39
1988	Rochester	Int'national	24	$176\frac{2}{3}$	12	8	.600	174	62	53	103	65	2.70
1988	Baltimore	American	3	25	2	0	1.000	9	2	2	18	9	0.72
	Major League Totals—1 Year		3	25	2	0	1.000	9	2	2	18	9	0.72

Selected by San Diego Padres' organization in 1st round (ninth player selected) of free-agent draft, January 11, 1983.
Selected by Baltimore Orioles' organization in secondary phase of free-agent draft, June 6, 1983.
†On disabled list, July 2 to August 28, 1984.
‡On disabled list, April 12 to May 11, 1985.
§On disabled list, July 5 to August 24, 1985.

DARRELL KEITH MILLER

Born February 26, 1959, at Washington, D. C.
Height, 6.02. Weight, 210.
Throws and bats righthanded.
Attended California State Poly University, Pomona, Calif.
Brother of Cheryl Miller, member of 1984 U.S. Olympic Gold Medal women's basketball team; and Reggie Miller, guard with Indiana Pacers.

Major League stolen bases: 1987 (1), 1988 (2). Total—3.

Year	Club	League	Pos.	G.	AB.	R.	H.	2B.	3B.	HR.	RBI.	B.A.	PO.	A.	E.	F.A.
1979	Idaho Falls	Pion.	C-1B	60	205	35	55	10	2	6	34	.268	254	40	12	.961
1980	Salinas	Calif.	C-1B-OF	64	195	26	56	6	3	4	28	.287	289	57	8	.977
1980	Salt Lake City	P. C.	C	30	101	10	30	2	2	0	11	.297	113	18	6	.956
1981	Holyoke	East.	C-OF-1B	126	443	61	117	26	9	10	62	.264	507	50	24	.959
1982	Holyoke†	East.	OF	119	450	76	118	25	*10	11	60	.262	187	8	8	.961
1983	Edmonton‡	P. C.	O-C-1-3	51	142	29	43	5	1	2	23	.303	146	24	8	.955
1984	Edmonton§	P. C.	C-OF-1B	92	328	65	107	19	9	12	67	.326	270	27	4	.987
1984	California	Amer.	1B-OF	17	41	5	7	0	0	0	1	.171	92	7	1	.990
1985	California x	Amer.	OF-C-3B	51	48	8	18	2	1	2	7	.375	39	3	2	.955
1985	Edmonton	P. C.	OF-C	17	71	10	20	3	1	1	6	.282	43	5	1	.980
1986	California	Amer.	OF-C	33	57	6	13	2	1	0	4	.228	30	3	0	1.000
1986	Edmonton	P. C.	OF-C-1B	63	212	37	65	8	7	8	30	.307	39	0	2	.951
1987	California y	Amer.	C-OF-3B	53	108	14	26	5	0	4	16	.241	131	15	2	.986
1988	Edmonton	P. C.	OF-C-1B	37	123	14	39	5	3	4	19	.317	108	9	4	.967
1988	California z	Amer.	C-OF	70	140	21	31	4	1	2	7	.221	229	18	4	.984
	Major League Totals—5 Years			224	394	54	95	13	3	8	35	.241	521	46	9	.984

Selected by California Angels' organization in 9th round of free-agent draft, June 5, 1979.
†On disabled list, May 6 to May 20, 1982.
‡On disabled list, May 4 to May 31, 1983.
§On disabled list, July 17 to August 7, 1984.
xOn disabled list, June 13 to July 5, 1985.
yOn disabled list, June 23 to July 18 and August 17 to September 8, 1987.
zOn disabled list, July 7 to July 22, 1988.

DAVID SCOTT MILLER
(Dave)

Born October 17, 1964, at Jacksonville, Fla.
Height, 6.03. Weight, 200.
Throws and bats righthanded.
Attended Pensacola Junior College, Pensacola, Fla., and University of Mississippi, University, Miss.

Tied for Carolina League lead in complete games with 8 in 1987.

Year	Club	League	G.	IP.	W.	L.	Pct.	H.	R.	ER.	SO.	BB.	ERA.
1986	Bradenton Braves	Gulf Coast	18	$40\frac{1}{3}$	3	2	.600	25	8	6	44	7	1.34
1986	Pulaski	Ap'lachian	4	5	2	0	1.000	5	3	3	4	5	5.40
1987	Durham	Carolina	30	*$205\frac{1}{3}$	*15	9	.625	188	92	82	*155	53	3.59
1988	Greenville	Southern	10	72	5	4	.556	59	26	20	50	19	2.50
1988	Richmond	Int'national	20	$115\frac{2}{3}$	11	6	.647	128	58	53	67	20	4.12

Selected by Kansas City Royals' organization in 3rd round of free-agent draft, January 17, 1984.
Signed as free agent by Atlanta Braves' organization, June 21, 1986.

KEITH ALAN MILLER

Born June 12, 1963, at Midland, Mich.
Height, 5.11. Weight, 180.
Throws and bats righthanded.
Attended Oral Roberts University, Tulsa, Okla.

Major League stolen bases: 1987 (8).
Tied for Texas League lead in being hit by pitch with 7 in 1986.

Year Club	League	Pos.	G.	AB.	R.	H.	2B.	3B.	HR.	RBI.	B.A.	PO.	A.	E.	F.A.
1985—Lynchburg	Carol.	3B-2B-OF	89	325	51	98	16	5	7	54	.302	103	203	25	.924
1985—Jackson	Texas	2B-SS	46	165	17	37	8	1	3	22	.224	108	132	8	.968
1986—Jackson†	Texas	2B	94	353	80	116	23	4	5	36	.329	198	272	19	.961
1987—Tidewater	Int.	2B-OF	53	202	29	50	9	1	6	22	.248	112	129	5	.980
1987—New York‡	Nat.	2B	25	51	14	19	2	2	0	1	.373	21	38	2	.967
1988—Tidewater	Int.	2-S-3-O	42	171	23	48	11	1	1	15	.281	81	111	12	.941
1988—New York	Nat.	2-S-3-O	40	70	9	15	1	1	1	5	.214	34	24	5	.921
Major League Totals—2 Years			65	121	23	34	3	3	1	6	.281	55	62	7	.944

Selected by Cleveland Indians' organization in 24th round of free-agent draft, June 5, 1981.
Selected by New York Yankees' organization in 2nd round of free-agent draft, June 4, 1984 (contract was later voided after it was discovered he had a pre-existing knee injury).
Signed as free agent by New York Mets' organization, September 6, 1984.
†On disabled list, April 8 to May 20, 1986.
‡On disabled list, June 29 to September 1, 1987; included rehabilitation disability assignment to Tidewater, August 21 to September 1, 1987.

NEAL KEITH MILLER

(Known by middle name.)
Born March 7, 1963, at Dallas, Tex.
Height, 5.11. Weight, 170.
Throws right and bats left and righthanded.
Attended Lubbock Christian College, Lubbock, Tex.

Led Eastern League second basemen in total chances with 657 in 1985.

Year Club	League	Pos.	G.	AB.	R.	H.	2B.	3B.	HR.	RBI.	B.A.	PO.	A.	E.	F.A.
1984—Bend	N'west	SS	3	12	1	2	0	0	0	0	.167	9	12	1	.955
1984—Peninsula	Carol.	3B-SS	65	226	44	73	8	5	0	36	.323	71	181	29	.897
1985—Reading	East.	2B	134	499	77	*147	24	7	6	59	.295	273	•355	•29	.956
1986—Portland	P. C.	2-3-O-S	36	130	15	32	8	1	0	11	.246	60	70	6	.956
1986—Reading	East.	2B	98	354	57	93	14	4	7	57	.263	220	262	*15	.970
1987—Maine	Int.	2B-OF-3B	122	383	61	112	16	4	16	54	.292	183	187	11	.971
1988—Maine	Int.	OF-2B-1B	59	200	38	56	14	1	3	23	.280	105	36	3	.979
1988—Philadelphia	Nat.	OF-3B-SS	47	48	4	8	3	0	0	6	.167	3	2	1	.833
Major League Totals—1 Year			47	48	4	8	3	0	0	6	.167	3	2	1	.833

Selected by Philadelphia Phillies' organization in 16th round of free-agent draft, June 4, 1984.

RANDALL ANDRE MILLIGAN
(Randy)

Born November 27, 1961, at San Diego, Calif.
Height, 6.02. Weight, 225.
Throws and bats righthanded.
Attended San Diego Mesa College, San Diego, Calif.

Major League stolen bases: 1988 (1).
Led International League batters in total bases with 272, bases on balls received with 91 and tied for lead in intentional bases on balls received with 10 in 1987.
Named Minor League Player of the Year by The Sporting News, 1987.
Named International League Player of the Year, 1987.

Year Club	League	Pos.	G.	AB.	R.	H.	2B.	3B.	HR.	RBI.	B.A.	PO.	A.	E.	F.A.
1981—Shelby	S. Atl.	OF-SS	130	406	90	115	16	6	7	58	.283	174	5	14	.927
1982—Lynchburg	Carol.	OF-1B	118	420	63	113	10	6	5	55	.269	341	12	11	.970
1983—Lynchburg	Carol.	1B-OF	106	349	60	102	13	5	5	56	.292	558	41	13	.979
1984—Jackson†	Texas	1B	62	193	32	53	5	0	9	34	.275	475	67	8	.985
1985—Jackson	Texas	1B	119	391	60	121	22	2	13	77	.309	726	49	11	.986
1986—Tidewater	Int.	1B	21	60	3	5	0	0	0	3	.083	60	4	1	.985
1986—Jackson	Texas	1B	78	269	53	85	11	3	7	53	.316	684	62	6	.992
1987—Tidewater	Int.	1B-OF	136	457	*99	149	28	4	29	*103	*.326	858	88	10	.990
1987—New York‡	Nat.	PH-PR	3	1	0	0	0	0	0	0	.000	0	0	0	.000
1988—Pittsburgh	Nat.	1B-OF	40	82	10	18	5	0	3	8	.220	213	15	3	.987
1988—Buffalo§	A. A.	1B-OF	63	221	37	61	15	3	2	30	.276	551	48	5	.992
Major League Totals—2 Years			43	83	10	18	5	0	3	8	.217	213	15	3	.987

Selected by New York Mets' organization in 1st round (third player selected) of free-agent draft, January 13, 1981.
†On disabled list, July 11, 1984 through remainder of season.
‡Traded with Pitcher Scott Henion to Pittsburgh Pirates for Catcher Mackey Sasser and Pitcher Tim Drummond, March 26, 1988.
§Traded to Baltimore Orioles for a player to be named later, November 9, 1988; Pittsburgh acquired Pitcher Pete Blohm to complete deal, December 7, 1988.

EDDIE JAMES MILNER JR.

Born May 21, 1955, at Columbus, O.
Height, 5.11. Weight, 170.
Throws and bats lefthanded.
Attended Muskingum College, New Concord, O., and received bachelor of science degree in business from Central State University, Wilberforce, O. in 1978.
Brother of Hobson Milner, 12th round selection of Minnesota Vikings in 1982 NFL draft; cousin of John Milner, first baseman-outfielder with New York Mets, Pittsburgh Pirates and Montreal Expos, 1971 through 1982.

Major League stolen bases: 1982 (18), 1983 (41), 1984 (21), 1985 (35), 1986 (18), 1987 (10), 1988 (2). Total—145.
Tied for Pioneer League lead in double plays by outfielders with 1 in 1976.
Named Florida State League Most Valuable Player, 1978.

Year Club	League	Pos.	G.	AB.	R.	H.	2B.	3B.	HR.	RBI.	B.A.	PO.	A.	E.	F.A.
1976—Billings	Pion.	OF	67	231	51	59	14	3	2	27	.255	*149	*12	7	.958
1977—Shelby	W. Carol.	OF	110	414	62	111	15	8	3	30	.268	254	10	10	.964
1978—Tampa	Fla. St.	OF	133	497	79	141	16	*16	8	44	.284	283	7	6	.980
1979—Indianapolis	A. A.	OF	30	98	9	18	0	2	0	5	.184	49	2	2	.962
1979—Nashville	South.	OF	104	369	70	97	12	12	11	51	.263	259	9	5	.982
1980—Indianapolis	A. A.	OF	130	468	63	118	11	7	5	37	.252	*363	6	7	.981
1980—Cincinnati	Nat.	PH-PR	6	3	1	0	0	0	0	0	.000	0	0	0	.000
1981—Indianapolis	A. A.	OF	127	453	69	130	14	6	3	42	.287	228	12	4	.984
1981—Cincinnati	Nat.	OF	8	5	0	1	1	0	0	1	.200	2	0	0	1.000
1982—Cincinnati†	Nat.	OF	113	407	61	109	23	5	4	31	.268	215	8	3	.987
1983—Cincinnati	Nat.	OF	146	502	77	131	23	6	9	33	.261	392	9	4	.990
1984—Cincinnati‡	Nat.	OF	117	336	44	78	8	4	7	29	.232	285	8	5	.983
1985—Cincinnati	Nat.	OF	145	453	82	115	19	7	3	33	.254	340	12	6	.983
1986—Cincinnati§	Nat.	OF	145	424	70	110	22	6	15	47	.259	292	6	3	.990
1987—San Francisco x	Nat.	OF	101	214	38	54	14	0	4	19	.252	135	0	1	.993
1987—Phoenix y	P. C.	OF	17	62	10	17	2	1	0	8	.274	38	0	0	1.000
1988—Nashville z	A. A.	OF-1B	18	70	10	15	2	0	0	3	.214	51	2	0	1.000
1988—Cincinnati a	Nat.	OF	23	51	3	9	1	0	0	2	.176	29	1	1	.968
Major League Totals—9 Years			804	2395	376	607	111	28	42	195	.253	1690	44	23	.987

Selected by Cincinnati Reds' organization in 21st round of free-agent draft, June 8, 1976.
†On disabled list, August 11 to September 7, 1982.
‡On disabled list, June 30 to August 6, 1984.
§Traded to San Francisco Giants for Pitchers Frank Williams, Timber Mead and Mike Villa, January 8, 1987.
xOn disabled list, April 17 to June 8, 1987; included rehabilitation disability assignment to Phoenix, May 24 to June 8, 1987.
yGranted free agency, November 9, 1987; signed by Cincinnati Reds, February 10, 1988.
zOn ineligible list, March 31 to May 28, 1988; then transferred to Cincinnati disabled list, May 29 to July 31, 1988; included rehabilitation disability assignment to Nashville, May 29 to June 19, 1988.
aReleased, July 31, 1988; re-signed by Reds' organization, August 5, 1988.

CHAMPIONSHIP SERIES RECORD

Year Club	League	Pos.	G.	AB.	R.	H.	2B.	3B.	HR.	RBI.	B.A.	PO.	A.	E.	F.A.
1987—San Francisco	Nat.	PR-O-PH	6	7	0	1	0	0	0	0	.143	8	0	0	1.000

GREGORY BRIAN MINTON
(Greg)

Born July 29, 1951, at Lubbock, Tex.
Height, 6.02. Weight, 207.
Throws right and bats left and righthanded.
Attended San Diego Mesa College, San Diego, Calif.

Major League saves: 1979 (4), 1980 (19), 1981 (21), 1982 (30), 1983 (22), 1984 (19), 1985 (4), 1986 (5), 1987 (11), 1988 (7). Total—142.
Led National League in intentional bases on balls issued with 20 in 1984 and 18 in 1985.
Led National League in games finished in relief with 44 in 1981 and 66 in 1982.
Tied for American League lead in intentional bases on balls issued with 10 in 1988.
Led Pacific Coast League in wild pitches with 18 in 1977.
Led Pacific Coast League in balks with 6 in 1975.

Year Club	League	G.	IP.	W.	L.	Pct.	H.	R.	ER.	SO.	BB.	ERA.
1970—Billings†	Pioneer	16	40	1	4	.200	37	23	14	36	16	3.15
1971—Waterloo	Midwest	27	124	11	6	.647	118	52	42	117	55	3.05
1972—San Jose‡	California	28	178	12	12	.500	182	117	78	153	77	3.94
1973—Phoenix	P. Coast	5	13	0	0	.000	11	6	6	4	8	4.15
1973—Amarillo	Texas	38	122	5	11	.313	138	87	61	77	48	4.50
1974—Fresno	California	13	96	10	1	.909	85	32	24	81	18	2.25
1974—Amarillo	Texas	6	29	1	4	.200	42	26	19	21	10	5.90
1975—Phoenix	P. Coast	42	177	10	6	.625	178	73	51	76	76	2.59
1975—San Francisco	National	4	17	1	1	.500	19	14	13	6	11	6.88
1976—San Francisco	National	10	26	0	3	.000	32	18	14	7	12	4.85
1976—Phoenix§	P. Coast	13	74	4	5	.444	91	57	46	31	32	5.59
1977—Phoenix	P. Coast	29	161	14	6	*.700	188	93	87	77	70	4.86
1977—San Francisco	National	2	14	1	1	.500	14	8	7	5	4	4.50
1978—Phoenix	P. Coast	14	92	7	4	.636	97	54	46	32	38	4.50
1978—San Francisco	National	11	16	0	1	.000	22	14	14	6	8	7.88
1979—San Francisco x	National	46	80	4	3	.571	59	25	16	33	27	1.80
1980—San Francisco	National	68	91	4	6	.400	81	28	25	42	34	2.47

Year Club	League	G.	IP.	W.	L.	Pct.	H.	R.	ER.	SO.	BB.	ERA.
1981—San Francisco	National	55	84	4	5	.444	84	28	27	29	36	2.89
1982—San Francisco	National	78	123	10	4	.714	108	29	25	58	42	1.83
1983—San Francisco	National	73	106⅔	7	11	.389	117	51	42	38	47	3.54
1984—San Francisco	National	74	124⅓	4	9	.308	130	60	52	48	57	3.76
1985—San Francisco	National	68	96⅔	5	4	.556	98	42	38	37	54	3.54
1986—San Francisco y	National	48	68⅔	4	4	.500	63	35	30	34	34	3.93
1987—San Francisco z	National	15	23⅓	1	0	1.000	30	9	9	9	10	3.47
1987—California a	American	41	76	5	4	.556	71	28	26	35	29	3.08
1988—Palm Springs b	California	2	4	0	0	.000	3	0	0	4	1	0.00
1988—California	American	44	79	4	5	.444	67	37	25	46	34	2.85
National League Totals—13 Years		552	870⅔	45	52	.464	857	361	312	352	376	3.23
American League Totals—2 Years		85	155	9	9	.500	138	65	51	81	63	2.96
Major League Totals—14 Years		637	1025⅔	54	61	.470	995	426	363	433	439	3.19

Selected by Kansas City Royals' organization in 3rd round of free-agent draft, January 17, 1970.

†Appeared in two games as an outfielder with one putout.

‡Traded to San Francisco Giants for Catcher Fran Healy, April 2, 1973.

§On disabled list, July 24 to August 5, 1976.

xOn disabled list, March 26 to May 31, 1979.

yOn disabled list, July 22 to August 14, 1986.

zReleased, May 28, 1987; signed by California Angels, June 1, 1987.

aGranted free agency, November 9, 1987; re-signed by Angels, December 3, 1987.

bOn California disabled list, March 26 to May 11, 1988; included rehabilitation disability assignment to Palm Springs, May 7 to May 11, 1988.

ALL-STAR GAME RECORD

Year League	IP.	W.	L.	Pct.	H.	R.	ER.	SO.	BB.	ERA.
1982—National	⅔	0	0	.000	0	0	0	0	1	0.00

PAUL THOMAS MIRABELLA

Born March 20, 1954, at Belleville, N. J.
Height, 6.02. Weight, 185.
Throws and bats lefthanded.
Attended Montclair State University, Upper Montclair, N. J.

Major League saves: 1978 (1), 1982 (3), 1984 (3), 1987 (2), 1988 (4). Total—13.

Tied for Pacific Coast League lead in balks with 4 in 1978.

Tied for Texas League lead in shutouts with 4 and games started by pitchers with 26 in 1977.

Tied for Western Carolinas League lead in balks with 5 in 1976.

Year Club	League	G.	IP.	W.	L.	Pct.	H.	R.	ER.	SO.	BB.	ERA.
1976—Asheville	W. Carol.	22	149	10	7	.588	149	77	66	*136	69	3.99
1977—Tulsa	Texas	26	176	12	7	.632	167	90	75	112	70	3.83
1978—Tucson	P. Coast	22	143	9	6	.600	158	77	63	85	68	3.97
1978—Texas†	American	10	28	3	2	.600	30	18	18	23	17	5.79
1979—Columbus	Int'national	22	144	11	7	.611	129	75	62	98	50	3.88
1979—New York‡	American	10	14	0	4	.000	16	15	14	4	10	9.00
1980—Syracuse	Int'national	4	31	1	2	.333	28	13	9	23	8	2.61
1980—Toronto	American	33	131	5	12	.294	151	73	63	53	66	4.33
1981—Syracuse	Int'national	22	153	11	7	.611	150	63	52	79	53	3.06
1981—Toronto§x	American	8	15	0	0	.000	20	16	12	9	7	7.20
1982—Texas y	American	40	50⅔	1	1	.500	46	28	27	29	22	4.80
1983—Rochester	Int'national	19	76⅓	3	5	.375	87	44	31	32	29	3.66
1983—Baltimore z	American	3	9⅔	0	0	.000	9	6	6	4	7	5.59
1983—Portland a	P. Coast	5	14⅓	0	1	.000	19	13	12	11	10	7.53
1984—Seattle	American	52	68	2	5	.286	74	39	33	41	32	4.37
1985—Calgary	P. Coast	53	68⅓	5	4	.556	84	34	31	42	29	4.08
1985—Seattle	American	10	13⅔	0	0	.000	9	4	2	8	4	1.32
1986—Seattle	American	8	6⅓	0	0	.000	13	7	6	6	3	8.53
1986—Calgary b	P. Coast	47	68⅓	3	4	.429	92	48	45	42	24	5.93
1987—Denver	Am. Assoc.	25	39	5	1	.833	39	11	10	28	10	2.31
1987—Milwaukee	American	29	29⅓	2	1	.667	30	20	16	14	16	4.91
1988—Denver	Am. Assoc.	8	9⅔	0	0	.000	9	3	1	7	4	0.93
1988—Milwaukee c	American	38	60	2	2	.500	44	12	11	33	21	1.65
Major League Totals—11 Years		241	425⅔	15	27	.357	442	238	208	224	205	4.40

Selected by Minnesota Twins' organization in 16th round of free-agent draft, June 4, 1975.

Selected by Texas Rangers' organization in secondary phase of free-agent draft, January 7, 1976.

†Traded with Pitchers Mike Griffin and Dave Righetti and Outfielders Juan Beniquez and Greg Jemison to New York Yankees for Pitchers Sparky Lyle, Larry McCall and Dave Rajsich, Catcher Mike Heath, Shortstop Domingo Ramos and cash, November 10, 1978.

‡Traded with First Baseman Chris Chambliss and Infielder Damaso Garcia to Toronto Blue Jays for Catcher Rick Cerone, Pitcher Tom Underwood and Outfielder Ted Wilborn, November 1, 1979.

§Traded to Chicago Cubs' organization for a player to be named later, December 28, 1981; Toronto Blue Jays' organization acquired Pitcher Dave Geisel to complete deal, March 25, 1982.

xTraded with a player to be named later and cash to Texas Rangers for Second Baseman Bump Wills, March 26, 1982; Texas organization acquired Pitcher Paul Semall to complete deal, April 21, 1982.

yReleased, March 26, 1983; signed by Rochester (Baltimore Orioles' organization), April 16, 1983.

zSold to Portland (Philadelphia Phillies' organization), August 12, 1983.

aGranted free agency, October 20, 1983; signed by Seattle Mariners, January 23, 1984.

bGranted free agency, October 15, 1986; signed by Denver (Milwaukee Brewers' organization), February 14, 1987.

cOn disabled list, August 15 to August 30, 1988.

JOHN KYLE MITCHELL

Born August 11, 1965, at Dickson, Tenn.
Height, 6.02. Weight, 195.
Throws and bats righthanded.
Brother of Charlie Mitchell, pitcher in Boston Red Sox' and Minnesota Twins' organization, 1982 through 1986.

Pitched 4-0 no-hit victory against Indianapolis, June 27, 1988 (first game).
Led Florida State League in wild pitches with 21 in 1984.
Named International League Pitcher of the Year, 1986.

Year Club	League	G.	IP.	W.	L.	Pct.	H.	R.	ER.	SO.	BB.	ERA.
1983—Elmira	NYP	16	75⅓	5	6	.455	78	57	41	72	41	4.90
1984—Winter Haven	Florida St.	27	*183⅔	16	9	.640	160	84	64	109	66	3.14
1985—New Britain†	Eastern	26	190⅓	12	8	.600	143	71	57	108	61	2.70
1986—Tidewater	Int'national	27	172⅓	12	9	.571	162	78	65	83	59	3.39
1986—New York	National	4	10	0	1	.000	10	4	4	2	4	3.60
1987—Tidewater	Int'national	8	48⅔	3	2	.600	44	24	18	16	20	3.33
1987—New York	National	20	111⅔	3	6	.333	124	64	51	57	36	4.11
1988—Tidewater	Int'national	27	*190	10	9	.526	164	76	60	65	45	2.84
1988—New York	National	1	1	0	0	.000	2	0	0	1	1	0.00
Major League Totals—3 Years		25	122⅔	3	7	.300	136	68	55	60	41	4.04

Selected by Boston Red Sox' organization in 7th round of free-agent draft, June 6, 1983.
†Traded with Pitchers Bob Ojeda, Tom McCarthy and Chris Bayer to New York Mets for Pitchers Calvin Schiraldi and Wes Gardner and Outfielders John Christensen and LaSchelle Tarver, November 13, 1985.

KEVIN DARRELL MITCHELL

Born January 13, 1962, at San Diego, Calif.
Height, 5.11. Weight, 210.
Throws and bats righthanded.

Major League stolen bases: 1986 (3), 1987 (9), 1988 (5). Total—17.
Led International League third basemen in assists with 215 in 1984.

Year Club	League	Pos.	G.	AB.	R.	H.	2B.	3B.	HR.	RBI.	B.A.	PO.	A.	E.	F.A.
1981—Kingsport	Appal.	3B-OF	62	221	39	74	9	2	7	45	.335	44	102	18	.890
1982—Lynchburg†	Carol.	3B	29	85	19	27	5	1	1	16	.318	11	33	10	.815
1983—Jackson	Texas	*3B-OF	120	441	75	132	25	2	15	85	.299	81	*224	21	.936
1984—Tidewater	Int.	3B-1B-OF	120	432	51	105	21	3	10	54	.243	114	220	22	.938
1984—New York	Nat.	3B	7	14	0	3	0	0	0	1	.214	1	4	1	.833
1985—Tidewater‡	Int.	*3B-1B	95	348	44	101	24	2	9	43	.290	56	209	*22	.923
1986—New York§	Nat.	O-S-3-1	108	328	51	91	22	2	12	43	.277	158	69	10	.958
1987—S.D. x-S.F.	Nat.	3B-OF-SS	131	464	68	130	20	2	22	70	.280	76	240	15	.955
1988—San Francisco	Nat.	3B-OF	148	505	60	127	25	7	19	80	.251	118	205	22	.936
Major League Totals—4 Years			394	1311	179	351	67	11	53	194	.268	353	518	48	.948

Signed as free agent by New York Mets' organization, November 16, 1980.
†On disabled list, July 21, 1982 through remainder of season.
‡On disabled list, July 12 to July 30, 1985.
§Traded with Outfielders Shawn Abner and Stanley Jefferson and Pitchers Kevin Armstrong and Kevin Brown to San Diego Padres for Outfielder Kevin McReynolds, Pitcher Gene Walter and Infielder Adam Ging, December 11, 1986.
xTraded with Pitchers Dave Dravecky and Craig Lefferts to San Francisco Giants for Third Baseman Chris Brown and Pitchers Keith Comstock, Mark Davis and Mark Grant, July 4, 1987.

CHAMPIONSHIP SERIES RECORD

Tied National League Championship Series record for most at-bats, seven-game Series (30), 1987.

Year Club	League	Pos.	G.	AB.	R.	H.	2B.	3B.	HR.	RBI.	B.A.	PO.	A.	E.	F.A.
1986—New York	Nat.	OF	2	8	1	2	0	0	0	0	.250	3	0	0	1.000
1987—San Francisco	Nat.	3B	7	30	2	8	1	0	1	2	.267	4	11	1	.938
Championship Series Totals—2 Years			9	38	3	10	1	0	1	2	.263	7	11	1	.947

WORLD SERIES RECORD

Year Club	League	Pos.	G.	AB.	R.	H.	2B.	3B.	HR.	RBI.	B.A.	PO.	A.	E.	F.A.
1986—New York	Nat.	PH-O-DH	5	8	1	2	0	0	0	0	.250	0	2	0	1.000

DALE ROBERT MOHORCIC

Name pronounced Muh-HORR-sick.

Born January 25, 1956, at Cleveland, O.
Height, 6.03. Weight, 220.
Throws and bats righthanded.
Attended Cuyahoga Community College (Metro), Cleveland, O., and Cleveland State University, Cleveland, O.

Tied major league record for most consecutive games pitched as relief pitcher (13), August 6 through 20, 1986.
Major league saves: 1986 (7), 1987 (16), 1988 (6). Total—29.
Tied for Northwest League lead in shutouts with 2 in 1978.

Year Club	League	G.	IP.	W.	L.	Pct.	H.	R.	ER.	SO.	BB.	ERA.
1978—Victoria†	Northwest	14	98	6	5	.545	84	39	22	73	36	2.02
1979—Dunedin‡	Florida St.	23	106	4	7	.364	134	59	52	52	27	4.42

Year	Club	League	G.	IP.	W.	L.	Pct.	H.	R.	ER.	SO.	BB.	ERA.
1980	—Salem	Carolina	47	111	7	5	.583	91	38	27	85	32	2.18
1981	—Portland	P. Coast	40	93	5	3	.625	103	54	45	39	41	4.35
1982	—Buffalo§	Eastern	44	57⅔	2	8	.200	71	41	32	40	23	4.99
1983	—Lynn	Eastern	18	34⅔	3	1	.750	35	20	14	13	17	3.63
1983	—Hawaii	P. Coast	15	69	6	6	.500	90	42	38	30	21	4.96
1984	—Hawaii x	P. Coast	9	57⅓	1	3	.250	67	29	25	21	17	3.92
1985	—Oklahoma City y	Amer. Assoc.	40	84⅔	3	7	.300	72	32	27	47	21	2.87
1986	—Oklahoma City	Amer. Assoc.	16	37⅔	4	4	.500	34	16	10	24	11	2.39
1986	—Texas	American	58	79	2	4	.333	86	25	22	29	15	2.51
1987	—Texas z	American	74	99⅓	7	6	.538	88	34	33	48	19	2.99
1988	—Texas ab-New York	American	56	74⅔	4	8	.333	83	42	35	44	29	4.22
Major League Totals—3 Years			188	253	13	18	.419	257	101	90	121	63	3.20

Signed as free agent by Victoria, June 11, 1978.
†Sold to Toronto Blue Jays' organization, September 25, 1978.
‡Released, January 8, 1980; signed by Pittsburgh Pirates' organization, April 5, 1980.
§On disabled list, May 27 through July 2, 1982.
xGranted free agency, October 15, 1984; signed by Oklahoma City (Texas Rangers' organization), May 19, 1985.
yGranted free agency, October 15, 1985; re-signed by Oklahoma City (Texas Rangers' organization), February 18, 1986.
zOn disabled list, August 12 to August 27, 1987.
aOn disabled list, March 26 to April 27, 1988.
bTraded to New York Yankees for Pitcher Cecilio Guante, August 30, 1988.

PAUL LEO MOLITOR

Born August 22, 1956, at St. Paul, Minn.
Height, 6.00. Weight, 175.
Throws and bats righthanded.
Attended University of Minnesota, Minneapolis, Minn.

Tied major league record for most stolen bases, inning (3), July 26, 1987, first inning.
Hit three home runs in a game, May 12, 1982.
Major League stolen bases: 1978 (30), 1979 (33), 1980 (34), 1981 (10), 1982 (41), 1983 (41), 1984 (1), 1985 (21), 1986 (20), 1987 (45), 1988 (41). Total—317.
Led American League third basemen in errors with 29 and double plays with 48 in 1982.
Named American League Rookie Player of the Year by The Sporting News, 1978.
Named Midwest League Most Valuable Player, 1977.
Received reported $100,000 bonus to sign with Milwaukee Brewers, 1977.
Named shortstop on The Sporting News College Baseball All-America Team, 1977.
Named designated hitter on The Sporting News American League All-Star Team, 1987.
Named designated hitter on The Sporting News American League Silver Slugger team, 1987 and 1988.

Year	Club	League	Pos.	G.	AB.	R.	H.	2B.	3B.	HR.	RBI.	B.A.	PO.	A.	E.	F.A.
1977	—Burlington	Midw.	SS	64	228	52	79	12	0	8	50	.346	83	207	28	.912
1978	—Milwaukee	Amer.	2B-SS-3B	125	521	73	142	26	4	6	45	.273	253	401	22	.967
1979	—Milwaukee	Amer.	2B-SS	140	584	88	188	27	16	9	62	.322	309	440	16	.979
1980	—Milwaukee†	Amer.	2B-SS-3B	111	450	81	137	29	2	9	37	.304	260	336	20	.968
1981	—Milwaukee‡	Amer.	OF	64	251	45	67	11	0	2	19	.267	119	4	3	.976
1982	—Milwaukee	Amer.	3B-SS	160	*666	*136	201	26	8	19	71	.302	134	350	32	.938
1983	—Milwaukee	Amer.	3B	152	608	95	164	28	6	15	47	.270	105	343	16	.966
1984	—Milwaukee§	Amer.	3B	13	46	3	10	1	0	0	6	.217	7	21	2	.933
1985	—Milwaukee x	Amer.	3B	140	576	93	171	28	3	10	48	.297	126	263	19	.953
1986	—Milwaukee y	Amer.	3B-OF	105	437	62	123	24	6	9	55	.281	86	171	15	.945
1987	—Milwaukee za	Amer.	3B-2B	118	465	*114	164	*41	5	16	75	.353	60	113	5	.972
1988	—Milwaukee	Amer.	3B-2B	154	609	115	190	34	6	13	60	.312	87	188	17	.942
Major League Totals—11 Years				1282	5213	905	1557	275	56	108	525	.299	1546	2630	167	.962

Selected by St. Louis Cardinals' organization in 28th round of free-agent draft, June 5, 1974.
Selected by Milwaukee Brewers' organization in 1st round (third player selected) of free-agent draft, June 7, 1977.
†On disabled list, June 24 to July 18, 1980.
‡On disabled list, May 3 to August 12, 1981.
§On disabled list, May 2, 1984 through remainder of season.
xOn disabled list, August 13 to August 28, 1985.
yOn disabled list, May 10 to May 30, June 2 to June 17 and June 19 to July 8, 1986.
zOn disabled list, April 30 to May 26 and June 27 to July 16, 1987.
aGranted free agency, November 9, 1987, re-signed by Brewers, January 5, 1988.

DIVISION SERIES RECORD

Year	Club	League	Pos.	G.	AB.	R.	H.	2B.	3B.	HR.	RBI.	B.A.	PO.	A.	E.	F.A.
1981	—Milwaukee	Amer.	OF	5	20	2	5	0	0	1	1	.250	12	0	0	1.000

CHAMPIONSHIP SERIES RECORD

Tied American League Championship Series record for most home runs, five-game Series (2), 1982.

Year	Club	League	Pos.	G.	AB.	R.	H.	2B.	3B.	HR.	RBI.	B.A.	PO.	A.	E.	F.A.
1982	—Milwaukee	Amer.	3B	5	19	4	6	1	0	2	5	.316	4	11	2	.882

WORLD SERIES RECORD

Established World Series records for most hits, game (5), October 12, 1982; most one-base hits, game (5), October 12, 1982.
Tied World Series records for most at-bats, nine-inning game (6), October 12, 1982; most hits, two consecutive games, one Series (7), October 12, 13, 1982.

Year	Club	League	Pos.	G.	AB.	R.	H.	2B.	3B.	HR.	RBI.	B.A.	PO.	A.	E.	F.A.
1982	—Milwaukee	Amer.	3B	7	31	5	11	0	0	0	3	.355	4	9	0	1.000

ALL-STAR GAME RECORD

Year League	Pos.	AB.	R.	H.	2B.	3B.	HR.	RBI.	B.A.	PO.	A.	E.	F.A.
1985—American	3B-OF	1	0	0	0	0	0	0	.000	0	0	0	.000
1988—American	2B	3	0	0	0	0	0	0	.000	1	2	0	1.000
All-Star Game Totals—2 Years		4	0	0	0	0	0	0	.000	1	2	0	1.000

Named to American League All-Star Team in 1980; replaced due to injury.

RICHARD MONTELEONE
(Rich)

Born March 22, 1963, at Tampa, Fla.
Height, 6.02. Weight, 217.
Throws and bats righthanded.

Led Appalachian League pitchers in home runs allowed with 8 in 1982.

Year Club	League	G.	IP.	W.	L.	Pct.	H.	R.	ER.	SO.	BB.	ERA.
1982—Bristol	Ap'lachian	12	71⅔	4	6	.400	66	41	31	52	23	3.89
1983—Lakeland	Florida St.	24	142⅓	9	8	.529	146	80	65	124	80	4.11
1983—Birmingham	Southern	3	15	1	1	.500	25	12	12	9	6	7.20
1984—Birmingham	Southern	19	123⅔	7	8	.467	116	69	64	74	67	4.66
1984—Evansville	Am. Assoc.	11	64	5	3	.625	64	33	32	42	36	4.50
1985—Nashville†	Am. Assoc.	27	145⅓	6	12	.333	149	89	82	97	87	5.08
1986—Calgary	P. Coast	39	158⅔	8	12	.400	177	108	93	101	*89	5.28
1987—Seattle	American	3	7	0	0	.000	10	5	5	2	4	6.43
1987—Calgary	P. Coast	51	65⅓	6	*13	.316	59	45	40	38	63	5.51
1988—Calgary‡-Edmonton	P. Coast	30	122⅓	4	7	.364	141	84	69	97	27	5.08
1988—California	American	3	4⅓	0	0	.000	4	0	0	3	1	0.00
Major League Totals—2 Years		6	11⅓	0	0	.000	14	5	5	5	5	3.97

Selected by Detroit Tigers' organization in 1st round (20th player selected) of free-agent draft, June 7, 1982.
†Traded to Seattle Mariners for Third Baseman Darnell Coles, December 12, 1985.
‡Released, May 9, 1988; signed by Edmonton (California Angels' organization), May 13, 1988.

JEFFREY THOMAS MONTGOMERY
(Jeff)

Born January 7, 1962, at Wellston, O.
Height, 5.11. Weight, 180
Throws and bats righthanded.
Received bachelor of science degree in computer science from
Marshall University, Huntington, W. Va., in 1984.

Major League saves: 1988 (1).
Tied for Florida State League lead in saves with 14 in 1984.

Year Club	League	G.	IP.	W.	L.	Pct.	H.	R.	ER.	SO.	BB.	ERA.
1983—Billings	Pioneer	20	44⅔	6	2	.750	31	13	12	90	13	2.42
1984—Tampa	Florida St.	31	44⅓	5	3	.625	29	15	12	56	30	2.44
1984—Vermont	Eastern	22	25⅓	2	0	1.000	14	7	6	20	24	2.13
1985—Vermont	Eastern	*53	101	5	3	.625	63	25	23	89	48	2.05
1986—Denver	Am. Assoc.	30	151⅔	11	7	.611	162	88	74	78	57	4.39
1987—Nashville	Am. Assoc.	24	139	8	5	.615	132	76	64	121	51	4.14
1987—Cincinnati†	National	14	19⅓	2	2	.500	25	15	14	13	9	6.52
1988—Omaha	Am. Assoc.	20	28⅓	1	2	.333	15	6	6	36	11	1.91
1988—Kansas City	American	45	62⅔	7	2	.778	54	25	24	47	30	3.45
National League Totals—1 Year		14	19⅓	2	2	.500	25	15	14	13	9	6.52
American League Totals—1 Year		45	62⅔	7	2	.778	54	25	24	47	30	3.45
Major League Totals—2 Years		59	82	9	4	.692	79	40	38	60	39	4.17

Selected by Cincinnati Reds' organization in 9th round of free-agent draft, June 6, 1983.
†Traded to Kansas City Royals for Outfielder Van Snider, February 15, 1988.

BRADLEY ALAN MOORE
(Brad)

Born June 21, 1964, at Loveland, Colo.
Height, 6.01. Weight, 185.
Throws and bats righthanded.
Attended Garden City Community College, Garden City, Kan.,
and Grand Canyon College, Phoenix, Ariz.

Year Club	League	G.	IP.	W.	L.	Pct.	H.	R.	ER.	SO.	BB.	ERA.
1986—Bend	Northwest	16	33⅔	2	5	.286	32	29	22	35	22	5.88
1987—Clearwater	Florida St.	53	67⅓	4	7	.364	63	23	15	42	21	2.00
1987—Reading	Eastern	9	18⅓	0	1	.000	12	2	2	13	4	0.98
1988—Reading	Eastern	57	70⅔	4	6	.400	57	30	24	39	33	3.06
1988—Philadelphia	National	5	5⅔	0	0	.000	4	0	0	2	4	0.00
Major League Totals—1 Year		5	5⅔	0	0	.000	4	0	0	2	4	0.00

Signed as free agent by Philadelphia Phillies' organization, June 25, 1986.

DONNIE RAY MOORE

Born February 13, 1954, at Lubbock, Tex.
Height, 6.00. Weight, 185.
Throws right and bats lefthanded.
Attended Ranger Junior College, Ranger, Tex.
Cousin of Hubie Brooks, outfielder with Montreal Expos.

Major League saves: 1978 (4), 1979 (1), 1982 (1), 1983 (6), 1984 (16), 1985 (31), 1986 (21), 1987 (5), 1988 (4). Total—89.

Led American Association in home runs allowed with 25 in 1976.

Led Texas League pitchers in games started with 27 and tied for lead in shutouts with 3 and home runs allowed with 16 in 1975.

Received reported $50,000 bonus to sign with Chicago Cubs, 1973.

Year Club	League	G.	IP.	W.	L.	Pct.	H.	R.	ER.	SO.	BB.	ERA.
1973—Bradenton Cubs	Gulf Coast	4	10	0	1	.000	9	5	4	6	6	3.60
1974—Key West†	Florida St.	26	174	11	12	.478	167	73	54	97	69	2.79
1974—Midland	Texas	5	22	0	4	.000	32	18	17	9	5	6.95
1975—Midland	Texas	28	•185	14	8	.636	191	79	61	123	67	2.97
1975—Chicago	National	4	9	0	0	.000	12	4	4	8	4	4.00
1976—Wichita	Am. Assoc.	24	152	7	11	.389	170	96	80	92	61	4.74
1977—Wichita	Am. Assoc.	11	66	4	4	.500	68	38	36	34	22	4.91
1977—Chicago	National	27	49	4	2	.667	51	27	22	34	18	4.04
1978—Chicago	National	71	103	9	7	.563	117	55	47	50	31	4.11
1979—Wichita	Am. Assoc.	5	29	1	3	.250	29	26	26	16	20	8.07
1979—Chicago‡	National	39	73	1	4	.200	95	46	42	43	25	5.18
1980—St. Louis	National	11	22	1	1	.500	25	15	15	10	5	6.14
1980—Springfield	Am. Assoc.	14	85	6	5	.545	74	32	29	49	32	3.07
1981—Springfield§xy	Am. Assoc.	21	108	8	6	.571	115	49	41	47	31	3.42
1981—Milwaukee	American	3	4	0	0	.000	4	3	3	2	4	6.75
1982—Richmond	Int'national	36	55	5	3	.625	51	17	14	45	18	2.29
1982—Atlanta	National	16	27⅔	3	1	.750	32	13	13	17	7	4.23
1983—Richmond	Int'national	12	16⅔	0	2	.000	12	6	6	9	7	3.24
1983—Atlanta z	National	43	68⅔	2	3	.400	72	30	28	41	10	3.67
1984—Atlanta ab	National	47	64⅓	4	5	.444	63	27	21	47	18	2.94
1985—California c	American	65	103	8	8	.500	91	28	22	72	21	1.92
1986—California d	American	49	72⅔	4	5	.444	60	28	24	53	22	2.97
1987—California e	American	14	26⅔	2	2	.500	28	12	8	17	13	2.70
1987—Palm Springs f	California	3	5	0	0	.000	5	0	0	4	4	0.00
1988—California g	American	27	33	5	2	.714	48	20	18	22	8	4.91
1988—Palm Springs h	California	5	8	0	0	.000	4	4	2	7	4	2.25
National League Totals—8 Years		258	416⅔	24	23	.511	467	217	192	250	118	4.15
American League Totals—5 Years		158	239⅓	19	17	.528	231	91	75	166	68	2.82
Major League Totals—13 Years		416	656	43	40	.518	698	308	267	416	186	3.66

Selected by Boston Red Sox' organization in 12th round of free-agent draft, June 6, 1972.

Signed as free agent by Chicago Cubs' organization, June 3, 1973.

†Appeared in two games as an outfielder with two putouts.

‡Traded to St. Louis Cardinals for Second Baseman Mike Tyson, October 17, 1979.

§On temporary inactive list, April 14 to May 11, 1981.

xSold conditionally to Milwaukee Brewers, September 3, 1981; returned, October 23, 1981.

yTraded to Atlanta Braves' organization for Pitcher Dan Morogiello, February 1, 1982.

zOn disabled list, August 3 to August 24, 1983.

aOn disabled list, April 19 to May 24, 1984.

bSelected by California Angels in player compensation pool draft, January 24, 1985. (California received compensation for Baltimore Orioles' signing free agent Outfielder Fred Lynn, a Type A player, December 11, 1984.)

cGranted free agency, November 12, 1985; re-signed by Angels, January 8, 1986.

dOn disabled list, May 25 to June 30, 1986.

eOn disabled list, May 29 to July 3 and July 9 to September 13, 1987; included rehabilitation disability assignment to Palm Springs, June 25 to July 3, 1987.

fGranted free agency, January 22, 1988; re-signed by Angels, February 9, 1988.

gOn disabled list, May 8 to June 18 and August 8 to August 26, 1988; included rehabilitation disability assignment to Palm Springs, May 30 to June 16, 1988.

hReleased, August 26, 1988.

CHAMPIONSHIP SERIES RECORD

Year Club	League	G.	IP.	W.	L.	Pct.	H.	R.	ER.	SO.	BB.	ERA.
1982—Atlanta	National	2	2⅔	0	0	.000	2	0	0	1	0	0.00
1986—California	American	3	5	0	1	.000	8	4	4	0	2	7.20
Championship Series Totals—2 Years		5	7⅔	0	1	.000	10	4	4	1	2	4.70

ALL-STAR GAME RECORD

Year League	IP.	W.	L.	Pct.	H.	R.	ER.	SO.	BB.	ERA.
1985—American	2	0	0	.000	0	0	0	1	0	0.00

MICHAEL WAYNE MOORE
(Mike)

Born November 26, 1959, at Eakly, Okla.
Height, 6.04. Weight, 205.
Throws and bats righthanded.
Attended Oral Roberts University, Tulsa, Okla.

Major League saves: 1986 (1), 1988 (1). Total—2.

Tied for American League lead in games started by pitchers with 37 in 1986.
Received reported $100,000 bonus to sign with Seattle Mariners, 1981.
Named righthanded pitcher on THE SPORTING NEWS College Baseball All-America Team, 1981.

Year Club	League	G.	IP.	W.	L.	Pct.	H.	R.	ER.	SO.	BB.	ERA.
1981—Lynn	Eastern	13	94	6	5	.545	83	42	38	81	34	3.64
1982—Seattle	American	28	144⅓	7	14	.333	159	91	86	73	79	5.36
1982—Salt Lake City	P. Coast	1	8	0	0	.000	9	4	4	6	5	4.50
1983—Seattle	American	22	128	6	8	.429	130	75	67	108	60	4.71
1983—Salt Lake City	P. Coast	11	82⅓	4	4	.500	78	48	33	80	54	3.61
1984—Seattle	American	34	212	7	17	.292	236	127	117	158	85	4.97
1985—Seattle	American	35	247	17	10	.630	230	100	95	155	70	3.46
1986—Seattle	American	38	266	11	13	.458	★279	141	127	146	94	4.30
1987—Seattle	American	33	231	9	★19	.321	★268	145	★121	115	84	4.71
1988—Seattle†	American	37	228⅔	9	15	.375	196	104	96	182	63	3.78
Major League Totals—7 Years		227	1457	66	96	.407	1498	783	709	937	535	4.38

Selected by St. Louis Cardinals' organization in 3rd round of free-agent draft, June 6, 1978.
Selected by Seattle Mariners' organization in 1st round (first player selected) of free-agent draft, June 8, 1981.
†Granted free agency, November 4, 1988; signed by Oakland Athletics, November 28, 1988.

BOBBY KEITH MORELAND

(Known by middle name.)

Born May 2, 1954, at Dallas, Tex.
Height, 6.00. Weight, 200.
Throws and bats righthanded.
Attended University of Texas, Austin, Tex.

Major League stolen bases: 1980 (3), 1981 (1), 1984 (1), 1985 (12), 1986 (3), 1987 (3), 1988 (2). Total—25.
Led American Association in sacrifice flies with 10 in 1978 and with 13 in 1979.
Led American Association catchers in double plays with 10 in 1978.
Led American Association in passed balls with 11 in 1979 and tied for lead with 10 in 1978.
Led Eastern League in passed balls with 18 in 1977.
Tied for Carolina League lead in double plays by third basemen with 19 in 1976.

Year Club	League	Pos.	G.	AB.	R.	H.	2B.	3B.	HR.	RBI.	B.A.	PO.	A.	E.	F.A.
1975—Spartanburg	W. Car.	3B	69	246	28	68	13	1	1	41	.276	52	128	17	.914
1976—Peninsula	Carol.	●3B-SS	78	294	38	83	12	2	4	47	.282	50	221	●26	.912
1976—Reading	East.	3B-2B	61	199	7	52	5	0	0	7	.261	62	99	13	.925
1977—Reading	East.	C-3B	104	401	61	131	19	1	8	55	.327	339	60	8	.980
1977—Oklahoma City	A. A.	C	7	13	3	1	0	0	0	1	.077	17	1	0	1.000
1978—Oklahoma City	A. A.	C-1-3-O	130	501	73	145	25	4	16	98	.289	641	75	13	.982
1978—Philadelphia	Nat.	C	1	2	0	0	0	0	0	0	.000	4	0	0	1.000
1979—Oklahoma City	A. A.	C-3B-OF	130	494	86	149	●34	3	20	109	.302	397	44	13	.971
1979—Philadelphia	Nat.	C	14	48	3	18	3	2	0	8	.375	71	3	0	1.000
1980—Philadelphia	Nat.	C-OF	62	159	13	50	8	0	4	29	.314	186	22	7	.967
1981—Philadelphia†	Nat.	C-3-1-O	61	196	16	50	7	0	6	37	.255	267	31	9	.971
1982—Chicago	Nat.	OF-C-3B	138	476	50	124	17	2	15	68	.261	384	38	8	.981
1983—Chicago	Nat.	OF-C	154	533	76	161	30	3	16	70	.302	244	7	6	.977
1984—Chicago	Nat.	O-1-3-C	140	495	59	138	17	3	16	80	.279	393	30	10	.977
1985—Chicago	Nat.	O-1-3-C	161	587	74	180	30	3	14	106	.307	313	29	13	.963
1986—Chicago	Nat.	O-3-C-1	156	586	72	159	30	0	12	79	.271	340	58	9	.978
1987—Chicago‡	Nat.	★3B-1B	153	563	63	150	29	1	27	88	.266	99	300	★28	.934
1988—San Diego§	Nat.	1B-OF-3B	143	511	40	131	23	0	5	64	.256	747	58	7	.991
Major League Totals—11 Years			1183	4156	466	1161	194	14	115	629	.279	3048	576	97	.974

Selected by Philadelphia Phillies' organization in 7th round of free-agent draft, June 4, 1975.
†Traded with Pitchers Dan Larson and Dickie Noles to Chicago Cubs for Pitcher Mike Krukow and cash, December 8, 1981.
‡Traded with Infielder Mike Brumley to San Diego Padres for Pitchers Rich Gossage and Ray Hayward, February 12, 1988.
§Traded with Infielder Chris Brown to Detroit Tigers for Pitcher Walt Terrell, October 28, 1988.

DIVISION SERIES RECORD

Year Club	League	Pos.	G.	AB.	R.	H.	2B.	3B.	HR.	RBI.	B.A.	PO.	A.	E.	F.A.
1981—Philadelphia	Nat.	C	4	13	2	6	0	0	1	3	.462	30	2	1	.970

CHAMPIONSHIP SERIES RECORD

Year Club	League	Pos.	G.	AB.	R.	H.	2B.	3B.	HR.	RBI.	B.A.	PO.	A.	E.	F.A.
1980—Philadelphia	Nat.	C-PH	2	1	0	0	0	0	0	1	.000	0	0	0	.000
1984—Chicago	Nat.	OF	5	18	3	6	2	0	0	2	.333	9	0	0	1.000
Championship Series Totals—2 Years			7	19	3	6	2	0	0	3	.316	9	0	0	1.000

WORLD SERIES RECORD

Year Club	League	Pos.	G.	AB.	R.	H.	2B.	3B.	HR.	RBI.	B.A.	PO.	A.	E.	F.A.
1980—Philadelphia	Nat.	DH	3	12	1	4	0	0	0	1	.333	0	0	0	.000

—DID YOU KNOW—

That in 1988, St. Louis' Jose Oquendo became the first National Leaguer to play all nine positions in the same season since Gene Paulette of the Cardinals in 1918?

MICHAEL THOMAS MORGAN
(Mike)

Born October 8, 1959, at Tulare, Calif.
Height, 6.02. Weight, 215.
Throws and bats righthanded.

Major League saves: 1986 (1), 1988 (1). Total—2.
Tied for International League lead in shutouts with 4 in 1984.
Received reported $50,000 bonus to sign with Oakland A's, 1978.

Year Club	League	G.	IP.	W.	L.	Pct.	H.	R.	ER.	SO.	BB.	ERA.
1978—Oakland	American	3	12	0	3	.000	19	12	10	0	8	7.50
1978—Vancouver	P. Coast	14	92	5	6	.455	109	67	57	31	54	5.58
1979—Ogden	P. Coast	13	101	5	5	.500	93	48	39	42	49	3.48
1979—Oakland	American	13	77	2	10	.167	102	57	51	17	50	5.96
1980—Ogden†‡	P. Coast	20	115	6	9	.400	135	79	69	46	77	5.40
1981—Nashville§	Southern	26	169	8	7	.533	164	97	83	100	83	4.42
1982—New York x	American	30	150⅓	7	11	.389	167	77	73	71	67	4.37
1983—Toronto y	American	16	45⅓	0	3	.000	48	26	26	22	21	5.16
1983—Syracuse	Int'national	5	19⅓	0	3	.000	20	12	12	17	13	5.59
1984—Syracuse z	Int'national	34	⋆185⅔	13	11	.542	167	•101	84	105	•100	4.07
1985—Seattle a	American	2	6	1	1	.500	11	8	8	2	5	12.00
1985—Calgary	P. Coast	1	2	0	0	.000	3	1	1	0	0	4.50
1986—Seattle	American	37	216⅓	11	•17	.393	243	122	109	116	86	4.53
1987—Seattle b	American	34	207	12	17	.414	245	117	107	85	53	4.65
1988—Baltimore c	American	22	71⅓	1	6	.143	70	45	43	29	23	5.43
1988—Rochester	Int'national	3	17	0	2	.000	19	10	9	7	6	4.76
Major League Totals—8 Years		157	785⅓	34	68	.333	905	464	427	342	313	4.89

Selected by Oakland A's organizaton in 1st round (fourth player selected) of free-agent draft, June 6, 1978.

†On disabled list, May 14 to June 27, 1980.

‡Traded to New York Yankees for Shortstop Fred Stanley and a player to be named later, November 3, 1980; Oakland A's acquired Second Baseman Brian Doyle to complete deal, November 17, 1980.

§On disabled list, April 9 to April 22, 1981.

xTraded with Outfielder-First Baseman Dave Collins, First Baseman Fred McGriff and a reported $400,000 to Toronto Blue Jays for Pitcher Dale Murray and Outfielder-Catcher Tom Dodd, December 9, 1982.

yOn disabled list, July 2 to August 23, 1983; included rehabilitation disability assignment to Syracuse, August 1 to August 18, 1983.

zDrafted by Seattle Mariners, December 3, 1984.

aOn disabled list, April 17, 1985 through remainder of season; included rehabilitation disability assignment to Calgary, July 19 to July 22, 1985.

bTraded to Baltimore Orioles for Pitcher Ken Dixon, December 9, 1987.

cOn disabled list, June 9 to July 19 and August 12, 1988 through remainder of season; included rehabilitation disability assignment to Rochester, June 30 to July 17, 1988.

RUSSELL LEE MORMAN
(Russ)

Born April 28, 1962, at Independence, Mo.
Height, 6.04. Weight, 215.
Throws and bats righthanded.
Attended Iowa Western Community College, Clarinda, Ia.,
and Wichita State University, Wichita, Kan.

Tied major league record for most hits, inning, first major league game (2), August 3, 1986 (fourth inning).
Major League stolen bases: 1986 (1).
Led Eastern League in slugging percentage with .512 in 1985.
Led Midwest League in game-winning RBIs with 15 in 1984.
Led American Association third basemen in double plays with 23 in 1986.
Led Eastern League first basemen in assists with 79 in 1985.
Named first baseman on THE SPORTING NEWS College Baseball All-America Team, 1983.

Year Club	League	Pos.	G.	AB.	R.	H.	2B.	3B.	HR.	RBI.	B.A.	PO.	A.	E.	F.A.
1983—Glens Falls	East.	1B	71	233	29	57	9	1	3	32	.245	591	43	7	.989
1984—Appleton	Midw.	1B-OF	122	424	68	111	17	7	7	80	.262	823	43	10	.989
1985—Glens Falls	East.	⋆1-3-O	119	422	64	131	24	5	17	81	.310	905	81	12	⋆.988
1985—Buffalo	A. A.	1B	21	64	16	19	3	1	7	14	.297	144	7	2	.987
1986—Buffalo	A. A.	3B-OF	106	365	52	97	17	2	13	57	.266	87	201	24	.923
1986—Chicago	Amer.	1B	49	159	18	40	5	0	4	17	.252	342	26	4	.989
1987—Hawaii	P. C.	1B-OF	89	294	52	79	19	2	9	53	.269	410	28	3	.993
1988—Vancouver	P. C.	1B-OF	69	257	40	77	8	1	5	45	.300	370	21	3	.992
1988—Chicago	Amer.	1B-OF	40	75	8	18	2	0	0	3	.240	114	5	2	.983
Major League Totals—2 Years			89	234	26	58	7	0	4	20	.248	456	31	6	.988

Selected by Kansas City Royals' organization in 7th round of free-agent draft, January 13, 1981.
Selected by Chicago White Sox' organization in 1st round (28th player selected) of free-agent draft, June 6, 1983.

JOHN DANIEL MORRIS

Born February 23, 1961, at Freeport, N.Y.
Height, 6.01. Weight, 185.
Throws and bats lefthanded.
Attended Seton Hall University, South Orange, N.J.

Major League stolen bases: 1986 (6), 1987 (5). Total—11.

Led Southern League outfielders in total chances with 343 in 1985.
Named Southern League Most Valuable Player, 1983.
Named outfielder on THE SPORTING NEWS College Baseball All-America Team, 1982.

Year	Club	League	Pos.	G.	AB.	R.	H.	2B.	3B.	HR.	RBI.	B.A.	PO.	A.	E.	F.A.
1982	—Fort Myers	Fla. St.	OF	45	137	21	39	7	2	2	17	.285	64	2	2	.971
1983	—Jacksonville	South.	OF	140	490	96	141	27	8	23	92	.288	260	8	3	*.989
1984	—Omaha	A. A.	OF	148	492	77	133	24	4	15	60	.270	*359	7	4	*.989
1985	—Omaha†-Louis.	A. A.	OF	130	466	64	117	25	6	5	50	.251	*330	11	2	*.994
1986	—Louisville‡	A. A.	OF	60	213	30	50	13	7	1	24	.235	132	6	2	.986
1986	—St. Louis	Nat.	OF	39	100	8	24	0	1	1	14	.240	68	0	1	.986
1987	—Louisville	A. A.	OF	14	47	13	16	5	2	3	12	.340	20	2	0	1.000
1987	—St. Louis	Nat.	OF	101	157	22	41	6	4	3	23	.261	86	0	1	.989
1988	—Louisville§	A. A.	OF	13	40	3	4	0	0	0	0	.100	8	0	0	1.000
1988	—St. Louis	Nat.	OF	20	38	3	11	2	1	0	3	.289	12	0	2	.857
Major League Totals—3 Years				160	295	33	76	8	6	4	40	.258	166	0	4	.976

Selected by Kansas City Royals' organization in 1st round (10th player selected) of free-agent draft, June 7, 1982.
†Traded to St. Louis Cardinals' organization for Outfielder Lonnie Smith, May 17, 1985.
‡On disabled list, May 7 to June 11 and June 28 to July 8, 1986.
§On St. Louis disabled list, March 20 to September 2, 1988; included rehabilitation disability assignment to Louisville, August 17 to September 2, 1988.

CHAMPIONSHIP SERIES RECORD

Year	Club	League	Pos.	G.	AB.	R.	H.	2B.	3B.	HR.	RBI.	B.A.	PO.	A.	E.	F.A.
1987	—St. Louis	Nat.	OF	2	3	0	0	0	0	0	0	.000	1	0	0	1.000

WORLD SERIES RECORD

Year	Club	League	Pos.	G.	AB.	R.	H.	2B.	3B.	HR.	RBI.	B.A.	PO.	A.	E.	F.A.
1987	—St. Louis	Nat.	OF	1	2	0	0	0	0	0	0	.000	2	0	0	1.000

JOHN SCOTT MORRIS
(Jack)

Born May 16, 1955, at St. Paul, Minn.
Height, 6.03. Weight, 200.
Throws and bats righthanded.
Attended Brigham Young University, Provo, Utah.

Established American League record for most consecutive starting assignments, lifetime (336).
Established American League records for most wild pitches, season (24), 1987; most seasons leading league, wild pitches (4).
Tied American League record for most wild pitches, game (5), August 3, 1987 (10 innings).
Pitched 4-0 no-hit victory against Chicago White Sox, April 7, 1984.
Led American League in shutouts with 6 in 1986.
Led American League in wild pitches with 18 in 1983, 14 in 1984, 15 in 1985 and 24 in 1987.
Named American League Pitcher of the Year by THE SPORTING NEWS, 1981.
Named righthanded pitcher on THE SPORTING NEWS American League All-Star Team, 1981.

Year	Club	League	G.	IP.	W.	L.	Pct.	H.	R.	ER.	SO.	BB.	ERA.
1976	—Montgomery	Southern	12	36	2	3	.400	37	31	25	18	36	6.25
1977	—Evansville	Am. Assoc.	20	135	6	7	.462	141	68	54	95	42	3.60
1977	—Detroit	American	7	46	1	1	.500	38	20	19	28	23	3.72
1978	—Detroit	American	28	106	3	5	.375	107	57	51	48	49	4.33
1979	—Evansville	Am. Assoc.	5	34	2	2	.500	22	13	9	28	18	2.38
1979	—Detroit	American	27	198	17	7	.708	179	76	72	113	59	3.27
1980	—Detroit	American	36	250	16	15	.516	252	125	116	112	87	4.18
1981	—Detroit	American	25	198	•14	7	.667	153	69	67	97	*78	3.05
1982	—Detroit	American	37	266⅓	17	16	.515	247	131	120	135	96	4.06
1983	—Detroit†	American	37	*293⅔	20	13	.606	257	117	109	*232	83	3.34
1984	—Detroit	American	35	240⅓	19	11	.633	221	108	96	148	87	3.60
1985	—Detroit‡	American	35	257	16	11	.593	212	102	95	191	110	3.33
1986	—Detroit§	American	35	267	21	8	.724	229	105	97	223	82	3.27
1987	—Detroit x	American	34	266	18	11	.621	227	111	100	208	93	3.38
1988	—Detroit	American	34	235	15	13	.536	225	115	103	168	83	3.94
Major League Totals—12 Years			370	2623⅓	177	118	.600	2347	1136	1045	1703	930	3.59

Selected by Detroit Tigers' organization in 5th round of free-agent draft, June 8, 1976.
†Appeared in seven games as a pinch-runner.
‡Appeared in one game as a pinch-runner.
§Granted free agency, November 12, 1986; re-signed by Tigers, December 19, 1986.
xGranted free agency, November 9, 1987; re-signed by Tigers, December 29, 1987.

CHAMPIONSHIP SERIES RECORD

Year	Club	League	G.	IP.	W.	L.	Pct.	H.	R.	ER.	SO.	BB.	ERA.
1984	—Detroit	American	1	7	1	0	1.000	5	1	1	4	1	1.29
1987	—Detroit	American	1	8	0	1	.000	6	6	6	7	3	6.75
Championship Series Totals—2 Years			2	15	1	1	.500	11	7	7	11	4	4.20

Appeared as pinch-runner for Detroit Tigers in one game of 1987 Championship Series.

WORLD SERIES RECORD

Established World Series record for most putouts, pitcher, five-game Series (5), 1984.
Tied World Series record for most wild pitches, game (2), October 13, 1984.

Year	Club	League	G.	IP.	W.	L.	Pct.	H.	R.	ER.	SO.	BB.	ERA.
1984	Detroit	American	2	18	2	0	1.000	13	4	4	13	3	2.00

ALL-STAR GAME RECORD

Year	League	IP.	W.	L.	Pct.	H.	R.	ER.	SO.	BB.	ERA.
1981	American	2	0	0	.000	2	0	0	2	1	0.00
1984	American	2	0	0	.000	2	0	0	2	1	0.00
1985	American	2⅔	0	1	.000	5	2	2	1	1	6.75
1987	American	2	0	0	.000	1	0	0	2	1	0.00
All-Star Game Totals—4 Years		8⅔	0	1	.000	10	2	2	7	4	2.08

WILLIAM HAROLD MORRIS
(Hal)

Born April 9, 1965, at Fort Rucker, Ala.
Height, 6.04. Weight, 200.
Throws and bats lefthanded.
Attended University of Michigan, Ann Arbor, Mich.

Year	Club	League	Pos.	G.	AB.	R.	H.	2B.	3B.	HR.	RBI.	B.A.	PO.	A.	E.	F.A.
1986	Oneonta	NYP	1B	36	127	26	48	9	2	3	30	.378	317	26	3	.991
1986	Albany†	East.	1B	25	79	7	17	5	0	0	4	.215	203	19	2	.991
1987	Albany	East.	1B-OF	135	*530	65	*173	31	4	5	73	.326	1086	79	17	.986
1988	Columbus	Int.	OF-1B	121	452	41	134	19	4	3	38	.296	543	26	8	.986
1988	New York	Amer.	OF	15	20	1	2	0	0	0	0	.100	7	0	0	1.000
Major League Totals—1 Year				15	20	1	2	0	0	0	0	.100	7	0	0	1.000

Selected by New York Yankees' organization in 8th round of free-agent draft, June 2, 1986.
†On disabled list, August 14, 1986 through remainder of season.

JAMES FORREST MORRISON
(Jim)

Born September 23, 1952, at Pensacola, Fla.
Height, 5.11. Weight, 185.
Throws and bats righthanded.
Attended Georgia Southern College, Statesboro, Ga.

Established major league record for fewest chances accepted by third baseman, season, 150 or more games (349), 1986.

Tied major league records for fewest three-base hits, most at-bats, season (0 and 604), 1980; most times caught stealing, inning (2), June 15, 1987, eighth inning.

Major League stolen bases: 1978 (1), 1979 (11), 1980 (9), 1981 (3), 1982 (2), 1983 (2), 1985 (3), 1986 (9), 1987 (10). Total—50.

Led American League second basemen in assists with 481, total chances with 932 and double plays with 117 in 1980.
Led Carolina League in total bases with 239 in 1975.
Led American Association third basemen in assists with 236 in 1977.
Led American Association third basemen in double plays with 22 in 1976.
Led Carolina League third basemen in assists with 311, errors with 32 and double plays with 35 in 1975.

Year	Club	League	Pos.	G.	AB.	R.	H.	2B.	3B.	HR.	RBI.	B.A.	PO.	A.	E.	F.A.
1974	Spartanburg	W. Car.	3B	3	8	1	3	1	0	1	3	.375	4	5	1	.900
1974	Rocky Mount	Carol.	3B	72	265	30	67	9	1	4	24	.253	54	157	19	.917
1975	Rocky Mount	Carol.	3B-SS	140	497	*98	143	24	6	*20	88	.288	135	331	35	.930
1976	Oklahoma City	A. A.	*3B-SS	126	422	79	122	17	6	18	71	.289	100	*239	24	.934
1977	Oklahoma City	A. A.	3B-2B-OF	127	452	72	133	23	4	12	71	.294	99	272	25	.937
1977	Philadelphia	Nat.	3B	5	7	3	3	0	0	0	1	.429	0	7	1	.875
1978	Oklahoma City	A. A.	2B-3B-1B	54	189	37	52	6	1	10	28	.275	111	134	10	.961
1978	Philadelphia	Nat.	2B-3B-OF	53	108	12	17	1	1	3	10	.157	88	97	6	.969
1979	Oklahoma City†	A. A.	2B-3B-OF	79	281	59	90	15	0	22	61	.320	129	226	17	.954
1979	Chicago	Amer.	2B-3B	67	240	38	66	14	0	14	35	.275	121	185	9	.971
1980	Chicago	Amer.	*2B-SS	162	604	66	171	40	0	15	57	.283	*422	482	*29	.969
1981	Chicago	Amer.	3B-2B	90	290	27	68	8	1	10	34	.234	64	200	12	.957
1982	Chicago‡	Amer.	3B	51	166	17	37	7	3	7	19	.223	19	87	10	.914
1982	Pittsburgh	Nat.	3-2-O-S	44	86	10	24	4	1	4	15	.279	17	43	2	.968
1983	Pittsburgh	Nat.	2B-3B-SS	66	158	16	48	7	2	6	25	.304	56	99	7	.957
1984	Pittsburgh	Nat.	3-2-S-1	100	304	38	87	14	2	11	45	.286	86	166	10	.962
1985	Pittsburgh	Nat.	3B-2B-OF	92	244	17	62	10	0	4	22	.254	73	121	5	.975
1986	Pittsburgh	Nat.	3B-2B-SS	154	537	58	147	35	4	23	88	.274	92	258	20	.946
1987	Pittsburgh§	Nat.	3B-SS-2B	96	348	41	92	22	1	9	46	.264	72	200	7	.975
1987	Detroit	Amer.	3-2-S-O-1	34	117	15	24	1	1	4	19	.205	27	51	2	.975
1988	Detroit x	Amer.	1-3-O-S	24	74	7	16	5	0	0	6	.216	31	2	1	.971
1988	Atlanta y	Nat.	3B-OF-P	51	92	6	14	2	0	2	13	.152	26	28	3	.947
National League Totals—9 Years				661	1884	201	494	95	11	62	265	.262	510	1019	61	.962
American League Totals—6 Years				428	1491	170	382	75	5	50	170	.256	684	1007	63	.964
Major League Totals—12 Years				1089	3375	371	876	170	16	112	435	.260	1194	2026	124	.963

Selected by Pittsburgh Pirates' organization in 5th round of free-agent draft, January 12, 1972.
Selected by Pittsburgh Pirates' organization in secondary phase of free-agent draft, June 6, 1972.
Selected by Philadelphia Phillies' organization in 5th round of free-agent draft, June 5, 1974.
†Traded to Chicago White Sox, July 10, 1979, completing deal in which Chicago traded Pitcher Jack Kucek to Philadelphia Phillies for a player to be named later, April 13, 1979.
‡Traded to Pittsburgh Pirates for Pitcher Eddie Solomon, June 14, 1982.

§Traded to Detroit Tigers for Third Baseman Darnell Coles and a player to be named later, August 7, 1987; Pittsburgh Pirates' organization acquired Pitcher Morris Madden to complete deal, August 12, 1987.
xReleased, June 6, 1988; signed by Atlanta Braves, June 10, 1988.
yGranted free agency, November 4, 1988.

CHAMPIONSHIP SERIES RECORD

Year	Club	League	Pos.	G.	AB.	R.	H.	2B.	3B.	HR.	RBI.	B.A.	PO.	A.	E.	F.A.
1978	Philadelphia	Nat.	PH	1	1	0	0	0	0	0	0	.000	0	0	0	.000
1987	Detroit	Amer.	DH-3B	2	5	1	2	0	0	0	0	.400	1	2	0	1.000
Championship Series Totals—2 Years				3	6	1	2	0	0	0	0	.333	1	2	0	1.000

PITCHING RECORD

Year	Club	League	G.	IP.	W.	L.	Pct.	H.	R.	ER.	SO.	BB.	ERA.
1988	Atlanta	National	3	3⅔	0	0	.000	3	0	0	1	2	0.00

GERALD MICHAEL MOSCREY JR.
(Mike)

Born December 15, 1967, at Dallas, Tex.
Height, 6.01. Weight, 195.
Throws left and bats righthanded.

Led Midwest League pitchers in games started with 29 and tied for lead in shutouts with 3 in 1988.

Year	Club	League	G.	IP.	W.	L.	Pct.	H.	R.	ER.	SO.	BB.	ERA.
1986	Billings	Pioneer	14	88⅔	5	6	.455	99	52	35	62	21	3.55
1987	Cedar Rapids	Midwest	19	94	8	4	.667	100	56	45	65	45	4.31
1988	Cedar Rapids	Midwest	29	190⅔	11	8	.579	163	83	58	143	80	2.74

Selected by Cincinnati Reds' organization in 4th round of free-agent draft, June 2, 1986.

LLOYD ANTHONY MOSEBY

Born November 5, 1959, at Portland, Ark.
Height, 6.03. Weight, 200.
Throws right and bats lefthanded.

Major League stolen bases: 1980 (4), 1981 (11), 1982 (11), 1983 (27), 1984 (39), 1985 (37), 1986 (32), 1987 (39), 1988 (31). Total—231.
Led Florida State League in total bases with 237 and tied for lead in being hit by pitch with 10 in 1979.
Led Pioneer League in being hit by pitch with 11 and tied for lead in caught stealing with 7 in 1978.
Named outfielder on THE SPORTING NEWS American League All-Star Team, 1983.
Named outfielder on THE SPORTING NEWS American League Silver Slugger team, 1983.

Year	Club	League	Pos.	G.	AB.	R.	H.	2B.	3B.	HR.	RBI.	B.A.	PO.	A.	E.	F.A.
1978	Medicine Hat	Pion.	OF	67	253	65	77	12	4	10	38	.304	76	3	6	.929
1979	Dunedin	Fla. St.	OF	129	446	*89	*148	23	6	18	84	.332	190	11	9	.957
1980	Syracuse	Int.	OF	37	146	28	47	8	6	3	19	.322	83	1	3	.966
1980	Toronto	Amer.	OF	114	389	44	89	24	1	9	46	.229	208	12	4	.982
1981	Toronto	Amer.	OF	100	378	36	88	16	2	9	43	.233	259	4	3	.989
1982	Toronto	Amer.	OF	147	487	51	115	20	9	9	52	.236	361	4	3	.992
1983	Toronto	Amer.	OF	151	539	104	170	31	7	18	81	.315	399	10	7	.983
1984	Toronto	Amer.	OF	158	592	97	166	28	•15	18	92	.280	473	8	5	.990
1985	Toronto	Amer.	OF	152	584	92	151	30	7	18	70	.259	394	7	8	.980
1986	Toronto	Amer.	OF	152	589	89	149	24	5	21	86	.253	371	6	6	.984
1987	Toronto	Amer.	OF	155	592	106	167	27	4	26	96	.282	294	7	6	.980
1988	Toronto†	Amer.	OF	128	472	77	113	17	7	10	42	.239	304	2	5	.984
Major League Totals—9 Years				1257	4622	696	1208	217	57	138	608	.261	3063	60	47	.985

Selected by Toronto Blue Jays' organization in 1st round (second player selected) of free-agent draft, June 6, 1978.
†On disabled list, July 31 to August 16, 1988.

CHAMPIONSHIP SERIES RECORD

Year	Club	League	Pos.	G.	AB.	R.	H.	2B.	3B.	HR.	RBI.	B.A.	PO.	A.	E.	F.A.
1985	Toronto	Amer.	OF	7	31	5	7	1	0	0	4	.226	16	0	0	1.000

ALL-STAR GAME RECORD

Year	League	Pos.	AB.	R.	H.	2B.	3B.	HR.	RBI.	B.A.	PO.	A.	E.	F.A.
1986	American	OF	0	0	0	0	0	0	0	.000	0	0	0	.000

JOHN WILLIAM MOSES

Born August 9, 1957, at Los Angeles, Calif.
Height, 5.10. Weight, 170.
Throws left and bats left and righthanded.
Attended Golden West College, Huntington Beach, Calif., and
University of Arizona, Tucson, Ariz.

Major League stolen bases: 1982 (5), 1983 (11), 1984 (1), 1985 (5), 1986 (25), 1987 (23), 1988 (11). Total—81.
Tied for American League lead in caught stealing with 18 in 1986.
Led Midwest League in caught stealing with 21 and bases on balls received with 103 in 1981.
Tied for Midwest League lead in sacrifice hits with 13 in 1981.
Led Eastern League outfielders in double plays with 6 in 1982.

Year	Club	League	Pos.	G.	AB.	R.	H.	2B.	3B.	HR.	RBI.	B.A.	PO.	A.	E.	F.A.
1980	—Bellingham	N'west	OF	60	227	55	60	5	2	2	32	.264	92	6	3	.970
1981	—Wausau	Midw.	OF	123	429	*102	120	24	3	3	48	.280	204	10	5	.977
1982	—Lynn	East.	OF	128	466	87	133	25	6	6	52	.285	259	*20	0	*1.000
1982	—Seattle	Amer.	OF	22	44	7	14	5	1	1	3	.318	16	2	1	.947
1983	—Seattle	Amer.	OF	93	130	19	27	4	1	0	6	.208	87	8	2	.979
1983	—Salt Lake City	P. C.	OF	16	65	14	17	4	0	0	10	.262	26	0	0	1.000
1984	—Chattanooga	South.	OF	53	182	27	46	6	3	0	12	.253	107	4	2	.982
1984	—Salt Lake City	P. C.	OF	70	276	45	76	11	5	0	27	.275	161	8	1	.994
1984	—Seattle	Amer.	OF	19	35	3	12	1	1	0	2	.343	26	1	0	1.000
1985	—Calgary	P. C.	OF-1B	113	473	75	152	*37	1	5	47	.321	316	12	4	.988
1985	—Seattle	Amer.	OF	33	62	4	12	0	0	0	3	.194	35	1	0	1.000
1986	—Calgary	P. C.	OF	39	148	31	48	3	1	3	18	.324	93	3	1	.990
1986	—Seattle	Amer.	OF-1B	103	399	56	102	16	3	3	34	.256	249	11	5	.981
1987	—Seattle†‡	Amer.	OF-1B	116	390	58	96	16	4	3	38	.246	271	7	4	.986
1988	—Portland	P. C.	OF	17	66	13	23	3	1	0	6	.348	40	0	0	1.000
1988	—Minnesota	Amer.	OF	105	206	33	65	10	3	2	12	.316	123	1	0	1.000
Major League Totals—7 Years				491	1266	180	328	52	13	9	98	.259	807	31	12	.986

Selected by Seattle Mariners' organization in 16th round of free-agent draft, June 3, 1980.
†Released, December 21, 1987; signed by Cleveland Indians, January 19, 1988.
‡Released, March 29, 1988; signed by Portland (Minnesota Twins' organization), April 5, 1988.

JAMIE MOYER

Born November 18, 1962, at Sellersville, Pa.
Height, 6.00. Weight, 170.
Throws and bats lefthanded.
Attended St. Joseph's University, Philadelphia, Pa.

Year	Club	League	G.	IP.	W.	L.	Pct.	H.	R.	ER.	SO.	BB.	ERA.
1984	—Geneva	NYP	14	*104⅔	●9	3	.750	59	27	22	*120	31	1.89
1985	—Winston-Salem	Carolina	12	94	8	2	.800	82	36	24	94	22	2.30
1985	—Pittsfield	Eastern	15	96⅔	7	6	.538	99	49	40	51	32	3.72
1986	—Pittsfield	Eastern	6	41	3	1	.750	27	10	4	42	16	0.88
1986	—Iowa	Am. Assoc.	6	42⅓	3	2	.600	25	14	12	25	11	2.55
1986	—Chicago	National	16	87⅓	7	4	.636	107	52	49	45	42	5.05
1987	—Chicago	National	35	201	12	15	.444	210	127	*114	147	97	5.10
1988	—Chicago†	National	34	202	9	15	.375	212	84	78	121	55	3.48
Major League Totals—3 Years			85	490⅓	28	34	.452	529	263	241	313	194	4.42

Selected by Chicago Cubs' organization in 6th round of free-agent draft, June 4, 1984.
†Traded with Outfielder Rafael Palmeiro and Pitcher Drew Hall to Texas Rangers for Pitchers Mitch Williams, Paul Kilgus and Steve Wilson, Infielders Curtis Wilkerson and Luis Benitez and Outfielder Pablo Delgado, December 5, 1988.

TERENCE JOHN MULHOLLAND
(Terry)

Born March 9, 1963, at Uniontown, Pa.
Height, 6.03. Weight, 200.
Throws left and bats righthanded.
Attended Marietta College, Marietta, O.

Led Pacific Coast League pitchers in games started with 29 in 1987.
Led Texas League in shutouts with 3 in 1985.

Year	Club	League	G.	IP.	W.	L.	Pct.	H.	R.	ER.	SO.	BB.	ERA.
1984	—Everett	Northwest	3	19	1	0	1.000	10	2	0	15	4	0.00
1984	—Fresno	California	9	42⅔	5	2	.714	32	17	14	39	36	2.95
1985	—Shreveport	Texas	26	176⅔	9	8	.529	166	79	57	122	87	2.90
1986	—Phoenix	P. Coast	17	111	8	5	.615	112	60	55	77	56	4.46
1986	—San Francisco	National	15	54⅔	1	7	.125	51	33	30	27	35	4.94
1987	—Phoenix	P. Coast	37	172⅓	7	12	.368	200	*124	●97	94	90	5.07
1988	—Phoenix	P. Coast	19	100⅔	7	3	.700	116	45	40	57	44	3.58
1988	—San Francisco†	National	9	46	2	1	.667	50	20	19	18	7	3.72
Major League Totals—2 Years			24	100⅔	3	8	.273	101	53	49	45	42	4.38

Selected by San Francisco Giants' organization in 1st round (24th player selected) of free-agent draft, June 4, 1984.
†On disabled list, August 1, 1988 through remainder of season.

STEVEN RANCE MULLINIKS

Name pronounced MUL-in-iks.

(Known by middle name.)

Born January 15, 1956, at Tulare, Calif.
Height, 6.00. Weight, 175.
Throws right and bats lefthanded.
Son of Harvey Mulliniks, pitcher in New York Yankees' organization, 1956 and 1957.

Major League stolen bases: 1977 (1), 1978 (2), 1982 (3), 1984 (2), 1985 (2), 1986 (1), 1987 (1), 1988 (1). Total—13.
Led American League third basemen in fielding percentage with .968 in 1984.
Led Pacific Coast League shortstops in fielding percentage with .968 in 1979.

Year	Club	League	Pos.	G.	AB.	R.	H.	2B.	3B.	HR.	RBI.	B.A.	PO.	A.	E.	F.A.
1974	Idaho Falls	Pion.	SS	66	202	28	44	8	3	0	24	.218	*110	*170	*33	.895
1975	Quad Cities	Midw.	SS	52	186	34	50	6	2	1	21	.269	82	136	17	.928
1975	Salinas	Calif.	SS-2B	59	209	38	54	8	0	0	10	.258	88	146	14	.944
1976	El Paso†	Texas	SS-2B	90	333	81	105	22	4	7	51	.315	140	247	20	.951
1977	Salt Lake City	P. C.	SS	58	220	48	68	17	3	11	51	.309	116	207	15	.956
1977	California	Amer.	SS	78	271	36	73	13	2	3	21	.269	112	229	13	.963
1978	Salt Lake City	P. C.	SS	34	127	34	39	6	2	3	21	.307	65	109	12	.935
1978	California	Amer.	SS	50	119	6	22	3	1	1	6	.185	68	93	8	.953
1979	Salt Lake City	P. C.	SS-2B	116	402	94	138	21	7	3	59	.343	204	331	17	.969
1979	California‡	Amer.	SS	22	68	7	10	0	0	1	8	.147	46	43	4	.957
1980	Kansas City	Amer.	SS-2B	36	54	8	14	3	0	0	6	.259	30	53	1	.988
1981	Kansas City§	Amer.	2B-SS-3B	24	44	6	10	3	0	0	5	.227	25	39	5	.928
1982	Toronto	Amer.	3B-SS	112	311	32	76	25	0	4	35	.244	69	154	14	.941
1983	Toronto	Amer.	3B-SS-2B	129	364	54	100	34	3	10	49	.275	77	185	7	.974
1984	Toronto	Amer.	3B-SS-2B	125	343	41	111	21	5	3	42	.324	67	152	8	.965
1985	Toronto	Amer.	3B	129	366	55	108	26	1	10	57	.295	75	162	7	*.971
1986	Toronto x	Amer.	*3B-2B	117	348	50	90	22	0	11	45	.259	60	176	6	*.975
1987	Toronto	Amer.	3B-SS	124	332	37	103	28	1	11	44	.310	29	137	13	.927
1988	Toronto y	Amer.	3B	119	337	49	101	21	1	12	48	.300	3	5	0	1.000
	Major League Totals—12 Years			1065	2957	381	818	199	14	66	366	.277	661	1428	86	.960

Selected by California Angels' organization in 3rd round of free-agent draft, June 5, 1974.

†On disabled list, May 4 to June 9 and September 2 to September 24, 1976.

‡Traded with First Baseman Willie Aikens to Kansas City Royals for Outfielder Al Cowens, Shortstop Todd Cruz and a player to be named later, December 6, 1979; California Angels acquired Pitcher Craig Eaton to complete deal, April 1, 1980.

§Traded to Toronto Blue Jays for Pitcher Phil Huffman, March 25, 1982.

xOn disabled list, August 6 to September 1, 1986.

yOn disabled list, April 12 to May 2, 1988.

CHAMPIONSHIP SERIES RECORD

Year	Club	League	Pos.	G.	AB.	R.	H.	2B.	3B.	HR.	RBI.	B.A.	PO.	A.	E.	F.A.
1985	Toronto	Amer.	PH-3B	5	11	1	4	1	0	1	3	.364	1	4	0	1.000

JERRY WAYNE MUMPHREY

Born September 9, 1952, at Tyler, Tex.
Height, 6.02. Weight, 200.
Throws right and bats left and righthanded.

Major League stolen bases: 1976 (22), 1977 (22), 1978 (14), 1979 (8), 1980 (52), 1981 (14), 1982 (11), 1983 (7), 1984 (15), 1985 (6), 1986 (2), 1987 (1). Total—174.

Led American Association in stolen bases with 44 and caught stealing with 21 in 1975.

Led Gulf Coast League batters in strikeouts with 45 in 1971.

Year	Club	League	Pos.	G.	AB.	R.	H.	2B.	3B.	HR.	RBI.	B.A.	PO.	A.	E.	F.A.
1971	Sarasota Cards	Gulf C.	OF	38	141	20	36	3	2	0	6	.255	52	1	3	.946
1972	Sarasota Cards	Gulf C.	OF	26	111	21	38	5	2	0	12	.342	63	2	0	1.000
1972	Cedar Rapids	Midw.	OF	11	33	6	6	2	0	0	1	.182	15	0	0	1.000
1972	St. Petersburg	Fla. St.	OF	17	44	7	15	2	1	0	1	.341	11	1	1	.923
1973	St. Petersburg	Fla. St.	OF	142	*556	*93	*159	20	●9	5	52	.286	210	6	4	982
1974	Arkansas	Tex.	OF	130	507	87	147	21	6	10	54	.290	209	11	9	.961
1974	St. Louis	Nat.	OF	5	2	2	0	0	0	0	0	.000	0	0	0	.000
1975	Tulsa	A. A.	OF	127	495	87	141	19	6	8	59	.285	248	7	6	.977
1975	St. Louis	Nat.	OF	11	16	2	6	2	0	0	1	.375	9	0	0	1.000
1976	Tulsa	A. A.	OF	19	68	14	23	9	1	1	8	.338	42	4	0	1.000
1976	St. Louis	Nat.	OF	112	384	51	99	15	5	1	26	.258	261	6	2	.993
1977	St. Louis	Nat.	OF	145	463	73	133	20	10	2	38	.287	291	8	9	.971
1978	St. Louis	Nat.	OF	125	367	41	96	13	4	2	37	.262	178	10	1	.995
1979	St. Louis †‡§	Nat.	OF	124	339	53	100	10	3	3	32	.295	180	3	3	.984
1980	San Diego x	Nat.	OF	160	564	61	168	24	3	4	59	.298	398	10	●11	.974
1981	New York	Amer.	OF	80	319	44	98	11	5	6	32	.307	219	5	●8	.966
1982	New York y	Amer.	OF	123	477	76	143	24	10	9	68	.300	336	5	5	.986
1983	New York z	Amer.	OF	83	267	41	70	11	4	7	36	.262	227	7	4	.983
1983	Houston	Nat.	OF	44	143	17	48	10	2	1	17	.336	103	1	1	.990
1984	Houston	Nat.	OF	151	524	66	152	20	3	9	83	.290	317	5	4	.988
1985	Houston a	Nat.	OF	130	444	52	123	25	2	8	61	.277	248	6	8	.969
1986	Chicago	Nat.	OF	111	309	37	94	11	2	5	32	.304	161	3	3	.982
1987	Chicago	Nat.	OF	118	309	41	103	19	2	13	44	.333	124	5	1	.992
1988	Chicago b	Nat.	OF	63	66	3	9	2	0	0	9	.136	5	0	0	1.000
	National League Totals—13 Years			1299	3930	499	1131	171	36	48	439	.288	2275	57	43	.982
	American League Totals—3 Years			286	1063	161	311	46	19	22	136	.293	782	17	17	.979
	Major League Totals—15 Years			1585	4993	660	1442	217	55	70	575	.289	3057	74	60	.981

Selected by St. Louis Cardinals' organization in 4th round of free-agent draft, June 8, 1971.

†On disabled list, March 29 to April 20, 1979.

‡Traded with Pitcher John Denny to Cleveland Indians for Outfielder Bobby Bonds, December 7, 1979.

§Traded by Cleveland Indians to San Diego Padres for Pitcher Bob Owchinko and Outfielder Jim Wilhelm, February 15, 1980.

xTraded with Pitcher John Pacella to New York Yankees for Outfielders Ruppert Jones and Joe Lefebvre and Pitchers Tim Lollar and Chris Welsh, April 1, 1981.

yOn disabled list, May 10 to June 21, 1982.

zTraded to Houston Astros for Outfielder Omar Moreno, August 10, 1983.

aTraded to Chicago Cubs for Outfielder Billy Hatcher and a player to be named later, December 16, 1985; Houston Astros' organization acquired Pitcher Steve Engel to complete deal, July 24, 1986.
bReleased, November 10, 1988.

DIVISION SERIES RECORD

Year	Club	League	Pos.	G.	AB.	R.	H.	2B.	3B.	HR.	RBI.	B.A.	PO.	A.	E.	F.A.
1981	—New York	Amer.	OF	5	21	2	2	0	0	0	0	.095	15	1	0	1.000

CHAMPIONSHIP SERIES RECORD

Year	Club	League	Pos.	G.	AB.	R.	H.	2B.	3B.	HR.	RBI.	B.A.	PO.	A.	E.	F.A.
1981	—New York	Amer.	OF	3	12	2	6	1	0	0	0	.500	4	0	0	1.000

WORLD SERIES RECORD

Year	Club	League	Pos.	G.	AB.	R.	H.	2B.	3B.	HR.	RBI.	B.A.	PO.	A.	E.	F.A.
1981	—New York	Amer.	OF	5	15	2	3	0	0	0	0	.200	6	0	0	1.000

ALL-STAR GAME RECORD

Year	League	Pos.	AB.	R.	H.	2B.	3B.	HR.	RBI.	B.A.	PO.	A.	E.	F.A.
1984	—National	PH	1	0	0	0	0	0	0	.000	0	0	0	.000

MICHAEL ANTHONY MUNOZ
(Mike)

Born July 12, 1965, at Baldwin Park, Calif.
Height, 6.02. Weight, 190.
Throws and bats lefthanded.
Attended California State Poly University, Pomona, Calif.

Year	Club	League	G.	IP.	W.	L.	Pct.	H.	R.	ER.	SO.	BB.	ERA.
1986	—Great Falls	Pioneer	14	81⅓	4	4	.500	85	44	29	49	38	3.21
1987	—Bakersfield	California	52	118	8	7	.533	125	68	49	80	43	3.74
1988	—San Antonio	Texas	56	71⅔	7	2	.778	63	18	8	71	24	1.00

Selected by Los Angeles Dodgers' organization in 3rd round of free-agent draft, June 2, 1986.

DALE BRYAN MURPHY

Born March 12, 1956, at Portland, Ore.
Height, 6.04. Weight, 215.
Throws and bats righthanded.
Attended Portland Community College, Portland, Ore. and Brigham Young University, Provo, Utah.

Tied major league records for most years leading league in games, outfielder (6); fewest double plays by outfielder, season, 150 or more games (0), 1983; fewest double plays by outfielder, season, for leader in double plays (4), 1981 and 1985.

Tied National League record for most intentional bases on balls by righthander, season (29), 1987.

Major League stolen bases: 1978 (11), 1979 (6), 1980 (9), 1981 (14), 1982 (23), 1983 (30), 1984 (19), 1985 (10), 1986 (7), 1987 (16), 1988 (3). Total—148.

Hit three home runs in a game, May 18, 1979.

Led National League in grounding into double plays with 24 in 1988.

Led National League in intentional bases on balls received with 29 in 1987.

Led National League in bases on balls received with 90 in 1985.

Led National League in total bases with 332 in 1984.

Led National League in slugging percentage with .540 in 1983 and .547 in 1984.

Led National League batters in strikeouts with 145 in 1978, 133 in 1980 and tied for lead with 141 in 1985.

Led National League first basemen in errors with 20 in 1978.

Tied for National League lead in double plays by outfielders with 4 in 1981 and 1985.

Tied for International League lead in total bases with 249 in 1977.

Led International League catchers in putouts with 510, passed balls with 14 and tied for lead in double plays with 7 in 1977.

Named National League Player of the Year by THE SPORTING NEWS, 1982 and 1983.

Named National League Most Valuable Player by Baseball Writers' Association of America, 1982 and 1983.

Named outfielder on THE SPORTING NEWS National League All-Star Team, 1982 through 1985.

Named outfielder on THE SPORTING NEWS National League All-Star fielding team, 1982 through 1986.

Named outfielder on THE SPORTING NEWS National League Silver Slugger team, 1982 through 1985.

Year	Club	League	Pos.	G.	AB.	R.	H.	2B.	3B.	HR.	RBI.	B.A.	PO.	A.	E.	F.A.
1974	—Kingsport	Appal.	C	54	181	28	46	7	0	5	31	.254	389	28	7	.983
1975	—Greenwood	W. Car.	C-1B	131	443	48	101	20	1	5	48	.228	723	81	18	.978
1976	—Savannah	South.	C	104	352	37	94	13	5	12	55	.267	444	40	10	.980
1976	—Richmond	Int.	C-OF	18	50	10	13	1	1	4	8	.260	60	9	4	.945
1976	—Atlanta	Nat.	C	19	65	3	17	6	0	0	9	.262	100	13	3	.974
1977	—Richmond	Int.	C-1B	127	466	71	142	●33	4	22	*90	.305	600	50	15	.977
1977	—Atlanta	Nat.	C	18	76	5	24	8	1	2	14	.316	114	11	6	.954
1978	—Atlanta	Nat.	1B-C	151	530	66	120	14	3	23	79	.226	1220	105	23	.983
1979	—Atlanta†	Nat.	1B-C	104	384	53	106	7	2	21	57	.276	812	57	20	.978
1980	—Atlanta	Nat.	OF-1B	156	569	98	160	27	2	33	89	.281	384	15	6	.985
1981	—Atlanta	Nat.	OF-1B	104	369	43	91	12	1	13	50	.247	264	11	5	.982
1982	—Atlanta	Nat.	OF	●162	598	113	168	23	2	36	●109	.281	407	6	9	.979
1983	—Atlanta	Nat.	OF	*162	589	131	178	24	4	36	*121	.302	373	10	6	.985
1984	—Atlanta	Nat.	OF	*162	607	94	176	32	8	●36	100	.290	369	10	5	.987
1985	—Atlanta	Nat.	OF	●162	616	*118	185	32	2	*37	111	.300	334	8	7	.980
1986	—Atlanta	Nat.	OF	160	614	89	163	29	7	29	83	.265	303	6	6	.981

Year	Club	League	Pos.	G.	AB.	R.	H.	2B.	3B.	HR.	RBI.	B.A.	PO.	A.	E.	F.A.
1987	—Atlanta	Nat.	OF	159	566	115	167	27	1	44	105	.295	325	14	8	.977
1988	—Atlanta	Nat.	OF	156	592	77	134	35	4	24	77	.226	340	15	3	.992
Major League Totals—13 Years				1675	6175	1005	1689	276	37	334	1004	.274	5345	281	107	.981

Selected by Atlanta Braves' organization in 1st round (fifth player selected) of free-agent draft, June 5, 1974.

†On disabled list, May 25 to July 19, 1979.

CHAMPIONSHIP SERIES RECORD

Year	Club	League	Pos.	G.	AB.	R.	H.	2B.	3B.	HR.	RBI.	B.A.	PO.	A.	E.	F.A.
1982	—Atlanta	Nat.	OF	3	11	1	3	0	0	0	0	.273	8	0	0	1.000

ALL-STAR GAME RECORD

Year	League	Pos.	AB.	R.	H.	2B.	3B.	HR.	RBI.	B.A.	PO.	A.	E.	F.A.
1980	—National	OF	1	0	0	0	0	0	0	.000	0	0	0	.000
1982	—National	OF	2	1	0	0	0	0	0	.000	2	0	0	1.000
1983	—National	OF	3	0	1	0	0	0	1	.333	0	0	0	.000
1984	—National	OF	3	1	2	0	0	1	1	.667	0	0	0	.000
1985	—National	OF	3	0	1	1	0	0	0	.333	1	0	0	1.000
1986	—National	OF	2	0	0	0	0	0	0	.000	2	0	0	1.000
1987	—National	OF	1	0	0	0	0	0	0	.000	1	0	0	1.000
All-Star Game Totals—7 Years			15	2	4	1	0	1	2	.267	6	0	0	1.000

DWAYNE KEITH MURPHY

Born March 18, 1955, at Merced, Calif.
Height, 6.01. Weight, 185.
Throws right and bats lefthanded.

Tied major league record for fewest double plays by outfielder, season, 150 or more games (0), 1980 and 1985.

Major League stolen bases: 1979 (15), 1980 (26), 1981 (10), 1982 (26), 1983 (7), 1984 (4), 1985 (4), 1986 (3), 1987 (4), 1988 (1). Total—100.

Led American League in sacrifice hits with 22 in 1980 and game-winning RBIs with 15 in 1981.

Led American League outfielders in total chances with 525 in 1980, 474 in 1982 and 494 in 1984.

Led Southern League in bases on balls received with 97 in 1977.

Tied for Southern League lead in double plays by outfielders with 4 in 1977.

Named outfielder on THE SPORTING NEWS American League All-Star Team, 1981.

Named outfielder on THE SPORTING NEWS American League All-Star fielding team, 1980 through 1985.

Year	Club	League	Pos.	G.	AB.	R.	H.	2B.	3B.	HR.	RBI.	B.A.	PO.	A.	E.	F.A.
1973	—Lewiston	N'west	OF	68	215	25	50	7	2	3	19	.233	102	*13	6	.950
1974	—Burlington†	Midw.	OF	53	150	16	33	6	2	2	10	.220	55	2	3	.959
1975	—Modesto	Calif.	OF	126	429	81	125	20	7	8	71	.291	250	7	9	.966
1976	—Chattanooga	South.	OF	68	200	32	52	6	0	1	23	.260	138	6	1	.993
1976	—Tucson	P. C.	OF	52	179	32	42	7	2	3	11	.235	125	6	4	.970
1977	—Chattanooga	South.	OF	132	406	53	104	11	9	5	53	.256	320	14	5	*.985
1978	—Vancouver	P. C.	OF-SS	42	148	35	39	4	1	7	17	.264	125	9	3	.978
1978	—Oakland	Amer.	OF	60	52	15	10	2	0	0	5	.192	49	1	0	1.000
1979	—Oakland‡	Amer.	OF	121	388	57	99	10	4	11	40	.255	322	10	4	.988
1980	—Oakland	Amer.	OF	159	573	86	157	18	2	13	68	.274	*507	13	5	.990
1981	—Oakland	Amer.	OF	107	390	58	98	10	3	15	60	.251	326	6	5	.985
1982	—Oakland	Amer.	*OF-SS	151	543	84	129	15	1	27	94	.238	*452	18	8	.983
1983	—Oakland§	Amer.	OF	130	471	55	107	17	2	17	75	.227	365	7	8	.979
1984	—Oakland	Amer.	OF	153	559	93	143	18	2	33	88	.256	*474	14	6	.988
1985	—Oakland	Amer.	OF	152	523	77	122	21	3	20	59	.233	432	6	5	.989
1986	—Oakland x	Amer.	OF	98	329	50	83	11	3	9	39	.252	276	6	2	.993
1986	—Modesto	Calif.	OF	2	5	1	1	1	0	0	0	.200	1	0	0	1.000
1986	—Madison	Midw.	OF	1	0	0	0	0	0	0	0	.000	1	0	0	1.000
1987	—Oakland y	Amer.	OF-1B-2B	82	219	39	51	7	0	8	35	.233	187	2	3	.984
1987	—Tacoma z	P. C.	OF	5	15	1	4	3	0	0	2	.267	6	0	0	1.000
1988	—Fresno a	Calif.	OF-1B	13	34	6	7	1	0	1	5	.206	25	4	1	.967
1988	—Toledo	Int.	OF	51	173	20	38	9	0	5	15	.220	112	0	2	.982
1988	—Detroit	Amer.	OF	49	144	14	36	5	0	4	19	.250	122	1	0	1.000
Major League Totals—11 Years				1262	4191	628	1035	134	20	157	582	.247	3512	84	46	.987

Selected by Oakland A's organization in 15th round of free-agent draft, June 5, 1973.

†On disabled list, July 16 to September 16, 1974.

‡On disabled list, June 21 to July 14, 1979.

§On disabled list, June 24 to July 11, 1983.

xOn disabled list, May 12 to July 5, 1986; included rehabilitation disability assignment to Modesto, July 1 to July 3, and to Madison, July 4, 1986.

yOn disabled list, April 24 to June 25 and July 18 to August 2, 1987; included rehabilitation disability assignment to Tacoma, June 16 to June 25, 1987.

zGranted free agency, November 9, 1987; signed by Fresno (Independent), May 20, 1988.

aReleased, June 5, 1988; signed by Detroit Tigers, June 5, 1988.

DIVISION SERIES RECORD

Year	Club	League	Pos.	G.	AB.	R.	H.	2B.	3B.	HR.	RBI.	B.A.	PO.	A.	E.	F.A.
1981	—Oakland	Amer.	OF	3	11	4	6	1	0	1	2	.545	13	0	0	1.000

CHAMPIONSHIP SERIES RECORD

Year	Club	League	Pos.	G.	AB.	R.	H.	2B.	3B.	HR.	RBI.	B.A.	PO.	A.	E.	F.A.
1981	—Oakland	Amer.	OF	3	8	0	2	1	0	0	1	.250	9	0	0	1.000

ROBERT ALBERT MURPHY JR.
(Rob)

Born May 26, 1960, at Miami, Fla.
Height, 6.02. Weight, 205.
Throws and bats lefthanded.
Attended University of Florida, Gainesville, Fla.

Major League saves: 1986 (1), 1987 (3), 1988 (3). Total—7.
Tied for Eastern League lead in saves with 15 in 1984.

Year Club	League	G.	IP.	W.	L.	Pct.	H.	R.	ER.	SO.	BB.	ERA.
1981—Tampa	Florida St.	25	105	6	8	.429	109	73	53	58	67	4.54
1982—Cedar Rapids	Midwest	31	89	3	7	.300	92	62	40	96	61	4.04
1983—Cedar Rapids	Midwest	36	140⅔	6	10	.375	120	66	52	137	69	3.33
1984—Vermont	Eastern	45	69⅔	2	3	.400	57	23	21	69	35	2.71
1985—Denver	Am. Assoc.	41	84	5	5	.500	94	55	43	66	57	4.61
1985—Cincinnati	National	2	3	0	0	.000	2	2	2	1	2	6.00
1986—Denver	Am. Assoc.	27	42⅔	3	4	.429	33	12	9	36	24	1.90
1986—Cincinnati	National	34	50⅓	6	0	1.000	26	4	4	36	21	0.72
1987—Cincinnati	National	87	100⅔	8	5	.615	91	37	34	99	32	3.04
1988—Cincinnati †	National	★76	84⅔	0	6	.000	69	31	29	74	38	3.08
Major League Totals—4 Years		199	238⅔	14	11	.560	188	74	69	210	93	2.60

Selected by Milwaukee Brewers' organization in 29th round of free-agent draft, June 6, 1978.
Selected by Cincinnati Reds' organization in secondary phase of free-agent draft, January 13, 1981.
†Traded with First Baseman Nick Esasky to Boston Red Sox for First Baseman Todd Benzinger, Pitcher Jeff Sellers and a player to be named later, December 13, 1988.

EDDIE CLARENCE MURRAY

Born February 24, 1956, at Los Angeles, Calif.
Height, 6.02. Weight, 224.
Throws right and bats left and righthanded.
Attended California State University, Los Angeles, Calif.
Brother of Rich Murray, first baseman with San Francisco Giants, 1980 and 1983;
Leon Murray, first baseman in San Franciso Giants' organization, 1970;
Charles Murray, minor league outfielder, 1962 through 1966
and 1969; and Venice Murray, first baseman in
San Francisco Giants' organization, 1978.

Tied major league record for most games, switch-hit home runs, season (2), 1982 and 1987.
Established American League records for most consecutive games, one or more hits by switch-hitter, season (22), 1984; most game-winning runs batted in, lifetime (117); most intentional bases on balls by switch-hitter, season (25), 1984.
Major League stolen bases: 1978 (6), 1979 (10), 1980 (7), 1981 (2), 1982 (7), 1983 (5), 1984 (10), 1985 (5), 1986 (3), 1987 (1), 1988 (5). Total—61.
Hit three home runs in a game, August 29, 1979 (second game), September 14, 1980 (13 innings) and August 26, 1985.
Switch-hit home runs in one game eight times: August 3, 1977, August 29, 1979 (two righthanded and one lefthanded); August 16, 1981, April 24, 1982, August 26, 1982, August 26, 1985 (two lefthanded and one righthanded), May 8, 1987 and May 9, 1987.
Led American League in bases on balls received with 107 and game-winning RBIs with 19 in 1984.
Led American League in intentional bases on balls received with 25 in 1984 and tied for lead with 18 in 1982.
Led American League first basemen in double plays with 152 in 1984, 146 in 1987 and tied for lead with 154 in 1985.
Led American League first basemen in total chances with 1,615 in 1978, 1,694 in 1984 and 1,526 in 1987.
Led American League first basemen in putouts with 1,504 in 1978.
Led Florida State League in total bases with 212 in 1974.
Led Florida State League first basemen in double plays with 113 in 1974.
Named American League Rookie of the Year by Baseball Writers' Association of America, 1977.
Named first baseman on The Sporting News American League All-Star Team, 1983.
Named first baseman on The Sporting News American League All-Star fielding team, 1982 through 1984.
Named first baseman on The Sporting News American League Silver Slugger team, 1983 and 1984.
Named Appalachian League Player of the Year, 1973.

Year Club	League	Pos.	G.	AB.	R.	H.	2B.	3B.	HR.	RBI.	B.A.	PO.	A.	E.	F.A.
1973—Bluefield	Appal.	1B	50	188	34	54	6	0	11	32	.287	421	14	13	.971
1974—Miami	Fla. St.	1B	131	460	64	133	★29	7	12	63	.289	★1114	★51	★25	.979
1974—Asheville	South.	1B	2	7	1	2	2	0	0	2	.286	17	0	0	1.000
1975—Asheville	South.	1B-3B	124	436	66	115	13	5	17	68	.264	637	58	15	.979
1976—Charlotte	South.	1B	88	299	46	89	15	2	12	46	.298	746	45	9	.989
1976—Rochester	Int.	1B-OF-3B	54	168	35	46	6	2	11	40	.274	291	13	5	.984
1977—Baltimore	Amer.	OF-1B	160	611	81	173	29	2	27	88	.283	482	20	4	.992
1978—Baltimore	Amer.	1B-3B	161	610	85	174	32	3	27	95	.285	1507	112	6	.996
1979—Baltimore	Amer.	1B	159	606	90	179	30	2	25	99	.295	★1456	107	10	.994
1980—Baltimore	Amer.	1B	158	621	100	186	36	2	32	116	.300	1369	77	9	.994
1981—Baltimore	Amer.	1B	99	378	57	111	21	2	●22	★78	.294	899	★91	1	★.999
1982—Baltimore	Amer.	1B	151	550	87	174	30	1	32	110	.316	1269	97	4	★.997
1983—Baltimore	Amer.	1B	156	582	115	178	30	3	33	111	.306	1393	114	10	.993
1984—Baltimore	Amer.	1B	●162	588	97	180	26	3	29	110	.306	★1538	★143	13	.992
1985—Baltimore	Amer.	1B	156	583	111	173	37	1	31	124	.297	1338	152	★19	.987
1986—Baltimore†	Amer.	1B	137	495	61	151	25	1	17	84	.305	1045	88	13	.989
1987—Baltimore	Amer.	1B	160	618	89	171	28	3	30	91	.277	1371	145	10	.993
1988—Baltimore‡	Amer.	1B	161	603	75	171	27	2	28	84	.284	867	106	11	.989
Major League Totals—12 Years			1820	6845	1048	2021	351	25	333	1190	.295	14534	1252	110	.993

Selected by Baltimore Orioles' organization in 3rd round of free-agent draft, June 5, 1973.

†On disabled list, July 10 to August 7, 1986.

‡Traded to Los Angeles Dodgers for Pitchers Brian Holton and Ken Howell and Shortstop Juan Bell, December 4, 1988.

CHAMPIONSHIP SERIES RECORD

Tied Championship Series record for most runs, game (4), October 7, 1983.

Tied American League Championship Series record for most bases on balls, four-game Series (5), 1979.

Year Club	League	Pos.	G.	AB.	R.	H.	2B.	3B.	HR.	RBI.	B.A.	PO.	A.	E.	F.A.
1979—Baltimore	Amer.	1B	4	12	3	5	0	0	1	5	.417	44	3	2	.959
1983—Baltimore	Amer.	1B	4	15	5	4	0	0	1	3	.267	34	3	1	.974
Championship Series Totals—2 Years			8	27	8	9	0	0	2	8	.333	78	6	3	.966

WORLD SERIES RECORD

Established World Series record for most double plays started by first baseman, game (2), October 11, 1979.

Year Club	League	Pos.	G.	AB.	R.	H.	2B.	3B.	HR.	RBI.	B.A.	PO.	A.	E.	F.A.
1979—Baltimore	Amer.	1B	7	26	3	4	1	0	1	2	.154	60	7	0	1.000
1983—Baltimore	Amer.	1B	5	20	2	5	0	0	2	3	.250	46	1	1	.979
World Series Totals—2 Years			12	46	5	9	1	0	3	5	.196	106	8	1	.991

ALL-STAR GAME RECORD

Year League	Pos.	AB.	R.	H.	2B.	3B.	HR.	RBI.	B.A.	PO.	A.	E.	F.A.
1981—American	PH-1B	2	0	0	0	0	0	0	.000	2	1	0	1.000
1982—American	PH-1B	1	0	0	0	0	0	0	.000	4	0	0	1.000
1983—American	1B	2	0	0	0	0	0	0	.000	4	0	0	1.000
1984—American	1B	2	0	1	1	0	0	0	.500	3	0	0	1.000
1985—American	1B	3	0	0	0	0	0	0	.000	5	2	0	1.000
All-Star Game Totals—5 Years		10	0	1	1	0	0	0	.100	18	3	0	1.000

Member of American League All-Star Team in 1978 and 1986; did not play.

JEFFREY JOSEPH MUSSELMAN
(Jeff)

Born June 21, 1963, at Doylestown, Pa.
Height, 6.00. Weight, 185.
Throws and bats lefthanded.

Received bachelor of arts degree in economics from Harvard University, Cambridge, Mass., in 1985.

Major League saves: 1987 (1).

Tied for Pioneer League lead in games started by pitchers with 15 in 1985.

Year Club	League	G.	IP.	W.	L.	Pct.	H.	R.	ER.	SO.	BB.	ERA.
1985—Medicine Hat	Pioneer	16	88	6	4	.600	75	41	39	96	44	3.99
1986—Ventura County	California	26	154⅔	7	7	.500	122	67	52	165	59	3.03
1986—Knoxville	Southern	7	41⅓	5	1	.833	33	17	13	38	25	2.83
1986—Toronto	American	6	5⅓	0	0	.000	8	7	6	4	5	10.13
1987—Toronto	American	68	89	12	5	.706	75	43	41	54	54	4.15
1988—Dunedin†	Florida St.	2	5⅔	0	0	.000	6	3	2	4	1	3.18
1988—Syracuse	Int'national	10	49	4	1	.800	42	20	16	31	17	2.94
1988—Toronto	American	15	85	8	5	.615	80	34	30	39	30	3.18
Major League Totals—3 Years		89	179⅓	20	10	.667	163	84	77	97	89	3.86

Selected by Toronto Blue Jays' organization in 6th round of free-agent draft, June 3, 1985.

†On Toronto disabled list, March 22 to June 15, 1988; included rehabilitation disability assignment to Dunedin, May 23 to May 27, 1988.

GREGORY RICHARD MYERS
(Greg)

Born April 14, 1966, at Riverside, Calif.
Height, 6.02. Weight, 200.
Throws right and bats lefthanded.

Led International League catchers in total chances with 698 in 1987.

Led California League catchers in total chances with 967 in 1986.

Year Club	League	Pos.	G.	AB.	R.	H.	2B.	3B.	HR.	RBI.	B.A.	PO.	A.	E.	F.A.
1984—Medicine Hat	Pion.	C	38	133	20	42	9	0	2	20	.316	216	24	4	.984
1985—Florence	S. Atl.	C	134	489	52	109	19	2	5	62	.223	551	61	7	*.989
1986—Ventura	Calif.	C	124	451	65	133	23	4	20	79	.295	*849	99	19	.980
1987—Syracuse	Int.	C	107	342	35	84	19	1	10	47	.246	*637	50	11	.984
1987—Toronto	Amer.	C	7	9	1	1	0	0	0	0	.111	24	1	0	1.000
1988—Syracuse†	Int.	C	34	120	18	34	7	1	7	21	.283	63	9	1	.986
Major League Totals—1 Year			7	9	1	1	0	0	0	0	.111	24	1	0	1.000

Selected by Toronto Blue Jays' organization in 3rd round of free-agent draft, June 4, 1984.

†On disabled list, June 17, 1988 through remainder of season.

—DID YOU KNOW—

That the San Diego Padres set a major league record April 13, 1987 when their first three batters (Marvell Wynne, Tony Gwynn and John Kruk) hit home runs to open a game against the Giants?

RANDALL KIRK MYERS
(Randy)

Born September 19, 1962, at Vancouver, Wash.
Height, 6.01. Weight, 208.
Throws and bats lefthanded.
Attended Clark College, Vancouver, Wash.

Major League saves: 1987 (6), 1988 (26). Total—32.
Tied for Carolina League lead in complete games with 7 in 1984.
Tied for South Atlantic League lead in games started by pitchers with 28 in 1983.
Tied for Appalachian League lead in games started by pitchers with 13 and balks with 3 in 1982.
Named Carolina League Pitcher of the Year, 1984.

Year Club	League	G.	IP.	W.	L.	Pct.	H.	R.	ER.	SO.	BB.	ERA.
1982—Kingsport	Ap'lachian	13	74⅓	6	3	.667	68	49	34	•86	69	4.12
1983—Columbia	S. Atlantic	28	173⅓	14	10	.583	146	94	70	164	108	3.63
1984—Lynchburg	Carolina	23	157	13	5	.722	123	46	36	171	61	*2.06
1984—Jackson	Texas	5	35	2	1	.667	29	14	8	35	16	2.06
1985—Jackson	Texas	19	120⅓	4	8	.333	99	61	53	116	69	3.96
1985—Tidewater	Int'national	8	44	1	1	.500	40	13	9	25	20	1.84
1985—New York	National	1	2	0	0	.000	0	0	0	2	1	0.00
1986—Tidewater	Int'national	45	65	6	7	.462	44	19	17	79	44	2.35
1986—New York	National	10	10⅔	0	0	.000	11	5	5	13	9	4.22
1987—New York	National	54	75	3	6	.333	61	36	33	92	30	3.96
1987—Tidewater	Int'national	5	7⅓	0	0	.000	6	4	4	13	4	4.91
1988—New York	National	55	68	7	3	.700	45	15	13	69	17	1.72
Major League Totals—4 Years		120	155⅔	10	9	.526	117	56	51	176	57	2.95

Selected by Cincinnati Reds' organization in 3rd round of free-agent draft, January 12, 1982.
Selected by New York Mets' organization in secondary phase of free-agent draft, June 7, 1982.

CHAMPIONSHIP SERIES RECORD

Tied Championship Series record for most games won, seven-game Series (2), 1988.

Year Club	League	G.	IP.	W.	L.	Pct.	H.	R.	ER.	SO.	BB.	ERA.
1988—New York	National	3	4⅔	2	0	1.000	1	0	0	0	2	0.00

ROBERT AUGUSTUS NELSON II
(Rob)

Born May 17, 1964, at Pasadena, Calif.
Height, 6.04. Weight, 215.
Throws and bats lefthanded.
Attended Mount San Antonio College, Walnut, Calif.

Led Pacific Coast League batters in strikeouts with 133 in 1987 and 130 in 1988.
Led Pacific Coast League in sacrifice flies with 13 in 1986.
Led Midwest League batters in strikeouts with 140 in 1984.
Led Pacific Coast League first basemen in total chances with 1,359 in 1986.
Led Midwest League first basemen in double plays with 111 and total chances with 1,279 in 1984.

Year Club	League	Pos.	G.	AB.	R.	H.	2B.	3B.	HR.	RBI.	B.A.	PO.	A.	E.	F.A.
1983—Idaho Falls	Pion.	1B	54	196	42	57	12	2	12	38	.291	418	32	6	.986
1984—Madison	Midw.	1B	136	487	71	120	25	2	19	85	.246	*1173	*89	17	.987
1985—Huntsville	South.	1B	140	499	68	116	25	0	32	98	.232	1101	86	*23	.981
1986—Tacoma	P. C.	1B	139	508	77	140	26	4	20	108	.276	*1228	*121	10	.992
1986—Oakland	Amer.	1B	5	9	1	2	1	0	0	0	.222	3	1	1	.800
1987—Oakland	Amer.	1B	7	24	1	4	1	0	0	0	.167	49	11	2	.968
1987—Tacoma†	P. C.	1B-OF	120	413	68	89	19	3	20	74	.215	971	70	7	.993
1987—San Diego	Nat.	1B	10	11	0	1	0	0	0	1	.091	14	0	0	1.000
1988—Las Vegas	P. C.	1B-OF	116	388	68	101	23	1	23	77	.260	632	50	6	.991
1988—San Diego	Nat.	1B	7	21	4	4	0	0	1	3	.190	48	5	1	.981
American League Totals—2 Years			12	33	2	6	2	0	0	0	.182	52	12	3	.955
National League Totals—2 Years			17	32	4	5	0	0	1	4	.156	62	5	1	.985
Major League Totals—3 Years			29	65	6	11	2	0	1	4	.169	114	17	4	.970

Selected by Houston Astros' organization in 27th round of free-agent draft, June 7, 1982.
Selected by Atlanta Braves' organization in secondary phase of free-agent draft, January 11, 1983.
Selected by Oakland A's organization in secondary phase of free-agent draft, June 6, 1983.
†Traded to San Diego Padres, September 8, 1987, completing deal in which San Diego traded Pitcher Storm Davis to Oakland Athletics for two players to be named later, August 30, 1987. San Diego acquired Pitcher Dave Leiper as partial completion of deal, August 31, 1987.

WAYLAND EUGENE NELSON II
(Gene)

Born December 3, 1960, at Tampa, Fla.
Height, 6.00. Weight, 172.
Throws and bats righthanded.

Major League saves: 1984 (1), 1985 (2), 1986 (6), 1987 (3), 1988 (3). Total—15.
Major League stolen bases: 1988 (1).
Led Florida State League in shutouts with 5 and complete games with 16 in 1980.

Year Club	League	G.	IP.	W.	L.	Pct.	H.	R.	ER.	SO.	BB.	ERA.
1978—Sarasota Rangers	Gulf Coast	14	52	5	0	•1.000	41	18	13	28	20	2.25
1979—Asheville†	W. Carol.	33	155	13	5	*.722	149	77	62	96	44	3.60
1980—Fort Lauderdale	Florida St.	27	196	*20	3	*.870	146	51	43	130	70	1.97
1981—New York‡	American	8	39	3	1	.750	40	24	21	16	23	4.85
1981—Fort Lauderdale	Florida St.	2	10	0	0	.000	9	6	6	8	5	5.40
1981—Columbus§	Int'national	5	32	4	0	1.000	25	9	9	37	14	2.53
1982—Seattle	American	22	122⅔	6	9	.400	133	70	63	71	60	4.62
1982—Salt Lake City	P. Coast	5	37⅔	1	3	.250	36	18	14	22	28	3.35
1983—Salt Lake City x	P. Coast	16	99	9	4	.692	115	65	57	74	28	5.18
1983—Seattle	American	10	32	0	3	.000	38	29	28	11	21	7.88
1984—Salt Lake City y	P. Coast	17	112	6	8	.429	138	75	70	89	54	5.63
1984—Chicago	American	20	74⅔	3	5	.375	72	38	37	36	17	4.46
1985—Chicago z	American	46	145⅔	10	10	.500	144	74	69	101	67	4.26
1986—Chicago a	American	54	114⅔	6	6	.500	118	52	49	70	41	3.85
1987—Oakland	American	54	123⅔	6	5	.545	120	58	54	94	35	3.93
1988—Oakland b	American	54	111⅓	9	6	.600	93	42	38	67	38	3.06
Major League Totals—8 Years		268	764	43	45	.489	758	387	359	466	302	4.23

Selected by Texas Rangers' organization in 29th round of free-agent draft, June 6, 1978.

†Traded with Pitcher Ray Fontenot to New York Yankees' organization for Pitchers Bob Polinsky, Neal Mersch and Mark Softy, October 8, 1979; completing deal in which New York traded Outfielder Mickey Rivers and three players to be named later to Texas Rangers for Third Baseman Amos Lewis and two players to be named later, August 1, 1979.

‡On disabled list, April 10 to May 4, 1981; included rehabilitation disability assignment to Ft. Lauderdale, April 17 to May 4, 1981.

§Traded with Pitcher Bill Caudill, a player to be named later and cash to Seattle Mariners for Pitcher Shane Rawley, April 1, 1982; Seattle organization acquired Outfielder Bobby Brown to complete deal, April 6, 1982.

xOn disabled list, June 25 to July 31, 1983.

yTraded with Pitcher Jerry Don Gleaton to Chicago White Sox for Pitcher Salome Barojas, June 27, 1984.

zHad one at-bat with no hits.

aTraded with a player to be named later to Oakland A's for Infielder Donnie Hill, December 11, 1986; Oakland acquired Pitcher Bruce Tanner to complete deal, December 18, 1986.

bAppeared in three games as a pinch-runner.

CHAMPIONSHIP SERIES RECORD

Tied Championship Series record for most games won, four-game Series (2), 1988.

Year Club	League	G.	IP.	W.	L.	Pct.	H.	R.	ER.	SO.	BB.	ERA.
1988—Oakland	American	2	4⅔	2	0	1.000	5	0	0	0	1	0.00

WORLD SERIES RECORD

Year Club	League	G.	IP.	W.	L.	Pct.	H.	R.	ER.	SO.	BB.	ERA.
1988—Oakland	American	3	6⅓	0	0	.000	4	1	1	3	3	1.42

GRAIG NETTLES

Born August 20, 1944, at San Diego, Calif.
Height, 6.00. Weight, 187.
Throws right and bats lefthanded.
Attended San Diego State College, San Diego, Calif.
Brother of Jim Nettles, outfielder with Minnesota, Detroit, Kansas City and Oakland, 1970 through 1972, 1974, 1979 and 1981; minor league coach, Oakland A's organization, 1982; and minor league manager in Oakland A's organization since 1983.

Established major league records for most assists by third baseman, season (412), and most double plays by third baseman, season (54), 1971.

Tied major league records for most home runs month of April (11), 1974; fewest three-base hits, season, 150 or more games (0), 1972 and 1973.

Established American League record for most home runs by third baseman, lifetime (319).

Tied American League record for most home runs, doubleheader (4), April 14, 1974.

Tied National League record for most home runs, six consecutive games (7), August 11 through 22, 1984.

Major League stolen bases: 1969 (1), 1970 (3), 1971 (7), 1972 (2), 1974 (1), 1975 (1), 1976 (11), 1977 (2), 1978 (1), 1979 (1), 1982 (1), 1987 (1). Total—32.

Led American League in sacrifice flies with 11 in 1975.

Led American League third basemen in total chances with 587 in 1971, 553 in 1973, 545 in 1974 and 539 in 1976.

Led American League third basemen in double plays with 54 in 1971, 30 in 1976 and tied for lead with 30 in 1978.

Led American League third basemen in assists with 383 in 1976.

Led Southern League third basemen in double plays with 34 in 1967 and led Pacific Coast League third basemen with 20 in 1968.

Named third baseman on THE SPORTING NEWS American League All-Star Team, 1975, 1977 and 1978.

Named third baseman on THE SPORTING NEWS American League All-Star fielding team, 1977 and 1978.

Year Club	League	Pos.	G.	AB.	R.	H.	2B.	3B.	HR.	RBI.	B.A.	PO.	A.	E.	F.A.
1966—Wis. Rapids	Midw.	2B-3B	117	413	84	111	19	6	*28	75	.269	240	245	28	.945
1967—Charlotte	South.	3B	140	499	69	116	18	4	•19	86	.232	107	*318	24	.947
1967—Minnesota	Amer.	PH	3	3	0	1	1	0	0	0	.333	0	0	0	.000
1968—Denver	P. C.	3B-OF-1B	130	451	84	134	17	•12	22	83	.297	125	266	17	.958
1968—Minnesota	Amer.	OF-3B-1B	22	76	13	17	2	1	5	8	.224	50	9	2	.967
1969—Minnesota†	Amer.	OF-3B	96	225	27	50	9	2	7	26	.222	88	44	2	.985
1970—Cleveland	Amer.	*3B-OF	157	549	81	129	13	1	26	62	.235	135	358	17	*.967
1971—Cleveland	Amer.	3B	158	598	78	156	18	1	28	86	.261	*159	*412	16	.973
1972—Cleveland‡	Amer.	3B	150	557	65	141	28	0	17	70	.253	114	*358	*21	.957
1973—New York	Amer.	3B	160	552	65	129	18	0	22	81	.234	117	*410	26	.953
1974—New York	Amer.	*3B-SS	155	566	74	139	21	1	22	75	.246	*147	377	21	.961

Year Club	League	Pos.	G.	AB.	R.	H.	2B.	3B.	HR.	RBI.	B.A.	PO.	A.	E.	F.A.
1975—New York	Amer.	3B	157	581	71	155	24	4	21	91	.267	135	*379	19	.964
1976—New York	Amer.	3B-SS	158	583	88	148	29	2	*32	93	.254	137	384	19	.965
1977—New York	Amer.	3B	158	589	99	150	23	4	37	107	.255	132	321	12	.974
1978—New York	Amer.	3B-SS	159	587	81	162	23	2	27	93	.276	110	326	11	.975
1979—New York	Amer.	3B	145	521	71	132	15	1	20	73	.253	110	339	16	.966
1980—New York§	Amer.	3B-SS	89	324	52	79	14	0	16	45	.244	59	183	10	.960
1981—New York	Amer.	3B	103	349	46	85	7	1	15	46	.244	63	214	8	.972
1982—New York x	Amer.	3B	122	405	47	94	11	2	18	55	.232	73	255	23	.934
1983—New York y	Amer.	3B	129	462	56	123	17	3	20	75	.266	78	273	16	.956
1984—San Diego	Nat.	3B	124	395	56	90	11	1	20	65	.228	93	201	20	.936
1985—San Diego	Nat.	3B	137	440	66	115	23	1	15	61	.261	122	229	15	.959
1986—San Diego z	Nat.	3B	126	354	36	77	9	0	16	55	.218	83	174	16	.941
1987—Atlanta ab	Nat.	3B-1B	112	177	16	37	8	1	5	33	.209	61	56	3	.975
1988—Montreal c	Nat.	3B-1B	80	93	5	16	4	0	1	14	.172	32	14	5	.902
American League Totals—17 Years			2121	7527	1014	1890	273	25	333	1086	.251	1707	4642	239	.964
National League Totals—5 Years			579	1459	179	335	55	3	57	228	.230	391	674	59	.948
Major League Totals—22 Years			2700	8986	1193	2225	328	28	390	1314	.248	2098	5316	298	.961

Selected by Minnesota Twins' organization in 4th round of free-agent draft, June 9, 1965.

†Traded with Pitchers Dean Chance and Robert L. Miller and Outfielder Ted Uhlaender to Cleveland Indians for Pitchers Luis Tiant and Stan Williams, December 12, 1969.

‡Traded with Catcher Jerry Moses to New York Yankees for Catcher-First Baseman John Ellis, Infielder Jerry Kenney and Outfielders Charlie Spikes and Rosendo Torres, November 27, 1972.

§On disabled list, July 27 to October 2, 1980.

xOn disabled list, April 26 to May 17, 1982.

yTraded to San Diego Padres for Pitcher Dennis Rasmussen and a player to be named later, March 30, 1984; New York Yankees' organization acquired Pitcher Darin Cloninger to complete deal, April 26, 1984.

zReleased, December 20, 1986; signed by Atlanta Braves, April 1, 1987.

aGranted free agency, November 9, 1987; signed by Braves' organization, December 6, 1987.

bSold to Montreal Expos, March 24, 1988.

cGranted free agency, November 4, 1988.

DIVISION SERIES RECORD

Year Club	League	Pos.	G.	AB.	R.	H.	2B.	3B.	HR.	RBI.	B.A.	PO.	A.	E.	F.A.
1981—New York	Amer.	3B	5	17	1	1	0	0	0	1	.059	7	7	0	1.000

CHAMPIONSHIP SERIES RECORD

Established Championship Series records for most hits, inning (2), October 14, 1981; most runs batted in, three-game Series (9), 1981.

Tied Championship Series record for most times reached first base safely, game (5), October 14, 1981.

Tied American League Championship Series records for most home runs, five-game Series (2), 1976; highest slugging average, three-game Series (.917), 1981; most Series, one or more home runs (4).

Year Club	League	Pos.	G.	AB.	R.	H.	2B.	3B.	HR.	RBI.	B.A.	PO.	A.	E.	F.A.
1969—Minnesota	Amer.	PH	1	1	0	1	0	0	0	0	1.000	0	0	0	.000
1976—New York	Amer.	3B	5	17	2	4	1	0	2	4	.235	5	14	0	1.000
1977—New York	Amer.	3B	5	20	1	3	0	0	0	1	.150	2	12	0	1.000
1978—New York	Amer.	3B	4	15	3	5	0	1	1	2	.333	6	7	0	1.000
1980—New York	Amer.	3B-PH	2	6	1	1	0	0	1	1	.167	0	2	0	1.000
1981—New York	Amer.	3B	3	12	2	6	2	0	1	9	.500	4	4	1	.889
1984—San Diego	Nat.	3B	4	14	1	2	0	0	0	2	.143	5	8	0	1.000
Championship Series Totals—7 Years			24	85	10	22	3	1	5	19	.259	22	47	1	.986

WORLD SERIES RECORD

Established World Series records for most double plays by third baseman, four-game Series (3), 1976; most assists by third baseman, six-game Series (20), 1977; highest fielding average by third baseman, six-game Series, most chances accepted (1.000 and 26), 1978; most double plays by third baseman, total Series (7); most double plays and double plays started by third baseman, six-game Series (3), 1978; most assists by third baseman, total Series (68); most chances accepted by third baseman, total Series (96).

Tied World Series records for most double plays started by third baseman, four-game Series (2), 1976; most double plays started, game (2), October 19, 1976; fewest chances accepted by third baseman, game (0), October 18, 1977.

Year Club	League	Pos.	G.	AB.	R.	H.	2B.	3B.	HR.	RBI.	B.A.	PO.	A.	E.	F.A.
1976—New York	Amer.	3B	4	12	0	3	0	0	0	2	.250	8	8	0	1.000
1977—New York	Amer.	3B	6	21	1	4	1	0	0	2	.190	2	20	1	.957
1978—New York	Amer.	3B	6	25	2	4	0	0	0	1	.160	8	18	0	1.000
1981—New York	Amer.	3B	3	10	1	4	1	0	0	0	.400	3	10	1	.929
1984—San Diego	Nat.	3B	5	12	2	3	0	0	0	2	.250	7	12	0	1.000
World Series Totals—5 Years			24	80	6	18	2	0	0	7	.225	28	68	2	.980

ALL-STAR GAME RECORD

Year League	Pos.	AB.	R.	H.	2B.	3B.	HR.	RBI.	B.A.	PO.	A.	E.	F.A.
1975—American	3B	4	0	1	0	0	0	0	.250	2	2	0	1.000
1977—American	3B	2	0	0	0	0	0	0	.000	0	1	0	1.000
1978—American†	3B	0	0	0	0	0	0	0	.000	0	1	0	1.000
1979—American	3B	1	0	1	0	0	0	0	1.000	1	2	0	1.000
1980—American	3B	2	0	0	0	0	0	0	.000	0	1	0	1.000
1985—National	3B	2	0	0	0	0	0	0	.000	0	1	0	1.000
All-Star Game Totals—6 Years		11	0	2	0	0	0	0	.182	3	8	0	1.000

†Originally replaced due to injury by Larry Hisle, then re-named to replace Reggie Jackson.

ALBERT DWAYNE NEWMAN
(Al)

Born June 30, 1960, at Kansas City, Mo.
Height, 5.09. Weight, 183.
Throws right and bats left and righthanded.
Attended Chaffey College, Alta Loma, Calif., and
San Diego State University, San Diego, Calif.

Major League stolen bases: 1985 (2), 1986 (11), 1987 (15), 1988 (12). Total—40.
Led Southern League in sacrifice hits with 18 in 1982.
Led Texas League shortstops in double plays with 58 in 1984.
Led Southern League second basemen in total chances with 776 in 1982.

Year Club	League	Pos.	G.	AB.	R.	H.	2B.	3B.	HR.	RBI.	B.A.	PO.	A.	E.	F.A.
1982—Memphis	South.	2B	142	494	85	136	16	8	1	41	.275	*356	•388	*32	.959
1983—Wichita	A. A.	2B	38	124	20	30	6	1	0	16	.242	73	96	5	.971
1983—Memphis†‡	South.	2B	52	194	18	49	5	2	0	13	.253	111	123	14	.944
1984—Beaumont§	Texas	SS	88	318	69	80	8	0	0	23	.252	138	250	27	.935
1984—Indianapolis	A. A.	2-3-O-S	37	123	13	37	3	0	0	11	.301	49	79	2	.985
1985—Indianapolis	A. A.	2B-SS	87	301	42	85	16	2	0	23	.282	144	250	10	.975
1985—Montreal	Nat.	2B-SS	25	29	7	5	1	0	0	1	.172	19	36	0	1.000
1986—Montreal x	Nat.	2B-SS	95	185	23	37	3	0	1	8	.200	98	161	11	.959
1987—Minnesota	Amer.	S-2-3-O	110	307	44	68	15	5	0	29	.221	120	225	5	.986
1988—Minnesota	Amer.	3B-SS-2B	105	260	35	58	7	0	0	19	.223	97	155	6	.977
National League Totals—2 Years			120	214	30	42	4	0	1	9	.196	117	197	11	.966
American League Totals—2 Years			215	567	79	126	22	5	0	48	.222	217	380	11	.982
Major League Totals—4 Years			335	781	109	168	26	5	1	57	.215	334	577	22	.976

Selected by California Angels' organization in 3rd round of free-agent draft, January 9, 1979.
Selected by Texas Rangers' organization in 3rd round of free-agent draft, January 8, 1980.
Selected by New York Mets' organization in secondary phase of free-agent draft, June 3, 1980.
Selected by Montreal Expos' organization in secondary phase of free-agent draft, June 8, 1981.
†On disabled list, July 23 to August 16, 1983.
‡Traded with Pitcher Scott Sanderson to San Diego Padres for Pitcher Gary Lucas, December 7, 1983.
§Traded to Montreal Expos' organization for Pitcher Greg Harris, July 20, 1984.
xTraded to Minnesota Twins for Pitcher Mike Shade, February 20, 1987.

CHAMPIONSHIP SERIES RECORD

Year Club	League	Pos.	G.	AB.	R.	H.	2B.	3B.	HR.	RBI.	B.A.	PO.	A.	E.	F.A.
1987—Minnesota	Amer.	2B	1	2	0	0	0	0	0	0	.000	0	1	0	1.000

WORLD SERIES RECORD

Year Club	League	Pos.	G.	AB.	R.	H.	2B.	3B.	HR.	RBI.	B.A.	PO.	A.	E.	F.A.
1987—Minnesota	Amer.	PR-2-PH	4	5	0	1	0	0	0	0	.200	1	2	0	1.000

FRANCIS ANDREW NEZELEK
(Andy)

Born October 24, 1965, at Endicott, N.Y.
Height, 6.06. Weight, 218.
Throws right and bats lefthanded.
Attended Bucknell University, Lewisburg, Pa.

Year Club	League	G.	IP.	W.	L.	Pct.	H.	R.	ER.	SO.	BB.	ERA.
1986—Pulaski	Ap'lachian	12	66⅓	2	4	.333	69	36	20	55	22	2.71
1987—Sumter	S. Atlantic	12	85	6	3	.667	56	24	17	67	12	1.80
1988—Greenville	Southern	26	133⅔	7	8	.467	133	77	65	89	45	4.38

Selected by Atlanta Braves' organization in 5th round of free-agent draft, June 2, 1986.

CARL EDWARD NICHOLS

Born October 14, 1962, at Los Angeles, Calif.
Height, 6.00. Weight, 192.
Throws and bats righthanded.

Led International League catchers in fielding percentage with .988, double plays with 9 and passed balls with 9 in 1987.
Led Southern League catchers in putouts with 693 and total chances with 818 in 1986.
Led California League catchers in total chances with 897 in 1984.
Led New York-Pennsylvania League catchers in assists with 47 and tied for lead in double plays with 6 in 1983.

Year Club	League	Pos.	G.	AB.	R.	H.	2B.	3B.	HR.	RBI.	B.A.	PO.	A.	E.	F.A.
1980—Bluefield	Appal.	C-1B-OF	37	85	24	18	2	2	0	10	.212	129	13	2	.986
1981—Miami	Fla. St.	C-1-S-3-O	16	31	1	6	0	0	0	3	.194	34	9	6	.878
1981—Hagerstown†	Carol.	C-O-S-2	38	81	8	22	4	0	1	6	.272	131	21	3	.981
1982—Macon	S. Atl.	C-OF-1B	84	257	33	55	10	2	0	30	.214	391	49	21	.954
1983—San Jose	Calif.	C-OF-3B	54	152	16	31	4	0	1	12	.204	204	39	17	.935
1983—Newark	NYP	C-O-3-S	66	217	40	63	14	0	5	26	.290	348	56	10	.976
1984—S.J.‡-Red.§	Calif.	*C-OF	121	389	53	88	14	2	4	54	.226	*769	*112	17	.981
1985—Charlotte	South.	C-OF-1B	115	331	45	78	11	2	2	37	.236	496	71	15	.984
1986—Charlotte	South.	*C-OF	118	439	63	118	26	1	14	72	.269	700	*110	16	.981
1986—Baltimore	Amer.	C	5	5	0	0	0	0	0	0	.000	11	0	0	1.000
1987—Rochester	Int.	C-OF	108	364	45	93	15	3	11	52	.255	617	65	9	.987
1987—Baltimore	Amer.	C	13	21	4	8	1	0	0	3	.381	39	3	0	1.000

Year	Club	League	Pos.	G.	AB.	R.	H.	2B.	3B.	HR.	RBI.	B.A.	PO.	A.	E.	F.A.
1988	Baltimore	Amer.	C-OF	18	47	2	9	1	0	0	1	.191	71	13	1	.988
1988	Rochester	Int.	C-OF-3B	75	193	20	44	7	1	3	16	.228	335	44	8	.979
Major League Totals—3 Years				36	73	6	17	2	0	0	4	.233	121	16	1	.993

Selected by Baltimore Orioles' organization in 4th round of free-agent draft, June 3, 1980.
†Loaned to Macon (Detroit Tigers' organization), April 8, 1982; returned, September 15, 1982.
‡Loaned to San Jose (Independent), April 10, 1984; returned, June 9, 1984.
§Loaned to Redwood (California Angels' organization), June 9, 1984; returned, September 10, 1984.

RODNEY LEA NICHOLS
(Rod)

Born December 29, 1964, at Burlington, Ia.
Height, 6.02. Weight, 190.
Throws and bats righthanded.
Attended University of New Mexico, Albuquerque, N.M.

Year	Club	League	G.	IP.	W.	L.	Pct.	H.	R.	ER.	SO.	BB.	ERA.
1985	Batavia	NYP	13	84	5	5	.500	74	40	28	93	33	3.00
1986	Waterloo†	Midwest	20	115⅓	8	5	.615	128	56	52	83	21	4.06
1987	Kinston	Carolina	9	56	4	2	.667	53	27	25	61	14	4.02
1987	Williamsport	Eastern	16	100	4	3	.571	107	53	41	60	33	3.69
1988	Kinston‡	Carolina	4	24	3	1	.750	26	13	12	19	15	4.50
1988	Colorado Springs	P. Coast	10	58⅔	2	6	.250	69	41	37	43	17	5.74
1988	Cleveland	American	11	69⅓	1	7	.125	73	41	39	31	23	5.06
Major League Totals—1 Year			11	69⅓	1	7	.125	73	41	39	31	23	5.06

Selected by Cleveland Indians' organization in 5th round of free-agent draft, June 3, 1985.
†On disabled list, July 12 to August 18, 1986.
‡On Cleveland disabled list, March 26 to May 12, 1988.

THOMAS EDWARD NIEDENFUER

Name pronounced NEED-un-fyoor.

(Tom)

Born August 13, 1959, at St. Louis Park, Minn.
Height, 6.05. Weight, 224.
Throws and bats righthanded.
Attended Washington State University, Pullman, Wash.
Husband of Judy Landers, television actress.

Major League saves: 1981 (2), 1982 (9), 1983 (11), 1984 (11), 1985 (19), 1986 (11), 1987 (14), 1988 (18). Total—95.

Year	Club	League	G.	IP.	W.	L.	Pct.	H.	R.	ER.	SO.	BB.	ERA.
1981	San Antonio	Texas	36	90	13	3	*.813	61	19	18	95	34	1.80
1981	Los Angeles	National	17	26	3	1	.750	25	11	11	12	6	3.81
1982	Albuquerque	P. Coast	4	10⅔	2	0	1.000	6	0	0	15	2	0.00
1982	Los Angeles	National	55	69⅔	3	4	.429	71	22	21	60	25	2.71
1983	Los Angeles	National	66	94⅔	8	3	.727	55	22	20	66	29	1.90
1984	Los Angeles†	National	33	47⅓	2	5	.286	39	14	13	45	23	2.47
1985	Los Angeles	National	64	106⅓	7	9	.438	86	32	32	102	24	2.71
1986	Los Angeles‡	National	60	80	6	6	.500	86	35	33	55	29	3.71
1987	Los Angeles§	National	15	16⅓	1	0	1.000	13	5	5	10	9	2.76
1987	Baltimore	American	45	52⅓	3	5	.375	55	32	29	37	22	4.99
1988	Baltimore x	American	52	59	3	4	.429	59	23	23	40	19	3.51
National League Totals—7 Years			310	440⅓	30	28	.517	375	141	135	350	145	2.76
American League Totals—2 Years			97	111⅓	6	9	.400	114	55	52	77	41	4.20
Major League Totals—8 Years			407	551⅔	36	37	.493	489	196	187	427	186	3.05

Selected by Los Angeles Dodgers' organization in 36th round of free-agent draft, June 7, 1977.
Signed as free agent by Los Angeles Dodgers' organization, August 14, 1980.
†On disabled list, July 16 to July 31 and August 5 to September 11, 1984.
‡On disabled list, August 19 to September 3, 1986.
§Traded to Baltimore Orioles for Outfielder John Shelby and Pitcher Brad Havens, May 22, 1987.
xGranted free agency, November 4, 1988; signed by Seattle Mariners, December 7, 1988.

DIVISION SERIES RECORD

Year	Club	League	G.	IP.	W.	L.	Pct.	H.	R.	ER.	SO.	BB.	ERA.
1981	Los Angeles	National	1	⅓	0	0	.000	1	0	0	1	1	0.00

CHAMPIONSHIP SERIES RECORD

Tied Championship Series record for most games lost, Series (2), 1985.

Year	Club	League	G.	IP.	W.	L.	Pct.	H.	R.	ER.	SO.	BB.	ERA.
1981	Los Angeles	National	1	⅓	0	0	.000	2	0	0	0	0	0.00
1983	Los Angeles	National	2	2	0	0	.000	0	0	0	3	1	0.00
1985	Los Angeles	National	3	5⅔	0	2	.000	5	4	4	5	2	6.35
Championship Series Totals—3 Years			6	8	0	2	.000	7	4	4	8	3	4.50

WORLD SERIES RECORD

Year	Club	League	G.	IP.	W.	L.	Pct.	H.	R.	ER.	SO.	BB.	ERA.
1981	Los Angeles	National	2	5	0	0	.000	3	2	0	0	1	0.00

JOSEPH FRANKLIN NIEKRO

Name pronounced NEE-krow.

(Joe)

Born November 7, 1944, at Martins Ferry, O.
Height, 6.01. Weight, 190.
Throws and bats righthanded.
Attended West Liberty State College, West Liberty, W. Va.
Brother of Phil Niekro, pitcher with Milwaukee-Atlanta Braves, New York Yankees, Cleveland Indians and Toronto Blue Jays, 1964 through 1987.

Pitched seven-inning, 2-0 perfect game against Tidewater, July 16, 1972 (second game).
Major League saves: 1971 (1), 1972 (1), 1973 (3), 1975 (4), 1977 (5). Total—14.
Led National League pitchers in games started with 38 in 1983 and 1984.
Led National League in wild pitches with 19 in 1982, 14 in 1983, 21 in 1985 and tied for lead with 19 in 1979.
Tied for National League lead in shutouts with 5 in 1979.
Named National League Pitcher of the Year by THE SPORTING NEWS, 1979.
Named righthanded pitcher on THE SPORTING NEWS National League All-Star Team, 1979.

Year Club	League	G.	IP.	W.	L.	Pct.	H.	R.	ER.	SO.	BB.	ERA.
1966—Treasure Valley	Pioneer	1	4	0	0	.000	4	0	0	7	1	0.00
1966—Quincy	Midwest	4	25	1	2	.333	17	7	3	14	6	1.08
1966—Dallas-Fort Worth	Texas	12	79	5	4	.556	71	28	22	50	15	2.51
1967—Chicago	National	36	170	10	7	.588	171	68	63	77	32	3.34
1968—Chicago	National	34	177	14	10	.583	204	93	85	65	59	4.32
1969—Chicago†-San Diego‡	National	41	221	8	18	.308	237	100	91	62	51	3.71
1970—Detroit	American	38	213	12	13	.480	221	107	96	101	72	4.06
1971—Detroit	American	31	122	6	7	.462	136	62	61	43	49	4.28
1972—Toledo§	Int'national	2	14	2	0	1.000	6	1	1	11	3	0.64
1972—Detroit	American	18	47	3	2	.600	62	20	20	24	8	3.83
1973—Toledo x	Int'national	26	143	7	10	.412	148	74	59	77	47	3.71
1973—Atlanta	National	20	24	2	4	.333	23	11	11	12	11	4.13
1974—Richmond	Int'national	30	52	8	1	.889	44	14	12	50	18	2.08
1974—Atlanta y	National	27	43	3	2	.600	36	19	17	31	18	3.56
1975—Iowa	Am. Assoc.	7	9	1	0	1.000	7	6	5	9	7	5.00
1975—Houston	National	40	88	6	4	.600	79	32	30	54	39	3.07
1976—Houston	National	36	118	4	8	.333	107	60	44	77	56	3.36
1977—Houston	National	44	181	13	8	.619	155	66	61	101	64	3.03
1978—Houston	National	35	203	14	14	.500	190	97	87	97	73	3.86
1979—Houston	National	38	264	•21	11	.656	221	102	88	119	107	3.00
1980—Houston	National	37	256	20	12	.625	268	119	101	127	79	3.55
1981—Houston	National	24	166	9	9	.500	150	60	52	77	47	2.82
1982—Houston	National	35	270	17	12	.586	224	79	74	130	64	2.47
1983—Houston	National	38	263⅔	15	14	.517	238	115	102	152	101	3.48
1984—Houston	National	38	248⅓	16	12	.571	223	104	84	127	89	3.04
1985—Houston z	National	32	213	9	12	.429	197	100	88	117	99	3.72
1985—New York a	American	3	12⅓	2	1	.667	14	8	8	4	8	5.84
1986—New York b	American	25	125⅔	9	10	.474	139	84	68	59	63	4.87
1987—New York c-Minnesota d	American	27	147	7	13	.350	155	101	87	84	64	5.33
1988—Minnesota e	American	5	11⅔	1	1	.500	16	13	13	7	9	10.03
National League Totals—16 Years		555	2906	181	157	.536	2723	1225	1078	1425	989	3.34
American League Totals—7 Years		147	678⅔	40	47	.460	743	395	353	322	273	4.68
Major League Totals—22 Years		702	3584⅔	221	204	.520	3466	1620	1431	1747	1262	3.59

Selected by Cleveland Indians' organization in 7th round of free-agent draft, January, 1966.
Selected by Chicago Cubs' organization in 3rd round of free-agent draft, June, 1966.
†Traded with Pitcher Gary Ross and Infielder Francisco Libran to San Diego Padres for Pitcher Dick Selma, April 24, 1969. Libran remained on Cubs' San Antonio farm team but became San Diego property.
‡Traded to Detroit Tigers for Pitcher Pat Dobson and Shortstop-Outfielder Dave Campbell, December 4, 1969.
§On disabled list, August 7 to September 1, 1972.
xSold on waivers to Atlanta Braves, August 7, 1973.
ySold to Houston Astros, April 5, 1975.
zTraded to New York Yankees for Pitcher Jim Deshaies and two players to be named later, September 15, 1985; Houston Astros' organization acquired Infielder Neder Horta, September 24, 1985, and Pitcher Dody Rather, January 11, 1986, to complete deal.
aGranted free agency, November 12, 1985; re-signed by Yankees, January 8, 1986.
bOn disabled list, June 29 to July 17, 1986.
cTraded with cash to Minnesota Twins for Catcher Mark Salas, June 7, 1987.
dGranted free agency, January 22, 1988; re-signed by Twins, February 9, 1988.
eReleased, May 4, 1988.

DIVISION SERIES RECORD

Year Club	League	G.	IP.	W.	L.	Pct.	H.	R.	ER.	SO.	BB.	ERA.
1981—Houston	National	1	8	0	0	.000	7	0	0	4	3	0.00

CHAMPIONSHIP SERIES RECORD

Established record for most years played in major leagues before playing in World Series (21).
Tied National League Championship Series record for most innings pitched, game (10), October 10, 1980.

Year Club	League	G.	IP.	W.	L.	Pct.	H.	R.	ER.	SO.	BB.	ERA.
1980—Houston	National	1	10	0	0	.000	6	0	0	2	1	0.00

Appeared as pinch-runner for Detroit Tigers in one game of 1972 Championship Series.

WORLD SERIES RECORD

Year	Club	League	G.	IP.	W.	L.	Pct.	H.	R.	ER.	SO.	BB.	ERA.
1987	—Minnesota	American	1	2	0	0	.000	1	0	0	1	1	0.00

ALL-STAR GAME RECORD

Member of National League All-Star Team for 1979 game; did not play.

JEFFREY SCOTT NIELSEN

(Known by middle name.)

Born December 18, 1958, at Salt Lake City, Utah.
Height, 6.01. Weight, 190.
Throws and bats righthanded.
Attended Brigham Young University, Provo, Utah.

Pitched 3-0 no-hit victory against Maine, June 8, 1988.
Major League saves: 1987 (2).
Tied for International League lead in shutouts with 3 in 1988.

Year	Club	League	G.	IP.	W.	L.	Pct.	H.	R.	ER.	SO.	BB.	ERA.
1983	—Bellingham	Northwest	2	13	2	0	1.000	11	4	3	13	2	2.08
1983	—Chattanooga†	Southern	13	63⅓	2	4	.333	81	49	45	24	27	6.39
1984	—Fort Lauderdale‡	Florida St.	4	16⅔	2	1	.667	16	8	2	7	5	1.08
1984	—Nashville	Southern	10	73⅔	6	3	.667	55	34	20	27	15	2.44
1984	—Columbus	Int'national	11	56⅔	5	4	.556	59	27	25	21	23	3.97
1985	—Albany§	Eastern	11	73⅓	6	1	.857	60	26	24	31	14	2.95
1986	—Fort Lauderdale	Florida St.	6	34⅓	4	0	1.000	32	12	8	10	9	2.10
1986	—Columbus	Int'national	19	116⅔	11	7	.611	123	52	45	44	38	3.47
1986	—New York x	American	10	56	4	4	.500	66	29	25	20	12	4.02
1987	—Hawaii	P. Coast	10	68	3	4	.429	74	36	30	21	30	3.97
1987	—Chicago y	American	19	66⅓	3	5	.375	83	48	46	23	25	6.24
1988	—Columbus	Int'national	25	172⅓	•13	6	.684	142	52	46	62	42	2.40
1988	—New York	American	7	19⅔	1	2	.333	27	16	15	4	13	6.86
Major League Totals—3 Years			36	142	8	11	.421	176	93	86	47	50	5.45

Selected by Seattle Mariners' organization in 6th round of free-agent draft, June 6, 1983.

†Traded with Pitcher Eric Parent to New York Yankees' organization for Infielder Larry Milbourne, February 14, 1984.

‡On disabled list, April 6 to April 23, 1984.

§On disabled list, May 30 to June 21 and June 27 to September 16, 1985.

xTraded with Infielder Mike Soper to Chicago White Sox for Pitcher Pete Filson and Infielder Randy Velarde, January 5, 1987.

yTraded with Pitcher Richard Dotson to New York Yankees for Outfielder Dan Pasqua, Catcher Mark Salas and Pitcher Steve Rosenberg, November 12, 1987.

THOMAS ANDREW NIETO

Name pronounced Nee-AY-toh.

(Tom)

Born October 27, 1960, at Downey, Calif.
Height, 6.01. Weight, 205.
Throws and bats righthanded.
Attended Cerritos College, Norwalk, Calif., and
Oral Roberts University, Tulsa, Okla.

Tied for American Association lead in being hit by pitch with 8 in 1983.

Year	Club	League	Pos.	G.	AB.	R.	H.	2B.	3B.	HR.	RBI.	B.A.	PO.	A.	E.	F.A.
1981	—Arkansas	Texas	C	62	184	12	33	2	0	2	19	.179	270	37	8	.975
1982	—Arkansas†	Texas	C	96	298	33	72	11	3	5	31	.242	466	58	3	*.994
1983	—Louisville	A. A.	C	115	383	44	104	17	1	5	52	.272	605	71	*15	.978
1984	—Louisville	A. A.	C	77	253	23	70	12	1	7	34	.277	446	43	8	.984
1984	—St. Louis	Nat.	C	33	86	7	24	4	0	3	12	.279	135	18	1	.994
1985	—St. Louis‡	Nat.	C	95	253	15	57	10	2	0	34	.225	384	28	4	.990
1986	—Montreal§	Nat.	C	30	65	5	13	3	1	1	7	.200	123	11	3	.978
1986	—Indianapolis x	A. A.	C	53	167	21	50	16	0	3	19	.299	295	25	9	.973
1987	—Minnesota y	Amer.	C	41	105	7	21	7	1	1	12	.200	210	17	1	.996
1987	—Portland	P. C.	C	38	110	10	25	5	0	0	3	.227	193	15	5	.977
1988	—Minnesota	Amer.	C	24	60	1	4	0	0	0	0	.067	108	6	1	.991
1988	—Portland z	P. C.	C	53	158	11	44	7	2	3	21	.278	276	25	6	.980
National League Totals—3 Years				158	404	27	94	17	3	4	53	.233	642	57	8	.989
American League Totals—2 Years				65	165	8	25	7	1	1	12	.152	318	23	2	.994
Major League Totals—5 Years				223	569	35	119	24	4	5	65	.209	960	80	10	.990

Selected by Minnesota Twins' organization in 31st round of free-agent draft, June 5, 1979.

Selected by Pittsburgh Pirates' organization in secondary phase of free-agent draft, January 8, 1980.

Selected by St. Louis Cardinals' organization in 3rd round of free-agent draft, June 8, 1981.

†On disabled list, June 19 to June 30, 1982.

‡Traded to Montreal Expos for Infielder Fred Manrique, March 31, 1986.

§On disabled list, August 21 to September 11, 1986; included rehabilitation disability assignment to Indianapolis, September 3 to September 10, 1986.

xTraded with Pitcher Jeff Reardon to Minnesota Twins for Pitchers Neal Heaton, Al Cardwood and Yorkis Perez and Catcher Jeff Reed, February 3, 1987.

yOn disabled list, May 18 to July 22, 1987; included rehabilitation disability assignment to Portland, July 12 to July 22, 1987.

zTraded with Second Baseman Tom Herr and Outfielder Eric Bullock to Philadelphia Phillies for Pitcher Shane Rawley and cash, October 24, 1988.

CHAMPIONSHIP SERIES RECORD

Year	Club	League	Pos.	G.	AB.	R.	H.	2B.	3B.	HR.	RBI.	B.A.	PO.	A.	E.	F.A.
1985	St. Louis	Nat.	C	1	3	1	0	0	0	0	0	.000	7	0	0	1.000

WORLD SERIES RECORD

Year	Club	League	Pos.	G.	AB.	R.	H.	2B.	3B.	HR.	RBI.	B.A.	PO.	A.	E.	F.A.
1985	St. Louis	Nat.	C	2	5	0	0	0	0	0	1	.000	23	1	0	1.000

JUAN MANUEL NIEVES

Born January 5, 1965, at Santurce, Puerto Rico.
Height, 6.03. Weight, 190.
Throws and bats lefthanded.

Pitched 7-0 no-hit victory against Baltimore Orioles, April 15, 1987.
Major League saves: 1988 (1).
Named Texas League Pitcher of the Year, 1985.
Received reported $150,000 bonus to sign with Milwaukee Brewers, 1983.

Year	Club	League	G.	IP.	W.	L.	Pct.	H.	R.	ER.	SO.	BB.	ERA.
1983	Beloit	Midwest	12	69⅓	7	1	.875	43	11	10	89	15	1.30
1984	Stockton	California	24	139⅔	10	3	.769	137	75	55	133	63	3.54
1985	El Paso	Texas	17	120	8	2	*.800	106	53	47	91	44	3.53
1985	Vancouver	P. Coast	12	68⅔	8	3	.727	56	30	29	54	44	3.80
1986	Milwaukee	American	35	184⅔	11	12	.478	224	124	101	116	77	4.92
1987	Milwaukee	American	34	195⅔	14	8	.636	199	112	106	163	100	4.88
1988	Milwaukee†	American	25	110⅓	7	5	.583	84	53	50	73	50	4.08
1988	Denver	Am. Assoc.	5	19⅔	0	2	.000	11	5	5	14	7	2.29
Major League Totals—3 Years			94	490⅔	32	25	.561	507	289	257	352	227	4.71

Signed as free agent by Milwaukee Brewers' organization, July 1, 1983.

†On disabled list, May 26 to July 28, 1988; included rehabilitation disability assignment to Denver, July 8 to July 27, 1988.

ALBERT SAMUEL NIPPER
(Al)

Born April 2, 1959, at San Diego, Calif.
Height, 6.00. Weight, 194.
Throws and bats righthanded.
Attended Northeast Missouri State University, Kirksville, Mo.

Major League saves: 1988 (1).
Led Florida State League in complete games with 15 in 1981.

Year	Club	League	G.	IP.	W.	L.	Pct.	H.	R.	ER.	SO.	BB.	ERA.
1980	Winter Haven	Florida St.	16	85	6	4	.600	82	29	24	48	49	2.54
1981	Winter Haven	Florida St.	29	*212	14	8	.636	191	59	40	139	60	*1.70
1982	Bristol†	Eastern	19	115	6	7	.462	108	50	47	66	45	3.68
1983	New Britain	Eastern	10	67	4	3	.571	46	26	21	42	25	2.82
1983	Pawtucket	Int'national	18	109⅓	9	4	.692	108	62	54	58	54	4.45
1983	Boston	American	3	16	1	1	.500	17	4	4	5	7	2.25
1984	Boston	American	29	182⅔	11	6	.647	183	86	79	84	52	3.89
1985	Boston‡	American	25	162	9	12	.429	157	83	73	85	82	4.06
1986	Boston§	American	26	159	10	12	.455	186	108	95	79	47	5.38
1987	Boston xy	American	30	174	11	12	.478	196	115	105	89	62	5.43
1988	Chicago z	National	22	80	2	4	.333	72	37	27	27	34	3.04
American League Totals—5 Years			113	693⅔	42	43	.494	739	396	356	342	250	4.62
National League Totals—1 Year			22	80	2	4	.333	72	37	27	27	34	3.04
Major League Totals—6 Years			135	773⅔	44	47	.484	811	433	383	369	284	4.46

Selected by Boston Red Sox' organization in 8th round of free-agent draft, June 3, 1980.

†On disabled list, June 26 to July 25, 1982.

‡On disabled list, March 25 to April 15, 1985; included rehabilitation disability assignment to Pawtucket, March 31 to April 15, 1985.

§On disabled list, May 19 to June 25, 1986.

xOn disabled list, July 20 to August 13, 1987.

yTraded with Pitcher Calvin Schiraldi to Chicago Cubs for Pitcher Lee Smith, December 8, 1987.

zOn disabled list, May 28 to June 23 and August 12 to September 2, 1988.

WORLD SERIES RECORD

Year	Club	League	G.	IP.	W.	L.	Pct.	H.	R.	ER.	SO.	BB.	ERA.
1986	Boston	American	2	6⅓	0	1	.000	10	5	5	2	2	7.11

—DID YOU KNOW—

That Tom Browning's September 16 perfect game was the first pitched in the National League since the Dodgers' Sandy Koufax hurled a 1-0 victory against the Cubs on September 9, 1965?

OTIS JUNIOR NIXON

Born January 9, 1959, at Evergreen, N.C.
Height, 6.02. Weight, 180.
Throws right and bats right and lefthanded.
Attended Louisburg College, Louisburg, N.C.
Brother of Donell Nixon, outfielder with San Francisco Giants.

Major League stolen bases: 1984 (12), 1985 (20), 1986 (23), 1987 (2), 1988 (46). Total—103.
Led International League in stolen bases with 94 and caught stealing with 29 in 1983.
Led Southern League in bases on balls received with 110 in 1981.
Led South Atlantic League in bases on balls received with 113 and stolen bases with 67 in 1980.
Led Appalachian League in bases on balls received with 57 in 1979.
Led International League outfielders in fielding percentage with .992, putouts with 363 and total chances with 371 in 1983.
Led Appalachian League third basemen in fielding percentage with .945, putouts with 52, assists with 120, and double plays with 12 in 1979.

Year	Club	League	Pos.	G.	AB.	R.	H.	2B.	3B.	HR.	RBI.	B.A.	PO.	A.	E.	F.A.
1979	—Paintsville	Appal.	3B-SS	63	203	58	58	10	3	1	25	.286	54	122	11	.941
1980	—Greensboro	S. Atl.	3B-SS	136	493	*124	137	12	5	3	48	.278	164	308	36	.929
1981	—Nashville	South.	SS	127	407	89	102	9	2	0	20	.251	198	348	*56	.907
1982	—Nashville	South.	SS-2B	72	283	47	80	3	2	0	20	.283	126	211	23	.936
1982	—Columbus	Int.	2B-SS	59	207	43	58	4	0	0	14	.280	104	169	14	.951
1983	—Columbus	Int.	OF-2B	138	*557	*129	*162	11	6	0	41	.291	385	24	4	.990
1983	—New York†	Amer.	OF	13	14	2	2	0	0	0	0	.143	14	1	1	.938
1984	—Cleveland	Amer.	OF	49	91	16	14	0	0	0	1	.154	81	3	0	1.000
1984	—Maine	Int.	OF	72	253	42	70	5	1	0	22	.277	206	7	1	.995
1985	—Cleveland	Amer.	OF	104	162	34	38	4	0	3	9	.235	129	5	4	.971
1986	—Cleveland	Amer.	OF	105	95	33	25	4	1	0	8	.263	90	3	3	.969
1987	—Cleveland	Amer.	OF	19	17	2	1	0	0	0	1	.059	21	0	0	1.000
1987	—Buffalo‡	A. A.	OF	59	249	51	71	13	4	2	23	.285	170	3	3	.983
1988	—Indianapolis	A. A.	OF	67	235	52	67	6	3	0	19	.285	130	1	1	.992
1988	—Montreal	Nat.	OF	90	271	47	66	8	2	0	15	.244	176	2	1	.994
	American League Totals—5 Years			290	379	87	80	8	1	3	19	.211	335	12	8	.977
	National League Totals—1 Year			90	271	47	66	8	2	0	15	.244	176	2	1	.994
	Major League Totals—6 Years			380	650	134	146	16	3	3	34	.225	511	14	9	.983

Selected by Cincinnati Reds' organization in 21st round of free-agent draft, June 6, 1978.
Selected by California Angels' organization in secondary phase of free-agent draft, January 9, 1979.
Selected by New York Yankees' organization in secondary phase of free-agent draft, June 5, 1979.
†Traded with Pitcher George Frazier and a player to be named later to Cleveland Indians for Third Baseman Toby Harrah and a player to be named later, February 5, 1984; New York organization acquired Pitcher Rick Browne and Cleveland organization acquired Pitcher Guy Elston to complete deal, February 8, 1984.
‡Granted free agency, October 15, 1987; signed by Indianapolis (Montreal Expos' organization), March 5, 1988.

ROBERT DONELL NIXON

(Known by middle name.)
Born December 31, 1961, at Evergreen, N. C.
Height, 6.01. Weight, 185.
Throws and bats righthanded.
Attended Louisburg College, Louisburg, N. C.
Brother of Otis Nixon, outfielder with Montreal Expos.

Tied major league record for most times caught stealing, inning (2), July 6, 1988 (sixth inning).
Major League stolen bases: 1987 (21), 1988 (11). Total—32.
Led Pacific Coast League in stolen bases with 46 in 1987.
Led Southern League in stolen bases with 102 in 1984.
Led California League in stolen bases with 144 and caught stealing with 24 in 1983.
Led Midwest League in stolen bases with 85 in 1982.

Year	Club	League	Pos.	G.	AB.	R.	H.	2B.	3B.	HR.	RBI.	B.A.	PO.	A.	E.	F.A.
1981	—Wausau†	Midw.	1B-2B-OF	59	204	35	58	7	2	5	26	.284	252	9	3	.989
1982	—Wausau	Midw.	*3B-1B	116	461	102	156	18	7	11	56	.338	*87	187	*49	.848
1982	—Lynn	Midw.	3B	6	24	5	7	2	1	0	1	.292	0	2	0	1.000
1983	—Bakersfield	Calif.	*3B-OF	135	542	*116	174	27	4	4	51	.321	98	249	*51	.872
1984	—Chattanooga	South.	OF-3B	140	536	99	144	25	5	4	57	.269	262	6	8	.971
1985	—Seattle‡	Amer.					(Did not play)									
1986	—Chattanooga§	South.	OF	4	18	2	6	1	0	0	0	.333	7	0	1	.875
1986	—Calgary	P. C.	OF	8	35	3	12	1	1	0	1	.343	15	2	0	1.000
1987	—Seattle	Amer.	OF	46	132	17	33	4	0	3	12	.250	76	1	0	1.000
1987	—Calgary	P. C.	OF-1B	82	328	72	106	18	1	5	52	.323	168	1	6	.966
1988	—Calgary x	P. C.	OF	40	160	28	45	7	0	3	10	.281	0	0	0	.000
1988	—San Francisco	Nat.	OF	59	78	15	27	3	0	0	6	.346	59	0	1	.983
	American League Totals—1 Year			46	132	17	33	4	0	3	12	.250	76	1	0	1.000
	National League Totals—1 Year			59	78	15	27	3	0	0	6	.346	59	0	1	.983
	Major League Totals—2 Years			105	210	32	60	7	0	3	18	.286	135	1	1	.993

Selected by Seattle Mariners' organization in 10th round of free-agent draft, June 3, 1980.
†On disabled list, July 7, 1981 through remainder of season.
‡On disabled list, April 8, 1985 through entire season.
§On Calgary disabled list, April 11 to August 1, 1986.
xTraded to San Francisco Giants, June 23, 1988, completing deal in which San Francisco traded Pitcher Rod Scurry to Seattle Mariners for a player to be named later, March 19, 1988.

MILCIADES ARTURO NOBOA JR.

Name pronounced Nah-BO-ah.

(Junior)

Born November 10, 1964, at Azua, D. R.
Height, 5.09. Weight, 160.
Throws and bats righthanded.

Major League stolen bases: 1984 (1), 1987 (1). Total—2.
Led Eastern League in sacrifice hits with 17 in 1984.
Led Midwest League in sacrifice hits with 18 in 1983.
Led Midwest League second basemen in putouts with 257 and double plays with 81 in 1983.

Year Club	League	Pos.	G.	AB.	R.	H.	2B.	3B.	HR.	RBI.	B.A.	PO.	A.	E.	F.A.
1981—Batavia	NYP	2B	50	162	15	49	8	0	0	6	.302	82	100	*18	.910
1982—Waterloo	Midw.	SS	121	385	69	96	12	5	0	23	.249	*207	306	46	.918
1983—Waterloo	Midw.	2B-SS	132	449	64	115	22	3	1	29	.256	260	355	24	.962
1984—Buffalo	East.	2B	117	383	55	97	18	4	1	45	.253	228	305	*18	.967
1984—Cleveland	Amer.	2B	23	11	3	4	0	0	0	0	.364	7	13	0	1.000
1985—Maine	Int.	2B	122	403	62	116	11	2	5	32	.288	270	379	14	.979
1986—Maine	Int.	2B-SS-3B	108	399	44	114	21	1	4	32	.286	160	252	13	.969
1987—Buffalo	A. A.	2B-SS-3B	43	149	26	47	6	2	0	14	.315	70	108	11	.942
1987—Cleveland†	Amer.	2B-SS-3B	39	80	7	18	2	1	0	7	.225	28	66	3	.969
1988—Edmonton	P. C.	2-S-O-3	50	159	24	47	6	1	0	17	.296	86	145	7	.971
1988—California‡	Amer.	2B-SS-3B	21	16	4	1	0	0	0	0	.063	8	24	1	.970
Major League Totals—3 Years			83	107	14	23	2	1	0	7	.215	43	103	4	.973

Signed as free agent by Cleveland Indians' organization, May 26, 1981.
†Traded to California Angels for Outfielder Ted Milner, March 30, 1988.
‡Granted free agency, October 15, 1988.

MATTHEW DODGE NOKES

(Matt)

Born October 31, 1963, at San Diego, Calif.
Height, 6.01. Weight, 185.
Throws right and bats lefthanded.

Major League stolen bases: 1987 (2).
Led Texas League catchers in double plays with 6 in 1985.
Led California League catchers in double plays with 9 in 1983.
Led Pioneer League in passed balls with 19 in 1981.
Tied for American Association lead in errors by catchers with 13 in 1986.
Named catcher on THE SPORTING NEWS American League All-Star Team, 1987.
Named catcher on THE SPORTING NEWS American League Silver Slugger team, 1987.

Year Club	League	Pos.	G.	AB.	R.	H.	2B.	3B.	HR.	RBI.	B.A.	PO.	A.	E.	F.A.
1981—Great Falls	Pion.	C	44	146	14	33	6	2	0	13	.226	288	35	*13	.961
1982—Clinton	Midw.	C	82	247	19	53	12	0	3	23	.215	363	41	13	.969
1983—Fresno	Calif.	C	125	429	62	138	26	6	14	82	.322	595	62	16	.976
1984—Shreveport	Texas	C	97	308	32	89	19	2	11	61	.289	400	31	8	.982
1985—Shreveport	Texas	C	105	344	52	101	24	1	14	56	.294	520	40	12	.979
1985—San Francisco†	Nat.	C	19	53	3	11	2	0	2	5	.208	84	2	2	.977
1986—Nashville	A. A.	C-1B-OF	125	428	55	122	25	4	10	71	.285	502	50	18	.968
1986—Detroit	Amer.	C	7	24	2	8	1	0	1	2	.333	43	2	0	1.000
1987—Detroit	Amer.	C-OF-3B	135	461	69	133	14	2	32	87	.289	600	32	5	.992
1988—Detroit	Amer.	C	122	382	53	96	18	0	16	53	.251	574	45	7	.989
National League Totals—1 Year			19	53	3	11	2	0	2	5	.208	84	2	2	.977
American League Totals—3 Years			264	867	124	237	33	2	49	142	.273	1217	79	12	.991
Major League Totals—4 Years			283	920	127	248	35	2	51	147	.270	1301	81	14	.990

Selected by San Francisco Giants' organization in 20th round of free-agent draft, June 8, 1981.
†Traded with Pitchers Dave LaPoint and Eric King to Detroit Tigers for Pitcher Juan Berenguer, Catcher Bob Melvin and a player to be named later, October 7, 1985; San Francisco Giants acquired Pitcher Scott Medvin to complete deal, December 11, 1985.

CHAMPIONSHIP SERIES RECORD

Year Club	League	Pos.	G.	AB.	R.	H.	2B.	3B.	HR.	RBI.	B.A.	PO.	A.	E.	F.A.
1987—Detroit	Amer.	PH-DH-C	5	14	2	2	0	0	1	2	.143	11	2	0	1.000

ALL-STAR GAME RECORD

Year League	Pos.	AB.	R.	H.	2B.	3B.	HR.	RBI.	B.A.	PO.	A.	E.	F.A.
1987—American	C	2	0	0	0	0	0	0	.000	8	0	0	1.000

DICKIE RAY NOLES

Born November 19, 1956, at Charlotte, N. C.
Height, 6.02. Weight, 190.
Throws and bats righthanded.

Major League saves: 1980 (6), 1985 (1), 1987 (4). Total—11.
Led Eastern League in hit batsmen with 15 in 1978.
Led Carolina League in games started by pitchers with 27 in 1977.
Led Western Carolinas League in hit batsmen with 13 in 1976.
Tied for Carolina League lead in hit batsmen with 11 in 1977.
Tied for Western Carolinas League lead in home runs allowed with 13 in 1976.

Year Club	League	G.	IP.	W.	L.	Pct.	H.	R.	ER.	SO.	BB.	ERA.
1975—Auburn	NYP	9	50	2	2	.500	49	30	20	31	27	3.60
1976—Spartanburg	W. Carol.	24	137	4	★16	.200	166	★110	★90	95	65	5.91
1977—Peninsula	Carolina	27	★199	10	11	.476	188	103	81	114	78	3.66
1978—Reading	Eastern	27	159	12	8	.600	177	100	75	78	72	4.25
1979—Oklahoma City†	Am. Assoc.	12	76	6	4	.600	69	38	33	48	28	3.91
1979—Philadelphia	National	14	90	3	4	.429	80	40	38	42	38	3.80
1979—Reading	Eastern	1	9	0	1	.000	7	5	4	2	4	4.00
1980—Philadelphia	National	48	81	1	4	.200	80	42	35	57	42	3.89
1981—Oklahoma City‡	Am. Assoc.	22	104	6	6	.500	85	45	38	82	46	3.29
1981—Philadelphia§	National	13	58	2	2	.500	57	30	27	34	23	4.19
1982—Chicago x	National	31	171	10	13	.435	180	99	84	85	61	4.42
1983—Chicago y	National	24	116⅓	5	10	.333	133	69	61	59	37	4.72
1983—Quad Cities	Midwest	3	12	0	1	.000	19	11	7	12	5	5.25
1984—Chicago z	National	21	50⅔	2	2	.500	60	29	29	14	16	5.15
1984—Texas	American	18	57⅔	2	3	.400	60	38	33	39	30	5.15
1985—Texas ab	American	28	110⅓	4	8	.333	129	67	62	59	33	5.06
1986—Cleveland c	American	32	54⅔	3	2	.600	56	33	31	32	30	5.10
1986—Maine d	Int'national	3	10	0	1	.000	11	6	5	4	4	4.50
1987—Chicago e	National	41	64⅓	4	2	.667	59	31	25	33	27	3.50
1987—Pittsfield f	Eastern	1	3	0	1	.000	4	2	2	5	1	6.00
1987—Iowa	Am. Assoc.	3	5	0	1	.000	8	6	6	3	3	10.80
1987—Detroit g	American	4	2	0	0	.000	2	1	1	0	1	4.50
1988—Rochester	Int'national	31	130	10	5	.667	124	57	45	59	31	3.12
1988—Baltimore	American	2	3⅓	0	2	.000	11	10	9	1	0	24.30
National League Totals—7 Years		192	631⅓	27	37	.422	649	340	299	324	244	4.26
American League Totals—5 Years		84	228	9	15	.375	258	149	136	131	94	5.37
Major League Totals—10 Years		276	859⅓	36	52	.409	907	489	435	455	338	4.56

Selected by Philadelphia Phillies' organization in 4th round of free-agent draft, June 4, 1975.

†On disabled list, April 13 to April 24, 1979.

‡Appeared as outfielder with no chances.

§Traded with Catcher Keith Moreland and Pitcher Dan Larson to Chicago Cubs for Pitcher Mike Krukow and cash, December 8, 1981.

xOn disabled list, June 13 to July 4, 1982.

yOn disabled list, April 12 to June 4, 1983; included rehabilitation disability assignment to Quad Cities, May 21 to June 4, 1983.

zTraded to Texas Rangers for two players to be named later, July 2, 1984; Chicago Cubs' organization acquired Pitcher Tim Henry and Infielder Jorge Gomez to complete deal, December 11, 1984.

aOn disabled list, June 24 to July 14, 1985.

bReleased, December 20, 1985; signed by Maine (Cleveland Indians' organization), February 8, 1986.

cOn disabled list, April 18 to June 18, 1986; included rehabilitation disability assignment to Maine, June 7 to June 18 1986.

dGranted free agency, November 12, 1986; signed by Chicago Cubs, April 6, 1987.

eOn disabled list, July 2 to August 21, 1987; included rehabilitation disability assignment to Pittsfield, August 10, and Iowa, August 14 to August 21, 1987.

fTraded to Detroit Tigers for a player to be named later, September 22, 1987; returned, October 23, 1987.

gGranted free agency, November 9, 1987; signed by Rochester (Baltimore Orioles' organization), April 2, 1988.

DIVISION SERIES RECORD

Year Club	League	G.	IP.	W.	L.	Pct.	H.	R.	ER.	SO.	BB.	ERA.
1981—Philadelphia	National	1	4	0	0	.000	4	2	2	5	2	4.50

CHAMPIONSHIP SERIES RECORD

Year Club	League	G.	IP.	W.	L.	Pct.	H.	R.	ER.	SO.	BB.	ERA.
1980—Philadelphia	National	2	2⅔	0	0	.000	1	0	0	0	3	0.00

WORLD SERIES RECORD

Year Club	League	G.	IP.	W.	L.	Pct.	H.	R.	ER.	SO.	BB.	ERA.
1980—Philadelphia	National	1	4⅔	0	0	.000	5	1	1	6	2	1.93

ERIC CARL NOLTE

Born April 28, 1964, at Canoga Park, Calif.
Height, 6.03. Weight, 200.
Throws and bats lefthanded.
Attended University of California, Los Angeles, Calif.

Tied for Northwest League lead in balks with 2 in 1985.

Year Club	League	G.	IP.	W.	L.	Pct.	H.	R.	ER.	SO.	BB.	ERA.
1985—Spokane	Northwest	14	76⅔	3	●8	.273	79	50	34	52	46	3.99
1986—Charleston	S. Atlantic	26	164	12	9	.571	154	80	71	121	68	3.90
1987—Reno	California	11	64	3	4	.429	76	38	31	47	24	4.36
1987—Wichita	Texas	10	75	4	2	.667	62	28	24	67	19	2.88
1987—San Diego	National	12	67⅓	2	6	.250	57	28	24	44	36	3.21
1988—San Diego	National	2	3	0	0	.000	3	2	2	1	2	6.00
1988—Las Vegas	P. Coast	27	128⅓	8	7	.533	168	97	86	68	53	6.03
Major League Totals—2 Years		14	70⅓	2	6	.250	60	30	26	45	38	3.33

Selected by Chicago Cubs' organization in 7th round of free-agent draft, June 7, 1982.

Selected by San Diego Padres' organization in 6th round of free-agent draft, June 3, 1985.

RANDALL WILLIAM NOSEK

(Randy)

Born January 8, 1967, at Omaha, Neb.
Height, 6.04. Weight, 215.
Throws and bats righthanded.

Year Club	League	G.	IP.	W.	L.	Pct.	H.	R.	ER.	SO.	BB.	ERA.
1986—Gastonia	S. Atlantic	12	52⅓	4	5	.444	56	41	35	37	49	6.02
1986—Bristol	Ap'lachian	11	63⅓	6	4	.600	58	38	32	48	45	4.55
1987—Fayetteville	S. Atlantic	16	77⅔	4	11	.267	69	63	40	57	63	4.64
1988—Lakeland	Florida St.	8	30⅔	0	4	.000	29	17	13	11	16	3.82

Selected by Detroit Tigers' organization in 1st round (26th player selected) of free-agent draft, June 3, 1985.

EDWIN NUNEZ (MARTINEZ)

Name pronounced NOON-yez.

Born May 27, 1963, at Humacao, Puerto Rico.
Height, 6.05. Weight, 240.
Throws and bats righthanded.

Major League saves: 1984 (7), 1985 (16), 1987 (12). Total—35.
Led Midwest League in complete games with 13 in 1981.

Year Club	League	G.	IP.	W.	L.	Pct.	H.	R.	ER.	SO.	BB.	ERA.
1979—Bellingham	Northwest	6	39	4	1	.800	39	14	9	30	5	2.08
1980—Wausau	Midwest	22	138	9	7	.563	145	71	57	91	58	3.72
1981—Wausau	Midwest	25	*186	*16	3	.842	143	61	51	*205	58	2.47
1982—Seattle†	American	8	35⅓	1	2	.333	36	18	18	27	16	4.58
1982—Salt Lake City‡	P. Coast	11	55⅓	4	3	.571	40	26	21	42	23	3.42
1983—Seattle	American	14	37	0	4	.000	40	21	18	35	22	4.38
1983—Salt Lake City§	P. Coast	14	77⅓	4	4	.500	99	70	61	52	36	7.10
1984—Salt Lake City x	P. Coast	18	27⅔	3	2	.600	24	12	11	26	12	3.58
1984—Seattle	American	37	67⅔	2	2	.500	55	26	24	57	21	3.19
1985—Seattle	American	70	90⅓	7	3	.700	79	36	31	58	34	3.09
1986—Seattle y	American	14	21⅔	1	2	.333	25	15	14	17	5	5.82
1986—Calgary	P. Coast	6	14	1	2	.333	19	13	11	17	4	7.07
1987—Seattle z	American	48	47⅓	3	4	.429	45	20	20	34	18	3.80
1988—Seattle	American	14	29⅓	1	4	.200	45	33	26	19	14	7.98
1988—Calgary a	P. Coast	3	15⅓	2	0	1.000	15	9	8	12	4	4.70
1988—New York	National	10	14	1	0	1.000	21	7	7	8	3	4.50
American League Totals—7 Years		205	328⅔	15	21	.417	325	169	151	247	130	4.13
National League Totals—1 Year		10	14	1	0	1.000	21	7	7	8	3	4.50
Major League Totals—7 Years		215	342⅔	16	21	.432	346	176	158	255	133	4.15

Signed as free agent by Seattle Mariners' organization, March 17, 1979.
†On disabled list, April 23 to May 15, 1982.
‡On disabled list, June 4 to June 29, 1982.
§On disabled list, June 30 to July 14, 1983.
xOn disabled list, May 12 to June 3, 1984.
yOn disabled list, April 5 to April 29 and May 1 to May 16, 1986.
zOn disabled list, May 20 to June 4, 1987.
aTraded to New York Mets for Pitcher Gene Walter, July 11, 1988.

JOSE NUNEZ

Born January 13, 1964, at Jarabocoa, D. R.
Height, 6.03. Weight, 185.
Throws and bats righthanded.

Year Club	League	G.	IP.	W.	L.	Pct.	H.	R.	ER.	SO.	BB.	ERA.
1984—Charleston	S. Atlantic	25	170	14	8	.636	*167	91	62	106	54	3.28
1985—Fort Myers†	Florida St.	11	44⅓	3	2	.600	32	14	12	23	12	2.44
1986—Memphis	Southern	13	48⅔	2	6	.250	52	43	29	36	51	5.36
1986—Fort Myers‡	Florida St.	14	87⅓	8	2	.800	73	31	24	59	32	2.47
1987—Toronto	American	37	97	5	2	.714	91	57	54	99	58	5.01
1988—Syracuse	Int'national	12	71⅓	5	4	.556	62	26	23	67	16	2.90
1988—Toronto§	American	13	29⅓	0	1	.000	28	11	10	18	17	3.07
Major League Totals—2 Years		50	126⅓	5	3	.625	119	68	64	117	75	4.56

Signed as free agent by Kansas City Royals' organization, November 11, 1983.
†On disabled list, May 30 to June 19 and July 1 to August 24, 1985.
‡Drafted by Toronto Blue Jays, December 8, 1986.
§On disabled list, June 3 to June 18, 1988.

KENNETH RAY OBERKFELL

Name pronounced OH-burk-fell.

(Ken)

Born May 4, 1956, at Maryville, Ill.
Height, 6.01. Weight, 210.
Throws right and bats lefthanded.
Attended Belleville Area Junior College, Belleville, Ill.

Major League stolen bases: 1979 (4), 1980 (4), 1981 (13), 1982 (11), 1983 (12), 1984 (2), 1985 (1), 1986 (7), 1987 (3), 1988 (4). Total—61.

Led National League third basemen in double plays with 23 and tied for lead in total chances with 338 in 1981.

Led National League second basemen in fielding percentage with .985 in 1979.

Year Club	League	Pos.	G.	AB.	R.	H.	2B.	3B.	HR.	RBI.	B.A.	PO.	A.	E.	F.A.
1975—Johnson City	Appal.	SS	17	54	15	19	3	0	1	8	.352	21	58	4	.952
1975—St. Petersburg	Fla. St.	SS	41	134	14	47	6	1	0	22	.351	71	107	6	.967
1976—Arkansas	Texas	2B-SS	128	456	64	131	19	2	3	47	.287	259	321	18	.970
1977—New Orleans	A. A.	2B-SS	120	418	67	105	18	5	4	32	.251	205	325	17	.969
1977—St. Louis	Nat.	2B	9	9	0	1	0	0	0	1	.111	3	4	0	1.000
1978—Springfield	A. A.	3B-2B-SS	64	242	41	69	13	4	6	38	.285	77	113	6	.969
1978—St. Louis	Nat.	2B-3B	24	50	7	6	1	0	0	0	.120	30	48	1	.987
1979—St. Louis	Nat.	2B-3B-SS	135	369	53	111	19	5	1	35	.301	223	343	9	.984
1980—St. Louis†	Nat.	2B-3B	116	422	58	128	27	6	3	46	.303	227	340	7	.988
1981—St. Louis	Nat.	3B-SS	102	376	43	110	12	6	2	45	.293	77	247	15	.956
1982—St. Louis‡	Nat.	*3B-2B	137	470	55	136	22	5	2	34	.289	80	305	11	*.972
1983—St. Louis	Nat.	*3B-2B-SS	151	488	62	143	26	5	3	38	.293	132	303	18	*.960
1984—St. L.§-Atl.x	Nat.	3B-2B-SS	100	324	38	87	19	2	1	21	.269	64	173	8	.967
1985—Atlanta	Nat.	3B-2B	134	412	30	112	19	4	3	35	.272	88	257	12	.966
1986—Atlanta	Nat.	3B-2B	151	503	62	136	24	3	5	48	.270	116	335	11	.976
1987—Atlanta y	Nat.	3B-2B	135	508	59	142	29	2	3	48	.280	89	265	7	.981
1988—Atl. z-Pit.	Nat.	3-2-S-1	140	476	49	129	22	4	3	42	.271	107	237	15	.958
Major League Totals—12 Years			1334	4407	516	1241	220	42	26	393	.282	1236	2857	114	.973

Signed as free agent by St. Louis Cardinals' organization, May 4, 1975.

†On disabled list, May 11 to June 20, 1980.

‡On disabled list, March 31 to April 23, 1982.

§Traded to Atlanta Braves for Pitcher Ken Dayley and First Baseman Mike Jorgensen, June 15, 1984.

xOn disabled list, August 27, 1984 through remainder of season.

yOn disabled list, June 26 to July 11, 1987.

zTraded with cash to Pittsburgh Pirates for a player to be named later, August 28, 1988; Atlanta Braves acquired Outfielder Tommy Gregg to complete deal, September 1, 1988.

CHAMPIONSHIP SERIES RECORD

Tied Championship Series record for most at-bats, three-game Series (15).

Year Club	League	Pos.	G.	AB.	R.	H.	2B.	3B.	HR.	RBI.	B.A.	PO.	A.	E.	F.A.
1982—St. Louis	Nat.	3B	3	15	1	3	0	0	0	2	.200	2	4	1	.857

WORLD SERIES RECORD

Year Club	League	Pos.	G.	AB.	R.	H.	2B.	3B.	HR.	RBI.	B.A.	PO.	A.	E.	F.A.
1982—St. Louis	Nat.	3B	7	24	4	7	1	0	0	1	.292	3	21	1	.960

CHARLES HUGH O'BRIEN
(Charlie)

Born May 1, 1961, at Tulsa, Okla.
Height, 6.02. Weight, 190.
Throws and bats righthanded.
Attended McClennan Community College, Waco, Tex., and Wichita State University, Wichita, Kan.

Year Club	League	Pos.	G.	AB.	R.	H.	2B.	3B.	HR.	RBI.	B.A.	PO.	A.	E.	F.A.
1982—Medford	N'west	C	17	60	11	17	3	0	3	14	.283	116	18	4	.971
1982—Modesto	Calif.	C	41	140	23	42	6	0	3	32	.300	239	44	5	.983
1983—Albany†	East.	C-1B	92	285	50	83	12	1	14	56	.291	478	82	11	.981
1984—Modesto‡	Calif.	C	9	32	8	9	2	0	1	5	.281	41	8	0	1.000
1984—Tacoma	P. C.	C-OF	69	195	33	44	11	0	9	22	.226	260	39	0	1.000
1985—Huntsville	South.	C	33	115	20	24	5	0	7	16	.209	182	29	5	.977
1985—Oakland	Amer.	C	16	11	3	3	1	0	0	1	.273	23	0	1	.958
1985—Modesto	Calif.	C	9	27	5	8	4	1	1	2	.296	33	8	1	.976
1985—Tacoma§	P. C.	C	18	57	5	9	4	0	0	7	.158	110	9	3	.975
1986—Vancouver	P. C.	C	6	17	1	2	0	0	0	1	.118	22	3	2	.926
1986—El Paso	Texas	C-OF-1B	92	336	72	109	20	3	15	75	.324	437	43	4	.992
1987—Denver	A. A.	C	80	266	37	75	12	1	8	35	.282	415	53	6	.987
1987—Milwaukee	Amer.	C	10	35	2	7	3	1	0	0	.200	78	11	0	1.000
1988—Denver	A. A.	C	48	153	16	43	5	0	4	25	.281	243	44	3	.990
1988—Milwaukee	Amer.	C	40	118	12	26	6	0	2	9	.220	210	20	2	.991
Major League Totals—3 Years			66	164	17	36	10	1	2	10	.220	311	31	3	.991

Selected by Texas Rangers' organization in 14th round of free-agent draft, June 6, 1978.

Selected by Seattle Mariners' organization in 21st round of free-agent draft, June 8, 1981.

Selected by Oakland A's organization in 5th round of free-agent draft, June 7, 1982.

†On disabled list, July 31, 1983 through remainder of season.

‡On Albany disabled list, April 13 to May 15, 1984.

§Traded with Infielder Steve Kiefer and Pitchers Mike Fulmer and Pete Kendrick to Milwaukee Brewers for Pitcher Moose Haas, March 30, 1986.

—DID YOU KNOW—

That Minnesota outfielder Kirby Puckett's .356 average in 1988 was the highest for a righthanded batter in the American League since Joe DiMaggio hit .357 for the Yankees in 1941?

PETER MICHAEL O'BRIEN
(Pete)

Born February 9, 1958, at Santa Monica, Calif.
Height, 6.02. Weight, 205.
Throws and bats lefthanded.
Attended Monterrey Peninsula College, Monterrey, Calif.; and
University of Nebraska, Lincoln, Neb.

Tied major league record for most double plays started by first baseman, nine-inning game (3), May 22, 1984.
Major League stolen bases: 1982 (1), 1983 (5), 1984 (3), 1985 (5), 1986 (4), 1988 (1). Total—19.
Led American League first basemen in assists with 120 in 1983.

Year Club	League	Pos.	G.	AB.	R.	H.	2B.	3B.	HR.	RBI.	B.A.	PO.	A.	E.	F.A.
1979—Sarasota Rangers	Gulf C.	1B	50	189	39	46	10	2	0	31	.243	★465	★44	7	.986
1980—Asheville	S. Atl.	1B	134	505	98	149	34	2	17	94	.295	★1227	★96	14	.990
1981—Tulsa	Texas	1B	110	382	57	109	19	3	17	78	.285	973	95	11	.990
1982—Denver	A. A.	OF-1B	128	477	92	148	21	1	25	102	.310	418	37	8	.983
1982—Texas	Amer.	OF-1B	20	67	13	16	4	1	4	13	.239	39	3	0	1.000
1983—Texas	Amer.	1B-OF	154	524	53	124	24	5	8	53	.237	1191	121	11	.992
1984—Texas	Amer.	1B-OF	142	520	57	149	26	2	18	80	.287	1271	105	11	.992
1985—Texas	Amer.	1B	159	573	69	153	34	3	22	92	.267	1457	98	8	.995
1986—Texas	Amer.	1B	156	551	86	160	23	3	23	90	.290	1224	115	11	.992
1987—Texas	Amer.	★1B-OF	159	569	84	163	26	1	23	88	.286	1233	★146	11	.992
1988—Texas†	Amer.	1B	156	547	57	149	24	1	16	71	.272	1346	140	8	.995
Major League Totals—7 Years			946	3351	419	914	161	16	114	487	.273	7761	728	60	.993

Selected by Texas Rangers' organization in 15th round of free-agent draft, June 5, 1979.
†Traded with Outfielder Oddibe McDowell and Second Baseman Jerry Browne to Cleveland Indians for Second Baseman Julio Franco, December 6, 1988.

RONALD JOHN OESTER

Name pronounced O-ster.

(Ron)

Born May 5, 1956, at Cincinnati, O.
Height, 6.02. Weight, 190.
Throws right and bats left and righthanded.

Major League stolen bases: 1980 (6), 1981 (2), 1982 (5), 1983 (2), 1984 (7), 1985 (5), 1986 (9), 1987 (2). Total—38.
Led National League second basemen in total chances with 861 in 1986.
Led American Association shortstops in double plays with 102 in 1978.
Led Eastern League shortstops in double plays with 84 in 1976.
Led Pioneer League shortstops in double plays with 27 in 1974.

Year Club	League	Pos.	G.	AB.	R.	H.	2B.	3B.	HR.	RBI.	B.A.	PO.	A.	E.	F.A.
1974—Billings	Pion.	SS	53	167	23	52	11	1	0	21	.311	87	141	27	.894
1975—Tampa	Fla. St.	SS	117	375	40	82	3	4	0	25	.219	174	358	34	.940
1976—Three Rivers	East.	SS	138	447	57	110	14	4	0	44	.246	★233	★408	38	.944
1977—Indianapolis	A. A.	SS	134	455	60	116	16	5	3	33	.255	203	★386	39	.938
1978—Indianapolis	A. A.	SS	●135	514	78	133	21	4	7	49	259	★300	★428	32	.958
1978—Cincinnati	Nat.	SS	6	8	1	3	0	0	0	1	.375	3	9	0	1.000
1979—Indianapolis	A. A.	SS	●136	509	62	143	19	6	2	33	.281	★244	397	31	.954
1979—Cincinnati	Nat.	SS	6	3	0	0	0	0	0	0	.000	1	2	0	1.000
1980—Cincinnati	Nat.	2B-SS-3B	100	303	40	84	16	2	2	20	.277	161	224	10	.975
1981—Cincinnati	Nat.	2B-SS	105	354	45	96	16	7	5	42	.271	213	341	11	.981
1982—Cincinnati	Nat.	2B-SS-3B	151	549	63	143	19	4	9	47	.260	304	403	22	.970
1983—Cincinnati	Nat.	2B	157	549	63	145	23	5	11	58	.264	315	413	17	.977
1984—Cincinnati	Nat.	2B-SS	150	553	54	134	26	3	3	38	.242	357	388	15	.980
1985—Cincinnati	Nat.	2B	152	526	59	155	26	3	1	34	.295	366	457	9	.989
1986—Cincinnati	Nat.	2B	153	523	52	135	23	2	8	44	.258	●367	475	19	.978
1987—Cincinnati†‡	Nat.	2B	69	237	28	60	9	6	2	23	.253	183	186	10	.974
1988—Nashville	A. A.	2B	12	37	4	7	1	0	0	3	.189	15	28	4	.915
1988—Chattanooga	South.	2B	14	46	5	14	2	0	1	6	.304	19	25	1	.978
1988—Cincinnati§	Nat.	2B-SS	54	150	20	42	7	0	0	10	.280	110	113	1	.996
Major League Totals—11 Years			1103	3755	425	997	165	32	41	317	.266	2380	3011	114	.979

Selected by Cincinnati Reds' organization in 9th round of free-agent draft, June 5, 1974.
†On disabled list, July 6, 1987 through remainder of season.
‡Released, October 21, 1987; re-signed by Reds' organization, January 29, 1988.
§Granted free agency, November 4, 1988; re-signed by Reds, December 2, 1988.

ROBERT MICHAEL OJEDA

Name pronounced Oh-HEED-a.

(Bob)

Born December 17, 1957, at Los Angeles, Calif.
Height, 6.01. Weight, 195.
Throws and bats lefthanded.
Attended College of the Sequoias, Visalia, Calif.

Major League saves: 1985 (1).
Tied for American League lead in shutouts with 5 in 1984.
Tied for International League lead in balks with 3 in 1980.

Tied for Florida State League lead in games started by pitchers with 29 in 1979.
Named International League Pitcher of the Year, 1981.

Year Club	League	G.	IP.	W.	L.	Pct.	H.	R.	ER.	SO.	BB.	ERA.
1978—Elmira	NYP	18	43	1	6	.143	45	32	23	35	43	4.81
1979—Winter Haven	Florida St.	29	200	15	7	.682	163	66	54	150	84	2.43
1980—Pawtucket	Int'national	19	123	6	7	.462	107	54	44	78	56	3.22
1980—Boston	American	7	26	1	1	.500	39	20	20	12	14	6.92
1981—Pawtucket	Int'national	25	173	12	9	.571	136	52	41	113	73	*2.13
1981—Boston	American	10	66	6	2	.750	50	25	23	28	25	3.14
1982—Boston†	American	22	78⅓	4	6	.400	95	53	49	52	29	5.63
1983—Boston	American	29	173⅔	12	7	.632	173	85	78	94	73	4.04
1984—Boston‡	American	33	216⅔	12	12	.500	211	106	96	137	96	3.99
1985—Boston§	American	39	157⅔	9	11	.450	166	74	70	102	48	4.00
1986—New York	National	32	217⅓	18	5	*.783	185	72	62	148	52	2.57
1987—New York x	National	10	46⅓	3	5	.375	45	23	20	21	10	3.88
1988—New York	National	29	190⅓	10	13	.435	158	74	61	133	33	2.88
American League Totals—6 Years		140	718⅓	44	39	.530	734	363	336	425	285	4.21
National League Totals—3 Years		71	454	31	23	.574	388	169	143	302	95	2.83
Major League Totals—9 Years		211	1172⅓	75	62	.547	1122	532	479	727	380	3.68

Signed as free agent by Boston Red Sox' organization, May 20, 1978.
†On disabled list, August 20 to September 10, 1982.
‡On disabled list, August 16 to September 1, 1984.
§Traded with Pitchers Tom McCarthy, John Mitchell and Chris Bayer to New York Mets for Pitchers Calvin Schiraldi and Wes Gardner and Outfielders John Christensen and LaSchelle Tarver, November 13, 1985.
xOn disabled list, May 11 to September 1, 1987.

CHAMPIONSHIP SERIES RECORD

Tied National League Championship Series record for most hits allowed, game (10), October 9, 1986.

Year Club	League	G.	IP.	W.	L.	Pct.	H.	R.	ER.	SO.	BB.	ERA.
1986—New York	National	2	14	1	0	1.000	15	4	4	6	4	2.57

WORLD SERIES RECORD

Year Club	League	G.	IP.	W.	L.	Pct.	H.	R.	ER.	SO.	BB.	ERA.
1986—New York	National	2	13	1	0	1.000	13	3	3	9	5	2.08

JOSEPH MELTON OLIVER
(Joe)

Born July 24, 1965, at Memphis, Tenn.
Height, 6.03. Weight, 215.
Throws and bats righthanded.

Led Florida State League catchers in assists with 84 and passed balls with 33 in 1985.
Led Midwest League catchers in passed balls with 30 and total chances with 855 in 1984.
Led Pioneer League catchers in putouts with 425, assists with 38 and total chances with 468 in 1983.

Year Club	League	Pos.	G.	AB.	R.	H.	2B.	3B.	HR.	RBI.	B.A.	PO.	A.	E.	F.A.
1983—Billings	Pion.	*C-1B	56	186	21	40	4	0	4	28	.215	426	39	5	*.989
1984—Cedar Rapids	Midw.	C	102	335	34	73	11	0	3	29	.218	*757	85	13	.985
1985—Tampa	Fla. St.	C-1B	112	386	38	104	23	2	7	62	.269	615	94	16	.978
1986—Vermont†	East.	C	84	282	32	78	18	1	6	41	.277	383	62	14	.969
1987—Vermont	East.	C-1B	66	236	31	72	13	2	10	60	.305	247	35	10	.966
1988—Nashville	A. A.	C	73	220	19	45	7	2	4	24	.205	413	37	7	.985
1988—Chattanooga	South.	C	28	105	9	26	6	0	3	12	.248	176	15	0	1.000

Selected by Cincinnati Reds' organization in 2nd round of free-agent draft, June 6, 1983.
†On disabled list, April 23 to May 6, 1986.

GREGG WILLIAM OLSON

Born October 11, 1966, at Omaha, Neb.
Height, 6.04. Weight, 211.
Throws and bats righthanded.
Attended Auburn University, Auburn, Ala.

Received reported $200,000 bonus to sign with Baltimore Orioles, 1988.
Named righthanded pitcher on The Sporting News College Baseball All-America Team, 1988.

Year Club	League	G.	IP.	W.	L.	Pct.	H.	R.	ER.	SO.	BB.	ERA.
1988—Hagerstown	Carolina	8	9	1	0	1.000	5	2	2	9	2	2.00
1988—Charlotte	Southern	8	15⅓	0	1	.000	24	13	10	22	6	5.87
1988—Baltimore	American	10	11	1	1	.500	10	4	4	9	10	3.27
Major League Totals—1 Year		10	11	1	1	.500	10	4	4	9	10	3.27

Selected by Baltimore Orioles' organization in 1st round (fourth player selected) of free-agent draft, June 1, 1988.

EDWARD R. OLWINE
(Ed)

Born May 28, 1958, at Greenville, O.
Height, 6.02. Weight, 170.
Throws left and bats righthanded.
Attended Morehead State University, Morehead, Ky.

Major League saves: 1986 (1), 1987 (1), 1988 (1). Total—3.
Led South Atlantic League in saves with 19 in 1981.

Year Club	League	G.	IP.	W.	L.	Pct.	H.	R.	ER.	SO.	BB.	ERA.
1980—Oneonta	NYP	6	9	2	1	.667	8	4	1	8	6	1.00
1980—Paintsville	Ap'lachian	13	35	5	2	.714	32	11	10	47	11	2.57
1980—Fort Lauderdale	Florida St.	2	1	0	0	.000	5	4	1	0	0	9.00
1981—Greensboro	S. Atlantic	51	75	8	5	.615	67	35	25	73	25	3.00
1982—Fort Lauderdale	Florida St.	39	67⅔	5	4	.556	70	32	25	48	21	3.33
1983—Nashville	Southern	29	82⅔	2	4	.333	90	53	40	66	38	4.35
1983—Columbus†	Int'national	8	10⅓	2	0	1.000	21	11	11	11	6	9.58
1984—Tidewater‡	Int'national	50	68	4	2	.667	47	26	18	50	25	2.38
1985—Tidewater§	Int'national	55	66	4	7	.364	60	23	21	50	26	2.86
1986—Richmond	Int'national	20	24⅔	2	0	1.000	18	2	2	15	9	0.73
1986—Atlanta	National	37	47⅔	0	0	.000	35	20	18	37	17	3.40
1987—Atlanta	National	27	23⅓	0	1	.000	25	16	13	12	8	5.01
1987—Richmond	Int'national	22	33	3	0	1.000	34	8	7	19	7	1.91
1988—Greenville x	Southern	9	14⅓	1	2	.333	17	15	13	6	6	8.16
1988—Atlanta	National	16	18⅔	0	0	.000	22	15	14	5	4	6.75
1988—Richmond y	Int'national	8	12	0	0	.000	10	2	2	9	5	1.50
Major League Totals—3 Years		80	89⅔	0	1	.000	82	51	45	54	29	4.52

Signed as free agent by New York Yankees' organization, June 15, 1980.
†Drafted by Tidewater (New York Mets' organization), December 6, 1983.
‡Drafted by Philadelphia Phillies, December 3, 1984; returned, March 28, 1985.
§Traded to Atlanta Braves' organization for Pitcher Mike Santiago, April 2, 1986.
xOn Atlanta disabled list, March 29 to June 29, 1988; included rehabilitation disability assignment to Greenville, June 7 to June 26, 1988.
yReleased, December 4, 1988.

THOMAS PATRICK O'MALLEY
(Tom)

Born December 25, 1960, at Orange, N. J.
Height, 6.00. Weight, 190.
Throws right and bats lefthanded.

Major League stolen bases: 1983 (2).
Led American Association third basemen in fielding percentage with .955 in 1988.
Led International League third basemen in putouts with 90 and fielding percentage with .964 in 1985.

Year Club	League	Pos.	G.	AB.	R.	H.	2B.	3B.	HR.	RBI.	B.A.	PO.	A.	E.	F.A.
1979—Great Falls	Pion.	2-S-O-3	42	119	13	29	6	1	1	20	.244	41	34	9	.893
1980—Fresno	Calif.	3B	122	435	67	125	20	9	3	74	.287	69	253	22	*.936
1981—Shreveport	Texas	3B	123	467	50	135	23	6	6	53	.289	94	237	15	.957
1982—Phoenix	P. C.	3B	26	96	23	43	11	1	3	15	.448	12	44	6	.903
1982—San Francisco†	Nat.	3B-SS-2B	92	291	26	80	12	4	2	27	.275	60	161	8	.965
1983—San Francisco	Nat.	3B	135	410	40	106	16	1	5	45	.259	70	213	18	.940
1984—Phoenix	P. C.	3B-1B	105	387	44	134	20	2	5	72	.346	227	134	15	.960
1984—San Francisco‡	Nat.	3B	13	25	2	3	0	0	0	0	.120	5	8	0	1.000
1984—Chicago§	Amer.	3B	12	16	0	2	0	0	0	3	.125	2	1	0	1.000
1985—Nashville x	A. A	3B	33	128	13	39	8	0	1	12	.305	16	62	9	.897
1985—Rochester	Int.	3B-1B	102	358	62	108	13	1	10	44	.302	92	207	11	.965
1985—Baltimore	Amer.	3B	8	14	1	1	0	0	1	2	.071	2	3	1	.833
1986—Rochester	Int.	3B-2B	59	212	36	65	10	0	9	30	.307	46	111	8	.952
1986—Baltimore y	Amer.	3B	56	181	19	46	9	0	1	18	.254	37	98	9	.938
1987—Oklahoma City	A. A.	3B	109	431	83	134	27	2	12	70	.311	*112	198	9	*.972
1987—Texas	Amer.	3B-2B	45	117	10	32	8	0	1	12	.274	21	56	3	.962
1988—Oklahoma City z	A. A.	3B-1B-2B	*138	522	68	152	26	4	9	72	.291	118	246	16	.958
1988—Montreal	Nat.	3B	14	27	3	7	0	0	0	2	.259	4	15	2	.905
National League Totals—4 Years			254	753	71	196	28	5	7	74	.260	139	397	28	.950
American League Totals—4 Years			121	328	30	81	17	0	3	35	.247	62	158	13	.944
Major League Totals—7 Years			375	1081	101	277	45	5	10	109	.256	201	555	41	.949

Selected by San Francisco Giants' organization in 16th round of free-agent draft, June 5, 1979.
†On disabled list, August 16 to September 6, 1982.
‡Traded to Chicago White Sox for two players to be named later, September 1, 1984; San Francisco Giants acquired Pitcher Mike Trujillo and First Baseman Pat Adams to complete deal, September 7, 1984.
§Released, April 1, 1985; signed by Nashville (Detroit Tigers' organization), April 8, 1985.
xTraded to Rochester (Baltimore Orioles' organization) for Catcher Luis Rosado, May 21, 1985.
yGranted free agency, October 15, 1986; signed by Texas Rangers' organization, December 3, 1986.
zTraded to Montreal Expos for a player to be named later, September 1, 1988; Texas Rangers' organization acquired First Baseman Jack Daugherty to complete deal, September 13, 1988.

RANDALL JEFFREY O'NEAL
(Randy)

Born August 30, 1960, at Ashland, Ky.
Height, 6.02. Weight, 195.
Throws and bats righthanded.
Attended Palm Beach Junior College, Lake Worth, Fla.,
and University of Florida, Gainesville, Fla.

Pitched seven-inning, 4-0 no-hit victory against Winter Haven, August 23, 1981 (first game).
Major League saves: 1985 (1), 1986 (2). Total—3.

Tied for American Association lead in balks with 6 in 1984.

Year Club	League	G.	IP.	W.	L.	Pct.	H.	R.	ER.	SO.	BB.	ERA.
1981—Lakeland	Florida St.	13	69	4	5	.444	59	27	22	31	18	2.87
1982—Birmingham	Southern	27	185	11	7	.611	169	83	70	105	71	3.41
1983—Evansville	Am. Assoc.	23	140⅓	8	10	.444	159	80	66	70	45	4.23
1984—Evansville	Am. Assoc.	25	166⅓	9	10	.474	152	82	66	110	59	3.57
1984—Detroit	American	4	18⅔	2	1	.667	16	7	7	12	6	3.38
1985—Nashville	Am. Assoc.	10	67⅔	5	4	.556	57	29	27	44	19	3.59
1985—Detroit	American	28	94⅓	5	5	.500	82	42	34	52	36	3.24
1986—Detroit	American	37	122⅔	3	7	.300	121	69	59	68	44	4.33
1986—Nashville†	Am. Assoc.	4	28⅓	1	2	.333	28	16	15	15	9	4.76
1987—Atlanta-St. Louis	National	17	66	4	2	.667	81	42	39	37	26	5.32
1987—Richmond‡	Int'national	1	5	0	1	.000	4	3	2	5	1	3.60
1987—Louisville	Am. Assoc.	7	47⅓	3	1	.750	54	27	24	19	10	4.56
1988—Louisville	Am. Assoc.	10	60⅔	3	5	.375	59	30	25	33	21	3.71
1988—St. Louis§x	National	10	53	2	3	.400	57	29	27	20	10	4.58
American League Totals—3 Years		69	235⅔	10	13	.435	219	118	100	132	86	3.82
National League Totals—2 Years		27	119	6	5	.545	138	71	66	57	36	4.99
Major League Totals—5 Years		96	354⅔	16	18	.471	357	189	166	189	122	4.21

Selected by Montreal Expos' organization in 4th round of free-agent draft, January 9, 1979.
Selected by Minnesota Twins' organization in secondary phase of free-agent draft, June 5, 1979.
Selected by Milwaukee Brewers' organization in secondary phase of free-agent draft, January 8, 1980.
Selected by Cincinnati Reds' organization in secondary phase of free-agent draft, June 3, 1980.
Selected by Detroit Tigers' organization in secondary phase of free-agent draft, June 8, 1981.
†Traded with Pitcher Chuck Cary to Atlanta Braves for Outfielders Terry Harper and Freddy Tiburcio, January 27, 1987.
‡Traded to St. Louis Cardinals' organization for Pitcher Joe Boever, July 25, 1987.
§On disabled list, June 10 to August 11, 1988; included rehabilitation disability assignment to Louisville, July 26 to August 11, 1988.
xGranted free agency, October 15, 1988.

PAUL ANDREW O'NEILL

Born February 25, 1963, at Columbus, O.
Height, 6.04. Weight, 210.
Throws and bats lefthanded.
Attended Otterbein College, Westerville, O.
Son of Charles W. O'Neill, minor league pitcher, 1945 through 1948.

Major League stolen bases: 1987 (2), 1988 (8). Total—10.
Tied for American Association lead in game-winning RBIs with 13 in 1985.
Led American Association outfielders in assists with 19 and double plays with 8 in 1985.

Year Club	League	Pos.	G.	AB.	R.	H.	2B.	3B.	HR.	RBI.	B.A.	PO.	A.	E.	F.A.
1981—Billings	Pion.	OF	66	241	37	76	7	2	3	29	.315	87	4	5	.948
1982—Cedar Rapids	Midw.	OF	116	386	50	105	19	2	8	71	.272	137	7	8	.947
1983—Tampa	Fla. St.	OF-1B	121	413	62	115	23	7	8	51	.278	218	14	10	.959
1983—Waterbury	East.	OF	14	43	6	12	0	0	0	6	.279	26	0	0	1.000
1984—Vermont	East.	OF	134	475	70	126	31	5	16	76	.265	246	5	7	.973
1985—Denver	A. A.	OB-1B	*137	*509	63	*155	*32	3	7	74	.305	248	20	7	.975
1985—Cincinnati	Nat.	OF	5	12	1	4	1	0	0	1	.333	3	1	0	1.000
1986—Cincinnati	Nat.	PH	3	2	0	0	0	0	0	0	.000	0	0	0	.000
1986—Denver†	A. A.	OF	55	193	20	49	9	2	5	27	.254	98	7	4	.963
1987—Cincinnati	Nat.	OF-1B-P	84	160	24	41	14	1	7	28	.256	90	2	4	.958
1987—Nashville	A. A.	OF	11	37	12	11	0	0	3	6	.297	19	1	0	1.000
1988—Cincinnati	Nat.	OF-1B	145	485	58	122	25	3	16	73	.252	410	13	6	.986
Major League Totals—4 Years			237	659	83	167	40	4	23	102	.253	503	16	10	.981

Selected by Cincinnati Reds' organization in 4th round of free-agent draft, June 8, 1981.
†On disabled list, May 10 to July 16, 1986.

PITCHING RECORD

Year Club	League	G.	IP.	W.	L.	Pct.	H.	R.	ER.	SO.	BB.	ERA.
1987—Cincinnati	National	1	2	0	0	.000	2	3	3	2	4	13.50

STEVEN ONTIVEROS
(Steve)

Born March 5, 1961, at Tularosa, N.M.
Height, 6.00. Weight, 180.
Throws and bats righthanded.
Received bachelor of science degree in physical education
from University of Michigan, Ann Arbor, Mich.

Major League saves: 1985 (8), 1986 (10), 1987 (1). Total—19.

Year Club	League	G.	IP.	W.	L.	Pct.	H.	R.	ER.	SO.	BB.	ERA.
1982—Medford	Northwest	4	8	1	0	1.000	3	0	0	9	4	0.00
1982—West Haven†	Eastern	16	27	2	2	.500	34	26	19	28	12	6.33
1983—Albany	Eastern	32	129⅔	8	4	.667	131	62	54	91	36	3.75
1984—Tacoma‡	P. Coast	2	11⅓	1	1	.500	18	11	10	6	5	7.94
1985—Madison	Midwest	5	30⅔	3	1	.750	23	10	7	26	6	2.05
1985—Tacoma§	P. Coast	15	33⅔	3	0	1.000	26	13	11	30	21	2.94
1985—Oakland	American	39	74⅔	1	3	.250	45	17	16	36	19	1.93

Year	Club	League	G.	IP.	W.	L.	Pct.	H.	R.	ER.	SO.	BB.	ERA.
1986—Oakland xy		American	46	72⅔	2	2	.500	72	40	38	54	25	4.71
1987—Tacoma z		P. Coast	1	3	0	0	.000	1	1	1	1	2	3.00
1987—Oakland		American	35	150⅔	10	8	.556	141	78	67	97	50	4.00
1988—Oakland abc		American	10	54⅔	3	4	.429	57	32	28	30	21	4.61
Major League Totals—4 Years			130	352⅔	16	17	.485	315	167	149	217	115	3.80

Selected by Oakland A's organization in 2nd round of free-agent draft, June 7, 1982.
†On temporarily inactive list, July 27 to August 6, 1982.
‡On disabled list, April 16 to August 8, 1984.
§On disabled list, April 16 to April 28, 1985.
xAppeared in one game as a pinch-runner.
yOn disabled list, July 24 to September 14, 1986.
zOn Oakland disabled list, March 30 to April 24, 1987; included rehabilitation disability assignment to Tacoma, April 21 to April 24, 1987.
aAppeared in two games as a pinch-runner.
bOn disabled list, June 12 to August 2 and August 3, 1988 through remainder of season.
cReleased, December 21, 1988.

JOSE MANUEL OQUENDO

Name pronounced Oh-KEN-doh.

Born July 4, 1963, at Rio Piedras, Puerto Rico.
Height, 5.10. Weight, 156.
Throws right and bats left and righthanded.

Major League stolen bases: 1983 (8), 1984 (10), 1986 (2), 1987 (4), 1988 (4). Total—28.
Led American Association in sacrifice hits with 15 in 1985.
Led International League in sacrifice hits with 14 in 1982.
Led Carolina League in sacrifice hits with 13 in 1980.
Led American Association shortstops in total chances with 591 in 1985.
Led Northwest League shortstops in errors with 40 in 1979.

Year	Club	League	Pos.	G.	AB.	R.	H.	2B.	3B.	HR.	RBI.	B.A.	PO.	A.	E.	F.A.
1979—Grays Harbor		N'west	*SS-2B	64	220	24	50	8	0	1	14	.227	90	177	*40	.870
1980—Lynchburg		Carol.	SS	109	301	38	51	10	3	0	26	.169	126	358	31	*.940
1981—Lynchburg		Carol.	SS	124	393	59	98	8	6	0	38	.249	169	390	23	*.961
1982—Tidewater		Int.	SS	114	337	40	72	8	3	0	22	.214	186	337	25	.954
1983—Tidewater		Int.	SS	13	34	3	4	0	0	0	3	.118	20	23	4	.915
1983—New York		Nat.	SS	120	328	29	70	7	0	1	17	.213	182	326	21	.960
1984—New York		Nat.	SS	81	189	23	42	5	0	0	10	.222	95	152	7	.972
1984—Tidewater†		Int.	SS	38	113	8	18	1	0	1	8	.159	54	111	2	.988
1985—Louisville		A. A.	SS	133	384	38	81	8	1	1	30	.211	*227	341	23	.961
1986—St. Louis		Nat.	S-2-3-O	76	138	20	41	4	1	0	13	.297	52	94	8	.948
1987—St. Louis		Nat.	I-O-P	116	248	43	71	9	0	1	24	.286	149	133	4	.986
1988—St. Louis		Nat.	I-O-C-P	148	451	36	125	10	1	7	46	.277	268	315	11	.981
Major League Totals—5 Years				541	1354	151	349	35	2	9	110	.258	746	1020	51	.972

Signed as free agent by New York Mets' organization, April 15, 1979.
†Traded with Pitcher Mark Jason Davis to St. Louis Cardinals' organization for Shortstop Argenis Salazar and Pitcher John Young, April 2, 1985.

CHAMPIONSHIP SERIES RECORD

Year	Club	League	Pos.	G.	AB.	R.	H.	2B.	3B.	HR.	RBI.	B.A.	PO.	A.	E.	F.A.
1987—St. Louis		Nat.	O-3B-PH	5	12	3	2	0	0	1	4	.167	7	0	0	1.000

WORLD SERIES RECORD

Year	Club	League	Pos.	G.	AB.	R.	H.	2B.	3B.	HR.	RBI.	B.A.	PO.	A.	E.	F.A.
1987—St. Louis		Nat.	OF-3B	7	24	2	6	0	0	0	2	.250	8	10	0	1.000

PITCHING RECORD

Year	Club	League	G.	IP.	W.	L.	Pct.	H.	R.	ER.	SO.	BB.	ERA.
1987—St. Louis		National	1	1	0	0	.000	4	3	3	0	1	27.00
1988—St. Louis		National	1	4	0	1	.000	4	2	2	1	6	4.50
Major League Totals—2 Years			2	5	0	1	.000	8	5	5	1	7	9.00

JESSE OROSCO

Name pronounced Oh-ROSS-koh.

Born April 21, 1957, at Santa Barbara, Calif.
Height, 6.02. Weight, 185.
Throws left and bats righthanded.
Attended Santa Barbara City College, Santa Barbara, Calif.

Major League saves: 1981 (1), 1982 (4), 1983 (17), 1984 (31), 1985 (17), 1986 (21), 1987 (16), 1988 (9). Total—116.
Led Appalachian League in intentional bases on balls issued with 5 in 1978.

Year	Club	League	G.	IP.	W.	L.	Pct.	H.	R.	ER.	SO.	BB.	ERA.
1978—Elizabethton†		Ap'lachian	20	40	4	4	.500	29	7	5	48	20	1.13
1979—Tidewater		Int'national	16	81	4	4	.500	82	45	35	55	43	3.89
1979—New York		National	18	35	1	2	.333	33	20	19	22	22	4.89
1980—Jackson		Texas	37	71	4	4	.500	52	36	29	85	62	3.68
1981—Tidewater		Int'national	46	87	9	5	.643	80	39	32	81	32	3.31
1981—New York		National	8	17	0	1	.000	13	4	3	18	6	1.59

Year	Club	League	G.	IP.	W.	L.	Pct.	H.	R.	ER.	SO.	BB.	ERA.
1982	—New York	National	54	109⅓	4	10	.286	92	37	33	89	40	2.72
1983	—New York	National	62	110	13	7	.650	76	27	18	84	38	1.47
1984	—New York	National	60	87	10	6	.625	58	29	25	85	34	2.59
1985	—New York	National	54	79	8	6	.571	66	26	24	68	34	2.73
1986	—New York‡	National	58	81	8	6	.571	64	23	21	62	35	2.33
1987	—New York§	National	58	77	3	9	.250	78	41	38	78	31	4.44
1988	—Los Angeles x	National	55	53	3	2	.600	41	18	16	43	30	2.72
	Major League Totals—9 Years		427	648⅓	50	49	.505	521	225	197	549	270	2.73

Selected by St. Louis Cardinals' organization in 7th round of free-agent draft, January 11, 1977.

Selected by Minnesota Twins' organization in 2nd round of free-agent draft, January 10, 1978.

†Traded to New York Mets, February 7, 1979, completing deal in which Minnesota Twins traded Pitcher Greg Field and a player to be named later to New York for Pitcher Jerry Koosman, December 8, 1978.

‡Appeared in one game as an outfielder with one putout.

§As part of an eight-player, three-team deal, New York Mets traded Pitcher Jesse Orosco to Oakland Athletics, December 11, 1987. Oakland then traded Orosco along with shortstop Alfredo Griffin and Pitcher Jay Howell to Los Angeles Dodgers for Pitchers Bob Welch, Matt Young and Jack Savage. Oakland then traded Savage along with Pitchers Wally Whitehurst and Kevin Tapani to New York.

xGranted free agency, November 4, 1988; signed by Cleveland Indians, December 3, 1988.

CHAMPIONSHIP SERIES RECORD

Established Championship Series record for most games won, Series (3), 1986.

Tied Championship Series record for most games pitched, seven-game Series (4), 1988.

Year	Club	League	G.	IP.	W.	L.	Pct.	H.	R.	ER.	SO.	BB.	ERA.
1986	—New York	National	4	8	3	0	1.000	5	3	3	10	2	3.38
1988	—Los Angeles	National	4	2⅓	0	0	.000	4	2	2	0	3	7.71
	Championship Series Totals—2 Years		8	10⅓	3	0	1.000	9	5	5	10	5	4.35

WORLD SERIES RECORD

Year	Club	League	G.	IP.	W.	L.	Pct.	H.	R.	ER.	SO.	BB.	ERA.
1986	—New York	National	4	5⅔	0	0	.000	2	0	0	6	0	0.00

ALL-STAR GAME RECORD

Year	League	IP.	W.	L.	Pct.	H.	R.	ER.	SO.	BB.	ERA.
1983	—National	⅓	0	0	.000	0	0	0	1	0	0.00

Member of National League All-Star Team in 1984; did not play.

JOSEPH MICHAEL ORSULAK

(Joe)

Born May 31, 1962, at Glen Ridge, N.J.
Height, 6.01. Weight, 186.
Throws and bats lefthanded.

Major League stolen bases: 1984 (3), 1985 (24), 1986 (24), 1988 (9). Total—60.

Led Pacific Coast League outfielders in total chances with 367 and double plays with 8 in 1983.

Tied for South Atlantic League lead in double plays by outfielders with 4 in 1981.

Year	Club	League	Pos.	G.	AB.	R.	H.	2B.	3B.	HR.	RBI.	B.A.	PO.	A.	E.	F.A.
1981	—Greenwood†	S. Atl.	OF	118	460	80	145	18	8	6	70	.315	249	16	4	★.985
1982	—Alexandria	Carol.	OF-1B	129	463	92	134	18	4	14	65	.289	286	7	10	.967
1983	—Hawaii	P. C.	OF	139	538	87	154	12	•13	10	58	.286	★341	•18	8	.978
1983	—Pittsburgh	Nat.	OF	7	11	0	2	0	0	0	1	.182	2	2	0	1.000
1984	—Hawaii	P. C.	OF	98	388	51	110	19	12	3	53	.284	258	6	2	.992
1984	—Pittsburgh	Nat.	OF	32	67	12	17	1	2	0	3	.254	41	1	0	1.000
1985	—Pittsburgh‡	Nat.	OF	121	397	54	119	14	6	0	21	.300	229	10	6	.976
1986	—Pittsburgh	Nat.	OF	138	401	60	100	19	6	2	19	.249	193	11	4	.981
1987	—Vancouver§x	P. C.	OF	39	143	20	33	6	1	1	12	.231	58	2	2	.968
1988	—Baltimore	Amer.	OF	125	379	48	109	21	3	8	27	.288	228	6	5	.979
	National League Totals—4 Years			298	876	126	238	34	14	2	44	.272	465	24	10	.980
	American League Totals—1 Year			125	379	48	109	21	3	8	27	.288	228	6	5	.979
	Major League Totals—5 Years			423	1255	174	347	55	17	10	71	.276	693	30	15	.980

Selected by Pittsburgh Pirates' organization in 6th round of free-agent draft, June 3, 1980.

†On temporarily inactive list, July 10 to July 27, 1981.

‡On disabled list, May 25 to June 9, 1985.

§On Pittsburgh disabled list, March 31 to May 22, 1987; included rehabilitation disability assignment to Vancouver, May 4 to May 22, 1987.

xTraded to Baltimore Orioles for Shortstop Terry Crowley Jr. and Third Baseman Rico Rossy, November 6, 1987.

ADALBERTO ORTIZ JR. (COLON)

Name pronounced Orr-TEEZ.

(Junior)

Born October 24, 1959, at Humacao, Puerto Rico.
Height, 5.11. Weight, 176.
Throws and bats righthanded.
Brother of Alexander Ortiz, minor league outfielder, 1978 and 1979.

Major League stolen bases: 1983 (1), 1984 (1), 1985 (1), 1988 (1). Total—4.

Led Pacific Coast League catchers in putouts with 744 and double plays with 17 in 1982.
Led Carolina League catchers in double plays with 12 in 1979.
Tied for Western Carolinas League lead in passed balls with 22 in 1978.

Year Club	League	Pos.	G.	AB.	R.	H.	2B.	3B.	HR.	RBI.	B.A.	PO.	A.	E.	F.A.
1977—Charleston†	W. Car.	C	21	53	2	14	3	0	0	10	.264	93	13	4	.964
1977—Bradenton Pir.	Gulf C.	C	34	118	11	24	5	1	1	12	.203	76	14	4	.957
1978—Charleston‡	W. Car.	C	41	122	12	26	4	0	1	16	213	198	44	7	.972
1979—Salem	Carol.	*C-1B	108	396	35	112	21	2	5	66	.283	632	*84	*17	.977
1980—Buffalo	East.	C	126	515	79	*178	25	1	12	78	*.346	497	91	16	.974
1980—Portland	P. C.	C	8	27	1	3	0	1	0	3	.111	42	10	0	1.000
1981—Portland	P. C.	C	105	346	49	93	14	7	2	46	.269	606	76	15	.978
1982—Portland	P. C.	*C-O-1	124	449	46	131	22	0	6	57	.292	751	*110	*19	.978
1982—Pittsburgh	Nat.	C	7	15	1	3	1	0	0	0	.200	27	3	0	1.000
1983—Pitt.§-N.Y.	Nat.	C	73	193	11	48	5	0	0	12	.249	293	31	11	.967
1984—New York x	Nat.	C	40	91	6	18	3	0	0	11	.198	136	13	3	.980
1985—Pittsburgh	Nat.	C	23	72	4	21	2	0	1	5	.292	115	14	2	.985
1986—Pittsburgh	Nat.	C	49	110	11	37	6	0	0	14	.336	165	13	3	.983
1987—Pittsburgh	Nat.	C	75	192	16	52	8	1	1	22	.271	313	39	9	.975
1988—Pittsburgh y	Nat.	C	49	118	8	33	6	0	2	18	.280	152	23	3	.983
Major League Totals—7 Years			316	791	57	212	31	1	4	82	.268	1201	136	31	.977

Signed as free agent by Pittsburgh Pirates' organization, January 18, 1977.
†On temporary inactive list, June 18 to June 22, 1977.
‡On disabled list, June 16 to September 5, 1978.
§Traded with Pitcher Art Ray to New York Mets for Outfielder Marvell Wynne and Pitcher Steve Senteney, June 14, 1983.
xDrafted by Pittsburgh Pirates, December 3, 1984.
yOn disabled list, July 28 to September 5, 1988.

ANGEL A. ORTIZ (TORRES)

Born December 12, 1967, at Juana Diaz, Puerto Rico.
Height, 6.03. Weight, 170.
Throws and bats lefthanded.

Tied for Appalachian League lead in games started by pitchers with 14 in 1987.

Year Club	League	G.	IP.	W.	L.	Pct.	H.	R.	ER.	SO.	BB.	ERA.
1986—Burlington	Ap'lachian	11	29	0	2	.000	24	13	10	26	14	3.10
1987—Burlington	Ap'lachian	14	83⅔	5	3	.625	68	45	31	85	46	3.33
1988—Waterloo	Midwest	15	98	5	5	.500	79	33	28	98	37	2.57

Signed as free agent by Cleveland Indians' organization, January 18, 1986.

DAVID ALAN OTTO
(Dave)

Born November 12, 1964, at Chicago, Ill.
Height, 6.07. Weight, 210.
Throws and bats lefthanded.
Attended University of Missouri, Columbia, Mo.

Year Club	League	G.	IP.	W.	L.	Pct.	H.	R.	ER.	SO.	BB.	ERA.
1985—Medford	Northwest	11	42⅓	2	2	.500	42	27	19	27	22	4.04
1986—Madison	Midwest	26	169	13	7	.650	154	72	50	125	71	2.66
1987—Madison	Midwest	1	3	0	0	.000	2	0	0	2	0	0.00
1987—Huntsville	Southern	9	50	4	1	.800	36	14	13	25	11	2.34
1987—Oakland	American	3	6	0	0	.000	7	6	6	3	1	9.00
1988—Tacoma	P. Coast	21	127⅔	4	9	.308	124	71	50	80	63	3.52
1988—Oakland	American	3	10	0	0	.000	9	2	2	7	6	1.80
Major League Totals—2 Years		6	16	0	0	.000	16	8	8	10	7	4.50

Selected by Baltimore Orioles' organization in 2nd round of free-agent draft, June 7, 1982.
Selected by Oakland A's organization in 2nd round of free-agent draft, June 3, 1985.

DAVE OWEN

Born April 25, 1958, at Cleburne, Tex.
Height, 6.01. Weight, 175.
Throws right and bats left and righthanded.
Attended University of Texas, Arlington, Tex.
Brother of Spike Owen, shortstop with Boston Red Sox.

Major League stolen bases: 1983 (1), 1984 (1), 1985 (1). Total—3.

Year Club	League	Pos.	G.	AB.	R.	H.	2B.	3B.	HR.	RBI.	B.A.	PO.	A.	E.	F.A.
1979—Sarasota Cubs	Gulf C.	SS	10	23	8	7	0	0	0	4	.304	17	26	7	.860
1979—Quad Cities	Midw.	SS	45	129	23	18	3	0	0	4	.140	56	139	11	.947
1980—Midland	Texas	SS	78	257	45	74	8	0	3	31	.288	96	213	32	.906
1980—Quad Cities	Midw.	SS	56	188	43	49	5	1	0	17	.261	88	155	17	.935
1981—Midland	Texas	SS-2B-3B	80	247	40	53	8	1	0	23	.215	109	205	26	.924
1982—Midland	Texas	SS-3B	125	427	59	135	12	9	4	40	.316	183	309	29	.944
1983—Iowa	A. A.	SS	126	425	67	110	21	3	6	39	.259	203	*431	25	*.962
1983—Chicago	Nat.	SS-3B	16	22	1	2	0	1	0	2	.091	10	29	0	1.000
1984—Iowa	A. A.	SS-2B-OF	43	136	18	31	5	1	1	9	.228	65	111	7	.962
1984—Chicago	Nat.	SS-3B-2B	47	93	8	18	2	2	1	10	.194	40	91	7	.949
1985—Iowa	A. A.	2-S-3-O	100	321	60	73	13	5	11	40	.227	157	280	7	.984

Year	Club	League	Pos.	G.	AB.	R.	H.	2B.	3B.	HR.	RBI.	B.A.	PO.	A.	E.	F.A.
1985	—Chicago†‡	Nat.	SS-3B-2B	22	19	6	7	0	0	0	4	.368	6	14	2	.909
1986	—Oklahoma City	A. A.	S-2-3-1-O	64	188	33	47	8	4	2	22	.250	100	119	10	.956
1987	—Okla. C.§-Omaha	A. A.	SS-3B-2B	93	276	36	63	8	7	2	31	.228	142	241	19	.953
1988	—Omaha	A. A.	SS-3B	115	352	44	94	11	4	3	34	.267	136	347	16	.968
1988	—Kansas City x	Amer.	SS	7	5	0	0	0	0	0	0	.000	7	9	1	.941
National League Totals—3 Years				85	134	15	27	2	3	1	16	.201	56	134	9	.955
American League Totals—1 Year				7	5	0	0	0	0	0	0	.000	7	9	1	.941
Major League Totals—4 Years				92	139	15	27	2	3	1	16	.194	63	143	10	.954

Selected by Chicago Cubs' organization in 10th round of free-agent draft, June 5, 1979.
†Traded to San Francisco Giants for Second Baseman Manny Trillo, December 11, 1985.
‡Released, March 24, 1986; signed by Texas Rangers' organization, March 27, 1986.
§Traded to Omaha (Kansas City Royals' organization) for a player to be named later, July 31, 1987; Texas Rangers acquired Pitcher Rufus Ellis to complete deal, October 13, 1987.
xGranted free agency, October 15, 1988.

LAWRENCE THOMAS OWEN
(Larry)

Born May 31, 1955, at Cleveland, O.
Height, 5.10. Weight, 190.
Throws and bats righthanded.
Attended Bowling Green State University, Bowling Green, O.

Led American Association catchers in double plays with 7 in 1988.
Led International League catchers in double plays with 11 in 1987.
Led International League catchers in total chances with 648 in 1984 and 593 in 1987.
Tied for International League lead in passed balls with 15 in 1979.

Year	Club	League	Pos.	G.	AB.	R.	H.	2B.	3B.	HR.	RBI.	B.A.	PO.	A.	E.	F.A.
1977	—Greenwood	W. Car.	C	61	170	26	48	9	2	3	24	.282	295	47	11	.969
1978	—Savannah	South.	C	112	364	35	78	9	1	11	45	.214	*545	*89	*25	.962
1978	—Richmond	Int.	C	14	40	2	10	1	0	0	3	.250	59	9	6	.919
1979	—Richmond	Int.	C	110	358	32	70	7	3	7	29	.196	*615	•73	*13	.981
1980	—Savannah	South.	C-3B	76	228	27	48	8	1	6	20	.211	304	44	7	.980
1981	—Savannah	South.	C	90	279	30	64	8	3	5	23	.229	450	77	*23	.958
1981	—Atlanta	Nat.	C	13	16	0	0	0	0	0	0	.000	23	4	1	.964
1982	—Richmond	Int.	C	58	178	21	37	5	0	5	26	.208	265	37	6	.981
1982	—Atlanta	Nat.	C	2	3	1	1	1	0	0	0	.333	2	1	0	1.000
1983	—Atlanta	Nat.	C	17	17	0	2	0	0	0	1	.118	30	2	1	.970
1983	—Richmond	Int.	C	5	12	4	5	0	1	1	2	.417	20	0	0	1.000
1984	—Richmond	Int.	C	94	314	33	76	13	0	7	45	.242	572	*62	*14	.978
1985	—Richmond	Int.	C	83	247	21	57	15	0	5	32	.231	436	65	12	.977
1985	—Atlanta	Nat.	C	26	71	7	17	3	0	2	12	.239	129	11	5	.966
1986	—Richmond†	Int.	C	98	265	32	52	13	0	3	21	.196	*511	*69	*13	.978
1987	—Kansas City	Amer.	C	76	164	17	31	6	0	5	14	.189	370	38	7	.983
1988	—Omaha	A. A.	C	62	196	35	42	10	0	9	30	.214	349	48	6	.985
1988	—Kansas City	Amer.	C	37	81	5	17	1	0	1	3	.210	168	13	2	.989
National League Totals—4 Years				58	107	8	20	4	0	2	13	.187	184	18	7	.967
American League Totals—2 Years				113	245	22	48	7	0	6	17	.196	538	51	9	.985
Major League Totals—6 Years				171	352	30	68	11	0	8	30	.193	722	69	16	.980

Selected by California Angels' organization in 18th round of free-agent draft, June 8, 1976.
Selected by Atlanta Braves' organization in 17th round of free-agent draft, June 7, 1977.
†Granted free agency, October 15, 1986; signed by Omaha (Kansas City Royals' organization), March 31, 1987.

SPIKE DEE OWEN

Born April 19, 1961, at Cleburne, Tex.
Height, 5.10. Weight, 165.
Throws right and bats left and righthanded.
Attended University of Texas, Austin, Tex.
Brother of Dave Owen, shortstop with Chicago Cubs and Kansas City Royals, 1983 through 1985 and 1988.

Tied modern major league record for most runs, game (6), August 21, 1986.
Major League stolen bases: 1983 (10), 1984 (16), 1985 (11), 1986 (4), 1987 (11). Total—52.
Led American League shortstops in total chances with 767 and double plays with 133 in 1986.
Named shortstop on The Sporting News College Baseball All-America Team, 1982.

Year	Club	League	Pos.	G.	AB.	R.	H.	2B.	3B.	HR.	RBI.	B.A.	PO.	A.	E.	F.A.
1982	—Lynn	East.	SS	78	241	32	64	9	2	1	27	.266	106	207	9	.972
1983	—Salt Lake City	P. C.	SS	72	256	58	68	8	9	1	32	.266	111	212	14	.958
1983	—Seattle	Amer.	SS	80	306	36	60	11	3	2	21	.196	122	233	11	.970
1984	—Seattle	Amer.	SS	152	530	67	130	18	8	3	43	.245	245	463	17	.977
1985	—Seattle†	Amer.	SS	118	352	41	91	10	6	6	37	.259	196	361	14	.975
1986	—Sea.‡-Bos.	Amer.	SS	154	528	67	122	24	7	1	45	.231	279	467	21	.973
1987	—Boston	Amer.	SS	132	437	50	113	17	7	2	48	.259	176	336	13	.975
1988	—Boston§	Amer.	SS	89	257	40	64	14	1	5	18	.249	102	192	10	.967
Major League Totals—6 Years				725	2410	301	580	94	32	19	212	.241	1120	2052	86	.974

Selected by Seattle Mariners' organization in 1st round (sixth player selected) of free-agent draft, June 7, 1982.
†On disabled list, July 15 to August 1, 1985.
‡Traded with Outfielder Dave Henderson to Boston Red Sox for Infielder Rey Quinones, a player to be named later and cash, August 19, 1986; as part of deal, Seattle Mariners claimed Pitchers Mike Brown and Mike Trujillo on waivers from Boston, August 22, 1986. Seattle acquired Outfielder John Christensen to complete deal, September 25, 1986.

§Traded with Pitcher Dan Gakeler to Montreal Expos for Pitcher John Dopson and Shortstop Luis Rivera, December 8, 1988.

CHAMPIONSHIP SERIES RECORD

Tied Championship Series record for most hits, two consecutive games, one Series (6), October 14 and 15, 1986.

Year	Club	League	Pos.	G.	AB.	R.	H.	2B.	3B.	HR.	RBI.	B.A.	PO.	A.	E.	F.A.
1986	—Boston	Amer.	SS	7	21	5	9	0	1	0	3	.429	12	21	5	.868
1988	—Boston	Amer.	PH	1	0	0	0	0	0	0	0	.000	0	0	0	.000
Championship Series Totals—2 Years				8	21	5	9	0	1	0	3	.429	12	21	5	.868

WORLD SERIES RECORD

Year	Club	League	Pos.	G.	AB.	R.	H.	2B.	3B.	HR.	RBI.	B.A.	PO.	A.	E.	F.A.
1986	—Boston	Amer.	SS	7	20	2	6	0	0	0	2	.300	10	13	0	1.000

PATRICK MICHAEL PACILLO

Name pronounced Puh-SILL-oh.

(Pat)

Born July 23, 1963, at Rutherford, N. J.
Height, 6.02. Weight, 210.
Throws and bats righthanded.
Attended Seton Hall University, South Orange, N. J.

Tied for American Association lead in shutouts with 2 in 1986.
Member of 1984 U.S. Olympic baseball team.

Year	Club	League	G.	IP.	W.	L.	Pct.	H.	R.	ER.	SO.	BB.	ERA.
1985	—Tampa	Florida St.	25	38⅔	8	1	.889	28	17	13	39	28	3.03
1985	—Vermont	Eastern	22	36⅔	0	4	.000	27	11	10	39	24	2.45
1986	—Denver	Am. Assoc.	25	148	11	6	.647	135	81	71	111	85	4.32
1987	—Nashville	Am. Assoc.	16	97⅔	8	4	.667	89	43	39	80	38	3.59
1987	—Cincinnati	National	12	39⅔	3	3	.500	41	30	27	23	19	6.13
1988	—Nashville-Indianapolis	Am. Assoc.	22	74⅔	3	4	.429	76	42	32	62	30	3.86
1988	—Cincinnati†‡	National	6	10⅔	1	0	1.000	14	7	6	11	4	5.06
Major League Totals—2 Years			18	50⅓	4	3	.571	55	37	33	34	23	5.90

Selected by Cincinnati Reds' organization in 1st round (fifth player selected) of free-agent draft, June 4, 1984.

†On disabled list, June 2 to June 23, 1988; included rehabilitation disability assignment to Nashville, June 22, 1988.

‡Traded with Outfielder Tracy Jones to Montreal Expos for Catcher Jeff Reed, Outfielder Herm Winningham and Pitcher Randy St. Claire, July 13, 1988.

MICHAEL TIMOTHY PAGLIARULO

Name pronounced Pal-ya-ROO-lo.

(Mike)

Born March 15, 1960, at Medford, Mass.
Height, 6.02. Weight, 195.
Throws right and bats lefthanded.
Attended University of Miami, Coral Gables, Fla.
Son of Charles Pagliarulo, infielder in Chicago Cubs' organization, 1958.

Major League stolen bases: 1986 (4), 1987 (1), 1988 (1). Total—6.
Led New York-Pennsylvania League in intentional bases on balls received with 8 in 1981.
Led Southern League third basemen in total chances with 433 in 1983.
Led New York-Pennsylvania League third basemen in total chances with 214 in 1981.

Year	Club	League	Pos.	G.	AB.	R.	H.	2B.	3B.	HR.	RBI.	B.A.	PO.	A.	E.	F.A.
1981	—Oneonta	NYP	3B	72	245	32	53	9	4	2	28	.216	40	*159	15	.930
1982	—Greensboro	S. Atl.	3B	123	403	79	113	22	0	22	79	.280	73	*278	27	.929
1983	—Nashville	South.	3B	135	450	82	117	19	4	19	80	.260	*98	*315	20	*.954
1984	—Columbus	Int.	3B-SS	58	146	24	31	5	1	7	25	.212	27	95	13	.904
1984	—New York	Amer.	3B	67	201	24	48	15	3	7	34	.239	44	106	7	.955
1985	—New York	Amer.	3B	138	380	55	91	16	2	19	62	.239	67	187	13	.951
1986	—New York	Amer.	3B-SS	149	504	71	120	24	3	28	71	.238	104	283	19	.953
1987	—New York	Amer.	3B-1B	150	522	76	122	26	3	32	87	.234	97	297	17	.959
1988	—New York†	Amer.	3B	125	444	46	96	20	1	15	67	.216	82	232	19	.943
Major League Totals—5 Years				629	2051	272	477	101	12	101	321	.233	394	1105	75	.952

Selected by New York Yankees' organization in 6th round of free-agent draft, June 8, 1981.

†On disabled list, July 25 to August 11, 1988.

THOMAS ALAN PAGNOZZI

(Tom)

Born July 30, 1962, at Tucson, Ariz.
Height, 6.01. Weight, 190.
Throws and bats righthanded.
Attended Central Arizona College, Coolidge, Ariz.,
and University of Arkansas, Fayetteville, Ark.
Brother of Tim Pagnozzi, shortstop in Philadelphia Phillies' organization, 1976;
and Mike Pagnozzi, pitcher in Baltimore Orioles' organization, 1975 through 1978.

Major League stolen bases: 1987 (1).

Year	Club	League	Pos.	G.	AB.	R.	H.	2B.	3B.	HR.	RBI.	B.A.	PO.	A.	E.	F.A.
1983	—Erie	NYP	C	45	168	28	52	9	1	6	22	.310	183	20	3	.985
1983	—Macon	S. Atl.	C	18	57	7	14	2	1	0	6	.246	125	18	8	.947
1984	—Springfield	Midw.	C	114	396	57	112	20	4	10	68	.283	667	*90	12	.984
1985	—Arkansas	Texas	C-1B	41	139	15	43	7	1	5	29	.309	243	27	1	.996
1985	—Louisville	A. A.	C	76	268	29	72	13	2	5	40	.269	266	25	4	.986
1986	—Louisville	A. A.	C	30	106	12	31	4	0	1	18	.292	160	19	3	.984
1987	—Louisville	A. A.	C-3B	84	320	53	100	20	2	14	71	.313	427	43	6	.987
1987	—St. Louis	Nat.	C-1B	27	48	8	9	1	0	2	9	.188	61	5	0	1.000
1988	—St. Louis	Nat.	1B-C-3B	81	195	17	55	9	0	0	15	.282	340	30	4	.989
Major League Totals—2 Years				108	243	25	64	10	0	2	24	.263	401	35	4	.991

Selected by Milwaukee Brewers' organization in 24th round of free-agent draft, January 12, 1982.
Selected by St. Louis Cardinals' organization in 8th round of free agent draft, June 6, 1983.

CHAMPIONSHIP SERIES RECORD

Year	Club	League	Pos.	G.	AB.	R.	H.	2B.	3B.	HR.	RBI.	B.A.	PO.	A.	E.	F.A.
1987	—St. Louis	Nat.	PH	1	1	0	0	0	0	0	0	.000	0	0	0	.000

WORLD SERIES RECORD

Year	Club	League	Pos.	G.	AB.	R.	H.	2B.	3B.	HR.	RBI.	B.A.	PO.	A.	E.	F.A.
1987	—St. Louis	Nat.	DH-PH	2	4	0	1	0	0	0	0	.250	0	0	0	.000

ROBERT REY PALACIOS

Name pronounced Pah-LAH-see-os.

(Known by middle name.)

Born November 8, 1962, at Brooklyn, N. Y.
Height, 5.10. Weight, 190.
Throws and bats righthanded.
Attended Kingsborough Community College, Brooklyn, N. Y.

Led International League in sacrifice flies with 9 in 1987.

Led International League catchers in putouts with 789, total chances with 890 and tied for lead in double plays with 7 and passed balls with 15 in 1988.

Led International League catchers in assists with 66 in 1987 and 82 in 1988.

Led International League catchers in errors with 19 in 1988 and tied for lead with 13 in 1987.

Led Eastern League catchers in putouts with 603, assists with 86, errors with 20, total chances with 709 and double plays with 8 in 1986.

Tied for Appalachian League lead in double plays by catchers with 2 in 1984.

Year	Club	League	Pos.	G.	AB.	R.	H.	2B.	3B.	HR.	RBI.	B.A.	PO.	A.	E.	F.A.
1983	—Bristol	Appal.	C	47	139	28	42	7	1	7	28	.302	187	22	7	.968
1984	—Lakeland†	Fla. St.	3B-1B-C	107	373	44	92	21	4	2	53	.247	285	105	19	.954
1985	—Lakeland	Fla. St.	C-1B	85	280	35	65	11	1	2	27	.232	410	45	13	.972
1985	—Birmingham	South.	C-3B-1B	35	110	14	29	4	0	2	16	.264	153	43	8	.961
1986	—Glens Falls	East.	C-3B-1B	135	461	66	116	20	4	16	66	.252	703	140	26	.970
1987	—Toledo	Int.	C-3-1-O	133	449	50	116	22	2	13	60	.258	569	122	22	.969
1988	—Toledo‡	Int.	C-1-O-2-3	132	409	38	94	26	1	5	27	.230	811	84	20	.978
1988	—Kansas City	Amer.	C-3B	5	11	2	1	0	0	0	0	.091	17	1	0	1.000
Major League Totals—1 Year				5	11	2	1	0	0	0	0	.091	17	1	0	1.000

Signed as free agent by Detroit Tigers' organization, August 16, 1982.
†On disabled list, April 17 to May 21, 1984.
‡Traded with Pitcher Mark Lee to Kansas City Royals for Pitcher Ted Power, August 31, 1988.

VICENTE PALACIOS (HERNANDEZ)

Name pronounced Pah-LAH-see-os.

(Vince)

Born July 19, 1963, at Mataloma, Mex.
Height, 6.03. Weight, 165.
Throws right and bats left and righthanded.

Led Pacific Coast League in shutouts with 5 in 1987.
Led Mexican League in balks with 3 in 1983.
Tied for Eastern League lead in balks with 4 in 1985.

Year	Club	League	G.	IP.	W.	L.	Pct.	H.	R.	ER.	SO.	BB.	ERA.
1982	—Veracruz	Mexican					(Did not play)						
1983	—Veracruz	Mexican	22	165⅓	12	6	.667	121	53	48	125	60	2.61
1984	—Veracruz†	Mexican	24	128	7	8	.468	117	64	50	120	79	3.52
1984	—Glens Falls	Eastern	5	25⅓	1	2	.333	23	12	7	10	11	2.49
1985	—Glens Falls‡	Eastern	8	39⅔	1	1	.500	44	25	21	20	29	4.76
1985	—Mexico City Reds	Mexican	13	74⅓	7	2	.778	86	44	32	49	44	3.87
1986	—Aguascalientes§xy	Mexican	23	138⅔	5	14	.263	157	75	68	121	78	4.41
1987	—Vancouver	P. Coast	27	*185	13	5	.722	140	63	53	*148	85	*2.58
1987	—Pittsburgh	National	6	29⅓	2	1	.667	27	14	14	13	9	4.30
1988	—Pittsburgh	National	7	24⅓	1	2	.333	28	18	18	15	15	6.66
1988	—Buffalo	Am. Assoc.	5	31⅔	3	0	1.000	26	7	7	23	5	1.99
Major League Totals—2 Years			13	53⅔	3	3	.500	55	32	32	28	24	5.37

Signed as free agent by Veracruz of Mexican League, April 23, 1982.
†Sold to Chicago White Sox' organization, July 20, 1984.
‡Loaned to Mexico City Reds of Mexican League, May 28, 1985; returned, September 3, 1985.

§Loaned to Aguascalientes of Mexican League, April 5, 1986; returned, September 1, 1986.
xReleased, November 10, 1986; signed by Pittsburgh Pirates' organization, December 4, 1986.
yDrafted by Milwaukee Brewers, December 8, 1986; returned, April 3, 1987.

DONN STEVEN PALL

Born January 11, 1962, at Chicago, Ill.
Height, 6.01. Weight, 180.
Throws and bats righthanded.
Received degree from University of Illinois, Champaign, Ill., in 1985.

Tied for Gulf Coast League lead in complete games with 4 and shutouts with 2 in 1985.

Year Club	League	G.	IP.	W.	L.	Pct.	H.	R.	ER.	SO.	BB.	ERA.
1985—Sarasota White Sox	Gulf Coast	13	★86	●7	5	.583	68	34	16	63	10	1.67
1986—Appleton	Midwest	11	78	5	5	.500	71	29	20	51	14	2.31
1986—Birmingham	Southern	21	73	3	4	.429	77	38	36	41	27	4.44
1987—Birmingham	Southern	30	158	8	11	.421	173	100	75	139	63	4.27
1988—Vancouver	P. Coast	44	72⅔	5	2	.714	61	21	18	41	20	2.23
1988—Chicago	American	17	28⅔	0	2	.000	39	11	11	16	8	3.45
Major League Totals—1 Year		17	28⅔	0	2	.000	39	11	11	16	8	3.45

Selected by Chicago White Sox' organization in 23rd round of free-agent draft, June 3, 1985.

RAFAEL CORRALES PALMEIRO

Name pronounced Pal-MAIR-oh.

Born September 24, 1964, at Havana, Cuba.
Height, 6.00. Weight, 180.
Throws and bats lefthanded.
Received degree in commercial art from Mississippi State University, Starkville, Miss.

Major League stolen bases: 1986 (1), 1987 (2), 1988 (12). Total—15.
Led Eastern League in total bases with 225, sacrifice flies with 13 and intentional bases on balls received with 13 in 1986.
Named outfielder on THE SPORTING NEWS College Baseball All-America Team, 1985.
Named Eastern League Most Valuable Player, 1986.

Year Club	League	Pos.	G.	AB.	R.	H.	2B.	3B.	HR.	RBI.	B.A.	PO.	A.	E.	F.A.
1985—Peoria	Midw.	OF	73	279	34	83	22	4	5	51	.297	113	7	1	.992
1986—Pittsfield	East.	OF	●140	509	66	★156	29	2	12	★95	.306	248	9	3	★.988
1986—Chicago	Nat.	OF	22	73	9	18	4	0	3	12	.247	34	2	4	.900
1987—Iowa	A. A.	OF-1B	57	214	36	64	14	3	11	41	.299	150	13	2	.988
1987—Chicago	Nat.	OF-1B	84	221	32	61	15	1	14	30	.276	176	9	1	.995
1988—Chicago†	Nat.	OF-1B	152	580	75	178	41	5	8	53	.307	322	11	5	.985
Major League Totals—3 Years			258	874	116	257	60	6	25	95	.294	532	22	10	.982

Selected by New York Mets' organization in 8th round of free-agent draft, June 7, 1982.
Selected by Chicago Cubs' organization in 1st round (22nd player selected) of free-agent draft, June 3, 1985.
†Traded with Pitchers Jamie Moyer and Drew Hall to Texas Rangers for Pitchers Mitch Williams, Paul Kilgus and Steve Wilson, Infielders Curtis Wilkerson and Luis Benitez and Outfielder Pablo Delgado, December 5, 1988.

ALL-STAR GAME RECORD

Year League	Pos.	AB.	R.	H.	2B.	3B.	HR.	RBI.	B.A.	PO.	A.	E.	F.A.
1988—National	PH-OF	0	0	0	0	0	0	0	.000	1	0	0	1.000

DAVID WILLIAM PALMER JR.

Born October 19, 1957, at Glens Falls, N.Y.
Height, 6.01. Weight, 205.
Throws and bats righthanded.

Pitched five-inning, 4-0 perfect game against St. Louis Cardinals, April 21, 1984 (second game).
Major League saves: 1979 (2).
Tied for Pioneer League lead in home runs allowed with 6 in 1976.

Year Club	League	G.	IP.	W.	L.	Pct.	H.	R.	ER.	SO.	BB.	ERA.
1976—Lethbridge	Pioneer	13	45	0	5	.000	58	49	36	44	28	7.20
1977—West Palm Beach	Florida St.	25	119	6	8	.429	120	49	38	88	44	2.87
1978—West Palm Beach	Florida St.	7	51	4	2	.667	44	23	11	58	4	1.94
1978—Memphis	Southern	19	130	8	10	.444	107	57	44	78	44	3.05
1978—Montreal	National	5	10	0	1	.000	9	4	3	7	2	2.70
1979—Montreal	National	36	123	10	2	.833	110	41	36	72	30	2.63
1980—Montreal†	National	24	130	8	6	.571	124	53	43	73	30	2.98
1981—West Palm Beach‡	Florida St.	3	11	0	0	.000	9	1	1	7	5	0.82
1981—Memphis	Southern	1	0	0	0	.000	0	1	1	0	1	0.00
1982—Memphis	Southern	9	51⅓	3	2	.600	38	21	20	44	33	3.51
1982—Montreal §	National	13	73⅔	6	4	.600	60	34	26	46	36	3.18
1983—West Palm Beach x	Florida St.					(Did not play)						
1984—Montreal y	National	20	105⅓	7	3	.700	101	45	45	66	44	3.84
1985—Montreal za	National	24	135⅔	7	10	.412	128	60	56	106	67	3.71
1986—Atlanta b	National	35	209⅔	11	10	.524	181	98	85	170	102	3.65
1987—Atlanta c	National	28	152⅓	8	11	.421	169	94	83	111	64	4.90
1987—Greenville d	Southern	1	5	1	0	1.000	3	0	0	6	3	0.00
1988—Philadelphia ef	National	22	129	7	9	.438	129	67	64	85	48	4.47
Major League Totals—9 Years		207	1068⅔	64	56	.533	1011	496	441	736	423	3.71

Selected by Montreal Expos' organization in 21st round of free-agent draft, June 8, 1976.
†On disabled list, July 21 to August 27, 1980.
‡On Montreal disabled list, March 25 to August 9, 1981; included rehabilitation disability assignment to West Palm Beach, May 6 to May 25, 1981.
§On disabled list, August 14 to September 27, 1982.
xOn Montreal disabled list, March 28 to September 20, 1983; included rehabilitation disability assignment to West Palm Beach, August 6 to August 26, 1983.
yOn disabled list, August 5 to September 1, 1984.
zOn disabled list, August 9 to September 1, 1985.
aGranted free agency, November 12, 1985; signed by Atlanta Braves' organizaton, February 13, 1986.
bGranted free agency, November 12, 1986; re-signed by Braves, December 19, 1986.
cOn disabled list, June 19 to July 25, 1987; included rehabilitation disability assignment to Greenville, July 21 to July 25, 1987.
dGranted free agency, November 9, 1987; signed by Philadelphia Phillies, December 18, 1987.
eOn disabled list, July 3 to July 18, 1988.
fReleased, October 13, 1988.

DEAN WILLIAM PALMER

Born December 27, 1968, at Tallahassee, Fla.
Height, 6.01. Weight, 175.
Throws and bats righthanded.

Year	Club	League	Pos.	G.	AB.	R.	H.	2B.	3B.	HR.	RBI.	B.A.	PO.	A.	E.	F.A.
1986	Sarasota Rangers	Gulf C.	3B	50	163	19	34	7	1	0	12	.209	25	75	13	.885
1987	Gastonia	S. Atl.	3B	128	484	51	104	16	0	9	54	.215	58	209	★59	.819
1988	Port Charlotte†	Fla. St.	3B	74	305	38	81	12	1	4	35	.266	49	144	28	.873

Selected by Texas Rangers' organization in 3rd round of free-agent draft, June 2, 1986.
†On disabled list, July 19, 1988 through remainder of season.

JAMES FRANKLIN PANKOVITS
(Jim)

Born August 6, 1955, at Pennington Gap, Va.
Height, 5.10. Weight, 175.
Throws and bats righthanded.
Attended University of South Carolina, Columbia, S.C.

Major League stolen bases: 1984 (2), 1985 (1), 1986 (1), 1987 (2), 1988 (2). Total—8.
Led Appalachian League second basemen in assists with 212 and double plays with 47 in 1976.
Named third baseman on THE SPORTING NEWS College Baseball All-America Team, 1976.

Year	Club	League	Pos.	G.	AB.	R.	H.	2B.	3B.	HR.	RBI.	B.A.	PO.	A.	E.	F.A.
1976	Covington	Appal.	2B	●70	275	50	68	9	2	5	31	.247	165	212	18	.954
1977	Cocoa†	Fla. St.	SS-3B	91	326	27	74	9	3	2	20	.227	2	3	0	1.000
1978	Columbus	South.	SS	137	509	67	122	19	7	10	43	.240	4	8	2	.857
1978	Charleston	Int.	2B	3	7	0	1	0	0	0	0	.143	5	3	0	1.000
1979	Columbus	South.	SS	92	346	53	91	10	3	10	45	.263	0	13	0	1.000
1979	Charleston	Int.	2B	22	59	7	10	3	1	0	3	.169	43	53	4	.960
1980	Tucson	P. C.	2B-3B-SS	64	213	36	53	8	4	2	26	.249	110	128	9	.964
1981	Tucson	P. C.	O-3-2-S	122	450	83	127	34	9	7	64	.282	93	75	22	.884
1982	Hawaii‡§	P. C.	3B-2B-OF	139	494	84	132	25	7	15	77	.267	192	162	22	.941
1983	Tucson	P. C.	2B	126	450	77	129	25	6	11	62	.287	215	322	25	.956
1984	Tucson	P. C.	2B	49	187	41	62	12	3	7	39	.332	103	176	8	.972
1984	Houston	Nat.	2B-SS-OF	53	81	6	23	7	0	1	14	.284	22	22	3	.936
1985	Houston x	Nat.	O-2-S-3	75	172	24	42	3	0	4	14	.244	81	38	2	.983
1986	Houston	Nat.	2B-OF-C	70	113	12	32	6	1	1	7	.283	42	58	4	.962
1987	Tucson	P. C.	2-3-1-O-S	34	101	17	33	7	2	4	25	.327	67	49	3	.975
1987	Houston	Nat.	2B-OF-3B	50	61	7	14	2	0	1	8	.230	19	15	0	1.000
1988	Houston y	Nat.	2B-3B-1B	68	140	13	31	7	1	2	12	.221	48	80	11	.921
Major League Totals—5 Years				316	567	62	142	25	2	9	55	.250	212	213	20	.955

Selected by Houston Astros' organization in 4th round of free-agent draft, June 8, 1976.
†On disabled list, May 22 to June 24, 1977.
‡Traded to Hawaii (San Diego Padres' organization) for Outfielder Doug Lulay, March 28, 1982.
§Granted free agency, October 22, 1982; re-signed by Astros' organization, January 23, 1983.
xOn disabled list, July 3 to July 18 and July 26 to August 22, 1985.
yReleased, November 17, 1988.

CHAMPIONSHIP SERIES RECORD

Year	Club	League	Pos.	G.	AB.	R.	H.	2B.	3B.	HR.	RBI.	B.A.	PO.	A.	E.	F.A.
1986	Houston	Nat.	PH	2	2	0	0	0	0	0	0	.000	0	0	0	.000

ALBERTO JUDAS PARDO
(Al)

Born September 8, 1962, at Oviedo, Spain.
Height, 6.02. Weight, 195.
Throws right and bats left and righthanded.
Attended Hillsborough Community College, Tampa, Fla.
Brother of Braulio Pardo, minor league catcher, 1980.

Led Southern League in game-winning RBIs with 17 in 1984.

Year	Club	League	Pos.	G.	AB.	R.	H.	2B.	3B.	HR.	RBI.	B.A.	PO.	A.	E.	F.A.
1980	—Bluefield	Appal.	C-1B	48	151	26	52	6	2	3	23	.344	66	8	0	1.000
1981	—Miami	Fla. St.	C	91	291	25	63	9	3	3	32	.216	396	41	6	.987
1981	—Hagerstown	Carol.	C	21	76	11	24	3	1	1	7	.316	37	7	2	.957
1982	—Hagerstown	Carol.	C-1B-OF	130	492	76	142	24	4	17	86	.289	685	74	11	.986
1983	—Rochester	Int.	C	69	220	25	56	11	2	1	31	.255	223	18	9	.964
1983	—Charlotte	South.	C	37	141	20	44	11	3	4	19	.312	129	18	4	.974
1984	—Charlotte	South.	C-OF-1B	138	483	72	128	23	2	13	81	.265	397	32	14	.968
1985	—Rochester	Int.	C	60	194	23	49	14	1	8	35	.253	258	19	6	.979
1985	—Baltimore	Amer.	C	34	75	3	10	1	0	0	1	.133	131	7	3	.979
1986	—Rochester	Int.	C	76	253	34	54	12	1	8	34	.213	321	27	3	.991
1986	—Baltimore†	Amer.	C	16	51	3	7	1	0	1	3	.137	70	5	1	.987
1987	—Richmond‡	Int.	C	16	47	8	10	3	0	2	5	.213	72	4	0	1.000
1987	—Jackson	Texas	1B-C	25	61	2	20	6	0	1	13	.328	58	7	1	.985
1988	—Tide.§-Maine	Int.	C-1B	59	153	13	39	8	0	4	21	.255	127	10	1	.993
1988	—Philadelphia	Nat.	C	2	2	0	0	0	0	0	0	.000	2	0	0	1.000
American League Totals—2 Years				50	126	6	17	2	0	1	4	.135	201	12	4	.982
National League Totals—1 Year				2	2	0	0	0	0	0	0	.000	2	0	0	1.000
Major League Totals—3 Years				52	128	6	17	2	0	1	4	.133	203	12	4	.982

Selected by Baltimore Orioles' organization in 2nd round of free-agent draft, June 3, 1980.
†Granted free agency, October 15, 1986; signed by Atlanta Braves' organization, November 17, 1986.
‡Released, June 8, 1987; signed by Jackson (New York Mets' organization), July 24, 1987.
§Sold to Maine (Philadelphia Phillies' organization), July 30, 1988.

JOHNNY ALFONSO PAREDES (ISAMBERT)

Born September 2, 1962, at Maracaibo, Venezuela.
Height, 5.11. Weight, 165.
Throws and bats righthanded.

Major League stolen bases: 1988 (5).

Year	Club	League	Pos.	G.	AB.	R.	H.	2B.	3B.	HR.	RBI.	B.A.	PO.	A.	E.	F.A.
1982	—Helena	Pioneer	3B-2B-SS	34	105	17	32	4	1	1	7	.305	28	63	7	.929
1983	—Spartanburg†	S. Atl.	3B-1B-2B	46	130	14	31	0	3	0	11	.238	98	59	11	.925
1984	—W. Palm Beach	Fla. St.	2B	112	438	64	111	11	1	0	32	.253	275	295	15	*.974
1985	—W. Palm Beach	Fla. St.	2B	101	322	65	84	7	4	2	34	.261	184	281	9	*.981
1985	—Jacksonville	South.	2B	21	73	11	23	2	0	0	5	.315	47	51	2	.980
1986	—Jacksonville	South.	O-S-2-3-1	122	472	86	135	15	5	6	34	.286	230	189	19	.957
1987	—Indianapolis	A. A.	2B	130	493	80	154	19	6	8	47	.312	234	387	14	.978
1988	—Indianapolis	A. A.	2B-3B	101	400	69	118	17	3	4	46	.295	220	275	10	.980
1988	—Montreal	Nat.	2B-OF	35	91	6	17	2	0	1	10	.187	46	77	3	.976
Major League Totals—1 Year				35	91	6	17	2	0	1	10	.187	46	77	3	.976

Signed as free agent by Philadelphia Phillies' organization, June 22, 1982.
†Released, September 19, 1983; signed by Gastonia (Montreal Expos' organization), January 12, 1984.

MARK ALAN PARENT

Born September 16, 1961, at Ashland, Ore.
Height, 6.05. Weight, 224.
Throws and bats righthanded.

Led Pacific Coast League catchers in fielding percentage with .988 in 1987.
Led Carolina League catchers in double plays with 16 in 1981.
Led Northwest League catchers in fielding percentage with .979 in 1980.

Year	Club	League	Pos.	G.	AB.	R.	H.	2B.	3B.	HR.	RBI.	B.A.	PO.	A.	E.	F.A.
1979	—Walla Walla	N'west	C-OF	40	126	8	24	4	0	1	11	.190	229	34	6	.978
1980	—Reno	Calif.	C	30	99	8	20	3	0	0	12	.202	128	23	2	.987
1980	—Grays Harbor	N'west	C-1B	66	230	29	55	11	2	7	32	.230	381	38	9	.979
1981	—Salem	Carol.	C	123	438	44	103	16	3	6	47	.235	*694	87	*28	.965
1982	—Amarillo	Texas	C	26	89	12	17	3	1	1	13	.191	100	6	2	.981
1982	—Salem	Carol.	C-1B	99	360	39	81	15	2	6	41	.225	475	64	12	.978
1983	—Beaumont†	Texas	C	81	282	38	71	22	1	7	33	.252	464	71	10	*.982
1984	—Beaumont‡	Texas	C-1B	111	380	52	109	24	3	7	60	.287	674	68	7	.991
1985	—Las Vegas	P. C.	C-1B	105	361	36	87	23	3	7	45	.241	586	54	6	.991
1986	—Las Vegas	P. C.	C-1B	86	267	29	77	10	4	5	40	.288	344	40	5	.987
1986	—San Diego	Nat.	C	8	14	1	2	0	0	0	0	.143	16	0	2	.889
1987	—Las Vegas	P. C.	C-1-3-O	105	387	50	113	23	2	4	43	.292	556	58	8	.987
1987	—San Diego	Nat.	C	12	25	0	2	0	0	0	2	.080	36	3	0	1.000
1988	—San Diego	Nat.	C	41	118	9	23	3	0	6	15	.195	203	15	3	.986
Major League Totals—3 Years				61	157	10	27	3	0	6	17	.172	255	18	5	.982

Selected by San Diego Padres' organization in 4th round of free-agent draft, June 5, 1979.
†On suspended list, August 27, 1983 through remainder of season.
‡On disabled list, September 4, 1984 through remainder of season.

—DID YOU KNOW—

That when Joe Magrane homered April 4 against Cincinnati, he became the first St. Louis Cardinal pitcher to hit a home run in a season opener since Jack Powell in 1901?

KELLY JAY PARIS

Born October 17, 1957, at Encinada, Calif.
Height, 6.00. Weight, 175.
Throws right and bats left and righthanded.
Brother of Brett Paris, infielder in San Francisco Giants' and
St. Louis Cardinals' organizations, 1975 and 1976.

Led Appalachian League in sacrifice flies with 7 in 1977.

Led Florida State League third basemen in double plays with 24 and tied for lead in errors with 29 in 1979.

Year Club	League	Pos.	G.	AB.	R.	H.	2B.	3B.	HR.	RBI.	B.A.	PO.	A.	E.	F.A.
1975—Sarasota Cards	Gulf C.	SS	34	123	14	29	2	0	2	13	.236	59	92	14	.915
1976—Johnson City†	Appal.	1B	●7°	247	40	68	7	3	5	30	.275	621	43	7	.990
1977—St. Petersburg‡	Fla. St.	1B-3B	44	124	14	22	3	0	0	9	.177	269	22	3	.990
1977—Johnson City‡	Appal.	1B-3B	51	169	32	53	8	1	2	28	.314	355	37	5	.987
1978—St. Petersburg	Fla. St.	1B	42	155	14	32	6	0	1	12	.206	319	23	5	.986
1978—Gastonia	W. Car.	1B-3B	79	297	48	75	9	3	2	20	.253	593	49	12	.982
1979—St. Petersburg	Fla. St.	3B-1B	118	388	52	110	15	3	2	53	.284	291	229	30	.945
1980—Arkansas	Texas	SS	116	399	63	120	28	3	4	49	.301	181	349	38	.933
1981—Springfield§	A. A.	SS-3B	90	292	38	78	10	1	6	31	.267	119	237	36	.908
1982—Louisville	A. A.	SS-3B-2B	129	482	71	158	32	5	11	83	.328	208	364	29	.952
1982—St. Louis x	Nat.	3B-2B	12	29	1	3	0	0	0	1	.103	9	25	4	.895
1983—Cincinnati	Nat.	3-2-S-1	56	120	13	30	6	0	0	7	.250	60	62	6	.953
1983—Indianapolis yz	A. A.	SS-2B-3B	8	35	9	11	1	0	2	9	.314	10	26	0	1.000
1984—Hawaii a	P. C.	SS-2B	127	460	65	115	26	3	10	58	.250	203	313	32	.942
1985—Rochester	Int.	S-2-3-O	126	440	69	121	25	2	18	67	.275	169	376	34	.941
1985—Baltimore	Amer.	2B	5	9	0	0	0	0	0	0	.000	3	3	1	.857
1986—Rochester b	Int.	3B-SS-2B	87	309	43	77	16	2	11	48	.249	92	204	16	.949
1986—Baltimore c	Amer.	3B	5	10	0	2	0	0	0	0	.200	0	6	1	.857
1987—					(Out of Organized Baseball)										
1988—Vancouver	P. C.	3B-SS-2B	89	359	41	102	32	3	5	52	.284	66	231	15	.952
1988—Chicago de	Amer.	1B-3B	14	44	6	11	0	0	3	6	.250	60	12	1	.986
National League Totals—2 Years			68	149	14	33	6	0	0	8	.221	69	87	10	.940
American League Totals—3 Years			24	63	6	13	0	0	3	6	.206	63	21	3	.966
Major League Totals—5 Years			92	212	20	46	6	0	3	14	.217	132	108	13	.949

Selected by St. Louis Cardinals' organization in 2nd round of free-agent draft, June 4, 1975.

†On temporarily inactive list, April 16 to May 7, 1976.

‡Batted as switchhitter.

§On disabled list, July 25, 1981 through remainder of season.

xTraded to Cincinnati Reds' organization for Pitcher James Strichek, March 31, 1983.

ySold to Chicago White Sox, November 28, 1983.

zReleased, March 21, 1984; signed by Pittsburgh Pirates' organization, March 28, 1984.

aGranted free agency, October 15, 1984; signed by Rochester (Baltimore Orioles' organization), November 12, 1984.

bOn disabled list, April 16 to May 14, 1986.

cGranted free agency, October 15, 1986; signed by Vancouver (Chicago White Sox' organization), December 24, 1987.

dOn disabled list, August 19, 1988 through remainder of season.

eReleased, November 8, 1988.

DAVID GENE PARKER
(Dave)

Born June 9, 1951, at Jackson, Miss.
Height, 6.05. Weight, 245.
Throws right and bats lefthanded.

Tied major league record for most home runs, month of October (4), 1985; fewest errors by outfielder, season, for leader in errors (9), 1986.

Major League stolen bases: 1973 (1), 1974 (3), 1975 (8), 1976 (19), 1977 (17), 1978 (20), 1979 (20), 1980 (10), 1981 (6), 1982 (7), 1983 (12), 1984 (11), 1985 (5), 1986 (1), 1987 (7). Total—147.

Led National League in grounding into double plays with 26 in 1985.

Led National League in total bases with 340 in 1978, 350 in 1985 and 304 in 1986.

Led National League in slugging percentage with .541 in 1975 and .585 in 1978.

Led National League in intentional bases on balls received with 23 in 1978 and tied for lead with 24 in 1985.

Tied for National League lead in game-winning RBIs with 16 in 1987.

Tied for National League lead in sacrifice flies with 9 in 1979.

Led National League outfielders in total chances with 430 and double plays with 9 in 1977.

Led Carolina League in total bases with 270 and stolen bases with 38 in 1972.

Tied for Gulf Coast League lead in total bases with 107 in 1970.

Named National League Player of the Year by The Sporting News, 1978.

Named National League Most Valuable Player by Baseball Writers' Association of America, 1978.

Named outfielder on The Sporting News National League All-Star Team, 1975, 1977, 1978, 1985 and 1986.

Named outfielder on The Sporting News National League All-Star fielding team, 1977 through 1979.

Named outfielder on The Sporting News National League Silver Slugger team, 1985 and 1986.

Named Carolina League Most Valuable Player, 1972.

Year Club	League	Pos.	G.	AB.	R.	H.	2B.	3B.	HR.	RBI.	B.A.	PO.	A.	E.	F.A.
1970—Bradenton Pir.	Gulf C.	●OF-P	61	239	34	75	8	3	●6	41	.314	92	11	●8	.928
1971—Waterbury	East.	OF	30	114	10	26	4	1	0	7	.228	43	5	6	.889
1971—Monroe	W. Car.	OF	71	268	49	96	16	4	11	48	.358	104	8	10	.918
1972—Salem	Carol.	OF	135	★523	★91	★162	★30	6	22	★101	★.310	★250	★20	★20	.931
1973—Charleston	Int.	OF	84	309	44	98	20	7	9	57	.317	144	11	7	.957
1973—Pittsburgh	Nat.	OF	54	139	17	40	9	1	4	14	.288	77	3	3	.964

Year	Club	League	Pos.	G.	AB.	R.	H.	2B.	3B.	HR.	RBI.	B.A.	PO.	A.	E.	F.A.
1974	—Pittsburgh†	Nat.	OF-1B	73	220	27	62	10	3	4	29	.282	154	8	4	.976
1975	—Pittsburgh	Nat.	OF	148	558	75	172	35	10	25	101	.308	311	7	9	.972
1976	—Pittsburgh	Nat.	OF	138	537	82	168	28	10	13	90	.313	294	13	*14	.956
1977	—Pittsburgh	Nat.	*OF-2B	159	637	107	*215	*44	8	21	88	*.338	*389	*26	*15	.965
1978	—Pittsburgh‡	Nat.	OF	148	581	102	194	32	12	30	117	*.334	302	12	*13	.960
1979	—Pittsburgh	Nat.	OF	158	622	109	193	45	7	25	94	.310	341	15	*15	.960
1980	—Pittsburgh	Nat.	OF	139	518	71	153	31	1	17	79	.295	235	14	9	.965
1981	—Pittsburgh§	Nat.	OF	67	240	29	62	14	3	9	48	.258	110	1	7	.941
1982	—Pittsburgh x	Nat.	OF	73	244	41	66	19	3	6	29	.270	108	2	5	.957
1983	—Pittsburgh y	Nat.	OF	144	552	68	154	29	4	12	69	.279	282	3	8	.973
1984	—Cincinnati	Nat.	OF	156	607	73	173	28	0	16	94	.285	296	6	8	.974
1985	—Cincinnati	Nat.	OF	160	635	88	198	*42	4	34	*125	.312	329	12	10	.972
1986	—Cincinnati	Nat.	OF	*162	637	89	174	31	3	31	116	.273	278	9	•9	.970
1987	—Cincinnati z	Nat.	OF-1B	153	589	77	149	28	0	26	97	.253	354	17	11	.971
1988	—Oakland a	Amer.	OF-1B	101	377	43	97	18	1	12	55	.257	63	5	3	.958
National League Totals—15 Years				1932	7316	1055	2173	425	69	273	1190	.297	3860	147	140	.966
American League Totals—1 Year				101	377	43	97	18	1	12	55	.257	63	5	3	.958
Major League Totals—16 Years				2033	7693	1098	2270	443	70	285	1245	.295	3923	152	143	.966

Selected by Pittsburgh Pirates' organization in 14th round of free-agent draft, June 4, 1970.
†On disabled list, June 7 to June 28 and July 5 to July 31, 1974.
‡On disabled list, July 1 to July 16, 1978.
§On disabled list, May 14 to May 29, 1981.
xOn disabled list, May 12 to June 7 and July 29 to September 7, 1982.
yGranted free agency, November 7, 1983; signed by Cincinnati Reds, December 7, 1983.
zTraded to Oakland A's for Pitchers Jose Rijo and Tim Birtsas, December 8, 1987.
aOn disabled list, July 5 to August 21, 1988.

CHAMPIONSHIP SERIES RECORD

Year	Club	League	Pos.	G.	AB.	R.	H.	2B.	3B.	HR.	RBI.	B.A.	PO.	A.	E.	F.A.
1974	—Pittsburgh	Nat.	OF-PH	3	8	0	1	0	0	0	0	.125	4	1	0	1.000
1975	—Pittsburgh	Nat.	OF	3	10	2	0	0	0	0	0	.000	13	1	0	1.000
1979	—Pittsburgh	Nat.	OF	3	12	2	4	0	0	0	2	.333	9	0	0	1.000
1988	—Oakland	Amer.	DH-OF	3	12	1	3	1	0	0	0	.250	1	0	1	.500
Championship Series Totals—4 Years				12	42	5	8	1	0	0	2	.190	27	2	1	.967

WORLD SERIES RECORD

Year	Club	League	Pos.	G.	AB.	R.	H.	2B.	3B.	HR.	RBI.	B.A.	PO.	A.	E.	F.A.
1979	—Pittsburgh	Nat.	OF	7	29	2	10	3	0	0	4	.345	13	1	1	.933
1988	—Oakland	Amer.	OF-DH	4	15	0	3	0	0	0	0	.200	4	0	0	1.000
World Series Totals—2 Years				11	44	2	13	3	0	0	4	.295	17	1	1	.947

ALL-STAR GAME RECORD

Established All-Star Game record for most assists by outfielder, game (2), July 17, 1979.

Year	League	Pos.	AB.	R.	H.	2B.	3B.	HR.	RBI.	B.A.	PO.	A.	E.	F.A.
1977	—National	OF	3	1	1	0	0	0	0	.333	2	0	0	1.000
1979	—National	OF	3	0	1	0	0	0	1	.333	0	2	0	1.000
1980	—National	OF	2	0	0	0	0	0	0	.000	0	0	0	.000
1981	—National	OF	3	1	1	0	0	1	1	.333	1	0	0	1.000
1985	—National	OF	2	0	0	0	0	0	0	.000	1	0	0	1.000
1986	—National	OF	2	0	1	0	0	0	0	.500	0	0	0	.000
All-Star Game Totals—6 Years			15	2	4	0	0	1	2	.267	4	2	0	1.000

PITCHING RECORD

Year	Club	League	G.	IP.	W.	L.	Pct.	H.	R.	ER.	SO.	BB.	ERA.
1970	—Bradenton Pirates	Gulf Coast	1	4	0	0	.000	7	2	2	2	1	4.50

RICHARD ALLEN PARKER
(Rick)

Born March 20, 1963, at Kansas City, Mo.
Height, 6.00. Weight, 185.
Throws and bats righthanded.
Attended Southwest Missouri State University, Springfield, Mo., and University of Texas, Austin, Tex.

Year	Club	League	Pos.	G.	AB.	R.	H.	2B.	3B.	HR.	RBI.	B.A.	PO.	A.	E.	F.A.
1985	—Bend	N'west	SS	55	205	45	51	9	1	2	20	.249	79	143	25	.899
1986	—Spartanburg	S. Atl.	SS	62	233	39	69	7	3	5	28	.296	87	169	18	.934
1986	—Clearwater	Fla. St.	SS	63	218	24	51	10	2	0	15	.234	94	197	21	.933
1987	—Clearwater	Fla. St.	2B-SS-3B	101	330	56	83	13	3	3	34	.252	130	234	27	.931
1988	—Reading	East.	3-O-1-2-S	116	362	50	93	13	3	3	47	.257	174	114	18	.941

Selected by Philadelphia Phillies' organization in 16th round of free-agent draft, June 3, 1985.

DEREK GAVIN PARKS

Born September 29, 1968, at Covina, Calif.
Height, 6.01. Weight, 195.
Throws and bats righthanded.

Led Southern League in being hit by pitch with 15 in 1988.
Led Appalachian League in passed balls with 17 in 1986.

Year	Club	League	Pos.	G.	AB.	R.	H.	2B.	3B.	HR.	RBI.	B.A.	PO.	A.	E.	F.A.
1986	Elizabethton	Appal.	C	62	224	39	53	10	1	10	40	.237	297	36	7	.979
1987	Kenosha	Midw.	C	129	466	70	115	19	2	24	94	.247	800	85	14	.984
1988	Orlando	South.	C	118	400	52	94	15	0	7	42	.235	616	66	7	.990

Selected by Minnesota Twins' organization in 1st round (10th player selected) of free-agent draft, June 2, 1986.

JEFFREY DALE PARRETT
(Jeff)

Born August 26, 1961, at Indianapolis, Ind.
Height, 6.03. Weight, 200.
Throws and bats righthanded.
Attended University of Kentucky, Lexington, Ky.

Major League saves: 1987 (6), 1988 (6). Total—12.

Year	Club	League	G.	IP.	W.	L.	Pct.	H.	R.	ER.	SO.	BB.	ERA.
1983	Paintsville	Ap'lachian	3	17	2	0	1.000	12	6	4	21	8	2.12
1983	Beloit	Midwest	10	47	2	2	.500	40	26	21	34	29	4.02
1984	Beloit	Midwest	29	91⅔	4	3	.571	76	50	46	95	71	4.52
1985	Stockton†	California	45	127⅔	7	4	.636	97	50	39	120	75	*2.75
1986	Montreal	National	12	20⅓	0	1	.000	19	11	11	21	13	4.87
1986	Indianapolis	Am. Assoc.	25	69	2	5	.286	54	44	38	76	35	4.96
1987	Montreal	National	45	62	7	6	.538	53	33	29	56	30	4.21
1987	Indianapolis	Am. Assoc.	20	22⅓	2	1	.667	15	5	5	17	13	2.01
1988	Montreal‡§	National	61	91⅔	12	4	.750	66	29	27	62	45	2.65
Major League Totals—3 Years			118	174	19	11	.633	138	73	67	139	88	3.47

Selected by Milwaukee Brewers' organization in 9th round of free-agent draft, June 6, 1983.
†Drafted by Montreal Expos, December 10, 1985.
‡On disabled list, July 16 to August 14, 1988.
§Traded with Pitcher Floyd Youmans to Philadelphia Phillies for Pitcher Kevin Gross, December 6, 1988.

LANCE MICHAEL PARRISH

Born June 15, 1956, at McKeesport, Pa.
Height, 6.03. Weight, 220.
Throws and bats righthanded.

Major League stolen bases: 1979 (6), 1980 (6), 1981 (2), 1982 (3), 1983 (1), 1984 (2), 1985 (2). Total—22.
Led American League in sacrifice flies with 13 in 1983.
Led American League catchers in double plays with 11 in 1984.
Led American League catchers in total chances with 772 in 1983.
Led American League in passed balls with 21 in 1979.
Led National League catchers in passed balls with 12 and tied for lead in double plays with 11 in 1988.
Tied for American League lead in passed balls with 17 in 1980.
Led Appalachian League batters in strikeouts with 92 in 1974.
Led American Association in double plays with 10 and passed balls with 21 in 1977.
Led Southern League in passed balls with 22 in 1976.
Led Florida State League catchers in double plays with 8 and passed balls with 31 in 1975.
Named catcher on THE SPORTING NEWS American League All-Star Team, 1982 and 1984.
Named catcher on THE SPORTING NEWS American League All-Star fielding team, 1983 through 1985.
Named catcher on THE SPORTING NEWS American League Silver Slugger team, 1980, 1982 through 1984 and 1986.

Year	Club	League	Pos.	G.	AB.	R.	H.	2B.	3B.	HR.	RBI.	B.A.	PO.	A.	E.	F.A.
1974	Bristol	Appal.	3B-OF	68	253	45	54	11	1	11	46	.213	36	83	22	.844
1975	Lakeland	Fla. St.	C	100	341	30	75	15	2	5	37	.220	460	50	7	.986
1976	Montgomery	South.	C	107	340	46	75	9	2	14	55	.221	*600	*79	11	*.984
1977	Evansville	A. A.	C	115	416	74	116	21	2	25	90	.279	*722	*82	11	*.987
1977	Detroit	Amer.	C	12	46	10	9	2	0	3	7	.196	76	6	0	1.000
1978	Detroit	Amer.	C	85	288	37	63	11	3	14	41	.219	353	39	5	.987
1979	Detroit	Amer.	C	143	493	65	136	26	3	19	65	.276	707	*79	9	.989
1980	Detroit	Amer.	C-1B-OF	144	553	79	158	34	6	24	82	.286	607	67	7	.990
1981	Detroit	Amer.	C	96	348	39	85	18	2	10	46	.244	407	40	3	.993
1982	Detroit	Amer.	C-OF	133	486	75	138	19	2	32	87	.284	627	76	8	.989
1983	Detroit	Amer.	C	155	605	80	163	42	3	27	114	.269	695	73	4	.995
1984	Detroit	Amer.	C	147	578	75	137	16	2	33	98	.237	720	67	7	.991
1985	Detroit	Amer.	C	140	549	64	150	27	1	28	98	.273	695	53	5	.993
1986	Detroit†‡	Amer.	C	91	327	53	84	6	1	22	62	.257	483	48	6	.989
1987	Philadelphia	Nat.	C	130	466	42	114	21	0	17	67	.245	724	66	9	.989
1988	Philadelphia§x	Nat.	C-1B	123	424	44	91	17	2	15	60	.215	640	73	9	.988
American League Totals—10 Years				1146	4273	577	1123	201	23	212	700	.263	5370	548	54	.991
National League Totals—2 Years				253	890	86	205	38	2	32	127	.230	1364	139	18	.988
Major League Totals—12 Years				1399	5163	663	1328	239	25	244	827	.257	6734	687	72	.990

Selected by Detroit Tigers' organization in 1st round (16th player selected) of free-agent draft, June 5, 1974.
†On disabled list, July 31 to September 29, 1986.
‡Granted free agency, November 12, 1986; signed by Philadelphia Phillies, March 13, 1987.
§On disabled list, July 13 to July 28, 1988.
xTraded to California Angels for Pitcher David Holdridge, October 3, 1988.

CHAMPIONSHIP SERIES RECORD

Year	Club	League	Pos.	G.	AB.	R.	H.	2B.	3B.	HR.	RBI.	B.A.	PO.	A.	E.	F.A.
1984	Detroit	Amer.	C	3	12	1	3	1	0	1	3	.250	21	2	0	1.000

WORLD SERIES RECORD

Year	Club	League	Pos.	G.	AB.	R.	H.	2B.	3B.	HR.	RBI.	B.A.	PO.	A.	E.	F.A.
1984	Detroit	Amer.	C	5	18	3	5	1	0	1	2	.278	30	3	1	.971

ALL-STAR GAME RECORD

Established All-Star Game record for most assists by catcher, game (3), July 13, 1982.

Year	League	Pos.	AB.	R.	H.	2B.	3B.	HR.	RBI.	B.A.	PO.	A.	E.	F.A.
1980	American	C	1	0	0	0	0	0	0	.000	0	0	0	.000
1982	American	C	2	0	1	1	0	0	0	.500	2	3	0	1.000
1983	American	C	2	0	0	0	0	0	0	.000	1	0	0	1.000
1984	American	C	2	0	0	0	0	0	0	.000	3	1	1	.800
1986	American	C	3	0	0	0	0	0	0	.000	4	0	0	1.000
1988	National	C	1	0	0	0	0	0	0	.000	0	0	0	.000
All-Star Game Totals—6 Years			11	0	1	1	0	0	0	.091	10	4	1	.933

Named to American League All-Star Team for 1985 game; replaced due to injury by Rich Gedman.

LARRY ALTON PARRISH

Born November 10, 1953, at Winter Haven, Fla.
Height, 6.03. Weight, 215.
Throws and bats righthanded.
Attended Seminole Community College, Sanford, Fla.

Tied major league records for most home runs, bases filled, month (3), July, 1982; most home runs, bases filled, week (3), July 4 through 10 (first game), 1982.

Major League stolen bases‘ 1975 (4), 1976 (2), 1977 (2), 1978 (2), 1979 (5), 1980 (2), 1982 (5), 1984 (2), 1986 (3), 1987 (3). Total—30.

Hit three home runs in a game, May 29, 1977, July 30, 1978, April 25, 1980 and April 29, 1985.

Tied for National League lead in double plays by third basemen with 35 in 1976.

Led Florida State League in sacrifice flies with 9 in 1973.

Led Eastern League third basemen in double plays with 32 in 1974.

Led Florida State League third basemen in putouts with 95 and assists with 285 in 1973.

Named Florida State League Most Valuable Player, 1973.

Year	Club	League	Pos.	G.	AB.	R.	H.	2B.	3B.	HR.	RBI.	B.A.	PO.	A.	E.	F.A.
1972	W. Palm B'ch	Fla. St.	OF	2	4	0	1	0	0	0	0	.250	2	0	0	1.000
1972	Jamestown	NYP	OF	62	223	32	58	4	3	4	28	.260	69	3	3	.960
1973	W. Palm B'ch	Fla. St.	★3B-SS	138	481	82	141	14	6	16	81	.293	100	292	32	★.925
1974	Quebec City	East.	3B	119	437	61	124	14	2	13	77	.284	★108	★277	●31	.925
1974	Montreal	Nat.	3B	25	69	9	14	5	0	0	4	.203	20	51	1	.986
1975	Montreal	Nat.	3B-SS-2B	145	532	50	146	32	5	10	65	.274	105	291	35	.919
1976	Montreal	Nat.	3B	154	543	65	126	28	5	11	61	.232	122	310	25	.945
1977	Montreal	Nat.	3B	123	402	50	99	19	2	11	46	.246	81	225	21	.936
1978	Montreal	Nat.	3B	144	520	68	144	39	4	15	70	.277	122	288	23	.947
1979	Montreal	Nat.	3B	153	544	83	167	39	2	30	82	.307	119	290	23	.947
1980	Montreal†	Nat.	3B	126	452	55	115	27	3	15	72	.254	106	231	18	.949
1981	Montreal‡	Nat.	3B	97	349	41	85	19	3	8	44	.244	★91	141	16	.935
1982	Texas	Amer.	OF-3B	128	440	59	116	15	0	17	62	.264	190	12	8	.962
1983	Texas	Amer.	OF	145	555	76	151	26	4	26	88	.272	215	11	9	.962
1984	Texas	Amer.	OF-3B	156	613	72	175	42	1	22	101	.285	155	35	4	.979
1985	Texas§	Amer.	OF-3B	94	346	44	86	11	1	17	51	.249	111	7	1	.992
1986	Texas x	Amer.	3B	129	464	67	128	22	1	28	94	.276	23	35	4	.935
1987	Texas	Amer.	3B-OF	152	557	79	149	22	1	32	100	.268	19	26	4	.918
1988	Tex.y-Bos.z	Amer.	1B	120	406	32	88	14	1	14	52	.217	221	25	3	.988
National League Totals—8 Years				967	3411	421	896	208	24	100	444	.263	866	1827	162	.943
American League Totals—7 Years				924	3381	429	893	152	9	156	548	.264	934	151	33	.970
Major League Totals—15 Years				1891	6792	850	1789	360	33	256	992	.263	1800	1978	195	.951

Signed as free agent by Montreal Expos' organization, May 21, 1972.

†On disabled list, June 2 to June 30, 1980.

‡Traded with First Baseman Dave Hostetler to Texas Rangers for First Baseman-Outfielder Al Oliver, March 31, 1982.

§On disabled list, July 6 to September 1, 1985.

xOn disabled list, May 20 to June 18, 1986.

yReleased, July 9, 1988; signed by Boston Red Sox, July 16, 1988.

zReleased, October 28, 1988.

DIVISION SERIES RECORD

Year	Club	League	Pos.	G.	AB.	R.	H.	2B.	3B.	HR.	RBI.	B.A.	PO.	A.	E.	F.A.
1981	Montreal	Nat.	3B	5	20	3	3	1	0	0	1	.150	7	6	0	1.000

CHAMPIONSHIP SERIES RECORD

Year	Club	League	Pos.	G.	AB.	R.	H.	2B.	3B.	HR.	RBI.	B.A.	PO.	A.	E.	F.A.
1981	Montreal	Nat.	3B	5	19	2	5	2	0	0	2	.263	3	13	1	.941
1988	Boston	Amer.	PH-DH-1	4	6	0	0	0	0	0	0	.000	7	0	0	1.000
Championship Series Totals—2 Years				9	25	2	5	2	0	0	2	.200	10	13	1	.958

ALL-STAR GAME RECORD

Year League	Pos.	AB.	R.	H.	2B.	3B.	HR.	RBI.	B.A.	PO.	A.	E.	F.A.
1979—National	3B	0	0	0	0	0	0	0	.000	0	0	0	.000
1987—American	PH	1	0	1	0	0	0	0	1.000	0	0	0	.000
All-Star Game Totals—2 Years		1	0	1	0	0	0	0	1.000	0	0	0	.000

DANIEL ANTHONY PASQUA

Name Pronounced PASS-quah.

(Dan)

Born October 17, 1961, at Yonkers, N. Y.
Height, 6.00. Weight, 205.
Throws and bats lefthanded.
Attended William Paterson College, Wayne, N.J.

Major League stolen bases: 1986 (2), 1988 (1). Total—3.
Led American League outfielders in fielding percentage with .996 in 1988.
Led International League in slugging percentage with .599 in 1985.
Led Southern League batters in strikeouts with 148 in 1984.
Named International League Player of the Year, 1985.
Named Appalachian League Player of the Year, 1982.

Year Club	League	Pos.	G.	AB.	R.	H.	2B.	3B.	HR.	RBI.	B.A.	PO.	A.	E.	F.A.
1982—Paintsville	Appal.	OF	60	239	43	72	10	2	*16	●63	.301	114	4	4	.967
1982—Oneonta	NYP	OF	4	17	3	5	1	0	2	4	.294	2	1	1	.750
1983—Fort Lauderdale	Fla. St.	OF	131	451	83	123	25	10	19	84	.273	213	8	5	.978
1983—Columbus	Int.	OF	1	3	0	0	0	0	0	0	.000	5	0	0	1.000
1984—Nashville	South.	OF	136	460	78	112	14	3	*33	91	.243	244	11	*12	.955
1985—Columbus	Int.	OF	78	287	52	92	16	5	18	69	.321	141	9	4	.974
1985—New York	Amer.	OF	60	148	17	31	3	1	9	25	.209	72	2	0	1.000
1986—Columbus	Int.	OF	32	110	25	32	3	3	6	20	.291	62	0	3	.954
1986—New York	Amer.	OF-1B	102	280	44	82	17	0	16	45	.293	172	4	2	.989
1987—New York	Amer.	OF-1B	113	318	42	74	7	1	17	42	.233	214	10	2	.991
1987—Columbus†	Int.	OF	23	85	16	29	6	0	6	15	.341	55	0	1	.982
1988—Chicago	Amer.	OF-1B	129	422	48	96	16	2	20	50	.227	316	14	2	.994
Major League Totals—4 Years			404	1168	151	283	43	4	62	162	.242	774	30	6	.993

Selected by New York Yankees' organization in 3rd round of free-agent draft, June 7, 1982.

†Traded with Catcher Mark Salas and Pitcher Steve Rosenberg to Chicago White Sox for Pitchers Richard Dotson and Scott Nielsen, November 12, 1987.

KENNETH BRIAN PATTERSON

(Ken)

Born July 8, 1964, at Costa Mesa, Calif.
Height, 6.04. Weight, 210.
Throws and bats lefthanded.
Attended McLennan Community College, Waco, Tex., and Baylor University, Waco, Tex.

Major League saves: 1988 (1).
Led New York-Pennsylvania League in shutouts with 4 in 1986.

Year Club	League	G.	IP.	W.	L.	Pct.	H.	R.	ER.	SO.	BB.	ERA.
1985—Oneonta	NYP	6	22⅓	2	2	.500	23	14	12	21	14	4.84
1986—Fort Lauderdale	Florida St.	5	18⅔	0	2	.000	30	20	16	13	16	7.71
1986—Oneonta†	NYP	15	100⅓	9	3	.750	67	25	15	102	45	*1.35
1987—Daytona Beach	Florida St.	9	42⅔	1	3	.250	46	34	30	36	31	6.33
1987—Hawaii	P. Coast	3	3⅓	0	0	.000	1	0	0	5	3	0.00
1988—Vancouver	P. Coast	55	86⅓	6	5	.545	64	37	31	89	36	3.23
1988—Chicago	American	9	20⅔	0	2	.000	25	11	11	8	7	4.79
Major League Totals—1 Year		9	20⅔	0	2	.000	25	11	11	8	7	4.79

Selected by Philadelphia Phillies' organization in 29th round of free-agent draft, June 7, 1982.
Selected by Baltimore Orioles' organization in secondary phase of free-agent draft, January 11, 1983.
Selected by Philadelphia Phillies' organization in secondary phase of free-agent draft, June 6, 1983.
Selected by New York Yankees' organization in 3rd round of free-agent draft, June 3, 1985.

†Traded with a player to be named later to Chicago White Sox for Infielder-Outfielder Jerry Royster and Infielder Mike Soper, August 26, 1987; White Sox acquired Pitcher Jeff Pries to complete deal, September 19, 1987.

DAVID LEE PAVLAS

(Dave)

Born August 12, 1962, at Frankfurt, West Germany.
Height, 6.07. Weight, 180.
Throws and bats righthanded.
Attended Rice University, Houston, Tex.

Named Carolina League Pitcher of the Year, 1986.

Year Club	League	G.	IP.	W.	L.	Pct.	H.	R.	ER.	SO.	BB.	ERA.
1985—Peoria	Midwest	17	110	8	3	.727	90	40	32	86	32	2.62
1986—Winston-Salem	Carolina	28	173⅓	14	6	.700	172	91	74	143	57	3.84
1987—Pittsfield†	Eastern	7	45	6	1	.857	49	25	19	27	17	3.80
1987—Tulsa	Texas	13	59⅔	1	6	.143	79	51	51	46	27	7.69
1988—Tulsa	Texas	26	77⅓	5	2	.714	52	26	17	69	18	1.98
1988—Oklahoma City	Am. Assoc.	13	52⅓	3	1	.750	59	29	26	40	28	4.47

Signed as free agent by Chicago Cubs' organization, December 15, 1984.

†Traded to Texas Rangers' organization, June 6, 1987, completing deal in which Texas traded Pitcher Mike Mason to Chicago Cubs for a player to be named later, May 15, 1987.

JOHN PAWLOWSKI

Born September 6, 1963, at Johnson City, N. Y.
Height, 6.02. Weight, 175.
Throws and bats righthanded.
Attended Clemson University, Clemson, S. C.

Tied for New York-Pennsylvania League lead in games started by pitchers with 14 in 1985.

Year Club	League	G.	IP.	W.	L.	Pct.	H.	R.	ER.	SO.	BB.	ERA.
1985—Niagara Falls	NYP	15	97	9	3	.750	74	41	23	82	35	2.13
1986—Peninsula	Carolina	8	48	5	2	.714	33	21	18	30	22	3.38
1986—Birmingham	Southern	23	106⅓	6	4	.600	111	67	58	58	47	4.91
1987—Birmingham	Southern	35	69	5	6	.455	69	44	36	57	38	4.70
1987—Chicago	American	2	3⅔	0	0	.000	7	2	2	2	3	4.91
1988—Chicago	American	6	14	1	0	1.000	20	14	13	10	3	8.36
1988—Vancouver	P. Coast	9	21⅓	0	0	.000	24	11	10	11	12	4.22
Major League Totals—2 Years		8	17⅔	1	0	1.000	27	16	15	12	6	7.64

Selected by Chicago White Sox' organization in 6th round of free-agent draft, June 3, 1985.

WILLIAM JOSEPH PECOTA
(Bill)

Born February 16, 1960, at Redwood City, Calif.
Height, 6.02. Weight, 190.
Throws and bats righthanded.
Attended De Anza College, Cupertino, Calif.

Major League stolen bases: 1987 (5), 1988 (7). Total—12.

Led American Association third basemen in assists with 217 and total chances with 337 in 1986.

Led American Association third basemen in total chances with 372 and double plays with 22 in 1985.

Led Southern League third basemen in total chances with 434 in 1984.

Year Club	League	Pos.	G.	AB.	R.	H.	2B.	3B.	HR.	RBI.	B.A.	PO.	A.	E.	F.A.
1981—Sara.Roy.-Blue	Gulf C.	C-3B-2B	61	208	*61	66	11	4	3	22	.317	112	45	6	.963
1982—Fort Myers	Fla. St.	3B	135	482	71	115	16	6	4	49	.239	109	243	15	.959
1983—Fort Myers	Fla. St.	3B	65	234	48	63	7	2	5	33	.269	46	114	7	.958
1983—Jacksonville	South.	3B-SS	72	260	38	63	9	1	5	25	.242	54	135	19	.909
1984—Memphis	South.	3B	145	543	84	131	19	2	9	50	.241	*142	267	25	*.942
1985—Omaha	A. A.	*3-S-O	130	409	47	98	17	3	1	34	.240	*111	*247	14	*.962
1986—Omaha	A. A.	3B-SS-OF	139	474	48	125	26	2	4	54	.264	125	238	11	.971
1986—Kansas City	Amer.	3B-SS	12	29	3	6	2	0	0	2	.207	7	31	1	.974
1987—Omaha	A. A.	3B-SS-2B	35	126	31	39	8	1	2	16	.310	38	78	8	.935
1987—Kansas City	Amer.	SS-3B-2B	66	156	22	43	5	1	3	14	.276	67	135	6	.971
1988—Kansas City	Amer.	I-O-C	90	178	25	37	3	3	1	15	.208	98	145	6	.976
Major League Totals—3 Years			168	363	50	86	10	4	4	31	.237	172	311	13	.974

Selected by Kansas City Royals' organization in 10th round of free-agent draft, January 13, 1981.

ALFREDO JOSE PEDRIQUE (GARCIA)
(Al)

Born August 11, 1960, at Aragua, Venezuela.
Height, 6.00. Weight, 155.
Throws and bats righthanded.

Major League stolen bases: 1987 (5).

Led International League shortstops in fielding percentage with .962, assists with 321, errors with 18, total chances with 478 and double plays with 74 in 1986.

Led Texas League shortstops in fielding percentage with .961 in 1984.

Year Club	League	Pos.	G.	AB.	R.	H.	2B.	3B.	HR.	RBI.	B.A.	PO.	A.	E.	F.A.
1978—Little Falls	NYP	SS	20	54	10	12	4	0	0	2	.222	25	48	6	.924
1979—Lynchburg	Carol.	SS	19	49	2	11	2	0	0	3	.224	22	63	6	.934
1979—Little Falls	NYP	SS-2B	33	92	3	21	0	2	0	11	.228	56	90	19	.885
1980—Lynchburg	Carol.	SS-2B-3B	105	321	37	79	3	2	0	24	.246	120	234	24	.937
1981—Jackson	Texas	SS-2B	115	379	39	91	9	0	0	25	.240	184	324	34	.937
1982—Jackson	Texas	SS	121	392	38	86	13	2	2	36	.219	189	370	23	*.960
1983—Jackson	Texas	SS-2B-3B	102	326	43	78	7	1	0	27	.239	182	292	20	.960
1984—Jackson†	Texas	SS-2B-3B	109	362	47	103	15	5	1	35	.285	198	281	21	.958
1985—Tidewater	Int.	S-3-1-2	110	325	39	82	17	2	2	24	.252	170	261	12	.973
1986—Tidewater	Int.	S-1-3-2	112	379	49	111	13	2	0	41	.293	189	340	19	.965
1987—N. Y.‡-Pitt.	Nat.	SS-2B-3B	93	252	24	74	10	1	1	27	.294	118	196	11	.966
1987—Tidewater	Int.	2-3-1-S	10	27	2	7	0	0	0	3	.259	14	17	0	1.000
1988—Pittsburgh	Nat.	SS-3B	50	128	7	23	5	0	0	4	.180	65	124	5	.974
1988—Buffalo§	A. A.	2B-SS-3B	61	218	23	67	14	2	1	22	.307	101	205	12	.962
Major League Totals—2 Years			143	380	31	97	15	1	1	31	.255	183	320	16	.969

Signed as free agent by New York Mets' organization, July 21, 1978.

†Granted free agency, October 15, 1984; re-signed by Mets' organization, November 12, 1984.

‡Traded with Outfielder Scott Little to Pittsburgh Pirates for Infielder-Outfielder Bill Almon, May 29, 1987.

§Released, November 20, 1988; signed by Detroit Tigers, December 5, 1988.

ALEJANDRO PENA (VASQUEZ)

Born June 25, 1959, at Cambiaso, Dominican Republic.
Height, 6.01. Weight, 205.
Throws and bats righthanded.

Major League saves: 1981 (2), 1983 (1), 1986 (1), 1987 (11), 1988 (12). Total—27.
Tied for National League lead in shutouts with 4 in 1984.
Led Pacific Coast League in saves with 22 in 1981.

Year Club	League	G.	IP.	W.	L.	Pct.	H.	R.	ER.	SO.	BB.	ERA.
1979—Clinton	Midwest	21	71	3	3	.500	53	39	33	57	44	4.18
1980—Vero Beach	Florida St.	35	73	10	3	.769	57	32	26	46	41	3.21
1981—Albuquerque	P. Coast	38	56	2	5	.286	36	12	10	40	21	1.61
1981—Los Angeles	National	14	25	1	1	.500	18	8	8	14	11	2.88
1982—Los Angeles	National	29	35⅔	0	2	.000	37	24	19	20	21	4.79
1982—Albuquerque	P. Coast	16	28⅔	1	1	.500	37	18	17	27	10	5.34
1983—Los Angeles	National	34	177	12	9	.571	152	67	54	120	51	2.75
1984—Los Angeles	National	28	199⅓	12	6	.667	186	67	55	135	46	★2.48
1985—Los Angeles†	National	2	4⅓	0	1	.000	7	5	4	2	3	8.31
1986—Vero Beach‡	Florida St.	4	15⅔	0	2	.000	22	15	13	11	4	7.47
1986—Los Angeles	National	24	70	1	2	.333	74	40	38	46	30	4.89
1987—Los Angeles§	National	37	87⅓	2	7	.222	82	41	34	76	37	3.50
1988—Los Angeles x	National	60	94⅓	6	7	.462	75	29	20	83	27	1.91
Major League Totals—8 Years		228	693	34	35	.493	631	281	232	496	226	3.01

Signed as free agent by Los Angeles Dodgers' organization, September 10, 1978.
†On disabled list, April 8 to September 5, 1985.
‡On Los Angeles disabled list, March 23 to May 26, 1986; included rehabilitation disability assignment to Vero Beach, May 2 to May 19, 1986.
§On disabled list, July 27 to August 17, 1987.
xGranted free agency, November 4, 1988; re-signed by Dodgers, November 7, 1988.

CHAMPIONSHIP SERIES RECORD

Year Club	League	G.	IP.	W.	L.	Pct.	H.	R.	ER.	SO.	BB.	ERA.
1981—Los Angeles	National	2	2⅓	0	0	.000	1	0	0	0	0	0.00
1983—Los Angeles	National	1	2⅔	0	0	.000	4	2	2	3	1	6.75
1988—Los Angeles	National	3	4⅓	1	1	.500	1	2	2	1	5	4.15
Championship Series Totals—3 Years		6	9⅓	1	1	.500	6	4	4	4	6	3.86

WORLD SERIES RECORD

Year Club	League	G.	IP.	W.	L.	Pct.	H.	R.	ER.	SO.	BB.	ERA.
1988—Los Angeles	National	2	5	1	0	1.000	2	0	0	7	1	0.00

ANTONIO FRANCISCO PENA (PADILLA)
(Tony)

Born June 4, 1957, at Monte Cristi, Dominican Republic.
Height, 6.00. Weight, 184.
Throws and bats righthanded.
Brother of Ramon Pena, pitcher in Detroit Tigers' organization; and related to Jose Pena, catcher in San Francisco Giants' organization.

Major League stolen bases: 1981 (1), 1982 (2), 1983 (6), 1984 (12), 1985 (12), 1986 (9), 1987 (6), 1988 (6). Total—54.
Tied for National League lead in grounding into double plays with 21 in 1986.
Led National League catchers in fielding percentage with .994 in 1988.
Led National League catchers in assists with 100 in 1985.
Led National League catchers in double plays with 15 in 1984.
Led National League catchers in total chances with 1,075 in 1983, 999 in 1984 and 1,034 in 1985.
Led Eastern League catchers in double plays with 14 in 1979.
Led Carolina League catchers in double plays with 9 in 1977.
Tied for Carolina League lead in passed balls with 16 in 1977.
Named catcher on The Sporting News National League All-Star Team, 1983.
Named catcher on The Sporting News National League All-Star fielding team, 1983 through 1985.

Year Club	League	Pos.	G.	AB.	R.	H.	2B.	3B.	HR.	RBI.	B.A.	PO.	A.	E.	F.A.
1976—Bradenton Pir.	Gulf C.	O-1-C-3	33	110	10	23	2	2	1	11	.209	108	14	4	.968
1976—Charleston	W. Car.	C	14	49	4	11	2	0	1	8	.224	64	7	2	.973
1977—Charleston	W. Car.	C	29	101	10	24	4	0	3	16	.238	172	19	6	.970
1977—Salem	Carol.	C	84	319	36	88	15	3	7	46	.276	★470	★66	★17	.969
1978—Shreveport	Texas	C	104	348	34	80	14	0	8	42	.230	637	54	★25	.965
1979—Buffalo	East.	C	134	515	89	161	16	4	34	97	.313	★768	★120	★26	.972
1980—Portland	P. C.	C	124	452	57	148	24	13	9	77	.327	★639	85	●23	.969
1980—Pittsburgh	Nat.	C	8	21	1	9	1	1	0	1	.429	38	2	2	.952
1981—Pittsburgh	Nat.	C	66	210	16	63	9	1	2	17	.300	286	41	5	.985
1982—Pittsburgh	Nat.	C	138	497	53	147	28	4	11	63	.296	763	89	16	.982
1983—Pittsburgh	Nat.	C	151	542	51	163	22	3	15	70	.301	★976	90	9	.992
1984—Pittsburgh	Nat.	C	147	546	77	156	27	2	15	78	.286	★895	★95	9	.991
1985—Pittsburgh	Nat.	C-1B	147	546	53	136	27	2	10	59	.249	925	102	12	.988
1986—Pittsburgh†	Nat.	★C-1B	144	510	56	147	26	2	10	52	.288	824	99	★18	.981
1987—St. Louis‡	Nat.	C-1B-OF	116	384	40	82	13	4	5	44	.214	624	51	8	.988
1987—Louisville	A. A.	C	2	8	0	3	0	0	0	0	.375	7	1	0	1.000
1988—St. Louis	Nat.	C-1B	149	505	55	133	23	1	10	51	.263	796	72	6	.993
Major League Totals—9 Years			1066	3761	402	1036	176	20	78	435	.275	6127	641	85	.988

Signed as free agent by Pittsburgh Pirates' organization, July 22, 1975.

†Traded to St. Louis Cardinals for Outfielder Andy Van Slyke, Catcher Mike LaValliere and Pitcher Mike Dunne, April 1, 1987.

‡On disabled list, April 11 to May 22, 1987; included rehabilitation disability assignment to Louisville, May 19 to May 22, 1987.

CHAMPIONSHIP SERIES RECORD

Year	Club	League	Pos.	G.	AB.	R.	H.	2B.	3B.	HR.	RBI.	B.A.	PO.	A.	E.	F.A.
1987—	St. Louis	Nat.	C	7	21	5	8	0	1	0	0	.381	55	5	0	1.000

WORLD SERIES RECORD

Year	Club	League	Pos.	G.	AB.	R.	H.	2B.	3B.	HR.	RBI.	B.A.	PO.	A.	E.	F.A.
1987—	St. Louis	Nat.	C-DH	7	22	2	9	1	0	0	4	.409	32	1	1	.971

ALL-STAR GAME RECORD

Year	League	Pos.	AB.	R.	H.	2B.	3B.	HR.	RBI.	B.A.	PO.	A.	E.	F.A.
1982—	National	PR-C	1	0	0	0	0	0	0	.000	3	0	0	1.000
1984—	National	C	0	0	0	0	0	0	0	.000	2	0	0	1.000
1985—	National	C	1	0	0	0	0	0	0	.000	4	1	0	1.000
1986—	National	PR	0	0	0	0	0	0	0	.000	0	0	0	.000
All-Star Game Totals—4 Years			2	0	0	0	0	0	0	.000	9	1	0	1.000

GERONIMO PENA

Born March 29, 1967, at Distrito Nacional, D. R.
Height, 6.01. Weight, 170.
Throws and bats righthanded.

Led South Atlantic League in stolen bases with 80 in 1987.

Led Appalachian League in intentional bases on balls received with 4 in 1986.

Led Florida State League second basemen in total chances with 723 and double plays with 103 in 1988.

Led South Atlantic League shortstops in putouts with 324, assists with 342, total chances with 695 and double plays with 80 in 1987.

Year	Club	League	Pos.	G.	AB.	R.	H.	2B.	3B.	HR.	RBI.	B.A.	PO.	A.	E.	F.A.
1986—	Johnson City	Appal.	2B	56	202	*55	60	7	4	3	20	.297	108	144	7	.973
1987—	Savannah	S. Atl.	*2B-SS	134	505	95	136	28	3	9	51	.269	325	343	*29	.958
1988—	St. Petersburg	Fla. St.	2B	130	484	82	125	25	10	4	35	.258	*301	*402	20	*.972

Signed as free agent by St. Louis Cardinals' organization, August 9, 1984.

HIPOLITO PENA

First name pronounced Ee-PO-lee-to.

Born January 30, 1964, at Cotui, Dominican Republic.
Height, 6.03. Weight, 165.
Throws and bats lefthanded.

Major League saves: 1986 (1), 1987 (1). Total—2.

Year	Club	League	G.	IP.	W.	L.	Pct.	H.	R.	ER.	SO.	BB.	ERA.
1981—	Butte	Pioneer	7	33	2	1	.667	21	17	10	22	33	2.73
1982—	Pikeville†‡	Ap'lachian	7	21⅓	0	2	.000	23	15	11	23	16	4.64
1983—	Aguascalientes	Mexican	17	39⅓	1	4	.200	26	25	19	18	23	4.35
1983—	Beloit§	Midwest	1	1	0	0	.000	0	0	0	0	2	0.00
1984—	Bradenton Pirates x	Gulf Coast	10	16⅓	1	1	.500	12	8	5	15	9	2.76
1985—	Miami	Florida St.	25	71⅓	2	4	.333	69	54	38	73	41	4.79
1985—	Prince William	Carolina	20	44	2	1	.667	31	14	14	63	21	2.86
1986—	Nashua	Eastern	31	99	7	4	.636	86	47	39	76	43	3.55
1986—	Pittsburgh	National	10	8⅓	0	3	.000	7	10	8	6	3	864
1987—	Vancouver	P. Coast	27	77⅓	5	6	.455	69	37	32	62	37	3.72
1987—	Pittsburgh y	National	16	25⅔	0	3	.000	16	14	13	16	26	4.56
1988—	Columbus	Int'national	50	104⅔	7	6	.538	84	51	45	109	55	3.87
1988—	New York	American	16	14⅓	1	1	.500	10	8	5	10	9	3.14
National League Totals—2 Years			26	34	0	6	.000	23	24	21	22	29	5.56
American League Totals—1 Year			16	14⅓	1	1	.500	10	8	5	10	9	3.14
Major League Totals—3 Years			42	48⅓	1	7	.125	33	32	26	32	38	4.84

Signed as free agent by Milwaukee Brewers' organization, May 30, 1981.

†On temporary inactive list, August 5 to September 2, 1982.

‡Loaned to Aguascalientes of Mexican League, April 2, 1983; returned June 19,1983.

§Released, July 1, 1983; signed by Pittsburgh Pirates' organization, June 21, 1984.

xLoaned to Miami (Independent), April 8, 1985; returned, July 2, 1985.

yTraded to New York Yankees for First Baseman Orestes Destrade, March 30, 1988.

JOSE LUIS PENA

Born April 24, 1965, at Bonao, Dominican Republic.
Height, 6.00. Weight, 190.
Throws and bats righthanded.
Related to Tony Pena, catcher with St. Louis Cardinals;
and Ramon Pena, pitcher in Detroit Tigers' organization.

Year	Club	League	Pos.	G.	AB.	R.	H.	2B.	3B.	HR.	RBI.	B.A.	PO.	A.	E.	F.A.
1983—	Great Falls	Pion.	C	30	81	7	19	0	0	0	8	.235	132	10	4	.973
1984—	Clinton	Midw.	C	70	222	20	39	8	0	3	26	.176	409	40	14	.970

Year	Club	League	Pos.	G.	AB.	R.	H.	2B.	3B.	HR.	RBI.	B.A.	PO.	A.	E.	F.A.
1985	—Clinton	Midw.	C	82	262	26	69	20	0	1	24	.263	321	43	10	.973
1986	—Clinton	Midw.	C	102	350	30	87	18	0	5	53	.249	483	57	5	.991
1987	—Fresno	Calif.	C	80	266	43	74	11	1	4	35	.278	254	46	8	.974
1988	—Shreveport	Texas	C	98	314	29	77	19	1	4	36	.245	539	50	10	.983

Signed as free agent by San Francisco Giants' organization, January 17, 1983.

TERRY LEE PENDLETON

Born July 16, 1960, at Los Angeles, Calif.
Height, 5.09. Weight, 178.
Throws right and bats left and righthanded.
Attended Oxnard College, Oxnard, Calif. and Fresno State University, Fresno, Calif.

Major League stolen bases: 1984 (20), 1985 (17), 1986 (24), 1987 (19), 1988 (3). Total—83.
Led National League third basemen in total chances with 524 in 1986 and 512 in 1987.
Led National League third basemen in double plays with 36 in 1986.
Led American Association third basemen in putouts with 88 and fielding percentage with .964 in 1984.
Named third baseman on THE SPORTING NEWS National League All-Star fielding team, 1987.

Year	Club	League	Pos.	G.	AB.	R.	H.	2B.	3B.	HR.	RBI.	B.A.	PO.	A.	E.	F.A.
1982	—Johnson City	Appal.	2B	43	181	38	58	14	•4	4	27	.320	79	105	17	.915
1982	—St. Petersburg	Fla. St.	2B	20	69	4	18	2	1	1	7	.261	41	51	2	.979
1983	—Arkansas†	Texas	2B	48	185	29	51	10	3	4	20	.276	94	135	7	.970
1984	—Louisville	A. A.	3B-2B	91	330	52	98	23	5	4	44	.297	91	157	10	.961
1984	—St. Louis	Nat.	3B	67	262	37	85	16	3	1	33	.324	59	155	13	.943
1985	—St. Louis‡	Nat.	3B	149	559	56	134	16	3	5	69	.240	129	361	18	.965
1986	—St. Louis	Nat.	★3B-OF	159	578	56	138	26	5	1	59	.239	★133	★371	20	.962
1987	—St. Louis	Nat.	3B	159	583	82	167	29	4	12	96	.286	117	★369	26	.949
1988	—St. Louis§	Nat.	3B	110	391	44	99	20	2	6	53	.253	75	239	12	.963
Major League Totals—5 Years				644	2373	275	623	107	17	25	310	.263	513	1495	89	.958

Selected by St. Louis Cardinals' organization in 7th round of free-agent draft, June 7, 1982.
†On disabled list, April 8 to May 23 and July 16 to September 5, 1983.
‡On disabled list June 15 to June 30, 1985.
§On disabled list, May 28 to June 24, 1988.

CHAMPIONSHIP SERIES RECORD

Year	Club	League	Pos.	G.	AB.	R.	H.	2B.	3B.	HR.	RBI.	B.A.	PO.	A.	E.	F.A.
1985	—St. Louis	Nat.	3B	6	24	2	5	1	0	0	4	.208	6	18	1	.960
1987	—St. Louis	Nat.	3B	6	19	3	4	0	1	0	1	.211	3	11	0	1.000
Championship Series Totals—2 Years				12	43	5	9	1	1	0	5	.209	9	29	1	.974

WORLD SERIES RECORD

Tied World Series record for most doubles, driving in three runs, game (1), October 20, 1985.

Year	Club	League	Pos.	G.	AB.	R.	H.	2B.	3B.	HR.	RBI.	B.A.	PO.	A.	E.	F.A.
1985	—St. Louis	Nat.	3B	7	23	3	6	1	1	0	3	.261	6	14	1	.952
1987	—St. Louis	Nat.	DH-PH	3	7	2	3	0	0	0	1	.429	0	0	0	.000
World Series Totals—2 Years				10	30	5	9	1	1	0	4	.300	6	14	1	.952

OSWALDO JOSE PERAZA

Born October 19, 1962, at Puerto Cabello, Venezuela.
Height, 6.04. Weight, 209.
Throws and bats righthanded.

Year	Club	League	G.	IP.	W.	L.	Pct.	H.	R.	ER.	SO.	BB.	ERA.
1981	—Bradenton Jays	Gulf Coast	2	1	0	0	.000	3	2	2	0	0	18.00
1982	—Bradenton Jays	Gulf Coast	2	5⅓	0	1	.000	3	1	1	7	2	1.69
1983	—Bradenton Jays	Gulf Coast	3	13⅔	0	1	.000	16	16	9	11	11	5.93
1984	—Florence	S. Atlantic	31	137⅓	8	7	.533	108	67	52	104	62	3.41
1985	—Kinston	Carolina	25	154⅔	6	10	.375	132	69	55	134	72	3.20
1985	—Knoxville	Southern	9	51	5	2	.714	53	31	23	28	30	4.06
1986	—Knoxville†	Southern	26	107⅓	7	4	.636	101	58	50	80	54	4.19
1986	—Syracuse	Int'national	2	2⅓	0	0	.000	3	3	3	2	4	11.57
1987	—Knoxville‡	Southern	28	132⅔	10	7	.588	122	63	46	105	33	3.12
1988	—Baltimore	American	19	86	5	7	.417	98	62	53	61	37	5.55
1988	—Rochester	Int'national	6	43⅔	3	0	1.000	35	14	14	36	9	2.89
Major League Totals—1 Year			19	86	5	7	.417	98	62	53	61	37	5.55

Signed as free agent by Toronto Blue Jays' organization, February 3, 1981.
†On disabled list, July 4 to August 14, 1986.
‡Traded with a player to be named later to Baltimore Orioles for Pitcher Mike Flanagan, August 31, 1987; Baltimore acquired Pitcher Jose Mesa to complete deal, September 4, 1987.

RECORD AS CATCHER

Year	Club	League	Pos.	G.	AB.	R.	H.	2B.	3B.	HR.	RBI.	B.A.	PO.	A.	E.	F.A.
1981	—Brad. Jays	Gulf C.	C-1-O-P	23	40	1	5	0	0	0	0	.125	59	6	8	.890
1982	—Brad. Jays	Gulf C.	★C-1B-P	51	156	20	34	2	0	2	13	.218	233	42	3	★.989

LEONARDO PEREZ
(Leo)

Born August 6, 1966, at Los Medina, Mayarit, Mexico.
Height, 6.00. Weight, 180.
Throws and bats righthanded.

Year Club	League	G.	IP.	W.	L.	Pct.	H.	R.	ER.	SO.	BB.	ERA.
1985—Leon	Mexican	20	51⅓	3	4	.429	65	51	44	23	42	7.71
1986—Leon	Mexican	20	67⅔	3	7	.300	90	62	53	34	43	7.05
1987—Leon†	Mexican	34	63⅔	3	4	.429	76	41	38	40	41	5.37
1987—Stockton	California	2	4⅓	0	0	.000	2	4	4	5	6	8.31
1988—Beloit	Midwest	22	122⅔	10	8	.556	96	45	28	124	31	2.05
1988—Stockton	California	1	7	0	0	.000	7	3	2	5	3	2.57

Signed as free agent by Leon (Mexican League), March 13, 1985.
†Sold to Milwaukee Brewers' organization, August, 1987.

MELIDO T. PEREZ

Born February 15, 1966, at San Cristobal, D. R.
Height, 6.04. Weight, 180.
Throws and bats righthanded.
Brother of Pascual Perez, pitcher with Montreal Expos; Dario Perez, pitcher in Kansas City Royals' organization; and Valerio Perez, pitcher in Kansas City Royals' organization, 1983 and 1984.

Led Midwest League in complete games with 13 in 1986.
Tied for Northwest League lead in games started by pitchers with 15, balks with 2 and home runs allowed with 13 in 1985.

Year Club	League	G.	IP.	W.	L.	Pct.	H.	R.	ER.	SO.	BB.	ERA.
1984—Charleston	S. Atlantic	16	89	5	7	.417	99	52	43	55	19	4.35
1985—Eugene	Northwest	17	101	6	7	.462	116	65	*61	88	35	5.44
1986—Burlington	Midwest	28	170⅓	10	12	.455	148	83	70	153	49	3.70
1987—Fort Myers	Florida St.	8	64⅓	4	3	.571	51	20	17	51	7	2.38
1987—Memphis	Southern	20	133⅔	8	5	.615	125	60	51	126	20	3.43
1987—Kansas City†	American	3	10⅓	1	1	.500	18	12	9	5	5	7.84
1988—Chicago	American	32	197	12	10	.545	186	105	83	138	72	3.79
Major League Totals—2 Years		35	207⅓	13	11	.542	204	117	92	143	77	3.99

Signed as free agent by Kansas City Royals' organization, July 22, 1983.
†Traded with Pitchers John Davis, Chuck Mount and Greg Hibbard to Chicago White Sox for Pitcher Floyd Bannister and Infielder Dave Cochrane, December 10, 1987.

PASCUAL GROSS PEREZ

Born May 17, 1957, at San Cristobal, Dominican Republic.
Height, 6.03. Weight, 180.
Throws and bats righthanded.
Brother of Melido Perez, pitcher with Chicago White Sox; Dario Perez, pitcher in Kansas City Royals' organization; and Valerio Perez, pitcher in Kansas City Royals' organization, 1983 and 1984.

Pitched five-inning, 1-0 no-hit victory against Philadelphia Phillies, September 24, 1988.
Tied for National League lead in balks with 10 in 1988.
Led Western Carolinas League in balks with 6 in 1977.
Tied for American Association lead in shutouts with 2 in 1987.
Tied for Carolina League lead in shutouts with 5 in 1978.
Named American Association Pitcher of the Year, 1987.

Year Club	League	G.	IP.	W.	L.	Pct.	H.	R.	ER.	SO.	BB.	ERA.
1976—Bradenton Pirates†	Gulf Coast	10	56	2	5	.286	51	41	29	34	35	4.66
1977—Charleston	W. Carol.	25	156	10	5	.667	153	80	69	96	60	3.98
1978—Salem	Carolina	24	152	11	7	.611	133	70	44	126	51	2.61
1978—Columbus	Int'national	1	5	0	0	.000	4	0	0	4	1	0.00
1979—Portland‡	P. Coast	20	103	9	7	.563	121	70	63	51	47	5.50
1980—Portland	P. Coast	24	160	12	10	.545	172	76	72	105	48	4.05
1980—Pittsburgh	National	2	12	0	1	.000	15	6	5	7	2	3.75
1981—Portland	P. Coast	5	31	1	2	.333	40	19	17	11	14	4.94
1981—Pittsburgh	National	17	86	2	7	.222	92	50	38	46	34	3.98
1982—Portland§	P. Coast	19	106⅓	4	9	.308	111	59	57	59	37	4.82
1982—Richmond	Int'national	5	43	5	0	1.000	32	7	6	27	8	1.26
1982—Atlanta	National	16	79⅓	4	4	.500	85	35	27	29	17	3.06
1983—Atlanta	National	33	215⅓	15	8	.652	213	88	82	144	51	3.43
1984—Atlanta x	National	30	211⅔	14	8	.636	208	96	88	145	51	3.74
1985—Atlanta yza	National	22	95⅓	1	13	.071	115	72	65	57	57	6.14
1986		(Out of Organized Baseball)										
1987—Indianapolis	Am. Assoc.	19	133	9	7	.563	128	65	56	125	34	*3.79
1987—Montreal	National	10	70⅓	7	0	1.000	52	21	18	58	16	2.30
1988—Montreal b	National	27	188	12	8	.600	133	59	51	131	44	2.44
1988—Indianapolis	Am. Assoc.	2	7⅔	0	0	.000	4	1	1	7	4	1.17
Major League Totals—8 Years		157	958	55	49	.529	913	427	374	617	272	3.51

Signed as free agent by Pittsburgh Pirates' organization, January 27, 1976.
†On suspended list, August 26 to August 28, 1976.
‡On disabled list, July 16 to August 14, 1979.

§Traded with a player to be named later to Atlanta Braves' organization for Pitcher Larry McWilliams, June 30, 1982; Atlanta organization acquired Shortstop Carlos Rios to complete deal, September 8, 1982.
xOn suspended list, April 3 to May 1, 1984.
yOn disabled list, May 5 to May 25, June 1 to June 22 and August 13 to September 3, 1985.
zOn suspended list, July 22, 1985; then transferred to restricted list, July 25 to August 4, 1985.
aReleased, April 1, 1986; signed by Indianapolis (Montreal Expos' organization), February 16, 1987.
bOn disabled list, May 8 to June 21, 1988; included rehabilitation disability assignment to Indianapolis, June 13 to June 21, 1988.

CHAMPIONSHIP SERIES RECORD

Year Club	League	G.	IP.	W.	L.	Pct.	H.	R.	ER.	SO.	BB.	ERA.
1982—Atlanta	National	2	8⅔	0	1	.000	10	5	5	4	2	5.19

ALL-STAR GAME RECORD

Year League	IP.	W.	L.	Pct.	H.	R.	ER.	SO.	BB.	ERA.
1983—National	⅔	0	0	.000	3	2	2	1	1	27.00

ANTONIO LLAMAS PEREZCHICA
(Tony)

Born April 20, 1966, at Mexicali, Mex.
Height, 5.11. Weight, 175.
Throws and bats righthanded.

Led Midwest League shortstops in total chances with 599 in 1985.

Year Club	League	Pos.	G.	AB.	R.	H.	2B.	3B.	HR.	RBI.	B.A.	PO.	A.	E.	F.A.
1984—Everett	N'west	SS	33	119	10	23	6	1	0	10	.193	45	73	18	.868
1985—Clinton	Midw.	SS	127	452	54	109	21	•8	4	40	.241	*224	332	43	.928
1986—Fresno	Calif.	SS-3B	126	452	65	126	30	8	9	54	.279	224	303	42	.926
1987—Shreveport	Texas	SS-2B	89	332	44	106	24	1	11	47	.319	144	258	16	.962
1988—Phoenix	P. C.	2B-SS-OF	134	517	79	158	18	•10	9	64	.306	255	381	29	.956
1988—San Francisco	Nat.	2B	7	8	1	1	0	0	0	1	.125	5	5	0	1.000
Major League Totals—1 Year			7	8	1	1	0	0	0	1	.125	5	5	0	1.000

Selected by San Francisco Giants' organization in 3rd round of free-agent draft, June 4, 1984.

JONATHAN SAMUEL PERLMAN
(Jon)

Born December 13, 1958, at Dallas, Tex.
Height, 6.03. Weight, 185.
Throws right and bats lefthanded.
Received bachelor of business administration degree in finance and management from Baylor University, Waco, Tex.

Led Texas League pitchers in games started with 30 in 1980.
Tied for Texas League lead in hit batsmen with 13 in 1982.

Year Club	League	G.	IP.	W.	L.	Pct.	H.	R.	ER.	SO.	BB.	ERA.
1979—Midland	Texas	18	96	4	8	.333	133	76	49	34	32	4.59
1980—Midland	Texas	30	200	13	7	.650	*230	115	95	78	76	4.28
1981—Iowa	Am. Assoc.	16	62	2	7	.222	74	53	44	16	37	6.39
1981—Midland	Texas	12	58	1	4	.200	90	62	49	29	22	7.60
1982—Midland	Texas	26	184⅓	•13	7	.650	196	89	75	81	50	3.66
1983—Iowa	Am. Assoc.	31	115⅔	4	11	.267	138	78	58	34	29	4.51
1984—Iowa	Am. Assoc.	24	147⅓	11	6	.647	131	69	62	61	51	3.79
1985—Iowa	Am. Assoc.	32	151⅓	7	12	.368	181	91	79	64	45	4.70
1985—Chicago†	National	6	8⅔	1	0	1.000	10	11	11	4	8	11.42
1986—Phoenix	P. Coast	45	117	7	3	.700	149	64	56	45	32	4.31
1987—Phoenix	P. Coast	52	89⅔	12	6	.667	93	36	28	49	37	2.81
1987—San Francisco‡	National	10	11⅓	0	0	.000	11	7	5	3	4	3.97
1988—Colorado Springs	P. Coast	22	30⅔	3	1	.750	31	16	11	19	11	3.23
1988—Cleveland§	American	10	19⅔	0	2	.000	25	12	12	10	11	5.49
1988—Williamsport x	Eastern	3	5⅓	0	1	.000	5	2	2	3	0	3.38
National League Totals—2 Years		16	20	1	0	1.000	21	18	16	7	12	7.20
American League Totals—1 Year		10	19⅔	0	2	.000	25	12	12	10	11	5.49
Major League Totals—3 Years		26	39⅔	1	2	.333	46	30	28	17	23	6.35

Selected by Chicago Cubs' organization in 5th round of free-agent draft, June 6, 1978.
Selected by Chicago Cubs' organization in 1st round (12th player selected) of free-agent draft, June 5, 1979.
†Released, October 8, 1985; signed by Phoenix (San Francisco Giants' organization), January 27, 1986.
‡Released, March 29, 1988; signed by Colorado Springs (Cleveland Indians' organization), April 7, 1988.
§On disabled list, July 9, 1988 through remainder of season; included rehabilitation disability assignment to Williamsport, August 16 to September 4, 1988.
xReleased, December 20, 1988.

GERALD JUNE PERRY

Born October 30, 1960, at Savannah, Ga.
Height, 6.00. Weight, 190.
Throws right and bats lefthanded.
Nephew of Dan Driessen, first baseman with Cincinnati Reds, Montreal Expos, San Francisco Giants, Houston Astros and St. Louis Cardinals, 1973 through 1987.

Major League stolen bases: 1984 (15), 1985 (9), 1987 (42), 1988 (29). Total—95.

Led International League in game-winning RBIs with 17 and tied for lead in intentional bases on balls received with 8 in 1986.

Led Carolina League first basemen in double plays with 109 in 1980.

Led Gulf Coast League first basemen in double plays with 46 in 1978.

Year Club	League	Pos.	G.	AB.	R.	H.	2B.	3B.	HR.	RBI.	B.A.	PO.	A.	E.	F.A.
1978—Bradenton Brav...	Gulf C.	1B	*55	191	32	51	*12	3	1	26	.267	*479	*37	6	*.989
1979—Greenwood...........	W. Car.	1B	109	400	69	133	17	4	9	71	*.333	881	59	19	.980
1980—Durham.................	Carol.	1B	138	497	102	124	19	5	15	92	.249	*1296	93	16	.989
1981—Savannah..............	South.	1B	137	476	71	132	18	3	19	84	.277	1221	86	18	.986
1982—Richmond.............	Int.	1B	133	492	94	146	22	4	15	92	.297	1110	94	•17	.986
1983—Richmond.............	Int.	1B	113	423	81	133	21	8	13	71	.314	943	88	11	.989
1983—Atlanta..................	Nat.	1B-OF	27	39	5	14	2	0	1	6	.359	55	0	1	.982
1984—Atlanta..................	Nat.	1B-OF	122	347	52	92	12	2	7	47	.265	550	28	12	.980
1985—Atlanta..................	Nat.	1B-OF	110	238	22	51	5	0	3	13	.214	541	37	9	.985
1986—Richmond.............	Int.	OF-1B	107	384	69	125	30	5	10	75	.326	394	25	7	.984
1986—Atlanta..................	Nat.	OF-1B	29	70	6	19	2	0	2	11	.271	24	1	2	.926
1987—Atlanta..................	Nat.	1B-OF	142	533	77	144	35	2	12	74	.270	1297	72	14	.990
1988—Atlanta†................	Nat.	1B	141	547	61	164	29	1	8	74	.300	1282	106	•17	.988
Major League Totals—6 Years................			571	1774	223	484	85	5	33	225	.273	3749	244	55	.986

Selected by Atlanta Braves' organization in 11th round of free-agent draft, June 6, 1978.

†On disabled list, June 19 to July 4, 1988.

ALL-STAR GAME RECORD

Year League	Pos.	AB.	R.	H.	2B.	3B.	HR.	RBI.	B.A.	PO.	A.	E.	F.A.
1988—National..	PH	1	0	0	0	0	0	0	.000	0	0	0	.000

WILLIAM PATRICK PERRY
(Pat)

Born February 4, 1959, at Taylorville, Ill.
Height, 6.01. Weight, 190.
Throws and bats lefthanded.
Attended Lincoln Land Community College, Springfield, Ill.

Major League saves: 1986 (2), 1987 (2), 1988 (1). Total—5.

Tied for Gulf Coast League lead in shutouts with 2 in 1978.

Year Club	League	G.	IP.	W.	L.	Pct.	H.	R.	ER.	SO.	BB.	ERA.
1978—Sarasota Astros.............................	Gulf Coast	12	35	2	4	.333	29	15	9	35	14	2.31
1979—Daytona Beach.............................	Florida St.	12	51	2	3	.400	64	31	30	30	16	5.29
1979—Sarasota Astros.............................	Gulf Coast	9	49	3	1	.750	55	21	20	24	16	3.67
1980—Daytona Beach.............................	Florida St.	22	115	9	5	.643	121	51	38	54	46	2.97
1981—Columbus..	Southern	27	51	3	1	.750	54	40	36	35	38	6.35
1981—Daytona Beach.............................	Florida St.	9	20	2	0	1.000	11	6	6	22	7	2.70
1982—Columbus†......................................	Southern	22	37⅔	4	0	1.000	32	19	17	28	18	4.06
1983—Columbus‡§....................................	Southern	11	49	5	2	.714	60	30	22	27	21	4.04
1983—Buffalo x...	Eastern	4	5⅓	0	0	.000	8	5	4	4	4	6.75
1983—Springfield......................................	Midwest	6	24⅓	1	1	.500	17	6	6	31	5	2.22
1984—Arkansas...	Texas	25	48⅔	4	2	.667	34	8	6	51	17	1.11
1984—Louisville..	Am. Assoc.	21	44⅔	4	3	.571	35	12	11	43	21	2.22
1985—Louisville..	Am. Assoc.	45	91	4	3	.571	56	33	24	63	39	2.37
1985—St. Louis...	National	6	12⅓	1	0	1.000	3	0	0	6	3	0.00
1986—St. Louis...	National	46	68⅔	2	3	.400	59	31	29	29	34	3.80
1986—Louisville..	Am. Assoc.	5	11	1	0	1.000	8	6	4	7	6	3.27
1987—St. Louis y-Cincinnati....................	National	57	81	5	2	.714	60	34	32	39	25	3.56
1988—Cincinnati z-Chicago a...................	National	47	58⅔	4	4	.500	61	32	27	35	16	4.14
1988—Iowa..	Am. Assoc.	2	3	0	0	.000	0	0	0	4	0	0.00
Major League Totals—4 Years............................		156	220⅔	12	9	.571	183	97	88	109	78	3.59

Selected by Houston Astros' organization in 2nd round of free-agent draft, January 10, 1978.

†On disabled list, May 6 to May 24 and August 1, 1982 through remainder of season.

‡On disabled list, May 24 to June 15, 1983.

§Released, June 24, 1983; signed by Buffalo (Cleveland Indians' organization), July 1, 1983.

xReleased, July 12, 1983; signed by Springfield (St. Louis Cardinals' organization), August 3, 1983.

yTraded to Cincinnati Reds for a player to be named later, August 31, 1987; St. Louis Cardinals acquired Pitcher Scott Terry to complete deal, September 3, 1987.

zTraded with cash to Chicago Cubs for First Baseman Leon Durham, May 19, 1988.

aOn disabled list, August 20 to September 10, 1988.

STEVEN BRADLEY PETERS
(Steve)

Born November 14, 1962, at Oklahoma City, Okla.
Height, 5.11. Weight, 173.
Throws and bats lefthanded.
Attended Seminole Junior College, Seminole, Okla.,
and University of Oklahoma, Norman, Okla.

Major League saves: 1987 (1).

Led Texas League in saves with 23 in 1987.

Year	Club	League	G.	IP.	W.	L.	Pct.	H.	R.	ER.	SO.	BB.	ERA.
1985	—Johnson City	Ap'lachian	3	19	3	0	1.000	5	1	1	30	3	0.47
1985	—St. Petersburg	Florida St.	10	64⅔	4	3	.571	52	21	18	60	29	2.51
1986	—Springfield	Midwest	15	103	10	1	*.909	78	32	29	99	36	2.53
1986	—Arkansas	Texas	10	49⅔	3	3	.500	50	25	21	32	15	3.81
1987	—Arkansas†	Texas	47	74⅓	4	4	.500	51	16	13	78	24	1.57
1987	—Louisville	Am. Assoc.	11	19	2	0	1.000	13	2	2	22	4	0.95
1987	—St. Louis	National	12	15	0	0	.000	17	3	3	11	6	1.80
1988	—St. Louis	National	44	45	3	3	.500	57	34	32	30	22	6.40
1988	—Louisville	Am Assoc.	22	27	1	1	.500	25	11	11	16	16	3.67
Major League Totals—2 Years			56	60	3	3	.500	74	37	35	41	28	5.25

Selected by Chicago White Sox' organization in 7th round of free-agent draft, January 11, 1983.
Selected by St. Louis Cardinals' organization in 5th round of free-agent draft, June 3, 1985.
†Appeared in one game as an outfielder with no chances.

ADAM CHARLES PETERSON

Born December 11, 1965, at Long Beach, Calif.
Height, 6.03. Weight, 190.
Throws and bats righthanded.

Year	Club	League	G.	IP.	W.	L.	Pct.	H.	R.	ER.	SO.	BB.	ERA.
1984	—Sarasota White Sox	Gulf Coast	12	43	1	4	.200	49	39	26	31	19	5.44
1985	—Niagara Falls	NYP	14	92⅓	7	6	.538	74	39	31	79	34	3.02
1986	—Peninsula	Carolina	24	147	9	8	.529	150	92	75	84	58	4.59
1986	—Birmingham	Southern	6	32⅓	1	3	.250	34	16	15	21	16	4.18
1987	—Birmingham	Southern	26	170⅔	12	9	.571	165	79	74	124	73	3.90
1987	—Chicago	American	1	4	0	0	.000	8	6	6	1	3	13.50
1988	—Vancouver	P. Coast	28	171	14	7	.667	161	69	63	103	81	3.32
1988	—Chicago	American	2	6	0	1	.000	6	9	9	5	6	13.50
Major League Totals—2 Years			3	10	0	1	.000	14	15	15	6	9	13.50

Selected by Chicago White Sox' organization in 5th round of free-agent draft, June 4, 1984.

EUGENE JAMES PETRALLI JR.
(Geno)

Born September 25, 1959, at Sacramento, Calif.
Height, 6.01. Weight, 180.
Throws right and bats lefthanded.
Attended Sacramento City College, Sacramento, Calif.
Son of Gene Petralli, minor league first baseman, 1948 through 1951 and 1953.

Established modern major league record for most passed balls, season (35), 1987.

Tied modern major league record for most passed balls, game (6), August 30, 1987; most passed balls, inning (4), August 22, 1987, seventh inning.

Major League stolen bases: 1983 (1), 1985 (1), 1986 (3). Total—5.

Led American League in passed balls with 35 in 1987 and 20 in 1988.

Led International League catchers in putouts with 633, assists with 86, errors with 19, double plays with 10 and total chances with 738 in 1982.

Tied for Pioneer League lead in passed balls with 27 in 1978.

Year	Club	League	Pos.	G.	AB.	R.	H.	2B.	3B.	HR.	RBI.	B.A.	PO.	A.	E.	F.A.
1978	—Medicine Hat†	Pion.	C-3B	65	242	42	68	14	5	2	40	.281	238	68	19	.942
1979	—Dunedin†‡	Fla. St.	C-3B-OF	52	184	18	53	13	0	1	24	.288	206	42	5	.980
1979	—Syracuse†	Int.	C	18	56	6	13	0	1	0	7	.232	67	12	1	.988
1980	—Knoxville†	South.	C-1B-OF	116	382	42	109	20	2	3	38	.285	569	82	18	.973
1981	—Syracuse‡§	Int.	C	45	151	17	40	11	0	0	16	.265	188	30	6	.973
1982	—Syracuse†	Int.	C-1B-3B	126	395	57	114	19	3	9	58	.289	674	89	20	.974
1982	—Toronto†	Amer.	C-3B	16	44	3	16	2	0	0	1	.364	51	4	1	.982
1983	—Syracuse†	Int.	C-1B	104	327	39	80	9	2	3	40	.245	541	68	7	.989
1983	—Toronto†	Amer.	C	6	4	0	0	0	0	0	0	.000	7	0	0	1.000
1984	—Toronto† x	Amer.	C	3	3	0	0	0	0	0	0	.000	1	1	0	1.000
1984	—Maine† y	Int.	C-O-1	23	83	9	18	3	0	0	5	.217	122	11	6	.957
1985	—Maine z	Int.	C	2	7	0	1	0	0	0	1	.143	12	1	1	.929
1985	—Oklahoma City	A. A.	C	27	80	11	21	8	0	1	5	.263	108	14	3	.976
1985	—Texas†	Amer.	C	42	100	7	27	2	0	0	11	.270	179	16	2	.990
1986	—Texas†	Amer.	C-3B-2B	69	137	17	35	9	3	2	18	.255	163	14	4	.978
1987	—Texas†	Amer.	C-3-1-2-O	101	202	28	61	11	2	7	31	.302	370	34	5	.988
1988	—Texas	Amer.	C-3-1-2	129	351	35	99	14	2	7	36	.282	421	54	10	.979
Major League Totals—7 Years				366	841	90	238	38	7	16	97	.283	1192	123	22	.984

Selected by Toronto Blue Jays' organization in 3rd round of free-agent draft, January 10, 1978.
†Switch-hitter.
‡On suspended list, April 13 to April 27, 1979.
§On disabled list, May 6 to June 1 and June 28 to August 18, 1981.
xSold to Maine (Cleveland Indians' organization), May 8, 1984.
yOn disabled list, July 11, 1984 through remainder of season.
zReleased, April 23, 1985; signed by Oklahoma City (Texas Rangers' organization), May 17, 1985.

DANIEL JOSEPH PETRY

Name pronounced PEE-tree.

(Dan)

Born November 13, 1958, at Palo Alto, Calif.
Height, 6.04. Weight, 215.
Throws and bats righthanded.

Led American League pitchers in games started with 38 and home runs allowed with 37 in 1983.

Year Club	League	G.	IP.	W.	L.	Pct.	H.	R.	ER.	SO.	BB.	ERA.
1976—Bristol	Ap'lachian	14	79	2	3	.400	54	42	33	51	★56	3.76
1977—Lakeland	Florida St.	25	145	10	11	.476	139	68	55	68	68	3.41
1978—Montgomery	Southern	14	92	6	7	.462	70	38	25	69	41	2.45
1978—Evansville	Am. Assoc.	13	71	4	3	.571	59	38	36	50	33	4.56
1979—Evansville	Am. Assoc.	15	91	4	3	.571	92	60	49	55	37	4.85
1979—Detroit	American	15	98	6	5	.545	90	46	43	43	33	3.95
1980—Evansville	Am. Assoc.	4	30	2	0	1.000	21	11	9	16	12	2.70
1980—Detroit	American	27	165	10	9	.526	156	82	72	88	83	3.93
1981—Detroit	American	23	141	10	9	.526	115	53	47	79	57	3.00
1982—Detroit	American	35	246	15	9	.625	220	98	88	132	100	3.22
1983—Detroit	American	38	266⅓	19	11	.633	256	126	116	122	99	3.92
1984—Detroit	American	35	233⅓	18	8	.692	231	94	84	144	66	3.24
1985—Detroit	American	34	238⅔	15	13	.536	190	98	89	109	81	3.36
1986—Detroit†	American	20	116	5	10	.333	122	78	60	56	53	4.66
1986—Lakeland	Florida St.	3	10⅓	1	1	.500	13	8	8	6	1	6.97
1987—Detroit‡	American	30	134⅔	9	7	.563	148	101	84	93	76	5.61
1988—California§	American	22	139⅔	3	9	.250	139	70	68	64	59	4.38
1988—Palm Springs	California	3	15	1	2	.333	19	14	11	11	11	6.60
Major League Totals—10 Years		279	1778⅔	110	90	.550	1667	846	751	930	707	3.80

Selected by Detroit Tigers' organization in 4th round of free-agent draft, June 8, 1976.

†On disabled list, June 6 to August 19, 1986; included rehabilitation disability assignment to Lakeland, July 30 to August 19, 1986.

‡Traded to California Angels for Outfielder Gary Pettis, December 5, 1987.

§On disabled list, June 26 to August 30, 1988; included rehabilitation disability assignment to Palm Springs, August 13 to August 30, 1988.

CHAMPIONSHIP SERIES RECORD

Year Club	League	G.	IP.	W.	L.	Pct.	H.	R.	ER.	SO.	BB.	ERA.
1984—Detroit	American	1	7	0	0	.000	4	2	2	4	1	2.57
1987—Detroit	American	1	3⅓	0	0	.000	1	1	0	1	0	0.00
Championship Series Totals—2 Years		2	10⅓	0	0	.000	5	3	2	5	1	1.74

WORLD SERIES RECORD

Year Club	League	G.	IP.	W.	L.	Pct.	H.	R.	ER.	SO.	BB.	ERA.
1984—Detroit	American	2	8	0	1	.000	14	8	8	4	5	9.00

ALL-STAR GAME RECORD

Year League	IP.	W.	L.	Pct.	H.	R.	ER.	SO.	BB.	ERA.
1985—American	⅓	0	0	.000	0	2	2	1	3	54.00

GARY GEORGE PETTIS

Born April 3, 1958, at Oakland, Calif.
Height, 6.01. Weight, 160.
Throws right and bats left and righthanded.
Attended Laney College, Oakland, Calif.
Brother of Stacey Pettis, outfielder in Pittsburgh Pirates' and California Angels' organizations, 1981 through 1987.

Tied major league record for most putouts by outfielder, game (12), June 4, 1985, 15 innings.
Tied American League record for most chances accepted by outfielder, game (12), June 4, 1985, 15 innings.
Major League stolen bases: 1983 (8), 1984 (48), 1985 (56), 1986 (50), 1987 (24), 1988 (44). Total—230.
Led American League outfielders in total chances with 478 in 1986.
Led Pacific Coast League in stolen bases with 53 in 1982.
Named outfielder on The Sporting News American League All-Star fielding team, 1985, 1986 and 1988.

Year Club	League	Pos.	G.	AB.	R.	H.	2B.	3B.	HR.	RBI.	B.A.	PO.	A.	E.	F.A.
1979—Idaho Falls	Pion.	3B-SS-2B	50	198	39	63	10	●10	3	26	.318	59	94	24	.864
1980—Salinas	Calif.	OF-SS-3B	118	393	71	94	15	3	2	31	.239	206	36	13	.949
1981—Holyoke	East.	OF	120	421	77	112	8	9	3	36	.266	237	5	4	.984
1982—Spokane	P. C.	OF	133	528	108	152	22	★14	1	59	.288	★345	9	6	★.983
1982—California	Amer.	OF	10	5	5	1	0	0	1	1	.200	5	1	0	1.000
1983—Edmonton	P. C.	OF	132	529	★138	151	27	8	11	52	.285	325	10	5	.985
1983—California	Amer.	OF	22	85	19	25	2	3	3	6	.294	49	5	1	.982
1984—California	Amer.	OF	140	397	63	90	11	6	2	29	.227	337	11	6	.983
1985—California†	Amer.	OF	125	443	67	114	10	8	1	32	.257	368	13	4	.990
1986—California	Amer.	OF	154	539	93	139	23	4	5	58	.258	★462	9	7	.985
1987—California	Amer.	OF	133	394	49	82	13	2	1	17	.208	344	2	7	.980
1987—Edmonton‡	P. C.	OF	8	16	6	2	1	0	0	1	.125	7	1	1	.889
1988—Detroit§	Amer.	OF	129	458	65	96	14	4	3	36	.210	361	5	5	.987
Major League Totals—7 Years			713	2321	361	547	73	27	16	179	.236	1926	46	30	.985

Selected by California Angels' organization in 6th round of free-agent draft, January 9, 1979.

†On disabled list, July 5 to July 31, 1985.
‡Traded to Detroit Tigers for Pitcher Dan Petry, December 5, 1987.
§On disabled list, July 30 to August 15, 1988.

CHAMPIONSHIP SERIES RECORD

Year	Club	League	Pos.	G.	AB.	R.	H.	2B.	3B.	HR.	RBI.	B.A.	PO.	A.	E.	F.A.
1986	California	Amer.	OF	7	26	4	9	1	0	1	4	.346	28	0	1	.966

KENNETH ALLEN PHELPS
(Ken)

Born August 6, 1954, at Seattle, Wash.
Height, 6.01. Weight, 204.
Throws and bats lefthanded.
Attended Washington State University, Pullman, Wash.; Mesa Community College, Mesa, Ariz., and received bachelor of science degree in physical education from Arizona State University, Tempe, Ariz.

Major League stolen bases: 1984 (3), 1985 (2), 1986 (2), 1987 (1), 1988 (1). Total—9.
Led American Association in total bases with 320 in 1982.
Led American Association in bases on balls received with 128 in 1980 and 108 in 1982.
Led Southern League in bases on balls received with 99 in 1978.
Tied for American Association lead in intentional bases on balls received with 12 in 1982.
Led American Association first basemen in double plays with 111 in 1979, 103 in 1980 and 108 in 1982.
Named American Association Most Valuable Player, 1982.

Year	Club	League	Pos.	G.	AB.	R.	H.	2B.	3B.	HR.	RBI.	B.A.	PO.	A.	E.	F.A.
1976	Sarasota Royals	Gulf C.	1B	28	98	20	29	6	3	3	28	.296	166	16	2	.989
1976	Waterloo	Midw.	1B	25	72	12	19	8	0	1	10	.264	205	12	3	.986
1977	Daytona Beach	Fla. St.	1B	40	145	22	50	7	0	5	32	.345	341	31	8	.979
1977	Jacksonville	South.	1B	81	262	30	51	6	3	5	40	.195	691	38	10	.986
1978	Jacksonville	South.	1B	124	381	65	94	20	0	16	61	.247	1028	66	16	.986
1979	Omaha	A. A.	1B	130	430	71	114	26	3	20	77	.265	*1129	80	*13	.989
1980	Omaha	A. A.	1B	133	442	80	130	30	3	23	72	.294	*1154	51	12	.990
1980	Kansas City	Amer.	1B	3	4	0	0	0	0	0	0	.000	14	0	0	1.000
1981	Kansas City	Amer.	1B	21	22	1	3	0	1	0	1	.136	4	1	0	1.000
1981	Omaha†	A. A.	1B	19	66	9	22	8	1	5	21	.333	169	15	2	.989
1982	Wichita	A. A.	1B	132	453	112	151	23	4	*46	*141	.333	1047	74	14	.988
1982	Montreal‡	Nat.	PH	10	8	0	2	0	0	0	0	.250	0	0	0	.000
1983	Seattle	Amer.	1B	50	127	10	30	4	1	7	16	.236	164	16	0	1.000
1983	Salt Lake City	P. C.	1B	74	270	81	92	29	6	24	82	.341	535	37	7	.988
1984	Seattle§	Amer.	1B	101	290	52	70	9	0	24	51	.241	72	4	1	.987
1984	Salt Lake City	P. C.	1B	12	45	7	14	3	0	3	13	.311	25	5	0	1.000
1985	Seattle	Amer.	1B	61	116	18	24	3	0	9	24	.207	31	2	0	1.000
1986	Seattle	Amer.	1B	125	344	69	85	16	4	24	64	.247	487	34	9	.983
1987	Seattle	Amer.	1B	120	332	68	86	13	1	27	68	.259	8	0	0	1.000
1988	Sea. x-N.Y.	Amer.	1B	117	297	54	78	13	0	24	54	.263	18	2	1	.952
American League Totals—8 Years				598	1532	272	376	58	7	115	278	.245	798	59	11	.987
National League Totals—1 Year				10	8	0	2	0	0	0	0	.250	0	0	0	.000
Major League Totals—9 Years				608	1540	272	378	58	7	115	278	.245	798	59	11	.987

Selected by Atlanta Braves' organization in 8th round of free-agent draft, June 6, 1972.
Selected by New York Yankees' organization in 1st round (11th player selected) of free-agent draft, January 9, 1974.
Selected by Philadelphia Phillies' organization in secondary phase of free-agent draft, June 5, 1974.
Selected by Kansas City Royals' organization in 15th round of free-agent draft, June 8, 1976.
†Traded to Montreal Expos' organization for Pitcher Grant Jackson, January 19, 1982.
‡Sold to Seattle Mariners, March 31, 1983.
§On disabled list, April 7 to May 18, 1984; included rehabilitation disability assignment to Salt Lake City, May 4 to May 18, 1984.
xTraded to New York Yankees for Outfielder Jay Buhner, Pitcher Rich Balabon and a player to be named later, July 21, 1988; Seattle Mariners acquired Pitcher Troy Evers to complete deal, October 12, 1988.

KEITH ANTHONY PHILLIPS
(Tony)

Born April 15, 1959, at Atlanta, Ga.
Height, 5.10. Weight, 175.
Throws right and bats right and lefthanded.
Attended New Mexico Military Institute, Roswell, N.M.

Tied major league record for most assists by second baseman, nine-inning game (12), July 6, 1986.
Major League stolen bases: 1982 (2), 1983 (16), 1984 (10), 1985 (3), 1986 (15), 1987 (7). Total—53.
Hit for the cycle, May 16, 1986.
Led Eastern League in being hit by pitch with 10 in 1981.
Led Southern League in bases on balls received with 98 in 1980.

Year	Club	League	Pos.	G.	AB.	R.	H.	2B.	3B.	HR.	RBI.	B.A.	PO.	A.	E.	F.A.
1978	W. Palm Beach†	Fla. St.	3B-SS-2B	32	54	8	9	0	0	0	3	.167	13	33	5	.902
1978	Jamestown	NYP	SS-2B-3B	52	152	24	29	5	2	1	17	.191	73	146	16	.932
1979	W. Palm Beach	Fla. St.	2B-SS	60	203	30	47	5	1	0	18	.232	120	156	21	.929
1979	Memphis	South.	SS-2B	52	156	31	44	4	2	3	11	.282	68	134	18	.914
1980	Memphis‡§	South.	*SS-2B	136	502	100	125	18	4	5	41	.249	226	408	*42	.938
1981	West Haven	East.	SS	131	461	79	114	25	3	9	64	.247	200	391	*33	.947
1981	Tacoma	P. C.	2B-SS	4	11	1	4	1	0	0	2	.364	8	10	0	1.000

Year	Club	League	Pos.	G.	AB.	R.	H.	2B.	3B.	HR.	RBI.	B.A.	PO.	A.	E.	F.A.
1982	—Tacoma	P. C.	SS	86	300	76	89	18	5	4	47	.297	138	236	30	.926
1982	—Oakland	Amer.	SS	40	81	11	17	2	2	0	8	.210	46	95	7	.953
1983	—Oakland	Amer.	SS-2B-3B	148	412	54	102	12	3	4	35	.248	218	383	30	.952
1984	—Oakland	Amer.	SS-2B-OF	154	451	62	120	24	3	4	37	.266	255	391	28	.958
1985	—Tacoma x	P. C.	3B-2B	20	69	9	9	1	0	0	5	.130	15	36	4	.927
1985	—Oakland	Amer.	3B-2B	42	161	23	45	12	2	4	17	.280	54	103	3	.981
1986	—Oakland y	Amer.	2-3-O-S	118	441	76	113	14	5	5	52	.256	191	326	13	.975
1987	—Oakland z	Amer.	2-3-S-O	111	379	48	91	20	0	10	46	.240	179	299	14	.972
1987	—Tacoma a	P. C.	2B-3B	7	26	5	9	2	1	1	6	.346	8	10	0	1.000
1988	—Tacoma	P. C.	S-O-2-3	16	59	10	16	0	0	2	8	.271	25	27	2	.963
1988	—Oakland b	Amer.	3-O-2-S-1	79	212	32	43	8	4	2	17	.203	84	80	10	.943
Major League Totals—7 Years				692	2137	306	531	92	19	29	212	.248	1027	1677	105	.963

Selected by Seattle Mariners' organization in 16th round of free-agent draft, June 7, 1977.

Selected by Montreal Expos' organization in secondary phase of free-agent draft, January 10, 1978.

†On temporary inactive list, April 11 to May 4, 1978.

‡Traded with cash to San Diego Padres for First Baseman Willie Montanez, August 31, 1980.

§Traded with Pitcher Eric Mustad and Infielder Kevin Bell to Oakland A's organization for Pitcher Bob Lacey and Pitcher Roy Moretti, March 27, 1981.

xOn Oakland disabled list, March 26 to August 22, 1985; included rehabilitation disability assignment to Tacoma, July 30 to August 5 and August 7 to August 20, 1985.

yOn disabled list, August 14 to October 3, 1986.

zOn disabled list, July 12 to August 28, 1987; included rehabilitation disability assignment to Tacoma, August 20 to August 28, 1987.

aReleased, December 21, 1987; re-signed by Athletics, March 9, 1988.

bOn disabled list, May 18 to July 8, 1988; included rehabilitation disability assignment to Tacoma, June 16 to July 4, 1988.

CHAMPIONSHIP SERIES RECORD

Year	Club	League	Pos.	G.	AB.	R.	H.	2B.	3B.	HR.	RBI.	B.A.	PO.	A.	E.	F.A.
1988	—Oakland	Amer.	OF-2B	2	7	0	2	1	0	0	0	.286	10	0	0	1.000

WORLD SERIES RECORD

Year	Club	League	Pos.	G.	AB.	R.	H.	2B.	3B.	HR.	RBI.	B.A.	PO.	A.	E.	F.A.
1988	—Oakland	Amer.	OF-2B	2	4	1	1	0	0	0	0	.250	3	5	0	1.000

JEFFREY MARK PICO
(Jeff)

Born February 12, 1966, at Antioch, Calif.
Height, 6.02. Weight, 170.
Throws and bats righthanded.

Tied major league record for pitching shutout, first major league game, May 31, 1988.

Major League saves: 1988 (1).

Tied for Appalachian League lead in games started by pitchers with 13 in 1984.

Year	Club	League	G.	IP.	W.	L.	Pct.	H.	R.	ER.	SO.	BB.	ERA.
1984	—Pikeville	Ap'lachian	13	73⅓	2	3	.400	65	35	27	46	29	3.31
1985	—Peoria	Midwest	27	179⅓	11	10	.524	186	76	61	109	56	3.06
1986	—Winston-Salem	Carolina	27	166	12	8	.600	165	75	59	116	54	3.20
1987	—Pittsfield	Eastern	12	79	4	4	.500	74	38	34	52	23	3.87
1987	—Iowa	Am. Assoc.	16	93⅔	6	5	.545	118	57	50	45	27	4.80
1988	—Iowa	Am. Assoc.	10	68⅓	5	2	.714	67	28	17	40	18	2.24
1988	—Chicago	National	29	112⅔	6	7	.462	108	57	52	57	37	4.15
Major League Totals—1 Year			29	112⅔	6	7	.462	108	57	52	57	37	4.15

Selected by Chicago Cubs' organization in 13th round of free-agent draft, June 4, 1984.

JAMES PARK PITTMAN

(Known by middle name.)

Born August 5, 1965, at Richmond, Ind.
Height, 6.00. Weight, 175.
Throws and bats righthanded.
Received degree from Ohio State University, Columbus, O.

Tied for California League lead in games started by pitchers with 29 in 1987.

Year	Club	League	G.	IP.	W.	L.	Pct.	H.	R.	ER.	SO.	BB.	ERA.
1986	—Elizabethton	Ap'lachian	8	44	3	1	.750	31	19	12	65	23	2.45
1987	—Visalia	California	31	161⅔	4	12	.250	109	81	59	*198	*138	3.28
1988	—Orlando	Southern	24	103⅔	8	7	.533	73	50	44	103	84	3.82

Selected by Minnesota Twins' organization in 4th round of free-agent draft, June 2, 1986.

DANIEL THOMAS PLESAC
(Dan)

Born February 4, 1962, at Gary, Ind.
Height, 6.05. Weight, 210.
Throws and bats lefthanded.
Attended North Carolina State University, Raleigh, N.C.

Major League saves: 1986 (14), 1987 (23), 1988 (30). Total—67.
Led Appalachian League pitchers in balks with 3 and tied for lead in games started with 14 in 1983.

Year Club	League	G.	IP.	W.	L.	Pct.	H.	R.	ER.	SO.	BB.	ERA.
1983—Paintsville	Ap'lachian	14	82⅓	*9	1	*.900	76	44	32	*85	57	3.50
1984—Stockton	California	16	108⅓	6	6	.500	106	51	40	101	50	3.32
1984—El Paso	Texas	7	39	2	2	.500	43	19	15	24	16	3.46
1985—El Paso	Texas	25	150⅓	12	5	.706	171	91	83	128	68	4.97
1986—Milwaukee	American	51	91	10	7	.588	81	34	30	75	29	2.97
1987—Milwaukee	American	57	79⅓	5	6	.455	63	30	23	89	23	2.61
1988—Milwaukee	American	50	52⅓	1	2	.333	46	14	14	52	12	2.41
Major League Totals—3 Years		158	222⅔	16	15	.516	190	78	67	216	64	2.71

Selected by St. Louis Cardinals' organization in 2nd round of free-agent draft, June 3, 1980.
Selected by Milwaukee Brewers' organization in 1st round (26th player selected) of free-agent draft, June 6, 1983.

ALL-STAR GAME RECORD

Year League	IP.	W.	L.	Pct.	H.	R.	ER.	SO.	BB.	ERA.
1987—American	1	0	0	.000	0	0	0	1	0	0.00
1988—American	⅓	0	0	.000	0	0	0	1	0	0.00
All-Star Game Totals—2 Years	1⅓	0	0	.000	0	0	0	2	0	0.00

ERIC VAUGHN PLUNK

Born September 3, 1963, at Wilmington, Calif.
Height, 6.05. Weight, 210.
Throws and bats righthanded.
Attended California State University at Dominguez Hills, Carson, Calif.

Major League saves: 1987 (2), 1988 (5). Total—7.
Led American League in balks with 6 in 1986.
Tied for Florida State League lead in shutouts with 4 in 1983 and balks with 7 in 1984.

Year Club	League	G.	IP.	W.	L.	Pct.	H.	R.	ER.	SO.	BB.	ERA.
1981—Bradenton Yankees	Gulf Coast	11	54	3	4	.429	56	29	23	47	20	3.83
1982—Paintsville	Ap'lachian	12	64	6	3	.667	63	35	33	59	30	4.64
1983—Fort Lauderdale†	Florida St.	20	125	8	10	.444	115	55	38	109	63	2.74
1984—Fort Lauderdale‡	Florida St.	28	176⅓	12	12	.500	153	85	56	*152	*123	2.86
1985—Huntsville	Southern	13	79⅓	8	2	.800	61	36	30	68	56	3.40
1985—Tacoma	P. Coast	11	53	0	5	.000	51	41	34	43	50	5.77
1986—Tacoma	P. Coast	6	32⅔	2	3	.400	25	18	17	31	33	4.68
1986—Oakland	American	26	120⅓	4	7	.364	91	75	71	98	102	5.31
1987—Oakland	American	32	95	4	6	.400	91	53	50	90	62	4.74
1987—Tacoma	P. Coast	24	34⅔	1	1	.500	21	8	6	56	17	1.56
1988—Oakland§	American	49	78	7	2	.778	62	27	26	79	39	3.00
Major League Totals—3 Years		107	293⅓	15	15	.500	244	155	147	267	203	4.51

Selected by New York Yankees' organization in 4th round of free-agent draft, June 8, 1981.
†On disabled list, August 11 to August 26, 1983.
‡Traded with Outfielder Stan Javier and Pitchers Jay Howell, Jose Rijo and Tim Birtsas to Oakland A's for Outfielder Rickey Henderson, Pitcher Bert Bradley and cash, December 5, 1984.
§On disabled list, July 2 to July 17, 1988.

CHAMPIONSHIP SERIES RECORD

Year Club	League	G.	IP.	W.	L.	Pct.	H.	R.	ER.	SO.	BB.	ERA.
1988—Oakland	American	1	⅓	0	0	.000	1	0	0	1	0	0.00

WORLD SERIES RECORD

Year Club	League	G.	IP.	W.	L.	Pct.	H.	R.	ER.	SO.	BB.	ERA.
1988—Oakland	American	2	1⅔	0	0	.000	0	0	0	3	0	0.00

GUSTAVO POLIDOR
(Gus)

Born October 26, 1961, at Caracas, Venezuela.
Height, 6.00. Weight, 184.
Throws and bats righthanded.

Led Pacific Coast League shortstops in fielding percentage with .986 in 1986.
Led Pacific Coast League shortstops in double plays with 93 in 1985 and tied for lead with 92 in 1986.
Led Pacific Coast League shortstops in total chances with 669 in 1985.
Tied for Eastern League lead in double plays by shortstops with 69 in 1983.

Year Club	League	Pos.	G.	AB.	R.	H.	2B.	3B.	HR.	RBI.	B.A.	PO.	A.	E.	F.A.
1981—Holyoke	East.	SS	130	479	46	119	17	3	2	47	.248	192	375	32	.947
1982—Holyoke†	East.	SS	56	208	17	47	7	0	2	23	.226	74	149	21	.914
1983—Nashua	East.	*SS-3B	105	329	32	69	7	2	0	21	.210	208	283	*37	.930
1984—Waterbury	East.	*SS-P	119	394	42	88	11	1	1	32	.223	*200	322	27	*.951
1985—Edmonton	P. C.	SS	132	460	56	131	18	7	2	51	.285	*250	*396	23	.966
1985—California	Amer.	SS-OF	2	1	1	1	0	0	0	0	1.000	0	2	0	1.000
1986—Edmonton	P. C.	S-2-1-3	119	476	72	143	27	5	5	61	.300	213	316	7	.987
1986—California	Amer.	2B-SS-3B	6	19	1	5	1	0	0	1	.263	10	13	0	1.000
1987—California	Amer.	SS-3B-2B	63	137	12	36	3	0	2	15	.263	46	92	2	.986
1988—California‡	Amer.	SS-3B-2B	54	81	4	12	3	0	0	4	.148	31	54	1	.988
1988—Edmonton§	P. C.	SS-1B	11	33	6	12	4	0	0	7	.364	20	23	2	.956
Major League Totals—4 Years			125	238	18	54	7	0	2	20	.227	87	161	3	.988

Signed as free agent by California Angels' organization, January 5, 1981.
†On disabled list, June 22 to July 14 and July 26, 1982 through remainder of season.
‡On disabled list, June 14 to July 1, 1988.
§Traded to Milwaukee Brewers for Catcher Bill Schroeder, December 7, 1988.

PITCHING RECORD

Year Club	League	G.	IP.	W.	L.	Pct.	H.	R.	ER.	SO.	BB.	ERA.
1984—Waterbury	Eastern	1	1	0	0	.000	0	0	0	0	1	0.00

LUIS ANDREW POLONIA (ALMONTE)

Born October 12, 1964, at Santiago City, D. R.
Height, 5.08. Weight, 155.
Throws and bats lefthanded.

Major League stolen bases: 1987 (29), 1988 (24). Total—53.
Led Pacific Coast League in caught stealing with 21 in 1986.
Led Midwest League in caught stealing with 24 in 1984.

Year Club	League	Pos.	G.	AB.	R.	H.	2B.	3B.	HR.	RBI.	B.A.	PO.	A.	E.	F.A.
1984—Madison†	Midw.	OF	135	*528	103	*162	21	10	8	64	.307	202	9	10	.955
1985—Huntsville†	South.	OF	130	515	82	149	15	*18	2	36	.289	236	13	12	.954
1986—Tacoma†	P. C.	OF	134	*549	98	*165	20	4	3	63	.301	*318	8	10	.970
1987—Tacoma†	P. C.	OF	14	56	18	18	1	2	0	8	.321	28	1	1	.967
1987—Oakland	Amer.	OF	125	435	78	125	16	10	4	49	.287	235	2	5	.979
1988—Tacoma†	P. C.	OF	65	254	58	85	13	5	2	27	.335	129	7	7	.951
1988—Oakland	Amer.	OF	84	288	51	84	11	4	2	27	.292	155	3	2	.988
Major League Totals—2 Years			209	723	129	209	27	14	6	76	.289	390	5	7	.983

Signed as free agent by Oakland A's organization, January 3, 1984.
†Switch-hitter.

CHAMPIONSHIP SERIES RECORD

Year Club	League	Pos.	G.	AB.	R.	H.	2B.	3B.	HR.	RBI.	B.A.	PO.	A.	E.	F.A.
1988—Oakland	Amer.	PR-O-PH	3	5	0	2	0	0	0	0	.400	2	0	0	1.000

WORLD SERIES RECORD

Year Club	League	Pos.	G.	AB.	R.	H.	2B.	3B.	HR.	RBI.	B.A.	PO.	A.	E.	F.A.
1988—Oakland	Amer.	PH-OF	3	9	1	1	0	0	0	0	.111	2	0	0	1.000

MARK STEVEN PORTUGAL

Born October 30, 1962, at Los Angeles, Calif.
Height, 6.00. Weight, 200.
Throws and bats righthanded.

Major League saves: 1986 (1), 1988 (3). Total—4.
Led Appalachian League in wild pitches with 12, home runs allowed with 11 and tied for lead in hit batsmen with 5 in 1981.

Year Club	League	G.	IP.	W.	L.	Pct.	H.	R.	ER.	SO.	BB.	ERA.
1981—Elizabethton	Ap'lachian	14	85	7	1	.875	65	41	35	65	39	3.71
1982—Wisconsin Rapids	Midwest	36	119	9	8	.529	110	62	53	95	62	4.01
1983—Visalia	California	24	131⅓	10	5	.667	142	77	61	132	84	4.18
1984—Orlando	Southern	27	196	14	7	.667	171	80	65	110	113	2.98
1985—Toledo†	Int'national	19	128⅔	8	5	.615	129	60	54	89	60	3.78
1985—Minnesota	American	6	24⅓	1	3	.250	24	16	15	12	14	5.55
1986—Toledo	Int'national	6	45	5	1	.833	34	15	13	30	23	2.60
1986—Minnesota	American	27	112⅔	6	10	.375	112	56	54	67	50	4.31
1987—Minnesota	American	13	44	1	3	.250	58	40	38	28	24	7.77
1987—Portland	P. Coast	17	102	1	10	.091	108	75	68	69	50	6.00
1988—Portland	P. Coast	3	19⅔	2	0	1.000	15	3	3	9	8	1.37
1988—Minnesota‡§	American	26	57⅔	3	3	.500	60	30	29	31	17	4.53
Major League Totals—4 Years		72	238⅔	11	19	.367	254	142	136	138	105	5.13

Signed as free agent by Minnesota Twins' organization, October 23, 1980.
†On disabled list, July 22 to August 2, 1985.
‡On disabled list, August 7 to August 28, 1988.
§Traded to Houston Astros for a player to be named later, December 4, 1988; Minnesota Twins' organization acquired Pitcher Todd McClure to complete deal, December 7, 1988.

ALONZO SIDNEY POWELL

Born December 12, 1964, at San Francisco, Calif.
Height, 6.02. Weight, 195.
Throws and bats righthanded.

Year Club	League	Pos.	G.	AB.	R.	H.	2B.	3B.	HR.	RBI.	B.A.	PO.	A.	E.	F.A.
1983—Clinton	Midw.	OF	36	113	14	22	5	1	0	9	.195	66	2	5	.932
1983—Great Falls	Pion.	OF-1B-3B	51	149	13	33	2	2	1	16	.221	127	15	8	.947
1984—Everett	N'west	1B	6	17	2	3	1	0	1	4	.176	38	2	3	.930
1984—Clinton†	Midw.	OF-1B-2B	47	149	22	37	3	2	1	10	.248	166	9	5	.972
1985—San Jose‡	Calif.	*OF-1B	136	473	79	122	27	6	9	62	.258	292	*21	10	.969
1986—W. Palm Beach	Fla. St.	OF	23	76	20	25	7	1	4	18	.329	56	1	0	1.000
1986—Jacksonville	South.	OF	105	402	67	121	21	5	15	80	.301	256	4	3	.989

Year	Club	League	Pos.	G.	AB.	R.	H.	2B.	3B.	HR.	RBI.	B.A.	PO.	A.	E.	F.A.
1987	Montreal	Nat.	OF	14	41	3	8	3	0	0	4	.195	13	0	0	1.000
1987	Indianapolis	A. A.	OF-1B	90	331	64	99	14	10	19	74	.299	163	6	5	.971
1988	Indianapolis §	A. A.	OF	88	282	31	74	18	3	4	39	.262	148	6	1	.994
Major League Totals—1 Year				14	41	3	8	3	0	0	4	.195	13	0	0	1.000

Signed as free agent by San Francisco Giants' organization, February 3, 1983.
†Loaned to San Jose (Independent), April 9, 1985; returned, September 10, 1985.
‡Traded with Pitcher George Riley to Montreal Expos' organization for Pitcher Bill Laskey, October 24, 1985.
§On disabled list, August 8, 1988 through remainder of season.

DENNIS CLAY POWELL

Born August 13, 1963, at Moultrie, Ga.
Height, 6.03. Weight, 200.
Throws left and bats righthanded.

Major League saves: 1985 (1).
Led Gulf Coast League in shutouts with 2 in 1983.

Year	Club	League	G.	IP.	W.	L.	Pct.	H.	R.	ER.	SO.	BB.	ERA.
1983	Bradenton Dodgers	Gulf Coast	11	74	8	2	.800	52	22	12	*103	23	1.46
1984	Vero Beach	Florida St.	4	26	1	1	.500	19	7	4	14	12	1.38
1984	San Antonio	Texas	24	168	9	8	.529	153	81	63	82	87	3.38
1985	Albuquerque	P. Coast	18	111⅔	9	0	1.000	106	40	34	55	48	2.74
1985	Los Angeles	National	16	29⅓	1	1	.500	30	19	17	19	13	5.22
1986	Los Angeles†	National	27	65⅓	2	7	.222	65	32	31	31	25	4.27
1986	Albuquerque‡	P. Coast	7	41⅔	3	3	.500	45	23	19	27	15	4.10
1987	Calgary	P. Coast	20	117⅓	4	8	.333	145	80	64	65	48	4.52
1987	Seattle	American	16	34⅓	1	3	.250	32	13	12	17	15	3.15
1988	Calgary	P. Coast	21	108	6	4	.600	116	57	50	81	49	4.17
1988	Seattle	American	12	18⅔	1	3	.250	29	20	18	15	11	8.68
National League Totals—2 Years			43	94⅔	3	8	.273	95	51	48	50	38	4.56
American League Totals—2 Years			28	53	2	6	.250	61	33	30	32	26	5.09
Major League Totals—4 Years			71	147⅔	5	14	.263	156	84	78	82	64	4.75

Signed as free agent by Los Angeles Dodgers' organization, May 17, 1983.
†On disabled list, April 30 to June 6, 1986.
‡Traded with Infielder Mike Watters to Seattle Mariners for Pitcher Matt Young, December 10, 1986.

TED HENRY POWER

Born January 31, 1955, at Guthrie, Okla.
Height, 6.04. Weight, 220.
Throws and bats righthanded.
Attended Kansas State University, Manhattan, Kan.

Major League saves: 1983 (2), 1984 (11), 1985 (27), 1986 (1). Total—41.

Year	Club	League	G.	IP.	W.	L.	Pct.	H.	R.	ER.	SO.	BB.	ERA.
1976	Lodi	California	13	51	1	3	.250	46	34	26	58	44	4.59
1977	San Antonio†	Texas	12	72	5	3	.625	51	35	31	60	55	3.88
1978	San Antonio‡	Texas	25	101	6	5	.545	92	57	45	97	75	4.01
1979	San Antonio	Texas	10	64	5	1	.833	69	44	37	52	43	5.20
1979	Albuquerque	P. Coast	18	101	5	5	.500	95	59	52	69	82	4.63
1980	Albuquerque	P. Coast	26	155	13	7	.650	160	93	78	113	95	4.53
1981	Albuquerque	P. Coast	27	187	*18	3	*.857	165	84	74	111	*103	3.56
1981	Los Angeles	National	5	14	1	3	.250	16	6	5	7	7	3.21
1982	Los Angeles	National	12	33⅔	1	1	.500	38	27	25	15	23	6.68
1982	Albuquerque§	P. Coast	14	73	5	4	.556	77	51	42	54	49	5.18
1983	Cincinnati	National	49	111	5	6	.455	120	62	56	57	49	4.54
1984	Cincinnati	National	*78	108⅔	9	7	.563	93	37	34	81	46	2.82
1985	Cincinnati	National	64	80	8	6	.571	65	27	24	42	45	2.70
1986	Cincinnati	National	56	129	10	6	.625	115	59	53	95	52	3.70
1987	Cincinnati x	National	34	204	10	13	.435	213	115	102	133	71	4.50
1988	Kansas City yz—Detroit a	American	26	99	6	7	.462	121	67	65	57	38	5.91
National League Totals—7 Years			298	680⅓	44	42	.512	660	333	299	430	293	3.96
American League Totals—1 Year			26	99	6	7	.462	121	67	65	57	38	5.91
Major League Totals—8 Years			324	779⅓	50	49	.505	781	400	364	487	331	4.20

Selected by Los Angeles Dodgers' organization in 5th round of free-agent draft, June 8, 1976.
†On disabled list, July 18 to July 29 and August 20 to September 4, 1977.
‡On disabled list, July 5 to July 21, 1978.
§Traded to Cincinnati Reds for cash and Infielder Michael James Ramsey, October 15, 1982.
xTraded with Shortstop Kurt Stillwell to Kansas City Royals for Pitcher Danny Jackson and Shortstop Angel Salazar, November 6, 1987.
yOn disabled list, June 18 to July 4, 1988.
zTraded to Detroit Tigers for Catcher Rey Palacios and Pitcher Mark Lee, August 31, 1988.
aGranted free agency, November 4, 1988; re-signed by Tigers, December 7, 1988.

—DID YOU KNOW—

That the Royals' George Brett led all designated hitters with a .333 batting average last season?

JAMES ARTHUR PRESLEY
(Jim)

Born October 23, 1961, at Pensacola, Fla.
Height, 6.01. Weight, 190.
Throws and bats righthanded.
Attended Pensacola Junior College, Pensacola, Fla.

Established major league record for fewest putouts by third baseman, season, 150 or more games (82), 1985.
Tied major league record for most home runs, opening day of season (2), April 8, 1986.
Major League stolen bases: 1984 (1), 1985 (2), 1987 (2), 1988 (3). Total—8.
Hit three home runs in a game, September 1, 1986.
Led American League third basemen in assists with 311 and total chances with 445 in 1987.
Led Eastern League in game-winning RBIs with 16 in 1982.
Led Midwest League in being hit by pitch with 12 in 1980.
Led Eastern League third basemen in assists with 247 and total chances with 365 in 1982.
Led Southern League third basemen in double plays with 29 in 1983.

Year Club	League	Pos.	G.	AB.	R.	H.	2B.	3B.	HR.	RBI.	B.A.	PO.	A.	E.	F.A.
1979—Bellingham	N'west	SS	48	138	20	27	4	1	1	12	.196	42	127	27	.862
1980—Wausau	Midw.	3-S-2-1	126	429	45	105	21	1	12	52	.245	161	235	22	.947
1981—Wausau	Midw.	3B	57	208	48	58	10	0	12	53	.279	32	105	9	.938
1981—Lynn	East.	3B-2B	64	210	32	54	7	1	8	36	.257	49	110	11	.935
1982—Lynn	East.	*3B-OF	133	462	65	123	24	0	22	79	.266	84	250	*35	.905
1983—Chattanooga	South.	3B-SS	131	461	70	122	31	5	14	90	.265	122	329	27	.944
1984—Salt Lake City	P. C.	3B	69	265	43	84	13	4	13	56	.317	53	140	12	.941
1984—Seattle	Amer.	3B	70	251	27	57	12	1	10	36	.227	48	113	7	.958
1985—Seattle	Amer.	3B	155	570	71	157	33	1	28	84	.275	82	335	17	.961
1986—Seattle	Amer.	3B	155	616	83	163	33	4	27	107	.265	110	308	15	.965
1987—Seattle	Amer.	3B-SS	152	575	78	142	23	6	24	88	.247	113	315	21	.953
1988—Seattle	Amer.	3B	150	544	50	125	26	0	14	62	.230	112	234	22	.940
Major League Totals—5 Years			682	2556	309	644	127	12	103	377	.252	465	1305	82	.956

Selected by Seattle Mariners' organization in 4th round of free-agent draft, June 5, 1979.

ALL-STAR GAME RECORD

Member of American League All-Star Team in 1986; did not play.

JOSEPH WALTER PRICE
(Joe)

Born November 29, 1956, at Inglewood, Calif.
Height, 6.04. Weight, 215.
Throws left and bats righthanded.
Attended Oklahoma State University, Stillwater, Okla., and
University of Oklahoma, Norman, Okla.

Major League saves: 1981 (4), 1982 (3), 1985 (1), 1987 (1), 1988 (4). Total—13.

Year Club	League	G.	IP.	W.	L.	Pct.	H.	R.	ER.	SO.	BB.	ERA.
1977—Billings	Pioneer	15	94	6	5	.545	83	50	39	97	42	3.73
1978—Tampa	Florida St.	23	165	10	4	.714	123	40	27	128	51	1.47
1978—Nashville	Southern	2	10	0	0	.000	7	3	3	10	3	2.70
1979—Nashville	Southern	22	109	6	6	.500	101	58	48	69	41	3.96
1980—Indianapolis	Am. Assoc.	11	79	4	4	.500	64	36	34	83	30	3.87
1980—Cincinnati	National	24	111	7	3	.700	95	45	44	44	37	3.57
1981—Cincinnati	National	41	54	6	1	.857	42	19	15	41	18	2.50
1982—Cincinnati	National	59	72⅔	3	4	.429	73	26	23	71	32	2.85
1983—Cincinnati†	National	21	144	10	6	.625	118	46	46	83	46	2.88
1984—Cincinnati	National	30	171⅔	7	13	.350	176	91	80	129	61	4.19
1985—Cincinnati‡	National	26	64⅔	2	2	.500	59	35	28	52	23	3.90
1986—Cincinnati§x	National	25	41⅔	1	2	.333	49	30	25	30	22	5.40
1987—Phoenix	P. Coast	17	61⅓	6	0	1.000	45	21	17	49	40	2.49
1987—San Francisco y	National	20	35	2	2	.500	19	10	10	42	13	2.57
1988—San Francisco z	National	38	61⅔	1	6	.143	59	33	27	49	27	3.94
Major League Totals—9 Years		284	756⅓	39	39	.500	690	335	298	541	279	3.55

Selected by Cincinnati Reds' organization in 4th round of free-agent draft, June 7, 1977.
†On disabled list, August 7 to September 1, 1983.
‡On disabled list, July 23 to August 8 and August 29 to September 13, 1985.
§On disabled list, July 17 to September 1, 1986.
xGranted free agency, November 12, 1986; signed by San Francisco Giants, February 5, 1987.
yGranted free agency, November 9, 1987; re-signed by San Francisco Giants, December 14, 1987.
zOn disabled list, May 9 to June 3 and August 17 to September 2, 1988.

CHAMPIONSHIP SERIES RECORD

Year Club	League	G.	IP.	W.	L.	Pct.	H.	R.	ER.	SO.	BB.	ERA.
1987—San Francisco	National	2	5⅔	1	0	1.000	3	0	0	7	1	0.00

—DID YOU KNOW—

That the Red Sox' Wade Boggs led the majors in on-base percentage with .476 in 1988?

THOMAS ALBERT PRINCE
(Tom)

Born August 13, 1964, at Kankakee, Ill.
Height, 5.11. Weight, 185.
Throws and bats righthanded.
Attended Kankakee Community College, Kankakee, Ill.

Led Eastern League catchers in double plays with 9 and total chances with 721 in 1987.
Led Carolina League catchers in total chances with 954 and passed balls with 15 in 1986.
Led South Atlantic League catchers in total chances with 930, double plays with 10 and passed balls with 27 in 1985.

Year	Club	League	Pos.	G.	AB.	R.	H.	2B.	3B.	HR.	RBI.	B.A.	PO.	A.	E.	F.A.
1984	Watertown	NYP	C-3B	23	69	6	14	3	0	2	13	.203	155	26	2	.989
1984	Bradenton Pir.	Gulf C.	C-1B	18	48	4	11	0	0	1	6	.229	75	16	4	.958
1985	Macon	S. Atl.	C	124	360	60	75	20	1	10	42	.208	*810	*101	*19	.980
1986	Prince William	Carol.	C	121	395	59	100	34	1	10	47	.253	*821	•113	20	.979
1987	Harrisburg	East.	C	113	365	41	112	23	2	6	54	.307	*622	*88	•11	.985
1987	Pittsburgh	Nat.	C	4	9	1	2	1	0	1	2	.222	14	3	0	1.000
1988	Buffalo	A. A.	C	86	304	35	79	16	0	14	42	.260	456	51	*12	.977
1988	Pittsburgh	Nat.	C	29	74	3	13	2	0	0	6	.176	108	8	2	.983
Major League Totals—2 Years				33	83	4	15	3	0	1	8	.181	122	11	2	.985

Selected by Atlanta Braves' organization in 8th round of free-agent draft, January 11, 1983.
Selected by Atlanta Braves' organization in secondary phase of free-agent draft, June 6, 1983.
Selected by Pittsburgh Pirates' organization in secondary phase of free-agent draft, January 17, 1984.

KIRBY PUCKETT

Born March 14, 1961, at Chicago, Ill.
Height, 5.08. Weight, 210.
Throws and bats righthanded.
Attended Bradley University, Peoria, Ill., and Triton College, River Grove, Ill.

Tied major league record for most at-bats, season, no sacrifice flies (680), 1986.
Tied modern major league record for most hits, first game in majors, nine innings (4), May 8, 1984.
Established American League record for most hits, two consecutive nine-inning games (10), August 29 and 30, 1987.
Major League stolen bases: 1984 (14), 1985 (21), 1986 (20), 1987 (12), 1988 (6). Total—73.
Collected six hits in one game, August 30, 1987.
Hit for the cycle, August 1, 1986.
Led American League in total bases with 358 in 1988.
Led American League outfielders in total chances with 492 in 1985 and 465 in 1988.
Led Appalachian League in total bases with 135 and tied for lead in stolen bases with 43 in 1982.
Led California League outfielders in double plays with 5 in 1983.
Named outfielder on THE SPORTING NEWS American League All-Star Team, 1986 through 1988.
Named outfielder on THE SPORTING NEWS American League All-Star fielding team, 1986 through 1988.
Named outfielder on THE SPORTING NEWS American League Silver Slugger team, 1986 through 1988.
Named California League Player of the Year, 1983.

Year	Club	League	Pos.	G.	AB.	R.	H.	2B.	3B.	HR.	RBI.	B.A.	PO.	A.	E.	F.A.
1982	Elizabethton	Appal.	OF	65	*275	*65	*105	15	3	3	35	*.382	133	*11	5	.966
1983	Visalia	Calif.	OF	138	*548	105	172	29	7	9	97	.314	253	*22	5	.982
1984	Toledo	Int.	OF	21	80	9	21	2	0	1	5	.263	35	1	3	.923
1984	Minnesota	Amer.	OF	128	557	63	165	12	5	0	31	.296	438	*16	3	.993
1985	Minnesota	Amer.	OF	161	*691	80	199	29	13	4	74	.288	*465	19	8	.984
1986	Minnesota	Amer.	OF	161	680	119	223	37	6	31	96	.328	429	8	6	.986
1987	Minnesota	Amer.	OF	157	624	96	•207	32	5	28	99	.332	341	8	5	.986
1988	Minnesota	Amer.	OF	158	*657	109	*234	42	5	24	121	.356	*450	12	3	.994
Major League Totals—5 Years				765	3209	467	1028	152	34	87	421	.320	2123	63	25	.989

Selected by Minnesota Twins' organization in 1st round (third player selected) of free-agent draft, January 12, 1982.

CHAMPIONSHIP SERIES RECORD

Tied Championship Series record for most at-bats, nine-inning game (6), October 12, 1987.
Established American League Championship Series record for most at-bats, five-game Series (24), 1987.

Year	Club	League	Pos.	G.	AB.	R.	H.	2B.	3B.	HR.	RBI.	B.A.	PO.	A.	E.	F.A.
1987	Minnesota	Amer.	OF	5	24	3	5	1	0	1	3	.208	7	0	0	1.000

WORLD SERIES RECORD

Tied World Series records for most at-bats, inning (2), October 18, 1987 (fourth inning); most runs (4) and most times reaching first base safely, game (batting 1.000) (5), October 24, 1987.

Year	Club	League	Pos.	G.	AB.	R.	H.	2B.	3B.	HR.	RBI.	B.A.	PO.	A.	E.	F.A.
1987	Minnesota	Amer.	OF	7	28	5	10	1	1	0	3	.357	15	1	1	.941

ALL-STAR GAME RECORD

Year	League	Pos.	AB.	R.	H.	2B.	3B.	HR.	RBI.	B.A.	PO.	A.	E.	F.A.
1986	American	OF	3	0	1	0	0	0	0	.333	5	0	0	1.000
1987	American	PH-OF	4	0	0	0	0	0	0	.000	1	0	0	1.000
1988	American	OF	1	0	0	0	0	0	0	.000	1	0	0	1.000
All-Star Game Totals—3 Years			8	0	1	0	0	0	0	.125	7	0	0	1.000

TERRANCE STEPHEN PUHL

Name pronounced Pool.

(Terry)

Born July 8, 1956, at Melville, Saskatchewan, Canada.
Height, 6.02. Weight, 197.
Throws right and bats lefthanded.

Established major league record for highest fielding percentage by outfielder, lifetime, 1,000 or more games (.993).

Tied major league records for highest fielding percentage by outfielder, season, 150 or more games (1.000), 1979; fewest errors by outfielder, season, 150 or more games (0), 1979.

Major League stolen bases: 1977 (10), 1978 (32), 1979 (30), 1980 (27), 1981 (22), 1982 (17), 1983 (24), 1984 (13), 1985 (6), 1986 (3), 1987 (1), 1988 (22). Total—207.

Year Club	League	Pos.	G.	AB.	R.	H.	2B.	3B.	HR.	RBI.	B.A.	PO.	A.	E.	F.A.
1974—Covington	Appal.	OF	59	211	42	60	11	0	0	21	.284	89	2	2	.978
1975—Dubuque	Midw.	OF-1B	104	346	57	115	10	2	0	28	.332	230	11	7	.971
1976—Columbus	South.	OF	28	98	13	28	5	0	1	14	.286	76	1	2	.975
1976—Memphis	Int.	OF	105	372	50	99	17	3	1	39	.266	191	5	3	.985
1977—Charleston	Int.	OF	78	285	53	87	12	6	4	33	.305	189	4	3	.985
1977—Houston	Nat.	OF	60	229	40	69	13	5	0	10	.301	119	3	1	.992
1978—Houston	Nat.	OF	149	585	87	169	25	6	3	35	.289	386	6	3	.992
1979—Houston	Nat.	OF	157	600	87	172	22	4	8	49	.287	352	7	0	*1.000
1980—Houston	Nat.	OF	141	535	75	151	24	5	13	55	.282	311	14	3	.991
1981—Houston	Nat.	OF	96	350	43	88	19	4	3	28	.251	185	5	0	•1.000
1982—Houston	Nat.	OF	145	507	64	133	17	9	8	50	.262	257	4	3	.989
1983—Houston	Nat.	OF	137	465	66	136	25	7	8	44	.292	220	4	2	.991
1984—Houston†	Nat.	OF	132	449	66	135	19	7	9	55	.301	213	6	3	.986
1985—Houston‡	Nat.	OF	57	194	34	55	14	3	2	23	.284	92	3	0	1.000
1986—Houston§	Nat.	OF	81	172	17	42	10	0	3	14	.244	65	0	0	1.000
1987—Houston	Nat.	OF	90	122	9	28	5	0	2	15	.230	48	0	1	.980
1988—Houston	Nat.	OF	113	234	42	71	7	2	3	19	.303	116	2	2	.983
Major League Totals—12 Years			1358	4442	630	1249	200	52	62	397	.281	2364	54	18	.993

Signed as free agent by Houston Astros' organization, September 19, 1973.

†On disabled list, April 13 to April 30, 1984.

‡On disabled list, April 22 to May 7, June 13 to June 28, July 19 to August 15 and August 26, 1985 through remainder of season.

§On disabled list, March 30 to April 15 and July 2 to July 23, 1986.

DIVISION SERIES RECORD

Year Club	League	Pos.	G.	AB.	R.	H.	2B.	3B.	HR.	RBI.	B.A.	PO.	A.	E.	F.A.
1981—Houston	Nat.	OF	5	21	2	4	1	0	0	0	.190	7	1	0	1.000

CHAMPIONSHIP SERIES RECORD

Tied Championship Series records for most at-bats, extra-inning game (6), October 8, 1980; most one-base hits, five-game Series (8), 1980.

Established National League Championship Series records for highest batting average, five-game Series (.526), 1980; most hits, five-game Series (10), 1980.

Tied National League Championship Series record for most hits, game (4), October 12, 1980.

Year Club	League	Pos.	G.	AB.	R.	H.	2B.	3B.	HR.	RBI.	B.A.	PO.	A.	E.	F.A.
1980—Houston	Nat.	PH-OF	5	19	4	10	2	0	0	3	.526	13	0	0	1.000
1986—Houston	Nat.	PH	3	3	0	2	0	0	0	0	.667	0	0	0	.000
Championship Series Totals—2 Years			8	22	4	12	2	0	0	3	.545	13	0	0	1.000

ALL-STAR GAME RECORD

Member of National League All-Star Team for 1978 game; did not play.

CHARLES MICHAEL PULEO

Name pronounced Puh-LAY-oh.

(Charlie)

Born February 7, 1955, at Glen Ridge, N. J.
Height, 6.03. Weight, 200.
Throws and bats righthanded.
Received bachelor of science degree in physical education and science from
Seton Hall University, South Orange, N. J. in 1977.

Pitched seven-inning, 3-0 no-hit victory against St. Petersburg, August 13, 1979 (second game).

Major League saves: 1982 (1), 1988 (1). Total—2.

Tied International League in complete games with 9 in 1986.

Year Club	League	G.	IP.	W.	L.	Pct.	H.	R.	ER.	SO.	BB.	ERA.
1978—Utica	NYP	16	104	10	3	.769	81	46	31	*125	48	2.68
1979—Dunedin	Florida St.	22	123	10	10	.500	126	72	61	77	61	4.46
1980—Knoxville†‡	Southern	19	108	8	7	.533	87	51	34	97	66	2.83
1981—Tidewater	Int'national	26	169	12	9	.571	132	74	65	133	73	3.46
1981—New York	National	4	13	0	0	.000	8	1	0	8	8	0.00
1982—New York§	National	36	171	9	9	.500	179	99	85	98	90	4.47
1983—Cincinnati x	National	27	143⅔	6	12	.333	145	86	78	71	91	4.89
1984—Wichita	Am. Assoc.	19	104⅓	8	9	.471	117	71	62	59	59	5.35
1984—Cincinnati	National	5	22	1	2	.333	27	15	14	6	15	5.73
1985—Denver y	Am. Assoc.	11	61	1	5	.167	70	42	31	40	37	4.57

Year Club	League	G.	IP.	W.	L.	Pct.	H.	R.	ER.	SO.	BB.	ERA.
1985—Richmond	Int'national	16	71	5	4	.556	50	23	22	63	37	2.79
1986—Richmond	Int'national	27	170	★14	7	.667	166	80	66	•124	76	3.79
1986—Atlanta	National	5	24⅓	1	2	.333	13	10	8	18	12	2.96
1987—Atlanta	National	35	123⅓	6	8	.429	122	63	58	99	40	4.23
1988—Atlanta	National	53	106⅓	5	5	.500	101	46	41	70	47	3.47
Major League Totals—7 Years		165	603⅔	28	38	.424	595	320	284	370	303	4.23

Selected by Detroit Tigers' organization in 13th round of free-agent draft, June 5, 1973.
Signed as free agent by Toronto Blue Jays' organization, March 14, 1978.
†On disabled list, April 24 to June 14, 1980.
‡Traded to New York Mets' organization, April 14, 1981; completing deal in which New York traded Pitcher Mark Bomback to Toronto Blue Jays for a player to be named later, April 6, 1981.
§Traded with Catcher Lloyd McClendon and Outfielder Jason Felice to Cincinnati Reds for Pitcher Tom Seaver, December 16, 1982.
xOn disabled list, March 20 to May 2, 1983.
ySold to Richmond (Atlanta Braves' organization), June 6, 1985.

LUIS RAUL QUINONES

Name pronounced Key-NO-nez.

Born April 28, 1962, at Ponce, Puerto Rico.
Height, 5.11. Weight, 175.
Throws right and bats left and righthanded.

Major League stolen bases: 1983 (1), 1986 (3), 1988 (1). Total—5.
Led Carolina League shortstops in double plays with 77 in 1981.
Tied for Northwest League lead in double plays by shortstops with 33 in 1980.

Year Club	League	Pos.	G.	AB.	R.	H.	2B.	3B.	HR.	RBI.	B.A.	PO.	A.	E.	F.A.
1980—Grays Harbor	N'west	SS	56	156	33	35	2	2	0	11	.224	70	157	24	.904
1981—Salem	Carol.	•SS-2B	123	455	64	102	10	4	7	37	.224	208	341	•53	.912
1982—Salem	Carol.	SS	41	173	32	48	1	4	5	28	.277	41	99	15	.903
1982—Amarillo†	Texas	SS	95	411	69	120	19	7	11	60	.292	164	288	31	.936
1983—Albany	East.	2B-OF-SS	56	213	35	51	5	0	6	23	.239	101	138	13	.948
1983—Oakland	Amer.	2-O-3-S	19	42	5	8	2	1	0	4	.190	22	24	1	.979
1983—Tacoma‡	P. C.	SS-OF-2B	45	133	14	35	3	1	2	14	.263	62	97	9	.946
1984—Maine	Int.	★SS-OF-2B	131	473	71	127	27	3	8	60	.268	217	330	★43	.927
1985—Maine§	Int.	SS-OF	14	45	4	8	2	1	1	2	.178	19	12	0	1.000
1985—Phoenix	P. C.	SS-2B-3B	85	304	46	78	13	7	8	47	.257	106	236	13	.963
1986—Phoenix	P. C.	SS	14	55	7	14	4	1	0	7	.255	23	37	3	.952
1986—San Francisco xy	Nat.	SS-3B-2B	71	106	13	19	1	3	0	11	.179	28	66	8	.922
1987—Iowa	A. A.	SS-2B	77	287	44	91	14	★12	11	62	.317	93	122	14	.939
1987—Chicago z	Nat.	SS-2B-3B	49	101	12	22	6	0	0	8	.218	35	58	3	.969
1988—Nashville	A. A.	SS-3B-1B	114	417	42	115	28	6	9	53	.276	164	285	25	.947
1988—Cincinnati	Nat.	SS-3B-2B	23	52	4	12	3	0	1	11	.231	15	37	2	.963
American League Totals—1 Year			19	42	5	8	2	1	0	4	.190	22	24	1	.979
National League Totals—3 Years			143	259	29	53	10	3	1	30	.205	78	161	13	.948
Major League Totals—4 Years			162	301	34	61	12	4	1	34	.203	100	185	14	.953

Signed as free agent by San Diego Padres' organization, April 28, 1980.
†Drafted by Oakland A's, December 6, 1982.
‡Traded to Cleveland Indians, December 8, 1983, completing deal in which Cleveland traded Catcher Jim Essian to Oakland A's for a player to be named later, December 5, 1983.
§Traded with Pitcher Mike Jeffcoat to San Francisco Giants' organization for Shortstop Johnnie LeMaster, May 7, 1985.
xReleased, November 10, 1986; signed by Tacoma (Oakland A's organization), January 22, 1987.
yTraded to Chicago Cubs for Third Baseman Ron Cey, January 30, 1987.
zTraded to Cincinnati Reds for Pitcher Bill Landrum, April 1, 1988.

REY FRANCISCO QUINONES

Name pronounced Key-NO-nez.

Born November 11, 1963, at Rio Piedras, Puerto Rico.
Height, 5.11. Weight, 185.
Throws and bats righthanded.

Major League stolen bases: 1986 (4), 1987 (1). Total—5.
Led Eastern League in being hit by pitch with 9 in 1985.
Led Carolina League in grounding into double plays with 20 in 1984.
Led Eastern League shortstops in double plays with 75 in 1985.
Led Carolina League shortstops in total chances with 718 and double plays with 84 in 1984.

Year Club	League	Pos.	G.	AB.	R.	H.	2B.	3B.	HR.	RBI.	B.A.	PO.	A.	E.	F.A.
1983—Elmira	NYP	SS	67	234	38	69	11	0	12	55	.295	107	226	27	.925
1984—Winston-Salem	Carol.	SS	132	458	53	128	★30	6	11	69	.279	★240	★428	★50	.930
1985—New Britain	East.	SS	134	439	67	113	19	5	9	50	.257	207	★402	★34	.947
1986—Pawtucket	Int.	SS	24	87	12	23	2	0	4	18	.264	35	67	4	.962
1986—Bos.†-Sea.	Amer.	SS	98	312	32	68	16	1	2	22	.218	143	247	24	.942
1987—Seattle	Amer.	SS	135	478	55	132	18	2	12	56	.276	204	384	★25	.959
1988—Seattle‡	Amer.	SS	140	499	63	124	30	3	12	52	.248	202	396	23	.963
Major League Totals—3 Years			373	1289	150	324	64	6	26	130	.251	549	1027	72	.956

Signed as free agent by Boston Red Sox' organization, September 8, 1982.

†Traded with a player to be named later and cash to Seattle Mariners for Infielder Spike Owen and Outfielder Dave Henderson, August 19, 1986; as part of deal, Seattle claimed Pitchers Mike Brown and Mike Trujillo on waivers from Boston Red Sox, August 22, 1986. Seattle acquired Outfielder John Christensen to complete deal, September 25, 1986.

‡On disqualified list, May 4 to May 8, 1988.

CARLOS NARCIS QUINTANA

Born August 26, 1965, at Estado Miranda, Venezuela.
Height, 6.02. Weight, 195.
Throws and bats righthanded.

Led International League outfielders in assists with 15 in 1988.

Year Club	League	Pos.	G.	AB.	R.	H.	2B.	3B.	HR.	RBI.	B.A.	PO.	A.	E.	F.A.
1985—Elmira	NYP	OF	65	220	27	61	8	0	4	35	.277	55	5	3	.952
1986—Greensboro	S. Atl.	OF-1B	126	443	97	144	19	4	11	81	.325	224	12	9	.963
1987—New Britain	East.	OF	56	206	31	64	11	3	2	31	.311	100	4	2	.981
1988—Pawtucket	Int.	OF-1B	131	471	67	134	25	3	16	66	.285	525	44	11	.981
1988—Boston	Amer.	OF	5	6	1	2	0	0	0	2	.333	4	0	0	1.000
Major League Totals—1 Year			5	6	1	2	0	0	0	2	.333	4	0	0	1.000

Signed as free agent by Boston Red Sox' organization, November 26, 1984.

JAMES PATRICK QUIRK
(Jamie)

Born October 22, 1954, at Whittier, Calif.
Height, 6.04. Weight, 200.
Throws right and bats lefthanded.
Attended Whittier College, Whittier, Calif.

Major League stolen bases: 1980 (3), 1987 (1), 1988 (1). Total—5.
Led American Association in passed balls with 23 in 1985.
Led American Association third basemen in double plays with 31 in 1975.
Led Pioneer League shortstops in double plays with 16 in 1972.

Year Club	League	Pos.	G.	AB.	R.	H.	2B.	3B.	HR.	RBI.	B.A.	PO.	A.	E.	F.A.
1972—Billings	Pion.	SS	55	208	29	53	9	4	5	37	.255	★63	★162	★28	★.889
1973—San Jose	Calif.	SS	132	429	58	99	12	7	8	45	.231	160	330	39	.926
1974—Jacksonville	South.	SS	46	163	16	37	7	2	3	21	.227	75	133	20	.912
1974—Omaha	A. A.	SS-3B-2B	53	203	27	57	10	2	10	31	.281	64	141	14	.936
1975—Omaha	A. A.	3B	127	445	62	122	23	4	13	64	.274	109	★254	16	★.958
1975—Kansas City	Amer.	OF-3B	14	39	2	10	0	0	1	5	.256	19	3	2	.917
1976—Kansas City†	Amer.	SS-3B-1B	64	114	11	28	6	0	1	15	.246	9	14	2	.920
1977—Milwaukee	Amer.	OF-3B	93	221	16	48	14	1	3	13	.217	19	4	2	.920
1978—Spokane‡	P. C.	3B-1B	97	343	58	100	20	2	12	63	.292	235	142	20	.950
1978—Kansas City§	Amer.	3B-SS	17	29	3	6	2	0	0	2	.207	11	16	2	.931
1979—Kansas City	Amer.	C-SS-3B	51	79	8	24	6	1	1	11	.304	16	9	1	.960
1980—Kansas City	Amer.	C-3-O-1	62	163	13	45	5	0	5	21	.276	78	66	8	.947
1981—Kansas City	Amer.	C-3-2-O	46	100	8	25	7	0	0	10	.250	63	23	4	.956
1982—Kansas City xy	Amer.	C-1-3-O	36	78	8	18	3	0	1	5	.231	110	12	0	1.000
1983—St. Louis za	Nat.	C-3B-SS	48	86	3	18	2	1	2	11	.209	68	13	6	.931
1984—Denver	A. A.	C-3-O-1-P	70	201	23	42	6	3	2	24	.209	212	67	11	.962
1984—Chi. b-Cle. c	Amer.	3B-C	4	3	1	1	0	0	1	2	.333	1	0	0	1.000
1985—Omaha	A. A.	C-1B-3B	104	324	33	79	5	1	8	48	.244	525	67	14	.977
1985—Kansas City d	Amer.	C-1B	19	57	3	16	3	1	0	4	.281	66	8	1	.987
1986—Kansas City e	Amer.	C-3-1-O	80	219	24	47	10	0	8	26	.215	303	64	4	.989
1987—Kansas City fg	Amer.	C-SS	109	296	24	70	17	0	5	33	.236	532	40	8	.986
1988—Kansas City h	Amer.	C-1B-3B	84	196	22	47	7	1	8	25	.240	412	34	8	.982
American League Totals—13 Years			679	1594	143	385	80	4	34	172	.242	1639	293	42	.979
National League Totals—1 Year			48	86	3	18	2	1	2	11	.209	68	13	6	.931
Major League Totals—14 Years			727	1680	146	403	82	5	36	183	.240	1707	306	48	.977

Selected by Kansas City Royals' organization in 1st round (18th player selected) of free-agent draft, June 6, 1972.

†Traded with Outfielder Jim Wohlford and a player to be named later to Milwaukee Brewers for Pitcher Jim Colborn and Catcher Darrell Porter, December 6, 1976; Milwaukee acquired Pitcher Bob McClure to complete deal, March 15, 1977.

‡Traded to Kansas City Royals for Pitcher Gerry Ako and cash, August 3, 1978.
§On disabled list, August 14 to September 5, 1978.
xOn disabled list, August 10 to September 1, 1982.
yGranted free agency, November 10, 1982; signed by St. Louis Cardinals, February 16, 1983.
zReleased, March 26, 1984; named St. Louis Cardinals coach, April 13, 1984.
aSigned by Chicago White Sox' organization, May 23, 1984.
bSold to Cleveland Indians, September 24, 1984.
cReleased, October 15, 1984; signed by Kansas City Royals' organization, February 25, 1985.
dGranted free agency, November 12, 1985; re-signed by Royals, November 27, 1985.
eGranted free agency, November 12, 1986; re-signed by Royals, December 17, 1986.
fOn disabled list, July 21 to August 5, 1987.
gGranted free agency, November 9, 1987; re-signed by Royals, January 25, 1988.
hGranted free agency, November 4, 1988; signed by New York Yankees, December 20, 1988.

CHAMPIONSHIP SERIES RECORD

Year	Club	League	Pos.	G.	AB.	R.	H.	2B.	3B.	HR.	RBI.	B.A.	PO.	A.	E.	F.A.
1976	—Kansas City	Amer.	PH-DH	4	7	1	1	0	1	0	2	.143	0	0	0	.000
1985	—Kansas City	Amer.	PH	1	1	0	0	0	0	0	0	.000	0	0	0	.000
Championship Series Totals—2 Years				5	8	1	1	0	1	0	2	.125	0	0	0	.000

PITCHING RECORD

Year	Club	League	G.	IP.	W.	L.	Pct.	H.	R.	ER.	SO.	BB.	ERA.
1984	—Denver	Am. Assoc.	2	2	0	0	.000	6	3	3	0	0	13.50

DANIEL RAYMOND QUISENBERRY

Name pronounced QUIZ-en-berry.

(Dan)

Born February 7, 1953, at Santa Monica, Calif.
Height, 6.02. Weight, 185.
Throws and bats righthanded.
Attended Orange Coast College, Costa Mesa, Calif., LaVerne College, LaVerne, Calif., and Fresno Pacific College, Fresno, Calif.

Established American League record for most saves, lifetime (238).

Major League saves: 1979 (5), 1980 (33), 1981 (18), 1982 (35), 1983 (45), 1984 (44), 1985 (37), 1986 (12), 1987 (8), 1988 (1). Total—238.

Led American League in games finished in relief with 68 in both 1980 and 1982, 62 in 1983 and 76 in 1985.

Led American League in saves with 35 in 1982, 45 in 1983, 44 in 1984, 37 in 1985 and tied for lead with 33 in 1980.

Tied for Southern League lead in saves with 15 in 1978.

Named American League Fireman of the Year by THE SPORTING NEWS, 1980 and 1982 through 1985.

Year	Club	League	G.	IP.	W.	L.	Pct.	H.	R.	ER.	SO.	BB.	ERA.
1975	—Waterloo	Midwest	20	44	3	2	.600	40	16	12	31	6	2.45
1975	—Jacksonville	Southern	6	8	0	1	.000	5	3	2	2	4	2.25
1976	—Jacksonville	Southern	9	12	0	1	.000	8	6	3	6	2	2.25
1976	—Waterloo	Midwest	34	42	2	1	.667	28	4	3	19	9	0.64
1977	—Jacksonville	Southern	33	74	3	1	.750	61	18	11	33	11	1.34
1978	—Jacksonville	Southern	48	64	4	2	.667	62	22	17	29	12	2.39
1979	—Omaha	Am. Assoc.	26	35	2	1	.667	29	15	14	16	10	3.60
1979	—Kansas City	American	32	40	3	2	.600	42	16	14	13	7	3.15
1980	—Kansas City	American	*75	128	12	7	.632	129	47	44	37	27	3.09
1981	—Kansas City	American	40	62	1	4	.200	59	16	12	20	15	1.74
1982	—Kansas City	American	72	136⅔	9	7	.563	126	43	39	46	12	2.57
1983	—Kansas City	American	*69	139	5	3	.625	118	35	30	48	11	1.94
1984	—Kansas City	American	72	129⅓	6	3	.667	121	39	38	41	12	2.64
1985	—Kansas City	American	*84	129	8	9	.471	142	41	34	54	16	2.37
1986	—Kansas City	American	62	81⅓	3	7	.300	92	30	25	36	24	2.77
1987	—Kansas City	American	47	49	4	1	.800	58	15	15	17	10	2.76
1988	—Kansas City†	American	20	25⅓	0	1	.000	32	11	10	9	5	3.55
1988	—St. Louis	National	33	38	2	0	1.000	54	26	26	19	6	6.16
American League Totals—10 Years			573	919⅔	51	44	.537	919	293	261	321	139	2.55
National League Totals—1 Year			33	38	2	0	1.000	54	26	26	19	6	6.16
Major League Totals—10 Years			606	957⅔	53	44	.546	973	319	287	340	145	2.70

Signed as free agent by Kansas City Royals' organization, June 7, 1975.
†Released, July 4, 1988; signed by St. Louis Cardinals, July 14, 1988.

DIVISION SERIES RECORD

Year	Club	League	G.	IP.	W.	L.	Pct.	H.	R.	ER.	SO.	BB.	ERA.
1981	—Kansas City	American	1	1	0	0	.000	1	0	0	0	0	0.00

CHAMPIONSHIP SERIES RECORD

Tied American League Championship Series record for most games pitched, seven-game Series (4), 1985.
Tied American League Championship Series record for most saves, total Series (2), 1985.

Year	Club	League	G.	IP.	W.	L.	Pct.	H.	R.	ER.	SO.	BB.	ERA.
1980	—Kansas City	American	2	4⅔	1	0	1.000	4	1	0	1	2	0.00
1984	—Kansas City	American	1	3	0	1	.000	2	2	1	1	1	3.00
1985	—Kansas City	American	4	4⅔	0	1	.000	7	4	2	3	0	3.86
Championship Series Totals—3 Years			7	12⅓	1	2	.333	13	7	3	5	3	2.19

WORLD SERIES RECORD

Established World Series records for most games pitched in relief, six-game Series (6), 1980; most games finished, six-game Series (6), 1980.

Year	Club	League	G.	IP.	W.	L.	Pct.	H.	R.	ER.	SO.	BB.	ERA.
1980	—Kansas City	American	6	10⅓	1	2	.333	10	6	6	0	3	5.23
1985	—Kansas City	American	4	4⅓	1	0	1.000	5	1	1	3	3	2.08
World Series Totals—2 Years			10	14⅔	2	2	.500	15	7	7	3	6	4.30

ALL-STAR GAME RECORD

Year	League	IP.	W.	L.	Pct.	H.	R.	ER.	SO.	BB.	ERA.
1982	—American	2	0	0	.000	3	1	1	1	0	4.50
1983	—American	1	0	0	.000	1	0	0	1	0	0.00
All-Star Game Totals—2 Years		3	0	0	.000	4	1	1	2	0	3.00

Member of American League All-Star Team in 1984; did not play.

JOHN ANDREW RABB

Born June 23, 1960, at Los Angeles, Calif.
Height, 6.01. Weight, 179.
Throws and bats righthanded.
Attended El Camino Junior College, Torrance, Calif.

Major League stolen bases: 1983 (1), 1984 (1). Total—2.
Led International League in being hit by pitch with 10 in 1985.
Led California League catchers in putouts with 661 and tied for lead in passed balls with 17 in 1980.
Tied for Texas League lead in double plays by catchers with 6 in 1981.

Year Club	League	Pos.	G.	AB.	R.	H.	2B.	3B.	HR.	RBI.	B.A.	PO.	A.	E.	F.A.
1978—Great Falls	Pion.	C-O-3-1	54	184	32	52	5	3	8	32	.283	185	22	6	.972
1979—Cedar Rapids	Midw.	C-OF	125	447	63	118	19	1	19	90	.264	384	50	15	.967
1980—Fresno	Calif.	*C-OF-3B	128	395	69	96	21	2	19	80	.243	*661	70	11	.985
1981—Shreveport	Texas	*C-OF	102	355	51	98	16	2	16	58	.276	533	42	*18	.970
1982—Phoenix	P. C.	C-OF	119	413	66	115	27	2	22	73	.278	552	55	16	.974
1982—San Francisco	Nat.	OF	2	2	0	1	0	1	0	0	.500	1	0	0	1.000
1983—Phoenix	P. C.	C-OF	62	216	50	74	11	1	10	51	.343	291	17	5	.984
1983—San Francisco	Nat.	C-OF	40	104	10	24	9	0	1	14	.231	176	13	5	.974
1984—San Francisco	Nat.	1B-OF-C	54	82	10	16	1	0	3	9	.195	107	7	3	.974
1985—Phoenix†	P. C.	OF	6	22	3	7	1	0	0	0	.318	13	0	1	.929
1985—Richmond	Int.	O-C-3-1	111	369	55	93	12	5	21	62	.252	151	5	5	.969
1985—Atlanta	Nat.	OF	3	2	0	0	0	0	0	0	.000	0	0	0	.000
1986—Richmond‡	Int.	OF	123	414	73	110	19	6	19	78	.266	85	3	1	989
1987—Richmond§	Int.	OF-3B-2B	121	403	57	91	15	3	20	50	.226	175	40	12	.947
1988—Calgary	P. C.	OF-1B	48	181	35	56	12	0	13	44	.309	165	17	5	.973
1988—Seattle x	Amer.	OF-1B	9	14	2	5	2	0	0	4	.357	5	0	0	1.000
National League Totals—4 Years			99	190	20	41	10	1	4	23	.216	284	20	8	.974
American League Totals—1 Year			9	14	2	5	2	0	0	4	.357	5	0	0	1.000
Major League Totals—5 Years			108	204	22	46	12	1	4	27	.225	289	20	8	.975

Selected by San Francisco Giants' organization in 11th round of free-agent draft, June 6, 1978.
†Traded to Atlanta Braves' organization for Catcher Alex Trevino, April 17, 1985.
‡Granted free agency, October 15, 1986; re-signed by Braves' organization, February 22, 1987.
§Granted free agency, October 15, 1987; signed by Calgary (Seattle Mariners' organization), January 19, 1988.
xOn ineligible list, August 4, 1988 through remainder of season.

ERIC HAROLD RAETHER
(Rick)

Born May 30, 1964, at Milwaukee, Wis.
Height, 6.04. Weight, 192.
Throws and bats righthanded.
Attended University of Miami, Coral Gables, Fla.

Year Club	League	G.	IP.	W.	L.	Pct.	H.	R.	ER.	SO.	BB.	ERA.
1986—Tulsa	Texas	21	33⅔	3	1	.750	24	12	12	21	12	3.21
1987—Charlotte	Florida St.	27	40⅔	2	1	.667	30	8	5	35	16	1.11
1987—Tulsa	Texas	31	34	3	3	.500	34	19	18	38	12	4.76
1988—Tulsa	Texas	46	56⅓	4	1	.800	35	8	6	40	28	0.96

Selected by California Angels' organization in 18th round of free-agent draft, June 3, 1985.
Selected by Texas Rangers' organization in 6th round of free-agent draft, June 2, 1986.

TIMOTHY RAINES
(Tim)

Born September 16, 1959, at Sanford, Fla.
Height, 5.08. Weight, 180.
Throws right and bats left and righthanded.
Brother of Ned Raines, minor league outfielder, 1978 through 1980.

Established major league records for highest stolen base percentage, lifetime, 300 or attempts (.870); most intentional bases on balls by switch-hitter, season (26), 1987.
Tied major league record for fewest double plays by outfielder, season, for leader in double plays (4), 1985.
Major League stolen bases: 1979 (2), 1980 (5), 1981 (71), 1982 (78), 1983 (90), 1984 (75), 1985 (70), 1986 (70), 1987 (50), 1988 (33). Total—544.
Switch-hit home runs in one game, July 16, 1988.
Hit for the cycle, August 16, 1987.
Led National League in stolen bases with 71 in 1981, 78 in 1982, 90 in 1983 and 75 in 1984.
Led National League outfielders in assists with 21 in 1983.
Led American Association in stolen bases with 77 in 1980.
Won THE SPORTING NEWS Gold Shoe Award, 1984.
Named outfielder on THE SPORTING NEWS National League All-Star Team, 1983 and 1986.
Named outfielder on THE SPORTING NEWS National League Silver Slugger team, 1986.
Named National League Rookie Player of the Year by THE SPORTING NEWS, 1981.
Named Minor League Player of the Year by THE SPORTING NEWS, 1980.

Year Club	League	Pos.	G.	AB.	R.	H.	2B.	3B.	HR.	RBI.	B.A.	PO.	A.	E.	F.A.
1977—Sarasota Expos	Gulf C.	2B-3B-OF	49	161	28	45	6	2	0	21	.280	79	72	13	.921
1978—W. Palm Beach†	Fla. St.	2B-SS	100	359	67	103	10	0	0	23	.287	219	273	24	.953
1979—Memphis	South.	2B	•145	552	*104	160	25	10	5	50	.290	*341	*413	*23	.970
1979—Montreal	Nat.	PR	6	0	3	0	0	0	0	0	.000	0	0	0	.000
1980—Denver	A. A.	2B	108	429	105	152	23	•11	6	64	*.354	226	338	16	.972

Year	Club	League	Pos.	G.	AB.	R.	H.	2B.	3B.	HR.	RBI.	B.A.	PO.	A.	E.	F.A.
1980	—Montreal	Nat.	2B-OF	15	20	5	1	0	0	0	0	.050	15	16	0	1.000
1981	—Montreal	Nat.	OF-2B	88	313	61	95	13	7	5	37	.304	162	8	4	.977
1982	—Montreal	Nat.	OF-2B	156	647	90	179	32	8	4	43	.277	293	126	8	.981
1983	—Montreal	Nat.	OF-2B	156	615	*133	183	32	8	11	71	.298	314	23	4	.988
1984	—Montreal	Nat.	OF-2B	160	622	106	192	•38	9	8	60	.309	420	8	6	.986
1985	—Montreal	Nat.	OF	150	575	115	184	30	13	11	41	.320	284	8	2	.993
1986	—Montreal‡	Nat.	OF	151	580	91	194	35	10	9	62	*.334	270	13	6	.979
1987	—Montreal	Nat.	OF	139	530	*123	175	34	8	18	68	.330	297	9	4	.987
1988	—Montreal§	Nat.	OF	109	429	66	116	19	7	12	48	.270	235	5	3	.988
Major League Totals—10 Years				1130	4331	793	1319	233	70	78	430	.305	2290	216	37	.985

Selected by Montreal Expos' organization in 5th round of free-agent draft, June 7, 1977.
†On disabled list, May 23 to June 5, 1978.
‡Granted free agency, November 12, 1986; re-signed by Expos, May 2, 1987.
§On disabled list, June 24 to July 9, 1988.

CHAMPIONSHIP SERIES RECORD

Year	Club	League	Pos.	G.	AB.	R.	H.	2B.	3B.	HR.	RBI.	B.A.	PO.	A.	E.	F.A.
1981	—Montreal	Nat.	OF	5	21	1	5	2	0	0	1	.238	9	0	0	1.000

ALL-STAR GAME RECORD

Year	League	Pos.	AB.	R.	H.	2B.	3B.	HR.	RBI.	B.A.	PO.	A.	E.	F.A.
1981	—National	PR-OF	0	0	0	0	0	0	0	.000	1	0	0	1.000
1982	—National	OF	1	0	0	0	0	0	0	.000	0	0	0	.000
1983	—National	OF	3	0	0	0	0	0	0	.000	2	0	0	1.000
1984	—National	OF	1	0	0	0	0	0	0	000	4	0	0	1.000
1985	—National	PH-OF	0	1	0	0	0	0	0	.000	0	0	0	.000
1986	—National	PH-OF	2	0	0	0	0	0	0	.000	1	0	0	1.000
1987	—National	OF	3	0	3	0	1	0	2	1.000	1	0	0	1.000
All-Star Game Totals—7 Years			10	1	3	0	1	0	2	.300	9	0	0	1.000

RAFAEL EMILIO RAMIREZ (PEGUERO)

Born February 18, 1959, at San Pedro de Macoris, Dominican Republic.
Height, 5.11. Weight, 190.
Throws and bats righthanded.

Tied major league records for most doubles, game (4), May 21, 1986, 13 innings; most double plays by shortstop, extra-inning game (6), June 27, 1982 (14 innings).

Established National League record for fewest putouts by shortstop, season, for leader in most putouts (251), 1984.

Major League stolen bases: 1980 (2), 1981 (7), 1982 (27), 1983 (16), 1984 (14), 1985 (2), 1986 (19), 1987 (6), 1988 (3). Total—96.

Led National League shortstops in double plays with 130 in 1982, 116 in 1983, 115 in 1985 and tied for lead with 94 in 1984.

Led National League shortstops in total chances with 866 in 1982 and 724 in 1984.

Year	Club	League	Pos.	G.	AB.	R.	H.	2B.	3B.	HR.	RBI.	B.A.	PO.	A.	E.	F.A.
1977	—Brad. Braves	Gulf C.	SS-OF	49	175	20	31	2	1	4	19	.177	52	94	32	.820
1978	—Greenwood	W. Car.	SS	81	282	54	77	15	3	6	46	.273	119	229	*43	.890
1978	—Savannah	South.	SS	38	131	14	27	4	0	2	13	.206	61	123	15	.925
1979	—Savannah†	South.	SS	113	386	47	80	17	3	10	39	.207	134	282	*38	.916
1980	—Richmond‡	Int.	SS	80	281	33	79	15	3	5	38	.281	117	294	23	.947
1980	—Atlanta	Nat.	SS	50	165	17	44	6	1	2	11	.267	63	140	11	.949
1981	—Atlanta	Nat.	SS	95	307	30	67	16	2	2	20	.218	181	306	*30	.942
1982	—Atlanta	Nat.	SS	157	609	74	169	24	4	10	52	.278	*300	528	*38	.956
1983	—Atlanta	Nat.	SS	152	622	82	185	13	5	7	58	.297	232	490	*39	.949
1984	—Atlanta	Nat.	SS	145	591	51	157	22	4	2	48	.266	*251	443	•30	.959
1985	—Atlanta	Nat.	SS	138	568	54	141	25	4	5	58	.248	214	451	*32	.954
1986	—Atlanta	Nat.	SS-3B-OF	134	496	57	119	21	1	8	33	.240	156	371	29	.948
1987	—Atlanta§ x	Nat.	SS-3B	56	179	22	47	12	0	1	21	.263	66	110	10	.946
1988	—Houston	Nat.	SS	155	566	51	156	30	5	6	59	.276	232	408	23	.965
Major League Totals—9 Years				1082	4103	438	1085	169	26	43	360	.264	1695	3247	242	.953

Signed as free agent by Atlanta Braves' organization, September 28, 1976.
†On disabled list, April 16 to April 27, 1979.
‡On disabled list, June 23 to July 17, 1980.
§On disabled list, July 2 to September 25, 1987.
xTraded with cash to Houston Astros for Third Baseman Ed Whited and Pitcher Mike Stoker, December 8, 1987.

CHAMPIONSHIP SERIES RECORD

Year	Club	League	Pos.	G.	AB.	R.	H.	2B.	3B.	HR.	RBI.	B.A.	PO.	A.	E.	F.A.
1982	—Atlanta	Nat.	SS	3	11	1	2	0	0	0	1	.182	5	11	1	.941

ALL-STAR GAME RECORD

Member of National League All-Star Team in 1984; did not play.

DOMINGO ANTONIO RAMOS

Born March 29, 1958, at Santiago, Dominican Republic.
Height, 5.10. Weight, 154.
Throws and bats righthanded.

Major League stolen bases: 1983 (3), 1984 (2). Total—5.
Tied for International League lead in sacrifice flies with 6 in 1981.

Year	Club	League	Pos.	G.	AB.	R.	H.	2B.	3B.	HR.	RBI.	B.A.	PO.	A.	E.	F.A.
1975	—Oneonta	NYP	SS-3B	49	166	29	39	4	1	0	21	.235	60	143	14	.935
1976	—Fort Lauderdale	Fla. St.	SS	103	328	34	79	11	3	0	29	.241	150	343	35	.934
1976	—Syracuse	Int.	SS	11	39	7	10	2	1	0	8	.256	13	20	2	.943
1977	—West Haven	East.	SS	129	431	55	106	18	6	2	50	.246	222	433	23	*.966
1978	—Tacoma	P. C.	SS	91	314	43	74	13	3	0	30	.236	155	290	28	.941
1978	—West Haven	East.	SS	40	134	16	34	2	2	1	13	.254	40	128	6	.966
1978	—New York†‡	Amer.	SS	1	0	0	0	0	0	0	0	.000	0	0	0	.000
1979	—Syr.§-Colum. x	Int.	SS	115	376	38	92	11	4	1	28	.245	211	323	26	.954
1980	—Syracuse	Int.	SS	84	319	45	80	8	4	4	27	.251	160	240	28	.935
1980	—Toronto	Amer.	SS-2B	5	16	0	2	0	0	0	0	.125	5	10	0	1.000
1981	—Syracuse y	Int.	SS-3B-2B	96	320	42	82	4	5	0	31	.256	158	248	19	.955
1982	—Salt Lake City	P. C.	SS	112	427	75	134	19	8	6	56	.314	174	288	19	.960
1982	—Seattle	Amer.	SS	8	26	3	4	2	0	0	1	.154	9	14	2	.920
1983	—Seattle	Amer.	2B-SS-3B	53	127	14	36	4	0	2	10	.283	51	109	8	.952
1984	—Seattle	Amer.	3-S-1-2	59	81	6	15	2	0	0	2	.185	51	49	5	.952
1985	—Seattle	Amer.	S-2-1-3	75	168	19	33	6	0	1	15	.196	87	119	10	.954
1986	—Seattle	Amer.	SS-2B-3B	49	99	8	18	2	0	0	5	.182	55	93	6	.961
1987	—Seattle z	Amer.	SS-3B-2B	42	103	9	32	6	0	2	11	.311	47	88	5	.964
1988	—Colo. Sp.a-Edm.	P. C.	3B-SS-2B	50	165	30	46	10	2	2	25	.279	45	107	9	.944
1988	—Clev.-Calif.b	Amer.	2-3-1-S-O	32	61	10	14	1	0	0	5	.230	37	43	1	.988
Major League Totals—9 Years				324	681	69	154	23	0	5	49	.226	342	525	37	.959

Signed as free agent by New York Yankees' organization, May 27, 1975.

†Traded with Pitchers Sparky Lyle, Larry McCall and Dave Rajsich, Catcher Mike Heath and cash to Texas Rangers for Outfielders Juan Beniquez and Greg Jemison and Pitchers Mike Griffin, Paul Mirabella and Dave Righetti, November 10, 1978.

‡Loaned to Toronto Blue Jays' organization, April 5, 1979.

§Loaned to New York Yankees' organization, July 30, 1979; returned to Texas Rangers, September 28, 1979.

xSold to Toronto Blue Jays, November 5, 1979.

yDrafted by Seattle Mariners, December 7, 1981.

zReleased, December 21, 1987; signed by Colorado Springs (Cleveland Indians' organization), February 1, 1988.

aReleased, August 5, 1988; signed by Edmonton (California Angels' organization), August 17, 1988.

bGranted free agency, November 4, 1988; signed by Iowa (Chicago Cubs' organization), December 14, 1988.

JAMES ODELL RANDALL
(Sap)

Born August 19, 1960, at Mobile, Ala.
Height, 5.11. Weight, 195.
Throws right and bats left and righthanded.
Attended Grambling State University, Grambling, La.

Tied for California League lead in double plays by outfielders with 6 in 1982.

Year	Club	League	Pos.	G.	AB.	R.	H.	2B.	3B.	HR.	RBI.	B.A.	PO.	A.	E.	F.A.
1981	—Salem	N'west	OF-1B	43	160	28	45	7	0	6	29	.281	102	7	6	.948
1982	—Redwood	Calif.	OF	135	504	64	138	27	4	11	74	.274	187	•23	*13	.942
1983	—Nashua	East	OF-1B	133	456	78	126	26	4	14	88	.276	407	54	15	.968
1984	—Edmonton	P. C.	1B-OF	119	426	61	121	17	7	11	71	.284	892	95	29	.971
1985	—Edmonton	P. C.	OF-1B	35	103	12	29	5	1	0	16	.282	50	2	1	.981
1985	—Midland	Texas	1B-OF	81	302	54	94	23	1	15	61	.311	452	25	14	.971
1986	—Midland	Texas	*1B-OF	123	468	90	155	23	2	22	93	.331	952	73	*12	.988
1987	—Edmonton†	P. C.	1B	13	34	6	11	5	0	1	5	.324	1	0	0	1.000
1988	—Vancouver	P. C.	OF-1B	112	402	65	110	24	6	11	61	.274	255	16	10	.964
1988	—Chicago‡	Amer.	1B-OF	4	12	1	0	0	0	0	1	.000	15	2	0	1.000
Major League Totals—1 Year				4	12	1	0	0	0	0	1	.000	15	2	0	1.000

Selected by California Angels' organization in 10th round of free-agent draft, June 8, 1981.

†Released, June 5, 1987; signed by Chicago White Sox, December 9, 1987.

‡Granted free agency, October 15, 1988.

WILLIAM LARRY RANDOLPH JR.
(Willie)

Born July 6, 1954, at Holly Hill, S. C.
Height, 5.11. Weight, 163.
Throws and bats righthanded.
Brother of Terry Randolph, defensive back with Green Bay Packers, 1977.

Tied major league record for most assists by second baseman in extra-inning game since 1900 (13), August 25, 1976 (19 innings).

Established American League record for most chances accepted by second baseman in extra-inning game (20), August 25, 1976 (19 innings).

Major League stolen bases: 1975 (1), 1976 (37), 1977 (13), 1978 (36), 1979 (33), 1980 (30), 1981 (14), 1982 (16), 1983 (12), 1984 (10), 1985 (16), 1986 (15), 1987 (11), 1988 (8). Total—252.

Led American League in bases on balls received with 119 in 1980.

Led American League second basemen in double plays with 128 in 1979 and 112 in 1984.

Led American League second basemen in total chances with 846 in 1979.

Led Eastern League in bases on balls received with 110 in 1974.

Led Western Carolinas League in bases on balls received with 90 and tied for lead in sacrifice flies with 8 in 1973.

Named second baseman on THE SPORTING NEWS American League All-Star Team, 1977, 1980 and 1987.

Named second baseman on THE SPORTING NEWS American League Silver Slugger team, 1980.

Year	Club	League	Pos.	G.	AB.	R.	H.	2B.	3B.	HR.	RBI.	B.A.	PO.	A.	E.	F.A.
1972	—Bradenton Pir.	Gulf C.	SS-OF	44	167	21	53	6	5	0	10	.317	85	116	24	.893
1973	—Charleston	W. Car.	2B	121	428	93	120	25	6	8	51	.280	*285	308	*24	.961
1974	—Thetford Mines	East.	2B	135	461	*103	117	28	6	12	53	.254	269	319	21	.966
1975	—Charleston	Int.	2B	91	313	41	106	13	5	7	42	.339	189	250	16	.965
1975	—Pittsburgh†	Nat.	2B-3B	30	61	9	10	1	0	0	3	.164	34	45	6	.929
1976	—New York	Amer.	2B	125	430	59	115	15	4	1	40	.267	307	415	19	.974
1977	—New York	Amer.	2B	147	551	91	151	28	11	4	40	.274	350	454	16	.980
1978	—New York‡	Amer.	2B	134	499	87	139	18	6	3	42	.279	296	400	16	.978
1979	—New York	Amer.	2B	153	574	98	155	15	13	5	61	.270	*355	*478	13	.985
1980	—New York	Amer.	2B	138	513	99	151	23	7	7	46	.294	361	401	19	.976
1981	—New York	Amer.	2B	93	357	59	83	14	3	2	24	.232	205	268	*11	.977
1982	—New York	Amer.	2B	144	553	85	155	21	4	3	36	.280	352	380	14	.981
1983	—New York§	Amer.	2B	104	420	73	117	21	1	2	38	.279	265	298	12	.979
1984	—New York	Amer.	2B	142	564	86	162	24	2	2	31	.287	334	419	13	.983
1985	—New York	Amer.	2B	143	497	75	137	21	2	5	40	.276	303	425	11	.985
1986	—New York x	Amer.	2B	141	492	76	136	15	2	5	50	.276	313	381	*20	.972
1987	—New York y	Amer.	2B	120	449	96	137	24	2	7	67	.305	286	338	12	.981
1988	—New York za	Amer.	2B	110	404	43	93	20	1	2	34	.230	254	339	7	.988
National League Totals—1 Year				30	61	9	10	1	0	0	3	.164	34	45	6	.929
American League Totals—13 Years				1694	6303	1027	1731	259	58	48	549	.275	3981	4996	183	.980
Major League Totals—14 Years				1724	6364	1036	1741	260	58	48	552	.274	4015	5041	189	.980

Selected by Pittsburgh Pirates' organization in 7th round of free-agent draft, June 6, 1972.

†Traded with Pitchers Ken Brett and Dock Ellis to New York Yankees for Pitcher Doc Medich, December 11, 1975.

‡On disabled list, June 23 to July 14, 1978.

§On disabled list, June 27 to July 12 and July 13 to August 5, 1983.

xGranted free agency, November 12, 1986; re-signed by Yankees, January 8, 1987.

yOn disabled list, July 15 to August 14, 1987.

zOn disabled list, June 10 to June 25 and August 3 to August 28, 1988.

aGranted free agency, October 24, 1988; signed by Los Angeles Dodgers, December 10, 1988.

DIVISION SERIES RECORD

Year	Club	League	Pos.	G.	AB.	R.	H.	2B.	3B.	HR.	RBI.	B.A.	PO.	A.	E.	F.A.
1981	—New York	Amer.	2B	5	20	0	4	0	0	0	1	.200	7	10	0	1.000

CHAMPIONSHIP SERIES RECORD

Year	Club	League	Pos.	G.	AB.	R.	H.	2B.	3B.	HR.	RBI.	B.A.	PO.	A.	E.	F.A.
1975	—Pittsburgh	Nat.	PH-PR-2	2	2	1	0	0	0	0	0	.000	0	1	0	1.000
1976	—New York	Amer.	2B	5	17	0	2	0	0	0	1	.118	8	14	0	1.000
1977	—New York	Amer.	2B	5	18	4	5	1	0	0	2	.278	13	9	0	1.000
1980	—New York	Amer.	2B	3	13	0	5	2	0	0	1	.385	2	9	0	1.000
1981	—New York	Amer.	2B	3	12	2	4	0	0	1	2	.333	12	12	0	1.000
Championship Series Totals—5 Years				18	62	7	16	3	0	1	6	.258	35	45	0	1.000

WORLD SERIES RECORD

Established World Series record for most bases on balls, six-game Series (9), 1981.

Tied World Series record for fewest chances accepted by second baseman, game (0), October 25, 1981.

Year	Club	League	Pos.	G.	AB.	R.	H.	2B.	3B.	HR.	RBI.	B.A.	PO.	A.	E.	F.A.
1976	—New York	Amer.	2B	4	14	1	1	0	0	0	0	.071	13	8	0	1.000
1977	—New York	Amer.	2B	6	25	5	4	2	0	1	1	.160	13	14	0	1.000
1981	—New York	Amer.	2B	6	18	5	4	1	1	2	3	.222	13	11	0	1.000
World Series Totals—3 Years				16	57	11	9	3	1	3	4	.158	39	33	0	1.000

ALL-STAR GAME RECORD

Established All-Star Game record for most assists by second baseman, nine-inning game (6), July 19, 1977.

Tied All-Star Game records for most at bats, nine-inning game (5), July 19, 1977; most errors, game (2), July 8, 1980.

Year	League	Pos.	AB.	R.	H.	2B.	3B.	HR.	RBI.	B.A.	PO.	A.	E.	F.A.
1977	—American	2B	5	0	1	0	0	0	1	.200	2	6	0	1.000
1980	—American	2B	4	0	2	0	0	0	0	.500	0	3	2	.600
1981	—American	2B	3	0	1	0	0	0	0	.333	0	5	0	1.000
1987	—American	2B	1	0	0	0	0	0	0	.000	0	1	0	1.000
All-Star Game Totals—4 Years			13	0	4	0	0	0	1	.308	2	15	2	.895

Named to American League All-Star Team for 1976 game; replaced due to injury.

DENNIS LEE RASMUSSEN

Born April 18, 1959, at Los Angeles, Calif.
Height, 6.07. Weight, 225.
Throws and bats lefthanded.
Attended Creighton University, Omaha, Neb.
Grandson of Wilbur Lee (Bill) Brubaker, infielder with Pittsburgh
Pirates and Boston Braves, 1932 through 1940 and 1943.

Led Eastern League in wild pitches with 18 in 1981.

Tied for International League lead in games started by pitchers with 28 in 1983.

Year	Club	League	G.	IP.	W.	L.	Pct.	H.	R.	ER.	SO.	BB.	ERA.
1980	—Salinas	California	11	76	4	6	.400	69	51	46	63	52	5.45
1981	—Holyoke	Eastern	24	156	8	12	.400	134	95	69	125	99	3.98

Year Club	League	G.	IP.	W.	L.	Pct.	H.	R.	ER.	SO.	BB.	ERA.
1982—Spokane†	P. Coast	27	171⅔	11	8	.579	166	110	96	162	*113	5.03
1983—Columbus‡	Int'national	28	181	•13	10	.565	161	106	92	*187	108	4.57
1983—San Diego§	National	4	13⅔	0	0	.000	10	5	3	13	8	1.98
1984—Columbus	Int'national	6	43⅔	4	1	.800	24	15	15	30	27	3.09
1984—New York	American	24	147⅔	9	6	.600	127	79	75	110	60	4.57
1985—New York	American	22	101⅔	3	5	.375	97	56	45	63	42	3.98
1985—Columbus	Int'national	7	45	0	3	.000	41	24	19	43	25	3.80
1986—New York	American	31	202	18	6	.750	160	91	87	131	74	3.88
1987—New York	American	26	146	9	7	.563	145	78	77	89	55	4.75
1987—Columbus x	Int'national	1	7	1	0	1.000	5	1	1	4	0	1.29
1987—Cincinnati	National	7	45⅓	4	1	.800	39	22	20	39	12	3.97
1988—Cincinnati y-San Diego	National	31	204⅔	16	10	.615	199	84	78	112	58	3.43
National League Totals—3 Years		42	263⅔	20	11	.645	248	111	101	164	78	3.45
American League Totals—4 Years		103	597⅓	39	24	.619	529	304	284	393	231	4.28
Major League Totals—6 Years		145	861	59	35	.628	777	415	385	557	309	4.02

Selected by Pittsburgh Pirates' organization in 18th round of free-agent draft, June 7, 1977.

Selected by California Angels' organization in 1st round (17th player selected) of free-agent draft, June 3, 1980.

†Traded to New York Yankees, November 24, 1982, completing deal in which New York traded Pitcher Tommy John to California Angels for a player to be named later, August 31, 1982.

‡Traded with Second Baseman Edwin Rodriguez to San Diego Padres, September 12, 1983, completing deal in which San Diego traded Pitcher John Montefusco to New York Yankees for two players to be named later, August 26, 1983.

§Traded with a player to be named later to New York Yankees' organization for Third Baseman Graig Nettles, March 30, 1984; New York organization acquired Pitcher Darin Cloninger to complete deal, April 26, 1984.

xTraded to Cincinnati Reds for Pitcher Bill Gullickson, August 26, 1987.

yTraded to San Diego Padres for Pitcher Candy Sierra, June 8, 1988.

SHANE WILLIAM RAWLEY

Born July 27, 1955, at Racine, Wis.
Height, 6.00. Weight, 185.
Throws left and bats righthanded.
Attended Indian Hills Community College, Centerville, Ia.

Major League saves: 1978 (4), 1979 (11), 1980 (13), 1981 (8), 1982 (3), 1983 (1). Total—40.

Led American League in intentional bases on balls issued with 16 in 1980.

Tied for National League lead in games started by pitchers with 36 in 1987.

Year Club	League	G.	IP.	W.	L.	Pct.	H.	R.	ER.	SO.	BB.	ERA.
1974—Sarasota Expos	Gulf Coast	2	12	0	1	.000	12	9	3	16	4	2.25
1974—Kinston	Carolina	5	19	0	2	.000	22	15	13	11	12	6.16
1975—West Palm Beach	Florida St.	24	165	8	12	.400	148	80	56	113	73	3.05
1976—Quebec City	Eastern	25	164	11	7	.611	143	55	49	113	79	2.69
1977—Denver†-Indianapolis‡§	Am. Assoc.	26	152	6	10	.375	150	89	80	92	68	4.74
1978—Seattle	American	52	111	4	9	.308	114	57	51	66	51	4.14
1979—Seattle x	American	48	84	5	9	.357	88	40	36	48	40	3.86
1980—Seattle	American	59	114	7	7	.500	103	44	42	68	63	3.32
1981—Spokane	P. Coast	3	6	0	0	.000	3	0	0	3	3	0.00
1981—Seattle yz	American	46	68	4	6	.400	64	31	30	35	38	3.97
1982—New York	American	47	164	11	10	.524	165	79	74	111	54	4.06
1983—New York	American	34	238⅓	14	14	.500	246	111	100	124	79	3.78
1984—New York ab	American	11	42	2	3	.400	46	33	29	24	27	6.21
1984—Philadelphia	National	18	120⅓	10	6	.625	117	55	51	58	27	3.81
1985—Philadelphia	National	36	198⅔	13	8	.619	188	82	73	106	81	3.31
1986—Philadelphia c	National	23	157⅔	11	7	.611	166	67	62	73	50	3.54
1987—Philadelphia	National	36	229⅔	17	11	.607	250	118	112	123	86	4.39
1988—Philadelphia de	National	32	198	8	16	.333	220	111	92	87	78	4.18
American League Totals—7 Years		297	821⅓	47	58	.448	826	395	362	476	352	3.97
National League Totals—5 Years		145	904⅓	59	48	.551	941	433	390	447	322	3.88
Major League Totals—11 Years		442	1725⅔	106	106	.500	1767	828	752	923	674	3.92

Selected by Los Angeles Dodgers' organization in 4th round of free-agent draft, January 9, 1974.

Selected by Montreal Expos' organization in secondary phase of free-agent draft, June 5, 1974.

†Traded with Pitcher Angel Torres to Cincinnati Reds' organization, May 27, 1977, completing deal in which Cincinnati traded Pitcher Santo Alcala to Montreal Expos for two players to be named later, May 21, 1977.

‡Appeared with Indianapolis in one game as an outfielder with no chances.

§Traded to Seattle Mariners for Outfielder Dave Collins, December 9, 1977.

xOn disabled list, June 30 to August 21, 1979.

yOn disabled list, April 1 to April 24, 1981; included rehabilitation disability assignment to Spokane, April 16 to April 24, 1981.

zTraded to New York Yankees for Pitchers Gene Nelson and Bill Caudill, a player to be named later and cash, April 1, 1982; Seattle Mariners' organization acquired Outfielder Bobby Brown to complete deal, April 6, 1982.

aOn disabled list, May 20 to June 4, 1984.

bTraded to Philadelphia Phillies for Pitcher Marty Bystrom and Outfielder Keith Hughes, June 30, 1984.

cOn disabled list, July 30, 1986 through remainder of season.

dOn disabled list, August 5 to August 28, 1988.

eTraded with cash to Minnesota Twins for Second Baseman Tom Herr, Catcher Tom Nieto and Outfielder Eric Bullock, October 24, 1988.

ALL-STAR GAME RECORD

Member of National League All-Star Team in 1986; did not play.

JOHNNY CORNELIUS RAY

Born March 1, 1957, at Chouteau, Okla.
Height, 5.11. Weight, 189.
Throws right and bats right and lefthanded.
Attended Northeastern Oklahoma A & M, Miami, Okla.; and
University of Arkansas, Fayetteville, Ark.

Tied major league record for fewest errors by second baseman, season, 150 or more games (5), 1986.
Major League stolen bases: 1982 (16), 1983 (18), 1984 (11), 1985 (13), 1986 (6), 1987 (4), 1988 (4). Total—72.
Tied for National League lead in grounding into double plays with 21 in 1986.
Led National League second basemen in total chances with 914 in 1982.
Named National League Rookie Player of the Year by THE SPORTING NEWS, 1982.
Named second baseman on THE SPORTING NEWS American League All-Star Team, 1988.
Named second baseman on THE SPORTING NEWS National League Silver Slugger team, 1983.

Year Club	League	Pos.	G.	AB.	R.	H.	2B.	3B.	HR.	RBI.	B.A.	PO.	A.	E.	F.A.
1979—Sarasota Astros	Gulf C.	3B-2B	37	132	25	41	8	1	3	25	.311	25	51	11	.874
1979—Daytona Beach	Fla. St.	3B-SS-2B	24	68	6	15	1	2	1	10	.221	21	38	8	.881
1980—Columbus	South.	2B-3B-OF	138	497	86	161	32	6	10	72	.324	203	331	24	.957
1981—Tucson†	P. C.	2B	131	525	111	183	*50	10	5	83	.349	309	369	19	.973
1981—Pittsburgh	Nat.	2B	31	102	10	25	11	0	0	6	.245	52	96	2	.987
1982—Pittsburgh	Nat.	2B	•162	647	79	182	30	7	7	63	.281	*381	*512	*21	.977
1983—Pittsburgh	Nat.	2B	151	576	68	163	•38	7	5	53	.283	319	452	13	.983
1984—Pittsburgh	Nat.	2B	155	555	75	173	•38	6	6	67	.312	331	400	12	.984
1985—Pittsburgh	Nat.	2B	154	594	67	163	33	3	7	70	.274	305	423	18	.976
1986—Pittsburgh	Nat.	2B	155	579	67	174	33	0	7	78	.301	280	479	5	.993
1987—Pittsburgh‡	Nat.	2B	123	472	48	129	19	3	5	54	.273	248	358	12	.981
1987—California	Amer.	2B	30	127	16	44	11	0	0	15	.346	52	90	2	.986
1988—California	Amer.	2B-OF	153	602	75	184	42	7	6	83	.306	269	328	20	.968
National League Totals—7 Years			931	3525	414	1009	202	26	37	391	.286	1916	2720	83	.982
American League Totals—2 Years			183	729	91	228	53	7	6	98	.313	321	418	22	.971
Major League Totals—8 Years			1114	4254	505	1237	255	33	43	489	.291	2237	3138	105	.981

Selected by Houston Astros' organization in 12th round of free-agent draft, June 5, 1979.

†Traded with two players to be named later to Pittsburgh Pirates for Second Baseman Phil Garner, August 31, 1981; Pittsburgh organization acquired Pitcher Randy Niemann and Outfielder Kevin Houston to complete deal, September 9, 1981.

‡Traded to California Angels for Third Baseman Billie Merrifield and a player to be named later, August 29, 1987; Pittsburgh Pirates acquired Pitcher Miguel Garcia to complete deal, September 3, 1987.

ALL-STAR GAME RECORD

Year League	Pos.	AB.	R.	H.	2B.	3B.	HR.	RBI.	B.A.	PO.	A.	E.	F.A.
1988—American	PH	1	0	0	0	0	0	0	.000	0	0	0	.000

RANDY MAX READY

Born January 8, 1960, at San Mateo, Calif.
Height, 5.11. Weight, 180.
Throws and bats righthanded.
Attended California State University, Hayward,
Calif., and Mesa College, Grand Junction, Colo.

Tied American League record for most innings played by third baseman, game (25), May 8, finished May 9, 1984 (fielded 24⅓ innings).
Major League stolen bases: 1986 (2), 1987 (7), 1988 (6). Total—15.
Led Pacific Coast League in bases on balls received with 99 in 1983.
Led Texas League in total bases with 281 in 1982.
Led Texas League third basemen in double plays with 27 and total chances with 456 in 1982.
Led Midwest League third basemen in double plays with 22 in 1981.

Year Club	League	Pos.	G.	AB.	R.	H.	2B.	3B.	HR.	RBI.	B.A.	PO.	A.	E.	F.A.
1980—Butte	Pion.	SS-2B-3B	61	226	*65	85	*23	4	8	50	*.376	86	174	22	.922
1981—Burlington	Midw.	3B	110	367	74	113	17	0	17	56	.308	72	216	21	*.932
1982—El Paso	Texas	3B	132	475	*122	*178	33	5	20	99	*.375	*115	*312	•29	.936
1983—Vancouver	P. C.	3B	116	407	82	134	28	1	13	59	.329	136	231	24	.939
1983—Milwaukee	Amer.	3B	12	37	8	15	3	2	1	6	.405	5	8	0	1.000
1984—Milwaukee	Amer.	3B	37	123	13	23	6	1	3	13	.187	29	76	6	.946
1984—Vancouver†	P. C.	2B-3B	43	151	48	49	7	4	3	18	.325	74	125	6	.971
1985—Milwaukee‡	Amer.	OF-3B-2B	48	181	29	48	9	5	1	21	.265	93	14	1	.991
1985—Vancouver	P. C.	OF-3B-2B	52	190	33	62	12	3	4	29	.326	60	35	7	.931
1986—Milwaukee§	Amer.	OF-2B-3B	23	79	8	15	4	0	1	4	.190	35	21	3	.949
1986—San Diego x	Nat.	3B	1	3	0	0	0	0	0	0	.000	0	2	1	.667
1986—Las Vegas y	P. C.	3B-OF	10	38	5	14	4	0	1	8	.368	12	10	0	1.000
1987—San Diego	Nat.	3B-2B-OF	124	350	69	108	26	6	12	54	.309	124	220	15	.958
1988—San Diego	Nat.	3B-2B-OF	114	331	43	88	16	2	7	39	.266	112	153	11	.960
American League Totals—4 Years			120	420	58	101	22	8	6	44	.240	162	119	10	.966
National League Totals—3 Years			239	684	112	196	42	8	19	93	.287	236	375	27	.958
Major League Totals—8 Years			359	1104	170	297	64	16	25	137	.269	398	494	37	.960

Selected by Milwaukee Brewers' organization in 5th round of free-agent draft, June 3, 1980.

†On disabled list, August 21, 1984 through remainder of season.

‡On disabled list, April 30 to June 19, 1985; included rehabilitation disability assignment to Vancouver, June 1 to June 19, 1985.

§Traded to San Diego Padres for a player to be named later, June 12, 1986; San Diego traded Infielder Tim Pyznarski to Milwaukee Brewers' organization to complete deal, October 29, 1986.
xOn disabled list, June 19 to July 7, 1986.
yOn disabled list, July 22, 1986 through remainder of season.

JEFFREY JAMES REARDON
(Jeff)

Born October 1, 1955, at Pittsfield, Mass.
Height, 6.00. Weight, 200.
Throws and bats righthanded.
Attended University of Massachusetts, Amherst, Mass.

Major League saves: 1979 (2), 1980 (6), 1981 (8), 1982 (26), 1983 (21), 1984 (23), 1985 (41), 1986 (35), 1987 (31), 1988 (42). Total—235.
Led National League in saves with 41 in 1985.
Led Carolina League in shutouts with 3 in 1977.
Named American League Co-Fireman of the Year by THE SPORTING NEWS, 1987.
Named National League Fireman of the Year by THE SPORTING NEWS, 1985.

Year Club	League	G.	IP.	W.	L.	Pct.	H.	R.	ER.	SO.	BB.	ERA.
1977—Lynchburg	Carolina	16	101	8	3	.727	89	42	37	60	30	3.30
1978—Jackson	Texas	28	163	*17	4	*.810	128	56	46	115	65	2.53
1979—Tidewater†	Int'national	30	69	5	2	.714	46	18	16	64	21	2.09
1979—New York	National	18	21	1	2	.333	12	7	4	10	9	1.71
1980—New York	National	61	110	8	7	.533	96	36	32	101	47	2.62
1981—New York‡-Montreal	National	43	70	3	0	1.000	48	17	17	49	21	2.19
1982—Montreal	National	75	109	7	4	.636	87	28	25	86	36	2.06
1983—Montreal	National	66	92	7	9	.438	87	34	31	78	44	3.03
1984—Montreal	National	68	87	7	7	.500	70	31	28	79	37	2.90
1985—Montreal	National	63	87⅔	2	8	.200	68	31	31	67	26	3.18
1986—Montreal§	National	62	89	7	9	.438	83	42	39	67	26	3.94
1987—Minnesota	American	63	80⅓	8	8	.500	70	41	40	83	28	4.48
1988—Minnesota	American	63	73	2	4	.333	68	21	20	56	15	2.47
National League Totals—8 Years		456	665⅔	42	46	.477	551	226	207	537	246	2.80
American League Totals—2 Years		126	153⅓	10	12	.455	138	62	60	139	43	3.52
Major League Totals—10 Years		582	819	52	58	.473	689	288	267	676	289	2.93

Selected by Montreal Expos' organization in 23rd round of free-agent draft, June 5, 1973.
Signed as free agent by New York Mets' organization, June 14, 1977.
†On disabled list, June 13 to June 24 and June 29 to July 26, 1979.
‡Traded with Outfielder Dan Norman to Montreal Expos for Outfielder Ellis Valentine, May 29, 1981.
§Traded with Catcher Tom Nieto to Minnesota Twins for Pitchers Neal Heaton, Al Cardwood and Yorkis Perez and Catcher Jeff Reed, February 3, 1987.

DIVISION SERIES RECORD

Year Club	League	G.	IP.	W.	L.	Pct.	H.	R.	ER.	SO.	BB.	ERA.
1981—Montreal	National	3	4⅓	0	1	.000	1	1	1	2	1	2.08

CHAMPIONSHIP SERIES RECORD

Tied Championship Series record for most saves, five-game Series (2), 1987.
Tied American League Championship Series records for most games pitched, five-game Series (4), 1987; most saves, total Series (2).

Year Club	League	G.	IP.	W.	L.	Pct.	H.	R.	ER.	SO.	BB.	ERA.
1981—Montreal	National	1	1	0	0	.000	3	3	3	0	0	27.00
1987—Minnesota	American	4	5⅓	1	1	.500	7	3	3	5	3	5.06
Championship Series Totals—2 Years		5	6⅓	1	1	.500	10	6	6	5	3	8.53

WORLD SERIES RECORD

Year Club	League	G.	IP.	W.	L.	Pct.	H.	R.	ER.	SO.	BB.	ERA.
1987—Minnesota	American	4	4⅔	0	0	.000	5	0	0	3	0	0.00

ALL-STAR GAME RECORD

Year League	IP.	W.	L.	Pct.	H.	R.	ER.	SO.	BB.	ERA.
1985—National	1	0	0	.000	1	0	0	1	0	0.00

Member of National League All-Star Team in 1986; did not play.
Member of American League All-Star Team in 1988; did not play.

JOSEPH RANDALL REDFIELD
(Joe)

Born January 14, 1961, at Doylestown, Pa.
Height, 6.02. Weight, 185.
Throws and bats righthanded.
Received degree from University of California, Santa Barbara, Calif.

Year Club	League	Pos.	G.	AB.	R.	H.	2B.	3B.	HR.	RBI.	B.A.	PO.	A.	E.	F.A.
1982—Little Falls	NYP	SS-3B	54	206	44	59	14	5	8	57	.286	100	130	26	.898
1983—Jackson	Texas	SS-OF-1B	36	127	16	25	4	1	2	12	.197	47	94	12	.922
1983—Lynchburg	Carol.	S-3-1-2-O	62	192	32	39	4	7	4	27	.203	115	103	15	.936
1984—Lynchburg	Carol.	3-S-2-1	122	428	80	115	18	7	11	58	.269	133	269	29	.933
1985—Jackson†	Texas	1B-3B-SS	39	73	12	10	4	0	1	5	.137	88	21	5	.956

Year	Club	League	Pos.	G.	AB.	R.	H.	2B.	3B.	HR.	RBI.	B.A.	PO.	A.	E.	F.A.
1985	—Tidewater	Int.	3B	4	10	0	3	1	0	0	0	.300	0	2	0	1.000
1985	—Lynchburg	Carol.	3B-2B	41	132	22	32	8	0	3	18	.242	37	76	7	.942
1986	—Jackson‡	Texas	3B	15	60	8	17	1	2	0	3	.283	10	19	4	.879
1986	—Charlotte§x	South.	3-S-1-O-2	95	344	65	102	16	4	14	49	.297	91	153	22	.917
1987	—Midland	Texas	3B-1B-2B	128	498	108	160	31	7	•30	•108	.321	132	137	23	.921
1988	—Edmonton	P. C.	3B-1B-OF	118	417	67	121	*38	1	3	52	.290	377	154	14	.974
1988	—California y	Amer.	3B	1	2	0	0	0	0	0	0	.000	0	1	0	1.000
	Major League Totals—1 Year			1	2	0	0	0	0	0	0	.000	0	1	0	1.000

Selected by New York Mets' organization in 9th round of free-agent draft, June 7, 1982.
†On disabled list, April 9 to May 9, 1985.
‡Traded to Baltimore Orioles for Third Baseman Rick Lockwood, April 25, 1986.
§Drafted by Richmond (Atlanta Braves' organization), December 8, 1986.
xTraded to California Angels for Pitcher Stan Cliburn, April 7, 1987.
yGranted free agency, October 15, 1988.

GARY EUGENE REDUS

Name pronounced REE-dus.
Born November 1, 1956, at Athens, Ala.
Height, 6.01. Weight, 185.
Throws and bats righthanded.

Major League stolen bases: 1982 (11), 1983 (39), 1984 (48), 1985 (48), 1986 (25), 1987 (52), 1988 (31). Total—254.
Led American Association in stolen bases with 54 and tied for lead in sacrifice flies with 9 in 1982.
Led Florida State League in total bases with 220 in 1980.
Led Pioneer League in total bases with 199, stolen bases with 42 and tied for lead in sacrifice flies with 6 in 1978.
Tied for Western Carolinas League lead in errors by second basemen with 20 in 1979.
Named Pioneer League Player of the Year, 1978.

Year	Club	League	Pos.	G.	AB.	R.	H.	2B.	3B.	HR.	RBI.	B.A.	PO.	A.	E.	F.A.
1978	—Billings	Pion.	2B	68	253	*100	*117	19	6	17	62	*.462	124	*185	*28	.917
1979	—Nashville	South.	OF	36	109	7	19	2	1	0	7	.174	74	3	3	.963
1979	—Greensboro	W. Car.	2B-OF	83	309	79	86	17	1	16	52	.278	172	193	21	.946
1980	—Tampa	Fla. St.	OF-3B-1B	128	452	78	136	18	9	16	68	.301	213	84	27	.917
1981	—Waterbury	East.	OF-1B	138	477	71	119	26	4	20	75	.249	667	34	14	.980
1982	—Indianapolis	A. A.	OF	122	439	112	146	29	9	24	93	.333	223	10	7	.971
1982	—Cincinnati	Nat.	OF	20	83	12	18	3	2	1	7	.217	29	3	1	.970
1983	—Cincinnati	Nat.	OF	125	453	90	112	20	9	17	51	.247	235	11	7	.972
1984	—Cincinnati	Nat.	OF	123	394	69	100	21	3	7	22	.254	200	6	7	.967
1985	—Cincinnati†	Nat.	OF	101	246	51	62	14	4	6	28	.252	140	3	2	.986
1986	—Philadelphia‡	Nat.	OF	90	340	62	84	22	4	11	33	.247	185	8	4	.980
1986	—Reading§	East.	OF	6	24	4	6	1	0	0	0	.250	11	1	1	.923
1987	—Chicago	Amer.	OF	130	475	78	112	26	6	12	48	.236	262	13	6	.979
1988	—Chicago x	Amer.	OF	77	262	42	69	10	4	6	34	.263	140	7	2	.987
1988	—Pittsburgh y	Nat.	OF	30	71	12	14	2	0	2	4	.197	42	2	2	.957
	National League Totals—6 Years			489	1587	296	390	82	22	44	145	.246	831	33	23	.974
	American League Totals—2 Years			207	737	120	181	36	10	18	82	.246	402	20	8	.981
	Major League Totals—7 Years			696	2324	416	571	118	32	62	227	.246	1233	53	31	.976

Selected by Boston Red Sox' organization in 17th round of free-agent draft, June 7, 1977.
Selected by Cincinnati Reds' organization in 15th round of free-agent draft, June 6, 1978.
†Traded with Pitcher Tom Hume to Philadelphia Phillies for Pitchers John Denny and Jeff Gray, December 11, 1985.
‡On disabled list, April 28 to July 1, 1986; included rehabilitation disability assignment to Reading, June 23 to June 30, 1986.
§Traded to Chicago White Sox for Pitcher Joe Cowley and cash, March 26, 1987.
xTraded to Pittsburgh Pirates for Outfielder Mike Diaz, August 19, 1988.
yGranted free agency, November 4, 1988; re-signed by Pirates, November 15, 1988.

DARREN DOUGLAS REED

Born October 16, 1965, at Ventura, Calif.
Height, 6.01. Weight, 190.
Throws and bats righthanded.
Attended Ventura College, Ventura, Calif.

Year	Club	League	Pos.	G.	AB.	R.	H.	2B.	3B.	HR.	RBI.	B.A.	PO.	A.	E.	F.A.
1984	—Oneonta	NYP	OF-C	40	113	17	26	7	0	2	9	.230	41	2	2	.956
1985	—Fort Lauderdale	Fla. St.	OF	100	369	63	117	21	4	10	61	.317	191	8	7	.966
1986	—Albany†	East.	OF	51	196	22	45	11	1	4	27	.230	78	2	5	.941
1987	—Albany	East.	OF	107	404	68	129	23	4	20	79	.319	174	6	4	.978
1987	—Columbus‡	Int.	OF	21	79	15	26	3	3	8	16	.329	33	2	1	.972
1988	—Tidewater	Int.	OF-C	101	345	31	83	26	0	9	47	.241	170	5	4	.978

Selected by Oakland A's organization in 10th round of free-agent draft, January 17, 1984.
Selected by New York Yankees' organization in secondary phase of free-agent draft, June 4, 1984.
†On disabled list, June 17, 1986 through remainder of season.
‡Traded with Catcher Phil Lombardi and Pitcher Steve Frey to New York Mets for Shortstop Rafael Santana and Pitcher Victor Garcia, December 11, 1987.

JEFFREY SCOTT REED
(Jeff)

Born November 12, 1962, at Joliet, Ill.
Height, 6.02. Weight, 190.
Throws right and bats lefthanded.
Brother of Curtis Reed, outfielder in San Diego Padres' and Chicago White Sox' organizations, 1977 through 1984.

Established modern National League record for most errors by catcher, inning (3), July 28, 1987, seventh inning.
Major League stolen bases: 1986 (1), 1988 (1). Total—2.
Led International League catchers in total chances with 720 in 1985.
Led Southern League catchers in total chances with 714 and double plays with 12 in 1983.
Led California League catchers in total chances with 758 and tied for lead in double plays with 9 in 1982.

Year Club	League	Pos.	G.	AB.	R.	H.	2B.	3B.	HR.	RBI.	B.A.	PO.	A.	E.	F.A.
1980—Elizabethton	Appal.	C	65	225	39	64	15	1	1	20	.284	269	*41	9	.972
1981—Wisconsin Rapids	Midw.	C	106	312	63	73	12	1	4	34	.234	547	*93	7	.989
1981—Orlando	South.	C	3	4	0	1	0	0	0	0	.250	4	1	0	1.000
1982—Visalia	Calif.	C	125	395	69	130	19	2	5	54	.329	*642	•106	10	.987
1983—Orlando	South.	C	118	379	52	100	16	5	6	45	.264	*618	*88	8	*.989
1983—Toledo	Int.	C	14	41	5	7	1	1	0	3	.171	77	6	1	.988
1984—Minnesota	Amer.	C	18	21	3	3	3	0	0	1	.143	41	2	1	.977
1984—Toledo	Int.	C	94	301	30	80	16	3	3	35	.266	546	43	5	*.992
1985—Toledo	Int.	C	122	404	53	100	15	3	5	36	.248	*627	*81	12	.983
1985—Minnesota	Amer.	C	7	10	2	2	0	0	0	0	.200	9	3	0	1.000
1986—Minnesota	Amer.	C	68	165	13	39	6	1	2	9	.236	332	19	2	.994
1986—Toledo†	Int.	C	25	71	10	22	5	3	1	14	.310	108	22	2	.985
1987—Montreal‡	Nat.	C	75	207	15	44	11	0	1	21	.213	357	36	12	.970
1987—Indianapolis	A. A.	C	5	17	0	3	0	0	0	0	.176	27	2	0	1.000
1988—Mont.§-Cinc.	Nat.	C	92	265	20	60	9	2	1	16	.226	468	38	3	.994
1988—Indianapolis	A. A.	C	8	22	1	7	3	0	0	1	.318	30	11	0	1.000
American League Totals—3 Years			93	196	18	44	9	1	2	10	.224	382	24	3	.993
National League Totals—2 Years			167	472	35	104	20	2	2	37	.220	825	74	15	.984
Major League Totals—5 Years			260	668	53	148	29	3	4	47	.222	1207	98	18	.986

Selected by Minnesota Twins' organization in 1st round (12th player selected) of free-agent draft, June 3, 1980.
†Traded with Pitchers Neal Heaton, Al Cardwood and Yorkis Perez to Montreal Expos for Pitcher Jeff Reardon and Catcher Tom Nieto, February 3, 1987.
‡On disabled list, April 20 to May 25, 1987; included rehabilitation disability assignment to Indianapolis, May 19 to May 25, 1987.
§Traded with Outfielder Herm Winningham and Pitcher Randy St. Claire to Cincinnati Reds for Outfielder Tracy Jones and Pitcher Pat Pacillo, July 13, 1988.

JERRY MAXWELL REED

Born October 8, 1955, at Bryson City, N.C.
Height, 6.01. Weight, 190.
Throws and bats righthanded.
Received bachelor of science degree in education from Western Carolina University, Cullowhee, N.C. in 1977.

Major League saves: 1985 (8), 1987 (7), 1988 (1). Total—16.
Tied for Eastern League lead in intentional bases on balls issued with 9 in 1979.

Year Club	League	G.	IP.	W.	L.	Pct.	H.	R.	ER.	SO.	BB.	ERA.
1977—Auburn	NYP	*32	56	3	5	.375	63	35	30	36	24	4.82
1978—Spartanburg	W. Carol.	39	66	7	2	.778	36	22	10	31	34	1.36
1978—Peninsula	Carolina	15	24	1	0	1.000	9	3	2	11	5	0.75
1979—Reading	Eastern	45	80	11	4	.733	67	25	17	37	28	1.91
1980—Oklahoma City	Am. Assoc.	33	97	6	5	.545	128	62	53	36	42	4.92
1980—Reading	Eastern	8	17	1	1	.500	17	6	6	10	10	3.18
1981—Reading	Eastern	56	80	5	4	.556	80	34	29	62	29	3.26
1981—Philadelphia	National	4	5	0	1	.000	7	4	4	5	6	7.20
1982—Oklahoma City	Am. Assoc.	25	131⅔	6	7	.462	135	78	64	73	59	4.37
1982—Philadelphia†	National	7	8⅔	1	0	1.000	11	6	5	1	3	5.19
1982—Cleveland	American	6	15⅔	1	1	.500	15	6	6	10	3	3.45
1983—Charleston	Int'national	21	145⅓	10	6	.625	141	70	58	57	67	3.59
1983—Cleveland	American	7	21⅓	0	0	.000	26	19	17	11	9	7.17
1984—Maine	Int'national	27	179⅓	12	6	.667	*193	86	72	77	57	3.61
1985—Maine	Int'national	14	95⅓	8	5	.615	88	41	36	47	37	3.40
1985—Cleveland‡	American	33	72⅓	3	5	.375	67	41	33	37	19	4.11
1986—Calgary	P. Coast	19	41	2	1	.667	45	24	21	20	17	4.61
1986—Seattle§	American	11	34⅔	4	0	1.000	38	13	12	16	13	3.12
1987—Seattle x	American	39	81⅔	1	2	.333	79	32	31	51	24	3.42
1987—Calgary	P. Coast	1	3	0	0	.000	1	0	0	3	0	0.00
1988—Seattle	American	46	86⅓	1	1	.500	82	42	38	48	33	3.96
National League Totals—2 Years		11	13⅔	1	1	.500	18	10	9	6	9	5.93
American League Totals—6 Years		142	312	10	9	.526	307	153	137	173	101	3.95
Major League Totals—7 Years		153	325⅔	11	10	.524	325	163	146	179	110	4.03

Selected by Minnesota Twins' organization in 11th round of free-agent draft, June 5, 1973.
Selected by Philadelphia Phillies' organization in 22nd round of free-agent draft, June 7, 1977.
†Traded with Pitcher Roy Smith and Outfielder Wil Culmer to Cleveland Indians for Pitcher John Denny, September 12, 1982.

‡Released, April 1, 1986; signed by Calgary (Seattle Mariners' organization), April 11, 1986.
§On disabled list, August 4, 1986 through remainder of season.
xOn disabled list, July 25 to August 20, 1987; included rehabilitation disability assignment to Calgary, August 16 to August 20, 1987.

JODY ERIC REED

Born July 26, 1962, at Tampa, Fla.
Height, 5.09. Weight, 160.
Throws and bats righthanded.
Attended Manatee Junior College, Bradenton, Fla., and received degree in criminology from Florida State University, Tallahassee, Fla., in 1985.

Major League stolen bases: 1987 (1), 1988 (1). Total—2.
Led Florida State League in bases on balls received with 94 in 1985.
Led International League shortstops in total chances with 683 and double plays with 86 in 1987.
Led Florida State League shortstops in double plays with 101 in 1985.

Year Club	League	Pos.	G.	AB.	R.	H.	2B.	3B.	HR.	RBI.	B.A.	PO.	A.	E.	F.A.
1984—Winter Haven	Fla. St.	SS	77	273	46	74	14	1	0	20	.271	128	271	26	.939
1985—Winter Haven	Fla. St.	SS	134	489	*95	157	25	1	0	45	*.321	*256	*478	37	*.952
1986—New Britain	East.	SS	60	218	33	50	12	1	0	11	.229	114	190	14	.956
1986—Pawtucket	Int.	SS	69	227	27	64	11	0	1	30	.282	115	222	12	.966
1987—Pawtucket	Int.	SS	136	510	77	151	22	2	7	51	.296	*236	*427	20	.971
1987—Boston	Amer.	SS-2B-3B	9	30	4	9	1	1	0	8	.300	11	26	0	1.000
1988—Boston†	Amer.	SS-2B-3B	109	338	60	99	23	1	1	28	.293	147	282	11	.975
Major League Totals—2 Years			118	368	64	108	24	2	1	36	.293	158	308	11	.977

Selected by Texas Rangers' organization in 3rd round of free-agent draft, January 12, 1982.
Selected by San Francisco Giants' organization in secondary phase of free-agent draft, June 7, 1982.
Selected by Texas Rangers' organization in secondary phase of free-agent draft, June 6, 1983.
Selected by Boston Red Sox' organization in 8th round of free-agent draft, June 4, 1984.
†Appeared in one game as a pinch-runner.

CHAMPIONSHIP SERIES RECORD

Year Club	League	Pos.	G.	AB.	R.	H.	2B.	3B.	HR.	RBI.	B.A.	PO.	A.	E.	F.A.
1988—Boston	Amer.	SS	4	11	0	3	1	0	0	0	.273	3	10	0	1.000

RICHARD ALLEN REED
(Rick)

Born August 16, 1964, at Huntington, W. Va.
Height, 6.00. Weight, 195.
Throws and bats righthanded.
Attended Marshall University, Huntington, W. Va.

Year Club	League	G.	IP.	W.	L.	Pct.	H.	R.	ER.	SO.	BB.	ERA.
1986—Bradenton Pirates	Gulf Coast	8	24	0	2	.000	20	12	10	15	6	3.75
1986—Macon	S. Atlantic	1	6⅓	0	0	.000	5	3	2	1	2	2.84
1987—Macon	S. Atlantic	46	93⅔	8	4	.667	80	38	26	92	29	2.50
1988—Salem	Carolina	15	72⅓	6	2	.750	56	28	22	73	17	2.74
1988—Harrisburg	Eastern	2	16	1	0	1.000	11	2	2	17	2	1.13
1988—Buffalo	Am. Assoc.	10	77	5	2	.714	62	15	14	50	12	1.64
1988—Pittsburgh	National	2	12	1	0	1.000	10	4	4	6	2	3.00
Major League Totals—1 Year		2	12	1	0	1.000	10	4	4	6	2	3.00

Selected by Pittsburgh Pirates' organization in 26th round of free-agent draft, June 2, 1986.

JESSIE THOMAS REID

Born June 1, 1962, at Honolulu, Haw.
Height, 6.01. Weight, 200.
Throws and bats lefthanded.

Year Club	League	Pos.	G.	AB.	R.	H.	2B.	3B.	HR.	RBI.	B.A.	PO.	A.	E.	F.A.
1980—Great Falls	Pion.	OF-1B	59	227	57	83	15	6	5	48	.366	137	7	4	.973
1981—Fresno	Calif.	OF-1B	124	426	68	105	15	3	1	40	.246	222	13	8	.967
1982—Fresno	Calif.	OF-1B	127	476	78	139	20	5	6	73	.292	385	27	14	.967
1983—Shreveport	Texas	OF	125	389	59	101	22	0	13	50	.260	157	7	4	.976
1984—Shreveport	Texas	OF	88	296	33	62	10	1	6	32	.209	129	9	2	.986
1984—Phoenix	P. C.	OF	36	121	13	28	5	0	1	9	.231	70	0	1	.986
1985—Fresno	Calif.	OF-1B	72	254	45	82	14	2	8	55	.323	139	6	4	.973
1985—Phoenix	P. C.	OF	54	179	26	47	6	3	7	32	.263	101	3	3	.972
1986—Phoenix	P. C.	OF	120	428	70	115	26	6	14	61	.269	227	5	7	.971
1987—Phoenix	P. C.	OF	128	433	83	117	22	5	16	84	.270	274	9	4	.986
1987—San Francisco	Nat.	OF	6	8	1	1	0	0	1	1	.125	3	0	0	1.000
1988—San Francisco	Nat.	PH	2	2	0	0	0	0	0	0	.000	0	0	0	.000
1988—Phoenix	P. C.	OF	111	381	62	105	21	6	18	72	.276	195	6	6	.971
Major League Totals—2 Years			8	10	1	1	0	0	1	1	.100	3	0	0	1.000

Selected by San Francisco Giants' organization in 1st round (seventh player selected) of free-agent draft, June 3, 1980.

KEVIN MICHAEL REIMER

Born June 28, 1964, at Macon, Ga.
Height, 6.02. Weight, 215.
Throws right and bats lefthanded.
Attended Orange Coast College, Costa Mesa, Calif.,
and California State University, Fullerton, Calif.
Son of Gerry Reimer, minor league first baseman-outfielder, 1958 through 1968.

Led Texas League in game-winning RBIs with 12 and tied for intentional bases on balls received with 9 in 1988.

Year Club	League	Pos.	G.	AB.	R.	H.	2B.	3B.	HR.	RBI.	B.A.	PO.	A.	E.	F.A.
1985—Burlington	Midw.	1B-OF	80	292	25	67	12	0	8	33	.229	685	29	15	.979
1986—Salem	Carol.	OF-1B	133	453	57	111	21	2	16	76	.245	412	27	32	.932
1987—Charlotte	Fla. St.	OF	74	271	36	66	13	7	6	34	.244	31	0	2	.939
1988—Tulsa	Texas	OF	133	486	74	147	30	*11	21	76	.302	63	1	7	.901
1988—Texas	Amer.	OF	12	25	2	3	0	0	1	2	.120	0	0	0	.000
Major League Totals—1 Year			12	25	2	3	0	0	1	2	.120	0	0	0	.000

Selected by Texas Rangers' organization in 11th round of free-agent draft, June 3, 1985.

RICHARD AVINA RENTERIA

Name pronounced Ren-ter-REE-ah.

(Rich)

Born December 25, 1961, at Harbor City, Calif.
Height, 5.09. Weight, 172.
Throws and bats righthanded.

Major League stolen bases: 1987 (1), 1988 (1). Total—2.
Led South Atlantic League third basemen in errors with 39 in 1981.
Tied for Carolina League in grounding into double plays with 19 in 1982.

Year Club	League	Pos.	G.	AB.	R.	H.	2B.	3B.	HR.	RBI.	B.A.	PO.	A.	E.	F.A.
1980—Bradenton Pir.	Gulf C.	3B-SS	46	176	19	40	6	1	2	23	.227	32	87	16	.882
1981—Greenwood	S. Atl.	3B-SS	127	510	90	146	19	5	4	48	.286	87	232	39	.891
1982—Alexandria	Carol.	2B	127	508	80	*168	24	5	14	*100	*.331	196	346	28	.951
1983—Lynn†	East.	3B	115	424	47	121	25	0	4	40	.285	83	170	19	.930
1984—Nashua	East.	2B	113	443	63	121	22	7	1	34	.273	208	283	12	.976
1984—Hawaii‡	P. C.	2B	19	77	8	19	3	1	0	11	.247	22	45	2	.971
1985—Mex. C. Tigers	Mex.	3B-2B	125	484	89	169	29	11	19	*125	.349	121	241	19	.950
1985—Hawaii	P. C.	2B	7	31	2	6	2	0	0	2	.194	5	15	0	1.000
1986—Hawaii	P. C.	3B-2B	112	389	51	122	20	9	1	51	.314	112	196	13	.960
1986—Pittsburgh§	Nat.	3B	10	12	2	3	1	0	0	1	.250	1	2	2	.600
1987—Seattle x	Amer.	2B-SS	12	10	2	1	1	0	0	0	.100	3	4	1	.875
1987—Calgary	P. C.	2B-SS-3B	69	267	41	79	14	3	1	32	.296	110	187	11	.964
1988—Seattle	Amer.	SS-3B-2B	31	88	6	18	9	0	0	6	.205	33	44	3	.963
1988—Calgary	P. C.	SS-2B-3B	24	87	15	23	6	1	4	10	.264	34	64	7	.933
National League Totals—1 Year			10	12	2	3	1	0	0	1	.250	1	2	2	.600
American League Totals—2 Years			43	98	8	19	10	0	0	6	.194	36	48	4	.955
Major League Totals—3 Years			53	110	10	22	11	0	0	7	.200	37	50	6	.935

Selected by Pittsburgh Pirates' organization in 1st round (20th player selected) of free-agent draft, June 3, 1980.
†On disabled list, May 10 to June 1, 1983.
‡Loaned to Mexico City Tigers, March 11, 1985; returned, August 21, 1985.
§Traded to Seattle Mariners for a player to be named later, December 5, 1986; Pittsburgh Pirates' organization acquired Pitcher Bob Siegel to complete deal, December 8, 1986.
xOn disabled list, April 2 to April 18, 1987.

RICKY EUGENE REUSCHEL

Name pronounced RUSH-ul.

(Rick)

Born May 16, 1949, at Quincy, Ill.
Height, 6.03. Weight, 240.
Throws and bats righthanded.
Attended Western Illinois University, Macomb, Ill.
Brother of Paul Reuschel, pitcher with Chicago Cubs and Cleveland Indians, 1975 through 1978.

Tied major league record for most putouts, pitcher, inning (3), April 25, 1975 (third inning).
Major League saves: 1975 (1), 1976 (1), 1977 (1), 1985 (1). Total—4.
Tied for National League lead in complete games with 12 and shutouts with 4 in 1987.
Tied for National League lead in hit batsmen with 8 in 1986.
Tied for National League lead in games started by pitchers with 38 in 1980 and 36 in 1988.
Tied for National League lead in sacrifice hits by batters with 19 in 1988.
Led Northern League pitchers in complete games with 7 and tied for lead in games started with 14 in 1970.
Named righthanded pitcher on THE SPORTING NEWS National League All-Star Team, 1977.
Named National League Comeback Player of the Year by THE SPORTING NEWS, 1985.
Named pitcher on THE SPORTING NEWS National League All-Star fielding team, 1985 and 1987.

Year Club	League	G.	IP.	W.	L.	Pct.	H.	R.	ER.	SO.	BB.	ERA.
1970—Huron	Northern	14	102	9	2	.818	96	52	40	88	22	3.52
1971—San Antonio†	Texas	16	121	8	4	.667	105	40	31	81	15	2.31
1972—Wichita	Am. Assoc.	12	102	9	2	.818	78	30	15	72	30	1.32
1972—Chicago	National	21	129	10	8	.556	127	46	42	87	29	2.93
1973—Chicago	National	36	237	14	15	.483	244	95	79	168	62	3.00

Year Club	League	G.	IP.	W.	L.	Pct.	H.	R.	ER.	SO.	BB.	ERA.
1974—Chicago	National	41	241	13	12	.520	262	130	115	160	83	4.29
1975—Chicago	National	38	234	11	*17	.393	244	116	97	155	67	3.73
1976—Chicago	National	38	260	14	12	.538	260	*117	100	146	64	3.46
1977—Chicago	National	39	252	20	10	.667	233	84	78	166	74	2.79
1978—Chicago	National	35	243	14	15	.483	235	98	92	115	54	3.41
1979—Chicago	National	36	239	18	12	.600	251	104	96	125	75	3.62
1980—Chicago	National	38	257	11	13	.458	*281	111	97	140	76	3.40
1981—Chicago‡	National	13	86	4	7	.364	87	40	33	53	23	3.45
1981—New York	American	12	71	4	4	.500	75	24	21	22	10	2.66
1982—New York§	American					(Did not play)						
1983—Columbus xy	Int'national	4	16	0	1	.000	21	9	9	7	6	5.06
1983—Quad Cities	Midwest	13	70⅔	3	4	.429	73	29	19	56	9	2.42
1983—Chicago	National	4	20⅔	1	1	.500	18	9	9	9	10	3.92
1984—Chicago za	National	19	92⅓	5	5	.500	123	57	53	43	23	5.17
1985—Hawaii	P. Coast	8	54	6	2	.750	52	18	15	46	12	2.50
1985—Pittsburgh	National	31	194	14	8	.636	153	58	49	138	52	2.27
1986—Pittsburgh	National	35	215⅔	9	16	.360	232	106	95	125	57	3.96
1987—Pittsburgh b-San Francisco	National	34	227	13	9	.591	207	91	78	107	42	3.09
1988—San Francisco	National	36	245	19	11	.633	242	88	85	92	42	3.12
National League Totals—16 Years		494	3172⅔	190	171	.526	3199	1350	1198	1829	833	3.40
American League Totals—1 Year		12	71	4	4	.500	75	24	21	22	10	2.66
Major League Totals—16 Years		506	3243⅔	194	175	.526	3274	1374	1219	1851	843	3.38

Selected by Chicago Cubs' organization in 3rd round of free-agent draft, June 4, 1970.

†On temporary inactive list, July 2, 1971; transferred to military list, July 8, 1971 through April 10, 1972.

‡Traded to New York Yankees for Pitcher Doug Bird, $400,000 and a player to be named later, June 12, 1981; Chicago Cubs acquired Pitcher Mike Griffin to complete deal, August 5, 1981.

§On disabled list, March 23, 1982 through remainder of season.

xOn New York disabled list, April 4 to June 9, 1983; included rehabilitation disability assignment to Columbus, May 23 to June 9, 1983.

yReleased, June 9, 1983; signed by Quad Cities (Chicago Cubs' organization), June 28, 1983.

zOn disabled list, March 27 to April 21 and August 23 to September 1, 1984.

aGranted free agency, November 8, 1984; signed by Pittsburgh Pirates' organization, February 28, 1985.

dTraded to San Francisco Giants for Pitchers Jeff Robinson and Scott Medvin, August 21, 1987.

DIVISION SERIES RECORD

Year Club	League	G.	IP.	W.	L.	Pct.	H.	R.	ER.	SO.	BB.	ERA.
1981—New York	American	1	6	0	1	.000	4	2	2	3	1	3.00

CHAMPIONSHIP SERIES RECORD

Tied National League Championship Series record for most earned runs allowed, seven-game Series (7), 1987.

Year Club	League	G.	IP.	W.	L.	Pct.	H.	R.	ER.	SO.	BB.	ERA.
1987—San Francisco	National	2	10	0	1	.000	15	8	7	2	2	6.30

WORLD SERIES RECORD

Year Club	League	G.	IP.	W.	L.	Pct.	H.	R.	ER.	SO.	BB.	ERA.
1981—New York	American	2	3⅔	0	0	.000	7	3	2	2	3	4.91

ALL-STAR GAME RECORD

Year League	IP.	W.	L.	Pct.	H.	R.	ER.	SO.	BB.	ERA.
1977—National	1	0	0	.000	1	0	0	0	0	0.00
1987—National	1⅓	0	0	.000	1	0	0	1	0	0.00
All-Star Game Totals—2 Years	2⅓	0	0	.000	2	0	0	1	0	0.00

JERRY REUSS

Name pronounced Royce.

Born June 19, 1949, at St. Louis, Mo.
Height, 6.05. Weight, 227.
Throws and bats lefthanded.
Attended Southern Illinois University, Carbondale, Ill., Central Missouri State College, Warrensburg, Mo., and University of California, Santa Barbara, Calif.

Tied major league record for most home runs allowed, bases filled, lifetime (9).
Pitched 8-0 no-hit victory against San Francisco Giants, June 27, 1980.
Major League saves: 1972 (1), 1976 (2), 1979 (3), 1980 (3), 1984 (1), 1986 (1). Total—11.
Led National League in shutouts with 6 in 1980.
Led National League in hit batsmen with 10 in 1972.
Tied for National League lead in games started by pitchers with 40 in 1973.
Led American Association pitchers in games started with 29 in 1969.
Led Texas League in wild pitches with 16 in 1968.
Named National League Comeback Player of the Year by THE SPORTING NEWS, 1980.
Received reported $30,000 bonus to sign with St. Louis Cardinals, 1967.

Year Club	League	G.	IP.	W.	L.	Pct.	H.	R.	ER.	SO.	BB.	ERA.
1967—Sarasota Cards	Gulf Coast	2	7	0	0	.000	7	6	4	6	3	5.14
1967—Cedar Rapids	Midwest	9	58	2	5	.286	44	20	12	63	19	1.86
1967—Tulsa	P. Coast	1	1	0	0	.000	2	6	6	1	4	54.00
1968—Arkansas	Texas	17	112	7	8	.467	75	43	27	86	45	2.17
1969—Tulsa	Am. Assoc.	30	*186	•13	11	.542	188	•112	84	*151	116	4.06
1969—St. Louis	National	1	7	1	0	1.000	2	0	0	3	3	0.00

Year	Club	League	G.	IP.	W.	L.	Pct.	H.	R.	ER.	SO.	BB.	ERA.
1970	Tulsa	Am. Assoc.	11	85	7	2	.778	69	26	20	69	28	2.12
1970	St. Louis	National	20	127	7	8	.467	132	62	58	74	49	4.11
1971	St. Louis†	National	36	211	14	14	.500	228	125	112	131	109	4.78
1972	Houston	National	33	192	9	13	.409	177	101	89	174	83	4.17
1973	Houston‡	National	41	279	16	13	.552	271	123	116	177	*117	3.74
1974	Pittsburgh	National	35	260	16	11	.593	259	115	101	105	101	3.50
1975	Pittsburgh	National	32	237	18	11	.621	224	73	67	131	78	2.54
1976	Pittsburgh	National	31	209	14	9	.609	209	98	82	108	51	3.53
1977	Pittsburgh	National	33	208	10	13	.435	225	109	95	116	71	4.11
1978	Pittsburgh§	National	23	83	3	2	.600	97	48	45	42	23	4.88
1979	Los Angeles	National	39	160	7	14	.333	178	88	63	83	60	3.54
1980	Los Angeles	National	37	229	18	6	.750	193	74	64	111	40	2.52
1981	Los Angeles	National	22	153	10	4	.714	138	44	39	51	27	2.29
1982	Los Angeles	National	39	254⅔	18	11	.621	232	98	88	138	50	3.11
1983	Los Angeles	National	32	223⅓	12	11	.522	233	94	73	143	50	2.94
1984	Los Angeles x	National	30	99	5	7	.417	102	51	42	44	31	3.82
1985	Los Angeles	National	34	212⅔	14	10	.583	210	78	69	84	58	2.92
1986	Los Angeles y	National	19	74	2	6	.250	96	57	48	29	17	5.84
1987	Los Angeles z-Cincinnati	National	8	36⅔	0	5	.000	54	32	31	12	12	7.61
1987	Nashville a	Am. Assoc.	2	12	0	2	.000	16	8	8	4	6	6.00
1987	California bc	American	17	82⅓	4	5	.444	112	60	48	37	17	5.25
1988	Chicago	American	32	183	13	9	.591	183	79	70	73	43	3.44
National League Totals—19 Years			545	3255⅓	194	168	.536	3260	1470	1282	1756	1030	3.54
American League Totals—2 Years			49	265⅓	17	14	.548	295	139	118	110	60	4.00
Major League Totals—20 Years			594	3520⅔	211	182	.537	3555	1609	1400	1866	1090	3.58

Selected by St. Louis Cardinals' organization in 2nd round of free-agent draft, June 6, 1967.
†Traded to Houston Astros for Pitchers Scipio Spinks and Lance Clemons, April 15, 1972.
‡Traded to Pittsburgh Pirates for Catcher Milt May, October 31, 1973.
§Traded to Los Angeles Dodgers for Pitcher Rick Rhoden, April 9, 1979.
xOn disabled list, June 8 to July 12, 1984.
yOn disabled list, July 17 to September 3, 1986.
zReleased, April 10, 1987; signed by Nashville (Cincinnati Reds' organization), April 18, 1987.
aReleased, June 14, 1987; signed by California Angels, June 19, 1987.
bOn disabled list, August 1 to August 16, 1987.
cGranted free agency, November 9, 1987; signed by Chicago White Sox, March 29, 1988.

DIVISION SERIES RECORD

Year	Club	League	G.	IP.	W.	L.	Pct.	H.	R.	ER.	SO.	BB.	ERA.
1981	Los Angeles	National	2	18	1	0	1.000	10	0	0	7	5	0.00

CHAMPIONSHIP SERIES RECORD

Established Championship Series records for most games lost, total Series (7); most runs allowed, inning (7), October 13, 1985 (second inning).

Tied Championship Series records for most runs allowed, total Series (25); most games lost, Series (2), 1974, 1983; most bases on balls, four-game Series (8), 1974.

Year	Club	League	G.	IP.	W.	L.	Pct.	H.	R.	ER.	SO.	BB.	ERA.
1974	Pittsburgh	National	2	9⅔	0	2	.000	7	4	4	3	8	3.72
1975	Pittsburgh	National	1	2⅔	0	1	.000	4	4	4	1	4	13.50
1981	Los Angeles	National	1	7	0	1	.000	7	4	4	2	1	5.14
1983	Los Angeles	National	2	12	0	2	.000	14	6	6	4	3	4.50
1985	Los Angeles	National	1	1⅔	0	1	.000	5	7	2	0	1	10.80
Championship Series Totals—5 Years			7	33	0	7	.000	37	25	20	10	17	5.45

WORLD SERIES RECORD

Year	Club	League	G.	IP.	W.	L.	Pct.	H.	R.	ER.	SO.	BB.	ERA.
1981	Los Angeles	National	2	11⅔	1	1	.500	10	5	5	8	3	3.86

ALL-STAR GAME RECORD

Year	League	IP.	W.	L.	Pct.	H.	R.	ER.	SO.	BB.	ERA.
1975	National	3	0	0	.000	3	0	0	2	0	0.00
1980	National	1	1	0	1.000	0	0	0	3	0	0.00
All-Star Game Totals—2 Years		4	1	0	1.000	3	0	0	5	0	0.00

GILBERTO R. REYES (POLANCO)

Name pronounced RAY-us.

(Gil)

Born December 10, 1963, at Santo Domingo, D. R.
Height, 6.02. Weight, 195.
Throws and bats righthanded.

Tied for Pacific Coast League lead in sacrifice flies with 8 in 1985.
Led Pacific Coast League catchers in assists with 64 in 1988.
Led Pacific Coast League in passed balls with 24 in 1985 and 17 in 1986.
Led Texas League catchers in total chances with 718, double plays with 13 and passed balls with 31 in 1984.
Tied for California League lead in assists by catchers with 106 and double plays with 9 in 1982.

Year	Club	League	Pos.	G.	AB.	R.	H.	2B.	3B.	HR.	RBI.	B.A.	PO.	A.	E.	F.A.
1980	—Lethbridge	Pion.	1B	6	11	0	2	0	0	0	1	.182	16	0	2	.889
1981	—Vero Beach	Fla. St.	1B-C	21	58	3	12	3	0	1	6	.207	71	6	2	.975
1981	—Lethbridge	Pion.	C-1B	44	155	28	40	9	0	6	24	.258	240	24	4	.985
1982	—Lodi	Calif.	C-3B	127	424	65	119	18	1	15	55	.281	493	106	20	.968
1983	—San Antonio†	Texas	C	33	124	10	35	7	0	1	16	.282	167	30	5	.975
1983	—Los Angeles	Nat.	C	19	31	1	5	2	0	0	0	.161	59	9	4	.944
1983	—Albuquerque	P. C.	C	20	62	8	19	1	2	2	15	.306	103	17	8	.938
1984	—San Antonio	Texas	C	120	433	55	131	16	2	10	78	.303	⋆598	⋆101	⋆19	.974
1984	—Los Angeles	Nat.	C	4	5	0	0	0	0	0	0	.000	5	0	0	1.000
1985	—Albuquerque	P. C.	⋆C-1B	111	366	35	97	20	0	6	54	.265	439	66	⋆21	.960
1985	—Los Angeles	Nat.	C	6	1	0	0	0	0	0	0	.000	6	4	0	1.000
1986	—Albuquerque	P. C.	C-1B	104	306	36	70	13	1	7	36	.229	423	69	14	.972
1987	—Albuquerque	P. C.	C-1B-P	89	265	42	72	18	2	5	46	.272	414	66	12	.976
1987	—Los Angeles	Nat.	C	1	0	0	0	0	0	0	0	.000	2	0	0	1.000
1988	—Albuquerque	P. C.	C-1B-3B	98	318	40	93	14	0	12	66	.292	459	70	16	.971
1988	—Los Angeles	Nat.	C	5	9	1	1	0	0	0	0	.111	16	0	0	1.000
Major League Totals—5 Years				35	46	2	6	2	0	0	0	.130	88	13	4	.962

Signed as free agent by Los Angeles Dodgers' organization, January 15, 1980.
†On disabled list, May 11 to June 1, 1983.

PITCHING RECORD

Year	Club	League	G.	IP.	W.	L.	Pct.	H.	R.	ER.	SO.	BB.	ERA.
1987	—Albuquerque	P. Coast	1	⅓	0	0	.000	0	0	0	1	1	0.00

GORDON CRAIG REYNOLDS

(Known by middle name.)

Born December 27, 1952, at Houston, Tex.
Height, 6.01. Weight, 175.
Throws right and bats lefthanded.
Attended Houston Baptist College, Houston, Tex.

Tied modern major league record for most three-base hits, game (3), May 16, 1981.

Major League stolen bases: 1977 (6), 1978 (9), 1979 (12), 1980 (2), 1981 (3), 1982 (3), 1984 (7), 1985 (4), 1986 (3), 1987 (5), 1988 (3). Total—57.

Led National League in sacrifice hits with 34 in 1979, 18 in 1981 and 16 in 1984.

Led National League shortstops in assists with 472 in 1984.

Tied for Gulf Coast League lead in sacrifice flies with 4 in 1971.

Led Carolina League shortstops in double plays with 81 in 1973 and tied for International League lead with 64 in 1975.

Year	Club	League	Pos.	G.	AB.	R.	H.	2B.	3B.	HR.	RBI.	B.A.	PO.	A.	E.	F.A.
1971	—Bradenton Pir.	Gulf C.	SS	48	192	26	61	8	0	0	16	.318	⋆87	112	⋆25	.888
1972	—Gastonia†	W. Car.	SS	41	146	18	35	4	1	0	9	.240	55	94	12	.925
1973	—Salem	Carol.	SS-2B	138	⋆558	75	⋆160	18	5	13	86	.287	200	395	50	.922
1973	—Charleston	Int.	SS-3B	4	14	2	3	0	0	0	0	.214	4	11	1	.938
1974	—Thetford Mines	East.	SS	64	234	31	66	7	0	6	29	.282	76	170	13	.950
1974	—Charleston‡	Int.	SS-2B	36	107	12	36	5	0	0	5	.336	40	71	3	.974
1975	—Charleston	Int.	SS	108	425	51	131	22	3	6	42	.308	151	287	26	.944
1975	—Pittsburgh	Nat.	SS	31	76	8	17	3	0	0	4	.224	43	82	4	.969
1976	—Charleston	Int.	SS-2B	126	497	57	144	18	1	2	47	.290	198	262	31	.937
1976	—Pittsburgh§	Nat.	SS-2B	7	4	1	1	0	0	1	1	.250	2	6	1	.889
1977	—Seattle	Amer.	SS	135	420	41	104	12	3	4	28	.248	197	397	28	.955
1978	—Seattle x	Amer.	SS	148	548	57	160	16	7	5	44	.292	243	461	29	.960
1979	—Houston	Nat.	SS	146	555	63	147	20	9	0	39	.265	208	428	23	.965
1980	—Houston	Nat.	SS	137	381	34	86	9	6	3	28	.226	162	362	17	.969
1981	—Houston	Nat.	SS	87	323	43	84	10	•12	4	31	.260	139	261	11	.973
1982	—Houston y	Nat.	SS-3B	54	118	16	30	2	3	1	7	.254	45	98	6	.960
1983	—Houston	Nat.	2-3-S-O	65	98	10	21	3	0	1	6	.214	37	57	3	.969
1984	—Houston	Nat.	SS-3B	146	527	61	137	15	11	6	60	.260	212	473	25	.965
1985	—Houston	Nat.	SS-2B	107	379	43	103	18	8	4	32	.272	159	319	11	.978
1986	—Houston	Nat.	S-1-3-O-P	114	313	32	78	7	3	6	41	.249	124	209	7	.979
1987	—Houston	Nat.	SS-3B	135	374	35	95	17	3	4	28	.254	160	292	14	.970
1988	—Houston z	Nat.	S-3-2-1	78	161	20	41	7	0	1	14	.255	88	81	9	.949
American League Totals—2 Years				283	968	98	264	28	10	9	72	.273	440	858	57	.958
National League Totals—12 Years				1107	3309	366	840	111	55	31	291	.254	1379	2668	131	.969
Major League Totals—14 Years				1390	4277	464	1104	139	65	40	363	.258	1819	3526	188	.966

Selected by Pittsburgh Pirates' organization in 1st round (22nd player selected) of free-agent draft, June 8, 1971.
†On disabled list, June 6 to August 30, 1972.
‡On disabled list, July 31 to August 21, 1974.
§Traded with Infielder Jim Sexton to Seattle Mariners for Pitcher Grant Jackson, December 7, 1976.
xTraded to Houston Astros for Pitcher Floyd Bannister, December 8, 1978.
yOn disabled list, April 11 to May 5, 1982.
zGranted free agency, November 4, 1988; re-signed by Astros, December 16, 1988.

DIVISION SERIES RECORD

Year	Club	League	Pos.	G.	AB.	R.	H.	2B.	3B.	HR.	RBI.	B.A.	PO.	A.	E.	F.A.
1981	—Houston	Nat.	PH-SS	2	3	1	1	0	0	0	0	.333	1	0	0	1.000

CHAMPIONSHIP SERIES RECORD

Year	Club	League	Pos.	G.	AB.	R.	H.	2B.	3B.	HR.	RBI.	B.A.	PO.	A.	E.	F.A.
1975	Pittsburgh	Nat.	SS	2	1	0	0	0	0	0	0	.000	0	0	1	.000
1980	Houston	Nat.	SS	4	13	2	2	1	0	0	0	.154	8	12	1	.952
1986	Houston	Nat.	SS-PH	4	12	1	4	0	0	0	0	.333	7	8	2	.882
Championship Series Totals—3 Years				10	26	3	6	1	0	0	0	.231	15	20	4	.897

ALL-STAR GAME RECORD

Year	League	Pos.	AB.	R.	H.	2B.	3B.	HR.	RBI.	B.A.	PO.	A.	E.	F.A.
1979	National	SS	2	0	0	0	0	0	0	.000	0	1	0	1.000

Named to American League All-Star Team for 1978 game; did not play.

PITCHING RECORD

Year	Club	League	G.	IP.	W.	L.	Pct.	H.	R.	ER.	SO.	BB.	ERA.
1986	Houston	National	1	1	0	0	.000	3	3	3	1	2	27.00

HAROLD CRAIG REYNOLDS

Born November 26, 1960, at Eugene, Ore.
Height, 5.11. Weight, 165.
Throws right and bats left and righthanded.
Attended San Diego State University, San Diego, Calif.; Canada College, Redwood City, Calif., and California State University, Long Beach, Calif.
Brother of Larry Reynolds, shortstop-outfielder in Texas Rangers' and St. Louis Cardinals' organizations, 1979 through 1984; and Don Reynolds, outfielder with San Diego Padres, 1978 and 1979; and minor league instructor in Seattle Mariners' organization, 1988.

Tied major league record for most assists by second baseman, nine-inning game (12), August 27, 1986.
Major League stolen bases: 1984 (1), 1985 (3), 1986 (30), 1987 (60), 1988 (35). Total—129.
Led American League in stolen bases with 60 in 1987.
Led American League in caught stealing with 20 in 1987 and 29 in 1988.
Led American League second basemen in double plays with 111 in 1986, 1987 and 1988.
Led American League second basemen in total chances with 874 in 1987 and 792 in 1988.
Led Pacific Coast League in sacrifice hits with 14 in 1983.
Led Eastern League in caught stealing with 20 in 1982.
Led Midwest League in stolen bases with 69 in 1981.
Tied for Pacific Coast League lead in caught stealing with 17 in 1984.
Led Pacific Coast League second basemen in double plays with 104 and total chances with 747 in 1984.
Led Pacific Coast League second basemen in putouts with 286 and total chances with 723 in 1983.
Led Midwest League second basemen in double plays with 82 in 1981.
Named second baseman on THE SPORTING NEWS American League All-Star fielding team, 1988.

Year	Club	League	Pos.	G.	AB.	R.	H.	2B.	3B.	HR.	RBI.	B.A.	PO.	A.	E.	F.A.
1981	Wausau	Midw.	2B-OF-3B	127	493	98	146	23	3	11	59	.296	259	386	27	.960
1982	Lynn	East.	2B	102	375	58	102	14	4	2	48	.272	202	232	19	.958
1983	Salt Lake City	P. C.	*2B-SS	136	534	84	165	20	9	1	72	.309	287	*410	*27	.963
1983	Seattle	Amer.	2B	20	59	8	12	4	1	0	1	.203	30	48	2	.975
1984	Salt Lake City	P. C.	2B	135	*558	94	165	22	6	3	54	.296	*326	*396	*25	*.967
1984	Seattle	Amer.	2B	10	10	3	3	0	0	0	0	.300	8	12	0	1.000
1985	Seattle	Amer.	2B	67	104	15	15	3	1	0	6	.144	69	123	8	.960
1985	Calgary	P. C.	2B	52	212	36	77	11	3	5	30	.363	119	171	13	.957
1986	Calgary	P. C.	2B	29	118	20	37	7	0	1	7	.314	64	83	4	.974
1986	Seattle	Amer.	2B	126	445	46	99	19	4	1	24	.222	278	415	16	.977
1987	Seattle	Amer.	2B	160	530	73	146	31	8	1	35	.275	*347	*507	*20	.977
1988	Seattle	Amer.	2B	158	598	61	169	26	●11	4	41	.283	303	*471	*18	.977
Major League Totals—6 Years				541	1746	206	444	83	25	6	107	.254	1035	1576	64	.976

Selected by San Diego Padres' organization in 5th round of free-agent draft, June 5, 1979.
Selected by Seattle Mariners' organization in secondary phase of free-agent draft, June 3, 1980.

ALL-STAR GAME RECORD

Year	League	Pos.	AB.	R.	H.	2B.	3B.	HR.	RBI.	B.A.	PO.	A.	E.	F.A.
1987	American	2B	3	0	0	0	0	0	0	.000	4	4	0	1.000
1988	American	2B	1	0	0	0	0	0	0	.000	1	1	0	1.000
All-Star Game Totals—2 Years			4	0	0	0	0	0	0	.000	5	5	0	1.000

ROBERT JAMES REYNOLDS
(R. J.)

Born April 19, 1960, at Sacramento, Calif.
Height, 6.00. Weight, 180.
Throws right and bats left and righthanded.
Attended Cosumnes River College, Sacramento, Calif.; and Sacramento City College, Sacramento, Calif.

Tied major league record for fewest errors by outfielder, season, for leader in errors (9), 1986.
Major League stolen bases: 1983 (5), 1984 (7), 1985 (18), 1986 (16), 1987 (14), 1988 (15). Total—75.
Led Texas League outfielders in double plays with 8 in 1983.
Led Florida State League outfielders in double plays with 6 and total chances with 395 in 1981.
Led California League outfielders in double plays with 6 in 1980.

Year	Club	League	Pos.	G.	AB.	R.	H.	2B.	3B.	HR.	RBI.	B.A.	PO.	A.	E.	F.A.
1980—Lodi		Calif.	OF	86	299	33	84	6	3	4	31	.281	188	10	12	.943
1981—Vero Beach		Fla. St.	OF	132	502	62	139	9	11	2	49	.277	*368	20	7	.982
1982—Lodi		Calif.	OF	108	403	67	126	19	3	6	35	.313	212	12	6	.974
1982—San Antonio		Texas	OF	3	12	3	2	0	0	1	2	.167	10	1	0	1.000
1983—San Antonio		Texas	OF	133	504	103	170	25	3	18	89	.337	255	•18	12	.958
1983—Los Angeles		Nat.	OF	24	55	5	13	0	0	2	11	.236	25	2	2	.931
1984—Albuquerque		P. C.	OF	47	199	38	69	10	4	3	30	.347	104	4	6	.947
1984—Los Angeles†		Nat.	OF	73	240	24	62	12	2	2	24	.258	104	4	3	.973
1985—L.A.‡§-Pitt.		Nat.	OF	104	337	44	95	15	7	3	42	.282	159	6	6	.965
1986—Pittsburgh		Nat.	OF	118	402	63	108	30	2	9	48	.269	190	2	•9	.955
1987—Pittsburgh		Nat.	OF	117	335	47	87	24	1	7	51	.260	134	7	1	.993
1988—Pittsburgh		Nat.	OF	130	323	35	80	14	2	6	51	.248	142	7	4	.974
Major League Totals—6 Years				566	1692	218	445	95	14	29	227	.263	754	28	25	.969

Selected by Los Angeles Dodgers' organization in 2nd round of free-agent draft, January 8, 1980.

†On disabled list, July 2 to July 17, 1984.

‡On disabled list, April 8 to April 23 and July 10 to August 2, 1985.

§Traded to Pittsburgh Pirates, September 3, 1985, as partial completion of deal in which Los Angeles Dodgers acquired Third Baseman Bill Madlock for three players to be named later, August 31, 1985; Pittsburgh acquired Outfielder Cecil Espy and First Baseman Sid Bream to complete deal, September 9, 1985.

RICHARD ALAN RHODEN

Name pronounced ROH-dun.

(Rick)

Born May 16, 1953, at Boynton Beach, Fla.
Height, 6.04. Weight, 203.
Throws and bats righthanded.

Pitched seven-inning, 1-0 no-hit victory against Phoenix, April 23, 1980 (first game).

Major League saves: 1983 (1).

Named pitcher on THE SPORTING NEWS National League Silver Slugger team, 1984 through 1986.

Year	Club	League	G.	IP.	W.	L.	Pct.	H.	R.	ER.	SO.	BB.	ERA.
1971—Daytona Beach		Florida St.	11	61	4	6	.400	59	32	27	67	29	3.98
1972—El Paso		Texas	13	87	6	4	.600	70	36	32	89	30	3.31
1972—Albuquerque		P. Coast	13	80	7	1	.875	83	41	34	55	34	3.83
1973—Albuquerque†		P. Coast	20	116	4	9	.308	117	66	58	68	70	4.50
1974—Albuquerque		P. Coast	26	178	9	10	.474	197	103	87	106	65	4.40
1974—Los Angeles		National	4	9	1	0	1.000	5	2	2	7	4	2.00
1975—Los Angeles		National	26	99	3	3	.500	94	40	34	40	32	3.09
1976—Los Angeles		National	27	181	12	3	.800	165	66	60	77	53	2.98
1977—Los Angeles		National	31	216	16	10	.615	223	98	90	122	63	3.75
1978—Los Angeles‡		National	30	165	10	8	.556	160	77	67	79	51	3.65
1979—Pittsburgh§		National	1	5	0	1	.000	5	4	4	2	2	7.20
1980—Portland		P. Coast	10	52	6	3	.667	47	22	17	24	21	2.94
1980—Pittsburgh		National	20	127	7	5	.583	133	58	54	70	40	3.83
1981—Pittsburgh		National	21	136	9	4	.692	147	66	59	76	53	3.90
1982—Pittsburgh		National	35	230⅓	11	14	.440	239	115	106	128	70	4.14
1983—Pittsburgh		National	36	244⅓	13	13	.500	256	95	84	153	68	3.09
1984—Pittsburgh		National	33	238⅓	14	9	.609	216	81	72	136	62	2.72
1985—Pittsburgh		National	35	213⅓	10	15	.400	254	•119	*106	128	69	4.47
1986—Pittsburgh x		National	34	253⅔	15	12	.556	211	82	80	159	76	2.84
1987—New York		American	30	181⅔	16	10	.615	184	84	78	107	61	3.86
1988—New York yz		American	30	197	12	12	.500	206	107	94	94	56	4.29
National League Totals—13 Years			333	2118	121	97	.555	2108	903	818	1177	643	3.48
American League Totals—2 Years			60	378⅔	28	22	.560	390	191	172	201	117	4.09
Major League Totals—15 Years			393	2496⅔	149	119	.556	2498	1094	990	1378	760	3.57

Selected by Los Angeles Dodgers' organization in 1st round (20th player selected) of free-agent draft, June 8, 1971.

†On disabled list, July 20 to August 15, 1973.

‡Traded to Pittsburgh Pirates for Pitcher Jerry Reuss, April 9, 1979.

§On disabled list, May 12 to October 4, 1979.

xTraded with Pitchers Cecilio Guante and Pat Clements to New York Yankees for Pitchers Doug Drabek, Brian Fisher and Logan Easley, November 26, 1986.

yOn disabled list, April 29 to May 21, 1988.

zAppeared in one game as starting designated hitter, grounding out and hitting sacrifice fly with a run batted in during two plate appearances.

CHAMPIONSHIP SERIES RECORD

Year	Club	League	G.	IP.	W.	L.	Pct.	H.	R.	ER.	SO.	BB.	ERA.
1977—Los Angeles		National	1	4⅓	0	0	.000	2	0	0	0	2	0.00
1978—Los Angeles		National	1	4	0	0	.000	2	1	1	3	1	2.25
Championship Series Totals—2 Years			2	8⅓	0	0	.000	4	1	1	3	3	1.08

WORLD SERIES RECORD

Year	Club	League	G.	IP.	W.	L.	Pct.	H.	R.	ER.	SO.	BB.	ERA.
1977—Los Angeles		National	2	7	0	1	.000	4	2	2	5	1	2.57

ALL-STAR GAME RECORD

Year	League	IP.	W.	L.	Pct.	H.	R.	ER.	SO.	BB.	ERA.
1976—National		1	0	0	.000	1	0	0	0	0	0.00

Member of National League All-Star Team in 1986; did not play.

KARL DERRICK RHODES

Born August 21, 1968, at Cincinnati, O.
Height, 5.11. Weight, 170.
Throws and bats lefthanded.

Year	Club	League	Pos.	G.	AB.	R.	H.	2B.	3B.	HR.	RBI.	B.A.	PO.	A.	E.	F.A.
1986	Sarasota Astros	Gulf C.	OF	★62	222	36	65	10	3	0	22	.293	113	6	0	★1.000
1987	Asheville	S. Atl.	OF	129	413	62	104	16	4	3	50	.252	163	14	9	.952
1988	Osceola	Fla. St.	OF-2B	132	452	69	128	4	2	1	34	.283	232	14	2	.992

Selected by Houston Astros' organization in 3rd round of free-agent draft, June 2, 1986.

JAMES EDWARD RICE
(Jim)

Born March 8, 1953, at Anderson, S. C.
Height, 6.02. Weight, 217.
Throws and bats righthanded.

Established major league record for most times grounding into double plays, season (36), 1984.

Tied major league records for most consecutive seasons leading major leagues, total bases (2); fewest double plays by outfielder, season, 150 or more games (0), 1986.

Tied American League records for most consecutive seasons leading league, total bases (3); most years leading league in grounding into double plays (3).

Major League stolen bases: 1975 (10), 1976 (8), 1977 (5), 1978 (7), 1979 (9), 1980 (8), 1981 (2), 1984 (4), 1985 (2), 1987 (1), 1988 (1). Total—57

Hit three home runs in a game, August 29, 1977 and August 29, 1983 (second game).

Led American League in grounding into double plays with 29 in 1982, 36 in 1984, 35 in 1985 and tied for lead with 31 in 1983.

Led American League in total bases with 382 in 1977, 406 in 1978, 369 in 1979 and 344 in 1983.

Led American League in slugging percentage with .593 in 1977 and .600 in 1978.

Led American League batters in strikeouts with 123 in 1976.

Led International League in total bases with 249 in 1974.

Led Florida State League in total bases with 240 in 1972.

Named American League Player of the Year by THE SPORTING NEWS, 1978.

Named American League Most Valuable Player by Baseball Writers' Association of America, 1978.

Named outfielder on THE SPORTING NEWS American League All-Star Team, 1975, 1977 through 1979, 1983 and 1986.

Named outfielder on THE SPORTING NEWS American League Silver Slugger team, 1983 and 1984.

Named Minor League Player of the Year by THE SPORTING NEWS, 1974.

Named International League Most Valuable Player, 1974.

Received reported $45,000 bonus to sign with Boston Red Sox, 1971.

Year	Club	League	Pos.	G.	AB.	R.	H.	2B.	3B.	HR.	RBI.	B.A.	PO.	A.	E.	F.A.
1971	Williamsport	NYP	OF	60	223	34	57	9	5	5	27	.256	86	2	6	.936
1972	Winter Haven	Fla. St.	OF	130	★491	★80	★143	20	13	17	87	.291	190	10	9	.957
1973	Bristol	East.	OF	119	423	66	134	25	4	27	93	★.317	169	13	12	.938
1973	Pawtucket	Int.	OF	10	37	7	14	2	0	4	10	.378	21	0	0	1.000
1974	Pawtucket	Int.	OF	117	430	69	145	21	4	★25	★93	★.337	181	10	11	.946
1974	Boston	Amer.	OF	24	67	6	18	2	1	1	13	.269	4	0	1	.800
1975	Boston	Amer.	OF	144	564	92	174	29	4	22	102	.309	162	6	0	1.000
1976	Boston	Amer.	OF	153	581	75	164	25	8	25	85	.282	199	8	7	.967
1977	Boston	Amer.	OF	160	644	104	206	29	15	★39	114	.320	83	4	4	.956
1978	Boston	Amer.	OF	★163	★677	121	★213	25	★15	★46	★139	.315	245	13	3	.989
1979	Boston	Amer.	OF	158	619	117	201	39	6	39	130	.325	241	8	4	.984
1980	Boston†	Amer.	OF	124	504	81	148	22	6	24	86	.294	233	10	3	.988
1981	Boston	Amer.	OF	108	★451	51	128	18	1	17	62	.284	237	9	3	.988
1982	Boston	Amer.	OF	145	573	86	177	24	5	24	97	.309	273	10	9	.969
1983	Boston	Amer.	OF	155	626	90	191	34	1	★39	●126	.305	339	21	6	.984
1984	Boston	Amer.	OF	159	657	98	184	25	7	28	122	.280	336	12	4	.989
1985	Boston	Amer.	OF	140	546	85	159	20	3	27	103	.291	236	8	9	.964
1986	Boston	Amer.	OF	157	618	98	200	39	2	20	110	.324	330	16	8	.977
1987	Boston	Amer.	OF	108	404	66	112	14	0	13	62	.277	155	12	4	.977
1988	Boston	Amer.	OF	135	485	57	128	18	3	15	72	.264	30	0	1	.968
Major League Totals—15 Years				2033	8016	1227	2403	363	77	379	1423	.300	3103	137	66	.980

Selected by Boston Red Sox' organization in 1st round (15th player selected) of free-agent draft, June 8, 1971.

†On disabled list, June 22 to July 27, 1980.

CHAMPIONSHIP SERIES RECORD

Established American League Championship Series record for most runs, seven-game Series (8), 1986.

Tied American League Championship Series record for most strikeouts, seven-game Series (8), 1986.

Year	Club	League	Pos.	G.	AB.	R.	H.	2B.	3B.	HR.	RBI.	B.A.	PO.	A.	E.	F.A.
1986	Boston	Amer.	OF	7	31	8	5	1	0	2	6	.161	13	1	0	1.000
1988	Boston	Amer.	DH	4	13	0	2	0	0	0	1	.154	0	0	0	.000
Championship Series Totals—2 Years				11	44	8	7	1	0	2	7	.159	13	1	0	1.000

WORLD SERIES RECORD

Tied World Series record for most at-bats, nine-inning game (6), October 19, 1986.

Year	Club	League	Pos.	G.	AB.	R.	H.	2B.	3B.	HR.	RBI.	B.A.	PO.	A.	E.	F.A.
1986	Boston	Amer.	OF	7	27	6	9	1	1	0	0	.333	16	2	0	1.000

ALL-STAR GAME RECORD

Tied All-Star Game record for most at bats, game (5), July 17, 1979.

Year League	Pos.	AB.	R.	H.	2B.	3B.	HR.	RBI.	B.A.	PO.	A.	E.	F.A.
1977—American	OF	2	0	1	0	0	0	0	.500	1	0	0	1.000
1978—American	OF	4	0	0	0	0	0	0	.000	2	0	0	1.000
1979—American	OF	5	0	1	1	0	0	0	.200	3	0	0	1.000
1983—American	OF	4	1	2	0	0	1	1	.500	1	0	0	1.000
1984—American	PH-OF	1	0	0	0	0	0	0	.000	1	0	0	1.000
1985—American	OF	3	0	0	0	0	0	0	.000	1	0	0	1.000
1986—American	PH	1	0	0	0	0	0	0	.000	0	0	0	.000
All-Star Game Totals—7 Years		20	1	4	1	0	1	1	.200	9	0	0	1.000

Named to American League All-Star Team in 1980; replaced due to injury.

RUSSELL EARL RICHARDS
(Rusty)

Born January 27, 1965, at Houston, Tex.
Height, 6.04. Weight, 200.
Throws right and bats lefthanded.
Attended Austin Community College, Austin, Tex.,
and University of Texas, Austin, Tex.

Year Club	League	G.	IP.	W.	L.	Pct.	H.	R.	ER.	SO.	BB.	ERA.
1986—Bradenton Braves	Gulf Coast	12	19⅓	0	0	.000	17	8	5	15	7	2.33
1987—Sumter	S. Atlantic	10	48	3	3	.500	45	28	17	39	17	3.19
1987—Durham	Carolina	22	125	6	10	.375	138	73	63	62	50	4.54
1988—Durham	Carolina	1	3⅓	1	0	1.000	0	0	0	3	0	0.00
1988—Greenville	Southern	28	147	10	7	.588	125	46	43	96	42	2.63

Selected by Philadelphia Phillies' organization in 7th round of free-agent draft, January 14, 1986.
Signed as free agent by Atlanta Braves' organization, June 19, 1986.

DANA JOSEPH RIDENOUR

Born November 15, 1965, at Panorama City, Calif.
Height, 6.02. Weight, 205.
Throws and bats righthanded.
Attended University of California, Los Angeles, Calif.

Year Club	League	G.	IP.	W.	L.	Pct.	H.	R.	ER.	SO.	BB.	ERA.
1986—Oneonta	NYP	23	34⅔	4	2	.667	21	6	6	47	11	1.56
1987—Fort Lauderdale	Florida St.	43	66	5	4	.556	38	14	13	90	34	1.77
1988—Albany	Eastern	30	43⅔	5	4	.556	29	19	19	56	29	3.92
1988—Columbus	Int'national	14	21⅓	1	2	.333	16	9	5	24	19	2.11

Selected by New York Yankees' organization in 16th round of free-agent draft, June 2, 1986.

DAVID ALLEN RIGHETTI

Name pronounced Ri-GET-tee.

(Dave)

Born November 28, 1958, at San Jose, Calif.
Height, 6.04. Weight, 210.
Throws and bats lefthanded.
Attended San Jose City College, San Jose, Calif.
Son of Leo Righetti, minor league infielder, 1944 through 1949 and 1951 through 1957;
Brother of Steven Righetti, third baseman in Texas Rangers' organization, 1977 through 1979.

Established major league record for most saves, season (46), 1986.
Pitched 4-0 no-hit victory against Boston Red Sox, July 4, 1983.
Major League saves: 1982 (1), 1984 (31), 1985 (29), 1986 (46), 1987 (31), 1988 (25). Total—163.
Led American League in saves with 46 and games finished in relief with 68 in 1986.
Named American League Co-Fireman of the Year by THE SPORTING NEWS, 1987.
Named American League Fireman of the Year by THE SPORTING NEWS, 1986.
Named American League Rookie Pitcher of the Year by THE SPORTING NEWS, 1981.
Named American League Rookie of the Year by Baseball Writers' Association of America, 1981.

Year Club	League	G.	IP.	W.	L.	Pct.	H.	R.	ER.	SO.	BB.	ERA.
1977—Asheville	W. Carol.	17	109	11	3	*.786	98	47	38	101	53	3.14
1978—Tulsa†‡	Texas	13	91	5	5	.500	66	40	32	127	49	3.16
1979—West Haven§	Eastern	11	69	4	3	.571	45	23	15	78	45	1.96
1979—Columbus x	Int'national	8	40	3	2	.600	22	13	13	44	19	2.93
1979—New York	American	3	17	0	1	.000	10	7	7	13	10	3.71
1980—Columbus	Int'national	24	142	6	10	.375	124	79	73	139	*101	4.63
1981—Columbus	Int'national	7	45	5	0	1.000	30	8	5	50	26	1.00
1981—New York	American	15	105	8	4	.667	75	25	24	89	38	2.06
1982—New York	American	33	183	11	10	.524	155	88	77	163	*108	3.79
1982—Columbus	Int'national	4	25⅔	1	0	1.000	22	11	8	33	12	2.81
1983—New York	American	31	217	14	8	.636	194	96	83	169	67	3.44
1984—New York y	American	64	96⅓	5	6	.455	79	29	25	90	37	2.34
1985—New York	American	74	107	12	7	.632	96	36	33	92	45	2.78
1986—New York	American	74	106⅔	8	8	.500	88	31	29	83	35	2.45
1987—New York z	American	60	95	8	6	.571	95	45	37	77	44	3.51
1988—New York	American	60	87	5	4	.556	86	35	34	70	37	3.52
Major League Totals—9 Years		414	1014	71	54	.568	878	392	349	846	421	3.10

Selected by Texas Rangers' organization in 1st round (ninth player selected) of free-agent draft, January 11, 1977.
†On disabled list, July 31 to September 2, 1978.

‡Traded with Pitchers Mike Griffin and Paul Mirabella and Outfielders Juan Beniquez and Greg Jemison to New York Yankees for Pitchers Sparky Lyle, Larry McCall and Dave Rajsich, Catcher Mike Heath, Shortstop Domingo Ramos and cash, November 10, 1978.

§On disabled list, May 21 to June 28, 1979.

xOn disabled list, June 28 to July 20 and August 2 to August 23, 1979.

yOn disabled list, June 17 to July 2, 1984.

zGranted free agency, November 9, 1987; re-signed by Yankees, December 23, 1987.

DIVISION SERIES RECORD

Year	Club	League	G.	IP.	W.	L.	Pct.	H.	R.	ER.	SO.	BB.	ERA.
1981	—New York	American	2	9	2	0	1.000	8	1	1	10	3	1.00

CHAMPIONSHIP SERIES RECORD

Year	Club	League	G.	IP.	W.	L.	Pct.	H.	R.	ER.	SO.	BB.	ERA.
1981	—New York	American	1	6	1	0	1.000	4	0	0	4	2	0.00

WORLD SERIES RECORD

Year	Club	League	G.	IP.	W.	L.	Pct.	H.	R.	ER.	SO.	BB.	ERA.
1981	—New York	American	1	2	0	0	.000	5	3	3	1	2	13.50

ALL-STAR GAME RECORD

Year	League	IP.	W.	L.	Pct.	H.	R.	ER.	SO.	BB.	ERA.
1986	—American	⅔	0	0	.000	2	0	0	0	0	0.00
1987	—American	⅓	0	0	.000	1	0	0	0	0	0.00
All-Star Game Totals—2 Years		1	0	0	.000	3	0	0	0	0	0.00

JOSE ANTONIO RIJO (ABREAU)

Name pronounced REE-ho.

Born May 13, 1965, at San Cristobal, Dominican Republic.
Height, 6.02. Weight, 200.
Throws and bats righthanded.
Son-in-law of Juan Marichal, Hall of Fame pitcher with San Francisco Giants, Boston Red Sox and Los Angeles Dodgers, 1960 through 1975; and scout for Oakland A's, 1983 through 1985.

Major League saves: 1984 (2),1986 (1). Total—3.
Led Pacific Coast League in balks with 11 in 1985.
Led Florida State League in complete games with 15 and tied for lead in shutouts with 4 in 1983.
Named Florida State League Most Valuable Player, 1983.

Year	Club	League	G.	IP.	W.	L.	Pct.	H.	R.	ER.	SO.	BB.	ERA.
1981	—Bradenton Yankees	Gulf Coast	11	22	3	3	.500	37	16	11	22	7	4.50
1982	—Paintsville	Ap'lachian	13	79⅓	8	4	.667	76	33	22	66	22	2.50
1983	—Fort Lauderdale	Florida St.	21	160⅓	*15	5	.750	129	38	30	152	43	*1.68
1983	—Nashville	Southern	5	40⅓	3	2	.600	31	12	12	32	22	2.68
1984	—New York	American	24	62⅓	2	8	.200	74	40	33	47	33	4.76
1984	—Columbus†	Int'national	11	65⅓	3	3	.500	67	35	32	47	40	4.41
1985	—Tacoma	P. Coast	24	149	7	10	.412	116	64	48	*179	*108	2.90
1985	—Oakland	American	12	63⅔	6	4	.600	57	26	25	65	28	3.53
1986	—Oakland	American	39	193⅔	9	11	.450	172	116	100	176	108	4.65
1987	—Oakland	American	21	82⅓	2	7	.222	106	67	54	67	41	5.90
1987	—Tacoma‡	P. Coast	9	54⅔	2	4	.333	44	27	24	67	28	3.95
1988	—Cincinnati §	National	49	162	13	8	.619	120	47	43	160	63	2.39
American League Totals—4 Years			96	402	19	30	.388	409	249	212	355	210	4.75
National League Totals—1 Year			49	162	13	8	.619	120	47	43	160	63	2.39
Major League Totals—5 Years			145	564	32	38	.457	529	296	255	515	273	4.07

Signed as free agent by New York Yankees' organization, August 1, 1980.

†Traded with Outfielder Stan Javier and Pitchers Jay Howell, Eric Plunk and Tim Birtsas to Oakland A's for Outfielder Rickey Henderson, Pitcher Bert Bradley and cash, December 5, 1984.

‡Traded with Pitcher Tim Birtsas to Cincinnati Reds for Outfielder Dave Parker, December 8, 1987.

§On disabled list, August 18 to September 8, 1988.

ERNEST RILES

Born October 2, 1960, at Bainbridge, Ga.
Height, 6.01. Weight, 180.
Throws right and bats lefthanded.
Attended Middle Georgia College, Cochran, Ga.

Major League stolen bases: 1985 (2), 1986 (7), 1987 (3), 1988 (3). Total—15.
Led California League in bases on balls received with 84 in 1982.
Led Texas League shortstops in total chances with 670 and double plays with 77 in 1983.
Led California League shortstops in double plays with 95 and tied for lead in total chances with 692 in 1982.

Year	Club	League	Pos.	G.	AB.	R.	H.	2B.	3B.	HR.	RBI.	B.A.	PO.	A.	E.	F.A.
1981	—Butte	Pion.	SS-3B-2B	67	256	63	89	11	2	4	43	.348	97	217	27	.921
1982	—Stockton	Calif.	SS	138	447	60	128	23	6	2	56	.286	204	*451	37	.947
1983	—El Paso	Texas	SS	130	476	109	166	31	3	13	91	*.349	*193	*445	32	*.952
1984	—Vancouver	P. C.	SS	123	424	59	113	19	7	3	54	.267	*190	316	17	.967
1985	—Vancouver	P. C.	SS	30	118	19	41	7	1	2	20	.347	47	120	6	.965
1985	—Milwaukee	Amer.	SS	116	448	54	128	12	7	5	45	.286	183	310	22	.957
1986	—Milwaukee	Amer.	SS	145	524	69	132	24	2	9	47	.252	212	327	20	.964
1987	—El Paso†	Texas	SS	41	153	45	52	10	0	6	24	.340	70	127	10	.952

Year	Club	League	Pos.	G.	AB.	R.	H.	2B.	3B.	HR.	RBI.	B.A.	PO.	A.	E.	F.A.
1987	—Milwaukee	Amer.	3B-SS	83	276	38	72	11	1	4	38	.261	76	152	13	.946
1988	—Milwaukee‡	Amer.	3B-SS	41	127	7	32	6	1	1	9	.252	36	64	4	.962
1988	—San Francisco	Nat.	3B-2B-SS	79	187	26	55	7	2	3	28	.294	46	133	3	.984
American League Totals—4 Years				385	1375	168	364	53	11	19	139	.265	507	853	59	.958
National League Totals—1 Year				79	187	26	55	7	2	3	28	.294	46	133	3	.984
Major League Totals—4 Years				464	1562	194	419	60	13	22	167	.268	553	986	62	.961

Selected by Seattle Mariners' organization in 21st round of free-agent draft, June 3, 1980.

Selected by Milwaukee Brewers' organization in secondary phase of free-agent draft, January 13, 1981.

†On Milwaukee disabled list, March 26 to June 3, 1987; included rehabilitation disability assignment to El Paso, May 13 to June 2, 1987.

‡Traded to San Francisco Giants for Outfielder Jeffrey Leonard, June 8, 1988.

CALVIN EDWIN RIPKEN JR.
(Cal)

Born August 24, 1960, at Havre de Grace, Md.
Height, 6.04. Weight, 225.
Throws and bats righthanded.
Son of Cal Ripken, minor league catcher, 1957 through 1962 and 1964; minor league manager, 1961 through 1974; scout, Baltimore Orioles, 1975; manager, Baltimore Orioles, 1987 through April 11, 1988; and coach with Baltimore Orioles, 1976 through 1986; brother of Billy Ripken, second baseman with Baltimore Orioles; and nephew of Bill Ripken, minor league outfielder, 1947 through 1949.

Established major league record for fewest stolen bases, season, most at-bats (0 and 663), 1983.
Established American League record for most assists by shortstop, season (583), 1984.
Major League stolen bases: 1982 (3), 1984 (2), 1985 (2), 1986 (4), 1987 (3), 1988 (2). Total—16.
Hit for the cycle, May 6, 1984.
Tied for American League lead in sacrifice flies with 10 in 1988.
Tied for American League lead in game-winning RBIs with 15 in 1986.
Led American League shortstops in total chances with 831 in 1983 and 906 in 1984.
Led American League shortstops in double plays with 113 in 1983, 122 in 1984 and 123 in 1985.
Tied for Southern League lead in sacrifice flies with 9 in 1980.
Led Southern League third basemen in fielding percentage with .933, putouts with 119, assists with 268, and double plays with 34 in 1980.
Tied for Appalachian League lead in double plays by shortstops with 31 in 1978.
Named Major League Player of the Year by THE SPORTING NEWS, 1983.
Named American League Player of the Year by THE SPORTING NEWS, 1983.
Named American League Most Valuable Player by Baseball Writers' Association of America, 1983.
Named American League Rookie Player of the Year by THE SPORTING NEWS, 1982.
Named American League Rookie of the Year by Baseball Writers' Association of America, 1982.
Named shortstop on THE SPORTING NEWS American League All-Star Team, 1983 through 1985.
Named shortstop on THE SPORTING NEWS Silver Slugger team, 1983 through 1986.

Year	Club	League	Pos.	G.	AB.	R.	H.	2B.	3B.	HR.	RBI.	B.A.	PO.	A.	E.	F.A.
1978	—Bluefield	Appal.	SS	63	239	27	63	7	1	0	24	.264	*92	204	*33	.900
1979	—Miami	Fla. St.	3B-SS-2B	105	393	51	119	*28	1	5	54	.303	149	260	30	.932
1979	—Charlotte	South.	3B	17	61	6	11	0	1	3	8	.180	13	26	3	.929
1980	—Charlotte	South.	3B-SS	•144	522	91	144	28	5	25	78	.276	151	341	35	.934
1981	—Rochester	Int.	3B-SS	114	437	74	126	31	4	23	75	.288	128	320	21	.955
1981	—Baltimore	Amer.	SS-3B	23	39	1	5	0	0	0	0	.128	13	30	3	.935
1982	—Baltimore	Amer.	SS-3B	160	598	90	158	32	5	28	93	.264	221	440	19	.972
1983	—Baltimore	Amer.	SS	•162	*663	*121	*211	*47	2	27	102	.318	272	*534	25	.970
1984	—Baltimore	Amer.	SS	•162	641	103	195	37	7	27	86	.304	*297	*583	26	.971
1985	—Baltimore	Amer.	SS	161	642	116	181	32	5	26	110	.282	*286	474	26	.967
1986	—Baltimore	Amer.	SS	162	627	98	177	35	1	25	81	.282	240	*482	13	.982
1987	—Baltimore	Amer.	SS	*162	624	97	157	28	3	27	98	.252	240	*480	20	.973
1988	—Baltimore	Amer.	SS	161	575	87	152	25	1	23	81	.264	*284	480	21	.973
Major League Totals—8 Years				1153	4409	713	1236	236	24	183	651	.280	1853	3503	153	.972

Selected by Baltimore Orioles' organization in 2nd round of free-agent draft, June 6, 1978.

CHAMPIONSHIP SERIES RECORD

Year	Club	League	Pos.	G.	AB.	R.	H.	2B.	3B.	HR.	RBI.	B.A.	PO.	A.	E.	F.A.
1983	—Baltimore	Amer.	SS	4	15	5	6	2	0	0	1	.400	7	11	0	1.000

WORLD SERIES RECORD

Year	Club	League	Pos.	G.	AB.	R.	H.	2B.	3B.	HR.	RBI.	B.A.	PO.	A.	E.	F.A.
1983	—Baltimore	Amer.	SS	5	18	2	3	0	0	0	1	.167	6	14	0	1.000

ALL-STAR GAME RECORD

Year	League	Pos.	AB.	R.	H.	2B.	3B.	HR.	RBI.	B.A.	PO.	A.	E.	F.A.
1983	—American	SS	0	0	0	0	0	0	0	.000	1	0	0	1.000
1984	—American	SS	3	0	0	0	0	0	0	.000	0	0	0	.000
1985	—American	SS	3	0	1	0	0	0	0	.333	2	1	0	1.000
1986	—American	SS	4	0	0	0	0	0	0	.000	0	1	0	1.000
1987	—American	SS	2	0	1	0	0	0	0	.500	0	5	0	1.000
1988	—American	SS	3	0	0	0	0	0	0	.000	1	4	0	1.000
All-Star Game Totals—6 Years			15	0	2	0	0	0	0	.133	4	11	0	1.000

WILLIAM OLIVER RIPKEN
(Billy)

Born December 16, 1964, at Havre de Grace, Md.
Height, 6.01. Weight, 183
Throws and bats righthanded.
Son of Cal Ripken Sr., minor league catcher, 1957 through 1962 and 1964; minor league manager, 1961 through 1974; scout, Baltimore Orioles, 1975; manager, Baltimore Orioles, 1987 through April 11, 1988; and coach with Baltimore Orioles, 1976 through 1986; brother of Cal Ripken, Jr., infielder with Baltimore Orioles; and nephew of Bill Ripken, minor league outfielder, 1947 through 1949.

Major League stolen bases: 1987 (4), 1988 (8). Total—12.
Tied for Southern League lead in grounding into double plays with 21 in 1986.
Led Southern League second basemen in total chances with 723 and double plays with 79 in 1986.

Year Club	League	Pos.	G.	AB.	R.	H.	2B.	3B.	HR.	RBI.	B.A.	PO.	A.	E.	F.A.
1982—Bluefield	Appal.	SS-3B-2B	27	45	8	11	1	0	0	4	.244	15	17	3	.914
1983—Bluefield	Appal.	SS-3B	48	152	24	33	6	0	0	13	.217	82	145	23	.908
1984—Hagerstown†	Carol.	SS-2B	115	409	48	94	15	3	2	40	.230	187	358	28	.951
1985—Charlotte	South.	SS	18	51	2	7	1	0	0	3	.137	18	52	4	.946
1985—Daytona Beach‡	Fla. St.	SS-3B-2B	67	222	23	51	11	0	0	18	.230	90	198	8	.973
1985—Hagerstown	Carol.	3B-2B	14	47	9	12	0	1	0	0	.255	14	37	2	.962
1986—Charlotte	South.	2B	141	530	58	142	20	3	5	62	.268	*305	*395	*23	.968
1987—Rochester	Int.	2B-SS	74	238	32	68	15	0	0	11	.286	154	200	9	.975
1987—Baltimore	Amer.	2B	58	234	27	72	9	0	2	20	.308	133	162	3	.990
1988—Baltimore	Amer.	2B-3B	150	512	52	106	18	1	2	34	.207	310	440	12	.984
Major League Totals—2 Years			208	746	79	178	27	1	4	54	.239	443	602	15	.986

Selected by Baltimore Orioles' organization in 11th round of free-agent draft, June 7, 1982.
†On disabled list, April 20 to May 3, 1984.
‡On disabled list, June 23 to July 6, 1985.

WALLACE REID RITCHIE
(Wally)

Born July 12, 1965, at Glendale, Calif.
Height, 6.02. Weight, 180.
Throws and bats lefthanded.
Attended Glendale College, Glendale, Calif., and Brigham Young University, Provo, Utah.

Major League saves: 1987 (3).

Year Club	League	G.	IP.	W.	L.	Pct.	H.	R.	ER.	SO.	BB.	ERA.
1985—Bend	Northwest	2	10	1	0	1.000	10	11	5	3	5	4.50
1985—Clearwater	Florida St.	14	46⅔	3	1	.750	49	30	18	24	12	3.47
1986—Clearwater	Florida St.	32	52	4	1	.800	40	15	13	39	16	2.22
1986—Reading	Eastern	28	30	4	1	.800	29	13	9	13	9	2.70
1987—Maine	Int'national	13	22	3	1	.750	17	6	5	16	8	2.05
1987—Philadelphia	National	49	62⅓	3	2	.600	60	27	26	45	29	3.75
1988—Philadelphia	National	19	26	0	0	.000	19	14	9	8	17	3.12
1988—Maine	Int'national	16	78⅔	4	5	.444	88	49	41	49	29	4.69
Major League Totals—2 Years		68	88⅓	3	2	.600	79	41	35	53	46	3.57

Selected by Philadelphia Phillies' organization in 4th round of free-agent draft, June 3, 1985.

KEVIN D. RITZ

Born June 8, 1965, at Eatonstown, N. J.
Height, 6.04. Weight, 195.
Throws and bats righthanded.
Attended Indian Hills Community College, Centerville, Ia.

Year Club	League	G.	IP.	W.	L.	Pct.	H.	R.	ER.	SO.	BB.	ERA.
1986—Gastonia	S. Atlantic	7	36⅓	1	2	.333	29	19	17	34	21	4.21
1986—Lakeland	Florida St.	18	85⅔	3	9	.250	114	60	53	39	45	5.57
1987—Glens Falls	Eastern	25	152⅔	8	8	.500	171	95	83	78	71	4.89
1988—Glens Falls	Eastern	26	136⅔	8	10	.444	115	68	58	75	70	3.82

Selected by San Francisco Giants' organization in 4th round of free-agent draft, January 9, 1985.
Selected by Detroit Tigers' organization in secondary phase of free-agent draft, June 3, 1985.

BIENVENIDO SANTANA RIVERA
(Ben)

Born January 11, 1969, at Dominican Republic.
Height, 6.06. Weight, 190.
Throws and bats righthanded.

Year Club	League	G.	IP.	W.	L.	Pct.	H.	R.	ER.	SO.	BB.	ERA.
1987—Bradenton Braves	Gulf Coast	16	49⅔	1	5	.167	55	26	18	29	19	3.26
1988—Sumter†	S. Atlantic	27	173⅓	9	11	.450	167	77	61	99	52	3.17

Signed as free agent by Atlanta Braves' organization, November 15, 1985.
†Drafted by Atlanta Braves, December 5, 1988.

LUIS ANTONIO RIVERA

Born January 3, 1964, at Cidra, Puerto Rico.
Height, 5.09. Weight, 165.
Throws and bats righthanded.

Major League stolen bases: 1986 (1), 1988 (3). Total—4.
Led American Association shortstops in double plays with 84 in 1987.
Led Southern League shortstops in total chances with 643 and double plays with 107 in 1985.
Led Florida State League shortstops in assists with 436, errors with 51, total chances with 704 and double plays with 95 in 1983.
Tied for Florida State League lead in total chances by shortstops with 626 in 1984.

Year Club	League	Pos.	G.	AB.	R.	H.	2B.	3B.	HR.	RBI.	B.A.	PO.	A.	E.	F.A.
1982—San Jose	Calif.	SS	130	476	53	123	20	3	3	49	.258	226	389	55	.918
1983—W. Palm Beach	Fla. St.	SS	129	419	63	95	18	5	5	53	.227	217	436	51	.928
1984—W. Palm Beach	Fla. St.	SS	124	439	54	100	23	0	6	43	.228	*198	*389	39	.938
1985—Jacksonville	South.	SS	138	*538	74	129	20	2	16	72	.240	*198	*412	33	.949
1986—Indianapolis	A. A.	SS	108	407	60	100	17	5	7	43	.246	178	330	24	.955
1986—Montreal	Nat.	SS	55	166	20	34	11	1	0	13	.205	64	119	9	.953
1987—Indianapolis	A. A.	SS	108	433	73	135	26	3	8	53	.312	190	291	18	.964
1987—Montreal	Nat.	SS	18	32	0	5	2	0	0	1	.156	9	27	3	.923
1988—Montreal†	Nat.	SS	123	371	35	83	17	3	4	30	.224	160	301	18	.962
Major League Totals—3 Years			196	569	55	122	30	4	4	44	.214	233	447	30	.958

Signed as free agent by Montreal Expos' organization, September 22, 1981.
†Traded with Pitcher John Dopson to Boston Red Sox for Shortstop Spike Owen and Pitcher Dan Gakeler, December 8, 1988.

LEON JOSEPH ROBERTS III
(Bip)

Born October 27, 1963, at Berkeley, Calif.
Height, 5.07. Weight, 160.
Throws right and bats left and righthanded.
Attended Chabot College, Hayward, Calif.; and University of Nevada, Las Vegas, Nev.

Major League stolen bases: 1986 (14).
Tied for Eastern League lead in stolen bases with 40 in 1985.
Led Carolina League second basemen in total chances with 654 and double plays with 91 in 1984.
Led South Atlantic League second basemen in fielding percentage with .962 and tied for lead in double plays with 76 in 1983.

Year Club	League	Pos.	G.	AB.	R.	H.	2B.	3B.	HR.	RBI.	B.A.	PO.	A.	E.	F.A.
1982—Bradenton Pir.	Gulf C.	2B	6	23	4	7	1	0	0	1	.304	14	15	0	1.000
1982—Greenwood	S. Atl.	2B	33	107	15	23	3	1	0	6	.215	52	82	7	.950
1983—Greenwood	S. Atl.	2B-SS	122	438	78	140	20	5	6	63	.320	273	311	24	.961
1984—Prince William	Carol.	2B	134	498	81	*150	25	5	8	77	.301	*282	352	20	*.969
1985—Nashua†‡	East.	2B	105	401	64	109	19	5	1	23	.272	217	249	•29	.941
1986—San Diego§	Nat.	2B	101	241	34	61	5	2	1	12	.253	166	172	10	.971
1987—Las Vegas	P. C.	2B-OF-3B	98	359	66	110	18	10	1	38	.306	147	150	8	.974
1988—Las Vegas	P. C.	3B-OF-2B	100	343	73	121	21	8	7	51	.353	103	130	17	.932
1988—San Diego	Nat.	2B-3B	5	9	1	3	0	0	0	0	.333	2	3	1	.833
Major League Totals—2 Years			106	250	35	64	5	2	1	12	.256	168	175	11	.969

Selected by Pittsburgh Pirates' organization in 5th round of free-agent draft, June 8, 1981.
Selected by Pittsburgh Pirates' organization in secondary phase of free-agent draft, June 7, 1982.
†On suspended list, June 30 to July 3, 1985.
‡Drafted by San Diego Padres, December 10, 1985.
§On disabled list, May 21 to June 5, 1986.

DOUGLAS SCOTT ROBERTSON
(Doug)

Born April 15, 1963, at Upland, Calif.
Height, 6.01. Weight, 185.
Throws and bats righthanded.
Attended California State University, Fullerton, Calif.

Led California League in games finished in relief with 51 and saves with 23 in 1988.
Led Northwest League in wild pitches with 12 in 1985.

Year Club	League	G.	IP.	W.	L.	Pct.	H.	R.	ER.	SO.	BB.	ERA.
1985—Everett	Northwest	13	81⅓	4	4	.500	77	56	40	85	59	4.43
1986—Clinton	Midwest	27	118⅓	3	10	.231	117	78	60	79	73	4.56
1987—Clinton	Midwest	28	164	8	12	.400	185	115	93	173	95	5.10
1988—San Jose	California	57	78⅓	7	5	.583	63	18	11	103	30	1.26

Selected by San Francisco Giants' organization in 3rd round of free-agent draft, June 3, 1985.

WILLIAM JOSEPH ROBIDOUX

Name pronounced ROW-ba-doe.

(Billy Jo)

Born January 13, 1964, at Ware, Mass.
Height, 6.01. Weight, 200.
Throws right and bats lefthanded.

Major League stolen bases: 1988 (1).

Led Texas League in total bases with 297 and slugging percentage with .577 in 1985.

Led Texas League first basemen in putouts with 1,025, assists with 68, fielding percentage with .988, total chances with 1,106 and double plays with 102 in 1985.

Named Texas League Most Valuable Player, 1985.

Year Club	League	Pos.	G.	AB.	R.	H.	2B.	3B.	HR.	RBI.	B.A.	PO.	A.	E.	F.A.
1982—Pikeville†	Appal.	3B-1B	54	167	28	48	10	1	0	13	.287	57	54	15	.881
1983—Beloit	Midw.	3B-1B-2B	126	435	70	138	30	1	10	61	.317	104	163	25	.914
1984—Stockton	Calif.	3B-1B	97	333	50	93	18	1	5	67	.279	323	98	15	.966
1985—El Paso	Texas	1B-OF-3B	133	515	*111	*176	*46	3	23	*132	*.342	1030	69	15	.987
1985—Milwaukee	Amer.	OF-1B	18	51	5	9	2	0	3	8	.176	64	6	0	1.000
1986—Milwaukee‡	Amer.	1B	56	181	15	41	8	0	1	21	.227	326	29	5	.986
1986—Beloit	Midw.	1B	7	16	3	4	2	0	0	2	.250	12	2	0	1.000
1986—El Paso	Texas	1B	30	114	30	37	9	0	10	34	.325	269	11	1	.996
1987—Milwaukee	Amer.	1B	23	62	9	12	0	0	0	4	.194	53	4	1	.983
1987—Denver§	A. A.	1B-3B	30	116	27	33	9	3	3	15	.284	184	14	5	.975
1988—Denver	A. A.	1B	70	240	43	70	24	0	8	42	.292	570	48	8	.987
1988—Milwaukee x	Amer.	1B	33	91	9	23	5	0	0	5	.253	212	25	4	.983
Major League Totals—4 Years			130	385	38	85	15	0	4	38	.221	655	64	10	.986

Selected by Milwaukee Brewers' organization in 6th round of free-agent draft, June 7, 1982.

†On disabled list, June 21 to July 1, 1982.

‡On disabled list, May 13 to June 11 and July 8 to August 20, 1986; included rehabilitation disability assignment to Beloit, June 4 to June 11, and to El Paso, August 1 to August 20, 1986.

§On disabled list, July 16, 1987 through remainder of season.

xGranted free agency, October 15, 1988; signed by Chicago White Sox, October 30, 1988.

DON ALLEN ROBINSON

Born June 8, 1957, at Ashland, Ky.
Height, 6.04. Weight, 231.
Throws and bats righthanded.

Major League saves: 1978 (1), 1980 (1), 1981 (2), 1984 (10), 1985 (3), 1986 (14), 1987 (19), 1988 (6). Total—56.

Tied for National League lead in home runs allowed with 26 in 1982.

Led Western Carolinas League in complete games with 11 in 1976.

Tied for Gulf Coast League lead in hit batsmen with 6 in 1975.

Named National League Rookie Pitcher of the Year by THE SPORTING NEWS, 1978.

Named pitcher on THE SPORTING NEWS National League Silver Slugger team, 1982.

Year Club	League	G.	IP.	W.	L.	Pct.	H.	R.	ER.	SO.	BB.	ERA.
1975—Bradenton Pirates	Gulf Coast	10	66	2	3	.400	51	23	18	*70	31	2.45
1976—Charleston	W. Carol.	25	*172	12	9	.571	146	79	62	132	64	3.24
1977—Shreveport	Texas	18	112	7	6	.538	113	58	51	103	41	4.06
1977—Columbus†	Int'national	1	5	1	0	1.000	7	0	0	3	1	0.00
1978—Pittsburgh	National	35	228	14	6	.700	203	98	88	135	57	3.47
1979—Pittsburgh	National	29	161	8	8	.500	171	74	69	96	52	3.86
1980—Pittsburgh‡	National	29	160	7	10	.412	157	74	71	103	45	3.99
1981—Pittsburgh§	National	16	38	0	3	.000	47	27	25	17	23	5.92
1982—Pittsburgh	National	38	227	15	13	.536	213	*123	108	165	103	4.28
1983—Pittsburgh x	National	9	36⅓	2	2	.500	43	21	18	28	21	4.46
1983—Lynn	Eastern	2	6⅔	0	1	.000	9	6	6	5	2	8.10
1984—Pittsburgh y	National	51	122	5	6	.455	99	45	41	110	49	3.02
1985—Pittsburgh	National	44	95⅓	5	11	.313	95	49	41	65	42	3.87
1986—Pittsburgh z	National	50	69⅓	3	4	.429	61	27	26	53	27	3.38
1986—Prince William	Carolina	3	12⅔	1	1	.500	13	7	1	13	1	0.71
1987—Pittsburgh a-San Francisco	National	67	108	11	7	.611	105	42	41	79	40	3.42
1988—San Francisco	National	51	176⅔	10	5	.667	152	63	48	122	49	2.45
Major League Totals—11 Years		419	1421⅔	80	75	.516	1346	643	576	973	508	3.65

Selected by Pittsburgh Pirates' organization in 3rd round of free-agent draft, June 4, 1975.

†On disabled list, July 28 to September 6, 1977.

‡On disabled list, March 31 to May 1, 1980.

§On disabled list, May 2 to June 6 and August 2 to August 26, 1981.

xOn disabled list, March 29 to June 10 and July 29 to September 2, 1983; included rehabilitation disability assignment to Lynn, April 29 to May 18, 1983.

yAppeared in one game as an outfielder with two putouts.

zOn disabled list, April 21 to June 7, 1986; included rehabilitation disability assignment to Prince William, May 24 to June 7, 1986.

aTraded to San Francisco Giants for Catcher Mackey Sasser and $50,000, July 31, 1987.

CHAMPIONSHIP SERIES RECORD

Year Club	League	G.	IP.	W.	L.	Pct.	H.	R.	ER.	SO.	BB.	ERA.
1979—Pittsburgh	National	2	2	1	0	1.000	0	0	0	3	1	0.00
1987—San Francisco	National	3	3	0	1	.000	3	3	3	3	0	9.00
Championship Series Totals—2 Years		5	5	1	1	.500	3	3	3	6	1	5.40

WORLD SERIES RECORD

Year Club	League	G.	IP.	W.	L.	Pct.	H.	R.	ER.	SO.	BB.	ERA.
1979—Pittsburgh	National	4	5	1	0	1.000	4	3	3	3	6	5.40

JEFFREY DANIEL ROBINSON
(Jeff)

Born December 13, 1960, at Santa Ana, Calif.
Height, 6.04. Weight, 200.
Throws and bats righthanded.
Attended California State University, Fullerton, Calif.

Tied major league record by striking out side on 9 pitches, September 7, 1987 (eighth inning).
Major League saves: 1986 (8), 1987 (14), 1988 (9). Total—31.
Tied for National League lead in hit batsmen with 7 in 1984.
Tied for Pacific Coast League lead in games started by pitchers with 29 in 1985.

Year Club	League	G.	IP.	W.	L.	Pct.	H.	R.	ER.	SO.	BB.	ERA.
1983—Fresno	California	14	94⅔	7	6	.538	88	35	24	78	21	2.28
1984—San Francisco	National	34	171⅔	7	15	.318	195	99	87	102	52	4.56
1985—Phoenix	P. Coast	29	161	9	9	.500	192	107	92	80	60	5.14
1985—San Francisco	National	8	12⅓	0	0	.000	16	11	7	8	10	5.11
1986—San Francisco†	National	64	104⅓	6	3	.667	92	46	39	90	32	3.36
1987—San Francisco‡-Pittsburgh	National	81	123⅓	8	9	.471	89	43	39	101	54	2.85
1988—Pittsburgh	National	75	124⅔	11	5	.688	113	44	42	87	39	3.03
Major League Totals—5 Years		262	536⅓	32	32	.500	505	243	214	388	187	3.59

Selected by Toronto Blue Jays' organization in 17th round of free-agent draft, June 5, 1979.
Selected by Detroit Tigers' organization in 14th round of free-agent draft, June 7, 1982.
Selected by San Francisco Giants' organization in 2nd round of free-agent draft, June 6, 1983.
†Appeared in one game as an outfielder with no chances.
‡Traded with Pitcher Scott Medvin to Pittsburgh Pirates for Pitcher Rick Reuschel, August 21, 1987.

JEFFREY MARK ROBINSON
(Jeff)

Born December 14, 1961, at Ventura, Calif.
Height, 6.06. Weight, 210.
Throws and bats righthanded.
Attended Azusa Pacific University, Azusa, Calif.

Year Club	League	G.	IP.	W.	L.	Pct.	H.	R.	ER.	SO.	BB.	ERA.
1983—Lakeland	Florida St.	11	50	2	5	.286	61	38	33	23	19	5.94
1984—Lakeland	Florida St.	10	61⅔	2	3	.400	62	30	23	33	26	3.36
1984—Birmingham	Southern	20	113	6	6	.500	111	64	59	47	56	4.70
1985—Birmingham†	Southern	22	115	4	8	.333	142	79	65	67	59	5.09
1986—Nashville	Am. Assoc.	25	150	10	7	.588	162	85	73	72	72	4.38
1987—Detroit	American	29	127⅓	9	6	.600	132	86	76	98	54	5.37
1988—Detroit‡	American	24	172	13	6	.684	121	61	57	114	72	2.98
Major League Totals—2 Years		53	299⅓	22	12	.647	253	147	133	212	126	4.00

Selected by San Diego Padres' organization in 40th round of free-agent draft, June 3, 1980.
Selected by Detroit Tigers' organization in 3rd round of free-agent draft, June 6, 1983.
†On disabled list, June 28 to July 10, 1985.
‡On disabled list, August 24, 1988 through remainder of season.

CHAMPIONSHIP SERIES RECORD

Year Club	League	G.	IP.	W.	L.	Pct.	H.	R.	ER.	SO.	BB.	ERA.
1987—Detroit	American	1	⅓	0	0	.000	1	0	0	0	0	0.00

RONALD DEAN ROBINSON
(Ron)

Born March 24, 1962, at Exeter, Calif.
Height, 6.04. Weight, 230.
Throws and bats righthanded.

Major League saves: 1985 (1), 1986 (14), 1987 (4). Total—19.

Year Club	League	G.	IP.	W.	L.	Pct.	H.	R.	ER.	SO.	BB.	ERA.
1980—Tampa	Florida St.	13	76	4	6	.400	76	32	28	44	16	3.32
1981—Cedar Rapids	Midwest	24	169	10	8	.556	136	58	42	165	55	2.24
1982—Waterbury	Eastern	32	178⅓	13	7	.650	166	78	65	149	65	3.28
1983—Waterbury	Eastern	20	142⅔	7	9	.438	132	66	57	82	60	3.60
1983—Indianapolis	Am. Assoc.	4	30⅔	4	0	1.000	22	13	11	20	7	3.23
1984—Wichita	Am. Assoc.	25	150⅓	9	6	.600	168	86	77	98	60	4.61
1984—Cincinnati	National	12	39⅔	1	2	.333	35	18	12	24	13	2.72
1985—Denver	Am. Assoc.	6	39⅔	2	1	.667	39	17	12	24	12	2.72
1985—Cincinnati	National	33	108⅓	7	7	.500	107	53	48	76	32	3.99
1986—Cincinnati	National	70	116⅔	10	3	.769	110	44	42	117	43	3.24
1987—Cincinnati	National	48	154	7	5	.583	148	71	63	99	43	3.68
1988—Cincinnati†	National	17	78⅔	3	7	.300	88	47	36	38	26	4.12
1988—Nashville	Am. Assoc.	2	3⅔	0	0	.000	4	3	3	4	3	7.36
Major League Totals—5 Years		180	497⅓	28	24	.538	488	233	201	354	157	3.64

Selected by Cincinnati Reds' organization in 1st round (19th player selected) of free-agent draft, June 3, 1980.
†On disabled list, June 25 to July 18 and July 20 to September 2, 1988; included rehabilitation disability assignment to Nashville, August 15 to September 2, 1988.

MICHAEL JOSEPH ROCHFORD
(Mike)

Born March 14, 1963, at Methuen, Mass.
Height, 6.04. Weight, 205.
Throws and bats lefthanded.
Attended Santa Fe Community College, Gainsville, Fla.

Led International League in balks with 5 in 1984.
Tied for Carolina League lead in games started by pitchers with 29 in 1983.

Year Club	League	G.	IP.	W.	L.	Pct.	H.	R.	ER.	SO.	BB.	ERA.
1982—Elmira	NYP	16	85⅔	6	4	.600	99	53	40	66	26	4.20
1983—Winston-Salem	Carolina	29	210⅓	16	11	.593	182	85	70	165	57	3.00
1984—Pawtucket	Int'national	31	141⅓	8	10	.444	156	88	77	73	59	4.90
1985—New Britain	Eastern	14	93⅓	8	5	.615	84	39	31	42	41	2.99
1985—Pawtucket	Int'national	12	72	5	2	.714	74	34	33	47	32	4.13
1986—Pawtucket	Int'national	28	170⅔	11	10	.524	178	76	67	70	50	3.53
1987—Pawtucket	Int'national	22	123⅔	8	8	.500	144	65	63	42	38	4.58
1988—Pawtucket	Int'national	52	81⅔	1	5	.167	68	30	28	47	29	3.09
1988—Boston	American	2	2⅓	0	0	.000	4	0	0	1	1	0.00
Major League Totals—1 Year		2	2⅓	0	0	.000	4	0	0	1	1	0.00

Selected by Boston Red Sox' organization in 1st round (17th player selected) of free-agent draft, January 12, 1982.

RICARDO RODRIGUEZ
(Rick)

Born September 21, 1960, at Oakland, Calif.
Height, 6.02. Weight, 200.
Throws and bats righthanded.
Attended Chabot College, Hayward, Calif., and University of California, Riverside, Calif.

Year Club	League	G.	IP.	W.	L.	Pct.	H.	R.	ER.	SO.	BB.	ERA.
1981—Modesto	California	11	63	2	5	.286	68	51	37	28	28	5.29
1982—Modesto†	California	15	105⅔	8	2	.800	100	38	32	70	41	2.73
1983—Tacoma‡	P. Coast	10	58	1	4	.200	61	32	25	25	28	3.88
1984—Modesto§	California	2	13⅓	0	0	.000	11	3	3	6	5	2.03
1984—Tacoma	P. Coast	6	16⅓	0	1	.000	21	17	16	9	7	8.82
1984—Albany	Eastern	10	42⅔	5	1	.833	59	33	25	29	19	5.27
1985—Modesto	California	16	103⅔	8	1	.889	103	42	38	50	41	3.30
1985—Huntsville	Southern	8	50	2	1	.667	40	18	13	25	13	2.34
1985—Tacoma	P. Coast	7	13⅓	0	1	.000	18	9	6	5	7	4.05
1986—Huntsville	Southern	9	16	0	0	.000	17	11	9	14	7	5.06
1986—Tacoma	P. Coast	26	139	7	8	.467	144	82	61	76	59	3.95
1986—Oakland	American	3	16⅓	1	2	.333	17	12	12	2	7	6.61
1987—Oakland	American	15	24⅓	1	0	1.000	32	8	8	9	15	2.96
1987—Tacoma x	P. Coast	21	92⅓	5	4	.556	90	39	34	52	36	3.31
1988—Colorado Springs	P. Coast	19	126⅔	8	6	.571	112	49	43	55	43	3.06
1988—Cleveland y	American	10	33	1	2	.333	43	28	26	9	17	7.09
Major League Totals—3 Years		28	73⅔	3	4	.429	92	48	46	20	39	5.62

Selected by Oakland A's organization in 2nd round of free-agent draft, June 8, 1981.
†On disabled list, May 15 to July 23, 1982.
‡On disabled list, April 10 to May 14 and July 1, 1983 through remainder of season.
§On Tacoma disabled list, April 7 to May 23 and June 12 to June 22, 1984.
xReleased, December 21, 1987; signed by Cleveland Indians, January 15, 1988.
yGranted free agency, October 15, 1988; signed by Chicago White Sox' organization, November 8, 1988.

RUBEN DARIO RODRIGUEZ (MARTINEZ)

Born August 4, 1964, at Cabrera, Dominican Republic.
Height, 6.00. Weight, 175.
Throws and bats righthanded.

Led Pacific Coast League catchers in double plays with 11 and passed balls with 22 in 1987.
Led Eastern League in passed balls with 17 in 1985.
Led Eastern League catchers in double plays with 10 in 1984.

Year Club	League	Pos.	G.	AB.	R.	H.	2B.	3B.	HR.	RBI.	B.A.	PO.	A.	E.	F.A.
1982—Greenwood†	S. Atl.	C	69	218	26	54	13	0	1	15	.248	351	60	19	.956
1983—Alexandria	Carol.	C-1B	79	254	19	58	14	1	4	31	.228	496	70	11	.981
1984—Nashua	East.	C	87	242	26	53	13	1	4	32	.219	409	58	11	.977
1985—Nashua	East.	C	104	341	28	73	9	4	3	40	.214	498	96	11	.982
1985—Hawaii	P. C.	C	1	4	0	1	0	0	0	0	.250	9	0	0	1.000
1986—Nashua	East.	C	53	169	17	31	10	2	0	12	.183	318	47	6	.984
1986—Hawaii	P. C.	C	30	108	11	28	5	2	0	15	.259	201	23	6	.974
1986—Pittsburgh	Nat.	C	2	3	0	0	0	0	0	0	.000	6	1	0	1.000
1987—Vancouver	P. C.	★C-P	88	285	24	63	5	4	1	28	.221	524	★69	11	.982
1988—Harrisburg	East.	C	48	160	12	44	7	1	0	19	.275	311	30	6	.983
1988—Buffalo	A. A.	C	24	82	4	21	3	1	0	2	.256	135	14	4	.974
1988—Pittsburgh	Nat.	C	2	5	1	1	0	1	0	1	.200	9	0	0	1.000
Major League Totals—2 Years			4	8	1	1	0	1	0	1	.125	15	1	0	1.000

Signed as free agent by Pittsburgh Pirates' organization, November 6, 1981.
†On disabled list, May 10 to May 25, 1982.

PITCHING RECORD

Year	Club	League	G.	IP.	W.	L.	Pct.	H.	R.	ER.	SO.	BB.	ERA.
1987	Vancouver	P. Coast	1	1	0	0	.000	1	2	2	0	3	18.00

GARY STEVEN ROENICKE

Name pronounced RENN-uh-kee.

Born December 5, 1954, at Covina, Calif.
Height, 6.03. Weight, 200.
Throws and bats righthanded.
Attended California Poly State University, Pomona, Calif., Whittier College, Whittier, Calif., and University of California at Los Angeles, Los Angeles, Calif.
Brother of Ron Roenicke, outfielder with Los Angeles Dodgers, Seattle Mariners, San Diego Padres, San Francisco Giants, Philadelphia Phillies and Cincinnati Reds, 1981 through 1988.

Major League stolen bases: 1979 (1), 1980 (2), 1981 (1), 1982 (6), 1983 (2), 1984 (1), 1985 (2), 1986 (1). Total—16.
Led American Association in being hit by pitch with 13 in 1977.
Led Florida State League in being hit by pitch with 11 in 1974.
Tied for Eastern League lead in being hit by pitch with 12 in 1975.
Tied for Florida State League lead in double plays by third basemen with 32 in 1974.
Named Eastern League Most Valuable Player, 1975.

Year	Club	League	Pos.	G.	AB.	R.	H.	2B.	3B.	HR.	RBI.	B.A.	PO.	A.	E.	F.A.
1973	Jamestown	NYP	3B	68	255	48	76	17	6	3	40	.298	*71	92	11	*.937
1974	W. Palm Beach	Fla. St.	3B-OF-1B	131	470	68	130	24	0	14	*82	.277	152	216	31	.922
1974	Quebec City	East.	3B	1	3	0	1	0	0	0	0	.333	1	2	0	1.000
1975	Quebec City	East.	OF	131	466	67	133	23	0	14	*74	.285	223	*22	10	.961
1976	Denver	A. A.	OF	77	252	56	73	11	5	12	44	.290	110	9	5	.960
1976	Montreal	Nat.	OF	29	90	9	20	3	1	2	5	.222	39	3	2	.955
1977	Denver†	A. A.	OF-3B-1B	124	448	87	144	31	4	11	72	.321	174	113	17	.944
1978	Rochester	Int.	OF-1B-3B	98	329	49	101	15	1	13	64	.307	219	25	2	.992
1978	Baltimore	Amer.	OF	27	58	5	15	3	0	3	15	.259	22	1	0	1.000
1979	Baltimore	Amer.	OF	133	376	60	98	16	1	25	64	.261	246	10	5	.981
1980	Baltimore‡	Amer.	OF	118	297	40	71	13	0	10	28	.239	197	8	0	*1.000
1981	Baltimore	Amer.	OF	85	219	31	59	16	0	3	20	.269	175	2	3	.983
1982	Baltimore	Amer.	OF-1B	137	393	58	106	25	1	21	74	.270	363	13	3	.992
1983	Baltimore	Amer.	OF-1B-3B	115	323	45	84	13	0	19	64	.260	219	9	3	.987
1984	Baltimore	Amer.	OF	121	326	36	73	19	1	10	44	.224	197	6	1	.995
1985	Baltimore§	Amer.	OF	114	225	36	49	9	0	15	43	.218	134	6	1	.993
1986	New York x	Amer.	OF-3B-1B	69	136	11	36	5	0	3	18	.265	46	6	0	1.000
1987	Atlanta	Nat.	OF-1B	67	151	25	33	8	0	9	28	.219	110	7	2	.983
1988	Atlanta y	Nat.	OF-1B	49	114	11	26	5	0	1	7	.228	53	0	0	1.000
American League Totals—9 Years				919	2353	322	591	119	3	109	370	.251	1599	61	16	.990
National League Totals—3 Years				145	355	45	79	16	1	12	40	.223	202	10	4	.981
Major League Totals—12 Years				1064	2708	367	670	135	4	121	410	.247	1801	71	20	.989

Selected by Montreal Expos' organization in 1st round (eighth player selected) of free-agent draft, June 5, 1973.
†Traded with Pitchers Joe Kerrigan and Don Stanhouse to Baltimore Orioles for Pitchers Rudy May, Randy Miller and Bryn Smith, December 7, 1977.
‡On disabled list, June 10 to July 15, 1980.
§Traded with a player to be named later to New York Yankees for Pitcher Rich Bordi and Infielder Rex Hudler, December 12, 1985; New York acquired Outfielder Leo Hernandez to complete deal, December 16, 1985.
xGranted free agency, November 12, 1986; signed by Atlanta Braves, January 23, 1987.
yReleased, July 26, 1988.

CHAMPIONSHIP SERIES RECORD

Tied Championship Series record for most consecutive games, one or more runs batted in, total Series (4).
Tied American League Championship Series record for most bases on balls, four-game Series (5), 1983.

Year	Club	League	Pos.	G.	AB.	R.	H.	2B.	3B.	HR.	RBI.	B.A.	PO.	A.	E.	F.A.
1979	Baltimore	Amer.	OF-PH	2	5	1	1	0	0	0	1	.200	3	1	0	1.000
1983	Baltimore	Amer.	OF-PH	3	4	4	3	1	0	1	4	.750	4	1	0	1.000
Championship Series Totals—2 Years				5	9	5	4	1	0	1	5	.444	7	2	0	1.000

WORLD SERIES RECORD

Year	Club	League	Pos.	G.	AB.	R.	H.	2B.	3B.	HR.	RBI.	B.A.	PO.	A.	E.	F.A.
1979	Baltimore	Amer.	OF-PH	6	16	1	2	1	0	0	0	.125	14	1	0	1.000
1983	Baltimore	Amer.	PH-OF	3	7	0	0	0	0	0	0	.000	2	1	0	1.000
World Series Totals—2 Years				9	23	1	2	1	0	0	0	.087	16	2	0	1.000

RONALD JON ROENICKE

Name pronounced RENN-uh-kee.

(Ron)

Born August 19, 1956, at Covina, Calif.
Height, 6.00. Weight, 180.
Throws left and bats left and righthanded.
Attended Mount San Antonio College, Walnut, Calif., and University of California, Los Angeles, Calif.
Brother of Gary Roenicke, outfielder with Montreal Expos, Baltimore Orioles, New York Yankees and Atlanta Braves, 1976 and 1978 through 1988.

Major League stolen bases: 1981 (1), 1982 (5), 1983 (9), 1985 (6), 1986 (2), 1987 (1). Total—24.

Led Pacific Coast League in on-base percentage with .464, bases on balls received with 110, and sacrifice flies with 16 in 1981.

Led Texas League outfielders in fielding percentage with .993 in 1979.

Year Club	League	Pos.	G.	AB.	R.	H.	2B.	3B.	HR.	RBI.	B.A.	PO.	A.	E.	F.A.
1977—Clinton	Midw.	OF-1B	76	250	35	64	12	0	5	25	.256	253	7	4	.985
1978—Lodi†	Calif.	OF	61	215	61	78	13	5	9	51	.363	100	8	6	.947
1978—San Antonio	Texas	OF	30	109	16	26	2	2	1	11	.239	51	4	2	.965
1979—San Antonio	Texas	OF-1B	130	464	82	140	24	6	13	69	.302	426	18	4	.991
1980—Albuquerque‡	P. C.	OF-1B	77	270	60	80	18	3	7	47	.296	167	9	8	.957
1981—Albuquerque	P. C.	OF-1B	126	411	100	130	23	9	15	94	.316	217	14	4	.983
1981—Los Angeles	Nat.	OF	22	47	6	11	0	0	0	0	.234	38	1	0	1.000
1982—Albuquerque	P. C.	OF	23	78	18	24	5	1	4	15	.308	14	1	0	1.000
1982—Los Angeles	Nat.	OF	109	143	18	37	8	0	1	12	.259	59	1	1	.984
1983—Los Angeles§	Nat.	OF	81	145	12	32	4	0	2	12	.221	75	1	1	.987
1983—Seattle x	Amer.	OF-1B	59	198	23	50	12	0	4	23	.253	168	13	2	.989
1984—Las Vegas y	P. C.	OF-1B	90	290	65	90	14	3	8	45	.310	161	7	1	.994
1984—San Diego z	Nat.	OF	12	20	4	6	1	0	1	2	.300	10	0	0	1.000
1985—Phoenix	P. C.	OF-1B	60	214	36	66	16	0	5	48	.308	130	6	1	.993
1985—San Francisco a	Nat.	OF	65	133	23	34	9	1	3	13	.256	63	0	1	.984
1986—Tacoma b	P. C.	OF	20	72	13	16	3	0	0	7	.222	33	1	1	.971
1986—Philadelphia	Nat.	OF	102	275	42	68	13	1	5	42	.247	181	3	2	.989
1987—Philadelphia	Nat.	OF	63	78	9	13	3	1	1	4	.167	26	1	1	.964
1987—Maine c	Int.	OF	38	124	15	30	10	0	1	15	.242	93	2	1	.990
1988—Nashville	A. A.	OF-1B	83	237	34	51	7	3	0	16	.215	150	4	1	.994
1988—Cincinnati d	Nat.	OF	14	37	4	5	1	0	0	5	.135	18	0	0	1.000
National League Totals—8 Years			468	878	118	206	39	3	13	90	.235	470	7	6	.988
American League Totals—1 Year			59	198	23	50	12	0	4	23	.253	168	13	2	.989
Major League Totals—8 Years			527	1076	141	256	51	3	17	113	.238	638	20	8	.988

Selected by Oakland A's organization in 7th round of free-agent draft, June 5, 1974.
Selected by Detroit Tigers' organization in secondary phase of free-agent draft, January 7, 1976.
Selected by Atlanta Braves' organization in secondary phase of free-agent draft, June 8, 1976.
Selected by Los Angeles Dodgers' organization in secondary phase of free agent draft, June 7, 1977.
†On disabled list, June 11 to July 17, 1978.
‡On disabled list, July 1 to August 27, 1980.
§Released, July 18, 1983; signed by Seattle Mariners, July 26, 1983.
xReleased, March 23, 1984; signed by Las Vegas (San Diego Padres' organization), April 5, 1984.
yOn disabled list, June 19 to July 29, 1984.
zReleased, March 30, 1985; signed by Phoenix (San Francisco Giants' organization), May 3, 1985.
aReleased, April 1, 1986; signed by Oakland A's organization, April 7, 1986.
bSold to Philadelphia Phillies, May 9, 1986.
cReleased, November 3, 1987; signed by Cincinnati Reds' organization, January 5, 1988.
dGranted free agency, October 15, 1988.

WORLD SERIES RECORD

Year Club	League	Pos.	G.	AB.	R.	H.	2B.	3B.	HR.	RBI.	B.A.	PO.	A.	E.	F.A.
1984—San Diego	Nat.	OF-PR	2	0	0	0	0	0	0	0	.000	0	0	0	.000

MICHAEL JOSEPH ROESLER

Name pronounced RESS-ler.

(Mike)

Born September 12, 1963, at Fort Wayne, Ind.
Height, 6.05. Weight, 195.
Throws and bats righthanded.
Attended Ball State University, Muncie, Ind.

Year Club	League	G.	IP.	W.	L.	Pct.	H.	R.	ER.	SO.	BB.	ERA.
1985—Billings	Pioneer	13	$88\frac{2}{3}$	8	2	.800	72	32	23	73	28	2.33
1986—Cedar Rapids	Midwest	32	163	9	13	.409	165	95	83	135	80	4.58
1987—Tampa	Florida St.	28	$36\frac{1}{3}$	7	2	.778	30	14	9	29	15	2.23
1987—Vermont	Eastern	22	$27\frac{1}{3}$	4	2	.667	28	10	10	19	10	3.29
1988—Chattanooga	Southern	16	$20\frac{1}{3}$	1	1	.500	16	5	5	13	8	2.21
1988—Nashville	Am. Assoc.	32	$41\frac{1}{3}$	3	2	.600	44	25	23	31	27	5.01

Selected by Cincinnati Reds' organization in 17th round of free-agent draft, June 3, 1985.

KENNETH SCOTT ROGERS

(Ken)

Born November 10, 1964, at Savannah, Ga.
Height, 6.01. Weight, 200.
Throws and bats lefthanded.

Year Club	League	G.	IP.	W.	L.	Pct.	H.	R.	ER.	SO.	BB.	ERA.
1982—Sarasota Rangers	Gulf Coast	2	3	0	0	.000	0	0	0	4	0	0.00
1983—Sarasota Rangers	Gulf Coast	15	$53\frac{1}{3}$	4	1	.800	40	21	14	36	20	2.36
1984—Burlington	Midwest	39	$92\frac{2}{3}$	4	7	.364	87	52	41	93	33	3.98
1985—Daytona Beach	Florida St.	6	10	0	1	.000	12	9	8	9	11	7.20
1985—Burlington	Midwest	33	95	2	5	.286	67	34	30	96	62	2.84
1986—Tulsa†	Texas	10	$26\frac{1}{3}$	0	3	.000	39	30	29	23	18	9.91
1986—Salem	Carolina	12	66	2	7	.222	75	54	46	46	26	6.27
1987—Charlotte	Florida St.	5	17	0	3	.000	17	13	9	14	8	4.76

Year	Club	League	G.	IP.	W.	L.	Pct.	H.	R.	ER.	SO.	BB.	ERA.
1987	—Tulsa	Texas	28	69	1	5	.167	80	51	41	59	35	5.35
1988	—Tulsa	Texas	13	83⅓	4	6	.400	73	43	37	76	34	4.00
1988	—Port Charlotte	Florida St.	8	35⅓	2	0	1.000	22	8	5	26	11	1.27

Selected by Texas Rangers' organization in 39th round of free-agent draft, June 7, 1982.
†On disabled list, April 12 to April 30, 1986.

EDGARDO ROMERO
(Ed)

Born December 9, 1957, at Santurce, Puerto Rico.
Height, 5.11. Weight, 180.
Throws and bats righthanded.
Attended Engineer College, Mayaquez, Puerto Rico.

Major League stolen bases: 1980 (2), 1983 (1), 1984 (3), 1985 (1), 1986 (2). Total—9.
Led Pacific Coast League shortstops in double plays with 97 in 1979.
Led Midwest League shortstops in total chances with 647 and double plays with 64 in 1976.

Year	Club	League	Pos.	G.	AB.	R.	H.	2B.	3B.	HR.	RBI.	B.A.	PO.	A.	E.	F.A.
1976	—Burlington	Midwest	SS	•129	462	58	101	23	1	1	32	.219	187	*419	41	.937
1977	—Holyoke	East.	SS	121	457	63	118	19	6	1	38	.258	203	372	41	.933
1977	—Milwaukee	Amer.	SS	10	25	4	7	1	0	0	2	.280	9	24	1	.971
1978	—Spokane	P. C.	SS-3B	129	440	73	123	27	2	4	52	.280	221	349	32	.947
1979	—Vancouver	P. C.	SS	139	515	65	134	26	6	0	39	.260	215	*414	26	.960
1980	—Vancouver	P. C.	SS-2B	50	172	19	47	7	1	0	16	.273	72	153	6	.974
1980	—Milwaukee	Amer.	SS-2B-3B	42	104	20	27	7	0	1	10	.260	60	102	12	.931
1981	—Milwaukee	Amer.	SS-3B-2B	44	91	6	18	3	0	1	10	.198	61	102	6	.964
1982	—Milwaukee	Amer.	2-S-3-O	52	144	18	36	8	0	1	7	.250	103	113	7	.969
1983	—Milwaukee	Amer.	S-O-3-2	59	145	17	46	7	0	1	18	.317	59	58	5	.959
1984	—Milwaukee	Amer.	3-S-2-1-O	116	357	36	90	12	0	1	31	.252	141	256	18	.957
1985	—Milwaukee†	Amer.	S-2-O-3	88	251	24	63	11	1	0	21	.251	157	219	8	.979
1986	—Boston	Amer.	S-3-2-O	100	233	41	49	11	0	2	23	.210	111	159	12	.957
1987	—Boston	Amer.	2-S-3-1	88	235	23	64	5	0	0	14	.272	122	151	6	.978
1988	—Boston‡	Amer.	3-S-2-1	31	75	3	18	3	0	0	5	.240	21	42	0	1.000
Major League Totals—10 Years				630	1660	192	418	68	1	7	141	.252	844	1226	75	.965

Signed as free agent by Milwaukee Brewers' organization, November 14, 1975.
†Traded to Boston Red Sox for Pitcher Mark Clear, December 11, 1985.
‡On disabled list, June 6 to July 21, 1988.

DIVISION SERIES RECORD

Year	Club	League	Pos.	G.	AB.	R.	H.	2B.	3B.	HR.	RBI.	B.A.	PO.	A.	E.	F.A.
1981	—Milwaukee	Amer.	2B	1	2	1	1	0	0	0	0	.500	2	2	0	1.000

CHAMPIONSHIP SERIES RECORD

Year	Club	League	Pos.	G.	AB.	R.	H.	2B.	3B.	HR.	RBI.	B.A.	PO.	A.	E.	F.A.
1986	—Boston	Amer.	PR-SS	1	2	0	0	0	0	0	0	.000	0	0	0	.000
1988	—Boston	Amer.	PR	1	0	0	0	0	0	0	0	.000	0	0	0	.000
Championship Series Totals—2 Years				2	2	0	0	0	0	0	0	.000	0	0	0	.000

WORLD SERIES RECORD

Year	Club	League	Pos.	G.	AB.	R.	H.	2B.	3B.	HR.	RBI.	B.A.	PO.	A.	E.	F.A.
1986	—Boston	Amer.	PR-SS	3	1	0	0	0	0	0	0	.000	0	1	0	1.000

KEVIN ANDREW ROMINE

Name pronounced Ro-MINE.

Born May 23, 1961, at Exeter, N.H.
Height, 5.11. Weight, 185.
Throws and bats righthanded.
Attended Orange Coast College, Costa Mesa, Calif., and
Arizona State University, Tempe, Ariz.

Major League stolen bases: 1985 (1), 1986 (2), 1988 (2). Total—5.
Tied for Eastern League lead in double plays by outfielders with 4 in 1983.
Named outfielder on THE SPORTING NEWS College Baseball All-America Team, 1982.

Year	Club	League	Pos.	G.	AB.	R.	H.	2B.	3B.	HR.	RBI.	B.A.	PO.	A.	E.	F.A.
1982	—Winter Haven	Fla. St.	OF	55	201	24	51	4	4	3	22	.254	97	6	3	.972
1983	—New Britain	East.	OF	132	467	74	122	26	5	11	80	.261	211	12	4	.982
1984	—Pawtucket†	Int.	OF	113	336	62	85	10	1	12	72	.253	202	12	5	.977
1985	—Pawtucket‡	Int.	OF	106	403	43	98	20	1	5	33	.243	246	9	8	.970
1985	—Boston	Amer.	OF	24	28	3	6	2	0	0	1	.214	20	1	0	1.000
1986	—Pawtucket	Int.	OF	71	257	30	75	8	3	4	32	.292	162	2	2	.988
1986	—Boston	Amer.	OF	35	35	6	9	2	0	0	2	.257	45	1	0	1.000
1987	—Pawtucket	Int.	OF	129	491	72	131	24	1	11	52	.267	311	6	3	.991
1987	—Boston	Amer.	OF	9	24	5	7	2	0	0	2	.292	10	1	0	1.000
1988	—Boston	Amer.	OF	57	78	17	15	2	1	1	6	.192	44	0	2	.957
1988	—Pawtucket	Int.	OF	41	148	18	53	6	1	4	26	.358	71	5	0	1.000
Major League Totals—4 Years				125	165	31	37	8	1	1	11	.224	119	3	2	.984

Selected by California Angels' organization in 3rd round of free-agent draft, January 8, 1980.

Selected by Philadelphia Phillies' organization in secondary phase of free-agent draft, June 3, 1980.
Selected by Boston Red Sox' organization in second round of free-agent draft, June 7, 1982.
†On disabled list, July 18 to July 31, 1984.
‡On disabled list, July 6 to July 17, 1985.

CHAMPIONSHIP SERIES RECORD

Year	Club	League	Pos.	G.	AB.	R.	H.	2B.	3B.	HR.	RBI.	B.A.	PO.	A.	E.	F.A.
1988	Boston	Amer.	PR	2	0	1	0	0	0	0	0	.000	0	0	0	.000

ROLANDO AUDLEY ROOMES

Born February 15, 1962, in Jamaica, West Indies.
Height, 6.03. Weight, 180.
Throws and bats righthanded.

Led American Association batters in strikeouts with 134 in 1988.
Led Eastern League batters in strikeouts with 135 in 1987.
Led Midwest League batters in strikeouts with 167 in 1983.
Led New York-Pennsylvania League outfielders in double plays with 4 in 1982.

Year	Club	League	Pos.	G.	AB.	R.	H.	2B.	3B.	HR.	RBI.	B.A.	PO.	A.	E.	F.A.
1980	Sarasota Cubs	Gulf C.	OF	19	48	11	7	1	0	2	3	.146	19	1	4	.833
1981	Sarasota Cubs	Gulf C.	OF	63	207	31	48	4	9	2	25	.232	80	7	5	.946
1982	Quad Cities	Midw.	OF	31	80	11	12	1	0	3	8	.150	50	1	3	.944
1982	Geneva	NYP	OF	65	251	57	80	11	3	22	59	.319	129	8	8	.945
1983	Quad Cities	Midw.	OF	122	416	47	89	6	4	9	40	.214	216	*22	14	.944
1984	Lodi	Calif.	OF	116	377	52	100	12	2	13	52	.265	194	11	8	.962
1985	Winston-Salem	Carol.	OF	131	433	57	105	19	6	13	51	.242	254	14	6	.978
1986	Winston-Salem	Carol.	OF	19	68	10	15	3	0	6	14	.238	22	0	0	1.000
1986	Pittsfield	East.	OF	79	191	24	52	5	3	7	42	.272	91	4	7	.931
1987	Pittsfield	East.	OF	129	503	100	155	19	*12	21	95	.308	268	13	6	.979
1988	Chicago	Nat.	OF	17	16	3	3	0	0	0	0	.188	5	0	1	.833
1988	Iowa†	A. A.	OF	112	419	65	126	19	5	16	66	.301	247	12	9	.966
Major League Totals—1 Year				17	16	3	3	0	0	0	0	.188	5	0	1	.833

Signed as free agent by Chicago Cubs' organization, July 14, 1980.
†Traded to Cincinnati Reds for Catcher Lloyd McClendon, December 9, 1988.

STEVEN ALAN ROSENBERG
(Steve)

Born October 31, 1964, at Brooklyn, N.Y.
Height, 6.00. Weight, 185.
Throws and bats lefthanded.
Attended University of Florida, Gainesville, Fla.

Major League saves: 1988 (1).

Year	Club	League	G.	IP.	W.	L.	Pct.	H.	R.	ER.	SO.	BB.	ERA.
1986	Oneonta	NYP	4	9	0	0	.000	4	1	1	10	2	1.00
1986	Fort Lauderdale	Florida St.	25	29⅔	6	1	.857	24	7	7	26	18	2.12
1987	Albany	Eastern	32	40	4	4	.500	33	11	10	24	12	2.25
1987	Columbus†	Int'national	21	35⅓	4	1	.800	43	17	16	27	18	4.08
1988	Vancouver	P. Coast	20	24⅓	2	0	1.000	15	9	9	17	11	3.33
1988	Chicago	American	33	46	0	1	.000	53	22	22	28	19	4.30
Major League Totals—1 Year			33	46	0	1	.000	53	22	22	28	19	4.30

Selected by New York Yankees' organization in 4th round of free-agent draft, June 2, 1986.
†Traded with Outfielder Dan Pasqua and Catcher Mark Salas to Chicago White Sox for Pitchers Richard Dotson and Scott Nielsen, November 12, 1987.

MARK JOSEPH ROSS

Born August 8, 1957, at Galveston, Tex.
Height, 6.00. Weight, 195.
Throws and bats righthanded.

Received bachelor of business degree in finance from Texas A&M University, College Station, Tex. in 1979.
Major League saves: 1985 (1).
Led Pacific Coast League in games finished in relief with 45 and saves with 20 in 1984.
Led Southern League in games finished in relief with 59, intentional bases on balls issued with 12 and tied for lead in saves with 22 in 1981.

Year	Club	League	G.	IP.	W.	L.	Pct.	H.	R.	ER.	SO.	BB.	ERA.
1979	Sarasota Astros	Gulf Coast	2	7	1	0	1.000	5	3	3	2	1	3.86
1980	Daytona Beach	Florida St.	30	58	5	3	.625	50	14	11	39	11	1.71
1980	Columbus	Southern	14	27	2	2	.500	30	11	11	13	4	3.67
1981	Columbus	Southern	*64	116	8	10	.444	103	35	29	70	32	*2.25
1982	Tucson	P. Coast	43	83	4	3	.571	106	55	45	35	32	4.88
1982	Houston	National	4	6	0	0	.000	3	1	1	4	0	1.50
1983	Columbus†	Southern	13	27⅓	1	1	.500	27	8	8	12	16	2.63
1983	Tucson	P. Coast	6	6⅓	0	2	.000	14	10	7	2	4	9.95
1984	Tucson	P. Coast	57	92	5	6	.455	88	35	30	32	24	2.93
1984	Houston	National	2	2⅓	1	0	1.000	1	0	0	1	0	0.00
1985	Tucson	P. Coast	46	77	8	5	.615	109	38	31	31	21	3.62

Year	Club	League	G.	IP.	W.	L.	Pct.	H.	R.	ER.	SO.	BB.	ERA.
1985	—Houston‡	National	8	13	0	2	.000	12	7	7	3	2	4.85
1986	—Tucson§	P. Coast	48	73⅓	5	5	.500	99	37	34	26	20	4.17
1987	—Vancouver	P. Coast	32	89⅓	5	6	.455	87	40	30	48	21	3.02
1987	—Pittsburgh x	National	1	1	0	0	.000	1	1	1	0	0	9.00
1988	—Syracuse	Int'national	17	99⅔	3	8	.273	101	50	40	57	19	3.61
1988	—Toronto y	American	3	7⅓	0	0	.000	5	6	4	4	4	4.91
National League Totals—4 Years			15	22⅓	1	2	.333	17	9	9	8	2	3.63
American League Totals—1 Year			3	7⅓	0	0	.000	5	6	4	4	4	4.91
Major League Totals—5 Years			18	29⅔	1	2	.000	22	15	13	12	6	3.94

Selected by Houston Astros' organization in 7th round of free-agent draft, June 5, 1979.
†On Tucson disabled list, April 11 to June 27, 1983.
‡Traded to St. Louis Cardinals for a player to be named later, December 9, 1985.
§Granted free agency, October 15, 1986; signed by Vancouver (Pittsburgh Pirates' organization), December 4, 1986.
xGranted free agency, October 15, 1987; signed by Syracuse (Toronto Blue Jays' organization), February 22, 1988.
yGranted free agency, October 15, 1988.

WADE LEE ROWDON

Born September 7, 1960, at Riverhead, N.Y.
Height, 6.02. Weight, 170.
Throws and bats righthanded.
Attended Stetson University, Deland, Fla.

Major League stolen bases: 1986 (2), 1988 (1). Total—3.
Led American Association in total bases with 230 in 1985.
Led Eastern League third basemen in fielding percentage with .940 in 1983.
Led Midwest League third basemen in total chances with 362 and double plays with 24 in 1982.

Year	Club	League	Pos.	G.	AB.	R.	H.	2B.	3B.	HR.	RBI.	B.A.	PO.	A.	E.	F.A.
1981	—Sarasota W. Sox	Gulf C.	SS	3	6	2	3	0	0	0	1	.500	1	3	0	1.000
1982	—Appleton†	Midw.	3B	126	433	75	123	19	8	12	79	.284	81	*264	17	*.953
1983	—Waterbury	East.	3B-2B-1B	135	480	62	112	29	1	21	76	.233	173	231	22	.948
1984	—Wichita	A. A.	SS-3B	144	479	78	120	30	4	16	72	.251	175	295	28	.944
1984	—Cincinnati	Nat.	SS-3B	4	7	0	2	0	0	0	0	.286	3	5	0	1.000
1985	—Denver	A. A.	3B-SS-2B	128	457	61	132	31	5	19	78	.289	148	277	25	.944
1985	—Cincinnati	Nat.	3B	5	9	2	2	0	0	0	2	.222	1	3	2	.667
1986	—Denver	A. A.	3-O-S-1	55	180	36	60	12	4	8	37	.333	56	48	11	.904
1986	—Cincinnati‡	Nat.	3-S-O-2	38	80	9	20	5	1	0	10	.250	22	34	6	.903
1987	—Iowa	A. A.	3-S-1-O	132	483	91	163	35	8	18	*113	.337	117	240	28	.927
1987	—Chicago§	Nat.	3B	11	31	2	7	1	1	1	4	.226	3	15	4	.818
1988	—Baltimore	Amer.	3B-OF	20	30	1	3	0	0	0	0	.100	7	14	1	.955
1988	—Rochester x	Int.	2B-SS-3B	86	329	41	83	17	4	7	33	.252	135	231	15	.961
National League Totals—4 Years				58	127	13	31	6	2	1	16	.244	29	57	12	.878
American League Totals—1 Year				20	30	1	3	0	0	0	0	.100	7	14	1	.955
Major League Totals—5 Years				78	157	14	34	6	2	1	16	.217	36	71	13	.892

Selected by Chicago White Sox' organization in 8th round of free-agent draft, June 8, 1981.
†Traded with Outfielder Leo Garcia to Cincinnati Reds' organization, September 7, 1982, completing deal in which Cincinnati traded Pitcher Jim Kern to Chicago White Sox for two players to be named later, August 23, 1982.
‡Traded to Chicago Cubs' organization, February 23, 1987, completing deal in which Chicago traded Pitcher Guy Hoffman to Cincinnati Reds for a player to be named later, February 17, 1987.
§Traded to Baltimore Orioles for Shortstop Nick Ramirez and Pitcher Tom Michno, March 29, 1988.
xReleased, November 14, 1988.

JERON KENNIS ROYSTER
(Jerry)

Born October 18, 1952, at Sacramento, Calif.
Height, 6.00. Weight, 165.
Throws and bats righthanded.
Attended Healds Business College, Sacramento, Calif.
Cousin of Ricky Reynolds, cornerback with Tampa Bay Buccaneers.

Major League stolen bases: 1973 (1), 1975 (1), 1976 (24), 1977 (28), 1978 (27), 1979 (35), 1980 (22), 1981 (7), 1982 (14), 1983 (11), 1984 (6), 1985 (6), 1986 (3), 1987 (4). Total—189.
Led National League third basemen in putouts with 156 in 1976.
Tied for National League lead in double plays by third basemen with 35 in 1976.
Tied for Pacific Coast League lead in stolen bases with 33 in 1975.
Led Pacific Coast League third basemen in fielding percentage with .962 in 1974.
Led Texas League third basemen in double plays with 26 in 1972.
Named Pacific Coast League Player of the Year in 1975.

Year	Club	League	Pos.	G.	AB.	R.	H.	2B.	3B.	HR.	RBI.	B.A.	PO.	A.	E.	F.A.
1971	—Bakersfield	Calif.	3B	7	20	2	2	1	0	0	2	.100	1	5	1	.857
1971	—Daytona Beach	Fla. St.	3B-SS-2B	111	371	68	100	13	7	8	42	.270	90	265	29	.925
1972	—El Paso	Texas	*3-S-O	127	479	*89	123	28	3	18	59	.257	103	209	*35	.899
1973	—Albuquerque	P. C.	3B-SS-OF	122	463	78	140	24	11	6	68	.302	167	222	24	.942
1973	—Los Angeles	Nat.	3B-2B	10	19	1	4	0	0	0	2	.211	3	14	3	.850
1974	—Albuquerque	P. C.	3B-2B-SS	125	458	69	126	19	1	10	65	.275	121	257	14	.964
1974	—Los Angeles	Nat.	2B-OF-3B	6	0	2	0	0	0	0	0	.000	0	3	0	1.000
1975	—Albuquerque	P. C.	SS-3B	133	487	*91	162	31	7	10	65	*.333	183	349	38	.933
1975	—Los Angeles†	Nat.	O-2-3-S	13	36	2	9	2	1	0	1	.250	12	15	2	.931
1976	—Atlanta	Nat.	3B-SS	149	533	65	132	13	1	5	45	.248	158	310	19	.961

Year Club	League	Pos.	G.	AB.	R.	H.	2B.	3B.	HR.	RBI.	B.A.	PO.	A.	E.	F.A.
1977—Atlanta	Nat.	3-S-2-O	140	445	64	96	10	2	6	28	.216	182	267	28	.941
1978—Atlanta	Nat.	SS-2B-3B	140	529	67	137	17	8	2	35	.259	284	376	23	.966
1979—Atlanta	Nat.	3B-2B	154	601	103	164	25	6	3	51	.273	261	405	22	.968
1980—Atlanta	Nat.	2B-3B-OF	123	392	42	95	17	5	1	20	.242	195	166	18	.953
1981—Atlanta	Nat.	3B-2B	64	93	13	19	4	1	0	9	.204	35	48	4	.954
1982—Atlanta	Nat.	3-O-2-S	108	261	43	77	13	2	2	25	.295	105	112	11	.952
1983—Atlanta‡	Nat.	3-2-O-S	91	268	32	63	10	3	3	30	.235	112	156	10	.964
1984—Atlanta§	Nat.	2-3-S-O	81	227	22	47	13	2	1	21	.207	99	162	9	.967
1985—San Diego	Nat.	2-3-S-O	90	249	31	70	13	2	5	31	.281	130	214	8	.977
1986—San Diego x	Nat.	3-S-2-O	118	257	31	66	12	0	5	26	.257	87	166	14	.948
1987—Chi.y-N. Y.z	Amer.	3-O-2-S	73	196	26	52	13	0	7	27	.265	66	75	4	.972
1988—Atlanta a	Nat.	O-3-2-S	68	102	8	18	3	0	0	1	.176	49	11	1	.984
National League Totals—15 Years			1355	4012	526	997	152	33	33	325	.249	1712	2425	172	.960
American League Totals—1 Year			73	196	26	52	13	0	7	27	.265	66	75	4	.972
Major League Totals—16 Years			1428	4208	552	1049	165	33	40	352	.249	1778	2500	176	.960

Signed as free agent by Los Angeles Dodgers' organization, August 21, 1970.

†Traded with Outfielder Jimmy Wynn, Second Baseman Lee Lacy and First Baseman-Outfielder Tom Paciorek to Atlanta Braves for Outfielder Dusty Baker and First Baseman-Third Baseman Ed Goodson, November 17, 1975.

‡On disabled list, August 19 to September 9, 1983.

§Granted free agency, November 8, 1984; signed by San Diego Padres, January 3, 1985.

xGranted free agency, November 12, 1986; signed by Chicago White Sox, January 21, 1987.

yTraded with Infielder Mike Soper to New York Yankees for Pitcher Ken Patterson and a player to be named later, August 26, 1987; Chicago White Sox acquired Pitcher Jeff Pries to complete deal, September 19, 1987.

zReleased, April 4, 1988; signed by Atlanta Braves, May 17, 1988.

aGranted free agency, November 4, 1988.

CHAMPIONSHIP SERIES RECORD

Year Club	League	Pos.	G.	AB.	R.	H.	2B.	3B.	HR.	RBI.	B.A.	PO.	A.	E.	F.A.
1982—Atlanta	Nat.	OF-3B	3	11	0	2	0	0	0	0	.182	4	0	0	1.000

DAVID MICHAEL RUCKER
(Dave)

Born September 1, 1957, at San Bernardino, Calif.
Height, 6.01. Weight, 185.
Throws and bats lefthanded.
Attended University of California, Los Angeles, Calif., and
LaVerne College, LaVerne, Calif.

Major League saves: 1985 (1).

Year Club	League	G.	IP.	W.	L.	Pct.	H.	R.	ER.	SO.	BB.	ERA.
1978—Bristol	Ap'lachian	3	7	1	0	1.000	10	5	4	7	2	5.14
1978—Lakeland	Florida St.	18	31	6	3	.667	26	13	11	18	13	3.19
1979—Montgomery	Southern	28	96	4	7	.364	97	56	49	64	66	4.59
1979—Evansville	Am. Assoc.	2	13	1	1	.500	11	4	4	8	1	2.77
1980—Evansville	Am. Assoc.	52	92	7	8	.467	94	53	35	53	52	3.42
1981—Detroit	American	2	4	0	0	.000	3	4	3	2	1	6.75
1981—Evansville	Am. Assoc.	35	67	7	4	.636	60	30	28	36	42	3.76
1982—Evansville	Am. Assoc.	30	58⅓	4	1	.800	53	27	22	42	29	3.39
1982—Detroit	American	27	64	5	6	.455	62	26	24	31	23	3.38
1983—Detroit	American	4	9	1	2	.333	18	17	17	6	8	17.00
1983—Evansville†	Am. Assoc.	18	29⅔	2	4	.333	25	12	11	30	21	3.34
1983—St. Louis	National	34	37	5	3	.625	36	14	10	22	18	2.43
1984—St. Louis‡	National	50	73	2	3	.400	62	23	17	38	34	2.10
1985—Portland	P. Coast	10	16	1	0	1.000	15	9	8	17	4	4.50
1985—Philadelphia	National	39	79⅓	3	2	.600	83	42	38	41	40	4.31
1986—Philadelphia	National	19	25	0	2	.000	34	19	16	14	14	5.76
1986—Portland§	P. Coast	12	69⅔	3	3	.500	71	39	33	36	26	4.26
1987—Oklahoma City x	Am. Assoc.	53	65⅔	3	2	.600	59	38	31	37	40	4.25
1988—Buffalo	Am. Assoc.	16	30⅔	0	1	.000	16	8	3	16	18	0.88
1988—Pittsburgh y	National	31	28⅓	0	2	.000	39	19	15	16	9	4.76
American League Totals—3 Years		33	77	6	8	.429	83	47	44	39	32	5.14
National League Totals—5 Years		173	242⅔	10	12	.455	254	117	96	131	115	3.56
Major League Totals—7 Years		206	319⅔	16	20	.444	337	164	140	170	147	3.94

Selected by Philadelphia Phillies' organization in 19th round of free-agent draft, June 4, 1975.

Selected by Detroit Tigers' organization in 16th round of free-agent draft, June 6, 1978.

†Traded to St. Louis Cardinals, July 5, 1983, completing deal in which St. Louis traded Pitcher Doug Bair to Detroit Tigers for a player to be named later, June 21, 1983.

‡Traded to Philadelphia Phillies' organization for Pitcher Bill Campbell and Shortstop Ivan DeJesus, April 6, 1985.

§Released, November 12, 1986; signed by Texas Rangers' organization, December 3, 1986.

xGranted free agency, October 15, 1987; signed by Buffalo (Pittsburgh Pirates' organization), February 9, 1988.

yReleased, October 13, 1988.

BRUCE WAYNE RUFFIN

Born October 4, 1963, at Lubbock, Tex.
Height, 6.02. Weight, 205.
Throws and bats lefthanded.
Attended University of Texas, Austin, Tex.

Major League stolen bases: 1988 (3).

Year Club	League	G.	IP.	W.	L.	Pct.	H.	R.	ER.	SO.	BB.	ERA.
1985—Clearwater	Florida St.	14	97	5	5	.500	87	33	31	74	34	2.88
1986—Reading	Eastern	16	90⅓	8	4	.667	89	41	33	68	26	3.29
1986—Philadelphia	National	21	146⅓	9	4	.692	138	53	40	70	44	2.46
1987—Philadelphia	National	35	204⅔	11	14	.440	236	118	99	93	73	4.35
1988—Philadelphia	National	55	144⅓	6	10	.375	151	86	71	82	80	4.43
Major League Totals—3 Years		111	495⅓	26	28	.481	525	257	210	245	197	3.82

Selected by Philadelphia Phillies' organization in 31st round of free-agent draft, June 7, 1982.
Selected by Philadelphia Phillies' organization in 2nd round of free-agent draft, June 3, 1985.

PAUL WILLIAM RUNGE

Name pronounced RUNG-ee.

Born May 21, 1958, at Kingston, N.Y.
Height, 6.00. Weight, 175.
Throws and bats righthanded.
Received degree from Jacksonville University, Jacksonville, Fla.

Major League stolen bases: 1984 (5).
Led International League in bases on balls received with 95 in 1982 and 92 in 1986.
Tied for International League lead in grounding into double plays with 16 in 1986.
Led International League second basemen in putouts with 269, assists with 383 and total chances with 663 in 1986.
Led International League second basemen in total chances with 747 in 1982.
Led International League shortstops in double plays with 67 in 1981.
Led Appalachian League shortstops in double plays with 38 in 1979.

Year Club	League	Pos.	G.	AB.	R.	H.	2B.	3B.	HR.	RBI.	B.A.	PO.	A.	E.	F.A.
1979—Kingsport	Appal.	SS	66	229	57	67	11	0	6	45	.293	*104	*194	*24	.925
1980—Durham	Carol.	SS	74	245	37	64	8	4	8	37	.261	105	280	25	.939
1980—Savannah	South.	SS	75	248	32	68	11	3	9	34	.274	115	196	17	.948
1981—Richmond	Int.	SS	134	426	49	98	20	5	9	41	.230	191	450	*35	.948
1981—Atlanta	Nat.	SS	10	27	2	7	1	0	0	2	.259	14	27	4	.911
1982—Richmond	Int.	2B	134	507	*106	142	25	6	15	71	.280	*318	412	•17	.977
1982—Atlanta	Nat.	PH-PR	4	2	0	0	0	0	0	0	.000	0	0	0	.000
1983—Richmond	Int.	2B	137	472	76	129	17	4	15	72	.273	269	392	14	.979
1983—Atlanta	Nat.	2B	5	8	0	2	0	0	0	1	.250	4	3	0	1.000
1984—Atlanta	Nat.	2B-SS-3B	28	90	5	24	3	1	0	3	.267	53	101	5	.969
1984—Richmond	Int.	2-3-S-1	91	301	44	72	9	3	8	41	.239	163	264	16	.964
1985—Atlanta	Nat.	3B-SS-2B	50	87	15	19	3	0	1	5	.218	15	66	7	.920
1986—Richmond	Int.	2B-SS	*138	458	76	126	27	1	6	59	.275	275	393	16	.977
1986—Atlanta	Nat.	2B	7	8	1	2	0	0	0	0	.250	5	12	0	1.000
1987—Richmond	Int.	2B-3B	70	235	34	65	11	3	3	21	.277	109	190	7	.977
1987—Atlanta	Nat.	3B-SS-2B	27	47	9	10	1	0	3	8	.213	15	27	2	.955
1988—Atlanta	Nat.	3B-2B-SS	52	76	11	16	5	0	0	7	.211	22	32	1	.982
Major League Totals—8 Years			183	345	43	80	13	1	4	26	.232	128	268	19	.954

Selected by Atlanta Braves' organization in 8th round of free-agent draft, June 5, 1979.

JEFFREY LEE RUSSELL
(Jeff)

Born September 2, 1961, at Cincinnati, O.
Height, 6.03. Weight, 210.
Throws and bats righthanded.
Attended Gulf Coast Community College, Panama City, Fla.

Major League saves: 1986 (2), 1987 (3). Total—5.

Year Club	League	G.	IP.	W.	L.	Pct.	H.	R.	ER.	SO.	BB.	ERA.
1980—Eugene	Northwest	13	90	6	5	.545	80	47	30	75	50	3.00
1981—Tampa	Florida St.	22	143	10	4	.714	109	51	32	92	48	2.01
1982—Waterbury†	Eastern	14	79⅔	6	4	.600	67	27	21	88	23	2.37
1983—Indianapolis	Am. Assoc.	18	119	5	5	.500	106	51	47	98	44	3.55
1983—Cincinnati	National	10	68⅓	4	5	.444	58	30	23	40	22	3.03
1984—Cincinnati	National	33	181⅔	6	*18	.250	186	97	86	101	65	4.26
1985—Denver‡§-Oklahoma City	Am. Assoc.	18	115⅓	7	4	.636	105	55	52	94	51	4.06
1985—Texas	American	13	62	3	6	.333	85	55	52	44	27	7.55
1986—Oklahoma City	Am. Assoc.	11	70⅔	4	1	.800	63	32	31	34	38	3.95
1986—Texas	American	37	82	5	2	.714	74	40	31	54	31	3.40
1987—Port Charlotte x	Florida St.	2	11	0	0	.000	8	3	3	3	5	2.45
1987—Oklahoma City	Am. Assoc.	4	6⅓	0	0	.000	5	1	1	5	1	1.42
1987—Texas	American	52	97⅓	5	4	.556	109	56	48	56	52	4.44
1988—Texas y	American	34	188⅔	10	9	.526	183	86	80	88	66	3.82
National League Totals—2 Years		43	250	10	23	.303	244	127	109	141	87	3.92
American League Totals—4 Years		136	430	23	21	.523	451	237	211	242	176	4.42
Major League Totals—6 Years		179	680	33	44	.429	695	364	320	383	263	4.24

Selected by Cincinnati Reds' organization in 5th round of free-agent draft, June 5, 1979.
†On disabled list, May 5 to June 10 and July 28, 1982 through remainder of season.
‡On disabled list, May 22 to June 10, 1985.
§Traded to Texas Rangers' organization, July 23, 1985, completing deal in which Texas traded Third Baseman Buddy Bell to Cincinnati Reds for Outfielder Duane Walker and a player to be named later, July 19, 1985.

xOn Texas disabled list, March 25 to May 15, 1987; included rehabilitation disability assignment to Port Charlotte, April 26 to May 4, and to Oklahoma City, May 5 to May 15, 1987.

yMade an out in only appearance as a pinch-hitter.

ALL-STAR GAME RECORD

Year	League	IP.	W.	L.	Pct.	H.	R.	ER.	SO.	BB.	ERA.
1988	American	1	0	0	.000	1	0	0	0	1	0.00

JOHN WILLIAM RUSSELL

Born January 5, 1961, at Oklahoma City, Okla.
Height, 6.00. Weight, 195.
Throws and bats righthanded.
Attended University of Oklahoma, Norman, Okla.

Major League stolen bases: 1985 (2).
Led National League in passed balls with 17 in 1986.
Tied for Pacific Coast League lead in passed balls with 13 in 1983.

Year	Club	League	Pos.	G.	AB.	R.	H.	2B.	3B.	HR.	RBI.	B.A.	PO.	A.	E.	F.A.
1982	Reading	East.	C-OF-1B	77	263	26	53	10	5	6	30	.202	354	44	12	.971
1983	Portland	P. C.	C-O-3	128	445	71	113	23	3	27	76	.254	551	58	12	.981
1984	Portland	P. C.	OF-1B-C	93	350	75	101	22	5	19	77	.289	182	18	5	.976
1984	Philadelphia	Nat.	OF-C	39	99	11	28	8	1	2	11	.283	51	1	0	1.000
1985	Philadelphia	Nat.	OF-1B	81	216	22	47	12	0	9	23	.218	170	9	4	.978
1985	Portland	P. C.	OF-C-1B	16	49	8	15	2	2	4	11	.306	24	1	1	.962
1986	Philadelphia	Nat.	C	93	315	35	76	21	2	13	60	.241	498	39	13	.976
1987	Philadelphia	Nat.	OF-C	24	62	5	9	1	0	3	8	.145	48	1	1	.980
1987	Maine	Int.	OF-C-3B	44	143	15	29	6	1	7	24	.203	107	14	2	.984
1988	Maine	Int.	C-O-3-1	110	394	50	90	18	0	13	52	.228	363	54	10	.977
1988	Philadelphia	Nat.	C	22	49	5	12	1	0	2	4	.245	77	9	5	.945
	Major League Totals—5 Years			259	741	78	172	43	3	29	106	.232	844	59	23	.975

Selected by Montreal Expos' organization in 4th round of free-agent draft, June 5, 1979.
Selected by Philadelphia Phillies' organization in 1st round (13th player selected) of free-agent draft, June 7, 1982.

LYNN NOLAN RYAN JR.

(Known by middle name.)

Born January 31, 1947, at Refugio, Tex.
Height, 6.02. Weight, 220.
Throws and bats righthanded.
Attended Alvin Junior College, Alvin, Tex.

Established major league records for most strikeouts, lifetime (4,775); most games, 15 or more strikeouts, lifetime (22); most games, 10 or more strikeouts, lifetime (181); most seasons, 300 or more strikeouts (5); most seasons, 200 or more strikeouts (12); most games, 10 or more strikeouts, season (23), 1973; most strikeouts, three consecutive games (including extra innings—27⅓) (47), August 12, 16 and 20, 1974; most strikeouts by losing pitcher, extra-inning game (19), August 20, 1974 (11 innings); most seasons leading league, bases on balls allowed (8); most bases on balls, lifetime (2,442); most no-hit games, lifetime (5).

Established modern major league records for most consecutive seasons, 300 or more strikeouts (3); most strikeouts, season (383), 1973.

Tied major league records for striking out side on nine pitches, April 19, 1968 (third inning) and July 9, 1972 (second inning); most no-hit games, season (2), 1973; most clubs shut out, season (8), 1972; most consecutive seasons leading major leagues, bases on balls allowed (3); most strikeouts, three consecutive nine-inning games (41), August 7, 12 and 16, 1974.

Established American League record for most games, 10 or more strikeouts, lifetime (114); most games, 15 or more strikeouts, lifetime (19).

Tied American League records for most consecutive strikeouts, game (8), July 9, 1972 and July 15, 1973; most strikeouts, two consecutive games (32), August 7 (13), 12 (19), 1974; most low-hit (no-hit and one-hit) games, season (3), 1973; most seasons leading league, errors by pitcher (4).

Pitched 5-0 no-hit victory against Los Angeles Dodgers, September 26, 1981.
Pitched 1-0 no-hit victory against Baltimore Orioles, June 1, 1975.
Pitched 4-0 no-hit victory against Minnesota Twins, September 28, 1974.
Pitched 6-0 no-hit victory against Detroit Tigers, July 15, 1973.
Pitched 3-0 no-hit victory against Kansas City Royals, May 15, 1973.
Major League saves: 1969 (1), 1970 (1), 1973 (1). Total—3.
Led National League in hit batsmen with 8 in 1982.
Led National League in wild pitches with 16 in 1981 and 15 in 1986.
Led American League in shutouts with 9 in 1972, 7 in 1976, and tied for lead with 5 in 1979.
Led American League in wild pitches with 18 in 1972, 21 in 1977 and 13 in 1978.
Tied for American League lead in complete games with 22 in 1977.
Tied for National League lead in sacrifice hits by hitters with 14 in 1985.
Led Western Carolinas League pitchers in games started with 28 in 1966.
Tied for Appalachian League lead in hit batsmen with 8 in 1965.
Named American League Pitcher of the Year by THE SPORTING NEWS, 1977.
Named righthanded pitcher on THE SPORTING NEWS American League All-Star Team, 1977.
Named Western Carolinas Pitcher of the Year, 1966.

Year	Club	League	G.	IP.	W.	L.	Pct.	H.	R.	ER.	SO.	BB.	ERA.
1965	Marion	Ap'lachian	13	78	3	6	.333	61	47	38	115	56	4.38
1966	Greenville	W. Carol.	29	183	*17	2	.895	109	59	51	*272	*127	2.51
1966	Williamsport	Eastern	3	19	0	2	.000	9	6	2	35	12	0.95
1966	New York	National	2	3	0	1	.000	5	5	5	6	3	15.00

Year Club	League	G.	IP.	W.	L.	Pct.	H.	R.	ER.	SO.	BB.	ERA.
1967—Winter Haven†	Florida St.	1	4	0	0	.000	1	1	1	5	2	2.25
1967—Jacksonville‡	Int'national	3	7	1	0	1.000	3	1	0	18	3	0.00
1968—New York§	National	21	134	6	9	.400	93	50	46	133	75	3.09
1969—New York	National	25	89	6	3	.667	60	38	35	92	53	3.54
1970—New York	National	27	132	7	11	.389	86	59	50	125	97	3.41
1971—New York x	National	30	152	10	14	.417	125	78	67	137	116	3.97
1972—California	American	39	284	19	16	.543	166	80	72	★329	★157	2.28
1973—California	American	41	326	21	16	.568	238	113	104	★383	★162	2.87
1974—California	American	42	★333	22	16	.579	221	127	107	★367	★202	2.89
1975—California	American	28	198	14	12	.538	152	90	76	186	132	3.45
1976—California	American	39	284	17	★18	.486	193	117	106	★327	★183	3.36
1977—California	American	37	299	19	16	.543	198	110	92	★341	★204	2.77
1978—California y	American	31	235	10	13	.435	183	106	97	★260	★148	3.71
1979—California z	American	34	223	16	14	.533	169	104	89	★223	114	3.59
1980—Houston	National	35	234	11	10	.524	205	100	87	200	★98	3.35
1981—Houston	National	21	149	11	5	.688	99	34	28	140	68	★1.69
1982—Houston	National	35	250⅓	16	12	.571	196	100	88	245	★109	3.16
1983—Houston a	National	29	196⅓	14	9	.609	134	74	65	183	101	2.98
1984—Houston b	National	30	183⅔	12	11	.522	143	78	62	197	69	3.04
1985—Houston	National	35	232	10	12	.455	205	108	98	209	95	3.80
1986—Houston c	National	30	178	12	8	.600	119	72	66	194	82	3.34
1987—Houston	National	34	211⅔	8	16	.333	154	75	65	★270	87	★2.76
1988—Houston d	National	33	220	12	11	.522	186	98	86	★228	87	3.52
National League Totals—14 Years		387	2365	135	132	.506	1810	969	848	2359	1140	3.23
American League Totals—8 Years		291	2182	138	121	.533	1520	847	743	2416	1302	3.06
Major League Totals—22 Years		678	4547	273	253	.519	3330	1816	1591	4775	2442	3.15

Selected by New York Mets' organization in 8th round of free-agent draft, June, 1965.

†On military list, January 3 to May 13, 1967.

‡On disabled list, July 16 to August 30, 1967.

§On disabled list, July 30 to August 30, 1968.

xTraded with Pitcher Don Rose, Outfielder Leroy Stanton and Catcher Francisco Estrada to California Angels for Infielder Jim Fregosi, December 10, 1971.

yOn disabled list, June 14 to July 5, 1978.

zGranted free agency, November 1, 1979; signed by Houston Astros, November 19, 1979.

aOn disabled list, March 25 to April 17 and May 3 to June 6, 1983.

bOn disabled list, June 2 to June 17 and June 18 to July 3, 1984.

cOn disabled list, June 1 to June 24 and July 28 to August 12, 1986.

dGranted free agency, November 4, 1988; signed by Texas Rangers, December 7, 1988.

DIVISION SERIES RECORD

Year Club	League	G.	IP.	W.	L.	Pct.	H.	R.	ER.	SO.	BB.	ERA.
1981—Houston	National	2	15	1	1	.500	6	4	3	14	3	1.80

CHAMPIONSHIP SERIES RECORD

Tied Championship Series record for most consecutive strikeouts, start of game (4), October 3, 1979.

Established National League Championship Series records for most runs and earned runs allowed, five-game Series (8), 1980; most hits allowed, five-game Series (16), 1980; most strikeouts, total Series, (46).

Established National League Championship Series record for most strikeouts by relief pitcher, game (7), October 6, 1969.

Year Club	League	G.	IP.	W.	L.	Pct.	H.	R.	ER.	SO.	BB.	ERA.
1969—New York	National	1	7	1	0	1.000	3	2	2	7	2	2.57
1979—California	American	1	7	0	0	.000	4	3	1	8	3	1.29
1980—Houston	National	2	13⅓	0	0	.000	16	8	8	14	3	5.40
1986—Houston	National	2	14	0	1	.000	9	6	6	17	1	3.86
Championship Series Totals—4 Years		6	41⅓	1	1	.500	32	19	17	46	9	3.70

WORLD SERIES RECORD

Year Club	League	G.	IP.	W.	L.	Pct.	H.	R.	ER.	SO.	BB.	ERA.
1969—New York	National	1	2⅓	0	0	.000	1	0	0	3	2	0.00

ALL-STAR GAME RECORD

Year League	IP.	W.	L.	Pct.	H.	R.	ER.	SO.	BB.	ERA.
1973—American	2	0	0	.000	2	2	2	2	2	9.00
1979—American	2	0	0	.000	5	3	3	2	1	13.50
1981—National	1	0	0	.000	0	0	0	1	0	0.00
1985—National	3	0	0	.000	2	0	0	2	2	0.00
All-Star Game Totals—4 Years	8	0	0	.000	9	5	5	7	5	5.63

Member of American League All-Star Team for the 1972 and 1975 games; did not play.

Named to American League All-Star Team to replace Frank Tanana for 1977 game; declined.

—DID YOU KNOW—

That when the Indians defeated the Blue Jays, 14-3, on April 9, 1987, it marked the first time two 300-game winners pitched for the same team in the same game in modern times? Phil Niekro, who won his 312th game, and Steve Carlton, who entered the contest with 323 victories, both pitched for Cleveland.

BRET WILLIAM SABERHAGEN

Born April 11, 1964, at Chicago Heights, Ill.
Height, 6.01. Weight, 185.
Throws and bats righthanded.

Major League saves: 1984 (1).
Named American League Pitcher of the Year by THE SPORTING NEWS, 1985.
Won American League Cy Young Memorial Award, 1985.
Named righthanded pitcher on THE SPORTING NEWS American League All-Star Team, 1985.
Named American League Comeback Player of the Year by THE SPORTING NEWS, 1987.

Year Club	League	G.	IP.	W.	L.	Pct.	H.	R.	ER.	SO.	BB.	ERA.
1983—Fort Myers	Florida St.	16	109⅔	10	5	.667	98	34	28	82	19	2.30
1983—Jacksonville	Southern	11	77⅓	6	2	.750	66	31	25	48	29	2.91
1984—Kansas City†	American	38	157⅔	10	11	.476	138	71	61	73	36	3.48
1985—Kansas City	American	32	235⅓	20	6	.769	211	79	75	158	38	2.87
1986—Kansas City‡	American	30	156	7	12	.368	165	77	72	112	29	4.15
1987—Kansas City	American	33	257	18	10	.643	246	99	96	163	53	3.36
1988—Kansas City	American	35	260⅔	14	16	.467	*271	122	110	171	59	3.80
Major League Totals—5 Years		168	1066⅔	69	55	.556	1031	448	414	677	215	3.49

Selected by Kansas City Royals' organization in 19th round of free-agent draft, June 7, 1982.
†Appeared in one game as a pinch-runner.
‡On disabled list, August 10 to September 1, 1986.

CHAMPIONSHIP SERIES RECORD

Year Club	League	G.	IP.	W.	L.	Pct.	H.	R.	ER.	SO.	BB.	ERA.
1984—Kansas City	American	1	8	0	0	.000	6	3	2	5	1	2.25
1985—Kansas City	American	2	7⅓	0	0	.000	12	5	5	6	2	6.14
Championship Series Totals—2 Years		3	15⅓	0	0	.000	18	8	7	11	3	4.11

WORLD SERIES RECORD

Year Club	League	G.	IP.	W.	L.	Pct.	H.	R.	ER.	SO.	BB.	ERA.
1985—Kansas City	American	2	18	2	0	1.000	11	1	1	10	1	0.50

ALL-STAR GAME RECORD

Year League	IP.	W.	L.	Pct.	H.	R.	ER.	SO.	BB.	ERA.
1987—American	3	0	0	.000	1	0	0	0	0	0.00

CHRISTOPHER ANDREW SABO
(Chris)

Born January 19, 1962, at Detroit, Mich.
Height, 6.00. Weight, 185.
Throws and bats righthanded.
Attended University of Michigan, Ann Arbor, Mich.

Tied major league record for most assists, third baseman, nine-inning game (11), April 7, 1988.
Major League stolen bases: 1988 (46).
Led National League third basemen in double plays with 31 in 1988.
Led Eastern League third basemen in assists with 236 in 1985.
Led Eastern League third basemen in fielding percentage with .943 in 1984.
Named National League Rookie of the Year by Baseball Writers' Association of America, 1988.
Named third baseman on THE SPORTING NEWS College Baseball All-America Team, 1983.

Year Club	League	Pos.	G.	AB.	R.	H.	2B.	3B.	HR.	RBI.	B.A.	PO.	A.	E.	F.A.
1983—Cedar Rapids	Midw.	3B	77	274	43	75	11	6	12	37	.274	43	130	9	.951
1984—Vermont	East.	3B-2B	125	441	44	94	19	1	5	38	.213	80	210	21	.932
1985—Vermont	East.	3B-SS	124	428	66	119	19	0	11	46	.278	97	236	18	.949
1986—Denver	A. A.	3B	129	432	83	118	26	2	10	60	.273	83	202	9	*.969
1987—Nashville	A. A.	3B	91	315	56	92	19	3	7	51	.292	43	137	12	.938
1988—Cincinnati	Nat.	*3B-SS	137	538	74	146	40	2	11	44	.271	75	318	14	*.966
Major League Totals—1 Year			137	538	74	146	40	2	11	44	.271	75	318	14	.966

Selected by Montreal Expos' organization in 30th round of free-agent draft, June 3, 1980.
Selected by Cincinnati Reds' organization in 2nd round of free-agent draft, June 6, 1983.

ALL-STAR GAME RECORD

Year League	Pos.	AB.	R.	H.	2B.	3B.	HR.	RBI.	B.A.	PO.	A.	E.	F.A.
1988—National	PR	0	0	0	0	0	0	0	.000	0	0	0	.000

MARK BRUCE SALAS

Name pronounced SAL-us.

Born March 8, 1961, at Montebello, Calif.
Height, 6.00. Weight, 205.
Throws right and bats lefthanded.

Major League stolen bases: 1986 (3).
Tied for Florida State League lead in sacrifice flies with 10 in 1981.
Tied for Appalachian League lead in passed balls with 10 in 1979.

Year Club	League	Pos.	G.	AB.	R.	H.	2B.	3B.	HR.	RBI.	B.A.	PO.	A.	E.	F.A.
1979—Johnson City	Appal.	C	53	144	23	35	4	2	5	23	.243	194	19	6	.973
1980—Gastonia	S. Atl.	C	98	267	42	67	8	3	9	46	.251	452	41	5	★.990
1981—St. Petersburg	Fla St.	●C-1B	100	321	26	78	9	2	2	52	.243	387	66	●13	.972
1982—Arkansas	Texas	C	27	76	4	17	4	0	0	5	.224	88	15	1	.990
1982—Louisville†	A. A.	C	7	22	1	4	0	0	0	1	.182	16	3	1	.950
1982—Nashville	South.	C	43	137	19	35	7	0	6	20	.255	267	24	7	.977
1983—Arkansas	Texas	C-OF	131	473	76	144	25	4	20	82	.304	334	41	4	.989
1984—Louisville	A. A.	C-OF	95	316	28	77	20	2	12	48	.244	260	28	7	.976
1984—St. Louis‡	Nat.	C-OF	14	20	1	2	1	0	0	1	.100	13	2	0	1.000
1985—Minnesota	Amer.	C	120	360	51	108	20	5	9	41	.300	529	39	5	.991
1986—Minnesota§	Amer.	C	91	258	28	60	7	4	8	33	.233	358	32	8	.980
1987—Minn. x-N. Y.	Amer.	C-OF	72	160	21	40	6	0	6	21	.250	258	16	1	.996
1987—Columbus y	Int.	C	12	43	5	10	1	0	2	4	.233	46	5	0	1.000
1988—Chicago	Amer.	C	75	196	17	49	7	0	3	9	.250	251	35	6	.979
National League Totals—1 Year			14	20	1	2	1	0	0	1	.100	13	2	0	1.000
American League Totals—4 Years			358	974	117	257	40	9	26	104	.264	1396	122	20	.987
Major League Totals—5 Years			372	994	118	259	41	9	26	105	.261	1409	124	20	.987

Selected by St. Louis Cardinals' organization in 18th round of free-agent draft, June 5, 1979.

†Loaned to Nashville (New York Yankees' organization), June 30, 1982; returned, September 13, 1982.

‡Drafted by Minnesota Twins, December 3, 1984.

§On disabled list, May 24 to June 17, 1986.

xTraded to New York Yankees for Pitcher Joe Niekro and cash, June 7, 1987.

yTraded with Outfielder Dan Pasqua and Pitcher Steve Rosenberg to Chicago White Sox for Pitchers Richard Dotson and Scott Nielsen, November 12, 1987.

ARGENIS ANTONIO SALAZAR
(Angel)

Born November 4, 1961, at El Tigre, Venezuela.
Height, 6.00. Weight, 173.
Throws and bats righthanded.

Major League stolen bases: 1984 (1), 1986 (1), 1987 (4). Total—6.

Tied for Pioneer League lead in double plays by shortstops with 45 in 1981.

Year Club	League	Pos.	G.	AB.	R.	H.	2B.	3B.	HR.	RBI.	B.A.	PO.	A.	E.	F.A.
1980—W. Palm Beach†	Fla. St.					(Did not play)									
1980—Calgary	Pion.	S-2-1-C	51	169	29	41	2	0	0	11	.243	60	126	17	.916
1981—Calgary	Pion.	SS	63	259	37	64	5	3	2	25	.247	89	★228	13	★.961
1982—W. Palm Beach	Fla. St.	SS	112	408	63	109	15	2	2	36	.267	176	★364	35	.939
1983—Wichita	A. A.	SS	98	341	47	103	23	7	1	54	.302	152	256	24	.944
1983—Montreal	Nat.	SS	36	37	5	8	1	1	0	1	.216	28	28	2	.966
1984—Montreal	Nat.	SS	80	174	12	27	4	2	0	12	.155	88	155	10	.960
1984—Indianapolis‡§	A. A.	SS-3B	50	156	11	43	8	1	1	14	.276	54	117	3	.983
1985—Tidewater xy	Int.	SS-2B	84	230	25	58	10	1	0	18	.252	119	244	16	.958
1986—Kansas City	Amer.	SS-2B	117	298	24	73	20	2	0	24	.245	121	284	9	.978
1987—Kansas City zab	Amer.	SS	116	317	24	65	7	0	2	21	.205	134	332	9	.981
1988—Chicago	Nat.	SS-2B-3B	34	60	4	15	1	1	0	1	.250	38	53	3	.968
National League Totals—3 Years			150	271	21	50	6	4	0	14	.185	154	236	15	.963
American League Totals—2 Years			233	615	48	138	27	2	2	45	.224	255	616	18	.980
Major League Totals—5 Years			383	886	69	188	33	6	2	59	.212	409	852	33	.974

Signed as free agent by Montreal Expos' organization, January 20, 1980.

†On temporarily inactive list, April 10 to June 1, 1980.

‡Selected by St. Louis Cardinals' organization in player compensation pool draft, January 24, 1985. (St. Louis received compensation for Atlanta Braves' signing of free agent Pitcher Bruce Sutter, a Type A player, December 7, 1984.)

§Traded with Pitcher John Young to New York Mets' organization for Shortstop Jose Oquendo and Pitcher Mark Jason Davis, April 2, 1985.

xOn disabled list, April 13 to April 27 and June 16 to July 2, 1985.

yTraded to Kansas City Royals for Pitcher Tony Ferreira, April 1, 1986.

zOn disabled list, August 12 to September 4, 1987.

aTraded with Pitcher Danny Jackson to Cincinnati Reds for Pitcher Ted Power and Shortstop Kurt Stillwell, November 6, 1987.

bReleased, March 28, 1988; signed by Chicago Cubs, March 31, 1988.

LUIS ERNESTO SALAZAR

Born May 19, 1956, at Barcelona, Venezuela.
Height, 5.09. Weight, 180.
Throws and bats righthanded.

Major League stolen bases: 1980 (11), 1981 (11), 1982 (32), 1983 (24), 1984 (11), 1985 (14), 1987 (3), 1988 (6). Total—112.

Led National League third basemen in errors with 26 and tied for lead in double plays with 28 in 1982.

Led Eastern League outfielders in putouts with 312 and tied for lead in double plays with 3 in 1979.

Year Club	League	Pos.	G.	AB.	R.	H.	2B.	3B.	HR.	RBI.	B.A.	PO.	A.	E.	F.A.
1974—Sarasota Royals†	Gulf C.	SS	2	4	0	1	0	0	0	1	.250	0	2	0	1.000
1976—Niagara Falls	NYP	SS-OF	42	151	18	36	3	4	1	17	.238	71	49	17	.876
1977—Salem	Carol.	SS-3B-2B	116	433	72	117	17	5	11	48	.270	157	294	45	.909
1978—Salem	Carol.	OF-3B-SS	126	472	55	138	20	4	3	49	.292	160	77	19	.926
1979—Buffalo	East.	OF-3B	★139	★561	★108	★181	17	5	27	86	.323	321	42	13	.965

Year	Club	League	Pos.	G.	AB.	R.	H.	2B.	3B.	HR.	RBI.	B.A.	PO.	A.	E.	F.A.
1980	Port.‡-Hawaii	P. C.	OF	127	497	91	157	23	15	9	64	.316	304	11	8	.975
1980	San Diego	Nat.	3B-OF	44	169	28	57	4	7	1	25	.337	39	88	7	.948
1981	San Diego	Nat.	3B-OF	109	400	37	121	19	6	3	38	.303	108	191	14	.955
1982	San Diego	Nat.	3B-SS-OF	145	524	55	127	15	5	8	62	.242	133	326	29	.941
1983	San Diego	Nat.	3B-SS	134	481	52	124	16	2	14	45	.258	122	274	21	.950
1984	San Diego§x	Nat.	3B-OF-SS	93	228	20	55	7	2	3	17	.241	87	97	6	.968
1985	Chicago	Amer.	OF-3B-1B	122	327	39	80	18	2	10	45	.245	180	57	10	.960
1986	Appleton y	Midw.	3B	21	79	9	16	1	0	2	4	.203	9	39	5	.906
1986	Chicago z	Amer.	DH-PH	4	7	1	1	0	0	0	0	.143	0	0	0	.000
1987	Las Vegas	P. C.	OF	4	17	2	5	2	0	1	3	.294	5	0	0	1.000
1987	San Diego a	Nat.	3-S-O-P-1	84	189	13	48	5	0	3	17	.254	56	95	9	.944
1988	Detroit	Amer.	O-S-3-2-1	130	452	61	122	14	1	12	62	.270	199	151	10	.972
National League Totals—6 Years				609	1991	205	532	66	22	32	204	.267	545	1071	86	.949
American League Totals—3 Years				256	786	101	203	32	3	22	107	.258	379	208	20	.967
Major League Totals—9 Years				865	2777	306	735	98	25	54	311	.265	924	1279	106	.954

Signed as free agent by Kansas City Royals' organization, November 29, 1973.

†Released, July 8, 1974; signed by Pittsburgh Pirates' organization, November 23, 1975.

‡Traded with Outfielder Rick Lancellotti to San Diego Padres' organization for Infielder Kurt Bevacqua and a player to be named later, August 4, 1980; Pittsburgh Pirates' organization acquired Pitcher Mark Lee to complete deal, August 12, 1980.

§On disabled list, May 15 to June 11, 1984.

xTraded with Pitchers Tim Lollar and Bill Long and Shortstop Ozzie Guillen to Chicago White Sox for Pitchers LaMarr Hoyt, Kevin Kristan and Todd Simmons, December 6, 1984.

yOn Chicago disabled list, April 4 to August 8, August 16 to September 1 and September 8, 1986 through remainder of season; included rehabilitation disability assignment to Appleton, July 17 to August 6, 1986.

zReleased, December 19, 1986; signed by San Diego Padres' organization, April 2, 1987.

aGranted free agency, October 20, 1987; signed by Toledo (Detroit Tigers' organization), February 20, 1988.

CHAMPIONSHIP SERIES RECORD

Year	Club	League	Pos.	G.	AB.	R.	H.	2B.	3B.	HR.	RBI.	B.A.	PO.	A.	E.	F.A.
1984	San Diego	Nat.	3B-PH-OF	3	5	0	1	0	1	0	0	.200	1	3	0	1.000

WORLD SERIES RECORD

Year	Club	League	Pos.	G.	AB.	R.	H.	2B.	3B.	HR.	RBI.	B.A.	PO.	A.	E.	F.A.
1984	San Diego†	Nat.	3B-OF	4	3	0	1	0	0	0	0	.333	1	0	0	1.000

†Also appeared as a pinch-runner and pinch-hitter.

PITCHING RECORD

Year	Club	League	G.	IP.	W.	L.	Pct.	H.	R.	ER.	SO.	BB.	ERA.
1987	San Diego	National	2	2	0	0	.000	2	1	1	0	1	4.50

JUAN MILTON SAMUEL

Name pronounced SAHM-well.

Born December 9, 1960, at San Pedro de Macoris, D.R.
Height, 5.11. Weight, 170.
Throws and bats righthanded.

Established major league records for most at-bats by righthander, season (701), 1984; fewest sacrifice hits, most at-bats, season (0 and 701), 1984.

Tied major league records for most consecutive seasons leading league in strikeouts (4), 1984 through 1987; most assists by second baseman, nine-inning game (12), April 20, 1985.

Established National League record for most at-bats, season (701), 1984.

Major League stolen bases: 1983 (3), 1984 (72), 1985 (53), 1986 (42), 1987 (35), 1988 (33). Total—238.

Led National League batters in strikeouts with 168 in 1984, 142 in 1986, 162 in 1987 and tied for lead with 141 in 1985.

Led National League second basemen in putouts with 343 and double plays with 92 in 1988.

Led National League second basemen in total chances with 826 in 1987.

Led Carolina League in total bases with 283 and tied for lead in being hit by pitch with 15 in 1982.

Led Northwest League batters in strikeouts with 87 and caught stealing with 10 in 1980.

Led Carolina League second basemen in double plays with 82 and total chances with 721 in 1982.

Led South Atlantic League second basemen in double plays with 82 and total chances with 737 in 1981.

Named second baseman on THE SPORTING NEWS National League All-Star Team, 1987.

Named second baseman on THE SPORTING NEWS National League Silver Slugger team, 1987.

Named National League Rookie Player of the Year by THE SPORTING NEWS, 1984.

Named Carolina League Most Valuable Player, 1982.

Year	Club	League	Pos.	G.	AB.	R.	H.	2B.	3B.	HR.	RBI.	B.A.	PO.	A.	E.	F.A.
1980	Cen. Oregon	N'west	2B	69	★298	66	84	11	2	17	44	.282	162	188	★30	.921
1981	Spartanburg	S. Atl.	2B	135	512	88	127	22	8	11	74	.248	★280	★409	★50	.932
1982	Peninsula	Carol.	2B	135	494	★111	158	29	6	28	94	.320	★244	★442	★35	.951
1983	Reading	East.	2B	47	184	36	43	10	0	11	39	.234	121	127	14	.947
1983	Portland	P. C.	2B	65	261	59	86	14	8	15	52	.330	110	168	15	.949
1983	Philadelphia	Nat.	2B	18	65	14	18	1	2	2	5	.277	44	54	9	.916
1984	Philadelphia	Nat.	2B	160	★701	105	191	36	●19	15	69	.272	388	438	★33	.962
1985	Philadelphia	Nat.	2B	161	★663	101	175	31	13	19	74	.264	★389	463	15	.983
1986	Philadelphia†	Nat.	2B	145	591	90	157	36	12	16	78	.266	290	440	★25	.967
1987	Philadelphia	Nat.	2B	160	★655	113	178	37	★15	28	100	.272	★374	434	★18	.978
1988	Philadelphia	Nat.	2B-OF-3B	157	629	68	153	32	9	12	67	.243	351	387	16	.979
Major League Totals—6 Years				801	3304	491	872	173	70	92	393	.264	1836	2216	116	.972

Signed as free agent by Philadelphia Phillies' organization, April 29, 1980.

†On disabled list, April 13 to May 2, 1986.

CHAMPIONSHIP SERIES RECORD

Year	Club	League	Pos.	G.	AB.	R.	H.	2B.	3B.	HR.	RBI.	B.A.	PO.	A.	E.	F.A.
1983	—Philadelphia	Nat.	PR	1	0	0	0	0	0	0	0	.000	0	0	0	.000

WORLD SERIES RECORD

Year	Club	League	Pos.	G.	AB.	R.	H.	2B.	3B.	HR.	RBI.	B.A.	PO.	A.	E.	F.A.
1983	—Philadelphia	Nat.	PR-PH	3	1	0	0	0	0	0	0	.000	0	0	0	.000

ALL-STAR GAME RECORD

Established All-Star Game record for most putouts by second baseman, game (7), July 14, 1987.
Tied All-Star Game record for most chances accepted by second baseman, game (9), July 14, 1987.

Year	League	Pos.	AB.	R.	H.	2B.	3B.	HR.	RBI.	B.A.	PO.	A.	E.	F.A.
1987	—National	2B	4	0	0	0	0	0	0	.000	7	2	0	1.000

Member of National League All-Star Team in 1984; did not play.

ROGER HOWARD SAMUELS

Born January 3, 1961, at San Jose, Calif.
Height, 6.05. Weight, 210.
Throws and bats lefthanded.
Attended Santa Clara University, Santa Clara, Calif.

Year	Club	League	G.	IP.	W.	L.	Pct.	H.	R.	ER.	SO.	BB.	ERA.
1983	—Auburn	NYP	6	33⅔	3	2	.600	33	19	13	21	19	3.48
1983	—Asheville	S. Atlantic	10	60	3	4	.429	60	33	27	47	30	4.05
1984	—Asheville	S. Atlantic	15	88⅓	4	5	.444	82	38	33	82	44	3.36
1984	—Daytona Beach	Florida St.	13	68⅓	5	4	.556	67	40	32	44	37	4.21
1985	—Columbus	Southern	33	147⅔	10	9	.526	132	73	65	85	82	3.96
1986	—Columbus†	Southern	38	77⅔	2	3	.400	76	49	44	56	46	5.10
1987	—Fresno	California	27	42⅔	1	2	.333	29	11	4	64	18	0.84
1987	—Shreveport	Texas	21	33⅓	3	1	.750	24	10	6	35	10	1.62
1988	—Phoenix	P. Coast	30	48	3	2	.600	34	16	14	33	15	2.63
1988	—San Francisco	National	15	23⅓	1	2	.333	17	10	9	22	7	3.47
Major League Totals—1 Year			15	23⅓	1	2	.333	17	10	9	22	7	3.47

Selected by Toronto Blue Jays' organization in 2nd round of free-agent draft, January 8, 1980.
Selected by Houston Astros' organization in 10th round of free-agent draft, June 6, 1983.
†Released, January 19, 1987; signed by Phoenix (San Francisco Giants' organization), February 6, 1987.

ISRAEL SANCHEZ JR.

Born August 20, 1963, at Falcon, Cuba.
Height, 5.09. Weight, 170.
Throws and bats lefthanded.

Major League saves: 1988 (1).

Year	Club	League	G.	IP.	W.	L.	Pct.	H.	R.	ER.	SO.	BB.	ERA.
1982	—Sarasota Royals	Gulf Coast	12	61	3	5	.375	63	41	31	49	36	4.57
1983	—Charleston	S. Atlantic	30	163	10	6	.625	172	92	65	130	70	3.59
1984	—Fort Myers†	Florida St.	14	66⅔	3	3	.500	62	30	27	63	29	3.65
1985	—Fort Myers‡	Florida St.	28	98⅓	8	6	.571	72	32	23	86	27	2.11
1986	—Memphis	Southern	28	184⅓	13	7	.650	190	97	71	141	55	3.47
1986	—Omaha	Am. Assoc.	1	3	0	1	.000	4	3	3	2	2	9.00
1987	—Omaha	Am. Assoc.	23	124⅔	5	12	.294	162	74	64	74	46	4.62
1988	—Omaha	Am. Assoc.	15	102	7	4	.636	102	36	33	85	36	2.91
1988	—Kansas City	American	19	35⅔	3	2	.600	36	20	18	14	18	4.54
Major League Totals—1 Year			19	35⅔	3	2	.600	36	20	18	14	18	4.54

Selected by Kansas City Royals' organization in 9th round of free-agent draft, June 7, 1982.
†On disabled list, May 26 to June 18 and June 29 to August 22, 1984.
‡On disabled list, April 12 to May 1, 1985.

REY FRANCISCO SANCHEZ (GUADALUPE)

Born October 5, 1967, at Rio Piedras, Puerto Rico.
Height, 5.10. Weight, 180.
Throws and bats righthanded.

Led Florida State League shortstops in total chances with 676 in 1988.
Led Gulf Coast League shortstops in fielding percentage with .932 in 1986.

Year	Club	League	Pos.	G.	AB.	R.	H.	2B.	3B.	HR.	RBI.	B.A.	PO.	A.	E.	F.A.
1986	—Sarasota Rangers	Gulf C.	SS-2B	52	169	27	49	3	1	0	23	.290	69	158	15	.938
1987	—Gastonia	S. Atl.	SS	50	160	19	35	1	2	1	10	.219	88	162	18	.933
1987	—Butte	Pion.	SS	49	189	36	69	10	6	0	25	.365	84	162	12	.953
1988	—Port Charlotte	Fla. St.	SS	128	418	60	128	6	5	0	38	.306	226	*415	35	.948

Selected by Texas Rangers' organization in 13th round of free-agent draft, June 2, 1986.

RYNE DEE SANDBERG

Born September 18, 1959, at Spokane, Wash.
Height, 6.02. Weight, 180.
Throws and bats righthanded.

Tied major league records for most assists by second baseman, nine-inning game (12), June 12, 1983; fewest errors by second baseman, season, 150 or more games (5), 1986.

Established National League record for highest fielding average by second baseman, season (.994), 1986.

Major League stolen bases: 1982 (32), 1983 (37), 1984 (32), 1985 (54), 1986 (34), 1987 (21), 1988 (25). Total—235.

Led National League second basemen in total chances with 914 in 1983, 870 in 1984 and 824 in 1988.

Led National League second basemen in assists with 571 and double plays with 126 in 1983.

Led Eastern League shortstops in fielding percentage with .964, assists with 386 and double plays with 81 in 1980.

Led Western Carolinas League shortstops in double plays with 80 in 1979.

Led Pioneer League shortstops in double plays with 39 in 1978.

Named Major League Player of the Year by The Sporting News, 1984.

Named National League Player of the Year by The Sporting News, 1984.

Named National League Most Valuable Player by Baseball Writers' Association of America, 1984.

Named second baseman on The Sporting News National League All-Star Team, 1984 and 1988.

Named second baseman on The Sporting News National League All-Star fielding team, 1983 through 1988.

Named second baseman on The Sporting News National League Silver Slugger team, 1984, 1985 and 1988.

Received reported $30,000 bonus to sign with Philadelphia Phillies, 1978.

Year Club	League	Pos.	G.	AB.	R.	H.	2B.	3B.	HR.	RBI.	B.A.	PO.	A.	E.	F.A.
1978—Helena	Pion.	SS	56	190	34	59	6	6	1	23	.311	92	*200	24	.924
1979—Spartanburg	W. Car.	SS	*138	*539	83	133	21	7	4	47	.247	134	*467	35	*.945
1980—Reading	East.	SS-3B	129	490	95	152	21	12	11	79	.310	156	388	20	.965
1981—Oklahoma City	A. A.	SS-2B	133	519	78	152	17	5	9	62	.293	229	396	21	.967
1981—Philadelphia†	Nat.	SS-2B	13	6	2	1	0	0	0	0	.167	7	7	0	1.000
1982—Chicago	Nat.	3B-2B	156	635	103	172	33	5	7	54	.271	136	373	12	.977
1983—Chicago	Nat.	*2B-SS	158	633	94	165	25	4	8	48	.261	330	572	13	*.986
1984—Chicago	Nat.	2B	156	636	*114	200	36	•19	19	84	.314	314	*550	6	*.993
1985—Chicago	Nat.	2B-SS	153	609	113	186	31	6	26	83	.305	353	501	12	.986
1986—Chicago	Nat.	2B	154	627	68	178	28	5	14	76	.284	309	*492	5	*.994
1987—Chicago‡	Nat.	2B	132	523	81	154	25	2	16	59	.294	294	375	10	.985
1988—Chicago	Nat.	2B	155	618	77	163	23	8	19	69	.264	291	*522	11	.987
Major League Totals—8 Years			1077	4287	652	1219	201	49	109	473	.284	2034	3392	69	.987

Selected by Philadelphia Phillies' organization in 20th round of free-agent draft, June 6, 1978.

†Traded with Shortstop Larry Bowa to Chicago Cubs for Shortstop Ivan DeJesus, January 27, 1982.

‡On disabled list, June 14, to July 11, 1987.

CHAMPIONSHIP SERIES RECORD

Year Club	League	Pos.	G.	AB.	R.	H.	2B.	3B.	HR.	RBI.	B.A.	PO.	A.	E.	F.A.
1984—Chicago	Nat.	2B	5	19	3	7	2	0	0	2	.368	13	18	1	.969

ALL-STAR GAME RECORD

Year League	Pos.	AB.	R.	H.	2B.	3B.	HR.	RBI.	B.A.	PO.	A.	E.	F.A.
1984—National	2B	4	0	1	0	0	0	0	.250	0	0	0	.000
1985—National	2B	1	1	0	0	0	0	0	.000	0	3	0	1.000
1986—National	2B	3	0	0	0	0	0	0	.000	0	2	1	.667
1987—National	2B	2	0	0	0	0	0	0	.000	0	2	0	1.000
1988—National	2B	4	0	1	0	0	0	0	.250	2	2	0	1.000
All-Star Game Totals—5 Years		14	1	2	0	0	0	0	.143	2	9	1	.917

SCOTT DOUGLAS SANDERSON

Born July 22, 1956, at Dearborn, Mich.
Height, 6.05. Weight, 198.
Throws and bats righthanded.
Attended Vanderbilt University, Nashville, Tenn.

Tied National League record for most consecutive home runs allowed, inning (3), July 11, 1982 (second inning).

Major League saves: 1979 (1), 1983 (1), 1986 (1), 1987 (2). Total—5.

Year Club	League	G.	IP.	W.	L.	Pct.	H.	R.	ER.	SO.	BB.	ERA.
1977—West Palm Beach	Florida St.	10	57	5	2	.714	58	22	17	37	23	2.68
1978—Memphis	Southern	9	58	5	3	.625	55	32	26	44	19	4.03
1978—Denver	Am. Assoc.	9	49	4	2	.667	47	35	33	36	30	6.06
1978—Montreal	National	10	61	4	2	.667	52	20	17	50	21	2.51
1979—Montreal	National	34	168	9	8	.529	148	69	64	138	54	3.43
1980—Montreal	National	33	211	16	11	.593	206	76	73	125	56	3.11
1981—Montreal	National	22	137	9	7	.563	122	50	45	77	31	2.96
1982—Montreal	National	32	224	12	12	.500	212	98	86	158	58	3.46
1983—Montreal†‡	National	18	81⅓	6	7	.462	98	50	42	55	20	4.65
1984—Chicago§	National	24	140⅔	8	5	.615	140	54	49	76	24	3.14
1984—Lodi	California	1	5	0	1	.000	7	2	2	2	0	3.60
1985—Chicago x	National	19	121	5	6	.455	100	49	42	80	27	3.12
1986—Chicago	National	37	169⅔	9	11	.450	165	85	79	124	37	4.19
1987—Chicago y	National	32	144⅔	8	9	.471	156	72	69	106	50	4.29
1988—Peoria z	Midwest	1	5	0	0	.000	4	1	0	3	0	0.00
1988—Iowa	Am. Assoc.	3	13⅓	1	0	1.000	13	7	7	4	2	4.73
1988—Chicago a	National	11	15⅓	1	2	.333	13	9	9	6	3	5.28
Major League Totals—11 Years		272	1473⅔	87	80	.521	1412	632	575	995	381	3.51

Selected by Kansas City Royals' organization in 11th round of free-agent draft, June 5, 1974.

Selected by Montreal Expos' organization in 3rd round of free-agent draft, June 7, 1977.

†On disabled list, July 5 to September 1, 1983.

‡Traded with Infielder Al Newman to San Diego Padres for Pitcher Gary Lucas, December 7, 1983; Traded by San Diego to Chicago Cubs for First Baseman Carmelo Martinez, Pitcher Craig Lefferts and Third Baseman Fritz Connally, December 7, 1983.

§On disabled list, June 1 to July 5, 1984; included rehabilitation disability assignment to Lodi, June 29 to July 5, 1984.
xOn disabled list, August 14, 1985 through remainder of season.
yOn disabled list, March 29 to April 24 and June 22 to July 7, 1987.
zOn Chicago disabled list, April 5 to August 23, 1988; included rehabilitation disability assignment to Peoria, June 25 to June 29, 1988; and Iowa, June 30 to July 11, 1988.
aGranted free agency, November 4, 1988; re-signed by Cubs, December 7, 1988.

DIVISION SERIES RECORD

Year Club	League	G.	IP.	W.	L.	Pct.	H.	R.	ER.	SO.	BB.	ERA.
1981—Montreal	National	1	2⅔	0	0	.000	4	4	2	2	2	6.75

CHAMPIONSHIP SERIES RECORD

Year Club	League	G.	IP.	W.	L.	Pct.	H.	R.	ER.	SO.	BB.	ERA.
1984—Chicago	National	1	4⅔	0	0	.000	6	3	3	2	1	5.79

ANDRES CONFESOR SANTANA

Born March 19, 1968, at San Pedro de Macoris, D.R.
Height, 5.11. Weight, 150.
Throws right and bats left and righthanded.

Led Pioneer League in stolen bases with 45 and caught stealing with 10 in 1987.
Led Midwest League in caught stealing with 23 in 1988.
Led Pioneer League shortstops in total chances with 337 in 1987.

Year Club	League	Pos.	G.	AB.	R.	H.	2B.	3B.	HR.	RBI.	B.A.	PO.	A.	E.	F.A.
1987—Pocatello	Pion.	SS	67	256	51	67	2	3	0	9	.262	94	*202	*41	.878
1988—Clinton	Midw.	SS	118	450	77	126	4	1	0	24	.280	154	301	50	.901
1988—Shreveport	Texas	SS	11	36	3	6	0	0	0	3	.167	20	29	1	.980

Signed as free agent by San Francisco Giants' organization, November 22, 1985.

RAFAEL FRANCISCO SANTANA (DeLaCRUZ)

Born January 31, 1958, at La Romana, Dominican Republic.
Height, 6.01. Weight, 156.
Throws and bats righthanded.

Established National League record for fewest assists by shortstop, season, 150 or more games (396), 1985.
Major League stolen bases: 1985 (1), 1987 (1), 1988 (1). Total—3.
Led New York-Pennsylvania League in sacrifice hits with 8 in 1977.
Led Texas League shortstops in fielding percentage with .955 and tied for lead in double plays with 79 in 1981.

Year Club	League	Pos.	G.	AB.	R.	H.	2B.	3B.	HR.	RBI.	B.A.	PO.	A.	E.	F.A.
1977—Oneonta	NYP	SS	60	157	26	41	5	0	0	23	.261	62	162	*27	.892
1978—Fort Lauderdale	Fla. St.	SS	131	431	37	111	8	5	0	35	.258	166	372	*48	.918
1979—Fort Lauderdale	Fla. St.	SS-3B-2B	133	472	62	124	9	6	0	41	.263	160	351	16	.970
1980—Nashville	South.	SS	86	275	33	64	4	3	0	20	.233	125	247	25	.937
1980—Fort Lauderdale†	Fla. St.	SS	51	168	20	38	2	0	1	17	.226	81	158	9	.964
1981—Arkansas	Texas	SS-3B-2B	110	326	34	76	14	3	0	19	.233	154	350	23	.956
1981—Springfield	A. A.	SS-3B	2	8	3	4	1	0	1	2	.500	1	8	3	750
1982—Louisville	A. A.	3B-2B-SS	121	430	65	123	15	3	3	53	.286	163	275	11	.976
1983—St. Louis	Nat.	2B-SS-3B	30	14	1	3	0	0	0	2	.214	3	8	4	.733
1983—Louisville‡	A. A.	3-2-S-1	45	167	19	47	9	1	0	20	.281	60	117	10	.947
1984—Tidewater	Int.	S-3-2-1	77	255	34	71	6	0	1	23	.278	107	232	14	.960
1984—New York§	Nat.	SS	51	152	14	42	11	1	1	12	.276	92	104	6	.970
1985—New York	Nat.	SS	154	529	41	136	19	1	1	29	.257	*301	396	25	.965
1986—New York	Nat.	SS-2B	139	394	38	86	11	0	1	28	.218	203	369	16	.973
1987—New York x	Nat.	SS	139	439	41	112	21	2	5	44	.255	213	396	17	.973
1988—New York	Amer.	SS	148	480	50	115	12	1	4	38	.240	202	421	22	.966
National League Totals—5 Years			513	1528	135	379	62	4	8	115	.248	812	1273	68	.968
American League Totals—1 Year			148	480	50	115	12	1	4	38	.240	202	421	22	.966
Major League Totals—6 Years			661	2008	185	494	74	5	12	153	.246	1014	1694	90	.968

Signed as free agent by New York Yankees' organization, August 31, 1976.
†Traded to St. Louis Cardinals for a player to be named later, February 16, 1981; New York Yankees' organization acquired Pitcher George Frazier to complete deal, June 7, 1981.
‡Released, January 17, 1984; signed by Tidewater (New York Mets' organization), January 17, 1984.
§On disabled list, August 25 to September 9, 1984.
xTraded with Pitcher Victor Garcia to New York Yankees for Outfielder Darren Reed, Catcher Phil Lombardi and Pitcher Steve Frey, December 11, 1987.

CHAMPIONSHIP SERIES RECORD

Year Club	League	Pos.	G.	AB.	R.	H.	2B.	3B.	HR.	RBI.	B.A.	PO.	A.	E.	F.A.
1986—New York	Nat.	SS	6	17	0	3	0	0	0	0	.176	13	18	0	1.000

WORLD SERIES RECORD

Year Club	League	Pos.	G.	AB.	R.	H.	2B.	3B.	HR.	RBI.	B.A.	PO.	A.	E.	F.A.
1986—New York	Nat.	SS	7	20	3	5	0	0	0	2	.250	11	17	1	.966

BENITO SANTIAGO (RIVERA)

Born March 9, 1965, at Ponce, P.R.
Height, 6.01. Weight, 185.
Throws and bats righthanded.

Established major league record for most consecutive games batted safely by rookie, season (34), August 25 through October 2, 1987.

Major League stolen bases: 1987 (21), 1988 (15). Total—36.
Tied for National League lead in double plays by catchers with 11 in 1988.
Led Pacific Coast League catchers in total chances with 655 in 1986.
Led Texas League in passed balls with 16 in 1985.
Led Florida State League catchers in double plays with 12 and passed balls with 26 in 1983.
Led National League in passed balls with 22 in 1987.
Named catcher on THE SPORTING NEWS National League All-Star Team, 1987.
Named catcher on THE SPORTING NEWS National League All-Star fielding team, 1988.
Named catcher on THE SPORTING NEWS National League Silver Slugger team, 1987 and 1988.
Named National League Rookie Player of the Year by THE SPORTING NEWS, 1987.
Named National League Rookie of the Year by Baseball Writers' Association of America, 1987.

Year Club	League	Pos.	G.	AB.	R.	H.	2B.	3B.	HR.	RBI.	B.A.	PO.	A.	E.	F.A.
1983—Miami	Fla. St.	C	122	429	34	106	25	3	5	56	.247	471	★69	★21	.963
1984—Reno	Calif.	C	114	416	64	116	20	6	16	83	.279	692	96	25	.969
1985—Beaumont†	Texas	★C-1B-3B	101	372	55	111	16	6	5	52	.298	525	★78	15	.976
1986—Las Vegas	P. C.	C	117	437	55	125	26	3	17	71	.286	★563	71	★21	.968
1986—San Diego	Nat.	C	17	62	10	18	2	0	3	6	.290	80	7	5	.946
1987—San Diego	Nat.	C	146	546	64	164	33	2	18	79	.300	817	80	★22	.976
1988—San Diego	Nat.	C	139	492	49	122	22	2	10	46	.248	725	★75	★12	.985
Major League Totals—3 Years			302	1100	123	304	57	4	31	131	.276	1622	162	39	.979

Signed as free agent by San Diego Padres' organization, September 1, 1982.
†On disabled list, June 21 to July 2, 1985.

NELSON GIL SANTOVENIA

Born July 27, 1961, at Pino del Rio, Cuba.
Height, 6.03. Weight, 220.
Throws and bats righthanded.
Attended Miami-Dade Community College (South), Miami, Fla., and University of Miami, Coral Gables, Fla.

Major League stolen bases: 1988 (2).
Led Southern League catchers in putouts with 785 and total chances with 867 in 1987.
Led Southern League in passed balls with 21 in 1983.
Tied for Southern League lead in double plays by catchers with 9 in 1984.

Year Club	League	Pos.	G.	AB.	R.	H.	2B.	3B.	HR.	RBI.	B.A.	PO.	A.	E.	F.A.
1982—W. Palm Beach	Fla. St.	C	40	118	8	29	4	0	1	12	.246	127	21	5	.967
1983—Memphis	South.	C	94	318	27	77	13	0	3	44	.242	490	69	★15	.974
1984—Jacksonville†	South.	C	90	255	27	55	9	0	5	29	.216	464	●64	4	.992
1985—Jacksonville	South.	C	57	184	15	40	6	0	2	15	.217	281	20	9	.971
1985—Indianapolis	A. A.	C	28	75	5	16	2	0	0	4	.213	135	20	1	.994
1986—Jacksonville	South.	C-OF	31	72	15	22	7	0	4	11	.306	97	14	1	.991
1986—Indianapolis	A. A.	C	18	57	6	12	1	0	1	2	.211	80	14	1	.989
1987—Jacksonville	South.	C-1B	117	394	56	110	17	0	19	63	.279	790	71	11	.987
1987—Montreal	Nat.	C	2	1	0	0	0	0	0	0	.000	1	0	0	1.000
1988—Indianapolis	A. A.	C	27	91	9	28	5	0	2	13	.308	198	23	3	.987
1988—Montreal‡	Nat.	C-1B	92	309	26	73	20	2	8	41	.236	465	63	9	.983
Major League Totals—2 Years			94	310	26	73	20	2	8	41	.235	466	63	9	.983

Selected by Philadelphia Phillies' organization in 29th round of free-agent draft, June 5, 1979.
Selected by Montreal Expos' organization in 3rd round of free-agent draft, June 8, 1981.
Selected by Montreal Expos' organization in secondary phase of free-agent draft, June 7, 1982.
†On suspended list, May 24 to May 31, 1984.
‡On disabled list, June 4 to June 20, 1988.

MACK DANIEL SASSER JR.
(Mackey)

Born August 3, 1962, at Fort Gaines, Ga.
Height, 6.01. Weight, 210.
Throws right and bats lefthanded.
Attended George C. Wallace Community College, Dothan, Ala., and Troy State University, Troy, Ala.

Led Texas League in intentional bases on balls received with 13 in 1986.
Led California League in total bases with 245 and tied for lead in game-winning RBIs with 16 in 1985.
Led Pacific Coast League catchers in putouts with 584, errors with 16 and total chances with 663 in 1987.
Led California League in passed balls with 19 in 1985.

Year Club	League	Pos.	G.	AB.	R.	H.	2B.	3B.	HR.	RBI.	B.A.	PO.	A.	E.	F.A.
1984—Clinton	Midw.	1-3-O-C	118	428	57	125	20	5	6	65	.292	526	95	17	.973
1984—Fresno	Calif.	OF-3B-1B	16	62	8	17	1	1	0	6	.274	24	15	4	.907
1985—Fresno	Calif.	O-C-1-3	133	497	79	168	27	4	14	102	.338	402	42	14	.969
1986—Shreveport	Texas	C-1B-OF	120	441	52	129	29	5	5	72	.293	577	66	10	.985
1987—Phoe.†-Vanc.	P. C.	C-3B-1B	115	400	53	127	24	1	3	56	.318	588	72	18	.973
1987—S.F.-Pitt.‡	Nat.	C	14	27	2	5	0	0	0	2	.185	29	0	0	1.000
1988—New York	Nat.	C-3B-OF	60	123	9	35	10	1	1	17	.285	235	17	6	.977
Major League Totals—2 Years			74	150	11	40	10	1	1	19	.267	264	17	6	.979

Selected by San Francisco Giants' organization in 5th round of free-agent draft, January 17, 1984.
†Traded with $50,000 to Pittsburgh Pirates' organization for Pitcher Don Robinson, July 31, 1987.
‡Traded with Pitcher Tim Drummond to New York Mets for First Baseman Randy Milligan and Pitcher Scott Henion, March 26, 1988.

CHAMPIONSHIP SERIES RECORD

Year	Club	League	Pos.	G.	AB.	R.	H.	2B.	3B.	HR.	RBI.	B.A.	PO.	A.	E.	F.A.
1988	New York	Nat.	PH-C	4	5	0	1	0	0	0	0	.200	2	0	0	1.000

RICHARD D. SAUVEUR
(Rich)

Born November 23, 1963, at Arlington, Va.
Height, 6.04. Weight, 170.
Throws and bats lefthanded.
Attended Manatee Junior College, Bradenton, Fla.

Led Eastern League in balks with 4 in 1984 and tied for lead with 4 in 1985.
Tied for Eastern League lead in games started by pitchers with 27 in 1987.
Tied for New York-Pennsylvania League lead in balks with 4 in 1983.

Year	Club	League	G.	IP.	W.	L.	Pct.	H.	R.	ER.	SO.	BB.	ERA.
1983	Watertown	NYP	16	93⅔	7	5	.593	80	41	24	73	31	2.31
1984	Prince William†	Carolina	10	54⅔	3	3	.500	43	22	19	54	31	3.13
1984	Nashua	Eastern	10	70⅔	5	3	.625	54	27	23	48	34	2.93
1985	Nashua	Eastern	25	157⅓	9	10	.474	146	73	62	85	78	3.55
1986	Nashua	Eastern	5	38	3	1	.750	21	5	5	28	11	1.18
1986	Hawaii‡	P. Coast	14	92	7	6	.538	73	40	31	68	45	3.03
1986	Pittsburgh	National	3	12	0	0	.000	17	8	8	6	6	6.00
1987	Harrisburg§x	Eastern	30	*195	13	6	.684	174	71	62	*160	96	2.86
1988	Jacksonville	Southern	8	6⅔	0	2	.000	7	5	3	8	5	4.05
1988	Indianapolis	Am. Assoc.	43	81⅓	7	4	.636	60	26	22	58	28	2.43
1988	Montreal	National	4	3	0	0	.000	3	2	2	3	2	6.00
Major League Totals—2 Years			7	15	0	0	.000	20	10	10	9	8	6.00

Selected by Pittsburgh Pirates' organization in 11th round of free-agent draft, January 11, 1983.
Selected by Pittsburgh Pirates' organization in secondary phase of free-agent draft, June 6, 1983.
†On disabled list, May 25 to July 5, 1984.
‡On disabled list, August 10 to September 5, 1986.
§Played one game at first base with two putouts.
xDrafted by Montreal Expos, December 7, 1987.

JOHN JOSEPH SAVAGE
(Jack)

Born April 22, 1964, at Louisville, Ky.
Height, 6.00. Weight, 185.
Throws and bats righthanded.
Attended University of Kentucky, Lexington, Ky.

Led Texas League in intentional bases on balls issued with 12 in 1987.
Led California League in intentional bases on balls with 11 in 1986.
Tied for Pioneer League lead in saves with 8 in 1985.

Year	Club	League	G.	IP.	W.	L.	Pct.	H.	R.	ER.	SO.	BB.	ERA.
1985	Great Falls	Pioneer	24	44⅔	5	1	.833	26	5	5	51	18	1.01
1986	Bakersfield	California	44	77⅔	5	8	.385	82	45	39	77	45	4.52
1987	San Antonio	Texas	49	69⅓	5	6	.455	64	22	20	67	31	2.60
1987	Albuquerque	P. Coast	13	15	0	4	.000	20	15	7	13	11	4.20
1987	Los Angeles†	National	3	3⅓	0	0	.000	4	1	1	0	0	2.70
1988	Tidewater	Int'national	43	88⅓	5	8	.385	67	37	31	46	37	3.16
Major League Totals—1 Year			3	3⅓	0	0	.000	4	1	1	0	0	2.70

Selected by New York Yankees' organization in 6th round of free-agent draft, June 6, 1983.
Selected by Los Angeles Dodgers' organization in 8th round of free-agent draft, June 3, 1985.
†As part of an eight-player three-team deal, New York Mets traded Pitcher Jesse Orosco to Oakland Athletics, December 11, 1987. Oakland then traded Orosco along with Shortstop Alfredo Griffin and Pitcher Jay Howell to Los Angeles Dodgers for Pitchers Bob Welch, Matt Young and Jack Savage. Oakland then traded Savage along with Pitchers Wally Whitehurst and Kevin Tapani to New York.

STEPHEN LOUIS SAX
(Steve)

Born January 29, 1960, at Sacramento, Calif.
Height, 5.11. Weight, 185.
Throws and bats righthanded.
Brother of David Sax, catcher with Los Angeles Dodgers and Boston Red Sox, 1982, 1983 and 1985 through 1987.

Major League stolen bases: 1981 (5), 1982 (49), 1983 (56), 1984 (34), 1985 (27), 1986 (40), 1987 (37), 1988 (42). Total—290.
Led National League in caught stealing with 30 in 1983.
Led Florida State League second basemen in double plays with 91 in 1980.
Named second baseman on THE SPORTING NEWS National League All-Star Team, 1986.
Named second baseman on THE SPORTING NEWS National League Silver Slugger team, 1986.
Named National League Rookie of the Year by Baseball Writers' Association of America, 1982.
Named Texas League Most Valuable Player, 1981.

Year	Club	League	Pos.	G.	AB.	R.	H.	2B.	3B.	HR.	RBI.	B.A.	PO.	A.	E.	F.A.
1978	Lethbridge	Pion.	SS	39	131	24	43	6	3	0	21	.328	21	40	9	.871
1979	Clinton	Midw.	OF-2B-3B	115	386	64	112	15	2	2	52	.290	111	75	18	.912

Year Club	League	Pos.	G.	AB.	R.	H.	2B.	3B.	HR.	RBI.	B.A.	PO.	A.	E.	F.A.
1980—Vero Beach	Fla. St.	★2B-OF	●139	●530	78	150	18	8	3	61	.283	★360	★438	20	★.976
1981—San Antonio	Texas	2B	115	485	94	168	23	3	8	52	★.346	255	298	17	.970
1981—Los Angeles	Nat.	2B	31	119	15	33	2	0	2	9	.277	64	93	4	.975
1982—Los Angeles	Nat.	2B	150	638	88	180	23	7	4	47	.282	347	452	19	.977
1983—Los Angeles	Nat.	2B	155	623	94	175	18	5	5	41	.281	331	399	★30	.961
1984—Los Angeles	Nat.	2B	145	569	70	138	24	4	1	35	.243	318	450	21	.973
1985—Los Angeles†	Nat.	★2B-3B	136	488	62	136	8	4	1	42	.279	330	358	★22	.969
1986—Los Angeles	Nat.	2B	157	633	91	210	43	4	6	56	.332	●367	432	16	.980
1987—Los Angeles	Nat.	2B-OF-3B	157	610	84	171	22	7	6	46	.280	343	420	14	.982
1988—Los Angeles ‡	Nat.	2B	160	★632	70	175	19	4	5	57	.277	276	429	14	.981
Major League Totals—8 Years			1091	4312	574	1218	159	35	30	333	.282	2376	3033	140	.975

Selected by Los Angeles Dodgers' organization in 9th round of free-agent draft, June 6, 1978.
†On disabled list, April 19 to May 4, 1985.
‡Granted free agency, November 4, 1988; signed by New York Yankees, November 23, 1988.

DIVISION SERIES RECORD

Year Club	League	Pos.	G.	AB.	R.	H.	2B.	3B.	HR.	RBI.	B.A.	PO.	A.	E.	F.A.
1981—Los Angeles	Nat.	2B	1	0	0	0	0	0	0	0	.000	0	0	0	.000

CHAMPIONSHIP SERIES RECORD

Established National League Championship Series records for most runs, seven-game Series (7), 1988; most singles, seven-game Series (8), 1988; most stolen bases, seven-game Series (5), 1988.

Tied National League Championship Series records for most at-bats, seven-game Series (30), 1988; most stolen bases, game (3), October 9, 1988 (12 innings).

Year Club	League	Pos.	G.	AB.	R.	H.	2B.	3B.	HR.	RBI.	B.A.	PO.	A.	E.	F.A.
1981—Los Angeles	Nat.	2B	1	0	0	0	0	0	0	0	.000	0	1	0	1.000
1983—Los Angeles	Nat.	2B	4	16	0	4	0	0	0	0	.250	11	12	0	1.000
1985—Los Angeles	Nat.	2B	6	20	1	6	3	0	0	1	.300	11	21	0	1.000
1988—Los Angeles	Nat.	2B	7	30	7	8	0	0	0	3	.267	12	22	0	1.000
Championship Series Totals—4 Years			18	66	8	18	3	0	0	4	.273	34	56	0	1.000

WORLD SERIES RECORD

Year Club	League	Pos.	G.	AB.	R.	H.	2B.	3B.	HR.	RBI.	B.A.	PO.	A.	E.	F.A.
1981—Los Angeles	Nat.	PH-PR-2	2	1	0	0	0	0	0	0	.000	0	0	0	.000
1988—Los Angeles	Nat.	2B	5	20	3	6	0	0	0	0	.300	11	11	0	1.000
World Series Totals—2 Years			7	21	3	6	0	0	0	0	.286	11	11	0	1.000

ALL-STAR GAME RECORD

Year League	Pos.	AB.	R.	H.	2B.	3B.	HR.	RBI.	B.A.	PO.	A.	E.	F.A.
1982—National	PR-2B	1	0	1	0	0	0	0	1.000	2	0	1	.667
1983—National	2B	3	1	1	0	0	0	1	.333	2	0	1	.667
1986—National	2B	1	0	1	0	0	0	1	1.000	0	1	0	1.000
All-Star Game Totals—3 Years		5	1	3	0	0	0	2	.600	4	1	2	.714

ROBERT GUY SCANLAN JR.
(Bob)

Born August 9, 1966, at Los Angeles, Calif.
Height, 6.07. Weight, 200.
Throws and bats righthanded.
Attended University of California, Los Angeles, Calif.

Led International League in wild pitches with 17 in 1988.

Year Club	League	G.	IP.	W.	L.	Pct.	H.	R.	ER.	SO.	BB.	ERA.
1984—Sarasota Phillies	Gulf Coast	13	33⅓	0	2	.000	43	31	24	17	30	6.48
1985—Spartanburg	S. Atlantic	26	152⅓	8	12	.400	160	95	70	108	53	4.14
1986—Clearwater	Florida St.	24	125⅔	8	12	.400	146	73	58	51	45	4.15
1987—Reading	Eastern	27	164	★15	5	.750	187	98	93	91	55	5.10
1988—Maine	Int'national	28	161	5	★18	.217	181	★110	★100	79	50	5.59

Selected by Philadelphia Phillies' organization in 25th round of free-agent draft, June 4, 1984.

DANIEL ERNEST SCHATZEDER

Name pronounced SHOT-zay-dur.

(Dan)

Born December 1, 1954, at Elmhurst, Ill.
Height, 6.00. Weight, 195.
Throws and bats lefthanded.
Received degree in business administration from University of Denver, Denver, Colo., in 1976.

Major League saves: 1979 (1), 1983 (2), 1984 (1), 1986 (2), 1988 (3). Total—9.

Year Club	League	G.	IP.	W.	L.	Pct.	H.	R.	ER.	SO.	BB.	ERA.
1976—West Palm Beach	Florida St.	10	64	5	3	.625	49	22	19	49	20	2.67
1976—Quebec City	Eastern	5	28	2	3	.400	38	16	14	19	10	4.50
1977—Quebec City	Eastern	8	62	5	3	.625	39	20	19	59	15	2.76
1977—Denver†	Am. Assoc.	9	36	2	2	.500	45	25	24	28	14	6.00
1977—Montreal	National	6	22	2	1	.667	16	6	6	14	13	2.45
1978—Denver	Am. Assoc.	4	28	3	0	1.000	24	11	9	19	11	2.89

Year	Club	League	G.	IP.	W.	L.	Pct.	H.	R.	ER.	SO.	BB.	ERA.
1978	—Montreal	National	29	144	7	7	.500	108	54	49	69	68	3.06
1979	—Montreal‡	National	32	162	10	5	.667	136	57	51	106	59	2.83
1980	—Detroit§	American	32	193	11	13	.458	178	88	86	94	58	4.01
1981	—Detroit x	American	17	71	6	8	.429	74	49	48	20	29	6.08
1982	—San Francisco y-Montreal	National	39	69⅓	1	6	.143	84	46	41	33	24	5.23
1982	—Phoenix	P. Coast	1	3⅔	0	0	.000	10	6	5	1	3	12.27
1983	—Montreal z	National	58	87	5	2	.714	88	34	31	48	25	3.21
1984	—Montreal	National	36	136	7	7	.500	112	44	41	89	36	2.71
1985	—Montreal a	National	24	104⅓	3	5	.375	101	52	44	64	31	3.80
1985	—Indianapolis	Am. Assoc.	1	3	0	0	.000	2	0	0	3	1	0.00
1986	—Montreal b-Philadelphia	National	55	88⅓	6	5	.545	81	43	32	47	35	3.26
1987	—Philadelphia c	National	26	37⅔	3	1	.750	40	21	17	28	14	4.06
1987	—Minnesota d	American	30	43⅔	3	1	.750	64	37	31	30	18	6.39
1988	—Cleveland e-Minnesota	American	25	26⅓	0	3	.000	34	21	19	17	7	6.49
1988	—Portland f	P. Coast	13	86⅔	6	4	.600	82	26	25	55	24	2.60
National League Totals—9 Years			305	850⅔	44	39	.530	766	357	312	498	305	3.30
American League Totals—4 Years			104	334	20	25	.444	350	195	184	161	112	4.96
Major League Totals—12 Years			409	1184⅔	64	64	.500	1116	552	496	659	417	3.77

Selected by Montreal Expos' organization in 3rd round of free-agent draft, June 8, 1976.
†On disabled list, July 5 to August 30, 1977.
‡Traded to Detroit Tigers for Outfielder Ron LeFlore, December 7, 1979.
§On disabled list, May 27 to June 17, 1980.
xTraded with Pitcher Mike Chris to San Francisco Giants for Outfielder Larry Herndon, December 9, 1981.
ySold to Montreal Expos, June 15, 1982.
zGranted free agency, November 7, 1983; re-signed by Expos, December 19, 1983.
aOn disabled list, June 21 to July 23 and August 7 to September 1, 1985; included rehabilitation disability assignment to Indianapolis, July 19 to July 23, 1985.
bTraded with Infielder Skeeter Barnes to Philadelphia Phillies for Infielder Tom Foley and Pitcher Lary Sorensen, July 24, 1986.
cTraded with cash to Minnesota Twins for Pitcher Danny Clay and Third Baseman Tom Schwarz, June 24, 1987.
dReleased, December 21, 1987; signed by Cleveland Indians, February 9, 1988.
eReleased, June 22, 1988; signed by Portland (Minnesota Twins' organization), June 27, 1988.
fGranted free agency, November 4, 1988.

CHAMPIONSHIP SERIES RECORD

Tied American League Championship Series record for most strikeouts by relief pitcher, game (5), October 10, 1987.

Year	Club	League	G.	IP.	W.	L.	Pct.	H.	R.	ER.	SO.	BB.	ERA.
1987	—Minnesota	American	2	4⅓	0	0	.000	2	0	0	5	0	0.00

WORLD SERIES RECORD

Year	Club	League	G.	IP.	W.	L.	Pct.	H.	R.	ER.	SO.	BB.	ERA.
1987	—Minnesota	American	3	4⅓	1	0	1.000	4	3	3	3	3	6.23

WILLIAM JOSEPH SCHERRER

Named pronounced SHURR-ur.

(Bill)

Born January 20, 1958, at Tonawanda, N. Y.
Height, 6.04. Weight, 180.
Throws and bats lefthanded.
Attended University of Nevada, Las Vegas, Nev.

Major League saves: 1983 (10), 1984 (1). Total—11.
Led American League in intentional bases on balls issued with 13 in 1985.
Tied for American Association lead in shutouts with 2 in 1982.
Tied for Northwest League lead in shutouts with 2 in 1978.

Year	Club	League	G.	IP.	W.	L.	Pct.	H.	R.	ER.	SO.	BB.	ERA.
1977	—Shelby	W. Carol.	27	158	9	9	.500	132	87	62	122	105	3.53
1978	—Shelby	W. Carol.	10	31	0	2	.000	27	19	14	18	26	4.06
1978	—Eugene	Northwest	13	84	6	4	.600	61	43	33	87	42	3.54
1979	—Tampa	Florida St.	25	159	12	3	.800	126	43	32	140	65	1.81
1980	—Waterbury	Eastern	25	151	7	8	.467	139	58	56	84	58	3.34
1981	—Waterbury	Eastern	50	119	5	9	.357	121	70	57	89	62	4.31
1982	—Tampa	Florida St.	7	47⅓	3	2	.600	37	13	12	45	18	2.28
1982	—Waterbury	Eastern	5	31	1	3	.250	30	15	13	18	15	3.77
1982	—Indianapolis	Am. Assoc.	19	88⅔	6	4	.600	68	43	40	81	32	4.06
1982	—Cincinnati	National	5	17⅓	0	1	.000	17	7	5	7	0	2.60
1983	—Cincinnati	National	73	92	2	3	.400	73	31	28	57	33	2.74
1984	—Cincinnati†	National	36	52⅓	1	1	.500	64	31	29	35	15	4.99
1984	—Wichita‡§	Am. Assoc.	10	16⅔	2	3	.400	16	6	6	14	11	3.24
1984	—Detroit	American	18	19	1	0	1.000	14	4	4	16	8	1.89
1985	—Detroit	American	48	66	3	2	.600	62	35	32	46	41	4.36
1986	—Nashville	Am. Assoc.	31	58⅔	5	2	.714	60	36	33	49	28	5.06
1986	—Detroit x	American	13	21	0	1	.000	19	19	17	16	22	7.29
1987	—Nashville	Am. Assoc.	33	29	4	1	.800	25	6	6	24	10	1.86
1987	—Cincinnati y	National	23	33	1	1	.500	43	17	16	24	16	4.36
1988	—Rochester-Maine	Int'national	10	12⅔	0	0	.000	8	1	1	11	6	0.71
1988	—Baltimore z	American	4	4	0	1	.000	8	6	6	3	3	13.50

Year Club	League	G.	IP.	W.	L.	Pct.	H.	R.	ER.	SO.	BB.	ERA.
1988—Philadelphia a	National	8	6⅔	0	0	.000	7	4	4	3	2	5.40
1988—Iowa b	Am. Assoc.	10	14⅔	1	0	1.000	23	12	8	12	7	4.91
National League Totals—5 Years		145	201⅓	4	6	.400	204	90	82	126	66	3.67
American League Totals—4 Years		83	110	4	4	.500	103	64	59	81	74	4.83
Major League Totals—7 Years		228	311⅓	8	10	.444	307	154	141	207	140	4.08

Selected by Cleveland Indians' organization in 6th round of free-agent draft, June 8, 1976.

Selected by Cincinnati Reds' organization in secondary phase of free-agent draft, January 11, 1977.

†On disabled list, April 18 to May 3, 1984.

‡On disabled list, July 31 to August 10, 1984.

§Traded to Detroit Tigers for cash and a player to be named later, August 27, 1984; Cincinnati Reds acquired Pitcher Carl Willis to complete deal, September 1, 1984.

xGranted free agency, October 15, 1986.

yReleased, October 27, 1987; signed by Rochester (Baltimore Orioles' organization), January 27, 1988.

zReleased, May 2, 1988; signed by Maine (Philadelphia Phillies' organization), June 25, 1988.

aReleased, August 1, 1988; signed by Iowa (Chicago Cubs' organization), August 8, 1988.

bGranted free agency, October 15, 1988.

WORLD SERIES RECORD

Year Club	League	G.	IP.	W.	L.	Pct.	H.	R.	ER.	SO.	BB.	ERA.
1984—Detroit	American	3	3	0	0	.000	5	1	1	0	0	3.00

CURTIS MONTAGUE SCHILLING

Born November 14, 1966, at Phoenix, Ariz.
Height, 6.04. Weight, 215.
Throws and bats righthanded.
Attended Yavapai College, Prescott, Ariz.

Year Club	League	G.	IP.	W.	L.	Pct.	H.	R.	ER.	SO.	BB.	ERA.
1986—Elmira	NYP	16	93⅔	7	3	.700	92	34	27	75	30	2.59
1987—Greensboro	S. Atlantic	29	184	8	★15	.348	179	96	78	★189	65	3.82
1988—New Britain †	Eastern	21	106	8	5	.615	91	44	35	62	40	2.97
1988—Charlotte	Southern	7	45⅓	5	2	.714	36	19	16	32	23	3.18
1988—Baltimore	American	4	14⅔	0	3	.000	22	19	16	4	10	9.82
Major League Totals—1 Year		4	14⅔	0	3	.000	22	19	16	4	10	9.82

Selected by Boston Red Sox' organization in 2nd round of free-agent draft, January 14, 1986.

†Traded with Outfielder Brady Anderson to Baltimore Orioles for Pitcher Mike Boddicker, July 29, 1988.

CALVIN DREW SCHIRALDI

Born June 16, 1962, at Houston, Tex.
Height, 6.05. Weight, 215.
Throws and bats righthanded.
Attended University of Texas, Austin, Tex.

Major League saves: 1986 (9), 1987 (6), 1988 (1). Total—16.

Named Texas League Pitcher of the Year, 1984.

Year Club	League	G.	IP.	W.	L.	Pct.	H.	R.	ER.	SO.	BB.	ERA.
1983—Jackson	Texas	7	38⅔	3	3	.500	41	28	25	26	29	5.82
1983—Lynchburg	Carolina	6	30⅓	4	1	.800	28	16	15	41	17	4.45
1984—Jackson	Texas	23	156⅓	•14	3	★.824	118	58	50	131	69	2.88
1984—Tidewater	Int'national	4	31⅓	3	1	.750	18	6	4	24	10	1.15
1984—New York	National	5	17⅓	0	2	.000	20	13	11	16	10	5.71
1985—Tidewater	Int'national	17	100⅓	4	5	.444	91	50	39	76	56	3.50
1985—New York†‡	National	10	26⅓	2	1	.667	43	27	26	21	11	8.89
1986—Pawtucket	Int'national	31	44	4	3	.571	32	19	14	59	20	2.86
1986—Boston	American	25	51	4	2	.667	36	8	8	55	15	1.41
1987—Boston§	American	62	83⅔	8	5	.615	75	45	41	93	40	4.41
1988—Chicago x	National	29	166⅓	9	13	.409	166	87	81	140	63	4.38
National League Totals—3 Years		44	210	11	16	.407	229	127	118	177	84	5.06
American League Totals—2 Years		87	134⅔	12	7	.632	111	53	49	148	55	3.27
Major League Totals—5 Years		131	344⅔	23	23	.500	340	180	167	325	139	4.36

Selected by Chicago White Sox' organization in 17th round of free-agent draft, June 3, 1980.

Selected by New York Mets' organization in 1st round (27th player selected) of free-agent draft, June 6, 1983.

†On disabled list, May 15 to May 30, 1985.

‡Traded with Pitcher Wes Gardner and Outfielders John Christensen and LaSchelle Tarver to Boston Red Sox for Pitchers Bob Ojeda, Tom McCarthy, John Mitchell and Chris Bayer, November 13, 1985.

§Traded with Pitcher Al Nipper to Chicago Cubs for Pitcher Lee Smith, December 8, 1987.

xOn disabled list, May 13 to May 28 and August 5 to August 20, 1988.

CHAMPIONSHIP SERIES RECORD

Tied American League Championship Series records for most games pitched, seven game Series (4), 1986; most strikeouts by a relief pitcher, game (5), October 15, 1986.

Year Club	League	G.	IP.	W.	L.	Pct.	H.	R.	ER.	SO.	BB.	ERA.
1986—Boston	American	4	6	0	1	.000	5	2	1	9	3	1.50

WORLD SERIES RECORD

Tied World Series record for most games lost, seven-game Series (2), 1986.

Year Club	League	G.	IP.	W.	L.	Pct.	H.	R.	ER.	SO.	BB.	ERA.
1986—Boston	American	3	4	0	2	.000	7	7	6	2	3	13.50

DAVID JOSEPH SCHMIDT
(Dave)

Born April 22, 1957, at Niles, Mich.
Height, 6.01. Weight, 194.
Throws and bats righthanded.
Attended Los Angeles Valley College, Van Nuys, Calif., and University of California, Los Angeles, Calif.

Major League saves: 1981 (1), 1982 (6), 1983 (2), 1984 (12), 1985 (5), 1986 (8), 1987 (1), 1988 (2). Total—37.

Year Club	League	G.	IP.	W.	L.	Pct.	H.	R.	ER.	SO.	BB.	ERA.
1979—Sarasota Rangers	Gulf Coast	7	30	2	2	.500	30	19	14	27	8	4.20
1980—Asheville	S. Atlantic	12	91	8	1	.889	76	32	20	67	13	1.98
1980—Tulsa	Texas	12	73	4	6	.400	90	42	36	46	28	4.44
1981—Tulsa	Texas	3	24	1	1	.500	17	5	5	17	6	1.88
1981—Texas	American	14	32	0	1	.000	31	11	11	13	11	3.09
1981—Wichita	Am. Assoc.	12	87	2	5	.286	90	47	47	49	26	4.86
1982—Texas	American	33	109⅔	4	6	.400	118	45	39	69	25	3.20
1983—Texas†	American	31	46⅓	3	3	.500	42	20	20	29	14	3.88
1984—Texas	American	43	70⅓	6	6	.500	69	30	20	46	20	2.56
1985—Texas‡	American	51	85⅔	7	6	.538	81	36	30	46	22	3.15
1986—Chicago§	American	49	92⅓	3	6	.333	94	37	34	67	27	3.31
1987—Baltimore	American	35	124	10	5	.667	128	57	52	70	26	3.77
1988—Baltimore	American	41	129⅔	8	5	.615	129	58	49	67	38	3.40
Major League Totals—8 Years		297	690	41	38	.519	692	294	255	407	183	3.33

Selected by Texas Rangers' organization in 26th round of free-agent draft, June 5, 1979.
†On disabled list, March 25 to May 1, 1983.
‡Traded with Infielder Wayne Tolleson to Chicago White Sox for Pitcher Ed Correa, Infielder Scott Fletcher and a player to be named later, November 25, 1985; Texas Rangers acquired Infielder Jose Mota to complete deal, December 12, 1985.
§Released, December 19, 1986; signed by Baltimore Orioles, January 22, 1987.

MICHAEL JACK SCHMIDT
(Mike)

Born September 27, 1949, at Dayton, O.
Height, 6.02. Weight, 203.
Throws and bats righthanded.
Received bachelor of arts degree in business administration from Ohio University, Athens, O. in 1971.

Established major league records for most total bases, extra-inning game (17), April 17, 1976 (10 innings); most home runs by third baseman, season (48), 1980; most home runs by third baseman, lifetime (503).

Tied major league records for most home runs, extra-inning game (4), April 17, 1976 (10 innings); most consecutive home runs, extra-inning game (4), April 17, 1976 (10 innings); most home runs, consecutive plate appearances (4), April 17, 1976 and July 6 and 7, 1979; most extra bases on long hits, game (12), April 17, 1976 (10 innings); most home runs, two consecutive games (5), April 17 and 18, 1976; most home runs, three consecutive games (6), April 17-20, 1976; most home runs, month of April (11), 1976; most consecutive seasons leading major leagues in strikeouts (3), 1974 through 1976; most home runs, month of October (4), 1980; most years leading league in double plays by third baseman (6).

Established National League records for most years, third baseman (17); most years leading league in home runs (8); most years leading league in extra bases on long hits (7); most assists, third baseman, season (404), 1974; fewest singles, season, 150 or more games (63), 1979; most games, third baseman, lifetime (2,170); most assists by third baseman, lifetime (4,974); most chances accepted, third baseman, lifetime (6,547); most double plays by third baseman, lifetime (442).

Tied National League records for most years leading league in runs batted in (4); most home runs, bases full, one month, 2, June, 1973; most home runs through July 31 (36), 1979; most home runs, five consecutive games, one or more homer each game (7), July 6 through 10, 1979; most consecutive years leading league in extra bases on long hits (3, performed twice); most consecutive years leading league in bases on balls (3); most years leading league in assists by third baseman (7).

Hit three home runs in a game, July 7, 1979 and June 14, 1987.

Hit home runs in all 12 National League parks, 1979.

Major League stolen bases: 1973 (8), 1974 (23), 1975 (29), 1976 (14), 1977 (15), 1978 (19), 1979 (9), 1980 (12), 1981 (12), 1982 (14), 1983 (7), 1984 (5), 1985 (1), 1986 (1), 1987 (2), 1988 (3). Total—174.

Led National League in intentional bases on balls received with 18 in 1981 and 25 in 1986.

Led National League in total bases with 306 in 1976, 342 in 1980 and 228 in 1981.

Led National League in slugging percentage with .546 in 1974, .624 in 1980, .644 in 1981 and .547 in 1982 and 1986.

Led National League batters in strikeouts with 138 in 1974, 180 in 1975, 149 in 1976 and 148 in 1983.

Led National League in bases on balls received with 120 in 1979, 73 in 1981, 107 in 1982 and 128 in 1983.

Led National League in sacrifice flies with 13 in 1980 and tied for lead with 9 in 1979.

Tied for National League lead in being hit by pitch with 11 in 1976.

Led National League third basemen in fielding percentage with .980 in 1986.

Led National League third basemen in total chances with 537 in 1976, 521 in 1977, 497 in 1980, 457 in 1982 and tied for lead with 338 in 1981 and 458 in 1983.

Led National League third basemen in double plays with 34 in 1978, 36 in 1979, 31 in 1980, 29 in 1983, 28 in 1987 and tied for lead with 28 in 1982.

Led National League third basemen in assists with 396 in 1977 and 332 in 1983.

Led Pacific Coast League batters in strikeouts with 145 in 1972.

Named National League Player of the Year by THE SPORTING NEWS, 1980 and 1986.

Named National League Most Valuable Player by Baseball Writers' Association of America, 1980, 1981 and 1986.

Named third baseman on THE SPORTING NEWS National League All-Star Team, 1974, 1976, 1977 and 1979 through 1984 and 1986.

Named third baseman on THE SPORTING NEWS National League All-Star fielding team, 1976 through 1984 and 1986.

Named third baseman on THE SPORTING NEWS National League Silver Slugger team, 1980 through 1984 and 1986.

Named shortstop on THE SPORTING NEWS College Baseball All-America Team, 1971.

Year Club	League	Pos.	G.	AB.	R.	H.	2B.	3B.	HR.	RBI.	B.A.	PO.	A.	E.	F.A.
1971—Reading	East.	SS-3B	74	237	27	50	7	1	8	31	.211	100	224	23	.934
1972—Eugene	P. C.	2B-3B-SS	131	436	80	127	23	6	26	91	.291	271	324	25	.960
1972—Philadelphia†	Nat.	3B-2B	13	34	2	7	0	0	1	3	.206	10	25	2	.946
1973—Philadelphia‡	Nat.	3-2-1-S	132	367	43	72	11	0	18	52	.196	119	256	18	.954
1974—Philadelphia	Nat.	3B	162	568	108	160	28	7	*36	116	.282	134	*404	26	.954
1975—Philadelphia	Nat.	3B-SS	158	562	93	140	34	3	*38	95	.249	139	390	26	.953
1976—Philadelphia	Nat.	3B	160	584	112	153	31	4	*38	107	.262	139	*377	21	.961
1977—Philadelphia	Nat.	3B-SS-2B	154	544	114	149	27	11	38	101	.274	109	401	20	.962
1978—Philadelphia	Nat.	3B-SS	145	513	93	129	27	2	21	78	.251	98	325	16	.964
1979—Philadelphia	Nat.	3B-SS	160	541	109	137	25	4	45	114	.253	115	363	23	.954
1980—Philadelphia	Nat.	3B	150	548	104	157	25	8	*48	*121	.286	98	*372	27	.946
1981—Philadelphia	Nat.	3B	102	354	*78	112	19	2	*31	*91	.316	74	*249	15	.956
1982—Philadelphia§	Nat.	3B	148	514	108	144	26	3	35	87	.280	110	*324	23	.950
1983—Philadelphia	Nat.	3B-SS	154	534	104	136	16	4	*40	109	.255	108	333	19	.959
1984—Philadelphia	Nat.	3B-1B-SS	151	528	93	146	23	3	●36	●106	.277	93	330	26	.942
1985—Philadelphia	Nat.	1B-3B-SS	158	549	89	152	31	5	33	93	.277	911	193	18	.984
1986—Philadelphia	Nat.	3B-1B	160	552	97	160	29	1	*37	*119	.290	347	238	8	.987
1987—Philadelphia x	Nat.	3B-1B-SS	147	522	88	153	28	0	35	113	.293	138	319	13	.972
1988—Philadelphia yz	Nat.	3B-1B	108	390	52	97	21	2	12	62	.249	76	223	19	.940
Major League Totals—17 Years			2362	8204	1487	2204	401	59	542	1567	.269	2818	5122	320	.961

Selected by Philadelphia Phillies' organization in 2nd round of free-agent draft, June 8, 1971.
†On disabled list, August 21 to September 2, 1972.
‡On disabled list, March 28 to April 21, 1973.
§On disabled list, April 14 to April 29, 1982.
xOn disabled list, May 26 to June 10, 1987.
yOn disabled list, August 13, 1988 through remainder of season.
zGranted free agency, November 4, 1988; re-signed by Phillies, December 7, 1988.

DIVISION SERIES RECORD

Year Club	League	Pos.	G.	AB.	R.	H.	2B.	3B.	HR.	RBI.	B.A.	PO.	A.	E.	F.A.
1981—Philadelphia	Nat.	3B	5	16	3	4	1	0	1	2	.250	6	10	1	.941

CHAMPIONSHIP SERIES RECORD

Established Championship Series record for most at-bats, five-game Series (24), 1980.

Tied Championship Series records for highest batting average, four-game Series (.467), 1983; most at-bats, extra-inning game (6), October 8, 1980; most two-base hits, total Series (7).

Year Club	League	Pos.	G.	AB.	R.	H.	2B.	3B.	HR.	RBI.	B.A.	PO.	A.	E.	F.A.
1976—Philadelphia	Nat.	3B	3	13	1	4	2	0	0	2	.308	4	9	1	.929
1977—Philadelphia	Nat.	3B	4	16	2	1	0	0	0	1	.063	4	15	0	1.000
1978—Philadelphia	Nat.	3B	4	15	1	3	2	0	0	1	.200	3	18	2	.913
1980—Philadelphia	Nat.	3B	5	24	1	5	1	0	0	1	.208	3	17	1	.952
1983—Philadelphia	Nat.	3B	4	15	5	7	2	0	1	2	.467	6	7	1	.929
Championship Series Totals—5 Years			20	83	10	20	7	0	1	7	.241	20	66	5	.945

WORLD SERIES RECORD

Tied World Series record for fewest chances accepted by third baseman, game (0), October 21, 1980.

Year Club	League	Pos.	G.	AB.	R.	H.	2B.	3B.	HR.	RBI.	B.A.	PO.	A.	E.	F.A.
1980—Philadelphia	Nat.	3B	6	21	6	8	1	0	2	7	.381	9	8	0	1.000
1983—Philadelphia	Nat.	3B	5	20	0	1	0	0	0	0	.050	1	10	1	.917
World Series Totals—2 Years			11	41	6	9	1	0	2	7	.220	10	18	1	.966

ALL-STAR GAME RECORD

Year League	Pos.	AB.	R.	H.	2B.	3B.	HR.	RBI.	B.A.	PO.	A.	E.	F.A.
1974—National	PH-3B	0	1	0	0	0	0	0	.000	0	1	0	1.000
1976—National	3B	1	0	0	0	0	0	0	.000	0	0	0	.000
1977—National	PR	0	0	0	0	0	0	0	.000	0	0	0	.000
1979—National	3B	3	2	2	1	1	0	1	.667	1	1	1	.667
1981—National	3B	4	1	2	1	0	1	2	.500	0	2	1	.667
1982—National	3B	1	0	0	0	0	0	0	.000	0	0	0	.000
1983—National	3B	3	0	0	0	0	0	0	.000	0	0	1	.000
1984—National	3B	3	0	0	0	0	0	0	.000	0	4	0	1.000
1986—National	3B	1	0	0	0	0	0	0	.000	0	0	0	.000
1987—National	3B	2	0	1	0	0	0	0	.500	0	1	0	1.000
All-Star Game Totals—10 Years		18	4	5	2	1	1	3	.278	1	9	3	.769

Named to National League All-Star Team in 1980; replaced due to injury by Ray Knight.

RICHARD CRAIG SCHOFIELD
(Dick)

Born November 21, 1962, at Springfield, Ill.
Height, 5.10. Weight, 175.
Throws and bats righthanded.
Son of John Richard (Dick) Schofield, infielder with St. Louis Cardinals, Pittsburgh, San Francisco, New York Yankees, Los Angeles Dodgers, Boston and Milwaukee Brewers, 1953 through 1971.

Major League stolen bases: 1984 (5), 1985 (11), 1986 (23), 1987 (19), 1988 (20). Total—78.
Led American League shortstops in double plays with 125 in 1988.

Led Pioneer League in bases on balls received with 68 in 1981.
Received reported $100,000 bonus to sign with California Angels, 1981.

Year	Club	League	Pos.	G.	AB.	R.	H.	2B.	3B.	HR.	RBI.	B.A.	PO.	A.	E.	F.A.
1981	—Idaho Falls	Pion.	★SS-2B	66	226	59	63	10	1	6	31	.279	★102	201	22	.932
1982	—Danville	Midw.	SS	92	308	80	111	21	★10	12	53	★.360	129	249	23	.943
1982	—Redwood	Calif.	SS	33	102	15	25	3	3	1	8	.245	35	103	3	.979
1982	—Spokane	P. C.	SS-3B	7	30	4	9	4	1	1	12	.300	7	20	0	1.000
1983	—Edmonton	P. C.	SS-3B	139	521	91	148	30	7	16	94	.284	220	402	30	.954
1983	—California	Amer.	SS	21	54	4	11	2	0	3	4	.204	24	67	7	.929
1984	—California†	Amer.	SS	140	400	39	77	10	3	4	21	.193	218	420	12	★.982
1985	—California	Amer.	SS	147	438	50	96	19	3	8	41	.219	261	397	25	.963
1986	—California	Amer.	SS	139	458	67	114	17	6	13	57	.249	246	389	18	.972
1987	—California‡	Amer.	★SS-2B	134	479	52	120	17	3	9	46	.251	205	351	9	★984
1988	—California	Amer.	SS	155	527	61	126	11	6	6	34	.239	278	492	13	★.983
Major League Totals—6 Years				736	2356	273	544	76	21	43	203	.231	1232	2116	84	.976

Selected by California Angels' organization in 1st round (third player selected) of free-agent draft, June 8, 1981.
†On disabled list, July 1 to July 24, 1984.
‡On disabled list, July 13 to August 11, 1987.

CHAMPIONSHIP SERIES RECORD

Year	Club	League	Pos.	G.	AB.	R.	H.	2B.	3B.	HR.	RBI.	B.A.	PO.	A.	E.	F.A.
1986	—California	Amer.	SS	7	30	4	9	1	0	1	2	.300	13	23	2	.947

MICHAEL RALPH SCHOOLER
(Mike)

Born August 10, 1962, at Anaheim, Calif.
Height, 6.03. Weight, 220.
Throws and bats righthanded.
Attended Golden West College, Huntington, Beach, Calif.,
and California State University, Fullerton, Calif.

Major League saves: 1988 (15).

Year	Club	League	G.	IP.	W.	L.	Pct.	H.	R.	ER.	SO.	BB.	ERA.
1985	—Bellingham	Northwest	10	55⅓	4	3	.571	42	24	18	48	15	2.93
1986	—Wausau	Midwest	26	166⅓	12	10	.545	166	83	62	171	44	3.35
1987	—Chattanooga	Southern	28	175	13	8	.619	183	87	77	144	48	3.96
1988	—Calgary	P. Coast	26	33⅔	4	4	.500	33	19	12	47	6	3.21
1988	—Seattle	American	40	48⅓	5	8	.385	45	21	19	54	24	3.54
Major League Totals—1 Year			40	48⅓	5	8	.385	45	21	19	54	24	3.54

Selected by Seattle Mariners' organization in 2nd round of free-agent draft, June 3, 1985.

ALFRED WILLIAM SCHROEDER III

Name pronounced SHRO-der.

(Bill)

Born September 7, 1958, at Baltimore, Md.
Height, 6.02. Weight, 200.
Throws and bats righthanded.
Attended Clemson University, Clemson, S. C.

Major League stolen bases: 1986 (1), 1987 (5). Total—6.
Led Pacific Coast League batters in strikeouts with 136 and game-winning RBIs with 15 in 1982.
Led California League batters in strikeouts with 141 in 1980.
Led Pioneer League in total bases with 170 in 1979.
Led California League catchers in total chances with 759 in 1980.
Tied for Pacific Coast League lead in passed balls with 13 in 1983.

Year	Club	League	Pos.	G.	AB.	R.	H.	2B.	3B.	HR.	RBI.	B.A.	PO.	A.	E.	F.A.
1979	—Butte	Pion.	C-1B	65	242	73	86	16	7	18	77	.355	474	50	9	.983
1980	—Stockton	Calif.	★C-1B	123	437	68	117	20	3	18	97	.268	669	96	7	★.991
1981	—El Paso	Texas	C-OF	95	335	41	87	20	2	15	61	.260	511	49	10	.982
1982	—Vancouver	P. C.	C	116	425	66	113	16	3	22	77	.266	569	77	7	★.989
1983	—Vancouver	P. C.	C	82	304	51	87	13	3	20	70	.286	399	68	6	★.987
1983	—Milwaukee	Amer.	C	23	73	7	13	2	1	3	7	.178	92	5	2	.980
1984	—Milwaukee	Amer.	C-1B	61	210	29	54	6	0	14	25	.257	277	24	4	.987
1985	—Milwaukee†	Amer.	C-1B	53	194	18	47	8	0	8	25	.242	216	23	3	.988
1986	—El Paso‡	Texas	C	8	26	5	6	3	0	1	2	.231	26	2	0	1.000
1986	—Milwaukee	Amer.	C-1B	64	217	32	46	14	0	7	19	.212	307	25	1	.997
1987	—Milwaukee	Amer.	C-1B	75	250	35	83	12	0	14	42	.332	373	27	2	.995
1988	—Milwaukee§	Amer.	C-1B	41	122	9	19	2	0	5	10	.156	197	21	0	1.000
1988	—Denver x	A. A.	C	6	17	4	4	2	1	0	3	.235	16	3	0	1.000
Major League Totals—6 Years				317	1066	130	262	44	1	51	128	.246	1462	125	12	.992

Selected by Milwaukee Brewers' organization in 8th round of free-agent draft, June 5, 1979.
†On disabled list, May 15 to June 14 and June 22 to July 19, 1985.
‡On Milwaukee disabled list, March 29 to May 4, 1986; included rehabilitation disability assignment to El Paso, April 24 to May 4, 1986.
§On disabled list, July 27 to August 15, 1988; included rehabilitation disability assignment to Denver, August 5 to August 12, 1988.
xTraded to California Angels for Infielder Gus Polidor, December 7, 1988.

RICHARD SPENCER SCHU

Name pronounced Shoo.

(Rick)

Born January 26, 1962, at Philadelphia, Pa.
Height, 6.00. Weight, 194.
Throws and bats righthanded.
Attended Sacramento City College, Sacramento, Calif.
Son of Ken Schu, minor league pitcher, 1955 and 1956.

Tied major league record for most doubles, inning (2), October 3, 1985, third inning.
Major League stolen bases: 1985 (8), 1986 (2), 1988 (6). Total—16.
Led Pacific Coast League third basemen in total chances with 390 in 1984.

Year Club	League	Pos.	G.	AB.	R.	H.	2B.	3B.	HR.	RBI.	B.A.	PO.	A.	E.	F.A.
1981—Bend	N'west	3B-2B-SS	68	258	41	69	10	0	2	42	.267	55	137	24	.889
1982—Spartanburg	S. Atl.	3B-2B-SS	125	429	78	117	28	1	12	60	.273	157	257	45	.902
1983—Peninsula	Carol.	3B-SS-2B	122	444	69	119	22	3	14	63	.268	82	252	30	.918
1983—Portland	P. C.	3B-SS	9	29	7	11	2	1	1	3	.379	6	12	2	.900
1984—Portland	P. C.	3B	140	552	70	166	35	•14	12	82	.301	*109	*254	*27	.931
1984—Philadelphia	Nat.	3B	17	29	12	8	2	1	2	5	.276	7	13	1	.952
1985—Portland	P. C.	SS-3B	42	150	19	42	8	3	4	22	.280	36	91	11	.920
1985—Philadelphia	Nat.	3B	112	416	54	105	21	4	7	24	.252	86	191	20	.933
1986—Philadelphia	Nat.	3B	92	208	32	57	10	1	8	25	.274	42	94	13	.913
1987—Philadelphia†‡	Nat.	3B-1B	92	196	24	46	6	3	7	23	.235	193	71	10	.964
1988—Baltimore§	Amer.	3B-1B	89	270	22	69	9	4	4	20	.256	94	110	11	.949
National League Totals—4 Years			313	849	122	216	39	9	24	77	.254	328	369	44	.941
American League Totals—1 Year			89	270	22	69	9	4	4	20	.256	94	110	11	.949
Major League Totals—5 Years			402	1119	144	285	48	13	28	97	.255	422	479	55	.942

Signed as free agent by Philadelphia Phillies' organization, November 25, 1980.

†On disabled list, August 19 to September 3, 1987.

‡Traded with Outfielders Jeff Stone and Keith Hughes to Baltimore Orioles for Outfielder Mike Young and a player to be named later, March 21, 1988; Philadelphia Phillies acquired Outfielder Frank Bellino to complete deal, June 14, 1988.

§On disabled list, April 22 to May 7, June 6 to June 21 and August 12 to August 29, 1988.

DONALD ARTHUR SCHULZE

Name pronounced SHULL-zee.

(Don)

Born September 27, 1962, at Roselle, Ill.
Height, 6.03. Weight, 230.
Throws and bats righthanded.

Led Gulf Coast League in complete games with 3 in 1980.
Tied for American Association lead in shutouts with 2 in 1983.

Year Club	League	G.	IP.	W.	L.	Pct.	H.	R.	ER.	SO.	BB.	ERA.
1980—Sarasota Cubs	Gulf Coast	12	66	2	7	.222	58	38	30	30	36	4.09
1981—Quad Cities†	Midwest	17	105	8	5	.615	89	33	27	61	51	2.31
1982—Salinas	California	24	165	13	7	.650	150	61	52	122	59	2.84
1983—Iowa	Am. Assoc.	25	168⅔	11	9	.550	170	88	80	103	63	4.27
1983—Chicago	National	4	14	0	1	.000	19	11	11	8	7	7.07
1984—Iowa	Am. Assoc.	13	79	5	5	.500	79	40	38	44	29	4.33
1984—Chicago‡	National	1	3	0	0	.000	8	4	4	2	1	12.00
1984—Maine	Int'national	2	9⅓	1	1	.500	14	12	9	7	3	8.68
1984—Cleveland	American	19	85⅔	3	6	.333	105	53	46	39	27	4.83
1985—Cleveland	American	19	94⅓	4	10	.286	128	75	63	37	19	6.01
1985—Maine	Int'national	15	115⅓	6	4	.600	105	41	34	45	29	2.65
1986—Cleveland§	American	19	84⅔	4	4	.500	88	48	47	33	34	5.00
1986—Maine	Int'national	3	10	0	1	.000	12	7	7	7	4	6.30
1987—Buffalo x	Am. Assoc.	5	22⅓	0	1	.000	33	25	24	13	12	9.67
1987—Tidewater	Int'national	15	89⅓	11	1	*.917	81	37	36	45	31	3.63
1987—New York yz	National	5	21⅔	1	2	.333	24	15	15	5	6	6.23
1988—Toledo a	Int'national	27	185⅓	10	13	.435	172	72	64	107	56	3.11
National League Totals—3 Years		10	38⅔	1	3	.250	51	30	30	15	14	6.98
American League Totals—3 Years		57	264⅔	11	20	.355	321	176	156	109	80	5.30
Major League Totals—5 Years		67	303⅓	12	23	.343	372	206	186	124	94	5.52

Selected by Chicago Cubs' organization in 1st round (11th player selected) of free-agent draft, June 3, 1980.

†On disabled list, June 22 to July 16, 1981.

‡Traded with Outfielders Mel Hall and Joe Carter and Pitcher Darryl Banks to Cleveland Indians for Catcher Ron Hassey and Pitchers Rick Sutcliffe and George Frazier, June 13, 1984.

§On disabled list, July 22 to September 1, 1986; included rehabilitation disability assignment to Maine, August 20 to September 1, 1986.

xTraded to Tidewater (New York Mets' organization) for Outfielder Ricky Nelson, May 11, 1987.

yGranted free agency, October 15, 1987; signed by Minnesota Twins, December 7, 1987.

zTraded to Detroit Tigers for Pitcher Karl Best, March 28, 1988.

aGranted free agency, October 15, 1988; signed by New York Yankees, November 17, 1988.

MICHAEL LORRI SCIOSCIA

Name pronounced SO-sha.
(Mike)
Born November 27, 1958, at Upper Darby, Pa.
Height, 6.02. Weight, 219.
Throws right and bats lefthanded.
Attended Pennsylvania State University, University Park, Pa.

Major League stolen bases: 1980 (1), 1982 (2), 1984 (2), 1985 (3), 1986 (3), 1987 (7). Total—18.
Led National League catchers in total chances with 1,016 in 1987.
Led National League in passed balls with 11 in 1981.
Tied for Pacific Coast League lead in being hit by pitch with 7 in 1979.
Led Pacific Coast League catchers in double plays with 19 and passed balls with 22 in 1979.
Led Midwest League catchers in errors with 20 and double plays with 12 in 1978.

Year Club	League	Pos.	G.	AB.	R.	H.	2B.	3B.	HR.	RBI.	B.A.	PO.	A.	E.	F.A.
1976—Bellingham	N'west.	C	46	151	25	42	6	0	7	26	.278	202	35	14	.944
1977—Clinton	Midw.	C-1B	121	364	58	92	20	1	7	44	.253	764	95	22	.975
1978—San Antonio†	Texas	C	58	204	29	61	16	0	2	34	.299	214	17	4	.983
1979—Albuquerque	P. C.	C	143	461	80	155	34	0	3	68	.336	*690	*86	*15	.981
1980—Albuquerque	P. C.	C	52	160	33	53	11	1	3	33	.331	207	19	5	.978
1980—Los Angeles‡	Nat.	C	54	134	8	34	5	1	1	8	.254	226	26	2	.992
1981—Los Angeles	Nat.	C	93	290	27	80	10	0	2	29	.276	493	48	7	.987
1982—Los Angeles	Nat.	C	129	365	31	80	11	1	5	38	.219	631	57	10	.986
1983—Los Angeles§	Nat.	C	12	35	3	11	3	0	1	7	.314	55	4	0	1.000
1984—Los Angeles x	Nat.	C	114	341	29	93	18	0	5	38	.273	701	64	12	.985
1985—Los Angeles	Nat.	C	141	429	47	127	26	3	7	53	.296	818	66	•13	.986
1986—Los Angeles y	Nat.	C	122	374	36	94	18	1	5	26	.251	756	64	15	.982
1987—Los Angeles z	Nat.	C	142	461	44	122	26	1	6	38	.265	*925	80	11	.989
1988—Los Angeles	Nat.	C	130	408	29	105	18	0	3	35	.257	748	63	7	.991
Major League Totals—9 Years			937	2837	254	746	135	7	35	272	.263	5353	472	77	.987

Selected by Los Angeles Dodgers' organization in 1st round (19th player selected) of free-agent draft, June 8, 1976.
†On disabled list, May 19 to August 4, 1978.
‡On disabled list, April 10 to April 20, 1980.
§On disabled list, May 15, 1983 through remainder of season.
xOn disabled list, May 6 to May 21, 1984.
yOn disabled list, June 10 to July 15, 1986.
zOn disabled list, June 1 to June 16, 1987.

DIVISION SERIES RECORD

Year Club	League	Pos.	G.	AB.	R.	H.	2B.	3B.	HR.	RBI.	B.A.	PO.	A.	E.	F.A.
1981—Los Angeles	Nat.	C	4	13	0	2	0	0	0	1	.154	21	3	0	1.000

CHAMPIONSHIP SERIES RECORD

Year Club	League	Pos.	G.	AB.	R.	H.	2B.	3B.	HR.	RBI.	B.A.	PO.	A.	E.	F.A.
1981—Los Angeles	Nat.	C	5	15	1	2	0	0	1	1	.133	27	1	0	1.000
1985—Los Angeles	Nat.	C	6	16	2	4	0	0	0	1	.250	31	4	1	.972
1988—Los Angeles	Nat.	C	7	22	3	8	1	0	1	2	.364	37	4	0	1.000
Championship Series Totals—3 Years			18	53	6	14	1	0	2	4	.264	95	9	1	.990

WORLD SERIES RECORD

Year Club	League	Pos.	G.	AB.	R.	H.	2B.	3B.	HR.	RBI.	B.A.	PO.	A.	E.	F.A.
1981—Los Angeles	Nat.	C-PH	3	4	1	1	0	0	0	0	.250	7	1	0	1.000
1988—Los Angeles	Nat.	C	4	14	0	3	0	0	0	1	.214	28	0	1	.966
World Series Totals—2 Years			7	18	1	4	0	0	0	1	.222	35	1	1	.973

MICHAEL WARREN SCOTT
(Mike)

Born April 26, 1955, at Santa Monica, Calif.
Height, 6.03. Weight, 215.
Throws and bats righthanded.
Attended Pepperdine University, Malibu, Calif.

Tied major league record for most strikeouts, inning (4), September 3, 1986 (fifth inning).
Pitched 2-0 no-hit victory against San Francisco Giants, September 25, 1986.
Major League saves: 1982 (3).
Tied for National League lead in games started by pitchers with 36 in 1987.
Tied for National League lead in shutouts with 5 in 1986.
Led Texas League in complete games with 14 and tied for lead in balks with 3 in 1977.
Tied for International League lead in games started by pitchers with 29 in 1978 and balks with 3 in 1980.
Named National League Pitcher of the Year by THE SPORTING NEWS, 1986.
Won National League Cy Young Memorial Award, 1986.
Named righthanded pitcher on THE SPORTING NEWS National League All-Star Team, 1986.

Year Club	League	G.	IP.	W.	L.	Pct.	H.	R.	ER.	SO.	BB.	ERA.
1976—Jackson	Texas	7	44	3	3	.500	34	20	14	19	14	2.86
1977—Jackson	Texas	25	*187	*14	10	.583	132	77	61	97	55	2.94
1977—Tidewater	Int'national	2	2	0	1	.000	4	5	4	0	3	18.00
1978—Tidewater	Int'national	29	192	10	10	.500	196	105	84	93	83	3.94
1979—Tidewater	Int'national	18	99	8	4	.667	103	37	35	40	27	3.18

Year Club	League	G.	IP.	W.	L.	Pct.	H.	R.	ER.	SO.	BB.	ERA.
1979—New York	National	18	52	1	3	.250	59	35	31	21	20	5.37
1980—Tidewater	Int'national	27	170	13	7	.650	165	69	56	88	64	2.96
1980—New York	National	6	29	1	1	.500	40	14	14	13	8	4.34
1981—New York	National	23	136	5	10	.333	130	65	59	54	34	3.90
1982—New York†	National	37	147	7	13	.350	185	100	84	63	60	5.14
1983—Houston‡	National	24	145	10	6	.625	143	67	60	73	46	3.72
1984—Houston	National	31	154	5	11	.313	179	96	80	83	43	4.68
1985—Houston	National	36	221⅔	18	8	.692	194	91	81	137	80	3.29
1986—Houston	National	37	*275⅓	18	10	.643	182	73	68	*306	72	*2.22
1987—Houston	National	36	247⅔	16	13	.552	199	94	89	233	79	3.23
1988—Houston§	National	32	218⅔	14	8	.636	162	74	71	190	53	2.92
Major League Totals—10 Years		280	1626⅓	95	83	.534	1473	709	637	1173	495	3.53

Selected by New York Mets' organization in 2nd round of free-agent draft, June 8, 1976.
†Traded to Houston Astros for Outfielder-First Baseman Danny Heep, December 10, 1982.
‡On disabled list, April 5 to May 4, 1983.
§On disabled list, June 22 to July 13, 1988.

CHAMPIONSHIP SERIES RECORD

Established Championship Series record for most complete games, Series (2), 1986.

Tied Championship Series record for most strikeouts, game (14), October 8, 1986.

Established National League Championship Series records for most innings pitched, six-game Series (18), 1986; most consecutive scoreless innings, Series (16), 1986; most strikeouts, Series (19), 1986.

Tied National League Championship Series record for most complete games, total Series (2); most consecutive scoreless innings, total Series (16).

Year Club	League	G.	IP.	W.	L.	Pct.	H.	R.	ER.	SO.	BB.	ERA.
1986—Houston	National	2	18	2	0	1.000	8	1	1	19	1	0.50

ALL-STAR GAME RECORD

Year League	IP.	W.	L.	Pct.	H.	R.	ER.	SO.	BB.	ERA.
1986—National	1	0	0	.000	1	1	1	2	0	9.00
1987—National	2	0	0	.000	1	0	0	1	0	0.00
All-Star Game Totals—2 Years	3	0	0	.000	2	1	1	3	0	3.00

WILLIAM SCOTT SCUDDER

(Known by middle name.)

Born February 14, 1968, at Paris, Tex.
Height, 6.02. Weight, 180.
Throws and bats righthanded.

Pitched 4-0 no-hit victory against Wausau, May 20, 1988.

Year Club	League	G.	IP.	W.	L.	Pct.	H.	R.	ER.	SO.	BB.	ERA.
1986—Billings	Pioneer	12	52⅔	1	3	.250	43	34	28	38	36	4.78
1987—Cedar Rapids	Midwest	26	153⅔	7	12	.368	129	86	70	128	76	4.10
1988—Cedar Rapids	Midwest	16	102⅓	7	3	.700	61	30	23	126	41	2.02
1988—Chattanooga	Southern	11	70	7	0	1.000	53	24	23	52	30	2.96

Selected by Cincinnati Reds' organization in 1st round (17th player selected) of free-agent draft, June 2, 1986.

RODNEY GRANT SCURRY

Name pronounced SKUR-ee.

(Rod)

Born March 17, 1956, at Sacramento, Calif.
Height, 6.02. Weight, 195.
Throws and bats lefthanded.

Cousin of Joe Rose, tight end with Miami Dolphins and Los Angeles Rams, 1980 through 1985 and 1987.

Pitched seven-inning, 2-0 no-hit victory against Richmond, July 25, 1977.
Major League saves: 1981 (7), 1982 (14), 1983 (7), 1984 (4), 1985 (3), 1986 (2), 1988 (2). Total—39.
Led Carolina League pitchers in games started with 26 in 1975.
Led New York-Pennsylvania League in hit batsmen with 7 in 1974.

Year Club	League	G.	IP.	W.	L.	Pct.	H.	R.	ER.	SO.	BB.	ERA.
1974—Niagara Falls	NYP	14	89	5	6	.455	55	36	34	102	*74	3.44
1975—Salem	Carolina	26	150	9	12	.429	128	79	61	143	118	3.66
1976—Shreveport	Texas	24	123	8	8	.500	120	71	53	83	83	3.88
1977—Shreveport	Texas	18	113	3	11	.214	97	54	36	111	48	2.87
1977—Columbus	Int'national	8	37	3	2	.600	30	31	19	39	32	4.62
1978—Columbus†	Int'national	16	63	3	3	.500	69	44	40	57	43	5.71
1978—Shreveport	Texas	5	29	1	4	.200	27	19	15	38	24	4.66
1979—Portland‡	P. Coast	35	122	5	5	.500	121	64	56	94	72	4.13
1980—Pittsburgh	National	20	38	0	2	.000	23	12	9	28	17	2.13
1981—Pittsburgh	National	27	74	4	5	.444	74	33	31	65	40	3.77
1982—Pittsburgh	National	76	103⅔	4	5	.444	79	26	20	94	64	1.74
1983—Pittsburgh	National	61	68	4	9	.308	63	45	42	67	53	5.56
1984—Pittsburgh§	National	43	46⅓	5	6	.455	28	14	13	48	22	2.53
1985—Pittsburgh x	National	30	47⅔	0	1	.000	42	22	17	43	28	3.21
1985—New York	American	5	12⅔	1	0	1.000	5	4	4	17	10	2.84
1986—New York y	American	31	39⅓	1	2	.333	38	18	16	36	22	3.66
1986—Fort Lauderdale za	Florida St.	7	7⅓	1	0	1.000	7	3	3	16	7	3.68

Year Club	League	G.	IP.	W.	L.	Pct.	H.	R.	ER.	SO.	BB.	ERA.
1987—Phoenix b	P. Coast	28	59⅔	3	3	.500	53	27	25	57	41	3.77
1988—Calgary	P. Coast	18	24⅓	2	1	.667	26	14	11	23	16	4.07
1988—Seattle c	American	39	31⅓	0	2	.000	32	16	14	33	18	4.02
National League Totals—6 Years		257	377⅔	17	28	.378	309	152	132	345	224	3.15
American League Totals—3 Years		75	83⅓	2	4	.333	75	38	34	86	50	3.67
Major League Totals—8 Years		332	461	19	32	.373	384	190	166	431	274	3.24

Selected by Pittsburgh Pirates' organization in 1st round (11th player selected) of free-agent draft, June 5, 1974.

†On disabled list, June 12 to July 11, 1978.

‡On disabled list, August 4 to August 14, 1979.

§On disabled list, April 7 to May 13 and August 5 to August 27, 1984.

xSold to New York Yankees, September 14, 1985.

yOn disabled list, May 13 to July 25, 1986; included rehabilitation disability assignment to Fort Lauderdale, July 7 to July 25, 1986.

zGranted free agency, November 12, 1986; re-signed by Yankees, December 6, 1986.

aReleased, March 27, 1987; signed by San Francisco Giants, June 4, 1987.

bTraded to Seattle Mariners for a player to be named later, March 19, 1988; San Francisco Giants acquired Outfielder Donell Nixon to complete deal, June 23, 1988.

cReleased, December 21, 1988.

RUDY CABALLERO SEANEZ

Born October 20, 1968, at Brawley, Calif.
Height, 6.00. Weight, 170.
Throws and bats righthanded.

Pitched 4-0 no-hit victory against Pulaski, August 2, 1986.

Year Club	League	G.	IP.	W.	L.	Pct.	H.	R.	ER.	SO.	BB.	ERA.
1986—Burlington	Ap'lachian	13	76	5	2	.714	59	37	27	56	32	3.20
1987—Waterloo†	Midwest	10	34⅔	0	4	.000	35	29	26	23	23	6.75
1988—Waterloo	Midwest	22	113⅓	6	6	.500	98	69	59	93	68	4.69

Selected by Cleveland Indians' organization in 4th round of free-agent draft, June 10, 1986.

†On disabled list, May 4 to July 11 and August 9 to August 29, 1987.

RAYMOND MARK SEARAGE
(Ray)

Born May 1, 1955, at Freeport, N.Y.
Height, 6.01. Weight, 180.
Throws and bats lefthanded.
Attended West Liberty State College, West Liberty, W. Va.

Major League saves: 1981 (1), 1984 (6), 1985 (1), 1986 (1), 1987 (2). Total—11.

Led International League in wild pitches with 14 in 1982.

Year Club	League	G.	IP.	W.	L.	Pct.	H.	R.	ER.	SO.	BB.	ERA.
1976—Sara. W. Sox-Sara. Cards	Gulf Coast	11	32	1	3	.250	24	17	15	31	22	4.22
1977—St. Petersburg	Florida St.	13	19	0	0	.000	11	7	6	12	12	2.84
1977—Johnson City	Ap'lachian	8	41	3	2	.600	38	23	22	27	21	4.83
1978—Gastonia	W. Carol.	39	110	8	3	.727	86	40	34	86	68	2.78
1979—Arkansas†	Texas	42	89	10	4	.714	73	27	22	63	46	2.22
1980—Tidewater	Int'national	19	30	1	0	1.000	35	24	23	20	20	6.90
1980—Jackson	Texas	14	70	4	5	.444	54	32	26	71	26	3.34
1981—Tidewater	Int'national	18	27	2	0	1.000	29	10	7	23	13	2.33
1981—New York‡	National	26	37	1	0	1.000	34	16	15	16	17	3.65
1982—Charleston§	Int'national	38	114	2	7	.222	112	73	62	87	87	4.89
1983—Charleston x	Int'national	31	134	7	7	.500	146	94	84	77	76	5.64
1984—Vancouver	P. Coast	33	76⅓	6	3	.667	62	29	26	59	44	3.07
1984—Milwaukee	American	21	38⅓	2	1	.667	20	3	3	29	16	0.70
1985—Milwaukee	American	33	38	1	4	.200	54	27	25	36	24	5.92
1985—Vancouver	P. Coast	23	26	2	0	1.000	22	10	7	31	12	2.42
1986—Milwaukee yz-Chicago	American	46	51	1	1	.500	44	20	19	36	28	3.35
1986—Vancouver	P. Coast	20	25	2	0	1.000	12	5	4	20	8	1.44
1987—Chicago	American	58	55⅔	2	3	.400	56	28	26	33	24	4.20
1987—Hawaii a	P. Coast	3	7⅓	0	1	.000	6	5	3	5	3	3.68
1988—Albuquerque	P. Coast	51	60	2	3	.400	62	39	34	58	25	5.10
National League Totals—1 Year		26	37	1	0	1.000	34	16	15	16	17	3.65
American League Totals—4 Years		158	183	6	9	.400	174	78	73	134	92	3.59
Major League Totals—5 Years		184	220	7	9	.438	208	94	88	150	109	3.60

Selected by St. Louis Cardinals' organization in 22nd round of free-agent draft, June 8, 1976.

†Traded to New York Mets' organization for Catcher Jody Davis, December 10, 1979.

‡Traded to Cleveland Indians for Shortstop Tom Veryzer, January 8, 1982.

§Traded on a conditional basis to San Diego Padres for a player to be named later, December 15, 1982; returned, March 28, 1983.

xGranted free agency, October 20, 1983; signed by Vancouver (Milwaukee Brewers' organization), November 4, 1983.

yLoaned to Buffalo (Chicago White Sox' organization), July 17, 1986; returned, July 23, 1986.

zTraded to Chicago White Sox for Pitcher Al Jones and Outfielder Tom Hartley, July 23, 1986.

aReleased, March 25, 1988; signed by Albuquerque (Los Angeles Dodgers' organization), April 5, 1988.

WILLIAM STEPHEN SEARCY
(Steve)

Born June 4, 1964, at Knoxville, Tenn.
Height, 6.01. Weight, 185.
Throws and bats lefthanded.
Attended University of Tennessee, Knoxville, Tenn.

Led International League in hit batsmen with 12 in 1988.
Tied for Eastern League lead in games started by pitchers with 27 in 1986.
Named International League Pitcher of the Year, 1988.

Year Club	League	G.	IP.	W.	L.	Pct.	H.	R.	ER.	SO.	BB.	ERA.
1985—Bristol	Ap'lachian	4	22	1	1	.500	15	6	5	24	2	2.05
1985—Birmingham	Southern	7	36⅔	2	2	.500	39	17	13	19	23	3.19
1986—Glens Falls	Eastern	27	172	11	6	.647	166	79	63	*139	74	3.30
1987—Toledo	Int'national	10	53⅓	3	4	.429	49	26	25	54	32	4.22
1988—Toledo	Int'national	27	170	•13	7	.650	131	61	49	*176	79	2.59
1988—Detroit	American	2	8	0	2	.000	8	6	5	5	4	5.63
Major League Totals—1 Year		2	8	0	2	.000	8	6	5	5	4	5.63

Selected by Detroit Tigers' organization in 3rd round of free-agent draft, June 3, 1985.

ROBERT BUSH SEBRA
Name pronounced SEBB-ruh.
(Bob)

Born December 11, 1961, at Ridgewood, N.J.
Height, 6.02. Weight, 195.
Throws and bats righthanded.
Attended University of Nebraska, Lincoln, Neb.

Tied for American Association lead in home runs allowed with 17 in 1985.
Named American Association Pitcher of the Year, 1988.

Year Club	League	G.	IP.	W.	L.	Pct.	H.	R.	ER.	SO.	BB.	ERA.
1983—Tri-Cities	Northwest	12	58⅓	4	3	.571	48	36	26	70	29	4.01
1984—Tulsa	Texas	17	100⅓	10	5	.667	86	45	38	90	41	3.41
1984—Oklahoma City	Am. Assoc.	9	53⅓	4	4	.500	37	23	20	38	25	3.38
1985—Oklahoma City	Am. Assoc.	22	138⅔	10	6	.625	121	62	59	84	57	3.83
1985—Texas†	American	7	20⅓	0	2	.000	26	17	17	13	14	7.52
1986—Indianapolis	Am. Assoc.	20	126	9	2	.818	108	59	48	91	70	3.43
1986—Montreal	National	17	91⅓	5	5	.500	82	39	36	66	25	3.55
1987—Montreal	National	36	177⅓	6	15	.286	184	99	87	156	67	4.42
1988—Indianapolis‡	Am. Assoc.	29	174⅓	12	6	.667	154	71	57	126	59	2.94
1988—Philadelphia	National	3	11⅓	1	2	.333	15	11	10	7	10	7.94
American League Totals—1 Year		7	20⅓	0	2	.000	26	17	17	13	14	7.52
National League Totals—3 Years		56	280	12	22	.353	281	149	133	229	102	4.28
Major League Totals—4 Years		63	300⅓	12	24	.333	307	166	150	242	116	4.50

Selected by Detroit Tigers' organization in 4th round of free-agent draft, June 3, 1980.
Selected by Texas Rangers' organization in 5th round of free-agent draft, June 6, 1983.
†Traded with Infielder Jim Anderson to Montreal Expos for Outfielder Pete Incaviglia, November 2, 1985.
‡Traded to Philadelphia Phillies for Pitcher Travis Chambers, September 1, 1988.

RALPH LAURENCE SEE
(Larry)

Born June 20, 1960, at Norwalk, Calif.
Height, 6.00. Weight, 200.
Throws and bats righthanded.
Attended Cerritos Junior College, Norwalk, Calif.

Led Texas League in being hit by pitch with 16 in 1983.
Tied for Pacific Coast League lead in total bases with 278 in 1986.
Led Pacific Coast League first basemen in fielding percentage with .993 in 1986.
Led Texas League third basemen in putouts with 98, errors with 38 and total chances with 327 in 1983.
Led Pioneer League third basemen in total chances with 196 and tied for lead in double plays with 10 in 1980.

Year Club	League	Pos.	G.	AB.	R.	H.	2B.	3B.	HR.	RBI.	B.A.	PO.	A.	E.	F.A.
1980—Lethbridge	Pion.	3B	68	252	41	87	19	2	4	44	.345	*55	*119	22	*.888
1981—Lodi†	Calif.					(Did not play)									
1982—Vero Beach	Fla. St.	3B	132	455	74	120	*29	1	12	•85	.264	*118	228	36	.906
1983—San Antonio	Texas	3B-1B	132	445	72	130	38	2	17	91	.292	150	195	39	.898
1984—Albuquerque	P. C.	3B-1B	58	217	32	63	11	1	8	44	.290	41	117	16	.908
1984—San Antonio	Texas	3B-1B	77	254	56	72	17	1	17	50	.283	85	137	26	.895
1985—San Antonio	Texas	1B	99	373	55	100	17	1	15	58	.268	879	57	•14	.985
1985—Albuquerque	P. C.	3B	23	77	7	20	3	1	3	9	.260	25	29	6	.900
1986—Albuquerque	P. C.	1B-3B	*142	536	83	155	*38	2	27	106	.289	1089	118	11	.991
1986—Los Angeles	Nat.	1B	13	20	1	5	2	0	0	2	.250	41	6	1	.979
1987—Albuquerque‡	P. C.	1B-3B	66	257	45	78	18	2	6	44	.304	608	42	8	.988
1987—Oklahoma City	A. A.	1B-3B	69	258	35	70	16	1	6	45	.271	524	54	9	.985
1988—Texas	Amer.	1B-C-3B	13	23	0	3	0	0	0	0	.130	13	1	1	.933

Year	Club	League	Pos.	G.	AB.	R.	H.	2B.	3B.	HR.	RBI.	B.A.	PO.	A.	E.	F.A.
1988	Okahoma City§	A. A.	1B-C-3B	89	329	34	86	18	2	12	55	.261	672	48	15	.980
National League Totals—1 Year				13	20	1	5	2	0	0	2	.250	41	6	1	.979
American League Totals—1 Year				13	23	0	3	0	0	0	0	.130	13	1	1	.933
Major League Totals—2 Years				26	43	1	8	2	0	0	2	.186	54	7	2	.968

Selected by San Diego Padres' organization in 5th round of free-agent draft, January 9, 1979.
Selected by Los Angeles Dodgers' organization in 3rd round of free-agent draft, January 8, 1980.
†On disabled list, April 10, 1981 through entire season.
‡Traded to Texas Rangers' organization for Second Baseman Jose Mota, June 25, 1987.
§Granted free agency, October 15, 1988; signed by Toledo (Detroit Tigers' organization), December 6, 1988.

JOSE ALTAGRACIA SEGURA (MOTA)

Born January 26, 1963, at Fundacion Barahona, D. R.
Height, 5.11. Weight 180.
Throws and bats righthanded.

Year	Club	League	G.	IP.	W.	L.	Pct.	H.	R.	ER.	SO.	BB.	ERA.
1981	Helena	Pioneer	25	35	2	3	.400	42	26	17	27	15	4.37
1982	Spartanburg	S. Atlantic	20	29	2	2	.500	32	28	25	17	18	7.76
1982	Bend	Northwest	24	36⅔	4	4	.500	27	16	7	43	28	1.72
1983	Spartanburg†	S. Atlantic	40	65⅔	1	6	.143	77	59	47	54	42	6.44
1984	Kinston	Carolina	16	97⅓	7	4	.636	88	48	43	55	35	3.98
1984	Knoxville	Southern	12	69	4	6	.400	75	47	34	26	47	4.43
1985	Kinston	Carolina	34	110⅓	4	•13	.235	109	62	51	73	69	4.16
1986	Knoxville‡	Southern	24	106⅔	4	7	.364	101	72	50	55	72	4.22
1987	Syracuse§	Int'national	43	107	5	8	.385	136	90	78	54	59	6.56
1988	Chicago	American	4	8⅔	0	0	.000	19	17	13	2	8	13.50
1988	Vancouver x	P. Coast	20	111	6	6	.500	127	69	56	39	60	4.54
Major League Totals—1 Year			4	8⅔	0	0	.000	19	17	13	2	8	13.50

Signed as free agent by Philadelphia Phillies' organization, June 22, 1981.
†Drafted by Syracuse (Toronto Blue Jays' organization), December 6, 1983.
‡On disabled list, July 14 to August 9, 1986.
§Granted free agency, October 15, 1987; signed by Chicago White Sox, January 29, 1988.
xReleased, November 20, 1988.

KEVIN LEE SEITZER

Born March 26, 1962, at Springfield, Ill.
Height, 5.11. Weight, 180.
Throws and bats righthanded.
Received bachelor of science degree in industrial electronics from
Eastern Illinois University, Charleston, Ill.

Major League stolen bases: 1987 (12), 1988 (10). Total—22.
Collected six hits in one game, August 2, 1987.
Led American League third basemen in errors with 22 in 1987.
Led South Atlantic League in bases on balls received with 118 in 1984.
Tied for American Association lead in being hit by pitch with 9 in 1986.
Led South Atlantic League third basemen in total chances with 409 in 1984.
Led Pioneer League third basemen in assists with 122 and total chances with 172 in 1983.
Named South Atlantic League Most Valuable Player, 1984.

Year	Club	League	Pos.	G.	AB.	R.	H.	2B.	3B.	HR.	RBI.	B.A.	PO.	A.	E.	F.A.
1983	Butte	Pion.	3B-SS	68	238	60	82	14	1	2	45	.345	52	124	21	.893
1984	Charleston	S. Atl.	3B	•141	489	*96	*145	26	5	8	79	.297	80	*279	*50	.878
1985	Fort Myers	Fla. St.	1B-3B	90	290	61	91	10	5	3	46	.314	569	88	9	.986
1985	Memphis	South.	3B-1B-OF	52	187	26	65	6	2	1	20	.348	79	51	10	.929
1986	Omaha	A. A.	OF-1B-3B	129	432	86	138	20	11	13	74	.319	338	39	9	.977
1986	Kansas City	Amer.	1B-OF-3B	28	96	16	31	4	1	2	11	.323	224	19	3	.988
1987	Kansas City	Amer.	3B-1B-OF	161	641	105	•207	33	8	15	83	.323	290	315	24	.962
1988	Kansas City	Amer.	*3B-OF	149	559	90	170	32	5	5	60	.304	93	297	*26	.938
Major League Totals—3 Years				338	1296	211	408	69	14	22	154	.315	607	631	53	.959

Selected by Kansas City Royals' organization in 11th round of free-agent draft, June 6, 1983.

ALL-STAR GAME RECORD

Year	League	Pos.	AB.	R.	H.	2B.	3B.	HR.	RBI.	B.A.	PO.	A.	E.	F.A.
1987	American	3B	2	0	0	0	0	0	0	.000	0	0	0	.000

JEFFREY DOYLE SELLERS
(Jeff)

Born May 11, 1964, at Compton, Calif.
Height, 6.00. Weight, 195.
Throws and bats righthanded.

Led Eastern League in shutouts with 5 and complete games with 15 in 1985.
Led Florida State League pitchers in games started with 29 in 1984.

Year	Club	League	G.	IP.	W.	L.	Pct.	H.	R.	ER.	SO.	BB.	ERA.
1982	Elmira	NYP	17	61⅔	1	4	.200	55	31	21	45	39	3.06
1983	Winter Haven	Florida St.	21	117⅔	8	9	.471	149	77	59	68	47	4.51
1984	Winter Haven	Florida St.	29	182	12	10	.545	182	87	69	94	80	3.41

Year	Club	League	G.	IP.	W.	L.	Pct.	H.	R.	ER.	SO.	BB.	ERA.
1985	—New Britain	Eastern	25	184⅔	•14	7	.667	165	67	57	115	67	2.78
1985	—Boston	American	4	22⅓	2	0	1.000	24	10	9	6	7	3.63
1986	—Pawtucket	Int'national	15	106	7	4	.636	95	50	44	74	59	3.74
1986	—Boston	American	14	82	3	7	.300	90	56	45	51	40	4.94
1987	—Boston	American	25	139⅔	7	8	.467	161	85	82	99	61	5.28
1987	—Pawtucket	Int'national	5	38	3	2	.600	36	13	10	35	19	2.37
1988	—Boston†	American	18	85⅔	1	7	.125	89	49	46	70	56	4.83
1988	—Pawtucket‡	Int'national	3	14⅔	1	1	.500	16	9	9	9	11	5.52
Major League Totals—4 Years			61	329⅔	13	22	.371	364	200	182	226	164	4.97

Selected by Boston Red Sox' organization in 8th round of free-agent draft, June 7, 1982.

†On disabled list, June 22 to August 9 and August 27 to September 11, 1988; included rehabilitation disability assignment to Pawtucket, July 24 to August 9, 1988.

‡Traded with First Baseman Todd Benzinger and a player to be named later to Cincinnati Reds for First Baseman Nick Esasky and Pitcher Rob Murphy, December 13, 1988.

DAVID SCOTT SERVICE

(Known by middle name.)

Born February 27, 1967, at Cincinnati, O.
Height, 6.06. Weight, 225.
Throws and bats righthanded.

Year	Club	League	G.	IP.	W.	L.	Pct.	H.	R.	ER.	SO.	BB.	ERA.
1986	—Spartanburg	S. Atlantic	14	58⅔	1	6	.143	68	44	38	49	34	5.83
1986	—Utica	NYP	10	70⅔	5	4	.556	65	30	21	43	18	2.67
1986	—Clearwater	Florida St.	4	25⅓	1	2	.333	20	10	9	19	15	3.20
1987	—Reading	Eastern	5	19⅔	0	3	.000	22	19	17	12	16	7.78
1987	—Clearwater	Florida St.	21	137⅔	13	4	.765	127	46	38	73	32	2.48
1988	—Reading	Eastern	10	56⅔	3	4	.429	52	25	18	39	22	2.86
1988	—Maine	Int'national	19	110⅓	8	8	.500	109	51	45	87	31	3.67
1988	—Philadelphia	National	5	5⅓	0	0	.000	7	1	1	6	1	1.69
Major League Totals—1 Year			5	5⅓	0	0	.000	7	1	1	6	1	1.69

Signed as free agent by Philadelphia Phillies' organization, August 24, 1985.

MICHAEL TYRONE SHARPERSON
(Mike)

Born October 4, 1961, at Orangeburg, S.C.
Height, 6.03. Weight, 185.
Throws and bats righthanded.
Attended DeKalb Community College South, Decatur, Ga.

Major League stolen bases: 1987 (2).
Led International League second basemen in putouts with 286 and total chances with 666 in 1985.
Led Southern League second basemen in total chances with 775 and double plays with 103 in 1984.
Tied for International League lead in double plays by third basemen with 16 in 1987.

Year	Club	League	Pos.	G.	AB.	R.	H.	2B.	3B.	HR.	RBI.	B.A.	PO.	A.	E.	F.A.
1982	—Florence	S. Atl.	SS-3B	111	326	51	83	16	1	3	33	.255	136	261	33	.923
1983	—Kinston†	Carol.	S-3-2-C	90	361	55	96	8	1	5	41	.266	148	286	19	.958
1984	—Knoxville	South.	2B	140	542	86	165	25	7	4	48	.304	*331	*423	21	.973
1985	—Syracuse	Int.	2B-SS	134	*536	*86	*155	19	*7	1	59	.289	291	372	17	.975
1986	—Syracuse	Int.	2B-3B	133	519	*86	*150	18	*9	4	45	.289	258	376	18	.972
1987	—Toronto	Amer.	2B	32	96	4	20	4	1	0	9	.208	64	69	4	.971
1987	—Syracuse‡	Int.	3B-2B	88	338	67	101	21	5	5	26	.299	81	152	8	.967
1987	—Los Angeles	Nat.	3B-2B	10	33	7	9	2	0	0	1	.273	4	28	1	.970
1988	—Albuquerque	P. C.	2B-3B-SS	56	210	55	67	10	2	0	30	.319	88	173	12	.956
1988	—Los Angeles	Nat.	2B-3B-SS	46	59	8	16	1	0	0	4	.271	19	31	2	.962
American League Totals—1 Year				32	96	4	20	4	1	0	9	.208	64	69	4	.971
National League Totals—2 Years				56	92	15	25	3	0	0	5	.272	23	59	3	.965
Major League Totals—2 Years				88	188	19	45	7	1	0	14	.239	87	128	7	.968

Selected by Pittsburgh Pirates' organization in 41st round of free-agent draft, June 5, 1979.
Selected by Montreal Expos' organization in secondary phase of free-agent draft, January 8, 1980.
Selected by Detroit Tigers' organization in 4th round of free-agent draft, January 13, 1981.
Selected by Toronto Blue Jays' organization in secondary phase of free-agent draft, June 8, 1981.
†On disabled list, August 14, 1983 through remainder of season.
‡Traded to Los Angeles Dodgers for Pitcher Juan Guzman, September 22, 1987.

CHAMPIONSHIP SERIES RECORD

Year	Club	League	Pos.	G.	AB.	R.	H.	2B.	3B.	HR.	RBI.	B.A.	PO.	A.	E.	F.A.
1988	—Los Angeles	Nat.	PH-S-3	2	1	0	0	0	0	0	1	.000	1	0	0	1.000

JEFFREY THOMAS SHAVER
(Jeff)

Born July 30, 1963, at Beaver Falls, Pa.
Height, 6.03. Weight, 185.
Throws and bats righthanded.
Attended Central Arizona College, Coolidge, Ariz.; Grand Canyon College, Phoenix, Ariz., and State University College of New York, Fredonia, N. Y.

Year Club	League	G.	IP.	W.	L.	Pct.	H.	R.	ER.	SO.	BB.	ERA.
1985—Medford	Northwest	15	95⅔	8	4	.667	66	39	27	81	48	2.54
1986—Madison	Midwest	26	163	10	5	.667	141	67	61	144	61	3.37
1987—Huntsville	Southern	23	140⅔	7	9	.438	147	69	53	85	51	3.39
1988—Tacoma	P. Coast	27	146⅔	7	10	.412	151	78	73	93	39	4.48
1988—Oakland	American	1	1	0	0	.000	0	0	0	0	0	0.00
Major League Totals—1 Year		1	1	0	0	.000	0	0	0	0	0	0.00

Selected by Oakland A's organization in 22nd round of free-agent draft, June 3, 1985.

JEFFREY LEE SHAW
(Jeff)

Born July 7, 1966, at Washington Court House, O.
Height, 6.02. Weight, 185.
Throws and bats righthanded.
Attended Cuyahoga Community College-Western Campus, Parma, O.

Led Midwest League pitchers in games started with 28 and shutouts with 4 in 1987.
Tied for Eastern League lead in games started by pitchers with 27 in 1988.

Year Club	League	G.	IP.	W.	L.	Pct.	H.	R.	ER.	SO.	BB.	ERA.
1986—Batavia	NYP	14	88⅔	8	4	.667	79	32	24	71	35	2.44
1987—Waterloo	Midwest	28	184⅓	11	11	.500	192	89	72	117	56	3.52
1988—Williamsport	Eastern	27	163⅔	5	*19	.208	•173	*94	66	61	75	3.63

Selected by Cleveland Indians' organization in 1st round (first player selected) of free-agent draft, January 14, 1986.

LARRY KENT SHEETS

Born December 6, 1959, at Staunton, Va.
Height, 6.03. Weight, 236.
Throws right and bats lefthanded.

Received degree in health and physical education from Eastern Mennonite College, Harrisonburg, Va. in 1986.
Major League stolen bases: 1986 (2), 1987 (1), 1988 (1). Total—4.
Led International League outfielders in double plays with 5 in 1984.

Year Club	League	Pos.	G.	AB.	R.	H.	2B.	3B.	HR.	RBI.	B.A.	PO.	A.	E.	F.A.
1978—Bluefield	Appal.	OF-1B	67	225	32	60	9	2	11	*48	.267	121	8	4	.970
1979—Miami†	Fla. St.						(Did not play)								
1979—Bluefield	Appal.	OF	3	12	2	4	2	0	0	2	.333	1	0	0	1.000
1980—Bluefield‡	Appal.	OF	37	124	29	47	9	1	*14	47	.379	40	3	2	.956
1980—Charlotte	South.	OF	13	48	1	9	4	0	0	5	.188	4	1	0	1.000
1981—Rochester§	Int.						(Did not play)								
1982—Rochester x	Int.						(Did not play)								
1982—Hagerstown y	Carol.	OF	88	324	46	96	21	0	18	59	.296	123	5	6	.955
1983—Charlotte	South.	OF-1B	138	503	72	145	*37	3	•25	87	.288	256	15	7	.975
1983—Rochester	Int.	OF	3	13	1	2	1	0	0	2	.154	5	0	1	.833
1984—Rochester	Int.	OF	134	431	76	130	26	4	13	67	.302	201	*19	2	.991
1984—Baltimore	Amer.	OF	8	16	3	7	1	0	1	2	.438	12	1	0	1.000
1985—Baltimore	Amer.	OF-1B	113	328	43	86	8	0	17	50	.262	12	1	1	.929
1986—Baltimore z	Amer.	O-1-3-C	112	338	42	92	17	1	18	60	.272	90	8	3	.970
1987—Baltimore	Amer.	OF-1B	135	469	74	148	23	0	31	94	.316	243	7	7	.973
1988—Baltimore	Amer.	OF-1B	136	452	38	104	19	1	10	47	.230	159	12	4	.977
Major League Totals—5 Years			504	1603	200	437	68	2	77	253	.273	516	29	15	.973

Selected by Baltimore Orioles' organization in 2nd round of free-agent draft, June 6, 1978.
†On suspended list, May 1 to August 29, 1979.
‡On restricted list, June 18 to June 23, 1980.
§On restricted list, April 14 to May 28 and June 18, 1981 through remainder of season.
xOn suspended list, April 13, 1982; then transferred to restricted list, April 23 to May 13, 1982.
yOn disabled list, August 23, 1982 through remainder of season.
zOn disabled list, June 30 to July 17, 1986.

GARY ANTONIAN SHEFFIELD

Born November 18, 1968, at Tampa, Fla.
Height, 5.11. Weight, 190.
Throws and bats righthanded.
Nephew of Dwight Gooden, pitcher with New York Mets.

Major League stolen bases: 1988 (3).
Led California League shortstops in double plays with 77 in 1987.
Led Pioneer League shortstops in double plays with 34 in 1986.
Named Minor League co-Player of the Year by THE SPORTING NEWS, 1988.

Year Club	League	Pos.	G.	AB.	R.	H.	2B.	3B.	HR.	RBI.	B.A.	PO.	A.	E.	F.A.
1986—Helena	Pion.	SS	57	222	53	81	12	2	15	*71	.365	97	149	24	.911
1987—Stockton	Calif.	SS	129	469	84	130	23	3	17	*103	.277	235	345	39	.937
1988—El Paso	Texas	SS-3B-OF	77	296	70	93	19	3	19	65	.314	130	206	23	.936
1988—Denver	A. A.	3B-SS	57	212	42	73	9	5	9	54	.344	54	97	8	.950
1988—Milwaukee	Amer.	SS	24	80	12	19	1	0	4	12	.238	39	48	3	.967
Major League Totals—1 Year			24	80	12	19	1	0	4	12	.238	39	48	3	.967

Selected by Milwaukee Brewers' organization in 1st round (sixth player selected) of free-agent draft, June 2, 1986.

JOHN T. SHELBY

Born February 23, 1958, at Lexington, Ky.
Height, 6.01. Weight, 175.
Throws right and bats right and lefthanded.
Attended Columbia State Community College, Columbia, Tenn.

Established National League record for most strikeouts by switch-hitter, season (128), 1988.
Major League stolen bases: 1981 (2), 1983 (15), 1984 (12), 1985 (5), 1986 (18), 1987 (16), 1988 (16). Total—84.
Led Florida State League outfielders in double plays with 7 in 1979.
Led Appalachian League outfielders in double plays with 3 in 1978.

Year Club	League	Pos.	G.	AB.	R.	H.	2B.	3B.	HR.	RBI.	B.A.	PO.	A.	E.	F.A.
1977—Bluefield	Appal.	OF	60	211	28	54	9	1	0	1	.256	90	•12	7	.936
1978—Miami	Fla. St.	OF	13	26	4	6	1	0	0	3	.231	14	2	2	.889
1978—Bluefield	Appal.	OF	64	248	49	70	9	1	6	25	.282	128	*11	6	.959
1979—Miami	Fla. St.	OF	132	478	50	96	11	6	3	38	.201	*252	•22	8	.972
1980—Charlotte	South.	OF	134	*560	66	135	27	11	6	51	.241	*361	21	*16	.960
1981—Charlotte	South.	OF	62	251	40	59	11	4	2	21	.235	120	3	10	.925
1981—Rochester	Int.	OF	76	326	42	86	21	8	3	32	.264	189	8	6	.970
1981—Baltimore	Amer.	OF	7	2	2	0	0	0	0	0	.000	1	0	0	1.000
1982—Rochester	Int.	OF	133	*548	92	153	26	6	16	52	.279	331	13	8	.977
1982—Baltimore	Amer.	OF	26	35	8	11	3	0	1	2	.314	20	1	0	1.000
1983—Baltimore	Amer.	OF	126	325	52	84	15	2	5	27	.258	200	9	4	.981
1984—Baltimore	Amer.	OF	128	383	44	80	12	5	6	30	.209	261	9	2	.993
1985—Rochester	Int.	OF	52	206	31	59	16	4	8	21	.286	124	4	1	.992
1985—Baltimore	Amer.	OF-2B	69	205	28	58	6	2	7	27	.283	148	4	3	.981
1986—Baltimore	Amer	OF	135	404	54	92	14	4	11	49	.228	222	5	5	.978
1987—Baltimore	Amer.	OF	21	32	4	6	0	0	1	3	.188	25	0	0	1.000
1987—Rochester†	Int.	OF	6	24	5	6	2	0	1	2	.250	14	0	0	1.000
1987—Los Angeles	Nat.	OF	120	476	61	132	26	0	21	69	.277	269	9	8	.972
1988—Los Angeles	Nat.	OF	140	494	65	130	23	6	10	64	.263	329	7	6	.982
American League Totals—7 Years			512	1386	192	331	50	13	31	138	.239	877	28	14	.985
National League Totals—2 Years			260	970	126	262	49	6	31	133	.270	598	16	14	.978
Major League Totals—8 Years			772	2356	318	593	99	19	62	271	.252	1475	44	28	.982

Selected by Baltimore Orioles' organization in 1st round (19th player selected) of free-agent draft, January 11, 1977.
†Traded with Pitcher Brad Havens to Los Angeles Dodgers for Pitcher Tom Niedenfuer, May 22, 1987.
‡On disabled list, April 22 to May 12, 1988.

CHAMPIONSHIP SERIES RECORD

Established Championship Series record for most strikeouts, seven-game Series (12), 1988.

Year Club	League	Pos.	G.	AB.	R.	H.	2B.	3B.	HR.	RBI.	B.A.	PO.	A.	E.	F.A.
1983—Baltimore	Amer.	OF-PH	3	9	1	2	0	0	0	0	.222	3	0	0	1.000
1988—Los Angeles	Nat.	OF	7	24	3	4	0	0	0	3	.167	19	0	0	1.000
Championship Series Totals—2 Years			10	33	4	6	0	0	0	3	.182	22	0	0	1.000

WORLD SERIES RECORD

Year Club	League	Pos.	G.	AB.	R.	H.	2B.	3B.	HR.	RBI.	B.A.	PO.	A.	E.	F.A.
1983—Baltimore	Amer.	PH-OF	5	9	1	4	0	0	0	1	.444	10	0	0	1.000
1988—Los Angeles	Nat.	OF	5	18	0	4	1	0	0	1	.222	14	0	0	1.000
World Series Totals—2 Years			10	27	1	8	1	0	0	2	.296	24	0	0	1.000

PATRICK ARTHUR SHERIDAN
(Pat)

Born December 4, 1957, at Ann Arbor, Mich.
Height, 6.03. Weight, 175.
Throws right and bats lefthanded.
Attended Eastern Michigan University, Ypsilanti, Mich.
Son of Arthur Sheridan, minor league pitcher, 1952 through 1956.

Major League stolen bases: 1983 (12), 1984 (19), 1985 (11), 1986 (9), 1987 (18), 1988 (8). Total—77.

Year Club	League	Pos.	G.	AB.	R.	H.	2B.	3B.	HR.	RBI.	B.A.	PO.	A.	E.	F.A.
1979—Fort Myers	Fla. St.	OF	67	235	25	66	4	3	0	16	.281	142	8	1	.993
1980—Fort Myers	Fla. St.	OF-C	20	79	17	32	1	0	1	13	.405	37	4	1	.976
1980—Jacksonville†	South.	OF	97	367	63	112	17	7	5	42	.305	201	7	9	.959
1981—Omaha‡	A. A.	OF	86	315	49	94	15	8	5	31	.298	193	2	3	.985
1981—Kansas City	Amer.	OF	3	1	0	0	0	0	0	0	.000	2	0	0	1.000
1982—Omaha§	A. A.	OF	41	135	8	34	8	1	0	13	.252	92	3	0	1.000
1983—Omaha	A. A.	OF	20	75	16	23	4	5	4	14	.307	53	2	0	1.000
1983—Kansas City	Amer.	OF	109	333	43	90	12	2	7	36	.270	237	6	3	.988
1984—Kansas City	Amer.	OF	138	481	64	136	24	4	8	53	.283	273	8	4	.986
1985—Kansas City x	Amer.	OF	78	206	18	47	9	2	3	17	.228	116	3	2	.983
1985—Omaha y	A. A.	OF	8	28	1	10	1	0	0	1	.357	8	1	0	1.000
1986—Nashville	A. A.	OF	9	35	4	10	2	0	1	5	.286	16	0	0	1.000
1986—Detroit	Amer.	OF	98	236	41	56	9	1	6	19	.237	172	1	4	.977
1987—Detroit	Amer.	OF	141	421	57	109	19	3	6	49	.259	236	6	6	.976
1988—Detroit	Amer.	OF	127	347	47	88	9	5	11	47	.254	203	2	4	.981
Major League Totals—7 Years			694	2025	270	526	82	17	41	221	.260	1239	26	23	.982

Selected by Cincinnati Reds' organization in 36th round of free-agent draft, June 8, 1976.
Selected by Kansas City Royals' organization in 3rd round of free-agent draft, June 5, 1979.

†On disabled list, May 16 to June 2, 1980.
‡On disabled list, May 25 to June 25, 1981.
§On disabled list, April 27 to June 25 and June 27 to July 19, 1982.
xOn disabled list, June 19 to July 4 and August 5 to September 3, 1985; included rehabilitation disability assignment to Omaha, August 26 to September 3, 1985.
yReleased, March 28, 1986; signed by Detroit Tigers, April 25, 1986.

CHAMPIONSHIP SERIES RECORD

Tied Championship Series record for most home runs by pinch-hitter, game (1), October 9, 1985.

Year Club	League	Pos.	G.	AB.	R.	H.	2B.	3B.	HR.	RBI.	B.A.	PO.	A.	E.	F.A.
1984—Kansas City	Amer.	OF	3	6	1	0	0	0	0	0	.000	9	0	1	.900
1985—Kansas City	Amer.	OF-PH	7	20	4	3	0	0	2	3	.150	13	0	0	1.000
1987—Detroit	Amer.	OF-PR	5	10	2	3	1	0	1	2	.300	7	1	0	1.000
Championship Series Totals—3 Years			15	36	7	6	1	0	3	5	.167	29	1	1	.968

WORLD SERIES RECORD

Year Club	League	Pos.	G.	AB.	R.	H.	2B.	3B.	HR.	RBI.	B.A.	PO.	A.	E.	F.A.
1985—Kansas City	Amer.	PH-OF	5	18	0	4	2	0	0	1	.222	6	0	0	1.000

STEPHEN MACK SHIELDS
(Steve)

Born November 30, 1958, in Etowah County, Ala.
Height, 6.05. Weight, 230.
Throws and bats righthanded.

Major League saves: 1987 (3).
Tied for International League lead in shutouts with 3 and hit batsmen with 8 in 1985.
Tied for Eastern League lead in complete games with 13 and shutouts with 3 in 1982.
Tied for Eastern League lead in intentional bases on balls issued with 10 in 1981.

Year Club	League	G.	IP.	W.	L.	Pct.	H.	R.	ER.	SO.	BB.	ERA.
1977—Elmira	NYP	15	81	1	6	.143	72	45	37	108	37	4.11
1978—Winter Haven†	Florida St.	14	51	3	3	.500	52	14	11	34	9	1.94
1979—Winston-Salem	Carolina	24	152	11	8	.579	149	78	51	152	80	3.02
1980—Bristol	Eastern	39	113	5	6	.455	128	79	61	63	77	4.86
1981—Bristol	Eastern	29	126	5	★14	.263	136	75	65	87	65	4.64
1982—Bristol	Eastern	29	170⅓	10	13	.435	172	100	67	125	71	3.54
1983—Pawtucket‡	Int'national	36	143	4	12	.250	171	94	74	115	63	4.66
1984—Richmond	Int'national	39	110	9	4	.692	122	69	58	101	39	4.75
1985—Richmond	Int'national	18	133	6	7	.462	110	53	39	88	54	2.64
1985—Atlanta	National	23	68	1	2	.333	86	46	39	29	32	5.16
1986—Richmond	Int'national	21	149⅓	9	8	.529	133	55	43	●124	55	2.59
1986—Atlanta§	National	6	12⅔	0	0	.000	13	10	10	6	7	7.11
1986—Kansas City x	American	3	8⅔	0	0	.000	3	3	2	2	4	2.08
1987—Seattle y	American	20	30	2	0	1.000	43	25	22	22	12	6.60
1987—Calgary z	P. Coast	16	24	3	2	.600	16	7	6	15	11	2.25
1988—Columbus	Int'national	17	25	0	1	.000	28	7	7	23	6	2.52
1988—New York	American	39	82⅓	5	5	.500	96	44	40	55	30	4.37
National League Totals—2 Years		29	80⅔	1	2	.333	99	56	49	35	39	5.47
American League Totals—3 Years		62	121	7	5	.583	142	72	64	79	46	4.76
Major League Totals—4 Years		91	201⅔	8	7	.533	241	128	113	114	85	5.04

Selected by Boston Red Sox' organization in 10th round of free-agent draft, June 7, 1977.
†On disabled list, April 10 to June 14, 1978.
‡Granted free agency, October 20, 1983; signed by Richmond (Atlanta Braves' organization), October 26, 1983.
§Traded to Kansas City Royals for Outfielder Darryl Motley, September 23, 1986.
xTraded with Pitcher Scott Bankhead and Outfielder Mike Kingery to Seattle Mariners for Outfielder Danny Tartabull and Pitcher Rick Luecken, December 19, 1986.
yOn disabled list, April 12 to May 12, 1987.
zGranted free agency, October 15, 1987; signed by New York Yankees, November 11, 1987.

CRAIG BARRY SHIPLEY

Born January 7, 1963, at Parramatta, Australia.
Height, 6.00. Weight, 170.
Throws right and bats left and righthanded.
Attended University of Alabama, University, Ala.

Year Club	League	Pos.	G.	AB.	R.	H.	2B.	3B.	HR.	RBI.	B.A.	PO.	A.	E.	F.A.
1984—Vero Beach†	Fla. St.	SS	85	293	56	82	11	2	0	28	.280	137	216	17	.954
1985—Albuquerque	P. C.	SS	124	414	50	100	9	2	0	30	.242	202	367	21	.964
1986—Albuquerque‡	P. C.	SS	61	203	33	59	8	2	0	16	.291	99	173	18	.938
1986—Los Angeles	Nat.	SS-2B-3B	12	27	3	3	1	0	0	4	.111	16	18	3	.919
1987—Albuquerque	P. C.	SS	49	139	17	31	6	1	1	15	.223	70	101	9	.950
1987—San Antonio	Texas	3B	33	127	14	30	5	3	2	9	.236	19	56	3	.962
1987—Los Angeles§	Nat.	SS-3B	26	35	3	9	1	0	0	2	.257	15	28	3	.935
1988—Jackson	Texas	SS	89	335	41	88	14	3	6	41	.263	141	266	16	.962
1988—Tidewater	Int.	2B-SS-3B	40	151	12	41	5	0	1	13	.272	54	110	2	.988
Major League Totals—2 Years			38	62	6	12	2	0	0	6	.194	31	46	6	.928

Signed as a free agent by Los Angeles Dodgers' organization, May 28, 1984.
†Batted righthanded.

‡On disabled list, May 5 to June 6, 1986.
§Traded to New York Mets for Catcher John Gibbons, April 1, 1988.

ERIC VAUGHN SHOW

Name rhymes with Chow.

Born May 19, 1956, at Riverside, Calif.
Height, 6.01. Weight, 190.
Throws and bats righthanded.
Attended University of California, Riverside, Calif.

Major League saves: 1981 (3), 1982 (3). Total—6.
Led Texas League in hit batsmen with 10 in 1980.

Year Club	League	G.	IP.	W.	L.	Pct.	H.	R.	ER.	SO.	BB.	ERA.
1978—Walla Walla	Northwest	11	60	5	2	.714	47	28	19	43	20	2.85
1979—Reno	California	28	169	13	9	.591	144	79	67	186	92	3.57
1980—Amarillo	Texas	26	166	12	6	.667	141	81	69	144	81	3.74
1981—Hawaii	P. Coast	34	85	7	3	.700	67	30	24	70	35	2.54
1981—San Diego	National	15	23	1	3	.250	17	9	8	22	9	3.13
1982—San Diego	National	47	150	10	6	.625	117	49	44	88	48	2.64
1983—San Diego	National	35	200⅔	15	12	.556	201	97	93	120	74	4.17
1984—San Diego	National	32	206⅔	15	9	.625	175	88	78	104	88	3.40
1985—San Diego	National	35	233	12	11	.522	212	95	80	141	87	3.09
1986—San Diego†	National	24	136⅓	9	5	.643	109	47	45	94	69	2.97
1987—San Diego	National	34	206⅓	8	16	.333	188	99	88	117	85	3.84
1988—San Diego	National	32	234⅔	16	11	.593	201	86	85	144	53	3.26
Major League Totals—8 Years		254	1390⅔	86	73	.541	1220	570	521	830	513	3.37

Selected by Minnesota Twins' organization in 36th round of free-agent draft, June 5, 1974.
Selected by San Diego Padres' organization in 18th round of free-agent draft, June 6, 1978.
†On disabled list, July 8 to July 31 and August 28, 1986 through remainder of season.

CHAMPIONSHIP SERIES RECORD

Tied National League Championship Series records for most runs and earned runs allowed, five-game Series (8), 1984.

Year Club	League	G.	IP.	W.	L.	Pct.	H.	R.	ER.	SO.	BB.	ERA.
1984—San Diego	National	2	5⅓	0	1	.000	8	8	8	2	4	13.50

WORLD SERIES RECORD

Year Club	League	G.	IP.	W.	L.	Pct.	H.	R.	ER.	SO.	BB.	ERA.
1984—San Diego	National	1	2⅔	0	1	.000	4	4	3	2	1	10.13

RUBEN ANGEL SIERRA (GARCIA)

Born October 6, 1965, at Rio Piedras, Puerto Rico.
Height, 6.01. Weight, 175.
Throws right and bats left and righthanded.

Major League stolen bases: 1986 (7), 1987 (16), 1988 (18). Total—41.
Switch-hit home runs in one game, September 13, 1986 and August 27, 1988.
Led American League in sacrifice flies with 12 in 1987.
Led American League outfielders in double plays with 6 in 1987.

Year Club	League	Pos.	G.	AB.	R.	H.	2B.	3B.	HR.	RBI.	B.A.	PO.	A.	E.	F.A.
1983—Sarasota Ran.†	Gulf C.	OF	48	182	26	44	7	3	1	26	.242	67	6	4	.948
1984—Burlington	Midw.	OF	•138	482	55	127	33	5	6	75	.263	239	18	*20	.928
1985—Tulsa	Texas	OF	*137	*545	63	138	34	*8	13	74	.253	234	12	*15	.943
1986—Oklahoma City	A. A.	OF	46	189	31	56	11	2	9	41	.296	114	4	2	.983
1986—Texas	Amer.	OF	113	382	50	101	13	10	16	55	.264	200	7	6	.972
1987—Texas	Amer.	OF	158	*643	97	169	35	4	30	109	.263	272	•17	11	.963
1988—Texas	Amer.	OF	156	615	77	156	32	2	23	91	.254	310	11	7	.979
Major League Totals—3 Years			427	1640	224	426	80	16	69	255	.260	782	35	24	.971

Signed as free agent by Texas Rangers' organization, November 21, 1982.
†Batted righthanded.

ULISES SIERRA (PIZARRO)
(Candy)

Born March 27, 1967, at Rio Piedras, Puerto Rico.
Height, 6.02. Weight, 190.
Throws and bats righthanded.

Pitched seven-inning, 2-0 no-hit victory against Modesto, June 15, 1984 (first game).

Year Club	League	G.	IP.	W.	L.	Pct.	H.	R.	ER.	SO.	BB.	ERA.
1983—Spokane	Northwest	23	37	1	5	.167	44	33	22	31	21	5.35
1984—Reno	California	28	135⅓	11	4	.733	133	67	56	106	57	3.72
1985—Beaumont	Texas	23	104⅓	3	6	.333	109	65	55	93	60	4.74
1986—Beaumont†	Texas	16	90⅔	4	5	.444	104	53	49	60	37	4.86
1987—Wichita	Texas	19	114	8	5	.615	120	57	50	89	42	3.95
1988—San Diego‡-Cincinnati	National	16	27⅔	0	1	.000	41	17	17	24	12	5.53
1988—Nashville	Am. Assoc.	13	73	5	5	.500	82	41	38	40	36	4.68
Major League Totals—1 Year		16	27⅔	0	1	.000	41	17	17	24	12	5.53

Signed as free agent by San Diego Padres' organization, May 29, 1983.
†On disabled list, May 27 to July 22, 1986.
§Traded to Cincinnati Reds for Pitcher Dennis Rasmussen, June 8, 1988.

TED LYLE SIMMONS

Born August 9, 1949, at Highland Park, Mich.
Height, 6.00. Weight, 200.
Throws right and bats left and righthanded.
Attended Wayne State University, Detroit, Mich. and
University of Michigan, Ann Arbor, Mich.

Established National League records for most home runs by switch-hitter, career (182); fewest errors by catcher, season, for leader in errors (15), 1975.

Established American League records for longest errorless game and most innings played by first baseman, game (25), May 8, finished May 9, 1984 (fielded 24⅓ innings).

Major League stolen bases: 1970 (2), 1971 (1), 1972 (1), 1973 (2), 1975 (1), 1977 (2), 1978 (1), 1980 (1), 1983 (4), 1984 (3), 1985 (1), 1986 (1), 1987 (1). Total—21.

Switch-hit home runs in one game three times: April 17, 1975, June 11, 1979 and May 2, 1982.
Led National League in intentional bases on balls received with 19 in 1976 and 25 in 1977.
Led National League in grounding into double plays with 29 in 1973.
Led National League catchers in putouts with 842 in 1972 and 888 in 1973.
Led National League catchers in assists with 78 in 1972 and 74 in 1973.
Led National League catchers in total chances with 928 in 1972, 975 in 1973 and 880 in 1975.
Led National League in passed balls with 25 in 1973, 28 in 1975 and 14 in 1979.
Led California League catchers in putouts with 984 in 1968.
Tied for California League lead in being hit by pitch with 9 in 1968.
Named catcher on THE SPORTING NEWS National League All-Star Team, 1977 through 1979.
Named catcher on THE SPORTING NEWS National League Silver Slugger team, 1980.
Named California League Most Valuable Player, 1968.
Received reported $50,000 bonus to sign with St. Louis Cardinals, 1967.

Year Club	League	Pos.	G.	AB.	R.	H.	2B.	3B.	HR.	RBI.	B.A.	PO.	A.	E.	F.A.
1967—Sarasota Cards	Gulf C.	C	6	20	5	7	1	1	2	8	.350	33	0	0	1.000
1967—Cedar Rapids	Midw.	OF-C	47	171	15	46	11	2	4	34	.269	119	8	3	.977
1968—Modesto	Calif.	*C-OF	136	493	86	163	30	2	28	*117	*.331	989	79	*16	.985
1968—St. Louis	Nat.	C	2	3	0	1	0	0	0	0	.333	3	1	0	1.000
1969—Tulsa	A. A.	C-3-O-1	129	499	80	158	33	4	16	88	.317	463	92	19	.967
1969—St. Louis†	Nat.	C	5	14	0	3	0	1	0	3	.214	22	0	1	.957
1970—Tulsa	A. A.	C	15	51	10	19	4	1	1	8	.373	99	7	0	1.000
1970—St. Louis	Nat.	C	82	284	29	69	8	2	3	24	.243	466	37	5	.990
1971—St. Louis‡	Nat.	C	133	510	64	155	32	4	7	77	.304	747	52	9	.989
1972—St. Louis	Nat.	C-1B	152	594	70	180	36	6	16	96	.303	967	93	13	.988
1973—St. Louis	Nat.	C-1B-OF	161	619	62	192	36	2	13	91	.310	932	78	14	.986
1974—St. Louis	Nat.	C-1B	152	599	66	163	33	6	20	103	.272	813	87	15	.984
1975—St. Louis	Nat.	*C-1B-OF	157	581	80	193	32	3	18	100	.332	818	64	*15	.983
1976—St. Louis	Nat.	C-1-O-3	150	546	60	159	35	3	5	75	.291	726	88	10	.988
1977—St. Louis	Nat.	C-OF	150	516	82	164	25	3	21	95	.318	683	75	10	.987
1978—St. Louis	Nat.	*C-OF	152	516	71	148	40	5	22	80	.287	703	*88	10	.988
1979—St. Louis§	Nat.	C	123	448	68	127	22	0	26	87	.283	606	69	10	.985
1980—St. Louis x	Nat.	C-OF	145	495	84	150	33	2	21	98	.303	528	71	10	.984
1981—Milwaukee	Amer.	C-1B	100	380	45	82	13	3	14	61	.216	333	41	8	.979
1982—Milwaukee	Amer.	C	137	539	73	145	29	0	23	97	.269	570	62	3	*.995
1983—Milwaukee y	Amer.	C	153	600	76	185	39	3	13	108	.308	395	41	11	.975
1984—Milwaukee	Amer.	1B-3B	132	497	44	110	23	2	4	52	.221	352	52	8	.981
1985—Milwaukee z	Amer.	1B-C-3B	143	528	60	144	28	2	12	76	.273	291	26	3	.991
1986—Atlanta	Nat.	1B-C-3B	76	127	14	32	5	0	4	25	.252	167	18	6	.969
1987—Atlanta	Nat.	1B-C-3B	73	177	20	49	8	0	4	30	.277	282	35	5	.984
1988—Atlanta ab	Nat.	1B-C	78	107	6	21	6	0	2	11	.196	140	14	3	.981
National League Totals—16 Years			1791	6136	776	1806	351	37	182	995	.294	8603	870	136	.986
American League Totals—5 Years			665	2544	298	666	132	10	66	394	.262	1941	222	33	.985
Major League Totals—21 Years			2456	8680	1074	2472	483	47	248	1389	.285	10544	1092	169	.986

Selected by St. Louis Cardinals' organization in 1st round (10th player selected) of free-agent draft, June 6, 1967.
†On military list, December 12, 1969 through May 9, 1970.
‡On military list, June 19 to July 4, 1971.
§On disabled list, June 25 to July 24, 1979.
xTraded with Pitchers Rollie Fingers and Pete Vuckovich to Milwaukee Brewers for Pitchers Lary Sorensen and Dave LaPoint and Outfielders Sixto Lezcano and David Green, December 12, 1980.
yGranted free agency, November 7, 1983; re-signed by Brewers, January 16, 1984.
zTraded to Atlanta Braves for Catcher Rick Cerone, Pitcher David Clay and Shortstop Flavio Alfaro, March 5, 1986.
aOn disabled list, June 7 to June 23, 1988.
bNamed Director of Player Development with St. Louis Cardinals, October 26, 1988.

DIVISION SERIES RECORD

Year Club	League	Pos.	G.	AB.	R.	H.	2B.	3B.	HR.	RBI.	B.A.	PO.	A.	E.	F.A.
1981—Milwaukee	Amer.	C	5	18	1	4	1	0	1	4	.222	23	2	1	.962

CHAMPIONSHIP SERIES RECORD

Year Club	League	Pos.	G.	AB.	R.	H.	2B.	3B.	HR.	RBI.	B.A.	PO.	A.	E.	F.A.
1982—Milwaukee	Amer.	C	5	18	3	3	0	0	0	1	.167	36	3	0	1.000

WORLD SERIES RECORD

Tied World Series record for fewest putouts by catcher, game (1), October 15, 1982.

Year	Club	League	Pos.	G.	AB.	R.	H.	2B.	3B.	HR.	RBI.	B.A.	PO.	A.	E.	F.A.
1982—	Milwaukee	Amer.	C	7	23	2	4	0	0	2	3	.174	28	2	1	.968

ALL-STAR GAME RECORD

Year	League	Pos.	AB.	R.	H.	2B.	3B.	HR.	RBI.	B.A.	PO.	A.	E.	F.A.
1973—	National	PH-C	1	0	0	0	0	0	0	.000	1	1	0	1.000
1977—	National	C	3	0	0	0	0	0	0	.000	5	0	0	1.000
1978—	National	C	3	0	1	0	0	0	0	.333	4	1	0	1.000
1981—	American	PH	1	0	1	0	0	0	1	1.000	0	0	0	.000
1983—	American	C	2	0	0	0	0	0	0	.000	4	0	0	1.000
All-Star Game Totals—5 Years			10	0	2	0	0	0	1	.200	14	2	0	1.000

Member of National League All-Star Team for 1972 and 1974 games; did not play.
Named to National League All-Star Team for 1979 game; replaced due to injury.

MATTHEW STEPHEN SINATRO
(Matt)

Born March 22, 1960, at West Hartford, Conn.
Height, 5.09. Weight, 174.
Throws and bats righthanded.

Major League stolen bases: 1981 (1).
Tied for Western Carolinas League lead in caught stealing with 15 in 1979.
Led Southern League catchers in total chances with 537 in 1984.
Led International League catchers in total chances with 710 in 1983.
Led Southern League catchers in double plays with 10 in 1980.

Year	Club	League	Pos.	G.	AB.	R.	H.	2B.	3B.	HR.	RBI.	B.A.	PO.	A.	E.	F.A.
1978—	Kingsport	Appal.	C	35	112	15	23	7	0	0	6	.205	198	26	2	.991
1979—	Greenwood	W. Car.	C	120	385	54	97	16	4	7	57	.252	639	69	11	.985
1980—	Savannah	South.	C	122	449	76	125	16	1	11	50	.278	514	70	15	.975
1981—	Richmond	Int.	C	121	430	43	101	13	2	6	53	.235	738	78	12	.986
1981—	Atlanta	Nat.	C	12	32	4	9	1	1	0	4	.281	56	10	0	1.000
1982—	Atlanta	Nat.	C	37	81	10	11	2	0	1	4	.136	112	25	0	1.000
1982—	Richmond	Int.	C	72	246	39	62	7	1	8	29	.252	423	53	5	.990
1983—	Richmond	Int.	C	110	365	36	77	11	1	4	41	.211	★642	60	8	.989
1983—	Atlanta	Nat.	C	7	12	0	2	0	0	0	2	.167	24	5	1	.967
1984—	Atlanta	Nat.	C	2	4	0	0	0	0	0	0	.000	4	0	0	1.000
1984—	Greenville†	South.	C	101	352	36	80	16	1	5	49	.227	★466	●64	7	.987
1985—	Greenville	South.	C	49	172	25	48	4	1	6	28	.279	265	49	7	.978
1985—	Richmond‡	Int.	C	24	67	7	19	3	0	1	8	.284	89	8	3	.970
1986—	Richmond§ x	Int.	C-3B	28	66	8	13	2	0	2	7	.197	124	18	2	.986
1986—	Buffalo y	A. A.	C	11	32	4	8	3	0	0	3	.250	60	7	4	.944
1987—	Tacoma	P. C.	C-3B-OF	79	215	30	54	13	0	5	32	.251	370	50	12	.972
1987—	Oakland z	Amer.	C	6	3	0	0	0	0	0	0	.000	4	0	0	1.000
1988—	Tacoma	P. C.	C-OF	77	234	28	54	8	1	2	23	.231	361	48	7	.983
1988—	Oakland a	Amer.	C	10	9	1	3	2	0	0	5	.333	21	2	0	1.000
National League Totals—4 Years				58	129	14	22	3	1	1	10	.171	196	40	1	.996
American League Totals—2 Years				16	12	1	3	2	0	0	5	.250	25	2	0	1.000
Major League Totals—6 Years				74	141	15	25	5	1	1	15	.177	221	42	1	.996

Selected by Atlanta Braves' organization in 2nd round of free-agent draft, June 6, 1978.
†Granted free agency, October 15, 1984; re-signed by Atlanta Braves' organization, December 11, 1984.
‡On disabled list, July 2 to August 1, 1985.
§On suspended list, July 6 to August 15, 1986.
xReleased, August 15, 1986; signed by Buffalo (Chicago White Sox' organization), August 20, 1986.
yGranted free agency, October 15, 1986; signed by Tacoma (Oakland Athletics' organization), April 1, 1987.
zReleased, October 15, 1987; re-signed by Athletics' organization, January 5, 1988.
aOn disabled list, August 19 to September 3, 1988.

DOUGLAS RANDALL SISK
(Doug)

Born September 26, 1957, at Renton, Wash.
Height, 6.02. Weight, 210.
Throws and bats righthanded.
Attended Green River Community College, Auburn, Wash. and received bachelor of science degree in criminal justice from Washington State University, Pullman, Wash.

Major League saves: 1982 (1), 1983 (11), 1984 (15), 1985 (2), 1986 (1), 1987 (3). Total—33.
Led Appalachian League pitchers in games started with 15 in 1980.

Year	Club	League	G.	IP.	W.	L.	Pct.	H.	R.	ER.	SO.	BB.	ERA.
1980—	Kingsport	Ap'lachian	15	★98	●8	5	.615	★91	46	29	41	45	2.66
1981—	Lynchburg	Carolina	36	83	3	2	.600	78	35	30	61	32	3.25
1981—	Jackson	Texas	14	25	3	0	1.000	23	11	10	15	12	3.60
1982—	Jackson	Texas	44	138	11	8	.611	136	59	41	53	58	★2.67
1982—	New York	National	8	8⅔	0	1	.000	5	1	1	4	4	1.04
1983—	New York	National	67	104⅓	5	4	.556	88	38	26	33	59	2.24
1984—	New York†	National	50	77⅔	1	3	.250	57	24	18	32	54	2.09
1985—	New York	National	42	73	4	5	.444	86	48	43	26	40	5.30

Year	Club	League	G.	IP.	W.	L.	Pct.	H.	R.	ER.	SO.	BB.	ERA.
1985—	Tidewater	Int'national	4	15	0	2	.000	15	12	12	4	13	7.20
1986—	Tidewater	Int'national	9	30	2	3	.400	34	16	14	19	9	4.20
1986—	New York	National	41	70⅔	4	2	.667	77	31	24	31	31	3.06
1987—	New York‡	National	55	78	3	1	.750	83	38	30	37	22	3.46
1988—	Baltimore§	American	52	94⅓	3	3	.500	109	43	39	26	45	3.72
1988—	Rochester x	Int'national	6	10⅔	0	2	.000	15	7	7	5	3	5.91
	National League Totals—6 Years		263	412⅓	17	16	.515	396	180	142	163	210	3.10
	American League Totals—1 Year		52	94⅓	3	3	.500	109	43	39	26	45	3.72
	Major League Totals—7 Years		315	506⅔	20	19	.513	505	223	181	189	255	3.22

Signed as free agent by New York Mets' organization, June 10, 1980.

†On disabled list, August 9 to August 29, 1984.

‡Traded to Baltimore Orioles for Pitcher Blaine Beatty and a player to be named later, December 8, 1987; New York Mets acquired Pitcher Greg Talamantez to complete deal, December 11, 1987.

§On disabled list, June 27 to July 22, 1988; included rehabilitation disability assignment to Rochester, July 3 to July 21, 1988.

xReleased, October 3, 1988.

CHAMPIONSHIP SERIES RECORD

Year	Club	League	G.	IP.	W.	L.	Pct.	H.	R.	ER.	SO.	BB.	ERA.
1986—	New York	National	1	1	0	0	.000	1	0	0	0	1	0.00

WORLD SERIES RECORD

Year	Club	League	G.	IP.	W.	L.	Pct.	H.	R.	ER.	SO.	BB.	ERA.
1986—	New York	National	1	⅔	0	0	.000	0	0	0	1	1	0.00

JOSEPH DOUGLAS SKALSKI
(Joe)

Born September 26, 1964, at Chicago, Ill.
Height, 6.03. Weight, 190.
Throws and bats righthanded.
Attended St. Xavier College, Chicago, Ill.

Led Pacific Coast League in home runs allowed with 30 and wild pitches with 14 in 1988.

Year	Club	League	G.	IP.	W.	L.	Pct.	H.	R.	ER.	SO.	BB.	ERA.
1986—	Batavia	NYP	14	104⅔	7	6	.538	79	34	23	*130	29	1.98
1986—	Waterloo	Midwest	2	12⅔	2	0	1.000	15	8	8	16	1	5.68
1987—	Williamsport†	Eastern	18	113⅔	8	7	.533	105	62	53	76	35	4.20
1987—	Buffalo	Am. Assoc.	5	18⅔	0	3	.000	30	21	21	18	12	10.13
1988—	Colorado Springs	P. Coast	29	159⅓	10	13	.435	186	*125	*116	117	64	6.55

Selected by Cleveland Indians' organization in 3rd round of free-agent draft, June 2, 1986.

†On disabled list, June 21 to July 17, 1987.

RAFEL CHARLES SKEETE

Born April 24, 1966, at St. Kitts, Netherlands Antilles.
Height, 5.10. Weight, 175.
Throws and bats lefthanded.

Led Southern League outfielders in total chances with 353 in 1988.

Year	Club	League	Pos.	G.	AB.	R.	H.	2B.	3B.	HR.	RBI.	B.A.	PO.	A.	E.	F.A.
1985—	Bluefield†‡	Appal.	OF	5	8	2	1	0	0	0	1	.125	3	0	1	.750
1986—	Newark	NYP	OF	16	41	6	10	1	0	0	2	.244	27	1	1	.966
1987—	Hagerstown	Carol.	OF	98	364	69	101	7	3	3	38	.277	234	6	11	.956
1987—	Charlotte	South.	OF	11	32	5	9	1	0	0	2	.281	15	3	1	.947
1988—	Charlotte	South.	OF	134	494	*89	117	18	1	3	29	.237	*332	10	11	.969

Signed as free agent by Baltimore Orioles' organization, February 22, 1985.

†On disabled list, July 8 to July 18, 1985.

‡On suspended lst, July 19, 1985 through remainder of season.

JOEL PATRICK SKINNER

Born February 21, 1961, at La Jolla, Calif.
Height, 6.04. Weight, 205.
Throws and bats righthanded.
Attended San Diego Mesa College, San Diego, Calif.
Son of Bob Skinner, outfielder-first baseman with Pittsburgh Pirates, Cincinnati Reds and St. Louis Cardinals, 1954 through 1966; manager, Philadelphia Phillies, 1968 and 1969, manager, San Diego Padres, 1977; coach, San Diego Padres, 1977; coach, California Angels, 1978; coach with Pittsburgh Pirates, 1979 through 1985; and coach with Atlanta Braves, 1986 through May 22, 1988.

Major League stolen bases: 1984 (1), 1986 (1). Total—2.

Led American Association batters in strikeouts with 115 and tied for lead in grounding into double plays with 16 in 1985.

Led American Association catchers in total chances with 698 and double plays with 13 in 1985.

Tied for South Atlantic League lead in double plays by catchers with 7 in 1980.

Year	Club	League	Pos.	G.	AB.	R.	H.	2B.	3B.	HR.	RBI.	B.A.	PO.	A.	E.	F.A.
1980—	Shelby	S. Atl.	C	100	324	36	73	15	2	7	27	.225	536	63	18	.971
1981—	Greenwood†‡	S. Atl.	C	117	428	48	114	25	2	11	63	.266	766	42	*22	.974
1982—	Glens Falls	East.	C	120	422	49	107	11	6	7	65	.254	726	80	12	.985

Year	Club	League	Pos.	G.	AB.	R.	H.	2B.	3B.	HR.	RBI.	B.A.	PO.	A.	E.	F.A.
1983—	Denver	A. A.	C	108	361	55	94	15	5	12	50	.260	550	54	5	.992
1983—	Chicago	Amer.	C	6	11	2	3	0	0	0	1	.273	20	4	1	.960
1984—	Denver§	A. A.	C	42	141	27	40	6	0	10	27	.284	255	24	5	.982
1984—	Chicago	Amer.	C	43	80	4	17	2	0	0	3	.213	171	11	2	.989
1985—	Buffalo	A. A.	C	115	390	47	94	13	0	12	59	.241	★623	★65	10	.986
1985—	Chicago	Amer.	C	22	44	9	15	4	1	1	5	.341	94	8	3	.971
1986—	Chi.x-N.Y.	Amer.	C	114	315	23	73	9	1	5	37	.232	507	37	9	.984
1987—	New York	Amer.	C	64	139	9	19	4	0	3	14	.137	232	18	4	.984
1987—	Columbus	Int.	C	49	178	19	43	10	2	6	27	.242	226	25	4	.984
1988—	New York	Amer.	C-OF-1B	88	251	23	57	15	0	4	23	.227	396	16	4	.990
Major League Totals—6 Years				337	840	70	184	34	2	13	83	.219	1420	94	23	.985

Selected by Pittsburgh Pirates' organization in 36th round of free-agent draft, June 5, 1979.

†On disabled list, June 1 to June 13, 1981.

‡Selected by Chicago White Sox' organization in player compensation pool draft, February 2, 1982. (Chicago received compensation for Philadelphia Phillies' signing of free agent Pitcher Ed Farmer, a Type A player, January 28, 1982.)

§On disabled list, July 23, 1984 through remainder of season.

xTraded with Outfielder-Designated Hitter Ron Kittle and Infielder Wayne Tolleson to New York Yankees for Catcher Ron Hassey, Shortstop Carlos Martinez and a player to be named later, July 30, 1986; New York traded Catcher Bill Lindsey to Chicago White Sox' organization to complete deal, December 24, 1986.

DONALD MARTIN SLAUGHT
(Don)

Born September 11, 1958, at Long Beach, Calif.
Height, 6.01. Weight, 190.
Throws and bats righthanded.
Attended El Camino College, Torrance, Calif., and received bachelor of science degree in economics from University of California, Los Angeles, Calif., in 1983.

Major League stolen bases: 1983 (3), 1985 (5), 1986 (3), 1988 (1). Total—12.

Year	Club	League	Pos.	G.	AB.	R.	H.	2B.	3B.	HR.	RBI.	B.A.	PO.	A.	E.	F.A.
1980—	Fort Myers	Fla. St.	C	50	176	13	46	9	0	2	16	.261	175	34	4	.981
1981—	Jacksonville	South.	C-1B	96	379	45	127	21	2	6	44	.335	482	61	9	.984
1981—	Omaha†	A. A.	C	22	71	10	21	4	0	2	8	.296	91	7	3	.970
1982—	Omaha‡	A. A.	C	53	206	29	55	10	1	4	16	.267	216	25	5	.980
1982—	Kansas City	Amer.	C	43	115	14	32	6	0	3	8	.278	156	7	1	.994
1983—	Kansas City§	Amer.	C	83	276	21	86	13	4	0	28	.312	299	18	12	.964
1984—	Kansas City x	Amer.	C	124	409	48	108	27	4	4	42	.264	547	44	11	.982
1985—	Texas y	Amer.	C	102	343	34	96	17	4	8	35	.280	550	33	6	.990
1986—	Texas z	Amer.	C	95	314	39	83	17	1	13	46	.264	533	40	4	.993
1986—	Oklahoma City	A. A.	C	3	12	2	4	1	0	0	1	.333	6	1	0	1.000
1987—	Texas a	Amer.	C	95	237	25	53	15	2	8	16	.224	429	39	7	.985
1988—	New York b	Amer.	C	97	322	33	91	25	1	9	43	.283	496	24	•11	.979
Major League Totals—7 Years				639	2016	214	549	120	16	45	218	.272	3010	205	52	.984

Selected by Milwaukee Brewers' organization in 19th round of free-agent draft, June 5, 1979.

Selected by Kansas City Royals' organization in 7th round of free-agent draft, June 3, 1980.

†On disabled list, August 16 to September 29, 1981.

‡On disabled list, April 21 to May 15, 1982.

§On disabled list, May 16 to June 1, 1983.

xTraded to Texas Rangers as part of a six-player, four-team deal in which Kansas City Royals acquired Catcher Jim Sundberg from Milwaukee Brewers, New York Mets' organization acquired Pitcher Frank Wills from Kansas City, Milwaukee acquired Pitcher Danny Darwin and a player to be named later from Texas and Pitcher Tim Leary from New York, January 18, 1985; Milwaukee organization acquired Catcher Bill Hance from Texas to complete deal, January 30, 1985.

yOn disabled list, August 9 to August 26, 1985.

zOn disabled list, May 18 to July 4, 1986; included rehabilitation disability assignment to Oklahoma City, July 1 to July 4, 1986.

aTraded to New York Yankees for a player to be named later, November 2, 1987; Texas Rangers acquired Pitcher Brad Arnsberg to complete deal, November 10, 1987.

bOn disabled list, May 15 to June 20, 1988.

CHAMPIONSHIP SERIES RECORD

Year	Club	League	Pos.	G.	AB.	R.	H.	2B.	3B.	HR.	RBI.	B.A.	PO.	A.	E.	F.A.
1984—	Kansas City	Amer.	C	3	11	0	4	0	0	0	0	.364	17	0	3	.850

CRAIG LEE SMAJSTRLA

Born June 19, 1962, at Houston, Tex.
Height, 5.08. Weight, 160.
Throws right and bats left and righthanded.

Year	Club	League	Pos.	G.	AB.	R.	H.	2B.	3B.	HR.	RBI.	B.A.	PO.	A.	E.	F.A.
1981—	Sarasota W. S.	Gulf C.	SS	40	110	15	37	1	0	0	4	.336	50	103	13	.922
1982—	Niagara Falls†	NYP	2B	63	270	38	82	11	★10	1	29	.304	129	★185	16	.952
1982—	Appleton†	Midw.	2B	8	29	5	7	2	0	0	2	.241	5	8	1	.929
1983—	Appleton†‡	Midw.	2B	93	330	42	91	16	4	0	24	.276	159	166	6	.982
1984—	Glens Falls†	East.	2B	133	497	78	131	18	6	4	41	.264	158	192	15	.959
1985—	G.F.§-Water.†	East.	3-2-S-O	124	470	84	130	20	5	0	43	.277	162	237	25	.941

Year	Club	League	Pos.	G.	AB.	R.	H.	2B.	3B.	HR.	RBI.	B.A.	PO.	A.	E.	F.A.
1986	—Waterbury†	East.	2B-OF	42	163	20	46	3	2	0	10	.282	80	60	2	.986
1986	—Maine†	Int.	2-3-S-O	90	319	42	93	9	3	0	20	.292	148	246	14	.966
1987	—Buffalo x	A. A.	2B-SS	111	432	63	122	19	4	7	51	.282	198	298	15	.971
1988	—Tucson	P. C.	*2B-SS	133	513	*89	159	30	5	4	56	.310	*295	342	16	*.975
1988	—Houston†y	Nat.	2B	8	3	2	0	0	0	0	0	.000	1	0	0	1.000
	Major League Totals—1 Year			8	3	2	0	0	0	0	0	.000	1	0	0	1.000

Selected by Chicago White Sox' organization in 4th round of free-agent draft, June 8, 1981.
†Batted left and righthanded.
‡On disabled list, May 1 to May 23, 1983.
§Traded to Waterbury (Cleveland Indians' organization), July 9, 1985, completing deal in which Cleveland traded Pitcher Tom Brennan to Chicago White Sox for a player to be named later, January 23, 1984.
xGranted free agency, October 15, 1987; signed by Tucson (Houston Astros' organization), November 27, 1987.
yReleased, November 17, 1988; re-signed by Astros' organization, December 14, 1988.

JOHN PATRICK SMILEY

Born March 17, 1965 at Phoenixville, Pa.
Height, 6.04. Weight, 195.
Throws and bats lefthanded.

Major League saves: 1987 (4).
Tied for Gulf Coast League lead in home runs allowed with 5 in 1983.

Year	Club	League	G.	IP.	W.	L.	Pct.	H.	R.	ER.	SO.	BB.	ERA.
1983	—Bradenton Pirates	Gulf Coast	12	65⅓	3	4	.429	69	45	43	42	27	5.92
1984	—Macon†	S. Atlantic	21	130	5	11	.313	119	73	57	73	41	3.95
1985	—Prince William	Carolina	10	56	2	2	.500	64	36	32	45	27	5.14
1985	—Macon	S. Atlantic	16	88⅔	3	8	.273	84	55	46	70	37	4.67
1986	—Prince William	Carolina	48	90	2	4	.333	64	35	31	93	40	3.10
1986	—Pittsburgh	National	12	11⅔	1	0	1.000	4	6	5	9	4	3.86
1987	—Pittsburgh	National	63	75	5	5	.500	69	49	48	58	50	5.76
1988	—Pittsburgh	National	34	205	13	11	.542	185	81	74	129	46	3.25
	Major League Totals—3 Years		109	291⅔	19	16	.543	258	136	127	196	100	3.92

Selected by Pittsburgh Pirates' organization in 12th round of free-agent draft, June 6, 1983.
†On disabled list, April 27 to May 27, 1984.

BRICK DUDLEY SMITH

Born May 2, 1959, at Charlotte, N. C.
Height, 6.04. Weight, 225.
Throws and bats righthanded.
Received bachelor of arts degree in communications from
Wake Forest University, Winston-Salem, N. C., in 1981.

Tied for Northwest League lead in game-winning RBIs with 7 in 1981.
Led Southern League first basemen in fielding percentage with .993 in 1984.

Year	Club	League	Pos.	G.	AB.	R.	H.	2B.	3B.	HR.	RBI.	B.A.	PO.	A.	E.	F.A.
1981	—Bellingham	N'west	1B	60	204	48	59	10	0	11	47	.289	510	35	9	.984
1982	—Bakersfield	Calif.	1B	96	348	59	90	20	1	12	58	.259	911	83	13	.987
1983	—Bakersfield	Calif.	1B	137	493	84	150	26	2	19	88	.304	1084	92	11	.990
1984	—Chattanooga†	South.	1B-C	100	334	36	83	13	0	5	35	.249	881	79	9	.991
1985	—Chattanooga‡	South.	1B-3B	80	275	38	72	7	0	8	37	.262	563	46	8	.987
1986	—Chattanooga	South.	1B-3B	128	474	80	163	*38	2	23	101	*.344	1023	94	7	.994
1987	—Calgary	P. C.	1B	84	314	47	82	15	0	11	48	.261	610	58	1	.999
1987	—Seattle	Amer.	1B	5	8	1	1	0	0	0	0	.125	24	2	1	.963
1988	—Calgary	P. C.	1B-3B	86	306	43	88	18	2	8	50	.288	704	63	4	.995
1988	—Seattle§	Amer.	1B	4	10	1	1	0	0	0	1	.100	27	4	0	1.000
	Major League Totals—2 Years			9	18	2	2	0	0	0	1	.111	51	6	1	.983

Selected by San Francisco Giants' organization in 11th round of free-agent draft, June 3, 1980.
Selected by Seattle Mariners' organization in 5th round of free-agent draft, June 8, 1981.
†On disabled list, August 10 to September 4, 1984.
‡On disabled list, April 11 to May 31, 1985
§Granted free agency, October 15, 1988.

BRYN NELSON SMITH

First name pronounced Brin.

Born August 11, 1955, at Marietta, Ga.
Height, 6.02. Weight, 205.
Throws and bats righthanded.
Attended Allan Hancock College, Santa Maria, Calif.

Major League saves: 1982 (3), 1983 (3). Total—6.
Tied for American Association lead in complete games with 9 in 1981.
Tied for Southern League lead in complete games with 16 in 1977 and 12 in 1980.
Named American Association Pitcher of the Year, 1981.

Year	Club	League	G.	IP.	W.	L.	Pct.	H.	R.	ER.	SO.	BB.	ERA.
1975	—Miami	Florida St.	26	139	11	7	.611	117	48	33	93	59	2.14
1976	—Miami	Florida St.	23	164	10	10	.500	140	72	51	119	62	2.80
1977	—Charlotte†	Southern	27	*206	*15	11	.577	*195	78	63	103	57	2.75
1978	—Denver	Am. Assoc.	11	54	0	6	.000	79	48	41	25	14	6.83

Year	Club	League	G.	IP.	W.	L.	Pct.	H.	R.	ER.	SO.	BB.	ERA.
1978—Memphis‡		Southern	11	69	4	6	.400	53	28	19	48	31	2.48
1979—Memphis		Southern	27	184	11	10	.524	175	80	69	115	74	3.38
1980—Memphis		Southern	27	181	10	9	.526	179	75	56	110	54	2.78
1981—Denver		Am. Assoc.	29	*183	*15	5	*.750	166	80	62	127	42	3.05
1981—Montreal		National	7	13	1	0	1.000	14	4	4	9	3	2.77
1982—Wichita		Am. Assoc.	3	23⅔	2	0	1.000	21	5	5	15	2	1.90
1982—Montreal		National	47	79⅓	2	4	.333	81	43	37	50	23	4.20
1983—Montreal		National	49	155⅓	6	11	.353	142	51	43	101	43	2.49
1984—Montreal		National	28	179	12	13	.480	178	72	66	101	51	3.32
1985—Montreal		National	32	222⅓	18	5	.783	193	85	72	127	41	2.91
1986—Montreal§		National	30	187⅓	10	8	.556	182	101	82	105	63	3.94
1987—West Palm Beach x		Florida St.	4	17⅔	0	2	.000	19	10	8	16	1	4.08
1987—Montreal y		National	26	150⅓	10	9	.526	164	81	73	94	31	4.37
1988—Montreal		National	32	198	12	10	.545	179	79	66	122	32	3.00
Major League Totals—8 Years			251	1184⅔	71	60	.542	1133	516	443	709	287	3.37

Selected by St. Louis Cardinals' organization in the 49th round of free-agent draft, June 5, 1973.

Signed as free agent by Baltimore Orioles' organization, December 18, 1974.

†Traded with Pitchers Rudy May and Randy Miller by Baltimore Orioles' organization to Montreal Expos' organization for Pitchers Don Stanhouse and Joe Kerrigan and Outfielder Gary Roenicke, December 7, 1977.

‡On disabled list, August 5 to August 17, 1978.

§Released, December 20, 1986; re-signed by Expos, February 27, 1987.

xOn Montreal disabled list, March 23 to May 1, 1987; included rehabilitation disability assignment to West Palm Beach, April 10, 1987.

yGranted free agency, November 9, 1987; re-signed by Expos, December 16, 1987.

DAVID STANLEY SMITH JR.
(Dave)

Born January 21, 1955, at San Francisco, Calif.
Height, 6.01. Weight, 195.
Throws and bats righthanded.
Attended San Diego State University, San Diego, Calif.

Major League saves: 1980 (10), 1981 (8), 1982 (11), 1983 (6), 1984 (5), 1985 (27), 1986 (33), 1987 (24), 1988 (27). Total—151.

Year	Club	League	G.	IP.	W.	L.	Pct.	H.	R.	ER.	SO.	BB.	ERA.
1976—Covington		Ap'lachian	15	97	5	5	.500	80	40	29	71	28	2.69
1977—Cocoa		Florida St.	14	93	7	5	.583	97	40	32	81	31	3.10
1977—Columbus		Southern	9	54	3	5	.375	52	2	21	29	24	3.50
1978—Columbus		Southern	26	181	10	13	.435	170	89	70	114	88	3.48
1979—Charleston		Int'national	34	160	7	8	.467	159	80	65	90	44	3.66
1980—Houston		National	57	103	7	5	.583	90	24	22	85	32	1.92
1981—Houston		National	42	75	5	3	.625	54	26	23	52	23	2.76
1982—Houston†		National	49	63⅓	5	4	.556	69	30	27	28	31	3.84
1983—Houston		National	42	72⅔	3	1	.750	72	32	25	41	36	3.10
1984—Houston		National	53	77⅓	5	4	.556	60	22	19	45	20	2.21
1985—Houston		National	64	79⅓	9	5	.643	69	26	20	40	17	2.27
1986—Houston		National	54	56	4	7	.364	39	17	17	46	22	2.73
1987—Houston‡		National	50	60	2	3	.400	39	13	11	73	21	1.65
1988—Houston		National	51	57⅓	4	5	.444	60	26	17	38	19	2.67
Major League Totals—9 Years			462	644	44	37	.543	552	216	181	448	221	2.53

Selected by Houston Astros' organization in 8th round of free-agent draft, June 8, 1976.

†On disabled list, June 27 to July 18, 1982.

‡Granted free agency, November 9, 1987; re-signed by Astros, January 8, 1988.

DIVISION SERIES RECORD

Year	Club	League	G.	IP.	W.	L.	Pct.	H.	R.	ER.	SO.	BB.	ERA.
1981—Houston		National	2	2⅓	0	0	.000	2	1	1	4	0	3.86

CHAMPIONSHIP SERIES RECORD

Year	Club	League	G.	IP.	W.	L.	Pct.	H.	R.	ER.	SO.	BB.	ERA.
1980—Houston		National	3	2⅓	1	0	1.000	4	1	1	4	2	3.86
1986—Houston		National	2	2	0	1	.000	2	2	2	2	3	9.00
Championship Series Totals—2 Years			5	4⅓	1	1	.500	6	3	3	6	5	6.23

ALL-STAR GAME RECORD

Member of National League All-Star Team in 1986; did not play.

GREGORY ALLEN SMITH
(Greg)

Born April 5, 1967, at Baltimore, Md.
Height, 5.11. Weight, 170.
Throws right and bats left and righthanded.

Led Midwest League shortstops in errors with 48 and tied for lead in putouts with 189 in 1987.

Year	Club	League	Pos.	G.	AB.	R.	H.	2B.	3B.	HR.	RBI.	B.A.	PO.	A.	E.	F.A.
1985	Wytheville	Appal.	SS	51	179	28	42	6	2	0	15	.235	56	160	24	.900
1986	Peoria	Midw.	SS-2B	53	170	24	43	6	3	2	26	.253	65	101	15	.917
1987	Peoria	Midw.	SS-2B	124	444	69	120	23	5	6	56	.270	193	347	49	.917
1988	Winston-Salem	Carol.	2B-1B	95	361	62	101	12	2	4	29	.280	162	236	16	.961

Selected by Chicago Cubs' organization in 2nd round of free-agent draft, June 3, 1985.

JOHN DWIGHT SMITH

(Known by middle name.)
Born November 8, 1963, at Tallahassee, Fla.
Height, 5.11. Weight, 175.
Throws right and bats lefthanded.
Attended Spartanburg Methodist College, Spartanburg, S.C.

Led Eastern League in total bases with 270, stolen bases with 60 and tied for lead in caught stealing with 18 in 1987.
Led Appalachian League in stolen bases with 47 in 1984.
Led Midwest League outfielders in total chances with 296 in 1986.
Tied for Appalachian League lead in double plays by outfielders with 3 in 1984.

Year	Club	League	Pos.	G.	AB.	R.	H.	2B.	3B.	HR.	RBI.	B.A.	PO.	A.	E.	F.A.
1984	Pikeville	Appal.	OF	61	195	42	46	6	2	1	17	.236	77	8	•9	.904
1985	Geneva	NYP	OF	73	232	44	67	11	2	4	32	.289	81	4	7	.924
1986	Peoria	Midw.	OF	124	471	92	146	22	*11	11	57	.310	*272	11	13	.956
1987	Pittsfield	East.	OF	130	498	*111	168	28	10	18	72	.337	214	8	•14	.941
1988	Iowa	A. A.	OF	129	505	76	148	26	3	9	48	.293	216	11	*15	.938

Selected by Toronto Blue Jays' organization in 3rd round of free-agent draft, January 17, 1984.
Selected by Chicago Cubs' organization in secondary phase of free-agent draft, June 4, 1984.

LEE ARTHUR SMITH

Born December 4, 1957, at Jamestown, La.
Height, 6.06. Weight, 245.
Throws and bats righthanded.
Attended Northwestern State University, Natchitoches, La.

Major League saves: 1981 (1), 1982 (17), 1983 (29), 1984 (33), 1985 (33), 1986 (31), 1987 (36), 1988 (29). Total—209.
Led National League in games finished in relief with 57 in 1985 and tied for lead with 56 in 1983.
Led National League in saves with 29 in 1983.
Tied for American Association lead in wild pitches with 16 in 1980.
Named National League co-Fireman of the Year by The Sporting News, 1983.

Year	Club	League	G.	IP.	W.	L.	Pct.	H.	R.	ER.	SO.	BB.	ERA.
1975	Bradenton Cubs	Gulf Coast	10	62	3	5	.375	35	23	16	35	*49	2.32
1976	Pompano Beach	Florida St.	26	101	4	8	.333	120	76	60	52	74	5.35
1977	Pompano Beach	Florida St.	26	130	10	4	.714	131	67	62	82	85	4.29
1978	Midland	Texas	30	155	8	10	.444	161	122	103	71	*128	5.98
1979	Midland	Texas	35	104	9	5	.643	122	65	57	46	85	4.93
1980	Wichita	Am. Assoc.	50	90	4	7	.364	70	49	37	63	56	3.70
1980	Chicago	National	18	22	2	0	1.000	21	9	7	17	14	2.86
1981	Chicago	National	40	67	3	6	.333	57	31	26	50	31	3.49
1982	Chicago	National	72	117	2	5	.286	105	38	35	99	37	2.69
1983	Chicago	National	66	103⅓	4	10	.286	70	23	19	91	41	1.65
1984	Chicago	National	69	101	9	7	.563	98	42	41	86	35	3.65
1985	Chicago	National	65	97⅔	7	4	.636	87	35	33	112	32	3.04
1986	Chicago†	National	66	90⅓	9	9	.500	69	32	31	93	42	3.09
1987	Chicago‡	National	62	83⅔	4	10	.286	84	30	29	96	32	3.12
1988	Boston	American	64	83⅔	4	5	.444	72	34	26	96	37	2.80
National League Totals—8 Years			458	682	40	51	.440	591	240	221	644	264	2.92
American League Totals—1 Year			64	83⅔	4	5	.444	72	34	26	96	37	2.80
Major League Totals—9 Years			522	765⅔	44	56	.440	663	274	247	740	301	2.90

Selected by Chicago Cubs' organization in 2nd round of free-agent draft, June 4, 1975.
†On disabled list, April 21 to May 6, 1986.
‡Traded to Boston Red Sox for Pitchers Al Nipper and Calvin Schiraldi, December 8, 1987.

CHAMPIONSHIP SERIES RECORD

Year	Club	League	G.	IP.	W.	L.	Pct.	H.	R.	ER.	SO.	BB.	ERA.
1984	Chicago	National	2	2	0	1	.000	3	2	2	3	0	9.00
1988	Boston	American	2	3⅓	0	1	.000	6	3	3	4	1	8.10
Championship Series Totals—2 Years			4	5⅓	0	2	.000	9	5	5	7	1	8.44

ALL-STAR GAME RECORD

Year	League	IP.	W.	L.	Pct.	H.	R.	ER.	SO.	BB.	ERA.
1983	National	1	0	0	.000	2	2	1	1	0	9.00
1987	National	3	1	0	1.000	2	0	0	4	0	0.00
All-Star Game Totals—2 Years		4	1	0	1.000	4	2	1	5	0	2.25

—DID YOU KNOW—

That the Pirates' Bobby Bonilla led the National League by hitting .329 on the road in 1988?

LEROY PURDY SMITH III
(Roy)

Born September 6, 1961, at Mt. Vernon, N.Y.
Height, 6.03. Weight, 217.
Throws and bats righthanded.
Attended Fordham University, Bronx, N.Y.

Tied for Carolina League lead in shutouts with 3 in 1980.
Named Carolina League Pitcher of the Year, 1980.

Year Club	League	G.	IP.	W.	L.	Pct.	H.	R.	ER.	SO.	BB.	ERA.
1979—Helena	Pioneer	5	36	5	0	1.000	21	16	10	42	16	2.50
1980—Peninsula	Carolina	27	163	*17	6	.739	101	54	47	134	63	2.60
1981—Reading	Eastern	27	161	11	8	.579	123	92	79	117	97	4.42
1982—Reading†	Eastern	26	166	10	8	.556	141	81	71	122	82	3.85
1983—Charleston	Int'national	27	155⅓	6	8	.429	166	101	89	95	75	5.16
1984—Maine	Int'national	12	80⅔	5	4	.556	77	47	39	48	29	4.35
1984—Cleveland	American	22	86⅓	5	5	.500	91	49	44	55	40	4.59
1985—Maine	Int'national	15	109⅓	10	4	.714	84	33	29	65	29	2.39
1985—Cleveland‡§	American	12	62⅓	1	4	.200	84	40	37	28	17	5.34
1986—Minnesota	American	5	10⅓	0	2	.000	13	8	8	8	5	6.97
1986—Toledo xy	Int'national	9	53⅔	2	1	.667	42	12	9	39	16	1.51
1987—Portland	P. Coast	24	166⅓	9	12	.429	176	84	70	106	41	3.79
1987—Minnesota	American	7	16⅓	1	0	1.000	20	10	9	8	6	4.96
1988—Portland	P. Coast	22	150	12	9	.571	152	82	72	110	31	4.32
1988—Minnesota	American	9	37	3	0	1.000	29	12	11	17	12	2.68
Major League Totals—5 Years		55	212⅓	10	11	.476	237	119	109	116	80	4.62

Selected by Philadelphia Phillies' organization in 3rd round of free-agent draft, June 5, 1979.
†Traded with Pitcher Jerry Reed and Outfielder Wil Culmer to Cleveland Indians for Pitcher John Denny, September 12, 1982.
‡On disabled list, July 3 to August 1, 1985; included rehabilitation disability assignment to Maine, July 27 to July 30, 1985.
§Traded with Pitcher Ramon Romero to Minnesota Twins for Pitchers Ken Schrom and Bryan Oelkers, January 7, 1986.
xOn disabled list, June 7 to July 3, 1986.
yReleased, December 20, 1986; re-signed by Minnesota Twins' organization, February 24, 1987.

LONNIE SMITH

Born December 22, 1955, at Chicago, Ill.
Height, 5.09. Weight, 170.
Throws and bats righthanded.

Tied major league record for fewest double plays by outfielder, season, for leader in double plays (4), 1983.
Tied modern National League record for most stolen bases, game, (5), September 4, 1982.
Major League stolen bases: 1978 (4), 1979 (2), 1980 (33), 1981 (21), 1982 (68), 1983 (43), 1984 (50), 1985 (52), 1986 (26), 1987 (9), 1988 (4). Total—312.
Led National League in being hit by pitch with 9 in 1982 and 1984 and tied for lead with 9 in 1983.
Tied for National League lead in caught stealing with 26 in 1982.
Tied for National League lead in double plays by outfielders with 4 in 1983.
Led International League in bases on balls received with 66 in 1988.
Led American Association in stolen bases with 66 and caught stealing with 19 in 1978.
Led Western Carolinas League in stolen bases with 56 and tied for lead in caught stealing with 14 in 1975.
Led American Association outfielders in double plays with 5 in 1978.
Named National League Rookie Player of the Year by THE SPORTING NEWS, 1980.
Named outfielder on THE SPORTING NEWS National League All-Star Team, 1982.

Year Club	League	Pos.	G.	AB.	R.	H.	2B.	3B.	HR.	RBI.	B.A.	PO.	A.	E.	F.A.
1974—Auburn	NYP	OF	61	210	48	60	10	4	5	27	.286	143	6	•9	.943
1975—Spartanburg	W. Car.	OF	131	465	*114	*150	23	4	7	40	.323	*317	9	11	.967
1976—Oklahoma City	A. A.	OF	134	483	*93	149	24	9	8	54	.308	200	4	*14	.936
1977—Oklahoma City	A. A.	OF	125	477	91	132	14	10	4	41	.277	231	8	*13	.948
1978—Oklahoma City†	A. A.	OF	125	480	103	151	20	5	7	43	.315	274	*21	*12	.961
1978—Philadelphia	Nat.	OF	17	4	6	0	0	0	0	0	.000	5	1	0	1.000
1979—Oklahoma City	A. A.	OF	110	451	*106	149	26	9	7	44	.330	268	13	*12	.959
1979—Philadelphia	Nat.	OF	17	30	4	5	2	0	0	3	.167	19	1	0	1.000
1980—Philadelphia	Nat.	OF	100	298	69	101	14	4	3	20	.339	121	2	4	.969
1981—Philadelphia‡	Nat.	OF	62	176	40	57	14	3	2	11	.324	91	10	3	.971
1982—St. Louis	Nat.	OF	156	592	*120	182	35	8	8	69	.307	303	•16	10	.970
1983—St. Louis§	Nat.	OF	130	492	83	158	31	5	8	45	.321	225	14	*15	.941
1984—St. Louis	Nat.	OF	145	504	77	126	20	4	6	49	.250	184	*18	•11	.948
1985—St. Louis x	Nat.	OF	28	96	15	25	2	2	0	7	.260	43	1	0	1.000
1985—Kansas City	Amer.	OF	120	448	77	115	23	4	6	41	.257	195	10	9	.958
1986—Kansas City yz	Amer.	OF	134	508	80	146	25	7	8	44	.287	245	5	9	.965
1987—Omaha	A. A.	OF	40	149	36	49	9	1	7	33	.329	51	1	3	.945
1987—Kansas City a	Amer.	OF	48	167	26	42	7	1	3	8	.251	52	2	5	.915
1988—Richmond	Int.	OF	93	290	58	87	13	5	9	51	.300	120	6	2	.984
1988—Atlanta	Nat.	OF	43	114	14	27	3	0	3	9	.237	59	2	2	.968
National League Totals—9 Years			698	2306	428	681	121	26	30	213	.295	1050	65	45	.961
American League Totals—3 Years			302	1123	183	303	55	12	17	93	.270	492	17	23	.957
Major League Totals—11 Years			1000	3429	611	984	176	38	47	306	.287	1542	82	68	.960

Selected by Philadelphia Phillies' organization in 1st round (third player selected) of free-agent draft, June 5, 1974.

†On disabled list, April 14 to April 25, 1978.

‡Traded with a player to be named later to Cleveland Indians for Catcher Bo Diaz, November 20, 1981; Traded by Cleveland to St. Louis Cardinals for Pitchers Lary Sorensen and Silvio Martinez, November 20, 1981. Cleveland organization acquired Pitcher Scott Munninghoff to complete first deal, December 9, 1981.

§On disabled list, June 11 to July 8, 1983.

xTraded to Kansas City Royals for Outfielder John Morris, May 17, 1985.

yOn disabled list, April 13 to May 4, 1986.

zGranted free agency, November 12, 1986; re-signed by Royals' organization, May 18, 1987.

aReleased, December 15, 1987; signed by Richmond (Atlanta Braves' organization), March 12, 1988.

DIVISION SERIES RECORD

Year	Club	League	Pos.	G.	AB.	R.	H.	2B.	3B.	HR.	RBI.	B.A.	PO.	A.	E.	F.A.
1981	Philadelphia	Nat.	OF	5	19	1	5	1	0	0	0	.263	6	1	0	1.000

CHAMPIONSHIP SERIES RECORD

Year	Club	League	Pos.	G.	AB.	R.	H.	2B.	3B.	HR.	RBI.	B.A.	PO.	A.	E.	F.A.
1980	Philadelphia	Nat.	PR-OF	3	5	2	3	0	0	0	0	.600	2	1	0	1.000
1982	St. Louis	Nat.	OF	3	11	1	3	0	0	0	1	.273	2	0	0	1.000
1985	Kansas City	Amer.	OF	7	28	2	7	2	0	0	1	.250	8	3	1	.917
Championship Series Totals—3 Years				13	44	5	13	2	0	0	2	.295	12	4	1	.941

WORLD SERIES RECORD

Tied World Series record for most clubs, total Series (3).

Year	Club	League	Pos.	G.	AB.	R.	H.	2B.	3B.	HR.	RBI.	B.A.	PO.	A.	E.	F.A.
1980	Philadelphia	Nat.	PR-O-DH	6	19	2	5	1	0	0	1	.263	4	1	0	1.000
1982	St. Louis	Nat.	OF-DH	7	28	6	9	4	1	0	1	.321	11	0	0	1.000
1985	Kansas City	Amer.	OF	7	27	4	9	3	0	0	4	.333	7	2	0	1.000
World Series Totals—3 Years				20	74	12	23	8	1	0	6	.311	22	3	0	1.000

ALL-STAR GAME RECORD

Year	League	Pos.	AB.	R.	H.	2B.	3B.	HR.	RBI.	B.A.	PO.	A.	E.	F.A.
1982	National	OF	0	0	0	0	0	0	0	.000	1	0	0	1.000

MICHAEL ANTHONY SMITH
(Mike)

Born February 23, 1961, at Jackson, Miss.
Height, 6.01. Weight, 195.
Throws right and bats right and lefthanded.
Attended Utica Junior College, Utica, Miss.

Major League saves: 1988 (1).

Led Florida State League in saves with 21 in 1982.

Year	Club	League	G.	IP.	W.	L.	Pct.	H.	R.	ER.	SO.	BB.	ERA.
1981	Billings	Pioneer	22	46	5	5	.500	39	21	7	52	19	1.37
1982	Tampa	Florida St.	48	80⅓	7	1	.875	55	17	11	80	42	1.23
1983	Waterbury†	Eastern	22	28⅔	2	5	.286	18	13	9	16	25	2.83
1984	Cincinnati	National	8	10⅓	1	0	1.000	12	6	6	7	5	5.23
1984	Wichita	Am. Assoc.	12	18	3	2	.600	17	8	8	20	13	4.00
1984	Vermont	Eastern	35	51	3	3	.500	51	28	19	49	20	3.35
1985	Denver	Am. Assoc.	47	68⅔	5	4	.556	65	40	37	67	38	4.85
1985	Cincinnati	National	2	3⅓	0	0	.000	2	2	2	2	1	5.40
1986	Denver‡-Indianapolis	Am. Assoc.	40	76⅔	6	3	.667	95	54	46	50	44	5.40
1986	Cincinnati§	National	2	3⅓	0	0	.000	7	5	5	1	1	13.50
1987	Indianapolis	Am. Assoc.	45	86⅓	4	4	.500	85	51	45	90	43	4.69
1988	Indianapolis	Am. Assoc.	32	63	5	1	.833	40	22	18	55	14	2.57
1988	Montreal x	National	5	8⅔	0	0	.000	6	3	3	4	5	3.12
Major League Totals—4 Years			17	25⅔	1	0	1.000	27	16	16	14	12	5.61

Signed as free agent by Cincinnati Reds' organization, May 11, 1981.

†On disabled list, June 28, 1983 through remainder of season.

‡Loaned to Indianapolis (Montreal Expos' organization), July 24, 1986; returned, September 10, 1986.

§Traded to Montreal Expos for a player to be named later, December 1, 1986; Cincinnati Reds' organization acquired Pitcher Bill Cutshall to complete deal, December 9, 1986.

xTraded to Baltimore Orioles for a player to be named later, November 14, 1988; Montreal Expos acquired Pitcher Doug Kline to complete deal, December 7, 1988.

MICHAEL ANTHONY SMITH
(Mike)

Born October 31, 1963, at San Antonio, Tex.
Height, 6.03. Weight, 180.
Throws and bats righthanded.
Attended Ranger Junior College, Ranger, Tex.

Led Southern League in hit batsmen with 10 in 1988.

Tied for Eastern League lead in games started by pitchers with 27 in 1987.

Tied for Midwest League lead in wild pitches with 19 in 1986.

Year	Club	League	G.	IP.	W.	L.	Pct.	H.	R.	ER.	SO.	BB.	ERA.
1984	Sarasota Reds	Gulf Coast	11	67	2	4	.333	65	33	27	65	24	3.63
1985	Billings	Pioneer	7	33⅔	2	2	.500	24	15	11	24	24	2.94

Year Club	League	G.	IP.	W.	L.	Pct.	H.	R.	ER.	SO.	BB.	ERA.
1985—Cedar Rapids	Midwest	8	44⅓	5	1	.833	38	20	16	28	22	3.25
1986—Cedar Rapids	Midwest	28	★191	10	10	.500	155	88	71	172	106	3.35
1987—Vermont	Eastern	27	171⅓	8	12	.400	152	78	64	104	★117	3.36
1988—Chattanooga†	Southern	28	194⅓	9	10	.474	160	90	69	141	★98	3.20

Selected by San Diego Padres' organization in 4th round of free-agent draft, January 11, 1983.
Selected by Cincinnati Reds' organization in 5th round of free-agent draft, January 17, 1984.
†Drafted by Baltimore Orioles, December 5, 1988.

OSBORNE EARL SMITH
(Ozzie)

Born December 26, 1954, at Mobile, Ala.
Height, 5.10. Weight, 155.
Throws right and bats left and righthanded.
Received degree from California Polytechnic State University, San Luis Obispo, Calif.

Established major league records for most assists by shortstop, season (621), 1980; most years with 500 or more assists by shortstop (8).

Tied major league records for most years leading league in assists by shortstop (7); most years leading league in chances accepted by shortstop (7); most double plays by shortstop, extra-inning game (6), August 25, 1979 (19 innings).

Tied National League records for most consecutive years leading league in assists by shortstop (4), 1979 through 1982; most years leading league in fielding average by shortstop, 100 or more games (6); highest fielding average by shortstop, season, 150 or more games (.987), 1987.

Tied modern National League record for most consecutive years leading league in fielding average by shortstop, 100 or more games (4), 1984 through 1987.

Major League stolen bases: 1978 (40), 1979 (28), 1980 (57), 1981 (22), 1982 (25), 1983 (34), 1984 (35), 1985 (31), 1986 (31), 1987 (43), 1988 (57). Total—403.

Led National League in sacrifice hits with 28 in 1978 and 23 in 1980.

Led National League shortstops in total chances with 933 in 1980, 658 in 1981, 844 in 1983, 827 in 1985, 771 in 1987 and 775 in 1988.

Led National League shortstops in double plays with 113 in 1980, 111 in 1987 and tied for lead with 94 in 1984 and 96 in 1986.

Led Northwest League in stolen bases with 30 in 1977.

Led Northwest League shortstops in double plays with 40 in 1977.

Named shortstop on THE SPORTING NEWS National League All-Star Team, 1982 and 1984 through 1987.

Named shortstop on THE SPORTING NEWS National League All-Star fielding team, 1980 through 1988.

Named shortstop on THE SPORTING NEWS National League Silver Slugger team, 1987.

Year Club	League	Pos.	G.	AB.	R.	H.	2B.	3B.	HR.	RBI.	B.A.	PO.	A.	E.	F.A.
1977—Walla Walla	N'west	SS	●68	★287	★69	87	10	2	1	35	.303	130	★254	23	★.943
1978—San Diego	Nat.	SS	159	590	69	152	17	6	1	46	.258	264	548	25	.970
1979—San Diego	Nat.	SS	156	587	77	124	18	6	0	27	.211	256	★555	20	.976
1980—San Diego	Nat.	SS	158	609	67	140	18	5	0	35	.230	★288	★621	24	.974
1981—San Diego†	Nat.	SS	●110	★450	53	100	11	2	0	21	.222	220	★422	16	★.976
1982—St. Louis	Nat.	SS	140	488	58	121	24	1	2	43	.248	279	★535	13	★.984
1983—St. Louis	Nat.	SS	159	552	69	134	30	6	3	50	.243	★304	519	21	.975
1984—St. Louis‡	Nat.	SS	124	412	53	106	20	5	1	44	.257	233	437	12	★.982
1985—St. Louis	Nat.	SS	158	537	70	148	22	3	6	54	.276	264	★549	14	★.983
1986—St. Louis	Nat.	SS	153	514	67	144	19	4	0	54	.280	229	453	15	★.978
1987—St. Louis	Nat.	SS	158	600	104	182	40	4	0	75	.303	245	★516	10	★.987
1988—St. Louis	Nat.	SS	153	575	80	155	27	1	3	51	.270	234	★519	22	.972
Major League Totals—11 Years			1628	5914	767	1506	246	43	16	500	.255	2816	5674	192	.978

Selected by Detroit Tigers' organization in 7th round of free-agent draft, June 8, 1976.
Selected by San Diego Padres' organization in 4th round of free-agent draft, June 7, 1977.
†Traded to St. Louis Cardinals for Shortstop Garry Templeton, February 11, 1982.
‡On disabled list, July 14 to August 19, 1984.

CHAMPIONSHIP SERIES RECORD

Established National League Championship Series records for highest batting average (.435) and most hits (10), six-game Series, 1985.

Tied National League Championship Series record for most singles, six-game Series (7), 1985.

Year Club	League	Pos.	G.	AB.	R.	H.	2B.	3B.	HR.	RBI.	B.A.	PO.	A.	E.	F.A.
1982—St. Louis	Nat.	SS	3	9	0	5	0	0	0	3	.556	4	11	0	1.000
1985—St. Louis	Nat.	SS	6	23	4	10	1	1	1	3	.435	6	16	0	1.000
1987—St. Louis	Nat.	SS	7	25	2	5	0	1	0	1	.200	10	19	1	.967
Championship Series Totals—3 Years			16	57	6	20	1	2	1	7	.351	20	46	1	.985

WORLD SERIES RECORD

Established World Series record for most putouts by shortstop, seven-game Series (22), 1982.

Tied World Series record for fewest chances accepted, shortstop, game (0), October 23, 1985.

Year Club	League	Pos.	G.	AB.	R.	H.	2B.	3B.	HR.	RBI.	B.A.	PO.	A.	E.	F.A.
1982—St. Louis	Nat.	SS	7	24	3	5	0	0	0	1	.208	22	17	0	1.000
1985—St. Louis	Nat.	SS	7	23	1	2	0	0	0	0	.087	10	16	1	.963
1987—St. Louis	Nat.	SS	7	28	3	6	0	0	0	2	.214	7	19	0	1.000
World Series Totals—3 Years			21	75	7	13	0	0	0	3	.173	39	52	1	.989

ALL-STAR GAME RECORD

Year League	Pos.	AB.	R.	H.	2B.	3B.	HR.	RBI.	B.A.	PO.	A.	E.	F.A.
1981—National	SS	0	0	0	0	0	0	0	.000	1	0	0	1.000

Year	League	Pos.	AB.	R.	H.	2B.	3B.	HR.	RBI.	B.A.	PO.	A.	E.	F.A.
1982—National		PR-SS	0	0	0	0	0	0	0	.000	0	1	0	1.000
1983—National		SS	2	1	1	0	0	0	0	.500	0	0	0	.000
1984—National		SS	3	0	0	0	0	0	0	.000	3	0	0	1.000
1985—National		SS	4	0	0	0	0	0	0	.000	1	3	0	1.000
1986—National		SS	1	0	0	0	0	0	0	.000	3	2	0	1.000
1987—National		SS	2	0	0	0	0	0	0	.000	3	2	1	.833
1988—National		SS	2	0	0	0	0	0	0	.000	1	4	0	1.000
All-Star Game Totals—8 Years			14	1	1	0	0	0	0	.071	12	12	1	.960

PETER JOHN SMITH
(Pete)

Born February 27, 1966, at Abington, Mass.
Height, 6.02. Weight, 185.
Throws and bats righthanded.

Year	Club	League	G.	IP.	W.	L.	Pct.	H.	R.	ER.	SO.	BB.	ERA.
1984—Sarasota Phillies		Gulf Coast	8	37	1	2	.333	28	11	6	35	16	1.46
1985—Clearwater†		Florida St.	26	153	12	10	.545	135	68	56	86	80	3.29
1986—Greenville		Southern	24	104⅔	1	8	.111	117	88	68	64	78	5.85
1987—Greenville		Southern	29	177⅓	9	9	.500	162	76	66	119	67	3.35
1987—Atlanta		National	6	31⅔	1	2	.333	39	21	17	11	14	4.83
1988—Atlanta		National	32	195⅓	7	15	.318	183	89	80	124	88	3.69
Major League Totals—2 Years			38	227	8	17	.320	222	110	97	135	102	3.85

Selected by Philadelphia Phillies' organization in 1st round (21st player selected) of free-agent draft, June 4, 1984.

†Traded with Catcher Ozzie Virgil to Atlanta Braves for Pitcher Steve Bedrosian and Outfielder Milt Thompson, December 10, 1985.

WILLIE EVERETT SMITH

Born January 27, 1967, at Savannah, Ga.
Height, 6.05. Weight, 225.
Throws and bats righthanded.

Year	Club	League	G.	IP.	W.	L.	Pct.	H.	R.	ER.	SO.	BB.	ERA.
1986—Bradenton Pirates		Gulf Coast	7	21⅔	1	0	1.000	16	8	6	13	6	2.49
1987—Bradenton Pirates		Gulf Coast	10	19⅓	2	1	.667	12	4	2	27	11	1.40
1987—Watertown		NYP	5	20⅓	2	0	1.000	15	13	10	24	10	4.43
1988—Augusta		S. Atlantic	30	48⅓	1	4	.200	35	20	16	48	29	2.98

Signed as free agent by Pittsburgh Pirates' organization, July 13, 1986.

ZANE WILLIAM SMITH

Born December 28, 1960, at Madison, Wis.
Height, 6.02. Weight, 195.
Throws and bats lefthanded.
Attended Indiana State University, Terre Haute, Ind.

Major League saves: 1986 (1).
Led National League hitters in sacrifice hits with 14 in 1987.
Tied for National League lead in games started by pitchers with 36 in 1987.
Named lefthanded pitcher on THE SPORTING NEWS National League All-Star Team, 1987.

Year	Club	League	G.	IP.	W.	L.	Pct.	H.	R.	ER.	SO.	BB.	ERA.
1982—Anderson		S. Atlantic	12	63	5	3	.625	65	53	48	32	34	6.86
1983—Durham		Carolina	27	170⅔	9	•15	.375	183	109	93	126	83	4.90
1984—Greenville		Southern	9	60	7	0	1.000	47	13	11	35	23	1.65
1984—Richmond		Int'national	19	123⅔	7	4	.636	113	62	57	68	65	4.15
1984—Atlanta		National	3	20	1	0	1.000	16	7	5	16	13	2.25
1985—Atlanta†		National	42	147	9	10	.474	135	70	62	85	80	3.80
1986—Atlanta		National	38	204⅔	8	16	.333	209	109	92	139	105	4.05
1987—Atlanta		National	36	242	15	10	.600	245	*130	110	130	91	4.09
1988—Atlanta‡		National	23	140⅓	5	10	.333	159	72	67	59	44	4.30
Major League Totals—5 Years			142	754	38	46	.452	764	388	336	429	333	4.01

Selected by Atlanta Braves' organization in 3rd round of free-agent draft, June 7, 1982.
†On disabled list, August 5 to September 1, 1985.
‡On disabled list, August 25, 1988 through remainder of season.

BILLY MIKE SMITHSON

(Known by middle name.)

Born January 21, 1955, at Centerville, Tenn.
Height, 6.08. Weight, 215.
Throws right and bats lefthanded.
Attended University of Tennessee, Knoxville, Tenn.

Led American League in hit batsmen with 15 in 1985.
Led American League in home runs allowed with 35 in 1984.
Tied for American League lead in games started by pitchers with 36 in 1984 and 37 in 1985.
Tied for International League lead in intentional bases on balls issued with 13 in 1980.

Year	Club	League	G.	IP.	W.	L.	Pct.	H.	R.	ER.	SO.	BB.	ERA.
1976—	Winter Haven	Florida St.	11	64	4	3	.571	63	27	22	29	20	3.09
1977—	Winter Haven	Florida St.	25	172	13	8	.619	170	56	53	92	41	2.77
1977—	Bristol	Eastern	1	3	0	1	.000	8	7	7	1	0	21.00
1978—	Bristol	Eastern	27	160	11	10	.524	178	92	81	86	76	4.56
1979—	Bristol	Eastern	*48	132	8	12	.400	128	82	69	89	53	4.70
1980—	Pawtucket	Int'national	*50	99	5	9	.357	95	50	32	73	45	2.91
1981—	Pawtucket†	Int'national	34	91	2	4	.333	74	44	39	82	45	3.86
1982—	Denver	Am. Assoc.	29	152⅔	11	7	.611	149	82	77	*144	47	4.54
1982—	Texas	American	8	46⅔	3	4	.429	51	26	26	24	13	5.01
1983—	Texas‡	American	33	223⅓	10	14	.417	233	102	97	135	71	3.91
1984—	Minnesota	American	36	252	15	13	.536	246	113	103	144	54	3.68
1985—	Minnesota	American	37	257	15	14	.517	264	134	*124	127	78	4.34
1986—	Minnesota	American	34	198	13	14	.481	234	123	105	114	57	4.77
1987—	Minnesota§	American	21	109	4	7	.364	126	76	72	53	38	5.94
1987—	Portland x	P. Coast	6	38	2	3	.400	36	22	21	31	17	4.97
1988—	Boston	American	31	126⅔	9	6	.600	149	87	84	73	37	5.97
1988—	Pawtucket y	Int'national	2	7	1	0	1.000	6	0	0	5	2	0.00
Major League Totals—7 Years			200	1212⅔	69	72	.489	1303	661	611	670	348	4.53

Selected by Boston Red Sox' organization in 5th round of free-agent draft, June 8, 1976.
†Traded to Texas Rangers' organization for Pitcher John Henry Johnson, April 9, 1982.
‡Traded with Pitcher John Butcher and Catcher Sam Sorce to Minnesota Twins for Outfielder Gary Ward, December 7, 1983.
§On disabled list, May 11 to June 8, 1987.
xReleased, December 21, 1987; signed by Pawtucket (Boston Red Sox' organization), January 18, 1988.
yGranted free agency, November 4, 1988; re-signed by Red Sox, December 19, 1988.

CHAMPIONSHIP SERIES RECORD

Year	Club	League	G.	IP.	W.	L.	Pct.	H.	R.	ER.	SO.	BB.	ERA.
1988—	Boston	American	1	2⅓	0	0	.000	3	0	0	1	0	0.00

JOHN ANDREW SMOLTZ

Born May 15, 1967, at Detroit, Mich.
Height, 6.03. Weight, 185.
Throws and bats righthanded.

Tied for Florida State League lead in balks with 6 in 1986.

Year	Club	League	G.	IP.	W.	L.	Pct.	H.	R.	ER.	SO.	BB.	ERA.
1986—	Lakeland †	Florida St.	17	96	7	8	.467	86	44	38	47	31	3.56
1987—	Glens Falls	Eastern	21	130	4	10	.286	131	89	82	86	81	5.68
1987—	Richmond	Int'national	3	16	0	1	.000	17	11	11	5	11	6.19
1988—	Richmond	Int'national	20	135⅓	10	5	.667	118	49	42	115	37	2.79
1988—	Atlanta	National	12	64	2	7	.222	74	40	39	37	33	5.48
Major League Totals—1 Year			12	64	2	7	.222	74	40	39	37	33	5.48

Selected by Detroit Tigers' organization in 22nd round of free-agent draft, June 3, 1985.
†Traded to Atlanta Braves for pitcher Doyle Alexander, August 12, 1987.

VAN VOORHEES SNIDER

Born August 11, 1963, at Birmingham, Ala.
Height, 6.03. Weight, 205.
Throws right and bats lefthanded.
Attended Gadsden State Junior College, Gadsden, Ala.

Led American Association in total bases with 259 and tied for lead in intentional bases on balls received with 9 in 1988.
Tied for Southern League lead in intentional bases on balls received with 9 in 1986.
Led South Atlantic League outfielders in double plays with 7 in 1983.
Tied for Pioneer League lead in double plays by outfielder with 2 in 1982.

Year	Club	League	Pos.	G.	AB.	R.	H.	2B.	3B.	HR.	RBI.	B.A.	PO.	A.	E.	F.A.
1982—	Butte	Pion.	OF	67	237	46	71	13	5	9	53	.300	99	*14	9	.926
1983—	Charleston	S. Atl.	OF	123	467	86	136	26	2	20	94	.291	207	17	*22	.911
1983—	Jacksonville	South.	OF	13	33	2	6	3	0	0	2	.182	28	0	2	.933
1984—	Memphis	South.	OF	132	488	52	120	23	9	7	62	.246	319	*24	4	*.988
1985—	Memphis†	South.	OF	85	292	43	69	15	4	8	39	.236	166	9	*13	.931
1986—	Memphis	South.	OF	134	492	79	133	27	5	26	81	.270	276	*23	6	.980
1986—	Omaha	A. A.	OF	4	13	5	4	2	1	0	3	.308	7	0	0	1.000
1987—	Omaha	A. A.	OF	70	244	26	50	9	1	9	27	.205	105	7	3	.974
1987—	Memphis ‡	South.	OF	45	174	25	57	10	7	9	40	.328	95	6	4	.962
1988—	Nashville	A. A.	OF	135	525	72	152	22	8	*23	73	.290	263	14	4	.986
1988—	Cincinnati	Nat.	OF	11	28	4	6	1	0	1	6	.214	15	0	0	1.000
Major League Totals—1 Year				11	28	4	6	1	0	1	6	.214	15	0	0	1.000

Signed as free agent by Kansas City Royals' organization, November 2, 1981.
†On disabled list, May 3 to July 1, 1985.
‡Traded to Cincinnati Reds' organization for Pitcher Jeff Montgomery, February 15, 1988.

JAMES CORY SNYDER

(Known by middle name.)

Born November 11, 1962, at Englewood, Calif.
Height, 6.03. Weight, 185.
Throws and bats righthanded.
Attended Brigham Young University, Provo, Utah.
Son of Jim Snyder, infielder in Milwaukee Braves' organization, 1961 and 1962.

Major League stolen bases: 1986 (2), 1987 (5), 1988 (5). Total—12.
Hit three home runs in a game, May 21, 1987.
Led Eastern League in total bases with 255, game-winning RBIs with 14 and sacrifice flies with 12 in 1985.
Led Eastern League third basemen in putouts with 132, total chances with 391 and double plays with 26 in 1985.
Named Eastern League Most Valuable Player, 1985.
Member of 1984 U.S. Olympic baseball team.
Named shortstop on THE SPORTING NEWS College Baseball All-America Team, 1984.

Year Club	League	Pos.	G.	AB.	R.	H.	2B.	3B.	HR.	RBI.	B.A.	PO.	A.	E.	F.A.
1985—Waterbury	East.	3B-SS	*139	512	77	144	25	1	*28	*94	.281	134	231	33	.917
1986—Maine	Int.	3B-SS	49	192	25	58	19	0	9	32	.302	46	87	8	.943
1986—Cleveland	Amer.	OF-SS-3B	103	416	58	113	21	1	24	69	.272	213	84	10	.967
1987—Cleveland	Amer.	OF-SS	157	577	74	136	24	2	33	82	.236	313	53	15	.961
1988—Cleveland	Amer.	OF	142	511	71	139	24	3	26	75	.272	314	*16	5	.985
Major League Totals—3 Years			402	1504	203	388	69	6	83	226	.258	840	153	30	.971

Selected by Cleveland Indians' organization in 1st round (fourth player selected) of free-agent draft, June 4, 1984.

LUIS SOJO

Born January 3, 1966, at Barquisimeto, Venezuela.
Height, 5.11. Weight, 175.
Throws and bats righthanded.

Year Club	League	Pos.	G.	AB.	R.	H.	2B.	3B.	HR.	RBI.	B.A.	PO.	A.	E.	F.A.
1986—				(Played in Dominican Republic League)											
1987—Myrtle Beach	S. Atl.	S-2-3-O	72	223	23	47	5	4	2	15	.211	104	123	14	.942
1988—Myrtle Beach	S. Atl.	SS	135	*536	83	*155	22	5	5	56	.289	191	407	28	.955

Signed as free agent by Toronto Blue Jays' organization, January 3, 1986.

JULIO CESAR SOLANO

Born January 8, 1960, at Agua Blanca, Dominican Republic.
Height, 6.01. Weight, 170.
Throws and bats righthanded.

Major League saves: 1988 (3).
Led South Atlantic League in hit batsmen with 11 and tied for lead in games started by pitchers with 27 and shutouts with 3 in 1982.

Year Club	League	G.	IP.	W.	L.	Pct.	H.	R.	ER.	SO.	BB.	ERA.
1980—Sarasota Astros-Orange	Gulf Coast	18	38	5	2	.714	31	16	11	29	23	2.61
1981—Sarasota Astros-Blue	Gulf Coast	17	74	4	4	.500	71	47	32	45	36	3.89
1982—Asheville	S. Atlantic	28	178	10	7	.588	165	89	70	163	116	3.54
1983—Houston	National	4	6	0	2	.000	5	5	4	3	4	6.00
1983—Tucson	P. Coast	29	161⅔	10	7	.588	183	104	89	123	71	4.95
1984—Tucson	P. Coast	17	80⅔	3	5	.375	74	41	23	55	37	2.57
1984—Houston	National	31	50⅔	1	3	.250	31	13	11	33	18	1.95
1985—Houston	National	20	33⅔	2	2	.500	34	13	13	17	13	3.48
1985—Tucson	P. Coast	23	31⅔	2	3	.400	25	16	14	23	21	3.98
1986—Tucson	P. Coast	27	71⅓	6	4	.600	64	24	15	54	27	1.89
1986—Houston	National	16	32	3	1	.750	39	28	27	21	22	7.59
1987—Tucson†	P. Coast	42	69	5	5	.500	71	40	34	45	45	4.43
1987—Houston‡	National	11	20	0	0	.000	25	17	17	12	9	7.65
1988—Seattle	American	17	22	0	0	.000	22	13	10	10	12	4.09
1988—Calgary	P. Coast	25	35	3	2	.600	32	19	19	23	17	4.89
National League Totals—5 Years		82	142⅓	6	8	.429	134	76	72	86	66	4.55
American League Totals—1 Year		17	22	0	0	.000	22	13	10	10	12	4.09
Major League Totals—6 Years		99	164⅓	6	8	.429	156	89	82	96	78	4.49

Signed as free agent by Houston Astros' organization, November 21, 1979.
†Played one game as an outfielder with no chances.
‡Traded to Seattle Mariners for Pitcher Doug Givler, September 30, 1987.

LARY ALAN SORENSEN

Born October 4, 1955, at Detroit, Mich.
Height, 6.02. Weight, 200.
Throws and bats righthanded.
Attended University of Michigan, Ann Arbor, Mich.

Major League saves: 1978 (1), 1980 (1), 1984 (1), 1987 (1), 1988 (2). Total—6.
Tied for American League lead in balks with 4 in 1984.
Tied for National League lead in balks with 5 in 1981.
Tied for Pacific Coast League lead in shutouts with 3 in 1977.
Tied for New York-Pennsylvania league lead in complete games with 7 and shutouts with 2 in 1976.

Year Club	League	G.	IP.	W.	L.	Pct.	H.	R.	ER.	SO.	BB.	ERA.
1976—Newark	NYP	13	75	6	2	.750	58	22	19	65	27	2.28
1976—Berkshire	Eastern	7	41	0	3	.000	44	19	15	25	16	3.29
1977—Spokane	P. Coast	12	72	5	5	.500	79	41	37	43	31	4.63
1977—Milwaukee	American	23	142	7	10	.412	147	72	69	57	36	4.37
1978—Milwaukee	American	37	281	18	12	.600	277	111	100	78	50	3.20
1979—Milwaukee	American	34	235	15	14	.517	250	113	104	63	42	3.98
1980—Milwaukee†	American	35	196	12	10	.545	242	91	80	54	45	3.67
1981—St. Louis‡	National	23	140	7	7	.500	149	59	51	52	26	3.28
1982—Cleveland	American	32	189⅓	10	15	.400	251	130	118	62	55	5.61
1983—Cleveland§	American	36	222⅔	12	11	.522	238	112	105	76	65	4.24
1984—Oakland x	American	46	183⅓	6	13	.316	240	117	100	63	44	4.91
1985—Chicago yz	National	45	82⅓	3	7	.300	86	44	39	34	24	4.26
1986—Portland a	P. Coast	17	102⅔	5	5	.500	112	59	43	37	32	3.77
1986—Indianapolis	Am. Assoc.	9	57	2	3	.400	51	25	20	20	17	3.16
1987—Montreal	National	23	47⅔	3	4	.429	56	32	25	21	12	4.72
1987—Indianapolis bc	Am. Assoc.	21	50⅓	2	2	.500	54	29	24	30	11	4.29
1988—Chattanooga d	Southern	7	18⅓	0	1	.000	18	7	6	12	4	2.95
1988—Phoenix	P. Coast	14	42⅓	4	2	.667	42	15	13	11	12	2.76
1988—San Francisco	National	12	16⅔	0	0	.000	24	13	9	9	3	4.86
American League Totals—7 Years		243	1449⅓	80	85	.485	1645	746	676	453	337	4.20
National League Totals—4 Years		103	286⅔	13	18	.419	315	148	124	116	65	3.89
Major League Totals—11 Years		346	1736	93	103	.474	1960	894	800	569	402	4.15

Selected by Milwaukee Brewers' organization in 8th round of free-agent draft, June 8, 1976.

†Traded with Outfielders Sixto Lezcano and David Green and Pitcher Dave LaPoint to St. Louis Cardinals for Pitchers Rollie Fingers and Pete Vuckovich and Catcher Ted Simmons, December 12, 1980.

‡Traded with Pitcher Silvio Martinez to Cleveland Indians for Outfielder Lonnie Smith, November 20, 1981.

§Granted free agency, November 7, 1983; signed by Oakland A's, January 23, 1984.

xReleased, October 16, 1984; signed by Chicago Cubs, December 13, 1984.

yReleased, December 20, 1985; re-signed by Cubs, January 26, 1986.

zReleased, March 26, 1986; signed by Portland (Philadelphia Phillies' organization), May 5, 1986.

aTraded with Infielder Tim Foley to Montreal Expos for Pitcher Dan Schatzeder and Infielder Skeeter Barnes, July 24, 1986.

bReleased, September 30, 1987; signed by Nashville (Cincinnati Reds' organization), January 18, 1988.

cReleased, March 28, 1988; re-signed by Reds' organization, April 17, 1988.

dReleased, May 5, 1988; signed by Phoenix (San Francisco Giants' organization), July 5, 1988.

eGranted free agency, November 4, 1988; re-signed by Giants' organization, December 7, 1988.

ALL-STAR GAME RECORD

Year League	IP.	W.	L.	Pct.	H.	R.	ER.	SO.	BB.	ERA.
1978—American	3	0	0	.000	1	0	0	0	0	0.00

PAUL ANTHONY SORRENTO

Born November 17, 1965, at Somerville, Mass.
Height, 6.02. Weight, 195.
Throws right and bats lefthanded.
Attended Florida State University, Tallahassee, Fla.

Year Club	League	Pos.	G.	AB.	R.	H.	2B.	3B.	HR.	RBI.	B.A.	PO.	A.	E.	F.A.
1986—Quad Cities	Midw.	OF	53	177	33	63	11	2	6	34	.356	83	7	1	.989
1986—Palm Springs	Calif.	OF	16	62	5	15	3	0	1	7	.242	16	1	1	.944
1987—Palm Springs	Calif.	OF	114	370	66	83	14	2	8	45	.224	123	10	4	.971
1988—Palm Springs †	Calif.	1B-OF	133	465	91	133	30	6	14	99	.286	719	55	18	.977

Selected by California Angels' organization in 4th round of free-agent draft, June 2, 1986.

†Traded with Pitchers Mike Cook and Rob Wassenaar to Minnesota Twins for Pitchers Bert Blyleven and Kevin Trudeau, November 3, 1988.

SAMUEL SOSA
(Sam)

Born November 10, 1968, at San Pedro de Macoris, D.R.
Height, 6.00. Weight, 165.
Throws and bats righthanded.

Led Gulf Coast League in total bases with 96 in 1986.

Tied for South Atlantic League lead in double plays by outfielders with 4 in 1987.

Year Club	League	Pos.	G.	AB.	R.	H.	2B.	3B.	HR.	RBI.	B.A.	PO.	A.	E.	F.A.
1986—Sarasota Rangers	Gulf C.	OF	61	229	38	63	*19	1	4	28	.275	92	9	●6	.944
1987—Gastonia	S. Atl.	OF	129	519	73	145	27	4	11	59	.279	183	12	17	.920
1988—Port Charlotte	Fla. St.	OF	131	507	70	116	13	*12	9	51	.229	227	11	7	.971

Signed as free agent by Texas Rangers' organization, July 30, 1985.

MARIO MELVIN SOTO

Born July 12, 1956, Bani, Dominican Republic.
Height, 6.00. Weight, 185.
Throws and bats righthanded.

Tied major league records for most strikeouts, inning (4), May 17, 1984 (third inning); most home runs allowed, inning (4), April 29, 1986 (fourth inning).

Major League saves: 1980 (4).

Led National League in complete games with 18 in 1983 and 13 in 1984.
Led National League in home runs allowed with 28 in 1983, 30 in 1985 and tied for lead with 13 in 1981.
Tied for National League lead in games started by pitchers with 25 in 1981.
Led Florida State League in balks with 6 in 1976.
Tied for American Association lead in balks with 6 in 1978.

Year Club	League	G.	IP.	W.	L.	Pct.	H.	R.	ER.	SO.	BB.	ERA.
1974—Billings†	Pioneer					(Did not play)						
1975—Eugene	Northwest	5	30	2	3	.400	33	21	14	11	18	4.20
1976—Tampa	Florida St.	26	*197	13	7	.650	142	54	41	*124	80	1.87
1977—Indianapolis	Am. Assoc.	18	123	11	5	.688	100	51	42	109	61	3.07
1977—Cincinnati	National	12	61	2	6	.250	60	38	36	44	26	5.31
1978—Indianapolis	Am. Assoc.	26	160	9	12	.429	129	102	89	121	95	5.01
1978—Cincinnati	National	5	18	1	0	1.000	13	5	5	13	13	2.50
1979—Indianapolis‡	Am. Assoc.	15	25	1	1	.500	20	11	11	38	18	3.96
1979—Cincinnati	National	25	37	3	2	.600	33	25	22	32	30	5.35
1980—Cincinnati	National	53	190	10	8	.556	126	72	65	182	84	3.08
1981—Cincinnati	National	25	175	12	9	.571	142	69	64	151	61	3.29
1982—Cincinnati	National	35	257⅔	14	13	.519	202	88	80	274	71	2.79
1983—Cincinnati	National	34	273⅔	17	13	.567	207	96	82	242	95	2.70
1984—Cincinnati	National	33	237⅓	18	7	.720	181	102	93	185	87	3.53
1985—Cincinnati	National	36	256⅔	12	15	.444	196	109	102	214	104	3.58
1986—Cincinnati§	National	19	105	5	10	.333	113	61	55	67	46	4.71
1987—Cincinnati x	National	6	31⅔	3	2	.600	34	18	18	11	12	5.12
1987—Sarasota Reds	Gulf Coast	2	11⅓	0	1	.000	11	8	3	5	2	2.38
1987—Nashville	Am. Assoc.	2	11⅓	0	2	.000	17	16	15	8	8	11.91
1988—Cincinnati yza	National	14	87	3	7	.300	88	49	45	34	28	4.66
1988—Bakersfield	California	1	3	0	1	.000	7	6	3	2	2	9.00
Major League Totals—12 Years		297	1730	100	92	.521	1395	732	667	1449	657	3.47

Signed as free agent by Cincinnati Reds' organization, December 3, 1973.
†On disabled list, July 1 to September 17, 1974.
‡On disabled list, April 13 to May 21, 1979.
§On disabled list, May 24 to June 8, June 20 to July 18 and August 16, 1986 through remainder of season.
xOn disabled list, April 5 to April 20 and May 22, 1987 through remainder of season; included rehabilitation disability assignment to Sarasota, August 5 to August 13, and to Nashville, August 14 to August 24, 1987.
yReleased, June 20, 1988; signed by Los Angeles Dodgers, June 27, 1988.
zOn Los Angeles disabled list, July 1 to September 26, 1988; included rehabilitation disability assignment to Bakersfield, August 23 to September 10, 1988.
aGranted free agency, November 4, 1988; re-signed by Dodgers' organization, December 7, 1988.

CHAMPIONSHIP SERIES RECORD

Year Club	League	G.	IP.	W.	L.	Pct.	H.	R.	ER.	SO.	BB.	ERA.
1979—Cincinnati	National	1	2	0	0	.000	0	0	0	1	0	0.00

ALL-STAR GAME RECORD

Year League	IP.	W.	L.	Pct.	H.	R.	ER.	SO.	BB.	ERA.
1982—National	2	0	0	.000	3	0	0	4	0	0.00
1983—National	2	0	1	.000	2	2	0	2	2	0.00
1984—National	2	0	0	.000	0	0	0	1	0	0.00
All-Star Game Totals—3 Years	6	0	1	.000	5	2	0	7	2	0.00

CHRIS EDWARD SPEIER

Name pronounced Spire.

Born June 28, 1950, at Alameda, Calif.
Height, 6.01. Weight, 180.
Throws and bats righthanded.
Attended University of Santa Barbara, Santa Barbara, Calif.

Major League stolen bases: 1971 (4), 1972 (9), 1973 (4), 1974 (3), 1975 (4), 1976 (2), 1977 (1), 1978 (1), 1981 (1), 1982 (1), 1983 (2), 1985 (1), 1986 (2), 1987 (4), 1988 (3). Total—42.
Hit for the cycle, July 20, 1978 and July 9, 1988.
Led Texas League shortstops in putouts with 223 and assists with 325 in 1970.
Named shortstop on THE SPORTING NEWS National League All-Star Team, 1972.

Year Club	League	Pos.	G.	AB.	R.	H.	2B.	3B.	HR.	RBI.	B.A.	PO.	A.	E.	F.A.
1970—Amarillo	Texas	SS-3B-OF	129	460	44	130	20	5	6	66	.283	224	327	38	.935
1971—San Francisco	Nat.	SS	157	601	74	141	17	6	8	46	.235	239	517	•33	.953
1972—San Francisco	Nat.	SS	150	562	74	151	25	2	15	71	.269	243	*517	20	.974
1973—San Francisco	Nat.	•SS-2B	153	542	58	135	17	4	11	71	.249	255	471	•33	.957
1974—San Francisco	Nat.	SS-2B	141	501	55	125	19	5	9	53	.250	215	453	21	.970
1975—San Francisco	Nat.	*SS-3B	141	487	60	132	30	5	10	69	.271	247	421	12	*.982
1976—San Francisco	Nat.	S-2-3-1	145	495	51	112	18	4	3	40	.226	241	464	19	.974
1977—S.F.†-Mont.	Nat.	SS	145	548	59	128	31	6	5	38	.234	239	455	23	.968
1978—Montreal	Nat.	SS	150	501	47	126	18	3	5	51	.251	245	467	18	.975
1979—Montreal‡	Nat.	SS	113	344	31	78	13	1	7	26	.227	194	355	17	.970
1980—Montreal	Nat.	SS-3B	128	388	35	103	14	4	1	32	.265	187	397	21	.965
1981—Montreal§	Nat.	SS	96	307	33	69	10	2	2	25	.225	175	280	17	.964
1982—Montreal	Nat.	SS	156	530	41	136	26	4	7	60	.257	291	405	13	.982
1983—Montreal x	Nat.	SS-3B-2B	88	261	31	67	12	2	2	22	.257	117	203	14	.958
1984—Mont. y-St.L. z	Nat.	SS-3B	63	158	10	27	7	1	3	9	.171	56	152	4	.981
1984—Minnesota ab	Amer.	SS	12	33	2	7	0	0	0	1	.212	14	28	1	.977

Year	Club	League	Pos.	G.	AB.	R.	H.	2B.	3B.	HR.	RBI.	B.A.	PO.	A.	E.	F.A.
1985—	Chicago	Nat.	SS-3B-2B	106	218	16	53	11	0	4	24	.243	87	177	11	.960
1986—	Chicago c	Nat.	3B-SS-2B	95	155	21	44	8	0	6	23	.284	62	106	3	.982
1987—	San Francisco	Nat.	2B-3B-SS	111	317	39	79	13	0	11	39	.249	118	229	4	.989
1988—	San Francisco	Nat.	2B-3B-SS	82	171	26	37	9	1	3	18	.216	70	142	3	.986
National League Totals—18 Years				2220	7086	761	1743	298	50	112	717	.246	3281	6211	286	.971
American League Totals—1 Year				12	33	2	7	0	0	0	1	.212	14	28	1	.977
Major League Totals—18 Years				2232	7119	763	1750	298	50	112	718	.246	3295	6239	287	.971

Selected by Washington Senators' organization in 11th round of free-agent draft, June 7, 1968.
Selected by San Francisco Giants' organization in secondary phase of free-agent draft, January 17, 1970.
†Traded to Montreal Expos for Shortstop Tim Foli, April 27, 1977.
‡On disabled list, July 8 to July 27, 1979.
§Granted free agency, November 13, 1981; re-signed by Expos, January 12, 1982.
xOn disabled list, May 29 to June 13, 1983.
yTraded with cash to St. Louis Cardinals for Infielder Mike Ramsey, July 1, 1984.
zTraded to Minnesota Twins for a player to be named later and cash, August 19, 1984; St. Louis Cardinals' organization acquired Pitcher Jay Pettibone to complete deal, October 2, 1984.
aOn disabled list, August 22 to September 7, 1984.
bGranted free agency, November 8, 1984; signed by Chicago Cubs, April 8, 1985.
cGranted free agency, November 12, 1986; signed by San Francisco Giants, December 12, 1986.

DIVISION SERIES RECORD

Year	Club	League	Pos.	G.	AB.	R.	H.	2B.	3B.	HR.	RBI.	B.A.	PO.	A.	E.	F.A.
1981—	Montreal	Nat.	SS	5	15	4	6	2	0	0	3	.400	16	15	0	1.000

CHAMPIONSHIP SERIES RECORD

Year	Club	League	Pos.	G.	AB.	R.	H.	2B.	3B.	HR.	RBI.	B.A.	PO.	A.	E.	F.A.
1971—	San Francisco	Nat.	SS	4	14	4	5	1	0	1	1	.357	3	14	1	.944
1981—	Montreal	Nat.	SS	5	16	0	3	0	0	0	0	.188	15	16	2	.939
1987—	San Francisco	Nat.	PH-2B	3	5	0	0	0	0	0	0	.000	1	3	0	1.000
Championship Series Totals—3 Years				12	35	4	8	1	0	1	1	.229	19	33	3	.945

ALL-STAR GAME RECORD

Year	League	Pos.	AB.	R.	H.	2B.	3B.	HR.	RBI.	B.A.	PO.	A.	E.	F.A.
1972—	National	SS	2	0	0	0	0	0	0	.000	1	5	0	1.000
1973—	National	SS	2	0	0	0	0	0	0	.000	1	1	0	1.000
All-Star Game Totals—2 Years			4	0	0	0	0	0	0	.000	2	6	0	1.000

Member of National League All-Star Team in 1974 game; did not play.

WILLIAM HARRY SPILMAN

(Known by middle name.)

Born July 18, 1954, at Albany, Ga.
Height, 6.01. Weight, 190.
Throws right and bats lefthanded.
Son of Harry Spilman, catcher in Los Angeles Dodgers' organization, 1952.

Major League stolen bases: 1987 (1).
Led Eastern League in total bases with 277 and intentional bases on balls received with 19 in 1977.
Named Eastern League Most Valuable Player, 1977.

Year	Club	League	Pos.	G.	AB.	R.	H.	2B.	3B.	HR.	RBI.	B.A.	PO.	A.	E.	F.A.
1974—	Billings	Pion.	1B-3B	54	178	29	55	12	2	2	30	.309	92	8	3	.971
1975—	Tampa	Fla. St.	1B	115	348	33	90	13	1	1	38	.259	946	56	•17	.983
1976—	Tampa	Fla. St.	1B	118	361	50	90	12	5	6	35	.249	986	70	16	.985
1977—	Three Rivers	East.	1B	133	493	*94	*184	*39	3	16	78	*.373	1095	78	7	.994
1978—	Indianapolis	A. A.	3B-1B	133	488	95	144	26	4	13	79	.295	262	184	23	.951
1978—	Cincinnati	Nat.	PH	4	4	1	1	0	0	0	0	.250	0	0	0	.000
1979—	Indianapolis	A. A.	3B-1B	71	267	42	77	13	3	3	27	.288	154	92	8	.969
1979—	Cincinnati	Nat.	1B-3B-OF	43	56	7	12	3	0	0	5	.214	64	11	0	1.000
1980—	Cincinnati	Nat.	1-3-O-C	65	101	14	27	4	0	4	19	.267	132	15	2	.987
1981—	Cinc.†-Hou.	Nat.	1B	51	58	9	14	1	0	0	4	.241	62	5	1	.985
1982—	Tucson	P. C.	1B-3B	53	190	34	63	16	3	6	33	.332	307	13	3	.991
1982—	Houston	Nat.	1B	38	61	7	17	2	0	3	11	.279	86	5	1	.989
1983—	Houston	Nat.	1B-C	42	78	7	13	3	0	1	9	.167	138	8	0	1.000
1984—	Houston‡	Nat.	1B-C	32	72	14	19	2	0	2	15	.264	143	9	3	.981
1985—	Houston§	Nat.	1B-C	44	66	3	9	1	0	1	4	.136	134	4	0	1.000
1986—	Detroit x	Amer.	3B-1B-C	24	49	6	12	2	0	3	8	.245	7	1	0	1.000
1986—	San Francisco y	Nat.	1-3-2-O-C	58	94	12	27	7	0	2	22	.287	140	17	2	.987
1987—	San Francisco	Nat.	3B-1B-C	83	90	5	24	5	0	1	14	.267	40	7	2	.959
1988—	S. F. z-Hou	Nat.	1B-C-OF	47	45	4	7	1	1	1	3	.156	24	3	1	.964
1988—	Phoe.-Tucs. a	P. C.	1B	20	64	12	21	4	1	4	17	.328	121	9	1	.992
National League Totals—11 Years				507	725	83	170	29	1	15	106	.234	963	84	12	.989
American League Totals—1 Year				24	49	6	12	2	0	3	8	.245	7	1	0	1.000
Major League Totals—11 Years				531	774	89	182	31	1	18	114	.235	970	85	12	.989

Signed as free agent by Cincinnati Reds' organization, June 25, 1974.
†Traded to Houston Astros for Second Baseman Rafael Landestoy, June 8, 1981.
‡On disabled list, July 16, 1984 through remainder of season.
§Granted free agency, November 12, 1985; signed by Nashville (Detroit Tigers' organization), February 18, 1986.

xReleased, June 12, 1986; signed by San Francisco Giants, June 13, 1986.
yGranted free agency, November 12, 1986; re-signed by Giants, December 12, 1986.
zReleased, August 11, 1988; signed by Tucson (Houston Astros' organization), August 17, 1988.
aGranted free agency, November 4, 1988.

DIVISION SERIES RECORD

Year	Club	League	Pos.	G.	AB.	R.	H.	2B.	3B.	HR.	RBI.	B.A.	PO.	A.	E.	F.A.
1981	Houston	Nat.	PH	1	1	0	0	0	0	0	0	.000	0	0	0	.000

CHAMPIONSHIP SERIES RECORD

Tied Championship Series record for most home runs by pinch-hitter, game (1), October 9, 1987.

Year	Club	League	Pos.	G.	AB.	R.	H.	2B.	3B.	HR.	RBI.	B.A.	PO.	A.	E.	F.A.
1979	Cincinnati	Nat.	PH	2	2	0	0	0	0	0	0	.000	0	0	0	.000
1987	San Francisco	Nat.	PH	3	2	1	1	0	0	1	1	.500	0	0	0	.000
Championship Series Totals—2 Years				5	4	1	1	0	0	1	1	.250	0	0	0	.000

PETER LOUIS STANICEK

Name pronounced Stan-i-sek.

(Pete)

Born April 18, 1963, at Harvey, Ill.
Height, 5.11. Weight, 185.
Throws right and bats left and righthanded.
Received degree from Stanford University, Stanford, Calif., in 1985.
Brother of Steve Stanicek, designated hitter with Milwaukee Brewers, 1987.

Major League stolen bases: 1987 (8), 1988 (12). Total—20.
Led Carolina League in being hit by pitch with 9 and stolen bases with 77 in 1986.
Led Carolina League second basemen in double plays with 50 in 1985.

Year	Club	League	Pos.	G.	AB.	R.	H.	2B.	3B.	HR.	RBI.	B.A.	PO.	A.	E.	F.A.
1985	Newark†	NYP	2B	69	255	39	64	12	1	2	25	.251	*162	198	9	.976
1986	Hagerstown	Carol.	2B	127	457	115	145	24	2	6	67	.317	240	357	19	.969
1987	Charlotte	South.	2B	88	337	78	106	18	4	8	50	.315	191	241	10	.977
1987	Rochester	Int.	2B	38	145	29	43	13	0	2	16	.297	71	90	7	.958
1987	Baltimore	Amer.	2B-3B	30	113	9	31	3	0	0	9	.274	37	46	4	.954
1988	Rochester	Int.	2B-OF	19	69	13	12	2	1	2	8	.174	36	40	5	.938
1988	Baltimore‡	Amer.	OF-2B	83	261	29	60	7	1	4	17	.230	149	24	4	.977
Major League Totals—2 Years				113	374	38	91	10	1	4	26	.243	186	70	8	.970

Selected by Baltimore Orioles' organization in 13th round of free-agent draft, June 4, 1984.
Selected by Baltimore Orioles' organization in 9th round of free-agent draft, June 3, 1985.
†Batted righthanded only.
‡On disabled list, May 29 to June 6, 1988.

ROBERT MICHAEL STANLEY

(Mike)

Born June 25, 1963, at Fort Lauderdale, Fla.
Height, 6.00. Weight, 185.
Throws and bats righthanded.
Attended University of Florida, Gainesville, Fla.

Major League stolen bases: 1986 (1), 1987 (3). Total—4.

Year	Club	League	Pos.	G.	AB.	R.	H.	2B.	3B.	HR.	RBI.	B.A.	PO.	A.	E.	F.A.
1985	Salem	Carol.	1B-C	4	9	2	5	0	0	0	3	.556	19	1	1	.952
1985	Burlington	Midw.	C-1B-OF	13	42	8	13	2	0	1	6	.310	45	2	0	1.000
1985	Tulsa	Texas	C-1-O-2	46	165	24	51	10	0	3	17	.309	289	18	6	.981
1986	Tulsa	Texas	C-1B-3B	67	235	41	69	16	2	6	35	.294	379	45	2	.995
1986	Texas	Amer.	3B-C-OF	15	30	4	10	3	0	1	1	.333	14	8	1	.957
1986	Oklahoma City	A. A.	C-3B-1B	56	202	37	74	13	3	5	49	.366	206	55	9	.967
1987	Oklahoma City	A. A.	C-1B	46	182	43	61	8	3	13	54	.335	277	32	2	.994
1987	Texas	Amer.	C-1B-OF	78	216	34	59	8	1	6	37	.273	389	26	7	.983
1988	Texas†	Amer.	C-1B-3B	94	249	21	57	8	0	3	27	.229	342	17	4	.989
Major League Totals—3 Years				187	495	59	126	19	1	10	65	.255	745	51	12	.985

Selected by Texas Rangers' organization in 16th round of free-agent draft, June 3, 1985.
†On disabled list, July 24 to August 14, 1988.

ROBERT WILLIAM STANLEY

(Bob)

Born November 10, 1954, at Portland, Me.
Height, 6.04. Weight, 225.
Throws and bats righthanded.

Established American League record for most innings pitched by relief pitcher, season (168⅓), 1982.
Major League saves: 1977 (3), 1978 (10), 1979 (1), 1980 (14), 1982 (14), 1983 (33), 1984 (22), 1985 (10), 1986 (16), 1988 (5). Total—128.
Led Eastern League in hit batsmen with 11 and tied for lead in games started by pitchers with 27 in 1976.
Led New York-Pennsylvania League pitchers in games started with 15 in 1974.
Tied for Florida State League lead in games started by pitchers with 26 in 1975.

Year Club	League	G.	IP.	W.	L.	Pct.	H.	R.	ER.	SO.	BB.	ERA.
1974—Elmira	NYP	15	86	6	6	.500	94	57	44	45	40	4.60
1975—Winter Haven	Florida St.	27	169	5	★17	.227	136	76	55	73	74	2.93
1976—Bristol†	Eastern	27	186	15	9	.625	176	76	55	78	83	2.66
1977—Boston	American	41	151	8	7	.533	176	74	67	44	43	3.99
1978—Boston	American	52	142	15	2	.882	142	50	41	38	34	2.60
1979—Boston	American	40	217	16	12	.571	250	110	96	56	44	3.98
1980—Boston	American	52	175	10	8	.556	186	75	66	71	52	3.39
1981—Boston	American	35	99	10	8	.556	110	46	42	28	38	3.82
1982—Boston	American	48	168⅓	12	7	.632	161	60	58	83	50	3.10
1983—Boston	American	64	145⅓	8	10	.444	145	56	46	65	38	2.85
1984—Boston	American	57	106⅔	9	10	.474	113	57	42	52	23	3.54
1985—Boston	American	48	87⅔	6	6	.500	76	30	28	46	30	2.87
1986—Boston	American	66	81⅓	6	6	.500	109	48	40	54	22	4.37
1987—Boston‡	American	34	152⅔	4	15	.211	198	96	85	67	42	5.01
1988—Boston§	American	57	101⅔	6	4	.600	90	41	36	57	29	3.19
1988—Winter Haven	Florida St.	2	10	0	1	.000	13	9	8	3	3	7.20
1988—Pawtucket	Int'national	4	11	1	0	1.000	7	1	1	6	5	0.82
Major League Totals—12 Years		594	1628⅔	110	95	.537	1756	743	647	661	445	3.58

Selected by Los Angeles Dodgers' organization in 9th round of free-agent draft, June 5, 1973.

Selected by Boston Red Sox' organization in secondary phase of free-agent draft, January 9, 1974.

†On disabled list, June 19 to June 24, 1976.

‡On disabled list, June 28 to July 16, 1987.

§On Boston disabled list, March 26 to May 12, 1988; included rehabilitation disability assignment to Winter Haven, April 20 to May 10, 1988.

CHAMPIONSHIP SERIES RECORD

Year Club	League	G.	IP.	W.	L.	Pct.	H.	R.	ER.	SO.	BB.	ERA.
1986—Boston	American	3	5⅔	0	0	.000	7	4	3	1	3	4.76
1988—Boston	American	2	1	0	0	.000	2	1	1	0	1	9.00
Championship Series Totals—2 Years		5	6⅔	0	0	.000	9	5	4	1	4	5.40

WORLD SERIES RECORD

Year Club	League	G.	IP.	W.	L.	Pct.	H.	R.	ER.	SO.	BB.	ERA.
1986—Boston	American	5	6⅓	0	0	.000	5	0	0	4	1	0.00

ALL-STAR GAME RECORD

Year League	IP.	W.	L.	Pct.	H.	R.	ER.	SO.	BB.	ERA.
1979—American	2	0	0	.000	1	1	1	0	0	4.50
1983—American	2	0	0	.000	2	0	0	0	0	0.00
All-Star Game Totals—2 Years	4	0	0	.000	3	1	1	0	0	2.25

DAVID EARL STAPLETON
(Dave)

Born October 16, 1961, at Miami, Ariz.
Height, 6.00. Weight, 180.
Throws and bats lefthanded.
Attended Grand Canyon College, Phoenix, Ariz.

Year Club	League	G.	IP.	W.	L.	Pct.	H.	R.	ER.	SO.	BB.	ERA.
1984—Beloit	Midwest	48	92⅔	9	6	.600	77	29	24	85	35	2.33
1985—Stockton	California	52	71	2	9	.182	68	32	20	58	26	2.54
1986—El Paso	Texas	38	68⅔	6	2	.750	75	34	24	37	22	3.15
1987—El Paso	Texas	4	10⅓	0	0	.000	9	2	2	10	2	1.74
1987—Denver	Am. Assoc.	44	129	11	3	.786	141	64	58	74	28	4.05
1987—Milwaukee	American	4	14⅔	2	0	1.000	13	3	3	14	3	1.84
1988—Milwaukee†‡	American	6	13⅔	0	0	.000	20	9	9	6	9	5.93
Major League Totals—2 Years		10	28⅓	2	0	1.000	33	12	12	20	12	3.81

Signed as free agent by Milwaukee Brewers' organization, September 22, 1983.

†On disabled list, May 12 to September 30, 1988.

‡Drafted by Houston Astros, December 5, 1988.

MATTHEW SCOTT STARK
(Matt)

Born January 21, 1965, at Whittier, Calif.
Height, 6.04. Weight, 225.
Throws and bats righthanded.

Led Southern League catchers in double plays with 12 in 1986.

Year Club	League	Pos.	G.	AB.	R.	H.	2B.	3B.	HR.	RBI.	B.A.	PO.	A.	E.	F.A.
1983—Medicine Hat	Pion.	C	60	206	29	58	6	0	8	49	.282	215	19	10	.959
1984—Florence†	S. Atl.	C	69	205	24	46	7	1	3	27	.224	383	36	12	.972
1985—Florence	S. Atl.	C	110	381	66	113	15	0	13	70	.297	392	36	17	.962
1985—Knoxville	South.	C	18	53	3	13	1	0	1	3	.245	85	8	4	.959
1986—Knoxville	South.	C	120	424	63	125	21	0	17	72	.295	665	73	16	.979
1987—Toronto‡	Amer.	C	5	12	0	1	0	0	0	0	.083	25	1	0	1.000
1987—Knoxville	South.	C	25	87	10	26	3	2	2	18	.299	18	3	0	1.000
1988—Knoxville§x	South.	C	97	334	37	89	17	1	11	54	.266	78	9	1	.989
Major League Totals—2 Years			5	12	0	1	0	0	0	0	.083	25	1	0	1.000

Selected by Toronto Blue Jays' organization in 1st round (ninth player selected) of free-agent draft, June 6, 1983.
†On disabled list, July 7, 1984 through remainder of season.
‡On disabled list, April 16 to May 6, 1987.
§On Toronto disabled list, March 22 to June 17, 1988; included rehabilitation disability assignment to Knoxville, May 28 to June 16, 1988.
xDrafted by Atlanta Braves, December 5, 1988.

RANDY ANTHONY ST. CLAIRE

Born August 23, 1960, at Glens Falls, N.Y.
Height, 6.02. Weight, 190.
Throws and bats righthanded.
Son of Ebba St. Claire, catcher with Boston Braves,
Milwaukee Braves and New York Giants, 1951 through 1954;
and brother of Steve St. Claire, outfielder in Montreal Expos' organization.

Major League saves: 1986 (1), 1987 (7). Total—8.
Led Southern League in intentional bases on balls issued with 14 in 1984.

Year Club	League	G.	IP.	W.	L.	Pct.	H.	R.	ER.	SO.	BB.	ERA.
1979—Calgary	Pioneer	6	33	1	2	.333	30	22	16	17	15	4.36
1980—Calgary	Pioneer	21	57	5	7	.417	65	36	27	51	23	4.26
1981—Jamestown	NYP	13	51	4	1	.800	53	22	11	36	17	1.94
1982—San Jose	California	9	61	2	5	.286	58	32	28	44	20	4.13
1982—West Palm Beach	Florida St.	19	65	3	8	.273	74	41	38	38	17	5.26
1983—West Palm Beach	Florida St.	42	98	5	7	.417	72	33	23	77	31	2.11
1984—Jacksonville	Southern	48	75	10	7	.588	64	35	24	56	29	2.88
1984—Indianapolis	Am. Assoc.	13	17⅔	1	1	.500	15	2	2	17	6	1.02
1984—Montreal	National	4	8	0	0	.000	11	4	4	4	2	4.50
1985—Indianapolis†	Am. Assoc.	11	19⅔	0	1	.000	21	5	4	11	3	1.83
1985—Montreal	National	42	68⅔	5	3	.625	69	32	30	25	26	3.93
1986—Indianapolis	Am. Assoc.	*57	99⅓	5	7	.417	105	49	44	72	29	3.99
1986—Montreal	National	11	19	2	0	1.000	13	5	5	21	6	2.37
1987—Montreal	National	44	67	3	3	.500	64	31	30	43	20	4.03
1987—Indianapolis	Am. Assoc.	18	20⅔	0	1	.000	12	5	5	15	12	3.82
1988—Montreal‡-Cincinnati	National	16	21	1	0	1.000	24	13	9	14	10	3.86
1988—Indianapolis-Nashville	Am. Assoc.	36	40⅓	0	3	.000	35	15	12	27	9	2.68
Major League Totals—5 Years		117	183⅔	11	6	.647	181	85	78	107	64	3.82

Signed as free agent by Montreal Expos' organization, September 9, 1978.
†On disabled list, May 7 to May 17, 1985.
‡Traded with Catcher Jeff Reed and Outfielder Herm Winningham to Cincinnati Reds for Outfielder Tracy Jones and Pitcher Pat Pacillo, July 13, 1988.

JAMES EARL STEELS
(Jim)

Born May 30, 1961, at Jackson, Miss.
Height, 5.10. Weight, 185.
Throws and bats lefthanded.
Attended Allan Hancock College, Santa Maria, Calif.

Major League stolen bases: 1987 (3), 1988 (2). Total—5.
Named Texas League Most Valuable Player, 1984.

Year Club	League	Pos.	G.	AB.	R.	H.	2B.	3B.	HR.	RBI.	B.A.	PO.	A.	E.	F.A.
1980—Reno†	Calif.	OF	73	285	42	86	8	4	3	27	.302	78	9	5	.946
1981—Amarillo	Texas	OF-1B	127	485	58	138	28	5	3	59	.285	206	14	8	.965
1982—Amarillo	Texas	1B	86	371	61	118	16	8	6	57	.318	789	61	*20	.977
1982—Hawaii	P. C.	OF-1B	52	196	33	49	10	6	4	26	.250	103	2	4	.963
1983—Las Vegas	P. C.	OF-1B	28	95	17	23	5	1	1	14	.242	47	4	0	1.000
1983—Beaumont	Texas	OF-1B	83	313	57	84	17	4	10	61	.268	188	10	7	.966
1984—Beaumont	Texas	OF-P-1B	127	474	90	161	26	10	12	81	*.340	195	15	5	.977
1985—Las Vegas‡	P. C.	OF	111	394	39	103	19	4	5	46	.261	163	12	3	.983
1986—Las Vegas	P. C.	OF	126	482	87	148	28	9	8	64	.307	228	●16	12	.953
1987—San Diego	Nat.	OF	62	68	9	13	1	1	0	6	.191	23	1	1	.960
1987—Las Vegas§	P. C.	OF-1B	15	53	12	17	3	1	0	5	.321	46	4	1	.980
1988—Oklahoma City	A. A.	OF-1B	37	144	21	45	7	2	0	11	.313	92	7	6	.943
1988—Texas x	Amer.	OF-1B	36	53	4	10	1	0	0	5	.189	41	2	1	.977
National League Totals—1 Year			62	68	9	13	1	1	0	6	.191	23	1	1	.960
American League Totals—1 Year			36	53	4	10	1	0	0	5	.189	41	2	1	.977
Major League Totals—2 Years			98	121	13	23	2	1	0	11	.190	64	3	2	.971

Selected by San Diego Padres' organization in 8th round of free-agent draft, June 5, 1979.
†On disabled list, April 29 to June 16, 1980.
‡On disabled list, July 6 to July 24, 1985.
§Granted free agency, October 15, 1987; signed by Texas Rangers, October 23, 1987.
xGranted free agency, October 15, 1988.

PITCHING RECORD

Year Club	League	G.	IP.	W.	L.	Pct.	H.	R.	ER.	SO.	BB.	ERA.
1984—Beaumont	Texas	3	4⅔	0	0	.000	3	4	4	2	10	7.71

TERRY LEE STEINBACH

Born March 2, 1962, at New Ulm, Minn.
Height, 6.01. Weight, 195.
Throws and bats righthanded.
Attended University of Minnesota, Minneapolis, Minn.
Brother of Tom Steinbach, outfielder in Seattle Mariners' organization, 1983.

Tied major league record by hitting home run in first major league at-bat, September 12, 1986.
Major League stolen bases: 1987 (1), 1988 (3). Total—4.
Led Southern League in passed balls with 22 in 1986.
Led Midwest League third basemen in double plays with 31 in 1984.
Led Northwest League third basemen in assists with 122 and tied for lead in errors with 17 in 1983.
Named Southern League Most Valuable Player, 1986.

Year Club	League	Pos.	G.	AB.	R.	H.	2B.	3B.	HR.	RBI.	B.A.	PO.	A.	E.	F.A.
1983—Medford	N'west	3B-OF-1B	62	219	42	69	16	0	6	38	.315	105	124	21	.916
1984—Madison	Midw.	3B-1B-P	135	474	57	140	24	6	11	79	.295	107	257	27	.931
1985—Huntsville	South.	C-3-1-O-P	128	456	64	124	31	3	9	72	.272	187	43	6	.975
1986—Huntsville	South.	C-1B-3B	138	505	113	164	33	2	24	*132	.325	620	73	14	.980
1986—Oakland	Amer.	C	6	15	3	5	0	0	2	4	.333	21	4	1	.962
1987—Oakland	Amer.	C-3B-1B	122	391	66	111	16	3	16	56	.284	642	44	10	.986
1988—Oakland†	Amer.	C-3-1-O	104	351	42	93	19	1	9	51	.265	536	58	9	.985
Major League Totals—3 Years			232	757	111	209	35	4	27	111	.276	1199	106	20	.985

Selected by Cleveland Indians' organization in 16th round of free-agent draft, June 3, 1980.
Selected by Oakland A's organization in 9th round of free-agent draft, June 6, 1983.
†On disabled list, May 6 to June 1, 1988.

CHAMPIONSHIP SERIES RECORD

Year Club	League	Pos.	G.	AB.	R.	H.	2B.	3B.	HR.	RBI.	B.A.	PO.	A.	E.	F.A.
1988—Oakland	Amer.	C	2	4	0	1	0	0	0	0	.250	12	0	0	1.000

WORLD SERIES RECORD

Year Club	League	Pos.	G.	AB.	R.	H.	2B.	3B.	HR.	RBI.	B.A.	PO.	A.	E.	F.A.
1988—Oakland	Amer.	C-DH	3	11	0	4	1	0	0	0	.364	11	3	0	1.000

ALL-STAR GAME RECORD

Year League	Pos.	AB.	R.	H.	2B.	3B.	HR.	RBI.	B.A.	PO.	A.	E.	F.A.
1988—American	C	1	1	1	0	0	1	2	1.000	3	1	1	.800

PITCHING RECORD

Year Club	League	G.	IP.	W.	L.	Pct.	H.	R.	ER.	SO.	BB.	ERA.
1984—Madison	Midwest	2	3	0	0	.000	2	4	3	0	4	9.00
1985—Huntsville	Southern	1	1	0	0	.000	0	0	0	0	0	0.00

PHILLIP RAYMOND STEPHENSON
(Phil)

Born September 19, 1960, at Guthrie, Okla.
Height, 6.01. Weight, 195.
Throws and bats lefthanded.
Received bachelor of arts degree in business management from Wichita State University, Wichita, Kan.
Brother of Gene Stephenson, baseball coach at Wichita State University.

Led American Association in slugging percentage with .566 and tied for lead in intentional bases on balls received with 9 in 1988.
Led Eastern League in bases on balls received with 114 in 1983 and 129 in 1986.
Tied for Eastern League lead in sacrifice flies with 10 in 1983.
Led American Association first basemen in double plays with 103 in 1988.
Led Eastern League first basemen in putouts with 1,164 and total chances with 1,332 in 1986.
Named first baseman on THE SPORTING NEWS College Baseball All-America Team, 1981.

Year Club	League	Pos.	G.	AB.	R.	H.	2B.	3B.	HR.	RBI.	B.A.	PO.	A.	E.	F.A.
1982—Modesto	Calif.	1B	64	212	39	60	14	2	5	26	.283	436	39	4	.992
1983—Albany	East.	•1B-OF	133	436	90	122	•30	3	19	77	.280	771	85	•14	.984
1984—Tacoma	P. C.	OF-1B	124	398	70	120	25	1	10	69	.302	418	40	9	.981
1985—Tacoma†	P. C.	OF-1B	56	171	30	36	11	0	5	24	.211	117	6	5	.961
1985—Midland‡	Texas	1B-OF	50	176	39	52	14	0	7	41	.295	340	27	3	.992
1986—Pittsfield	East.	*1B-OF-P	•140	423	72	115	29	2	12	68	.272	1165	*163	5	*.996
1987—Iowa	A. A.	1B-OF	105	298	53	91	24	2	10	56	.305	735	71	10	.988
1988—Iowa	A. A.	1B	118	426	69	125	28	11	22	81	.293	925	*88	10	.990

Selected by Montreal Expos' organization in 5th round of free-agent draft, June 8, 1981.
Selected by Oakland A's organization in 3rd round of free-agent draft, June 7, 1982.
†Loaned to Midland (California Angels' organization), July 7, 1985; returned, September 10, 1985.
‡Traded with Third Baseman Bob Bathe to Oakland A's for Second Baseman Gary Jones and Pitcher John Cox, January 17, 1986.

PITCHING RECORD

Year Club	League	G.	IP.	W.	L.	Pct.	H.	R.	ER.	SO.	BB.	ERA.
1986—Pittsfield	Eastern	3	4	0	0	.000	1	0	0	1	2	0.00

DeWAIN LEE STEVENS

(Known by middle name.)

Born July 10, 1967, at Kansas City, Mo.
Height, 6.04. Weight, 205.
Throws and bats lefthanded.

Tied for Northwest League lead in game-winning RBIs with 8 in 1986.
Led Texas League outfielders in errors with 12 in 1988.
Led California League first basemen in putouts with 1,028, assists with 66 and fielding percentage with .986 in 1987.

Year	Club	League	Pos.	G.	AB.	R.	H.	2B.	3B.	HR.	RBI.	B.A.	PO.	A.	E.	F.A.
1986—	Salem	N'west	OF-1B	72	267	45	75	18	2	6	47	.281	231	18	5	.980
1987—	Palm Springs	Calif.	1B-OF	140	532	82	130	29	2	19	97	.244	1031	68	18	.984
1988—	Midland	Texas	OF-1B	116	414	79	123	26	2	23	76	.297	217	16	14	.943

Selected by California Angels' organization in 1st round (22nd player selected) of free-agent draft, June 2, 1986.

DAVID KEITH STEWART
(Dave)

Born February 19, 1957, at Oakland, Calif.
Height, 6.02. Weight, 200.
Throws and bats righthanded.
Attended Merritt College, Oakland, Calif., and California State University, Hayward, Calif.

Major League saves: 1981 (6), 1982 (1), 1983 (8), 1985 (4). Total—19.
Led American League pitchers in games started with 37, balks with 16 and tied for lead in complete games with 14 in 1988.
Led Pacific Coast League pitchers in games started with 29 in 1980.
Tied for Texas League lead in games started by pitchers with 28 in 1978.
Tied for Midwest League lead in complete games with 15, shutouts with 3 and balks with 3 in 1977.
Named righthanded pitcher on THE SPORTING NEWS American League All-Star Team, 1988.

Year	Club	League	G.	IP.	W.	L.	Pct.	H.	R.	ER.	SO.	BB.	ERA.
1975—	Bellingham	Northwest	22	49	0	5	.000	59	46	30	37	49	5.51
1976—	Danville	Midwest	4	10	0	2	.000	17	20	18	10	16	16.20
1976—	Bellingham	Northwest	24	50	1	1	.500	47	35	28	53	58	5.04
1977—	Clinton	Midwest	24	176	*17	4	*.810	152	52	42	144	72	2.15
1977—	Albuquerque	P. Coast	1	6	1	0	1.000	4	3	3	3	6	4.50
1978—	San Antonio	Texas	28	*193	14	12	.538	181	99	79	130	97	3.68
1978—	Los Angeles	National	1	2	0	0	.000	1	0	0	1	0	0.00
1979—	Albuquerque	P. Coast	28	170	11	12	.478	198	112	99	105	81	5.24
1980—	Albuquerque	P. Coast	31	*202	•15	10	.600	189	94	83	125	89	3.70
1981—	Los Angeles	National	32	43	4	3	.571	40	13	12	29	14	2.51
1982—	Los Angeles	National	45	146⅓	9	8	.529	137	72	62	80	49	3.81
1983—	Los Angeles†	National	46	76	5	2	.714	67	28	25	54	33	2.96
1983—	Texas	American	8	59	5	2	.714	50	15	14	24	17	2.14
1984—	Texas	American	32	192⅓	7	14	.333	193	106	101	119	87	4.73
1985—	Texas‡	American	42	81⅓	0	6	.000	86	53	49	64	37	5.42
1985—	Philadelphia	National	4	4⅓	0	0	.000	5	4	3	2	4	6.23
1986—	Philadelphia§	National	8	12⅓	0	0	.000	15	9	9	9	4	6.57
1986—	Tacoma	P. Coast	1	3	0	0	.000	4	1	0	3	1	0.00
1986—	Oakland	American	29	149⅓	9	5	.643	137	67	62	102	65	3.74
1987—	Oakland	American	37	261⅓	•20	13	.606	224	121	107	205	105	3.68
1988—	Oakland	American	37	*275⅔	21	12	.636	240	111	99	192	110	3.23
	National League Totals—6 Years		136	284	18	13	.581	265	126	111	175	104	3.52
	American League Totals—6 Years		185	1019	62	52	.544	930	473	432	706	421	3.82
	Major League Totals—9 Years		321	1303	80	65	.552	1195	599	543	881	525	3.75

Selected by Los Angeles Dodgers' organization in 16th round of free-agent draft, June 4, 1975.
†Traded with a player to be named later to Texas Rangers for Pitcher Rick Honeycutt, August 19, 1983; Texas acquired Pitcher Ricky Wright to complete deal, September 16, 1983.
‡Traded to Philadelphia Phillies for Pitcher Rick Surhoff, September 13, 1985.
§Released, May 9, 1986; signed by Tacoma (Oakland A's organization), May 23, 1986.

DIVISION SERIES RECORD

Year	Club	League	G.	IP.	W.	L.	Pct.	H.	R.	ER.	SO.	BB.	ERA.
1981—	Los Angeles	National	2	⅔	0	2	.000	4	3	3	1	0	40.50

CHAMPIONSHIP SERIES RECORD

Year	Club	League	G.	IP.	W.	L.	Pct.	H.	R.	ER.	SO.	BB.	ERA.
1988—	Oakland	American	2	13⅓	1	0	1.000	9	2	2	11	6	1.35

WORLD SERIES RECORD

Year	Club	League	G.	IP.	W.	L.	Pct.	H.	R.	ER.	SO.	BB.	ERA.
1981—	Los Angeles	National	2	1⅔	0	0	.000	1	0	0	1	2	0.00
1988—	Oakland	American	2	14⅓	0	1	.000	12	7	5	5	5	3.14
	World Series Totals—2 Years		4	16	0	1	.000	13	7	5	6	7	2.81

—DID YOU KNOW—

That John Shelby's 24-game batting streak was the longest in the majors in 1988?

DAVID ANDREW STIEB

Name pronounced Steeb.

(Dave)

Born July 22, 1957, at Santa Ana, Calif.
Height, 6.00. Weight, 195.
Throws and bats righthanded.
Attended Santa Ana College, Santa Ana, Calif., and
Southern Illinois University, Carbondale, Ill.
Brother of Steve Stieb, catcher in Atlanta Braves' organization, 1979 through 1981.

Tied major league record for most consecutive one-hit games (2), September 24 and 30, 1988.
Tied American League record for most low-hit (no-hit and one-hit) games, season (3), 1988.
Major League saves: 1986 (1).
Led American League in hit batsmen with 14 in 1983, 11 in 1984, 15 in 1986 and tied for lead with 11 in 1981.
Led American League in complete games with 19 and shutouts with 5 in 1982.
Named American League Pitcher of the Year by THE SPORTING NEWS, 1982.
Named righthanded pitcher on THE SPORTING NEWS American League All-Star Team, 1982.
Named outfielder on THE SPORTING NEWS College Baseball All-America Team, 1978.

Year Club	League	G.	IP.	W.	L.	Pct.	H.	R.	ER.	SO.	BB.	ERA.
1978—Dunedin	Florida St.	4	26	2	0	1.000	23	10	6	8	1	2.08
1979—Dunedin	Florida St.	8	51	5	0	1.000	54	30	24	38	28	4.24
1979—Syracuse	Int'national	7	51	5	2	.714	39	15	12	20	14	2.12
1979—Toronto	American	18	129	8	8	.500	139	70	62	52	48	4.33
1980—Toronto†	American	34	243	12	15	.444	232	108	100	108	83	3.70
1981—Toronto	American	25	184	11	10	.524	148	70	65	89	61	3.18
1982—Toronto	American	38	*288⅓	17	14	.548	*271	116	104	141	75	3.25
1983—Toronto	American	36	278	17	12	.586	223	105	94	187	93	3.04
1984—Toronto	American	35	*267	16	8	.667	215	87	84	198	88	2.83
1985—Toronto	American	36	265	14	13	.519	206	89	73	167	96	*2.48
1986—Toronto‡	American	37	205	7	12	.368	239	128	108	127	87	4.74
1987—Toronto	American	33	185	13	9	.591	164	92	84	115	87	4.09
1988—Toronto‡	American	32	207⅓	16	8	.667	157	76	70	147	79	3.04
Major League Totals—10 Years		324	2251⅔	131	109	.546	1994	941	844	1331	797	3.37

Selected by Toronto Blue Jays' organization in 5th round of free-agent draft, June 6, 1978.
†Appeared in one game as outfielder with no chances.
‡Appeared in one game as a pinch-runner.

CHAMPIONSHIP SERIES RECORD

Tied Championship Series record for most games started, Series (3), 1985.
Established American League Championship Series record for most bases on balls (10), seven-game Series, 1985.

Year Club	League	G.	IP.	W.	L.	Pct.	H.	R.	ER.	SO.	BB.	ERA.
1985—Toronto	American	3	20⅓	1	1	.500	11	7	7	18	10	3.10

ALL-STAR GAME RECORD

Tied All-Star Game record for most wild pitches, inning and game (2), July 8, 1980 (seventh inning).

Year League	IP.	W.	L.	Pct.	H.	R.	ER.	SO.	BB.	ERA.
1980—American	1	0	0	.000	1	1	0	0	2	0.00
1981—American	1⅔	0	0	.000	1	0	0	1	1	0.00
1983—American	3	1	0	1.000	0	1	0	4	1	0.00
1984—American	2	0	1	.000	3	2	1	2	0	4.50
1985—American	1	0	0	.000	0	0	0	2	1	0.00
1988—American	1	0	0	.000	1	0	0	0	0	0.00
All-Star Game Totals—6 Years	9⅔	1	1	.500	6	4	1	9	5	0.93

RECORD AS OUTFIELDER

Year Club	League	Pos.	G.	AB.	R.	H.	2B.	3B.	HR.	RBI.	B.A.	PO.	A.	E.	F.A.
1978—Dunedin	Fla. St.	OF-P	35	99	10	19	3	0	1	9	.192	85	7	3	.968

KURT ANDREW STILLWELL

Born June 4, 1965, at Glendale, Calif.
Height, 5.11. Weight, 175.
Throws right and bats left and righthanded.
Son of Ron Stillwell, infielder with Washington Senators, 1961 and 1962.

Major League stolen bases: 1986 (6), 1987 (4), 1988 (6). Total—16.

Year Club	League	Pos.	G.	AB.	R.	H.	2B.	3B.	HR.	RBI.	B.A.	PO.	A.	E.	F.A.
1983—Billings	Pion.	SS	65	250	47	81	10	1	2	44	.324	73	137	*30	.875
1984—Cedar Rapids	Midw.	SS	112	382	63	96	15	1	4	33	.251	156	245	25	.941
1985—Denver†	A. A.	SS-3B	59	182	28	48	7	4	1	22	.264	103	135	25	.905
1986—Cincinnati	Nat.	SS	104	279	31	64	6	1	0	26	.229	107	205	16	.951
1986—Denver	A. A.	SS	10	30	2	7	0	0	0	2	.233	14	21	5	.875
1987—Cincinnati‡	Nat.	SS-2B-3B	131	395	54	102	20	7	4	33	.258	144	247	23	.944
1988—Kansas City	Amer.	SS	128	459	63	115	28	5	10	53	.251	170	349	13	.976
National League Totals—2 Years			235	674	85	166	26	8	4	59	.246	251	452	39	.947
American League Totals—1 Year			128	459	63	115	28	5	10	53	.251	170	349	13	.976
Major League Totals—3 Years			363	1133	148	281	54	13	14	112	.248	421	801	52	.959

Selected by Cincinnati Reds' organization in 1st round (second player selected) of free-agent draft, June 6, 1983.

†On disabled list, August 9, 1985 through remainder of season.

‡Traded with Pitcher Ted Power to Kansas City Royals for Pitcher Danny Jackson and Shortstop Angel Salazar, November 6, 1987.

ALL-STAR GAME RECORD

Year League	Pos.	AB.	R.	H.	2B.	3B.	HR.	RBI.	B.A.	PO.	A.	E.	F.A.
1988—American	SS	0	0	0	0	0	0	0	.000	1	0	0	1.000

TIMOTHY PAUL STODDARD
(Tim)

Born January 24, 1953, at East Chicago, Ind.
Height, 6.07. Weight, 250.
Throws and bats righthanded.
Attended North Carolina State University, Raleigh, N. C.

Major League saves: 1979 (3), 1980 (26), 1981 (7), 1982 (12), 1983 (9), 1984 (7), 1985 (1), 1987 (8), 1988 (3). Total—76.
Tied for Southern League lead in wild pitches with 17 in 1977.

Year Club	League	G.	IP.	W.	L.	Pct.	H.	R.	ER.	SO.	BB.	ERA.
1975—Knoxville	Southern	31	66	3	4	.429	66	40	31	37	43	4.23
1975—Chicago	American	1	1	0	0	.000	2	1	1	0	0	9.00
1976—Knoxville	Southern	20	140	9	8	.529	147	55	45	62	60	2.89
1976—Iowa†	Am. Assoc.	12	29	0	2	.000	37	20	18	20	15	5.59
1977—Charlotte	Southern	36	174	10	7	.588	175	75	62	94	66	3.21
1978—Rochester‡	Int'national	45	76	7	3	.700	80	28	22	70	32	2.61
1978—Baltimore	American	8	18	0	1	.000	22	17	12	14	8	6.00
1979—Baltimore§	American	29	58	3	1	.750	44	12	11	47	19	1.71
1980—Baltimore	American	64	86	5	3	.625	72	27	24	64	38	2.51
1981—Baltimore	American	31	37	4	2	.667	38	16	16	32	18	3.89
1982—Baltimore xy	American	50	56	3	4	.429	53	26	25	42	29	4.02
1982—Rochester	Int'national	5	6	0	0	.000	2	1	1	6	2	1.50
1983—Baltimore za	American	47	57⅔	4	3	.571	65	39	39	50	29	6.09
1984—Chicago b	National	58	92	10	6	.625	77	41	39	87	57	3.82
1985—San Diego	National	44	60	1	6	.143	63	35	31	42	37	4.65
1986—San Diego c	National	30	45⅓	1	3	.250	33	20	19	47	34	3.77
1986—New York	American	24	49⅓	4	1	.800	41	23	21	34	23	3.83
1987—Fort Lauderdale d	Florida St.	2	2	0	0	.000	1	0	0	1	0	0.00
1987—New York	American	57	92⅔	4	3	.571	83	38	36	78	30	3.50
1988—New York ef	American	28	55	2	2	.500	62	41	39	33	27	6.38
American League Totals—10 Years		339	510⅔	29	20	.592	482	240	224	394	221	3.95
National League Totals—3 Years		132	197⅓	12	15	.444	173	96	89	176	128	4.06
Major League Totals—12 Years		471	708	41	35	.539	655	336	313	570	349	3.98

Selected by Texas Rangers' organization in 24th round of free-agent draft, June 5, 1974.

Selected by Chicago White Sox' organization in secondary phase of free-agent draft, January 9, 1975.

†Released, March 28, 1977; signed by Charlotte (Baltimore Orioles' organization), April 8, 1977.

‡On disabled list, June 15 to July 9, 1978.

§On disabled list, July 21 to September 1, 1979.

xOn disabled list, March 31 to May 5, 1982; included rehabilitation disability assignment to Rochester, April 27 to May 5, 1982.

yOn disabled list, September 7, 1982 through remainder of season.

zTraded to Oakland A's for Third Baseman Wayne Gross, December 9, 1983.

aTraded to Chicago Cubs for Pitcher Stan Kyles and a player to be named later, March 26, 1984; Oakland A's acquired Outfielder Stan Boderick to complete deal, March 31, 1984.

bGranted free agency, November 8, 1984; signed by San Diego Padres, January 8, 1985.

cTraded to New York Yankees for Pitcher Ed Whitson, July 9, 1986.

dOn New York Yankees disabled list, March 28 to April 15, 1987; included rehabilitation disability assignment to Fort Lauderdale, April 10, 1987.

eOn disabled list, May 22 to June 12, 1988.

fReleased, August 14, 1988.

CHAMPIONSHIP SERIES RECORD

Year Club	League	G.	IP.	W.	L.	Pct.	H.	R.	ER.	SO.	BB.	ERA.
1984—Chicago	National	2	2	0	0	.000	1	2	1	2	2	4.50

WORLD SERIES RECORD

Year Club	League	G.	IP.	W.	L.	Pct.	H.	R.	ER.	SO.	BB.	ERA.
1979—Baltimore	American	4	5	1	0	1.000	6	3	3	3	1	5.40

MICHAEL ROBERT STOKER
(Mike)

Born November 11, 1966, at Las Vegas, Nev.
Height, 6.03. Weight, 195.
Throws and bats righthanded.

Year Club	League	G.	IP.	W.	L.	Pct.	H.	R.	ER.	SO.	BB.	ERA.
1986—Sarasota Astros	Gulf Coast	13	80⅓	6	5	.545	53	24	16	66	39	1.79
1987—Asheville†	S. Atlantic	25	164	13	5	.722	129	60	53	124	86	2.91
1988—Durham	Carolina	26	147	8	6	.571	113	75	64	111	101	3.92

Signed as free agent by Houston Astros' organization, May 19, 1986.

†Traded with Third Baseman Ed Whited to Atlanta Braves for Shortstop Rafael Ramirez, December 8, 1987.

JEFFERY GLEN STONE
(Jeff)

Born December 26, 1960, at Kennett, Mo.
Height, 6.00. Weight, 180.
Throws right and bats lefthanded.
Twin brother of Jerome Stone, outfielder in Philadelphia Phillies organization, 1984 through 1985.

Major League stolen bases: 1983 (4), 1984 (27), 1985 (15), 1986 (19), 1987 (3), 1988 (4). Total—72.
Led Carolina League in stolen bases with 94 in 1982.
Led South Atlantic League in being hit by pitch with 15 and stolen bases with 123 in 1981.
Led South Atlantic League outfielders in total chances with 290 in 1981.
Named Eastern League Most Valuable Player, 1983.

Year Club	League	Pos.	G.	AB.	R.	H.	2B.	3B.	HR.	RBI.	B.A.	PO.	A.	E.	F.A.
1980—Central Oregon	N'west	OF	55	241	52	63	12	4	0	19	.261	116	4	4	.968
1981—Spartanburg	S. Atl.	OF	134	516	★108	143	13	9	3	53	.277	★264	11	15	.948
1982—Peninsula	Carol.	OF	★137	★559	110	166	18	★13	2	50	.297	●276	9	8	.973
1983—Reading†	East.	OF	125	492	★109	156	25	10	9	67	.317	226	6	9	.963
1983—Philadelphia	Nat.	OF	9	4	2	3	0	2	0	3	.750	0	0	0	.000
1984—Portland	P. C.	OF	82	355	59	109	15	●14	7	34	.307	194	7	12	.944
1984—Philadelphia‡	Nat.	OF	51	185	27	67	4	6	1	15	.362	75	1	7	.916
1985—Philadelphia	Nat.	OF	88	264	36	70	4	3	3	11	.265	82	4	3	.966
1985—Portland	P. C.	OF	67	252	58	83	16	8	2	28	.329	103	6	6	.948
1986—Portland	P. C.	OF	31	118	25	40	4	1	2	9	.339	60	0	1	.984
1986—Philadelphia	Nat.	OF	82	249	32	69	6	4	6	19	.277	103	8	2	.982
1987—Maine	Int.	OF	40	151	22	35	6	2	1	10	.232	89	1	2	.978
1987—Philadelphia§ x	Nat.	OF	66	125	19	32	7	1	1	16	.256	32	3	0	1.000
1988—Baltimore y	Amer.	OF	26	61	4	10	1	0	0	1	.164	23	3	1	.963
1988—Rochester z	Int.	OF	71	267	39	74	12	5	3	27	.277	102	9	3	.974
National League Totals—5 Years			296	827	116	241	21	16	11	64	.291	292	16	12	.963
American League Totals—1 Year			26	61	4	10	1	0	0	1	.164	23	3	1	.963
Major League Totals—6 Years			322	888	120	251	22	16	11	65	.283	315	19	13	.963

Signed as free agent by Philadelphia Phillies' organization, August 26, 1979.
†On disabled list, May 11 to May 21, 1983.
‡On disabled list, July 7 to August 6, 1984; included rehabilitation disability assignment to Portland, August 2 to August 6, 1984.
§On disabled list, June 16 to July 20, 1987; included rehabilitation disability assignment to Maine, July 1 to July 20, 1987.
xTraded with Infielder Rick Schu and Outfielder Keith Hughes to Baltimore Orioles for Outfielder Mike Young and a player to be named later, March 21, 1988; Philadelphia Phillies acquired Outfielder Frank Bellino to complete deal, June 14, 1988.
yOn disabled list, April 29 to June 12, 1988; included rehabilitation disability assignment to Rochester, May 24 to June 12, 1988.
zReleased, December 5, 1988.

MELVIN LEON STOTTLEMYRE JR.
(Mel)

Born December 28, 1963, at Prosser, Wash.
Height, 6.00. Weight 190.
Throws and bats righthanded.
Attended University of Nevada, Las Vegas, Nev.
Son of Mel Stottlemyre Sr., pitcher with the New York Yankees, 1964 through 1974; minor league pitching instructor, Seattle Mariners' organization, 1977 through 1981; and coach with the New York Mets since 1984; nephew of Jeff Stottlemyre, pitcher in Seattle Mariners' organization, 1980 through 1983; and brother of Todd Stottlemyre, pitcher with Toronto Blue Jays.

Year Club	League	G.	IP.	W.	L.	Pct.	H.	R.	ER.	SO.	BB.	ERA.
1985—Asheville†	S. Atlantic	14	78⅔	5	4	.556	65	33	24	70	38	2.75
1986—Osceola	Florida St.	9	35⅔	0	7	.000	48	38	31	25	26	7.82
1986—Asheville	S. Atlantic	7	34⅓	3	1	.750	32	13	8	28	12	2.10
1987—Columbus‡-Memphis	Southern	20	127⅓	7	6	.538	125	68	61	85	41	4.31
1988—Memphis§	Southern	7	45	3	2	.600	41	18	12	29	14	2.40

Selected by Seattle Mariners' organization in 28th round of free-agent draft, June 7, 1982.
Selected by Houston Astros' organization in secondary phase of free-agent draft, January 9, 1985.
†On disabled list, July 23, 1985 through remainder of season.
‡Traded to Kansas City Royals' organization for Shortstop Buddy Biancalana, July 29, 1987.
§On disabled list, May 20, 1988 through remainder of season.

TODD VERNON STOTTLEMYRE

Born May 20, 1965, at Yakima, Wash.
Height, 6.03. Weight, 190.
Throws right and bats lefthanded.
Attended Yakima Valley College, Yakima, Wash.
Son of Mel Stottlemyre Sr., pitcher with New York Yankees, 1964 through 1974; minor league pitching instructor, Seattle Mariners' organization, 1977 through 1981; and coach with New York Mets since 1984; nephew of Jeff Stottlemyre, pitcher in Seattle Mariners' organization, 1980 through 1983; and brother of Mel Stottlemyre Jr., pitcher in Kansas City Royals' organization.

Led International League pitchers in games started with 34 in 1987.

Year	Club	League	G.	IP.	W.	L.	Pct.	H.	R.	ER.	SO.	BB.	ERA.
1986—	Ventura County	California	17	103⅔	9	4	.692	76	39	28	104	36	2.43
1986—	Knoxville	Southern	18	99	8	7	.533	93	56	46	81	49	4.18
1987—	Syracuse	Int'national	34	186⅔	11	•13	.458	189	•103	★92	143	★87	4.44
1988—	Toronto	American	28	98	4	8	.333	109	70	62	67	46	5.69
1988—	Syracuse	Int'national	7	48⅓	5	0	1.000	36	12	11	51	8	2.05
	Major League Totals—1 Year		28	98	4	8	.333	109	70	62	67	46	5.69

Selected by New York Yankees' organization in 5th round of free-agent draft, June 6, 1983.
Selected by St. Louis Cardinals' organization in secondary phase of free-agent draft, January 9, 1985.
Selected by Toronto Blue Jays' organization in secondary phase of free-agent draft, June 3, 1985.

LESTER PAUL STRAKER
(Les)

Born October 10, 1959, at Ciudad Bolivar, Venezuela.
Height, 6.01. Weight, 193.
Throws and bats righthanded.
Attended Oriente University, Bolivar, Venezuela.

Major League saves: 1988 (1).
Pitched 4-0 no-hit victory against Winter Haven, July 17, 1982.
Led Southern League in complete games with 12 and tied for lead in shutouts with 3 in 1985.
Tied for Pioneer League lead in shutouts with 1 in 1978.

Year	Club	League	G.	IP.	W.	L.	Pct.	H.	R.	ER.	SO.	BB.	ERA.
1977—	Eugene	Northwest	7	26	1	2	.333	25	10	8	18	20	2.77
1978—	Billings	Pioneer	12	69	7	2	.778	46	29	18	54	37	2.35
1979—	Greensboro	W. Carol.	29	141	7	10	.412	123	83	62	121	75	3.96
1980—	Cedar Rapids	Midwest	34	135	6	5	.545	135	74	56	89	66	3.73
1981—	Waterbury†	Eastern	19	45	1	5	.167	50	35	32	33	34	6.40
1982—	Tampa	Florida St.	25	154⅓	9	9	.500	137	58	44	99	60	2.57
1983—	Waterbury‡§	Eastern	3	10	0	2	.000	16	10	10	5	6	9.00
1984—	Albany x	Eastern	28	95⅔	6	5	.545	97	55	45	60	43	4.23
1985—	Orlando	Southern	27	★193	16	6	.727	164	75	66	106	79	3.08
1986—	Toledo y	Int'national	18	107⅓	6	7	.462	102	46	41	50	44	3.44
1987—	Minnesota	American	31	154⅓	8	10	.444	150	79	75	76	59	4.37
1988—	Minnesota z	American	16	82⅔	2	5	.286	86	39	36	23	25	3.92
1988—	Portland	P. Coast	4	19⅔	0	0	.000	19	12	7	13	8	3.20
	Major League Totals—2 Years		47	237	10	15	.400	236	118	111	99	84	4.22

Signed as free agent by Cincinnati Reds' organization, February 10, 1977.
†On Tampa disabled list, August 3, 1981 through remainder of season.
‡On disabled list, May 5, 1983 through remainder of season.
§Granted free agency, October 20, 1983; signed by Tacoma (Oakland A's organization), November 26, 1983.
xReleased, December 12, 1984; signed by Orlando (Minnesota Twins' organization), January 10, 1985.
yOn disabled list, April 11 to May 23, 1986.
zOn disabled list, April 18 to May 4 and June 14 to September 1, 1988; included rehabilitation disability assignment to Portland, August 11 to August 30, 1988.

CHAMPIONSHIP SERIES RECORD

Year	Club	League	G.	IP.	W.	L.	Pct.	H.	R.	ER.	SO.	BB.	ERA.
1987—	Minnesota	American	1	2⅔	0	0	.000	3	5	5	1	4	16.88

WORLD SERIES RECORD

Year	Club	League	G.	IP.	W.	L.	Pct.	H.	R.	ER.	SO.	BB.	ERA.
1987—	Minnesota	American	2	9	0	0	.000	9	4	4	6	3	4.00

JOSEPH DOUGLAS STRANGE
(Doug)

Born April 13, 1964, at Greenville, S.C.
Height, 6.02. Weight, 170.
Throws right and bats left and righthanded.
Attended North Carolina State University, Raleigh, N.C.

Led Florida State League third basemen in putouts with 116 and tied for lead in double plays with 20 in 1986.

Year	Club	League	Pos.	G.	AB.	R.	H.	2B.	3B.	HR.	RBI.	B.A.	PO.	A.	E.	F.A.
1985—	Bristol	Appal.	OF-2B-3B	65	226	43	69	16	1	6	45	.305	84	59	11	.929
1986—	Lakeland	Fla. St.	3B-1B	126	466	59	119	29	4	2	63	.255	202	215	37	.919
1987—	Glens Falls†	East.	3-2-O-S	115	431	63	130	31	1	13	70	.302	110	214	20	.942
1987—	Toledo	Int.	3B	16	45	7	11	2	0	1	5	.244	14	28	3	.933
1988—	Toledo	Int.	3B-SS-1B	82	278	23	56	8	2	6	19	.201	52	126	13	.932
1988—	Glens Falls	East.	3B	57	218	32	61	11	1	1	36	.280	45	112	12	.929

Selected by Detroit Tigers' organization in 7th round of free-agent draft, June 3, 1985.
†Batted righthanded only.

DARRYL EUGENE STRAWBERRY

Born March 12, 1962, at Los Angeles, Calif.
Height, 6.06. Weight, 195.
Throws and bats lefthanded.
Brother of Michael Strawberry, outfielder in Los Angeles Dodgers' organization, 1980 and 1981.

Hit three home runs in a game, August 5, 1985.
Major League stolen bases: 1983 (19), 1984 (27), 1985 (26), 1986 (28), 1987 (36), 1988 (29). Total—165.
Led National League in slugging percentage with .545 in 1988.
Led Texas League in slugging percentage with .602, bases on balls received with 100 and caught stealing with 22 in 1982.
Named outfielder on THE SPORTING NEWS National League All-Star Team, 1988.
Named outfielder on THE SPORTING NEWS National League Silver Slugger team, 1988.
Named National League Rookie Player of the Year by THE SPORTING NEWS, 1983.
Named National League Rookie of the Year by Baseball Writers' Association of America, 1983.
Named Texas League Most Valuable Player, 1982.
Received reported $210,000 bonus to sign with New York Mets, 1980.

Year Club	League	Pos.	G.	AB.	R.	H.	2B.	3B.	HR.	RBI.	B.A.	PO.	A.	E.	F.A.
1980—Kingsport	Appal.	OF	44	157	27	42	5	2	5	20	.268	55	4	3	.952
1981—Lynchburg	Carol.	OF	123	420	84	107	22	6	13	78	.255	173	8	13	.933
1982—Jackson	Texas	OF	129	435	93	123	19	9	*34	97	.283	211	8	9	.961
1983—Tidewater	Int.	OF	16	57	12	19	4	1	3	13	.333	22	0	4	.846
1983—New York	Nat.	OF	122	420	63	108	15	7	26	74	.257	232	8	4	.984
1984—New York	Nat.	OF	147	522	75	131	27	4	26	97	.251	276	11	6	.980
1985—New York†	Nat.	OF	111	393	78	109	15	4	29	79	.277	211	5	2	.991
1986—New York	Nat.	OF	136	475	76	123	27	5	27	93	.259	226	10	6	.975
1987—New York	Nat.	OF	154	532	108	151	32	5	39	104	.284	272	6	8	.972
1988—New York	Nat.	OF	153	543	101	146	27	3	*39	101	.269	297	4	9	.971
Major League Totals—6 Years			823	2885	501	768	143	28	186	548	.266	1514	44	35	.978

Selected by New York Mets' organization in 1st round (first player selected) of free-agent draft, June 3, 1980.
†On disabled list, May 12 to June 28, 1985.

CHAMPIONSHIP SERIES RECORD

Established National League Championship Series record for most strikeouts, six-game Series (12), 1986.
Tied National League Championship Series record for most at-bats, seven-game Series (30), 1988.

Year Club	League	Pos.	G.	AB.	R.	H.	2B.	3B.	HR.	RBI.	B.A.	PO.	A.	E.	F.A.
1986—New York	Nat.	OF	6	22	4	5	1	0	2	5	.227	9	0	0	1.000
1988—New York	Nat.	OF	7	30	5	9	2	0	1	6	.300	11	0	0	1.000
Championship Series Totals—2 Years			13	52	9	14	3	0	3	11	.269	20	0	0	1.000

WORLD SERIES RECORD

Year Club	League	Pos.	G.	AB.	R.	H.	2B.	3B.	HR.	RBI.	B.A.	PO.	A.	E.	F.A.
1986—New York	Nat.	OF	7	24	4	5	1	0	1	1	.208	19	0	0	1.000

ALL-STAR GAME RECORD

Tied All-Star Game record for most putouts and chances accepted by right fielder, game (4), July 12, 1988.

Year League	Pos.	AB.	R.	H.	2B.	3B.	HR.	RBI.	B.A.	PO.	A.	E.	F.A.
1984—National	OF	2	0	1	0	0	0	0	.500	0	0	0	.000
1985—National	OF	1	2	1	0	0	0	0	1.000	3	0	0	1.000
1986—National	OF	2	0	1	0	0	0	0	.500	1	0	0	1.000
1987—National	OF	2	0	0	0	0	0	0	.000	0	0	0	.000
1988—National	OF	4	0	1	0	0	0	0	.250	4	0	0	1.000
All-Star Game Totals—5 Years		11	2	4	0	0	0	0	.364	8	0	0	1.000

FRANKLIN LEE STUBBS

Born October 21, 1960, at Laurinburg, N.C.
Height, 6.02. Weight, 218.
Throws and bats lefthanded.
Attended Virginia Tech., Blacksburg, Va.

Major League stolen bases: 1984 (2), 1986 (7), 1987 (8), 1988 (11). Total—28.
Led National League first basemen in fielding percentage with .994 in 1987.
Named first baseman on THE SPORTING NEWS College Baseball All-America Team, 1982.

Year Club	League	Pos.	G.	AB.	R.	H.	2B.	3B.	HR.	RBI.	B.A.	PO.	A.	E.	F.A.
1982—Vero Beach†	Fla. St.	1B	16	54	6	11	1	1	3	5	.204	134	3	3	.979
1983—San Antonio	Texas	1B-OF	47	173	35	54	8	3	12	52	.312	425	23	5	.989
1983—Albuquerque	P. C.	OF-1B	76	267	49	74	16	3	16	58	.277	106	3	6	.948
1984—Albuquerque	P. C.	OF-1B	29	108	26	35	5	5	6	24	.324	36	4	2	.952
1984—Los Angeles	Nat.	1B-OF	87	217	22	42	2	3	8	17	.194	417	37	4	.991
1985—Albuquerque	P. C.	1B-OF	132	421	86	118	23	5	32	93	.280	945	87	14	.987
1985—Los Angeles	Nat.	1B	10	9	0	2	0	0	0	2	.222	11	0	0	1.000
1986—Los Angeles	Nat.	OF-1B	132	420	55	95	11	1	23	58	.226	244	14	7	.974
1987—Los Angeles‡	Nat.	1B-OF	129	386	48	90	16	3	16	52	.233	830	79	5	.995
1988—Los Angeles	Nat.	1B-OF	115	242	30	54	13	0	8	34	.223	530	57	13	.978
Major League Totals—5 Years			473	1274	155	283	42	7	55	163	.222	2032	187	29	.987

Selected by Los Angeles Dodgers' organization in 1st round (19th player selected) of free-agent draft, June 7, 1982.
†On disabled list, July 5, 1982 through remainder of season.
‡On disabled list, August 3 to August 24, 1987.

CHAMPIONSHIP SERIES RECORD

Year Club	League	Pos.	G.	AB.	R.	H.	2B.	3B.	HR.	RBI.	B.A.	PO.	A.	E.	F.A.
1988—Los Angeles	Nat.	1B-PH	4	8	0	2	0	0	0	0	.250	16	2	0	1.000

WORLD SERIES RECORD

Year Club	League	Pos.	G.	AB.	R.	H.	2B.	3B.	HR.	RBI.	B.A.	PO.	A.	E.	F.A.
1988—Los Angeles	Nat.	1B	5	17	3	5	2	0	0	2	.294	34	0	0	1.000

JAMES HOWARD SUNDBERG
(Jim)

Born May 18, 1951, at Galesburg, Ill.
Height, 6.00. Weight, 196.
Throws and bats righthanded.
Attended University of Iowa, Iowa City, Iowa.

Tied major league records for most seasons leading league in assists by catcher (6); most assists by catcher, inning (3), September 3, 1976 (fifth inning); fewest errors by catcher, season (4), 1979.

Established American League record for highest fielding percentage by catcher, season (.995), 1979.

Tied American League record for most games, catcher, season (155), 1975.

Major League stolen bases: 1974 (2), 1975 (3), 1977 (2), 1978 (2), 1979 (3), 1980 (2), 1981 (2), 1982 (2), 1984 (1), 1986 (1). Total—20.

Led American League in passed balls with 8 in 1981 and 16 in 1982.

Led American League catchers in total chances with 909 in 1975, 822 in 1976, 909 in 1977, 863 in 1978, 833 in 1979 and 936 in 1980.

Led American League catchers in double plays with 15 in 1974, 11 in 1976 and 15 in 1982.

Tied for American League lead in passed balls with 17 in 1980.

Tied for American League lead in double plays by catchers with 12 in 1977 and 14 in 1978.

Named catcher on THE SPORTING NEWS American League All-Star Team, 1978 and 1981.

Named catcher on THE SPORTING NEWS American League All-Star fielding team, 1976 through 1981.

Year Club	League	Pos.	G.	AB.	R.	H.	2B.	3B.	HR.	RBI.	B.A.	PO.	A.	E.	F.A.
1973—Pittsfield	East.	C	91	242	39	72	14	0	5	40	.298	449	52	3	★.994
1974—Texas	Amer.	C	132	368	45	91	13	3	3	36	.247	722	69	8	.990
1975—Texas	Amer.	C	155	472	45	94	9	0	6	36	.199	★791	★101	17	.981
1976—Texas	Amer.	C	140	448	33	102	24	2	3	34	.228	★719	★96	7	★.991
1977—Texas	Amer.	C	149	453	61	132	20	3	6	65	.291	★801	★103	5	★.994
1978—Texas	Amer.	C	149	518	54	144	23	6	6	58	.278	★769	★91	3	★.997
1979—Texas	Amer.	C	150	495	50	136	23	4	5	64	.275	★754	75	4	★.995
1980—Texas	Amer.	C	151	505	59	138	24	1	10	63	.273	★853	★76	7	.993
1981—Texas	Amer.	★C-OF	102	339	42	94	17	2	3	28	.277	465	★52	2	★.996
1982—Texas	Amer.	C-OF	139	470	37	118	22	5	10	47	.251	612	69	6	.991
1983—Texas†	Amer.	C	131	378	30	76	14	0	2	28	.201	618	56	5	.993
1984—Milwaukee‡§	Amer.	C	110	348	43	91	19	4	7	43	.261	556	55	3	★.995
1985—Kansas City	Amer.	C	115	367	38	90	12	4	10	35	.245	572	41	5	.992
1986—Kansas City x	Amer.	C	140	429	41	91	9	1	12	42	.212	686	46	4	★.995
1987—Chicago	Nat.	C	61	139	9	28	2	0	4	15	.201	273	34	2	.994
1988—Chicago y	Nat.	C	24	54	8	13	1	0	2	9	.241	88	7	0	1.000
1988—Texas z	Amer.	C	38	91	13	26	4	0	4	13	.286	141	9	0	1.000
American League Totals—14 Years			1801	5681	591	1423	233	35	87	592	.250	9059	939	76	.992
National League Totals—2 Years			85	193	17	41	3	0	6	24	.212	361	41	2	.995
Major League Totals—15 Years			1886	5874	608	1464	236	35	93	616	.249	9420	980	78	.993

Selected by Oakland A's organization in 14th round of free-agent draft, June 5, 1969.

Selected by Texas Rangers' organization in 8th round of free-agent draft, June 6, 1972.

Selected by Texas Rangers' organization in secondary phase of free-agent draft, January 10, 1973.

†Traded to Milwaukee Brewers for Catcher Ned Yost and Pitcher Dan Scarpetta, December 8, 1983.

‡On disabled list, August 6 to September 1, 1984.

§Traded to Kansas City Royals as part of a six-player, four-team deal in which Texas Rangers acquired Catcher Don Slaught from Kansas City, New York Mets' organization acquired Pitcher Frank Wills from Kansas City, Milwaukee Brewers acquired Pitcher Danny Darwin and a player to be named later from Texas and Pitcher Tim Leary from New York, January 18, 1985; Milwaukee organization acquired Catcher Bill Hance from Texas to complete deal, January 30, 1985.

xTraded to Chicago Cubs for Outfielder Thad Bosley and Pitcher Dave Gumpert, March 30, 1987.

yReleased, July 15, 1988; signed by Texas Rangers, July 21, 1988.

zGranted free agency, November 4, 1988.

CHAMPIONSHIP SERIES RECORD

Year Club	League	Pos.	G.	AB.	R.	H.	2B.	3B.	HR.	RBI.	B.A.	PO.	A.	E.	F.A.
1985—Kansas City	Amer.	C	7	24	3	4	1	1	1	6	.167	41	2	1	.977

WORLD SERIES RECORD

Year Club	League	Pos.	G.	AB.	R.	H.	2B.	3B.	HR.	RBI.	B.A.	PO.	A.	E.	F.A.
1985—Kansas City	Amer.	C	7	24	6	6	2	0	0	1	.250	47	3	0	1.000

ALL-STAR GAME RECORD

Year League	Pos.	AB.	R.	H.	2B.	3B.	HR.	RBI.	B.A.	PO.	A.	E.	F.A.
1978—American	C	0	0	0	0	0	0	0	.000	2	1	0	1.000
1984—American	C	1	0	0	0	0	0	0	.000	6	0	0	1.000
All-Star Game Totals—2 Years		1	0	0	0	0	0	0	.000	8	1	0	1.000

Member of American League All-Star Team in 1974 game; did not play.

WILLIAM JAMES SURHOFF
(B. J.)

Born August 4, 1964, at Bronx, N.Y.
Height, 6.01. Weight, 190.
Throws right and bats lefthanded.
Attended University of North Carolina, Chapel Hill, N.C.
Son of Dick Surhoff, forward with New York Knicks and Milwaukee Hawks of the National Basketball Association, 1952-53 and 1953-54; and brother of Rich Surhoff, pitcher with Philadelphia Phillies and Texas Rangers, 1985.

Major League stolen bases: 1987 (11), 1988 (21). Total—32.
Tied for Pacific Coast League lead in double plays by catchers with 10 in 1986.
Named College Player of the Year by THE SPORTING NEWS, 1985.
Member of 1984 U. S. Olympic baseball team.
Named catcher on THE SPORTING NEWS College Baseball All-America Team, 1985.

Year Club	League	Pos.	G.	AB.	R.	H.	2B.	3B.	HR.	RBI.	B.A.	PO.	A.	E.	F.A.
1985—Beloit	Midw.	C	76	289	39	96	13	4	7	58	.332	475	44	3	.994
1986—Vancouver	P. C.	C	116	458	71	141	19	3	5	59	.308	539	70	7	★.989
1987—Milwaukee	Amer.	C-3B-1B	115	395	50	118	22	3	7	68	.299	648	56	11	.985
1988—Milwaukee	Amer.	C-3-1-S-O	139	493	47	121	21	0	5	38	.245	550	94	8	.988
Major League Totals—2 Years			254	888	97	239	43	3	12	106	.269	1198	150	19	.986

Selected by New York Yankees' organization in 5th round of free-agent draft, June 7, 1982.
Selected by Milwaukee Brewers' organization in 1st round (first player selected) of free-agent draft, June 3, 1985.

RICHARD LEE SUTCLIFFE
(Rick)

Born June 21, 1956, at Independence, Mo.
Height, 6.07. Weight, 215.
Throws right and bats lefthanded.
Brother of Terry Sutcliffe, pitcher in Los Angeles Dodgers' organization, 1979 through 1981.

Tied major league record for fewest games won, season, for leader (18), 1987.
Major League saves: 1980 (5), 1982 (1). Total—6.
Led National League in intentional bases on balls issued with 14 in 1987.
Led California League pitchers in games started with 28 in 1975.
Tied for Northwest League lead in shutouts with 2 in 1974.
Named National League Pitcher of the Year by THE SPORTING NEWS, 1984.
Won National League Cy Young Memorial Award, 1984.
Named righthanded pitcher on THE SPORTING NEWS National League All-Star Team, 1984.
Named National League Comeback Player of the Year by THE SPORTING NEWS, 1987.
Named National League Rookie Pitcher of the Year by THE SPORTING NEWS, 1979.
Named National League Rookie of the Year by Baseball Writers' Association of America, 1979.
Received reported $80,000 bonus to sign with Los Angeles Dodgers, 1974.

Year Club	League	G.	IP.	W.	L.	Pct.	H.	R.	ER.	SO.	BB.	ERA.
1974—Bellingham	Northwest	17	95	10	3	.769	79	42	35	69	48	3.32
1975—Bakersfield	California	28	193	8	★16	.333	★214	★115	★89	91	68	4.15
1976—Waterbury	Eastern	30	187	10	11	.476	★187	90	66	121	45	3.18
1976—Los Angeles	National	1	5	0	0	.000	2	0	0	3	1	0.00
1977—Albuquerque†	P. Coast	17	77	3	10	.231	96	67	55	48	63	6.43
1978—Albuquerque	P. Coast	30	184	13	6	.684	179	101	91	99	92	4.45
1978—Los Angeles	National	2	2	0	0	.000	2	0	0	0	1	0.00
1979—Los Angeles	National	39	242	17	10	.630	217	104	93	117	97	3.46
1980—Los Angeles	National	42	110	3	9	.250	122	73	68	59	55	5.56
1981—Los Angeles‡§	National	14	47	2	2	.500	41	24	21	16	20	4.02
1982—Cleveland	American	34	216	14	8	.636	174	81	71	142	98	★2.96
1983—Cleveland	American	36	243⅓	17	11	.607	251	131	116	160	102	4.29
1984—Cleveland x	American	15	94⅓	4	5	.444	111	60	54	58	46	5.15
1984—Chicago y	National	20	150⅓	16	1	★.941	123	53	45	155	39	2.69
1985—Chicago z	National	20	130	8	8	.500	119	51	46	102	44	3.18
1986—Chicago a	National	28	176⅔	5	14	.263	166	92	91	122	96	4.64
1987—Chicago	National	34	237⅓	★18	10	.643	223	106	97	174	106	3.68
1988—Chicago b	National	32	226	13	14	.481	232	97	97	144	70	3.86
National League Totals—10 Years		232	1326⅓	82	68	.547	1247	600	558	892	529	3.79
American League Totals—3 Years		85	553⅔	35	24	.593	536	272	241	360	246	3.92
Major League Totals—12 Years		317	1880	117	92	.560	1783	872	799	1252	775	3.83

Selected by Los Angeles Dodgers' organization in 1st round (21st player selected) of free-agent draft, June 5, 1974.
†On disabled list, May 3 to May 24, 1977.
‡On disabled list, August 14 to September 5, 1981.
§Traded with Second Baseman Jack Perconte to Cleveland Indians for Outfielder Jorge Orta, Catcher Jack Fimple and Pitcher Larry White, December 9, 1981.
xTraded with Catcher Ron Hassey and Pitcher George Frazier to Chicago Cubs for Outfielders Mel Hall and Joe Carter and Pitchers Don Schulze and Darryl Banks, June 13, 1984.
yGranted free agency, November 8, 1984; re-signed by Cubs, December 14, 1984.
zOn disabled list, May 20 to June 7, July 8 to July 23 and July 29 to September 27, 1985.
aOn disabled list, June 30 to August 3, 1986.
bOn disabled list, May 21 to June 11, 1988.

CHAMPIONSHIP SERIES RECORD

Tied Championship Series records for hitting home run in first Series at-bat, October 2, 1984; most home runs hit by pitcher, total Series (1); most bases on balls, five-game Series (8), 1984.

Year Club	League	G.	IP.	W.	L.	Pct.	H.	R.	ER.	SO.	BB.	ERA.
1984—Chicago	National	2	13⅓	1	1	.500	9	6	5	10	8	3.38

ALL-STAR GAME RECORD

Year League	IP.	W.	L.	Pct.	H.	R.	ER.	SO.	BB.	ERA.
1987—National	2	0	0	.000	1	0	0	0	1	0.00

Member of American League All-Star Team in 1983; did not play.

HOWARD BRUCE SUTTER

Name pronounced SUIT-er.

(Known by middle name.)

Born January 8, 1953, at Lancaster, Pa.
Height, 6.02. Weight, 195.
Throws and bats righthanded.

Tied major league record by striking out side on 9 pitches, September 8, 1977 (ninth inning).
Established National League records for most saves, lifetime (300); most saves, season (45), 1984.
Tied National League records for most consecutive strikeouts by relief pitcher, game (6), September 8, 1977.
Major League saves: 1976 (10), 1977 (31), 1978 (27), 1979 (37), 1980 (28), 1981 (25), 1982 (36), 1983 (21), 1984 (45), 1985 (23), 1986 (3), 1988 (14). Total—300.
Led National League in saves with 37 in 1979, 28 in 1980, 25 in 1981, 36 in 1982 and 45 in 1984.
Led National League in games finished in relief with 63 in 1984.
Tied for Texas League lead in saves with 13 in 1975.
Won National League Cy Young Memorial Award, 1979.
Named National League Fireman of the Year by THE SPORTING NEWS, 1979, 1981, 1982 and 1984.

Year Club	League	G.	IP.	W.	L.	Pct.	H.	R.	ER.	SO.	BB.	ERA.
1972—Bradenton Cubs	Gulf Coast	2	5	0	0	.000	3	0	0	4	0	0.00
1973—Quincy	Midwest	40	85	3	3	.500	94	52	39	76	27	4.13
1974—Key West†	Florida St.	18	40	1	5	.167	26	9	6	50	13	1.35
1974—Midland	Texas	8	25	1	2	.333	22	6	4	14	6	1.44
1975—Midland	Texas	41	67	5	7	.417	64	26	16	50	21	2.15
1976—Wichita	Am. Assoc.	7	12	2	1	.667	9	3	2	16	4	1.50
1976—Chicago	National	52	83	6	3	.667	63	27	25	73	26	2.71
1977—Chicago‡	National	62	107	7	3	.700	69	21	16	129	23	1.35
1978—Chicago	National	64	99	8	10	.444	82	44	35	106	34	3.18
1979—Chicago	National	62	101	6	6	.500	67	29	25	110	32	2.23
1980—Chicago§	National	60	102	5	8	.385	90	35	30	76	34	2.65
1981—St. Louis	National	48	82	3	5	.375	64	24	24	57	24	2.63
1982—St. Louis	National	70	102⅓	9	8	.529	88	38	33	61	34	2.90
1983—St. Louis	National	60	89⅓	9	10	.474	90	45	42	64	30	4.23
1984—St. Louis x	National	71	122⅔	5	7	.417	109	26	21	77	23	1.54
1985—Atlanta	National	58	88⅓	7	7	.500	91	46	44	52	29	4.48
1986—Atlanta y	National	16	18⅔	2	0	1.000	17	9	9	16	9	4.34
1987—Atlanta z	National					(Did not play)						
1988—Atlanta a	National	38	45⅓	1	4	.200	49	26	24	40	11	4.76
Major League Totals—12 Years		661	1040⅔	68	71	.489	879	370	328	861	309	2.84

Selected by Washington Senators' organization in 21st round of free-agent draft, June 4, 1970.
Signed as free agent by Chicago Cubs' organization, September 9, 1971.
†On disabled list, May 22 to July 28, 1974.
‡On disabled list, August 2 to August 23, 1977.
§Traded to St. Louis Cardinals for Third Baseman Ken Reitz, Outfielder-First Baseman Leon Durham and a player to be named later, December 9, 1980; Chicago Cubs acquired Third Baseman Tye Waller to complete deal, December 22, 1980.
xGranted free agency, November 8, 1984; signed by Atlanta Braves, December 7, 1984 (Shortstop Argenis Salazar selected from player compensation pool by St. Louis Cardinals' organization, January 24, 1985).
yOn disabled list, May 28, 1986 through remainder of season.
zOn disabled list, March 25, 1987 through entire season.
aOn disabled list, July 24 to August 19, 1988.

CHAMPIONSHIP SERIES RECORD

Year Club	League	G.	IP.	W.	L.	Pct.	H.	R.	ER.	SO.	BB.	ERA.
1982—St. Louis	National	2	4⅓	1	0	1.000	0	0	0	1	0	0.00

WORLD SERIES RECORD

Year Club	League	G.	IP.	W.	L.	Pct.	H.	R.	ER.	SO.	BB.	ERA.
1982—St. Louis	National	4	7⅔	1	0	1.000	6	4	4	6	3	4.70

ALL-STAR GAME RECORD

Year League	IP.	W.	L.	Pct.	H.	R.	ER.	SO.	BB.	ERA.
1978—National	1⅔	1	0	1.000	0	0	0	2	0	0.00
1979—National	2	1	0	1.000	2	0	0	3	2	0.00
1980—National	2	0	0	.000	0	0	0	1	1	0.00
1981—National	1	0	0	.000	0	0	0	1	0	0.00
All-Star Game Totals—4 Years	6⅔	2	0	1.000	2	0	0	7	3	0.00

Member of National League All-Star Team in 1984; did not play.
Named to National League All-Star Team in 1977; replaced due to injury.

DONALD HOWARD SUTTON

(Don)

Born April 2, 1945, at Clio, Ala.
Height, 6.01. Weight, 190.
Throws and bats righthanded.
Attended Gulf Coast Community College, Panama City, Fla.;
Mississippi College, Clinton, Miss.; University of Southern California, Los Angeles, Calif.;
and Whittier College, Whittier, Calif.

Established major league records for most consecutive games lost to one club, lifetime (13), 1966 through 1969, (vs. Chicago); most years and most consecutive years with 100 or more strikeouts (21).

Tied National League record for most consecutive home runs allowed, inning (3), May 27, 1980 (third inning).

Tied modern National League record for most one-hit games, lifetime (5).

Major League saves: 1971 (1), 1979 (1), 1980 (1). Total—3.

Led National League pitchers in games started with 40 in 1974.

Led National League in shutouts with 9 in 1972.

Tied for National League lead in balks with 3 in 1968.

Named National League Rookie Pitcher of the Year by THE SPORTING NEWS, 1966.

Named righthanded pitcher on THE SPORTING NEWS National League All-Star Team, 1976.

Named Texas League Player of the Year, 1965.

Year Club	League	G.	IP.	W.	L.	Pct.	H.	R.	ER.	SO.	BB.	ERA.
1965—Santa Barbara	California	10	84	8	1	.889	59	18	14	101	15	1.50
1965—Albuquerque	Texas	21	165	15	6	*.714	151	60	51	138	30	2.78
1966—Los Angeles	National	37	226	12	12	.500	192	82	75	209	52	2.99
1967—Los Angeles	National	37	233	11	15	.423	223	106	102	169	57	3.94
1968—Spokane	P. Coast	2	16	1	1	.500	11	2	2	19	5	1.13
1968—Los Angeles	National	35	208	11	15	.423	179	64	60	162	59	2.60
1969—Los Angeles	National	41	293	17	18	.486	269	123	113	217	91	3.47
1970—Los Angeles	National	38	260	15	13	.536	251	127	•118	201	78	4.08
1971—Los Angeles	National	38	265	17	12	.586	231	85	75	194	55	2.55
1972—Los Angeles	National	33	273	19	9	.679	186	78	63	207	63	2.08
1973—Los Angeles	National	33	256	18	10	.643	196	78	69	200	56	2.43
1974—Los Angeles	National	40	276	19	9	.679	241	111	99	179	80	3.23
1975—Los Angeles	National	35	254	16	13	.552	202	87	81	175	62	2.87
1976—Los Angeles	National	35	268	21	10	.677	231	98	91	161	82	3.06
1977—Los Angeles	National	33	240	14	8	.636	207	93	85	150	69	3.19
1978—Los Angeles	National	34	238	15	11	.577	228	109	94	154	54	3.55
1979—Los Angeles	National	33	226	12	15	.444	201	109	96	146	61	3.82
1980—Los Angeles†	National	32	212	13	5	.722	163	56	52	128	47	*2.21
1981—Houston	National	23	159	11	9	.550	132	51	46	104	29	2.60
1982—Houston‡	National	27	195	13	8	.619	169	75	65	139	46	3.00
1982—Milwaukee	American	7	54⅔	4	1	.800	55	21	20	36	18	3.29
1983—Milwaukee	American	31	220⅓	8	13	.381	209	109	100	134	54	4.08
1984—Milwaukee§	American	33	212⅔	14	12	.538	224	103	89	143	51	3.77
1985—Oakland x-California y	American	34	226	15	10	.600	221	101	97	107	59	3.86
1986—California	American	34	207	15	11	.577	192	93	86	116	49	3.74
1987—California z	American	35	191⅔	11	11	.500	199	101	100	99	41	4.70
1988—Los Angeles ab	National	16	87⅓	3	6	.333	91	44	38	44	30	3.92
National League Totals—18 Years		600	4169⅓	257	198	.565	3592	1576	1422	2939	1071	3.07
American League Totals—6 Years		174	1112⅓	67	58	.536	1100	528	492	635	272	3.98
Major League Totals—23 Years		774	5281⅔	324	256	.559	4692	2104	1914	3574	1343	3.26

Signed as free agent by Los Angeles Dodgers' organization, September 11, 1964.

†Granted free agency, October 23, 1980; signed by Houston Astros, December 4, 1980.

‡Traded to Milwaukee Brewers for three players to be named later, August 30, 1982; Houston Astros acquired Pitchers Frank DiPino and Mike Madden and Outfielder Kevin Bass to complete deal, September 3, 1982.

§Traded to Oakland A's for Pitchers Ray Burris, Eric Barry and a player to be named later, December 7, 1984; Milwaukee Brewers' organization acquired Pitcher Ed Myers to complete deal, March 25, 1985.

xTraded to California Angels for two players to be named later, September 10, 1985; Oakland A's organization acquired Pitcher Robert Sharpnack and Outfielder Jerome Nelson to complete deal, September 25, 1985.

yGranted free agency, November 12, 1985; re-signed by Angels, December 5, 1985.

zReleased, October 30, 1987; signed by Los Angeles Dodgers, January 5, 1988.

aOn disabled list, June 29 to August 9, 1988; included rehabilitation disability assignment to Bakersfield, July 23 to August 9, 1988.

bReleased, August 10, 1988.

CHAMPIONSHIP SERIES RECORD

Established Championship Series records for most consecutive scoreless innings, Series (15⅔), 1974; most innings pitched, four-game Series (17), 1974.

Tied Championship Series records for most games won, Series (2), 1974; most games won, total Series (4).

Established National League Championship Series record for most consecutive scoreless innings, total Series (15⅔).

Tied National League Championship Series records for most games won, total Series (3); most complete games, total Series (2); most strikeouts four-game Series (13), 1974.

Year Club	League	G.	IP.	W.	L.	Pct.	H.	R.	ER.	SO.	BB.	ERA.
1974—Los Angeles	National	2	17	2	0	1.000	7	1	1	13	2	0.53
1977—Los Angeles	National	1	9	1	0	1.000	9	1	1	4	0	1.00
1978—Los Angeles	National	1	5⅔	0	1	.000	7	7	4	0	2	6.35
1982—Milwaukee	American	1	7⅔	1	0	1.000	8	3	3	9	2	3.52
1986—California	American	2	9⅔	0	0	.000	6	2	2	4	1	1.86
Championship Series Totals—5 Years		7	49	4	1	.800	37	14	11	30	7	2.02

WORLD SERIES RECORD

Tied World Series records for most consecutive home runs allowed, inning (2), October 16, 1977 (eighth inning); most runs allowed, six-game Series (10), 1978.

Year Club	League	G.	IP.	W.	L.	Pct.	H.	R.	ER.	SO.	BB.	ERA.
1974—Los Angeles	National	2	13	1	0	1.000	9	4	4	12	3	2.77
1977—Los Angeles	National	2	16	1	0	1.000	17	7	7	6	1	3.94
1978—Los Angeles	National	2	12	0	2	.000	17	10	10	8	4	7.50
1982—Milwaukee	American	2	10⅓	0	1	.000	12	11	9	5	1	7.84
World Series Totals—4 Years		8	51⅓	2	3	.400	55	32	30	31	9	5.26

ALL-STAR GAME RECORD

Year League	IP.	W.	L.	Pct.	H.	R.	ER.	SO.	BB.	ERA.
1972—National	2	0	0	.000	1	0	0	2	0	0.00
1973—National	1	0	0	.000	0	0	0	0	0	0.00
1975—National	2	0	0	.000	3	0	0	1	0	0.00
1977—National	3	1	0	1.000	1	0	0	4	1	0.00
All-Star Game Totals—4 Years	8	1	0	1.000	5	0	0	7	1	0.00

DALE CURTIS SVEUM

Name pronounced Swaim.
Born November 23, 1963, at Richmond, Calif.
Height, 6.03. Weight, 185.
Throws right and bats left and righthanded.

Major League stolen bases: 1986 (4), 1987 (2), 1988 (1). Total—7.
Hit three home runs in a game, July 17, 1987.
Switch-hit home runs in one game, July 17, 1987 and June 12, 1988.
Led American League third basemen in errors with 26 in 1986.
Led Texas League in total bases with 256 in 1984.
Led Texas League third basemen in putouts with 111 in 1984.
Led California League third basemen in assists with 261 in 1983.

Year Club	League	Pos.	G.	AB.	R.	H.	2B.	3B.	HR.	RBI.	B.A.	PO.	A.	E.	F.A.
1982—Pikeville	Appal.	SS-3B	58	223	29	52	13	1	2	21	.233	84	158	36	.871
1983—Stockton	Calif.	3B-SS	135	533	70	139	26	5	5	70	.261	105	281	40	.906
1984—El Paso	Texas	*3B-SS	131	523	92	*172	*41	8	9	84	.329	113	259	*30	.925
1985—Vancouver	P. C.	3B-SS	122	415	42	98	17	3	6	48	.236	81	200	26	.915
1986—Vancouver	P. C.	3B	28	105	16	31	3	2	1	23	.295	22	54	4	.950
1986—Milwaukee†	Amer.	3B-SS-2B	91	317	35	78	13	2	7	35	.246	92	179	30	.900
1987—Milwaukee	Amer.	SS-2B	153	535	86	135	27	3	25	95	.252	242	396	23	.965
1988—Milwaukee	Amer.	SS-2B	129	467	41	113	14	4	9	51	.242	209	375	*27	.956
Major League Totals—3 Years			373	1319	162	326	54	9	41	181	.247	543	950	80	.949

Selected by Milwaukee Brewers' organization in 1st round (25th player selected) of free-agent draft, June 7, 1982.
†On disabled list, July 23 to August 9, 1986.

RUSSELL HOWARD SWAN
(Russ)

Born January 3, 1964, at Fremont, Calif.
Height, 6.04. Weight, 210.
Throws and bats lefthanded.
Attended Spokane Falls Community College, Spokane, Wash., and Texas A&M University, College Station, Tex.

Year Club	League	G.	IP.	W.	L.	Pct.	H.	R.	ER.	SO.	BB.	ERA.
1986—Everett	Northwest	7	46	5	0	1.000	30	17	11	45	22	2.15
1986—Clinton	Midwest	7	43⅔	3	3	.500	36	18	15	37	8	3.09
1987—Fresno	California	12	64	6	3	.667	54	40	27	59	29	3.80
1988—San Jose	California	11	76⅔	7	0	1.000	53	28	19	62	26	2.23

Selected by Houston Astros' organization in 2nd round of free-agent draft, January 17, 1984.
Selected by Seattle Mariners' organization in secondary phase of free-agent draft, June 4, 1984.
Selected by San Francisco Giants' organization in 9th round of free-agent draft, June 2, 1986.

WILLIAM CHARLES SWIFT
(Bill)

Born December 27, 1961, at Portland, Maine.
Height, 6.00. Weight, 180.
Throws and bats righthanded.
Attended University of Maine, Orono, Maine.

Member of 1984 U.S. Olympic baseball team.

Year Club	League	G.	IP.	W.	L.	Pct.	H.	R.	ER.	SO.	BB.	ERA.
1985—Chattanooga†	Southern	7	39	2	1	.667	34	16	16	21	21	3.69
1985—Seattle	American	23	120⅔	6	10	.375	131	71	64	55	48	4.77
1986—Seattle	American	29	115⅓	2	9	.182	148	85	70	55	55	5.46
1986—Calgary	P. Coast	10	57	4	4	.500	57	33	25	29	22	3.95
1987—Calgary‡	P. Coast	5	18⅓	0	0	.000	32	22	18	5	13	8.84
1988—Seattle	American	38	174⅔	8	12	.400	199	99	89	47	65	4.59
Major League Totals—3 Years		90	410⅔	16	31	.340	478	255	223	157	168	4.89

Selected by Minnesota Twins' organization in 2nd round of free-agent draft, June 6, 1983.
Selected by Seattle Mariners' organization in 1st round (second player selected) of free-agent draft, June 4, 1984.
†On disabled list, May 6 to May 21, 1985.
‡On disabled list, April 22, 1987 through remainder of season.

—DID YOU KNOW—

That the Twins led all of baseball last year with two triple plays?

FOREST GREGORY SWINDELL
(Greg)

Born January 2, 1965, at Fort Worth, Tex.
Height, 6.03. Weight, 225.
Throws left and bats righthanded.
Attended University of Texas, Austin, Tex.

Named lefthanded pitcher on THE SPORTING NEWS College Baseball All-America Team, 1985 and 1986.

Year Club	League	G.	IP.	W.	L.	Pct.	H.	R.	ER.	SO.	BB.	ERA.
1986—Waterloo	Midwest	3	18	2	1	.667	12	2	2	25	3	1.00
1986—Cleveland	American	9	61⅔	5	2	.714	57	35	29	46	15	4.23
1987—Cleveland†	American	16	102⅓	3	8	.273	112	62	58	97	37	5.10
1988—Cleveland	American	33	242	18	14	.563	234	97	86	180	45	3.20
Major League Totals—3 Years		58	406	26	24	.520	403	194	173	323	97	3.83

Selected by Cleveland Indians' organization in 1st round (second player selected) of free-agent draft, June 2, 1986.
†On disabled list, June 30, 1987 through remainder of season.

JEFFREY JON TABAKA
(Jeff)

Born January 17, 1964, at Barberton, O.
Height, 6.00. Weight, 190.
Throws left and bats righthanded.
Attended Kent State University, Kent, O.

Year Club	League	G.	IP.	W.	L.	Pct.	H.	R.	ER.	SO.	BB.	ERA.
1986—Jamestown	NYP	13	52⅓	2	4	.333	51	31	25	57	34	4.30
1987—West Palm Beach	Florida St.	28	95	8	6	.571	90	46	44	71	58	4.17
1988—West Palm Beach†	Florida St.	16	95	7	5	.583	71	38	18	52	34	1.71

Selected by Montreal Expos' organization in 2nd round of free-agent draft, June 2, 1986.
†Drafted by Philadelphia Phillies, December 5, 1988.

PATRICK SEAN TABLER
(Pat)

Born February 2, 1958, at Hamilton, O.
Height, 6.02. Weight, 200.
Throws and bats righthanded.

Major League stolen bases: 1983 (2), 1984 (3), 1986 (3), 1987 (5), 1988 (3). Total—16.
Led Southern League in game-winning RBIs with 13 in 1980.
Led American Association third basemen in total chances with 361 in 1982.
Tied for American Association lead in sacrifice flies with 9 in 1982.

Year Club	League	Pos.	G.	AB.	R.	H.	2B.	3B.	HR.	RBI.	B.A.	PO.	A.	E.	F.A.
1976—Oneonta	NYP	3B-OF	65	238	27	55	3	0	1	20	.231	79	71	12	.926
1977—Fort Lauderdale	Fla. St.	3B	110	391	35	93	7	1	1	36	.238	87	209	*35	.894
1978—Fort Lauderdale	Fla. St.	1B-3B-OF	138	455	56	124	9	5	5	70	.273	855	88	15	.984
1979—Fort Lauderdale	Fla. St.	O-3-2-1	75	247	39	78	12	4	2	33	.316	102	41	11	.929
1979—West Haven	East.	2B-OF	56	190	33	57	15	3	6	36	.300	124	169	13	.958
1980—Nashville	South.	2B	136	479	82	142	38	8	16	83	.296	262	361	*27	.958
1981—Columbus†‡	Int.	2B-3B	52	179	41	53	14	3	11	33	.296	66	116	14	.929
1981—Iowa	A. A.	2B	63	222	41	68	13	3	6	37	.306	110	141	4	.984
1981—Chicago	Nat.	2B	35	101	11	19	3	1	1	5	.188	70	93	3	.982
1982—Iowa	A. A.	*3B-1B	129	441	89	151	32	*11	17	105	.342	*112	*215	*34	.906
1982—Chicago§x	Nat.	3B	25	85	9	20	4	2	1	7	.235	23	33	3	.949
1983—Charleston	Int.	3B	4	14	2	3	0	1	0	2	.214	2	4	3	.667
1983—Cleveland	Amer.	OF-3B-2B	124	430	56	125	23	5	6	65	.291	197	55	11	.958
1984—Cleveland	Amer.	1-O-3-2	144	473	66	137	21	3	10	68	.290	532	89	7	.989
1985—Cleveland	Amer.	1B-3B-2B	117	404	47	111	18	3	5	59	.275	744	77	14	.983
1986—Cleveland y	Amer.	1B	130	473	61	154	29	2	6	48	.326	846	84	9	.990
1986—Maine	Int.	DH	3	12	5	3	1	0	0	1	.250	0	0	0	.000
1987—Cleveland	Amer.	1B	151	553	66	170	34	3	11	86	.307	650	75	●12	.984
1988—Clev. z-K.C.	Amer.	OF-1B-3B	130	444	53	125	22	3	2	66	.282	182	10	5	.975
National League Totals—2 Years			60	186	20	39	7	3	2	12	.210	93	126	6	.973
American League Totals—6 Years			796	2777	349	822	147	19	40	392	.296	3151	390	58	.984
Major League Totals—8 Years			856	2963	369	861	154	22	42	404	.291	3244	516	64	.983

Selected by New York Yankees' organization in 1st round (16th player selected) of free-agent draft, June 8, 1976.
†Loaned to Iowa (Chicago Cubs' organization), June 12, 1981; returned, August 19, 1981.
‡Acquired on waivers by Chicago Cubs for two players to be named later, August 19, 1981; New York Yankees acquired Pitcher Bill Caudill, April 1, 1982, and New York organization acquired Pitcher Jay Howell, August 2, 1982, to complete deal.
§Traded with Pitchers Dick Tidrow and Randy Martz and Infielder Scott Fletcher to Chicago White Sox for Pitchers Steve Trout and Warren Brusstar, January 25, 1983.
xTraded to Cleveland Indians for Shortstop Jerry Dybzinski, April 1, 1983.
yOn disabled list, June 11 to June 30, 1986; included rehabilitation disability assignment to Maine, June 26 to June 30, 1986.
zTraded to Kansas City Royals for Pitcher Bud Black, June 3, 1988.

ALL-STAR GAME RECORD

Year League	Pos.	AB.	R.	H.	2B.	3B.	HR.	RBI.	B.A.	PO.	A.	E.	F.A.
1987—American	PH	1	0	0	0	0	0	0	.000	0	0	0	.000

FRANK DARYL TANANA

Name rhymes with Banana.

Born July 3, 1953, at Detroit, Mich.
Height, 6.03. Weight, 195.
Throws and bats lefthanded.
Attended California State University, Fullerton, Calif.
Son of Frank Richard Tanana, minor league outfielder, 1952 through 1956.

Tied American League record for most consecutive hits allowed, start of game (5), May 18, 1980.
Led American League in balks with 8 in 1978 and tied for lead with 4 in 1984.
Led American League in shutouts with 7 in 1977.
Led Texas League in complete games with 15 in 1973.
Named American League Rookie Pitcher of the Year by THE SPORTING NEWS, 1974.
Named lefthanded pitcher on THE SPORTING NEWS American League All-Star Team, 1976 and 1977.
Named Texas League Pitcher of the Year, 1973.

Year Club	League	G.	IP.	W.	L.	Pct.	H.	R.	ER.	SO.	BB.	ERA.
1971—Idaho Falls†	Pioneer	....	....	....	....	......	....	....	....	....	....	......
1972—Quad Cities	Midwest	19	129	7	2	.778	111	48	40	134	57	2.79
1973—El Paso	Texas	26	★206	16	6	.727	170	72	62	★197	63	2.71
1973—Salt Lake City	P. Coast	2	14	1	0	1.000	11	5	4	15	2	2.57
1973—California	American	4	26	2	2	.500	20	11	9	22	8	3.12
1974—California	American	39	269	14	19	.424	262	104	93	180	77	3.11
1975—California	American	34	257	16	9	.640	211	80	75	★269	73	2.63
1976—California	American	34	288	19	10	.655	212	88	78	261	73	2.44
1977—California	American	31	241	15	9	.625	201	72	68	205	61	★2.54
1978—California	American	33	239	18	12	.600	239	108	97	137	60	3.65
1979—California‡	American	18	90	7	5	.583	93	44	39	46	25	3.90
1980—California§	American	32	204	11	12	.478	223	107	94	113	45	4.15
1981—Boston x	American	24	141	4	10	.286	142	70	63	78	43	4.02
1982—Texas	American	30	194⅓	7	●18	.280	199	102	91	87	55	4.21
1983—Texas	American	29	159⅓	7	9	.438	144	70	56	108	49	3.16
1984—Texas	American	35	246⅓	15	15	.500	234	117	89	141	81	3.25
1985—Texas y-Detroit	American	33	215	12	14	.462	220	112	102	159	57	4.27
1986—Detroit	American	32	188⅓	12	9	.571	196	95	87	119	65	4.16
1987—Detroit z	American	34	218⅔	15	10	.600	216	106	95	146	56	3.91
1988—Detroit	American	32	203	14	11	.560	213	105	95	127	64	4.21
Major League Totals—16 Years		474	3180	188	174	.519	3025	1391	1231	2198	892	3.48

Selected by California Angels' organization in 1st round (13th player selected) of free-agent draft, June 8, 1971.
†Appeared in one game as pinch-runner (did not pitch due to a sore arm).
‡On disabled list, July 9 to September 4, 1979.
§Traded with Pitcher Jim Dorsey and Outfielder Joe Rudi to Boston Red Sox for Outfielder Fred Lynn and Pitcher Steve Renko, January 23, 1981.
xGranted free agency, November 13, 1981; signed by Texas Rangers, January 6, 1982.
yTraded to Detroit Tigers for Pitcher Duane James, June 20, 1985.
zGranted free agency, November 9, 1987.

CHAMPIONSHIP SERIES RECORD

Year Club	League	G.	IP.	W.	L.	Pct.	H.	R.	ER.	SO.	BB.	ERA.
1979—California	American	1	5	0	0	.000	6	2	2	3	2	3.60
1987—Detroit	American	1	5⅓	0	1	.000	6	4	3	1	4	5.06
Championship Series Totals—2 Years		2	10⅓	0	1	.000	12	6	5	4	6	4.35

ALL-STAR GAME RECORD

Year League	IP.	W.	L.	Pct.	H.	R.	ER.	SO.	BB.	ERA.
1976—American	2	0	0	.000	3	3	3	0	1	6.00

Named to American League All-Star Team for the 1977 game; replaced due to injury.
Named to American League All-Star Team for 1978 game; did not play.

KEVIN RAY TAPANI

Born February 18, 1964, at Des Moines, Ia.
Height, 6.00. Weight, 180.
Throws and bats righthanded.
Received degree in finance from Central Michigan University, Mt. Pleasant, Mich., in 1987.

Year Club	League	G.	IP.	W.	L.	Pct.	H.	R.	ER.	SO.	BB.	ERA.
1986—Medford	Northwest	2	8⅓	1	0	1.000	6	3	0	9	3	0.00
1986—Modesto	California	11	69	6	1	.857	74	26	19	44	22	2.48
1986—Huntsville	Southern	1	6	1	0	1.000	8	4	4	2	1	6.00
1986—Tacoma	P. Coast	1	2⅓	0	1	.000	5	6	4	1	1	15.43
1987—Modesto†	California	24	148⅓	10	7	.588	122	74	62	121	60	3.76
1988—St. Lucie	Florida St.	3	19	1	0	1.000	17	5	3	11	4	1.42
1988—Jackson	Texas	24	62⅓	5	1	.833	46	23	19	35	19	2.74

Selected by Chicago Cubs' organization in 9th round of free-agent draft, June 3, 1985.
Selected by Oakland Athletics' organization in 2nd round of free-agent draft, June 2, 1986.
†As part of an eight-player, three-team deal, New York Mets traded Pitcher Jesse Orosco to Oakland Athletics, December 11, 1987. Oakland then traded Orosco along with Shortstop Alfredo Griffin and Pitcher Jay Howell to Los Angeles Dodgers for Pitchers Bob Welch, Matt Young and Jack Savage. Oakland then traded Savage along with Pitchers Wally Whitehurst and Kevin Tapani to New York.

DANILO TARTABULL (MORA)
(Danny)

Born October 30, 1962, at Miami, Fla.
Height, 6.01. Weight, 205.
Throws and bats righthanded.
Son of Jose Tartabull, outfielder with Kansas City A's, Boston Red Sox and Oakland A's, 1962 through 1970; and minor league manager in Houston Astros' organization, 1982 through 1984.

Major League stolen bases: 1985 (1), 1986 (4), 1987 (9), 1988 (8). Total—22.
Led American League in game-winning RBIs with 21 in 1987.
Led Pacific Coast League in slugging percentage with .615 and total bases with 291 in 1985.
Led Pacific Coast League shortstops in errors with 35 in 1985.
Led Pacific Coast League shortstops in double plays with 68 in 1984.
Led Florida State League third basemen in errors with 29 in 1981.
Named Pacific Coast League Player of the Year, 1985.
Named Florida State League Most Valuable Player, 1981.

Year Club	League	Pos.	G.	AB.	R.	H.	2B.	3B.	HR.	RBI.	B.A.	PO.	A.	E.	F.A.
1980—Billings	Pion.	3B-OF-2B	59	157	33	47	10	0	2	27	.299	34	54	14	.863
1981—Tampa	Fla. St.	3B-2B	127	422	86	131	*28	10	14	81	*.310	150	248	39	.911
1982—Waterbury†	East.	2B	126	409	64	93	17	3	17	63	.227	237	306	*32	.944
1983—Chattanooga	South.	2B	128	481	95	145	32	7	13	66	.301	252	405	23	.966
1984—Salt Lake City	P. C.	SS	116	418	69	127	22	9	13	73	.304	181	333	24	.955
1984—Seattle	Amer.	SS-2B	10	20	3	6	1	0	2	7	.300	8	21	2	.935
1985—Calgary	P. C.	SS-3B	125	473	102	142	14	3	*43	*109	.300	181	399	36	.942
1985—Seattle	Amer.	SS-3B	19	61	8	20	7	1	1	7	.328	28	43	4	.947
1986—Seattle‡§	Amer.	OF-2B-3B	137	511	76	138	25	6	25	96	.270	233	111	18	.950
1987—Kansas City	Amer.	OF	158	582	95	180	27	3	34	101	.309	228	11	6	.976
1988—Kansas City	Amer.	OF	146	507	80	139	38	3	26	102	.274	227	8	9	.963
Major League Totals—5 Years			470	1681	262	483	98	13	88	313	.287	724	194	39	.959

Selected by Cincinnati Reds' organization in 3rd round of free-agent draft, June 3, 1980.
†Selected by Seattle Mariners' organization in player compensation pool draft, January 20, 1983. (Seattle received compensation for Chicago White Sox' signing of free-agent Pitcher Floyd Bannister, December 13, 1982.)
‡On disabled list, May 15 to May 30, 1986.
§Traded with Pitcher Rick Luecken to Kansas City Royals for Pitchers Scott Bankhead and Steve Shields and Outfielder Mike Kingery, December 10, 1986.

STUART DOUGLAS TATE
(Stu)

Born June 17, 1962, at Huntsville, Ala.
Height, 6.03. Weight, 205.
Throws and bats righthanded.
Attended Columbia State Community College, Columbia, Tenn.;
John C. Calhoun Community College, Decatur, Ala.,
and Auburn University, Auburn University, Ala.

Year Club	League	G.	IP.	W.	L.	Pct.	H.	R.	ER.	SO.	BB.	ERA.
1984—Everett	Northwest	10	10⅓	1	2	.333	9	7	7	15	11	6.10
1984—Clinton	Midwest	17	24⅔	1	1	.500	22	9	8	26	12	2.92
1985—Fresno	California	34	123	9	6	.600	112	73	59	118	86	4.32
1986—Shreveport	Texas	36	63⅔	5	1	.833	56	33	24	57	41	3.39
1987—Shreveport	Texas	34	83	5	5	.500	75	41	35	75	57	3.80
1988—Shreveport	Texas	24	40	3	2	.600	27	11	9	45	18	2.03
1988—Phoenix	P. Coast	27	47⅓	2	4	.333	50	38	31	45	30	5.89

Selected by San Francisco Giants' organization in 8th round of free-agent draft, June 4, 1984.

EDWARD KENNETH TAUBENSEE
(Eddie)

Born October 31, 1968, at Beeville, Tex.
Height, 6.03. Weight, 200.
Throws right and bats lefthanded.

Led Pioneer League in passed balls with 19 in 1987.
Tied for South Atlantic League lead in double plays by catchers with 7 in 1988.

Year Club	League	Pos.	G.	AB.	R.	H.	2B.	3B.	HR.	RBI.	B.A.	PO.	A.	E.	F.A.
1986—Sarasota Reds	Gulf C.	C-1B	35	107	8	21	3	0	1	11	.196	208	27	8	.967
1987—Billings	Pion.	C	55	162	24	43	7	0	5	28	.265	344	29	6	.984
1988—Greensboro	S. Atl.	C	103	330	36	85	16	1	10	41	.258	640	70	15	.979
1988—Chattanooga	South.	C	5	12	2	2	0	0	1	1	.167	17	5	1	.957

Selected by Cincinnati Reds organization in 6th round of free-agent draft, June 2, 1986.

TERRY DERRELL TAYLOR

Born July 28, 1964, at Crestview, Fla.
Height, 6.01. Weight, 180.
Throws and bats righthanded.
Son of Tommy Taylor, pitcher in Cincinnati Reds' organization, 1957 and 1958.

Led Southern League in wild pitches with 16 in 1986.
Tied for Southern League lead in hit batsmen with 16 in 1985.

Year	Club	League	G.	IP.	W.	L.	Pct.	H.	R.	ER.	SO.	BB.	ERA.
1982	—Bellingham	Northwest	14	86⅔	6	4	.600	75	53	42	61	54	4.36
1983	—Wausau	Midwest	24	130⅔	9	9	.500	131	94	79	118	79	5.44
1984	—Salinas	California	17	104⅓	7	6	.538	87	48	34	73	55	2.93
1985	—Chattanooga	Southern	28	165⅓	4	15	.211	171	*114	*97	107	96	5.28
1986	—Chattanooga	Southern	27	177	12	8	.600	164	88	79	*164	90	4.02
1987	—Calgary	P. Coast	25	138	10	3	.769	131	69	56	107	90	3.65
1988	—Calgary	P. Coast	24	134	11	9	.550	151	89	84	97	*90	5.64
1988	—Seattle	American	5	23	0	1	.000	26	17	16	9	11	6.26
Major League Totals—1 Year			5	23	0	1	.000	26	17	16	9	11	6.26

Selected by Seattle Mariners' organization in 4th round of free-agent draft, June 7, 1982.

WILFREDO ARISTIDES TEJADA (ANDUJAR)

Named pronounced Tay-HA-duh.

(Wil)

Born November 12, 1962, at Santo Domingo, D.R.
Height, 6.00, Weight, 185.
Throws and bats righthanded.
Attended Universidad Autonoma, Santo Domingo, D.R.

Tied for South Atlantic League lead in being hit by pitch with 12 in 1983.

Year	Club	League	Pos.	G.	AB.	R.	H.	2B.	3B.	HR.	RBI.	B.A.	PO.	A.	E.	F.A.
1982	—Helena	Pion.	C	26	57	4	11	3	0	0	4	.193	152	17	8	.955
1983	—Spartanburg	S. Atl.	C	90	273	33	68	14	2	2	29	.249	483	63	13	.977
1984	—Peninsula	Carol.	C	45	127	13	34	6	1	2	16	.268	262	27	11	.963
1984	—Reading	East.	C	28	72	7	24	7	0	0	15	.333	107	22	9	.935
1985	—Reading†	East.	C-1B	69	210	24	57	7	0	3	25	.271	295	30	4	.988
1986	—Jacksonville	South.	C	107	382	49	103	11	5	13	46	.270	576	65	*19	.971
1986	—Montreal	Nat.	C	10	25	1	6	1	0	0	2	.240	40	8	0	1.000
1987	—Indianapolis	A. A.	C	91	299	28	74	10	1	3	29	.247	568	53	●12	.981
1988	—Indianapolis	A. A.	C	59	172	16	40	11	1	1	19	.233	339	37	3	.992
1988	—Montreal‡	Nat.	C	8	15	1	4	2	0	0	2	.267	37	1	0	1.000
Major League Totals—2 Years				18	40	2	10	3	0	0	4	.250	77	9	0	1.000

Signed as free agent by Philadelphia Phillies' organization, June 10, 1982.
†Drafted by Indianapolis (Montreal Expos' organization), December 11, 1985.
‡Traded to San Francisco Giants for Shortstop Angel Escobar, November 20, 1988.

KENTON CHARLES TEKULVE

Name pronounced Tuh-KULL-vee.

(Kent)

Born March 5, 1947, at Cincinnati, O.
Height, 6.04. Weight, 190.
Throws and bats righthanded.
Received bachelor of science degree in physical education
from Marietta College, Marietta, O.

Tied major league records for most intentional bases on balls allowed, season (23), 1982; most consecutive games won by relief pitcher, three consecutive games (3), May 6, 7, 9, 1980.

Established National League records for most games pitched, lifetime (1,013); most games finished lifetime (618); most innings by relief pitcher, lifetime (1,384⅓).

Major League saves: 1975 (5), 1976 (9), 1977 (7), 1978 (31), 1979 (31), 1980 (21), 1981 (3), 1982 (20), 1983 (18), 1984 (13), 1985 (14), 1986 (4), 1987 (3), 1988 (4). Total—183.

Led National League in intentional bases on balls issued with 20 in 1979, 23 in 1982 and tied for lead with 16 in 1980.

Led National League in games finished in relief with 65 in 1978, 67 in 1979 and tied for lead with 56 in 1983.

Year	Club	League	G.	IP.	W.	L.	Pct.	H.	R.	ER.	SO.	BB.	ERA.
1969	—Geneva	NYP	9	53	6	2	.750	40	15	10	60	22	1.70
1970	—Salem	Carolina	41	79	4	6	.400	68	29	17	75	51	1.94
1971	—Salem	Carolina	47	75	11	5	.688	77	36	29	62	31	3.48
1971	—Waterbury	Eastern	2	3	0	0	.000	3	0	0	0	2	0.00
1972	—Sherbrooke	Eastern	31	72	7	6	.538	61	24	21	54	22	2.63
1972	—Charleston	Int'national	9	22	2	1	.667	22	10	10	9	10	4.09
1973	—Sherbrooke	Eastern	*57	94	●12	4	*.750	70	24	16	89	35	1.53
1974	—Charleston	Int'national	35	60	6	3	.667	50	20	15	38	21	2.25
1974	—Pittsburgh	National	8	9	1	1	.500	12	6	6	6	5	6.00
1975	—Charleston	Int'national	24	71	5	4	.556	47	23	14	46	19	1.77
1975	—Pittsburgh	National	34	56	1	2	.333	43	20	14	28	23	2.25
1976	—Pittsburgh	National	64	103	5	3	.625	91	30	28	68	25	2.45
1977	—Pittsburgh	National	72	103	10	1	.909	89	41	35	59	33	3.06
1978	—Pittsburgh	National	*91	135	8	7	.533	115	44	35	77	55	2.33
1979	—Pittsburgh†	National	*94	134	10	8	.556	109	46	41	75	49	2.75
1980	—Pittsburgh	National	78	93	8	12	.400	96	39	35	47	40	3.39
1981	—Pittsburgh	National	45	65	5	5	.500	61	19	18	34	17	2.49
1982	—Pittsburgh	National	*85	128⅔	12	8	.600	113	47	41	66	46	2.87
1983	—Pittsburgh‡	National	76	99	7	5	.583	78	27	18	52	36	1.64
1984	—Pittsburgh	National	72	88	3	9	.250	86	30	26	36	33	2.66
1985	—Pittsburgh §-Philadelphia	National	61	75⅔	4	10	.286	74	35	30	40	30	3.57
1986	—Philadelphia	National	73	110	11	5	.688	99	35	31	57	25	2.54
1987	—Philadelphia	National	*90	105	6	4	.600	96	38	36	60	29	3.09

Year	Club	League	G.	IP.	W.	L.	Pct.	H.	R.	ER.	SO.	BB.	ERA.
1988—Philadelphia xy		National	70	80	3	7	.300	87	34	32	43	22	3.60
Major League Totals—15 Years			1013	1384⅓	94	87	.519	1249	491	426	748	468	2.77

Signed as free agent by Pittsburgh Pirates' organization, July 16, 1969.
†Appeared in one game as an outfielder with one putout.
‡Granted free agency, November 7, 1983; re-signed by Pirates, December 22, 1983.
§Traded to Philadelphia Phillies for Pitchers Al Holland and Frankie Griffin, April 20, 1985.
xOn disabled list, June 11 to June 30, 1988.
yReleased, December 7, 1988.

CHAMPIONSHIP SERIES RECORD

Year	Club	League	G.	IP.	W.	L.	Pct.	H.	R.	ER.	SO.	BB.	ERA.
1975—Pittsburgh		National	2	1⅓	0	0	.000	3	1	1	2	1	6.75
1979—Pittsburgh		National	2	2⅔	0	0	.000	2	1	1	2	2	3.38
Championship Series Totals—2 Years			4	4	0	0	.000	5	2	2	4	3	4.50

WORLD SERIES RECORD

Established World Series record for most saves, seven-game Series (3), 1979.

Year	Club	League	G.	IP.	W.	L.	Pct.	H.	R.	ER.	SO.	BB.	ERA.
1979—Pittsburgh		National	5	9⅓	0	1	.000	4	3	3	10	3	2.89

ALL-STAR GAME RECORD

Member of National League All-Star Team in 1980; did not play.

GARRY LEWIS TEMPLETON

Born March 24, 1956, at Lockney, Tex.
Height, 5.11. Weight, 190.
Throws right and bats left and righthanded.
Brother of Ken Templeton, outfielder in Oakland A's organization, 1972 through 1974; son of Spiavia Templeton, former infielder in the Negro Leagues.

Tied major league records by collecting 100 or more hits righthanded and lefthanded, season, 1979; most consecutive seasons leading league, three-base hits (3), 1977 through 1979; most intentional bases on balls, game (4), July 5, 1985 (12 innings).

Tied modern major league record for most three-base hits by switch hitter, season, (19), 1979; most intentional bases on balls, game (4), July 5, 1985 (12 innings).

Major League stolen bases: 1976 (11), 1977 (28), 1978 (34), 1979 (26), 1980 (31), 1981 (8), 1982 (27), 1983 (16), 1984 (8), 1985 (16), 1986 (10), 1987 (14), 1988 (8). Total—237.

Led National League in intentional bases on balls received with 23 in 1984 and tied for lead with 24 in 1985.
Led National League shortstops in total chances with 848 in 1978 and 851 in 1979.
Led National League shortstops in double plays with 108 in 1978.
Tied for National League lead in caught stealing with 24 in 1977.
Tied for National League lead in double plays by shortstops with 102 in 1979.
Named shortstop on THE SPORTING NEWS National League All-Star Team, 1977, 1979 and 1980.
Named shortstop on THE SPORTING NEWS National League Silver Slugger team, 1980 and 1984.
Received reported $40,000 bonus to sign with St. Louis Cardinals, 1974.

Year	Club	League	Pos.	G.	AB.	R.	H.	2B.	3B.	HR.	RBI.	B.A.	PO.	A.	E.	F.A.
1974—Sarasota Cards		Gulf C.	SS	18	71	11	19	1	0	3	10	.268	15	41	3	.949
1974—St. Petersburg		Fla. St.	SS	23	95	3	20	1	0	0	2	.211	42	64	7	.938
1975—St. Petersburg		Fla. St.	SS	82	349	50	92	7	8	1	32	.264	130	253	29	.930
1975—Arkansas		Texas	SS	42	177	36	71	9	4	2	20	.401	60	131	18	.914
1976—Tulsa		A. A.	*S-3-O	106	443	65	142	24	*15	6	38	.321	*178	319	34	.936
1976—St. Louis		Nat.	SS	53	213	32	62	8	2	1	17	.291	111	172	24	.922
1977—St. Louis		Nat.	SS	153	621	94	200	19	*18	8	79	.322	285	453	32	.958
1978—St. Louis		Nat.	SS	155	647	82	181	31	*13	2	47	.280	*285	523	*40	.953
1979—St. Louis		Nat.	SS	154	672	105	*211	32	*19	9	62	.314	*292	525	*34	.960
1980—St. Louis†		Nat.	SS	118	504	83	161	19	9	4	43	.319	223	451	*29	.959
1981—St. Louis‡§		Nat.	SS	80	333	47	96	16	8	1	33	.288	160	272	18	.960
1982—San Diego		Nat.	SS	141	563	76	139	25	8	6	64	.247	220	422	26	.961
1983—San Diego x		Nat.	SS	126	460	39	121	20	2	3	40	.263	219	355	24	.960
1984—San Diego		Nat.	SS	148	493	40	127	19	3	2	35	.258	225	407	26	.960
1985—San Diego		Nat.	SS	148	546	63	154	30	2	6	55	.282	245	460	23	.968
1986—San Diego		Nat.	SS	147	510	42	126	21	2	2	44	.247	207	358	20	.966
1987—San Diego		Nat.	SS	148	510	42	113	13	5	5	48	.222	*253	447	20	.972
1988—San Diego y		Nat.	SS-3B	110	362	35	90	15	7	3	36	.249	170	316	16	.968
Major League Totals—13 Years				1681	6434	780	1781	268	98	52	603	.277	2895	5161	332	.960

Selected by St. Louis Cardinals' organization in 1st round (13th player selected) of free-agent draft, June 5, 1974.
†On disabled list, July 24 to August 14 and August 24 to September 8, 1980.
‡On suspended list, August 26, 1981; then transferred to disabled list, August 28 to September 14, 1981.
§Traded to San Diego Padres for Shortstop Ozzie Smith, February 11, 1982.
xOn disabled list, April 28 to May 17, 1983.
yGranted free agency, November 4, 1988; re-signed by Padres, December 6, 1988.

CHAMPIONSHIP SERIES RECORD

Year	Club	League	Pos.	G.	AB.	R.	H.	2B.	3B.	HR.	RBI.	B.A.	PO.	A.	E.	F.A.
1984—San Diego		Nat.	SS	5	15	2	5	1	0	0	2	.333	19	11	1	.968

WORLD SERIES RECORD

Year	Club	League	Pos.	G.	AB.	R.	H.	2B.	3B.	HR.	RBI.	B.A.	PO.	A.	E.	F.A.
1984—San Diego		Nat.	SS	5	19	1	6	1	0	0	0	.316	8	11	0	1.000

ALL-STAR GAME RECORD

Year League	Pos.	AB.	R.	H.	2B.	3B.	HR.	RBI.	B.A.	PO.	A.	E.	F.A.
1977—National	SS	1	1	1	1	0	0	0	1.000	1	2	1	.750
1985—National	PH	1	0	1	0	0	0	0	1.000	0	0	0	.000
All-Star Game Totals—2 Years		2	1	2	1	0	0	0	1.000	1	2	1	.750

Named to National League All-Star Team for 1979 game; declined.

CHARLES WALTER TERRELL

Name pronounced TEAR-el.

(Walt)

Born May 11, 1958, at Jeffersonville, Ind.
Height, 6.02. Weight, 205.
Throws right and bats lefthanded.
Received degree from Morehead State University, Morehead, Ky. in 1980.

Tied for International League lead in intentional bases on balls issued with 9 in 1982.
Named International League Pitcher of the Year, 1983.

Year Club	League	G.	IP.	W.	L.	Pct.	H.	R.	ER.	SO.	BB.	ERA.
1980—Sarasota Rangers	Gulf Coast	7	38	3	2	.600	20	11	6	23	12	1.42
1980—Asheville	S. Atlantic	3	8	1	1	.500	11	9	6	5	8	6.75
1981—Tulsa†	Texas	27	174	•15	7	.682	158	74	60	123	63	3.10
1982—Tidewater‡	Int'national	21	138⅔	7	8	.467	130	69	61	74	72	3.96
1982—New York	National	3	21	0	3	.000	22	12	8	8	14	3.43
1983—Tidewater	Int'national	12	86⅔	10	1	★.909	76	34	30	58	44	3.12
1983—New York	National	21	133⅔	8	8	.500	123	57	53	59	55	3.57
1984—New York§	National	33	215	11	12	.478	232	99	84	114	80	3.52
1985—Detroit	American	34	229	15	10	.600	221	107	98	130	95	3.85
1986—Detroit	American	34	217⅓	15	12	.556	199	116	110	93	98	4.56
1987—Detroit	American	35	244⅔	17	10	.630	254	123	110	143	94	4.05
1988—Lakeland x	Florida St.	2	9⅔	1	1	.500	13	7	7	6	1	6.52
1988—Detroit y	American	29	206⅓	7	16	.304	199	101	91	84	78	3.97
National League Totals—3 Years		57	369⅔	19	23	.452	377	168	145	181	149	3.53
American League Totals—4 Years		132	897⅓	54	48	.529	873	447	409	450	365	4.10
Major League Totals—7 Years		189	1267	73	71	.507	1250	615	554	631	514	3.94

Selected by New York Mets' organization in 15th round of free-agent draft, June 5, 1979.
Selected by Texas Rangers' organization in 33rd round of free-agent draft, June 3, 1980.
†Traded with Pitcher Ron Darling to New York Mets' organization for Outfielder Lee Mazzilli, April 1, 1982.
‡On disabled list, July 19 to August 2, 1982.
§Traded to Detroit Tigers for Third Baseman Howard Johnson, December 7, 1984.
xOn Detroit disabled list, April 1 to April 30, 1988; included rehabilitation disability assignment to Lakeland, April 16 to April 26, 1988.
yTraded to San Diego Padres for Infielders Chris Brown and Keith Moreland, October 28, 1988.

CHAMPIONSHIP SERIES RECORD

Year Club	League	G.	IP.	W.	L.	Pct.	H.	R.	ER.	SO.	BB.	ERA.
1987—Detroit	American	1	6	0	0	.000	7	6	6	4	4	9.00

SCOTT RAY TERRY

Born November 21, 1959, at Hobbs, N.M.
Height, 5.11. Weight, 195.
Throws and bats righthanded.
Received degree from Southwestern University, Georgetown, Tex., in 1982.

Major League saves: 1988 (3).
Led American Association in complete games with 10 in 1987.
Led Eastern League in shutouts with 6 in 1984.
Tied for American Association lead in games started by pitchers with 28 and wild pitches with 14 in 1985.

Year Club	League	G.	IP.	W.	L.	Pct.	H.	R.	ER.	SO.	BB.	ERA.
1983—Tampa	Florida St.	30	59⅓	3	3	.500	60	34	28	52	30	4.25
1984—Vermont	Eastern	20	144	14	3	★.824	110	31	24	100	43	★1.50
1984—Wichita†	Am. Assoc.	2	9⅓	0	0	.000	13	6	6	6	7	5.79
1985—Denver	Am. Assoc.	28	178⅔	11	12	.478	★203	★105	★88	101	76	4.43
1986—Denver	Am. Assoc.	10	19⅓	1	2	.333	22	13	5	13	8	2.33
1986—Cincinnati	National	28	55⅔	1	2	.333	66	40	38	32	32	6.14
1987—Nashville‡	Am. Assoc.	27	★181⅔	11	10	.524	199	94	80	91	48	3.96
1987—St. Louis	National	11	13⅓	0	0	.000	13	5	5	9	8	3.38
1988—St. Louis §	National	51	129⅓	9	6	.600	119	48	42	65	34	2.92
1988—Louisville	Am. Assoc.	3	5	0	0	.000	2	0	0	1	1	0.00
Major League Totals—3 Years		90	198⅓	10	8	.556	198	93	85	106	74	3.86

Selected by Cincinnati Reds' organization in 12th round of free-agent draft, June 3, 1980.
†On disabled list, August 8 to September 18, 1984.
‡Traded to St. Louis Cardinals, September 3, 1987, completing deal in which St. Louis traded Pitcher Pat Perry to Cincinnati Reds for a player to be named later, August 31, 1987.
§On disabled list, June 27 to July 24, 1988; included rehabilitation disability assignment to Louisville, July 18 to July 24, 1988.

RECORD AS OUTFIELDER

Year	Club	League	Pos.	G.	AB.	R.	H.	2B.	3B.	HR.	RBI.	B.A.	PO.	A.	E.	F.A.
1980	—Billings	Pion.	OF	67	251	39	65	9	3	4	45	.259	104	•10	5	.958
1981	—Cedar Rapids	Midw.	OF	113	351	32	68	9	0	5	31	.194	147	5	5	.968
1982	—Cedar Rapids	Midw.	OF	108	335	50	85	16	3	12	54	.254	156	10	8	.954
1983	—Tampa	Fla. St.	OF-P	66	105	14	25	6	2	0	12	.238	60	16	3	.962

MICKEY LEE TETTLETON

Born September 16, 1960, at Oklahoma City, Okla.
Height, 6.02. Weight, 214.
Throws right and bats left and righthanded.
Attended Oklahoma State University, Stillwater, Okla.

Major League stolen bases: 1985 (2), 1986 (7), 1987 (1). Total—10.
Switch-hit home runs in one game, June 13, 1988.
Tied for Eastern League lead in intentional bases on balls received with 8 in 1984.

Year	Club	League	Pos.	G.	AB.	R.	H.	2B.	3B.	HR.	RBI.	B.A.	PO.	A.	E.	F.A.
1981	—Modesto	Calif.	C-OF-1B	48	138	28	34	3	0	5	19	.246	235	31	14	.950
1982	—Modesto†	Calif.	C-OF	88	253	44	63	18	0	8	37	.249	424	36	8	.983
1983	—Modesto	Calif.	C-OF	124	378	55	92	18	2	7	62	.243	582	46	11	.983
1984	—Albany	East.	*C-O-1-3-S	86	281	32	65	18	0	5	47	.231	368	42	3	*.993
1984	—Oakland	Amer.	C	33	76	10	20	2	1	1	5	.263	112	10	1	.992
1985	—Oakland‡	Amer.	C	78	211	23	53	12	0	3	15	.251	344	24	4	.989
1985	—Modesto	Calif.	C	4	14	1	3	3	0	0	2	.214	20	1	0	1.000
1986	—Oakland§	Amer.	C	90	211	26	43	9	0	10	35	.204	463	32	8	.984
1986	—Modesto	Calif.	C	15	42	14	10	1	0	2	8	.238	40	3	2	.956
1987	—Oakland x	Amer.	C-1B	82	211	19	41	3	0	8	26	.194	435	29	6	.987
1987	—Modesto y	Calif.	C	3	11	4	4	1	0	2	2	.364	5	0	0	1.000
1988	—Rochester	Int.	C-OF	19	41	9	10	3	1	1	4	.244	71	7	3	.963
1988	—Baltimore	Amer.	C	86	283	31	74	11	1	11	37	.261	361	31	3	.992
Major League Totals—5 Years				369	992	109	231	37	2	33	118	.233	1715	126	22	.988

Selected by Oakland A's organization in 5th round of free-agent draft, June 8, 1981.
†On disabled list, July 16 to August 13, 1982.
‡On disabled list, August 4 to August 25, 1985; included rehabilitation disability assignment to Modesto, August 21 to August 25, 1985.
§On disabled list, May 9 to June 16, 1986; included rehabilitation disability assignment to Modesto, May 23 to June 13, 1986.
xOn disabled list, July 22 to August 6, 1987; included rehabilitation disability assignment to Modesto, August 2 to August 6, 1987.
yReleased, March 28, 1988; signed by Rochester (Baltimore Orioles' organization), April 5, 1988.

TIMOTHY SHAWN TEUFEL

Name pronounced TUFF-el.

(Tim)

Born July 7, 1958, at Greenwich, Conn.
Height, 6.00. Weight, 175.
Throws and bats righthanded.
Attended St. Petersburg Junior College, St. Petersburg, Fla., and Clemson University, Clemson, S. C.

Established American League record for fewest double plays by second baseman, season, 150 or more games (81), 1984.
Major League stolen bases: 1984 (1), 1985 (4), 1986 (1), 1987 (3). Total—9.
Led International League second basemen in putouts with 304, assists with 394, total chances with 711 and double plays with 109 in 1983.
Named International League Player of the Year, 1983.
Named second baseman on THE SPORTING NEWS College Baseball All-America Team, 1980.

Year	Club	League	Pos.	G.	AB.	R.	H.	2B.	3B.	HR.	RBI.	B.A.	PO.	A.	E.	F.A.
1980	—Orlando	South.	2B	86	287	38	76	15	3	11	47	.265	196	246	17	.963
1981	—Orlando	South.	2B	128	416	69	103	21	5	17	60	.248	312	376	20	.972
1982	—Orlando	South.	2B	100	340	52	96	12	4	9	56	.282	231	185	15	.965
1982	—Toledo	Int.	2B	45	149	25	42	10	4	6	20	.282	99	139	3	.988
1983	—Toledo	Int.	2B-SS	136	471	103	152	27	6	27	100	.323	306	401	14	.981
1983	—Minnesota	Amer.	2B-SS	21	78	11	24	7	1	3	6	.308	47	58	1	.991
1984	—Minnesota	Amer.	2B	157	568	76	149	30	3	14	61	.262	315	*485	13	.984
1985	—Minnesota†	Amer.	2B	138	434	58	113	24	3	10	50	.260	237	352	12	.980
1986	—New York	Nat.	2B-1B-3B	93	279	35	69	20	1	4	31	.247	143	174	9	.972
1987	—New York‡	Nat.	2B-1B	97	299	55	92	29	0	14	61	.308	139	214	11	.970
1988	—New York §	Nat.	2B-1B	90	273	35	64	20	0	4	31	.234	175	213	7	.982
American League Totals—3 Years				316	1080	145	286	61	7	27	117	.265	599	895	26	.983
National League Totals—3 Years				280	851	125	225	69	1	22	123	.264	457	601	27	.975
Major League Totals—6 Years				596	1931	270	511	130	8	49	240	.265	1056	1496	53	.980

Selected by Milwaukee Brewers' organization in 16th round of free-agent draft, June 6, 1978.
Selected by Chicago White Sox' organization in secondary phase of free-agent draft, June 5, 1979.
Selected by Minnesota Twins' organization in 2nd round of free-agent draft, June 3, 1980.
†Traded with Outfielder Pat Crosby to New York Mets for Outfielder Billy Beane and Pitchers Bill Latham and Joe Klink, January 16, 1986.
‡On disabled list, June 16 to July 1, 1987.
§On disabled list, May 17 to June 11, 1988.

CHAMPIONSHIP SERIES RECORD

Year	Club	League	Pos.	G.	AB.	R.	H.	2B.	3B.	HR.	RBI.	B.A.	PO.	A.	E.	F.A.
1986	—New York	Nat.	2B	2	6	0	1	0	0	0	0	.167	2	8	0	1.000
1988	—New York	Nat.	2B	1	3	0	0	0	0	0	0	.000	1	3	0	1.000
Championship Series Totals—2 Years				3	9	0	1	0	0	0	0	.111	3	11	0	1.000

WORLD SERIES RECORD

Year	Club	League	Pos.	G.	AB.	R.	H.	2B.	3B.	HR.	RBI.	B.A.	PO.	A.	E.	F.A.
1986	—New York	Nat.	2B	3	9	1	4	1	0	1	1	.444	3	3	1	.857

ROBERT ALAN TEWKSBURY
(Bob)

Born November 30, 1960, at Concord, N. H.
Height, 6.04. Weight, 200.
Throws and bats righthanded.
Attended Rutgers University, New Brunswick, N.J., and St. Leo College, St. Leo, Fla.

Led Florida State League in shutouts with 5 and tied for lead in complete games with 13 in 1982.

Year	Club	League	G.	IP.	W.	L.	Pct.	H.	R.	ER.	SO.	BB.	ERA.
1981	—Oneonta	NYP	14	85	7	3	.700	85	43	34	62	37	3.40
1982	—Fort Lauderdale	Florida St.	24	182⅓	*15	4	.789	146	46	38	92	47	*1.88
1983	—Fort Lauderdale†	Florida St.	2	16	2	0	1.000	6	1	0	5	1	0.00
1983	—Nashville	Southern	7	51	5	1	.833	49	20	16	15	10	2.82
1984	—Nashville‡	Southern	26	172	11	9	.550	185	69	54	78	42	2.83
1985	—Albany§	Eastern	17	106⅔	6	5	.545	101	48	42	63	19	3.54
1985	—Columbus	Int'national	6	44	3	0	1.000	27	5	5	21	5	1.02
1986	—New York	American	23	130⅓	9	5	.643	144	58	48	49	31	3.31
1986	—Columbus	Int'national	2	10	1	0	1.000	6	3	3	4	2	2.70
1987	—New York x	American	8	33⅓	1	4	.200	47	26	25	12	7	6.75
1987	—Columbus	Int'national	11	74⅔	6	1	.857	68	23	21	32	11	2.53
1987	—Chicago y	National	7	18	0	4	.000	32	15	13	10	13	6.50
1988	—Iowa	Am. Assoc.	10	67	4	2	.667	73	28	28	43	10	3.76
1988	—Chicago za	National	1	3⅓	0	0	.000	6	5	3	1	2	8.10
American League Totals—2 Years			31	163⅔	10	9	.526	191	84	73	61	38	4.01
National League Totals—2 Years			8	21⅓	0	4	.000	38	20	16	11	15	6.75
Major League Totals—3 Years			39	185	10	13	.435	229	104	89	72	53	4.33

Selected by New York Yankees' organization in 19th round of free-agent draft, June 8, 1981.
†On disabled list, April 8 to June 7, 1983.
‡On disabled list, April 9 to April 27, 1984.
§On disabled list, June 10 to June 25, 1985.
xTraded with Pitchers Rich Scheid and Dean Wilkins to Chicago Cubs for Pitcher Steve Trout, July 13, 1987.
yOn disabled list, August 13, 1987 through remainder of season.
zOn disabled list, May 22 to June 12, 1988.
aGranted free agency, October 15, 1988.

ROBERT THOMAS THIGPEN
(Bobby)

Born July 17, 1963, at Tallahassee, Fla.
Height, 6.03. Weight, 195.
Throws and bats righthanded.
Attended Seminole Community College, Sanford, Fla., and
Mississippi State University, Starkville, Miss.

Major League saves: 1986 (7), 1987 (16), 1988 (34). Total—57.
Led American League in games finished in relief with 59 in 1988.
Led Southern League in hit batsmen with 11 in 1986.

Year	Club	League	G.	IP.	W.	L.	Pct.	H.	R.	ER.	SO.	BB.	ERA.
1985	—Niagara Falls	NYP	28	52⅓	2	3	.400	30	12	10	74	19	1.72
1985	—Appleton	Midwest	1	2⅔	1	0	1.000	1	0	0	4	1	0.00
1986	—Birmingham	Southern	25	159⅔	8	11	.421	182	97	83	90	54	4.68
1986	—Chicago	American	20	35⅔	2	0	1.000	26	7	7	20	12	1.77
1987	—Chicago	American	51	89	7	5	.583	86	30	27	52	24	2.73
1987	—Hawaii	P. Coast	9	52⅔	2	3	.400	72	38	36	17	14	6.15
1988	—Chicago	American	68	90	5	8	.385	96	38	33	62	33	3.30
Major League Totals—3 Years			139	214⅔	14	13	.519	208	75	67	134	69	2.81

Selected by Milwaukee Brewers' organization in 7th round of free-agent draft, January 11, 1983.
Selected by Chicago White Sox' organization in 4th round of free-agent draft, June 3, 1985.

ANDRES PERES THOMAS

Born November 10, 1963, at Santo Domingo, Dominican Republic.
Height, 6.01. Weight, 185.
Throws and bats righthanded.

Major League stolen bases: 1986 (4), 1987 (6), 1988 (7). Total—17.
Led National League shortstops in double plays with 90 in 1988.

Year	Club	League	Pos.	G.	AB.	R.	H.	2B.	3B.	HR.	RBI.	B.A.	PO.	A.	E.	F.A.
1982	—Bradenton Brav.	Gulf C.	SS	44	143	18	37	2	1	1	14	.259	61	136	20	.908
1983	—Anderson	S. Atl.	SS	61	251	33	79	8	4	1	20	.315	61	197	24	.915

Year	Club	League	Pos.	G.	AB.	R.	H.	2B.	3B.	HR.	RBI.	B.A.	PO.	A.	E.	F.A.
1983	—Durham	Carol.	SS	70	290	17	72	14	0	2	41	.248	107	222	32	.911
1984	—Durham†	Carol.	SS	114	460	64	121	18	4	7	44	.263	156	361	34	.938
1985	—Greenville	South.	SS-OF	114	458	53	114	18	4	9	59	.249	155	339	31	.941
1985	—Richmond	Int.	SS	11	28	3	5	0	0	1	6	.179	15	30	3	.938
1985	—Atlanta	Nat.	SS	15	18	6	5	0	0	0	2	.278	6	17	2	.920
1986	—Atlanta	Nat.	SS	102	323	26	81	17	2	6	32	.251	143	290	19	.958
1987	—Atlanta‡	Nat.	SS	82	324	29	75	11	0	5	39	.231	128	276	20	.953
1988	—Atlanta	Nat.	SS	153	606	54	153	22	2	13	68	.252	230	456	•29	.959
Major League Totals—4 Years				352	1271	115	314	50	4	24	141	.247	507	1039	70	.957

Signed as free agent by Atlanta Braves' organization, December 16, 1981.
†On suspended list, August 28, 1984 through remainder of season.
‡On disabled list, April 20 to May 13 and August 10, 1987 through remainder of season.

MILTON BERNARD THOMPSON
(Milt)

Born January 5, 1959, at Washington, D.C.
Height, 5.11. Weight, 170.
Throws right and bats lefthanded.
Attended Howard University, Washington, D.C.

Major League stolen bases: 1984 (14), 1985 (9), 1986 (19), 1987 (46), 1988 (17). Total—105.
Led International League outfielders in total chances with 341 in 1984.
Led Southern League in stolen bases with 68 and caught stealing with 19 in 1982.
Led Southern League outfielders in total chances with 336 in 1982.

Year	Club	League	Pos.	G.	AB.	R.	H.	2B.	3B.	HR.	RBI.	B.A.	PO.	A.	E.	F.A.
1979	—Greenwood	W. Car.	OF	53	145	31	27	4	1	2	16	.186	85	8	3	.969
1979	—Kingsport	Appal.	OF	26	94	22	31	8	4	1	11	.330	58	4	1	.984
1980	—Durham	Carol.	OF	68	255	49	74	12	3	2	36	.290	159	8	5	.971
1980	—Savannah	South.	OF	71	278	35	83	7	3	1	15	.299	133	11	6	.960
1981	—Savannah	South.	OF	140	493	92	135	18	2	4	31	.274	226	17	8	.968
1982	—Savannah	South.	OF	•144	526	83	132	20	7	6	45	.251	*312	10	14	.958
1982	—Richmond	Int.	OF	3	6	2	1	0	0	0	0	.167	4	0	0	1.000
1983	—Richmond	Int.	OF	12	32	12	8	1	0	0	3	.250	30	0	1	.968
1983	—Savannah	South.	OF-1B	115	386	84	117	21	4	5	36	.303	295	15	7	.978
1984	—Richmond	Int.	OF	134	503	•91	145	11	3	4	40	.288	*317	13	11	.968
1984	—Atlanta	Nat.	OF	25	99	16	30	1	0	2	4	.303	37	6	2	.956
1985	—Richmond	Int.	OF	82	312	52	98	10	1	2	22	.314	209	3	4	.981
1985	—Atlanta†	Nat.	OF	73	182	17	55	7	2	0	6	.302	78	2	3	.964
1986	—Philadelphia	Nat.	OF	96	299	38	75	7	1	6	23	.251	212	1	2	.991
1986	—Portland	P. C.	OF	41	161	26	56	10	2	1	16	.348	101	1	1	.990
1987	—Philadelphia	Nat.	OF	150	527	86	159	26	9	7	43	.302	354	4	4	.989
1988	—Philadelphia‡	Nat.	OF	122	378	53	109	16	2	2	33	.288	278	5	5	.983
Major League Totals—5 Years				466	1485	210	428	57	14	17	109	.288	959	18	16	.984

Selected by Atlanta Braves' organization in 2nd round of free-agent draft, January 9, 1979.
†Traded with Pitcher Steve Bedrosian to Philadelphia Phillies for Catcher Ozzie Virgil and Pitcher Pete Smith, December 10, 1985.
‡Traded to St. Louis Cardinals for Catcher Steve Lake and Outfielder Curt Ford, December 16, 1988.

ROBERT RANDALL THOMPSON
(Rob)

Born May 10, 1962, at West Palm Beach, Fla.
Height, 5.11. Weight, 170.
Throws and bats righthanded.
Attended Palm Beach Junior College, Lake Worth, Fla.,
and University of Florida, Gainesville, Fla.

Major League stolen bases: 1986 (12), 1987 (16), 1988 (14). Total—42.
Established major league record for most times caught stealing, game (4), June 27, 1986, 12 innings.
Led National League in sacrifice hits with 18 in 1986.
Named National League Rookie Player of the Year by THE SPORTING NEWS, 1986.
Led Texas League second basemen in putouts with 291, total chances with 664 and double plays with 91 in 1985.

Year	Club	League	Pos.	G.	AB.	R.	H.	2B.	3B.	HR.	RBI.	B.A.	PO.	A.	E.	F.A.
1983	—Fresno	Calif.	2B	64	220	33	57	8	1	4	23	.259	118	185	11	.965
1984	—Fresno	Calif.	2B-SS-3B	102	325	53	81	11	0	8	43	.249	182	280	24	.951
1985	—Shreveport	Texas	*2B-SS	121	449	85	117	20	7	9	40	.261	292	366	12	*.982
1986	—San Francisco	Nat.	2B-SS	149	549	73	149	27	3	7	47	.271	255	451	17	.976
1987	—San Francisco†	Nat.	2B	132	420	62	110	26	5	10	44	.262	246	341	17	.972
1988	—San Francisco	Nat.	2B	138	477	66	126	24	6	7	48	.264	255	365	14	.978
Major League Totals—3 Years				419	1446	201	385	77	14	24	139	.266	756	1157	48	.976

Selected by Oakland A's organization in 2nd round of free-agent draft, January 12, 1982.
Selected by Seattle Mariners' organization in secondary phase of free-agent draft, June 7, 1982.
Selected by San Francisco Giants' organization in secondary phase of free-agent draft, June 6, 1983.
†On disabled list, April 28 to May 13, 1987.

CHAMPIONSHIP SERIES RECORD

Year	Club	League	Pos.	G.	AB.	R.	H.	2B.	3B.	HR.	RBI.	B.A.	PO.	A.	E.	F.A.
1987	—San Francisco	Nat.	2B-PH	7	20	4	2	0	1	1	2	.100	11	19	1	.968

ALL-STAR GAME RECORD

Named to National League All-Star Team for 1988 game; replaced due to injury by Bob Walk.

RICHARD WILLIAM THON
(Dickie)

Born June 20, 1958, at South Bend, Ind.
Height, 5.11. Weight, 175.
Throws and bats righthanded.
Grandson of Fred Thon, minor league pitcher, 1940.

Tied National League record for fewest triples, season, for league leader in triples (10), 1982.
Major League stolen bases: 1980 (7), 1981 (6), 1982 (37), 1983 (34), 1985 (8), 1986 (6), 1987 (3), 1988 (19). Total—120.
Led National League in game-winning RBIs with 18 in 1983.
Named shortstop on THE SPORTING NEWS National League All-Star Team, 1983.
Named shortstop on THE SPORTING NEWS National League Silver Slugger team, 1983.

Year Club	League	Pos.	G.	AB.	R.	H.	2B.	3B.	HR.	RBI.	B.A.	PO.	A.	E.	F.A.
1976—Quad Cities	Midw.	SS	69	246	46	68	11	4	1	32	.276	96	193	32	.900
1977—Salinas	Calif.	SS	56	225	48	71	13	2	4	44	.316	95	162	13	.952
1977—Salt Lake City	P. C.	SS	77	274	47	79	9	3	8	43	.288	129	242	26	.935
1978—Salt Lake City	P. C.	2B-SS	130	439	67	113	17	3	1	47	.257	273	380	26	.962
1979—Salt Lake City	P. C.	SS-2B	38	162	25	47	3	1	2	21	.290	70	120	11	.945
1979—California	Amer.	2B-SS-3B	35	56	6	19	3	0	0	8	.339	38	46	8	.913
1980—Salt Lake City	P. C.	2B-SS	40	155	28	61	14	2	2	28	.394	81	107	12	.940
1980—California†	Amer.	S-2-3-1	80	267	32	68	12	2	0	15	.255	70	124	10	.951
1981—Houston	Nat.	2B-SS-3B	49	95	13	26	6	0	0	3	.274	53	63	6	.951
1982—Houston	Nat.	SS-3B-2B	136	496	73	137	31	*10	3	36	.276	183	412	17	.972
1983—Houston	Nat.	SS	154	619	81	177	28	9	20	79	.286	258	*533	28	.966
1984—Houston‡	Nat.	SS	5	17	3	6	0	1	0	1	.353	8	13	0	1.000
1985—Houston§x	Nat.	SS	84	251	26	63	6	1	6	29	.251	106	218	11	.967
1986—Houston y	Nat.	SS	106	278	24	69	13	1	3	21	.248	142	210	10	.972
1987—Tucson z	P. C.	SS	14	48	10	13	4	0	0	6	.271	22	40	7	.899
1987—Houston ab	Nat.	SS	32	66	6	14	1	0	1	3	.212	21	53	6	.925
1988—San Diego	Nat.	SS-2B-3B	95	258	36	68	12	2	1	18	.264	84	171	12	.955
American League Totals—2 Years			115	323	38	87	15	2	0	23	.269	108	170	18	.939
National League Totals—8 Years			661	2080	262	560	97	24	34	190	.269	855	1673	90	.966
Major League Totals—10 Years			776	2403	300	647	112	26	34	213	.269	963	1843	108	.963

Signed as free agent by California Angels' organization, November 23, 1975.
†Traded to Houston Astros for Pitcher Ken Forsch, April 1, 1981.
‡On disabled list, April 9, 1984 through remainder of season.
§On disabled list, May 19 to June 8, 1985.
xGranted free agency, November 12, 1985; re-signed by Astros, January 7, 1986.
yOn disabled list, June 6 to June 23, 1986.
zOn Houston restricted list, April 3 to April 18, 1987; then transferred to disabled list, April 19 to May 10, 1987; included rehabilitation disability assignment to Tucson, April 19 to May 8, 1987.
aOn disqualified list, July 4, 1987 through remainder of season.
bGranted free agency, November 9, 1987; signed by San Diego Padres, February 18, 1988.

DIVISION SERIES RECORD

Year Club	League	Pos.	G.	AB.	R.	H.	2B.	3B.	HR.	RBI.	B.A.	PO.	A.	E.	F.A.
1981—Houston	Nat.	SS-PH	4	11	0	2	0	0	0	0	.182	5	10	1	.938

CHAMPIONSHIP SERIES RECORD

Year Club	League	Pos.	G.	AB.	R.	H.	2B.	3B.	HR.	RBI.	B.A.	PO.	A.	E.	F.A.
1979—California	Amer.	PR-SS	1	0	1	0	0	0	0	0	.000	0	0	0	.000
1986—Houston	Nat.	SS-PH	6	12	1	3	0	0	1	1	.250	6	9	0	1.000
Championship Series Totals—2 Years			7	12	2	3	0	0	1	1	.250	6	9	0	1.000

ALL-STAR GAME RECORD

Year League	Pos.	AB.	R.	H.	2B.	3B.	HR.	RBI.	B.A.	PO.	A.	E.	F.A.
1983—National	PH-SS	3	0	1	0	0	0	0	.333	0	2	0	1.000

LOUIS THORNTON JR.
(Lou)

Born April 26, 1963, at Montgomery, Ala.
Height, 6.00. Weight, 175.
Throws right and bats lefthanded.

Major League stolen bases: 1985 (1).
Led Appalachian League outfielders in errors with 9 in 1982.

Year Club	League	Pos.	G.	AB.	R.	H.	2B.	3B.	HR.	RBI.	B.A.	PO.	A.	E.	F.A.
1981—Kingsport	Appal.	1B	48	153	23	32	7	0	2	17	.209	338	43	16	.960
1982—Kingsport	Appal.	OF-1B-3B	57	210	29	44	9	2	5	29	.210	182	7	13	.940
1983—Columbia	S. Atl.	OF	119	448	80	120	24	6	11	73	.268	193	18	11	.950
1984—Lynchburg†	Carolina	OF-1B	131	505	78	139	25	7	6	67	.275	250	13	11	.960
1985—Toronto	Amer.	OF	56	72	18	17	1	1	1	8	.236	44	0	2	.957
1986—Syracuse‡	Int.	OF	64	231	34	60	4	2	2	28	.260	114	5	4	.967
1987—Syracuse	Int.	OF	122	464	64	123	10	5	9	47	.265	199	6	10	.953
1987—Toronto	Amer.	OF	12	2	5	1	0	0	0	0	.500	0	0	0	.000

Year	Club	League	Pos.	G.	AB.	R.	H.	2B.	3B.	HR.	RBI.	B.A.	PO.	A.	E.	F.A.
1988—	Syracuse	Int.	OF-3B	69	246	23	51	12	3	4	22	.207	106	31	12	.919
1988—	Toronto§	Amer.	OF	11	2	1	0	0	0	0	0	.000	1	0	0	1.000
Major League Totals—3 Years				79	76	24	18	1	1	1	8	.237	45	0	2	.957

Selected by New York Mets' organization in 19th round of free-agent draft, June 8, 1981.
†Drafted by Toronto Blue Jays, December 3, 1984.
‡On disabled list, May 29 to September 1, 1986.
§Granted free agency, October 15, 1988.

CHAMPIONSHIP SERIES RECORD

Year	Club	League	Pos.	G.	AB.	R.	H.	2B.	3B.	HR.	RBI.	B.A.	PO.	A.	E.	F.A.
1985—	Toronto	Amer.	PR	2	0	1	0	0	0	0	0	.000	0	0	0	.000

GARY MONTEZ THURMAN JR.

Born November 12, 1964, at Indianapolis, Ind.
Height, 5.10. Weight, 175.
Throws and bats righthanded.

Major League stolen bases: 1987 (7), 1988 (5). Total—12.
Led American Association in stolen bases with 58 in 1987.
Led Florida State League in stolen bases with 70 in 1985.
Led Gulf Coast League batters in strikeouts with 58 in 1983.
Tied for South Atlantic League lead in caught stealing with 17 in 1984.
Led Gulf Coast League outfielders in total chances with 143 in 1983, South Atlantic League outfielders with 329 in 1984 and Florida State League outfielders with 396 in 1985.
Tied for American Association lead in double plays by outfielders with 6 in 1987.

Year	Club	League	Pos.	G.	AB.	R.	H.	2B.	3B.	HR.	RBI.	B.A.	PO.	A.	E.	F.A.
1983—	Sarasota Royals	Gulf C.	OF	59	203	32	52	8	2	0	19	.256	★127	★13	3	.979
1984—	Charleston	S. Atl.	OF	129	478	71	109	6	8	6	51	.228	★311	5	13	.960
1985—	Fort Myers	Fla. St.	OF	134	453	68	137	9	9	0	45	.302	★368	18	10	.975
1986—	Memphis	South.	OF	131	525	88	164	24	12	7	62	.312	277	5	11	.962
1986—	Omaha	A. A.	OF	3	2	1	1	0	0	0	0	.500	2	0	0	1.000
1987—	Omaha	A. A.	OF	115	450	88	132	14	9	8	39	.293	283	11	●8	.974
1987—	Kansas City	Amer.	OF	27	81	12	24	2	0	0	5	.296	61	5	2	.971
1988—	Omaha	A. A.	OF	106	422	77	106	12	6	3	40	.251	195	16	6	.972
1988—	Kansas City	Amer.	OF	35	66	6	11	1	0	0	2	.167	36	1	2	.949
Major League Totals—2 Years				62	147	18	35	3	0	0	7	.238	97	6	4	.963

Selected by Kansas City Royals' organization in 1st round (21st player selected) of free-agent draft, June 6, 1983.

MARK ANTHONY THURMOND

Born September 12, 1956, at Houston, Tex.
Height, 6.00. Weight, 190.
Throws and bats lefthanded.
Received bachelor of science degree in finance from
Texas A&M University, College Station, Tex. in 1979.

Major League saves: 1985 (2), 1986 (3), 1987 (5), 1988 (3). Total—13.
Named lefthanded pitcher on THE SPORTING NEWS National League All-Star Team, 1984.
Tied for Texas League lead in games started by pitchers with 27 in 1981.

Year	Club	League	G.	IP.	W.	L.	Pct.	H.	R.	ER.	SO.	BB.	ERA.
1979—	Amarillo	Texas	17	62	3	5	.375	89	52	39	46	31	5.66
1980—	Amarillo†	Texas	26	156	10	9	.526	164	80	67	125	61	3.87
1981—	Amarillo	Texas	27	193	12	5	.706	202	86	70	128	56	3.26
1982—	Hawaii	P. Coast	28	194⅓	12	10	.545	202	88	77	106	58	3.57
1983—	Las Vegas	P. Coast	19	63	6	1	.857	63	28	23	38	24	3.29
1983—	San Diego	National	21	115⅓	7	3	.700	104	40	34	49	33	2.65
1984—	San Diego	National	32	178⅔	14	8	.636	174	70	59	57	55	2.97
1985—	San Diego	National	36	138⅓	7	11	.389	154	70	61	57	44	3.97
1986—	San Diego‡	National	17	70⅔	3	7	.300	96	58	51	32	27	6.50
1986—	Detroit	American	25	51⅔	4	1	.800	44	13	11	17	17	1.92
1987—	Detroit§	American	48	61⅔	0	1	.000	83	32	29	21	24	4.23
1988—	Baltimore	American	43	74⅔	1	8	.111	80	43	38	29	27	4.58
1988—	Rochester	Int'national	8	54⅓	5	3	.625	40	22	16	25	18	2.65
National League Totals—4 Years			106	503	31	29	.517	528	238	205	195	159	3.67
American League Totals—3 Years			116	188	5	10	.333	207	88	78	67	68	3.73
Major League Totals—6 Years			222	691	36	39	.480	735	326	283	262	227	3.69

Selected by San Diego Padres' organization in 24th round of free-agent draft, June 6, 1978.
Selected by San Diego Padres' organization in 5th round of free-agent draft, June 5, 1979.
†On disabled list, July 5 to July 16, 1980.
‡Traded to Detroit Tigers for Pitcher Dave LaPoint, July 9, 1986.
§Traded to Baltimore Orioles for Third Baseman Ray Knight, February 27, 1988.

CHAMPIONSHIP SERIES RECORD

Year	Club	League	G.	IP.	W.	L.	Pct.	H.	R.	ER.	SO.	BB.	ERA.
1984—	San Diego	National	1	3⅔	0	1	.000	7	4	4	1	2	9.82
1987—	Detroit	American	1	⅓	0	0	.000	0	0	0	0	0	0.00
Championship Series Totals—2 Years			2	4	0	1	.000	7	4	4	1	2	9.00

WORLD SERIES RECORD

Year	Club	League	G.	IP.	W.	L.	Pct.	H.	R.	ER.	SO.	BB.	ERA.
1984	San Diego	National	2	5⅓	0	1	.000	12	6	6	2	3	10.13

JAY LINDSEY TIBBS

Born January 4, 1962, at Birmingham, Ala.
Height, 6.01. Weight, 175.
Throws and bats righthanded.

Year	Club	League	G.	IP.	W.	L.	Pct.	H.	R.	ER.	SO.	BB.	ERA.
1980	Kingsport	Ap'lachian	12	76	3	7	.300	88	54	37	45	32	4.38
1981	Lynchburg	Carolina	15	72	2	7	.222	89	65	55	41	34	6.88
1981	Shelby	W. Carol.	13	89	4	8	.333	87	56	38	57	33	3.84
1982	Lynchburg†	Carolina	7	38⅓	2	4	.333	42	28	24	31	23	5.63
1982	Jackson	Texas	1	3⅓	0	0	.000	2	1	0	3	1	0.00
1983	Lynchburg‡	Carolina	28	203⅔	14	8	.636	172	94	66	170	96	2.92
1984	Jackson	Texas	6	37⅓	1	2	.333	28	15	13	31	19	3.13
1984	Tidewater§	Int'national	8	41⅓	3	5	.375	44	27	24	27	23	5.23
1984	Wichita	Am. Assoc.	4	27⅔	3	0	1.000	22	13	11	14	8	3.58
1984	Cincinnati	National	14	100⅔	6	2	.750	87	34	32	40	33	2.86
1985	Cincinnati	National	35	218	10	16	.385	216	111	95	98	83	3.92
1985	Denver x	Am. Assoc.	4	31⅔	1	2	.333	20	10	8	15	12	2.27
1986	Montreal	National	35	190⅓	7	9	.438	181	96	84	117	70	3.97
1987	Montreal	National	19	83	4	5	.444	95	55	46	54	34	4.99
1987	Indianapolis y	Am. Assoc.	12	81⅓	5	5	.500	64	31	27	55	22	2.99
1988	Rochester	Int'national	4	25⅓	3	1	.750	22	12	8	18	9	2.84
1988	Baltimore	American	30	158⅔	4	15	.211	184	103	95	82	63	5.39
National League Totals—4 Years			103	592	27	32	.458	579	296	257	309	220	3.91
American League Totals—1 Year			30	158⅔	4	15	.211	184	103	95	82	63	5.39
Major League Totals—5 Years			133	750⅔	31	47	.397	763	399	352	391	283	4.22

Selected by New York Mets' organization in 2nd round of free-agent draft, June 3, 1980.
†On disabled list, July 21 to August 29, 1982.
‡Drafted by Philadelphia Phillies, December 5, 1983; returned, March 29, 1984.
§Traded with Third Baseman Eddie Williams and Pitcher Matt Bullinger to Cincinnati Reds' organization for Pitcher Bruce Berenyi, June 15, 1984.
xTraded with Pitchers Andy McGaffigan and John Stuper and Catcher Dann Bilardello to Montreal Expos for Pitcher Bill Gullickson and Catcher Sal Butera, December 19, 1985.
yTraded with Pitcher Al Cardwood to Baltimore Orioles for Pitchers John Hoover, Doug Cinnella and Rick Carriger, February 16, 1988.

KERRY JEROME TILLMAN
(Rusty)

Born August 29, 1960, at Jacksonville, Fla.
Height, 6.00. Weight, 190.
Throws and bats righthanded.
Attended Florida Junior College, Temple Terrace, Fla.

Major League stolen bases: 1986 (2).

Year	Club	League	Pos.	G.	AB.	R.	H.	2B.	3B.	HR.	RBI.	B.A.	PO.	A.	E.	F.A.
1979	Little Falls	NYP	OF	6	22	4	7	0	1	0	4	.318	4	1	0	1.000
1979	Grays Harbor	N'west	OF	60	217	33	64	10	1	3	30	.295	140	7	5	.967
1980	Lynchburg	Carol.	OF	135	526	94	166	27	11	8	79	.316	173	10	5	*.973
1981	Jackson	Texas	OF-1B	122	464	66	129	21	4	6	59	.278	126	8	4	.971
1982	Tidewater	Int.	OF	108	404	60	130	10	6	5	54	.322	156	10	3	.982
1982	New York	Nat.	OF	12	13	4	2	1	0	0	0	.154	2	0	0	1.000
1983	Tidewater	Int.	OF	126	483	67	123	20	7	8	63	.255	220	13	7	.971
1984	Tidewater†	Int.	OF-3B	44	151	17	33	5	1	3	13	.219	56	8	2	.970
1984	Denver ‡	A. A.	OF	75	255	43	78	6	3	9	43	.306	114	8	5	.961
1985	Las Vegas	P. C.	O-1-3-P	115	412	66	139	27	7	12	75	.337	193	7	6	.971
1986	L.V.§-Tac.	P. C.	OF	74	261	42	82	19	2	3	42	.314	128	6	1	.993
1986	Oakland xy	Amer.	OF	22	39	6	10	1	0	1	6	.256	20	0	1	.952
1987	Phoenix	P. C.	OF	94	304	50	96	12	2	10	52	.316	99	6	6	.946
1988	Phoenix	P. C.	1B-OF-3B	113	421	62	124	25	4	12	71	.295	492	36	9	.983
1988	San Francisco z	Nat.	OF	4	4	1	1	0	0	1	3	.250	1	0	0	1.000
National League Totals—2 Years				16	17	5	3	1	0	1	3	.176	3	0	0	1.000
American League Totals—1 Year				22	39	6	10	1	0	1	6	.256	20	0	1	.952
Major League Totals—3 Years				38	56	11	13	2	0	2	9	.232	23	0	1	.958

Selected by New York Mets' organization in 10th round of free-agent draft, January 9, 1979.
†Loaned to Denver (Chicago White Sox' organization), June 14, 1984; returned, September 16, 1984.
‡Traded to San Diego Padres' organization for Outfielder-First Baseman Rick Lancellotti, March 31, 1985.
§Traded to Oakland A's organization for Pitcher Bob Stoddard and Outfielder Kevin Russ, April 18, 1986.
xOn disabled list, August 29 to September 13, 1986.
yReleased, March 20, 1987; signed by San Francisco Giants' organization, April 26, 1987.
zGranted free agency, October 15, 1988.

PITCHING RECORD

Year	Club	League	G.	IP.	W.	L.	Pct.	H.	R.	ER.	SO.	BB.	ERA.
1985	Las Vegas	P. Coast	1	1	0	0	.000	5	6	3	1	1	27.00

RONALD IRVIN TINGLEY
(Ron)

Born May 27, 1959, at Presque Isle, Maine.
Height, 6.02. Weight, 180.
Throws and bats righthanded.

Year	Club	League	Pos.	G.	AB.	R.	H.	2B.	3B.	HR.	RBI.	B.A.	PO.	A.	E.	F.A.
1977	Walla Walla	N'west	OF	21	33	8	5	0	0	1	3	.152	5	2	0	1.000
1978	Walla Walla	N'west	OF-C	43	140	22	29	2	0	2	21	.207	149	16	8	.954
1979	Santa Clara	Calif.	C-OF-P	52	143	11	29	4	1	0	17	.203	258	42	8	.974
1979	Amarillo	Texas	C-OF	30	90	16	23	4	1	1	6	.256	133	17	4	.974
1980	Reno†	Calif.	C-OF	65	204	37	61	3	3	3	35	.299	333	46	10	.974
1981	Amarillo	Texas	C-1B-OF	116	379	72	109	9	*10	13	60	.288	607	47	11	.983
1982	Hawaii	P. C.	C	115	362	45	95	13	8	6	42	.262	540	77	12	.981
1982	San Diego	Nat.	C	8	20	0	2	0	0	0	0	.100	40	4	2	.957
1983	Las Vegas	P. C.	C	92	294	44	83	15	6	10	48	.282	449	55	12	.977
1984	Salt Lake City‡§	P. C.	C	3	2	1	1	0	0	1	1	.500	3	0	0	1.000
1985	Calgary x	P. C.	C-OF	83	277	36	70	11	3	11	47	.253	399	51	10	.978
1986	Rich.y-Maine	Int.	C	58	174	13	35	2	1	3	13	.201	280	23	6	.981
1987	Buffalo	A. A.	C-1B-3B	57	167	27	45	8	5	5	30	.269	306	37	6	.983
1988	Colorado Springs	P. C.	C	44	130	11	37	5	1	3	20	.285	234	22	0	1.000
1988	Cleveland	Amer.	C	9	24	1	4	0	0	1	2	.167	48	6	0	1.000
National League Totals—1 Year				8	20	0	2	0	0	0	0	.100	40	4	2	.957
American League Totals—1 Year				9	24	1	4	0	0	1	2	.167	48	6	0	1.000
Major League Totals—2 Years				17	44	1	6	0	0	1	2	.136	88	10	2	.980

Selected by San Diego Padres' organization in 10th round of free-agent draft, June 7, 1977.
†On disabled list, April 10 to April 29, 1980.
‡On disabled list, April 7 to August 10, 1984.
§Granted free agency, October 15, 1984; signed by Calgary (Seattle Mariners' organization), January 15, 1985.
xGranted free agency, October 15, 1985; signed by Richmond (Atlanta Braves' organization), November 19, 1985.
yReleased, June 19, 1986; signed by Maine (Cleveland Indians' organization), June 23, 1986.

PITCHING RECORD

Year	Club	League	G.	IP.	W.	L.	Pct.	H.	R.	ER.	SO.	BB.	ERA.
1979	Santa Clara	California	1	1	0	0	.000	4	5	1	2	2	9.00

FREDDIE LEE TOLIVER
(Fred)

Born February 3, 1961, at Natchez, Miss.
Height, 6.01. Weight, 170.
Throws and bats righthanded.

Major League saves: 1985 (1).

Year	Club	League	G.	IP.	W.	L.	Pct.	H.	R.	ER.	SO.	BB.	ERA.
1979	Oneonta	NYP	13	77	*10	2	.833	46	28	18	71	66	2.10
1980	Fort Lauderdale	Florida St.	3	8	0	2	.000	14	15	13	4	10	14.63
1980	Greensboro†	S. Atlantic	20	126	6	8	.429	98	60	40	96	89	2.86
1981	Greensboro‡§	S. Atlantic	17	80	5	3	.625	67	38	31	62	56	3.49
1982	Cedar Rapids	Midwest	23	115	6	7	.462	114	77	54	117	66	4.23
1982	Indianapolis	Am. Assoc.	4	20⅔	2	2	.500	20	10	9	19	13	3.92
1983	Indianapolis	Am. Assoc.	26	166⅔	8	10	.444	151	93	84	112	*110	4.54
1984	Wichita	Am. Assoc.	32	164	11	6	.647	142	90	88	113	*116	4.83
1984	Cincinnati	National	3	10	0	0	.000	7	2	1	4	7	0.90
1985	Denver xy	Am. Assoc.	19	122⅓	11	3	.786	113	50	44	84	56	3.24
1985	Philadelphia	National	11	25	0	4	.000	27	15	13	23	17	4.68
1986	Portland	P. Coast	6	26⅔	1	3	.250	31	23	22	15	14	7.43
1986	Philadelphia z	National	5	25⅔	0	2	.000	28	14	10	20	11	3.51
1987	Maine	Int'national	22	124⅔	6	9	.400	114	70	64	80	67	4.62
1987	Philadelphia a	National	10	30⅓	1	1	.500	34	19	19	25	17	5.64
1988	Portland	P. Coast	13	95	7	2	.778	79	42	33	54	35	3.13
1988	Minnesota	American	21	114⅔	7	6	.538	116	57	54	69	52	4.24
National League Totals—4 Years			29	91	1	7	.125	96	50	43	72	52	4.25
American League Totals—1 Year			21	114⅔	7	6	.538	116	57	54	69	52	4.24
Major League Totals—5 Years			50	205⅔	8	13	.381	212	107	97	141	104	4.24

Selected by New York Yankees' organization in 3rd round of free-agent draft, June 5, 1979.
†On disabled list, May 23 to June 6, 1980.
‡On disabled list, April 9 to May 27, 1981.
§Traded to Cincinnati Reds' organization, December 10, 1981, completing deal in which Cincinnati traded Outfielder Ken Griffey to New York Yankees for Pitcher Brian Ryder and a player to be named later, November 4, 1981.
xOn disabled list, July 5 to August 10, 1985.
yTraded to Philadelphia Phillies, August 27, 1985, completing deal in which Philadelphia traded Catcher Bo Diaz and Pitcher Greg Simpson to Cincinnati Reds for Shortstop Tom Foley, Catcher Alan Knicely, a player to be named later and cash, August 8, 1985.
zOn disabled list, May 30 to June 25 and July 8, 1986 through remainder of season.
aTraded to Minnesota Twins for Catcher Chris Calvert, February 5, 1988.

JIMMY WAYNE TOLLESON

(Known by middle name.)

Born September 22, 1955, at Spartanburg, S. C.
Height, 5.09. Weight, 160.
Throws right and bats left and righthanded.
Received degree from Western Carolina University, Cullowhee, N. C., in 1978.
Brother of Mike Tolleson, outfielder in Cleveland Indians' organization, 1984.

Major League stolen bases: 1981 (2), 1982 (1), 1983 (33), 1984 (22), 1985 (21), 1986 (17), 1987 (5), 1988 (1). Total—102.

Year Club	League	Pos.	G.	AB.	R.	H.	2B.	3B.	HR.	RBI.	B.A.	PO.	A.	E.	F.A.
1978—Asheville	W. Car.	3B-SS	70	212	35	57	4	1	0	21	.269	85	175	20	.929
1979—Tulsa	Texas	SS	130	418	43	98	9	7	1	36	.234	179	413	*41	.935
1980—Tulsa	Texas	SS	131	452	69	124	19	7	1	30	.274	161	395	31	.947
1981—Wichita	A. A.	3-S-2-O	107	375	58	98	9	4	3	38	.261	96	259	15	.959
1981—Texas	Amer.	3B-SS	14	24	6	4	0	0	0	1	.167	5	8	0	1.000
1982—Texas	Amer.	SS-3B-2B	38	70	6	8	1	0	0	2	.114	47	70	5	.959
1982—Denver	A. A.	SS	71	266	48	64	9	3	4	27	.241	97	195	6	.980
1983—Texas	Amer.	2B-SS	134	470	64	122	13	2	3	20	.260	268	372	17	.974
1984—Texas	Amer.	2-S-3-O	118	338	35	72	9	2	0	9	.213	195	287	10	.980
1985—Texas†	Amer.	SS-2B-3B	123	323	45	101	9	5	1	18	.313	149	255	14	.967
1986—Chi.‡-N.Y.	Amer.	S-3-2-O	141	475	61	126	16	5	3	43	.265	147	327	14	.971
1987—New York§	Amer.	SS-3B	121	349	48	77	4	0	1	22	.221	162	326	15	.970
1988—Fort Lauderdale x	Fla. St.	SS	4	18	2	5	0	0	0	5	.278	6	13	2	.905
1988—Columbus	Int.	SS-3B	8	27	4	5	0	0	0	1	.185	7	20	1	.964
1988—New York y	Amer.	2B-3B-SS	21	59	8	15	2	0	0	5	.254	28	54	3	.965
Major League Totals—8 Years			710	2108	273	525	54	14	8	120	.249	1001	1699	78	.972

Selected by Pittsburgh Pirates' organization in 12th round of free-agent draft, June 7, 1977.
Selected by Texas Rangers' organization in 8th round of free-agent draft, June 6, 1978.

†Traded with Pitcher Dave Schmidt to Chicago White Sox for Pitcher Ed Correa, Infielder Scott Fletcher and a player to be named later, November 25, 1985; Texas Rangers acquired Infielder Jose Mota to complete deal, December 12, 1985.

‡Traded with Outfielder-Designated Hitter Ron Kittle and Catcher Joel Skinner to New York Yankees for Catcher Ron Hassey, Shortstop Carlos Martinez and a player to be named later, July 30, 1986; New York traded Catcher Bill Lindsey to Chicago White Sox' organization to complete deal, December 24, 1986.

§On disabled list, August 19 to September 3, 1987.

xOn New York disabled list, April 4 to June 10, June 20 to July 14, July 17 to August 11 and August 14 to September 11, 1988; included rehabilitation disability assignment to Fort Lauderdale, April 16 to April 24, and to Columbus, May 19 to May 28, 1988.

yGranted free agency, November 4, 1988; re-signed by Yankees, December 18, 1988.

KELVIN CURTIS TORVE

Born January 10, 1960, at Rapid City, S.D.
Height, 6.03. Weight, 185.
Throws right and bats lefthanded.
Received bachelor of science degreee in marketing from Oral Roberts University, Tulsa, Okla.

Led Texas League in intentional bases on balls received with 11 and tied for lead in sacrifice flies with 9 in 1982.

Year Club	League	Pos.	G.	AB.	R.	H.	2B.	3B.	HR.	RBI.	B.A.	PO.	A.	E.	F.A.
1981—Clinton	Midw.	1B	57	211	27	55	10	0	1	27	.261	538	41	4	.993
1982—Shreveport	Texas	1B	127	449	66	137	29	7	15	84	.305	1040	*96	17	.985
1983—Phoenix	P. C.	1B	115	392	58	102	21	5	4	54	.260	730	53	10	.987
1984—Shreveport†	Texas	1B-SS	114	316	59	94	21	5	16	62	.297	668	58	4	.995
1985—Charlotte	South.	1B-OF	134	482	85	140	•34	1	15	77	.290	1077	68	9	.992
1986—Rochester	Int.	1B	109	356	39	86	16	1	4	41	.242	555	51	5	.992
1987—Rochester‡	Int.	1B	86	252	27	66	10	0	9	32	.262	632	48	3	.996
1988—Portland	P. C.	1B	103	385	58	116	28	2	9	47	.301	864	62	2	*.998
1988—Minnesota	Amer.	1B	12	16	1	3	0	0	1	2	.188	14	1	0	1.000
Major League Totals—1 Year			12	16	1	3	0	0	1	2	.188	14	1	0	1.000

Selected by San Francisco Giants' organization in 2nd round of free-agent draft, June 8, 1981.

†Traded to Baltimore Orioles' organization for Pitcher Tommy Alexander, April 9, 1985.

‡Granted free agency, October 15, 1987; signed by Portland (Minnesota Twins' organization), January 18, 1988.

JAMES JOSEPH TRABER
(Jim)

Born December 26, 1961, at Columbus, O.
Height, 6.00. Weight, 213.
Throws and bats lefthanded.
Attended Oklahoma State University, Stillwater, Okla.

Major League stolen bases: 1988 (1).
Tied for International League lead in intentional bases on balls received with 10 in 1987.
Led Appalachian League in game-winning RBIs with 10 in 1982.
Led Carolina League first basemen in putouts with 1,006, double plays with 96 and total chances with 1,070 in 1983.
Led Appalachian League first basemen in double plays with 44 and total chances with 581 in 1982.

Year Club	League	Pos.	G.	AB.	R.	H.	2B.	3B.	HR.	RBI.	B.A.	PO.	A.	E.	F.A.
1982—Bluefield	Appal.	1B	61	235	41	76	18	3	9	•63	.323	*540	*34	7	.988
1982—Hagerstown	Carol.	OF-1B	7	26	1	9	2	0	0	2	.346	12	0	0	1.000

Year	Club	League	Pos.	G.	AB.	R.	H.	2B.	3B.	HR.	RBI.	B.A.	PO.	A.	E.	F.A.
1983	Hagerstown	Carol.	*1B-OF	128	449	73	123	22	1	14	79	.274	1012	54	10	*.991
1984	Hagerstown†	Carol.	1B-OF	48	165	33	59	15	0	2	29	.358	361	30	7	.982
1984	Charlotte	South.	1B	75	296	50	104	17	2	16	56	.351	663	44	7	.990
1984	Baltimore	Amer.	DH-PH	10	21	3	5	0	0	0	2	.238	0	0	0	.000
1985	Rochester‡	Int.	OF-1B	80	279	32	74	13	2	7	37	.265	220	22	4	.984
1986	Rochester	Int.	1B-OF	87	323	46	90	19	2	12	55	.279	592	56	3	.995
1986	Baltimore	Amer.	1B-OF	65	212	28	54	7	0	13	44	.255	243	23	5	.982
1987	Rochester	Int.	OF-1B	127	482	69	132	31	3	21	71	.274	491	27	8	.985
1988	Baltimore	Amer.	1B-OF	103	352	25	78	6	0	10	45	.222	481	59	6	.989
1988	Rochester	Int.	1B	38	144	17	41	10	0	6	23	.285	344	31	5	.987
Major League Totals—3 Years				178	585	56	137	13	0	23	91	.234	724	82	11	.987

Selected by Baltimore Orioles' organization in 21st round of free-agent draft, June 7, 1982.
†On suspended list, June 7 to June 17, 1984.
‡On disabled list, May 21 to July 8, 1985.

ALAN STUART TRAMMELL

Name pronounced TRAM-mull.

Born February 21, 1958, at Garden Grove, Calif.
Height, 6.00. Weight, 175.
Throws and bats righthanded.

Major League stolen bases: 1978 (3), 1979 (17), 1980 (12), 1981 (10), 1982 (19), 1983 (30), 1984 (19), 1985 (14), 1986 (25), 1987 (21), 1988 (7). Total—177.
Led American League in sacrifice hits with 16 in 1981 and 15 in 1983.
Named American League Comeback Player of the Year by THE SPORTING NEWS, 1983.
Named shortstop on THE SPORTING NEWS American League All-Star Team, 1987 and 1988.
Named shortstop on THE SPORTING NEWS American League All-Star fielding team, 1980, 1981, 1983 and 1984.
Named shortstop on THE SPORTING NEWS American League Silver Slugger team, 1987 and 1988.
Named Southern League Most Valuable Player, 1977.

Year	Club	League	Pos.	G.	AB.	R.	H.	2B.	3B.	HR.	RBI.	B.A.	PO.	A.	E.	F.A.
1976	Bristol	Appal.	SS	41	140	27	38	2	2	0	7	.271	59	131	12	.941
1976	Montgomery	South.	SS	21	56	4	10	0	0	0	2	.179	40	64	2	.981
1977	Montgomery	South.	SS	134	454	78	132	9	*19	3	50	.291	188	397	27	.956
1977	Detroit	Amer.	SS	19	43	6	8	0	0	0	0	.186	15	34	2	.961
1978	Detroit	Amer.	SS	139	448	49	120	14	6	2	34	.268	239	421	14	.979
1979	Detroit	Amer.	SS	142	460	68	127	11	4	6	50	.276	245	388	26	.961
1980	Detroit	Amer.	SS	146	560	107	168	21	5	9	65	.300	225	412	13	.980
1981	Detroit	Amer.	SS	105	392	52	101	15	3	2	31	.258	181	347	9	.983
1982	Detroit	Amer.	SS	157	489	66	126	34	3	9	57	.258	259	459	16	.978
1983	Detroit	Amer.	SS	142	505	83	161	31	2	14	66	.319	236	367	13	.979
1984	Detroit†	Amer.	SS	139	555	85	174	34	5	14	69	.314	180	314	10	.980
1985	Detroit	Amer.	SS	149	605	79	156	21	7	13	57	.258	225	400	15	.977
1986	Detroit	Amer.	SS	151	574	107	159	33	7	21	75	.277	238	445	22	.969
1987	Detroit	Amer.	SS	151	597	109	205	34	3	28	105	.343	222	421	19	.971
1988	Detroit ‡	Amer.	SS	128	466	73	145	24	1	15	69	.311	195	355	11	.980
Major League Totals—12 Years				1568	5694	884	1650	272	46	133	678	.290	2460	4363	170	.976

Selected by Detroit Tigers' organization in 2nd round of free-agent draft, June 8, 1976.
†On disabled list, July 9 to July 31, 1984.
‡On disabled list, June 29 to July 17, 1988.

CHAMPIONSHIP SERIES RECORD

Year	Club	League	Pos.	G.	AB.	R.	H.	2B.	3B.	HR.	RBI.	B.A.	PO.	A.	E.	F.A.
1984	Detroit	Amer.	SS	3	11	2	4	0	1	1	3	.364	1	8	0	1.000
1987	Detroit	Amer.	SS	5	20	3	4	1	0	0	2	.200	6	9	1	.938
Championship Series Totals—2 Years				8	31	5	8	1	1	1	5	.258	7	17	1	.960

WORLD SERIES RECORD

Tied World Series records for batting in all club's runs, game, most (4), October 13, 1984; most hits, five-game Series (9), 1984.

Year	Club	League	Pos.	G.	AB.	R.	H.	2B.	3B.	HR.	RBI.	B.A.	PO.	A.	E.	F.A.
1984	Detroit	Amer.	SS	5	20	5	9	1	0	2	6	.450	8	9	1	.944

ALL-STAR GAME RECORD

Year	League	Pos.	AB.	R.	H.	2B.	3B.	HR.	RBI.	B.A.	PO.	A.	E.	F.A.
1980	American	SS	0	0	0	0	0	0	0	.000	0	0	0	.000
1985	American	SS	1	0	0	0	0	0	0	.000	0	0	0	.000
1987	American	PH	1	0	0	0	0	0	0	.000	0	0	0	.000
All-Star Game Totals—3 Years			2	0	0	0	0	0	0	.000	0	0	0	.000

Named to American League All-Star Team for 1984 game; replaced due to injury by Alfredo Griffin.
Named to American League All-Star Team for 1988 game; replaced due to injury by Cal Ripken Jr.

JOHN HOWARD TRAUTWEIN

Born August 7, 1962, at Lafayette Hills, Pa.
Height, 6.03. Weight, 195.
Throws and bats righthanded.
Received bachelor of arts degree in chemistry from Northwestern University, Evanston, Ill.
Son of Jack Trautwein, minor league pitcher, 1950 through 1954.

Year Club	League	G.	IP.	W.	L.	Pct.	H.	R.	ER.	SO.	BB.	ERA.
1984—Helena†	Pioneer	19	35⅔	3	4	.429	27	14	13	39	14	3.28
1985—West Palm Beach	Florida St.	35	66⅔	3	5	.375	52	20	16	54	22	2.16
1986—Jacksonville	Southern	12	23	2	1	.667	24	19	18	14	25	7.04
1986—West Palm Beach	Florida St.	10	17	1	2	.333	23	12	11	13	6	5.82
1986—Burlington	Midwest	21	36⅓	3	2	.600	29	9	8	39	10	1.98
1987—Jacksonville‡	Southern	56	106⅔	*15	4	.789	92	43	34	85	42	2.87
1988—Boston	American	9	16	0	1	.000	26	17	16	8	9	9.00
1988—Pawtucket	Int'national	4	9	0	1	.000	4	2	2	7	6	2.00
Major League Totals—1 Year		9	16	0	1	.000	26	17	16	8	9	9.00

Signed as free agent by Helena (Independent), June 13, 1984.
†Sold to Jamestown (Montreal Expos' organization), October 17, 1984.
‡Drafted by Boston Red Sox, December 7, 1987.

HUGH JEFFERY TREADWAY
(Jeff)

Born January 22, 1963, at Columbus, Ga.
Weight, 5.11. Weight, 170.
Throws right and bats lefthanded.
Attended Middle Georgia College, Cochran, Ga.,
and University of Georgia, Athens, Ga.

Major League stolen bases: 1987 (1), 1988 (2). Total—3.

Year Club	League	Pos.	G.	AB.	R.	H.	2B.	3B.	HR.	RBI.	B.A.	PO.	A.	E.	F.A.
1984—Tampa	Fla. St.	3B-2B	119	372	44	115	16	0	0	44	.309	128	184	25	.926
1985—Vermont	East.	2B	129	431	63	130	17	1	2	49	.302	271	332	15	.976
1986—Vermont	East.	2B	33	122	18	41	8	1	1	16	.336	68	102	5	.971
1986—Denver	A. A.	2B-3B	72	204	20	67	11	4	3	23	.328	75	153	6	.974
1987—Nashville	A. A.	2B	123	409	66	129	28	5	7	59	.315	236	362	12	*.980
1987—Cincinnati	Nat.	2B	23	84	9	28	4	0	2	4	.333	44	48	4	.958
1988—Cincinnati †	Nat.	2B-3B	103	301	30	76	19	4	2	23	.252	189	253	8	.982
Major League Totals—2 Years			126	385	39	104	23	4	4	27	.270	233	301	12	.978

Selected by Montreal Expos' organization in 18th round of free-agent draft, January 13, 1981.
Signed as free agent by Cincinnati Reds' organization, January 29, 1984.
†On disabled list, August 28 to September 24, 1988.

ALEJANDRO TREVINO (CASTRO)
(Alex)

Born August 26, 1957, at Monterrey, Nuevo Leon, Mex.
Height, 5.11. Weight, 179.
Throws and bats righthanded.
Attended University of Nuevo Leon, Monterrey, Mex.
Brother of Bobby Trevino, outfielder with California Angels, 1968; manager, Tabasco, 1977, Tampico, 1979, and Toluca, 1980.

Major League stolen bases: 1979 (2), 1981 (3), 1982 (3), 1984 (5), 1987 (1), 1988 (5). Total—19.
Led Midwest League catchers in putouts with 847 and assists with 102 in 1977.
Led Carolina League in passed balls with 18 in 1976.

Year Club	League	Pos.	G.	AB.	R.	H.	2B.	3B.	HR.	RBI.	B.A.	PO.	A.	E.	F.A.
1973—Victoria†	Mx. Cen.	C-OF	12	26	3	6	1	0	0	2	.231	26	5	1	.969
1974—Marion	Appal.	C-SS	12	16	0	1	0	0	0	1	.063	15	0	0	1.000
1975—Marion	Appal.	C-2B-OF	22	60	10	12	1	0	0	3	.200	96	8	6	.963
1976—Lynchburg	Carol.	C-3-2-S	94	284	17	57	11	2	0	31	.201	400	130	18	.967
1977—Wausau	Midw.	C-2-1-3	128	422	57	100	10	0	2	36	.237	865	110	15	.985
1978—Tidewater	Int.	C-3B	87	262	44	77	13	2	5	37	.294	303	68	11	.971
1978—New York	Nat.	C-3B	6	12	3	3	0	0	0	0	.250	12	4	0	1.000
1979—New York	Nat.	C-3B-2B	79	207	24	56	11	1	0	20	.271	229	71	9	.971
1980—New York	Nat.	C-3B-2B	106	355	26	91	11	2	0	37	.256	450	76	16	.970
1981—New York‡	Nat.	C-2-O-3	56	149	17	39	2	0	0	10	.262	215	25	9	.964
1982—Cincinnati	Nat.	*C-3B	120	355	24	89	10	3	1	33	.251	725	61	*17	.979
1983—Cincinnati	Nat.	C-3B-2B	74	167	14	36	8	1	1	13	.216	359	32	5	.987
1984—Cinc.§-Atl.	Nat.	C	85	272	36	66	16	0	3	28	.243	403	61	5	.989
1985—Atl. x-S.F. y	Nat.	C-3B	57	157	17	34	10	1	6	19	.217	299	19	7	.978
1986—Los Angeles	Nat.	C-1B	89	202	31	53	13	0	4	26	.262	304	46	11	.970
1987—Los Angeles z	Nat.	C-OF-3B	72	144	16	32	7	1	3	16	.222	206	22	3	.987
1988—Tucson	P. C.	C-OF-3B	15	45	5	10	3	1	0	3	.222	39	10	2	.961
1988—Houston a	Nat.	C-OF	78	193	19	48	17	0	2	13	.249	360	24	9	.977
Major League Totals—11 Years			822	2213	227	547	105	9	20	215	.247	3562	441	91	.978

Signed as free agent by Victoria, May 16, 1973.
†Sold to New York Mets' organization, May 22, 1974.
‡Traded with Pitchers Jim Kern and Greg Harris to Cincinnati Reds for Outfielder George Foster, February 10, 1982.
§Traded to Atlanta Braves for player to be named later, April 24, 1984; deal settled with reported $50,000 in July, 1984.
xTraded to San Francisco Giants for Catcher-Outfielder John Rabb, April 17, 1985.
yTraded to Los Angeles Dodgers for Outfielder Candy Maldonado, December 11, 1985.
zReleased, April 4, 1988; signed by Tucson (Houston Astros' organization), April 12, 1988.
aGranted free agency, November 4, 1988; re-signed by Astros, December 21, 1988.

JESUS MANUEL TRILLO (MARCANO)

Name pronounced TREE-yo.

(Manny)

Born December 25, 1950, at Caritito, Monagas, Venezuela.
Height, 6.01. Weight, 164.
Throws and bats righthanded.
Attended Colegio Libertador Bolivar, Maturin, Monagas, Venz.

Established major league records for most consecutive errorless games by second baseman, season (89), 1982; most consecutive errorless chances accepted by second baseman, season (479), 1982.

Major League stolen bases: 1975 (1), 1976 (17), 1977 (3), 1979 (4), 1980 (8), 1981 (10), 1982 (8), 1983 (1), 1985 (2), 1988 (2). Total—56.

Led National League second basemen in double plays with 99 in 1978.

Led National League second basemen in total chances with 822 in 1977 and 878 in 1978.

Led Pacific Coast League second basemen in double plays with 113 in 1973.

Named second baseman on The Sporting News National League All-Star Team, 1980 through 1982.

Named second baseman on The Sporting News National League All-Star fielding team, 1979, 1981 and 1982.

Named second baseman on The Sporting News National League Silver Slugger team, 1980 and 1981.

Year Club	League	Pos.	G.	AB.	R.	H.	2B.	3B.	HR.	RBI.	B.A.	PO.	A.	E.	F.A.
1968—Huron†	North.	SS-3B-C	35	92	8	24	2	1	0	4	.261	35	48	5	.943
1969—Spartanburg‡	W. Car.	3-C-S-2	83	275	41	77	18	0	1	26	.280	188	98	12	.960
1970—Birmingham	South.	3B-2B-SS	84	241	26	63	10	1	2	19	.261	101	130	14	.943
1971—Birmingham§	South.	3B-SS	107	371	37	104	18	1	5	44	.280	110	212	31	.912
1972—Iowa	A. A.	3B-2B-SS	133	509	67	153	27	6	9	53	.301	176	304	28	.945
1973—Tucson	P. C.	*2B-OF	135	519	76	162	25	7	8	78	.312	*304	*373	19	*.973
1973—Oakland	Amer.	2B	17	12	0	3	2	0	0	3	.250	15	17	2	.941
1974—Tucson	P. C.	2B	85	320	31	81	19	1	2	39	.253	198	256	12	.974
1974—Oakland x	Amer.	2B	21	33	3	5	0	0	0	2	.152	31	43	4	.949
1975—Chicago	Nat.	*2B-SS	154	545	55	135	12	2	7	70	.248	350	*509	*29	.967
1976—Chicago	Nat.	*2B-SS	158	582	42	139	24	3	4	59	.239	350	*527	17	.981
1977—Chicago	Nat.	2B	152	504	51	141	18	5	7	57	.280	330	*467	*25	.970
1978—Chicago y	Nat.	2B	152	552	53	144	17	5	4	55	.261	354	*505	19	.978
1979—Philadelphia z	Nat.	2B	118	431	40	112	22	1	6	42	.260	270	368	10	.985
1980—Philadelphia a	Nat.	2B	141	531	68	155	25	9	7	43	.292	*360	467	11	.987
1981—Philadelphia	Nat.	2B	94	349	37	100	14	3	6	36	.287	*245	286	7	.987
1982—Philadelphia b	Nat.	2B	149	549	52	149	24	1	0	39	.271	343	441	5	*.994
1983—Cleveland cd	Amer.	2B	88	320	33	87	13	1	1	29	.272	172	269	5	.989
1983—Montreal e	Nat.	2B	31	121	16	32	8	0	2	16	.264	57	86	3	.979
1984—San Francisco f	Nat.	2B-3B	98	401	45	102	21	1	4	36	.254	218	294	6	.988
1985—San Francisco g	Nat.	2B-3B	125	451	36	101	16	2	3	25	.224	263	361	13	.980
1986—Chicago h	Nat.	3B-1B-2B	81	152	22	45	10	0	1	19	.296	114	63	5	.973
1987—Chicago i	Nat.	1-3-2-S	108	214	27	63	8	0	8	26	.294	301	53	4	.989
1988—Chicago j	Nat.	1-3-2-S	76	164	15	41	5	0	1	14	.250	177	81	3	.989
American League Totals—3 Years			126	365	36	95	15	1	1	34	.260	218	329	11	.980
National League Totals—14 Years			1637	5546	559	1459	224	32	60	537	.263	3732	4508	157	.981
Major League Totals—16 Years			1763	5911	595	1554	239	33	61	571	.263	3950	4837	168	.981

Signed as free agent by Philadelphia Phillies' organization, January 26, 1968.

†On disabled list, August 16 to September 3, 1968.

‡Drafted by Birmingham (Oakland Athletics' organization), December 1, 1969.

§On disabled list, May 1 to May 20, 1971.

xTraded with Pitchers Darold Knowles and Bob Locker to Chicago Cubs for First Baseman-Outfielder Billy Williams, October 23, 1974.

yTraded with Outfielder Greg Gross and Catcher Dave Rader to Philadelphia Phillies for Outfielder Jerry Martin, Catcher Barry Foote, Second Baseman Ted Sizemore and Pitchers Derek Botelho and Henry Mack, February 23, 1979.

zOn disabled list, May 4 to June 16, 1979.

aOn disabled list, April 20 to May 7, 1980.

bTraded with Outfielder George Vukovich, Infielder Julio Franco, Pitcher Jay Baller and Catcher Jerry Willard to Cleveland Indians for Outfielder Von Hayes, December 9, 1982.

cOn disabled list, July 24 to August 8, 1983.

dTraded to Montreal Expos for outfielder Don Carter and cash, August 17, 1983.

eGranted free agency, November 7, 1983; signed by San Francisco Giants, December 20, 1983.

fOn disabled list, May 13 to July 7, 1984.

gTraded to Chicago Cubs for Infielder Dave Owen, December 11, 1985.

hOn disabled list, June 3 to July 11, 1986.

iGranted free agency, November 9, 1987; re-signed by Cubs, December 7, 1987.

jGranted free agency, November 4, 1988; signed by Cincinnati Reds, December 21, 1988

DIVISION SERIES RECORD

Year Club	League	Pos.	G.	AB.	R.	H.	2B.	3B.	HR.	RBI.	B.A.	PO.	A.	E.	F.A.
1981—Philadelphia	Nat.	2B	5	16	1	3	0	0	0	1	.188	15	10	0	1.000

CHAMPIONSHIP SERIES RECORD

Year Club	League	Pos.	G.	AB.	R.	H.	2B.	3B.	HR.	RBI.	B.A.	PO.	A.	E.	F.A.
1974—Oakland	Amer.	PR	1	0	1	0	0	0	0	0	.000	0	0	0	.000
1980—Philadelphia	Nat.	2B	5	21	1	8	2	1	0	4	.381	18	25	1	.977
Championship Series Totals—2 Years			6	21	2	8	2	1	0	4	.381	18	25	1	.977

WORLD SERIES RECORD

Year Club	League	Pos.	G.	AB.	R.	H.	2B.	3B.	HR.	RBI.	B.A.	PO.	A.	E.	F.A.
1980—Philadelphia	Nat.	2B	6	23	4	5	2	0	0	2	.217	14	25	1	.975

ALL-STAR GAME RECORD

Year League	Pos.	AB.	R.	H.	2B.	3B.	HR.	RBI.	B.A.	PO.	A.	E.	F.A.
1977—National	2B	1	0	0	0	0	0	0	.000	0	1	0	1.000
1981—National	2B	2	0	0	0	0	0	0	.000	1	1	0	1.000
1982—National	2B	2	0	1	0	0	0	0	.500	0	1	0	1.000
1983—American	2B	3	1	1	0	0	0	0	.333	3	1	0	1.000
All-Star Game Totals—4 Years		8	1	2	0	0	0	0	.250	4	4	0	1.000

STEVEN RUSSELL TROUT
(Steve)

Born July 30, 1957, at Detroit, Mich.
Height, 6.04. Weight, 190.
Throws and bats lefthanded.
Son of Paul (Dizzy) Trout, pitcher with Detroit Tigers, Boston Red Sox and Baltimore Orioles, 1939 through 1952 and 1957.

Major League saves: 1979 (4).

Led American League in hit batsmen with 9 in 1980.

Year Club	League	G.	IP.	W.	L.	Pct.	H.	R.	ER.	SO.	BB.	ERA.
1976—Sarasota White Sox	Gulf Coast	9	38	1	3	.250	28	18	11	35	29	2.61
1977—Appleton	Midwest	21	111	6	8	.429	113	66	50	101	66	4.05
1977—Iowa	Am. Assoc.	5	24	0	4	.000	27	16	15	14	11	5.63
1978—Knoxville	Southern	12	71	8	3	.727	46	16	13	48	33	1.65
1978—Iowa	Am. Assoc.	9	55	3	4	.429	57	36	32	38	22	5.24
1978—Chicago	American	4	22	3	0	1.000	19	10	10	11	11	4.09
1979—Iowa	Am. Assoc.	4	27	3	1	.750	24	10	9	12	19	3.00
1979—Chicago	American	34	155	11	8	.579	165	77	67	76	59	3.89
1980—Chicago	American	32	200	9	16	.360	229	102	82	89	49	3.69
1981—Chicago	American	20	125	8	7	.533	122	53	48	54	38	3.46
1982—Chicago†	American	25	120⅓	6	9	.400	130	76	57	62	50	4.26
1983—Chicago	National	34	180	10	14	.417	217	105	93	80	59	4.65
1984—Chicago‡	National	32	190	13	7	.650	205	80	72	81	59	3.41
1985—Chicago§	National	24	140⅔	9	7	.563	142	57	53	44	63	3.39
1986—Chicago	National	37	161	5	7	.417	184	88	85	69	78	4.75
1987—Chicago x	National	11	75	6	3	.667	72	27	25	32	27	3.00
1987—Peoria y	Midwest	1	8	1	0	1.000	6	0	0	6	0	0.00
1987—New York z	American	14	46⅓	0	4	.000	51	36	34	27	37	6.60
1988—Seattle a	American	15	56⅓	4	7	.364	86	53	49	14	31	7.83
1988—Calgary	P. Coast	3	15⅔	0	2	.000	15	5	2	2	2	1.15
American League Totals—7 Years		144	725	41	51	.446	802	407	347	333	275	4.31
National League Totals—5 Years		138	746⅔	43	38	.531	820	357	328	306	286	3.95
Major League Totals—11 Years		282	1471⅔	84	89	.486	1622	764	675	639	561	4.13

Selected by Chicago White Sox' organization in 1st round (eighth player selected) of free-agent draft, June 8, 1976.

†Traded with Pitcher Warren Brusstar to Chicago Cubs for Pitchers Dick Tidrow and Randy Martz and Infielders Scott Fletcher and Pat Tabler, January 25, 1983.

‡Granted free agency, November 8, 1984; re-signed by Cubs, December 7, 1984.

§On disabled list, July 23 to August 23, 1985.

xOn disabled list, May 4 to June 16, 1987; included rehabilitation disability assignment to Peoria, June 11, 1987.

yTraded to New York Yankees for Pitchers Bob Tewksbury, Rich Scheid and Dean Wilkins, July 13, 1987.

zTraded with Outfielder Henry Cotto to Seattle Mariners for Pitchers Lee Guetterman, Clay Parker and Wade Taylor, December 22, 1987.

aOn disabled list, May 8 to June 21 and August 12 to September 2, 1988; included rehabilitation disability assignment to Calgary, June 3 to June 18, 1988.

CHAMPIONSHIP SERIES RECORD

Year Club	League	G.	IP.	W.	L.	Pct.	H.	R.	ER.	SO.	BB.	ERA.
1984—Chicago	National	2	9	1	0	1.000	5	2	2	3	3	2.00

MICHAEL ANDREW TRUJILLO

Name pronounced Tru-HEEY-O.

(Mike)

Born January 12, 1960, at Denver, Colo.
Height, 6.01. Weight, 180.
Throws and bats righthanded.
Received degree from University of Northern Colorado, Greeley, Colo., in 1984.

Major League saves: 1985 (1), 1986 (1), 1987 (1). Total—3.

Led International League in games finished in relief with 36 and tied for lead in intentional bases on balls issued with 6 in 1986.

Led Midwest League pitchers in games started with 29 and tied for lead in complete games with 11 in 1983.

Year Club	League	G.	IP.	W.	L.	Pct.	H.	R.	ER.	SO.	BB.	ERA.
1982—Sarasota White Sox	Gulf Coast	1	7⅓	0	0	.000	1	2	1	6	4	1.23
1982—Niagara Falls	NYP	12	79	5	4	.556	54	33	21	100	25	2.39
1983—Appleton	Midwest	29	*198⅔	15	8	.652	146	75	53	148	63	2.40
1984—Glens Falls	Eastern	20	121⅔	13	3	.813	107	47	32	69	25	2.37
1984—Denver†‡	Am. Assoc.	8	30	2	5	.286	38	27	26	9	20	7.80
1985—Boston	American	27	84	4	4	.500	112	55	45	19	23	4.82
1986—Pawtucket	Int'national	42	84⅔	8	9	.471	76	29	25	45	27	2.66

Year Club	League	G.	IP.	W.	L.	Pct.	H.	R.	ER.	SO.	BB.	ERA.
1986—Boston§-Seattle	American	14	47	3	2	.600	39	17	17	23	21	3.26
1987—Seattle	American	28	65⅔	4	4	.500	70	46	45	36	26	6.17
1987—Calgary x	P. Coast	5	27⅔	3	1	.750	25	8	7	21	9	2.28
1988—Toledo	Int'national	18	106⅓	4	10	.286	102	42	37	54	42	3.13
1988—Detroit	American	6	12⅓	0	0	.000	11	7	7	5	5	5.11
Major League Totals—4 Years		75	209	11	10	.524	232	125	114	83	75	4.91

Selected by Chicago White Sox' organization in 7th round of free-agent draft, June 7, 1982.

†Traded with First Baseman Pat Adams to San Francisco Giants, September 7, 1984, completing deal in which San Francisco traded Infielder Tom O'Malley to Chicago White Sox for two players to be named later, September 1, 1984.

‡Drafted by Boston Red Sox, December 3, 1984.

§Claimed with Pitcher Mike Brown on waivers by Seattle Mariners from Boston Red Sox, August 22, 1986, as part of deal in which Seattle traded Infielder Spike Owen and Outfielder Dave Henderson to Boston for Infielder Rey Quinones, a player to be named later and cash, August 19, 1986. Seattle acquired Outfielder John Christensen to complete deal, September 25, 1986.

xReleased, March 28, 1988; signed by Toledo (Detroit Tigers' organization), March 31, 1988.

JOHN THOMAS TUDOR

Born February 2, 1954, at Schenectady, N.Y.
Height, 6.00. Weight, 185.
Throws and bats lefthanded.
Attended North Shore Community College, Beverly, Mass. and received bachelor of science degree in criminal justice from Georgia Southern College, Statesboro, Ga.

Pitched seven-inning, 2-0 no-hit victory against Reading, June 28, 1977.
Major League saves: 1981 (1).
Led National League in shutouts with 10 in 1985.
Named lefthanded pitcher on THE SPORTING NEWS National League All-Star Team, 1985.

Year Club	League	G.	IP.	W.	L.	Pct.	H.	R.	ER.	SO.	BB.	ERA.
1976—Winston-Salem	Carolina	25	82	5	2	.714	77	26	25	76	28	2.74
1977—Bristol	Eastern	27	115	6	5	.545	113	57	45	78	35	3.52
1977—Pawtucket	Int'national	4	4	1	1	.500	5	1	1	1	3	2.25
1978—Pawtucket	Int'national	26	105	7	4	.636	100	46	36	83	56	3.09
1979—Pawtucket	Int'national	25	163	10	11	.476	145	73	53	103	52	2.93
1979—Boston	American	6	28	1	2	.333	39	23	20	11	9	6.43
1980—Pawtucket	Int'national	12	74	4	5	.444	67	36	30	51	33	3.65
1980—Boston	American	16	92	8	5	.615	81	35	31	45	31	3.03
1981—Boston	American	18	79	4	3	.571	74	44	40	44	28	4.56
1982—Boston	American	32	195⅔	13	10	.565	215	90	79	146	59	3.63
1983—Boston†	American	34	242	13	12	.520	236	122	110	136	81	4.09
1984—Pittsburgh‡	National	32	212	12	11	.522	200	81	77	117	56	3.27
1985—St. Louis	National	36	275	21	8	.724	209	68	59	169	49	1.93
1986—St. Louis§	National	30	219	13	7	.650	197	81	71	107	53	2.92
1987—St. Louis x	National	16	96	10	2	.833	100	43	41	54	32	3.84
1987—Louisville	Am. Assoc.	2	8	1	0	1.000	11	8	7	3	1	7.88
1988—St. Louis yz-Los Angeles	National	30	197⅔	10	8	.556	189	60	51	87	41	2.32
American League Totals—5 Years		106	636⅔	39	32	.549	645	314	280	382	208	3.96
National League Totals—5 Years		144	999⅔	66	36	.647	895	333	299	534	231	2.69
Major League Totals—10 Years		250	1636⅓	105	68	.607	1540	647	579	916	439	3.18

Selected by New York Mets' organization in 21st round of free-agent draft, June 4, 1975.

Selected by Boston Red Sox' organization in secondary phase of free-agent draft, January 7, 1976.

†Traded to Pittsburgh Pirates for Outfielder Mike Easler, December 6, 1983.

‡Traded with Outfielder Brian Harper to St. Louis Cardinals for Outfielder-First Baseman George Hendrick and Catcher Steve Barnard, December 12, 1984.

§On disabled list, September 16, 1986 through remainder of season.

xOn disabled list, April 20 to July 30, 1987; included rehabilitation disability assignment to Louisville, July 22 to July 30, 1987.

yOn disabled list, March 26 to April 25, 1988.

zTraded to Los Angeles Dodgers for Infielder Pedro Guerrero, August 16, 1988.

CHAMPIONSHIP SERIES RECORD

Established National League Championship Series record for most bases on balls, Series (5), 1987.
Tied National League Championship Series record for most hits allowed, game (10), October 7, 1987.

Year Club	League	G.	IP.	W.	L.	Pct.	H.	R.	ER.	SO.	BB.	ERA.
1985—St. Louis	National	2	12⅔	1	1	.500	10	5	4	8	3	2.84
1987—St. Louis	National	2	15⅓	1	1	.500	16	5	3	12	5	1.76
1988—Los Angeles	National	1	5	0	0	.000	8	4	4	1	1	7.20
Championship Series Totals—3 Years		5	33	2	2	.500	34	14	11	21	9	3.00

WORLD SERIES RECORD

Year Club	League	G.	IP.	W.	L.	Pct.	H.	R.	ER.	SO.	BB.	ERA.
1985—St. Louis	National	3	18	2	1	.667	15	6	6	14	7	3.00
1987—St.Louis	National	2	11	1	1	.500	15	7	7	8	3	5.73
1988—Los Angeles	National	1	1⅓	0	0	.000	0	0	0	1	0	0.00
World Series Totals—3 Years		6	30⅓	3	2	.600	30	13	13	23	10	3.86

SHANE LEE TURNER

Born January 8, 1963, at Los Angeles, Calif.
Height, 5.10. Weight, 180.
Throws right and bats lefthanded.
Attended California State University, Fullerton, Calif.

Year Club	League	Pos.	G.	AB.	R.	H.	2B.	3B.	HR.	RBI.	B.A.	PO.	A.	E.	F.A.
1985—Oneonta	NYP	*SS-2B	64	228	35	56	7	3	0	26	.246	109	164	15	*.948
1986—Fort Lauderdale†	Fla. St.	SS	66	222	48	71	12	2	2	36	.320	121	200	16	.953
1987—Columbus	Int.	SS	25	76	10	17	0	2	0	7	.224	35	53	8	.917
1987—Alb.‡-Read.	East.	3B-2B-SS	94	356	69	119	19	7	4	55	.334	106	172	9	.969
1988—Maine	Int.	3-S-2-O	38	117	10	21	3	1	0	9	.179	38	100	9	.939
1988—Reading	East.	3B-2B-SS	78	295	52	88	11	6	3	21	.298	102	150	10	.962
1988—Philadelphia	Nat.	3B-SS	18	35	1	6	0	0	0	1	.171	8	14	1	.957
Major League Totals—1 Year			18	35	1	6	0	0	0	1	.171	8	14	1	.957

Selected by New York Yankees' organization in 6th round of free-agent draft, June 3, 1985.
†On disabled list, June 3 to June 14 and July 5, 1986 through remainder of season.
‡Traded with Outfielder Keith Hughes to Philadelphia Phillies' organization for Outfielder Mike Easler, June 10, 1987.

WILLIE CLAY UPSHAW

Born April 27, 1957, at Blanco, Tex.
Height, 6.00. Weight, 185.
Throws and bats lefthanded.
Cousin of Gene Upshaw, guard with Oakland Raiders, 1967 through 1981;
and currently executive director of NFL Players Association; and Marvin Upshaw,
lineman with Cleveland Browns, Kansas City Chiefs and St. Louis Cardinals, 1968 through 1976.

Tied major league record for most errors by first baseman, inning (3), July 1, 1986 (fifth inning).
Major League stolen bases: 1978 (4), 1980 (1), 1981 (2), 1982 (8), 1983 (10), 1984 (10), 1985 (8), 1986 (23), 1987 (10), 1988 (12). Total—88.
Led American League first basemen in total chances with 1,556 in 1982.

Year Club	League	Pos.	G.	AB.	R.	H.	2B.	3B.	HR.	RBI.	B.A.	PO.	A.	E.	F.A.
1975—Oneonta	NYP	OF	29	91	8	8	1	0	0	4	.088	7	1	0	1.000
1976—Fort Lauderdale	Fla. St.	OF	84	263	20	60	6	0	3	22	.228	22	0	0	1.000
1977—Fort Lauderdale	Fla. St.	1B-OF	87	335	38	92	13	7	3	29	.275	358	31	14	.965
1977—West Haven†	East.	OF-1B	41	157	20	47	5	2	4	22	.299	40	0	4	.909
1978—Toronto	Amer.	OF-1B	95	224	26	53	8	2	1	17	.237	131	4	7	.951
1979—Syracuse	Int.	OF-1B	140	526	71	131	25	8	12	68	.249	544	24	14	.976
1980—Syracuse	Int.	OF-1B	100	358	55	91	13	7	9	52	.254	355	19	7	.982
1980—Toronto	Amer.	1B-OF	34	61	10	13	3	1	1	5	.213	51	7	1	.983
1981—Toronto	Amer.	1B-OF	61	111	15	19	3	1	4	10	.171	72	6	0	1.000
1982—Toronto	Amer.	1B	160	580	77	155	25	7	21	75	.267	*1438	101	*17	.989
1983—Toronto	Amer.	1B	160	579	99	177	26	7	27	104	.306	1294	117	*21	.985
1984—Toronto	Amer.	1B	152	569	79	158	31	9	19	84	.278	1246	103	14	.990
1985—Toronto	Amer.	1B	148	501	79	138	31	5	15	65	.275	1157	104	10	.992
1986—Toronto	Amer.	1B	155	573	85	144	28	6	9	60	.251	1314	131	12	.992
1987—Toronto‡	Amer.	1B	150	512	68	125	22	4	15	58	.244	1169	127	9	.993
1988—Cleveland§	Amer.	1B	149	493	58	121	22	3	11	50	.245	1162	102	*12	.991
Major League Totals—10 Years			1264	4203	596	1103	199	45	123	528	.262	9034	802	103	.990

Selected by New York Yankees' organization in 5th round of free-agent draft, June 4, 1975.
†Drafted by Toronto Blue Jays, December 5, 1977.
‡Sold to Cleveland Indians, March 25, 1988.
§Granted free agency, November 4, 1988; signed by Daiei Hawks of Japanese Baseball League, December 6, 1988.

CHAMPIONSHIP SERIES RECORD

Year Club	League	Pos.	G.	AB.	R.	H.	2B.	3B.	HR.	RBI.	B.A.	PO.	A.	E.	F.A.
1985—Toronto	Amer.	1B	7	26	2	6	2	0	0	1	.231	53	7	1	.984

JOSE ALTA URIBE

(Name pronounced Yoo-REE-bay.)
(Formerly known as Jose Alta Gonzalez.)

Born January 21, 1960, at San Cristobal, D. R.
Height, 5.10. Weight, 165.
Throws right and bats left and righthanded.

Major League stolen bases: 1984 (1), 1985 (8), 1986 (22), 1987 (12), 1988 (14). Total—57.
Led American Association in sacrifice hits with 14 in 1983.
Led American Association shortstops in total chances with 720 and double plays with 96 in 1984.
Led American Association shortstops in total chances with 664 and double plays with 90 in 1983.
Led Texas League shortstops in double plays with 88 in 1982.

Year Club	League	Pos.	G.	AB.	R.	H.	2B.	3B.	HR.	RBI.	B.A.	PO.	A.	E.	F.A.
1981—St. Petersburg†	Fla. St.	SS	128	463	54	124	15	2	0	40	.268	171	*387	32	.946
1982—Arkansas	Texas	SS	123	465	73	115	17	7	0	41	.247	185	385	36	.941
1982—Louisville	A. A.	SS	8	28	5	10	2	0	0	4	.357	15	18	1	.971
1983—Louisville	A. A.	SS	122	423	64	120	19	6	3	44	.284	206	425	*33	.950
1984—Louisville	A. A.	SS	145	484	68	135	20	2	3	46	.279	*233	*455	*32	*.956
1984—St. Louis‡	Nat.	SS-2B	8	19	4	4	0	0	0	3	.211	7	15	1	.957
1985—San Francisco	Nat.	SS-2B	147	476	46	113	20	4	3	26	.237	209	438	26	.961
1986—San Francisco	Nat.	SS	157	453	46	101	15	1	3	43	.223	249	444	16	.977

Year	Club	League	Pos.	G.	AB.	R.	H.	2B.	3B.	HR.	RBI.	B.A.	PO.	A.	E.	F.A.
1987—	San Francisco§	Nat.	SS	95	309	44	90	16	5	5	30	.291	145	286	13	.971
1988—	San Francisco x	Nat.	SS	141	493	47	124	10	7	3	35	.252	212	404	19	.970
	Major League Totals—5 Years			548	1750	187	432	61	17	14	137	.247	822	1587	75	.970

Signed as free agent by New York Yankees' organization, February 18, 1977.

†Released, July 5, 1977; signed by St. Louis Cardinals' organization, August 18, 1980.

‡Traded with First Basemen David Green and Gary Rajsich and Pitcher Dave LaPoint to San Francisco Giants for Outfielder-First Baseman Jack Clark, February 1, 1985.

§On disabled list, April 11 to April 30, May 5 to May 20 and May 28 to July 4, 1987.

xOn disabled list, May 31 to June 16, 1988.

CHAMPIONSHIP SERIES RECORD

Year	Club	League	Pos.	G.	AB.	R.	H.	2B.	3B.	HR.	RBI.	B.A.	PO.	A.	E.	F.A.
1987—	San Francisco	Nat.	SS	7	26	1	7	1	0	0	2	.269	11	20	1	.969

FRANK VALDEZ

Born October 12, 1968, at Santo Domingo, Dominican Republic.
Height, 6.01. Weight, 160.
Throws and bats righthanded.

Year	Club	League	Pos.	G.	AB.	R.	H.	2B.	3B.	HR.	RBI.	B.A.	PO.	A.	E.	F.A.
1986—	Elizabethton	Appal.	SS	16	40	6	8	2	0	0	6	.200	13	24	8	.822
1987—	Elizabethton	Appal.	3B-SS-OF	61	227	28	52	8	0	5	28	.229	70	109	18	.909
1988—	Kenosha	Midw.	3B	115	424	49	118	30	2	8	60	.278	89	222	33	.904

Signed as free agent by Minnesota Twins' organization, March 19, 1986.

SERGIO SANCHEZ VALDEZ

Born September 7, 1965, at Elias Pina, D.R.
Height, 6.01. Weight, 190.
Throws and bats righthanded.

Tied for American Association lead in shutouts with 2 in 1987.
Tied for Florida State League lead in shutouts with 4 in 1986.
Tied for New York-Pennsylvania League lead in games started by pitchers with 15 in 1985.

Year	Club	League	G.	IP.	W.	L.	Pct.	H.	R.	ER.	SO.	BB.	ERA.
1983—	Calgary	Pioneer	13	72⅔	6	3	.667	88	55	45	41	31	5.57
1984—	West Palm Beach†	Florida St.	5	11⅓	0	0	.000	15	11	11	6	8	8.74
1984—	Jamestown	NYP	13	76	2	7	.222	78	47	34	46	33	4.03
1985—	Utica	NYP	15	105⅔	6	5	.545	98	53	36	86	36	3.07
1986—	West Palm Beach	Florida St.	24	145⅔	*16	6	.727	119	48	40	108	46	2.47
1986—	Montreal	National	5	25	0	4	.000	39	20	19	20	11	6.84
1987—	Indianapolis	Am. Assoc.	27	158⅓	10	7	.588	191	108	90	*128	64	5.12
1988—	Indianapolis	Am. Assoc.	14	84	5	4	.556	80	38	32	61	28	3.43
	Major League Totals—1 Year		5	25	0	4	.000	39	20	19	20	11	6.84

Signed as free agent by Montreal Expos' organizaton, June 18, 1983.

†On disabled list, May 17 to June 3, 1984.

FERNANDO VALENZUELA (ANGUAMEA)

Name pronounced Val-en-ZWAY-luh.

Born November 1, 1960, at Navajoa, Sonora, Mexico.
Height, 5.11. Weight, 202.
Throws and bats lefthanded.

Tied modern major league record for most shutout games won or tied, rookie year (8), 1981.
Tied National League record for fewest assists by pitcher, season, for leader in assists (47), 1986.
Major League saves: 1980 (1), 1988 (1). Total—2.
Led National League in wild pitches with 14 in 1987.
Led National League in complete games with 11 in 1981, 20 in 1986 and tied for lead with 12 in 1987.
Led National League in shutouts with 8 in 1981.
Tied for National League lead in games started by pitchers with 25 in 1981.
Led Mexican Center League in wild pitches with 13 in 1978.
Named Major League Player of the Year by The Sporting News, 1981.
Named National League Pitcher of the Year by The Sporting News, 1981.
Won National League Cy Young Memorial Award, 1981.
Named National League Rookie Pitcher of the Year by The Sporting News, 1981.
Named National League Rookie of the Year by Baseball Writers' Association of America, 1981.
Named lefthanded pitcher on The Sporting News National League All-Star Team, 1981 and 1986.
Named pitcher on The Sporting News National League All-Star fielding team, 1986.
Named pitcher on The Sporting News National League Silver Slugger team, 1981 and 1983.

Year	Club	League	G.	IP.	W.	L.	Pct.	H.	R.	ER.	SO.	BB.	ERA.
1978—	Guanajuato	Mex. Cent.	16	93	5	6	.455	88	46	23	*91	46	2.23
1979—	Yucatan†	Mexican	26	181	10	12	.455	157	68	50	141	70	2.49
1979—	Lodi	California	3	24	1	2	.333	21	10	3	18	3	1.13
1980—	San Antonio	Texas	27	174	13	9	.591	156	70	60	*162	70	3.10
1980—	Los Angeles	National	10	18	2	0	1.000	8	2	0	16	5	0.00
1981—	Los Angeles	National	25	*192	13	7	.650	140	55	53	*180	61	2.48
1982—	Los Angeles‡	National	37	285	19	13	.594	247	105	91	199	83	2.87
1983—	Los Angeles	National	35	257	15	10	.600	245	*122	107	189	99	3.75
1984—	Los Angeles	National	34	261	12	17	.414	218	109	88	240	*106	3.03

Year	Club	League	G.	IP.	W.	L.	Pct.	H.	R.	ER.	SO.	BB.	ERA.
1985	—Los Angeles	National	35	272⅓	17	10	.630	211	92	74	208	101	2.45
1986	—Los Angeles	National	34	269⅓	*21	11	.656	226	104	94	242	85	3.14
1987	—Los Angeles	National	34	251	14	14	.500	*254	120	111	190	*124	3.98
1988	—Los Angeles§	National	23	142⅓	5	8	.385	142	71	67	64	76	4.24
	Major League Totals—9 Years		267	1948	118	90	.567	1691	780	685	1528	740	3.16

†Sold to Los Angeles Dodgers' organization, July 6, 1979.
‡Appeared in one game as an outfielder with no chances.
§On disabled list, July 31 to September 26, 1988.

DIVISION SERIES RECORD

Year	Club	League	G.	IP.	W.	L.	Pct.	H.	R.	ER.	SO.	BB.	ERA.
1981	—Los Angeles	National	2	17	1	0	1.000	10	2	2	10	3	1.06

CHAMPIONSHIP SERIES RECORD

Established National League Championship Series records for most bases on balls (10) and most strikeouts (13), six-game Series, 1985; most bases on balls, game (8), October 14, 1985.

Year	Club	League	G.	IP.	W.	L.	Pct.	H.	R.	ER.	SO.	BB.	ERA.
1981	—Los Angeles	National	2	14⅔	1	1	.500	10	4	4	10	5	2.45
1983	—Los Angeles	National	1	8	1	0	1.000	7	1	1	5	4	1.13
1985	—Los Angeles	National	2	14⅓	1	0	1.000	11	3	3	13	10	1.88
	Championship Series Totals—3 Years		5	37	3	1	.750	28	8	8	28	19	1.95

WORLD SERIES RECORD

Year	Club	League	G.	IP.	W.	L.	Pct.	H.	R.	ER.	SO.	BB.	ERA.
1981	—Los Angeles	National	1	9	1	0	1.000	9	4	4	6	7	4.00

ALL-STAR GAME RECORD

Tied All-Star Game record for most consecutive strikeouts, game (5), July 15, 1986.

Year	League	IP.	W.	L.	Pct.	H.	R.	ER.	SO.	BB.	ERA.
1981	—National	1	0	0	.000	2	0	0	0	0	0.00
1982	—National	⅔	0	0	.000	0	0	0	0	2	0.00
1984	—National	2	0	0	.000	2	0	0	3	0	0.00
1985	—National	1	0	0	.000	0	0	0	1	1	0.00
1986	—National	3	0	0	.000	1	0	0	5	0	0.00
	All-Star Game Totals—5 Years	7⅔	0	0	.000	5	0	0	9	3	0.00

Member of National League All-Star Team in 1983; did not play.

DAVID VALLE

Name pronounced Valley.

(Dave)

Born October 30, 1960, at Bayside, N. Y.
Height, 6.02. Weight, 200.
Throws and bats righthanded.
Brother of John Valle, minor league outfielder, 1972 through 1984.

Major League stolen bases: 1987 (2).

Led Northwest League catchers in double plays with 6 and tied for lead in passed balls with 23 in 1978.

Year	Club	League	Pos.	G.	AB.	R.	H.	2B.	3B.	HR.	RBI.	B.A.	PO.	A.	E.	F.A.
1978	—Bellingham	N'west	C	57	167	12	34	2	0	2	21	.204	*338	65	10	.976
1979	—Alexandria†	Carol.	C	58	169	17	36	5	0	6	25	.213	290	44	11	.968
1980	—San Jose	Calif.	C	119	430	81	126	14	0	12	70	.293	570	*102	17	.975
1981	—Lynn‡	East.	C	93	318	38	82	16	0	11	54	.258	445	56	6	.988
1982	—Salt Lake City	P. C.	C-1B	75	234	28	49	11	1	4	28	.209	347	49	11	.973
1983	—Chattanooga§	South.	C-1B	53	176	20	42	11	0	3	22	.239	239	24	4	.985
1984	—Salt Lake City x	P. C.	C	86	284	54	79	13	1	12	54	.278	433	34	6	.987
1984	—Seattle	Amer.	C	13	27	4	8	1	0	1	4	.296	56	5	0	1.000
1985	—Seattle y	Amer.	C	31	70	2	11	1	0	0	4	.157	117	7	3	.976
1985	—Calgary	P. C.	C	42	131	17	45	8	0	6	26	.344	202	11	1	.995
1986	—Calgary	P. C.	C	105	353	71	110	21	2	21	72	.312	404	61	6	.987
1986	—Seattle	Amer.	C-1B	22	53	10	18	3	0	5	15	.340	90	3	2	.979
1987	—Seattle z	Amer.	C-1B-OF	95	324	40	83	16	3	12	53	.256	422	34	5	.989
1988	—Seattle a	Amer.	C-1B	93	290	29	67	15	2	10	50	.231	490	47	6	.989
	Major League Totals—5 Years			254	764	85	187	36	5	28	126	.245	1175	96	16	.988

Selected by Seattle Mariners' organization in 2nd round of free-agent draft, June 6, 1978.
†On disabled list, July 26 to August 25, 1979.
‡On disabled list, June 24 to July 3, 1981.
§On disabled list, April 13 to June 20 and June 27 to July 7, 1983.
xOn disabled list, May 4 to May 17 and June 9 to June 25, 1984.
yOn disabled list, April 26 to July 19, 1985; included rehabilitation disability assignment to Calgary, June 26 to July 12, 1985.
zOn disabled list, April 17 to May 7, 1987.
aOn disabled list, July 23 to September 2, 1988.

PITCHING RECORD

Year	Club	League	G.	IP.	W.	L.	Pct.	H.	R.	ER.	SO.	BB.	ERA.
1980	—San Jose	California	1	1	0	0	.000	1	0	0	2	2	0.00

EDWARD JOHN VANDE BERG
(Ed)

Born October 26, 1958, at Redlands, Calif.
Height, 6.01. Weight, 170.
Throws left and bats righthanded.
Attended San Bernardino Valley, San Bernardino, Calif. and Arizona State University, Tempe, Ariz.

Major League saves: 1982 (5), 1983 (5), 1984 (7), 1985 (3), 1988 (2). Total—22.
Named American League Rookie Pitcher of the Year by THE SPORTING NEWS, 1982.

Year Club	League	G.	IP.	W.	L.	Pct.	H.	R.	ER.	SO.	BB.	ERA.
1980—Bellingham	Northwest	14	101	9	0	*1.000	82	40	32	78	46	2.85
1981—Spokane	P. Coast	49	62	4	3	.571	62	33	26	49	29	3.77
1982—Seattle	American	*78	76	9	4	.692	54	21	20	60	32	2.37
1983—Seattle	American	68	64⅓	2	4	.333	59	32	24	49	22	3.36
1984—Seattle†	American	50	130⅓	8	12	.400	165	76	69	71	50	4.76
1985—Seattle‡	American	76	67⅔	2	1	.667	71	30	28	34	31	3.72
1986—Los Angeles§	National	60	71⅓	1	5	.167	83	32	27	42	33	3.41
1987—Cleveland xy	American	55	72⅓	1	0	1.000	96	42	41	40	21	5.10
1988—Oklahoma City	Am. Assoc.	26	46⅓	3	2	.600	41	20	19	47	11	3.69
1988—Texas z	American	26	37	2	2	.500	44	19	17	18	11	4.14
American League Totals—6 Years		353	447⅔	24	23	.511	489	220	199	272	167	4.00
National League Totals—1 Year		60	71⅓	1	5	.167	83	32	27	42	33	3.41
Major League Totals—7 Years		413	519	25	28	.472	572	252	226	314	200	3.92

Selected by San Diego Padres' organization in 3rd round of free-agent draft, January 10, 1978.
Selected by St. Louis Cardinals' organization in secondary phase of free-agent draft, June 6, 1978.
Selected by Seattle Mariners' organization in 13th round of free-agent draft, June 3, 1980.
†Appeared in one game as a pinch-runner.
‡Traded to Los Angeles Dodgers for Catcher Steve Yeager, December 11, 1985.
§Released, December 20, 1986; signed by Cleveland Indians, January 27, 1987.
xGranted free agency, November 9, 1987; signed by Texas Rangers, February 2, 1988.
yReleased, March 29, 1988; re-signed by Rangers, April 8, 1988.
zGranted free agency, November 4, 1988; re-signed by Rangers, December 21, 1988.

ANDREW JAMES VAN SLYKE
(Andy)

Born December 21, 1960, at Utica, N.Y.
Height, 6.02. Weight, 190.
Throws right and bats lefthanded.

Tied Major League record for fewest double plays by outfielder, season, for leader in double plays (4), 1985.
Major League stolen bases: 1983 (21), 1984 (28), 1985 (34), 1986 (21), 1987 (34), 1988 (30). Total—168.
Led National League in sacrifice flies with 13 in 1988.
Led National League outfielders in total chances with 422 in 1988.
Tied for National League lead in double plays by outfielders with 4 in 1985 and 6 in 1987.
Named National League Player of the Year by THE SPORTING NEWS, 1988.
Named outfielder on THE SPORTING NEWS National League All-Star Team, 1988.
Named outfielder on THE SPORTING NEWS National League All-Star fielding team, 1988.
Named outfielder on THE SPORTING NEWS National League Silver Slugger team, 1988.
Received reported $50,000 bonus to sign with St. Louis Cardinals, 1979.

Year Club	League	Pos.	G.	AB.	R.	H.	2B.	3B.	HR.	RBI.	B.A.	PO.	A.	E.	F.A.
1979—Johnson City†	Appal.						(Did not play)								
1980—Gastonia	S. Atl.	OF	126	426	62	115	15	4	8	59	.270	177	16	•16	.923
1981—St. Petersburg‡	Fla. St.	OF	94	282	42	62	11	3	1	25	.220	168	10	5	.973
1982—Arkansas	Texas	OF	123	416	83	116	13	*11	16	70	.279	266	17	7	.976
1983—Louisville	A. A.	3B-1B-OF	54	220	52	81	21	4	6	41	.368	201	78	16	.946
1983—St. Louis	Nat.	OF-3B-1B	101	309	51	81	15	5	8	38	.262	203	59	6	.978
1984—St. Louis	Nat.	OF-3B-1B	137	361	45	88	16	4	7	50	.244	357	82	8	.982
1985—St. Louis	Nat.	OF-1B	146	424	61	110	25	6	13	55	.259	237	13	1	.996
1986—St. Louis§	Nat.	OF-1B	137	418	48	113	23	7	13	61	.270	415	34	8	.982
1987—Pittsburgh	Nat.	OF-1B	157	564	93	165	36	11	21	82	.293	338	10	4	.989
1988—Pittsburgh	Nat.	OF	154	587	101	169	23	*15	25	100	.288	*406	12	4	.991
Major League Totals—6 Years			832	2663	399	726	138	48	87	386	.273	1956	210	31	.986

Selected by St. Louis Cardinals' organization in 1st round (sixth player selected) of free-agent draft, June 5, 1979.
†On disabled list, June 8, 1979 through remainder of season.
‡On disabled list, April 10 to May 14, 1981.
§Traded with Catcher Mike LaValliere and Pitcher Mike Dunne to Pittsburgh Pirates for Catcher Tony Pena, April 1, 1987.

CHAMPIONSHIP SERIES RECORD

Year Club	League	Pos.	G.	AB.	R.	H.	2B.	3B.	HR.	RBI.	B.A.	PO.	A.	E.	F.A.
1985—St. Louis	Nat.	OF-PR	5	11	1	1	0	0	0	1	.091	6	0	0	1.000

WORLD SERIES RECORD

Year Club	League	Pos.	G.	AB.	R.	H.	2B.	3B.	HR.	RBI.	B.A.	PO.	A.	E.	F.A.
1985—St. Louis	Nat.	O-PH-PR	6	11	0	1	0	0	0	0	.091	8	0	0	1.000

ALL-STAR GAME RECORD

Year League	Pos.	AB.	R.	H.	2B.	3B.	HR.	RBI.	B.A.	PO.	A.	E.	F.A.
1988—National	OF	2	0	0	0	0	0	0	.000	2	0	0	1.000

GARY ANDREW VARSHO

Born June 20, 1961, at Marshfield, Wis.
Height, 5.11. Weight, 190.
Throws right and bats lefthanded.
Attended University of Wisconsin, Oshkosh, Wis.

Major League stolen bases: 1988: (5).
Led American Association in caught stealing with 17 in 1987.
Led Eastern League in stolen bases with 45 in 1986 and tied for lead with 40 in 1985.
Led Texas League second basemen in total chances with 650 in 1984.
Led California League second basemen in double plays with 71 in 1983.

Year Club	League	Pos.	G.	AB.	R.	H.	2B.	3B.	HR.	RBI.	B.A.	PO.	A.	E.	F.A.
1982—Quad Cities	Midw.	2B	76	271	52	68	9	4	3	40	.251	190	180	14	.964
1983—Salinas	Calif.	2B	131	490	69	129	16	*13	3	57	.263	284	339	•33	.950
1984—Midland	Texas	2B	128	429	65	112	15	6	8	50	.261	*286	335	*29	.955
1985—Pittsfield	East.	1B-OF	115	418	62	101	14	6	3	37	.242	670	51	6	.992
1986—Pittsfield †	East.	OF-1B-2B	107	399	75	106	18	5	13	44	.266	213	14	6	.974
1987—Iowa	A. A.	OF	132	504	87	152	23	9	9	48	.302	227	18	6	.976
1988—Iowa	A. A.	OF	66	234	46	65	16	5	4	26	.278	120	6	2	.984
1988—Chicago	Nat.	OF	46	73	6	20	3	0	0	5	.274	29	0	3	.906
Major League Totals—1 Year			46	73	6	20	3	0	0	5	.274	29	0	3	.906

Selected by Chicago Cubs' organization in 5th round of free-agent draft, June 7, 1982.
†On disabled list, August 13, 1986 through remainder of season.

AGUEDO VASQUEZ

Born February 5, 1967, at Puerto Plata, Dominican Republic.
Height, 5.10. Weight 160.
Throws and bats righthanded.

Led Florida State League in saves with 33 and games finished in relief with 51 in 1988.

Year Club	League	G.	IP.	W.	L.	Pct.	H.	R.	ER.	SO.	BB.	ERA.
1987—Sarasota Royals	Gulf Coast	3	2	1	0	1.000	1	0	0	0	2	0.00
1987—Fort Myers	Florida St.	8	15⅔	0	1	.000	24	12	11	7	8	6.32
1988—Baseball City	Florida St.	*62	80⅔	3	2	.600	54	26	15	68	30	1.67
1988—Omaha	Am. Assoc.	2	4	0	0	.000	9	4	4	1	2	9.00

Signed as free agent by Kansas City Royals' organization, November 23, 1985.

LUIS EDUARDO VASQUEZ

Born March 23, 1967, at Estrada Bolivar, Venezuela.
Height, 6.01. Weight, 170.
Throws and bats righthanded.

Year Club	League	G.	IP.	W.	L.	Pct.	H.	R.	ER.	SO.	BB.	ERA.
1985—Elmira	NYP	18	57⅓	2	4	.333	50	28	22	42	24	3.45
1986—Winter Haven	Florida St.	31	159⅓	15	3	•.833	145	65	60	92	58	3.39
1987—New Britain	Eastern	10	61	3	2	.600	63	23	19	26	19	2.80
1988—New Britain	Eastern	15	112⅓	3	9	.250	87	46	31	97	28	2.48
1988—Pawtucket	Int'national	12	75⅓	5	4	.556	74	37	30	73	15	3.58

Signed as free agent by Boston Red Sox' organization, January 24, 1985.

DeWAYNE MATHEW VAUGHN

Born July 22, 1959, at Oklahoma City, Okla.
Height, 6.01. Weight, 175.
Throws and bats righthanded.
Received degree from University of Oklahoma, Norman, Okla., in 1981.

Year Club	League	G.	IP.	W.	L.	Pct.	H.	R.	ER.	SO.	BB.	ERA.
1981—Little Falls	NYP	1	1	0	0	.000	2	0	0	0	1	0.00
1981—Shelby	S. Atlantic	12	29	1	3	.250	27	17	10	18	10	3.10
1982—Lynchburg	Carolina	20	45⅓	1	5	.167	52	34	26	36	30	5.16
1983—Jackson	Texas	12	61	3	7	.300	76	51	44	28	23	6.49
1983—Lynchburg	Carolina	13	88	8	3	.727	100	40	33	61	20	3.38
1984—Jackson †	Texas	16	104⅓	6	4	.600	104	40	26	58	20	2.24
1985—Jackson ‡	Texas	24	124⅔	9	7	.563	133	59	48	58	35	3.47
1986—Tidewater §	Int'national	25	125	6	8	.429	128	56	53	58	41	3.82
1987—Tidewater x	Int'national	50	122	4	4	.500	103	40	36	72	39	*2.66
1988—Texas	American	8	15⅓	0	0	.000	24	15	13	8	4	7.63
1988—Oklahoma City y	Am. Assoc.	14	86	4	6	.400	105	51	46	45	22	4.81
Major League Totals—1 Year		8	15⅓	0	0	.000	24	15	13	8	4	7.63

Signed as free agent by New York Mets' organization, July 18, 1981.
†On disabled list, April 20 to June 11, 1984.
‡On disabled list, April 9 to April 22 and June 10 to June 21, 1985.
§On disabled list, April 11 to April 22, 1986.
xGranted free agency, October 15, 1987; signed by Oklahoma City (Texas Rangers' organization), November 12, 1987.
yGranted free agency, October 15, 1988.

GREGORY LAMONT VAUGHN
(Greg)

Born July 3, 1965, at Sacramento, Calif.
Height, 6.00. Weight, 195.
Throws and bats righthanded.
Attended Sacramento City College, Sacramento, Calif.,
and University of Miami, Coral Gables, Fla.

Led Texas League in total bases with 279 in 1988.
Led Midwest League in total bases with 292 in 1987.
Named Midwest League co-Most Valuable Player, 1987.

Year Club	League	Pos.	G.	AB.	R.	H.	2B.	3B.	HR.	RBI.	B.A.	PO.	A.	E.	F.A.
1986—Helena	Pion.	OF	66	258	64	75	13	2	16	54	.291	99	5	3	.972
1987—Beloit	Midw.	OF	139	492	*120	150	31	6	*33	105	.305	247	11	10	.963
1988—El Paso	Texas	OF	131	505	*104	152	*39	2	*28	*105	.301	216	12	7	.970

Selected by St. Louis Cardinals' organization in 5th round of free-agent draft, January 17, 1984.
Selected by Milwaukee Brewers' organization in secondary phase of free-agent draft, June 4, 1984.
Selected by Pittsburgh Pirates' organization in secondary phase of free-agent draft, January 9, 1985.
Selected by California Angels' organization in secondary phase of free-agent draft, June 3, 1985.
Selected by Milwaukee Brewers' organization in secondary phase of free-agent draft, June 2, 1986.

RANDY LEE VELARDE

Bor November 24, 1962, at Midland, Tex.
Height, 6.00. Weight, 185.
Throws and bats righthanded.
Attended Lubbock Christian College, Lubbock, Tex.

Major League stolen bases: 1988 (1).
Led Midwest League shortstops in errors with 52 in 1986.

Year Club	League	Pos.	G.	AB.	R.	H.	2B.	3B.	HR.	RBI.	B.A.	PO.	A.	E.	F.A.
1985—Niagara Falls	NYP	O-S-2-3	67	218	28	48	7	3	1	16	.220	124	117	15	.941
1986—Appleton	Midw.	SS-3B-OF	124	417	55	105	31	4	11	50	.252	205	300	54	.903
1986—Buffalo†	A. A.	SS	9	20	2	4	1	0	0	2	.200	9	28	3	.925
1987—Albany	East.	SS-OF	71	263	40	83	20	2	7	32	.316	128	254	17	.957
1987—Columbus	Int.	SS	49	185	21	59	10	6	5	33	.319	100	164	16	.943
1987—New York	Amer.	SS	8	22	1	4	0	0	0	1	.182	8	20	2	.933
1988—Columbus	Int.	SS-2B-3B	78	293	39	79	23	4	5	37	.270	123	271	25	.940
1988—New York	Amer.	2B-SS-3B	48	115	18	20	6	0	5	12	.174	72	98	8	.955
Major League Totals—2 Years			56	137	19	24	6	0	5	13	.175	80	118	10	.952

Selected by Chicago White Sox' organization in 19th round of free-agent draft, June 3, 1985.
†Traded with Pitcher Pete Filson to New York Yankees for Pitcher Scott Nielsen and Infielder Mike Soper, January 5, 1987.

DAVID SCOTT VERES
(Dave)

Born October 19, 1966, at Montgomery, Ala.
Height, 6.02. Weight, 195.
Throws and bats righthanded.
Attended Mount Hood Community College, Gresham, Ore.

Tied for California League lead in wild pitches with 29 in 1987.
Tied for Northwest League lead in games started by pitchers with 15 in 1986.

Year Club	League	G.	IP.	W.	L.	Pct.	H.	R.	ER.	SO.	BB.	ERA.
1986—Medford	Northwest	15	77⅓	5	2	.714	58	38	28	60	57	3.26
1987—Modesto	California	26	148⅓	8	9	.471	124	90	79	124	108	4.79
1988—Modesto	California	19	125	4	11	.267	100	61	46	91	78	3.31
1988—Huntsville	Southern	8	39	3	4	.429	50	20	18	17	15	4.15

Selected by Oakland Athletics' organization in 4th round of free-agent draft, January 14, 1986.

RANDOLPH RUHLAND VERES
(Randy)

Born November 25, 1965, at San Francisco, Calif.
Height, 6.03. Weight, 190.
Throws and bats righthanded.
Attended Sacramento City College, Sacramento, Calif.

Year Club	League	G.	IP.	W.	L.	Pct.	H.	R.	ER.	SO.	BB.	ERA.
1985—Helena	Pioneer	13	77⅓	7	4	.636	66	43	33	67	36	3.84
1986—Beloit†	Midwest	23	113⅓	4	12	.250	132	78	49	87	52	3.89
1987—Beloit	Midwest	21	127	10	6	.625	132	63	44	98	52	3.12
1988—Stockton	California	20	110	8	4	.667	94	54	41	96	77	3.35
1988—El Paso	Texas	6	39⅓	3	2	.600	35	18	16	31	12	3.66

Selected by New York Mets' organization in 32nd round of free-agent draft, June 4, 1984.
Selected by Milwaukee Brewers' organization in secondary phase of free-agent draft, January 9, 1985.
†On disabled list, August 17, 1986 through remainder of season.

FRANK JOHN VIOLA JR.

Name pronounced Vy-OH-luh.

Born April 19, 1960, at Hempstead, N.Y.
Height, 6.04. Weight, 209.
Throws and bats lefthanded.
Attended St. John's University, Jamaica, N.Y.

Tied for American League lead in games started by pitchers with 37 in 1986.
Named American League Pitcher of the Year by THE SPORTING NEWS, 1988.
Won American League Cy Young Memorial Award, 1988.
Named lefthanded pitcher on THE SPORTING NEWS American League All-Star Team, 1988.

Year Club	League	G.	IP.	W.	L.	Pct.	H.	R.	ER.	SO.	BB.	ERA.
1981—Orlando	Southern	17	97	5	4	.556	112	47	37	50	33	3.43
1982—Toledo	Int'national	8	58	2	3	.400	61	27	25	34	18	3.88
1982—Minnesota	American	22	126	4	10	.286	152	77	73	84	38	5.21
1983—Minnesota	American	35	210	7	15	.318	242	*141	*128	127	92	5.49
1984—Minnesota	American	35	257⅔	18	12	.600	225	101	92	149	73	3.21
1985—Minnesota	American	36	250⅔	18	14	.563	262	*136	114	135	68	4.09
1986—Minnesota	American	37	245⅔	16	13	.552	257	136	123	191	83	4.51
1987—Minnesota	American	36	251⅔	17	10	.630	230	91	81	197	66	2.90
1988—Minnesota	American	35	255⅓	*24	7	*.774	236	80	75	193	54	2.64
Major League Totals—7 Years		236	1597	104	81	.562	1604	762	686	1076	474	3.87

Selected by Kansas City Royals' organization in 16th round of free-agent draft, June 6, 1978.
Selected by Minnesota Twins' organization in 2nd round of free-agent draft, June 8, 1981.

CHAMPIONSHIP SERIES RECORD

Year Club	League	G.	IP.	W.	L.	Pct.	H.	R.	ER.	SO.	BB.	ERA.
1987—Minnesota	American	2	12	1	0	1.000	14	8	7	9	5	5.25

WORLD SERIES RECORD

Year Club	League	G.	IP.	W.	L.	Pct.	H.	R.	ER.	SO.	BB.	ERA.
1987—Minnesota	American	3	19⅓	2	1	.667	17	8	8	16	3	3.72

ALL-STAR GAME RECORD

Year League	IP.	W.	L.	Pct.	H.	R.	ER.	SO.	BB.	ERA.
1988—American	2	1	0	1.000	0	0	0	1	0	0.00

OSVALDO JOSE VIRGIL JR.
(Ozzie)

Born December 7, 1956, at Mayaguez, P. R.
Height, 6.01. Weight, 195.
Throws and bats righthanded.
Son of Ozzie Virgil, infielder-catcher with New York N.L., Detroit, Kansas City, Baltimore, Pittsburgh and San Francisco, 1956 through 1958, 1960 through 1962, 1965, 1966 and 1969; coach, San Francisco Giants, 1970 through 1972, 1974 and 1975; scout, San Francisco Giants, 1973; coach, Montreal Expos, 1976 through 1981; coach, San Diego Padres, 1982 through 1985; and coach with Seattle Mariners, 1986 through June 6, 1988.

Major League stolen bases: 1984 (1), 1986 (1), 1988 (2). Total—4.
Led Carolina League in total bases with 234 in 1978.
Named Carolina League Most Valuable Player, 1978.

Year Club	League	Pos.	G.	AB.	R.	H.	2B.	3B.	HR.	RBI.	B.A.	PO.	A.	E.	F.A.
1976—Auburn	NYP	C	39	113	10	16	1	2	1	10	.142	153	14	5	.971
1977—Spartanburg	W. Car.	C	107	365	53	103	21	1	14	54	.282	502	*68	18	.969
1978—Peninsula	Carol.	C	126	409	79	124	21	1	*29	*98	.303	581	45	8	.987
1979—Reading	East.	C	128	429	57	99	17	1	8	66	.231	532	64	12	.980
1980—Reading	East.	C-1B	135	456	92	123	15	2	28	*104	.270	592	62	16	.976
1980—Philadelphia	Nat.	C	1	5	1	1	1	0	0	0	.200	4	0	0	1.000
1981—Oklahoma City†	A. A.	C	83	275	41	63	11	2	11	44	.229	201	28	4	.983
1981—Philadelphia	Nat.	C	6	6	0	0	0	0	0	0	.000	2	0	0	1.000
1982—Philadelphia	Nat.	C	49	101	11	24	6	0	3	8	.238	173	14	7	.964
1983—Philadelphia	Nat.	C	55	140	11	30	7	0	6	23	.214	228	24	9	.966
1984—Philadelphia	Nat.	C	141	456	61	119	21	2	18	68	.261	722	58	6	.992
1985—Philadelphia‡	Nat.	C	131	426	47	105	16	3	19	55	.246	667	52	4	*.994
1986—Atlanta	Nat.	C	114	359	45	80	9	0	15	48	.223	682	93	13	.984
1987—Atlanta	Nat.	C	123	429	57	106	13	1	27	72	.247	654	74	8	.989
1988—Atlanta§	Nat.	C	107	320	23	82	10	0	9	31	.256	448	45	5	.990
Major League Totals—9 Years			727	2242	256	547	83	6	97	305	.244	3580	360	52	.987

Selected by Philadelphia Phillies' organization in 6th round of free-agent draft, June 8, 1976.
†On disabled list, April 14 to April 27 and June 2 to June 29, 1981.
‡Traded with Pitcher Pete Smith to Atlanta Braves for Pitcher Steve Bedrosian and Outfielder Milt Thompson, December 10, 1985.
§Granted free agency, November 4, 1988.

CHAMPIONSHIP SERIES RECORD

Year Club	League	Pos.	G.	AB.	R.	H.	2B.	3B.	HR.	RBI.	B.A.	PO.	A.	E.	F.A.
1983—Philadelphia	Nat.	PH	1	1	0	0	0	0	0	0	.000	0	0	0	.000

WORLD SERIES RECORD

Year	Club	League	Pos.	G.	AB.	R.	H.	2B.	3B.	HR.	RBI.	B.A.	PO.	A.	E.	F.A.
1983	Philadelphia	Nat.	PH-C	3	2	0	1	0	0	0	1	.500	1	0	0	1.000

ALL-STAR GAME RECORD

Year	League	Pos.	AB.	R.	H.	2B.	3B.	HR.	RBI.	B.A.	PO.	A.	E.	F.A.
1985	National	C	1	0	1	0	0	0	2	1.000	3	0	0	1.000
1987	National	C	2	1	1	0	0	0	0	.500	7	0	0	1.000
All-Star Game Totals—2 Years			3	1	2	0	0	0	2	.667	10	0	0	1.000

JOSE LUIS VIZCAINO (PIMENTAL)

Born March 26, 1968, at Palenque, Dominican Republic.
Height, 6.01. Weight, 150.
Throws right and bats left and righthanded.

Led Gulf Coast League shortstops in double plays with 23 in 1987.

Year	Club	League	Pos.	G.	AB.	R.	H.	2B.	3B.	HR.	RBI.	B.A.	PO.	A.	E.	F.A.
1987	Sarasota Dodgers	Gulf C.	SS-1B	49	150	26	38	5	1	0	12	.253	73	107	13	.933
1988	Bakersfield	Calif.	SS	122	433	77	126	11	4	0	38	.291	185	340	30	.946

Signed as free agent by Los Angeles Dodgers' organization, February 18, 1986.

OMAR ENRIQUE VIZQUEL

Born May 15, 1967, at Caracas, Venezuela.
Height, 5.09. Weight, 155.
Throws right and bats left and righthanded.

Led Midwest League shortstops in fielding with .969 in 1986.

Year	Club	League	Pos.	G.	AB.	R.	H.	2B.	3B.	HR.	RBI.	B.A.	PO.	A.	E.	F.A.
1984	Butte†	Pion.	SS-2B	15	45	7	14	2	0	0	4	.311	13	29	5	.894
1985	Bellingham†	N'west	SS-2B	50	187	24	42	9	0	5	17	.225	85	175	19	.932
1986	Wausau†	Midw.	SS-2B	105	352	60	75	13	2	4	28	.213	153	328	16	.968
1987	Salinas†	Calif.	SS-2B	114	407	61	107	12	8	0	38	.263	81	295	25	.938
1988	Vermont†	East.	SS	103	374	54	95	18	2	2	35	.254	173	268	19	*.959
1988	Calgary	P. C.	SS	33	107	10	24	2	3	1	12	.224	43	92	6	.957

Signed as free agent by Seattle Mariners' organization, April 1, 1984.
†Batted righthanded.

HECTOR RAUL WAGNER

Born November 26, 1968, at Los Mamelles, Santo Domingo, D.R.
Height, 6.03. Weight, 185.
Throws and bats righthanded.

Year	Club	League	G.	IP.	W.	L.	Pct.	H.	R.	ER.	SO.	BB.	ERA.
1987	Sarasota Royals	Gulf Coast	13	53	1	3	.250	63	26	18	28	12	3.06
1988	Eugene	Northwest	15	85⅔	4	•9	.308	76	46	35	67	28	3.68

Signed as free agent by Kansas City Royals' organization, May 13, 1986.

JAMES WALEWANDER

Name pronounced WHALE-wonn-der.

(Jim)

Born May 2, 1961, at Chicago, Ill.
Height, 5.10. Weight, 160.
Throws right and bats left and righthanded.
Attended Iowa State University, Ames, Iowa.

Major League stolen bases: 1987 (2), 1988 (11). Total—13.
Led Appalachian League in stolen bases with 35 in 1983.
Led Florida State League second basemen in total chances with 698 in 1985.
Led Florida State League second basemen in putouts with 329 in 1984.
Led Appalachian League second basemen in assists with 188, total chances with 325 and double plays with 33 in 1983.

Year	Club	League	Pos.	G.	AB.	R.	H.	2B.	3B.	HR.	RBI.	B.A.	PO.	A.	E.	F.A.
1983	Bristol	Appal.	2B-SS	•73	*285	56	91	14	2	4	28	.319	140	222	16	.958
1984	Lakeland	Fla. St.	2B-SS-3B	137	502	70	136	16	2	0	36	.271	342	341	23	.967
1985	Lakeland	Fla. St.	2B	129	499	80	141	13	7	0	36	.283	267	*417	14	.980
1985	Birmingham	South.	2B	14	45	3	13	0	1	0	2	.289	22	33	1	.982
1986	Glens Falls	East.	2B-3B-SS	124	440	59	107	10	6	1	31	.243	207	291	18	.965
1987	Toledo	Int.	2B	59	210	27	57	9	1	0	12	.271	129	139	12	.957
1987	Detroit	Amer.	2B-3B-SS	53	54	24	13	3	1	1	4	.241	26	58	1	.988
1988	Detroit	Amer.	2B-SS-3B	88	175	23	37	5	0	0	6	.211	125	154	6	.979
1988	Toledo	Int.	2B	4	11	4	5	2	0	0	2	.455	12	10	1	.957
Major League Totals—2 Years				141	229	47	50	8	1	1	10	.218	151	212	7	.981

Selected by Detroit Tigers' organization in 9th round of free-agent draft, June 6, 1983.

ROBERT VERNON WALK

(Bob)

Born November 26, 1956, at Van Nuys, Calif.
Height, 6.04. Weight, 217.
Throws and bats righthanded.
Attended College of the Canyons, Valencia, Calif.

Major League saves: 1986 (2).

Led National League in wild pitches with 13 in 1988.

Led Pacific Coast League in complete games with 12 in 1985.

Led International League in complete games with 11 and tied for lead in games started by pitchers with 28 and home runs allowed with 22 in 1983.

Led Carolina League in hit batsmen with 13 in 1978.

Year Club	League	G.	IP.	W.	L.	Pct.	H.	R.	ER.	SO.	BB.	ERA.
1977—Spartanburg	W. Carol.	15	99	6	9	.400	90	55	40	66	46	3.64
1977—Peninsula	Carolina	8	36	0	2	.000	44	31	17	23	20	4.25
1978—Peninsula	Carolina	26	187	13	8	.619	147	58	44	150	64	2.12
1979—Reading	Eastern	24	185	12	7	.632	156	62	46	*135	77	*2.24
1980—Oklahoma City	Am. Assoc.	8	49	5	1	.833	39	21	16	36	17	2.94
1980—Philadelphia†	National	27	152	11	7	.611	163	82	77	94	71	4.56
1981—Atlanta‡	National	12	43	1	4	.200	41	25	22	16	23	4.60
1981—Richmond	Int'national	4	22	2	1	.667	18	7	6	13	11	2.45
1982—Atlanta	National	32	164⅓	11	9	.550	179	101	89	84	59	4.87
1983—Richmond	Int'national	28	*185	11	12	.478	179	*119	*107	123	102	5.21
1983—Atlanta§	National	1	3⅔	0	0	.000	7	3	3	4	2	7.36
1984—Hawaii	P. Coast	18	127⅓	9	5	.643	100	39	32	85	42	*2.26
1984—Pittsburgh x	National	2	10⅓	1	1	.500	8	5	3	10	4	2.61
1985—Hawaii	P. Coast	24	173	*16	5	.762	143	57	51	124	61	*2.65
1985—Pittsburgh	National	9	58⅔	2	3	.400	60	27	24	40	18	3.68
1986—Pittsburgh	National	44	141⅔	7	8	.467	129	66	59	78	64	3.75
1987—Pittsburgh	National	39	117	8	2	.800	107	52	43	78	51	3.31
1988—Pittsburgh y	National	32	212⅔	12	10	.545	183	75	64	81	65	2.71
Major League Totals—8 Years		198	903⅓	53	44	.546	877	436	384	485	357	3.83

Selected by California Angels' organization in 5th round of free-agent draft, January 9, 1975.

Selected by Philadelphia Phillies' organization in 5th round of free-agent draft, January 7, 1976.

Selected by Philadelphia Phillies' organization in secondary phase of free-agent draft, June 8, 1976.

†Traded to Atlanta Braves for Outfielder Gary Matthews, March 25, 1981.

‡On disabled list, May 26 to August 9, 1981.

§Released, March 26, 1984; signed by Pittsburgh Pirates' organization, April 3, 1984.

xOn disabled list, July 23, 1984 through remainder of season.

yGranted free agency, November 4, 1988; re-signed by Pirates, November 27, 1988.

CHAMPIONSHIP SERIES RECORD

Year Club	League	G.	IP.	W.	L.	Pct.	H.	R.	ER.	SO.	BB.	ERA.
1982—Atlanta	National	1	1	0	0	.000	2	1	1	1	1	9.00

WORLD SERIES RECORD

Year Club	League	G.	IP.	W.	L.	Pct.	H.	R.	ER.	SO.	BB.	ERA.
1980—Philadelphia	National	1	7	1	0	1.000	8	6	6	3	3	7.71

ALL-STAR GAME RECORD

Year League	IP.	W.	L.	Pct.	H.	R.	ER.	SO.	BB.	ERA.
1988—National	⅓	0	0	.000	0	0	0	0	0	0.00

CLEOTHA WALKER

(Chico)

Born November 25, 1957, at Jackson, Miss.
Height, 5.09. Weight, 170.
Throws right and bats left and righthanded.

Major League stolen bases: 1980 (3), 1985 (1), 1986 (15), 1987 (11). Total—30.

Led American Association in total bases with 258, caught stealing with 22 and tied for lead in game-winning RBIs with 11 and stolen bases with 67 in 1986.

Led International League in intentional bases on balls received with 9 in 1984.

Led Eastern League in caught stealing with 16 in 1979.

Led American Association outfielders in assists with 16 in 1986.

Tied for International League lead in double plays by second basemen with 74 in 1980.

Year Club	League	Pos.	G.	AB.	R.	H.	2B.	3B.	HR.	RBI.	B.A.	PO.	A.	E.	F.A.
1976—Elmira	NYP	2B	22	28	9	5	1	2	0	1	.179	9	18	3	.900
1977—Elmira	NYP	2B-SS	64	227	26	50	4	3	1	14	.220	122	196	15	.955
1978—Winter Haven	Fla. St.	SS-3B-2B	133	480	66	134	10	6	3	52	.279	172	380	42	.929
1979—Bristol†	East.	2B	123	498	75	132	19	*12	8	57	.265	252	357	23	.964
1980—Pawtucket	Int.	2B	139	536	59	146	18	7	8	52	.272	252	*394	*21	.969
1980—Boston	Amer.	2B	19	57	3	12	0	0	1	5	.211	15	31	2	.958
1981—Pawtucket	Int.	OF-2B-3B	138	535	50	148	21	5	17	68	.277	209	178	13	.968
1981—Boston	Amer.	2B	6	17	3	6	0	0	0	2	.353	4	10	0	1.000
1982—Pawtucket	Int.	O-2-3-S	133	494	71	124	22	2	15	66	.251	209	48	11	.959
1983—Pawtucket	Int.	3-O-S-2	125	442	78	119	18	1	18	56	.269	122	126	16	.939
1983—Boston	Amer.	OF	4	5	2	2	0	2	0	1	.400	4	1	0	1.000
1984—Pawtucket	Int.	2B-OF-3B	130	499	●91	131	26	5	18	51	.263	223	241	20	.959

Year	Club	League	Pos.	G.	AB.	R.	H.	2B.	3B.	HR.	RBI.	B.A.	PO.	A.	E.	F.A.
1984—	Boston‡	Amer.	2B	3	2	0	0	0	0	0	1	.000	0	1	0	1.000
1985—	Iowa	A. A.	OF-3B	89	331	47	94	17	8	5	46	.284	177	6	5	.973
1985—	Chicago	Nat.	OF-2B	21	12	3	1	0	0	0	0	.083	4	0	0	1.000
1986—	Iowa	A. A.	OF-2B	138	530	97	•158	30	11	16	65	.298	286	38	8	.976
1986—	Chicago	Nat.	OF	28	101	21	28	3	2	1	7	.277	42	1	2	.956
1987—	Chicago	Nat.	OF-3B	47	105	15	21	4	0	0	7	.200	37	0	1	.974
1987—	Iowa§	A. A.	O-2-3-S	90	315	64	77	13	3	8	31	.244	146	80	8	.967
1988—	Edmonton	P. C.	OF-2B	79	304	58	88	17	4	7	39	.289	174	5	7	.962
1988—	California x	Amer.	OF-2B-3B	33	78	8	12	1	0	0	2	.154	33	20	2	.964
American League Totals—5 Years				65	159	16	32	1	2	1	11	.201	56	63	4	.967
National League Totals—3 Years				96	218	39	50	7	2	1	14	.229	83	1	3	.966
Major League Totals—8 Years				161	377	55	82	8	4	2	25	.218	139	64	7	.967

Selected by Boston Red Sox' organization in 22nd round of free-agent draft, June 8, 1976.
†On disabled list, August 22 to September 19, 1979.
‡Granted free agency, October 15, 1984; signed by Iowa (Chicago Cubs' organization), November 9, 1984.
§Traded to California Angels for Pitcher Todd Fischer, October 16, 1987.
xGranted free agency, October 15, 1988.

DUANE ALLEN WALKER

Born March 13, 1957, at Pasadena, Tex.
Height, 6.00. Weight, 185.
Throws and bats lefthanded.
Attended San Jacinto College, Pasadena, Tex.

Major League stolen bases: 1982: (9), 1983 (6), 1984 (7), 1985 (2). Total—24.
Led American Association in bases on balls received with 87 in 1987.

Year	Club	League	Pos.	G.	AB.	R.	H.	2B.	3B.	HR.	RBI.	B.A.	PO.	A.	E.	F.A.
1976—	Tampa	Fla. St.	OF	29	91	9	19	1	0	0	3	.209	36	5	2	.953
1976—	Eugene	N'west	OF	46	172	41	49	11	5	10	24	.285	51	5	3	.949
1977—	Tampa	Fla. St.	OF	122	466	67	116	13	7	2	37	.249	180	12	3	.985
1978—	Nashville	South.	OF	103	288	38	69	15	3	2	31	.240	133	7	5	.966
1979—	Nashville	South.	OF	143	545	97	165	28	*15	9	57	.303	237	9	12	.953
1980—	Indianapolis	A. A.	OF	109	351	41	87	16	4	6	30	.248	169	14	9	.953
1981—	Indianapolis	A. A.	OF	130	450	80	127	22	1	19	80	.282	213	3	6	.973
1982—	Indianapolis	A. A.	OF	36	115	21	33	6	1	4	19	.287	68	3	2	.973
1982—	Cincinnati	Nat.	OF	86	239	26	52	10	0	5	22	.218	110	7	1	.992
1983—	Cincinnati	Nat.	OF	109	225	14	53	12	1	2	29	.236	104	4	5	.956
1984—	Cincinnati †	Nat.	OF	83	195	35	57	10	3	10	28	.292	110	3	6	.950
1985—	Cincinnati ‡	Nat.	OF	37	48	5	8	2	1	2	6	.167	15	0	2	.882
1985—	Texas §x	Amer.	OF	53	132	14	23	2	0	5	11	.174	51	6	0	1.000
1986—	Tucson y	P. C.	OF	81	251	38	75	20	5	4	40	.299	122	5	2	.984
1986—	Louisville z	A. A.	OF	32	107	18	29	7	2	3	12	.271	60	2	2	.969
1987—	Louisville a	A. A.	OF	102	311	63	91	29	4	16	69	.293	111	4	3	.975
1988—	Louisville	A. A.	OF	31	76	7	21	6	0	1	18	.276	16	3	0	1.000
1988—	St. Louis b	Nat.	OF-1B	24	22	1	4	1	0	0	3	.182	2	0	0	1.000
National League Totals—5 Years				339	729	81	174	35	5	19	88	.239	341	14	14	.962
American League Totals—1 Year				53	132	14	23	2	0	5	11	.174	51	6	0	1.000
Major League Totals—5 Years				392	861	95	197	37	5	24	99	.229	392	20	14	.967

Selected by San Francisco Giants' organization in 34th round of free-agent draft, June 4, 1975.
Selected by Cincinnati Reds' organization in secondary phase of free-agent draft, January 7, 1976.
†On disabled list, May 18 to June 4 and August 5 to September 1, 1984.
‡Traded with a player to be named later to Texas Rangers for Third Baseman Buddy Bell, July 19, 1985; Texas organization acquired Pitcher Jeff Russell to complete deal, July 23, 1985.
§Released, December 20, 1985; re-signed by Rangers, January 17, 1986.
xReleased, March 27, 1986; signed by Tucson (Houston Astros' organization), April 3, 1986.
yReleased, August 1, 1986; signed by Louisville (St. Louis Cardinals' organization), August 3, 1986.
zGranted free agency, October 15, 1986; re-signed by Cardinals' organization, December 1, 1986.
aGranted free agency, October 15, 1987; re-signed by Cardinals' organization, February 1, 1988.
bGranted free agency, October 15, 1988.

GREGORY LEE WALKER
(Greg)

Born October 6, 1959, at Douglas, Ga.
Height, 6.03. Weight, 210.
Throws right and bats lefthanded.

Major League stolen bases: 1983 (2), 1984 (8), 1985 (5), 1986 (1), 1987 (2). Total—18.
Led Midwest League first basemen in double plays with 108 in 1980.

Year	Club	League	Pos.	G.	AB.	R.	H.	2B.	3B.	HR.	RBI.	B.A.	PO.	A.	E.	F.A.
1977—	Auburn†	NYP	1B	33	98	12	25	1	2	2	8	.255	5	0	0	1.000
1978—	Spartanburg	W. Car.	1B-3B-C	100	341	51	71	16	2	11	47	.208	538	50	13	.978
1979—	Peninsula‡	Carol.	1B	122	446	59	125	*27	4	10	61	.280	973	53	19	.982
1980—	Appleton	Midw.	1B	135	464	88	130	20	3	21	*98	.280	*1298	*88	10	*.993
1981—	Glens Falls	East.	1B	135	508	*117	*163	*33	2	22	86	.321	*1215	77	11	.992
1982—	Edmonton§	P. C.	1B	35	117	18	41	8	0	3	12	.350	94	11	0	1.000
1982—	Chicago	Amer.	DH	11	17	3	7	2	1	2	7	.412	0	0	0	.000
1983—	Chicago	Amer.	1B	118	307	32	83	16	3	10	55	.270	426	19	7	.985
1984—	Chicago	Amer.	1B	136	442	62	130	29	2	24	75	.294	791	51	4	.995

Year	Club	League	Pos.	G.	AB.	R.	H.	2B.	3B.	HR.	RBI.	B.A.	PO.	A.	E.	F.A.
1985—Chicago		Amer.	1B	★163	601	77	155	38	4	24	92	.258	1217	97	8	.994
1986—Chicago x		Amer.	1B	78	282	37	78	10	6	13	51	.277	670	57	5	.993
1987—Chicago		Amer.	1B	157	566	85	145	33	2	27	94	.256	★1402	80	9	.994
1988—Chicago y		Amer.	1B	99	377	45	93	22	1	8	42	.247	935	41	7	.993
Major League Totals—7 Years				672	2592	341	691	150	19	108	416	.267	5441	345	40	.993

Selected by Philadelphia Phillies' organization in 20th round of free-agent draft, June 7, 1977.
†On disabled list, June 21, 1977 through remainder of season.
‡Drafted by Iowa (Chicago White Sox' organization), December 4, 1979.
§On disabled list, April 23 to July 27, 1982.
xOn disabled list, April 15 to May 14 and August 3, 1986 through remainder of season.
yOn disabled list, July 30, 1988 through remainder of season.

CHAMPIONSHIP SERIES RECORD

Year	Club	League	Pos.	G.	AB.	R.	H.	2B.	3B.	HR.	RBI.	B.A.	PO.	A.	E.	F.A.
1983—Chicago		Amer.	PH-1B	2	3	0	1	0	0	0	0	.333	7	1	0	1.000

LARRY KENNETH ROBERT WALKER

Born December 1, 1966, at Maple River, British Columbia, Canada.
Height, 6.02. Weight, 185.
Throws right and bats lefthanded.

Tied for Southern League lead in game-winning RBIs with 19 in 1987.

Year	Club	League	Pos.	G.	AB.	R.	H.	2B.	3B.	HR.	RBI.	B.A.	PO.	A.	E.	F.A.
1985—Utica		NYP	1B-3B	62	215	24	48	8	2	2	26	.223	354	62	8	.981
1986—Burlington		Midw.	OF-3B	95	332	67	96	12	6	29	74	.289	106	51	10	.940
1986—W. Palm Beach		Fla. St.	OF	38	113	20	32	7	5	4	16	.283	44	5	0	1.000
1987—Jacksonville		South.	OF	128	474	91	136	25	7	26	83	.287	263	9	9	.968
1988—Jacksonville †		South.					(Did not play)									

Signed as free agent by Montreal Expos' organization, November 14, 1984.
†On disabled list, April 4, 1988 through entire season.

MICHAEL AARON WALKER
(Mike)

Born June 23, 1965, at Houston, Tex.
Height, 6.03. Weight, 205.
Throws and bats righthanded.
Attended University of Houston, Houston, Tex.

Year	Club	League	G.	IP.	W.	L.	Pct.	H.	R.	ER.	SO.	BB.	ERA.
1986—Watertown		NYP	16	103⅓	4	●10	.286	★116	★71	★52	81	46	4.53
1987—Harrisburg		Eastern	4	15	0	2	.000	20	17	15	9	9	9.00
1987—Salem		Carolina	21	135⅔	12	5	.706	140	67	56	91	57	3.71
1988—Salem		Carolina	5	37	2	2	.500	42	17	13	29	9	3.16
1988—Harrisburg		Eastern	13	74⅓	2	7	.222	76	40	29	47	15	3.51
1988—Buffalo		Am. Assoc.	8	55	2	3	.400	52	18	17	26	8	2.78

Selected by Pittsburgh Pirates' organization in 2nd round of free-agent draft, June 2, 1986.

MICHAEL CHARLES WALKER
(Mike)

Born October 4, 1966, at Brooksville, Fla.
Height, 6.01. Weight, 175.
Throws and bats righthanded.
Attended Seminole Community College, Sanford, Fla.

Led Eastern League pitchers in wild pitches with 17 and tied for lead in games started with 27 in 1988.
Led Midwest League in complete games with 8 in 1987.

Year	Club	League	G.	IP.	W.	L.	Pct.	H.	R.	ER.	SO.	BB.	ERA.
1986—Burlington		Ap'lachian	14	70⅓	4	6	.400	75	★65	●46	42	45	5.89
1987—Waterloo		Midwest	23	145⅓	11	7	.611	133	74	58	144	68	3.59
1987—Kingston		Carolina	3	20⅔	3	0	1.000	17	7	6	19	14	2.61
1988—Williamsport		Eastern	28	★164⅓	★15	7	.682	162	82	68	★144	74	3.72
1988—Cleveland		American	3	8⅔	0	1	.000	8	7	7	7	10	7.27
Major League Totals—1 Year			3	8⅔	0	1	.000	8	7	7	7	10	7.27

Selected by Montreal Expos' organization in 14th round of free-agent draft, June 4, 1984.
Selected by Montreal Expos' organization in secondary phase of free-agent draft, January 9, 1985.
Selected by Cleveland Indians' organization in 2nd round of free-agent draft, January 14, 1986.

TIMOTHY CHARLES WALLACH
(Tim)

Born September 14, 1957, at Huntington Park, Calif.
Height, 6.03. Weight, 200.
Throws and bats righthanded.
Attended Saddleback Junior College, Mission Viejo, Calif., and
California State University, Fullerton, Calif.

Tied major league record by hitting home run in first major league at-bat, September 6, 1980.
Major League stolen bases: 1982 (6), 1984 (3), 1985 (9), 1986 (8), 1987 (9), 1988 (2). Total—37.
Hit three home runs in a game, May 4, 1987.

Led National League in being hit by pitch with 10 in 1986.
Tied for National League lead in game-winning RBIs with 16 in 1987.
Led National League third basemen in putouts with 123 in 1988.
Led National League third basemen in total chances with 515 in 1984 and 549 in 1985.
Led National League third basemen in double plays with 29 in 1984, 34 in 1985 and tied for lead with 31 in 1988.
Led American Association in total bases with 295, game-winning RBIs with 16 and tied for lead in sacrifice flies with 9 in 1980.
Named third baseman on THE SPORTING NEWS National League All-Star Team, 1985 and 1987.
Named third baseman on THE SPORTING NEWS National League All-Star fielding team, 1985 and 1988..
Named third baseman on THE SPORTING NEWS National League Silver Slugger team, 1985 and 1987.
Named College Player of the Year by THE SPORTING NEWS College Baseball All-America Team, 1979.

Year Club	League	Pos.	G.	AB.	R.	H.	2B.	3B.	HR.	RBI.	B.A.	PO.	A.	E.	F.A.
1979—Memphis	South.	1B-3B	75	257	50	84	16	4	18	51	.327	290	35	4	.988
1980—Denver	A. A.	3B-OF-1B	134	512	103	144	29	7	36	124	.281	222	147	21	.946
1980—Montreal	Nat.	OF-1B	5	11	1	2	0	0	1	2	.182	12	0	0	1.000
1981—Montreal	Nat.	OF-1B-3B	71	212	19	50	9	1	4	13	.236	207	31	1	.996
1982—Montreal	Nat.	★3-O-1	158	596	89	160	31	3	28	97	.268	★132	287	23	.948
1983—Montreal	Nat.	3B	156	581	54	156	33	3	19	70	.269	★151	262	19	.956
1984—Montreal	Nat.	★3B-SS	160	582	55	143	25	4	18	72	.246	★162	★332	21	.959
1985—Montreal	Nat.	3B	155	569	70	148	36	3	22	81	.260	★148	★383	18	.967
1986—Montreal	Nat.	3B	134	480	50	112	22	1	18	71	.233	94	270	16	.958
1987—Montreal	Nat.	★3B-P	153	593	89	177	★42	4	26	123	.298	★128	292	21	.952
1988—Montreal	Nat.	3B-2B	159	592	52	152	32	5	12	69	.257	124	329	18	.962
Major League Totals—9 Years			1151	4216	479	1100	230	24	148	598	.261	1158	2189	137	.961

Selected by California Angels' organization in 8th round of free-agent draft, June 6, 1978.
Selected by Montreal Expos' organization in 1st round (10th player selected) of free-agent draft, June 5, 1979.

DIVISION SERIES RECORD

Year Club	League	Pos.	G.	AB.	R.	H.	2B.	3B.	HR.	RBI.	B.A.	PO.	A.	E.	F.A.
1981—Montreal	Nat.	OF	4	4	1	1	1	0	0	0	.250	4	0	0	1.000

CHAMPIONSHIP SERIES RECORD

Year Club	League	Pos.	G.	AB.	R.	H.	2B.	3B.	HR.	RBI.	B.A.	PO.	A.	E.	F.A.
1981—Montreal	Nat.	PH	1	1	0	0	0	0	0	0	.000	0	0	0	.000

ALL-STAR GAME RECORD

Year League	Pos.	AB.	R.	H.	2B.	3B.	HR.	RBI.	B.A.	PO.	A.	E.	F.A.
1984—National	3B	1	0	0	0	0	0	0	.000	0	0	0	.000
1985—National	3B	2	1	1	1	0	0	0	.500	1	1	0	1.000
1987—National	3B	3	0	0	0	0	0	0	.000	0	2	0	1.000
All-Star Game Totals—3 Years		6	1	1	1	0	0	0	.167	1	3	0	1.000

PITCHING RECORD

Year Club	League	G.	IP.	W.	L.	Pct.	H.	R.	ER.	SO.	BB.	ERA.
1987—Montreal	National	1	1	0	0	.000	1	0	0	0	0	0.00

DENNIS MARTIN WALLING
(Denny)

Born April 17, 1954, at Neptune, N.J.
Height, 6.01. Weight, 185.
Throws right and bats lefthanded.
Attended Brookdale Community College, Lincroft, N.J., and
Clemson University, Clemson, S.C.
Brother of Gregory Walling, minor league outfielder, 1967.

Major League stolen bases: 1978 (9), 1979 (3), 1980 (4), 1981 (2), 1982 (4), 1983 (2), 1984 (7), 1985 (5), 1986 (1), 1987 (5), 1988 (2). Total—44.
Named outfielder on THE SPORTING NEWS College Baseball All-America Team, 1975.

Year Club	League	Pos.	G.	AB.	R.	H.	2B.	3B.	HR.	RBI.	B.A.	PO.	A.	E.	F.A.
1975—Oakland	Amer.	OF	6	8	0	1	1	0	0	2	.125	3	0	0	1.000
1976—Chattanooga	South.	OF	115	369	48	95	15	5	9	42	.257	241	8	2	★.992
1976—Oakland	Amer.	OF	3	11	1	3	0	0	0	0	.273	8	0	1	.889
1977—San Jose†‡	P. C.	OF	3	10	1	3	0	0	0	4	.300	8	0	0	1.000
1977—Charleston	Int.	OF	29	89	17	31	4	1	4	14	.348	66	0	0	1.000
1977—Houston	Nat.	OF	6	21	1	6	0	1	0	6	.286	14	0	0	1.000
1978—Houston	Nat.	OF	120	247	30	62	11	3	3	36	.251	140	4	3	.980
1979—Houston	Nat.	OF	82	147	21	48	8	4	3	31	.327	65	2	1	.985
1980—Houston	Nat.	1B-OF	100	284	30	85	6	5	3	29	.299	525	31	6	.989
1981—Houston	Nat.	1B-OF	65	158	23	37	6	0	5	23	.234	226	9	2	.992
1982—Houston	Nat.	OF-1B	85	146	22	30	4	1	1	14	.205	167	11	1	.994
1983—Houston§	Nat.	1B-3B-OF	100	135	24	40	5	3	3	19	.296	134	29	6	.964
1984—Houston x	Nat.	3B-1B-OF	87	249	37	70	11	5	3	31	.281	116	102	7	.969
1985—Houston	Nat.	3B-1B-OF	119	345	44	93	20	1	7	45	.270	326	124	12	.974
1986—Houston	Nat.	3B-OF-1B	130	382	54	119	23	1	13	58	.312	108	161	9	.968
1987—Houston y	Nat.	3B-1B-OF	110	325	45	92	21	4	5	33	.283	175	119	10	.967
1988—Hou. za-St.L.	Nat.	3B-OF-1B	84	234	22	56	13	2	1	21	.239	73	112	9	.954
1988—Tucson	P. C.	3B	5	16	2	3	1	0	0	4	.188	4	10	1	.933
American League Totals—2 Years			9	19	1	4	1	0	0	2	.210	11	0	1	.917
National League Totals—12 Years			1088	2673	353	738	128	30	47	346	.276	2069	704	66	.977
Major League Totals—14 Years			1097	2692	354	742	129	30	47	348	.276	2080	704	67	.976

Selected by San Francisco Giants' organization in 8th round of free-agent draft, June 5, 1974.
Selected by Oakland A's organization in secondary phase of free-agent draft, June 4, 1975.
†On disabled list, April 18 to June 15, 1977.
‡Traded with cash to Houston Astros' organization for Outfielder Willie Crawford, June 15, 1977.
§Granted free agency, November 7, 1983; re-signed by Astros, December 20, 1983.
xOn disabled list, May 2 to May 24, 1984.
yOn disabled list, March 28 to April 17, 1987.
zOn disabled list, June 20 to August 6, 1988; included rehabilitation disability assignment to Tucson, July 29 to August 3, 1988.
aTraded to St. Louis Cardinals for Pitcher Bob Forsch, August 31, 1988.

DIVISION SERIES RECORD

Year	Club	League	Pos.	G.	AB.	R.	H.	2B.	3B.	HR.	RBI.	B.A.	PO.	A.	E.	F.A.
1981	—Houston	Nat.	PH-1B	3	6	0	2	0	0	0	1	.333	6	1	1	.875

CHAMPIONSHIP SERIES RECORD

Year	Club	League	Pos.	G.	AB.	R.	H.	2B.	3B.	HR.	RBI.	B.A.	PO.	A.	E.	F.A.
1980	—Houston	Nat.	1-O-PH	3	9	2	1	0	0	0	2	.111	6	0	0	1.000
1986	—Houston	Nat.	3B-PH	5	19	1	3	1	0	0	2	.158	3	6	0	1.000
Championship Series Totals—2 Years				8	28	3	4	1	0	0	4	.143	9	6	0	1.000

GENE WINSTON WALTER

Born November 22, 1960, at Chicago, Ill.
Height, 6.04. Weight, 200.
Throws and bats lefthanded.
Attended Morton College, Cicero, Ill., and received degree from Eastern Kentucky University, Richmond, Ky.

Major League saves: 1985 (3), 1986 (1) Total—4.

Year	Club	League	G.	IP.	W.	L.	Pct.	H.	R.	ER.	SO.	BB.	ERA.
1982	—Walla Walla	Northwest	17	72⅔	4	4	.500	73	55	39	61	46	4.83
1983	—Miami	Florida St.	42	121⅓	6	13	.316	114	73	51	105	61	3.78
1984	—Miami	Florida St.	9	59	3	5	.375	43	22	15	70	27	2.29
1984	—Beaumont	Texas	34	76	7	3	.700	53	25	22	71	40	2.61
1985	—Las Vegas†	P. Coast	45	95	7	5	.583	75	34	29	107	35	2.75
1985	—San Diego	National	15	22	0	2	.000	12	6	5	18	8	2.05
1986	—San Diego‡	National	57	98	2	2	.500	89	47	42	84	49	3.86
1987	—New York	National	21	19⅔	1	2	.333	18	10	7	11	13	3.20
1987	—Tidewater	Int'national	33	49⅓	1	4	.200	37	33	27	43	23	4.93
1988	—New York§	National	19	16⅔	0	1	.000	21	9	7	14	11	3.78
1988	—Seattle	American	16	26⅓	1	0	1.000	21	16	15	13	15	5.13
1988	—Calgary	P. Coast	8	8⅔	0	0	.000	9	5	2	11	1	2.08
National League Totals—4 Years			112	156⅓	3	7	.300	140	72	61	127	81	3.51
American League Totals—1 Year			16	26⅓	1	0	1.000	21	16	15	13	15	5.13
Major League Totals—4 Years			128	182⅔	4	7	.364	161	88	76	140	96	3.74

Selected by Montreal Expos' organization in 25th round of free-agent draft, June 8, 1981.
Selected by San Diego Padres' organization in 29th round of free-agent draft, June 7, 1982.
†Appeared in one game as an outfielder with one putout.
‡Traded with Outfielder Kevin McReynolds and Infielder Adam Ging to New York Mets for Outfielders Shawn Abner, Stanley Jefferson and Kevin Mitchell and Pitchers Kevin Armstrong and Kevin Brown, December 11, 1986.
§Traded to Seattle Mariners for Pitcher Edwin Nunez, July 11, 1988.

JEROME O'TERRELL WALTON

Born July 8, 1965, at Newnan, Ga.
Height, 6.01. Weight, 175.
Throws and bats righthanded.
Attended Enterprise State Junior College, Enterprise, Ala.

Led Midwest League in caught stealing with 25 in 1987.
Led Appalachian League outfielders in putouts with 128, total chances with 131 and tied for lead in double plays with 2 in 1986.

Year	Club	League	Pos.	G.	AB.	R.	H.	2B.	3B.	HR.	RBI.	B.A.	PO.	A.	E.	F.A.
1986	—Wytheville	Appal.	OF-3B	62	229	48	66	7	4	5	34	.288	130	7	3	.979
1987	—Peoria	Midw.	OF	128	472	102	158	24	11	6	38	.335	255	9	7	.974
1988	—Pittsfield	East.	OF	120	414	64	137	26	2	3	49	.331	270	11	2	★.993

Selected by Chicago Cubs' organization in 2nd round of free-agent draft, January 14, 1986.

GARY LAMELL WARD

Born December 6, 1953, at Los Angeles, Calif.
Height, 6.02. Weight, 202.
Throws and bats righthanded.
Father of Agee Ward, forward at Fullerton State.

Major League stolen bases: 1981 (5), 1982 (13), 1983 (8), 1984 (7), 1985 (26), 1986 (12), 1987 (9). Total—80.
Hit for the cycle, September 18, 1980 (first game).
Led American League outfielders in double plays with 4 in 1981.
Led New York-Pennsylvania League first basemen in errors with 12 in 1973.
Tied for Midwest League lead in assists by outfielders with 18 in 1974.

Year Club	League	Pos.	G.	AB.	R.	H.	2B.	3B.	HR.	RBI.	B.A.	PO.	A.	E.	F.A.
1973—Geneva	NYP	1B-OF-3B	61	211	36	57	13	1	10	38	.270	336	20	14	.962
1974—Wisconsin Rapids	Midw.	OF-1B	126	*467	*104	122	12	5	26	78	.261	184	19	11	.949
1975—Orlando	South.	OF-C	124	438	45	117	18	5	8	71	.267	204	10	4	.982
1976—Orlando	South.	OF	132	475	50	119	17	2	9	65	.251	235	●16	●10	.962
1977—Tacoma	P. C.	OF-3B	125	413	62	97	15	8	8	43	.235	212	34	10	.961
1978—Toledo	Int.	*O-1-3	139	511	82	150	20	12	14	79	.294	260	6	*13	.953
1979—Toledo	Int.	OF	134	506	75	133	16	9	13	67	.263	323	12	●11	.968
1979—Minnesota	Amer.	DH-PH	10	14	2	4	0	0	0	1	.286	0	0	0	.000
1980—Toledo†	Int.	OF-1B	128	496	82	140	22	8	13	66	.282	269	14	8	.973
1980—Minnesota	Amer.	OF	13	41	11	19	6	2	1	10	.463	14	0	0	1.000
1981—Minnesota	Amer.	OF	85	295	42	78	7	6	3	29	.264	185	8	5	.975
1982—Minnesota	Amer.	OF	152	570	85	165	33	7	28	91	.289	343	13	4	.989
1983—Minnesota‡	Amer.	OF	157	623	76	173	34	5	19	88	.278	374	*24	9	.978
1984—Texas	Amer.	OF	155	602	97	171	21	7	21	79	.284	376	11	5	.987
1985—Texas	Amer.	OF	154	593	77	170	28	7	15	70	.287	304	11	10	.969
1986—Texas§	Amer.	OF	105	380	54	120	15	2	5	51	.316	237	8	1	.996
1987—New York	Amer.	OF-1B	146	529	65	131	22	1	16	78	.248	318	10	3	.991
1988—New York	Amer.	OF-1B-3B	91	231	26	52	8	0	4	24	.225	220	5	2	.991
Major League Totals—10 Years			1068	3878	535	1083	174	37	112	521	.279	2371	90	39	.984

Signed as free agent by Minnesota Twins' organization, August 29, 1972.

†On disabled list, April 16 to April 26, 1980.

‡Traded to Texas Rangers for Pitchers Mike Smithson and John Butcher and Catcher Sam Sorce, December 7, 1983.

§Granted free agency, November 12, 1986; signed by New York Yankees, December 24, 1986.

ALL-STAR GAME RECORD

Year League	Pos.	AB.	R.	H.	2B.	3B.	HR.	RBI.	B.A.	PO.	A.	E.	F.A.
1983—American	PH	1	0	0	0	0	0	0	.000	0	0	0	.000
1985—American	PH	1	0	0	0	0	0	0	.000	0	0	0	.000
All-Star Game Totals—2 Years		2	0	0	0	0	0	0	.000	0	0	0	.000

ROY DUANE WARD

(Known by middle name.)
Born May 28, 1964, at Parkview, N.M.
Height, 6.04. Weight, 205.
Throws and bats righthanded.

Major League saves: 1988 (15).

Year Club	League	G.	IP.	W.	L.	Pct.	H.	R.	ER.	SO.	BB.	ERA.
1982—Bradenton Braves	Gulf Coast	8	45⅔	2	3	.400	45	25	23	31	24	4.53
1982—Anderson	S. Atlantic	5	23⅔	1	2	.333	24	16	14	18	15	5.32
1983—Durham	Carolina	28	178⅓	11	13	.458	165	103	85	115	75	4.29
1984—Greenville†	Southern	21	104⅔	4	9	.308	108	71	58	54	57	4.99
1985—Greenville	Southern	28	150	11	10	.524	141	83	70	100	*105	4.20
1985—Richmond	Int'national	5	5⅓	0	1	.000	8	9	7	3	8	11.81
1986—Atlanta	National	10	16	0	1	.000	22	13	13	8	8	7.31
1986—Richmond‡-Syracuse	Int'national	20	117⅔	7	5	.583	125	56	52	67	52	3.98
1986—Toronto	American	2	2	0	1	.000	3	4	3	1	4	13.50
1987—Toronto	American	12	11⅔	1	0	1.000	14	9	9	10	12	6.94
1987—Syracuse	Int'national	46	76⅓	2	2	.500	59	35	33	67	42	3.89
1988—Toronto	American	64	111⅔	9	3	.750	101	46	41	91	60	3.30
National League Totals—1 Year		10	16	0	1	.000	22	13	13	8	8	7.31
American League Totals—3 Years		78	125⅓	10	4	.714	118	59	53	102	76	3.81
Major League Totals—3 Years		88	141⅓	10	5	.667	140	72	66	110	84	4.20

Selected by Atlanta Braves' organization in 1st round (ninth player selected) of free-agent draft, June 7, 1982.

†On disabled list, May 7 to May 29 and July 14 to August 7, 1984.

‡Traded to Toronto Blue Jays for Pitcher Doyle Alexander, July 6, 1986.

CLAUDELL WASHINGTON

Born August 31, 1954, at Los Angeles, Calif.
Height, 6.02. Weight, 195.
Throws and bats lefthanded.
Brother of Don Washington, outfielder in Los Angeles Dodgers' and Oakland A's organizations, 1975 through 1977.

Hit three home runs in a game, July 14, 1979 and June 22, 1980.

Major League stolen bases: 1974 (6), 1975 (40), 1976 (37), 1977 (21), 1978 (5), 1979 (19), 1980 (21), 1981 (12), 1982 (33), 1983 (31), 1984 (21), 1985 (14), 1986 (10), 1987 (10), 1988 (15). Total—295.

Led Midwest League in total bases with 218 in 1973.

Year Club	League	Pos.	G.	AB.	R.	H.	2B.	3B.	HR.	RBI.	B.A.	PO.	A.	E.	F.A.
1972—C's Bay-N. Bend	N'west.	OF	33	111	13	31	3	2	2	15	.279	37	1	6	.864
1973—Burlington	Midw.	OF	108	447	*92	144	25	5	13	81	.322	149	10	*15	.914
1974—Birmingham	South.	OF	74	294	64	106	23	3	11	55	.361	116	5	13	.903
1974—Oakland	Amer.	OF	73	221	16	63	10	5	0	19	.285	63	2	1	.985
1975—Oakland	Amer.	OF	148	590	86	182	24	7	10	77	.308	305	8	7	.978
1976—Oakland†‡	Amer.	●OF	134	490	65	126	20	6	5	53	.257	276	10	●11	.963
1977—Texas§	Amer.	OF	129	521	63	148	31	2	12	68	.284	255	11	6	.978
1978—Tex. x-Chi. y	Amer.	OF	98	356	34	90	16	5	6	33	.253	170	6	8	.957

Year	Club	League	Pos.	G.	AB.	R.	H.	2B.	3B.	HR.	RBI.	B.A.	PO.	A.	E.	F.A.
1979	—Chicago	Amer.	OF	131	471	79	132	33	5	13	66	.280	256	7	7	.974
1980	—Chicago z	Amer.	OF	32	90	15	26	4	2	1	12	.289	41	1	3	.933
1980	—New York a	Nat.	OF	79	284	38	78	16	4	10	42	.275	123	12	3	.978
1981	—Atlanta b	Nat.	OF	85	320	37	93	22	3	5	37	.291	145	5	1	.993
1982	—Atlanta	Nat.	OF	150	563	94	150	24	6	16	80	.266	221	9	12	.950
1983	—Atlanta	Nat.	OF	134	496	75	138	24	8	9	44	.278	218	8	6	.974
1984	—Atlanta c	Nat.	OF	120	416	62	119	21	2	17	61	.286	170	4	6	.967
1985	—Atlanta	Nat.	OF	122	398	62	110	14	6	15	43	.276	122	3	5	.962
1986	—Atlanta de	Nat.	OF	40	137	17	37	11	0	5	14	.270	44	1	2	.957
1986	—New York f	Amer.	OF	54	135	19	32	5	0	6	16	.237	66	0	1	.985
1987	—New York g	Amer.	OF	102	312	42	87	17	0	9	44	.279	166	3	2	.988
1988	—New York h	Amer.	OF	126	455	62	140	22	3	11	64	.308	309	5	5	.984
American League Totals—10 Years				1027	3641	481	1026	182	35	73	452	.282	1907	53	51	.975
National League Totals—7 Years				730	2614	385	725	132	29	77	321	.277	1043	42	35	.969
Major League Totals—15 Years				1757	6255	866	1751	314	64	150	773	.280	2950	95	86	.973

Signed as free agent by Oakland A's organization, July 7, 1972.
†On disabled list, August 16 to September 1, 1976.
‡Traded to Texas Rangers for Pitcher Jim Umbarger, Infielder Rodney Scott and cash estimated at $100,000, March 26, 1977.
§On disabled list, May 27 to June 11, 1977.
xTraded with Outfielder Rusty Torres and cash to Chicago White Sox for Outfielder Bobby Bonds, May 16, 1978.
yOn disabled list, May 22 to June 16, 1978.
zTraded to New York Mets for Pitcher Jesse Anderson, June 7, 1980.
aGranted free agency, October 31, 1980; signed by Atlanta Braves, November 15, 1980.
bOn disabled list, June 5 to August 9, 1981.
cOn disabled list, May 30 to June 14, 1984.
dOn disabled list, May 18 to June 16, 1986.
eTraded with Shortstop Paul Zuvella to New York Yankees for Outfielder Ken Griffey, June 30, 1986.
fGranted free agency, November 12, 1986; re-signed by Yankees, December 7, 1986.
gOn disabled list, May 18 to June 2, 1987.
hGranted free agency, October 24, 1988.

CHAMPIONSHIP SERIES RECORD

Year	Club	League	Pos.	G.	AB.	R.	H.	2B.	3B.	HR.	RBI.	B.A.	PO.	A.	E.	F.A.
1974	—Oakland	Amer.	OF-PH	4	11	1	3	1	0	0	0	.273	11	0	0	1.000
1975	—Oakland	Amer.	OF-DH	3	12	1	3	1	0	0	1	.250	1	0	2	.333
1982	—Atlanta	Nat.	OF	3	9	0	3	0	0	0	0	.333	5	1	0	1.000
Championship Series Totals—3 Years				10	32	2	9	2	0	0	1	.281	17	1	2	.900

WORLD SERIES RECORD

Tied World Series record for most positions played, Series (3), 1974 (all three outfield positions).

Year	Club	League	Pos.	G.	AB.	R.	H.	2B.	3B.	HR.	RBI.	B.A.	PO.	A.	E.	F.A.
1974	—Oakland	Amer.	OF-PH	5	7	1	4	0	0	0	0	.571	3	0	0	1.000

ALL-STAR GAME RECORD

Year	League	Pos.	AB.	R.	H.	2B.	3B.	HR.	RBI.	B.A.	PO.	A.	E.	F.A.
1975	—American	PR-OF	1	0	1	0	0	0	0	1.000	1	0	0	1.000
1984	—National	OF	2	0	1	1	0	0	0	.500	1	0	0	1.000
All-Star Game Totals—2 Years			3	0	2	1	0	0	0	.667	2	0	0	1.000

RONALD WASHINGTON
(Ron)

Born April 29, 1952, at New Orleans, La.
Height, 5.11. Weight, 160.
Throws and bats righthanded.
Attended Manatee Junior College, Bradenton, Fla.

Major League stolen bases: 1977 (1), 1981 (4), 1982 (3), 1983 (10), 1984 (1), 1985 (5), 1986 (1), 1988 (3). Total—28.

Year	Club	League	Pos.	G.	AB.	R.	H.	2B.	3B.	HR.	RBI.	B.A.	PO.	A.	E.	F.A.
1971	—Sara. Royals†	Gulf C.	C	38	127	29	37	2	•6	1	23	.291	★213	23	3	★.987
1972	—Waterloo	Midw.	C-OF-3B	76	241	37	55	3	1	1	30	.228	424	48	8	.983
1973	—Waterloo	Midw.	SS	85	289	35	80	13	5	6	34	.277	130	198	29	.919
1974	—San Jose‡	Calif.	2B-SS-C	109	425	49	104	16	3	2	41	.245	233	266	33	.938
1975	—Jacksonville§	South.	2-3-S-1	96	267	22	61	7	1	0	20	.228	133	199	22	.938
1976	—Waterbury x	East.	3B-2B	115	436	61	128	9	10	4	32	.294	170	249	26	.942
1977	—San Antonio y	Texas	SS	39	158	24	44	8	4	0	13	.278	78	92	12	.934
1977	—Albuquerque	P. C.	SS	85	359	71	116	17	8	8	59	.323	204	250	★33	.932
1977	—Los Angeles	Nat.	SS	10	19	4	7	0	0	0	1	.368	4	14	3	.857
1978	—Albuquerque z	P. C.	3B	31	122	26	42	10	3	5	32	.344	23	58	8	.910
1979	—Aguila	Mex.	3B	42	165	22	43	3	3	0	14	.261	35	96	10	.929
1979	—Tidewater a	Int.	3B-SS	83	273	18	72	13	4	1	26	.264	77	157	13	.947
1980	—Toledo	Int.	3B-2B-SS	114	407	62	117	•31	5	3	36	.287	131	268	30	.930
1981	—Toledo	Int.	3B-OF-SS	138	★544	84	157	27	8	15	54	.289	130	287	26	.941
1981	—Minnesota	Amer.	SS-OF	28	84	8	19	3	1	0	5	.226	64	80	8	.947
1982	—Minnesota	Amer.	SS-2B-3B	119	451	48	122	17	6	5	39	.271	201	269	13	.973
1983	—Minnesota	Amer.	SS-2B-3B	99	317	28	78	7	3	4	26	.246	140	246	16	.960
1984	—Minnesota	Amer.	SS-2B-3B	88	197	25	58	11	5	3	23	.294	77	134	4	.981

Year	Club	League	Pos.	G.	AB.	R.	H.	2B.	3B.	HR.	RBI.	B.A.	PO.	A.	E.	F.A.
1985—	Minnesota	Amer.	S-2-3-1	70	135	24	37	6	4	1	14	.274	55	100	7	.957
1986—	Minnesota	Amer.	2B-SS-3B	48	74	15	19	3	0	4	11	.257	12	20	2	.941
1986—	Toledo b	Int.	2B-3B-SS	49	198	22	53	6	1	3	19	.268	79	112	9	.955
1987—	Rochester	Int.	2-S-3-O	70	272	50	87	17	1	15	43	.320	42	84	6	.955
1987—	Baltimore c	Amer.	3-2-O-S	26	79	7	16	3	1	1	6	.203	19	42	0	1.000
1988—	Cleveland d	Amer.	SS-3B-2B	69	223	30	57	14	2	2	21	.256	95	162	17	.938
National League Totals—1 Year				10	19	4	7	0	0	0	1	.368	4	14	3	.857
American League Totals—8 Years				547	1560	185	406	64	22	20	145	.260	663	1053	67	.962
Major League Totals—9 Years				557	1579	189	413	64	22	20	146	.262	667	1067	70	.961

Signed as free agent by Kansas City Royals' organization, July 17, 1970.
†On military list, September 30, 1971 through March 3, 1972.
‡On temporary inactive list, July 4 to July 25, 1974.
§On disabled list, June 19 to June 30, 1975.
xTraded to Los Angeles Dodgers' organization for Catcher Steve Patchin, November 2, 1976.
yOn temporary inactive list, April 12 to April 22, 1977.
zOn disabled list, May 12 to June 26 and July 17 to September 10, 1978.
aTraded to Minnesota Twins' organization for Infielder Wayne Caughey, March 26, 1980.
bReleased, March 30, 1987; signed by Baltimore Orioles' organization, April 6, 1987.
cReleased, December 21, 1987; signed by Colorado Springs (Cleveland Indians' organization), December 28, 1987.
dGranted free agency, November 4, 1988.

MARK THOMAS WASINGER

Born August 4, 1961, at Monterey, Calif.
Height, 6.00. Weight, 165.
Throws and bats righthanded.
Received bachelor of science degree in leisure studies from
Old Dominion University, Norfolk, Va. in 1986.

Major League stolen bases: 1987 (2).
Led Texas League in sacrifice hits with 16 in 1984.
Led Texas League second basemen in fielding percentage with .977 in 1984.
Named second baseman on THE SPORTING NEWS College Baseball All-America Team, 1983.

Year	Club	League	Pos.	G.	AB.	R.	H.	2B.	3B.	HR.	RBI.	B.A.	PO.	A.	E.	F.A.
1982—	Reno	Calif.	2B	60	220	36	70	18	0	2	32	.318	108	184	9	.970
1983—	Reno	Calif.	2B	83	308	46	102	13	5	4	53	.331	164	241	9	.978
1984—	Beaumont†	Texas	2B-SS	106	362	54	103	20	0	3	48	.285	220	358	14	.976
1985—	Beaumont	Texas	3B-2B-SS	114	411	71	124	13	0	8	52	.302	93	240	22	.938
1986—	Las Vegas	P. C.	2B-3B	103	378	68	116	22	5	1	34	.307	136	241	11	.972
1986—	San Diego	Nat.	3B-2B	3	8	0	0	0	0	0	1	.000	2	2	3	.571
1987—	L.V.‡-Phoe.	P. C.	3-2-S-O	50	170	28	38	4	2	1	16	.224	45	74	7	.944
1987—	San Francisco	Nat.	3B-2B-SS	44	80	16	22	3	0	1	3	.275	21	50	1	.986
1988—	Phoe.-C.S.	P. C.	O-3-2-S	58	196	26	57	12	0	0	15	.291	64	53	7	.944
1988—	San Francisco§x	Nat.	3B	3	2	1	0	0	0	0	0	.000	0	0	0	.000
Major League Totals—3 Years				50	90	17	22	3	0	1	4	.244	23	52	4	.949

Selected by San Diego Padres' organization in 3rd round of free-agent draft, June 7, 1982.
†On disabled list, May 16 to May 27 and August 31, 1984 through remainder of season.
‡Traded with Pitcher Tom Meagher to San Francisco Giants' organization for Pitcher Colin Ward and Infielder Steve Miller, April 25, 1987.
§Released, July 15, 1988; signed by Colorado Springs (Cleveland Indians' organization), July 17, 1988.
xGranted free agency, October 15, 1988; re-signed by Indians, November 16, 1988.

DARREN KEITH WATKINS

Born August 30, 1966, at Everett, Wash.
Height, 6.01. Weight, 185.
Throws and bats righthanded.

Year	Club	League	Pos.	G.	AB.	R.	H.	2B.	3B.	HR.	RBI.	B.A.	PO.	A.	E.	F.A.
1986—	Sarasota Royals	Gulf C.	OF	24	72	8	17	3	2	0	7	.236	41	3	2	.957
1987—	Appleton	Midw.	OF	12	18	3	2	0	0	0	1	.111	4	0	1	.800
1987—	Eugene	N'west	OF	40	136	25	25	2	1	0	11	.184	73	7	2	.976
1988—	Appleton	Midw.	OF	96	366	42	97	8	8	4	46	.265	188	6	9	.956
1988—	Baseball City	Fla. St.	OF	17	54	9	12	0	1	0	7	.222	33	0	0	1.000

Selected by Kansas City Royals' organization in 29th round of free-agent draft, June 3, 1985.

ROGER TIMOTHY WATKINS
(Tim)

Born August 14, 1964, at Ogden, Utah.
Height, 6.04. Weight, 210.
Throws and bats righthanded.
Attended Mississippi College, Clinton, Miss.

Year	Club	League	G.	IP.	W.	L.	Pct.	H.	R.	ER.	SO.	BB.	ERA.
1985—	Billings	Pioneer	17	65	1	3	.250	71	44	35	41	26	4.85
1986—	Tampa†	Florida St.	22	45⅔	3	3	.500	47	37	25	33	31	4.93
1987—	Beloit	Midwest	18	71⅔	5	5	.500	55	40	29	71	38	3.64
1987—	Stockton	California	25	57⅓	7	1	.875	30	14	11	63	26	1.73
1988—	Denver	Am. Assoc.	47	68	6	3	.667	62	36	31	50	35	4.10

Selected by Cincinnati Reds' organization in 8th round of free-agent draft, June 3, 1985.
†Sold to Beloit (Milwaukee Brewers' organization), December 15, 1986.

GARY ANTHONY WAYNE

Born November 30, 1962, at Dearborn, Mich.
Height, 6.03. Weight, 185.
Throws and bats lefthanded.
Attended University of Michigan, Ann Arbor, Mich.

Led Florida State League in saves with 25 in 1986.

Year Club	League	G.	IP.	W.	L.	Pct.	H.	R.	ER.	SO.	BB.	ERA.
1984—West Palm Beach	Florida St.	13	74⅓	3	5	.375	70	38	32	46	49	3.87
1985—Jacksonville	Southern	21	102	3	12	.200	108	67	60	62	70	5.29
1985—West Palm Beach	Florida St.	8	30⅔	2	2	.500	37	23	19	18	22	5.58
1986—West Palm Beach	Florida St.	47	61⅓	2	5	.286	48	16	11	55	25	1.61
1987—Jacksonville	Southern	56	80⅓	5	1	.833	56	23	21	78	35	2.35
1988—Indianapolis†‡	Am. Assoc.	8	7⅓	0	0	.000	9	5	5	6	3	6.14

Selected by Oakland A's organization in 23rd round of free-agent draft, June 6, 1983.
Selected by Montreal Expos' organization in 4th round of free-agent draft, June 4, 1984.
†On disabled list, April 7 to August 24, 1988.
‡Drafted by Minnesota Twins, December 5, 1988.

LEONARD IRELL WEBSTER

Born February 10, 1965, at New Orleans, La.
Height, 5.09. Weight, 185.
Throws and bats righthanded.
Attended Grambling State University, Grambling, La.

Led Midwest League in game-winning RBIs with 14 in 1988.
Named Midwest League Most Valuable Player, 1988.

Year Club	League	Pos.	G.	AB.	R.	H.	2B.	3B.	HR.	RBI.	B.A.	PO.	A.	E.	F.A.
1986—Kenosha	Midw.	C	22	65	2	10	2	0	0	8	.154	87	9	0	1.000
1986—Elizabethton	Appal.	C	48	152	29	35	4	0	3	14	.230	88	11	3	.971
1987—Kenosha	Midw.	C	52	140	17	35	7	0	3	17	.250	228	29	5	.981
1988—Kenosha	Midw.	C	129	465	82	134	23	2	11	87	.288	606	96	14	.980

Selected by Minnesota Twins' organization in 16th round of free-agent draft, June 7, 1982.
Selected by Minnesota Twins' organization in 21st round of free-agent draft, June 3, 1985.

MITCHELL DEAN WEBSTER
(Mitch)

Born May 16, 1959, at Larned, Kan.
Height, 6.01. Weight, 185.
Throws left and bats left and righthanded.

Tied major league record for fewest double plays by outfielder, season, 150 or more games (0), 1987.
Major League stolen bases: 1985 (15), 1986 (36), 1987 (33), 1988 (22). Total—106.
Led International League outfielders in double plays with 5 and total chances with 385 in 1982.

Year Club	League	Pos.	G.	AB.	R.	H.	2B.	3B.	HR.	RBI.	B.A.	PO.	A.	E.	F.A.
1977—Lethbridge	Pion	OF	55	168	45	59	4	0	0	31	.351	81	3	8	.913
1978—Clinton	Midw.	OF	45	157	18	38	3	1	0	9	.242	92	6	7	.933
1978—Lethbridge	Pion.	OF	55	182	58	58	5	1	0	18	.319	77	3	0	*1.000
1979—Clinton†	Midw.	OF	123	473	95	*154	17	7	2	40	*.326	*272	10	10	.966
1980—Syracuse	Int.	OF	49	161	23	35	4	2	1	12	.217	112	3	5	.958
1980—Kinston	Carol.	OF	65	258	43	76	7	3	0	28	.295	129	8	5	.965
1981—Knoxville	South.	OF	140	554	89	163	26	6	1	42	.294	317	7	10	.970
1982—Syracuse	Int.	OF	137	513	95	144	21	7	13	68	.281	*367	16	2	*.995
1983—Syracuse	Int.	OF-1B	135	462	77	120	26	8	9	45	.260	266	16	10	.966
1983—Toronto	Amer.	OF	11	11	2	2	0	0	0	0	.182	5	0	0	1.000
1984—Toronto	Amer.	OF-1B	26	22	9	5	2	1	0	4	.227	16	0	2	.889
1984—Syracuse	Int.	OF	95	360	60	108	22	5	3	25	.300	239	7	7	.972
1985—Toronto	Amer.	OF	4	1	0	0	0	0	0	0	.000	0	0	0	.000
1985—Syracuse‡	Int.	OF	47	189	32	52	5	3	3	23	.275	83	10	1	.989
1985—Montreal	Nat.	OF	74	212	32	58	8	2	11	30	.274	133	3	1	.993
1986—Montreal	Nat.	OF	151	576	89	167	31	*13	8	49	.290	325	12	8	.977
1987—Montreal	Nat.	OF	156	588	101	165	30	8	15	63	.281	266	8	5	.982
1988—Mont.§-Chi.	Nat.	OF	151	523	69	136	16	8	6	39	.260	322	3	6	.982
American League Totals—3 Years			41	34	11	7	2	1	0	4	.206	21	0	2	.913
National League Totals—4 Years			532	1899	291	526	85	31	40	181	.277	1046	26	20	.982
Major League Totals—6 Years			573	1933	302	533	87	32	40	185	.276	1067	26	22	.980

Selected by Los Angeles Dodgers' organization in 23rd round of free-agent draft, June 7, 1977.
†Drafted by Syracuse (Toronto Blue Jays' organization), December 4, 1979.
‡Traded to Montreal Expos for a player to be named later, June 22, 1985; Toronto Blue Jays' organization acquired Pitcher Cliff Young to complete deal, September 10, 1985.
§Traded to Chicago Cubs for Outfielder Dave Martinez, July 14, 1988.

DANNY KEITH WEEMS

Born August 26, 1966, at Greenville, Tenn.
Height, 6.03. Weight, 175.
Throws and bats righthanded.

Pitched 3-0 no-hit victory against Greensboro, June 3, 1987 (first game).

Year	Club	League	G.	IP.	W.	L.	Pct.	H.	R.	ER.	SO.	BB.	ERA.
1985	—Pulaski	Ap'lachian	13	55⅓	3	4	.429	65	43	38	20	26	6.18
1986	—Sumter	S. Atlantic	8	10	0	3	.000	15	11	11	7	10	9.90
1986	—Bradenton Braves	Gulf Coast	15	64⅓	3	5	.375	73	34	27	39	12	3.78
1987	—Charleston, W. Va.	S. Atlantic	28	164⅔	5	8	.385	159	91	62	100	58	3.39
1988	—Durham	Carolina	31	*191⅓	13	8	.619	168	85	70	98	74	3.29

Selected by Atlanta Braves' organization in 28th round of free-agent draft, June 4, 1984.

WILLIAM EDWARD WEGMAN
(Bill)

Born December 19, 1962, at Cincinnati, O.
Height, 6.05. Weight, 200.
Throws and bats righthanded.

Led Pacific Coast League in home runs allowed with 21 in 1985.
Led California League in balks with 5 and tied for lead in complete games with 15 and shutouts with 4 in 1983.

Year	Club	League	G.	IP.	W.	L.	Pct.	H.	R.	ER.	SO.	BB.	ERA.
1981	—Butte	Pioneer	14	82	6	5	.545	94	51	38	47	44	4.17
1982	—Beloit	Midwest	25	179⅔	12	6	.667	176	77	56	129	38	2.81
1983	—Stockton	California	24	186⅔	*16	5	.762	149	33	27	135	45	*1.30
1984	—El Paso	Texas	10	64	4	5	.444	62	25	19	42	15	2.67
1984	—Vancouver†	P. Coast	6	27⅔	0	3	.000	30	11	6	16	8	1.95
1985	—Vancouver	P. Coast	28	188	10	11	.476	187	93	84	113	52	4.02
1985	—Milwaukee	American	3	17⅔	2	0	1.000	17	8	7	6	3	3.57
1986	—Milwaukee‡	American	35	198⅓	5	12	.294	217	120	113	82	43	5.13
1987	—Milwaukee§	American	34	225	12	11	.522	229	113	106	102	53	4.24
1988	—Milwaukee xy	American	32	199	13	13	.500	207	104	91	84	50	4.12
Major League Totals—4 Years			104	640	32	36	.471	670	345	317	274	149	4.46

Selected by Milwaukee Brewers' organization in 5th round of free-agent draft, June 8, 1981.
†On disabled list, June 18 to August 11, 1984.
‡Appeared in two games as a pinch-runner.
§On disabled list, August 7 to August 22, 1987.
xAppeared in one game as a pinch-runner.
yOn disabled list, May 21 to June 7, 1988.

WALTER WILLIAM WEISS JR.
(Walt)

Born November 28, 1963, at Tuxedo, N. Y.
Height, 6.00. Weight, 175.
Throws right and bats left and righthanded.
Attended University of North Carolina, Chapel Hill, N. C.

Major League stolen bases: 1987 (1), 1988 (4). Total—5.
Named American League Rookie Player of the Year by THE SPORTING NEWS, 1988.
Named American League Rookie of the Year by Baseball Writers' Association of America, 1988.

Year	Club	League	Pos.	G.	AB.	R.	H.	2B.	3B.	HR.	RBI.	B.A.	PO.	A.	E.	F.A.
1985	—Pocatello	Pion.	SS	40	158	19	49	9	3	0	21	.310	51	126	11	.941
1985	—Modesto	Calif.	SS	30	122	17	24	4	1	0	7	.197	36	97	7	.950
1986	—Madison	Midw.	SS	84	322	50	97	15	5	2	54	.301	143	251	20	.952
1986	—Huntsville	South.	SS	46	160	19	40	2	1	0	13	.250	72	142	11	.951
1987	—Huntsville	South.	SS	91	337	43	96	16	2	1	32	.285	152	259	17	.960
1987	—Oakland	Amer.	SS	16	26	3	12	4	0	0	1	.462	8	30	1	.974
1987	—Tacoma	P. C.	SS	46	179	35	47	4	3	0	17	.263	76	140	11	.952
1988	—Oakland	Amer.	SS	147	452	44	113	17	3	3	39	.250	254	431	15	.979
Major League Totals—2 Years				163	478	47	125	21	3	3	40	.262	262	461	16	.978

Selected by Baltimore Orioles' organization in 10th round of free-agent draft, June 7, 1982.
Selected by Oakland A's organization in 1st round (11th player selected) of free-agent draft, June 3, 1985.

CHAMPIONSHIP SERIES RECORD

Year	Club	League	Pos.	G.	AB.	R.	H.	2B.	3B.	HR.	RBI.	B.A.	PO.	A.	E.	F.A.
1988	—Oakland	Amer.	SS	4	15	2	5	2	0	0	2	.333	7	10	0	1.000

WORLD SERIES RECORD

Year	Club	League	Pos.	G.	AB.	R.	H.	2B.	3B.	HR.	RBI.	B.A.	PO.	A.	E.	F.A.
1988	—Oakland	Amer.	SS	5	16	1	1	0	0	0	0	.063	5	11	1	.941

ROBERT LYNN WELCH
(Bob)

Born November 3, 1956, at Detroit, Mich.
Height, 6.03. Weight, 195.
Throws and bats righthanded.
Attended Eastern Michigan University, Ypsilanti, Mich.

Major League saves: 1978 (3), 1979 (5). Total—8.
Tied for National League lead in shutouts with 4 in 1987.

Year Club	League	G.	IP.	W.	L.	Pct.	H.	R.	ER.	SO.	BB.	ERA.
1977—San Antonio	Texas	14	71	4	5	.444	94	44	35	56	17	4.44
1978—Albuquerque	P. Coast	11	69	5	1	.833	72	33	29	53	19	3.78
1978—Los Angeles	National	23	111	7	4	.636	92	28	25	66	26	2.03
1979—Los Angeles	National	25	81	5	6	.455	82	42	36	64	32	4.00
1980—Los Angeles	National	32	214	14	9	.609	190	85	78	141	79	3.28
1981—Los Angeles	National	23	141	9	5	.643	141	56	54	88	41	3.45
1982—Los Angeles†	National	36	235⅔	16	11	.593	199	94	88	176	81	3.36
1983—Los Angeles	National	31	204	15	12	.556	164	73	60	156	72	2.65
1984—Los Angeles	National	31	178⅔	13	13	.500	191	86	75	126	58	3.78
1985—Los Angeles‡	National	23	167⅓	14	4	.778	141	49	43	96	35	2.31
1985—Vero Beach	Florida St.	3	17	0	0	.000	15	4	4	9	1	2.12
1986—Los Angeles	National	33	235⅔	7	13	.350	227	95	86	183	55	3.28
1987—Los Angeles§	National	35	251⅔	15	9	.625	204	94	90	196	86	3.22
1988—Oakland	American	36	244⅔	17	9	.654	237	107	99	158	81	3.64
National League Totals—10 Years		292	1820	115	86	.572	1631	702	635	1292	565	3.14
American League Totals—1 Year		36	244⅔	17	9	.654	237	107	99	158	81	3.64
Major League Totals—11 Years		328	2064⅔	132	95	.581	1868	809	734	1450	646	3.20

Selected by Chicago Cubs' organization in 14th round of free-agent draft, June 5, 1974.
Selected by Los Angeles Dodgers' organization in 1st round (20th player selected) of free-agent draft, June 7, 1977.
†Appeared in one game as outfielder with no chances.
‡On disabled list, April 29 to June 5, 1985; included rehabilitation disability assignment to Vero Beach, May 21 to June 5, 1985.
§As part of an eight-player, three-team deal, New York Mets traded Pitcher Jesse Orosco to Oakland Athletics, December 11, 1987. Oakland then traded Orosco along with Shortstop Alfredo Griffin and Pitcher Jay Howell to Los Angeles Dodgers for Pitchers Bob Welch, Matt Young and Jack Savage. Oakland then traded Savage along with Pitchers Wally Whitehurst and Kevin Tapani to New York.

DIVISION SERIES RECORD

Year Club	League	G.	IP.	W.	L.	Pct.	H.	R.	ER.	SO.	BB.	ERA.
1981—Los Angeles	National	1	1	0	0	.000	0	0	0	1	1	0.00

CHAMPIONSHIP SERIES RECORD

Tied Championship Series record for most bases on balls, inning (4), October 12, 1985 (first inning).

Year Club	League	G.	IP.	W.	L.	Pct.	H.	R.	ER.	SO.	BB.	ERA.
1978—Los Angeles	National	1	4⅓	1	0	1.000	2	1	1	5	0	2.08
1981—Los Angeles	National	3	1⅔	0	0	.000	2	1	1	2	0	5.40
1983—Los Angeles	National	1	1⅓	0	1	.000	0	2	1	0	2	6.75
1985—Los Angeles	National	1	2⅔	0	1	.000	5	4	2	2	6	6.75
1988—Oakland	American	1	1⅔	0	0	.000	6	5	5	0	2	27.00
Championship Series Totals—5 Years		7	11⅔	1	2	.333	15	13	10	9	10	7.71

WORLD SERIES RECORD

Year Club	League	G.	IP.	W.	L.	Pct.	H.	R.	ER.	SO.	BB.	ERA.
1978—Los Angeles	National	3	4⅓	0	1	.000	4	3	3	6	2	6.23
1981—Los Angeles	National	1	0	0	0	.000	3	2	2	0	1	....
1988—Oakland	American	1	5	0	0	.000	6	1	1	8	3	1.80
World Series Totals—3 Years		5	9⅓	0	1	.000	13	6	6	14	6	5.79

ALL-STAR GAME RECORD

Year League	IP.	W.	L.	Pct.	H.	R.	ER.	SO.	BB.	ERA.
1980—National	3	0	0	.000	5	2	2	4	1	6.00

BRAD EUGENE WELLMAN

Born August 17, 1959, at Lodi, Calif.
Height, 6.00. Weight, 170.
Throws and bats righthanded.
Attended Chabot College, Hayward, Calif.
Brother-in-law of Tom Candiotti, pitcher with Cleveland Indians.

Major League stolen bases: 1983 (5), 1984 (10), 1985 (5), 1988 (1). Total—21.

Year Club	League	Pos.	G.	AB.	R.	H.	2B.	3B.	HR.	RBI.	B.A.	PO.	A.	E.	F.A.
1979—Sarasota Royals	Gulf C.	SS	48	170	24	44	6	0	2	24	.259	79	159	20	.922
1980—Fort Myers	Fla. St.	2B-SS	105	390	67	130	15	7	1	39	.333	175	301	27	.946
1981—Jacksonville	South	2B-SS	135	498	72	131	25	2	6	47	.263	286	368	25	.963
1982—Omaha†	A. A.	2B	6	24	5	7	3	0	1	3	.292	14	23	0	1.000
1982—Phoenix	P. C.	2B-3B	102	339	64	110	19	7	4	42	.324	201	257	14	.970
1982—San Francisco	Nat.	2B	6	4	1	1	0	0	0	0	.250	0	1	0	1.000
1983—Phoenix	P. C.	2B-SS	45	167	32	52	6	4	2	28	.311	79	123	4	.981
1983—San Francisco	Nat.	2B-SS	82	182	15	39	3	0	1	16	.214	94	167	9	.967
1984—Phoenix	P. C.	2B	43	159	26	47	8	1	0	11	.296	91	123	6	.973
1984—San Francisco	Nat.	2B-SS-3B	93	265	23	60	9	1	2	25	.226	151	258	11	.974
1985—San Francisco‡	Nat.	2B-3B-SS	71	174	16	41	11	1	0	16	.236	66	107	9	.951
1986—San Francisco	Nat.	SS-3B-2B	12	13	0	2	0	0	0	1	.154	3	10	0	1.000
1986—Phoenix§	P. C.	2B-SS-3B	79	262	31	74	17	1	2	30	.282	145	221	13	.966
1987—Albuquerque	P. C.	S-2-3-1-C	88	317	50	97	11	5	2	38	.306	123	253	18	.954
1987—Los Angeles xy	Nat.	3B-SS-2B	3	4	1	1	0	0	0	1	.250	3	3	0	1.000

Year	Club	League	Pos.	G.	AB.	R.	H.	2B.	3B.	HR.	RBI.	B.A.	PO.	A.	E.	F.A.
1988—Kansas City		Amer.	2B-SS-3B	71	107	11	29	3	0	1	6	.271	67	101	6	.966
National League Totals—6 Years				267	642	56	144	23	2	3	59	.224	317	546	29	.967
American League Totals—1 Year				71	107	11	29	3	0	1	6	.271	67	101	6	.966
Major League Totals—7 Years				338	749	67	173	26	2	4	65	.231	384	647	35	.967

Signed as free agent by Kansas City Royals' organization, August 27, 1978.

†Traded to San Francisco Giants' organization, April 19, 1982, completing deal in which San Francisco traded Pitchers Vida Blue and Bob Tufts to Kansas City Royals for Pitchers Atlee Hammaker, Craig Chamberlain and Renie Martin and a player to be named later, March 30, 1982.

‡On disabled list, May 30 to June 28, 1985.

§Granted free agency, October 15, 1986; signed by Albuquerque (Los Angeles Dodgers' organization), December 5, 1986.

xOn disabled list, August 3 to September 2, 1987; included rehabilitation disability assignment to Albuquerque, August 18 to September 2, 1987.

yGranted free agency, October 15, 1987; signed by Kansas City Royals, October 26, 1987.

DAVID LEE WELLS

Born May 20, 1963, at Torrance, Calif.
Height, 6.04. Weight, 225.
Throws and bats lefthanded.

Major League saves: 1987 (1), 1988 (4). Total—5.

Year	Club	League	G.	IP.	W.	L.	Pct.	H.	R.	ER.	SO.	BB.	ERA.
1982—Medicine Hat		Pioneer	12	64⅓	4	3	.571	71	42	37	53	32	5.18
1983—Kinston		Carolina	25	157	6	5	.545	141	81	65	115	71	3.73
1984—Kinston		Carolina	7	42	1	6	.143	51	29	22	44	19	4.71
1984—Knoxville†		Southern	8	59	3	2	.600	58	22	17	34	17	2.59
1985—Syracuse‡		Int'national					(Did not play)						
1986—Florence		S. Atlantic	4	12⅔	0	0	.000	7	6	5	14	9	3.55
1986—Ventura		California	5	19	2	1	.667	13	5	4	26	4	1.89
1986—Knoxville§		Southern	10	40	1	3	.250	42	24	18	32	18	4.05
1986—Syracuse		Int'national	3	3⅔	0	1	.000	6	4	4	2	1	9.82
1987—Syracuse		Int'national	43	109⅓	4	6	.400	102	49	47	106	32	3.87
1987—Toronto		American	18	29⅓	4	3	.571	37	14	13	32	12	3.99
1988—Toronto		American	41	64⅓	3	5	.375	65	36	33	56	31	4.62
1988—Syracuse		Int'national	6	5⅔	0	0	.000	7	1	0	8	2	0.00
Major League Totals—2 Years			59	93⅔	7	8	.467	102	50	46	88	43	4.42

Selected by Toronto Blue Jays' organization in 2nd round of free-agent draft, June 7, 1982.

†On disabled list, June 28, 1984, through remainder of season.

‡On disabled list, April 10, 1985, through entire season.

§On disabled list, July 7 to August 20, 1986.

DAVID LEE WEST
(Dave)

Born September 1, 1964, at Memphis, Tenn.
Height, 6.06. Weight, 220.
Throws and bats lefthanded.

Won 3-0 no-hit victory against Spartanburg, August 14, 1985.

Led New York-Pennsylvania League in wild pitches with 16 in 1984.

Tied for Texas League lead in shutouts with 2 in 1987.

Year	Club	League	G.	IP.	W.	L.	Pct.	H.	R.	ER.	SO.	BB.	ERA.
1983—Sarasota Mets		Gulf Coast	12	53⅔	2	4	.333	41	28	17	56	52	2.85
1984—Columbia		S. Atlantic	12	60⅔	3	5	.375	41	47	42	60	68	6.23
1984—Little Falls		NYP	13	62	6	4	.600	43	35	23	79	62	3.34
1985—Columbia		S. Atlantic	26	150	10	9	.526	105	97	76	194	★111	4.56
1986—Lynchburg		Carolina	13	75	1	6	.143	76	50	43	70	53	5.16
1986—Columbia		S. Atlantic	13	92⅔	10	3	.769	74	41	30	101	56	2.91
1987—Jackson		Texas	25	166⅔	10	7	.588	152	67	52	★186	★81	2.81
1988—Tidewater		Int'national	23	160⅓	12	4	★.750	106	42	32	143	★97	★1.80
1988—New York		National	2	6	1	0	1.000	6	2	2	3	3	3.00
Major League Totals—1 Year			2	6	1	0	1.000	6	2	2	3	3	3.00

Selected by New York Mets' organization in 4th round of free-agent draft, June 6, 1983.

JOHN KARL WETTELAND

Born August 21, 1966, at San Mateo, Calif.
Height, 6.02. Weight, 195.
Throws and bats righthanded.
Attended College of San Mateo, San Mateo, Calif.

Led Texas League in wild pitches with 22 in 1988.

Tied for Florida State League lead in home runs allowed with 11 and wild pitches with 17 in 1987.

Year	Club	League	G.	IP.	W.	L.	Pct.	H.	R.	ER.	SO.	BB.	ERA.
1985—Great Falls		Pioneer	11	20⅔	1	1	.500	17	10	9	23	15	3.92
1986—Bakersfield		California	15	67	0	7	.000	71	50	43	38	46	5.78
1986—Great Falls		Pioneer	12	69⅓	4	3	.571	70	51	42	59	40	5.45
1987—Vero Beach†		Florida St.	27	175⅔	12	7	.632	150	81	61	144	92	3.13
1988—San Antonio		Texas	25	162⅓	10	8	.556	141	74	70	140	•77	3.88

Selected by New York Mets' organization in 12th round of free-agent draft, June 4, 1984.
Selected by Los Angeles Dodgers' organization in secondary phase of free-agent draft, January 9, 1985.
†Drafted by Detroit Tigers, December 7, 1987; returned, March 29, 1988.

LOUIS RODMAN WHITAKER
(Lou)

Born May 12, 1957, at Brooklyn, N.Y.
Height, 5.11. Weight, 160.
Throws right and bats lefthanded.

Major League stolen bases: 1977 (2), 1978 (7), 1979 (20), 1980 (8), 1981 (5), 1982 (11), 1983 (17), 1984 (6), 1985 (6), 1986 (13), 1987 (13), 1988 (2). Total—110.

Led American League second basemen in total chances with 811 and double plays with 120 in 1982.

Led Florida State League second basemen in double plays with 30 in 1976.

Named second baseman on THE SPORTING NEWS American League All-Star Team, 1983 and 1984.

Named second baseman on THE SPORTING NEWS American League All-Star fielding team, 1983 through 1985.

Named second baseman on THE SPORTING NEWS American League Silver Slugger team, 1983 through 1985 and 1987.

Named American League Rookie of the Year by Baseball Writers' Association of America, 1978.

Named Florida State League Most Valuable Player, 1976.

Year Club	League	Pos.	G.	AB.	R.	H.	2B.	3B.	HR.	RBI.	B.A.	PO.	A.	E.	F.A.
1975—Bristol	Appal.	3B-SS	42	114	17	27	6	1	1	17	.237	38	82	16	.882
1976—Lakeland	Fla. St.	3B	124	343	★70	129	12	5	1	62	.297	★99	★267	★30	★.924
1977—Montgomery†	South.	2B	107	396	★81	111	13	4	3	48	.280	208	285	15	.970
1977—Detroit	Amer.	2B	11	32	5	8	1	0	0	2	.250	17	18	0	1.000
1978—Detroit	Amer.	2B	139	484	71	138	12	7	3	58	.285	301	458	17	.978
1979—Detroit‡	Amer.	2B	127	423	75	121	14	8	3	42	.286	280	369	9	.986
1980—Detroit	Amer.	2B	145	477	68	111	19	1	1	45	.233	340	428	12	.985
1981—Detroit	Amer.	2B	●109	335	48	88	14	4	5	36	.263	227	★354	9	.985
1982—Detroit	Amer.	2B	152	560	76	160	22	8	15	65	.286	331	★470	10	★.988
1983—Detroit	Amer.	2B	161	643	94	206	40	6	12	72	.320	299	447	13	.983
1984—Detroit	Amer.	2B	143	558	90	161	25	1	13	56	.289	290	405	15	.979
1985—Detroit	Amer.	2B	152	609	102	170	29	8	21	73	.279	314	414	11	.985
1986—Detroit	Amer.	2B	144	584	95	157	26	6	20	73	.269	276	421	11	.984
1987—Detroit	Amer.	2B	149	604	110	160	38	6	16	59	.265	275	416	17	.976
1988—Detroit	Amer.	2B	115	403	54	111	18	2	12	55	.275	218	284	8	.984
Major League Totals—12 Years			1547	5712	888	1591	258	57	121	636	.279	2968	4484	132	.983

Selected by Detroit Tigers' organization in 5th round of free-agent draft, June 4, 1975.
†On disabled list, May 3 to May 14, 1977.
‡On disabled list, June 13 to June 28, 1979.

CHAMPIONSHIP SERIES RECORD

Year Club	League	Pos.	G.	AB.	R.	H.	2B.	3B.	HR.	RBI.	B.A.	PO.	A.	E.	F.A.
1984—Detroit	Amer.	2B	3	14	3	2	0	0	0	0	.143	5	6	0	1.000
1987—Detroit	Amer.	2B	5	17	4	3	0	0	1	1	.176	11	14	0	1.000
Championship Series Totals—2 Years			8	31	7	5	0	0	1	1	.161	16	20	0	1.000

WORLD SERIES RECORD

Tied World Series record for most runs, five-game Series (6), 1984.

Year Club	League	Pos.	G.	AB.	R.	H.	2B.	3B.	HR.	RBI.	B.A.	PO.	A.	E.	F.A.
1984—Detroit	Amer.	2B	5	18	6	5	2	0	0	0	.278	15	18	0	1.000

ALL-STAR GAME RECORD

Year League	Pos.	AB.	R.	H.	2B.	3B.	HR.	RBI.	B.A.	PO.	A.	E.	F.A.
1983—American	PH-2B	1	1	1	0	1	0	2	1.000	1	0	0	1.000
1984—American	2B	3	0	2	1	0	0	0	.667	0	5	0	1.000
1985—American	2B	2	0	0	0	0	0	0	.000	1	1	0	1.000
1986—American	2B	2	1	1	0	0	1	2	.500	0	3	0	1.000
All-Star Game Totals—4 Years		8	2	4	1	1	1	4	.500	2	9	0	1.000

Named to American League All-Star Team for 1987 game; replaced due to injury by Harold Reynolds.

DEVON MARKES WHITE

First name pronounced De-VON.
Born December 29, 1962, at Kingston, Jamaica.
Height, 6.02. Weight, 178.
Throws right and bats left and righthanded.

Established major league record for most strikeouts by switch-hitter, season (135), 1987.
Major League stolen bases: 1985 (3), 1986 (6), 1987 (32), 1988 (17). Total—58.
Switch-hit home runs in one game, June 23, 1987.
Led American League outfielders in total chances with 449 in 1987.
Led Pacific Coast League in stolen bases with 42 in 1986.
Led Pacific Coast League outfielders in total chances with 339 in 1986.
Led California League outfielders in total chances with 351 in 1984.
Led Midwest League outfielders in total chances with 286 in 1983.
Named outfielder on THE SPORTING NEWS American League All-Star fielding team, 1988.

Year	Club	League	Pos.	G.	AB.	R.	H.	2B.	3B.	HR.	RBI.	B.A.	PO.	A.	E.	F.A.
1981	—Idaho Falls	Pion.	OF-3B-1B	30	106	10	19	2	0	0	10	.179	33	10	3	.935
1982	—Danville†	Midw.	OF	57	186	21	40	6	1	1	11	.215	89	3	8	.920
1983	—Peoria	Midw.	OF	117	430	69	109	17	6	13	66	.253	267	8	11	.962
1983	—Nashua	East.	OF	17	70	11	18	7	2	0	2	.257	37	0	3	.925
1984	—Redwood	Calif.	OF	138	520	101	147	25	5	7	55	.283	★322	16	13	.963
1985	—Midland	Texas	OF	70	260	52	77	10	4	4	35	.296	176	10	4	.979
1985	—Edmonton	P. C.	OF	66	277	53	70	16	5	4	39	.253	205	6	2	.991
1985	—California	Amer.	OF	21	7	7	1	0	0	0	0	.143	10	1	0	1.000
1986	—Edmonton‡	P. C.	OF	112	461	84	134	25	10	14	60	.291	317	●16	6	.982
1986	—California	Amer.	OF	29	51	8	12	1	1	1	3	.235	49	0	2	.961
1987	—California	Amer.	OF	159	639	103	168	33	5	24	87	.263	★424	16	9	.980
1988	—California§	Amer.	OF	122	455	76	118	22	2	11	51	.259	364	7	9	.976
Major League Totals—4 Years				331	1152	194	299	56	8	36	141	.260	847	24	20	.978

Selected by California Angels' organization in 6th round of free-agent draft, June 8, 1981.
†On suspended list, June 11 to June 12 and July 19, 1982 through remainder of season.
‡On disabled list, May 12 to May 22, 1986.
§On disabled list, May 7 to June 10, 1988.

CHAMPIONSHIP SERIES RECORD

Year	Club	League	Pos.	G.	AB.	R.	H.	2B.	3B.	HR.	RBI.	B.A.	PO.	A.	E.	F.A.
1986	—California	Amer.	OF-PR	4	2	2	1	0	0	0	0	.500	3	0	0	1.000

FRANK WHITE JR.

Born September 4, 1950, at Greenville, Miss.
Height, 5.11. Weight, 190.
Throws and bats righthanded.
Attended Manatee Junior College, Bradenton, Fla., and
Longview Community College, Lee's Summit, Mo.

Hit for the cycle, September 26, 1979 and August 3, 1982.

Major League stolen bases: 1973 (3), 1974 (3), 1975 (11), 1976 (20), 1977 (23), 1978 (13), 1979 (28), 1980 (19), 1981 (4), 1982 (10), 1983 (13), 1984 (5), 1985 (10), 1986 (4), 1987 (1), 1988 (7). Total—174.

Led American League second basemen in total chances with 849 in 1985.

Led Gulf Coast League in stolen bases with 18 in 1971.

Led Gulf Coast League shortstops in double plays with 27 in 1971.

Named second baseman on THE SPORTING NEWS American League All-Star Team, 1978.

Named second baseman on THE SPORTING NEWS American League All-Star fielding team, 1977 through 1982, 1986 and 1987.

Named second baseman on THE SPORTING NEWS American League Silver Slugger team, 1986.

Year	Club	League	Pos.	G.	AB.	R.	H.	2B.	3B.	HR.	RBI.	B.A.	PO.	A.	E.	F.A.
1971	—Sara. Royals	Gulf C.	SS	50	158	31	39	6	3	1	21	.247	70	★149	17	★.928
1972	—San Jose	Calif.	SS	49	187	44	55	7	2	10	26	.294	77	138	14	.939
1972	—Jacksonville	South.	SS	91	333	34	84	12	2	2	23	.252	124	306	31	.933
1973	—Omaha	A. A.	2B-SS	86	348	49	92	19	2	4	32	.264	163	221	21	.948
1973	—Kansas City	Amer.	SS-2B	51	139	20	31	6	1	0	5	.223	71	121	12	.941
1974	—Kansas City	Amer.	2B-SS-3B	99	204	19	45	6	3	1	18	.221	119	189	12	.963
1975	—Kansas City	Amer.	2-S-3-C	111	304	43	76	10	2	7	36	.250	182	275	12	.974
1976	—Kansas City	Amer.	2B-SS	152	446	39	102	17	6	2	46	.229	296	479	23	.971
1977	—Kansas City	Amer.	★2B-SS	152	474	59	116	21	5	5	20	.245	310	437	8	★.989
1978	—Kansas City	Amer.	2B	143	461	66	127	24	6	7	50	.275	325	385	16	.978
1979	—Kansas City†	Amer.	2B	127	467	73	124	26	4	10	48	.266	317	332	12	.982
1980	—Kansas City	Amer.	2B	154	560	70	148	23	4	7	60	.264	395	448	10	.988
1981	—Kansas City	Amer.	2B	94	364	35	91	17	1	9	38	.250	226	263	6	.988
1982	—Kansas City	Amer.	2B	145	524	71	156	45	6	11	56	.298	★361	389	★17	.978
1983	—Kansas City	Amer.	2B	146	549	52	143	35	6	11	77	.260	★390	442	8	★.990
1984	—Kansas City‡	Amer.	2B	129	479	58	130	22	5	17	56	.271	299	425	11	.985
1985	—Kansas City	Amer.	2B	149	563	62	140	25	1	22	69	.249	342	★490	★17	.980
1986	—Kansas City	Amer.	2B-SS-3B	151	566	76	154	37	3	22	84	.272	317	441	10	.987
1987	—Kansas City	Amer.	2B	154	563	67	138	32	2	17	78	.245	320	458	10	.987
1988	—Kansas City	Amer.	2B	150	537	48	126	25	1	8	58	.235	293	426	4	★.994
Major League Totals—16 Years				2107	7200	858	1847	371	56	156	829	.257	4563	6000	188	.983

Signed as free agent by Kansas City Royals' organization, July 2, 1970.
†On disabled list, May 9 to June 11, 1979.
‡On disabled list, July 6 to July 21, 1984.

DIVISION SERIES RECORD

Year	Club	League	Pos.	G.	AB.	R.	H.	2B.	3B.	HR.	RBI.	B.A.	PO.	A.	E.	F.A.
1981	—Kansas City	Amer.	2B	3	11	1	2	0	0	0	0	.182	5	6	1	.917

CHAMPIONSHIP SERIES RECORD

Year	Club	League	Pos.	G.	AB.	R.	H.	2B.	3B.	HR.	RBI.	B.A.	PO.	A.	E.	F.A.
1976	—Kansas City	Amer.	2B-PR	4	8	2	1	0	0	0	0	.125	6	11	0	1.000
1977	—Kansas City	Amer.	2B	5	18	1	5	1	0	0	2	.278	13	16	0	1.000
1978	—Kansas City	Amer.	2B	4	13	1	3	0	0	0	2	.231	9	12	0	1.000
1980	—Kansas City	Amer.	2B	3	11	3	6	1	0	1	3	.545	9	10	1	.950
1984	—Kansas City	Amer.	2B	3	11	1	1	0	0	0	0	.091	7	3	0	1.000
1985	—Kansas City	Amer.	2B	7	25	1	5	0	0	0	3	.200	9	28	0	1.000
Championship Series Totals—6 Years				26	86	9	21	2	0	1	10	.244	53	80	1	.993

WORLD SERIES RECORD

Tied World Series records for fewest runs, Series (0), 1980; most at-bats, nine-inning game, no hits (5), October 18, 1980; most unassisted double plays by second baseman, game (1), October 17, 1980; fewest chances accepted, second baseman, game (0), October 20, 1985.

Year	Club	League	Pos.	G.	AB.	R.	H.	2B.	3B.	HR.	RBI.	B.A.	PO.	A.	E.	F.A.
1980	Kansas City	Amer.	2B	6	25	0	2	0	0	0	0	.080	13	21	2	.944
1985	Kansas City	Amer.	2B	7	28	4	7	3	0	1	6	.250	10	20	0	1.000
World Series Totals—2 Years				13	53	4	9	3	0	1	6	.170	23	41	2	.970

ALL-STAR GAME RECORD

Tied All-Star Game record for most home runs by pinch-hitter, game (1), July 15, 1986.

Year	League	Pos.	AB.	R.	H.	2B.	3B.	HR.	RBI.	B.A.	PO.	A.	E.	F.A.
1978	American	2B	1	0	0	0	0	0	0	.000	1	2	0	1.000
1979	American	2B	2	0	0	0	0	0	0	.000	2	2	0	1.000
1981	American	PR-2B	1	0	0	0	0	0	0	.000	1	0	0	1.000
1982	American	2B	1	0	0	0	0	0	0	.000	2	1	0	1.000
1986	American	PH-2B	2	1	1	0	0	1	1	.500	1	1	0	1.000
All-Star Game Totals—5 Years			7	1	1	0	0	1	1	.143	7	6	0	1.000

EDWARD MORRIS WHITED
(Ed)

Born February 9, 1964, at Bristol, Pa.
Height, 6.03. Weight, 195.
Throws and bats righthanded.
Attended Rider College, Lawrenceville, N.J.

Led Southern League in bases on balls received with 97 in 1988.
Led South Atlantic League in game-winning RBIs with 18 in 1987.
Led South Atlantic League third basemen in fielding percentage with .944 in 1987.
Named South Atlantic League Most Valuable Player, 1988.

Year	Club	League	Pos.	G.	AB.	R.	H.	2B.	3B.	HR.	RBI.	B.A.	PO.	A.	E.	F.A.
1986	Auburn	NYP	3B-1B	61	219	34	64	15	1	5	36	.292	286	82	15	.961
1987	Asheville†	S. Atl.	3B-1B-2B	128	440	97	142	★37	0	28	★126	★.323	107	250	19	.949
1988	Greenville	South.	3B	132	428	81	108	11	4	16	62	.252	73	264	33	.911

Selected by Houston Astros' organization in 18th round of free-agent draft, June 2, 1986.
†Traded with Pitcher Mike Stoker to Atlanta Braves for Shortstop Rafael Ramirez, December 8, 1987.

WALTER RICHARD WHITEHURST
(Wally)

Born April 11, 1964, at Shreveport, La.
Height, 6.03. Weight, 180.
Throws and bats righthanded.
Attended University of New Orleans, New Orleans, La.

Tied for Southern League lead in shutouts with 3 in 1987.
Tied for Midwest League lead in shutouts with 4 in 1986.
Tied for Northwest League lead in hit batsmen with 7 and balks with 2 in 1985.

Year	Club	League	G.	IP.	W.	L.	Pct.	H.	R.	ER.	SO.	BB.	ERA.
1985	Medford	Northwest	14	88	7	5	.583	92	51	35	●91	29	3.58
1985	Modesto	California	2	10	1	0	1.000	10	3	2	5	5	1.80
1986	Madison	Midwest	8	61	6	1	.857	42	8	4	57	16	0.59
1986	Huntsville	Southern	19	104⅔	9	5	.643	114	66	54	54	46	4.64
1987	Huntsville†	Southern	28	183⅓	11	10	.524	192	104	81	106	42	3.98
1988	Tidewater	Int'national	26	165	10	11	.476	145	65	56	113	32	3.05

Selected by Oakland A's organization in 3rd round of free-agent draft, June 3, 1985.

†As part of an eight-player, three-team deal, New York Mets traded Pitcher Jesse Orosco to Oakland Athletics, December 11, 1987. Oakland then traded Orosco along with Shortstop Alfredo Griffin and Pitcher Jay Howell to Los Angeles Dodgers for Pitchers Bob Welch, Matt Young and Jack Savage. Oakland then traded Savage along with Pitchers Wally Whitehurst and Kevin Tapani to New York.

MARK ANTHONY WHITEN

Born November 25, 1966, at Pensacola, Fla.
Height, 6.03. Weight, 210.
Throws and bats righthanded.
Attended Pensacola Junior College, Pensacola, Fla.

Led South Atlantic League in being hit by pitch with 16 and tied for lead in intentional bases on balls received with 10 in 1987.

Tied for Pioneer League lead in being hit by pitch with 6 in 1986.

Led South Atlantic League outfielders in total chances with 322 and tied for lead in double plays by outfielders with 4 in 1987.

Year	Club	League	Pos.	G.	AB.	R.	H.	2B.	3B.	HR.	RBI.	B.A.	PO.	A.	E.	F.A.
1986	Medicine Hat	Pion.	OF	●70	270	53	81	16	3	10	44	.300	111	9	★10	.923
1987	Myrtle Beach	S. Atl.	OF	★139	494	90	125	22	5	15	64	.253	★292	★18	12	.963
1988	Dunedin	Fla. St.	OF	99	385	61	97	8	5	7	37	.252	200	★21	9	.961
1988	Knoxville	South.	OF	28	108	20	28	3	1	2	9	.259	62	3	4	.942

Selected by Toronto Blue Jays' organization in 5th round of free-agent draft, January 14, 1986.

EDDIE LEE WHITSON
(Ed)

Born May 19, 1955, at Johnson City, Tenn.
Height, 6.03. Weight, 195.
Throws and bats righthanded.

Major League saves: 1978 (4), 1979 (1), 1982 (2), 1983 (1). Total—8.
Led National League in home runs allowed with 36 in 1987.
Led Carolina League in complete games with 16 in 1976.
Led Western Carolinas League in hit batsmen with 15 in 1975.

Year Club	League	G.	IP.	W.	L.	Pct.	H.	R.	ER.	SO.	BB.	ERA.
1974—Bradenton Pirates	Gulf Coast	8	44	1	4	.200	45	28	21	25	15	4.30
1975—Charleston	W. Carol.	24	142	8	★15	.348	140	★96	★80	120	99	5.07
1976—Salem	Carolina	26	★203	●15	9	.625	168	75	57	★186	65	2.53
1977—Columbus	Int'national	26	175	8	13	.381	175	74	65	120	68	3.34
1977—Pittsburgh	National	5	16	1	0	1.000	11	6	6	10	9	3.38
1978—Columbus	Int'national	7	51	2	2	.500	56	25	21	55	10	3.71
1978—Pittsburgh	National	43	74	5	6	.455	66	31	27	64	37	3.28
1979—Pittsburgh†-San Francisco	National	37	158	7	11	.389	151	83	72	93	75	4.10
1980—San Francisco	National	34	212	11	13	.458	222	88	73	90	56	3.10
1981—San Francisco‡	National	22	123	6	9	.400	130	61	55	65	47	4.02
1982—Cleveland§	American	40	107⅔	4	2	.667	91	43	39	61	58	3.26
1983—San Diego x	National	31	144⅓	5	7	.417	143	73	69	81	50	4.30
1983—Las Vegas	P. Coast	3	12	1	0	1.000	15	9	9	11	5	6.75
1984—San Diego y	National	31	189	14	8	.636	181	72	68	103	42	3.24
1985—New York	American	30	158⅔	10	8	.556	201	100	86	89	43	4.88
1986—New York za	American	14	37	5	2	.714	54	37	31	27	23	7.54
1986—San Diego	National	17	75⅓	1	7	.125	85	48	47	46	37	5.59
1987—San Diego	National	36	205⅔	10	13	.435	197	113	108	135	64	4.73
1988—San Diego	National	34	205⅓	13	11	.542	202	93	86	118	45	3.77
National League Totals—10 Years		290	1403	73	85	.462	1388	668	611	805	462	3.92
American League Totals—3 Years		84	303⅓	19	12	.613	346	180	156	177	124	4.63
Major League Totals—12 Years		374	1706⅓	92	97	.487	1734	848	767	982	586	4.05

Selected by Pittsburgh Pirates' organization in 6th round of free-agent draft, June 5, 1974.
†Traded with Pitchers Fred Breining and Al Holland to San Francisco Giants for Infielders Bill Madlock and Lenny Randle and Pitcher Dave Roberts, June 28, 1979.
‡Traded to Cleveland Indians for Second Baseman Duane Kuiper, November 16, 1981.
§Traded to San Diego Padres for Pitcher Juan Eichelberger and First Baseman-Outfielder Broderick Perkins, November 18, 1982.
xOn disabled list, April 18 to May 28, 1983; included rehabilitation disability assignment to Las Vegas, May 10 to May 28, 1983.
yGranted free agency, November 8, 1984; signed by New York Yankees, December 27, 1984.
zOn disabled list, April 30 to May 21, 1986.
aTraded to San Diego Padres for Pitcher Tim Stoddard, July 9, 1986.

CHAMPIONSHIP SERIES RECORD

Year Club	League	G.	IP.	W.	L.	Pct.	H.	R.	ER.	SO.	BB.	ERA.
1984—San Diego	National	1	8	1	0	1.000	5	1	1	6	2	1.13

WORLD SERIES RECORD

Year Club	League	G.	IP.	W.	L.	Pct.	H.	R.	ER.	SO.	BB.	ERA.
1984—San Diego	National	1	⅔	0	0	.000	5	3	3	0	0	40.50

ALL-STAR GAME RECORD

Member of National League All-Star Team in 1980; did not play.

LEO ERNEST WHITT
(Ernie)

Born June 13, 1952, Detroit, Mich.
Height, 6.02. Weight, 200.
Throws right and bats lefthanded.
Attended Macomb County Community College, Warren, Mich.

Major League stolen bases: 1980 (1), 1981 (5), 1982 (3), 1983 (1), 1985 (3), 1988 (4). Total—17.
Hit three home runs in a game, September 14, 1987.
Led American League catchers in total chances with 863 in 1987.
Led International League in passed balls with 16 in 1978.
Led Eastern League catchers in fielding percentage with .992 in 1974.
Tied for Carolina League lead in double plays by catchers with 7 in 1973.
Named catcher on The Sporting News American League All-Star Team, 1988.

Year Club	League	Pos.	G.	AB.	R.	H.	2B.	3B.	HR.	RBI.	B.A.	PO.	A.	E.	F.A.
1972—Williamsport	NYP	1B	1	4	1	2	1	0	0	0	.500	8	1	0	1.000
1972—Winter Haven	Fla. St.	C-1B-OF	31	82	3	15	1	1	0	7	.183	151	14	5	.971
1973—Winston-Salem	Carol.	C-OF-1B	130	424	63	123	23	3	1	50	.290	686	70	15	.980
1974—Bristol	East.	C-OF-1B	111	385	55	96	10	1	9	56	.249	557	50	6	.990
1975—Bristol†	East.	C-OF	82	252	29	64	9	1	2	19	.254	357	36	7	.982
1976—Bristol	East.	C	26	87	12	19	2	3	1	10	.218	127	25	1	.993
1976—Rhode Island	Int.	C-1-O-3	90	304	33	81	16	2	7	42	.266	487	59	9	.984
1976—Boston‡	Amer.	C	8	18	4	4	2	0	1	3	.222	24	0	0	1.000

Year Club	League	Pos.	G.	AB.	R.	H.	2B.	3B.	HR.	RBI.	B.A.	PO.	A.	E.	F.A.
1977—Charleston	Int.	C-3B	29	94	12	24	6	0	0	7	.255	129	28	7	.957
1977—Toronto§	Amer.	C	23	41	4	7	3	0	0	6	.171	62	4	0	1.000
1978—Syracuse	Int.	C-1B-OF	121	399	50	98	16	3	12	53	.246	673	79	7	.991
1978—Toronto	Amer.	C	2	4	0	0	0	0	0	0	.000	7	1	0	1.000
1979—Syracuse	Int.	*C-OF-3B	114	382	32	95	18	4	7	43	.249	494	69	3	*.995
1980—Toronto	Amer.	C	106	295	23	70	12	2	6	34	.237	436	56	7	.986
1981—Toronto	Amer.	C	74	195	16	46	9	0	1	16	.236	297	46	3	.991
1982—Toronto	Amer.	C	105	284	28	74	14	2	11	42	.261	406	30	8	.982
1983—Toronto	Amer.	C	123	344	53	88	15	2	17	56	.256	554	50	5	.992
1984—Toronto x	Amer.	C	124	315	35	75	12	1	15	46	.238	583	40	4	.994
1985—Toronto	Amer.	C	139	412	55	101	21	2	19	64	.245	649	38	8	.988
1986—Toronto yz	Amer.	C	131	395	48	106	19	2	16	56	.268	709	41	7	.991
1987—Toronto	Amer.	C	135	446	57	120	24	1	19	75	.269	*803	55	5	.994
1988—Toronto	Amer.	C	127	398	63	100	11	2	16	70	.251	643	43	4	.994
Major League Totals—12 Years			1097	3147	386	791	142	14	121	468	.251	5173	404	51	.991

Selected by Boston Red Sox' organization in 15th round of free-agent draft, June 6, 1972.

†On disabled list, April 11 to June 13, 1975.

‡Selected by Toronto Blue Jays in American League expansion draft, November 5, 1976.

§On disabled list, August 17 to September 27, 1977.

xOn disabled list, June 16 to July 1, 1984.

yOn disabled list, April 15 to April 30, 1986; included rehabilitation disability assignment to Syracuse, April 28 to April 30, 1986.

zGranted free agency, November 12, 1986; re-signed by Blue Jays, January 8, 1987.

CHAMPIONSHIP SERIES RECORD

Year Club	League	Pos.	G.	AB.	R.	H.	2B.	3B.	HR.	RBI.	B.A.	PO.	A.	E.	F.A.
1985—Toronto	Amer.	C	7	21	1	4	1	0	0	2	.190	50	3	0	1.000

ALL-STAR GAME RECORD

Year League	Pos.	AB.	R.	H.	2B.	3B.	HR.	RBI.	B.A.	PO.	A.	E.	F.A.
1985—American	C	0	0	0	0	0	0	0	.000	2	0	0	1.000

CURTIS VERNON WILKERSON
(Curt)

Born April 26, 1961, at Petersburg, Va.
Height, 5.09. Weight, 160.
Throws right and bats left and righthanded.

Major League stolen bases: 1983 (3), 1984 (12), 1985 (14), 1986 (9), 1987 (6), 1988 (9). Total—53.

Tied for Texas League lead in sacrifice hits with 11 in 1982.

Year Club	League	Pos.	G.	AB.	R.	H.	2B.	3B.	HR.	RBI.	B.A.	PO.	A.	E.	F.A.
1980—Sarasota Rangers	Gulf C.	SS-2B	37	105	15	20	2	0	0	8	.190	38	86	17	.879
1981—Asheville	S. Atl.	SS-2B	106	333	45	68	7	3	0	19	.204	188	372	28	.952
1982—Burlington	Midw.	SS-2B	56	198	18	50	6	0	0	13	.253	78	159	16	.937
1982—Tulsa	Texas	SS	72	266	32	71	6	3	2	14	.267	102	225	18	.948
1983—Oklahoma City†	A. A.	SS	89	343	51	107	19	4	3	31	.312	135	272	19	.955
1983—Texas	Amer.	SS-2B-3B	16	35	7	6	0	1	0	1	.171	18	31	1	.980
1984—Texas	Amer.	SS-2B	153	484	47	120	12	0	1	26	.248	227	391	30	.954
1985—Texas	Amer.	SS-2B	129	360	35	88	11	6	0	22	.244	165	328	21	.959
1986—Texas	Amer.	2B-SS	110	236	27	56	10	3	0	15	.237	125	199	13	.961
1987—Texas	Amer.	SS-2B-3B	85	138	28	37	5	3	2	14	.268	79	98	6	.967
1988—Texas‡	Amer.	2B-SS-3B	117	338	41	99	12	5	0	28	.293	186	299	15	.970
Major League Totals—6 Years			610	1591	185	406	50	18	3	106	.255	800	1346	86	.961

Selected by Texas Rangers' organization in 4th round of free-agent draft, June 3, 1980.

†On disabled list, May 19 to June 21, 1983.

‡Traded with Pitchers Mitch Williams, Paul Kilgus and Steve Wilson, Infielder Luis Benitez and Outfielder Pablo Delgado to Chicago Cubs for Outfielder Rafael Palmeiro and Pitchers Jamie Moyer and Drew Hall, December 5, 1988.

DEAN ALLAN WILKINS

Born August 24, 1966, at Chicago, Ill.
Height, 6.01. Weight, 170.
Throws and bats righthanded.
Attended San Diego Mesa College, San Diego, Calif.

Led Eastern League in saves with 26 and games finished in relief with 49 in 1988.

Year Club	League	G.	IP.	W.	L.	Pct.	H.	R.	ER.	SO.	BB.	ERA.
1986—Oneonta	NYP	15	83⅓	9	0	*1.000	64	32	29	80	24	3.13
1987—Fort Lauderdale	Florida St.	15	105⅔	8	5	.615	95	41	32	76	39	2.73
1987—Albany†	Eastern	2	12	0	0	.000	18	11	9	8	1	6.75
1987—Winston-Salem	Carolina	13	50⅓	4	4	.500	49	31	23	29	24	4.11
1988—Pittsfield	Eastern	•59	71⅔	5	7	.417	53	25	13	59	30	1.63

Selected by New York Yankees' organization in 2nd round of free-agent draft, January 14, 1986.

†Traded with Pitchers Rick Scheid and Bob Tewksbury to Chicago Cubs for Pitcher Steve Trout, July 13, 1987.

WILLIAM CARL WILKINSON
(Bill)

Born August 10, 1964, at Greybull, Wyo.
Height, 5.10. Weight, 160.
Throws left and bats righthanded.
Brother of Brian Wilkinson, pitcher in Seattle Mariners' organization.

Major League saves: 1987 (10), 1988 (2). Total—12.

Year Club	League	G.	IP.	W.	L.	Pct.	H.	R.	ER.	SO.	BB.	ERA.
1983—Bellingham	Northwest	13	63⅔	4	5	.444	54	41	24	87	54	3.39
1984—Wausau	Midwest	19	103⅓	6	4	.600	79	47	38	117	52	3.31
1985—Salinas	California	9	59⅔	6	1	.857	47	19	18	75	23	2.72
1985—Calgary†	P. Coast	9	57⅓	5	1	.833	44	21	17	42	25	2.67
1985—Seattle	American	2	6	0	2	.000	8	9	9	5	6	13.50
1986—Calgary‡	P. Coast	23	143	8	8	.500	146	82	76	86	51	4.78
1987—Seattle§	American	56	76⅓	3	4	.429	61	33	31	73	21	3.66
1988—Seattle x	American	30	31	2	2	.500	28	14	12	25	15	3.48
1988—Calgary	P. Coast	21	23⅔	0	4	.000	31	28	24	20	20	9.13
Major League Totals—3 Years		88	113⅓	5	8	.385	97	56	52	103	42	4.13

Selected by Seattle Mariners' organization in 4th round of free-agent draft, June 6, 1983.
†On disabled list, July 18, 1985 through remainder of season.
‡On disabled list, July 26, 1986 through remainder of season.
§On disabled list, July 19 to August 5, 1987.
xOn disabled list, May 13 to June 21, 1988; included rehabilitation disability assignment to Calgary, May 29 to June 15, 1988.

EDWARD LAQUAN WILLIAMS
(Eddie)

Born November 1, 1964, at Shreveport, La.
Height, 6.00. Weight, 175.
Throws and bats righthanded.

Led Pacific Coast League in being hit by pitch with 12 in 1988.
Led American Association in being hit by pitch with 15 in 1987.
Led Midwest League in being hit by pitch with 15 in 1985.
Led American Association third basemen in total chances with 352 and double plays with 24 in 1987.
Named Midwest League Most Valuable Player, 1985.

Year Club	League	Pos.	G.	AB.	R.	H.	2B.	3B.	HR.	RBI.	B.A.	PO.	A.	E.	F.A.
1983—Little Falls	NYP	3B	50	190	30	50	6	2	6	28	.263	50	53	13	.888
1984—Columbia†	S. Atl.	3B	43	152	17	28	4	2	3	24	.184	24	76	16	.862
1984—Tampa	Fla. St.	3B	50	138	20	35	8	0	2	16	.254	25	43	11	.861
1985—Cedar Rapids‡	Midw.	3B	119	406	71	106	13	3	20	83	.261	83	204	33	.897
1986—Cleveland	Amer.	OF	5	7	2	1	0	0	0	1	.143	0	0	0	.000
1986—Waterbury	East.	3B	62	214	24	51	10	0	7	30	.238	39	100	15	.903
1987—Buffalo	A. A.	★3B-SS	131	488	90	142	29	2	22	85	.291	88	★237	★27	.923
1987—Cleveland	Amer.	3B	22	64	9	11	4	0	1	4	.172	17	37	1	.982
1988—Colorado Springs	P. C.	3B-SS-1B	101	365	53	110	24	3	12	58	.301	93	177	29	.903
1988—Cleveland	Amer.	3B	10	21	3	4	0	0	0	1	.190	3	18	0	1.000
Major League Totals—3 Years			37	92	14	16	4	0	1	6	.174	20	55	1	.987

Selected by New York Mets' organization in 1st round (fourth player selected) of free-agent draft, June 6, 1983.
†Traded with Pitchers Matt Bullinger and Jay Tibbs to Cincinnati Reds for Pitcher Bruce Berenyi, June 15, 1984.
‡Drafted by Cleveland Indians, December 10, 1985.

FRANK LEE WILLIAMS

Born February 13, 1958, at Seattle, Wash.
Height, 6.01. Weight, 205.
Throws and bats righthanded.
Attended Shoreline Community College, Seattle, Wash., and Lewis-Clark State College, Lewiston, Ida.

Major League saves: 1984 (3), 1986 (1), 1987 (2), 1988 (1). Total—7.
Led California League in hit batsmen with 18 in 1980 and 13 in 1981.
Led Pioneer League in hit batsmen with 9 in 1979.
Tied for Texas League lead in hit batsmen with 13 in 1982.
Tied for California League lead in complete games with 14 in 1981.

Year Club	League	G.	IP.	W.	L.	Pct.	H.	R.	ER.	SO.	BB.	ERA.
1979—Great Falls	Pioneer	13	91	6	•7	.462	85	53	34	81	53	3.36
1980—Fresno	California	21	114	12	3	.800	105	53	42	80	70	3.32
1981—Fresno	California	27	187	14	9	.609	170	81	70	170	85	3.37
1982—Shreveport	Texas	27	169⅔	11	9	.550	143	96	74	145	99	3.93
1983—Shreveport	Texas	21	42	7	2	.778	22	14	8	54	25	1.71
1983—Phoenix	P. Coast	25	47⅔	5	3	.625	45	22	19	37	24	3.59
1984—San Francisco	National	61	106⅓	9	4	.692	88	49	42	91	51	3.55
1985—San Francisco	National	49	73	2	4	.333	65	39	34	54	35	4.19
1985—Phoenix	P. Coast	9	13⅔	1	1	.500	10	8	6	10	14	3.95
1986—Phoenix	P. Coast	27	38	1	1	.500	28	10	9	41	17	2.13
1986—San Francisco†	National	36	52⅓	3	1	.750	35	8	7	33	21	1.20
1987—Cincinnati	National	85	105⅔	4	0	1.000	101	37	27	60	39	2.30

Year	Club	League	G.	IP.	W.	L.	Pct.	H.	R.	ER.	SO.	BB.	ERA.
1988—Cincinnati		National	60	62⅔	3	2	.600	59	24	18	43	35	2.59
1988—Nashville‡		Am. Assoc.	2	3	0	0	.000	3	3	3	1	2	9.00
Major League Totals—5 Years			291	400	21	11	.656	348	157	128	281	181	2.88

Selected by San Francisco Giants' organization in 11th round of free-agent draft, June 5, 1979.

†Traded with Pitchers Timber Mead and Mike Villa to Cincinnati Reds for Outfielder Eddie Milner, January 8, 1987.

‡Released, December 21, 1988.

KENNETH ROYAL WILLIAMS
(Ken)

Born April 6, 1964, at Berkeley, Calif.
Height, 6.01. Weight, 187.
Throws and bats righthanded.
Attended Stanford University, Stanford, Calif.

Major League stolen bases: 1986 (1), 1987 (21), 1988 (6). Total—28.

Received reported $165,000 bonus to sign with Chicago White Sox, 1982.

Year	Club	League	Pos.	G.	AB.	R.	H.	2B.	3B.	HR.	RBI.	B.A.	PO.	A.	E.	F.A.
1982—Sarasota W. Sox		Gulf C.	OF	31	104	19	31	2	1	1	11	.298	61	2	0	1.000
1983—Appleton		Midw.	OF	124	415	60	96	18	2	12	53	.231	218	10	10	.958
1984—Appleton		Midw.	OF	38	147	23	42	11	2	5	26	.286	58	5	2	.969
1984—Glens Falls		East.	OF	97	309	35	76	7	5	8	47	.246	173	10	5	.973
1985—Glens Falls		East.	OF	133	*520	*87	130	16	6	16	66	.250	296	*20	*14	.958
1986—Buffalo		A. A.	OF	50	189	21	40	4	2	4	15	.212	100	8	1	.991
1986—Birmingham		South.	OF	68	272	41	90	16	5	6	40	.331	192	3	8	.961
1986—Chicago		Amer.	OF	15	31	2	4	0	0	1	1	.129	18	1	0	1.000
1987—Hawaii		P. C.	OF	35	134	19	36	4	4	3	14	.269	75	1	2	.974
1987—Chicago		Amer.	OF	116	391	48	110	18	2	11	50	.281	303	5	6	.981
1988—Chicago†		Amer.	OF-3B	73	220	18	35	4	2	8	28	.159	87	69	17	.902
1988—Vancouver		P. C.	OF	16	60	8	15	2	1	1	7	.250	23	0	0	1.000
Major League Totals—3 Years				204	642	68	149	22	4	20	79	.232	408	75	23	.955

Selected by Chicago White Sox' organization in 3rd round of free-agent draft, June 7, 1982.

†On disabled list, May 25 to June 30, 1988.

MATTHEW DERRICK WILLIAMS
(Matt)

Born November 28, 1965, at Bishop, Calif.
Height, 6.02. Weight, 205.
Throws and bats righthanded.
Attended University of Nevada, Las Vegas, Nev.

Major League stolen bases: 1987 (4).

Named shortstop on The Sporting News College Baseball All-America Team, 1986.

Year	Club	League	Pos.	G.	AB.	R.	H.	2B.	3B.	HR.	RBI.	B.A.	PO.	A.	E.	F.A.
1986—Everett		N'west	SS	4	17	3	4	0	1	1	10	.235	5	10	2	.882
1986—Clinton		Midw.	SS	68	250	32	60	14	3	7	29	.240	89	150	10	.960
1987—Phoenix		P. C.	3B-2B-SS	56	211	36	61	15	2	6	37	.289	53	136	14	.931
1987—San Francisco		Nat.	SS-3B	84	245	28	46	9	2	8	21	.188	110	234	9	.975
1988—Phoenix		P. C.	3-S-2-O	82	306	45	83	19	1	12	51	.271	56	173	13	.946
1988—San Francisco		Nat.	3B-SS	52	156	17	32	6	1	8	19	.205	48	108	7	.957
Major League Totals—2 Years				136	401	45	78	15	3	16	40	.195	158	342	16	.969

Selected by New York Mets organization in 27th round of free-agent draft, June 6, 1983.

Selected by San Francisco Giants organization in 1st round (third player selected) of free-agent draft, June 2, 1986.

MITCHELL STEVEN WILLIAMS
(Mitch)

Born November 17, 1964, at Santa Ana, Calif.
Height, 6.04. Weight, 200.
Throws and bats lefthanded.
Brother of Bruce Williams, pitcher in Milwaukee Brewers' organization, 1981 through 1985.

Major League saves: 1986 (8), 1987 (6), 1988 (18). Total—32.

Established major league record for most games pitched by rookie (80), 1986.

Led Northwest League pitchers in wild pitches with 14 and tied for lead in games started with 14 and balks with 2 in 1983.

Year	Club	League	G.	IP.	W.	L.	Pct.	H.	R.	ER.	SO.	BB.	ERA.
1982—Walla Walla		Northwest	12	58⅓	3	4	.429	37	37	31	66	*72	4.78
1983—Reno		California	11	58	1	7	.125	58	56	46	44	60	7.14
1983—Spokane		Northwest	14	92⅓	7	6	.538	84	51	•46	87	55	4.48
1984—Reno†‡		California	26	164	9	8	.529	163	113	91	165	127	4.99
1985—Salem		Carolina	22	99	6	9	.400	57	64	60	138	*117	5.45
1985—Tulsa		Texas	6	33	2	2	.500	17	24	17	37	48	4.64
1986—Texas		American	*80	98	8	6	.571	69	39	39	90	79	3.58
1987—Texas		American	85	108⅔	8	6	.571	63	47	39	129	94	3.23
1988—Texas§x		American	67	68	2	7	.222	48	38	35	61	47	4.63
Major League Totals—3 Years			232	274⅔	18	19	.486	180	124	113	280	220	3.70

Selected by San Diego Padres' organization in 8th round of free-agent draft, June 7, 1982.
†Drafted by Texas Rangers, December 3, 1984; returned, April 6, 1985.
‡Traded to Texas Rangers for Third Baseman Randy Asadoor, April 6, 1985.
§On suspended list, May 2 to May 4, 1988.
xTraded with Pitchers Paul Kilgus and Steve Wilson, Infielders Curtis Wilkerson and Luis Benitez and Outfielder Pablo Delgado to Chicago Cubs for Outfielder Rafael Palmeiro and Pitchers Jamie Moyer and Drew Hall, December 5, 1988.

REGINALD DEWAYNE WILLIAMS
(Reggie)

Born August 29, 1960, at Memphis, Tenn.
Height, 5.11. Weight, 185.
Throws and bats righthanded.
Received bachelor of science degree in business
from Southern University, New Orleans, La.

Major League stolen bases: 1985 (1), 1986 (9), 1987 (1). Total—11.

Year Club	League	Pos.	G.	AB.	R.	H.	2B.	3B.	HR.	RBI.	B.A.	PO.	A.	E.	F.A.
1982—Lethbridge	Pion.	OF	67	253	40	76	8	2	3	33	.300	*141	12	7	.956
1983—Vero Beach†	Fla. St.	OF	81	293	53	83	11	3	4	32	.283	142	3	8	.948
1984—Vero Beach‡	Fla. St.	OF	60	222	31	53	5	2	0	19	.239	87	5	1	.989
1985—San Antonio	Texas	OF	120	436	73	127	17	4	10	53	.291	209	14	11	.953
1985—Los Angeles	Nat.	OF	22	9	4	3	0	0	0	0	.333	8	1	1	.900
1986—Los Angeles	Nat.	OF	128	303	35	84	14	2	4	32	.277	179	5	3	.984
1986—Albuquerque	P. C.	OF	11	44	6	13	1	1	1	4	.295	18	0	0	1.000
1987—Albuquerque	P. C.	OF	58	166	24	51	8	3	1	17	.307	58	2	1	.984
1987—Los Angeles§	Nat.	OF	39	36	6	4	0	0	0	4	.111	21	0	2	.913
1988—Colorado Springs	P. C.	OF	114	456	72	134	27	5	6	58	.294	220	7	8	.966
1988—Cleveland x	Amer.	OF	11	31	7	7	2	0	1	3	.226	13	1	0	1.000
National League Totals—3 Years			189	348	45	91	14	2	4	36	.261	208	6	6	.973
American League Totals—1 Year			11	31	7	7	2	0	1	3	.226	13	1	0	1.000
Major League Totals—4 Years			200	379	52	98	16	2	5	39	.259	221	7	6	.974

Selected by St. Louis Cardinals' organization in 6th round of free-agent draft, June 8, 1981.
Selected by Los Angeles Dodgers' organization in 13th round of free-agent draft, June 7, 1982.
†On disabled list, June 22 to August 11, 1983.
‡On disabled list, April 6 to June 28, 1984.
§Traded to Cleveland Indians for Pitcher Greg LaFever, April 5, 1988.
xReleased, December 20, 1988.

MARK ALAN WILLIAMSON

Born July 21, 1959, at Corpus Christi, Tex.
Height, 6.00. Weight, 171.
Throws and bats righthanded.
Attended Grossmont College, El Cajon, Calif., and received degree in mechanical engineering from San Diego State University, San Diego, Calif.

Major League saves: 1987 (3), 1988 (2). Total—5.
Led American League in intentional bases on balls issued with 15 in 1987.
Tied for Pacific Coast League lead in saves with 16 in 1986.
Tied for California League lead in intentional bases on balls issued with 10 in 1984.

Year Club	League	G.	IP.	W.	L.	Pct.	H.	R.	ER.	SO.	BB.	ERA.
1982—Reno	California	26	41	7	5	.583	34	24	20	30	18	4.39
1983—Beaumont	Texas	47	82⅔	6	3	.667	90	45	37	39	30	4.03
1984—Reno	California	56	93	10	12	.455	105	41	30	69	23	2.90
1985—Beaumont	Texas	42	78⅔	10	9	.526	72	27	25	64	23	2.86
1986—Las Vegas†	P. Coast	*65	104⅓	10	3	*.769	103	47	39	81	36	3.36
1987—Baltimore	American	61	125	8	9	.471	122	59	56	73	41	4.03
1987—Rochester	Int'national	1	4	0	1	.000	6	3	3	1	1	6.75
1988—Baltimore	American	37	117⅔	5	8	.385	125	70	64	69	40	4.90
1988—Rochester	Int'national	12	29⅔	2	3	.400	38	11	11	25	5	3.34
Major League Totals—2 Years		98	242⅔	13	17	.433	247	129	120	142	81	4.45

Selected by Kansas City Royals' organization in 12th round of free-agent draft, June 8, 1981.
Selected by San Diego Padres' organization in 4th round of free-agent draft, June 7, 1982.
†Traded with Catcher Terry Kennedy to Baltimore Orioles for Pitcher Storm Davis, October 30, 1986.

CARL BLAKE WILLIS

Born December 28, 1960, at Danville, Va.
Height, 6.03. Weight, 210.
Throws right and bats lefthanded.
Attended University of North Carolina, Wilmington, N.C.

Major League saves: 1984 (1), 1985 (1). Totals—2.

Year Club	League	G.	IP.	W.	L.	Pct.	H.	R.	ER.	SO.	BB.	ERA.
1983—Bristol	Ap'lachian	2	2⅔	0	1	.000	0	1	1	3	4	3.38
1983—Lakeland	Florida St.	4	9⅔	3	0	1.000	6	0	0	7	5	0.00
1983—Birmingham	Southern	14	20⅓	3	1	.750	16	9	9	13	7	3.98
1984—Evansville	Am. Assoc.	40	60⅓	5	3	.625	59	26	25	27	20	3.73
1984—Detroit†	American	10	16	0	2	.000	25	13	13	4	5	7.31
1984—Cincinnati	National	7	9⅔	0	1	.000	8	4	4	3	2	3.72

Year	Club	League	G.	IP.	W.	L.	Pct.	H.	R.	ER.	SO.	BB.	ERA.
1985	—Cincinnati	National	11	13⅔	1	0	1.000	21	18	14	6	5	9.22
1985	—Denver‡	Am. Assoc.	37	78	4	4	.500	82	39	36	27	30	4.15
1986	—Denver	Am. Assoc.	20	32⅔	1	3	.250	29	22	17	16	16	4.68
1986	—Cincinnati	National	29	52⅓	1	3	.250	54	29	26	24	32	4.47
1987	—Nashville§	Am. Assoc.	53	83⅔	6	4	.600	97	39	31	54	30	3.33
1988	—Vancouver	P. Coast	40	64	4	4	.500	77	36	30	44	16	4.22
1988	—Chicago	American	6	12	0	0	.000	17	12	11	6	7	8.25
American League Totals—2 Years			16	28	0	2	.000	42	25	24	10	12	7.71
National League Totals—3 Years			47	75⅔	2	4	.333	83	51	44	33	39	5.23
Major League Totals—4 Years			63	103⅔	2	6	.250	125	76	68	43	51	5.90

Selected by San Francisco Giants' organization in 31st round of free-agent draft, June 7, 1982.
Selected by Detroit Tigers' organization in 23rd round of free-agent draft, June 6, 1983.
†Traded to Cincinnati Reds, September 1, 1984, completing deal in which Cincinnati traded Pitcher Bill Scherrer to Detroit Tigers for cash and a player to be named later, August 27, 1984.
‡Drafted by California Angels, December 10, 1985; returned, April 6, 1986.
§Traded to Chicago White Sox for Outfielder Darrell Pruitt, January 19, 1988.

FRANK LEE WILLS JR.

Born October 26, 1958, at New Orleans, La.
Height, 6.02. Weight, 200.
Throws and bats righthanded.
Attended Tulane University, New Orleans, La.

Pitched seven-inning, 1-0 no-hit victory against Tacoma, May 31, 1985 (first game).
Major League saves: 1985 (1), 1986 (4), 1987 (1). Total—6.
Tied for Southern League lead in wild pitches with 15 in 1981.
Named righthanded pitcher on THE SPORTING NEWS College Baseball All-America Team, 1980.

Year	Club	League	G.	IP.	W.	L.	Pct.	H.	R.	ER.	SO.	BB.	ERA.
1980	—Sarasota Royals-Blue	Gulf Coast	4	23	2	0	1.000	18	7	5	20	8	1.96
1980	—Charleston	S. Atlantic	9	57	2	5	.286	59	33	23	48	32	3.63
1981	—Jacksonville	Southern	27	192	9	14	.391	199	104	85	174	91	3.98
1982	—Omaha	Am. Assoc.	41	107⅓	7	10	.412	110	71	62	77	*81	5.20
1983	—Jacksonville	Southern	8	54⅓	5	2	.714	44	19	15	40	23	2.48
1983	—Omaha	Am. Assoc.	16	95	4	11	.267	96	56	50	65	45	4.74
1983	—Kansas City	American	6	34⅔	2	1	.667	35	17	16	23	15	4.15
1984	—Omaha	Am. Assoc.	15	89⅔	7	4	.636	75	32	28	69	49	2.81
1984	—Kansas City†‡§	American	10	37	2	3	.400	39	21	21	21	13	5.11
1985	—Calgary	P. Coast	9	46⅓	4	3	.571	44	27	25	31	25	4.86
1985	—Seattle x	American	24	123	5	11	.313	122	85	82	67	68	6.00
1986	—Maine y	Int'national	22	31⅓	4	3	.571	37	10	10	21	10	2.87
1986	—Cleveland	American	26	40⅓	4	4	.500	43	23	22	32	16	4.91
1987	—Buffalo	Am. Assoc.	36	56⅔	3	2	.600	53	28	21	45	22	3.34
1987	—Cleveland z	American	6	5⅓	0	1	.000	3	3	3	4	7	5.06
1988	—Syracuse	Int'national	25	80⅔	6	4	.600	70	40	29	53	25	3.24
1988	—Toronto a	American	10	20⅔	0	0	.000	22	12	12	19	6	5.23
Major League Totals—6 Years			82	261	13	20	.394	264	161	156	166	125	5.38

Selected by Kansas City Royals' organization in 1st round (16th player selected) of free-agent draft, June 3, 1980.
†On disabled list, August 1 to August 16, 1984.
‡Traded to New York Mets' organization as part of a six-player, four-team deal in which Kansas City Royals acquired Catcher Jim Sundberg from Milwaukee Brewers, Texas Rangers acquired Catcher Don Slaught from Kansas City, Milwaukee acquired Pitcher Danny Darwin and a player to be named later from Texas and Pitcher Tim Leary from New York, January 18, 1985; Milwaukee organization acquired Catcher Bill Hance from Texas to complete deal, January 30, 1985.
§Traded to Seattle Mariners' organization for Pitcher Wray Bergendahl, March 29, 1985.
xReleased, March 20, 1986; signed by Maine (Cleveland Indians' organization), March 27, 1986.
yOn disabled list, May 4 to May 31, 1986.
zReleased, March 29, 1988; signed by Knoxville (Toronto Blue Jays' organization), April 7, 1988.
aReleased, October 28, 1988.

GLENN DWIGHT WILSON

Born December 22, 1958, at Baytown, Tex.
Height, 6.01. Weight, 190.
Throws and bats righthanded.
Attended Sam Houston State University, Huntsville, Tex.

Tied major league record for fewest double plays by outfielder, season, for leader in double plays (4), 1985.
Major League stolen bases: 1982 (2), 1983 (1), 1984 (7), 1985 (7), 1986 (5), 1987 (3), 1988 (1). Total—26.
Led National League outfielders in assists with 18 in 1987.
Led National League outfielders in double plays with 5 in 1986 and tied for lead with 4 in 1985.
Received reported $60,000 bonus to sign with Detroit Tigers, 1980.
Named third baseman on THE SPORTING NEWS College Baseball All-America Team, 1980.

Year	Club	League	Pos.	G.	AB.	R.	H.	2B.	3B.	HR.	RBI.	B.A.	PO.	A.	E.	F.A.
1980	—Montgomery	South.	3B	77	284	36	75	16	2	7	31	.264	56	189	*33	.881
1981	—Birmingham	South.	OF	124	496	77	152	24	6	18	82	.306	292	18	5	.984
1981	—Evansville	A. A.	OF-1B	10	37	5	9	2	0	2	7	.243	16	2	0	1.000
1982	—Detroit	Amer.	OF	84	322	39	94	15	1	12	34	.292	215	8	3	.987
1982	—Evansville†	A. A.	OF	42	165	24	46	7	2	10	33	.279	96	6	3	.971
1983	—Detroit‡	Amer.	OF	144	503	55	135	25	6	11	65	.268	225	12	3	.988
1984	—Philadelphia	Nat.	OF-3B	132	341	28	82	21	3	6	31	.240	153	7	7	.958

Year	Club	League	Pos.	G.	AB.	R.	H.	2B.	3B.	HR.	RBI.	B.A.	PO.	A.	E.	F.A.
1985	—Philadelphia	Nat.	OF	161	608	73	167	39	5	14	102	.275	343	*18	*12	.968
1986	—Philadelphia	Nat.	OF	155	584	70	158	30	4	15	84	.271	331	*20	4	.989
1987	—Philadelphia§	Nat.	*OF-P	154	569	55	150	21	2	14	54	.264	315	19	*11	.968
1988	—Seattle x	Amer.	OF	78	284	28	71	10	1	3	17	.250	140	4	3	.980
1988	—Pittsburgh y	Nat.	OF	37	126	11	34	8	0	2	15	.270	66	1	1	.985
American League Totals—3 Years				306	1109	122	300	50	8	26	116	.271	580	24	9	.985
National League Totals—5 Years				639	2228	237	591	119	14	51	286	.265	1208	65	35	.973
Major League Totals—7 Years				945	3337	359	891	169	22	77	402	.267	1788	89	44	.977

Selected by Detroit Tigers' organization in 1st round (18th player selected) of free-agent draft, June 3, 1980.

†On disabled list, May 27 to June 9 and June 17 to June 27, 1982.

‡Traded with Catcher-First Baseman John Wockenfuss to Philadelphia Phillies for First Baseman Dave Bergman and Pitcher Willie Hernandez, March 24, 1984.

§Traded with Outfielder Dave Brundage and Pitcher Mike Jackson to Seattle Mariners for Outfielder Phil Bradley and Pitcher Tim Fortugno, December 9, 1987.

xTraded to Pittsburgh Pirates for Outfielder Darnell Coles, July 22, 1988.

yOn disabled list, August 5 to August 20, 1988.

ALL-STAR GAME RECORD

Year	League	Pos.	AB.	R.	H.	2B.	3B.	HR.	RBI.	B.A.	PO.	A.	E.	F.A.
1985	—National	PH	1	0	0	0	0	0	0	.000	0	0	0	.000

PITCHING RECORD

Year	Club	League	G.	IP.	W.	L.	Pct.	H.	R.	ER.	SO.	BB.	ERA.
1987	—Philadelphia	National	1	1	0	0	.000	0	0	0	1	0	0.00

STEPHEN DOUGLAS WILSON
(Steve)

Born December 13, 1964, at Victoria, British Columbia, Can.
Height, 6.04. Weight, 195.
Throws and bats lefthanded.
Attended University of Portland, Portland, Ore.

Played semi-pro baseball with Alaska Goldpanners.

Year	Club	League	G.	IP.	W.	L.	Pct.	H.	R.	ER.	SO.	BB.	ERA.
1985	—Burlington	Midwest	21	72⅔	3	5	.375	71	44	37	76	27	4.58
1986	—Tulsa	Texas	24	136⅔	7	13	.350	117	83	74	95	*103	4.87
1987	—Charlotte	Florida St.	20	107	9	5	.643	81	41	29	80	44	2.44
1988	—Tulsa	Texas	25	165⅓	15	7	.682	147	72	58	132	53	3.16
1988	—Texas†	American	3	7⅔	0	0	.000	7	5	5	1	4	5.87
Major League Totals—1 Year			3	7⅔	0	0	.000	7	5	5	1	4	5.87

Selected by Texas Rangers' organization in 4th round of free-agent draft, June 3, 1985.

†Traded with Pitchers Mitch Williams and Paul Kilgus, Infielders Curtis Wilkerson and Luis Benitez and Outfielder Pablo Delgado to Chicago Cubs for Outfielder Rafael Palmeiro and Pitchers Jamie Moyer and Drew Hall, December 5, 1988.

TREVOR KIRK WILSON

Born June 7, 1966, at Torrance, Calif.
Height, 6.00. Weight, 175.
Throws and bats lefthanded.
Attended Oregon State University, Corvallis, Ore.

Tied for Northwest League lead in balks with 2 in 1985.

Year	Club	League	G.	IP.	W.	L.	Pct.	H.	R.	ER.	SO.	BB.	ERA.
1985	—Everett	Northwest	17	55⅓	2	4	.333	67	36	26	50	26	4.23
1986	—Clinton	Midwest	34	130⅔	6	11	.353	126	70	62	84	64	4.27
1987	—Clinton	Midwest	26	161⅓	10	6	.625	130	60	36	146	77	2.01
1988	—Shreveport	Texas	12	72⅔	5	4	.556	55	19	15	53	23	1.86
1988	—Phoenix	P. Coast	11	51⅔	2	3	.400	49	35	29	49	33	5.05
1988	—San Francisco	National	4	22	0	2	.000	25	14	10	15	8	4.09
Major League Totals—1 Year			4	22	0	2	.000	25	14	10	15	8	4.09

Selected by San Francisco Giants' organization in 8th round of free-agent draft, June 3, 1985.

WILLIAM HAYWARD WILSON
(Mookie)

Born February 9, 1956, at Bamberg, S. C.
Height, 5.10. Weight, 170.
Throws right and bats right and lefthanded.
Attended Spartanburg Methodist College, Spartanburg, S. C.,
and University of South Carolina, Columbia, S. C.
Brother of John Wilson, outfielder in New York Mets' organization, 1982 through 1987; and
Phil Wilson, outfielder in Minnesota Twins' organization.

Major League stolen bases: 1980 (7), 1981 (24), 1982 (58), 1983 (54), 1984 (46), 1985 (24), 1986 (25), 1987 (21), 1988 (15). Total—274.

Led National League outfielders in double plays with 6 in 1984.

Year	Club	League	Pos.	G.	AB.	R.	H.	2B.	3B.	HR.	RBI.	B.A.	PO.	A.	E.	F.A.
1977	—Wausau	Midw.	OF	68	245	50	71	10	2	6	32	.290	150	8	9	.946

Year	Club	League	Pos.	G.	AB.	R.	H.	2B.	3B.	HR.	RBI.	B.A.	PO.	A.	E.	F.A.
1978	—Jackson	Texas	OF	132	497	72	145	13	*15	7	72	.292	282	10	7	.977
1979	—Tidewater	Int.	OF	*141	529	84	141	22	10	5	36	.267	317	11	7	.979
1980	—Tidewater	Int.	OF	132	515	*92	*152	11	*14	4	44	.295	*350	11	7	.981
1980	—New York	Nat.	OF	27	105	16	26	5	3	0	4	.248	72	1	2	.973
1981	—New York	Nat.	OF	92	328	49	89	8	8	3	14	.271	226	3	4	.983
1982	—New York	Nat.	OF	159	639	90	178	25	9	5	55	.279	415	12	5	.988
1983	—New York	Nat.	OF	152	*638	91	176	25	6	7	51	.276	422	5	7	.984
1984	—New York	Nat.	OF	154	587	88	162	28	10	10	54	.276	396	8	4	.990
1985	—New York†	Nat.	OF	93	337	56	93	16	8	6	26	.276	216	0	8	.964
1986	—Tidewater	Int.	OF	9	31	4	8	1	0	0	4	.258	19	1	0	1.000
1986	—New York‡	Nat.	OF	123	381	61	110	17	5	9	45	.289	228	7	5	.979
1987	—New York	Nat.	OF	124	385	58	115	19	7	9	34	.299	205	3	8	.963
1988	—New York	Nat.	OF	112	378	61	112	17	5	8	41	.296	200	4	5	.976
Major League Totals—9 Years				1036	3778	570	1061	160	61	57	324	.281	2380	43	48	.981

Selected by Los Angeles Dodgers' organization in 4th round of free-agent draft, January 7, 1976.
Selected by New York Mets' organization in 2nd round of free-agent draft, June 7, 1977.
†On disabled list, July 2 to September 1, 1985.
†On New York disabled list, March 30 to May 9, 1986; included rehabilitation disability assignment to Tidewater, April 26 to May 9, 1986.

CHAMPIONSHIP SERIES RECORD

Tied Championship Series record for most at-bats, game (7), October 15, 1986 (16 innings).

Year	Club	League	Pos.	G.	AB.	R.	H.	2B.	3B.	HR.	RBI.	B.A.	PO.	A.	E.	F.A.
1986	—New York	Nat.	OF	6	26	2	3	0	0	0	1	.115	16	1	0	1.000
1988	—New York	Nat.	OF-PH	4	13	2	2	0	0	0	1	.154	6	0	0	1.000
Championship Series Totals—2 Years				10	39	4	5	0	0	0	2	.128	22	1	0	1.000

WORLD SERIES RECORD

Year	Club	League	Pos.	G.	AB.	R.	H.	2B.	3B.	HR.	RBI.	B.A.	PO.	A.	E.	F.A.
1986	—New York	Nat.	OF	7	26	3	7	1	0	0	0	.269	15	2	0	1.000

WILLIE JAMES WILSON

Born July 9, 1955, at Montgomery, Ala.
Height, 6.03. Weight, 195.
Throws right and bats left and righthanded.

Established major league records for most at-bats season (705), 1980; most at-bats by switch-hitter, season (705), 1980.

Tied major league records by collecting 100 or more hits righthanded and lefthanded, season, 1980; for most hits by switch-hitter, season (230), 1980.

Established American League records for most triples by switch-hitter, season (21), 1985; highest stolen base percentage, lifetime, 300 or more attempts (.841).

Tied American League records for most years leading league in triples (5); most consecutive stolen bases without caught stealing (32), July 23 through September 23, 1980; fewest times caught stealing, season, 50 or more stolen bases (8), 1983.

Major League stolen bases: 1976 (2), 1977 (6), 1978 (46), 1979 (83), 1980 (79), 1981 (34), 1982 (37), 1983 (59), 1984 (47), 1985 (43), 1986 (34), 1987 (59), 1988 (35). Total—564.

Switch-hit home runs in one game, June 15, 1979.

Led American League in stolen bases with 83 in 1979.

Led Gulf Coast League in stolen bases with 24 in 1974, Midwest League with 76 in 1975 and American Association with 74 in 1977.

Led Midwest League in being hit by pitch with 13 in 1975.

Named outfielder on THE SPORTING NEWS American League All-Star fielding team, 1980.

Named outfielder on THE SPORTING NEWS American League Silver Slugger team, 1980 and 1982.

Named Midwest League Most Valuable Player, 1975.

Received reported $90,000 bonus to sign with Kansas City Royals, 1974.

Year	Club	League	Pos.	G.	AB.	R.	H.	2B.	3B.	HR.	RBI.	B.A.	PO.	A.	E.	F.A.
1974	—Sarasota Royals	Gulf C.	OF	47	155	30	39	3	5	1	14	.252	92	8	4	.962
1975	—Waterloo	Midw.	OF	127	486	92	*132	18	4	8	73	.272	249	•17	*17	.940
1976	—Jacksonville	South.	OF	107	388	54	98	13	6	1	35	.253	273	5	8	.972
1976	—Kansas City	Amer.	OF	12	6	0	1	0	0	0	0	.167	6	1	1	.875
1977	—Omaha	A. A.	OF	132	495	67	139	10	6	4	47	.281	*278	7	11	.963
1977	—Kansas City	Amer.	OF	13	34	10	11	2	0	0	1	.324	24	0	1	.960
1978	—Kansas City	Amer.	OF	127	198	43	43	8	2	0	16	.217	171	6	4	.978
1979	—Kansas City	Amer.	OF	154	588	113	185	18	13	6	49	.315	384	12	6	.985
1980	—Kansas City	Amer.	OF	161	*705	*133	*230	28	•15	3	49	.326	482	9	6	.988
1981	—Kansas City	Amer.	OF	102	439	54	133	10	7	1	32	.303	299	*14	4	.987
1982	—Kansas City	Amer.	OF	136	585	87	194	19	*15	3	46	*.332	215	8	3	.987
1983	—Kansas City†‡	Amer.	OF	137	576	90	159	22	8	2	33	.276	354	3	9	.975
1984	—Kansas City	Amer.	OF	128	541	81	163	24	9	2	44	.301	383	6	4	.990
1985	—Kansas City	Amer.	OF	141	605	87	168	25	*21	4	43	.278	378	4	2	.995
1986	—Kansas City	Amer.	OF	156	631	77	170	20	7	9	44	.269	408	4	3	.993
1987	—Kansas City	Amer.	OF	146	610	97	170	18	*15	4	30	.279	342	3	1	*.997
1988	—Kansas City	Amer.	OF	147	591	81	155	17	•11	1	37	.262	365	1	4	.989
Major League Totals—13 Years				1560	6109	953	1782	211	123	35	424	.292	3811	71	48	.988

Selected by Kansas City Royals' organization in 1st round (18th player selected) of free-agent draft, June 5, 1974.
†On disabled list, August 21 to September 6, 1983.
‡On suspended list, December 15, 1983 through May 15, 1984.

DIVISION SERIES RECORD

Year	Club	League	Pos.	G.	AB.	R.	H.	2B.	3B.	HR.	RBI.	B.A.	PO.	A.	E.	F.A.
1981	—Kansas City	Amer.	OF	3	13	0	4	0	0	0	1	.308	6	0	0	1.000

CHAMPIONSHIP SERIES RECORD

Year	Club	League	Pos.	G.	AB.	R.	H.	2B.	3B.	HR.	RBI.	B.A.	PO.	A.	E.	F.A.
1978	—Kansas City	Amer.	PR-OF	3	4	0	1	0	0	0	0	.250	2	0	0	1.000
1980	—Kansas City	Amer.	OF	3	13	2	4	2	1	0	4	.308	6	1	0	1.000
1984	—Kansas City	Amer.	OF	3	13	0	2	0	0	0	0	.154	10	0	0	1.000
1985	—Kansas City	Amer.	OF	7	29	5	9	0	0	1	2	.310	12	0	0	1.000
Championship Series Totals—4 Years				16	59	7	16	2	1	1	6	.271	30	1	0	1.000

WORLD SERIES RECORD

Established World Series record for most strikeouts, six-game and any length Series (12), 1980.
Tied World Series record for most at bats, inning (2), October 18, 1980 (first inning).

Year	Club	League	Pos.	G.	AB.	R.	H.	2B.	3B.	HR.	RBI.	B.A.	PO.	A.	E.	F.A.
1980	—Kansas City	Amer.	OF	6	26	3	4	1	0	0	0	.154	15	1	0	1.000
1985	—Kansas City	Amer.	OF	7	30	2	11	0	1	0	3	.367	19	1	0	1.000
World Series Totals—2 Years				13	56	5	15	1	1	0	3	.268	34	2	0	1.000

ALL-STAR GAME RECORD

Year	League	Pos.	AB.	R.	H.	2B.	3B.	HR.	RBI.	B.A.	PO.	A.	E.	F.A.
1982	—American	OF	2	0	0	0	0	0	0	.000	1	0	0	1.000
1983	—American	OF	1	0	1	1	0	0	1	1.000	2	0	0	1.000
All-Star Game Totals—2 Years			3	0	1	1	0	0	1	.333	3	0	0	1.000

DAVID MARK WINFIELD
(Dave)

Born October 3, 1951, at St. Paul, Minn.
Height, 6.06. Weight, 220.
Throws and bats righthanded.
Received degree from University of Minnesota, Minneapolis, Minn.

Major League stolen bases: 1974 (9), 1975 (23), 1976 (26), 1977 (16), 1978 (21), 1979 (15), 1980 (23), 1981 (11), 1982 (5), 1983 (15), 1984 (6), 1985 (19), 1986 (6), 1987 (5), 1988 (9). Total—209.

Led National League in total bases with 333 and intentional bases on balls received with 24 in 1979.
Named outfielder on The Sporting News American League All-Star Team, 1982 through 1984.
Named outfielder on The Sporting News National League All-Star Team, 1979.
Named outfielder on The Sporting News American League All-Star fielding team, 1982 through 1985 and 1987.
Named outfielder on The Sporting News National League All-Star fielding team, 1979 and 1980.
Named outfielder on The Sporting News American League Silver Slugger team, 1981 through 1985.
Received reported $100,000 bonus to sign with San Diego Padres, 1973.
Selected by Atlanta Hawks in 5th round (79th player selected) of 1973 NBA draft.
Selected by Utah Stars in 6th round (58th player selected) of 1973 ABA draft.
Selected by Minnesota Vikings in 17th round (429th player selected) of 1973 NFL draft.
Named outfielder on The Sporting News College Baseball All-America Team, 1973.

Year	Club	League	Pos.	G.	AB.	R.	H.	2B.	3B.	HR.	RBI.	B.A.	PO.	A.	E.	F.A.
1973	—San Diego	Nat.	OF-1B	56	141	9	39	4	1	3	12	.277	65	1	3	.957
1974	—San Diego	Nat.	OF	145	498	57	132	18	4	20	75	.265	276	11	•12	.960
1975	—San Diego	Nat.	OF	143	509	74	136	20	2	15	76	.267	302	9	9	.972
1976	—San Diego	Nat.	OF	137	492	81	139	26	4	13	69	.283	304	*15	6	.982
1977	—San Diego	Nat.	OF	157	615	104	169	29	7	25	92	.275	368	15	11	.972
1978	—San Diego	Nat.	OF-1B	158	587	88	181	30	5	24	97	.308	328	8	7	.980
1979	—San Diego	Nat.	OF	159	597	97	184	27	10	34	*118	.308	344	14	5	.986
1980	—San Diego†	Nat.	OF	162	558	89	154	25	6	20	87	.276	273	20	4	.987
1981	—New York	Amer.	OF	105	388	52	114	25	1	13	68	.294	196	1	3	.985
1982	—New York‡	Amer.	OF	140	539	84	151	24	8	37	106	.280	279	*17	8	.974
1983	—New York	Amer.	OF	152	598	99	169	26	8	32	116	.283	313	5	7	.978
1984	—New York§	Amer.	OF	141	567	106	193	34	4	19	100	.340	306	3	2	.994
1985	—New York	Amer.	OF	155	633	105	174	34	6	26	114	.275	316	13	3	.991
1986	—New York	Amer.	OF-3B	154	565	90	148	31	5	24	104	.262	292	9	5	.984
1987	—New York	Amer.	OF	156	575	83	158	22	1	27	97	.275	253	6	3	.989
1988	—New York	Amer.	OF	149	559	96	180	37	2	25	107	.322	276	3	3	.989
National League Totals—8 Years				1117	3997	599	1134	179	39	154	626	.284	2260	93	57	.976
American League Totals—8 Years				1152	4424	715	1287	233	35	203	812	.291	2231	57	34	.985
Major League Totals—16 Years				2269	8421	1314	2421	412	74	357	1438	.287	4491	150	91	.981

Selected by Baltimore Orioles' organization in 40th round of free-agent draft, June 5, 1969.
Selected by San Diego Padres' organization in 1st round (fourth player selected) of free-agent draft, June 5, 1973.
†Granted free agency, October 22, 1980; signed by New York Yankees, December 15, 1980.
‡On disabled list, May 20 to June 4, 1982.
§On disabled list, April 16 to May 1, 1984.

DIVISION SERIES RECORD

Year	Club	League	Pos.	G.	AB.	R.	H.	2B.	3B.	HR.	RBI.	B.A.	PO.	A.	E.	F.A.
1981	—New York	Amer.	OF	5	20	2	7	3	0	0	0	.350	10	1	0	1.000

CHAMPIONSHIP SERIES RECORD

Year	Club	League	Pos.	G.	AB.	R.	H.	2B.	3B.	HR.	RBI.	B.A.	PO.	A.	E.	F.A.
1981	—New York	Amer.	OF	3	13	2	2	1	0	0	2	.154	6	0	0	1.000

WORLD SERIES RECORD

Tied World Series record for fewest runs, Series (0), 1981.

Year	Club	League	Pos.	G.	AB.	R.	H.	2B.	3B.	HR.	RBI.	B.A.	PO.	A.	E.	F.A.
1981	New York	Amer.	OF	6	22	0	1	0	0	0	1	.045	13	1	0	1.000

ALL-STAR GAME RECORD

Established All-Star Game record for most doubles, lifetime (7).
Tied All-Star Game record for most at-bats, game (5), July 17, 1979.
Tied All-Star Game record for most consecutive games, one or more hits (7).

Year	League	Pos.	AB.	R.	H.	2B.	3B.	HR.	RBI.	B.A.	PO.	A.	E.	F.A.
1977	National	OF	2	0	2	1	0	0	2	1.000	1	0	0	1.000
1978	National	OF	2	1	1	0	0	0	0	.500	1	0	0	1.000
1979	National	OF	5	1	1	1	0	0	1	.200	3	0	0	1.000
1980	National	OF	2	0	0	0	0	0	1	.000	2	0	0	1.000
1981	American	OF	4	0	0	0	0	0	0	.000	0	1	0	1.000
1982	American	OF	2	0	1	0	0	0	0	.500	0	0	0	.000
1983	American	OF	3	2	3	1	0	0	1	1.000	3	0	0	1.000
1984	American	OF	4	0	1	1	0	0	0	.250	2	1	0	1.000
1985	American	OF	3	0	1	0	0	0	0	.333	0	0	0	.000
1986	American	OF	1	1	1	1	0	0	0	1.000	0	0	0	.000
1987	American	OF	5	0	1	1	0	0	0	.200	2	0	0	1.000
1988	American	OF	3	1	1	1	0	0	0	.333	1	0	0	1.000
All-Star Game Totals—12 Years			36	6	13	7	0	0	5	.361	15	2	0	1.000

JAMES FRANCIS WINN

(Jim)

Born September 23, 1959, at Stockton, Calif.
Height, 6.03. Weight, 215.
Throws and bats righthanded.
Attended John Brown University, Siloam Springs, Ark.

Major League saves: 1984 (1), 1986 (3), 1987 (6). Total—10.

Year	Club	League	G.	IP.	W.	L.	Pct.	H.	R.	ER.	SO.	BB.	ERA.
1981	Bradenton Pirates	Gulf Coast	1	4	0	0	.000	1	0	0	6	0	0.00
1981	Buffalo	Eastern	12	65	2	5	.286	60	40	33	44	23	4.57
1982	Buffalo†	Eastern	3	6⅔	0	2	.000	6	7	4	7	5	5.40
1982	Alexandria	Carolina	7	28	1	2	.333	31	17	12	20	11	3.86
1983	Pittsburgh	National	7	11	0	0	.000	12	9	9	3	6	7.36
1983	Hawaii	P. Coast	31	38⅔	0	1	.000	49	23	17	22	22	3.96
1984	Hawaii	P. Coast	21	44⅔	6	1	.857	44	19	17	28	28	3.43
1984	Pittsburgh	National	9	18⅔	1	0	1.000	19	8	8	11	9	3.86
1985	Hawaii	P. Coast	7	42⅔	5	2	.714	31	19	16	33	20	3.38
1985	Pittsburgh	National	30	75⅔	3	6	.333	77	45	44	22	31	5.23
1986	Pittsburgh‡	National	50	88	3	5	.375	85	44	35	70	38	3.58
1987	Chicago§	American	56	94	4	6	.400	95	54	50	44	62	4.79
1988	Portland	P. Coast	22	29⅓	2	3	.400	32	14	13	21	12	3.99
1988	Minnesota x	American	9	21	1	0	1.000	33	15	14	9	10	6.00
National League Totals—4 Years			96	193⅓	7	11	.389	193	106	96	106	84	4.47
American League Totals—2 Years			65	115	5	6	.455	128	69	64	53	72	5.01
Major League Totals—6 Years			161	308⅓	12	17	.414	321	175	160	159	156	4.67

Selected by Pittsburgh Pirates' organization in 1st round (14th player selected) of free-agent draft, June 8, 1981.
†On disabled list, April 12 to May 24 and June 8 to July 16, 1982.
‡Traded to Chicago White Sox for a player to be named later, March 27, 1987; Pittsburgh Pirates acquired Outfielder John Cangelosi to complete deal, March 30, 1987.
§Released, March 25, 1988; signed by Portland (Minnesota Twins' organization), April 5, 1988.
xOn disabled list, August 15 to September 1, 1988.

HERMAN S. WINNINGHAM JR.

(Herm)

Born December 1, 1961, at Orangeburg, S.C.
Height, 5.11. Weight, 175.
Throws right and bats lefthanded.
Attended DeKalb Community College South, Decatur, Ga.

Major League stolen bases: 1984 (2), 1985 (20), 1986 (12), 1987 (29), 1988 (12). Total—75.

Year	Club	League	Pos.	G.	AB.	R.	H.	2B.	3B.	HR.	RBI.	B.A.	PO.	A.	E.	F.A.
1981	Kingsport	Appal.	OF	58	204	44	52	7	4	2	14	.255	128	3	2	★.985
1982	Lynchburg	Carol.	OF	120	430	65	127	20	5	6	61	.295	235	6	5	.980
1983	Jackson	Texas	OF	78	288	54	102	13	6	4	41	.354	157	5	6	.964
1983	Tidewater†	Int.	OF	29	113	18	30	5	2	1	11	.265	70	1	3	.959
1984	Tidewater	Int.	OF	115	406	50	114	20	3	3	47	.281	228	8	4	.983
1984	New York‡	Nat.	OF	14	27	5	11	1	1	0	5	.407	7	0	0	1.000
1985	Montreal§	Nat.	OF	125	312	30	74	6	5	3	21	.237	229	6	4	.983
1985	Indianapolis	A. A.	OF	11	35	3	6	0	0	0	2	.171	22	0	1	.957
1986	Montreal	Nat.	OF-SS	90	185	23	40	6	3	4	11	.216	97	2	2	.980
1986	Indianapolis	A. A.	OF	51	201	35	54	5	7	4	24	.269	106	3	1	.991
1987	Montreal	Nat.	OF	137	347	34	83	20	3	4	41	.239	225	5	6	.975
1988	Mont. x-Cinc.	Nat.	OF	100	203	16	47	3	4	0	21	.232	128	1	1	.992

Year	Club	League	Pos.	G.	AB.	R.	H.	2B.	3B.	HR.	RBI.	B.A.	PO.	A.	E.	F.A.
1988	Indianapolis	A. A.	OF	3	10	2	2	0	1	0	1	.200	6	0	0	1.000
	Major League Totals—5 Years			466	1074	108	255	36	16	11	99	.237	686	14	13	.982

Selected by Pittsburgh Pirates' organization in 38th round of free-agent draft, June 5, 1979.
Selected by Milwaukee Brewers' organization in secondary phase of free-agent draft, January 8, 1980.
Selected by Montreal Expos' organization in secondary phase of free-agent draft, June 3, 1980.
Selected by New York Mets' organization in secondary phase of free-agent draft, January 13, 1981.
†On disabled list, August 9 to September 20, 1983.
‡Traded with Infielder Hubie Brooks, Catcher Mike Fitzgerald and Pitcher Floyd Youmans to Montreal Expos for Catcher Gary Carter, December 10, 1984.
§On disabled list, June 24 to July 13, 1985; included rehabilitation disability assignment to Indianapolis, July 4 to July 13, 1985.
xTraded with Catcher Jeff Reed and Pitcher Randy St. Claire to Cincinnati Reds for Outfielder Tracy Jones and Pitcher Pat Pacillo, July 13, 1988.

MICHAEL ATWATER WITT
(Mike)

Born July 20, 1960, at Fullerton, Calif.
Height, 6.07. Weight, 198.
Throws and bats righthanded.
Attending Cypress Junior College, Cypress, Calif.

Pitched 1-0 perfect game against Texas Rangers, September 30, 1984.
Major League saves: 1983 (5).
Tied for American League lead in hit batsmen with 11 in 1981.

Year	Club	League	G.	IP.	W.	L.	Pct.	H.	R.	ER.	SO.	BB.	ERA.
1978	Idaho Falls	Pioneer	13	86	7	1	.875	88	45	34	79	26	3.56
1979	Salinas	California	30	141	8	10	.444	156	96	80	94	70	5.11
1980	Salinas	California	13	90	7	3	.700	85	30	21	76	35	2.10
1980	El Paso	Texas	12	70	5	5	.500	72	53	45	64	39	5.79
1981	California	American	22	129	8	9	.471	123	60	47	75	47	3.28
1982	California	American	33	179⅔	8	6	.571	177	77	70	85	47	3.51
1983	California	American	43	154	7	14	.333	173	90	84	77	75	4.91
1984	California	American	34	246⅔	15	11	.577	227	103	95	196	84	3.47
1985	California	American	35	250	15	9	.625	228	115	99	180	98	3.56
1986	California	American	34	269	18	10	.643	218	95	85	208	73	2.84
1987	California†	American	36	247	16	14	.533	252	128	110	192	84	4.01
1988	California	American	34	249⅔	13	16	.448	263	*130	115	133	87	4.15
	Major League Totals—8 Years		271	1725	100	89	.529	1661	798	705	1146	595	3.68

Selected by California Angels' organization in 4th round of free-agent draft, June 6, 1978.
†Granted free agency, November 9, 1987; re-signed by Angels, December 22, 1987.

CHAMPIONSHIP SERIES RECORD

Year	Club	League	G.	IP.	W.	L.	Pct.	H.	R.	ER.	SO.	BB.	ERA.
1982	California	American	1	3	0	0	.000	2	2	2	3	2	6.00
1986	California	American	2	17⅔	1	0	1.000	13	5	5	8	2	2.55
	Championship Series Totals—2 Years		3	20⅔	1	0	1.000	15	7	7	11	4	3.05

ALL-STAR GAME RECORD

Member of American League All-Star Team in 1986 and 1987; did not play.

ROBERT ANDREW WITT
(Bobby)

Born May 11, 1964, at Canton, Mass.
Height, 6.02. Weight, 205.
Throws and bats righthanded.
Attended University of Oklahoma, Norman, Okla.

Tied major league record for most strikeouts, inning (4), August 2, 1987, second inning.
Led American League in wild pitches with 22 in 1986 and tied for lead with 16 in 1988.
Named as righthanded pitcher on THE SPORTING NEWS College Baseball All-America Team, 1985.
Member of 1984 U.S. Olympic baseball team.

Year	Club	League	G.	IP.	W.	L.	Pct.	H.	R.	ER.	SO.	BB.	ERA.
1985	Tulsa	Texas	11	35	0	6	.000	26	26	25	39	44	6.43
1986	Texas	American	31	157⅔	11	9	.550	130	104	96	174	*143	5.48
1987	Texas†‡	American	26	143	8	10	.444	114	82	78	160	*140	4.91
1987	Oklahoma City	Am. Assoc.	1	5	1	0	1.000	5	5	5	2	3	9.00
1987	Tulsa	Texas	1	5	0	1	.000	5	9	3	2	6	5.40
1988	Texas	American	22	174⅓	8	10	.444	134	83	76	148	101	3.92
1988	Oklahoma City	Am. Assoc.	11	76⅔	4	6	.400	69	42	37	70	47	4.34
	Major League Totals—3 Years		79	475	27	29	.482	378	269	250	482	384	4.74

Selected by Cincinnati Reds' organization in 7th round of free-agent draft, June 7, 1982.
Selected by Texas Rangers' organization in 1st round (third player selected) of free-agent draft, June 3, 1985.
†On disabled list, May 21 to June 20, 1987; included rehabilitation disability assignment to Oklahoma City, June 7 to June 12, and Tulsa, June 13, 1987.
‡Struck out in only at-bat.

EDWARD DAVID WOJNA

Name pronounced WOHJ-nuh.

(Ed)

Born August 20, 1960, at Bridgeport, Conn.
Height, 6.01. Weight, 187.
Throws and bats righthanded.
Attended Indian River Community College, Fort Pierce, Fla.

Led Eastern League in hit batsmen with 9 in 1983.
Tied for Pacific Coast League lead in wild pitches with 16 in 1984.

Year Club	League	G.	IP.	W.	L.	Pct.	H.	R.	ER.	SO.	BB.	ERA.
1981—Spartanburg	S. Atlantic	27	178	11	13	.458	181	•107	•82	130	69	4.15
1982—Peninsula	Carolina	27	176⅔	12	8	.600	156	79	57	116	49	2.90
1983—Reading†	Eastern	28	161⅔	13	7	.650	147	80	66	83	78	3.67
1984—Las Vegas	P. Coast	29	159⅓	14	8	.636	182	99	90	95	81	5.08
1985—Las Vegas	P. Coast	18	111⅓	5	8	.385	121	63	55	66	43	4.45
1985—San Diego	National	15	42	2	4	.333	53	35	27	18	19	5.79
1986—Las Vegas	P. Coast	25	175⅓	12	7	.632	181	81	70	102	50	3.59
1986—San Diego	National	7	39	2	2	.500	42	19	14	19	16	3.23
1987—San Diego	National	5	18⅓	0	3	.000	25	12	12	13	6	5.89
1987—Las Vegas‡	P. Coast	18	96	7	5	.583	97	50	43	47	42	4.03
1988—Vancouver	P. Coast	21	124	10	6	.625	112	55	45	73	36	3.27
Major League Totals—3 Years		27	99⅓	4	9	.308	120	66	53	50	41	4.80

Selected by Baltimore Orioles' organization in 6th round of free-agent draft, January 8, 1980.

Selected by Philadelphia Phillies' organization in secondary phase of free-agent draft, June 3, 1980.

†Traded with Pitchers Marty Decker, Darren Burroughs and Lance McCullers to San Diego Padres, September 20, 1983, as partial completion of deal in which San Diego traded Outfielder Sixto Lezcano and a player to be named later to Philadelphia Phillies for four players to be named later, August 31, 1983; Philadelphia organization acquired Pitcher Steve Fireovid to complete deal, October 11, 1983.

‡Traded to Chicago White Sox for a player to be named later, October 5, 1987; San Diego Padres acquired Pitcher Joel McKeon to complete deal, February 11, 1988..

MICHAEL CARY WOODARD

(Mike)

Born March 2, 1960, at Melrose Park, Ill.
Height, 5.09. Weight, 155.
Throws right and bats lefthanded.

Major League stolen bases: 1985 (6), 1986 (7), 1988 (1). Total—14.
Led Eastern League in stolen bases with 54 in 1982.
Led Eastern League in caught stealing with 23 in 1981.
Led Pacific Coast League second basemen in total chances with 702 and double plays with 89 in 1985.
Led Northwest League second basemen in double plays with 34 in 1978.

Year Club	League	Pos.	G.	AB.	R.	H.	2B.	3B.	HR.	RBI.	B.A.	PO.	A.	E.	F.A.
1978—Bend	N'west	2B	62	231	45	79	8	1	0	12	.342	141	136	•20	.933
1979—Modesto	Calif.	2B	118	431	90	124	8	3	2	31	.288	230	253	*30	.942
1980—Modesto	Calif.	2B-OF	73	289	52	86	8	1	0	32	.298	177	165	19	.947
1980—West Haven†	East.	2B	6	13	2	0	0	0	0	0	.000	8	9	2	.895
1981—West Haven	East.	2B	133	427	59	96	9	3	1	25	.225	249	299	19	.967
1982—West Haven‡	East.	2B-3B	104	348	55	95	13	1	1	43	.273	198	208	13	.969
1983—Tacoma	P. C.	2B-SS-3B	122	323	45	78	7	1	0	27	.241	120	236	12	.967
1984—Albany	East.	2B	23	96	19	34	2	0	0	9	.354	62	72	6	.957
1984—Tacoma§	P. C.	2B-OF-SS	95	325	47	89	8	2	1	17	.274	191	229	6	.986
1985—Phoenix	P. C.	2B	140	*573	85	*181	16	9	3	63	.316	*283	*404	15	.979
1985—San Francisco	Nat.	2B	24	82	12	20	1	0	0	9	.244	49	46	1	.990
1986—Phoenix	P. C.	2B-3B	62	248	45	79	7	2	0	27	.319	116	165	8	.972
1986—San Francisco	Nat.	2B-3B-SS	48	79	14	20	2	1	1	5	.253	28	43	2	.973
1987—San Francisco	Nat.	2B	10	19	0	4	1	0	0	1	.211	13	15	0	1.000
1987—Phoe.x-Tuc.y	P. C.	2B-3B-OF	104	381	56	95	10	5	0	36	.250	207	263	18	.963
1988—Vancouver	P. C.	2B-OF-3B	94	367	63	122	12	•10	1	40	.332	190	217	9	.978
1988—Chicago z	Amer.	2B	18	45	3	6	0	1	0	4	.133	41	37	2	.975
National League Totals—3 Years			82	180	26	44	4	1	1	15	.244	90	104	3	.985
American League Totals—1 Year			18	45	3	6	0	1	0	4	.133	41	37	2	.975
Major League Totals—4 Years			100	225	29	50	4	2	1	19	.222	131	141	5	.982

Selected by Oakland A's organization in 4th round of free-agent draft, June 6, 1978.

†On disabled list, July 8, 1980 through remainder of season.

‡On disabled list, July 4 to July 14 and July 20 to July 31, 1982.

§Granted free agency, October 15, 1984; signed by Phoenix (San Francisco Giants' organization), November 20, 1984.

xReleased, June 29, 1987; signed by Houston Astros' organization, July 2, 1987.

yGranted free agency, October 15, 1987; signed by Vancouver (Chicago White Sox' organization), November 21, 1987.

zGranted free agency, October 15, 1988.

TRACY MICHAEL WOODSON

Born October 5, 1962, at Richmond, Va.
Height, 6.03. Weight, 215.
Throws and bats righthanded.
Attended North Carolina State University, Raleigh, N. C.

Major League stolen bases: 1987 (1), 1988 (1). Total—2.
Led Texas League third basemen in total chances with 413 in 1986.
Led Florida State League third basemen in putouts with 111, fielding percentage with .926 and total chances with 408 in 1985.

Year Club	League	Pos.	G.	AB.	R.	H.	2B.	3B.	HR.	RBI.	B.A.	PO.	A.	E.	F.A.
1984—Vero Beach	Fla. St.	1B	76	256	29	56	9	0	4	36	.219	630	38	9	.987
1985—Vero Beach	Fla. St.	3B-1B	138	504	55	126	30	4	9	62	.250	131	270	30	.930
1986—San Antonio	Texas	*3B-SS	131	495	65	133	27	3	18	90	.269	*135	259	22	*.947
1987—Los Angeles	Nat.	3B-1B	53	136	14	31	8	1	1	11	.228	58	58	4	.967
1987—Albuquerque	P. C.	3B-1B	67	259	37	75	13	2	5	44	.290	285	90	15	.962
1988—Albuquerque	P. C.	1-3-2-S	85	313	46	100	21	1	17	73	.319	493	131	14	.978
1988—Los Angeles	Nat.	3B-1B	65	173	15	43	4	1	3	15	.249	160	60	6	.973
Major League Totals—2 Years			118	309	29	74	12	2	4	26	.239	218	118	10	.971

Selected by Los Angeles Dodgers' organization in 3rd round of free-agent draft, June 4, 1984.

CHAMPIONSHIP SERIES RECORD

Year Club	League	Pos.	G.	AB.	R.	H.	2B.	3B.	HR.	RBI.	B.A.	PO.	A.	E.	F.A.
1988—Los Angeles	Nat.	PH-1B	3	4	0	1	0	0	0	0	.250	3	0	0	1.000

WORLD SERIES RECORD

Year Club	League	Pos.	G.	AB.	R.	H.	2B.	3B.	HR.	RBI.	B.A.	PO.	A.	E.	F.A.
1988—Los Angeles	Nat.	PH-1B	4	4	0	0	0	0	0	1	.000	6	1	0	1.000

ROBERT JOHN WOODWARD
(Rob)

Born September 28, 1962, at Hanover, N.H.
Height, 6.03. Weight, 212.
Throws and bats righthanded.

Led International League in shutouts with 4 in 1986.
Led Eastern League pitchers in hit batsmen with 12 and tied for lead in games started with 27 in 1984.
Tied for Carolina League lead in games started by pitchers with 29 in 1983.

Year Club	League	G.	IP.	W.	L.	Pct.	H.	R.	ER.	SO.	BB.	ERA.
1981—Elmira	NYP	12	77	4	3	.571	77	38	29	47	23	3.39
1982—Winter Haven	Florida St.	27	126⅔	7	9	.438	140	85	72	50	62	5.12
1983—Winston-Salem	Carolina	30	197⅔	13	11	.542	177	103	91	157	100	4.14
1984—New Britain	Eastern	28	166	10	•12	.455	167	87	73	100	65	3.96
1985—New Britain	Eastern	12	86⅓	7	5	.583	71	42	34	54	36	3.54
1985—Pawtucket	Int'national	15	82⅔	3	8	.273	79	46	41	70	41	4.46
1985—Boston	American	5	26⅔	1	0	1.000	17	8	5	16	9	1.69
1986—Pawtucket	Int'national	18	127⅔	9	6	.600	114	55	45	73	42	3.17
1986—Boston	American	9	35⅔	2	3	.400	46	26	21	14	11	5.30
1987—Boston	American	9	37	1	1	.500	53	33	29	15	15	7.05
1987—Pawtucket	Int'national	21	136	12	8	.600	134	65	53	82	62	3.51
1988—Pawtucket	Int'national	47	44⅓	1	4	.200	44	20	19	53	24	3.86
1988—Boston	American	1	⅔	0	0	.000	2	1	1	0	1	13.50
Major League Totals—4 Years		24	100	4	4	.500	118	68	56	45	36	5.04

Selected by Boston Red Sox' organization in 3rd round of free-agent draft, June 8, 1981.

TODD ROLAND WORRELL

Name pronounced Wor-RELL.

Born September 28, 1959, at Arcadia, Calif.
Height, 6.05. Weight, 210.
Throws and bats righthanded.
Received bachelor of science degree in Christian education from
Biola College, La Mirada, Calif.

Established major league record for most saves by rookie (36), 1986.
Major League saves: 1985 (5), 1986 (36), 1987 (33), 1988 (32). Total—106.
Led National League in games finished in relief with 60, saves with 36 and intentional bases on balls issued with 16 in 1986.
Named National League Rookie Pitcher of the Year by THE SPORTING NEWS, 1986.
Named National League Rookie of the Year by Baseball Writers' Association of America, 1986.
Named National League Fireman of the Year by THE SPORTING NEWS, 1986.
Named righthanded pitcher on THE SPORTING NEWS College Baseball All-America Team, 1982.

Year Club	League	G.	IP.	W.	L.	Pct.	H.	R.	ER.	SO.	BB.	ERA.
1982—Erie	NYP	9	51⅔	4	1	.800	52	23	19	57	15	3.31
1983—Louisville	Am. Assoc.	15	79⅔	4	2	.667	76	49	42	46	42	4.74
1983—Arkansas	Texas	10	70⅓	5	2	.714	57	33	24	74	37	3.07
1984—Arkansas	Texas	18	100⅓	3	10	.231	109	72	50	88	67	4.49
1984—St. Petersburg	Florida St.	8	47⅓	3	2	.600	41	22	11	33	24	2.09
1985—Louisville	Am. Assoc.	34	127⅔	8	6	.571	114	59	51	*126	47	3.60
1985—St. Louis	National	17	21⅔	3	0	1.000	17	7	7	17	7	2.91
1986—St. Louis†	National	74	103⅔	9	10	.474	86	29	24	73	41	2.08
1987—St. Louis‡	National	75	94⅔	8	6	.571	86	29	28	92	34	2.66
1988—St. Louis	National	68	90	5	9	.357	69	32	30	78	34	3.00
Major League Totals—4 Years		234	310	25	25	.500	258	97	89	260	116	2.58

Selected by St. Louis Cardinals' organization in 1st round (21st player selected) of free-agent draft, June 7, 1982.
†Appeared in two games as an outfielder with no chances.
‡Appeared in one game as an outfielder with no chances.

CHAMPIONSHIP SERIES RECORD

Year Club	League	G.	IP.	W.	L.	Pct.	H.	R.	ER.	SO.	BB.	ERA.
1985—St. Louis	National	4	6⅓	1	0	1.000	4	1	1	3	2	1.42
1987—St. Louis	National	3	4⅓	0	0	.000	4	1	1	6	1	2.08
Championship Series Totals—2 Years		7	10⅔	1	0	1.000	8	2	2	9	3	1.69

Appeared as an outfielder in one game of 1987 Championship Series.

WORLD SERIES RECORD

Tied World Series record for most consecutive strikeouts, game (6), October 24, 1985.

Year Club	League	G.	IP.	W.	L.	Pct.	H.	R.	ER.	SO.	BB.	ERA.
1985—St. Louis	National	3	4⅔	0	1	.000	4	2	2	6	2	3.86
1987—St. Louis	National	4	7	0	0	.000	6	1	1	3	4	1.29
World Series Totals—2 Years		7	11⅔	0	1	.000	10	3	3	9	6	2.31

ALL-STAR GAME RECORD

Year League	IP.	W.	L.	Pct.	H.	R.	ER.	SO.	BB.	ERA.
1988—National	1	0	0	.000	0	0	0	0	0	0.00

CRAIG RICHARD WORTHINGTON

Born April 17, 1965, at Los Angeles, Calif.
Height, 6.00. Weight, 190.
Throws and bats righthanded.
Attended Cerritos College, Norwalk, Calif.

Major League stolen bases: 1988 (1).
Led Carolina League in game-winning RBIs with 16 in 1986.
Led International League third basemen in total chances with 310 in 1987 and 319 in 1988.
Tied for International League lead in double plays by third basemen with 16 in 1987.
Named International League Player of the Year, 1988.

Year Club	League	Pos.	G.	AB.	R.	H.	2B.	3B.	HR.	RBI.	B.A.	PO.	A.	E.	F.A.
1985—Bluefield	Appal.	3B	39	129	33	44	9	1	7	20	.341	32	68	12	.893
1986—Hagerstown	Carol.	3B	132	480	85	144	35	1	15	*105	.300	92	249	32	.914
1987—Rochester	Int.	3B	109	383	46	99	14	1	7	50	.258	*79	*211	*20	*.935
1988—Rochester	Int.	*3B-SS	121	430	53	105	25	1	16	73	.244	*91	209	19	.940
1988—Baltimore	Amer.	3B	26	81	5	15	2	0	2	4	.185	20	53	3	.961
Major League Totals—1 Year			26	81	5	15	2	0	2	4	.185	20	53	3	.961

Selected by New York Mets' organization in 6th round of free-agent draft, January 17, 1984.
Selected by Houston Astros' organization in secondary phase of free-agent draft, June 4, 1984.
Selected by Chicago Cubs' organization in secondary phase of free-agent draft, January 9, 1985.
Selected by Baltimore Orioles' organization in secondary phase of free-agent draft, June 3, 1985.

RICHARD JAMES WRONA
(Rick)

Born December 10, 1963, at Tulsa, Okla.
Height, 6.00. Weight, 180.
Throws and bats righthanded.
Attended Wichita State University, Wichita, Kan.

Year Club	League	Pos.	G.	AB.	R.	H.	2B.	3B.	HR.	RBI.	B.A.	PO.	A.	E.	F.A.
1985—Peoria†	Midw.	C	6	16	2	4	1	0	0	2	.250	31	1	2	.941
1985—Winston-Salem†	Carol.	C	20	49	4	11	4	0	0	2	.224	90	10	3	.971
1986—Winston-Salem	Carol.	C-O-3-1	91	267	43	68	15	0	4	32	.255	464	74	11	.980
1987—Pittsfield	East.	C-1B	70	218	22	48	10	3	1	25	.220	299	49	9	.975
1988—Pittsfield	East.	C	5	6	0	0	0	0	0	1	.000	11	1	0	1.000
1988—Iowa	A. A.	C	83	193	28	51	9	0	2	23	.264	347	36	7	.982
1988—Chicago	Nat.	C	4	6	0	0	0	0	0	0	.000	11	0	1	1.000
Major League Totals—1 Year			4	6	0	0	0	0	0	0	.000	11	1	0	1.000

Selected by Chicago Cubs' organization in 5th round of free-agent draft, June 3, 1985.
†Batted left and righthanded.

HAROLD DELANO WYNEGAR JR.

Name pronounced WY-nuh-ger.

(Butch)

Born March 14, 1956, at York, Pa.
Height, 6.00. Weight, 194.
Throws right and bats left and righthanded.

Major League stolen bases: 1977 (2), 1978 (1), 1979 (2), 1980 (3), 1983 (1), 1984 (1). Total—10.
Led American League catchers in double plays with 13 in 1980.
Led California League in bases on balls received with 142 in 1975.
Led Appalachian League catchers in double plays with 9 in 1974.
Named American League Rookie Player of the Year by THE SPORTING NEWS, 1976.

Year	Club	League	Pos.	G.	AB.	R.	H.	2B.	3B.	HR.	RBI.	B.A.	PO.	A.	E.	F.A.
1974	—Elizabethton	Appal.	C	60	191	32	66	10	0	8	51	*.346	344	39	5	*.987
1975	—Reno	Calif.	C	•139	468	106	147	18	6	19	*112	.314	*734	*99	9	*.989
1976	—Minnesota	Amer.	C	149	534	58	139	21	2	10	69	.260	650	78	*16	.978
1977	—Minnesota	Amer.	C-3B	144	532	76	139	22	3	10	79	.261	676	84	5	.993
1978	—Minnesota	Amer.	C-3B	135	454	36	104	22	1	4	45	.229	582	70	8	.988
1979	—Minnesota	Amer.	C	149	504	74	136	20	0	7	57	.270	653	65	6	.992
1980	—Minnesota	Amer.	C	146	486	61	124	18	3	5	57	.255	670	72	9	.988
1981	—Minnesota†	Amer.	C	47	150	11	37	5	0	0	10	.247	162	24	1	.995
1982	—Minn.‡-N.Y.§	Amer.	C	87	277	36	74	12	1	4	28	.267	523	26	5	.991
1983	—New York x	Amer.	C	94	301	40	89	18	2	6	42	.296	480	29	8	.985
1984	—New York	Amer.	C	129	442	48	118	13	1	6	45	.267	757	59	6	.993
1985	—New York yz	Amer.	C	102	309	27	69	15	0	5	32	.223	547	34	6	.990
1986	—New York abc	Amer.	C	61	194	19	40	4	1	7	29	.206	325	22	2	.994
1987	—California de	Amer.	C	31	92	4	19	2	0	0	5	.207	162	12	1	.994
1988	—California fg	Amer.	C	27	55	8	14	4	1	1	8	.255	94	8	2	.981
Major League Totals—13 Years				1401	4330	498	1102	176	15	65	506	.255	6281	583	75	.989

Selected by Minnesota Twins' organization in 2nd round of free-agent draft, June 5, 1974.
†On disabled list, April 6 to May 16 and August 26 to September 11, 1981.
‡Traded with Pitcher Roger Erickson to New York Yankees for Infielder Larry Milbourne and Pitchers John Pacella and Pete Filson, May 12, 1982.
§On disabled list, July 25 to September 1, 1982.
xOn disabled list, May 12 to May 27, 1983.
yOn disabled list, June 18 to July 18 and July 22 to August 2, 1985.
zGranted free agency, November 12, 1985; re-signed by Yankees, January 8, 1986.
aOn disabled list, April 21 to May 6, 1986.
bOn restricted list, August 1, 1986 through remainder of season.
cTraded to California Angels for Pitcher Ron Romanick and a player to be named later, December 19, 1986; New York Yankees' organization acquired Pitcher Alan Mills to complete deal, June 22, 1987.
dOn disabled list, May 12 to June 26 and July 28, 1987 through remainder of season.
eGranted free agency, January 22, 1988; re-signed by Angels, February 9, 1988.
fOn disabled list, May 26, 1988 through remainder of season.
gReleased, October 6, 1988.

ALL-STAR GAME RECORD

Year	League	Pos.	AB.	R.	H.	2B.	3B.	HR.	RBI.	B.A.	PO.	A.	E.	F.A.
1976	—American	PH	0	0	0	0	0	0	0	.000	0	0	0	.000
1977	—American	C	2	1	1	0	0	0	0	.500	3	0	0	1.000
All-Star Game Totals—2 Years			2	1	1	0	0	0	0	.500	3	0	0	1.000

MARVELL WYNNE

Name pronounced Win.

Born December 17, 1959, at Chicago, Ill.
Height, 5.11. Weight, 185.
Throws and bats lefthanded.

Major League stolen bases: 1983 (12), 1984 (24), 1985 (10), 1986 (11), 1987 (11), 1988 (3). Total—71.
Led South Atlantic League in total bases with 256 in 1980.
Led South Atlantic League outfielders in assists with 17 in 1980.
Tied for International League lead in game-winning RBIs with 14 in 1982.
Tied for Gulf Coast League lead in being hit by pitch with 5 in 1979.

Year	Club	League	Pos.	G.	AB.	R.	H.	2B.	3B.	HR.	RBI.	B.A.	PO.	A.	E.	F.A.
1979	—Sarasota Royals	Gulf C.	OF	50	190	21	54	6	4	4	28	.284	108	9	4	.967
1980	—Charleston†	S. Atl.	OF-2B-3B	137	*547	106	152	20	*15	18	98	.278	281	19	13	.958
1981	—Jackson	Texas	OF	127	497	69	142	29	2	4	50	.286	267	21	6	.980
1982	—Tidewater	Int.	OF	130	512	76	118	15	7	10	65	.230	283	13	12	.961
1983	—Tidewater‡	Int.	OF	51	175	32	50	13	1	3	29	.286	114	5	2	.983
1983	—Pittsburgh	Nat.	OF	103	366	66	89	16	2	7	26	.243	223	3	4	.983
1984	—Pittsburgh	Nat.	OF	154	653	77	174	24	11	0	39	.266	373	8	4	.990
1985	—Pittsburgh§x	Nat.	OF	103	337	21	69	6	3	2	18	.205	229	7	3	.987
1986	—San Diego	Nat.	OF	137	288	34	76	19	2	7	37	.264	203	3	3	.986
1987	—San Diego y	Nat.	OF	98	188	17	47	8	2	2	24	.250	100	2	2	.981
1988	—San Diego	Nat.	OF	128	333	37	88	13	4	11	42	.264	216	5	3	.987
Major League Totals—6 Years				723	2165	252	543	86	24	29	186	.251	1344	28	19	.986

Signed as free agent by Kansas City Royals' organization, September 3, 1978.
†Traded with Pitcher John Skinner to New York Mets' organization for Pitcher Juan Berenguer, March 31, 1981.
‡Traded with Pitcher Steve Senteney to Pittsburgh Pirates for Catcher Junior Ortiz and Pitcher Arthur Ray, June 14, 1983.
§On disabled list, April 20 to May 5 and June 3 to June 18, 1985.
xTraded to San Diego Padres for Pitcher Bob Patterson, April 3, 1986.
yOn disabled list, June 10 to June 25, 1987.

ERIC GIRARD YELDING

Born February 22, 1965, at Montrose, Ala.
Height, 6.01. Weight, 170.
Thows and bats righthanded.
Attended Chipola Junior College, Marianna, Fla.

Led International League in stolen bases with 59 and caught stealing with 23 in 1988.
Led Carolina League in stolen bases with 62 and caught stealing with 26 in 1985.

Led Pioneer League in caught stealing with 11 in 1984.
Led International League second basemen in errors with 21 in 1988.
Led California League shortstops in total chances with 573 in 1986.

Year Club	League	Pos.	G.	AB.	R.	H.	2B.	3B.	HR.	RBI.	B.A.	PO.	A.	E.	F.A.
1984—Medicine Hat	Pion.	OF	67	*304	61	94	14	6	4	29	.309	99	9	13	.893
1985—Kinston	Carol.	OF	135	526	59	137	14	4	2	31	.260	310	10	9	.973
1986—Ventura County	Calif.	SS	131	*560	83	157	14	7	4	40	.280	*231	284	*58	.899
1987—Myrtle Beach	S. Atl.	SS	88	357	53	109	12	2	1	31	.305	126	226	45	.887
1987—Knoxville	South.	SS	39	150	23	30	6	1	0	7	.200	64	92	14	.918
1988—Syracuse†	Int.	2B-SS	•138	*556	•69	139	15	2	1	38	.250	222	310	35	.938

Selected by Toronto Blue Jays' organization in 1st round (19th player selected) of free-agent draft, January 17, 1984.
†Drafted by Chicago Cubs, December 5, 1988.

RICHARD MARTIN YETT
(Rich)

Born October 6, 1962, at Pomona, Calif.
Height, 6.02. Weight, 187.
Throws and bats righthanded.

Major League saves: 1986 (1), 1987 (1). Total—2.
Led International League in wild pitches with 16 in 1985.

Year Club	League	G.	IP.	W.	L.	Pct.	H.	R.	ER.	SO.	BB.	ERA.
1980—Elizabethton	Ap'lachian	10	52	3	4	.429	46	30	25	35	19	4.33
1981—Wisconsin Rapids	Midwest	25	164	12	6	.667	147	87	67	121	77	3.68
1982—Visalia	California	27	196⅔	16	9	.640	183	98	80	121	97	3.66
1983—Orlando†	Southern	24	162	8	10	.444	153	82	68	93	78	3.78
1984—Toledo	Int'national	26	174⅔	12	9	.571	159	71	63	129	66	3.25
1985—Minnesota	American	1	⅓	0	0	.000	1	1	1	0	2	27.00
1985—Toledo‡-Maine	Int'national	25	165	9	11	.450	162	82	76	99	*101	4.15
1986—Maine	Int'national	1	6	0	0	.000	7	3	3	2	2	4.50
1986—Cleveland	American	39	78⅔	5	3	.625	84	48	45	50	37	5.15
1987—Cleveland	American	37	97⅔	3	9	.250	96	63	57	59	49	5.25
1987—Buffalo	Am. Assoc.	7	44⅓	3	3	.500	38	17	15	33	18	3.05
1988—Cleveland§	American	23	134⅓	9	6	.600	146	72	69	71	55	4.62
1988—Williamsport	Eastern	1	3⅓	0	1	.000	6	6	3	4	3	8.10
1988—Colorado Springs	P. Coast	2	8	0	1	.000	10	8	8	5	3	9.00
Major League Totals—4 Years		100	311	17	18	.486	327	184	172	180	143	4.98

Selected by Minnesota Twins' organization in 26th round of free-agent draft, June 3, 1980.
†On disabled list, April 8 to April 25, 1983.
‡Traded to Cleveland Indians' organization, September 17, 1985, completing deal in which Cleveland traded Pitcher Bert Blyleven to Minnesota Twins for Pitcher Curt Wardle, Outfielder Jim Weaver, Infielder Jay Bell and a player to be named later, August 1, 1986.
§On disabled list, June 14 to July 18, 1988; included rehabilitation disability assignment to Williamsport, June 29 to July 18, 1988.

FLOYD EVERETT YOUMANS JR.

Name pronounced YOH-muns.

Born May 11, 1964, at Tampa, Fla.
Height, 6.01. Weight, 200.
Throws and bats righthanded.

Year Club	League	G.	IP.	W.	L.	Pct.	H.	R.	ER.	SO.	BB.	ERA.
1982—Kingsport	Ap'lachian	10	39⅓	2	4	.333	35	39	27	31	39	6.18
1983—Columbia	S. Atlantic	23	134⅓	12	3	.800	112	77	51	117	73	3.42
1984—Lynchburg	Carolina	7	39⅔	5	2	.714	31	19	16	45	27	3.63
1984—Jackson†‡	Texas	16	86	6	7	.462	75	47	44	87	74	4.60
1985—Jacksonville	Southern	14	85⅔	7	3	.700	65	35	32	86	57	3.36
1985—Montreal	National	14	77	4	3	.571	57	27	21	54	49	2.45
1985—Indianapolis	Am. Assoc.	6	37⅔	3	2	.600	19	14	13	38	26	3.11
1986—Montreal	National	33	219	13	12	.520	145	93	86	202	*118	3.53
1987—Montreal§	National	23	116⅓	9	8	.529	112	63	60	94	47	4.64
1987—Jacksonville	Southern	1	6	1	0	1.000	4	2	2	6	3	3.00
1988—Montreal x	National	14	84	3	6	.333	64	35	30	54	41	3.21
1988—Indianapolis y	Am. Assoc.	1	3	0	0	.000	2	1	1	1	1	3.00
Major League Totals—4 Years		84	496⅓	29	29	.500	378	218	197	404	255	3.57

Selected by New York Mets' organization in 2nd round of free-agent draft, June 7, 1982.
†On disabled list, June 11 to June 21, 1984.
‡Traded with Infielder Hubie Brooks, Catcher Mike Fitzgerald and Outfielder Herm Winningham to Montreal Expos for Catcher Gary Carter, December 10, 1984.
§On disabled list, May 4 to May 19, June 10 to June 30 and August 16 to September 1, 1987; included rehabilitation disability assignment to Jacksonville, June 26 to June 30, 1987.
xOn ineligible list, June 25 to August 24, 1988; then transferred to disabled list, August 25 to September 14, 1988; included rehabilitation disability assignment to Indianapolis, August 25 to September 13, 1988.
yTraded with Pitcher Jeff Parrett to Philadelphia Phillies for Pitcher Kevin Gross, December 6, 1988.

CURTIS ALLEN YOUNG
(Curt)

Born April 16, 1960, at Saginaw, Mich.
Height, 6.01. Weight, 175.
Throws left and bats righthanded.
Attended Central Michigan University, Mt. Pleasant, Mich.

Led California League pitchers in games started with 28 in 1982.

Year Club	League	G.	IP.	W.	L.	Pct.	H.	R.	ER.	SO.	BB.	ERA.
1981—Medford	Northwest	8	53	2	2	.500	45	27	25	49	32	4.25
1981—Modesto	California	5	31	2	1	.667	28	15	12	22	16	3.48
1982—Modesto	California	28	205	15	8	.652	189	90	79	162	81	3.47
1983—Tacoma	P. Coast	27	158⅔	12	9	.571	175	94	89	109	52	5.05
1983—Oakland	American.	8	9	0	1	.000	17	17	16	5	5	16.00
1984—Tacoma	P. Coast	14	95⅓	6	4	.600	88	45	40	61	28	3.78
1984—Oakland	American	20	108⅔	9	4	.692	118	53	49	41	31	4.06
1985—Oakland†	American	19	46	0	4	.000	57	38	37	19	22	7.24
1985—Modesto	California	2	5⅔	0	0	.000	7	4	3	3	6	4.76
1985—Tacoma	P. Coast	3	15	2	0	1.000	10	7	6	8	7	3.60
1986—Tacoma	P. Coast	4	27	4	0	1.000	16	7	6	28	6	2.00
1986—Oakland	American	29	198	13	9	.591	176	88	76	116	57	3.45
1987—Oakland‡§	American	31	203	13	7	.650	194	102	92	124	44	4.08
1988—Oakland	American	26	156⅓	11	8	.579	162	77	72	69	50	4.14
Major League Totals—6 Years		133	721	46	33	.582	724	375	342	374	209	4.27

Selected by Oakland A's organization in 4th round of free-agent draft, June 8, 1981.

†On disabled list, May 3 to July 5, 1985; included rehabilitation disability assignment to Modesto, June 29 to July 5, 1985.

‡On disabled list, June 30 to July 20, 1987.

§Had one at-bat with no hits.

CHAMPIONSHIP SERIES RECORD

Year Club	League	G.	IP.	W.	L.	Pct.	H.	R.	ER.	SO.	BB.	ERA.
1988—Oakland	American	1	1⅓	0	0	.000	1	1	0	2	0	0.00

WORLD SERIES RECORD

Year Club	League	G.	IP.	W.	L.	Pct.	H.	R.	ER.	SO.	BB.	ERA.
1988—Oakland	American	1	1	0	0	.000	1	0	0	0	0	0.00

GERALD ANTHONY YOUNG

Born October 22, 1964, in Tele, Honduras.
Height, 6.02. Weight, 185.
Throws right and bats left and righthanded.

Major League stolen bases: 1987 (26), 1988 (65). Total—91.
Tied for National League lead in caught stealing with 27 in 1988.
Led Southern League in stolen bases with 54 and caught stealing with 27 in 1986.
Tied for Appalachian League lead in being hit by pitch with 6 in 1982.
Led Appalachian League shortstops in errors with 38 in 1982.
Tied for Florida State League lead in double plays by outfielders with 5 in 1985.

Year Club	League	Pos.	G.	AB.	R.	H.	2B.	3B.	HR.	RBI.	B.A.	PO.	A.	E.	F.A.
1982—Kingsport	Appal.	SS-2B-3B	59	197	27	35	6	1	0	15	.178	79	170	39	.865
1983—Sarasota Mets	Gulf C.	OF-SS	56	177	34	42	7	2	1	14	.237	88	9	7	.933
1984—Columbia†	S. Atl.	OF	124	396	69	84	14	3	1	52	.212	254	7	4	.985
1985—Osceola	Fla. St.	OF	133	474	88	121	20	9	3	48	.255	251	11	5	.981
1986—Columbus	South.	OF	136	539	101	151	30	4	9	62	.280	317	22	13	.963
1987—Tucson	P. C.	OF	86	340	59	99	15	5	2	31	.291	232	7	7	.972
1987—Houston	Nat.	OF	71	274	44	88	9	2	1	15	.321	143	5	3	.980
1988—Houston	Nat.	OF	149	576	79	148	21	9	0	37	.257	357	10	3	.992
Major League Totals—2 Years			220	850	123	236	30	11	1	52	.278	500	15	6	.988

Selected by New York Mets' organization in 5th round of free-agent draft, June 7, 1982.

†Traded with Infielder Manny Lee to Houston Astros, August 31, 1984, as partial completion of deal in which New York Mets acquired Infielder Ray Knight for three players to be named later, August 28, 1984; Houston acquired Pitcher Mitch Cook to complete deal, September 10, 1984.

MATTHEW JOHN YOUNG
(Matt)

Born August 9, 1958, at Pasadena, Calif.
Height, 6.03. Weight, 205.
Throws and bats lefthanded.
Attended Pasadena City College, Pasadena, Calif., and
University of California, Los Angeles, Calif.

Major League saves: 1985 (1), 1986 (13), 1987 (11). Total—25.

Year Club	League	G.	IP.	W.	L.	Pct.	H.	R.	ER.	SO.	BB.	ERA.
1980—Bellingham	Northwest	12	73	4	5	.444	73	46	40	53	62	4.93
1981—Lynn	Eastern	14	81	3	9	.250	80	47	36	57	38	4.00
1982—Salt Lake City	P. Coast	29	176	12	10	.545	192	113	91	118	75	4.65
1983—Seattle	American	33	203⅔	11	15	.423	178	86	74	130	79	3.27
1984—Seattle†	American	22	113⅓	6	8	.429	141	81	72	73	57	5.72

Year	Club	League	G.	IP.	W.	L.	Pct.	H.	R.	ER.	SO.	BB.	ERA.
1984	—Salt Lake City	P. Coast	6	41⅔	6	0	1.000	32	9	7	37	20	1.51
1985	—Seattle	American	37	218⅓	12	*19	.387	242	135	119	136	76	4.91
1986	—Seattle‡	American	65	103⅔	8	6	.571	108	50	44	82	46	3.82
1987	—Los Angeles§	National	47	54⅓	5	8	.385	62	30	27	42	17	4.47
1988	—Oakland xy	American					(Did not play)						
American League Totals—4 Years			157	639	37	48	.435	669	352	309	421	258	4.35
National League Totals—1 Year			47	54⅓	5	8	.385	62	30	27	42	17	4.47
Major League Totals—5 Years			204	693⅓	42	56	.429	731	382	336	463	275	4.36

Selected by Boston Red Sox' organization in 2nd round of free-agent draft, January 10, 1978.
Selected by Seattle Mariners' organization in 2nd round of free-agent draft, June 3, 1980.
†On disabled list, July 4 to July 29, 1984.
‡Traded to Los Angeles Dodgers for Pitcher Dennis Powell and Infielder Mike Watters, December 10, 1986.
§As part of an eight-player, three-team deal, New York Mets traded Pitcher Jesse Orosco to Oakland Athletics, December 11, 1987. Oakland then traded Orosco along with Shortstop Alfredo Griffin and Pitcher Jay Howell to Los Angeles Dodgers for Pitchers Bob Welch, Matt Young and Jack Savage. Oakland then traded Savage along with Pitchers Wally Whitehurst and Kevin Tapani to New York.
xOn disabled list, April 3, 1988 through entire season.
yReleased, December 21, 1988.

ALL-STAR GAME RECORD

Year	League	IP.	W.	L.	Pct.	H.	R.	ER.	SO.	BB.	ERA.
1983	—American	1	0	0	.000	0	0	0	1	0	0.00

MICHAEL DARREN YOUNG
(Mike)

Born March 20, 1960, at Oakland, Calif.
Height, 6.02. Weight, 206.
Throws right and bats left and righthanded.
Attended St. Mary's College, Moraga, Calif.; and Chabot College, Hayward, Calif.

Tied major league record for most extra-inning home runs, game (2), May 28, 1987, 10th and 12th innings.
Switch-hit home runs in one game, August 13, 1985.
Major League stolen bases: 1983 (1), 1984 (6), 1985 (1), 1986 (3), 1987 (10). Total—21.
Led International League batters in strikeouts with 140 in 1982.
Tied for Florida State League lead in double plays by outfielders with 4 in 1980.

Year	Club	League	Pos.	G.	AB.	R.	H.	2B.	3B.	HR.	RBI.	B.A.	PO.	A.	E.	F.A.
1980	—Miami	Fla. St.	OF	115	393	72	105	13	8	5	52	.267	212	*17	7	.970
1981	—Miami	Fla. St.	OF	63	235	32	81	19	6	3	34	.345	135	7	1	.993
1981	—Charlotte	South.	OF	75	275	58	88	16	3	12	45	.320	190	5	5	.975
1981	—Rochester	Int.	OF	1	3	0	1	0	0	0	0	.000	1	0	0	1.000
1982	—Rochester	Int.	OF	137	502	86	133	22	11	16	62	.265	291	7	11	.964
1982	—Baltimore	Amer.	OF	6	2	2	0	0	0	0	0	.000	1	0	0	1.000
1983	—Rochester	Int.	OF	102	373	62	106	14	8	14	66	.284	198	4	6	.971
1983	—Baltimore	Amer.	OF	25	36	5	6	2	1	0	2	.167	25	1	2	.929
1984	—Rochester	Int.	OF	20	72	17	24	6	1	4	15	.333	39	0	3	.929
1984	—Baltimore	Amer.	OF	123	401	59	101	17	2	17	52	.252	216	4	4	.982
1985	—Baltimore	Amer.	OF	139	450	72	123	22	1	28	81	.273	190	6	5	.975
1986	—Baltimore	Amer.	OF	117	369	43	93	15	1	9	42	.252	149	1	6	.962
1986	—Rochester	Int.	OF	32	97	14	27	2	0	5	21	.278	58	3	2	.968
1987	—Rochester†	Int.	DH	7	25	4	8	0	1	2	5	.320	0	0	0	.000
1987	—Baltimore‡	Amer.	OF	110	363	46	87	10	1	16	39	.240	117	0	3	.975
1988	—Philadelphia§	Nat.	OF	75	146	13	33	14	0	1	14	.226	76	0	5	.938
1988	—Milwaukee	Amer.	OF	8	14	2	0	0	0	0	0	.000	0	0	0	.000
American League Totals—6 Years				418	1272	183	323	56	5	54	177	.254	581	12	17	.972
National League Totals—1 Year				75	146	13	33	14	0	1	14	.226	76	0	5	.938
Major League Totals—6 Years				493	1418	196	356	70	5	55	191	.251	657	12	22	.968

Selected by Cleveland Indians' organization in 7th round of free-agent draft, June 6, 1978.
Selected by Baltimore Orioles' organization in secondary phase of free-agent draft, January 8, 1980.
†On Baltimore disabled list, March 23 to May 13, 1987; included rehabilitation disability assignment to Rochester, May 5 to May 13, 1987.
‡Traded with a player to be named later to Philadelphia Phillies for Infielder Rick Schu and Outfielders Jeff Stone and Keith Hughes, March 21, 1988; Philadelphia acquired Outfielder Frank Bellino to complete deal, June 14, 1988.
§Traded to Milwaukee Brewers for Pitcher Alex Madrid, August 24, 1988.

JOEL RANDOLPH YOUNGBLOOD III

Born August 28, 1951, at Houston, Tex.
Height, 5.11. Weight, 175.
Throws and bats righthanded.

Established major league record for most clubs, one or more hits for, one day (2), August 4, 1982.
Tied major league record for most clubs played, one day (2), August 4, 1982.
Major League stolen bases: 1976 (1), 1977 (1), 1978 (4), 1979 (18), 1980 (14), 1981 (2), 1982 (2), 1983 (7), 1984 (5), 1985 (3), 1986 (1), 1987 (1), 1988 (1). Total—60.
Led National League third basemen in errors with 36 in 1984.
Led National League outfielders in double plays with 6 in 1980.
Led Northern League second basemen in errors with 19 in 1970.
Tied for Northern League lead in being hit by pitch with 5 in 1970.

Year	Club	League	Pos.	G.	AB.	R.	H.	2B.	3B.	HR.	RBI.	B.A.	PO.	A.	E.	F.A.
1970—	Tampa	Fla. St.	SS	17	54	7	12	0	0	0	3	.222	22	40	9	.873
1970—	Sioux Falls	North.	2B-3B-SS	65	236	27	53	11	1	0	17	.225	110	134	26	.904
1971—	Tampa	Fla. St.	3B-SS-OF	136	443	75	113	25	4	5	44	.255	159	207	26	.934
1972—	Three Rivers	East.	OF-3B	104	366	57	106	15	5	12	60	.290	118	80	30	.868
1973—	Indianapolis	A. A.	OF-SS-3B	124	451	88	143	24	9	11	50	.317	136	112	28	.899
1974—	Indianapolis†	A. A.	OF	103	316	55	90	17	4	13	49	.285	115	6	4	.968
1975—	Indianapolis	A. A.	OF-2B	123	418	65	110	21	●9	6	51	.263	201	13	7	.968
1976—	Cincinnati‡	Nat.	1-O-C-2	55	57	8	11	1	1	0	1	.193	15	3	1	.947
1977—	St. L.§-N.Y.	Nat.	2B-OF-3B	95	209	17	51	13	1	0	12	.244	107	94	8	.962
1978—	New York	Nat.	O-2-3-S	113	266	40	67	12	8	7	30	.252	160	96	13	.952
1979—	New York	Nat.	OF-2B-3B	158	590	90	162	37	5	16	60	.275	337	57	9	.978
1980—	New York	Nat.	OF-3B-2B	146	514	58	142	26	2	8	69	.276	318	65	13	.967
1981—	New York x	Nat.	OF	43	143	16	50	10	2	4	25	.350	70	6	3	.962
1982—	N.Y. y-Mont. z	Nat.	O-2-S-3	120	292	37	70	14	0	3	29	.240	149	23	7	.961
1983—	San Francisco	Nat.	2B-3B-OF	124	373	59	109	20	3	17	53	.292	147	182	19	.945
1984—	San Francisco	Nat.	3B-OF-2B	134	469	50	119	17	1	10	51	.254	102	206	37	.893
1985—	San Francisco a	Nat.	OF-3B	95	230	24	62	6	0	4	24	.270	103	6	6	.948
1986—	San Francisco	Nat.	O-1-3-2-S	97	184	20	47	12	0	5	28	.255	68	14	3	.965
1987—	San Francisco b	Nat.	OF-3B	69	91	9	23	3	0	3	11	.253	24	3	0	1.000
1988—	San Francisco c	Nat.	OF	83	123	12	31	4	0	0	16	.252	48	0	1	.980
	Major League Totals—13 Years			1332	3541	440	944	175	23	77	409	.267	1648	755	120	.952

Selected by Cincinnati Reds' organization in 2nd round of free-agent draft, January 17, 1970.
†On disabled list, June 7 to June 19, 1974.
‡Traded to St. Louis Cardinals for Pitcher Bill Caudill, March 28, 1977.
§Traded to New York Mets for Shortstop Mike Phillips, June 15, 1977.
xOn disabled list, June 6 to August 1 and August 15 to September 15, 1981.
yTraded to Montreal Expos for a player to be named later, August 4, 1982; New York Mets' organization acquired Pitcher Tom Gorman to complete deal, August 14, 1982.
zGranted free agency, November 10, 1982; signed by San Francisco Giants, February 7, 1983.
aReleased, December 20, 1985; re-signed by Giants, March 20, 1986.
bGranted free agency, November 9, 1987; re-signed by Giants, December 1, 1987.
cGranted free agency, November 4, 1988; signed by Cincinnati Reds, December 21, 1988.

ALL-STAR GAME RECORD

Year	League	Pos.	AB.	R.	H.	2B.	3B.	HR.	RBI.	B.A.	PO.	A.	E.	F.A.
1981—	National	PH	1	0	0	0	0	0	0	.000	0	0	0	.000

ROBIN R. YOUNT

Born September 16, 1955, at Danville, Ill.
Height, 6.00. Weight, 180.
Throws and bats righthanded.
Brother of Larry Yount, pitcher with Houston Astros, 1971.

Major League stolen bases: 1974 (7), 1975 (12), 1976 (16), 1977 (16), 1978 (16), 1979 (11), 1980 (20), 1981 (4), 1982 (14), 1983 (12), 1984 (14), 1985 (10), 1986 (14), 1987 (19), 1988 (22). Total—207.
Hit for the cycle, June 12, 1988.
Led American League in total bases with 367 and slugging percentage with .578 in 1982.
Led American League outfielders in fielding percentage with .997 in 1986.
Led American League shortstops in double plays with 104 and total chances with 831 in 1976.
Named Major League Player of the Year by The Sporting News, 1982.
Named American League Player of the Year by The Sporting News, 1982.
Named American League Most Valuable Player by Baseball Writers' Association of America, 1982.
Named shortstop on The Sporting News American League All-Star Team, 1978, 1980 and 1982.
Named shortstop on The Sporting News American League All-Star fielding team, 1982.
Named shortstop on The Sporting News American League Silver Slugger team, 1980 and 1982.

Year	Club	League	Pos.	G.	AB.	R.	H.	2B.	3B.	HR.	RBI.	B.A.	PO.	A.	E.	F.A.
1973—	Newark	NYP	SS	64	242	29	69	15	3	3	25	.285	43	85	18	.877
1974—	Milwaukee	Amer.	SS	107	344	48	86	14	5	3	26	.250	148	327	19	.962
1975—	Milwaukee	Amer.	SS	147	558	67	149	28	2	8	52	.267	273	402	★44	.939
1976—	Milwaukee	Amer.	●SS-OF	●161	638	59	161	19	3	2	54	.252	●290	510	31	.963
1972—	Milwaukee	Amer.	SS	154	605	66	174	34	4	4	49	.288	256	449	29	.964
1978—	Milwaukee†	Amer.	SS	127	502	66	147	23	9	9	71	.293	246	453	30	.959
1979—	Milwaukee	Amer.	SS	149	577	72	154	26	5	8	51	.267	267	517	25	.969
1980—	Milwaukee	Amer.	SS	143	611	121	179	★49	10	23	87	.293	239	455	28	.961
1981—	Milwaukee	Amer.	SS	96	377	50	103	15	5	10	49	.273	161	370	8	★.985
1982—	Milwaukee	Amer.	SS	156	635	129	★210	●46	12	29	114	.331	253	★489	24	.969
1983—	Milwaukee	Amer.	SS	149	578	102	178	42	★10	17	80	.308	256	420	19	.973
1984—	Milwaukee	Amer.	SS	160	624	105	186	27	7	16	80	.298	199	402	18	.971
1985—	Milwaukee	Amer.	OF-1B	122	466	76	129	26	3	15	68	.277	267	5	8	.971
1986—	Milwaukee	Amer.	OF-1B	140	522	82	163	31	7	9	46	.312	365	9	2	.995
1987—	Milwaukee	Amer.	OF	158	635	99	198	25	9	21	103	.312	380	5	5	.987
1988—	Milwaukee	Amer.	OF	★162	621	92	190	38	●11	13	91	.306	444	12	2	.996
	Major League Totals—15 Years			2131	8293	1234	2407	443	102	187	1021	.290	4044	4825	289	.968

Selected by Milwaukee Brewers' organization in 1st round (third player selected) of free-agent draft, June 5, 1973.
†On disabled list, March 28 to May 3, 1978.

DIVISION SERIES RECORD

Year	Club	League	Pos.	G.	AB.	R.	H.	2B.	3B.	HR.	RBI.	B.A.	PO.	A.	E.	F.A.
1981—	Milwaukee	Amer.	SS	5	19	4	6	0	1	0	1	.316	6	16	1	.957

CHAMPIONSHIP SERIES RECORD

Year	Club	League	Pos.	G.	AB.	R.	H.	2B.	3B.	HR.	RBI.	B.A.	PO.	A.	E.	F.A.
1982	Milwaukee	Amer.	SS	5	16	1	4	0	0	0	0	.250	11	12	1	.958

WORLD SERIES RECORD

Established World Series record for most games, Series, four or more hits (2), 1982.
Tied World Series record for most at-bats, nine-inning game (6), October 12, 1982.

Year	Club	League	Pos.	G.	AB.	R.	H.	2B.	3B.	HR.	RBI.	B.A.	PO.	A.	E.	F.A.
1982	Milwaukee	Amer.	SS	7	29	6	12	3	0	1	6	.414	20	19	3	.929

ALL-STAR GAME RECORD

Year	League	Pos.	AB.	R.	H.	2B.	3B.	HR.	RBI.	B.A.	PO.	A.	E.	F.A.
1980	American	SS	2	0	0	0	0	0	0	.000	3	2	0	1.000
1982	American	SS	3	0	0	0	0	0	0	.000	0	2	0	1.000
1983	American	SS	2	1	0	0	0	0	1	.000	0	1	0	1.000
All-Star Game Totals—3 Years			7	1	0	0	0	0	1	.000	3	5	0	1.000

TODD EDWARD ZEILE

Born September 9, 1965, at Van Nuys, Calif.
Height, 6.01. Weight, 190.
Throws and bats righthanded.
Attended University of California, Los Angeles, Calif.

Led New York-Pennsylvania League in sacrifice flies with 6 in 1986.
Led Texas League catchers in putouts with 687 and total chances with 761 in 1988.
Tied for New York-Pennsylvania League lead in double plays by catchers with 7 in 1986.
Named Midwest League Co-Most Valuable Player, 1987.

Year	Club	League	Pos.	G.	AB.	R.	H.	2B.	3B.	HR.	RBI.	B.A.	PO.	A.	E.	F.A.
1986	Erie	NYP	C	70	248	40	64	14	1	14	★63	.258	407	★66	8	.983
1987	Springfield	Midw.	C-3B	130	487	94	142	24	4	25	★106	.292	867	79	14	.985
1988	Arkansas	Texas	C-OF-1B	129	430	95	117	33	2	19	75	.272	697	66	10	.987

Selected by Kansas City Royals' organization in 30th round of free-agent draft, June 6, 1983.
Selected by St. Louis Cardinals' organization in 2nd round of free-agent draft, June 2, 1986.

PAUL ZUVELLA

Name pronounced Zoo-VELL-uh.

Born October 31, 1958, at San Mateo, Calif.
Height, 6.00. Weight, 178.
Throws and bats righthanded.
Received bachelor of arts degree in communications
from Stanford University, Stanford, Calif.

Major League stolen bases: 1985 (2).
Led International League in being hit by pitch with 8 in 1984.
Led International League shortstops in total chances with 644 and double plays with 85 in 1984.
Led Southern League shortstops in total chances with 661 in 1981.

Year	Club	League	Pos.	G.	AB.	R.	H.	2B.	3B.	HR.	RBI.	B.A.	PO.	A.	E.	F.A.
1980	Bradenton Brav.	Gulf C.	SS	2	8	0	1	0	0	0	1	.125	4	9	1	.929
1980	Durham†	Carol.	SS	48	149	21	47	7	0	2	19	.315	58	140	12	.943
1981	Savannah	South.	SS	138	485	61	145	17	2	11	68	.299	220	★406	35	.947
1982	Richmond	Int.	SS	133	455	63	128	15	2	9	54	.281	245	335	22	.963
1982	Atlanta	Nat.	SS	2	1	0	0	0	0	0	0	.000	0	4	1	.800
1983	Richmond	Int.	SS	117	415	53	119	13	2	6	64	.287	169	324	18	★.965
1983	Atlanta	Nat.	SS	3	5	0	0	0	0	0	0	.000	1	2	1	.750
1984	Richmond	Int.	SS	127	462	77	140	18	●6	6	55	.303	★219	★409	16	★.975
1984	Atlanta	Nat.	2B-SS	11	25	2	5	1	0	0	1	.200	13	21	0	1.000
1985	Richmond	Int.	SS	8	32	3	7	0	0	1	3	.219	10	30	3	.930
1985	Atlanta	Nat.	2B-SS-3B	81	190	16	48	8	1	0	4	.253	112	173	8	.973
1986	Rich.‡-Col.	Int.	SS-2B	89	334	56	101	13	1	2	31	.302	149	231	10	.974
1986	New York	Amer.	SS	21	48	2	4	1	0	0	2	.083	30	54	3	.966
1987	New York	Amer.	2B-SS-3B	14	34	2	6	0	0	0	0	.176	20	25	0	1.000
1987	Columbus§	Int.	SS-2B	69	269	47	81	15	4	2	25	.301	131	178	11	.966
1988	Colorado Springs	P. C.	SS-2B	68	232	33	67	11	3	1	28	.289	105	190	16	.949
1988	Cleveland	Amer.	SS	51	130	9	30	5	1	0	7	.231	77	112	8	.959
National League Totals—4 Years				97	221	18	53	9	1	0	5	.240	126	200	10	.970
American League Totals—3 Years				86	212	13	40	6	1	0	9	.189	127	191	11	.967
Major League Totals—7 Years				183	433	31	93	15	2	0	14	.215	253	391	21	.968

Selected by Milwaukee Brewers' organization in 11th round of free-agent draft, June 5, 1979.
Selected by Atlanta Braves' organization in 15th round of free-agent draft, June 3, 1980.
†On disabled list, August 27, 1980 through remainder of season.
‡Traded with Outfielder Claudell Washington to New York Yankees for Outfielder Ken Griffey, June 30, 1986.
§Granted free agency, October 15, 1987; signed by Colorado Springs (Cleveland Indians' organization), January 8, 1988.

—DID YOU KNOW—

That the Tigers led the majors in 1988 with five grand slams?

Major League Managers

GEORGE LEE ANDERSON
(Sparky)
Detroit Tigers

Born February 22, 1934, at Bridgewater, S. D.
Height, 5.09. Weight, 168.
Threw and batted righthanded.

Major League stolen bases: 1959 (6).
Led International League in sacrifice hits with 15 in 1960.
Led Western League in sacrifice hits with 20 in 1954.
Tied for Texas League lead in sacrifice hits with 22 in 1955.
Led Texas League second basemen in double plays with 117 in 1955, Pacific Coast League with 135 in 1957 and International League with 104 in 1958 and 89 in 1960.
Led California League shortstops in double plays with 83 in 1953.

Year Club	League	Pos.	G.	AB.	R.	H.	2B.	3B.	HR.	RBI.	B.A.	PO.	A.	E.	F.A.
1953—Santa Barbara	Calif.	SS	•141	*598	98	157	21	4	5	55	.263	*277	395	32	.955
1954—Pueblo	West.	2B	147	497	72	147	13	5	0	62	.296	*397	432	20	•.976
1955—Fort Worth	Texas	2B	158	594	86	158	24	1	0	42	.266	*456	*469	18	*.981
1956—Montreal	Int.	2B	140	453	65	135	17	5	0	47	.298	372	391	15	.981
1957—Los Angeles	P. C.	*•2B-SS	•168	619	74	161	15	0	2	35	.260	*524	*488	•15	*.985
1958—Montreal†	Int.	2B	•155	580	78	156	35	5	2	56	.269	*387	*464	10	*.983
1959—Philadelphia	Nat.	2B	152	477	42	104	9	3	0	34	.218	343	403	12	.984
1960—Toronto	Int.	2B	148	543	67	123	11	5	5	21	.227	319	*416	12	.984
1961—Toronto	Int.	2B	97	275	30	66	17	0	0	22	.240	189	203	6	.985
1962—Toronto	Int.	2B	124	432	56	111	18	2	2	38	.257	282	327	8	*.987
1963—Toronto	Int.	2B	116	358	56	89	12	5	3	25	.249	226	256	6	*.988
Major League Totals—1 Year			152	477	42	104	9	3	0	34	.218	343	403	12	.984

†Recalled by Los Angeles Dodgers; traded to Philadelphia Phillies for Pitchers Jim Golden and Gene Snyder and Outfielder Eldon (Rip) Repulski, December 23, 1958.

RECORD AS MANAGER

Named American League Manager of the Year by THE SPORTING NEWS, 1987.

Year Club	League	Position	W.	L.
1964—Toronto	Int.	Fifth	80	72
1965—Rock Hill	W. Carol.	Eighth	24	40
(Second Half)		†First	35	23
1966—St. Petersburg	Fla. St.	Second	42	24
(Second Half)		‡First	49	21
1967—Modesto	Calif.	§Second	38	32
(Second Half)		xFirst	41	29
1968—Asheville	South.	First	86	54
1970—Cincinnati	Nat.	First(W)	102	60
1971—Cincinnati	Nat.	yFourth(W)	79	83
1972—Cincinnati	Nat.	First(W)	95	59
1973—Cincinnati	Nat.	First(W)	99	63
1974—Cincinnati	Nat.	Second(W)	98	64
1975—Cincinnati	Nat.	First(W)	108	54
1976—Cincinnati	Nat.	First(W)	102	60

Year Club	League	Position	W.	L.
1977—Cincinnati	Nat.	Second(W)	88	74
1978—Cincinnati	Nat.	Second(W)	92	69
1979—Detroit z	Amer.	Fifth(E)	56	50
1980—Detroit	Amer.	Fifth(E)	84	78
1981—Detroit a	Amer.		60	49
1982—Detroit	Amer.	Fourth(E)	83	79
1983—Detroit	Amer.	Second(E)	92	70
1984—Detroit	Amer.	First(E)	104	58
1985—Detroit	Amer.	Third(E)	84	77
1986—Detroit	Amer.	Third(E)	87	75
1987—Detroit	Amer.	First (E)	98	64
1988—Detroit	Amer.	Second (E)	88	74
American League Totals—10 Years			836	674
National League Totals—9 Years			863	586
Major League Totals—19 Years			1699	1260

†Won playoff against Salisbury (First Half winner), two games to none.
‡Lost playoff against Leesburg (First Half winner), three games to two.
§Tied for position with Santa Barbara.
xLost playoff against San Jose (First Half winner), two games to none.
yTied for position with Houston Astros.
zReplaced Les Moss (and interim manager Dick Tracewski) with club in fifth place (record of 29-26), June 14, 1979.
aFirst Half. . . . Fourth (E) (record of 31-26); Second Half. . . . Third (E) (record of 29-23).
Coach, San Diego Padres, 1969.
Manager, American League All-Star Team, 1985.
Manager, National League All-Star Team, 1971, 1973, 1976 and 1977.
Coach, National League All-Star Team, 1974.
Coach, American League All-Star Team, 1982 and 1984.

CHAMPIONSHIP SERIES RECORD

Year Club	League	W.	L.
1970—Cincinnati	National	3	0
1972—Cincinnati	National	3	2
1973—Cincinnati	National	2	3
1975—Cincinnati	National	3	0
1976—Cincinnati	National	3	0
1984—Detroit	American	3	0
1987—Detroit	American	1	4
Championship Series Totals—7 Years		18	9

WORLD SERIES RECORD

Year Club	League	W.	L.
1970—Cincinnati	National	1	4
1972—Cincinnati	National	3	4
1975—Cincinnati	National	4	3
1976—Cincinnati	National	4	0
1984—Detroit	American	4	1
World Series Totals—5 Years		16	12

—DID YOU KNOW—

That the Pirates' Andy Van Slyke hit more triples (15) in 1988 than the entire New York Yankees team (12)?

ROGER LEE CRAIG
San Francisco Giants

Born February 17, 1931, at Durham, N. C.
Height, 6.04. Weight, 196.
Threw and batted righthanded.
Attended North Carolina State College, Raleigh, N. C.

Tied major league record for most 1-0 games lost, season (5), 1963.
Tied National League record for most consecutive losses, season (18), May 4 through August 4, 1963, inclusive.
Tied for National League lead in shutouts with 4 in 1959.

Year Club	League	G.	IP.	W.	L.	Pct.	H.	R.	ER.	SO.	BB.	ERA.
1950—Newport News	Piedmont	6	19	0	1	.000	22	17	15	7	23	7.11
1950—Valdosta	Ga.-Fla.	23	167	14	7	.667	136	86	58	152	150	3.13
1951—Newport News	Piedmont	38	21	14	11	.560	175	109	90	119	*175	3.67
1952-53—Elmira	Eastern					(In Military Service)						
1954—Elmira	Eastern	3	2	0	0	.000	4	6	2	1	2	9.00
1954—Pueblo	Western	6	14	1	1	.500	14	17	15	8	19	9.64
1954—Newport News	Piedmont	20	125	8	3	.727	107	44	35	108	56	2.50
1955—Montreal	Int'national	22	117	10	2	.833	105	48	46	68	64	3.54
1955—Brooklyn	National	21	91	5	3	.625	81	37	28	48	43	2.77
1956—Brooklyn	National	35	199	12	11	.522	169	90	82	109	87	3.71
1957—Brooklyn	National	32	111	6	9	.400	102	58	57	69	47	4.62
1958—Los Angeles	National	9	32	2	1	.667	30	20	16	16	12	4.50
1958—St. Paul	Am. Assoc.	28	182	5	•17	.227	180	100	79	119	77	3.91
1959—Spokane	P. Coast	14	96	6	7	.462	86	39	34	46	26	3.19
1959—Los Angeles	National	29	153	11	5	.688	122	49	35	76	45	2.06
1960—Los Angeles	National	21	116	8	3	.727	99	48	42	69	43	3.26
1961—Los Angeles†	National	40	113	5	6	.455	130	87	77	63	52	6.13
1962—New York	National	42	233	10	*24	.294	261	133	117	118	70	4.52
1963—New York‡	National	46	236	5	*22	.185	249	117	99	108	58	3.78
1964—St. Louis§	National	39	166	7	9	.438	180	76	60	84	35	3.25
1965—Cincinnati x	National	40	64	1	4	.200	74	33	26	30	25	3.66
1966—Philadelphia	National	14	23	2	1	.667	31	15	14	13	5	5.48
1966—Seattle	P. Coast	6	22	0	1	.000	15	11	6	11	9	2.45
1968—Albuquerque	Texas	1	4	0	0	.000	3	0	0	2	2	0.00
Major League Totals—12 Years		368	1537	74	98	.430	1528	763	653	803	522	3.82

†Selected by New York Mets in National League expansion draft, October 10, 1961.
‡Traded to St. Louis Cardinals for Pitcher Bill Wakefield and Outfielder George Altman, November 4, 1963.
§Traded to Cincinnati Reds with Outfielder Charlie James for Pitcher Bob Purkey and a player to be named later, December 14, 1964.
xReleased by Cincinnati Reds and signed by Philadelphia Phillies, April 11, 1966.

WORLD SERIES RECORD

Year Club	League	G.	IP.	W.	L.	Pct.	H.	R.	ER.	SO.	BB.	ERA.
1955—Brooklyn	National	1	6	1	0	1.000	4	2	2	4	5	3.00
1956—Brooklyn	National	2	6	0	1	.000	10	8	8	4	3	12.00
1959—Los Angeles	National	2	9⅓	0	1	.000	15	9	9	8	5	8.68
1964—St. Louis	National	2	5	1	0	1.000	2	0	0	9	3	0.00
World Series Totals—3 Years		7	26⅓	2	2	.500	31	19	19	25	16	6.49

RECORD AS MANAGER

Year Club	League	Position	W.	L.
1968—Albuquerque	Texas	Second(W)	70	69
1978—San Diego	Nat.	Fourth(W)	84	78
1979—San Diego	Nat.	Fifth(W)	68	93
1985—San Francisco†	Nat.	Sixth(W)	6	12
1986—San Francisco	Nat.	Third(W)	83	79
1987—San Francisco	Nat.	First(W)	90	72
1988—San Francisco	Nat.	Fourth(W)	83	79
Major League Totals—6 Years			414	413

†Replaced Jim Davenport with club in sixth place (record of 56-88), September 18, 1985.
Scout, Los Angeles Dodgers, 1967; coach, San Diego Padres, 1969 through 1972; minor league pitching instructor, Los Angeles Dodgers, 1973; coach, Houston Astros, 1974 and 1975; coach, San Diego Padres, 1976 and 1977; named manager of Padres (replacing Alvin Dark), March 21, 1978; coach, Detroit Tigers, 1980 through 1983; scout, Detroit Tigers, March 2, 1985 through September 18, 1985.
Coach, National League All-Star Team, 1987 and 1988.

CHAMPIONSHIP SERIES RECORD

Year Club	League	W.	L.
1987—San Francisco	National	3	4

—DID YOU KNOW—

That the Los Angeles Dodgers' pitching staff compiled a 1.000 batting average in the 1988 World Series? Orel Hershiser was 3 for 3 in Game 2, pinch-hitters were used for the pitchers in Game 1, and Games 3, 4 and 5 were played in Oakland, where the designated hitter rule was used.

HOWARD RODNEY EDWARDS
(Doc)

(Given nickname by servicemen who started calling him 'Doc' after being discharged from Medical Corps and attending school near a Marine base.)

Cleveland Indians

Born December 10, 1937, at Red Jacket, W. Va.
Height, 6.02. Weight, 215.
Threw and batted righthanded.
Attended Mira Costa College, Oceanside, Calif.
Served in U. S. Navy Medical Corps, 1954 through 1957.

Year Club	League	Pos.	G.	AB.	R.	H.	2B.	3B.	HR.	RBI.	B.A.	PO.	A.	E.	F.A.
1958—North Platte	Neb. St.	C	42	131	24	47	6	1	3	29	.359	253	18	9	.968
1959—Selma	Ala.-Fla.	C	90	303	33	102	15	1	4	53	.337	534	*47	11	*.981
1960—Burlington	Carol.	C	128	458	54	128	11	1	8	48	.279	*855	72	*24	.975
1961—Salt Lake City	P. C.	*C-1B	120	402	51	133	14	5	5	54	.331	*666	*51	7	.990
1962—Cleveland	Amer.	C	53	143	13	39	6	0	3	9	.273	223	16	2	.992
1963—Clev.†-K. C.	Amer.	C	81	271	22	68	14	0	6	35	.251	421	33	6	.987
1964—Kansas City	Amer.	C-1B	97	294	25	66	10	0	5	28	.224	522	37	8	.986
1965—K. C.‡-N. Y.	Amer.	C	51	120	4	22	3	0	1	9	.183	230	18	3	.988
1965—Toledo§	Int.	C	20	63	5	20	5	0	0	7	.317	74	5	0	1.000
1966—Portland x	P. C.	C	116	376	28	98	3	0	4	38	.261	627	55	6	.991
1967—Oklahoma City y	P. C.	C	95	288	23	63	9	2	2	25	.219	577	39	4	.994
1968—San Diego	P. C.	C	83	270	17	70	6	0	0	20	.259	496	40	6	.989
1969—Eugene za	P. C.	C	73	237	16	63	13	0	2	31	.266	390	32	3	•.993
1970—Philadelphia bc	Nat.	C	35	78	5	21	0	0	0	6	.269	177	19	6	.970
American League Totals—4 Years			282	828	64	195	33	0	15	81	.236	1396	104	19	.987
National League Totals—1 Year			35	78	5	21	0	0	0	6	.269	177	19	6	.970
Major League Totals—5 Years			317	906	69	216	33	0	15	87	.238	1573	123	25	.985

†Traded with $100,000 to Kansas City Athletics for Catcher Jose Azcue and Shortstop Dick Howser, May 25, 1963.
‡Traded to New York Yankees for Catcher John Blanchard and Pitcher Roland Sheldon, May 3, 1965.
§Traded to Portland (Cleveland Indians' organization) for Outfielder Lu Clinton, January 14, 1966.
xSold to Oklahoma City (Houston Astros' organization), January 3, 1967.
yDrafted by San Diego (Philadelphia Phillies' organization), November 28, 1967.
zPlayer-coach.
aReleased as player and signed as coach with Philadelphia Phillies, October 3, 1969.
bReleased as coach and signed as player with Philadelphia Phillies, June 6, 1970.
cReleased as player and signed as coach with Philadelphia Phillies, October 7, 1970.

RECORD AS MANAGER

Named International League Manager of the Year, 1983.
Named Eastern League Manager of the Year, 1973.

Year Club	League	Position	W.	L.
1973—West Haven	East.	Second(A)	72	66
1974—West Haven	East.	Fourth(A)	58	79
1975—Midland	Texas	†First(W)	81	53
1976—Wichita	A. A.	Fourth(W)	56	79
1977—Quebec City	East.	Second(C)	65	70
1978—Denver	A. A.	Second(W)	64	71
1979—Rochester	Int.	Eighth	53	86
1980—Rochester	Int.	‡Third	74	65
1981—Rochester	Int.	Fourth	69	70
1982—Charleston	Int.	Eighth	59	81
1983—Charleston	Int.	§Third	74	66
1984—Maine	Int.	xSecond	77	59
1985—Maine	Int.	ySecond	76	63
1987—Cleveland z	Amer.	Seventh(E)	30	45
1988—Cleveland	Amer.	Sixth(E)	78	84
Major League Totals—2 Years			108	129

†Named Co-champion with Lafayette when best-of-five playoff series was tied 2-2 when weather forced cancellation of final game.
‡Lost playoff to Toledo, three games to one.
§Lost playoff to Richmond, three games to none.
xWon playoff from Toledo, three games to none; lost championship playoff from Pawtucket, three games to two.
yLost playoff to Tidewater, three games to two.
zReplaced Pat Corrales with club in seventh place (record of 31-56), July 16, 1987.
Coach, Philadelphia Phillies, beginning of 1970 through June 9, 1970, 1971 and 1972; coach, Cleveland Indians, June 13, 1985 through July 16, 1987.

GEORGE DALLAS GREEN JR.

(Known by middle name.)

New York Yankees

Born August 4, 1934, at Newport, Del.
Height, 6.05. Weight, 210.
Threw right and batted lefthanded.
Attended University of Delaware, Newark, Del.

Year Club	League	G.	IP.	W.	L.	Pct.	H.	R.	ER.	SO.	BB.	ERA.
1955—Reidsville	Carolina	7	17	1	1	.500	25	22	19	8	16	10.06
1955—Mattoon	M-O. V.	11	55	4	3	.571	43	29	21	85	42	3.44
1956—Salt Lake City	Pioneer	33	239	17	12	.586	182	126	95	*226	*187	3.58
1957—Miami	Int'national	2	6	0	1	.000	6	8	7	5	4	10.50
1957—High Point-Thomasville	Carolina	25	159	12	9	.571	143	84	71	147	92	4.02
1958—Miami	Int'national	31	159	7	10	.412	135	73	66	103	70	3.74

Year Club	League	G.	IP.	W.	L.	Pct.	H.	R.	ER.	SO.	BB.	ERA.
1959—Buffalo	Int'national	17	101	9	5	.643	94	39	33	72	28	2.94
1960—Buffalo	Int'national	11	75	3	4	.429	72	35	28	44	26	3.36
1960—Philadelphia	National	23	109	3	6	.333	100	54	49	51	44	4.05
1961—Philadelphia	National	42	128	2	4	.333	160	77	69	51	47	4.85
1962—Philadelphia	National	37	129	6	6	.500	145	58	55	58	43	3.84
1963—Philadelphia	National	40	120	7	5	.583	134	53	43	68	38	3.23
1964—Arkansas†	P. Coast	7	48	4	1	.800	46	15	14	34	9	2.63
1964—Philadelphia	National	25	42	2	1	.667	63	31	27	21	14	5.79
1965—Washington‡	American	6	14	0	0	.000	14	6	5	6	3	3.21
1965—Arkansas	P. Coast	23	172	12	7	.632	180	81	70	119	36	3.66
1966—San Diego§	P. Coast	26	184	14	9	.609	200	91	78	90	28	3.82
1966—New York x	National	4	5	0	0	.000	6	3	3	1	2	5.40
1967—Reading y	Eastern	8	66	6	2	.750	59	20	13	42	12	1.77
1967—Philadelphia z	National	8	15	0	0	.000	25	16	15	12	6	9.00
National League Totals—7 Years		179	548	20	22	.476	633	292	261	262	194	4.29
American League Totals—1 Year		6	14	0	0	.000	14	6	5	6	3	3.21
Major League Totals—8 Years		185	562	20	22	.476	647	298	266	268	197	4.26

†Sold to Washington Senators, April 11, 1965.
‡Returned to Philadelphia Phillies' organization, May 11, 1965.
§Sold to New York Mets' organization, July 22, 1966.
xReturned to Philadelphia Phillies' organization, August 10, 1966.
yPlayer-coach.
zReleased, September 22, 1967.

RECORD AS MANAGER

Named Appalachian League Manager of the Year, 1969.

Year Club	League	Position	W.	L.
1968—Huron	North.	Fifth	26	43
1969—Pulaski	Appal.	First(N)	38	28
1979—Philadelphia†	Nat.	Fourth(E)	19	11
1980—Philadelphia	Nat.	First(E)	91	71
1981—Philadelphia‡	Nat.		59	48
Major League Totals—3 Years			169	130

†Replaced Danny Ozark with club in fifth place (record of 65-67), August 31, 1979.
‡First Half .... First (E) (record of 34-21); Second Half .... Third (E) (record of 25-27).

Assistant farm director, Philadelphia Phillies, 1970 through June 2, 1972; Director of Minor Leagues, Philadelphia Phillies, June 2, 1972 to August 31, 1979; General Manager, Chicago Cubs, 1982 through 1987.

Manager, National League All-Star Team, 1981.

DIVISION SERIES RECORD

Year Club	League	W.	L.
1981—Philadelphia	National	2	3

CHAMPIONSHIP SERIES RECORD

Year Club	League	W.	L.
1980—Philadelphia	National	3	2

WORLD SERIES RECORD

Year Club	League	W.	L.
1980—Philadelphia	National	4	2

DORREL NORMAN ELVERT HERZOG
(Relly or Whitey)

(Named "Relly" by mother from his first name; "Whitey" by Bill Speith, McAlester sportscaster, because of light hair.)

St. Louis Cardinals

Born November 9, 1931, at New Athens, Ill.
Height, 5.11. Weight, 187.
Threw and batted lefthanded.

Major League stolen bases: 1956 (8), 1957 (1), 1959 (1), 1961 (1), 1962 (2). Total—13.

Year Club	League	Pos.	G.	AB.	R.	H.	2B.	3B.	HR.	RBI.	B.A.	PO.	A.	E.	F.A.
1949—McAlester	Soo. St.	OF	96	398	53	111	19	7	0	31	.279	222	14	0	★1.000
1950—McAlester	Soo. St.	OF	132	467	107	164	36	10	4	85	.351	272	15	7	★.976
1951—Norfolk	Pied.	OF	5	17	5	1	0	0	0	2	.059	13	0	1	.926
1951—Joplin	W. A.	OF-1B	113	418	99	119	14	8	7	48	.285	454	19	9	.981
1952—Beaumont	Texas	OF	35	121	11	24	4	1	0	9	.198	83	3	5	.945
1952—Quincy	I. I. I.	OF	68	225	53	65	9	6	7	44	.289	131	9	5	.966
1952—Kansas City	A. A.	OF-1B	14	27	5	8	1	0	1	5	.296	21	1	1	.957
1953-54—						(In Military Service.)									
1955—Denver†	A. A.	OF-1B	149	515	101	149	24	7	21	98	.289	324	10	4	.988
1956—Washington	Amer.	OF-1B	117	421	49	103	13	7	4	35	.245	274	10	7	.976
1957—Washington	Amer.	OF	36	78	7	13	3	0	0	4	.167	53	0	1	.981
1957—Miami	Int.	OF	77	257	48	70	14	5	2	25	.272	114	5	4	.967
1958—Wash.‡-K.C.	Amer.	OF-1B	96	101	11	23	1	2	0	9	.228	146	6	3	.981
1959—Kansas City	Amer.	OF-1B	38	123	25	36	7	1	1	9	.293	87	2	3	.967

Year	Club	League	Pos.	G.	AB.	R.	H.	2B.	3B.	HR.	RBI.	B.A.	PO.	A.	E.	F.A.
1960	Kansas City§	Amer.	OF-1B	83	252	43	67	10	2	8	38	.266	137	6	4	.973
1961	Baltimore	Amer.	OF	113	323	39	94	11	6	5	35	.291	143	2	0	1.000
1962	Baltimore x	Amer.	OF	99	263	34	70	13	1	7	35	.266	132	4	3	.978
1963	Detroit	Amer.	1B-OF	52	53	5	8	2	1	0	7	.151	44	1	1	.978
Major League Totals—8 Years				634	1614	213	414	60	20	25	172	.257	1016	31	22	.979

†Traded to Washington Senators with Pitcher Bob Wiesler, Catcher Lou Berberet, Second Baseman Herb Plews and Outfielder Dick Tettelbach for pitcher Maury McDermott and Shortstop Bob Kline (assigned to the Yankees' American Association farm club—Denver). Other players in deal assigned February 8, 1956; Herzog, April 2, 1956.

‡Sold to Kansas City Athletics, May 14, 1958.

§Traded to Baltimore Orioles with Outfielder Russ Snyder and a player to be named at later date, for Pitcher Jim Archer, Catcher Clint Courtney, First Baseman Bob Boyd, Infielder Wayne Causey and Outfielder Al Pilarcik, January 24, 1961; Courtney returned to the Orioles, April 15, 1961, to complete deal.

xTraded to Detroit Tigers with Catcher Gus Triandos for Catcher Dick Brown, November 26, 1962.

RECORD AS MANAGER

Named Man of the Year by THE SPORTING NEWS, 1982.
Named Major League Manager of the Year by THE SPORTING NEWS, 1982.

Year	Club	League	Position	W.	L.
1973	Texas†	Amer.	Sixth(W)	47	91
1974	California‡	Amer.	Sixth(W)	2	2
1975	Kansas City§	Amer.	Second(W)	41	25
1976	Kansas City	Amer.	First(W)	90	72
1977	Kansas City	Amer.	First(W)	102	60
1978	Kansas City	Amer.	First(W)	92	70
1979	Kansas City	Amer.	Second(W)	85	77
1980	St. Louis xy	Nat.	Fourth(E)	38	35
1981	St. Louis z	Nat.		59	43
1982	St. Louis	Nat.	First(E)	92	70
1983	St. Louis	Nat.	Fourth(E)	79	83
1984	St. Louis	Nat.	Third(E)	84	78
1985	St. Louis	Nat.	First(E)	101	61
1986	St. Louis	Nat.	Third(E)	79	82
1987	St. Louis	Nat.	First(E)	95	67
1988	St. Louis	Nat.	Fifth(E)	76	86
National League Totals—9 Years				703	605
American League Totals—7 Years				459	397
Major League Totals—16 Years				1162	1002

†Replaced by Billy Martin, September 8, 1973 (Del Wilber served as interim manager, September 7).
‡Served as interim manager, June 27 to June 30, 1974 after Dick Williams replaced Bobby Winkles, June 26.
§Replaced Jack McKeon with club in second place (record of 50-46), July 24, 1975.
xReplaced Ken Boyer (and interim manager Jack Krol) with club in sixth place (record of 18-33), June 9, 1980.
yNamed General Manager, August 28, 1980, with Red Schoendienst serving as manager remainder of season.
zFirst Half. . . . Second(E) (record of 30-20); Second Half. . . . Second(E) (record of 29-23).

Scout, Kansas City Athletics, 1964.; coach, Kansas City Athletics, 1965; New York Mets, 1966; California Angels, 1974 and part of 1975.

Director of Player Development, New York Mets, 1967 through 1972.
Manager, National League All-Star Team, 1983, 1986 and 1988.
Coach, American League All-Star Team, 1973, 1974 and 1978.

CHAMPIONSHIP SERIES RECORD

Year	Club	League	W.	L.
1976	Kansas City	American	2	3
1977	Kansas City	American	2	3
1978	Kansas City	American	1	3
1982	St. Louis	National	3	0
1985	St. Louis	National	4	2
1987	St. Louis	National	4	3
Championship Series Totals—6 Years			16	14

WORLD SERIES RECORD

Year	Club	League	W.	L.
1982	St. Louis	National	4	3
1985	St. Louis	National	3	4
1987	St. Louis	National	3	4
World Series Totals—3 Years			10	11

ARTHUR HENRY HOWE JR.
(Art)
Houston Astros

Born December 15, 1946, at Pittsburgh, Pa.
Height, 6.01. Weight, 185.
Threw and batted righthanded.
Received bachelor of science degree in business administration from University of Wyoming, Laramie, Wyo. in 1969.

Major League stolen bases: 1975 (1), 1978 (2), 1979 (3), 1980 (1), 1981 (1), 1982 (2). Total—10.
Led International League third basemen in errors with 22 and double plays with 24 in 1972.
Tied for Carolina League lead in putouts by third basemen with 95 in 1971.

Year	Club	League	Pos.	G.	AB.	R.	H.	2B.	3B.	HR.	RBI.	B.A.	PO.	A.	E.	F.A.
1971	Salem	Carol.	3B-SS	114	382	77	133	27	7	12	79	*.348	110	221	21	.940
1972	Charleston†	Int.	3B-2B-SS	109	365	68	99	21	3	14	53	.271	105	248	24	.936
1973	Charleston‡	Int.	3B-2B-SS	119	372	50	85	20	1	8	44	.228	141	229	21	.946
1974	Charleston	Int.	3B	60	207	26	70	17	4	8	36	.338	35	90	9	.933
1974	Pittsburgh	Nat.	3B-SS	29	74	10	18	4	1	1	5	.243	11	49	4	.938

Year	Club	League	Pos.	G.	AB.	R.	H.	2B.	3B.	HR.	RBI.	B.A.	PO.	A.	E.	F.A.
1975	Charleston	Int.	3B-2B	11	42	4	15	1	3	0	3	.357	15	23	1	.974
1975	Pittsburgh§	Nat.	3B-SS	63	146	13	25	9	0	1	10	.171	19	89	7	.939
1976	Memphis	Int.	3B-1B	74	259	50	92	21	3	12	59	.355	93	120	14	.934
1976	Houston	Nat.	3B-2B	21	29	0	4	1	0	0	0	.138	17	16	1	.970
1977	Houston	Nat.	2B-3B-SS	125	413	44	109	23	7	8	58	.264	213	333	8	.986
1978	Houston	Nat.	2B-3B-1B	119	420	46	123	33	3	7	55	.293	240	302	13	.977
1979	Houston	Nat.	2B-3B-1B	118	355	32	88	15	2	6	33	.248	188	261	7	.985
1980	Houston	Nat.	1-3-2-S	110	321	34	91	12	5	10	46	.283	598	86	10	.986
1981	Houston	Nat.	3B-1B	103	361	43	107	22	4	3	36	.296	67	206	9	.968
1982	Houston x	Nat.	3B-1B	110	365	29	87	15	1	5	38	.238	344	174	7	.987
1983	Houston yz	Nat.					(Did not play)									
1984	St. Louis	Nat.	3-1-2-S	89	139	17	30	5	0	2	12	.216	71	80	3	.981
1985	St. Louis a	Nat.	1B-3B	4	3	0	0	0	0	0	0	.000	5	1	0	1.000
Major League Totals—12 Years				891	2626	268	682	139	23	43	293	.260	1773	1597	69	.980

Signed as free agent by Pittsburgh Pirates' organization, June, 1971.

†On disabled list, August 17 to September 2, 1972.

‡On disabled list, April 13 to May 6, 1973.

§Traded to Houston Astros, January 6, 1976, completing deal in which Houston traded Second Baseman Tommy Helms to Pittsburgh Pirates for a player to be named later, December 12, 1975.

xOn disabled list, May 12 to June 19, 1982.

yOn disabled list, March 27, 1983 through remainder of season.

zGranted free agency, November 7, 1983; signed by St. Louis Cardinals, March 21, 1984.

aReleased, April 22, 1985.

DIVISION SERIES RECORD

Year	Club	League	Pos.	G.	AB.	R.	H.	2B.	3B.	HR.	RBI.	B.A.	PO.	A.	E.	F.A.
1981	Houston	Nat.	3B	5	17	1	4	0	0	1	1	.235	6	9	0	1.000

CHAMPIONSHIP SERIES RECORD

Year	Club	League	Pos.	G.	AB.	R.	H.	2B.	3B.	HR.	RBI.	B.A.	PO.	A.	E.	F.A.
1974	Pittsburgh	Nat.	PH	1	1	0	0	0	0	0	0	.000	0	0	0	.000
1980	Houston	Nat.	1B-PH	5	15	0	3	1	1	0	2	.200	29	3	0	1.000
Championship Series Totals—2 Years				6	16	0	3	1	1	0	2	.188	29	3	0	1.000

RECORD AS MANAGER

Coach, Texas Rangers, May 21, 1985 through 1988.

DAVID ALLEN JOHNSON
(Dave)
New York Mets

Born January 30, 1943, at Orlando, Fla.
Height, 6.01. Weight, 182.
Threw and batted righthanded.
Attended Texas A&M University, College Station, Tex., received bachelor of science degree in mathematics from Trinity University, San Antonio, Tex., and attended Johns Hopkins University, Baltimore, Md.

Established major league record for most home runs by second baseman, season, (42), 1973.

Tied major league records for fewest triples, season (150 or more games), (0), 1973; most home runs, bases filled, season, pinch-hitter (2), 1978.

Major League stolen bases: 1965 (3), 1966 (3), 1967 (4), 1968 (7), 1969 (3), 1970 (2), 1971 (3), 1972 (1), 1973 (5), 1974 (1), 1977 (1). Total—33.

Tied for American League lead in sacrifice flies with 8 in 1967.

Led National League second basemen in total chances with 877 and tied for lead in double plays with 106 in 1973.

Led American League second basemen in double plays with 103 in 1971.

Led California League shortstops in double plays with 63 in 1962.

Named National League Comeback Player of the Year by THE SPORTING NEWS, 1973.

Named second baseman on THE SPORTING NEWS National League All-Star Team, 1973.

Named second baseman on THE SPORTING NEWS American League All-Star Team, 1970.

Named second baseman on THE SPORTING NEWS American League All-Star fielding team, 1969 through 1971.

Year	Club	League	Pos.	G.	AB.	R.	H.	2B.	3B.	HR.	RBI.	B.A.	PO.	A.	E.	F.A.
1962	Stockton	Calif.	SS	97	343	58	106	18	•12	10	63	.309	135	307	40	★.917
1963	Elmira	East.	SS-2B	63	233	47	76	11	6	13	42	.326	115	155	12	.957
1963	Rochester	Int.	2B-OF	63	211	31	52	9	3	6	22	.246	141	138	11	.962
1964	Rochester	Int.	2B-SS	•155	590	87	156	29	14	19	73	.264	326	445	39	.952
1965	Baltimore	Amer.	3B-2B-SS	20	47	5	8	3	0	0	1	.170	11	37	3	.941
1965	Rochester	Int.	SS	52	193	29	58	9	3	4	22	.301	96	161	10	.963
1966	Baltimore	Amer.	★2B-SS	131	501	47	129	20	3	7	56	.257	294	357	★20	.970
1967	Baltimore	Amer.	2B-3B	148	510	62	126	30	3	10	64	.247	344	351	14	.980
1968	Baltimore	Amer.	2B-SS	145	504	50	122	24	4	9	56	.242	294	370	15	.978
1969	Baltimore	Amer.	2B-SS	142	511	52	143	34	1	7	57	.280	358	370	12	.984
1970	Baltimore	Amer.	•2B-SS	149	530	68	149	27	1	10	53	.281	•382	391	8	.990
1971	Baltimore	Amer.	2B	142	510	67	144	26	1	18	72	.282	361	367	12	.984
1972	Baltimore†	Amer.	2B	118	376	31	83	22	3	5	32	.221	286	307	6	★.990
1973	Atlanta	Nat.	2B	157	559	84	151	25	0	43	99	.270	383	464	★30	.966
1974	Atlanta	Nat.	1B-2B	136	454	56	114	18	0	15	62	.251	789	231	11	.989
1975	Atlanta‡	Nat.	PH	1	1	0	1	1	0	0	1	1.000	0	0	0	.000
1975	Yomiuri	Central	3B-SS	91	289	29	57	7	0	13	38	.197	85	157	11	.957

Year Club	League	Pos.	G.	AB.	R.	H.	2B.	3B.	HR.	RBI.	B.A.	PO.	A.	E.	F.A.
1976—Yomiuri§	Central	2B-3B-1B	108	371	48	102	16	2	26	74	.275	226	28	11	.979
1977—Philadelphia x	Nat.	1B-2B-3B	78	156	23	50	9	1	8	36	.321	299	31	0	1.000
1978—Phil. y-Chi. z	Nat.	3B-2B-1B	68	138	19	32	3	1	4	20	.232	61	63	11	.919
1979—Miami	Int.-Am.	1B	10	25	7	6	2	0	1	2	.240	Figures Unavailable			
American League Totals—8 Years			995	3489	382	904	186	16	66	391	.259	2330	2550	90	.982
National League Totals—5 Years			440	1308	182	348	56	2	70	218	.266	1532	789	52	.978
Major League Totals—13 Years			1435	4797	564	1252	242	18	136	609	.261	3862	3339	142	.981

†Traded with Pitchers Pat Dobson and Roric Harrison and Catcher Johnny Oates to Atlanta Braves for Catcher Earl Williams and Infielder Taylor Duncan, November 30, 1972.

‡Released, April 11, 1975; signed by Yomiuri Giants of Japanese Baseball League.

§Released, January 21, 1977; signed as free agent with Philadelphia Phillies, February 3, 1977.

xOn disabled list, June 15 to July 1, 1977.

yTraded to Chicago Cubs for Pitcher Larry Anderson, August 6, 1978.

zReleased, October 17, 1978.

CHAMPIONSHIP SERIES RECORD

Tied American League Championship Series record for most home runs, three-game Series (2), 1970.

Year Club	League	Pos.	G.	AB.	R.	H.	2B.	3B.	HR.	RBI.	B.A.	PO.	A.	E.	F.A.
1969—Baltimore	Amer.	2B	3	13	2	3	0	0	0	0	.231	5	11	0	1.000
1970—Baltimore	Amer.	2B	3	11	4	4	0	0	2	4	.364	11	4	0	1.000
1971—Baltimore	Amer.	2B	3	10	2	3	2	0	0	0	.300	5	6	1	.917
1977—Philadelphia	Nat.	1B	1	4	0	1	0	0	0	2	.250	8	0	0	1.000
Championship Series Totals—4 Years			10	38	8	11	2	0	2	6	.289	29	21	1	.980

WORLD SERIES RECORD

Established World Series record for highest fielding average by second baseman, four-game Series (1.000 with 24 chances), 1966.

Year Club	League	Pos.	G.	AB.	R.	H.	2B.	3B.	HR.	RBI.	B.A.	PO.	A.	E.	F.A.
1966—Baltimore	Amer.	2B	4	14	1	4	1	0	0	1	.286	12	12	0	1.000
1969—Baltimore	Amer.	2B	5	16	1	1	0	0	0	0	.063	8	15	0	1.000
1970—Baltimore	Amer.	2B	5	16	2	5	2	0	0	2	.313	15	9	0	1.000
1971—Baltimore	Amer.	2B	7	27	1	4	0	0	0	3	.148	18	12	0	1.000
World Series Totals—4 Years			21	73	5	14	3	0	0	6	.192	53	48	0	1.000

ALL-STAR GAME RECORD

Year League	Pos.	AB.	R.	H.	2B.	3B.	HR.	RBI.	B.A.	PO.	A.	E.	F.A.
1968—American	2B	1	0	0	0	0	0	0	.000	1	1	0	1.000
1970—American	2B	5	0	1	0	0	0	0	.200	5	1	0	1.000
1973—National	2B	1	0	0	0	0	0	0	.000	1	1	0	1.000
All-Star Game Totals—3 Years		7	0	1	0	0	0	0	.143	7	3	0	1.000

Named to American League All-Star Team for 1969 game; replaced due to injury.

RECORD AS MANAGER

Year Club	League	Position	W.	L.
1979—Miami	Inter-Amer.	First	43	17
(Second Half)		First	8	4
1981—Jackson	Texas	†First(E)	39	27
(Second Half)		Third(E)	29	39
1983—Tidewater	Int.	‡Fourth	71	68
1984—New York	Nat.	Second(E)	90	72

Year Club	League	Position	W.	L.
1985—New York	Nat.	Second(E)	98	64
1986—New York	Nat.	First(E)	108	54
1987—New York	Nat.	Second(E)	92	70
1988—New York	Nat.	First(E)	100	60
Major League Totals—5 Years			488	320

†Defeated Tulsa, two games to one, and San Antonio (finals), three games to none, for championship.

‡Defeated Columbus, three games to two, and Richmond (finals), three games to one, for championship.

Manager, National League All-Star Team, 1987.

Coach, National League All-Star Team, 1986.

Instructor, New York Mets' organization, 1982.

CHAMPIONSHIP SERIES RECORD

Year Club	League	W.	L.
1986—New York	National	4	2
1988—New York	National	3	4
Championship Series Totals—2 Years		7	6

WORLD SERIES RECORD

Year Club	League	W.	L.
1986—New York	National	4	3

JAY THOMAS KELLY
(Tom)
Minnesota Twins

Born August 15, 1950, at Graceville, Minn.
Height, 5.11. Weight, 185.
Threw and batted lefthanded.
Attended Mesa Community College, Mesa, Ariz., and Monmouth College, West Long Branch, N. J.
Son of Joe Kelly, former pitcher in St. Louis Cardinals' and New York Giants' organizations.

Led International League in bases on balls received with 91 in 1978.
Led New York-Pennsylvania League in stolen bases with 16 in 1968.
Led Pacific Coast League outfielders in double plays with 6 in 1972.

Year	Club	League	Pos.	G.	AB.	R.	H.	2B.	3B.	HR.	RBI.	B.A.	PO.	A.	E.	F.A.
1968—Newark		NYP	OF	65	218	50	69	11	4	2	10	.317	*144	*9	3	.981
1969—Clinton		Midw.	OF	100	269	47	60	10	2	6	35	.223	158	15	4	.977
1970—Jacksonville†‡		South.	OF-1B	93	266	33	64	10	1	8	38	.241	204	19	4	.982
1971—Charlotte		South.	1B-OF	100	303	50	89	17	0	6	41	.294	508	38	9	.984
1972—Tacoma		P. C.	OF-1B	132	407	76	114	19	2	10	52	.280	282	19	10	.968
1973—Tacoma		P. C.	OF-1B	114	337	67	87	10	2	17	49	.258	200	20	6	.973
1974—Tacoma		P. C.	OF-1B	115	357	68	110	16	0	18	69	.308	514	41	3	.985
1975—Tacoma		P. C.	OF-1B	62	202	38	51	5	0	9	29	.252	185	12	6	.970
1975—Minnesota§		Amer.	1B-OF	49	127	11	23	5	0	1	11	.181	360	28	6	.985
1976—Rochester		Int.	OF-1B	127	405	71	117	19	3	18	70	.289	323	28	4	.989
1977—Tacoma xyz		P. C.	1B-OF-P	113	363	80	99	12	1	12	64	.273	251	15	6	.978
1978—Toledo ab		Int.	1B-OF	119	325	47	74	13	0	10	49	.228	556	46	5	.992
Major League Totals—1 Year				49	127	11	23	5	0	1	11	.181	360	28	6	.985

†On temporary inactive list, April 16 to April 20, April 25 to April 30 and August 21, 1970 through remainder of season.

‡Released, April 6, 1971; signed by Charlotte (Minnesota Twins' organization), April 28, 1971.

§Loaned to Rochester (Baltimore Orioles' organization), April 5, 1976; returned, September 22, 1976.

xOn temporary inactive list, April 15 to April 19, 1977.

yPlayer-manager.

zOn disabled list, July 25 to August 4, 1977.

aPlayer-coach.

bReleased, December 18, 1978.

PITCHING RECORD

Year	Club	League	G.	IP.	W.	L.	Pct.	H.	R.	ER.	SO.	BB.	ERA.
1977—Tacoma		P. Coast	1	3	0	0	.000	2	2	2	0	3	6.00

RECORD AS MANAGER

Named Southern League Manager of the Year, 1981.
Named California League Co-Manager of the Year, 1980.
Named California League Manager of the Year, 1979.

Year	Club	League	Position	W.	L.
1977—Tacoma†		P. Coast	Third(W)	28	26
1979—Visalia		Calif.	‡First(S)	44	26
	(Second Half)		Second(S)	42	28
1980—Visalia		Calif.	Fourth(S)	27	43
	(Second Half)		§First(S)	44	26
1981—Orlando		South.	xFirst(E)	42	27
	(Second Half)		Third(E)	37	36
1982—Orlando		South.	Fifth(E)	31	38
	(Second Half)		Second(E)	43	32
1986—Minnesota y		Amer.	Sixth(W)	12	11
1987—Minnesota		Amer.	First(W)	85	77
1988—Minnesota		Amer.	Second(W)	91	71
Major League Totals—3 Years				188	159

†Replaced Del Wilber (record of 40-49), June, 1977.

‡Lost to San Jose, two games to one in semifinals.

§Defeated Fresno, two games to none in semifinals, and lost to Stockton, three games to none for championship.

xDefeated Savannah, three games to one in semifinals, and defeated Nashville, three games to one for championship.

yReplaced Ray Miller with club in seventh place (record of 59-80), September 12, 1986.

Manager, American League All-Star Team, 1988.

Coach, Minnesota Twins, 1983 through September 11, 1986.

CHAMPIONSHIP SERIES RECORD

Year	Club	League	W.	L.
1987—Minnesota		American	4	1

WORLD SERIES RECORD

Year	Club	League	W.	L.
1987—Minnesota		American	4	3

ANTHONY LaRUSSA JR.

(Tony)

Oakland Athletics

Born October 4, 1944, at Tampa, Fla.
Height, 6.00. Weight, 185.
Threw and batted righthanded.
Attended University of Tampa, Tampa, Fla., and received degree in industrial management from University of Southern Florida, Tampa, Fla.; and received law degree from Florida State University, Tallahassee, Fla. in 1980.

Led International League in being hit by pitch with 11 in 1972.
Received reported $50,000 bonus to sign with Kansas City A's, 1962.

Year	Club	League	Pos.	G.	AB.	R.	H.	2B.	3B.	HR.	RBI.	B.A.	PO.	A.	E.	F.A.
1962—Daytona Beach		Fla. St.	SS	64	225	37	58	7	0	1	32	.258	135	173	38	.890
1962—Binghamton		East.	SS-2B	12	43	3	8	0	0	0	4	.186	20	27	8	.855
1963—Kansas City		Amer.	SS-2B	34	44	4	11	1	1	0	1	.250	29	25	2	.964
1964—Lewiston†		N'west	2B-SS	90	329	50	77	22	1	1	25	.234	188	218	18	.958
1965—Birmingham‡		South.	2B	75	259	24	50	11	2	1	18	.193	202	161	21	.945
1966—Modesto		Calif.	2B	81	316	67	92	20	1	7	54	.291	201	212	20	.954
1966—Mobile		South.	2B	51	170	20	50	9	4	4	26	.294	117	133	10	.962
1967—Birmingham§		South.	2B	41	139	12	32	6	1	5	22	.230	88	120	5	.977

Year Club	League	Pos.	G.	AB.	R.	H.	2B.	3B.	HR.	RBI.	B.A.	PO.	A.	E.	F.A.
1968—Oakland	Amer.	PH	5	3	0	1	0	0	0	0	.333	0	0	0	.000
1968—Vancouver	P. C.	2B	122	455	55	109	16	8	5	29	.240	249	321	14	*.976
1969—Iowa	A. A.	2B	67	235	37	72	11	1	4	27	.306	177	222	15	.964
1969—Oakland	Amer.	PH	8	8	0	0	0	0	0	0	.000	0	0	0	.000
1970—Iowa	A. A.	2B	22	88	13	22	5	0	2	5	.250	52	59	3	.974
1970—Oakland	Amer.	2B	52	106	6	21	4	1	0	6	.198	67	89	5	.969
1971—Iowa	A. A.	2-3-S-O	28	107	21	31	5	1	2	11	.290	70	85	2	.987
1971—Oakland x	Amer.	2B-SS-3B	23	8	3	0	0	0	0	0	.000	8	7	2	.882
1971—Atlanta	Nat.	2B	9	7	1	2	0	0	0	0	.286	8	6	1	.933
1972—Richmond y	Int.	2B	122	389	68	120	13	2	10	42	.308	305	289	20	.967
1973—Wichita	A. A.	2B-1B-3B	106	392	82	123	16	0	5	75	.314	423	213	26	.961
1973—Chicago z	Nat.	PR	1	0	1	0	0	0	0	0	.000	0	0	0	.000
1974—Charleston a	Int.	2B	139	457	50	119	17	1	8	35	.260	262	*378	17	.974
1975—Denver	A. A.	3-O-S-2	118	354	87	99	23	2	7	46	.280	95	91	10	.949
1976—Iowa bc	A. A.	INF-O-P	107	332	53	86	11	0	4	34	.259	132	160	22	.930
1977—New Orleans de	A. A.	2B-3B	50	128	17	24	2	2	3	6	.188	66	87	7	.956
American League Totals—5 Years			122	169	13	33	5	2	0	7	.195	104	121	9	.962
National League Totals—2 Years			10	7	2	2	0	0	0	0	.286	8	6	1	.933
Major League Totals—6 Years			132	176	15	35	5	2	0	7	.199	112	127	10	.960

†On disabled list, May 9 to September 8, 1964.
‡On disabled list, June 3 to July 15, 1965.
§On disabled list, April 12 to May 6 and July 3 to September 5, 1967.
xSold to Atlanta Braves, August 14, 1971.
yTraded to Chicago Cubs for Pitcher Tom Phoebus, October 20, 1972.
zSold to Pittsburgh Pirates' organization.
aReleased, April 4, 1975; signed by Chicago White Sox' organization, April 7, 1975.
bOn disabled list, August 8 to August 18, 1976.
cSold to St. Louis Cardinals' organization, December 13, 1976.
dNamed coach, June 20, 1977.
eReleased, September 29, 1977.

PITCHING RECORD

Year Club	League	G.	IP.	W.	L.	Pct.	H.	R.	ER.	SO.	BB.	ERA.
1976—Iowa	Am. Assoc.	3	3	0	0	.000	3	1	1	0	0	3.00

RECORD AS MANAGER

Tied major league record for most clubs managed, season (2), 1986.
Named Major League Manager of the Year by THE SPORTING NEWS, 1983.
Named American League Manager of the Year, 1988.

Year Club	League	Position	W.	L.
1978—Knoxville	South.	First(W)	49	21
(Second Half)†		Third(W)	4	4
1979—Iowa‡	A. A.	Second(E)	54	52
1979—Chicago§	Amer.	Fifth(W)	27	27
1980—Chicago	Amer.	Fifth(W)	70	90
1981—Chicago x	Amer.		54	52
1982—Chicago	Amer.	Third(W)	87	75
1983—Chicago	Amer.	First(W)	99	63
1984—Chicago	Amer.	yFifth(W)	74	88
1985—Chicago	Amer.	Third(W)	85	77
1986—Chicago z	Amer.	Sixth(W)	26	38
1986—Oakland a	Amer.	bThird(W)	45	34
1987—Oakland	Amer.	Third(W)	81	81
1988—Oakland	Amer.	First(W)	104	58
Major League Totals—10 Years			752	683

†Replaced by Joe Jones, July 3, 1978.
‡Replaced by Joe Sparks, August 3, 1979.
§Replaced Don Kessinger with club in fifth place (record of 46-60), August 3, 1979.
xFirst Half. . . . Third (W) (record 31-22); Second Half. . . . Sixth (W) (record of 23-30).
yTied for position with Seattle Mariners.
zReplaced by interim manager Doug Rader, June 20, 1986.
aReplaced manager Jackie Moore (record of 29-44) and interim manager Jeff Newman (record of 2-8) with club in seventh place (combined record of 31-52), July 7, 1986.
bTied for position with Kansas City Royals.
Coach, Chicago White Sox, July 3 through remainder of 1978 season.
Coach, American League All-Star Team, 1984 and 1987.

CHAMPIONSHIP SERIES RECORD

Year Club	League	W.	L.
1983—Chicago	American	1	3
1988—Oakland	American	4	0
Championship Series Totals—2 Years		5	3

WORLD SERIES RECORD

Year Club	League	W.	L.
1988—Oakland	American	1	4

THOMAS CHARLES LASORDA

Name pronounced Luh-SORR-duh.

(Tom)

Los Angeles Dodgers

Born September 22, 1927, at Norristown, Pa.
Height, 5.09. Weight, 195.
Threw and batted lefthanded.

Tied National League record by making three wild pitches in an inning, first inning, May 5, 1955.
Led International League in complete games with 16 and tied for lead in shutouts with 5 in 1958.
Led Canadian-American League in wild pitches with 20 in 1948 and led International League with 14 in 1953.
Named International League Pitcher of the Year, 1958.

Year Club	League	G.	IP.	W.	L.	Pct.	H.	R.	ER.	SO.	BB.	ERA.
1945—Concord	N. C. St.	27	121	3	12	.200	115	84	55	91	100	4.09
1946-47—†	E. Shore					(In Military Service)						
1948—Schenectady‡§	Can.-Am.	32	192	9	12	.429	180	122	99	195	153	4.64
1949—Greenville	Sally	45	178	7	7	.500	141	81	58	151	138	2.93
1950—Montreal	Int'national	31	146	9	4	.692	136	73	60	85	82	3.70
1951—Montreal	Int'national	31	165	12	8	.600	145	75	64	80	87	3.49
1952—Montreal	Int'national	33	182	14	5	.737	156	90	74	77	93	3.66
1953—Montreal	Int'national	36	208	17	8	.680	171	77	65	122	94	2.81
1954—Montreal	Int'national	23	154	14	5	.737	142	66	60	75	79	3.51
1954—Brooklyn	National	4	9	0	0	.000	8	5	5	5	5	5.00
1955—Brooklyn	National	4	4	0	0	.000	5	6	6	4	6	13.50
1955—Montreal x	Int'national	22	143	9	8	.529	125	58	52	92	62	3.27
1956—Kansas City y	American	18	45	0	4	.000	40	38	31	28	45	6.20
1956—Denver	Am. Assoc.	16	83	3	4	.429	94	54	46	54	34	4.99
1957—Denver z	Am. Assoc.	6	17	0	2	.000	29	25	23	8	6	12.18
1957—Los Angeles	P. Coast	29	132	7	10	.412	134	73	57	72	59	3.90
1958—Montreal	Int'national	34	*230	*18	6	.750	191	77	64	126	76	2.50
1959—Montreal	Int'national	29	188	12	8	.600	192	93	80	64	77	3.83
1960—Montreal a	Int'national	12	45	2	5	.286	79	48	41	17	24	8.20
American League Totals—1 Year		18	45	0	4	.000	40	38	31	28	45	6.20
National League Totals—2 Years		8	13	0	0	.000	13	11	11	9	11	7.62
Major League Totals—3 Years		26	58	0	4	.000	53	49	42	37	56	6.52

†On National Defense list, May 14, 1946 through February 2, 1948.
‡On disabled list, July 9 to July 19, 1948.
§Drafted by Nashua (Brooklyn Dodgers' organization) from Philadelphia Phillies' organization, November 24, 1948.
xSold by Brooklyn Dodgers' organization to Kansas City Athletics for an estimated $35,000, March 2, 1956.
yTraded to New York Yankees for Pitcher Wally Burnette and cash, July 11, 1956.
zSold by New York Yankees' organization to Brooklyn Dodgers' organization, May 26, 1957.
aReleased, July 9, 1960.

RECORD AS MANAGER

Named National League co-Manager of the Year, 1988.
Named Minor League Manager of the Year by THE SPORTING NEWS, 1970.
Named Pacific Coast League co-Manager of the Year, 1970.
Named Pioneer League Manager of the Year, 1967.

Year Club	League	Position	W.	L.
1965—Pocatello	Pion.	†Second	33	33
1966—Ogden	Pion.	First	39	27
1967—Ogden	Pion.	First	41	25
1968—Ogden	Pion.	First	39	25
1969—Spokane	P. C.	Second(N)	71	73
1970—Spokane	P. C.	‡First(N)	94	52
1971—Spokane	P. C.	Third(N)	69	76
1972—Albuquerque	P. C.	§First(E)	92	56
1976—Los Angeles x	Nat.	Second(W)	2	2
1977—Los Angeles	Nat.	First(W)	98	64
1978—Los Angeles	Nat.	First(W)	95	67
1979—Los Angeles	Nat.	Third(W)	79	83
1980—Los Angeles	Nat.	Second(W)	92	71
1981—Los Angeles y	Nat.		63	47
1982—Los Angeles	Nat.	Second(W)	88	74
1983—Los Angeles	Nat.	First(W)	91	71
1984—Los Angeles	Nat.	Fourth(W)	79	83
1985—Los Angeles	Nat.	First(W)	95	67
1986—Los Angeles	Nat.	Fifth(W)	73	89
1987—Los Angeles	Nat.	Fourth(W)	73	89
1988—Los Angeles	Nat.	First(W)	94	67
Major League Totals—13 Years			1022	874

†Tied for position with Magic Valley.
‡Won championship playoff against Hawaii, four games to none.
§Won championship playoff against Eugene, three games to one.
xReplaced retiring Walter Alston with club in second place (record of 90-68), September 29, 1976.
yFirst Half. . . . First(W) (record of 36-21); Second Half. . . . Fourth(W) (record of 27-26).
Scout, Los Angeles Dodgers, 1961 through 1965; manager Los Angeles farm team in Arizona Instructional League, 1969; coach, Los Angeles Dodgers, 1973 through 1976.
Manager, National League All-Star Team, 1978, 1979 and 1982.
Coach, National League All-Star Team, 1977, 1983, 1984 and 1986.

DIVISION SERIES RECORD

Year Club	League	W.	L.
1981—Los Angeles	National	3	2

CHAMPIONSHIP SERIES RECORD

Year Club	League	W.	L.
1977—Los Angeles	National	3	1
1978—Los Angeles	National	3	1
1981—Los Angeles	National	3	2
1983—Los Angeles	National	1	3
1985—Los Angeles	National	2	4
1988—Los Angeles	National	4	3
Championship Series Totals—6 Years		16	14

WORLD SERIES RECORD

Year Club	League	W.	L.
1977—Los Angeles	National	2	4
1978—Los Angeles	National	2	4
1981—Los Angeles	National	4	2
1988—Los Angeles	National	4	1
World Series Totals—4 Years		12	11

JAMES KENNETH LEFEBVRE

Name pronounced Luh-FEE-ver.

(Jim)

Seattle Mariners

Born January 7, 1943, at Inglewood, Calif.
Height, 6.00. Weight, 185.
Threw right and batted right and lefthanded.

Led California League second basemen in double plays with 79 in 1962.
Led Northwest League second basemen in double plays with 109 in 1963.
Named National League Rookie of the Year by Baseball Writers' Association of America, 1965.

Year Club	League	Pos.	G.	AB.	R.	H.	2B.	3B.	HR.	RBI.	B.A.	PO.	A.	E.	F.A.
1962—Reno	Calif.	2B	138	541	139	177	33	4	39	130	.327	345	313	27	.961
1963—Salem	N'west	2B	139	474	82	134	29	9	17	92	.283	*316	327	*35	.948
1964—Spokane†	P. C.	2B	55	200	26	53	10	1	6	31	.265	123	126	8	.969
1965—Los Angeles	Nat.	2B	157	544	57	136	21	4	12	69	.250	349	429	24	.970
1966—Los Angeles	Nat.	2B-3B	152	544	69	149	23	3	24	74	.274	268	389	16	.976
1967—Los Angeles	Nat.	3B-2B-1B	136	494	51	129	18	5	8	50	.261	173	321	18	.965
1968—Los Angeles	Nat.	2-3-O-1	84	286	23	69	12	1	5	31	.241	179	161	8	.977
1969—Los Angeles	Nat.	3B-2B-1B	95	275	29	65	15	2	4	44	.236	154	185	6	.983
1970—Los Angeles	Nat.	2B-3B-1B	109	314	33	79	15	1	4	44	.252	168	212	6	.984
1971—Los Angeles	Nat.	2B-3B	119	388	40	95	14	2	12	68	.245	247	274	9	.983
1972—Los Angeles‡	Nat.	2B-3B	70	169	11	34	8	0	5	24	.201	70	99	4	.977
1973—Lotte	Pac.	1-2-3-O	111	400	50	106	12	2	29	63	.265	763	77	7	.992
1974—Lotte	Pac.	1B-3B	82	279	37	79	12	2	14	52	.283	580	32	4	.994
1975—Lotte	Pac.	1B	47	151	13	39	5	0	9	24	.258	252	13	0	1.000
1976—Lotte	Pac.	1B	90	268	22	65	8	0	8	37	.243	506	32	3	.994
Major League Totals—8 Years			922	3014	313	756	126	18	74	404	.251	1608	2070	91	.976

†On military list, March 15 to July 18, 1964.
‡Released, November 27, 1972; signed with Lotte Orions of Japanese Baseball League.

WORLD SERIES RECORD

Year Club	League	Pos.	G.	AB.	R.	H.	2B.	3B.	HR.	RBI.	B.A.	PO.	A.	E.	F.A.
1965—Los Angeles	Nat.	2B	3	10	2	4	0	0	0	0	.400	3	7	1	.909
1966—Los Angeles	Nat.	2B	4	12	1	2	0	0	1	1	.167	10	10	0	1.000
World Series Totals—2 Years			7	22	3	6	0	0	1	1	.273	13	17	1	.968

ALL-STAR GAME RECORD

Year League	Pos.	AB.	R.	H.	2B.	3B.	HR.	RBI.	B.A.	PO.	A.	E.	F.A.
1966—National	2B	2	0	0	0	0	0	0	.000	2	0	0	1.000

RECORD AS MANAGER

Named Pacific Coast League Manager of the Year, 1985 and 1986.

Year Club	League	Position	W.	L.
1978—Lethbridge	Pion.	Fifth	33	35
1985—Phoenix	P. C.	Second(S)	37	33
(Second Half)		†First(S)	43	29
1986—Phoenix	P. C.	‡First(S)	43	28
(Second Half)		Second(S)	38	33

†Defeated Hawaii, three games to none in semifinals; lost to Vancouver, three games to none, for championship.
‡Lost to Las Vegas, three games to two in semifinals.

Coach, Lotte Orions, 1977; coach, Los Angeles Dodgers, September 24, 1978 through 1979; coach, San Francisco Giants, 1980 and 1982; Director of Player Development, San Francisco Giants, 1983 and 1984; coach, Oakland Athletics, 1987 and 1988.

JAMES RICHARD LEYLAND

Named pronounced LEE-lund.

(Jim)

Pittsburgh Pirates

Born December 15, 1944, at Toledo, O.
Height, 5.11. Weight, 170.
Threw and batted righthanded.

Year Club	League	Pos.	G.	AB.	R.	H.	2B.	3B.	HR.	RBI.	B.A.	PO.	A.	E.	F.A.
1964—Lakeland†	Fla. St.	C	52	129	8	25	0	1	0	8	.194	268	17	6	.979
1964—Cocoa Tigers	Rookie	C	24	52	2	12	1	1	0	4	.231	122	15	3	.979
1965—Jamestown	NYP	C-3B-P	82	211	18	50	7	2	1	21	.237	318	36	6	.983
1966—Rocky Mount	Carol.	C	67	173	24	42	6	0	0	16	.243	369	23	1	.997
1967—Montgomery	South.	C	62	171	11	40	3	0	1	16	.234	350	25	6	.984
1968—Montgomery	South.	C-3B-SS	81	264	19	51	3	0	1	20	.193	511	43	7	.988
1969—Montgomery	South.	C	16	39	1	8	0	0	0	1	.205	64	6	3	.959
1969—Lakeland	Fla. St.	C-P	60	179	20	43	8	0	1	16	.240	321	28	4	.989
1970—Montgomery‡	South.	C	2	3	0	0	0	0	0	0	.000	6	0	1	.857

Signed as free agent by Detroit Tigers' organization, September 21, 1963.
†On disabled list, June 15 to June 27, 1964.
‡Player-coach.

PITCHING RECORD

Year	Club	League	G.	IP.	W.	L.	Pct.	H.	R.	ER.	SO.	BB.	ERA.
1965	—Jamestown	NYP	1	2	0	0	.000	2	0	0	1	0	0.00
1969	—Lakeland	Florida St.	1	2	0	0	.000	4	2	2	1	0	9.00

RECORD AS MANAGER

Named National League co-Manager of the Year, 1988.
Named American Association Manager of the Year, 1979.
Named Florida State League Manager of the Year, 1977 and 1978.

Year	Club	League	Position	W.	L.
1971	—Bristol	Appal.	Third(S)	31	35
1972	—Clinton	Midw.	Fifth(N)	22	41
	(Second Half)		Fourth(N)	27	36
1973	—Clinton	Midw.	Second(N)	36	26
	(Second Half)		†First(N)	37	25
1974	—Montgomery	South.	Third(W)	61	76
1975	—Clinton	Midw.	Fourth(S)	29	31
	(Second Half)		Second(S)	38	30
1976	—Lakeland	Fla. St.	‡Second(N)	74	64
1977	—Lakeland	Fla. St.	§First(N)	85	53
1978	—Lakeland	Fla. St.	Fourth(N)	31	38
	(Second Half)		xFirst(N)	47	22
1979	—Evansville	A. A.	yFirst(E)	78	58
1980	—Evansville	A. A.	Second(E)	61	74
1981	—Evansville	A. A.	zFirst(E)	73	63
1986	—Pittsburgh	Nat.	Sixth(E)	64	98
1987	—Pittsburgh	Nat.	aFourth(E)	80	82
1988	—Pittsburgh	Nat.	Second(E)	85	75
	Major League Totals—3 Years			229	255

†Lost playoff to Wisconsin Rapids, two games to none.
‡Defeated Miami, two games to none in semifinals, and defeated Tampa, two games to none for championship.
§Defeated Miami, two games to none in semifinals, and defeated St. Petersburg, three games to one for championship.
xDefeated St. Petersburg, one game to none for Northern Division championship, and lost to Miami, two games to one for championship.
yDefeated Oklahoma City, four games to two for championship.
zLost to Denver, three games to one in semifinals.
aTied for position with Philadelphia Phillies.
Coach, Detroit Tigers' organization, 1970 through June 5, 1971; Coach, Chicago White Sox, 1982 through 1985.

NICOLAS TOMAS LEYVA
(Nick)
Philadelphia Phillies

Born August 16, 1953, at Ontario, Calif.
Height, 5.11. Weight, 165.
Threw and batted righthanded.
Attended University of La Verne, La Verne, Calif.

Year	Club	League	Pos.	G.	AB.	R.	H.	2B.	3B.	HR.	RBI.	B.A.	PO.	A.	E.	F.A.
1975	—Sarasota Cards	Gulf C.	3B-SS	4	18	3	5	2	0	0	4	.278	8	11	4	.826
1975	—St. Petersburg	Fla. St.	3B-SS	47	157	16	42	8	2	0	21	.268	48	105	7	.956
1976	—St. Petersburg	Fla. St.	3B-SS	70	237	32	66	11	0	2	28	.278	69	128	7	.966
1976	—Arkansas	Texas	2B-3B-SS	48	153	16	38	4	1	3	26	.248	60	87	6	.961
1977	—Arkansas†	Texas	I-O-P	84	213	24	57	4	2	3	30	.268	102	119	11	.953

Selected by St. Louis Cardinals' organization in 24th round of free-agent draft, June 4, 1975.
†Released, December 12, 1977.

PITCHING RECORD

Year	Club	League	G.	IP.	W.	L.	Pct.	H.	R.	ER.	SO.	BB.	ERA.
1977	—Arkansas	Texas	2	4	0	0	.000	6	5	0	0	0	0.00

RECORD AS MANAGER

Named Texas League Manager of the Year, 1983.

Year	Club	League	Position	W.	L.
1978	—Johnson City	Appal.	Second	37	33
1979	—Johnson City	Appal.	Fifth	25	43
1980	—Gastonia†	S. Atl.	Third(N)	37	33
	(Second Half)		Second(N)	37	33
1981	—St. Petersburg	Fla. St.	Third(N)	33	36
	(Second Half)		Second(N)	36	27
1982	—St. Petersburg‡	Fla. St.	Fourth(N)	26	30
1982	—Arkansas§	Texas	Third(E)	12	7
	(Second Half)		Second(E)	38	31
1983	—Arkansas	Texas	Fourth(E)	30	38
	(Second Half)x		First(E)	39	29

†Lost playoffs to Greensboro, two games to one.
‡Manager through May 31, 1982.
§Shared first half managing duties with Gaylen Pitts.
xLost playoffs to Jackson, two games to none.
Coach, St. Louis Cardinals, 1984 through 1988.

JOHN ALOYSIUS McKEON
(Jack)
San Diego Padres

Born November 23, 1930, at South Amboy, N. J.
Height, 5.08. Weight, 205.
Threw and batted righthanded.
Attended Holy Cross College, Worcester, Mass., Seton Hall University, South Orange, N.J., and received bachelor of arts degree in physical education and science from Elon College, Elon, N.C.

Brother of Bill McKeon, minor league catcher, 1952 through 1954, 1956 and 1957; scout, Kansas City Royals, 1969 and 1970; and scout, San Diego Padres since 1981; father-in-law of Greg Booker, pitcher with San Diego Padres.

Led Carolina League catchers in double plays with 17 in 1953.
Led Alabama State League catchers in double plays with 9 in 1949.

Year Club	League	Pos.	G.	AB.	R.	H.	2B.	3B.	HR.	RBI.	B.A.	PO.	A.	E.	F.A.
1949—Greenville	Ala. St.	C	116	390	54	98	12	1	1	49	.251	*806	65	13	*.985
1950—York	Int.	C	1	3	....	1	....	....	....	....	.333	figures unavailable			
1950—Gloversville	C.-Am.	C	72	209	18	45	5	0	0	14	.215	281	30	15	.954
1951—		(In Military Service)													
1952—Hutchinson	W. Assn.	C	116	358	42	78	10	1	4	40	.218	756	68	11	.987
1953—Burlington	Carol.	C	140	474	46	86	19	2	6	52	.181	*836	*82	21	.978
1954—Burlington	Carol.	C	17	30	1	4	0	0	0	2	.133	60	9	0	1.000
1954—Hutchinson†	W. Assn.	C	46	140	18	29	5	0	1	13	.207	273	33	4	.987
1955—Fay.-Greens‡	Carol.	C	59	172	20	29	3	0	1	17	.169	292	20	6	.981
1956—Missoula§	Pion.	C	113	370	44	63	8	0	0	29	.170	630	78	9	.987
1957—Missoula§	Pion.	C	102	299	37	65	7	0	4	40	.217	645	55	10	.986
1958—Missoula§	Pion.	C	108	354	49	93	16	0	8	51	.263	739	64	12	.985
1959—Fox Cities	Three-I	C	11	20	1	2	0	0	0	1	1.000	figures unavailable			

†Released by Pittsburgh Pirates' organization, September 28, 1954.
‡Played 10 games with Fayetteville, 5 games with Greensboro, and was a player-manager with Fayetteville for 44 games.
§Player-manager.

PITCHING RECORD

Year Club	League	G.	IP.	W.	L.	Pct.	H.	R.	ER.	SO.	BB.	ERA.
1956—Missoula	Pioneer	8	....	0	0	.000	....	....	....	....	....	....
1957—Missoula	Pioneer	6	....	0	0	.000	....	....	....	....	....	....
1958—Missoula	Pioneer	2	....	0	0	.000	....	....	....	....	....	....

RECORD AS MANAGER

Named American Association Manager of the Year, 1969 and 1970.
Named Carolina League Manager of the Year, 1961.
Named Pioneer League Manager of the Year, 1958.

Year Club	League	Position	W.	L.
1955—Fayetteville†	Carol.	Third	70	67
1956—Missoula	Pion.	Seventh	61	71
1957—Missoula	Pion.	Sixth	26	35
(Second Half)		Third	36	29
1958—Missoula	Pion.	Fourth	34	29
(Second Half)		Third	36	30
1959—Fox Cities	Three-I	Seventh	26	39
(Second Half)		Fourth	33	28
1960—Wilson	Carol.	Third	36	34
(Second Half)		Second	37	31
1961—Wilson	Carol.	First	41	28
(Second Half)		First	42	28
1962—Vancouver	P. C.	Seventh	72	79
1963—Dallas-Ft. W	P. C.	Third(S)	79	79
1964—Atlanta‡	Int.	Eighth	19	42
1968—H. Pt.-Thom.	Carol.	§Second(W)	69	71

Year Club	League	Position	W.	L.
1969—Omaha	A. A.	First	85	55
1970—Omaha	A. A.	xFirst(E)	73	65
1971—Omaha	A. A.	Third(E)	69	70
1972—Omaha	A. A.	Second (E)	71	69
1973—Kansas City	Amer.	Second(W)	88	74
1974—Kansas City	Amer.	Fifth(W)	77	85
1975—Kansas City y	Amer.	Second(W)	50	46
1976—Richmond	Int.	Fourth	69	71
1977—Oakland z	Amer.	aFifth(W)	26	27
1978—Oakland b	Amer.	Fourth(W)	45	78
1980—Denver	A. A.	Third	62	73
1988—San Diego c	Nat.	Third(W)	67	48
American League Totals—5 Years			286	310
National League Totals—1 Year			67	48
Major League Totals—6 Years			353	358

†Replaced Aaron Robinson on June 11, 1955, and replaced by John Sanford on August 6, 1955 because of hand injury with team tied for first (record is for full season).
‡Replaced by Peter Appleton, June 21, 1964.
§Defeated Greensboro, one game to none in quarterfinals; defeated Lynchburg, two games to none in semifinals; and defeated Raleigh-Durham, two games to one for championship.
xDefeated Denver, four games to one for championship; lost Junior World Series to Syracuse, four games to one.
yReplaced by Whitey Herzog, July 24, 1975.
zReplaced by Bobby Winkles, June 10, 1977.
aTied for position with Kansas City Royals.
bReplaced Bobby Winkles with club in first place (record of 24-15), May 23, 1978.
cReplaced Larry Bowa with club in fifth place (record of 16-30), May 28, 1988.
Managed Sampson Air Force Base team to Air Force Championship, 1951.
Scout, Minnesota Twins, 1965 through 1967; coach, Oakland A's, beginning of 1978 season through May 22, 1978; scout and Assistant to General Manager, San Diego Padres, 1980; and Vice-President of Baseball Operations, San Diego Padres, 1981 through 1988.

JOSEPH MICHAEL MORGAN
(Joe)
Boston Red Sox

Born November 19, 1930, at Walpole, Mass.
Height, 5.10. Weight, 180.
Threw and batted lefthanded.
Received bachelor of science degree in history and government from Boston College, Chestnut Hill, Mass., in 1953.

Named International League Player of the Year, 1964.

Year Club	League	Pos.	G.	AB.	R.	H.	2B.	3B.	HR.	RBI.	B.A.	PO.	A.	E.	F.A.
1952—Hartford	East.	SS-3B	72	258	23	59	6	0	3	18	.228	141	237	22	.945
1953—Evansville†	I.I.I.	SS	78	301	53	74	10	5	4	29	.246	157	228	24	.941
1954-55—‡		(In U. S. Army)													

Year Club	League	Pos.	G.	AB.	R.	H.	2B.	3B.	HR.	RBI.	B.A.	PO.	A.	E.	F.A.
1956—Jacksonville	S. Atl.	SS	132	476	85	143	24	8	9	45	.300	209	421	37	.945
1957—Atlanta	S. A.	SS	149	551	111	174	31	8	12	77	.316	278	446	29	.961
1958—Wichita	A. A.	3B-SS	133	442	60	111	22	4	11	49	.251	120	271	23	.944
1959—Milwaukee	Nat.	2B	13	23	2	5	1	0	0	1	.217	9	12	2	.913
1959—Louisville§	A. A.	OF-3B	82	305	54	96	26	6	8	47	.315	134	22	5	.969
1959—Kansas City	Amer.	3B	20	21	2	4	0	1	0	3	.190	1	2	0	1.000
1960—Louisville x	A. A.	3B	55	174	35	49	5	2	4	29	.282	39	96	4	.971
1960—Philadelphia y	Nat.	3B	26	83	5	11	2	2	0	2	.133	24	42	2	.971
1960—Cleveland	Amer.	3B-OF	22	47	6	14	2	0	2	4	.298	11	22	4	.892
1961—Cleveland z	Amer.	OF	4	10	0	2	0	0	0	0	.200	6	0	0	1.000
1961—Charleston	Int.	3B	118	405	59	117	21	2	8	46	.289	79	184	15	.946
1962—Atlanta	Int.	3B-OF	142	474	70	132	15	4	16	70	.278	183	105	15	.950
1963—Atlanta	Int.	1B-OF-3B	131	406	61	114	12	3	12	70	.281	507	101	12	.981
1964—Jacksonville	Int.	3B-1B	143	476	77	138	24	4	16	66	.290	283	220	19	.964
1964—St. Louis	Nat.	PH	3	3	0	0	0	0	0	0	.000	0	0	0	.000
1965—J'cks'nv'lle abcde	Int.	3B-OF	93	270	31	56	8	2	5	24	.207	81	71	7	.956
1966—Raleigh	Carol.	3B	112	331	48	90	10	3	9	62	.272	66	169	10	.959
National League Totals—3 Years			42	109	7	16	3	2	0	3	.147	33	54	4	.956
American League Totals—3 Years			46	78	8	20	2	1	2	7	.256	18	24	4	.913
Major League Totals—4 Years			88	187	15	36	5	3	2	10	.193	51	78	8	.942

Signed as free agent by Boston Braves' organization, June 20, 1952.
†On restricted list, February 5 to June 12, 1953.
‡On National Defense Service list, November 17, 1953 through December 2, 1955.
§Sold to Kansas City A's, August 20, 1959; returned to Milwaukee Braves, April 15, 1960.
xTraded to Philadelphia Phillies for Shortstop Alvin Dark, June 23, 1960.
ySold to Cleveland Indians, August 9, 1960.
zTraded with cash and a player to be named later to St. Louis Cardinals for Outfielder Bob Nieman, May 10, 1961; St. Louis acquired Pitcher Mike Lee to complete deal, September 25, 1961.
aOn disabled list, April 17 to July 27, 1965.
bNon-player-coach, July 9 to July 16, 1965.
cPlayer-coach, July 17, 1965 through remainder of season.
dOn temporary inactive list, August 20, 1965 through remainder of season.
eReleased, January 11, 1966; signed by Raleigh (Pittsburgh Pirates' organization) as a player-manager, January 12, 1966.

RECORD OF MANAGER

Named Minor League Manager of the Year by THE SPORTING NEWS, 1973.
Named International League Manager of the Year, 1973 and 1977.
Named Eastern League Manager of the Year, 1969.
Named Carolina League Manager of the Year, 1966.

Year Club	League	Position	W.	L.
1966—Raleigh	Carol.	Third (W)	71	66
1967—Raleigh	Carol.	†First(E)	77	65
1968—York	East.	Fifth	58	82
1969—York	East.	‡First	89	50
1970—Columbus	Int.	§Second	81	59
1971—Charleston	Int.	xThird	78	62
1973—Charleston	Int.	yFirst(N)	85	60
1974—Pawtucket	Int.	Fourth(N)	57	87
1975—Pawtucket	Int.	Eighth	53	87
1976—Pawtucket	Int.	Fifth	68	70
1977—Pawtucket	Int.	zFirst	80	60
1978—Pawtucket	Int.	aSecond	81	59
1979—Pawtucket	Int.	Fifth	66	74
1980—Pawtucket	Int.	Seventh	62	77
1981—Pawtucket	Int.	Sixth	67	73
1982—Pawtucket	Int.	Fifth	67	71
1988—Boston b	Amer.	First(E)	46	31
Major League Totals—1 Year			46	31

†Defeated Rocky Mount, one game to none in quarterfinals, and lost to Tidewater, two games to none in semifinals.
‡Losing to Pittsfield, one game to none in semifinals when playoffs were cancelled.
§Defeated Rochester, three games to two in semifinals, and lost to Syrcause, three games to one for championship.
xLost to Tidewater, three games to none in semifinals.
yDefeated Rochester, three games to none for championship, and lost to Pawtucket, three games to two for Governor's Cup.
zDefeated Richmond, three games to one in semifinals, and lost to Charleston, four games to none in Governor's Cup.
aDefeated Toledo, three games to two in semifinals, and lost to Richmond, four games to three for Governor's Cup.
bReplaced John McNamara with club in fourth place (record of 43-42), July 14, 1988.
Scout, Boston Red Sox, 1983 and 1984.
Coach, Pittsburgh Pirates, 1972; coach, Boston Red Sox, 1985 through July 13, 1988.

CHAMPIONSHIP SERIES RECORD

Year Club	League	W.	L.
1988—Boston	American	0	4

RUSSELL EUGENE NIXON
(Russ)
Atlanta Braves

Born February 19, 1935, at Cleves, O.
Height, 6.01. Weight, 185.
Threw right and batted lefthanded.
Attended University of Cincinnati, Cincinnati, O.
Twin brother of Roy Nixon, first baseman in Cleveland Indians' organization, 1953 through 1957.
Led Florida State League catchers in double plays with 14 and passed balls with 23 in 1954.

Year	Club	League	Pos.	G.	AB.	R.	H.	2B.	3B.	HR.	RBI.	B.A.	PO.	A.	E.	F.A.
1953	—Green Bay	Wis. St.	C-OF	43	137	17	46	6	5	0	30	.336	213	22	6	.975
1954	—Jack'ville Beach	Fla. St.	C	125	465	114	180	★36	12	6	96	★.387	★821	★95	22	.977
1955	—Keokuk	I.I.I.	C	94	358	66	138	29	2	5	77	★.385	★718	47	10	●.987
1956	—Indianapolis	A. A.	C	105	320	38	102	19	5	4	44	.319	402	37	9	.980
1957	—Cleveland	Amer.	C	62	185	15	52	7	1	2	18	.281	268	31	5	.984
1958	—Cleveland	Amer.	C	113	376	42	113	17	4	9	46	.301	499	31	5	.991
1959	—Cleveland	Amer.	C	82	258	23	62	10	3	1	29	.240	374	31	6	.985
1960	—Clev.†-Boston	Amer.	C	105	354	30	101	22	3	6	39	.285	488	34	6	.989
1961	—Boston	Amer.	C	87	242	24	70	12	2	1	19	.289	330	21	9	.975
1962	—Boston‡	Amer.	C	65	151	11	42	7	2	1	19	.278	201	7	0	1.000
1963	—Boston	Amer.	C	98	287	27	77	18	1	5	30	.268	483	22	4	.992
1964	—Boston	Amer.	C	81	163	10	38	7	0	1	20	.233	273	11	3	.990
1965	—Boston	Amer.	C	59	137	11	37	5	1	0	11	.270	200	10	4	.981
1965	—Toronto§	Int.	C	31	93	10	30	3	2	0	14	.323	195	11	3	.986
1966	—Minnesota	Amer.	C	51	90	5	25	2	1	0	7	.260	137	5	2	.986
1967	—Minnesota x	Amer.	C	74	170	16	40	6	1	1	22	.235	306	26	2	.994
1968	—Pittsfield y	East.	C-OF	41	137	15	29	3	2	0	13	.212	214	23	3	.988
1968	—Boston za	Amer.	C	29	85	1	13	2	0	0	6	.153	147	6	1	.994
Major League Totals—12 Years				906	2504	215	670	115	19	27	266	.268	3708	238	47	.988

Signed as free agent by Cleveland Indians' organization, June 18, 1953.

†Traded with Outfielder Carroll Hardy to Boston Red Sox for Pitcher Ted Bowsfield and Outfielder Marty Keough, June 13, 1960. (Indians had traded Nixon to Red Sox for First Baseman Jim Marshall and Catcher Stan White, March 16, 1960, but deal was cancelled by Commissioner Ford Frick on March 25 because of White's request for voluntary retirement.)

‡On disabled list, May 20 to June 20, 1962.

§Traded with Infielder Chuck Schilling to Minnesota Twins for Pitcher Dick Stigman and a player to be named later, April 6, 1966; Boston Red Sox acquired First Baseman Jose Calero to complete deal, April 17, 1966.

xReleased, April 8, 1968; signed as free agent by Pittsfield (Boston Red Sox' organization), April 8, 1968.

yOn disabled list, June 25 to July 16, 1968.

zDrafted by Chicago White Sox, December 2, 1968.

aReleased, April 5, 1969.

RECORD AS MANAGER

Year	Club	League	Position	W.	L.
1970	—Sioux Falls	North.	Sixth	24	46
1971	—Tampa	Fla. St.	Second(W)	79	61
1972	—Tampa	Fla. St.	Second(W)	66	64
1973	—Tampa	Fla. St.	Fourth(N)	73	71
1974	—Tampa	Fla. St.	†First(N)	68	64
1975	—Tampa	Fla. St.	Second(N)	72	59
1982	—Cincinnati‡	Nat.	Sixth(W)	27	43
1983	—Cincinnati	Nat.	Sixth(W)	74	88
1988	—Greenville	South.	First§	22	21
1988	—Atlanta x	Nat.	Sixth(W)	42	79
Major League Totals—3 Years				143	210

†Lost to West Palm Beach, two games to none in semifinals.

‡Replaced John McNamara with club in sixth place (record of 34-58), July 21, 1982.

§Tied for position.

xReplaced Chuck Tanner with club in sixth place (record of 12-27), May 22, 1988.

Coach, Cincinnati Reds' organization, April 15 to June 1, 1970; coach, Cincinnati Reds, 1976 through July 20, 1982; coach, Montreal Expos, 1984; coach, Pittsburgh Pirates, 1985; coach, Atlanta Braves, 1986 and 1987.

DOUGLAS LEE RADER
(Doug)
California Angels

Born July 30, 1944, at Chicago, Ill.
Height, 6.03. Weight, 230.
Threw and batted righthanded.
Attended Illinois Wesleyan University, Bloomington, Ill.

Led National League third basemen in total chances with 479 in 1972.

Led National League third basemen in putouts with 147 in 1970.

Led National League third basemen in double plays with 39 in 1970 and tied for lead with 31 in 1972.

Named third baseman on The Sporting News National League All-Star fielding team, 1970 through 1973.

Received reported $25,000 bonus to sign with Houston Astros, 1964.

Year	Club	League	Pos.	G.	AB.	R.	H.	2B.	3B.	HR.	RBI.	B.A.	PO.	A.	E.	F.A.
1965	—Durham	Carol.	3B-OF	112	330	44	69	14	1	14	38	.209	111	185	21	.934
1966	—Amarillo	Texas	3B	138	527	85	★153	21	12	16	74	.290	102	240	27	.927
1967	—Oklahoma City	P. C.	3B	75	273	40	80	23	5	9	44	.293	47	110	12	.929
1967	—Houston	Nat.	1B-3B	47	162	24	54	10	4	2	26	.333	270	33	8	.974
1968	—Houston	Nat.	3B-1B	98	333	42	89	16	4	6	43	.267	130	171	22	.932
1969	—Houston	Nat.	3B-1B	155	569	62	140	25	3	11	83	.246	140	307	26	.945
1970	—Houston	Nat.	★3B-1B	156	576	90	145	25	3	25	87	.252	149	★357	18	★.966
1971	—Houston	Nat.	3B	135	484	51	118	21	4	12	56	.244	93	275	●21	.946
1972	—Houston	Nat.	3B	152	533	70	131	24	7	22	90	.237	119	★340	20	.958
1973	—Houston	Nat.	3B	154	574	79	146	26	0	21	89	.254	★134	296	★25	.945
1974	—Houston	Nat.	3B	152	533	61	137	27	3	17	78	.257	128	347	17	.965
1975	—Houston†	Nat.	★3B-SS	129	448	41	100	23	2	12	48	.223	114	259	11	★.971
1976	—San Diego	Nat.	3B	139	471	45	121	22	4	9	55	.257	109	318	20	.955
1977	—San Diego‡	Nat.	3B	52	170	19	46	8	3	5	27	.271	43	104	6	.961
1977	—Toronto§	Amer.	3B-1B-OF	96	313	47	75	18	2	13	40	.240	97	106	7	.967
National League Totals—11 Years				1369	4873	584	1227	227	37	142	682	.252	1429	2807	194	.956
American League Totals—1 Year				96	313	47	75	18	2	13	40	.240	97	106	7	.967
Major League Totals—11 Years				1465	5186	631	1302	245	39	155	722	.251	1526	2913	201	.957

Signed as free agent by Houston Colt .45s' organization, September 13, 1964.
†Traded to San Diego Padres for Pitchers Joe McIntosh and Larry Hardy, December 11, 1975.
‡Sold to Toronto Blue Jays, June 8, 1977.
§Released, March 18, 1978.

RECORD AS MANAGER

Year	Club	League	Position	W.	L.
1980	Hawaii	P. C.	First(N)	40	25
	(Second Half)		Third(N)	36	40
1981	Hawaii	P. C.	First(N)	35	31
	(Second Half)		Third(N)	37	34
1982	Hawaii	P. C.	Second(S)	36	35
	(Second Half)		Third(S)	37	36
1983	Texas	Amer.	Third(W)	77	85
1984	Texas	Amer.	Seventh(W)	69	92
1985	Texas†	Amer.	Seventh(W)	9	23
1986	Chicago‡	Amer.	Fifth(W)	1	1
Major League Totals—4 Years				156	201

†Replaced by Bobby Valentine, May 16, 1985.
‡Served as interim manager, June 20 and June 21, 1986 before Jim Fregosi replaced Tony LaRussa, June 22, 1986.
Coach, San Diego Padres, 1979; Coach, Chicago White Sox, 1986 and 1987; scout, California Angels, 1988.

FRANK ROBINSON
Baltimore Orioles

Born August 31, 1935, at Beaumont, Tex.
Height, 6.01. Weight, 194.
Threw and batted righthanded.
Attended Xavier University, Cincinnati, O.

Established major league record for most consecutive seasons leading league, intentional bases on balls (4), 1961 through 1964 (tied in 1962).

Established modern major league record for most times hit by pitch, rookie season (20), 1956.

Tied major league records for most home runs, bases filled, game (2), June 26, 1970; most home runs, bases filled, two successive at bats (2), June 26, 1970; most runs batted in, two successive innings (8), June 26, 1970 (fifth and sixth innings); fewest putouts, first baseman, game (0), July 1, 1971; most home runs, rookie season (38), 1956; most years leading league, intentional bases on balls, since 1955 (4).

Hit three home runs in a game, August 22, 1959.

Hit for the cycle, May 2, 1959.

Won American League Triple Crown, 1966.

Led National League in slugging percentage with .595 in 1960, .611 in 1961 and .624 in 1962.

Led American League in total bases with 367 and in slugging percentage with .637 in 1966.

Led American League in being hit by pitch with 13 in 1969.

Led National League in being hit by pitch with 20 in 1956, 8 in 1959, 9 in 1960, 11 in 1962, 14 in 1963 and 18 in 1965.

Led National League in intentional bases on balls received with 23 in 1961, 20 in 1963, 20 in 1964 and tied for lead with 16 in 1962.

Led National League in sacrifice flies with 10 in 1961.

Led National League first basemen in double plays with 111 in 1959.

Tied for American League lead in sacrifice flies with 7 in 1966.

Named Major League Player of the Year by THE SPORTING NEWS, 1966.

Named American League Player of the Year by THE SPORTING NEWS, 1966.

Named American League Most Valuable Player by Baseball Writers' Association of America, 1966.

Named National League Player of the Year by THE SPORTING NEWS, 1961.

Named National League Most Valuable Player by Baseball Writers' Association of America, 1961.

Named National League Rookie of the Year by THE SPORTING NEWS, 1956.

Named National League Rookie of the Year by Baseball Writers' Association of America, 1956.

Named outfielder on THE SPORTING NEWS American League All-Star Team, 1966 and 1967.

Named outfielder on THE SPORTING NEWS National League All-Star Team, 1961 and 1962.

Named outfielder on THE SPORTING NEWS National League All-Star fielding team, 1958.

Elected to Hall of Fame, 1982.

Year	Club	League	Pos.	G.	AB.	R.	H.	2B.	3B.	HR.	RBI.	B.A.	PO.	A.	E.	F.A.
1953	Ogden	Pion.	OF-3B-1B	72	270	70	94	20	6	17	83	.348	105	28	18	.881
1954	Tulsa	Texas	2B-3B	8	30	4	8	0	0	0	1	.267	17	15	1	.970
1954	Columbia	Sally	OF-3B-2B	132	491	★112	165	32	9	25	110	.336	258	63	18	.947
1955	Columbia	Sally	OF-1B	80	243	50	64	15	7	12	52	.263	203	3	4	.981
1956	Cincinnati	Nat.	OF	152	572	★122	166	27	6	38	83	.290	323	5	8	.976
1957	Cincinnati	Nat.	OF-1B	150	611	97	197	29	5	29	75	.322	487	36	6	.989
1958	Cincinnati	Nat.	OF-3B	148	554	90	149	25	6	31	83	.269	314	24	6	.983
1959	Cincinnati	Nat.	1B-OF	146	540	106	168	31	4	36	125	.311	1049	78	18	.984
1960	Cincinnati	Nat.	1B-OF-3B	139	464	86	138	33	6	31	83	.297	775	62	10	.988
1961	Cincinnati	Nat.	OF-3B	153	545	117	176	32	7	37	124	.323	284	15	3	.990
1962	Cincinnati	Nat.	OF	162	609	★134	208	★51	2	39	136	.342	315	10	2	.994
1963	Cincinnati	Nat.	OF-1B	140	482	79	125	19	3	21	91	.259	238	13	4	.984
1964	Cincinnati	Nat.	OF	156	568	103	174	38	6	29	96	.306	279	7	4	.986
1965	Cincinnati†	Nat.	OF	156	582	109	172	33	5	33	113	.296	282	5	3	.990
1966	Baltimore	Amer.	OF-1B	155	576	★122	182	34	2	★49	★122	★.316	282	6	5	.983
1967	Baltimore	Amer.	OF-1B	129	479	83	149	23	7	30	94	.311	207	8	2	.991
1968	Baltimore	Amer.	OF-1B	130	421	69	113	27	1	15	52	.268	193	5	7	.966
1969	Baltimore	Amer.	OF-1B	148	539	111	166	19	5	32	100	.308	367	19	5	.987
1970	Baltimore	Amer.	OF-1B	132	471	88	144	24	1	25	78	.306	262	11	4	.986
1971	Baltimore‡	Amer.	OF-1B	133	455	82	128	16	2	28	99	.281	449	20	11	.977
1972	Los Angeles§	Nat.	OF	103	342	41	86	6	1	19	59	.251	168	6	6	.967
1973	California	Amer.	OF	147	534	85	142	29	0	30	97	.266	38	3	1	.976
1974	Calif. x-Cleve.	Amer.	1B-OF	144	477	81	117	27	3	22	68	.245	23	0	1	.958
1975	Cleveland yz	Amer.	DH-PH	49	118	19	28	5	0	9	24	.237	0	0	0	.000

Year	Club	League	Pos.	G.	AB.	R.	H.	2B.	3B.	HR.	RBI.	B.A.	PO.	A.	E.	F.A.
1976	—Cleveland yab	Amer.	1B-OF	36	67	5	15	0	0	3	10	.224	11	0	0	1.000
National League Totals—11 Years				1605	5869	1084	1759	324	51	343	1068	.300	4514	261	70	.986
American League Totals—10 Years				1203	4137	745	1184	204	21	243	744	.286	1832	72	36	.981
Major League Totals—21 Years				2808	10006	1829	2943	528	72	586	1812	.294	6346	333	106	.984

†Traded to Baltimore Orioles for Outfielder Dick Simpson and Pitchers Milt Pappas and Jack Baldschun, December 9, 1965.

‡Traded with Pitcher Pete Richert to Los Angeles Dodgers for Pitchers Doyle Alexander and Bob O'Brien, Catcher Sergio Robles and First Baseman-Outfielder Royle Stillman, December 2, 1971.

§Traded with Infielders Billy Grabarkewitz and Bob Valentine and Pitchers Bill Singer and Mike Strahler to California Angels for Third Baseman Ken McMullen and Pitcher Andy Messersmith, November 28, 1972.

xReleased on waivers to Cleveland Indians, September 12, 1974; Indians assigned Outfielder Rusty Torres and Catcher Ken Suarez to Angels, December 4, 1974, to complete deal.

yPlayer-manager.

zOn disabled list, July 4 to July 23, 1975.

aOn disabled list, April 4 to April 26, 1976.

bReleased October 5, 1976.

CHAMPIONSHIP SERIES RECORD

Tied Championship Series records for hitting home run in first Championship Series at bat, October 4, 1969; most at bats, inning (2), October 3, 1970 (fourth inning).

Year	Club	League	Pos.	G.	AB.	R.	H.	2B.	3B.	HR.	RBI.	B.A.	PO.	A.	E.	F.A.
1969	—Baltimore	Amer.	OF	3	12	1	4	2	0	1	2	.333	2	0	1	.667
1970	—Baltimore	Amer.	OF	3	10	3	2	0	0	1	2	.200	2	0	0	1.000
1971	—Baltimore	Amer.	OF	3	12	2	1	1	0	0	1	.083	7	0	0	1.000
Championship Series Totals—3 Years				9	34	6	7	3	0	2	5	.206	11	0	1	.917

WORLD SERIES RECORD

Tied World Series record for most times hit by pitcher, game (2), October 8, 1961; most times hit by pitch, total Series (3); most times home run won 1-0 game (1), October 9, 1966; most putouts and chances accepted game by right fielder (7), October 14, 1969.

Year	Club	League	Pos.	G.	AB.	R.	H.	2B.	3B.	HR.	RBI.	B.A.	PO.	A.	E.	F.A.
1961	—Cincinnati	Nat.	OF	5	15	3	3	2	0	1	4	.200	5	0	0	1.000
1966	—Baltimore	Amer.	OF	4	14	4	4	0	1	2	3	.286	6	0	0	1.000
1969	—Baltimore	Amer.	OF	5	16	2	3	0	0	1	1	.188	13	0	0	1.000
1970	—Baltimore	Amer.	OF	5	22	5	6	0	0	2	4	.273	7	0	0	1.000
1971	—Baltimore	Amer.	OF	7	25	5	7	0	0	2	2	.280	12	0	0	1.000
World Series Totals—5 Years				26	92	19	23	2	1	8	14	.250	43	0	0	1.000

ALL-STAR GAME RECORD

Year	League	Pos.	AB.	R.	H.	2B.	3B.	HR.	RBI.	B.A.	PO.	A.	E.	F.A.
1956	—National	OF	2	0	0	0	0	0	0	.000	1	0	0	1.000
1957	—National	OF	2	0	1	0	0	0	0	.500	5	0	0	1.000
1959	—National (second game)	1B	3	1	3	0	0	1	1	1.000	3	0	1	.750
1961	—National (first game)	OF	1	0	1	0	0	0	0	1.000	2	0	0	1.000
1962	—National (second game)	OF	3	0	0	0	0	0	0	.000	1	0	0	1.000
1965	—National	PH	1	0	0	0	0	0	0	.000	0	0	0	.000
1966	—American	OF	4	0	0	0	0	0	0	.000	2	0	0	1.000
1969	—American	OF	2	0	0	0	0	0	0	.000	0	0	0	.000
1970	—American	OF	3	0	0	0	0	0	0	.000	1	0	0	1.000
1971	—American	OF	2	1	1	0	0	1	2	.500	2	0	0	1.000
1974	—American	PH	1	0	0	0	0	0	0	.000	0	0	0	.000
All-Star Game Totals—11 Years			24	2	6	0	0	2	3	.250	17	0	1	.944

Member of National League All-Star Team in 1959 (first game) and 1961 (second game); did not play.

Named to American League Team for 1967 game; replaced due to injury.

RECORD AS MANAGER

Year	Club	League	Position	W.	L.
1975	—Cleveland	Amer.	Fourth(E)	79	80
1976	—Cleveland	Amer.	Fourth(E)	81	78
1977	—Cleveland†	Amer.	Sixth(E)	26	31
1978	—Rochester‡	Int.	Sixth	58	64
1981	—San Francisco§	Nat.		56	55
1982	—San Francisco	Nat.	Third(W)	87	75
1983	—San Francisco	Nat.	Fifth(W)	79	83
1984	—San Francisco x	Nat.	Sixth(W)	42	64
1988	—Baltimore y	Amer.	Seventh(E)	54	101
National League Totals—4 Years				264	277
American League Totals—4 Years				240	290
Major League Totals—8 Years				504	567

†Replaced by Jeff Torborg, June 19, 1977.

‡Replaced interim manager Al Widmar (replacing Ken Boyer), May 8, 1978.

§First Half . . . Fifth (W) (record of 27-32); Second Half . . . Third (W) (record of 29-23).

xReplaced by interim manager Danny Ozark, August 5, 1984.

yReplaced Cal Ripken with club in seventh place (record of 0-6), April 12, 1988.

Coach, California Angels, July 11 through remainder of 1977 season; Coach, Baltimore Orioles, beginning of 1978 season through May 8, 1978, 1979, 1980 and 1985 through 1987; and Special Assistant to the President, Baltimore Orioles, beginning of 1988 through April 11, 1988.

Coach, American League All-Star Team, 1980.

ROBERT LEROY RODGERS
(Bob or Buck)
Montreal Expos

Born August 16, 1938, at Delaware, O.
Height, 6.01. Weight, 190.
Threw right and batted left and righthanded.
Attended Ohio Wesleyan University, Delaware, O., and Ohio Northern University, Ada, O.

Established American League record for most games, by catcher, rookie season (150), 1962.
Tied American League record for fewest assists by catcher, season, 150 or more games (73), 1962.
Major League stolen bases: 1962 (1), 1963 (2), 1964 (4), 1965 (4), 1966 (3), 1967 (1), 1968 (2). Total—17.
Led American League catchers in double plays with 14 in 1962 and 14 in 1964.

Year Club	League	Pos.	G.	AB.	R.	H.	2B.	3B.	HR.	RBI.	B.A.	PO.	A.	E.	F.A.
1956—Jamestown	Pony	OF	48	153	28	36	8	1	6	26	.235	43	6	3	.942
1957—Erie	NYP	*C-OF	114	430	79	127	26	4	12	80	.295	568	*77	*25	.963
1958—Lancaster	East.	C	19	63	8	16	3	0	3	8	.254	111	11	2	.984
1958—Idaho Falls	Pion.	*C-OF	99	378	73	115	15	6	12	74	.304	524	45	*20	.966
1959—Birmingham	South.	C	3	13	1	1	0	1	0	2	.077	28	0	1	.966
1959—Knoxville	Sally	*C-OF	105	355	53	102	18	6	7	55	.287	565	60	*13	.980
1960—Denver	A. A.	C	23	84	12	20	7	1	3	12	.238	127	15	4	.973
1960—Birmingham	South.	C	93	313	36	77	14	1	5	38	.246	456	*68	7	.987
1961—Dallas-Ft. W.†	A. A.	C	124	427	55	122	22	3	3	62	.286	*595	*70	11	.984
1961—Los Angeles	Amer.	C	16	56	8	18	2	0	2	13	.321	71	11	3	.965
1962—Los Angeles	Amer.	C	155	565	65	146	34	6	6	61	.258	826	73	●10	.989
1963—Los Angeles	Amer.	C	100	300	24	70	6	0	4	23	.233	416	48	*10	.979
1964—Los Angeles	Amer.	C	148	514	38	125	18	3	4	54	.243	884	*87	*13	.987
1965—California	Amer.	C	132	411	33	86	14	3	1	32	.209	682	52	7	.991
1966—California	Amer.	C	133	454	45	107	20	3	7	48	.236	662	*69	6	.992
1967—California	Amer.	*C-OF	139	429	29	94	13	3	6	41	.219	728	*73	7	.991
1968—California	Amer.	C	91	258	13	49	6	0	1	14	.190	407	50	7	.985
1969—Hawaii	P. C.	C-3B	44	145	15	37	5	0	0	12	.255	215	26	4	.984
1969—California	Amer.	C	18	49	4	9	1	0	0	2	.196	74	9	0	1.000
1975—Salinas‡	Calif.	PH	4	3	1	1	0	0	0	0	.333	0	0	0	.000
1977—El Paso§	Texas	PH	1	0	0	0	0	0	0	0	.000	0	0	0	.000
Major League Totals—9 Years			932	3033	259	704	114	18	31	288	.232	4750	472	63	.988

†Selected by Los Angeles Angels from Detroit Tigers in American League expansion draft, December 14, 1960.
‡Player-manager, August 24 through September 15, 1975.
§Player-manager, July 15 through August 14, 1977.

RECORD AS MANAGER

Named National League Manager of the Year by THE SPORTING NEWS, 1987.
Named Minor League Manager of the Year by THE SPORTING NEWS, 1984.
Named American Association Manager of the Year, 1984.
Named Texas League Manager of the Year, 1977.

Year Club	League	Position	W.	L.
1975—Salinas	Calif.	Fifth	35	35
(Second Half)		Sixth	32	38
1977—El Paso	Texas	First(W)	38	24
(Second Half)		†First(W)	40	28
1980—Milwaukee‡	Amer.	Third(E)	39	31
1981—Milwaukee§	Amer.		62	47
1982—Milwaukee x	Amer.	yFifth(E)	23	24
1984—Indianapolis	A. A.	zFirst	91	63

Year Club	League	Position	W.	L.
1985—Montreal	Nat.	Third(E)	84	77
1986—Montreal	Nat.	Fourth(E)	78	83
1987—Montreal	Nat.	Third(E)	91	71
1988—Montreal	Nat.	Third(E)	81	81
American League Totals—3 Years			124	102
National League Totals—4 Years			334	312
Major League Totals—7 Years			458	414

†Lost league championship to Arkansas, two games to none.
‡Began season as interim manager for ill George Bamberger who returned June 6, 1980, with club in second place (record of 26-21); named manager when Bamberger retired with club tied for fourth place (record of 73-66), September 7, 1980.
§First Half . . . Third (E) (record of 31-25); Second Half . . . First (E) (record of 31-22).
xReplaced by Harvey Kuenn, June 2, 1982.
yTied for position with Baltimore Orioles.
zLost semifinal playoff series to Louisville, four games to two.
Coach, National League All-Star Team, 1988.
Coach, Minnesota Twins, 1970 through 1974; San Francisco Giants, 1976; Milwaukee Brewers, 1978 through 1980.

DIVISION SERIES RECORD

Year Club	League	W.	L.
1981—Milwaukee	American	2	3

PETER EDWARD ROSE
(Pete)
Cincinnati Reds

Born April 14, 1941, at Cincinnati, O.
Height, 5.11. Weight, 203.
Threw right and batted right and lefthanded.
Brother of David Rose, pitcher in Cincinnati Reds' organization, 1967 and 1968; and father of Pete Rose II, infielder in Baltimore Orioles' organization.

Established major league records for most games, lifetime (3,562); most singles, lifetime (3,215); most seasons and most consecutive seasons, 100 or more games (23); most seasons, 200 or more hits (10); most seasons, 150 or more games (17); most at-bats, lifetime (14,053); most plate appearances, lifetime (15,890); most consecutive seasons, 600 or more at-bats (13); most seasons, 600 or more at-bats (17); most plate appearances, season (771), 1974; most hits, lifetime (4,256); most doubles by switch-hitter, season (51), 1978.

Tied major league records for most consecutive seasons leading major leagues in runs scored (3); fewest sacrifice flies, season, most at-bats (0 and 680), 1973; most hits by switch-hitter, season (230), 1973; most games, first baseman, season (162), 1980 and 1982; most stolen bases, inning (3), May 11, 1980, seventh inning.

Established National League records for most years and most consecutive years played (24); most years playing in all clubs' games (10); most runs, lifetime (2,165); most seasons leading league, hits (7); most doubles, lifetime (746); most singles by switch-hitter, season (181), 1973; fewest stolen bases, season, most at-bats (0 and 662), 1975; most times five or more hits in one game, lifetime (10).

Tied National League records for most consecutive games, one or more hits, season (44), 1978; most seasons leading league in at-bats (4).

Established modern National League record for most 20-game hitting streaks, lifetime (7).

Tied modern National League records for most seasons leading league in fielding percentage by outfielder, 100 or more games (3); most consecutive years leading league in fielding percentage by outfielder, 100 or more games (2).

Major League stolen bases: 1963 (13), 1964 (4), 1965 (8), 1966 (4), 1967 (11), 1968 (3), 1969 (7), 1970 (12), 1971 (13), 1972 (10), 1973 (10), 1974 (2), 1976 (9), 1977 (16), 1978 (13), 1979 (20), 1980 (12), 1981 (4), 1982 (8), 1983 (7), 1984 (1), 1985 (8), 1986 (3). Total—198.

Hit three home runs in a game, April 29, 1978.

Switch-hit home runs in one game two times: August 30, 1966 and August 2, 1967.

Tied for National League lead in being hit by pitch with 6 in 1980.

Led Florida State League in total bases with 246 in 1961.

Named Player of the Decade for 1970-79 by The Sporting News.

Named Man of the Year by The Sporting News, 1985.

Named National League Player of the Year by The Sporting News, 1968.

Named National League Most Valuable Player by Baseball Writers' Association of America, 1973.

Named National League Rookie Player of the Year by The Sporting News, 1963.

Named National League Rookie of the Year by Baseball Writers' Association of America, 1963.

Named first baseman on The Sporting News National League All-Star Team, 1981.

Named third baseman on The Sporting News National League All-Star Team, 1978.

Named outfielder on The Sporting News National League All-Star Team, 1968 and 1973.

Named second baseman on The Sporting News National League All-Star Team, 1965 and 1966.

Named outfielder on The Sporting News National League All-Star fielding team, 1969 and 1970.

Named first baseman on The Sporting News National League Silver Slugger team, 1981.

Year Club	League	Pos.	G.	AB.	R.	H.	2B.	3B.	HR.	RBI.	B.A.	PO.	A.	E.	F.A.
1960—Geneva	NYP	2B	85	321	60	89	8	5	1	43	.277	198	193	*36	.916
1961—Tampa	Fla. St.	2B	130	484	105	*160	20	*30	2	77	.331	256	294	21	.963
1962—Macon	Sally	2B	139	540	*136	178	31	*17	9	71	.330	317	368	24	.966
1963—Cincinnati†	Nat.	2B-OF	157	623	101	170	25	9	6	41	.273	360	366	22	.971
1964—Cincinnati	Nat.	2B	136	516	64	139	13	2	4	34	.269	263	301	12	.979
1965—Cincinnati	Nat.	2B	162	*670	117	*209	35	11	11	81	.312	*382	403	20	.975
1966—Cincinnati	Nat.	2B-3B	156	654	97	205	38	5	16	70	.313	409	374	18	.978
1967—Cincinnati	Nat.	OF-2B	148	585	86	176	32	8	12	76	.301	287	93	11	.972
1968—Cincinnati‡	Nat.	●O-2-1	149	626	94	●210	42	6	10	49	*.335	270	●20	3	.990
1969—Cincinnati	Nat.	OF-2B	156	627	●120	218	33	11	16	82	*.348	317	10	4	.988
1970—Cincinnati	Nat.	OF	159	649	120	●205	37	9	15	52	.316	309	8	1	*.997
1971—Cincinnati	Nat.	OF	160	632	86	192	27	4	13	44	.304	306	13	2	●.994
1972—Cincinnati	Nat.	OF	*154	*645	107	*198	31	11	6	57	.307	330	●15	2	.994
1973—Cincinnati	Nat.	OF	160	*680	115	*230	36	8	5	64	*.338	343	15	3	.992
1974—Cincinnati	Nat.	OF	*163	652	*110	185	*45	7	3	51	.284	346	11	1	*.997
1975—Cincinnati	Nat.	3B-OF	●162	662	*112	210	*47	4	7	74	.317	161	230	14	.965
1976—Cincinnati	Nat.	*3B-OF	162	665	*130	*215	*42	6	10	63	.323	115	293	13	*.969
1977—Cincinnati	Nat.	3B	●162	*655	95	204	38	7	9	64	.311	98	268	16	.958
1978—Cincinnati§	Nat.	3B-OF-1B	159	655	103	198	*51	3	7	52	.302	135	256	15	.963
1979—Philadelphia	Nat.	1B-3B-2B	163	628	90	208	40	5	4	59	.331	1429	93	10	.993
1980—Philadelphia	Nat.	1B	162	655	95	185	*42	1	1	64	.282	1427	*123	5	*.997
1981—Philadelphia	Nat.	1B	107	431	73	*140	18	5	0	33	.325	929	91	4	.996
1982—Philadelphia	Nat.	1B	●162	634	80	172	25	4	3	54	.271	1428	123	8	.995
1983—Philadelphia x	Nat.	1B-OF	151	493	52	121	14	3	0	45	.245	827	74	10	.989
1984—Mont. y-Cin.	Nat.	1B-OF	121	374	43	107	15	2	0	34	.286	530	53	8	.986
1985—Cincinnati	Nat.	1B	119	405	60	107	12	2	2	46	.264	870	73	5	.995
1986—Cincinnati za	Nat.	1B	72	237	15	52	8	2	0	25	.219	523	43	6	.990
Major League Totals—24 Years			3562	14053	2165	4256	746	135	160	1314	.303	12394	3349	213	.987

Signed as free agent by Cincinnati Reds' organization, July 8, 1960.

†On military list, October 1, 1963 through March 14, 1964.

‡On disabled list, July 6 to July 27, 1968.

§Granted free agency, November 2, 1978; signed by Philadelphia Phillies, December 5, 1978.

xReleased, October 19, 1983; signed by Montreal Expos, January 20, 1984.

yTraded to Cincinnati Reds for Infielder Tom Lawless, August 16, 1984.

zOn disabled list, April 3 to April 23, 1986.

aReleased as player, November 11, 1986.

DIVISION SERIES RECORD

Year Club	League	Pos.	G.	AB.	R.	H.	2B.	3B.	HR.	RBI.	B.A.	PO.	A.	E.	F.A.
1981—Philadelphia	Nat.	1B	5	20	1	6	1	0	0	2	.300	29	8	0	1.000

CHAMPIONSHIP SERIES RECORD

Established Championship Series records for most positions played, total Series (4); most consecutive games, one or more hits (15); most hits, total Series (45); most one-base hits, total Series (34); most hits, two consecutive Series (17), 1972 and 1973.

Tied Championship Series records for most times on winning club (6); most one-base hits, five-game Series (8), 1980; most two-base hits, total Series (7); most two-base hits, five-game Series (4), 1972.

Established National League Championship Series records for most games, total Series (28); most Series, played all games (7); highest batting average, total Series, 50 or more at-bats (.381); most at-bats, total Series (118); most runs, total Series (17); most total bases, total Series (63).

Tied National League Championship Series records for most Series, one or more hits (7); most total bases, five-game Series (15), 1973.

Year Club	League	Pos.	G.	AB.	R.	H.	2B.	3B.	HR.	RBI.	B.A.	PO.	A.	E.	F.A.
1970—Cincinnati	Nat.	OF	3	13	1	3	0	0	0	1	.231	3	0	0	1.000
1972—Cincinnati	Nat.	OF	5	20	1	9	4	0	0	2	.450	10	0	0	1.000
1973—Cincinnati	Nat.	OF	5	21	3	8	1	0	2	2	.381	10	1	0	1.000
1975—Cincinnati	Nat.	3B	3	14	3	5	0	0	1	2	.357	2	1	0	1.000
1976—Cincinnati	Nat.	3B	3	14	3	6	2	1	0	2	.429	2	5	1	.875
1980—Philadelphia	Nat.	1B	5	20	3	8	0	0	0	2	.400	53	7	0	1.000
1983—Philadelphia	Nat.	1B	4	16	3	6	0	0	0	0	.375	29	2	0	1.000
Championship Series Totals—7 Years			28	118	17	45	7	1	3	11	.381	109	16	1	.992

WORLD SERIES RECORD

Tied World Series records for most positions played, total Series (4); most double plays by first baseman, six-game Series (8), 1980; most double plays by first baseman, nine-inning game (4), October 15, 1980; most times awarded first base on catcher's interference, game (1), October 10, 1970; most times home run as leadoff batter in game (1), October 20, 1972.

Year Club	League	Pos.	G.	AB.	R.	H.	2B.	3B.	HR.	RBI.	B.A.	PO.	A.	E.	F.A.
1970—Cincinnati	Nat.	OF	5	20	2	5	1	0	1	2	.250	14	1	1	.938
1972—Cincinnati	Nat.	OF	7	28	3	6	0	0	1	2	.214	14	1	0	1.000
1975—Cincinnati	Nat.	3B	7	27	3	10	1	1	0	2	.370	7	9	0	1.000
1976—Cincinnati	Nat.	3B	4	16	1	3	1	0	0	1	.188	6	3	0	1.000
1980—Philadelphia	Nat.	1B	6	23	2	6	1	0	0	1	.261	49	6	0	1.000
1983—Philadelphia	Nat.	PH-1B-OF	5	16	1	5	1	0	0	1	.313	26	4	0	1.000
World Series Totals—6 Years			34	130	12	35	5	1	2	9	.269	116	24	1	.993

ALL-STAR GAME RECORD

Established All-Star Game record for most positions played, total games (5).

Year League	Pos.	AB.	R.	H.	2B.	3B.	HR.	RBI.	B.A.	PO.	A.	E.	F.A.
1965—National	2B	2	0	0	0	0	0	0	.000	2	4	0	1.000
1967—National	2B	1	0	0	0	0	0	0	.000	1	0	0	1.000
1969—National	OF	1	0	0	0	0	0	0	.000	2	0	0	1.000
1970—National	OF	3	1	1	0	0	0	0	.333	3	0	0	1.000
1971—National	OF	0	0	0	0	0	0	0	.000	0	0	0	.000
1973—National	OF	3	1	0	0	0	0	0	.000	1	0	0	1.000
1974—National	OF	2	0	0	0	0	0	0	.000	1	0	0	1.000
1975—National	OF	4	0	2	0	0	0	1	.500	4	0	0	1.000
1976—National	3B	3	1	2	0	1	0	0	.667	0	1	20	1.000
1977—National	PH-3B	2	0	0	0	0	0	0	.000	0	1	0	1.000
1978—National	3B	4	0	1	1	0	0	0	.250	1	0	0	1.000
1979—National	PH-1B	2	0	0	0	0	0	0	.000	2	0	0	1.000
1980—National	PH	1	0	0	0	0	0	0	.000	0	0	0	.000
1981—National	1B	3	0	1	0	0	0	0	.333	5	0	0	1.000
1982—National	1B	1	0	0	0	0	0	1	.000	4	0	0	1.000
1985—National	PH	1	0	0	0	0	0	0	.000	0	0	0	.000
All-Star Game Totals—16 Years		33	3	7	1	1	0	2	.212	26	6	0	1.000

Named to National League All-Star Team for 1968 game; replaced due to injury.

RECORD AS MANAGER

Year Club	League	Position	W.	L.
1984—Cincinnati†	Nat.	Fifth (W)	19	22
1985—Cincinnati	Nat.	Second (W)	89	72
1986—Cincinnati	Nat.	Second (W)	86	76
1987—Cincinnati	Nat.	Second (W)	84	78
1988—Cincinnati‡	Nat.	Second(W)	87	74
Major League Totals—5 Years			365	322

†Replaced Vern Rapp with club in fifth place (record of 51-70), August 16, 1984.
‡On suspension, May 2 to May 31, 1988 (Replaced by Tommy Helms, who had a record of 12-15).

JEFFREY ALLEN TORBORG
(Jeff)
Chicago White Sox

Born November 26, 1941, at Westfield, N. J.
Height, 6.00. Weight, 195.
Threw and batted righthanded.
Received bachelor of science degree in education from Rutgers University, New Brunswick, N. J.; and received master's degree in athletic administration from Montclair State College, Montclair, N. J.
Father of Doug Torborg, pitcher in Pittsburgh Pirates' organization.

Received reported $100,000 bonus to sign with Los Angeles Dodgers, 1963.

Year	Club	League	Pos.	G.	AB.	R.	H.	2B.	3B.	HR.	RBI.	B.A.	PO.	A.	E.	F.A.
1963	—Albuquerque	Texas	C	64	184	19	41	10	3	1	18	.223	349	27	6	.984
1964	—Los Angeles	Nat.	C	28	43	4	10	1	1	0	4	.233	80	4	2	.977
1965	—Los Angeles	Nat.	C	56	150	8	36	5	1	3	13	.240	300	19	3	.991
1966	—Los Angeles	Nat.	C	46	120	4	27	3	0	1	13	.225	269	17	4	.986
1967	—Los Angeles	Nat.	C	76	196	11	42	4	1	2	12	.214	413	30	5	.989
1968	—Los Angeles	Nat.	C	37	93	2	15	2	0	0	4	.161	206	20	2	.991
1969	—Los Angeles	Nat.	C	51	124	7	23	4	0	0	7	.185	251	26	1	.996
1970	—Los Angeles†	Nat.	C	64	134	11	31	8	0	1	17	.231	275	16	5	.983
1971	—California‡	Amer.	C	55	123	6	25	5	0	0	5	.203	208	17	3	.987
1972	—California§	Amer.	C	59	153	5	32	3	0	0	8	.209	383	28	1	.998
1973	—California xyz	Amer.	C	102	255	20	56	7	0	1	18	.220	611	37	6	.991
National League Totals—7 Years				358	860	47	184	27	3	7	70	.214	1794	132	22	.989
American League Totals—3 Years				216	531	31	113	15	0	1	31	.213	1202	82	10	.990
Major League Totals—10 Years				574	1391	78	297	42	3	8	101	.214	2996	214	32	.990

†Sold to California Angels, March 13, 1971.
‡On disabled list, June 25 to July 27, 1971.
§On disabled list, May 21 to June 13, 1972.
xOn disabled list, July 13 to August 10, 1973.
yTraded to St. Louis Cardinals for Pitcher John Andrews, December 6, 1973.
zReleased, March 25, 1974.

RECORD AS MANAGER

Year	Club	League	Position	W.	L.
1977	—Cleveland†	Amer.	Fifth(E)	45	59
1978	—Cleveland	Amer.	Sixth(E)	69	90
1979	—Cleveland‡	Amer.	Sixth(E)	43	52
Major League Totals—3 Years				157	201

†Replaced Frank Robinson with club in sixth place (record of 26-31), June 19, 1977.
§Replaced by Dave Garcia, July 23, 1979.
Coach, Cleveland Indians, 1975 to June 18, 1977; coach, New York Yankees, July 26, 1979 through 1988.

THOMAS LYNN TREBELHORN
(Tom)
Milwaukee Brewers

Born January 27, 1948, at Portland, Ore.
Height, 5.11. Weight, 178.
Threw right and batted lefthanded.
Received bachelor of science degree in history and teaching from Portland State University, Portland, Ore. in 1970.

Led Northwest League catchers in fielding percentage with .997 in 1971.
Led National League catchers in double plays with 5 in 1970.
Tied for Northwest League lead in double plays by catchers with 3 in 1972.

Year	Club	League	Pos.	G.	AB.	R.	H.	2B.	3B.	HR.	RBI.	B.A.	PO.	A.	E.	F.A.
1970	—Bend	N'west	C-3-2-O	68	198	33	48	4	1	4	32	.242	296	48	12	.966
1971	—Bend	N'west	C-OF	51	149	28	47	13	3	3	38	.315	282	33	2	.994
1972	—Walla Walla†	N'west	C	42	124	17	25	5	1	2	20	.202	272	19	4	.986
1973	—Birmingham	South.	3B-C-1B	33	89	9	18	5	0	2	13	.202	87	31	8	.937
1973	—Burlington	Midw.	C-1B	43	146	23	33	6	0	2	20	.226	298	25	5	.985
1974	—Birmingham	South.	C-3B	8	9	1	2	1	0	0	0	.222	13	1	1	.933
1974	—Lewiston‡§	N'west	P	7	2	0	0	0	0	0	0	.000	1	2	0	1.000

Signed as free agent by Hawaii (Pacific Coast League), June 4, 1970.
†Sold to Oakland A's organization, September 2, 1972.
‡Player-coach.
§Released, June 17, 1975.

PITCHING RECORD

Year	Club	League	G.	IP.	W.	L.	Pct.	H.	R.	ER.	SO.	BB.	ERA.
1974	—Lewiston	Northwest	5	12	1	0	1.000	7	1	1	2	2	0.75

RECORD AS MANAGER

Year	Club	League	Position	W.	L.
1975	—Boise	N'west	Third(S)	39	39
1976	—Boise	N'west	Third(S)	33	38
1977	—Modesto	Calif.	Fourth	31	39
	(Second Half)		Sixth	22	48
1979	—Batavia	NYP	Third(W)	37	34
1982	—Portland	P. C.	Fifth(N)	32	39
	(Second Half)		Fifth(N)	33	40
1983	—Hawaii	P. C.	†Fourth(S)	32	40
	(Second Half)		Second(S)	40	31
1985	—Vancouver‡	P. C.	Second(N)	38	34
	(Second Half)		First(N)	41	30
1986	—Milwaukee§	Amer.	Sixth(E)	6	3
1987	—Milwaukee	Amer.	Third(E)	91	71
1988	—Milwaukee	Amer.	xThird(E)	87	75
Major League Totals—3 Years				184	149

†Tied for position with Phoenix.
‡Won division championship from Calgary, three games to none; won league championship from Phoenix, three games to none.
§Replaced retiring manager George Bamberger with club in sixth place (record of 71-81), September 26, 1986.
xTied for position with Toronto Blue Jays.
Coach, American League All-Star Team, 1988.
Coach, Cleveland Indians' organization, 1978; coach, Pittsburgh Pirates' organization, 1980 and 1981; coach, Milwaukee Brewers, 1984 and beginning of 1986 season through September 25, 1986.

ROBERT JOHN VALENTINE
(Bobby)
Texas Rangers

Born May 13, 1950, at Stamford, Conn.
Height, 5.10. Weight, 185.
Threw and batted righthanded.
Attended Arizona State University, Tempe, Ariz., and University of Southern California, Los Angeles, Calif.
Son-in-law of Ralph Branca, pitcher with Brooklyn Dodgers, Detroit Tigers
and New York Yankees, 1944 through 1954 and 1956.

Major League stolen bases: 1971 (5), 1972 (5), 1973 (6), 1974 (8), 1975 (1), 1978 (1), 1979 (1). Total—27.
Led Pioneer League in stolen bases with 20 in 1968.
Led Pacific Coast League in total bases with 324, sacrifice flies with 10 and double plays by shortstops with 106 in 1970.
Led Pioneer League outfielders in putouts with 107 and tied for lead in assists with 8 in 1987.
Named Pacific Coast League Player of the Year, 1970.

Year Club	League	Pos.	G.	AB.	R.	H.	2B.	3B.	HR.	RBI.	B.A.	PO.	A.	E.	F.A.
1968—Odgen	Pion.	OF-SS	62	224	★62	63	14	4	6	26	.281	111	10	6	.953
1969—Spokane	P. C.	★SS-OF	111	402	61	104	19	5	3	35	.259	166	254	★38	.917
1969—Los Angeles	Nat.	PR	5	0	3	0	0	0	0	0	.000	0	0	0	.000
1970—Spokane	P. C.	★SS-2B	●146	★621	★122	★211	★39	★16	14	80	★.340	★217	474	★54	.928
1971—Spokane	P. C.	SS	7	30	7	10	2	0	1	2	.333	13	18	3	.912
1971—Los Angeles	Nat.	S-3-2-O	101	281	32	70	10	2	1	25	.249	123	176	16	.949
1972—Los Angeles†	Nat.	2-3-O-S	119	391	42	107	11	2	3	32	.274	178	245	23	.948
1973—California‡	Amer.	SS-OF	32	126	12	38	5	2	1	13	.302	63	75	6	.958
1974—California§x	Amer.	OF-SS-3B	117	371	39	97	10	3	3	39	.261	160	116	17	.942
1975—Charleston	Int.	3B	56	175	27	41	4	0	1	17	.234	44	74	6	.952
1975—Salt Lake City	P. C.	1-O-3-2	46	147	29	45	6	1	0	17	.306	92	14	3	.972
1975—California y	Amer.	1B-3B-OF	26	57	5	16	2	0	0	5	.281	27	1	2	.933
1975—San Diego	Nat.	OF	7	15	1	2	0	0	1	1	.133	4	0	0	1.000
1976—Hawaii	P. C.	1-O-3-S	120	395	67	120	23	2	13	89	.304	578	47	4	.994
1976—San Diego	Nat.	OF-1B	15	49	3	18	4	0	0	4	.367	55	6	0	1.000
1977—S.D.z-N.Y.	Nat.	SS-1B-3B	86	150	13	23	4	0	2	13	.153	119	64	3	.984
1978—New York a	Nat.	2B-3B	69	160	17	43	7	0	1	18	.269	78	109	6	.969
1979—Seattle b	Amer.	S-O-2-3-C	62	98	9	27	6	0	0	7	.276	32	38	2	.972
National League Totals—7 Years			402	1046	111	263	36	4	8	93	.251	557	600	48	.960
American League Totals—4 Years			237	652	65	178	23	5	4	64	.273	282	230	27	.950
Major League Totals—10 Years			639	1698	176	441	59	9	12	157	.260	839	830	75	.957

Selected by Los Angeles Dodgers' organization in 1st round (fifth player selected) of free-agent draft, June 7, 1968.
†Traded with Infielder Billy Grabarkewitz, Outfielder Frank Robinson and Pitchers Bill Singer and Mike Strahler to California Angels for Pitcher Andy Messersmith and Third Baseman Ken McMullen, November 28, 1972.
‡On disabled list, May 17, 1973 through remainder of season.
§On disabled list, May 29 to June 13, 1974.
xLoaned to Charleston (Pittsburgh Pirates' organization), April 4, 1975; returned, June 20, 1975.
yTraded with a player to be named later to San Diego Padres for Pitcher Gary Ross, September 17, 1975; San Diego acquired Infielder Rudy Meoli to complete deal, November 4, 1975.
zTraded with Pitcher Paul Siebert to New York Mets for Infielder-Outfielder Dave Kingman, June 15, 1977.
aReleased, March 26, 1979; signed by Seattle Mariners, April 10, 1979.
bGranted free agency, November 1, 1979.

RECORD AS MANAGER

Year Club	League	Position	W.	L.
1985—Texas†	Amer.	Seventh(W)	53	76
1986—Texas	Amer.	Second(W)	87	75
1987—Texas	Amer.	‡Sixth(W)	75	87
1988—Texas	Amer.	Sixth(W)	70	91
Major League Totals—4 Years			285	329

†Replaced Doug Rader with club in seventh place (record of 9-23), May 16, 1985.
‡Tied for position with California Angels.
Coach, American League All-Star Team, 1988.
Scout and minor league instructor, San Diego Padres, 1981; minor league instructor, New York Mets, 1982; coach, New York Mets, 1983 through May 15, 1985.

JOHN DAVID WATHAN
Kansas City Royals

Born October 4, 1949, at Cedar Rapids, Ia.
Height, 6.02. Weight, 205.
Threw and batted righthanded.
Attended University of San Diego, San Diego, Calif., and
Mount Mercy College, Cedar Rapids, Ia.

Major League stolen bases: 1977 (2), 1978 (2), 1979 (2), 1980 (17), 1981 (11), 1982 (36), 1983 (28), 1984 (6), 1985 (1). Total—105.

Year Club	League	Pos.	G.	AB.	R.	H.	2B.	3B.	HR.	RBI.	B.A.	PO.	A.	E.	F.A.
1971—San Jose	Calif.	C-OF	64	215	37	56	11	2	1	29	.260	438	31	14	.971
1971—Waterloo	Midw.	C-OF-1B	43	147	31	41	4	4	3	21	.279	282	18	1	.997
1972—San Jose†	Calif.	C-1B-3B	48	148	25	40	8	0	4	15	.270	324	31	3	.992
1972—Omaha	A. A.	C	18	51	8	15	1	1	0	2	.294	94	5	1	.990

Year	Club	League	Pos.	G.	AB.	R.	H.	2B.	3B.	HR.	RBI.	B.A.	PO.	A.	E.	F.A.
1972	—Jacksonville	South.	C	16	54	6	17	3	1	0	3	.315	111	7	4	.967
1973	—Jacksonville‡	South.	C-1B-3B	65	233	20	58	8	3	5	34	.249	294	28	4	.988
1974	—Jacksonville	South.	1B-OF-C	120	428	63	105	14	2	7	47	.245	760	50	7	.991
1975	—Omaha	A. A.	C-OF	104	360	42	109	14	4	8	46	.303	532	45	10	.983
1976	—Omaha§	A. A.	C-OF	24	84	4	13	5	0	0	6	.155	128	14	4	.973
1976	—Kansas City	Amer.	C-1B	27	42	5	12	1	0	0	5	.286	63	4	1	.985
1977	—Kansas City	Amer.	C-1B	55	119	18	39	5	3	2	21	.328	156	9	2	.988
1978	—Kansas City x	Amer.	1B-C	67	190	19	57	10	1	2	28	.300	385	28	2	.995
1979	—Kansas City	Amer.	1B-C-OF	90	199	26	41	7	3	2	28	.206	336	24	3	.992
1980	—Kansas City	Amer.	C-OF-1B	126	453	57	138	14	7	6	58	.305	472	33	8	.984
1981	—Kansas City	Amer.	C-OF-1B	89	301	24	76	9	3	1	19	.252	316	28	7	.980
1982	—Kansas City y	Amer.	C-1B	121	448	79	121	11	3	3	51	.270	482	40	10	.981
1983	—Kansas City	Amer.	C-1B-OF	128	437	49	107	18	3	2	32	.245	615	58	9	.987
1984	—Kansas City	Amer.	C-1B-OF	97	171	17	31	7	1	2	10	.181	304	31	6	.982
1985	—Kansas City z	Amer.	C-1B	60	145	11	34	8	1	1	9	.234	259	29	4	.986
Major League Totals—10 Years				860	2505	305	656	90	25	21	261	.262	3388	284	52	.986

Selected by Kansas City Royals' organization in 4th round of free-agent draft, January 13, 1971.
†On disabled list, May 5 to May 30, 1972.
‡On disabled list, May 25 to June 28, 1973.
§On disabled list, July 29 to September 1, 1976.
xOn disabled list, June 16 to July 7, 1978.
yOn disabled list, July 6 to August 10, 1982.
zReleased and signed as coach, April 7, 1986.

DIVISION SERIES RECORD

Year	Club	League	Pos.	G.	AB.	R.	H.	2B.	3B.	HR.	RBI.	B.A.	PO.	A.	E.	F.A.
1981	—Kansas City	Amer.	C	3	10	1	3	0	0	0	0	.300	11	4	1	.938

CHAMPIONSHIP SERIES RECORD

Tied American League Championship Series record for most positions played, total Series (3).

Year	Club	League	Pos.	G.	AB.	R.	H.	2B.	3B.	HR.	RBI.	B.A.	PO.	A.	E.	F.A.
1976	—Kansas City	Amer.	C	1	0	0	0	0	0	0	0	.000	0	0	0	.000
1977	—Kansas City	Amer.	C-1-D-PH	4	6	0	0	0	0	0	0	.000	19	0	0	1.000
1978	—Kansas City	Amer.	1B	1	3	0	0	0	0	0	0	.000	7	0	0	1.000
1980	—Kansas City	Amer.	OF-PH	3	6	1	0	0	0	0	0	.000	7	0	0	1.000
1984	—Kansas City	Amer.	PR-DH	1	1	0	0	0	0	0	0	.000	0	0	0	.000
Championship Series Totals—5 Years				10	16	1	0	0	0	0	0	.000	33	0	0	1.000

WORLD SERIES RECORD

Year	Club	League	Pos.	G.	AB.	R.	H.	2B.	3B.	HR.	RBI.	B.A.	PO.	A.	E.	F.A.
1980	—Kansas City	Amer.	PH-OF-C	3	7	1	2	0	0	0	1	.286	7	1	0	1.000
1985	—Kansas City	Amer.	PH-PR	2	1	0	0	0	0	0	0	.000	0	0	0	.000
World Series Totals—2 Years				5	8	1	2	0	0	0	1	.250	7	1	0	1.000

RECORD AS MANAGER

Year	Club	League	Position	W.	L.
1987	—Omaha	A. A.	Seventh†	64	76
1987	—Kansas City‡	Amer.	Second(W)	21	15
1988	—Kansas City	Amer.	Third(W)	84	77
Major League Totals—2 Years				105	92

†Tied for position with Nashville.
‡Replaced manager Billy Gardner with club in fourth place (record of 62-64), August 27, 1987.
Coach, Kansas City Royals, 1986.

JAMES FRANCIS WILLIAMS
(Jimy)
Toronto Blue Jays

Born October 4, 1943, at Santa Maria, Calif.
Height, 5.11. Weight, 170.
Threw and batted righthanded.
Received bachelor of science degree in agribusiness from Fresno State College, Fresno, Calif.

Year	Club	League	Pos.	G.	AB.	R.	H.	2B.	3B.	HR.	RBI.	B.A.	PO.	A.	E.	F.A.
1965	—Waterloo†	Midw.	SS	115	435	64	125	19	3	2	31	.287	173	*312	26	*.949
1966	—St. Louis‡	Nat.	SS-2B	13	11	1	3	0	0	0	1	.273	2	5	0	1.000
1967	—Arkansas	Texas	SS	28	101	8	21	1	1	0	8	.208	49	80	2	.985
1967	—Tulsa	P. C.	SS	61	164	18	37	2	0	1	21	.226	87	156	26	.903
1967	—St. Louis§	Nat.	SS	1	2	0	0	0	0	0	0	.000	6	1	0	1.000
1968	—Indianapolis x	P. C.	SS-2B	120	403	38	91	19	5	2	34	.226	198	323	27	.951
1969	—Vancouver y	P. C.	3B-OF-SS	35	66	7	17	1	1	0	9	.258	17	23	2	.952
1970	—Buf. z-Winn.	Int.	SS-2B-3B	109	361	49	83	15	0	3	18	.230	178	244	30	.934
1971	—Winn. ab-Tide. c	Int.	SS-3B-2B	105	327	40	84	7	4	5	31	.257	120	219	22	.939
1975	—El Paso de	Texas	DH	6	17	3	2	0	0	0	2	.118	0	0	0	.000
Major League Totals—2 Years				14	13	1	3	0	0	0	1	.231	8	6	0	1.000

†Drafted by St. Louis Cardinals from Toronto (Boston Red Sox' organization), November 29, 1965.
‡In military service, July 24, 1966 through remainder of season.
§Traded with Catcher Pat Corrales to Cincinnati Reds for Catcher John Edwards, February 8, 1968.
xRecalled by Cincinnati Reds; selected by Montreal Expos from Cincinnati in expansion draft, October 14, 1968.
yOn disabled list, May 13 to May 30 and June 24 to September 2, 1969.
zFranchise transferred from Buffalo to Winnipeg, June 4, 1970.
aOn suspended list, June 7 to June 16, 1971.
bSold to New York Mets' organization, June 16, 1971.
cOn temporary inactive list, August 12 to August 16, 1971.
dPlayer-manager.
eOn disabled list, May 15 to July 17 and July 29 to August 20, 1975.

RECORD AS MANAGER

Named Pacific Coast League Manager of the Year, 1976 and 1979.

Year Club	League	Position	W.	L.
1974—Quad Cities	Midw.	First(S)	33	26
(Second Half)		†Third(S)	32	32
1975—El Paso	Texas	Third(W)	62	71
1976—Salt Lake City	P. C.	‡First(E)	90	54
1977—Salt Lake City	P. C.	Second(E)	74	65
1978—Springfield	A. A.	Third(E)	70	66
1979—Salt Lake City	P. C.	Fourth(S)	34	40
(Second Half)		§First(S)	46	28
1986—Toronto	Amer.	Fourth(E)	96	76
1987—Toronto	Amer.	Second(E)	96	66
1988—Toronto	Amer.	xThird(E)	87	75
Major League Totals—3 Years			269	217

†Lost playoff to Danville, two games to one.
‡Lost championship playoff to Hawaii, three games to two.
§Won playoff from Albuquerque, two games to none; won championship playoff from Hawaii, three games to none.
xTied for position with Milwaukee Brewers.
Coach, Toronto Blue Jays, 1980 through 1985.

DONALD WILLIAM ZIMMER
(Don)
Chicago Cubs

Born January 17, 1931, at Cincinnati, O.
Height, 5.10. Weight, 188.
Threw and batted righthanded.
Father of Tom Zimmer, minor league catcher in St. Louis Cardinals' organization, 1971 through 1975; coach, St. Louis Cardinals' organization, 1975; coach, St. Louis Cardinals, 1976; player-manager with Victoria in Lone Star League (Independent), 1977; manager with Butte in Pioneer League (Co-op), 1978; manager in Pittsburgh Pirates' organization, 1979; manager in California Angels' organization, 1980; and scout for San Francisco Giants since 1981.

Named American Association Rookie of the Year, 1953.

Year Club	League	Pos.	G.	AB.	R.	H.	2B.	3B.	HR.	RBI.	B.A.	PO.	A.	E.	F.A.
1949—Cambridge	E. Shore	SS	71	304	56	69	14	3	4	30	.227	162	171	27	.925
1950—Hornell	Pony	*SS-3B	123	518	*146	163	34	5	*23	122	.315	*269	*367	45	*.934
1951—Elmira	East.	SS	137	546	94	149	28	2	9	70	.273	*326	414	38	*.951
1952—Mobile	South.	SS	153	613	107	190	32	7	17	91	.310	*355	*517	*52	.944
1953—St. Paul†	A. A.	SS	81	320	57	96	14	4	23	63	.300	165	264	21	.953
1954—St. Paul	A. A.	SS	73	268	54	78	9	6	17	53	.291	152	200	16	.957
1954—Brooklyn	Nat.	SS	24	33	3	6	0	1	0	0	.182	14	32	3	.939
1955—Brooklyn	Nat.	2B-SS-3B	88	280	38	67	10	1	15	50	.239	184	207	12	.970
1956—Brooklyn‡	Nat.	SS-3B-2B	17	20	4	6	1	0	0	2	.300	10	11	1	.955
1957—Brooklyn	Nat.	3B-SS-2B	84	269	23	59	9	1	6	19	.219	114	186	15	.952
1958—Los Angeles	Nat.	S-3-2-O	127	455	52	119	15	2	17	60	.262	281	395	26	.963
1959—Los Angeles§	Nat.	SS-3B-2B	97	249	21	41	7	1	4	28	.165	120	240	10	.973
1960—Chicago	Nat.	2-3-S-O	132	368	37	95	16	7	6	35	.258	211	274	16	.968
1961—Chicago x	Nat.	2B-3B-OF	128	477	57	120	25	4	13	40	.252	284	332	20	.969
1962—N.Y. y-Cinn. z	Nat.	3B-2B-SS	77	244	19	52	12	2	2	17	.213	77	129	11	.949
1963—Los Angeles a	Nat.	3B-2B-SS	22	23	4	5	1	0	1	2	.217	3	14	2	.895
1963—Washington	Amer.	3B-2B	83	298	37	74	12	1	13	44	.248	90	177	18	.937
1964—Washington	Amer.	3-O-C-2	121	341	38	84	16	2	12	38	.246	72	144	10	.956
1965—Washington b	Amer.	C-3B-2B	95	226	20	45	6	0	2	17	.199	181	81	12	.956
1966—Toei	Pacific	3B-SS	87	203	14	37	2	0	9	20	.182	101	143	11	.957
1967—Knoxville	South	P-3-1-C	25	49	2	10	3	0	0	5	.204	21	12	6	.846
1967—Buffalo	Int.	3B-OF	16	33	2	6	2	0	1	2	.182	4	9	3	.813
American League Totals—3 Years			299	865	95	203	34	3	27	99	.235	343	402	40	.949
National League Totals—10 Years			796	2418	258	570	96	19	64	253	.236	1298	1820	116	.964
Major League Totals—12 Years			1095	3283	353	773	130	22	91	352	.235	1641	2222	156	.961

†On disabled list, July 7, 1953 through remainder of season.
‡On disabled list, June 23, 1956 through remainder of season.
§Traded to Chicago Cubs for Pitcher Ron Perranoski, Infielder John Goryl, Outfielder Lee Handley and reported $25,000, April 8, 1960.

xSelected by New York Mets in Expansion Draft, October 10, 1961.
yTraded to Cincinnati Reds for Pitcher Robert G. Miller and Third Baseman Cliff Cook, May 6, 1962.
zTraded to Los Angeles Dodgers for Pitcher Scott Breeden, January 24, 1963.
aSold to Washington Senators, June 24, 1963.
bReleased, November 19, 1965; signed by Toei Flyers of Japanese Baseball League.

WORLD SERIES RECORD

Year	Club	League	Pos.	G.	AB.	R.	H.	2B.	3B.	HR.	RBI.	B.A.	PO.	A.	E.	F.A.
1955	Brooklyn	Nat.	2B	4	9	0	2	0	0	0	2	.222	4	8	2	.857
1959	Los Angeles	Nat.	SS	1	1	0	0	0	0	0	0	.000	0	1	0	1.000
World Series Totals—2 Years				5	10	0	2	0	0	0	2	.200	4	9	2	.867

ALL-STAR GAME RECORD

Year	League	Pos.	AB.	R.	H.	2B.	3B.	HR.	RBI.	B.A.	PO.	A.	E.	F.A.
1961	National (first game)	2B	1	0	0	0	0	0	0	.000	0	0	1	.000

PITCHING RECORD

Year	Club	League	G.	IP.	W.	L.	Pct.	H.	R.	ER.	SO.	BB.	ERA.
1967	Knoxville	Southern	12	27	0	0	.000	33	15	14	8	7	4.67

RECORD AS MANAGER

Year	Club	League	Position	W.	L.
1967	Knoxville	South.	†Sixth	26	46
1967	Buffalo	Int.	Seventh	33	40
1968	Indianapolis	P. C.	Fifth(E)	66	78
1969	Key West	Fla. St.	‡Third(S)	67	63
1972	San Diego§	Nat.	Sixth(W)	54	88
1973	San Diego	Nat.	Sixth(W)	60	102
1976	Boston x	Amer.	Third(E)	42	34
1977	Boston	Amer.	ySecond(E)	97	64
1978	Boston	Amer.	Second(E)	99	64
1979	Boston	Amer.	Third (E)	91	69
1980	Boston z	Amer.	aThird(E)	82	73
1981	Texas b	Amer.		57	48
1982	Texas c	Amer.	Sixth(W)	38	58
1988	Chicago	Nat.	Fourth(E)	77	85
American League Totals—7 Years				506	410
National League Totals—3 Years				191	275
Major League Totals—10 Years				697	685

†Transferred by Cincinnati Reds' organization from Knoxville to Buffalo, July 5, 1967.
‡Tied for position with Pompano Beach.
§Replaced Preston Gomez with club in fourth place (record of 4-7), April 27, 1972.
xReplaced Darrell Johnson with club in fifth place (record of 41-45), July 19, 1976.
yTied for position with Baltimore Orioles.
zReplaced by interim manager Johnny Pesky, October 1, 1980.
aTied for position with Milwaukee Brewers.
bFirst Half. . . . Second (W) (record of 33-22); Second Half. . . . Third (W) (record of 24-26).
cReplaced by Darrell Johnson, July 29, 1982.

Coach, Montreal Expos, 1971; San Diego Padres, 1972; Boston Red Sox, 1974 to July, 1976; coach, New York Yankees, 1983 and June 16, 1986 through remainder of season; coach, Chicago Cubs, 1984 through June 12, 1986; coach, San Francisco Giants, 1987.

Coach, American League All-Star Team, 1978 and 1981.

PLAYER MOVES

The following player deals involve players in the Register with the transactions occurring after January 4, 1989 and included January 9.

ACKER, JIM: Re-signed by Atlanta Braves, January 6, 1989.
BELL, BUDDY: Signed by Texas Rangers, January 9, 1989.
GUANTE, CECILIO: Re-signed by Texas Rangers, January 6, 1989.
LEA, CHARLIE: Re-signed by Minnesota Twins, January 6, 1989.
MADISON, SCOTTI: Signed by Nashville (Cincinnati Reds' organization), January 4, 1989.
NOBOA, JUNIOR: Signed by Indianapolis (Montreal Expos' organization), January 4, 1989.
SUNDBERG, JIM: Re-signed by Texas Rangers, January 6, 1989.

1989 Hall of Fame Enshrinees

JOHNNY LEE BENCH

Born December 7, 1947, at Oklahoma City, Okla.
Height, 6.01. Weight, 210.
Threw and batted righthanded.

Established major league records for most games, catcher, rookie season (154), 1968; most home runs by catcher, lifetime (327).

Tied major league records for most consecutive seasons leading league in sacrifice flies (2); fewest passed balls, season, 100 or more games (0), 1975; most bases on balls, game (5), July 22, 1979; most consecutive years by catcher, with 100 or more games (13).

Established National League record for most years by catcher, with 100 or more games (13).

Tied National League records for most home runs, five consecutive games (7), May 30 through June 3, 1972; most home runs through July 31 (36), 1970; most seasons leading league in sacrifice flies (3); most two-base hits by catcher, season (40), 1968.

Hit three home runs in a game, July 26, 1970, May 9, 1973 and May 29, 1980.
Hit home runs in all 12 National League parks, 1972.
Led National League in total bases with 315 in 1974.
Led National League in sacrifice flies with 11 in 1970, 12 in 1972 and tied for lead with 10 in 1973.
Led National League in intentional bases on balls received with 23 in 1972.
Led National League catchers in putouts with 651, total chances with 713 and fielding percentage with .997 in 1976.
Led National League catchers in double plays with 16 in 1974.
Led National League in passed balls with 18 in 1968.
Led International League catchers in assists with 70 in 1967.
Named Major League Player of the Year by The Sporting News, 1970.
Named National League Player of the Year by The Sporting News, 1970.
Named National League Most Valuable Player by Baseball Writers' Association of America, 1970 and 1972.
Named catcher on The Sporting News National League All-Star Team, 1968, 1969, 1970, 1972, 1973, 1974 and 1975.
Named catcher on The Sporting News National League All-Star fielding team, 1968 through 1977.
Named National League Rookie Player of the Year by The Sporting News, 1968.
Named National League Rookie of the Year by Baseball Writers' Association of America, 1968.
Named Minor League Player of the Year by The Sporting News, 1967.
Named Carolina League Player of the Year, 1966.
Named to Hall of Fame, 1989.

Year Club	League	Pos.	G.	AB.	R.	H.	2B.	3B.	HR.	RBI.	B.A.	PO.	A.	E.	F.A.
1965—Tampa	Fla. St.	C-OF	68	214	29	53	13	1	2	35	.248	415	40	6	.987
1966—Peninsula	Carol.	C	98	350	59	103	16	0	22	68	.294	692	•87	★17	.979
1966—Buffalo†‡	Int.	C	1	0	0	0	0	0	0	0	.000	2	0	0	1.000
1967—Buffalo§	Int.	C-3-O-1	98	344	39	89	17	2	23	68	.259	577	82	13	.981
1967—Cincinnati	Nat.	C	26	86	7	14	3	1	1	6	.163	175	16	1	.995
1968—Cincinnati	Nat.	C	154	564	67	155	40	2	15	82	.275	★942	★102	9	.991
1969—Cincinnati x	Nat.	C	148	532	83	156	23	1	26	90	.293	793	76	7	.992
1970—Cincinnati	Nat.	C-O-1-3	158	605	97	177	35	4	★45	★148	.293	854	78	15	.984
1971—Cincinnati y	Nat.	C-O-1-3	149	562	80	134	19	2	27	61	.238	735	67	10	.988
1972—Cincinnati	Nat.	C-O-1-3	147	538	87	145	22	2	★40	★125	.270	791	63	10	.988
1973—Cincinnati	Nat.	C-O-1-3	152	557	83	141	17	3	25	104	.253	757	63	6	.993
1974—Cincinnati	Nat.	C-3B-1B	160	621	108	174	38	2	33	★129	.280	794	123	9	.990
1975—Cincinnati	Nat.	C-OF-1B	142	530	83	150	39	1	28	110	.283	646	52	8	.989
1976—Cincinnati	Nat.	C-OF-1B	135	465	62	109	24	1	16	74	.234	655	60	4	.994
1977—Cincinnati	Nat.	C-O-1-3	142	494	67	136	34	2	31	109	.275	735	69	11	.987
1978—Cincinnati	Nat.	C-1B-OF	120	393	52	102	17	1	23	73	.260	680	53	9	.988
1979—Cincinnati	Nat.	C-1B	130	464	73	128	19	0	22	80	.276	632	69	10	.986
1980—Cincinnati	Nat.	C	114	360	52	90	12	0	24	68	.250	505	39	5	.991
1981—Cincinnati z	Nat.	1B-C	52	178	14	55	8	0	8	25	.309	375	28	7	.983
1982—Cincinnati	Nat.	3B-1B-C	119	399	44	103	16	0	13	38	.258	108	159	19	.934
1983—Cincinnati a	Nat.	3-1-C-O	110	310	32	79	15	2	12	54	.255	292	74	10	.973
Major League Totals—17 Years			2158	7658	1091	2048	381	24	389	1376	.267	10469	1191	150	.987

Selected by Cincinnati Reds' organization in 2nd round of free-agent draft, June 21, 1965.
†On disabled list, July 31 to September 6, 1966.
‡On military list, November 7, 1966 through April 9, 1967.
§On temporary inactive list, July 29 to August 14, 1967.
xOn military list, July 11 to July 18, 1969.
yOn military list, June 13 to June 17, 1971.
zOn disabled list, May 29 to August 22, 1981.
aOn voluntarily retired list, October 19, 1983.

CHAMPIONSHIP SERIES RECORD

Established Championship Series record for most Series, one or more home runs (5).
Tied Championship Series record for most games, total Series, one club (22).
Established National League Championship Series record for most long hits, total Series (11).
Tied National League Championship Series records for most Series played, one club (6); most three-base hits, total Series (2).

Year Club	League	Pos.	G.	AB.	R.	H.	2B.	3B.	HR.	RBI.	B.A.	PO.	A.	E.	F.A.
1970—Cincinnati	Nat.	C	3	9	2	2	0	0	1	1	.222	20	3	0	1.000
1972—Cincinnati	Nat.	C	5	18	3	6	1	1	1	2	.333	28	3	1	.969
1973—Cincinnati	Nat.	C	5	19	1	5	2	0	1	1	.263	31	2	0	1.000
1975—Cincinnati	Nat.	C	3	13	1	1	0	0	0	0	.077	18	4	0	1.000
1976—Cincinnati	Nat.	C	3	12	3	4	1	0	1	1	.333	11	4	0	1.000
1979—Cincinnati	Nat.	C	3	12	1	3	0	1	1	1	.250	17	2	0	1.000
Championship Series Totals—6 Years			22	83	11	21	4	2	5	6	.253	125	18	1	.993

WORLD SERIES RECORD

Tied World Series records for most double plays by catcher, total Series (6); most double plays by catcher, Series (3), 1975; one or more hits, each game, four-game Series, 1976.

Year	Club	League	Pos.	G.	AB.	R.	H.	2B.	3B.	HR.	RBI.	B.A.	PO.	A.	E.	F.A.
1970	Cincinnati	Nat.	C	5	19	3	4	0	0	1	3	.211	36	3	0	1.000
1972	Cincinnati	Nat.	C	7	23	4	6	1	0	1	1	.261	41	7	1	.980
1975	Cincinnati	Nat.	C	7	29	5	6	2	0	1	4	.207	44	6	0	1.000
1976	Cincinnati	Nat.	C	4	15	4	8	1	1	2	6	.533	18	2	0	1.000
World Series Totals—4 Years				23	86	16	24	4	1	5	14	.279	139	18	1	.994

ALL-STAR GAME RECORD

Tied All-Star Game records for most strikeouts, nine-inning game (3), July 14, 1970; most putouts by catcher, game (10), July 15, 1975; most chances accepted by catcher, game (11), July 15, 1975.

Year	League	Pos.	AB.	R.	H.	2B.	3B.	HR.	RBI.	B.A.	PO.	A.	E.	F.A.
1968	National	C	0	0	0	0	0	0	0	.000	2	0	0	1.000
1969	National	C	3	2	2	0	0	1	2	.667	4	0	0	1.000
1970	National	C	3	0	0	0	0	0	0	.000	5	1	0	1.000
1971	National	C	4	1	2	0	0	1	2	.500	5	0	0	1.000
1972	National	C	2	0	1	0	0	0	0	.500	3	0	0	1.000
1973	National	C	3	1	1	0	0	1	1	.333	3	0	0	1.000
1974	National	C	3	1	2	0	0	0	0	.667	7	0	1	.875
1975	National	C	4	0	1	0	0	0	1	.250	10	1	0	1.000
1976	National	C	2	0	1	0	0	0	0	.500	1	0	0	1.000
1977	National	C	2	0	0	0	0	0	0	.000	4	0	0	1.000
1980	National	C	1	0	0	0	0	0	0	.000	5	0	0	1.000
1983	National	PH	1	0	0	0	0	0	0	.000	0	0	0	.000
All-Star Game Totals—12 Years			28	5	10	0	0	3	6	.357	49	2	1	.981

Named to National League All-Star Team for 1978 game; replaced due to injury by Biff Pocoroba.
Named to National League All-Star Team for 1979 game; replaced due to injury by John Stearns.

CARL MICHAEL YASTRZEMSKI

Name pronounced Yah-STREM-skee.

Born August 22, 1939, at Southampton, N. Y.
Height, 5.11. Weight, 185.
Threw right and batted lefthanded.
Attended University of Notre Dame, Notre Dame, Ind., and received bachelor of science degree in business administration from Merrimack College, North Andover, Mass.
Father of Mike Yastrzemski, outfielder in Chicago White Sox' organization.

Established major league records for lowest batting average, season, leader in batting (.301), 1968; most years leading league in assists by outfielders (7) 1977; most times grounded into double play by lefthanded batter, season (30), 1964.

Tied major league records for most seasons, one club (23), most consecutive seasons, one club (23); fewest triples, season, 150 or more games (0), 1970; fewest double plays by outfielder, season, for leader in double plays (4), 1971; most home runs, two consecutive games (5), May 19 and 20, 1976; highest fielding percentage by outfielder, season, 100 or more games (1.000), 1977.

Established American League records for most games, lifetime (3,308); most seasons, 100 or more games (22); most at-bats, lifetime (11,988); most plate appearances, lifetime (13,990); most intentional bases on balls, lifetime (190); most consecutive seasons, 100 or more games (20); most times grounded into double play, lifetime (323).

Won American League Triple Crown, 1967.

Hit three home runs in a game, May 19, 1976.

Hit for the cycle, May 14, 1965.

Led American League in sacrifice flies with 9 in 1972.

Led American League in total bases with 360 in 1967 and 335 in 1970.

Led American League in slugging percentage with .536 in 1965, .622 in 1967 and .592 in 1970.

Led American League in bases on balls received with 95 in 1963 and 119 in 1968.

Led American League in grounding into double plays with 27 in 1962 and 30 in 1964.

Led American League outfielders in assists with 17 in 1969, 16 in 1977 and tied for lead with 19 in 1964.

Tied for American League lead in sacrifice flies with 11 in 1977.

Tied for American League lead in double plays by outfielders with 4 in 1971.

Named Major League Player of the Year by THE SPORTING NEWS, 1967.

Named American League Player of the Year by THE SPORTING NEWS, 1967.

Named American League Most Valuable Player by Baseball Writers' Association of America, 1967.

Named outfielder on THE SPORTING NEWS American League All-Star Team, 1963, 1965 and 1967.

Named outfielder on THE SPORTING NEWS American League All-Star fielding team, 1963, 1965, 1967 through 1969, 1971 and 1977.

Named Carolina League Most Valuable Player, 1959.

Received reported $100,000 bonus to sign with Boston Red Sox, 1958.

Named to Hall of Fame, 1989.

Year	Club	League	Pos.	G.	AB.	R.	H.	2B.	3B.	HR.	RBI.	B.A.	PO.	A.	E.	F.A.
1959	Raleigh	Carol.	★2B-SS	120	451	87	★170	★34	6	15	100	★.377	★255	284	★45	★.923
1960	Minneapolis	A. A.	OF	148	570	84	★193	36	8	7	69	.339	243	18	5	.981
1961	Boston	Amer.	OF	148	583	71	155	31	6	11	80	.266	248	12	10	.963
1962	Boston	Amer.	OF	160	646	99	191	43	6	19	94	.296	329	★15	★11	.969
1963	Boston	Amer.	OF	151	570	91	★183	★40	3	14	68	★.321	283	★18	6	.980
1964	Boston	Amer.	OF-3B	151	567	77	164	29	9	15	67	.289	372	24	11	.973
1965	Boston	Amer.	OF	133	494	78	154	●45	3	20	72	.312	222	11	3	.987
1966	Boston	Amer.	OF	160	594	81	165	★39	2	16	80	.278	310	★15	5	.985
1967	Boston	Amer.	OF	161	579	★112	★189	31	4	●44	★121	★.326	297	13	7	.978

Year	Club	League	Pos.	G.	AB.	R.	H.	2B.	3B.	HR.	RBI.	B.A.	PO.	A.	E.	F.A.
1968	—Boston	Amer.	OF-1B	157	539	90	162	32	2	23	74	★.301	315	13	3	.991
1969	—Boston	Amer.	OF-1B	●162	603	96	154	28	2	40	111	.255	427	38	6	.987
1970	—Boston	Amer.	1B-OF	161	566	★125	186	29	0	40	102	.329	816	64	14	.984
1971	—Boston	Amer.	OF	148	508	75	129	21	2	15	70	.254	281	★16	2	.993
1972	—Boston†	Amer.	OF-1B	125	455	70	120	18	2	12	68	.264	498	43	8	.985
1973	—Boston	Amer.	1B-3B-OF	152	540	82	160	25	4	19	95	.296	979	119	18	.984
1974	—Boston	Amer.	1B-OF	148	515	★93	155	25	2	15	79	.301	806	46	6	.993
1975	—Boston	Amer.	1B-OF	149	543	91	146	30	1	14	60	.269	1217	88	5	.996
1976	—Boston	Amer.	1B-OF	155	546	71	146	23	2	21	102	.267	922	55	4	.996
1977	—Boston	Amer.	★OF-1B	150	558	99	165	27	3	28	102	.296	344	22	0	★1.000
1978	—Boston	Amer.	OF-1B	144	523	70	145	21	2	17	81	.277	523	49	5	.991
1979	—Boston	Amer.	1B-OF	147	518	69	140	28	1	21	87	.270	529	56	4	.993
1980	—Boston	Amer.	OF-1B	105	364	49	100	21	1	15	50	.275	225	13	4	.983
1981	—Boston	Amer.	1B	91	338	36	83	14	1	7	53	.246	353	34	3	.992
1982	—Boston	Amer.	1B-OF	131	459	53	126	22	1	16	72	.275	119	10	0	1.000
1983	—Boston‡	Amer.	1B-OF	119	380	38	101	24	0	10	56	.266	22	1	0	1.000
Major League Totals—23 Years				3308	11988	1816	3419	646	59	452	1844	.285	10437	775	135	.988

Signed as free agent by Boston Red Sox' organization, November 29, 1958.
†On supplemental disabled list, May 10 to June 9, 1972.
‡On voluntarily retired list, October 25, 1983.

CHAMPIONSHIP SERIES RECORD

Year	Club	League	Pos.	G.	AB.	R.	H.	2B.	3B.	HR.	RBI.	B.A.	PO.	A.	E.	F.A.
1975	—Boston	Amer.	OF	3	11	4	5	1	0	1	2	.455	7	2	0	1.000

WORLD SERIES RECORD

Year	Club	League	Pos.	G.	AB.	R.	H.	2B.	3B.	HR.	RBI.	B.A.	PO.	A.	E.	F.A.
1967	—Boston	Amer.	OF	7	25	4	10	2	0	3	5	.400	16	2	0	1.000
1975	—Boston	Amer.	OF-1B	7	29	7	9	0	0	0	4	.310	35	1	0	1.000
World Series Totals—2 Years				14	54	11	19	2	0	3	9	.352	51	3	0	1.000

ALL-STAR GAME RECORD

Tied All-Star Game records for most hits, game (4), July 14, 1970; most one-base hits, game (3), July 14, 1970; most home runs by pinch-hitter, game (1), July 15, 1975.

Year	League	Pos.	AB.	R.	H.	2B.	3B.	HR.	RBI.	B.A.	PO.	A.	E.	F.A.
1963	—American	OF	2	0	0	0	0	0	0	.000	1	0	0	1.000
1967	—American	OF	4	0	3	1	0	0	0	.750	2	0	0	1.000
1968	—American	OF	4	0	0	0	0	0	0	.000	0	0	0	.000
1969	—American	OF	1	0	0	0	0	0	0	.000	1	0	0	1.000
1970	—American	OF-1B	6	1	4	1	0	0	1	.667	8	0	0	1.000
1971	—American	OF	3	0	0	0	0	0	0	.000	0	0	0	.000
1972	—American	OF	3	0	0	0	0	0	0	.000	3	0	0	1.000
1974	—American	1B	1	0	0	0	0	0	0	.000	5	0	0	1.000
1975	—American	PH	1	1	1	0	0	1	3	1.000	0	0	0	.000
1976	—American	OF	2	0	0	0	0	0	0	.000	0	0	0	.000
1977	—American	OF	2	0	0	0	0	0	0	.000	0	0	0	.000
1979	—American	1B	3	0	2	0	0	0	1	.667	5	1	0	1.000
1982	—American	PH	1	0	0	0	0	0	0	.000	0	0	0	.000
1983	—American	PH	1	0	0	0	0	0	0	.000	0	0	0	.000
All-Star Game Totals—14 Years			34	2	10	2	0	1	5	.294	25	1	0	1.000

Member of American League All-Star Team in 1966; did not play.
Named to American League All-Star Teams for 1965, 1973 and 1978 games; replaced due to injury.